Glencoe
Literature
The Reader's Choice

British Literature

PROGRAM CONSULTANTS

Jeffrey D. Wilhelm, PhD

Douglas Fisher, PhD

Beverly Ann Chin, PhD

Jacqueline Jones Royster, DA

McGraw Hill Glencoe

New York, New York   Columbus, Ohio   Chicago, Illinois   Woodland Hills, California

ACKNOWLEDGMENTS

Grateful acknowledgment is given authors, publishers, photographers, museums, and agents for permission to reprint the following copyrighted material. Every effort has been made to determine copyright owners. In case of any omissions, the Publisher will be pleased to make suitable acknowledgments in future editions.

Acknowledgments continued on page R108.

 **Glencoe**

The **McGraw·Hill** Companies

Send all inquiries to:
Glencoe/McGraw-Hill
8787 Orion Place
Columbus, OH 43240-4027

ISBN-13: (student edition) 978-0-07-845482-0
ISBN-10: (student edition) 0-07-845482-4
ISBN-13: (teacher edition) 978-0-07-845606-0
ISBN-10: (teacher edition) 0-07-845606-1

Printed in the United States of America.

3 4 5 6 7 8 9 027/055 12 11 10 09 08 07

Senior Program Consultants

Jeffrey D. Wilhelm, PhD, a former middle and secondary school English and reading teacher, is currently Professor of Education at Boise State University. He is the author or coauthor of numerous articles and several books on the teaching of reading and literacy, including award-winning titles such as *You Gotta BE the Book* and *Reading Don't Fix No Chevys*. He also works with local schools as part of the Adolescent Literacy Project and recently helped establish the National Writing Project site at Boise State University.

Douglas Fisher, PhD, is Professor of Language and Literacy Education and Director of Professional Development at San Diego State University, where he teaches English language development and literacy. He also serves as Director of City Heights Educational Pilot, which won the Christa McAuliffe Award from the American Association of State Colleges and Universities. He has published numerous articles on reading and literacy, differentiated instruction, and curriculum design. He is coauthor of the book *Improving Adolescent Literacies: Strategies That Work* and coeditor of the book *Inclusive Urban Schools*.

Program Consultants

Beverly Ann Chin, PhD, is Professor of English, Director of the English Teaching Program, former Director of the Montana Writing Project, and former Director of Composition at the University of Montana in Missoula. She currently serves as a Member at Large of the Conference of English Leadership. Dr. Chin is a nationally recognized leader in English language arts standards, curriculum, and assessment. Formerly a high school teacher and an adult education reading teacher, Dr. Chin has taught in English language arts education at several universities and has received awards for her teaching and service.

Jacqueline Jones Royster, DA, is Professor of English and Senior Vice Provost and Executive Dean of the Colleges of Arts and Sciences at The Ohio State University. She is currently on the Writing Advisory Committee of the National Commission on Writing and serves as chair for both the Columbus Literacy Council and the Ohioana Library Association. In addition to the teaching of writing, Dr. Royster's professional interests include the rhetorical history of African American women and the social and cultural implications of literate practices. She has contributed to and helped to edit numerous books, anthologies, and journals.

TEACHER REVIEWERS

The following teachers contributed to the review of *Glencoe Literature*.

Bridget M. Agnew
St. Michael School
Chicago, Illinois

Monica Anzaldua Araiza
Dr. Juliet V. Garcia Middle School
Brownsville, Texas

Katherine R. Baer
Howard County Public Schools
Ellicott City, Maryland

Tanya Baxter
Roald Amundsen High School
Chicago, Illinois

Danielle R. Brain
Thomas R. Proctor Senior High
   School
Utica, New York

Yolanda Conder
Owasso Mid-High School
Owasso, Oklahoma

Gwenn de Mauriac
The Wiscasset Schools
Wiscasset, Maine

Courtney Doan
Bloomington High School
Bloomington, Illinois

Susan M. Griffin
Edison Preparatory School
Tulsa, Oklahoma

Cindi Davis Harris
Helix Charter High School
La Mesa, California

Joseph F. Hutchinson
Toledo Public Schools
Toledo, Ohio

Ginger Jordan
Florien High School
Florien, Louisiana

Dianne Konkel
Cypress Lake Middle School
Fort Myers, Florida

Melanie A. LaFleur
Many High School
Many, Louisiana

Patricia Lee
Radnor Middle School
Wayne, Pennsylvania

Linda Copley Lemons
Cleveland High School
Cleveland, Tennessee

Heather S. Lewis
Waverly Middle School
Lansing, Michigan

Sandra C. Lott
Aiken Optional School
Alexandria, Louisiana

Connie M. Malacarne
O'Fallon Township High School
O'Fallon, Illinois

Lori Howton Means
Edward A. Fulton Junior High
   School
O'Fallon, Illinois

Claire C. Meitl
Howard County Public Schools
Ellicott City, Maryland

Patricia P. Mitcham
Mohawk High School
   (Retired)
New Castle, Pennsylvania

Lisa Morefield
South-Western Career Academy
Grove City, Ohio

Kevin M. Morrison
Hazelwood East High School
St. Louis, Missouri

Jenine M. Pokorak
School Without Walls Senior
   High School
Washington, DC

Susan Winslow Putnam
Butler High School
Matthews, North Carolina

Paul C. Putnoki
Torrington Middle School
Torrington, Connecticut

Jane Thompson Rae
Cab Calloway High School of
   the Arts
Wilmington, Delaware

Stephanie L. Robin
N. P. Moss Middle School
Lafayette, Louisiana

Ann C. Ryan
Lindenwold High School
Lindenwold, New Jersey

Pamela Schoen
Hopkins High School
Minnetonka, Minnesota

Megan Schumacher
Friends' Central School
Wynnewood, Pennsylvania

Fareeda J. Shabazz
Paul Revere Elementary School
Chicago, Illinois

Molly Steinlage
Brookpark Middle School
Grove City, Ohio

Barry Stevenson
Garnet Valley Middle School
Glen Mills, Pennsylvania

Paul Stevenson
Edison Preparatory School
Tulsa, Oklahoma

Kathy Thompson
Owasso Mid-High School
Owasso, Oklahoma

How to Use *The Reader's Choice* xxxvi
Literary Maps 0
Scavenger Hunt 3

UNIT ONE ## The Anglo-Saxon Period and the Middle Ages 449–1485 4
Part 1: The Epic Warrior..19
Part 2: The Power of Faith...81
Part 3: The World of Romance 171

UNIT TWO ## The English Renaissance 1485–1650 236
Part 1: Humanists and Courtiers..251
Part 2: A Bard for the Ages 291
Part 3: The Sacred and the Secular...413

UNIT THREE ## From Puritanism to the Enlightenment 1640–1780 500
Part 1: The Civil War, the Commonwealth, and the Restoration..............515
Part 2: The English Enlightenment and Neoclassicism.......................563

UNIT FOUR ## The Triumph of Romanticism 1750–1837 692
Part 1: The Stirrings of Romanticism...707
Part 2: Nature and the Imagination 779
Part 3: The Quest for Truth and Beauty 841

UNIT FIVE ## The Victorian Age 1837–1901 906
Part 1: Optimism and the Belief in Progress 921
Part 2: Realism and Naturalism 963

UNIT SIX ## The Modern Age 1901–1950 1028
Part 1: Class, Colonialism, and the Great War 1043
Part 2: Modernism 1105
Part 3: World War II and Its Aftermath 1165

UNIT SEVEN ## An International Literature 1950–Present 1226
Part 1: The British Isles: Making and Remaking Traditions 1241
Part 2: Around the World: Extending and Evaluating Traditions 1283

Reference Section

Literary Terms Handbook R1
Reading Handbook R20
Foldables™ R26
Writing Handbook R30
Business Writing R42
Language Handbook R46
Test-Taking Skills Handbook R61

Glossary/Glosario R64
Academic Word List R82
Index of Skills R85
Index of Authors and Titles R100
Index of Art and Artists R104
Acknowledgments R108

CONTENTS

UNIT ONE The Anglo-Saxon Period and the Middle Ages 449–1485 4

Timeline 6

By the Numbers 8

Being There 9

Historical, Social, and Cultural Forces............ 10

Big Ideas 12

from **The Battle of Maldon** ....Poem 13

from **The Creation of Adam and Eve** ....Drama 15

Sir Thomas Malory   from **Le Morte d'Arthur** ....Legend 17

Wrap-Up 18

Part 1 **The Epic Warrior** 19

Literary History: The Epic and the Epic Hero 20

Anonymous   from **Beowulf** ....Epic 22

"my hands
Alone shall fight for me, struggle for life
Against the monster. God must decide
Who will be given to death's cold grip."

—Beowulf

Comparing Literature *Across Time and Place* 54

Anonymous   **The Death of Humbaba** ....Epic 55
from **Gilgamesh**

J. R. R. Tolkien   from **The Battle of the Pelennor Fields** ....Novel 58
from **The Lord of the Rings: The Return of the King**

Gareth Hinds   from **The Collected Beowulf** ....Graphic Novel 62

Tristram Hunt   **TIME:** A Brief History of Heroes .... Feature Article 69

Vocabulary Workshop: Word Origins and Word Parts:
Understanding Anglo-Saxon Derivations 73

Anonymous   *The Seafarer* .... Poem 74

Part 2   The Power of Faith 81

The Venerable Bede   from *The Ecclesiastical History
of the English People* .... Nonfiction 82

Literary History: The Development of English 90

Geoffrey Chaucer   from *The Canterbury Tales*

from *The Prologue* .... Poem 92

from *The Pardoner's Tale* .... Poem 116

from *The Wife of Bath's Tale* .... Poem 124

*"they were pilgrims all
That towards Canterbury meant to ride."*

—Geoffrey Chaucer

Jeff Chu   **TIME:** The Roads Now Taken .... Feature Article 142

Margery Kempe   from *The Book of Margery Kempe* .... Autobiography 145

Grammar Workshop: Language Usage: Correcting Verb Tense 151

Literary History: Miracle and Morality Plays 152

Anonymous   from *Everyman* .... Drama 154

Part 3 The World of Romance 171

Anonymous	from *Sir Gawain and the Green Knight* ....Romance 172		
Barbara Tuchman	**Historical Perspective:** from *A Distant Mirror* ....Nonfiction 193		
Sir Thomas Malory	from *Le Morte d'Arthur* ....Legend 196		

> *"King Arthur smote Sir Mordred under the shield with a thrust of his spear on through the body more than a fathom."*
>
> —Sir Thomas Malory

Vocabulary Workshop: Context Clues: Determining the Meaning of Unfamiliar Words...207

Literary History: The Ballad Tradition...208

Anonymous	*Sir Patrick Spens* ....Ballad 210		
Anonymous	*Bonny Barbara Allan*....................................Ballad 213		
Anonymous	*Get Up and Bar the Door* ....Ballad 215		

Writing Workshop: Descriptive Essay: Describing a Character 218

Penelope Lively	PROFESSIONAL MODEL: from *A House Unlocked* ....Memoir 219	

Speaking, Listening, and Viewing Workshop: Presenting a Photo-Essay 226

Literature of the Time...228

Test Preparation and Practice 230

The Venerable Bede	from *The Ecclesiastical History of the English People* ....Nonfiction 230	

UNIT TWO The English RENAISSANCE *1485–1650* **236**

Timeline 238

By the Numbers 240

Being There 241

Historical, Social, and Cultural Forces 242

Big Ideas 244

Sir Philip Sidney   from **A Defence of Poesie** .... Essay 245

William Shakespeare   from **Richard III** .... Drama 247

John Donne   **Batter my heart, three-personed God** .... Poem 249

Wrap-Up 250

PART 1 Humanists and Courtiers 251

Literary History: The Development of the Sonnet 252

Francesco Petrarch   **Sonnet XII** .... Poem 253

Elizabeth I   **On Monsieur's Departure** .... Poem 254

Speech to the Troops at Tilbury .... Speech 257

Sir Thomas Wyatt   **The Lover Showeth How He Is Forsaken** .... Poem 259

Whoso List to Hunt .... Poem 262

Edmund Spenser   **Sonnet 30** .... Poem 265

Sonnet 75 .... Poem 268

Sir Philip Sidney   **Sonnet 31** .... Poem 270

Sonnet 39 .... Poem 273

Christopher Marlowe   **The Passionate Shepherd to His Love** .... Poem 275

Sir Walter Raleigh   **The Nymph's Reply to the Shepherd** .... Poem 279

Sir Francis Bacon   **Of Studies** .... Essay 283

Grammar Workshop: Language Usage: Making Subjects
and Verbs Agree 290

PART 2   *A Bard for the Ages* 291

William Shakespeare   *Sonnet 116* .... Poem 292

Sonnet 130 .... Poem 296

Sonnet 73 .... Poem 298

Sonnet 29 .... Poem 299

Fear No More the Heat o' the Sun .... Song 301

Blow, Blow, Thou Winter Wind .... Song 303

To be, or not to be from **Hamlet** .... Soliloquy 305

> "To be, or not to be—that is the question.
> Whether 'tis nobler in the mind to suffer
> The slings and arrows of outrageous fortune,
> Or to take arms against a sea of troubles,
> And by opposing end them."
>
> —William Shakespeare

All the world's a stage from **As You Like It** .... Soliloquy 308

Our revels now are ended from **The Tempest** .... Soliloquy 310

Literary History: Shakespeare's Theater 314

The Tragedy of Macbeth .... Drama 316

Daniel Rosenthal   **Visual Perspective:** **Throne of Blood** from **Shakespeare on Screen** .... Essay 406

William A. Henry III   **TIME:** Midsummer Night's Spectacle .... Arts Feature 410

PART 3 *The Sacred and the Secular* 413

The King James Version of the Bible	from **Genesis** .... Sacred Text 414	
	Psalm 23 .... Sacred Text 421	
Aemilia Lanyer	**Eve's Apology** .... Poem 424	

Literary History: The Metaphysical Poets 428

John Donne	**Song** .... Poem 430
	A Valediction: Forbidding Mourning .... Poem 433
	Death Be Not Proud .... Poem 435
	Meditation 17 .... Nonfiction 438

"Who bends not his ear to any bell which upon any occasion rings? but who can remove it from that bell which is passing a piece of himself out of this world?"

—John Donne

Vocabulary Workshop: Analogies: Understanding Relationships Between Words 444

Ben Jonson	**On My First Son** .... Poem 445
	Song: To Celia .... Poem 449

Literary History: The Cavalier Poets 452

Comparing Literature *Across Time and Place* 454

Robert Herrick	**To the Virgins, to Make Much of Time** .... Poem 455
Horace	**Carpe Diem** .... Poem 459
Pierre de Ronsard	**To Hélène** .... Poem 460
Omar Khayyám	from the **Rubáiyát** .... Poems 461

Sir John Suckling   *The Constant Lover* ....Poem 464

                       Why So Pale and Wan, Fond Lover? ....Poem 467

Richard Lovelace   *To Lucasta, Going to the Wars* ....Poem 469

                       To Althea, from Prison ....Poem 472

Andrew Marvell   *To His Coy Mistress* ....Poem 474

Writing Workshop: Literary Research Paper:
Writing a Historical Investigation 480

Speaking, Listening, and Viewing Workshop:
Delivering a Multimedia Presentation 490

Literature of the Time 492

Test Preparation and Practice 494

Sir Francis Bacon   from *Of Cunning* ....Essay 494

UNIT THREE

From PURITANISM *to the* ENLIGHTENMENT 1640–1780 500

Timeline 502

By the Numbers 504

Being There 505

Historical, Social, and Cultural Forces 506

Big Ideas 508

John Milton   from *Areopagitica* ....Essay 509

John Wilmot   from *A Satire Against Mankind* ....Poem 511

Alexander Pope   from the *Odyssey* ....Epic 513

Wrap-Up 514

Part 1 THE CIVIL WAR, THE COMMONWEALTH, AND THE RESTORATION 515

John Milton	*How Soon Hath Time*	Poem	516
	When I Consider How My Light Is Spent	Poem	518
	from *Paradise Lost*	Epic	520
John Bunyan	from *The Pilgrim's Progress*	Fiction	532

Vocabulary Workshop: Language Resources: Using a Thesaurus 541

Aphra Behn	*On Her Loving Two Equally*	Poem	542
John Dryden	from *An Essay of Dramatic Poesy*	Essay	546
Samuel Pepys	from *The Diary of Samuel Pepys*	Diary	552

Part 2 THE ENGLISH ENLIGHTENMENT AND NEOCLASSICISM 563

Jonathan Swift	*A Modest Proposal*	Essay	564
	from *Gulliver's Travels*		
	from *A Voyage to Lilliput*	Novel	575
	from *A Voyage to Brobdingnag*	Novel	580
Alexander Pope	*Epigrams*	Epigrams	586

*"Good nature and good sense must ever join;
To err is human, to forgive, divine."*

—Alexander Pope

from *An Essay on Man* .... Poem 590

from *The Rape of the Lock* .... Mock-Epic 593

Lady Mary Wortley
Montagu *Letter to Her Daughter* .... Letter 602

Vocabulary Workshop: Denotation and Connotation:
Using a Semantic Chart 611

Literary History: The Essay 612

Joseph Addison and
Sir Richard Steele from *The Spectator* .... Essay 614

Comparing Literature *Across Time and Place* 621

Daniel Defoe from *A Journal of the Plague Year* .... Historical Fiction 622

Richard Preston from *The Demon in the Freezer* .... Magazine Article 629

Thucydides from *History of the Peloponnesian War* .... History 635

Albert Camus from *The Plague* .... Novel 639

Christine Gorman **TIME:** Death By Mosquito .... Science Article 644

Samuel Johnson from *A Dictionary of the English Language* .... Nonfiction 648

Letter to Lord Chesterfield .... Letter 654

Grammar Workshop: Language Usage: Correcting
Pronoun-Antecedent Agreement 658

James Boswell from *The Life of Samuel Johnson* .... Biography 659

W. Jackson Bate **Historical Perspective:** from *Samuel Johnson* .... Biography 670

Writing Workshop: Persuasive Essay:
Taking a Stand on an Issue 674

Winston Churchill PROFESSIONAL MODEL: *War Speech,
September 3, 1939* .... Speech 675

Speaking, Listening, and Viewing Workshop:
Delivering a Persuasive Speech 682

Literature of the Time 684

Test Preparation and Practice 686

Jonathan Swift from *The Battle of the Books* .... Satire 686

UNIT FOUR

The Triumph of

ROMANTICISM *1750–1837* 692

Timeline		694
By the Numbers		696
Being There		697
Historical, Social, and Cultural Forces		698
Big Ideas		700

William Blake — from **Proverbs of Hell** from **The Marriage of Heaven and Hell** ....Poem 701

William Wordsworth — from the **Preface to Lyrical Ballads** ....Essay 703

Percy Bysshe Shelley — from **A Defense of Poetry** ....Essay 705

Wrap-Up 706

PART 1 *The Stirrings of Romanticism* 707

Thomas Gray — **Elegy Written in a Country Churchyard** ....Poem 708

Robert Burns — **John Anderson, My Jo** ....Poem 717

To a Mouse ....Poem 720

Auld Lang Syne ....Poem 722

Mary Wollstonecraft — from **A Vindication of the Rights of Woman** ....Essay 725

"I wish to persuade women to endeavor to acquire strength, both of mind and body, and to convince them that the soft phrases, susceptibility of heart, delicacy of sentiment, and refinement of taste are almost synonymous with epithets of weakness . . ."

—Mary Wollstonecraft

Vocabulary Workshop: Word Origins and Word Parts:
Understanding Greek and Latin Roots, Prefixes, and Suffixes 735

Jeff Chu **TIME:** Raising Their Voices .... Feature Article 736

Fanny Burney from *The Diary of Fanny Burney* .... Diary 742

Grammar Workshop: Sentence Structure:
Avoiding Dangling Modifiers 753

William Blake *A Poison Tree* .... Poem 754

The Lamb .... Poem 757

The Tyger .... Poem 758

London .... Poem 760

The Chimney Sweeper from *Songs of Innocence* .... Poem 761

The Chimney Sweeper from *Songs of Experience* .... Poem 762

Literary History: The Two Sides of Blake 766

Jane Austen from *Pride and Prejudice* .... Novel 768

PART 2 *Nature and the Imagination* 779

William Wordsworth *The World Is Too Much with Us* .... Poem 780

It Is a Beauteous Evening, Calm and Free .... Poem 783

My Heart Leaps Up .... Poem 783

Composed Upon Westminster Bridge, September 3, 1802 .... Poem 784

Lines Composed a Few Miles Above Tintern Abbey .... Poem 786

Dorothy Wordsworth from *The Journals of Dorothy Wordsworth* .... Journal 795

Samuel Taylor
Coleridge *Kubla Khan* .... Poem 799

The Rime of the Ancient Mariner .... Poem 804

"Water, water, everywhere,
And all the boards did shrink;
Water, water, everywhere,
Nor any drop to drink."

—Samuel Taylor Coleridge

| Bruce Chatwin | **Historical Perspective:** from **In Patagonia** | Nonfiction | 829 |
| Mary Shelley | from the **Introduction to Frankenstein** | Novel | 833 |

PART 3 *The Quest for Truth and Beauty* 841

George Gordon, Lord Byron	**She Walks in Beauty**	Poem	842
	from **Childe Harold's Pilgrimage**	Poem	845
	Literary History: The Byronic Hero		848
Percy Bysshe Shelley	**Ozymandias**	Poem	850

"'My name is Ozymandias, king of kings:
Look on my works, ye Mighty, and despair!"

—Percy Bysshe Shelley

	Ode to the West Wind	Poem	854
	To a Skylark	Poem	858
John Keats	**La Belle Dame sans Merci**	Poem	865
	When I Have Fears That I May Cease to Be	Poem	869
	Ode on a Grecian Urn	Poem	871

Comparing Literature *Across Time and Place* 875

John Keats   *To Autumn* ....Poem 876

Matsuo Bashō   *Haiku for Four Seasons* ....Haiku 880

Countee Cullen   *To John Keats, Poet, At Springtime* ....Poem 882

Annie Dillard   *Untying the Knot* from *Pilgrim at Tinker Creek* ....Nonfiction 884

Writing Workshop: Reflective Essay: Reflecting
on a Poetic Theme 888

Robin Becker   PROFESSIONAL MODEL: from *Wordsworth* ....Essay 889

Speaking, Listening, and Viewing Workshop:
Delivering a Reflective Presentation on a Poetic Theme 896

Literature of the Time 898

Test Preparation and Practice 900

Mary Wollstonecraft from *A Vindication of the Rights of Woman* ....Essay 900

UNIT FIVE   The Victorian Age 1837–1901 906

Timeline 908

By the Numbers 910

Being There 911

Historical, Social, and Cultural Forces...............................912

Big Ideas 914

Thomas Carlyle   from *Past and Present* ....Nonfiction 915

Charles Dickens   from *Hard Times* ....Novel 917

Thomas Hardy   *The Subalterns* ....Poem 919

Wrap-Up 920

Part 1   Optimism and the Belief in Progress 921

Alfred, Lord Tennyson from *In Memoriam A. H. H.* ....Poem 922

Crossing the Bar ....Poem 928

Tears, Idle Tears from **The Princess** ....Poem 929

Ulysses ....Poem 931

Comparing Literature **Across Time and Place** 938

Elizabeth Barrett Browning   *Sonnet 43* ....Poem 939

Edna St. Vincent Millay   *Love Is Not All: It Is Not Meat nor Drink* ....Poem 943

Simone de Beauvoir   *Simone de Beauvoir to Nelson Algren* ....Letter 944

John Lennon and Paul McCartney   *In My Life* ....Song 946

Paul Gray   **TIME:** What Is Love? ....Science Article 948

Gerard Manley Hopkins   *Pied Beauty* ....Poem 951

Spring and Fall: To a Young Child ....Poem 954

Lewis Carroll   *Jabberwocky* ....Poem 956

"'Beware the Jabberwock, my son!
The jaws that bite, the claws that catch!
Beware the Jubjub bird, and shun
The frumious Bandersnatch!'"

—Lewis Carroll

Wanda Coleman   **Literary Perspective:** *Jabberwocky* ....Essay 960

Part 2 Realism and Naturalism 963

Literary History: The Age of the Novel 964

Charlotte Brontë   from **Jane Eyre** ....Novel 966

Grammar Workshop: Sentence Structure:
Using Adverb Clauses 978

Robert Browning *My Last Duchess* ....Poem 979

Charles Dickens from *Oliver Twist* ....Novel 984

Vocabulary Workshop: Word Origins: Understanding
Political and Historical Terms...993

Matthew Arnold *Dover Beach* ....Poem 994

"*And we are here as on a darkling plain*
Swept with confused alarms of struggle and flight,
Where ignorant armies clash by night."
—Matthew Arnold

A. E. Housman *To an Athlete Dying Young*......................................Poem 998

When I Was One-and-Twenty...Poem 1001

Thomas Hardy *The Darkling Thrush* ....Poem 1003

The Man He Killed..Poem 1006

"*Ah, Are You Digging on My Grave?*" ....Poem 1007

Writing Workshop: Literary Analysis: Analyzing a Poem 1010

David Perkins PROFESSIONAL MODEL: from *Hardy and the*
Poetry of Isolation ....Essay 1011

Speaking, Listening, and Viewing Workshop:
Delivering an Oral Response to Literature..1018

Literature of the Time...1020

Test Preparation and Practice 1022

Charles Dickens from *The New Railway* from *Dombey and Son*...................Novel 1022

UNIT SIX — THE MODERN AGE

1901–1950 1028

Timeline 1030

By the Numbers 1032

Being There 1033

Historical, Social, and Cultural Forces 1034

Big Ideas 1036

Vera Brittain — from *Testament of Youth* .... Memoir 1037

James Joyce — from *Ulysses* .... Novel 1039

George Orwell — from *George Orwell's Wartime Diary* .... Diary 1041

Wrap-Up 1042

PART 1 — Class, Colonialism, and the Great War 1043

Comparing Literature *Across Time and Place* 1044

Katherine Mansfield — *A Cup of Tea* .... Short Story 1045

Bessie Head — *Village People* .... Essay 1054

The King James Version of the Bible — *The Parable of Lazarus and the Rich Man* .... Parable 1057

from the *Qur'an* .... Sacred Text 1059

Aparisim Ghosh — **TIME:** *Down and Out in Europe* .... News Article 1062

Literary History: The Modern British Short Story 1066

Rudyard Kipling — *Miss Youghal's Sais* .... Short Story 1068

George Orwell — *Shooting an Elephant* .... Essay 1077

Grammar Workshop: Sentence Structure: Using Coordinating Conjunctions 1088

Rupert Brooke — *The Soldier* .... Poem 1089

Siegfried Sassoon — *Dreamers* .... Poem 1093

Wilfred Owen — *Dulce et Decorum Est* .... Poem 1097

Paul Fussell — **Historical Perspective:** from *The Great War and Modern Memory* .... Nonfiction 1101

PART 2   Modernism 1105

William Butler Yeats   *The Lake Isle of Innisfree*.................Poem 1106

When You Are Old ....Poem 1108

Sailing to Byzantium...............................Poem 1110

The Second Coming ....Poem 1112

> *"Turning and turning in the widening gyre*
> *The falcon cannot hear the falconer;*
> *Things fall apart; the center cannot hold"*
>
> —William Butler Yeats

T. S. Eliot   *Preludes* ....Poem 1117

D. H. Lawrence   *The Rocking-Horse Winner* ....Short Story 1122

James Joyce   *Araby* ....Short Story 1138

Vocabulary Workshop: Word Parts: Understanding
Unfamiliar Math and Science Terms.......................1148

Virginia Woolf   from **A Room of One's Own**................Essay 1149

from **Mrs. Dalloway** ....Novel 1156

PART 3   World War II and Its Aftermath 1165

Winston Churchill   *Be Ye Men of Valor* ....Speech 1166

Vocabulary Workshop: Denotation and Connotation:
Recognizing Loaded Words 1173

Elizabeth Bowen   *The Demon Lover* ....Short Story 1174

W. H. Auden	*Musée des Beaux Arts*	Poem	1184
	The Unknown Citizen	Poem	1187
Graham Greene	*A Shocking Accident*	Short Story	1192
	Grammar Workshop: Sentence Structure: Avoiding Run-on Sentences		1199
Dylan Thomas	*Fern Hill*	Poem	1200
	Do Not Go Gentle into That Good Night	Poem	1204
	Writing Workshop: Short Story: Creating and Resolving a Conflict		1208
R. K. Narayan	PROFESSIONAL MODEL: *A Snake in the Grass*	Short Story	1209
	Speaking, Listening, and Viewing Workshop: Delivering an Oral Interpretation of a Short Story		1216
	Literature of the Time		1218
	Test Preparation and Practice		1220
Virginia Woolf	*Old Mrs. Grey*	Essay	1220

UNIT SEVEN — An International Literature 1950–Present 1226

	Timeline		1228
	By the Numbers		1230
	Being There		1231
	Historical, Social, and Cultural Forces		1232
	Big Ideas		1234
Ted Hughes	*Thistles*	Poem	1235
Philip Larkin	*Homage to a Government*	Poem	1237
Salman Rushdie	from *Midnight's Children*	Novel	1239
	Wrap-Up		1240

Part 1 The British Isles: Making and Remaking Traditions 1241

| Stevie Smith | *Not Waving but Drowning* ....Poem ....1242 |
| Penelope Lively | *At the Pitt-Rivers* ....Short Story ....1246 |

Comparing Literature *Across Time and Place* 1257

Seamus Heaney	*Follower* ....Poem 1258
Li-Young Lee	*Mnemonic* ....Poem 1262
Michael Ondaatje	*Photograph* from *Running in the Family* ....Memoir 1264

| Ted Hughes | *Wind* ....Poem ....1267 |
| Harold Pinter | *That's All* ....Drama ....1271 |

Literary History: British Drama—From the Drawing Room to the Kitchen Sink...1276

| Eavan Boland | *What We Lost* ....Poem ....1278 |

Part 2 Around the World: Extending and Evaluating Traditions 1283

| Doris Lessing | *A Mild Attack of Locusts* ....Short Story ....1284 |
| Nadine Gordimer | *The Train from Rhodesia* ....Short Story ....1295 |

"The train had cast the station like a skin.
It called out to the sky, I'm coming, I'm coming;
and again, there was no answer."

—Nadine Gordimer

| Chinua Achebe | *Dead Men's Path*...............................Short Story ....1304 |

Vocabulary Workshop: Distinct Meanings: Understanding Homophones.................................1312

Wole Soyinka *Telephone Conversation* ....Poem 1313

Janet Frame *Two Sheep* ....Fable 1318

Grammar Workshop: Mechanics: Using Commas with
Nonessential Elements 1326

Derek Walcott from *Tales of the Islands* ....Poem 1327

V. S. Naipaul *B. Wordsworth* ....Short Story 1331

Salman Rushdie **Literary Perspective:** from *Imaginary Homelands* ....Essay 1340

Anita Desai *Games at Twilight* ....Short Story 1344

Margaret Atwood *Elegy for the Giant Tortoises* ....Poem 1355

Christopher John Farley **TIME:** Music Goes Global ....Music Profile 1360

Writing Workshop: Critical Review: Evaluating a Literary Work 1364

Selden Rodman PROFESSIONAL MODEL: from *Catfish Row, Trinidad* ....Essay 1365

Speaking, Listening, and Viewing Workshop:
Delivering a Critical Review 1372

Literature of the Time 1374

Test Preparation and Practice 1376

Derek Walcott *Winding Up* ....Poem 1376

Reference Section

Literary Terms Handbook	R1	**Business Writing**	R42
Reading Handbook	R20	**Language Handbook**	R46
Vocabulary Development	R20	Grammar Glossary	R46
Comprehension Strategies	R21	Mechanics	R53
Literary Response	R23	Spelling	R58
Analysis and Evaluation	R24	**Test-Taking Skills Handbook**	R61
Foldables™	R26	**Glossary/Glosario**	R64
Writing Handbook	R30	**Academic Word List**	R82
The Writing Process	R30	**Index of Skills**	R85
Using the Traits of Strong Writing	R33	**Index of Authors and Titles**	R100
Writing Modes	R35	**Index of Art and Artists**	R104
Research Paper Writing	R36	**Acknowledgments**	R108

SELECTIONS BY GENRE

Short Story

A Cup of Tea 1045
Katherine Mansfield

Miss Youghal's *Sais* 1068
Rudyard Kipling

The Rocking-Horse Winner 1122
D. H. Lawrence

Araby 1138
James Joyce

The Demon Lover 1174
Elizabeth Bowen

A Shocking Accident 1192
Graham Greene

A Snake in the Grass 1209
R. K. Narayan

At the Pitt-Rivers 1246
Penelope Lively

A Mild Attack of Locusts 1284
Doris Lessing

The Train from Rhodesia 1295
Nadine Gordimer

Dead Men's Path 1304
Chinua Achebe

B. Wordsworth 1331
V. S. Naipaul

Games at Twilight 1344
Anita Desai

Fiction

from **The Pilgrim's Progress** 532
John Bunyan

from **A Journal of the Plague Year** 622
Daniel Defoe

from **The Battle of the Books** 686
Jonathan Swift

Fable

Two Sheep 1318
Janet Frame

Legend

from **Le Morte d'Arthur** 17, 196
Sir Thomas Malory

Novel Excerpt

from **The Battle of the Pelennor Fields** *from*
**The Lord of the Rings: The Return
of the King** 58
J. R. R. Tolkien

from **Gulliver's Travels** 575
Jonathan Swift

from **The Plague** 639
Albert Camus

from **Pride and Prejudice** 768
Jane Austen

from the **Introduction to Frankenstein** 833
Mary Shelley

from **Hard Times** 917
Charles Dickens

from **Jane Eyre** 966
Charlotte Brontë

from **Oliver Twist** 984

from **The New Railway** *from* **Dombey
and Son** 1022
Charles Dickens

from **Ulysses** 1039
James Joyce

from **Mrs. Dalloway** 1156
Virginia Woolf

from **Midnight's Children** 1239
Salman Rushdie

Graphic Novel

from **The Collected Beowulf** 62
Gareth Hinds

Poetry

from **The Battle of Maldon** 13

The Seafarer 74

from **The Canterbury Tales**
from **The Prologue** 92
from **The Pardoner's Tale** 116

from The Wife of Bath's Tale 124
Geoffrey Chaucer

Sir Patrick Spens 210
Bonny Barbara Allan 213
Get Up and Bar the Door 215
Batter my heart, three-personed God 249
John Donne

Sonnet XII 253
Francesco Petrarch

On Monsieur's Departure 254
Elizabeth I

The Lover Showeth How He Is Forsaken 259
Whoso List to Hunt 262
Sir Thomas Wyatt

Sonnet 30 265
Sonnet 75 268
Edmund Spenser

Sonnet 31 270
Sonnet 39 273
Sir Philip Sidney

The Passionate Shepherd to His Love 275
Christopher Marlowe

The Nymph's Reply to the Shepherd 279
Sir Walter Raleigh

Sonnet 116 292
Sonnet 130 296
Sonnet 73 298
Sonnet 29 299
William Shakespeare

Eve's Apology 424
Aemilia Lanyer

Song 430
A Valediction: Forbidding Mourning 433
Death Be Not Proud 435
John Donne

On My First Son 445
Song: To Celia 449
Ben Jonson

To the Virgins, to Make Much of Time 455
Robert Herrick

Carpe Diem 459
Horace

To Hélène 460
Pierre de Ronsard

from the Rubáiyát 461
Omar Khayyám

The Constant Lover 464
Why So Pale and Wan, Fond Lover? 467
Sir John Suckling

To Lucasta, Going to the Wars 469
To Althea, from Prison 472
Richard Lovelace

To His Coy Mistress 474
Andrew Marvell

from A Satire Against Mankind 511
John Wilmot

How Soon Hath Time 516
When I Consider How My Light Is Spent 518
John Milton

On Her Loving Two Equally 542
Aphra Behn

Epigrams 586
from An Essay on Man 590
Alexander Pope

from Proverbs of Hell *from the* Marriage
of Heaven and Hell 701
William Blake

Elegy Written in a Country Churchyard 708
Thomas Gray

John Anderson, My Jo 717
To a Mouse 720
Auld Lang Syne 722
Robert Burns

A Poison Tree 754
The Lamb 757
The Tyger 758
London 760

The Chimney Sweeper *from*
Songs of Innocence.................................761
The Chimney Sweeper *from*
Songs of Experience 762
   William Blake

The World Is Too Much with Us 780
It Is a Beauteous Evening, Calm and Free 783
My Heart Leaps Up 783
Composed Upon Westminster Bridge,
September 3, 1802 784
Lines Composed a Few Miles Above
Tintern Abbey....................................786
   William Wordsworth

Kubla Khan 799
The Rime of the Ancient Mariner 804
   Samuel Taylor Coleridge

She Walks in Beauty...............................842
from Childe Harold's Pilgrimage 845
   George Gordon, Lord Byron

Ozymandias 850
Ode to the West Wind 854
To a Skylark......................................858
   Percy Bysshe Shelley

La Belle Dame sans Merci 865
When I Have Fears That I May
Cease to Be.......................................869
Ode on a Grecian Urn 871
To Autumn...876
   John Keats

Haiku for Four Seasons............................880
   Matsuo Bashō

To John Keats, Poet, At Springtime................882
   Countee Cullen

The Subalterns....................................919
   Thomas Hardy

from In Memoriam A. H. H........................922
Crossing the Bar..................................928
Tears, Idle Tears *from* The Princess.............929
Ulysses...931
   Alfred, Lord Tennyson

Sonnet 43 939
   Elizabeth Barrett Browning

Love Is Not All: It Is Not Meat
nor Drink 943
   Edna St. Vincent Millay

Pied Beauty 951
Spring and Fall: To a Young Child.................954
   Gerard Manley Hopkins

Jabberwocky.......................................956
   Lewis Carroll

My Last Duchess...................................979
   Robert Browning

Dover Beach.......................................994
   Matthew Arnold

To an Athlete Dying Young 998
When I Was One-and-Twenty 1001
   A. E. Housman

The Darkling Thrush 1003
The Man He Killed.................................1006
"Ah, Are You Digging on My Grave?"................1007
   Thomas Hardy

The Soldier.......................................1089
   Rupert Brooke

Dreamers 1093
   Siegfried Sassoon

Dulce et Decorum Est..............................1097
   Wilfred Owen

The Lake Isle of Innisfree........................1106
When You Are Old 1108
Sailing to Byzantium 1110
The Second Coming.................................1112
   William Butler Yeats

Preludes 1117
   T. S. Eliot

Musée des Beaux Arts 1184
The Unknown Citizen...............................1187
   W. H. Auden

Fern Hill 1200
Do Not Go Gentle into That Good Night 1204
   Dylan Thomas
Thistles 1235
   Ted Hughes
Homage to a Government 1237
   Philip Larkin
Not Waving but Drowning 1242
   Stevie Smith
Follower 1258
   Seamus Heaney
Mnemonic 1262
   Li-Young Lee
Wind 1267
   Ted Hughes
What We Lost 1278
   Eavan Boland
Telephone Conversation 1313
   Wole Soyinka
from Tales of the Islands 1327
   Derek Walcott
Elegy for the Giant Tortoises 1355
   Margaret Atwood
Winding Up 1376
   Derek Walcott

Epic or Mock-Epic

from Beowulf 22
The Death of Humbaba *from* Gilgamesh 55
from the Odyssey 513
   Alexander Pope
from Paradise Lost 520
   John Milton
from The Rape of the Lock 593
   Alexander Pope

Romance

from Sir Gawain and the Green Knight 172

Song

Fear No More the Heat o' the Sun 301
Blow, Blow, Thou Winter Wind 303
   William Shakespeare

In My Life 946
   John Lennon and Paul McCartney

Drama

from The Creation of Adam and Eve 15
from Everyman 154
from Richard III 247
To be, or not to be *from* Hamlet 305
All the world's a stage *from* As You Like It 308
Our revels now are ended *from*
The Tempest 310
The Tragedy of Macbeth 316
   William Shakespeare
That's All 1271
   Harold Pinter

Sacred Text

from Genesis 414
Psalm 23 421
The Parable of Lazarus and the Rich Man 1057
   The King James Version of the Bible
from the Qur'an 1059

Nonfiction and Informational Text

Essay

from The Ecclesiastical History
of the English People 82, 230
   The Venerable Bede
from A Distant Mirror 193
   Barbara Tuchman
from A Defence of Poesie 245
   Sir Philip Sidney
Of Studies 283
   Sir Francis Bacon
Throne of Blood *from* Shakespeare
on Screen 406
   Daniel Rosenthal
Meditation 17 438
   John Donne
from Of Cunning 494
   Sir Francis Bacon

from **Areopagitica**........................509
John Milton

from **An Essay of Dramatic Poesy**....................546
John Dryden

A Modest Proposal...................564
Jonathan Swift

from **The Spectator**......................614
Joseph Addison and Sir Richard Steele

from **The Demon in the Freezer**.....................629
Richard Preston

from **History of the Peloponnesian War**...........635
Thucydides

from **A Dictionary of the English Language**......648
Samuel Johnson

from the **Preface to Lyrical Ballads**....................703
William Wordsworth

from **A Defense of Poetry**...................705
Percy Bysshe Shelley

from **A Vindication of the Rights
of Woman**......................725, 900
Mary Wollstonecraft

from **In Patagonia**....................829
Bruce Chatwin

Untying the Knot *from* **Pilgrim
at Tinker Creek**...................884
Annie Dillard

from **Wordsworth**.....................889
Robin Becker

from **Past and Present**...........................915
Thomas Carlyle

Jabberwocky.....................960
Wanda Coleman

from **Hardy and the Poetry of Isolation**..........1011
David Perkins

Village People.....................1054
Bessie Head

Shooting an Elephant......................1077
George Orwell

from **The Great War and
Modern Memory**....................1101
Paul Fussell

from **A Room of One's Own**....................1149
Virginia Woolf

Old Mrs. Grey.....................1220
Virginia Woolf

from **Imaginary Homelands**...................1340
Salman Rushdie

from **Catfish Row, Trinidad**...................1365
Selden Rodman

Biography, Autobiography, or Memoir

from **The Book of Margery Kempe**.....................145
Margery Kempe

from **A House Unlocked**.......................219
Penelope Lively

from **The Life of Samuel Johnson**.....................659
James Boswell

from **Samuel Johnson**.........................670
W. Jackson Bate

from **Testament of Youth**.....................1037
Vera Brittain

Photograph *from* **Running in the Family**.........1264
Michael Ondaatje

Letter, Journal, or Diary

from **The Diary of Samuel Pepys**......................552
Samuel Pepys

Letter to Her Daughter.......................602
Lady Mary Wortley Montagu

Letter to Lord Chesterfield.................654
Samuel Johnson

from **The Diary of Fanny Burney**......................742
Fanny Burney

from **The Journals of Dorothy Wordsworth**......795
Dorothy Wordsworth

Simone de Beauvoir to Nelson Algren.............944
Simone de Beauvoir

from **George Orwell's Wartime Diary**.................1041
George Orwell

Speech

Speech to the Troops at Tilbury......................257
Elizabeth I

War Speech, September 3, 1939.....................675

Be Ye Men of Valor...........................1166
Winston Churchill

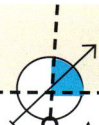

PERSPECTIVES

Award-winning nonfiction book excerpts and primary source documents

Historical Perspective:
from A Distant Mirror 193
Barbara Tuchman

Visual Perspective: Throne of Blood *from*
Shakespeare on Screen 406
Daniel Rosenthal

Historical Perspective:
from Samuel Johnson 670
W. Jackson Bate

Historical Perspective: *from* In Patagonia 829
Bruce Chatwin

Literary Perspective: Jabberwocky 960
Wanda Coleman

Historical Perspective: *from* The Great War
and Modern Memory 1101
Paul Fussell

Literary Perspective:
from Imaginary Homelands 1340
Salman Rushdie

TIME

High-interest, informative magazine articles

A Brief History of Heroes 69
Tristram Hunt

The Roads Now Taken 142
Jeff Chu

Midsummer Night's Spectacle 410
William A. Henry III

Death By Mosquito 644
Christine Gorman

Raising Their Voices 736
Jeff Chu

What Is Love? 948
Paul Gray

Down and Out in Europe 1062
Aparisim Ghosh

Music Goes Global 1360
Christopher John Farley

Comparing Literature
Across Time and Place

UNIT ONE

from Beowulf 22
The Death of Humbaba *from* Gilgamesh 55
from The Battle of the Pelennor Fields *from*
The Lord of the Rings: The Return
of the King 58
J. R. R. Tolkien
from The Collected Beowulf 62
Gareth Hinds

UNIT TWO

To the Virgins, to Make Much of Time 455
Robert Herrick
Carpe Diem 459
Horace
To Hélène 460
Pierre de Ronsard
from the Rubáiyát 461
Omar Khayyám

FEATURES

UNIT THREE

from **A Journal of the Plague Year** 622
  Daniel Defoe
from **The Demon in the Freezer** 629
  Richard Preston
from **History of the Peloponnesian War** 635
  Thucydides
from **The Plague** 639
  Albert Camus

UNIT FOUR

To Autumn 876
  John Keats
Haiku for Four Seasons 880
  Matsuo Bashō
To John Keats, Poet, At Springtime 882
  Countee Cullen
Untying the Knot *from* **Pilgrim
at Tinker Creek** 884
  Annie Dillard

UNIT FIVE

Sonnet 43 939
  Elizabeth Barrett Browning
Love Is Not All: It Is Not Meat nor Drink 943
  Edna St. Vincent Millay
Simone de Beauvoir to Nelson Algren 944
  Simone de Beauvoir
In My Life 946
  John Lennon and Paul McCartney

UNIT SIX

A Cup of Tea 1045
  Katherine Mansfield
Village People 1054
  Bessie Head
The Parable of Lazarus and the Rich Man 1057
  The King James Version of the Bible
from the **Qur'an** 1059

UNIT SEVEN

Follower 1258
  Seamus Heaney
Mnemonic 1262
  Li-Young Lee
Photograph *from* **Running in the Family** 1264
  Michael Ondaatje

LITERARY HISTORY

The Epic and the Epic Hero 20
The Development of English 90
Miracle and Morality Plays 152
The Ballad Tradition 208
The Development of the Sonnet 252
Shakespeare's Theater 314
The Metaphysical Poets 428
The Cavalier Poets 452
The Essay 612
The Two Sides of Blake 766
The Byronic Hero 848
The Age of the Novel 964
The Modern British Short Story 1066
British Drama—From the Drawing Room
to the Kitchen Sink 1276

LITERATURE OF THE TIME

For Independent Reading

Unit 1 228
Unit 2 492
Unit 3 684
Unit 4 898
Unit 5 1020
Unit 6 1218
Unit 7 1374

TEST PREPARATION AND PRACTICE

Unit 1 230
Unit 2 494
Unit 3 686
Unit 4 900
Unit 5 1022
Unit 6 1220
Unit 7 1376

SKILLS WORKSHOPS

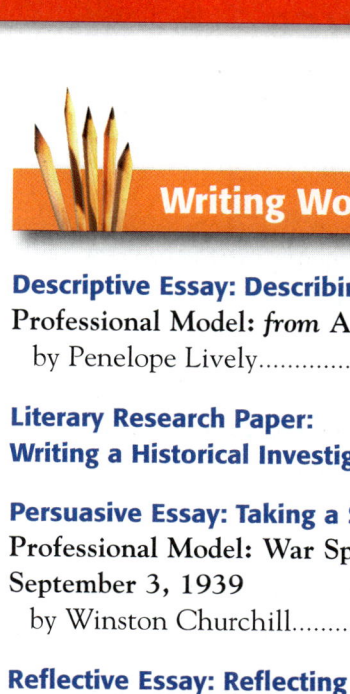

Writing Workshops

Descriptive Essay: Describing a Character
Professional Model: *from* A House Unlocked
 by Penelope Lively.............................218

Literary Research Paper:
Writing a Historical Investigation.....................480

Persuasive Essay: Taking a Stand on an Issue
Professional Model: War Speech,
September 3, 1939
 by Winston Churchill............................674

Reflective Essay: Reflecting on a Poetic Theme
Professional Model: *from* Wordsworth
 by Robin Becker 888

Literary Analysis: Analyzing a Poem
Professional Model: *from* Hardy and the
Poetry of Isolation
 by David Perkins.................................1010

Short Story: Creating and Resolving a Conflict
Professional Model: A Snake in the Grass
 by R. K. Narayan 1208

Critical Review: Evaluating a Literary Work
Professional Model: *from* Catfish Row,
Trinidad
 by Selden Rodman................................1364

Speaking, Listening, and Viewing Workshops

Presenting a Photo-Essay.....................226
Delivering a Multimedia Presentation...............490
Delivering a Persuasive Speech 682
Delivering a Reflective Presentation
 on a Poetic Theme.........................896
Delivering an Oral Response to Literature 1018
Delivering an Oral Interpretation
 of a Short Story 1216
Delivering a Critical Review...................1372

Grammar Workshops

Language Usage: Correcting Verb Tense...........151
Language Usage: Making Subjects
 and Verbs Agree 290
Language Usage: Correcting
 Pronoun-Antecedent Agreement.....................658
Sentence Structure: Avoiding
 Dangling Modifiers 753
Sentence Structure:
 Using Adverb Clauses.................................978
Sentence Structure:
 Using Coordinating Conjunctions.................1088
Sentence Structure:
 Avoiding Run-on Sentences 1199
Mechanics: Using Commas
 with Nonessential Elements............................1326

Vocabulary Workshops

Word Origins and Word Parts: Understanding
 Anglo-Saxon Derivations...................................73
Context Clues: Determining the Meaning
 of Unfamiliar Words 207
Analogies: Understanding Relationships
 Between Words 444
Language Resources: Using a Thesaurus..........541
Denotation and Connotation: Using
 a Semantic Chart 611
Word Origins and Word Parts:
 Understanding Greek and Latin Roots,
 Prefixes, and Suffixes..735
Word Origins: Understanding Political
 and Historical Terms...993
Word Parts: Understanding Unfamiliar
 Math and Science Terms..................................1148
Denotation and Connotation:
 Recognizing Loaded Words...............................1173
Distinct Meanings:
 Understanding Homophones.............................1312

Why do I need this book?

Glencoe Literature, The Reader's Choice is more than just a collection of stories, poems, nonfiction articles, and other literary works. Every unit is built around **Big Ideas,** concepts that you will want to think about, talk about, and maybe even argue about. Big Ideas help you become part of an important conversation. You can join in lively discussions about who we are, where we have been, and where we are going.

Organization

The literature selections you will read are organized chronologically into seven units spanning the Anglo-Saxon period to the present.

Each unit contains the following:

A **UNIT INTRODUCTION** provides you with the background information to help make your reading experience more meaningful.

- The **TIMELINE** helps you keep track of major literary and historical events.

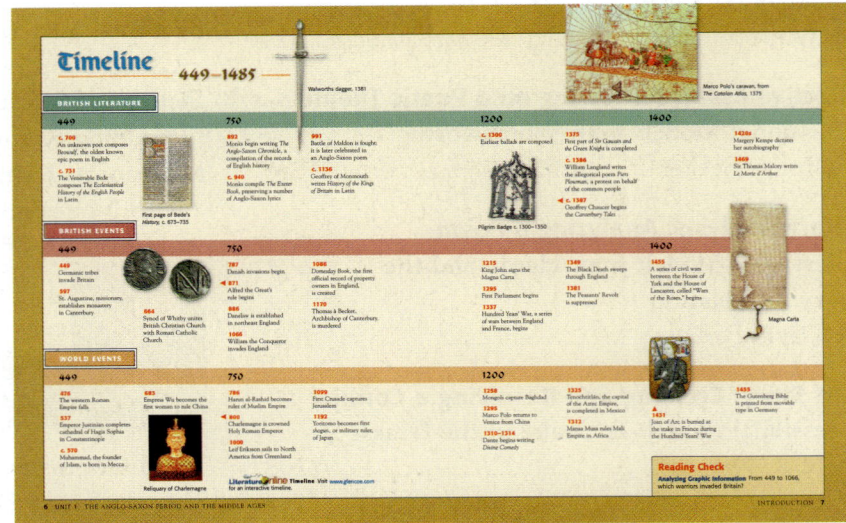

- **BY THE NUMBERS** shows you figures and key data at a glance.
- **BEING THERE** gives you a glimpse of the geography related to the literary period.
- **HISTORICAL, CULTURAL, AND SOCIAL FORCES** explains the influences that shape a specific literary period.
- **BIG IDEAS** target three concepts that you can trace as you read the literary selections.

LITERATURE SELECTIONS follow each Unit Introduction. The selections are organized as follows.

Reading and Thinking

The main selections in your textbook are arranged in three parts.

• Start with **BEFORE YOU READ.** Learn valuable background information about the selection and preview the skills and strategies that will guide your reading.

MEET THE AUTHOR presents a detailed biography of the writer whose work you will read and analyze.

LITERATURE PREVIEW and **READING PREVIEW** list the basic tools you will use to read and analyze the selection.

• Next, read the **LITERATURE SELECTION.** As you flip through the selections, you will notice that parts of the text are highlighted in different colors. At the bottom of the page are color-coded questions that relate to the highlighted text. Yellow represents a *Big Idea*, magenta represents a *Literary Element*, and blue represents a *Reading Strategy*. These questions will help you gain a better understanding of the text.

AFTER YOU READ

RESPONDING AND THINKING CRITICALLY

Respond

1. Can you sympathize with the feelings of the speaker in "On Monsieur's Departure"? Why or why not?

Recall and Interpret

2. (a)According to the first stanza of the poem, what feelings has the speaker been forced to hide? (b)What reasons might she have for hiding them?

3. (a)In the second stanza of the poem, to what does the speaker compare her feelings? (b)What does the second stanza reveal about her feelings for Monsieur?

4. (a)According to the opening lines of "Speech to the Troops at Tilbury," what warning have some of Elizabeth's advisors given her? (b)According to Elizabeth, why does she ignore their advice? (c)What effect do you think Elizabeth hopes to have on her audience by opening her speech in this way?

Analyze and Evaluate

5. In your opinion, what image in the poem is most effective in conveying the speaker's feelings? Explain your answer.

6. How does knowing the identity of the poem's author deepen your understanding of the conflict that the poem describes?

7. (a)In her speech, what does Elizabeth say she will do rather than see her country dishonored? (b)Against what criticism of her ruling ability is she defending herself? (c)Do you think this is an adequate defense? Explain your answer.

Connect

8. On the basis of this poem and other things you have read or heard about, do you think a ruler's duty and loyalty to his or her country should take precedence over his or her personal feelings and private life? Explain.

9. **Big Idea** **Humanists and Courtiers** In what ways do these two works demonstrate the idea that the English were beginning to focus more on secular subjects than on the more religious subjects of the past?

LITERARY ANALYSIS

Literary Element Tone

Just as a queen's attitude can set the tone of her court, a writer's attitude toward subject matter or audience sets the tone of a literary work.

What evidence can you find in "Speech to the Troops at Tilbury" that Elizabeth I's attitude toward her audience is one of deep respect?

Interdisciplinary Activity: Art

Make an illustration to accompany either Elizabeth's poem or speech. You may imitate the style of the Elizabethan period, as seen in the picture of Elizabeth, or use another abstract style. Try to convey the emotions expressed in the written work.

Literature Online **Web Activities** For eFlashcards, Selection Quick Checks, and other Web activities, go to www.glencoe.com.

READING AND VOCABULARY

Reading Strategy Analyzing Text Structure

Elizabeth I uses comparison and contrast to make her points in both the poem and the speech.

Partner Activity With a partner, list three examples of the use of comparison and contrast in the poem and the speech. Then discuss how this structure adds to the emotional impact of the poem.

Vocabulary Practice

Practice with Synonyms Identify the synonym for each vocabulary word below.

1. concord	a. agreement	b. rejoice
2. mute	a. small	b. silent
3. suppressed	a. surprised	b. subdued
4. treachery	a. betrayal	b. treasure
5. valor	a. courage	b. cowardice

258 UNIT 2 THE ENGLISH RENAISSANCE

LITERARY ANALYSIS

Literary Element Tragedy

Traditionally, the **tragic hero** is a person of high rank who, out of hubris, or an exaggerated sense of power and pride, violates a human, natural, or divine law. By breaking that law, the hero poses a threat to society, causing the suffering or death of family members, friends, and associates. In the last act of a traditional tragedy, the tragic hero is punished, and order is restored.

1. In your opinion, what causes Macbeth's downfall—a tragic flaw, errors in judgment, forces beyond his control, or a combination of these factors? Support your opinion with evidence from the play.

2. Do you think Macbeth's death sets everything right again? Give reasons for your opinion.

3. Is Lady Macbeth also a tragic hero? Why or why not?

Review: Irony

As you learned on page 116, **irony** is a contrast or a discrepancy between expectation and reality. Irony can take several forms: **verbal irony** occurs when a person says one thing while meaning another; **situational irony** exists when the outcome of a situation is the opposite of what someone expected; **dramatic irony** occurs when the audience or reader knows something that the characters do not know.

Partner Activity Meet with another classmate to discuss Shakespeare's use of irony in *Macbeth*. Use a diagram like the one below to record examples of irony.

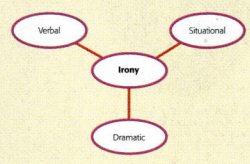

READING AND VOCABULARY

Reading Strategy Analyzing Cause-and-Effect Relationships

By determining why something occurred and what happened as a result, you can more effectively interpret, analyze, and evaluate events in the plot. Review the diagram you created on page 388 and then answer the following questions.

1. According to the Doctor, what is the cause of Lady Macbeth's mental breakdown?

2. Ultimately, what effect does Duncan produce by naming his son Malcolm heir to the throne?

Vocabulary Practice

Practice with Context Clues Choose the vocabulary word that best fits each sentence.

1. José's _____ in spelling amazed his class.
   a. antidote   b. prowess   c. siege

2. We must search for the _____ to counter the venom of that snakebite.
   a. usurper   b. purge   c. antidote

3. The family of the company's deceased president accused his power-hungry successor of being a/an _____.
   a. usurper   b. antidote   c. siege

4. The invaders laid _____ to the castle, hoping to force its inhabitants to surrender.
   a. prowess   b. siege   c. purge

5. The dictator planned a/an _____ to eliminate his political foes.
   a. purge   b. siege   c. antidote

Academic Vocabulary

Here is a word from the vocabulary list on page R86.

react (rē akt´) *v.* to respond to a stimulus; be affected by an event, influence, etc.

Practice and Apply
How do Macbeth's followers **react** to the news that the English army has surrounded Dunsinane?

404 UNIT 2 THE ENGLISH RENAISSANCE

- Wrap up the selection with **AFTER YOU READ.** Explore what you have learned through a wide range of reading, thinking, vocabulary, and writing activities.

Vocabulary

VOCABULARY WORDS that may be new or difficult are chosen from most selections. They are introduced on the **BEFORE YOU READ** page. Each word is accompanied by its pronunciation, its part of speech, its definition, and the page number on which it appears. The vocabulary word is also used in a sample sentence. Vocabulary words are highlighted in the Literature Selection.

VOCABULARY PRACTICE On the **AFTER YOU READ** pages, you will be able to practice using the vocabulary words in an exercise. This exercise will show you how to apply a vocabulary strategy to understand new or difficult words.

ACADEMIC VOCABULARY Many of the **AFTER YOU READ** pages will also introduce you to one or two words that are frequently used in academic work. You will be prompted to apply the definitions of these words to answer questions about the selection that you have just read.

Writing Workshops

Each unit in *Glencoe Literature, The Reader's Choice* includes a Writing Workshop. The workshop walks you through the writing process as you work on an extended piece of writing related to the unit.

- You will create writing goals and apply strategies to meet them.
- You will pick up tips and polish your critical skills as you analyze professional and workshop models.
- You will focus on mastering specific aspects of writing, including organization, grammar, and vocabulary.
- You will use a rubric to evaluate your own writing.

Revising

Use the rubric below to evaluate your writing.

Rubric: Writing an Effective Short Story

- ☑ Do you present and resolve a conflict?
- ☑ Do you create a clear series of events?
- ☑ Do you build up tension or intensify the conflict, present a clear climax, and end with a satisfying resolution?
- ☑ Do you present events in chronological order and link them with transitions?
- ☑ Do you use a consistent point of view?
- ☑ Do you use dialogue to reveal characters or advance the plot?

Test Preparation and Practice

At the end of each unit, you will be tested on the literature, reading, and vocabulary skills you have just learned. Designed to simulate standardized tests, this test will give you the practice you need to succeed while providing an assessment of how you have met the unit objectives.

Test Preparation and Practice

English–Language Arts

Reading: Nonfiction

Carefully read the following passage. Use context clues to help define any words with which you are unfamiliar. Pay close attention to the use of figurative language, argument, and tone. Then, on a separate sheet of paper, answer the questions that follow.

from "Of Cunning" by Sir Francis Bacon

We take cunning for a sinister or crooked wisdom. And certainly there is a great difference between a cunning man and a wise man; not only in point of honesty, but in point of ability. . . .

. . . I knew a counsellor and secretary, that never came to Queen Elizabeth of England with bills to sign, but he would always first put her into some discourse of estate, that she might the less mind the bills. . . .

In things that are tender and unpleasing, it is good to break the ice by some whose words are of less weight, and to reserve the more weighty voice to come in as by chance, so that he may be asked the question upon the other's speech. . . .

I knew one that, when he wrote a letter, he would put that which was most material in the postscript, as if it had been a by-matter.

I knew another that, when he came to have speech, he would pass over that that he intended most; and go forth, and come back again, and speak of it as of a thing that he had almost forgot. . . .

It is a point of cunning, to let fall those words in a man's own name, which he would have another man learn and use, and thereupon take advantage. I knew two that were competitors for the

Organizing Information

Graphic organizers—such as Foldables™, diagrams, and charts—help you keep your information and ideas organized.

FOLDABLES Study Organizer

THREE-POCKET BOOK

Big Idea 1   Big Idea 2   Big Idea 3

You might try using this graphic organizer to keep track of the three Big Ideas in this unit.

LITERARY MAP OF LONDON

Faber & Faber
T. S. Eliot works as editor

RUSSELL SQUARE

E. M. Forster writes

Charles Dickens writes

Gray's Inn
Francis Bacon studies law

BLOOMSBURY

Harold Monro's Poetry Bookshop

HIGH HOLBORN

Also in London

- Francis Bacon, George G. Byron, Geoffrey Chaucer, Daniel Defoe, Robert Herrick, Ben Jonson, John Keats, John Milton, Harold Pinter, Edmund Spenser, Mary Wollstonecraft, Virginia Woolf born

- Aphra Behn, Lewis Carroll, T. S. Eliot, Aemilia Lanyer, Alexander Pope, Stevie Smith, John Suckling write

- Graham Greene childhood

John Donne studies law

Lincoln's Inn

WEST END

Button's Coffee House
Joseph Addison and Richard Steele publish

Royal Opera House

William Blake born

Elizabeth B. Browning family home

SOHO

Turk's Head Tavern
Samuel Johnson's "Club" meets

Thomas Davies's bookshop
James Boswell and Samuel Johnson meet

David Garrick home

Harold Pinter's plays performed

River

Royal Academy of Arts

William Blake studies
Pre-Raphaelite Brotherhood forms

WHITEHALL

Royal Society of London

TRAFALGAR SQUARE

George B. Shaw writes

National Theatre

ST. JAMES'S SQUARE

Green Park

St. James's Park

Prime Minister's house

No. 10 Downing Street

CITY OF WESTMINSTER

Cabinet War Rooms

Buckingham Palace

Queen Victoria's home

Winston Churchill's WWII broadcasts on BBC

Westminster Hall

Houses of Parliament
Joseph Addison, Francis Bacon, George G. Byron, Winston Churchill, Andrew Marvell, Samuel Pepys serve as members

Westminster Abbey
William Caxton's first printing press
Samuel Pepys's "The Coronation of Charles II"
Robert Browning, Geoffrey Chaucer, John Dryden, Elizabeth I, Thomas Hardy, James I, Samuel Johnson, Rudyard Kipling, Edmund Spenser, Alfred Tennyson buried

Westminster School

Ben Jonson, John Dryden study

Joseph Conrad writes

HOLBORN

Samuel Johnson home

Newgate Prison
Thomas Malory writes in jail

Rhymer's Club

Samuel Johnson writes dictionary

John Donne preaches

St. Paul's Cathedral

CITY OF LONDON

St. Mary of Bethlehem Hospital (Bedlam)

ALDGATE

T. S. Eliot works as a banker

Lloyd's

Alexander Pope writes

Daniel Defoe observes plague

Samuel Pepys writes

Thames

Shakespeare writes

Shakespeare's plays performed

Globe Theatre

Southwark Cathedral

Tower of London

St. Katherine's

Thomas Wyatt, Walter Raleigh write in jail
John Suckling attempts rescue of the Earl of Strafford

Tabard Inn
Chaucer's *Canterbury Tales* start

Guy's Hospital

John Keats studies medicine

SOUTHWARK

GREATER LONDON

Hemel Hempstead
St. Albans
Potters Bar
Cheshunt
Epping
Amersham
Watford
Borehamwood
Loughton
Brentwood
Wembley
Tottenham
Hampstead
Ilford
LONDON
Kensington
Stratford
Richmond
Chelsea
Southwark
Catford
Tilbury
Windsor
Dartford
Gravesend
Twickenham
Streatham
Chertsey
Woking
Orpington
Epsom
Tatsfield
Sevenoaks
Leatherhead
Caterham
Guildford
Dorking
Reigate
Tonbridge
East Grinstead

LAMBETH

North Sea

ATLANTIC OCEAN

King Duncan's palace

Forres

Inverness

Macbeth slain

Dunsinane

Aberdeen

SCOTLAND

Sir Patrick Spens drowns
George G. Byron childhood

Dundee

James Boswell born
Wilfred Owen meets
Siegfried Sassoon (WWI)

Dumferling

Greenock

Glasgow

Edinburgh

Ayrshire

Robert Burns's poetry

Newcastle Upon Tyne

Venerable Bede writes

Jarrow

Caedmon's hymns

Londonderry

Seamus Heaney born

Carlisle

Middlesbrough

NORTHERN IRELAND

Belfast

William Wordsworth's poetry
Dorothy Wordsworth's journal

LAKE DISTRICT

Whitby

William B. Yeats's childhood

Sligo

Cambridge University

Francis Bacon | Andrew Marvell
Rupert Brooke | John Milton
George G. Byron | Samuel Pepys
Samuel T. Coleridge | Siegfried Sassoon
John Dryden | Edmund Spenser
Thomas Gray | John Suckling
Robert Herrick | Alfred Tennyson
Christopher Marlowe | William Wordsworth
 | Thomas Wyatt

Irish Sea

IRELAND

York

Andrew Marvell born

W. H. Auden born

Winestead
Kingston

Blackpool

Haworth

Leeds

Brontës born

Dublin

Bolton

Manchester

Sheffield

Birkenhead

Liverpool

Edmund Spenser writes

Limerick

Kilcolman

Clonmel

Laurence Sterne born

Cork

Frank O'Connor born

Jonathan Swift preaches
Gerard M. Hopkins teaches
Eavan Boland, Elizabeth Bowen,
James Joyce, Richard Steele,
Jonathan Swift, William B.
Yeats born

Gawain vs. Green Knight

Newstead

Nottingham

George G. Byron home

King's Lynn (Bishop's Lynn)

Eastwood

ENGLAND

Norwich

D. H. Lawrence born

Samuel Johnson born

Lichfield

Rupert Brooke born

John Bunyan born

Fanny Burney born
Margery Kempe writes

Birmingham

Cambridge

Ipswich

John Dryden born

Rugby

Aldwinkle

Elstow

Shakespeare born

Stratford-upon-Avon

KINGDOM

Lady Mary W. Montagu writes
Alexander Pope writes

WALES

Jane Austen writes

Oxford

Elizabeth I palace

London

Thomas Wyatt born

Swansea

Newport

Bristol

Thames

Richmond

Allington

Canterbury

Dylan Thomas's poetry

Cardiff

Bath

Twickenham

Maidstone

Matthew Arnold's "Dover Beach"

Wordsworth's Tintern Abbey

Samuel T. Coleridge writes *Rime of the Ancient Mariner*

Nether Stowey

Southampton

Chaucer's *Canterbury Tales*
Christopher Marlowe born
Richard Lovelace home

Exeter Book written

Mary Shelley buried

Exeter

Dorchester

Portsmouth

Bournemouth

King Arthur born

East Budleigh

English Channel

Tintagel

Plymouth

Thomas Hardy writes

Walter Raleigh born

Oxford University

Joseph Addison | Penelope Lively
W. H. Auden | Richard Lovelace
Lewis Carroll | V. S. Naipaul
John Donne | Walter Raleigh
T. S. Eliot | Percy B. Shelley
Graham Greene | Philip Sidney
Gerard M. Hopkins | Richard Steele
A. E. Housman | Jonathan Swift
Samuel Johnson | J. R. R. Tolkien

FRANCE

Miles
0 25 50 75 100

0 50 100
Kilometers

Glencoe's Reader's Choice contains a wealth of information. The trick is to know where to look to access all of that information. If you go through this scavenger hunt, either alone or with teachers or parents, you will quickly learn how the textbook is organized and how to get the most out of your reading and study time.

Let's get started!

1. How many units and parts are there in this book?

2. What is the difference between the Glossary and the Index?

3. There is a section on Test-Taking Strategies in the Reference Section in the back of the textbook. Where else in the book can you find help for test preparation?

4. In what special feature would you find biographical information about a specific author?

5. If you wanted to find all of the selections in the book that are short stories, where would you look?

6. If you wanted to find a definition of the term *allegory,* where would you look?

7. Where can you find the Big Ideas for each unit of the book?

8. The Web site for the book is referred to throughout the book. What sort of information does the Web site contain that might help you?

9. Which of the book's main features will provide you with the strategies for developing your writing skills?

After you answer all the questions, meet with a partner or a small group to compare answers.

Duke William and His Fleet Cross the Channel to Pevensey, from *the Bayeux Tapestry,* c. 1000–1082. French School. Wool embroidery on linen. Musée de la Tapisserie, Bayeux, France.

The Anglo-Saxon Period
and the Middle Ages

449–1485

Looking Ahead

British literature developed in an era characterized by foreign invasions and social turbulence. Germanic tribes left northern Europe and invaded the island of Britain. The dialects spoken by these tribes, now separated by water from the European mainland, evolved into a separate language called English. Writers used that language to create works of great power and beauty—works that formed the foundation of British literature.

Keep the following questions in mind as you read:

➡ How did foreign invasions affect British history and culture?

➡ Why was the Roman Catholic Church important to medieval culture?

➡ What cultural forces does the medieval romance reflect?

OBJECTIVES

In learning about the Anglo-Saxon Period and the Middle Ages, you will focus on the following:

- analyzing the characteristics of various literary periods and how issues of those periods influenced the writers
- clarifying understanding of informational texts by creating diagrams
- evaluating how a historical period shapes literary characters, plots, settings, and themes
- connecting literature to historical contexts, current events, and your own experiences

Timeline

449–1485

Walworths dagger, 1381

BRITISH LITERATURE

449

c. 700
An unknown poet composes *Beowulf*, the oldest known epic poem in English

c. 731
The Venerable Bede composes *The Ecclesiastical History of the English People* in Latin

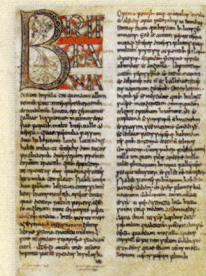

First page of Bede's *History*, c. 673–735

750

892
Monks begin writing *The Anglo-Saxon Chronicle*, a compilation of the records of English history

c. 940
Monks compile *The Exeter Book*, preserving a number of Anglo-Saxon lyrics

991
Battle of Maldon is fought; it is later celebrated in an Anglo-Saxon poem

c. 1136
Geoffrey of Monmouth writes *History of the Kings of Britain* in Latin

---

BRITISH EVENTS

449

449
Germanic tribes invade Britain

597
St. Augustine, missionary, establishes monastery in Canterbury

664
Synod of Whitby unites British Christian Church with Roman Catholic Church

750

787
Danish invasions begin

◀ **871**
Alfred the Great's rule begins

886
Danelaw is established in northeast England

1066
William the Conqueror invades England

1086
Domesday Book, the first official record of property owners in England, is created

1170
Thomas à Becket, Archbishop of Canterbury, is murdered

WORLD EVENTS

449

476
The western Roman Empire falls

537
Emperor Justinian completes cathedral of Hagia Sophia in Constantinople

c. 570
Muhammad, the founder of Islam, is born in Mecca

683
Empress Wu becomes the first woman to rule China

Reliquary of Charlemagne

750

786
Harun al-Rashid becomes ruler of Muslim Empire

◀ **800**
Charlemagne is crowned Holy Roman Emperor

1000
Leif Eriksson sails to North America from Greenland

1099
First Crusade captures Jerusalem

1192
Yoritomo becomes first *shogun*, or military ruler, of Japan

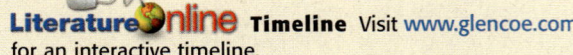

Literature Online Timeline Visit www.glencoe.com for an interactive timeline.

Marco Polo's caravan, from *The Catalan Atlas*, 1375

1200　　　　　　　　　　　　　　　**1400**

c. 1300
Earliest ballads are composed

Pilgrim Badge c. 1300–1350

1375
First part of *Sir Gawain and the Green Knight* is completed

c. 1386
William Langland writes the allegorical poem *Piers Plowman*, a protest on behalf of the common people

 c. 1387
Geoffrey Chaucer begins the *Canterbury Tales*

1420s
Margery Kempe dictates her autobiography

1469
Sir Thomas Malory writes *Le Morte d'Arthur*

1400

1215
King John signs the Magna Carta

1295
First Parliament begins

1337
Hundred Years' War, a series of wars between England and France, begins

1349
The Black Death sweeps through England

1381
The Peasants' Revolt is suppressed

1455
A series of civil wars between the House of York and the House of Lancaster, called "Wars of the Roses," begins

Magna Carta

1200

1258
Mongols capture Baghdad

1295
Marco Polo returns to Venice from China

1310–1314
Dante begins writing *Divine Comedy*

1325
Tenochtitlán, the capital of the Aztec Empire, is completed in Mexico

1312
Mansa Musa rules Mali Empire in Africa

▲ **1431**
Joan of Arc is burned at the stake in France during the Hundred Years' War

1455
The Gutenberg Bible is printed from movable type in Germany

Reading Check

Analyzing Graphic Information From 449 to 1066, which warriors invaded Britain?

By the Numbers

MEDIEVAL WEALTH

The household goods of a wealthy thirteenth-century butcher in the English town of Colchester included the following:

- one trestle table (with boards stored in a corner except at mealtimes)
- probably some settles, or stools
- two silver spoons
- one cup
- one tablecloth and two towels
- one brass cauldron
- one brass dish
- one trivet, or three-legged stand
- one iron candlestick
- one washing-basin and pitcher
- two beds
- two gowns
- one cloak
- two barrels

PEASANT'S WHEEL OF LIFE

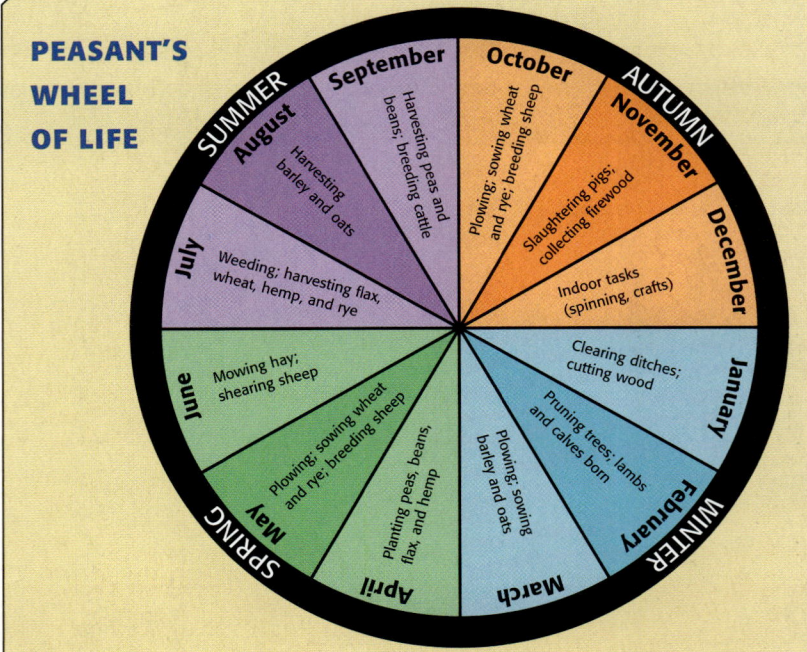

In the Middle Ages, the life of English peasants was a cycle of recurring labor. The seasons largely determined peasant activities, with each season bringing new tasks. Harvest time in August and September was especially laborious. A good harvest of grains for making bread and brewing ale was crucial to survival in the winter months.

WERGILD

In Anglo-Saxon society, blood feuds avenged wrongdoings, but claimed many lives. To avoid revenge from the slain man's kin, one could pay them *wergild,* or "man-price," a sum of money that reflected the deceased's importance. In Wessex, a fixed scale was observed:

- nobleman or member of the warrior class: 1200 shillings
- free peasant: 200 shillings

DOMESDAY BOOK

Commissioned in 1085 by William the Conqueror, the first draft of the Domesday Book contained census-type records for 13,418 English estates for tax purposes. William later imposed Danegeld, a tax to pay for defense against Viking invasions.

THE BLACK DEATH

During the first wave of the plague in 1349, approximately 300 people died each day within a square mile in London. Before the Black Death had run its course, it ravaged Europe, killing between one-third and one-half of the population.

PERCENTAGE OF LAND OWNED IN ENGLAND IN THE ELEVENTH CENTURY, According to the Domesday Book

- King and his family   17%
- Barons, Lords, and Church Tenants   54%*

- Bishops and Abbots   26%

* About a dozen barons controlled a quarter of the land in England.

Being There

Britain is the largest of a group of islands off the northwest coast of Europe. The fertile soil and mild climate of Britain's southern lowlands attracted a series of invaders, who established small kingdoms that eventually merged into a single nation. Some of the displaced native peoples fled west and north to the highlands of Wales and Scotland.

July: harvest, sowing, c. 16th century. British Library, London.

Three Men Digging and Sowing, c. 1025–1050. Anglo-Saxon Calendar. British Library, London.

June: Jousting and a game with hobby horses, c. 1520–30. From the workshop of Simon Bening. British Library, London

Literature Online **Maps in Motion** Visit www.glencoe.com for an interactive map.

Reading Check

Analyzing Graphic Information:

1. On the basis of *wergild,* how valuable was a nobleman in comparison to a free peasant?

2. In which months of the year did medieval peasants harvest crops?

3. Where were most of the towns located in medieval England?

The Anglo-Saxon Period and the Middle Ages

449–1485

Historical, Social, and Cultural Forces

The Anglo-Saxons

In A.D. 43 the Romans conquered the Celtic tribes of southern Britain and introduced a standard of living more advanced than any the Celtic tribes had ever known. Early in the fifth century, however, when the Roman Empire began to fall, the Roman legions left Britain to defend Rome, and the Britons became easy prey to invaders. In 449 the Angles, Saxons, and Jutes—Germanic tribes collectively referred to as "Anglo-Saxons"—began invading Britain's eastern shores.

Battle Between Britons and the Invaders. From *Life, Passion and Miracles of St. Edmund, King and Martyr.* England, c. 1130. The Pierpont Morgan Library, New York.

The Britons—according to legends, led by a king named Arthur—won a few victories against the invaders. Gradually, however, the Anglo-Saxon warriors, clothed in animal skins and wielding spears, drove the Britons into the mountains and took the land for their own. It was a bloody beginning for the nation that would come to be known as England.

These Germanic invaders took over the southeastern part of the island and called it "Angle-land." They formed small tribal kingdoms, supported themselves through farming and hunting, and believed in many different gods. Only toward the end of the seventh century, when Christianity was firmly established, did a unified civilization emerge.

Vikings and Normans

During the eighth and ninth centuries, other Germanic tribes attacked Britain. Danes and Norsemen took to the seas in an attempt to win Britain by force. By the middle of the ninth century, most of England had fallen to the invaders. However, the tide turned in 878 when Alfred, the Saxon king of Wessex, led his warriors to victory over the Danes in the Battle of Edington. Alfred went on to capture London and, eventually, much of England. For these and other feats, Alfred was called "the Great." During the next century, Alfred's son and grandson won back all of England from the Danes, and at last the country was at peace.

These peaceful times, however, were short-lived. When King Edward died in 1066, William, Duke of Normandy (a region in northwest France also settled by the Vikings), laid claim to the English throne. When the English council of elders chose Harold II as king, William retaliated by attacking and defeating the Anglo-Saxons at the Battle of Hastings. He emerged as the first Norman king of England, ending the Anglo-Saxon era.

Feudal England

Following the Norman Conquest, the Anglo-Saxons became the subjects of the Norman aristocracy. William the Conqueror introduced to England the continental social, economic, and political system called *feudalism*. Under that system, land (the real wealth of the nation) was divided among noble overlords, or barons. Lesser lords, called knights, pledged their wealth and services to the overlords, who, in return, provided use of the land. At the lowest end of the social scale were the serfs, peasants pledged to the lord of the manor and bound to the land.

> *"To no one will we sell, to no one deny or delay right or justice."*
>
> —King John, from *Magna Carta*

Feudal relationships sometimes erupted in heated conflicts. In the early 1200s, King John, needing money for military campaigns, imposed heavy financial burdens on his barons without consulting them. In 1215 a group of those barons forced the unpopular King John to agree to a Great Charter, or the Magna Carta. By this document, he agreed not to raise taxes without the consent of the barons. Many see in this curtailment of royal power the beginning of constitutional government in England, including the right to trial by jury.

War and Plague

The fourteenth century was a dark time in British history. Beginning in 1337, the English and French waged a series of wars for control of lands in France. Known as the Hundred Years' War, that conflict drained England financially. However, the ensuing break with France helped England develop a national identity independent of French influence.

In the midst of the Hundred Years' War, an epidemic called the Black Death swept through Europe. This plague first struck England in 1348, with new outbreaks occurring during the next decades. The Black Death eventually killed almost a third of England's people. This massive loss of life eroded the feudal system. Still, towns and cities continued to grow. The resulting shift in power from the landed aristocracy to an urban middle class set the stage for a new era: the Renaissance.

PREVIEW **Big Ideas** **of the Anglo-Saxon Period and the Middle Ages**

1 The Epic Warrior

Anglo-Saxon culture expressed a brooding vision of a failing human world beset by dark forces. Against these grim conditions emerged the epic warrior, motivated by the desire for undying fame.

See pages 12–13.

2 The Power of Faith

The Christian church shaped the culture of medieval England, influencing all aspects of life: politics, warfare, education, business, art, literature, folkways, and recreation.

See pages 14–15.

3 The World of Romance

In medieval England, the upper classes enjoyed romantic tales about legendary heroes such as King Arthur and his knights. The popular ballad was the imaginative literature of the common people.

See pages 16–17.

A complex society such as that in the modern United States offers a wide range of heroic types. The Anglo-Saxons, however, recognized only a single heroic type: the warrior, who embodied the qualities valued by the tribes who settled on Britain's shores. Courage was an important virtue because, by demonstrating courage, a warrior could achieve fame and immortality. Loyalty to one's tribal lord was also important, as was wisdom in making decisions and guiding others. Physical strength was crucial to overcoming one's enemies.

In a mostly illiterate society, such songs served as literary entertainment. To the warriors who listened to them, these heroic songs also provided models to emulate and a goal to pursue: namely, to win fame and be remembered after death for one's deeds.

> "He who earns praise / Has under heaven the greatest glory."
>
> —Widsith, the Minstrel

A Warrior Society

For the early Anglo-Saxons, warfare was a way of life; their tribal organization, values, and beliefs—as well as their poetry—reflected that reality. Tribes consisted of warrior families led by a nobleman who, in turn, served a chief or overlord. An Anglo-Saxon ruler was primarily a warlord who protected his people from attacks and led his followers on expeditions. The warlord and his followers formed a close-knit group known as a *comitatus*. Warlords rewarded the bravest of their followers with treasure. (One of the most common epithets for a lord or ruler was "ring-giver.") In return, warriors showed absolute loyalty to their leader. The Roman historian Tacitus described the fierce loyalty of the Germanic warriors from whom the Anglo-Saxons were descended: "On the field of battle it is a disgrace to a chief to be surpassed in courage by his followers, and to the followers not to equal the courage of their chief. And to leave a battle alive after their chief has fallen means lifelong infamy and shame."

Oral Literature

The Anglo-Saxons brought their Germanic language, religion, culture, and oral literary traditions to Britain. Anglo-Saxon storytellers created heroic songs describing warriors' great deeds and celebrating qualities such as strength, courage, and loyalty, which they believed could save the people from the evils that threatened them. Minstrels known as *scops* (shōps) performed these songs during the banquets held at the mead-halls of Anglo-Saxon rulers. (Mead is an alcoholic beverage made from fermented honey.)

Germanic and Christian Traditions

The two most important influences on Anglo-Saxon, or Old English, literature were the Germanic tradition and the Christian religion. Anglo-Saxon literary tradition was deeply rooted in the dark, heroic tales of Germanic mythology, which depict a tragic world in which even the gods ultimately perish. Since Germanic religious beliefs held no promise of an afterlife, the warrior's primary goal was to achieve fame in this life. The coming of Christianity, with its omnipotent God and promise of eternal life, did not so much replace this stark Germanic mythology as coexist with it. In works such as *Beowulf* (see pages 24–50), the poet combines both Germanic and Christian elements. For example, Grendel is described as both a troll-like creature and a descendant of Cain, the first biblical murderer.

Importance of *Wyrd*

Because of constant intertribal warfare and the primitive state of science and medicine, life in early Anglo-Saxon times was strife-ridden and brief. As a result, the early Anglo-Saxons believed that fate, which they called *wyrd*, controlled human destiny and that one's ultimate and inescapable fate was death. The hero's only appropriate response was to face this somber destiny with courage. Beowulf's last words express the Germanic view of wyrd: "Fate has swept our race away, / Taken warriors in their strength and led them / To the death that was waiting. And now I follow them."

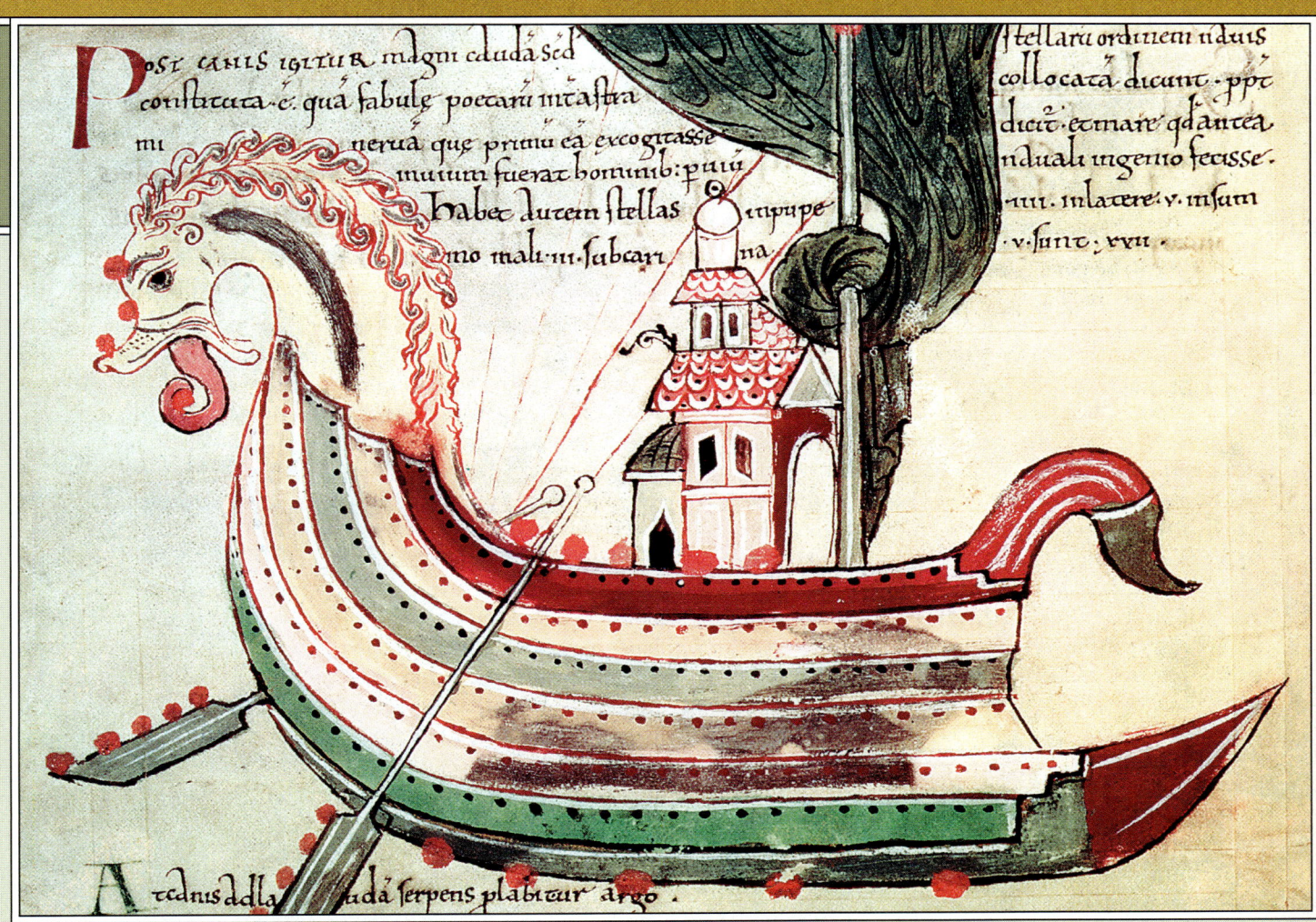

A Dragon Ship from a manuscript, c. 10th century. Anglo-Saxon. Vellum. British Museum, London.

In 991 Viking raiders defeated an Anglo-Saxon force, killing its leader and many of his followers. In a heroic song written a few years later, a poet commemorated the Anglo-Saxon force's heroic last stand.

from *The Battle of Maldon*

The strife was stern, warriors were steadfast,
Bold in battle; fighters fell
Weary with wounds. Death covered earth.
Oswold and Ealdwald all the while,
Both the brothers, marshalled their men;
Bade friend and kinsmen endure in combat
And never weaken, but wield the sword.
Byrhtwold encouraged them, brandishing buckler,
Aged companion shaking ash-spear;
Stout were the words he spoke to his men:
"Heart must be braver, courage the bolder,

Mood the stouter as our strength grows less!
Here on the ground my good lord lies
Gory with wounds. Always will he regret it
Who now from this battle thinks to turn back.
I am old in years; I will never yield,
But here at the last beside my lord,
By the leader I love I think to lie."

Reading Check

Interpreting Which values of the Anglo-Saxons does this passage from *The Battle of Maldon* reflect?

It has been observed that a community's tallest buildings reveal its dominant values. On the basis of this standard, modern skyscrapers strikingly indicate the importance of commercial values in U.S. society. By contrast, in medieval English cities, the tallest buildings were towering stone cathedrals, which symbolized the importance of the Roman Catholic Church in the life of the people. The first English cathedral was built in Canterbury between 1070 and 1180, beginning a period of more than four hundred years of cathedral-building. These awesome and towering cathedrals were artistic masterpieces created by the most talented architects, masons, artists, and craftspeople of the time to celebrate the glory of God.

Christianizing England

In 596 Pope Gregory I sent missionaries to convert the Anglo-Saxons to Christianity. By the year 650, most of England was Christian in name, though many people retained some pagan beliefs and traditions. Meanwhile, Celtic monks from Ireland had brought Christianity to other parts of England, establishing England's first monastery on the island of Lindisfarne off its coast. With Christianity came the glimmerings of education and culture. By the eighth century, Anglo-Saxon culture reached its peak in the Northumbrian monasteries that produced decorated books, known as illuminated manuscripts. Some of them, including the Book of Durrow and the Lindisfarne Gospels, rank among the most beautiful works of art in the Middle Ages.

Monasteries

As Christianity spread throughout Anglo-Saxon England, some men and women chose to dedicate their lives to work and prayer. These men (known as monks) and women (known as nuns) joined religious orders, which varied greatly in their rules for communal living. Some religious orders were very strict, demanding poverty, fasting, absolute obedience, and manual labor.

English monks established libraries and schools within their monasteries, where they emphasized the importance of the written word—especially of the Bible. Working as scribes, Anglo-Saxon monks copied manuscripts by hand, thereby preserving much of the classical and Anglo-Saxon literature that survives today. The Venerable Bede and other monks also composed their own scholarly literature, which represents the first written literature in England. The earliest important work of this kind was Bede's *Ecclesiastical History of the English People* (see page 82), which offers a remarkably complete picture of early Anglo-Saxon life and times. However, like most monastic scholars of the era, Bede composed his *History* in Latin, the language of church scholarship. It was Alfred the Great, the era's most important political leader, who first encouraged the widespread use of Old English in written literature. Alfred's greatest achievement in this regard was *The Anglo-Saxon Chronicle*, an Old English history in prose and poetry.

Pilgrimages

One way to express religious devotion in the Middle Ages was to undertake a pilgrimage, or journey, to a sacred site. If English pilgrims could not go on pilgrimages to Jerusalem, Rome, or the famous shrine at Santiago de Compostela in Spain, they could still visit various holy sites in their own country. One of the most important destinations for English pilgrims was Canterbury Cathedral, where in 1170 Archbishop Thomas à Becket had been slain. The pilgrims described in Chaucer's *Canterbury Tales* (see page 92) are journeying to this holy site to seek blessings from the martyred archbishop.

Religious Drama

In a time when few people could read, the church used sermons, stained-glass windows, and popular entertainment to teach the truths and historical events of religion. English drama developed from enactments of biblical stories during church services on feast days such as Palm Sunday and Easter. Eventually, these dramatic scenes moved from the cathedral to the village green and finally to pageant wagons. The church would often have common people, such as members of a bakers' guild, dress up like characters in the Old and the New Testaments.

In several cities in England, these plays were well attended, and as a result complete cycles developed, beginning with the creation of the world and concluding with the last judgment. These plays were known as **mystery plays** because they were performed by the guilds (at that time *mystery* meant "trade" or "craft"). Less realistic dramas called **morality plays** were also popular. Featuring allegorical figures representing good, evil, and other abstract qualities, these plays presented moral lessons.

The following passage comes from a cycle of mystery plays performed in the city of York.

from *The Creation of Adam and Eve*

GOD: In paradise shall ye sam won;   **sam won:** together dwell
Of earthly thing get ye no need.
Ill and good both shall ye con;   **con:** know
I shall you learn your life to lead.

ADAM: Ah, Lord since we shall do no thing
But lof thee for thy great goodness,   **lof:** love
We shall obey to thy bidding,
And fulfil it both more and less.

EVE: His sign since he has on us set
Before all other thing, certain,
Him for to lof we shall not let,   **let:** stop
And worship him with might and main.

GOD: At heaven and earth first I began,
And six days wrought ere I would rest;
My work is ended now at man:
All likes me well, but this the best.

Stained glass window panel, Canterbury Cathedral, 12th century. Panel in the west window depicts Adam digging. Canterbury Cathedral, UK.

Reading Check

Analyzing Cause and Effect How did the lack of literacy in the Middle Ages indirectly lead to the emergence of drama in England?

The World of Romance

For many people today, the knight in shining armor is emblematic of the Middle Ages. This is partly because of the enduring popularity of medieval romances. Featuring brave knights courting lovely maidens, noble women wearing pointed headdresses, castles containing moats and drawbridges, minstrels wandering, and common folk enjoying tournaments and pageantry, the romance created striking, albeit mostly imaginary, portraits of medieval life.

The Knight

Constant warfare characterized life in the Middle Ages, with troops of heavily armed warriors, or knights, fighting one another for supremacy. These knights enjoyed great social prestige and formed the nucleus of the feudal aristocracy, which was based on the relationship between lords and vassals. In exchange for tracts of land, vassals pledged to fulfill various obligations to their lords, the foremost of which was military service.

Trained as warriors but with few other responsibilities, knights had little to do but fight. When not engaged in actual warfare, knights provided sport and entertainment for others by participating in showy tournaments, which gave them the opportunity to practice fighting and improve their skills. However, even these mock battles were dangerous and sometimes fatal. By 1500 the nature of jousting changed to encourage a safer form of entertainment. The church also attempted to regulate knightly violence by outlawing fighting on Sundays and holidays.

Chivalry and Courtly Love

In the eleventh and twelfth centuries, under the influence of the church, an ideal of civilized behavior, called chivalry, gradually took hold among the nobility of Europe. The term *chivalry* derives from the French word *chevalier,* meaning "horseman." Chivalry referred to the code of ethics that knights were obliged to uphold. According to that code, knights strove to be honorable, generous, brave, skillful in battle, respectful to women, and protective of widows and orphans. This romantic attitude would affect much of the literature of the period, especially the songs and stories. Although only partly successful, the code of chivalry did help to civilize the conduct of knights and to elevate the status of women.

Closely allied to the code of chivalry, courtly love described the relationship between a knight and a courtly lady, who was usually married to someone else. In medieval times, upper-class marriage was rarely a love match between a man and a woman. It was instead a commercial arrangement involving an exchange of property or goods or an alliance of families. However, courtly love, as popularized in the songs and poems of the troubadours in southern France, proclaimed the transcendent value of passionate love and the all-consuming devotion of a knight toward his lady—the kind of relationship, for example, shared by Sir Lancelot and Guinevere in the Arthurian legends.

> *"Whither has not flying fame spread and familiarized the name of Arthur the Briton, even as far as the empire of Christendom extends?"*
>
> —Alain de Lille

The Rise of Romance

Originating in France in the 1100s, the romance became the most popular literary genre in medieval England. Most romances describe the adventures of legendary knights and celebrate chivalry and courtly love. Working in both verse and prose, many English writers produced romances about the legendary King Arthur and his knights of the Round Table. The most highly regarded verse romance in English is *Sir Gawain and the Green Knight*, written in the 1300s by an unidentified poet. It blends Celtic themes (such as elfland) and the Anglo-Saxon poetic device of alliteration (which was old-fashioned by this time)

King Arthur with a shield, from *A Chronicle of England,* c. 1300–1325. British Library, London.

from *Le Morte d'Arthur*
by Sir Thomas Malory

So [Arthur and Merlin] rode till they came to a lake, the which was a fair water and broad, and in the midst of the lake Arthur was ware of an arm clothed in white samite, that held a fair sword in that hand. Lo! said Merlin, yonder is that sword that I spake of. With that they saw a damosel going upon the lake. What damosel is that? said Arthur. That is the Lady of the Lake, said Merlin; and within that lake is a rock, and therein is as fair a place as any on earth, and richly beseen; and this damosel will come to you anon, and then speak ye fair to her that she will give you that sword. Anon withal came the damosel unto Arthur, and saluted him, and he her again. Damosel, said Arthur, what sword is that, that yonder the arm holdeth above the water? I would it were mine, for I have no sword. Sir Arthur, king, said the damosel, that sword is mine, and if ye will give me a gift when I ask it you, ye shall have it. By my faith, said Arthur, I will give you what gift ye will ask. Well! said the damosel, go ye into yonder barge, and row yourself to the sword, and take it and the scabbard with you, and I will ask my gift when I see my time. So Sir Arthur and Merlin alit and tied their horses to two trees, and so they went into the ship, and when they came to the sword that the hand held, Sir Arthur took it up by the handles, and took it with him, and the arm and the hand went under the water.

in a seriocomic tale of a quest undertaken by King Arthur's finest knight. Around 1470, as the Middle Ages were waning, Sir Thomas Malory retold the entire cycle of Arthurian legends in *Le Morte d'Arthur* ("The Death of Arthur"), a superb work of Middle English prose.

Reading Check

Comparing and Contrasting How would you compare medieval knights with Anglo-Saxon warriors?

Wrap-Up

Why It Matters

The centuries between the Anglo-Saxon invasions and the end of the Hundred Years' War witnessed many watershed events in British history. The Anglo-Saxon invasion brought the Germanic traditions that influenced British culture and society. It also introduced the Germanic language, many words of which still form the basic vocabulary of English-speakers throughout the world.

The Norman Conquest brought French language, culture, and institutions that profoundly affected society in medieval England. By establishing basic political rights, the Magna Carta became the foundation of law and government first in Great Britain and later in the United States.

The Romantic movement of the late 1800s and early 1900s found one of its primary sources of inspiration in medieval romances. One category of romance literature—the legends of King Arthur—remains popular to this day.

 Literature Online **Big Ideas** Link to Web resources to further explore the Big Ideas at www.glencoe.com.

Cultural Links

→ The Anglo-Saxon epic *Beowulf* inspired the novel *Grendel*, by the modern American writer John Gardner, which tells the story from the monster's point of view.

→ Geoffrey Chaucer's *Canterbury Tales* is an example of a literary form used worldwide: a collection of tales within a frame story. Other notable examples of frame tales include the *Metamorphoses* by Ovid, and *The Arabian Nights*.

→ Based on earlier versions of the Arthurian legend, Sir Thomas Malory's *Le Morte d'Arthur*, in turn, inspired Alfred, Lord Tennyson's *The Idylls of the King* and T. H. White's *The Once and Future King*.

 **THREE-TAB BOOK**

You might try using this study organizer to keep track of the big ideas in this unit.

Connect to Today → Use what you have learned about the period to do one of these activities.

1. Speaking/Listening Translations of Old English and Middle English works, such as *Beowulf* and *Sir Gawain and the Green Knight,* vary considerably. Working with other students, present an oral reading of three or four translations of the same passage from either of these works. Then discuss how the translations differ in emphasis and literary quality.

2. Visual Literacy Research one of the illuminated manuscripts created in medieval monasteries, such as the Book of Kells. Then create a visual display for your class, presenting photocopies of some of the most remarkable pages. Include explanations of how the manuscript was produced and descriptions of its stylistic features.

OBJECTIVES
- Present an oral reading.
- Create a visual display.

Literature Online **Study Central** Visit www.glencoe.com and click on Study Central to review the Anglo-Saxon Period and the Middle Ages.

Part 1

The Epic Warrior

Detail of the Gundestrup cauldron, c. 100 B.C. Silver. National Museum, Copenhagen, Denmark.

"Fate often spares the undoomed warrior if his courage holds good."

—*Beowulf*

The Epic and the Epic Hero

> "*That mighty protector of men
> Meant to hold the monster till its life
> Leaped out . . .*"
>
> —from *Beowulf*

Peopple are living in fear as an evil force threatens to destroy the land. Then a superhero appears. Brave, strong, and good, the hero defeats the evil force and saves the land and its people. You know this story well. It is one of the most widely told stories in literature as well as one of the oldest. In times past, the deeds of the superhero were told in the form of an **epic**—a long narrative poem that recounts, in formal language, the exploits of a larger-than-life hero. Ancient epic poets and their audiences viewed the epic as the early history of their people.

The earliest epics date back to a time when most people were illiterate. Recited by poets, probably with musical accompaniment, these epics were the movies of their day. Audiences were enthralled by monsters, perilous journeys, and fierce battles. Some of the early epics were eventually written down. Of most, we have only fragments, but a few complete epics have survived. Historians and anthropologists look at epics as cultural records of the societies that produced them.

"I will proclaim to the world the deeds of Gilgamesh."

—*The Epic of Gilgamesh*

The epic is found in cultures around the world, thus indicating the timeless and universal human need to transmit legends from one generation to another. The earliest epic is the *Epic of Gilgamesh* (see pages 56–57), composed by the Sumerians in one of the ancient languages of Mesopotamia (present-day Iraq). It tells of the great deeds of Gilgamesh, a legendary king who had ruled hundreds of years earlier. Centuries later, the ancient Greeks had their epics:

the *Iliad* and the *Odyssey*. The Spanish had *The Song of El Cid*; the French, *The Song of Roland*; and the Anglo-Saxons, *Beowulf*. Modern heroes such as Superman and Luke Skywalker continue the epic tradition today.

Tyr, sky-god of the Germanic tribes, with chained animal, 6th century. Bronze. Torslunda parish, Oland, Sweden. Statens Historiska Museet, Stockholm.

Epic Form

More than a thousand years after *Gilgamesh*, the ancient Greek poet Homer established the standard features of the epic form in Western literature with the *Iliad* and the *Odyssey*. These features include:

- poetic lines that have regular meter and rhythm and formal, elevated, or even lofty language
- main characters who have heroic or superhuman qualities
- gods or godlike beings who intervene in the events
- action on a huge scale, often involving the fates of entire peoples
- stories that begin *in medias res* (Latin for "in the middle of things") or at a critical point in the action

The classical Greek epics also established the use of certain literary devices. One of these is the **epithet,** a word or brief phrase often used to characterize a particular person, place, or thing. For example, the goddess Athena is "gray-eyed" and the sea is "wine-dark." Standardized comparisons known as **kennings** perform a similar function in the Anglo-Saxon epic *Beowulf*. For example, a king is a "ring-giver" and the sea is the "whale-road." Both epithets and kennings helped epic poets mold their ideas to their poetic forms.

The Epic Hero

The epic hero is a man—women take subordinate roles in traditional epics—of high social status whose fate affects the destiny of his people. Epic plots typically involve supernatural events, long periods of time, distant journeys, and life-and-death struggles between good and evil. Through physical strength, skill as a warrior, nobility of character, and quick wits, the epic hero almost always defeats his enemies, be they human or demonic. The hero is rarely modest, and boasting is almost a ritual in epics.

The epic hero embodies the ideals and values of his people. Odysseus, for example, displays the Greek ideal *arête*, or all-around excellence. He is a great warrior, a cunning leader, a clever speaker, and highly skilled at everything from sailing to plowing. Rooted in ancient Germanic tradition, the values celebrated in *Beowulf* include courage, endurance, and loyalty. The last word of the poem, which describes Beowulf as "most eager for fame," touches on one of the most universal and enduring characteristics of heroes, from Gilgamesh to today's comic book and movie heroes.

Grendel, 1908 from *Brave Beowulf*. British Library, London.

Literature Online **Literary History** For more about the epic and epic heroes, go to www.glencoe.com.

RESPONDING AND THINKING CRITICALLY

1. In your opinion, what are today's epics? How do modern audiences differ from ancient ones in their responses to epics?

2. Identify three characteristics that we might expect today's epic heroes to exhibit.

3. Which characteristics of the traditional epic hero might be difficult for readers today to accept?

4. How are epithets and kennings similar and different?

OBJECTIVES
- Analyze the epic and the epic hero.
- Connect to historical context of literature.

from *Beowulf*

MEET THE *BEOWULF*-POET

It is a curious fact that some of the world's greatest literature has come to us from an unknown hand. *Beowulf* ranks high among such literature. It is the oldest of the surviving national epics produced in Western Europe after the fall of Rome. It is one of Europe's first literary works to be composed in the vernacular, or the language of the people, rather than in Latin, the language of church scholarship. Like other national epics—Spain's *The Song of El Cid* and France's *Song of Roland*, for example—*Beowulf* relates the deeds of a great national hero. That hero arose from the Anglo-Saxons' ancestral home on the European mainland where legends about him were part of the oral tradition of the Germanic tribes.

> *"The newly Christian understanding of the world which operates in the poet's designing mind displaces him from his imaginative at-homeness in the world of his poem—a pagan Germanic society governed by a heroic code of honor."*
>
> —Seamus Heaney

Anglo-Saxon Poet Beginning in the 400s, those Germanic tribes, later known collectively as the Anglo-Saxons, invaded and settled the territory that later would become known as England. They brought their songs and legends about heroes with them, passed down from one *scop* (shōp), or oral poet, to another and reshaped with each performance. In the early eighth century, scholars believe, an Anglo-Saxon poet thoroughly versed in the scops' stock of legends, historical accounts, and poetic devices composed *Beowulf*. By that time, the Anglo-Saxons had converted to Christianity, and the Vikings had not yet begun their invasions in England. The *Beowulf*-poet was clearly a Christian, for his poem contains references to the Bible and many expressions of a deep religious faith. He was also well educated, displaying knowledge of Greek and Roman mythology and familiarity with the *Aeneid*, the great Latin epic by the ancient Roman poet Virgil.

It is uncertain whether the *Beowulf*-poet composed the poem orally and later transcribed it, or wrote it down in the form in which we now have it. But at some time the poem was written down, and Christian scribes made a copy of it in the late tenth century. It is their manuscript that has survived over the years, despite various misadventures, including a fire in 1731 that destroyed some of the lines. Today, the *Beowulf* manuscript, which consists of about 3,200 lines, is carefully preserved in the British Library in London.

In his groundbreaking essay "*Beowulf*: The Monsters and the Critics," J. R. R. Tolkien stated that the *Beowulf*-poet presented a vision of the past, "pagan but noble and fraught with a deep significance—a past that itself had depth and reached back into a dark antiquity of sorrow." By vividly imagining that pagan past, the *Beowulf*-poet created an inspiring tale of courage—and the first great heroic poem in the English language.

Literature Online **Author Search** For more about the *Beowulf*-poet, go to www.glencoe.com.

Connecting to the Epic

In *Beowulf,* the poet describes the exploits of a larger-than-life hero. As you read, think about these questions:

- Who are some heroes or role models in society today?
- What qualities do these heroes have in common?

Building Background

Imagine a time when war bands from northern Europe regularly raided one another's shores to loot and burn settlements; when great warriors feasted, drank, and bragged of their bloody conquests in huge banquet halls; when kings bestowed riches upon their bravest warriors to retain their allegiance; and when people believed in monsters and dragons. That time was the sixth century—the period in which *Beowulf* is set.

The story of *Beowulf* is not set in England, however. The story takes place in Scandinavia, and it involves the Geats (gēts), a tribe from southern Sweden, and the Danes, a tribe from Denmark.

Setting Purposes for Reading

Big Idea The Epic Warrior

In the primitive world of the early Anglo-Saxons, the hero held a place of great importance. As you read, consider the heroic qualities that Beowulf displays.

Literary Element Conflict

Conflict is the central struggle between two opposing forces in a story or drama. An **external conflict** exists when a character struggles against some outside force, such as another person or nature. An **internal conflict** is a struggle within the mind of a character. As you read *Beowulf,* notice the conflicts in which the hero is involved.

- See Literary Terms Handbook, p. R4.

Literature Online Interactive Literary Elements Handbook To review or learn more about the literary elements, go to www.glencoe.com.

Reading Strategy Identifying Sequence

Identifying sequence is finding the logical order of ideas or events in a text. In *Beowulf,* the poet retells three principal episodes in the hero's life. As you read, identify the sequence of events in each episode.

Reading Tip: Taking Notes Use a graphic organizer like the one started below to record the order of events in each episode.

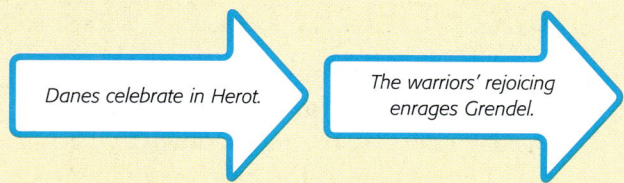

Danes celebrate in Herot. → The warriors' rejoicing enrages Grendel. →

Vocabulary

lament (lə ment′) *n.* expression of sorrow; song or literary composition that mourns a loss or death; p. 25 *The mother's lament for her child brought tears to my eyes.*

forged (fôrjd) *adj.* formed or shaped, often with blows or pressure after heating; p. 25 *By hammering and bending the white hot iron, the blacksmith forged an axle.*

shroud (shroud) *n.* burial cloth; p. 30 *The bodies of the slain were wrapped in shrouds.*

infamous (in′ fə məs) *adj.* having a bad reputation; notorious; p. 31 *The pirate was infamous for his brutal treatment of prisoners.*

writhing (rīth′ ing) *adj.* twisting, as in pain; p. 31 *Whining and writhing, the wounded dog rolled its head from side to side.*

Vocabulary Tip: Analogies An analogy is a type of comparison that is based on the relationships between things or ideas.

OBJECTIVES
In studying this selection, you will focus on the following:
- relating literature to historical periods
- analyzing conflict
- identifying sequence

from BEOWULF

Translated by Burton Raffel

GRENDEL ATTACKS THE DANES

A powerful monster, living down
In the darkness, growled in pain, impatient
As day after day the music rang
Loud in that hall,° the harp's rejoicing
5 Call and the poet's clear songs, sung
Of the ancient beginnings of us all, recalling
The Almighty making the earth, shaping
These beautiful plains marked off by oceans,
Then proudly setting the sun and moon
10 To glow across the land and light it;
The corners of the earth were made lovely with trees
And leaves, made quick with life, with each
Of the nations who now move on its face. And then
As now warriors sang of their pleasure:
15 So Hrothgar's men lived happy in his hall
Till the monster stirred, that demon, that fiend,
Grendel, who haunted the moors, the wild
Marshes, and made his home in a hell
Not hell but earth. He was spawned° in that slime,
20 Conceived by a pair of those monsters born
Of Cain,° murderous creatures banished
By God, punished forever for the crime
Of Abel's death. The Almighty drove
Those demons out, and their exile was bitter,
25 Shut away from men; they split
Into a thousand forms of evil—spirits
And fiends, goblins, monsters, giants,
A brood forever opposing the Lord's
Will, and again and again defeated.

30 Then, when darkness had dropped, Grendel
Went up to Herot, wondering what the warriors
Would do in that hall when their drinking was done.
He found them sprawled in sleep, suspecting
Nothing, their dreams undisturbed. The monster's
35 Thoughts were as quick as his greed or his claws:

4 hall: The Danish King Hrothgar's mead hall, Herot.

19 spawned: born. Usually, *spawned* refers to the production of young by fish, amphibians, or other water-dwelling creatures.
21 Cain: According to the Bible (Genesis 4:8), *Cain,* the eldest son of Adam and Eve, murdered his brother, Abel.

He slipped through the door and there in the silence
Snatched up thirty men, smashed them
Unknowing in their beds and ran out with their bodies,
The blood dripping behind him, back
40 To his lair,° delighted with his night's slaughter.
    At daybreak, with the sun's first light, they saw
How well he had worked, and in that gray morning
Broke their long feast with tears and **laments**
For the dead. Hrothgar, their lord, sat joyless
45 In Herot, a mighty prince mourning
The fate of his lost friends and companions,
Knowing by its tracks that some demon had torn
His followers apart. He wept, fearing
The beginning might not be the end. And that night
50 Grendel came again, so set
On murder that no crime could ever be enough,
No savage assault quench his lust
For evil. Then each warrior tried
To escape him, searched for rest in different
55 Beds, as far from Herot as they could find,
Seeing how Grendel hunted when they slept.
Distance was safety; the only survivors
Were those who fled him. Hate had triumphed.
    So Grendel ruled, fought with the righteous,
60 One against many, and won; so Herot
Stood empty, and stayed deserted for years,
Twelve winters of grief for Hrothgar, king
Of the Danes, sorrow heaped at his door
By hell-**forged** hands. His misery leaped
65 The seas, was told and sung in all
Men's ears: how Grendel's hatred began,
How the monster relished his savage war
On the Danes, keeping the bloody feud
Alive, seeking no peace, offering
70 No truce, accepting no settlement, no price
In gold or land, and paying the living
For one crime only with another. No one
Waited for reparation° from his plundering claws:

40 **lair:** den of a wild animal.

Viking pendants from Sweden

73 **reparation:** payment or action done to make amends for a wrong or an injury.

Literary Element **Conflict** *What does the conflict between the Danes and Grendel symbolize?*

Reading Strategy **Identifying Sequence** *By the time Hrothgar's grief is told and sung, what events have occurred in the poem? List them in order.*

Vocabulary

lament (lə ment′) *n.* expression of sorrow; song or literary composition that mourns a loss or death
forged (fôrjd) *adj.* formed or shaped, often with blows or pressure after heating

That shadow of death hunted in the darkness,
75 Stalked Hrothgar's warriors, old
And young, lying in waiting, hidden
In mist, invisibly following them from the edge
Of the marsh, always there, unseen.
   So mankind's enemy continued his crimes,
80 Killing as often as he could, coming
Alone, bloodthirsty and horrible. Though he lived
In Herot, when the night hid him, he never
Dared to touch king Hrothgar's glorious
Throne, protected by God.

THE COMING OF BEOWULF

85   So the living sorrow of Healfdane's son°
Simmered, bitter and fresh, and no wisdom
Or strength could break it: that agony hung
On king and people alike, harsh
And unending, violent and cruel, and evil.
90   In his far-off home Beowulf, Higlac's
Follower° and the strongest of the Geats—greater
And stronger than anyone anywhere in this world—
Heard how Grendel filled nights with horror
And quickly commanded a boat fitted out,
95 Proclaiming that he'd go to that famous king,
Would sail across the sea to Hrothgar,
Now when help was needed. None
Of the wise ones regretted his going, much
As he was loved by the Geats: the omens were good,
100 And they urged the adventure on. So Beowulf
Chose the mightiest men he could find,
The bravest and best of the Geats, fourteen
In all, and led them down to their boat;
He knew the sea, would point the prow°
105 Straight to that distant Danish shore.
   Then they sailed, set their ship
Out on the waves, under the cliffs.
Ready for what came they wound through the currents,
The seas beating at the sand, and were borne
110 In the lap of their shining ship, lined
With gleaming armor, going safely
In that oak-hard boat to where their hearts took them.
The wind hurried them over the waves,
The ship foamed through the sea like a bird
115 Until, in the time they had known it would take,
Standing in the round-curled prow they could see

85 **Healfdane's son:** Hrothgar.

90–91 **Higlac's Follower:** Higlac, king of the Geats, is Beowulf's uncle. *Higlac's follower,* then, refers to Beowulf.

104 **prow:** the bow, or forwardmost part of a ship.

Big Idea **The Epic Warrior** *What are your first impressions of Beowulf?*

Sparkling hills, high and green,
Jutting up over the shore, and rejoicing
In those rock-steep cliffs they quietly ended
120   Their voyage. Jumping to the ground, the Geats
Pushed their boat to the sand and tied it
In place, mail shirts° and armor rattling
As they swiftly moored their ship. And then
They gave thanks to God for their easy crossing.
125   High on a wall a Danish watcher
Patrolling along the cliffs saw
The travelers crossing to the shore, their shields
Raised and shining; he came riding down,
Hrothgar's lieutenant, spurring his horse,
130   Needing to know why they'd landed, these men
In armor. Shaking his heavy spear
In their faces he spoke:
                    "Whose soldiers are you,
You who've been carried in your deep-keeled ship°
135   Across the sea-road to this country of mine?
Listen! I've stood on these cliffs longer
Than you know, keeping our coast free
Of pirates, raiders sneaking ashore
From their ships, seeking our lives and our gold.
140   None have ever come more openly—
And yet you've offered no password, no sign
From my prince, no permission from my people for your landing
Here. Nor have I ever seen,
Out of all the men on earth, one greater
145   Than has come with you; no commoner carries
Such weapons, unless his appearance, and his beauty,
Are both lies. You! Tell me your name,
And your father's; no spies go further onto Danish
Soil than you've come already. Strangers,
150   From wherever it was you sailed, tell it,
And tell it quickly, the quicker the better,
I say, for us all. Speak, say
Exactly who you are, and from where, and why."

    Their leader answered him, Beowulf unlocking
155   Words from deep in his breast:
                        "We are Geats,
Men who follow Higlac. My father
Was a famous soldier, known far and wide
As a leader of men. His name was Edgetho.
160   His life lasted many winters;

122 mail shirts: a type of flexible body armor usually made of linked metal loops.

134 deep-keeled ship: a ship that possesses a deep bottom—the *keel* being the main piece of timber that runs the length of the bottom of the ship to support the ship's frame.

The so-called "Sigurd's helmet." Vendel period, 7th c. From the Vendel boat grave, Uppland. Upplandsmuseet, Uppsala, Sweden.

Big Idea   The Epic Warrior *How do the watchman's words help characterize Beowulf?*

Wise men all over the earth surely
Remember him still. And we have come seeking
Your prince, Healfdane's son, protector
Of this people, only in friendship: instruct us,
165 Watchman, help us with your words! Our errand
Is a great one, our business with the glorious king
Of the Danes no secret; there's nothing dark
Or hidden in our coming. You know (if we've heard
The truth, and been told honestly) that your country
170 Is cursed with some strange, vicious creature
That hunts only at night and that no one
Has seen. It's said, watchman, that he has slaughtered
Your people, brought terror to the darkness. Perhaps
Hrothgar can hunt, here in my heart,
175 For some way to drive this devil out—
If anything will ever end the evils
Afflicting your wise and famous lord.
Here he can cool his burning sorrow.
Or else he may see his suffering go on
180 Forever, for as long as Herot towers
High on your hills."
                    The mounted officer
Answered him bluntly, the brave watchman:
    "A soldier should know the difference between words
185 And deeds, and keep that knowledge clear
In his brain. I believe your words, I trust in
Your friendship. Go forward, weapons and armor
And all, on into Denmark. I'll guide you
Myself—and my men will guard your ship,
190 Keep it safe here on our shores,
Your fresh-tarred boat, watch it well,
Until that curving prow carries
Across the sea to Geatland a chosen
Warrior who bravely does battle with the creature
195 Haunting our people, who survives that horror
Unhurt, and goes home bearing our love."
    Then they moved on. Their boat lay moored,
Tied tight to its anchor. Glittering at the top
Of their golden helmets wild boar heads gleamed,
200 Shining decorations, swinging as they marched,
Erect like guards, like sentinels, as though ready
To fight. They marched, Beowulf and his men
And their guide, until they could see the gables
Of Herot, covered with hammered gold

First folio of the oldest surviving
Beowulf manuscript. Cotton
Vitellius A.xv. By permission of the
British Library, London.

Literary Element **Conflict** *According to Beowulf, what are Hrothgar's options?*

Reading Strategy **Identifying Sequence** *What happens before Beowulf and his followers leave their ship?*

205 And glowing in the sun—that most famous of all dwellings,
Towering majestic, its glittering roofs
Visible far across the land.
Their guide reined in his horse, pointing
To that hall, built by Hrothgar for the best
210 And bravest of his men; the path was plain,
They could see their way.

                Beowulf arose, with his men
Around him, ordering a few to remain
With their weapons, leading the others quickly
215 Along under Herot's steep roof into Hrothgar's
Presence. Standing on that prince's own hearth,
Helmeted, the silvery metal of his mail shirt
Gleaming with a smith's high art, he greeted
The Danes' great lord:
220   "Hail, Hrothgar!
Higlac is my cousin° and my king; the days
Of my youth have been filled with glory. Now Grendel's
Name has echoed in our land: sailors
Have brought us stories of Herot, the best
225 Of all mead-halls, deserted and useless when the moon
Hangs in skies the sun had lit,
Light and life fleeing together.
My people have said, the wisest, most knowing
And best of them, that my duty was to go to the Danes'
230 Great king. They have seen my strength for themselves,
Have watched me rise from the darkness of war,
Dripping with my enemies' blood. I drove
Five great giants into chains, chased
All of that race from the earth. I swam
235 In the blackness of night, hunting monsters
Out of the ocean, and killing them one
By one; death was my errand and the fate
They had earned. Now Grendel and I are called
Together, and I've come. Grant me, then,
240 Lord and protector of this noble place,
A single request! I have come so far,
Oh shelterer of warriors and your people's loved friend,
That this one favor you should not refuse me—
That I, alone and with the help of my men,
245 May purge all evil from this hall. I have heard,
Too, that the monster's scorn of men
Is so great that he needs no weapons and fears none.
Nor will I. My lord Higlac
Might think less of me if I let my sword

221 **cousin:** in this case, used broadly to mean any relative.

Ship full of Viking warriors. 10th century artifact.

250 Go where my feet were afraid to, if I hid
Behind some broad linden° shield: my hands
Alone shall fight for me, struggle for life
Against the monster. God must decide
Who will be given to death's cold grip.

255 Grendel's plan, I think, will be
What it has been before, to invade this hall
And gorge his belly with our bodies. If he can,
If he can. And I think, if my time will have come,
There'll be nothing to mourn over, no corpse to
     prepare

260 For its grave: Grendel will carry our bloody
Flesh to the moors, crunch on our bones
And smear torn scraps of our skin on the walls
Of his den. No, I expect no Danes
Will fret about sewing our **shrouds**, if he wins.

265 And if death does take me, send the hammered
Mail of my armor to Higlac, return
The inheritance I had from Hrethel, and he
From Wayland.° Fate will unwind as it must!"

THE BATTLE WITH GRENDEL

    Out from the marsh, from the foot of misty
270 Hills and bogs, bearing God's hatred,
Grendel came, hoping to kill
Anyone he could trap on this trip to high Herot.
He moved quickly through the cloudy night,
Up from his swampland, sliding silently

275 Toward that gold-shining hall. He had visited Hrothgar's
Home before, knew the way—
But never, before nor after that night,
Found Herot defended so firmly, his reception
So harsh. He journeyed, forever joyless,

280 Straight to the door, then snapped it open,
Tore its iron fasteners with a touch
And rushed angrily over the threshold.
He strode quickly across the inlaid
Floor, snarling and fierce: his eyes

285 Gleamed in the darkness, burned with a gruesome
Light. Then he stopped, seeing the hall
Crowded with sleeping warriors, stuffed
With rows of young soldiers resting together.
And his heart laughed, he relished the sight,

290 Intended to tear the life from those bodies
By morning; the monster's mind was hot

251 linden: made from the wood of a linden tree.

267–268 inheritance . . . Wayland: The inheritance is the armor that Wayland, a blacksmith of Germanic legend, forged for Hrethel, Beowulf's grandfather and former king of the Geats.

Page of text with a dragon illustration on vellum. 15th century. Flemish School, 43 x 31 cm. Musée Condé, Chantilly, France.

With the thought of food and the feasting his belly
Would soon know. But fate, that night, intended
Grendel to gnaw the broken bones
295 Of his last human supper. Human
Eyes were watching his evil steps,
Waiting to see his swift hard claws.
Grendel snatched at the first Geat
He came to, ripped him apart, cut
300 His body to bits with powerful jaws.
Drank the blood from his veins and bolted
Him down, hands and feet; death
And Grendel's great teeth came together,
Snapping life shut. Then he stepped to another
305 Still body, clutched at Beowulf with his claws,
Grasped at a strong-hearted wakeful sleeper
—And was instantly seized himself, claws
Bent back as Beowulf leaned up on one arm.
　　That shepherd of evil, guardian of crime,
310 Knew at once that nowhere on earth
Had he met a man whose hands were harder;
His mind was flooded with fear—but nothing
Could take his talons° and himself from that tight
Hard grip. Grendel's one thought was to run
315 From Beowulf, flee back to his marsh and hide there:
This was a different Herot than the hall he had emptied.
But Higlac's follower remembered his final
Boast and, standing erect, stopped
The monster's flight, fastened those claws
320 In his fists till they cracked, clutched Grendel
Closer. The **infamous** killer fought
For his freedom, wanting no flesh but retreat,
Desiring nothing but escape; his claws
Had been caught, he was trapped. That trip to Herot
325 Was a miserable journey for the **writhing** monster!
　　The high hall rang, its roof boards swayed,
And Danes shook with terror. Down
The aisles the battle swept, angry

8th century bronze mounting in the form of a dragon without wings, possibly from a bridle. Bronze, gilded. Sweden.

313 **talons:** the sharp, hooked claws on birds of prey and some other animals.

Reading Strategy　Identifying Sequence *What future event in the story do these lines foreshadow?*

Literary Element　Conflict *How does Beowulf differ from other warriors whom Grendel has attacked?*

Big Idea　The Epic Warrior *What motivates Beowulf in his time of need?*

Vocabulary

infamous (in´ fə məs) *adj.* having a bad reputation; notorious
writhing (rīth´ ing) *adj.* twisting, as in pain

And wild. Herot trembled, wonderfully
330　Built to withstand the blows, the struggling
　　　Great bodies beating at its beautiful walls;
　　　Shaped and fastened with iron, inside
　　　And out, artfully worked, the building
　　　Stood firm. Its benches rattled, fell
335　To the floor, gold-covered boards grating
　　　As Grendel and Beowulf battled across them.
　　　Hrothgar's wise men had fashioned Herot
　　　To stand forever; only fire,
　　　They had planned, could shatter what such skill had put
340　Together, swallow in hot flames such splendor
　　　Of ivory and iron and wood. Suddenly
　　　The sounds changed, the Danes started
　　　In new terror, cowering in their beds as the terrible
　　　Screams of the Almighty's enemy sang
345　In the darkness, the horrible shrieks of pain
　　　And defeat, the tears torn out of Grendel's
　　　Taut throat, hell's captive caught in the arms
　　　Of him who of all the men on earth
　　　Was the strongest.

350　　　　　　　　　That mighty protector of men
　　　Meant to hold the monster till its life
　　　Leaped out, knowing the fiend was no use
　　　To anyone in Denmark. All of Beowulf's
　　　Band had jumped from their beds, ancestral
355　Swords raised and ready, determined
　　　To protect their prince if they could. Their courage
　　　Was great but all wasted: they could hack at Grendel
　　　From every side, trying to open
　　　A path for his evil soul, but their points
360　Could not hurt him, the sharpest and hardest iron
　　　Could not scratch at his skin, for that sin-stained demon
　　　Had bewitched all men's weapons, laid spells
　　　That blunted every mortal man's blade.
　　　And yet his time had come, his days
365　Were over, his death near; down
　　　To hell he would go, swept groaning and helpless
　　　To the waiting hands of still worse fiends.
　　　Now he discovered—once the afflictor
　　　Of men, tormentor of their days—what it meant
370　To feud with Almighty God: Grendel

A helmet made of iron, bronze, and silver from the Sutton Hoo ship burial.

Reading Strategy **Identifying Sequence** *What events have occurred since Grendel entered Herot this night?*

Big Idea **The Epic Warrior** *What heroic traits do Beowulf's followers show?*

Saw that his strength was deserting him, his claws
Bound fast, Higlac's brave follower tearing at
His hands. The monster's hatred rose higher,
But his power had gone. He twisted in pain,
375 And the bleeding sinews° deep in his shoulder
Snapped, muscle and bone split
And broke. The battle was over, Beowulf
Had been granted new glory: Grendel escaped,
But wounded as he was could flee to his den,
380 His miserable hole at the bottom of the marsh,
Only to die, to wait for the end
Of all his days. And after that bloody
Combat the Danes laughed with delight.
He who had come to them from across the sea,
385 Bold and strong-minded, had driven affliction
Off, purged Herot clean. He was happy,
Now, with that night's fierce work; the Danes
Had been served as he'd boasted he'd serve them; Beowulf,
A prince of the Geats, had killed Grendel,
390 Ended the grief, the sorrow, the suffering
Forced on Hrothgar's helpless people
By a bloodthirsty fiend. No Dane doubted
The victory, for the proof, hanging high
From the rafters where Beowulf had hung it, was the monster's
395 Arm, claw and shoulder and all.

　　And then, in the morning, crowds surrounded
Herot, warriors coming to that hall
From faraway lands, princes and leaders
Of men hurrying to behold the monster's
400 Great staggering tracks. They gaped with no sense
Of sorrow, felt no regret for his suffering,
Went tracing his bloody footprints, his beaten
And lonely flight, to the edge of the lake
Where he'd dragged his corpselike way, doomed
405 And already weary of his vanishing life.
The water was bloody, steaming and boiling
In horrible pounding waves, heat
Sucked from his magic veins; but the swirling
Surf had covered his death, hidden
410 Deep in murky darkness his miserable
End, as hell opened to receive him.
　　Then old and young rejoiced, turned back
From that happy pilgrimage, mounted their hard-hooved
Horses, high-spirited stallions, and rode them
415 Slowly toward Herot again, retelling

375 **sinews**: bands of tissue, or tendons, that connect muscle and bone.

Norse chessmen, from a Viking hoard, Isle of Lewis, Scotland.

Literary Element　**Conflict**　*Why does Beowulf hang Grendel's arm in the rafters?*

Beowulf's bravery as they jogged along.
And over and over they swore that nowhere
On earth or under the spreading sky
Or between the seas, neither south nor north,
420 Was there a warrior worthier to rule over men.

THE BATTLE WITH GRENDEL'S MOTHER

The night after Grendel's defeat, his mother, a monster who lives at the bottom of a cold, dark lake, goes to Herot to avenge her son's death. She kills Hrothgar's closest friend, retrieves Grendel's arm from the rafters where Beowulf had hung it, and returns to her lake. When Beowulf hears of this, he pursues her.

He leaped into the lake, would not wait for anyone's
Answer; the heaving water covered him
Over. For hours he sank through the waves;
At last he saw the mud of the bottom.
425 And all at once the greedy she-wolf
Who'd ruled those waters for half a hundred
Years discovered him, saw that a creature
From above had come to explore the bottom
Of her wet world. She welcomed him in her claws,
430 Clutched at him savagely but could not harm him,
Tried to work her fingers through the tight
Ring-woven mail on his breast, but tore
And scratched in vain. Then she carried him, armor
And sword and all, to her home; he struggled
435 To free his weapon, and failed. The fight
Brought other monsters swimming to see
Her catch, a host of sea beasts who beat at
His mail shirt, stabbing with tusks and teeth
As they followed along. Then he realized, suddenly,
440 That she'd brought him into someone's battle-hall,
And there the water's heat could not hurt him,
Nor anything in the lake attack him through
The building's high-arching roof. A brilliant
Light burned all around him, the lake
445 Itself like a fiery flame.
                Then he saw
The mighty water witch, and swung his sword,
His ring-marked blade, straight at her head;
The iron sang its fierce song,

Hinged clasp from the Sutton Hoo ship burial. Seventh century.

Reading Strategy   Identifying Sequence *Summarize what happens the morning after Beowulf's triumph.*

Big Idea   The Epic Warrior *What might Beowulf's journey to the she-wolf's lair symbolize?*

450   Sang Beowulf's strength. But her guest
      Discovered that no sword could slice her evil
      Skin, that Hrunting° could not hurt her, was useless
      Now when he needed it. They wrestled, she ripped
      And tore and clawed at him, bit holes in his helmet,
455   And that too failed him; for the first time in years
      Of being worn to war it would earn no glory;
      It was the last time anyone would wear it. But Beowulf
      Longed only for fame, leaped back
      Into battle. He tossed his sword aside,
460   Angry; the steel-edged blade lay where
      He'd dropped it. If weapons were useless he'd use
      His hands, the strength in his fingers. So fame
      Comes to the men who mean to win it
      And care about nothing else! He raised
465   His arms and seized her by the shoulder; anger
      Doubled his strength, he threw her to the floor.
      She fell, Grendel's fierce mother, and the Geats'
      Proud prince was ready to leap on her. But she rose
      At once and repaid him with her clutching claws,
470   Wildly tearing at him. He was weary, that best
      And strongest of soldiers; his feet stumbled
      And in an instant she had him down, held helpless.
      Squatting with her weight on his stomach, she drew
      A dagger, brown with dried blood, and prepared
475   To avenge her only son. But he was stretched
      On his back, and her stabbing blade was blunted
      By the woven mail shirt he wore on his chest.
      The hammered links held; the point
      Could not touch him. He'd have traveled to the bottom of
         the earth,
480   Edgetho's son, and died there, if that shining
      Woven metal had not helped—and Holy
      God, who sent him victory, gave judgment
      For truth and right, Ruler of the Heavens,
      Once Beowulf was back on his feet and fighting.

485   Then he saw, hanging on the wall, a heavy
      Sword, hammered by giants, strong
      And blessed with their magic, the best of all weapons
      But so massive that no ordinary man could lift
      Its carved and decorated length. He drew it
490   From its scabbard,° broke the chain on its hilt,°

452 **Hrunting:** sword that a Danish warrior had lent to Beowulf.

Silver Viking figurine

490 **scabbard:** a case that protects a sword's blade. **hilt:** the sword's handle, which protrudes from the scabbard.

Big Idea   **The Epic Warrior** *What qualities of Beowulf does this passage reveal?*

Big Idea   **The Epic Warrior** *What does this description imply about Beowulf's strength?*

And then, savage, now, angry
And desperate, lifted it high over his head
And struck with all the strength he had left,
Caught her in the neck and cut it through,
495 Broke bones and all. Her body fell
To the floor, lifeless, the sword was wet
With her blood, and Beowulf rejoiced at the sight.
    The brilliant light shone, suddenly,
As though burning in that hall, and as bright as Heaven's
500 Own candle, lit in the sky. He looked
At her home, then following along the wall
Went walking, his hands tight on the sword,
His heart still angry. He was hunting another
Dead monster, and took his weapon with him
505 For final revenge against Grendel's vicious
Attacks, his nighttime raids, over
And over, coming to Herot when Hrothgar's
Men slept, killing them in their beds,
Eating some on the spot, fifteen
510 Or more, and running to his loathsome moor
With another such sickening meal waiting
In his pouch. But Beowulf repaid him for those visits,
Found him lying dead in his corner,
Armless, exactly as that fierce fighter
515 Had sent him out from Herot, then struck off
His head with a single swift blow. The body
Jerked for the last time, then lay still.
    The wise old warriors who surrounded Hrothgar,
Like him staring into the monster's lake,
520 Saw the waves surging and blood
Spurting through. They spoke about Beowulf,
All the graybeards, whispered together
And said that hope was gone, that the hero
Had lost fame and his life at once, and would never
525 Return to the living, come back as triumphant
As he had left; almost all agreed that Grendel's
Mighty mother, the she-wolf, had killed him.
The sun slid over past noon, went further
Down. The Danes gave up, left
530 The lake and went home, Hrothgar with them.

Viking keys.

The Geats stayed, sat sadly, watching,
Imagining they saw their lord but not believing
They would ever see him again.
                                    —Then the sword
535 Melted, blood-soaked, dripping down
Like water, disappearing like ice when the world's
Eternal Lord loosens invisible
Fetters and unwinds icicles and frost
As only He can, He who rules
540 Time and seasons, He who is truly
God. The monsters' hall was full of
Rich treasures, but all that Beowulf took
Was Grendel's head and the hilt of the giants'
Jeweled sword; the rest of that ring-marked
545 Blade had dissolved in Grendel's steaming
Blood, boiling even after his death.
And then the battle's only survivor
Swam up and away from those silent corpses;
The water was calm and clean, the whole
550 Huge lake peaceful once the demons who'd lived in it
Were dead.
                    Then that noble protector of all seamen°
Swam to land, rejoicing in the heavy
Burdens he was bringing with him. He
555 And all his glorious band of Geats
Thanked God that their leader had come back unharmed;
They left the lake together. The Geats
Carried Beowulf's helmet, and his mail shirt.
Behind them the water slowly thickened
560 As the monsters' blood came seeping up.
They walked quickly, happily, across
Roads all of them remembered, left
The lake and the cliffs alongside it, brave men
Staggering under the weight of Grendel's skull,
565 Too heavy for fewer than four of them to handle—
Two on each side of the spear jammed through it—
Yet proud of their ugly load and determined
That the Danes, seated in Herot, should see it.
Soon, fourteen Geats arrived
570 At the hall, bold and warlike, and with Beowulf,
Their lord and leader, they walked on the mead-hall
Green. Then the Geats' brave prince entered
Herot, covered with glory for the daring
Battles he had fought; he sought Hrothgar

552 that noble protector of all seamen: Beowulf. This phrase recalls an account Beowulf tells earlier in the epic and sums up in lines 234–238, in which he boasts of having slain sea monsters and thus prevented them from attacking other seamen.

Carved dragon-head post from the ship burial at Oseberg, c. A.D. 850 Viking Ship Museum, Bygdoy, Norway.

Big Idea **The Epic Warrior** *What traits do Beowulf's followers show here?*

Literary Element **Conflict** *What does this detail suggest about Beowulf's conflict with the monsters?*

575   To salute him and show Grendel's head.
He carried that terrible trophy by the hair,
Brought it straight to where the Danes sat,
Drinking, the queen among them. It was a weird
And wonderful sight, and the warriors stared.

THE BATTLE WITH THE DRAGON

Beowulf presents Hrothgar with the jeweled hilt of the magic sword. In recognition of Beowulf's heroic services to Denmark, Hrothgar proclaims the Danes and the Geats to be allies. The following morning, Beowulf sets sail for Geatland. After he arrives in his homeland, he meets with his uncle, Higlac, the king, to recount the slayings of the monsters and to convey Hrothgar's pledge of friendship.

580   Afterwards, in the time when Higlac was dead
And Herdred, his son, who'd ruled the Geats
After his father, had followed him into darkness—
Killed in battle with the Swedes, who smashed
His shield, cut through the soldiers surrounding
585   Their king—then, when Higd's one son°
Was gone, Beowulf ruled in Geatland,
Took the throne he'd refused, once,°
And held it long and well. He was old
With years and wisdom, fifty winters
590   A king, when a dragon awoke from its darkness
And dreams and brought terror to his people. The beast
Had slept in a huge stone tower, with a hidden
Path beneath; a man stumbled on
The entrance, went in, discovered the ancient
595   Treasure, the pagan jewels and gold
The dragon had been guarding, and dazzled and greedy
Stole a gem-studded cup, and fled.
But now the dragon hid nothing, neither
The theft nor itself; it swept through the darkness,
600   And all Geatland knew its anger.

      But the thief had not come to steal; he stole,
And roused the dragon, not from desire
But need. He was someone's slave, had been beaten
By his masters, had run from all men's sight,
605   But with no place to hide; then he found the hidden
Path, and used it. And once inside,
Seeing the sleeping beast, staring as it
Yawned and stretched, not wanting to wake it,
Terror-struck, he turned and ran for his life,

585 Higd's one son: Herdred, the son of Queen Higd and King Higlac.

587 Beowulf . . . took the throne he'd refused, once: The widowed queen, fearful that her son would be unable to defend Geatland against invaders, had offered Beowulf the throne; but he chose to support Herdred, the rightful heir.

Reading Strategy **Identifying Sequence** *What events precede the dragon's attack on the Geats?*

610   Taking the jeweled cup.
                      That tower
      Was heaped high with hidden treasure, stored there
      Years before by the last survivor
      Of a noble race, ancient riches
615   Left in the darkness as the end of a dynasty
      Came. Death had taken them, one
      By one, and the warrior who watched over all
      That remained mourned their fate, expecting,
      Soon, the same for himself, knowing
620   The gold and jewels he had guarded so long
      Could not bring him pleasure much longer. He brought
      The precious cups, the armor and the ancient
      Swords, to a stone tower built
      Near the sea, below a cliff, a sealed
625   Fortress with no windows, no doors, waves
      In front of it, rocks behind. Then he spoke:
         "Take these treasures, earth, now that no one
      Living can enjoy them. They were yours, in the beginning;
      Allow them to return. War and terror
630   Have swept away my people, shut
      Their eyes to delight and to living, closed
      The door to all gladness. No one is left
      To lift these swords, polish these jeweled
      Cups: no one leads, no one follows. These hammered
635   Helmets, worked with gold, will tarnish
      And crack; the hands that should clean and polish them
      Are still forever. And these mail shirts, worn
      In battle, once, while swords crashed
      And blades bit into shields and men,
640   Will rust away like the warriors who owned them.
      None of these treasures will travel to distant
      Lands, following their lords. The harp's
      Bright song, the hawk crossing through the hall
      On its swift wings, the stallion tramping
645   In the courtyard—all gone, creatures of every
      Kind, and their masters, hurled to the grave!"
        And so he spoke, sadly, of those
      Long dead, and lived from day to day,
      Joyless, until, at last, death touched
650   His heart and took him too. And a stalker
      In the night, a flaming dragon, found
      The treasure unguarded; he whom men fear
      Came flying through the darkness, wrapped in fire,
      Seeking caves and stone-split ruins°
655   But finding gold. Then it stayed, buried

Pendant of a Viking. Statens Historiska Museum, Stockholm, Sweden.

654 Seeking caves and stone-split ruins: It was believed that dragons made their dens in caves and stone burial mounds.

Literary Element   **Conflict** *What does this passage suggest about Beowulf's upcoming conflict with the dragon?*

Itself with heathen silver and jewels
It could neither use nor ever abandon.
　So mankind's enemy, the mighty beast,
Slept in those stone walls for hundreds
660　Of years; a runaway slave roused it,
Stole a jeweled cup and bought
His master's forgiveness, begged for mercy
And was pardoned when his delighted lord took the present
He bore, turned it in his hands and stared
665　At the ancient carvings. The cup brought peace
To a slave, pleased his master, but stirred
A dragon's anger. It turned, hunting
The thief's tracks, and found them, saw
Where its visitor had come and gone. He'd survived,
670　Had come close enough to touch its scaly
Head and yet lived, as it lifted its cavernous
Jaws, through the grace of almighty God
And a pair of quiet, quick-moving feet.
The dragon followed his steps, anxious
675　To find the man who had robbed it of silver
And sleep; it circled around and around
The tower, determined to catch him, but could not,
He had run too fast, the wilderness was empty.
The beast went back to its treasure, planning
680　A bloody revenge, and found what was missing,
Saw what thieving hands had stolen.
Then it crouched on the stones, counting off
The hours till the Almighty's candle went out,
And evening came, and wild with anger
685　It could fly burning across the land, killing
And destroying with its breath. Then the sun was gone,
And its heart was glad: glowing with rage
It left the tower, impatient to repay
Its enemies. The people suffered, everyone
690　Lived in terror, but when Beowulf had learned
Of their trouble his fate was worse, and came quickly.

　Vomiting fire and smoke, the dragon
Burned down their homes. They watched in horror
As the flames rose up: the angry monster
695　Meant to leave nothing alive. And the signs
Of its anger flickered and glowed in the darkness,
Visible for miles, tokens of its hate
And its cruelty, spread like a warning to the Geats

Helmet from a Vendel boat grave.
Seventh century.

Literary Element　Conflict *How do the dragon's motives differ from those of Grendel?*

Reading Strategy　Identifying Sequence *What is ironic about this sequence of events?*

700 Who had broken its rest. Then it hurried back
To its tower, to its hidden treasure, before dawn
Could come. It had wrapped its flames around
The Geats; now it trusted in stone
Walls, and its strength, to protect it. But they would not.
    Then they came to Beowulf, their king, and announced
705 That his hall, his throne, the best of buildings,
Had melted away in the dragon's burning
Breath. Their words brought misery, Beowulf's
Sorrow beat at his heart: he accused
Himself of breaking God's law, of bringing
710 The Almighty's anger down on his people.
Reproach pounded in his breast, gloomy
And dark, and the world seemed a different place.
But the hall was gone, the dragon's molten
Breath had licked across it, burned it
715 To ashes, near the shore it had guarded. The Geats
Deserved revenge; Beowulf, their leader
And lord, began to plan it, ordered
A battle-shield shaped of iron, knowing that
Wood would be useless, that no linden shield
720 Could help him, protect him, in the flaming heat
Of the beast's breath. That noble prince
would end his days on earth, soon,
Would leave this brief life, but would take the dragon
With him, tear it from the heaped-up treasure
725 It had guarded so long. And he'd go to it alone,
Scorning to lead soldiers against such
An enemy: he saw nothing to fear, thought nothing
Of the beast's claws, or wings, or flaming
Jaws—he had fought, before, against worse
730 Odds, had survived, been victorious, in harsher
Battles, beginning in Herot, Hrothgar's
Unlucky hall.

And Beowulf uttered his final boast:
    "I've never known fear; as a youth I fought
735 In endless battles. I am old, now,
But I will fight again, seek fame still,
If the dragon hiding in his tower dares
To face me."
                Then he said farewell to his followers,
740 Each in his turn, for the last time:
    "I'd use no sword, no weapon, if this beast
Could be killed without it, crushed to death
Like Grendel, gripped in my hands and torn

Viking pendant from Sweden

Big Idea **The Epic Warrior** *What does this passage reveal about Beowulf as a ruler of his people?*

BEOWULF **41**

Limb from limb. But his breath will be burning
745 Hot, poison will pour from his tongue.
I feel no shame, with shield and sword
And armor, against this monster: when he comes to me
I mean to stand, not run from his shooting
Flames, stand till fate decides
750 Which of us wins. My heart is firm,
My hands calm: I need no hot
Words. Wait for me close by, my friends.
We shall see, soon, who will survive
This bloody battle, stand when the fighting
755 Is done. No one else could do
What I mean to, here, no man but me
Could hope to defeat this monster. No one
Could try. And this dragon's treasure, his gold
And everything hidden in that tower, will be mine
760 Or war will sweep me to a bitter death!"
    Then Beowulf rose, still brave, still strong,
And with his shield at his side, and a mail shirt on his breast,
Strode calmly, confidently, toward the tower, under
The rocky cliffs: no coward could have walked there!
765 And then he who'd endured dozens of desperate
Battles, who'd stood boldly while swords and shields
Clashed, the best of kings, saw
Huge stone arches and felt the heat
Of the dragon's breath, flooding down
770 Through the hidden entrance, too hot for anyone
To stand, a streaming current of fire
And smoke that blocked all passage. And the Geats'
Lord and leader, angry, lowered
His sword and roared out a battle cry,
775 A call so loud and clear that it reached through
The hoary rock, hung in the dragon's
Ear.° The beast rose, angry,
Knowing a man had come—and then nothing
But war could have followed. Its breath came first.
780 A steaming cloud pouring from the stone,
Then the earth itself shook. Beowulf
Swung his shield into place, held it
In front of him, facing the entrance. The dragon

Viking amulet in the shape of a cross with a dragon's head. 8th century, silver. National Museum of Iceland, Reykjavik.

775–777 A call . . . ear: The dragon hears the echoing sound of Beowulf's battle cry.

Big Idea **The Epic Warrior** *How would you contrast Beowulf's and Hrothgar's responses to attack?*

Literary Element Conflict *Is Beowulf being foolhardy or noble in deciding to fight alone? Explain.*

Reading Strategy Identifying Sequence *What effect does this sequence of events create?*

Coiled and uncoiled, its heart urging it
785 Into battle. Beowulf's ancient sword
Was waiting, unsheathed, his sharp and gleaming
Blade. The beast came closer; both of them
Were ready, each set on slaughter. The Geats'
Great prince stood firm, unmoving, prepared
790 Behind his high shield, waiting in his shining
Armor. The monster came quickly toward him,
Pouring out fire and smoke, hurrying
To its fate. Flames beat at the iron
Shield, and for a time it held, protected
795 Beowulf as he'd planned; then it began to melt,
And for the first time in his life that famous prince
Fought with fate against him, with glory
Denied him. He knew it, but he raised his sword
And struck at the dragon's scaly hide.
800 The ancient blade broke, bit into
The monster's skin, drew blood, but cracked
And failed him before it went deep enough, helped him
Less than he needed. The dragon leaped
With pain, thrashed and beat at him, spouting
805 Murderous flames, spreading them everywhere.
And the Geats' ring-giver did not boast of glorious
Victories in other wars: his weapon
Had failed him, deserted him, now when he needed it
Most, that excellent sword. Edgetho's
810 Famous son stared at death,
Unwilling to leave this world, to exchange it
For a dwelling in some distant place—a journey
Into darkness that all men must make, as death
Ends their few brief hours on earth.
815   Quickly, the dragon came at him, encouraged
As Beowulf fell back; its breath flared,
And he suffered, wrapped around in swirling
Flames—a king, before, but now
A beaten warrior. None of his comrades
820 Came to him, helped him, his brave and noble
Followers; they ran for their lives, fled
Deep in a wood. And only one of them
Remained, stood there, miserable, remembering,
As a good man must, what kinship should mean.

825   His name was Wiglaf, he was Wexstan's son
And a good soldier; his family had been Swedish,°

Vendel brooch

826 **his family had been Swedish:**
Wiglaf, though of Swedish descent,
considers himself to be a Geat. It was not
unusual for a warrior from one people to
serve the chief or king of another people.

Big Idea **The Epic Warrior** *What does this passage reveal about Beowulf?*

Big Idea **The Epic Warrior** *How does this passage show the bond of kinship in Anglo-Saxon culture?*

Once. Watching Beowulf, he could see
How his king was suffering, burning. Remembering
Everything his lord and cousin had given him,
830   Armor and gold and the great estates
Wexstan's family enjoyed, Wiglaf's
Mind was made up; he raised his yellow
Shield and drew his sword—an ancient
Weapon that had once belonged to Onela's
835   Nephew, and that Wexstan had won,° killing
The prince when he fled from Sweden, sought safety
With Herdred, and found death. And Wiglaf's father
Had carried the dead man's armor, and his sword,
To Onela, and the king had said nothing, only
840   Given him armor and sword and all,
Everything his rebel nephew had owned
And lost when he left this life. And Wexstan
Had kept those shining gifts, held them
For years, waiting for his son to use them,
845   Wear them as honorably and well as once
His father had done; then Wexstan died
And Wiglaf was his heir, inherited treasures
And weapons and land. He'd never worn
That armor, fought with that sword, until Beowulf
850   Called him to his side, led him into war.
But his soul did not melt, his sword was strong;
The dragon discovered his courage, and his weapon,
When the rush of battle brought them together.
   And Wiglaf, his heart heavy, uttered
855   The kind of words his comrades deserved:
   "I remember how we sat in the mead-hall, drinking
And boasting of how brave we'd be when Beowulf
Needed us, he who gave us these swords
And armor: all of us swore to repay him,
860   When the time came, kindness for kindness
—With our lives, if he needed them. He allowed us to join him,
Chose us from all his great army, thinking
Our boasting words had some weight, believing
Our promises, trusting our swords. He took us
865   For soldiers, for men. He meant to kill
This monster himself, our mighty king,
Fight this battle alone and unaided,
As in the days when his strength and daring dazzled
Men's eyes. But those days are over and gone

833–835 an ancient weapon . . . that Wexstan had won: Wexstan killed the rebellious nephew of Onela, the king of Sweden, in battle. Wexstan was therefore entitled to the nephew's sword.

Study of a Dragon's Head after Michelangelo. John Ruskin (1819–1900). Ink on paper. Abbot Hall Art Gallery, Kendal, Cumbria, UK.

Reading Strategy   **Identifying Sequence** *What sequence of events led to Wiglaf's receiving his armor and sword?*

Big Idea   **The Epic Warrior** *What does this passage reveal about the relationship between a chief and his followers?*

870 And now our lord must lean on younger
Arms. And we must go to him, while angry
Flames burn at his flesh, help
Our glorious king! By almighty God,
I'd rather burn myself than see
875 Flames swirling around my lord.
And who are we to carry home
Our shields before we've slain his enemy
And ours, to run back to our homes with Beowulf
So hard-pressed here? I swear that nothing
880 He ever did deserved an end
Like this, dying miserably and alone,
Butchered by this savage beast: we swore
That these swords and armor were each for us all!"
    Then he ran to his king, crying encouragement
885 As he dove through the dragon's deadly fumes:
    "Belovèd Beowulf, remember how you boasted,
Once, that nothing in the world would ever
Destroy your fame: fight to keep it,
Now, be strong and brave, my noble
890 King, protecting life and fame
Together. My sword will fight at your side!"
    The dragon heard him, the man-hating monster,
And was angry; shining with surging flames
It came for him, anxious to return his visit.
895 Waves of fire swept at his shield
And the edge began to burn. His mail shirt
Could not help him, but before his hands dropped
The blazing wood Wiglaf jumped
Behind Beowulf's shield; his own was burned
900 To ashes. Then the famous old hero, remembering
Days of glory, lifted what was left
Of Nagling, his ancient sword, and swung it
With all his strength, smashed the gray
Blade into the beast's head. But then Nagling
905 Broke to pieces, as iron always
Had in Beowulf's hands. His arms
Were too strong, the hardest blade could not help him,
The most wonderfully worked. He carried them to war
But fate had decreed that the Geats' great king
910 Would be no better for any weapon.
    Then the monster charged again, vomiting
Fire, wild with pain, rushed out
Fierce and dreadful, its fear forgotten.

Statue, Bergen, Norway

Literary Element   Conflict *How might Wiglaf's actions affect the fight?*

Literary Element   Conflict *What is ironic about Beowulf's strength?*

Watching for its chance it drove its tusks
915 Into Beowulf's neck; he staggered, the blood
Came flooding forth, fell like rain.

    And then when Beowulf needed him most
Wiglaf showed his courage, his strength
And skill, and the boldness he was born with. Ignoring
920 The dragon's head, he helped his lord
By striking lower down. The sword
Sank in; his hand was burned, but the shining
Blade had done its work, the dragon's
Belching flames began to flicker
925 And die away. And Beowulf drew
His battle-sharp dagger: the blood-stained old king
Still knew what he was doing. Quickly, he cut
The beast in half, slit it apart.
It fell, their courage had killed it, two noble
930 Cousins had joined in the dragon's death.
Yet what they did all men must do
When the time comes! But the triumph was the last
Beowulf would ever earn, the end
Of greatness and life together. The wound
935 In his neck began to swell and grow;
He could feel something stirring, burning
In his veins, a stinging venom, and knew
The beast's fangs had left it. He fumbled
Along the wall, found a slab
940 Of stone, and dropped down; above him he saw
Huge stone arches and heavy posts,
Holding up the roof of that giant hall.
Then Wiglaf's gentle hands bathed
The blood-stained prince, his glorious lord,
945 Weary of war, and loosened his helmet.
    Beowulf spoke, in spite of the swollen,
Livid wound, knowing he'd unwound
His string of days on earth, seen
As much as God would grant him; all worldly
950 Pleasure was gone, as life would go,
Soon:
        "I'd leave my armor to my son,
Now, if God had given me an heir,
A child born of my body, his life
955 Created from mine. I've worn this crown
For fifty winters: no neighboring people
Have tried to threaten the Geats, sent soldiers
Against us or talked of terror. My days
Have gone by as fate willed, waiting
960 For its word to be spoken, ruling as well
As I knew how, swearing no unholy oaths,
Seeking no lying wars. I can leave

Viking axe. Nationalmuseet, Copenhagen.

This life happy; I can die, here,
Knowing the Lord of all life has never
965 Watched me wash my sword in blood
Born of my own family. Belovèd
Wiglaf, go, quickly, find
The dragon's treasure: we've taken its life,
But its gold is ours, too. Hurry,
970 Bring me ancient silver, precious
Jewels, shining armor and gems,
Before I die. Death will be softer,
Leaving life and this people I've ruled
So long, if I look at this last of all prizes."

975   Then Wexstan's son went in, as quickly
As he could, did as the dying Beowulf
Asked, entered the inner darkness
Of the tower, went with his mail shirt and his sword.
Flushed with victory he groped his way,
980 A brave young warrior, and suddenly saw
Piles of gleaming gold, precious
Gems, scattered on the floor, cups
And bracelets, rusty old helmets, beautifully
Made but rotting with no hands to rub
985 And polish them. They lay where the dragon left them;
It had flown in the darkness, once, before fighting
Its final battle. (So gold can easily
Triumph, defeat the strongest of men,
No matter how deep it is hidden!) And he saw,
990 Hanging high above, a golden
Banner, woven by the best of weavers
And beautiful. And over everything he saw
A strange light, shining everywhere,
On walls and floor and treasure. Nothing
995 Moved, no other monsters appeared;
He took what he wanted, all the treasures
That pleased his eye, heavy plates
And golden cups and the glorious banner,
Loaded his arms with all they could hold.
1000 Beowulf's dagger, his iron blade,
Had finished the fire-spitting terror
That once protected tower and treasures
Alike; the gray-bearded lord of the Geats
Had ended those flying, burning raids
1005 Forever.

Brooch, 9th century. Goldwork.

Big Idea   The Epic Warrior   Why does Beowulf believe that he has been a good king?

Big Idea   The Epic Warrior   Why does the treasure mean so much to Beowulf?

Then Wiglaf went back, anxious
To return while Beowulf was alive, to bring him
Treasure they'd won together. He ran,
hoping his wounded king, weak
1010 And dying, had not left the world too soon.
Then he brought their treasure to Beowulf, and found
His famous king bloody, gasping
For breath. But Wiglaf sprinkled water
Over his lord, until the words
1015 Deep in his breast broke through and were heard.
Beholding the treasure he spoke, haltingly:
    "For this, this gold, these jewels, I thank
Our Father in Heaven, Ruler of the Earth—
For all of this, that His grace has given me,
1020 Allowed me to bring to my people while breath
Still came to my lips. I sold my life
For this treasure, and I sold it well. Take
What I leave, Wiglaf, lead my people,
Help them; my time is gone. Have
1025 The brave Geats build me a tomb,
When the funeral flames° have burned me, and build it
Here, at the water's edge, high
On this spit of land, so sailors can see
This tower, and remember my name, and call it
1030 Beowulf's tower, and boats in the darkness
And mist, crossing the sea, will know it."
    Then that brave king gave the golden
Necklace from around his throat to Wiglaf,
Gave him his gold-covered helmet, and his rings,
1035 And his mail shirt, and ordered him to use them well:
    "You're the last of all our far-flung family.
Fate has swept our race away,
Taken warriors in their strength and led them
To the death that was waiting. And now I follow them."
1040   The old man's mouth was silent, spoke
No more, had said as much as it could;
He would sleep in the fire, soon. His soul
Left his flesh, flew to glory.

    And when the battle was over Beowulf's followers
1045 Came out of the wood, cowards and traitors,
Knowing the dragon was dead. Afraid,
While it spit its fires, to fight in their lord's
Defense, to throw their javelins and spears,

1026 funeral flames: It was the custom to cremate the bodies of the dead on a pile of flammable materials known as a funeral pyre.

Bronze helmet, late Bronze Age (800–400 BC), from Veksoe-bog, Denmark. National Museum, Copenhagen.

Big Idea **The Epic Warrior** *Why does Beowulf plan the tower so carefully?*

Reading Strategy **Identifying Sequence** *Beowulf's followers return to their leader after, not during, the battle. What can you conclude about them?*

They came like shamefaced jackals, their shields
1050 In their hands, to the place where the prince lay dead,
And waited for Wiglaf to speak. He was sitting
Near Beowulf's body, wearily sprinkling
Water in the dead man's face, trying
To stir him. He could not. No one could have kept
1055 Life in their lord's body, or turned
Aside the Lord's will: world
And men and all move as He orders,
And always have, and always will.
    Then Wiglaf turned and angrily told them
1060 What men without courage must hear.
Wexstan's brave son stared at the traitors,
His heart sorrowful, and said what he had to:
    "I say what anyone who speaks the truth
Must say. Your lord gave you gifts,
1065 Swords and the armor you stand in now;
You sat on the mead-hall benches, prince
And followers, and he gave you, with open hands,
Helmets and mail shirts, hunted across
The world for the best of weapons. War
1070 Came and you ran like cowards, dropped
Your swords as soon as the danger was real.
Should Beowulf have boasted of your help, rejoiced
In your loyal strength? With God's good grace
He helped himself, swung his sword
1075 Alone, won his own revenge.
The help I gave him was nothing, but all
I was able to give; I went to him, knowing
That nothing but Beowulf's strength could save us,
And my sword was lucky, found some vital
1080 Place and bled the burning flames
Away. Too few of his warriors remembered
To come, when our lord faced death, alone.
And now the giving of swords, of golden
Rings and rich estates, is over,
1085 Ended for you and everyone who shares
Your blood: when the brave Geats hear
How you bolted and ran none of your race
Will have anything left but their lives. And death
Would be better for them all, and for you, than the kind
1090 Of life you can lead, branded with disgrace!"

Viking longship candleholder.

THE FUNERAL FIRE

    A huge heap of wood was ready,
Hung around with helmets, and battle

Big Idea **The Epic Warrior** *Why did the Anglo-Saxons regard cowardice as particularly shameful?*

Shields, and shining mail shirts, all
As Beowulf had asked. The bearers brought
1095 Their belovèd lord, their glorious king,
And weeping laid him high on the wood.
Then the warriors began to kindle that greatest
Of funeral fires; smoke rose
Above the flames, black and thick,
1100 And while the wind blew and the fire
Roared they wept, and Beowulf's body
Crumbled and was gone. The Geats stayed,
Moaning their sorrow, lamenting their lord:
A gnarled old woman, hair wound
1105 Tight and gray on her head, groaned
A song of misery, of infinite sadness
And days of mourning, of fear and sorrow
To come, slaughter and terror and captivity.
And Heaven swallowed the billowing smoke.
1110   Then the Geats built the tower, as Beowulf
Had asked, strong and tall, so sailors
Could find it from far and wide; working
For ten long days they made his monument,
Sealed his ashes in walls as straight
1115 And high as wise and willing hands
Could raise them. And the riches he and Wiglaf
Had won from the dragon, rings, necklaces,
Ancient, hammered armor—all
The treasures they'd taken were left there, too,
1120 Silver and jewels buried in the sandy
Ground, back in the earth, again
And forever hidden and useless to men.
And then twelve of the bravest Geats
Rode their horses around the tower,
1125 Telling their sorrow, telling stories
Of their dead king and his greatness, his glory,
Praising him for heroic deeds, for a life
As noble as his name. So should all men
Raise up words for their lords, warm
1130 With love, when their shield and protector leaves
His body behind, sends his soul
On high. And so Beowulf's followers
Rode, mourning their belovèd leader,
Crying that no better king had ever
1135 Lived, no prince so mild, no man
So open to his people, so deserving of praise.

Visitors from Overseas. Nikolai
Roerich. Tretyakov Gallery,
Moscow, Russia.

Big Idea   **The Epic Warrior** *What does the hero's death mean to his people?*

RESPONDING AND THINKING CRITICALLY

Respond

1. What are your impressions of Beowulf? Explain.

Recall and Interpret

2. (a)Describe where Grendel lives and the nature of his origins. (b)What do the details about Grendel's origins and dwelling place add to your impression of him?

3. (a)Summarize what happens during the battle between Grendel and Beowulf. (b)How does learning about Grendel's fears and feelings during the battle affect your impression of the monster?

4. (a)Why does Grendel's mother try to kill Beowulf? Describe their struggle and its outcome. (b)After the struggle with Grendel's mother, why does Beowulf search for Grendel? Why does he feel the way he does?

5. (a)Why does Beowulf believe he must fight the dragon? (b)Summarize the outcome of the battle.

6. (a)Why does Wiglaf come to Beowulf's aid in his fight with the dragon? (b)In what ways are Beowulf and Wiglaf similar? In what ways are they different?

Analyze and Evaluate

7. Given the fact that most of Beowulf's men abandon him during his fight with the dragon, what might this indicate about the future of the kingdom?

8. For which character did you feel the most sympathy? What strategies did the poet use to create sympathy for that character?

9. A **symbol** is a person, thing, or event that stands for something else, often an idea or concept. What might Beowulf symbolize? What might Grendel and the dragon represent?

Connect

10. [Big Idea] **The Epic Warrior** From the description of Beowulf's character, what traits do you think the Anglo-Saxons considered heroic?

VISUAL LITERACY: Graphic Organizer

Creating a Storyboard

One way to visualize the flow of events in an epic poem is to create a **storyboard**—a series of sketches depicting the most important events in sequence. Each sketch illustrates a single scene or action.

Group Activity With a group of classmates, list details about the setting, characters, and events in a selected passage from the poem. For example, review lines 658–693, and then add details to the third column in the chart below:

Then turn your chart into a storyboard, or a series of cartoon panels, to illustrate the events. Consider how graphic storytelling increases your understanding of the poem.

Setting	Characters	Events
inside the dragon's lair	• a runaway slave • a sleeping dragon	The dragon sleeps inside stone walls.

Literary Element | Conflict

An **external conflict** exists when a character struggles against some outside force, such as another person, nature, society, or fate. An **internal conflict** is a struggle that takes place within the mind of a character who is torn between opposing feelings, desires, or goals.

1. Which of Beowulf's external conflicts seems the most challenging? Explain.

2. In lines 707–717, what internal conflict does Beowulf face? How does he resolve it?

Review: Epic Hero

As you learned on page 21, an **epic hero** is typically a person of high social status who usually embodies the ideals of his people.

Group Activity An epic hero is defined by his or her society. How might Beowulf, an Anglo-Saxon epic hero, behave in our society? What kinds of jobs might he hold? With a group of your classmates, discuss Beowulf's main character traits—both good and bad. Create a diagram like the one below to record your observations. Then discuss how Beowulf might act in present-day situations as well as how others might regard him. Share your conclusions with the rest of your class.

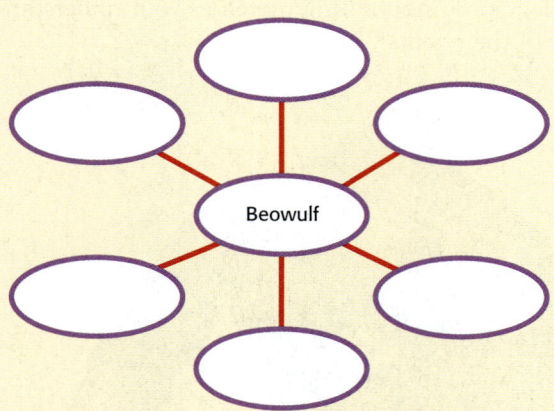

Reading Strategy | Identifying Sequence

Identifying the sequence of events is an important step in determining an author's purpose for writing. In *Beowulf,* the hero fights three monsters in succession: Grendel, Grendel's mother, and the fire-breathing dragon.

1. What does the poet suggest about Beowulf's challenges by using this sequence of battles?

2. How would you contrast Beowulf in youth with Beowulf in old age?

3. Why might the poet show Beowulf fighting monsters but not other human beings?

Vocabulary | Practice

Practice with Analogies Complete each analogy below.

1. hammer : forge :: chisel :
   a. paint **b.** sand **c.** sculpt

2. pain : writhing :: cold :
   a. warming **b.** skiing **c.** shivering

3. criminal : infamous :: philanthropist :
   a. reputable **b.** careful **c.** joyous

4. cheer : celebrate :: lament :
   a. rejoice **b.** mourn **c.** criticize

5. pajamas : nap :: shroud :
   a. burial **b.** wedding **c.** convalescence

Academic Vocabulary

Here are two words from the vocabulary list on page R82. These words will help you think, write, and talk about the selection.

concept (kon′ sept) *n.* a general idea based on knowledge or experience

policy (po′ lə sē) *n.* a consistent plan of action

Practice and Apply
1. What **concept** of fate influences Beowulf?
2. What **policy** does Beowulf follow as king of the Geats?

Writing About Literature

Analyze Settings In the first part of *Beowulf*, Grendel attacks Herot, Hrothgar's hall. In the last part of the epic, the dragon destroys Beowulf's hall. In a brief essay, analyze the significance of the two settings. What does Herot mean to Hrothgar and the Danish people? What does the destruction of Beowulf's hall represent? Use details from the poem to support your explanation.

As you draft, write from start to finish. Follow the writing path shown here to help organize your essay and keep your writing on track.

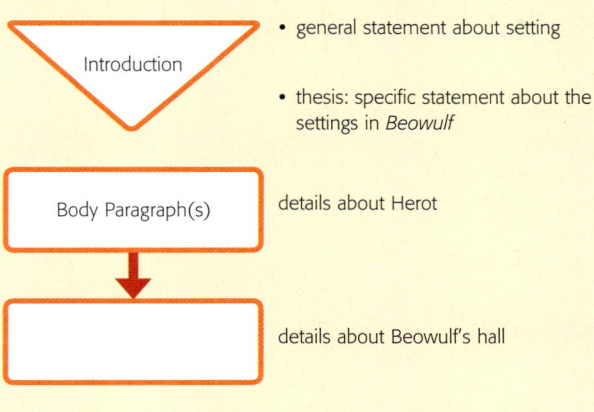

Introduction
- general statement about setting
- thesis: specific statement about the settings in *Beowulf*

Body Paragraph(s)
- details about Herot
- details about Beowulf's hall

Conclusion
- restatement of thesis in different words
- related insight about the symbolic use of setting

After you finish your draft, meet with a peer reviewer to evaluate each other's work and suggest revisions. Then proofread and edit your draft for errors in spelling, grammar, and punctuation.

Performing

With a small group, choose a section of *Beowulf* to perform for your class. Decide among you who will read the narrative, who will play each character, and whether one of you will provide musical accompaniment. Rehearse as if you were trying to capture the attention of banqueters in a grand mead hall. Take full advantage of rhythms and other dramatic devices built into the poem. When you feel you're ready, perform for the class.

Literature Online Web Activities For eFlashcards, Selection Quick Checks, and other Web activities, go to www.glencoe.com.

The *Beowulf*-Poet's Language and Style

Using Possessive Pronouns A possessive pronoun takes the place of the possessive form of a noun. In *Beowulf*, the poet often uses possessive pronouns to emphasize meaning and create rhythm:

"A child born of **my** body, **his** life
Created from **mine**." (lines 954–955)

Afraid,/ While it spit **its** fires, to fight in **their** lord's
Defense, . . . (lines 1046–1048)

And then twelve of the bravest Geats
Rode **their** horses around the tower, . . .
(lines 1123–1124)

Possessive pronouns act as adjectives when they modify nouns. In the first example above, the possessive pronouns *my* and *his* modify the nouns *body* and *life,* respectively. Notice that possessive pronouns do not contain apostrophes. Take particular note that the possessive pronoun *its* has no apostrophe. It is a common error to mistake *its* and the contraction *it's (it is).* In the following sentence, the pronoun and the contraction are used correctly: *It's* the theft of a cup from *its* hoard that outrages the dragon.

Possessive pronouns have person and number, as shown in the chart below.

Possessive Pronouns		
	Singular	Plural
First Person	my, mine	our, ours
Second Person	your, yours	your, yours
Third Person	his her, hers its	their, theirs

Activity Create a chart of your own in which you list other examples of possessive pronouns in the poem and identify the words that each modifies.

Revising Check

Possessive Pronouns With a partner, review your essay on analyzing setting. Look for places where using possessive pronouns could strengthen the style. Revise your essay accordingly.

Comparing Literature *Across Time and Place*

Connecting to the Reading Selections

Throughout history, writers from different cultures have explored the terrifying intrusion of dark forces into human life and the heroic struggles to destroy those forces. The four writers compared here—the *Beowulf*-poet, the creator of *Gilgamesh*, J. R. R. Tolkien, and Gareth Hinds—portray this timeless conflict between good and evil.

c. A.D. 700

from *Beowulf* .... epic 22
Strength, self-sacrifice, and heroic spirit

Mesopotamia, c. 2000 B.C.

"The Death of Humbaba"
from *Gilgamesh* .... epic 55
The bonds of friendship

Middle Earth

J. R. R. Tolkien
"The Battle of the Pelennor Fields"
from *The Lord of the Rings:*
The Return of the King .... fantasy 58
Loyalty to a fallen king

Gareth Hinds
from ***The Collected Beowulf*** .... graphic novel 62

COMPARING THE Big Idea The Epic Warrior

Epic warriors face life-threatening challenges. Their responses to these challenges define them as heroes and help characterize them as individuals. The *Beowulf*-poet, the creator of *Gilgamesh*, J. R. R. Tolkien, and Gareth Hinds all portray larger-than-life warriors who struggle against the forces of evil.

COMPARING Heroes' Goals

From Odysseus and Beowulf to Batman and Luke Skywalker, the superhero represents goodness and nobility. Heroes' personal goals motivate them to take risks, pursue adventures, and perform great deeds. These goals not only drive the plot of the story but suggest the **theme**, or the writer's message about life.

COMPARING Cultures

The values of a culture find expression in its art, music, and literature. The heroes in these stories embody the values cherished by their respective cultures.

The Death of Humbaba
from *Gilgamesh*

Building Background

The epic of *Gilgamesh* was lost for more than two thousand years. Only because of an ancient king named Assurbanipal (ä´ sər bä´ nə päl´) and an accidental discovery by a British archeologist do we know it today.

From 668 to 627 B.C., Assurbanipal reigned over the ancient empire of Assyria. During his reign, Assurbanipal sent men out to find ancient texts at such historical sites of learning as Babylon, Uruk, and Nippur. He then asked that these texts be translated into Akkadian Semitic, the language of his empire. *Gilgamesh* was one of the works found and was transcribed onto clay tablets, which were then stored in Assurbanipal's library at Nineveh.

Thousands of years later, in 1839, a British traveler named Austen Henry Layard, on his way to Ceylon (today known as Sri Lanka), stopped to investigate some mounds in Mesopotamia. What was intended as a brief delay became the work of years for Layard, as the mounds eventually proved to be the buried library of Assurbanipal. Here, among nearly twenty-five thousand broken tablets, Layard unearthed the text of *Gilgamesh*.

Who Was Gilgamesh? Gilgamesh was an actual king who lived sometime between 2800 and 2500 B.C. and reigned over the ancient Sumerian city-state of Uruk (o͞o´ rook), located in what is now southeastern Iraq. During the first several hundred years following Gilgamesh's death, people recited tales of his adventures as separate stories. Then, sometime between 2000 and 1600 B.C., storytellers began to string these tales together, forming the work that is now known as the epic of *Gilgamesh*. The following selection is taken from that epic.

Context At the point in the epic in which the tale reprinted here begins, Gilgamesh's

Seventh century BC cuneiform tablet.

ambition to build great walls and temples to glorify his name has driven him to the forest for building materials. There, he and his friend, Enkidu, plan to chop down a great cedar tree. However, they both believe that these precious trees are guarded by supernatural forces that will attempt to block their efforts—the greatest of these forces being Humbaba, a giant who serves the gods and protects the woods with his own physical strength and magical powers. Therefore, Gilgamesh has asked the sun-god Shamash for protection and has promised, in return, to build a great temple for him.

from Gilgamesh
The Death of Humbaba

Retold by Herbert Mason

Statue of a Hero Taming a Lion.
722–705 B.C. From the palace of Sargon II,
King of Assur in Khorsabad. Height: 445 cm.
Louvre Museum, Département des
Antiquités Orientales, Paris.

At dawn Gilgamesh raised his ax
And struck at the great cedar.
When Humbaba heard the sound of falling trees,
He hurried down the path that they had seen
5   But only he had traveled. Gilgamesh felt weak
At the sound of Humbaba's footsteps and called to Shamash
Saying, I have followed you in the way decreed;
Why am I abandoned now? Suddenly the winds
Sprang up. They saw the great head of Humbaba
10   Like a water buffalo's bellowing down the path,
His huge and clumsy legs, his flailing arms
Thrashing at phantoms in his precious trees.
His single stroke could cut a cedar down
And leave no mark on him. His shoulders,
15   Like a porter's under building stones,
Were permanently bent by what he bore;
He was the slave who did the work for gods
But whom the gods would never notice.
Monstrous in his contortion, he aroused
20   The two almost to pity.
But pity was the thing that might have killed.
It made them pause just long enough to show
How pitiless he was to them. Gilgamesh in horror saw
Him strike the back of Enkidu and beat him to the ground
25   Until he thought his friend was crushed to death.
He stood still watching as the monster leaned to make
His final strike against his friend, unable
To move to help him, and then Enkidu slid
Along the ground like a ram making its final lunge
30   On wounded knees. Humbaba fell and seemed
To crack the ground itself in two, and Gilgamesh,
As if this fall had snapped him from his daze,
Returned to life

The Demon Humbaba.
1800 B.C., Sippar.

And stood over Humbaba with his ax
35   Raised high above his head watching the monster plead
In strangled sobs and desperate appeals
The way the sea contorts under a violent squall.¹
I'll serve you as I served the gods, Humbaba said;
I'll build you houses from their sacred trees.

40   Enkidu feared his friend was weakening
And called out: Gilgamesh! Don't trust him!
As if there were some hunger in himself
That Gilgamesh was feeling
That turned him momentarily to yearn
45   For someone who would serve, he paused;
And then he raised his ax up higher
And swung it in a perfect arc
Into Humbaba's neck. He reached out
To touch the wounded shoulder of his friend,

50   And late that night he reached again
To see if he was yet asleep, but there was only
Quiet breathing. The stars against the midnight sky
Were sparkling like mica² in a riverbed.
In the slight breeze
55   The head of Humbaba was swinging from a tree.

---

1. A *squall* is a sudden, violent storm.
2. *Mica* is a mineral that sparkles in the light.

Quickwrite ....

In what ways is Gilgamesh a heroic character? What qualities make him seem to be an ordinary human being? Write a brief essay exploring his character.

from *The Battle of the Pelennor Fields*
from *The Lord of the Rings: The Return of the King*

Building Background

While grading papers in 1928, J. R. R. Tolkien (tōl′ kēn) came across a page left blank by a student. On this blank page, Tolkien scribbled, "In a hole in the ground there lived a hobbit." From that sentence evolved his vastly popular children's fantasy, *The Hobbit.* This novel in turn helped Tolkien crystallize his musings about an imaginary realm—Middle Earth, later the setting for the most influential body of fantasy writing in the twentieth century.

Born in South Africa, John Ronald Reuel Tolkien moved with his family to England at the age of four after his father's death. A devout Roman Catholic, like his mother, Tolkien served in World War I and afterward became a professor of English language and literature at Oxford University. His academic achievements included an edition of *Sir Gawain and the Green Knight* and an acclaimed lecture, "*Beowulf*: The Monsters and the Critics," which greatly influenced subsequent studies of that epic.

An Imaginary World In his spare time, Tolkien continued developing his intricate, fictional world, complete with its own language, history, geography, and characters—including dwarves and elves. He created much of his early fantasy writing to entertain his four children. Included in these writings is *The Hobbit*, which was published in 1937. As an extension of this popular work, Tolkien continued developing the story of Middle Earth into *The Lord of the Rings*, published seventeen years later. Because of its length, this work was originally divided into three volumes: *The Fellowship of the Ring, The Two Towers*, and *The Return of the King.* Into this modern fantasy epic, Tolkien wove elements drawn from the heroic traditions of the Germanic and Celtic peoples.

In the United States, *The Lord of the Rings* became a cult classic on college campuses when it was published in paperback in 1965. In the late 1990s, New Zealand-born film director Peter Jackson

began adapting Tolkien's work in the form of a trilogy for the screen. Jackson's film version of *The Lord of the Rings: The Return of the King* won eleven Oscars, including Best Picture, in 2004.

Context At the point in *The Lord of the Rings* in which this episode occurs, the conflict between the forces of good and evil is nearing its climax. The Dark Lord, Sauron, has sent his vast armies to besiege the city of Minas Tirith. The leader of Sauron's forces is the Lord of the Nazgûl, a spectral demon astride a huge, foul, dragonlike steed. Among those defending the city are the Rohirrim, the mounted warriors of the Mark of Rohan, led by their aged king, Théoden. Unknown to Théoden, his beloved niece, Éowyn, disguised as the warrior Dernhelm, has accompanied his troops. With her is Merry, a Hobbit.

J. R. R. Tolkien was born in 1892 and died in 1973.

Literature Online **Author Search** For more about J. R. R. Tolkien, go to www.glencoe.com.

from
The Battle of the Pelennor Fields

J. R. R. Tolkien

Théoden King of the Mark had reached the road from the Gate to the River, and he turned towards the City that was now less than a mile distant. He slackened his speed a little, seeking new foes, and his knights came about him, and Dernhelm was with them. Ahead nearer the walls Elfhelm's[1] men were among the siege-engines, hewing, slaying, driving their foes into the fire-pits. Well nigh all the northern half of the Pelennor[2] was overrun, and there camps were blazing, orcs[3] were flying towards the River like herds before the hunters; and the Rohirrim went hither and thither at their will. But they had not yet overthrown the siege, nor won the Gate. Many foes stood before it, and on the further half of the plain were other hosts still unfought. Southward beyond the road lay the main force of the Haradrim,[4] and there their horsemen were gathered about the standard[5] of their chieftain. And he looked out, and in the growing light he saw the banner of the king, and that it was far ahead of the battle with few men about it. Then he was filled with a red wrath and shouted aloud, and displaying his standard, black serpent upon scarlet, he came against the white horse and the green with great press of men; and the drawing of the scimitars of the Southrons was like a glitter of stars.

Then Théoden was aware of him, and would not wait for his onset, but crying to Snowmane[6] he charged headlong to greet him. Great was the clash of their meeting. But the white fury of the Northmen burned the hotter, and more skilled was their knighthood with long spears and bitter. Fewer were they but they clove through the Southrons like a fire-bolt in a forest. Right through the press drove Théoden Thengel's son, and his spear was shivered as he threw down their chieftain. Out swept his sword, and he spurred to the standard, hewed[7] staff and bearer; and the black serpent foundered.[8] Then all that was left unslain of their cavalry turned and fled far away.

But lo! suddenly in the midst of the glory of the king his golden shield was dimmed. The new morning was blotted from the sky. Dark fell about him. Horses reared and screamed. Men cast from the saddle lay groveling on the ground.

1. *Elfhelm* is one of the Rohirrim.
2. The *Pelennor* is the region immediately around Minas Tirith.
3. *Orcs* are troll-like beings who form one of the principal groups serving the Dark Lord.
4. The *Haradrim* are the men of Harad, a region to the south, who serve Sauron. They are also known as *Southrons*.
5. A *standard* is a banner or emblem.

6. *Snowmane* is Théoden's horse.
7. *Hewed* means "cut."
8. *Foundered* means "fell."

"To me! To me!" cried Théoden. "Up, Eorlingas![9] Fear no darkness!" But Snowmane wild with terror stood up on high, fighting with the air, and then with a great scream he crashed upon his side: a black dart had pierced him. The king fell beneath him.

The great shadow descended like a falling cloud. And behold! it was a winged creature: if bird, then greater than all other birds, and it was naked, and neither quill nor feather did it bear, and its vast pinions[10] were as webs of hide between horned fingers; and it stank. A creature of an older world maybe it was, whose kind, lingering in forgotten mountains cold beneath the Moon, outstayed their day, and in hideous eyrie[11] bred this last untimely brood, apt to evil. And the Dark Lord took it, and nursed it with fell[12] meats, until it grew beyond the measure of all other things that fly; and he gave it to his servant to be his steed. Down, down it came, and then, folding its fingered webs, it gave a croaking cry, and settled upon the body of Snowmane, digging in its claws, stooping its long naked neck.

Upon it sat a shape, black-mantled, huge and threatening. A crown of steel he bore, but between rim and robe naught was there to see, save only a deadly gleam of eyes: the Lord of the Nazgûl. To the air he had returned, summoning his steed ere the darkness failed, and now he was come again, bringing ruin, turning hope to despair, and victory to death. A great black mace[13] he wielded.

But Théoden was not utterly forsaken. The knights of his house lay slain about him, or else mastered by the madness of their steeds were borne far away. Yet one stood there still: Dernhelm the young, faithful beyond fear; and he wept, for he had loved his lord as a father. Right through the charge Merry had been borne unharmed behind him, until the Shadow came; and then Windfola[14] had thrown them in his ter-

ror, and now ran wild upon the plain. Merry crawled on all fours like a dazed beast, and such a horror was on him that he was blind and sick.

"King's man! King's man!" his heart cried within him. "You must stay by him. As a father you shall be to me, you said." But his will made no answer, and his body shook. He dared not open his eyes or look up.

Then out of the blackness in his mind he thought that he heard Dernhelm speaking; yet now the voice seemed strange, recalling some other voice that he had known.

"Begone, foul dwimmerlaik, lord of carrion![15] Leave the dead in peace!"

A cold voice answered: "Come not between the Nazgûl and his prey! Or he will not slay thee in thy turn. He will bear thee away to the houses of lamentation, beyond all darkness, where thy flesh shall be devoured, and thy shriveled mind be left naked to the Lidless Eye."

A sword rang as it was drawn. "Do what you will; but I will hinder it, if I may."

"Hinder me? Thou fool. No living man may hinder me!"

Then Merry heard of all sounds in that hour the strangest. It seemed that Dernhelm laughed, and the clear voice was like the ring of steel. "But no living man am I! You look upon a woman. Éowyn I am, Éomund's daughter. You stand between me and my lord and kin. Begone,

---

9. The *Eorlingas* are the men of Rohan, whose ancestor was Eorl.
10. *Pinions* means "wings."
11. *Eyrie* means "nest."
12. *Fell* means "deadly."
13. A *mace* is a war-club.
14. *Windfola* is Dernhelm's horse.

15. *Carrion* refers to the flesh of dead people and animals.

if you be not deathless! For living or dark undead, I will smite you, if you touch him."

The winged creature screamed at her, but the Ringwraith made no answer, and was silent, as if in sudden doubt. Very amazement for a moment conquered Merry's fear. He opened his eyes and the blackness was lifted from them. There some paces from him sat the great beast, and all seemed dark about it, and above it loomed the Nazgûl Lord like a shadow of despair. A little to the left facing them stood she whom he had called Dernhelm. But the helm of her secrecy had fallen from her, and her bright hair, released from its bonds, gleamed with pale gold upon her shoulders. Her eyes grey as the sea were hard and fell, and yet tears were on her cheek. A sword was in her hand, and she raised her shield against the horror of her enemy's eyes.

Éowyn it was, and Dernhelm also. For into Merry's mind flashed the memory of the face that he saw at the riding from Dunharrow: the face of one that goes seeking death, having no hope. Pity filled his heart and great wonder, and suddenly the slow-kindled courage of his race awoke. He clenched his hand. She should not die, so fair, so desperate! At least she should not die alone, unaided.

The face of their enemy was not turned towards him, but still he hardly dared to move, dreading lest the deadly eyes should fall on him. Slowly, slowly he began to crawl aside; but the Black Captain, in doubt and malice intent upon the woman before him, heeded him no more than a worm in the mud.

Suddenly the great beast beat its hideous wings, and the wind of them was foul. Again it leaped into the air, and then swiftly fell down upon Éowyn, shrieking, striking with beak and claw.

Still she did not blench:[16] maiden of the Rohirrim, child of kings, slender but as a steel-blade, fair but terrible. A swift stroke she dealt, skilled and deadly. The outstretched neck she clove asunder,[17] and the hewn head fell like a stone. Backward she sprang as the huge shape crashed to ruin, vast wings outspread, crumpled on the earth; and with its fall the shadow passed away. A light fell about her, and her hair shone in the sunrise.

Out of the wreck rose the Black Rider, tall and threatening, towering above her. With a cry of hatred that stung the very ears like venom he let fall his mace. Her shield was shivered in many pieces, and her arm was broken; she stumbled to her knees. He bent over her like a cloud, and his eyes glittered; he raised his mace to kill.

But suddenly he too stumbled forward with a cry of bitter pain, and his stroke went wide, driving into the ground. Merry's sword had stabbed him from behind, shearing through the black mantle, and passing up beneath the hauberk[18] had pierced the sinew behind his mighty knee.

"Éowyn! Éowyn!" cried Merry. Then tottering, struggling up, with her last strength she drove her sword between crown and mantle, as the great shoulders bowed before her. The sword broke sparkling into many shards. The crown rolled away with a clang. Éowyn fell forward upon her fallen foe. But lo! the mantle and hauberk were empty. Shapeless they lay now on the ground, torn and tumbled; and a cry went up into the shuddering air, and faded to a shrill wailing, passing with the wind, a voice bodiless and thin that died, and was swallowed up, and was never heard again in that age of this world. ❧

---

16. *Blench* means "turn white," as with fear.

17. *Asunder* means "in half."
18. A *hauberk* is a long coat of chain armor.

Discussion Starter ·····································

What background knowledge of *The Lord of the Rings* did you bring to your reading of this selection? How would you account for the enduring popularity of Tolkien's epic?

THE COLLECTED
BEOWULF

GARETH HINDS

BEFORE YOU READ

Building Background

There have been several comic book versions of *Beowulf* in recent years. Certainly the most elegant is the graphic novel by American illustrator Gareth Hinds, who first issued his *Beowulf* in three comic books that each presents one of the hero's combats in the epic. Hinds's *The Collected Beowulf* appeared in 2003.

In a recent interview, Hinds explained his choice of *Beowulf* as a subject for a graphic novel by saying that he "wanted to do a superhero book, without the modern superhero conventions." For the text of his graphic novel, Hinds used a 1910 translation of *Beowulf* by Francis Gummere, which he felt provides a sense, "to the greatest extent possible in modern English, that you were actually reading the Old English poem." The excerpt you are about to read shows Beowulf's arrival in Denmark.

GARETH HINDS **63**

Hither have fared to thee far-come men
o'er the paths of ocean, people of Geatland;
and the stateliest there by his sturdy band
is Beowulf named. This boon they seek,
that they, my master, may with thee
have speech at will.
In weeds of the warrior worthy they,
methinks, of our liking; their leader most surely,
a hero that hither his henchmen has led.

I knew him of yore in his youthful days;
his aged father was Ecgtheow named,
to whom, at home, gave Hrethel the Geat
his only daughter. Their offspring bold
fares hither to aid a steadfast ally.
And seamen, too, have said me this--
who carried my gifts to the Geatish court,
thither for thanks,--he has thirty men's
heft of grasp in the gripe of his hand,
the bold-in-battle one.

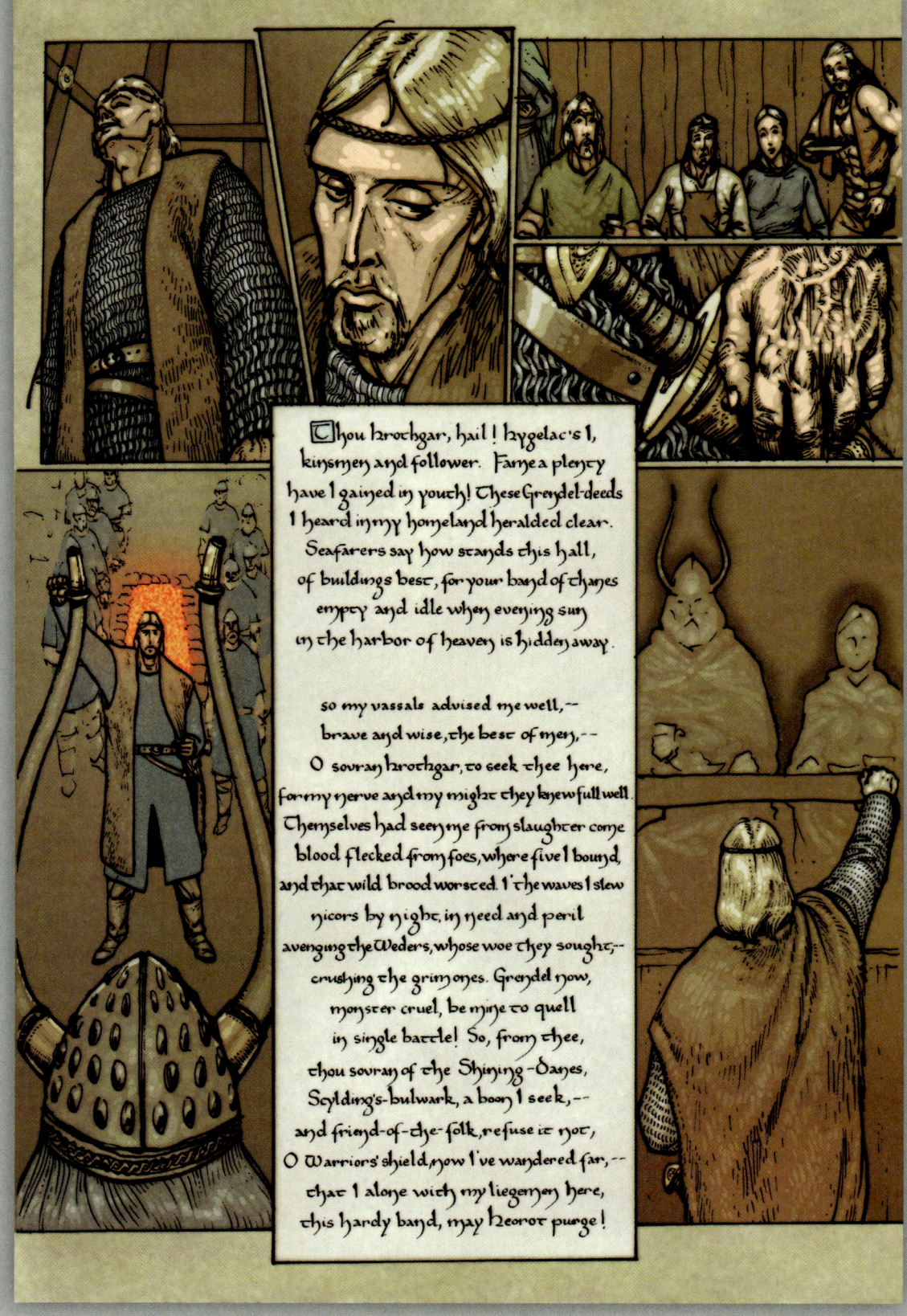

Thou Hrothgar, hail! Hygelac's I,
kinsmen and follower. Fame a plenty
have I gained in youth! These Grendel-deeds
I heard in my homeland heralded clear.
Seafarers say how stands this hall,
of buildings best, for your band of thanes
empty and idle, when evening sun
in the harbor of heaven is hidden away.

So my vassals advised me well,—
brave and wise, the best of men,—
O sovran Hrothgar, to seek thee here,
for my nerve and my might they knew full well.
Themselves had seen me from slaughter come
blood flecked from foes, where five I bound,
and that wild brood worsted. I' the waves I slew
nicors by night, in need and peril
avenging the Weders, whose woe they sought,—
crushing the grim ones. Grendel now,
monster cruel, be mine to quell
in single battle! So, from thee,
thou sovran of the Shining-Danes,
Scylding's-bulwark, a boon I seek,—
and friend-of-the-folk, refuse it not,
O Warriors' shield, now I've wandered far,—
that I alone with my liegemen here,
this hardy band, may Heorot purge!

Discussion Starter

Comic books use various conventions, such as panels to organize narrative. Discuss how Hinds uses this graphic convention to effectively present part of the story of Beowulf.

Wrap-Up: Comparing Literature Across Time and Place

- *Beowulf*
- "The Death of Humbaba" from *Gilgamesh*
- "The Battle of the Pelennor Fields" from *The Lord of the Rings: The Return of the King*
  by J. R. R. Tolkien
- from *The Collected Beowulf*
  by Gareth Hinds

COMPARING THE [Big Idea] The Epic Warrior

Partner Activity With a partner, review the following quotations. Then discuss the particular challenges faced by each epic warrior. Which warrior strikes you as most heroic in his or her response to these challenges? Support your interpretation with additional evidence from the selections.

> "The monster came quickly toward him,
> Pouring out fire and smoke . . .
> And for the first time in his life that famous
>   prince
> Fought with fate against him, with glory
> Denied him. He knew it, but he raised his
>   sword
> And struck at the dragon's scaly hide."
>
> —"The Battle with the Dragon" from *Beowulf*

> "Out of the wreck rose the Black Rider, tall and threatening, towering above her. With a cry of hatred that stung the very ears like venom he let fall his mace. Her shield was shivered in many pieces, and her arm was broken; she stumbled to her knees."
>
> —"The Battle of the Pelennor Fields" from *The Lord of the Rings: The Return of the King*

> "They saw the great head of Humbaba /
> Like a water buffalo's bellowing down the path, / His huge and clumsy legs, his flailing arms / Thrashing at phantoms in his precious trees."
>
> —"The Death of Humbaba"" from *Gilgamesh*

> ". . . but with gripe alone must I front the fiend and fight for life, foe against foe. Then faith be his in the doom of the Lord, whom death shall take."
>
> —from *The Collected Beowulf*

COMPARING Heroes' Goals

Group Discussion With a small group, compare the personal goals of Beowulf (in the epic and the graphic novel), Gilgamesh, and Éowyn. Discuss the following questions:

1. Why does each hero put himself or herself at risk?
2. What other motives surface during the course of each hero's struggle?

COMPARING Cultures

Visual Display Create a visual display, such as a chart or a collage, to accompany one of these selections. In your display, present images that depict the culture in the selection you chose. Use the Internet and library materials as research sources.

OBJECTIVES
- Compare and contrast authors' messages.
- Analyze epic warriors.
- Compare and contrast cultures.

TIME

A Brief History of
HEROES

What does it mean to be a hero? Definitions of heroism have changed through the ages, but are there certain qualities that all heroes have in common?

By TRISTRAM HUNT

MOST OF US HAVE OUR OWN DEFINITION OF heroism—we think we know a hero when we see one. History and literature are filled with both epic and ordinary heroes, but pinning down the attributes of a hero is a challenge. Your hero may not look much like mine. So it's worth asking: Are there certain unchallengeable characteristics that have defined heroism across the ages? Do today's heroes share personality traits with heroes of the past? Or are heroes shaped mostly by circumstance? Although most would agree that there are some timeless, universal qualities known as heroic, throughout history the idea of the hero has fluctuated and evolved to suit the culture of the times.

THE RENAISSANCE HERO

The modern concept of the hero would not have been possible without the Renaissance, a period in European history that saw a revived interest in the classical art, literature, and learning of ancient Greece and Rome. Previously, the Middle Ages had not looked favorably upon man's achievements. Living under the shadow of human sin, the Roman Catholic scholars of medieval Europe stressed the afterlife. Greatness came from God, not man, so the true heroes of Christendom were the martyrs, missionaries, and priests preparing for salvation.

The Renaissance challenged this bleak vision. Part of the challenge came from 14th-century Italy's rediscovery of classical literature. The writings of the Roman historian Tacitus, the biographies of the Greek philosopher Plutarch, but above all, the letters and speeches of the Roman orator Cicero opened the classical world anew. What they all emphasized was man's capacity for greatness.

In the 14th century, it was the Italian poet Francesco Petrarca, known as Petrarch, who ushered in the new humanism, a philosophy that focused on human values and capabilities. What excited Petrarch was the classical tradition of education. The aim of education, according to Cicero, was not to teach a narrow range of technical skills, like those needed to practice a trade, but rather to cultivate the single, noble virtue of manliness. During the Renaissance, this classical idea of *virtus* (moral excellence and goodness) went on to inspire many advice books outlining what was needed to become a well-rounded man. A manly man was proficient in warfare, scholarship, government, literature, and even the art of love. In the city-states of 15th-century Italy arose a new belief in human potential. The modern hero was born, and the ideal of the Renaissance man remains a heroic value today.

From this Renaissance culture—this new stress on the capabilities and virtue of man—came a series of histories in the late 14th century that recounted the inspirational lives of great men. Petrarch's *De Viris Illustribus* (On Famous Men) ignored saints and martyrs, concentrating instead on the achievements of generals and statesmen. For Petrarch, heroism demanded the purposeful display of *virtus:* from Romulus, the founder of Rome, to the war leader Scipio, Petrarch celebrated heroes who conquered fortune, beat the odds and rose to the top.

There was, however, one dissenting voice: that of the Florentine diplomat Niccolò Machiavelli. He ridiculed Cicero's lofty sentiments about *virtus.* In his book, *The Prince* (1513), Machiavelli turned these Renaissance ideas on their head. Where Petrarch had stressed the virtues of justice, mercy, and honesty in great men, Machiavelli offered the more ruthless concepts of realpolitik, which focuses on the advancement of individual interests—be they the interests of a person or nation. Machiavelli's heroes were those

who thought it was better to be feared than loved; who practiced cruelty rather than charity; who didn't base their conduct on firm principles or values, but on the winds of fortune. Machiavelli's hero was not the valiant General Scipio, but the scheming, manipulative prince Cesare Borgia. This notion of antiheroism represented a shocking reversal of thinking and secured Machiavelli his everlasting notoriety (and it finds its echo today in some scheming statesmen and princes of industry).

THE HERO OF ROMANTICISM

Yet Petrarch's more benevolent vision of classical heroism continued to dominate European culture for centuries to come. Only in the 18th century did the well-rounded Renaissance man finally fall out of fashion. The philosophers of Europe's Enlightenment period had little time for the vanity of personal greatness. As part of a movement that considered reason the highest virtue, these thinkers instead advocated the heroism of humanity. A scientific approach to social problems and a belief in universal human progress were to be honored, not the petty achievements of politicians and conquerors, or "celebrated villains," as the French writer Voltaire called them.

Inevitably, the impersonal equality of the Enlightenment produced a reaction: Romanticism. Beginning in the late 1790s with the writings of Johann von Schiller, August von Schlegel, and Novalis, the early German Romantics criticized the elevation of logic and reason above feeling. Instead, through art, literature, music, and love they celebrated the inner emotions and creative development of the human spirit. The Romantics believed in man's natural goodness and the call of individuals to develop their personality to the full. If the

Renaissance tradition had emphasized military glory and outward achievement, the German Romantics emphasized the uniqueness of each meaningful experience. The heroes of the day were not warriors but poets, dreamers, philosophers, and rebels. Britain's Lord Byron (1788–1824) managed to embody it all: author, lover, and revolutionary. Through the work of writers such as William Wordsworth, Samuel Taylor Coleridge, and Robert Southey, British culture became steeped in Romanticism, which stressed individual imagination and rebellion against social conventions and injustice. In France, Victor Hugo, author of *Les Misérables* and *The Hunchback of Notre-Dame,* championed the human spirit in the face of all adversity. And Italy awaited its own Romantic hero in the form of revolutionary Giuseppe Garibaldi, who fought to unify Italy.

THE VICTORIAN HERO

But it was the Victorian author Thomas Carlyle who turned the countercultural Romantic hero into the Great Man of history. A painfully tortured genius, Carlyle found in the humanism of the Romantics a refuge from his own brutal, mechanical age. For Carlyle, the Britain of the Industrial Revolution was a petty, soulless society run by technocrats lacking any conception of greatness.

In 1840, he delivered a series of lectures, titled *On Heroes, Hero-Worship, and the Heroic in History,* lamenting this cultural poverty and championing the role of great men in history. From the prophet Muhammad to William Shakespeare to Martin Luther to Napoleon Bonaparte, Carlyle argued, "Universal History, the history of what man has accomplished in this world, is at bottom the History of the Great Men who have worked here." For Carlyle, heroic conduct was not a skill that could be taught, as Renaissance thinkers had hoped. It was something individuals were gifted with. Moreover, heroes were not people to be emulated, but rather demigods to be acknowledged as possessing greater power. It was a potentially dangerous idea, but one that struck a chord in Victorian Britain and led to such national saviors of the 20th century as Winston Churchill and General de Gaulle.

THE QUIET HERO OF THE 19TH CENTURY

Yet even as Carlyle praised his Great Men, there emerged an alternative: the earnest heroism of middle-class virtue. Where the Renaissance hero achieved greatness in battle and the Romantic hero turned his back on society, the 19th-century hero quietly did his duty. As the British lecturer Samuel Smiles put it in his global best seller, *Self-Help,* "Many are the lives of men unwritten, which have nevertheless as powerfully influenced civilization and progress as the more fortunate Great whose names are recorded in biography." Heroism had become democratized, and the earnest, unpublicized work of those who provided people with their basic needs was now considered heroic.

As the democratic 20th century dawned, there was an ever-stronger emphasis on those whom history forgot. For the traditional marks of heroism had passed over the worthy lives of millions. Some seemed even to believe that every human being was intrinsically heroic. The late-19th-century Russian anarchist Alexander Herzen suggested that it was "quite enough to be simply a human being, to have something to tell." British writer, Virginia Woolf remarked: "Since so much is known that used to be unknown, the question now inevitably asks itself, whether the lives of great

GREAT MEN
Clockwise from top left: Would Machiavelli and Petrarch have recognized Shakespeare and Luther as heroes?

(tl bl)CORBIS, (tr br)Bridgeman Art Library

men only should be recorded. Is not anyone who has lived a life, and left a record of that life, worthy of biography—the failures as well as the successes, the humble as well as the illustrious? And what is greatness? And what smallness?" It was up to modern biographers to set up new standards of merit and "new heroes for our admiration."

THE 20TH-CENTURY HERO

As the 20th century progressed, many felt the need to reject heroism altogether. Carlyle's Great Man had morphed into German philosopher Friedrich Nietzsche's Super-Man with devastating global consequences. The warmongering of European statesmen led British novelist E.M. Forster to condemn hero-worship as "a dangerous vice." For Forster, one of democracy's merits was that "it does not . . . produce that unmanageable type of citizen known as the Great Man," but "produces instead different kinds of small men—a much finer achievement."

Small heroes seemed absolutely necessary in the face of Adolf Hitler. The thinkers of the mid-20th century fled from the idea of connecting militarism with greatness. Even during wartime, the British novelist George Orwell felt able to write in 1944, "The English people have no love of military glory and not much admiration for great men." Orwell did not assign to heroism semidivine greatness or classical *virtus;* instead he admired "a moral quality which must be vaguely described as decency."

THE MULTICULTURAL MEDIA AGE HERO

Heroism today is even more complex. The lack of privacy that mass media demands means that personal failings can, in the public imagination, often overshadow great acts. Today, John F. Kennedy is as much remembered for his love life as for the achievements of his presidency. The cult of celebrity often threatens to undermine true heroism. On the other hand, some celebrities, like the British actress Emma Thompson and U2's Bono, have used their fame to further the public good.

Perhaps most problematic—and most encouraging—is that few modern Western states are uniform societies that can instinctively rally around "national heroes." An educated, multicultural citizenry rarely shares a common idea of heroism—

CORBIS

Getty Images

Are modern figures, such as Kennedy and David Beckham, authentic heroes or just celebrities of the media age?

which is why everyday people like Fadéla Amara, a French woman of Algerian descent fighting for women's rights, and Hasan Saltik, a half-Turkish, half-Kurdish man who's been persecuted for trying to preserve Kurdish music, can be singled out as heroes. At the same time, when Hicham El Guerrouj, Morocco's star runner wins an Olympic medal after years of struggle, how many among us can fully resist sharing the national pride?

The tension between multiculturalism and national pride is precisely why it's important to focus on the qualities which all heroes share. Perhaps that's why when people today think about heroes, many choose an encompassing definition of heroism based on merit and humanity; one that seeks to recognize the often forgotten achievements of ordinary people; and one that values overcoming adversity and celebrates selfless acts to help others.

—**Updated 2005, from TIME, October 11, 2004**

RESPONDING AND THINKING CRITICALLY

Respond

1. Which ideas in this article did you find most interesting? Why?

Recall and Interpret

2. (a)Which people were regarded as heroes during the Middle Ages? (b)What shift occurred that affected people's view of heroes during the Renaissance?

3. (a)What accomplishments distinguished the Renaissance man? (b)How did Machiavelli challenge the Renaissance ideal of a hero?

4. (a)Which faculty did people during the Enlightenment value the most? (b)What faculty did the Romantics emphasize instead?

Analyze and Evaluate

5. How does Thomas Carlyle's view of heroism differ from Virginia Woolf's?

6. How well do you think the writer supports the thesis, or main idea, of this article? Explain.

7. Review the chart you made on page 69. Which of the ideas presented in this article most enhances your understanding of contemporary issues? Explain.

Connect

8. How does this article affect your understanding of the epic warriors featured in Unit One: Beowulf, Gilgamesh, and Éowyn? Support your answer with evidence from this article and the selections.

Vocabulary Workshop

Word Origins and Word Parts

Understanding Anglo-Saxon Derivations

"Then, when darkness had dropped, Grendel
Went up to Herot, wondering what the warriors
Would do in that hall when their drinking was done."

—*Beowulf*, lines 30–32

Connecting to Literature Some of the words in the modern English translation of *Beowulf* are derived from Anglo-Saxon words. In the above quotation, the word *darkness* comes from the Old English root *deorc* (dark), *wondering* from *wundor* (to wonder), *drinking* from *drincan* (to drink), and *do* and *done* both come from the root *dōn* (to act). Knowing Anglo-Saxon, or Old English, word parts can make analyzing unfamiliar language much easier.

Anglo-Saxon Word Parts

Below is a chart listing some common Anglo-Saxon word parts and their meanings.

Prefix or Suffix	Meaning	Example Words
a-	in a condition	asleep
be-	completely, thoroughly	befuddle
for-	completely	forsake
un-	reverse	unfold
-ful	full of	plentiful
-ly	in the manner of	quickly
-ness	state, condition	likeness
-ship	quality, state, or condition	kinship
-some	having the quality of	burdensome

Exercise

Read the following sentences from *Beowulf*. Using the chart above, determine which word or words contain an Old English suffix or prefix. Explain how each word is derived from Old English.

1. "Of Cain, murderous creatures banished / By God, punished forever for the crime / Of Abel's death." (lines 21–23)
2. "That agony hung / On king and people alike, harsh / And unending, violent and cruel, and evil." (lines 87–89)
3. "In the lap of their shining ship, lined / With gleaming armor, going safely." (lines 110–111)

► **Vocabulary Terms**

Anglo-Saxon word parts originated in Anglo-Saxon England and remain a part of our vocabulary.

► **Test-Taking Tip**

You can identify unfamiliar words more easily in a test-taking situation by memorizing a few common word parts, such as the ones listed in the chart.

► **Reading Handbook**

For more about word origins and word parts, see Reading Handbook, p. R20.

eFlashcards For eFlashcards and other vocabulary activities, go to www.glencoe.com.

OBJECTIVES
- Understand Anglo-Saxon word parts.
- Determine the meanings of unfamiliar words.

Connecting to the Poem

In "The Seafarer," a sailor laments the hardships he has faced at sea. Yet the sailor also feels drawn to sea life, accepting his fate. As you read the poem, think about the following questions:

- What is fate? Do you feel it plays a role in your life?
- How do you deal with circumstances that are both unavoidable and unpleasant?

Building Background

Created by an unknown writer, "The Seafarer" is representative of the somewhat grim Anglo-Saxon worldview. The Anglo-Saxons believed that a person's *wyrd*, or fate, was unavoidable: all roads led inescapably to death. In "The Seafarer," this view is united with Christianized notions of heaven and God.

Some scholars, noting that the tone of the poem changes dramatically in line 64, believe that a monk added to the last sections of the poem to create a work more religious in tone. Other scholars argue that "The Seafarer" is the work of one poet.

Setting Purposes for Reading

Big Idea The Epic Warrior

As you read, notice how the speaker combines descriptions of the failed human world with the "hope of Heaven."

Literary Element Mood

Mood is the emotional quality of a work of literature. A number of elements may contribute to creating mood, such as a writer's choice of language, subject matter, setting, and tone, as well as sound devices such as rhyme, rhythm, and meter. As you read, examine how the poet creates a somber, mournful mood.

- See Literary Terms Handbook, p. R11.

Literature Online **Interactive Literary Elements Handbook** To review or learn more about the literary elements, go to www.glencoe.com.

Reading Strategy Making Inferences About Theme

To **make inferences about theme** means to make a reasonable guess about the main idea of a literary work and express it as a general statement about life. In many works, the theme is implied, not stated explicitly.

Reading Tip: Taking Notes Use a chart like the one below to record the inferences you draw from the details presented in the poem.

Detail	Inference About Theme
Line 86 Those powers have vanished.	The human world is impermanent.

Vocabulary

admonish (ad mon′ ish) *v.* to warn; to reprimand; p. 76 *The teacher was forced to repeatedly admonish his class for their lack of effort.*

rancor (rang′ kər) *n.* bitter malice or resentment; p. 77 *The rancor Herman felt was visible in the scowl on his face.*

flourish (flur′ ish) *v.* to exist at the peak of development or achievement; to thrive; p. 77 *With enough water and sun, the plants should flourish.*

blanch (blanch) *v.* to turn white or become pale; p. 78 *The chemicals that the painter was using, while safe, were causing her skin to blanch.*

Vocabulary Tip: Analogies Analogies are comparisons based on a similarity between things that are otherwise dissimilar. To complete an analogy, decide on the relationship represented by the first pair of words. Then, apply that relationship to the second set of words.

OBJECTIVES
In studying this selection, you will focus on the following:
- analyzing literary periods
- analyzing mood
- making inferences about theme

Three ceramic tiles depicting a ship sailing at sunset. William De Morgan. The De Morgan Centre, London.

The Seafarer

Translated by Burton Raffel

This tale is true, and mine. It tells
How the sea took me, swept me back
And forth in sorrow and fear and pain,
Showed me suffering in a hundred ships,
5   In a thousand ports, and in me. It tells
Of smashing surf when I sweated in the cold
Of an anxious watch,° perched in the bow°
As it dashed under cliffs. My feet were cast
In icy bands, bound with frost,
10   With frozen chains, and hardship groaned
Around my heart. Hunger tore
At my sea-weary soul. No man sheltered
On the quiet fairness of earth can feel
How wretched I was, drifting through winter
15   On an ice-cold sea, whirled in sorrow,
Alone in a world blown clear of love,
Hung with icicles. The hailstorms flew.
The only sound was the roaring sea,
The freezing waves. The song of the swan
20   Might serve for pleasure, the cry of the sea-fowl,
The death-noise of birds instead of laughter,
The mewing of gulls instead of mead.
Storms beat on the rocky cliffs and were echoed
By icy-feathered terns° and the eagle's screams;

7 watch: a period of time during a day on a ship in which a crew member is on duty. **bow:** the front section of the ship

24 terns: seabirds that resemble small gulls and have forked tails

Literary Element **Mood** *How do these images contribute to the poem's mood?*

25　No kinsman could offer comfort there,
　　To a soul left drowning in desolation.
　　　　　　And who could believe, knowing but
　　The passion of cities, swelled proud with wine
　　And no taste of misfortune, how often, how wearily,
30　I put myself back on the paths of the sea.
　　Night would blacken; it would snow from the north;
　　Frost bound the earth and hail would fall,
　　The coldest seeds. And how my heart
　　Would begin to beat, knowing once more
35　The salt waves tossing and the towering sea!
　　The time for journeys would come and my soul
　　Called me eagerly out, sent me over
　　The horizon, seeking foreigners' homes.
　　　　　　But there isn't a man on earth so proud,
40　So born to greatness, so bold with his youth,
　　Grown so brave, or so graced by God,
　　That he feels no fear as the sails unfurl,
　　Wondering what Fate has willed and will do.
　　No harps ring in his heart, no rewards,
45　No passion for women, no worldly pleasures,
　　Nothing, only the ocean's heave;
　　But longing wraps itself around him.
　　Orchards blossom, the towns bloom,
　　Fields grow lovely as the world springs fresh,
50　And all these **admonish** that willing mind
　　Leaping to journeys, always set
　　In thoughts traveling on a quickening tide.
　　So summer's sentinel,° the cuckoo, sings
　　In his murmuring voice, and our hearts mourn
55　As he urges. Who could understand,
　　In ignorant ease, what we others suffer
　　As the paths of exile stretch endlessly on?
　　　　　　And yet my heart wanders away,
　　My soul roams with the sea, the whales'
60　Home, wandering to the widest corners
　　Of the world, returning ravenous with desire,
　　Flying solitary, screaming, exciting me
　　To the open ocean, breaking oaths
　　On the curve of a wave.

53 **sentinel:** one who keeps guard

Norman soldiers crossing the English channel, from "La Vie de Saint Aubin d'Angers," 11th century. French School. Vellum. Bibliotheque Nationale, Paris.

Baroque Harmony in the Ice Off the Labrador Coast, 1929. Dora Carrington. Tinsel painting on glass, 3½ in. x 5 in. Private collection.

                    Thus the joys of God
65   Are fervent° with life, where life itself
     Fades quickly into the earth. The wealth
     Of the world neither reaches to Heaven nor remains.
     No man has ever faced the dawn
     Certain which of Fate's three threats
70   Would fall: illness, or age, or an enemy's
     Sword, snatching the life from his soul.
     The praise the living pour on the dead
     Flowers from reputation: plant
     An earthly life of profit reaped
75   Even from hatred and **rancor,** of bravery
     Flung in the devil's face, and death
     Can only bring you earthly praise
     And a song to celebrate a place
     With the angels, life eternally blessed
80   In the hosts of Heaven.
                         The days are gone
     When the kingdoms of earth **flourished** in glory;
     Now there are no rulers, no emperors,
     No givers of gold, as once there were,

65 **fervent:** Here, *fervent* means "glowing" or "burning."

Reading Strategy **Making Inferences About Theme** *How do these lines help you make inferences about the poem's theme?*

Big Idea **The Epic Warrior** *What do lines 80–83 suggest about the era in which "The Seafarer" was composed?*

Vocabulary

rancor (rang′ ker) *n.* bitter malice or resentment
flourish (flur′ ish) *v.* to exist at the peak of development or achievement; to thrive

When wonderful things were worked among them
85 And they lived in lordly magnificence.
Those powers have vanished, those pleasures are dead.
The weakest survives and the world continues,
Kept spinning by toil. All glory is tarnished,
The world's honor ages and shrinks,
90 Bent like the men who mold it. Their faces
Blanch as time advances, their beards
Wither and they mourn the memory of friends.
The sons of princes, sown in the dust.
The soul stripped of its flesh knows nothing
95 Of sweetness or sour, feels no pain,
Bends neither its hand nor its brain. A brother
Opens his palms and pours down gold
On his kinsman's grave, strewing his coffin
With treasures intended for Heaven, but nothing
100 Golden shakes the wrath of God
For a soul overflowing with sin, and nothing
Hidden on earth rises to Heaven.
          We all fear God. He turns the earth,
He set it swinging firmly in space,
105 Gave life to the world and light to the sky.
Death leaps at the fools who forget their God.
He who lives humbly has angels from Heaven
To carry him courage and strength and belief.
A man must conquer pride, not kill it,
110 Be firm with his fellows, chaste for himself,
Treat all the world as the world deserves,
With love or with hate but never with harm,
Though an enemy seek to scorch him in hell,
Or set the flames of a funeral pyre°
115 Under his lord. Fate is stronger
And God mightier than any man's mind.
Our thoughts should turn to where our home is,
Consider the ways of coming there,
Then strive for sure permission for us
120 To rise to that eternal joy,
That life born in the love of God
And the hope of Heaven. Praise the Holy
Grace of Him who honored us,
Eternal, unchanging creator of earth. Amen.

The Coming of the Norsemen in 1000 AD, 20th century. Mabelle Linnea Holmes. Tapestry. Jamestown-Yorktown Educational Trust, VA.

114 funeral pyre: a heap of flammable material on which a dead body is burned

---

Reading Strategy **Making Inferences About Theme** *What can you infer about the theme from these lines?*

Vocabulary

blanch (blanch) *v.* to turn white or become pale

RESPONDING AND THINKING CRITICALLY

Respond

1. Which images in the poem did you find the most memorable? Explain.

Recall and Interpret

2. (a)What hardships of life at sea does the speaker describe at the beginning of the poem (lines 1–26)? (b)What mood do these lines create?

3. (a)What pleasures of life on the land does the speaker mention? (b)In your opinion, does the speaker long for a comfortable life on land or does he willingly go to sea? Explain.

4. (a)What does the speaker say is different about life in his time as compared with life in the past? (b)What does the speaker's attitude about the past suggest about his feelings for the time in which he lives?

Analyze and Evaluate

5. (a)How does the sea function literally and figuratively in the poem? (b)In what ways is the sea an effective symbol?

6. (a)What change do you notice in the focus and tone midway through the poem? (b)Which half of the poem do you prefer? Explain.

7. How does the poem's imagery help to convey the speaker's conflicted emotions?

Connect

8. **Big Idea** **The Epic Warrior** In what ways does this poem capture the brooding worldview of the Anglo-Saxons?

LITERARY ANALYSIS

Literary Element Mood

While there are many contributing factors to a literary work's **mood**, imagery is one of the most significant elements. Frequent use of dark, strange, or repellent images can help create a bleak mood. Lighthearted images help create a pleasant mood. However, authors sometimes use images as a counterpoint to the prevailing mood of a piece. By including images that conflict with the mood, authors can create more complicated or ironic works.

1. What is the principal mood of "The Seafarer"?

2. Identify several images from the poem that contribute to this mood.

3. Are there any images that conflict with the principal mood of the piece? List any that you find.

Review: Conflict

As you learned on page 23, **conflict** refers to the central struggle between two opposing forces in a story or drama. There are two main types of conflict that can occur in a work of literature. **External conflict** exists when a character struggles against an outside force, such as a war or nature. **Internal conflict** is present when a struggle takes place within the mind of a character. In "The Seafarer," the speaker experiences both types of conflict.

Partner Activity Meet with another classmate to discuss the speaker's conflicts, the causes of these conflicts, and how they affect the poem's mood. Be sure to cite textual evidence during your discussion to support your claims.

Reading Strategy Making Inferences About Theme

The theme of a literary work can have multiple, interrelated parts. The theme of "The Seafarer," for example, has several aspects. The conflict within the speaker, as well as the speaker's feelings about fate and eternity, all contribute different elements to the poem's broader theme.

1. What is the theme of "The Seafarer"?

2. In support of your theme, list three important details from the poem and the inferences you drew from them.

Vocabulary Practice

Practice with Analogies Choose the word that best completes each analogy.

1. supported : flourished :: neglected :
   - **a.** aged
   - **b.** regretted
   - **c.** deteriorated
   - **d.** promoted

2. white : blanch :: red :
   - **a.** examine
   - **b.** embarrass
   - **c.** blush
   - **d.** beet

3. urge : encourage :: admonish :
   - **a.** warn
   - **b.** praise
   - **c.** admire
   - **d.** amuse

4. irritation : rancor :: fondness :
   - **a.** love
   - **b.** apathy
   - **c.** anger
   - **d.** cowardice

Academic Vocabulary

Here are two words from the vocabulary list on page R82.

derive (di rīv′) *v.* to reach a conclusion based on logic or reasoning; to deduce

ensure (en shoor′) *v.* to confirm or make certain

Practice and Apply

1. What lessons about life could a reader **derive** from "The Seafarer"?

2. What does the poem's speaker suggest is **ensured** for all earthly things?

Writing About Literature

Respond to Mood What feelings did you have as you read "The Seafarer"? Did you experience a range of emotions? Was one emotion stronger than the others? Write a brief essay in which you describe how the mood of "The Seafarer" affected your emotions. Use examples from the poem to support your position.

Before you begin drafting, it is important to take notes to guide the writing of your response. Look over the poem again and record any impressions that strike you, as well as the poem's main ideas and your response to those ideas. Also, write down quotations that evoke the emotions you experienced while reading the poem. Compile your notes in an outline, like the one below.

> I. Poem's main ideas
>   A. Life is impermanent.
>   B.
> II. My impressions and responses to main ideas
>   A.
>   B.
> III. Supporting quotations
>   A. Line 89: "The world's honor ages and shrinks"
>   B.

After you complete your draft, meet with a peer reviewer to evaluate each other's work and to suggest revisions. Then proofread and edit your draft for errors in spelling, grammar, and punctuation.

Internet Connection

A number of universities have Web pages devoted to the study of Old English verse. To hear Old English poetry read aloud, and to read other Old English elegies, search the Web, using the key words "Old English verse."

Literature Online Web Activities For eFlashcards, Selection Quick Checks, and other Web activities, go to www.glencoe.com.

Part 2

The Power of Faith

Lydgate and the Canterbury Pilgrims Leaving Canterbury (detail), from *the Troy Book and the Siege of Thebes*, c. 1412–1422. Vellum. British Library, London.

"And specially, from every shire's end
Of England, down to Canterbury they wend
To seek the holy blissful martyr, quick
To give his help to them when they were sick."

—Geoffrey Chaucer, *The Canterbury Tales*

from *The Ecclesiastical History of the English People*

MEET THE VENERABLE BEDE

About the same time that a scop may have been singing in a hushed mead-hall about the heroic deeds of Beowulf, a monk named Bede was studying and writing in the equally quiet library of a monastery. Whereas the gifted scop remained forever nameless, this monk's name became known throughout the world.

A Life of Religious Study When Bede was a boy of seven, he went to study and live in a monastery at Wearmouth, England. About two years later, Bede moved to a monastery in Jarrow, just a short distance away. There he remained for the rest of his life, devoting himself to religion and scholarly pursuits.

> *"It has ever been my delight to learn or teach or write."*
>
> —Bede

A man of great learning, Bede had far-ranging interests that included religion, poetry, grammar, music, art, mathematics, and science. His passion for calculating time and dates led him to use a method of dating still in use today. This method starts from the birth of Jesus in the year A.D. 1 (A.D. stands for the Latin *Anno Domini*, "the year of our Lord"). Bede's use of this form of dating in his histories helped to popularize it.

Bede wrote in Latin, the language of religion and learning, rather than in Old English, the language of the people. With almost forty volumes bearing his name, Bede is the first important writer of prose in England and is considered the father of English history. Bede's masterpiece, *The Ecclesiastical History of the English People*, documents the influence of the church on the development of English civilization.

Writing History Fortunately for us, Bede was a talented storyteller. His histories are far more than mere chronicles of events; they present meticulously researched stories of conquests, saints, missionaries, and monasteries. To write his great works, Bede did research in the library of the monastery, sent letters all over the world, and spoke with artists and scholars from afar who visited the monastery. Bede reveals in his histories how people actually lived, providing most of what we know about life in Britain between the years 46 and 731.

Except for visits to York and Lindisfarne, Bede never left Jarrow. Nevertheless, his reputation spread widely. About a century after his death, he was given the title "Venerable" to honor his wisdom and piety. In 1899 he was declared a saint of the Catholic Church. Historian Kemp Malone writes of Bede's legacy, "Bede makes every effort to be accurate. He admits wonders only after he has investigated them and found them well authenticated. His standards of verification are not ours, of course. If today a victim of snakebite were to drink down some scrapings of Irish books and get well, we should not conclude that the scrapings had worked the cure."

Bede was born in 672 or 673 and died in 735.

Literature Online **Author Search** For more about the Venerable Bede, go to www.glencoe.com.

Connecting to the Chronicle

Have you ever had to face a major change in your life? In *The Ecclesiastical History of the English People*, two men face miraculous changes. As you read the excerpts, consider what can cause people to make major life changes.

Building Background

The Anglo-Saxon invasions of the mid-fifth century overthrew the Christian society of Celtic Britain. Nearly 150 years later in 596, Pope Gregory I sent missionaries to convert the Anglo-Saxons. By about 650, Anglo-Saxon England was largely Christianized.

The first selection from Bede's *Ecclesiastical History* takes place during the early 600s. In it, Edwin, who has recently conquered his enemies to become king of Northumbria in northern England, is discussing Christianity with Paulinus, his wife's religious counselor. The second selection takes place in the late 600s in Whitby, England. It tells of the miraculous talent of Caedmon, the first poet to use Old English verse forms to recite religious poetry.

Setting Purposes for Reading

Big Idea   The Power of Faith

As you read the excerpts, note how the power of faith played a role in the lives of people living in Anglo-Saxon England.

Literary Element   Historical Narrative

A **historical narrative** is a factual account of events that occurred in the past. It is usually presented chronologically and seeks to provide a detailed, accurate description of life in a particular time period. As you read the two excerpts from *The Ecclesiastical History of the English People*, identify the features that make it a historical narrative.

- See Literary Terms Handbook, p. R8.

Reading Strategy   Summarizing

A summary is a brief restatement, in one's own words, of the main ideas and events in a literary work. **Summarizing** what you have read is an excellent tool for understanding and remembering a passage.

....

Reading Tip: Taking Notes When you read, stop periodically to summarize and record important ideas and events. Create a chart to organize your notes.

Main Event or Idea	Summary
Paulinus visits the king.	

Vocabulary

expound (iks pound′) *v.* to set forth in detail, explain; p. 86 *I didn't understand the theory, so I asked the teacher to expound its meaning.*

diligently (dil′ ə jənt lē) *adv.* persistently; p. 86 *After diligently submitting many applications, I finally found a job.*

aspire (əs pīr′) *v.* to strive for; p. 87 *I practice the guitar often because I aspire to become a famous musician.*

frivolous (friv′ ə ləs) *adj.* not serious, silly; p. 87 *His frivolous manner made him seem incapable of taking on anything responsibly.*

Vocabulary Tip: Word Origins Word origins, or **etymologies,** refer to the history and development of words. Word origins are included in dictionary entries.

Literature Online Interactive Literary Elements Handbook To review or learn more about the literary elements, go to www.glencoe.com.

OBJECTIVES
In studying this selection, you will focus on the following:
- exploring the history of English literature
- evaluating historical narrative
- summarizing text

A Scribe Writing, 12th century. Latin (Durham). Illumination from
Bede's *Life and Miracles of St. Cuthbert.* British Library, London

from

THE ECCLESIASTICAL HISTORY OF THE ENGLISH PEOPLE

The Venerable Bede
Translated by Bertram Colgrave

The Anglo-Saxons Embrace Christianity

King Edwin hesitated to accept the word of God which Paulinus preached but, as we have said, used to sit alone for hours at a time, earnestly debating within himself what he ought to do and what religion he should follow. One day Paulinus came to him and, placing his right hand on the king's head, asked him if he recognized this sign.

The king began to tremble and would have thrown himself at the bishop's feet but Paulinus raised him up and said in a voice that seemed familiar, "First you have escaped with God's help from the hands of the foes you feared; secondly you have acquired by His gift the kingdom you desired; now, in the third place, remember your own promise; do not delay in fulfilling it but receive the faith and keep the commandments of Him who rescued you from your earthly foes and raised you to the honor of an earthly kingdom. If from henceforth you are willing to follow His will which is made known to you through me, He will also rescue you from the everlasting torments of the wicked and make you a partaker with Him of His eternal kingdom in heaven."

When the king had heard his words, he answered that he was both willing and bound to accept the faith which Paulinus taught. He said, however, that he would confer about this with his loyal chief men and his counsellors so that, if they agreed with him, they might all be consecrated together in the waters of life. Paulinus agreed, and the king did as he had said. A meeting of his council was held, and each one was asked in turn what he thought of this doctrine[1] hitherto unknown to them and this new worship of God which was being proclaimed.

Coifi, the chief of the priests, answered at once, "Notice carefully, King, this doctrine which is

---

1. A *doctrine* is a body of principles taught or advocated, as of a religion or a government.

Reading Strategy Summarizing *Summarize the argument that Paulinus makes in the following speech.*

Literary Element Historical Narrative *In what way is this detail characteristic of a historical narrative?*

Illuminated manuscript page. Kungl. Bernadotte-Biblioteket, The Royal Collection, Sweden.

now being **expounded** to us. I frankly admit that, for my part, I have found that the religion which we have hitherto held has no virtue nor profit in it. None of your followers has devoted himself more earnestly than I have to the worship of our gods, but nevertheless there are many who receive greater benefits and greater honor from you than I do and are more successful in all their undertakings. If the gods had any power, they would have helped me more readily, seeing that I have always served them with greater zeal.[2] So it follows that if, on examination, these new doctrines which have now been explained to us are found to be better and more effectual, let us accept them at once without any delay."

---

2. *Zeal* means "enthusiastic devotion."

Reading Strategy Summarizing *Summarize Coifi's attitude toward religion.*

Vocabulary

expound (iks pound′) *v.* to set forth in detail; explain

Another of the king's chief men agreed with this advice and with these wise words and then added, "This is how the present life of man on earth, King, appears to me in comparison with that time which is unknown to us. You are sitting feasting with your eldermen and thanes[3] in winter time; the fire is burning on the hearth in the middle of the hall and all inside is warm, while outside the wintry storms of rain and snow are raging; and a sparrow flies swiftly through the hall. It enters in at one door and quickly flies out through the other. For the few moments it is inside, the storm and wintry tempest cannot touch it, but after the briefest moment of calm, it flits from your sight, out of the wintry storm and into it again. So this life of man appears but for a moment; what follows or indeed what went before, we know not at all. If this new doctrine brings us more certain information, it seems right that we should accept it." Other elders and counsellors of the king continued in the same manner, being divinely prompted to do so.

Coifi added that he would like to listen still more carefully to what Paulinus himself had to say about God. The king ordered Paulinus to speak, and when he had said his say, Coifi exclaimed, "For a long time now I have realized that our religion is worthless; for the more **diligently** I sought the truth in our cult, the less I found it. Now I confess openly that the truth shines out clearly in this teaching which can bestow on us the gift of life, salvation, and eternal happiness. Therefore, I advise your Majesty that we should promptly abandon and commit to the flames the temples and the altars which we have held sacred without reaping any benefit." Why need I say more? The king publicly accepted the gospel which Paulinus preached, renounced idolatry, and confessed his faith in

---

3. *Eldermen* are advisers; *thanes* are nobles.

Big Idea The Power of Faith *What point do you think Bede is making about the afterlife by relating this parable of the sparrow?*

Literary Element Historical Narrative *How might a modern historian represent this scene differently?*

Vocabulary

diligently (dil′ ə jənt lē) *adv.* persistently

Christ. When he asked the high priest of their religion which of them should be the first to profane[4] the altars and the shrines of the idols, together with their precincts, Coifi answered, "I will; for through the wisdom the true God has given me no one can more suitably destroy those things which I once foolishly worshipped, and so set an example to all." And at once, casting aside his vain superstitions, he asked the king to provide him with arms and a stallion; and mounting it, he set out to destroy the idols. Now a high priest of their religion was not allowed to carry arms or to ride except on a mare. So, girded with a sword, he took a spear in his hand, and mounting the king's stallion, he set off to where the idols were. The common people who saw him thought he was mad. But as soon as he approached the shrine, without any hesitation he profaned it by casting the spear which he held into it; and greatly rejoicing in the knowledge of the worship of the true God, he ordered his companions to destroy and set fire to the shrine and all the enclosures. The place where the idols once stood is still shown, not far from York, to the east, over the river Derwent. Today it is called Goodmanham, the place where the high priest, through the inspiration of the true God, profaned and destroyed the altars which he himself had consecrated.[5]

Caedmon[6]
Translated by Leo Sherley-Price

In this monastery of Whitby there lived a brother[7] whom God's grace made remarkable. So skilful was he in composing religious and devotional songs, that he could quickly turn whatever passages of Scripture were explained to him into delightful and moving poetry in his own English tongue. These verses of his stirred the hearts of many folk to despise the world and

Kneeling crusader with his horse behind him (page from Westminster Psalter), 13th Century. Illuminated manuscript. The British Library, London.

aspire to heavenly things. Others after him tried to compose religious poems in English, but none could compare with him, for he received this gift of poetry as a gift from God and did not acquire it through any human teacher. For this reason he could never compose any **frivolous** or profane[8] verses, but only such as had a religious theme fell fittingly from his devout lips. And although he followed a secular[9] occupation until well advanced in years, he had never learned anything about poetry: indeed, whenever all those present at a feast took it in turns to sing and entertain the company, he would get up from table and go home directly he saw the harp approaching him.

---

4. *Profane* means "to treat with disrespect; to desecrate."
5. *Consecrated* means "set apart as sacred."
6. *Caedmon* (kad′mən)
7. A *brother* is a member of a religious community who is not a priest or a monk.

Big Idea The Power of Faith *What historical fact about religion do Coifi's actions illustrate?*

---

8. Here, *profane* means "worldly."
9. *Secular* means "not religious."

Vocabulary

aspire (əs pīr′) *v.* to strive for
frivolous (friv′ ə ləs) *adj.* not serious; silly

On one such occasion he had left the house in which the entertainment was being held and went out to the stable, where it was his duty to look after the beasts that night. He lay down there at the appointed time and fell asleep, and in a dream he saw a man standing beside him who called him by name. "Caedmon," he said, "sing me a song." "I don't know how to sing," he replied. "It is because I cannot sing that I left the feast and came here." The man who addressed him then said: "But you shall sing to me." "What should I sing about?" he replied. "Sing about the Creation of all things," the other answered. And Caedmon immediately began to sing verses in praise of God the Creator that he had never heard before, and their theme ran thus: "Let us praise the Maker of the kingdom of heaven, the power and purpose of our Creator, and the acts of the Father of glory. Let us sing how the eternal God, the Author of all marvels, first created the heavens for the sons of men as a roof to cover them, and how their almighty Protector gave them the earth for their dwelling place." This is the general sense, but not the actual words that Caedmon sang in his dream; for however excellent the verses, it is impossible to translate them from one language into another[10] without losing much of their beauty and dignity. When Caedmon awoke, he remembered everything that he had sung in his dream, and soon added more verses in the same style to the glory of God.

Early in the morning he went to his superior the reeve,[11] and told him about this gift that he had received. The reeve took him before the abbess,[12] who ordered him to give an account of his dream and repeat the verses in the presence of many learned men, so that they might decide their quality and origin. All of them agreed that Caedmon's gift had been given him by our Lord, and when they had explained to him a passage of scriptural history or doctrine, they asked him to render[13] it into verse if he could. He promised to do this, and returned next morning with excellent verses as they had ordered him. The abbess was delighted that God had given such grace to the man, and advised him to abandon secular life and adopt the monastic state. And when she had admitted him into the Community as a brother, she ordered him to be instructed in the events of sacred history.[14] So Caedmon stored up in his memory all that he learned, and after meditating on it, turned it into such melodious verse that his delightful renderings turned his instructors into his audience. He sang of the creation of the world, the origin of the human race, and the whole story of Genesis. He sang of Israel's departure from Egypt, their entry into the land of promise, and many other events of scriptural history. He sang of the Lord's Incarnation, Passion, Resurrection, and Ascension into heaven, the coming of the Holy Spirit, and the teaching of the Apostles. He also made many poems on the terrors of the Last Judgement, the horrible pains of Hell, and the joys of the kingdom of heaven. In addition to these, he composed several others on the blessings and judgements of God, by which he sought to turn his hearers from delight in wickedness, and to inspire them to love and do good. For Caedmon was a deeply religious man, who humbly submitted to regular discipline, and firmly resisted all who tried to do evil, thus winning a happy death. ❧

---

10. Caedmon's poetry was translated from *one language into another*—from Old English to Latin.
11. A *reeve* is the manager of a manor or farm.
12. An *abbess* is the head of a convent or monastery.

Reading Strategy Summarizing *Put the "general sense" of Caedmon's song into your own words.*

---

13. *Render* means "to express in another form."
14. [*The abbess . . . history.*] The abbess is delighted with Caedmon's gift and advises him to join the monastery and learn the narratives of the Bible.

Big Idea The Power of Faith *What does Bede mean by a "happy death"?*

RESPONDING AND THINKING CRITICALLY

Respond

1. After reading the selections, what questions would you like to ask Bede? Why?

Recall and Interpret

2. (a)What arguments convince Edwin to convert to Christianity? (b)What does Edwin's reaction to the arguments reveal about his personality?

3. (a)Summarize the **analogy**, or comparison, made by one of the king's chief men. (b)What do the sparrow and the storm symbolize?

4. (a)Why does Coifi volunteer to be the first person to profane the shrine? (b)Why might the "common people" be impressed by Coifi's actions?

5. (a)What is Caedmon's life like before his dream? (b)How does it change after the dream?

Analyze and Evaluate

6. (a)Which of Paulinus's arguments for conversion did you find the most convincing? Explain. (b)Which of the arguments by Edwin's advisers did you find the most convincing? Explain.

7. (a)Analyze the poem that came to Caedmon in his dream. To what is heaven compared? (b)Why is Caedmon's dream considered to be a miracle?

Connect

8. (a)Why was a humble poet such as Caedmon so revered in his time? (b)Do you think that a poet could be regarded as equally important today? Explain.

9. **Big Idea** **The Power of Faith** How do the events in the two excerpts from *The Ecclesiastical History* portray the power of faith in England during the Anglo-Saxon period?

LITERARY ANALYSIS

Literary Element **Historical Narrative**

A **historical narrative** tells the story of real people and events during a particular time and place. For this reason, a historical narrative contains many details about the period that it describes. These details are intended to present an objective rendering of reality.

1. In your opinion, do the excerpts from Bede's *Ecclesiastical History* fit the above definition of a historical narrative? Explain.

2. Although historians try to be objective, they are nevertheless influenced by the time in which they live. What biases, prejudices, or other "blind spots" might have colored Bede's work?

Listening and Speaking

With three other students, read aloud the excerpt about the conversion of Edwin. Each student should choose one of these "parts": Paulinus, Coifi, the unnamed counselor, and the narrator. After rehearsing your parts, do a dramatic reading of the selection for the class.

READING AND VOCABULARY

Reading Strategy **Summarizing**

The best summaries can easily be understood by someone who has not read the selection being summarized.

1. What are the main ideas or events in the first excerpt, "The Anglo-Saxons Embrace Christianity"?

2. What are the main ideas and events in the second excerpt, "Caedmon"?

Vocabulary **Practice**

Practice with Word Origins Match each vocabulary word with its corresponding Latin root. Use a dictionary for assistance.

1. expound   **a.** *aspirare,* "to breathe upon"

2. diligently   **b.** *frivolus,* "of little weight"

3. aspire   **c.** *exponere,* "to explain"

4. frivolous   **d.** *diligere,* "to esteem"

Literature Online **Web Activities** For eFlashcards, Selection Quick Checks, and other Web activities, go to www.glencoe.com.

The Development of English

> "One cannot but be impressed by the amazing hospitality of the English language."
>
> —Robert Burchfield

MODERN ENGLISH BEGAN AS *ENGLISC*, THE speech of a scattered population of Anglo-Saxon peoples on an island off the European coast. Today, English is a global language spoken by perhaps a billion people around the world. This is largely due to the political power and cultural influence of the British Empire and the United States. However, it is also the result of the simplicity that English grammar has acquired during its long history. Modern English passed through two major stages, Old English and Middle English.

Old English: 450–1150

The Anglo-Saxons spoke various Germanic dialects, a mixture of which are the basis of Old English, the form of the English language used from the mid-400s to the early 1100s. To present-day readers of English, Old English looks like a foreign language, as these lines from the Old English epic poem *Beowulf* show:

Dā cōm of mōre   *under mist-hleoþum*
Grendel gongan,   *Godes yrre bær*

(translation)
Then out of the marsh,   *under mist-covered cliffs,*
Grendel stalked   *bearing God's wrath*

Old English had a significant effect on Modern English. Although less than one percent of the words—4,500 out of 500,000—in the *Oxford English Dictionary* are from Old English, these words form our most basic (*man, wife, work, Friday, house*) and functional (*to, for, but, and*) vocabulary. One computer analysis revealed that all of the hundred most commonly used English words are of Anglo-Saxon origin.

Interior of Scriptorium, School of Segovia. Spanish School. Oil on panel. Museo Lazaro Galdiano, Madrid, Spain.

By the 600s, Christian scribes had further developed English by replacing the ancient Germanic characters known as runes with the Old English alphabet of twenty-four letters. The scribes who transcribed *Beowulf* around the year 1000 used this alphabet.

Middle English: 1150–1500

Between 450 and 1200, Latin, Danish, Old Norse, and Norman French fed the growing English language. After the Norman Conquest in 1066, England's new aristocracy spoke French. Well-educated people needed to know three languages, however: French for dealing with the nobility or the courts; Latin for the church, business, and scholarship; and English for communication with the majority of the common people. French had a strong influence on English. Many French words were introduced into the language that was becoming Middle English, and many Old English words were dropped. In fact, French increased the English vocabulary by a staggering 10,000 words, 7,500 of which are still in use. Today, almost half of Modern English's vocabulary comes from Latin and French. French influence also led to the gradual simplification of English grammar and spelling. Middle English slowly developed into a language somewhat similar to the English used today.

Linguistic diversity, however, remained so great during this period that people in one part of England could often not understand people who lived in another part. Over time, the dialect spoken in London—the language in which Geoffrey Chaucer wrote—eventually became the standard. Compare these opening lines of his *Canterbury Tales* with the passage from *Beowulf* quoted earlier.

Whan that Aprille with his shoures soote
The droghte of March hath perced to the roote,
And bathed every veyne in swich licour
Of which vertu engendred is the flour;
Whan Zephirus eek with his sweete breeth
Inspired hath in every holt and heeth
The tendre croppes, and the yonge sonne
Hath in the Ram his halve cours yronne,
And smale foweles maken melodye,
That slepen al the nyght with open ye
(So priketh hem nature in hir corages);
Thanne longen folk to goon on pilgrimages,
And palmeres for to seken straunge strondes,
To ferne halwes, kowthe in sondry londes;
And specially from every shires ende
Of Engelond to Caunterbury they wende,
The hooly blisful martir for to seke,
That hem hath holpen when that they were seeke.

Illuminated page from St. Luke's Gospel taken from Lindisfarne Gospels, c. 695.

Literature Online Literary History For more about the development of English, go to www.glencoe.com.

RESPONDING AND THINKING CRITICALLY

1. What most surprises you about the development of the English language? Explain.

2. Why do you think Old English remained an important influence on the development of English even after the Norman Conquest?

3. Why do you think the form of Middle English used in the London region became the standard form?

4. In what ways is the passage from *The Canterbury Tales* more accessible to a modern reader than the passage from *Beowulf*?

OBJECTIVES
- Trace the development of the English language.
- Connect to historical context of literature.

from *The Canterbury Tales*

MEET GEOFFREY CHAUCER

Geoffrey Chaucer has often been called the father of English poetry. In "The Prologue" to *The Canterbury Tales*, Chaucer presents a portrait gallery virtually unparalleled in English literature. It offers a catalogue of the virtues, vices, and idiosyncrasies of a diverse cross section of medieval English society that still resonates for modern readers.

A Man of the World Chaucer understood how a variety of people spoke and acted. This knowledge proved invaluable to his writing. Chaucer's father was a prosperous middle-class wine merchant, and the young Chaucer was likely exposed to the colorful banter of the characters who frequented the London docks. Chaucer became a page in the royal household while still a teenager. Despite the lowly duties of the job, such as running errands, the position offered Chaucer exposure to a world of fine manners and high-born people. In 1359 he went to France to fight in the Hundred Years' War. Taken prisoner, he was ransomed in the following year with money contributed by King Edward himself.

> "Although Chaucer's invented personages are now six hundred years old, they are flesh and blood today; they are, in fact, the people whom we have known all our lives."
>
> —Louis Untermeyer

Public Servant While in his twenties, Chaucer was made a court official, an appointment that was the start of many years of public service. During his

Initial with a portrait of Chaucer holding a book. English illumination, c.1400.

career, he traveled abroad on diplomatic missions to France, Spain, and Italy and became familiar with the literature and culture of these countries. Thereafter he held a variety of governmental posts.

Despite his busy professional duties, Chaucer managed to write a large body of work. His early poetry, influenced by the French medieval tradition, includes the *Book of the Duchess* and the *Roman of the Rose*. Later he wrote the *Parliament of Fowls* and the masterful *Troilus and Cressida*. Chaucer's most mature writing, crafted while he was in his forties, includes the *Legend of Good Women* and *The Canterbury Tales*.

Literary Innovator *The Canterbury Tales* is considered Chaucer's masterpiece for several reasons. First, it marks the beginning of a new tradition— Chaucer was the first writer to use English in a major literary work. Before him, literature was composed in French or Latin. Secondly, because *The Canterbury Tales* focuses on an assortment of people who are thrown together on a journey, it gives a lifelike and engaging picture of the various strata of English society during the 1300s. Finally, it is an outstanding literary achievement. Chaucer created approximately 17,000 lines of vivid poetry that still entertain readers six centuries later.

Geoffrey Chaucer was born about 1342 and died in 1400.

Connecting to the Poem

Have you ever wondered about fellow travelers on a trip and imagined what their lives are like? As you read "The Prologue" to *The Canterbury Tales,* think about to what extent you can judge a person's character from his or her profession, appearance, and manners.

Building Background

In *The Canterbury Tales,* Chaucer uses a **frame story,** which is a plot structure that includes the telling of a story within a story. The pilgrims' contest and journey, narrated in "The Prologue," is the frame story. The various tales told by the pilgrims on their journey comprise the stories within the frame.

Chaucer's English was not the same English that we use today. He wrote in what is now known as Middle English, the language that resulted when Old English was infused with the Old French imported by the Norman invaders. The version of *The Canterbury Tales* that you will read is a modern English translation. To sample Chaucer's Middle English, read the famous opening lines of "The Prologue" in the Literary History feature on page 91.

Setting Purposes for Reading

Big Idea **The Power of Faith**

As you read "The Prologue," note the various ways in which the pilgrims interpret and act upon the requirements of their religious faith.

Literary Element **Characterization**

Characterization refers to the methods a writer uses to reveal the values and personalities of his or her characters. A writer may make explicit statements about a character or may reveal a character indirectly through well-chosen words, thoughts, and actions.

• See Literary Terms Handbook, p. R3.

Literature Online **Interactive Literary Elements Handbook** To review or learn more about the literary elements, go to www.glencoe.com.

Reading Strategy **Paraphrasing**

When you **paraphrase,** you put a text you have read into your own words. Paraphrasing is a useful strategy to help you review the content of complex passages. A paraphrase differs from a summary in that a summary is always shorter than the original, while a paraphrase may be approximately the same length as the original.

Reading Tip: Finding Subjects and Verbs You may find it helpful, especially when paraphrasing long, complex sentences or passages, to search for the simple subject and simple predicate in a sentence. Use a standard sentence diagram to find the subject and predicate of sentences in "The Prologue."

Vocabulary

solicitous (sə lis′ ə təs) *adj.* full of concern; p. 98 *The store owner was especially solicitous toward Helen because her accident occurred on store property.*

estimable (es′ tə mə bəl) *adj.* deserving of esteem; admirable; p. 102 *The estimable volunteers raised five thousand dollars.*

discreet (dis krēt′) *adj.* having or showing careful judgment in speech and action; prudent; p. 102 *The talk show guest was discreet and did not criticize his fellow actors.*

disdainful (dis dān′ fəl) *adj.* feeling or showing contempt; scornful; p. 107 *Even though he had come from an impoverished background, Robert was often disdainful toward the homeless.*

prevarication (pri var′ ə kā shən) *n.* the act of evading the truth; a lie; p. 111 *You had better tell the truth; your prevarication will only get you into more trouble.*

Vocabulary Tip: Synonyms Words that have the same or nearly the same meaning are called synonyms. The words *fame* and *renown,* for example, are synonyms. Note that synonyms are always the same part of speech.

OBJECTIVES
In studying this selection, you will focus on the following:
• analyzing literary periods
• analyzing characterization
• paraphrasing text

First page of the *Canterbury Tales.* Illuminated manuscript, early 15th century.

from The Canterbury Tales

Geoffrey Chaucer
Translated by Nevill Coghill

from The Prologue

When in April the sweet showers fall
And pierce the drought of March to the root, and all
The veins are bathed in liquor of such power
As brings about the engendering of the flower,
5 When also Zephyrus° with his sweet breath
Exhales an air in every grove and heath
Upon the tender shoots, and the young sun
His half-course in the sign of the *Ram*° has run,
And the small fowl are making melody
10 That sleep away the night with open eye
(So nature pricks them and their heart engages)
Then people long to go on pilgrimages
And palmers° long to seek the stranger strands
Of far-off saints, hallowed° in sundry° lands,
15 And specially, from every shire's end
Of England, down to Canterbury they wend
To seek the holy blissful martyr,° quick
To give his help to them when they were sick.
    It happened in that season that one day
20 In Southwark, at *The Tabard,*° as I lay
Ready to go on pilgrimage and start
For Canterbury, most devout at heart,
At night there came into that hostelry°

5 Zephyrus (ze′ fə rəs): Greek mythological god of the west wind, which brings mild weather.

8 Ram: the constellation Aries and the first sign of the zodiac. Evidence suggests that the pilgrimage began on April 11, 1387.

13 palmers: pilgrims who wore palm leaves as a sign that they had visited the Holy Land.
14 hallowed: regarded as sacred or holy. **sundry:** various.

17 martyr: Thomas à Becket, archbishop of Canterbury, who was murdered in 1170.

20 Southwark (sə′ thərk): area just across the river Thames from London; today, part of Greater London. **The Tabard** (tab′ ərd): an inn in Southwark.
23 hostelry (hos′ təl rē): inn.

Reading Strategy **Paraphrasing** *Paraphrase the opening lines (1–12) that introduce the subject of the poem.*

Some nine and twenty in a company
25 Of sundry folk happening then to fall
In fellowship, and they were pilgrims all
That towards Canterbury meant to ride.
The rooms and stables of the inn were wide;
They made us easy, all was of the best.
30 And, briefly, when the sun had gone to rest,
I'd spoken to them all upon the trip
And was soon one with them in fellowship,
Pledged to rise early and to take the way
To Canterbury, as you heard me say.
35   But none the less, while I have time and space,
Before my story takes a further pace,
It seems a reasonable thing to say
What their condition was, the full array°
Of each of them, as it appeared to me,
40 According to profession and degree,
And what apparel they were riding in;
And at a Knight I therefore will begin.
There was a *Knight*, a most distinguished man,
Who from the day on which he first began
45 To ride abroad had followed chivalry,
Truth, honor, generousness and courtesy.
He had done nobly in his sovereign's° war
And ridden into battle, no man more,
As well in Christian as in heathen places,
50 And ever honored for his noble graces.
    When we took Alexandria,° he was there.
He often sat at table in the chair
Of honor, above all nations, when in Prussia.
In Lithuania he had ridden, and Russia,
55 No Christian man so often, of his rank.
When, in Granada, Algeciras sank
Under assault, he had been there, and in
North Africa, raiding Benamarin;
In Anatolia he had been as well
60 And fought when Ayas and Attalia fell,
For all along the Mediterranean coast
He had embarked with many a noble host.°
In fifteen mortal battles he had been
And jousted° for our faith at Tramissen
65 Thrice in the lists,° and always killed his man.
This same distinguished knight had led the van
Once with the Bey of Balat,° doing work
For him against another heathen Turk;
He was of sovereign value in all eyes.

38 array: a large grouping or collection.

47 sovereign's: ruler's; king's or queen's.

51 Alexandria: This and the place names that immediately follow are sites of wide-ranging military campaigns and crusades by medieval Christians against the Muslims and other non-Christians.

62 host: army.

64 jousted: fought in formal combat as part of a knightly tournament.
65 lists: the fenced areas where jousts were held.
67 Bey of Balat: a Turkish governor.

Reading Strategy Paraphrasing *What does the narrator intend to do?*

The Pilgrimage to Canterbury, 1806–1807. Thomas Stothard. Oil on wood, 31.8 x 95.2 cm. Tate Gallery, London.

70   And though so much distinguished, he was wise
     And in his bearing modest as a maid.
     He never yet a boorish° thing had said

72 **boorish:** crude; bad-mannered.

     In all his life to any, come what might;
     He was a true, a perfect gentle-knight.
75   Speaking of his equipment, he possessed
     Fine horses, but he was not gaily dressed.
     He wore a fustian° tunic stained and dark

77 **fustian:** coarse, heavy fabric of cotton and linen.

     With smudges where his armor had left mark;
     Just home from service, he had joined our ranks
80   To do his pilgrimage and render thanks.
         He had his son with him, a fine young *Squire,*
     A lover and cadet, a lad of fire
     With locks as curly as if they had been pressed.
     He was some twenty years of age, I guessed.
85   In stature he was of a moderate length,
     With wonderful agility and strength.
     He'd seen some service with the cavalry
     In Flanders and Artois and Picardy°

88 **Flanders . . . Picardy:** historic regions of Belgium, Holland, and northern France.

     And had done valiantly in little space
90   Of time, in hope to win his lady's grace.
     He was embroidered like a meadow bright
     And full of freshest flowers, red and white.
     Singing he was, or fluting all the day;

Literary Element   Characterization *What qualities does the speaker admire in the Knight?*

Literary Element   Characterization *How does the Squire's character differ from that of the Knight?*

He was as fresh as is the month of May.
95 Short was his gown, the sleeves were long and wide;
He knew the way to sit a horse and ride.
He could make songs and poems and recite,
Knew how to joust and dance, to draw and write.
He loved so hotly that till dawn grew pale
100 He slept as little as a nightingale.
Courteous he was, lowly and serviceable,
And carved to serve his father at the table.
     There was a *Yeoman°* with him at his side,
No other servant; so he chose to ride.
105 This Yeoman wore a coat and hood of green,
And peacock-feathered arrows, bright and keen
And neatly sheathed, hung at his belt the while
—For he could dress his gear in yeoman style,
His arrows never drooped their feathers low—
110 And in his hand he bore a mighty bow.
His head was like a nut, his face was brown.
He knew the whole of woodcraft up and down.
A saucy brace° was on his arm to ward
It from the bow-string, and a shield and sword
115 Hung at one side, and at the other slipped
A jaunty dirk,° spear-sharp and well-equipped.
A medal of St. Christopher° he wore
Of shining silver on his breast, and bore
A hunting-horn, well slung and burnished clean,
120 That dangled from a baldrick° of bright green.
He was a proper forester, I guess.
     There also was a *Nun,* a Prioress,°
Her way of smiling very simple and coy.
Her greatest oath was only "By St. Loy!"°
125 And she was known as Madam Eglantyne.

103 **Yeoman** (yō′ mən): nobleman's attendant.

113 **brace:** leather guard worn on the archer's forearm.

116 **dirk:** a small dagger.
117 **St. Christopher:** patron saint of travelers.

120 **baldrick:** shoulder belt.

122 **Prioress:** the nun ranking next below the head nun in an abbey.
124 **St. Loy:** St. Eligius, patron saint of goldsmiths and jewelers, known for his good looks and sumptuous attire.

And well she sang a service,° with a fine
Intoning through her nose, as was most seemly,
And she spoke daintily in French, extremely,
After the school of Stratford-atte-Bowe;°
130   French in the Paris style she did not know.
At meat her manners were well taught withal;
No morsel from her lips did she let fall,
Nor dipped her fingers in the sauce too deep;
But she could carry a morsel up and keep
135   The smallest drop from falling on her breast.
For courtliness she had a special zest,
And she would wipe her upper lip so clean
That not a trace of grease was to be seen
Upon the cup when she had drunk; to eat,
140   She reached a hand sedately for the meat.
She certainly was very entertaining,
Pleasant and friendly in her ways, and straining
To counterfeit a courtly kind of grace,
A stately bearing fitting to her place,
145   And to seem dignified in all her dealings.
As for her sympathies and tender feelings,
She was so charitably **solicitous**
She used to weep if she but saw a mouse
Caught in a trap, if it were dead or bleeding.
150   And she had little dogs she would be feeding
With roasted flesh, or milk, or fine white bread.
And bitterly she wept if one were dead
Or someone took a stick and made it smart;
She was all sentiment and tender heart.
155   Her veil was gathered in a seemly way,
Her nose was elegant, her eyes glass-gray;
Her mouth was very small, but soft and red,
Her forehead, certainly, was fair of spread,
Almost a span° across the brows, I own;
160   She was indeed by no means undergrown.
Her cloak, I noticed, had a graceful charm.
She wore a coral trinket on her arm,
A set of beads, the gaudies° tricked in green,
Whence hung a golden brooch of brightest sheen
165   On which there first was graven a crowned A,

126 service: daily prayers.

129 Stratford-atte-Bowe: a nunnery near London where provincial, rather than courtly, French was taught.

159 span: nine inches. A broad forehead was a sign of beauty in Chaucer's day.

163 gaudies: large beads used in counting prayers.

Big Idea   **The Power of Faith** *Does the Prioress conform to your conception of a high-ranking member of the church? Explain.*

Literary Element   **Characterization** *What is your opinion of the Prioress's "charity" toward animals? Explain.*

Vocabulary

solicitous (sə lis′ ə təs) *adj.* full of concern

Bird's eye view of Canterbury. Georg Braun and Franz Hogenberg. Copper engraving. Civitates Orbis Terrarum, Cologne, Germany.

And lower, *Amor vincit omnia.*°
    Another *Nun*, the secretary at her cell,
Was riding with her, and *three Priests* as well.
    A *Monk* there was, one of the finest sort
170 Who rode the country; hunting was his sport.
A manly man, to be an Abbot° able;
Many a dainty horse he had in stable.
His bridle, when he rode, a man might hear
Jingling in a whistling wind as clear,
175 Aye, and as loud as does the chapel bell
Where my lord Monk was Prior of the cell.°
The Rule of good St. Benet or St. Maur°
As old and strict he tended to ignore;
He let go by the things of yesterday
180 And took the modern world's more spacious way.
He did not rate that text at a plucked hen
Which says that hunters are not holy men
And that a monk uncloistered° is a mere
Fish out of water, flapping on the pier,
185 That is to say a monk out of his cloister.
That was a text he held not worth an oyster;
And I agreed and said his views were sound;
Was he to study till his head went round
Poring over books in cloisters? Must he toil
190 As Austin° bade and till the very soil?
Was he to leave the world upon the shelf?
Let Austin have his labor to himself.
    This Monk was therefore a good man to horse;
Greyhounds he had, as swift as birds, to course.°
195 Hunting a hare or riding at a fence
Was all his fun, he spared for no expense.
I saw his sleeves were garnished at the hand
With fine grey fur, the finest in the land,
And on his hood, to fasten it at his chin

166 Amor vincit omnia (ä′ môr′ win′ kit ôm′ nē ə): Latin for "Love conquers all."

171 Abbot: the head of a monastery.

176 Prior of the cell: head of a subordinate monastery.
177 St. Benet or St. Maur: French versions of St. Benedict, who established the rules of European monasticism, and St. Maurus, one of his followers. Monastic life is governed by strict rules requiring poverty, chastity, and obedience.

183 uncloistered: not *cloistered,* or retired or secluded from the world, as most monks were.

190 Austin: English version of St. Augustine (A.D. 354–430), church father who instructed monks to avoid idleness by performing manual labor.

194 to course: for hunting.

200   He had a wrought-gold cunningly fashioned pin;
      Into a lover's knot it seemed to pass.
      His head was bald and shone like looking-glass;
      So did his face, as if it had been greased.
      He was a fat and personable priest;
205   His prominent eyeballs never seemed to settle.
      They glittered like the flames beneath a kettle;
      Supple his boots, his horse in fine condition.
      He was a prelate° fit for exhibition,
      He was not pale like a tormented soul.
210   He liked a fat swan best, and roasted whole.
      His palfrey° was as brown as is a berry.
         There was a *Friar*, a wanton° one and merry,
      A Limiter,° a very festive fellow.
      In all Four Orders° there was none so mellow,
215   So glib with gallant phrase and well-turned speech.
      He'd fixed up many a marriage, giving each
      Of his young women what he could afford her.
      He was a noble pillar to his Order.
      Highly beloved and intimate was he
220   With County folk° within his boundary,
      And city dames of honor and possessions;
      For he was qualified to hear confessions,
      Or so he said, with more than priestly scope;
      He had a special license from the Pope.
225   Sweetly he heard his penitents at shrift°
      With pleasant absolution,° for a gift.
      He was an easy man in penance-giving
      Where he could hope to make a decent living;
      It's a sure sign whenever gifts are given
230   To a poor Order that a man's well shriven,°
      And should he give enough he knew in verity
      The penitent repented in sincerity.
      For many a fellow is so hard of heart
      He cannot weep, for all his inward smart.
235   Therefore instead of weeping and of prayer
      One should give silver for a poor Friar's care.
      He kept his tippet° stuffed with pins for curls,
      And pocket-knives, to give to pretty girls.
      And certainly his voice was gay and sturdy,
240   For he sang well and played the hurdy-gurdy.°
      At sing-songs he was champion of the hour.
      His neck was whiter than a lily-flower

---

208 prelate: high-ranking clergyman.

211 palfrey: a horse that is saddled and ready for riding.
212 wanton: lively, but here, also meaning morally lax.
213 Limiter: friar licensed to beg in a certain district.
214 Four Orders: referring to the four religious orders in which friars lived by begging: Dominicans, Franciscans, Carmelites, and Augustinians.

220 County folk: the wealthy and socially prominent rural landowners.

225 shrift: confession.
226 absolution: formal forgiveness.

230 well shriven: completely forgiven, through confession, of his sins.

237 tippet: hood.

240 hurdy-gurdy: stringed instrument played by turning a hand crank.

Reading Strategy   Paraphrasing *Paraphrase the Monk's philosophy of life.*

Big Idea   **The Power of Faith** *How does the Friar represent the corruption in the medieval church?*

But strong enough to butt a bruiser down.
He knew the taverns well in every town
245 And every innkeeper and barmaid too
Better than lepers, beggars and that crew,
For in so eminent a man as he
It was not fitting with the dignity
Of his position, dealing with a scum
250 Of wretched lepers; nothing good can come
Of commerce with such slum-and-gutter dwellers,
But only with the rich and victual-sellers.
But anywhere a profit might accrue
Courteous he was and lowly of service too.
255 Natural gifts like his were hard to match.
He was the finest beggar of his batch,
And, for his begging-district, paid a rent;
His brethren did no poaching where he went.
For though a widow mightn't have a shoe,
260 So pleasant was his holy how-d'ye-do
He got his farthing° from her just the same
Before he left, and so his income came
To more than he laid out. And how he romped,
Just like a puppy! He was ever prompt
265 To arbitrate disputes on settling days°
(For a small fee) in many helpful ways,
Not then appearing as your cloistered scholar
With threadbare habit hardly worth a dollar,
But much more like a Doctor or a Pope.
270 Of double-worsted was the semi-cope°
Upon his shoulders, and the swelling fold
About him, like a bell about its mold
When it is casting, rounded out his dress.
He lisped a little out of wantonness
275 To make his English sweet upon his tongue.
When he had played his harp, or having sung,
His eyes would twinkle in his head as bright
As any star upon a frosty night.
This worthy's name was Hubert, it appeared.
280   There was a *Merchant* with a forking beard
And motley° dress; high on his horse he sat,
Upon his head a Flemish° beaver hat
And on his feet daintily buckled boots.
He told of his opinions and pursuits
285 In solemn tones, he harped on his increase
Of capital; there should be sea-police
(He thought) upon the Harwich-Holland ranges;°
He was expert at dabbling in exchanges.

The Monk, c.15th century. Facsimile of Ellesmere Chaucer illuminated manuscript. The Victoria and Albert Museum, London.

261 **farthing:** old British coin.
265 **settling days:** days on which disputes could be settled out of court.
270 **semi-cope:** short robe. A robe made of double worsted, a fine woolen fabric, would be a luxury unsuitable for a friar.

281 **motley:** many-colored or varied.
282 **Flemish:** from Flanders, a region of northwestern Europe.

287 **Harwich-Holland ranges:** North Sea shipping lanes between Harwich (har′ ij), an English port, and Holland.

Big Idea **The Power of Faith** *How does the Friar misuse his position and power within the church?*

This **estimable** Merchant so had set
290   His wits to work, none knew he was in debt,
He was so stately in administration,
In loans and bargains and negotiation.
He was an excellent fellow all the same;
To tell the truth I do not know his name.
295   An *Oxford Cleric*, still a student though,
One who had taken logic long ago,
Was there; his horse was thinner than a rake,
And he was not too fat, I undertake,
But had a hollow look, a sober stare;
300   The thread upon his overcoat was bare.
He had found no preferment° in the church
And he was too unworldly to make search
For secular employment. By his bed
He preferred having twenty books in red
305   And black, of Aristotle's° philosophy,
Than costly clothes, fiddle or psaltery.°
Though a philosopher, as I have told,
He had not found the stone for making gold.°
Whatever money from his friends he took
310   He spent on learning or another book
And prayed for them most earnestly, returning
Thanks to them thus for paying for his learning.
His only care was study, and indeed
He never spoke a word more than was need,
315   Formal at that, respectful in the extreme,
Short, to the point, and lofty in his theme.
A tone of moral virtue filled his speech
And gladly would he learn, and gladly teach.
      A *Sergeant at the Law*° who paid his calls,
320   Wary and wise, for clients at St. Paul's°
There also was, of noted excellence.
Discreet he was, a man to reverence,°
Or so he seemed, his sayings were so wise.
He often had been Justice of Assize°
325   By letters patent,° and in full commission.
His fame and learning and his high position

301 **preferment:** position; sponsorship.

305 **Aristotle's:** referring to the Greek philosopher (384–322 B.C.).
306 **psaltery** (sôl′ tər ē): stringed musical instrument played by plucking.
308 **stone . . . gold:** Medieval alchemists believed that there existed a "philosopher's stone" capable of turning ordinary metals into gold.

319 **Sergeant at the Law:** lawyer appointed by the king to serve as a judge.
320 **St. Paul's:** London cathedral outside which lawyers often met clients when the courts were closed.
322 **reverence:** respect deeply.

324 **Assize:** traveling law court.

325 **letters patent:** royal documents commissioning Assize judges.

Literary Element   Characterization   *How is the Merchant characterized as a hypocrite?*

Literary Element   Characterization   *How does the character of the Cleric contrast with that of the Friar?*

Vocabulary

estimable (es′ tə mə bəl) *adj.* deserving of esteem; admirable
discreet (dis krēt′) *adj.* having or showing careful judgment in speech and action; prudent

Had won him many a robe and many a fee.
There was no such conveyancer° as he;
All was fee-simple° to his strong digestion,
330 Not one conveyance could be called in question.
Though there was nowhere one so busy as he,
He was less busy than he seemed to be.
He knew of every judgment, case and crime
Ever recorded since King William's° time.
335 He could dictate defenses or draft deeds;
No one could pinch a comma from his screeds°
And he knew every statute off by rote.
He wore a homely parti-colored coat,
Girt with a silken belt of pin-stripe stuff;
340 Of his appearance I have said enough.
    There was a *Franklin*° with him, it appeared;
White as a daisy-petal was his beard.
A sanguine° man, high-colored and benign,°
He loved a morning sop° of cake in wine.
345 He lived for pleasure and had always done,
For he was Epicurus'° very son,
In whose opinion sensual delight
Was the one true felicity in sight.
As noted as St. Julian° was for bounty
350 He made his household free to all the County.
His bread, his ale were finest of the fine
And no one had a better stock of wine.
His house was never short of bake-meat pies,
Of fish and flesh, and these in such supplies
355 It positively snowed with meat and drink
And all the dainties that a man could think.
According to the seasons of the year
Changes of dish were ordered to appear.
He kept fat partridges in coops, beyond,
360 Many a bream and pike° were in his pond.
Woe to the cook unless the sauce was hot
And sharp, or if he wasn't on the spot!
And in his hall a table stood arrayed
And ready all day long, with places laid.
365 As Justice at the Sessions none stood higher;°
He often had been Member for the Shire.°
A dagger and a little purse of silk
Hung at his girdle, white as morning milk.
As Sheriff° he checked audit, every entry.
370 He was a model among landed gentry.
    A *Haberdasher*,° a *Dyer*, a *Carpenter*,
A *Weaver* and a *Carpet-maker* were

328 **conveyancer:** The Sergeant specializes in land sales and leases as well as property disputes.
329 **fee-simple:** property owned outright.

334 **King William's:** referring to William the Conqueror, king of England from 1066 to 1087.
336 **screeds:** long, tiresome writings.

341 **Franklin:** wealthy landowner.

343 **sanguine:** cheerful; optimistic. **benign:** of a kind or gentle disposition.
344 **sop:** piece.

346 **Epicurus':** referring to the Greek philosopher (341?–270 B.C.) who taught that the goal of life was real and enduring pleasure, in the sense of peace of mind–a view of pleasure commonly mischaracterized as mere gratification of physical appetites.
349 **St. Julian:** patron saint of hospitality.
360 **bream and pike:** kinds of fishes.
365 **Justice . . . higher:** When a justice of the peace heard a case, he was the presiding judge.
366 **Member . . . Shire:** representative of his county in Parliament.
369 **Sheriff:** royal tax collector.
371 **Haberdasher:** one who sells men's clothing.

The Man of Law, (detail from *The Canterbury Tales*), 15th century. English School. Huntington Library and Art Gallery, San Marino, CA.

Reading Strategy **Paraphrasing** *What motivates the Franklin? Paraphrase lines 345–348.*

Among our ranks, all in the livery
Of one impressive guild-fraternity.°
375 They were so trim and fresh their gear would pass
For new. Their knives were not tricked out with brass
But wrought with purest silver, which avouches
A like display on girdles and on pouches.
Each seemed a worthy burgess,° fit to grace
380 A guild-hall with a seat upon the dais.
Their wisdom would have justified a plan
To make each one of them an alderman;°
They had the capital and revenue,
Besides their wives declared it was their due.
385 And if they did not think so, then they ought;
To be called *"Madam"* is a glorious thought,
And so is going to church and being seen
Having your mantle° carried, like a queen.
　　　They had a *Cook* with them who stood alone
390 For boiling chicken with a marrow-bone,
Sharp flavoring-powder and a spice for savor.
He could distinguish London ale by flavor,
And he could roast and seethe and broil and fry,
Make good thick soup and bake a tasty pie.
395 But what a pity—so it seemed to me,
That he should have an ulcer° on his knee.
As for blancmange,° he made it with the best.
　　　There was a *Skipper* hailing from far west;
He came from Dartmouth, so I understood.
400 He rode a farmer's horse as best he could,
In a woolen gown that reached his knee.
A dagger on a lanyard falling free
Hung from his neck under his arm and down.
The summer heat had tanned his color brown,
405 And certainly he was an excellent fellow.
Many a draught of vintage, red and yellow,
He'd drawn at Bordeaux,° while the trader snored.
The nicer rules of conscience he ignored.
If, when he fought, the enemy vessel sank,
410 He sent his prisoners home; they walked the plank.
As for his skill in reckoning his tides,
Currents and many another risk besides,
Moons, harbors, pilots, he had such dispatch
That none from Hull to Carthage° was his match.
415 Hardy he was, prudent in undertaking;
His beard in many a tempest had its shaking,
And he knew all the havens as they were
From Gottland to the Cape of Finisterre,

373–374 livery . . . guild-fraternity:
The five tradesmen all belong to the same
fraternal trade organization and wear its
livery, or identifying uniform.

379 burgess: citizen or freeman of a
British borough; townsman.

382 alderman: high-ranking member of
the town council.
388 mantle: cloak; cape.
396 ulcer: open sore.
397 blancmange (blə mänj´): white
pudding made of milk, rice, and
seasonings.

The Physician, (detail from *The
Canterbury Tales*). Private Collection.

407 vintage . . . Bordeaux: Bordeaux
(bôr dō´), France, was famous for its red
and white (here, "yellow") wine.

414 Hull to Carthage: These and the
place names that immediately follow
indicate how widely the Skipper has
traveled.

Literary Element　　**Characterization** *Given this information, how is line
405 ironic?*

And every creek in Brittany and Spain;
420 The barge he owned was called *The Maudelayne*.
     A *Doctor* too emerged as we proceeded;
No one alive could talk as well as he did
On points of medicine and of surgery,
For, being grounded in astronomy,°
425 He watched his patient closely for the hours
When, by his horoscope, he knew the powers
Of favorable planets, then ascendent,
Worked on the images for his dependent.
The cause of every malady you'd got
430 He knew, and whether dry, cold, moist or hot;°
He knew their seat, their humor and condition.
He was a perfect practicing physician.
These causes being known for what they were,
He gave the man his medicine then and there.
435 All his apothecaries° in a tribe
Were ready with the drugs he would prescribe
And each made money from the other's guile;°
They had been friendly for a goodish while.
He was well-versed in Aesculapius° too
440 And what Hippocrates and Rufus knew
And Dioscorides, now dead and gone,
Galen and Rhazes, Hali, Serapion,
Averroes, Avicenna, Constantine,
Scotch Bernard, John of Gaddesden, Gilbertine.
445 In his own diet he observed some measure;
There were no superfluities for pleasure,
Only digestives, nutritives and such.
He did not read the Bible very much.
In blood-red garments, slashed with bluish gray
450 And lined with taffeta, he rode his way;
Yet he was rather close as to expenses
And kept the gold he won in pestilences.°
Gold stimulates the heart, or so we're told.
He therefore had a special love of gold.
455   A worthy *woman* from beside *Bath*° city
Was with us, somewhat deaf, which was a pity.
In making cloth she showed so great a bent
She bettered those of Ypres and of Ghent.°
In all the parish not a dame dared stir
460 Towards the altar steps in front of her,
And if indeed they did, so wrath was she
As to be quite put out of charity.
Her kerchiefs were of finely woven ground;°
I dared have sworn they weighed a good ten pound,

424 astronomy: in Chaucer's day, astrology. The planets' positions supposedly determined the best time to treat a patient.

430 dry, cold, moist or hot: In Chaucer's day people believed that the body was composed of four elements: earth (said to be dry and cold), water (cold and moist), air (hot and moist), and fire (hot and dry). Excess of one element could lead to illness.
435 apothecaries: druggists.

437 guile: cunning; deceit; slyness.

439 Aesculapius (es´ kyə lā´ pē əs): This and the names that immediately follow identify medical experts from ancient times to Chaucer's day.

452 pestilences: plagues.

455 Bath: city in southwestern England.

458 Ypres (ē´ prə) ... **Ghent:** Flemish cities known for weaving and wool making.

463 ground: a composite fabric.

Literary Element **Characterization** *What information in lines 435–454 about the Doctor contradicts the characterization in line 432?*

465 The ones she wore on Sunday, on her head.
     Her hose were of the finest scarlet red
     And gartered tight; her shoes were soft and new.
     Bold was her face, handsome, and red in hue.
     A worthy woman all her life, what's more
470 She'd had five husbands, all at the church door,
     Apart from other company in youth;
     No need just now to speak of that, forsooth.
     And she had thrice been to Jerusalem,°
     Seen many strange rivers and passed over them;
475 She'd been to Rome and also to Boulogne,
     St. James of Compostella and Cologne,
     And she was skilled in wandering by the way.
     She had gap-teeth, set widely, truth to say.
     Easily on an ambling horse she sat
480 Well wimpled° up, and on her head a hat
     As broad as is a buckler° or a shield;
     She had a flowing mantle that concealed
     Large hips, her heels spurred sharply under that.
     In company she liked to laugh and chat
485 And knew the remedies for love's mischances,
     An art in which she knew the oldest dances.
         A holy-minded man of good renown
     There was, and poor, the *Parson* to a town,
     Yet he was rich in holy thought and work.
490 He also was a learned man, a clerk,
     Who truly knew Christ's gospel and would preach it
     Devoutly to parishioners, and teach it.
     Benign and wonderfully diligent,
     And patient when adversity was sent
495 (For so he proved in much adversity)
     He hated cursing to extort a fee,
     Nay rather he preferred beyond a doubt
     Giving to poor parishioners round about
     Both from church offerings and his property;
500 He could in little find sufficiency.°
     Wide was his parish, with houses far asunder,
     Yet he neglected not in rain or thunder,
     In sickness or in grief, to pay a call
     On the remotest, whether great or small,
505 Upon his feet, and in his hand a stave.
     This noble example to his sheep he gave
     That first he wrought, and afterwards he taught;

473 **Jerusalem:** This and the place names immediately following were famous pilgrimage sites during the Middle Ages.

480 **wimpled:** A wimple is a cloth that covers the head and neck.
481 **buckler:** small round shield.

500 **He . . . sufficiency:** He required little to satisfy his own needs..

The Parson, detail from *The Canterbury Tales*, by Geoffrey Chaucer, c.1342–1400. English School. Vellum. Huntington Library and Art Gallery, San Marino, CA.

Big Idea **The Power of Faith** *How were religion and traveling linked in the Middle Ages?*

Literary Element **Characterization** *What qualifies the Wife of Bath as an expert on love?*

And it was from the Gospel he had caught
Those words, and he would add this figure too,
510 That if gold rust, what then will iron do?
For if a priest be foul in whom we trust
No wonder that a common man should rust;

The true example that a priest should give
Is one of cleanness, how the sheep should live.
515 He did not set his benefice to hire°
And leave his sheep encumbered in the mire
Or run to London to earn easy bread
By singing masses for the wealthy dead,
Or find some Brotherhood and get enrolled.
520 He stayed at home and watched over his fold
So that no wolf should make the sheep miscarry.
He was a shepherd and no mercenary.
Holy and virtuous he was, but then
Never contemptuous of sinful men,
525 Never **disdainful,** never too proud or fine,
But was discreet in teaching and benign.
His business was to show a fair behavior
And draw men thus to Heaven and their Savior,
Unless indeed a man were obstinate;
530 And such, whether of high or low estate,
He put to sharp rebuke, to say the least.
I think there never was a better priest.
He sought no pomp or glory in his dealings,
No scrupulosity° had spiced his feelings.
535 Christ and His Twelve Apostles and their lore
He taught, but followed it himself before.
    There was a *Plowman* with him there, his brother;
Many a load of dung one time or other
He must have carted through the morning dew.
540 He was an honest worker, good and true,
Living in peace and perfect charity,
And, as the gospel bade him, so did he,
Loving God best with all his heart and mind
And then his neighbor as himself, repined
545 At no misfortune, slacked for no content,
For steadily about his work he went

515 **set . . . hire:** pay someone else to perform clerical duties.

534 **scrupulosity:** here, overly careful attention to social niceties.

Literary Element Characterization *How does this proverb contrast the Parson's character with that of other clerics, such as the Monk and the Friar?*

Big Idea The Power of Faith *How does the Plowman demonstrate the ideals of the Christian religion?*

Vocabulary

disdainful (dĭs dān′ fəl) *adj.* feeling or showing contempt; scornful

To thrash his corn, to dig or to manure
Or make a ditch; and he would help the poor
For love of Christ and never take a penny
550 If he could help it, and, as prompt as any,
He paid his tithes° in full when they were due
On what he owned, and on his earnings too.
He wore a tabard smock° and rode a mare.
   There was a *Reeve,*° also a *Miller,* there,
555 A College *Manciple* from the Inns of Court,°
A papal *Pardoner* and, in close consort,°
A Church-Court *Summoner,*° riding at a trot,
And finally myself—that was the lot.
   The *Miller* was a chap of sixteen stone,°
560 A great stout fellow big in brawn and bone.
He did well out of them, for he could go
And win the ram at any wrestling show.
Broad, knotty and short-shouldered, he would boast
He could heave any door off hinge and post,
565 Or take a run and break it with his head.
His beard, like any sow or fox, was red
And broad as well, as though it were a spade;
And, at its very tip, his nose displayed
A wart on which there stood a tuft of hair
570 Red as the bristles in an old sow's ear.
His nostrils were as black as they were wide.
He had a sword and buckler at his side,
His mighty mouth was like a furnace door.
A wrangler and buffoon, he had a store
575 Of tavern stories, filthy in the main.
His was a master-hand at stealing grain.
He felt it with his thumb and thus he knew
Its quality and took three times his due—
A thumb of gold, by God, to gauge an oat!
580 He wore a hood of blue and a white coat.
He liked to play his bagpipes up and down
And that was how he brought us out of town.
   The *Manciple* came from the Inner Temple;°
All caterers might follow his example
585 In buying victuals; he was never rash
Whether he bought on credit or paid cash.
He used to watch the market most precisely
And got in first, and so he did quite nicely.
Now isn't it a marvel of God's grace
590 That an illiterate fellow can outpace
The wisdom of a heap of learned men?
His masters—he had more than thirty then—

The Friar, detail from *The Canterbury Tales.* 15th century. English School. Huntington Library and Art Gallery, San Marino, CA.

551 tithes (tīthz): offerings made to the church consisting of one-tenth of a person's income.
553 tabard smock: loose jacket of heavy fabric.
554 Reeve: manager of a landowner's estate.
555 Manciple . . . Court: administrator in charge of providing food for the lawyers who lived and trained at London's Inns of Court.
556 Pardoner: church employee licensed by the pope to dispense papal pardons, which released people from punishment for sins, and to collect money for church charities. **consort:** accompaniment.
557 Summoner: layman charged with summoning sinners before a church court.
559 sixteen stone: 224 pounds. A stone is a British unit of weight equal to 14 pounds.

583 Inner Temple: one of the four Inns of Court.

Literary Element   **Characterization** *Given the characterization of the Miller, what sort of tale would you expect him to tell when his time comes?*

All versed in the abstrusest° legal knowledge,
Could have produced a dozen from their College
595 Fit to be stewards in land and rents and game
To any Peer° in England you could name,
And show him how to live on what he had
Debt-free (unless of course the Peer were mad)
Or be as frugal as he might desire,
600 And make them fit to help about the Shire
In any legal case there was to try;
And yet this Manciple could wipe their eye.°
    The *Reeve* was old and choleric° and thin;
His beard was shaven closely to the skin,
605 His shorn hair came abruptly to a stop
Above his ears, and he was docked on top
Just like a priest in front; his legs were lean,
Like sticks they were, no calf was to be seen.
He kept his bins and garners° very trim;
610 No auditor could gain a point on him.
And he could judge by watching drought and rain
The yield he might expect from seed and grain.
His master's sheep, his animals and hens,
Pigs, horses, dairies, stores and cattle-pens
615 Were wholly trusted to his government.
He had been under contract to present
The accounts, right from his master's earliest years.
No one had ever caught him in arrears.
No bailiff, serf or herdsman dared to kick,
620 He knew their dodges, knew their every trick;
Feared like the plague he was, by those beneath.
He had a lovely dwelling on a heath,
Shadowed in green by trees above the sward.°
A better hand at bargains than his lord,
625 He had grown rich and had a store of treasure
Well tucked away, yet out it came to pleasure
His lord with subtle loans or gifts of goods,
To earn his thanks and even coats and hoods.
When young he'd learnt a useful trade and still
630 He was a carpenter of first-rate skill.
The stallion-cob he rode at a slow trot
Was dapple-gray and bore the name of Scot.
He wore an overcoat of bluish shade
And rather long; he had a rusty blade
635 Slung at his side. He came, as I heard tell,
From Norfolk, near a place called Baldeswell.
His coat was tucked under his belt and splayed.
He rode the hindmost of our cavalcade.

593 **abstrusest:** hardest to understand.

596 **stewards . . . To any Peer:** estate managers for any nobleman.

602 **wipe their eye:** get the better of or outdo them.
603 **choleric:** easily irritated or angered.

609 **garners:** buildings for storing grain.

623 **sward:** grassland; lawn.

Reading Strategy **Paraphrasing** *Paraphrase Chaucer's description of the Reeve in lines 603–638.*

There was a *Summoner* with us at that Inn,
640 His face on fire, like a cherubin,°
For he had carbuncles.° His eyes were narrow,
He was as hot and lecherous as a sparrow.
Black scabby brows he had, and a thin beard.
Children were afraid when he appeared.
645 No quicksilver, lead ointment, tartar creams,
No brimstone, no boracic,° so it seems,
Could make a salve that had the power to bite,
Clean up or cure his whelks° of knobby white
Or purge the pimples sitting on his cheeks.
650 Garlic he loved, and onions too, and leeks,
And drinking strong red wine till all was hazy.
Then he would shout and jabber as if crazy,
And wouldn't speak a word except in Latin
When he was drunk, such tags° as he was pat in;
655 He only had a few, say two or three,
That he had mugged up° out of some decree;
No wonder, for he heard them every day.
And, as you know, a man can teach a jay°
To call out "Walter" better than the Pope.
660 But had you tried to test his wits and grope
For more, you'd have found nothing in the bag.
Then *"Questio quid juris"*° was his tag.
He was a noble varlet° and a kind one,
You'd meet none better if you went to find one.

665   He and a gentle *Pardoner* rode together,
A bird from Charing Cross° of the same feather,
Just back from visiting the Court of Rome.
He loudly sang *"Come hither, love, come home!"*
The Summoner sang deep seconds to this song,
670 No trumpet ever sounded half so strong.
This Pardoner had hair as yellow as wax,
Hanging down smoothly like a hank of flax.
In driblets fell his locks behind his head
Down to his shoulders which they overspread;
675 Thinly they fell, like rat-tails, one by one.
He wore no hood upon his head, for fun;
The hood inside his wallet° had been stowed,
He aimed at riding in the latest mode;
But for a little cap his head was bare
680 And he had bulging eye-balls, like a hare.
He'd sewed a holy relic° on his cap;
His wallet lay before him on his lap,
Brimful of pardons come from Rome, all hot.

640 cherubin: one of the angels who, in medieval art, usually had flame-colored faces.
641 carbuncles: large pimples and patches of red skin, often seen as a sign of lechery or drunkenness in Chaucer's time.

645–646 quicksilver . . . boracic: medieval skin medicines.

648 whelks: pustules.

654 tags: brief quotations.

656 mugged up: memorized.

658 jay: a bird that can be taught to mimic human speech but cannot understand what it says.

662 Questio quid juris: Latin for "The question is, what point of the law applies?"
663 varlet: rascal.

666 Charing Cross: district of London.

677 wallet: pack; knapsack.

681 relic: an object cherished for its association with a saint or holy person.

Reading Strategy Paraphrasing *What does the speaker say about the Summoner's knowledge and intelligence? Paraphrase lines 660–662.*

He had the same small voice a goat has got.
685 His chin no beard had harbored, nor would harbor,
Smoother than ever chin was left by barber.
I judge he was a gelding, or a mare.
As to his trade, from Berwick down to Ware
There was no pardoner of equal grace,
690 For in his trunk he had a pillow-case
Which he asserted was Our Lady's veil.
He said he had a gobbet° of the sail
St. Peter had the time when he made bold
To walk the waves, till Jesu Christ took hold.°
695 He had a cross of metal set with stones
And, in a glass, a rubble of pigs' bones.
And with these relics, any time he found
Some poor up-country parson to astound,
In one short day, in money down, he drew
700 More than the parson in a month or two,
And by his flatteries and **prevarication**
Made monkeys of the priest and congregation.
But still to do him justice first and last
In church he was a noble ecclesiast.°
705 How well he read a lesson or told a story!
But best of all he sang an Offertory,°
For well he knew that when that song was sung
He'd have to preach and tune his honey-tongue
And (well he could) win silver from the crowd.
710 That's why he sang so merrily and loud.
    Now I have told you shortly, in a clause,
The rank, the array, the number and the cause
Of our assembly in this company
In Southwark, at that high-class hostelry
715 Known as *The Tabard*, close beside *The Bell*.°
And now the time has come for me to tell
How we behaved that evening; I'll begin
After we had alighted at the Inn,
Then I'll report our journey, stage by stage,
720 All the remainder of our pilgrimage.
But first I beg of you, in courtesy,
Not to condemn me as unmannerly
If I speak plainly and with no concealings

---

692 gobbet: large piece.

693–694 St. Peter . . . hold: In the Christian Bible (Matthew 14:29–31), Jesus extended a helping hand to Peter when Peter walked on the water and became afraid.

704 ecclesiast (i klē′ zē əst′): clergyman.

706 Offertory: song accompanying the collection of the offering in church.

715 The Bell: another inn.

Big Idea   **The Power of Faith** *How does the Pardoner abuse his holy office and take advantage of the religious faith of his victims?*

Reading Strategy   Paraphrasing *Paraphrase the speaker's disclaimer in lines 721–723.*

Vocabulary

prevarication (pri var′ ə kā′ shən) *n.* the act of evading the truth; a lie

GEOFFREY CHAUCER   **111**

And give account of all their words and dealings,
725 Using their very phrases as they fell.
For certainly, as you all know so well,
He who repeats a tale after a man
Is bound to say, as nearly as he can,
Each single word, if he remembers it,
730 However rudely spoken or unfit,
Or else the tale he tells will be untrue,
The things pretended and the phrases new.
He may not flinch although it were his brother,
He may as well say one word as another.
735 And Christ Himself spoke broad° in Holy Writ,
Yet there is no scurrility° in it,
And Plato° says, for those with power to read,
"The word should be as cousin to the deed."
Further I beg you to forgive it me
740 If I neglect the order and degree
And what is due to rank in what I've planned.
I'm short of wit as you will understand.

Our *Host* gave us great welcome; everyone
Was given a place and supper was begun.
745 He served the finest victuals° you could think,
The wine was strong and we were glad to drink.
A very striking man our Host withal,
And fit to be a marshal in a hall.°
His eyes were bright, his girth a little wide;
750 There is no finer burgess in Cheapside.°
Bold in his speech, yet wise and full of tact,
There was no manly attribute he lacked,
What's more he was a merry-hearted man.
After our meal he jokingly began
755 To talk of sport, and, among other things
After we'd settled up our reckonings,
He said as follows: "Truly, gentlemen,
You're very welcome and I can't think when
—Upon my word I'm telling you no lie—
760 I've seen a gathering here that looked so spry,
No, not this year, as in this tavern now.
I'd think you up some fun if I knew how.
And, as it happens, a thought has just occurred
To please you, costing nothing, on my word.
765 You're off to Canterbury—well, God speed!
Blessed St. Thomas° answer to your need!
And I don't doubt, before the journey's done
You mean to while the time in tales and fun.

735 **broad:** bluntly; plainly.
736 **scurrility:** coarseness; indecency.
737 **Plato:** Greek philosopher (427?–347? B.C.).
745 **victuals** (vit′ əlz): food.
748 **marshal in a hall:** a manager in charge of making the arrangements for a banquet.

Pilgrims. Illustration from *the Troy Book and the Siege of Thebes.*

750 **Cheapside:** in Chaucer's day, London's main business district.

766 **St. Thomas:** here, St. Thomas à Becket.

Literary Element **Characterization** *How does the speaker characterize himself in this passage? How is his self-portrait here consistent with the way he has portrayed himself throughout "The Prologue"?*

Indeed, there's little pleasure for your bones
770 Riding along and all as dumb° as stones.
So let me then propose for your enjoyment,
Just as I said, a suitable employment.
And if my notion suits and you agree
And promise to submit yourselves to me
775 Playing your parts exactly as I say
Tomorrow as you ride along the way,
Then by my father's soul (and he is dead)
If you don't like it you can have my head!
Hold up your hands, and not another word."
780   Well, our opinion was not long deferred,
It seemed not worth a serious debate;
We all agreed to it at any rate
And bade him issue what commands he would.
"My lords," he said, "now listen for your good,
785   And please don't treat my notion with disdain.
This is the point. I'll make it short and plain.
Each one of you shall help to make things slip
By telling two stories on the outward trip
To Canterbury, that's what I intend,
790 And, on the homeward way to journey's end
Another two, tales from the days of old;
And then the man whose story is best told,
That is to say who gives the fullest measure
Of good morality and general pleasure,
795 He shall be given a supper, paid by all,
Here in this tavern, in this very hall,
When we come back again from Canterbury.
And in the hope to keep you bright and merry
I'll go along with you myself and ride
800 All at my own expense and serve as guide.
I'll be the judge, and those who won't obey
Shall pay for what we spend upon the way.
Now if you all agree to what you've heard
Tell me at once without another word,
805 And I will make arrangements early for it."
       Of course we all agreed, in fact we swore it
Delightedly, and made entreaty° too
That he should act as he proposed to do,
Become our Governor in short, and be
810 Judge of our tales and general referee,
And set the supper at a certain price.

770 **dumb:** silent.

807 **entreaty:** an enthusiastic request.

Reading Strategy   Paraphrasing *What "notion" does the Host propose in lines 785–805?*

We promised to be ruled by his advice
Come high, come low; unanimously thus
We set him up in judgment over us.
815 More wine was fetched, the business being done;
We drank it off and up went everyone
To bed without a moment of delay.
    Early next morning at the spring of day
Up rose our Host and roused us like a cock,
820 Gathering us together in a flock,
And off we rode at slightly faster pace
Than walking to St. Thomas' watering-place;°
And there our Host drew up, began to ease
His horse, and said, "Now, listen if you please,
825 My lords! Remember what you promised me.
If evensong and matins will agree°
Let's see who shall be first to tell a tale.
And as I hope to drink good wine and ale
I'll be your judge. The rebel who disobeys,
830 However much the journey costs, he pays.
Now draw for cut and then we can depart;
The man who draws the shortest cut shall start.
My Lord the Knight," he said, "step up to me
And draw your cut, for that is my decree.
835 And come you near, my Lady Prioress,
And you, Sir Cleric, drop your shamefastness,
No studying now! A hand from every man!"
Immediately the draw for lots began
And to tell shortly how the matter went,
840 Whether by chance or fate or accident,
The truth is this, the cut fell to the Knight,
Which everybody greeted with delight.
And tell his tale he must, as reason was
Because of our agreement and because
845 He too had sworn. What more is there to say?
For when this good man saw how matters lay,
Being by wisdom and obedience driven
To keep a promise he had freely given,
He said, "Since it's for me to start the game,
850 Why, welcome be the cut in God's good name!
Now let us ride, and listen to what I say."
And at the word we started on our way
And in a cheerful style he then began
At once to tell his tale, and thus it ran.

822 **St. Thomas' watering-place:** a brook two miles from London.

826 **If evensong . . . agree:** literally referring to evening and morning prayer services; here meaning, "if what you said last night is what you mean this morning."

Thomas Becket is consecrated Archbishop of Canterbury. 14th century illuminated manuscript. From the Queen Mary Psalter.

Literary Element Characterization *What character traits of the Host have gained him the trust of the pilgrims?*

Reading Strategy Paraphrasing *How does the Host decide who will tell the first tale? Paraphrase lines 838-841.*

RESPONDING AND THINKING CRITICALLY

Respond

1. (a)Which characters remind you in some way of people you know? Explain. (b)Do any of the characters seem unrealistic to you? Explain.

Recall and Interpret

2. (a)Where are the pilgrims traveling and for what reason? (b)How is the time of year in which they are traveling meaningful?

3. (a)What narrative point of view does the speaker use? (b)How does this point of view affect the information you learn about the other pilgrims?

4. (a)What information does the speaker give about himself? (b)Does the speaker seem to fit in with the band of pilgrims? Explain.

Analyze and Evaluate

5. (a)Categorize the twenty-nine pilgrims according to their roles in fourteenth-century English society. Use the following categories: 1) Trades or Professions; 2) Church; 3) Feudal System. (b)How well do these people represent the whole of medieval society? Are any groups of people missing?

6. (a)Which character appeals to you the most? Why? (b)Which character appeals to you the least? Why?

Connect

7. (a)How do people today amuse themselves on trips? (b)How do these activities compare with the amusements of Chaucer's time?

8. **Big Idea** **The Power of Faith** How does the Christian faith in the Middle Ages inform the whole of "The Prologue" to *The Canterbury Tales*?

LITERARY ANALYSIS

Literary Element Characterization

In **direct characterization**, the writer makes explicit statements about a character. In **indirect characterization**, the writer reveals a character through the character's words, thoughts, actions, and appearance, as well as through what other characters say or think about the character.

1. (a)Find an example of direct characterization in "The Prologue." (b)Find an example of indirect characterization.

2. (a)What details does the speaker use to describe the Knight and the Squire? (b)What do the speaker's descriptions suggest about these characters?

Writing About Literature

Explore Author's Purpose Scholars have noted that "The Prologue" is an *estates satire,* a type of medieval literary work that pokes fun at the professions and classes, or "estates" of society, in order to expose their flaws. What flaws is Chaucer exposing in secular society and within the church? Write several paragraphs in which you analyze "The Prologue" as an estates satire.

READING AND VOCABULARY

Reading Strategy Paraphrasing

When you paraphrase a passage, you restate it in your own words.

1. Write the simple subjects and predicates of the two clauses in lines 23–27.

2. Paraphrase Chaucer's description of the Manciple in lines 583–602.

Vocabulary Practice

Practice with Synonyms Find the synonyms for each vocabulary word from "The Prologue" listed in the first column below.

1. discreet	**a.** careless	**b.** careful
2. disdainful	**a.** scornful	**b.** friendly
3. estimable	**a.** lowly	**b.** admirable
4. prevarication	**a.** truth	**b.** falsehood
5. solicitous	**a.** helpful	**b.** aloof

Literature Online **Web Activities** For eFlashcards, Selection Quick Checks, and other Web activities, go to www.glencoe.com.

from *The Pardoner's Tale*

Connecting to the Poem

In "The Pardoner's Tale," three young men allow their greed to destroy them. As you read, think about the following questions:

- How far would you go to attain great wealth?
- Is there any goal or reward that would tempt you to betray one of your friends?

Building Background

In the Middle Ages, church representatives called pardoners were licensed by the pope to preach and to collect money for specific goals, such as building a church. A pardoner could also grant indulgences, which were gifts of divine mercy to repentant sinners. Through such indulgences, sinners received pardon, or release, from the pain of punishment. By Chaucer's time, corrupt pardoners sold indulgences for personal profit rather than granting them to the deserving penitents in return for a voluntary donation to a church charity. "The Pardoner's Tale" is an **exemplum**—a brief story used as an example to teach a moral lesson.

Setting Purposes for Reading

Big Idea **The Power of Faith**

As you read, notice how the sins of greed and betrayal lead to moral chaos and self-destruction.

Literary Element **Irony**

Irony is a contrast or discrepancy between expectation and reality. **Situational irony** exists when an occurrence is the opposite of a character's expectations. **Dramatic irony** occurs when readers or audiences have information unknown to the characters. **Verbal irony** occurs when a character says one thing while meaning another. As you read "The Pardoner's Tale," look for all three types of irony.

- See Literary Terms Handbook, p. R9.

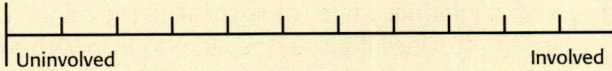 **Interactive Literary Elements Handbook** To review or learn more about the literary elements, go to www.glencoe.com.

Reading Strategy **Analyzing Tone**

Tone expresses an author's attitude toward his or her subject as conveyed through such elements as word choice, sentence structure, and figures of speech. A writer's tone may convey a variety of attitudes, such as sympathy, irony, objectivity, humor, or sadness.

Reading Tip: Analyzing Objectivity How emotionally involved or objective a speaker is can contribute to the speaker's tone. As you read, use a continuum similar to the one below to denote the tone of a passage.

Uninvolved   Involved

Vocabulary

adversary (ad′ vər ser′ ē) *n.* opponent; enemy; p. 117 *Louise and Frank were worthy adversaries at playing Scrabble because each had an extensive vocabulary.*

prudent (prōōd′ ənt) *adj.* cautious; careful; p. 120 *Be prudent in divulging your Social Security number because it can be misused by an unscrupulous person.*

gratify (grat′ə fī′) *v.* to satisfy; indulge; p. 121 *Grandfather likes to gratify his sweet tooth with chocolate ice cream.*

deftly (deft′ lē) *adv.* skillfully; nimbly; p. 122 *Working in the bakery window, the pizza chef deftly spun the dough into a large circle.*

Vocabulary Tip: Context Clues Clues to the meanings of unfamiliar words can often be found in the surrounding text.

OBJECTIVES
In studying this selection, you will focus on the following:
- analyzing literary genres
- analyzing irony
- analyzing tone

Manuscript illumination of a pharmacy with the scientist and philosopher Ibn Sina. From the *Cannon Mayor.*

from The Pardoner's Tale

It's of three rioters° I have to tell
Who, long before the morning service bell,°
Were sitting in a tavern for a drink.
And as they sat, they heard the hand-bell clink
5   Before a coffin going to the grave;°
One of them called the little tavern-knave°
And said "Go and find out at once—look spry!—
Whose corpse is in that coffin passing by;
And see you get the name correctly too."
10   "Sir," said the boy, "no need, I promise you;
Two hours before you came here I was told.
He was a friend of yours in days of old,
And suddenly, last night, the man was slain,
Upon his bench, face up, dead drunk again.
15   There came a privy° thief, they call him Death,
Who kills us all round here, and in a breath
He speared him through the heart, he never stirred.
And then Death went his way without a word.
He's killed a thousand in the present plague,°
20   And, sir, it doesn't do to be too vague
If you should meet him; you had best be wary.
Be on your guard with such an **adversary**,
Be primed to meet him everywhere you go,
That's what my mother said. It's all I know."
25   The publican° joined in with, "By St. Mary,

1   **rioters:** those given to unrestrained revelry and debauchery.
2   **long before . . . bell:** long before 9 A.M.

4–5   **hand-bell . . . grave:** During this time, a bell was rung next to the coffin in a funeral procession.
6   **tavern-knave:** serving boy.

15   **privy:** secretive.

19   **killed . . . plague:** In 1348 and 1349 at least a third of the population of England perished from the plague called the Black Death.

25   **publican:** tavernkeeper or innkeeper.

Reading Strategy   **Analyzing Tone**   *How would you describe the tone of the tavern-knave's report?*

Vocabulary

adversary (ad′vər ser′ē) *n.* opponent; enemy

What the child says is right; you'd best be wary,
This very year he killed, in a large village
A mile away, man, woman, serf at tillage,°
Page in the household, children—all there were.
30 Yes, I imagine that he lives round there.
It's well to be prepared in these alarms,
He might do you dishonor." "Huh, God's arms!"
The rioter said, "Is he so fierce to meet?
I'll search for him, by Jesus, street by street.
35 God's blessed bones! I'll register a vow!
Here, chaps! The three of us together now,
Hold up your hands, like me, and we'll be brothers
In this affair, and each defend the others,
And we will kill this traitor Death, I say!
40 Away with him as he has made away
With all our friends. God's dignity! Tonight!"
    They made their bargain, swore with appetite,
These three, to live and die for one another
As brother-born might swear to his born brother.
45 And up they started in their drunken rage
And made towards this village which the page
And publican had spoken of before.
Many and grisly were the oaths they swore,
Tearing Christ's blessed body to a shred;°
50 "If we can only catch him, Death is dead!"
    When they had gone not fully half a mile,
Just as they were about to cross a stile,°
They came upon a very poor old man
Who humbly greeted them and thus began,
55 "God look to you, my lords, and give you quiet!"
To which the proudest of these men of riot
Gave back the answer, "What, old fool? Give place!
Why are you all wrapped up except your face?
Why live so long? Isn't it time to die?"
60   The old, old fellow looked him in the eye
And said, "Because I never yet have found,
Though I have walked to India, searching round
Village and city on my pilgrimage,
One who would change his youth to have my age.
65 And so my age is mine and must be still
Upon me, for such time as God may will.
    "Not even Death, alas, will take my life;

28 **tillage:** plowing.

49 **Tearing . . . shred:** Their swearing included such expressions as "God's arms" (line 32) and "God's blessed bones" (line 35).
52 **stile:** a stairway used to climb over a wall or fence.

Literary Element Irony *What is ironic about the rioters' resolution?*

Reading Strategy Analyzing Tone *In what tone does the rioter answer the "poor old man"?*

Big Idea The Power of Faith *How does the old man show his religious faith?*

The Pardoner (detail). Illumination from Geoffrey Chaucer's *The Canterbury Tales*. The Huntington Art Collection, San Marino, CA.

So, like a wretched prisoner at strife
Within himself, I walk alone and wait
70 About the earth, which is my mother's gate,°
Knock-knocking with my staff from night to noon
And crying, 'Mother, open to me soon!
Look at me, mother, won't you let me in?
See how I wither, flesh and blood and skin!
75 Alas! When will these bones be laid to rest?
Mother, I would exchange—for that were best—
The wardrobe in my chamber, standing there
So long, for yours! Aye, for a shirt of hair°
To wrap me in!' She has refused her grace,
80 Whence comes the pallor of my withered face.
　　"But it dishonored you when you began
To speak so roughly, sir, to an old man,
Unless he had injured you in word or deed.
It says in holy writ, as you may read,
85 'Thou shalt rise up before the hoary° head
And honor it.' And therefore be it said
'Do no more harm to an old man than you,
Being now young, would have another do
When you are old'—if you should live till then.
90 And so may God be with you, gentlemen,
For I must go whither I have to go."
　　"By God," the gambler said, "you shan't do so,
You don't get off so easy, by St. John!
I heard you mention, just a moment gone,
95 A certain traitor Death who singles out
And kills the fine young fellows hereabout.
And you're his spy, by God! You wait a bit.
Say where he is or you shall pay for it,
By God and by the Holy Sacrament!
100 I say you've joined together by consent
To kill us younger folk, you thieving swine!"
　　"Well, sirs," he said, "if it be your design
To find out Death, turn up this crooked way
Towards that grove, I left him there today
105 Under a tree, and there you'll find him waiting.
He isn't one to hide for all your prating.
You see that oak? He won't be far to find.
And God protect you that redeemed mankind,
Aye, and amend° you!" Thus that ancient man.
110 　　At once the three young rioters began
To run, and reached the tree, and there they found
A pile of golden florins on the ground,
New-coined, eight bushels of them as they thought.
No longer was it Death those fellows sought,

70 **mother's gate:** entrance to the grave.

78 **shirt of hair:** usually a rough shirt worn as self-punishment; here, a shroud

85 **hoary:** whitened with age.

Chaucer, the Knight and the Squire from "The Pardoner's Prologue" of *The Canterbury Tales.* Harry Mileham (1873–1957). Private Collection.
Viewing the Art: Of the figures shown here, in your opinion which would be Chaucer? What about this character's body language leads you to that conclusion?

109 **amend:** improve.

Literary Element　Irony　*What is ironic about the rioters' discovery?*

115 For they were all so thrilled to see the sight,
The florins were so beautiful and bright,
That down they sat beside the precious pile.
The wickedest spoke first after a while.
"Brothers," he said, "you listen to what I say.
120 I'm pretty sharp although I joke away.
It's clear that Fortune° has bestowed this treasure
To let us live in jollity and pleasure.
Light come, light go! We'll spend it as we ought.
God's precious dignity! Who would have thought
125 This morning was to be our lucky day?
    "If one could only get the gold away,
Back to my house, or else to yours, perhaps—
For as you know, the gold is ours, chaps—
We'd all be at the top of fortune, hey?
130 But certainly it can't be done by day.
People would call us robbers—a strong gang,
So our own property would make us hang.
No, we must bring this treasure back by night
Some **prudent** way, and keep it out of sight.
135 And so as a solution I propose
We draw for lots and see the way it goes;
The one who draws the longest, lucky man,
Shall run to town as quickly as he can
To fetch us bread and wine—but keep things dark°—
140 While two remain in hiding here to mark
Our heap of treasure. If there's no delay,
When night comes down we'll carry it away,
All three of us, wherever we have planned."
    He gathered lots and hid them in his hand
145 Bidding them draw for where the luck should fall.
It fell upon the youngest of them all,
And off he ran at once towards the town.
    As soon as he had gone the first sat down
And thus began a parley° with the other:
150 "You know that you can trust me as a brother;
Now let me tell you where your profit lies;
You know our friend has gone to get supplies
And here's a lot of gold that is to be
Divided equally amongst us three.

121 **Fortune:** fate.

139 **keep things dark:** act in secret; don't give us away.

149 **parley** (pär′ lē): a discussion, as with an enemy.

Big Idea **The Power of Faith** *How does the rioters' deduction illustrate a perversion of Christian faith?*

Vocabulary

prudent (pro͞od′ ənt) *adj.* cautious; careful

155 Nevertheless, if I could shape things thus
So that we shared it out—the two of us—
Wouldn't you take it as a friendly act?"
"But how?" the other said. "He knows the fact
That all the gold was left with me and you;
160 What can we tell him? What are we to do?"
"Is it a bargain," said the first, "or no?
For I can tell you in a word or so
What's to be done to bring the thing about."
"Trust me," the other said, "you needn't doubt
165 My word. I won't betray you, I'll be true."
"Well," said his friend, "you see that we are two,
And two are twice as powerful as one.
Now look; when he comes back, get up in fun
To have a wrestle; then, as you attack,
170 I'll up and put my dagger through his back
While you and he are struggling, as in game;
Then draw your dagger too and do the same.
Then all this money will be ours to spend,
Divided equally of course, dear friend.
175 Then we can **gratify** our lusts and fill
The day with dicing at our own sweet will."
Thus these two miscreants° agreed to slay
The third and youngest, as you heard me say.
The youngest, as he ran towards the town,
180 Kept turning over, rolling up and down
Within his heart the beauty of those bright
New florins, saying, "Lord, to think I might
Have all that treasure to myself alone!
Could there be anyone beneath the throne
185 Of God so happy as I then should be?"
And so the Fiend, our common enemy,
Was given power to put it in his thought
That there was always poison to be bought,
And that with poison he could kill his friends.
190 To men in such a state the Devil sends
Thoughts of this kind, and has a full permission
To lure them on to sorrow and perdition;°
For this young man was utterly content
To kill them both and never to repent.
195 And on he ran, he had no thought to tarry,

Florin, a coin of the
thirteenth century

177 **miscreants** (mis′ krē ənts):
evildoers, villains.

192 **perdition:** damnation.

Literary Element   Irony *What ironic thread runs through the dialogue among the three rioters?*

Big Idea   The Power of Faith *What point about the Devil is the Pardoner expressing here?*

Vocabulary

gratify (grat′ ə fī′) *v.* to satisfy; indulge

Came to the town, found an apothecary
And said, "Sell me some poison if you will,
I have a lot of rats I want to kill
And there's a polecat too about my yard
200 That takes my chickens and it hits me hard;
But I'll get even, as is only right,
With vermin that destroy a man by night."

The chemist answered, "I've a preparation
Which you shall have, and by my soul's salvation
205 If any living creature eat or drink
A mouthful, ere he has the time to think,
Though he took less than makes a grain of wheat,
You'll see him fall down dying at your feet;
Yes, die he must, and in so short a while
210 You'd hardly have the time to walk a mile,
The poison is so strong, you understand."

This cursed fellow grabbed into his hand
The box of poison and away he ran
Into a neighboring street, and found a man
215 Who lent him three large bottles. He withdrew
And **deftly** poured the poison into two.
He kept the third one clean, as well he might,
For his own drink, meaning to work all night
Stacking the gold and carrying it away.
220 And when this rioter, this devil's clay,
Had filled his bottles up with wine, all three,
Back to rejoin his comrades sauntered he.

Why make a sermon of it? Why waste breath?
Exactly in the way they'd planned his death
225 They fell on him and slew him, two to one.
Then said the first of them when this was done,
"Now for a drink. Sit down and let's be merry,
For later on there'll be the corpse to bury."
And, as it happened, reaching for a sup,
230 He took a bottle of poison up
And drank; and his companion, nothing loth,°
Drank from it also, and they perished both.

There is, in Avicenna's long relation°
Concerning poison and its operation,
235 Trust me, no ghastlier section to transcend
What these two wretches suffered at their end.
Thus these two murderers received their due,
So did the treacherous young poisoner too.

231 **nothing loth:** very willingly.

233 **Avicenna's** (av′ ə sen′ əz) **long relation:** a medieval book on medicines by the Arab physician Avicenna (980–1037), which contains a chapter on poisons.

Reading Strategy Analyzing Tone *How would you describe the Pardoner's tone in relating the deaths of the last two rioters?*

Vocabulary

deftly (deft′ lē) *adv.* skillfully; nimbly

RESPONDING AND THINKING CRITICALLY

Respond

1. (a)Were you surprised by the way the tale ends? Why or why not? (b)Would any other ending have been as satisfactory? Explain.

Recall and Interpret

2. (a)What are the three rioters doing at the beginning of the story? (b)What do the opening lines imply about the character of the rioters? (c)Why might an exemplum employ such characters?

3. (a)How does the rioters' treatment of the tavern-knave and the old man characterize the rioters? (b)How does the old man characterize himself?

4. (a)When the rioters go in search of Death, what do they find under the oak tree? (b)What symbolic association about greed might Chaucer be making here?

Analyze and Evaluate

5. (a)Why do you think Chaucer decided to **personify**, or give human qualities to, Death in this tale? (b)Do you find this personification to be an effective literary device? Explain.

6. (a)What do you think is the moral of this exemplum? (b)Do you find it ironic that the Pardoner has told a moralistic tale? Explain.

Connect

7. **Big Idea** **The Power of Faith** In what way does this tale illustrate the power of faith in medieval society?

LITERARY ANALYSIS

Literary Element Irony

"The Pardoner's Tale" contains examples of verbal irony, situational irony, and dramatic irony.

1. One rioter says, "We'll be brothers in this affair, and each defend the others." How is this an example of verbal irony?

2. When the rioters find the treasure, the "wickedest" says that Fortune gave it to them so that they could live "in jollity and pleasure." How is this an example of situational irony?

3. What example of dramatic irony occurs near the end of the tale?

Literary Criticism

In line 15, Death is described as a "privy thief." Scholar Stephen A. Barney notes that this description refers to a passage from the Bible: "The day of the Lord shall so come, as a thief in the night" (I Thessalonians 5:2). Meet in a small group to discuss what this reference to Judgment Day adds to the tale.

Literature Online **Web Activities** For eFlashcards, Selection Quick Checks, and other Web activities, go to www.glencoe.com.

READING AND VOCABULARY

Reading Strategy Analyzing Tone

The **tone** of a work may include the moral outlook that the writer conveys through the voice of the narrator.

Partner Activity With a partner, discuss the moral tone of "The Pardoner's Tale." Do you think the tone is appropriate? Explain.

Vocabulary Practice

Practice with Context Clues Identify the context clue that helps you determine the meaning of each underlined word below.

1. Tom's adversary in the game was his greatest opponent yet.
   a. game   **b.** greatest   **c.** opponent

2. Sheila was prudent; she saved her money.
   a. Sheila   **b.** saved   **c.** money

3. To gratify my hunger, I ate until I was full.
   a. hunger   **b.** ate   **c.** full

4. She deftly typed without making any mistakes.
   a. without   **b.** typed   **c.** mistakes

LITERATURE PREVIEW

READING PREVIEW

Connecting to the Poem

When you have a disagreement with someone, how do you resolve the issue? "The Wife of Bath's Tale" revolves around an argument about what women want. As you read the tale, think about the following questions:

- What does it mean to have mastery over another human being?
- What are the benefits of submitting oneself to the superior arguments of another?

Building Background

That the Wife has had five husbands would not have seemed remarkable to Chaucer's contemporaries. In the Middle Ages, a woman with property was very eligible. What they might have found remarkable—because women were considered inferior to men—is the Wife's success in governing her husbands. Another remarkable feature about the Wife is her high degree of education given that women of the time received no schooling beyond Bible studies and domestic training.

Setting Purposes for Reading

Big Idea **The Power of Faith**

The Wife's tale is set in the shadowy margin between the pagan and Christian worlds. As you read, think about which events belong to each of these worlds.

Literary Element **Humor**

The quality of a literary work that makes characters and their situations seem funny, amusing, or ludicrous is called **humor.** Humor often ridicules human failings and reveals the irony found in many predicaments. Types of humor range widely, from puns and word play to broad satire, sarcasm, parody, and subtle wit.

- See Literary Terms Handbook, p. R8.

Literature Online **Interactive Literary Elements Handbook** To review or learn more about the literary elements, go to www.glencoe.com.

Reading Strategy **Evaluating Argument**

Argument is a type of persuasive writing or speaking in which logic or reason is used to influence a reader's or listener's ideas or actions. Unlike other forms of persuasion, argument does not resort to emotional appeals.

Reading Tip: Analyzing Arguments Near the climax of "The Wife of Bath's Tale," the knight makes a series of accusations and the old woman responds with a series of arguments. Use a chart similar to the one below to keep track of their exchanges.

Knight's Accusations	Old Woman's Arguments
The old woman is not a gentlewoman.	Gentility is a gift from God, not one's ancestry, and is manifested in virtuous behavior.

Vocabulary

reprove (ri proōv′) *v.* to scold or correct, usually gently or out of kindness; p. 126 *Felicia's mother reproved her for not sharing her toys.*

concede (kən sēd′) *v.* to admit as true; acknowledge; p. 128 *Reuben had to concede that Charles's fundraising scheme was best.*

disperse (dis purs′) *v.* to scatter about; distribute widely; p. 132 *After the family reunion, all the relatives dispersed to their homes around the country.*

arrogance (ar′ ə gəns) *n.* overbearing pride or self-importance; p. 134 *In his arrogance, the ruler built a monument to himself.*

suffice (sə fīs′) *v.* to be enough for; p. 137 *You said you hoped for rain; will this downpour suffice?*

Vocabulary Tip: Analogies To complete an analogy, apply the relationship represented by the first pair of words to the second pair of words.

OBJECTIVES
In studying this selection, you will focus on the following:
- understanding historical and cultural context
- analyzing humor
- evaluating argument

from The Wife of Bath's Tale

*The Wife of Bath prefaces her tale by saying that she has a
right to speak of the woes of marriage since she has had considerable experience in the matter. Apparently, the object of marriage for her is to have mastery over her husband, "who shall be
both my debtor and my slave." To support this view, she cites
part of a statement by St. Paul that grants a wife power over
her husband's body. This prompts the Pardoner to interrupt.*

> The Pardoner started up, and thereupon
> 'Madam,' he said, 'by God and by St John,
> That's noble preaching no one could surpass!
> I was about to take a wife; alas!
> 5   Am I to buy it on my flesh so dear?
> There'll be no marrying for me this year!'
>   'You wait,' she said, 'my story's not begun.
> You'll taste another brew before I've done;
> You'll find it doesn't taste as good as ale;
> 10 And when I've finished telling you my tale
> Of tribulation in the married life
> In which I've been an expert as a wife,
> That is to say, myself have been the whip.
> So please yourself whether you want to sip
> 15 At that same cask of marriage I shall broach.
> Be cautious before making the approach,

Literary Element   Humor *What is humorous in this exchange between the Wife
and the Pardoner?*

For I'll give instances, and more than ten.
And those who won't be warned by other men,
By other men shall suffer their correction,
20 So Ptolemy° has said, in this connection.
You read his *Almagest*; you'll find it there.
        'Madam, I put it to you as a prayer,'
The Pardoner said, 'go on as you began!
Tell us your tale, spare not for any man.
25 Instruct us younger men in your technique.'
'Gladly,' she said, 'if you will let me speak,
But still I hope the company won't **reprove** me
Though I should speak as fantasy may move me,
And please don't be offended at my views;
30 They're really only offered to amuse.

The Wife proceeds to tell a series of vivid private anecdotes of her five marriages, supposedly as exempla of her beliefs about relationships. She boasts of how she controlled her first three husbands by always making them feel at fault. Her last two husbands proved less cooperative. The fourth cheated on her, and the most she could do to retaliate was to pretend to be interested in other men. The fifth would beat her, and yet she loved him most, because "he was disdainful in his love." A scholar, he would try to educate her to be submissive by forcing her to listen to authoritative readings on wicked women. This finally provoked her to start a brawl. In the end, she made him burn the texts and surrender his mastery to her, and from then on, she says, she was kind and true to him and he to her. In the tale that follows, it is the wife who subjects the husband to a course of education.

When good King Arthur ruled in ancient days
(A king that every Briton loves to praise)
This was a land brim-full of fairy folk.
The Elf-Queen and her courtiers joined and broke
35 Their elfin dance on many a green mead,°
Or so was the opinion once, I read,
Hundreds of years ago, in days of yore.
But no one now sees fairies any more.
For now the saintly charity and prayer
40 Of holy friars seem to have purged the air;
They search the countryside through field and stream
As thick as motes° that speckle a sun-beam,
Blessing the halls, the chambers, kitchens, bowers,

20 **Ptolemy** (tä′ lə mē): Claudius Ptolemaeus was a second-century Greek astronomer whose work the *Almagest* served as the definitive textbook for medieval astronomers. The proverb in the preceding lines was added by someone else to a particular edition of the *Almagest.*

35 **mead:** meadow.

42 **motes:** particles of dust.

Big Idea **The Power of Faith** *How has Christianity supplanted paganism in King Arthur's day?*

Vocabulary

reprove (ri prōōv′) *v.* to scold or correct, usually gently or out of kindness

The City Weir, Bath, Looking Towards Walcot, 18th century. Thomas Ross. Oil on canvas, 91.5 x 121.5 cm. Victoria Art Gallery, Bath and North East Somerset Council, England.

Cities and boroughs, castles, courts and towers,
45 Thorpes,° barns and stables, outhouses and dairies,
And that's the reason why there are no fairies.
Wherever there was wont to walk° an elf
To-day there walks the holy friar himself
As evening falls or when the daylight springs,
50 Saying his mattins and his holy things,
Walking his limit round from town to town.
Women can now go safely up and down
By every bush or under every tree;
There is no other incubus° but he,
55 So there is really no one else to hurt you
And he will do no more than take your virtue.
    Now it so happened, I began to say,
Long, long ago in good King Arthur's day,
There was a knight who was a lusty liver.
60 One day as he came riding from the river
He saw a maiden walking all forlorn
Ahead of him, alone as she was born.
And of that maiden, spite of all she said,
By very force he took her maidenhead.
65   This act of violence made such a stir,
So much petitioning to the king for her,
That he condemned the knight to lose his head
By course of law. He was as good as dead
(It seems that then the statutes took that view)
70 But that the queen, and other ladies too,
Implored° the king to exercise his grace
So ceaselessly, he gave the queen the case
And granted her his life, and she could choose

45 **Thorpes:** villages.

47 **wont to walk:** habitually walked.

54 **incubus:** evil spirit that attacks women in their sleep.

71 **implored:** pleaded with.

Whether to show him mercy or refuse.
75   The queen returned him thanks with all her might,
And then she sent a summons to the knight
At her convenience, and expressed her will:
'You stand, for such is the position still,
In no way certain of your life,' said she,
80   'Yet you shall live if you can answer me:
What is the thing that women most desire?
Beware the axe and say as I require.
   'If you can't answer on the moment, though,
I will **concede** you this: you are to go
85   A twelvemonth and a day to seek and learn
Sufficient answer, then you shall return.
I shall take gages° from you to extort
Surrender of your body to the court.'
   Sad was the knight and sorrowfully sighed,
90   But there! All other choices were denied,
And in the end he chose to go away
And to return after a year and day
Armed with such answer as there might be sent
To him by God. He took his leave and went.
95   He knocked at every house, searched every place,
Yes, anywhere that offered hope of grace.
What could it be that women wanted most?
But all the same he never touched a coast,
Country or town in which there seemed to be
100   Any two people willing to agree.
   Some said that women wanted wealth and treasure,
'Honour,' said some, some 'Jollity and pleasure,'
Some 'Gorgeous clothes' and others 'Fun in bed,'
'To be oft widowed and remarried,' said
105   Others again, and some that what most mattered
Was that we should be cosseted° and flattered.
That's very near the truth, it seems to me;
A man can win us best with flattery.
To dance attendance on us, make a fuss,
110   Ensnares° us all, the best and worst of us.
   Some say the things we most desire are these:
Freedom to do exactly as we please,
With no one to reprove our faults and lies,
Rather to have one call us good and wise.
115   Truly there's not a woman in ten score°
Who has a fault, and someone rubs the sore,

87 **gages:** valuable items pledged in support of a promise, such as money posted for bail.

15th-Century Manuscript Illumination of a Knight from the Codex Capodilista.

106 **cosseted:** pampered.

110 **ensnares:** captures or traps.

115 **ten score:** two hundred.

Big Idea **The Power of Faith** *How does the knight expect ultimately to free himself through faith?*

Vocabulary

concede (kən sēd′) *v.* to admit as true; acknowledge

Knight Visiting His Lady, 1475 (detail). Artist unknown.
Manuscript illumination.

But she will kick if what he says is true;
You try it out and you will find so too.
However vicious we may be within
120　We like to be thought wise and void of sin.
Others assert we women find it sweet
When we are thought dependable, discreet
And secret, firm of purpose and controlled,
Never betraying things that we are told.
125　But that's not worth the handle of a rake;
Women conceal a thing? For Heaven's sake!
Remember Midas? Will you hear the tale?
　　Among some other little things, now stale,
Ovid° relates that under his long hair
130　The unhappy Midas grew a splendid pair
Of ass's ears; as subtly as he might,
He kept his foul deformity from sight;
Save for his wife, there was not one that knew.
He loved her best, and trusted in her too.
135　He begged her not to tell a living creature
That he possessed so horrible a feature.
And she—she swore, were all the world to win,
She would not do such villainy and sin
As saddle her husband with so foul a name;
140　Besides to speak would be to share the shame.
Nevertheless she thought she would have died
Keeping this secret bottled up inside;
It seemed to swell her heart and she, no doubt,
Thought it was on the point of bursting out.
145　　Fearing to speak of it to woman or man,
Down to reedy marsh she quickly ran

129　Ovid: Roman poet (43 B.C.?–A.D. 17) best known for the *Metamorphoses,* a collection of ancient tales written in verse.

Literary Element　**Humor** *What is the Wife making fun of here?*

Illustration of a Knight and Horse in Armor by Friedrich Martin von Reibisch. Stapleton Collection.

And reached the sedge.° Her heart was all on fire
And, as a bittern° bumbles in the mire,
She whispered to the water, near the ground,
'Betray me not, O water, with thy sound!
To thee alone I tell it: it appears
My husband has a pair of ass's ears!
Ah! My heart's well again, the secret's out!
I could no longer keep it, not a doubt.'
And so you see, although we may hold fast°
A little while, it must come out at last,
We can't keep secrets; as for Midas, well,
Read Ovid for his story°; he will tell.
   This knight that I am telling you about
Perceived at last he never would find out
What it could be that women loved the best.
Faint was the soul within his sorrowful breast,
As home he went, he dared no longer stay;
His year was up and now it was the day.
   As he rode home in a dejected mood
Suddenly, at the margin of a wood,

147 sedge: any of a family of marsh plants.
148 bittern: heron.

155 hold fast: restrain firmly.

158 Read . . . story: In the *Metamorphoses,* the marsh weeds whisper Midas's secret whenever the wind blows.

Reading Strategy **Evaluating Argument** *Is Ovid's tale convincing proof of the Wife's argument that women cannot keep secrets? Explain.*

He saw a dance upon the leafy floor
Of four and twenty ladies, nay, and more.
Eagerly he approached, in hope to learn
170 Some words of wisdom ere he should return;
But lo! Before he came to where they were,
Dancers and dance all vanished into air!
There wasn't a living creature to be seen
Save one old woman crouched upon the green.
175 A fouler-looking creature I suppose
Could scarcely be imagined. She arose
And said, 'Sir knight, there's no way on from here.
Tell me what you are looking for, my dear,
For peradventure° that were best for you;
180 We old, old women know a thing or two.'
    'Dear Mother,' said the knight, 'alack the day!
I am as good as dead if I can't say
What thing it is that women most desire;
If you could tell me I would pay your hire.'
185 'Give me your hand,' she said, 'and swear to do
Whatever I shall next require of you
—If so to do should lie within your might—
And you shall know the answer before night.'
'Upon my honour,' he answered, 'I agree.'
190 'Then,' said the crone,° 'I dare to guarantee
Your life is safe; I shall make good my claim.
Upon my life the queen will say the same.
Show me the very proudest of them all
In costly coverchief or jewelled caul°
195 That dare say no to what I have to teach.
Let us go forward without further speech.'
And then she crooned her gospel in his ear
And told him to be glad and not to fear.
    They came to court. This knight, in full array,
200 Stood forth and said, 'O Queen, I've kept my day
And kept my word and have my answer ready.'
    There sat the noble matrons and the heady
Young girls, and widows too, that have the grace
Of wisdom, all assembled in that place,
205 And there the queen herself was throned to hear
And judge his answer. Then the knight drew near
And silence was commanded through the hall.
    The queen gave order he should tell them all
What thing it was that women wanted most.
210 He stood not silent like a beast or post,
But gave his answer with the ringing word
Of a man's voice and the assembly heard:

179 **peradventure:** perhaps.

190 **crone:** withered old woman.

194 **caul:** net cap worn in the hair and sometimes ornamented.

Big Idea **The Power of Faith** *How does the knight's encounter at the edge of the wood evoke the pagan world?*

'My liege and lady, in general,' said he,
'A woman wants the self-same sovereignty°
215 Over her husband as over her lover,
And master him; he must not be above her.
That is your greatest wish, whether you kill
Or spare me; please yourself. I wait your will.'
    In all the court not one that shook her head
220 Or contradicted what the knight had said;
Maid, wife and widow cried, 'He's saved his life!'
    And on the word up started the old wife,
The one the knight saw sitting on the green,
And cried, 'Your mercy, sovereign lady queen!
225 Before the court **disperses,** do me right!
'Twas I who taught this answer to the knight,
For which he swore, and pledged his honour to it,
That the first thing I asked of him he'd do it,
So far as it should lie within his might.
230 Before this court I ask you then, sir knight,
To keep your word and take me for your wife;
For well you know that I have saved your life.
If this be false, deny it on your sword!'
    'Alas!' he said, 'Old lady, by the Lord
235 I know indeed that such was my behest,°
But for God's love think of a new request,
Take all my goods, but leave my body free.'
'A curse on us,' she said, 'If I agree!
I may be foul, I may be poor and old,
240 Yet will not choose to be, for all the gold
That's bedded in the earth or lies above,
Less than your wife, nay, than your very love!'
    'My love?' said he. 'By heaven, my damnation!
Alas that any of my race and station
245 Should ever make so foul a misalliance!'°
Yet in the end his pleading and defiance
All went for nothing, he was forced to wed.
He takes his ancient wife and goes to bed.
    Now peradventure some may well suspect
250 A lack of care in me since I neglect
To tell of the rejoicing and display
Made at the feast upon their wedding-day.

214 **sovereignty:** power to rule another person or group of people.

235 **behest:** command.

245 **misalliance:** marriage between people unsuitable for each other.

Reading Strategy **Evaluating Argument** *What criterion do the women use to evaluate the knight's answer?*

Literary Element **Humor** *Do you see any humor in the knight's predicament? Explain.*

Vocabulary

disperse (dis purs′) *v.* to scatter about; distribute widely

Month of May: May Dance and Game of Small Papers, c. 1459. Artist unknown. From the Hours of the Duchess of Burgundy. Musée Condé, Chantilly, France.

I have but a short answer to let fall;
I say there was no joy or feast at all,
255 Nothing but heaviness of heart and sorrow.
He married her in private on the morrow
And all day long stayed hidden like an owl,
It was such torture that his wife looked foul.
     Great was the anguish churning in his head
260 When he and she were piloted to bed;
He wallowed back and forth in desperate style.
His ancient wife lay smiling all the while;
At last she said, 'Bless us! Is this, my dear,
How knights and wives get on together here?
265 Are these the laws of good King Arthur's house?
Are knights of his all so contemptuous?
I am your own beloved and your wife,
And I am she, indeed, that saved your life;
And certainly I never did you wrong.
270 Then why, this first of nights, so sad a song?
You're carrying on as if you were half-witted.

Literary Element **Humor** *How is the old woman making fun of the knight? Why does she appear to be unoffended by his aversion to her age and appearance?*

Say, for God's love, what sin have I committed?
I'll put things right if you will tell me how.'
        'Put right?' he cried. 'That never can be now!
275 Nothing can ever be put right again!
You're old, and so abominably plain,
So poor to start with, so low-bred to follow;
It's little wonder if I twist and wallow!
God, that my heart would burst within my breast!'
280   'Is that,' said she, 'the cause of your unrest?'
        'Yes, certainly,' he said, 'and can you wonder?'
        'I could set right what you suppose a blunder,
That's if I cared to, in a day or two,
If I were shown more courtesy by you.
285 Just now,' she said, 'you spoke of gentle birth,
Such as descends from ancient wealth and worth.
If that's the claim you make for gentlemen
Such **arrogance** is hardly worth a hen.
Whoever loves to work for virtuous ends,
290 Public and private, and who most intends
To do what deeds of gentleness he can,
Take him to be the greatest gentleman.
Christ wills we take our gentleness from Him,
Not from a wealth of ancestry long dim,
295 Though they bequeath their whole establishment
By which we claim to be of high descent.
Our fathers cannot make us a bequest
Of all those virtues that became them best
And earned for them the name of gentlemen,
300 But bade us follow them as best we can.
        'Thus the wise poet of the Florentines,
Dante° by name, has written in these lines,
For such is the opinion Dante launches;
"Seldom arises by these slender branches°
305 Prowess of men, for it is God, no less,
Wills us to claim of Him our gentleness."
For of our parents nothing can we claim
Save temporal° things, and these may hurt and maim.
        'But everyone knows this as well as I;
310 For if gentility° were implanted by
The natural course of lineage down the line,
Public or private, could it cease to shine
In doing the fair work of gentle deed?

Pilgrims Going to Canterbury,
13th century. Artist unknown.
Stained glass. Canterbury
Cathedral, Kent, UK.

302 **Dante Alighieri:** (dän′tā
ä′lə gyär′ē) Italian poet (1265–1321),
author of the *Divine Comedy.*
304 **slender branches:** branches of the
family tree.

308 **temporal:** worldly.

310 **gentility:** courteous behavior
befitting a person of noble birth.

Reading Strategy **Evaluating Argument** *Summarize and evaluate
the old woman's argument against the knight's accusation that she is not
a gentlewoman.*

Vocabulary

arrogance (ar′ə gəns) *n.* overbearing pride or self-importance

No vice or villainy could then bear seed.
315 'Take fire and carry it to the darkest house
Between this kingdom and the Caucasus,°
And shut the doors on it and leave it there,
It will burn on, and it will burn as fair
As if ten thousand men were there to see,
320 For fire will keep its nature and degree,
I can assure you, sir, until it dies.
        'But gentleness, as you will recognize,
Is not annexed° in nature to possessions.
Men fail in living up to their professions;
325 But fire never ceases to be fire.
God knows you'll often find, if you enquire,
Some lording full of villainy and shame.
If you would be esteemed for the mere name
Of having been by birth a gentleman
330 And stemming from some virtuous, noble clan,
And do not live yourself by gentle deed
Or take your father's noble code and creed,
You are no gentleman, though duke or earl.
Vice and bad manners are what make a churl.°
335 'Gentility is only the renown
For bounty that your fathers handed down,
Quite foreign to your person, not your own;
Gentility must come from God alone.
That we are gentle comes to us by grace
340 And by no means is it bequeathed with place.
        'Reflect how noble (says Valerius)°
Was Tullius surnamed Hostilius,
Who rose from poverty to nobleness.
And read Boethius,° Seneca° no less,
345 Thus they express themselves and are agreed:
"Gentle is he that does a gentle deed."
And therefore, my dear husband, I conclude
That even if my ancestors were rude,
Yet God on high—and so I hope He will—
350 Can grant me grace to live in virtue still,
A gentlewoman only when beginning
To live in virtue and to shrink from sinning.
        'As for my poverty which you reprove,
Almighty God Himself in whom we move,
355 Believe and have our being, chose a life
Of poverty, and every man or wife

316 **Caucasus:** Caucasus Mountains, in southeastern Europe.

323 **annexed:** attached as a quality or consequence.

334 **churl:** discourteous, ill-bred person.

341 **Valerius Maximus:** Roman author (c. 20 B.C.–A.D. 50), whose work was widely popular as a source for writers.

344 **Boethius:** (bō ē′ thē əs) Roman philosopher and statesman (c. 480–c. 524), best known for his Consolation of Philosophy, written while he was imprisoned for treason. **Seneca:** Roman playwright and philosopher (4 B.C.?–A.D. 65).

Big Idea **The Power of Faith** *How does the old woman use the power of faith to support her argument?*

Big Idea **The Power of Faith** *How does the old woman's first argument against the knight's accusation of poverty illustrate her religious faith?*

Chaucer at the Court of Edward III, 1856–1868. Ford Madox Brown. Oil on canvas, 123.2 x 99.1 cm. Tate Gallery, London

Nay, every child can see our Heavenly King
Would never stoop to choose a shameful thing.
No shame in poverty if the heart is gay,
360 As Seneca and all the learned say.
He who accepts his poverty unhurt
I'd say is rich although he lacked a shirt.
But truly poor are they who whine and fret
And covet what they cannot hope to get.
365 And he that, having nothing, covets not,
Is rich, though you may think he is a sot.°
    'True poverty can find a song to sing.
Juvenal° says a pleasant little thing:
"The poor can dance and sing in the relief
370 Of having nothing that will tempt a thief."
Though it be hateful, poverty is good,
A great incentive to a livelihood,
And a great help to our capacity
For wisdom, if accepted patiently.
375 Poverty is, though wanting in estate,
A kind of wealth that none calumniate.°
Poverty often, when the heart is lowly,
Brings one to God and teaches what is holy,

366 **sot:** habitual drunkard.

368 **Juvenal:** Roman poet and satirist (A.D. 60?–127?).

376 **calumniate:** utter false and vicious statements.

Reading Strategy **Evaluating Argument** *The old woman has cited Dante, Valerius, Boethius, Seneca, and now Juvenal. How well do these citations support her argument?*

Gives knowledge of oneself and even lends
380 A glass° by which to see one's truest friends.
And since it's no offence, let me be plain;
Do not rebuke my poverty again.

'Lastly you taxed me, sir, with being old.
Yet even if you never had been told
385 By ancient books, you gentlemen engage,
Yourselves in honour to respect old age.
To call an old man "father" shows good breeding,
And this could be supported from my reading.

'You say I'm old and fouler than a fen.°
390 You need not fear to be a cuckold,° then.
Filth and old age, I'm sure you will agree,
Are powerful wardens over chastity.
Nevertheless, well knowing your delights,
I shall fulfil your worldly appetites.

395 'You have two choices; which one will you try?
To have me old and ugly till I die,
But still a loyal, true, and humble wife
That never will displease you all her life,
Or would you rather I were young and pretty
400 And chance your arm what happens in a city
Where friends will visit you because of me,
Yes, and in other places too, maybe.
Which would you have? The choice is all your own.'

The knight thought long, and with a piteous groan
405 At last he said, with all the care in life,
'My lady and my love, my dearest wife,
I leave the matter to your wise decision.
You make the choice yourself, for the provision
Of what may be agreeable and rich
410 In honour to us both, I don't care which;
Whatever pleases you **suffices** me.'

'And have I won the mastery?' said she,
'Since I'm to choose and rule as I think fit?'
'Certainly, wife,' he answered her, 'that's it.'

380 **glass:** mirror.

389 **fen:** lowland wholly or partly covered with water.
390 **cuckold:** man whose wife is unfaithful to him.

Reading Strategy Evaluating Argument *Summarize the six reasons the old woman uses to support her argument that poverty is beneficial.*

Reading Strategy Evaluating Argument *Summarize and evaluate the old woman's argument that the knight should not scorn her for being old and ugly.*

Literary Element Humor *Do you find any humor in the knight's response to the choice offered him by the old woman? Explain.*

Vocabulary

suffice (sə fīs′) *v.* to be enough for

Month of April, Wedding Procession. Grimani Breviary. Biblioteca Marciana, Venice, Italy.

415   'Kiss me,' she cried. 'No quarrels! On my oath
      And word of honour, you shall find me both,
      That is, both fair and faithful as a wife;
      May I go howling mad and take my life
      Unless I prove to be as good and true
420   As ever wife was since the world was new!
      And if to-morrow when the sun's above
      I seem less fair than any lady-love,
      Than any queen or empress east or west,
      Do with my life and death as you think best.
425   Cast up the curtain, husband. Look at me!'
          And when indeed the knight had looked to see,
      Lo, she was young and lovely, rich in charms.
      In ecstasy he caught her in his arms,
      His heart went bathing in a bath of blisses
430   And melted in a hundred thousand kisses,
      And she responded in the fullest measure
      With all that could delight or give him pleasure.
          So they lived ever after to the end
      In perfect bliss; and may Christ Jesus send
435   Us husbands meek and young and fresh in bed,
      And grace to overbid them when we wed.
      And—Jesu hear my prayer!—cut short the lives
      Of those who won't be governed by their wives;
      And all old, angry niggards of their pence,°
440   God send them soon a very pestilence!

439 niggards: misers. **pence:** pennies.

138   UNIT 1   THE ANGLO-SAXON PERIOD AND THE MIDDLE AGES

RESPONDING AND THINKING CRITICALLY

Respond

1. Do you think the knight gets what he deserves? Explain.

Recall and Interpret

2. (a)What question does the knight have to answer in order to save his life? (b)How do you think the knight feels when he provides the queen with the correct answer? Explain.

3. (a)What bargain does the old woman make with the knight? (b)What is the ironic connection between the answer to the queen's question and the requirement that the old woman demands of the knight?

4. (a)Summarize the ending of "The Wife of Bath's Tale." (b)What lesson does the ending teach?

Analyze and Evaluate

5. (a)How does the old woman get the knight to change his attitude toward marrying her? (b)Do you find her method convincing? Explain.

6. (a)Through her arguments, what is the old woman ultimately demanding that the knight acknowledge? (b)How does the knight's acknowledgment transform both the knight and the old woman?

7. Do you think Chaucer's portrayal of the Wife indicates that he was ahead of his time in his view of women? Why or why not?

Connect

8. In your opinion, is the lesson that the Wife teaches relevant to today's world? Explain.

9. **Big Idea** **The Power of Faith** To what extent does "The Wife of Bath's Tale" illustrate the power of Christian faith?

DAILY LIFE AND CULTURE

The Medieval Pilgrimage

A pilgrimage is a journey made to a holy place, or shrine, to venerate it, ask for supernatural aid, or to fulfill a religious obligation. The shrines were specific locations made holy by the birth, life, or death of a prophet or saint. In medieval England the most popular pilgrimage was the one made each year to Canterbury Cathedral. The cathedral achieved renown as the place where Archbishop Thomas à Becket was murdered by agents of King Henry II in

1170 during a struggle for power between church and state. Becket was made a saint in 1173, and in the following year Henry II was forced to do penance at the saint's tomb.

The journey from London to Canterbury was not an easy one, but it afforded a challenging adventure. It was expensive because the pilgrims had to stay at inns along the way. Also, they had to endure the hardships of life on horseback over unpaved roads for several days on their way to Canterbury and back.

1. Of Chaucer's 29 pilgrims, which ones strike you as making this pilgrimage for spiritual reasons?

2. Do any of the pilgrims seem to be making this journey for other reasons? Explain.

12th century plan of
Canterbury Cathedral.

Literary Element — Humor

Among the types of humor that Chaucer uses in "The Wife of Bath's Tale" are exaggeration, understatement, and incongruity. Incongruity involves the juxtaposition of two or more jarring or unexpected pieces of information.

1. How is the Wife's reply to the Pardoner in line 26 of "The Wife of Bath's Tale" an example of understatement?

2. How is the Wife's account of the way in which friars have banished fairies (lines 38–46) an example of exaggeration?

3. How is the Wife's comment on friars in lines 55–56 an example of incongruity?

Review: Characterization

As you learned on page 93, **characterization** refers to the various methods a writer uses to develop the personality of a character.

Partner Activity Meet with another classmate to discuss the character of the knight in "The Wife of Bath's Tale." Use a graphic organizer similar to the one below to describe his character at several points during the tale. Write your description under the heading in the first column and cite the knight's words or actions that support your descriptions in the second column. When you finish filling in your chart, summarize how the knight changes throughout the tale.

Character Description	Words or Actions
At the beginning: The knight is immoral and violent.	"By very force he took her maidenhead."
On his quest:	
After he is freed:	
After he is married:	
At the end:	

Reading Strategy — Evaluating Argument

In "The Wife of Bath's Tale," the old woman reforms the knight by presenting a series of arguments to refute his accusations.

1. What accusations does the knight make against the old woman?

2. What arguments does the old woman use to answer the knight's accusations?

3. How persuasive do you find the old woman's arguments? Explain.

Vocabulary — Practice

Practice with Analogies Complete each analogy below. Use a dictionary if you need help.

1. reprove : fault :: applaud :
   a. honor   **b.** good deed   **c.** smile

2. concede : deny :: trust :
   a. honor   **b.** payment   **c.** doubt

3. disperse : scatter :: spoil :
   a. ruin   **b.** robbery   **c.** improve

4. arrogance : attitude :: wave :
   a. greet   **b.** enjoyment   **c.** gesture

5. suffice : lack :: raise :
   a. lower   **b.** crops   **c.** bonus

Academic Vocabulary

Here are two words from the vocabulary list on page R82. These words will help you think, write, and talk about the selection.

scheme (skēm) *n.* a systematic plan for achieving some object or end

acquire (ə kwīr′) *v.* to get or gain by one's own efforts or actions

Practice and Apply

1. Do you think the old woman has a **scheme** to save the knight even before the knight meets her by the wood? Explain.

2. What does the knight **acquire** at the end of the tale?

Writing About Literature

Analyze Theme Both "The Pardoner's Tale" and "The Wife of Bath's Tale" belong to the subgenre known as the **exemplum,** which is a tale used to illustrate a moral truth, or theme. Choose either tale and write an essay that analyzes its moral, or theme.

Plan carefully before you begin to write. As its name suggests, an exemplum is an "example," so you will need to show how the tale contains examples of the moral truth embodied in the theme. You can use a graphic organizer similar to the one below to organize your thoughts.

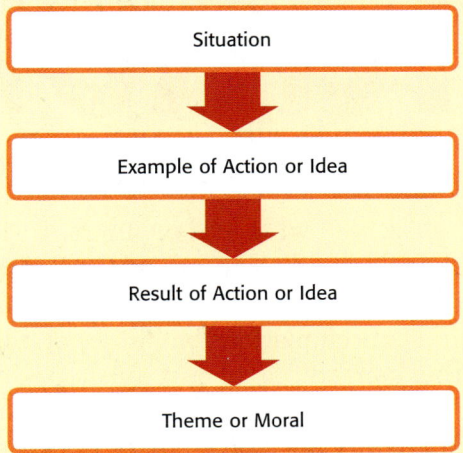

After you complete your draft, meet with a peer reviewer to evaluate each other's work and to suggest revisions. Then proofread and edit your draft for errors in spelling, grammar, and punctuation.

Literature Groups

Imagine you are creating a movie of one of the excerpts from *The Canterbury Tales* that you have just read. In your group, create a casting list detailing the traits you are looking for in the characters. Then cast the main parts with people from film, television, or your life. Share your list with the class and explain why you chose the people you did.

Chaucer's Language and Style

Using Indefinite Pronouns A pronoun ordinarily takes the place of a noun. However, sometimes pronouns refer to persons, places, and things in a more general way than nouns do. These are called **indefinite pronouns** because they do not take the place of specific nouns. Here are some examples from "The Prologue":

" . . . *all* was of the best." (line 29)
"*It* seems a reasonable thing to say . . ." (line 37)
"*He* who repeats a tale . . ." (line 727)

More indefinite pronouns are listed below:

anybody	none
both	no one
each	nothing
either	one
everyone	others
everything	plenty
few	several
many	something

Activity Use half of the indefinite pronouns listed above in original sentences about the pilgrims preparing to leave for Canterbury. Take care that you use these words as pronouns, not as adjectives or other parts of speech. For example, in "*Many* pilgrims were going to Canterbury," *many* is an adjective; in "*Many* were going to Canterbury," *many* is a pronoun.

Revising Check

Indefinite Pronouns Review and revise your word choice in the essay you wrote for the Writing About Literature feature. Have you used any indefinite pronouns? Have you used them correctly?

Media Link to *The Canterbury Tales*

TIME

The Roads Now Taken

It's a secular age, but Europeans still go on quests, treks, and pilgrimages to test their limits and nourish their souls.

By JEFF CHU

THE BENEDICTINE MONKS WERE FED UP. BY 1420, TRAFFIC was so bad inside England's Canterbury Cathedral that the Benedictines were constantly being diverted from their duties and contemplations by hordes of pilgrims. Ever since the martyrdom of Archbishop Thomas Becket 250 years earlier, people had been flocking here—to the grand seat of English Christianity and the scene of Becket's murder. They came to ask for Becket's saintly help in personal problems and to plead for healing and good health. This was all good and holy of the pilgrims, but who could hear themselves pray with all these visitors tramping around?

So the monks built a tunnel under the stairs at the center of the church, a sort of express lane to the spot where Becket was killed. Over the years, thousands of faithful shuffled through the cool, stone corridor, but gradually, what with King Henry VIII's break with Roman Catholicism, the Reformation, and later, creeping secularization, the pilgrims' numbers shrank to the point that the passageway became more useful as a broom closet. In 2004, however, officials at Canterbury reopened the tunnel. This time the passageway wasn't for Benedictines and pilgrims. It was for tourists, their digital cameras in hand, visiting one of the most famous cathedrals in England.

Where have all the pilgrims gone? They serve as a barometer for the values of an age. Their habits tell us about the spiritual state of a people. What temples do they worship in? To whom do they pay their tithes and offerings? Where do they seek their soul food? The fashionable answer is to say that faith in Europe is nearly extinct. Some theologians call the Continent "post-Christian." But the truth is that neither faith nor pilgrimage is dead in Europe.

Xurxo Lobato

THE HARD WAY On Spain's Camino de Santiago, pilgrims battle blisters, fatigue, and the elements over hundreds of miles of ancient trail.

Spiritual Experiences

TIME decided to hitch a ride with modern-day pilgrims to find out what moves people today—how travel helps test physical limits and nourish the spirit. Yes, there are still religious roamers out there: the constantly faithful Muslims, whose visits to Mecca have given us a word for a center of shared interest that draws people from all over; the Christians who walk the great pilgrim's way of El Camino de Santiago in Spain.

But in a secular age, the spiritual impulse is more likely to show itself in a cycling or mountain-climbing adventure, or the quiet contem-

plation of an English garden. Mass worship may take place in a football stadium. Many of today's most secular pilgrimages have a ritualistic quality that makes them part of the ancient tradition. It is what the Very Rev. Robert Willis, dean of Canterbury, calls the search for "blessing and enrichment. In pilgrimage, body, mind, and spirit come together in an individual quest," he says. "Jesus was always walking, walking, walking—all the way to Calvary." Our quest need not be so momentous: "Any journey that adds a mini-jigsaw piece to the puzzle of you can be a mini-pilgrimage."

Part of the joy of pilgrimage is a spirit of community that comes from identifying with something bigger than oneself. The pilgrim who sets out solo shares a bond with others who journey on the same path: the aches, the pains, and the triumphs. "The experience is very much about helping other pilgrims," says Abbot Christopher Dillon of Ireland's Glenstal Abbey, who walked the rugged Camino last year and hosts occasional pilgrims at his monastery in County Limerick. "There is great companionship on the road." That's the whole point of the Volksmarches, the communal hikes in Germany that attract thousands every year. The preservation of generational bonds is at the heart of the pilgrimages made to the battlefields of Europe, where families go to honor ancestors they never knew but will never forget.

A Journey into the Soul

And yet each pilgrim is utterly alone, because a pilgrimage is a trip not just to a physical place but also into a person's soul. So one can travel to Stratford-upon-Avon to celebrate Shakespeare's writings, be surrounded by thousands of other Shakespeare lovers, and yet be absolutely alone with one's own epiphanies about the Bard's works.

The traditional may argue that only a religious person is a true pilgrim, but as Phil Cousineau, the author of *The Art of Pilgrimage,* says, "The phenomenon of pilgrimage tends to hold up a mirror to what is sacred for the times." The world has changed, and so has pilgrimage. There will also always be those who label it foolishness, whether you embark with a belief in an unseen God's promise of salvation or in the

Shamil Zhumatov/Reuters

Kent News & Pictures

PILGRIMS' PROGRESS Muslims pray en route to Mecca (top); tourists pose at Canterbury.

power of a pair of devilish stilettos, as the amazingly committed shoppers at the Prada outlet in Montevarchi, Italy, do. A modern miracle—say, a game-winning goal that curled magnetically into the net at a world championship soccer match—works as much magic for some as the reenactment of medieval ones does for others. Faith is not rational. You can't argue a doubter into belief or force anyone onto the pilgrim's path.

In Chaucer's *Canterbury Tales,* the Prioress wears a brooch inscribed *Amor vincit omnia* (Love conquers all). This is true, not least, of pilgrimage. The love that drives it springs from faith, from mockery-proof loyalty, from unwavering belief in the power of a religion, or a great idea, or even a beautiful game. The pilgrim is no ordinary traveler. His map is in the heart.

—Updated 2005, from TIME International, July 5/12, 2004

RESPONDING AND THINKING CRITICALLY

Respond

1. How have your ideas about pilgrimages changed after reading the article?

Recall and Interpret

2. (a)Why did the number of Canterbury pilgrims dwindle? (b)Why is this relevant to the article?

3. (a)How does the Very Rev. Robert Willis define a "mini-pilgrimage"? (b)Why do you think people go on these mini-pilgrimages?

4. According to the article, what are some examples of secular pilgrimages that people go on?

Analyze and Evaluate

5. How do religious and secular pilgrimages differ? How are they alike?

6. How do you think the writer feels about the shift from religious to secular pilgrimages? Cite specific examples from the text to support your opinion.

Connect

7. Have you ever been on a religious or secular pilgrimage? If so, how did that experience affect you?

8. Think about the pilgrimage of the Wife of Bath. What does her journey have in common with the pilgrimages discussed in this article?

from *The Book of Margery Kempe*

MEET MARGERY KEMPE

Daughter of a mayor, wife of a tax collector, and mother of fourteen children, Margery Kempe might seem a conventional woman of the 1400s; however, she was anything but typical. She was a mystic, a pilgrim, and the author of the first English-language autobiography.

Born into a prosperous family in Norfolk, England, Kempe had both money and status. She married John Kempe at twenty and soon after, during a serious illness, had an intense religious experience that, she believed, restored her health.

In the following years, Kempe dedicated her energy to her children and two business ventures—a brewery and a mill. When both businesses failed, she decided to change her life. At the age of forty, Kempe devoted her life entirely to Christ. She took a vow of chastity and received permission from an archbishop to wear white clothes and receive weekly communion.

> "This is a short account of someone who had high status and worldly reputation but was later drawn to our Lord by severe poverty, sickness, humiliation . . ."
>
> —Margery Kempe, from *The Book of Margery Kempe*

Spiritual Pilgrim After a visit to Canterbury, Kempe began her life as a pilgrim. She traveled first to Jerusalem and then to Rome. Her spells of excessive sobbing, however, annoyed both priests and fellow travelers. After her return to England, she set out on a pilgrimage to Spain and then journeyed to Germany and Northern Europe. Later, she visited sacred sites in England.

The Exorcism of the Demon. Master of Saint Severin. Museo Horne, Florence, Italy.

Despite Kempe's devotion and her claims to mysticism, or the direct experience of the reality of God, she made some church officials uneasy. She was arrested and tried for the heresy of Lollardy but was acquitted. The Lollards were supporters of John Wycliffe, a priest and Oxford scholar who was highly critical of the church and some of its practices. The church, in turn, attempted to suppress followers of Wycliffe.

Staunch in Her Faith Given to spells of "boisterous crying," mystical visions, and spontaneous preaching against all "merriment," Kempe had few friends, but her faith in God and in her calling remained unshaken. Nothing is known of the last years of her life. Medical experts have commented on her excessive weeping and shouting. Feminists have pondered her situation as a medieval woman in a male-dominated society. Theologians have studied the descriptions of her visions and marveled at her devotion. Though she related many details about her life in her autobiography, she remains an enigma to the modern world.

Margery Kempe was born about 1373 and died in 1439 or 1440.

Literature Online **Author Search** For more about Margery Kempe, go to www.glencoe.com.

Connecting to the Autobiography

If you were to write the story of your life, what events would you include? In this selection, Margery Kempe describes a turning point in her life. As you read the selection, think about the following questions:

- Which autobiographies have you enjoyed reading?
- Why do you think people write autobiographies?

Building Background

Although Margery Kempe wanted to record the events of her life so that others might learn from them, she, like most women of her time, was illiterate. Therefore, Kempe dictated her autobiography to a scribe, possibly her eldest son. Unfortunately, he had poor handwriting and an even poorer grasp of English grammar, and he died before the manuscript was completed. The autobiography was then revised by a priest, who had to "sett a peyr of spectacles on hys nose" in order to accomplish the task. *The Book of Margery Kempe,* lost for centuries, was rediscovered in 1934 and published in its entirety for the first time in 1936.

Setting Purposes for Reading

Big Idea The Power of Faith

As you read, consider what this selection reveals about the importance of the church in medieval life.

Literary Element Autobiography

An **autobiography** is a person's account of his or her own life. Told from the first-person point of view, autobiographies can offer revealing insights into a person's view of herself or himself. As you read, consider what the details in this autobiography reveal about Margery Kempe's personality.

- See Literary Terms Handbook, p. R2.

Literature Online Interactive Literary Elements Handbook To review or learn more about the literary elements, go to www.glencoe.com.

Reading Strategy Analyzing Cause-and-Effect Relationships

When you **analyze cause-and-effect relationships,** you look for the causes, or reasons, why something happened and relate them to the effects or results. Writers often signal cause-and-effect relationships, using words such as *therefore, because, subsequently,* and *consequently.* Identifying these relationships will help you better understand the connections between events.

Reading Tip: Using a Cause-Effect Organizer Use a chart to record cause-and-effect relationships.

Cause	Effect
Something troubles Kempe's conscience.	She sends for her priest.

Vocabulary

divulge (di vulj´) v. to make known; disclose; p. 148 *Though many people knew the secret, no one divulged it.*

slander (slan´ dər) v. to utter false or malicious statements about; p. 148 *By spreading rumors and telling lies, he slandered his former friend.*

instigation (in´stə gā´ shən) n. the act of inciting or urging on; p. 148 *At the instigation of the leader, the crowd shouted and stamped their feet.*

restrain (ri strān´) v. to hold back; restrict; p. 149 *The owner used a leash to restrain his dog.*

composure (kəm pō´ zhər) n. a calm or tranquil state of mind; p. 149 *After barely avoiding a head-on collision, we could not regain our composure.*

Vocabulary Tip: Antonyms Antonyms are words that have opposite or nearly opposite meanings. The words *bright* and *dim* are antonyms.

OBJECTIVES
In studying this selection, you will focus on the following:
- understanding the historical period
- analyzing an autobiography
- examining cause-and-effect relationships

Saint Bernard exorcising an evil spirit, Panel from the
Altar of Saint Bernard. 1500. Jörg Breu the Elder.
Tempera on Wood.

from The Book of
Margery Kempe

Margery Kempe

Chapter 1

When I was twenty, or a little older, I was married to a well-respected burgess,[1] and, things being what they are, I quickly found myself pregnant. During the pregnancy and up to the time the child was born I suffered from severe attacks of illness; and then, what with the labor of giving birth on top of my previous illness, I despaired of my life and thought that I would not survive.

At that point I sent for my priest, because I had something on my conscience which I had never before **divulged** in my life. For I was constantly hindered by my enemy, the devil, who was always telling me that so long as I was in good health I had no need to make confession; I should just do penance[2] by myself, in private, and God, in his all-sufficient mercy, would forgive me for everything.

And therefore I often did harsh penances, restricting myself to bread and water; I also did other godly deeds, praying devoutly but never revealing my guilty secret in the course of confession.

But when I was ever sick or out of spirits, the devil whispered to me that I would be damned because I had not been absolved of[3] that special sin. Therefore, not expecting to survive the birth of my child, I sent for my priest, as I've already told you, fully intending to be absolved for everything I had done in my life.

But when I was on the point of revealing my long-concealed secret, my confessor[4] was a little too hasty with me; he began to tell me off in no uncertain terms, before I had even covered all I meant to say; and after that, try as he might, he couldn't get me to say a word.

Eventually, what with my fear of damnation on one hand and the priest's sharp tongue on the other, I became insane, and for half a year, eight weeks and a few days I was prodigiously[5] plagued and tormented by spirits.

During that time I saw (or I believed I saw) devils opening their mouths as if to swallow me, and revealing waves of fire that were burning inside their bodies. Sometimes they grabbed at me, sometimes they threatened me; they tugged and pulled me, night and day for a whole eight months. They also bayed[6] at me fearsomely, and told me to forsake the church and its faith and deny my God, his mother, and all the saints in heaven.

They told me to deny my good works and all my good qualities, and turn my back on my father, my mother, and all my friends. And that's what I did: I **slandered** my husband, my friends, and my own self. I said many wicked and cruel things; I was empty of any virtue or goodness; I was bent on every wickedness; I said and did whatever the spirits tempted me to say and do. At their **instigation** I would have destroyed myself many times over and been damned to hell; and as if to show determination I bit my own hand so savagely that the mark has been visible ever since.

---

1. A *burgess* is a citizen of an English borough, or town.
2. *Penance* is a religious act, such as praying, done to show sorrow or repentance for sin.
3. *Absolved of* means "pardoned for."
4. The *confessor* was the priest to whom Kempe confessed.

5. *Prodigiously* means "strangely."
6. *Bayed* means "shouted" or "roared."

The birth of Louis, son of Isabella, future Louis VIII the Good, in 1187. From "Histoire des nobles princes de Hainaut", late 15th century. Jacques de Guise Bibliotheque Municipale, Boulogne-sur-Mer, France.

What's more, I used my nails (for I had no other instrument) to scratch myself viciously, ripping the skin on my chest near my heart. And if I'd had my own way I would have done even more to myself, but I was bound and **restrained** by force day and night. I suffered from these and other temptations for such a long while that people thought I'd never recover or even survive, but then something happened: as I lay by myself, without my attendants, our merciful Lord Jesus Christ—ever to be trusted! his name be praised!—never forsaking his servant in a time of need, appeared to me—his creature who had forsaken him—in human form, the most pleasing, most beautiful, loveliest sight that human eyes could ever behold. Dressed in a mantle[7] of purple

silk, he sat by the bed, looking at me with so much holiness in his face that I felt myself inwardly fortified. And he spoke to me in the following way:

"Daughter, why have you abandoned me, when I never thought to abandon you?"

And instantly, as he spoke these words, I swear that I saw the air open up as brightly as any shaft of lightning. And he rose up into the air, not very fast or quickly but with grace and ease, so that I could clearly see him in the air until it closed again.

And at once my **composure** and mental faculties came back to me, just as they had been before, and I begged my husband, as soon as he came, for the keys of the cellar so that I could get myself food and drink as I had done in the past. My maids and attendants advised him not to hand over any keys; they said I would only give away any such stores[8] as we had, for they thought that I was beside myself.

Nevertheless, my husband, who was always kind and sympathetic to me, ordered them to give me the keys; and I got myself food and drink, insofar as my physical health would allow me to do so. And I recognized my friends, the members of my household, and all the others who came to see the act of mercy which our Lord Jesus Christ had performed on me. Blessed may he be, who is always close to us in our troubles. When people think he is far away, he is right beside them, full of grace.

Afterwards, I returned to all my other household duties, doing everything in a quite level-headed and sober way but not really knowing the call of our Lord.[9] ❧

---

7. A *mantle* is a long sleeveless garment worn over other clothes.

---

8. Here, *stores* refers to food stored for future use.

9. *Not . . . our Lord* indicates that Kempe had not yet devoted herself fully to God.

Big Idea **The Power of Faith** *To what does Kempe credit the restoration of her mental faculties?*

RESPONDING AND THINKING CRITICALLY

Respond

1. What questions would you like to ask Margery Kempe?

Recall and Interpret

2. (a)Why does Kempe refuse to tell her secret to the priest? (b)What does this refusal reveal about her character?

3. (a)How does Kempe's illness affect her personality? (b)Why was she "restrained by force"?

4. (a)Describe the vision that changes the course of Kempe's illness. (b)Why was that vision a turning point in her life? Explain.

Analyze and Evaluate

5. Which **images** in the selection did you find the most powerful? Why?

6. In your opinion, would the selection be more interesting if Kempe had revealed her secret to readers? Explain why or why not.

7. Poet William Wordsworth once wrote, "From the body of one guilty deed, / A thousand ghostly fears, and haunting thoughts, proceed!" Would Kempe agree with this statement? Support your answer with evidence from the selection.

Connect

8. **Big Idea** **The Power of Faith** Which of the church's teachings about confession and Jesus profoundly affect Kempe's life? Explain.

LITERARY ANALYSIS

Literary Element Autobiography

Autobiographies not only provide details about the author's personality but usually impart information about the society in which the author lived.

1. What did you learn about medieval life in an English town from reading this selection?

2. From the details Kempe chose to include in this excerpt, what values do you think were most important to her?

Writing About Literature

Analyze Genre Elements Writers of autobiographies treat literary elements in distinctive ways. In a brief essay, analyze how Kempe handles the following elements in the selection: point of view, characterization, motivation, description, sequence of events, historical and social context, and theme. Support your analysis with examples from the text.

Literature Online **Web Activities** For eFlashcards, Selection Quick Checks, and other Web activities, go to www.glencoe.com.

READING AND VOCABULARY

Reading Strategy Analyzing Cause-and-Effect Relationships

To understand this selection, you must consider the reasons why Margery Kempe and the people in her life act as they do. Review the **cause-and-effect** chart you filled in as you read the selection.

1. What caused Kempe to inflict pain on herself?

2. After her recovery, why do her attendants advise her husband not to give her the keys to the cellar?

3. Why does her husband disregard this advice?

Vocabulary Practice

Practice with Antonyms Choose the antonym for each vocabulary word below.

1. divulge   **a.** conceal   **b.** reveal

2. slander   **a.** malign   **b.** flatter

3. instigation   **a.** urging   **b.** impediment

4. restrain   **a.** release   **b.** restrict

5. composure   **a.** distress   **b.** poise

Grammar Workshop

Language Usage

Correcting Verb Tense

"And at once my composure and mental faculties came back to me, just as they had been before . . . "

> —Margery Kempe, from *The Book of Margery Kempe*

Connecting to Literature The **tenses** of a verb are different forms that help show time. Margery Kempe uses the past tense form *came* to describe events at a particular past time. Then she uses the past perfect form *had been* to describe an earlier situation. In your writing and speaking, using the correct verb tense informs your audience of when an event occurred and helps the audience keep track of a sequence of events.

Here are some ways to recognize and solve problems with verb tense.

Problem 1 A verb ending is incorrect or missing.
Margery Kempe confess to her priest before giving birth.
Mental illness torment Kempe for more than eight months.

Solution Add *-ed* to a regular verb to form its past tense or past participle.
Margery Kempe confessed to her priest before giving birth.
Mental illness tormented Kempe for more than eight months.

Problem 2 The past tense and the past participle forms are confused.
She had wrote her autobiography in order to describe her faith.

Solution Irregular verbs may have different past tense and past participle forms. For example, the past tense of *write* is *wrote*; the past participle of *write* is *written*.
She had written her autobiography in order to describe her faith.

Exercise

A. Revise for Clarity Rewrite the following sentences, correcting any errors in verb form.

1. Margery Kempe travel on several religious pilgrimages.
2. Like Kempe, the Venerable Bede record English history.
3. Chaucer, Kempe, and Bede had influence society.
4. Kempe stay in bed most of the time when she was ill.

B. Partner Activity Write a short paragraph that contains four incorrect verb tenses. Exchange papers with a partner. Revise the paragraph to correct any errors.

▶ **Verb Tenses**

Verb Tenses are the different forms verbs take to indicate when an action occurred.

▶ **Test-Taking Tip**

To identify the correct verb tense in a test-taking situation, think about how different verb forms would sound in the sentence. Often, an irregular verb will sound incorrect if you add an *-ed*.

▶ **Language Handbook**

For more about verb tenses, see Language Handbook, p. R51.

eWorkbooks To link to the Grammar and Language eWorkbook, go to www.glencoe.com.

OBJECTIVES
- Understand and use correct verb tenses.
- Recognize rules of grammar and language.

Miracle and Morality Plays

THE PRIME ENTERTAINERS IN ANGLO-SAXON Britain were storytellers and singing poets. Not until later medieval times did drama as public entertainment take hold. Like most forms of culture in those times, the theater had its beginnings in religion.

Rise of Medieval Drama

Though the church had condemned plays as immoral in 692, it revived theater later in the Middle Ages for religious purposes. Medieval theater developed in the early 900s from the annual cycle of the church liturgy (religious rites) that presented events in the life of Christ. It began as a dialogue about Christ's Resurrection performed by priests at Easter services. Later, clerical plays presented the events of Christmas and the Epiphany—the revelation of God to humankind in the form of Jesus—(the latter including a mechanical star of Bethlehem).

Miracle and Mystery Plays

By the 1100s, the church had developed religious drama in order to teach Bible stories and the lives of saints to a mostly illiterate populace. Originally, members of the clergy performed these plays in church sanctuaries, acting out the parts of biblical characters or saints. These short, one-act dramas were called **miracle plays,** after the miracles performed by the saints. Later, after the performances were taken over by the trade guilds known as "mysteries" (from *mystery,* meaning "trade" or "craft," related to the modern English word *ministry*), they became known as **mystery plays.**

Although based on religious subjects, medieval drama included elements of secular humor. In *Noah's Flood,* for example, Noah has an easy time building the ark but a difficult time persuading his wife to get aboard.

Noah: Wife in this castle we shall be kept:
My children and thou I would in leaped!
Wife: In faith, Noe, I had as lief thou had slept,
for all thy frankishfare [nonsense]
For I will not do after thy rede [advice].
Noah: Good wife, do as I thee bid.
Wife: By Christ not, or I see more need,

The Beginnings of the Christmas Play, cover of The Illustrated London News, 1935. Muriel Broderick.

Though thou stand all the day and rave.
Noah: Lord, that women be crabbed aye!
And never are meek, that I dare say.

As time went on, the plays grew more popular and the costumes and settings more elaborate—so much so that the churches could no longer hold such large audiences. The dramas moved outdoors and their production was taken over by the trade guilds. Guild members made scenery, props, and costumes and loaded them onto wagons (known as "pageants") so that the plays could be performed at fairs, in marketplaces, at crossroads and, if the producers were lucky, in the great halls of castles, where people paid good money for entertainment.

Guild records indicate that performances featured music, dancing, and comedy. Some performances

Stage set of Mystery play, c.1547. Hubert Cailleau. Wash gouache, ink. Bibliothèque Nationale, Paris.

even included special effects. For example, to depict the drowning of the Pharaoh's army in the Red Sea, stagehands covered the actors with a large blue cloth, shaking it to imitate the movement of waves. No feast days were complete without miracle plays, and everyone turned out for these performances. Audiences were anything but silent—cheers greeted heroes and saints, while villains such as Lucifer and Herod were enthusiastically booed and hissed.

Gradually, these short plays began to be presented in day-long cycles, beginning with the story of the creation of the world and ending with the story of Christ. By the late 1300s, cycles that lasted for several days were being performed on wagon stages throughout such English towns as York and Wakefield. As time passed, plays were not limited to biblical stories in cycles. A non-cycle play, *Robin Hood and the Sheriff of Nottingham*, was often presented at May Day festivals.

The Morality Play

In the early 1400s, a corps of professional actors arose who performed **morality plays**—plays that dramatized points of religious doctrine. Morality plays, as their name implies, centered on the moral struggles of everyday people. The characters in these plays had names such as Patience, Greed, and Good Works, and their dialogue was designed to teach people important lessons about salvation and the struggle between virtue and vice. As the popularity of morality plays grew, their staging became more sophisticated, while their subject matter moved from the church to the secular world. The morality plays established a theater tradition in England that eventually led to the plays of William Shakespeare and George Bernard Shaw.

Literature Online **Literary History** For more about miracle and morality plays, go to www.glencoe.com.

RESPONDING AND THINKING CRITICALLY

1. What do you think would have been the most interesting features of medieval theater?

2. In what way was the church involved in both the decline and revival of theater in medieval Europe?

3. Why do you think the guilds gradually took over the production of medieval theater?

4. In what way are morality plays more closely linked to modern drama than miracle plays?

OBJECTIVES
• Analyze the development of British drama.

• Analyze the characteristics of miracle and morality plays.

Connecting to the Play

Do all human beings have certain characteristics in common? If you were to create a character for a play who was meant to represent all people, think about the traits your character would have. As you read *Everyman*, think about the following questions:

- Which characteristics are common to everyone, regardless of class, religion, race, age, or era?
- Why might a story that explores the characteristics of an "everyman" remain popular for centuries?

Building Background

Everyman is probably based on the Flemish play *Elckerlijc* (Everyman), which was first printed in 1495. (Flemish is the language of Flanders, a historical region of northwestern Europe that today is part of France, Belgium, and the Netherlands.) The two anonymous plays are connected by their similar reflection of northern European religious thought at the end of the fifteenth century. Both are based on the orthodox teachings of the Christian Church but hint at the need for reform—an issue that was present in late fifteenth-century English sermons and lyrics.

Setting Purposes for Reading

Big Idea The Power of Faith

As you read, keep in mind the function of morality plays in medieval England and the influence of the church.

Literary Element Allegory

An **allegory** is a work of fiction or drama in which the elements—characters, settings, and plot—symbolize ideas, qualities, or figures beyond themselves. The overall purpose of an allegory is to teach a moral lesson. As you read the play, explore what the characters symbolize and how their actions and words help to teach a moral lesson.

- See Literary Terms Handbook, p. R1.

Reading Strategy Recognizing Author's Purpose

When you **recognize an author's purpose**, you identify the author's intent in writing a piece of literature. To recognize an author's purpose, look for clues to help you infer if the author wrote to persuade, inform, explain, or entertain.

Reading Tip: Creating a Checklist As you read, use a checklist to record evidence of the four purposes listed above.

Vocabulary

reckoning (rek′ ən ing) *n.* a settlement of accounts; p. 156 *Some people feel they will be called to a spiritual reckoning when they die.*

perceive (pər sēv′) *v.* to become aware of; comprehend; p. 156 *Elsa had to return to her crumbled town to perceive the full damage of the earthquake.*

respite (res′ pit) *n.* a delay or extension; p. 158 *Saul felt he needed a respite from studying to remain alert during exam time.*

adversity (ad vur′ sə tē) *n.* a state of hardship; misfortune; p. 163 *The boy had faced much adversity while growing up, but he was determined not to give up hope.*

Vocabulary Tip: Word Parts Greek, Latin, and Anglo-Saxon roots may appear in combination with prefixes, suffixes, or both. Recognizing them can help you to unlock the meaning of unfamiliar words.

 **Interactive Literary Elements Handbook** To review or learn more about the literary elements, go to www.glencoe.com.

OBJECTIVES
In studying this selection, you will focus on the following:
- analyzing literary periods
- analyzing allegory
- recognizing author's purpose

from Everyman

The Triumph of Death, 15th century. Flemish. Musée du Berry, Bourges, France.

CHARACTERS

GOD	CONFESSION
MESSENGER	BEAUTY
DEATH	STRENGTH
EVERYMAN	DISCRETION
FELLOWSHIP	FIVE WITS
GOODS	ANGEL
GOOD DEEDS	DOCTOR
KNOWLEDGE	

Here beginneth a treatise how the High Father of Heaven sendeth Death to summon every creature to come and give account of their lives in this world, and is in manner of a moral play.

MESSENGER.   I pray you all give your audience
And hear this matter with reverence,
By figure° a moral play:
The Summoning of Everyman called it is,
5   That of our lives and ending shows
How transitory we be all day.°
This matter is wondrous precious,
But the intent of it is more gracious,
And sweet to bear away.
10   The story saith: Man, in the beginning,
Look well, and take good heed to the ending,
Be you never so gay!
Ye think sin in the beginning full sweet,
Which in the end causeth the soul to weep,
15   When the body lieth in clay.
Here shall you see how Fellowship and Jollity,
Both Strength, Pleasure, and Beauty,
Will fade from thee as flower in May;
For ye shall hear how our Heaven King
20   Calleth Everyman to a general **reckoning**:
Give audience, and hear what he doth say.

[*Exit* MESSENGER.]

[*Enter* GOD.]

GOD.   I **perceive**, here in my majesty,
How that all creatures be to me unkind,

3 **By figure:** in form

6 **all day:** always

Reading Strategy   Recognizing Author's Purpose *Why might the author have the Messenger mention the full title of the play and what the play "shows"?*

Vocabulary

reckoning (rek′ ən ing) *n.* a settlement of accounts
perceive (pər sēv′) *v.* to become aware of; comprehend

Living without dread in worldly prosperity.
25 Of ghostly° sight the people be so blind,
Drowned in sin, they know me not for their God;
In worldly riches is all their mind,
They fear not my righteousness, the sharp rod. . . .
Every man liveth so after his own pleasure,
30 And yet of their life they be nothing sure:
I see the more that I them forbear,
The worse they be from year to year.
All that liveth appaireth° fast;
Therefore, I will, in all the haste,
35 Have a reckoning of every man's person; . . .
On every man living without fear.
Where art thou, Death, thou mighty messenger?

[*Enter* DEATH.]

DEATH. Almighty God, I am here at your will,
Your commandment to fulfill.

40 GOD. Go thou to Everyman,
And show him, in my name,
A pilgrimage he must on him take,
Which he in no wise may escape;
And that he bring with him a sure reckoning
45 Without delay or any tarrying.

[GOD *withdraws*.]

DEATH. Lord, I will in the world go run overall,°
And cruelly outsearch both great and small;
Every man will I beset° that liveth beastly,
Out of God's laws, and dreadeth not folly. . . .
50 Lo, yonder I see Everyman walking.
Full little he thinketh on my coming;
His mind is on fleshly lusts and his treasure,
And great pain it shall cause him to endure
Before the Lord, Heaven King.

[*Enter* EVERYMAN.]

55 Everyman, stand still! Whither art thou going
Thus gaily? Hast thou thy Maker forget?°

EVERYMAN. Why askest thou?
Wouldest thou wit?°

DEATH. Yea sir; I will show you:
60 In great haste I am sent to thee
From God out of his majesty.

Last Judgment. 1452. Petrus Christus. Right wing of a triptych, oil on oak panel, 134 x 56 cm. Gemaeldegalerie, Staatliche Museen zu Berlin, Germany.

25 **ghostly:** spiritual
33 **appaireth:** degenerate
46 **overall:** everywhere
48 **beset:** attack

56 **forget:** forgotten

58 **wit:** know

Big Idea **The Power of Faith** *Why might a speech like God's have been familiar to an audience at an early performance of* Everyman?

Literary Element **Allegory** *How does the author reveal that Everyman is a symbol for "every man"?*

EVERYMAN. What, sent to me?

DEATH.   Yea, certainly.
65   Though thou have forgot him here,
        He thinketh on thee in the heavenly sphere,
        As, ere we depart, thou shalt know.

EVERYMAN. What desireth God of me?

DEATH.   That shall I show thee:
        A reckoning he will needs have
70   Without any longer **respite**.

EVERYMAN.   To give a reckoning longer leisure I crave;
        This blind° matter troubleth my wit.°

DEATH.   On thee thou must take a long journey;
        Therefore, thy book of count° with thee thou bring,
75   For turn again thou cannot by no way.
        And look thou be sure of thy reckoning,
        For before God thou shalt answer, and show
        Thy many bad deeds and, good but a few;
        How thou hast spent thy life, and in what wise,
80   Before the chief Lord of Paradise. . . .

EVERYMAN.   Full unready I am such reckoning to give.
        I know thee not. What messenger art thou?

DEATH.   I am Death, that no man dreadeth,°
        For every man I rest,° and no man spareth;
85   For it is God's commandment
        That all to me should be obedient.

EVERYMAN.   O Death, thou comest when I had thee least in
            mind!
        In thy power it lieth me to save;
        Yet of my good° will I give thee, if thou will be kind—
90   Yea, a thousand pound shalt thou have—
        And defer this matter till another day.

DEATH.   Everyman, it may not be, by no way.
        I set not by° gold, silver, nor riches,
        Nor by pope, emperor, king, duke, nor princes;
95   For, and° I would receive gifts great,
        All the world I might get;
        But my custom is clean contrary.

"Totenkasel". Chasuble for funeral mass, with a skeleton triumphant above broken crowns, sceptres and papal tiara, c. 1630. Velvet, embroidery, applique. 118 x 78 cm. Abbey, Kremsmuenster, Austria.

72 **blind:** unclear. **wit:** mind
74 **count:** accounts
83 **no man dreadeth:** dreads no man
84 **rest:** arrest

89 **good:** worldly goods

93 **I set not by:** I care not for

95 **and:** if

Big Idea **The Power of Faith** *What does Death's statement tell you about the beliefs of many Christians in the Middle Ages?*

Reading Strategy **Recognizing Author's Purpose** *What is Everyman doing here, and why would the author want to include such a passage?*

Vocabulary

respite (res′ pit) *n.* a delay or extension

I give thee no respite. Come hence, and not tarry.

EVERYMAN.   Alas, shall I have no longer respite?
100   I may say Death giveth no warning!
To think on thee, it maketh my heart sick,
For all unready is my book of reckoning.
But twelve year and I might have abiding,
My counting-book I would make so clear
105   That my reckoning I should not need to fear.°
Wherefore, Death, I pray thee, for God's mercy,
Spare me till I be provided of remedy.

DEATH.   Thee availeth not to cry, weep, and pray;
But haste thee lightly° that thou were gone that journey,
110   And prove° thy friends if thou can;
For, wit thou well, the tide abideth no man,
And in the world each living creature
For Adam's sin must die of nature.

EVERYMAN.   Death, if I should this pilgrimage take,
115   And my reckoning surely make,
Show me, for saint° charity,
Should I not come again shortly?

DEATH.   No, Everyman; and thou be once there,
Thou mayst never more come here,
120   Trust me verily.°

EVERYMAN.   O gracious God in the high seat celestial,
Have mercy on me in this most need!
Shall I have no company from this vale terrestrial°
Of mine acquaintance, that way me to lead?

125   DEATH.   Yea, if any be so hardy
That would go with thee and bear thee company.
Hie° thee that thou were gone to God's magnificence,
Thy reckoning to give before his presence.
What, weenest° thou thy life is given thee,
130   And thy worldly goods also?

EVERYMAN.   I had wend so, verily.

DEATH.   Nay, nay, it was but lent thee;
For as soon as thou art go,
Another a while shall have it, and then go therefro,
135   Even as thou hast done.
Everyman, thou art mad! Thou hast thy wits five,°
And here on earth will not amend thy life;
For suddenly I do come.

EVERYMAN.   O wretched caitiff,° whither shall I flee,
140   That I might scape° this endless sorrow?
Now, gentle Death, spare me till tomorrow
That I may amend me
With good advisement.°

DEATH.   Nay, thereto I will not consent,
145   Nor no man will I respite;

---

105 But twelve year . . . need to fear:
If I had twelve more years, I could improve my record.

109 lightly: quickly

110 prove: seek help from

116 saint: holy

120 verily: truly

123 terrestrial: earthly

127 Hie: hurry

129 weenest: think

136 thy wits five: The five wits were sense, imagination, fantasy, estimation, and memory.

139 caitiff: coward

140 scape: escape

143 advisement: preparation

But to the heart suddenly I shall smite
Without any advisement.
And now out of thy sight I will me hie;
See thou make thee ready shortly,
150   For thou mayst say this is the day
That no man living may scape away.

[*Exit* DEATH.]

EVERYMAN.   Alas, I may well weep with sighs deep!
Now have I no manner of company
To help me in my journey and me to keep;°
155   And also my writing° is full unready. . . .
To whom were I best my complaint to make?
What and I to Fellowship thereof spake,
And showed him of this sudden chance?
For in him is all mine affiance;°
160   We have in the world so many a day
Be good friends in sport and play.
I see him yonder, certainly.
I trust that he will bear me company;
Therefore to him will I speak to ease my sorrow.
165   Well met, good Fellowship, and good morrow!

FELLOWSHIP.   Everyman, good morrow, by this day!
Sir, why lookest thou so piteously?
If anything be amiss, I pray thee me say,
That I may help to remedy.

170   EVERYMAN.   Yea, good Fellowship, yea;
I am in great jeopardy.

FELLOWSHIP.   My true friend, show to me your mind;
I will not forsake thee to my life's end,
In the way of good company.

175   EVERYMAN.   That was well spoken, and lovingly.

FELLOWSHIP.   Sir, I must needs know your heaviness;°
I have pity to see you in any distress.
If any have you wronged, ye shall revenged be:
Though I on the ground be slain for thee—
180   Though that I know before that I should die.

EVERYMAN.   Verily, Fellowship, gramercy.°

FELLOWSHIP.   Tush! by thy thanks I set not a straw.
Show me your grief and say no more. . . .

EVERYMAN.   Ye speak like a good friend; I believe you well.
185   I shall deserve° it, and I may.

---

154 keep: guard

155 writing: the record of Everyman's accounts

159 affiance: trust

176 heaviness: sorrow

181 gramercy: many thanks

185 deserve: repay

Reading Strategy Recognizing Author's Purpose *What point is the author emphasizing about Death?*

Literary Element Allegory *What does the character Fellowship represent?*

Young Girl and the Angel of Death.
c. 1900. Adrian Stokes. Musée
d'Orsay, Paris, France.

FELLOWSHIP.   I speak of no deserving, by this day!
            For he that will say, and nothing do,
            Is not worthy with good company to go;
            Therefore show me the grief of your mind,
190   As to your friend most loving and kind.

EVERYMAN.   I shall show you how it is:
            Commanded I am to go a journey,
            A long way, hard and dangerous,
            And give a strait count,° without delay,
195   Before the high Judge, Adonai.°
            Wherefore, I pray you, bear me company,
            As ye have promised, in this journey.

FELLOWSHIP.   That is matter, indeed. Promise is duty;

            But, and I should take such a voyage on me,
200   I know it well, it should be to my pain;
            Also it maketh me afeard, certain.
            But let us take counsel here as well as we can,
            For your words would fear° a strong man.

EVERYMAN.   Why, ye said if I had need
205   Ye would me never forsake, quick° ne dead,
            Though it were to hell, truly.

FELLOWSHIP.   So I said, certainly,
            But such pleasures° be set aside, the sooth° to say;
            And also, if we took such a journey,
210   When should we come again?

EVERYMAN.   Nay, never again, till the day of doom.°

FELLOWSHIP.   In faith, then will not I come there! . . .

194 **strait count:** strict account
195 **Adonai:** God

203 **fear:** frighten

205 **quick:** living

208 **pleasures:** pleasantries. **sooth:** truth

211 **day of doom:** judgment day

Literary Element   **Allegory** *What is Fellowship's response to Everyman's request? What does Fellowship's response suggest about the "journey"?*

Allegory of Death (In Ictu Oculi). Juan de Valdes Leal. Hopital de la Caridad, Seville, Spain.

EVERYMAN.   Whither away, Fellowship? Will thou forsake me?

FELLOWSHIP.   Yea, by my fay!° To God I betake° thee.

214 **fay:** faith. **betake:** commend

215   EVERYMAN.   Farewell, good Fellowship; for thee my heart is
          sore.
          Adieu forever! I shall see thee no more.

FELLOWSHIP.   In faith, Everyman, farewell now at the ending;
          For you I will remember that parting is mourning.

[*Exit* FELLOWSHIP.] . . .

*Everyman next appeals to Kindred and Cousin, but they, too, refuse
to accompany him on his journey.*

EVERYMAN.   My kinsmen promised me faithfully
220   For to abide with me steadfastly,
          And now fast away do they flee:
          Even so Fellowship promised me.
          What friend were best me of to provide?°
          I lose my time here longer to abide,°

223 **me of to provide:** to provide
myself with
224 **abide:** stay

Literary Element   **Allegory** *On an allegorical level, what does Fellowship
reveal about the limits of his character?*

225   Yet in my mind a thing there is:
      All my life I have loved riches;
      If that my Good° now help me might,
      He would make my heart full light.
      I will speak to him in this distress—
230   Where art thou, my Goods and riches?

      [GOODS *speaks from a corner.*]

      GOODS.   Who calleth me? Everyman? What! hast thou haste?
      I lie here in corners, trussed° and piled so high,
      And in chests I am locked so fast,
      Also sacked in bags. Thou mayst see with thine eye
235   I cannot stir; in packs low I lie.
      What would ye have? Lightly me say.°

      EVERYMAN.   Come hither, Good, in all the haste thou may,
      For of counsel I must desire thee.

      GOODS.   Sir, and ye in the world have sorrow or **adversity,**
240   That can I help you to remedy shortly.

      EVERYMAN.   It is another disease° that grieveth me;
      In this world it is not, I tell thee so.
      I am sent for another way to go,
      To give a strait count general
245   Before the highest Jupiter of all;
      And all my life I have had joy and pleasure in thee,
      Therefore, I pray thee, go with me;
      For, peradventure,° thou mayst before God Almighty
      My reckoning help to clean and purify;
250   For it is said ever among
      That money maketh all right that is wrong.

      GOODS.   Nay, Everyman, I sing another song.
      I follow no man in such voyages;
      For, and I went with thee,
255   Thou shouldst fear much the worse for me;
      For because on me thou did set thy mind,
      Thy reckoning I have made blotted and blind,
      That thine account thou cannot make truly;
      And that hast thou for the love of me.

260   EVERYMAN.   That would grieve me full sore,
      When I should come to that fearful answer.
      Up, let us go thither together.

---

227 Good: worldly goods

232 trussed: tied up

236 Lightly me say: Tell me quickly

241 disease: trouble

248 peradventure: perhaps

Reading Strategy   Recognizing Author's Purpose *What might be the author's purpose in describing Goods this way?*

Vocabulary

adversity (ad vur′ sə tē) *n.* a state of hardship; misfortune

GOODS.   Nay, not so! I am too brittle, I may not endure;
              I will follow no man one foot, be ye sure.

265   EVERYMAN.   Alas, I have thee loved, and had great pleasure
              All my life-days on goods and treasure.

GOODS.   That is to thy damnation, without leasing,°
              For my love is contrary to the love everlasting;
              But if thou had me loved moderately during,°
270   As to the poor to give part of me,
              Then shouldst thou not in this dolor° be,
              Nor in this great sorrow and care.

EVERYMAN.   Lo, now was I deceived ere I was ware,°
              And all I may wite° my spending of time;

275   GOODS.   What, weenest thou that I am thine?

EVERYMAN.   I had wend so.

GOODS.   Nay, Everyman, I say no.
              As for a while I was lent thee;
              A season thou hast had me in prosperity.
280   My condition is man's soul to kill;
              If I save one, a thousand I do spill.
              Weenest thou that I will follow thee?
              Nay, not from this world, verily. . . .

EVERYMAN.   Ah, Good, thou hast had long my heartly love;
285   I gave thee that which should be the Lord's above.
              But wilt thou not go with me indeed?
              I pray thee truth to say.

GOODS.   No, so God me speed!
              Therefore farewell, and have good day.

              [*Exit* GOODS.] . . .

Everyman calls next on his Good Deeds.

290   EVERYMAN.   I think that I shall never speed°
              Till that I go to my Good Deed.
              But, alas, she is so weak
              That she can neither go nor speak;
              Yet will I venture on her now.
295   My Good Deeds, where be you?

              [GOOD DEEDS *speaks from the ground.*]

267	**leasing:** lying
269	**during:** during life
271	**dolor:** sorrow
273	**ware:** aware
274	**wite:** blame on
290	**speed:** prosper

Big Idea   **The Power of Faith** *How is the value of charity reflected by Goods?*

Literary Element   **Allegory** *What does Goods's statement reveal about the limits of his character?*

GOOD DEEDS.   Here I lie, cold in the ground;
                Thy sins hath me sore bound,
                That I cannot stir.

EVERYMAN.   O Good Deeds, I stand in fear!
300   I must you pray of counsel,
                For help now should come right well.°

GOOD DEEDS.   Everyman, I have understanding
                That ye be summoned account to make
                Before Messiah, of Jerusalem King;
305   And you do by me,° that journey with you will I take.

EVERYMAN.   Therefore, I come to you, my moan to make;
                I pray you that ye will go with me.

GOOD DEEDS.   I would full fain,° but I cannot stand, verily.

EVERYMAN.   Why, is there anything on you fall?°

310 GOOD DEEDS.   Yea, sir, I may thank you of all;
                If ye had perfectly cheered° me,
                Your book of count full ready had be.
                Look, the books of your works and deeds eke!°
                Behold how they lie under the feet,
315   To your soul's heaviness.

EVERYMAN.   Our Lord Jesus, help me!
                For one letter here I cannot see.

GOOD DEEDS.   There is a blind reckoning° in time of distress. . . .

EVERYMAN.   Good Deeds, your counsel I pray you give me.

320 GOOD DEEDS.   That shall I do verily.
                Though that on my feet I may not go,
                I have a sister that shall with you also,
                Called Knowledge, which shall with you abide
                To help you make that dreadful reckoning. . . .

**Knowledge escorts Everyman to Confession. Everyman then does
penance for his sins and receives contrition.** *Good Deeds is thus
restored to health. Good Deeds and Knowledge advise Everyman to
call on Discretion, Strength, Beauty, and Five Wits to help him on his
journey. When Everyman and the others reach his grave, all but Good
Deeds and Knowledge refuse to accompany him further and leave.*

325   EVERYMAN.   O Jesu, help! All hath forsaken me.

301 **come right well:** be welcome

305 **And you do by me:** If you do as I suggest

308 **fain:** gladly

309 **fall:** befallen

311 **cheered:** nourished

313 **eke:** also

318 **There is a blind reckoning:** The record is difficult to read.

Reading Strategy   Recognizing Author's Purpose *How does the author describe Good Deeds, and what is the situation meant to symbolize?*

Big Idea   The Power of Faith *How does Knowledge help Everyman? What does this suggest about the relationship between knowledge and the Christian church at the time?*

GOOD DEEDS.   Nay, Everyman; I will bide with thee.
    I will not forsake thee indeed;
    Thou shalt find me a good friend at need.

EVERYMAN.   Gramercy, Good Deeds! Now may I true friends see.
330   They have forsaken me, every one;
    I loved them better than my Good Deeds alone.
    Knowledge, will ye forsake me also?

KNOWLEDGE.   Yea, Everyman, when ye to death shall go;
    But not yet, for no manner of danger.

335 EVERYMAN.   Gramercy, Knowledge, with all my heart.

KNOWLEDGE.   Nay, yet I will not from hence depart
    Till I see where ye shall become.°

EVERYMAN.   Methink, alas, that I must be gone
    To make my reckoning and my debts pay,
340   For I see my time is nigh spent away.
    Take example, all ye that this do hear or see,
    How they that I loved best do forsake me,
    Except my Good Deeds that bideth truly.

GOOD DEEDS.   All earthly things is but vanity:
345   Beauty, Strength, and Discretion do man forsake,
    Foolish friends, and kinsmen, that fair spake—
    All fleeth save Good Deeds, and that am I.

EVERYMAN.   Have mercy on me, God most mighty;
    And stand by me, thou mother and maid, holy Mary.

350 GOOD DEEDS.   Fear not; I will speak for thee.

EVERYMAN.   Here I cry God mercy.

GOOD DEEDS.   Short° our end, and minish° our pain;
    Let us go and never come again.

EVERYMAN.   Into thy hands, Lord, my soul I commend;
355   Receive it, Lord, that it be not lost.
    As thou me boughtest,° so me defend,
    And save me from the fiend's boast,
    That I may appear with that blessed host
    That shall be saved at the day of doom.
360   *In manus tuas,*° of mights most
    Forever, *commendo spiritum meum.*°

  [*He sinks into his grave.*]

KNOWLEDGE.   Now hath he suffered that we all shall endure;
    The Good Deeds shall make all sure.

---

337 Till I see where ye shall become: till I see what will become of you

352 Short: shorten. **minish:** diminish

356 boughtest: redeemed

360 In manus tuas: into your hands
361 commendo spiritum meum: I commend my spirit.

Reading Strategy   **Recognizing Author's Purpose** *Who is Everyman addressing here, and what might be the author's purpose for the address?*

Literary Element   **Allegory** *What does this statement imply about the character of Good Deeds?*

365

Now hath he made ending;
Methinketh that I hear angels sing,
And make great joy and melody
Where Everyman's soul received shall be.

ANGEL.   Come, excellent elect spouse,° to Jesu!
Hereabove thou shalt go
370 Because of thy singular virtue.
Now the soul is taken the body fro,
Thy reckoning is crystal clear.
Now shalt thou into the heavenly sphere,
Unto the which all ye shall come
375 That liveth well before the day of doom.

[*Enter* DOCTOR.]

DOCTOR.   This moral men may have in mind.
Ye hearers, take it of worth, old and young,
And forsake Pride, for he deceiveth you in the end;
And remember Beauty, Five Wits, Strength, and Discretion,
380 They all at the last do every man forsake,
Save his Good Deeds there doth he take.
But beware, for and they be small
Before God, he hath no help at all;
None excuse may be there for every man.
385 Alas, how shall he do then?
For after death, amends may no man make,
For then mercy and pity doth him forsake.
If his reckoning be not clear when he doth come,
God will say, "*Ite, maledicti, in ignem eternum.*"°
390 And he that hath his account whole and sound,
High in heaven he shall be crowned;
Unto which place God bring us all thither,
That we may live body and soul together.
Thereto help the Trinity!
395 Amen, say ye, for saint charity.

THUS ENDETH THIS MORAL PLAY OF EVERYMAN

368 spouse: soul

389 Ite, maledicti, in ignem eternum: Depart, ye cursed, into everlasting fire.

Literary Element   Allegory   *What moral lesson does the play teach?*

Heaven from the Last Judgment, 15th Century (detail). Fra Angelico. Tempera on panel. Museo di San marco dell'Angelico, Florence, Italy.

RESPONDING AND THINKING CRITICALLY

Respond

1. Did you find yourself identifying with Everyman—his needs, his fears, his weaknesses? Explain.

Recall and Interpret

2. (a)At the beginning of the play, what does the Messenger say that *Everyman* will be about? (b)How do the Messenger's words (lines 1–21) further the purpose of the play?

3. (a)Why does God send Death to visit Everyman? (b)In what ways are the relationships between God, Death, and Everyman similar to those between the playwright, messenger, and audience?

4. (a)How would you summarize the reaction of the character called Goods to Everyman's plea for help? (b)What does the dialogue between Goods and Everyman reveal about people living in medieval times?

Analyze and Evaluate

5. Everyman learns that, like Goods, neither Fellowship nor Knowledge will accompany him in death. What is the effect of showing that none of these characters, whether good or bad, will accompany Everyman in death?

6. (a)What is the effect of using symbolic figures instead of real characters in the play? (b)How would the play be different if the characters were round instead of flat?

7. (a)What is the effect of ending the play at Everyman's death? (b)Does this ending express hope or despair for the human condition? Explain.

Connect

8. In your opinion, how effective are morality plays or similar messages today? Explain.

9. **Big Idea** **The Power of Faith** How does a morality play like *Everyman* promote religious faith?

VISUAL LITERACY: Fine Art

Death and *Everyman*

The paintings of Joseph Wright of Derby reflect a fusion of science and art. Wright's artwork reveals the influence of both the Enlightenment of the eighteenth century and Romanticism of the late eighteenth and early nineteenth centuries. Rather than religious truths, the Enlightenment sought rational, empirical knowledge. Romanticism valued the expression of emotion and individuality. *The Old Man and Death* portrays an emotional, symbolic image of a man personally confronting Death. Death, however, is personified almost scientifically, as a realistic skeleton—the most obvious evidence of human mortality. The painting is based on Aesop's fable of the same name, in which an old laborer carelessly wishes that Death would take him, sparing him from his toil.

1. (a)What is the old man's reaction to Death in the painting? (b)How does *Everyman* describe a similar encounter?

2. How do you think the artist's purpose for *The Old Man and Death* might contrast with the author's purpose for *Everyman*?

The Old Man and Death 1773. Joseph Wright of Derby (1734–1797). Oil on canvas, 40 in x 50 ¹/₁₆ in. Wadsworth Atheneum, Hartford, CT.

Literary Element Allegory

In an **allegory**, all or most of the characters, settings, and events symbolize ideas, qualities, or figures beyond themselves in order to teach a moral lesson. In *Everyman*, as in most other allegories, the names of characters indicate the abstract quality that they represent. Typically, an allegory can be read on both a literal level and a figurative level. For example, the exchange between Fellowship and Everyman is both a portrayal of one friend's refusal to help another and a representation of the loneliness of death.

1. What abstract ideas and figures do the characters in *Everyman* represent?

2. Choose a short scene between Everyman and Death or another character. Explain the literal and figurative meanings of the scene.

Review: Mood

As you learned on page 74, **mood** refers to the emotional quality or atmosphere of a literary work. For example, moods can be somber, mysterious, peaceful, or joyous. A writer's choice of language, subject matter, setting, and tone, as well as such sound devices as rhyme and rhythm, contribute to the mood.

Partner Activity Meet with a partner to discuss the prevailing atmosphere, or mood, of *Everyman*. Create a graphic like the one below and fill it in with examples from the selection to help determine the mood. Then in the bottom triangle write what the mood is.

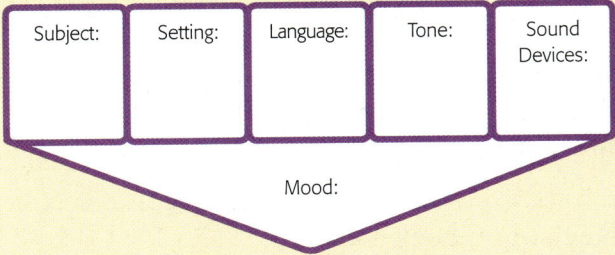

Subject: | Setting: | Language: | Tone: | Sound Devices:

Mood:

Reading Strategy Recognizing Author's Purpose

Everyman, like most morality plays, has an explicit purpose: to teach a moral lesson to the audience. In *Everyman,* the Messenger appears onstage alone to reveal this purpose before the action begins.

1. What does the author wish to achieve by having the Messenger reveal the purpose of the play in the opening lines?

2. How might the author's purpose be revealed differently in a play written today?

Vocabulary Practice

Practice with Word Parts Choose the correct answer for each question below. Use a dictionary if you need help.

1. Which word comes from the Middle English word *reknen*?
   a. reckoning   **b.** respite   **c.** perceive

2. Which word comes from the Latin word *advertere*, meaning "to turn toward"?
   a. respite   **b.** adversity   **c.** perceive

3. Which word comes from the Latin word *percipere*, meaning "to see all the way through"?
   a. adversity   **b.** perceive   **c.** reckoning

4. Which word comes from the Latin word *respicere*, meaning "to look back"?
   a. perceive   **b.** adversity   **c.** respite

Academic Vocabulary

Here are two words from the vocabulary list on page R82.

strategy (strat′ ə jē) *n.* a plan of action

foundation (foun dā′shən) *n.* the basis on which something stands or is supported

Practice and Apply

1. What reading **strategies** could you use to understand the events in *Everyman*?

2. What historical **foundation** contributed to the importance of *Everyman*?

Writing About Literature

Explore Author's Purpose It is unknown whether *Everyman* was originally written to be staged. Since its creation, however, it has been translated, adapted, and performed, and it is still staged today. Write a review of this excerpt from *Everyman*. Include a brief plot summary, a statement of the purpose of the play, and an evaluation of the play's effectiveness in meeting that purpose. Support your evaluation with specific examples from the play.

Before you draft, outline the parts of your review.

> I.   Plot Summary
> II. Statement of Purpose
> III. Evaluation
>   A. Supporting Idea 1
>   B. Supporting Idea 2
>   C. Supporting Idea 3
> IV. Conclusion

After you complete your draft, exchange papers with a partner to review each other's work. Then proofread and edit your draft for errors in spelling, grammar, and punctuation.

Performing

With one or two classmates, choose a scene from *Everyman* to perform. Rehearse your parts, keeping in mind the idea or figure your character represents. Make your voice and gestures fit your part. Then perform the scene for the rest of the class.

Everyman's Language and Style

Using Adjectives The author of *Everyman* uses a variety of **adjectives**—words that modify nouns or pronouns by limiting their meaning. Adjectives tell what kind, which, how many, or how much.

Notice that the adjectives in columns two and three of the chart are familiar words that add information but contribute little to the style of the writing. Adjectives that tell what kind are often more colorful and precise.

What kind?	Which?	How many or how much?
moral play	*our* lives	*all* creatures
dreadful reckoning	*their* mind	*twelve* years
worldly riches	*every* man	*any* respite

An adjective can come before or after the word it modifies. In the following passage, notice the position of the italicized adjectives in relation to the boldface nouns they modify.

> "That is to *thy* **damnation**, without leasing,
>
> For *my* **love** is contrary to the **love** *everlasting*"

Activity Scan *Everyman* to find colorful adjectives. Think about what those adjectives contribute to the style of the play.

Revising Check

Adjectives Work with a partner to review your use of adjectives in your review of *Everyman*. Look for opportunities to use colorful adjectives to make your style more lively. In addition, look for ways to clarify your ideas with adjectives.

Literature Online **Web Activities** For eFlashcards, Selection Quick Checks, and other Web activities, go to www.glencoe.com.

The World of Romance

Roman de Tristan: Tournament, c. 15th century.

"On a great festival such as this [King Arthur] would eat no meat till he had heard some strange tale of adventure, of the deeds of princes, or feats of arms, some great wonder which he might listen to and believe."

—*Sir Gawain and the Green Knight*

from *Sir Gawain and the Green Knight*

Connecting to the Story

In Anglo-Saxon England, knights such as Sir Gawain were expected to uphold the highest standards of honor. As you read the selection, think about how you define honor.

Building Background

The author of *Sir Gawain and the Green Knight* is unknown to us, but scholars have pieced together clues to the poet's identity. Because of the dialect in which *Sir Gawain* is written, scholars have concluded that it was composed in northwest England about 1370. The poet's sophisticated technique and his knowledge of French and Latin point to an educated man who was familiar with the ways of the aristocracy.

Some writers have characterized Sir Gawain as a ruthless, bloodthirsty warrior; others have emphasized his nobility and courage. The tale of the Green Knight represents the latter category, because in it Sir Gawain is shown to possess the ideal traits of a knight at the Round Table: strength, skill, courage, humility, courtesy, and loyalty.

Setting Purposes for Reading

Big Idea **The World of Romance**

Sir Gawain and the Green Knight is set in an imaginary medieval world of enchanted castles and perilous quests. Read to learn about the challenges Sir Gawain faces in a test of honor.

Literary Element Archetype

An **archetype** is a character type, a setting, an image, or a story pattern that appears frequently in literature across many cultures. Read to see how many archetypes you can identify.

• See Literary Terms Handbook, p. R1.

Literature Online Interactive Literary Elements Handbook To review or learn more about the literary elements, go to www.glencoe.com.

Reading Strategy Monitoring Comprehension

When you read, stop periodically to check your **comprehension**, or understanding, of the story. To get the most from your reading, you should be able to recall and summarize key ideas, characters, and events.

Reading Tip: Taking Notes As you read, jot down notes on important characters and events. Use a chart similar to the one below to get started.

Character or Event	Significance
Sir Gawain accepts a challenge from the Green Knight.	Gawain is risking his life and his honor for the king.

Vocabulary

copiously (kō′pē əs lē) *adv.* plentifully; p. 175 *The seashells were scattered copiously around the beach after they had been washed in at high tide.*

intrepid (in trep′ id) *adj.* fearless; courageous; p. 177 *The intrepid woman dashed back into the burning house to save the family dog.*

dauntless (dônt′ lis) *adj.* daring; not easily discouraged; p. 186 *Dauntless despite the loss of his supplies, the explorer pressed forward.*

blithe (blīth) *adj.* carefree; lighthearted; p. 187 *I wish we could be children again, when we were naively blithe.*

Vocabulary Tip: Synonyms Words that have the same or nearly the same meaning are called synonyms. Synonyms are always the same part of speech.

OBJECTIVES
In studying this selection, you will focus on the following:
• understanding characteristics of medieval romance
• analyzing archetypes and conflict
• reviewing and summarizing to monitor comprehension

Translating *Gawain*

Translators of *Sir Gawain* face tremendous challenges in trying to capture the style and subtleties of meaning found in the original text. Each translator will meet those challenges in different ways. To provide a sense of those differences, the opening part of this selection is presented in two translations. Below, you will find the first twenty-four lines as translated by John Gardner. Then on the next page you will find a longer translation of the work by Brian Stone.

Translated by John Gardner

Splendid that knight errant° stood in a splay of green,
And green, too, was the mane of his mighty destrier;°
Fair fanning tresses enveloped the fighting man's shoulders,
And over his breast hung a beard as big as a bush;
5   The beard and the huge mane burgeoning° forth from his head
Were clipped off clean in a straight line over his elbows,
And the upper half of each arm was hidden underneath
As if covered by a king's chaperon,° closed round the neck.
The mane of the marvelous horse was much the same,
10   Well crisped° and combed and carefully pranked with knots,°
Threads of gold interwoven with the glorious green,
Now a thread of hair, now another thread of gold;
The tail of the horse and the forelock were tricked the
       same way,
And both were bound up with a band of brilliant green
15   Adorned with glittering jewels the length of the dock,°
Then caught up tight with a thong° in a criss-cross knot
Where many a bell tinkled brightly, all burnished° gold.
So monstrous a mount, so mighty a man in the saddle
Was never once encountered on all this earth
20   till then;
            His eyes, like lightning, flashed,
            And it seemed to many a man,
            That any man who clashed
            With him would not long stand.

1 knight errant: a knight who wanders the land, searching for adventure.
2 destrier (des′ trē ər): war horse.

5 burgeoning (bər′ jən ing): sprouting; growing.

8 chaperon (sha′ pə rōn): hood.

10 crisped: curled. **pranked with knots:** decorated with bows.

15 dock: the fleshy part of a horse's tail.
16 thong: a narrow strip of leather used for binding.
17 burnished: polished or rubbed smooth.

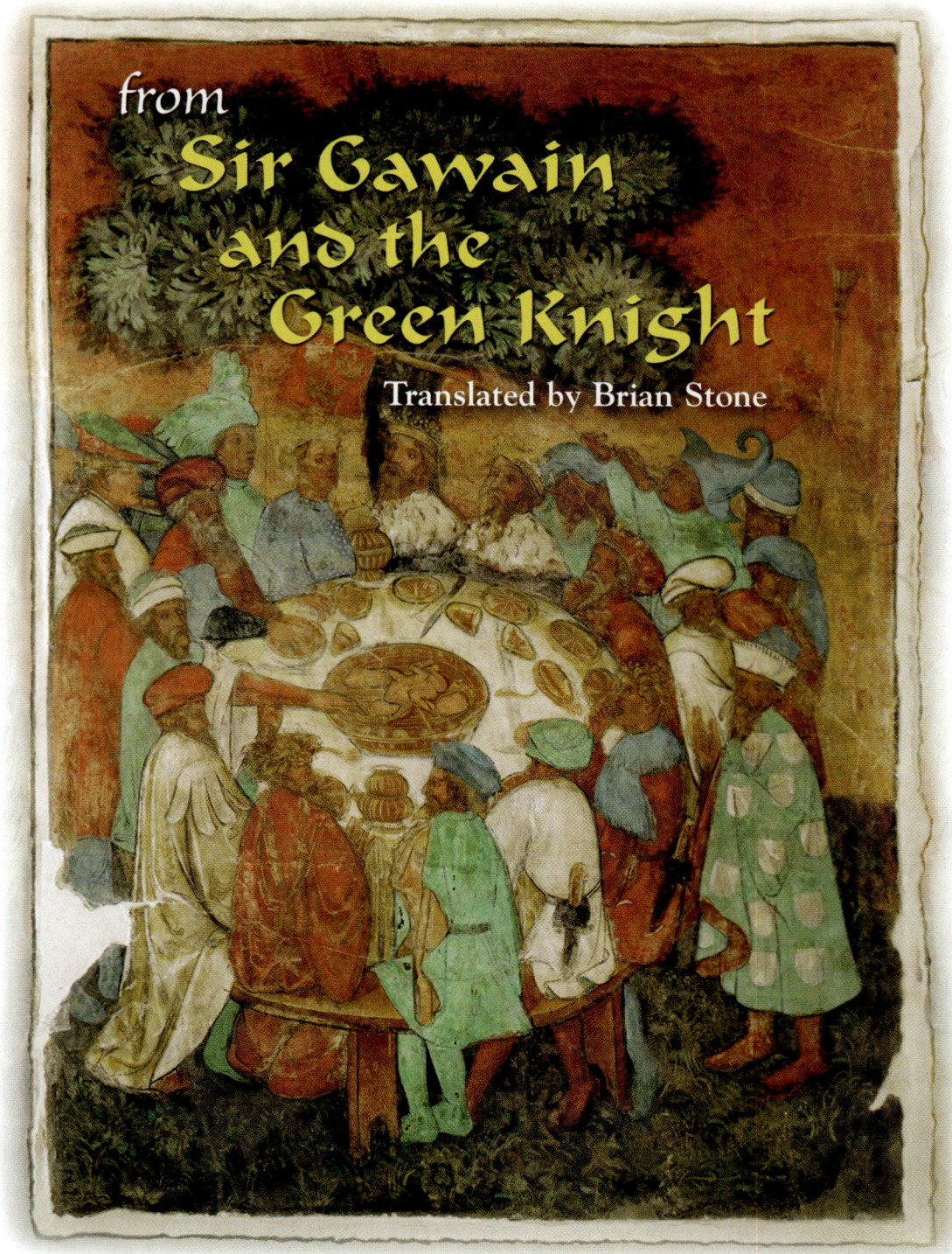

from

Sir Gawain and the Green Knight

Translated by Brian Stone

King Arthur and his knights sit at the Round Table, 14th century fresco. Runkelstein Castle, South Tyrol, Italy.

Yes, garbed all in green was the gallant rider,
And the hair of his head was the same hue as his horse,
And floated finely like a fan round his shoulders;
And a great bushy beard on his breast flowing down,
5   With the heavy hair hanging from his head,
Was shorn below the shoulder, sheared right round,
So that half his arms were under the encircling hair,

Covered as by a king's cape, that closes at the neck.
The mane of that mighty horse, much like the beard,
10 Well crisped and combed, was **copiously** plaited
With twists of twining gold, twinkling in the green,
First a green gossamer, a golden one next.
His flowing tail and forelock followed suit,
And both were bound with bands of bright green,
15 Ornamented to the end with exquisite stones,
While a thong running through them threaded on high
Many bright golden bells, burnished and ringing.
Such a horse, such a horseman, in the whole wide world
Was never seen or observed by those assembled before,
20   Not one.
              Lightning like he seemed
              And swift to strike and stun.
              His dreadful blows, men deemed,
              Once dealt, meant death was done.

25 Yet hauberk° and helmet had he none,
Nor plastron° nor plate-armor proper to combat,
Nor shield for shoving, nor sharp spear for lunging;
But he held a holly cluster° in one hand, holly
That is greenest when groves are gaunt and bare,
30 And an axe in his other hand, huge and monstrous,
A hideous helmet-smasher for anyone to tell of;
The head of that axe was an ell-rod° long.
Of green hammered gold and steel was the socket,
And the blade was burnished bright, with a broad edge,
35 Acutely honed° for cutting, as keenest razors are.
The grim man gripped it by its great strong handle,
Which was wound with iron all the way to the end,
And graven° in green with graceful designs.
A cord curved round it, was caught at the head,
40 Then hitched to the haft° at intervals in loops,
With costly tassels attached thereto in plenty
On bosses° of bright green embroidered richly.
In he rode, and up the hall, this man,
Driving towards the high dais,° dreading no danger.
45 He gave no one a greeting, but glared over all.
His opening utterance was, "Who and where
Is the governor of this gathering? Gladly would I
Behold him with my eyes and have speech with him."

25 **hauberk** (hô′ bərk′): a long shirt of chain mail worn as armor.
26 **plastron**: a metal breastplate worn under a hauberk.
28 **holly cluster**: Holly represents good luck and shows that the knight comes in peace.

32 **ell-rod**: almost four feet.

35 **honed**: sharpened.

38 **graven**: carved.

40 **haft**: handle.

42 **bosses**: raised decorations.

44 **dais** (dā′ əs): raised platform.

Big Idea **The World of Romance** *How can you tell from the description in lines 1–20 that the "gallant rider" is a knight?*

Vocabulary

copiously (kō′ pē əs lē) *adv.* plentifully

King Arthur and the knights of the Round Table.

50　　He frowned;
　　　Took note of every knight
　　　As he ramped and rode around;
　　　Then stopped to study who might
　　　Be the noble most renowned.

　　　The assembled folk stared, long scanning the fellow,
55　For all men marveled what it might mean
　　　That a horseman and his horse should have such a color
　　　As to grow green as grass, and greener yet, it seemed,
　　　More gaudily glowing than green enamel on gold.
　　　Those standing studied him and sidled towards him
60　With all the world's wonder as to what he would do.
　　　For astonishing sights they had seen, but such a one never;
　　　Therefore a phantom from Fairyland the folk there deemed him.
　　　So even the doughty° were daunted° and dared not reply,
　　　All sitting stock-still, astounded by his voice.
65　Throughout the high hall was a hush like death;
　　　Suddenly as if all had slipped into sleep, their voices were
　　　　　　At rest;
　　　　　Hushed not wholly for fear,
　　　　　But some at honor's behest;°
70　　　But let him whom all revere
　　　　　Greet that gruesome guest.

　　　For Arthur sensed an exploit before the high dais,
　　　And accorded him courteous greeting, no craven° he,
　　　Saying to him, "Sir knight, you are certainly welcome.
75　I am head of this house:° Arthur is my name.
　　　Please deign to dismount and dwell with us
　　　Till you impart your purpose, at a proper time."
　　　"May he that sits in heaven help me," said the knight,
　　　"But my intention was not to tarry in this turreted hall.
80　But as your reputation, royal sir, is raised up so high,
　　　And your castle and cavaliers° are accounted the best,
　　　The mightiest of mail-clad men in mounted fighting,
　　　The most warlike, the worthiest the world has bred,
　　　Most valiant to vie with in virile contests,
85　And as chivalry is shown here, so I am assured,
　　　At this time, I tell you, that has attracted me here.
　　　By this branch that I bear, you may be certain
　　　That I proceed in peace, no peril seeking;
　　　For had I fared forth in fighting gear,
90　My hauberk and helmet, both at home now,
　　　My shield and sharp spear, all shining bright,
　　　And other weapons to wield, I would have brought;

63 **doughty** (dou′ tē): courageous, valiant. **daunted:** fearful.

69 **behest:** command.

73 **craven:** coward.

75 **this house:** Arthur's court at Camelot.

81 **cavaliers:** knights.

Literary Element　　Archetype　*What might the Green Knight's color represent?*

However, as I wish for no war here, I wear soft clothes.
But if you are as bold as brave men affirm,
95 You will gladly grant me the good sport I demand
                    By right."
            Then Arthur answer gave:
            "If you, most noble knight,
            Unarmored combat crave,
100   We'll fail you not in fight."

"No, it is not combat I crave, for come to that,
On this bench only beardless boys are sitting.
If I were hasped° in armor on a high steed,
No man among you could match me, your might being meagre.
105 So I crave in this court a Christmas game,
For it is Yuletide and New Year, and young men abound here.
If any in this household is so hardy in spirit,
Of such mettlesome° mind and so madly rash
As to strike a strong blow in return for another,
110 I shall offer to him this fine axe freely;
This axe, which is heavy enough, to handle as he please.
And I shall bide the first blow, as bare as I sit here.
If some **intrepid** man is tempted to try what I suggest,
Let him leap towards me and lay hold of this weapon,
115 Acquiring clear possession of it, no claim from me ensuing.
Then shall I stand up to his stroke, quite still on this floor—
So long as I shall have leave to launch a return blow
                    Unchecked.
            Yet he shall have a year
120   And a day's reprieve,° I direct.
            Now hasten and let me hear
            Who answers, to what effect."

"By heaven," then said Arthur, "what you ask is foolish,
But as you firmly seek folly, find it you shall.
125 No good man here is aghast at your great words.
Hand me your axe now, for heaven's sake,
And I shall bestow the boon° you bid us give."
He sprang towards him swiftly, seized it from his hand,

Gawain. From "Le Roman de Lancelot du Lac", 14th century. The Pierpont Morgan Library, New York.

103 **hasped:** fastened.
108 **mettlesome:** spirited; plucky.

120 **reprieve:** a postponement or temporary relief from danger.

127 **boon:** favor.

Reading Strategy Monitoring Comprehension *What impression do you have of the Green Knight so far?*

Reading Strategy Monitoring Comprehension *What "game" is the Green Knight proposing?*

Vocabulary

intrepid (in trep′ id) *adj.* fearless; courageous

And fiercely the other fellow footed the floor.
130 Now Arthur had his axe, and holding it by the haft
Swung it about sternly, as if to strike with it.
The strong man stood before him, stretched to his full height,
Higher than any in the hall by a head and more.
Stern of face he stood there, stroking his beard,
135 Turning down his tunic in a tranquil manner,
Less unmanned° and dismayed by the mighty strokes
Than if a banqueter at the bench had brought him a drink
        Of wine.
            Then Gawain at Guinevere's side
140   Bowed and spoke his design:
            "Before all, King, confide
            This fight to me. May it be mine."

"If you would, worthy lord," said Gawain to the King,
"Bid me stir from this seat and stand beside you,
145 Allowing me without lese-majesty° to leave the table,
And if my liege lady° were not displeased thereby,
I should come there to counsel you before this court of nobles.
For it appears unmeet° to me, as manners go,
When your hall hears uttered such a haughty request,
150 Though you gladly agree, for you to grant it yourself,
When on the benches about you many such bold men sit,
Under heaven, I hold, the highest-mettled,
There being no braver knights when battle is joined.
I am the weakest, the most wanting in wisdom, I know,
155 And my life, if lost, would be least missed, truly.
Only through your being my uncle, am I to be valued;
No bounty but your blood in my body do I know.
And since this affair is too foolish to fall to you,
And I first asked it of you, make it over to me;
160 And if I fail to speak fittingly, let this full court judge
            Without blame."
            Then wisely they whispered of it,
            And after, all said the same:
            That the crowned King should be quit,
165   And Gawain given the game.

❧

"By God," said the Green Knight, "Sir Gawain, I rejoice
That I shall have from your hand what I have asked for here.
And you have gladly gone over, in good discourse,°
The covenant° I requested of the King in full,
170 Except that you shall assent, swearing in truth,

Sir Gawain presents himself to Arthur and Guinevere, from Cotton Nero A.x. 1410. Artist Unknown. British Library, London.

Literary Element Archetype *What archetypal characteristics do you see in Gawain and the Green Knight?*

To seek me yourself, in such place as you think
To find me under the firmament, and fetch your payment
For what you deal me today before this dignified gathering."
"How shall I hunt for you? How find your home?"
175 Said Gawain, "By God that made me, I go in ignorance;
Nor, knight, do I know your name or your court.
But instruct me truly thereof, and tell me your name,
And I shall wear out my wits to find my way there;
Here is my oath on it, in absolute honor!"
180 "That is enough this New Year, no more is needed,"
Said the gallant in green to Gawain the courteous,
"To tell you the truth, when I have taken the blow
After you have duly dealt it, I shall directly inform you
About my house and my home and my own name.
185 Then you may keep your covenant, and call on me,
And if I waft you no words, then well may you prosper,
Stay long in your own land and look for no further
        Trial.
        Now grip your weapon grim;
190   Let us see your fighting style."
        "Gladly," said Gawain to him,
        Stroking the steel the while.

On the ground the Green Knight graciously stood,
With head slightly slanting to expose the flesh.
195 His long and lovely locks he laid over his crown,
Baring the naked neck for the business now due.
Gawain gripped his axe and gathered it on high,
Advanced the left foot before him on the ground,
And slashed swiftly down on the exposed part,
200 So that the sharp blade sheared through, shattering the bones,
Sank deep in the sleek flesh, split it in two,
And the scintillating° steel struck the ground.
The fair head fell from the neck, struck the floor,
And people spurned it° as it rolled around.
205 Blood spurted from the body, bright against the green.
Yet the fellow did not fall, nor falter one whit,
But stoutly sprang forward on legs still sturdy,
Roughly reached out among the ranks of nobles,
Seized his splendid head and straightway lifted it.
210 Then he strode to his steed, snatched the bridle,
Stepped into the stirrup and swung aloft,

202 **scintillating:** sparkling, brilliant.

204 **spurned it:** here, fended it off with their feet.

Big Idea The World of Romance *What does this oath reveal about the values of this time?*

Big Idea The World of Romance *What does this supernatural event suggest about the elements of medieval romance?*

The Headless Green Knight in Arthur's Hall, from Cotton Nero A.x. 1410. Artist Unknown.
British Library, London.
Viewing the Art: How does the artist's depiction of the Green Knight compare with your
impressions of him?

Holding his head in his hand by the hair.
He settled himself in the saddle as steadily
As if nothing had happened to him, though he had

215   No head.
       He twisted his trunk about,
       That gruesome body that bled;
       He caused much dread and doubt
       By the time his say was said.

220 For he held the head in his hand upright,
Pointed the face at the fairest in fame° on the dais;
And it lifted its eyelids and looked glaringly,
And menacingly said with its mouth as you may now hear:
"Be prepared to perform what you promised, Gawain;

225 Seek faithfully till you find me, my fine fellow,
According to your oath in this hall in these knights' hearing.
Go to the Green Chapel without gainsaying° to get
Such a stroke as you have struck. Strictly you deserve
That due redemption on the day of New Year.

230 As the Knight of the Green Chapel I am known to many;
Therefore if you ask for me, I shall be found.
So come, or else be called coward accordingly!"
Then he savagely swerved, sawing at the reins,
Rushed out at the hall door, his head in his hand,

235 And the flint-struck fire flew up from the hooves.
What place he departed to no person there knew,
Nor could any account be given of the country he had come
    from.
         What then?
       At the Green Knight Gawain and King

240   Grinned and laughed again;
       But plainly approved the thing
       As a marvel in the world of men.

As the end of the next year approaches, Sir Gawain sets out on his horse Gringolet to seek the Green Knight. After fruitless searching and many adventures, he arrives at a castle whose lord, Bercilak, can direct him to the Green Chapel nearby. Gawain is invited to stay until his appointment. The lord proposes a game: he will give Gawain the winnings of his hunt each day in return for whatever Gawain has won while staying in his castle. For two days, while the lord is hunting, the lady of the castle attempts to seduce Gawain, but Gawain nobly rejects her advances. He accepts only a kiss each day which he exchanges with the lord in return for his hunting spoils. On the third day, Gawain continues to resist the lady, but she presses him to accept one small gift by which to remember her.

221 fairest in fame: Guinevere.

227 gainsaying: contradicting, opposing.

Reading Strategy   Monitoring Comprehension *How do you think Sir Gawain feels now about his oath to the Green Knight?*

Knight receiving tokens from his lady love whilst preparing for tournament, from facsimile of the *Manesse Codex,* 1305–40. German manuscript. University Library, Heidelberg, Germany.

She proffered him a rich ring wrought in red gold,
With a sparkling stone set conspicuously in it,
245 Which beamed as brilliantly as the bright sun;
You may well believe its worth was wonderfully great.
But the courteous man declined it and quickly said,
"Before God, gracious lady, no giving just now!
Not having anything to offer, I shall accept nothing."
250 She offered it him urgently and he refused again,
Fast affirming his refusal on his faith as a knight.
Put out by this repulse, she presently said,
"If you reject my ring as too rich in value,
Doubtless you would be less deeply indebted to me
255 If I gave you my girdle,° a less gainful gift."
She swiftly slipped off the cincture° of her gown
Which went round her waist under the wonderful mantle,
A girdle of green silk with a golden hem,
Embroidered only at the edges, with hand-stitched ornament.
260 And she pleaded with the prince in a pleasant manner
To take it notwithstanding° its trifling worth;
But he told her that he could touch no treasure at all,
Not gold nor any gift, till God gave him grace
To pursue to success the search he was bound on.
265 "And therefore I beg you not to be displeased:
Press no more your purpose, for I promise it never
                    Can be.
              I owe you a hundredfold
              For grace you have granted me;
270   And ever through hot and cold
              I shall stay your devotee."

255 **girdle:** belt or sash.
256 **cincture:** belt, sash.

261 **notwithstanding:** in spite of.

"Do you say 'no' to this silk?" then said the beauty,
"Because it is simple in itself? And so it seems.
Lo! It is little indeed, and so less worth your esteem.
275 But one who was aware of the worth twined in it
Would appraise its properties as more precious perhaps,
For the man that binds his body with this belt of green,
As long as he laps it closely about him,
No hero under heaven can hack him to pieces,
280 For he cannot be killed by any cunning on earth."
Then the prince pondered, and it appeared to him
A precious gem to protect him in the peril appointed him
When he gained the Green Chapel to be given checkmate:°
It would be a splendid stratagem° to escape being slain.
285 Then he allowed her to solicit° him and let her speak.
She pressed the belt upon him with potent words
And having got his agreement, she gave it him gladly,
Beseeching him for her sake to conceal it always,
And hide it from her husband with all diligence.
290 That never should another know of it, the noble swore
            Outright.
        Then often his thanks gave he
        With all his heart and might,
        And thrice by then had she
295   Kissed the constant knight.

*The time comes for Gawain to keep his appointment with the Green
Knight. He dresses carefully, wrapping the green sash around his waist,
and sets off with a guide, who leaves him as they near the Green Chapel.*

        Then he gave the spur to Gringolet and galloped down the path,
        Thrust through a thicket there by a bank,
        And rode down the rough slope right into the ravine.
        Then he searched about, but it seemed savage and wild,
300   And no sign did he see of any sort of building;
        But on both sides banks, beetling° and steep,
        And great crooked crags, cruelly jagged;
        The bristling barbs of rock seemed to brush the sky.
        Then he held in his horse, halted there,
305   Scanned on every side in search of the chapel.
        He saw no such thing anywhere, which seemed remarkable,
        Save, hard by in the open, a hillock of sorts,
        A smooth-surfaced barrow° on a slope beside a stream
        Which flowed forth fast there in its course,
310   Foaming and frothing as if feverishly boiling.
        The knight, urging his horse, pressed onwards to the mound,
        Dismounted manfully and made fast to a lime-tree

283 checkmate: total defeat, which is inescapable and indefensible.
284 stratagem: a clever, often underhanded scheme.
285 solicit: persuade.

301 beetling: overhanging.

308 barrow: a mound of earth, often over a grave.

Literary Element   **Archetype** *Why might the lady be considered a literary archetype?*

Knight on horseback, from series of frescoes of tournaments. 14th century. Museo Civico, San Gimignano, Italy.

The reins, hooking them round a rough branch;
Then he went to the barrow, which he walked round, inspecting,
315   Wondering what in the world it might be.
It had a hole in each end and on either side,
And was overgrown with grass in great patches.
All hollow it was within, only an old cavern
Or the crevice of an ancient crag: he could not explain it
320   Aright.
      "O God, is the Chapel Green
      This mound?" said the noble knight.
      "At such might Satan be seen
      Saying matins° at midnight."

325   "Now certainly the place is deserted," said Gawain,
"It is a hideous oratory,° all overgrown,
And well graced for the gallant garbed in green
To deal out his devotions in the Devil's fashion.
Now I feel in my five wits, it is the Fiend himself
330   That has tricked me into this tryst, to destroy me here.
This is a chapel of mischance—checkmate to it!

324 matins (ma′ tənz): here, a liturgical prayer traditionally beginning at midnight.

326 oratory: a place of prayer.

It is the most evil holy place I ever entered."
With his high helmet on his head, and holding his lance,
He roamed up to the roof of that rough dwelling.
335   Then from that height he heard, from a hard rock
On the bank beyond the brook, a barbarous noise.
What! It clattered amid the cliffs fit to cleave° them apart,
As if a great scythe° were being ground on a grindstone there.
What! It whirred and it whetted like water in a mill.
340   What! It made a rushing, ringing din, rueful° to hear.
"By God!" then said Gawain, "that is going on,
I suppose, as a salute to myself, to greet me
          Hard by.
    God's will be warranted:
345   'Alas!' is a craven cry.
    No din shall make me dread
    Although today I die."

Then the courteous knight called out clamorously,
"Who holds sway here and has an assignation° with me?
350   For the good knight Gawain is on the ground here.
If anyone there wants anything, wend your way hither fast,
And further your needs either now, or not at all."
"Bide there!" said one on the bank above his head,
"And you shall swiftly receive what I once swore to give you."
355   Yet for a time he continued his tumult° of scraping,
Turning away as he whetted,° before he would descend.
Then he thrust himself round a thick crag through a hole,
Whirling round a wedge of rock with a frightful weapon,
A Danish axe duly honed for dealing the blow,
360   With a broad biting edge, bow-bent along the handle,
Ground on a grindstone, a great four-foot blade—
No less, by that love-lace gleaming so brightly!
And the gallant in green was garbed as at first,
His looks and limbs the same, his locks and beard;
365   Save that steadily on his feet he strode on the ground,
Setting the handle to the stony earth and stalking beside it.
He would not wade through the water when he came to it,
But vaulted over on his axe, then with huge strides
Advanced violently and fiercely along the field's width
370   On the snow.
    Sir Gawain went to greet
    The knight, not bowing low.
    The man said, "Sir so sweet,
    You honor the trysts you owe."

375   "Gawain," said the green knight, "may God guard you!

---

337 cleave: split.

338 scythe (sīth): a tool used for mowing or reaping, consisting of a long curved blade and a long bent handle.

340 rueful: mournful.

349 assignation: an appointment for a meeting.

355 tumult (tōō məlt): a noisy commotion; disturbance.

356 whetted: sharpened.

Reading Strategy   Monitoring Comprehension *What is happening here, and what is its effect on the story?*

You are welcome to my dwelling, I warrant you,
And you have timed your travel here as a true man ought.
You know plainly the pact we pledged between us:
This time a twelvemonth ago you took your portion,
380　　And now at this New Year I should nimbly requite° you.
And we are on our own here in this valley
With no seconds° to sunder° us, spar° as we will.
Take your helmet off your head, and have your payment here.
And offer no more argument or action than I did
385　　When you whipped off my head with one stroke."
"No," said Gawain, "by God who gave me a soul,
The grievous gash to come I grudge you not at all;
Strike but the one stroke and I shall stand still
And offer you no hindrance; you may act freely,
390　　　　　　　I swear."
　　　　　Head bent, Sir Gawain bowed,
　　　　　And showed the bright flesh bare.
　　　　　He behaved as if uncowed,°
　　　　　Being loth° to display his care.

395　　Then the gallant in green quickly got ready,
Heaved his horrid weapon on high to hit Gawain,
With all the brute force in his body bearing it aloft,
Swinging savagely enough to strike him dead.
Had it driven down as direly as he aimed,
400　　The daring **dauntless** man would have died from the blow.
But Gawain glanced up at the grim axe beside him
As it came shooting through the shivering air to shatter him,
And his shoulders shrank slightly from the sharp edge.
The other suddenly stayed the descending axe,
405　　And then reproved the prince with many proud words:
"You are not Gawain," said the gallant, "whose greatness is such
That by hill or hollow no army ever frightened him;
For now you flinch for fear before you feel harm.
I never did know that knight to be a coward.
410　　I neither flinched nor fled when you let fly your blow,
Nor offered any quibble in the house of King Arthur.
My head flew to my feet, but flee I did not.
Yet you quail° cravenly though unscathed so far.
So I am bound to be called the better man
415　　　　　　　Therefore."
　　　　　Said Gawain, "Not again

380　**requite:** repay.

382　**second:** an official attendant of a contestant in a duel. **sunder:** separate. **spar:** fight.

393　**uncowed:** not frightened by threats.
394　**loth:** reluctant.
413　**quail:** flinch.

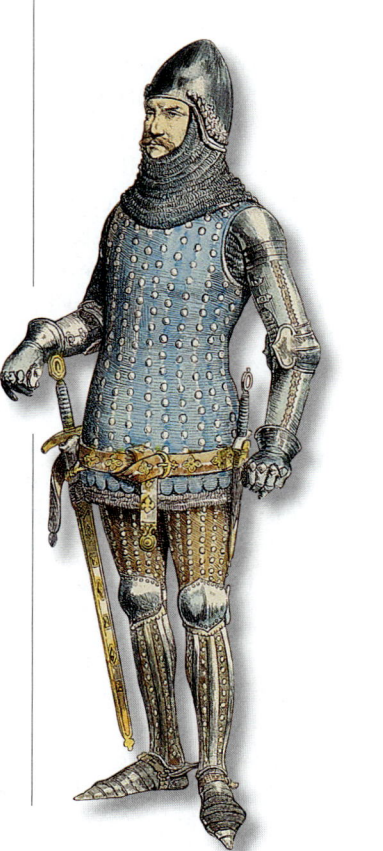

Knight. Artist Unknown. Antique hand-colored print.

Big Idea　**The World of Romance** *Why does the Green Knight use the word* coward *to insult Sir Gawain?*

Vocabulary

dauntless (dônt′ lis) *adj.* daring; not easily discouraged

Shall I flinch as I did before;
But if my head pitch to the plain,
It's off for evermore.

420 "But be brisk, man, by your faith, and bring me to the point;
Deal me my destiny and do it out of hand,
For I shall stand your stroke, not starting at all
Till your axe has hit me. Here is my oath on it."
"Have at you then!" said the other, heaving up his axe,
425 Behaving as angrily as if he were mad.
He menaced him mightily, but made no contact,
Smartly withholding his hand without hurting him.
Gawain waited unswerving, with not a wavering limb,
But stood still as a stone or the stump of a tree
430 Gripping the rocky ground with a hundred grappling roots.
Then again the green knight began to gird:°

431 gird: get ready.

"So now you have a whole heart I must hit you.
May the high knighthood which Arthur conferred
Preserve you and save your neck, if so it avail you!"
435 Then said Gawain, storming with sudden rage,
"Thrash on, you thrustful fellow, you threaten too much.
It seems your spirit is struck with self-dread."
"Forsooth,"° the other said, "You speak so fiercely

438 Forsooth: in truth.

I will no longer lengthen matters by delaying your business,
440   I vow."
                 He stood astride to smite,°

441 smite: strike.

Lips pouting, puckered brow.
No wonder he lacked delight
Who expected no help now.

445 Up went the axe at once and hurtled down straight
At the naked neck with its knife-like edge.
Though it swung down savagely, slight was the wound,
A mere snick on the side, so that the skin was broken.
Through the fair fat to the flesh fell the blade,
450 And over his shoulders the shimmering blood shot to the ground.
When Sir Gawain saw his gore glinting on the snow,
He leapt feet close together a spear's length away,
Hurriedly heaved his helmet on to his head,
And shrugging his shoulders, shot his shield to the front,
455 Swung out his bright sword and said fiercely,
(For never had the knight since being nursed by his mother
Been so buoyantly happy, so **blithe** in this world)

Reading Strategy   **Monitoring Comprehension**   *What has happened on the Green Knight's third strike?*

Vocabulary

blithe (blīth) *adj.* carefree; lighthearted

"Cease your blows, sir, strike me no more.
I have sustained a stroke here unresistingly,
460 And if you offer any more I shall earnestly reply.
Resisting, rest assured, with the most rancorous
Despite.°
The single stroke is wrought
To which we pledged our plight°
465 In high King Arthur's court:
Enough now, therefore, knight!"

The bold man stood back and bent over his axe,
Putting the haft to earth, and leaning on the head.
He gazed at Sir Gawain on the ground before him,
470 Considering the spirited and stout way he stood,
Audacious° in arms; his heart warmed to him.
Then he gave utterance gladly in his great voice,
With resounding speech saying to the knight,
"Bold man, do not be so bloodily resolute.°
475 No one here has offered you evil discourteously,
Contrary to the covenant made at the King's court.
I promised a stroke, which you received: consider yourself paid.
I cancel all other obligations of whatever kind.
If I had been more active, perhaps I could
480 Have made you suffer by striking a savager stroke.
First in foolery I made a feint° at striking,
Not rending° you with a riving cut—and right I was,
On account of the first night's covenant we accorded;
For you truthfully kept your trust in troth with me,
485 Giving me your gains, as a good man should.
The further feinted blow was for the following day,
When you kissed my comely wife, and the kisses came to me:
For those two things, harmlessly I thrust twice at you
Feinted blows.
490 Truth for truth's the word;
No need for dread, God knows.
From your failure at the third
The tap you took arose.

"For that braided belt you wear belongs to me.
495 I am well aware that my own wife gave it you.
Your conduct and your kissings are completely known to me,
And the wooing by my wife—my work set it on.
I instructed her to try you, and you truly seem
To be the most perfect paladin° ever to pace the earth.
500 As the pearl to the white pea in precious worth,
So in good faith is Gawain to other gay knights.

Imperial crown of the Holy Roman Empire.

461–462 **rancorous Despite:** bitter ill will or malice.
464 **plight:** promise.
471 **Audacious:** daring; bold.
474 **resolute:** determined.

481 **feint** (fānt): here, a deceptive action designed to draw attention away from one's real purpose.
482 **rending:** tearing apart.

499 **paladin:** a model of chivalry.

Literary Element   **Archetype** *At this point in the story, how has the lady developed into an archetype?*

But here your faith failed you, you flagged° somewhat, sir,
Yet it was not for a well-wrought thing, nor for wooing either,
But for love of your life, which is less blameworthy."

502 **flagged:** grew weak.

505 The other strong man stood considering this a while,
So filled with fury that his flesh trembled,
And the blood from his breast burst forth in his face
As he shrank for shame at what the chevalier° spoke of.

508 **chevalier:** knight.

The first words the fair knight could frame were:
510 "Curses on both cowardice and covetousness!
Their vice and villainy are virtue's undoing."
Then he took the knot, with a twist twitched it loose,
And fiercely flung the fair girdle to the knight.
"Lo! There is the false thing, foul fortune befall it!
515 I was craven about our encounter, and cowardice taught me
To accord with covetousness and corrupt my nature
And the liberality and loyalty belonging to chivalry.
Now I am faulty and false and found fearful always.
In the train of treachery and untruth go woe
520   And shame.
        I acknowledge, knight, how ill
        I behaved, and take the blame.
        Award what penance you will:
        Henceforth I'll shun ill-fame."

525 Then the other lord laughed and politely said,
==In my view you have made amends for your misdemeanor;==
You have confessed your faults fully with fair acknowledgment,
And plainly done penance at the point of my axe.
You are absolved° of your sin and as stainless now

529 **absolved:** forgiven.

530 As if you had never fallen in fault since first you were born.
As for the gold-hemmed girdle, I give it you, sir,
Seeing it is as green as my gown. Sir Gawain, you may
Think about this trial when you throng in company
With paragons° of princes, for it is a perfect token,°

534 **paragons:** models of perfection.
token: keepsake or souvenir.

535 At knightly gatherings, of the great adventure at the Green
      Chapel.
You shall come back to my castle this cold New Year,
And we shall revel° away the rest of this rich feast;
              Let us go."

537 **revel:** make merry.

        Thus urging him, the lord
540   Said, "You and my wife, I know
        We shall bring to clear accord,
        Though she was your fierce foe."

Big Idea   **The World of Romance** *How does Sir Gawain exhibit both heroism and humbleness?*

RESPONDING AND THINKING CRITICALLY

Respond

1. Were you surprised by the Green Knight's actions at the end of the story? Why or why not?

Recall and Interpret

2. (a)In your own words, state the challenge that the Green Knight offers the members of the Round Table. (b)Do you think the Green Knight is meant to be viewed as evil? Use evidence from the text to support your opinion.

3. (a)Why does Sir Gawain consider himself the knight best qualified to accept the Green Knight's challenge? (b)Why do you think King Arthur allows Sir Gawain to take up the challenge?

4. (a)Why does Sir Gawain refuse the lady's gift of a gold ring but accept her green silk girdle? (b) In the final line of the selection, the Green Knight claims that his wife was Sir Gawain's "fierce foe." In what ways might the lady be considered Sir Gawain's foe?

5. (a)During the incident at the Green Chapel, what reasons does the Green Knight give for the three blows of the axe? (b)What was Sir Gawain's real test? Did he pass? Explain.

Analyze and Evaluate

6. (a)Compare the two translations of the opening section of the poem on pages 173–175. How are they both similar and different? (b)Which of these translations do you prefer? Why?

7. (a)How realistic is the character of Sir Gawain? (b)Explain why the author may have developed his character the way he did.

Connect

8. **Big Idea** **The World of Romance** Do you think Sir Gawain is a hero, both by today's standards and by the expectations of knightly behavior in Sir Gawain's time? Why or why not?

PRIMARY VISUAL ARTIFACT

A Knight's Armor

In *Sir Gawain and the Green Knight*, many of the characters wear elaborate armor to protect themselves in battle. Early knights wore simple *hauberks* (hô′ bərk′), knee-length suits of chain mail. Mail was a netting made of interlocking metal rings; a single suit might contain 200,000 rings. Mail armor was both flexible and strong, but it was also heavy, weighing about thirty pounds, and it offered little protection from some weapons, such as the longbow. During the 1300s and 1400s, armor improved. New types of furnaces allowed metalsmiths to create lightweight yet strong steel plates.

Group Activity What were the advantages and disadvantages of armor as it changed over time? Discuss this question with your classmates. Refer to the image and captions on the right and cite evidence from the selection to support your answers.

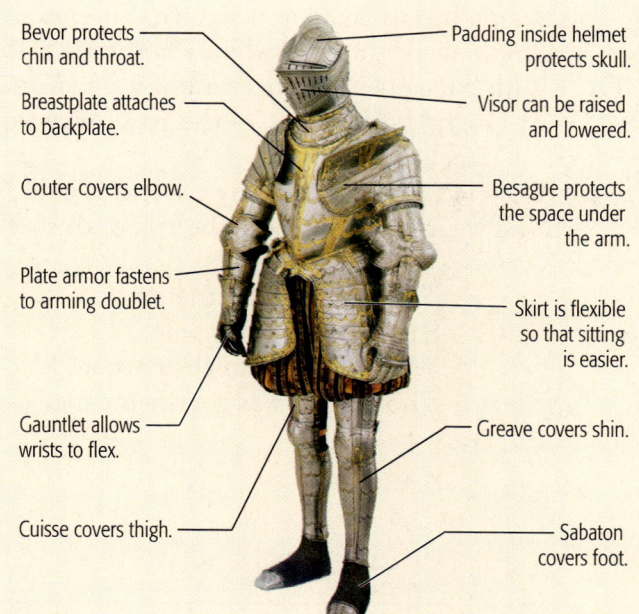

Bevor protects chin and throat.

Breastplate attaches to backplate.

Couter covers elbow.

Plate armor fastens to arming doublet.

Gauntlet allows wrists to flex.

Cuisse covers thigh.

Padding inside helmet protects skull.

Visor can be raised and lowered.

Besague protects the space under the arm.

Skirt is flexible so that sitting is easier.

Greave covers shin.

Sabaton covers foot.

Literary Element Archetype

An **archetype** represents a pattern that has recurred in literature throughout time. Because the audience is already familiar with what archetypes represent, they often evoke a strong response from the reader.

1. What archetypes are present in *Sir Gawain and the Green Knight*?

2. In what ways are archetypes used to further the plot of the poem?

Review: Conflict

As you learned on page 23, **conflict** is the central struggle between two opposing forces in a story or drama. An **external conflict** exists when a character struggles against some outside force. Many stories, such as *Sir Gawain and the Green Knight*, feature conflict between the **protagonist**, or central character, and the **antagonist**, a person or force that opposes the protagonist. An antagonist may try to prevent the protagonist from doing something or may simply have beliefs that contradict those of the protagonist.

Partner Activity Meet with another classmate to discuss the conflicts in *Sir Gawain and the Green Knight*. With your partner, create a web diagram like the one below. Fill in the diagram, listing each antagonist and conflict Sir Gawain must face throughout the story.

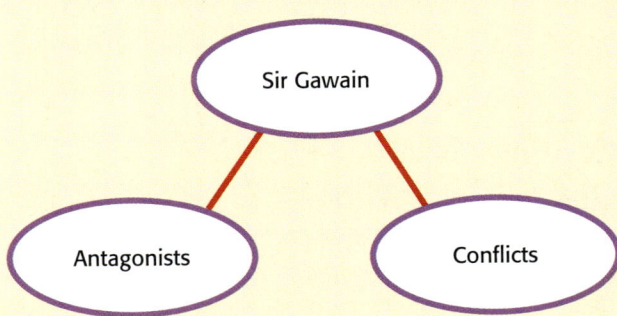

Reading Strategy Monitoring Comprehension

When reading challenging material, you will need to reread the text to gain a better understanding of it. You should be able to summarize important ideas after your first reading so that you can pay closer attention to supporting details in your second reading.

1. Summarize the conflicts in *Sir Gawain and the Green Knight* and how each is ultimately resolved.

2. Imagine that you saw the Green Knight in King Arthur's court. How would you describe his initial appearance? Include as many details from the text as possible.

Vocabulary Practice

Practice with Synonyms Match each vocabulary word below with its synonym. Use a dictionary if you need help.

1. intrepid   **a.** carefree

2. copious   **b.** unflinching

3. dauntless   **c.** bold

4. blithe   **d.** profuse

Academic Vocabulary

Here are two words from the vocabulary list on page R82.

achieve (ə chēv′) *v.* to accomplish; to complete a goal

version (vur′ zhən) *n.* an account that varies from the original

Practice and Apply
1. What does the Green Knight's test **achieve**?
2. Which **version** of the *Sir Gawain* translation do you consider more effective and why?

Writing About Literature

Analyze Sound Devices Alliteration is a literary sound device in which a writer repeats an initial consonant sound in order to create a desired effect. Alliteration is often used to emphasize certain words or to create a musical quality. The author of *Sir Gawain and the Green Knight* makes extensive use of alliteration throughout the text, as evidenced in the first lines of the poem:

> "Yes, **g**arbed all in **g**reen was the **g**allant rider,
> And the **h**air of **h**is **h**ead was the same **h**ue as **h**is **h**orse,
> And **f**loated **f**inely like a **f**an round his shoulders . . . "

In a brief essay, analyze the overall effect achieved by the author's use of alliteration. Consider why the author might want to emphasize certain words. Before you begin writing, select additional passages from *Sir Gawain* that make use of alliteration. Read the passages aloud, making an effort to emphasize the repeated consonant sounds. Note how the effect of the poem is heightened when it is read orally in this manner. Use a chart like the one below to compile your notes.

Passage	Alliteration	Effect
Lines 217–218	body, bled dread, doubt	

After completing your draft, meet with a peer reviewer to evaluate each other's work and to suggest revisions. Then proofread your draft for errors in spelling, grammar, and punctuation.

Internet Connection

Use the Internet to learn more about King Arthur, the knights of the Round Table, and the world of Camelot. Trace the origins of the Arthurian legend and determine for yourself just how "real" a figure Arthur was. You may also wish to find tales that do not depict Sir Gawain as the humble and noble soul of the Green Knight tale.

Language and Style of *Sir Gawain and the Green Knight*

Using Action Verbs In *Sir Gawain and the Green Knight,* both transitive and intransitive action verbs contribute to translator Brian Stone's style. A **transitive verb** is a verb that has a receiver of the action, a word or words that answer the question *what?* or *whom?* of the action verb. In the active voice, that word or words are called an object. An **intransitive verb** is a verb that has no receiver of the action, or object.

> "Those standing *studied him* and *sidled* towards him
> With all the world's wonder as to what he would do."

In this sentence, the action verb *studied* is transitive, because it is followed by the object *him,* which answers the question *whom?* The action verb *sidled* is intransitive; that is, what follows it does not answer the question *whom?* or *what?*

Notice some of Stone's most effective verb choices.

Transitive Verb/Object	Intransitive Verb
twisted/[the] trunk	dwell
caused/dread and doubt	spurted

Activity Scan pages 174–189 to locate examples of action verbs that create suspense and move the story forward. In a chart of your own, list transitive verbs and their objects in one column and intransitive verbs in a second column.

Revising Check

Action Verbs Action verbs can increase the effectiveness of your writing. With a partner, review your essay on *Sir Gawain and the Green Knight.* Revise your writing by varying your choice of transitive and intransitive action verbs.

Literature Online Web Activities For eFlashcards, Selection Quick Checks, and other Web activities, go to www.glencoe.com.

Informational Text

from A DISTANT MIRROR

Barbara Tuchman

National Book Award Winner

Building Background

Barbara Tuchman was one of the foremost historians of the twentieth century. She was twice awarded the Pulitzer Prize, first for *The Guns of August*, a compelling history of the first month of fighting during World War I, and then again for *Stilwell and the American Experience in China, 1911–1945*, which describes Chinese-American relations before and during World War II. In this excerpt from *A Distant Mirror*, a brilliant survey of the plague-and-war-ridden fourteenth century, Tuchman discusses the development and effects of chivalry on medieval European society.

Set a Purpose for Reading

Read to learn how the historical realities of chivalry and knighthood differ from the descriptions of them in medieval romances.

Reading Strategy

Analyzing Historical Context

Analyzing historical context involves gathering background information and exploring the social forces that influenced the writing of a literary work. As you read, take notes on the historical context for *Sir Gawain and the Green Knight*. Use a two-column chart like the one below.

Literary Work	Historical Context
World of Gawain	World of the fourteenth century

C hivalry was a moral system, governing the whole of noble life. It developed at the same time as the great crusades of the 12th century as a code intended to fuse the religious and martial spirits and somehow bring the fighting man into accord with Christian theory. A moral gloss was needed that would allow the Church to tolerate the warriors in good conscience and the warriors to pursue their own values in spiritual comfort. With the help of Benedictine thinkers,[1] a code evolved that put the knight's sword arm in the service, theoretically, of justice, right, piety, the Church, the widow, the orphan, and the oppressed.

Chivalry could not be contained by the Church, and bursting through the pious veils, it developed its own principles. Prowess, that combination of courage, strength, and skill that made a chevalier *preux*,[2] was the prime essential. Honor and loyalty, together with courtesy—meaning the kind of behavior that has since come to be called "chivalrous"—were the ideals, and so-called courtly love the presiding genius.[3] Designed to make the knight more polite and to

---

1. *Benedictine thinkers* refers to monks of the Order of Saint Benedict.
2. *Chevalier* is French for "knight." *Preux* means "valiant" in French.
3. Here, *genius* means "guiding principle."

Scene from the *Battle of Crecy*, 1346. From "Les Chroniques de France." British Library, London.

"Unconquered Knight" of the late 14th century. "They expose themselves to every peril; they give up their bodies to the adventure of life in death. Moldy bread or biscuit, meat cooked or uncooked; today enough to eat and tomorrow nothing, little or no wine, water from a pond or a butt,[7] bad quarters, the shelter of a tent or branches, a bad bed, poor sleep with their armor still on their backs, burdened with iron, the enemy an arrow-shot off. 'Ware! Who goes there? To arms! To arms!' With the first drowsiness, an alarm; at dawn, the trumpet. 'To horse! To horse! Muster! Muster!' As lookouts, as sentinels,[8] keeping watch by day and by night, fighting without cover, as foragers,[9] as scouts, guard after guard, duty after duty. 'Here they come! Here! They are so many—No, not as many as that—This way—that—Come this side—Press them there—News! News! They come back hurt, they have prisoners—no, they bring none back. Let us go! Let us go! Give no ground! On!' Such is their calling."

Horrid wounds were part of the calling. In one combat Don Pero Niño was struck by an arrow that "knit together his gorget[10] and his neck," but he fought on against the enemy on the bridge. "Several lance stumps were still in his shield and it was that which hindered him most." A bolt[11] from a crossbow "pierced his nostrils most painfully whereat he was dazed, but his daze lasted but a little time." He pressed forward, receiving many sword blows on head and shoulders which "sometimes hit the bolt embedded in his nose making him suffer great pain." When weariness on both sides brought the battle to an end, Pero Niño's

lift the tone of society, courtly love required its disciple to be in a chronically amorous[4] condition, on the theory that he would thus be rendered[5] more courteous, gay, and gallant, and society in consequence more joyous.

Prowess was not mere talk, for the function of physical violence required real stamina. To fight on horseback or foot wearing 55 pounds of plate armor, to crash in collision with an opponent at full gallop while holding horizontal an eighteen-foot lance half the length of an average telephone pole, to give and receive blows with sword or battle-ax that could cleave[6] a skull or slice off a limb at a stroke, to spend half of life in the saddle through all weathers and for days at a time, was not a weakling's work. Hardship and fear were part of it. "Knights who are at the wars . . . are forever swallowing their fear," wrote the companion and biographer of Don Pero Niño, the

---

4. *Amorous* means "to be in love."
5. Here, *rendered* means "made."
6. *Cleave* means "to cut" or "to slash."

7. Here, *butt* means "ditch."
8. *Sentinels* are guards.
9. *Foragers* are scavengers.
10. A *gorget* is a piece of armor worn around the neck.
11. Here, *bolt* refers to a type of small arrow.

shield "was tattered and all in pieces; his sword blade was toothed like a saw and dyed with blood . . . his armor was broken in several places by lance-heads of which some had entered the flesh and drawn blood, although the coat was of great strength." Prowess was not easily bought.

In the performance of his function, the knight must be prepared, as John of Salisbury[12] wrote, "to shed your blood for your brethren"—he meant brethren in the universal sense—"and, if needs must, to lay down your life." Many were thus prepared, though perhaps more from sheer love of battle than concern for a cause. Blind King John of Bohemia[13] met death in that way. He loved fighting for its own sake, not caring whether the conflict was important.

As an ally of Philip VI,[14] at the head of 500 knights, the sightless King fought the English

---

12. *John of Salisbury* (1115–1180) was a writer, historian, secretary to two archbishops of Canterbury, and the Bishop of Chartres.
13. *King John of Bohemia* (1296–1346) was a popular heroic figure who ruled from 1311 until his death at the Battle of Crécy in France.
14. *Philip VI* (1293–1350) was king of France from 1328 until his death.

through Picardy,[15] always rash and in the avant-garde. At Crécy he asked his knights to lead him deeper into the battle so that he might strike further blows with his sword. Twelve of them tied their horses' reins together and, with the King at their head, advanced into the thick of the fight, "so far as never to return." His body was found next day among his knights, all slain with their horses still tied together.

Fighting filled the noble's need of something to do, a way to exert himself. It was his substitute for work. His leisure time was spent chiefly in hunting, otherwise in games of chess, backgammon, and dice, in songs, dances, pageants, and other entertainments. Long winter evenings were occupied listening to the recital of interminable[16] verse epics. The sword offered the workless noble an activity with a purpose, one that could bring him honor, status, and, if he was lucky, gain. ❧

---

15. *Picardy* is a region of northern France.
16. *Interminable* means "never-ending."

RESPONDING AND THINKING CRITICALLY

Respond

1. How have your ideas about knights and chivalry changed as a result of reading this excerpt?

Recall and Interpret

2. How does this excerpt define chivalry?

3. (a)According to Tuchman, why did chivalry develop? (b)Why do you think chivalry eventually took on a life of its own and burst "through [its] pious veils"?

4. (a)Why did Blind King John fight so many battles? (b)What does this suggest to you about chivalry?

Analyze and Evaluate

5. (a)What assertions does Tuchman make about the life of a knight? (b)How does she support these assertions?

6. Overall, do you think the author has a positive or a negative view of chivalry? Cite specific examples to support your opinion.

7. (a)Compare and contrast this passage's depiction of chivalry and knighthood with the depiction of them in *Sir Gawain and the Green Knight.* (b)Which depiction seems more accurate?

Connect

8. The portrayal of chivalry and knighthood in medieval tales is often not accurate. Despite this, do you think that these myths and legends are important? Explain.

OBJECTIVES
- Read to enhance understanding of history and British culture.
- Analyze the influences of historical context that shape elements of a literary work.
- Connect a literary work, including character, plot, and setting, to the historical context.

BARBARA TUCHMAN   **195**

Le Morte d' Arthur

MEET SIR THOMAS MALORY

"Syr Thomas Maleore, knyght" reads the name of the author on the first printing of *Le Morte d'Arthur* in 1485. That simple listing tells everything that is definitely known about the author, for there was more than one Thomas Malory. Most evidence suggests, however, that the writer was the hot-blooded Thomas Malory who represented Warwickshire in Parliament in 1445 and spent much of his later life in jail.

Knighthood and Prison Malory lived in troubled times. Though his family held land and was well respected, he found himself supporting the wrong side—the Lancasters—during the Wars of the Roses, a bloody, drawn-out conflict to determine which family would rule England. That conflict pitted the House of Lancaster, whose symbol was a red rose, against the House of York, whose symbol was a white rose. A long list of crimes was attributed to Malory, from extortion and attempted murder to cattle rustling. In one notorious incident, he escaped from prison by swimming across a moat and then attacked a nearby abbey that he believed was holding possessions stolen from him. Malory's behavior outraged King Edward IV, who specifically excluded him from four general pardons for criminals, issued between 1468 and 1470.

> "It is as if the book were the production of no one mind, nor even of a score of successive minds, nor even of any one place or time, but were a rolling body of British-Norman legend."
>
> —David Masson

Literature Online **Author Search** For more about Sir Thomas Malory, go to www.glencoe.com.

How Morgan le Fay Gave a Shield to Sir Tristram, 1893-1894. Aubrey Vincent Beardsley. Illustration.

Le Morte d'Arthur Malory was in jail when he composed the great English prose work that related the heroic adventures of King Arthur and his knights of the Round Table. The narrative is a reworking of English, French, and Latin tales. Malory translated and organized the diverse body of Arthurian romance that had developed in England and France since Anglo-Saxon times. In the process, he created the first prose masterpiece in English.

Malory died in jail and was buried in the Chapel of St. Francis at Grey Friars. After his death, his manuscript was published by William Caxton, the man who introduced the printing press to England. Caxton gave the work its famous title, *Le Morte d'Arthur*, which is French for "The Death of Arthur." Caxton's title highlighted the story's tragic end.

Never before had a work of English prose matched the elegance and force of English verse. Through the centuries, *Le Morte d'Arthur* has influenced the imaginations of many writers. As American novelist and satirist Mark Twain said, "From time to time I dipped into old Sir Thomas Malory's enchanting book, and fed at its rich feast of prodigies and adventures, breathed in the fragrance of its obsolete names, and dreamed again."

Sir Thomas Malory was born about 1405 and died in 1471.

Connecting to the Story

What would it be like to foresee the future? In this selection, King Arthur has a dream that reveals the future to him. Do you think dreams can foretell the future?

Building Background

Was there a real King Arthur? Historical documents, as well as archaeological remains from Cadbury Castle in England, hint that in the early 500s a Celtic chieftain named Arthur fought against the invading Germanic tribes. A vast oral literature developed around Arthur and by the time the stories were written down, truth and fiction had been forever entwined.

In Malory's *Le Morte d'Arthur,* King Arthur creates the brotherhood of the Round Table, an assembly of knights including Sir Lancelot and Sir Gawain, Arthur's nephew, who pledge loyalty to Arthur and to the code of chivalry. As the selection begins, Arthur prepares for battle against his illegitimate son, Mordred, who has raised an army against him.

Setting Purposes for Reading

Big Idea The World of Romance

In his writing, Malory sought to recapture the Arthurian romantic ideals. As you read, consider the ideals that King Arthur and his knights represent.

Literary Element Legend

A **legend** is a tale that is based on history and handed down from one generation to the next. Usually, a legend celebrates the heroic qualities of a national or cultural leader. As you read, notice the characteristic qualities of a legend in this story.

- See Literary Terms Handbook, p. R9.

Literature Online Interactive Literary Elements Handbook To review or learn more about the literary elements, go to www.glencoe.com.

Reading Strategy Activating Prior Knowledge

Reading is an interactive process. When you recall information and personal experiences that are uniquely your own while you are reading, you draw on your personal background. By thus **activating prior knowledge,** and combining it with the words on a page, you create meaning in a selection. As you read, use what you already know about King Arthur to help you understand the story.

Reading Tip: Taking Notes Use a chart to connect your prior knowledge to specific events in the story.

Prior Knowledge	Events in the Story
Sir Lancelot was King Arthur's bravest knight.	Gawain warns Arthur to wait for Lancelot to defeat Mordred.

Vocabulary

doleful (dōl´fəl) *adj.* sad; p. 201 *The wind in the trees made a doleful sound.*

peril (per´əl) *n.* risk of injury, loss, or destruction; p. 201 *Police officers face great perils in chasing hit-and-run drivers.*

jeopardy (jep´ər dē) *n.* danger; p. 203 *The fire in the warehouse put nearby buildings in jeopardy.*

brandish (bran´dish) *v.* to shake or swing threateningly, as a weapon; p. 203 *Pretending he was a knight, the boy brandished a plastic sword.*

Vocabulary Tip: Analogies Analogies are comparisons based on relationships between ideas. To complete an analogy, determine the relationship between the ideas represented by the first pair of words. Then apply that relationship to the second pair.

OBJECTIVES

In studying this selection, you will focus on the following:
- analyzing literary periods
- analyzing legends and archetypes
- activating prior knowledge

Battle between King Arthur and Mordred. English. Lambeth Palace Library, London.

from
Le Morte d'Arthur

Sir Thomas Malory

I

Upon Trinity Sunday[1] at night King Arthur dreamed a wonderful dream, and that was this: it seemed that he saw upon a platform a chair and the chair was fastened to a wheel; thereupon King Arthur sat in the richest cloth of gold that might be made. And the king thought that under him, far from him, was hideous deep black water; therein were all manner of serpents and worms and wild beasts, foul and horrible. Suddenly the king thought the wheel turned upside-down and he fell among the serpents, and every beast caught him by a limb. The king cried out as he lay in his bed and slept, "Help, help!"

Then knights, squires,[2] and yeomen[3] awakened the king, and he was so dazed that he knew not where he was. He stayed awake until it was nigh day and then he fell to slumbering again, not sleeping but not thoroughly awake. Then it seemed to the king that Sir Gawain actually came unto him with a number of fair ladies.

When King Arthur saw him he cried, "Welcome, my sister's son; I thought that ye were dead. And now that I see thee alive, much am I beholden unto almighty Jesus. Ah, fair nephew, what are these ladies that have come hither with you?"

"Sir," said Sir Gawain, "all those are ladies for whom I have fought when I was a living man. And all these are those whom I did battle for in righteous quarrels; at their devout prayer, because I did battle for them righteously, God hath given them the grace to bring me hither unto you. Thus God hath given me leave to warn you away from your death: for if ye fight to-morn with Sir Mordred, as ye have both agreed, doubt ye not that ye shall be slain, and the most part of your people on both sides. Through the great grace and goodness that almighty Jesus hath unto you, and through pity for you and many other good men who would be slain there, God in His special grace hath sent me to you to give you warning that in no wise[4] should ye do battle to-morn; but ye should make a treaty for a month. And make this offer generously to-morn so as to

---

1. *Trinity Sunday* is the eighth Sunday after Easter.
2. *Squires* assisted knights.
3. *Yeomen* were attendants to nobles.

---

4. Here, *wise* means "way."

St. Bedivere returns Excalibur to the lake at the death of King Arthur, early 14th century. Illuminated manuscript.

assure the delay, for within a month Sir Lancelot shall come with all his noble knights and rescue you worshipfully and slay Sir Mordred and all who ever will hold with him."

Then Sir Gawain and all the ladies vanished; at once the king called upon his knights, squires, and yeoman and charged them quickly to fetch his noble lords and wise bishops unto him. When they had come the king told them of his vision and what Sir Gawain had said to him: that if he fought on the morn, he would be slain. Then the king commanded and charged Sir Lucan le Butler, his brother Sir Bedivere, and two bishops to make a treaty in any way for a month with Sir Mordred: "And spare not; offer him lands and goods, as much as ye think best."

They departed and came to Sir Mordred, where he had a grim host[5] of a hundred thousand men. There they entreated Sir Mordred a long time, and at the last it was agreed for Sir Mordred to have Cornwall and Kent during King Arthur's days and all England after the king's days.

II

Then they agreed that King Arthur and Sir Mordred should meet between their two hosts, and that each of them should bring fourteen persons with him. They came back with this word to King Arthur.

Then he said, "I am glad that this is done." So he went into the field.

When King Arthur prepared to depart for the meeting in the field he warned all his host that if they should see any sword drawn, "see that ye come on fiercely and slay that traitor Sir Mordred, for I in no wise trust him."

---

5. Here, *host* means "army."

King Arthur and His Knights Around the Table. Manuscript on vellum. Bibliotheque Nationale, Paris.

In like wise Sir Mordred warned his host: "If ye see any sword drawn, see that ye come on fiercely and then slay all who stand before you, for in no way will I trust in this treaty; I know well that my father wishes to be avenged upon me."

So they met for their appointment and were thoroughly agreed and accorded;[6] wine was fetched and they drank together. Just then an adder came out of a little heath-bush and stung a knight on the foot. When the knight felt the sting, he looked down and saw the adder; at once he drew his sword to slay the adder, and thought to cause no harm. But when the hosts on both sides saw that sword drawn, they blew trumpets and horns and shouted grimly, and the two hosts rushed toward each other.

Then King Arthur mounted his horse and said, "Alas, this unhappy day!" So he rode to join his party, and Sir Mordred did in like wise. And never since was there seen a more **doleful** battle in any Christian land, for there was great rushing and riding, thrusting and striking, and many a grim word was spoken by each side, and many a deadly stroke was dealt. But King Arthur rode steadily throughout the army of Sir Mordred many times and did full nobly, as a noble king should; never at any time did he weaken. And Sir Mordred did his duty that day and put himself in great **peril.** Thus they fought all the long day, and no knight ever stinted[7] till he was laid to the cold earth. So they fought on till it was near night, and by that time there were a hundred thousand who lay dead upon the ground. Then King Arthur was madly wroth[8] out of measure, when he saw that so many of his people were slain. When the king looked about him he

was aware that of all his host and of all his good knights no more were left alive but two: one was Sir Lucan le Butler, and the other his brother Sir Bedivere; and they were both sorely wounded.

"Jesus, mercy!" said the king. "Where are all my noble knights? Alas, that ever I should see this doleful day! For now I have come to my end. But would to God that I knew where that traitor Sir Mordred, who hath caused all this mischief, is."

Then King Arthur looked about and saw where Sir Mordred stood leaning upon his sword among a great heap of dead men. "Now give me my spear," said King Arthur to Sir Lucan, "for yonder I have spied the traitor who hath wrought all this woe."

"Sir, let him be," said Sir Lucan, "for he brings ill fortune. And if ye can pass through this unlucky day, ye shall be right well revenged upon him. Good lord, remember your night's dream and what the spirit of Sir Gawain told you last night. God in His great goodness hath preserved you so far. Therefore for God's sake, my lord, leave off now; for, blessed be God, ye have won the field: here we three are alive, but with Sir Mordred no one is alive. Therefore if ye leave off now, this wicked day of destiny is over."

"Now betide[9] me death, betide me life," said the king, "now that I see him yonder alone, he shall never escape my hands! For I shall never have him at better avail."[10]

"God speed you well!" said Sir Bedivere.

Then the king got his spear in both his hands and ran toward Sir Mordred, crying, "Traitor, now has thy death-day come!"

When Sir Mordred heard King Arthur he ran toward him with his sword drawn in his hand. Then King Arthur smote[11] Sir Mordred under the shield with a thrust of his spear on through the body more than a fathom. When Sir Mordred felt that he had his death-wound, he thrust himself with all his might up to the handguard of King Arthur's spear; and right so, holding his sword in both his hands, he smote his father King Arthur upon the side of the head so that the sword pierced the helmet and the brain-pan. Therewith Sir Mordred fell stark dead to the earth; and the noble King Arthur fell to the

---

6. *Accorded* means "reconciled."
7. Here, *stinted* means "ceased" or "stopped."
8. *Wroth* means "angered."

9. *Betide* means "come to."
10. Here, *avail* means "advantage."
11. *Smote* means "struck."

earth and there he swooned often, and Sir Lucan and Sir Bedivere lifted him up each time. So they led him, weak between them, to a little chapel not far from the sea, and when the king was there he seemed reasonably comfortable.

Then they heard people cry out in the field.

"Now go thou, Sir Lucan," said the king, "and let me know what that noise in the field betokens."[12]

So Sir Lucan departed slowly, for he was grievously wounded in many places; as he went he saw and noticed by the moonlight how plunderers and robbers had come into the field to plunder and to rob many a full noble knight of brooches and beads, of many a good ring, and of many a rich jewel. And whoever was not fully dead, the robbers slew them for their armor and their riches. When Sir Lucan understood this work, he came back to the king as quickly as he could and told him all that he had heard and seen.

"Therefore, by my counsel," said Sir Lucan, "it is best that we bring you to some town."

III

"I would it could be so," said the king, "but I cannot stand, my head aches so. Ah, Sir Lancelot, this day have I sorely missed thee! And alas, that ever I was against thee! For now I have my death, whereof Sir Gawain warned me in my dream."

Then Sir Lucan took up the king on one side and Sir Bedivere did so on the other side, and in the lifting the king swooned. Also with the lifting, Sir Lucan fell into a swoon and part of his guts fell out of his body, and therewith the noble knight's heart burst. When the king awoke he beheld Sir Lucan, how he lay foaming at the mouth, and how part of his guts lay at his feet.

"Alas," said the king, "this is to me a full heavy sight to see this noble duke die so for my

12. *Betokens* means "foretells."

sake; for he wished to help me, he who had more need of help than I. Alas, he would not complain, his heart was so set upon helping me. Now Jesus have mercy upon his soul!"

Then Sir Bedivere wept for the death of his brother.

"Leave this mourning and weeping," said the king, "for all this will not avail me. For wit thou well,[13] if I might live myself the death of Sir Lucan would grieve me evermore, but my time passeth on fast. Therefore take thou here Excalibur, my good sword, and go with it to yonder water's side; when thou comest there, I charge thee to throw my sword into that water and come again and tell me what thou saw there."

"My lord," said Sir Bedivere, "your command shall be done, and quickly I shall bring you word back."

So Sir Bedivere departed. And along the way he beheld that noble sword, that the pommel and the haft were all of precious stones. Then he said to himself, "If I throw this rich sword into the water, thereof shall never come good, but only harm and loss." Then Sir Bedivere hid Excalibur under a tree, and as soon as he might he came again unto the king and said that he had been at the water and had thrown the sword into the water.

"What saw thou there?" said the king.

"Sir," he said, "I saw nothing but waves and winds."

"That is untruly said by thee," said the king. "Therefore go thou quickly again and do my command. As thou art dear to me, spare not but throw it in."

Then Sir Bedivere returned again and took the sword in his hand, and again he thought it a sin and a shame to throw away that noble sword. So once more he hid the sword and returned again and told the king that he had been at the water and done his command.

"What saw thou there?" said the king.

13. The expression *wit thou well* means "heed what I say."

Reading Strategy **Activating Prior Knowledge** *Why is Excalibur so important to King Arthur?*

Then King Arthur smote Sir Mordred under the shield with a thrust of his spear on through the body more than a fathom.

The Death of Arthur. John Mulcaster Carrick.
Viewing the Art: How does this painting compare with how you imagine this scene?

"Sir," he said, "I saw nothing but waves and winds."

"Ah, traitor untrue," said King Arthur, "now hast thou betrayed me twice! Who would have thought that thou who hast been to me so lief[14] and dear and thou who art called a noble knight would betray me for the richness of this sword? But now go again quickly; thy long tarrying[15] putteth me in great **jeopardy** of my life, for I have taken cold. And unless thou do now as I bid thee, if ever I may see thee again I shall slay thee with my own hands; for thou would for my rich sword see me dead."

Then Sir Bedivere departed and went to the sword and quickly took it up and went to the water's side, and there he bound the girdle[16] about the hilt;[17] then he threw the sword as far into the water as he might. And there came an arm and a hand above the water which caught it and shook and **brandished** it thrice and then vanished with the sword into the water. So Sir Bedivere came back to the king and told him what he saw.

"Alas," said the king, "help me hence, for I fear that I have tarried over-long."

Then Sir Bedivere took the king upon his back and so went with him to the water's side. When they reached there they saw a little barge which waited fast by the bank with many fair

---

14. *Lief* means "beloved."
15. *Tarrying* means "delaying."

Big Idea **The World of Romance** *In addition to betraying King Arthur, what does Bedivere betray by lying to his king?*

Vocabulary

jeopardy (je′ pər dē) *n.* danger

---

16. The *girdle* is the sash around a sword's handle.
17. The *hilt* is the handle, also called the haft, of the sword.

Vocabulary

brandish (bran′ dish) *v.* to shake or swing threateningly, as a weapon

ladies in it. Among them all was a queen, and they all had black hoods; they all wept and shrieked when they saw King Arthur.

"Now put me into that barge," said the king.

Sir Bedivere did so gently, and three queens received him there with great mourning and put him down; in one of their laps King Arthur laid his head. Then that queen said, "Ah, dear brother, why have ye tarried so long from me? Alas, this wound on your head hath caught over-much cold."

So they rowed from the land and Sir Bedivere beheld all those ladies go from him. Then Sir Bedivere cried, "Ah, my lord Arthur, what shall become of me, now that ye go from me and leave me here alone among my enemies?"

"Comfort thyself," said the king, "and do as well as thou may, for in me is no more trust to trust in. I must go into the Vale of Avalon[18] to heal me of my grievous wound. And if thou hear nevermore of me, pray for my soul!"

But ever the queens and ladies wept and shrieked, so that it was a pity to hear. As soon as Sir Bedivere had lost sight of the barge, he wept and wailed and then took to the forest and walked all night. And in the morning he was aware of a chapel and a hermitage[19] between two ancient woods.

Then Sir Bedivere was glad, and thither he went. When he came into the chapel he saw where a hermit lay grovelling on all fours fast[20] by a tomb that was newly made. When the hermit saw Sir Bedivere he knew him at once, for he was the Bishop of Canterbury whom Sir Mordred recently put to flight.

"Sir," said Sir Bedivere, "what man is interred[21] there whom you pray so earnestly for?"

"Fair son," said the hermit, "I know not truly but by deeming.[22] But this night at midnight a number of ladies came here and brought hither a dead corpse and prayed me to bury him. And

here they offered a hundred tapers[23] and they gave me a thousand besants."[24]

"Alas," said Sir Bedivere, "that was my lord King Arthur who here lieth buried in this chapel." Then Sir Bedivere swooned and when he awoke he prayed the hermit that he might remain with him always, there to live with fasting and prayers. "For hence I will never go," said Sir Bedivere, "of my own will. But all the days of my life I will be here to pray for my lord Arthur."

"Ye are welcome to me here," said the hermit, "for I know you better than ye think I do. Ye are Sir Bedivere the Bold, and the full noble duke Sir Lucan le Butler was your brother."

Then Sir Bedivere told the hermit all, as ye have heard before, and he remained with the hermit who was earlier the Bishop of Canterbury. There he put on poor clothes and served the hermit full humbly in fasting and in prayers.

Thus, concerning Arthur I find no more written in books which are authorized. Nor did I ever hear or read more with true certainty concerning his death. . . .

Yet some men say in many parts of England that King Arthur is not dead, but was taken by the will of our Lord Jesus into another place. And men say that he shall come again and shall win the Holy Cross. Yet I will not say that it shall be so; rather, I would say that here in this world he changed his form of life. But many men say that there is written upon his tomb this line:

HERE LIES ARTHUR, THE ONCE AND FUTURE KING.

---

23. *Tapers* are candles.
24. *Besants* are gold coins.

Big Idea **The World of Romance** *What chivalric ideals does Bedivere's decision reflect?*

Literary Element Legend *Why does the writer conclude the story with this statement?*

---

18. *Avalon* is a legendary island paradise.
19. A *hermitage* is the home of a hermit, a person who lives in solitude for religious reasons.
20. Here, *fast* means "near."
21. *Interred* means "buried."
22. *Deeming* is guessing.

RESPONDING AND THINKING CRITICALLY

Respond

1. What are your impressions of King Arthur and the decisions that he makes? Explain.

Recall and Interpret

2. (a)Summarize the content of Arthur's dreams. (b)What might the overturned chair symbolize? What might the serpents represent?

3. (a)What accident triggers the battle between the two armies? (b)What part does Arthur and Mordred's mutual distrust play in triggering the battle?

4. (a)What does Arthur ask Sir Bedivere to do with his sword, Excalibur? (b)What do Bedivere's actions regarding Excalibur reveal about his character?

Analyze and Evaluate

5. (a)What motivates Arthur to fight Mordred to the death? (b)In your opinion, is Arthur's decision wise? Why or why not?

6. (a)How would you describe the **mood** of this selection? Does it change as the story progresses? Explain. (b)What details does Malory use to achieve this mood?

7. Evaluate Malory's use of **dialogue.** How does it help develop the characters? How does it help move the narrative along?

Connect

8. | Big Idea | **The World of Romance** In the literature of medieval Europe, King Arthur came to represent the ideal of chivalry. In what ways does he embody this ideal?

LITERARY ANALYSIS

| Literary Element | Legend

A **legend** is different from a myth in that a legend has fewer supernatural elements and more historical truth than a myth does. Because legends are stories of the people, they are often expressions of the spirit, values, or character of the culture that creates them.

1. Find examples in the selection that contribute to the perception of King Arthur as a legendary hero. Explain your choices.

2. In your opinion, why has the legend of King Arthur endured?

Review: Archetype

As you learned on page 172, an **archetype** is a character type, a setting, an image, or a story pattern that occurs frequently in literature across many cultures.

Partner Activity Meet with another classmate to identify and discuss archetypal elements in this selection. Working with your partner, list these archetypes and the emotional responses they evoke in a chart like the one below.

Archetypes	Emotional Responses

Reading Strategy Activating Prior Knowledge

To read effectively, you must **activate your prior knowledge** of people, places, history, languages, and literature. For example, while reading *Le Morte d'Arthur*, you might recall other portrayals of King Arthur and his knights in movies, art, fiction, or poetry. Drawing upon this prior knowledge can help you identify the qualities that distinguish Malory's story.

1. What prior knowledge about King Arthur did you bring to your reading of this story?

2. What makes Malory's portrayal of King Arthur different from other portrayals of him?

Vocabulary Practice

Practice with Analogies Choose the pair of words that best completes each analogy below. Use a dictionary if you need help.

1. **safety : jeopardy ::**
   a. peace : harmony   **c.** joy : sorrow
   b. affection : regard

2. **whimper : doleful ::**
   a. crash : accidental   **c.** laugh : amused
   b. shriek : distant

3. **danger : peril ::**
   a. fear : cowardice   **c.** luck : diligence
   b. weakness : frailty

4. **sword : brandish ::**
   a. pencil : write   **c.** marathon : sprint
   b. student : teach

Academic Vocabulary

Here is a word from the vocabulary list on page R82.

proceed (prə sēd') *v.* to go forward; to continue

Practice and Apply
How does Sir Bedivere **proceed** after King Arthur commands him to throw Excalibur into the water?

Writing About Literature

Evaluate Contemporary Relevance The modern American novelist John Steinbeck suggested that movie and television westerns bear similarities to the world of King Arthur, especially their heroes and villains. In what ways do you think Arthurian legends are relevant to the modern world? Write a brief essay in which you evaluate the contemporary relevance of these legends. Use examples from *Le Morte d'Arthur* to support your position. As you draft, follow the writing plan shown below.

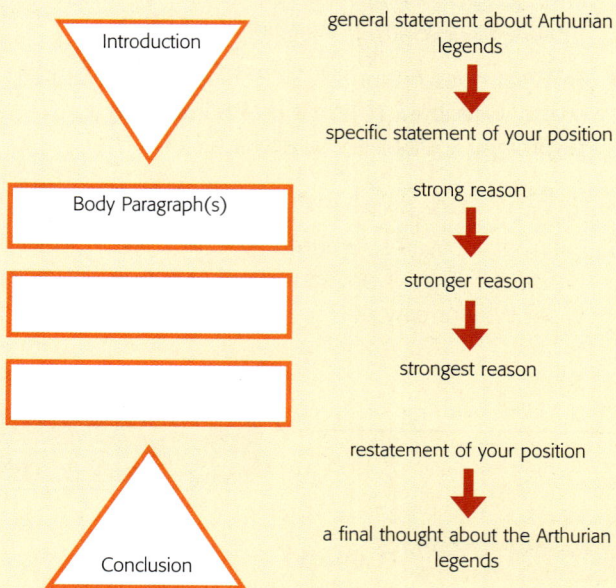

After you complete your draft, meet with a peer reviewer to evaluate each other's work and to suggest revisions. Then proofread and edit your draft for errors in spelling, grammar, and punctuation.

Interdisciplinary Activity: Psychology

There is an ancient belief that dreams can predict the future, as King Arthur thought in *Le Morte d'Arthur*. Using library and Internet resources, find out more about dream analysis, including archetypes common to many people's dreams. In an oral report, present your findings to the rest of your class.

Literature Online **Web Activities** For eFlashcards, Selection Quick Checks, and other Web activities, go to www.glencoe.com.

Vocabulary Workshop

Context Clues

Determining the Meaning of Unfamiliar Words

"Welcome, my sister's son; I thought that ye were dead. And now that I see thee alive, much am I beholden unto almighty Jesus."

—Sir Thomas Malory, from *Le Morte d'Arthur*

Connecting to Literature Sometimes an unfamiliar word's **context,** or the words that surround that word, can provide clues to the word's meaning. For example, in the line above, you can infer the meaning of *beholden* from its context. Because Arthur is happy that his nephew is alive, you can infer that Arthur feels indebted or grateful to Jesus for saving Gawain.

Types of Context Clues

- The context can provide an **example** of the word.
  The boy took the teacher's remark literally. *When she said, "We'll take the bull by the horns," he looked around for a bull.*

- A **contrast** implies that an unfamiliar word is the opposite of a familiar one.
  It is difficult to use literal *language to talk about being in love; people tend to talk about love by using figurative language and imagery.*

- A **restatement** of the word in context rewords it in a more familiar way.
  In poetry, a literal style seems out of place; however, in an essay, a matter-of-fact style is appropriate.*

- An unfamiliar word may be used as a **synonym** for another term.
  Nancy was so literal that she thought every comment I made was exact.

Exercise

For each item below, use context clues to determine the meaning of the underlined word. Identify which type of context clue you used.

1. Sir Gawain was sent to Arthur to quickly warn him of the <u>portending</u> danger of the next day's battle.
   a. impending **b.** bold **c.** horrifying **d.** pleasant

2. *Sir Gawain and the Green Knight* and *Le Morte d'Arthur* are <u>indigenous</u> English writings because they were written in England.
   a. rich **b.** native **c.** rare **d.** fictitious

3. In *Le Morte d'Arthur,* Malory shaped a loose group of Arthurian legends into a single, <u>homogeneous</u> narrative.
   a. unexpected **b.** complicated **c.** multiple **d.** unified

The Ballad Tradition

"O I fear ye are poisoned, Lord
   Randall, my son!
O I fear ye are poisoned, my
   handsome young man!"
"O yes, I am poisoned; Mother,
   make my bed soon,
For I'm sick at the heart, and I fain
   would lie doon."

—from "Lord Randall"

Robin Hood, Will Scarlet and Little John, 17th century. Ballad in woodcut form.

SIX CENTURIES AGO, MOST PEOPLE IN THE BRITISH Isles were unable to read or write. For entertainment, they relied upon traveling minstrels and local storytellers. These musicians and poets created **folk ballads**, or rhymed verse that is recited or sung, out of local stories and tall tales. During the Middle Ages, balladeers often resembled today's journalists; many ballads recounted actual events. Similar to the American Blues, folk ballads contain common tropes and characteristics. The typical ballad usually deals with one of the following topics:

- murderous acts and the desire for revenge
- tragic accidents and sudden disasters
- heroic deeds and quests for honor
- jealous sweethearts and unrequited love

For example, the stanza from "Lord Randall," quoted above, tells of a young man poisoned by his sweetheart.

The Ballad's Influence

Most of the English and Scottish ballads we know today date from after the fifteenth century. The authors of these ballads are unknown. In fact, a given ballad may exist in any number of versions, because of the memories and personal tastes of the many different people who passed it on from generation to generation. Ballads were first collected and published in the late eighteenth and early nineteenth centuries, most notably by Thomas Percy in *Reliques of Ancient English Poetry* (1765) and Sir Walter Scott in *Minstrelsy of the Scottish Border* (1802–1803). Samuel Coleridge, John Keats, and other Romantic poets were inspired by such collections of folk and medieval literature. These authors began to write **literary ballads**, or ballads that are written in imitation of folk ballads and have a known author.

Robin Hood—Ballad Hero

One of the most enduringly popular and widespread ballad themes is that of the noble outlaw. Robin Hood, the legendary bandit of Sherwood Forest who robbed from the rich and gave to the poor, became the hero of a cycle of ballads. The earliest of the surviving Robin Hood ballads date from the fifteenth and sixteenth centuries. In the same tradition, recent ballads have immortalized the American outlaw Jesse James as a modern Robin Hood.

"Then bold Robin Hood drew forth bugle horn,
  And he blew it both loud and shrill,
  And direct thereupon he espied Little John
  Come running a-down the hill."

—"Robin Hood and the Tanner"

Characteristics of the Folk Ballad

English and Scottish ballads share many characteristics:

- *Dramatization of a single incident.* The story begins abruptly, often in the middle of the action. Little attention is paid to characterization, background exposition, or description.

- *Little reflection or expression of sentiment.* Ballads focus on telling a story rather than what people thought or felt about the events.

- *Dialogue or questions and answers that further the story.* Typically, the tales are told through the speech of the characters rather than by a first-person narrator.

- *A strong, simple beat and an uncomplicated rhyme scheme or pattern.* The literary ballad differs from the folk ballad; it has a set metrical pattern and rhyme scheme. Coleridge's *The Rime of the Ancient Mariner* (pp. 805–826) is an example.

- *Use of refrain, repeated regularly throughout the ballad, often at the end of a stanza to emphasize ideas and add to the musical quality of the verse.* Ballads often employ incremental repetition, in which a line is repeated with small but significant changes as the poem approaches its climax. For an example, see "Sir Patrick Spens" (page 211), lines 33 and 37.

- *Use of a burden, or a complete lyrical stanza that is repeated after a narrative stanza.* Some ballads use a burden rather than a refrain. A burden is like a modern chorus. It allowed listeners to join in and gave singers time to remember verses.

Robin Hood, Holding a Bow and Arrow, ca. 1650. Woodcut.

- *The tendency to suggest rather than directly state.* Although sparsely told, ballads often contain sharp psychological portraits and much folk wisdom.

- *Stories that are often based on actual events.* These incidents—shipwrecks, murders, accidental deaths—might make headlines today.

The best of the folk ballads are among the most haunting narrative poems in British literature. They are still popular today, particularly among Irish folk singers. In the twentieth century, musical artists such as Bob Dylan and B. B. King employed variations of this storied lyrical form. The universal themes and compelling rhythms and rhymes of ballads continue to inspire and entertain.

Literature Online Literary History For more about the ballad tradition, go to www.glencoe.com.

RESPONDING AND THINKING CRITICALLY

1. Given the content of most ballads, what conclusions might you draw about the people who created them and the people who enjoyed them?

2. Why do you think musicians and poets continue to write and perform ballads?

3. (a) Who was the audience for most of the early folk ballads? (b) Why do you think Robin Hood became the hero of many of these ballads?

OBJECTIVES
- Analyze ballads.
- Connect literature to historical context.

Connecting to the Poems

Think about some of your favorite popular songs. As you read the ballads that follow, consider what makes certain songs memorable and why they appeal to many people.

Building Background

During medieval times, English and Scottish popular ballads were passed down orally and communally, from generation to generation and from region to region. Ballads were often sung to the accompaniment of a lute, rebec (rē′ bek), or other stringed instrument.

All three of the ballads you are about to read are Scottish.

- "Sir Patrick Spens" tells the story of sailors sent on an ill-fated voyage. It may be based on actual events from the thirteenth century.
- "Bonny Barbara Allan" tells a familiar, tragic story of disappointment in love.
- "Get Up and Bar the Door" is a comic ballad about married life—a favorite target of medieval humor.

Setting Purposes for Reading

Big Idea **The World of Romance**

As you read, notice how these ballads romanticize heroic and tragic stories of the period.

Literary Element **Ballad Stanza**

The **ballad stanza** is a quatrain, or four-line stanza. The first and third lines have four stressed syllables; the second and fourth lines have three. Only the second and fourth lines rhyme, and repetition of part or full lines is common. As you read these ballads, notice how each stanza follows or diverges from the ballad stanza form.

• See Literary Terms Handbook, p. R2.

Literature Online **Interactive Literary Elements Handbook** To review or learn more about the literary elements, go to www.glencoe.com.

Reading Strategy **Responding to Characters**

Responding to characters means thinking about how the characters in a selection make the reader or the audience feel. As you read these ballads, focus on the actions and dialogue of the characters to form your responses to them.

....

Reading Tip: Making a Response-Evidence Chart
As you read, respond to the characters. Then provide the evidence that informed your response.

> Character: The king from "Sir Patrick Spens"
> Response: The king is selfish and capricious.
>
> Evidence:
>
> The king ignores the dangers of sailing at a time of year when storms are frequent.

Vocabulary

dwell (dwel) *v.* to live as a resident; p. 213 *Before moving to London, Sayed dwelled in a small town.*

foremost (fôr′ mōst′) *adj.* ahead of all others or in the first position; p. 216 *As the foremost authority in his field, he was the obvious choice for department chair.*

....

Vocabulary Tip: Analogies An analogy is a comparison demonstrated in terms of a relationship between a pair of words.

OBJECTIVES
In studying these selections, you will focus on the following:
- analyzing literary periods
- analyzing ballad stanzas
- responding to characters

Tantallon Castle with the Bass Rock, c. 1816. Alexander Nasmyth. Oil on canvas, 92 x 122.3 cm. National Gallery of Scotland, Edinburgh.

Sir Patrick Spens

The king sits in Dumferling[1] town,
    Drinking the blude-red wine:
"O where will I get guid sailor,
    To sail this ship of mine?"

5 Up and spake an eldern knight
    Sat at the king's right knee:
"Sir Patrick Spens is the best sailor
    That sails upon the sea."

The king has written a braid[2] letter,
10   And signed it wi' his hand,
And sent it to Sir Patrick Spens
    Was walking on the sand.

The first line that Sir Patrick read,
    A loud laugh laughed he;
15 The next line that Sir Patrick read,
    A tear blinded his ee.

---

1. *Dumferling* is a town in Scotland—the site of a favorite home of Scottish kings.
2. *Braid* means "broad; emphatic."

Literary Element **Ballad Stanza** *How does this quatrain maintain the rhythm and rhyme of the ballad stanza?*

"O wha[3] is this has done this deed,
    This ill deed done to me,
To send me out this time o' the year,
20   To sail upon the sea!

Make haste, make haste, my merry men all,
    Our guid ship sails the morn:"
"O say na sae,[4] my master dear,
    For I fear a deadly storm.

25   "Late late yestreen I saw the new moon,
    Wi' the auld moon in her arm,[5]
And I fear, I fear, my dear master,
    That we will come to harm."

O our Scots nobles were right laith[6]
30   To weet[7] their cork-heeled shoone;[8]
But long owre[9] a' the play were played,
    Their hats they swam aboon.[10]

O long, long may their ladies sit,
    Wi' their fans into their hand,
35   Or eir they see Sir Patrick Spens
    Come sailing to the land.

O long, long may the ladies stand
    Wi' their gold kems[11] in their hair,
Waiting for their ain dear lords,
35   For they'll see them na mair.

Half o'er, half o'er to Aberdour,[12]
    It's fifty fathoms deep,
And there lies guid Sir Patrick Spens,
    Wi' the Scots lords at his feet.

---

3. *Wha* means "who."
4. *Na sae* means "not so."
5. *The new moon . . . arm* describes a bright crescent moon with the rest of the moon shining faintly.
6. *Laith* means "loath" or "unwilling."
7. *Weet* means "wet."
8. *Shoone* are shoes.
9. *Owre* means "before."
10. *Aboon* means "above."
11. *Kems* are combs.
12. *Aberdour* is a small town on the Scottish coast.

Reading Strategy   **Responding to Characters** *What does this quatrain reveal about Sir Patrick, and how would you now respond to his character?*

Big Idea   **The World of Romance** *How does this image reflect the romanticized tales and legends of the time?*

At Harvest Time, 1880. Jules Bastien-Lepage. Oil on canvas, 81.3 x 105.4 cm. Sotheby's, New York, NY.

Bonny Barbara Allan

It was in and about the Martinmas[1] time,
    When the green leaves were a falling,
That Sir John Graeme, in the West Country,
    Fell in love with Barbara Allan.

5   He sent his men down through the town,
    To the place where she was **dwelling**:
"O haste and come to my master dear,
    Gin[2] ye be Barbara Allan."

O hooly,[3] hooly rose she up,
10   To the place where he was lying,

---

1. *Martinmas* (St. Martin's Day) is celebrated on November 11.
2. *Gin* means "if."
3. *Hooly* means "slowly."

Literary Element   **Ballad Stanza** *Does this quatrain follow the typical rhyme scheme of the ballad stanza? How might singing or reciting the ballad contribute to the rhyme in a way that simply seeing it on the page might not?*

Vocabulary

dwell (dwel) *v.* to live as a resident

And when she drew the curtain by,
    "Young man, I think you're dying."

"O it's I'm sick, and very, very sick,
    And 'tis a' for Barbara Allan:"
15 "O the better for me ye's[4] never be,
    Though your heart's blood were a spilling.

"O dinna ye mind,[5] young man," said she,
    "When ye was in the tavern a drinking,
That ye made the healths gae[6] round and round,
20   And slighted Barbara Allan?"

He turned his face unto the wall,
    And death was with him dealing:
"Adieu, adieu, my dear friends all,
    And be kind to Barbara Allan."

25 And slowly, slowly raise she up,
    And slowly, slowly left him,
And sighing said, she coud not stay,
    Since death of life had reft[7] him.

She had not gane[8] a mile but twa[9]
30   When she heard the dead-bell[10] ringing,
And every jow[11] that the dead-bell geid,[12]
    It cry'd, "Woe to Barbara Allan!"

"O mother, mother, make my bed!
    O make it saft and narrow!
35 Since my love died for me today,
    I'll die for him tomorrow."

---

4. *Ye's* means "you shall."
5. *Dinna ye mind* means "don't you remember."
6. *Healths gae* means "toasts go."
7. *Reft* means "deprived."
8. *Gane* means "gone."
9. *Twa* means "two."
10. A *dead-bell* is a church bell rung when someone dies.
11. *Jow* means "stroke."
12. *Geid* means "gave."

Reading Strategy **Responding to Characters** *Knowing that Graeme slighted Barbara Allan publicly, how might you respond to his character after these last words?*

Big Idea **The World of Romance** *How does Barbara Allan's final action reflect the attitudes toward romantic love that were popular during medieval times?*

Cottage and Pond, Moonlight, c. 1780. Thomas Gainsborough. Oil on glass, 28 x 33.6 cm. Victoria and Albert Museum, London.

Get Up and Bar the Door

It fell about the Martinmas time,
   And a gay time it was then,
When our goodwife got puddings[1] to make,
   And she's boiled them in the pan.

5   The wind sae cauld blew south and north
   And blew into the floor;
Quoth our goodman to our goodwife,
   "Gae out and bar the door."

"My hand is in my hussyfskap,[2]
10   Goodman, as ye may see;
An it should nae[3] be barred this hundred year,
   It s' no be barred for me."

They made a paction[4] tween them twa,
   They made it firm and sure,
15   That the first word whaeer[5] should speak
   Should rise and bar the door.

Then by there came two gentlemen,
   At twelve o'clock at night,
And they could neither see house nor hall,
20   Nor coal nor candle-light.

---

1. *Puddings* are sausages.
2. *Hussyfskap* means "household chores."
3. [*An . . . nae*] means "if it should not."
4. A *paction* is an agreement.
5. *Whaeer* means "whoever."

"Now whether is this a rich man's house,
   Or whether is it a poor?"
But neer a word wad ane o' them speak,
   For barring of the door.

25   And first they[6] ate the white puddings,
   And then they ate the black;
Tho muckle[7] thought the goodwife to hersel,
   Yet neer a word she spake.

Then said the one unto the other,
30   "Here, man, tak ye my knife;
Do ye tak aff the auld man's beard,
   And I'll kiss the goodwife."

"But there's nae water in the house,
   And what shall we do then?"
35   "What ails ye at the pudding-broo[8]
   That boils into the pan?"

O up then started our goodman,
   An angry man was he:
"Will ye kiss my wife before my een
40   And scad[9] me wi' pudding-bree?"[10]

Then up and started our goodwife,
   Gied three skips on the floor:
"Goodman, you've spoken the **foremost** word,
   Get up and bar the door!"

---

6. *They* refers to the two gentlemen.
7. *Muckle* means "a great deal."
8. *[What ails . . . broo]* means "What's wrong with using the pudding broth?"
9. *Scad* means "scald."
10. *Bree* means "broth."

Literary Element Ballad Stanza *How does this quatrain maintain or diverge from the traditional ballad stanza form?*

Big Idea The World of Romance *How are the ideals of heroism, chivalry, and romantic love portrayed in this ballad?*

Reading Strategy Responding to Characters *What is your response to the wife's comment?*

Vocabulary

foremost (fôr´ mōst´) *adj.* ahead of all others or in the first position

RESPONDING AND THINKING CRITICALLY

Respond

1. Which ballad did you like best, and what in particular impressed you about that ballad?

Recall and Interpret

2. (a)Contrast the two settings mentioned in the ballad "Sir Patrick Spens." Where is the king? Where is Sir Patrick? (b)How does the contrast help define the two characters?

3. (a)What does Barbara Allan ask her mother to do for her? (b)What does her request suggest about her true feelings for John Graeme?

4. (a)In "Get Up and Bar the Door," what excuse does the wife give to her husband for not barring the door herself? (b)Is this her real reason? Explain.

Analyze and Evaluate

5. Do you think Sir Patrick did the right thing? Support your answer with details from the ballad.

6. How might "Bonny Barbara Allan" have been more or less effective if the writer had included the characters' thoughts and emotions?

7. What techniques does the writer use to create the humorous tone in "Get Up and Bar the Door"? Support your answer with details from the poem.

Connect

8. **Big Idea** **The World of Romance** How is marriage in "Get Up and Bar the Door" shown to be at odds with the ideals of the medieval period?

LITERARY ANALYSIS

Literary Element **Ballad Stanza**

Repetition of lines, phrases, and words is common in ballads. Such repetition is often used to emphasize a particular tone or theme or to maintain the rhythm of the ballad within or between stanzas.

1. In "Sir Patrick Spens," how does the repetition in the fourth stanza contribute to the emotional effect of the ballad?

2. (a)How is the expression "bar the door" expressed throughout "Get Up and Bar the Door"? (b)What effect does this imprecise repetition have on the poem?

Writing About Literature

Analyze Genre Elements Each ballad is a narrative poem that tells a story—often one based on actual events. Refer to page 209 to help you recall the other distinguishing features of ballads. Paraphrase in prose form one of the three ballads you read. Then write a brief essay to explain what the ballad gains or loses by being paraphrased.

Literature Online **Web Activities** For eFlashcards, Selection Quick Checks, and other Web activities, go to www.glencoe.com.

READING AND VOCABULARY

Reading Strategy **Responding to Characters**

A **dynamic character** grows and changes, whereas a **static character** remains basically unchanged, even though things happen to him or her.

1. In "Sir Patrick Spens," decide whether the king and Sir Patrick are dynamic characters or static ones. How can you tell?

2. Are the husband and wife in "Get Up and Bar the Door" dynamic characters or static ones? How do you know?

Vocabulary **Practice**

Practice with Analogies Complete each analogy below.

1. resident : dwell :: architect :
   a. design   **c.** building
   b. build   **d.** architecture

2. foremost : paramount :: peak :
   a. climb   **c.** nadir
   b. valley   **d.** pinnacle

Writing Workshop

Descriptive Essay

 ### Describing a Character

> "He had his son with him, a fine young Squire,
> A lover and a cadet, a lad of fire
> With locks as curly as if they had been pressed.
> He was some twenty years of age, I guessed."
>
> —Geoffrey Chaucer, from *The Canterbury Tales*

Connecting to Literature Throughout *The Canterbury Tales*, Chaucer describes each pilgrim's most distinguishing characteristics—in the process both revealing the pilgrim's character and creating a vivid, lasting impression. Similarly, when writing a descriptive essay about a character, you choose details that will make the person you are describing believable and memorable to your audience. To write a successful essay, follow the goals and strategies of descriptive essay writing.

Rubric: Features of Descriptive Essays

Goals	Strategies
To identify and describe a real or fictional character	☑ Focus on the distinguishing characteristics of a character to make him or her memorable to others.
To use descriptive details	☑ Vividly describe the character's physical features. Use sensory details and figurative language to enhance your description.
To elaborate on the character's qualities	☑ Describe the character's thoughts, attitudes, and behavior. Use anecdotes and dialogue to bring the character to life.
To create a lasting impression for an audience	☑ Organize your essay in a clear, effective order. Include only important details that contribute to the dominant impression.

The Writing Process

In this workshop, you will follow the stages of the writing process. At any stage, you may think of new ideas to include and better ways to express them. Feel free to return to earlier stages as you write.

Prewriting

- - - - - - - - - - - - -

Drafting

- - - - - - - - - - - - -

Revising

- - - - - - - - - - - - -

➡ Focus Lesson: Elaborating with Descriptive Details

Editing and Proofreading

➡ Focus Lesson: Using Semicolons

Presenting

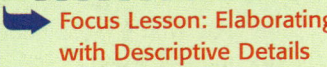
Writing Models For models and other writing activities, go to www.glencoe.com.

OBJECTIVES
Write a descriptive essay about a memorable character. Use description and elaboration to create a vivid, lasting picture of the character for your audience.

> **Assignment**
>
> Write a vivid descriptive essay about a person (real or fictional) in which you make that person memorable to others. As you move through the stages of the writing process, keep your audience and purpose in mind.
>
> ---
>
> **Audience:** peers, classmates, and teacher
>
> **Purpose:** to create a vivid and memorable impression of your character

Analyzing a Professional Model

In the following selection, Booker Prize–winning author Penelope Lively describes her grandmother and the woman's seemingly steadfast convictions despite changing times. As you read the following passage, notice how Lively uses vivid details and controls the reader's impression of her subject. Pay close attention to the comments in the margin; they point out features that you might want to include in your own descriptive essay.

From *A House Unlocked* by Penelope Lively

When I summon up the late 1940s, the vision is a profoundly confusing one. There is a sense in which I am still there, a lumpen teenager, gripped by the roller-coaster emotions of that turbulent period in life. I am too tall, too tongue-tied, my hair is frizzy, my legs unshapely. I wear glasses and, down here in Somerset, where such things matter, I am no good on a horse. On the other hand, Golsoncott is the safe haven, the calm security from which I can mull over my own deficiencies, take stock of a perplexing world and undergo the slow metamorphosis into adult life.

All the while, my grandmother is an abiding presence—brisk, merry, unshakeable in her convictions. On public occasions, I take shelter behind her rock-solid confidence in the society with which she is familiar. She knows what to say when and to whom, she is never stuck for a comment or an opinion, she is deft about such stultifying embarrassments as how to locate the lavatory in an unfamiliar environment. I was devoted to her, and still am. But I was beginning to question her assumptions: about religion, about social structure. We argued—good-humoredly. For my part,

Introduction

Give your readers important background information to set the stage for your character description.

Subject

Choose an interesting character to describe.

I was increasingly less certain that she was right about everything, though that in no way diminished my regard for her; she saw me as a normally disaffected schoolgirl who would come round to a proper outlook in due course.

Descriptive Details
Use vivid details and sensory images to describe the character.

In my head, my grandmother is always aged around seventy. Her grey hair is set in neat rolls and confined within an invisible net. She wears a tweed skirt, a blouse and cardigan in winter, linen dresses in summer. Lisle stockings, always. A large hessian apron is tied round her waist for garden-

Elaboration
Elaborate on your description to reveal a character's behavior, attitudes, and emotions, bringing him or her to "life" for your readers.

ing, its pockets bristling with secateurs, raffia, pruning knife. When I hugged her I could feel the carapace of her corset, never discarded, even in the hottest weather. For the evening, she changed into a long red velveteen house-coat, worn with a rope of ivory beads. Her presence seemed to animate the house. When she was out, the whole place went very still; when she was at home, her brisk step rang on the stairs and along the passages, you heard her humming and singing, you heard her laughter. She could share a joke, and had a sense of the ridiculous. But there was an implacable code of conduct, and minefields on all sides. Good manners were considered paramount—the decent consideration of each towards all. Excessive behavior or bad language

Elaboration
Use anecdotes that tell about important moments in the character's life.

brought instant disapproval: once, a young woman visitor, inflamed by sherry, tossed a cushion across the Golsoncott drawing-room to a friend, and was never invited to the house again. My grandmother became tight-lipped at any sexual inference. On another occasion, when she was in her eighties, we had to leave a concert in the interval because a couple in the row in front had been kissing. Sheltered from the tabloid press, and listening only to BBC Home Service and Third Programme, she was immune to much of the changing climate of the fifties, let alone the sixties. But occasionally the licence of the times filtered through to her; her condemnation was absolute and unrelenting. Skimpy clothing on women was a particular affront. The

Conclusion
Use dialogue to leave a lasting impression of the character.

miniskirt made public outings an ordeal. But then, bizarrely, she rounded on the ankle-length skirts and coats of the seventies: "Ridiculous! Why go back to all that clutter!"

Reading–Writing Connection Think about the writing techniques that you just encountered and try them out in the descriptive essay you write.

Prewriting

Gather Ideas As you ponder subjects to write about, think of people who have made a significant impression on you or your life. Or, if you prefer, create a fictional character that would leave your audience with a lasting impression.

Choose a Subject Use the following criteria to help you choose a memorable character to describe.

▶ **Choose a familiar subject** It is easier to write vividly about a subject you know or remember well. Think about someone who has influenced you directly. If you are making up a character, fully imagine the physical traits, attitudes, behaviors, and speech that you will need to make that character believable.

▶ **Choose a meaningful subject** Choose a character who is meaningful to you personally. Consider what specifically makes that character memorable to you and how to leave your audience with a similar impression.

▶ **Choose a complex subject or a new approach** To hold your readers' interest, choose a subject who is unusual or multifaceted and will give you something fresh to describe. Try to choose a character that may not be obviously important to you (or one that might be important but for unexpected reasons). For example, an eccentric neighbor from your childhood may have made a strong impression on you or your life.

Organize Details Visualize the character you have chosen, concentrating on his or her most striking characteristics. To organize your description, arrange the important details in a graphic organizer like the one shown below.

Character	Character Traits
Grandpa Bob	is a good listener, loves animals, loves the outdoors, is timid
Lisbeth, my neighbor	is friendly, funny, a good gardener, a great storyteller
Marco	is a great best friend, loyal, funny; loves soccer

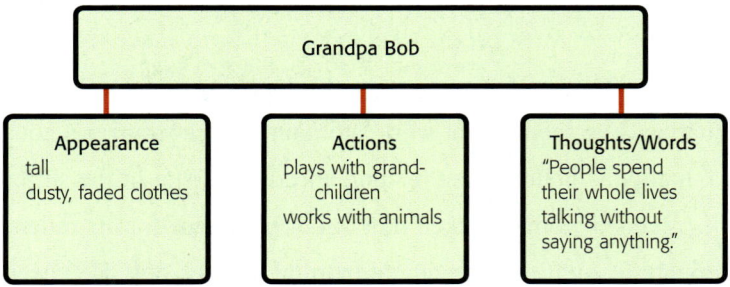

Make an Impression Before you begin drafting, clarify the overall impression you want to create for your audience. What makes the character special to you? This unique perspective is the *point* of your description. The overall impression you want to create will help you decide which details to include and which to omit.

Talk About Your Ideas To help develop a natural writing voice and a conversational tone, describe your character aloud to a partner. Check to ensure that your partner's impression of your character matches the one you want to convey, and note which details you should add or delete.

Drafting

Bring Your Character to Life Using your plan as a guide, begin drafting your descriptive essay. Refer often to the notes you made earlier but feel free to add new ideas that come to you as you write. Occasionally look back at your unfinished draft and check to be sure that the details you include contribute to the overall impression you want to give your readers.

Analyzing a Workshop Model

Here is a final draft of a descriptive essay. Read the essay and answer the questions in the margin. Use the answers to these questions to guide you as you write.

Descriptive Details

What type of details make Grandpa Bob believable?

Subject

What makes this character an interesting subject?

Elaboration

How does this anecdote reveal Grandpa's character?

Dialogue

How does including dialogue help make the character convincing?

Elaboration

How might noting this gesture make the description of Grandpa more vivid?

Gruff Grandpa Bob

Standing about six feet tall in cowboy boots, wearing a faded bandana below his bronzed, weathered face, my grandpa Bob looks as if he belongs outdoors. His clothes always seem faintly dusty, even right after they have been washed, and his hair is bleached and wild from decades in the sun and wind. When he steps inside, the smell of hay and damp soil rises from his clothes like steam. He likes to keep his coat on and his walking stick near, just in case he has to go outside quickly, and he never sits down unless he's eating—sometimes not even then. As my grandpa himself would admit, he gets along better with animals than most people. Most people tend to keep their distance from him.

He has lived in Montana for much of his life, making house calls as the local veterinarian. I've seen him at work, stomping into a stranger's house or barn with hardly a "hello," often rushing ahead in pursuit of the suffering animal. One offended woman kicked him out of her house for his rudeness. Grandpa, though, wouldn't leave without helping her sick dog. He paced for half an hour on the woman's porch; finally she let him in. "What's more important," he said frankly, "making small talk with someone or healing her poor dog?" Although he usually makes people nervous, their pets relax in his presence. I've seen spooked horses calmed with a few of his firm words or his careful touch. Even stray cats allow him to check behind their ears for fleas. When they see him on the street, people approach him to thank him—sometimes years later—for coming out after midnight to set a horse's leg or to perform emergency surgery on a dog. He reddens and looks down at the sidewalk with his hands thrust deep in the pockets of his faded jeans."All right, then,"

he says, nodding shyly. "All right." Then he makes a dash for his truck.

He tried to retire when he turned sixty-five, but people kept calling him. My grandma wanted him to have more time for himself, but I think she knew it wouldn't last. "Oh, just go," she would tell him. "You'll drive yourself crazy moping around here."

My grandparents have been married for forty-five years, although I've rarely caught them having a typical conversation together. My grandma does most of the talking, but Grandpa never seems to grow tired of her company. Even though he inevitably grumbles under his breath every time Grandma tells him to take off his muddy boots when he comes inside (and she does tell him, every time), you can tell by the way he looks at her and listens to her that he respects her completely. If she's happy, he'll shoot her a wink when he thinks no one's looking; if she's upset, he'll reach across the table and softly enclose her tiny, shaking hand between his own callused palms.

In his quiet way, Grandpa is a supportive father. He gives my dad and his brothers a hand—whether it's as someone to listen to their troubles or just someone to help paint the garage. Despite his gruff reputation, he's also a great grandpa. Unlike most adults, he isn't afraid to run around the fields and play with his grandchildren or let us watch him work on an animal he's treating. He knows how to keep a secret and can get me to talk about a problem that I want to discuss but don't have the nerve to bring up.

Now that he's in his seventies, he's traded in his walking stick for a cane. Most of the townspeople are used to him by now, but the new ones are often a little shocked when they first meet him. "People spend their whole lives talking without saying anything," he once told me. "They might accomplish something worthwhile if they just listened to someone else for a minute." I couldn't agree more.

Descriptive Details

Why might the writer have chosen to focus on Grandpa's actions here, rather than his thoughts or words?

Conversational Tone

Why might the writer have chosen a conversational tone for this descriptive essay?

Organization

Why does the writer describe Grandpa's more sensitive traits at the end, rather than at the beginning of the essay?

Dominant Impression

How does the conclusion help give the audience a lasting impression of Grandpa?

Revising

Peer Review Once you complete your draft, exchange papers with a partner. Have your partner note any areas that could use more vivid details, dialogue, or other elaboration. Then have your partner tell his or her impression of your subject. If the impression is not what you intended, discuss ways to clarify your description.

Use the rubric below to help you evaluate and strengthen your essay.

Traits of Strong Writing

Ideas message or theme and the details that develop it

Organization arrangement of main ideas and supporting details

Voice writer's unique way of using tone and style

Word Choice vocabulary a writer uses to convey meaning

Sentence Fluency rhythm and flow of sentences

Conventions correct spelling, grammar, usage, and mechanics

Presentation the way words and design elements look on a page

For more information on using the Traits of Strong Writing, see pages R33–R34 in the Writing Handbook.

Rubric: Writing an Effective Descriptive Essay
☑ Do you describe a meaningful character?
☑ Do you describe a complex subject or present a fresh perspective on a common subject?
☑ Do you use descriptive details to show the character's appearance, attitudes, and behavior?
☑ Do you elaborate on the character's qualities, including sensory details, dialogue, figurative language, and anecdotes to bring your character to life?
☑ Do you leave your readers with a clear and memorable impression?

► **Focus Lesson**

Elaborating with Descriptive Details

After you delete unimportant or distracting details from your essay, focus on elaborating with details to help make your character seem as real to your audience as he or she is to you. Think of sensory details—such as sounds, smells, and textures—to enhance physical descriptions. Describe actions and gestures that reveal personality and emotion. For example, instead of *saying* that someone is anxious, *show* the character pacing or fidgeting. Use dialogue and anecdotes to develop your character further, as in the example below.

Draft:

He gets embarrassed and doesn't say much.

Revision:

He reddens and <u>looks down at the sidewalk with his hands thrust deep in the pockets</u>[1] of his faded jeans. <u>"All right, then," he says, nodding shyly. "All right."</u>[2] Then he <u>makes a dash for his truck.</u>[3]

1: Describe gestures that reveal emotion.

2: Use dialogue to reveal attitudes and personality.

3: Describe actions that show the character's thoughts.

Editing and Proofreading

Get It Right When you have completed the final draft of your essay, proofread it for errors in grammar, usage, mechanics, and spelling. Refer to the Language Handbook, pages R46–R60, as a guide.

▶ **Focus Lesson**

Using Semicolons

One use of a semicolon (;) is to join main clauses. In this construction, a semicolon can always take the place of a period. Often semicolons are used instead of periods to connect short, choppy sentences, particularly when the sentences are parallel in construction. Like conjunctions, semicolons can also be used to correct comma splices. Use semicolons sparingly to add variety to your writing.

Problem: Comma splice

If she's happy, he'll shoot her a wink when he thinks no one's looking, if she's upset, he'll reach across the table and softly enclose her tiny, shaking hand between his own callused palms.

Solution: To avoid a comma splice, join two main clauses with a semicolon.

If she's happy, he'll shoot her a wink when he thinks no one's looking; if she's upset, he'll reach across the table and softly enclose her tiny, shaking hand between his own callused palms.

Problem: Short, choppy sentences

He paced for half an hour on the woman's porch. Finally she let him in.

Solution: Connect short, choppy sentences with a semicolon.

He paced for half an hour on the woman's porch; finally she let him in.

Presenting

Finishing Touches Before handing in your revised descriptive essay, be sure that it is typed or neatly handwritten and that you turn in the correct, revised version. Check to see that you have followed your teacher's general guidelines, including length, spacing, font size, and margin requirements. After you turn in your final draft, consider sharing your description with your subject or with people who know him or her.

Writer's Portfolio

Place a clean copy of your descriptive essay in your portfolio to review later.

Speaking, Listening, and Viewing Workshop

Photo-Essay

Presenting a Photo-Essay

"He had his son with him, a fine young Squire,
a lover and cadet, a lad of fire
with locks as curly as if they had been pressed."

—Geoffrey Chaucer, *The Canterbury Tales*

Connecting to Literature In "The Prologue" to *The Canterbury Tales,* Chaucer describes his characters in great detail. As one critic comments, "Not a whisper, not a wart, is omitted." Artists have since used Chaucer's description to create images of what the Squire or the Knight may have looked like, as seen in the images on this page.

The Squire, detail from *The Canterbury Tales,* 15th c. English School. Vellum. Huntington Library and Art Gallery, San Marino, CA.

You can also use images to describe or represent a person. In a photo-essay, an artist combines photographs, images, and artifacts to represent a person or time in history. The images in a photo-essay should show the audience why the person represented is interesting and noteworthy.

> **Finding the Right Image**
> Photo-essays often include other kinds of images besides photographs. You can also use drawings, illustrations, or visuals such as posters or collages.

> ▶ **Assignment**   **Plan and deliver a photo-essay about someone you admire.**

The Prioress, detail from *The Canterbury Tales,* 15th c. English School. Vellum. Huntington Library and Art Gallery, San Marino, CA.

The Manciple, detail from *The Canterbury Tales,* 15th c. English School. Vellum. Huntington Library and Art Gallery, San Marino, CA.

The Canon's Yeoman, detail from *The Canterbury Tales,* 15th c. English School. Vellum. Huntington Library and Art Gallery, San Marino, CA.

Planning Your Presentation

Think about what it is you want to convey about the person you are presenting to the audience. Then consider what images can best communicate that message. Just like a written essay, a photo-essay needs to have a main idea. Ask yourself: Why is this person interesting to me? Your presentation should show how the person you are presenting has influenced history, society, or your life. You can brainstorm ideas for appropriate images by making a list or chart.

Follow these guidelines when presenting an art essay or photo-essay.

- Research your subject well and present a clear main idea.
- Support your ideas with well-chosen images, examples, stories, and anecdotes.
- Decide how you will showcase your work. Will you use an easel, sheets of poster board, a slide projector, or a computer presentation? How will you organize your images?

Creating Meaning in Visual Media

The pictures you choose to include in your photo-essay need to convey emotion and feeling to the audience. Your images should be unusual and visually striking in order to stand out among everyday images. In addition, consider whether your images would convey your main idea more effectively if some were manipulated. For example, you might want to enlarge an important image, crop an image to focus on a part of it, or create a **montage,** that is, an image made up of several different images, to present several aspects of your subject at once.

Techniques for Delivering a Photo-Essay

Verbal Techniques	Nonverbal Techniques
☑ **Volume** Speak loudly and slowly enough so that your audience can understand the background information you provide.	☑ **Eye Contact** Make frequent eye contact with the audience; however, you should also look at the photographs or art to draw attention to important details.
☑ **Pace** Allow the audience enough time to view and react to each piece of your essay before moving on to the next photograph.	☑ **Gestures** Use gestures to emphasize ideas in your essay when appropriate.
☑ **Tone** Define any terms your audience may be unfamiliar with; describe any places your audience may not have visited.	☑ **Display** Show your images prominently enough so that your entire audience can see them clearly.

Rehearsing

You do not need to memorize your presentation of a photo-essay. However, you should practice and familiarize yourself with what you intend to say so that you will feel comfortable when presenting.

OBJECTIVES
- Connect visual media to personal experience.
- Speak effectively to explain and justify ideas to peers.

For Independent Reading

BEFORE THE ADVENT OF CHRISTIANITY IN BRITAIN, THERE WERE NO BOOKS. THE FIRST BOOKS were produced in monasteries where Anglo-Saxon monks copied religious texts written in Latin onto vellum, a fine parchment made from the skin of a calf. Printing did not come to England until 1476, when William Caxton set up a wooden printing press in a shop near Westminster Abbey. Even with this advance, few people of the time could read. They could listen, however, and traveling minstrels and members of the clergy created a great body of oral literature in order to teach and entertain. Much of this literature was eventually written down.

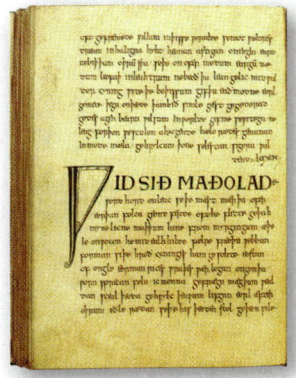

Anglo-Saxon Riddles

We know about Old English riddles today due to their inclusion in the Exeter Book (shown above), which Leofric, the first bishop of Exeter, willed to the library of Exeter Cathedral in southwestern England before his death in 1072. The book contains thirty-one poems and ninety-five riddles. Try to guess the answer to the following riddle. (A *lay* is a short poem meant to be sung.)

> A moth ate words; a marvelous event
> I thought it when I heard about that wonder,
> A worm had swallowed some man's lay, a thief
> In darkness had consumed the mighty saying
> With its foundation firm. The thief was not
> One whit the wiser when he ate those words.

Anglo-Saxon riddles can be quite clever as evidenced by the answer to the one above—a bookworm.

Heroic Poems

Old English poetry often is about brave deeds, allegiance to a military leader, and accounts of victories or, sometimes, defeats. "The Battle of Maldon" is one such poem, inspired by a battle between invading Danes and English defenders in 991. The beginning and ending of the poem no longer exist, but enough remains for readers to visualize what happened during that battle in southeastern England. The English army, led by Byrtnoth, lost the battle. Byrtnoth was killed, and his most faithful men fought on until they, too, were killed. Some soldiers fled the battle, however, and are condemned by the unknown poet.

When William Caxton began printing in 1476, many forms of English existed and there was no standardized spelling. The following anecdote expresses Caxton's frustration over the various words being used for *eggs*.

" . . . *Sheffelde, a mercer, cam in-to an hows and axed for mete; and specyally he axyed after eggys; and the good wyf answerde, that she coude speke no frenshe. And the merchaunt was angry, for he also coude speke no frenshe, but wolde haue hadde 'egges' and she vunderstode hym not. And theene at laste another sayd that he wolde haue 'eyren' then the good wyf sayd that she vunderstod hym wel. Loo, what sholde a man in thyse dayes now wryte, 'egges' or 'eyren'?*"

—William Caxton

Lyrics and Carols

Lyrics and carols were both popular literary forms during the Middle Ages. A *lyric* is a short poem or verse that may or may not be sung. One of the earliest lyrics is "Sumer is icumen in," commonly known as "The Cuckoo Song," written in Middle English by an unknown poet.

A carol is a song of praise or joy. Although today carols are often associated only with Christmas, in medieval times carols could be sung on or about any occasion. "The Agincourt Carol" is a famous one that celebrates the victory of King Henry V at Agincourt in Normandy in 1415.

From the Glencoe Literature Library

Beowulf

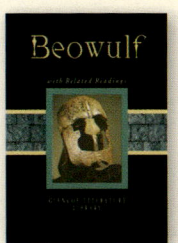

This powerful Anglo-Saxon epic follows Beowulf, the greatest of the Geat warriors through various adventures including his battle with Grendel, Grendel's mother, and his final encounter with a dragon before his death.

The Canterbury Tales

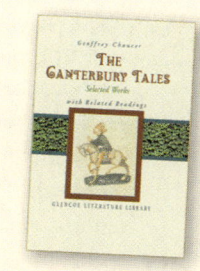

In *The Canterbury Tales*, a group of men and women meet at an inn to begin a pilgrimage to the shrine of Thomas à Becket in Canterbury. The inn's host suggests that they while away their time on the long journey by telling stories. Chaucer presents an array of colorful characters who vary widely in social standing, occupation, morality, and wit. The pilgrims come to life through the narrator's vivid descriptions and through the tales they tell.

Test Preparation and Practice

English–Language Arts

Reading: Nonfiction

Carefully read the following passage. Use context clues to help you define any words with which you are unfamiliar. Pay close attention to cause-and-effect relationships, the conflicts described, and the tone. Then, on a separate sheet of paper, answer the questions that follow.

from *The Ecclesiastical History of the English People* by the Venerable Bede

line

From that time, the south part of Britain, destitute of armed soldiers, of martial stores, and of all its active youth, which had been led away by the rashness of the tyrants, never to return . . . suffered many years under two very savage foreign nations, the Scots from the west, and the Picts from the north. We call these foreign nations, not on account of their being seated out of Britain, but because
5 they were remote from that part of it which was possessed by the Britons . . .

On account of the irruption of these nations, the Britons sent messengers to Rome with letters in mournful manner . . . An armed legion was immediately sent them, which, arriving in the island, and engaging the enemy, slew a great multitude of them, drove the rest out of the territories of their allies, and having delivered them from their cruel oppressors, advised them to build a wall between the two
10 seas across the island, that it might secure them, and keep off the enemy; and thus they returned home with great triumph . . .

But the former enemies, when they perceived that the Roman soldiers were gone, immediately coming by sea, broke into the borders, trampled and overran all places, and like men mowing ripe corn, bore down all before them. Hereupon messengers are again sent to Rome, imploring aid . . . A
15 legion is accordingly sent again, and, arriving unexpectedly in autumn, made great slaughter of the enemy . . . Then the Romans declared to the Britons, that they could not for the future undertake such troublesome expeditions for their sake, advising them rather to handle their weapons like men, and undertake themselves the charge of engaging their enemies, who would not prove too powerful for them, unless they were deterred by cowardice; and, thinking that it might be some help to the
20 allies, whom they were forced to abandon, they built a strong stone wall from sea to sea . . . This famous wall, which is still to be seen, was built at the public and private expense, the Britons also lending their assistance. It is eight feet in breadth, and twelve in height, in a straight line from east to west, as is still visible to beholders . . .

After their departure, the Scots and Picts, understanding that they had declared they would come
25 no more, speedily returned, and growing more confident than they had been before, occupied all the northern and farthest part of the island, as far as the wall . . . At last, the Britons, forsaking their cities and wall, took to flight and were dispersed. The enemy pursued, and the slaughter was greater than

on any former occasion; for the wretched natives were torn in pieces by their enemies, as lambs are torn by wild beasts. Thus, being expelled their dwellings and possessions, they saved themselves from

30   starvation, by robbing and plundering one another, adding to the calamities occasioned by foreigners . . . till the whole country was left destitute of food, except such as could be procured in the chase.

1. According to Bede, what caused the lack of an active youth in Britain?
   A. The youth had gone to sea.
   B. The youth had been killed in battles with the Scots and Picts.
   C. The people were destitute.
   D. The people were afraid to fight.
   E. Tyrants took them away.

2. For what reason does Bede claim that the Scots and Picts were "foreign nations"?
   A. They lived in a remote part of the island.
   B. They were invaders.
   C. They were from outside Britain.
   D. They were not Christian.
   E. They were Nordic raiders.

3. Which of the following was an immediate effect of the first invasion of Britain described in the passage?
   A. The Picts and Scots were slaughtered.
   B. The Britons sent messengers to Rome.
   C. The Romans abandoned the Britons.
   D. The Romans were forced to flee.
   E. A defensive wall was built to defend the Britons.

4. According to the context, what does the word *slew*, in line 8, mean?
   A. chased
   B. killed
   C. overran
   D. frightened
   E. removed

5. According to Bede, what caused the Scots and Picts to return?
   A. The defensive wall was never built.
   B. The Britons were unable to defend themselves.
   C. There were too few resources in their own countries.
   D. They realized that the Romans had departed.
   E. They wished to join the Romans.

6. According to the context, what does the word *imploring*, in line 14, mean?
   A. refusing
   B. expecting
   C. issuing
   D. begging
   E. remembering

7. According to the context, what does the word *deterred*, in line 19, mean?
   A. frightened
   B. ashamed
   C. restrained
   D. amused
   E. reassured

8. Why did the Scots and Picts become "more confident than they had been before"?
   A. They had overcome Roman defenses.
   B. They knew that the Romans would not return.
   C. They had captured the northernmost part of the island.
   D. The Britons had abandoned their cities.
   E. The Britons had demonstrated their inability to fight.

9. To what does Bede compare the Scots and Picts?
   A. Britons
   B. Romans
   C. wild beasts
   D. lambs
   E. the natives

10. According to Bede, how did some Britons save themselves?
   A. They joined the Scots and Picts.
   B. They robbed other Britons.
   C. They fled to Rome.
   D. They defeated the invaders.
   E. They built a defensive wall.

11. From the context, what do you conclude that the word *calamities*, in line 30, means?
  A. wars
  B. friendships
  C. illnesses
  D. deaths
  E. disasters

12. Which group or individual is the main protagonist in this passage?
  A. the Romans
  B. the Picts
  C. the Scots
  D. the Britons
  E. Bede

13. Which of the following best describes the main external conflict represented in this passage?
  A. man against man
  B. man against nature
  C. man against society
  D. man against fate
  E. man against the divine

14. What is the overall tone of this passage?
  A. angry
  B. ironic
  C. authoritative
  D. skeptical
  E. sarcastic

15. From this selection, what do you conclude the author's main purpose was?
  A. to inform
  B. to persuade
  C. to instruct
  D. to entertain
  E. to tell a story

Literature Online **Unit Assessment** To prepare for the Unit test, go to www.glencoe.com.

232 UNIT 1   THE ANGLO-SAXON PERIOD AND THE MIDDLE AGES

Vocabulary Skills: Sentence Completion

For each item in the Vocabulary Skills section, choose the word or words that best complete the sentence.

1. Both the aristocracy and the peasantry faced great _____ during the Medieval period.
   A. composure
   B. adversity
   C. respite
   D. arrrogance
   E. adversary

2. The _____ Viking raiders were known throughout Europe for their unmerciful violence.
   A. solicitous
   B. discreet
   C. infamous
   D. forged
   E. writhing

3. During England's Anglo-Saxon period, seafaring was filled with _____ and misery.
   A. reckoning
   B. instigation
   C. prevarication
   D. shroud
   E. peril

4. Knights during the Medieval period were expected to be gallant and to _____ to attain the chivalrous ideal.
   A. blanch
   B. aspire
   C. slander
   D. dwell
   E. divulge

5. Anglo-Saxon poetry is filled with _____ imagery that conveys the themes of loss and misery.
   A. doleful
   B. estimable
   C. blithe
   D. intrepid
   E. frivolous

6. The clergy and the nobility were required at various times to _____ the unwieldy power of the monarch.
   A. perceive
   B. brandish
   C. concede
   D. restrain
   E. flourish

7. The two _____ causes of death during the 1300s were war and the bubonic plague.
   A. dauntless
   B. diligent
   C. disdainful
   D. discreet
   E. foremost

8. Intense _____ culminated in the brutal Hundred Years' War.
   A. rancor
   B. jeopardy
   C. lament
   D. composure
   E. arrogance

9. The power of the church _____ during the Medieval period like at no other time.
   A. expounded
   B. admonished
   C. flourished
   D. divulged
   E. slandered

10. Those who _____ in Europe's monasteries dedicated their lives to work and prayer.
    A. dispersed
    B. dwelled
    C. blanched
    D. perceived
    E. brandished

Grammar and Writing Skills: Paragraph Improvement

Read carefully through the opening paragraphs from the first draft of a student's descriptive essay. Pay close attention to the writer's use of verb tense, commas, and pronouns. Then, on a separate sheet of paper, answer the questions below.

(1) *My father is one of the most amazing men I have ever met.* (2) *Hes a big guy.* (3) *At over six feet tall, with big suntanned hands that look like baseball mitts, and dark green eyes, dad cuts an impressive figure.* (4) *He was a fisherman, a painter, and (perhaps most important of all) the person who saved my little brother's life.*

(5) *When I was fifteen, my father, my brother John, and I are all on an extended fishing trip in the boundary waters, near the Canadian border.* (6) *Its a wonderful part of the world, lush and clean.* (7) *We had planned to be gone for a little over two weeks, camping, fishing, canoeing, and trying with little luck to stay dry.* (8) *"What's the weather going to be like this time of year?"* (9) *I asked, as we loaded up the van.* (10) *"Cold, and probably rainy," Dad replied he wasn't lying.*

(11) *For the first five days there was a constant drizzle, the temperature never climbed above 50 degrees.* (12) *Then, on the sixth day, rain started lashing down and thunder could be heard at a distance.* (13) *The wind picked up.* (14) *The temperature dropped considerably.* (15) *As the weather rolls in, we huddled in our canoe, trying to catch that night's dinner.* (16) *None of us had expected this, it arrived so suddenly.*

1. Which of the following is the best revision of sentence 2?
   A. He was a big guy.
   B. My father and I are big guys.
   C. We are big guys.
   D. He's a big guy.
   E. He's that big of a guy.

2. Which of the following is the best revision of sentence 4?
   A. He was a fisherman, a painter; and (perhaps most important of all) the person who saved my little brother's life.
   B. He is a fisherman, a painter, and (perhaps most important of all) the person who saved my little brother's life.
   C. He was a fisherman, and a painter.
   D. He was a fisherman, and a painter, and (perhaps most important of all) the person who saved my little brother's life.
   E. We were fishermen, painters, and people who saved my little brother's life.

3. Which of the following is the best revision of sentence 5?
   A. When I was fifteen, my father, my brother John, and me are all on an extended fishing trip in the boundary waters, near the Canadian border.
   B. When I was fifteen, my father, my brother John, and I are all on an extended fishing trip.
   C. When I was fifteen, my father, my brother John, and me are all on an extended fishing trip.
   D. My father, my brother John, and I are all on an extended fishing trip in the boundary waters, near the Canadian border.
   E. When I was fifteen, my father, my brother John, and I were all on an extended fishing trip in the boundary waters, near the Canadian border.

4. Which of the following is the best revision of sentence 6?
  A. It's a wonderful part of the world, lush and clean.
  B. Its a wonderful part of the world; lush and clean.
  C. It was a wonderful part of the world, lush and clean.
  D. Its a wonderful part of the world.
  E. A wonderful part of the world, its lush and clean.

5. Which of following is the best revision of sentence 10?
  A. "Cold, and probably rainy," Dad replied, he wasn't lying.
  B. "Cold, and probably rainy."
  C. "Cold, and probably rainy," Dad replied. He wasn't lying.
  D. Cold, and probably rainy, Dad replied and he wasn't lying.
  E. My dad replied, and he wasn't lying.

6. Which of the following errors appears in sentence 11?
  A. run-on sentence
  B. misplaced modifier
  C. fragment
  D. incorrect verb tense
  E. incorrect parallelism

7. To improve sentence fluency, which of the following sentences in the third paragraph might be enhanced by combining them with a semicolon?
  A. 11 and 12
  B. 12 and 13
  C. 13 and 14
  D. 14 and 15
  E. 15 and 16

8. Which of the following is the best revision of sentence 15?
  A. As the weather rolls in, we huddled in our canoe.
  B. The weather rolled in, we huddled in our canoe.
  C. The weather rolls in. We huddled in our canoe. We tried to catch that night's dinner.
  D. We huddled in our canoe, trying to catch that night's dinner.
  E. As the weather rolled in, we huddled in our canoe, trying to catch that night's dinner.

9. Which of the following is the best revision of sentence 16?
  A. None of us expected this, it arrived suddenly.
  B. None of us had expected this, it had arrived so suddenly.
  C. None of us had expected this, it was arriving so suddenly.
  D. None of us had expected this; it arrived so suddenly.
  E. None of us had expected this.

10. While writing the concluding paragraphs of this draft, what information should the writer include?
  A. a description of how the father saved John's life
  B. a description of the types of fish that can be caught in the boundary waters
  C. a description of John's appearance
  D. a statement on the importance of family relationships
  E. further description of the father's appearance

Essay

Write a descriptive essay in which you explore the character of a person who has had an important influence on your life. How did you first come to know this person? In what ways has he or she influenced you? As you write, keep in mind that your essay will be checked for **ideas, organization, voice, word choice, sentence fluency, conventions,** and **presentation.**

The Family of Henry VIII: An Allegory of the Tudor Succession, c. 1570–75. Lucas de Heere.
Oil on panel. National Museum and Gallery of Wales, Cardiff.

The English RENAISSANCE

1485–1650

Looking Ahead

Near the end of the 1400s, a cultural movement known as the Renaissance, which had begun in Italy a century earlier, reached England. Although the next one hundred and fifty years in England were marked by bitter conflicts at home and military threats from abroad, they also produced some of the greatest works of English literature, notably William Shakespeare's plays and the King James Bible.

Keep the following questions in mind as you read:

➤➤ What were the characteristics of Renaissance humanism?

➤➤ How is humanism reflected in Shakespeare's works?

➤➤ How did the metaphysical and Cavalier poets respond to the religious conflicts of their time?

OBJECTIVES
In learning about the English Renaissance, you will focus on the following:

- analyzing the characteristics of various literary periods and how the issues influenced the writers of those periods
- evaluating the influences of the historical period that shaped literary characters, plots, settings, and themes
- connecting literature to historical contexts, current events, and your own experiences

Timeline
1485–1650

Dr. Faustus, 17th c. engraving.

BRITISH LITERATURE

1475

1476
William Caxton establishes the first printing press in England

c. 1500
Everyman, a morality play, is first performed

1516
Sir Thomas More writes *Utopia* ▶

1549
Book of Common Prayer is published

1550

1557
Tottel's Miscellany, an early collection of English songs and sonnets, is published

1564
William Shakespeare is born

1576
First professional playhouse opens in London

c. 1582
Sir Philip Sidney writes *Astrophel and Stella*

1590
Sir Edmund Spenser publishes the first part of *The Faerie Queene*

1597
Sir Francis Bacon's first essays are published

1599
The Globe Theatre, home of Shakespeare's company, is founded

BRITISH EVENTS

1475

1485
Wars of the Roses end; Henry VII begins reign (until 1509)

1509
Henry VIII begins reign (until 1547)

1534
Henry VIII breaks with Roman Catholic Church ▶

1547
Edward VI begins reign (until 1553)

1550

1553
Mary I begins reign (until 1558)

1558
Elizabeth I begins reign (until 1603)

1580
Sir Francis Drake circumnavigates the globe

Queen Elizabeth I medal c. 1588

1588
English navy defeats Spanish Armada

WORLD EVENTS

1475

1492
Columbus reaches New World

1498
Vasco Da Gama reaches India

1517
Martin Luther posts his *Ninety-Five Theses,* criticizing abuses in the church and spearheading the Protestant Reformation

1520
Suleiman the Magnificent becomes ruler of Ottoman Empire

1543
Nicholas Copernicus publishes his heliocentric theory ▶

1545
Council of Trent begins Catholic Counter-Reformation

1550

1556
Akbar becomes ruler of Mughal Empire

1580
Michel de Montaigne publishes *Essais (Essays)*

1600

1604
Christopher Marlowe's
Doctor Faustus is published

1609
Shakespeare's sonnets
are published

1610–1611
John Donne writes
Holy Sonnets

▲
1611
King James Bible
is published

1616
William Shakespeare dies

1623
First Folio, Shakespeare's
collected works,
is published

1640

1642
Theaters are closed by
order of the Puritans

1648
Robert Herrick publishes
Hesperides

Map of Virginia, c. 1590

1600

1600
East India Company
is chartered

1603
Elizabeth I dies; James I
begins reign (until 1625)

1605
Gunpowder Plot
is uncovered

1607
Jamestown colony
is established ▶

1616
William Harvey discovers
the circulation of the blood

1625
Charles I begins reign
(until 1649)

1642
Civil war erupts

1649
Charles I is beheaded;
Oliver Cromwell becomes
Lord Protector

1600

1603
Edo (Tokyo) becomes new
capital of Tokugawa Japan

1605
Miguel de Cervantes
writes *Don Quixote, Part I*

1606
Dutch painter Rembrandt
is born

▲
1609
Galileo constructs his
first telescope

1619
First enslaved Africans
arrive in America

1624
Japan prohibits European
contact

1640

1644
Ming Dynasty ends in China

Hizen ware, c. 17th century

Literature Online Timeline Visit www.glencoe.com
for an interactive timeline.

Reading Check

Analyzing Graphic Information Who ruled England
longer, Queen Elizabeth I or King James I?

By the Numbers

The Spanish Armada

In 1588, during the reign of Elizabeth I, England became one of the great sea powers of the world. In that year, Philip II, king of Spain and the most powerful ruler on the Continent, sent his renowned Spanish Armada, a huge fleet of warships, to fight England's small navy. Philip II sought to overthrow England's Protestant monarch and restore the supremacy of the Roman Catholic Church in England. The English navy won an impressive victory, aided by the inhospitable climate of the English seas. The defeated survivors of the "invincible Armada" returned to Spain, and England's mastery over the seas was unchallenged thereafter.

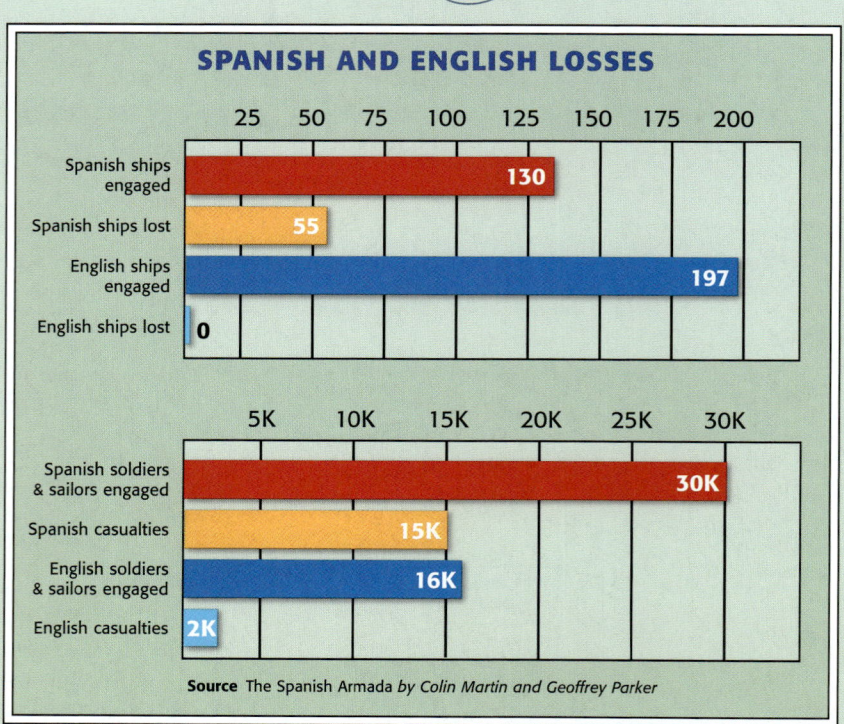

SPANISH AND ENGLISH LOSSES

	25	50	75	100	125	150	175	200
Spanish ships engaged					130			
Spanish ships lost	55							
English ships engaged								197
English ships lost	0							

	5K	10K	15K	20K	25K	30K
Spanish soldiers & sailors engaged						30K
Spanish casualties			15K			
English soldiers & sailors engaged			16K			
English casualties	2K					

Source *The Spanish Armada by Colin Martin and Geoffrey Parker*

HOLIDAYS

A 1552 act prohibited work on Sundays and listed 23 feast day holidays, with 11 more days off at Easter, Whitsun (the seventh Sunday after Easter), and Christmas.

EXECUTIONS

In Tudor England, executions for treason—which sometimes meant professing a religion that was out of favor—were not uncommon. According to a recent study, Henry VIII executed 308 people for treason between 1532 and 1540. Mary I, Henry's Catholic daughter, executed 132 for that crime during her five-year reign. Later, Elizabeth I, Henry's Protestant daughter, executed 183 traitors during her long reign.

LONDON'S POPULATION

During this period, plague frequently swept through the city of London. Epidemics occurred in 1498, 1535, 1543, 1563, 1589, 1593 (over 10,000 deaths), 1603 (over 25,000 deaths), 1625 (over 26,000 deaths), and 1636. Despite these deaths, the population of London grew steadily. In 1500 approximately 50,000 people lived in London; a century later, approximately four times as many inhabitants lived there.

THEATER PRICES

The Globe and other outdoor playhouses held approximately 3,000 spectators. The "groundlings," who stood in the large central courtyard, paid a penny to enter—roughly equivalent to the price of a movie ticket today; those who wished to sit in the covered galleries paid from two pennies to a shilling.

EARNING POWER

During Shakespeare's time, approximately 2 percent of the population controlled most of the nation's land and wealth. The incomes for some members of this upper class reached nearly $94,000 a year. Yeomen—free, land-owning farmers—earned from $94 to $188 a year. A teacher earned about $28.80 a year; a laborer, a shilling, or about 9 cents, a day.

Being There

A *Musicians at Wadley House,* detail from *The Life and Death of Sir Henry Unton,* c. 1596. English School. Oil on panel. National Portrait Gallery, London.

By the early 1600s, England, Scotland, and Wales were politically united under King James I. London, the hub of the nation's economy, was now one of the great capitals of Europe with a population exceeding 100,000. Tudor and Stuart monarchs lived in gorgeous palaces in or near London. Many writers spent their entire lives working in London or its suburbs.

B *The Southeast Prospect of Hampton Court, Herefordshire,* c. 1699. Leonard Knyff. Oil on canvas, 58½ x 84½ in. Yale Center for British Art, Paul Mellon Collection, New Haven, CT.

C *A Fete at Bermondsey,* c. 1570. Joris Hoefnagel. Hatfield House, Hertfordshire, England.

Literature Online **Maps in Motion** Visit www.glencoe.com for an interactive map.

Reading Check

Analyzing Graphic Information:

1. In 1588, what percentage of the ships in the Spanish Armada were lost?

2. At the Globe Theatre, how many times more was the highest price of admission than the lowest one?

3. About how many miles from London is Shakespeare's birthplace, Stratford-upon-Avon?

The English
RENAISSANCE
1485–1650

Historical, Social, and Cultural Forces

Tudor England

When Henry VII, a Tudor, became king of England in 1485, he was starting a new royal line. His defeat of Richard III and his marriage to a member of the House of York had ended the thirty-year civil war known as the Wars of the Roses. Under the Tudor monarchs—Henry VII, Henry VIII, Edward VI, Mary I, and Elizabeth I—broad changes swept through England. Religious and political conflicts divided the country. But by the late 1500s, a burst of creative energy brought a golden age to England.

The Renaissance

As England became an economic and naval power, it was also influenced by a cultural movement known as the Renaissance. Beginning in Italy in the fourteenth century, the Renaissance ("rebirth" in French) later swept into France, Holland, and the other nations of Western Europe, including England. This period marked the transition between the Middle Ages and the modern world and was characterized by a renewed interest in science, art, and all learning that had flourished in ancient Greece and Rome.

Throughout the Middle Ages, many pre-Christian literary masterpieces gathered dust in monastery libraries, and their cultural value went largely unnoticed. In the early Renaissance, however, scholars such as the Italian poet Francesco Petrarch (pe´trärk) rediscovered those classical works. Dazzled by what he had found, Petrarch was angry at earlier generations who had "permitted the fruit of other minds, and the writings that their ancestors had produced by toil and application, to perish through insufferable neglect."

Sea Battle Between the Spanish Armada and English Naval Forces, 1600. Hendrik Cornelisz Vroom. Oil on canvas, 91 x 153 cm. Landesmuseum Ferdinandeum, Innsbruck, Austria.

Humanism

An era of intellectual inquiry and artistic activity, the Renaissance produced a new movement called humanism. Proclaiming the unlimited potential of human beings to accomplish great feats in this world, humanism fostered remarkable achievements in the arts and sciences. This emphasis on humanity's, rather than God's, importance also threatened the authority of the Roman Catholic Church, thereby laying the groundwork for the Protestant Reformation.

In general, humanists relished new ideas and shared a lively interest in the affairs of this world, not the afterlife. Political and scientific questions intrigued them as did philosophical and religious ones. People painted, sculpted, and composed music as never before. The act of reading classical works emphasized the ability of the individual to think independently without guidance from higher authorities.

The French writer Michel de Montaigne (mon tän´) exemplified the new humanistic ideal. In 1571 he retired from public life to devote himself to reading and reflection on subjects that piqued his curiosity. Modeling his skeptical, independent quest for truth on that of the ancient Greek philosopher Socrates, Montaigne took as his mantra the question, *"Que sais-je?"* ("What do I know?"). To explore that question, he wrote brief prose discussions, which he called *essais*, meaning "attempts."

Beginning in the late 1300s with Geoffrey Chaucer, English writers who traveled abroad brought back to England not only new books but new ideas. Foreign works were translated into English, and humanistic values and methods of inquiry took root. Printing presses such as William Caxton's disseminated ideas far more quickly, widely, and inexpensively than had the hand-copied manuscripts of the medieval monasteries. By the late 1540s, when the eminent schoolmaster Roger Ascham became the tutor of the future Queen Elizabeth, it had become important to write, as he put it, "English matter in the English tongue for English men." The stage was set for a magnificent flowering of literary creativity.

The Protestant Reformation

During the early 1500s, a religious revolution that had begun in central Europe was spreading across the continent. It was called the Protestant Reformation and was a protest against the powerful Roman Catholic Church that significantly influenced the social, political, and economic structure of sixteenth-century Europe. In 1517 the German monk Martin Luther helped spur on this movement by protesting against the sale of indulgences and certain other perceived abuses of the Roman Catholic Church. His protests helped trigger a widespread rejection of the pope's authority in Europe.

By 1530 Henry VIII had reasons to align himself and England with the Protestants. He wanted his marriage to Catherine of Aragon annulled because she had not given him a male heir. When the pope in Rome refused, Henry VIII broke with the Roman Catholic Church, proclaiming himself the sole head of the Church of England, or the Anglican Church. This split led to bitter and long-lasting conflicts among religious factions in England that lasted until the end of the 1600s. When Henry VIII's Catholic daughter, Mary I, became queen, she executed Protestants; later, Henry VIII's Protestant daughter, Elizabeth I, executed Catholics. In an attempted invasion in 1588 launched by Philip II, the Catholic monarch of Spain, Elizabeth I's navy defeated the Spanish Armada. England thus remained Protestant under Elizabeth I and her cousin, James I.

 PREVIEW **Big Ideas** of the English Renaissance

1 Humanists and Courtiers	**2** A Bard for the Ages	**3** The Sacred and the Secular
To the humanists, human endeavor had dignity and worth in its own right. Influenced by that idea, English writers began to shift their focus from otherworldly concerns and concentrate on secular subjects, such as love, politics, science, and philosophy. **See pages 244–245.**	William Shakespeare, a singular genius, wrote poems and plays that represent the full flowering of the English Renaissance. His works focus on individuals: heroes and villains who grapple with painful dilemmas. **See pages 246–247.**	The English Renaissance was an age of extreme contrasts. It produced literature that includes devotional meditations as well as witty reflections on time, transience, and erotic love. The contrast between the sacred and the secular was sharply drawn. **See pages 248–249.**

Unlike scholars in the Middle Ages, the humanists of the Renaissance focused on this world. Many of their studies—including grammar, rhetoric, and logic—reflect this shift in emphasis. For example, medieval scholars believed the form of words revealed part of the essential meaningfulness of God's creation. Renaissance scholars, on the other hand, were curious about how human languages were related to one another.

Humanism in England

Living up to its name, humanism depended more on personal contact than on systematic instruction at schools and universities. The friendships formed by humanists—in private study with one another, in the royal courts where they served as political advisers, and in their personal correspondence—inspired many significant works in this period. Reading humanist works often seems like overhearing a conversation between friends.

> "Nature herself prescribes a life of joy (that is, pleasure)."
>
> —Thomas More, *Utopia*

Sir Thomas More, lord chancellor of England, and Desiderius Erasmus of Holland shared one of the most remarkable of these friendships. Whenever he visited London, Erasmus lived in More's home. There, he wrote his best-known work, *The Praise of Folly*, which he dedicated to his English friend. Erasmus considered More, with his cultivated intellect, sparkling wit, deep learning, and broad culture, to be the ideal humanist, calling him *"omnium horarum homo,"* which is usually translated as "a man for all seasons." More's most celebrated work, his satire *Utopia* (1516), presents his vision of an ideal society, freed from convention and ruled by reason. More coined the title of this work from Greek words that mean "no place."

Elizabeth I and Her Court

Queen Elizabeth I, Henry VIII's second daughter, came to the throne in 1558. Famous for her wit and eloquence, she knew Greek, Latin, and several modern languages and loved music, dancing, and the theater. Her long reign of forty-five years was marked by religious conflicts, political intrigue, and threats of war. She turned England into a great sea power capable of defeating the feared Spanish Armada. With a nimble intelligence and strong personality, she also supported a flourishing period of cultural achievement. Elizabeth's court served as a forum for daring displays of wit that the queen greatly admired—and in which she skillfully participated. Her favorites, privileged members of the court, exemplified the qualities she most admired. Sir Walter Raleigh, for example, combined many occupations: soldier and sailor, explorer of Virginia and Guiana, poet and scientist, possible spy. He began to write his *History of the World* while imprisoned in the Tower of London by Elizabeth's successor, her cousin James I.

The Court of James I

When Elizabeth I died in 1603, the throne passed peacefully to her cousin James, king of Scotland and a member of the Stuart family that would rule England through most of the 1600s. Thus James VI of Scotland became James I of England; all of Britain (England, Scotland, and Wales) was at last ruled by one monarch. Elizabeth I had been worldly and practical; James I, however, was theological and disputatious. He commissioned the translation of the Bible into English, still known as the King James Bible, a masterpiece of English prose. He wrote on a variety of subjects, including witchcraft and government, and argued for the divine right of kings. Like Elizabeth I, James I enjoyed theatrical performances. In fact, he admired one troupe of players so much that he gave it his patronage, commissioning it to give special performances at court. Formerly known as the Lord Chamberlain's Men, the King's Men included William Shakespeare, whose tragedy *Macbeth* was first performed before the king in 1605.

Edward Herbert, 1st Baron Herbert of Cherbury, c. 1610–14. Isaac Oliver. Vellum mounted on card, 9¹⁄₁₀ x 7¹⁄₁₀ in. Powis Castle, Wales.

In the early 1580s, Sir Philip Sidney wrote a defense of literature in response to Puritan attacks claiming that all art was immoral.

from A *Defence of Poesie* by Sir Philip Sidney

Now therin of all sciences (I speak still of human, and according to the humane conceits) is our poet the monarch. For he doth not only show the way, but giveth so sweet a prospect into the way, as will entice any man to enter into it. Nay, he doth, as if your journey should lie through a fair vineyard, at the very first give you a cluster of grapes, that, full of that taste, you may long to pass further. He beginneth not with obscure definitions, which must blur the margent with interpretations, and load the memory with doubtfulness; but he cometh to you with words set in delightful proportion, . . . and with a tale forsooth he cometh unto you, with a tale which holdeth children from play, and old men from the chimney corner. And, pretending no more, doth intend the winning of the mind from wickedness to virtue: even as the child is often brought to take most wholesome things by hiding them in such other as have a pleasant taste. . . . So is it in men (most of which are childish in the best things, till they be cradled in their graves): glad they will be to hear the tales of Hercules, Achilles, Cyrus, and Aeneas; and, hearing them, must needs hear the right description of wisdom, valor, and justice.

Reading Check

Interpreting According to Sidney, how does poetry fulfill a moral purpose?

William Shakespeare, poet and playwright, is said to be the world's favorite author. No other playwright's works have been produced so often and read so widely in so many different countries. On the one hand, little is known about Shakespeare as a person. He left behind no letters or manuscripts to provide clues about his personality or the inner workings of his mind. On the other hand, Shakespeare imbued the characters in his plays with such rich humanity that they live on the page and on the stage, still inspiring readers and theater audiences more than four hundred years after their creation.

> *"Soul of the age! / The applause! delight! the wonder of our stage!"*
>
> —Ben Jonson

Shakespeare's Theaters

No one knows when Shakespeare first arrived in London, but his name first appears in London theatrical records as an actor and a playwright. His career in the theater proved profitable for him. Around 1610, he had earned enough money to leave London and retire to an estate in the small country town of Stratford-upon-Avon, where he had grown up. His fortune, however, did not come directly from his plays. An astute businessman, Shakespeare was a shareholder, or part owner, in one of London's most popular acting companies, the Lord Chamberlain's Men. In 1599 the company built the Globe Theatre, the most famous of Elizabethan theaters.

Located on the disreputable south bank of the river Thames, the Globe was designed to provide inexpensive entertainment for approximately three thousand spectators. Built roughly in the shape of an O, this playhouse was open to the air. Galleries of seats and areas for standing ringed three-quarters of the platform stage. Above the stage a sign depicted the Greek hero Hercules carrying the world on his shoulders and bore the Latin inscription *"Totus mundus agit histrionem"* ("The whole world plays the actor")—or as Shakespeare wrote in his comedy *As You Like It*, "All the world's a stage."

Shakespeare was also a shareholder in the Blackfriars Theatre, a more intimate and expensive playhouse. Closer to the center of London and attracting a wealthier audience, the Blackfriars was roofed and provided candlelight for evening performances. For this playhouse, Shakespeare wrote plays that targeted a more sophisticated audience.

Shakespeare's Learning

Alluding to Shakespeare's lack of higher learning, Ben Jonson wrote that Shakespeare had "small Latin and less Greek." In fact, while there is no indication that Shakespeare knew any Greek at all, Latin works by the poet Ovid and the playwrights Plautus and Seneca, which he read at the local grammar school in Stratford-upon-Avon, deeply influenced him. Shakespeare imaginatively incorporated much of what he read into his plays. For example, in one of his essays, the French writer Montaigne praises the simple culture of some Native Americans as described by early French explorers. In his play *The Tempest,* Shakespeare transforms Montaigne's description into a vision of an ideal society.

Shakespeare's Humanism

Shakespeare's ability to absorb and transform different kinds of material—from political issues of the day to events from Roman and English history—reflects a humanistic ideal. His plays often focus on characters who seek to fulfill their potential. They are constantly probing and striving, demonstrating their wit at court, displaying their courage on the battlefield, falling in love and writing poetry, or devising plots to bring about their deepest desires, whether loving or vengeful. No other writer has seen more deeply into the many manifestations of human nature. In an uncanny way, Shakespeare understands why people behave the way they do. Young and old, women and men, good and evil, beggars and kings—all live in his plays.

David Garrick as Richard III, 1745. William Hogarth. Oil on canvas, 75 x 98⅕ in. Walker Art Gallery, National Museums, Liverpool.

The power of Shakespeare's imagination informs his understanding of even his villains' complexities. In the following passage from Richard III, *the title character vows to become a villain because of his physical repugnance and the unhappiness it has brought him.*

from *Richard III,* Act 1, scene 1 by William Shakespeare

Now is the winter of our discontent
Made glorious summer by this sun of York;
And all the clouds that loured upon our house
In the deep bosom of the ocean buried.
Now are our brows bound with victorious wreaths;
Our bruiséd arms hung up for monuments;
Our stern alarums changed to merry meetings;
Our dreadful marches to delightful measures.
Grim-visaged war hath smoothed his wrinkléd front;
And now, instead of mounting barbéd steeds
To fright the souls of fearful adversaries,
He capers nimbly in a lady's chamber
To the lascivious pleasing of a lute.
But I, that am not shaped for sportive tricks,
Nor made to court an amorous looking-glass;
I, that am rudely stamped, and want love's majesty
To strut before a wanton ambling nymph;

I, that am curtailed of this fair proportion,
Cheated of feature by dissembling Nature,
Deformed, unfinished, sent before my time
Into this breathing world, scarce half made up,
And that so lamely and unfashionable
That dogs bark at me as I halt by them;
Why I, in this weak piping time of peace,
Have no delight to pass away the time,
Unless to spy my shadow in the sun
And descant on mine own deformity:
And therefore, since I cannot prove a lover,
To entertain these fair well-spoken days,
I am determinéd to prove a villain
And hate the idle pleasures of these days.

Reading Check

Interpreting How does Richard's speech reflect Shakespeare's humanism?

The Sacred and the Secular

Should limits be imposed on the quest for knowledge? That question was as relevant in the Renaissance as it is today. With its emphasis on investigation rather than revelation, humanism inevitably roused the concern of religious authorities. Not all humanists, however, saw a contradiction between religious faith and free inquiry. After all, had not God endowed human beings with intelligence?

Humanism and Religion

Sir Thomas More's humanism, for example, was grounded in the Roman Catholic religion. He never allowed public affairs, however important, to distract him from private prayer and charities dear to his heart. He ran his home as a school for his daughters, whom he educated in Christian and classical subjects. It was a matter of conscience—his opposition to Henry VIII's intended divorce—that led to his execution for treason, ordered by the very king whom he had served so well. As he was about to be beheaded, More defined his relationship to both the sacred and secular realms: "The King's good servant, but God's first."

> "As thou readest therefore think that every syllable pertaineth to thine own self, and suck out the pith of the scripture, and arm thyself against all assaults."
>
> —William Tyndale

The Bible in English

Many Renaissance writers who did not associate with humanists such as More nonetheless were eager to wrest the control of learning from religious authorities. An important way to do so was to bring the Christian sacred writings down from the pulpit and into people's homes. The new printing presses made translations of the Bible into modern languages relatively affordable. By 1522 Martin Luther had translated the New Testament into German. In the 1520s and 1530s, William Tyndale, one of the leaders of the Protestant Reformation in England, followed Luther's example by translating the Bible into English. He sought to bring the words of scripture into the hearts and minds of individual readers.

These "assaults" were real. The penalties for translating the Bible without official approval from either the pope or—after Henry VIII took control of the Church of England—the government were often deadly. Tyndale was burned at the stake for heresy in 1536. Ironically, the scholars who later worked on the official translation of the Bible, the King James Version (see page 416), borrowed heavily from Tyndale's work.

Metaphysical and Cavalier Poets

Growing up as a Catholic in Protestant England, the poet John Donne learned early about the dangers of religious conflict. In his youth, however, Donne wrote witty poems about romantic love. Many of his contemporaries also delighted in writing about subjects far removed from the entangled and divisive religious issues of the day. Donne was the most notable of a group of writers later referred to as the metaphysical poets (see page 428). Poets such as Donne and Andrew Marvell shared a strong sense of the contradictions inherent in life, such as that between the beauty of the sensual world and the ravages of time.

In 1625 King James I was succeeded by his son, Charles I, whose court was more pleasure-loving than his father's had been. His courtiers were called cavaliers, after the Italian word for *knight*. They still aspired to the grace and elegance of Renaissance gallantry, but they cared little for its high seriousness and Christian chivalry. The Cavalier Poets (see page 452), such as Robert Herrick, Sir John Suckling, and Richard Lovelace, wrote lyrical poems of great polish, sophistication, wit, and raciness. They celebrated earthly pleasures, especially quick-blooming love, and lamented its inevitable fading.

Vanitas, Self Portrait of the Artist, Still Life, c. 17th century. David Bailly. Stedelijk Museum de Lakenhal, Leiden, The Netherlands.

Batter my heart, three-personed God by John Donne

Batter my heart, three-personed God; for, you
As yet but knock, breathe, shine, and seek to mend;
That I may rise, and stand, o'erthrow me, and bend
Your force to break, blow, burn and make me new.
I, like an usurped town, to another due,
Labor to admit you, but oh, to no end,
Reason your viceroy in me, me should defend,
But is captived, and proves weak or untrue,
Yet dearly I love you, and would be loved fain,
But am betrothed unto your enemy:
Divorce me, untie, or break that knot again,
Take me to you, imprison me, for I
Except you enthral me, never shall be free,
Nor ever chaste, except you ravish me.

Reading Check

Interpreting How does the word choice in this sonnet reflect both the sacred and the secular?

Wrap-Up

Why It Matters

The value that humanism placed on human experience has permanently altered the way people judge the world. Moreover, humanism's emphasis on intellectual questioning and direct observation gave birth to modern scientific methods. As Sir Francis Bacon wrote, "Knowledge is power."

The literature of the English Renaissance—particularly the plays of William Shakespeare—is one of the pinnacles of world culture. The reign of Elizabeth I also witnessed the beginning of England's three-hundred-year transformation from a small island nation into a global empire ruling one quarter of the world. The growth of the British Empire, in turn, spread the influence of English culture to most corners of the world.

The cultural products of the Protestant Reformation including the *Book of Common Prayer* and the King James Bible, have enriched the spiritual lives and the language of countless English speakers throughout the world.

 **Big Ideas** Link to Web resources to further explore the Big Ideas at www.glencoe.com.

Cultural Links

➤➤ Shakespeare's plays and poems continue to enthrall audiences: on stage and on film, in adaptations into operas and hip-hop musicals, in historically faithful productions with male actors playing female parts, and in iconoclastic productions set in inner-city slums and high-rise penthouses. Biographies and novels about Shakespeare appear frequently, attesting to his undiminished appeal.

➤➤ The King James Bible has profoundly influenced the development of the English language, introducing many phrases into the language that are still in use. These phrases include "fall flat on his face," "a man after my own heart," "to pour one's heart out," and "the land of the living."

FOLDABLES **Study Organizer** **BOUND BOOK**

Try using this organizer to explore your personal responses to the poetry, play, and nonfiction.

Reader-Response Journal

Connect to Today ➤ Use what you have learned about the period to do one of these activities.

1. Speaking/Listening The hero of the Renaissance was a multi-talented individual skilled in many fields, from writing sonnets to fighting battles. Does this ideal still have value in the modern world? With a small group of classmates, discuss whether modern concepts of specialization and teamwork have rendered the Renaissance person obsolete.

2. Visual Literacy From paintings and drawings in her own time to films and television programs today, Elizabeth I has been one of the most widely depicted monarchs of all time. Working with a group of your classmates, create a gallery of different representations of Elizabeth I that show different facets of her personality and her public role.

OBJECTIVES
- Hold a discussion.
- Create a visual display.

 Study Central Visit www.glencoe.com and click on Study Central to review the English Renaissance.

PART 1

Humanists
and Courtiers

Queen Elizabeth I Being Carried in Procession, c. 1601. Robert Peake. Oil on canvas, 51.97 x 75 in. Private collection.

"I have taken all knowledge to be my province."

—Sir Francis Bacon

The Development of the Sonnet

T HE WORD *SONNET* COMES FROM THE ITALIAN *sonetto*, meaning "a little sound or song." For more than seven hundred years, poets have used these highly structured fourteen-line poems to explore such issues as the fleeting nature of love and profound questions of mortality.

During the 1300s, Italian poet Francesco Petrarch (1304–1374) popularized the sonnet. By the end of the sixteenth century, poets throughout much of Europe were writing sonnets. Many of the most recognizable poems in history were written in sonnet form. Romantic poet William Wordsworth wrote that the sonnet was the key with which "Shakespeare unlocked his heart."

Meter and Rhyme Patterns

Traditional sonnets have fourteen lines, each of which is written in **iambic pentameter.** That is, each line has five metric units, or feet, and each foot

Portrait of Frances Howard, Countess of Essex and Somerset, c. 16–17th century. Isaac Oliver. Victoria and Albert Museum, London.

consists of an unstressed syllable (marked ˘) followed by a stressed syllable (marked ´). The rhythm of a line of iambic pentameter is shown in this example from Spenser's Sonnet 30:

My love is like to ice, and I to fire

Sonnets also have set rhyme schemes, based on the last word in each line. To identify the rhyme scheme of a poem, begin with the first line and assign letters, in alphabetical order, to each new sound at the end of each line. Lines that end in the same sound should be assigned the same letter. In Sidney's Sonnet 39, for example, the rhyme scheme for the first four lines would be *abab*.

Come sleep! O sleep, the certain knot of peace,	*a*
The baiting place of wit, the balm of woe,	*b*
The poor man's wealth, the prisoner's release,	*a*
The indifferent judge between the high and low	*b*

Sonnet Forms

There are three major sonnet forms: the **Italian,** or **Petrarchan;** the **English,** or **Shakespearean;** and the **Spenserian.**

Henry Percy, 9th Earl of Northumberland. Nicholas Hilliard, (1547–1619). Rijksmuseum, Amsterdam.

SONNET XII

by Francesco Petrarch
translated by Marion Shore

Octave: problem or situation is described.

If my life find strength enough to fight
the grievous battle of each passing day,
that I may meet your gaze, years from today,
lady, when your eyes have lost their light,
   and when your golden curls have turned to white,
and vanished are your wreaths and green array,
and when your youthful hue has fled away,
whose beauty makes me tremble in its sight,

Turn

Sestet: problem or situation is resolved.

   perhaps then Love will overcome my fears
enough that I may let my secret rise
and tell you what I've suffered all these years;
and if no flame be kindled in your eyes,
at least I may be granted for my tears
the comfort of a few belated sighs.

The Italian Sonnet The Italian sonnet is often called the Petrarchan sonnet after Francesco Petrarch, the poet who made it famous. Many of Petrarch's sonnets are about unrequited love, a common topic for sonnets that follow this form.

In an Italian sonnet, the first eight lines (called an **octave**) present a problem or situation. The last six lines (called a **sestet**) provide an answer or resolution to the problem. The switch from problem to resolution is called the turn. The octave of a typical Italian sonnet has the rhyme scheme *abbaabba*, and the sestet follows either *cdecde* or *cdcdcd*, as shown above.

The English Sonnet The English sonnet is also called the Shakespearean sonnet because Shakespeare was the master of this sonnet form. English sonnets are divided into three **quatrains** (groups of four lines, with each containing its own

rhyme scheme) and one **couplet** (a group of two lines). The rhyme scheme is usually *abab cdcd efef gg*. The English form allows for a more detailed development of the question or problem in the first three quatrains, but it demands a quick summary and solution in the couplet.

The Spenserian Sonnet Edmund Spenser crafted his own version of the sonnet. Like the Shakespearean sonnet, the Spenserian version has three quatrains and a couplet, but it follows the rhyme scheme *abab bcbc cdcd ee*. This interlocking rhyme scheme pushes the sonnet toward the final couplet, in which the writer typically makes a key point or comment.

Literature Online **Literary History** For more about sonnets, go to www.glencoe.com.

RESPONDING AND THINKING CRITICALLY

1. Read Sonnet XII above. What is the "puzzle" of the poem, or the issue that the speaker is exploring?

2. How is the situation resolved in the sestet?

3. Why do you think some modern poets still write in the highly structured sonnet form as well as in free verse?

OBJECTIVES
- Appreciate the sonnet as a classic type of poetic expression.
- Identify the characteristics of a sonnet and distinguish between Italian, English, and Spenserian sonnets.

On Monsieur's Departure and Speech to the Troops at Tilbury

MEET ELIZABETH I

Queen Elizabeth I had a turbulent youth. When she was only two, her father, King Henry VIII, had her mother, Anne Boleyn, beheaded. Elizabeth had four stepmothers over the next ten years. Thanks to Catherine Parr, Henry's sixth wife, Elizabeth received a rigorous education. When Elizabeth was fourteen, her father died. Her ten-year-old half brother, Edward, ascended the throne but died six years later, and Elizabeth's half sister, Mary, came to power. Mary, a devout Catholic, sought to purge Protestantism from the nation. Her executions of Protestants as rebels or heretics earned her the nickname Bloody Mary. Elizabeth, a Protestant, was compelled to observe Catholicism or risk execution. Upon Mary's death in 1558, Elizabeth took the throne. She was only twenty-five at the time, but her study of languages, history, and philosophy had prepared her to be a great ruler.

Religious Tensions Elizabeth's first major act as queen was to issue a proclamation called the Act of Supremacy, passed in 1559, which re-established the Church of England as the nation's official religion. With this decree, Elizabeth began to guide the nation toward a more moderate stance that would enable both Protestants and Catholics to practice their religions peacefully. This position was unpopular with the extremists of both groups, who would rather have punished, or even killed, those who did not share their convictions.

Elizabeth's Catholic cousin, Mary Queen of Scots, was one of these extremists. Mary's opinions were important because she was next in line for the English throne. If Elizabeth died without producing an heir, Mary would become the next queen of England, but Mary did not seem to be willing to wait for Elizabeth to die of natural causes to acquire this position. Shortly after she settled in England in 1568, Mary was linked to two attempts on the queen's life. In 1570, Pope Pius V, unhappy with Elizabeth's religious policies, tried to aid Mary by excommunicating

Elizabeth and declaring that English Catholics did not have to obey their queen's dictates. The pope's decree, though, only rallied England's citizens to support Elizabeth more strongly.

> *"Though God hath raised me high, yet this I count the glory of my crown: that I have reigned with your loves."*
>
> —Elizabeth I, from *"The Golden Speech"*

Political Savvy Over the next fifteen years, Protestants pressured Elizabeth to execute the Queen of Scots, make a politically favorable marriage, and produce a Protestant heir. Instead, Elizabeth simply kept Mary prisoner until a third assassination attempt in 1587 prompted her to order Mary's execution. As for making a favorable marriage, Elizabeth turned that possibility into a brilliant political maneuver. By hinting at a possible marriage to King Philip II of Spain, Elizabeth stalled him from attacking England until she had built a stronger nation with which to resist a Spanish invasion.

Elizabeth ruled with authority and intelligence. During the course of her forty-five-year reign, she demonstrated a shrewdness for politics that enabled her to establish a united kingdom. She enhanced the country's wealth and power and saw England emerge as a major naval power. She even managed to write a few poems.

Elizabeth I was born in 1533, became queen in 1558, and died in 1603.

Literature Online **Author Search** For more about Elizabeth I, go to www.glencoe.com.

Connecting to the Texts

The poem and speech that follow display two sides of the queen: one bound by love and one bound by duty. As you read the selections, consider these questions:

- Have you ever had to balance feelings of love and duty?
- How did you decide which emotion was more important?

Building Background

Although Elizabeth chose not to marry, tradition links her romantically to the Earl of Leicester, a member of her Privy Council and the "lieutenant general" to whom she refers in the speech you are about to read. She was also linked to the ambitious Earl of Essex, whom she eventually had executed for treason. Among her foreign suitors was the Duke of Alençon, a young Frenchman whom the English public disliked. Alençon was most likely the "Monsieur" of the poem you are about to read.

Elizabeth delivered the Speech to the Troops at Tilbury to the land forces assembled at Tilbury, in Essex, to prevent the invasion of the Spanish Armada, a fleet of warships sent by Philip II. The Armada was defeated at sea and never reached England, a miraculous victory thought to be a sign of God's special favor to Elizabeth and England.

Setting Purposes for Reading

Big Idea **Humanists and Courtiers**

As you read, notice how Elizabeth I is focused on secular subjects, such as love and politics, rather than on otherworldly concerns, such as religion.

Literary Element **Tone**

Tone is the author's attitude toward the subject matter or audience. A writer conveys tone through elements such as word choice, punctuation, sentence structure, and figures of speech. A work's tone can be described as formal, informal, serious, playful, sympathetic, objective, humorous, and so on. As you read, note the tones that Elizabeth I uses in her poem and speech.

- See Literary Terms Handbook, p. R18.

Reading Strategy Analyzing Text Structure

Analyzing text structure means studying the way an author organizes material and presents ideas. In the poem "On Monsieur's Departure," Elizabeth I explores her feelings through a series of contrasting images.

Reading Tip: Analyzing Contrasting Images As you read the poem, record examples of the speaker's state of mind on a chart like this one. When you have finished, evaluate the effect of these contrasts.

Image	Contrasting Image
grieving	not showing emotion

Vocabulary

mute (mūt) *adj.* unable to speak; refraining from producing vocal sounds; p. 256 *Izzy was struck mute by the beauty of the scene.*

suppressed (sə presd´) *adj.* subdued; held back; p. 256 *Andy's suppressed emotions finally bubbled to the surface.*

treachery (treach´ ər ē) *n.* willful betrayal of trust; treason; p. 257 *The soldier's treachery caused great losses in the war.*

concord (kon´ kôrd) *n.* an agreement of interests or feelings; p. 257 *The political concord between the two nations helped them achieve similar goals.*

valor (val´ ər) *n.* courage and boldness, as in battle; bravery; p. 257 *Because of his valor, Dana received the Medal of Honor.*

Vocabulary Tip: Synonyms Synonyms are words that have the same or nearly the same meaning.

Literature Online **Interactive Literary Elements Handbook** To review or learn more about the literary elements, go to www.glencoe.com.

OBJECTIVES

In studying these selections, you will focus on the following:
- relating literature to the historical period
- understanding tone
- analyzing text structure

On Monsieur's Departure

Elizabeth I

Elizabeth I, 1575. Artist unknown.
Oil on panel, 113 x 78.7 cm.
National Portrait Gallery, London.

> I grieve and dare not show my discontent,
> I love and yet am forced to seem to hate,
> I do, yet dare not say I ever meant,
> I seem stark mute but inwardly do prate.[1]
>
> 5   I am and not, I freeze and yet am burned,
>   Since from myself another self I turned.
>
> My care[2] is like my shadow in the sun,
> Follows me flying, flies when I pursue it,
> Stands and lies by me, doth what I have done.
> 10 His too familiar care doth make me rue it.[3]
>   No means I find to rid him from my breast,
>   Till by the end of things it be suppressed.
>
> Some gentler passion slide into my mind,
> For I am soft and made of melting snow;
> 15 Or be more cruel, love, and so be kind.
> Let me float or sink, be high or low.
>   Or let me live with some more sweet content,
>   Or die and so forget what love ere meant.

---

1. *Prate* means "chatter."
2. Here, *care* means "sorrow."
3. *[His . . . it]* can be restated as "His superficial sorrow makes me regret my own sorrow."

Reading Strategy   Analyzing Text Structure *How do the contrasting elements in these lines lend intensity to the poem?*

Literary Element   Tone *How would you describe the author's attitude toward her subject?*

Vocabulary

mute (mūt) *adj.* unable to speak; refraining from producing vocal sounds
suppressed (sə presd′) *adj.* subdued; held back

Speech to the Troops at Tilbury

Elizabeth I

My loving people,

　We have been persuaded by some that are careful of[1] our safety, to take heed how we commit our selves to armed multitudes, for fear of **treachery**; but I assure you I do not desire to live to distrust my faithful and loving people. Let tyrants fear, I have always so behaved myself that, under God, I have placed my chiefest strength and safeguard in the loyal hearts and good-will of my subjects; and therefore I am come amongst you, as you see, at this time, not for my recreation and disport, but being resolved, in the midst and heat of the battle, to live or die amongst you all; to lay down for my God, and for my kingdom, and my people, my honor and my blood, even in the dust. I know I have the body but of a weak and feeble woman; but I have the heart and stomach[2] of a king, and of a king of England too,[3] and think foul scorn that Parma[4] or Spain, or any prince of Europe, should dare to invade the borders of my realm; to which rather than any dishonor shall grow by me, I myself will take up arms, I myself will be your general, judge, and rewarder of every one of your virtues in the field. I know already, for your forwardness you have deserved rewards and crowns;[5] and We do assure you in the word of a prince, they shall be duly paid you. In the mean time, my lieutenant general[6] shall be in my stead, than whom never prince commanded a more noble or worthy subject; not doubting but by your obedience to my general, by your **concord** in the camp, and your **valor** in the field, we shall shortly have a famous victory over those enemies of my God, of my kingdom, and of my people. ❧

---

1. *Careful of* means "anxious about."
2. Here, *stomach* means "courage."
3. This statement alludes to the concept of the king's (or queen's) two bodies, the one natural and mortal, the other political and immortal.
4. The dukedom of Parma, in northern Italy, was an ally of Spain in the effort to invade England.
5. A *crown* was an English monetary unit.
6. Elizabeth's *lieutenant general* is Robert Dudley, Earl of Leicester. In addition to leading her armies, he was Elizabeth's favorite courtier. He was once rumored to be her lover and potential husband.

Big Idea **Humanists and Courtiers** *What evidence in this passage points to a shift from otherworldly concerns to a concentration on secular subjects?*

Vocabulary

treachery (treach′ ər ē) *n.* willful betrayal of trust; treason

concord (kon′ kôrd) *n.* an agreement of interests or feelings

valor (val′ ər) *n.* courage and boldness, as in battle; bravery

RESPONDING AND THINKING CRITICALLY

Respond

1. Can you sympathize with the feelings of the speaker in "On Monsieur's Departure"? Why or why not?

Recall and Interpret

2. (a)According to the first stanza of the poem, what feelings has the speaker been forced to hide? (b)What reasons might she have for hiding them?

3. (a)In the second stanza of the poem, to what does the speaker compare her feelings? (b)What does the second stanza reveal about her feelings for Monsieur?

4. (a)According to the opening lines of Speech to the Troops at Tilbury, what warning have some of Elizabeth's advisers given her? (b)According to Elizabeth, why does she ignore their advice? (c)What effect do you think Elizabeth hopes to have on her audience by opening her speech in this way?

Analyze and Evaluate

5. In your opinion, what image in the poem is most effective in conveying the speaker's feelings? Explain your answer.

6. How does knowing the identity of the poem's author deepen your understanding of the conflict that the poem describes?

7. (a)In her speech, what does Elizabeth say she will do rather than see her country dishonored? (b)Against what criticism of her ability as a ruler is she defending herself? (c)Do you think this is an adequate defense? Explain your answer.

Connect

8. On the basis of this poem and other things you have read or heard about, do you think a ruler's duty and loyalty to his or her country should take precedence over his or her personal feelings and private life? Explain.

9. **Big Idea** **Humanists and Courtiers** In what ways do these two works demonstrate the idea that the English were beginning to focus more on secular subjects than on the more religious subjects of the past?

LITERARY ANALYSIS

Literary Element **Tone**

Just as a queen's attitude can set the tone of her court, a writer's attitude toward subject matter or audience can set the tone of a literary work.

What evidence can you find in Speech to the Troops at Tilbury that Elizabeth I's attitude toward her audience is one of deep respect?

Interdisciplinary Activity: Art

Make an illustration to accompany either Elizabeth's poem or speech. You may imitate the style of the Elizabethan period, as seen in the portraits of Elizabeth, or you may use an abstract style. Try to convey the emotions expressed in the written work.

Literature Online **Web Activities** For eFlashcards, Selection Quick Checks, and other Web activities, go to www.glencoe.com.

READING AND VOCABULARY

Reading Strategy **Analyzing Text Structure**

Elizabeth I uses comparison and contrast to make her points in both the poem and the speech.

Partner Activity With a partner, list three examples of the use of comparison and contrast in the poem and the speech. Then discuss how this structure adds to the emotional impact of the poem.

Vocabulary **Practice**

Practice with Synonyms Identify the synonym for each vocabulary word below.

1. concord	**a.** agreement	**b.** rejoice
2. mute	**a.** small	**b.** silent
3. suppressed	**a.** surprised	**b.** subdued
4. treachery	**a.** betrayal	**b.** treasure
5. valor	**a.** courage	**b.** cowardice

The Lover Showeth How He Is Forsaken and Whoso List to Hunt

MEET SIR THOMAS WYATT

Sir Thomas Wyatt, the well-known poet and diplomat, was imprisoned and faced execution twice during the stormy reign of Henry VIII, but both times the fickle king had a change of heart.

Diplomatic Career Wyatt was born in Kent and received his education at St. John's College in Cambridge. Later, he took up his service to the king, and over the years he was assigned to a number of diplomatic posts. Wyatt's diplomatic voyages took him to France, Spain, the Netherlands, and Italy. It was during his first trip to Italy in 1527 that he experienced the Renaissance firsthand. He also came into contact with the sonnets of Petrarch. Wyatt had never before seen this particular form of poetry, and he was deeply impressed. Soon he began writing sonnets of his own, which he took back to England with him. The sonnet took English culture by storm and had a profound and lasting effect upon English poetry.

Wyatt also wrote traditional English lyrics that were sung in the royal court to the accompaniment of a lute. Like many English nobles of his time, he had little interest in publishing his work. Instead, he circulated handwritten copies of his verses among his fellow courtiers. Printed versions did not appear until years after Wyatt's death.

> *"For when this song is sung and past,*
> *My lute, be still, for I have done."*
>
> —Sir Thomas Wyatt

Uneasy Relations As Wyatt's reputation as a poet developed, his relationship with King Henry became more and more difficult. Wyatt's friendship with Henry's second wife, Anne Boleyn, led him into trouble. Henry was suspicious by nature, and the fact that Wyatt was known to have been well acquainted with Boleyn before her marriage to the king did not help matters.

In 1536 Henry threw Wyatt into prison and threatened him with execution. Fortunately for Wyatt, the king relented. Henry still may have needed Wyatt's diplomatic services. Thomas Cromwell, Wyatt's close friend who was also a top adviser to the king, also may have intervened. But it is just as likely that the king was persuaded by Wyatt's brilliant speeches in his own defense. In any case, Wyatt escaped beheading and was allowed to return to royal service. (Anne Boleyn would not be so lucky. She was imprisoned and beheaded in 1536 on charges that she was unfaithful.)

Despite his stormy relationship with the king, Wyatt continued to work as a diplomat. His next diplomatic post, from 1537 until 1539, was as the English ambassador to Charles V's court in Spain. However, Wyatt's fortunes took a downward turn in 1541 when he was imprisoned once again—on charges of treason. Though he spent only two months in jail this time, he would never again enjoy the king's favor.

In 1542 Wyatt set out on what would be his final diplomatic errand for Henry VIII. It was a long and difficult ride, and along the way Wyatt contracted a fever. He died shortly thereafter. Fifteen years after Wyatt's death, printer Richard Tottel published ninety-seven of Wyatt's poems in the now-famous anthology *Songs and Sonnets*, which today is usually referred to as *Tottel's Miscellany*. Despite his life's many difficulties, Wyatt won a place in English literary history.

Sir Thomas Wyatt was born about 1503 and died in 1542.

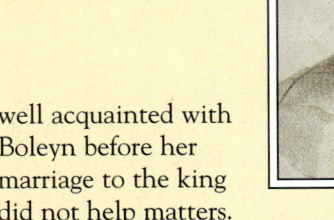 **Author Search** For more about Sir Thomas Wyatt, go to www.glencoe.com.

Connecting to the Poems

Sir Thomas Wyatt wrote many songs and poems about unrequited love. Think of some popular songs about unrequited love that you have heard. What do these songs have in common with one another?

Building Background

Wyatt patterned many of his poems on sonnets about unrequited love written by the fourteenth-century Italian poet Francesco Petrarch. "Whoso List to Hunt" was inspired by Petrarch's Sonnet 190. Petrarch was thought to be in love with a woman named Laura, who was married. In this sonnet, the speaker sees a beautiful doe bearing a warning from Caesar that no one should dare touch her. Petrarch based his poem on the story that the Roman dictator Julius Caesar kept tame deer that wore collars around their necks inscribed with the words *noli me tangere,* meaning "touch me not." Wyatt no doubt drew upon Petrarch's poetry and this story in particular to write his famous sonnet "Whoso List to Hunt." Wyatt likely knew quite a bit about the subject of love in his own right, however. Literary scholars claim that Wyatt wrote "Whoso List to Hunt" about Anne Boleyn, Henry VIII's future wife.

Setting Purposes for Reading

Big Idea Humanists and Courtiers

As you read the two poems, notice the poet's references to human nature, the animal kingdom, and the earthly conditions of love and loss.

Literary Element Figurative Language

Figurative language is used for descriptive effect, often to imply ideas or emotions indirectly. Figurative expressions are not meant to be interpreted literally. As you study the two poems by Sir Thomas Wyatt, notice how the author uses figurative language to compare animals and human beings to make his points.

- See Literary Terms Handbook, p. R6.

Literature Online **Interactive Literary Elements Handbook** To review or learn more about the literary elements, go to www.glencoe.com.

Reading Strategy Clarifying Meaning

Clarifying meaning means focusing on difficult sections of a text in order to understand them better. If you don't clarify a confusing passage, you may not understand the ideas and information that come later. As you read through these two poems, reread confusing sections slowly and ask yourself questions about what you do not understand.

Reading Tip: Restating Meaning You can sometimes clarify the meaning of a poem by putting it into your own words.

Ask yourself...

What happens in this line or stanza?

_____

How can I state this idea clearly and simply?

_____

Vocabulary

flee (flē) *v.* to run away; p. 261 *We had to flee the fire.*

stalking (stô′ king) *v.* tracking; pursuing; p. 261 *The neighbor's cat was stalking a bird.*

meek (mēk) *adj.* mild; gentle; p. 261 *She had a meek expression on her face when she apologized.*

continual (kən tin′ ū əl) *adj.* ongoing; repeated frequently; p. 261 *The continual ringing of the telephone annoyed me.*

bitter (bit′ ər) *adj.* hard to bear; causing pain; p. 261 *He was bitter about his brother's accusations.*

Vocabulary Tip: Analogies Analogies are comparisons based on relationships between words or ideas.

OBJECTIVES
In studying these selections, you will focus on the following:
- analyzing literary periods
- interpreting figurative language
- clarifying meaning through rereading

The LOVER
Showeth How He Is Forsaken

Sir Thomas Wyatt

They **flee** from me, that sometime did me seek
With naked foot **stalking** within my chamber.
Once have I seen them gentle, tame, and **meek**
That now are wild, and do not once remember
5   That sometime they have put themselves in danger
To take bread at my hand, and now they range,
Busily seeking in **continual** change.

Thankèd be fortune, it hath been otherwise,
Twenty times better; but once especial,[1]
10 In thin array, after a pleasant guise,[2]
When her loose gown did from her shoulders fall,
And she me caught in her arms long and small,[3]
And therewithal, so sweetly did me kiss
And softly said, "Dear heart, how like you this?"

15 It was no dream, for I lay broad awaking.[4]
But all is turned now, through my gentleness,
Into a **bitter** fashion of forsaking.
And I have leave[5] to go, of her goodness,
And she also to use newfangleness.[6]
20 But since that I unkindly so am servèd,
How like you this, what hath she now deservèd?

A Young Man Leaning Against a Tree Among Roses, 1587. Nicholas Hilliard. Body color on vellum, 13.5 x 7.3 cm.

---

1. *Especial* here means "especially."
2. *Guise* has two meanings: it can mean either "manner" or "form of dress."
3. Wyatt uses *small* here to mean "slender."
4. *Broad awaking* means "wide awake."
5. *Leave* is another word for *permission.*
6. *Newfangleness,* or *newfangledness,* means "attraction to novelty."

Big Idea   **Humanists and Courtiers** *How does this detail reflect the humanistic trend guiding the English Renaissance?*

Reading Strategy   **Clarifying Meaning** *Reread this stanza and study the footnotes. How would you rephrase these two lines?*

Vocabulary

flee (flē) *v.* to run away
stalking (stô′ king) *v.* tracking; pursuing
meek (mēk) *adj.* mild; gentle
continual (kən tin′ ū əl) *adj.* ongoing; repeated frequently
bitter (bit′ ər) *adj.* hard to bear; causing pain

Whoso List to Hunt

Sir Thomas Wyatt

Whoso list[1] to hunt, I know where is an hind,[2]
But as for me, alas, I may no more.
The vain travail[3] hath wearied me so sore
I am of them that farthest cometh behind.
5 Yet may I, by no means, my wearied mind
Draw from the deer, but as she fleeth afore,
Fainting[4] I follow. I leave off therefore,
Since in a net I seek to hold the wind.

Whoso list her hunt, I put him out of doubt,[5]
10 As well as I, may spend his time in vain.
And graven[6] with diamonds in letters plain
There is written, her fair neck round about,
"Noli me tangere, for Caesar's I am,
And wild for to hold, though I seem tame."

Anne Boleyn, c. 1530. Artist unknown. Oil on panel, 54.3 x 41.6 in. National Portrait Gallery, London.

---

1. *List* means "desires"
2. A *hind* is a female deer.
3. *Travail* means "hard work."
4. Here, *fainting* means "growing weak."
5. *I put him out of doubt* means "I assure him (that he)."
6. *Graven* means "carved."

Reading Strategy Clarifying Meaning *Restate these lines in your own words. What is the speaker trying to say?*

Literary Element Figurative Language *Given what you know about Wyatt's life, who might the tame deer and Caesar represent?*

RESPONDING AND THINKING CRITICALLY

Respond

1. What advice might you offer the speakers in "Whoso List to Hunt" and in "The Lover Showeth How He Is Forsaken"?

Recall and Interpret

2. (a)In "The Lover Showeth How He Is Forsaken," how has the treatment of the speaker changed over time? (b)Why does the speaker feel this has happened?

3. (a)In "The Lover Showeth How He Is Forsaken," what has happened between the speaker and his beloved in the third stanza? (b)How does he seem to feel about her by the end of the poem?

4. (a)In the first stanza of "Whoso List to Hunt," how does the speaker characterize his hunting of the hind? (b)What can you tell about the speaker's feelings from this stanza?

5. (a)What advice does the speaker in "Whoso List to Hunt" give to others who might wish to hunt the hind? (b)What does the last line of the poem suggest to you about the hind?

Analyze and Evaluate

6. (a)To what does the speaker compare his past loves in "The Lover Showeth How He Is Forsaken"? (b)Why might he use such a comparison?

7. (a)What attributes do you associate with deer? (b)In "Whoso List to Hunt," do you think deer hunting is an effective metaphor to convey the speaker's feelings? Explain.

Connect

8. In your opinion, does the attitude of the speaker in "The Lover Showeth How He Is Forsaken" reflect what many people might feel in a similar situation? Why or why not?

9. For whom do you feel more sympathy—the speaker in "The Lover Showeth How He Is Forsaken" or the woman he describes? Explain your reaction.

10. **Big Idea** **Humanists and Courtiers** (a)"Whoso List to Hunt" may have been read in King Henry VIII's court. How do you think the king and his followers might have responded to the poem? (b)Do you think it was unwise for Wyatt to have written the poem? Explain.

LITERARY ANALYSIS

Literary Element Figurative Language

Figurative language often includes the use of metaphor, a figure of speech that compares or equates two unlike things to help readers perceive an underlying similarity between the two. Reread the two poems and consider the metaphoric comparisons the poet makes.

1. The speaker in "The Lover Showeth How He Is Forsaken" claims "That sometime they have put themselves in danger / To take bread at my hand, and now they range, / Busily seeking in continual change." What comparison does the speaker make here? Explain.

2. The speaker in "Whoso List to Hunt" says "I leave off therefore, / Since in a net I seek to hold the wind." What does this metaphor represent? Is it an effective metaphor? Explain.

Review: Tone

As you learned on page 255, **tone** is the author's attitude toward his or her subject matter or the audience. Tone is conveyed through elements such as word choice, punctuation, sentence structure, and figures of speech. A writer's tone might convey a variety of attitudes, including sympathy, objectivity, or humor.

Partner Activity Create a chart for each poem like the one below. Working with a partner, fill in the chart with words that help convey a particular tone.

Word choice	Tone
"alas, I may no more?"	discouraged, sad

Reading Strategy Clarifying Meaning

Use a chart like this one to help you clarify the lines below from "Whoso List to Hunt" and "The Lover Showeth How He Is Forsaken."

Line	Questions	I would rephrase this line:
"Whoso list to hunt, I know where is an hind."	What does "list" mean in this context? What is a "hind"?	"Whoever wants to hunt, I know where there is a deer."

1. "They flee from me, that sometime did me seek / With naked foot stalking within my chamber." ("The Lover Showeth How He Is Forsaken," lines 1–2)

2. "The vain travail hath wearied me so sore / I am of them that farthest cometh behind." ("Whoso List to Hunt," lines 3–4)

Vocabulary Practice

Practice with Analogies Choose the word that best completes each analogy.

1. danger : flee :: joke :
   a. laugh **b.** fear **c.** hurry

2. stalking : hunter :: flying :
   a. doctor **b.** pilot **c.** obese

3. meek : mild :: joyous :
   a. happy **b.** terrier **c.** book

4. continual : intermittent :: serious :
   a. flippant **b.** ambitious **c.** solemn

5. bitter : hurt :: suspicious :
   a. questionable **b.** trustworthy **c.** jovial

Literature Online Web Activities For eFlashcards, Selection Quick Checks, and other Web activities, go to www.glencoe.com.

Writing About Literature

Analyze Genre Elements Sir Thomas Wyatt often used the Petrarchan form of the sonnet, in which fourteen lines are divided into two stanzas: the eight-line octave and the six-line sestet. The sonnet form establishes certain expectations. For example, the sestet usually responds to the question or situation posed by the octave, as in "Whoso List to Hunt." Write a brief essay in which you analyze the elements of Wyatt's sonnet. Examine the octave, the turn of the poem, and the sestet. Use evidence from the poem to support your observations.

As you draft, write from start to finish. Follow the writing path shown here to help you organize your essay and stay on track.

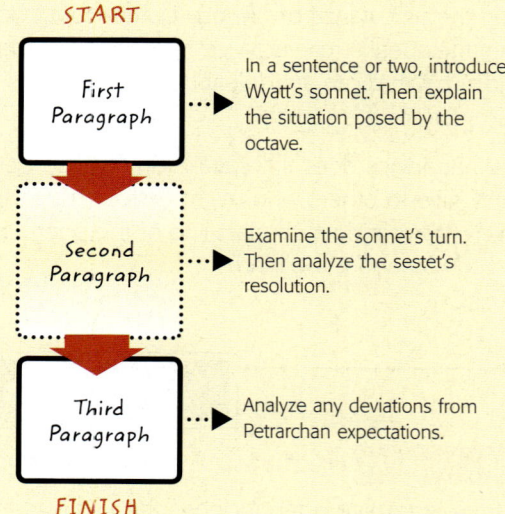

START

| First Paragraph | In a sentence or two, introduce Wyatt's sonnet. Then explain the situation posed by the octave. |

| Second Paragraph | Examine the sonnet's turn. Then analyze the sestet's resolution. |

| Third Paragraph | Analyze any deviations from Petrarchan expectations. |

FINISH

After you complete your draft, meet with a peer reviewer to evaluate your work and suggest revisions. Then proofread and edit your draft for errors in spelling, grammar, and punctuation.

Literary Criticism

The critic Jocst Daalder comments that "much of [Wyatt's] verse is about the loss of, or betrayal of, trust." Review "Whoso List to Hunt" and "The Lover Showeth How He Is Forsaken" for evidence that supports or refutes Daalder's comment. Would you consider the betrayal of trust to be a central theme in either poem? Write a brief response to Daalder's criticism in which you state your opinion on the issue.

Sonnet 30 and Sonnet 75

MEET EDMUND SPENSER

In his day, Edmund Spenser was considered one of the greatest poets of England and the first major English writer since Chaucer. He rose from humble beginnings to become a respected literary figure who received a life pension from Queen Elizabeth I after he personally presented his work to her.

Student and Diplomat Spenser was the son of a cloth maker. He attended the Merchant Taylors' School in London as a "poor boy" before going to Cambridge University as a scholarship student, where he received his bachelor of arts and master of arts degrees. Shortly after leaving Cambridge, Spenser published *The Shepheardes Calender,* a collection of twelve short pastoral poems, one for each month of the year. The **pastoral** is a traditional English verse form that idealizes the rural pleasures of shepherds and innocent country people living in harmony with nature.

In 1580 Spenser was hired as secretary to Arthur Lord Grey, the harsh Lord Deputy of Ireland, who attempted to crush the frequent Irish rebellions against English rule. In war-ravaged Ireland, Spenser made his fortune by acquiring the lands of defeated Irish rebels. He eventually settled at Kilcolman Castle near the city of Cork.

> "Sleep after toil, port after stormy seas,
> Ease after war, death after life does
>   greatly please."
>
> —Edmund Spenser

Major Poet and Courtier In Ireland, Spenser began his most famous work, the great Elizabethan epic, *The Faerie Queene.* The poem, divided into books, is more than a thousand pages long. It depicts heroism in an enchanted world of dragons, monsters, and other marvels. Spenser planned for his epic to have twelve books, but he completed only six. Each book has as its hero a knight who performs noble deeds for a glorious fairy queen, based on Queen Elizabeth.

Spenser became friendly with Sir Walter Raleigh, a favorite courtier of Queen Elizabeth's. Raleigh took Spenser to London, introduced him at court, and helped him publish the first three books of *The Faerie Queen* in 1590. The work was a resounding success, and three more books followed in 1596.

Unrest at Home Returning to Ireland in 1591, Spenser faced another rebellion. As a supporter of English rule, he was a natural target of the rebels, who set fire to Kilcolman Castle. Spenser and his family escaped, but many of his papers were destroyed, possibly including additional books of *The Faerie Queene.* He returned to London but died soon afterward and was buried near Chaucer in the Poets' Corner in Westminster Abbey. At the funeral, admiring fellow poets are said to have honored Spenser by dropping verse tributes into his open grave.

Edmund Spenser was probably born in 1552 or 1553 and died in 1599.

Literature Online Author Search For more about Edmund Spenser, go to www.glencoe.com.

Connecting to the Poems

Consider the depictions of romantic love that you have seen in paintings and literature, on television, and in movies. As you read the poems, think about the following questions:

- How does the depiction of romantic love in Spenser's sonnets differ from the depiction of romantic love in modern mass media?
- Does the desire to immortalize one's beloved in a work of art motivate poets and artists today?

Building Background

After the death of his first wife, Spenser began courting an Anglo-Irish gentlewoman named Elizabeth Boyle. Spenser composed a marriage ode called *Epithalamion,* which was inspired by the traditional marriage odes written in Latin and French. He also wrote an accompanying series of eighty-nine sonnets, which he called *Amoretti,* or "little love songs." *Amoretti* was probably about his courtship of Elizabeth, whom he married in 1594. The sonnets follow a narrative sequence and tell the story of a turbulent romance. Both Sonnet 30 and Sonnet 75 are from *Amoretti* and exemplify the Spenserian sonnet form, which Spenser invented.

Setting Purposes for Reading

Big Idea **Humanists and Courtiers**

As you read, note how the two sonnets illustrate the humanist ideals of courtly love and the power of art.

Literary Element **Rhyme Scheme**

A **rhyme scheme** is the pattern of end rhymes in a stanza of a poem. To identify the rhyme scheme, assign a letter, in alphabetical order, to each new end rhyme. For example, the rhyme scheme for these opening lines from Sonnet LIV by Edmund Spenser is *abab:*

Of this world's theatre in which we **stay,**	*a*
My love, like the spectator, idly **sits,**	*b*
Beholding me, that all the pageants **play,**	*a*
Disguising diversely my troubled **wits.**	*b*

- See Literary Terms Handbook, p. R15.

Reading Strategy **Connecting to Personal Experience**

Connecting to personal experience means applying the ideas, feelings, or events in a work of literature to aspects of your life.

Reading Tip: Taking Notes Use a chart like the one below to record similarities between the expressions of romantic love in the poems and your experiences at various times in your life.

Expression of Love	My Experience

Vocabulary

congeal (kən jēl´) *v.* harden; thicken; p. 267 *After several hours in the refrigerator, the gravy congealed.*

vain (vān) *adj.* conceited; excessively pleased with oneself; p. 268 *Although the actor was handsome, he was not vain.*

mortal (môrt´ əl) *adj.* destined to die; p. 268 *All human beings are mortal.*

subdue (səb dōō´) *v.* conquer; overcome; quiet; p. 268 *The army could not subdue the enemy.*

Vocabulary Tip: Word Origins Dictionary entries often include the **etymology,** or origin and history, of words. Study the following example: **sonnet** [It *sonetto,* fr OProv *sonet* little song, fr L *sonus* sound]. This entry tells you that the word *sonnet* can be traced back to its Latin origin through Italian and Old Provençal.

Literature Online **Interactive Literary Elements Handbook** To review or learn more about the literary elements, go to www.glencoe.com.

OBJECTIVES

In studying these selections, you will focus on the following:
- analyzing literary periods and genres
- identifying rhyme scheme
- connecting literature to personal experience

Sonnet 30

Edmund Spenser

Unrequited Love. Colored print. O'Shea Gallery, London.

My love is like to ice, and I to fire;
How comes it then that this her cold so great
Is not dissolv'd through my so hot desire,
But harder grows the more I her entreat?[1]
5   Or how comes it that my exceeding heat
Is not delayed[2] by her heart frozen cold,
But that I burn much more in boiling sweat,
And feel my flames augmented manifold?[3]
What more miraculous thing may be told,
10 That fire, which all things melts, should harden ice,
And ice, which is **congealed** with senseless cold,
Should kindle fire by wonderful device?
Such is the power of love in gentle mind,
That it can alter all the course of kind.[4]

---

1. *Entreat* means "beg."
2. In this context, *delayed* means "lessened."
3. *Augmented manifold* means "increased greatly."
4. *Kind* means "nature."

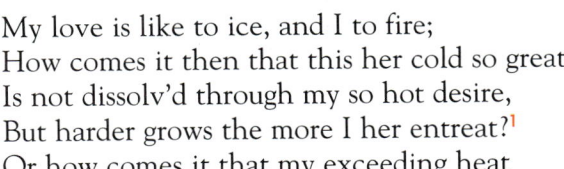

Literary Element Rhyme Scheme *How does the concluding rhyming couplet summarize the contradictions in the poem?*

Vocabulary

congeal (kən jēl´) *v.* harden; thicken

Sonnet 75

Edmund Spenser

Paolo and Francesca. Jean Auguste Dominique Ingres. Oil on wood. Musée Condé, Chantilly, France.

One day I wrote her name upon the strand,[1]
But came the waves and washèd it away:
Again I wrote it with a second hand,
But came the tide, and made my pains his prey.
5 "**Vain** man," said she, "that dost in vain assay,[2]
A **mortal** thing so to immortalize,
For I myself shall like to this decay,
And eke[3] my name be wipèd out likewise."
"Not so," quod[4] I, "let baser things devise[5]
10 To die in dust, but you shall live by fame:
My verse your virtues rare shall eternize,[6]
And in the heavens write your glorious name,
Where whenas death shall all the world **subdue,**
Our love shall live, and later life renew."

---

1. *Strand* means "beach."
2. *Assay* means "try."
3. *Eke* means "also."
4. *Quod* means "said."
5. *Devise* means "plan."
6. *Eternize* means "make eternal."

Big Idea **Humanists and Courtiers** *What humanist theme of the Elizabethan period does this line express?*

Vocabulary

vain (vān) *adj.* conceited; excessively pleased with oneself
mortal (môrt′ əl) *adj.* destined to die
subdue (səb′ dōō) *v.* conquer; overcome; quiet

RESPONDING AND THINKING CRITICALLY

Respond

1. In your opinion, which sonnet is more idealistic? Explain.

Recall and Interpret

2. (a)In Sonnet 30, to what does the speaker compare his and his beloved's feelings? (b)What do these comparisons indicate about the feelings of the two people?

3. (a)Paraphrase the question the speaker asks in lines 5–8 of Sonnet 30. (b)What does this question indicate about the speaker's love?

4. (a)What **paradox,** or apparent contradiction, does the speaker point out in lines 9–12 of Sonnet 30? (b)Is the paradox resolved? Explain.

5. (a)How does the speaker's beloved respond to the speaker's actions in Sonnet 75? (b)What do you think she means by what she says?

6. (a)What does the end of Sonnet 75 suggest about the power of poetry? (b)What contrast does the speaker emphasize in the concluding couplet?

Analyze and Evaluate

7. Assuming that these two sonnets are about the same speaker and the same woman, has their relationship changed between Sonnet 30 and Sonnet 75? Explain.

8. (a)Which sonnet employs a narrative structure? Which sonnet employs a comparison-contrast structure? (b)In your opinion, which sonnet is more effective as a love poem? Explain.

Connect

9. **Big Idea** **Humanists and Courtiers** How does Spenser reconcile humanism and religion at the end of Sonnet 75?

LITERARY ANALYSIS

Literary Element **Rhyme Scheme**

A poem's **rhyme scheme** is its pattern of end rhymes in each stanza.

1. Identify the rhyme scheme of Sonnet 30 and Sonnet 75.

2. (a)Where does the couplet, or pair of successive rhyming lines, appear in each sonnet? (b)What does Spenser accomplish in these rhyming couplets?

Writing About Literature

Compare and Contrast Tone Tone is a writer's attitude toward a subject. Tone is conveyed through such elements as word choice, punctuation, sentence structure, and figures of speech. Write a brief essay comparing and contrasting the tone of Sonnet 30 and Sonnet 75. Use examples from the sonnets to support your points.

Literature Online **Web Activities** For eFlashcards, Selection Quick Checks, and other Web activities, go to www.glencoe.com.

READING AND VOCABULARY

Reading Strategy **Connecting to Personal Experience**

Spenser's sonnets are in the courtly love tradition. Among the conventions of this tradition are the lover's idealization of the beloved and the desire of the lover to immortalize his beloved in verse.

1. How do the conventions, or rituals, of modern love differ from those of sixteenth-century courtly love?

2. Do you think the desire to achieve lasting fame motivates writers and artists today? Explain.

Vocabulary **Practice**

Practice with Word Origins Match each vocabulary word with its corresponding Latin root.

1. congealed   **a.** *mors,* meaning "death"

2. vain   **b.** *subdere,* meaning "to subject"

3. mortal   **c.** *vanus,* meaning "empty"

4. subdue   **d.** *congelare,* meaning "to freeze"

Sonnet 31 and Sonnet 39

MEET SIR PHILIP SIDNEY

Sir Philip Sidney was truly a Renaissance man—someone who can do a variety of things exceptionally well—like so many of the great figures of the Renaissance. Sidney was a brilliant courtier whose refined, aristocratic behavior made him for a time a particular favorite of Queen Elizabeth's. He also was a statesman, a brave soldier, a noted patron of the arts, and a gifted writer of both poetry and prose.

Educated by private tutors until he was ten, Sidney then entered Shrewsbury School, where he met his lifelong friend Fulke Greville, who later became his biographer. Sidney studied at Oxford from 1568 to 1571 but left before receiving a degree because of an outbreak of the plague. He completed his education by traveling abroad, visiting cities such as Paris, Frankfurt, Venice, and Vienna.

> *"They are never alone that are accompanied with noble thoughts."*
>
> —Sir Philip Sidney

Literary Renown Sidney's diverse talents are reflected in his writings. He has been called the "father of English literary criticism" for his extended essay *The Defence of Poesie*, an eloquent argument against Puritan charges that poetry is immoral. His romance the *Arcadia* is one of the finest imaginative prose works of Elizabethan times. Sidney is best known, however, for his sonnet sequence *Astrophel and Stella*, first published in 1591. In this work, which includes 108 sonnets and eleven songs, Sidney examines love from many different perspectives.

Like most members of the upper class, Sidney wrote for himself and his friends; only a few of his works were published during his lifetime. He spent his time traveling, encouraging other writers (including Edmund Spenser), and volunteering for causes in which he believed.

Tragic Death In 1585 Sidney was appointed governor of Flushing, an important English fortress in the Netherlands. There, at age thirty-one, while fighting alongside Dutch Protestants in their battle against Spanish Catholics in the Netherlands, he was seriously wounded by a musket shot that shattered his thighbone. Even in this debilitated state, Sidney was the picture of gentility. Just as he was about to take a drink, he saw a soldier nearby who was dying and offered his drink to the man, saying, "Thy necessity is greater than mine." Sidney succumbed to infection and died twenty-six days after being wounded. His death caused much grief in England. Queen Elizabeth and her subjects mourned the passing of this poet, the embodiment of Renaissance nobility.

Sir Philip Sidney was born in 1554 and died in 1586.

Literature Online Author Search For more about Sir Philip Sidney, go to www.glencoe.com.

Connecting to the Sonnets

What effects might unrequited love have on one's emotional state and sleep patterns? These two sonnets by Sir Philip Sidney are about love and heartbreak. As you read the sonnets, think about the following questions:

- Why do people sometimes associate moonlight and the moon with love and romance?
- How would you describe a sleep that followed a long period of wakefulness?
- Why do so many songs concern love and heartbreak?

Building Background

These two sonnets are from *Astrophel and Stella*, which is a **sonnet sequence,** or a series of sonnets interrelated by content or theme. In Sidney's sonnets, the speaker is called Astrophel, from the Greek for "star-lover." His beloved is called Stella, from the Latin for "star." A star, like the poet's beloved, is beautiful, bright, and fascinating, and Astrophel is the admirer of that star from afar. The real Stella was Penelope Devereux, to whom Sidney was briefly engaged. Though the engagement was broken off, and Devereux's family required her to marry the wealthy Lord Rich, Stella and Astrophel are forever wed in Sidney's sonnet sequence.

Setting Purposes for Reading

Big Idea **Humanists and Courtiers**

As you read, notice that these sonnets focus on romantic passion rather than religious concerns.

Literary Element **Apostrophe**

Apostrophe is a figure of speech in which a writer addresses an absent person, an inanimate object, or an idea as if it were present and capable of understanding. Often, the word *O* is used in apostrophe, as in lines 1 and 9 of Sidney's Sonnet 31. As you read, notice the use of apostrophe and consider its effects.

- See Literary Terms Handbook, p. R1.

Literature Online **Interactive Literary Elements Handbook** To review or learn more about the literary elements, go to www.glencoe.com.

Reading Strategy — Examining Denotation and Connotation

The **denotation** of a word is its direct meaning or dictionary definition. A word's **connotations** are the ideas and emotions associated with it. Connotations may be positive, negative, or neutral. For example, if you want to compliment a friend on her ability to save money, you would be wise to call her *thrifty* rather than *cheap*.

Reading Tip: Taking Notes Use word webs to list words from Sidney's sonnets and their connotations.

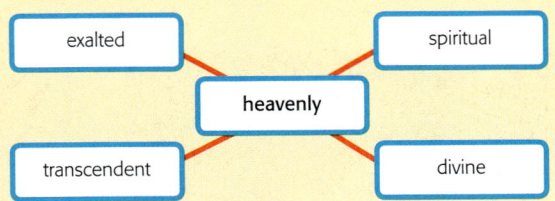

exalted — heavenly — spiritual
transcendent — heavenly — divine

Vocabulary

wan (won) *adj.* pale; p. 272 *Her wan complexion and watery eyes revealed that she was ill.*

languish (lang′gwish) *adj.* dispirited; lacking vitality; p. 272 *After a long stay in the hospital, he felt droopy and languished.*

deem (dēm) *v.* regard as; consider; p. 272 *Marla's essay was deemed worthy of publication.*

scorn (skôrn) *v.* to reject as contemptible or unworthy; p. 272 *Heather and Jillian scorn those who do not belong to their social circle.*

balm (bäm) *n.* a healing ointment; a soothing application; p. 273 *The balm brought immediate relief to his chafed neck.*

Vocabulary Tip: Analogies Analogies are comparisons based on relationships between words and ideas. To complete an analogy, decide on the relationship between the ideas represented by the first two words. Then apply that relationship to the second set.

OBJECTIVES
In studying these selections, you will focus on the following:
- analyzing literary periods
- analyzing apostrophe
- examining denotation and connotation

Sonnet 31

from *Astrophel and Stella*

Sir Philip Sidney

Astronomical Observation: Venus. Donato Creti. Pinacoteca, Vatican Museums.

With how sad steps, O Moon, thou climb'st the skies!
How silently, and with how **wan** a face!
What, may it be that even in heavenly place
That busy archer his sharp arrows tries?[1]

5 Sure, if that long-with-love-acquainted eyes
Can judge of love, thou feel'st a lover's case,
I read it in thy looks; thy **languished** grace,
To me, that feel the like, thy state descries.[2]
Then, even of fellowship, O Moon, tell me,

10 Is constant love **deemed** there but want of wit?[3]
Are beauties there as proud as here they be?
Do they above love to be loved, and yet
Those lovers **scorn** whom that love doth possess?
Do they call virtue there ungratefulness?

---

1. The *busy archer* is Cupid, the Roman god of love.
2. *Descries* is another word for "reveals."
3. Here, *wit* refers to intelligence.

Literary Element Apostrophe *What does the speaker imagine that he and the Moon have in common?*

Reading Strategy Examining Denotation and Connotation *What does the word* fellowship *suggest about the speaker's attitude toward the Moon?*

Vocabulary

wan (won) *adj.* pale
languish (lang´ gwish) *adj.* dispirited; lacking vitality
deem (dēm) *v.* regard as; consider
scorn (skôrn) *v.* to reject as contemptible or unworthy

Sonnet 39
from Astrophel and Stella

Sir Philip Sidney

Come sleep! O sleep, the certain knot of peace,
The baiting place[1] of wit, the **balm** of woe,
The poor man's wealth, the prisoner's release,
The indifferent judge between the high and low;
5   With shield of proof[2] shield me from out the prease[3]
Of those fierce darts Despair at me doth throw;
Oh make in me those civil wars to cease;
I will good tribute pay, if thou do so.
Take thou of me smooth pillows, sweetest bed,
10 A chamber deaf to noise and blind to light,
A rosy garland and a weary head;
And if these things, as being thine by right,
Move not thy heavy grace, thou shalt in me,
Livelier than elsewhere, Stella's image see.

The Soul Of The Rose, 1908. John William Waterhouse R.A. Oil on canvas. Private collection.

---

1. A *baiting place* is a place of refreshment.
2. Here, *proof* is proven strength.
3. *Prease* means "crowd."

Big Idea   Humanists and Courtiers   *Why does the speaker offer sleep these worldly gifts?*

Vocabulary

balm (bäm) *n.* a healing ointment; a soothing application

RESPONDING AND THINKING CRITICALLY

Respond

1. What advice would you give to the speakers of these sonnets? Explain.

Recall and Interpret

2. (a)In Sonnet 31, what human qualities does the speaker attribute to the moon? (b)What does this use of **personification** reveal about the speaker's emotional state?

3. (a)Paraphrase the questions that the speaker asks in lines 10–14 in Sonnet 31. (b)What do these questions imply about the object of the speaker's love?

4. (a)In lines 1–4 of Sonnet 39, to what things does the speaker compare sleep? (b)What do these **metaphors** reveal about the speaker's attitude toward sleep?

Analyze and Evaluate

5. When a line of poetry consists of one-syllable words, readers are forced to read it slowly. How does the slow pace support the meaning of lines 1–2 in Sonnet 31?

6. Poets strive to choose exactly the right word to convey meaning. In what way is the phrase "fierce darts" in line 6 of Sonnet 39 appropriate?

7. How well do you think these sonnets capture the emotional state of a rejected lover? Explain.

Connect

8. **Big Idea** **Humanists and Courtiers** In what ways do these sonnets reflect humanist concerns?

LITERARY ANALYSIS

Literary Element Apostrophe

In poetry, **apostrophe** and **personification** are figures of speech that often go hand in hand. For example, in these sonnets, Sidney addresses the moon and sleep and then gives them human qualities. Poets often use apostrophe to achieve a sense of emotional immediacy.

1. In Sonnet 39, how does the apostrophe help reveal the speaker's emotional state?

2. In what ways are your thoughts and feelings about sleep similar to or different from the speaker's? Explain.

3. If you were to write a poem about a sleepless night, whom or what would you address? Why?

Writing About Literature

Respond to Imagery The word pictures that writers create in order to evoke emotional responses in the reader comprise a work's **imagery.** What images linger in your mind after reading these sonnets? Write one or two paragraphs in which you list those images and describe the mood they create.

Literature Online **Web Activities** For eFlashcards, Selection Quick Checks, and other Web activities, go to www.glencoe.com.

READING AND VOCABULARY

Reading Strategy Examining Denotation and Connotation

Paying attention to words' **connotations** can provide you with clues about the author's attitude toward his or her subject.

1. Select three words from Sonnet 31 and explain how their connotations enhance your understanding of the speaker.

2. In Sonnet 39, what does the phrase "balm of woe" suggest?

Vocabulary Practice

Practice with Analogies Choose the word that best completes each analogy below.

1. silent : loud :: languished :
   a. energetic   b. lethargic
2. scare : frighten :: deem :
   a. earn   b. evaluate
3. praise : scold :: scorn :
   a. display   b. accept
4. loyal : faithful :: wan :
   a. pastel   b. sickly
5. ice : chill :: balm :
   a. relieve   b. lacerate

The Passionate Shepherd to His Love

MEET CHRISTOPHER MARLOWE

Nineteenth-century poet Alfred, Lord Tennyson wrote, "If Shakespeare is the dazzling sun of this mighty period, Marlowe is certainly the morning star." Born two months before William Shakespeare, Christopher Marlowe, with his innovative verse and shocking tragedies, led the way for Shakespeare and other Elizabethan writers. Though his literary career spanned only six years, Marlowe is considered by many critics to be the father of English drama. With the premiere of *Tamburlaine the Great*, blank verse, which Ben Jonson called Marlowe's "mighty line," became the staple of Elizabethan writing.

> *"Nature that fram'd us of four elements,*
> *Warring within our breasts for regiment,*
> *Doth teach us all to have aspiring minds."*
>
> —Christopher Marlowe, *Tamburlaine*

From Humble Beginnings Born in 1564, Marlowe was the son of a shoemaker. At age seventeen, he received a scholarship to attend Cambridge. While there, Marlowe was recruited by Sir Francis Walsingham to serve as a secret agent for Queen Elizabeth—a path that led to trouble.

Marlowe was nearly denied his master of arts because the university found his lengthy absences suspicious and potentially heretical. However, a letter from the Privy Council righted the situation: "it was not Her Majesty's pleasure that anyone employed, as he [Marlowe] had been, in matters touching the benefit of his country, should be defamed by those that are ignorant in th' affairs he went about." Some believe his "affairs" helped uncover the most dangerous conspiracy to assassinate the queen.

Poetry and Drama While at Cambridge, Marlowe translated Ovid's *Amores* into English by using blank verse and rhyming pentameter couplets. He also wrote *Tamburlaine*, the play that launched him into the London spotlight in 1587. Marlowe's plays, including *The Tragicall History of Dr. Faustus*, *Edward II*, *The Massacre at Paris*, and *The Jew of Malta*, provide a social framework and reveal his feelings about Queen Elizabeth's rule, as well as his deep awareness of corruption through power, the darkness of individual suffering, the danger of greed, and the need for social responsibility.

A Dramatic Ending While in London, Marlowe met dramatist Thomas Kyd, an acquaintance that would later prove fatal. In 1593 Kyd was arrested by officers of the court. Papers denying the divinity of Jesus Christ and referring to the Roman Catholic Church had been found in Kyd's room. Under torture and duress, Kyd professed his innocence and claimed the papers belonged to Marlowe and had been merely "shuffled" into his. Marlowe was arrested on May 20, 1593, on the charges of atheism and blasphemy.

Ten days later, Marlowe was stabbed in the eye and died at the lodging house of Dame Eleanor Bull in Deptford. Marlowe had spent the afternoon with three other men, all of whom were associated with Sir Francis Walsingham, head of the queen's secret service. The circumstances of his death have been debated for centuries. Some believe the murder was the result of a dispute over a bill, but many believe Marlowe was assassinated.

In six short years, Marlowe changed English drama. In his play *As You Like It*, Shakespeare alluded to Marlowe and his work as "a great reckoning in a little room."

Christopher Marlowe was born in 1564 and died in 1593.

Literature Online **Author Search** For more about Christopher Marlowe, go to www.glencoe.com.

Connecting to the Poem

Marlowe chose to look outside his own world and use an idealized rural setting and a simple shepherd to write about the joys of love. As you read the poem, think about the images you would use to describe love.

Building Background

Written in the pastoral tradition, "The Passionate Shepherd to His Love" was not meant to be realistic, but instead an idealized celebration of "the natural life." By promoting humble contentment with nature, Marlowe's poem suggests the dissatisfaction of urban people yearning for the lost innocence of a simpler time and place.

Considered one of the greatest pastoral poems ever written, "The Passionate Shepherd to His Love" inspired several responses from other poets, including John Donne, Robert Herrick, and Sir Walter Raleigh.

Setting Purposes for Reading

Big Idea Humanists and Courtiers

As you read, consider how the exaggerated style and setting of "The Passionate Shepherd to His Love" reflects the shift in focus from otherworldly concerns to secular subjects like love, politics, and science.

Literary Element Point of View

The standpoint from which a poem is told is called **point of view.** In first-person point of view the speaker uses *I* and *me.* In third-person point of view the speaker is an observer, not a participant in the action. "The Passionate Shepherd to His Love" uses first-person point of view. The speaker is a humble shepherd, not a sophisticated city dweller like Marlowe. While reading the poem, consider how Marlowe uses this point of view to speak about the joys of love.

- See Literary Terms Handbook, p. R13.

Literature Online Interactive Literary Elements Handbook To review or learn more about the literary elements, go to www.glencoe.com.

Reading Strategy Analyzing Sound Devices

Sound devices are techniques used to enhance a poem's sense of rhythm, to emphasize particular sounds, or to add to the musical quality of poetry. One sound device is **alliteration,** or the repetition of consonant sounds at the beginnings of words. As you read "The Passionate Shepherd to His Love," notice the effect of alliteration and how it might be used to reinforce meaning or tone and create a musical effect.

Reading Tip: Taking Notes Use a chart like the one below to record the lines in which Marlowe uses alliteration. Then explain the effect of alliteration on the poem's rhythm, tone, and meaning.

Alliteration	Effects

Shepherd Piping to a Shepherdess, 1747–1750. Francois Boucher. 94 x 142 cm. Wallace Collection, London.

OBJECTIVES
In studying this selection, you will focus on the following:
- relating literature to the historical period
- analyzing point of view in poetry
- analyzing sound devices

The Passionate Shepherd to His Love

Christopher Marlowe

Come live with me, and be my love,
And we will all the pleasures prove[1]
That valleys, groves, hills, and fields,
Woods or steepy mountain yields.

5   And we will sit upon the rocks,
Seeing the shepherds feed their flocks,
By shallow rivers to whose falls
Melodious birds sing madrigals.[2]

And I will make thee beds of roses,
10 And a thousand fragrant posies,
A cap of flowers, and a kirtle[3]
Embroidered all with leaves of myrtle.

A gown made of the finest wool,
Which from our pretty lambs we pull,
15 Fair lined slippers for the cold,
With buckles of the purest gold.

A belt of straw and ivy buds,
With coral clasps and amber studs.
And if these pleasures may thee move,
20 Come live with me and be my love.

The shepherd swains[4] shall dance and sing
For thy delight each May morning;
If these delights thy mind may move,
Then live with me and be my love.

---

1. Marlowe uses *prove* here to mean "experience."
2. *Madrigals* are harmonious songs.
3. A *kirtle* is a dress.
4. *Swains* means "youths."

Reading Strategy   Analyzing Sound Devices
How does the alliteration in this line contribute to the effect of the poem?

Camellia Japonica, 1793. Pierre Joseph Redoute. Watercolor, 38.6 x 27.7 cm. Fitzwillliam Museum, University of Cambridge.

RESPONDING AND THINKING CRITICALLY

Respond

1. Does this poem reflect your idea of love? Why or why not?

Recall and Interpret

2. (a)What does the shepherd ask of his beloved in the first stanza? (b)What does he tell her they will do if she accepts his request?

3. (a)What things does the shepherd promise to give his beloved? (b)What do these promises tell you about the shepherd and his love for the woman?

4. (a)Describe the kind of life the couple would have according to the shepherd. (b)Is this a realistic possibility? Explain.

Analyze and Evaluate

5. In this poem, Marlowe uses rhymes at the ends of each pair of lines. (a)What effect does this use of rhyme have on the tone of the poem? (b)What might Marlowe be trying to emphasize with his rhymes?

6. Do you find the shepherd's words persuasive? Why or why not?

Connect

7. **Big Idea** **Humanists and Courtiers** Marlowe's work, like that of many of his contemporaries, reflects ideas about love, politics, and philosophy. While the main subjects of this poem are love and the simple life, the poem also suggests other ideas. How might the ideas of this poem reflect the politics and society of the time?

LITERARY ANALYSIS

Literary Element **Point of View**

Marlowe wrote his poem from the **point of view** of the shepherd, who is attempting to persuade his love to live with him. This poem inspired many responses from other poets.

1. Why might Marlowe have chosen to write from the point of view of the shepherd?

2. What point of view might other poets have used when writing their responses?

Writing About Literature

Analyze Mood The **mood** of a literary work is its emotional quality or atmosphere. A writer's choice of language, subject matter, setting, and tone, as well as sound devices and rhythm, contributes to a work's mood. Read the poem again, and make a list of the literary elements Marlowe uses to create the mood of this poem. Then use your list to write a paragraph or two about how these elements work together to create the mood.

Literature Online **Web Activities** For eFlashcards, Selection Quick Checks, and other Web activities, go to www.glencoe.com.

READING AND VOCABULARY

Reading Strategy **Analyzing Sound Devices**

Marlowe uses **alliteration** to reinforce the poem's meaning and tone. Review the chart you made.

1. Marlowe uses the alliteration of *live* and *love* in the poem's first line and in the last lines of the fifth and sixth stanzas. What does the repetition of this alliteration contribute to the poem's mood?

2. (a)Cite the examples of alliteration in the last stanza. (b)Why might Marlowe have employed alliteration to this extent in the last stanza?

Academic Vocabulary

Here is a word from the vocabulary list on page R82. This word will help you think, write, and talk about the selection.

motive (mō´ tiv) *n.* a reason, desire, or other impulse

Practice and Apply
What is the shepherd's **motive** in the poem?

The Nymph's Reply to the Shepherd

MEET SIR WALTER RALEIGH

Sir Walter Raleigh was a soldier, explorer, colonizer, courtier, poet, scientist, and historian—perhaps the best example of a Renaissance man to emerge from the Elizabethan Age. He was described as "the most romantic figure of the most romantic age in the annals of English history" by biographer Hugh de Selincourt. Like Christopher Marlowe, Raleigh was brilliant and ambitious. He is credited as the father of both the British Empire and modern historical writing. He also introduced the potato to Ireland and tobacco to England. Even so, Raleigh experienced several spectacular failures. In his lifetime, he went from a war hero, favorite of the queen, and most loved man in England to a heretic accused of high treason and a prisoner of the court for more than a decade.

> *"We should begin by such a parting light*
> *To write the story of all ages past,*
> *And end the same before th' approaching night."*
>
> —Sir Walter Raleigh, *Ocean to Cynthia*

Quest for Excellence Raleigh began his career as a soldier and persuaded Elizabeth and her council to sponsor a voyage that established the first English colony—named Virginia after Queen Elizabeth, the Virgin Queen—in the hope of furthering England's position in the New World. However, his attempt to found a colony at Roanoke Island failed, as did most of his later overseas enterprises, such as his quest to find gold in Guiana.

Literary Man A patron of poets, Raleigh was also a poet himself. Fellow poet Edmund Spenser, whom Raleigh brought to Elizabeth's court from Ireland, claimed Raleigh's verse was "the sommers Nightingale." Critics, however, disagree about Raleigh's stature as a poet. Some argue that he "ranks even better amongst the minor poets of his time" and is indeed "extraordinary by any standards," while others label him "sometimes a Poet, not often."

The authenticity of some poems credited to Raleigh has been debated, but much of his best work simply disappeared or was left unsigned. Like many court poets, he resisted the "stigma of print." However, his remaining poems, his many papers, and his only book, *The History of the World,* mark Raleigh as a gifted writer who deserves his place in English literature.

Imprisonment When Raleigh secretly married one of the queen's ladies-in-waiting, Elizabeth turned on him and sent him to the Tower of London. He was briefly released, but after James I came to power in 1603, Raleigh was falsely accused of treason and sentenced to death. He remained in the Tower for the rest of his life, and it was there that he wrote his long, incomplete book *The History of the World.* He was to dedicate it to the Prince of Wales, his most powerful supporter, who is said to have declared, "None but my father would keep such a bird in a cage." The prince died in 1612 before he could help Raleigh, who was finally beheaded in 1618. As he examined his executioner's ax, Raleigh remarked, "This is a sharp medicine, but it is a cure for all diseases." His final words, as the executioner hesitated, were "Strike, man!"

Sir Walter Raleigh was born in 1552 and died in 1618.

Literature Online **Author Search** For more about Sir Walter Raleigh, go to www.glencoe.com.

Connecting to the Poem

Whether someone has been in love or not, everyone has a view of love and what love is and should be. What is your view of love? Are you romantic? Are you realistic? Or are you a little bit of both?

Building Background

As a favorite of Queen Elizabeth I, Raleigh was honored with both land and power. As a courtier, many of his poems were written for and about Elizabeth. At first they praised the queen in an attempt to advance his position in court, secure funds for his expeditions, and express his love for her. But after his dismissal from court, his poems about her turned dark and expressed his despair over her betrayal and rejection.

His most celebrated poem, "The Nymph's Reply to the Shepherd," is a response to Christopher Marlowe's pastoral poem "The Passionate Shepherd to His Love" (see page 277). Raleigh's nymph rejects each worldly pleasure the shepherd offers. The themes of the poem echo the themes that appeared in many of his works—the swiftness of time's passage, the vanity of youth, the corruption of society through greed and power, the inevitability of death, and the lies of lovers.

Setting Purposes for Reading

Big Idea **Humanists and Courtiers**

Like Christopher Marlowe and other sixteenth-century writers, Raleigh explored love, politics, science, and philosophy in his writing and in his life. As you read "The Nymph's Reply to the Shepherd," note the ways in which Raleigh addresses some of these issues.

Literary Element **Author's Purpose**

An author's intent when writing a literary work is called the **author's purpose.** Authors typically write to persuade, to inform, to explain, to entertain, or to describe. As you read, consider what Raleigh's purpose was in responding to Marlowe's poem.

- See Literary Terms Handbook, p. R2.

Reading Strategy **Comparing and Contrasting Speakers**

The **speaker** of a poem is similar to the narrator in a work of prose. The speaker's words communicate a particular tone toward the subject of the work. The nymph—the shepherd's love—is the speaker in Raleigh's poem, and she responds to the pleas of Marlowe's shepherd. As you read, pay attention to how the nymph's point of view is similar to or different from that of the shepherd in Marlowe's poem.

....

Reading Tip: Comparing and Contrasting In each stanza of Raleigh's poem, the nymph counters the shepherd's proposals in Marlowe's poem. Read both poems stanza by stanza, and use a chart like the one below to compare and contrast each speaker's point of view.

Stanza	Nymph	Shepherd
1.		
2.		
3.		
4.		
5.		
6.		
7.		

Literature Online **Interactive Literary Elements Handbook** To review or learn more about the literary elements, go to www.glencoe.com.

OBJECTIVES
In studying this selection, you will focus on the following:
- analyzing literary periods
- understanding and analyzing author's purpose
- comparing and contrasting speakers and points of view

The Nymph's Reply to the Shepherd

Sir Walter Raleigh

Shepherd and Shepherdess. Abraham Bloemaert. Oil on canvas.
Collection of the Earl of Pembroke, Wilton House, Wilts, UK.

If all the world and love were young,
And truth in every shepherd's tongue,
These pretty pleasures might me move,
To live with thee and be thy love.

5   Time drives the flocks from field to fold,[1]
When rivers rage, and rocks grow cold,
And Philomel[2] becometh dumb,
The rest complains of cares to come.

The flowers do fade, and wanton[3] fields
10 To wayward winter reckoning yields;
A honey tongue, a heart of gall,[4]
Is fancy's spring but sorrow's fall.

Thy gowns, thy shoes, thy beds of roses,
Thy cap, thy kirtle, and thy posies,
15 Soon break, soon wither, soon forgotten;
In folly ripe, in reason rotten.

Thy belt of straw and ivy buds,
Thy coral clasps and amber studs,
All these in me no means can move
20 To come to thee and be thy love.

But could youth last, and love still breed,
Had joys no date[5] nor age no need,
Then these delights my mind might move
To live with thee and be thy love.

---

1. The flocks are driven to a *fold,* or sheep enclosure.
2. *Philomel* was the nightingale, named after Princess Philomela, of Greek mythology, who was turned into a nightingale by the gods.
3. *Wanton* means "ample" or "luxuriant."
4. Here, *gall* is bitterness.
5. Raleigh uses *date* to mean "end."

Literary Element   Author's Purpose *How do these lines help to establish Raleigh's purpose?*

Reading Strategy   Comparing and Contrasting Speakers *Compare lines 13–15 with lines 9–16 in "The Passionate Shepherd to His Love." How do the speakers' tones differ?*

RESPONDING AND THINKING CRITICALLY

Respond

1. Has your view of love changed after reading this poem? Why or why not?

Recall and Interpret

2. (a)What does the nymph imply about the shepherd in the first stanza? (b)How would you describe the tone of this stanza?

3. (a)How does the nymph characterize all the treasures the shepherd offers? (b)What does the nymph's response to the shepherd reveal about her view of life?

4. (a)What does the nymph say might convince her to love the shepherd? (b)Does it seem likely that she will ever love the shepherd? Explain.

Analyze and Evaluate

5. Is Raleigh's response to "The Passionate Shepherd to His Love" a pastoral poem? Explain.

6. (a)Would the meaning of this poem be different if you had not already read "The Passionate Shepherd to His Love"? Explain. (b)How does reading these two poems together increase the impact of the poems?

7. How does Raleigh use imagery to express the nymph's views of life and the shepherd's promises?

Connect

8. **Big Idea** **Humanists and Courtiers** At this time, writers were focusing on the concerns of love, politics, science, and philosophy. (a)What do you think the theme of Raleigh's poem is? (b)How does the theme reflect Raleigh's views on these worldly subjects? Explain.

LITERARY ANALYSIS

Literary Element Author's Purpose

An **author's purpose** can be to persuade, to describe, to inform, to explain, or to entertain. Raleigh's "The Nymph's Reply to the Shepherd" is the most famous response to Marlowe's "The Passionate Shepherd to His Love."

1. Why might Raleigh have written a response to Marlowe's poem?

2. Why did Raleigh use the same meter and references that are in Marlowe's poem?

Listening and Speaking

Work with partners to create a script to introduce Raleigh's and Marlowe's poems and offer some background information. Then practice reading the poems aloud in a call-and-response fashion (first the shepherd's stanza and then the nymph's corresponding stanza). With your group, perform your scripted version of the poems for your class.

Literature Online **Web Activities** For eFlashcards, Selection Quick Checks, and other Web activities, go to www.glencoe.com.

READING AND VOCABULARY

Reading Strategy Comparing and Contrasting Speakers

The nymph in Raleigh's poem responds to each of the shepherd's pleas, and her responses establish the tone of the poem.

1. How does the nymph's tone compare to the shepherd's tone?

2. What words or phrases help you determine the nymph's tone?

Academic Vocabulary

Here is a word from the vocabulary list on page R82. This word will help you think, write, and talk about the selection.

amend (ə mend′) *v.* change or modify; to correct errors

Practice and Apply
How does the nymph **amend** the shepherd's statements about love?

Of Studies

MEET SIR FRANCIS BACON

P oet and playwright Ben Jonson called Sir Francis Bacon "one of the greatest men, and most worthy of admiration, that had been in many ages." Not everyone, however, shared this high opinion. The physician William Harvey, for example, said that Bacon had "the eye of a viper."

Political Rise and Fall Bacon was born in London, the son of a civil servant in Queen Elizabeth's court. After attending Trinity College, Cambridge, and training as a lawyer, Bacon held a series of government posts and was knighted in 1603. As a supporter of King James I, Bacon rose to the position of Lord Chancellor of England, the highest honor in the British legal profession. However, Bacon's good fortune soured in 1621, when at the peak of his career he was convicted of taking bribes to support his extravagant lifestyle. After resigning in disgrace, Bacon devoted himself to scholarly pursuits.

> "I have taken all knowledge to be my province."
>
> —Sir Francis Bacon

Scientist and Philosopher A true Renaissance man, Bacon contributed to many diverse fields: philosophy, biology, physics, chemistry, and architecture. He also wrote a digest of British laws, a history of Great Britain, and biographies of Tudor monarchs. In his writings *Advancement of Learning* and *De Dignitate et Augmentis Scientiarum*, he presented a thorough systematization of the whole range of human knowledge. Scientists today owe their reliance on the inductive method of reasoning to Bacon, who promoted the idea that generalizations should be based on facts. That idea, while obvious today, was revolutionary during Bacon's

lifetime, when scholars still preferred deductive reasoning—moving from generalizations to specifics instead of vice versa.

In addition, Bacon introduced the concept of hypotheses to scientists, arguing that scientists needed to make initial assumptions before beginning their experiments. He also pioneered the idea of a scientific research establishment that would work collaboratively in a methodical fashion to give material benefits to humankind. This innovative idea eventually led to the founding of Britain's Royal Society, an organization dedicated to the pursuit and advancement of scientific endeavors.

Bacon even died in the service of science. At the age of sixty-five, he impulsively decided while riding in his carriage to test the powers of refrigeration. Bacon exited the carriage to collect snow, which he stuffed into a dead hen. Unfortunately, he caught a chill in the process and took ill. Bacon died from bronchitis a few days later.

Acclaimed Stylist Of all Bacon's writings, the most popular remains his *Essays and Counsels,* which he first published in 1597. This work was a landmark in English prose composition. Bacon packed his essays with insights and shrewd observations about human nature. Much of what he wrote about his age applies equally well to modern times. His style is aphoristic: that is, it includes pithy sentences that express simple truths or nuggets of practical wisdom. This characteristic has earned him literary immortality: he remains one of the most quotable authors in the English language.

Sir Francis Bacon was born in 1561 and died in 1626.

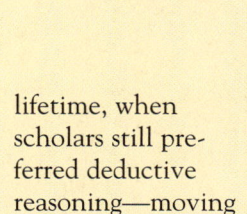 **Author Search** For more about Sir Francis Bacon, go to www.glencoe.com.

Connecting to the Essay

How and why do you study? What benefits do reading and studying offer? In the essay "Of Studies," Sir Francis Bacon discusses the value of reading and studying. As you read the essay, think about these questions:

- How do you choose what to read?
- What do you gain from reading?
- Is it possible to read or study too much?

Building Background

The **essay,** a brief prose composition exploring a single subject, was a development of the Renaissance. The French philosopher Montaigne (mon tän´) published a collection of his writings on selected topics that he called *Essais* (or "attempts"). Bacon borrowed this title for his own first published essays and thus became the "father" of the English essay, the first English writer to make use of this new literary form and shape it to his own taste. Unlike the personal essays of Montaigne, the Baconian essay is objective, compact, and logical.

Setting Purposes for Reading

Big Idea **Humanists and Courtiers**

As you read, notice how this essay reflects the Renaissance focus on secular concerns.

Literary Element **Parallelism**

The use of words, phrases, or sentences that have similar grammatical structures is called **parallelism.** Consider the following example:

Sir Francis Bacon was **a distinguished scientist** and **an elegant stylist.**

The boldfaced phrases are parallel, with each one consisting of an indefinite article followed by an adjective and then a noun.

- See Literary Terms Handbook, p. R12.

Literature Online **Interactive Literary Elements Handbook** To review or learn more about the literary elements, go to www.glencoe.com.

Reading Strategy **Determining Main Idea and Supporting Details**

Determining an author's main idea is finding the most important thought in a paragraph or a selection. An essay typically states or implies a **thesis,** or main idea, which is developed through the use of **supporting details,** such as examples, reasons, or facts.

Reading Tip: Using an Idea Web As you read, make a web like the one below. List supporting details around the middle circle. Then, after reading, write the main idea suggested by the supporting details.

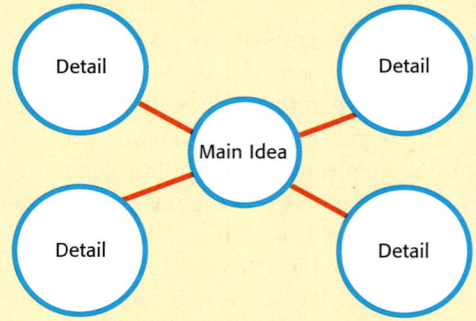

Vocabulary

discourse (dis´ kôrs´) *n.* verbal communication in speech or writing; p. 285 *His discourse left the audience bored and somewhat confused.*

execute (ek´ sə kūt´) *v.* to carry out; to put into effect; p. 285 *To execute her orders, the housekeeper polished the silverware with extreme care.*

sloth (slôth) *n.* laziness; p. 285 *His sloth prevented him from completing the required courses.*

impediment (im ped´ ə mənt) *n.* an obstacle; p. 286 *Her limited income was an impediment to a lavish lifestyle.*

Vocabulary Tip: Word Parts You can often figure out the meaning of an unfamiliar word by analyzing its parts.

OBJECTIVES

In studying this selection, you will focus on the following:
- analyzing literary periods
- analyzing parallelism
- identifying the main idea and supporting details

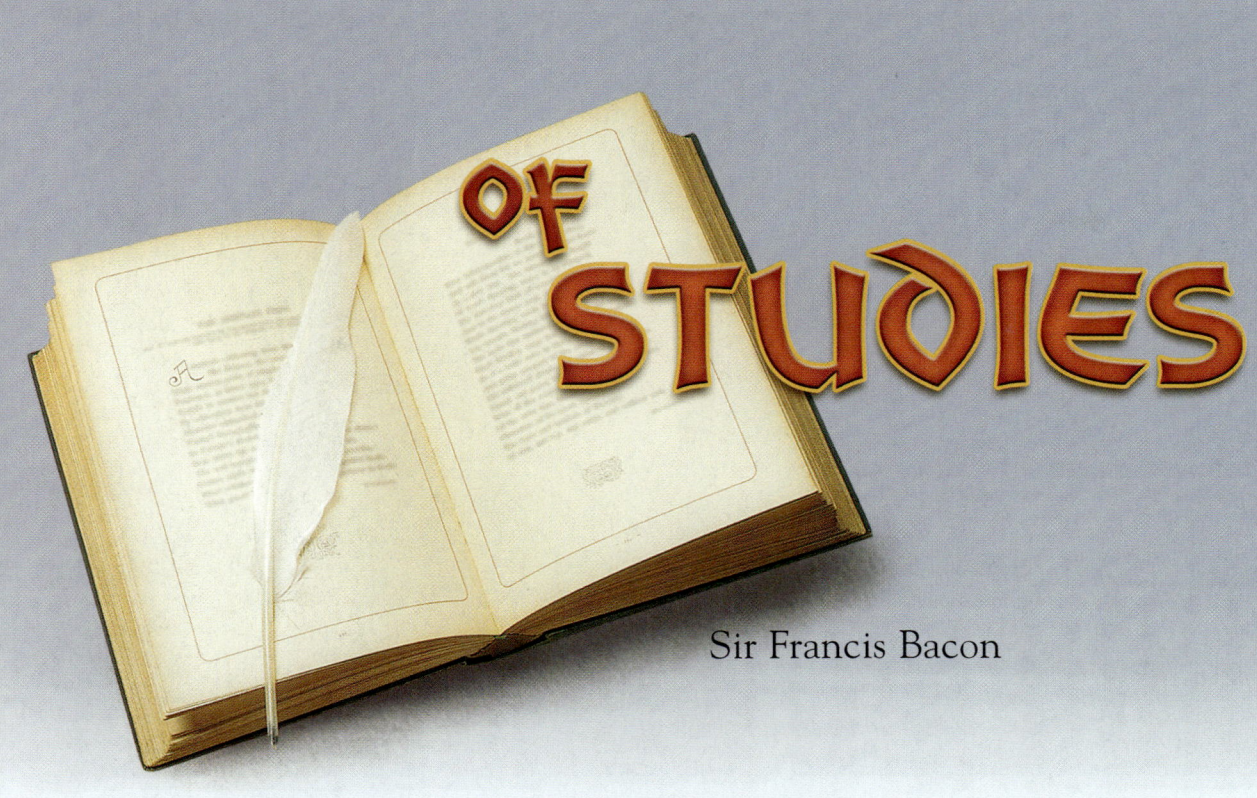

OF STUDIES

Sir Francis Bacon

Studies serve for delight, for ornament, and for ability. Their chief use for delight is in privateness and retiring; for ornament, is in **discourse;** and for ability, is in the judgment and disposition of business. For expert men can **execute,** and perhaps judge of particulars, one by one; but the general counsels, and the plots and marshaling of affairs, come best from those that are learned. To spend too much time in studies is **sloth;** to use them too much for ornament, is affectation;[1] to make judgment wholly by their rules, is the humor[2] of a scholar. They perfect nature, and are perfected by experience: for natural abilities are like natural plants, that need proyning[3] by study; and studies themselves do give forth directions too much at large, except they be bounded in by experience. Crafty men contemn[4] studies, simple men admire them, and wise men use them; for they teach not their own use; but that is a wisdom without them and above them, won by observation. Read not to contradict and confute;[5] nor to believe and take for granted; nor to find talk and discourse; but to weigh and consider. Some books are to be tasted, others to be swallowed, and some few to be chewed and digested; that is, some books are to be read only in parts; others to be read, but not curiously;[6] and some few to be read wholly, and with diligence and

---

1. *Affectation* is artificial behavior meant to be impressive.
2. Here, *humor* means "whim."

Vocabulary

discourse (dis´ kôrs´) *n.* verbal communication in speech or writing
execute (ek´ sə kūt´) *v.* to carry out; to put into effect
sloth (slôth) *n.* laziness

---

3. *Proyning* means "pruning."
4. *Contemn* means "to view with scorn or contempt."
5. *Confute* means "prove wrong."
6. *Curiously* means "carefully."

Still Life with Inkstand and Books, 1702. Edwaert Collier. Oil on canvas. Private collection.

attention. Some books also may be read by deputy, and extracts made of them by others; but that would be only in the less important arguments, and the meaner sort of books, else distilled books[7] are like common distilled waters,[8] flashy[9] things. Reading maketh a full man; conference[10] a ready man; and writing an exact man. And therefore, if a man write little, he had need have a great memory; if he confer little, he had need have a present wit;[11] and if he read little, he had need have much cunning, to seem to know that he doth not. Histories make men wise; poets witty; the mathematics subtile; natural philosophy deep; moral grave; logic and rhetoric[12] able to contend. *Abeunt studia in mores.*[13] Nay, there is no stond[14] or **impediment** in the wit but may be wrought out by fit studies; like as diseases of the body may have appropriate exercises. Bowling is good for the stone and reins;[15] shooting for the lungs and breast; gentle walking for the stomach; riding for the head; and the like. So if a man's wit be wandering, let him study the mathematics; for in demonstrations, if his wit be called away never so little, he must begin again. If his wit be not apt to distinguish or find differences, let him study the Schoolmen;[16] for they are *cymini sectores.*[17] If he be not apt to beat over[18] matters, and to call up one thing to prove and illustrate another, let him study the lawyers' cases. So every defect of the mind may have a special receipt.[19]

---

7. *Distilled books* are books that have been abridged, or condensed.
8. *Distilled waters* are homemade remedies.
9. *Flashy* means "tasteless."
10. A *conference* is a conversation.
11. A *present wit* is a quick, alert mind.
12. *Rhetoric* is the skill of speaking or writing effectively or persuasively.
13. *Abeunt studia in mores* is Latin for "Studies affect people's behavior."

Literary Element Parallelism *What are the parallel structures in this sentence?*

14. *Stond* means "obstruction."
15. *Stone and reins* are kidney stones and other kidney disorders.
16. *Schoolmen* refers to medieval philosophers.
17. *Cymini sectores* is Latin for "hairsplitters" (literally, "seedsplitters").
18. *Beat over* means "reason through."
19. Here, *receipt* means "remedy."

Vocabulary

impediment (im ped′ ə mənt) *n.* an obstruction; an obstacle

RESPONDING AND THINKING CRITICALLY

Respond

1. Did Bacon change your opinion of studies? Why or why not?

Recall and Interpret

2. (a)According to Bacon, what are the three main benefits of study, and what danger can result from each benefit? (b)Why do people need more than knowledge to make wise decisions?

3. (a)What is the proper attitude and purpose Bacon advises readers to take toward their books? (b)What does this advice tell you about Bacon's attitude toward learning?

4. (a)Summarize the benefits Bacon mentions for studying history, poetry, mathematics, philosophy, logic, and rhetoric. (b)What do these benefits have in common?

Analyze and Evaluate

5. Bacon believes that spending "too much time in studies is sloth." What might be his reasons for that belief? Explain why you agree or disagree with him.

6. (a)How valid is Bacon's statement that some books should be tasted, some swallowed, and some chewed and digested? Explain your response. (b)In your opinion, should this essay be tasted, swallowed, or chewed and digested? Support your evaluation.

Connect

7. **Big Idea** **Humanists and Courtiers** Why might this essay have appealed to young people during the Renaissance?

VISUAL LITERACY: Graphic Organizer

Creating a Concept Map

In "Of Studies," Bacon presents his insights about learning. Though brief, this essay is complex and dense in meaning. By creating a concept map, you can organize the ideas that Bacon presents. A concept map is a visual representation that enables you to process information quickly.

Group Activity With a small group, complete the concept map below by filling in the empty boxes. Then discuss your findings.

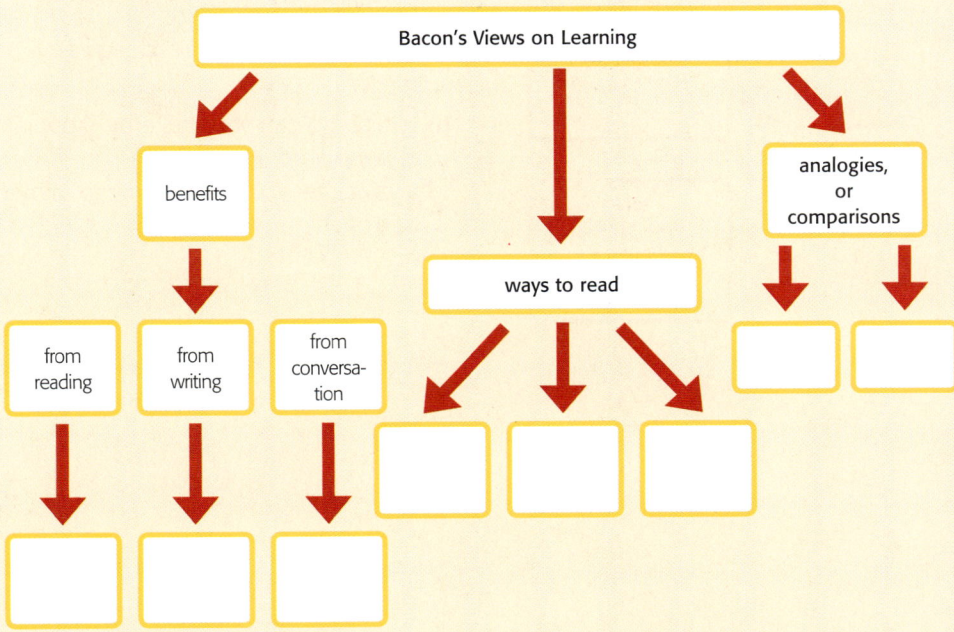

Bacon's Views on Learning

benefits

analogies, or comparisons

ways to read

from reading

from writing

from conversation

Literary Element Parallelism

Parallelism affects a piece of writing in many ways. It helps words flow together; it calls attention to important ideas; it balances different ideas in a composition; and it sets up a cadence, or rhythm. In "Of Studies," for example, Bacon writes:

"Studies serve **for delight, for ornament,** and **for ability.**"

In the example above, the sentence contains three phrases, with each phrase beginning with the preposition *for* followed by a noun.

1. Find three more examples of parallelism in "Of Studies."

2. Explain how Bacon's use of parallelism helps emphasize his ideas.

Review: Author's Purpose

As you learned on page 280, **author's purpose** refers to an author's intent in writing a literary work. An author typically writes to accomplish one or more of the following purposes: to persuade, to instruct, to inform or explain, to entertain, to describe, or to tell a story.

Partner Activity With another classmate, discuss Bacon's purposes for writing this essay. To present your evidence, create a web like the one below. Fill it in with an example for each item listed.

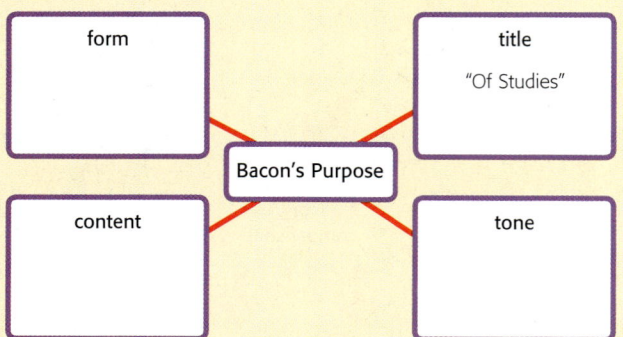

form

title
"Of Studies"

Bacon's Purpose

content

tone

Reading Strategy Determining Main Idea and Supporting Details

In order to figure out a text's main idea, note passages that express important points. Then try to sum up the thesis, or main idea. Refer to the web you created on page 284 as you answer the following questions:

1. Choose one idea from Bacon's essay that you find persuasive or interesting. Explain why it appeals to you.

2. Which idea seems to be at the heart of Bacon's views about studies?

3. Are Bacon's ideas still relevant today? Explain your reasoning.

Vocabulary Practice

Practice with Word Parts Use a dictionary and your knowledge of word parts to answer the following questions.

1. The root of the word *discourse* is *currere,* which means "to run." What is the literal meaning of *discourse*?
   a. a running back   **c.** a running together
   b. a running about

2. What does the prefix *ex-* in the word *execute* mean?
   a. former   **c.** out
   b. away

3. Which suffix changes *sloth* from a noun to an adjective?
   a. *-ly*   **c.** *-able*
   b. *-ful*

4. What verb can you make by dropping the suffix in *impediment*?
   a. impede   **c.** impediments
   b. imped

Writing About Literature

Evaluate Rhetorical Devices In "Of Studies," Bacon's style features a startling conciseness of expression, sentence rhythm, and rich, powerful phrases. To achieve those effects, Bacon uses **parallelism** and other rhetorical devices, such as **repetition,** or the use of the same words, phrases, or sentences again and again, and **analogy,** a comparison based on a similarity between things that are otherwise dissimilar.

Write a brief essay in which you discuss these rhetorical devices and evaluate their effectiveness. As you draft, write from start to finish. Develop your ideas in the order shown in the outline below.

> I. Introduction
> II. Body Paragraph
>   A. Examples of parallelism
>   B. Evaluation of this device
> III. Body Paragraph
>   A. Examples of repetition
>   B. Evaluation of this device
> IV. Body Paragraph
>   A. Examples of analogy
>   B. Evaluation of this device
> V. Conclusion

After completing your draft, meet with a peer reviewer to evaluate each other's work and to suggest revisions. Then edit and proofread your draft for errors in spelling, grammar, and punctuation.

Learning for Life

With a partner, plan an advertising campaign to promote reading in your community. Make a poster and write a public-service announcement for radio or television. Share your poster and announcement with your class.

Literature Online **Web Activities** For eFlashcards, Selection Quick Checks, and other Web activities, go to www.glencoe.com.

Bacon's Language and Style

Using Semicolons A semicolon (;) is a punctuation mark used to separate the main clauses in a compound sentence. Notice the following examples from "Of Studies":

"To spend too much time in studies is sloth; to use them too much for ornament, is affectation; to make judgment wholly by their rules, is the humor of a scholar."

"Some books are to be tasted, others to be swallowed, and some few to be chewed and digested; that is, some books are to be read only in parts; others to be read, but not curiously; and some few to be read wholly, and with diligence and attention."

In the first example, the semicolons help call attention to the parallel structures as they separate main clauses not joined by a comma and a coordinating conjunction (*and, but, or, nor, so, yet,* or *for*). In the second example, a semicolon precedes the expression *that is,* which introduces explanatory details. By convention, certain expressions and conjunctive adverbs separating two main clauses are preceded by a semicolon:

Conjunctive Adverbs	Expressions
therefore	for example
moreover	in fact
however	that is
consequently	on the other hand

Also, in the second example, notice the semicolons after the words *parts* and *curiously.* Those semicolons separate items in a series that already contain commas.

Activity Review "Of Studies" to identify other examples of sentences containing semicolons. For each example, explain the reason for that use of a semicolon.

Revising Check

Semicolons Review your essay on analyzing rhetorical devices. Look for places where semicolons could improve it.

Grammar Workshop

Language Usage

▶ **Subjects and Verbs**

A **subject** tells who or what a sentence is about. A **verb** tells the action that a subject takes.

▶ **Test-Taking Tip**

Avoid using forms of the verb *to be* when possible. Instead, write in the active voice.

Indefinite Pronouns	
Singular	**Plural**
another	both
anyone	many
everyone	few
one	several
each	others
either	
neither	
anything	

▶ **Language Handbook**

For more about subjects and verbs, see Language Handbook, p. R51.

Literature Online
eWorkbooks To link to the Grammar and Language eWorkbook, go to www.glencoe.com.

OBJECTIVES
- Understand subject-verb agreement.
- Recognize singular and plural subjects.

Making Subjects and Verbs Agree

"Crafty men contemn studies, simple men admire them, and wise men use them."
—Sir Francis Bacon, from "Of Studies"

Connecting to Literature In every sentence and clause, the subject and verb must agree; that is, if the **subject**—who or what is doing something—is singular, the **verb** that describes the action must also be singular. If the subject is plural, the verb must be plural. In the sample sentence above, *men* is the subject of each clause, so the verbs *contemn, admire,* and *use* must be in plural form. You can avoid many subject-verb agreement errors in your own writing by following the guidelines below.

Common Agreement Problems

Problem 1 A predicate nominative differs in number from the subject.
Reading and learning <u>was</u> Sir Francis Bacon's passion.

Solution Ignore the predicate nominative and make the verb agree with the subject, in this case, *reading and learning*.
Reading and learning <u>were</u> Sir Francis Bacon's passion.

Problem 2 A compound subject is joined by *or* or *nor*.
Neither "Of Studies" nor Bacon's other works <u>teaches</u> us that learning is the same for every person.

Solution Make the verb agree with the part of the compound subject that is closer to it.
Neither "Of Studies" nor Bacon's other works <u>teach</u> us that learning is the same for every person.

Problem 3 An indefinite pronoun is the subject.
Everyone <u>have encountered</u> a hobby to "chew up and digest."

Solution Determine whether the indefinite pronoun is singular or plural and make the verb agree with it.
Everyone <u>has encountered</u> a hobby to "chew up and digest."

Exercise

Correct Agreement. Correct any errors in subject-verb agreement. If there are none, write *no errors*.

1. Neither Bacon nor other writers has put the full value of learning into words.
2. Everyone have interests and subjects to pursue.
3. Histories or philosophy is important to study.
4. Studies is a labor of love for those who wish to learn.

PART 2

A Bard for the Ages

Detail of a Portrait of William Shakespeare, 1623. Martin Droeshout. Engraving.

"O! for a Muse of fire, that would ascend
The brightest heaven of invention."

—William Shakespeare, *Henry V*

Shakespeare's Poetry

MEET WILLIAM SHAKESPEARE

William Shakespeare is the most celebrated English poet and dramatist of all time. Nearly four centuries after his death, his works continue to delight readers and audiences around the world. In fact, Shakespeare's writings are more widely read and more often quoted than any other works ever written, except the Bible. Yet, while Shakespeare's literature endures, we know very little about the man himself. The meager information we do have about Shakespeare's life has been pieced together from anecdotes, gossip, clues found in his poems and plays, legal documents, entries in the public record, and the memorials and reminiscences by his fellow writers.

Early Life Shakespeare was born in the small town of Stratford-upon-Avon. His father, John Shakespeare, was a prosperous glove maker, butcher, and tradesman who also filled several local government positions, including high bailiff (the equivalent of mayor). His mother, Mary Arden, was the daughter of a wealthy landowner. William Shakespeare was the third of at least eight children born to this well-to-do couple. He was their first son and their first child to survive past childhood. As a young boy, Shakespeare likely attended the local grammar school, studying Latin and classical literature.

When Shakespeare was about thirteen, however, his father started to lose his social standing and to have serious financial problems. Shakespeare was forced to leave school in order to work to help support his family. Just what type of work he did remains unknown, but he may have apprenticed as a butcher. Shakespeare may also have served for a time as a schoolmaster in the country, where he would have acquired the familiarity with outdoor sports, such as hunting, hawking, and falconry, that manifests itself throughout his literary works.

At the age of eighteen, Shakespeare married a twenty-six-year-old local woman named Anne Hathaway and began a family of his own. The couple had a daughter, Susanna, and twins, Hamnet and Judith. Sadly, Hamnet died at the age of eleven.

The London Theater Scene Shakespeare moved to London to pursue a career in the theater, but, according to poet William Davenant, he arrived without friends or money. His first "theater job" actually consisted of tending the horses of theater patrons—the equivalent of parking cars at a theater today. Nevertheless, his wit attracted the attention of the actors, who apparently thought him clever enough to improve a few of their plays (revising plays to add scenes or to bring them up to date was a common practice at the time), and the actors eventually recommended him for a job. If Davenant's tale is true, this is how Shakespeare got his chance to write for the stage—and to act in small parts as well.

Dramatic Success The production of *Henry VI* in 1592 appears to have been Shakespeare's first theatrical success. Later, he wrote and published two long narrative poems, which became immediate favorites: *Venus and Adonis* and *The Rape of Lucrece*. He dedicated these works to a newfound patron and friend, the young Earl of Southampton. The earl, upon reaching maturity and thereby gaining

The Room in Which Shakespeare Was Born, 1853. Henry Wallis. Oil on board, 29.2 x 41.9 cm. Tate Gallery, London.

access to his fortune, expressed his thanks for these dedications by giving Shakespeare a large sum of money, which enabled him to become partial owner of a theatrical company, the Lord Chamberlain's Men. As part owner, Shakespeare became the main playwright for the troupe.

The playhouse in which they had been performing, called simply the "Theatre," was torn down and rebuilt in a larger, more splendid form south of the Thames River. This new playhouse, opened in 1599, was called the Globe, which is the name still associated with Shakespearean theater today.

Building a Career and an Estate By the time the Globe opened, Shakespeare had earned enough money to enable him to purchase several properties and a large estate for his family in Stratford, although he continued to live primarily in London. By 1599 the thirty-five-year-old playwright was producing two plays a year and drawing tremendous audiences as well as critical acclaim. A literary handbook of the time calls Shakespeare "most excellent" in both comedy and tragedy and "the most passionate among us to bewail and bemoan the perplexities of love."

> *"He was not of an age, but for all time!"*
>
> —Ben Jonson

The Pinnacle of Genius Shakespeare's greatest creative period had just begun in 1599. Between 1601 and 1607, he wrote the tragic masterpieces *Hamlet, Othello, Macbeth,* and *King Lear.* He also wrote comedies that were darker and more complex than his previous works. As well as performing in the Globe, the Lord Chamberlain's Men performed several times at the courts of Elizabeth I and James I. In fact, James's patronage enabled the troupe to call itself the King's Men. Besides their performances at court, the King's Men also performed after 1609 in an indoor, heated, and candle-lit playhouse called the Blackfriars Theatre. Their performances in this aristocratic venue proved much more profitable than those in the Globe.

Shakespeare's finest plays, though much admired by his contemporaries, achieved less literary status than his narrative and lyrical poems in his lifetime. During Shakespeare's career, his reputation as a great writer was based mainly on his nondramatic poems and on his sonnets. Shakespeare published his sonnets in 1609, although he had actually written and circulated the bulk of them in handwritten form in the 1590s.

In 1610, for reasons not known to us today, Shakespeare moved back to Stratford, where he lived comfortably as a semi-retired gentleman, writing fewer plays than before. Among these was a supreme romance, *The Tempest,* in which the main character's farewell speech (see page 310) is generally regarded as Shakespeare's farewell to writing and perhaps to life. He died in Stratford on his fifty-second birthday.

William Shakespeare was born in 1564 and died in 1616.

Literature Online **Author Search** For more about William Shakespeare, go to www.glencoe.com.

Connecting to the Poems

In the two sonnets you are about to read, the speaker comments on the nature of love and the way in which one's love is expressed. As you read these sonnets, think about the following questions:

- What is the essence of true love?
- To what extent is it possible to express one's love in words?

Building Background

Sonnet sequences became fashionable long before Shakespeare's time. Writing a sonnet was one way for a poet to demonstrate mastery of the technical aspects of writing poetry. But writing a sonnet was also a way for the poet to demonstrate his or her creative ingenuity. Sonnets often relied heavily on the literary conventions of a young man pining away because his love was unrequited, or of eternal love shared between two people in an idealized setting, such as a shepherd and shepherdess in a pastoral setting. A poet might demonstrate ingenuity either by composing clever variations on these conventions or by parodying them. A **parody** is a humorous imitation of a literary work that aims to point out its shortcomings.

Setting Purposes for Reading

Big Idea A Bard for the Ages

Shakespeare was a deep thinker and a learned man as well as a great poet. As you read, notice how he uses the sonnet form to express his philosophy about love and human relationships.

Literary Element Simile and Metaphor

Simile and **metaphor** are figures of speech that make comparisons between two seemingly unlike things or ideas in order to suggest an underlying similarity between them. A simile differs from a metaphor in that the words *like* or *as* are used to express the comparison. In other words, the comparison in a metaphor is implicit, while the comparison in a simile is explicit.

- See Literary Terms Handbook, pp. R10 and R16.

Reading Strategy Analyzing Figures of Speech

A **figure of speech** is a specific kind of figurative language, such as metaphor, simile, personification, or symbol. Figures of speech are not to be taken literally; they express a truth beyond the literal level. To analyze figures of speech in a literary work, first identify and explain the various types, and then determine how they contribute to the meaning of the selection as a whole.

Reading Tip: Taking Notes Use a chart to record the figures of speech in Sonnets 116 and 130.

Figure of Speech	Type	Meaning

Vocabulary

alteration (ôl´ tə rā´ shən) *n.* change; modification; p. 295 *Although I was gone for only a short time, I noticed a subtle alteration in the mood of the party.*

tempest (tem´ pist) *n.* a violent storm; a violent outburst or disturbance; p. 295 *The tempest left many people homeless.*

doom (do͞om) *n.* that which cannot be escaped; death, ruin, or destruction; p. 295 *The residents fearfully awaited the hurricane and its doom.*

tread (tred) *v.* to walk or step upon; p. 296 *Please do not tread on the flower beds.*

Vocabulary Tip: Synonyms Synonyms are words that have the same or nearly the same meanings. Note that synonyms are always the same part of speech.

Literature Online Interactive Literary Elements Handbook To review or learn more about the literary elements, go to www.glencoe.com.

OBJECTIVES
In studying these selections, you will focus on the following:
- analyzing literary genres
- understanding metaphor and simile
- analyzing figures of speech

Promenading Noblemen. Central section from the Garden of Love at the court of Philippe III the Good, Duke of Burgundy (1396—1467), in the gardens of Hesdin Castle in 1432, 15th century. Anonymous. Chateaux de Versailles et de Trianon, France.

SONNET 116

William Shakespeare

Let me not to the marriage of true minds
Admit impediments;[1] love is not love
Which alters when it **alteration** finds,
Or bends with the remover to remove.[2]
5   Oh no, it is an ever-fixèd mark[3]
That looks on **tempests** and is never shaken;
It is the star to every wand'ring bark,[4]
Whose worth's unknown, although his height be taken.
Love's not Time's fool, though rosy lips and cheeks
10 Within his bending sickle's compass[5] come,
Love alters not with his brief hours and weeks,
But bears it out even to the edge of **doom**.[6]
    If this be error and upon me proved,
    I never writ, nor no man ever loved.

1. *Impediments* means "obstacles." The speaker is referring to the traditional Christian marriage service in which the clergy member says, "If any of you know cause or just impediment why these persons should not be joined together . . ."
2. *[Bends . . . to remove]* means the person changes when his or her sweetheart is inconstant.
3. *Mark* refers to a landmark that sailors can see from the water and that is used as a navigational guide.
4. A *bark* is a boat.
5. Here, *compass* means "range."
6. *The edge of doom* refers to the end of the world.

Literary Element   Simile and Metaphor   *Explain the metaphor in this line. What is being compared?*

Vocabulary

alteration (ôl′ tə rā′ shən) *n.* change; modification

tempest (tem′ pist) *n.* a violent storm; a violent outburst or disturbance

doom (do͞om) *n.* that which cannot be escaped; death, ruin, or destruction

A Girl at a Window Holding a Bunch of Grapes. Attributed to Hieronymus van der Mij. Oil on panel, 43.5 x 34 cm. Sotheby's, London.

SONNET 130

William Shakespeare

My mistress' eyes are nothing like the sun;
Coral is far more red than her lips' red;
If snow be white, why then her breasts are dun;[1]
If hairs be wires, black wires grow on her head.
5 I have seen roses damask'd,[2] red and white,
But no such roses see I in her cheeks,
And in some perfumes is there more delight
Than in the breath that from my mistress reeks.[3]
I love to hear her speak, yet well I know
10 That music hath a far more pleasing sound;
I grant I never saw a goddess go,[4]
My mistress when she walks **treads** on the ground.
And yet, by heaven, I think my love as rare
As any she belied with false compare.[5]

1. *Dun* is dull gray.

2. Something that is *damasked* is multicolored.

3. Here, *reeks* simply means "is exhaled."

4. Here, *go* means "walk."

5. *[As any . . . compare]* means "As any woman misrepresented with false comparisons."

Big Idea **A Bard for the Ages** *What philosophical insight is Shakespeare expressing in this couplet?*

Vocabulary

tread (tred) *v.* to walk or step upon

RESPONDING AND THINKING CRITICALLY

Respond

1. After reading Sonnet 130, what was your initial response to the speaker's description of his beloved?

Recall and Interpret

2. (a)List two things that the speaker says love is not in Sonnet 116. (b)List two things that the speaker says love is.

3. (a)In your own words, summarize the two main points the speaker makes about the nature of love in Sonnet 116. (b)What is the speaker implying about failed relationships?

4. (a)How does the speaker in Sonnet 130 describe the woman he loves? (b)Does his description tell you his real opinion of her? Refer to lines from the poem to support your answer.

Analyze and Evaluate

5. (a)What is the speaker's main point in lines 1–12 of Sonnet 116? (b)In your opinion, is the couplet a convincing conclusion to the poem? Explain.

6. (a)What sort of poetry does Sonnet 130 mock or criticize? (b)What message about love is implied in this criticism?

7. (a)How would you describe the tone of Sonnet 130? (b)In your opinion, is the tone appropriate for a love poem? Explain.

Connect

8. **Big Idea** **A Bard for the Ages** What can you infer about Shakespeare's philosophy of life from Sonnets 116 and 130?

LITERARY ANALYSIS

Literary Element **Simile and Metaphor**

Sonnet 116 makes its points through a series of implicit comparisons, or **metaphors.** Sonnet 130 parodies, or makes fun of, a series of explicit comparisons, or **similes.** Note that the word *like* appears in the first simile in line 1 of Sonnet 130 and is understood, or implied, in all of the similes that follow.

1. Explain the metaphor in lines 5–6 of Sonnet 116.

2. (a)List the "negative similes," or what the speaker says his beloved is *not,* in Sonnet 130. (b)Identify the only example of metaphor in this poem.

Literary Criticism

Some scholars see Sonnet 116 as a definition of true love; others view the sonnet as an argument offering proof of the existence of true love. In a paragraph, explain which view you think more accurately represents the poem.

Literature Online **Web Activities** For eFlashcards, Selection Quick Checks, and other Web activities, go to www.glencoe.com.

READING AND VOCABULARY

Reading Strategy **Analyzing Figures of Speech**

In Sonnet 116, Shakespeare uses symbol and personification. A **symbol** is something that exists on a literal level and also represents something beyond itself. **Personification** is the attribution of human qualities to something inhuman.

1. What examples of personification are included in lines 9–10 of Sonnet 116?

2. What might the sickle in line 10 of Sonnet 116 symbolize?

Vocabulary **Practice**

Practice with Synonyms Match each vocabulary word in the left column with its synonym in the right column.

1. alteration   **a.** step
2. doom   **b.** storm
3. tempest   **c.** tragic fate
4. tread   **d.** change

Literary Element Simile

A **simile** is a figure of speech that uses *like* or *as* to compare two seemingly unlike things. Not every statement with *like* or *as* is a simile—the comparison must be between things that are basically different and must create greater understanding about what is being compared. For example, "My love is like a rose" is a simile; "My backpack is like your tote bag" is not a simile.

• See Literary Terms Handbook, p. R16.

Reading Strategy Drawing Conclusions About Speaker's Meaning

A **conclusion** is a general statement based on a number of specific examples. To be valid, a conclusion must make good sense and should not go beyond the evidence.

Reading Tip: Making Adjustments Be prepared to adjust your original conclusion to reflect the information you learn as you read. Your final conclusions might be different from what you originally expected.

SONNET 73

William Shakespeare

That time of year thou mayst in me behold
When yellow leaves, or none, or few, do hang
Upon those boughs which shake against the cold,
Bare ruin'd choirs,[1] where late the sweet birds sang.
5 In me thou seest the twilight of such day
As after sunset fadeth in the west,
Which by and by[2] black night doth take away,
Death's second self, that seals up all in rest.
In me thou seest the glowing of such fire
10 That on the ashes of his youth doth lie,
As the death-bed whereon it must expire,
Consum'd with that which it was nourish'd by.[3]
    This thou perceiv'st, which makes thy love more strong,
    To love that well, which thou must leave ere long.

1. *Choirs* is a reference to the place in a church where the choir sings.

2. *By and by* means "presently" or "soon."

3. *[Consum'd . . . by]* is an image that suggests that the fire was choked by the ashes of the wood that previously fueled its flame. The speaker means he has been consumed by life.

Reading Strategy Drawing Conclusions About Speaker's Meaning *What conclusion about himself does the speaker state in lines 1–4? Explain.*

Double Portrait, c. 1502. Giorgione (Giorgio da Castelfranco). Oil on canvas, 77 x 66.5 cm. Palazzo Venezia, Rome.

SONNET 29

William Shakespeare

When in disgrace with Fortune and men's eyes
I all alone beweep my outcast state,
And trouble deaf heaven with my bootless cries,[1]
And look upon myself and curse my fate,
5 Wishing me like to one more rich in hope,
Featur'd like him, like him with friends possess'd,[2]
Desiring this man's art, and that man's scope,[3]
With what I most enjoy contented least;
Yet in these thoughts myself almost despising,
10 Haply[4] I think on thee, and then my state,[5]
Like to the lark at break of day arising
From sullen earth, sings hymns at heaven's gate,
   For thy sweet love rememb'red such wealth brings
   That then I scorn to change my state with kings.

---

1. *Bootless cries* are vain or futile cries.
2. The speaker compares himself to three different men in lines 5–7.
3. Here, *scope* means "mental power."
4. *Haply* means "by chance."
5. *State,* here and in line 14, refers to the speaker's condition or position in life.

Literary Element   Simile *Are lines 5–6 an example of a simile? Explain.*

RESPONDING AND THINKING CRITICALLY

Respond

1. What emotions did you experience after reading Sonnet 73? After reading Sonnet 29?

Recall and Interpret

2. (a)To what three things does the speaker compare himself in Sonnet 73? (b)What do you think these three things symbolize, or represent?

3. (a)What does the speaker complain about in the first part of Sonnet 29? (b)Based on the early lines of the poem, what kind of person would you say the speaker is?

4. (a)How does the final couplet of Sonnet 29 relate to the rest of the poem? (b)How would you characterize the speaker after reading the entire poem?

Analyze and Evaluate

5. (a)How would you describe the tone of Sonnet 73? (b)What details create that tone?

6. (a)What reasons does the speaker in Sonnet 29 give for his change in mood? (b)Do you find the transition in the speaker's mood convincing? Explain.

Connect

7. What do these two sonnets have in common with Sonnets 116 and 130?

8. **Big Idea** **A Bard for the Ages** Based on these two sonnets, how would you describe the value Shakespeare puts on human relationships?

LITERARY ANALYSIS

Literary Element Simile

A **simile** is a comparison between two basically unlike things that uses *like* or *as.* The comparison is meant to create greater understanding of what is being compared.

1. (a)What is the simile in lines 9–12 of Sonnet 29? (b)What understanding of the speaker and his "state" do you gain from this comparison?

2. Write a simile that expresses the speaker's attitude toward himself in lines 1–4 of Sonnet 73.

Writing About Literature

Analyze Couplets In her analysis of Shakespeare's sonnets, scholar Helen Vendler calls "the significant words from the body of the poem that are repeated in the couplet . . . the Couplet Tie. These words are usually thematically central, and to see Shakespeare's careful reiteration of them is to be directed in one's interpretation by them." In a brief essay, analyze the "couplet ties" in Sonnets 73 and 29. How do they direct your interpretations of the sonnets? Cite specific details from the poems to support your response.

Literature Online **Web Activities** For eFlashcards, Selection Quick Checks, and other Web activities, go to www.glencoe.com.

READING AND VOCABULARY

Reading Strategy Drawing Conclusions About Speaker's Meaning

A **conclusion** is a general statement about a number of specific examples.

1. What conclusion does the speaker come to in the couplet of Sonnet 73?

2. What conclusion can you draw about the emotional state of the speaker in the first eight lines of Sonnet 29?

Academic Vocabulary

Here are two words from the vocabulary list on page R82.

conclude (kən klōōd′) *v.* to decide by reasoning; to infer; to end

previous (prē′ vē əs) *adj.* going before in time or order; prior

Practice and Apply

1. What can you **conclude** about the structure of a Shakespearean sonnet from these examples?

2. Do you find literature of the Renaissance easier to relate to than that of **previous** ages? Explain.

Connecting to the Songs

During the English Renaissance, the average life expectancy was much shorter than it is today. Plague, famine, and unhealthy living conditions made death a constant companion. Thus, Shakespeare's contemporaries had no qualms about reading poems or hearing songs about death. As you read these songs, think about the following questions:

- What are the topics of two of your favorite songs?
- How might emotions be expressed more powerfully through song than through speech?

Building Background

Shakespeare used songs in his plays to heighten the drama, making what is merry merrier or what is sad sadder. Shakespeare's plays were not musicals, however. In a modern musical, songs tend to be character driven and sometimes even fill out entire scenes. In Shakespeare's plays, the songs are more likely to be meditations on the action sung by minor characters.

Unfortunately, most of the original music that was written to accompany these songs has been lost—if it was ever written down in the first place. However, we do know a great deal about what Elizabethan music sounded like, and using that information, many composers since Shakespeare have set his lyrics to music.

Setting Purposes for Reading

Big Idea **A Bard for the Ages**

As you read, think about how people of the time would have responded to dirges in a tragedy or a romantic comedy.

Literary Element **Theme**

Theme is the central idea about life in a story, song, poem, or play. Some works have a stated theme, which is expressed explicitly. Other works have an implied theme, which is revealed gradually through events, dialogue, or description.

- See Literary Terms Handbook, p. R18.

Reading Strategy **Responding to Tone**

An author's attitude toward his or her subject matter or the audience is called **tone.** Tone is conveyed through word choice, punctuation, sentence structure, and figures of speech. Literary characters may also express tone. As you read, note how understanding tone can help you identify a work's theme.

Reading Tip: Noting Tone of Voice Tone in literature is akin to tone of voice in conversation. To help discover a literary tone, think of how the speaker's voice would sound if the words were spoken aloud.

Vocabulary

tyrant (tī′ rənt) n. a cruel, oppressive ruler; a ruler with unlimited power; p. 302 *Beverly complained that getting his own way all the time had turned her little brother into a tyrant.*

censure (sen′ shər) n. strong disapproval; condemnation as wrong; p. 302 *The alderman called upon the city council to issue an official censure of the mayor for her objectionable remarks.*

keen (kēn) adj. having a sharp edge or point; p. 303 *Tom kept a keen edge on the knife he used to take on camping trips.*

folly (fol′ ē) n. foolishness; an irrational and useless undertaking; p. 303 *Going ahead with the picnic after thunderstorms had been predicted was sheer folly.*

Vocabulary Tip: Word Origins Word origins, also called **etymologies,** can be found in most dictionaries. They tell what language a word comes from, its original meaning, and often how it passed from one language into another.

Literature Online **Interactive Literary Elements Handbook** To review or learn more about the literary elements, go to www.glencoe.com.

OBJECTIVES
In studying these selections, you will focus on the following:
- analyzing literary genres
- analyzing theme
- responding to tone

In the play Cymbeline, *Imogen, the daughter of King Cymbeline, is falsely accused of adultery. To clear herself, she wears a man's disguise. Falling ill, she takes a drug that puts her into a deathlike coma. The characters Guiderius and Arviragus (actually Imogen's brothers, also in disguise) express their sorrow for this "most rare boy." Believing Imogen to be dead, they sing this funeral dirge.*

Fear No More the Heat o' the Sun

William Shakespeare

Fear no more the heat o' the sun,
Nor the furious winter's rages,
Thou thy worldly task hast done,
Home art gone, and ta'en thy wages.
5   Golden lads and girls all must,
As[1] chimney-sweepers, come to dust.

Fear no more the frown o' the great,
Thou art past the **tyrant's** stroke;
Care no more to clothe and eat,
10   To thee the reed is as the oak.
The scepter, learning, physic,[2] must
All follow this and come to dust.

Fear no more the lightning-flash
Nor the all-dreaded thunder-stone.[3]
15   Fear not slander, **censure** rash.
Thou hast finish'd joy and moan.
All lovers young, all lovers must
Consign[4] to thee and come to dust.

No exorciser harm thee.
20   Nor no witchcraft charm thee.
Ghost unlaid forbear[5] thee.
Nothing ill come near thee.
Quiet consummation[6] have,
And renownèd be thy grave.

1. The speaker uses *as* to mean "like."

2. *Scepter, learning,* and *physic* refer to kings, scholars, and doctors.

3. The sound of thunder was thought to be caused by falling stones. Hence they were called *thunder-stones.*

4. *Consign* means "submit."

5. *Forbear* means "leave alone."

6. *Consummation* means "fulfillment."

Literary Element   **Theme** *What topic will the theme of this poem comment upon?*

Big Idea   **A Bard for the Ages** *How do these lines reflect Shakespeare's interest in the supernatural?*

Vocabulary

tyrant (tī′ rənt) *n.* a cruel, oppressive ruler; a ruler with unlimited power

censure (sen′ shər) *n.* strong disapproval; condemnation as wrong

In As You Like It, *the former Duke Senior, whose title has been usurped by his younger brother, has been living in exile in the Forest of Arden, where he enjoys the simple delights of nature— as opposed to the treachery of life at court. With him are Lord Amiens and other former attendants. This song occurs when the former duke requests Amiens to "Give us some music."*

Blow, Blow, Thou Winter Wind

William Shakespeare

Blow, blow, thou winter wind,
Thou art not so unkind
   As man's ingratitude;
Thy tooth is not so **keen**,
5   Because thou art not seen,
   Although thy breath be rude.
Heigh-ho! sing, heigh-ho! unto the green holly,
Most friendship is feigning,[1] most loving mere folly.
   Then, heigh-ho, the holly!
10   This life is most jolly.

Freeze, freeze, thou bitter sky,
That dost not bite so nigh[2]
   As benefits forgot;
Though thou the waters warp,[3]
15   Thy sting is not so sharp
   As friend remembered not.
Heigh-ho! sing, heigh-ho! unto the green holly,
Most friendship is feigning, most loving mere **folly**.
   Then, heigh-ho, the holly!
20   This life is most jolly.

---

1. *Feigning* means "pretending."
2. *Nigh* means "near."
3. *Warp* means "make rough by freezing."

Reading Strategy   **Responding to Tone**   *Do these two lines express the same tone? Explain.*

Vocabulary

keen (kēn) *adj.* having a sharp edge or point
folly (fol′ ē) *n.* foolishness; an irrational and useless undertaking

Winter, c. 1820. William Blake. Tempera on pine, 90.2 x 29.7 cm. Tate Gallery, London.

RESPONDING AND THINKING CRITICALLY

Respond

1. Which lines from the songs did you find most memorable or powerful? Explain.

Recall and Interpret

2. (a)According to "Fear No More the Heat o' the Sun," what things should the person addressed "fear no more"? (b)Why are these things no longer frightening?

3. (a)In "Fear No More . . ." what happens to all the "golden lads and girls," "the scepter, learning, physic," and the "lovers"? (b)What do "the scepter, learning, physic" in line 11 represent? (c)Why might the speaker have mentioned these particular people in a dirge for a young woman?

4. (a)According to "Blow, Blow, Thou Winter Wind," what is more unkind than the winter wind? (b)What has a sharper sting than ice water? Explain.

Analyze and Evaluate

5. (a)Explain the **pun** presented in the lines, "Golden lads and girls all must, / As chimney-sweepers, come to dust" from "Fear No More . . . ." (b)Given the context of the song, does this wordplay seem appropriate? Explain.

6. (a)In the last stanza of "Fear No More . . .," what does the speaker wish for the person being addressed? (b)Do you think this song is meant to be consoling? Explain.

7. (a)According to the **refrain**, how does "Blow, Blow, Thou Winter Wind" characterize love and friendship? (b)How do the words of this song contrast with its purpose?

Connect

8. **Big Idea** **A Bard for the Ages** In what way does "Fear No More the Heat o' the Sun" express a particularly Elizabethan attitude toward death?

LITERARY ANALYSIS

Literary Element **Theme**

A **theme** is a central idea about life in a literary work. Some works have a stated theme, while in other works the theme is implied. In addition, some themes are universal and can be found in literature all over the world.

1. (a)What is the theme of "Fear No More the Heat o' the Sun"? (b)Is this theme universal? Explain.

2. (a)Is the theme of "Blow, Blow, Thou Winter Wind" stated or implied? (b)What is the theme?

Interdisciplinary Activity: Music

Although the original music to Shakespeare's songs has been lost, that has not stopped composers over the centuries from setting his lyrics to music. Choose one of Shakespeare's songs to set to music. You might use a guitar, piano, computer program, or your own voice. As you compose, try to capture the tone of the lyric.

Literature Online **Web Activities** For eFlashcards, Selection Quick Checks, and other Web activities, go to www.glencoe.com.

READING AND VOCABULARY

Reading Strategy **Responding to Tone**

Tone is an author's or character's attitude toward his or her subject matter or audience.

How would you describe the tone of "Fear No More the Heat o' the Sun" and "Blow, Blow, Thou Winter Wind"?

Vocabulary **Practice**

Practice with Word Origins Use a dictionary to answer the following questions.

1. Which word comes from Old English?
   a. keen   **b.** censure   **c.** tyrant

2. Which word comes directly from Latin?
   a. tyrant   **b.** censure   **c.** folly

3. Which word comes from Middle English through French and Latin?
   a. censure   **b.** keen   **c.** folly

4. Which word has a Greek origin?
   a. censure   **b.** tyrant   **c.** keen

Shakespeare's Soliloquies

LITERATURE PREVIEW	READING PREVIEW

Connecting to the Texts

Have you ever wondered what your life means? Shakespeare's characters often voice their indecisiveness. As you read, think about the following questions:

- What prompts a person to wonder about life?
- How does anyone ever come to a real conclusion about such questions?

Building Background

Asides and soliloquies were commonly used in Elizabethan theater. In an **aside,** a character speaks to the audience or to another character in a voice that the audience can hear, but that other characters onstage are not supposed to hear. In a **soliloquy,** a character, alone onstage, reveals his or her private thoughts and feelings as if thinking aloud.

In *Hamlet,* the ghost of Hamlet's father, the former king, has urged Hamlet to avenge his murder. But Hamlet hesitates because he is unsure he has seen a true ghost and is uncertain how he should go about killing his uncle, the murderer, who now occupies his father's throne. Hamlet then wonders whether it would be better to be dead and free from care.

Setting Purposes for Reading

Big Idea A Bard for the Ages

As you read, watch for major themes that reveal ideas that are important in Elizabethan drama.

Literary Element Voice

The distinctive use of language that conveys the author's or speaker's personality to the reader or viewer is called **voice.** Voice is determined by elements of style such as word choice and tone. As you read the speeches, look for the distinctive voices of the speakers.

- See Literary Terms Handbook, p. R19.

Literature Online **Interactive Literary Elements Handbook** To review or learn more about the literary elements, go to www.glencoe.com.

Reading Strategy Drawing Conclusions About Theme

A **conclusion** is a general statement drawn from specific examples. **Theme** is the overall meaning about life in a work of literature. To draw a conclusion about theme, consider what has happened, how the characters feel about it, and how you—the reader or audience member—are supposed to feel about it.

Reading Tip: Taking Notes As you read the following speeches and soliloquies, jot down your conclusions in a chart like the one below.

Selection	Conclusions

Vocabulary

calamity (kə lam′ ə tē) *n.* disaster; extreme misfortune; p. 307 *It was a calamity when the levees broke and the river flooded the city.*

awry (ə rī′) *adj.* wrong; in a faulty way; p. 307 *All our careful vacation plans went awry when the airport was closed.*

oblivion (ə bliv′ ē ən) *n.* a state of forgetting; p. 309 *Jesse was in a state of oblivion after her surgery.*

pageant (paj′ ənt) *n.* an elaborately staged drama or spectacular exhibition; p. 310 *Our community staged a grand historical pageant.*

infirmity (in fur′ mə tē) *n.* weakness; state of being feeble or unable; p. 310 *Russell didn't let his infirmity ruin his life.*

Vocabulary Tip: Context Clues You can often find clues to the meaning of an unfamiliar word by looking at words and phrases around it.

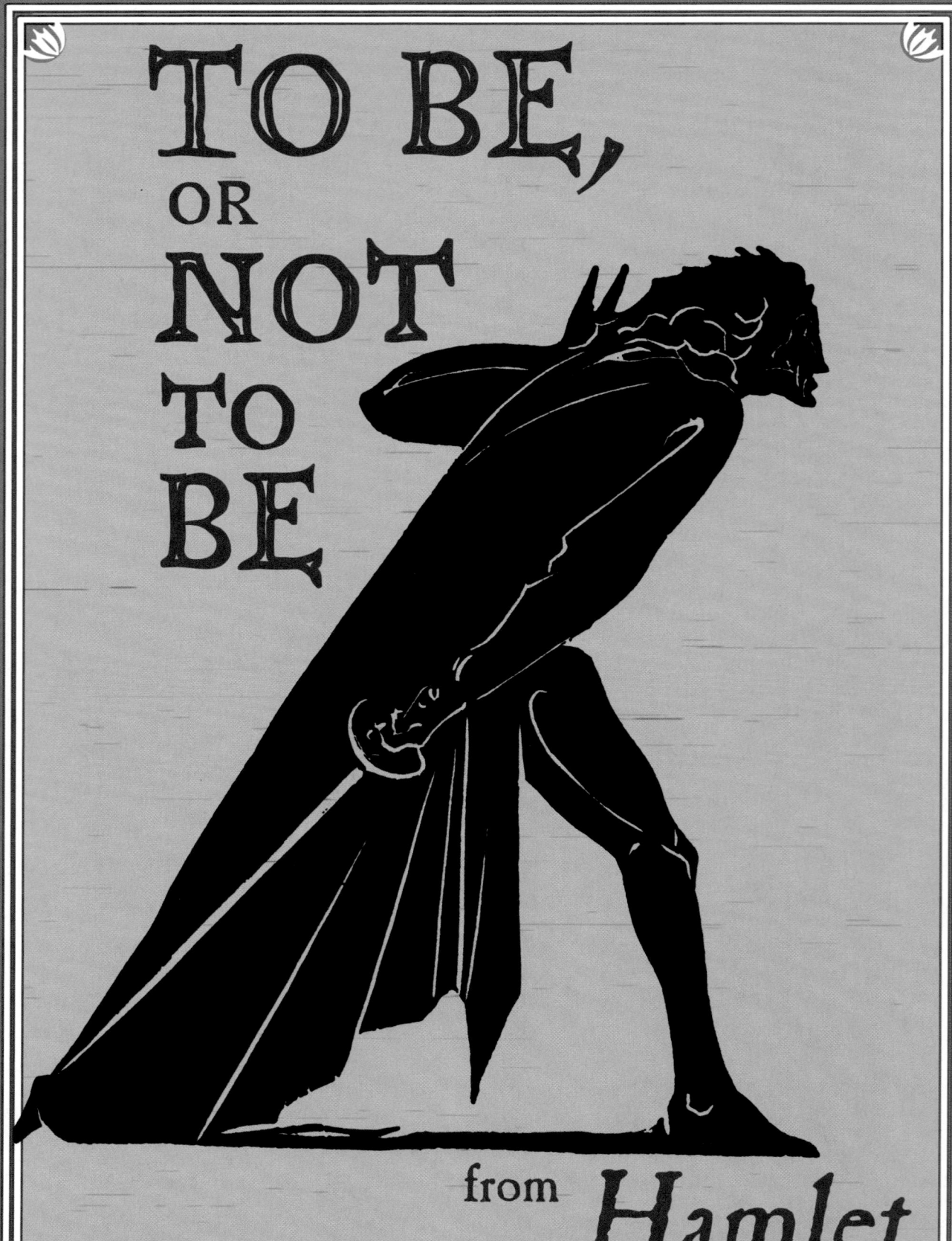

TO BE,
OR
NOT
TO BE

from *Hamlet*

William Shakespeare

Hamlet.

> To be, or not to be—that is the question.
> Whether 'tis nobler in the mind to suffer
> The slings and arrows of outrageous fortune,
> Or to take arms against a sea of troubles,
> 5 And by opposing end them. To die, to sleep—
> No more, and by a sleep to say we end
> The heartache and the thousand natural shocks
> That flesh is heir to. 'Tis a consummation
> Devoutly to be wished. To die, to sleep,
> 10 To sleep—perchance to dream. Aye, there's the rub,[1]
> For in that sleep of death what dreams may come
> When we have shuffled off this mortal coil[2]
> Must give us pause. There's the respect
> That makes **calamity** of so long life.
> 15 For who would bear the whips and scorns of time,
> The oppressor's wrong, the proud man's contumely,[3]
> The pangs of despised love, the law's delay,
> The insolence of office, and the spurns
> That patient merit of the unworthy takes,[4]
> 20 When he himself might his quietus make
> With a bare bodkin?[5] Who would fardels[6] bear,
> To grunt and sweat under a weary life,
> But that the dread of something after death,
> The undiscovered country from whose bourn[7]
> 25 No traveler returns, puzzles the will,
> And makes us rather bear those ills we have
> Than fly to others that we know not of?
> Thus conscience does make cowards of us all,
> And thus the native hue[8] of resolution
> 30 Is sicklied o'er with the pale cast of thought,
> And enterprises of great pitch[9] and moment
> With this regard their currents turn **awry**
> And lose the name of action. . . .

1. Here, *rub* refers to an obstacle.

2. *Coil* means "turmoil."

3. *Contumely* refers to abuse.

4. The phrase *of the unworthy takes* means "receives from unworthy persons."
5. A *bare bodkin* is a dagger out of its sheath.
6. *Fardels* are "burdens."
7. Here, *bourn* means "boundary."

8. *Native hue* means "natural color."

9. Here, *pitch* means "height."

Reading Strategy Drawing Conclusions About Theme *What conclusion can you draw from lines 21–28 about Hamlet's fear of death?*

Vocabulary

calamity (kə lam′ ə tē) *n.* disaster; extreme misfortune
awry (ə rī′) *adj.* wrong; in a faulty way

All the world's a stage
from *As You Like It*

William Shakespeare

In As You Like It, *the former Duke, whose title has been usurped by his younger brother, has been living in exile in the Forest of Arden. With him are Jaques, a melancholy lord, and other former attendants. The former Duke has just commented that the "wide and universal theater" of the world presents scenes sadder than theirs. Jaques picks up on the word* theater *in this meditation on life.*

Jaques.

All the world's a stage
And all the men and women merely players:
They have their exits and their entrances;
And one man in his time plays many parts,
5 His acts being seven ages. At first the infant,
Mewling¹ and puking in the nurse's arms.
And then the whining school-boy, with his satchel
And shining morning face, creeping like snail
Unwillingly to school. And then the lover,
10 Sighing like furnace, with a woeful ballad
Made to his mistress' eyebrow. Then a soldier,
Full of strange oaths, and bearded like the pard,²
Jealous in honor,³ sudden⁴ and quick in quarrel,
Seeking the bubble reputation
15 Even in the cannon's mouth. And then the justice,
In fair round belly with good capon lin'd,
With eyes severe, and beard of formal cut,
Full of wise saws⁵ and modern instances;
And so he plays his part. The sixth age shifts
20 Into the lean and slipper'd pantaloon,⁶
With spectacles on nose and pouch on side,
His youthful hose, well sav'd, a world too wide
For his shrunk shank;⁷ and his big manly voice,
Turning again toward childish treble, pipes
25 And whistles in his sound. Last scene of all,
That ends this strange eventful history,
Is second childishness and mere **oblivion**,
Sans⁸ teeth, sans eyes, sans taste, sans everything.

1. *Mewling* is a catlike cry.

2. The phrase *bearded like the pard* means the soldier had a moustache like a leopard's.
3. *Jealous in honor* means "being easily angered in matters of honor."
4. Here, *sudden* means "rash" or "impetuous."
5. Here, *saws* mean "sayings."

6. A *pantaloon* is a stock character in Italian comedy, usually portrayed as a ridiculous, helpless old man.
7. Here, *shank* means "calf."

8. *Sans* is French for "without."

Literary Element   Voice *How would you describe Jaques's voice in these lines?*

Vocabulary

oblivion (ə bliv′ ē ən) *n.* a state of forgetting

French and Italian comedians, 1670. Anonymous. Canvas. Comedie Francaise, Paris.

In The Tempest, *Prospero had been the Duke of Milan, but his brother conspired against him to steal the dukedom and kill Prospero. Instead, Prospero and his daughter, Miranda, ended up shipwrecked on an island. Years later, Prospero, who is also a powerful magician, has caused the wreck of another ship, one bearing Ferdinand, Prince of Naples. Hoping that Miranda and Ferdinand will fall in love, Prospero has just staged an elaborate show in which island spirits, portraying Roman goddesses, bless their union.*

Our revels now are ended
from The Tempest

William Shakespeare

Prospero.
    Our revels[1] now are ended. These our actors,
    As I foretold you, were all spirits and
    Are melted into air, into thin air;
    And, like the baseless fabric of this vision,[2]
5   The cloud-capped towers, the gorgeous palaces,
    The solemn temples, the great globe[3] itself,
    Yea, all which it inherit,[4] shall dissolve,
    And, like this insubstantial **pageant** faded,
    Leave not a rack[5] behind. We are such stuff
10 As dreams are made on,[6] and our little life
    Is rounded[7] with a sleep. Sir, I am vexed.
    Bear with my weakness. My old brain is troubled.
    Be not disturbed with my **infirmity**.
    If you be pleased, retire into my cell
15 And there repose. A turn or two I'll walk
    To still my beating[8] mind.

1. *Revels* refers to entertainment, specifically the pageant the spirits recently presented in the play.
2. This phrase refers to the flimsy theater edifice or background.
3. *Great globe* refers to the Globe Theatre in London, where Shakespeare worked and performed.
4. *Which it inherit* means "those who will occupy it."
5. A *rack* is a small part of a cloud.
6. Here, *on* means "of."
7. Here, *rounded* means "surrounded," (that is, before birth and after death).
8. Here, *beating* means "disrupted" or "agitated."

Big Idea **A Bard for the Ages** *How does Prospero's speech reflect the Elizabethan concern with impermanence and death?*

Vocabulary

pageant (paj′ ənt) *n.* an elaborately staged drama or spectacular exhibition

infirmity (in fur′ mə tē) *n.* weakness; state of being feeble or unable

RESPONDING AND THINKING CRITICALLY

Respond

1. Does Hamlet, Jaques, or Prospero come closest to your own views on life and death? Explain.

Recall and Interpret

2. (a)In "To be, or not to be," what do you think Hamlet means by "the slings and arrows of outrageous fortune" in line 3? Give some examples mentioned in the text. (b)What does Hamlet mean by the "undiscovered country" in line 24?

3. (a)What, according to Hamlet, is "Devoutly to be wished"? (b)What is wrong with that "consummation"?

4. (a)What are the "many parts" everyone must play, according to Jaques in "All the world's a stage"? (b)What does he mean by "second childishness"?

5. (a)In "Our revels now are ended," how does Prospero explain the disappearance of the actors? (b)What does he say corresponds in real life with the vision he has just shown?

Analyze and Evaluate

6. (a)Which lines in "To be, or not to be" suggest that Hamlet is contemplating suicide? (b)Why does he *not* take such a drastic step?

7. Hamlet is wondering if he should murder his uncle, the king. How does the possibility of death affect his decision in lines 29–33?

8. (a)In "All the world's a stage," does Jaques seem to respect the people who play "many parts"? Explain. (b)What does he mean by "strange, eventful history"? Is he being sarcastic? Explain.

Connect

9. Do you think most people agree with Hamlet about fearing death? Explain.

10. **Big Idea** **A Bard for the Ages** What do these three speeches and soliloquies have in common, in terms of a philosophy of life and death?

VISUAL LITERACY: Graphic Organizer

Using a Text Diagram

Putting aspects of a literary selection into visual form can enrich your understanding of them. Construct a diagram to order the "seven ages" in Jaques's "All the world's a stage." First copy this graphic organizer below on a separate piece of paper. Then complete it, using words and phrases from Jaques's speech.

Seven Ages of Mankind	
Age	Characteristics
1.	
2.	
3.	
4.	
5.	
6.	
7.	

Group Activity Discuss the following questions with classmates. Refer to the diagram you created and cite evidence from the text to support your answers.

1. Why do you think Jaques outlines seven ages? In your estimation, how old are the people represented in each? Decide on a range of ages for each of the seven categories.

2. Are there some stages you feel are missing or are different in today's culture from the ones that Jaques presents? Create your own diagram presenting the stages of life. Create a storyboard with illustrations if you prefer.

Literary Element Voice

Voice is the distinctive use of language that conveys a speaker's personality to the reader or viewer. Voice is determined by elements of style such as word choice and tone.

1. Describe Hamlet's voice in "To be, or not to be." Is he speaking personally and with a sense of immediacy, or objectively and with a sense of detachment?

2. Compare Hamlet's voice to that of Jaques in "All the world's a stage."

Review: Figurative Language

As you learned on page 260, **figurative language** is language used for descriptive effect or to convey ideas and emotions. Figurative expressions are not literally true but express some truth beyond the literal level. Three common types of figurative language are simile, metaphor, and personification. A **simile** is a comparison that uses words such as *like* or *as,* whereas a **metaphor** directly states a comparison without using these words. **Personification** is a figure of speech in which a nonhuman thing is given human characteristics.

Partner Activity Meet with a classmate to discuss the following questions.

1. What kind of figurative language is the phrase "all the world's a stage"?

2. Does the phrase "all the world's a stage" provide insight into the world, the stage, or both? Explain.

Prospero. Henry Fuseli. York Art Gallery, UK.

Reading Strategy Drawing Conclusions About Theme

A **conclusion** is a general statement drawn from specific examples. A conclusion about theme should take into account what has happened, how the characters feel about it, and how the audience is supposed to respond.

1. Hamlet asks the question, "To be, or not to be?" Does he come to a conclusion? Explain.

2. Use the examples given in "All the world's a stage" to come to a conclusion about Jaques's philosophy: *All the world's a stage, and all the men and women merely players; therefore _____ .*

Vocabulary Practice

Practice with Context Clues In the following sentences, choose the word or phrase that best helps you understand the underlined word.

1. We expected to win the championship, but the game turned into a real calamity and we lost by twenty points.
   a. expected   **c.** turned
   b. championship **d.** lost by twenty points

2. The play started to go awry in the first scene when the lead actor forgot his lines.
   a. play   **c.** lead actor
   b. first scene   **d.** forgot his lines

3. After his concussion, Jim was in a state of oblivion for awhile. He couldn't remember his own name.
   a. concussion   **c.** awhile
   b. state   **d.** couldn't remember

4. The school put on a pageant, or exhibition, to celebrate the coming of spring.
   a. school   **c.** celebrate
   b. exhibition   **d.** spring

5. My grandmother has to walk with a cane, but she refuses to let that infirmity stop her active life.
   a. grandmother   **c.** refuses
   b. walk with a cane **d.** active life

Writing About Literature

Compare and Contrast Motifs A motif is an element repeated throughout a literary work that contributes to, or is related to, the theme. A motif may be a word, phrase, image, description, idea, or other element.

In "To be, or not to be," "All the world's a stage," and "Our revels now are ended," *dreams* and *theater* are recurring motifs. Write a brief essay in which you compare and contrast how these motifs are developed in the three speeches and soliloquies. Can you reach a conclusion about what these motifs meant to Shakespeare?

Before you draft, look back at the selections and see how the motifs of dreams and theater are treated in each. Organize your essay in the following way.

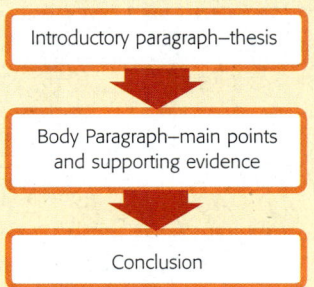

Introductory paragraph—thesis

Body Paragraph—main points and supporting evidence

Conclusion

After you complete your draft, meet with a peer reviewer to evaluate each other's work and to suggest improvements. Then proofread your essay for errors in spelling, grammar, and punctuation.

Internet Connection

As you've discovered, Shakespeare spoke and wrote an English different from the one you speak and write. Find out more about Shakespeare's English by doing an Internet search. Start with the keywords *Shakespeare* and *language.* Look especially for sites operated by educational institutions. Prepare a brief report for your class in which you select and present some of the information you find.

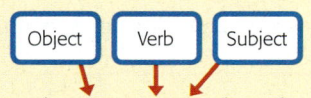 **Web Activities** For eFlashcards, Selection Quick Checks, and other Web activities, go to www.glencoe.com.

Shakespeare's Language and Style

Using Inversion In his sonnets, songs, speeches, and soliloquies, Shakespeare often inverts the word order of his lines and sentences. In writing, **inversion** is a reversal of the usual word order in a sentence for emphasis or variety. For example, in standard sentence construction, a subject comes before a verb, followed by an object. When the word order is inverted, the verb comes before the subject or an object comes before the verb:

Object   Verb   Subject

". . . no such roses see I in her cheeks" (Sonnet 130)

Notice some examples of Shakespeare's inversions:

Example of Inversion	Reason or Effect
1. "thou mayst in me behold" (Sonnet 73)	1. retains rhyme (behold/cold)
2. "For thy sweet love rememb'red such wealth brings" (Sonnet 29)	2. retains rhyme (brings/kings)
3. "Thy sting is not so sharp / As friend remembered not." ("Blow, Blow, Thou Winter Wind")	3. emphasizes negative (not)

Activity What is inverted in these examples from Shakespeare? On a separate piece of paper, write the sentence elements in standard order.

1. "This thou perceiv'st . . ." (Sonnet 73)

2. "A turn or two I'll walk . . ." ("Our revels now are ended")

3. ". . . love is not love / Which alters when it alteration finds . . ." (Sonnet 116)

Revising Check

Inversion In today's Standard English, writers rarely invert word order unless they are writing poetry or are intentionally using it to create emphasis. With a partner, go through your paper on motif to make sure you use standard word order. If you use inversion, make sure it is used intentionally.

Shakespeare's Theater

> *"The cause of plagues is sinne, if you look to it well: and the cause of sinne are playes: therefore the cause of plagues are playes."*
>
> —Thomas White, *Sermon*, 1576

The Globe Theatre. Medieval woodcut. London.

IN 1558, THE FIRST YEAR OF ELIZABETH I'S REIGN, there were no playhouses in England. Actors, or "players," performed wherever they could find an audience—often in the open courtyards of London inns. Much to the distress of the mostly Puritan city council, who believed that "playacting" was a violation of the biblical commandment against idolatry, these performances attracted large and often rowdy crowds. In 1574 the Common Council of London issued an order banishing players from London. To get around the order, actor James Burbage and his company of players leased land in nearby Shoreditch, where they built the first public playhouse in England. Completed in 1576, the "Theater" was an immediate success. Several other theaters soon followed.

The Globe

To theater-lovers today, one early English playhouse stands out from all the rest—the Globe, home to many of Shakespeare's plays. Built in 1599, the first Globe was, quite literally, a rebirth of the Theater. When Burbage had trouble renewing his lease, he had the Theater disassembled. The timber was carted over the Thames River to Bankside and was used to build the Globe. Although no trace of the original Globe remains today, surviving maps, construction contracts, and plays of the time have helped scholars piece together a fairly clear picture of what it looked like in its day.

This Wooden O

In *Henry V,* the first play to be performed at the Globe, Shakespeare referred to the theater as "this wooden O."

From that description and others, scholars believe that the Globe was a circular structure, formed by three-tiered, thatch-roofed galleries that served as seating. These galleries overlooked an open courtyard, into which jutted a raised platform stage. At the back of the main stage was a small curtained inner stage used for indoor scenes. Above the main stage stood a two-tiered gallery. The first tier was used to stage balcony and bedroom scenes; the second, to house musicians.

Lords and Groundlings

Plays were usually performed in the afternoon before a diverse audience of about two thousand people. Members of the nobility and the rising middle class generally sat in the galleries. Less well-to-do spectators, called "groundlings," could stand and watch from the courtyard for only a penny. Their close proximity to the stage made for an intimate theatrical experience, but it also made for a noisy one. Accounts of the time suggest that the groundlings did not hesitate to shout comments to the actors onstage and that vendors selling snacks circulated throughout the audience during performances.

Theatrical Conventions

Certain theatrical conventions that seemed natural to Elizabethans might strike today's audiences as strange. For example, most of Shakespeare's characters speak in **blank verse**—unrhymed lines of iambic pentameter. In this verse form, each line is divided into five units, or feet, with stress falling on every second syllable. Because the rhythm of blank verse mimics the natural rhythm of spoken English, it is especially appropriate for dialogue.

Because acting was considered to be too indelicate for women, female roles were played by boys—apprentices to the company of players. Costumes were usually colorful and elaborate versions of regular Elizabethan dress, whether worn for *Macbeth*, set in the eleventh century, or for *Julius Caesar*, set in 44 B.C. Scenery was almost nonexistent. A single tree might stand for a forest, or a chair for a throne room. Shakespeare made up for the lack of scenery by giving characters descriptive passages to help the audience visualize the scenes.

The Elizabethan stage had no front curtain, so the beginning of a play was announced by the blaring of trumpets, and the start of a new scene was signaled by the entrance of the appropriate characters. Given the lack of scenery changes and intermissions, Elizabethan productions probably moved quickly. Scholars estimate that a typical performance of a Shakespearean play lasted only two hours, as opposed to the three or more hours that it usually takes to perform his plays today.

The Red Bull Playhouse, 1672. Francis Kirkman. Frontpiece. Clerkenwell, London.

The Globe's Comeback

The original Globe Theatre was destroyed in 1613 when the explosion of a cannon intended to mark the entrance of the king during a performance of *Henry VIII* accidentally set the thatched roof on fire. Within an hour, the entire theater burned to the ground. Rebuilt the following year, the Globe stood until 1644, when it was torn down to clear the land for new housing.

Thanks to the late U.S. actor Sam Wanamaker, the Globe made a comeback in 1997. Wanamaker founded the new Globe, a working replica of the original. It stands on the south bank of the Thames River in London and opened, like the original, with a production of *Henry V*. After more than three centuries, Shakespeare's "wooden O" has come full circle.

Literature Online **Literary History** For more about Shakespeare's theater, go to www.glencoe.com.

RESPONDING AND THINKING CRITICALLY

1. Why do you think Elizabethan audiences found drama so appealing?

2. Why might the Puritans have thought that playacting violated the biblical commandment against idolatry?

3. Why do you think Elizabethan plays were performed during the afternoon in an open courtyard?

OBJECTIVES
- Analyze the development of English drama.
- Identify the conventions of Shakespearean theater.

Macbeth, Act 1

Connecting to the Play

In *The Tragedy of Macbeth,* Shakespeare examines the lust for power and its terrible consequences. As you read, think about why some people seek power at all costs.

Building Background

For the basic story of this play, Shakespeare turned to one of the most popular books of the time, Raphael Holinshed's *Chronicles of England, Scotland, and Ireland* (1587). Shakespeare read about Duncan, who reigned from 1034 to 1040, and Macbeth, who reigned from 1040 to 1057. The real Macbeth gained the throne with the help of other noblemen who were dissatisfied with King Duncan, a young and ineffective ruler.

Always fascinated by psychological truth, Shakespeare altered his source material to gain dramatic power. In Shakespeare's hands, the historical Macbeth becomes a **tragic hero**—a character, usually of high status, who suffers a downfall as a result of a fatal character flaw, errors in judgment, or forces beyond human control.

Setting Purposes for Reading

Big Idea A Bard for the Ages

Shakespeare explored human nature in its many manifestations. As you read, notice the characters' motivations and their universal appeal.

Literary Element Atmosphere

Atmosphere is the general mood, or emotional quality, of a literary work. Playwrights create atmosphere primarily through details, such as those of setting, that are conveyed through the dialogue. As you read, consider the mood and notice the details that create it.

• See Literary Terms Handbook, p. R2.

Literature Online Interactive Literary Elements Handbook To review or learn more about the literary elements, go to www.glencoe.com.

Reading Strategy Applying Background Knowledge

Background knowledge refers to what you already know about the historical, social, and cultural forces that help shape a literary work. Background information about Shakespeare and his times is found in the unit introduction on pages 246–247, the Literary History feature on Shakespeare's theater on pages 314–315, the biography of Shakespeare on pages 292–293, and the Building Background section on this page. Also use the side-column notes, which provide help with unfamiliar words and complicated sentence structures, to add to your background knowledge while reading particular passages. By applying what you already know to what you are reading, you create meaning and enrich your understanding.

Vocabulary

direful (dīr′ fəl) *adj.* terrible; dreadful; p. 320 *She claimed that the house was haunted because of direful events that happened long ago.*

prophetic (prə fet′ ik) *adj.* having the quality of foretelling future events; p. 324 *With prophetic skill, he predicted the final score of the baseball game.*

repentance (ri pent′ əns) *n.* feeling of sorrow for wrongdoing; remorse; p. 327 *Justin expressed deep repentance for breaking the window.*

plenteous (plen′ tē əs) *adj.* abundant; fruitful; p. 328 *The potluck dinner featured plenteous main courses but only two desserts.*

peerless (pēr′ lis) *adj.* unrivaled; without equal; p. 329 *Grandpa is peerless when it comes to reciting Shakespearean passages from memory.*

Vocabulary Tip: Word Parts Suffixes are word parts added to the end of a root or a base word to change its meaning and sometimes its part of speech.

OBJECTIVES
In studying this selection, you will focus on the following:
• analyzing literary periods

• analyzing atmosphere
• applying background knowledge

The Tragedy of
Macbeth

William Shakespeare

Macbeth and the Three Witches. John Wootton. Oil on canvas. Private Collection.

CAST OF CHARACTERS

DUNCAN: King of Scotland

MALCOLM: Duncan's older son and heir to the throne

DONALBAIN: Duncan's younger son

MACBETH: Thane of Glamis, a Scottish noble and general in King Duncan's army

LADY MACBETH: Macbeth's wife

BANQUO: a thane of Scotland and general in King Duncan's army

FLEANCE: Banquo's son

MACDUFF: Thane of Fife, a Scottish noble

LADY MACDUFF: Macduff's wife

SON OF MACDUFF AND LADY MACDUFF

LENNOX
ROSS
MENTEITH } thanes and nobles of Scotland
ANGUS
CAITHNESS

SIWARD: Earl of Northumberland and general of the English forces

YOUNG SIWARD: Siward's son

SEYTON: an officer attending Macbeth

THREE WITCHES

HECATE: leader of the witches

PORTER

OLD MAN

THREE MURDERERS

ENGLISH DOCTOR

SCOTTISH DOCTOR

CAPTAIN: an officer serving Duncan

GENTLEWOMAN: an attendant to Lady Macbeth

APPARITIONS

LORDS, GENTLEMEN, OFFICERS, SOLDIERS, MESSENGERS, ATTENDANTS, SERVANTS

SETTING: *Scotland and England during the eleventh century.*

ACT 1

SCENE 1. Scotland. An open place.

[*In the midst of a great storm of thunder and lightning,* THREE WITCHES *appear in a deserted, outdoor place.*]

    FIRST WITCH. When shall we three meet again?
      In thunder, lightning, or in rain?

    SECOND WITCH. When the hurlyburly's° done,
      When the battle's lost and won.

5   **THIRD WITCH.** That will be ere° the set of sun.

    FIRST WITCH. Where the place?

    SECOND WITCH.   Upon the heath.°

    THIRD WITCH. There to meet with Macbeth.

    FIRST WITCH. I come, Graymalkin.°

    SECOND WITCH. Paddock° calls.

    THIRD WITCH.   Anon!°

10   **ALL.** Fair is foul, and foul is fair.°
      Hover through the fog and filthy air.

    [*The* WITCHES *exit.*]

SCENE 2. A military camp near Forres, a town about a hundred miles north of Edinburgh in Scotland.

[*From offstage come the sounds of men fighting, weapons clashing, and trumpets blaring.* DUNCAN, *King of Scotland, enters with his two teenage sons.* MALCOLM, *the older, who is heir to the throne, and* DONALBAIN, *the younger. With them are a Scottish nobleman,* LENNOX, *and other attendants. They meet a* CAPTAIN *bleeding from wounds received in battle between the king's army and the forces of his two rivals, Macdonwald and the Thane of Cawdor.*]

    KING. What bloody man is that? He can report,
      As seemeth by his plight, of the revolt
      The newest state.

    MALCOLM.   This is the sergeant
      Who like a good and hardy soldier fought
5   'Gainst my captivity.° Hail, brave friend!
      Say to the king the knowledge of the broil°
      As thou didst leave it.

---

3 hurlyburly: commotion.

5 ere: before.

6 heath: uncultivated land covered by small shrubs.

8 Graymalkin: gray cat (the name of a familiar, or spirit in animal form, that serves a witch).
9 Paddock: toad (another familiar).
Anon: right away!
10 In Shakespeare's time, many people believed that witches reversed normal values and practices, considering ugliness beautiful and vice versa.

1–3 The wounded officer (**sergeant**) has returned to King Duncan's military camp near Forres. Duncan hopes he can report on the progress of the rebellion.

5 'Gainst my captivity: to keep me from being captured.
6 broil: battle.

Reading Strategy Applying Background Knowledge *Why might the witches want to meet Macbeth?*

Literary Element Atmosphere *What do these lines suggest about the world of this play?*

CAPTAIN.   Doubtful it stood,
As two spent swimmers, that do cling together
And choke their art.° The merciless Macdonwald—
10   Worthy to be a rebel for to that
The multiplying villainies of nature
Do swarm upon him°—from the Western Isles°
Of kerns and gallowglasses° is supplied;
And Fortune, on his damnèd quarrel smiling,
15   Showed like a rebel's whore:° but all's too weak:
For brave Macbeth—well he deserves that name—
Disdaining Fortune, with his brandished steel,
Which smoked with bloody execution,
Like valor's minion° carved out his passage
20   Till he faced the slave;
Which nev'r shook hands, nor bade farewell to him,
Till he unseamed him from the nave to th' chops,°
And fixed his head upon our battlements.

KING. O valiant cousin!° Worthy gentleman!

25   CAPTAIN. As whence the sun 'gins his reflection°
Shipwracking storms and **direful** thunders break,
So from that spring whence comfort seemed to come
Discomfort swells.° Mark, King of Scotland, mark:
No sooner justice had, with valor armed,
30   Compelled these skipping kerns to trust their heels
But the Norweyan lord,° surveying vantage,°
With furbished arms and new supplies of men,
Began a fresh assault.

KING.   Dismayed not this
Our captains, Macbeth and Banquo?

CAPTAIN.   Yes;
35   As sparrows eagles,° or the hare the lion.
If I say sooth,° I must report they were
As cannons overcharged with double cracks;°
So they doubly redoubled strokes upon the foe.
Except° they meant to bathe in reeking wounds,
40   Or memorize another Golgotha,°
I cannot tell—
But I am faint; my gashes cry for help.

KING. So well thy words become thee as thy wounds;
They smack of honor both. Go get him surgeons.

[*As the* CAPTAIN *exits with the help of attendants, noblemen* ROSS *and*
ANGUS *enter.*]

45   Who comes here?

MALCOLM.   The worthy Thane° of Ross.

8–9 **As . . . art:** like two tired swimmers who hinder their skill by clinging to each other.

10–12 **Worthy . . . him:** well suited to be a rebel, since he is infested with evil qualities.
12 **Western Isles:** the Hebrides, off Scotland's west coast.
13 **kerns and gallowglasses:** lightly armed Irish foot soldiers and horsemen armed with axes.
14–15 **Fortune . . . whore:** Fortune, approving Macdonwald's cause, appeared to favor the rebel.
19 **minion:** favorite.

21–22 **Which . . . chops:** Macbeth didn't part from Macdonwald until he had cut him open from his navel to his jaw.
24 **cousin:** kinsman (Macbeth and Duncan were both grandsons of King Malcolm).
25 **sun 'gins his reflection:** sun rises.

25–28 **As . . . swells:** The Captain says that Macdonwald's defeat was only a break in the storm.

31 **Norweyan lord:** Sweno, King of Norway. **surveying vantage:** seeing an opportunity for attack.

35 **As sparrows eagles:** as much as sparrows frighten eagles.
36 **sooth:** truth.
37 **cracks:** explosive charges.

39 **Except:** unless.
40 **memorize . . . Golgotha:** make the field as notorious for slaughter as Golgotha, where Christ was crucified.

45 **Thane:** a Scottish title of nobility.

Vocabulary

direful (dīr′ fəl) *adj.* terrible; dreadful

LENNOX. What a haste looks through his eyes! So should he look

That seems to° speak things strange.

ROSS. God save the king!

KING. Whence cam'st thou, worthy Thane?

ROSS. From Fife, great
King;
Where the Norweyan banners flout the sky
50 And fan our people cold.°
Norway° himself, with terrible° numbers,
Assisted by that most disloyal traitor
The Thane of Cawdor, began a dismal° conflict;
Till that Bellona's bridegroom, lapped in proof,°
55 Confronted him with self-comparisons,°
Point against point rebellious, arm 'gainst arm,
Curbing his lavish° spirit: and, to conclude,
The victory fell on us.

KING. Great happiness!

ROSS. That now
Sweno, the Norways' king, craves composition;°
60 Nor would we deign him burial of his men
Till he disbursèd, at Saint Colme's Inch,°
Ten thousand dollars° to our general use.

KING. No more that Thane of Cawdor shall deceive
Our bosom interest:° go pronounce his present° death,
65 And with his former title greet Macbeth.

ROSS. I'll see it done.

KING. What he hath lost, noble Macbeth hath won.

[*They exit.*]

SCENE 3. A heath.

[*It is thundering as the* THREE WITCHES *wait on a desolate heath for* MACBETH *and* BANQUO. *The two generals are on their way to* KING DUNCAN'*s palace at* Forres.]

FIRST WITCH. Where hast thou been, sister?

SECOND WITCH. Killing swine.°

THIRD WITCH. Sister, where thou?

FIRST WITCH. A sailor's wife had chestnuts in her lap,
5 And mounched, and mounched, and mounched.

---

47 **seems to:** seems about to.

50 **fan . . . cold:** filled the Scots with cold fear.
51 **Norway:** the King of Norway. **terrible:** terrifying.
53 **dismal:** ominous.
54 **Bellona's . . . proof:** Ross refers to Macbeth as the husband of Bellona—Roman goddess of war—clad in tested armor (**proof**).
55 **Confronted . . . self-comparisons:** faced him with equal courage and skill.
57 **lavish:** insolent.

59 **craves composition:** begs for terms of peace.

61 **Saint Colme's Inch:** Inchcolm, an island in the Firth of Forth.
62 **dollars:** currency that first came into use in the early sixteenth century, about five hundred years after Macbeth's time.
64 **Our . . . interest:** my dearest concerns. **present:** immediate.

2 **Killing swine:** It was commonly believed that witches killed domestic animals.

Literary Element **Atmosphere** *Which phrases in this passage increase the sense of foreboding?*

Reading Strategy **Applying Background Knowledge** *What do you predict will happen to the former Thane of Cawdor?*

The Witches in Macbeth, c. 1841–2. Alexandre Gabriel Decamps. The Wallace Collection, London.

Viewing the Art: How does this depiction of the witches compare with your impression of them thus far?

"Give me," quoth I.
"Aroint thee,° witch!" the rump-fed ronyon° cries.
Her husband's to Aleppo gone, master o' th' Tiger:
But in a sieve I'll thither sail,
10 And, like a rat without a tail,
I'll do, I'll do, and I'll do.°

SECOND WITCH. I'll give thee a wind.

FIRST WITCH. Th' art kind.

THIRD WITCH. And I another.

15 **FIRST WITCH.** I myself have all the other;
And the very ports they blow,
All the quarters that they know
I' th' shipman's card.°
I'll drain him dry as hay:
20 Sleep shall neither night nor day
Hang upon his penthouse lid;°
He shall live a man forbid:°
Weary sev'nights° nine times nine
Shall he dwindle, peak,° and pine:
25 Though his bark cannot be lost,°
Yet it shall be tempest-tossed.
Look what I have.

SECOND WITCH. Show me, show me.

7 Aroint thee: Go away! **rump-fed ronyon:** fat-rumped, scabby creature.

8–11 The First Witch says she will take revenge by doing mischief against the woman's husband, who is captain of the Tiger, a ship heading toward the Middle Eastern city of Aleppo. Witches could supposedly use a leaky sieve for a boat and assume the shape of any animal, although the tail would be missing.

12–18 I'll . . . shipman's card: Witches were thought to control winds. The First Witch plans to use this power to block the Tiger from entering a port.
18 shipman's card: a compass or navigational chart.
21 penthouse lid: eyelid.
22 forbid: cursed.
23 sev'nights: weeks.
24 peak: grow peaked or emaciated.
25 Though . . . lost: Although I cannot sink his ship.

FIRST WITCH. Here I have a pilot's thumb,
30 Wracked as homeward he did come.

[*The sound of a drum is heard offstage.*]

THIRD WITCH. A drum, a drum!
Macbeth doth come.

ALL. The weird° sisters, hand in hand,
Posters of° the sea and land,
35 Thus do go about, about:
Thrice to thine, and thrice to mine,
And thrice again, to make up nine.
Peace! The charm's wound up.

[*MACBETH and BANQUO enter.*]

MACBETH. So foul and fair a day I have not seen.°

40 **BANQUO.** How far is 't called° to Forres? What are these
So withered, and so wild in their attire,
That look not like th' inhabitants o' th' earth,
And yet are on 't? Live you, or are you aught
That man may question? You seem to understand me,
45 By each at once her choppy° finger laying
Upon her skinny lips. You should be women,
And yet your beards forbid me to interpret
That you are so.

MACBETH. Speak, if you can: what are you?

FIRST WITCH. All hail, Macbeth! Hail to thee, Thane of
Glamis!

50 **SECOND WITCH.** All hail, Macbeth! Hail to thee, Thane of
Cawdor!

THIRD WITCH. All hail, Macbeth, that shalt be King hereafter!

[*MACBETH is startled by the WITCHES' greeting; BANQUO notices and addresses him.*]

BANQUO. Good sir, why do you start,° and seem to fear
Things that do sound so fair? [*To the WITCHES.*] I' th' name
of truth,
Are ye fantastical,° or that indeed
55 Which outwardly ye show? My noble partner
You greet with present grace° and great prediction
Of noble having° and of royal hope,
That he seems rapt withal:° to me you speak not.
If you can look into the seeds of time,

---

33 **weird:** connected with or determining fate.
34 **Posters of:** swift travelers over.

39 **So . . . seen:** Macbeth refers to the foulness of the weather and the fairness of his victory, which echoes the witches' chant in Act 1, scene 1, line 10.
40 **is 't called:** is it said to be.

45 **choppy:** chapped.

52 **start:** act startled.

54 **fantastical:** imaginary.

56 **present grace:** current honor (the title Thane of Glamis).
57 **noble having:** possession of further titles.
58 **rapt withal:** carried away with it.

Literary Element Atmosphere *What happens to mortals who displease the witches?*

Literary Element Atmosphere *What effect does Shakespeare create by having Macbeth's first words in the play echo the witches' chant in scene 1?*

60	And say which grain will grow and which will not,
	Speak then to me, who neither beg nor fear
	Your favors nor your hate.°

FIRST WITCH. Hail!

SECOND WITCH. Hail!

| 65 | **THIRD WITCH.** Hail! |

FIRST WITCH. Lesser than Macbeth, and greater.

SECOND WITCH. Not so happy,° yet much happier.

THIRD WITCH. Thou shalt get° kings, though thou be none.
So all hail, Macbeth and Banquo!

| 70 | **FIRST WITCH.** Banquo and Macbeth, all hail! |

MACBETH. Stay, you imperfect° speakers, tell me more:
By Sinel's° death I know I am Thane of Glamis;
But how of Cawdor? The Thane of Cawdor lives,
A prosperous gentleman; and to be King
| 75 | Stands not within the prospect of belief, |
No more than to be Cawdor. Say from whence
You owe° this strange intelligence?° Or why
Upon this blasted° heath you stop our way
With such **prophetic** greeting? Speak, I charge you.

61–62 **beg . . . hate:** beg your favors nor fear your hatred.

67 **happy:** fortunate.

68 **get:** beget, father.

71 **imperfect:** incomplete.
72 **Sinel:** Macbeth's father.

77 **owe:** own, possess.
intelligence: information.
78 **blasted:** blighted.

Vocabulary

prophetic (prə fet′ ik) *adj.* having the quality of foretelling future events

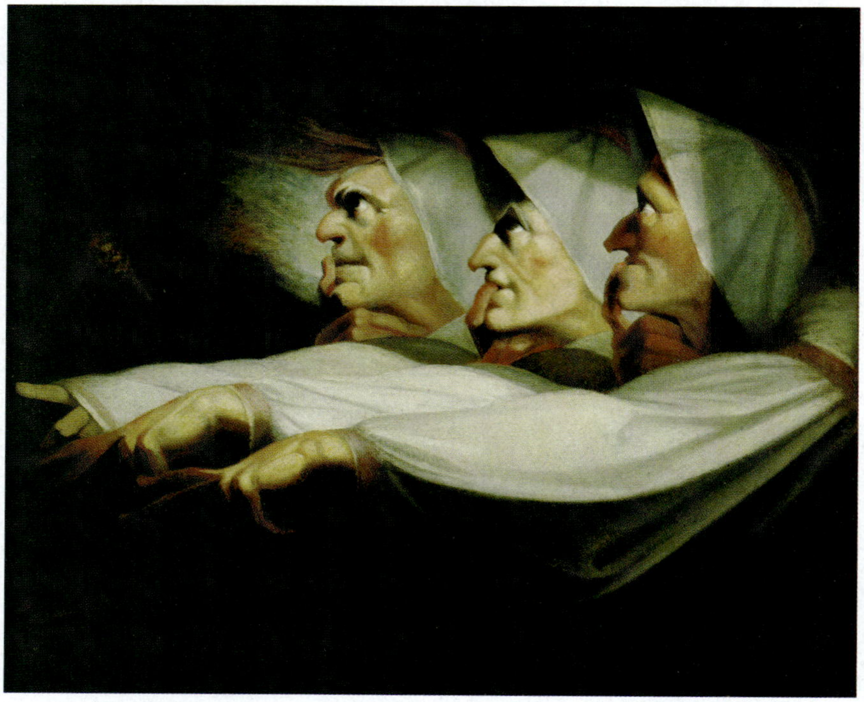

Three Witches, 1783. Henry Fuseli. Oil on canvas, 75 x 90.5 cm.
Royal Shakespeare Theater Collection, London.

[*The witches vanish.*]

80   **BANQUO.** The earth hath bubbles as the water has,
      And these are of them. Whither are they vanished?

    MACBETH. Into the air, and what seemed corporal° melted°
      As breath into the wind. Would° they had stayed!

    BANQUO. Were such things here as we do speak about?
85   Or have we eaten on the insane root°
      That takes the reason prisoner?

    MACBETH. Your children shall be kings.

    BANQUO.   You shall be King.

    MACBETH. And Thane of Cawdor too. Went it not so?

    BANQUO. To th' selfsame tune and words. Who's here?

[*ROSS and ANGUS enter.*]

90   **ROSS.** The King hath happily received, Macbeth,
      The news of thy success; and when he reads°
      Thy personal venture in the rebels' fight,
      His wonders and his praises do contend
      Which should be thine or his.° Silenced with that,
95   In viewing o'er the rest o' th' selfsame day,
      He finds thee in the stout Norweyan ranks,
      Nothing afeard of what thyself didst make,
      Strange images of death.° As thick as tale
      Came post with post,° and every one did bear
100   Thy praises in his kingdom's great defense,
      And poured them down before him.

    ANGUS.   We are sent
      To give thee, from our royal master, thanks;
      Only to herald° thee into his sight,
      Not pay thee.

105   **ROSS.** And for an earnest° of a greater honor,
      He bade me, from him, call thee Thane of Cawdor;
      In which addition,° hail, most worthy Thane!
      For it is thine.

    BANQUO. [*Aside.*] What, can the devil speak true?

    MACBETH. The Thane of Cawdor lives: why do you dress me
110   In borrowed robes?

    ANGUS.   Who° was the thane lives yet,
      But under heavy judgment bears that life
      Which he deserves to lose. Whether he was combined°
      With those of Norway, or did line° the rebel
      With hidden help and vantage, or that with both
115   He labored in his country's wrack,° I know not;

---

82 **corporal:** flesh and blood.
melted: vanished.
83 **Would:** I wish.

85 **insane root:** A number of plants, such as henbane and hemlock, were believed to cause insanity.

91 **reads:** considers.

93–94 **His . . . his:** His astonishment, which leaves him speechless, conflicts with his desire to praise Macbeth.

97–98 **Nothing . . . death:** Not at all afraid of dying as he killed.
98–99 **As thick . . . post:** As fast as could be counted came messenger after messenger.

103 **herald:** conduct.

105 **earnest:** a small payment made as a pledge.

107 **addition:** title.

110 **Who:** he who.

112 **combined:** in conspiracy.
113 **line:** support, strengthen.

115 **wrack:** ruin.

Reading Strategy   Applying Background Knowledge *How does Banquo interpret the apparition of the witches?*

But treasons capital,° confessed and proved,
Have overthrown him.

MACBETH. [*Aside.*]   Glamis, and Thane of Cawdor:
The greatest is behind.° [*Addressing* ROSS *and* ANGUS.]
    Thanks for your pains.
[*Aside to* BANQUO.] Do you not hope your children shall be
    kings,
120 When those that gave the Thane of Cawdor to me
Promised no less to them?

BANQUO. [*Aside to* MACBETH.] That, trusted home,°
Might yet enkindle you unto° the crown,
Besides the Thane of Cawdor. But 'tis strange:
And oftentimes, to win us to our harm,
125 The instruments of darkness tell us truths,
Win us with honest trifles, to betray 's
In deepest consequence.°
Cousins, a word, I pray you.

[BANQUO *speaks privately to the two noblemen while* MACBETH *expresses his thoughts in an aside.*]

MACBETH.   Two truths are told,
As happy prologues to the swelling act
130 Of the imperial theme.°—I thank you, gentlemen—

[MACBETH *interrupts himself to speak to* ROSS *and* BANQUO; *he then continues his aside.*]

This supernatural soliciting°
Cannot be ill, cannot be good. If ill,
Why hath it given me earnest of success,
Commencing in a truth? I am Thane of Cawdor:
135 If good, why do I yield to that suggestion
Whose horrid image doth unfix my hair
And make my seated heart knock at my ribs,
Against the use of nature?° Present fears
Are less than horrible imaginings.°
140 My thought, whose murder yet is but fantastical,
Shakes so my single state of man that function
Is smothered in surmise, and nothing is
But what is not.°

BANQUO. [*Speaking to* ROSS *about* MACBETH.] Look,
how our partner's rapt.

MACBETH. [*Aside.*] If chance will have me King, why, chance
may crown me,

---

116 **capital:** punishable by death.

118 **behind:** still to come.

121 **home:** fully.
122 **enkindle you unto:** enflame your hopes for.

123–127 **But . . . consequence:** Banquo says that demonic forces often win our confidence by making trivial predictions that come true.

128–130 **Two . . . theme:** Macbeth uses theatrical terms to describe his career, which will reach a climax when he becomes king.

131 **supernatural soliciting:** the witches' tempting or suggesting.

135–138 **If . . . nature:** Macbeth says that the thought of murdering Duncan causes his hair to stand on end and his firmly-placed (**seated**) heart to pound— symptoms of fear contrary to his nature.
138–139 **Present . . . imaginings:** Fears of something that presently exists are less powerful than fears of imaginary horrors.
140–143 **My . . . not:** Macbeth says that the imaginary murder in his thoughts has caused such inner turmoil that he can no longer act. The only thing that seems real to him is this unreal murder.

Big Idea **A Bard for the Ages** *What does Shakespeare reveal about Banquo's character in these lines?*

Literary Element **Atmosphere** *How do Macbeth's words echo the witches' lines?*

Without my stir.°

BANQUO.   New honors come upon him,
Like our strange garments, cleave not to their mold
But with the aid of use.°

MACBETH. [*Aside.*]   Come what come may,
Time and the hour runs through the roughest day.

BANQUO. Worthy Macbeth, we stay upon your leisure.°

150 **MACBETH.** Give me your favor. My dull brain was wrought
With things forgotten.° Kind gentlemen, your pains
Are registered where every day I turn
The leaf to read them. Let us toward the King.
[*Aside to* BANQUO.] Think upon what hath chanced, and at
    more time,°
155 The interim having weighed it,° let us speak
Our free hearts° each to other.

BANQUO.   Very gladly.

MACBETH. Till then, enough. Come, friends.

[*They all exit together.*]

SCENE 4. The palace at Forres.

[*At* KING DUNCAN's *palace at Forres, the king and his two sons,* MALCOLM
and DONALBAIN, *enter to a fanfare of trumpets. They are accompanied by*
LENNOX *and other attendants.*]

KING. Is execution done on Cawdor? Are not
Those in commission° yet returned?

MALCOLM.   My liege,
They are not yet come back. But I have spoke
With one that saw him die, who did report
5 That very frankly he confessed his treasons,
Implored your Highness' pardon and set forth
A deep **repentance**: nothing in his life
Became him like the leaving it. He died
As one that had been studied° in his death,
10 To throw away the dearest thing he owed°
As 'twere a careless° trifle.

KING.   There's no art
To find the mind's construction in the face:°
He was a gentleman on whom I built
An absolute trust.

Big Idea **A Bard for the Ages** *How does Malcolm's description of
Cawdor's death reveal Shakespeare's humanism?*

Vocabulary

repentance (ri pent′ əns) *n.* feeling of sorrow for wrongdoing;
remorse

Side notes:

145 **stir:** taking action.

146–147 **Like . . . use:** like new clothes that do not fit comfortably until worn for a while.

149 **stay . . . leisure:** we are waiting for you at your convenience.

150–151 **Give . . . forgotten:** Macbeth asks for their pardon. He excuses his inattentiveness by saying that he was trying to remember something.

154 **at more time:** when we have more leisure time.
155 **The interim . . . it:** having considered it in the meantime.
156 **Our free hearts:** our minds freely.

2 **Those in commission:** those charged with carrying out the execution.

9 **studied:** rehearsed.
10 **owed:** owned.
11 **careless:** worthless.

11–12 **There's . . . face:** There's no way to read a person's thoughts by looking at his or her face.

[MACBETH, BANQUO, ROSS, *and* ANGUS *enter. The* KING *addresses* MACBETH.]

O worthiest cousin!
15 The sin of my ingratitude even now
Was heavy on me: thou art so far before,°
That swiftest wing of recompense is slow
To overtake thee. Would thou hadst less deserved,
That the proportion both of thanks and payment
20 Might have been mine!° Only I have left to say,
More is thy due than more than all can pay.°

MACBETH.   The service and the loyalty I owe,
In doing it, pays itself. Your Highness' part
Is to receive our duties: and our duties
25 Are to your throne and state children and servants;
Which do but what they should, by doing every thing
Safe toward your love and honor.°

KING.   Welcome hither.
I have begun to plant thee, and will labor
To make thee full of growing. Noble Banquo,
30 That hast no less deserved, nor must be known
No less to have done so,° let me enfold° thee
And hold thee to my heart.

BANQUO.   There if I grow,
The harvest is your own.

KING.   My **plenteous** joys,
Wanton° in fullness, seek to hide themselves
35 In drops of sorrow. Sons, kinsmen, thanes,
And you whose places are the nearest,° know,
We will establish our estate upon
Our eldest, Malcolm, whom we name hereafter
The Prince of Cumberland: which honor must
40 Not unaccompanied invest him only,
But signs of nobleness, like stars, shall shine
On all deservers.° From hence to Inverness,°
And bind us further to you.°

MACBETH.   The rest is labor, which is not used for you.°
45 I'll be myself the harbinger,° and make joyful
The hearing of my wife with your approach;
So, humbly take my leave.

KING.   My worthy Cawdor!

16 **before:** ahead.

18–20 **Would . . . mine:** I wish you deserved less, so that I could repay you amply.
21 **than more . . . pay:** than it would be possible to pay.

23–27 **Your . . . honor:** Macbeth compares the relationship between kings and their subjects to that between parents and children or masters and servants. By doing everything possible to protect Duncan, his subjects are merely fulfilling their obligations.
30–31 **That hast . . . so:** who is no less worthy and whose deeds must be acknowledged.
31 **enfold:** embrace.

34 **Wanton:** unrestrained.

36 **whose . . . nearest:** who are by birth closest to the throne.
37–42 **We . . . deservers:** The King (using the royal "we") announces that his eldest son, Malcolm, will succeed him to the throne. He gives Malcolm a new title and says that other deserving subjects will also receive honors. In Scotland at this time, the crown was not hereditary.
42 **Inverness:** the location of Macbeth's castle.
43 **bind us further to you:** make me even more indebted to Macbeth for his hospitality.
44 **The rest . . . you:** Any leisure not devoted to you is labor.
45 **harbinger:** an officer who precedes royalty to arrange reception for a visit.

Reading Strategy   **Applying Background Knowledge** *Read the side note about kingship and heredity. Why might Macbeth think that he should be named Duncan's heir?*

Vocabulary

plenteous (plen′ tē əs) *adj.* abundant; fruitful

MACBETH. [*Aside.*] The Prince of Cumberland! That is a step
On which I must fall down, or else o'erleap,
50   For in my way it lies.° Stars, hide your fires;
Let not light see my black and deep desires:
The eye wink at the hand;° yet let that be
Which the eye fears, when it is done, to see.

[*MACBETH exits.*]

KING. True, worthy Banquo; he is full so valiant,°
55   And in his commendations° I am fed;
It is a banquet to me. Let's after him,
Whose care is gone before to bid us welcome.
It is a **peerless** kinsman.

[*They all exit to a flourish of trumpets.*]

SCENE 5. The castle at Inverness.

[*In* MACBETH'*s castle at Inverness,* LADY MACBETH *appears alone, reading a letter from her husband.*]

LADY MACBETH. [*Reads.*] "They met me in the day of success;
and I have learned by the perfect'st report° they have more
in them than mortal knowledge. When I burned in desire
to question them further, they made themselves air, into
5   which they vanished. Whiles I stood rapt in the wonder of
it, came missives° from the King, who all-hailed me 'Thane
of Cawdor'; by which title, before, these weird sisters
saluted me, and referred me to the coming on of time, with
'Hail, King that shalt be!' This have I thought good to
10   deliver° thee, my dearest partner of greatness, that thou
mightst not lose the dues of rejoicing,° by being ignorant of
what greatness is promised thee. Lay it to thy heart, and
farewell."
Glamis thou art, and Cawdor, and shalt be
15   What thou art promised. Yet do I fear thy nature;
It is too full o' th' milk of human kindness°
To catch the nearest way.° Thou wouldst be great,
Art not without ambition, but without
The illness° should attend it. What thou wouldst highly,°
20   That wouldst thou holily;° wouldst not play false,
And yet wouldst wrongly win. Thou'dst have, great Glamis,

48–50 **The . . . lies:** Macbeth realizes that he will not become king by "chance" (see Act 1, scene 3, line 144).
52 **The eye . . . hand:** Let my eyes be blind to my hand's deed.

54 **he . . . valiant:** Macbeth is as valiant as you say he is.
55 **his commendations:** commendations of him.

2 **perfect'st report:** best intelligence.

6 **missives:** messengers.

10 **deliver:** communicate to.
11 **lose . . . rejoicing:** be deprived of your rightful joy.

16 **milk . . . kindness:** natural feelings of compassion or loyalty.
17 **catch . . . way:** take the quickest means to the throne (that is, killing Duncan).
19 **illness:** wickedness, ruthlessness.
wouldst highly: would greatly like.
20 **wouldst thou holily:** you would like to have virtuously.

Literary Element   Atmosphere *How does this image reinforce the mood of the play?*

Big Idea   A Bard for the Ages *What does Shakespeare reveal about Macbeth's relationship with his wife in the phrase "my dearest partner of greatness"?*

Vocabulary

peerless (pēr′ lis) *adj.* unrivaled; without equal

That which cries "Thus thou must do" if thou have it;
And that which rather thou dost fear to do
Than wishest should be undone.° Hie thee hither,
25   That I may pour my spirits in thine ear,
And chastise° with the valor of my tongue
All that impedes thee from the golden round°
Which fate and metaphysical° aid doth seem
To have thee crowned withal.

[A MESSENGER *enters.*]

                                    What is your tidings?

30   MESSENGER. The King comes here tonight.

LADY MACBETH.   Thou'rt mad to
        say it!
    Is not thy master with him, who, were 't so,
    Would have informed for preparation?°

    MESSENGER. So please you, it is true. Our thane is coming.
    One of my fellows had the speed of him,°
35   Who, almost dead for breath, had scarcely more
    Than would make up his message.

LADY MACBETH.   Give him tending;
    He brings great news. [*The* MESSENGER *exits.*]
                                    The raven° himself is hoarse
    That croaks the fatal entrance of Duncan
    Under my battlements. Come, you spirits
40   That tend on mortal° thoughts, unsex me here,
    And fill me, from the crown° to the toe, top-full
    Of direst cruelty! Make thick my blood,
    Stop up th' access and passage to remorse,°
    That no compunctious visitings of nature°
45   Shake my fell purpose,° nor keep peace between
    Th' effect and it!° Come to my woman's breasts,
    And take my milk for gall,° you murd'ring ministers,°
    Wherever in your sightless° substances
    You wait on nature's mischief!° Come, thick night,
50   And pall thee in the dunnest smoke° of hell,
    That my keen knife see not the wound it makes,
    Nor heaven peep through the blanket of the dark,
    To cry "Hold, hold!"

[MACBETH *enters.*]

                                    Great Glamis! Worthy Cawdor!
    Greater than both, by the all-hail hereafter!
55   Thy letters have transported me beyond

Literary Element Atmosphere *How does the image of the hoarse raven contribute to the atmosphere?*

Literary Element Atmosphere *Which images in these lines reinforce the ominous mood?*

21–24 Thou'dst . . . undone: What you want requires you to do certain things, and you fear taking such action rather than wishing the action were not taken.
26 chastise: reprimand.
27 golden round: crown.
28 metaphysical: supernatural.

32 informed for preparation: sent word to prepare for the guest.

34 had . . . him: sped ahead of him.

37 raven: traditionally a bird of ill omen.

40 mortal: murderous.
41 crown: top of the head.

43 remorse: compassion.
44 compunctious . . . nature: natural feelings of pity.
45 fell purpose: cruel intentions.
45–46 nor . . . it: nor prevent my intentions from being carried out.
47 take . . . gall: exchange my milk for bile (traditionally associated with envy and hatred). **ministers:** agents.
48 sightless: invisible.
49 wait . . . mischief: serve evil.
50 pall . . . smoke: cover yourself in the darkest smoke.

Ellen Terry as Lady Macbeth, 1880s. John Singer Sargent. Oil on canvas, 221.0 x 114.3 cm. Tate Gallery, London.

Viewing the Art: What does this painting suggest about Lady Macbeth's desires?

This ignorant present,° and I feel now
The future in the instant.°

MACBETH.   My dearest love,
Duncan comes here tonight.

LADY MACBETH.   And when goes hence?

MACBETH. Tomorrow, as he purposes.

LADY MACBETH.   O, never
60   Shall sun that morrow see!
Your face, my Thane, is as a book where men
May read strange matters. To beguile the time,
Look like the time;° bear welcome in your eye,
Your hand, your tongue: look like th' innocent flower,
65   But be the serpent under 't. He that's coming
Must be provided for: and you shall put
This night's great business into my dispatch;°
Which shall to all our nights and days to come
Give solely sovereign sway° and masterdom.

70   MACBETH. We will speak further.

LADY MACBETH.   Only look up clear.°
To alter favor ever is to fear.°
Leave all the rest to me.

[They exit.]

SCENE 6. Outside the castle at Inverness.

[*Outside* MACBETH's *castle oboes sound to announce the arrival of royalty.*
KING DUNCAN *and his sons enter with a group of Scottish noblemen,*
including BANQUO, LENNOX, MACDUFF, ROSS, *and* ANGUS. *It is nighttime,*
and they are attended by servants with torches.]

KING. This castle hath a pleasant seat;° the air
Nimbly and sweetly recommends itself
Unto our gentle senses.

BANQUO.   This guest of summer,
The temple-haunting martlet, does approve
5   By his loved mansionry that the heaven's breath
Smells wooingly here.° No jutty, frieze,
Buttress, nor coign of vantage, but this bird
Hath made his pendent bed and procreant cradle.°
Where they most breed and haunt, I have observed
10   The air is delicate.

[LADY MACBETH *enters to welcome her guests.*]

KING.   See, see, our honored hostess!
The love that follows us sometime is our trouble,
Which still we thank as love. Herein I teach you

---

56 **this ignorant present:** this present
unaware of the future.
57 **instant:** present.

62–63 **To beguile . . . time:** To deceive
the occasion, put on an appearance
appropriate to the occasion.

67 **dispatch:** management.

69 **solely sovereign sway:** absolute
power.

70 **look up clear:** appear undisturbed.
71 **To alter . . . fear:** Changing one's
usual appearance always arouses
suspicion.

1 **seat:** location.

3–6 **This . . . here:** The house martin, a
bird that often nests in churches, proves
by building its nest here that the place is
heavenly.
6–8 **No jutty . . . cradle:** There is no
projecting part of a building, decorative
band on a wall, supporting structure, or
convenient corner where this bird has
not made its suspended bed and nest for
offspring.

Literary Element   **Atmosphere** *What is ironic about Banquo's*
comments about Macbeth's castle?

How you shall bid God 'ield us for your pains
And thank us for your trouble.°

LADY MACBETH.   All our service
15   In every point twice done, and then done double,
Were poor and single business° to contend
Against those honors deep and broad wherewith
Your Majesty loads our house: for those of old,
And the late dignities heaped up to them,
20   We rest your hermits.°

KING.   Where's the Thane of Cawdor?
We coursed him at the heels,° and had a purpose
To be his purveyor:° but he rides well,
And his great love, sharp as his spur, hath holp° him
To his home before us. Fair and noble hostess,
25   We are your guest tonight.

LADY MACBETH.   Your servants ever
Have theirs, themselves, and what is theirs, in compt,
To make their audit at your Highness' pleasure,
Still to return your own.°

KING.   Give me your hand.
Conduct me to mine host: we love him highly,
30   And shall continue our graces towards him.
By your leave, hostess.

[LADY MACBETH *and the* KING *go into the castle.*]

SCENE 7. The castle at Inverness.

[*In a torch-lit room in* MACBETH'*s castle, music is heard. A steward,
followed by other servants carrying dishes of food, crosses the stage. As they
exit,* MACBETH *enters.*]

MACBETH.   If it were done° when 'tis done, then 'twere well
It were done quickly. If th' assassination
Could trammel up the consequence, and catch,
With his surcease success; that but this blow
5   Might be the be-all and the end-all—here,
But here, upon this bank and shoal of time,
We'd jump the life to come.° But in these cases
We still have judgment here; that we but teach
Bloody instructions, which, being taught, return
10   To plague th' inventor:° this even-handed justice
Commends° th' ingredients of our poisoned chalice°
To our own lips. He's here in double trust:
First, as I am his kinsman and his subject,
Strong both against the deed; then, as his host,
15   Who should against his murderer shut the door,
Not bear the knife myself. Besides, this Duncan

11–14 **The . . . trouble:** The King says
that he sometimes finds love inconve-
nient, but he still is grateful for it. He
jokingly suggests that this will teach
Lady Macbeth to be thankful for the
trouble she is taking as his hostess.
16 **single business:** trivial service.

20 **We . . . hermits:** We will devote ourselves to praying for you.

21 **coursed . . . heels:** pursued him
closely.
22 **purveyor:** an officer who travels
ahead of a king or nobleman to make
advance preparations.
23 **holp:** helped.

25–28 **Your . . . own:** Your servants
forever hold their dependents, themselves, and their possessions in trust for
you, and are always ready to open their
accounts to you and return what is yours.

1 **were done:** were over and done with.

2–7 **If . . . come:** Macbeth says that if he
could achieve his goals merely by killing
Duncan, without any consequences here
on earth, he would risk whatever
consequences awaited him in the next
world.
8–10 **We still . . . inventor:** We are
always punished in this life, in that our
bloody deeds provide an example for
others to act against us.
11 **Commends:** offers. **chalice:** cup.

Reading Strategy   Applying Background Knowledge   *What do
subjects owe their king? What do hosts owe their guests?*

Hath borne his faculties° so meek, hath been
So clear° in his great office, that his virtues
Will plead like angels trumpet-tongued against
20   The deep damnation of his taking-off;°
And pity, like a naked newborn babe,
Striding the blast,° or heaven's cherubin° horsed
Upon the sightless couriers° of the air,
Shall blow the horrid deed in every eye,
25   That tears shall drown the wind. I have no spur
To prick the sides of my intent, but only
Vaulting ambition, which o'erleaps itself
And falls on th' other°—

[*LADY MACBETH enters.*]

How now! What news?

LADY MACBETH. He has almost supped. Why have you left the
chamber?

30   **MACBETH.** Hath he asked for me?

LADY MACBETH.   Know you not he has?

MACBETH. We will proceed no further in this business:
He hath honored me of late, and I have bought°
Golden opinions from all sorts of people,
Which would be worn now in their newest gloss,
35   Not cast aside so soon.

LADY MACBETH.   Was the hope drunk
Wherein you dressed yourself? Hath it slept since?
And wakes it now, to look so green and pale°
At what it did so freely? From this time
Such I account thy love. Art thou afeard
40   To be the same in thine own act and valor
As thou art in desire? Wouldst thou have that
Which thou esteem'st the ornament of life,°
And live a coward in thine own esteem,
Letting "I dare not" wait upon "I would,"
45   Like the poor cat i' th' adage?°

MACBETH.   Prithee, peace!
I dare do all that may become a man;
Who dares do more is none.

LADY MACBETH.   What beast was 't then
That made you break° this enterprise to me?
When you durst do it, then you were a man;
50   And to be more than what you were, you would
Be so much more the man. Nor time nor place
Did then adhere, and yet you would make both.
They have made themselves, and that their fitness now
Does unmake you.° I have given suck, and know

---

17 **borne his faculties:** used his powers.
18 **clear:** blameless.

20 **taking-off:** murder.

22 **striding the blast:** bestriding the trumpet's blow. **cherubin:** angels.
23 **sightless couriers:** invisible messengers (the wind).

25–28 **I . . . other:** Macbeth says that his only motivation is ambition, which he compares to a rider that makes a horse fall after leaping too high over an obstacle.

32 **bought:** acquired.

37 **green and pale:** sickly.

42 **ornament of life:** the crown.

45 **Like . . . adage:** Lady Macbeth refers to an old saying about a cat that wanted to eat fish but wouldn't get its paws wet to catch them.

48 **break:** reveal.

51–54 **Nor time . . . you:** You were willing when neither time nor place was suitable, and now that everything has fallen into place, the convenience has unnerved you.

55 How tender 'tis to love the babe that milks me:
I would, while it was smiling in my face,
Have plucked my nipple from his boneless gums,
And dashed the brains out, had I so sworn as you
Have done to this.

MACBETH.   If we should fail?

LADY MACBETH.   We fail?
60 But screw your courage to the sticking-place,°
And we'll not fail. When Duncan is asleep—
Whereto the rather° shall his day's hard journey
Soundly invite him—his two chamberlains
Will I with wine and wassail° so convince,°
65 That memory, the warder of the brain,
Shall be a fume, and the receipt of reason
A limbeck only:° when in swinish sleep
Their drenchèd natures lies as in a death,
What cannot you and I perform upon
70 Th' unguarded Duncan, what not put upon
His spongy° officers, who shall bear the guilt
Of our great quell?°

MACBETH.   Bring forth men-children only;
For thy undaunted mettle° should compose
Nothing but males. Will it not be received,
75 When we have marked with blood those sleepy two
Of his own chamber, and used their very daggers,
That they have done 't?

LADY MACBETH.   Who dares receive it other,°
As° we shall make our griefs and clamor roar
Upon his death?

MACBETH.   I am settled,° and bend up
80 Each corporal agent° to this terrible feat.
Away, and mock the time° with fairest show:
False face must hide what the false heart doth know.

[*They exit.*]

60 **But . . . sticking-place:** only summon up all your courage. **sticking place:** a notch on a crossbow that holds the string when it has been tightened for firing.
62 **Whereto the rather:** to which all the sooner.
64 **wassail:** "carousing" or "spiced ale." **convince:** overcome.

65–67 **memory . . . only:** Memory, the guardian of the brain, shall become only a vapor, and the brain only the part of a still through which vapors pass.

71 **spongy:** soaked with alcohol.
72 **quell:** murder.

73 **undaunted mettle:** brave spirit.

77 **receive it other:** take it otherwise.
78 **As:** since.

79 **settled:** resolved.
79–80 **bend . . . agent:** exert every power in my body.
81 **mock the time:** deceive the present occasion.

Literary Element   **Atmosphere** *How does this image contribute to the atmosphere?*

Big Idea   **A Bard for the Ages** *How does Shakespeare show a change in Macbeth's character at this point in the play?*

RESPONDING AND THINKING CRITICALLY

Respond

1. What is your impression of Macbeth and Lady Macbeth?

Recall and Interpret

2. (a)What predictions do the witches make about Macbeth's future? About Banquo's? (b)How does Macbeth's reaction differ from Banquo's?

3. (a)What conflict arises in Macbeth after the first prediction proves true? (b)What does this inner conflict reveal about his character?

4. (a)Which trait of her husband's does Lady Macbeth fear will prevent him from securing the Scottish throne? (b)What does this tell you about Lady Macbeth's character?

Analyze and Evaluate

5. A **soliloquy** is a dramatic device in which a character, alone on the stage, reveals his or her private thoughts and feelings as if thinking aloud. What does Macbeth's soliloquy in scene 7 reveal about him?

6. (a)Summarize the arguments that Lady Macbeth uses to convince her husband to murder Duncan. (b)Do these arguments appeal to Macbeth's reason, his emotions, or both? Explain your answer.

7. (a)Review the scenes in which the witches appear. What might the witches symbolize, or stand for? (b)What is their effect on Macbeth?

8. (a)How would you describe the relationship between Macbeth and Lady Macbeth? (b)In your opinion, who is more responsible for the plot against Duncan—Macbeth or Lady Macbeth? Support your opinion with evidence from the play.

Connect

9. **Big Idea** **A Bard for the Ages** How does Shakespeare make Macbeth a character with whom the audience can sympathize?

LITERARY ANALYSIS

Literary Element Atmosphere

In this play, Shakespeare uses the witches to establish the **atmosphere,** or emotional quality of the work.

1. Describe the atmosphere created by the witches' dialogue in scenes 1 and 3.

2. If you were producing scene 1 of *Macbeth* today, how would you establish the atmosphere?

Writing About Literature

Evaluate Author's Craft In a play, a character's comment that is heard by the audience but not by other characters onstage is called an **aside.** Analyze Shakespeare's use of the aside in scene 3. In a few paragraphs, explain what Macbeth's asides reveal about him and how your impression of Macbeth would change if they were omitted.

Literature Online **Web Activities** For eFlashcards, Selection Quick Checks, and other Web activities, go to www.glencoe.com.

READING AND VOCABULARY

Reading Strategy Applying Background Knowledge

Applying what you know to what you are reading helps you make connections that increase your understanding of a drama. Which pieces of background information were most useful to you in reading Act 1?

Vocabulary Practice

Practice with Word Parts For each vocabulary word below, identify the suffix and then choose the correct meaning. Use a dictionary if you need help.

1. direful   **a.** that which   **b.** full of
2. prophetic   **a.** characteristic of **b.** without
3. repentance   **a.** study of   **b.** quality of
4. plenteous   **a.** full of   **b.** not
5. peerless   **a.** one who   **b.** without

LITERATURE PREVIEW

Building Background

In all probability, *Macbeth* was first performed in 1606 at the Globe and then at the king's court. To Shakespeare's audience, a play that depicted the horrors of regicide would have hit close to home. The dating of the play places it in the aftermath of one of the most disturbing events in English history, the Gunpowder Plot of 1605.

The Gunpowder Plot involved a conspiracy by Catholic extremists to blow up King James I and his Protestant government at the opening of Parliament on November 5. On the night before the plan was to be carried out, a conspirator, Guy Fawkes, was arrested with thirty-six barrels of gunpowder in a cellar beneath the House of Lords. He and the other conspirators sought to restore a Catholic regime in England under King James I's child, Princess Elizabeth, with a Spanish invasion to follow.

That these events affected Shakespeare is evident in the allusions to equivocation, or deceptive testimony, in the porter's speech in scene 3 of this act. The famous Jesuit, Father Garnet, who was tried and executed for his role in the Gunpowder Plot, had made a speech defending equivocation as a legitimate means to avoid self-incrimination.

Literary Element Motif

A **motif** (mō tēf´) is a significant phrase, description, or image that is repeated throughout a literary work and related to its theme. For example, in Act 1 of *Macbeth,* two important motifs are the supernatural, associated with the witches, and the shedding of blood, associated with the wounded captain who reports Macbeth's exploits in battle. As you read Act 2, notice how these motifs recur. Also look for other motifs that Shakespeare introduces and develops.

- See Literary Terms Handbook, p. R11.

Literature Online **Interactive Literary Elements Handbook** To review or learn more about the literary elements, go to www.glencoe.com.

READING PREVIEW

Reading Strategy Evaluating Credibility

Evaluating credibility involves making a judgment about whether a character is knowledgeable and truthful. As you read, consider whether the characters' statements in this act are convincing.

Reading Tip: Using a Checklist Use a checklist like the one below to evaluate the characters' credibility.

☑ Under what circumstances is the statement made?

☑ Does the character have something to hide?

☑ Does the character have anything to gain or lose?

☑ Can the statement be corroborated by events or by other characters?

☑ Does the statement make logical sense?

Vocabulary

stealthy (stel´ thē) *adj.* secret; sly; p. 339 *The stealthy figure crept down the alley.*

surfeited (sur´ fit əd) *adj.* overfed; overcome by excess drinking, eating, etc.; p. 340 *After devouring the last two slices of pizza, I felt surfeited.*

provoke (prə vōk´) *v.* to call forth; to stir to action or feeling; p. 344 *His imaginative excuses for his late assignments usually provoked mild laughter.*

scruple (skrōō´ pəl) *n.* a moral or ethical principle that restrains action; p. 347 *Her scruples prevented her from resorting to dishonest means.*

predominance (pri dom´ ə nəns) *n.* the state of being most important, common, or noticeable; p. 348 *A predominance of children packed the theater for the animated film.*

Vocabulary Tip: Word Origins Knowing the origins, or etymologies, of words can help you build vocabulary and figure out the meanings of unfamiliar words.

OBJECTIVES
In studying this selection, you will focus on the following:
- analyzing literary periods
- analyzing motifs
- evaluating credibility

ACT 2

SCENE 1. The castle at Inverness.

[It is late at night as BANQUO *and his son,* FLEANCE, *both guests of* MACBETH's, *enter the courtyard of the castle.* FLEANCE *carries a torch to light the way.]*

BANQUO. How goes the night, boy?

FLEANCE. The moon is down; I have not heard the clock.

BANQUO. And she goes down at twelve.

FLEANCE.   I take't, 'tis later, sir.

BANQUO. Hold, take my sword. There's husbandry° in heaven.
5   Their candles° are all out. Take thee that° too.
A heavy summons° lies like lead upon me,
And yet I would not sleep. Merciful powers,
Restrain in me the cursèd thoughts that nature
Gives way to in respose!

*[*MACBETH *and a servant carrying a torch enter.]*

                    Give me my sword!
10   Who's there?

MACBETH. A friend.

BANQUO. What, sir, not yet at rest? The King's a-bed:
He hath been in unusual pleasure, and
Sent forth great largess to your offices:°
15   This diamond he greets your wife withal,
By the name of most kind hostess; and shut up°
In measureless content.

MACBETH.   Being unprepared,
Our will became the servant to defect,
Which else should free have wrought.°

BANQUO.   All's well.
20   I dreamed last night of the three weird sisters:
To you they have showed some truth.

MACBETH.   I think not of them.
Yet, when we can entreat an hour to serve,°
We would spend it in some words upon that business,
If you would grant the time.

BANQUO.   At your kind'st leisure.

25   **MACBETH.** If you shall cleave to my consent, when 'tis,°
It shall make honor for you.

---

4 husbandry: thrift.
5 candles: stars. **that:** perhaps his shield, cloak, or dagger.
6 summons: weariness calling him to sleep.

14 largess . . . offices: gifts to your servants' quarters.

16 shut up: concluded (his remarks).

17–19 Being . . . wrought: Our lack of preparation hindered us from entertaining as lavishly as we would have liked.

22 entreat . . . serve: arrange a suitable hour.

25 cleave . . . 'tis: support my position when the time comes.

Literary Element   Motif *Which motifs can you identify in this passage?*

Reading Strategy   Evaluating Credibility *Is Macbeth telling the truth? Do you think Banquo believes him? Explain.*

BANQUO.   So I lose none°
    In seeking to augment it, but still keep
    My bosom franchised and allegiance clear,°
    I shall be counseled.°

MACBETH.   Good repose the while!

30 **BANQUO.** Thanks, sir. The like to you!

[*BANQUO and FLEANCE exit.*]

MACBETH. [*To the servant.*] Go bid thy mistress, when my
        drink° is ready,
    She strike upon the bell. Get thee to bed.

[*The servant exits. MACBETH, alone, imagines that he sees a bloody
dagger.*]

    Is this a dagger which I see before me,
    The handle toward my hand? Come, let me clutch thee.
35 I have thee not, and yet I see thee still.
    Art thou not, fatal vision, sensible
    To feeling° as to sight, or art thou but
    A dagger of the mind, a false creation,
    Proceeding from the heat-oppressèd° brain?
40 I see thee yet, in form as palpable
    As this which now I draw.
    Thou marshal'st me° the way that I was going;
    And such an instrument I was to use.
    Mine eyes are made the fools o' th' other senses,
45 Or else worth all the rest.° I see thee still;
    And on thy blade and dudgeon° gouts° of blood,
    Which was not so before. There's no such thing.
    It is the bloody business which informs°
    Thus to mine eyes. Now o'er the one half-world
50 Nature seems dead, and wicked dreams abuse°
    The curtained° sleep; witchcraft celebrates
    Pale Hecate's offerings;° and withered murder,
    Alarumed by his sentinel, the wolf,
    Whose howl's his watch, thus with his **stealthy** pace,
55 With Tarquin's ravishing strides, towards his design
    Moves like a ghost.° Thou sure and firm-set earth,
    Hear not my steps, which way they walk, for fear
    Thy very stones prate of° my whereabout,

---

26 **So . . . none:** as long as I lose no honor.

28 **My . . . clear:** my heart free from guilt and my loyalty unstained.
29 **I . . . counseled:** I am ready to listen to you.

31 **drink:** posset (a hot, spiced bedtime drink).

36–37 **sensible . . . feeling:** capable of being perceived by touch.

39 **heat-oppressèd:** fevered.

42 **marshal'st me:** leads me.

44–45 **Mine . . . rest:** Either my eyes alone are deceived, or they correctly perceive what the other senses have missed.
46 **dudgeon:** handle. **gouts:** drops.
48 **informs:** takes shape.
50 **abuse:** deceive.
51 **curtained:** enclosed with bed curtains.
52 **Hecate's offerings:** rituals dedicated to Hecate, goddess of witchcraft (described as pale because she is associated with the moon).
52–56 **withered . . . ghost:** Murder, alerted by the wolf's howl of the night's progress, moves toward his victim as silently as a ghost. (Tarquin was a Roman tyrant infamous for his rape of Lucrece.)
58 **prate of:** chatter about.

Reading Strategy Evaluating Credibility *Is this dagger real or a figment of Macbeth's imagination? Explain.*

Literary Element Motif *What might this image foreshadow?*

Vocabulary

stealthy (stel´ thē) *adj.* secret; sly

And take the present horor from the time,
60 Which now suits with it.° Whiles I threat,° he lives:
Words to the heat of deeds too cold breath gives.°

[*A bell rings.*]

I go, and it is done: the bell invites me.°
Hear it not, Duncan, for it is a knell
That summons thee to heaven, or to hell.

[*MACBETH exits.*]

SCENE 2. The castle at Inverness.

[*Later the same night* LADY MACBETH *enters the empty courtyard of the castle.*]

LADY MACBETH.   That which hath made them drunk hath made me bold;
What hath quenched them hath given me fire. Hark!
Peace!
It was the owl that shrieked,° the fatal bellman,°
Which gives the stern'st good night. He° is about it.
5 The doors are open, and the **surfeited** grooms°
Do mock their charge° with snores. I have drugged their possets,
That death and nature do contend about them,
Whether they live or die.°

MACBETH.   [*Calling from within.*] Who's there? What, ho?

LADY MACBETH.   Alack, I am afraid they have awaked
10 And 'tis not done! Th' attempt and not the deed
Confounds° us. Hark! I laid their daggers ready;
He° could not miss 'em. Had he° not resembled
My father as he slept, I had done 't.°

[*MACBETH enters, his hands covered with blood.*]

My husband!

MACBETH.   I have done the deed. Didst thou not hear a noise?

15 **LADY MACBETH.**   I heard the owl scream and the crickets cry.°
Did not you speak?

MACBETH.   When?

58–60 Thy . . . it: Macbeth doesn't want his footsteps to interrupt the dead silence, which he finds appropriate for the crime he is about to commit.
60 threat: threaten.
61 Words . . . gives: Talking cools off one's urge to take action.
62 the . . . me: The bell is Lady Macbeth's signal for Macbeth to go to Duncan's room.

3 the owl that shrieked: considered an omen of death. **bellman:** a watchman who rang a bell to sound the hours at night, announce a death, or signal that a prisoner would soon be executed.
4 He: Macbeth.
5 grooms: servants.
6 mock their charge: make a mockery of their duty.
6–8 I . . . die: Lady Macbeth says that she has so strongly drugged their bedtime drinks that they are in a deathlike sleep.

11 Confounds: ruins.
12 He: Macbeth. **he:** Duncan.
13 I had done 't: I would have killed him.

15 crickets cry: another omen of death.

Big Idea   **A Bard for the Ages** *How does Shakespeare show a change in Macbeth by the end of this soliloquy?*

Reading Strategy   **Evaluating Credibility** *How would you compare this statement with Lady Macbeth's previous statements about killing the king in Act I?*

Vocabulary

surfeited (sur´ fit əd) *adj.* overfed; overcome by excess drinking, eating, etc.

Lady Macbeth Seizing the Daggers, 1812. Henry Fuseli. Tate Gallery, London.

LADY MACBETH.   Now.

MACBETH.   As I descended?

LADY MACBETH. Ay.

MACBETH. Hark!
  Who lies i' th' second chamber?

LADY MACBETH.   Donalbain.

20 **MACBETH.** [*Looking at his hands.*] This is a sorry° sight.   20 **sorry:** miserable.

LADY MACBETH. A foolish thought, to say a sorry sight.

MACBETH. There's one did laugh in 's sleep, and one cried
    "Murder!"
  That they did wake each other. I stood and heard them.
  But they did say their prayers, and addressed them   24–25 **addressed . . . sleep:** fell back
25   Again to sleep.°   asleep. **two:** Malcolm and Donalbain, King
                                                                               Duncan's sons.
LADY MACBETH. There are two° lodged together.

MACBETH.   One cried "God bless us!" and "Amen" the other,
As° they had seen me with these hangman's hands:°
List'ning their fear, I could not say "Amen,"
When they did say "God bless us!"

LADY MACBETH.   Consider it not so deeply.

30   **MACBETH.**   But wherefore° could not I pronounce "Amen"?
I had most need of blessing, and "Amen"
Stuck in my throat.

LADY MACBETH.   These deeds must not be thought
After these ways; so,° it will make us mad.

MACBETH.   Methought I heard a voice cry "Sleep no more!
35   Macbeth does murder sleep"—the innocent sleep,
Sleep that knits up the raveled sleave° of care,
The death of each day's life, sore labor's bath,
Balm° of hurt minds, great nature's second course,°
Chief nourisher in life's feast—

LADY MACBETH.   What do you mean?

40   **MACBETH.**   Still it cried "Sleep no more!" to all the house:
"Glamis hath murdered sleep, and therefore Cawdor
Shall sleep no more: Macbeth shall sleep no more."

LADY MACBETH.   Who was it that thus cried? Why, worthy
Thane,
You do unbend° your noble strength, to think
45   So brainsickly of things. Go get some water,
And wash this filthy witness° from your hand.
Why did you bring these daggers from the place?
They must lie there: go carry them, and smear
The sleepy grooms with blood.

MACBETH.   I'll go no more.
50   I am afraid to think what I have done;
Look on 't again I dare not.

LADY MACBETH.   Infirm of purpose!°
Give me the daggers. The sleeping and the dead
Are but as pictures.° 'Tis the eye of childhood
That fears a painted devil. If he do bleed,
55   I'll gild° the faces of the grooms withal,
For it must seem their guilt.

[As LADY MACBETH exits, knocking is heard offstage.]

MACBETH.   Whence is that knocking?
How is 't with me, when every noise appalls me?
What hands are here? Ha! They pluck out mine eyes!

Literary Element	**Motif** *In what way has Macbeth murdered sleep?*

27 As: as if. **hangman's hands:** bloodstained hands. (After an execution, the executioner would cut the victim's body into pieces.)

30 wherefore: why.

33 so: if we do so.

36 raveled sleave: tangled threads.

38 Balm: healing ointment. **second course:** main (and most nourishing) course of a meal.

44 unbend: relax, weaken.

46 witness: evidence.

51 Infirm of purpose: Feebly determined!

53 but as pictures: merely like pictures (because they do not move).

55 gild: smear, paint.

Will all great Neptune's ocean wash this blood

60   Clean from my hand? No; this my hand will rather
The multitudinous seas incarnadine,°
Making the green one red.

[*LADY MACBETH returns.*]

LADY MACBETH.   My hands are of your color, but I shame
To wear a heart so white. [*Knocking within.*] I hear a
knocking
65   At the south entry. Retire we to our chamber.
A little water clears us of this deed:
How easy is it then! Your constancy
Hath left you unattended.° [*Knock.*] Hark! more knocking.
Get on your nightgown, lest occasion call us
70   And show us to be watchers.° Be not lost
So poorly in your thoughts.

MACBETH.   To know my deed, 'twere best not know myself.°
[*Knock.*]
Wake Duncan with thy knocking! I would thou couldst!

[*They exit.*]

SCENE 3. The castle at Inverness.

[*The setting is the same as above, except that now it is early morning and a drunken* PORTER, *or doorkeeper, enters and crosses the courtyard to open the castle gate.*]

PORTER.   Here's a knocking indeed! If a man were porter of
hell gate, he should have old° turning the key. [*Knocking
is heard offstage.*] Knock, knock, knock! Who's there, i'
th' name of Beelzebub?° Here's a farmer, that hanged
5   himself on th' expectation of plenty.° Come in time! Have
napkins enow° about you; here you'll sweat for 't.
[*Knock.*] Knock, knock! Who's there, in th' other devil's
name? Faith, here's an equivocator,° that could swear in
both the scales against either scale; who committed
10   treason enough for God's sake, yet could not equivocate
to heaven. O, come in, equivocator. [*Knock.*] Knock,
knock, knock! Who's there? Faith, here's an English tailor
come hither for stealing out of a French hose:° come in,
tailor. Here you may roast your goose.° [*Knock.*] Knock,
15   knock; never at quiet! What are you? But this place is too
cold for hell. I'll devil-porter it no further. I had thought

61 **The . . . incarnadine:** turn the vast seas blood red.

67–68 **Your . . . unattended:** Your firmness of purpose has deserted you.

70 **show . . . watchers:** reveal that we have been awake all night.

72 **To know . . . myself:** If I am aware of my crime, it would be best for me to remain in this daze.

1–16 **Here's . . . further:** As the Porter goes to open the castle gate, he imagines himself admitting lost souls through the gates of hell.
2 **old:** plenty of.
4 **Beelzebub:** a devil.
4–5 **a farmer . . . plenty:** a farmer who hoarded grain in anticipation of higher prices, then hanged himself when crops turned out to be plentiful.
6 **napkins enow:** handkerchiefs enough (to wipe up your sweat in hell).
8 **equivocator:** one who gives deceptive testimony by using words that have more than one meaning.

13 **stealing . . . hose:** stealing cloth from a supply provided for a customer's French breeches.
14 **roast your goose:** heat your pressing iron.

Literary Element   Motif *With which words spoken by Macbeth does the phrase "a little water" contrast?*

Reading Strategy   Evaluating Credibility *The porter pretends that he is guarding the entrance to hell. What is ironic about the porter's fiction?*

to have let in some of all professions that go the primrose
way to th' everlasting bonfire.° [*Knock.*] Anon, anon! [*The
PORTER opens the gate.*] I pray you, remember the porter.°

[*MACDUFF and LENNOX enter through the gate.*]

20   **MACDUFF.** Was it so late, friend, ere you went to bed,
        That you do lie so late?

    PORTER. Faith, sir, we were carousing till the second cock:°
        and drink, sir, is a great provoker of three things.

    MACDUFF. What three things does drink especially **provoke**?

25   **PORTER.** Marry, sir, nose-painting, sleep, and urine. Lechery,
        sir, it provokes and unprovokes: it provokes the desire, but it
        takes away the performance. Therefore much drink may be
        said to be an equivocator with lechery: it makes him and it
        mars him; it sets him on and it takes him off; it persuades
30   him and disheartens him, makes him stand to and not stand
        to; in conclusion, equivocates him in a sleep, and, giving him
        the lie, leaves him.

    MACDUFF. I believe drink gave thee the lie° last night.

    PORTER. That it did, sir, i' the very throat° on me: but I
35   requited° him for his lie, and, I think, being too strong
        for him, though he took up my legs sometime, yet I made
        a shift to cast him.°

    MACDUFF. Is thy master stirring?

[*MACBETH enters in his dressing gown.*]

    Our knocking has awaked him; here he comes.

40   **LENNOX.** Good morrow, noble sir.

    MACBETH.   Good morrow, both.

    MACDUFF. Is the king stirring, worthy Thane?

    MACBETH.   Not yet.

    MACDUFF. He did command me to call timely° on him:
        I have almost slipped the hour.°

    MACBETH.   I'll bring you to him.

    MACDUFF. I know this is a joyful trouble to you;
45   But yet 'tis one.

    MACBETH. The labor we delight in physics pain.°
        This is the door.

    MACDUFF.   I'll make so bold to call,
        For 'tis my limited service.°

[*MACDUFF goes to wake KING DUNCAN.*]

17–18 primrose . . . bonfire: flowery path to hell.

19 I . . . porter: The Porter asks for a tip.

22 second cock: three o'clock in the morning.

33 gave . . . lie: laid you out (as in wrestling).
34 i' the very throat: an expression used to call someone a liar.
35 requited: repaid.

37 cast him: "throw him off" or "vomit him up."

42 timely: early.
43 slipped the hour: let the hour slip by.

46 The . . . pain: The labor we enjoy cures any discomfort associated with it.

48 limited service: assigned duty.

Vocabulary

provoke (prə vōk′) *v.* to call forth; to stir to action or feeling

LENNOX. Goes the king hence today?

MACBETH. He does: he did
  appoint so.°

50 **LENNOX.** The night has been unruly. Where we lay,
  Our chimneys were blown down, and, as they say,
  Lamentings heard i' the air, strange screams of death,
  And prophesying with accents terrible
  Of dire combustion° and confused events
55 New hatched to th' woeful time: the obscure bird°
  Clamored the livelong night. Some say, the earth
  Was feverous and did shake.°

MACBETH. 'Twas a rough night.

LENNOX. My young remembrance cannot parallel
  A fellow to it.

[*MACDUFF returns, appearing very shaken.*]

60 **MACDUFF.** O horror, horror, horror! Tongue nor heart
  Cannot conceive nor name thee.

MACBETH AND LENNOX. What's the matter?

MACDUFF. Confusion° now hath made his masterpiece.
  Most sacrilegious murder hath broke ope
  The Lord's anointed temple,° and stole thence
65 The life o' th' building.

MACBETH. What is 't you say? The life?

LENNOX. Mean you his Majesty?

MACDUFF. Approach the chamber, and destroy your sight
  With a new Gorgon:° do not bid me speak;
  See, and then speak yourselves. Awake, awake!

[*MACBETH and LENNOX rush off. MACDUFF comes forward, still upset and shouting.*]

70 Ring the alarum bell. Murder and Treason!
  Banquo and Donalbain! Malcolm! Awake!
  Shake off this downy sleep, death's counterfeit,
  And look on death itself! Up, up, and see
  The great doom's image!° Malcolm! Banquo!
75 As from your graves rise up, and walk like sprites,°
  To countenance° this horror. Ring the bell.

[*A bell begins to ring offstage as LADY MACBETH enters.*]

Literary Element **Motif** *Which motifs in lines 51–57 reinforce the atmosphere created in earlier scenes?*

---

49 **appoint so:** plan to do so.

54 **combustion:** confusion.
55 **obscure bird:** bird of darkness (the owl).
56–57 **the earth . . . shake:** Earthquakes were commonly associated with political unrest.

62 **Confusion:** destruction.

64 **The . . . temple:** the King's body.

68 **Gorgon:** a mythological monster whose gaze turned an onlooker to stone.

74 **great doom's image:** an image of doomsday.
75 **sprites:** ghosts.
76 **countenance:** look upon.

LADY MACBETH.   What's the business,
    That such a hideous trumpet calls to parley
    The sleepers of the house? Speak, speak!

MACDUFF.   O gentle lady,
80   'Tis not for you to hear what I can speak:
    The repetition, in a woman's ear,
    Would murder as it fell.

[*BANQUO enters.*]

                            O Banquo, Banquo!
    Our royal master's murdered.

LADY MACBETH.   Woe, alas!
    What, in our house?

BANQUO.   Too cruel anywhere.
85   Dear Duff, I prithee, contradict thyself,
    And say it is not so.

[*MACBETH and LENNOX return with ROSS.*]

MACBETH.   Had I but° died an hour before this chance,°
    I had lived a blessèd time; for from this instant
    There's nothing serious in mortality:°
90   All is but toys.° Renown and grace is dead,°
    The wine of life is drawn, and the mere lees°
    Is left this vault° to brag of.

[*MALCOLM and DONALBAIN, still in their nightclothes, enter.*]

DONALBAIN.   What is amiss?

MACBETH.   You are, and do not know 't.
    The spring, the head, the fountain of your blood
95   Is stopped; the very source of it is stopped.

MACDUFF.   Your royal father's murdered.

MALCOLM.   O, by whom?

LENNOX.   Those of his chamber, as it seemed, had done 't:
    Their hands and faces were all badged° with blood;
    So were their daggers, which unwiped we found
100   Upon their pillows. They stared, and were distracted.°
    No man's life was to be trusted with them.

MACBETH.   O, yet I do repent me of my fury,
    That I did kill them.

MACDUFF.   Wherefore did you so?°

MACBETH.   Who can be wise, amazed,° temp'rate and furious,
105   Loyal and neutral, in a moment? No man.
    The expedition° of my violent love
    Outrun the pauser,° reason. Here lay Duncan,
    His silver skin laced with his golden blood,

87 **but:** only. **chance:** event.

89 **serious in mortality:** important in life.
90 **toys:** trifles. **Renown . . . dead:** Fame and fortune are dead.
91 **lees:** dregs.
92 **vault:** "wine vault" or "the earth vaulted by heaven."

98 **badged:** marked.

100 **distracted:** insane.

103 **Wherefore . . . so:** Why did you do so?
104 **amazed:** bewildered.

106 **expedition:** haste.
107 **pauser:** delayer.

And his gashed stabs looked like a breach in nature
110 For ruin's wasteful entrance:° there, the murderers,
Steeped in the colors of their trade, their daggers
Unmannerly breeched with gore.° Who could refrain,
That had a heart to love, and in that heart
Courage to make 's° love known?

LADY MACBETH.   Help me hence, ho!

[*LADY MACBETH faints.*]

115 **MACDUFF.** Look to the lady.

MALCOLM. [*Aside to DONALBAIN.*] Why do we hold our
          tongues,
That most may claim this argument for ours?°

DONALBAIN. [*Aside to MALCOLM.*] What should be spoken
          here,
Where our fate, hid in an auger-hole,
May rush, and seize us?° Let's away:
120 Our tears are not yet brewed.

MALCOLM. [*Aside to DONALBAIN.*] Nor our strong sorrow
Upon the foot of motion.°

BANQUO.   Look to the lady.

[*LADY MACBETH, faint, is carried out.*]

And when we have our naked frailties hid,°
That suffer in exposure, let us meet
And question° this most bloody piece of work,
125 To know it further. Fears and **scruples** shake us.
In the great hand of God I stand, and thence
Against the undivulged pretense I fight
Of treasonous malice.°

MACDUFF.   And so do I.

ALL.   So all.

MACBETH. Let's briefly put on manly readiness,°
130 And meet i' th' hall together.

109–110 And . . . entrance: Macbeth compares Duncan's wounds to a gap in a defensive wall that allows destructive forces to enter.
112 breeched with gore: covered with blood.
114 's: his.

116 That . . . ours: who are most concerned with this matter.

117–119 What . . . us: Donalbain advises against speaking up in the castle, where deadly fate may ambush them from any tiny hole.
120–121 Nor . . . motion: Nor has our great sorrow begun to express itself.

122 when . . . hid: "when we have replaced our nightclothes with proper clothing" or "when we have covered our naked grief."
124 question: examine.

126–128 In the . . . malice: Placing myself in God's hands, I will fight against the undisclosed purpose of this treason.

129 put . . . readiness: prepare ourselves for taking action.

Reading Strategy Evaluating Credibility *Why does Lady Macbeth faint?*

Big Idea A Bard for the Ages *How does Shakespeare use this speech to show the difference in character between Banquo and Macbeth?*

Vocabulary

scruple (skrσ̄σ′ pəl) *n.* a moral or ethical principle that restrains action

ALL.   Well contented.

[*Everyone exits except* MALCOLM *and* DONALBAIN.]

    MALCOLM. What will you do? Let's not consort° with them.
        To show an unfelt sorrow is an office°
        Which the false man does easy. I'll to England.

    DONALBAIN. To Ireland, I; our separated fortune
135   Shall keep us both the safer. Where we are
        There's daggers in men's smiles; the near in blood,
        The nearer bloody.°

    MALCOLM.   This murderous shaft that's shot
        Hath not yet lighted,° and our safest way
        Is to avoid the aim. Therefore to horse;
140   And let us not be dainty of leave-taking,
        But shift away.° There's warrant in that theft
        Which steals itself when there's no mercy left.°

[*They exit.*]

SCENE 4. The castle at Inverness.

[*The nobleman* ROSS *and an* OLD MAN *enter the courtyard.*]

    OLD MAN. Threescore and ten° I can remember well:
        Within the volume of which time I have seen
        Hours dreadful and things strange, but this sore° night
        Hath trifled former knowings.

    ROSS.   Ha, good father,
5   Thou seest the heavens, as troubled with man's act,
        Threatens his bloody stage.° By th' clock 'tis day,
        And yet dark night strangles the traveling lamp:°
        Is 't night's **predominance**, or the day's shame,
        That darkness does the face of earth entomb,
10   When living light should kiss it?

    OLD MAN.   'Tis unnatural,
        Even like the deed that's done. On Tuesday last
        A falcon, tow'ring in her pride of place,°
        Was by a mousing owl hawked at° and killed.

    ROSS. And Duncan's horses—a thing most strange and
        certain—
15   Beauteous and swift, the minions of their race,°

---

131 **consort:** associate.
132 **office:** task.

136–137 **the near . . . bloody:** The more closely one is related (to Duncan), the more likely one is to be murdered.
138 **lighted:** reached its target.

140–141 **let . . . away:** Let us not be polite about taking leave, but instead slip off unnoticed.
141–142 **There's . . . left:** stealing away is justified in these merciless times.

1 **Threescore and ten:** seventy years.

3 **sore:** dreadful.

6 **his bloody stage:** the earth.
7 **traveling lamp:** the sun.

12 **tow'ring . . . place:** circling at the height of its ascent.
13 **Was by . . . at:** was attacked by an owl, which normally preys on mice.

15 **minions of their race:** best of their breed.

Literary Element   Motif *What does this unnatural event suggest?*

Vocabulary

predominance (pri dom′ ə nəns) *n.* the state of being most important, common, or noticeable

Conway Castle. John Varley (1778–1842). Watercolor, 27.7 x 42.1 cm. Agnew & Sons, London.

Viewing the Art: Does the scene depicted in the painting better reflect your image of King Duncan's palace at Forres or Macbeth's castle at Inverness? Give reasons for your answer.

Turned wild in nature, broke their stalls, flung out,
Contending 'gainst obedience, as they would make
War with mankind.

OLD MAN. 'Tis said they eat° each other.

ROSS. They did so, to th' amazement of mine eyes,
20   That looked upon 't.

[*MACDUFF enters.*]

        Here comes the good Macduff.
How goes the world, sir, now?

MACDUFF.   Why, see you not?

ROSS. Is 't known who did this more than bloody deed?

MACDUFF. Those that Macbeth hath slain.

ROSS.   Alas, the day!
What good could they pretend?°

MACDUFF.   They were suborned:°

18 **eat:** ate.

24 **What . . . pretend:** What did they intend to gain by it? **suborned:** secretly hired to commit evil.

<blockquote>

25   Malcolm and Donalbain, the king's two sons,
  Are stol'n away and fled, which puts upon them
  Suspicion of the deed.

ROSS.   'Gainst nature still.°
  Thriftless° ambition, that will ravin up°
  Thine own life's means! Then 'tis most like
30   The sovereignty will fall upon Macbeth.

MACDUFF.   He is already named, and gone to Scone
  To be invested.°

ROSS.   Where is Duncan's body?

MACDUFF.   Carried to Colmekill,°
  The sacred storehouse of his predecessors
35   And guardian of their bones.

ROSS.   Will you to Scone?

MACDUFF.   No, cousin, I'll to Fife.°

ROSS.   Well, I will thither.

MACDUFF.   Well, may you see things well done there. Adieu,
  Lest our old robes sit easier than our new!°

ROSS.   Farewell, father.

40   **OLD MAN.**   God's benison° go with you, and with those
  That would make good of bad, and friends of foes!

[*They exit.*]

</blockquote>

---

27 **'Gainst nature still:** even more unnatural.
28 **Thriftless:** wasteful. **ravin up:** swallow greedily.

31–32 **already . . . invested:** already chosen and has gone to Scone, the traditional Scottish coronation site, to be crowned.
33 **Colmekill:** Iona, a small island off Scotland's coast where kings were buried.

36 **Fife:** Macduff is Thane of Fife.

38 **Lest . . . new:** in case the old rule suits us better than the new.

40 **benison:** blessing.

Reading Strategy   Evaluating Credibility   *Why does Macduff refuse to attend Macbeth's coronation?*

Literary Element   Motif   *How does the image of ill-fitting robes sum up the action so far?*

Gentleman's Doublet and Hose, 1548. German School. Textile. Staatliche Kunstsammlungen Dresden, Germany.

RESPONDING AND THINKING CRITICALLY

Respond

1. What images did you find most powerful in Act 2? Why?

Recall and Interpret

2. (a)In scene 1, what reasons does Banquo give to explain why he has been unable to sleep? (b)How do his thoughts and actions compare with Macbeth's?

3. (a)What does the "dagger soliloquy" in scene 1 reveal about Macbeth's state of mind? (b)Why might Shakespeare have chosen to have Macbeth reveal his feelings in a soliloquy rather than in a speech to another character?

4. (a)How does Lady Macbeth get blood on her hands? (b)What does her reaction to the blood reveal about her character?

5. (a)Why do Duncan's sons decide to leave Scotland after their father's murder? (b)What **conflicts** might they cause for Macbeth in the future?

Analyze and Evaluate

6. (a)In your opinion, who is more responsible for Duncan's murder—Macbeth or Lady Macbeth? Why? (b)Contrast Macbeth's and Lady Macbeth's reactions so far to their murderous deed.

7. (a)Why do you think Shakespeare chose to have the murder of Duncan occur offstage rather than in front of the audience? (b)If the murder had occurred onstage, how do you think the audience would feel about Macbeth?

8. Macbeth's motive for killing Duncan is "vaulting ambition." In your opinion, what could Macbeth have done to keep his ambitions in check?

Connect

9. **Big Idea** **A Bard for the Ages** How does Shakespeare demonstrate his deep understanding of human nature in this act? Consider Macbeth's conflicted feelings about murdering Duncan.

LITERARY ANALYSIS

Literary Element Motif

By developing **motifs**, playwrights reinforce key elements, making them resonate in the minds of the audience.

1. How does Shakespeare develop the motif of the supernatural in Act 2?

2. Explain how the motif of blood dominates Act 2.

3. What does Macbeth say about sleep? How might the motif of sleep develop in the rest of the play?

Writing About Literature

Evaluate Author's Craft Shakespeare often uses **comic relief,** or humor meant to provide relief from emotional intensity. In a brief essay, analyze how the Porter's speech in scene 3 serves as comic relief in *Macbeth.*

READING AND VOCABULARY

Reading Strategy Evaluating Credibility

When you **evaluate credibility,** you express a judgment about whether a character's assertions are convincing on the basis of evidence in the text.

In scene 3, lines 102–114, Macbeth explains his motives for killing Duncan's attendants. Is Macbeth's explanation convincing? Explain.

Vocabulary Practice

Practice with Word Origins Match each vocabulary word with the meaning of its origin.

1. stealthy		**a.** to steal
2. provoke		**b.** source of uneasiness
3. scruple		**c.** to do
4. surfeited		**d.** to rule
5. predominance		**e.** to call forth

Building Background

Macbeth first appeared in the First Folio of 1623, a collection of Shakespeare's plays compiled by John Heminge and Henry Condell, two of his Globe colleagues, after the playwright's death. Except for *A Comedy of Errors,* written in the early 1590s, *Macbeth* is the shortest of Shakespeare's plays. As with *Othello,* there is no subplot; the poetry is unusually dense, terse, interwoven, often staccato, and suggestive of terror—for which brevity is most effective.

A masterpiece of compression, *Macbeth* is a study of the power of evil. During the 1500s and 1600s, belief in the existence of witchcraft was widespread. King James I even wrote a book on the subject, titled *Demonologie,* in which he argued that witchcraft and other forms of sorcery were a threat to society. According to some scholars, the prominence of witchcraft and the supernatural in the plot of *Macbeth* is evidence that Shakespeare was using this play to secure the king's approval.

Literary Element Foil

A **foil** is a minor character whose attitudes, beliefs, and behavior differ significantly from those of a main character. Through these differences, the foil helps highlight specific attributes—both good and bad—of the main character. One example of a foil in literature is the character of Enkidu, who is Gilgamesh's foil in the epic of *Gilgamesh* (see page 55). As you read, notice the character or characters that function as Macbeth's foil.

- See Literary Terms Handbook, p. R7.

Literature Online Interactive Literary Elements Handbook To review or learn more about the literary elements, go to www.glencoe.com.

Reading Strategy Analyzing Argument

Argument is a form of persuasion. To persuade the reader to accept the main idea, or **thesis,** the writer must present convincing evidence, which may include facts, examples, and well-supported opinions. The characters in *Macbeth* often construct arguments, citing reasons for acting and thinking the way they do.

Reading Tip: Taking Notes Use a chart to record the thesis and evidence in the characters' arguments.

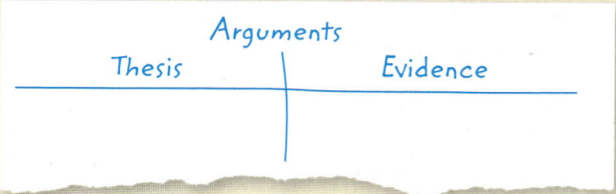

Arguments

| Thesis | Evidence |

Vocabulary

indissoluble (in′ di sol′ yə bəl) *adj.* incapable of being broken; permanent; p. 353 *The team members play as an indissoluble unit.*

incensed (in sensd′) *v.* to make enraged; filled with anger; p. 356 *The mistreatment of animals incensed her.*

jovial (jō′ vē al) *adj.* full of good humor; genial and playful; p. 358 *Always good-natured and jovial with his nephews, he enjoys telling them jokes.*

appall (ə pôl′) *v.* to fill with horror and shock; p. 362 *The images of poverty and starvation in that documentary appall sensitive viewers.*

amends (ə mendz′) *n.* something done or given to make up for injury, loss, etc.; p. 365 *Luke offered to replant the flowers to make amends for trampling them.*

Vocabulary Tip: Antonyms Antonyms are words that have opposite or nearly opposite meanings.

OBJECTIVES

In studying this selection, you will focus on the following:
- analyzing literary periods
- understanding foil characters
- analyzing argument

ACT 3

SCENE 1. The palace at Forres.

[BANQUO *is alone in a room in the royal palace at Forres.*]

BANQUO. Thou° hast it now: King, Cawdor, Glamis, all,
As the weird women promised, and I fear
Thou play'dst most foully for 't. Yet it was said
It should not stand in thy posterity,°
5   But that myself should be the root and father
Of many kings. If there come truth from them—
As upon thee, Macbeth, their speeches shine—
Why, by the verities on thee made good,°
May they not be my oracles as well
10   And set me up in hope? But hush, no more!

[*A trumpet sounds as* MACBETH, *the new king, and* LADY MACBETH
enter. They are accompanied by LENNOX, ROSS, *other* LORDS, LADIES,
and ATTENDANTS.]

MACBETH. Here's our chief guest.

LADY MACBETH.   If he had been forgotten,°
It had been as° a gap in our great feast,
And all-thing° unbecoming.

MACBETH. Tonight we hold a solemn supper,° sir,
15   And I'll request your presence.

BANQUO.   Let your Highness
Command upon me, to the which my duties
Are with a most **indissoluble** tie
For ever knit.°

MACBETH. Ride you this afternoon?

BANQUO.   Ay, my good lord.

20   MACBETH. We should have else desired your good advice
(Which still hath been both grave and prosperous)°
In this day's council; but we'll take tomorrow.°
Is 't far you ride?

BANQUO. As far, my lord, as will fill up the time
25   'Twixt this and supper. Go not my horse the better,
I must become a borrower of the night
For a dark hour or twain.°

MACBETH.   Fail not our feast.

Reading Strategy **Analyzing Argument** *Why does Banquo claim
that his descendants will be kings?*

Vocabulary

indissoluble (in′ di sol′ yə bəl) *adj.* incapable of being broken;
permanent

---

1 **Thou:** Macbeth.

4 **stand in thy posterity:** continue with
your descendants.

8 **by . . . good:** judging by the truths
regarding you that have been confirmed.

11 **forgotten:** absent, neglected.
12 **It . . . as:** it would have been like.
13 **all-thing:** wholly.

14 **solemn supper:** formal banquet.

18 **knit:** bound.

21 **still . . . prosperous:** always has been
sober and profitable.
22 **but . . . tomorrow:** Macbeth (now
using the royal "we") says that he can
wait until tomorrow.

25–27 **Go . . . twain:** Unless my horse
runs faster than I expect, I must ride an
hour or two after sunset.

BANQUO. My lord, I will not.

MACBETH. We hear our bloody cousins° are bestowed
30 In England and in Ireland, not confessing
Their cruel parricide,° filling their hearers
With strange invention.° But of that tomorrow,
When therewithal we shall have cause of state
Craving us jointly.° Hie° you to horse. Adieu,
35 Till you return at night. Goes Fleance with you?

BANQUO. Ay, my good lord: our time does call upon 's.°

MACBETH. I wish your horses swift and sure of foot,
And so I do commend° you to their backs.
Farewell. [*BANQUO exits.*]
40 Let every man be master of his time
Till seven at night. To make society
The sweeter welcome, we will keep ourself
Till suppertime alone. While° then, God be with you!

[*Everyone exits except MACBETH and a SERVANT.*]

Sirrah,° a word with you: attend those men
45 Our pleasure?°

ATTENDANT. They are, my lord, without the palace gate.

MACBETH. Bring them before us.

[*The SERVANT exits, leaving MACBETH alone.*]

To be thus is nothing, but to be safely thus°—
Our fears in Banquo stick deep,
50 And in his royalty of nature° reigns that
Which would be feared. 'Tis much he dares;
And, to° that dauntless temper° of his mind,
He hath a wisdom that doth guide his valor
To act in safety. There is none but he
55 Whose being I do fear: and under him
My genius is rebuked,° as it is said
Mark Antony's was by Caesar. He chid° the sisters,
When first they put the name of King upon me,
And bade them speak to him; then prophetlike
60 They hailed him father to a line of kings.
Upon my head they placed a fruitless° crown
And put a barren scepter in my gripe,°
Thence to be wrenched with an unlineal hand,°
No son of mine succeeding. If 't be so,
65 For Banquo's issue have I filed° my mind;
For them the gracious Duncan have I murdered;
Put rancors° in the vessel of my peace
Only for them, and mine eternal jewel°
Given to the common enemy of man,°

29 **cousins:** Malcolm and Donalbain.

31 **parricide:** murder of a parent or close relative.
32 **invention:** lies.

33–34 **therewithal . . . jointly:** In addition to that, we will have matters of state requiring the attention of both of us.
34 **Hie:** hurry.
36 **our . . . upon 's:** We should depart soon.
38 **commend:** entrust.

43 **While:** until.

44 **Sirrah:** a term of address to a social inferior.
44–45 **attend . . . pleasure:** Are those men waiting to serve me?

48 **To . . . thus:** To be king is nothing unless one's rule is secure.

50 **royalty of nature:** regal nature.

52 **to:** in addition to. **dauntless temper:** fearless disposition.

56 **genius is rebuked:** inner spirit is repressed.
57 **chid:** scolded.

61 **fruitless:** barren, childless.
62 **gripe:** grip.
63 **with an unlineal hand:** by someone not related to me.

65 **filed:** defiled.

67 **rancors:** bitterness.
68 **eternal jewel:** soul.
69 **common . . . man:** devil.

Literary Element **Foil** *Why does Macbeth perceive Banquo as a threat?*

70 To make them kings, the seeds of Banquo kings!
    Rather than so, come, fate, into the list,°
    And champion me to th' utterance!° Who's there?

[*The* SERVANT *returns with two* MURDERERS, *and* MACBETH *addresses
the* SERVANT.]

    Now go to the door, and stay there till we call.

[*The* SERVANT *exits.*]

    Was it not yesterday we spoke together?

75 FIRST MURDERER. It was, so please your Highness.

    MACBETH.   Well then, now
    Have you considered of my speeches? Know
    That it was he° in the times past, which held you
    So under fortune,° which you thought had been
    Our innocent self: this I made good to you
80 In our last conference; passed in probation° with you,
    How you were born in hand,° how crossed; the
        instruments,°
    Who wrought with them, and all things else that might
    To half a soul° and to a notion° crazed
    Say "Thus did Banquo."

    FIRST MURDERER.   You made it known to us.

85 MACBETH. I did so; and went further, which is now
    Our point of second meeting. Do you find
    Your patience so predominant in your nature,
    That you can let this go? Are you so gospeled,°
    To pray for this good man and for his issue,°
90 Whose heavy hand hath bowed you to the grave
    And beggared yours° for ever?

    FIRST MURDERER.   We are men, my liege.

    MACBETH. Ay, in the catalogue ye go for° men;
    As hounds and greyhounds, mongrels, spaniels, curs,
    Shoughs,° water-rugs° and demi-wolves,° are clept°
95 All by the name of dogs: the valued file°
    Distinguishes the swift, the slow, the subtle,
    The housekeeper, the hunter, every one
    According to the gift which bounteous nature
    Hath in him closed,° whereby he does receive
100 Particular addition, from the bill

71 **list:** field of combat.
72 **champion . . . utterance:** fight me to the death.

77 **he:** Banquo.
78 **under fortune:** in poverty.

80 **passed in probation:** went through the proof.
81 **born in hand:** deceived. **instruments:** means.

83 **half a soul:** a half-wit. **notion:** mind.

88 **gospeled:** schooled in the Gospels (which urge us to love our enemies).
89 **issue:** children.

91 **beggared yours:** impoverished your descendants.

92 **go for:** are counted as.

94 **Shoughs:** shaggy-haired dogs. **water-rugs:** rough-haired water dogs. **demi-wolves:** crossbreeds between wolf and dog. **clept:** called.
95 **valued file:** list of traits.

99 **closed:** enclosed.

Reading Strategy Analyzing Argument *What is the thesis of Macbeth's argument?*

Reading Strategy Analyzing Argument *Whom does Macbeth echo by arguing this way?*

Reading Strategy Analyzing Argument *What idea does Macbeth convey through this analogy?*

That writes them all alike:° and so of men.
Now if you have a station in the file,°
Not i' th' worst rank of manhood, say 't,
And I will put that business in your bosoms
105 Whose execution takes your enemy off,
Grapples you to the heart and love of us,
Who wear our health but sickly in his life,
Which in his death were perfect.°

SECOND MURDERER.   I am one, my liege,
Whom the vile blows and buffets of the world
110 Hath so **incensed** that I am reckless what
I do to spite the world.

FIRST MURDERER.   And I another
So weary with disasters, tugged with fortune,
That I would set° my life on any chance,
To mend it or be rid on 't.°

MACBETH.   Both of you
115 Know Banquo was your enemy.

BOTH MURDERERS.   True, my lord.

MACBETH. So is he mine, and in such bloody distance
That every minute of his being thrusts
Against my near'st of life:° and though I could
With barefaced power sweep him from my sight
120 And bid my will avouch it,° yet I must not,
For certain friends that are both his and mine,
Whose loves I may not drop, but wail his fall°
Who I myself struck down: and thence it is
That I to your assistance do make love,°
125 Masking the business from the common eye
For sundry weighty reasons.

SECOND MURDERER.   We shall, my lord,
Perform what you command us.

FIRST MURDERER.   Though our lives—

MACBETH. Your spirits shine through you. Within this hour at
    most
I will advise you where to plant yourselves,
130 Acquaint you with the perfect spy o' th' time,
The moment on 't;° for 't must be done tonight,
And something° from the palace; always thought°
That I require a clearness:° and with him—
To leave no rubs° nor botches in the work—

100–101 **Particular . . . alike:** a special designation that distinguishes him from the general category of dog.
102 **station in the file:** standing in the ranks.

106–108 **Grapples . . . perfect:** Macbeth says that their murder of Banquo will place them firmly in his affection. He is ill while Banquo lives but will be healthy again once he is dead.

113 **set:** risk.
114 **on 't:** of it.

116–118 **and . . . life:** Macbeth compares Banquo to a fencer standing dangerously close to him. Banquo's very existence is like a sword thrust against Macbeth's heart.
120 **bid . . . it:** offer my desire for Banquo's death as justification for killing him.
122 **but wail his fall:** but instead cry over his death.
124 **to your . . . love:** court your assistance.

130–131 **perfect . . . on 't:** precise instructions regarding exactly when to act.
132 **something:** at some distance.
always thought: it being understood at all times.
133 **clearness:** freedom from suspicion.
134 **rubs:** flaws.

Reading Strategy **Analyzing Argument** *Is Macbeth's argument for not ordering Banquo's execution convincing? Explain.*

Vocabulary

incensed (in sensd′) *v.* to make enraged; filled with anger

Macbeth instructing the murderers employed to kill Banquo. George Cattermole. Watercolor on paper. Victoria & Albert Museum, London.

135   Fleance his son, that keeps him company,
     Whose absence is no less material to me°
     Than is his father's, must embrace the fate
     Of that dark hour. Resolve yourselves apart:°
     I'll come to you anon.

     BOTH MURDERERS.   We are resolved, my lord.

140   **MACBETH.** I'll call upon you straight.° [*The* MURDERERS *exit.*]
     Abide within.
     It is concluded: Banquo, thy soul's flight,
     If it find heaven, must find it out tonight. [MACBETH
     exits.]

SCENE 2. The palace at Forres.

[LADY MACBETH *and a* SERVANT *enter another room in the palace.*]

     LADY MACBETH. Is Banquo gone from court?

     SERVANT. Ay, madam, but returns again tonight.

     LADY MACBETH. Say to the King, I would attend his leisure
     For a few words.

     SERVANT.   Madam, I will. [*The* SERVANT *exits to*
     summon MACBETH.]

     LADY MACBETH.   Nought's had, all's spent,
5   Where our desire is got without content:°
     'Tis safer to be that which we destroy
     Than by destruction dwell in doubtful° joy.

     [MACBETH *enters.*]

     How now, my lord! Why do you keep alone,
     Of sorriest fancies your companions making,
10   Using those thoughts which should indeed have died
     With them they think on? Things without all remedy
     Should be without regard:° what's done is done.

136 Whose . . . me: whose death is no less important to me.

138 Resolve . . . apart: Make up your minds in private.

140 straight: immediately.

4–5 Nought's . . . content: We possess nothing and squander everything when we are not satisfied after getting what we wished for.
7 doubtful: apprehensive, suspicious.

11–12 Things . . . regard: You shouldn't dwell upon matters beyond remedy.

MACBETH. We have scorched° the snake, not killed it:
 She'll close° and be herself, whilst our poor malice°
15 Remains in danger of her former tooth.°
 But let the frame of things disjoint, both the worlds
  suffer,°
 Ere we will eat our meal in fear, and sleep
 In the affliction of these terrible dreams
 That shake us nightly: better be with the dead,
20 Whom we, to gain our peace, have sent to peace,
 Than on the torture of the mind to lie
 In restless ecstasy.° Duncan is in his grave;
 After life's fitful fever he sleeps well.
 Treason has done his worst: nor steel, nor poison,
25 Malice domestic,° foreign levy,° nothing,
 Can touch him further.

LADY MACBETH. Come on.
 Gentle my lord, sleek o'er your rugged looks;
 Be bright and **jovial** among your guests tonight.

MACBETH. So shall I, love; and so, I pray, be you:
30 Let your remembrance apply to Banquo;
 Present him eminence, both with eye and tongue:°
 Unsafe the while, that we must lave
 Our honors in these flattering streams°
 And make our faces vizards° to our hearts,
35 Disguising what they are.

LADY MACBETH. You must leave this.

MACBETH. O, full of scorpions is my mind, dear wife!
 Thou know'st that Banquo, and his Fleance, lives.

LADY MACBETH. But in them nature's copy's not eterne.°

MACBETH. There's comfort yet; they are assailable.
40 Then be thou jocund.° Ere the bat hath flown
 His cloistered flight, ere to black Hecate's summons
 The shard-borne beetle with his drowsy hums
 Hath rung night's yawning peal,° there shall be done
 A deed of dreadful note.

LADY MACBETH. What's to be done?

45 **MACBETH.** Be innocent of the knowledge, dearest chuck,°
 Till thou applaud the deed. Come, seeling° night,

---

13 **scorched:** wounded.
14 **close:** heal. **poor malice:** feeble power to harm.
15 **in . . . tooth:** in as much danger from her tooth as before she was wounded.
16 **But . . . suffer:** but let the universe fall apart, and let both heaven and earth perish.

22 **ecstasy:** frenzy.

25 **Malice domestic:** civil war. **foreign levy:** troops sent from abroad.

31 **Present . . . tongue:** Pay respect to him with both looks and speech.

32–33 **Unsafe . . . streams:** We are vulnerable at the moment, so we must wash our reputations in these streams of flattery.
34 **vizards:** masks.

38 **in . . . eterne:** They do not have eternal life.

40 **jocund:** merry.

40–43 **Ere . . . peal:** before sunset (when the bat begins its flight and the winged beetle's droning announces nightfall).

45 **chuck:** a term of endearment.
46 **seeling:** eye-closing.

Big Idea **A Bard for the Ages** *What does Shakespeare convey about Macbeth's state of mind with this image?*

Big Idea **A Bard for the Ages** *How does Shakespeare signal a change in Macbeth's relationship with his wife in these lines?*

Vocabulary

jovial (jō′ vē al) *adj.* full of good humor; genial and playful

Scarf up° the tender eye of pitiful day,
And with thy bloody and invisible hand
Cancel and tear to pieces that great bond°
50   Which keeps me pale! Light thickens, and the crow
Makes wing to th' rooky° wood.
Good things of day begin to droop and drowse,
While night's black agents to their preys do rouse.
Thou marvel'st at my words: but hold thee still;
55   Things bad begun make strong themselves by ill:
So, prithee, go with me. [*They exit together.*]

SCENE 3. Outside the palace at Forres.

[*Some distance from the palace, the two assassins wait to attack* BANQUO *and* FLEANCE. *They are joined by a mysterious* THIRD MURDERER.]

FIRST MURDERER. But who did bid thee join with us?

THIRD MURDERER.   Macbeth.°

SECOND MURDERER. He needs not our mistrust; since he delivers°
Our offices° and what we have to do
To the direction just.°

FIRST MURDERER.   Then stand with us.
5   The west yet glimmers with some streaks of day.
Now spurs the lated° traveler apace°
To gain the timely inn,° and near approaches
The subject of our watch.

THIRD MURDERER.   Hark! I hear horses.

BANQUO. [*Calls from offstage.*] Give us a light there, ho!

SECOND MURDERER.   Then 'tis he. The rest
10   That are within the note of expectation°
Already are i' th' court.

FIRST MURDERER.   His horses go about.°

THIRD MURDERER. Almost a mile: but he does usually—
So all men do—from hence to th' palace gate
Make it their walk.

[BANQUO *and* FLEANCE, *carrying a torch, enter on foot.*]

SECOND MURDERER. A light, a light!

THIRD MURDERER.   'Tis he.

FIRST MURDERER.   Stand to 't.

15   BANQUO. It will be rain tonight.

FIRST MURDERER.   Let it come down.

[*They attack* BANQUO.]

Big Idea **A Bard for the Ages** *Why do you think Shakespeare hides the identity of this mysterious third murderer?*

47 **Scarf up:** blindfold.

49 **that great bond:** Banquo's and Fleance's lease on life.

51 **rooky:** black and full of rooks (birds similar to crows).

1 **Macbeth:** This third murderer is probably a spy sent by Macbeth to make sure the other murderers carry out his orders.
2 **delivers:** reports.
3 **offices:** duties.
4 **To . . . just:** in exact accordance with our instructions.

6 **lated:** belated. **apace:** at a swift pace.
7 **gain . . . inn:** reach a welcome inn.

10 **within . . . expectation:** included on the list of expected guests.

11 **go about:** take a roundabout route (rather than heading directly to the palace).

BANQUO. O, treachery! Fly, good Fleance, fly, fly, fly!

[*FLEANCE escapes*.]

Thou mayst revenge. O slave! [*BANQUO dies*.]

THIRD MURDERER. Who did strike out the light?

FIRST MURDERER.   Was 't not the way?°

THIRD MURDERER. There's but one down; the son is fled.

20   **SECOND MURDERER.** We have lost best half of our affair.

FIRST MURDERER. Well, let's away and say how much is done.

[*The MURDERERS exit*.]

18 **Was . . . way:** Was it not the right course of action?

SCENE 4. The palace at Forres.

[*A banquet has been prepared in a hall of the royal palace. MACBETH and LADY MACBETH enter with ROSS, LENNOX, and other LORDS and their ATTENDANTS.*]

MACBETH. You know your own degrees; sit down:°
 At first and last, the hearty welcome.

LORDS. Thanks to your Majesty.

MACBETH. Ourself will mingle with society
5   And play the humble host.
 Our hostess keeps her state,° but in best time
 We will require° her welcome.

LADY MACBETH. Pronounce it for me, sir, to all our friends,
 For my heart speaks they are welcome.

[*The first MURDERER enters and stands near the door.*]

1 **You . . . down:** At state banquets, guests were seated according to their ranks (**degrees**).

6 **keeps her state:** remains in the chair designated for the queen.
7 **require:** request.

10   **MACBETH.** See, they encounter thee with their hearts' thanks.
 Both sides are even:° here I'll sit i' th' midst:
 Be large in mirth; anon we'll drink a measure°
 The table round. [*He goes to the MURDERER at the door.*]
  There's blood upon thy face.

MURDERER. 'Tis Banquo's then.

11 **Both sides are even:** There are equal numbers on both sides of the table.
12 **measure:** toast.

15   **MACBETH.** 'Tis better thee without than he within.°
 Is he dispatched?

MURDERER. My lord, his throat is cut; that I did for him.

MACBETH. Thou art the best o' th' cutthroats.
 Yet he's good that did the like for Fleance;
20   If thou didst it, thou art the nonpareil.°

MURDERER. Most royal sir, Fleance is 'scaped.

MACBETH. [*Aside.*] Then comes my fit° again: I had else been
  perfect,
 Whole as the marble, founded as the rock,
 As broad and general as the casing air:°

15 **'Tis . . . within:** It is better on your face than in his body.

20 **nonpareil:** one without equal.

22 **fit:** violent disorder.

24 **As broad . . . air:** as free and unrestrained as the surrounding air.

Literary Element   Foil   *How do Banquo's dying words leave a lasting impression of his character in the mind of the audience?*

The Banquet Scene from Macbeth, 1840s. Daniel Maclise. Oil on canvas. The Garrick Club, London.

Viewing the Art: How does the painting reflect the chaos caused by Macbeth's mad ramblings?

25 But now I am cabined, cribbed, confined, bound in	
To saucy° doubts and fears. [*To the* MURDERER.]—But	26 **saucy:** insolent.
Banquo's safe?	
MURDERER. Ay, my good lord: safe in a ditch he bides,°	27 **bides:** remains.
With twenty trenchèd° gashes on his head,	28 **trenchèd:** cut.
The least a death to nature.°	29 **a death to nature:** enough to kill a man.
MACBETH. Thanks for that.	
30 [*Aside*.] There the grown serpent lies; the worm that's fled	
Hath nature that in time will venom breed,	
No teeth for th' present. [*To the* MURDERER.]—Get thee gone.	
Tomorrow	
We'll hear ourselves° again. [*The* MURDERER *exits*.]	33 **hear ourselves:** discuss the matter.
LADY MACBETH. My royal lord,	
You do not give the cheer.° The feast is sold	34 **give the cheer:** provide your guests with hospitality.
35 That is not often vouched, while 'tis a-making,	
'Tis given with welcome.° To feed were best at home;	34–36 **The feast . . . welcome:** A feast where the guests are not made to feel welcome is no better than a meal sold at an inn.
From thence,° the sauce to meat is ceremony;°	37 **From thence:** away from home. **ceremony:** courtesy.
Meeting were bare without it.	
[*The* GHOST OF BANQUO *enters and sits in* MACBETH's *place*.]	
MACBETH. Sweet remembrancer!	
Now good digestion wait on° appetite,	39 **wait on:** serve.
40 And health on both!	

Literary Element   **Foil** *Why does the thought of Banquo's son make Macbeth uneasy?*

LENNOX. May 't please your Highness sit.

MACBETH. Here had we now our country's honor roofed,°
Were the graced person of our Banquo present—
Who may I rather challenge for unkindness
Than pity for mischance!°

ROSS. His absence, sir,
45 Lays blame upon his promise. Please 't your Highness
To grace us with your royal company?

[MACBETH *looks at his chair and sees the* GHOST.]

MACBETH. The table's full.

LENNOX. Here is a place reserved, sir.

MACBETH. Where?

LENNOX. [*Indicating the place where* MACBETH *sees the* GHOST.]
Here, my good lord. What is 't that moves your Highness?

50 **MACBETH.** Which of you have done this?°

LORDS. What, my good lord?

MACBETH. Thou canst not say I did it. Never shake
Thy gory locks at me.

ROSS. Gentlemen, rise, his Highness is not well.

LADY MACBETH. Sit, worthy friends. My lord is often thus,
55 And hath been from his youth. Pray you, keep seat.
The fit is momentary; upon a thought°
He will again be well. If much you note him,
You shall offend him and extend his passion.°
Feed, and regard him not. [*To* MACBETH.]—Are you a man?

60 **MACBETH.** Ay, and a bold one, that dare look on that
Which might **appall** the devil.

LADY MACBETH. O proper stuff!°
This is the very painting of your fear.
This is the air-drawn dagger which, you said,
Led you to Duncan. O, these flaws° and starts,
65 Impostors to true fear, would well become
A woman's story at a winter's fire,
Authorized by her grandam.° Shame itself!
Why do you make such faces? When all's done,
You look but on a stool.

MACBETH. Prithee, see there!
70 Behold! Look! Lo! [*To the* GHOST.] How say you?
Why, what care I? If thou canst nod, speak too.

Literary Element Foil *Why does the ghost of Banquo sit in Macbeth's place?*

Vocabulary

appall (ə pôl′) *v.* to fill with horror and shock

---

41 **Here . . . roofed:** we would now have all of Scotland's noblemen under one roof.

43–44 **Who . . . mischance:** Macbeth says that he hopes Banquo's absence is caused by discourtesy rather than an accident.

50 **done this:** killed Banquo.

56 **upon a thought:** in a moment.

58 **extend his passion:** prolong his suffering.

61 **proper stuff:** nonsense.

64 **flaws:** emotional outbursts.

67 **Authorized . . . grandam:** passed down from her grandmother.

If charnel houses° and our graves must send
Those that we bury back, our monuments
Shall be the maws of kites.° [*The* GHOST *vanishes*.]

LADY MACBETH.   What, quite unmanned in folly?

75 **MACBETH.** If I stand here, I saw him.

LADY MACBETH.   Fie, for shame!

MACBETH. Blood hath been shed ere now, i' th' olden time,
Ere humane statute purged the gentle weal;°
Ay, and since too, murders have been performed
Too terrible for the ear. The times has been
80 That, when the brains were out, the man would die,
And there an end; but now they rise again,
With twenty mortal murders on their crowns,°
And push us from our stools. This is more strange
Than such a murder is.

LADY MACBETH.   My worthy lord,
85 Your noble friends do lack you.

MACBETH.   I do forget.
Do not muse at me, my most worthy friends;
I have a strange infirmity, which is nothing
To those that know me. Come, love and health to all!
Then I'll sit down. Give me some wine, fill full.

[*The* GHOST *reappears*, *but* MACBETH *does not notice him at once*.]

90 I drink to th' general joy o' th' whole table,
And to our dear friend Banquo, whom we miss;
Would he were here! To all and him we thirst,°
And all to all.

LORDS.   Our duties, and the pledge.

MACBETH. [*To the* GHOST.] Avaunt!° and quit my sight! Let
the earth hide thee!
95 Thy bones are marrowless, thy blood is cold;
Thou hast no speculation° in those eyes
Which thou dost glare with.

LADY MACBETH.   Think of this, good peers,
But as a thing of custom;° 'tis no other.
Only it spoils the pleasure of the time.

100 **MACBETH.** What man dare, I dare.
Approach thou like the rugged Russian bear,
The armed rhinoceros, or th' Hyrcan° tiger;
Take any shape but that,° and my firm nerves
Shall never tremble. Or be alive again,

72 **charnel houses:** buildings where bones dug up from old graves were stored.
73–74 **our . . . kites:** our tombs will be the stomachs of birds of prey.

77 **Ere . . . weal:** before human laws cleansed the community of violence.

82 **mortal . . . crowns:** deadly wounds on their heads.

92 **thirst:** wish to drink.

94 **Avaunt:** Begone!

96 **speculation:** vision.

98 **thing of custom:** a customary occurrence.

102 **Hyrcan:** from Hyrcania, an ancient province near the Caspian Sea.
103 **that:** Banquo's shape.

Big Idea **A Bard for the Ages** *What does Shakespeare suggest about the power of evil in this passage?*

Literary Element **Foil** *What is ironic about Macbeth's speech?*

The Banquet (Act 3 scene 4), *Macbeth* production at the Princess's Theatre, 1901. Victoria & Albert Museum, London.

105 And dare me to the desert° with thy sword.
If trembling I inhabit then, protest me
The baby of a girl.° Hence, horrible shadow!
Unreal mock'ry, hence! [*The* GHOST *vanishes again.*]
                    Why, so: being gone,
I am a man again. Pray you, sit still.

110 **LADY MACBETH.** You have displaced the mirth, broke the good meeting,
With most admired disorder.°

    MACBETH.   Can such things be,
And overcome° us like a summer's cloud,
Without our special wonder? You make me strange
Even to the disposition that I owe,°

115 When now I think you can behold such sights,
And keep the natural ruby of your cheeks,
When mine is blanched with fear.

    ROSS.   What sights, my lord?

    LADY MACBETH. I pray you, speak not: he grows worse and worse;
Question enrages him: at once, good night.

120 Stand not upon the order of your going,°
But go at once.

    LENNOX.   Good night; and better health
Attend his Majesty!

    LADY MACBETH.   A kind good night to all!

[*Everyone exits except* MACBETH *and* LADY MACBETH.]

    MACBETH. It will have blood, they say: blood will have blood.
Stones have been known to move and trees to speak;

125 Augures and understood relations have
By maggot-pies and choughs and rooks brought forth
The secret'st man of blood.° What is the night?

    LADY MACBETH. Almost at odds with morning,° which is which.

105 **the desert:** an uninhabited place.

106–107 **If . . . girl:** If I tremble, then call me a baby girl.

111 **admired disorder:** amazing lack of self-control.

112 **overcome:** pass over.

113–114 **You . . . owe:** You make me feel like a stranger to my own nature.

120 **Stand . . . going:** Do not wait to leave in order of your rank.

125–127 **Augures . . . blood:** Macbeth says that the cries of magpies (**maggot-pies**) and birds of the crow family (**choughs**) have provided omens and revealed hidden relationships that exposed even the most concealed murderers.
128 **Almost . . . morning:** almost midnight.

MACBETH. How say'st thou, that Macduff denies his person
130   At our great bidding?

LADY MACBETH.   Did you send to him, sir?

MACBETH. I hear it by the way, but I will send:
    There's not a one of them but in his house
    I keep a servant fee'd.° I will tomorrow,
    And betimes° I will, to the weird sisters:
135   More shall they speak, for now I am bent° to know
    By the worst means the worst. For mine own good
    All causes shall give way.° I am in blood
    Stepped in so far that, should I wade no more,
    Returning were as tedious as go o'er.°
140   Strange things I have in head that will to hand,°
    Which must be acted ere they may be scanned.°

LADY MACBETH. You lack the season of all natures,° sleep.

MACBETH. Come, we'll to sleep. My strange and self-abuse°
    Is the initiate fear that wants hard use.°
145   We are yet but young in deed.

  [*They exit.*]

SCENE 5. A heath.

[*There is thunder and lightning on a heath as the* THREE WITCHES *enter and meet* HECATE, *the goddess of witchcraft.*]

FIRST WITCH. Why, how now, Hecate! you look angerly.

HECATE. Have I not reason, beldams° as you are,
    Saucy and overbold? How did you dare
    To trade and traffic with Macbeth
5   In riddles and affairs of death;
    And I, the mistress of your charms,
    The close contriver° of all harms,
    Was never called to bear my part,
    Or show the glory of our art?
10   And, which is worse, all you have done
    Hath been but for a wayward son,
    Spiteful and wrathful; who, as others do,
    Loves for his own ends, not for you.
    But make **amends** now: get you gone,

---

133 fee'd: paid to inform me.
134 betimes: early.
135 bent: determined.

136–137 For mine . . . way: My own welfare takes precedence over all other interests.
139 go o'er: reaching the other shore.
140 will to hand: demand to be carried out.
141 scanned: examined.
142 season of all natures: preservative of all living things.
143 strange and self-abuse: remarkable self-delusion.
144 the initiate . . . use: the fear of a beginner who needs to be hardened by experience.

2 beldams: hags.

7 close contriver: secret plotter.

Literary Element   **Foil** *Why does Macbeth begin to suspect Macduff?*

Big Idea   **A Bard for the Ages** *How does Shakespeare suggest that Macbeth's character is beginning to crumble in these lines?*

Vocabulary

amends (ə mendz′) *n.* something done or given to make up for injury, loss, etc.

15   And at the pit of Acheron°
        Meet me i' th' morning: thither he
        Will come to know his destiny.
        Your vessels and your spells provide,
        Your charms and everything beside.
20   I am for th' air; this night I'll spend
        Unto a dismal° and a fatal end:
        Great business must be wrought ere noon.
        Upon the corner of the moon
        There hangs a vap'rous drop profound;°
25   I'll catch it ere it come to ground:
        And that distilled by magic sleights°
        Shall raise such artificial sprites°
        As by the strength of their illusion
        Shall draw him on to his confusion.°
30   He shall spurn fate, scorn death, and bear
        His hopes 'bove wisdom, grace, and fear:
        And you all know security°
        Is mortals' chiefest enemy.

[*Music and a song are heard offstage.* HECATE *is called away.*]

        Hark! I am called; my little spirit,° see,
35   Sits in a foggy cloud and stays for me.

[HECATE *exits.*]

        FIRST WITCH. Come, let's make haste; she'll soon be back
            again.

[*The* WITCHES *exit quickly.*]

SCENE 6. The palace at Forres.

[LENNOX *and another* LORD *enter a room in the palace.*]

        LENNOX. My former speeches have but hit° your thoughts,
            Which can interpret farther.° Only I say
            Things have been strangely borne.° The gracious Duncan
            Was pitied of Macbeth: marry,° he was dead.°
5   And the right-valiant Banquo walked too late;
            Whom, you may say, if 't please you, Fleance killed,
            For Fleance fled. Men must not walk too late.
            Who cannot want the thought,° how monstrous
            It was for Malcolm and for Donalbain
10   To kill their gracious father? Damnèd fact!°
            How it did grieve Macbeth! Did he not straight,
            In pious rage, the two delinquents tear,
            That were the slaves of drink and thralls° of sleep?
            Was not that nobly done? Ay, and wisely too;
15   For 'twould have angered any heart alive

Side notes:

15 **Acheron:** a river in the underworld in Greek mythology.

21 **dismal:** disastrous.

24 **profound:** with important qualities.

26 **sleights:** devices.
27 **artificial sprites:** spirits created by magic arts.

29 **confusion:** ruin.

32 **security:** overconfidence.

34 **little spirit:** Hecate's helper.

1 **but hit:** only agreed with.
2 **interpret further:** draw further conclusions.
3 **borne:** managed.
3–4 **The . . . dead:** Here, Lennox begins to mock Macbeth's explanations of the recent deaths.
4 **marry:** by the Virgin Mary (a mild oath similar to *indeed*).
8 **Who . . . thought:** who cannot help thinking.

10 **fact:** deed, crime.

13 **thralls:** slaves.

Big Idea **A Bard for the Ages** *Why does Shakespeare include these lines?*

To hear the men deny 't. So that I say
He has borne all things well:° and I do think
That, had he Duncan's sons under his key—
As, an 't° please heaven, he shall not—they should find
20 What 'twere to kill a father. So should Fleance.
But, peace! for from broad words,° and 'cause he failed
His presence at the tyrant's feast, I hear,
Macduff lives in disgrace. Sir, can you tell
Where he bestows himself?

LORD.   The son of Duncan,
25 From whom this tyrant holds the due of birth,°
Lives in the English court, and is received
Of the most pious Edward° with such grace
That the malevolence of fortune nothing
Takes from his high respect.° Thither Macduff
30 Is gone to pray the holy King, upon his aid
To wake Northumberland° and warlike Siward;°
That by the help of these, with Him above
To ratify the work, we may again
Give to our tables meat, sleep to our nights,
35 Free from our feasts and banquets bloody knives,°
Do faithful homage and receive free honors:°
All which we pine for now. And this report
Hath so exasperate the King° that he
Prepares for some attempt of war.

LENNOX.   Sent he to Macduff?

40 **LORD.** He did: and with an absolute "Sir, not I,"
The cloudy messenger turns me his back,
And hums, as who should say "You'll rue the time
That clogs me with this answer."°

LENNOX.   And that well might
Advise him to a caution, t' hold what distance
45 His wisdom can provide.° Some holy angel
Fly to the court of England and unfold°
His message ere he come, that a swift blessing
May soon return to this our suffering country
Under a hand accursed!

LORD.   I'll send my prayers with him.

[*They exit.*]

---

17 **borne . . . well:** managed everything cunningly.

19 **an 't:** if it.

21 **from broad words:** as a result of unrestrained speech.

25 **holds . . . birth:** withholds his birthright (the throne).

27 **Edward:** Edward the Confessor, King of England from 1042–1066.

28–29 **That . . . respect:** that Malcolm's misfortune has not diminished the great respect he is shown.

29–31 **Thither . . . Siward:** The Lord says that Macduff has gone to ask Edward to arouse Siward, Earl of **Northumberland** (a northern English county), to fight on Malcolm's behalf.

35 **Free . . . knives:** free our feasts and banquets from bloody knives.

36 **free honors:** the honors of free men (not enslaved to a tyrant).

38 **exasperate the King:** angered Macbeth.

40–43 **with an . . . answer:** When Macduff refused to obey the order to appear before Macbeth, the gloomy messenger turned and made a noise expressing his indignation and suggesting that Macduff will regret burdening him with such a response.

44–45 **Advise . . . provide:** warn him to be cautious and keep a safe distance from Macbeth.

46 **unfold:** reveal.

RESPONDING AND THINKING CRITICALLY

Respond

1. Did any of the events in Act 3 surprise you? Explain why or why not.

Recall and Interpret

2. (a)Describe the murder plot that Macbeth devises against Banquo. (b)How is it different from the murder plot against Duncan? What do these differences suggest to you about Macbeth's character?

3. (a)Which intended victim of Macbeth's plot manages to escape? (b)What conflicts might this character cause for Macbeth in the future?

4. (a)Describe Macbeth's behavior during the feast scene. (b)How might his guests' opinion of him have been affected by this behavior?

5. (a)What does Macbeth do when he learns of Macduff's opposition to him? (b)What importance might Macduff have in Acts 4 and 5?

Analyze and Evaluate

6. What signs are there in this act that Macbeth's conscience is troubling him?

7. (a)What does Lennox's sarcastic tone in scene 6, lines 1–24, suggest about Macbeth's future as king? (b)Does his tone seem realistic here? Explain.

8. How has the relationship between Macbeth and Lady Macbeth changed in this act?

Connect

9. **Big Idea** **A Bard for the Ages** Many critics believe that another author may have written scene 5 after Shakespeare's death. In your opinion, does the scene enhance the play? Explain why or why not.

LITERARY ANALYSIS

Literary Element **Foil**

A **foil** character serves two main purposes: to highlight flaws in the main character's personality and to suggest what the main character might have been like if these flaws had not been present.

1. In what significant ways is Banquo similar to and different from Macbeth?

2. What flaws in Macbeth's character do these differences help reveal?

Writing About Literature

Respond to Plot Macbeth finds himself in deeper and deeper trouble as the play progresses. If you could talk to him as a trusted friend or confidant, what advice would you offer? Do you think he would take it? In your opinion, do most people heed their friends' advice? In two paragraphs, describe what you would say to Macbeth and explain why you think it is good advice. In a third paragraph, write your thoughts about giving and receiving advice.

READING AND VOCABULARY

Reading Strategy **Analyzing Argument**

In this act, Macbeth persuades two desperate men to do his killing for him. Does Macbeth succeed in convincing the murderers to kill Banquo primarily through the strength of his argument or the force of his emotional appeal? Explain.

Vocabulary **Practice**

Practice with Antonyms Find the antonym for each vocabulary word listed in the first column.

1. amends   **a.** retribution   **b.** abuse

2. appall   **a.** soothe   **b.** distress

3. incensed   **a.** charmed   **b.** outraged

4. jovial   **a.** amusing   **b.** morose

5. indissoluble   **a.** fragile   **b.** ironclad

Literature Online **Web Activities** For eFlashcards, Selection Quick Checks, and other Web activities, go to www.glencoe.com.

LITERATURE PREVIEW	READING PREVIEW

Building Background

This act begins with the famous Cauldron Scene in which the witches prepare a ghastly brew. According to critic D. J. Palmer, "This scene is the climactic point of the play's use of spectacle: the cauldron itself is an image traditionally associated with hell, and each of the three Apparitions in turn rises and descends from within it. The presentation of these sights by the witches to Macbeth is a diabolical parody of the emblematic pageants and allegorical masques with which royalty was greeted and honored in Shakespeare's day, often at a banquet."

Shakespeare's audience would have had well-developed notions of what witches looked like and how they acted. Traditionally, witches were thought of as grotesque hags. Followers of Hecate, the goddess of witchcraft, witches were possessed by Familiars, or minor spirits of evil.

Literary Element Plot

The **plot** is the sequence of events in a narrative work. The plot may begin with **exposition**, or the introduction of the characters, setting, and conflict. The **rising action** adds complications to the conflicts, leading to the **climax**, or emotional high point. The climax gives way rapidly to its logical result in the **falling action**, and finally to the **resolution** (sometimes called the **dénouement**) in which the final outcome is revealed.

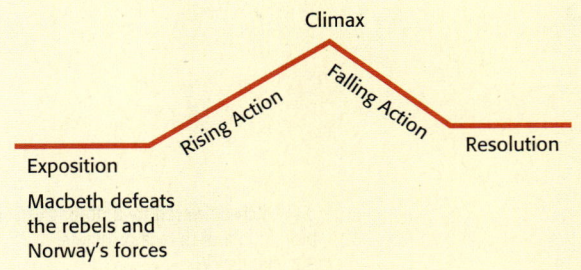

Climax

Rising Action

Falling Action

Exposition

Resolution

Macbeth defeats the rebels and Norway's forces

- See Literary Terms Handbook, p. R13.

Literature Online Interactive Literary Elements Handbook To review or learn more about the literary elements, go to www.glencoe.com.

Reading Strategy Making and Verifying Predictions

Predicting is making an educated guess about what will happen in a selection. When you predict, you use your prior knowledge and the clues you gather from the selection to create an expectation for what you will read. As you read, adjust or change your predictions if they don't fit what you learn.

Reading Tip: Predicting Use a chart to list clues from the play and the predictions you make.

Clues	Predictions
An apparition warns Macbeth about Macduff.	Macbeth vows to kill Macduff.

Vocabulary

pernicious (pər nish′ əs) *adj.* destructive; deadly; p. 375 *Parents feared that pernicious fumes from the toxic dump were harming their children.*

exploit (eks′ ploit) *n.* bold deed; p. 376 *Reading about the exploits of heroes reveals the true meaning of courage.*

redress (ri dres′) *v.* to set right; to remedy; p. 379 *Victims of injustice may go to court to redress their grievances.*

avarice (av′ ər is) *n.* greed; p. 381 *King Midas's avarice prompted his wish that everything he touched be turned into gold.*

pertain (pər tān′) *v.* to be connected to or have relevance to; p. 385 *The committee addressed only those questions that pertained to the proposal.*

Vocabulary Tip: Synonyms Words that have the same or nearly the same meaning are called synonyms.

OBJECTIVES
In studying this selection, you will focus on the following:
- analyzing literary periods
- analyzing plot
- making and verifying predictions

ACT 4

SCENE 1. A deserted place.

[It is thundering as the THREE WITCHES *enter and stand around a large caldron, or pot, in their deserted meeting place.]*

    FIRST WITCH. Thrice the brinded cat hath mewed.

    SECOND WITCH. Thrice and once the hedge-pig whined.°

    THIRD WITCH. Harpier° cries. 'Tis time, 'tis time.

    FIRST WITCH. Round about the caldron go:
5   In the poisoned entrails throw.

[The WITCHES *circle the caldron, and as each mentions an item, she throws it into the pot.]*

        Toad, that under cold stone
        Days and nights has thirty-one
        Swelt'red venom sleeping got,°
        Boil thou first i' th' charmèd pot.

10   **ALL.** Double, double, toil and trouble;
        Fire burn and caldron bubble.

    SECOND WITCH. Fillet of a fenny snake,°
        In the caldron boil and bake;
        Eye of newt and toe of frog,
15   Wool of bat and tongue of dog,
        Adder's fork° and blindworm's° sting,
        Lizard's leg and howlet's° wing,
        For a charm of pow'rful trouble,
        Like a hell-broth boil and bubble.

20   **ALL.** Double, double, toil and trouble;
        Fire burn and caldron bubble.

    THIRD WITCH. Scale of dragon, tooth of wolf,
        Witch's mummy, maw and gulf°
        Of the ravined° salt-sea shark,
25   Root of hemlock digged i' th' dark,
        Liver of blaspheming Jew,
        Gall of goat, and slips of yew
        Slivered in the moon's eclipse,
        Nose of Turk and Tartar's lips,
30   Finger of birth-strangled babe
        Ditch-delivered by a drab,°
        Make the gruel thick and slab:°
        Add thereto a tiger's chaudron,°
        For th' ingredients of our caldron.

35   **ALL.** Double, double, toil and trouble;
        Fire burn and caldron bubble.

1–2 Thrice . . . whined: The witches respond to the calls of their familiars, which include a striped (**brinded**) cat and a hedgehog (**hedge-pig**).
3 Harpier: one of the familiar spirits attending the witches. *Harpier* is derived from *harpy*, a birdlike monster of classical mythology.

6–8 that under . . . got: which has sweated venom for thirty-one days while sleeping under a cold stone.

12 Fillet . . . snake: a slice of a snake found in marshland.

16 Adder's fork: snake's forked tongue.
blindworm: a limbless lizard once thought to be poisonous.
17 howlet: small owl.

23 maw and gulf: stomach and gullet.
24 ravined: glutted with prey.

31 Ditch-delivered by a drab: given birth to in a ditch by a prostitute.
32 slab: sticky.
33 chaudron: entrails.

Literary Element   **Plot** *Why do you think Shakespeare shows the witches performing their satanic rites at this stage of the rising action?*

SECOND WITCH. Cool it with a baboon's blood,
    Then the charm is firm and good.

[HECATE, *goddess of witches, enters and addresses the other*
THREE WITCHES.]

HECATE. O, well done! I commend your pains;
40   And everyone shall share i' th' gains:
    And now about the caldron sing,
    Like elves and fairies in a ring,
    Enchanting all that you put in.

[*Music and a song are heard offstage*. HECATE *exits*.]

SECOND WITCH. By the pricking of my thumbs,°
45   Something wicked this way comes:
      Open, locks,
      Whoever knocks!

> 44 **By . . . thumbs:** I can tell by the tingling in my thumbs.

[MACBETH *enters*.]

MACBETH. How now, you secret, black, and midnight hags!
    What is 't you do?

ALL.   A deed without a name.

50 **MACBETH.** I conjure you, by that which you profess,°
    Howe'er you come to know it, answer me:
    Though you untie the winds and let them fight
    Against the churches; though the yesty° waves
    Confound° and swallow navigation up;
55   Though bladed corn° be lodged° and trees blown down;
    Though castles topple on their warders' heads;
    Though palaces and pyramids do slope°
    Their heads to their foundations; though the treasure
    Of nature's germens° tumble all together,
60   Even till destruction sicken, answer me
    To what I ask you.

> 50 **by . . . profess:** by the art you claim to have skill in.
>
> 53 **yesty:** foamy.
> 54 **Confound:** destroy.
> 55 **bladed corn:** unripe grain.
> **lodged:** beaten down by wind.
>
> 57 **slope:** bend.
>
> 59 **nature's germens:** the seeds of all life.

FIRST WITCH.   Speak.

SECOND WITCH.   Demand.

THIRD WITCH.   We'll answer.

FIRST WITCH. Say, if th' hadst rather hear it from our mouths,
    Or from our masters?

MACBETH.   Call 'em, let me see 'em.

FIRST WITCH. Pour in sow's blood, that hath eaten
65   Her nine farrow;° grease that's sweaten°
    From the murderer's gibbet° throw
    Into the flame.

> 65 **nine farrow:** litter of nine piglets.
> **sweaten:** sweated.
> 66 **gibbet:** gallows.

Reading Strategy Making and Verifying Predictions *What do you predict Macbeth will ask the witches?*

Macbeth and the Witches, 1780. George Romney. Folger Shakespeare Library, Washington, DC.

Viewing the Art: How does the painting compare with your vision of the scene?

ALL.　　　　　　　Come, high or low,
　Thyself and office° deftly show!

[*Thunder is heard as the* FIRST APPARITION, *the armored head of a warrior, appears.*]

MACBETH.　Tell me, thou unknown power—

FIRST WITCH.　　　　　　　He knows thy thought:
70　Hear his speech, but say thou nought.

FIRST APPARITION.°　Macbeth! Macbeth! Macbeth! Beware
　　Macduff!
　Beware the Thane of Fife. Dismiss me: enough.

[*The* FIRST APPARITION *disappears.*]

MACBETH.　Whate'er thou art, for thy good caution thanks:
　Thou has harped° my fear aright. But one word more—

75　**FIRST WITCH.**　He will not be commanded. Here's another,
　More potent than the first.

[*More thunder as the* SECOND APPARITION, *a Bloody Child, appears.*]

SECOND APPARITION.°　Macbeth! Macbeth! Macbeth!

MACBETH.　Had I three ears, I'd hear thee.

SECOND APPARITION.　Be bloody, bold, and resolute! Laugh to
　　scorn
80　The pow'r of man, for none of woman born
　Shall harm Macbeth.

[*The* SECOND APPARITION *disappears.*]

MACBETH.　Then live, Macduff: what need I fear of thee?
　But yet I'll make assurance double sure,
　And take a bond of fate.° Thou shalt not live;
85　That I may tell pale-hearted fear it lies,
　And sleep in spite of thunder.

[*Thunder sounds as the* THIRD APPARITION, *a Crowned Child with a tree in his hand, appears.*]

　　　　　　　What is this,
　That rises like the issue of a king,°
　And wears upon his baby-brow the round
　And top of sovereignty?°

ALL.　　　　　　　Listen, but speak not to 't.

90　**THIRD APPARITION.°**　Be lion-mettled, proud, and take no care
　Who chafes, who frets, or where conspirers are:
　Macbeth shall never vanquished be until
　Great Birnam Wood to high Dunsinane Hill
　Shall come against him.°

[*The* THIRD APPARITION *disappears.*]

MACBETH.　　　　　　　That will never be.
95　Who can impress° the forest, bid the tree
　Unfix his earth-bound root? Sweet bodements,° good!

---

68 **office:** your function.

71 **First Apparition:** The first of three ghosts whose appearance foretells Macbeth's downfall, this helmeted head probably symbolizes his confrontation with Macduff.

74 **harped:** guessed.

77 **Second Apparition:** This ghost probably represents Macduff at birth.

84 **take . . . fate:** get a guarantee from fate (by killing Macduff).

87 **rises . . . king:** rises in the likeness of a king's child.

88–89 **round . . . sovereignty:** crown.

90 **Third Apparition:** This ghost likely represents Malcolm, Duncan's son and designated heir to the throne.

92–94 **Macbeth . . . him:** Macbeth shall never be conquered until the forest of Great Birnam marches to his castle on Dunsinane Hill.

95 **impress:** force into service.
96 **bodements:** prophecies.

Macbeth and the Witches,
1834–35. Joseph Anton
Koch. Landesmuseum
Ferdinandeum, Innsbruck,
Austria.

Rebellious dead, rise never, till the Wood
Of Birnam rise, and our high-placed Macbeth
Shall live the lease of nature, pay his breath
100   To time and mortal custom.° Yet my heart
Throbs to know one thing. Tell me, if your art
Can tell so much: shall Banquo's issue ever
Reign in this kingdom?

ALL.   Seek to know no more.

MACBETH. I will be satisfied. Deny me this,
105   And an eternal curse fall on you! Let me know
Why sinks that caldron? And what noise is this?

[*Oboes are heard.*]

FIRST WITCH. Show!

SECOND WITCH. Show!

THIRD WITCH. Show!

110   **ALL.** Show his eyes, and grieve his heart;
Come like shadows, so depart!

[*A pantomime passes across the stage. In the show are the apparitions
of eight kings, representing the eight Stuart kings of Scotland. The
eighth king, representing James I of England, has a mirror in his hand.*
BANQUO'S GHOST *appears at the end of the procession.*]

99–100 live . . . custom: live out his
natural life and die a normal death.

Reading Strategy Making and Verifying Predictions *What do you
think Macbeth will do after hearing the apparitions' prophecies?*

MACBETH. Thou art too like the spirit of Banquo. Down!
Thy crown does sear mine eyelids. And thy hair,
Thou other gold-bound brow, is like the first.
115 A third is like the former. Filthy hags!
Why do you show me this? A fourth! Start, eyes!
What, will the line stretch out to th' crack of doom?
Another yet! A seventh! I'll see no more.
And yet the eighth° appears, who bears a glass
120 Which shows me many more; and some I see
That twofold balls and treble scepters carry:
Horrible sight! Now I see 'tis true;
For the blood-boltered° Banquo smiles upon me,
And points at them for his.°

[*The* APPARITIONS *in the pantomime vanish.*]

What, is this so?

125 **FIRST WITCH.** Ay, sir, all this is so. But why
Stands Macbeth thus amazedly?
Come, sisters, cheer we up his sprites,
And show the best of our delights:
I'll charm the air to give a sound,
130 While you perform your antic round,°
That this great king may kindly say
Our duties did his welcome pay.

[*Music plays as the* WITCHES *dance and vanish.*]

MACBETH. Where are they? Gone? Let this **pernicious** hour
Stand aye accursed° in the calendar!
135 Come in, without there!°

[*LENNOX enters.*]

LENNOX. What's your Grace's will?

MACBETH. Saw you the weird sisters?

LENNOX. No, my lord.

MACBETH. Came they not by you?

LENNOX. No indeed, my lord.

MACBETH. Infected be the air whereon they ride,
And damned all those that trust them! I did hear
140 The galloping of horse. Who was 't came by?

119–121 The **eighth** king is James VI of Scotland, who in 1603 became James I of England. He holds a magic mirror that shows future generations of Scottish rulers, some of them bearing coronation symbols of the Scottish and British thrones (**twofold balls** and **treble scepters**). James was descended from Banquo.
123 blood-boltered: having hair matted with blood.
124 his: his descendants.

130 antic round: fantastic circle dance.

134 Stand aye accursed: remain forever cursed.
135 without there: you who stands outside.

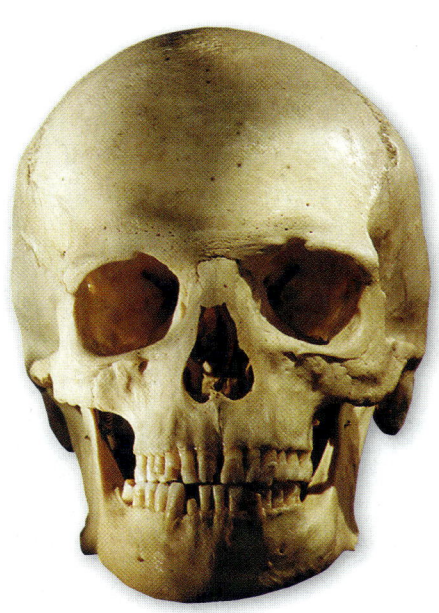

Reading Strategy **Making and Verifying Predictions** *How do you know that the prophecy about Banquo's descendants has come true?*

Vocabulary

pernicious (pər nish′ əs) *adj.* destructive; deadly

LENNOX. 'Tis two or three, my lord, that bring you word
Macduff is fled to England.

MACBETH.   Fled to England?

LENNOX. Ay, my good lord.

MACBETH. [*Aside.*] Time, thou anticipat'st° my dread **exploits**.
145   The flighty purpose never is o'ertook
Unless the deed go with it.° From this moment
The very firstlings of my heart shall be
The firstlings of my hand.° And even now,
To crown my thoughts with acts, be it thought and done:°
150   The castle of Macduff I will surprise;°
Seize upon Fife; give to th' edge o' th' sword
His wife, his babes, and all unfortunate souls
That trace him in his line.° No boasting like a fool;
This deed I'll do before this purpose cool:
155   But no more sights!—Where are these gentlemen?
Come, bring me where they are.

[*MACBETH exits with LENNOX.*]

SCENE 2. MACDUFF's castle at Fife.

[*In Fife, on the southeast coast of Scotland, LADY MACDUFF, her son, and ROSS enter a room in MACDUFF's castle. LADY MACDUFF is upset and angry with her husband for leaving Scotland.*]

LADY MACDUFF. What had he done, to make him fly the land?°

ROSS. You must have patience, madam.

LADY MACDUFF.   He had none:
His flight was madness. When our actions do not,
Our fears do make us traitors.°

ROSS.   You know not
5   Whether it was his wisdom or his fear.

LADY MACDUFF. Wisdom! To leave his wife, to leave his babes,
His mansion and his titles,° in a place
From whence himself does fly? He loves us not;
He wants the natural touch:° for the poor wren,

---

144 **anticipat'st:** prevent by acting in advance.
145–146 **The flighty . . . it:** Our intentions are so fleeting that they escape unless accompanied by immediate action.
146–148 **From . . . hand:** From now on, the first impulses of my heart will be matched by the actions of my hand.
149 **be it . . . done:** Let it be done immediately.
150 **surprise:** capture.
153 **trace . . . line:** follow in his lineage.

1 **fly the land:** flee the country.

3–4 **When . . . traitors:** Even when we are innocent of treason, our fears make us behave like traitors.

7 **titles:** possessions.

9 **wants . . . touch:** lacks natural feelings.

Literary Element   Plot *How does Macduff's escape frustrate Macbeth's plans?*

Reading Strategy   Making and Verifying Predictions *Do you think that Macduff's family will be able to save their lives? Explain.*

Literary Element   Plot *Why has Macduff fled Scotland without telling his wife?*

Vocabulary

exploit (eks′ ploit) *n.* bold deed

10　The most diminutive of birds, will fight,
Her young ones in her nest, against the owl.
All is the fear and nothing is the love;
As little is the wisdom, where the flight
So runs against all reason.

ROSS.　　　　　　　　　　My dearest coz,°
15　I pray you, school° yourself. But, for your husband,
He is noble, wise, judicious, and best knows
The fits o' th' season.° I dare not speak much further:
But cruel are the times, when we are traitors
And do not know ourselves;° when we hold rumor
20　From what we fear, yet know not what we fear,°
But float upon a wild and violent sea
Each way and move. I take my leave of you.
Shall not be long but I'll be here again.
Things at the worst will cease, or else climb upward
25　To what they were before. [*He addresses* MACDUFF's *son.*]
　　My pretty cousin,
Blessing upon you!

LADY MACDUFF.　Fathered he is, and yet he's fatherless.

ROSS.　I am so much a fool, should I stay longer,
It would be my disgrace and your discomfort.°
30　I take my leave at once.

[*ROSS exits.*]

LADY MACDUFF.　　　　　Sirrah, your father's dead:
And what will you do now? How will you live?

SON.　As birds do, mother.

LADY MACDUFF.　　　　　What, with worms and flies?

SON.　With what I get, I mean; and so do they.

LADY MACDUFF.　Poor bird! thou'dst never fear the net nor
　　lime,°
35　The pitfall° nor the gin.°

SON.　Why should I, mother? Poor birds they are not set for.°
My father is not dead, for all your saying.

LADY MACDUFF.　Yes, he is dead: how wilt thou do for a
　　father?

SON.　Nay, how will you do for a husband?

40　LADY MACDUFF.　Why, I can buy me twenty at any market.

SON.　Then you'll buy 'em to sell° again.

LADY MACDUFF.　Thou speak'st with all thy wit, and yet, i'
　　faith,
With wit enough for thee.°

---

14 **coz:** cousin, kinswoman.
15 **school:** control.

17 **fits o' th' season:** violent disorders of the time.
18–19 **we are . . . ourselves:** We are considered traitors but do not know of any treason we have committed.
19–20 **when . . . fear:** when we believe rumors merely because we are afraid.

29 **It . . . discomfort:** I would disgrace myself and embarrass you by weeping.

34 **lime:** birdlime, a sticky substance smeared on branches to catch birds.
35 **pitfall:** trap. **gin:** snare.
36 **Poor . . . for:** People do not set traps for birds of little value.

41 **sell:** betray.

43 **wit . . . thee:** considerable understanding for a child.

Big Idea **A Bard for the Ages** *What mood does Shakespeare create here through the dialogue between Lady Macduff and her son?*

SON. Was my father a traitor, mother?

45 **LADY MACDUFF.** Ay, that he was.

SON. What is a traitor?

LADY MACDUFF. Why, one that swears and lies.°

SON. And be all traitors that do so?

LADY MACDUFF. Every one that does so is a traitor, and must
be hanged.

50 **SON.** And must they all be hanged that swear and lie?

LADY MACDUFF. Every one.

SON. Who must hang them?

LADY MACDUFF. Why, the honest men.

SON. Then the liars and swearers are fools; for there are liars
55 and swearers enow° to beat the honest men and hang up
them.

LADY MACDUFF. Now, God help thee, poor monkey! But how
wilt thou do for a father?

SON. If he were dead, you'd weep for him. If you would not,°
it were a good sign that I should quickly have a new
father.

60 **LADY MACDUFF.** Poor prattler, how thou talk'st!

[A MESSENGER *enters.*]

MESSENGER. Bless you, fair dame! I am not to you known,
Though in your state of honor I am perfect.°
I doubt° some danger does approach you nearly:°
If you will take a homely° man's advice,
65 Be not found here; hence, with your little ones.
To fright you thus, methinks I am too savage;
To do worse to you were fell cruelty,
Which is too nigh your person.° Heaven preserve you!
I dare abide° no longer.

[The MESSENGER *exits quickly.*]

LADY MACDUFF. Whither should I fly?
70 I have done no harm. But I remember now
I am in this earthly world, where to do harm
Is often laudable, to do good sometime
Accounted dangerous folly. Why then, alas,
Do I put up that womanly defense,
75 To say I have done no harm?—What are these faces?

[The MURDERERS *hired by* MACBETH *enter.*]

MURDERER. Where is your husband?

LADY MACDUFF. I hope, in no place so unsanctified
Where such as thou mayst find him.

---

47 **swears and lies:** takes an oath and breaks it.

55 **enow:** enough.

58 **would not:** did not care to weep.

62 **in . . . perfect:** I am fully aware of your noble rank.
63 **doubt:** fear. **nearly:** closely.
64 **homely:** humble.

66–68 **To . . . person:** The messenger says that even frightening her like this is too savage. Any action taken against her would be fierce (**fell**) cruelty, and such cruelty is all too near.
69 **abide:** stay.

MURDERER.   He's a traitor.

SON. Thou li'st, thou shag-eared° villain!

MURDERER.   What, you egg!°

[*The* MURDERER *stabs the child.*]

80   Young fry of treachery!°

SON.   He has killed me, mother:
        Run away, I pray you!

[*The* BOY *dies as* LADY MACDUFF *runs off crying,* "Murder!" *The*
MURDERERS *pursue her.*]

SCENE 3. The palace of the King of England.

[MACDUFF *has come to England in an attempt to ally himself with*
MALCOLM, *KING DUNCAN's older son and rightful heir to the Scottish*
crown. MACDUFF *and* MALCOLM *enter and meet in front of the palace of*
Edward the Confessor, the devoutly religious king of England.]

MALCOLM. Let us seek out some desolate shade, and there
        Weep our sad bosoms empty.

MACDUFF.   Let us rather
        Hold fast the mortal sword,° and like good men
        Bestride our down-fall'n birthdom.° Each new morn

5   New widows howl, new orphans cry, new sorrows
        Strike heaven on the face, that it resounds
        As if it felt with Scotland and yelled out
        Like syllable of dolor.°

MALCOLM.   What I believe, I'll wail;
        What know, believe; and what I can **redress**,

10   As I shall find the time to friend,° I will.
        What you have spoke, it may be so perchance.°
        This tyrant, whose sole° name blisters our tongues,
        Was once thought honest:° you have loved him well;
        He hath not touched you yet. I am young; but something

15   You may deserve of him through me;° and wisdom°
        To offer up a weak, poor, innocent lamb
        T' appease an angry god.

MACDUFF. I am not treacherous.

Reading Strategy | Making and Verifying Predictions *What do you*
think Macduff will do when he learns that his son has been murdered?

Literary Element | Plot *Dramatic irony occurs when the audience*
knows something that the characters do not. What is ironic about
Macduff's statement?

Vocabulary

redress (ri dres´) *v.* to set right; to remedy

---

79 shag-eared: hairy-eared. **egg:** a term
of reproach for an impertinent boy.

80 Young . . . treachery: traitor's
offspring.

3 Hold . . . sword: keep a firm grip on
the deadly sword.
4 Bestride . . . birthdom: protectively
stand over our ruined native land.

8 Like . . . dolor: a similar cry of sorrow.

10 to friend: to be favorable to me.
11 may be so perchance: may perhaps
be true.
12 sole: mere.
13 honest: honorable.

14–15 something . . . me: You may be
rewarded by betraying me to Macbeth.
15 and wisdom: it would be wise.

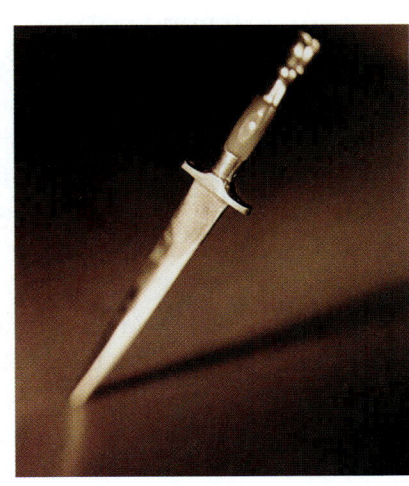

MALCOLM.   But Macbeth is.
A good and virtuous nature may recoil
20   In an imperial charge.° But I shall crave your pardon;
That which you are, my thoughts cannot transpose:°
Angels are bright still, though the brightest° fell:
Though all things foul would wear the brows of grace,
Yet grace must still look so.°

MACDUFF.   I have lost my hopes.

MALCOLM.   Perchance even there where I did find my
25   doubts.°
Why in that rawness left you wife and child,
Those precious motives, those strong knots of love,
Without leave-taking?° I pray you,
Let not my jealousies be your dishonors,
30   But mine own safeties.° You may be rightly just°
Whatever I shall think.

MACDUFF.   Bleed, bleed, poor country:
Great tyranny, lay thou thy basis sure,
For goodness dare not check thee:° wear thou thy wrongs;°
The title is affeered.° Fare thee well, lord:
35   I would not be the villain that thou think'st
For the whole space that's in the tyrant's grasp
And the rich East to boot.

MALCOLM.   Be not offended:
I speak not as in absolute fear of you.
I think our country sinks beneath the yoke;
40   It weeps, it bleeds, and each new day a gash
Is added to her wounds. I think withal°
There would be hands uplifted in my right;°
And here from gracious England° have I offer
Of goodly thousands: but, for all this,
45   When I shall tread upon the tyrant's head,
Or wear it on my sword, yet my poor country
Shall have more vices than it had before,
More suffer, and more sundry ways° than ever,
By him that shall succeed.

MACDUFF.   What° should he be?

50   **MALCOLM.**   It is myself I mean, in whom I know
All the particulars of vice so grafted°
That, when they shall be opened,° black Macbeth
Will seem as pure as snow, and the poor state
Esteem him as a lamb, being compared
55   With my confineless harms.°

MACDUFF.   Not in the legions
Of horrid hell can come a devil more damned
In evils to top Macbeth.

MALCOLM.   I grant him bloody,
Luxurious,° avaricious, false, deceitful,

19–20 A good . . . charge: A good man may fall away from his virtuous nature when pressured by a royal command.
21 transpose: change.
22 the brightest: Lucifer, the angel cast down from heaven for rebelling against God.
23–24 Though . . . so: Even if everything evil put on the appearance of virtue, virtue would still appear like itself.
25 doubts: suspicions.

25–28 Perchance . . . leave-taking: Malcolm says that he became suspicious of Macduff because Macduff left his family behind in a vulnerable state (**rawness**), which might suggest that he really is allied with Macbeth.
29–30 Let . . . safeties: Do not take my suspicions as attacks on your honor but rather as precautions for my safety.
30 rightly just: completely honorable.
32–33 lay . . . thee: You can establish yourself safely, for virtue is afraid to stop you.
33 wear . . . wrongs: Display your ill-gotten gains.
34 afeered: legally confirmed.

41 withal: in addition.
42 right: cause.
43 gracious England: the gracious King of England.

48 More . . . ways: shall suffer more and in more varied ways.

49 What: who.

51 grafted: implanted.
52 opened: exposed, in bloom.

55 confineless harms: boundless evils.

58 Luxurious: lecherous.

Sudden,° malicious, smacking of every sin

60 That has a name: but there's no bottom, none,
In my voluptuousness: your wives, your daughters,
Your matrons and your maids, could not fill up
The cistern of my lust, and my desire
All continent° impediments would o'erbear,°

65 That did oppose my will. Better Macbeth
Than such an one to reign.

MACDUFF.   Boundless intemperance°
In nature° is a tyranny; it hath been
Th' untimely emptying of the happy throne,
And fall of many kings. But fear not yet

70 To take upon you what is yours: you may
Convey your pleasures in a spacious plenty,°
And yet seem cold,° the time you may so hoodwink.°
We have willing dames enough. There cannot be
That vulture in you, to devour so many

75 As will to greatness dedicate themselves,
Finding it so inclined.

MALCOLM.   With this there grows
In my most ill-composed affection° such
A stanchless **avarice** that, were I King,
I should cut off the nobles for their lands,

80 Desire his° jewels and this other's house:
And my more-having would be as a sauce
To make me hunger more, that I should forge
Quarrels unjust against the good and loyal,
Destroying them for wealth.

MACDUFF.   This avarice

85 Sticks deeper, grows with more pernicious root
Than summer-seeming° lust, and it hath been
The sword° of our slain kings. Yet do not fear.
Scotland hath foisons° to fill up your will
Of your mere own.° All these are portable,

90 With other graces weighed.°

MALCOLM. But I have none: the king-becoming graces,
As justice, verity, temp'rance, stableness,
Bounty, perseverance, mercy, lowliness,
Devotion, patience, courage, fortitude,

95 I have no relish° of them, but abound
In the division of each several crime,°
Acting it many ways. Nay, had I pow'r, I should

Big Idea **A Bard for the Ages** *What does Shakespeare reveal about Malcolm's character in lines 58–66?*

Vocabulary

avarice (av′ ər is) *n.* greed

---

59 Sudden: violent.

64 continent: restraining. **would o'erbear:** would be overwhelmed.

66 Boundless intemperance: unrestrained lust.
67 nature: human nature.

71 Convey . . . plenty: secretly indulge your pleasures in great abundance.
72 cold: lacking in sexual desire. **the time . . . hoodwink:** In this way you may blindfold the age.

77 affection: character.

80 his: one man's.

86 summer-seeming: youthful, transitory.
87 sword: cause of overthrow.
88 foisons: abundant supplies.
89 Of . . . own: merely from your royal property.
89–90 All . . . weighed: All of these flaws are bearable when balanced against other virtuous qualities.

95 relish: trace.
96 division . . . crime: different forms of each particular crime.

Caregg Cennen Castle. John Samuel Raven (1829–1877). Oil on canvas, 42½ x 62¾ in. Private collection.

Viewing the Art: How would you describe the mood of this painting? How does it compare to the mood of this act?

        Pour the sweet milk of concord into hell,
        Uproar the universal peace, confound°

100   All unity on earth.

    MACDUFF.   O Scotland, Scotland!

    MALCOLM. If such a one be fit to govern, speak:
    I am as I have spoken.

    MACDUFF.   Fit to govern!
    No, not to live. O nation miserable!
    With an untitled° tyrant bloody-sceptered,

105   When shalt thou see thy wholesome days again,
    Since that the truest issue° of thy throne
    By his own interdiction° stands accursed,
    And does blaspheme his breed?° Thy royal father
    Was a most sainted king: the queen that bore thee,

110   Oft'ner upon her knees than on her feet,
    Died every day she lived.° Fare thee well!
    These evils thou repeat'st upon thyself
    Hath banished me from Scotland. O my breast,
    Thy hope ends here!

99 confound: destroy.

104 untitled: having no right to the throne.

106 issue: offspring.
107 interdiction: declaration against himself.
108 blaspheme . . . breed: slander his ancestry.

109–111 the queen . . . lived: Macduff says that Malcolm's mother lived every day as if preparing for heaven, spending more time on her knees in prayer than on her feet.

Literary Element   **Plot** *Why does Macduff describe Malcolm's parents this way?*

MALCOLM.   Macduff, this noble passion,
115   Child of integrity, hath from my soul
       Wiped the black scruples, reconciled my thoughts
       To thy good truth and honor. Devilish Macbeth
       By many of these trains° hath sought to win me
       Into his power; and modest wisdom° plucks me
120   From over-credulous haste: but God above
       Deal between thee and me! For even now
       I put myself to thy direction, and
       Unspeak mine own detraction;° here abjure
       The taints and blames I laid upon myself,
125   For° strangers to my nature. I am yet
       Unknown to woman, never was forsworn,°
       Scarcely have coveted what was mine own,
       At no time broke my faith, would not betray
       The devil to his fellow, and delight
130   No less in truth than life. My first false speaking
       Was this upon myself. What I am truly,
       Is thine and my poor country's to command:
       Whither indeed, before thy here-approach,°
       Old Siward,° with ten thousand warlike men,
135   Already at a point,° was setting forth.
       Now we'll together, and the chance of goodness
       Be like our warranted quarrel!° Why are you silent?

MACDUFF.   Such welcome and unwelcome things at once
       'Tis hard to reconcile.

[An ENGLISH DOCTOR enters.]

140   MALCOLM.   Well, more anon. Comes the King forth,
              I pray you?

DOCTOR.   Ay, sir. There are a crew of wretched souls
       That stay his cure:° their malady convinces
       The great assay of art;° but at his touch,
       Such sanctity hath heaven given his hand,
145   They presently amend.°

MALCOLM.   I thank you, doctor.

[The DOCTOR exits.]

MACDUFF.   What's the disease he means?

MALCOLM.   'Tis called the evil:°
       A most miraculous work in this good King,
       Which often since my here-remain° in England

---

118 **trains:** lures, traps.
119 **modest wisdom:** prudence.

123 **mine own detraction:** my
slander of myself.

125 **For:** as.
126 **was forsworn:** broke my oath.

133 **here-approach:** arrival.
134 **Old Siward:** the Earl of
Northumberland (general of the English
forces).
135 **at a point:** in readiness.
136–137 **we'll . . . quarrel:** We will go
forth together, and may our chance of
success be equal to the justness of our
cause.

142 **stay his cure:** wait to be healed by
him (Edward the Confessor was reputed
to have special healing powers).
142–143 **convinces . . . art:** defeats
the greatest efforts of medical science.
145 **presently amend:** recover
immediately.

146 **the evil:** scrofula, a skin disease
known as "the King's evil" because the
King's touch would supposedly cure it.
148 **here-remain:** stay here.

Literary Element   **Plot** *How does the dialogue between Macduff and Malcolm advance the plot?*

Big Idea   **A Bard for the Ages** *What does this ability suggest about how subjects should regard their king?*

I have seen him do. How he solicits heaven,
150 Himself best knows: but strangely visited people,
All swoll'n and ulcerous, pitiful to the eye,
The mere° despair of surgery, he cures,
Hanging a golden stamp° about their necks,
Put on with holy prayers: and 'tis spoken,
155 To the succeeding royalty he leaves
The healing benediction.° With this strange virtue°
He hath a heavenly gift of prophecy,
And sundry blessings hang about his throne
That speak him full of grace.

[*ROSS enters.*]

MACDUFF.   See, who comes here?

160 **MALCOLM.** My countryman; but yet I know him not.

MACDUFF. My ever gentle° cousin, welcome hither.

MALCOLM. I know him now: good God, betimes remove
The means that makes us strangers!

ROSS.   Sir, amen.

MACDUFF. Stands Scotland where it did?

ROSS.   Alas, poor country!
165 Almost afraid to know itself! It cannot
Be called our mother but our grave, where nothing
But who knows nothing is once seen to smile;°
Where sighs and groans, and shrieks that rend the air,
Are made, not marked; where violent sorrow seems
170 A modern ecstasy.° The dead man's knell
Is there scarce asked for who,° and good men's lives
Expire before the flowers in their caps,
Dying or ere they sicken.

MACDUFF.   O, relation
Too nice,° and yet too true!

MALCOLM.   What's the newest grief?

175 **ROSS.** That of an hour's age doth hiss the speaker;°
Each minute teems° a new one.

MACDUFF.   How does my wife?

ROSS. Why, well.

MACDUFF.   And all my children?

ROSS.   Well too.

MACDUFF. The tyrant has not battered at their peace?

ROSS. No; they were well at peace when I did leave 'em.

180 **MACDUFF.** Be not a niggard° of your speech: how goes 't?

ROSS. When I came hither to transport the tidings,
Which I have heavily borne, there ran a rumor
Of many worthy fellows that were out;°

152 **mere:** utter.
153 **stamp:** coin.

155–156 **To . . . benediction:** He will pass on the power of healing to his descendants.
156 **With . . . virtue:** in addition to this remarkable power.

161 **gentle:** noble.

166–167 **where . . . smile:** where no one ever smiles except for those who are oblivious to everything.

170 **modern ecstasy:** common emotion.
170–171 **The dead . . . who:** People rarely ask for whom the funeral bells toll (because they ring so often).

174 **nice:** exact, precisely detailed.

175 **That . . . speaker:** If one describes a tragedy that occurred an hour ago, listeners hiss because the news is so old.
176 **teems:** brings forth.

180 **niggard:** miser.

183 **out:** in open rebellion.

Which was to my belief witnessed the rather,
185 For that I saw the tyrant's power afoot.°
Now is the time of help. Your eye° in Scotland
Would create soldiers, make our women fight,
To doff° their dire distresses.

MALCOLM.   Be 't their comfort
We are coming thither. Gracious England hath
190 Lent us good Siward and ten thousand men;
An older and a better soldier none
That Christendom gives out.

ROSS.   Would I could answer
This comfort with the like! But I have words
That would be howled out in the desert air,
195 Where hearing should not latch° them.

MACDUFF.   What concern they?
The general cause or is it a fee-grief°
Due to some single breast?

ROSS.   No mind that's honest
But in it shares some woe, though the main part
Pertains to you alone.

MACDUFF.   If it be mine,
200 Keep it not from me, quickly let me have it.

ROSS. Let not your ears despise my tongue for ever,
Which shall possess them with the heaviest sound
That ever yet they heard.

MACDUFF.   Humh! I guess at it.

ROSS. Your castle is surprised; your wife and babes
205 Savagely slaughtered. To relate the manner,
Were, on the quarry° of these murdered deer,
To add the death of you.

MALCOLM.   Merciful heaven!
What, man! Ne'er pull your hat upon your brows;°
Give sorrow words. The grief that does not speak
210 Whispers the o'er-fraught heart,° and bids it break.

MACDUFF. My children too?

ROSS.   Wife, children, servants, all
That could be found.

MACDUFF.   And I must be from thence!
My wife killed too?

184–185 **Which . . . afoot:** which I am ready to believe because I saw Macbeth's forces on the march.
186 **Your eye:** the sight of you.
188 **doff:** put off.

195 **latch:** catch.

196 **fee-grief:** personal grief.

206 **quarry:** heap of game slain in a hunt.

208 **pull . . . brows:** a conventional gesture of grieving.

210 **Whispers . . . heart:** whispers to the overburdened heart.

Reading Strategy **Making and Verifying Predictions** *What do you predict Ross is going to reveal?*

Vocabulary

pertain (pər tān′) *v.* to be connected to or have relevance to

ROSS.   I have said.

MALCOLM.   Be comforted.
        Let's make us med'cines of our great revenge,
215   To cure this deadly grief.

        MACDUFF. He° has no children. All my pretty ones?
        Did you say all? O hell-kite!° All?
        What, all my pretty chickens and their dam°
        At one fell swoop?

220   MALCOLM. Dispute it° like a man.

        MACDUFF.   I shall do so;
        But I must also feel it as a man.
        I cannot but remember° such things were,
        That were most precious to me. Did heaven look on,
        And would not take their part? Sinful Macduff,
225   They were all struck for thee! Naught° that I am,
        Not for their own demerits but for mine
        Fell slaughter on their souls. Heaven rest them now!

        MALCOLM. Be this the whetstone of your sword. Let grief
        Convert to anger; blunt not the heart, enrage it.

230   MACDUFF. O, I could play the woman with mine eyes,
        And braggart with my tongue! But, gentle heavens,
        Cut short all intermission;° front to front°
        Bring thou this fiend of Scotland and myself;
        Within my sword's length set him. If he 'scape,
235   Heaven forgive him too!

        MALCOLM.   This time goes manly.
        Come, go we to the King. Our power is ready;
        Our lack is nothing but our leave.° Macbeth
        Is ripe for shaking, and the pow'rs above
        Put on their instruments.° Receive what cheer you may.
240   The night is long that never finds the day.

        [*They all exit.*]

216 He: may refer to Malcolm (who does not understand the depth of Macduff's grief because he has no children) or to Macbeth (who could not have performed such a deed if he had children).
217 hell-kite: infernal bird of prey.
218 dam: mother.
220 Dispute it: resist your grief.

222 but remember: help but remember that.

225 Naught: wicked man.

232 intermission: delay. **front to front:** face to face.

237 Our lack . . . leave: All we have left to do is take leave of the king.

239 Put . . . instruments: arm themselves.

Literary Element   Plot *Why does Macduff blame himself for the murder of his family?*

Reading Strategy   Making and Verifying Predictions *Do you think it is possible for Macbeth to escape punishment for his crimes? Explain.*

RESPONDING AND THINKING CRITICALLY

Respond

1. Which scene in this act did you find the most memorable? Why?

Recall and Interpret

2. (a)What information does Macbeth gather from the witches' apparitions? (b)How does this information spur Macbeth to commit more murders?

3. (a)Describe the characters of Lady Macduff and her son. (b)Why do you think Lady Macduff calls her husband a traitor and tells her son, ". . . your father's dead"?

4. (a)In scene 3, how does Malcolm test Macduff's loyalty? (b)What does this test tell you about Macduff and Malcolm?

Analyze and Evaluate

5. (a)How might the fate of Lady Macduff and her son affect an audience's opinion of Macbeth? (b)Do you think the murder of Macduff's son should take place offstage? Explain why or why not.

6. (a)In your opinion, to what extent are the witches responsible for Macbeth's moral decay? (b)How much of the responsibility falls on Macbeth himself? Explain.

Connect

7. **Big Idea** **A Bard for the Ages** As Malcolm points out, King Edward was believed to have "healing hands." Why might Shakespeare have focused upon Edward as a healer?

LITERARY ANALYSIS

Literary Element **Plot**

Several incidents make up the **plot** of a drama, which consists of a beginning, a middle, and an end.

1. How would you contrast Macbeth's meeting with the witches in this act with their first meeting on the heath?

2. Macduff is the thane who first discovers Duncan's murdered body. What events in the rising action transform him into a figure of nemesis, or retribution?

Learning for Life

Macbeth desperately wants to be king, but he proves himself to be unworthy of the position. In your opinion, which characters in the play (aside from Duncan) would actually be right for the job? Assess their qualifications by completing a chart like the one below. Who is the most qualified person?

Character	Skills	Personality

READING AND VOCABULARY

Reading Strategy **Making and Verifying Predictions**

Predicting gives you a reason to read: namely, to find out if your predictions match the events in the plot. Review the chart you made on page 369 and then answer the following questions.

1. Which of your predictions were accurate? Explain.

2. What do you predict will happen to Macbeth in Act 5? Why do you think so?

Vocabulary **Practice**

Practice with Synonyms Find the synonym for each vocabulary word listed in the first column. Use a dictionary or thesaurus if you need help.

1. avarice   **a.** covetousness   **b.** generosity

2. exploit   **a.** debate   **b.** action

3. pernicious   **a.** fatal   **b.** irritable

4. pertain   **a.** digress   **b.** relate

5. redress   **a.** compensate   **b.** overlook

Macbeth, *Act 5*

LITERATURE PREVIEW

Building Background

This act opens with a famous sleepwalking scene, a particular favorite of most actresses portraying Lady Macbeth. Somnambulism (**som nam′ byə li′ zəm**) is an abnormal condition of sleep in which actions such as walking are performed. Since sleepwalkers are not completely aware of their surroundings, they can easily injure themselves by falling down or bumping into things. When sleepwalkers later awaken, they may have little or no recollection of what they did while asleep. In adults, sleepwalking is considered symptomatic of a troubled personality. Shakespeare obviously knew about this condition and relished its theatrical possibilities. His depiction of Lady Macbeth's symptoms is medically accurate. These symptoms indicate that Lady Macbeth, formerly so commanding and calculating, now is haunted by guilt. As the Doctor observes, "Infected minds / To their deaf pillows will discharge their secrets."

Literary Element Tragedy

A **tragedy** is a literary work in which the main character, or hero, suffers a downfall as a result of a tragic flaw—a character weakness, an error in judgment, or forces beyond human control, such as fate. The **tragic hero** is usually a high-ranking character who ultimately gains some kind of insight into himself or herself even though he or she experiences defeat, and oftentimes death. *Macbeth* is considered to be one of Shakespeare's finest tragedies. As you read, think about the qualities of a tragedy that *Macbeth* reflects.

- See Literary Terms Handbook, p. R18.

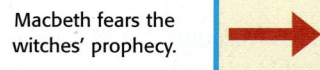 **Interactive Literary Elements Handbook** To review or learn more about the literary elements, go to www.glencoe.com.

READING PREVIEW

Reading Strategy Analyzing Cause-and-Effect Relationships

A **cause** is an action or event that makes something happen; an **effect** is the result of that action or event. You analyze cause-and-effect relationships whenever you try to answer the question "Why?"

Reading Tip: Noting Causes and Effects As you read, use a diagram to help you identify cause-and-effect relationships.

| Macbeth fears the witches' prophecy. | → | Macbeth orders the murderers to kill Fleance. |

Vocabulary

purge (purj) *n.* the process of getting rid of impurities or undesirable elements; p. 393 *The mayor organized a purge to rid the government of dishonest workers.*

antidote (an′ ti dōt′) *n.* a medicine used to counteract the effects of a poison; any counteracting remedy; p. 394 *He called the emergency room, seeking an antidote to the poison.*

siege (sēj) *n.* blockade; the surrounding of a fortified place by an opposing army intending to invade it; p. 396 *The siege of Troy continued for ten years before the Greeks captured the city.*

prowess (prou′ is) *n.* superior ability; skill; p. 401 *Pelé's prowess on the soccer field has earned him international acclaim.*

usurper (ū surp′ ər) *n.* one who seizes the power, position, or rights of another by force; p. 402 *The usurper forced the elected president from office, seizing control of the government.*

Vocabulary Tip: Context Clues You can often figure out the meaning of an unfamiliar word by looking for clues in the context.

OBJECTIVES
In studying this selection, you will focus on the following:
- analyzing literary periods
- understanding tragedy and the tragic hero
- analyzing cause-and-effect relationships

ACT 5

SCENE 1. MACBETH's castle at Dunsinane.

[*It is late at night in* MACBETH's *castle at Dunsinane. A* GENTLEWOMAN *who serves* LADY MACBETH *enters with a* SCOTTISH PHYSICIAN.]

DOCTOR. I have two nights watched° with you, but can perceive no truth in your report. When was it she last walked?°

GENTLEWOMAN. Since his Majesty went into the field,° I have
5   seen her rise from her bed, throw her nightgown upon her, unlock her closet,° take forth paper, fold it, write upon 't, read it, afterwards seal it, and again return to bed; yet all this while in a most fast sleep.

DOCTOR. A great perturbation in nature,° to receive at once
10   the benefit of sleep and do the effects of watching!° In this slumb'ry agitation, besides her walking and other actual performances, what, at any time, have you heard her say?

GENTLEWOMAN. That, sir, which I will not report after her.

15 **DOCTOR.** You may to me, and 'tis most meet° you should.

GENTLEWOMAN. Neither to you nor anyone, having no witness to confirm my speech.

[LADY MACBETH *enters, carrying a candlestick*.]

     Lo you, here she comes! This is her very guise,° and, upon my life, fast asleep! Observe her; stand close.°

20 **DOCTOR.** How came she by that light?

GENTLEWOMAN. Why, it stood by her. She has light by her continually. 'Tis her command.

[LADY MACBETH *moves across the stage, unaware that others are watching her*.]

DOCTOR. You see, her eyes are open.

GENTLEWOMAN. Ay, but their sense° are shut.

25 **DOCTOR.** What is it she does now? Look, how she rubs her hands.

GENTLEWOMAN. It is an accustomed action with her, to seem thus washing her hands: I have known her continue in this a quarter of an hour.

---

1 **watched:** stayed awake.

3 **walked:** sleepwalked.

4 **into the field:** joined the army on the battlefield.

6 **closet:** private cabinet.

9 **perturbation in nature:** disruption of natural functions.
10 **effects of watching:** actions one does while awake.

15 **meet:** proper.

18 **guise:** custom.
19 **close:** hidden.

24 **sense:** power of perception.

Reading Strategy   Analyzing Cause-and-Effect Relationships *Why has Macbeth gone into the field?*

Reading Strategy   Analyzing Cause-and-Effect Relationships *Why do you think Lady Macbeth goes through the motions of washing her hands while fast asleep?*

30   **LADY MACBETH.**   Yet here's a spot.

DOCTOR.   Hark! she speaks. I will set down what comes from her, to satisfy° my remembrance the more strongly.

LADY MACBETH.   [*She sets down the candlestick and rubs her hands as if she were washing them.*] Out, damned spot!
Out, I say! One: two: why, then 'tis time to do 't.° Hell
35   is murky. Fie, my lord, fie! A soldier, and afeard? What
need we fear who knows it, when none can call our
pow'r to accompt?° Yet who would have thought the old
man to have had so much blood in him?

DOCTOR.   Do you mark that?

40   **LADY MACBETH.**   The Thane of Fife had a wife. Where is she
now? What, will these hands ne'er be clean? No more o'
that, my lord, no more o' that! You mar all with this starting.°

DOCTOR.   Go to,° go to! You have known what you
should not.

45   **GENTLEWOMAN.**   She has spoke what she should not, I am sure
of that. Heaven knows what she has known.

LADY MACBETH.   Here's the smell of the blood still. ==All the
perfumes of Arabia will not sweeten this little hand.== Oh,
oh, oh!

50   **DOCTOR.**   What a sigh is there! The heart is sorely charged.°

GENTLEWOMAN.   I would not have such a heart in my bosom
for the dignity° of the whole body.

DOCTOR.   Well, well, well—

GENTLEWOMAN.   Pray God it be, sir.

55   **DOCTOR.**   This disease is beyond my practice. Yet I have
known those which have walked in their sleep who
have died holily in their beds.

LADY MACBETH.   Wash your hands; put on your nightgown;
look not so pale! I tell you yet again, Banquo's buried.
60   He cannot come out on 's° grave.

DOCTOR.   Even so?

LADY MACBETH.   To bed, to bed! There's knocking at the gate.
Come, come, come, come, give me your hand! What's
done cannot be undone. To bed, to bed, to bed!

[*LADY MACBETH exits.*]

65   **DOCTOR.**   Will she go now to bed?

GENTLEWOMAN.   Directly.

Big Idea   **A Bard for the Ages** *How does Shakespeare use this
image to reveal Lady Macbeth's change in character?*

---

32 satisfy: support.

34 One . . . do 't: Lady Macbeth, counting out the chimes of a clock, imagines it is the night when Duncan was murdered.
36–37 call . . . accompt: force anyone as powerful as us to answer for our crimes.

42 starting: sudden fits.

43 Go to: an exclamation expressing disapproval (addressed to Lady Macbeth).

50 charged: burdened.

52 dignity: worth.

60 on 's: of his.

Lady Macbeth Sleepwalking, 1784. Henry Fuseli. Oil on canvas, 87 x 63 in. Louvre Museum, Paris.

Viewing the Art: What does Lady Macbeth's expression tell you about her emotional state?

DOCTOR. Foul whisp'rings are abroad. Unnatural deeds
Do breed unnatural troubles. Infected minds
To their deaf pillows will discharge their secrets.
70 More needs she the divine° than the physician.
God, God forgive us all! Look after her;
Remove from her the means of all annoyance,°
And still° keep eyes upon her. So good night.
My mind she has mated° and amazed my sight:
75 I think, but dare not speak.

GENTLEWOMAN.   Good night, good doctor.

[*They exit.*]

SCENE 2. In the countryside, near Dunsinane.

[*Soldiers enter with the Scottish noblemen* MENTEITH, CAITHNESS, ANGUS, *and* LENNOX. *The soldiers are carrying drums and flags. They are all on the way to join forces with an approaching English army to rebel against* MACBETH.]

MENTEITH. The English pow'r° is near, led on by Malcolm,
His uncle Siward and the good Macduff.
Revenges burn in them; for their dear causes
Would to the bleeding and the grim alarm
5 Excite the mortified man.°

ANGUS.   Near Birnam Wood
Shall we well° meet them; that way are they coming.

CAITHNESS. Who knows if Donalbain be with his brother?

LENNOX. For certain, sir, he is not. I have a file°
Of all the gentry: there is Siward's son,
10 And many unrough° youths that even now
Protest their first of manhood.°

MENTEITH.   What does the tyrant?

CAITHNESS. Great Dunsinane he strongly fortifies.
Some say he's mad; others, that lesser hate him,
Do call it valiant fury: but, for certain,
15 He cannot buckle his distempered cause
Within the belt of rule.°

ANGUS.   Now does he feel
His secret murders sticking on his hands;
Now minutely revolts upbraid his faith-breach.°
Those he commands move only in command,
20 Nothing in love. Now does he feel his title
Hang loose about him, like a giant's robe
Upon a dwarfish thief.

Literary Element   **Tragedy** *What does Angus's comment reveal about Macbeth?*

---

70 **divine:** priest.

72 **annoyance:** injury.
73 **still:** always.
74 **mated:** bewildered.

1 **pow'r:** army.

3–5 **their dear . . . man:** Their grave cause would arouse a dead man to bloodshed and grim warfare.
6 **well:** no doubt.

8 **file:** list.

10 **unrough:** beardless.
11 **Protest . . . manhood:** proclaim the beginning of their manhood.

15–16 **He . . . rule:** Like a man who cannot buckle his belt because he is bloated with disease, Macbeth cannot impose order on his diseased cause.
18 **minutely . . . faith-breach:** Revolts occurring every minute upbraid his disloyalty.

MENTEITH.   Who then shall blame
His pestered° senses to recoil and start,
When all that is within him does condemn
25   Itself for being there?

CAITHNESS.   Well, march we on,
To give obedience where 'tis truly owed.
Meet we the med'cine of the sickly weal,°
And with him pour we, in our country's **purge**,
Each drop of us.°

LENNOX.   Or so much as it needs
30   To dew the sovereign flower and drown the weeds.°
Make we our march towards Birnam.

[*They march off.*]

SCENE 3. The castle at Dunsinane.

[MACBETH, *the* DOCTOR, *and attendants enter a room in Dunsinane Castle.*]

MACBETH.   Bring me no more reports; let them fly all!°
Till Birnam Wood remove to Dunsinane
I cannot taint° with fear. What's the boy Malcolm?
Was he not born of woman? The spirits that know
5   All mortal consequences° have pronounced me thus:
"Fear not, Macbeth; no man that's born of woman
Shall e'er have power upon thee." Then fly, false thanes,
And mingle with the English epicures.°
The mind I sway by° and the heart I bear
10   Shall never sag with doubt nor shake with fear.

[*A* SERVANT *enters.*]

The devil damn thee black, thou cream-faced loon!°
Where got'st thou that goose look?

SERVANT.   There is ten thousand—

MACBETH.   Geese, villain?

SERVANT.   Soldiers, sir.

MACBETH.   Go prick thy face and over-red thy fear,°
15   Thou lily-livered boy. What soldiers, patch?°
Death of thy soul! Those linen° cheeks of thine
Are counselors to fear.° What soldiers, whey-face?

---

23 **pestered:** troubled.

27 **med'cine . . . weal:** physician of our ailing commonwealth (Malcolm).

28–29 **pour . . . us:** Let us shed all our blood to restore Scotland's health.

30 **To . . . weeds:** to water the royal flower (Malcolm) and drown the evil (Macbeth).

1 **let . . . all:** Let all of the thanes desert me.

3 **taint:** become infected.

5 **All mortal consequences:** everything that will happen to human beings.

8 **epicures:** gluttons (The Scots, who typically ate plain food, often disapproved of English eating habits.)
9 **I sway by:** that directs me.

11 **loon:** stupid fellow.

14 **over-red thy fear:** cover your white-faced fear with redness.
15 **patch:** fool.
16 **linen:** pale as linen.
17 **Are . . . fear:** advise others to be afraid.

Literary Element   Tragedy *Which of Macbeth's qualities does this passage reveal?*

Vocabulary

purge (purj) *n.* the process of getting rid of impurities or undesirable elements

SERVANT. The English force, so please you.

MACBETH. Take thy face hence.

[*The SERVANT exits.*]

                            Seyton!°—I am sick at heart,
20   When I behold—Seyton, I say!—This push°
      Will cheer me ever, or disseat° me now.
      I have lived long enough. My way of life
      Is fall'n into the sear,° the yellow leaf,
      And that which should accompany old age,
25   As° honor, love, obedience, troops of friends,
      I must not look to have; but, in their stead,
      Curses not loud but deep, mouth-honor,° breath,
      Which the poor heart would fain° deny, and dare not.
      Seyton!

[*SEYTON enters.*]

30   SEYTON. What's your gracious pleasure?

MACBETH.   What news more?

SEYTON. All is confirmed, my lord, which was reported.

MACBETH. I'll fight, till from my bones my flesh be hacked.
      Give me my armor.

SEYTON.   'Tis not needed yet.

MACBETH. I'll put it on.
35   Send out moe° horses, skirr° the country round.
      Hang those that talk of fear. Give me mine armor.
      How does your patient, doctor?

DOCTOR.   Not so sick, my lord,
      As she is troubled with thick-coming fancies
      That keep her from her rest.

MACBETH.   Cure her of that.
40   Canst thou not minister to a mind diseased,
      Pluck from the memory a rooted sorrow,
      Raze out° the written troubles of the brain,
      And with some sweet oblivious **antidote**
      Cleanse the stuffed bosom of that perilous stuff
45   Which weighs upon the heart?

DOCTOR.   Therein the patient
      Must minister to himself.

19 **Seyton:** Macbeth's trusted officer.
20 **push:** effort.
21 **disseat:** dethrone.

23 **the sear:** a withered state.

25 **As:** such as.

27 **mouth-honor:** lip service.
28 **fain:** gladly.

35 **moe:** more. **skirr:** scour.

42 **Raze out:** erase.

Literary Element   Tragedy *How do these lines reinforce Macbeth's stature as a hero?*

Vocabulary

antidote (an′ ti dōt′) *n.* a medicine used to counteract the effects of a poison; any counteracting remedy

MACBETH. Throw physic° to the dogs, I'll none of it.
Come, put mine armor on. Give me my staff.
Seyton, send out—Doctor, the thanes fly from me—

50 Come, sir, dispatch.° If thou couldst, doctor, cast
The water of my land,° find her disease
And purge it to a sound and pristine health,
I would applaud thee to the very echo,
That should applaud again—Pull 't off,° I say—

55 What rhubarb, senna,° or what purgative drug,
Would scour these English hence? Hear'st thou of them?

DOCTOR. Ay, my good lord; your royal preparation
Makes us hear something.

MACBETH.   Bring it° after me.
I will not be afraid of death and bane°

60 Till Birnam Forest come to Dunsinane.

DOCTOR. [*Aside.*] Were I from Dunsinane away and clear,
Profit again should hardly draw me here.

[*They exit.*]

SCENE 4. In the countryside, near Birnam Wood.

[*A group of soldiers and noblemen enter marching. Among them are a drummer, flagbearer,* MALCOLM, MACDUFF, MENTEITH, CAITHNESS, ANGUS, *and* SIWARD, *the general sent by the King of England, and his son,* YOUNG SIWARD.]

MALCOLM. Cousins, I hope the days are near at hand
That chambers will be safe.°

MENTEITH.   We doubt it nothing.°

SIWARD. What wood is this before us?

MENTEITH.   The Wood of Birnam.

MALCOLM. Let every soldier hew him down a bough
5 And bear 't before him. Thereby shall we shadow°
The numbers of our host,° and make discovery°
Err in report of us.

SOLDIERS.   It shall be done.

SIWARD. We learn no other but° the confident tyrant
Keeps still in Dunsinane, and will endure
10 Our setting down before 't.°

47 **physic:** medicine.

50 **dispatch:** be quick (addressed to an attendant).
50–51 **cast . . . land:** diagnose the ailment of my country.

54 **Pull 't off:** remove this piece of armor (which was put on incorrectly).
55 **senna:** a purgative drug.

58 **it:** the rest of his armor.
59 **bane:** destruction.

2 **That . . . safe:** when we may be safe in our bedchambers. **nothing:** not at all.

5 **shadow:** conceal.
6 **host:** army. **discovery:** Macbeth's scouts.

8 **no other but:** only that.

9–10 **will . . . 't:** will not try to prevent us from laying siege to it.

Reading Strategy Analyzing Cause-and-Effect Relationships *Why does Macbeth not fear the forces aligned against him?*

Reading Strategy Analyzing Cause-and-Effect Relationships *How will this action reveal the flaw in Macbeth's interpretation of the witches' prophecy?*

MALCOLM.   'Tis his main hope,
For where there is advantage to be given
Both more and less° have given him the revolt,
And none serve with him but constrainèd things°
Whose hearts are absent too.

MACDUFF.   Let our just censures
15   Attend the true event,° and put we on
Industrious soldiership.

SIWARD.   The time approaches,
That will with due decision make us know
What we shall say we have and what we owe.°
Thoughts speculative their unsure hopes relate,
20   But certain issue strokes must arbitrate:°
Towards which advance the war.°

[*They march off.*]

SCENE 5. The castle at Dunsinane.

[*Inside Dunsinane Castle,* MACBETH, SEYTON, *and other soldiers, including a drummer and flagbearer, prepare for battle.*]

MACBETH.   Hang out our banners on the outward walls.
The cry is still "They come!" Our castle's strength
Will laugh a **siege** to scorn. Here let them lie
Till famine and the ague° eat them up.
5   Were they not forced with those that should be ours,°
We might have met them dareful,° beard to beard,
And beat them backward home.

[*A cry is heard within the castle.*]

                                        What is that noise?

SEYTON.   It is the cry of women, my good lord.

[*SEYTON exits.*]

MACBETH.   I have almost forgot the taste of fears:
10   The time has been, my senses would have cooled
To hear a night-shriek, and my fell of hair°
Would at a dismal treatise° rouse and stir
As life were in 't. I have supped full with horrors.
Direness,° familiar to my slaughterous thoughts,
15   Cannot once start me.

Reading Strategy   Analyzing Cause-and-Effect Relationships   *How have Macbeth's crimes affected his conscience?*

Vocabulary

siege (sēj) *n.* blockade; the surrounding of a fortified place by an opposing army intending to invade it

---

Side notes (right column):

12 **more and less:** noblemen and commoners.
13 **constrainèd things:** people who have no choice.

14–15 **Let . . . event:** Let us reserve our judgment of this matter until the battle is over.

17–18 **with due . . . owe:** distinguish our claims from what we really own.

19–20 **Thoughts . . . arbitrate:** Speculation may express unsure hopes, but certain outcomes must be decided in battle.
21 **war:** army.

4 **ague:** fever.
5 **forced . . . ours:** reinforced with deserters or rebels.
6 **met them dareful:** confronted them defiantly.

11 **my . . . hair:** the hair on my scalp.
12 **dismal treatise:** dreadful story.

14 **Direness:** horror.

The Death of Lady Macbeth. Dante Charles Gabriel Rossetti. Pen and ink on paper, 30.7 x 35.8 cm. Ashmolean Museum, University of Oxford, UK.

[*SEYTON returns.*]

Wherefore was that cry?

SEYTON. The Queen, my lord, is dead.

MACBETH. She should have died hereafter;°
There would have been a time for such a word.°
Tomorrow, and tomorrow, and tomorrow
20 Creeps in this petty pace from day to day,
To the last syllable of recorded time;
And all our yesterdays have lighted fools
The way° to dusty death. Out, out, brief candle!
Life's but a walking shadow,° a poor player
25 That struts and frets his hour upon the stage
And then is heard no more. It is a tale
Told by an idiot, full of sound and fury
Signifying nothing.

[*A MESSENGER enters.*]

Thou com'st to use thy tongue; thy story quickly!

30 **MESSENGER.** Gracious my lord,
I should report that which I say I saw,
But know not how to do 't.

17 **She . . . hereafter:** She should have died at a later time (not when I'm preoccupied with urgent matters).
18 **word:** message that the queen is dead.

22–23 **lighted . . . way:** illuminated the path that fools take.
24 **shadow:** insubstantial image, actor.

Literary Element **Tragedy** *What does this comparison suggest about Macbeth's view of life?*

MACBETH. Well, say, sir.

MESSENGER. As I did stand my watch upon the hill,
I looked toward Birnam, and anon, methought,
35   The wood began to move.

MACBETH. Liar and slave!

MESSENGER. Let me endure your wrath, if 't be not so.
Within this three mile may you see it coming;
I say a moving grove.

MACBETH. If thou speak'st false,
Upon the next tree shalt thou hang alive,
40   Till famine cling° thee. If thy speech be sooth,°
I care not if thou dost for me as much.
I pull in resolution,° and begin
To doubt th' equivocation of the fiend
That lies like truth:° "Fear not, till Birnam Wood
45   Do come to Dunsinane!" And now a wood
Comes toward Dunsinane. Arm, arm, and out!
If this which he avouches° does appear,
There is nor flying hence nor° tarrying here.
I 'gin to be aweary of the sun,
50   And wish th' estate° o' th' world were now undone.
Ring the alarum bell! Blow wind, come wrack!°
At least we'll die with harness° on our back.

[*They all exit.*]

SCENE 6. In the countryside, near the castle at Dunsinane.

[*MALCOLM, SIWARD, MACDUFF, and their soldiers, hidden by the tree boughs they are carrying, advance toward Dunsinane Castle.*]

MALCOLM. Now near enough. Your leavy° screens throw
     down,
And show like those you are. You, worthy uncle,°
Shall, with my cousin, your right noble son,
Lead our first battle.° Worthy Macduff and we
5   Shall take upon 's what else remains to do,
According to our order.

SIWARD. Fare you well.
Do we but find the tyrant's power° tonight,
Let us be beaten, if we cannot fight.

MACDUFF. Make all our trumpets speak; give them all breath,
10   Those clamorous harbingers° of blood and death.

[*Blaring trumpets and the sound of battle are heard as they exit.*]

---

40 cling: wither. **sooth:** the truth.

42 pull in resolution: restrain my confidence.

43–44 doubt . . . truth: mistrust the deceptive language of the devil, who tells apparent truths in order to deceive.

47 he avouches: the Messenger assures is true.

48 nor . . . nor: neither . . . nor.

50 estate: established order.
51 wrack: ruin.
52 harness: armor.

1 leavy: leafy.

2 uncle: Siward.

4 battle: battalion.

7 power: forces.

10 harbingers: forerunners announcing someone's approach.

Literary Element   Tragedy *What does this speech reveal about Macbeth's character?*

SCENE 7. In the countryside, near the castle at Dunsinane.

[*On another part of the battlefield outside the castle,* MACBETH *enters.*]

> MACBETH. They have tied me to a stake; I cannot fly,
> But bearlike, I must fight the course.° What's he
> That was not born of woman? Such a one
> Am I to fear, or none.

[*YOUNG SIWARD enters and challenges MACBETH.*]

5   YOUNG SIWARD. What is thy name?

> MACBETH.   Thou'lt be afraid to hear it.

> YOUNG SIWARD. No; though thou call'st thyself a hotter name
> Than any is in hell.

> MACBETH.   My name's Macbeth.

> YOUNG SIWARD. The devil himself could not pronounce a title
> More hateful to mine ear.

> MACBETH.   No, nor more fearful.

10   YOUNG SIWARD. Thou liest, abhorrèd tyrant; with my sword
> I'll prove the lie thou speak'st.

[*They fight, and* YOUNG SIWARD *is slain.*]

> MACBETH.   Thou wast born of woman.
> But swords I smile at, weapons laugh to scorn,
> Brandished by man that's of a woman born.

[*MACBETH exits as the sounds of battle mount.* MACDUFF *enters.*]

> MACDUFF. That way the noise is. Tyrant, show thy face!
15   If thou be'st slain and with no stroke of mine,
> My wife and children's ghosts will haunt me still.°
> I cannot strike at wretched kerns,° whose arms
> Are hired to bear their staves.° Either thou, Macbeth,
> Or else my sword, with an unbattered edge,
20   I sheathe again undeeded.° There thou shouldst be;
> By this great clatter, one of greatest note
> Seems bruited.° Let me find him, Fortune!
> And more I beg not.

[*More battle sounds are heard as* MACDUFF *exits.* MALCOLM *and* OLD SIWARD *enter.*]

> SIWARD. This way, my lord. The castle's gently rend'red:°
25   The tyrant's people on both sides do fight;
> The noble thanes do bravely in the war;

---

2 **bearlike . . . course:** Like a bear tied to a stake, I must fight off this round of attack. (Macbeth's metaphor refers to bear-baiting, a popular entertainment in which bears were tied to stakes and surrounded by vicious dogs.)

16 **still:** always.
17 **kerns:** hired Irish soldiers.
18 **bear their staves:** carry their spears.

20 **undeeded:** unused.

21–22 **By this . . . bruited:** The noise seems to announce the presence of someone of the highest rank.

24 **gently rend'red:** surrendered without resistance.

Literary Element **Tragedy** *What does Macbeth suggest about himself in this passage?*

Big Idea **A Bard for the Ages** *How does Shakespeare set apart Macduff's motives from those of Macbeth's other opponents?*

The day almost itself professes yours,
And little is to do.

MALCOLM.   We have met with foes
That strike beside us.°

SIWARD.   Enter, sir, the castle.

[*They exit as the sounds of battle continue.*]

29 **strike beside us:** fight on our side.

SCENE 8. Near the castle at Dunsinane.

[*MACBETH enters in another part of the battlefield, still ready to fight to the end despite overwhelming opposition.*]

MACBETH.   Why should I play the Roman fool, and die
On mine own sword?° Whiles I see lives,° the gashes
Do better upon them.

[*MACDUFF enters.*]

1–2 **play . . . sword:** commit suicide like a Roman was supposed to do when faced with defeat. **lives:** other living beings.

MACDUFF.   Turn, hell-hound, turn!

MACBETH.   Of all men else I have avoided thee.
5   But get thee back! My soul is too much charged°
With blood of thine already.

5 **charged:** burdened.

MACDUFF.   I have no words:
My voice is in my sword, thou bloodier villain
Than terms can give thee out!°

[*They fight.*]

8 **Than . . . out:** than words can describe.

MACBETH.   Thou losest labor:
As easy mayst thou the intrenchant air
10   With thy keen sword impress as make me bleed:°
Let fall thy blade on vulnerable crests;
I bear a charmèd life, which must not yield
To one of woman born.

9–10 **As easy . . . bleed:** You can as easily mark the invulnerable air with your sword as make me bleed.

MACDUFF.   Despair° thy charm,
And let the angel° whom thou still hast served
15   Tell thee, Macduff was from his mother's womb
Untimely ripped.°

13 **Despair:** lose hope in.
14 **angel:** fallen angel, demon.

MACBETH.   Accursèd be that tongue that tells me so,
For it hath cowed my better part of man!°
And be these juggling fiends no more believed,
20   That palter° with us in a double sense;
That keep the word of promise to our ear,
And break it to our hope. I'll not fight with thee.

15–16 Macduff tells Macbeth that he was prematurely removed from his mother's womb (presumably because she died) and therefore is not "of woman born."
18 **cowed . . . man:** intimidated my courage.
20 **palter:** use trickery.

MACDUFF.   Then yield thee, coward,
And live to be the show and gaze o' th' time:°

24 **show . . . time:** spectacle of the age.

Literary Element   **Tragedy** *Does Macbeth feel remorse for having murdered Macduff's family? Explain.*

25 We'll have thee, as our rarer monsters are,
    Painted upon a pole,° and underwrit,
    "Here may you see the tyrant."

MACBETH.   I will not yield,
    To kiss the ground before young Malcolm's feet,
    And to be baited° with the rabble's curse.
30 Though Birnam Wood be come to Dunsinane,
    And thou opposed,° being of no woman born,
    Yet I will try the last.° Before my body
    I throw my warlike shield. Lay on, Macduff;
    And damned be him that first cries "Hold, enough!"

[*They exit, fighting. More trumpet blasts and battle cries are heard. They reenter fighting, and* MACBETH *is slain.* MACDUFF *removes* MACBETH's *body. After he leaves,* MALCOLM, OLD SIWARD, ROSS, *various thanes and soldiers, including a drummer and flagbearer, enter.*]

35 MALCOLM. I would the friends we miss were safe arrived.

    SIWARD. Some must go off;° and yet, by these I see,
        So great a day as this is cheaply bought.

    MALCOLM. Macduff is missing, and your noble son.

    ROSS. Your son, my lord, has paid a soldier's debt:
40   He only lived but till he was a man;
        The which no sooner had his **prowess** confirmed
        In the unshrinking station where he fought,
        But like a man he died.°

    SIWARD.   Then he is dead?

    ROSS. Ay, and brought off the field. Your cause of sorrow
45   Must not be measured by his worth, for then
        It hath no end.

    SIWARD.   Had he his hurts before?°

    ROSS. Ay, on the front.

    SIWARD.   Why then, God's soldier be he!
        Had I as many sons as I have hairs,
        I would not wish them to a fairer death:
50   And so his knell is knolled.

    MALCOLM.   He's worth more sorrow,
        And that I'll spend for him.

    SIWARD.   He's worth no more:
        They say he parted well and paid his score:
        And so God be with him! Here comes newer comfort.

Literary Element Tragedy *What is your final impression of Macbeth?*

Vocabulary

prowess (prou′ is) *n.* superior ability; skill

Side notes:

25–26 We'll . . . pole: Macduff says that Macbeth will be treated like a sideshow freak, with his picture displayed on a pole to attract spectators.

29 baited: taunted.

31 opposed: opposing me.
32 try the last: try my fate to the end.

36 go off: die.

41–43 The which . . . died: He died just as he had confirmed his manhood through his steadfast fighting.

46 hurts before: wounds on the front of his body (received while facing the enemy).

Group of musicians preceding the celebratory procession (detail). 14th–15th Century. Artist Unknown. Fresco. Castello di Manta Asti, Italy.

[MACDUFF *enters with* MACBETH's *head.*]

MACDUFF. Hail, King! for so thou art: behold, where stands
55 Th' **usurper's** cursèd head. The time is free.°
I see thee compassed with thy kingdom's pearl,°
That speak my salutation in their minds,
Whose voices I desire aloud with mine:
Hail, King of Scotland!

ALL. Hail, King of Scotland!

[*There is a trumpet flourish.*]

60 **MALCOLM.** We shall not spend a large expense of time
Before we reckon with your several loves,°
And make us even with you. My thanes and kinsmen,
Henceforth be earls, the first that ever Scotland
In such an honor named. What's more to do,
65 Which would be planted newly with the time°—
As calling home our exiled friends abroad
That fled the snares of watchful tyranny,
Producing forth the cruel ministers°
Of this dead butcher and his fiendlike queen,
70 Who, as 'tis thought, by self and violent hands
Took off her life—this, and what needful else
That calls upon us, by the grace of Grace°
We will perform in measure, time, and place:°
So thanks to all at once and to each one,
75 Whom we invite to see us crowned at Scone.

[*They all exit to a flourish of trumpets.*]

55 **The time is free:** Our age is liberated from tyranny.
56 **compassed . . . pearl:** surrounded by the noblest in the kingdom.

61 **reckon . . . loves:** count up the acts of friendship that each of you has performed and reward your loyalty.

64–65 **What's . . . time:** what remains to be done at the beginning of this new era.

68 **producing . . . ministers:** bringing to justice the cruel agents.

72 **Grace:** God.
73 **in . . . place:** with restraint and in the appropriate time and place.

Literary Element Tragedy *What is the resolution of this tragedy?*

Vocabulary

usurper (ū surp′ ər) *n.* one who seizes the power, position, or rights of another by force

RESPONDING AND THINKING CRITICALLY

Respond

1. Was the ending of *Macbeth* what you thought it would be? Explain why or why not.

Recall and Interpret

2. (a)Summarize the statements Lady Macbeth makes while sleepwalking. (b)What does she say that incriminates her and Macbeth in the murders?

3. (a)What does the sleepwalking scene reveal about Lady Macbeth's state of mind? (b)What might Lady Macbeth's hand movements mean?

4. (a)How do Caithness and Angus describe Macbeth's state of mind? (b)What does Macbeth say and do in Act 5 that confirms their descriptions?

Analyze and Evaluate

5. (a)How does Macbeth react when he is told that his wife is dead? (b)What metaphors does Macbeth use in his soliloquy after her death? (c)What do these metaphors reveal about Macbeth's state of mind?

6. Do Macbeth and Lady Macbeth exchange personalities as the play progresses? Use evidence from the play to support your opinion.

7. (a)Describe how the Apparitions' prophecies are fulfilled in Act 5. (b)What dramatic function do these prophecies serve in Acts 4 and 5? (c)How would the acts change if the prophecies were omitted?

Connect

8. **Big Idea** **A Bard for the Ages** Poet and playwright Ben Jonson, a contemporary of Shakespeare's, wrote that Shakespeare was "not of an age, but for all time." In your opinion, what does *Macbeth* have to offer today's audiences? Explain.

DAILY LIFE AND CULTURE

Eleventh-Century Scotland

During the Middle Ages, the period in which *Macbeth* is set, society in Scotland was organized under the feudal system. The king awarded land grants, or fiefs, to important nobles in return for their pledge of a specified number of armed soldiers in times of war. Fiefdoms, or manors, consisted of a castle, a church, a village, and the surrounding farmland.

Most medieval houses consisted of one or two rooms with thatched roofs and dirt floors. They were dark, damp, and cold places. In the center of one room, a fire blazing in an open hearth provided warmth. Windows, which were small openings without glass, had wooden shutters that were put up at night or in foul weather.

Life in a castle revolved around a great hall, a large one-room structure with a high ceiling. At the end of the hall opposite the main entrance was a raised platform, or dais, where the nobles reclined. In early times the nobles slept in the hall behind the dais, with curtains or screens separating their sleeping quarters.

Kitchens were separate rooms or separate buildings, and bathrooms—if they were indoors—contained chamber pots or latrines that opened directly into a moat or river or onto the ground outside.

Partner Activity With a classmate, answer the following questions.

1. What was life like in a Scottish manor?

2. What distinguished the upper classes from the lower classes in medieval Scotland?

Conway Castle, 19th Century.

LITERARY ANALYSIS

Literary Element **Tragedy**

Traditionally, the **tragic hero** is a person of high rank who, out of hubris, or an exaggerated sense of power and pride, violates a human, natural, or divine law. By breaking that law, the hero poses a threat to society, causing the suffering or death of family members, friends, and associates. In the last act of a traditional tragedy, the tragic hero is punished, and order is restored.

1. In your opinion, what causes Macbeth's downfall— a tragic flaw, errors in judgment, forces beyond his control, or a combination of these factors? Support your opinion with evidence from the play.

2. Do you think Macbeth's death sets everything right again? Give reasons for your opinion.

3. Is Lady Macbeth also a tragic hero? Why or why not?

Review: Irony

As you learned on page 116, **irony** is a contrast or a discrepancy between expectation and reality. Irony can take several forms: **verbal irony** occurs when a person says one thing while meaning another; **situational irony** exists when the outcome of a situation is the opposite of what someone expected; **dramatic irony** occurs when the audience or reader knows something that the characters do not know.

Partner Activity Meet with a classmate to discuss Shakespeare's use of irony in *Macbeth*. Use a diagram like the one below to record examples of irony.

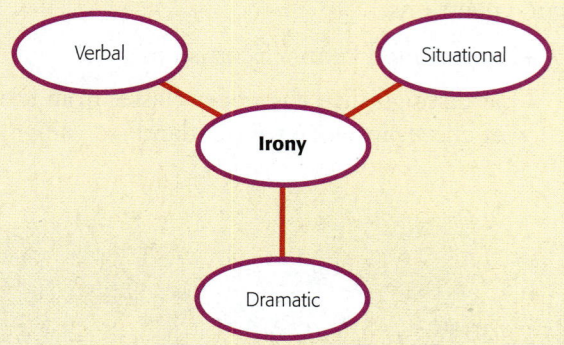

READING AND VOCABULARY

Reading Strategy **Analyzing Cause-and-Effect Relationships**

By determining why something occurred and what happened as a result, you can more effectively interpret, analyze, and evaluate events in the plot. Review the diagram you created on page 388 and then answer the following questions.

1. According to the Doctor, what is the cause of Lady Macbeth's mental breakdown?

2. Ultimately, what effect does Duncan produce by naming his son Malcolm heir to the throne?

Vocabulary **Practice**

Practice with Context Clues Choose the vocabulary word that best fits each sentence.

1. José's _____ in spelling amazed his class.
   a. antidote   **b.** prowess   **c.** siege

2. We must search for the _____ to counter the venom of that snakebite.
   a. usurper   **b.** purge   **c.** antidote

3. The family of the company's deceased president accused his power-hungry successor of being a/an _____.
   a. usurper   **b.** antidote   **c.** siege

4. The invaders laid _____ to the castle, hoping to force its inhabitants to surrender.
   a. prowess   **b.** siege   **c.** purge

5. The dictator planned a/an _____ to eliminate his political foes.
   a. purge   **b.** siege   **c.** antidote

Academic Vocabulary

Here is a word from the vocabulary list on page R82.

react (rē akt´) *v.* to respond to a stimulus; to be affected by an event, influence, etc.

Practice and Apply
How do Macbeth's followers **react** to the news that the English army has surrounded Dunsinane?

Writing About Literature

Respond to Character Many of Shakespeare's tragic heroes utter magnificent dying speeches that convey truths about life and death. Macbeth is not given that opportunity, but you can write a speech for him. If you wish, try to imitate Shakespeare's style of **blank verse**, or lines written in unrhymed iambic pentameter.

First, imagine the confrontation: Macbeth and Macduff are fighting fiercely with their swords. Macduff inflicts a final blow and then pauses, realizing that Macbeth is mortally wounded. What might Macbeth then say? Here are some possible questions that Macbeth might address:

- What were his hopes and dreams? What were his greatest mistakes?

- How does he feel about dying childless?

- What emotions does he harbor toward Macduff?

- What does he think will become of Scotland after his death?

If you choose to write in Shakespearean blank verse, here's a hint. Iambic pentameter closely resembles the natural flow of English speech. You can first try writing your speech in prose and then convert it to poetry. To do so, break each line after ten syllables. Then go back through each line to make the beat regular, with each unstressed syllable followed by a stressed syllable. You may need to substitute certain words or alter the syntax to achieve smoothly flowing lines of verse.

Literary Criticism

Scholar Faith Nostbakken asks, "What are those three characters who begin [the] play? Fates? Old hags? Mad people? Evil tempters? Prophets? Macbeth's personal demons?" How would you answer her question? Write a letter to Nostbakken giving her your opinion of the weird sisters and of their function in the play. Provide evidence from the play to support your ideas.

Literature Online Web Activities For eFlashcards, Selection Quick Checks, and other Web activities, go to www.glencoe.com.

Shakespeare's Language and Style

Using Appropriate Diction A key element of style, diction refers to an author's word choice, or use of appropriate words. In *Macbeth*, Shakespeare gives each character a distinct way of speaking. For example, compare these speeches by different characters in *Macbeth*:

Duncan:

"We will establish our estate upon
Our eldest, Malcolm, whom we name hereafter
The Prince of Cumberland: which honor must
Not unaccompanied invest him only,
But signs of nobleness, like stars, shall shine
On all deservers."

Porter:

"Here's a knocking indeed! If a man were porter of hell gate, he should have old turning the key. Knock, knock, knock! Who's there, i' th' name of Beelzebub? Here's a farmer. . . . Have napkins enow about you; here you'll sweat for 't . . . Anon, anon!"

Character	Diction
Duncan	• use of the royal plural pronouns *we* and *our* instead of *I* and *my* • use of political terms ("establish our estate")
Porter	• use of colloquialisms ("I' th' name of Beelzebub") • use of informal speech ("Anon, anon!")

Activity One of the most poignant passages is that in which Macbeth reacts to his wife's death (beginning "She should have died hereafter . . ."). With a partner, create a chart that analyzes the diction in this passage, including the use of monosyllabic words, imagery, and figurative language.

Revising Check

Appropriate Words With a partner, review the diction in the "dying words" speech you wrote for Macbeth. Look for places where you can substitute words that are more appropriate to Macbeth's character and his situation. Revise your draft to improve the diction.

THRONE OF BLOOD

from *Shakespeare on Screen*

Daniel Rosenthal

Building Background

Shakespeare's *Macbeth* has inspired a wide range of artists from various cultures. For instance, the Italian composer Giuseppe Verdi and the Russian composer Dmitri Shostakovich both wrote operas based on the play. *Macbeth* has even been interpreted in the styles of Japanese Kabuki and Chinese Beijing opera. One of the best-known treatments of *Macbeth* is the 1957 Japanese film *Throne of Blood*, created by one of Japan's greatest directors, Akira Kurosawa. During his career, Kurosawa won many film awards. In 1990 the Academy of Motion Picture Arts and Sciences recognized his achievements with a special Oscar. In the following section from his book *Shakespeare on Screen*, Daniel Rosenthal describes Kurosawa's adaptation of Shakespeare's famous tragedy.

Set a Purpose for Reading

Analyze how Kurosawa adapts *Macbeth* in *Throne of Blood*.

Reading Strategy

Comparing and Contrasting Genres

As you read the text and examine the photographs, **compare and contrast** the play *Macbeth* with the film *Throne of Blood*. Use a two-column chart like the one below to note their similarities and differences.

Macbeth	Throne of Blood
Set in 11th-century Scotland	Set in 15th-century Japan

The ambitious general Washizu (Toshiro Mifune) and his ruthless wife Asaji (Isuzu Yamada) ponder their next move.

Washizu, the Macbeth figure in *Throne of Blood* has all of his Shakespearean counterpart's courage, but none of his eloquence[1]. This wild-eyed samurai[2] (Toshiro Mifune at his fiercest) rarely says more than a dozen words at a time, and his language is as plain as the floorboards of his castle. There is no poetry in *Throne of Blood*'s sparse dialogue, and little subtlety in its characterization, but its pace, atmosphere and imagery have a power that is absolutely Shakespearean.

The Bard's evocation of 11th-century Scotland and Kurosawa's depiction of late 15th-century Japan are both marked by bestial omens and foul weather. In *Throne of Blood* a horse's wild behavior presages[3] its master's murder; galloping warriors are buffeted by howling wind and driving rain, or shrouded in fog or mist. The music of Shakespeare's verse is replaced by the woodwind and percussion of Masaru Sato's distinctively Japanese score.

Washizu's story is told in flashback, beginning with a shot of the monument that marks the site

---

1. *Eloquence* means "powerful speech."
2. A *samurai* is a noble warrior of medieval and early modern Japan.
3. *Presages* means "foreshadows."

of Cobweb Castle, as a male chorus sings of its destruction. Next, we see the impregnable[4] castle in its former glory, as Tsuzuki (the Duncan figure) learns of heroic exploits by Washizu and his best friend, Miki (Minoru Chiaki as a jovial, trusting Banquo), against Inui (the King of Norway) and the treacherous Fujimaki (the thane of Cawdor).

Meanwhile, in a marvelously dynamic and eerie sequence, Washizu and Miki become lost in the maze-like Cobweb Forest, and meet an aged "evil spirit" (Chieko Naniwa). Her white make-up resembles the ghost-masks of Noh theater[5] (the ancient Japanese form that Kurosawa adored), and she prophecies in the husky, expressionless tones of Noh actors: Washizu, commander of Fort One, will rule North Mansion and then Cobweb Castle. Miki will

---

4. *Impregnable* means "unconquerable."
5. *Noh theater* is a highly stylized form of Japanese drama that developed in the fourteenth and fifteenth centuries. Noh plays are performed by actors wearing symbolic masks.

take over Fort One, and his son will eventually rule the castle.

Tsuzuki installs Washizu and his wife, Asaji, in North Mansion, and Kurosawa immediately uses Noh to associate Asaji (the mesmerizing Isuzu Yamada) so closely with the forest spirit that the suspicion arises they are in league together. Yamada's long, oval face is like a Noh mask, she walks heel to toe, like Noh actors, and adopts an expressionless voice to suit Asaji's pitiless ambition. She convinces the unambitious Washizu that Tsuzuki and Miki are plotting his death and that he must strike while Tsuzuki is their guest.

Here, Kurosawa devises a night-time sequence of such stealth that it perfectly distills the dreadful tension of Duncan's murder in *Macbeth*. For seven minutes, in the build-up to and bloody aftermath of the crime, no words are spoken—nor are they necessary: the horror of the deed is writ large on Mifune and Yamada's faces.

The "guilty" flight of Kunimaru, Tsuzuki's son, and Noriyasu (Macduff) makes Washizu lord of the castle, and from now on the script begins to

After having his comrade Miki killed, Washizu imagines he sees his ghost at a banquet.

Tormented by guilt, Asaji sees blood on her hands.

Noh Mask of a Young Woman. Japanese, 19th century. Leeds Museum and Art Galleries, Great Britain.

work devastating variations on *Macbeth*. With no children of his own, Washizu has agreed to let Miki's son, Yoshiteru, inherit the castle, but then Asaji suddenly announces that she is pregnant: Washizu *will* have an heir, so Miki and Yoshiteru must die.

Kurosawa now pulls off a unique feat: improving on Shakespeare by *not* showing a murder that is invariably depicted on stage. Miki's horse refuses to be saddled, but he ignores this omen and sets off for Washizu's feast. The horse gallops, riderless, back into Fort One, showing that Miki is dead; his dazed ghost's appearance during the feast provides confirmation.

A final reckoning

Months pass, Asaji has a stillborn child, and the realization that Yoshiteru (who escaped his

father's assassin) will still inherit prompts a self-mocking shout from Washizu: "Fool! Fool!"—the closest Mifune gets to a soliloquy.

With Asaji madly washing Tsuzuki's invisible blood from her hands, and his enemies preparing to attack, Washizu rides back to the spirit, who guarantees him invincibility[6] "until Cobweb Forest comes to Cobweb Castle."

He reassures his soldiers with this promise, but when they see an army of pines approaching through the mist, we get the last, greatest twist on *Macbeth*: Washizu is killed by his own men. Dozens of arrows whistle into his armor, until one last arrow transfixes his neck and he collapses. Beyond the gates, Noriyasu's men prepare

6. *Invincibility* is the characteristic of being impossible to defeat.

In the violent climax of *Throne of Blood,*
Washizu is killed by his own men.

to raze the castle and the screen fades back to its opening image of the monument.

Astonishingly, on its first release, Kurosawa's film was dismissed by *The New York Times* for an "odd amalgamation[7] of cultural contrasts [that] hits the occidental[8] funnybone." However, by 1965, Britain's *Sight and Sound* magazine was making a bold and not unreasonable claim for *Throne of Blood* as the only work that "completely succeeded in transforming a play of Shakespeare's into a film." ❧

---

7. *Amalgamation* means "blending."

8. *Occidental* means "relating to Europe and the Western Hemisphere."

RESPONDING AND THINKING CRITICALLY

Respond

1. After reading Rosenthal's article and examining the images from Akira Kurosawa's film, which title do you think captures the mood of the play more—*Macbeth* or *Throne of Blood*? Explain.

Recall and Interpret

2. (a)List the various ways in which Kurosawa's film departs from Shakespeare's play. (b)Examine the image above of the dying Washizu. Why do you think Kurosawa changed this aspect of the play?

3. (a)What is Asaji's makeup modeled on? (b)Review the image of Asaji staring at her hands on page 408. How would you describe her face?

Analyze and Evaluate

4. In his film, Kurosawa uses a flashback; he begins the film with Cobweb Castle in ruins and then presents the events that brought about the castle's decline. What effect do you think this flashback has on the action of the film?

5. What aspects of *Macbeth* do you think Kurosawa's film is most successful in capturing? Explain.

Connect

6. Why do you think artists from other cultures have been so eager to interpret and adapt Shakespeare's *Macbeth*?

7. *Throne of Blood* is an example of one film adaptation of *Macbeth.* (a)If you were writing your own version of the play for the screen, what other settings might you use? (b)What aspects of the plot would you change?

OBJECTIVES
- Compare and contrast works of art.
- Apply critical viewing skills to nonprint media.
- Analyze how a work of art reflects cultural heritage.

Preview the Article

"Midsummer Night's Spectacle" examines the popularity of outdoor Shakespeare performances during the summer.

1. Read the title of the article. What clues does the word *spectacle* give you about the content of the article?

2. Read the *deck,* or the sentences in large type that appear to the left of the title. What problem or problems do you think the article will examine?

Set a Purpose for Reading

Read to learn how a playwright from the English Renaissance continues to entertain and inspire modern audiences.

Reading Strategy

Distinguishing Fact from Opinion
A **fact** is a statement that can be proved true. An **opinion** is a personal judgment that cannot be proved true. When you **distinguish fact from opinion,** you determine which statements represent facts and which represent opinions.

As you read, create a chart to record examples of facts and opinions you find throughout "Midsummer Night's Spectacle."

Statement	Fact or Opinion	How I Know

OBJECTIVES
- Distinguish fact from opinion.
- Connect literary works to the contemporary world.

TIME

Shakespeare is a reliable summer hit, especially performed outdoors.

So why is he a hard sell under a roof in winter?

Midsummer Night's Spectacle

By **WILLIAM A. HENRY III**

AS TWILIGHT SLIPS OVER THE HILLY COLLEGE TOWN OF Ashland, Oregon, the sweet summer evening seems too balmy for whiling away indoors, even to the vacationing crowds who have journeyed to attend the theater here. Fortunately, they need not choose between pleasures. Night after night, vividly costumed Shakespeare—preceded by the singing of madrigals and heralded by a flag raising and trumpet fanfare from the topmost gables of a Tudor stagehouse—unfolds here beneath a starry sky.

The scene takes place at the Oregon Shakespeare Festival (OSF), the largest regional theater in the United States and one of the oldest (it was founded in 1935). The theater is a three-stage jamboree built on a love of Shakespeare that draws almost 400,000 spectators a year. Ninety percent of those are from more than 125 miles away. With minor variations, this scene also takes place at dozens of outdoor theaters around the country, including one in an inner-city park in Louisville, Kentucky, and another on the grounds of a legendary mansion alongside the Hudson River in New York. According to Felicia Londre, former secretary of the Shakespeare Theater Association of America, the United States has about 100 outdoor Shakespeare festivals. Some, like Ashland's and New York City's Shakespeare in the Park, have grown into major institutions offering varied repertoires. Others operate just a few weeks a year. Nearly all rely on a lot of novice, non-union actors. But almost all are thriving.

A Passion for the Bard

Americans seemingly cannot get enough of Shakespeare in open air during the summer—though they are conspicuously less eager to see the Bard's work indoors at other times of the year. For many theatergoers, the experience of Shakespeare outdoors takes on an almost sacred character. When Richard Devin, the artistic director of the Colorado Shakespeare Festival, moved a summer's staging of Shakespeare's *The Winter's Tale* to a new indoor space and installed an adaptation of Richard Brinsley

David Cooper

Sheridan's *The Rivals* outdoors, he quickly realized he had goofed. Not only did *The Rivals* prove an unusually tough sell, but subscribers wrote in fury. "They told me they would never come to Shakespeare indoors or accept another writer outdoors," Devin says. "They spoke of Shakespeare's universality and of what it meant to see these plays under the stars with their children. They felt we were stealing an irreplaceable opportunity from them."

Other theater executives have noted a similar audience passion for Shakespeare. Even his less-popular "problem" plays, which many people consider both difficult to produce and to watch, have more box-office appeal than masterpieces by almost anyone else. Says Bill Patton, OSF's former executive director, who oversaw its growth for many years:

"Some of Shakespeare's popularity may be that it's certified as good for you, so audiences can congratulate themselves on their intellectuality, even though this was popular entertainment for its time and still is. Also the plays are taught in school, so people feel familiar with them."

Swordplay Sells

Actors and directors tend to be ambivalent about staging the Bard outdoors. Only a dozen or so of his 37 plays consistently succeed outdoors both artistically and at the box office, and those mainly when staged in broad strokes. By common consent, the lighter comedies and the more swashbuckling histories fare best because they depend less on language that is easily lost in the night air and more on pageantry and action. Intimate texts and

subtle, groundbreaking performances tend not to work in the wide and windy spaces.

Soliloquies cannot compete with swordplay. Jerry Turner, who spent almost 20 years as OSF's artistic director, refused to schedule Othello outdoors because he felt its intimate story and rich language were ill-suited to that setting. But after OSF erected a stadium-like "acoustic shell" that surrounded the stage with tiers of balconies while leaving it open to the sky, Turner finally consented to try Othello outdoors. The flat and tedious result bore out his original judgment— although critics said much of the blame went to the bland performances of the three principal actors.

Some artistic directors claim to find great value in working outdoors. Says Jack O'Brien of San Diego's Old Globe Theater:

ALL'S WELL THAT ENDS WELL IN COLORADO: The experience takes on an almost sacred character.

David Blue

Michal Daniel

COMEDY OF ERRORS: Making merry in New York's Central Park

"The shows are usually at their fairest and least phony outside. It's hard to stand next to a tree and speak archly. Even when we are doing Shakespeare indoors, I have often taken the cast outside during tech week and had a complete run-through just to get in touch with that honesty." O'Brien thinks of Shakespeare's earlier plays, almost all work outdoors, while his later ones mostly don't: "You can see in his poetry the adaptation from an open theater to a more enclosed one—the way, for example, he speaks of light or time of day."

The former head of the New York Shakespeare Festival, JoAnne Akalaitis, speaks enthusiastically about the "magic" of Shakespeare in Central Park: "Shakespeare in the park is part of the essence of being a cultural person in New York City. It is relaxed, warm, open, and democratic. The upsides are the wind and clouds, the informality, coupled with the power that comes with that much massed humanity." She adds dryly, "The downside is the body miking." Or at least, it was. For years, the Central Park sound system was notoriously tinny, and actors could not seem to avoid hitting their mikes when they scuffled, so every few minutes the audience heard what sounded like thunder. Today, however, the introduction of a more sophisticated sound system has largely solved that problem.

Another downside is the sheer size of the stage and audience, which can sometimes tempt film stars, fearful of understatement, into almost operatic acting. But whatever the shortcomings of these productions, audiences seem to want Shakespeare outdoors more than ever. New troupes spring up each year as producers discover what OSF's founder, Angus Bowmer, learned in 1935. He staged boxing matches as a way to help pay for his outdoor Shakespeare shows. The boxing lost money. From the start, the Shakespeare turned a profit.

Updated 2005, from TIME, August 24, 1992

RESPONDING AND THINKING CRITICALLY

Respond

1. What did you find interesting or unusual about outdoor Shakespeare festivals?

Recall and Interpret

2. (a)Why do Shakespeare's plays appeal to audiences, according to former OSF director Bill Patton? (b)How does this explain why audiences might feel protective of Shakespeare's work?

3. (a)What kind of plays typically succeed in outdoor Shakespeare festivals? (b)Why do you think they succeed?

Analyze and Evaluate

4. (a)Why do you think the writer chose to quote theater and artistic directors instead of theater patrons? (b)How might "Midsummer Night's Spectacle" be different if these quotes were removed, or if only theater patrons were quoted?

5. (a)Give one example of an instance in which the writer presents an opinion as fact. (b)In what way is the writer biased, or partial to one particular view or opinion?

Connect

6. In your opinion, are Shakespeare's plays best performed outdoors? Explain. Think about how the plays were originally performed in Shakespeare's time and what has changed since then.

The Sacred and the Secular

Allegory of Fleeting Time, c. 1634. Antonio Pereda. Kunsthistorisches Museum, Vienna, Austria.

"I write of groves, of twilights, and I sing
The court of Mab, and of the Fairy King.
I write of hell; I sing (and ever shall)
Of heaven, and hope to have it after all."

—Robert Herrick, "The Argument of His Book"

from the *King James Version of the Bible*

The Bible is a collection of writings belonging to the sacred literature of Judaism and Christianity. Although most people think of the Bible as a single book, it is actually a collection of books. In fact, the word *Bible* comes from the Greek words *ta biblia*, meaning "the little books." The Hebrew Bible, also called the *Tanakh*, contains the sacred writings of the Jewish people and chronicles their history. The Christian Bible was originally written in Greek. It contains most of the same texts as the Hebrew Bible, as well as twenty-seven additional books called the New Testament. The many books of the Bible were written at different times and contain various types of writing—including history, law, stories, songs, proverbs, sermons, prophecies, and letters.

The Creation of Heaven and Earth (detail from the Chaos), 1200. Mosaic. Monreale Cathedral, Sicily.

> *"I perceived how that it was impossible to establish the lay people in any truth except the Scripture were plainly laid before their eyes in their mother tongue."*
>
> —William Tyndale

From Latin to English Before the Protestant Reformation began in the early 1500s, the Christian Bible was ordinarily read in Latin. As a result, few people had direct knowledge of the Bible. One of the most important goals of Protestant leaders, such as Martin Luther, was to translate the Bible into the languages that common people could read. In 1525 the English Protestant William Tyndale completed his translation of the New Testament, the first English version of the Bible to be printed. Tyndale's work on the Hebrew Bible ended abruptly, however, when authorities banned his translation and executed him for heresy.

Other English translations appeared soon after, notably the Great Bible of Miles Coverdale; the Geneva Bible, translated by a group of English Protestants living in Switzerland; and the Rheims-Douay Bible, translated by English Roman Catholics living in France. By 1603, when James I became king of England, at least seven English translations of the Bible were in use. In 1604 a conference of churchmen proposed that the English Bible be revised. King James agreed and gathered a group of forty-seven scholars to create a new English Bible. The group was instructed to correct the Bishops' Bible—a version of Coverdale's Great Bible—by comparing it with the original Hebrew and Greek texts. These scholars turned to Tyndale's masterful prose in preparing their new version. The result of their efforts, first printed in 1611, was the King James—or Authorized—Version of the Holy Bible.

The Legacy of the King James Bible

For centuries, the King James Bible was not only the most widely read English Bible, but the most widely read English book. Thus it exerted an enormous stabilizing influence on the English language, which had been changing steadily since the Norman Conquest in 1066. The language and style of the King James Version of the Bible have had a profound influence on English language and literature up to the present day.

Connecting to the Selections

The King James Version of the Bible has long been admired for its simplicity and beauty. As you read the selections, ask yourself why the King James Bible became the first widely accepted translation.

Building Background

The Bible opens with the book of Genesis. This title is derived from the Greek word *gignesthai*, meaning "to be born." The book of Genesis begins with God's creation of the world. Genesis is the first of five books known as the *Pentateuch* (pen′ tə tōōk), Greek for "five books." These books narrate the early history of the Jewish people and present their religious laws. The Jewish people refer to these five books as the *Torah* (Hebrew for "law"). The King James Version of the Bible is written chiefly in prose, but some portions use poetry. In fact, the book of Psalms consists of poems intended to be sung. The 150 psalms, or songs of praise, form the last part of the Hebrew Bible, called the Writings. Many of the psalms are traditionally attributed to King David, who ruled Israel from about 1000 to 962 B.C.

Setting Purposes for Reading

Big Idea The Sacred and the Secular

As you read, think about the effects this translation might have had on laypeople, who could now read the Bible on their own.

Literary Element Style

Style is the way language is used to convey an idea or concept. It involves word choice and the length and arrangement of sentences, as well as the use of figurative language and imagery. As you read, note how the translators of the King James Bible use repetition and other devices to create a distinct style.

- See Literary Terms Handbook, p. R17.

Literature Online **Interactive Literary Elements Handbook** To review or learn more about the literary elements, go to www.glencoe.com.

Reading Strategy Analyzing Text Structure

Analyzing text structure—the organization of ideas within a work—can help you to understand the logic and message of a text. Recognizing the pattern of organization will focus your attention on important ideas in a selection. Some basic types of text structures include chronological order (order of time), cause-and-effect order, comparison-contrast order, and spatial order.

Reading Tip: Taking Notes Use a chart like the one below to identify clues to the text's structure.

Genesis	
Clue Words or Phrases	Type of Connection

Vocabulary

abundantly (ə bun′ dənt lē) *adv.* plentifully; p. 417 *The storeroom was packed with provisions, ensuring that we would be abundantly provided for during the long winter.*

replenish (ri plen′ ish) *v.* to refill or make complete again; to add a new supply to; p. 417 *Seeing the nearly empty candy bowl, the hostess replenished it, filling the bowl to the rim.*

beguile (bi gīl′) *v.* to mislead by trickery; to deceive; p. 420 *The sly suitor beguiled the naive heiress with flattery.*

enmity (en′ mə tē) *n.* ill will; hostility; p. 420 *The cruel girl's bullying earned her the enmity of all her classmates.*

Vocabulary Tip: Synonyms Words that have the same or nearly the same meaning are called synonyms. Synonyms are always the same part of speech.

OBJECTIVES
In studying these selections, you will focus on the following:
- analyzing literary periods
- analyzing style and parallelism
- analyzing text structure

from Genesis

from the King James version of the Bible

Elohim Creating Adam, 1805. William Blake. Watercolor on paper, 431 x 536 cm.
Tate Gallery, London.

Chapter 1

In the beginning God created the heaven and the earth. And the earth was without form and void; and darkness was upon the face of the deep. And the spirit of God moved upon the face of the waters. And God said, "Let there be light": and there was light. And God saw the light, that it was good: and God divided the light from the darkness. And God called the light Day, and the darkness he called Night. And the evening and the morning were the first day.

Reading Strategy   Analyzing Text Structure *What does this phrase tell you about how the story is structured?*

Reading Strategy   Analyzing Text Structure *What is created on the first day of Genesis?*

And God said, "Let there be a firmament[1] in the midst of the waters, and let it divide the waters from the waters." And God made the firmament, and divided the waters which were under the firmament from the waters which were above the firmament: and it was so. And God called the firmament Heaven. And the evening and the morning were the second day.

And God said, "Let the waters under the heaven be gathered together unto one place, and let the dry land appear": and it was so. And God called the dry land Earth; and the gathering together of the waters called he Seas: and God saw that it was good. And God said, "Let the earth bring forth grass, the herb[2] yielding seed, and the fruit tree yielding fruit after his kind,[3] whose seed is in itself, upon the earth": and it was so. And the earth brought forth grass, and herb yielding seed after his kind, and the tree yielding fruit, whose seed was in itself, after his kind: and God saw that it was good. And the evening and the morning were the third day.

And God said, "Let there be lights in the firmament of the heaven to divide the day from the night; and let them be for signs, and for seasons, and for days, and years: and let them be for lights in the firmament of the heaven to give light upon the earth": and it was so. And God made two great lights; the greater light to rule the day, and the lesser light to rule the night: he made the stars also. And God set them in the firmament of the heaven to give light upon the earth, and to rule over the day and over the night, and to divide the light from the darkness: and God saw that it was good. And the evening and the morning were the fourth day.

And God said, "Let the waters bring forth **abundantly** the moving creature that hath life,

and fowl that may fly above the earth in the open firmament of heaven." And God created great whales, and every living creature that moveth, which the waters brought forth abundantly, after their kind, and every winged fowl after his kind: and God saw that it was good. And God blessed them, saying, "Be fruitful, and multiply, and fill the waters in the seas, and let fowl multiply in the earth." And the evening and the morning were the fifth day.

And God said, "Let the earth bring forth the living creature after his kind, cattle, and creeping thing, and beast of the earth after his kind": and it was so. And God made the beast of the earth after his kind, and cattle after their kind, and every thing that creepeth upon the earth after his kind: and God saw that it was good.

And God said, "Let us make man in our image, after our likeness: and let them have dominion[4] over the fish of the sea, and over the fowl of the air, and over the cattle, and over all the earth, and over every creeping thing that creepeth upon the earth." So God created man in his own image, in the image of God created he him; male and female created he them. And God blessed them, and God said unto them, "Be fruitful, and multiply, and **replenish** the earth, and subdue it: and have dominion over the fish of the sea, and over the fowl of the air, and over every living thing that moveth upon the earth."

And God said, "Behold, I have given you every herb bearing seed, which is upon the face of all the earth, and every tree, in which is the fruit of a tree yielding seed; to you it shall be for meat.[5] And to every beast of the earth, and to every fowl of the air, and to every thing that creepeth upon the earth, wherein

---

1. The *firmament* is the atmosphere surrounding the earth.
2. Here, *herb* refers to vegetation.
3. *After his kind* means "like itself."

Literary Element Style *These sentences are repeated with slight variations throughout the first chapter of Genesis. How do these repetitions help you to understand what is happening in the text?*

Vocabulary

abundantly (ə bun′ dənt lē) *adv.* plentifully

---

4. *Dominion* means "authority" or "power to rule."
5. *Meat* refers to food in general.

Reading Strategy Analyzing Text Structure *What does this sentence tell you about how this text is organized?*

Reading Strategy Analyzing Text Structure *On the sixth day, what is the order of creation?*

Vocabulary

replenish (ri plen′ ish) *v.* to refill or make complete again; to add a new supply to

Creation of the Animals, Grabow Altarpiece, left inner wing, exterior, 1410. Master Bertram of Minden. Tempera on wood, 80 x 51 cm. Hamburg Kunsthalle Collection, Germany.

there is life, I have given every green herb for meat": and it was so.

And God saw every thing that he had made, and behold, it was very good. And the evening and the morning were the sixth day.

Chapter 2

Thus the heavens and the earth were finished, and all the host[6] of them. And on the seventh day God ended his work which he had made; and he rested on the seventh day from all his work which he had made. And God blessed the seventh day, and sanctified it: because that in it he had rested from all his work which God created and made.

These are the generations of the heavens and of the earth when they were created, in the day that the Lord God made the earth and the heavens, and every plant of the field before it was in the earth, and every herb of the field before it grew: for the Lord God had not caused it to rain upon the earth, and there was not a man to till the ground. But there went up a mist from the earth, and watered the whole face of the ground. And the Lord God formed man of the dust of the ground, and breathed into his nostrils the breath of life; and man became a living soul.

And the Lord God planted a garden eastward in Eden; and there he put the man whom he had formed. And out of the ground made the Lord God to grow every tree that is pleasant to the sight, and good for food; the tree of life also in the midst of the garden, and the tree of knowledge of good and evil. . . .

And the Lord God took the man, and put him into the garden of Eden to dress it and to keep it. And the Lord God commanded the man, saying, "Of every tree of the garden thou mayest freely eat: but of the tree of knowledge of good and evil, thou shalt not eat of it: for in the day that thou eatest thereof thou shalt surely die."

And the Lord God said, "It is not good that the man should be alone; I will make him a help meet for him."[7] And out of the ground the Lord God formed every beast of the field, and every fowl of the air; and brought them unto Adam to see what he would call them: and whatsoever Adam called every living creature, that was the name thereof. And Adam gave names to all cattle, and to the fowl of the air, and to every beast of the field; but for Adam there was not found a help meet for him.

And the Lord God caused a deep sleep to fall upon Adam, and he slept: and he took one of his ribs, and closed up the flesh instead thereof; and the rib, which the Lord God had taken from man, made he a woman, and brought her unto the man.

And Adam said, "This is now bone of my bones, and flesh of my flesh: she shall be called Woman, because she was taken out of Man."

Therefore shall a man leave his father and his mother, and shall cleave unto[8] his wife: and they shall be one flesh. And they were both naked, the man and his wife, and were not ashamed.

Chapter 3

Now the serpent was more subtle than any beast of the field which the Lord God had made. And he said unto the woman, "Yea, hath God said, 'Ye shall not eat of every tree of the garden'?"

And the woman said unto the serpent, "We may eat of the fruit of the trees of the garden: but of the fruit of the tree which is in the midst of the garden, God hath said, 'Ye shall not eat of it, neither shall ye touch it, lest ye die.' "

And the serpent said unto the woman, "Ye shall not surely die: for God doth know that in the day ye eat thereof, then your eyes shall be opened, and ye shall be as gods, knowing good and evil."

And when the woman saw that the tree was good for food, and that it was pleasant to the eyes, and a tree to be desired to make one wise,

---

6. *Host* refers to the great number of living things on the earth.

Big Idea The Sacred and the Secular *What religious and secular traditions are linked to this passage?*

Reading Strategy Analyzing Text Structure *At this point in the narrative, why does the text go back and explain how people were created?*

---

7. *Help meet for him* means, in this case, "wife."
8. *Cleave unto* means "cling to" or "be faithful to."

she took of the fruit thereof, and did eat, and gave also unto her husband with her; and he did eat. And the eyes of them both were opened, and they knew that they were naked; and they sewed fig leaves together, and made themselves aprons.

And they heard the voice of the Lord God walking in the garden in the cool of the day: and Adam and his wife hid themselves from the presence of the Lord God amongst the trees of the garden.

And the Lord God called unto Adam, and said unto him, "Where art thou?"

And he said, "I heard thy voice in the garden, and I was afraid, because I was naked; and I hid myself."

And he said, "Who told thee that thou wast naked? Hast thou eaten of the tree, whereof I commanded thee that thou shouldest not eat?"

And the man said, "The woman whom thou gavest to be with me, she gave me of the tree, and I did eat."

And the Lord God said unto the woman, "What is this that thou hast done?"

And the woman said, "The serpent **beguiled** me, and I did eat."

And the Lord God said unto the serpent, "Because thou hast done this, thou art cursed above all cattle, and above every beast of the field; upon thy belly shalt thou go, and dust shalt thou eat all the days of thy life: and I will put **enmity** between thee and the woman, and between thy seed and her seed; it shall bruise thy head, and thou shalt bruise his heel."

Unto the woman he said, "I will greatly multiply thy sorrow and thy conception;[9] in sorrow thou shalt bring forth children; and thy desire shall be to thy husband, and he shall rule over thee."

And unto Adam he said, "Because thou hast hearkened unto the voice of thy wife, and hast eaten of the tree, of which I commanded thee, saying, 'Thou shalt not eat of it': cursed is the ground for thy sake; in sorrow shalt thou eat of it all the days of thy life; thorns also and thistles shall it bring forth to thee; and thou shalt eat the herb of the field; in the sweat of thy face shalt thou eat bread, till thou return unto the ground; for out of it wast thou taken: for dust thou art, and unto dust shalt thou return."

And Adam called his wife's name Eve; because she was the mother of all living. Unto Adam also and to his wife did the Lord God make coats of skins, and clothed them.

And the Lord God said, "Behold, the man is become as one of us, to know good and evil: and now, lest he put forth his hand, and take also of the tree of life, and eat, and live forever": therefore the Lord God sent him forth from the garden of Eden, to till the ground from whence he was taken. So he drove out the man; and he placed at the east of the garden of Eden cherubim,[10] and a flaming sword which turned every way, to keep the way of[11] the tree of life. ❧

---

9. *Conception,* as used here, refers to childbirth.
10. *Cherubim* are a class of angels.
11. *Keep the way of* means "guard."

Reading Strategy Analyzing Text Structure *Does this curse apply to the present or the future?*

Literary Element Style *What is the effect of the repetition of the word* dust?

Vocabulary

beguile (bi gīl´) *v.* to mislead by trickery; to deceive
enmity (en´ mə tē) *n.* ill will; hostility

Psalm 23

from the King James *version of the* Bible

Agnus Dei, Lamb of God, fresco from crypt of Anagni Cathedral, 13th century. Anagni Cathedral, Italy.

The Lord is my shepherd; I shall not want.[1]

2   He maketh me to lie down in green pastures: he leadeth me beside the still waters.

3   He restoreth my soul: he leadeth me in the paths of righteousness for his name's sake.

4   Yea, though I walk through the valley of the shadow of death, I will fear no evil: for thou art with me; thy rod and thy staff they comfort me.

5   Thou preparest a table before me in the presence of mine enemies: thou anointest my head with oil; my cup runneth over.

6   Surely goodness and mercy shall follow me all the days of my life; and I will dwell in the house of the Lord for ever.

---

1. *Want* means "be in need of anything."

Reading Strategy   **Analyzing Text Structure**   *What does this comparison add to the earlier comparison of the Lord to a shepherd?*

Big Idea   **The Sacred and the Secular**   *Why does this psalm end with a reference to the future?*

RESPONDING AND THINKING CRITICALLY

Respond

1. Which selection did you enjoy more? Explain.

Recall and Interpret

2. (a)In your own words, describe the things God creates each day in Genesis. (b)Why are man and woman created last?

3. (a)According to Genesis, why do Adam and Eve disobey God and eat from the "tree of knowledge of good and evil"? (b)What causes Adam and Eve to be ashamed of their nakedness and afraid of God?

4. (a)What different punishments does God impose on Adam, Eve, and the serpent? (b)As a result of their actions, what do Adam and Eve lose?

5. (a)In Psalm 23, what is "the valley of the shadow of death"? (b)Why does the speaker "fear no evil"?

6. In the last verse of Psalm 23, what does the speaker conclude?

Analyze and Evaluate

7. (a)In Genesis, what does "the tree of life" symbolize, or stand for? (b)What does "the tree of knowledge of good and evil" symbolize?

8. (a)To what does the speaker compare the Lord in Psalm 23? (b)What do these metaphors suggest about the relationship between the speaker of the psalm and God?

Connect

9. **Big Idea** **The Sacred and the Secular** The last four paragraphs from chapter 2 of Genesis are often read at wedding ceremonies. Why might they be suitable for a wedding?

10. **Big Idea** **The Sacred and the Secular** (a)What message does Psalm 23 contain that is particularly comforting? (b)During what occasions might it be appropriate for someone to read this psalm?

LITERARY ANALYSIS

Literary Element | Style

One component of **style** is word choice. Compare the following three translations of a passage from Psalm 23.

- "You spread a table for me in full view of my enemies; / You anoint my head with oil; / my drink is abundant." (*Tanakh*, Jewish Publication Society)

- "Thou spreadest a table for me in the sight of my enemies; / thou hast richly bathed my head with oil, / and my cup runs over." (New English Bible)

- "Thou preparest a table before me in the presence of mine enemies; thou anointest my head with oil; my cup runneth over." (King James Bible)

1. Study the following phrases from the three passages: "in full view of," "in the sight of," and "in the presence of." Do you think the difference in wording reflects an important distinction in meaning? Explain.

2. Compare "my drink is abundant" with "my cup runneth over." What connotations does each phrase suggest?

Review: Parallelism

As you learned on page 284, **parallelism** is the use of a series of words, phrases, or sentences that have similar grammatical structures. For example, the following phrases are parallel: "Let the waters under the heaven be gathered" and "Let the dry land appear." Parallelism shows the relationship between ideas and helps emphasize thoughts.

Partner Activity With a partner, answer these questions.

1. Identify an example of parallelism in Genesis and explain what it adds to the telling of the story.

2. Find two examples of parallelism in Psalm 23 and explain how they contribute to the impact of the psalm.

READING AND VOCABULARY

Reading Strategy Analyzing Text Structure

There are four basic types of text structures:

- **Chronological order** means that a text is structured in sequence from beginning to end.

- **Cause-and-effect order** means that a text is structured around causal relationships.

- **Comparison-contrast order** means that a text is structured in a way that shows similarities and differences between various ideas or events.

- **Spatial order** means that the events of a text do not have a particular chronology. Instead, like the parts of a painting, they are all present at the same time.

In addition, there are often several organizational methods at work within the same text. For example, a text might proceed mainly in chronological order but demonstrate cause-and-effect relationships at the same time. Use the notes that you took while reading to help you answer the following questions.

1. How is Genesis structured? Explain.

2. How is Psalm 23 structured? Explain.

Vocabulary Practice

Practice with Synonyms Identify the synonym for each vocabulary word listed in the first column. Use a dictionary or a thesaurus if you need help.

1. **abundantly**   **a.** bountifully   **b.** boisterously

2. **replenish**   **a.** relinquish   **b.** restock

3. **beguile**   **a.** destroy   **b.** delude

4. **enmity**   **a.** indifference   **b.** hatred

WRITING AND EXTENDING

Writing About Literature

Compare and Contrast Theme The selections you have just read present two different views of the relationship between God and humans. Write an essay explaining how these two selections present contrasting views and express different themes. Begin with a brief statement identifying the topic of your essay. End with a brief summary of the main points of your discussion and offer an additional insight, if appropriate. Organize the body of your essay in either of the following ways:

A. 1. Relationship between God and humans in Genesis

     2. Relationship between God and humans in Psalm 23

     3. Similarities and differences between Genesis and Psalm 23

B. 1. Similarities in Genesis and Psalm 23 in God's relationship with humans

     2. Differences in Genesis and Psalm 23 in God's relationship with humans

     3. Significance of similarities and differences

As you draft, write from start to finish. After you finish writing, meet with a classmate to evaluate each other's work and to suggest revisions. Then proofread and edit your draft for errors in spelling, grammar, and punctuation.

Further Reading

- If you would like to see more examples of the ways in which translations differ, read Genesis and Psalm 23 in the New English Bible and other versions of the Bible.

- The Sermon on the Mount, recorded in the Christian Bible, contains many thoughts and expressions that have been quoted throughout the centuries and are commonly referred to in our contemporary culture. You might enjoy reading the first sixteen verses of Matthew, chapter 5, in the King James Version of the Bible to see how many of these references you recognize.

Literature Online Web Activities For eFlashcards, Selection Quick Checks, and other Web activities, go to www.glencoe.com.

Eve's Apology

MEET AEMILIA LANYER

In 1611, the same year that the King James Bible and three of Shakespeare's plays were published, forty-two-year-old Aemilia Lanyer (lən yēr′) published her landmark book of poetry, *Salve Deus Rex Judaeorum*. It was one of the first books of poetry ever published by an Englishwoman and the first such book dedicated exclusively to women patrons.

Source of the Book The book was remarkable for another reason as well. In it, according to scholar Susanne Woods, Lanyer is "attacking the vanity and blindness of men and justifying women's right to be free of masculine subjugation" at a time when few women dared to do so. Lanyer excused her boldness with the claim that her title, which means "Hail, God, King of the Jews," came to her in a dream. She said that this was "a significant token, that I was appointed to perform this Worke."

Detail from the Annunciation, c.1430–32. Fra Angelico. Oil on panel. Prado, Madrid, Spain.

> *"Do not the thing*
> *that goes against thy heart."*
>
> —Aemilia Lanyer,
> *from* Salve Deus Rex Judaeorum

Ironically, Lanyer may have owed some credit for her accomplishments to her father, Baptista Bassano, a musician at the English royal court. Although her father died when she was only seven, he left her with money and connections to people at the royal court who exposed her to ideas and rhetorical techniques that developed her mind and her art. She had a relationship with Lord Hunsdon, a member of Queen Elizabeth's court and a patron to Shakespeare's theater company. When Lanyer's relationship with Hunsdon ended, she married Alfonso Lanyer, a court musician.

An educated woman, Lanyer may have known Shakespeare himself, as well as Ben Jonson and Edmund Spenser. In fact, there is some evidence that Lanyer is the so-called Dark Lady whom Shakespeare addresses in many of his sonnets.

A Woman's Vision Lanyer was a friend of the Countess of Cumberland, a patron of the arts and Lanyer's patron as well. The Countess was one of the many women to whom Lanyer dedicated her book. Part of Lanyer's book contains what is known as a country-house poem, "The Description of Cooke-ham," which was the home of the Countess of Cumberland and her daughter. According to Woods, the poem "presents a woman's vision of an ideal life in harmony with nature in which neither men nor class distinctions mar conversation and song under a lovely oak tree with a wonderful view of the countryside."

Aemilia Lanyer was born in 1569 and died in 1645.

Literature Online **Author Search** For more about Aemilia Lanyer, go to www.glencoe.com.

Connecting to the Poem

Writers often question well-known and widely accepted literary texts and the characters they portray. In doing so, they provide fresh insight into those texts. As you read this poem, think about these questions:

- What were Eve's actions in the Genesis accounts of the Garden of Eden?
- Do you think Eve should be blamed for God's decision to banish the first couple from Eden?

Building Background

In the Bible, the book of Genesis tells how God created Adam, placed him in the Garden of Eden, and commanded him not to eat fruit from the tree of knowledge. God then created Eve to be Adam's companion. The two lived contentedly until Eve, tempted by a serpent, ate from the forbidden tree and gave the fruit to Adam, who ate as well. As punishment, God banished Adam and Eve from the garden.

The word *apology* in the title of Lanyer's poem does not mean that Eve is sorry for her actions or is accepting the blame for them. As it is used here, *apology* refers to a defense or justification of Eve's actions.

Setting Purposes for Reading

Big Idea **The Sacred and the Secular**

Some humanists believed that faith could be combined with the spirit of inquiry. As you read the selection, decide whether Lanyer was this kind of humanist.

Literary Element **Argument**

Argument is a type of persuasive writing in which logic or reason is used to try to influence the reader's ideas or actions. In an argument, a writer states an opinion and supports that opinion by using carefully presented facts and reasoning. Arguments may also appeal to the reader's emotions. During the English Renaissance, writers often presented arguments in the form of poems. As you read, decide which arguments are based on reason and which on emotion.

- See Literary Terms Handbook, p. R2.

Reading Strategy **Drawing Conclusions About Author's Beliefs**

A **conclusion** is a general statement about the information you have on a subject. You should back up your conclusions with supporting details. As you read, look for details that suggest what Aemilia Lanyer believes.

Reading Tip: Summarizing When you draw conclusions about parts of a poem, summarize the meaning of each stanza in a sentence or two. Then you can more easily draw conclusions about the whole work. Use a chart like the one below.

Stanza	Summary
1.	
2.	
3.	
4.	

Vocabulary

endure (en door´) *v.* bear; tolerate; put up with; p. 426 *It was hard to endure the pain in my knee when I fell.*

discretion (dis kresh´ ən) *n.* good judgment; p. 426 *When I asked her whether I should reveal the secret, she left it to my discretion.*

Vocabulary Tip: Context Clues When you come across an unfamiliar word or phrase, look at the surrounding words and phrases for clues.

Literature Online **Interactive Literary Elements Handbook** To review or learn more about the literary elements, go to www.glencoe.com.

OBJECTIVES
In studying this selection, you will focus on the following:
- analyzing literary periods
- identifying and analyzing arguments
- drawing conclusions about author's beliefs

Eve's Apology

from Salve Deus Rex Judaeorum

Aemilia Lanyer

The Temptress, 1995. Christian Pierre. Acrylic on masonite, 48 x 32 in. Private collection.

But surely Adam cannot be excused;
Her fault, though great, yet he was most to blame.
What weakness offered, strength might have refused;
Being lord of all, the greater was his shame;
5   Although the serpent's craft had her abused,
God's holy word ought all his actions frame;[1]
     For he was lord and king of all the earth
     Before poor Eve had either life or breath,

Who being framed[2] by God's eternal hand
10   The perfectest man that ever breathed on earth,
And from God's mouth received that strait[3] command,
The breach[4] whereof he knew was present death;
Yea, having power to rule both sea and land,
Yet with one apple won to lose that breath
15   Which God had breathèd in his beauteous face,
     Bringing us all in danger and disgrace;

And then to lay the fault on patience's back,
That we (poor women) must **endure** it all;
We know right well he did **discretion** lack,
20   Being not persuaded thereunto at all.
If Eve did err, it was for knowledge sake;
The fruit being fair persuaded him to fall.
     No subtle serpent's falsehood did betray him;
     If he would eat it, who had power to stay[5] him?

25   Not Eve, whose fault was only too much love,
Which made her give this present to her dear,
That what she tasted he likewise might prove,[6]
Whereby his knowledge might become more clear;
He never sought her weakness to reprove[7]
30   With those sharp words which he of God did hear;
     Yet men will boast of knowledge, which he took
     From Eve's fair hand, as from a learnèd book.

---

1. *Frame* means "determine."
2. Here, *framed* means "formed."
3. *Strait* means "strict."
4. A *breach* is a violation.
5. *Stay* means "prevent."
6. *Prove* means "discover by experience."
7. *Reprove* means "condemn."

Vocabulary

endure (en door´) *v.* bear; tolerate; put up with

discretion (dis kresh´ ən) *n.* good judgment

Literary Element   **Argument** *Explain why this is or is not a persuasive argument.*

RESPONDING AND THINKING CRITICALLY

Respond

1. What is your opinion of Adam after reading this poem? Why?

Recall and Interpret

2. In the first stanza, who does the speaker say is most to blame for Adam and Eve's sin? Why?

3. (a)According to the second stanza, what did Adam know would result from disobeying God's command? (b)What else results from his actions?

4. (a)In the third stanza, what reasons does the speaker give for Eve's error and Adam's fall? (b)What do these reasons imply about Eve and Adam?

Analyze and Evaluate

5. (a)In the fourth stanza, what reasons does the speaker give to argue that Eve's actions were more excusable than Adam's? (b)How effectively do you think these reasons support the argument? Explain.

6. What is your reaction to lines 31–32 about the source of men's knowledge?

7. Do you think this apology would be more or less effective if the speaker were Eve herself? Explain.

Connect

8. In your opinion, are two people who commit the same act always equally responsible for their actions? Explain.

9. **Big Idea** The Sacred and the Secular How do you think the attitudes about women during Lanyer's time might have affected her opinions and writing?

LITERARY ANALYSIS

Literary Element Argument

Writers often rely on different persuasive techniques in order to convince the reader to think in a certain way. In her poem, Lanyer uses **emotional appeals,** or words and phrases that arouse strong emotions in the reader.

1. Restate the main points of the argument in "Eve's Apology." Do you think it is an effective argument? Why or why not?

2. List two or three passages in which the speaker appeals to the reader's emotions. Do these appeals enhance her argument? Give reasons for your answer.

Writing About Literature

Respond to Argument How do you think Adam might have responded to "Eve's Apology"? When actors or politicians fall out of favor with the public, think about what strategies they use to regain favor. Using these persuasive strategies, write an argument from Adam's point of view in which you justify his actions in the Garden of Eden.

Literature Online **Web Activities** For eFlashcards, Selection Quick Checks, and other Web activities, go to www.glencoe.com.

READING AND VOCABULARY

Reading Strategy Drawing Conclusions About Author's Beliefs

When you draw a conclusion, you make a general statement about something you have read or found. What conclusion can you draw about Lanyer's beliefs, based on this poem?

Vocabulary Practice

Practice with Context Clues For each item below, identify a context clue that could help you to figure out the meaning of the underlined word.

1. I got up and walked out. I couldn't <u>endure</u> another minute of that terrible movie.
   a. walked out **b.** movie **c.** minute

2. Hank often uses poor judgment. His brother Jim has much more <u>discretion</u>.
   a. brother **b.** often **c.** poor judgment

The Metaphysical Poets

> *"The metaphysical poets were men of learning, and to show their learning was their whole endeavor. . . . Their thoughts are often new, but seldom natural."*
>
> —Samuel Johnson

Vanitas. French School. Louvre, Paris.

THE TERM *METAPHYSICAL POETS* IS GENERALLY applied to a distinctive group of seventeenth-century English poets, including John Donne, George Herbert, Richard Crashaw, and Andrew Marvell. Their poetry was marked by highly complex extended metaphors, avoidance of smooth or regular meter, and a fondness for unconventional imagery often drawn from philosophy, theology, science, or the arts.

The eighteenth-century Neoclassicist writer Samuel Johnson (see page 648), who was highly critical of the "unnatural" images and rhythms of John Donne's verse, gave it the name "metaphysical poetry," a term that has since been used by Donne's admirers as well as by his detractors. Johnson used the term to describe poetry that dealt with philosophical, abstract, and highly theoretical topics.

The Metaphysical Style

Although the metaphysical poets derived inspiration from the rich legacy of Elizabethan verse, their poetry was in part a reaction against the stylized conventions of the sixteenth-century sonnet sequence. Instead of using regular meters and "poetic" images drawn from nature, poets such as Donne often used irregular rhythms and unusual, often startling, figurative language. Donne's tone is less formal and his word choice is simpler than those of most Elizabethan poets, but his verse makes far greater demands on the reader's intellect. Donne's poetry often includes an elaborate metaphor, a witty argument, or a complex philosophical speculation.

The Characteristics of Metaphysical Poetry

Like the Elizabethan poets, the metaphysical poets wrote about love and the physical attraction between men and women, but they were also attracted to darker or more somber subjects, such as death, the brevity of human life, and the individual's relationship with God. A philosophical approach to everyday subjects and experience expressed in a witty, conversational style is a hallmark of metaphysical poetry. The similarities and differences between the Elizabethan and metaphysical styles may be summarized as follows:

- **Use of Argument** Like much Elizabethan verse, metaphysical poetry often takes the form of an argument, but the argument in a metaphysical poem appeals to the intellect as well as to emotions.
- **Use of Conceits** Elizabethan poets were fond of **conceits**, or elaborate extended metaphors. Often these conceits compared the beauty of a woman to the beauty of a natural object, such as a star. The metaphysical poets took the use of

conceits a significant step further, creating arresting comparisons between very dissimilar objects or ideas that demand thought and imagination to unravel. For example, in "A Valediction: Of Weeping," Donne compares the tears on a man's face to newly minted coins.

- **Use of Language** Elizabethan poets usually wrote in a "high style," using melodious words, elegant phrasing, and poetic inversions of typical speech patterns. By contrast, the metaphysical poets often wrote in a "plain style" that more closely resembled speech. To see the difference between these two styles, compare the opening lines of the following two poems. The first excerpt exemplifies high style, and the second excerpt exemplifies plain style.

"With how sad steps, O Moon, thou climb'st the skies!"
—Sir Philip Sidney, Sonnet 31

"For God's sake hold your tongue, and let me love"
—John Donne, "The Canonization"

- **Use of Unconventional Forms** Most Elizabethan poets were content with traditional forms, including rhyme and meter. To Samuel Johnson's aesthetic discomfort, the metaphysical poets did not always follow these conventions. The meter of lines did not always scan with regularity, rhyme schemes could not always be predicted, the vocabulary and syntax were not elevated, and some of the topics seemed scandalous. The result, however, is a directness of language that often arrests and captivates the reader.

Portrait of a Lady, c. 17th century. English School. Private collection.

The Legacy of the Metaphysical Poets

Because of the different literary tastes during the Neoclassical, Romantic, and Victorian periods, metaphysical poetry was undervalued throughout the eighteenth and nineteenth centuries. Eventually, poets such as William Butler Yeats, T. S. Eliot, and W. H. Auden praised the metaphysical poets for their ability to appeal to the mind as well as to the heart. In the early twentieth century, when Modernist poets were overturning the values and conventions of Romanticism in literature, metaphysical poetry was at last praised and recognized for its substantial contributions to English literature.

Literature Online **Literary History** For more about the metaphysical poets, go to www.glencoe.com.

RESPONDING AND THINKING CRITICALLY

1. In your opinion, should poetry primarily appeal to intellect or to emotions? Explain.

2. Why might Samuel Johnson have considered metaphysical poetry to be "unnatural"?

3. In what ways did the metaphysical poets anticipate Modernist poetry?

OBJECTIVES
- Analyze historical movements and periods in English literature.
- Understand the characteristics of metaphysical poetry.

Donne's Works

MEET JOHN DONNE

In life and in art, John Donne forged a unique path. Donne was a contemplative and religious man. Gifted with a nimble mind and astonishing talent, Donne created intimate portrayals of human relationships and of the physical world, but his foremost passion was for God. He believed that human suffering was transient, that the afterlife was real, and that people had a duty to confront their own mortality with courage. The poems and sermons in which Donne expressed his views are considered to be some of the most glorious works of English literature.

Ambitious Youth Donne was born into an affluent Roman Catholic family at a time when anti-Catholic sentiment ran high. When he was four, his father died. At twelve, Donne began studies at Oxford, continuing later at Cambridge, but as a result of his Catholicism, he received degrees from neither school. Donne would not make the oath to the Protestant Queen Elizabeth that was a requirement for graduation.

After traveling in Spain and Italy, the young Donne studied law in London. Perhaps to prove his patriotism and help pave the way for a government career, Donne then joined the Earl of Essex on two daring military expeditions against Spain. On his return to England in 1597, Donne secured the position of secretary to government minister Sir Thomas Egerton. By this time, Donne had abandoned Catholicism and joined the Church of England.

As Egerton's secretary, Donne met many important people with whom he made himself popular. His career flourished until 1601. That year, he met, fell in love, and eloped with Egerton's seventeen-year-old niece, Anne More. Anne's father, furious, responded by having Donne fired from his post and thrown into jail. Though his time there was brief, Donne lost all hope of a government career, his wife lost her dowry, and, suddenly without funds, the couple was forced to live on the charity of Anne's cousin.

Poet and Minister To occupy his time after being fired, Donne studied and wrote essays on theology and poems about love and religion. He supported his growing family with odd jobs, writing, and the charity of friends. His allies, moved by the power of his religious poems, urged him to enter the Anglican ministry. At forty-three he did just that, and he soon became a chaplain to King James I.

Two years later, Donne's wife died in childbirth. Grief-stricken, he poured himself into preaching with passionate intensity. The force and eloquence of these sermons helped lead to his appointment, at the age of forty-nine, to the deanship of the prestigious St. Paul's Cathedral in London.

> "Donne's verses are like the peace of God: they pass all understanding."
>
> —King James I

In February of 1631, Donne, who was already ill with the cancer that would kill him, gave his final sermon at court. Many believe that he intended it to be his own funeral sermon. By the time Donne died, he was considered the greatest preacher in England.

John Donne was born in 1572 and died in 1631.

Literature Online **Author Search** For more about John Donne, go to www.glencoe.com.

Connecting to the Poems

Think about a time when you had to say good-bye to someone who was important to you. What did you say, write, or do? In these poems, Donne claims that there are limits to the power of loss and death. As you read the poems, think about how you deal with loss in your own life.

Building Background

Most scholars agree that Donne wrote two of his best-loved poems just before leaving on a diplomatic mission to France. While Donne was planning the trip, his wife, Anne, had a premonition that something bad would happen while he was away. She urged him to stay home, and at first Donne heeded her warnings, but his friends eventually convinced him to go. Sensitive to his wife's suffering, Donne wrote "Song" and "A Valediction: Forbidding Mourning" to comfort her. A valediction is a farewell statement. "Death Be Not Proud" was written soon after the death of Donne's wife.

Setting Purposes for Reading

Big Idea **The Sacred and the Secular**

As you read, think about how Donne's religious beliefs affect his description of earthly events.

Literary Element **Meter**

Meter is the regular pattern of stressed and unstressed syllables that gives a line of poetry a predictable rhythm. The basic unit of meter is known as a **foot**, consisting of one or two stressed syllables (marked ´) and/or one or two unstressed syllables (marked ˘). As you read Donne's poems, pay attention to their rhythms and the way in which the stressed and unstressed syllables in each poem are arranged.

- See Literary Terms Handbook, p. R10.

Literature Online **Interactive Literary Elements Handbook** To review or learn more about the literary elements, go to www.glencoe.com.

Reading Strategy **Analyzing Figures of Speech**

Figurative language is language that is not meant to be interpreted literally. It is used for descriptive effect, often to imply ideas indirectly. A **figure of speech** is a specific device or kind of figurative language such as **metaphor**, **personification**, or **simile**.

- A **metaphor** makes a comparison between two unlike things to help readers perceive the first thing more vividly (as in *the stars are torches*).
- **Personification** gives human qualities to objects, animals, or ideas (as in *the trees are patient*).
- A **simile** compares two unlike things, using the words "like" or "as" (as in *the moon is like a purse*).

Reading Tip: Taking Notes As you read the poems, record figures of speech in a chart like the one shown. Write down your thoughts about the feeling or meaning each figure of speech suggests to you.

Figure of Speech	What the figure of speech communicates

Vocabulary

jest (jest) *n.* an utterance or act offered humorously or mockingly; p. 432 *When I said that I would not clean the house, Mom knew my remark was in jest.*

refined (ri fīnd´) *adj.* freed from imperfections; improved; p. 434 *Refined sugar has been processed to remove unwanted particles.*

Vocabulary Tip: Synonyms Synonyms are words that have the same or similar meanings. Note that synonyms are always the same part of speech.

OBJECTIVES
In studying these selections, you will focus on the following:
- analyzing literary genres
- analyzing meter and theme
- analyzing figures of speech

SONG

John Donne

A Market Scene with Fruit and Vegetable Sellers. Frederick van Valkenborch (1570–1623). Oil on canvas. Private collection.

Sweetest love, I do not go,
    For weariness of thee,
Nor in hope the world can show
    A fitter love for me,
5   But since that I
Must die at last, 'tis best,
To use[1] myself in **jest**
    Thus by feigned[2] deaths to die.

Yesternight the sun went hence,
10   And yet is here today,
He hath no desire nor sense,
    Nor half so short a way:
        Then fear not me,
But believe that I shall make
15 Speedier journeys, since I take
    More wings and spurs than he.

O how feeble is man's power,
    That if good fortune fall,
Cannot add another hour,
20   Nor a lost hour recall!

        But come bad chance,
And we join to it our strength,
And we teach it art and length,
    Itself o'er us to advance.

25 When thou sigh'st, thou sigh'st not wind,
    But sigh'st my soul away,
When thou weep'st, unkindly kind,
    My life's blood doth decay.
        It cannot be
30 That thou lov'st me as thou say'st,
If in thine my life thou waste,
    That art the best of me.

Let not thy divining heart
    Forethink me any ill,
35 Destiny may take thy part,
    And may thy fears fulfill,
        But think that we
Are but turned aside to sleep;
They who one another keep
40   Alive, ne'er parted be.

---

1. Here, *use* means "condition" or "prepare."
2. *Feigned* means "imagined" or "pretended" in this context.

Vocabulary

jest (jest) *n.* an utterance or act offered humorously or mockingly

Reading Strategy **Analyzing Figures of Speech** *Why does the speaker compare the sighs of his beloved to his soul?*

A Valediction:
Forbidding Mourning

John Donne

Ptolemy of Alexandria, c. 130 A.D. Illustration from *Margarita Philosophica*, 1535. Science Museum, London.

As virtuous men pass mildly away,
    And whisper to their souls to go,
Whilst some of their sad friends do say,
    "The breath goes now," and some say, "No";

5 So let us melt[1] and make no noise,
    No tear-floods nor sigh-tempests move;
'Twere profanation[2] of our joys
    To tell the laity[3] our love.

Moving of the earth[4] brings harms and fears,
10   Men reckon what it did and meant;
But trepidation of the spheres,[5]
    Though greater far, is innocent.[6]

Dull sublunary lovers' love,
    Whose soul[7] is sense,[8] cannot admit
15 Absence, because it doth remove
    Those things which elemented[9] it.

---

1. *Melt* means "part."
2. *Profanation* means "desecration, debasement, or sacrilege."
3. *Laity* are usually people who are not members of the clergy but here may be intended to mean "outsiders" or to refer to anyone besides the speaker and the speaker's beloved.
4. *Moving of the earth* is a reference to earthquakes.
5. *Trepidation of the spheres* refers to a shuddering motion attributed to the eighth sphere in Ptolemy's model of the universe.
6. Here, *innocent* means "harmless."
7. Here, *soul* refers to essence.
8. *Sense* means "physical perceptions."
9. *Elemented* means "composed."

Literary Element   **Meter** *What pattern of stressed and unstressed syllables do you hear in these two lines?*

But we, by a love so much **refined**
    That ourselves know not what it is,
Inter-assurèd[10] of the mind;
20   Care less, eyes, lips, and hands to miss.

Our two souls, therefore, which are one,
    Though I must go, endure not yet
A breach,[11] but an expansion,
    Like gold to airy thinness beat.[12]

25 If they be two, they are two so
    As stiff twin compasses[13] are two:
Thy soul, the fixed foot, makes no show
    To move, but doth if the other do.

And though it in the center sit,
30   Yet when the other far doth roam,
It leans and hearkens after it,
    And grows erect as that comes home.

Such wilt thou be to me, who must,
    Like the other foot, obliquely[14] run:
35 Thy firmness[15] makes my circle[16] just,
    And makes me end where I begun.

---

10. *Inter-assurèd* means "mutually assured."
11. A *breach* is a break.
12. *Like . . . beat* refers to gold leaf, which is made by beating gold into tissue-thin pieces. Baser metals would break up under the beating.
13. *Twin compasses* are the two legs of a geometrical compass.
14. *Obliquely* means "off course."
15. *Firmness* implies faithfulness or perfection.
16. The *circle,* which has neither a beginning nor an end, is a symbol of perfection.

Reading Strategy Analyzing Figures of Speech *Why does the poet compare people in love to the legs of a compass in this stanza?*

Vocabulary

refined (ri fīnd´) *adj.* freed from imperfections; improved

Saint Ursula dreams of her coming martyrdom, announced by an angel, 1494. Vittore Carpaccio. Oil on canvas, 274 x 267 cm. Accademia, Venice, Italy.

DEATH
BE NOT PROUD

John Donne

Death, be not proud, though some have called thee
Mighty and dreadful, for thou art not so;
For those whom thou think'st thou dost overthrow
Die not, poor Death, nor yet canst thou kill me.
5 From rest and sleep, which but thy pictures[1] be,
Much pleasure, then from thee much more must flow,
And soonest our best men with thee do go,
Rest of their bones, and soul's delivery.[2]
Thou art slave to fate, chance, kings, and desperate men,
10 And dost with poison, war, and sickness dwell,
And poppy[3] or charms can make us sleep as well
And better than thy stroke; why swell'st thou then?[4]
One short sleep past, we wake eternally,
And death shall be no more; Death, thou shalt die.

---

1. *Pictures,* or images, of rest and sleep are similar to images of death.
2. *Soul's delivery* likely means "soul's salvation."
3. *Poppy* is a source of opium, which is a narcotic drug that can produce sleep.
4. *Why swell'st thou then?* can be restated as "Why do you swell with pride?"

Big Idea   **The Sacred and the Secular** *What consolation do these lines suggest?*

RESPONDING AND THINKING CRITICALLY

Respond

1. What ideas from the poems did you find most powerful or surprising? Explain.

Recall and Interpret

2. (a)In "Song," how does the speaker try to reassure his beloved in the first stanza? (b)What does the speaker mean by "[t]hus by feigned deaths to die"?

3. (a)In "Song," how is the speaker similar to and different from the sun? (b)Why might the speaker make this comparison?

4. (a)In the first two stanzas of "A Valediction: Forbidding Mourning," to what does the speaker compare his separation from his lover? (b)What do the words "profanation" and "laity" imply about his feelings?

5. (a)In "A Valediction," when sublunary lovers are absent from each other, what happens to their love, according to lines 13–16? (b)In contrast to the sublunary lovers, what kind of love does the speaker claim he and his beloved share (in lines 17–20)?

6. (a)In "Death Be Not Proud," what does the speaker tell Death in the first four lines? (b)To what does the speaker compare Death in line five? (c)What can you infer about the speaker's attitude toward Death, based on the first eight lines?

7. (a)How is Death "slave to fate, chance, kings, and desperate men"? (b)According to lines 13–14, when will Death die?

Analyze and Evaluate

8. (a)In "Song," what is the speaker saying about the power people have over good and bad luck? (b)Do you agree with his views on the subject? Explain.

9. (a)Why should the parting of two people in love not be a cause for mourning, according to "A Valediction: Forbidding Mourning"? (b)How persuasive did you find the speaker of the poem? Explain.

10. **Tone** is the attitude of the author toward the subject of a literary work. (a)How would you describe the tone of "Death Be Not Proud"? (b)What standard ideas about death are contradicted by the poem? Support your answer.

Connect

11. **Big Idea** **The Sacred and the Secular** These poems explore life, death, and love. According to the poems, what is fleeting? What is eternal? Explain what the poems suggest about Donne's views of the sacred and the secular.

LITERARY ANALYSIS

Literary Element Meter

Meter is the pattern of stressed and unstressed syllables that gives a line of poetry a predictable rhythm. Within a poem, a poet may choose to vary the meter to create certain effects. For instance, if the reader has come to expect a line to be written in a certain rhythm, the introduction of a new rhythm may help to heighten the poem's drama.

- On a sheet of paper, copy out "Song" or "A Valediction: Forbidding Mourning." Then mark the stressed and unstressed syllables. Note how many syllables occur in each line of the poem. (a)How regular is the meter of the poem you chose? (b)Why might the poet have chosen such a meter? Explain.

Review: Theme

As you learned on page 301, the **theme** of a work is its central insight about life or human nature.

Partner Activity Meet with a classmate and discuss the themes of these three poems. For each poem, state the theme in one or two sentences. Then list evidence that supports your description of the theme. When you are done, compare and contrast the themes of the three poems.

Literature Online **Web Activities** For eFlashcards, Selection Quick Checks, and other Web activities, go to www.glencoe.com.

Reading Strategy Analyzing Figures of Speech

In these poems, **figures of speech**, such as metaphors and similes, are used by Donne to create a variety of effects. They help to create tone, to vividly portray feelings, and to suggest fresh ideas. To convey meaning, Donne also uses **personification**—a figure of speech in which human qualities are given to objects, animals, or concepts.

1. (a)Explain one metaphor in "Song." What does the metaphor compare? (b)What meaning does the metaphor contribute to the poem?

2. (a)Explain the simile in lines 21–24 of "A Valediction: Forbidding Mourning." (b)What is the simile comparing? What is the deeper meaning of the simile?

3. What does the poem "Death Be Not Proud" achieve by personifying death? Explain.

Vocabulary Practice

Practice with Synonyms For each vocabulary word from Donne's poems, choose the word's synonym.

1. jest   **a.** clown   **b.** quip

2. refined   **a.** improved   **b.** degraded

Academic Vocabulary

Here are two words from the vocabulary list on page R82.

communicate (kə mū′ ni kāt′) *v.* to transmit ideas or emotions; to make something clear or understood

contribute (kən trib′ ūt) *v.* to add something to; to help cause something

Practice and Apply

1. What message does the poem "Song" **communicate** about parting?

2. What does the metaphor of the compass **contribute** to the meaning of "A Valediction: Forbidding Mourning"?

Writing About Literature

Analyze Tone Tone is the attitude that a writer expresses toward his or her subject matter. When we speak, we choose a tone of voice to convey underlying attitudes such as humor, formality, anger, or sadness. Similarly, poets carefully choose their words in order to set a tone. Over the course of a poem, the tone may stay consistent, or it may shift at points.

Write a brief essay about the tone of Donne's poem "Song." Begin by reviewing the poem and jotting down any words or phrases—such as figures of speech—that give you insights into the tone. Also take notes about the poem's **imagery**, the descriptions that appeal to the senses.

Use your notes to begin constructing your essay. You might organize your essay like this.

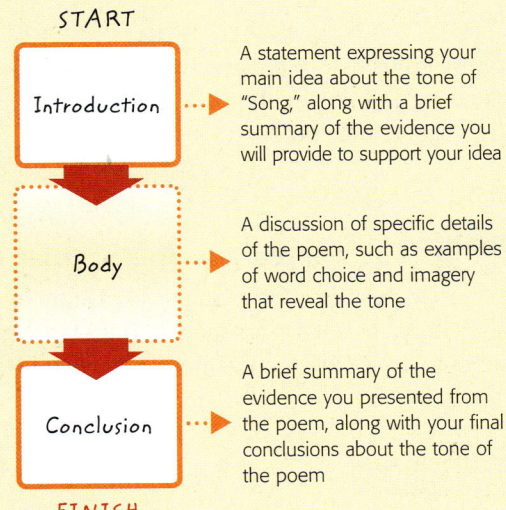

START

Introduction ····▶ A statement expressing your main idea about the tone of "Song," along with a brief summary of the evidence you will provide to support your idea

Body ····▶ A discussion of specific details of the poem, such as examples of word choice and imagery that reveal the tone

Conclusion ····▶ A brief summary of the evidence you presented from the poem, along with your final conclusions about the tone of the poem

FINISH

After you complete your draft, meet with a partner to evaluate each other's work and to suggest revisions. Then proofread and edit your draft for errors in spelling, grammar, and punctuation.

Learning for Life

Sooner or later, every person must face the death of a loved one. John Donne wrote "Death Be Not Proud" after the death of his wife, perhaps as a way to deal with his grief. What are some ways people can work through their complicated emotions after a loved one's death? Share your thoughts with a partner.

LITERATURE PREVIEW

READING PREVIEW

Connecting to the Meditation

Feelings of alienation and isolation are frequent issues in today's world. People in Donne's time faced the same emotions and often turned to religion for support. As you read Meditation 17, think about the following questions:

- In what ways do you feel connected to society as a whole?
- How can society function as a support system for those in need?

Building Background

At the age of fifty-one, while dean of St. Paul's Cathedral, Donne became seriously ill. After his recovery, he wrote a series of prose meditations—short sermons expressing his private reflections on this experience—including Meditation 17.

The central imagery in Meditation 17 refers to the ancient custom of ringing the bells of the village church to signal that someone was about to die.

Setting Purposes for Reading

Big Idea The Sacred and the Secular

As you read, note that even though Meditation 17 is a sermon, it contains secular imagery and metaphors. Think about why Donne chose these particular figures of speech.

Literary Element Metaphysical Conceit

A **metaphysical conceit** is an intellectual comparison that can develop a wide range of ideas and capture a broad range of emotions. As you read this sermon, pay attention to how Donne uses metaphysical conceits to advance an argument about mortality and salvation.

- See Literary Terms Handbook, p. R10.

Literature Online **Interactive Literary Elements Handbook** To review or learn more about the literary elements, go to www.glencoe.com.

Reading Strategy Making Inferences About Theme

The **theme** of a work is its overall message about life or human nature. Often, readers can discover the theme by making inferences, or educated guesses, based on details in the work. As you read, think about what overall message about life and death Donne's sermon is trying to convey.

Reading Tip: Taking Notes As you read Meditation 17, use a chart like the one below to help you make inferences about the sermon's theme.

Details	Inference About Theme
"all mankind is of one author and is one volume"	Everyone belongs to God and is a part of the same whole.

Vocabulary

congregation (kong′ grə gā′ shən) *n.* a group of people who gather for religious worship; p. 439 *The minister greeted his congregation before beginning the sermon.*

covetousness (kuv′ it əs nəs) *n.* great desire for something belonging to another; p. 440 *Greta wanted her sister's purse; she was guilty of covetousness.*

contemplation (kon′ təm plā′ shən) *n.* careful thought or consideration; meditation; p. 440 *Tom sat under the oak tree deep in contemplation.*

Vocabulary Tip: Analogies An analogy is a type of comparison that is based on the relationships between things or ideas.

OBJECTIVES
In studying this selection, you will focus on the following:
- analyzing literary genres
- analyzing metaphysical conceits
- making inferences about theme

Dance of Death, 16th century. Print. Private Collection.

Meditation 17

John Donne

Nunc lento sonitu dicunt, Morieris.
Now this bell, tolling softly for another, says to me, Thou must die.

Perchance he for whom this bell tolls may be so ill as that he knows not it tolls for him; and perchance I may think myself so much better than I am, as that they who are about me and see my state may have caused it to toll for me, and I know not that.

The church is catholic,[1] universal, so are all her actions; all that she does belongs to all. When she baptizes a child, that action concerns me; for that child is thereby connected to that head[2] which is my head too, and ingrafted into that body[3] whereof I am a member. And when she buries a man, that action concerns me: all mankind is of one author and is one volume; when one man dies, one chapter is not torn out of the book, but translated into a better language; and every chapter must be so translated. God employs several translators; some pieces are translated by age, some by sickness, some by war, some by justice; but God's hand is in every translation, and his hand shall bind up all our scattered leaves[4] again for that library where every book shall lie open to one another.

As therefore the bell that rings to a sermon calls not upon the preacher only, but upon the **congregation** to come, so this bell calls us all; but how much more me, who am brought so near the door by this sickness. There was a contention as

---

4. *Leaves,* in this context, are pages.

Literary Element **Metaphysical Conceit** *What two things is Donne comparing here?*

Reading Strategy **Making Inferences About Theme** *What does Donne mean when he says the death bell "calls us all"?*

Vocabulary

congregation (kong′ grə gā′ shən) *n.* a group of people who gather for religious worship

---

1. When Donne says the church is *catholic,* he means that it embraces all humankind.
2. *Head* stands for Christ, the head of the church.
3. *Body* stands for the church.

far as a suit[5] (in which piety[6] and dignity, religion and estimation,[7] were mingled) which of the religious orders should ring to prayers first in the morning; and it was determined that they should ring first that rose earliest. If we understand aright the dignity of this bell that tolls for our evening prayer, we would be glad to make it ours by rising early, in that application, that it might be ours as well as his whose indeed it is.

The bell doth toll for him that thinks it doth; and though it intermit[8] again, yet from that minute that that occasion wrought upon him, he is united to God.

Who casts not up his eye to the sun when it rises? but who takes off his eye from a comet when that breaks out? Who bends not his ear to any bell which upon any occasion rings? but who can remove it from that bell which is passing a piece of himself out of this world?

No man is an island, entire of itself; every man is a piece of the continent, a part of the main.[9] If a clod be washed away by the sea, Europe is the less, as well as if a promontory[10] were, as well as if a manor of thy friend's or of thine own were. Any man's death diminishes me, because I am involved in mankind, and therefore never send to know for whom the bell tolls; it tolls for thee.

Neither can we call this a begging of misery or a borrowing of misery, as though we were not miserable enough of ourselves but must fetch in more from the next house, in taking upon us the misery of our neighbors. Truly it were an excusable **covetousness** if we did; for affliction[11] is a treasure, and scarce any man hath enough of it. No man hath affliction enough that is not matured and ripened by it, and made fit for God by that affliction. If a man carry treasure in bullion,[12] or in a wedge of gold, and have none coined into current moneys, his treasure will not defray him[13] as he travels. Tribulation[14] is treasure in the nature of it, but it is not current money in the use of it, except we get nearer and nearer our home, heaven, by it. Another man may be sick too, and sick to death, and this affliction may lie in his bowels as gold in a mine and be of no use to him; but this bell that tells me of his affliction digs out and applies that gold to me, if by this consideration of another's danger I take mine own into **contemplation** and so secure myself by making my recourse[15] to my God, who is our only security. ◆

> *"No man is an island, entire of itself; every man is a piece of the continent, a part of the main."*

---

5. A *contention as far as a suit* is a dispute or controversy that resulted in a lawsuit.
6. *Piety* means "religious devotion."
7. *Estimation* refers to self-esteem here.
8. *Intermit* means "pause."
9. *Main* is a shortening of *mainland*.
10. A *promontory* is a ridge of land extending out into a body of water.

11. *Affliction* means "pain; misery; or suffering."
12. *Bullion* is precious metal in the form of bars or ingots.
13. *Defray him* means "pay his costs."
14. *Tribulation* is misery or suffering.
15. *Recourse* is an appeal for help or protection.

Big Idea **The Sacred and the Secular** *What is Donne's attitude toward earthly troubles?*

Literary Element **Metaphysical Conceit** *According to Donne, what good is the "gold" of a dying person's affliction?*

Vocabulary

covetousness (kuv′ it əs nəs) *n.* great desire for something belonging to another

contemplation (kon′ təm plā′ shən) *n.* careful thought or consideration; meditation

RESPONDING AND THINKING CRITICALLY

Respond

1. Which passages triggered the strongest reactions in you as you read this sermon? Why?

Recall and Interpret

2. (a)Paraphrase Donne's words in the first paragraph. (b)In your opinion, what is Donne's message in this paragraph?

3. (a)According to Donne, in what ways is humanity like a "piece of the continent"? (b)What do you think is the main point Donne makes in the sixth paragraph? State this point in your own words.

4. (a)What act would be "an excusable covetousness"? Why? (b)Explain in your own words why Donne says "affliction is a treasure."

Analyze and Evaluate

5. (a)In the last paragraph, what does Donne think he will gain from "consideration of another's danger"?

(b)What do you think Donne would have liked his parishioners to do when they heard a bell toll? Support your answer with details from the selection.

6. Donne's statement that "No man is an island, entire of itself" is very famous. (a)What does Donne mean by this statement? (b)How do other statements by Donne lead to the conclusion that "no man is an island"? Explain.

Connect

7. **Big Idea** **The Sacred and the Secular** (a)What images from the secular world does Donne use to advance his argument about the sacred? (b)Why do you think Donne uses these secular images? Explain.

YOU'RE THE CRITIC: Different Viewpoints

How Deep Is Donne?

T. S. Eliot and C. S. Lewis were two of the twentieth century's most celebrated writers and critics. Their views about the depth and emotional complexity of Donne's poetry sharply differed. Read the two excerpts from their literary criticism below.

"One of the characteristics of Donne which wins him, I fancy, his interest for the present age, is his fidelity to emotion as he finds it; his recognition of the complexity of feeling and its rapid alterations . . ."
—T. S. Eliot

"Paradoxical as it may seem, Donne's poetry is too simple to satisfy. Its complexity is all on the surface—an intellectual and fully conscious complexity that we soon come to the end of. . . . There are puzzles in his work, but we can solve them all if we are clever enough; there is none of the depth and ambiguity of real experience in him . . ."
—C. S. Lewis

Group Activity Discuss the following questions with classmates. Refer to the critics' comments and cite evidence from Donne's poems and prose for support.

1. (a)What is the reasoning behind Lewis's claim that Donne's poetry is "too simple"? (b)For what reason does Eliot claim that Donne is still of "interest for the present age"? (c)With which critic do you agree? Explain.

2. To what is Lewis referring when he says that Donne's work contains "puzzles"? Explain.

Literary Element Metaphysical Conceit

A **conceit** is an elaborate metaphor or simile that makes a comparison between two significantly different things. The comparison may seem far-fetched at first but, when examined, gains clarity and persuasion. The conceit not only brings together two entirely different images or ideas but then develops the comparison in details, so as to highlight the similarities. A **metaphysical conceit** creates an abstract or intellectual comparison rather than one based on nature.

1. (a)What conceit does Donne develop extensively in the second paragraph of Meditation 17? (b)How does this conceit help explain Donne's ideas about death and faith?

2. Summarize the main points of the conceit Donne develops in the last paragraph of Meditation 17.

3. Which conceit in this sermon do you feel was the most evocative or powerful? Support your answer.

Review: Motif

As you learned on page 337, a **motif** is a significant phrase, description, or image that is repeated throughout a literary work and that provides an insight into the work's theme.

Group Activity With a group of classmates, try to identify all of the motifs that appear in this sermon. Create a list of them on the board. Then discuss why Donne chose to repeat the words, phrases, and images that he did. How do these repeated ideas and images affect the broader argument of his sermon? How do they affect the sermon's emotional power?

Reading Strategy Making Inferences About Theme

The **theme** of a work is its overall message about life or human nature. Donne develops his theme by using a number of conceits. These conceits help the reader to see different ways of arriving at the same idea.

1. What is the theme of this meditation?

2. Understanding Donne's conceits can be like unraveling a puzzle. Why could it be argued that the labor of understanding Donne's conceits helps to reinforce his theme? Explain.

Vocabulary Practice

Practice with Analogies Choose the vocabulary word from Meditation 17 that best completes each analogy.

1. **worshipper : congregation :: student :**
   a. chorus **b.** audience **c.** class

2. **contemplation : thoughts :: behavior :**
   a. actions **b.** answers **c.** ideas

3. **covetousness : greed :: rivalry :**
   a. pride **b.** competition **c.** hate

Academic Vocabulary

Here are two words from the vocabulary list on page R82.

behalf (bi haf′) *n.* interest, benefit, support, or defense

aid (ād) *v.* to support, assist, or help

Practice and Apply

1. On **behalf** of whom does Donne claim the bell tolls?

2. To whom do you think this sermon can provide the most **aid**?

Writing About Literature

Evaluate Argument Throughout this sermon, Donne uses a variety of techniques, including metaphysical conceits and the repetition of motifs, in order to advance his argument. Write a brief essay in which you explain what Donne is arguing for, what details he provides in the service of his argument, and how effective you found his argument.

Before you begin drafting, compile the evidence that you intend to use in support of your main points. Organize the evidence in an outline like the one below.

I. Introduction

  A. Thesis statement—a concise statement of your overall evaluation of Donne's argument

  B. Brief summary of the ideas that led you to adopt your position

II. Main Idea

  A. Supporting Detail

    1. *"never send to know for whom the bell tolls; it tolls for thee"*

  B. Supporting Detail

  C. Supporting Detail

III. Main Idea

  A. Supporting Detail

  B. Supporting Detail

    1. *"Who casts not up his eye to the sun when it rises?"*

  C. Supporting Detail

IV. Conclusion

  A. A restatement of your thesis and final thoughts about the effectiveness of the sermon

After you complete your draft, meet with a peer reviewer to evaluate each other's work and to suggest revisions. Then proofread and edit your draft for errors in spelling, grammar, and punctuation.

Literary Criticism

Scholar James Dorrill asserts that the tolling bell "signaled for Donne a moral lesson which . . . touched every member of the human community." What do you think that moral lesson is? Write a short paragraph in which you restate this moral lesson in your own words.

Donne's Language and Style

Using Correlative Conjunctions A conjunction is a word that joins single words or groups of words. For example, *and*, *but*, *yet*, and, *or* are all conjunctions. Correlative conjunctions work in pairs to join words and groups of words of equal weight in a sentence. They are useful because they allow the writer to construct complicated sentences in which the relationships between words or groups of words remain clear. Donne uses correlative conjunctions to construct complicated, grammatically sound, and rhetorically powerful sentences.

*"**As** therefore the bell that rings to a sermon calls not upon the preacher only, but upon the congregation to come, **so** this bell calls us all."*

Below is a list of the most commonly used correlative conjunctions:

Correlative Conjunctions	
both . . . and	neither . . . nor
either . . . or	not only . . . but (also)
just as . . . so	whether . . . or

Activity Working with a partner, write three sentences about Meditation 17 that use correlative conjunctions. Use different correlative conjunctions in each sentence.

Revising Check

Correlative Conjunctions Work with a partner to review and revise your use of correlative conjunctions in your essay about Meditation 17.

Literature Online Web Activities For eFlashcards, Selection Quick Checks, and other Web activities, go to www.glencoe.com.

Vocabulary Workshop

Analogies

▶ **Vocabulary Terms**

An **analogy** is a type of comparison based on the relationships between pairs of things or ideas.

▶ **Test-Taking Tip**

To complete analogies in a test-taking situation, think about the relationship between the first pair of words. Then, try to find a similar relationship in the answer choices.

▶ **Reading Handbook**

For more about vocabulary development, see Reading Handbook, p. R20.

Understanding Relationships Between Words

"No man is an island, entire of itself; every man is a piece of the continent, a part of the main."

—John Donne, from Meditation 17

Connecting to Literature When John Donne compared the bond between human beings to the relationship between an island and the mainland, he created one of the most famous analogies in all of literature. An **analogy** is a comparison based on a similarity between things that are otherwise dissimilar. To complete an analogy on a test, you must select from a list the pair of words that represents the same relationship as the first pair given.

Strategy A good strategy for completing analogies is to make up a sentence using the first pair of words that establishes a clear relationship between the ideas they represent. For example, read the item below.

> **stanza : poem ::**
> **a.** flag : anthem   **c.** mural : painting
> **b.** story : building   **d.** program : recital

To determine the relationship represented by the first pair of words, you might use them in a sentence like this one: "Stanzas are the parts that make up a poem." Only pair *b* could also work in the sentence you created: "Stories are the parts that make up a building."

Analogies can be based on a variety of relationships.

Relationship	Example
Association or Usage	A *farmer* is associated with or uses a *plow*.
Part/Whole	A *leg* is a part of a *compass*.
Example/Class	*Asia* is a *continent*.
Synonym or Antonym	*Affliction* is a synonym for *suffering*.

OBJECTIVES
• Understand and complete analogies.
• Learn about the types of relationships between words.

Exercise

Complete the following analogies.

1. congregation : sermon ::
   a. audience : play
   b. horse : polo
   c. fans : spectators

2. pressure : force ::
   a. weight : gravity
   b. velocity : speed
   c. suction : grip

On My First Son and Song: To Celia

MEET BEN JONSON

Picture a fiery-tempered man with a "mountain belly," a "rocky face," and a thumb that had been branded to show he'd once killed a man. Seat him in a tavern called the Mermaid, discussing the art of poetry with a group of young writers who so idolized him that they called themselves the "Sons of Ben." Add to this the fact that, in the prime of his career, this man was more respected for his work than his contemporary William Shakespeare was for his, and you might just begin to appreciate Ben Jonson.

Soldier, Scholar, Playwright Jonson was born in or near London in 1572. As a boy, Jonson was educated at the Westminster School of London, but, unable to afford a university education, he went on to become a mostly self-taught scholar. His first job was as apprentice to a bricklayer; then he went into the army. It wasn't until his early twenties that he joined a theater company and began acting and writing.

> "Talking and eloquence are not the same: to speak, and to speak well, are two things. A fool may talk, but a wise man speaks."
>
> —Ben Jonson

Jonson's first major literary success was a play entitled *Every Man in His Humor*. It was produced when he was only twenty-six and featured Shakespeare in a leading role. Both critics and audiences loved it.

Almost overnight, however, Jonson nearly lost everything. He killed a fellow actor in a duel and wound up sentenced to death. He managed to escape hanging only through "benefit of clergy"—that is, by proving that he could read Latin—and was thus entitled to a trial in the more lenient church court. The court overturned the civil court's death sentence, but Jonson received a brand on his thumb as a convicted felon.

Poet Laureate Jonson was a proud man, and many people found him arrogant and argumentative. He also could be both warm-hearted and fearless.

Throughout his lifetime, Jonson's outspoken nature got him into trouble with the law, his critics, and many of his friends and colleagues. However, his literary career flourished. By 1616, his plays and other works were so popular that King James I gave the forty-four-year-old Jonson a lifetime pension—making him England's first poet laureate.

Yet this honor would turn out to be one of Jonson's last great career successes. Shortly after becoming poet laureate, he decided to spend a year away from London's literary scene. When he returned, he found himself unable to reclaim his former prominence in literary circles. Apparently, what Jonson liked to write had gone out of style.

Jonson suffered a stroke in 1628. After his death in 1637, Jonson was buried at Westminster Abbey under a tombstone that reads "O rare Ben Jonson."

Ben Jonson was born in 1572 and died in 1637.

Literature Online Author Search For more about Ben Jonson, go to www.glencoe.com.

Connecting to the Poems

Have you or someone you know ever lost a beloved family member or friend? If so, what emotions do you associate with that experience? What might you say to someone coping with this type of loss? As you read "On My First Son," ask yourself what this poem reveals about Jonson's views on paternal love and loss.

Building Background

Jonson wrote two of his finest elegies for his own children. He expresses his grief over his infant daughter Mary's death in his poem "On My First Daughter." In his elegy "On My First Son," he mourns the passing of his son, Benjamin, who died of the plague in 1603 on his seventh birthday.

Jonson's songs and poems were often inspired by his reading of classical texts. To create his "Song: To Celia," for example, Jonson actually reworked prose passages from the letters, or *Epistles*, of Philostratus, a third-century Greek philosopher. Though "Song: To Celia" first appeared in Jonson's collection *The Forrest* in 1616, it was set to music a century later by British composer Thomas Arne. The song was published under the title "Drink to Me Only with Thine Eyes." It became wildly popular and even today it continues to be printed in songbooks and recorded by well-known performers.

Setting Purposes for Reading

Big Idea **The Sacred and the Secular**

During the English Renaissance, much of poetic literature consisted of devotional meditations as well as witty reflections on time, transience, and love. As you read Jonson's two poems, note the very different ways in which these themes are expressed.

Literary Element **Elegy**

An **elegy** is a poem mourning a death or other great loss. The subject is often the transience of life. As you read "On My First Son," consider the points the poet makes about sorrow, grief, and the fleeting nature of human existence.

• See Literary Terms Handbook, p. R5.

Reading Strategy **Questioning**

Questioning is asking yourself what information in a selection is important. Questioning also involves regularly asking yourself whether you have understood what you've read. When you ask questions as you read, you're reading strategically. As you answer your questions, you're making sure that you're getting the gist of a text. Ask yourself the following questions as you read "On My First Son":

• Is this idea important? Why?
• Do I understand what this is about?
• How does this relate to what I already know?

Reading Tip: Asking Questions Good readers seldom take anything an author says for granted. As they read, they constantly ask "Why?" to check their understanding. As you read, fill in the answers to the questions in the chart below.

Question	Answer
1. Why does the speaker begin with the word "Farewell"?	
2. Why does the speaker feel as if he is paying a debt?	
3. Why does the speaker vow not to love anything too much in the future?	

Literature Online **Interactive Literary Elements Handbook** To review or learn more about the literary elements, go to www.glencoe.com.

OBJECTIVES
In studying these selections, you will focus on the following:
• analyzing literary genres

• analyzing elegy, lyric poetry, and rhyme scheme
• clarifying material through questioning
• making inferences

Barbet and His Son. Henri François Riesener. Oil on canvas. Musée des Beaux-Arts, Rouen, France.

On My First Son

Ben Jonson

Farewell, thou child of my right hand,[1] and joy;
　My sin was too much hope of thee, loved boy.
Seven years thou wert lent to me, and I thee pay,[2]
　Exacted by thy fate, on the just day.[3]
5　O, could I lose all father now![4] For why
　Will man lament the state he should envy?
To have so soon 'scaped world's and flesh's rage,
　And, if no other misery, yet age?
Rest in soft peace, and, asked, say here doth lie
10　Ben Jonson his[5] best piece of poetry;
For whose sake, henceforth, all his vows be such,
　As what he loves may never like too much.

---

1. *Child of my right hand* is the literal translation of the Hebrew name Benjamin, which was the name of Jonson's son.
2. *I thee pay* means "pay thee back."
3. Here, *just* may mean "exact," or it could mean "complete in amount." In Jonson's day, loans were often made for a period of seven years, and Jonson's son had completed exactly seven years of life on the day he died.
4. *Lose all father now* means "give up all thoughts of being a father."
5. *Ben Jonson his* means "Ben Jonson's."

Literary Element　Elegy　*Why might the speaker envy his dead son?*

RESPONDING AND THINKING CRITICALLY

Respond

1. What personal tastes, traits, or achievements would you like included if someone were to write an elegy for you?

Recall and Interpret

2. (a)What does Jonson say was his sin and the price he pays for it? (b)Given these statements, how do you think Jonson is handling his son's death?

3. (a)How old was Jonson's son when he died? (b)How does the boy's youth add some relief to the sorrow Jonson expresses?

Analyze and Evaluate

4. Why might Jonson still lament his son's death despite the fact that he also envies his son?

5. (a)What will Jonson do from now on for the sake of his dead son? Why? (b)In your opinion, what is the difference between loving and liking?

6. At the end of the poem, Jonson says his son is his best piece of poetry. What does this **epitaph**, or brief description, tell you about his feelings for the boy?

Connect

7. **Big Idea** **The Sacred and the Secular** How does Jonson address both the sacred and the secular in his response to his son's death?

LITERARY ANALYSIS

Literary Element **Elegy**

The **elegy** has a long tradition dating from Latin and Greek literature. In ancient times, *elegy* referred not to the content of a poem but to its meter, or pattern of stressed and unstressed syllables. Today, however, an elegy is a serious, formal poem of lament or sorrow. Most elegies mourn a death or other great loss, but some contemplate common truths or life's smaller tragedies.

1. List some of the words and phrases from "On My First Son" that express the qualities of an elegy.

2. How would you describe the tone of the poem? What elements create the tone?

Writing About Literature

Respond to Theme It has been said that the death of a son or daughter is the most difficult kind of grief a human being can bear. Keeping this in mind, create an epitaph for Jonson's son Benjamin.

Literature Online **Web Activities** For eFlashcards, Selection Quick Checks, and other Web activities, go to www.glencoe.com.

READING AND VOCABULARY

Reading Strategy **Questioning**

To increase your understanding of a literary work, you should read it more than once. Continue to ask questions each time you read. After you read "On My First Son," try to answer the following questions. If you can't answer all the questions, read the poem at least once more and try again.

1. What is the work about? Who is it about?

2. What parts of this poem do you find confusing?

3. If you could talk to the poet, what would you ask him?

Academic Vocabulary

Here is a word from the vocabulary list on page R82.

require (ri kwīr′) *v.* to make a claim by right or authority

Practice and Apply
At the end of the poem, what does Jonson **require** of himself for the future?

Literary Element Lyric Poetry

A **lyric** is a poem that expresses a speaker's personal thoughts and feelings. Lyric poems are usually short and highly musical. The form is thought to have originated in ancient Greece, where the words were sung to the music of a lyre, a stringed instrument similar to a harp. Over time, people began to speak lyrics as opposed to singing them. As you read "Song: To Celia," notice the strong rhythm created by its brief lines.

• See Literary Terms Handbook, p. R10.

Reading Strategy Making Inferences

Authors don't always directly state what they want you to understand in a selection. By providing clues and interesting details, they imply certain information. When readers combine those clues with their own background and knowledge, they are **making inferences**. In "Song: To Celia," Jonson does not directly state his theme. As you read, look for verbal clues that will allow you to make an inference about Jonson's views on love and attraction.

Song: To Celia

Ben Jonson

Drink to me only with thine eyes,
   And I will pledge with mine;
Or leave a kiss but in the cup,
   And I'll not look for wine.
5 The thirst that from the soul doth rise
   Doth ask a drink divine;
But might I of Jove's nectar[1] sup,
   I would not change[2] for thine.
I sent thee late[3] a rosy wreath,
10 Not so much honoring thee,
As giving it a hope that there
   It could not withered be.
But thou thereon did'st only breathe,
   And sent'st it back to me;
15 Since when it grows, and smells, I swear,
   Not of itself, but thee.

---

1. *Jove's nectar* refers to ambrosia, the drink of the gods in Greek mythology, which supposedly kept them immortal.
2. *Change* means "exchange."
3. *Late* means "recently."

Reading Strategy Making Inferences *What is the speaker saying about Celia's reaction to his gift?*

Two Lovers, c. 1525. Paris Bordone. Pinacoteca di Brera, Milan, Italy.

RESPONDING AND THINKING CRITICALLY

Respond

1. Which Jonson poem appeals to you more—"Song: To Celia" or "On My First Son"? Why?

Recall and Interpret

2. (a)What would the speaker sacrifice for a kiss? (b)How valuable is Celia's kiss? Explain.

3. (a)What reason does the speaker give for sending the wreath? (b)What is he implying about Celia?

Analyze and Evaluate

4. (a)How would you describe the speaker's feelings for Celia? (b)Do you think Celia returns his feelings? Explain.

5. (a)If you were Celia, would you trust the speaker's love to last? (b)What details make you think as you do?

6. (a)What can you infer about the speaker's personality? (b)What advice would you give to him?

Connect

7. Why do you think this song has remained popular for so many years?

8. **Big Idea** **The Sacred and the Secular** What sacred elements do you find in Jonson's expression of his love for Celia?

LITERARY ANALYSIS

Literary Element **Lyric Poetry**

Because of its musicality, lyric poetry is often memorable. **Meter**, or the arrangement of stressed and unstressed syllables in a line of verse, is often an important element in the creation of lyric poetry's musical effects. Before answering the questions, review the terms used to describe meter on page R1.

1. How many stressed syllables are there in the third line of "Song: To Celia?" How many are there in the fourth?

2. Try to describe the meter in these two lines using the correct terms.

Review: Rhyme Scheme

As you learned on page 266, **rhyme scheme** is the pattern that end rhymes form in a stanza or a poem. Rhyme scheme is designated by the assignment of a different letter of the alphabet for each new rhyme. The first five lines of "Song: To Celia" use an *abcba* rhyme scheme. On a separate sheet of paper, fill in the blanks to show the complete poem's rhyme scheme.

Drink to me only with thine eyes (a)
    And I will pledge with mine; (b)
Or leave a kiss but in the cup, (c)
    And I'll not look for wine. (b)
The thirst that from the soul doth rise (a)
    Doth ask a drink divine; ( )
But might I of Jove's nectar sup, ( )
    I would not change for thine. ( )
I sent thee late a rosy wreath, (d)
    Not so much honoring thee, (e)
As giving it a hope that there (f)
    It could not withered be. ( )
But thou thereon did'st only breathe, ( )
    And sent'st it back to me; ( )
Since when it grows, and smells, I swear, ( )
    Not of itself, but thee. ( )

What is the poem's complete rhyme scheme?

READING AND VOCABULARY

Reading Strategy Making Inferences

Use the text and a chart like the one below to help you make inferences about the speaker's intent in "Song: To Celia."

Quote	Question	Answer
"Drink to me only with thine eyes"	What does he actually want her to do?	He wants her to notice and pay attention to him.

1. **Quote:** "The thirst that from the soul doth rise / Doth ask a drink divine;"

   Question:

   Answer:

2. **Quote:** "But might I of Jove's nectar sup, / I would not change for thine."

   Question:

   Answer:

Academic Vocabulary

Here are two words from the vocabulary list on page R82.

contrast (kon′ trast) *n.* juxtaposition of dissimilar elements

apparent (ə par′ ənt) *adj.* clear to the senses as real or true

Practice and Apply

1. Write one sentence to describe the **contrast** between the speaker's feelings for Celia and Celia's feelings for the speaker.
2. Do you think Celia's return of the speaker's rose wreath made her feelings for him **apparent**? Why or why not?

WRITING AND EXTENDING

Writing About Literature

Evaluate Sound Devices In "Song: To Celia," Jonson uses **alliteration**, the repetition of consonant sounds at the beginnings of words, to reinforce meaning and to create a musical effect. Look at lines 5 and 6:

> The thirst that from the soul doth rise
>   Doth ask a drink divine;

Say the lines aloud several times. Notice where the natural rhythms fall.

Reread the poem paying close attention to Jonson's use of alliteration. What does alliteration add to the poem? How well does Jonson use this sound device? Write a brief essay in which you evaluate the effectiveness of Jonson's use of alliteration in "Song: To Celia." Use evidence from the poem in support of your position.

After you complete your draft, meet with a peer reviewer to evaluate each other's work and to suggest revisions. Then proofread and edit your draft for errors in spelling, grammar, and punctuation.

Performing

Search on the Internet for a copy of the Thomas Arne song "Drink to Me Only with Thine Eyes." Work with a partner to learn the song. Try to capture some kind of emotional quality based on the lyrics. You might make the song comic or play it seriously. Use gestures to enhance the lyrics. Take turns performing the song with your partner. Give each other tips on what works and what doesn't. Then perform the song for the class.

Literature Online Web Activities For eFlashcards, Selection Quick Checks, and other Web activities, go to www.glencoe.com.

The Cavalier Poets

"*Dum loquimur, fugerit invida Aetas; carpe diem, quam minimum credula postero.*"

"*As we speak, envious time runs away; seize the day, put very little faith in tomorrow.*"

—Horace,
Odes, Book 1.11

THE METAPHYSICAL POETS CAME MOSTLY FROM the middle class; but their contemporaries, the Cavalier poets, were often aristocrats. Some came from such distinguished families that they were welcomed at the court of King Charles I; others served the king as soldiers. Like his predecessors Elizabeth and James, Charles surrounded himself with well-educated, able, versatile young men who were witty writers and conversationalists. Some were literary followers of Ben Jonson, a brilliant poet and dramatist who had been a rival and friend of Shakespeare's. The most gifted of the "Tribe," or "Sons of Ben," were Sir John Suckling, Robert Herrick, and Richard Lovelace.

Long before the French word *cavalier* came to describe these poets, it simply denoted a horseman, especially a mounted warrior, such as a knight. During Charles I's reign, however, *cavalier* became a political term. Supporters of the monarchy were called Cavaliers or Royalists. Their opponents, who supported the Puritan-dominated Parliament, were called Roundheads (because of their closely cropped hair). The personal style of the Cavaliers, which featured long, flowing hair and elaborate dress, contrasted sharply with that of the austerely garbed Roundheads.

Features of Cavalier Poetry

As writers affiliated with the court, the Cavalier poets generally intended to entertain their audience rather than instruct it. Their poetry displays a number of typical features:

Conversational Style Influenced by the works of John Donne and Ben Jonson, the Cavaliers cultivated a conversational style based on natural speech patterns. "I sing of brooks, of blossoms, birds, and bowers; / Of April, May, of June, and July flowers" begins one of Herrick's poems.

Elaborate Conceits Some of the Cavalier poets shared Donne's fondness for elaborate conceits. In "The Garden," Andrew Marvell describes a garden and then implicitly compares it to the Garden of Eden. Still, the majority of the Cavaliers' poems were less obscure and more accessible than those of the metaphysical poets.

Meditative Tone The majority of the Cavaliers' poems seem controlled; at times the poets seem indifferent or self-mocking—as Suckling does when he writes, "I must confess, when I did part from you, / I could not force an artificial dew [tears] / Upon my cheeks . . . "

Classicism Most of the "Sons of Ben" shared Jonson's admiration for the poetry of the ancient Greeks and Romans. Cavalier poetry is rich in classical allusions, such as the names of Greek and Roman gods— demonstrating that readers were clearly expected to

A Cavalier, c. 1629—1667. Edward Bower. Oil on canvas. Dunster Castle, Somerset, England.

be well versed in such classical works. Furthermore, forms of the poems are often based on classical models, such as the odes of Horace, the satires of Juvenal, and *eclogues,* short pastoral poems often written as dialogues between shepherds.

Regular Poetic Form The Cavaliers' use of regular rhythmic patterns, carefully structured stanzas, and simple but eloquent language also reflects this classical influence. The Cavalier poets welcomed the tidy order of regular meter and rhyme scheme. Widely used by Marvell and others, the **heroic couplet** consists of two lines of rhymed iambic pentameter. Lovelace favored the four- or eight-line stanza with either an *abab* or *aabb* rhyme scheme. Such regularity, of course, allowed the poems to be set to music.

Carpe Diem The classical influence can also be seen in the Cavaliers' choices of subject. Love was a popular theme, and some Cavaliers wrote about idealized love and addressed their poems to women to whom they gave such classical names as Julia, Althea, and Lucasta. Others, reflecting on the uncertainty and brevity of life, wrote poems that expressed a precept known as *carpe diem* (Latin for "seize the day"). This expression, drawn from the famous line of the Roman poet Horace, urges readers to make the most of every moment—a sensible strategy, given the uncertainty of life during the English Civil War. Herrick wrote, "Gather ye rosebuds, while ye may, / Old time is still a-flying"; other poets wrote variations on this theme.

The Cavalier poets did not shrink, either, from writing sarcastic commentaries on the pursuit of coy beauties. The seemingly amazed speaker in a Suckling poem exclaims, "Out upon it! I have loved / Three whole days together; / And am like to love three more, / If it prove fair weather."

Charles I of England, c. 17th century. Anthony van Dyck. Louvre, Paris.

Political and Poetical Fortunes

As King Charles's fortunes changed, so did those of the Cavalier poets. In 1649, after civil wars between Royalists and Parliamentarians had thrown the country into chaos, a parliamentary court sentenced Charles to death. When Puritan leader Oliver Cromwell was declared head of the newly formed Commonwealth, the Cavalier poets fell into disgrace. Some fled London; others were arrested and imprisoned. Suckling is thought to have committed suicide; Lovelace died in poverty and obscurity. Only Herrick lived to see the restoration of the monarchy in 1660 when Charles II, son of the executed King Charles I, was crowned.

Literature Online **Literary History** For more about the Cavalier poets, go to www.glencoe.com.

RESPONDING AND THINKING CRITICALLY

1. What characteristics of Cavalier poetry do you expect to enjoy the most? Why?

2. Why might the *carpe diem* philosophy have appealed to the Cavalier poets as a theme?

3. Do you think that a witty poem can make a serious comment about human nature? Explain.

OBJECTIVES
• Understand the characteristics of Cavalier poetry.
• Connect literature to historical context.

Comparing Literature *Across Time and Place*

Connecting to the Reading Selections

Have you ever been too preoccupied with the past or the future to enjoy the present? The four writers compared here—Robert Herrick, Horace, Pierre de Ronsard, and Omar Khayyám—urge readers to "seize the day" and warn against missing youthful opportunities that may never come again.

Devonshire, England, 1620

Robert Herrick
To the Virgins, to Make Much of Time...........poem.............**455**
A warning against wasted youth

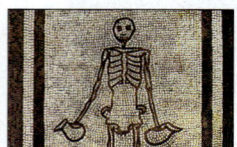

Rome, 23 B.C.

Horace
Carpe Diem..ode..............**459**
Treating each moment as the last

Paris, 1570

Pierre de Ronsard
To Hélène ....sonnet..............**460**
A lament for missed opportunities

Persia, 1110

Omar Khayyám
from the **Rubáiyát** ....ruba'i **461**
The ideal of earthly joy

COMPARING THE [Big Idea] The Sacred and the Secular

These four selections span sixteen centuries, yet they all express secular ideas about human mortality, such as the brevity of life and the uncertainty of the future. By ignoring the possibility of an afterlife, these poets encourage the pursuit of life's immediate pleasures.

COMPARING Universal Theme

The dual sense of the sweetness and brevity of human life is one of the earliest themes in literature. *Carpe diem,* a recurring literary motif that originated in Horace's odes, emphasizes an awareness of the transience of life and the permanent oblivion of death. Acceptance of these realities frees people to make the most of life and to seek pleasure and happiness in the present.

COMPARING Cultures

Herrick at the worldly court of Restoration England, Horace amid the political turmoil of ancient Rome, Ronsard among the refined aristocrats of Renaissance France, and Khayyám immersed in the scientifically advanced society of twelfth-century Persia—all these writers reflected, within these diverse cultures, a shared disillusionment with traditional religion and a humanistic spirit that valued intellectual inquiry and the pursuit of earthly happiness.

To the Virgins, to Make Much of Time

MEET ROBERT HERRICK

Although Robert Herrick has become one of the most celebrated Cavalier poets of the seventeenth century, literary success escaped him during his lifetime. Born the son of a goldsmith in London, Herrick spent six years as an apprentice to his uncle. Eventually, however, he abandoned the goldsmith trade to enroll at Saint John's College, Cambridge, at the age of twenty-two. After graduation, Herrick was drawn to London's literary circles. Ben Jonson, the city's literary giant, served as his mentor, father figure, and subject of several poems. Economic pressure eventually forced Herrick to abandon his leisurely literary life and accept a position as a vicar, or assistant priest, in Devonshire, a rural hamlet far from the excitement of London.

> *"It takes great wit and interest and energy to be happy. . . . It is the greatest feat man has to accomplish."*
>
> —Robert Herrick

Country Life As he gradually adapted to the country lifestyle, Herrick found poetic inspiration in his daily life and household. He wrote poems to his pet pig, his cat, his spaniel Tracy, his maid Prudence, and his neighbors. Many of his best-known poems are about rural life and festivals. He also composed 158 poems addressed to imaginary mistresses with exotic names, such as Anthea and Electra. But despite the relative peace and solitude of life in the country, Herrick was affected by political strife. Herrick was an Anglican priest and a supporter of King Charles I, the subject of some of his poems. When civil war broke out and the Puritans came to power, royalists like Herrick were expelled from their positions. After losing his post

as vicar, Herrick returned to London at the age of fifty-seven, having composed more than 1,400 poems.

Literary Labors and Disappointment Herrick had hoped to publish his poems and reestablish a literary reputation in London, but he found the literary scene there less receptive than he had expected. He was disappointed to discover that the London of his youth had irreversibly changed—Ben Jonson had died, and Herrick's literary circle had dispersed. Nonetheless, Herrick became one of the first poets to collect and publish nearly all of his poetry in one carefully organized volume. This massive collection contained two parts: the first, entitled *Noble Numbers,* contained religious poems, and the second, entitled *Hesperides*—referring to mythical nymphs who guarded an apple tree that bore golden fruit—contained his secular poems. Unfortunately for Herrick, critics largely ignored his poetry until the nineteenth century. After the Restoration ended Puritan rule, Herrick returned to his post at Devonshire at the age of seventy-one, where he remained until his death. He never composed poems again.

Herrick is now recognized as one of the foremost followers of Ben Jonson, but he also established a solid reputation as a poet in his own right. His poems are unique in their ability to explore serious philosophical questions of life and death in short, playful lyrics.

Robert Herrick was born in 1591 and died in 1674.

Literature Online **Author Search** For more about Robert Herrick, go to www.glencoe.com.

Connecting to the Poem

In this poem, Herrick advises the young to take advantage of their opportunities. As you read, think about the following questions:

- What have your family or friends advised you to take advantage of while you are still young?
- Have you ever regretted a missed opportunity?

Building Background

The *carpe diem* attitude of Cavalier poets such as Herrick reflects a literary response to the political and religious upheaval of the seventeenth century. Political disputes resulted from the struggle for power between Parliament, which wanted more authority, and the monarchy, which held to the theory that kings rule by a "divine right" bestowed by God, not by Parliament's consent. Religious disputes between Anglicans and Puritans intensified the conflict.

Setting Purposes for Reading

Big Idea **The Sacred and the Secular**

Although Herrick was an Anglican priest, much of his poetry expresses a secular point of view. As you read, try to determine the secular values that the speaker espouses.

Literary Element **Carpe Diem**

Carpe diem is a Latin phrase meaning "seize the day"; in other words, "make the most of each moment." The Roman poet Horace first made this phrase famous in one of his odes (see page 459), and the idea has been a motif, or recurring element, in literature throughout the ages. Lyric poets particularly enjoyed writing *carpe diem* poems in the 1600s and 1700s. In such poems, the speaker emphasizes the brevity of life—often with the purpose of persuading a young woman to yield to love before her beauty fades. As you read the poem, identify the images and figures of speech that convey the *carpe diem* motif.

- See Literary Terms Handbook, p. R3.

Reading Strategy **Evaluating Argument**

Argument is a type of persuasive writing in which logic, reason, or evidence is used to influence a reader's beliefs or actions. **Evaluating argument** means judging the validity of the writer's logic and the adequacy of his or her reasoning and evidence. You first need to understand what the author wants to convince you of and how he or she intends to convince you. Try to determine how tone, persuasive techniques, and the potential biases of the author affect the argument. Also look for fallacies in logic, such as emotional appeals or appeals to authority. In this poem, Herrick presents an argument intended to convince his audience to adopt a certain attitude toward life. As you read the poem, consider the following questions:

- What is the speaker in the poem trying to convince his audience to believe in or to do?
- What are the main points of the speaker's argument?
- Do you find this argument effective, or convincing?

Reading Tip: Taking Notes Use a chart similar to the one below to evaluate specific arguments in the poem.

Argument	My Evaluation

Passage:
"Gather ye rosebuds,
  while ye may,
Old time is still a-flying:
And this same flower that
  smiles today
Tomorrow will be dying."	

 **Interactive Literary Elements Handbook** To review or learn more about the literary elements, go to www.glencoe.com.

OBJECTIVES
In studying this selection, you will focus on the following:
- analyzing literary periods and movements
- analyzing the motif of *carpe diem*
- evaluating argument

Flora, detail from the Primavera, c. 1478.
Sandro Botticelli. Tempera on panel.
Galleria degli Uffizi, Florence, Italy.

To the Virgins, to Make Much of Time

Robert Herrick

Gather ye rosebuds, while ye may,
  Old time is still a-flying:
And this same flower that smiles today
  Tomorrow will be dying.

5 The glorious lamp of heaven, the sun,
  The higher he's a-getting,
The sooner will his race be run,
  And nearer he's to setting.

The age is best which is the first,
10 When youth and blood are warmer;
But being spent, the worse, and worst
  Times still succeed the former.

Then be not coy, but use your time,
  And, while ye may, go marry:
15 For having lost but once your prime
  You may forever tarry.[1]

---

1. *Tarry* means "linger" or "wait."

Literary Element   **Carpe Diem**   *How does the figurative language in this stanza convey the* carpe diem *motif?*

Big Idea   **The Sacred and the Secular**   *How does this statement illustrate a secular belief of the Cavalier poets?*

RESPONDING AND THINKING CRITICALLY

Respond

1. What do you think of the speaker's suggestions in this poem? Explain.

Recall and Interpret

2. (a)A **symbol** stands both for itself and something beyond itself. What symbol represents the pleasures of youth in the first stanza? (b)What message is the speaker trying to convey in this stanza?

3. (a)In the second stanza, what metaphor does the speaker use to describe the sun? (b)How does the path of the sun reinforce the speaker's message?

4. (a)What conclusion does the speaker reach in the last stanza? (b)How could you restate the last two lines?

Analyze and Evaluate

5. (a)What is the speaker's attitude toward youth and aging in the third stanza? (b)Do you agree with his assessment?

6. (a)What philosophy of life is expressed in this poem? (b)Do you agree with the speaker's philosophy? Explain.

Connect

7. How might this poem have a different significance for women today than it did in the seventeenth century?

8. **Big Idea** **The Sacred and the Secular** What does the fact that Herrick, an Anglican priest, wrote poetry extolling the sensual pleasures of marriage tell us about the age and the society in which he lived?

LITERARY ANALYSIS

Literary Element Carpe Diem

The term *carpe diem,* usually translated as "seize the day," comes from the Latin word *carpere,* meaning "to pluck, grab, or harvest."

1. (a)What evidence of the *carpe diem* theme do you find in the poem? (b)How might you summarize the speaker's attitude toward life and death?

2. In stanzas 1–2, the speaker uses the wilting flower and the rising and setting sun to represent a single day. What is the significance of this figurative repetition?

Writing About Literature

Analyze Sound Devices In the poem "To the Virgins, to Make Much of Time," Herrick uses a consistent metrical pattern. Scan the poem to determine how many feet, or beats, are in each line (a foot contains one stressed syllable and one or more unstressed syllables). Then figure out what type of foot (see page R1) Herrick uses. Write a brief essay in which you analyze how the poem's meter influences its tone and contributes to its overall message.

Literature Online Web Activities For eFlashcards, Selection Quick Checks, and other Web activities, go to www.glencoe.com.

READING AND VOCABULARY

Reading Strategy Evaluating Argument

A formal argument contains a proposition, which is the statement that must be proved. In a poem, the proposition may be expressed in figurative language.

1. (a)In your own words, state the proposition in "To the Virgins, to Make Much of Time." (b)Summarize the reasons and examples that the speaker uses to support the proposition.

2. Do you think the speaker's argument is convincing? Explain.

Academic Vocabulary

Here is a word from the vocabulary list on page R82.

explicit (eks plis′ it) *adj.* clearly stated or defined

Practice and Apply

In which line is the speaker's advice to the virgins most **explicit**?

BEFORE YOU READ

Building Background

Born in 65 B.C., Horace, the son of a freed slave, managed to acquire an excellent education in Rome and Athens. After the political turmoil that followed the assassination of Julius Caesar, Horace began his literary career. His poetry won him the admiration of Virgil, who, in 38 B.C., introduced Horace to the influential patron Maecenas. Octavian (who became the emperor Augustus Caesar) also took notice of Horace, eventually helping him to become Rome's leading poet.

Horace's **odes**—elaborate lyrics often addressed to a person, event, or force of nature—are rich in the *carpe diem* spirit. Denying the existence of an afterlife, he famously said, "Seize the day, put no trust in the morrow!" Influenced by the Greek philosophers Epicurus and Aristotle, Horace believed in the "golden mean," a lifestyle driven by the pursuit of pleasure and the avoidance of the pain that results from excessive self-indulgence. Horace died in 8 B.C.

Literature Online **Author Search** For more about Horace, go to www.glencoe.com.

Carpe Diem

Horace
translated by Thomas Hawkins

Skull, symbol of death, surrounded by symbolic objects. Mosaic from Pompeii. Museo Archeologico Nazionale, Naples, Italy.

Strive not, Leuconoe[1], to know what end
The gods above to me or thee will send:
Nor with astrologers consult at all,
That thou mayst better know what can befall;
5 Whether thou liv'st more winters; or thy last
Be this, which Tyrrhen[2] waves 'gainst rocks do cast.
Be wise! Drink free, and in so short a space
Do not protracted hopes of life embrace:
Whilst we are talking, envious time doth slide;
10 This day's thine own; the next may be denied.

---

1. *Leuconoe* (lyōō kō′ nō ē) is a friend of the poet.
2. *Tyrrhen* (tir′ ēn) is a reference to the Tyrrhenian Sea, a part of the Mediterranean, southwest of Italy.

Quickwrite

In "Carpe Diem," the speaker advises the reader to ignore the future because it is uncertain. Do you agree with this advice? How does it apply to your goals in life? Write a paragraph expressing your views.

Building Background

Revered during the Renaissance, Pierre de Ronsard earned a reputation as the "Prince of French Poets." Influenced by Horace and Virgil, he wrote odes that combined experimental forms with complex rhymes and classical allusions. He also excelled in the composition of Petrarchan sonnets.

Born in France in 1524, Ronsard later suffered an illness that left him partially deaf. He turned his attention to literature, taking minor orders in the church to support himself. He became part of the literary movement *la Pléiade* (plē əd), which strove to

create French poetry that would rival classical verse. The following poem is from Ronsard's collection *Sonnets pour Hélène* (1578), which reflects the profound melancholy that dominated Ronsard as he approached his death in 1585. This poem influenced the twentieth-century Irish poet William Butler Yeats, who wrote an adaptation of it called "When You Are Old" (see page 1108).

Literature Online Author Search For more about Pierre de Ronsard, go to www.glencoe.com.

Saint Magdalen Reading, 16th century.
Master of the Female Half-Figures. Oil on wood, 54 x 42 cm. Louvre, Paris.

To Hélène

Pierre de Ronsard
translated by Robert Hollander

When you are very old, in evening candlelight,
Moved closer to the coals and carding out your wool,[1]
You'll sing my songs and marvel that you were such a fool:
"O Ronsard did praise me when I was young and bright."

5   Then you'll have no handmaid to help you pass the night,
Spinning while your gossip leads her into lull,
Until you say my name and her rousèd eyes grow full
In wonder of your glory in what Ronsard did write.

When I am in the earth, poor ghost without his bones,
10   A sleeper in the shade of myrtle trees and stones,
Then you, beside the hearth, old and crouched and gray,
Will yearn for all that's lost, repenting your disdain.
Live it well, I pray you, today won't come again:
Gather up the roses before they fall away.

---

1. *Carding out your wool* refers to the act of combing strands of wool to untangle them before spinning them into thread.

Discussion Starter ....

Is this poem an encouragement to a young woman to "seize the day," or is it a lament for an old woman who has missed her opportunity for love? Discuss this question in a small group.

Building Background

Although Omar Khayyám (kī yäm′) is now the best-known Persian poet in Western civilization, he was better known during his lifetime for his brilliant achievements in mathematics and astronomy.

Manuscripts of the *Rubáiyát* (r$\overline{oo}$′ bī ät′) were not found until two hundred years after Khayyám's death, in 1123. Seventy-five of the 158 quatrains have come down to us in a translation made in 1859 by the Englishman Edward FitzGerald. His translation is considered to be a free, rather than a literal, translation.

Rubáiyát is plural for *ruba'i,* or "quatrain," which is the essential unit of Persian verse. Each ruba'i has an *aaba* rhyme scheme and expresses a complete thought: the first two lines pose a situation or problem, the third line creates suspense, and the fourth line offers a resolution. The *Rubáiyát* is complex and meditative, and Khayyám offers a secular rather than a religious solution to the problem of existing in an uncertain world.

Literature Online **Author Search** For more about Omar Khayyám, go to www.glencoe.com.

from the Rubáiyát

Omar Khayyám
translated by Edward FitzGerald

2

Dreaming when dawn's left hand was in the sky
I heard a voice within the tavern cry,
    "Awake, my little ones, and fill the cup
Before life's liquor in its cup be dry."

20

Ah! my belovéd, fill the cup that clears
Today of past regrets and future fears—
    Tomorrow?—Why, tomorrow I may be
Myself with yesterday's sev'n thousand years.

23

Ah, make the most of what we yet may spend,
Before we too into the dust descend;
    Dust into dust, and under dust, to lie,
Sans wine, sans song, sans singer and—sans end!

Bird and Scene of Lovers With an Attendant. Persia. Seattle Art Museum, WA.

26

Oh, come with old Khayyám, and leave the wise
To talk; one thing is certain, that life flies;
   One thing is certain, and the rest is lies;
The flower that once has blown for ever dies.

34

Then to this earthen bowl did I adjourn
My lip the secret well of life to learn:
   And lip to lip it murmur'd—"While you live,
Drink!—for once dead you never shall return."

37

One moment in annihilation's waste,
One moment, of the well of life to taste—
   The stars are setting, and the caravan
Starts for the dawn of nothing—Oh, make haste!

38

Ah, fill the cup:—what boots it to repeat
How time is slipping underneath our feet:
   Unborn tomorrow and dead yesterday,
Why fret about them if today be sweet!

39

How long, how long, in infinite pursuit
Of this and that endeavor and dispute?
   Better be merry with the fruitful grape
Than sadden after none, or bitter, fruit.

Quickwrite

Throughout the quatrains excerpted here, Khayyám repeats the image of filling and drinking from a cup. How does this image symbolize Khayyám's message? Using evidence from the text, write your response in a paragraph.

Wrap-up: Comparing Literature Across Time and Place

- **To the Virgins, to Make Much of Time**
  by Robert Herrick
- **Carpe Diem**
  by Horace
- **To Hélène**
  by Pierre de Ronsard
- **from the Rubáiyát**
  by Omar Khayyám

COMPARING THE `Big Idea` The Sacred and the Secular

Group Activity With a small group, read each of the following quotations. Then discuss how each quotation expresses a secular worldview and either implicitly or explicitly rejects a sacred worldview. Cite evidence from the poems to support your answers.

*"Gather ye rosebuds, while ye may,
Old time is still a-flying:"*

— Herrick, "To the Virgins, to Make Much of Time"

*"Be wise! Drink free, and in so short a space
Do not protracted hopes of life embrace . . ."*

— Horace, "Carpe Diem"

*"Live it well, I pray you, today won't come again:
Gather up the roses before they fall away."*

— Ronsard, "To Hélène"

*"One thing is certain, and the rest is lies;
The flower that once has blown for ever dies."*

— Khayyám, the *Rubáiyát*

Lady in a White Cap, c. 15th century. Hans Holbein the Younger.

COMPARING Universal Theme

Writing The four selections by Herrick, Horace, Ronsard, and Khayyám insist that one should make every moment count. Literature from many periods explores the attempt to defeat the ravages of time by living as if each moment is the last. How might the writing of literature be an attempt to defeat the ravages of time? In a brief essay, compare the poets' messages and the way in which they confront the fleeting nature of life through verse.

COMPARING Cultures

Partner Activity Despite writing in different cultures and time periods, Herrick, Horace, Ronsard, and Khayyám developed similar responses to the process of aging and humans' inevitable mortality. With a partner, discuss how historical and cultural context might have affected each of the poet's themes.

OBJECTIVES
- Relate literature to historical context.
- Compare and contrast authors' messages.
- Compare and contrast universal themes from different cultures and time periods.

Suckling's Poetry

MEET SIR JOHN SUCKLING

Imagine inheriting an immense fortune at the age of eighteen. What kind of life would you lead? When John Suckling came into his inheritance, he promptly left college to live as a gambler, big spender, and playboy, taking a grand tour of continental Europe and seeking glory as a gentleman soldier there.

Early Years Suckling was born on February 10, 1609, in Middlesex. In 1613, when Suckling was only four years old, his mother died. In 1623 Suckling enrolled in Trinity College in Cambridge. Three years later, while Suckling was still a student, his father died, leaving Suckling with the fortune that allowed him to pursue his life of extravagance. Shortly afterward, Suckling was admitted to Gray's Inn, one of four legal societies that, by tradition, govern the right of barristers to practice law in England's courts. For a while, Suckling pursued a military career, joining the army of Swedish king Gustavus Adolphus during the Thirty Years' War.

A Sparkling Wit Upon returning to England, Suckling became "famous at court for his accomplishments and ready, sparkling wit," according to his friend Sir William Davenant. In fact, he became so well liked that King Charles I knighted him when he was merely twenty-one. Regarded by many critics as the most famous member of the Cavalier poets, Suckling used his "sparkling wit" to write popular dramas, long ballads, and prose works, but he is best known today for his short, sprightly songs and verses. Suckling's attitude toward these songs and verses—casual diversions rather than things to be taken seriously—is reflected in the poems themselves. Their tone has been described as witty, light, mocking, lacking depth, and flippant. Yet, according to English critic Robin Skelton, they illustrate an admirable quality common to Cavalier poetry: the ability "to celebrate the minor pleasures and sadnesses of life."

> "I hold that perfect joy makes all our parts
> As joyful as our hearts."
>
> —Sir John Suckling, from
> "If You Refuse Me Once and Think Again"

Politics, Intrigue, and Death In 1639 Suckling led a troop in the king's thwarted expedition against Scotland. Suckling outfitted his soldiers in brightly colored uniforms with plumed hats and provided them with horses at his own expense. As it turned out, however, the troop's poor performance and gaudy costumes became the subject of much ridicule. Two years later, Suckling made a mistake that neither his wit nor his money could correct. He joined a conspiracy to rescue the Earl of Strafford, one of the king's chief deputies, whom Parliament had imprisoned in the Tower of London. The rescue mission failed, and Suckling fled to Paris. There, early in 1642, at the age of thirty-three, he died under mysterious circumstances. According to one theory, he was murdered by a servant; according to another, he poisoned himself.

Sir John Suckling was born in 1609 and died in 1642.

Literature Online **Author Search** For more about Sir John Suckling, go to www.glencoe.com.

Connecting to the Poems

Witty means "clever and amusing." These two poems by Suckling contain witty observations on the subject of love. As you read, think about the types of remarks you consider witty—Puns? Jokes? Exaggerations? Sarcasm?

Building Background

During the seventeenth century, most marriages were based on financial considerations and were arranged by the parents of the prospective bride and groom—often when the children were quite young. A family's wealth and status might depend upon the daughter's making an advantageous marriage. As a result, many young women were already engaged by the time they were old enough to inspire declarations of love. In order to retain their value as marital partners, these women may have felt it necessary to publicly ignore lovesick suitors' pleas for attention.

Setting Purposes for Reading

Big Idea The Sacred and the Secular

As you read, think about how these poems express the poet's witty reflections on amorous love.

Literary Element Form

Form is the structure of a literary work. The form of a poem is determined by the number of stanzas (groups of lines that form a unit), the number and length of lines within a stanza, the rhythmic patterns, and the rhyme scheme (or lack of it). **Rhythm** is achieved by arranging stressed and unstressed syllables within a line to create a pattern of beats. **Rhyme** is achieved by repeating the stressed vowel sounds and any succeeding sounds in two or more words. Any or all of these elements can be employed to help convey or reinforce meaning in a poem.

• See Literary Terms Handbook, p. R7.

Literature Online **Interactive Literary Elements Handbook** To review or learn more about the literary elements, go to www.glencoe.com.

Reading Strategy Applying Background Knowledge

The ideas expressed in Suckling's poems were shaped in part by the attitudes and customs of the world in which he lived. Becoming familiar with those attitudes and customs and their influence on Suckling can help you gain a better understanding of his poetry.

Reading Tip: Taking Notes Reread the biography of Suckling on page 464 and the Building Background feature on this page, noting details that describe attitudes and customs of his time. Use a chart like the one shown here to jot down some of those details. As you read the poems, look for ideas that may have been influenced by the attitudes and customs you have noted. Add these examples to your chart.

Attitudes and Customs	Illustrated in Poems
1. Cavalier poems are casual diversions—not to be taken seriously.	1. "If it prove fair weather" suggests that the speaker's commitment is not serious.
2.	2.

Vocabulary

constant (kon′ stənt) *adj.* never stopping, continuous; faithful, steadfast; p. 466 *Lydia remained constant to her brother, defending him against the neighbor's accusations.*

spite (spīt) *n.* desire to annoy or harm; ill will; p. 466 *The hateful spite, which caused the envious critic to make fun of the painting, hurt the artist.*

prevail (pri vāl′) *v.* be in general use; succeed; p. 467 *Supporters of the tax increase trusted that the practical reasons for it would prevail.*

Vocabulary Tip: Synonyms Words that have the same or nearly the same meaning are called synonyms.

OBJECTIVES
In studying these selections, you will focus on the following:
• analyzing the characteristics of secular poetry
• analyzing poetic forms
• applying background knowledge to literary works

The Constant Lover

Sir John Suckling

The Love Song. Alexei Stiepanoff. Eaton Gallery, Princes Arcade, London.

Out upon it![1] I have loved
    Three whole days together;
And am like to love three more,
    If it prove fair weather.

5 Time shall molt away[2] his wings,
    Ere[3] he shall discover
In the whole wide world again
    Such a **constant** lover.

But the **spite** on 't is, no praise
10   Is due at all to me:
Love with me had made no stays,
    Had it any been but she.

Had it any been but she,
    And that very face,
15 There had been at least ere this
    A dozen dozen in her place.

---

1. *Out upon it!* is a Renaissance slang expression of impatience and displeasure with oneself.
2. *Molt away* means "shed."
3. *Ere* means "before."

Literary Element Form *How does the rhyme scheme of the third stanza differ from that of the other three stanzas?*

Big Idea The Sacred and the Secular *Explain the wit employed in the fourth stanza.*

Vocabulary

constant (kon′ stənt) *adj.* never stopping, continuous; faithful, steadfast

spite (spīt) *n.* desire to annoy or harm; ill will

Why So Pale and Wan, Fond Lover?

Sir John Suckling

*Portrait of Francis Russell, the Marquess of Tavistock,
1767. Sir Joshua Reynolds. Oil on canvas.*

Why so pale and wan,[1] fond[2] lover?
  Prithee,[3] why so pale?
Will, when looking well can't move her,
  Looking ill **prevail**?
5   Prithee, why so pale?

Why so dull and mute, young sinner?
  Prithee, why so mute?
Will, when speaking well can't win her,
  Saying nothing do 't?
10   Prithee, why so mute?

Quit, quit, for shame, this will not move:
  This cannot take her.
If of herself she will not love,
  Nothing can make her:
15   The devil take her!

---

1. *Wan* means "sickly" or "pale."
2. *Fond,* in Suckling's time, meant "foolish."
3. At the time Suckling wrote this poem, *Prithee* meant "please."

Reading Strategy   Applying Background Knowledge
*How do Suckling's observations in this poem illustrate the
Cavaliers' attitudes?*

Vocabulary

prevail (pri vāl′) *v.* be in general use; succeed

RESPONDING AND THINKING CRITICALLY

Respond

1. Did you enjoy Suckling's wit in these two poems? Why or why not?

Recall and Interpret

2. (a)In "The Constant Lover," how long has the speaker been in love? How much longer will he be in love "if it prove fair weather"? (b)What do these statements suggest about the speaker's love?

3. (a)What does the speaker claim in the second stanza of "The Constant Lover"? (b)**Irony** is the contrast between appearance and reality. What is ironic about the speaker's claim?

4. (a)Paraphrase the speaker's questions in "Why So Pale and Wan, Fond Lover?" (lines 3–4 and lines 8–9). (b)What point might the speaker be trying to make by asking these questions?

5. (a)In addition to "pale and wan," how else does the speaker describe the suitor in line 1? (b)Why might the speaker in this poem view the suitor in this way?

Analyze and Evaluate

6. (a)One definition of *passion* is "very strong love." What do you think the "Why So Pale . . ." speaker's attitude is toward passion? (b)What do you think the suitor's attitude is toward passion? (c)Do you agree with the speaker, the suitor, or neither? Why?

Connect

7. **Big Idea** **The Sacred and the Secular** What types of wit does Suckling use in these two poems?

LITERARY ANALYSIS

Literary Element **Form**

In these two poems, Suckling employs specific rhythmic patterns, rhymes and near rhymes, and the grouping of stanzas to help convey his observations.

Partner Activity Meet with a classmate to study the poems. Then answer these questions:

1. How does the sequence of stanzas in "The Constant Lover" help convey meaning?

2. (a)Identify the rhyme scheme of "Why So Pale and Wan, Fond Lover?" Find two examples of slant rhyme (words that nearly rhyme but do not exactly rhyme). (b)Why might Suckling have created these slant rhymes?

Writing About Literature

Compare and Contrast Tone Tone is an author's attitude toward his or her subject matter. In a brief essay compare and contrast the two speakers of these poems and explain how the attitudes they reveal affect the tone of each poem.

READING AND VOCABULARY

Reading Strategy **Applying Background Knowledge**

Suckling's poems reflect the attitudes and customs of the world in which he lived.

In what ways do both of these poems express the attitudes of the Cavalier poets toward the writing of poetry and the subject matter in that poetry?

Vocabulary **Practice**

Practice with Synonyms Identify the synonym for each vocabulary word listed in the first column.

1. constant   **a.** variable   **b.** loyal

2. spite   **a.** annoyance   **b.** arrogance

3. prevail   **a.** prevent   **b.** win

Literature Online Web Activities For eFlashcards, Selection Quick Checks, and other Web activities, go to www.glencoe.com.

Lovelace's Poetry

MEET RICHARD LOVELACE

Richard Lovelace seemed destined to lead a charmed life. As a handsome, wealthy young aristocrat studying at Oxford University, he caught the notice of King Charles I and Queen Henrietta Maria. He so impressed them that they arranged for him to receive an honorary degree and join their court. There, his literary talent, love of the fine arts, and superb horsemanship made him a favorite. Unfortunately, his affiliation with the king also led to his downfall.

A Renaissance Gentleman Richard Lovelace was probably born in the Netherlands, where his father was stationed with the king's military. Sadly, he died in action when Lovelace was a young boy. Lovelace eventually returned to England and attended school at Charterhouse and Oxford. While studying at Oxford, Lovelace wrote *The Scholar*, a comedy that was performed at the school in 1636. At court, Lovelace epitomized the ideal of the Renaissance gentleman: he was a lover, soldier, wit, musician, and poet. From 1639 to 1640, he participated in the king's military campaign in Scotland. In 1642, at the age of twenty-four, Lovelace led a march petitioning Parliament to grant the king broader powers. Parliamentary leaders responded by briefly imprisoning him. It was during this imprisonment that Lovelace wrote "To Althea, from Prison."

Punishment and Poverty In 1646 Lovelace offered his services to King Louis XIV of France and was wounded during a battle at Dunkirk. When King Charles I was arrested in 1648, Lovelace was arrested again—this time to prevent him from leading a revolt to rescue the king. During this second imprisonment, he wrote "To Lucasta, Going to the Wars." After King Charles I was beheaded in 1649, Lovelace was released from prison, but by then he had exhausted his fortune. During the height of his popularity and influence at court, Lovelace had worn clothes made from fabrics of gold and silver. According to biographer Anthony à Wood, Lovelace, after leaving prison for the second time, was reduced to wearing ragged clothes, living in run-down lodgings, and accepting charity. He spent his last years in ill health— a victim of tuberculosis—and is believed to have died in the squalor of Gunpowder Alley, London, at age thirty-nine.

> *"Thus richer than untempted Kings are we,*
> *That asking nothing, nothing need:*
> *Though Lord of all what Seas embrace; yet he*
> *That wants himself, is poor indeed."*
>
> —Richard Lovelace
> from "The Grasshopper"

Enduring Fame Literary historians are divided in their opinion of Lovelace's body of poetry. One scholar has even suggested that it would have been better if most of Lovelace's poems "had remained in manuscript and perished with his two plays." Most critics agree, however, that "To Lucasta, Going to the Wars" and "To Althea, from Prison" are worthy of the enduring fame they have achieved.

Richard Lovelace was born in 1618 and died in 1657 or 1658.

Literature Online Author Search For more about Richard Lovelace, go to www.glencoe.com.

Connecting to the Poems

Sacrificing one's freedom or love for a higher calling or obligation is a difficult deed. As you read the following poems, think about these questions:

- What might cause you to sacrifice your freedom or love?
- How might the memory of loved ones help you in a time of crisis?

Building Background

Lovelace wrote "To Althea, from Prison" in 1642, during his first imprisonment, and "To Lucasta, Going to the Wars" in 1648, during his second imprisonment. Both poems appear in *Lucasta*, one of two collections that contain the bulk of Lovelace's literary legacy. The Lucasta who lends her name to these two volumes is said to have been Lucy Sacherevell. After hearing that Lovelace had died of wounds at Dunkirk, she married someone else. Lovelace prepared *Lucasta* for publication during his second imprisonment. Parliamentary leaders of the time held up its publication to silence Lovelace, whom they considered to be a political enemy.

Setting Purposes for Reading

Big Idea The Sacred and the Secular

As you read, think about how these poems express the poet's secular notions of love, honor, and freedom.

Literary Element Paradox

A **paradox** is a statement that appears to be contradictory but is actually true, either in fact or in a figurative sense. For example, the popular expression "less is more" states a paradox. As you read these two poems, look for statements or ideas that express paradoxes.

- See Literary Terms Handbook, p. R12.

Literature Online Interactive Literary Elements Handbook To review or learn more about the literary elements, go to www.glencoe.com.

Reading Strategy Paraphrasing

When you **paraphrase**, you put something you have read or heard into your own words. Paraphrasing is a useful strategy for breaking down difficult text and making it easier to understand.

Reading Tip: Taking Notes As you read these two poems, try paraphrasing each stanza. Write down your paraphrases in a chart like the one shown here.

"To Lucasta, Going to the Wars"	"To Althea, from Prison"
Stanza 1: Please don't think I'm being mean by leaving you to go off to war.	Stanza 1:
Stanza 2:	Stanza 2:
Stanza 3:	Stanza 3:
	Stanza 4:

Vocabulary

chaste (chāst) *adj.* pure; virtuous; modest; p. 471 *Felicity's chaste behavior made it difficult for her parents to believe that she would deceive them.*

inconstancy (in kon′ stən sē) *n.* changeable nature; disloyalty; p. 471 *Nora's inconstancy in the past caused the board to doubt her.*

unconfined (un kən fīnd′) *adj.* not shut in; unrestricted; p. 472 *Because some files were confidential, the reporter's request for unconfined access to the firm's records was denied.*

allaying (ə lā′ ing) *adj.* putting at rest; relieving; p. 472 *Once again the concerned mother used allaying tactics to try to dispel her child's fears.*

Vocabulary Tip: Context Clues You can often figure out the meaning of a new word by looking at its context—the other words and sentences that surround it.

OBJECTIVES
In studying these selections, you will focus on the following:
- analyzing the characteristics of secular poetry
- identifying paradoxical statements
- using paraphrasing to review and understand content

To Lucasta, Going to the Wars

Richard Lovelace

Tell me not, sweet, I am unkind,
   That from the nunnery
Of thy **chaste** breast and quiet mind
   To war and arms I fly.

5 True, a new mistress now I chase,
   The first foe in the field;
And with a stronger faith embrace
   A sword, a horse, a shield.

  Yet this **inconstancy** is such
10   As you too shall adore;
I could not love thee, dear, so much,
   Loved I not honor more.

Thomas Brown at the Battle of Dettingen, 27th June, 1743. English School. Oil on canvas. Private collection.

Big Idea **The Sacred and the Secular** *What qualities of a Renaissance gentleman and Cavalier poet does the speaker exhibit in these lines?*

Vocabulary

chaste (chāst) *adj.* pure; virtuous; modest
inconstancy (in kon′ stən sē) *n.* changeable nature; disloyalty

To Althea, from Prison

Richard Lovelace

When Love with **unconfinéd** wings
    Hovers within my gates;
And my divine Althea brings
    To whisper at the grates:
5 When I lie tangled in her hair,
    And fettered[1] to her eye;
The gods that wanton[2] in the air,
    Know no such liberty.

When flowing cups run swiftly round
10 With no **allaying** Thames,[3]
Our careless heads with roses bound,
    Our hearts with loyal flames;
When thirsty grief in wine we steep,
    When healths[4] and drafts[5] go free,
15 Fishes that tipple[6] in the deep,
    Know no such liberty.

When (like committed linnets[7]) I
    With shriller throat shall sing
The sweetness, mercy, majesty,
20 And glories of my king;
When I shall voice aloud, how good
    He is, how great should be;
Enlargéd[8] winds that curl the flood,[9]
    Know no such liberty.

25 Stone walls do not a prison make,
    Nor iron bars a cage;
Minds innocent and quiet take
    That for a hermitage;[10]
If I have freedom in my love,
30 And in my soul am free;
Angels alone that soar above,
    Enjoy such liberty.

1. *Fettered* means "bound."
2. *Wanton* means "play."
3. Cups that *run swiftly round, / with no allaying Thames* are goblets of wine that have not been diluted with water from the Thames (temz), the river that supplied London with drinking water.
4. *Healths* are toasts.
5. *Drafts* are drinks.
6. Here, *tipple* means "drink."
7. *Committed linnets* are caged birds.
8. In this context, *enlargéd* means "released."
9. *Flood* refers to the sea.
10. A *hermitage* is a private retreat or dwelling place.

Reading Strategy   **Paraphrasing** *Untangle the syntax of this stanza and explain the passage in your own words. What do the "flowing cups" run around?*

Vocabulary

unconfined (un kən fīnd´) *adj.* not shut in; unrestricted
allaying (ə lā´ing) *adj.* putting at rest; relieving

RESPONDING AND THINKING CRITICALLY

Respond

1. Which lines from the poems did you find most memorable? Why?

Recall and Interpret

2. (a)In "To Lucasta, Going to the Wars," who is the "new mistress" whom the speaker is chasing? (b)Why might the poet have chosen to compare this new love to his love for Lucasta?

3. (a)In "To Lucasta," what three things does the speaker "with a stronger faith embrace"? (b)What does his loyalty to these things suggest about his values?

4. (a)In "To Althea, from Prison," each of the first three stanzas begins with a description of an occasion associated with freedom. What are these occasions? (b)Why might these occasions make the speaker feel free?

5. (a)Sum up the speaker's attitude about imprisonment. (b)What are the only freedoms he claims to need?

Analyze and Evaluate

6. (a)In "To Lucasta," what reasons does the speaker give for going to war? (b)Do you think these are valid reasons?

7. (a)After reading "To Althea, from Prison," how do you think Lovelace would define freedom? (b)Do you agree with this definition? Explain.

Connect

8. **Big Idea** **The Sacred and the Secular** (a)What courtly attitudes are important to the speaker in each of these poems? (b)Do you think these attitudes are still important today?

LITERARY ANALYSIS

Literary Element **Paradox**

Lovelace's statement "Stone walls do not a prison make" is a **paradox**. Stone walls can imprison the speaker physically, but they cannot imprison his mind and soul.

1. Find and explain the two central paradoxes in "To Lucasta, Going to the Wars."

2. In "To Althea, from Prison," what paradoxes are implied in the first three stanzas? How do these paradoxes build to the paradox in the last stanza?

Interdisciplinary Activity: History

Richard Lovelace was imprisoned in the Gatehouse, Westminster, in 1642 and in Peterhouse Prison, Aldersgate, in 1648. Use the Internet and/or your local library to research information about prison conditions in these institutions during the seventeenth century. Prepare a report detailing what you learn.

Literature Online **Web Activities** For eFlashcards, Selection Quick Checks, and other Web activities, go to www.glencoe.com.

READING AND VOCABULARY

Reading Strategy **Paraphrasing**

Look back at the **paraphrases** you created as you read. What elements are missing from your paraphrases? In what ways do these elements contribute to your appreciation of the two poems?

Vocabulary **Practice**

Practice with Context Clues For each item below, identify a context clue that could help you to figure out the meaning of the underlined word.

1. The chaste, or pure, expression on little Emily's face was deceiving.
   a. pure   **b.** expression   **c.** deceiving

2. After two days in prison, he was happy to be unconfined at last.
   a. two days   **b.** happy   **c.** in prison

3. Susan changed her mind hourly; such inconstancy made it difficult to please her.
   a. changed   **b.** difficult   **c.** please her

4. The doctor was successful in allaying his pain.
   a. successful   **b.** pain   **c.** doctor

To His Coy Mistress

MEET ANDREW MARVELL

Andrew Marvell's legacy has been, like that of many other poets from his era, mixed. Initially considered one of the great political satirists of his day, he is now mostly remembered for his love lyrics. During his life, Marvell brilliantly adapted his thought and art—moving with the political, religious, and artistic currents of the day. In so doing, Marvell was able to remain active and alive, producing what is now considered some of the best-loved poetry of his century.

> *"The world in all doth but two nations bear—*
> *The good, the bad; and these mixed everywhere."*
>
> —Andrew Marvell

Young Scholar Marvell was born in 1621 and educated at the University of Cambridge. He received his degree in 1639, though, as a result of his father's death two years later, his academic career came to an early end. In all likelihood, Marvell spent the next five years overseas working as a tutor.

Marvell began making favorable connections at the age of twenty-nine when he became tutor to the daughter of Sir Thomas Fairfax, Lord-General of Oliver Cromwell's Parliamentary army. At first, Marvell was opposed to the Cromwell government, but became very supportive, eventually writing such laudatory poems as "An Horatian Ode upon Cromwell's Return from Ireland" and "On the Death of O. C." By age thirty-four, Marvell was tutoring William Dutton, a boy for whom Cromwell himself was guardian. Four years later, he advanced his career further by becoming assistant to the Latin secretary for the Puritan Commonwealth: famed poet and essayist John Milton.

Parliamentarian and Poet In 1659 Marvell was elected to Parliament, in which he served for the remainder of his life. That next year, King Charles II was restored to the throne. Many supporters of the Puritan cause were imprisoned or killed. Astonishingly, Marvell managed to stay well positioned. This is doubly miraculous considering that Marvell was also writing scathing attacks on the monarchy, parodies of the king's speeches, and strongly opinionated political pamphlets and religious tracts.

The reprisals against supporters of the Commonwealth were indeed harsh. Cromwell's body was exhumed from its resting place at Westminster Abbey and put on display, various leaders were captured and executed, and prominent literary figures, including Milton, were forced into hiding. While the historical record is unclear, it is possible that Marvell intervened, saving the poet's life, thus allowing Milton to write his masterpiece, *Paradise Lost*.

When Marvell died in 1678, none of his poems had yet been printed. Even after their initial publication, Marvell was, for some time, still generally remembered as a political satirist. It wasn't until the nineteenth and twentieth centuries that Marvell's lyrics became widely read and appreciated.

Andrew Marvell was born in 1621 and died in 1678.

Literature Online Author Search For more about Andrew Marvell, go to www.glencoe.com.

Connecting to the Poem

How should we treat our knowledge of our inevitable decline and death? What effect does it have on our daily lives? The speaker in Marvell's poem attempts to use the fleeting nature of life as a persuasive tool. As you read the poem, think about the following questions:

- In what ways can life's limitedness provide an appropriate perspective on our daily lives?
- When might this perspective be unhelpful?

Building Background

"To His Coy Mistress" first appeared in print after Marvell's death, in a volume entitled *Miscellaneous Poems*. Mary Palmer, Marvell's housekeeper, arranged for the book's publication and referred to Marvell as her husband in its preface. Palmer claimed to be his wife by virtue of a secret marriage. Her claim was hotly disputed, however, giving rise to a lengthy lawsuit. Many people believe that she had the book published simply to give the appearance of being a devoted wife.

Setting Purposes for Reading

Big Idea **The Sacred and the Secular**

As you read Marvell's poem, notice how the speaker uses philosophical and religious notions to advance his secular argument.

Literary Element **Hyperbole**

Hyperbole is a figure of speech that uses exaggeration to express strong emotion, make a point, or evoke humor. For example, when students say that "the lecture went on forever," they are using exaggeration to make their point and to generate a humorous effect.

- See Literary Terms Handbook, p. R8.

Reading Strategy Previewing

To **preview** means to look over a selection before you read. Previewing lets you begin to see what you already know and what you'll need to know. To preview "To His Coy Mistress," look at the poem's title, illustrations, headings, and captions.

Reading Tip: Taking Notes After scanning the text, the title, and the images associated with the text, write down predictions about the content and theme of the poem. Then, after you have finished reading, verify or modify your predictions. Use a chart like this.

Predictions	Verify or Modify
The poem's title suggests that it will be addressed to a young woman.	This prediction was correct.

Vocabulary

hue (hū) *n.* color, shade, or tint; p. 477
The sky was full of many magnificent hues.

strife (strīf) *n.* unrest or violent conflict; p. 477
The city was engulfed in uncontrollable strife.

Vocabulary Tip: Analogies Analogies compare pairs of words based on the relationship between each pair's meaning. Analogies can be based on different kinds of relationships: synonyms, antonyms, association, a part to its whole, an example to its class, or an object and its characteristics.

 **Interactive Literary Elements Handbook** To review or learn more about the literary elements, go to www.glencoe.com.

OBJECTIVES
In studying this selection, you will focus on the following:
- analyzing literary periods
- analyzing hyperbole and *carpe diem*
- previewing a text

The Stolen Kiss. Jean-Honore Fragonard. Oil on canvas. Hermitage Museum, St. Petersburg, Russia.

To His Coy Mistress

Andrew Marvell

     Had we but world enough, and time,
This coyness,[1] lady, were no crime.
We would sit down, and think which way
To walk, and pass our long love's day.
5 Thou by the Indian Ganges'[2] side
Shouldst rubies find; I by the tide
Of Humber[3] would complain.[4] I would
Love you ten years before the flood,[5]
And you should, if you please, refuse
10 Till the conversion of the Jews.[6]

1. *Coyness* may be modesty or flirtatious, playful evasiveness.
2. The *Ganges* is a great river in northern India.
3. The *Humber* is a muddy river in Marvell's hometown of Hull.
4. Here, *complain* means to write love complaints, or songs lamenting the cruelty of love.
5. By *flood,* the speaker means the flooding of the world associated with Noah in the biblical book of Genesis.
6. In Marvell's time, Christians believed that Jews would convert to Christianity just before the world's end.

Reading Strategy   Previewing *What do these first two lines suggest to you about the content of this poem?*

My vegetable love[7] should grow
Vaster than empires, and more slow;
An hundred years should go to praise
Thine eyes, and on thy forehead gaze;
15   Two hundred to adore each breast,
But thirty thousand to the rest;
An age at least to every part,
And the last age should show your heart.
For, lady, you deserve this state,[8]
20   Nor would I love at lower rate.
    But at my back I always hear
Time's wingèd chariot hurrying near;
And yonder all before us lie
Deserts of vast eternity.
25   Thy beauty shall no more be found,
Nor, in thy marble vault, shall sound
My echoing song; then worms shall try
That long-preserved virginity,
And your quaint honor turn to dust,
30   And into ashes all my lust.
The grave's a fine and private place,
But none, I think, do there embrace.
    Now, therefore, while the youthful **hue**
Sits on thy skin like morning dew,
35   And while thy willing soul transpires
At every pore with instant fires,
Now let us sport us while we may,
And now, like amorous birds of prey,
Rather at once our time devour
40   Than languish in his slow-chapped[9] power.
Let us roll all our strength and all
Our sweetness up into one ball,
And tear our pleasures with rough **strife**
Thorough[10] the iron gates of life:
45   Thus, though we cannot make our sun
Stand still, yet we will make him run.

7. *Vegetable love* is love that grows slowly and passively, like a plant.

8. Here, *state* means "dignity."

9. *Slow-chapped* means "slow-jawed," suggesting the image of time slowly chewing.

10. *Thorough* means "through."

ANDREW MARVELL   **477**

RESPONDING AND THINKING CRITICALLY

Respond

1. (a)What are your reactions to the speaker in this poem? (b)What might you like to say to him?

Recall and Interpret

2. (a)According to the speaker, what is his sweetheart's crime? (b)Why do you think he regards this as a crime?

3. (a)What are some of the things the speaker claims he would do if he had unlimited time? (b)How do these claims help the speaker's argument?

4. (a)What image of time does the speaker present in lines 21–22? (b)What do you think he means to suggest with this image?

Analyze and Evaluate

5. (a)Summarize the main parts of the speaker's argument. (b)In your opinion, is this a convincing argument? Why or why not?

6. (a)What is the poem's rhyme scheme? (b)What effect do the rhymes have on the poem?

7. (a)Restate the speaker's recommendations in the poem's final paragraph, lines 33–46. How is this portion of the poem different from the rest of the poem? (b)Why is this an effective way to end the poem?

Connect

8. **Big Idea** **The Sacred and the Secular** What details can you identify in this poem that undercut the common religious beliefs of the time?

LITERARY ANALYSIS

Literary Element **Hyperbole**

Humor is an integral part of **hyperbole**. When hyperbole appears in literature, it is often used expressly for this purpose. Like hyperbole, which exaggerates facts or circumstances, **understatement** can be employed in a similar way. Understatement is language that makes something seem less important than it really is. Like hyperbole, it can add humor or direct the reader's attention to something the author wants to emphasize.

1. What understatement appears in lines 31–32? In what ways is this example an effective use of the device?

2. Why might hyperbole and understatement be effective techniques to use together?

Review: Carpe Diem

As you learned on page 456, **carpe diem** is a Latin phrase meaning "seize the day"; in other words, "make the most out of every moment." In *carpe diem* poems, the speaker emphasizes the shortness of life.

Partner Activity "To His Coy Mistress" uses *carpe diem* as a motif. Throughout the poem, the speaker makes many references to the passing of time and urges his mistress to seize the day. Working with a partner, identify three images that further the speaker's message and explain how they support the *carpe diem* motif.

The Stolen Kiss (detail). Jean-Honoré Fragonard.

READING AND VOCABULARY

Reading Strategy Previewing

Previewing is the first step when navigating a text that you have never encountered before. It allows you, as a reader, to make predictions about that text and to set a purpose for your reading. While previewing, you are often able to determine the genre, the subject, and perhaps even the theme of a literary work. Review the chart you made while you were previewing the poem, and then answer the following questions.

1. In general, were your predictions about "To His Coy Mistress" correct? Explain.

2. Why might previewing be somewhat ineffective when attempting to predict the theme of a literary work?

Vocabulary Practice

Practice with Analogies Choose the word that best completes each analogy. To complete an analogy, decide on the relationship represented by the first pair of words. Then apply that relationship to the second set of words.

1. **color : hue :: loudness :**
   a. feeling **b.** hearing **c.** sound

2. **war : strife :: connection :**
   a. disorder **b.** bond **c.** disruption

Academic Vocabulary

Here are two words from the vocabulary list on page R82.

exploit (iks′ ploit′) *v.* to take advantage of or to make use of

paradigm (par′ ə dīm) *n.* an example, ideal, or model on which something is based

Practice and Apply

1. How does the speaker in "To His Coy Mistress" try to **exploit** his mistress's fear of mortality?

2. In what ways does Marvell invert the Puritan **paradigm** in this poem?

WRITING AND EXTENDING

Writing About Literature

Evaluate Author's Craft Throughout this poem, the speaker uses a variety of metaphors and similes to enhance his argument. How well does Marvell use this figurative language? How do these devices function in the poem? Write a brief essay in which you evaluate the poet's use of similes and metaphors. Use evidence from the poem to support your position.

Before you begin drafting, it is important to determine what your thesis statement will be. To do this, begin by rereading the poem, noting anything that comes to mind and recording any metaphors and similes in the poem that strike you as particularly effective or ineffective. Compile a list and add your analysis and evaluation of each example. Use a two-column chart like the one below.

Example	Analysis and Evaluation
"like amorous birds of prey"	intends to convey urgency; this is an effective simile

After you complete your draft, meet with a peer reviewer to evaluate each other's work and to suggest revisions. Then proofread and edit your draft for errors in spelling, grammar, and punctuation.

Literature Groups

In your opinion, is "To His Coy Mistress" mostly about love or mostly about time? With your classmates, form two groups, each taking a side. Find lines and phrases from the poem that support your position. Then present your ideas to the other group and listen to their argument. Together, reach a consensus about the main message of the poem. Share your decision and reasons with the rest of the class.

Literature Online **Web Activities** For eFlashcards, Selection Quick Checks, and other Web activities, go to www.glencoe.com.

Writing Workshop

Literary Research Paper

 Writing a Historical Investigation

"We have been persuaded by some that are careful of our safety, to take heed how we commit our selves to armed multitudes, for fear of treachery; but I assure you I do not desire to live to distrust my faithful and loving people."

—Queen Elizabeth I, from "Speech to the Troops at Tilbury"

Connecting to Literature Queen Elizabeth I's speech at Tilbury, a primary source from the English Renaissance, gives modern readers a sense of the personal and historical context of the attack of the Spanish Armada in 1588. In a **literary research paper,** you investigate the connections between literature and its historical context based on both primary and secondary sources. You then draw your own conclusions about the significance of the literature and its context. Use the goals and strategies below to write a successful literary research paper.

Rubric: Features of Literary Research Papers

Goals		Strategies
To form a thesis statement	☑	Clarify the focus of your essay
To provide historical context	☑	Draw connections between the historical context and the literary text
To organize your research logically	☑	Write well-structured paragraphs, along with a clear introduction, body, and conclusion
To elaborate main ideas with supporting evidence	☑	Gather information from a variety of sources. Quote, paraphrase, and summarize information and credit sources
To synthesize information and draw new conclusions	☑	Combine ideas from different sources that lead to fresh insights

The Writing Process

In this workshop, you will follow the stages of the writing process. At any stage, you may think of new ideas to include and better ways to express them. Feel free to return to earlier stages as you write.

Prewriting

- - - - - - - - - - - - - -

Drafting

- - - - - - - - - - - - - -

Revising

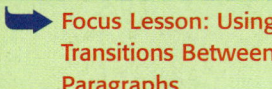 Focus Lesson: Using Transitions Between Paragraphs

Editing and Proofreading

- - - - - - - - - - - - - -

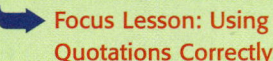 Focus Lesson: Using Quotations Correctly

Presenting

- - - - - - - - - - - - - -

Writing Models For models and other writing activities, go to www.glencoe.com.

OBJECTIVES
Write a literary research paper to investigate relationships between a historical period and a literary text from that time. Consider a variety of relevant perspectives from primary and secondary sources, and draw conclusions based on well-documented research.

> ### Assignment
>
> Write a literary research paper in which you investigate the relationship between a literary text and its historical context. As you move through the stages of the writing process, keep your audience and purpose in mind.
>
> **Audience:** other students and people familiar with your chosen literary text
>
> **Purpose:** to investigate a connection between a literary text and its historical context

Prewriting

Explore Ideas As you read through Unit Two, did you wonder how Queen Elizabeth's speech at Tilbury affected the battle or what a performance of *Macbeth* would have been like in Shakespeare's time? Consider literary texts that interest you and explore the relationship between a text and the history, culture, and author that shaped it.

▶ **Ask Questions** Consider which modern perspectives or historical information may shed new light on a literary text. Think of questions you want to answer and use your curiosity to guide your research.

▶ **Narrow Your Topic** Once you have a general topic that interests you, narrow the topic to fit the scope of the assignment. Too broad a topic will be overwhelming and difficult to focus, whereas too narrow a topic may not provide enough varied, reliable sources. Revise the question guiding your research until its scope fits that of the assignment.

Gather Research Now try to answer your research questions. Search through a combination of sources, such as online databases, general reference books, periodicals, the Internet, historical records, and documents. Ask a librarian for additional ideas.

▶ **Get a General Overview** Familiarize yourself with background information from reference books and the Internet to get a general understanding of your topic. This research may point you toward other relevant sources.

▶ **Consult a Variety of Sources with Diverse Perspectives** Include information from several sources and different viewpoints. Primary sources are original documents—such as letters, newspaper articles, historical records, and interviews—from the time period. Secondary sources are written by people who did not personally experience or influence the time or event. Include relevant information on your topic from a variety of literary and historical perspectives.

▶ **Use Reliable Sources** As you conduct your research, evaluate the credibility of your sources to make sure that they are not outdated, biased, or inaccurate. Both primary and secondary sources can be biased or inaccurate. For example, memoirs may promote personal agendas, and a magazine article may reflect an author's biases.

Real-World Connection

You might apply your research skills to planning a trip to a college campus or to learning about job opportunities at a company.

Journalists' Questions

Create a cluster diagram like the one below to explore different ways to approach a research idea. Fill in the center with an idea and write a relevant question beginning with each word surrounding the center. Then choose the most intriguing question as a starting point for further development of a topic.

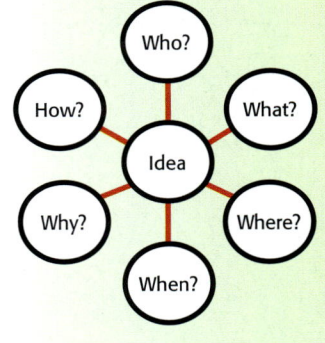

Take Notes As you look through sources, jot down important ideas, facts, and quotations. Whether you record your notes on note cards, in a notebook, or on separate computer files, keep your information organized. Record full publishing information for each source (see page R30) and assign it a number or the author's last name. Then use this number or name to label any notes taken from the source. This identification technique will save you time and will help you compile your works-cited list later.

> BIBLIOGRAPHY NOTE CARD
>
> Wells, Stanley   2
> Shakespeare: A Life in Drama
> New York: W. W. Norton & Company, 1995
> Wilmette Public Library
> 822.33 WE

Attention: Plagiarism

Plagiarism is using another writer's words or ideas without giving proper credit. Rewrite information in your own words and cite the source.

► **Quote** Record direct quotations word for word, including punctuation. Use direct quotations sparingly—for emphasis or to make a point.

► **Paraphrase** Restate someone else's idea in your own words. If you substitute a few of your own words in a direct quotation and call it a paraphrase, you have commited plagiarism because most of the words are still the source's words, not yours.

► **Summarize** Condense information to its key points.

> SUMMARY NOTE CARD
>
> Shakespeare: A Life in Drama   2
> Shakespeare focused on writing dialogue
> rather than on stage directions.
> (summary) page 28

Write a Thesis and Make an Outline Write a thesis statement to sum up the main idea based on your research. The thesis will guide your report. (Keep in mind, though, that you will probably revise your thesis as you gain new insights while writing.) Finally, use your notes to help you make an outline, including only the information that is relevant to your thesis. Choose an effective way to order the main ideas in your outline and keep related ideas together.

Drafting

Tie It All Together To begin drafting, follow your outline, revising the order of ideas as necessary. Remember that writing a research paper is more than just reporting facts and quotations. Interweave your historical research with specific quotations from literary texts, drawing your own conclusions for the reader. Show how each of your main points relates to your thesis and explain important relationships.

Analyzing a Workshop Model

Here is a final draft of a literary research paper. Read the paper and pay close attention to the comments in the margin. They point out features that you might want to include in your own paper. Then answer the questions in the margin and use the answers to guide you as you write your own draft.

Shakespeare: Man of the Theater

Readers of Shakespeare's plays, such as *Macbeth*, will better appreciate his scripts if they consider the historical background of the Elizabethan theater and Shakespeare's versatile role as a man of the theater. As Stanley Wells points out, Shakespeare "was a man of the theatre in at least three different senses: as a business man, as an actor, and as a playwright" (23). *Macbeth* serves as a model to illustrate Shakespeare's broad range of talents—directing, producing, staging, performing, and writing.

At the height of his career, Shakespeare was writing plays with a single Elizabethan stage in mind: the Globe Theatre in London. Although he began his career writing for many different playhouses, he wrote his most famous plays, including *Macbeth*, for the Globe. Shakespeare, one of the Globe's co-owners, helped build the theater in 1599 (Gurr 18).

The Globe was a round outdoor venue enclosed in wood. Although the stage was built so that the actors were in shadow rather than under direct sunlight (Gurr 22), there was no way to adjust the lighting onstage to suggest nighttime or a stormy setting. In addition, Shakespeare's plays had no intermissions or breaks when an act or scene changed (Gurr 38). Because of the lack of scenery, intervals, and controlled lighting, Shakespeare had to rely mainly on dialogue to indicate setting and passage of time. He compensated for such lacks by writing highly descriptive poetry to

Thesis Statement

State your thesis—the main idea that you will develop in your research paper. How does a thesis statement help guide readers?

Supporting Evidence: Details

Use factual details that help readers visualize descriptions of real people, places, and things. What do you picture here?

Supporting Evidence: Quotations

Include literary quotations as examples to illustrate your historical research. Would paraphrases or summaries of the lines be as effective? Explain.

Organization

Write well-structured paragraphs that relate to the thesis. How does this paragraph build on the thesis introduced in the first paragraph?

Summarize

Summarize information when you want to condense it to key points and details. Why would the writer choose to summarize here?

"paint the set" (Papp and Kirkland 138). For example, in *Macbeth*, Act 3, scene 2, Macbeth describes the approaching night to Lady Macbeth:

> Come, seeling night,
> Scarf up the tender eye of pitiful day,
> And with thy bloody and invisible hand
> Cancel and tear to pieces that great bond
> Which keeps me pale! Light thickens, and the crow
> Makes wing to th' rooky wood.
> Good things of day begin to droop and drowse,
> While night's black agents to their preys do rouse.

These lines help the audience envision the setting changing from dawn to dusk while revealing Macbeth's increasing remorse for Duncan's murder.

Shakespeare's stage directions, though sparse, also help overcome the limitations of the Elizabethan stage. In addition to suggesting entrances and exits, the stage directions often include predictable sounds to summon particular characters. In *Macbeth*, for example, thunder always introduces the witches and apparitions, a trumpet flourish summons royalty and authority figures, and the drum signals the march of soldiers. The bell is a more sinister signal that also becomes a clue for the audience. After the bell rings in Act 2, scene 1, Macbeth says, "I go, and it is done; the bell invites me. / Hear it not, Duncan, for it is a knell, / That summons thee to heaven, or to hell." The summons of the bell is echoed later in the act, after Macduff finds Duncan's corpse and cries, "Ring the alarum bell! Murder and Treason! . . . Ring the bell" (II.iii). Ironically, once the bell rings, Lady Macbeth wakes and cries, "What's the business, / That such a hideous trumpet calls to parley / The sleepers of the house?" (II.iii).

With the exception of some key stage directions, what most contemporary audiences notice is Shakespeare's *lack* of specific direction in the existing plays. Because of Shakespeare's active involvement in the production of his plays, such directions were not needed at the time the plays were written. Shakespeare would have had an intimate knowledge of his company and which types of roles his talented actors could best perform. From evidence in early manuscripts, it appears that he wrote certain characters with specific actors from his company in mind (Wells 28). When his company, the Chamberlain's Men, began performing at the Globe, "Shakespeare was at the height of his powers, and his confidence in his colleagues was, by any standard, unusual" (Thompson 184).

In addition, Shakespeare as playwright was likely to be the director of his plays, guiding the actors toward his vision of the performance (Papp and Kirkland 149; Wells 29). Based on the number of plays performed and the lack of rehearsal time, one can conclude that Shakespeare's main focus was on dialogue, rather than on "prescribing the gestures, facial expressions, and actions that should accompany the words," even when such cues established meaning (Wells 28). This focus on dialogue to the exclusion of stage directions results in an openness to interpretation for modern readers, actors, and directors (Wells 28). For Shakespeare, though, who knew his actors and knew he himself would be involved in rehearsal, the method was simply more practical. Unlike modern performers, Shakespeare's did not need detailed stage directions. Shakespeare could expect an accurate performance because of his personal collaboration with the actors.

Like stage directions, Shakespeare's dialogue was also influenced by the practical concerns of the Elizabethan stage. First, to succeed, a play had to draw an audience. Alfred Harbage notes: "Unlike some other audiences existing in and near his time, Shakespeare's audience was literally popular, ascending through each gradation from potboy to prince. It was the one to which he had been conditioned early and for which he never ceased to write" (159). In addition, unlike modern audiences, Elizabethan audiences reacted more to the auditory than to the visual. Many of those who attended the Globe were illiterate, and a play's dialogue, like a church's sermon or a storytelling, became a type of learning (Gurr 26; "All About Shakespeare" 5–6). For Elizabethan audiences, "the central feature of the plays was speech" (Gurr 26). The nuances of dialogue would not be lost on an Elizabethan audience, and Shakespeare could use particular diction and rhythms to reveal character (Sutherland 119).

For example, note the distinctions between the characters' language in *Macbeth*. Because most of the characters in *Macbeth* are royalty or of the nobility, they speak in blank verse (Nostbakken 15). On the other hand, the drunken Porter, a servant, speaks in prose. The witches speak in verse that often rhymes, emphasizing a chantlike quality. Although blank verse sounds more eloquent than prose, writing mainly blank verse was also a practical maneuver; its consistent rhythm made the lines easier for the

Supporting Evidence: Quotations

Use direct quotations to emphasize important information or to make a point. Why is this information effective as a direct quotation?

Secondary Source

Use a variety of primary and secondary sources. Why might a secondary source be more effective than a primary source in illustrating this point?

actors to memorize (Papp and Kirkland 169). Any change from blank verse to prose or vice versa became a signal to the audience. For example, Lady Macbeth speaks prose instead of her usual blank verse in Act 5, scene 1:

> To bed, to bed! There's knocking at the gate. Come, come, come, come, give me your hand! What's done cannot be undone. To bed, to bed, to bed!

Here Lady Macbeth is sleepwalking. Her repetitive, uncontrolled prose reveals her changed state and exposes how the murder has affected her character (Nostbakken 15).

Despite Shakespeare's attention to dialogue, as a "man of the theater" his focus was on a play's successful performance, not on its polished written form. Lines were revised during the rehearsal process, and recent critics argue that whole parts were added or deleted during rehearsal as needed (Wells 29; Nostbakken 13–14). In addition, because of a lack of copyright laws during the time and the attitude that stage plays were not serious literature, printing plays was not a priority for most playwrights (Papp and Kirkland 139). To people involved in theater during Elizabethan times, a stage play was a "passing event," not a "literary text" (Papp and Kirkland 140). About half of Shakespeare's plays were printed before his death, although "there is nothing to suggest that he did anything either to prepare the plays for reading or to see them through the press" (Wells 30). The written plays served as guides, but the true accomplishment was the live performance.

To understand Shakespeare's *Macbeth* today, one must keep in mind the particular theater for which Shakespeare was writing. By understanding the Elizabethan stage, the needs of its audience, and Shakespeare's personal involvement in the production of his plays, modern readers, audiences, and directors gain insight into Shakespeare's artistry. The stage informed every aspect of his plays; to read Shakespeare's plays as part of the Elizabethan world enriches the theatergoer's experience.

Conclusion

Summarize your main points and add related insight in your conclusion. What does or does not make this conclusion effective?

Works Cited

"All About Shakespeare."
http://www.pbs.org/standarddeviantstv/transcript_shakespeare.html.

Gurr, Andrew, with John Orrell. Rebuilding Shakespeare's Globe.
New York: Routledge/A Theatre Arts Book, 1989.

Harbage, Alfred. Shakespeare's Audience. New York and London:
Columbia University Press, 1969.

Nostbakken, Faith. Understanding Macbeth: A Student Casebook to Issues,
Sources, and Historical Documents. Westport, CT: Greenwood Press,
1997.

Papp, Joseph, and Elizabeth Kirkland. Shakespeare Alive! New York: Bantam,
1988.

Sutherland, James. "How the Characters Talk." In James Sutherland and Joel
Hurstfield. Shakespeare's World. New York: St. Martin's Press, 1964.

Thompson, Peter. "English Renaissance and Restoration Theatre."
In John Russell Brown, ed. The Oxford Illustrated History of
Theatre. Oxford: Oxford University Press, 1995.

Wells, Stanley. Shakespeare: A Life in Drama. New York:
W. W. Norton & Company, 1995.

Reliable Sources

Use a variety of reliable sources. What indicates that this source is probably reliable?

Variety of Sources

Use a variety of sources, such as books, encyclopedias, the Internet, newspapers, letters, and historical records. When might a writer use an encyclopedia?

Sian Thomas stars as Lady Macbeth in The Royal Shakespeare Company production of *Macbeth.*

Revising

Revising

Traits of Strong Writing

Ideas message or theme and the details that develop it

Organization arrangement of main ideas and supporting details

Voice writer's unique way of using tone and style

Word Choice vocabulary a writer uses to convey meaning

Sentence Fluency rhythm and flow of sentences

Conventions correct spelling, grammar, usage, and mechanics

Presentation the way words and design elements look on a page

For more information on using the Traits of Strong Writing, see pages R33–R34 of the Writing Handbook.

Peer Review Exchange drafts with a partner to help you identify strengths and weaknesses in your research papers. Both you and your partner should note any passages that seem unclear, irrelevant, or out of place. Return the papers and discuss ways to improve them. Refer to the traits of strong writing as you revise.

Use the rubric below to help you evaluate your writing.

Rubric: Writing an Effective Literary Research Paper
☑ Do you begin with a strong, clear thesis statement to guide your paper?
☑ Do you provide historical context and draw connections between this context and the literary text?
☑ Do you include a main idea and supporting details in each paragraph?
☑ Do you support main points with well-documented details, facts, and examples from a variety of sources?
☑ Do you quote, paraphrase, and summarize information correctly and cite sources accurately?
☑ Do you include a clear introduction, body, and conclusion?
☑ Do you synthesize information and draw your own conclusions?

▶ **Focus Lesson**

Using Transitions Between Paragraphs

Transitions show the relationship between ideas. Guide your readers by carefully choosing transitional words and phrases to show the relationships between paragraphs and to improve the overall flow of your paper. You can also repeat in one paragraph key words and phrases from an earlier one to create a link between ideas in your paper.

Draft:

Unlike modern performers, Shakespeare's did not need detailed stage directions. Shakespeare could expect an accurate performance because of his personal collaboration with the actors.

Shakespeare's dialogue was influenced by the practical concerns of the Elizabethan stage.

Revision:

Unlike modern performers, Shakespeare's did not need detailed stage directions. Shakespeare could expect an accurate performance because of his personal collaboration with the actors.

Like stage directions,[1] Shakespeare's dialogue was also[2] influenced by the practical concerns of the Elizabethan stage.

1: Repeat key phrases to show the relationship between paragraphs.

2: Use transitional words to show relationships and improve flow.

Editing and Proofreading

Get It Right Proofread your final draft for errors in grammar, usage, mechanics, and spelling. Refer to the Language Handbook, pages R46–R60, as a guide.

> **Focus Lesson**

Using Quotations Correctly

Check direct quotations for accuracy.

Problem: The direct quotation is not accurately quoted.

"As Stanley Wells points out, Shakespeare was a man of the theatre in at least three different senses: as a business man, as an actor, and as a playwright" (23).

Solution: Place quotation marks around the direct quotation only.

As Stanley Wells points out, Shakespeare "was a man of the theatre in at least three different senses: as a business man, as an actor, and as a playwright" (23).

Presenting

Appearance Matters Check to see that you have followed your teacher's general guidelines, including length, spacing, font size, and margin requirements.

Give Due Credit

Cite sources within your paper as closely to the end of the borrowed information as possible, usually before a period or comma. The citation consists of the author's last name and the page number(s) within parentheses: (Wells 28). Give full source information on the works-cited page.

Writer's Portfolio

Place a clean copy of your literary research paper in your portfolio to review later.

Speaking, Listening, and Viewing Workshop

Multimedia Presentation

Delivering a Multimedia Presentation

Connecting to Literature When Shakespeare staged his masterpieces, there were limits to what could be portrayed onstage. At the Globe Theatre, there was no scenery available, no artificial lighting, and limited performance space. To portray a distant location or a dramatic scene, therefore, Shakespeare wrote powerful dialogue and called for stylish costumes and believable props. Throughout history, people have used various media to transport audiences to places they have never been, often providing "front-row seats" to events audiences could never have experienced otherwise.

A combination of art and literature can both teach and entertain. In a **multimedia exhibit**, text, sound, visuals, and artifacts all communicate ideas about a topic. Multimedia exhibits should educate viewers while evoking emotions and opinions—often strong ones. For example, a multimedia exhibit designed to persuade others to preserve the South American rain forest might display photographs of environmental damage, a video of an ecology lecture, or a chart that records vital medical resources that come from the Amazon region. In this workshop, rely on a variety of materials related to the subject to achieve your purpose.

> **Assignment** Plan and present a multimedia exhibit.

Planning Your Presentation

The purpose of a multimedia exhibit is to convey information about an issue or an event and to leave a lasting impression on viewers. Make the most of the multimedia format as you plan and present your exhibit.

- Research your subject well and be prepared to answer any questions the audience may ask.
- Use the most striking images and text you can find to appeal to your audience. Your presentation is only as strong as its impact on viewers.
- Decide how you will organize your images, such as chronologically or by categories. Draw or sketch a layout of your exhibit.
- Include a variety of media, such as text, art, and photographs. Technology—such as a computer slideshow or an overhead projector—can be a plus. Ask your teacher what technology is available in the classroom.
- Most important, choose a topic you feel strongly about and would like to share with others.

Techniques for Delivering a Multimedia Exhibit

Verbal Techniques	Nonverbal Techniques
☑ **Volume** Speak loudly and slowly so the audience can hear the background information you provide.	☑ **Eye Contact** Establish and maintain eye contact with your audience as you present.
☑ **Pace** Allow the audience enough time to view each piece of your exhibit. If your multimedia exhibit is powerful, the audience will want time to react to and reflect on it.	☑ **Order** Present your ideas in a concise and logical order that properly develops the main idea of your presentation.
☑ **Mood** Decide what tone and mood are appropriate for your exhibit. For example, an exhibit on the Vietnam War would probably convey a serious tone and be thought provoking.	☑ **Display** Prominently display your exhibit. Ensure that nothing blocks text or images.

Analyzing the Model

Examine the photographs on page 490. What makes these photographs stand out above everyday images? How do these multimedia images make you feel?

Working Together

Because you may be completing your multimedia exhibits in groups, it will be important to choose a topic that interests each team member. Remember that each participant should contribute to both planning and presenting the exhibit.

OBJECTIVES
- Present a multimedia exhibit.
- Connect multimedia to your personal experience.

For Independent Reading

DURING THE ENGLISH RENAISSANCE, LYRIC POETRY AND DRAMA FLOURISHED, REACHING unsurpassable heights. Yet, throughout the sixteenth century, aristocratic poets such as Sir Thomas Wyatt and Sir Philip Sidney rarely published their own poems. Rather these poets circulated their poetry among friends. Eventually, however, printers gathered these poems and published collections, or anthologies, called "miscellanies." In 1557 Richard Tottel published his *Miscellany*, and for the first time the general public had widespread access to written poetry. People also read works by Richard Hakluyt (hak′ lōot), an English clergyman and geographer who collected prose accounts of travel adventures. His most important work was *The Principal Navigations, Voyages, and Discoveries of the English Nation*, an anthology published in 1589. Another major work of the English Renaissance was the *Book of Common Prayer*, which was first published in 1549 and came into prominence as a result of the English Reformation.

Tottel's Miscellany

compiled by Richard Tottel (1557)

Tottel's book is usually considered the first printed collection of English poetry. It contains sonnets by Sir Thomas Wyatt; Henry Howard, Earl of Surrey; and several others. The book originally entitled *The Book of Songs and Sonnets* is more commonly known as *Tottel's Miscellany*. Tottel was aware that his collection might have its share of naysayers. In a message to readers, he tried to forestall criticism by writing, "If perhaps some mislike the stateliness of style removed from the rude skill of common ears: I ask help of the learned to defend their learned friends, the authors of this work." Despite his concerns, Tottel's book was successful.

Book of Common Prayer

by Thomas Cranmer and others (1549)

By the end of King Edward VI's short-lived reign in 1553, Protestant churchgoers were familiar with the *Book of Common Prayer*. This book was based on the Latin liturgy and compiled in large part by Thomas Cranmer, the archbishop of Canterbury. It was written in English which allowed people to read the prayers for themselves. In 1549 the Act of Uniformity specified that only the *Book of Common Prayer* could be used in church services. This heightened the already heated tension between Protestants and Catholics created by King Henry VIII's split from the Catholic Church. A major revision was published in 1552, and the book has been revised from time to time ever since.

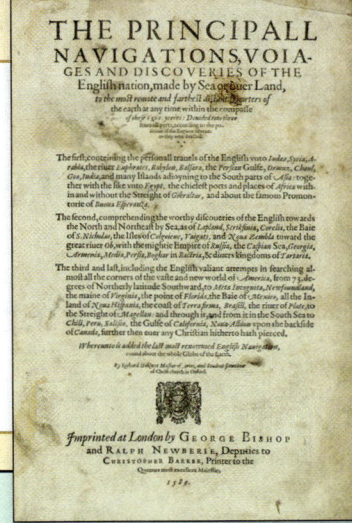

"*Hakluyt's Voyages is the prose epic of the English people. As Shakespeare's characters are giants, so too are Hakluyt's. As Shakespeare's language is vigorous and colorful, so too is the language of the Voyages. As Shakespeare's plays reflect the mind and spirit of his age, so too does Hakluyt's monumental work. The collection is Elizabethan in its vitality and scope, with all the greatness attributable to that age; at the same time it is more—in its panorama of the revealed birth of an empire and the opening of the globe, the Voyages has no equivalent in the English language.*"

—Irwin R. Blacker, Introduction to Hakluyt's *Voyages*, 1965

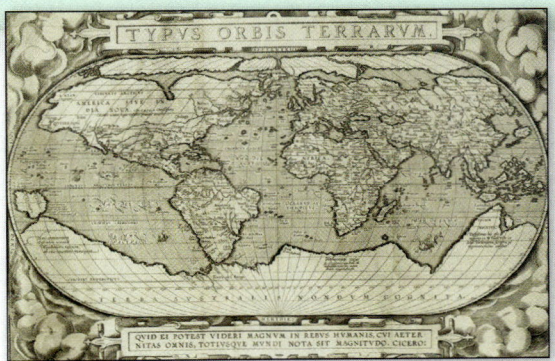

The Principal Navigations, Voyages, and Discoveries of the English Nation

compiled by Richard Hakluyt (1589)

Richard Hakluyt, a clergyman, collected accounts from adventurous sailors, explorers, and merchants who traveled all over the world. His book includes accounts from such famous globe-trotters as Sir Francis Drake, Sir Martin Frobisher, and Sir Walter Raleigh. Hakluyt wrote that his purpose was to save the texts "which long have lain miserably scattered in musty corners, and . . . hidden in misty darkness, and were very like for the greatest part to have been buried in perpetual oblivion." When he discovered a text in a language other than English, he translated it and included the original. His book helped to document England's growing relationship to the sea as a global highway while informing readers about valuable markets and astonishing lands.

From the Glencoe Literature Library

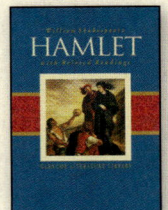

Hamlet

by William Shakespeare

Probably Shakespeare's best-known work, *Hamlet* is a brilliant study of revenge, madness, and appearance versus reality.

A Midsummer Night's Dream

by William Shakespeare

A Midsummer Night's Dream follows young lovers into a magical forest, where a mischievous elf causes comedy and chaos.

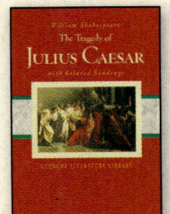

The Tragedy of Julius Caesar

by William Shakespeare

Julius Caesar relates the story of Julius Caesar's murder and the intrigues and ambitions of his supporters and enemies.

Reading: Nonfiction

Carefully read the following passage. Use context clues to help define any words with which you are unfamiliar. Pay close attention to the use of figurative language, argument, and tone. Then, on a separate sheet of paper, answer the questions that follow.

from *"Of Cunning"* by Sir Francis Bacon

line

We take cunning for a sinister or crooked wisdom. And certainly there is a great difference between a cunning man and a wise man; not only in point of honesty, but in point of ability. . . .

5   . . . I knew a counsellor and secretary, that never came to Queen Elizabeth of England with bills to sign, but he would always first put her into some discourse of estate, that she might the less mind the bills. . . .

10   In things that are tender and unpleasing, it is good to break the ice by some whose words are of less weight, and to reserve the more weighty voice to come in as by chance, so that he may be asked the question upon the other's speech. . . .

15   I knew one that, when he wrote a letter, he would put that which was most material in the postscript, as if it had been a by-matter.

I knew another that, when he came to have speech, he would pass over that that he intended
20   most; and go forth, and come back again, and speak of it as of a thing that he had almost forgot. . . .

It is a point of cunning, to let fall those words in a man's own name, which he would have another man learn and use, and thereupon take
25   advantage. I knew two that were competitors for the secretary's place in Queen Elizabeth's time, and yet kept good quarter between themselves; and would confer one with another upon the business; and the one of them said, That to be a secretary in

30 the *declination of a monarchy* was a ticklish thing,
and that he did not affect it: the other straight caught
up those words and discoursed with divers of his
friends, that he had no reason to desire to be
secretary in the *declination of a monarchy.* The

35 first man took hold of it, and found means it was
told the Queen; who, hearing of a *declination of a
monarchy,* took it so ill as she would never after hear
of the other's suit. . . .

Some have in readiness so many tales and
40 stories, as there is nothing they would insinuate, but
they can wrap it into a tale; which serveth both to
keep themselves more in guard, and to make others
carry it with more pleasure.

It is a good point of cunning for a man to
45 shape the answer he would have in his own words
and propositions; for it makes the other party stick
the less.

It is strange how long some men will lie in
wait to speak somewhat they desire to say; and how
50 far about they will fetch; and how many other
matters they will beat over, to come near it. It is a
thing of great patience, but yet of much use. . . .

But these small wares and petty points of
cunning are infinite; and it were a good deed to
55 make a list of them; for that nothing doth more hurt
in a state than that cunning men pass for wise.

But certainly some there are that know the
resorts and falls of business, that cannot sink into
the main of it; like a house that hath convenient
60 stairs and entries, but never a fair room. . . . Some
build rather upon the abusing of others, and (as we
now say) *putting tricks upon them,* than upon
soundness of their own proceedings.

1. In the opening paragraph, what is the principal
distinction that Bacon makes between cunning
people and wise people?
A. The cunning are evil; the wise are not.
B. The cunning are different from the wise in
ability and honesty.
C. The wise will always rise to the top ranks of
their professions.
D. The wise are less honest and have less ability
than the cunning.

2. From the context, what do you conclude that the
word *tender* means in line 10?
F. young
G. loving
H. gentle
J. sensitive

3. Why might the letter writer put the "most material" information in a postscript?
  A. to cause the reader to ignore it
  B. to make it more likely to be read
  C. to downplay the importance of the information
  D. to increase the importance of the information

4. From the context, what do you conclude that the word *material* means in line 16?
  F. important
  G. matter
  H. textile
  J. assured

5. For what reason did one of the competitors claim that being a "secretary in the *declination of a monarchy* was a ticklish thing"?
  A. He did not wish to compete any longer.
  B. He wanted to upset the queen.
  C. He wanted to trick his competitor and become secretary.
  D. He wanted to trick the queen so that his competitor would become secretary.

6. According to Bacon, why is it useful to present information in the form of a story?
  F. to make the information seem less important
  G. to guard the speaker and make the information more pleasant to hear
  H. to confuse the listener through the distortion and manipulation of facts
  J. to bore the listener with unimportant information

7. Why might it be "of much use" to "wait to speak"?
  A. to upset the listener
  B. to prevent the listener from speaking
  C. to allow the speaker to pass as wise
  D. to wait for the appropriate moment

8. What reason does Bacon give for listing the "small wares" of cunning?
  F. to create a definitive list
  G. to make the tools of the cunning available to everyone
  H. to hurt the state
  J. to pass on this information because doing so is a good deed

9. According to Bacon, what is the most hurtful thing to a state?
  A. that the wise pass for the cunning
  B. that the cunning pass for the wise
  C. that the petty points of cunning become infinite
  D. that the state itself becomes cunning

10. What literary device is most evident in the sentence beginning in line 57?
  F. simile
  G. metaphor
  H. motif
  J. apostrophe

11. From the context, what do you conclude that the word *fair* means in line 60?
  A. pale
  B. reasonable
  C. attractive
  D. dark

12. What is the overall tone of this passage?
  F. angry
  G. ironic
  H. knowing
  J. skeptical

13. What is the main idea of this passage?
  A. There are many different kinds of cunning.
  B. The wise and the cunning are essentially the same kind of people.
  C. The wise are less adept than the cunning.
  D. The cunning are different from the wise in ability and honesty.

14. On the basis of this passage, with which of the following statements would Bacon be most likely to agree?
  F. There is no such thing as wisdom.
  G. The cunning have many tools.
  H. The cunning always outwit the wise.
  J. The cunning are not intelligent.

Literature Online **Unit Assessment** To prepare for the Unit test, go to www.glencoe.com.

Vocabulary Skills: Sentence Completion

For each question in the Vocabulary Skills section, choose the word or words that best complete the sentence.

1. Although many were executed for _____ in Tudor England, their actual crime was holding religious beliefs different from those of the monarch.
   A. spite
   B. calamity
   C. treachery
   D. impediment

2. The humanists believed that limited skill in language, especially in rhetoric, was almost an _____.
   F. infirmity
   G. enmity
   H. tread
   J. discretion

3. Many Renaissance thinkers believed that learning and quiet contemplation rather than _____ between people could completely remake society.
   A. discourse
   B. hue
   C. folly
   D. sloth

4. There is nearly _____ recognition of Shakespeare's literary _____ among scholars.
   F. constant . . . virtues
   G. vain . . . tempest
   H. continual . . . strife
   J. bitter . . . balm

5. Many in Tudor England, including King James I, believed that supernatural forces could trick or _____ the unsuspecting into performing evil acts.
   A. scorn
   B. beguile
   C. replenish
   D. prevail

6. There was almost _____ violence between Catholics and Protestants in England and Europe throughout the Reformation.
   F. wan
   G. suppressed
   H. vain
   J. continual

7. Before the beginning of the Renaissance, the classics of ancient Greece and Rome had _____ in near obscurity.
   A. subdued
   B. scorned
   C. executed
   D. languished

8. Though barely able to _____ the grief he felt after his wife's death, Donne transformed his sorrow into powerful sermons and verse.
   F. deem
   G. censure
   H. endure
   J. congeal

9. Little _____ existed between writers who envied one another's talents and position.
   A. concord
   B. valor
   C. inconstancy
   D. alteration

10. Some poets of the period, including Donne, attempted to strike a balance between the impermanent, _____ world and the divine.
    F. meek
    G. mute
    H. wan
    J. mortal

Grammar and Writing Skills: Paragraph Improvement

In the following excerpt from a student draft of a literary research paper, some phrases are underlined. The number beneath each underlined phrase corresponds to a numbered question on the next page, which prompts you to replace the underlined phrase. If you think the original should not be changed, choose "NO CHANGE."

Throughout the passage, boxed numbers also appear. These numbers refer to questions about specific paragraphs or to the essay as a whole. When these questions are about a paragraph's sentence order, each sentence in the paragraph is numbered.

Both the boxed numbers and the numbers beneath underlined phrases refer to question numbers, *not* to the sequence of sentences or paragraphs.

Read the passage through once before you begin to answer the questions. As you read, pay close attention to the writer's use of **verb tense, quotation marks,** and **transitions.** Write your answers on a separate sheet of paper.

> Over the past four hundred years, literary critics have had mixed responses to the works of the Metaphysical poets. Some have found their use of conceits, or extended comparisons, labored or unnecessarily complex. Others, including poet T. S. Eliot, has been
> _____
> 1
> deeply affected by these poems' intellectual and emotional capacity. Often, those most critical of these works argue that they create unnatural, or forced, relationships between unlike things. 2 The best poets of this group did not create unnatural conceits, just that which was unexpected.
>
> This movement—which included John Donne, Andrew Marvell, and George Herbert,
> _____
> 3
> among others—were not simply generating complex and irregular poems to confuse readers.
> They were openly rejecting the formality found in the previous generation's work. Complicated
> _____
> 4
> conceits, irregular meter and rhyme, and unexpected intellectual maneuvers were not generally
> found in the works of sixteenth-century poets. These were revolutionary changes that did not sit
> well with some later critics. "[T]heir amplifications had no limits, wrote Samuel Johnson." He
> _____
> 5
> goes on to state that "they left not only reason but fancy behind them; and produced
> combinations of confused magnificence, that not only could not be credited, but could not be
> imagined."
>
> 6 [1] Eliot, in particular, would argue with the claim that these writers created a
> _____
> 7
> "confused magnificence." [2] Many would disagree with Johnson's assessment. [3] Eliot
> _____
> 8
> believed that these writers created a finely tuned poetry, he saw in them great clarity. 9
> _____
> 10

1. **A.** NO CHANGE
   B. Others, including poet T. S. Eliot, have been deeply affected by these poems' capacity.
   C. Others, including poet T. S. Eliot, was deeply affected by these poems' capacity.
   D. Poet T. S. Eliot has been deeply affected by these poems' intellectual and emotional capacity.

2. Which of the following transition words or phrases would work best at the start of this sentence?
   F. first
   G. for instance
   H. therefore
   J. yet

3. **A.** NO CHANGE
   B. This movement, which included John Donne, Andrew Marvell, and George Herbert, among others, were not simply generating complex and irregular poems to confuse readers.
   C. This movement—which included John Donne, Andrew Marvell, and George Herbert, among others—was not simply generating complex and irregular poems to confuse readers.
   D. This movement was not simply generating complex and irregular poems to confuse readers.

4. **F.** NO CHANGE
   G. Complicated conceits were not generally found in the works of sixteenth-century poets.
   H. Complicated conceits and irregular meter were not generally found in the works of sixteenth-century poets.
   J. Complicated conceits, irregular meter and rhyme, and unexpected intellectual maneuvers was not generally found.

5. **A.** NO CHANGE
   B. [T]heir amplifications had no limits, wrote Samuel Johnson.

   C. "[T]heir amplifications had no limits, Samuel Johnson wrote."
   D. "[T]heir amplifications had no limits," wrote Samuel Johnson.

6. Which of the following sentence sequences would make this paragraph logical?
   F. 1, 3, 2
   G. 2, 1, 3
   H. 3, 2, 1
   J. 2, 3, 1

7. **A.** NO CHANGE
   B. Eliot would argue with the claim that these writers created a "confused magnificence."
   C. Eliot, in particular, would argue with the claim that these writers created a confused magnificence.
   D. Eliot in particular would argue.

8. **F.** NO CHANGE
   G. Eliot believed that these writers created a finely tuned poetry; he saw in them great clarity.
   H. Eliot believed these writers created clarity.
   J. He believed that these writers created a finely tuned poetry.

9. Which of the following would be most appropriate at this point in paragraph 3?
   A. another quotation from Johnson
   B. a quotation from Eliot that demonstrates his position
   C. a quotation from Donne
   D. a restatement of the thesis

10. Which of the following must the writer include while completing this essay?
    F. footnotes
    G. quotations from Donne, Marvell, and Herbert
    H. examples of Metaphysical conceits
    J. examples of sixteenth-century poetry

Essay

T. S. Eliot claimed that it was not enough for poets to look into their hearts but that they also had to look "into the cerebral cortex, the nervous system, and the digestive tracts." Write a short essay in which you examine the use of imagery, or other literary devices, in a poem from this unit. As you write, keep in mind that your essay will be checked for **ideas, organization, voice, word choice, sentence fluency, conventions,** and **presentation.**

Dr. Johnson at Cave's the Publisher, 1854. Henry Wallis. Oil on canvas, 19½ x 23½ in. Private collection.

From PURITANISM to the ENLIGHTENMENT

1640–1780

Looking Ahead

In the 1640s, religious and political conflict between King Charles I and the largely Puritan supporters of Parliament led to civil war, the execution of the king, and a decade of stern Puritan rule. Following the return of the monarchy in 1660, Parliament kept much of its power, but Restoration culture reveled in a witty, worldly reaction against Puritan severity. During the same period, a scientific revolution was blossoming into the Enlightenment, an intellectual movement whose participants reexamined all aspects of life in the light of reason.

Keep the following questions in mind as you read:

➤➤ What were the essential features of Puritanism?

➤➤ What factors contributed to the outbreak of the English civil war?

➤➤ What were the goals of the English Enlightenment?

OBJECTIVES

In learning about Puritanism and the English Enlightenment, you will focus on the following:

- analyzing the characteristics of various literary periods and the issues that influenced the writers of those periods
- evaluating the influences of the historical period that shaped literary characters, plots, settings, and themes
- connecting literature to historical contexts, current events, and your own experiences

TIMELINE
1640–1780

Satan Smitten by Michael in Milton's *Paradise Lost.*

BRITISH LITERATURE

1640

1644
John Milton publishes *Areopagitica*

1660
Samuel Pepys begins his diary

1663
Drury Lane Theatre opened

1667
John Milton publishes *Paradise Lost*

1668
John Dryden becomes poet laureate

1678
John Bunyan publishes *Pilgrim's Progress* ▶

1680

1709
The Tatler begins publication

1711
The Spectator begins publication

1714
Alexander Pope publishes *The Rape of the Lock*

1719
Daniel Defoe publishes *Robinson Crusoe*

BRITISH EVENTS

1640

1647
George Fox founds Quakers

1660
Charles II restored to throne

1662
Royal Society founded

1665
Plague ravages London

1666
Great Fire of London occurs

Sir Isaac Newton's telescope

1680

1685
Charles II dies; James II becomes king

1687
Newton publishes theory of gravitation

1688
Glorious Revolution occurs

1707
England and Scotland unite as Great Britain ▶

1710
Sir Christopher Wren completes St. Paul's Cathedral

1714
Ruling House of Hanover founded by George I

WORLD EVENTS

1640

1644
Haiku master Matsuo Bashō born

1650 ▼
Taj Mahal completed in India

1657
Fire destroys much of Japanese capital, Edo (Tokyo)

1661
Louis XIV begins Palace of Versailles in France

1661
Emperor K'ang-hsi rules China

1668
Anton van Leeuwenhoek develops simple microscope

1680

1680
Molière's theater company becomes the Comédie Française

1682
LaSalle claims Louisiana for France

1683
Ottoman Turks besiege Vienna

c. 1697
Ashanti Empire formed in Africa ▼

Literature Online Timeline Visit www.glencoe.com for an interactive timeline.

Robert Lovelace Preparing to Abduct Clarissa Harlow, c. 18th century. Francis Hayman. Oil on canvas, 25 x 30 in. Southampton City Art Gallery, Hampshire, UK.

1720

1720
Alexander Pope completes translation of the *Iliad*

1726
Jonathan Swift publishes *Gulliver's Travels*

1728
Alexander Pope publishes *The Dunciad*

1729
Jonathan Swift publishes *A Modest Proposal*

1734
Alexander Pope publishes *An Essay on Man*

1747–1748
Samuel Richardson publishes *Clarissa*

1755
Samuel Johnson publishes *A Dictionary of the English Language*

1760

1763
Boswell meets Johnson

1768
Encyclopaedia Britannica begins publication

1776
Edward Gibbon publishes first volume of *The Decline and Fall of the Roman Empire*

1720

1721
Smallpox inoculation introduced by Lady Mary Wortley Montagu

1732
Covent Garden Theatre opens

1735
William Hogarth completes his engraving of *A Rake's Progress*

1742
George Frideric Handel's *Messiah* first performed

1746
Defeat at Culloden Moor ends Jacobite Rebellion ▶

1752
Britain adopts Gregorian calendar

1757
Victory at Plassey begins British rule of India

1760

1768
Royal Academy of Arts founded

1720

1722
Safavid Empire ends in Persia

1727
Coffee first planted in Brazil

1749
German composer Johann Sebastian Bach completes *The Art of the Fugue*

1752
Ben Franklin invents the lightning rod

1755
Earthquake destroys Lisbon in Portugal

1756
Seven Years' War begins in Europe

1759
French writer Voltaire publishes *Candide*

1760

1762
Catherine II becomes ruler of Russia ▶

1775
American Revolution begins

Reading Check

Analyzing Graphic Information During this period, what three cities suffered major disasters?

BY THE NUMBERS

The Great Fire of London

On September 2, 1666, fire broke out in a London bakery. During the next four days it spread, destroying much of the city. Fortunately, the flames spread slowly, which enabled Londoners to escape. As a result, few people were killed; contemporary records indicate only five deaths from the fire. Damage to buildings and property, however, was considerable; 100,000 Londoners were homeless.

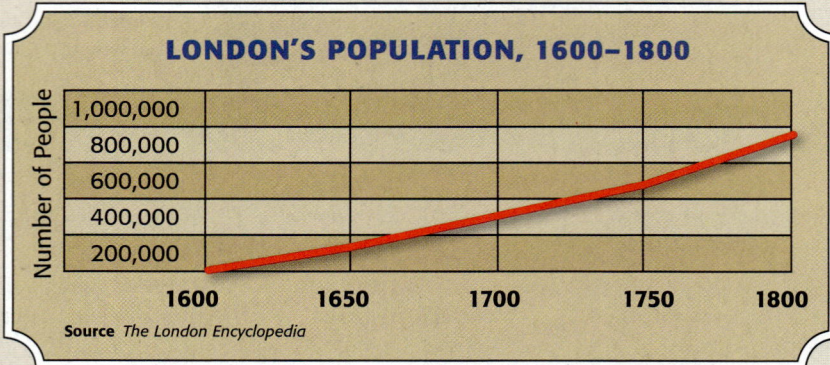

LONDON'S POPULATION, 1600–1800

Number of People: 1,000,000 / 800,000 / 600,000 / 400,000 / 200,000

Years: 1600 · 1650 · 1700 · 1750 · 1800

Source *The London Encyclopedia*

BUILDINGS DESTROYED:

- 13,200 houses
- 4 river bridges
- 3 city gates
- St. Paul's Cathedral
- 87 parish churches
- 6 chapels
- 52 company (guild or trade association) halls
- Royal Exchange
- Custom House
- Newgate and several other prisons

COST OF REBUILDING:

- Houses: nearly 4 million pounds
- Other public buildings: 2 million pounds
- St. Paul's Cathedral: 2 million pounds

PUNISHMENT FOR SWEARING

Under the Puritan Commonwealth, swearing in public was an offense punishable by the payment of a fine, which varied according to the social rank of the offender. A duke paid 30 shillings; a baron paid 20 shillings; a squire paid 10 shillings; and a commoner paid 3 shillings and fourpence.

TEA AND COFFEE

Drinking tea became popular in England during the Restoration. At that time, it was a very costly drink: a pound of tea cost 10 pounds. By 1700 the price was reduced to one pound, but this was still a big expense for ordinary British families, whose annual income ranged between 15 and 50 pounds a year. The first coffeehouse opened in London in 1652. By 1663 London had 82 coffeehouses; by 1700 the number had grown to somewhere between 500 and 2000.

TRAVEL RATES

In the late 1600s, stagecoaches could travel at a maximum speed of 3 to 4 miles per hour. By 1719 express coaches could travel a distance of 60 miles a day. In 1765 a coach pulled by 6 horses made the trip from London to the port of Dover, a distance of 84 miles, in one day.

THE SLAVE TRADE

In 1672 a group of merchants from London formed the Royal African Company to engage in the West African slave trade. The Royal African Company transported an average of 5000 Africans a year between 1680 and 1686 to the sugar plantations of the West Indies. In 1698, when the company lost its monopoly, the slave trade expanded greatly. In the first 9 years of unrestricted trade, the British port of Bristol alone transported over 160,000 Africans to slavery. Daniel Defoe estimated that British ships were transporting 40,000 to 50,000 Africans a year, who were then sold for an average price of 25 pounds per person.

BEING THERE

In 1707 the Act of Union established the state of Great Britain, composed of England and Scotland. Wales had been a part of England since the mid-1500s. In 1666 the Great Fire of London destroyed much of the city. Once London was rebuilt, however, it continued to grow throughout the 1700s, becoming Europe's largest city by 1750.

A *In a London Coffee House,* c. 1700. Engraving.

B *Family Party,* c. 18th century. William Hogarth. Private collection.

C *Earl and Countess of Ossory and their Children at Ampthill Park,* 1777. Benjamin Killingbeck. Private collection, Ackermann and Johnson Ltd, London.

Literature Online Maps in Motion Visit www.glencoe.com for an interactive map.

Reading Check

Analyzing Graphic Information:

1. How many times greater was London's population in 1800 than it had been in 1600?

2. Using Daniel Defoe's figures, what was the total value of the slaves transported each year by British ships?

3. Why would a port city like Portsmouth be especially vulnerable to the spread of plague?

From PURITANISM
to the ENLIGHTENMENT

1640–1780

Historical, Social, and Cultural Forces

The Divine Right of Kings

When James I succeeded to the English throne, he firmly upheld the principle of the divine right of kings, the belief that the regent derives power directly from God. James was not interested in reforming the Church of England, but rather in making his subjects conform to its practices. Catholics were forbidden to celebrate Mass, and Puritans could not gather for religious meetings. Many religious dissidents left England. Catholics tended to emigrate to the European continent, particularly France and Italy. The Puritans first found a home in Holland, and later voyaged to North America, where they established the Plymouth Colony in 1620 in present-day Massachusetts.

The Pilgrim Fathers: Departure of a Puritan Family for New England, 1856. Charles West Cope. Oil on canvas, 87²/₁₀ x 113²/₁₀ in. National Gallery of Victoria, Melbourne, Australia.

Growing Conflict

When James's son Charles I came to the throne in 1625, people who hoped for a more tolerant ruler were disappointed. The new king had taken to heart his father's example of ruling by divine right. Because of his belief that he would be committing a grave sin in surrendering part of his authority, Charles disregarded Parliament's opinions on economic spending and commanded his subjects to observe a form of Anglican ritual that was offensive to Puritans and other dissidents. By 1629, with Parliament and the king unable to agree on religious and economic matters, Charles dissolved Parliament and did not call it back for eleven years.

During the "eleven years' tyranny," grievances on both sides mounted. By the time Charles recalled Parliament in 1640, it was too late for any permanent compromise. Parliament called for a new constitution that included their demands to control all church and military matters and appoint ministers and judges. The king moved his court from London to the northern city of York. The ideological battle lines were drawn; by August 1642, war had begun.

Civil War

The English civil war was fought between Royalist Cavaliers loyal to the king and the Puritan Roundheads (so called because their hair was cut short, unlike the long-haired courtiers). Over time, Parliament proved victorious, due largely to the New Model Army of Oliver Cromwell, a military genius and Puritan extremist. In April 1646, Charles surrendered himself to the Scots, who turned him over to Parliament in exchange for a large ransom.

By this time, the Parliamentary forces wanted to do away with the monarchy. The court that tried Charles accused him of being a "Tyrant, Traitor and Murderer; and a public enemy to the good people of this nation." The trial was controversial; many people who had fought against Charles were reluctant to resort to execution. Nonetheless, the death sentence was passed, and the king was publicly beheaded. A week after his death, Parliament abolished the monarchy.

> "This is none other but the hand of God; and to him alone belongs the glory."
>
> —Oliver Cromwell

The Commonwealth

Cromwell became the Lord Protector of the country. Until his death in 1658, Cromwell imposed strict Puritanical rules on public behavior and religious worship. He closed theaters, banned dancing and music, caused all religious icons to be destroyed as "graven images," and forbade the celebration of Christmas.

The Restoration

In 1660 the English Parliament that had ordered the execution of Charles I invited his son Charles II to return from exile and reclaim the throne. With the restoration of the monarchy, many old entertainments were restored. The theaters were reopened, public festivals were celebrated, and new fashions in clothes, food, and ideas flooded in from the European continent. Intellectual life began to flourish once more and set the stage for the burgeoning Enlightenment that took hold in England during the following century.

The Enlightenment and Neoclassicism

The Enlightenment was a European philosophical and literary movement that in England is often called "The Age of Reason." It is characterized by a profound faith in the power of human reason and a devotion to clarity of thought. Other hallmarks of the age were a skeptical attitude toward traditional religion, best represented by the Scottish philosopher David Hume, and a surge of scientific discovery.

A related literary movement was Neoclassicism, which reached its pinnacle in the poetry, prose, and criticism of Samuel Johnson. Its major tenet was the conviction that the classical authors of ancient Greece and Rome had perfected the rules and norms that should govern the writing of literature for all time.

PREVIEW | Big Ideas | # Puritanism to the Enlightenment

1 Puritanism and the Civil War

In the early 1640s, conflicts between the Anglican supporters of the monarchy and the Puritan supporters of Parliament brought about the English civil war. Many English writers of the period took sides in the struggle between Parliament and the king.

See pages 508–509.

2 The Restoration

After ten years of stern Puritan rule, the re-establishment of the British monarchy under King Charles II was greeted with enthusiasm. British literary culture of the Restoration was marked by a witty, cynical tone and an emphasis on worldly values.

See pages 510–511.

3 The English Enlightenment & Neoclassicism

Beginning in the late 1600s, weariness with extremism resulted in the Enlightenment, an intellectual movement that accepted reason as the supreme authority. In the eighteenth century, Neoclassicists sought to revive the literary principles of ancient Greece and Rome.

See pages 512–513.

Puritanism and the Civil War

The Royalists and the Puritans, who would battle each other in the English civil war, both believed that all authority came from God. But they violently disagreed about how God's authority showed itself in the world, and this fierce dispute led to war.

What Was Puritanism?

Puritanism was a radical form of Calvinistic Protestantism whose adherents acknowledged only the "pure" word of God as revealed in their interpretations of the Bible. Puritans also shared the central goal of purifying the Church of England by eradicating the doctrines and rites that were retained from Catholicism.

The best thinkers among the Puritans embraced a liberal stance in politics that balanced their religious intolerance. John Milton, a democrat and pamphleteer for the anti-Royalist forces, spoke for "the true warfaring Christian" in his famous essay *Areopagitica*: "I cannot praise a fugitive and cloistered virtue, unexercised and unbreathed, that never sallies out and sees her adversary, but slinks out of the race, where that immortal garland is to be run for, not without dust and heat." Puritans such as Milton valued civil liberties and were zealous in defending their beliefs.

Religious Conflict

At least since the time of Elizabeth I, Puritans and other nonconformists (a blanket term for any Protestants who did not conform to the rites of the official Church of England) had been a thorn in the side of the monarch. James I had difficulties with Parliament, especially over government funding and foreign relations. James encouraged closer ties with Catholic Spain, even when Spain was at war with Protestant Holland. The House of Commons, with a large Puritan contingent, preferred to wage a Puritan crusade. James arrested some of his Parliamentary opponents; the Commons made a protest asserting their liberties. Charles I inherited both his father's autocratic beliefs and his problems with Parliament. Ultimately, the English civil war began over questions of authority—who had it and how it should be divided.

The Civil War

At the beginning of the war, the Royalist forces won some impressive victories, particularly because of the strength of their cavalry. Under the leadership of Oliver Cromwell, however, the Parliamentary army turned the tide. At the Battle of Naseby in June 1645, a miscalculation by the king and his cavalry commander, coupled with brilliant maneuvers by Cromwell, turned the battle into a Puritan victory.

Three and a half years later, in January 1649, Parliament tried the king for treason and condemned him to death. With the fall of the axe, the Puritans demonstrated that the former subjects wielded the sovereignty now. The moan from the assembled crowd, however, suggested that many were deeply divided and fearful. Some dipped handkerchiefs in the king's blood to preserve as relics.

Puritan Rule

Cromwell was a complex leader, leaving a legacy to be both admired and deplored. He preached and practiced religious toleration—except for Catholics. Any "graven images," which Cromwell associated with Catholicism, were destroyed. Throughout England, baptismal fonts, statues of saints, ceiling and altar decorations—the devotional art of centuries—were smashed. With the stability that Cromwell's government provided, the economy prospered, but there was little pleasure or entertainment in a country where public music was banned and theaters were closed. What had begun as a noble experiment in liberty ended in a military dictatorship.

After Cromwell's death in 1658, his son Richard briefly attempted to rule as Lord Protector, but he was ousted by the military, which disbanded Parliament and ruled incompetently. When order was restored by some of the king's old enemies, there seemed only one solution. In May 1660, Charles II returned triumphant, riding through London accompanied by a supportive army as he made his way to the palace of Whitehall, the scene of his father's execution twelve years before.

Cromwell Dissolving the Long Parliament, Benjamin West. Oil on canvas. Montclair Art Museum, NJ.

In 1644, responding to a recent government order imposing censorship, John Milton published his essay Areopagitica, *a defense of freedom of the press.*

from *Areopagitica* by John Milton

I deny not, but that it is of greatest concernment in the Church and Commonwealth, to have a vigilant eye how books demean themselves as well as men; and thereafter to confine, imprison, and do sharpest justice on them as malefactors. For books are not absolutely dead things, but do contain a potency of life in them to be as active as that soul was whose progeny they are; nay, they do preserve as in a vial the purest efficacy and extraction of that living intellect that bred them. I know they are as lively, and as vigorously productive, as those fabulous dragon's teeth, and being sown up and down, may chance to spring up armed men. And yet, on the other hand, unless wariness be used, as good almost kill a man as kill a good book: who kills a man kills a reasonable creature, God's image; but he who destroys a good book, kills reason itself, kills the image of God, as it were in the eye. Many a man lives a burden to the earth; but a good book is the precious life-blood of a master spirit, embalmed and treasured up on purpose to a life beyond life. 'Tis true, no age can restore a life, whereof perhaps there is no great loss; and revolutions of ages do not oft recover the loss of a rejected truth, for the want of which whole nations fare the worse.

Reading Check

Analyzing Cause and Effect What made Cromwell an unpopular ruler?

W e all know the sense of relief we feel when an arduous task is done or a difficult experience is finally over. After twenty years of turmoil, England was ready for a return to good times.

The Restoration Court

As he traveled through England to reclaim his throne, Charles II was greeted by many spontaneous outpourings of joy from the people. Writers and artists who looked forward to the renewal of royal patronage for their work were quick to praise his return. John Dryden, a young poet who had written a poem celebrating Cromwell's greatness, now wrote poems celebrating the king's return. In 1668 Charles made Dryden England's first official poet laureate.

Charles was a far cry from both his father and Oliver Cromwell. Known as the merry monarch, the good-natured Charles enjoyed pleasures of all kinds, from courtly entertainments to his royal mistresses. Trying to break the cycle of retribution which had plagued England for so long, Charles forgave many of his father's old enemies. His mercy did not extend, how-ever, to most of the judges at his father's trial and signers of the order of execution. Cromwell's body, which had been buried in the Tower of London, was dug up, beheaded, and reburied in a common pit.

Public Pleasures

Charles II's taste for pleasure was shared by many of his subjects, whose lives had been dreary under Puritan rule. Holidays such as Christmas were cele-brated once more, horse races—and betting—started up again, and music and evening masquerade parties filled public pleasure gardens such as Vauxhall. Charles also reopened the theaters. Audiences had an insatiable appetite for comedies about the fash-ionable manners of the age. Bawdy, witty, and amoral, these Restoration dramas by such play-wrights as William Congreve, William Wycherley, and George Farquhar reflect a cynical frivolity in matters of love and money.

The plays seemed all the more scandalous because the new theaters allowed women to appear on the stage for the first time. One of the most popular playwrights of the day was Aphra Behn, the first woman in England to make her living as a professional writer. Behn was often accused of lewdness, but there is no doubt that her vivacious comedies reflected the pleasure-loving attitude and *carpe diem* spirit of the Restoration.

The new licentiousness of public behavior was not universally shared. Puritans and others spoke out against the irreverence of the age. But dissenting too loudly could lead to jail, as it did in the case of John Bunyan, who spent more than twelve years impris-oned for his defiant Puritanism.

Plague and Fire

Perhaps the Puritans viewed the twin disasters of plague and fire as a punishment from God for what they perceived to be the immorality and corruption of the age. But the outbreak of the bubonic plague in 1665 disproportionately affected the poor. The College of Physicians ordered houses in which plague appeared to be nailed shut, leaving all the inhabitants to their fate. Wealthy people could engineer their escape and pay to leave London. So many victims died that bodies were buried in communal pits rather than in individual plots. The official number of the dead was more than 68,000; with the addition of people not usually included on official lists, such as Quakers and Jews, the actual number was probably more than 100,000.

Unlike the plague, the Great Fire of London equally affected both the rich and the poor. The fire raged for four days and continued to smolder for almost two months. An area about one and one-half miles long by a half mile wide was completely destroyed, includ-ing most of old London within its medieval walls. The king, who had shown great personal courage and intelligence in fighting the fire, took a vigorous inter-est in rebuilding the city—in fire-resistant stone—on an elegant and systematic scale. He placed his plan in the hands of Sir Christopher Wren, an astronomer by training, who proved to be the greatest civic architect England has ever produced.

John Rose Presenting the First English-Grown Pineapple to Charles II, 1675. Hendrick Danckerts. Oil.

One of the most brilliant and notorious members of the Restoration was John Wilmot, Earl of Rochester.

from *A Satire Against Mankind* by John Wilmot

Were I (who to my cost already am
One of those strange, prodigious creatures, man)
A spirit free to choose, for my own share,
What case of flesh and blood I pleased to wear,
I'd be a dog, a monkey, or a bear,
Or anything but that vain animal
Who is so proud of being rational.
   The senses are too gross, and he'll contrive
A sixth to contradict the other five,
And before certain instinct will prefer
Reason, which fifty times for one does err;
Reason, an *ignis fatuus* in the mind,
Which, leaving light of nature, sense, behind,
Pathless and dangerous wandering ways it takes
Through error's fenny bogs and thorny brakes;
Whilst the misguided follower climbs with pain

Mountains of whimseys, heaped in his own brain;
Stumbling from thought to thought falls headlong down
   Into doubt's boundless sea, where, like to drown,
Books bear him up a while, and make him try
To swim with bladders of philosophy;
In hopes still to o'ertake the escaping light,—
The vapor dances in his dazzling sight
Till, spent, it leaves him to eternal night.
Then old age and experience, hand in hand,
Lead him to death and make him understand,
After a search so painful and so long,
That all his life he has been in the wrong.
Huddled in dirt the reasoning engine lies,
Who was so proud, so witty, and so wise.

Reading Check

Comparing and Contrasting How did the attitude toward the arts during the Restoration differ from that during the Puritan Commonwealth?

English Enlightenment and Neoclassicism

Can humans understand the complexities of the natural world without the aid of divine revelation? Many eighteenth-century intellectuals were Deists, who believed that God manifests himself, not through the Bible or supernatural forces, but through the grandeur of his creation. Therefore, the way to know God is to use reason and observation to study the laws that govern the physical universe. This Enlightenment way of thinking led to a creative outburst of scientific inquiry and intellectual freedom that was unprecedented in the Western world.

A Scientific Revolution

Soon after his restoration to the throne, Charles II granted a charter to a group of "natural philosophers," or scientists, who were inspired by Francis Bacon's inductive approach to knowledge. The group became known as the Royal Society of London for the Promotion of Natural Knowledge. Early members included the astronomer and architect Christopher Wren, the chemist Robert Boyle, the astronomer Edmund Halley, and above all Isaac Newton, who made revolutionary advances in physics, mathematics, optics, and astronomy. Because of Newton, the mechanical workings of the universe were no longer considered mysterious, but instead could be understood by humans.

The Rule of Reason

In their study of nature, the members of the Royal Society emphasized the importance of experiment and observation. Nature was their sole authority. The Royal Society's Latin motto, *nullius in verba*, means "on the word of no one." Communicating their learning to others in a clear and accurate manner was a vital part of their methodology. They started the first scientific journal, *Philosophical Transactions*, which is still published today, to disseminate the discoveries of their members. Their plain style has influenced English prose—particularly in science, philosophy, and journalism—to this day.

The Rule of the Ancients

Just as the members of the Royal Society were concerned with extracting universal laws of nature from the diverse data of the real world, so too philosophers and poets set themselves the task of identifying universal laws of human nature. They believed that nature was rational and orderly, and that these underlying patterns were harmonious and beautiful. Poetry, no less than physics, was governed by natural, not man-made, laws. Therefore, the purpose of art was to imitate nature.

> *"Those RULES of old discovered, not devised*
> *Are Nature still, but Nature methodized."*
>
> —Alexander Pope, *Essay on Criticism*

By "rules of old," Pope was referring to the literary norms established by classical Greek and Roman authors that eighteenth-century writers began to apply in their own work. Neoclassical writers turned to ancient texts, such as Aristotle's *Poetics*, because they believed those texts explained the natural laws that govern, for example, why audiences laugh at comic characters or feel pity and terror for the downfall of a tragic hero.

The satirist Jonathan Swift gave literary life to the conflict between the ancients and the moderns in his satire *The Battle of the Books*, which contains the story of a spider and a bee in a library. The modern spider spins "dirt and poison" out of its own entrails; the ancient bee goes to the most fragrant flowers of nature to find the "sweetness and light" out of which it makes its honey. The poem ends with a ferocious battle between ancients, such as Homer and Aristotle, and moderns, such as Dryden and Milton. Pope, Swift, and other writers believed that satire could spur improvements in moral and social behavior. Satire, by pointing out our faults and vices, can induce us to live a more balanced, moderate, and harmonious life.

Covent Garden Market, 1737. Balthazar Nebot. Tate Gallery, London.

Alexander Pope's admiration for ancient Greek and Roman culture inspired one of his greatest achievements, the translation of the epics of Homer. In the following passage from Pope's Neoclassical translation of the Odyssey, the goddess Pallas Athena aids Odysseus in the destruction of his enemies by displaying her shield, the aegis, which inspires terror in all who see it.

from the **Odyssey, Book 22,** translated by Alexander Pope

Now *Pallas* shines confess'd; aloft she spreads
The arm of vengeance o'er their guilty heads;
The dreadful *Aegis* blazes in their eye;
Amaz'd they see, they tremble, and they fly:
Confus'd, distracted, thro' the rooms they fling,
  Like oxen madden'd by the breeze's sting,
When sultry days, and long, succeed the gentle spring.
Not half so keen, fierce vulturs of the chace
Stoop from the mountains on the feather'd race,

When the wide field extended snares beset,
With conscious dread they shun the quiv'ring net:
No help, no flight; but wounded ev'ry way,
Headlong they drop: the fowlers seize their prey.
On all sides thus they double wound on wound,
In prostrate heaps the wretches beat the ground,
Unmanly shrieks precede each dying groan,
And a red deluge floats the reeking stone.

Reading Check

Interpreting Why did Neoclassical writers believe that art should imitate nature?

WRAP-UP

Why It Matters

During this time, the British press and freedom of thought and expression became increasingly less restricted. British intellectual life was more and more marked by the desire to share information, explore new ideas, and to fight about them in print rather than on the battlefield.

The thinkers of the English Enlightenment helped to shape the ideals of the American Revolution and the U.S. government. John Locke's theory of natural rights is a key element in the Declaration of Independence. Arguments against the authoritarian rule of the king by intellectuals such as Milton, Locke, and Thomas Hobbes influenced the writers of *The Federalist Papers*, a series of articles supporting ratification of the U.S. Constitution.

The ideas of the scientific revolution and the Enlightenment laid the foundation for a modern worldview based on rationalism and secularism. The widespread use of the scientific method—the systematic procedures for collecting and analyzing evidence—was crucial to the development of modern science. The intellectuals of the Enlightenment advocated the rights of the individual, paving the way for the rise of democracy in the 1800s and 1900s.

Literature Online **Big Ideas** Link to Web resources to further explore the Big Ideas at www.glencoe.com.

Cultural Links

>> English Puritanism was a basic element in the development of American colonial literature. Pilgrim leader William Bradford advocated the use of a plain style that became an enduring influence on American literature.

>> John Milton's Satan in *Paradise Lost* is an archetypal rebel who influenced such characters as the monster in Mary Shelley's *Frankenstein* and Captain Ahab in Herman Melville's *Moby-Dick*.

>> Jonathan Swift's *Gulliver's Travels* has added several words to the English language, such as *Lilliputian* (tiny) and *Yahoo* (crude person).

You might try using this study organizer to jot down questions you have about the readings in this unit.

 **LAYERED-LOOK BOOK**

Reader's Questions

Who?

What?

Where?

When?

Why?

Connect to Today   >> Use what you have learned about the period to do one of these activities.

1. Speaking/Listening Milton's argument for the freedom of the press was grounded in his religious beliefs in the freedom of the individual conscience. What reasons do journalists today give when they argue against censorship? Working with other students, research contemporary issues involving freedom of the press and hold a panel discussion to examine the questions they raise.

2. Visual Literacy Make a chart to contrast the strengths and weaknesses of the Puritan Commonwealth and the Restoration monarchy. Illustrate the chart using seventeenth-century British art.

OBJECTIVES
- Hold a panel discussion.
- Construct a chart.

 Study Central Visit www.glencoe.com and click on Study Central to review Puritanism and the English Enlightenment.

Part 1

The Civil War, the Commonwealth, and the Restoration

After van Dyck: Triple Portrait of King Charles I, c. 17th century. Henry Stone. Victoria and Albert Museum, London.

"None can love freedom but good men;
the rest love not freedom but license, which never
hath more scope than under tyrants."

—John Milton, *The Tenure of Kings and Magistrates*

Milton's Poetry

MEET JOHN MILTON

John Milton recognized his potential as a writer at an early age. In fact, he had so much confidence in his literary talents that by the age of twenty-one he had declared it his intention to become a "great poet." The intensity of his work and the large scale of his subject matter helped him live up to this intention. He once expressed that his goal was to "justify the ways of God to men."

Early Success Milton was born in London on December 9, 1608. His early education took place at St. Paul's School, and his earliest attempts at poetry were rhymed retellings of Psalms 114 and 136. In April 1625, he became a student of Christ's College in Cambridge. His serious nature and piety made him unpopular with many of his more fun-loving classmates, but he eventually gained their respect, as well as the high esteem of his teachers. After graduating, Milton spent six years at his father's country home, reading extensively and writing several highly regarded works, including *Lycidas,* a poem about the death of a classmate, which is considered one of the finest elegies in the English language. When he was about thirty, Milton left his father's estate and traveled to Italy to meet the artists, scholars, philosophers, and scientists whose works he had been studying. They too hailed him as a brilliant young poet, further fueling his ambitions.

Political Pursuits However, political conflicts at home caused him to cut his trip short. Swept up in the religious and political turmoil of the time, he gave up all his other pursuits to write pamphlets in defense of religious and civil freedoms. Milton believed that power resided in the people, who delegated it to the king. He also believed that the people had a right to overthrow a king who abused that power. During this time, Milton also suffered several tragedies, including the deaths of his first and second wives, the deaths of all but three of his children, and, at the age of forty-four, the loss of his eyesight.

The Epic Poems Not until 1660 was Milton free to devote himself to writing the epic poems he had planned so many years earlier. Unfortunately, the events leading to his "free time" were less than ideal. When the Puritan government was dissolved and King Charles II ascended the throne, Milton was arrested as a traitor. Influential friends managed to save him from likely execution, but he was forced to retire and pay heavy fines that left him nearly penniless. Blind, poverty-stricken, and bitterly disappointed by the collapse of the Commonwealth, Milton returned to his first love, poetry.

> *"Yet some there be that by due steps aspire*
> *To lay their just hands on that golden key*
> *That opes the palace of Eternity."*
>
> —John Milton, from *Il Penseroso*

In the years before his death, and with the help of paid assistants, family members, and friends, he published *Paradise Lost,* his great epic masterpiece about Adam and Eve's fall from grace. He later published *Paradise Regained,* a shorter epic that tells of Christ's temptation in the wilderness.

John Milton was born in 1608 and died in 1674.

Literature Online **Author Search** For more about John Milton, go to www.glencoe.com.

Connecting to the Poems

People routinely set goals for themselves. How well do you follow through on the goals you set or the goals others suggest to you? In these poems, Milton reflects on his goals and limitations at opposite ends of his life. As you read the selections, ask yourself what you hope to accomplish after you leave school and begin a career.

Building Background

Milton wrote twenty-four sonnets between 1630 and 1658. The two that follow are autobiographical, and Milton employed the Italian, or Petrarchan, sonnet form in both (see page 252). In an **Italian sonnet,** an **octave** (the first eight lines) is followed by a **sestet** (the last six lines); both follow prescribed rhyme schemes. This type of sonnet traditionally presents a problem or situation in the octave, then provides an answer or resolution in the sestet. The switch from problem to resolution is called the "turn" in the poem. In "How Soon Hath Time," Milton expresses his thoughts and feelings on his twenty-third birthday. In "When I Consider How My Light Is Spent," which he composed twenty years later, he writes about the issues that concerned him after having just gone blind.

Setting Purposes for Reading

Big Idea Puritanism and the Civil War

As you read these poems, look for evidence that might help explain Milton's religious devotion and his identification with the Puritan cause.

Literary Element Personification

Personification is a figure of speech in which an animal, object, force of nature, or idea is given human characteristics. By presenting something such as the wind, the passing of time, or the virtue of patience as a person, a writer is able to intensify certain ideas. As you read the poems that follow, look for Milton's use of personification.

● See Literary Terms Handbook, p. R13.

Literature Online **Interactive Literary Elements Handbook** To review or learn more about the literary elements, go to www.glencoe.com.

Reading Strategy Identifying Problem and Solution

The Italian sonnet form is conducive to presenting a problem and a solution. Review the information about this type of sonnet in the Building Background section on this page. Then, as you read the poems, keep in mind the pattern of an Italian sonnet to help you identify both the problem and the solution in each poem.

Reading Tip: Using Details to Summarize Look for details in the poems that point to the problem, as well as details that lead to the solution. Then, in your own words, summarize the problem and the solution. Use a chart like the one shown here to help you organize your thoughts.

"How Soon Hath Time"	"When I Consider . . ."
Details Related to Problem	Details Related to Problem
1. twenty-third birthday	1. light is spent
2.	2.
3.	3.
Summary of Problem:	Summary of Problem:
Details Related to Solution	Details Related to Solution
1.	1.
2.	2.
3.	3.
Summary of Solution:	Summary of Solution:

OBJECTIVES
In studying these selections, you will focus on the following:
● analyzing the characteristics of Puritan poetry
● identifying personification
● identifying problems and solutions in literary works

How Soon Hath Time

John Milton

How soon hath Time, the subtle thief of youth,
  Stolen on his wing my three and twentieth year!
  My hasting days fly on with full career,[1]
  But my late spring no bud or blossom showeth.
5 Perhaps my semblance[2] might deceive the truth,
  That I to manhood am arrived so near,
  And inward ripeness doth much less appear,
  That some more timely-happy spirits endueth.[3]
  Yet be it less or more, or soon or slow,
10 It shall be still[4] in strictest measure even[5]
  To that same lot,[6] however mean[7] or high,
  Toward which Time leads me, and the will of Heaven;
  All is, if I have grace to use it so,
  As ever in my great Taskmaster's eye.

1. *Career* means "speed."

2. *Semblance* means "outward appearance."

3. *Endueth* means "endow."

4. *Still* means "always."
5. *Even* means "equal" or "adequate."
6. *Lot* means "fate."
7. *Mean* in this context means "low in status or quality."

When I Consider How My Light Is Spent

John Milton

When I consider how my light is spent
  Ere half my days in this dark world and wide,
  And that one talent[1] which is death to hide,
  Lodged with me useless, though my soul more bent
5 To serve therewith my Maker, and present
  My true account, lest He returning chide.
  "Doth God exact day-labor, light denied?"
  I fondly[2] ask. But Patience, to prevent
  That murmur, soon replies, "God doth not need
10 Either man's work or His own gifts. Who best
  Bear His mild yoke, they serve Him best. His state
  Is kingly. Thousands at His bidding speed
  And post o'er land and ocean without rest;
  They also serve who only stand and wait."

1. By using the word *talent*, Milton alludes to the biblical parable of the talents, in which a servant is scolded for hiding his master's *talent*, or money, in the earth instead of putting it to good use while the master was away (Matthew 25:14–30).
2. *Fondly* means "foolishly."

Reading Strategy **Identifying Problem and Solution** *What thought is expressed in this line? How does this thought relate to the problem presented in the poem?*

Literary Element **Personification** *What quality is personified in the last seven lines of this poem? How does this personification contribute to the theme of the poem?*

RESPONDING AND THINKING CRITICALLY

Respond

1. Do you share the concern Milton expresses in either of these poems? Why or why not?

Recall and Interpret

2. (a)In "How Soon Hath Time," how does the speaker personify time in line 1? (b)What does this depiction suggest about the speaker's attitude toward the passing of time?

3. (a)In "How Soon Hath Time," to what season does the speaker compare his twenty-third year? (b)What might the lack of "buds" and "blossoms" symbolize?

4. (a)What thoughts are expressed in lines 4–8 of "How Soon Hath Time"? What thoughts are expressed in lines 9–14? (b)Based on these lines, what appears to be the speaker's main concern, and how does he answer this concern?

5. (a)In "When I Consider . . . ," what is the speaker thinking about in line 1? (b)In your own words, explain why he is worried about his situation.

6. (a)What does the speaker ask in line 7 of "When I Consider . . ."? (b)What might he mean by this?

Analyze and Evaluate

7. Considering Milton's ambition to become a great poet, do you think the disappointment he expresses in "How Soon Hath Time" was justified? Why or why not?

8. In both poems, what is the standard by which the speaker seems to measure the value of his life?

Connect

9. **Big Idea** **Puritanism and the Civil War** What is the main aspect of faith that the speaker is struggling with in "When I Consider . . ."?

LITERARY ANALYSIS

Literary Element **Personification**

You may encounter the use of **personification** in everyday contexts: *"Chemistry, my nemesis, is holding me back from making the honor roll." "The swirling wind taunted the field-goal kicker."* In these examples, nonhuman entities are given human characteristics.

1. What is implied about time in line 8 of "How Soon Hath Time"? What is said about time in lines 11 and 12?

2. How is patience personified in "When I Consider . . ."?

Writing About Literature

Evaluate Contemporary Relevance In "When I Consider . . ." Milton expresses a deep concern that his blindness will prevent him from serving God through his poetry. In an essay, discuss some of the problems facing people with disabilities and the measures that could be taken to reduce or eliminate these problems.

Literature Online **Web Activities** For eFlashcards, Selection Quick Checks, and other Web activities, go to www.glencoe.com.

READING AND VOCABULARY

Reading Strategy **Identifying Problem and Solution**

Each of these poems presents a **problem** (something that concerns the speaker) and offers a **solution** (how the speaker responds to or answers his concern).

1. (a)In your own words, state the problem and the solution in both poems. (b)What details helped you identify each problem and solution?

2. How does the form and structure of each poem help reveal both the problem and the solution?

Academic Vocabulary

Here is a word from the vocabulary list on page R82.

adult (ə dult´) *adj.* grown-up; mature

Practice and Apply
What **adult** concern worried Milton as a young man embarking on a career as a poet?

LITERATURE PREVIEW

Connecting to the Poem

Satan has been featured in countless books, plays, movies, and other art forms, but perhaps nowhere has Satan been portrayed more powerfully than in Milton's *Paradise Lost.* As you read this excerpt, think about how you picture Satan and hell based on books you have read or movies you have seen.

Building Background

Milton spent his entire adult life planning to write something of the magnitude of his 10,565-line poem *Paradise Lost.* This epic relates the story of Adam and Eve as told in the biblical book of Genesis. In this story, Satan tempts Adam and Eve to commit the "original sin." By eating the forbidden fruit from the tree of knowledge, Adam and Eve disobey God, fall from God's grace, and are banished from the Garden of Eden. This story, known as the Fall, permitted Milton to construct vivid heroes and villains and to glorify not just a nation, but God. As background to the story, Milton describes hell at the time Satan and the other rebellious angels were first driven from heaven. They find themselves in a place of darkness and never-ending fire. Satan vows to continue the war against God, to seek ways to do evil to spite Him, and to rule over hell.

Setting Purposes for Reading

Big Idea **Puritanism and the Civil War**

As you read, think about the ways in which this poem reflects Milton's Puritan beliefs.

Literary Element **Allusion**

An **allusion** is a reference to a well-known person, place, event, written work, or work of art. Discovering the meaning of an allusion can often be essential to understanding part or all of a work of literature. As you read the excerpt from *Paradise Lost,* look for examples of allusions. Some are explained in the marginal notes. Check a dictionary or an encyclopedia for the meanings of those that are not explained.

• See Literary Terms Handbook, p. R1.

READING PREVIEW

Reading Strategy **Visualizing**

Visualizing is picturing a writer's ideas or descriptions in your mind's eye. Visualizing is a good way to understand and remember information in a text. In *Paradise Lost,* Milton creates exceptionally vivid pictures.

....

Reading Tip: Picturing the Descriptions Carefully read how Milton describes people, places, and things in this excerpt. Jot down especially vivid descriptions. Next to each one, in your own words, describe the picture it evokes.

Vocabulary

transgress (trans gres′) *v.* to break or violate a law; to go beyond a limit; p. 522 *If she achieved revenge, Sonja knew she would be transgressing one of the Ten Commandments.*

deluge (del′ ūj) *n.* something that overwhelms as if by a flood; p. 523 *The radio host's comments provoked a deluge of angry letters.*

discern (di surn′) *v.* to perceive; to detect; p. 523 *Peering over the top of a hill, the lost climber discerned a narrow road in the valley.*

myriad (mir′ ē əd) *n.* a great or countless number; p. 524 *Battling the locusts was a futile task; myriads of them—wave after wave—swarmed down on the crops.*

subterranean (sub tə rā′ nē ən) *adj.* below the earth's surface; underground; p. 528 *A subterranean stream flowed beneath the rocky land.*

Vocabulary Tip: Antonyms Words that are opposite in meaning are called antonyms. Note that antonyms are always the same part of speech.

Literature Online **Interactive Literary Elements Handbook** To review or learn more about the literary elements, go to www.glencoe.com.

OBJECTIVES

In studying this selection, you will focus on the following:
• analyzing the characteristics of Puritanism

• identifying allusions
• using visualizing to understand poetry

from Paradise Lost

John Milton

from Book I

Of man's first disobedience and the fruit
Of that forbidden tree whose mortal taste
Brought death into the world and all our woe,
With loss of Eden, till one greater Man°
5 Restore us and regain the blissful seat,
Sing, Heavenly Muse,° that on the secret top
Of Oreb or of Sinai° didst inspire
That shepherd° who first taught the chosen seed°
In the beginning how the Heavens and Earth
10 Rose out of Chaos;° or if Sion hill°
Delight thee more and Siloa's brook° that flowed
Fast° by the oracle of God, I thence
Invoke thy aid to my adventurous song,
That with no middle flight intends to soar
15 Above the Aonian mount° while it pursues
Things unattempted yet in prose or rhyme.
And chiefly thou, O Spirit, that dost prefer
Before all temples the upright heart and pure,
Instruct me, for thou knowest; thou from the first
20 Wast present and with mighty wings outspread
Dovelike sat'st brooding on the vast abyss

4 greater Man: Christ

6 Heavenly Muse: In Greek mythology, the Muses were nine goddesses who presided over the arts and sciences and were believed to be sources of inspiration. Milton calls on the Holy Spirit to help him compose his epic.
7 Oreb (ôr′ ĕb) **. . . Sinai** (sī′ nī): two names for the peak in Egypt where Moses was said to have received the word of God
8 shepherd: Moses. **the chosen seed:** the Jewish people
10 Chaos: infinite space; formless matter. **Sion hill:** hill in Jerusalem on which the palace of David and the Temple were built, usually spelled *Zion* today
11 Siloa's brook: a stream near Jerusalem
12 Fast: near
15 Aonian mount: Mount Helicon, home of the Muses

Reading Strategy **Visualizing** *Read the side note on Oreb and Sinai. How do you picture "the secret top"? The Old Testament account describes God descending "in fire" with smoke ascending. How does this information help you picture Milton's description?*

Big Idea **Puritanism and the Civil War** *What help does Milton ask of God? Why does he seek this help?*

And mad'st it pregnant: what in me is dark
Illumine; what is low raise and support;
That, to the height of this great argument,
25 I may assert° Eternal Providence
And justify the ways of God to men.
    Say first, for Heaven hides nothing from thy view,
Nor the deep tract of Hell, say first what cause
Moved our grand° parents in that happy state,
30 Favored of Heaven so highly, to fall off
From their Creator and **transgress** his will
For one restraint,° lords of the world besides.
Who first seduced them to that foul revolt?
The infernal Serpent; he it was whose guile,°
35 Stirred up with envy and revenge, deceived
The mother of mankind what time° his pride
Had cast him out from Heaven with all his host
Of rebel angels, by whose aid, aspiring
To set himself in glory above his peers,
40 He trusted to have equaled the Most High,
If he opposed, and with ambitious aim
Against the throne and monarchy of God,
Raised impious war in Heaven and battle proud
With vain attempt. Him the Almighty Power
45 Hurled headlong flaming from the ethereal° sky,
With hideous ruin and combustion, down
To bottomless perdition,° there to dwell
In adamantine° chains and penal fire,
Who durst defy the Omnipotent to arms.
50   Nine times the space that measures day and night
To mortal men, he with his horrid crew
Lay vanquished, rolling in the fiery gulf,
Confounded,° though immortal. But his doom
Reserved him to more wrath, for now the thought
55 Both of lost happiness and lasting pain
Torments him. Round he throws his baleful° eyes

25 assert: defend

29 grand: first (Adam and Eve)

32 one restraint: that they should not eat the fruit of the tree of knowledge of good and evil
34 guile: deceit

36 what time: when

45 ethereal: heavenly, celestial

47 perdition: damnation
48 adamantine: unyielding

53 Confounded: damned

56 baleful: evil

Literary Element **Allusion** *Who is the Serpent? Why does Milton refer to him in this way?*

Big Idea **Puritanism and the Civil War** *Recall Milton's belief that power belonged to all the people, who delegate it to a king. Why might Milton have been particularly disdainful of someone who aspires "to set himself in glory above his peers"?*

Reading Strategy **Visualizing** *What elements in this description of Satan's descent to hell in lines 44–48 evoke especially vivid pictures in your mind?*

Vocabulary

transgress (trans gres′) *v.* to break or violate a law; to go beyond a limit

Judgement of Adam and Eve, 1807. William Blake. Pen and watercolor on paper, 25 x 20.2 cm. The Huntington Library, Art Collections and Botanical Gardens, San Marino, CA.

That witnessed huge affliction and dismay
Mixed with obdurate° pride and steadfast hate.
At once, as far as angels' ken,° he views
60 The dismal situation waste and wild:
A dungeon horrible, on all sides round
As one great furnace flamed; yet from those flames
No light, but rather darkness visible
Served only to discover sights of woe,
65 Regions of sorrow, doleful shades, where peace
And rest can never dwell, hope never comes
That comes to all; but torture without end
Still urges and a fiery **deluge,** fed
With ever-burning sulfur unconsumed.
70 Such place Eternal Justice had prepared
For those rebellious, here their prison ordained
In utter darkness, and their portion set
As far removed from God and light of Heaven
As from the center thrice to the utmost pole.°
75 O how unlike the place from whence they fell!
There the companions of his fall, o'erwhelmed
With floods and whirlwinds of tempestuous fire,
He soon **discerns,** and weltering° by his side,

58 **obdurate:** stubborn or unyielding
59 **ken:** sight

74 **center . . . pole:** three times the distance from Earth's center to the outermost point of the universe

78 **weltering:** tossing, writhing

One next himself in power and next in crime,
80   Long after known in Palestine, and named
Beelzebub.° To whom the archenemy,
And thence in Heaven called Satan, with bold words
Breaking the horrid silence, thus began:
    "If thou beest he—but O, how fallen! how changed
85   From him who in the happy realms of light,
Clothed with transcendent brightness, didst outshine
Myriads, though bright—if he whom mutual league,
United thoughts and counsels, equal hope
And hazard in the glorious enterprise,
90   Joined with me once, now misery hath joined
In equal ruin: into what pit thou seest
From what height fallen! so much the stronger proved
He with his thunder; and till then who knew
The force of those dire arms? Yet not for those,
95   Nor what the potent Victor in his rage
Can else inflict, do I repent or change,
Though changed in outward luster, that fixed mind
And high disdain from sense of injured merit,
That with the Mightiest raised me to contend,
100   And to the fierce contention brought along
Innumerable force of spirits armed
That durst dislike his reign and, me preferring,
His utmost power with adverse power opposed
In dubious battle on the plains of Heaven,
105   And shook his throne. What though the field be lost?
All is not lost; the unconquerable will,
And study of revenge, immortal hate,
And courage never to submit or yield:
And what is else not to be overcome?
110   That glory never shall his wrath or might
Extort from me. To bow and sue for grace
With suppliant knee and deify his power,
Who from the terror of this arm so late
Doubted° his empire, that were low indeed;
115   That were an ignominy° and shame beneath
This downfall; since by fate the strength of gods
And this empyreal° substance cannot fail;

81 Beelzebub: Though the name is often used to mean Satan himself, Milton uses it for another fallen angel, Satan's second in command.

Satan in his Original Glory, 1805. William Blake. Watercolor on paper, 42.9 x 33.9 cm. Tate Gallery, London.
Viewing the Art: Does this painting help you understand what Satan lost when he was thrown out of heaven? Explain why or why not.

114 Doubted: feared for
115 ignominy: disgrace or dishonor

117 empyreal: heavenly; therefore, nonmaterial and indestructible

Reading Strategy   **Visualizing** *Based on Satan's description, how do you picture Beelzebub before his banishment from heaven?*

Big Idea   **Puritanism and the Civil War** *What does Satan consider to be "low indeed," "ignominy and shame"? How might Milton's attitude toward Satan here connect to his feelings about tyrannical monarchs?*

Vocabulary

myriad (mir′ ē əd) *n.* a great or countless number

Since, through experience of this great event,
In arms not worse, in foresight much advanced,
120 We may with more successful hope resolve
To wage by force or guile eternal war,
Irreconcilable to our grand Foe,
Who now triumphs, and in the excess of joy
Sole reigning holds the tyranny of Heaven."
125   So spake the apostate° Angel, though in pain,
Vaunting° aloud, but racked with deep despair;
And him thus answered soon his bold compeer:°
"O Prince, O Chief of many thronèd Powers,
That led the embattled Seraphim° to war
130 Under thy conduct and, in dreadful deeds
Fearless, endangered Heaven's perpetual King
And put to proof his high supremacy,
Whether upheld by strength or chance or fate,
Too well I see and rue the dire event,
135 That with sad overthrow and foul defeat
Hath lost us Heaven, and all this mighty host
In horrible destruction laid thus low,
As far as gods and heavenly essences
Can perish: for the mind and spirit remains
140 Invincible, and vigor° soon returns,
Though all our glory extinct, and happy state
Here swallowed up in endless misery.
But what if he our Conqueror (whom I now
Of force believe almighty, since no less
145 Than such could have o'erpowered such force as ours)
Have left us this our spirit and strength entire,
Strongly to suffer and support our pains,
That we may so suffice his vengeful ire
Or do him mightier service as his thralls°
150 By right of war, whate'er his business be,
Here in the heart of Hell to work in fire
Or do his errands in the gloomy deep?
What can it then avail, though yet we feel
Strength undiminished, or eternal being
155 To undergo eternal punishment?"
  Whereto with speedy words the Archfiend replied:
"Fallen Cherub,° to be weak is miserable,
Doing or suffering: but of this be sure,
To do aught good never will be our task,
160 But ever to do ill our sole delight,
As being the contrary to his high will
Whom we resist. If then his providence
Out of our evil seek to bring forth good,

125 **apostate:** renegade

126 **Vaunting:** boasting

127 **compeer:** companion; peer

129 **Seraphim:** the highest-ranking angels

140 **vigor:** strength, power

149 **thralls:** slaves

157 **Cherub:** angel

Big Idea **Puritanism and the Civil War** *In this passage, Milton clearly defines the nature of the battle between Satan and God. What is that battle?*

Our labor must be to pervert that end
165 And out of good still° to find means of evil,
Which ofttimes may succeed so as perhaps
Shall grieve him, if I fail not,° and disturb
His inmost counsels from their destined aim.
But see! The angry Victor hath recalled
170 His ministers of vengeance and pursuit
Back to the gates of Heaven: the sulfurous hail
Shot after us in storm, o'erblown hath laid
The fiery surge that from the precipice
Of Heaven received us falling; and the thunder,
175 Winged with red lightning and impetuous rage,
Perhaps hath spent his shafts and ceases now
To bellow through the vast and boundless deep.
Let us not slip° the occasion, whether scorn
Or satiate° fury yield it from our Foe.
180 Seest thou yon dreary plain, forlorn and wild,
The seat of desolation, void of light,
Save what the glimmering of these livid flames
Casts pale and dreadful? Thither let us tend
From off the tossing of these fiery waves,
185 There rest, if any rest can harbor there,
And reassembling our afflicted powers,°
Consult how we may henceforth most offend
Our Enemy, our own loss how repair,
How overcome this dire calamity,
190 What reinforcement we may gain from hope,
If not what resolution from despair."
   Thus Satan, talking to his nearest mate,
With head uplift above the wave and eyes
That sparkling blazed, his other parts besides
195 Prone on the flood, extended long and large,
Lay floating many a rood,° in bulk as huge
As whom the fables name of monstrous size,
Titanian, or Earthborn, that warred on Jove,
Briareos or Typhon, whom the den
200 By ancient Tarsus° held, or that sea beast
Leviathan,° which God of all his works
Created hugest that swim the ocean stream:
Him, haply slumbering on the Norway foam,
The pilot of some small night-foundered skiff,°

165 **still:** always

167 **if I fail not:** if I am not mistaken

178 **slip:** lose
179 **satiate:** satisfied

186 **afflicted powers:** stricken forces; overthrown armies

196 **rood:** unit of measure equaling about a quarter of an acre
197–200 **fables . . . Tarsus:** In Greek mythology, Zeus (the Roman Jove) successfully battled the Titans with the help of the earthborn giant Briareos; Typhon of Tarsus was a monstrous serpent who attacked Zeus.
201 **Leviathan:** a biblical sea monster

204 **skiff:** boat

Reading Strategy Visualizing *Picture the scene that Satan describes as the forces of God retreat to heaven. What does it look like?*

Reading Strategy Visualizing *Describe where Satan decides to go to escape the "fiery waves." Why might Milton have chosen this location as an appropriate place for Satan's purpose?*

The Fallen Angels Entering Pandemonium, 1851. John Martin. Oil on canvas, 622 x 765 mm. Tate Gallery, London.

Viewing the Art: How does this painting capture the atmosphere of hell as described by Milton?

205 Deeming some island, oft, as seamen tell,
With fixèd anchor in his scaly rind,
Moors by his side under the lee while night
Invests the sea and wishèd morn delays.
So stretched out huge in length the Archfiend lay,
210 Chained on the burning lake, nor ever thence
Had risen or heaved his head, but that the will
And high permission of all-ruling Heaven
Left him at large to his own dark designs,
That with reiterated crimes he might
215 Heap on himself damnation while he sought
Evil to others, and enraged might see
How all his malice served but to bring forth
Infinite goodness, grace, and mercy, shown
On man by him seduced, but on himself
220 Treble confusion, wrath, and vengeance poured.
  Forthwith upright he rears from off the pool
His mighty stature; on each hand the flames,
Driven backward, slope their pointing spires and, rolled
In billows, leave in the midst a horrid vale.
225 Then with expanded wings he steers his flight
Aloft, incumbent° on the dusky air

226 **incumbent:** lying or resting

Literary Element   **Allusion** *To what does Milton compare Satan?*

Reading Strategy   **Visualizing** *Picture the scene Milton describes in lines 221–224. Where might you see a creature like this in contemporary literature, media, or art?*

That felt unusual weight, till on dry land
He lights—if it were land that ever burned
With solid, as the lake with liquid, fire,
230   And such appeared in hue as when the force
Of **subterranean** wind transports a hill
Torn from Pelorus,° or the shattered side
Of thundering Etna, whose combustible°
And fueled entrails, thence conceiving fire
235   Sublimed° with mineral fury, aid the winds
And leave a singèd bottom all involved°
With stench and smoke. Such resting found the sole
Of unblest feet. Him followed his next mate,
Both glorying to have scaped the Stygian° flood
240   As gods and by their own recovered strength,
Not by the sufferance of supernal° power.
    "Is this the region, this the soil, the clime,"
Said then the lost Archangel, "this the seat
That we must change for Heaven, this mournful gloom
245   For that celestial light? Be it so, since he
Who now is sovereign can dispose and bid
What shall be right: farthest from him is best;
Whom reason hath equaled, force hath made supreme
Above his equals. Farewell, happy fields,
250   Where joy forever dwells! Hail, horrors! Hail,
Infernal world! and thou, profoundest Hell,
Receive thy new possessor—one who brings
A mind not to be changed by place or time.
The mind is its own place, and in itself
255   Can make a Heaven of Hell, a Hell of Heaven.
What matter where, if I be still the same,
And what I should be, all but less than He
Whom thunder hath made greater? Here at least
We shall be free; the Almighty hath not built
260   Here for his envy, will not drive us hence:
Here we may reign secure, and in my choice
To reign is worth ambition, though in Hell:
Better to reign in Hell than serve in Heaven."

232 Pelorus: a cape in Sicily
233 combustible: capable of igniting and burning

235 Sublimed: vaporized
236 involved: enveloped

239 Stygian: hellish. *Stygian* is the adjective form of *Styx*, the name of the river that, in Greek mythology, flows through the Underworld.
241 supernal: heavenly

Literary Element   Allusion *Mount Etna is an active volcano in Sicily. Why is it an appropriate allusion here?*

Big Idea   Puritanism and the Civil War *What declaration does Satan make in this passage? How is this a capstone, or a finishing touch, to his rebellion against God?*

Vocabulary

subterranean (subʹ tə rāʹ nē ən) *adj.* below the surface of the earth; underground

RESPONDING AND THINKING CRITICALLY

Respond

1. What was your reaction to Milton's descriptions of Satan and hell?

Recall and Interpret

2. (a)According to the introduction (lines 1–26), what is the purpose of the poem? (b)Why might Milton have chosen to include a direct statement of purpose at the beginning of the poem?

3. (a)Why have Satan and his followers been cast out of heaven? (b)How does the fall of Adam and Eve parallel the fall of Satan and his followers? How does it differ?

4. (a)What reason does Satan give for choosing to "reign in Hell" rather than "serve in Heaven"? (b)Do you think Satan really believes that it does not matter where he reigns, or is he merely trying to "save face"? Support your answer with reasons.

Analyze and Evaluate

5. (a)What function does Beelzebub serve in the poem? (b)Compare and contrast the characters of Beelzebub and Satan. Cite specific descriptions or incidents that show their similarities or differences.

6. (a)According to Milton, what is Satan's role in the fall of Adam and Eve? (b)Does this view of Satan's role change your impression of the story of Adam and Eve? Explain your answer.

7. (a)Satan suffers a fall from grace through his own actions. What is his "fatal flaw"? (b)How does Satan compare with other evil characters you've encountered in books or movies?

Connect

8. **Big Idea** **Puritanism and the Civil War** In what ways is the content of this poem influenced both by Milton's desire to serve God and by his support of Parliament's battle against Charles I?

VISUAL LITERACY: Fine Art

Depicting the Underworld

The dark, supernatural forces presented in Milton's *Paradise Lost* have been illustrated by various artists—including Gustave Doré (1832–1883), John Martin (see page 527), and the poet and artist William Blake (see pages 523–524). Because Milton drew from the Bible in writing his epic poem, the art that depicts *Paradise Lost* is deeply symbolic, with stark representations of good and evil—including the role of Satan in the battle between heaven and hell. In his engraving *Satan's Flight Through Chaos,* which is based on *Paradise Lost,* Doré shows, in rich textures, Satan's tense wings and tormented posture as he clings to a crag.

Group Activity Discuss these questions with your classmates.

1. How does this engraving contribute to your visualization of the scenes in *Paradise Lost*?

2. Look back at Blake's watercolor, *Satan in his Original Glory,* on page 524. How does that image of Satan contrast with Doré's?

Satan's Flight Through Chaos, 1866. Gustave Dore. Engraving.

Literary Element   Allusion

An author often makes an **allusion** in order to point out a similarity between his or her work and the work of another author. In line 6 of *Paradise Lost* ("Sing, Heavenly Muse . . . "), Milton makes an allusion when he calls on the "Heavenly Muse" for inspiration. Ancient Greek poetry often began with a prayer to the Muses. To readers of Milton's time, most of whom were familiar with classical poetry, this allusion places *Paradise Lost* in the classical tradition of calling upon a higher power for guidance while writing. Review the excerpt from *Paradise Lost* to remind yourself of the allusions in it. Then answer the following questions:

1. How do the numerous references to Greek mythology enrich the themes expressed in *Paradise Lost*? Give specific examples from the poem to support your opinion.

2. What other allusions did you find in the poem? Explain their significance in the context in which they are mentioned.

Review: Conflict

As you learned on page 23, **conflict** is the central struggle between two opposing forces in a story, drama, or narrative poem. An **external conflict** exists when a character struggles against some outside force, such as another person, nature, society, or fate. An **internal conflict** is a struggle that takes place within the mind of a character who is torn between opposing feelings, desires, or goals. The conflict builds until the story reaches a climax, which is the point of greatest emotional intensity.

Partner Activity With a partner, answer these questions:

1. Identify the conflict in this excerpt from *Paradise Lost*. Is this conflict external or internal? Explain why.

2. (a)How does Milton develop this conflict? (b)At what point does the conflict reach its climax?

3. Within the confines of this excerpt, what is the outcome of the conflict?

Reading Strategy   Visualizing

Through the use of vivid description an author helps the reader not only to picture the setting but also to understand more clearly the actions and ideas that are presented. Part of the greatness of *Paradise Lost* is its ability to evoke powerfully vivid pictures in the reader's mind. Review lines 50–69 ("Nine times the space . . . sulfur unconsumed."), and think about how you visualize this scene. Then answer the following questions:

1. (a)Where are the rebellious angels? Describe the position and movement of their bodies. (b)Describe Satan. What torments him?

2. How do you picture Milton's rendering of hell?

3. The word *doleful* means "dreary" or "dismal." The word *shade* has numerous meanings, including "not in the sunshine," "place of obscurity or seclusion," and "ghost" or "spirit." How does this information contribute to your picture of hell?

Vocabulary   Practice

Practice with Antonyms Identify the antonym for each vocabulary word listed below.

1. transgress   **a.** obey   **b.** sin

2. discern   **a.** perceive   **b.** ignore

3. subterranean   **a.** terrestrial   **b.** under

4. myriad   **a.** multitude   **b.** few

5. deluge   **a.** trickle   **b.** flood

Academic Vocabulary

Here are two words from the vocabulary list on page R82.

initial (i nish′ əl) *adj.* first; earliest

react (rē akt′) *v.* act back; act in response

Practice and Apply
1. What was Satan's **initial** response to finding himself in hell?
2. After discussing his predicament with Beelzebub, how does Satan **react** to his situation?

Writing About Literature

Analyze Setting In *Paradise Lost,* Milton frequently refers to light and darkness in his descriptions of heaven and hell. Write a brief essay in which you quote some of these references and write your thoughts about what light and darkness symbolize in the poem. Begin your essay by stating the main point you wish to make about Milton's use of light and darkness as symbols. In the body of your essay, develop your main point with examples from the poem. Devote one paragraph to each example you present and explain how the example illustrates your main point. Include at least three examples in your essay. In the last paragraph, summarize your main point and offer a brief evaluation of the effectiveness of Milton's descriptions. Use a graphic organizer like the one shown here to help you organize your ideas.

Introduction

Present your interpretation of how Milton uses light and darkness in the poem. Preview the examples you will show.

Body Paragraphs

Quote examples and explain how they support your interpretation.

Conclusion

Briefly summarize your analysis and consider offering a related insight.

As you draft your essay, write from start to finish. Express your ideas in the order shown in the graphic organizer. After completing your draft, meet with a peer reviewer to evaluate each other's work and to suggest revisions. Then edit and proofread your draft for errors in spelling, grammar, and punctuation.

Interdisciplinary Activity: Anthropology/ Sociology

In the Christian tradition, the snake has long been a symbol of evil. How do other traditions or cultures view snakes? Use library or Internet resources to investigate what this reptile symbolizes to various cultures, ancient or modern, then report your findings to the rest of the class. Photocopy or print out any artwork that will help you explain the snake's symbolic significance. Use the artwork as a visual aid during your report.

Milton's Language and Style

Using Spatial Order in Descriptions In *Paradise Lost,* Milton presents a number of scenes that are highly visual. One way he organizes these passages is through **spatial order**—a pattern of details that are presented in the order in which the eye sees them (left to right, top to bottom, far to near, and so on). Consider lines 221–226.

> Forthwith upright he rears from off the pool
> His mighty stature; on each hand the flames,
> Driven backward, slope their pointing spires and, rolled
> In billows, leave in the midst a horrid vale.
> Then with expanded wings he steers his flight
> Aloft, incumbent on the dusky air

Notice how the words that represent spatial order in the passage provide a sense of movement.

Spatial Order	Movement Shown
upright	Satan emerges from the pool.
backward	Fire trails off Satan's hands.
aloft	Satan raises himself into the sky.

Activity Identify other examples of spatial order in *Paradise Lost.* Discuss why they are significant in the poem. Evaluate how spatial order is expressed in the examples and then try expressing it more clearly or in more detail. You might sketch out a particular scene on paper to see how you understand its spatial order.

Revising Check

Spatial Order Spatial order, or presenting details by their location, can help make writing more vivid by creating a sense of movement. With a partner, go through your analysis essay on *Paradise Lost* and note places where spatial order would make your essay clearer and more engaging. Think of your essay as a movie camera "panning" to show scenes from the selection. Revise your draft to include spatial order in your descriptions.

Literature Online Web Activities For eFlashcards, Selection Quick Checks, and other Web activities, go to www.glencoe.com.

from *The Pilgrim's Progress*

MEET JOHN BUNYAN

Few English authors sprang from more humble beginnings than John Bunyan. Born in the quiet little village of Elstow, Bunyan was the son of a poverty-stricken tinker—a mender of pots and pans. He received only a basic education, leaving school at an early age to learn his father's trade and to contribute to the family income. Yet Bunyan went on to write more than fifteen books, among them the most widely read prose work of the seventeenth century, *The Pilgrim's Progress*. This achievement was just one of many in a remarkable life. In fact, according to nineteenth-century historian Thomas Babbington Macauley, "[D]uring the latter half of the seventeenth century, there were only two minds which possessed the imaginative faculty in a very eminent degree. One of those minds produced [John Milton's] *Paradise Lost*, the other *The Pilgrim's Progress*."

Puritan Beliefs As a teenager, Bunyan served in the Puritan-dominated Parliamentary army, fighting against supporters of the monarchy. He was discharged at the age of nineteen and married soon thereafter. His new wife introduced him to a series of religious texts including *The Plain Man's Pathway to Heaven* and *The Practice of Piety*. Moved by these books of Puritan religious philosophy, Bunyan joined a nonconformist (Puritan) church and began studying the Bible. While still in his twenties, he became one of England's best-known nonconformist preachers. This brought him into direct conflict with another religious group, the Quakers. His first writings, *Some Gospel Truths Opened* and *A Vindication*, were created to oppose Quaker beliefs.

> "[W]ords easy to be understood do often hit the mark, when high and learned ones do only pierce the air."
>
> —John Bunyan

Setbacks and Achievements After the Puritan government was dissolved, Bunyan fell upon hard times. At age thirty-two he was arrested for preaching without a license. Refusing to renounce his faith, Bunyan spent twelve years in a Bedford prison, during which time he wrote nine books, including his autobiography and several books of spiritual instruction. He also began work on *The Pilgrim's Progress*.

Bunyan was pardoned and released from prison at age forty-four. He returned to preaching and was appointed the pastor of the same church he had been affiliated with before his imprisonment. However, sentiments against nonconformist religious groups continued to run high, and after only four years, Bunyan was again arrested and imprisoned for his beliefs. While serving his second sentence, Bunyan completed *The Pilgrim's Progress*, a work that would come to be considered a masterpiece of the plain English prose style. In 1678 the first part of this book was published, and in 1684 the work was published in its entirety.

John Bunyan was born in 1628 and died in 1688.

Literature Online **Author Search** For more about John Bunyan, go to www.glencoe.com.

Connecting to the Selection

In this excerpt from *The Pilgrim's Progress*, you will see the role vanity plays in the life of a town, its fair, and the central characters. As you read, think about some ways in which people display their vanity.

Building Background

From the late sixteenth to the early eighteenth century, the word *Puritan* described a number of Protestant faiths. Puritanism was a type of religious belief rather than a specific church denomination. Puritans were united in the belief that all existing churches had been corrupted by pagan cultures and distorted by the power vested in kings and popes. They believed that common church practices needed to be purified. Their argument was that purification was only possible through strict belief in and interpretation of the Bible.

Setting Purposes for Reading

Big Idea Puritanism and the Civil War

As you read, notice how Bunyan employs the Puritan themes of good versus evil and destruction versus salvation. Particularly note how Bunyan portrays worldly greed as leading to corruption.

Literary Element Allegory

An **allegory** is a narrative or dramatic work in which almost all the characters, settings, and events are symbols representing abstract ideas. The overall purpose of an allegory is to teach a moral lesson. In simpler allegories, the characters and settings are often given names that clarify the abstract qualities they represent. *The Pilgrim's Progress* focuses on a character named Christian and the obstacles he must overcome during his pilgrimage to the Celestial City. During his journey, Christian meets Faithful, who decides to join him. One of the stopovers they make is at a fair in the town of Vanity.

• See Literary Terms Handbook, p. R1.

Literature Online Interactive Literary Elements Handbook To review or learn more about the literary elements, go to www.glencoe.com.

Reading Strategy Summarizing

A **summary** is a brief restatement, in one's own words, of the main ideas and events in a literary work. In a selection such as "Vanity Fair," separate main ideas from supporting details to help you better understand the meaning of the text.

Reading Tip: Restating Information Summarizing small sections at a time can help you better understand a difficult selection. Use a chart to restate important information from the story.

Paragraph	Summary
Paragraph 1 (pg. 534) Then I saw in my dream that...	The narrator dreams that Christian and Faithful encounter a town called Vanity. The town has a fair that runs all year long. The fair sells vanity.

Vocabulary

diverse (di vurs′) *adj.* markedly different; p. 535 *People of all ages and ethnicities made up the diverse crowd at the concert.*

indictment (in dīt′ mənt) *n.* a formal accusation; p. 537 *The documentary film offered a searing indictment of the effects of cigarette smoking.*

reconciled (rek′ ən sīld) *adj.* brought to acceptance of; p. 537 *The elderly couple could not be reconciled to the loss of their farm.*

Vocabulary Tip: Word Parts When you come across an unfamiliar word, you can often break it down into parts—prefix, root, and suffix—for clues to its meaning.

OBJECTIVES
In studying this selection, you will focus on the following:
• analyzing literary periods
• analyzing allegory and characterization
• summarizing information

from The Pilgrim's Progress

John Bunyan

Vanity Fair

Then I saw in my dream that, when they[1] were got out of the wilderness, they presently saw a town before them, and the name of that town is Vanity; and at the town there is a fair kept, called Vanity Fair. It is kept all the year long. It beareth the name of Vanity Fair because the town where it is kept is lighter than vanity and also because all that is there sold, or that cometh thither, is vanity. As is the saying of the wise, "All that cometh is vanity."

This fair is no new-erected business, but a thing of ancient standing. I will show you the original of it.

Almost five thousand years ago there were pilgrims walking to the Celestial City, as these two honest persons are; and Beelzebub, Apollyon, and Legion,[2] with their companions, perceiving by the path that the pilgrims made that their way to the city lay through this town of Vanity, they contrived here to set up a fair, a fair wherein should be sold all sorts of vanity, and that it should last all the year long. Therefore, at this fair are all such merchandise sold as houses, lands, trades, places, honors, preferments,[3] titles, countries, kingdoms, lusts, pleasures, and delights of all sorts, as harlots, wives, husbands, children, masters, servants, lives, blood, bodies, souls, silver, gold, pearls, precious stones, and what not.

And, moreover, at this fair there is at all times to be seen jugglings, cheats, games, plays, fools, apes, knaves, and rogues, and that of every kind.

Here are to be seen, too, and that for nothing, thefts, murders, adulteries, false swearers, and that of a blood-red color.

And as in other fairs of less moment, there are the several rows and streets under their proper names, where such and such wares are vended; so here likewise you have the proper places, rows, streets (namely, countries and kingdoms), where the wares of this fair are soonest to be found. Here is the Britain Row, the French Row, the Italian Row, the Spanish Row, the German Row, where several sorts of vanities are to be sold. But as in other fairs some one commodity is as the chief of all the fair, so the ware of Rome[4] and her merchandise is greatly promoted in this fair; only our English nation, with some others, have taken a dislike thereat.

Now, as I said, the way to the Celestial City lies just through this town where this lusty[5] fair is kept; and he that would go to the city, and yet not go through this town, must needs "go out of the world." The Prince of princes[6] himself, when here, went through this town to his own country, and that upon a fair day, too; yea, and, as I think,

---

1. *They* refers to Christian and Faithful.
2. *Beelzebub, Apollyon,* and *Legion* are devils.
3. Appointments to government or church positions were called *preferments.*

4. *Rome* refers to the Roman Catholic Church.
5. Here, *lusty* means "merry."
6. *The Prince of princes* is a reference to Christ, who was tempted in the wilderness, as described in the Bible (Matthew 4:1–11).

Reading Strategy **Summarizing** *Who originally established the fair and why did they decide to locate it in the town of Vanity?*

Big Idea **Puritanism and the Civil War** *Given that Bunyan and the Puritans believed that greed led to corruption, why do you think Bunyan named the fair's streets after powerful countries?*

Literary Element **Allegory** *What does the merchandise sold at the fair represent?*

Literary Element **Allegory** *What does the Celestial City symbolize?*

it was Beelzebub, the chief lord of this fair, that invited him to buy of his vanities; yea, would have made him lord of the fair would he but have done him reverence as he went through the town. Yea, because he was such a person of honor, Beelzebub had him from street to street and showed him all the kingdoms of the world in a little time that he might, if possible, allure the Blessed One to cheapen[7] and buy some of his vanities; but he had no mind to the merchandise and, therefore, left the town without laying out so much as one farthing upon these vanities. This fair, therefore, is an ancient thing of long standing, and a very great fair.

Now these pilgrims, as I said, must needs go through this fair. Well, so they did; but, behold, even as they entered into the fair, all the people in the fair were moved, and the town itself, as it were, in a hubbub about them, and that for several reasons.

First, the pilgrims were clothed with such kind of raiment[8] as was **diverse** from the raiment of any that traded in that fair. The people, therefore, of the fair made a great gazing upon them: some said they were fools; some they were bedlams;[9] and some they were outlandish[10] men.

Secondly, and as they wondered at their apparel, so they did likewise at their speech; for few could understand what they said. They naturally spoke the language of Canaan,[11] but they that kept the fair were the men of this world; so that, from one end of the fair to the other, they seemed barbarians each to the other.

Thirdly, but that which did not a little amuse the merchandisers was that these pilgrims set very light by their wares; they cared not so much as to look upon them; and if they called upon them to buy, they would put their fingers in their ears and cry, "Turn away mine eyes from beholding vanity," and look upwards, signifying that their trade and traffic was in heaven.

One chanced mockingly, beholding the carriage of the men, to say unto them, "What will ye buy?" But they, looking gravely upon him, answered, "We buy the truth." At that there was an occasion taken to despise the men the more; some mocking, some taunting, some speaking reproachfully, and some calling upon others to smite them. At last things came to a hubbub and great stir in the fair, insomuch that all order was confounded. Now was word presently brought to the great one of the fair, who quickly came down and deputed some of his most trusty friends to take these men into examination, about whom the fair was almost overturned. So the men were brought to examination; and they that sat upon[12] them asked them whence they came, whither they went, and what they did there in such an unusual garb? The men told them that they were pilgrims and strangers in the world and that they were going to their own country, which was the heavenly Jerusalem, and that they had given no occasion to the men of the town, nor yet to the merchandisers, thus to abuse them and to let[13] them in their journey, except it was for that, when one asked them what they would buy, they said they would buy the truth. But they that were appointed to examine them did not believe them to be any other than bedlams and mad or else such as came to put all things into a confusion in the fair. Therefore, they took them and beat them and besmeared them with dirt and then put them into the cage, that they might be made a spectacle to all the men of the fair.

There, therefore, they lay for some time and were made the objects of any man's sport or malice or revenge, the great one of the fair laughing still at all that befell them. But the men being patient and not rendering railing[14] for railing, but contrariwise, blessing, and giving

---

7. Bunyan uses *cheapen* to mean "inquire the price of."
8. Clothing is also called *raiment*.
9. People who were considered insane were called *bedlams. Bedlam* is a shortened form of *St. Mary's of Bethlehem,* an asylum in London.
10. Here, *outlandish* means "foreign."
11. Hebrew is the *language of Canaan,* the Promised Land.

Big Idea Puritanism and the Civil War *How does the townspeople's reaction to the pilgrims reflect the Puritan experience during Bunyan's lifetime?*

Vocabulary

diverse (di vurs´) *adj.* markedly different

---

12. Here, *sat upon* means "tried."
13. *Let* means "hinder."
14. *Railing* is bitter speech or strong criticism.

Reading Strategy Summarizing *What causes this disturbance?*

O, The Roast Beef of Olde England, 1748. William Hogarth.
Oil on canvas, 78.7 cm. x 94.6 cm. Tate Gallery, London.

good words for bad and kindness for injuries done, some men in the fair that were more observing and less prejudiced than the rest began to check and blame the baser sort for their continual abuses done by them to the men; they,[15] therefore, in angry manner, let fly at them again, counting them as bad as the men in the cage and telling them that they seemed confederates and should be made partakers of their misfortunes. The other replied that, for aught they could see, the men were quiet and sober and intended nobody any harm and that there were many that traded in their fair that were more worthy to be put into the cage, yea, and pillory,[16] too, than were the men they had abused. Thus, after diverse words had passed on both sides, the men behaving themselves all the while very wisely and soberly before them, they fell to some blows among themselves and did harm one to another. Then were these two poor men brought before their examiners again and there charged as being guilty of the late hubbub that had been in the fair. So they beat them pitifully and hanged irons upon them and led them in chains up and down the fair for an example and a terror to others, lest any should speak in their behalf or join themselves unto them. But Christian and Faithful behaved themselves yet more wisely and received the ignominy and shame that was cast upon them with so much meekness and patience that it won to their side, though but few in comparison of the rest, several of the men in the fair. This put the other party yet into greater rage, insomuch that they concluded[17] the death of these two men. Wherefore they threatened that neither cage nor irons should serve their turn, but that they should die for the abuse they had done and for deluding the men of the fair.

15. *They* refers to the baser ones.
16. A *pillory* is an instrument for public punishment consisting of a wooden board with holes in which to lock the offender's head and hands.

17. *Concluded* means "decided on."

Reading Strategy Summarizing *Why have Christian and Faithful been condemned to die?*

Then were they remanded to the cage again until further order should be taken with them. So they put them in and made their feet fast in the stocks. . . .[18]

Then a convenient time being appointed, they brought them forth to their trial in order to their condemnation. When the time was come, they were brought before their enemies and arraigned. The judge's name was Lord Hate-good. Their **indictment** was one and the same in substance, though somewhat varying in form; the contents whereof were this:

"That they were enemies to and disturbers of their trade; that they had made commotions and divisions in the town and had won a party to their own most dangerous opinions, in contempt of the law of their prince." . . .

Then went the jury out, whose names were Mr. Blind-man, Mr. No-good, Mr. Malice, Mr. Love-lust, Mr. Live-loose, Mr. Heady, Mr. High-mind, Mr. Enmity, Mr. Liar, Mr. Cruelty, Mr. Hate-light, and Mr. Implacable—who every one gave in his private verdict against [Faithful] among themselves and afterward unanimously concluded to bring him in guilty before the judge. And first, among themselves, Mr. Blind-man, the foreman, said, "I see clearly that this man is a heretic." Then said Mr. No-good, "Away with such a fellow from the earth." "Ay," said Mr. Malice, "for I hate the very looks of him." Then said Mr. Love-lust, "I could never endure him." "Nor I," said Mr. Live-loose, "for he would always be condemning my way." "Hang him, hang him," said Mr. Heady. "A sorry scrub,"[19] said Mr. High-mind. "My heart riseth against him," said Mr. Enmity. "He is a rogue," said Mr. Liar. "Hanging is too good for him," said Mr. Cruelty. "Let's dispatch him out of the way," said Mr. Hate-light. Then said Mr. Implacable, "Might I have all the world given me, I could not be **reconciled** to him; therefore, let us forthwith bring him in guilty of death." And so they did; therefore, he was presently condemned to be had from the place where he was to the place from whence he came and there to be put to the most cruel death that could be invented.

They, therefore, brought him out, to do with him according to their law; and first they scourged[20] him, then they buffeted[21] him, then they lanced his flesh with knives; after that they stoned him with stones, then pricked him with their swords; and last of all they burned him to ashes at the stake. Thus came Faithful to his end.

Now I saw that there stood behind the multitude a chariot and a couple of horses,[22] waiting for Faithful, who, so soon as his adversaries had dispatched him, was taken up into it and straightway was carried up through the clouds with sound of trumpet, the nearest way to the celestial gate.

But as for Christian, he had some respite and was remanded back to prison. So he there remained for a space; but He that overrules all things, having the power of their rage in his own hand, so wrought it about[23] that Christian for that time escaped them and went his way. ❧

---

18. The *stocks* were an instrument for public punishment consisting of a heavy wooden frame with holes in which to lock the offender's legs.

19. An insignificant person was called a *scrub*.
20. *Scourged* means "whipped."
21. *Buffeted* means "punched."
22. The image of the *chariot and a couple of horses* is an allusion to the biblical story of Elijah, who ascended to heaven in a chariot of fire.
23. *Wrought it about* means "arranged it."

Literary Element Allegory *Why might someone named "Mr. Live-loose" fear the condemnation of others?*

Literary Element Allegory *What fate awaits Faithful and why?*

Vocabulary

indictment (in dīt′ mənt) *n.* a formal accusation

Vocabulary

reconciled (rek′ ən sīld) *adj.* brought to acceptance of

RESPONDING AND THINKING CRITICALLY

Respond

1. If you could talk to John Bunyan, what questions would you ask him?

Recall and Interpret

2. (a)How do Christian and Faithful react to the fair? (b)What are they willing to buy? (c)What does this suggest about their values?

3. (a)How do the townspeople of Vanity know that the pilgrims are foreigners? (b)What does their response to the pilgrims indicate about Bunyan's view of Christians in the world?

4. (a)Throughout the humiliation and violence to which they are subjected, how do Faithful and Christian behave? (b)What causes the citizens of Vanity to begin fighting among themselves? (c)Who is blamed for the fighting?

Analyze and Evaluate

5. (a)What might the town of Vanity symbolize, or represent? (b)How does this reflect Bunyan's Puritan beliefs?

6. (a)Sum up the theme, or central message, of the allegory. (b)What might be lost if Bunyan had expressed this theme directly, in the form of an essay?

Connect

7. (a)Today's fairs are very different from the fairs of Bunyan's time. If Bunyan were writing today, what contemporary setting might he choose? (b)How would it compare with Vanity Fair?

8. **Big Idea** **Puritanism and the Civil War** How might Christian and Faithful reflect Bunyan's spiritual beliefs?

DAILY LIFE AND CULTURE

Country Fairs

During Bunyan's time, a typical English village held a weekly market where people sold and traded food and other goods. A village fair, however, was a more elaborate annual event. It was typically held on a set date, usually in honor of a holy saint. Some fairs lasted only one day, while others remained open for a week or more. They were typically loud bustling occasions with street performers and merchants hawking their wares. Merchandise might include textiles, livestock, baked goods, fruits and vegetables, crafts, and more. Like county fairs today, English village fairs often featured games of chance in which players could win prizes. These winnings—usually small porcelain boxes or figurines—were referred to as *fairings*.

1. In a small group, use the Internet or the library to learn more about historical reenactments or re-creations of English fairs. Share your findings with your class.

2. In your opinion, is Bunyan's depiction of the fair accurate? Explain.

Southwark Fair, 1733. William Hogarth. Oil on canvas. Private collection.

Literary Element Allegory

An **allegory** is a story with two meanings—a literal meaning and a symbolic meaning. The underlying symbolic meaning has moral, social, religious, or political significance. Characters in an allegory are often personifications of abstract concepts such as charity, greed, or envy. Think about the names Bunyan uses for his characters. Specifically, reread the list of jurors' names and pronouncements on page 537 and then answer the following questions.

1. (a)How are the names of the jurors fitting?
(b)What do the names of the judge and jury members suggest about the nature of Christian and Faithful's trial?

2. What do Christian and Faithful represent?

3. Create a few names that could be used in a modern allegory. These names can be humorous, but should describe either a stereotype or a distinct personality.

Review: Characterization

As you learned on page 93, **characterization** is a broad term for the methods a writer uses to reveal the personality and motivations of a character. In **direct characterization**, the narrator explicitly tells the reader about a character's personality. In **indirect characterization**, the character's personality is suggested through his or her actions, speech, thoughts, and physical appearance and by the reactions of other characters to him or her.

Partner Activity With a partner, discuss what you know about the characters Faithful and Christian in "Vanity Fair." On a sheet of paper, create a diagram like the one below. Then find a strong example of each method of characterization used to portray the two pilgrims.

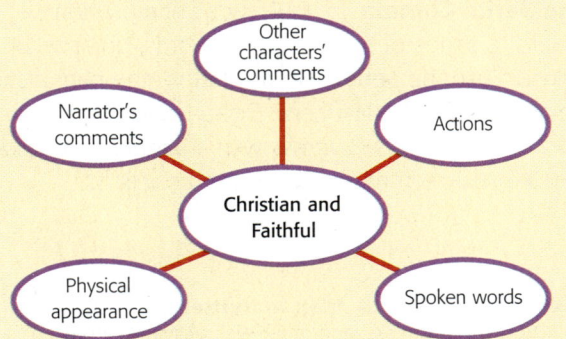

Reading Strategy Summarizing

Summarizing helps you to recap the action of a story and to identify main ideas. Review your notes and the chart you made for the Reading Strategy on page 533 to answer the following questions.

1. What conflict do Faithful and Christian encounter?

2. Is this conflict avoidable? Explain.

3. What is the result of this conflict?

Vocabulary Practice

Practice with Word Parts In "Vanity Fair," Christian and Faithful receive an *indictment* and a guilty *verdict*. At the heart of these two words is the Latin root *dict*. Knowing the meaning of word parts can help you figure out the definitions of words. Identify the meaning of the underlined part of each vocabulary word below. Use a dictionary if necessary.

1. <u>di</u>verse	**a.** two or twice	**b.** candid
2. in<u>dict</u>ment	**a.** to hang	**b.** to state
3. <u>re</u>conciled	**a.** meeting	**b.** hidden

Academic Vocabulary

Here are two words from the vocabulary list on page R82. These words will help you think, write, and talk about the selection.

principle (prin′ sə pəl) *n.* a rule or code of conduct

impose (im pōz′) *v.* to establish or apply by reason of authority

Practice and Apply

1. Name one way in which the people at Vanity Fair acted against the Pilgrims' **principles**.

2. Why did the court **impose** such harsh sentences on Christian and Faithful?

Writing About Literature

Analyze Genre Elements "Vanity Fair," like other allegories, employs a variety of symbols. A **symbol** is a person, animal, place, object, or event within a text that represents something on a figurative level. In a brief essay, examine the literal meaning of "Vanity Fair" by summarizing the story's events. Then describe the symbolic meaning of those events by explaining what the characters and their actions represent. Remember that these elements should support the theme of the allegory.

Before you draft your essay, use the following chart to help you organize your ideas.

Events

List the major events of the story in chronological order.

1. The Pilgrims arrive in the town of Vanity.

2. The people of Vanity notice the Pilgrims are different from them.

3.

Characters

Present your interpretation of the two main characters and what they represent.

Setting

Explain your symbolic interpretation of Vanity Fair.

When you're done writing, proofread your essay for errors in spelling, grammar, and punctuation.

Learning for Life

When some of the townspeople come to the defense of Christian and Faithful, the rest of the town turns against these "confederates" and a fight erupts. With a group of classmates, imagine that you have been called in to settle the argument between the two sides. Briefly describe each side's point of view; then explain what you would say or do to help the two sides reach a peaceful resolution.

Bunyan's Language and Style

Using the Serial Comma In the opening paragraphs of "Vanity Fair," Bunyan builds a case against the town of Vanity and its fair by listing several of its negative traits. Bunyan uses lists to provide both a clear picture and a strong point of view:

"And, moreover, at this fair there is at all times to be seen jugglings, cheats, games, plays, fools, apes, knaves, and rogues, and that of every kind."

"Here are to be seen, too, and that for nothing, thefts, murders, adulteries, false swearers, and that of a blood-red color."

Notice the way Bunyan uses commas when listing a series of items.

Series	Example from "Vanity Fair"
• Words	• " . . . gold, pearls, precious stones, and what not."
• Phrases	• "Here is the Britain Row, the French Row, the Italian Row . . . "
• Clauses	• " . . . some taunting, some speaking reproachfully, and some calling upon others to smite them."

Activity Notice how Bunyan arranges his lists so as to put harmless elements such as "jugglings" and "games" next to more negative elements such as "knaves" and "rogues." By doing so, he underscores the idea that even things that appear harmless may not be. Scan the story and write down other examples of lists that create cumulative expressions that convey the questionable morals of the citizens of Vanity.

Revising Check

The Serial Comma In your own writing, whenever you list a series of three or more words, phrases, or clauses, use the **serial comma** before the conjunction *and* preceding the last item. Exchange your essay about *The Pilgrim's Progress* with a partner and check that the serial comma has been used correctly.

 Literature Online Web Activities For eFlashcards, Selection Quick Checks, and other Web activities, go to www.glencoe.com.

Vocabulary Workshop

Language Resources

Using a Thesaurus

"Therefore, at this fair are all such merchandise sold as houses, lands, trades, places, honors, preferments, titles, countries, kingdoms, lusts, pleasures, and delights of all sorts."

—John Bunyan, from *The Pilgrim's Progress*

Connecting to Literature In this passage, the narrator describes Vanity Fair as a place with "pleasures, and delights of all sorts." *Pleasures* and *delights* are **synonyms**, or words with similar meanings. While some synonyms are practically interchangeable, many have subtly different associations, or connotations. For example, the word *pleasures* refers to general gratification, while *delights* suggests extraordinary enjoyment. Recognizing such differences in synonyms can improve your reading, writing, listening, and speaking.

Most dictionaries list and explain the differences among some synonyms, but for many words you will need to consult a thesaurus. A **thesaurus** is a specialized dictionary of synonyms and antonyms, or words with opposite meanings. Thesauruses are available in many formats—CD-ROM, Internet, word-processing software, and print—and can be organized either traditionally by concept or dictionary style.

Traditional Style

Probably the best-known traditional thesaurus is *Roget's Thesaurus*. To find a synonym for the adjective *loud*, for example, you would look it up in the alphabetical index. This listing includes several entries, including *loud-sounding* and *gaudy*, with page references. On those pages, you would find synonyms related, respectively, to the basic concepts *loudness* and *vulgarity*.

Dictionary Style

This type of thesaurus presents words in alphabetical order, exactly as in a dictionary. Each word is followed by several synonyms, which are listed by parts of speech. The entry also refers the reader to other related words, such as *audible* and *noisy*, in the case of *loud*.

Exercise

Using a thesaurus, find at least two synonyms for each underlined word. Then, working in small groups, discuss the connotations of each synonym.

1. Vanity Fair failed to tempt the <u>pious</u> pilgrims.
2. Each jury member in *The Pilgrim's Progress* has a name that <u>describes</u> him.
3. Christian and Faithful are both rewarded for their <u>kind</u> acts.
4. Christian <u>broke free</u> from the prison and continued his <u>trip</u> as a pilgrim.
5. Religion <u>often</u> played a <u>large</u> role in eighteenth-century British literature.

▶ **Vocabulary Terms**

A **thesaurus** is a reference guide used to find words with similar meanings, or **synonyms**.

▶ **Test-Taking Tip**

To decide whether two words are synonyms, first identify the part of speech of each word. Synonyms are always the same part of speech.

▶ **Reading Handbook**

For more about using reference materials, see Reading Handbook, p. R20.

eFlashcards For eFlashcards and other vocabulary activities, go to www.glencoe.com.

OBJECTIVES
- Use research tools such as a thesaurus.
- Analyze connotations.

On Her Loving Two Equally

MEET APHRA BEHN

Poet, novelist, playwright, and sometime spy—Aphra Behn (ä´ frä bän) was England's first professional female writer. Extraordinarily prolific, Behn wrote about the social and political topics of her time. She was a versatile and talented literary craftsperson.

> "All women together ought to let flowers fall upon the tomb of Aphra Behn, for it was she who earned them the right to speak their minds."
>
> —Virginia Woolf

Much of Behn's early life is a mystery. Accounts vary as to when she was born, who her parents were, and even what her real name was. She was probably born in 1640 in Kent. At twenty-three, she likely traveled to Surinam (Dutch Guiana), an English sugar colony in the West Indies, although why and with whom is unclear. She returned to England the next year and married a London merchant named Behn. However, he died just a year or two after their marriage—probably from the bubonic plague.

The King's Spy Ironically, the first documented facts of Behn's life concern her work as a spy for King Charles II. Shortly after being widowed, Behn, in need of an income, arrived in Holland as an official spy to see what she could learn of Dutch military plans. At the time, England was engaged in trade wars with the Dutch. Although she obtained valuable information about a planned Dutch invasion, the king's agents did not pay her fully for it, and she was forced to borrow money to return to England. As a result, she spent part of 1668 in a London debtors' prison.

This prison experience spurred Behn to do something that no other woman had yet tried—earn a living from writing. In 1670 she wrote a romantic melodrama called *The Forc'd Marriage*—and it was a success. Encouraged, Behn continued writing plays, producing fifteen more in the next twelve years and becoming a minor celebrity in the process. *The Rover, Part I,* her most successful play, is set in Naples during the carnival season. It starred the famous actress Nell Gwyn.

Early English Novelist In 1682 Behn was arrested for writing a play containing a satirical attack on the Duke of Monmouth, an illegitimate son of Charles II, and angering the king. Behn decided to take a break from writing for the stage and turned to writing poetry and fiction. Drawing upon her acquaintance with an enslaved African prince in Surinam, she wrote one of the first novels by an English author, *Oroonoko; or the History of the Royal Slave*. It was published a year before she died at the age of forty-eight.

Behn's literary contributions were undervalued during her lifetime primarily because of her gender. Although she wrote for money, she also sought recognition and acclaim. "I value fame as much as if I had been born a *Hero*," she wrote, "and if you rob me of that, I can retire from the ungrateful World, and scorn its fickle Favours."

Aphra Behn was probably born in 1640 and died in 1689.

Literature Online Author Search For more about Aphra Behn, go to www.glencoe.com.

Connecting to the Poem

As the title suggests, the speaker in Aphra Behn's poem finds herself "loving" two suitors equally. As you read the poem, think about the following questions:

- Have you ever had to choose between two people you cared about? How did you make your choice?
- Is it possible to be in love with two people at the same time?

Building Background

During Charles II's reign, a new kind of comedy called the comedy of manners became the vogue. In these plays, the heroes and heroines were shameless characters who waltzed in and out of one another's arms, exchanging witty remarks sparkling with innuendo.

In real life, however, women of the time could not behave nearly as freely as those stage characters did and still be respected. For example, Behn was often labeled immoral merely for writing comedies that depicted amorous situations similar to those found in the plays of male authors. Yet, throughout her career, Behn refused to modify her works to conform to the double standard. In 1684 she wrote "On Her Loving Two Equally" after having spent more than a dozen years writing and defending her plays against charges of immorality.

Setting Purposes for Reading

Big Idea The Restoration

The literary culture of the Restoration was marked by a witty, cynical tone and an emphasis on worldly values. As you read, notice how this poem reflects that culture.

Literary Element Inversion

Inversion is the reversal of the typical word order in a prose sentence or a line of poetry. For example, in the sentence "Thee I love," the direct object *thee* precedes rather than follows the subject and the verb. As you read, look for instances of inversion.

- See Literary Terms Handbook, p. R9.

Reading Strategy Questioning

Questioning is the process of asking questions as you read about things you do not understand. When you ask questions, you are reading strategically. With a partner, take turns reading stanzas of the poem aloud. Pause after each stanza to ask questions and to discuss difficult lines and passages. Reread those passages, first silently and then aloud.

....

Reading Tip: Taking Notes As you read, have a running conversation with yourself. Use a chart to record your questions and answers.

Questions	Answers
Who are the speaker's two suitors?	Damon and Alexis.

Vocabulary

passion (pash′ ən) *n.* powerful emotion; love; p. 544 *Macbeth's ruling passion was ambition.*

subdue (səb dōō′) *v.* to conquer; p. 544 *The army subdued the rebels before leaving the field.*

mourn (môrn) *v.* to show or feel sadness; grieve; p. 544 *We still mourn the loss of our beloved uncle.*

....

Vocabulary Tip: Antonyms Antonyms are words that have opposite or nearly opposite meanings. For example, the words *reduce* and *gain* are antonyms. Note that antonyms are always the same part of speech.

Literature Online **Interactive Literary Elements Handbook** To review or learn more about the literary elements, go to www.glencoe.com.

OBJECTIVES
In studying this selection, you will focus on the following:
- analyzing literary periods
- analyzing inversion in a poem
- using questioning as a reading strategy

Two Strings to her Bow, 1887. John Pettie. Oil on canvas, 84 x 120.8 cm. Art Gallery and Museum, Kelvingrove, Glasgow, Scotland.

On Her Loving Two Equally

Aphra Behn

How strong does my **passion** flow,
Divided equally twixt[1] two?
Damon had ne'er[2] **subdued** my heart
Had not Alexis took his part;
5   Nor could Alexis powerful prove,
Without my Damon's aid, to gain my love.

When my Alexis present is,
Then I for Damon sigh and **mourn**;
But when Alexis I do miss,
10   Damon gains nothing but my scorn.
But if it chance they both are by,[3]
For both alike I languish, sigh, and die.

Cure then, thou mighty wingéd god,[4]
This restless fever in my blood;
15   One golden-pointed dart take back:
But which, O Cupid, wilt thou take?
If Damon's, all my hopes are crossed;
Or that of my Alexis, I am lost.

1. *Twixt* means "between."
2. *Ne'er* means "never."

3. The word *by* means "near."

4. The *wingéd god* is Cupid, Roman god of love. Cupid shoots darts of gold or lead into the hearts of lovers. A golden-pointed dart would supposedly generate true love, while a leaden dart would generate false love.

Literary Element   **Inversion**   *How would you write this clause in normal word order?*

Vocabulary

passion (pash′ ən) *n.* powerful emotion; love
subdue (səb doō′) *v.* to conquer
mourn (môrn) *v.* to show or feel sadness; grieve

RESPONDING AND THINKING CRITICALLY

Respond

1. If you were a close friend of the speaker in the poem, what advice would you give her? Why?

Recall and Interpret

2. (a)According to the first stanza, why does the speaker find it hard to make up her mind? (b)What is ironic about the way her two rival suitors affect her?

3. (a)What does the speaker do when she is alone with Alexis? (b)What does she feel when she spends time alone with Damon?

4. (a)What does the speaker do when she is near both men? (b)What do the words she uses to describe her state at such times suggest about her personality and how she views her situation? Explain.

Analyze and Evaluate

5. What do you think the speaker really wants from Cupid? Explain.

6. (a)What is the speaker's **tone,** or attitude toward her subject? (b)How well does her word choice support that tone? Explain.

7. Why might this poem be considered a satire? What might it be satirizing? Use details from the poem to explain your answer.

Connect

8. **Big Idea** **The Restoration** In what ways is this poem a product of the Restoration? Consider the poem's subject matter and purpose.

LITERARY ANALYSIS

Literary Element Inversion

Poets use **inversion,** or the placing of parts of speech out of their normal positions, to emphasize certain words or phrases or to maintain the rhyme scheme or the meter. For example, a poet might place a verb before its subject, as in "there *go I*"; an adjective after its noun, as in "the *ocean wide*"; or a main verb after a direct object, as in "so sweetly did *me kiss.*"

1. Identify two inversions in Behn's poem. For each, tell what Behn inverts, or reverses.

2. Choose one inversion and tell why, in your opinion, Behn reverses the words or phrases.

Internet Connection

Using Internet sources, investigate the influence Behn had on women in the theater, female novelists, the development of the novel, or the antislavery movement. Present your findings in an oral report to your class.

Literature Online **Web Activities** For eFlashcards, Selection Quick Checks, and other Web activities, go to www.glencoe.com.

READING AND VOCABULARY

Reading Strategy Questioning

Questioning is a strategy that helps you create meaning while reading and reflecting on a poem. By asking questions, you deepen your understanding of a poem and the poet's intentions.

1. When was the strategy of questioning most helpful to you in reading this poem?

2. How would you evaluate the speaker of this poem? Is she really torn between her two suitors or does she keep them both waiting because she likes having more than one admirer? Explain.

Vocabulary Practice

Practice with Antonyms Identify the antonym for each vocabulary word from "On Her Loving Two Equally" listed below. Use a dictionary or thesaurus if you need help.

1. passion   **a.** fervor   **b.** apathy

2. subdue   **a.** overcome   **b.** yield

3. mourn   **a.** rejoice   **b.** lament

from *An Essay of Dramatic Poesy*

MEET JOHN DRYDEN

Samuel Johnson considered John Dryden "the father of English criticism," and the view still holds today. Dryden wrote *An Essay of Dramatic Poesy* using sound judgment and an informal style that resembles ordinary speech, making it one of the first English prose works to sound distinctly "modern."

> *"The employment of a poet is like that of a curious gunsmith, or watchmaker: the iron or silver is not his own; but they are the least part of that which gives the value: the price lies wholly in the workmanship."*
>
> —John Dryden

Favorable Beginnings Although John Dryden believed himself "slow and dull" in conversation, he wrote some of the most biting satires of his age. During his lifetime he also became an accomplished poet, playwright, and translator.

The oldest of fourteen children born to a prosperous Puritan family in 1631, Dryden attended Westminster school, studying the Greek and Roman classics—subjects that would inform his own writing as an adult. In 1654 Dryden earned his bachelor of arts degree from Trinity College in Cambridge, England. After his father died and left him a small inheritance, however, Dryden abandoned his academic career and moved to London. In 1654 he began working as secretary to Oliver Cromwell's Lord Chamberlain. Dryden wrote the poem *Heroic Stanzas* in 1659 as a memorial commemorating Cromwell's death. That work helped establish Dryden's reputation in London literary circles as a public poet. Later his poetry involving King Charles II would earn him the position of poet laureate.

Politics and Satire

In 1681 political tension mounted, and Dryden began writing satirical verse in an effort to support King Charles II. In 1682 Dryden's famous *MacFlecknoe* appeared in print, published anonymously and reportedly without his consent. Four years earlier Dryden had written *MacFlecknoe* as an attack against Whig playwright Thomas Shadwell. The basis of the scathing verse satire is a dispute between Shadwell and Dryden over Ben Jonson's wit. Dryden ridicules Shadwell's reverence for Jonson, representing him as heir to the kingdom of poetic dullness. *MacFlecknoe* was so successful that Shadwell's reputation never fully recovered.

At this time, Dryden began to examine his personal religious views, which led to his conversion to Catholicism in 1685. This conversion was advantageous because a Catholic king, James II, had just assumed the throne. However, when William and Mary (both Protestants) replaced James II three years later, Dryden lost his post as poet laureate to his rival Shadwell. He returned to his work of writing plays, translations, and criticism until his death in 1700.

John Dryden was born in 1631 and died in 1700.

Literature Online **Author Search** For more about John Dryden, go to www.glencoe.com.

Connecting to the Essay

Think about a time you reviewed or recommended a book or film to a friend and what qualities caught your attention. *An Essay of Dramatic Poesy* includes a critical review of several English dramatists. As you read from the essay, think about the following questions:

- What makes a particular writer's work great?
- How might literary criticism benefit literature overall?

Building Background

Dryden's first major critical work, *An Essay of Dramatic Poesy*, defends British drama against the champions of both ancient classical drama and the neoclassical French theater. It is written as a dialogue among four friends who have rowed down the River Thames to hear the English navy fight the Dutch fleets near the Suffolk coast. When the friends realize that the British have been victorious, they talk about the bad commemorative poems the victory will prompt. This in turn leads to a larger discussion of drama. In the excerpt here, the character who most closely resembles Dryden presents fairly radical opinions on several English dramatists including William Shakespeare, the team of Beaumont and Fletcher, and Ben Jonson.

Setting Purposes for Reading

Big Idea Puritanism and the Civil War

As you read, consider how the political and religious conflicts of the time may have influenced the form and content of Dryden's work.

Literary Element Essay

An **essay** is a short piece of nonfiction writing on any topic that communicates an idea or opinion. A personal or **informal essay** entertains while it informs, usually in light, conversational style.

- See Literary Terms Handbook, p. R6.

Literature Online Interactive Literary Elements Handbook To review or learn more about the literary elements, go to www.glencoe.com.

Reading Strategy Monitoring Comprehension

When you **monitor comprehension,** you stop to think about whether you understand what you are reading.

Reading Tip: Asking Questions To make sure you understand what you're reading, ask yourself questions. For nonfiction such as essays, ask and answer questions about the subject and main idea of each paragraph. Use a chart like the one below.

Paragraph	What is the subject?	What is the main idea?
Paragraph 1	Shakespeare	

Vocabulary

insipid (in sip′ id) *adj.* lacking interest; dull; p. 548 *Not only was the topic of the article uninteresting, the writing style was flat and insipid.*

bombast (bom′ bast) *n.* pretentious language; p. 548 *The man often filled his speeches with bombast to make up for his lack of true knowledge.*

esteem (es tēm′) *n.* favorable opinion; p. 549 *John Dryden was a writer held in high esteem during and after his lifetime.*

superfluous (soo pur′ floo əs) *adj.* beyond what is necessary; p. 549 *Once she cut out the superfluous material from the article, only a few paragraphs remained.*

monarch (mon′ ərk) *n.* one who rules over a state or a territory, usually by hereditary right, as a king or a queen; p. 550 *Charles I was not the first monarch to be beheaded.*

Vocabulary Tip: Word Origins Etymology is the study of a word's history and origins.

OBJECTIVES
In studying this selection, you will focus on the following:
- analyzing literary periods
- analyzing informal essays
- monitoring comprehension

from An Essay of Dramatic Poesy

John Dryden

To begin, then, with Shakespeare. He was the man who, of all modern and perhaps ancient poets, had the largest and most comprehensive soul. All the images of nature were still[1] present to him, and he drew them, not laboriously, but luckily; when he describes anything, you more than see it, you feel it, too. Those who accuse him to have wanted[2] learning give him the greater commendation: he was naturally learned; he needed not the spectacles of books to read nature; he looked inwards, and found her there. I cannot say he is everywhere alike; were he so, I should do him injury to compare him with the greatest of mankind. He is many times flat, **insipid**; his comic wit degenerating into clenches,[3] his serious swelling into **bombast.** But he is always great when some great occasion is presented to him; no man can say he ever had a fit subject for his wit[4] and did not then raise himself as high above the rest of poets *quantum lenta solent inter virburna cupressi.*[5] The consideration of this made Mr. Hales of Eton[6] say that there was no subject of which any poet ever writ but he would produce it much better done in Shakespeare; and however others are now generally preferred before him, yet the age wherein he lived, which had contemporaries with him Fletcher and Jonson, never equaled them to him in their

---

1. Here, *still* means "always" or "constantly."
2. As it is used here, *wanted* means "lacked" or "needed."

Vocabulary

insipid (in sip´ id) *adj.* lacking interest; dull

---

3. *Clenches* are puns.
4. Here, *wit* refers to intellectual powers or imagination.
5. The Latin phrase *[quantum . . . cupressi]* means "as cypresses customarily rise above more yielding shrubs."
6. *Mr. Hales of Eton* (1584–1656) was a scholar who taught at Oxford University and at Eton, a private school for boys, and was much admired by Ben Jonson and Sir John Suckling.

Vocabulary

bombast (bom´ bast) *n.* pretentious language

Shakespeare and His Friends. John Faed (1820–1902). Oil on canvas, 37 x 45 cm. Private collection.

Viewing the Art: How does the artist's representation of Shakespeare reflect Dryden's opinion of him?

esteem; and in the last king's[7] court, when Ben's reputation was at highest, Sir John Suckling, and with him the greater part of the courtiers, set our Shakespeare far above him.

Beaumont and Fletcher, of whom I am next to speak, had, with the advantage of Shakespeare's wit, which was their precedent, great natural gifts, improved by study. . . . Their plots were generally more regular than Shakespeare's, espe-cially those which were made before Beaumont's death; and they understood and imitated the conversation of gentlemen much better, whose wild debaucheries and quickness of wit in repar-tees no poet before them could paint as they have done. Humor, which Ben Jonson derived from particular persons, they made it not their business to describe; they represented all the pas-sions very lively, but above all, love. I am apt to believe the English language in them arrived to its highest perfection; what words have since been taken in are rather **superfluous** than ornamental. Their plays are now the most pleasant and frequent entertainments of the

---

7. *The last king* was Charles I.

Big Idea **Puritanism and the Civil War** *How does this reference reflect the influence of politics on writers of the time?*

Vocabulary

esteem (es tēm′) *n.* favorable opinion

Vocabulary

superfluous (soo pur′ floo əs) *adj.* beyond what is necessary

stage, two of theirs being acted through the year for one of Shakespeare's or Jonson's. The reason is because there is a certain gaiety in their comedies and pathos in their more serious plays, which suits generally with all men's humors. Shakespeare's language is likewise a little obsolete, and Ben Jonson's wit comes short of theirs.

As for Jonson, to whose character I am now arrived, if we look upon him while he was himself (for his last plays were but his dotage), I think him the most learned and judicious writer which any theater ever had. He was a most severe judge of himself, as well as others. One cannot say he wanted wit, but rather that he was frugal of it. In his works you find little to retrench or alter. Wit and language and humor also in some measure we had before him, but something of art was wanting to the drama till he came. He managed his strength to more advantage than any who preceded him. You seldom find him making[8] love in any of his scenes or endeavoring to move the passions; his genius was too sullen and saturnine[9] to do it gracefully, especially when he knew he came after those who had performed both to such a height. Humor was his proper sphere; and in that he delighted most to represent mechanic people.[10] He was deeply conversant in the ancients, both Greek and Latin, and he borrowed boldly from them; there is scarce a poet or historian among the Roman authors of those times whom he has not translated in *Sejanus*

and *Catiline*.[11] But he has done his robberies so openly that one may see he fears not to be taxed by any law. He invades authors like a **monarch**; and what would be theft in other poets is only victory in him. With the spoils of these writers, he so represents old Rome to us, in its rites, ceremonies, and customs, that if one of their poets had written either of his tragedies, we had seen[12] less of it than in him. If there was any fault in his language, 'twas that he weaved it too closely and laboriously, in his comedies especially. Perhaps, too, he did a little too much Romanize our tongue, leaving the words which he translated almost as much Latin as he found them; wherein, though he learnedly followed their language, he did not enough comply with the idiom of ours. If I would compare him with Shakespeare, I must acknowledge him the more correct poet, but Shakespeare the greater wit. Shakespeare was the Homer,[13] or father, of our dramatic poets; Jonson was the Virgil,[14] the pattern of elaborate writing. I admire him, but I love Shakespeare. ∾

---

8. Here, *making* means "depicting."
9. *Saturnine* means "having a gloomy or morose nature."
10. *Mechanic people* are artisans, or people who work with their hands.

Reading Strategy Monitoring Comprehension *What is the main idea of the second paragraph? Which clues help you understand this paragraph in the context of the previous one?*

---

11. *Sejanus* (si jān′ əs) and *Catiline* (kat ə līn′) are tragedies by Jonson.
12. Here, *had seen* means "would have seen."
13. *Homer* composed the *Iliad* and the *Odyssey*, the first important epics in Western literature, in the oral tradition.
14. *Virgil* wrote the epic poem *Aeneid* centuries after Homer composed his works. However, Virgil composed his epic as a written manuscript.

Literary Element Essay *What about this passage suggests it is a part of an informal essay?*

Reading Strategy Monitoring Comprehension *What does Dryden mean by this statement, and how does it contribute to the main conclusion he reaches in the selection?*

Vocabulary

monarch (mon′ ərk) *n.* one who rules over a state or a territory, usually by hereditary right, as a king or a queen

RESPONDING AND THINKING CRITICALLY

Respond

1. What is the difference between admiring and loving a writer?

Recall and Interpret

2. (a)What does Dryden say about Shakespeare's lack of formal education? (b)What do his words tell you about his opinion of Shakespeare?

3. (a)Identify two faults Dryden finds in Shakespeare's work and two favorable observations he makes. (b)Why does Dryden point out Shakespeare's faults?

4. (a)In comparing Jonson and Shakespeare, what does Dryden note about each? (b)In your own words, explain the distinction Dryden is making.

Analyze and Evaluate

5. (a)What is the effect of Dryden citing the opinion of "Mr. Hales of Eton" and that of Sir John Suckling? (b)How might citing those opinions make his argument more effective?

6. (a)What is the tone of this essay? (b)Is it appropriate? Why or why not?

Connect

7. Name a modern author about whose work you could say, "you more than see it, you feel it, too." Explain your answer.

8. **Big Idea** **Puritanism and the Civil War** Given Dryden's political affiliations, why might he have used Sir John Suckling as a reference on page 549 instead of another poet? Refer to pages 464 and 546 if you need help.

LITERARY ANALYSIS

Literary Element **Essay**

A **formal essay** is serious and impersonal, and is usually written to instruct or persuade. Typically, a formal essay is serious in tone and develops a main idea in a logical, highly organized way. By contrast, an **informal essay,** such as Dryden's, is characterized by its light, conversational style. Informal, or personal, essays often entertain while they inform.

1. (a)What is the point, or main idea, of the essay? (b)When is it stated, if at all?

2. How do the voice, tone, and point of view of the essay suggest it is informal rather than formal? Give specific examples from the text.

Literature Groups

In a small group, make a list of the qualities Dryden values in a dramatic work. Next, discuss your ideas from the Connecting to the Essay feature on page 547. Using ideas from that discussion, agree upon a set of qualities you would use to evaluate a film, television show, or play. Share these qualities with other groups.

READING AND VOCABULARY

Reading Strategy **Monitoring Comprehension**

To help with comprehension, think about the essay as a whole: how it is organized and how the larger parts fit together to support the main point.

1. How is the selection organized?

2. (a)What might be the reason to start and end with Shakespeare? (b)How does this organization reinforce Dryden's main point?

Vocabulary **Practice**

Practice with Word Origins Match each word below with the definition of its origin.

1. monarch		**a.** cotton	
2. bombast		**b.** savory	
3. insipid		**c.** running over	
4. esteem		**d.** worth	
5. superfluous		**e.** ruler	

Literature Online **Web Activities** For eFlashcards, Selection Quick Checks, and other Web activities, go to www.glencoe.com.

from *The Diary of Samuel Pepys*

MEET SAMUEL PEPYS

In his day Samuel Pepys (pēps) was primarily recognized for his contributions to the British navy. Today he is more appreciated for his colorful and informative diary. Unnoticed for more than one hundred years after Pepys's death, the diary provides vivid accounts of some of the most stirring events of the seventeenth century, as well as an intimate portrait of Pepys himself.

"The instinct to live for the moment lyrically and at the same time prudently is seen nowhere better than in the Diary of Samuel Pepys."

—George Sherburn

A Distinguished Career Pepys was the fifth son of a London tailor. He attended Cambridge University on a scholarship, eventually earning a master's degree. Pepys worked as personal secretary to his influential cousin Admiral Edward Montagu, but admitted that his role as a public servant was due to "chance without merit." In 1660 Montagu brought Pepys along on a journey to Holland to bring back the exiled king Charles II and restore him to the English throne. Pepys was later appointed to a position as a clerk in the navy office, and through successive promotions he became secretary to the admiralty, the navy's top-ranking official. During his tenure, he instituted countless changes and doubled the navy's fighting strength—increasing the number of battleships from thirty to fifty-nine and the firepower from 1,730 guns to 4,492—thus transforming a poorly organized navy into a major military powerhouse.

In 1679 Pepys won election to Parliament, but suffered a setback when he was falsely accused of passing secrets to the French. He was imprisoned in the Tower of London, but the charges were soon dropped. In 1684 he was again secretary of the admiralty and remained in that post until the Glorious Revolution of 1688.

Literary Legacy As a New Year's resolution, Pepys began his diary on January 1, 1660. While he probably never intended that the diary be published, he took great care with it. Much of the diary is transcribed from rough notes and carefully bound in six volumes. He wrote with extreme honesty and passion, whether he was recording his observations while witnessing important historical events or merely reflecting upon his personal interests—in music, theater, wine, clothes, and books—as well as his jealousies, weaknesses, desires, career advancements, and accumulation of wealth. His eye for detail and his vivid accounts afford a realistic glimpse into the events of the Restoration.

Pepys's diary is historically important and a literary success because he crafted his narrative with the care of a novelist, possibly with an audience in mind. According to biographer Richard Ollard: "The *Diary* is a great work, as literature, as history, as a psychological document and as a key to what has been known as the English character in an age of national cultures perhaps soon to become extinct. It is thus almost impossible to exaggerate its value and importance."

Samuel Pepys was born in 1633 and died in 1703.

Literature Online **Author Search** For more about Samuel Pepys, go to www.glencoe.com.

Connecting to the Diary

Many people keep diaries to record important events in their lives. As you read Pepys's diary, consider the following questions:

- What recent events would you record in a diary?
- What type of people would you include?

Building Background

Pepys began keeping a diary in 1660 and ended it nine years later because of failing eyesight. During the nearly ten years he kept his diary, he recorded vivid eyewitness accounts of such events as the restoration of King Charles II and the fire that ravaged the city in 1666. He also recorded intimate details about his personal experiences, safeguarding his privacy by writing his entries in a combination of shorthand and secret code.

On September 2, 1666, a fire broke out in the residence of the king's baker. Violent winds quickly spread the flames. The Great Fire of London raged for four days, devastating four-fifths of the central city. Thirteen thousand homes were destroyed.

Setting Purposes for Reading

Big Idea The Restoration

As you read, look for ways in which Pepys's entries reflect the new sense of freedom and the enjoyment of life that many writers of the Restoration felt.

Literary Element Diary

A **diary** is an individual's private, day-to-day account of personal thoughts, feelings, and experiences written for his or her own use rather than for publication. While reading Pepys's diary entries, consider what types of people, events, and details Pepys decided to capture and how they express his unique voice.

- See Literary Terms Handbook, p. R4.

Literature Online Interactive Literary Elements **Handbook** To review or learn more about the literary elements, go to www.glencoe.com.

Reading Strategy Drawing Conclusions About Author's Beliefs

Through close examination of an author's choice of details, tone, word choice, and use of figurative language, a reader can **draw conclusions**—or make general statements—about the author's beliefs. As you read Pepys's diary entries, look for evidence in the text that can enable you to draw accurate conclusions about his beliefs.

Reading Tip: Taking Notes As you read, use a chart to record your conclusions about Pepys's beliefs.

Clues in Text	Conclusions
"And a great pleasure it was to see the Abbey . . ."	Pepys was a royalist.

Vocabulary

cavalcade (kav´ əl kād´) *n.* a ceremonial procession; p. 555 *The men and women in the cavalcade wore elaborate robes.*

loath (lōth) *adj.* reluctant; unwilling; p. 556 *We were loath to leave the theater before the final encore.*

quench (kwench) *v.* to put out; to extinguish; p. 557 *The strong winds made it extremely difficult to quench the flames.*

malicious (mə lish´ əs) *adj.* deliberately harmful; p. 559 *John attacked his brother with malicious intent.*

Vocabulary Tip: Analogies An analogy is a relationship between two pairs of words. Some common relationships are synonyms, cause and effect, and part to the whole. For example, an analogy based on cause and effect is: deluge : flood :: fire : smoke.

OBJECTIVES
In studying this selection, you will focus on the following:
- analyzing literary movements and periods
- analyzing the diary as a literary form
- drawing conclusions about an author's beliefs

from
The Diary of Samuel Pepys

Samuel Pepys

The Coronation of Charles II

APRIL 23, 1661. Coronation Day. About four I rose and got to the Abbey,[1] where I followed Sir J. Denham, the surveyor, with some company that he was leading in. And with much ado, by the favor of Mr. Cooper, his man, did get up into a great scaffold[2] across the north end of the Abbey, where with a great deal of patience I sat from past four till eleven before the King came in. And a great pleasure it was to see the Abbey raised in the middle, all covered with red, and a throne (that is a chair) and footstool on the top of it; and all the officers of all kinds, so much as the very fiddlers, in red vests.

At last comes in the dean and prebends[3] of Westminster, with the bishops (many of them in cloth-of-gold copes[4]), and after them the nobility, all in their Parliament robes, which was a most magnificent sight. Then the Duke,[5] and the King with a scepter (carried by my Lord Sandwich) and sword and mond[6] before him, and the crown, too. The King in his robes, bare-headed, which was very fine. And after all had placed themselves, there was a sermon and the service; and then in the choir at the high altar, the King passed through all the ceremonies of the coronation, which to my great grief I and most in the Abbey could not see. The crown being put upon his head, a great shout begun, and he came forth to the throne, and there passed more ceremonies: as taking the oath and having things read to him by the bishop; and his lords (who put on their caps as soon as the King put on his crown) and bishops come and kneeled before him. And three times

---

1. The *Abbey* is Westminster Abbey, the London church that is the traditional site of coronations.
2. A *scaffold* is a raised platform.
3. The *dean* and *prebends* (pre′ bəndz) are high church officials.
4. *Copes* are long capes worn by church officials during processions and other religious ceremonies.
5. The *Duke* is the Duke of York—the king's brother and later King James II.
6. A *mond* is a ball of gold or other precious material with a cross on top, representing the globe of Earth. It is meant to be a symbol of royal power.

Reading Strategy Drawing Conclusions About Author's Beliefs *What conclusions can you draw about Pepys's political sympathies based on his descriptions of the coronation?*

Charles II's entry into London on the day before his Coronation in 1661. Dirck Stoop (1618–1686). Oil on canvas, 64 x 199 cm. Museum of London.

the King at Arms[7] went to the three open places on the scaffold and proclaimed that if anyone could show any reason why Charles Stuart should not be King of England, that now he should come and speak. And a general pardon also was read by the Lord Chancellor, and medals flung up and down by my Lord Cornwallis, of silver, but I could not come by any. But so great a noise that I could make but little of the music; and indeed, it was lost to everybody . . . .

I went out a little while before the King had done all his ceremonies and went round the Abbey to Westminster Hall,[8] all the way within rails, and ten thousand people, with the ground covered with blue cloth; and scaffolds all the way. Into the hall I got, where it was very fine with hangings and scaffolds one upon another full of brave[9] ladies; and my wife in one little one on the right hand. Here I stayed walking up and down, and at last, upon one of the side stalls, I stood and saw the King come in with all the persons (but the soldiers) that were yesterday in

the **cavalcade;** and a most pleasant sight it was to see them in their several robes. And the King came in with his crown on, and his scepter in his hand, under a canopy borne up by six silver staves,[10] carried by barons of the Cinque Ports,[11] and little bells at every end.

And after a long time, he got up to the farther end, and all set themselves down at their several tables; and that was also a brave sight; and the King's first course carried up by the Knights of the Bath. And many fine ceremonies there was of the herald's leading up people before him and bowing; and my Lord of Albemarle's going to the kitchen and eat a bit of the first dish that was to go to the King's table. But, above all, was these three Lords, Northumberland and Suffolk and the Duke of Ormond, coming before the courses on horseback and staying so all dinnertime, and at last to bring up [Dymock] the King's champion,[12] all in armor on horseback, with his spear and target carried

---

7. The *King at Arms* is the chief herald, an officer whose duties include making royal proclamations and arranging public processions and ceremonies.
8. *Westminster Hall* is the court of justice.
9. As it is used here, *brave* means "finely dressed."

10. *Staves* is the plural of *staff.*
11. *Cinque* (singk) *Ports* are the five seaports along the English Channel that jointly provided England's naval defense.
12. At coronations, the *King's champion* ceremoniously defended the new king's title to the crown. This office had been held by the *Dymock* family since Richard II was crowned in 1377.

Literary Element Diary *What words of approval used on page 554 does Pepys repeat here? In your opinion, does this repetition enhance or detract from Pepys's style?*

Vocabulary

cavalcade (kav′ əl kād′) *n.* a ceremonial procession

before him. And a herald proclaims, "That if any dare deny Charles Stuart to be lawful King of England, here was a champion that would fight with him"; and with these words, the champion flings down his gauntlet, and all this he do three times in his going up towards the King's table. At last when he is come, the King drinks to him and then sends him the cup, which is of gold, and he drinks it off and then rides back again with the cup in his hand. I went from table to table to see the bishops and all others at their dinner and was infinitely pleased with it. And at the Lords' table, I met with William Howe, and he spoke to my Lord[13] for me, and he did give me four rabbits and a pullet, and so I got it, and Mr. Creed and I got Mr. Michell to give us some bread, and so we at a stall eat it, as everybody else did what they could get. I took a great deal of pleasure to go up and down and look upon the ladies and to hear the music of all sorts, but above all, the twenty-four violins.

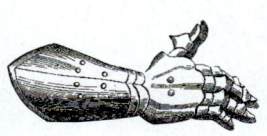

The London Fire

SEPTEMBER 2, 1666. Lord's Day.[14] Some of our maids sitting up late last night to get things ready against our feast today, Jane called us up about three in the morning to tell us of a great fire they saw in the city. So I rose and slipped on my nightgown and went to her window and thought it to be on the back side of Mark Lane at the farthest; but, being unused to such fires as followed, I thought it far enough off and so went to bed again and to sleep. About seven rose again to dress myself and there looked out at the window and saw the fire not so much as it was

and further off. So to my closet[15] to set things to rights after yesterday's cleaning.

By and by Jane comes and tells me that she hears that above three hundred houses have been burned down tonight by the fire we saw and that it is now burning down all Fish Street, by London Bridge.[16] So I made myself ready presently and walked to the Tower[17] and there got up upon one of the high places, Sir J. Robinson's little son going up with me; and there I did see the houses at the end of the bridge all on fire and an infinite great fire on this and the other side the end of the bridge, which, among other people, did trouble me for poor little Michell and our Sarah[18] on the bridge. So down, with my heart full of trouble, to the lieutenant of the Tower, who tells me that it begun this morning in the King's baker's house in Pudding Lane and that it hath burned St. Magnus's Church and most part of Fish Street already. So I down to the waterside and there got a boat and through bridge and there saw a lamentable fire. Poor Michell's house, as far as the Old Swan,[19] already burned that way, and the fire running further, that in a very little time it got as far as the Steel Yard, while I was there. Everybody endeavoring to remove their goods and flinging into the river or bringing them into lighters[20] that lay off; poor people staying in their houses as long as till the very fire touched them and then running into boats or clambering from one pair of stairs by the waterside to another. And among other things, the poor pigeons, I perceive, were **loath** to leave their houses, but hovered about the windows

---

13. *My Lord* is Edward Montagu, the Earl of Sandwich, who was Pepys's cousin and lifelong patron.
14. *Lord's Day* is Sunday.

15. A *closet* was a private room used especially for study or prayer.
16. *London Bridge* was the only bridge over the Thames River at that time. It was lined with shops and houses.
17. The *Tower* of London actually consists of a group of buildings on the Thames River constructed as a fortress and later used as a royal residence and prison.
18. *Sarah* was a maid whom Mrs. Pepys fired on December 5, 1662. Pepys still cared about her well-being.
19. Betty *Michell* was a former love interest of Pepys who lost her house in the fire. The *Old Swan* was a tavern near London Bridge.
20. *Lighters* are large, open barges.

Vocabulary

loath (lōth) *adj.* reluctant; unwilling

The Great Fire of London, 1666. After Waggoner. Oil on canvas, 46.9 x 72.4 cm. Guildhall Art Gallery, Corporation of London.
Viewing the Art: How does the artist's visual representation of the Great Fire compare with Pepys's written account?

and balconies till they were, some of them burned, their wings, and fell down. Having stayed, and in an hour's time seen the fire rage every way, and nobody, to my sight, endeavoring to **quench** it, but to remove their goods, and leave all to the fire, and having seen it get as far as the Steel Yard, and the wind mighty high and driving it into the City; and everything, after so long a drought, proving combustible, even the very stones of churches, and among other things the poor steeple by which pretty Mrs. —— lives, and whereof my old schoolfellow Elborough is parson, taken fire in the very top and there burned till it fell down. I to Whitehall[21] (with a gentleman with me who desired to go off from the Tower, to see the fire, in my boat); to

---

21. *Whitehall* was the king's residence in Westminster, London, as well as the location of several government offices.

Reading Strategy Drawing Conclusions About Author's Beliefs *Pepys uses the word* poor *three times in this paragraph. What conclusions can you draw about Pepys's social consciousness?*

Vocabulary

quench (kwench) *v.* to put out; to extinguish

Whitehall, and there up to the King's closet in the Chapel, where people come about me, and I did give them an account dismayed them all, and word was carried in to the King. So I was called for and did tell the King and Duke of York what I saw, and that unless his Majesty did command houses to be pulled down, nothing could stop the fire. They seemed much troubled, and the King commanded me to go to my Lord Mayor from him and command him to spare no houses, but to pull down before the fire every way. The Duke of York bid me tell him that if he would have any more soldiers, he shall; and so did my Lord Arlington afterwards, as a great secret. Here meeting with Captain Cocke, I in his coach, which he lent me, and Creed with me to Paul's,[22] and there walked along Watling Street, as well as I could, every creature coming away laden with goods to save, and here and there sick people carried away in beds.

---

22. *Paul's* is St. Paul's Cathedral, which was destroyed in the fire and later rebuilt.

Literary Element Diary *Why do you think Pepys includes this detail about his conversation with the king in his diary?*

Extraordinary good goods carried in carts and on backs. At last met my Lord Mayor in Canning Street, like a man spent, with a handkerchief about his neck. To the King's message he cried, like a fainting woman, "Lord! What can I do? I am spent: people will not obey me. I have been pulling down houses, but the fire overtakes us faster than we can do it." That he needed no more soldiers and that, for himself, he must go and refresh himself, having been up all night.

So he left me, and I him, and walked home, seeing people all almost distracted, and no manner of means used to quench the fire. The houses, too, so very thick thereabouts and full of matter for burning, as pitch and tar, in Thames Street; and warehouses of oil and wines and brandy and other things. Here I saw Mr. Isaake Houblon, the handsome man, prettily dressed and dirty, at his door at Dowgate, receiving some of his brothers' things, whose houses were on fire, and, as he says, have been removed twice already; and he doubts (as it soon proved) that they must be in a little time removed from his house also, which was a sad consideration. And to see the churches all filling with goods by people who themselves should have been quietly there at this time.

By this time it was about twelve o'clock; and so home and there find my guests, which was Mr. Wood and his wife, Barbary Sheldon, and also Mr. Moone: she mighty fine, and her husband, for aught I see, a likely man. But Mr. Moone's design and mine, which was to look over my closet and please him with the sight thereof, which he hath long desired, was wholly disappointed; for we were in great trouble and disturbance at this fire, not knowing what to think of it. However, we had an extraordinary good dinner, and as merry as at this time we could be. While at dinner, Mrs. Batelier come to enquire after Mr. Woolfe and Stanes (who, it seems, are related to them), whose houses in Fish Street are all burned, and they in a sad condition. She would not stay in the fright. Soon as dined, I and Moone away and walked through the City, the streets full of nothing but people and horses and carts laden with goods,

ready to run over one another, and removing goods from one burned house to another. They now removing out of Canning Street (which received goods in the morning) into Lombard Street and further; and among others I now saw my little goldsmith, Stokes, receiving some friend's goods, whose house itself was burned the day after. We parted at Paul's; he home, and I to Paul's Wharf, where I had appointed a boat to attend me, and took in Mr. Carcasse and his brother, whom I met in the street, and carried them below and above bridge to and again to see the fire, which was now got further, both below and above, and no likelihood of stopping it. Met with the King and Duke of York in their barge, and with them to Queenhithe, and there called Sir Richard Browne to them. Their order was only to pull down houses apace,[23] and so below bridge at the waterside; but little was or could be done, the fire coming upon them so fast. Good hopes there was of stopping it at the Three Cranes above, and at Buttolph's Wharf below bridge, if care be used; but the wind carries it into the City, so as we know not by the waterside what it do there. River full of lighters and boats taking in goods, and good goods swimming in the water, and only I observed that hardly one lighter or boat in three that had the goods of a house in but there was a pair of virginals in it.

Having seen as much as I could now, I away to Whitehall by appointment and there walked to St. James's Park and there met my wife and Creed and Wood and his wife and walked to my boat; and there upon the water again, and to the fire up and down, it still increasing, and the wind great. So near the fire as we could for smoke; and all over the Thames, with one's face in the wind, you were almost burned with a shower of firedrops. This is very true; so as houses were burned by these drops and flakes

---

Big Idea **The Restoration** *How does this comment capture the spirit of the Restoration?*

23. *Apace* means "swiftly."

of fire, three or four, nay, five or six houses, one from another. When we could endure no more upon the water, we to a little alehouse on the Bankside, over against the Three Cranes, and there stayed till it was dark almost and saw the fire grow; and as it grew darker, appeared more and more and in corners and upon steeples and between churches and houses as far as we could see up the hill of the City in a most horrid **malicious** bloody flame, not like the fine flame of an ordinary fire. Barbary and her husband away before us. We stayed till, it being darkish, we saw the fire as only one entire arch of fire from this to the other side the bridge and in a bow up the hill for an arch of above a mile long: it made me weep to see it. The churches, houses, and all on fire and flaming at once; and a horrid noise the flames made and the cracking of houses at their ruin.

So home with a sad heart, and there find everybody discoursing and lamenting the fire; and poor Tom Hater come with some few of his goods saved out of his house, which is burned upon Fish Street Hill. I invited him to lie at my house and did receive his goods, but was deceived in his lying there, the news coming every moment of the growth of the fire; so as we were forced to begin to pack up our own goods and prepare for their removal and did by moonshine (it being brave dry and moonshine and warm weather) carry much of my goods into the garden, and Mr. Hater and I did remove my money and iron chests into my cellar, as thinking that the safest place. And got my bags of gold into my office, ready to carry away, and my chief papers of accounts also there, and my tallies[24] into a box by themselves. So great was our fear, as Sir W. Batten hath carts come out of the country to fetch away his goods this night. We did put Mr. Hater, poor man, to bed a little; but he got but very little rest, so much noise being in my house, taking down of goods.

3RD.[25] About four o'clock in the morning, my Lady Batten sent me a cart to carry away all my money and plate[26] and best things to Sir W. Rider's at Bednall Green. Which I did, riding myself in my nightgown in the cart; and, Lord! to see how the streets and the highways are crowded with people running and riding and getting of carts at any rate to fetch away things. I find Sir W. Rider tired with being called up all night, and receiving things from several friends. His house full of goods, and much of Sir W. Batten's and Sir W. Pen's. I am eased at my heart to have my treasure so well secured. Then home, with much ado to find a way, nor any sleep all this night to me nor my poor wife.

London Traffic Jam, 19th Century. Gustave Doré. Engraving.

24. *Tallies* were sticks marked with notches representing amounts of money. The tallies served as records of money paid or owed.
25. The abbreviation *3rd* refers to the date, September 3.
26. *Plate* refers to tableware or decorative objects made of a precious metal, such as silver or gold.

Literary Element Diary *How has the tone of this diary entry changed as the fire continued to spread?*

Reading Strategy Drawing Conclusions About Author's Beliefs *Pepys itemizes the belongings that he chose to save from the fire. What does this list of items tell you about Pepys?*

Vocabulary

malicious (mə lish′ əs) *adj.* deliberately harmful

RESPONDING AND THINKING CRITICALLY

Respond

1. What were your reactions to the events Pepys describes?

Recall and Interpret

2. (a)Where does Pepys go to see the coronation of Charles II? (b)What is Pepys's attitude toward the king's restoration?

3. (a)Describe the events and sights that Pepys records about his time at Westminster Hall. (b)How do these descriptions reflect his personality and interests?

4. (a)When Pepys first views the fire burning in the distance, what does he do? Why? (b)How does his later attitude toward the fire compare with his initial reaction?

5. (a)When Pepys explores the burning city, what does he notice that most people are doing?

(b)What is Pepys's opinion of people's behavior during the fire?

Analyze and Evaluate

6. (a)Explain the mood of Pepys's account of the night of September 2 and early the next morning. (b)What techniques does he use to create this mood?

7. (a)What does Pepys do at twelve o'clock on the night of the fire? (b)What is your opinion of his behavior?

Connect

8. **Big Idea** **The Restoration** After the repressive years of Puritan rule, the Restoration gave writers a renewed sense of freedom. How does Pepys's account of the king's coronation illustrate the exhilarating atmosphere that characterized the Restoration?

PRIMARY VISUAL ARTIFACT

British Crown Jewels

The British Crown Jewels, dating back to the eleventh century, are the regalia used during the coronation ceremony. These treasures, including the royal crowns, scepters, orb, swords, anointing spoon and ampulla (a container used to hold consecrated wine or holy oil), have symbolic religious connotations because the sovereign is also the head of the Church of England.

In 1661 Charles II was crowned at Westminster Abbey (where William I was crowned) and escorted to the Coronation Chair (used since 1300) by his men who carried the Crown Jewels. When Charles was crowned with St. Edward's Crown, he held the Scepter with the Cross and the Scepter with the Dove, which symbolized the Holy Ghost. He also carried the orb (or mond), which represented royal power and Christian sovereignty. The swords represented mercy, spiritual justice, temporal justice, and royal authority. Finally, after Charles took the oath, the Archbishop of Canterbury anointed him with the ampulla and spoon.

1. (a)Why do you think Pepys describes the coronation ceremony and the Crown Jewels? (b)How were the jewels vital to this coronation?

2. Imagine you are writing a diary entry about seeing the Crown Jewels. Study the image on this page and include a description of the Crown Jewels.

Literary Element Diary

Pepys's diary entries offer valuable insight and impressions of historic events, such as the Great Fire, and candid pictures of everyday life. In his description of the coronation of Charles II, Pepys touches on both personal and historical details in his observations.

1. Find two other passages from Pepys's diary in which he reveals his personal feeling about a historical figure or event.

2. Identify a detail Pepys observes during the Great Fire of London that you would probably not find in a history book.

3. If Pepys had known his diary might be read or even published, how might it have been different? Explain.

Review: Tone

As you learned on page 255, **tone** refers to the author's attitude toward his or her subject matter or the audience. Tone is conveyed through elements such as word choice, punctuation, sentence structure, and figures of speech. A writer's tone may convey a variety of attitudes, such as sympathy, irony, sadness, or despair.

Partner Activity Work with a partner to discuss the similarities and differences in Pepys's tone when he presents his account of the coronation and his account of the Great Fire of London. Create a chart similar to the one below to compare and contrast words, phrases, and devices that Pepys uses to convey his tone.

Textual Evidence	Description of Tone
Coronation: "And a great pleasure it was to see the Abbey raised in the middle, all covered with red . . ."	festive, jubilant
Great Fire of London: "So down, with my heart full of trouble, to the lieutenant of the Tower . . ."	ominous, sad

Reading Strategy Drawing Conclusions About Author's Beliefs

In his description of the coronation and the Great Fire, Pepys interjects comments that give the reader insight into his personal beliefs.

1. What conclusion can you draw about Pepys's attitude toward King Charles II and the coronation ceremony?

2. Based on his description of people's actions during the fire, what conclusion can you draw about Pepys's attitude toward material wealth?

Vocabulary Practice

Practice with Analogies Choose the word that best completes each analogy below.

1. laundry : wash :: fire :
   a. quench   **b.** climb   **c.** shout
2. parade : holiday :: cavalcade :
   a. battle   **b.** ceremony   **c.** rodeo
3. courteous : polite :: malicious :
   a. tactful   **b.** flattering   **c.** spiteful
4. sarcastic : sincere :: loath :
   a. eager   **b.** indifferent   **c.** scornful

Academic Vocabulary

Here are two words from the vocabulary list on page R82.

context (kon′ tekst) *n.* parts surrounding a word, sentence, or passage that help determine its meaning

community (kə mū′ nə tē) *n.* people with shared interests living in a particular area; a unified body of individuals

Practice and Apply

1. In describing the coronation, Pepys wrote, "And a general pardon also was read by the Lord Chancellor." What is the historical **context** that explains the significance of this observation?

2. How did Pepys's **community** react to the Great Fire of London?

Writing About Literature

Respond to Imagery Pepys creates vivid **imagery** by using sensory details and closely observed descriptions to capture the characters, setting, and events he chronicles. Choose an event you have recently witnessed that is rich in sensory detail. Then, using Pepys's style as your model, write a diary entry that employs vivid imagery derived from your observation of the event.

To help you organize your diary entry, use the following outline.

I. **Beginning**

    A. Set the scene for the event.
    B. Tell when and where the event took place.
    C. Explain how and why you were in a position to witness the event.

II. **Middle**

    A. Choose an organizing principle that suits the event; you may decide to describe the event chronologically or spatially.
    B. Create vivid imagery from sensory details in your description of the event.

III. **End**

    A. Tell why this event made a strong impression on you.
    B. Summarize your thoughts and feelings about the event.

After you complete your diary entry, meet with a peer reviewer to evaluate each other's work and to suggest revisions. Then proofread and edit your entry for errors in spelling, grammar, and punctuation.

Performing

With a small group of classmates, dramatize a section of one of Pepys's diary entries. Use details and dialogue from the entry, but feel free to write additional dialogue of your own. Consider adding a narrator who can reveal Pepys's thoughts.

Pepys's Language and Style

Using Infinitives In his diary, Pepys uses infinitives and infinitive phrases to eliminate unnecessary words; to communicate his goals, wishes, and plans; and to make a clear relationship between actions and purposes or between ideas.

- An **infinitive** is a verb form that is usually preceded by the word *to* (*to go, to laugh*). An infinitive can function as a noun (*The objective is to defeat the other team*), as an adjective (*This is the best car to drive*), or as an adverb (*She was ready to volunteer*).

- An **infinitive phrase** is made up of an infinitive and its modifiers and complements. In a sentence, an infinitive phrase can be a subject, adjective, adverb, object, or predicate nominative.

Consider these examples from the selection:

Part of Speech	Example	Explanation
noun	"Their order was only **to pull** down houses apace"	predicate nominative of subject identifies *order*
adjective	"Lady Batten sent me a cart **to carry** away all my money"	modifies *cart*
adverb	"While at dinner, Mrs. Batelier come **to enquire** after Mr. Woolfe and Stanes"	modifies *come*

Activity Create a chart of your own, listing at least one more example from the selection of an infinitive used as a noun, an adjective, and an adverb. Be sure to explain how each infinitive functions in the sentence.

Revising Check

Split Infinitives Most students have been taught to never split infinitives, which means to insert words between the *to* and the verb. Today, however, most grammar experts consider it acceptable to split infinitives if it makes the sentence clearer and easier to read. Remember that an infinitive is *to* + verb, and a prepositional phrase is *to* + noun. With a partner, review the diary entry you wrote. Check for split infinitives, and decide whether they should be revised.

THE ENGLISH ENLIGHTENMENT AND NEOCLASSICISM

The Orrery, c. 1766. Joseph Wright of Derby. Oil on canvas. Derby Museum and Art Gallery, UK.

"Why, Sir, you find no man, at all intellectual, who is willing to leave London. No, Sir, when a man is tired of London, he is tired of life; for there is in London all that life can afford."

—Samuel Johnson

Swift's Works

MEET JONATHAN SWIFT

Jonathan Swift is generally thought to be the greatest prose writer of the eighteenth century and one of the world's finest satirists. He was a writer whom many considered a misanthrope (one who hates humankind) because his writings were deeply critical of humanity. It was, however, his deep love for humanity that caused him to criticize it, and his dream was to cure the ills of his age through humor.

Swift was born in Dublin, Ireland, of English parents. He had a difficult childhood. Before Swift was born, his father died, leaving the family so poor that his mother was forced to send her infant son to live with an uncle. Swift showed signs of brilliance early on—he could read when he was only three. At the age of six, he was sent to Kilkenny School, which was then the best school in Ireland. However, depression kept Swift from doing well in school, and later he barely graduated from Dublin's Trinity College.

> *"Satire is a sort of glass, wherein beholders do generally discover everybody's face but their own."*
>
> —Jonathan Swift

Early Writing Swift's education as a writer began at the age of twenty-two, when Sir William Temple, a retired diplomat living near London, hired him to be his secretary. Temple was also a noted author, and Swift learned a great deal about writing from him and benefited from exposure to his rich library. Temple helped Swift obtain an M.A. degree from the University of Oxford. Through Temple, Swift also gained the notice of King William III, who suggested that he pursue a career in the Church of England. Swift became an Anglican priest and, while in his late twenties, served in Ireland. However, Swift was unhappy with his post and returned to Temple's employment.

It was in Temple's house that Swift first composed awkward odes in the classical style of the ancient Greek poet Pindar. Then, realizing that he had a gift for humorous prose, he composed two of his acclaimed satires: *A Tale of a Tub*, which ridiculed the extravagances of religion, literature, and academia; and *The Battle of the Books*, which presented a mock debate between ancient and modern authors.

After Temple's death in 1699, Swift returned to Ireland to serve as pastor in a small Protestant parish. His works had caught the eye of other authors, and he was invited to write essays for *The Tatler*, a popular English periodical. These essays and a series of political pamphlets enhanced his fame and showed that he was well informed about current events in both Ireland and England.

Master Satirist In 1713 Queen Anne appointed Swift dean of St. Patrick's Cathedral in Dublin, a post that he continued to hold for more than thirty years until his death. While living in Ireland, he wrote his satirical masterpiece, *Gulliver's Travels*.

Swift died at the age of seventy-eight, bequeathing money to help build a hospital. The generosity of spirit, deep learning, and humane humor that informs his works are his rich legacy to the literary tradition.

Jonathan Swift was born in 1667 and died in 1745.

Literature Online **Author Search** For more about Jonathan Swift, go to www.glencoe.com.

Connecting to the Selections

In these selections, Jonathan Swift uses his writing to spotlight serious social problems. As you read, think about how you might persuade others to do something about problems in your community.

Building Background

In *A Modest Proposal,* first published in Dublin in 1729, Swift draws attention to economic conditions in Ireland. In the early 1700s that country experienced desperate times. Ireland was ruled by England, and English laws limited Ireland's ability to trade with other countries. Ireland could buy certain products only from England and only at high prices. English landlords, who owned much of Ireland's best land, charged exorbitant rents.

The narrator of *Gulliver's Travels* is Lemuel Gulliver, a doctor on a Royal Navy ship who washes up on the shores of several fictional countries. Upon returning to England, he is painfully aware of his country's flaws. The name *Gulliver* is a spoof on the word *gullible,* which means "easily persuaded or tricked."

Setting Purposes for Reading

Big Idea The English Enlightenment and Neoclassicism

As you read, consider how *A Modest Proposal* reflects reason, one of the core values of the Enlightenment.

Literary Element Satire

A Modest Proposal is a **satire**—a literary work that uses irony, humor, and other techniques to point out problems and criticize the people who are causing them. As you read, look for examples of these techniques.

- See Literary Terms Handbook, p. R15.

Literature Online **Interactive Literary Elements Handbook** To review or learn more about the literary elements, go to www.glencoe.com.

Reading Strategy Analyzing Text Structure

When you **analyze text structure,** you identify the pattern of organization that a writer uses to present his or her ideas. As you read, consider why Swift chose problem and solution as the pattern of organization in this essay.

Reading Tip: Taking Notes Use a graphic organizer to record information about the text structure as you read.

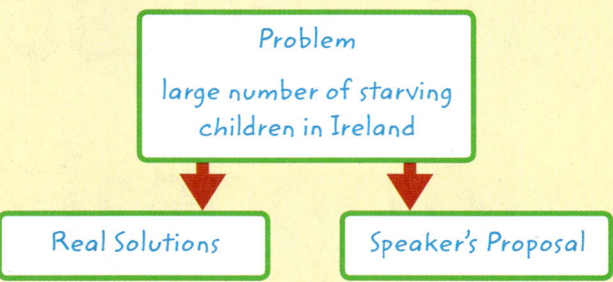

Problem
large number of starving children in Ireland

Real Solutions

Speaker's Proposal

Vocabulary

sustenance (sus′ tə nəns) *n.* food or items that support life; p. 566 *The volunteers gave the hurricane victims sustenance to restore their strength.*

deference (def′ ər əns) *n.* courteous respect; p. 569 *His deep admiration and deference for the teacher showed.*

digress (dī′ gres) *v.* to stray from the main subject; p. 570 *Please stay on the topic and do not digress to other subjects.*

conjecture (kən jek′ chər) *v.* to infer from inconclusive evidence; to guess; p. 575 *The fire chief conjectured that a frayed wire may have caused the blaze.*

magnitude (mag′ nə tōōd′) *n.* greatness of size or extent; p. 580 *A seismograph is used to measure and record the magnitude of earthquakes.*

Vocabulary Tip: Synonyms Words that are the same or nearly the same in meaning are called synonyms.

OBJECTIVES

In studying these selections, you will focus on the following:
- analyzing literary periods
- understanding satire
- analyzing text structure
- understanding parody
- making inferences about theme

A Modest Proposal

Jonathan Swift

Waifs and Strays, 1882. Joseph Clark. Oil on canvas, 102 x 84 cm. Sotheby's, London.

FOR PREVENTING THE CHILDREN OF POOR PEOPLE FROM BEING A *BURTHEN*[1] *TO THEIR PARENTS* OR THE COUNTRY, AND FOR MAKING THEM BENEFICIAL TO THE PUBLIC.

It is a melancholy object to those who walk through this great town,[2] or travel in the country, when they see the *streets,* the *roads,* and *cabin doors* crowded with *beggars* of the female sex, followed by three, four, or six children, *all in rags,* and importuning every passenger for an alms.[3] These *mothers,* instead of being able to work for their honest livelihood, are forced to employ all their time in strolling to beg <u>sustenance</u> for their *helpless infants* who, as they grow up, either turn *thieves* for want[4] of work or leave their *dear Native Country to fight for the Pretender*[5] in Spain or sell themselves to the Barbadoes.[6]

I think it is agreed by all parties that this prodigious number of children, in the arms or on the backs or at the *heels* of their *mothers,* and frequently of their fathers, is, *in the present deplorable state of the kingdom,* a very great additional grievance; and, therefore, whoever could

---

1. A *burthen* is a burden.
2. The *town* referred to here is Dublin, Ireland.
3. [*Importuning . . . alms*] means "asking every passerby for a handout."

Vocabulary

<u>sustenance</u> (sus´ tə nəns) *n.* food or items that support life

4. Here, *want* means "lack."
5. *The Pretender* was a name given to James Edward Stuart (1688–1766), the son of England's deposed king, James II. James Edward had the loyalty and sympathy of the Irish people because he was Roman Catholic.
6. [*Sell . . . Barbadoes*] is a reference to the many Irish people who hoped to escape poverty by traveling to the West Indies. They obtained passage by agreeing to work as indentured servants.

find out a fair, cheap, and easy method of making these children sound and useful members of the commonwealth would deserve so well of the public as to have his statue set up for a preserver of the nation.

But my intention is very far from being confined to provide only for the children of *professed beggars;* it is of a much greater extent and shall take in the whole number of infants at a certain age who are born of parents in effect as little able to support them as those who demand our charity in the streets.

As to my own part, having turned my thoughts for many years upon this important subject, and maturely weighed the several *schemes of other projectors,* I have always found them grossly mistaken in their computation. It is true a child *just dropped from its dam*[7] may be supported by her milk for a solar year with little other nourishment, at most not above the value of two shillings, which the mother may certainly get, or the value in *scraps,* by her lawful occupation of *begging.* And it is exactly at one year old that I propose to provide for them in such a manner as, instead of being a charge upon their *parents* or the *parish,* or *wanting food and raiment*[8] for the rest of their lives, they shall, on the contrary, contribute to the feeding and partly to the clothing of many thousands.

There is likewise another great advantage in my scheme, that it will prevent those *voluntary abortions,* and that horrid practice of *women murdering their bastard children,* alas! too frequent among us, sacrificing the *poor innocent babes,* I doubt, more to avoid the expense than the shame, which would move tears and pity in the most savage and inhuman breast.

---

7. A *dam* is a mother. The word is normally used only to refer to animals.
8. *Raiment* is clothing.

Reading Strategy Analyzing Text Structure *What does this passage tell you about conditions in Ireland?*

Big Idea The English Enlightenment and Neoclassicism *What characteristics does the speaker display in this paragraph?*

Reading Strategy Analyzing Text Structure *What details in this paragraph suggest that poverty is an urgent problem?*

The number of souls in this kingdom being usually reckoned one million and a half, of these I calculate there may be about two hundred thousand couples whose wives are breeders, from which number I subtract thirty thousand couples who are able to maintain their own children, although I apprehend there cannot be so many under *the present distresses of the kingdom,* but this being granted, there will remain a hundred and seventy thousand breeders. I again subtract fifty thousand for those women who miscarry or whose children die by accident or disease within the year. There only remain a hundred and twenty thousand children of poor parents annually born. The question, therefore, is how this number shall be reared and provided for, which, as I have already said, under the present situation of affairs is utterly impossible by all the methods hitherto proposed, for we can *neither employ them in handicraft or agriculture;* we neither build houses (I mean in the country) nor cultivate land. They can very seldom pick up a livelihood *by stealing* till they arrive at six years old, except where they are of towardly parts,[9] although I confess they learn the rudiments much earlier, during which time they can, however, be properly looked upon only as *probationers,*[10] as I have been informed by a principal gentleman in the County of Cavan, who protested to me that he never knew above one or two instances under the age of six, even in a part of the kingdom *so renowned for the quickest proficiency in that art.*

I am assured by our merchants that a boy or a girl, before twelve years old, is no saleable commodity, and even when they come to this age, they will not yield above three pounds, or three pounds and half-a-crown at most, on the Exchange, which cannot turn to account[11] either to the parents or the kingdom, the charge of nutriment and rags having been at least four times that value.

I shall now therefore humbly propose my own thoughts, which I hope will not be liable to the least objection.

---

9. *Towardly parts* means "promising talent."
10. *Probationers* are apprentices.
11. *Turn to account* means "be profitable."

Literary Element Satire *What does the term* breeders *suggest?*

Applicants for Admission to a Casual Ward, 1874. Sir Luke Fildes. Oil on canvas, 54 x 96 cm. Royal Holloway and Bedford New College, Surrey, England.

Viewing the Art: What do the people in the painting have in common with the people described in *A Modest Proposal*?

I have been assured by a very knowing American of my acquaintance in London that a young healthy child, well nursed, is at a year old a most delicious, nourishing, and wholesome food, whether *stewed, roasted, baked,* or *boiled,* and I make no doubt that it will equally serve in a *fricassee,* or a *ragout.*[12]

I do, therefore, humbly offer it to *public consideration* that, of the hundred and twenty thousand children already computed, twenty thousand may be reserved for breed, whereof only one-fourth part to be males, which is more than we allow to *sheep, black cattle,* or *swine;* and my reason is that these children are seldom the fruits of marriage, *a circumstance not much regarded by our savages;* therefore *one male* will be sufficient to serve *four females.* That the remaining hundred thousand may at a year old be offered in sale to the *persons of quality* and *fortune* through the kingdom, always advising the mother to let them suck plentifully of the last month, so as to render them plump and fat for a

good table. A child will make two dishes at an entertainment for friends, and when the family dines alone, the fore or hind quarter will make a reasonable dish and, seasoned with a little pepper or salt, will be very good boiled on the fourth day, especially in *winter.*

I have reckoned upon a medium, that a child just born will weigh twelve pounds and, in a solar year, if tolerably nursed, increaseth to twenty-eight pounds.

I grant this food will be somewhat dear,[13] and therefore very *proper for landlords,* who, as they have already devoured most of the parents, seem to have the best title to the children.

Infants' flesh will be in season throughout the year, but more plentiful in *March,* and a little before and after, for we are told by a grave author,[14] an eminent French physician, that *fish being a prolific diet,* there are more children born in *Roman Catholic countries* about nine months after *Lent* than at any other season; therefore,

12. *Fricassee* and *ragout* are types of meat stews.

Literary Element Satire *What does the speaker imply about his American acquaintance?*

13. Here, *dear* means "expensive."
14. The *grave author* is François Rabelais, a French satirist.

Big Idea The English Enlightenment and Neoclassicism *Despite the speaker's proposal, what details in this paragraph suggest that he is logical?*

reckoning a year after *Lent*, the markets will be more glutted than usual because the number of *Popish*[15] infants is at least three to one in this kingdom, and therefore it will have one other collateral advantage by lessening the number of *Papists*[16] among us.

I have already computed the charge of nursing a beggar's child (in which list I reckon all *cottagers*, *labourers*, and four-fifths of the *farmers*) to be about two shillings *per annum*, rags included, and I believe no gentleman would repine[17] to give ten shillings for the *carcass of a good fat child*, which, as I have said, will make four dishes of excellent nutritive meat when he hath only some particular friend or his own family to dine with him. Thus the Squire will learn to be a good landlord and grow popular among his tenants; the mother will have eight shillings net profit and be fit for work till she produces another child.

Those who are more thrifty (*as I must confess the times require*) may flay[18] the carcass, the skin of which, artificially[19] dressed, will make admirable *gloves for ladies* and *summer boots for fine gentlemen*.

As to our City of Dublin, shambles[20] may be appointed for this purpose in the most convenient parts of it, and butchers, we may be assured, will not be wanting, although I rather recommend buying the children alive and dressing them hot from the knife, as we do *roasting pigs*.

A very worthy person, *a true lover of his country*, and whose virtues I highly esteem, was lately pleased, in discoursing on this matter, to offer a refinement upon my scheme. He said that many gentlemen of this kingdom, having of late destroyed their deer, he conceived that the want of venison might be well supplied by the bodies of young lads and maidens not exceeding fourteen years of age, nor under twelve, so great a number of both sexes in every country being now ready to starve for want of work and service,[21] and these to be disposed of by their parents, if alive, or otherwise by their nearest relations. But with due **deference** to so excellent a friend and so deserving a patriot, I cannot be altogether in his sentiments; for as to the males, my American acquaintance assured me from frequent experience that their flesh was generally tough and lean, like that of our schoolboys, by continual exercise, and their taste disagreeable, and to fatten them would not answer the charge. Then as to the females, it would, I think, with humble submission, *be a loss to the public* because they soon would become breeders themselves. And besides, it is not improbable that some scrupulous people might be apt to censure such a practice (although indeed very unjustly) as a little bordering upon cruelty, which, I confess, hath always been with me the strongest objection against any project, however so well intended.

But in order to justify my friend, he confessed that this expedient[22] was put into his head by the famous *Psalmanazar*,[23] a native of the island Formosa, who came from thence to London above twenty years ago and in conversation told my friend that in his country when any young person happened to be put to death, the executioner sold the carcass to *persons of quality* as a prime dainty, and that in his time, the body of a plump girl of fifteen, who was crucified for an attempt to poison the emperor, was sold to his Imperial *Majesty's Prime Minister of State* and other great *Mandarins*[24] of the Court, *in joints from the gibbet*,[25] at four hundred crowns. Neither, indeed, can I deny that if the same use were made of several plump young girls in this town, who, without

---

15. *Popish* means "Roman Catholic."
16. *Papists* are Roman Catholics.
17. *Repine* means "complain."
18. To *flay* is to strip off the skin.
19. Here, *artificially* means "skillfully."
20. *Shambles* were slaughterhouses.

Literary Element   Satire *What examples of irony do you see in this paragraph?*

---

21. *Service* is work as a servant.
22. *Expedient* means "a means to an end."
23. George *Psalmanazar* was a French impostor who pretended to be from Formosa (now Taiwan) and wrote about incidences of cannibalism there.
24. *Mandarins* are powerful people.
25. *Joints from the gibbet* are pieces of meat from the gallows.

Literary Element   Satire *What is ironic about the speaker's saying that he is against cruel plans?*

Vocabulary

deference (def′ ər əns) *n.* courteous respect

one single groat to their fortunes, cannot stir abroad without a chair and appear at the *playhouse* and *assemblies* in foreign fineries, which they never will pay for, the kingdom would not be the worse.

Some persons of a desponding spirit are in great concern about that vast number of poor people who are aged, diseased, or maimed, and I have been desired to employ my thoughts what course may be taken to ease the nation of so grievous an encumbrance. But I am not in the least pain upon that matter because it is very well known that they are every day *dying* and *rotting* by *cold* and *famine* and *filth* and *vermin* as fast as can be reasonably expected. And as to the younger labourers, they are now in almost as hopeful a condition. They cannot get work and consequently pine away for want of nourishment to a degree that if at any time they are accidentally hired to common labour, they have not strength to perform it; and thus the country and themselves are happily delivered from the evils to come.

I have too long **digressed** and therefore shall return to my subject. I think the advantages by the proposal which I have made are obvious and many, as well as of the highest importance.

For *first*, as I have already observed, it would greatly lessen the *number of Papists*, with whom we are yearly overrun, being the principal breeders of the nation as well as our most dangerous enemies and who stay at home on purpose with a design to *deliver the kingdom to the Pretender*, hoping to take their advantage by the absence of *so many good Protestants*, who have chosen rather to leave their country than stay at home and pay tithes against their conscience to an *Episcopal curate.*[26]

Secondly, the poorer tenants will have something valuable of their own, which by law may be made liable to distress[27] and help to pay their landlord's rent, their corn and cattle being already seized and money a thing unknown.

Thirdly, whereas the maintenance of a hundred thousand children, from two years old and upwards, cannot be computed at less than ten shillings a piece *per annum,* the nation's stock will be thereby increased fifty thousand pounds *per annum,* besides the profit of a new dish introduced to the tables of all *gentlemen of fortune* in the kingdom who have any refinement in taste; and the money will circulate among ourselves, the goods being entirely of our own growth and manufacture.

Fourthly, the constant breeders, besides the gain of eight shillings *sterling per annum* by the sale of their children, will be rid of the charge of maintaining them after the first year.

Fifthly, this food would likewise bring great *custom to taverns,* where the vintners[28] will certainly be so prudent as to procure the best receipts[29] for dressing it to perfection and consequently have their houses frequented by all the *fine gentlemen,* who justly value themselves upon their knowledge in good eating; and a skillful cook, who understands how to oblige his guests, will contrive to make it as expensive as they please.

Sixthly, this would be a great inducement to marriage, which all wise nations have either encouraged by rewards or enforced by laws and penalties. It would increase the care and tenderness of mothers toward their children when they were sure of a settlement for life to the poor babes, provided in some sort by the public to their annual profit instead of expense. We should see an honest emulation[30] among the married women, *which of them could bring the fattest child to the market.* Men would

---

26. *[Protestants . . . curate]* Swift is attacking Protestants who have left Ireland and thus avoided paying tithes to the Anglican Church. A *tithe* is one-tenth of a person's annual income.

27. *Distress* is seizure of property for payment of debt.
28. *Vintners* are wine merchants.
29. Here, *receipts* are recipes.
30. Here, *emulation* means "competition."

Literary Element Satire *How does the language contribute to the irony in this paragraph?*

Vocabulary

digress (dī′ gres) *v.* to stray from the main subject

Reading Strategy Analyzing Text Structure *Whom does the speaker identify as the cause of Ireland's misery?*

Reading Strategy Analyzing Text Structure *How does Swift suggest that the speaker's plan is ridiculous?*

become as *fond* of their wives, during the time of their pregnancy, as they are now of their *mares* in foal, their *cows* in calf, or *sows* when they are ready to farrow,[31] nor offer to beat or kick them (as it is too frequent a practice) for fear of a miscarriage.

Many other advantages might be enumerated: for instance, the addition of some thousand carcasses in our exportation of barrelled beef; the propagation of *swine's flesh* and improvement in the art of making good *bacon,* so much wanted among us by the great destruction of *pigs,* too frequent at our tables, which are no way comparable in taste or magnificence to a well-grown, fat yearling child, which, roasted whole, will make a considerable figure at a *Lord Mayor's feast* or any other public entertainment. But this and many others I omit, being studious of brevity.

Supposing that one thousand families in this city would be constant customers for infants' flesh, besides others who might have it at merry-meetings, particularly weddings and christenings, I compute that Dublin would take off annually about twenty thousand carcasses, and the rest of the kingdom (where probably they will be sold somewhat cheaper) the remaining eighty thousand.

I can think of no one objection that will possibly be raised against this proposal, unless it should be urged that the number of people will be thereby much lessened in the kingdom. This I freely own, and it was indeed one principal design in offering it to the world. I desire the reader will observe that I calculate my remedy *for this one individual Kingdom of IRELAND and for no other that ever was, is, or, I think, ever can be upon earth.* Therefore, let no man talk to me of

Irish Emigrants. John Joseph Barker. Oil on canvas, 255 x 185.2 cm. Victoria Art Gallery, Bath and North East Somerset Council, UK.

other expedients: *of taxing our absentees*[32] *at five shillings a pound; of using neither clothes, nor household furniture, except what is of our own growth and manufacture; of utterly rejecting the materials and instruments that promote foreign luxury; of curing the expensiveness of pride, vanity, idleness, and gaming in our women; of introducing a vein of parsimony,*[33] *prudence, and temperance; of learning to love our Country, wherein we differ even from LAPLANDERS and the inhabitants of TOPINAMBOO;*[34] *of quitting our animosities and factions; . . . of being a little cautious not to sell our country and consciences for nothing; of teaching landlords to have at least one degree of mercy toward*

---

31. *Farrow* means "produce piglets."

---

32. In this context, *absentees* are English people who own land in Ireland but refuse to live on it.
33. *Parsimony* (pär′ sə mō′ nē) is thriftiness.
34. *Topinamboo* was an area in Brazil.

their tenants; lastly, of putting a spirit of honesty, *industry, and skill into our shopkeepers, who, if a resolution could now be taken to buy only our native goods, would immediately unite to cheat and exact upon us in the price, the measure, and the goodness, nor could ever yet be brought to make one fair proposal of just dealing, though often and earnestly invited to it.*

Therefore, I repeat, let no man talk to me of these and the like expedients till he hath at least some glimpse of hope that there will ever be some hearty and sincere attempt to put them in practice.

But as to myself, having been wearied out for many years with offering vain, idle, visionary thoughts, and at length utterly despairing of success, I fortunately fell upon this proposal, which, as it is wholly new, so it hath something solid and real, of no expense and little trouble, full in our own power, and whereby we can incur no danger in *disobliging England*. For this kind of commodity will not bear exportation, the flesh being of too tender a consistence to admit a long continuance in salt, *although perhaps I could name a country which would be glad to eat up our whole nation without it.*

After all, I am not so violently bent upon my own opinion as to reject any offer proposed by wise men, which shall be found equally innocent, cheap, easy, and effectual. But before something of that kind shall be advanced in contradiction to my scheme, and offering a better, I desire the author, or authors, will be pleased maturely to consider two points. *First,* as things now stand, how they will be able to find food and raiment for a hundred thousand useless mouths and backs. And *secondly,* there being a round million of creatures in human figure throughout this kingdom, whose whole subsistence[35] put into a common stock would leave them in debt two millions of pounds *sterling*; adding those who are beggars by profession to the bulk of farmers, cottagers, and labourers with their wives and children, who are beggars in effect; I desire those *politicians* who dislike my overture and may perhaps be so bold to attempt an answer, that they will first ask the parents of these mortals whether they would not at this day think it a great happiness to have been sold for food at a year old in the manner I prescribe and thereby have avoided such a perpetual scene of misfortunes as they have since gone through by the *oppression of landlords*, the impossibility of paying rent without money or trade, the want of common sustenance, with neither house nor clothes to cover them from the inclemencies of the weather, and the most inevitable prospect of entailing[36] the like or greater miseries upon their breed for ever.

I profess in the sincerity of my heart that I have not the least personal interest in endeavouring to promote this necessary work, having no other motive than the *public good of my country, by advancing our trade, providing for infants, relieving the poor, and giving some pleasure to the rich.* I have no children by which I can propose to get a single penny, the youngest being nine years old and my wife past childbearing. ❧

> "I have not the least personal interest in endeavouring to promote this necessary work, having no other motive than the *public good of my country*"

Reading Strategy | Analyzing Text Structure *Why does the speaker include these "other expedients"?*

Reading Strategy | Analyzing Text Structure *To which country does the speaker allude?*

---

35. *Whole subsistence* is all their possessions.
36. *Entailing* means "passing on to the next generation."

RESPONDING AND THINKING CRITICALLY

Respond

1. What were your reactions to the suggestions in *A Modest Proposal*? Explain your answer.

Recall and Interpret

2. (a)What problem does the speaker describe in the opening paragraphs of *A Modest Proposal*? (b)Does the speaker mainly analyze the causes of Ireland's problem or the effects? Why is it to the speaker's advantage not to analyze both?

3. (a)What solution to the problem does the speaker propose? (b)In your opinion does Swift expect readers to take the speaker's solution seriously? Explain.

4. (a)What objection to the proposal does the speaker think readers might raise? How does he answer that objection? (b)In your opinion, does the speaker understand the real reasons that readers might object to his proposal? Explain.

Analyze and Evaluate

5. (a)List six advantages the speaker claims for his proposal. (b)How well does the speaker support these advantages?

6. (a)Summarize at least two other solutions that the speaker lists and rejects. (b)What is **ironic** about the speaker's rejection of these solutions?

7. Evaluate the title *A Modest Proposal.* In your opinion, is it effective or not? Support your evaluation.

Connect

8. **Big Idea** **The English Enlightenment and Neoclassicism** In writing *A Modest Proposal*, Swift adopted a **persona**, a mask or voice through which an author speaks. What Enlightenment characteristics do you see in Swift's persona?

LITERARY ANALYSIS

Literary Element **Satire**

Satire aims to expose the vices, follies, or flaws of a person or group of people by making them seem ridiculous. Satirists' main weapon is humor, which they create through devices such as **exaggeration** and its opposite, **understatement.** In *A Modest Proposal,* for example, Swift exaggerates the economists' indifference toward the Irish and understates the impact of his proposal by his use of the word *modest.* By creating a narrator who supports a position opposite to his own, Swift also employs **irony,** another common satiric device.

1. Why might satire be an effective instrument for social change?

2. What other examples of exaggeration and understatement can you find in *A Modest Proposal*? Whom or what do these statements ridicule?

3. What is ironic about the conclusion of *A Modest Proposal*?

Review: Author's Purpose

As you learned on page 280, **author's purpose** refers to an author's intent in writing a literary work. An author typically writes to accomplish one or more of the following purposes: to persuade, to instruct, to inform or explain, to entertain, to describe, or to tell a story.

Partner Activity Meet with a partner to discuss Swift's purpose in writing *A Modest Proposal*. First, in a few words, describe the tone of the work; then quote a specific statement from the work to illustrate your description. Conclude your analysis by briefly explaining how the tone of the pamphlet helps it to fulfill its purpose.

1. What was Swift's purpose in writing this essay?

2. How does the tone of the pamphlet help fulfill that purpose?

Reading Strategy Analyzing Text Structure

The structure of *A Modest Proposal* is fairly straightforward. The speaker describes the problem, states and supports a proposal, refutes objections, and dismisses alternate solutions. Ironically, Swift really favors the alternate solutions that his speaker dismisses. Review the graphic organizer you created on page 565 and then answer the questions below.

1. What do the speaker's alternate solutions have in common?

2. Why do you think Swift used problem and solution as the method of organization in this essay?

Vocabulary Practice

Practice with Synonyms Choose the correct synonym for each vocabulary word below. Use a dictionary if you need help.

1. **sustenance**
   a. livelihood   **b.** neglect   **c.** shelter
2. **deference**
   a. dishonor   **b.** obedience   **c.** respect
3. **digress**
   a. deviate   **b.** maintain   **c.** insist

Academic Vocabulary

Here are two words from the vocabulary list on page R82.

perceive (pər sēv′) *v.* to become aware of; apprehend

period (pēr′ ē əd) *n.* an interval of time between one event and another

Practice and Apply

1. How does Swift **perceive** the English landlords in this essay?
2. Which characteristics of the **period** does this essay reflect?

Literature Online **Web Activities** For eFlashcards, Selection Quick Checks, and other Web activities, go to www.glencoe.com.

Writing About Literature

Evaluate Author's Craft Swift wrote *A Modest Proposal* in reaction to unjust English economic policies. The essay is highly satirical, causing some readers to misinterpret Swift's message and take his words at face value. What strategies does Swift use to let his readers know his intentions? In a brief essay, explain how Swift achieves his purpose by examining the essay's diction and style, paying special attention to the author's use of italics. As you draft, follow the plan below to help organize your essay.

After you complete your draft, meet with a peer reviewer to evaluate each other's work and to suggest revisions. Then proofread and edit your draft for errors in spelling, grammar, and punctuation.

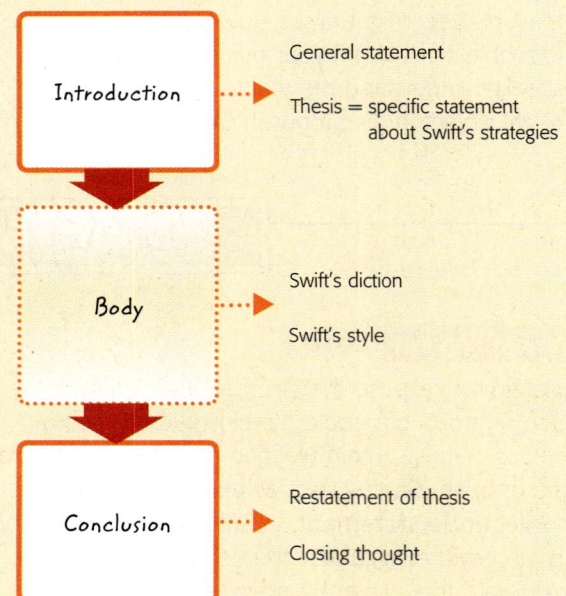

Introduction → General statement
Thesis = specific statement about Swift's strategies

Body → Swift's diction
Swift's style

Conclusion → Restatement of thesis
Closing thought

Learning for Life

Create a pamphlet in which you propose a solution to a problem facing your community. Begin with a short description of the problem and its negative effects, present the solution and its advantages, and then describe any objections readers might have and answer them. Like Swift, be satiric in your writing. Share your proposal with others in your class, and ask whether your proposal persuaded them that your solution would work.

Literary Element Parody

A **parody** is a humorous imitation of a literary work that aims to point out the work's shortcomings. Parodies usually imitate some defining characteristic of the work's style. *Gulliver's Travels* is in part a parody of early eighteenth-century travel books, which delighted in describing exotic places and people.

- See Literary Terms Handbook, p. R13.

Reading Strategy Making Inferences About Theme

Inferring is using your reason and experience to guess at what an author does not say directly. Most works have an **implied theme**, which you must infer by considering all the elements of a story and asking what message about life the author conveys.

Reading Tip: Identifying Clues As you read, look for clues about the theme. Notice descriptions, dialogue, events, and relationships that might tell you something about the author's message.

from Gulliver's Travels Jonathan Swift

from A Voyage to Lilliput

I lay down on the grass, which was very short and soft, where I slept sounder than ever I remember to have done in my life, and as I reckoned, above nine hours; for when I awaked, it was just daylight. I attempted to rise, but was not able to stir: for as I happened to lie on my back, I found my arms and legs were strongly fastened on each side to the ground; and my hair, which was long and thick, tied down in the same manner. I likewise felt several slender ligatures across my body, from my armpits to my thighs. I could only look upwards; the sun began to grow hot, and the light offended my eyes. I heard a confused noise about me, but in the posture I lay, could see nothing except the sky.

In a little time I felt something alive moving on my left leg, which advancing gently forward over my breast, came almost up to my chin; when bending my eyes downwards as much as I could, I perceived it to be a human creature not six inches high, with a bow and arrow in his hands, and a quiver at his back. In the meantime, I felt at least forty more of the same kind (as I **conjectured**) following the first. I was in the utmost astonishment and roared so loud that they all ran back in a fright; and some of them, as I was afterwards told, were hurt with the falls they got by leaping from my sides upon the ground. However, they soon returned; and

Vocabulary

conjecture (kən jek′ chər) *v.* to infer from inconclusive evidence; to guess

one of them, who ventured so far as to get a full sight of my face, lifting up his hands and eyes by way of admiration, cried out in a shrill but distinct voice, *Hekinah Degul.* The others repeated the same words several times, but I then knew not what they meant. I lay all this while, as the reader may believe, in great uneasiness. At length, struggling to get loose, I had the fortune to break the strings and wrench out the pegs that fastened my left arm to the ground; for by lifting it up to my face, I discovered the methods they had taken to bind me; and at the same time, with a violent pull, which gave me excessive pain, I a little loosened the strings that tied down my hair on the left side; so that I was just able to turn my head about two inches. But the creatures ran off a second time before I could seize them; whereupon there was a great shout in a very shrill accent; and after it ceased, I heard one of them cry aloud, *Tolgo Phonac;* when in an instant I felt above a hundred arrows discharged on my left hand, which pricked me like so many needles; and besides, they shot another flight into the air, as we do bombs in Europe. . . .

I had reason to believe I might be a match for the greatest armies they could bring against me if they were all of the same size with him that I saw. But fortune disposed otherwise of me. When the people observed I was quiet, they discharged no more arrows; but by the noise increasing, I knew their numbers were greater; and about four yards from me, over against my right ear, I heard a knocking for above an hour, like people at work; when turning my head that way, as well as the pegs and strings would permit me, I saw a stage erected about a foot and a half from the ground, capable of holding four of the inhabitants, with two or three ladders to mount it: from

> "In an instant I felt above a hundred arrows discharged on my left hand, which pricked me like so many needles"

whence one of them, who seemed to be a person of quality,[1] made me a long speech, whereof I understood not one syllable. . . .

He appeared to be of a middle age and taller than any of the other three who attended him, whereof one was a page,[2] who held up his train[3] and seemed to be somewhat longer than my middle finger. The other two stood one on each side to support him. He acted every part of an orator; and I could observe many periods of threatenings and others of promises, pity, and kindness.

I answered in a few words, but in the most submissive manner, lifting up my left hand and both my eyes to the sun, as calling him for a witness; and being almost famished with hunger, having not eaten a morsel for some hours before I left the ship, I found the demands of nature so strong upon me that I could not forbear showing my impatience (perhaps against the strict rules of decency) by putting my finger frequently on my mouth to signify that I wanted food. The *Hurgo* (for so they call a great lord, as I afterwards learned) understood me very well. He descended from the stage and commanded that several ladders should be applied to my sides, on which above a hundred of the inhabitants mounted and walked towards my mouth, laden with baskets full of meat, which had been provided and sent thither by the King's orders upon the first intelligence he received of me. I observed there was the flesh of several animals but could not distinguish them by the taste. There were shoulders, legs, and loins shaped like those of mutton, and very well dressed, but smaller than the wings of a lark. I ate them by two or three at a mouthful and took three loaves at a time, about the bigness of musket

---

1. Here, a *person of quality* is a nobleman.
2. A *page* is a court servant.
3. Here, a *train* is a long extension at the back of a robe that trails behind the wearer.

Big Idea **The English Enlightenment and Neoclassicism** *What does Swift suggest about the Europeans?*

Reading Strategy **Making Inferences About Theme** *What does the fact that a stage was erected suggest about the "person of quality"?*

Gulliver is tied down by the people of Lilliput, 1726. From *The Coloured Picture Book for the Nursery.*

bullets. They supplied me as fast as they could, showing a thousand marks of wonder and astonishment at my bulk and appetite. . . .

Because the reader may perhaps be curious to have some idea of the style and manner of expression peculiar to that people, as well as to know the articles upon which I recovered my liberty, I have made a translation of the whole instrument, word for word, as near as I was able, which I here offer to the public.

GOLBASTO MOMAREN EVLAME GURDILO SHEFIN MULLY ULLY GUE, most mighty Emperor of Lilliput, delight and terror of the universe, whose dominions extend five thousand *blustrugs* (about twelve miles in circumference) to the extremities of the globe; monarch of all monarchs, taller than the sons of men; whose feet press down to the center, and whose head strikes against the sun; at whose nod the princes of the earth shake their knees; pleasant as the spring, comfortable as the summer, fruitful as autumn, dreadful as winter. His most sublime Majesty proposeth to the Man-Mountain, lately arrived at our celestial dominions, the following articles, which by a solemn oath he shall be obliged to perform.

First, the Man-Mountain shall not depart from our dominions without our license under our great seal.

Secondly, he shall not presume to come into our metropolis without our express order, at which time the inhabitants shall have two hours warning to keep within their doors.

Thirdly, the said Man-Mountain shall confine his walks to our principal high roads and not offer to walk or lie down in a meadow or field of corn.

Fourthly, as he walks the said roads, he shall take the utmost care not to trample upon the bodies of any of our loving subjects, their horses, or carriages; nor take any of our said subjects into his hands without their own consent.

Fifthly, if an express require extraordinary dispatch, the Man-Mountain shall be obliged to carry in his pocket the messenger and horse, a six days' journey once in every moon, and return the said messenger back (if so required) safe to our Imperial Presence.

Sixthly, he shall be our ally against our enemies in the island of Blefuscu and do his utmost to destroy their fleet, which is now preparing to invade us.

Seventhly, that the said Man-Mountain shall, at his times of leisure, be aiding and assisting to our workmen, in helping to raise certain great stones, towards covering the wall of the principal park and other of our royal buildings.

Eighthly, that the said Man-Mountain shall, in two moons' time, deliver in an exact survey of the circumference of our dominions, by a computation of his own paces round the coast.

Lastly, that upon his solemn oath to observe all the above articles, the said Man-Mountain shall have a daily allowance of meat and drink, sufficient for the support of 1,728 of our subjects, with free access to our Royal Person and other marks of our favor. Given at our Palace at Belfaborac the twelfth day of the ninety-first moon of our reign.

I swore and subscribed to these articles with great cheerfulness and content, although some of them were not so honorable as I could have wished. . . .

One morning, about a fortnight[4] after I had obtained my liberty, Reldresal, Principal Secretary (as they style him) of Private Affairs, came to my house attended only by one servant. He ordered his coach to wait at a distance and desired I would give him an hour's audience, which I readily consented to on account of his quality and personal merits, as well as of the many good offices he had done me during my solicitations at court. I offered to lie down that he might the more conveniently reach my ear, but he chose rather to let me hold him in my hand during our conversation. He began with compliments on my liberty, said he might pretend to some merit in it, but, however, added that if it had not been for the present situation of things at court, perhaps I might not have obtained it so soon. "For," said he, "as flourishing a condition as we appear to be in to foreigners, we labor under two mighty evils: a violent faction at home and the danger of an invasion by a most potent enemy from abroad. As to the first, you are to understand that for about seventy moons past there have been two struggling parties in this empire, under the names of Tramecksan and Slamecksan, from the high and low heels on their shoes, by which they distinguish themselves. It is alleged, indeed, that the high heels are most agreeable to our ancient constitution: but however this be, his Majesty hath determined to make use of only low heels in the administration of the government and all offices in the gift of the Crown, as you cannot but observe; and particularly, that his Majesty's Imperial heels are lower at least by a *drurr* than any of his court (*drurr* is a measure about the fourteenth part of an inch). The animosities[5] between these two parties run so high that they will neither eat nor drink nor talk with each other. We compute the Tramecksan, or High-Heels, to exceed us in number; but the power is wholly on our side. We apprehend[6] his Imperial Highness, the Heir to the Crown, to have some tendency toward the High-Heels; at least we can plainly discover one of his heels higher than the other, which gives him a hobble in his gait. Now, in the midst of these intestine[7] disquiets, we are threatened with an invasion from the island of Blefuscu, which is the other great empire of the universe, almost as large and powerful as this of his Majesty. For as to what we have heard you affirm, that there are other kingdoms and states in the world inhabited by human creatures as large as yourself, our philosophers are in much doubt and would rather conjecture that you dropped from the moon or one of the stars because it is certain that an hundred mortals of your bulk would, in a short time, destroy all the fruits and cattle of his Majesty's dominions. Besides, our histories of six thousand moons make no mention of any other regions than the two great empires of Lilliput and Blefuscu, which two mighty powers have, as I was going to tell you,

---

4. A *fortnight* is two weeks.

5. *Animosity* means "a feeling of hostility or hatred."
6. *Apprehend* means "to perceive."
7. *Intestine*, here, means "internal."

Literary Element Parody *What might Swift be parodying with this lengthy document?*

Big Idea The English Enlightenment and Neoclassicism *What does Swift imply about political parties in England, namely the Tories and the Whigs?*

Reading Strategy Making Inferences About Theme *What generalization is Swift making about people when he has the Lilliputian philosophers doubt Gulliver's claims?*

been engaged in a most obstinate war for six and thirty moons past. It began upon the following occasion. It is allowed on all hands that the primitive way of breaking eggs before we eat them was upon the larger end. But his present Majesty's grandfather, while he was a boy, going to eat an egg and breaking it according to the ancient practice, happened to cut one of his fingers. Whereupon the Emperor his father published an edict,[8] commanding all his subjects, upon great penalties, to break the smaller end of their eggs. The people so highly resented this law that, our histories tell us, there have been six rebellions raised on that account; wherein one Emperor lost his life, and another his crown. These civil commotions were constantly fomented[9] by the monarchs of Blefuscu; and when they were quelled,[10] the exiles always fled for refuge to that empire. It is computed that eleven thousand persons have, at several times, suffered death rather than submit to break their eggs at the smaller end. Many hundred large volumes have been published upon this controversy: but the books of the Big-Endians have been long forbidden, and the whole party rendered incapable by law of holding employments. During the course of these troubles, the emperors of Blefuscu did frequently expostulate by their ambassadors, accusing us of making a schism[11] in religion by offending against a fundamental doctrine of our great prophet Lustrog, in the fifty-fourth chapter of the Brundrecal (which is their Alcoran).[12] This, however, is thought to be a mere strain upon the text, for the words are these: *that all true believers shall break their eggs at the convenient end;* and which is the convenient end seems, in my humble opinion, to be left to every man's conscience, or at least in the power of the chief magistrate to determine. Now the Big-Endian exiles have found so much credit in the Emperor of Blefuscu's court, and so much private assistance and encouragement from their party here at home, that a bloody war has been carried on between the two empires for six and thirty

Gulliver capturing the fleet of the Blefuscudians, enemies of his Lilliputian hosts, 1911. A. E. Jackson. Chromolithograph from an edition of Jonathan Swift's *Gulliver's Travels* (London & New York, 1911). Private collection.

moons with various success, during which time we have lost forty capital ships and a much greater number of smaller vessels, together with thirty thousand of our best seamen and soldiers; and the damage received by the enemy is reckoned to be somewhat greater than ours. However, they have now equipped a numerous fleet and are just preparing to make a descent upon us, and his Imperial Majesty, placing great confidence in your valor and strength, has commanded me to lay this account of his affairs before you."

I desired the Secretary to present my humble duty to the Emperor and to let him know that

---

8. An *edict* is an official command.
9. *Fomented* means "incited."
10. *Quelled* means "subdued."
11. A *schism* is a division.
12. The *Alcoran* is the Koran, Islam's sacred text.

Big Idea The English Enlightenment and Neoclassicism *How does Swift's portrayal of Reldresal satirize government officials? Consider Reldresal's tone in this passage.*

I thought it would not become me, who was a foreigner, to interfere with parties; but I was ready, with the hazard of my life, to defend his person and state against all invaders.

After leaving Lilliput, Gulliver goes on a second voyage, which ends with his being marooned in Brobdingnag. Everything in this imaginary country is twelve times larger than normal. As a result, Gulliver learns firsthand what it is like to feel small.

from
A Voyage to Brobdingnag

It is the custom that every Wednesday (which, as I have before observed, was their Sabbath) the King and Queen, with the royal issue of both sexes, dine together in the apartment of his Majesty, to whom I was now become a favorite; and at these times my little chair and table were placed at his left hand, before one of the saltcellars. This prince took a pleasure in conversing with me, inquiring into the manners, religion, laws, government, and learning of Europe; wherein I gave him the best account I was able. His apprehension was so clear, and his judgment so exact, that he made very wise reflections and observations upon all I said. But, I confess, that after I had been a little too copious[13] in talking of my own beloved country, of our trade, and wars by sea and land, of our schisms in religion, and parties in the state; the prejudices of his education prevailed so far that he could not forbear taking me up in his right hand and, stroking me gently with the other, after a hearty fit of laughing, asked me whether I were a Whig or a Tory.[14] Then turning to his first minister, who waited behind him with a white staff, near as tall as the mainmast of the *Royal Sovereign*, he observed how contemptible a thing was human grandeur, which could be mimicked by such

Visual Vocabulary
The *Royal Sovereign* was one of the largest British warships of Swift's day.

diminutive insects as I. "And yet," said he, "I dare engage, those creatures have their titles and distinctions of honor, they contrive little nests and burrows that they call houses and cities; they make a figure in dress and equipage; they love, they fight, they dispute, they cheat, they betray." And thus he continued on, while my color came and went several times with indignation to hear our noble country, the mistress of arts and arms, the scourge of France, the arbitress of Europe, the seat of virtue, piety, honor, and truth, the pride and envy of the world, so contemptuously treated.

But as I was not in a condition to resent injuries, so, upon mature thoughts, I began to doubt whether I were injured or no. For after having been accustomed several months to the sight and converse of this people and observed every object upon which I cast my eyes to be of proportionable **magnitude,** the horror I had first conceived from their bulk and aspect was so far worn off that if I had then beheld a company of English lords and ladies in their finery and birthday clothes, acting their several parts in the most courtly manner of strutting and bowing and prating,[15] to say the truth, I should have been strongly tempted to laugh as much at them as this King and his grandees[16] did at me. . . .

He was perfectly astonished with the historical account I gave him of our affairs during the last century, protesting it was only a heap of conspiracies, rebellions, murders, massacres, revolutions, banishments, the very worst effects that avarice,[17] faction, hypocrisy, perfidiousness,[18] cruelty, rage, madness, hatred, envy, lust, malice, and ambition could produce.

---

15. *Prating* means "chattering" or "babbling."
16. *Grandees* are important people.
17. *Avarice* is greed.
18. *Perfidiousness* is treachery.

Reading Strategy Making Inferences About Theme
What is ironic about this passage?

Literary Element Parody *What advantage does Swift derive by using Gulliver as his persona in this parody?*

Vocabulary

magnitude (mag′ nə tōōd) *n.* greatness of size or extent

---

13. Here, *copious* means "wordy."
14. A *Whig* and a *Tory* were members of the two main political parties in Britain.

Gulliver walking about on the table at the inn as Glumdalcitch, his "little" Brobdingnagian nurse, commanded him, 1911. A. E. Jackson. Chromolithograph from an edition of Jonathan Swift's *Gulliver's Travels* (London & New York, 1911).

Viewing the Art: From their facial expressions, how do you think the Brobdingnagians feel about Gulliver?

His Majesty in another audience was at the pains to recapitulate the sum of all I had spoken; compared the questions he made with the answers I had given; then taking me into his hands, and stroking me gently, delivered himself in these words, which I shall never forget, nor the manner he spoke them in. My little friend Grildrig, you have made a most admirable panegyric[19] upon your country. You have clearly proved that ignorance, idleness, and vice are the proper ingredients for qualifying a legislator; that laws are best explained, interpreted, and applied by those whose interest and abilities lie in perverting, confounding, and eluding them. I observe among you

some lines of an institution, which in its original might have been tolerable; but these half erased, and the rest wholly blurred and blotted by corruptions. It doth not appear from all you have said how any one perfection is required towards the procurement of any one station among you; much less that men are ennobled on account of their virtue, that priests are advanced for their piety or learning, soldiers for their conduct or valor, judges for their integrity, senators for the love of their country, or counselors for their wisdom. As for yourself (continued the King), who have spent the greatest part of your life in traveling, I am well disposed to hope you may hitherto have escaped many vices of your country. But, by what I have gathered from your own relation, and the answers I have with much pains wrung and extorted from you, I cannot but conclude the bulk of your natives to be the most pernicious[20] race of little odious vermin that nature ever suffered to crawl upon the surface of the earth.

Nothing but an extreme love of truth could have hindered me from concealing this part of my story. It was in vain to discover my resentments, which were always turned into ridicule; and I was forced to rest with patience while my noble and most beloved country was so injuriously treated. I am heartily sorry as any of my readers can possibly be that such an occasion was given; but this prince happened to be so curious and inquisitive upon every particular that it could not consist either with gratitude or good manners to refuse giving him what satisfaction I was able. Yet thus much I may be allowed to say in my own vindication, that I artfully eluded many of his questions and gave to every point a more favorable turn by many degrees than the strictness of truth would allow. For I have always born that laudable partiality to my own country, which Dionysius Halicarnassensis[21] with so much justice recommends to a historian. I would hide the frailties and deformities of my

---

19. A *panegyric* (pa´ nə jir´ ik) is a speech of praise.

20. *Pernicious* means "destructive" or "malicious."
21. *Dionysius Halicarnassensis* was a Greek writer who lived in Rome and tried to persuade the conquered Greeks to submit to the Romans. Swift is being ironic.

Big Idea **The English Enlightenment and Neoclassicism** *In what way is the king a man of reason?*

political mother and place her virtues and beauties in the most advantageous light. This was my sincere endeavor in those many discourses I had with that mighty monarch, although it unfortunately failed of success. . . .

But great allowances should be given to a King who lives wholly secluded from the rest of the world and must therefore be altogether unacquainted with the manners and customs that most prevail in other nations, the want of which knowledge will ever produce many prejudices and a certain narrowness of thinking, from which we and the politer countries of Europe are wholly exempted. And it would be hard indeed if so remote a prince's notions of virtue and vice were to be offered as a standard for all mankind.

To confirm what I have now said and further to show the miserable effects of a confined education, I shall here insert a passage which will hardly obtain belief. In hopes to ingratiate myself further into his Majesty's favor, I told him of an invention discovered between three and four hundred years ago to make a certain powder, into a heap of which the smallest spark of fire falling, would kindle the whole in a moment, although it were as big as a mountain, and make it all fly up in the air together, with a noise and agitation greater than thunder. That a proper quantity of this powder rammed into a hollow tube of brass or iron, according to its bigness, would drive a ball of iron or lead with such violence and speed as nothing was able to sustain its force. That the largest balls thus discharged would not only destroy whole ranks of an army at once but batter the strongest walls to the ground, sink down ships with a thousand men in each to the bottom of the sea; and when linked together by a chain, would cut through masts and rigging, divide hundreds of bodies in the middle, and lay all waste before them. That we often put this powder into large hollow balls of iron and discharged them by an engine into some city we were besieging, which would rip up the pavements, tear the houses to pieces, burst and throw splinters on every side, dashing out the brains of all who came near. That I knew the ingredients very well, which were cheap and common; I understood the manner of compounding them and could direct his workmen how to make those tubes of a size proportionable to all other things in his Majesty's kingdom, and the largest need not be above two hundred feet long; twenty or thirty of which tubes, charged with the proper quantity of powder and balls, would batter down the walls of the strongest town in his dominions in a few hours or destroy the whole metropolis if ever it should pretend to dispute his absolute commands. This I humbly offered to his Majesty as a small tribute of acknowledgment in return of so many marks that I had received of his royal favor and protection.

> "The King was struck with horror at the description I had given of those terrible engines and the proposal I had made."

The King was struck with horror at the description I had given of those terrible engines and the proposal I had made. He was amazed how so impotent and groveling an insect as I (these were his expressions) could entertain such inhuman ideas and in so familiar a manner as to appear wholly unmoved at all the scenes of blood and desolation, which I had painted as the common effects of those destructive machines, whereof, he said, some evil genius, enemy to mankind, must have been the first contriver. As for himself, he protested that although few things delighted him so much as new discoveries in art or in nature, yet he would rather lose half his kingdom than be privy to such a secret, which he commanded me, as I valued my life, never to mention any more. ❧

Reading Strategy Making Inferences About Theme
What is ironic about Gulliver making allowances for the king?

Reading Strategy Making Inferences About Theme
How does Swift expect the reader to react to Gulliver's description of gunpowder?

RESPONDING AND THINKING CRITICALLY

Respond

1. Which country do you prefer, Lilliput or Brobdingnag? Why?

Recall and Interpret

2. (a)Describe the Lilliputians' initial reaction to Gulliver. (b)Why do they treat him as they do? What does their behavior suggest about human nature?

3. (a)Summarize the Lilliputian emperor's command concerning eggs and the controversy it causes. (b)What point about human behavior does Swift make in his description of the Lilliputian egg controversy?

4. (a)What does the king of Brobdingnag think of the English? (b)Gulliver is physically smaller than the king of Brobdingnag and his people. In what other sense is Gulliver shown to be "small"?

Analyze and Evaluate

5. (a)What does the king's reaction to the technology Gulliver describes suggest about the Brobdingnagians? (b)What does the king's reaction suggest about people who use the technology?

6. Do you believe that Swift shared the views of the Lilliputians, of the Brobdingnagians, or of Gulliver? Explain.

7. What parts of Gulliver's experiences did you find humorous? What techniques did Swift use to create this humor?

Connect

8. **Big Idea** **The English Enlightenment and Neoclassicism** Satire is a literary form that flourished during the Enlightenment. In your opinion, is Swift's use of satire more or less effective than simple, direct criticism? Why?

YOU'RE THE CRITIC: Different Viewpoints

Was Swift a Misanthrope?

Jonathan Swift has often been accused of hating people in general because of his savage satires. But was he really a misanthrope? Read the two excerpts of literary criticism below. A. L. Rowse published a biography of Swift in 1975. William Makepeace Thackeray, who lived in the nineteenth century, was born too late to have known Swift, but he had strong opinions about him.

"What Swift detested was the nonsensical belief that men as a whole were rational—their behavior showed that this was not true. At the utmost, they were capable of reason; then why don't they act on it more? . . . The evidences of men's refusal to use what reason they have got were all round him, especially in Ireland, and Swift was right to highlight the evidences of their idiocy. He was a moralist and a preacher: he was right to bring home to them again and again the consequences of their folly— how otherwise can, or will, the fools learn?"

—A. L. Rowse

"If you had been his inferior in [talent or ability] . . . , his equal in mere social station, he would have bullied, scorned, and insulted you; if, undeterred by his great reputation, you had met him like a man, he would have quailed before you, and not had the pluck to reply, and gone home, and years after written a foul epigram about you—watched for you in a sewer, and come out to assail you with a coward's blow and a dirty bludgeon."

—William Makepeace Thackeray

Group Activity Discuss the following questions with classmates. Refer to the criticisms and cite evidence from Swift's work or his biography on page 564.

1. (a)What is the difference of opinion between Thackeray and Rowse? (b)Which critic seems closest to understanding Swift? Explain.

2. In your opinion, was Swift a misanthrope or was he a realist about humans? Explain.

Literary Element **Parody**

A parodist imitates some defining feature of a work, such as its style or subject matter, exaggerating it for comic effect. *Gulliver's Travels,* Swift's **parody** of travel books, even included maps of Gulliver's imaginary voyages and a picture and biography of Lemuel Gulliver, surgeon on a merchant ship.

1. What features of government documents does Swift parody in the Lilliputians' eight commandments to Gulliver?

2. (a)In your opinion, does Swift romanticize the Lilliputians and Brobdingnagians? (b)Why might Swift have chosen to portray them as he does?

Review: Irony

As you learned on page 116, **irony** is a contrast or discrepancy between expectation and reality. **Verbal irony** exists when a person says one thing while meaning another; **situational irony** exists when the outcome of a situation is the opposite of what someone expected.

Partner Activity Meet with another classmate to discuss Swift's use of irony in *Gulliver's Travels.* Working with your partner, create a web diagram like the one below and fill it in with an example of each kind of irony.

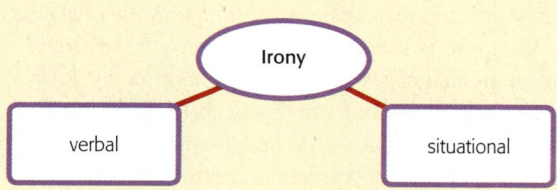

Portrait of Jonathan Swift. Francis Bindon. Oil on canvas. Royal Hospital Chelsea, London.

Reading Strategy **Making Inferences About Theme**

It is important to distinguish the topics of a work from its **theme** or themes. *Gulliver's Travels* includes many topics, such as human folly, corruption, politics, and several others. A **theme** is the message a writer shares about one of a work's topics. For example, "It is absurd for humans to take pride in gunpowder" is one of Swift's themes, or messages.

1. How would you state another important theme of *Gulliver's Travels*?

2. To support your theme, list three important details from these excerpts and the inferences about the theme that you drew from them.

Vocabulary **Practice**

Practice with Synonyms Identify the correct synonym for each vocabulary word below. Use a dictionary if you need help.

1. **conjecture**
    a. guess   **b.** doubt   **c.** verify

2. **magnitude**
    a. level   **b.** size   **c.** capacity

Academic Vocabulary

Here are two words from the vocabulary list on page R82.

function (fungk′ shən) *n.* specific role or duty

tradition (trə dish′ ən) *n.* custom or behavior followed by a people from generation to generation

Practice and Apply

1. What is the **function** of the Principal Secretary of Private Affairs in *Gulliver's Travels*?

2. How concerned with **tradition** are the Lilliputians?

Writing About Literature

Evaluate Author's Craft Creating a persona can be an effective way for an author to express opinions without revealing whether he or she agrees with them. If questioned, an author can always plead innocent to the most outrageous views expressed by the persona or another character. How effective is Gulliver as a persona for conveying Swift's satiric views? Write a brief essay stating your position and defending your evaluation with evidence from the selection.

As you draft, follow the writing path shown here to help you organize your essay.

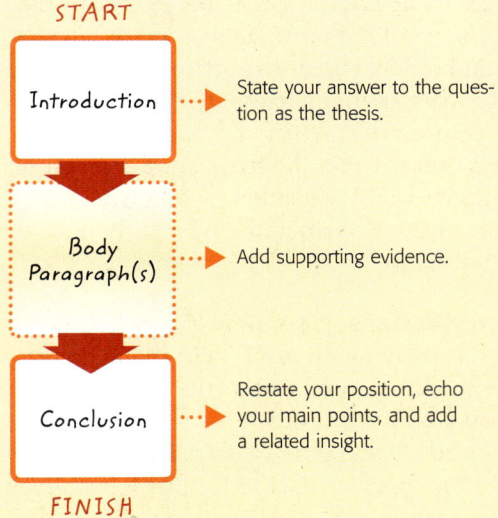

START

Introduction ····▶ State your answer to the question as the thesis.

Body Paragraph(s) ····▶ Add supporting evidence.

Conclusion ····▶ Restate your position, echo your main points, and add a related insight.

FINISH

After you complete your draft, meet with a peer reviewer to evaluate each other's work and to suggest revisions. Then proofread and edit your draft for errors in spelling, grammar, and punctuation.

Listening and Speaking

The story of *Gulliver's Travels* has been made into films and animated cartoons. Rent a movie or cartoon version of *Gulliver's Travels* and take notes on its presentation of Gulliver's experiences in Lilliput and Brobdingnag. How does the video presentation differ from what you expected based on your reading? Use your notes to write a brief review, and then present it to your class.

Literature Online Web Activities For eFlashcards, Selection Quick Checks, and other Web activities, go to www.glencoe.com.

Swift's Language and Style

Using Formal Language for Humorous Effect The language in *Gulliver's Travels* is extremely formal, with serious and dignified **diction**, or word choice. Writers of satire sometimes use lofty language to create humorous effects. For example, in the following passage Swift's language conveys the pretensions of the Lilliputian emperor:

"First, the Man-Mountain shall not depart from our dominions without our license under our great seal.

Secondly, he shall not presume to come into our metropolis without our express order, at which time the inhabitants shall have two hours warning to keep within their doors. . . .

Eighthly, that the said Man-Mountain shall, in two moons' time, deliver in an exact survey of the circumference of our dominions, by a computation of his own paces round the coast."

The chart below lists examples of lofty expressions in this passage and simple ones that might replace them:

Lofty Expressions	Simple Expressions
depart from our dominions	leave the country
not presume to come into our metropolis without our express order	not try to visit our city without permission
the inhabitants	the people

Activity Add other examples of lofty expressions in this passage to the chart above. For each one, substitute a simple phrase.

Revising Check

The Right Word Diction, or word choice, is important to consider when revising your own writing. With a partner, go through your essay to evaluate the author's craft and look for places where simpler language would strengthen your writing by making it clearer and more direct. Revise your draft to improve the diction.

Pope's Works

MEET ALEXANDER POPE

Although Alexander Pope became the first English writer to earn his living solely by writing literature, the odds were against him from birth. He was chronically ill from a young age and received little formal education. In addition, he was Roman Catholic when England was ruled by Protestants. Yet, Pope overcame his obstacles to become one of England's most respected satiric poets and quotable authors.

> "Nor fame I slight, nor her favors call;
> She comes unlook'd for, if she comes
>   at all."

> —Alexander Pope

Overcoming Odds Though a literary giant, Pope was well under five feet tall. Tuberculosis of the spine stunted his growth in childhood, leaving him disabled and an object of ridicule for the rest of his life. As a Catholic, Pope was barred from attending England's universities or holding a government office—the source of income for many writers of the time. He read widely on his own, however, perfecting his language skills by translating foreign works into English. Encouraged by his father, Pope developed an early talent for poetry. While still a teenager, he wrote a series of nature poems, his "Pastorals," which were solicited for publication by the time he was eighteen.

At twenty-three, Pope wrote *An Essay on Criticism.* The poem earned him some powerful enemies, as many critics were outraged that such a young writer would dare attack the literary establishment in print. However, the simple language and learned observations of the poem impressed many influential writers including Joseph Addison, Richard Steele, and Jonathan Swift. The next year, Pope followed this early success with another:

The Rape of the Lock, a satiric poem that pokes fun at the vanity of fashionable society. This poem and others reflect the attitudes that moved Pope to write satire, namely, that the age he lived in was in need of correction. Pope, a neoclassicist, felt that the moral, artistic, and societal ills of his time could be mended by following the example of the Roman and Greek authors of classical civilization.

Wit and Warfare Pope himself noted, "The life of a wit is a warfare on earth." He endured criticism from less talented writers his entire life, many of whom attacked not only his writing, but his religious beliefs and physical handicaps as well. In his thirties, Pope returned to his first love, Greek poetry, translating the *Iliad* and the *Odyssey* into modern verse. After announcing his intention to translate the *Iliad,* he was met with great resistance. Among others, Addison—who had turned against Pope for political reasons—attempted to thwart the success of the translation. The attempts failed, however. In fact, the translations sold so well that Pope was able to lease an estate outside of London called Twickenham (twi′ kə nəm). While there, he continued writing, all the while defending himself against his enemies.

Pope's friends remained loyal throughout his life. His later works, such as *An Essay on Man,* display a thoughtfulness that even his enemies later came to respect.

Alexander Pope was born in 1688 and died in 1744.

Literature Online **Author Search** For more about Alexander Pope, go to www.glencoe.com.

Connecting to the Selections

Pope's verse is rich in epigrams—brief, witty poems or sayings that sum up a philosophical or moral point. As you read, think about expressions or sayings you have learned from older generations. How would you paraphrase them?

Building Background

Pope was influenced by the style and structure of classical poetry. As a Neoclassicist, Pope valued order, balance, and clarity over emotion. The precedents set by the best of the ancient Greek and Roman authors guided the Neoclassicists. For example, the epistles of the ancient Roman poet Horace inspired *An Essay on Man,* Pope's philosophical poem that defines humankind's place in the universe.

A **verse epistle** is a poem addressed to a patron or friend (often in the form of a letter) that uses a conversational style. An **epigram** sums up a moral or philosophical point using exact, compressed language.

Setting Purposes for Reading

Big Idea The English Enlightenment and Neoclassicism

As you read the selections from Pope, notice how reason dominates his beliefs and opinions.

Literary Element Heroic Couplet

A **heroic couplet** is a pair of rhymed lines in iambic pentameter that work together to express an idea or point. A heroic couplet is based on the poetic form used by ancient Greek and Roman poets in their heroic epics. The following passage from *An Essay on Man* forms a heroic couplet:

> And, spite of pride, in erring reason's spite,
> One truth is clear, Whatever is, is right.

As you read the selections, look for other heroic couplets.

- See Literary Terms Handbook, p. R8.

Literature Online **Interactive Literary Elements Handbook** To review or learn more about the literary elements, go to www.glencoe.com.

Reading Strategy Paraphrasing

When you **paraphrase,** you restate something in your own words. As you read the selections from Pope, try to paraphrase his message, or point.

Reading Tip: Using a Paraphrase Chart Use a chart to record complex epigrams and to paraphrase their meaning in your own words.

Epigram	Paraphrase
p. 589 "Be thou the first true merit to befriend; His praise is lost, who stays till all commend."	One should compliment what is done well without waiting until others do so first.

Vocabulary

commend (kə mend´) *v.* to praise; to express approval of; p. 589 *The association held a banquet to commend the accomplishments of its members.*

discord (dis´ kôrd) *n.* a lack of agreement or harmony; p. 589 *The blaring music, harsh lighting, and general discord of the restaurant made the customers uncomfortable.*

disabuse (dis´ ə būz´) *v.* to free from a falsehood or misconception; p. 590 *I have been trying to disabuse my little brother of the idea that he is the center of the world.*

Vocabulary Tip: Context Clues You can often find clues to the meaning of an unfamiliar word by looking at words and phrases that surround the word. Context clues may be examples, definitions, synonyms, or other kinds of clues.

OBJECTIVES
In studying these selections, you will focus on the following:
- analyzing literary periods
- analyzing heroic couplets and the essay
- paraphrasing

Epigrams

Alexander Pope

from An Essay on Criticism

'Tis with our judgments as our watches, none
Go just alike, yet each believes his own.

❧

One science only will one genius fit;
So vast is art, so narrow human wit.

❧

A little learning is a dangerous thing;
Drink deep, or taste not the Pierian spring:[1]
There shallow drafts intoxicate the brain,
And drinking largely sobers us again.

❧

In wit, as Nature, what affects our hearts
Is not the exactness of peculiar parts;
'Tis not a lip or eye we beauty call,
But the joint force and full result of all.

❧

True wit is Nature to advantage dressed;
What oft was thought, but ne'er so well
  expressed.

❧

Words are like leaves; and where they most
  abound,
Much fruit of sense beneath is rarely found.

The Ship of Fools. Hieronymus Bosch. Louvre, Paris.

---

1. The *Pierian spring* is a reference to a sacred spring in Greek mythology. It can also mean "a source of inspiration."

Big Idea **The English Enlightenment and Neoclassicism** *What does this epigram mean, and how is it connected with the ideas of the Enlightenment?*

Literary Element **Heroic Couplet** *What characteristics of these lines make them a heroic couplet?*

In words, as fashions, the same rule will hold;
Alike fantastic, if too new or old:
Be not the first by whom the new are tried,
Nor yet the last to lay the old aside.

True ease in writing comes from art, not chance,
As those move easiest who have learned to dance.
'Tis not enough no harshness gives offense,
The sound must seem an echo to the sense.

Avoid extremes; and shun the fault of such,
Who still are pleased too little or too much.

Regard not then if wit be old or new,
But blame the false, and value still the true.

We think our fathers fools, so wise we grow;
Our wiser sons, no doubt, will think us so.

Be thou the first true merit to befriend;
His praise is lost, who stays till all **commend**.

Good nature and good sense must ever join;
To err is human, to forgive, divine.

For fools rush in where angels fear to tread.

from Moral Essays

'Tis education forms the common mind,
Just as the twig is bent, the tree's inclined.

from An Essay on Man

Hope springs eternal in the human breast:
Man never is, but always to be blest.

All Nature is but art, unknown to thee;
All chance, direction, which thou canst not see;
All **discord**, harmony not understood;
All partial evil, universal good:
And, spite of pride, in erring reason's spite,
One truth is clear, Whatever is, is right.

Vice is a monster of so frightful mien,
As, to be hated, needs but to be seen;
Yet seen too oft, familiar with her face,
We first endure, then pity, then embrace.

A wit's a feather, and a chief's a rod;
An honest man's the noblest work of God.

Reading Strategy Paraphrasing *How would you paraphrase this epigram from* An Essay on Man?

Vocabulary

commend (kə mend´) *v.* to praise; to express approval of

Vocabulary

discord (dis´ kôrd) *n.* a lack of agreement or harmony

ALEXANDER POPE **589**

from An Essay on Man

Alexander Pope

from Epistle II

Know then thyself, presume not God to scan;
The proper study of mankind is man.
Placed on this isthmus[1] of a middle state,
A being darkly wise, and rudely great:
5   With too much knowledge for the skeptic[2] side,
With too much weakness for the stoic's[3] pride,
He hangs between; in doubt to act, or rest;
In doubt to deem himself a god, or beast;
In doubt his mind or body to prefer;
10   Born but to die, and reasoning but to err;
Alike in ignorance, his reason such,
Whether he thinks too little, or too much:
Chaos of thought and passion, all confused;
Still[4] by himself abused, or **disabused**;
15   Created half to rise, and half to fall;
Great lord of all things, yet a prey to all;
Sole judge of truth, in endless error hurled:
The glory, jest, and riddle of the world!

---

1. An *isthmus* (is′ məs) is a narrow strip of land connecting two larger pieces of land.
2. A *skeptic* is a person who tends to be suspicious about the statements of others.
3. A *stoic* is a person who appears to be unaffected by pain or pleasure.
4. Here, *still* means "always."

Literary Element **Heroic Couplet** *What is the point of this couplet? What makes it a heroic couplet?*

Big Idea **The English Enlightenment and Neoclassicism**
Which ideas presented in these lines reflect attitudes of the Enlightenment? Which contradict ideas of the Enlightenment?

Vocabulary

disabuse (dis′ ə būz′) *v.* to free from a falsehood or misconception

The Thinker. Auguste Rodin. Bronze, h. 49 cm. Musee des Beaux-Arts, Lyon, France.

RESPONDING AND THINKING CRITICALLY

Respond

1. Which of Pope's sayings did you find particularly true or fitting? Explain.

Recall and Interpret

2. (a)According to the epigrams, which human qualities does Pope consider most important? (b)How can you tell that these are important to him?

3. (a)How would you describe Pope's attitude toward learning as conveyed in the epigrams? (b)Cite two examples that support your view.

4. (a)In your own words, explain the attitude expressed toward human nature in the excerpt from *An Essay on Man.* (b)What view of human nature do Pope's epigrams seem to suggest? Support your answer with examples from the text.

Analyze and Evaluate

5. (a)What is the **theme,** or comment about life, of the excerpt from *An Essay on Man*? (b)Which phrases help contribute to this theme?

6. (a)**Parallelism** is the use of words, phrases, or sentences that have similar grammatical structures. What instances of parallelism occur in the excerpt from *An Essay on Man*? (b)How does parallelism contribute to the overall effect of the poem?

Connect

7. In *An Essay on Man*, Pope remarks that humans are "the glory, jest, and riddle of the world." What historical examples portray humans as "the glory," "jest," or "riddle" of the world?

8. **Big Idea** The English Enlightenment and Neoclassicism Write your own epigram (as a heroic couplet) based on the attitudes of the English Enlightenment and Neoclassicism.

LITERARY ANALYSIS

Literary Element Heroic Couplet

The **heroic couplet** was the most common poetic measure used during the Neoclassical period. Pope and other poets of the time often wrote heroic couplets as **closed couplets**. A closed couplet forms the end of a sentence or phrase. In addition, the first line of a closed couplet is often **end-stopped**; that is, it contains a complete thought and requires a semicolon, colon, or period at its conclusion. In addition, many of the couplets have a **caesura**, or pause, usually positioned near the middle of a line and often indicated by a comma.

1. Which lines from the epigrams do not form closed heroic couplets?

2. How do the caesuras help emphasize the meaning of *An Essay on Man*? Give examples to support your answer.

Review: Essay

As you learned on page 547, an **essay** is a short nonfiction piece that communicates an idea. An essay usually follows a basic structure: main idea or thesis followed by supporting details, followed by a conclusion. Although *An Essay on Man* is written in verse, it follows the structure of an essay.

Partner Activity With a partner, use quotations from the excerpt from *An Essay on Man* to briefly explain its structure. Use the following graphic organizer to help clarify your thoughts.

Thesis: → Supporting Details: → Conclusion:

Reading Strategy Paraphrasing

To maintain the rhyme scheme (*aa, bb*), meter (iambic pentameter), and form (couplet) of a heroic couplet, the word order is often presented in an irregular way. This can make it difficult to identify the main idea. To **paraphrase** the theme of a couplet, first "translate" the couplet, rearranging the word order as necessary.

1. (a)In the third epigram from *An Essay on Man,* what does "her face" refer to? (b)What do we "endure," "pity," and "embrace"? (c)What is the message or theme of the epigram?

2. (a)In the excerpt from *An Essay on Man,* who does "He" refer to in line 7? (b)Who is the "Great lord of all things" (line 16)?

Vocabulary Practice

Practice with Context Clues In the following sentences, choose the context clue that best helps you understand the underlined word.

1. Because the whole class did well on the annual test, the principal wants to <u>commend</u> you.
   a. whole class   c. test
   b. did well   d. principal
2. Even though the school band produced nothing but <u>discord</u> at the start of the year, they were in perfect harmony for the holiday concert.
   a. band   c. start
   b. produced d. harmony
3. Until the Middle Ages, people thought Earth was the center of the universe, but science eventually <u>disabused</u> them of that false belief.
   a. Middle Ages   c. center
   b. earth   d. false belief

Academic Vocabulary

Here is a word from the vocabulary list on page R82.

<u>structure</u> (struk′ chər) *n.* the arrangement of parts or elements as related to the whole

Practice and Apply
What is the basic **structure** of an essay?

Writing About Literature

Respond to Theme Think about a time when you or someone you know could have benefited from the advice in one of Pope's epigrams. Write a brief personal essay to describe the situation. Begin by quoting the epigram and explaining the message or theme it expresses in your own words. Then briefly describe the personal situation in which Pope's advice would have been helpful.

As you draft, write from start to finish. Follow the writing path shown here to help organize your essay.

Introduction:
1. Quote the epigram.
2. Paraphrase the epigram.
3. Briefly describe your personal situation.

Body Paragraph(s):
1. Explain your personal situation in more detail.
2. Show how the epigram relates to your personal situation.

Conclusion:
1. Sum up your main points.
2. Add any related insight.

After you complete your draft, meet with a peer reviewer to evaluate each other's work and to suggest revisions. Then proofread and edit your draft for errors in spelling, grammar, and punctuation.

Literature Groups

The excerpt from *An Essay on Man* is built around contradictory statements. With a small group, find five pairs of contrasting ideas. Discuss how these contrasts help develop the theme of the work and present your conclusions to the class.

Literature⌐nline Web Activities For eFlashcards, Selection Quick Checks, and other Web activities, go to www.glencoe.com.

LITERATURE PREVIEW

Connecting to the Poem

What makes a story really funny? Think of comedies you have enjoyed in movies or on TV. Do comedies you enjoy use exaggeration? Understatement? Sarcasm? Silly situations? As you read the poem, think about what techniques can make a story funny.

Building Background

The Rape of the Lock, one of Pope's greatest comic poems, was based on an actual event. A wealthy baron named Lord Petre had cut a lock of hair from the beautiful Arabella Fermor's head and refused to give it back. A great scandal ensued. At the urging of his friend John Caryll, Pope created a miniature masterpiece of satire out of the event.

Setting Purposes for Reading

Big Idea The English Enlightenment and Neoclassicism

Part of Neoclassicism involved admiration for Greek and Roman civilization. As you read the poem, notice how Pope uses references to classical mythology to comment on his subject.

Literary Element Mock-Epic

The **mock-epic** is an imitation epic, or long narrative poem, that describes trivial subjects in a way that mimics the elaborate form and style of the classical epic. It often makes fun of a society by showing how that society falls short of the standards set in the classical heroic epic. The characters, events, and linguistic structures that are traditional in classical epics, such as Homer's *Iliad* and Virgil's *Aeneid,* form the basis of this type of literature. Epic or heroic poetry typically includes a brave hero who overcomes great trials, a major battle scene, a discussion of the hero's weapon, gods who participate in or direct the action, and epic similes in which things are compared at great length. As you read the poem, examine how Pope uses the mock-epic form to poke fun at society.

- See Literary Terms Handbook, p. R10.

READING PREVIEW

Reading Strategy Interpreting Imagery

To interpret is to use your own understanding of the world to decide what something means. When you **interpret imagery,** you decide what the "word pictures" and sensory details of a selection mean. As you read *The Rape of the Lock,* use your prior knowledge to help you determine the meaning of Pope's images.

Imagery:		Prior Knowledge:		Interpretation:
• "Two-edged weapon" • "glitt'ring forfex" • "Steel could . . . strike to dust th' imperial powers of Troy . . . thy hairs should feel / The conquering force of unresisted steel?"	**+**	Pope uses epic conventions to describe trivial events (mockepic); Pope is a master of satire.	**=**	Pope describes the battle weapon as if it were a steel sword that inspired fear. It is actually a pair of scissors.

Vocabulary

stratagem (strat′ ə jəm) *n.* a deception; a military tactic designed to surprise an enemy; p. 595 *The soldiers decided that an ambush was the only stratagem likely to defeat their powerful enemy.*

confound (kən found′) *v.* to confuse; to defeat or overthrow; p. 597 *Lars had little physical strength, but he was always able to confound his opponent in a chess match.*

Vocabulary Tip: Analogies An analogy is a comparison that shows similarities between things that are otherwise dissimilar. Analogies often help explain something unfamiliar by comparing it to something familiar.

Literature Online **Interactive Literary Elements Handbook** To review or learn more about the literary elements, go to www.glencoe.com.

OBJECTIVES
In studying this selection, you will focus on the following:
- analyzing literary genres
- analyzing a mock-epic and allusion
- interpreting imagery

from The Rape of the Lock

Alexander Pope

from Canto III

The Battle of the Beaux and the Belles, drawing for the eighth illustration from "Rape of the Lock", 1896. Aubrey Beardsley. 25.7 x 17.6 cm. Pen and ink on paper. The Barber Institute of Fine Arts, University of Birmingham.

Close by those meads,° for ever crown'd with flowers,
Where Thames with pride surveys his rising towers,
There stands a structure of majestic frame,°
Which from the neighb'ring Hampton takes its name.
5   Here Britain's statesmen oft the fall foredoom
Of foreign tyrants, and of nymphs at home;
Here thou, great ANNA!° whom three realms obey,
Dost sometimes counsel take—and sometimes tea.
    Hither the heroes and the nymphs resort,
10 To taste a while the pleasures of a court;
In various talk th' instructive hours they pass'd,
Who gave the ball, or paid the visit last;
One speaks the glory of the British Queen,
And one describes a charming Indian screen;
15 A third interprets motions, looks, and eyes;
At every word a reputation dies.
Snuff, or the fan, supply each pause of chat,
With singing, laughing, ogling, *and all that*.
    Meanwhile, declining from the noon of day,
20 The sun obliquely shoots his burning ray;
The hungry judges soon the sentence sign,
And wretches hang that jurymen may dine. . . .
Belinda now, whom thirst of fame invites,
Burns to encounter two adventurous knights,
25 At ombre° singly to decide their doom;
And swells her breast with conquests yet to come. . . .
The nymph exulting fills with shouts the sky;
The walls, the woods, and long canals reply.
   O thoughtless mortals! ever blind to fate,
30 Too soon dejected, and too soon elate.

---

1 meads: meadows—often wet, grassy lands.
3 structure . . . frame: Pope is referring to Hampton Court, the royal palace.
7 Anna: Queen Anne, who ruled Great Britain and Ireland and claimed to rule France; thus, "whom three realms obey."

25 Ombre: a card game.

Literary Element   Mock-Epic *What makes Pope's description of Queen Anne humorous and satirical?*

Reading Strategy   Interpreting Imagery *What is happening in this image? What does the image suggest about this society?*

Sudden, these honors shall be snatch'd away,
And cursed for ever this victorious day.
   For lo! the board with cups and spoons is crown'd,°
The berries crackle, and the mill turns round:
35 On shining altars of Japan they raise
The silver lamp; the fiery spirits blaze:
From silver spouts the grateful liquors glide,
While China's earth receives the smoking tide:
At once they gratify their scent and taste,
40 And frequent cups prolong the rich repast.
Straight hover round the fair her airy band;
Some, as she sipp'd, the fuming liquor fann'd,
Some o'er her lap their careful plumes display'd,
Trembling, and conscious of the rich brocade.
45 Coffee (which makes the politician wise,
And see through all things with his half-shut eyes)
Sent up in vapors to the baron's brain
New **stratagems**, the radiant lock to gain.
Ah cease, rash youth! desist ere 'tis too late,
50 Fear the just gods, and think of Scylla's fate!°
Changed to a bird, and sent to flit in air,
She dearly pays for Nisus' injured hair!
   But when to mischief mortals bend their will,
How soon they find fit instruments of ill!
55 Just then, Clarissa° drew with tempting grace
A two-edged weapon from her shining case:
So ladies, in romance, assist their knight,
Present the spear, and arm him for the fight.
He takes the gift with reverence and extends
60 The little engine° on his fingers' ends;
This just behind Belinda's neck he spread,
As o'er the fragrant steams she bends her head.
Swift to the lock a thousand sprites repair,
A thousand wings, by turns, blow back the hair;
65 And thrice they twitch'd the diamond in her ear;
Thrice she look'd back, and thrice the foe drew near.
Just in that instant, anxious Ariel sought
The close recesses of the virgin's thought:
As on the nosegay in her breast reclin'd,
70 He watch'd th' ideas rising in her mind,

33 the board . . . tide: The *board* refers to the tray on which coffee will be served. Lines 33–38 describe the preparation and serving of coffee. The *berries* (beans) crackle when they are roasted and then are ground in the mill. The *altars of Japan* are lacquered tables. The *smoking tide* is coffee, and it is poured into *China's earth*, or Chinese porcelain cups.

50 Scylla's (si′ lə) **fate:** refers to the classical myth about Scylla, who plucked out one of her father Nisus's hairs, on which the safety of the kingdom depended. As punishment, she was turned into a bird.

55 Clarissa: a female character in the poem who disapproves of Belinda's vanity.

60 engine: device.

Big Idea   **The English Enlightenment and Neoclassicism** *How does this warning reflect the inspiration of classical mythology?*

Literary Element   Mock-Epic *What is actually happening here? Which conventions of epic poetry does Pope employ in this passage?*

Vocabulary

stratagem (strat′ ə jəm) *n.* a deception; a military tactic designed to surprise an enemy

Madame de Pompadour. Francois Boucher. Oil on canvas. Louvre, Paris.

Sudden he view'd, in spite of all her art,
An earthly lover lurking at her heart.
Amazed, confused, he found his power expired,
Resign'd to fate, and with a sigh retired.
75 The peer now spreads the glitt'ring forfex° wide,
T' inclose the lock; now joins it, to divide.
Ev'n then, before the fatal engine closed,
A wretched sylph too fondly interposed;
Fate urged the shears, and cut the sylph in twain,
80 (But airy substance soon unites again)
The meeting points the sacred hair dissever
From the fair head, forever, and forever!
    Then flash'd the living lightning from her eyes,
And screams of horror rend th' affrighted skies.
85 Not louder shrieks to pitying Heaven are cast,
When husbands or when lap-dogs breathe their last;
Or when rich China vessels, fall'n from high,
In glitt'ring dust and painted fragments lie!
    "Let wreaths of triumph° now my temples twine,
90 (The victor cried) the glorious prize is mine!

75 **forfex:** scissors.

89 **Wreaths of triumph:** the wreaths that ancient Greek victors wore on their heads.

Reading Strategy Interpreting Imagery *What action is being described in this passage? How does the paradoxical language contribute to the effect of the image?*

While fish in streams, or birds delight in air,
Or in a coach and six° the British fair,
As long as *Atalantis*° shall be read,
Or the small pillow grace a lady's bed,
95 While visits° shall be paid on solemn days,
When numerous wax-lights in bright order blaze,
While nymphs take treats, or assignations give,
So long my honor, name, and praise shall live!"
What Time would spare, from steel receives its date
100 And monuments, like men, submit to fate!
Steel could the labor of the gods destroy,
And strike to dust th' imperial powers of Troy;°
Steel could the works of mortal pride **confound**,
And hew triumphal arches to the ground.
105 What wonder then, fair nymph! thy hairs should feel
The conquering force of unresisted steel?

*In Canto IV, Umbriel, a "melancholy sprite," travels to the under-
world to gather a vial of "soft sobs, melting griefs, and flowing tears"
and a bag of "sighs, sobs, and passions." When Umbriel returns, he
empties the vial and bag over Belinda and her friend. Belinda then
tells the Baron that he shouldn't have taken the lock. The Baron,
however, ignores her lament.*

from Canto V

"To arms, to arms!" the fierce virago° cries,
And swift as lightning to the combat flies.
All side in parties, and begin th' attack:
110 Fans clap, silks rustle, and tough whalebones crack;
Heroes' and heroines' shouts confusedly rise,
And bass and treble voices strike the skies.
No common weapons in their hands are found,
Like Gods they fight, nor dread a mortal wound. . . .
115 ⠀⠀See fierce Belinda on the baron flies,
With more than usual lightning in her eyes:
Nor fear'd the chief th' unequal fight to try,
Who sought no more than on his foe to die.
But his bold lord with manly strength endued,
120 She with one finger and a thumb subdued:
Just where the breath of life his nostrils drew,
A charge of snuff the wily virgin threw;

92 coach and six: a prestigious carriage with six horses.

93 *Atalantis:* a popular gossipy romance in which real society people were thinly disguised as fictional characters.

95 visits: the regular evening visits that were a serious ritual for the society lady. The society lady would be accompanied by servants carrying **wax-lights**.

102 steel . . . Troy: According to legend, the swords of the ancient Greeks conquered Troy.

107 virago: a "female warrior," in this case, Belinda.

Literary Element ⠀Mock-Epic ⠀*How does Pope make use of the conventions of epic poetry in this passage? What is the effect?*

Vocabulary

confound (kən found′) *v.* to confuse; to defeat or overthrow

The gnomes direct, to every atom just,
The pungent grains of titillating dust.
125 Sudden, with starting tears each eye o'erflows,
And the high dome re-echoes to his nose.
    "Now meet thy fate," incensed Belinda cried,
And drew a deadly bodkin° from her side. . . .
    "Boast not my fall, (he cried) insulting foe!
130 Thou by some other shalt be laid as low.
Nor think, to die dejects my lofty mind:
All that I dread is leaving you behind!
Rather than so, ah let me still survive,
And burn in Cupid's flames—but burn alive."
135   "Restore the lock!" she cries; and all around
"Restore the lock!" the vaulted roofs rebound.
Not fierce Othello° in so loud a strain
Roar'd for the handkerchief that caused his pain.
But see how oft ambitious aims are cross'd,
140 And chiefs contend till all the prize is lost!
The lock, obtain'd with guilt, and kept with pain,
In every place is sought, but sought in vain:
With such a prize no mortal must be blest,
So Heaven decrees! with Heaven who can contest?
145   Some thought it mounted to the lunar sphere,
Since all things lost on earth are treasured there.
There heroes' wits are kept in pond'rous vases,
And beaux' in snuff-boxes and tweezer-cases.
There broken vows, and death-bed alms are found,
150 And lovers' hearts with ends of riband° bound. . . .
    But trust the Muse—she saw it upward rise,
Though mark'd by none but quick, poetic eyes. . . .
A sudden star it shot through liquid air,
And drew behind a radiant trail of hair. . . .
155   Then cease, bright nymph! to mourn thy ravish'd hair,
Which adds new glory to the shining sphere!
Not all the tresses that fair head can boast
Shall draw such envy as the lock you lost.
For, after all the murders of your eye,
160 When, after millions slain, yourself shall die;
When those fair suns shall set, as set they must,
And all those tresses shall be laid in dust;
This lock, the Muse shall consecrate to fame,
And 'midst the stars inscribe Belinda's name.

❧

128 bodkin: a dagger. Here, it refers to a hairpin that is shaped like a dagger.

137 Othello: This allusion to Shakespeare's play *Othello* (Act III, scene 4) refers to Othello's demanding to see the handkerchief he had given his wife, believing her to have given it to another man and thus having been unfaithful.

150 Riband (ri bənd'): decorative ribbon.

Literary Element Mock-Epic *What does the juxtaposition of these two lines about what is kept in the "lunar sphere" reveal about the characters at Hampton Court?*

Reading Strategy Interpreting Imagery *After Belinda's lock of hair is lost, what happens to it?*

RESPONDING AND THINKING CRITICALLY

Respond

1. How effective was Pope's use of satire in revealing the personalities of his characters?

Recall and Interpret

2. (a)Reread lines 9–16. How would you interpret the society that Pope describes? (b)What is Pope's **tone,** or attitude toward his subject, in these lines?

3. (a)Reread lines 33–38. What is being described? (b)What does the descriptive language suggest about how the characters perceive the event?

4. (a)How is Belinda "raped" of her lock? (b)What does her reaction reveal about her?

Analyze and Evaluate

5. (a)What is the Baron's reaction after the lock is cut? (b)What is the effect of revealing the Baron's reaction in his own words?

6. Read the side note about Scylla in line 50. What does this allusion imply about the Baron's plan?

7. What is the effect of juxtaposing the death of husbands and lap dogs in the comparison to Belinda's grief in lines 85–86?

Connect

8. (a)What examples of satire have you encountered in your own life? (b)How can satire be more painful than a direct insult?

9. **Big Idea** The English Enlightenment and Neoclassicism How does Pope's interest in Greek and Roman history inform his attitude toward high society in *The Rape of the Lock*?

DAILY LIFE AND CULTURE

Hampton Court

Queen Anne often visited Hampton Court and hired artists and craftsmen to finish several improvements there, particularly to the Queen's Drawing Room, where she entertained. While it was an honor to be hired by royalty and to have one's work displayed at the palace, the artists and craftsmen often suffered from Anne's "aversion to paying bills."

Anne's frugal tendency carried over to entertaining at Hampton Court as well. As Jonathan Swift

remarked after dining there, "I dined at Her Majesty's best table in England . . . [it] is the only mark of magnificence or royal hospitality that I can see in the royal household." However, lack of lavish entertaining did not keep visitors away from the palace. One group staying at Hampton Court was playing cards while drinking coffee. When one of the ladies, Miss Arabella Fermor, took a drink, a lock of her hair fell into her cup. Another visitor, Lord Petre, grabbed a pair of scissors and snipped the unruly strand. Arabella's anger heightened when he refused to return the lock, and she left the palace offended. Pope wrote *The Rape of the Lock* as an attempt to heal the "pain" of the event by immortalizing Arabella's story through verse.

Group Activity Discuss the following questions with classmates.

1. What might have made Queen Anne's frugality particularly frustrating to her creditors?

2. (a)How is Belinda portrayed by Pope? (b)How do you think Arabella would have felt about Pope's mock-epic?

Hampton Court (after Jean Rigaud's Hampton Court). 1751. Artist Unknown. Engraving. Private Collection.

Literary Element Mock-Epic

The **mock-epic** mimics the elevated style and form of epic poetry to describe trivial events in a humorous way. Literary epics are highly conventional poems, and the mock-epic, likewise, includes these epic conventions: the hero is of national or cosmic significance; the setting is broad, often worldwide or even cosmic; the action involves superhuman battle feats; the gods or other supernatural beings take interest in these battles; and the epic poem is narrated in a grand, ceremonial style that includes allusions and epic similes.

1. What type of diction, or word choice, does Pope use throughout *The Rape of the Lock*? Give examples from the selection that illustrate his style.

2. How does the setting and action of Pope's poem reflect or mimic the conventions of epic poetry?

3. Who is the hero of the poem? How can you tell?

Review: Allusion

As you learned on page 520, an **allusion** is a reference to a well-known character, place, or situation from history, music, art, or another work of literature. Epic (and mock-epic) poetry is typically full of allusions that contribute to a grand, elevated style. Several of Pope's allusions relate to figures from Greek myth. A **myth** is a traditional story by an unknown author that deals with gods, heroes, and supernatural events.

Partner Activity Meet with a group of classmates and identify the allusions in *The Rape of the Lock*. Then, record the allusions you find, give their meanings, and try to interpret their significance in Pope's poem. Use a chart like the one below.

Allusion	Meaning	Significance in Poem
"Scylla's fate" (line 50)	Scylla plucked out one of her father Nisus's hairs, on which the safety of the kingdom depended. As punishment, she was turned into a bird.	The speaker warns the Baron not to cut the lock, reminding him of the destruction a similar act caused Scylla. But Scylla's act cost a kingdom; the Baron's act is trivial by comparison.

Reading Strategy Interpreting Imagery

Much of Pope's vivid imagery is figurative rather than literal. **Figurative language** is not literally true but expresses some truth beyond the literal level. In the poem, note how Pope uses elaborate, figurative language to describe mundane people and situations. Also notice how such descriptions satirize the subjects being described.

1. (a) Reread lines 33–38. How is the coffee service described? (b) What type of figurative language is used in the lines? (c) How do these images affect your understanding of the characters in the poem?

2. Reread the final twelve lines of the poem. Which images are figurative?

Vocabulary Practice

Practice with Analogies For each analogy, decide what the relationship is between the first pair of words. Then apply that relationship to the second pair.

1. stratagem : enemy :: vaccine :
   a. doctor   c. medicine
   b. disease   d. patient

2. reply : respond :: confound :
   a. enemy   c. advocate
   b. quandary   d. confuse

Academic Vocabulary

Here are two words from the vocabulary list on page R82.

indicate (in′ di kāt′) v. to demonstrate or point out

assume (ə sōōm′) v. to undertake, take on, or adopt

Practice and Apply
1. What features of *The Rape of the Lock* **indicate** that the poem is satirical?
2. What role does Belinda **assume** after the lock has been cut?

Writing About Literature

Evaluate Author's Craft Throughout *The Rape of the Lock,* Pope juxtaposes the monumental and the trivial—sometimes in the same line—to achieve an ironic and often humorous effect. For example:

"Not louder shrieks to pitying Heaven are cast, When husbands or when lap-dogs breathe their last"

Write a brief essay in which you evaluate Pope's juxtaposition of the trivial with the monumental and its effect on the theme of the poem. Use evidence from the poem to support your ideas.

Before you begin drafting, identify examples from the poem that illustrate the juxtaposition of the monumental and the trivial. Then analyze what effect the juxtaposition has on the theme, keeping in mind Pope's overall message in writing the poem. Use a graphic organizer like the one below to help you organize your essay.

Introduction:
Present your interpretation of Pope's use of juxtaposition and its effect on theme.

Body Paragraphs:
Present main points to support your thesis. Support your main points with textual evidence and examples.

Conclusion:
Summarize your position and main points. Add any related insight.

After you complete your draft, exchange papers with a partner. Review each other's work and suggest revisions. Finally, proofread and edit your draft for errors in spelling, grammar, and punctuation.

Performing

In a small group, designate one student as narrator, one to pantomime Belinda, and one to pantomime the Baron. First, have the narrator practice reading lines 75–126 aloud, with the characters pantomiming and speaking their parts. After members are comfortable with their roles, you can pantomime the scene in front of the class.

Pope's Language and Style

Comparing with Antithesis In *The Rape of the Lock,* Pope often juxtaposes lines or phrases to emphasize how they compare, or, more frequently, contrast. **Antithesis** is a specific type of contrast that uses parallelism to emphasize a contrast in meaning between two adjacent lines or phrases. Consider the following example:

"The hungry judges soon the sentence sign, And wretches hang that jurymen may dine . . . "

Notice the parallel structure of each phrase: *wretches hang* (plural noun + verb), followed by *jurymen may dine* (plural noun + verb). The parallel structure underscores the sharp contrast in meaning, particularly the juxtaposition of the significant death sentence opposed to the trivial afternoon meal.

Notice some of Pope's antitheses:

Antithesis	Contrast Emphasized
1. "Of foreign tyrants, and of nymphs at home" (line 6)	1. The parallelism emphasizes the force and distance of the "foreign tyrants" and the gentleness and closeness of the "nymphs at home."
2. "Thrice she look'd back, and thrice the foe drew near" (line 66)	2. The parallelism and repetition emphasize the contrasting images of Belinda's looking backward and the Baron's advancing forward.

Activity Create a similar chart of your own. Identify other antitheses from *The Rape of the Lock,* and explain how parallelism emphasizes the contrast in meaning.

Revising Check

Antithesis Review the essay you wrote about juxtaposition in *Rape of the Lock*. See if you can use antithesis to emphasize contrasts you are trying to point out. In addition, consider adding a discussion of one of Pope's antitheses to benefit your argument.

Letter to Her Daughter

MEET LADY MARY WORTLEY MONTAGU

Lady Mary Wortley Montagu went after what she wanted in life—even when that meant defying social customs. For example, although the custom of the time was for women to receive less education than men, the young Lady Montagu sneaked a Latin dictionary and grammar book from her family's library and secretly taught herself the language. She defied convention again at twenty-three, when she chose not to marry the man her father had selected for her and eloped instead with the man she loved, Edward Wortley Montagu, a member of Parliament.

Life in Turkey When her husband was appointed ambassador to Turkey at Constantinople (now Istanbul) in 1716, Lady Montagu embraced the culture, learning Turkish, visiting mosques, and even getting to know harem women. She noticed the effectiveness of the Turkish practice of immunizing children against smallpox, a disease that had marred her beauty when she was a young woman. She then had both her son and daughter immunized. When her husband was recalled to England in 1718, she pushed English doctors to adopt this immunization practice—and succeeded, overcoming the considerable prejudice against women offering advice to doctors. She recorded her observations about life in Turkey in *Turkish Embassy Letters*.

> "What fire, what ease, what knowledge of Europe and Asia."
>
> —Edward Gibbon

Lady Montagu was acquainted with several distinguished writers of her day. For a time, she was particularly friendly with Alexander Pope (both lived in Twickenham, west of London), who was evidently infatuated with her. He even commissioned an artist to paint her portrait in Turkish costume. For reasons unclear, they had a falling out, which occasioned much bitterness on both sides. While living in Twickenham, Lady Montagu wrote essays and composed a series of letters dealing with feminism.

Living Abroad By this time, Lady Montagu's relationship with her husband had become formal and impersonal. After twenty-five years of marriage, during which she had raised a son and daughter, Lady Montagu separated from her husband and left England. She lived abroad in Italy and France for more than twenty years. On a visit to the continent, the Reverend Joseph Spence met her for the first time in Rome and wrote this assessment of her character: "She is one of the most shining characters in the world, but shines like a comet; she is all irregularity, and always wandering; the most wise, most imprudent; loveliest, most disagreeable; best-natured, cruelest woman in the world."

Lady Montagu is best known for her witty and informative correspondence. Her letters to her daughter are full of vivid details and practical advice. Lady Montagu died of cancer at the age of seventy-three, shortly after returning to England.

Lady Mary Wortley Montagu was born in 1689 and died in 1762.

Literature Online Author Search For more about Lady Mary Wortley Montagu, go to www.glencoe.com.

Connecting to the Letter

In the following letter, Lady Montagu gives advice to her daughter. As you read the letter, think about the following questions:

- How do letters differ from other forms of communication?
- What was the best piece of advice you ever received?

Building Background

During the eighteenth century, writing letters was the primary form of long-distance communication. Lady Montagu's colorful correspondence chronicled everything from her adventures in Turkey to her exploits in Europe. These letters are remarkable literary accomplishments. However, Montagu's daughter, the Countess of Bute, tried to keep them out of print for fear that they would bring embarrassment to the family. Lady Montagu had been separated from her husband and family for seventeen years when in 1753 she wrote the following letter to her daughter from Italy.

Setting Purposes for Reading

Big Idea The English Enlightenment and Neoclassicism

The Enlightenment valued reason as the supreme authority in matters of opinion, belief, and conduct. As you read this letter, consider how it reflects the importance of reason.

Literary Element Extended Metaphor

Metaphors are figures of speech that compare two unlike things to help readers see underlying similarities between them. **Extended metaphors** compare two things in various ways throughout a paragraph, stanza, or selection. For example, a writer might develop a comparison between a country at war and a ship at sea. As you read, notice this technique and consider its effects.

- See Literary Terms Handbook, p. R6.

Literature Online **Interactive Literary Elements Handbook** To review or learn more about the literary elements, go to www.glencoe.com.

Reading Strategy Analyzing Argument

Argument is a type of persuasive writing in which logic or reason is used to try to influence the reader's ideas or actions. In an argument, a writer states opinions and supports them with facts and reasons. When you analyze an argument, you identify the writer's opinions and the supporting evidence.

Reading Tip: Taking Notes As you read, use a chart like the one below to record Montagu's opinions and reasons.

Opinions	Support
"Your children should be endowed with an uncommon share of good sense."	My family and my husband's have produced several intelligent people.

Vocabulary

edifice (ed´ ə fis) *n.* a building, especially a large one; p. 604 *The new apartment complex is an edifice that towers over the neighborhood.*

diversion (di vur´ zhən) *n.* an amusement; an entertainment; p. 605 *We tried to think of diversions to occupy the noisy preschoolers.*

inveterate (in vet´ ə rit) *adj.* firmly established; deep-rooted; p. 606 *Her inveterate love for gossip made her the town busybody.*

elate (i lāt´) *v.* to make happy; p. 608 *Winning the lottery elated that struggling family.*

Vocabulary Tip: Context Clues To figure out the meaning of an unfamiliar word, look for clues in the context, or the surrounding words. For example, consider the sentence "The epistle to the Romans is the longest letter in the Bible." The word *letter* helps you figure out the meaning of *epistle*, a formal and elegant letter.

OBJECTIVES
In studying this selection, you will focus on the following:
- analyzing literary periods

- analyzing extended metaphor and author's purpose
- analyzing an argument

Letter to Her Daughter

Lady Mary Wortley Montagu

January 28, 1753

Dear Child,

    You have given me a great deal of satisfaction by your account of your eldest daughter. I am particularly pleased to hear she is a good arithmetician; it is the best proof of understanding. The knowledge of numbers is one of the chief distinctions between us and brutes. If there is anything in blood, you may reasonably expect your children should be endowed with an uncommon share of good sense. Mr. Wortley's family and mine have both produced some of the greatest men that have been born in England. I mean Admiral Sandwich and my great-grandfather who was distinguished by the name of Wise William. I have heard Lord Bute's father mentioned as an extraordinary genius (though he had not many opportunities of showing it), and his uncle the present Duke of Argyle has one of the best heads I ever knew.

    I will therefore speak to you as supposing Lady Mary not only capable but desirous of learning. In that case, by all means let her be indulged in it. You will tell me I did not make it a part of your education. Your prospect was very different from hers, as you had no defect either in mind or person to hinder, and much in your circumstances to attract, the highest offers. It seemed your business to learn how to live in the world, as it is hers to know how to be easy out of it. It is the common error of builders and parents to follow some plan they think beautiful (and perhaps is so) without considering that nothing is beautiful that is misplaced. Hence we see so many **edifices** raised that the raisers can never inhabit, being too large for their fortunes. Vistas are laid open over barren heaths, and apartments contrived for a coolness very agreeable in Italy but killing in the north of Britain. Thus every woman endeavors to breed her daughter a fine lady,

---

Literary Element   **Extended Metaphor**   *How are parents similar to builders?*

Vocabulary

edifice (ed′ ə fis) *n.* a building, especially a large one

qualifying her for a station in which she will never appear, and at the same time incapacitating her for that retirement to which she is destined. Learning (if she has a real taste for it) will not only make her contented but happy in it. No entertainment is so cheap as reading, nor any pleasure so lasting. She will not want new fashions nor regret the loss of expensive **diversions** or variety of company if she can be amused with an author in her closet. To render this amusement extensive, she should be permitted to learn the languages. I have heard it lamented[1] that boys lose so many years in mere learning of words. This is no objection to a girl, whose time is not so precious. She cannot advance herself in any profession and has, therefore, more hours to spare; and as you say her memory is good, she will be very agreeably employed this way.

> *True knowledge consists in knowing things, not words.*

There are two cautions to be given on this subject: first, not to think herself learned when she can read Latin or even Greek. Languages are more properly to be called vehicles of learning than learning itself, as may be observed in many schoolmasters, who though perhaps critics in grammar are the most ignorant fellows upon earth. True knowledge consists in knowing things, not words. I would wish her no further a linguist than to enable her to read books in their originals, that are often corrupted and always injured by translations. Two hours' application every morning will bring this about much sooner than you can imagine, and she will have leisure enough besides to run over the English poetry, which is a more important part of a woman's education than it is generally supposed. Many a young damsel has been ruined by a fine copy of verses, which she would have laughed at if she had known it had been stolen from Mr. Waller.[2] I remember when I was a girl, I saved one of my companions from destruction, who communicated to me an epistle[3] she was quite charmed with. As she had a natural good taste, she observed the lines were not so smooth as Prior's or Pope's,[4] but had more thought and spirit than any of theirs. She was wonderfully delighted with such a demonstration of her lover's sense and passion, and not a little

---

1. *Lamented* means "regretted."
2. *Mr. Waller* was an English poet.
3. An *epistle* is a letter.
4. *Prior* (Matthew Prior) and *Pope* (Alexander Pope) were both English poets.

Reading Strategy **Analyzing Argument** *Why does Montagu include this detail about schoolmasters?*

Vocabulary

diversion (di vur′ zhən) *n.* an amusement; an entertainment

pleased with her own charms, that had force enough to inspire such elegancies. In the midst of this triumph, I showed her they were taken from Randolph's *Poems,* and the unfortunate transcriber was dismissed with the scorn he deserved. To say truth, the poor plagiary[5] was very unlucky to fall into my hands; that author, being no longer in fashion, would have escaped anyone of less universal reading than myself. You should encourage your daughter to talk over with you what she reads, and as you are very capable of distinguishing, take care she does not mistake pert folly for wit and humor, or rhyme for poetry, which are the common errors of young people, and have a train of ill consequences.

The second caution to be given her (and which is most absolutely necessary) is to conceal whatever learning she attains, with as much solicitude as she would hide crookedness or lameness. The parade of it can only serve to draw on her the envy, and consequently the most **inveterate** hatred of all he and she fools, which will certainly be at least three parts in four of all her acquaintance. The use of knowledge in our sex (beside the amusement of solitude) is to moderate the passions and learn to be contented with a small expense, which are the certain effects of a studious life and, it may be, preferable even to that fame which men have engrossed to themselves and will not suffer us to share. You will tell me I have not observed this rule myself, but you are mistaken; it is only inevitable accident that has given me any reputation that way. I have always carefully avoided it and ever thought it a misfortune.

The explanation of this paragraph would occasion a long digression, which I will not trouble you with, it being my present design only to say what I think useful for the instruction of my granddaughter, which I have much at heart. If she has the same inclination (I should say passion) for learning that I was born with, history, geography, and philosophy will furnish her with materials to pass away cheerfully a longer life than is allotted to mortals. I believe there are few heads capable of making Sir Isaac Newton's calculations, but the result of them is not difficult to be understood by a moderate capacity. Do not fear this should make her affect the character of Lady——— or Lady——— or Mrs.———. Those women are ridiculous, not because they have learning but because they have it not. One thinks herself a complete historian after reading Echard's *Roman History,*[6] another a profound philosopher having got by heart some of Pope's unintelligible essays, and a third an able divine[7] on the strength of Whitefield's sermons.[8] Thus you hear them screaming politics and controversy.

---

5. A *plagiary* is one who plagiarizes, or copies another's work and passes it off as one's own.
6. *Roman History* is a work by the English historian Lawrence Echard.
7. A *divine* is a theologian, or student of religion.
8. *Whitefield's sermons* refers to the writings of George Whitefield, a well-known English preacher of the time.

Reading Strategy Analyzing Argument *What is the point of this anecdote?*

Reading Strategy Analyzing Argument *What does this reference to Newton add to the author's argument?*

Vocabulary

inveterate (in vet′ ə rit) *adj.* firmly established; deep-rooted

An Interior at Hampton Court. James D. Wingfield (1832–1872). Oil on canvas. Haynes
Fine Art Gallery, Broadway, England.

Viewing the Art: With whom might you identify the woman standing at the right, Lady
Montagu or her daughter? Explain.

It is a saying of Thucydides:[9] Ignorance is bold, and knowledge reserved. Indeed, it is impossible to be far advanced in it without being more humbled by a conviction of human ignorance than **elated** by learning.

At the same time I recommend books, I neither exclude work nor drawing. I think it as scandalous for a woman not to know how to use a needle as for a man not to know how to use a sword. I was once extreme fond of my pencil, and it was a great mortification[10] to me when my father turned off my master,[11] having made a considerable progress for the short time I learned. My overeagerness in the pursuit of it had brought a weakness on my eyes that made it necessary to leave it off, and all the advantage I got was the improvement of my hand. I see by hers that practice will make her a ready writer. She may attain it by serving you for a secretary when your health or affairs make it troublesome to you to write yourself, and custom will make it an agreeable amusement to her. She cannot have too many for that station in life which will probably be her fate. The ultimate end of your education was to make you a good wife (and I have the comfort to hear that you are one); hers ought to be to make her happy in a virgin state. I will not say it is happier, but it is undoubtedly safer than any marriage. In a lottery where there is (at the lowest computation) ten thousand blanks to a prize, it is the most prudent choice not to venture.

I have always been so thoroughly persuaded of this truth that notwithstanding the flattering views I had for you (as I never intended you a sacrifice to my vanity) I thought I owed you the justice to lay before you all the hazards attending matrimony. You may recollect I did so in the strongest manner. Perhaps you may have more success in the instructing your daughter. She has so much company at home she will not need seeking it abroad, and will more readily take the notions you think fit to give her. As you were alone in my family, it would have been thought a great cruelty to suffer you no companions of your own age, especially having so many near relations, and I do not wonder their opinions influenced yours. I was not sorry to see you not determined on a single life, knowing it was not your father's intention, and contented myself with endeavoring to make your home so easy that you might not be in haste to leave it.

I am afraid you will think this a very long and insignificant letter. I hope the kindness of the design will excuse it, being willing to give you every proof in my power that I am your most affectionate mother,

M. Wortley

---

9. *Thucydides* was an ancient Greek historian.
10. *Mortification* means "humiliation."
11. *Turned off my master* means "dismissed my tutor."

Big Idea **The English Enlightenment and Neoclassicism** *What does this reference to Thucydides suggest about the Neoclassical period?*

Reading Strategy **Analyzing Argument** *Why does Lady Montagu want her granddaughter to be made aware of the drawbacks of marriage?*

Vocabulary

elate (i lāt′) *v.* to make happy

RESPONDING AND THINKING CRITICALLY

Respond

1. What ideas in this letter surprised you the most? Why?

Recall and Interpret

2. (a)What is Montagu's reaction to the news that her granddaughter is good at arithmetic? (b)What reason does she give for feeling this way?

3. (a)What term does Montagu use to describe Latin and Greek? (b)What might she mean by this?

4. (a)Besides being taught to read books, what else does Montagu believe her granddaughter's education should include? (b)What does this tell you about women's education during this period?

Analyze and Evaluate

5. (a)If Montagu were advising her daughter on the education of a grandson, in what ways might her advice differ? (b)Are there similar differences between men's and women's education today? Explain.

6. In your opinion, would Montagu have agreed with Alexander Pope's **aphorism** "A little learning is a dangerous thing"? Why or why not?

Connect

7. (a)Describe the life Montagu recommends for her granddaughter. (b)Would you like to lead such a life? Explain.

8. **Big Idea** **The English Enlightenment and Neoclassicism** The English Enlightenment was a movement that championed reason, science, and self-improvement. How does Montagu's letter reflect the values of that movement?

LITERARY ANALYSIS

Literary Element **Extended Metaphor**

In the second paragraph of her letter, Montagu presents an **extended metaphor** in which she points out the error commonly committed by both builders and parents. She then presents several common consequences of this error in terms of building, leaving the reader to infer the comparable mistakes in parenting each is meant to symbolize.

1. Identify three results of poor planning by builders that Montagu describes.

2. Explain how one of these building problems might relate to parenting.

Review: Author's Purpose

As you learned on page 280, **author's purpose** refers to an author's intent in writing a literary work. An author typically writes to accomplish one of the following purposes: to persuade, to inform or explain, to entertain, to describe, or to tell a story. Once you determine an author's intent, you can better evaluate what you are reading and respond appropriately.

Group Activity With a small group of your classmates, discuss Montagu's main purpose for writing this letter. Consider the title of the letter, its form and content, and Montagu's tone. Create a web like the one below to organize your thoughts.

Reading Strategy Analyzing Argument

In this letter, Montagu gives advice about her grand-daughter's education and voices her opinions about marriage and the life of a single woman.

1. What reason does Montagu give for recommending that her granddaughter be taught "to conceal whatever learning she attains"?

2. How does she support her opinion that her grand-daughter should remain single?

3. How does she justify having prepared her own daughter for marriage?

Vocabulary Practice

Practice with Context Clues For each sentence below, identify the context clues that best help you determine the meaning of the underlined vocabulary words.

1. Grandmother lived in an impressive Victorian <u>edifice</u> located on a large plot of land.
   a. grandmother   **b.** lived in

2. After giving up hope, we were <u>elated</u> to find her diamond ring lying in the birdbath.
   a. giving up hope   **b.** diamond ring

3. It seems that a bird called a magpie, an <u>inveterate</u> and practiced thief, had flown off with her ring.
   a. magpie   **b.** practiced

4. This act of thievery was a <u>diversion</u> for the bird, but a cause of acute anxiety for Grandmother.
   a. bird   **b.** anxiety

Academic Vocabulary

Here is a word from the vocabulary list on page R82.

<u>assess</u> (ə ses′) *v.* to evaluate or appraise

Practice and Apply
How would you assess the strengths of Montagu's letter?

Writing About Literature

Compare and Contrast Ideas In this letter, Montagu expresses her opinions about education and marriage. The audience for this letter is her daughter, who undoubtedly had her own views on those very topics—views that you can infer by reading between the lines of her mother's letter. Write a brief essay comparing and contrasting Montagu's views with her daughter's. First, fill in a Venn diagram to help you identify similarities and differences.

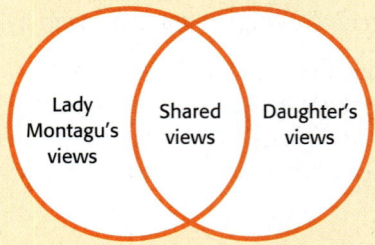

Lady Montagu's views | Shared views | Daughter's views

Your essay should include an introduction, a body, and a conclusion. The chart below lists two basic ways of organizing your body paragraphs.

Feature Approach	Subject Approach

Feature 1: Education
  A. Montagu's views
  B. her daughter's views
 	
Feature 2: Marriage
  A. Montagu's views
  B. her daughter's views
	Subject A: Montagu's views
	  A. Education
	  B. Marriage
	
	Subject B: her daughter's views
	  A. Education
	  B. Marriage

After you complete your draft, meet with a peer reviewer to evaluate each other's work and to suggest revisions. Then proofread and edit your draft for errors in spelling, grammar, and punctuation.

Learning for Life

Montagu proposes an education that will prepare her granddaughter for the future life she is likely to lead. Consider your own future and the skills you will need for it. Draft a letter to a family member or friend in which you present a plan for a year of studies and experiences that will best prepare you for your future.

Literature Online Web Activities For eFlashcards, Selection Quick Checks, and other Web activities, go to www.glencoe.com.

Vocabulary Workshop

Denotation and Connotation

Using a Semantic Chart

"Learning (if she has a real taste for it) will not only make her contented but happy in it."

— Lady Mary Wortley Montagu, from "Letter to Her Daughter"

Connecting to Literature In her letter, Montagu says that learning will make her granddaughter *contented* and *happy*. These words have similar **denotations**, or dictionary definitions, but subtly different **connotations**, or emotional associations. While each word has positive connotations, *happy* suggests a more active and highly charged emotional state than does *contented*. In using both words, Lady Montagu expresses the broad positive effect of education on her granddaughter's life.

To compare the connotations of words with similar denotations, try creating a semantic chart like the one below. Here's how:

- Write the words you're comparing in the left-hand column of the chart.
- Check a dictionary or thesaurus for the denotations and connotations of each word.
- Write the denotations and connotations in the columns at the top of the chart.
- If a word conveys the denotation or connotation at the top of the chart, put a check in the corresponding box. If it doesn't, put a zero. If you're not sure, write a question mark.

	Positive feeling	Fulfillment	Mental approval	Intense emotion	Overwhelming emotion
Contented	✓	✓	✓	0	0
Happy					
Satisfied					
Joyful					
Exuberant					

Exercise

1. Complete this semantic chart on a separate sheet of paper. Share your finished chart with your classmates and discuss which words best convey Montagu's feelings about her granddaughter's education.
2. Find three or four similar words used to describe a character in another selection in Unit 3, Part 2. Create a semantic chart for these words. Share and compare charts with your classmates.

The Essay

> *"The essay is a literary device for saying almost everything about almost anything."*
>
> —Aldous Huxley

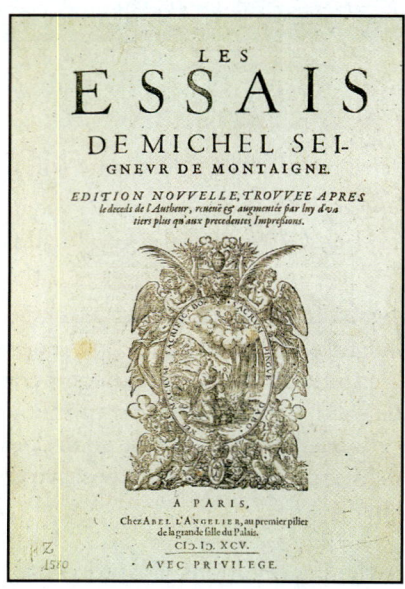

Title page from the 1595 first edition of Michel de Montaigne's *Les Essais.*

AN ESSAY IS A WORK OF PROSE NONFICTION that discusses, formally or informally, any topic. Because of the wide scope and variety of the essay, modern author E. B. White believed the essay to be a misunderstood literary genre, a "second-class citizen" in the world of letters. Yet, the essay in all its forms has remained immensely popular throughout the nearly six centuries since its humble origins.

Michel de Montaigne

Another distinguished contemporary essayist, Joseph Epstein, calls the birth of the personal essay a "happy accident of literature." In 1580 a forty-seven-year-old French lawyer, courtier, country gentleman, and writer named Michel de Montaigne (män tän´) published a volume of short prose works that exhibited his wide interests and learning. Although his early life had been dedicated to public affairs, most of the writings in this collection were short and personal, with unpretentious titles, such as "Of Idleness," "Of Smells and Odors," and "Of Books." To distinguish them from the more methodical, scholarly writings, known as *treatises,* which were common at the time, Montaigne called his works *essais,* a French word for "attempts." By coining this term for his literary musings, Montaigne is generally considered to be the father of the modern essay.

Sir Francis Bacon

In the 1590s, English philosopher and writer Francis Bacon, only seventeen years younger than Montaigne and clearly familiar with his work, used the term *essay* in the titles of several of his own commentaries on various subjects, such as truth, adversity, and the married versus the single life. Bacon also wrote about

both personal and universal topics, but he chose a more formal and objective style than Montaigne's. Bacon wrote essays closer to treatises, which are systematic examinations of scholarly subjects in such areas as philosophy, religion, and science. His essays usually begin with a thesis that is followed by supporting arguments. To support his thesis, Bacon offered extensive quotations from ancient writers, as well as short observations of his own. These concise statements (or aphorisms), which express an observation about human experience, are a hallmark of Bacon's style.

From these beginnings, the essay evolved into two distinct forms: the formal and the informal. Soon other writers were using the term *essay* for compositions in which they expressed their viewpoints on specific topics.

The Formal Essay

A **formal essay** is a prose composition in which an author writes as an impersonal, objective authority on a particular subject, with the purpose of instructing or persuading his or her readers. Using the third-person point of view instead of the first-person, the author strikes a serious tone and develops a main idea, or **thesis**, in a logical, highly organized way. Two eighteenth-century writers, Daniel Defoe and Samuel Johnson, were famous practitioners of the formal essay. Charles Lamb and William Hazlitt continued the formal essay tradition into the nineteenth century, as did Samuel Taylor Coleridge, Thomas De Quincey, Matthew Arnold, and John Stuart Mill. In the twentieth century, the formal essay was a mainstay in such fields as history, literature, and the natural and social sciences. In newspapers today, most editorials and many opinion pieces are formal essays.

The Informal Essay

By contrast, the **informal** or **personal essay** has a lighter tone, is less structured, and typically includes personal details and humor conveyed in a conversational style. Although writers may compose informal essays to instruct or persuade, they often write primarily to entertain their readers. For example, in the eighteenth century, Joseph Addison and Richard Steele wrote and published many instructive yet humorously satirical essays in *The Tatler* and *The Spectator* on such topics as marriage, education, and the folly and extravagance of the times. Nineteenth- and twentieth-century writers, including Robert Louis Stevenson, Max Beerbohm, G. K. Chesterton, Virginia Woolf, and George Orwell, contributed brilliantly to the personal essay form. Their essays address subjects ranging from the important to the trivial, in both cases providing fresh insights on life.

The formal essay has changed little since Bacon. The informal essay, however, has changed greatly. Novelist and essayist Cynthia Ozick thinks that one reason for this change might be the essayist's adaptations of fictional techniques, "including revelations, moments of suspense, moments of climax, moments of

Young Ladies' Finishing School. Thomas Rowlandson. Museum of London.
Viewing the Art: A finishing school is a school for girls that emphasizes proper social behavior. What is this illustration satirizing?

crescendo," as well as dialogue and detail. Another reason for the essay's renewed popularity may be the number and variety of forums for the personal essay in both print and electronic media—most recently in a multitude of blogs on the Internet.

Literature Online **Literary History** For more about the essay, go to www.glencoe.com.

RESPONDING AND THINKING CRITICALLY

1. (a) What are the two basic types of essay? (b) With which early essayists is each associated?

2. How would you categorize the many essays that you have written for school during the last several years? Are they primarily formal or informal?

3. (a) Name some of the techniques that modern essayists have adapted from fiction. (b) How do these techniques affect your appreciation of essays?

OBJECTIVES
- Connect literature to historical contexts and personal experience.
- Analyze qualities of the essay.
- Analyze the development of the English essay.

from *The Spectator*

Joseph Addison

MEET JOSEPH ADDISON AND SIR RICHARD STEELE

Joseph Addison and Sir Richard Steele were about as opposite as they could be. Addison was serious, reserved, and sensible. Steele was brash, outgoing, and always in debt. Nevertheless, the two formed one of the most successful literary partnerships of all time.

Childhood Friends Addison and Steele, both born in the same year, began a friendship as boys at London's Charterhouse School and continued their friendship at Oxford University. They stayed in contact after impetuous Steele left school without a degree to make a career in the army, while scholarly Addison remained behind to earn a master's degree.

> "[Bring] philosophy out of the closets and libraries, schools and colleges, to dwell in the clubs and assemblies, at tea-tables and in coffee-houses."
>
> —*The Spectator* (March 1711)

Sir Richard Steele

Literary Collaboration Their literary collaboration did not begin until the two were in their thirties. By that time, Steele had become disillusioned with the army, achieved some acclaim as a playwright, and served as the primary writer for the London *Gazette*. Addison, meanwhile, had also made a reputation for himself in the literary world and launched a promising diplomatic career. Their partnership began in 1709, when Steele decided to publish an essay-based periodical he called

The Tatler and invited his friend Addison to contribute. Steele's purpose was to "expose the false arts of life, to pull off the disguises of cunning, vanity, and affectation, and recommend a general simplicity in our dress, our discourse, and our behavior." *The Tatler* was a hybrid newspaper, literary review, and magazine of philosophical essays. As editor, Steele assumed the sardonic persona of Isaac Bickerstaff, a fictional character created by Jonathan Swift in order to perpetrate a literary hoax.

The Spectator Addison and Steele's collaboration continued in 1711, when Steele discontinued *The Tatler* for political reasons, and they launched a new, nonpolitical, essay-based periodical they called *The Spectator*. The authors succeeded so superbly in their mission "to enliven morality with wit, and to temper wit with morality" that this periodical immediately became a popular favorite. Despite the success of the magazine, the two parted ways in 1712 and later quarreled as a result of a political disagreement.

Although the pair's accomplishments included knighthood for Steele and a position as secretary of state for Addison, the two men are best remembered for their essays and their brief literary collaboration.

Joseph Addison was born in 1672 and died in 1719.

Richard Steele was born in 1672 and died in 1729.

Literature Online **Author Search** For more about Joseph Addison and Sir Richard Steele, go to www.glencoe.com.

Connecting to the Essays

The following essays from *The Spectator* satirize the manners and fashions of the society in which Addison and Steele lived. As you read, think about the following questions:

- How do you stay informed of news and trends?
- If you had the chance to write a newspaper column about modern life, what topics would you write about?

Building Background

In Addison and Steele's time, much like today, Londoners loved to gather in coffeehouses to gossip and discuss their reactions to controversial topics of the day. Many of their most heated conversations were inspired by pieces from *The Spectator*. As a result, the essays of Addison and Steele had an important influence on the manners and culture of the time.

Addison and Steele are credited with having invented the **periodical essay**, an informal essay that appears in a periodical publication such as a magazine or newspaper. The essay was usually about a topic that was the talk of the town. The topic might be a political issue one day and a play or a new mode of fashion the next.

Setting Purposes for Reading

Big Idea The English Enlightenment and Neoclassicism

As you read, think about how the Enlightenment emphasis on reason motivated writers to satirize irrational and hypocritical behavior.

Literary Element Style

Style is a writer's individual, characteristic way of writing. An author creates style through expressive qualities that distinguish his or her work, including word choice, sentence structure, and figures of speech. Style can reveal an author's attitude and purpose for writing.

- See Literary Terms Handbook, p. R17.

Literature Online Interactive Literary Elements Handbook To review or learn more about the literary elements, go to www.glencoe.com.

Reading Strategy Making Generalizations

When you draw conclusions about a text based on specific examples, ideas, or anecdotes, you are **making generalizations**. A generalization is an observation or statement that may relate universal themes and ideas to a text. To make generalizations, ask yourself questions such as the following: What is the author suggesting about the characters or about life in general? How does this literary work relate to my prior knowledge and background information?

Reading Tip: Taking Notes As you read, make generalizations by drawing conclusions from specific examples, ideas, or anecdotes in the text.

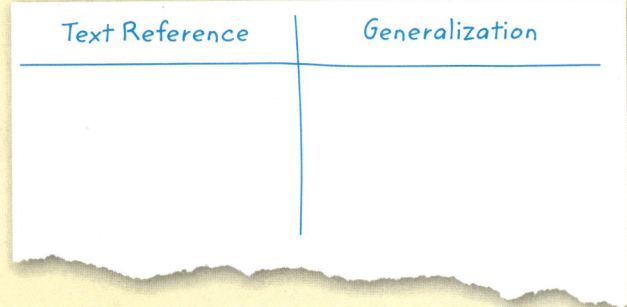

Text Reference	Generalization

OBJECTIVES
In studying these selections, you will focus on the following:
- analyzing literary genres

- analyzing an author's style
- making generalizations about a text

Sir Roger de Coverley and Addison with "The Saracen's Head", a scene from "The Spectator", 1867. William Powell Frith. Oil on canvas, 38.1 x 45.7 cm. Guildhall Art Gallery, Corporation of London, UK.

from The Spectator

Sir Roger de Coverley

Sir Richard Steele

Friday, March 2, 1711

The first of our society is a gentleman of Worcestershire, of ancient descent, a baronet, his name Sir Roger de Coverley. His great-grandfather was inventor of that famous country-dance[1] which is called after him. All who know that shire[2] are very well acquainted with the parts and merits of Sir Roger. He is a gentleman that is very singular in his behavior, but his singularities[3] proceed from his good sense and are contradictions to the manners of the world only as he thinks the world is in the wrong. However, this humor creates him no enemies, for he does nothing with sourness or obstinacy; and his being unconfined to modes and forms makes him but the readier and more capable to please and oblige all who know him. When he is in town, he lives in Soho Square.[4] It is said he keeps hisself a bachelor by reason he was crossed in love by a perverse,[5] beautiful widow of the next county to him. Before this disappointment, Sir Roger was what you call a fine gentleman, had often supped with my Lord Rochester and Sir George Etherege,[6] fought a duel upon his first coming to town, and kicked Bully Dawson[7] in a public coffeehouse for calling him "youngster."

---

1. *That famous country-dance* is a dance called the Roger of Coverley, dating from 1685.
2. A *shire* is a county.
3. *Singularities* are unique or peculiar features.

4. *Soho Square* is a fashionable district in the center of London.
5. Here, *perverse* means "willfully determined; contrary."
6. *Lord Rochester* and *Sir George Etherege* are John Wilmot, Earl of Rochester, a notorious Restoration poet, and Sir George Etherege, a playwright.
7. *Bully Dawson* was a notorious swindler.

Big Idea **The English Enlightenment and Neoclassicism** *What Enlightenment value is attributed to Sir Roger in this passage?*

Literary Element Style *What aspect of Steele's style indicates that he is satirizing the conventional notions of an English gentleman?*

But being ill used by the above-mentioned widow, he was very serious for a year and a half; and though, his temper being naturally jovial, he at last got over it, he grew careless of himself and never dressed afterwards. He continues to wear a coat and doublet of the same cut that were in fashion at the time of his repulse,[8] which, in his merry humors, he tells us, has been in and out[9] twelve times since he first wore it. . . . He is now in his fifty-sixth year, cheerful, gay, and hearty; keeps a good house both in town and country; a great lover of mankind; but there is such a mirthful cast in his behavior that he is rather beloved than esteemed. His tenants grow rich, his servants look satisfied, all the young women profess love to him, and the young men are glad of his company; when he comes into a house, he calls the servants by their names and talks all the way upstairs to a visit. I must not omit that Sir Roger is a justice of the quorum;[10] that he fills the chair at a quarter-session[11] with great abilities; and three months ago gained universal applause by explaining a passage in the Game Act.[12]

---

8. *Repulse* means "rejection," referring to his rejection by the widow.
9. When Steele writes *in and out,* he means "in and out of fashion."

10. *A justice of the quorum* is a justice of the peace.
11. In a county court, a meeting held four times a year is called a *quarter-session.*
12. The *Game Act* was a law governing hunting.

Reading Strategy Making Generalizations *What generalization can you make about Sir Roger from this statement?*

Coffee-House in Salisbury Market-Place.

Customers in the coffee house in Salisbury market-place. Thomas Rowlandson. Reproduced in *The Graphic,* Christmas number. 1891.

Country Manners   Joseph Addison

Tuesday, July 17, 1711

The first and most obvious reflections which arise in a man who changes the city for the country are upon the different manners of the people whom he meets with in those two different scenes of life. By manners, I do not mean morals, but behavior and good breeding, as they show themselves in the town and in the country. And here, in the first place, I must observe a very great revolution that has happened in this article of good breeding. Several obliging deferences, condescensions, and submissions, with many outward forms and ceremonies that accompany them, were first of all brought up among the politer part of mankind, who lived in courts and cities and distinguished themselves from the rustic part of the species (who on all occasions acted bluntly and naturally) by such a mutual **complaisance** and intercourse of civilities. These forms of conversation by degrees multiplied and grew troublesome; the modish[1] world found too great a constraint in them and have, therefore, thrown most of them aside. Conversation, like the Romish religion,[2] was so encumbered with show and ceremony that it stood in need of a reformation to retrench its superfluities and restore it to its natural good sense and beauty. At present, therefore, an unconstrained carriage and a certain openness of behavior are the height of good breeding. The fashionable world is grown free and easy; our manners sit more loose upon us; nothing is so modish as an agreeable **negligence**. In a word, good breeding shows itself most where to an ordinary eye it appears the least.

If after this we look on the people of mode in the country, we find in them the manners of the last age. They have no sooner fetched themselves up to the fashion of the polite world but the town has dropped them and are nearer to the first state of nature than to those refinements which formerly reigned in the court and still prevail in the country. One may now know a man that never conversed in the world by his excess of good breeding. A polite country squire[3] shall make you as many bows in half an hour as would serve a courtier[4] for a week. There is infinitely more to do about place and precedence in a meeting of justices' wives than in an assembly of duchesses.

This rural politeness is very troublesome to a man of my temper, who generally takes the chair that is next me and walks first or last, in the front or in the rear, as chance directs. I have known my friend Sir Roger's dinner almost cold before the company could adjust the ceremonial and be prevailed upon to sit down; and have heartily pitied my old friend when I have seen him forced to pick and cull[5] his guests, as they sat at the several parts of his table, that he might drink their healths according to their respective ranks and qualities. Honest Will Wimble, who I should have thought had been altogether uninfected with ceremony, gives me abundance of trouble in this particular. Though he has been fishing all the morning, he will not help himself at dinner till I am served. When we are going out of the hall, he runs behind me; and last night, as we were walking in the fields, stopped short at a stile till I came up to it and, upon my making signs to him to get over, told me, with a serious smile, that sure I believed they had no manners in the country.

There has happened another revolution in the

Visual Vocabulary
A *stile* is a set of steps passing over a fence.

---

1. *Modish* means "stylish" or "fashionable."
2. The *Romish religion* is Roman Catholicism.

3. A *squire* is a gentleman and landowner.
4. A *courtier* is an attendant at a royal court.
5. *Cull* means "choose."

Vocabulary

complaisance (kəm plā′ səns) *n.* a willingness to please, be gracious, or be courteous
negligence (neg′ li jəns) *n.* an air of careless ease or casualness

Reading Strategy   Making Generalizations   *Based on Addison's analysis, what generalizations can you make about the difference between city manners and country manners?*

Literary Element   Style   *What effect does Addison's use of personal pronouns, such as* my *and* me, *have on this essay?*

Lloyd's Coffee House, London, 1798.
William Holland. Intaglio print.

point of good breeding, which relates to the conversation among men of mode and which I cannot but look upon as very extraordinary. It was certainly one of the first distinctions of a well-bred man to express everything that had the most remote appearance of being obscene in modest terms and distant phrases; whilst the clown, who had no such delicacy of conception and expression, clothed his ideas in those plain homely terms that are the most obvious and natural. This kind of good manners was perhaps carried to an excess, so as to make conversation too stiff, formal, and precise; for which reason (as hypocrisy in one age is generally succeeded by atheism in another) conversation is in a great measure relapsed into the first extreme; so that at present several of our men of the town, and particularly those who have been polished in France, make use of the most coarse, uncivilized words in our language and utter themselves often in such a manner as a clown would blush to hear.

This infamous piece of good breeding, which reigns among the coxcombs[6] of the town, has not yet made its way into the country; and as it is impossible for such an **irrational** way of

conversation to last long among a people that make any profession of religion or show of modesty, if the country gentlemen get into it, they will certainly be left in the lurch. Their good breeding will come too late to them, and they will be thought a parcel of lewd clowns, while they fancy themselves talking together like men of wit and pleasure.

As the two points of good breeding which I have hitherto insisted upon regard behavior and conversation, there is a third which turns upon dress. In this too the country are very much behindhand. The rural beaus are not yet got out of the fashion that took place at the time of the Revolution[7] but ride about the country in red coats and laced hats, while the women in many parts are still trying to outvie one another in the height of their headdresses.

But a friend of mine who is now upon the western circuit, having promised to give me an account of the several modes and fashions that prevail in the different parts of the nation through which he passes, I shall defer the enlarging upon this last topic till I have received a letter from him, which I expect every post. ❧

---

6. *Coxcombs* are vain, foolish people.

7. *Revolution* refers to the Glorious Revolution of 1688, in which William III and Mary II took the throne of England from King James II without any bloodshed.

Reading Strategy Making Generalizations *What is Addison both explaining and predicting in this sentence?*

RESPONDING AND THINKING CRITICALLY

Respond

1. What are your impressions of Sir Roger de Coverley and the country folk?

Recall and Interpret

2. (a)Describe Sir Roger's odd traits. (b)Do you think Steele is being ironic when he attributes these "singularities" to Sir Roger's "good sense"?

3. (a)What disappointment did Sir Roger suffer? (b)How has it affected him?

4. (a)Summarize the basic difference that Addison describes between polite behavior in the country and in the city. (b)Why is Addison troubled by the "rural politeness" he experiences?

Analyze and Evaluate

5. In what ways is the description of Sir Roger meant to be a **caricature,** or exaggeration, of certain individual qualities for ridiculous effect?

6. (a)How is "Country Manners" a satire? (b)What do Addison's observations suggest about his opinion of city dwellers and country folk?

Connect

7. **Big Idea** **The English Enlightenment and Neoclassicism** The Enlightenment was an age of satire in which human follies were ridiculed. In your opinion, is satire a popular literary form today? Explain.

LITERARY ANALYSIS

Literary Element Style

Although Addison and Steele's eighteenth-century English may occasionally seem long-winded to modern readers, it was an elegant and familiar **style** that was popular in its day.

1. What elements of style do Addison and Steele use to create a sense of informality in their essays?

2. In "Sir Roger de Coverley," what different effect would Steele have produced if he had used the word *assaulted* instead of *kicked* in his description of what Sir Roger did to Bully Dawson?

3. In "Country Manners," what is the effect of Addison's analogy between "Romish religion" and polite conversation?

Writing About Literature

Respond to Character From the point of view of a modern-day Mr. or Ms. Spectator, write a brief informal essay about a current political figure. Feel free to use humor and other elements of the informal style. You might try to publish your essay in your school newspaper.

READING AND VOCABULARY

Reading Strategy Making Generalizations

When you make generalizations about essays, such as the excerpts from *The Spectator*, you need to support your generalizations with evidence from the text.

Partner Activity With a partner, discuss your reading of "Sir Roger de Coverley." What generalization can you make about Steele's attitude toward class distinctions in eighteenth-century society?

Vocabulary Practice

Practice with Antonyms Identify the antonym for each vocabulary word listed in the first column.

1. complaisance   **a.** deference   **b.** rudeness

2. negligence   **a.** indifference   **b.** diligence

3. irrational   **a.** logical   **b.** rash

Literature Online **Web Activities** For eFlashcards, Selection Quick Checks, and other Web activities, go to www.glencoe.com.

Comparing Literature Across Time and Place

Connecting to the Reading Selections

Pandemics, or epidemics that affect multiple countries, have changed the course of civilization. Although modern vaccines have saved innumerable lives from diseases such as smallpox and bubonic plague, new threats such as the avian (bird) flu are raising alarms across the world. Could a catastrophe on the scale of the influenza epidemic of 1918–1919, which killed twenty-five million people, happen again?

England, 1722

Daniel Defoe

from *A Journal of the Plague Year* .... historical fiction **622**

Grieving at the burial pit

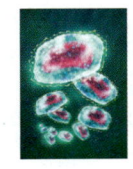

United States, 2002

Richard Preston

from "*The Demon in the Freezer*" .... magazine article **629**

The amazingly thin line between safety and catastrophe

Classical Greece, c. 420 B.C.

Thucydides

from *History of the Peloponnesian War* .... history **635**

Reading into the power of epidemic

French Algeria, 1947

Albert Camus

from *The Plague* .... novel **639**

Carrying on, numb with life

COMPARING THE Big Idea The English Enlightenment and Neoclassicism

In the 1700s, the works of such writers as Defoe often showed how the past repeats itself, sometimes unexpectedly. The importance of learning from history and the attempt to find order in chaos are strong features in the works here by Defoe, Preston, Thucydides, and Camus.

COMPARING Style

Style expresses both a writer's personality and a certain way of seeing the world. Note how the style of these selections contributes to the writers' messages.

COMPARING Cultures

The tragedies that strike various cultures often serve as warnings for future generations and as lessons to remind people of the precarious nature of life.

from *A Journal of the Plague Year*

MEET DANIEL DEFOE

Spy, satirist, journalist, merchant, and writer, Daniel Defoe bounced back and forth between bankruptcy and prosperity, prison and political favor, throughout his life. Even in his dimmest moments, he was known to keep his sense of humor. Once, as a punishment for publishing a controversial pamphlet, he was sentenced to the pillory, a wooden device used for public punishment that locked the prisoner's head and hands. For the occasion, Defoe composed and distributed a poem, "Hymn to the Pillory"—a mock-Pindaric ode that inspired audience members to decorate the pillory with flowers.

> *"The best of men cannot suspend*
> *their fate:*
> *The good die early, and the bad*
> *die late."*
>
> —Daniel Defoe

Early Schemes As the son of a Protestant Dissenter (someone who defied the Church of England), Defoe attended the Reverend Charles Morton's academy for Dissenters at Newington Green in hopes of becoming a Presbyterian minister. Here he developed his clear writing style.

Trade and commerce fascinated Defoe, leading him to abandon his plans for the ministry to become a merchant instead. His downfall was a weakness for risky business ventures. Defoe's various enterprises in hosiery, brickmaking, and breeding civets (cat-like mammals that secrete a musk-like substance used to make perfume) all failed. At age twenty-five, he joined a rebellion against the Roman Catholic King James II in which six hundred rebels died, but Defoe escaped. Three years later, the king fled to France, and

Defoe became the leading pamphleteer and political informant for Protestant King William III. Despite his royal connections, however, Defoe's troubles continued. He wrote a satire, *The Shortest Way with the Dissenters*, which was intended to ridicule the suppression of dissent. However, both Anglicans and Dissenters missed the point. Defoe was later jailed, but he was soon released by the Earl of Oxford, Robert Harley, for whom Defoe became a spy.

Literary Breakthrough Defoe's breakthrough work wasn't published until he was sixty—the first part of *The Life and Adventures of Robinson Crusoe*. Defoe presented this fictional work as a memoir; it is loosely based on the real-life adventures of Alexander Selkirk, a Scottish sailor who was marooned on one of the Juan Fernández Islands, off the coast of Chile, and lived there alone from October 1704 to February 1709.

Defoe again applied his journalistic method to fiction when, in 1721, reports reached London of a plague outbreak in continental Europe. Many people still remembered with horror the Great Plague of 1664 and 1665 that killed more than 75,000 of London's estimated population of 460,000. Aware of the public's fear and fascination with the epidemic, Defoe wrote *A Journal of the Plague Year*, which was presented as a first-hand account of the Great Plague. Literary critic Maximillian E. Novak points out that "Defoe never forgot that history was something that happened to masses of people, not just to Kings and Queens."

Daniel Defoe was born in 1660 and died in 1731.

Literature Online **Author Search** For more about Daniel Defoe, go to www.glencoe.com.

Connecting to the Story

In the following selection, Defoe describes the powerful effect the Great Plague of London had on people. As you read, think about how you would feel if you witnessed a major disaster, such as a hurricane. How might this affect the rest of your life?

Building Background

The bubonic plague first appeared in Europe in 1347. By 1351 it had killed twenty-four million people—one-fourth of Europe's population. It became known as the Black Death for the way victims appeared in the final stages of their illness—as the victims' respiratory systems failed, their bodies turned dark purple. The plague still exists, and small outbreaks have occurred as recently as 1994. Scientists now know that the plague is caused by tiny, rod-shaped bacteria called *Yersinia pestis,* which is spread by fleas that live on rats. Scientists have developed vaccines and antibiotics to combat any further outbreaks.

Setting Purposes for Reading

Big Idea The English Enlightenment and Neoclassicism

As you read, consider how Defoe's portrayal of a past outbreak of the plague fits into the concerns associated with the English Enlightenment and Neoclassicism.

Literary Element Historical Fiction

Historical fiction sets characters against the backdrop of a period other than the author's own. This type of fiction often blends actual historical people with fictitious ones and realistic details with symbolic ones. As you read the excerpt from *A Journal of the Plague Year,* notice how the fictional narrative is grounded in history.

- See Literary Terms Handbook, p. R8.

Literature Online **Interactive Literary Elements Handbook** To review or learn more about the literary elements, go to www.glencoe.com.

Reading Strategy Connecting to Contemporary Issues

Connecting means linking what you read to events in your own life or to other selections you have read. Associating details from literature with those from current events can help you further understand what you read. As you read, think about how the emergence of viruses today, such as Ebola and SARS, relates to Defoe's narrative about the plague.

Reading Tip: Making Connections As you read, identify things from your experience or other things you've read that link to Defoe's selection.

Detail in selection	Detail from my experience	Connection

Vocabulary

confining (kən′ fīn ing) *adj.* restricting; limiting; p. 625 *The confining nature of the assignment frustrated Juan.*

oppressed (ə prest′) *adj.* burdened; weighed down; p. 626 *Jim felt oppressed with sadness after his cousin's funeral.*

defy (di fī′) *v.* to resist; to refuse to cooperate with; p. 627 *Mrs. Johnson warned Betty not to defy her authority in the classroom.*

prodigious (prə dij′ əs) *adj.* great in size, number, or degree; enormous; p. 627 *The prodigious accomplishments of the Elizabethan theater were a testament to the importance that Queen Elizabeth I placed on drama.*

Vocabulary Tip: Word Parts Breaking down a word into its parts—prefix, root, and suffix—can help you understand the meaning of unfamiliar words.

OBJECTIVES
In studying this selection, you will focus on the following:
- relating literature to historical events
- analyzing historical fiction
- connecting to contemporary issues

from *A Journal of the Plague Year*

Daniel Defoe

Death on a Pale Horse, 1867. Gustave Doré. Illustration. This image is an illustration of "Plague," one of the four horsemen of the Apocalypse mentioned in the Book of Revelations in the Christian Bible.

1 went all the first part of the time freely about the streets, though not so freely as to run myself into apparent danger, except when they dug the great pit in the churchyard of our parish[1] of Aldgate. A terrible pit it was, and I could not resist my curiosity to go and see it. As near as I may judge, it was about forty feet in length, and about fifteen or sixteen feet broad, and at the time I first looked at it, about nine feet deep; but it was said they dug it near twenty feet deep afterwards in one part of it, till they could go no deeper for the water; for they had, it seems, dug several large pits before this. For though the plague was long a-coming to our parish, yet, when it did come, there was no parish in or about London where it raged with such violence as in the two parishes of Aldgate and Whitechapel.

I say they had dug several pits in another ground, when the distemper[2] began to spread in our parish, and especially when the dead carts began to go about, which was not, in our parish, till the beginning of August. Into these pits they had put perhaps fifty or sixty bodies each; then they made larger holes, wherein they buried all that the cart brought in a week, which, by the middle to the end of August, came to from two hundred to four hundred a week; and they could not well dig them larger, because of the order of the magistrates[3] **confining** them to leave no bodies within six feet of the surface; and the water coming on at about seventeen or eighteen feet, they could not well, I say, put more in one pit. But now, at the beginning of September, the plague raging in a dreadful manner, and the number of burials in our parish increasing to more than was ever buried in any parish about London of no larger extent, they ordered this dreadful gulf to be dug, for such it was, rather than a pit.

They had supposed this pit would have supplied them for a month or more when they dug it, and some blamed the churchwardens for suffering[4] such a frightful thing, telling them they were making preparations to bury the whole parish, and the like; but time made it appear the churchwardens knew the condition of the parish better than they did, for, the pit being finished the fourth of September, I think, they began to bury in it the sixth, and by the twentieth, which was just two weeks, they had thrown into it 1,114 bodies when they were obliged to fill it up, the bodies being then come to lie within six feet of the surface. I doubt not but there may be some ancient persons alive in the parish who can justify[5] the fact of this and are able to show even in what place of the churchyard the pit lay better than I can. The mark of it also was many years to be seen in the churchyard on the surface, lying in length parallel with the passage which goes by the west wall of the churchyard out of Houndsditch, and turns east again into Whitechapel, coming out near the Three Nuns' Inn.

It was about the tenth of September that my curiosity led, or rather drove, me to go and see this pit again, when there had been near four hundred people buried in it; and I was not content to see it in the daytime, as I had done before, for then there would have been nothing to have been seen but the loose earth; for all the bodies that were thrown in were immediately covered with earth by those they called the buriers, which at other times were called bearers; but I resolved to go in the night and see some of them thrown in.

---

1. In England, a *parish* is a subdivision of a county.
2. *Distemper* is a disease—in this case, the plague.
3. *Magistrates* are officers empowered to administer laws.

Reading Strategy Connecting to Contemporary Issues
How is this tendency shown in contemporary society?

Vocabulary

confining (kən´ fīn ing) *adj.* restricting; limiting

---

4. As used here, *suffering* means "permitting."
5. *Justify* means "verify."

Big Idea The English Enlightenment and Neoclassicism *How does the narrator's comment in this sentence link to the intellectual movements of Defoe's time?*

There was a strict order to prevent people coming to those pits, and that was only to prevent infection. But after some time that order was more necessary, for people that were infected and near their end, and delirious also, would run to those pits, wrapped in blankets or rugs, and throw themselves in, and, as they said, bury themselves. I cannot say that the officers suffered any willingly to lie there; but I have heard that in a great pit in Finsbury, in the parish of Cripplegate, it lying open then to the fields, for it was not then walled about, [people] came and threw themselves in, and expired there, before they threw any earth upon them; and that when they came to bury others and found them there, they were quite dead, though not cold.

This may serve a little to describe the dreadful condition of that day, though it is impossible to say anything that is able to give a true idea of it to those who did not see it, other than this, that it was indeed very, very, very dreadful, and such as no tongue can express.

I got admittance into the churchyard by being acquainted with the sexton[6] who attended; who, though he did not refuse me at all, yet earnestly persuaded me not to go, telling me very seriously, for he was a good, religious, and sensible man, that it was indeed their business and duty to venture, and to run all hazards,[7] and that in it they might hope to be preserved; but that I had no apparent call to it but my own curiosity, which, he said, he believed I would not pretend was sufficient to justify my running that hazard. I told him I had been pressed in my mind to go, and that perhaps it might be an instructing sight, that might not be without its uses. "Nay," says the good man, "if you will venture upon that score,[8] name of God go in; for, depend upon it, it

will be a sermon to you, it may be, the best that ever you heard in your life. 'Tis a speaking sight," says he, "and has a voice with it, and a loud one, to call us all to repentance"; and with that he opened the door and said, "Go, if you will."

His discourse had shocked my resolution a little, and I stood wavering for a good while, but just at that interval I saw two links come over from the end of the Minories,[9] and heard the bellman,[10] and then appeared a dead cart, as they called it, coming over the streets; so I could no longer resist my desire of seeing it, and went in. There was nobody, as I could perceive at first, in the churchyard, or going into it, but the buriers and the fellow that drove the cart, or rather led the horse and cart; but when they came up to the pit they saw a man go to and again,[11] muffled up in a brown cloak, and making motions with his hands under his cloak, as if he was in great agony, and the buriers immediately gathered about him, supposing he was one of those poor delirious or desperate creatures that used to pretend, as I have said, to bury themselves. He said nothing as he walked about, but two or three times groaned very deeply and loud, and sighed as he would break his heart.

Visual Vocabulary
Links are torches.

When the buriers came up to him they soon found he was neither a person infected and desperate, as I have observed above, or a person distempered[12] in mind, but one **oppressed** with a dreadful weight of grief indeed, having his wife and several of his children all in the cart that

---

6. The *sexton* was responsible for maintaining church property and for digging graves for churchyard burials.
7. *Hazards* are risks.
8. *Upon that score* means "for that reason."

9. *The Minories* is a street in London.
10. The *bellman* was the town crier, who rang a bell to attract attention. Part of his job was to announce deaths.
11. *To and again* means "to and fro."
12. Here, *distempered* means "deranged."

Flight of the Townspeople into the Country to Escape from the Plague, A.D. 1630. Hand-colored woodcut from *A Looking-glass for Town and Country;* broadside in the collection of the Society of Antiquaries.
Viewing the Art: What might the skeleton and the cart represent? What does this scene have in common with Defoe's account?

was just come in with him, and he followed in an agony and excess of sorrow. He mourned heartily, as it was easy to see, but with a kind of masculine grief that could not give itself vent by tears; and calmly **defying** the buriers to let him alone, said he would only see the bodies thrown in and go away, so they left importuning[13] him. But no sooner was the cart turned round and the bodies shot into the pit promiscuously,[14] which was a surprise to him, for he at least expected they would have been decently laid in, though indeed he was afterwards convinced that was impracticable;[15] I say, no sooner did he see the sight but he cried out aloud, unable to contain himself. I could not hear what he said, but he went backward two or three steps and fell down in a swoon. The buriers ran to him and took him up, and in a little while he came to himself, and they led him away to the Pie Tavern over against the end of Houndsditch, where, it seems, the man was known, and where they took care of him. He looked into the pit again as he went away, but the buriers had covered the bodies so immediately with throwing in earth, that though

there was light enough, for there were lanterns, and candles in them, placed all night round the sides of the pit, upon heaps of earth, seven or eight, or perhaps more, yet nothing could be seen.

This was a mournful scene indeed, and affected me almost as much as the rest; but the other was awful and full of terror. The cart had in it sixteen or seventeen bodies; some were wrapped up in linen sheets, some in rags, some little other than naked, or so loose that what covering they had fell from them in the shooting out of the cart, and they fell quite naked among the rest; but the matter was not much to them, or the indecency much to any one else, seeing they were all dead, and were to be huddled together into the common grave of mankind, as we may call it, for here was no difference made, but poor and rich went together; there was no other way of burials, neither was it possible there should, for coffins were not to be had for the **prodigious** numbers that fell in such a calamity as this. ❧

13. *Left importuning* means "stopped troubling."
14. Here, *promiscuously* means "casually" or "indiscriminately."
15. *Impracticable* means "not feasible."

Vocabulary

defy (di fī´) *v.* to resist; to refuse to cooperate with

Literary Element Historical Fiction *How do the details and the characterization of the cloaked man in the preceding two paragraphs contribute to the story?*

Reading Strategy Connecting to Contemporary Issues *What contemporary disasters have caused similar shortages?*

Vocabulary

prodigious (prə di´ jəs) *adj.* great in size, number, or degree; enormous

AFTER YOU READ

RESPONDING AND THINKING CRITICALLY

Respond

1. Which of the narrator's observations moved you the most? Why did this particular observation affect you?

Recall and Interpret

2. (a)Why was the great pit dug in the churchyard of the parish? (b)Why might people have been upset to see such a large pit being dug?

3. (a)Why did the initial order forbidding people to see the pit become more necessary as time passed? (b)What do the actions of the plague-infected people tell you about their state of mind?

4. (a)Describe the type of burial that is given to plague victims in the churchyard. (b)What does this say about the nature of death?

Analyze and Evaluate

5. (a)How do the statistics and factual details add to the account? (b)Which details were most powerful?

6. (a)Describe the **tone** of this selection. (b)Do you find it appropriate for the subject? Explain.

Connect

7. How might the lives of the survivors have been affected by the devastation of the plague?

8. **Big Idea** The English Enlightenment and Neoclassicism How does Defoe portray religion in the time of the plague?

LITERARY ANALYSIS

Literary Element **Historical Fiction**

Writers of **historical fiction** sometimes present history through the eyes of a real figure from the past. Some scholars believe Defoe used an actual diary from the time of the plague for reference and that the narrator is modeled after Defoe's uncle, Henry Foe.

1. What details from *A Journal of the Plague Year* could you investigate to check Defoe's accuracy?

2. Why might Defoe have chosen to write his account as fiction, rather than nonfiction?

Writing About Literature

Evaluate Author's Craft How well do you think Defoe tells the story of the plague? Much of *A Journal of the Plague Year* hinges on the narrator, who speaks from a first-person point of view. Write a brief essay analyzing the effectiveness of the first-person point of view in the selection.

READING AND VOCABULARY

Reading Strategy **Connecting to Contemporary Issues**

Defoe's portrayal of the plague has resonance in today's world—both for the problems caused by disasters that create large death tolls in poor, impoverished areas and for the danger of emergent viruses that could cause new epidemics.

Partner Activity Meet with a classmate to discuss the connections to contemporary issues you made while reading the selection by Defoe.

Vocabulary **Practice**

Practice with Word Parts Match each vocabulary word with the definition of its root.

1. confining   **a.** "to press against"

2. oppressed   **b.** "omen"

3. defy   **c.** "end"

4. prodigious   **d.** "to trust"

Literature Online **Web Activities** For eFlashcards, Selection Quick Checks, and other Web activities, go to www.glencoe.com.

BEFORE YOU READ

Building Background

Richard Preston has gained literary recognition for journalism and nonfiction books that tell dramatic stories about scientific subjects. He gained wide attention for his best-selling 1994 book *The Hot Zone*, in which he traces the Ebola virus from a cave in Africa to a lab in Virginia. Preston's nonfiction works employ techniques of fiction not usually associated with scientific writing, including shifts in perspectives and voice and use of rising action.

The following excerpt is from "The Demon in the Freezer," an article in the *New Yorker* magazine that Preston expanded into a book in 2002. It deals with smallpox at both the microscopic level in the labo-ratory and at the global level of how viruses can alter the course of history, including the potential for bioterrorism. In this excerpt, Preston details the history of smallpox and an outbreak in the 1970s that was thwarted before it could extend past the borders of Yugoslavia. The disease has been primarily wiped out, except for a few samples of the virus stored in known government laboratories and perhaps other clandestine locations.

Literature Online Author Search For more about Richard Preston, go to www.glencoe.com.

from The Demon in the Freezer

Richard Preston

A Maryland facility prepares to manufacture the smallpox virus. Though the disease is eradicated, post 9/11 fears of bio-weapon attacks are causing the US government to renew aging supplies of the vaccine. May 2, 2001. Rockville, Maryland.

The smallpox virus first became entangled with the human species somewhere between three thousand and twelve thousand years ago—possibly in Egypt at the time of the Pharaohs. Somewhere on earth at roughly that time, the virus jumped out of an unknown animal into its first human victim, and began to spread. Viruses are parasites that multiply inside the cells of their hosts, and they are the smallest life forms. Smallpox developed a deep affinity for human beings. It is thought to have killed more people than any other infectious disease, including the Black Death of the Middle Ages.

It was declared eradicated from the human species in 1979, after a twelve-year effort by a team of doctors and health workers from the World Health Organization. Smallpox now exists only in laboratories.

Smallpox is explosively contagious, and it travels through the air. Virus particles in the mouth become airborne when the host talks. If you inhale a single particle of smallpox, you can come down with the disease. After you've been infected, there is a typical incubation period of ten days. During that time, you feel normal. Then the illness hits with a spike of fever, a backache, and vomiting, and a bit later tiny red spots appear all over the body. The spots turn into blisters, called pustules, and the pustules enlarge, filling with pressurized opalescent pus. The eruption of pustules is sometimes called the splitting of the dermis. The skin doesn't break, but splits horizontally, tearing away from its underlayers. The pustules become hard, bloated sacs the size of peas, encasing the body with pus, and the skin resembles a cobblestone street.

The pain of the splitting is extraordinary. People lose the ability to speak, and their eyes can squeeze shut with pustules, but they remain alert. Death comes with a breathing arrest or a heart attack or shock or an immune-system storm, though exactly how smallpox kills a person is not known. There are many mysteries about the smallpox virus. Since the seventeenth century, doctors have understood that if the pustules merge into sheets across the body the victim will usually die: the virus has split the whole skin. If the victim survives, the pustules turn into scabs and fall off, leaving scars. This is known as ordinary smallpox.

Some people develop extreme smallpox, which is loosely called black pox. Doctors separate black pox into two forms—flat smallpox and hemorrhagic smallpox. In a case of flat smallpox, the skin remains smooth and doesn't pustulate, but it darkens until it looks charred, and it can slip off the body in sheets. In hemorrhagic smallpox, black, unclotted blood oozes or runs from the mouth and other body orifices. Black pox is close to a hundred per cent fatal. If any sign of it appears in the body, the victim will almost certainly die. Fatal smallpox can destroy the body's entire skin—both the exterior skin and the interior skin that lines the passages of the body.

Smallpox virus's scientific name is variola. It means "spotted" in Latin, and it was given to the disease by a medieval bishop. The virus,

"The pustules become hard, bloated sacs the size of peas, encasing the body with pus, and the skin resembles a cobblestone street."

as a life form, comes in two subspecies: *Variola minor* and *Variola major*. Minor is a weak mutant, and was first described in 1863 by doctors in Jamaica. People usually survive it. Classic major kills one out of three people if they haven't been vaccinated or if they've lost their immunity. The death rate with major can go higher—how much higher no one knows. *Variola major* killed half of its victims in an outbreak in Canada in 1924, and presumably many of them developed black pox. Smallpox is less contagious than measles but more contagious than mumps. It tends to go around until it has infected nearly everyone.

The man who is most widely credited with the eradication of smallpox from the human species is a doctor named Donald Ainslie Henderson. Everyone calls him D. A. Henderson. He was the director of the World Health Organization's Smallpox Eradication Unit from its inception, in 1966, to 1977, just before the last case occurred. Smallpox killed at least three hundred million people in the twentieth century. During that time, humanity was largely immune to smallpox, which is not the case today. When D. A. Henderson arrived on the scene in 1966, two million people a year were dying of smallpox. In the years since the eradication effort began, Henderson and his team have effectively saved more than fifty million lives.

On February 15, 1972, a thirty-eight-year-old Muslim clergyman returned to his home town of Damnjane, in Kosovo, Yugoslavia, after he'd been on a pilgrimage to Mecca, stopping at holy sites in Iraq. I will call him the Pilgrim. A photograph of the Pilgrim shows a man who looks well educated, has an intelligent face, and is wearing a clipped mustache and a beret. He had travelled by bus for his entire journey. The

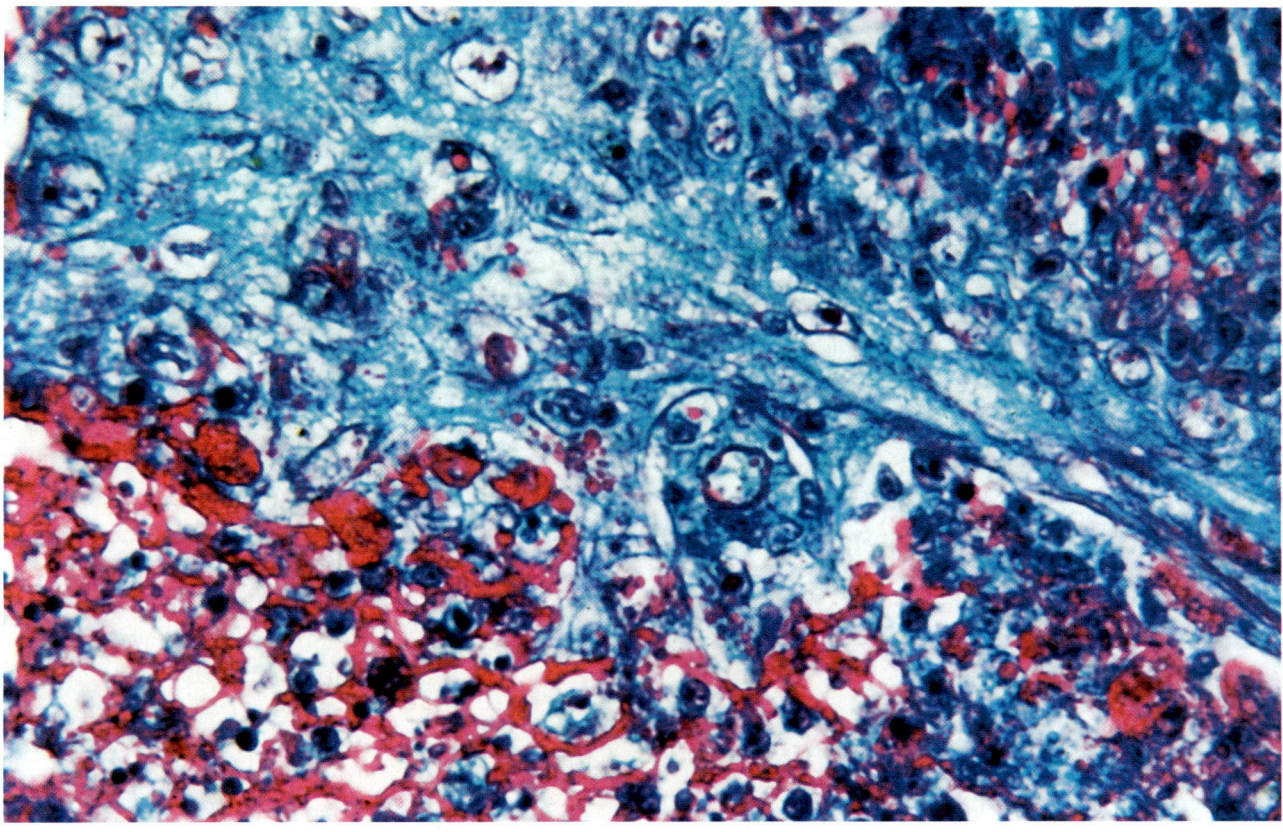

A micrograph shows the changes caused to human skin tissue due to the infection of the smallpox virus. Smallpox is a potentially fatal disease which is only preventable by vaccination.

morning after his return home, he woke up feeling achy. At first, he thought he was tired from the long bus ride, but then he realized that he had caught a bug. He shivered for a day or two, and developed a red rash brought on by his fever, but quickly recovered. He had been vaccinated for smallpox two months earlier. Indeed, the Yugoslav medical authorities had been vaccinating the population of Yugoslavia relentlessly for more than fifty years, and the country was considered to be thoroughly immunized. The last case of smallpox in Yugoslavia had occurred in 1930.

The Pilgrim's family members and friends came to visit him. They wanted to hear about his trip, and he enjoyed telling them about it. Meanwhile, variola particles were leaking out of raw spots in the back of his throat and mixing with his saliva. When he spoke, tiny droplets of saliva, too small to be seen, drifted around him in a droplet cloud. If the person is throwing off a lethal virus, the cloud becomes a hot zone that can extend ten feet in all directions. Although the raw spots in the Pilgrim's throat amounted to a tiny surface of virus emission, smaller than a postage stamp, in a biological sense it was as hot as the surface of the sun, and it put enough smallpox into the air to paralyze Yugoslavia.

Variola particles are built to survive in the air. They are rounded-off rectangles that have a knobby, patterned surface—a gnarly hand-grenade look. Some experts call the particles bricks. The whole brick is made of a hundred different proteins, assembled and interlocked in a three-dimensional puzzle, which nobody has ever figured out. Virus experts feel that the structure of a smallpox particle is almost breathtakingly beautiful and deeply mathematical—one of the unexplored wonders of the viral universe. The structure protects the virus's genetic material: a long strand of DNA coiled in the center of the brick.

RICHARD PRESTON **631**

Pox bricks are the largest viruses. If a smallpox brick were the size of a real brick then a cold-virus particle would be a blueberry sitting on the brick. But smallpox particles are still extremely small; about three million smallpox bricks laid down in rows would pave the period at the end of this sentence. A smallpox victim emits several bricks in each invisible droplet of saliva that spews into the air when the person speaks or coughs. When an airborne smallpox particle lands on a mucus membrane in someone's throat or lung, it sticks. It enters a cell and begins to make copies of itself. For one to three weeks, the virus spreads from cell to cell, amplifying silently in the body. No one has discovered exactly where the virus hides during its incubation phase. Probably it gets into the lymph cells, confusing the immune system, and victims are said to experience terrible dreams.

On February 21st, when the Pilgrim had been feeling achy for almost a week, a thirty-year-old man, a schoolteacher, who is known to experts as Ljatif M., arrived in Djakovica, a few miles from the Pilgrim's town, to enroll in the Higher Institute of Education. Doctors who later investigated the schoolteacher's case never found out how he had come in contact with the Pilgrim. One of them must have ended up in the other's town. Possibly they stood next to each other in a shop—something like that.

On March 3rd, Ljatif developed a fever. Two days later, he went to a local medical center, where doctors gave him penicillin for his fever. Antibiotics have no effect on a virus. Then his skin broke with dark spots. He felt worse, and a few days later his brother took him by bus to a hospital in the town of Cacak, about a hundred miles away. The dark spots were by this time merging into blackened, mottled splashes, which the doctors in Cacak didn't recognize. Ljatif became sicker. Finally, he was transferred by ambulance to Belgrade, where he was admitted to the Dermatology and Venereal Diseases Department of the city's main hospital. By then, his skin may have turned almost black in patches. We don't have access to his clinical reports, so I am describing a generalized extreme smallpox of the kind Ljatif had.

Inside the cells of the host, smallpox bricks pile up as if they were coming off a production line. Some of the particles develop tails. The tails are pieces of the cell's protein, which the virus steals from the cell for its own use. The tailed smallpox particles look like comets or spermatozoa. They begin to twist and wriggle, and they corkscrew through the cell, propelled by their tails toward the cell's outer membrane. They bump up against the inside of the cell membrane, and their heads make lumps, and the cell horripilates.[1] Then something wonderful happens. Finger tubes begin to extend from the cell. The tubes grow longer. The cell turns into a Koosh ball. Inside each finger tube is a smallpox comet. The fingers lengthen until they touch and join nearby cells, and the smallpox comets squirm through the finger tubes into the next cell. The comets are protected from attack by the immune system, because they stay inside the finger tubes, where antibodies and killer white blood cells can't reach them. Then the Koosh ball explodes. Out pour heaps of bricks that don't have tails. These smallpox particles are wrapped in a special armor, like hand grenades. They float away, still protected by their armor, and they stick to other cells and go inside them, and those cells turn into Koosh balls. Each infected cell releases up to a hundred thousand virus particles, and they are added to the quadrillions of particles replicating in the universe of the ruined host.

> *"Finger tubes begin to extend from the cell. The tubes grow longer. The cell turns into a Koosh ball. Inside each finger tube is a smallpox comet."*

---

1. *Horripilate* means "to bristle, as when one gets goose bumps."

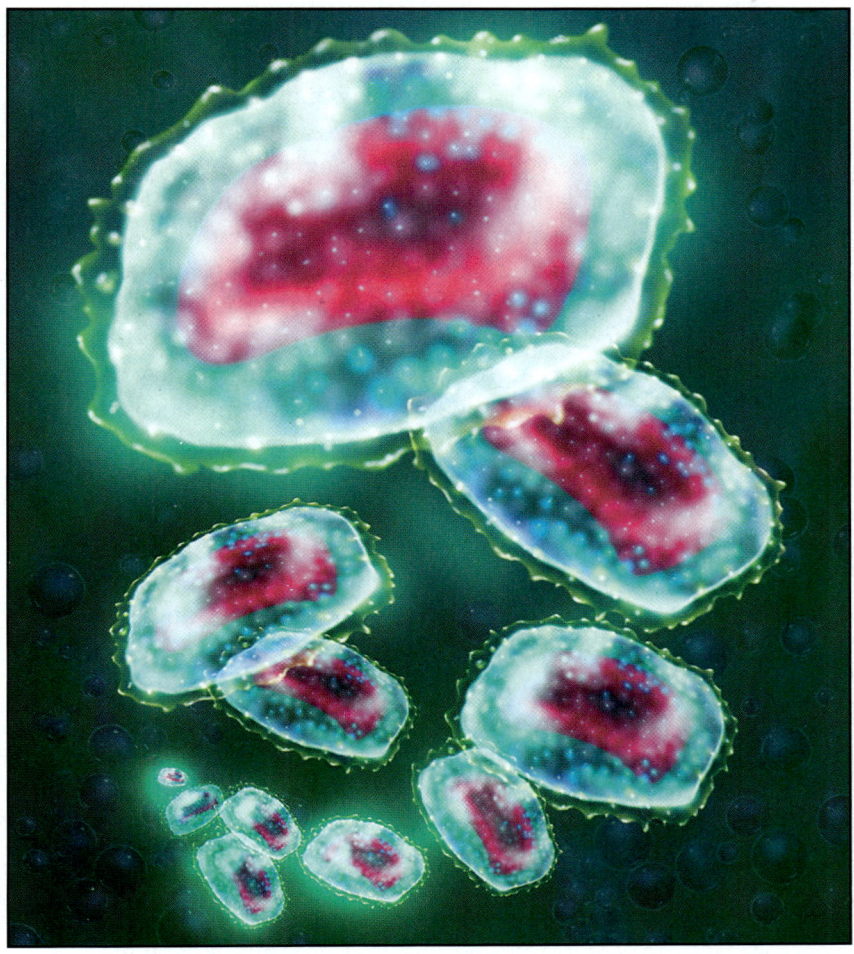

Smallpox virus

During the day of March 10th, Ljatif suffered catastrophic hemorrhages into the intestines. His intestines filled up with blood, and he expelled quarts of it, staining the sheets black, and he developed grave anemia from blood loss. For some unknown reason, black-pox patients remain conscious, in a kind of paralyzed shock, and they seem acutely aware of what is happening nearly up to the point of death—"a peculiar state of apprehension and mental alertness that were said to be unlike the manifestations of any other infectious disease," in the words of the Big Red Book of Smallpox. We can imagine that Ljatif was extremely frightened and witnessed his hemorrhages with a sense that his insides were coming apart. During the final phase of a smallpox intestinal bleedout, the lining of the intestines or the rectum can slip off. All we know about Ljatif is that his bleeds were unstoppable, that he was rushed to the Surgical Clinic of the Belgrade hospital, and that he died in the evening. The duty physician listed the cause of death as a bad reaction to penicillin.

"These hemorrhagic smallpox cases put an incredible amount of virus into the air," D. A. Henderson said. Some of the doctors and nurses who treated Ljatif were doomed. Indeed, Ljatif had seeded smallpox across Yugoslavia. Investigators later found that while he was in the hospital in Cacak he infected eight other patients and a nurse. The nurse died. One of the patients was a schoolboy, and he was sent home, where he broke with smallpox and infected his mother, and she died. In the Belgrade hospital, Ljatif infected twenty-seven more people, including seven nurses and doctors. Those victims infected five more people. Ljatif directly infected a total of thirty-eight people. They caught the virus by breathing the air near him. Eight of them died.

Meanwhile, the Pilgrim's smallpox travelled in waves through Yugoslavia. A rising tide of

Ljatif's skin had become blackened, mottled, and silky to the touch, and sheets of small blood blisters may have peppered his face. In a case of black pox, variola shocks the immune system so that it can't produce pus. Small blood vessels were leaking and breaking in his skin, and blood was seeping under the surface. His skin had developed large areas of continuous bruises.

On March 9th, the Belgrade doctors showed Ljatif to students and staff as a case that demonstrated an unusual reaction to penicillin. (In fact, a very bad reaction to penicillin can look like this.) Ljatif's eyes may have turned dark red. In hemorrhagic smallpox, one or two large hemorrhages appear in each eye, in the white encircling the iris, making the eyes look as if they could sag or leak blood. The eyes never do leak, but the blood in the eyes darkens, until the whites can sometimes seem almost black.

smallpox typically comes in fourteen-day waves—a wave of cases, a lull down to zero, and then a much bigger wave, another lull down to zero, then a huge and terrifying wave. The waves reflect the incubation periods, or generations, of the virus. Each wave or generation is anywhere from ten to twenty times as large as the last, so the virus grows exponentially and explosively, gathering strength like some kind of biological tsunami. This is because each infected person infects an average of ten to twenty more people. By the end of March, 1972, more than a hundred and fifty cases had occurred.

The Pilgrim had long since recovered. He didn't even know that he had started the outbreak. By then, however, Yugoslav doctors knew that they were dealing with smallpox, and they sent an urgent cable to the World Health Organization, asking for help.

Luckily, Yugoslavia had an authoritarian Communist government, under Josip Broz Tito, and he exercised full emergency powers. His government mobilized the Army and imposed strong measures to stop people from travelling and spreading the virus. Villages were closed by the Army, roadblocks were thrown up, public meetings were prohibited, and hotels and apartment buildings were made into quarantine wards to hold people who had had contact with smallpox cases. Ten thousand people were locked up in these buildings by the Yugoslav military. The daily life of the country came to a shocked halt. At the same time, all the countries surrounding Yugoslavia closed their borders with it, to prevent any travellers from coming out. Yugoslavia was cut off from the world. There were twenty-five foci of smallpox in the country. The virus had leapfrogged from town to town, even though the population had been heavily vaccinated. The Yugoslav authorities, helped by the W.H.O., began a massive campaign to revaccinate every person in Yugoslavia against smallpox; the population was twenty-one million. "They gave eighteen million doses in ten days," D. A. Henderson said. A person's immunity begins to grow immediately after the vaccination; it takes full effect within a week.

At the beginning of April, Henderson flew to Belgrade, where he found government officials in a state of deep alarm. The officials expected to see thousands of blistered, dying, contagious people streaming into hospitals any day. Henderson sat down with the Minister of Health and examined the statistics. He plotted the cases on a time line, and now he could see the generations of smallpox—one, two, three waves, each far larger than the previous one. Henderson had seen such waves appear many times before as smallpox rippled and amplified through human populations. Reading the viral surf with a practiced eye, he could see the start of the fourth wave. It was not climbing as steeply as he had expected. This meant that the waves had peaked. The outbreak was declining. Because of the military roadblocks, people weren't travelling, and the government was vaccinating everyone as fast as possible. "The outbreak is near an end," he declared to the Minister of Health. "I don't think you'll have more than ten additional cases." There were about a dozen: Henderson was right—the fourth wave never really materialized. The outbreak had been started by one man with the shivers. It was ended by a military crackdown and vaccination for every citizen. ❧

Discussion Starter ······································

In this excerpt, Richard Preston details the effects of smallpox ravaging an individual, while also showing the effects that these microscopic particles can have on a whole country. He also notes that, with the ease of travel in today's world, a virus can quickly cross international borders. What precautions do you think governments and the medical community should take to avert an epidemic? How far should the public's "right to know" extend in these matters? Discuss these questions with a group of classmates.

Building Background

Considered the greatest Greek historian, Thucydides was an Athenian general who recorded the battles during the Peloponnesian War between Athens and Sparta. Thucydides was born sometime between 460 B.C. and 454 B.C. and probably saw first-hand the great plague that struck Athens around 430 B.C. Thucydides lost his post as general after the Spartans sacked a key city under his watch. He was then exiled. This gave him time to write the *History of the Peloponnesian War,* which is divided into eight books.

The Peloponnesian War between the great city-states Athens and Sparta was fought between 431 B.C. and 404 B.C. Nearly every other city-state in Greece was allied in some way in the war. Sparta eventually emerged victorious from the twenty-seven-year war, ending the zenith of classical Greek culture that was reached in Athens. In this passage, Thucydides describes the medical symptoms of the plague that ravaged Athens and also reports on the devastating effects the plague had on Athenian morale, spirit, and behavior.

Literature Online Author Search For more about Thucydides, go to www.glencoe.com.

from
History of the Peloponnesian War

Thucydides
translated by Rex Warner

At the beginning of the following summer the Peloponnesians and their allies, with two-thirds of their total forces as before, invaded Attica, again under the command of the Spartan King Archidamus, the son of Zeuxidamus. Taking up their positions, they set about the devastation of the country.

They had not been many days in Attica before the plague first broke out among the Athenians. Previously attacks of the plague had been reported from many other places in the neighborhood of Lemnos and elsewhere, but there was no record of the disease being so virulent anywhere else or causing so many deaths as it did in Athens. At the beginning the doctors were quite incapable of treating the disease because of their ignorance of the right methods. In fact mortality among the doctors was the highest of all, since they came more frequently in contact with the sick. Nor was any other human art or science of any help at all. Equally useless were prayers made in the temples, consultation of oracles, and so forth; indeed, in the end people were so overcome by their sufferings that they paid no further attention to such things.

The plague originated, so they say, in Ethiopia in upper Egypt, and spread from there into Egypt itself and Libya and much of the territory of the

King of Persia. In the city of Athens it appeared suddenly, and the first cases were among the population of Piraeus, so that it was supposed by them that the Peloponnesians had poisoned the reservoirs. Later, however, it appeared also in the upper city, and by this time the deaths were greatly increasing in number. As to the question of how it could first have come about or what causes can be found adequate to explain its powerful effect on nature, I must leave that to be considered by other writers, with or without medical experience. I myself shall merely describe what it was like, and set down the symptoms, knowledge of which will enable it to be recognized, if it should ever break out again. I had the disease myself and saw others suffering from it.

That year, as is generally admitted, was particularly free from all other kinds of illness, though those who did have any illness previously all caught the plague in the end. In other cases, however, there seemed to be no reason for the attacks. People in perfect health suddenly began to have burning feelings in the head; their eyes became red and inflamed; inside their mouths there was bleeding from the throat and tongue, and the breath became unnatural and unpleasant. The next symptoms were sneezing and hoarseness of voice, and before long the pain settled on the chest and was accompanied by coughing. Next the stomach was affected with stomach-aches and with vomitings of every kind of bile that has been given a name by the medical profession, all this being accompanied by great pain and difficulty. In most cases there were attacks of ineffectual retching,[1] producing violent spasms; this sometimes ended with this

> "**W**ords indeed fail one when one tries to give a general picture of this disease; and as for the sufferings of individuals, they seemed almost beyond the capacity of human nature to endure."

stage of the disease, but sometimes continued long afterwards. Externally the body was not very hot to the touch, nor was there any pallor:[2] the skin was rather reddish and livid, breaking out into small pustules and ulcers. But inside there was a feeling of burning, so that people could not bear the touch even of the lightest linen clothing, but wanted to be completely naked, and indeed most of all would have liked to plunge into cold water. Many of the sick who were uncared for actually did so, plunging into the water-tanks in an effort to relieve a thirst which was unquenchable; for it was just the same with them whether they drank much or little. Then all the time they were afflicted with insomnia and the desperate feeling of not being able to keep still.

In the period when the disease was at its height, the body, so far from wasting away, showed surprising powers of resistance to all the agony, so that there was still some strength left on the seventh or eighth day, which was the time when, in most cases, death came from the internal fever. But if people survived this critical period, then the disease descended to the bowels, producing violent ulceration and uncontrollable diarrhea, so that most of them died later as a result of the weakness caused by this. For the disease, first settling in the head, went on to affect every part of the body in turn, and even when people escaped its worst effects it still left its traces on them by fastening upon the extremities of the body. It affected the genitals, the fingers, and the toes, and many of those who recovered lost the use of these members; some, too, went blind. There were some also who, when they first began to get

---

1. *Retching* means "vomiting."

2. *Pallor* means "paleness."

Funeral Stele of a Young Woman, ca. 460 BCE. Classical Greek. Marble, h. 52.30 in. Antikensammlung, Staatliche Museen zu Berlin, Germany.

better, suffered from a total loss of memory, not knowing who they were themselves and being unable to recognize their friends.

Words indeed fail one when one tries to give a general picture of this disease; and as for the sufferings of individuals, they seemed almost beyond the capacity of human nature to endure. Here in particular is a point where this plague showed itself to be something quite different from ordinary diseases: though there were many dead bodies lying about unburied, the birds and animals that eat human flesh either did not come near them or, if they did taste the flesh, died of it afterwards. Evidence for this may be found in the fact that there was a complete disappearance of all birds of prey: they were not to be seen either round the bodies or anywhere else. But dogs, being domestic animals, provided the best opportunity of observing this effect of the plague.

These, then, were the general features of the disease, though I have omitted all kinds of peculiarities which occurred in various individual cases. Meanwhile, during all this time there was no serious outbreak of any of the usual kinds of illness; if any such cases did occur, they ended in the plague. Some died in neglect, some in spite of every possible care being taken of them. As for a recognized method of treatment, it would be true to say that no such thing existed: what did good in some cases did harm in others. Those with naturally strong constitutions were no better able than the weak to resist the disease, which carried away all alike, even those who were treated and dieted with the greatest care. The most terrible thing of all was the despair into which people fell when they realized that they had caught the plague; for they would immediately adopt an attitude of utter hopelessness, and, by giving in in this way, would lose their powers of resistance. Terrible, too, was the sight of people dying like sheep through having caught the disease as a result of nursing others. This indeed caused more deaths than anything else. For when people were afraid to visit the sick, then they died with no one to look after them; indeed, there were many houses in which all the inhabitants perished through lack of any attention. When, on the other hand, they did visit the sick, they lost their own lives, and this was particularly true of those who made it a point of honor to act properly. Such people felt ashamed to think of their own safety and went into their friends' houses at times when even the members of the household were so overwhelmed by the weight of their calamities that they had actually given up the usual practice of making laments for the dead. Yet still the ones who felt most pity for the sick and the dying were those who had had the plague themselves and had recovered from it. They knew what it was like and at the same time felt themselves to be safe, for no one caught the disease twice, or, if he did, the second attack was never fatal. Such people were congratulated on all sides, and they themselves were so elated at the time of their recovery that they fondly imagined that they could never die of any other disease in the future.

A factor which made matters much worse than they were already was the removal of people from the country into the city, and this particularly affected the incomers. There were no houses for them, and, living as they did during the hot season in badly ventilated huts, they died like flies. The bodies of the dying were heaped one on top of the other, and half-dead creatures could be seen staggering about in the streets or flocking around the fountains in their desire for water. The temples in which they took up their quarters were full of the dead bodies of people who had died inside them. For the catastrophe was so overwhelming that men, not knowing what would happen next to them, became indifferent to every rule of religion or of law. All the funeral ceremonies which used to be observed were now disorganized, and they buried the dead as best they could. Many people, lacking the necessary means of burial because so many deaths had already occurred in their households, adopted the most shameless methods. They would arrive first at a funeral pyre that had been made by others, put their own dead upon it and set it alight; or, finding another pyre burning, they would throw the corpse that they were carrying on top of the other one and go away.

In other respects also Athens owed to the plague the beginnings of a state of unprecedented lawlessness. Seeing how quick and abrupt were the changes of fortune which came to the rich who suddenly died and to those who had previously been penniless but now inherited their wealth, people now began openly to venture on acts of self-indulgence which before then they used to keep dark. Thus they resolved to spend their money quickly and to spend it on pleasure, since money and life alike seemed equally ephemeral. As for what is called honor, no one showed himself willing to abide by its laws, so doubtful was it whether one would survive to enjoy the name for it. It was generally agreed that what was both honorable and valuable was the pleasure of the moment and everything that might conceivably contribute to that pleasure. No fear of god or law of man had a restraining influence. As for the gods, it seemed to be the same thing whether one worshipped them or not, when one saw the good and the bad dying indiscriminately. As for offences against human law, no one expected to live long enough to be brought to trial and punished: instead everyone felt that already a far heavier sentence had been passed on him and was hanging over him, and that before the time for its execution arrived it was only natural to get some pleasure out of life. ❧

Quickwrite

Thucydides describes the despair felt by Athenians who endured the plague. This despair is expressed sometimes in somber, isolated depression, other times through lawlessness and loose morals. How do you think humans should respond in times such as the one detailed in Thucydides' historical account? Write a paragraph explaining your views.

BEFORE YOU READ

Building Background

Albert Camus rose to literary fame from the poor quarters of Algiers, Algeria, presenting themes of absurdity while also proclaiming that the world needed justice. In 1947 he published his novel *The Plague,* which was an immediate best seller. Camus won the Nobel Prize in Literature in 1957 when he was forty-three. He died tragically in an automobile accident three years later.

The Plague is set in the Algerian port of Oran in the early 1940s. At the time Camus wrote it, he himself was apart from his wife, who was in the city of Oran. Camus was in a mountain village in France, seeking treatment for tuberculosis. While he was there, German troops tightened their control of the region, and Camus was not allowed to return home. "Caught like rats!" he wrote in his journal.

In the book, Camus depicts Oran as a dull city, with hardworking but complacent and materialistic citizens who are ill-prepared for disaster. The plot begins when Dr. Bernard Rieux steps on a dead rat. Soon scores of rats are crawling out into the open, ready to die. The citizens' annoyance turns to alarm when they realize that the cause of the dying rats is an outbreak of the bubonic plague. The city declares a state of emergency and seals itself off from nearly all contact, and Rieux works tirelessly to combat the epidemic. The novel has a mysterious point of view. Only in the last chapter does the narrator reveal that he is Doctor Rieux.

Literature Online **Author Search** For more about Albert Camus, go to **www.glencoe.com.**

Allegory of the Plague. A Biccherna book cover, 1437. Kunstgewerbemuseum, Staatliche Museen zu Berlin, Germany.

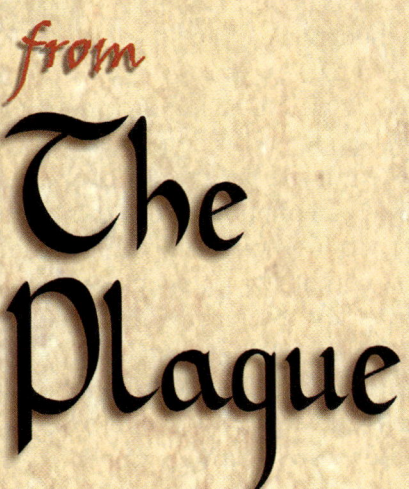

from

The Plague

Albert Camus

translated by Stuart Gilbert

The truth is that nothing is less sensational than pestilence,[1] and by reason of their very duration great misfortunes are monotonous. In the memories of those who lived through them, the grim days of plague do not stand out like vivid flames, ravenous and inextinguishable, beaconing a troubled sky, but rather like the slow, deliberate progress of some monstrous thing crushing out all upon its path.

No, the real plague had nothing in common with the grandiose imaginings that had haunted Rieux's mind at its outbreak. It was, above all, a shrewd, unflagging adversary; a skilled organizer, doing his work thoroughly and well. That, it may be said in passing, is why, so as not to play false to the facts, and, still more, so as not to play false to himself, the narrator has aimed at objectivity. He has made hardly any changes for the sake of artistic effect, except those elementary adjustments needed to present his narrative in a more or less coherent form. And in deference to this scruple he is constrained to admit that, though the chief source of distress, the deepest as well as the most widespread, was separation—and it is his duty to say more about it as it existed in the later stages of the plague—it cannot be denied that even this distress was coming to lose something of its poignancy.

Was it that our fellow citizens, even those who had felt the parting from their loved ones most keenly, were getting used to doing without them? To assume this would fall somewhat short of the truth. It would be more correct to say that they were wasting away emotionally as well as physically. At the beginning of the plague they had a vivid recollection of the absent ones and bitterly felt their loss. But though they could clearly recall the face, the smile and voice of the beloved, and this or that occasion when (as they now saw in retrospect) they had been supremely happy, they had trouble in picturing what he or she might be doing at the moment when they conjured up these memories, in a setting so hopelessly remote. In short, at these moments memory played its part, but their imagination failed them. During the second phase of the plague their memory failed them, too. Not that they had forgotten the face itself, but—what came to the same thing—it had lost fleshly substance and they no longer saw it in memory's mirror.

Thus, while during the first weeks they were apt to complain that only shadows remained to them of what their love had been and meant, they now came to learn that even shadows can waste away, losing the faint hues of life that memory may give. And by the end of their long sundering they had also lost the power of imagining the intimacy that once was theirs or understanding what it can be to live with someone whose life is wrapped up in yours.

In this respect they had adapted themselves to the very condition of the plague, all the more potent for its mediocrity. None of us was capable any longer of an exalted emotion; all had trite, monotonous feelings. "It's high time it stopped," people would say, because in time of calamity the obvious thing is to desire its end, and in fact they wanted it to end. But when making such remarks, we felt none of the passionate yearning or fierce resentment of the early phase; we merely voiced one of the few clear ideas that lingered in the twilight of our minds. The furious revolt of the first weeks had given place to a vast despondency, not to be taken for resignation, though it was none the less a sort of passive and provisional acquiescence.[2]

Our fellow citizens had fallen into line, adapted themselves, as people say, to the situation, because there was no way of doing otherwise. Naturally

---

1. *Pestilence* refers to the bubonic plague.

2. *Acquiescence* means "giving up."

they retained the attitudes of sadness and suffering, but they had ceased to feel their sting. Indeed, to some, Dr. Rieux among them, this precisely was the most disheartening thing: that the habit of despair is worse than despair itself. Hitherto those who were parted had not been utterly unhappy; there was always a gleam of hope in the night of their distress; but that gleam had now died out. You could see them at street corners, in cafés or friends' houses, listless, indifferent, and looking so bored that, because of them, the whole town seemed like a railway waiting-room. Those who had jobs went about them at the exact tempo of the plague, with dreary perseverance. Everyone was modest. For the first time exiles from those they loved had no reluctance to talk freely about them, using the same words as everybody else, and regarding their deprivation from the same angle as that from which they viewed the latest statistics of the epidemic. This change was striking, since until now they had jealously withheld their personal grief from the common stock of suffering; now they accepted its inclusion. Without memories, without hope, they lived for the moment only. Indeed, the here and now had come to mean everything to them. For there is no denying that the plague had gradually killed off in all of us the faculty not of love only but even of friendship. Naturally enough, since love asks something of the future, and nothing was left us but a series of present moments.

However, this account of our predicament gives only the broad lines. Thus, while it is true that all who were parted came ultimately to this state, we must add that all did not attain it simultaneously; moreover, once this utter apathy had fallen on them, there were still flashes of lucidity, broken lights of memory that rekindled in the exiles a younger, keener sensibility. This happened when, for instance, they fell to making plans implying that the plague had ended. Or

> "The town was peopled with sleepwalkers, whose trance was broken only on the rare occasions when at night their wounds, to all appearance closed, suddenly reopened."

when, quite unexpectedly, by some kindly chance, they felt a twinge of jealousy, none the less acute for its objectlessness. Others, again, had sudden accesses of energy and shook off their languor on certain days of the week—for obvious reasons, on Sundays and Saturday afternoons, because these had been devoted to certain ritual pleasures in the days when the loved ones were still accessible. Sometimes the mood of melancholy that descended on them with the nightfall acted as a sort of warning, not always fulfilled, however, that old memories were floating up to the surface. That evening hour which for believers is the time to look into their consciences is hardest of all hours on the prisoner or exile who has nothing to look into but the void. For a moment it held them in suspense; then they sank back into their lethargy, the prison door had closed on them once again.

Obviously all this meant giving up what was most personal in their lives. Whereas in the early days of the plague they had been struck by the host of small details that, while meaning absolutely nothing to others, meant so much to them personally, and thus had realized, perhaps for the first time, the uniqueness of each man's life; now, on the other hand, they took an interest only in what interested everyone else, they had only general ideas, and even their tenderest affections now seemed abstract, items of the common stock. So completely were they dominated by the plague that sometimes the one thing they aspired to was the long sleep it brought, and they caught themselves thinking: "A good thing if I get plague and have done with it!" But really they were asleep already; this whole period was for them no more than a long night's slumber. The town was peopled with sleepwalkers, whose trance was broken only on the rare occasions when at night their wounds, to all appearance closed, suddenly reopened. Then, waking with a start, they would run their fingers over the wounds with a sort of absentminded curiosity, twisting their lips, and in a flash their grief blazed up again, and abruptly there rose before them the mournful visage of their love. In the morning they harked back to normal conditions—in other words, the plague.

What impression, it may be asked, did these exiles of the plague make on the observer? The answer is simple; they made none. Or, to put it differently, they looked like everybody else, nondescript. They shared in the torpor of the town and in its puerile[3] agitations. They lost every trace of a critical spirit, while gaining an air of *sang-froid*.[4] You could see, for instance, even the most intelligent among them making a show like all the rest of studying the newspapers or listening to the radio, in the hope apparently of finding some reason to believe the plague would shortly end. They seemed to derive fantastic hopes or equally exaggerated fears from reading the lines that some journalist has scribbled at random, yawning with boredom at his desk. Meanwhile they drank their beer, nursed their sick, idled, or doped themselves with work, filed documents in offices, or played the phonograph at home without betraying any difference from the rest of us. In other words, they had ceased to choose for themselves; plague had leveled out discrimination. This could be seen by the way nobody troubled about the quality of the clothes or food he bought. Everything was taken as it came.

And, finally, it is worth noting that those who were parted ceased to enjoy the curious privilege that had been theirs at the outset. They had lost love's egoism and the benefit they derived from it. Now, at least, the position was clear: this calamity was everybody's business. What with the gunshots echoing at the gates, the punctual thuds of rubber stamps marking the rhythm of lives and deaths, the files and fires, the panics and formalities, all alike were pledged to an ugly but recorded death, and, amidst noxious fumes and the muted clang of ambulances, all of us ate the same sour bread of exile, unconsciously waiting for the same reunion, the same miracle of peace regained. No doubt our love persisted, but in practice it served nothing; it was an inert mass within us, sterile as crime or a life sentence. It had declined on a patience that led nowhere, a dogged expectation. Viewed from this angle, the attitude of some of our fellow citizens resembled that of the long queues one saw outside the food-shops. There was the same resignation, the same long-sufferance, inexhaustible and without illusions. The only difference was that the mental state of the food-seekers would need to be raised to a vastly higher power to make it comparable with the gnawing pain of separation, since this latter came from a hunger fierce to the point of insatiability.

In any case, if the reader would have a correct idea of the mood of these exiles, we must conjure up once more those dreary evenings sifting down through a haze of dust and golden light upon the treeless streets filled with teeming crowds of men and women. For, characteristically, the sound that rose toward the terraces still bathed in the last glow of daylight, now that the noises of vehicles and motors—the sole voice of cities in ordinary times—had ceased, was but one vast rumor of low voices and incessant footfalls, the drumming of innumerable soles timed to the eerie whistling of the plague in the sultry air above, the sound of a huge concourse of people marking time, a never ending, stifling drone that, gradually swelling, filled the town from end to end, and evening after evening gave its truest, mournfulest expression to the blind endurance that had ousted love from all our hearts. ❧

Quickwrite

Camus once wrote, "A novel is never anything but a philosophy expressed in images." He also never disguised the fact that *The Plague,* in part, is an allegorical novel about the fascist occupation of Europe.

How do you interpret the imagery in this selection? What questions do the images raise about the purpose of human suffering, the role of humanity in the universe, and the meaning of life? Write a brief essay on this topic, citing evidence from the text to support your points.

---

3. *Puerile* means "childish."
4. *Sang-froid* means "composure in tense situations."

- from *A Journal of the Plague Year* by Daniel Defoe
- from "The Demon in the Freezer" by Richard Preston
- from *History of the Peloponnesian War* by Thucydides
- from *The Plague* by Albert Camus

COMPARING THE Big Idea The English Enlightenment and Neoclassicism

Writing Reason and a vigorous intellectual quest to find the answers for the cause of things highlight the age of the English Enlightenment and Neoclassicism. In a brief essay, describe how Defoe, Preston, Thucydides, and Camus explore both the seeming randomness of epidemics and the causes and effects they identify in the coming of the disease.

COMPARING Style

Group Activity How do the styles of Defoe, Preston, Thucydides, and Camus compare and contrast? Review the quotations below and then meet with a group to describe the style of each writer and the purpose each style serves. Consider diction, sentence length and rhythm, and imagery in your discussion. Support your views with evidence from the selections.

> "He said nothing as he walked about, but two or three times groaned very deeply and loud, and sighed as he would break his heart."
>
> —Defoe, *A Journal of The Plague Year*

> "Inside the cells of the host, smallpox bricks pile up as if they were coming off a production line. Some of the particles develop tails."
>
> —Preston, "The Demon in the Freezer"

> "I myself shall merely describe what it was like, and set down the symptoms, knowledge of which will enable it to be recognized, if it should ever break out again. I had the disease myself and saw others suffering from it."
>
> —Thucydides, *History of the Peloponnesian War*

> ". . . the drumming of innumerable soles timed to the eerie whistling of the plague in the sultry air above, the sound of a huge concourse of people marking time, a never ending, stifling drone . . ."
>
> —Camus, *The Plague*

COMPARING Cultures

Speaking and Listening Defoe, Preston, Thucydides, and Camus write about different cultures, yet they present evidence about the similar physical and psychological toll exacted by disease. With a group, research the cultures explored in each selection (seventeenth-century England, 1970s era Yugoslavia, ancient Greece, and 1940s era Algeria). Present a report to the class about how the culture of one of the selections expands your understanding of the selection.

OBJECTIVES
- Connect literature to historical periods.
- Compare and contrast authors' messages.
- Evaluate writers' style and purpose.
- Compare works from different eras and cultures.

TIME

Malaria is killing millions. But it can be cured. Why isn't that happening?

Death By Mosquito

By CHRISTINE GORMAN

AS CURRENT TRENDS MAKE CLEAR, AIDS IS SURPASSING the Black Death as the most devastating plague ever to afflict the human race. But all the well-deserved attention paid to AIDS over the past few years has overshadowed the rapid comeback of a second, nearly-as-deadly plague—malaria. Statistics suggest that malaria sickened 300 million people in 2003 and killed 3 million—most of them under age 5. What makes the malaria deaths particularly tragic is that malaria can be cured.

Countries in sub-Saharan Africa have suffered the brunt of this assault, but nations in temperate zones, including the United States, are not immune. A malaria outbreak in Florida that hospitalized seven people in 2003 was the first widespread transmission of the disease on U.S. soil in nearly 20 years. The cause was almost certainly a parasite that hopped a ride in a human, or a mosquito on an international flight or ship, since none of the patients had recently traveled overseas.

There is reason for hope, however. Doctors have made remarkable progress over the past few years in the treatment of drug-resistant malaria by combining several compounds—the most powerful of which comes from an ancient Chinese herbal remedy that cures 90% of patients in three days. Meanwhile, community groups, nonprofit organizations, and gov-ernments are redoubling efforts to control the mosquitoes that cause the disease through insecticide-treated nets and the indoor spraying of antimosquito pesticides. Certainly the need for action has never been clearer.

Researchers believe the average number of cases of malaria per year in Africa has quadrupled since the 1980s. A study in the journal Lancet reported that the death rate due to malaria has at least doubled among children in eastern and southern Africa. And some rural areas have seen a heartbreaking 11-fold jump in deaths. Says malaria expert Dr. Christa Hook, "In many ways, it's a kind of silent Holocaust."

Recognition of malaria's toll on the global economy is also growing. Economist Jeffrey Sachs of Columbia University estimates that countries hit hardest by the most severe form of malaria have annual economic growth rates 1.3 percentage points lower than those in which malaria is not a serious problem. In other words, fighting malaria is good for business—as many companies with overseas operations have long understood.

Understanding the Disease

To better understand why malaria has become such a threat and what can be done to stop the disease, it helps to know a little biology. Malaria is caused by four closely related parasites, some of which have a particular fondness for anopheles mosquitoes. The parasites enter the bloodstream when an infected mosquito bites a human. Then they multiply inside the host's liver and red blood cells. (That's why pregnant women, who make lots of blood to nourish their growing fetus, are especially vulnerable.) Eventually the red blood cells burst with a new generation of parasites, causing fever, shivering, pain, and sometimes death. The cycle of transmission is complete when another mosquito bites an infected person and picks up more parasites.

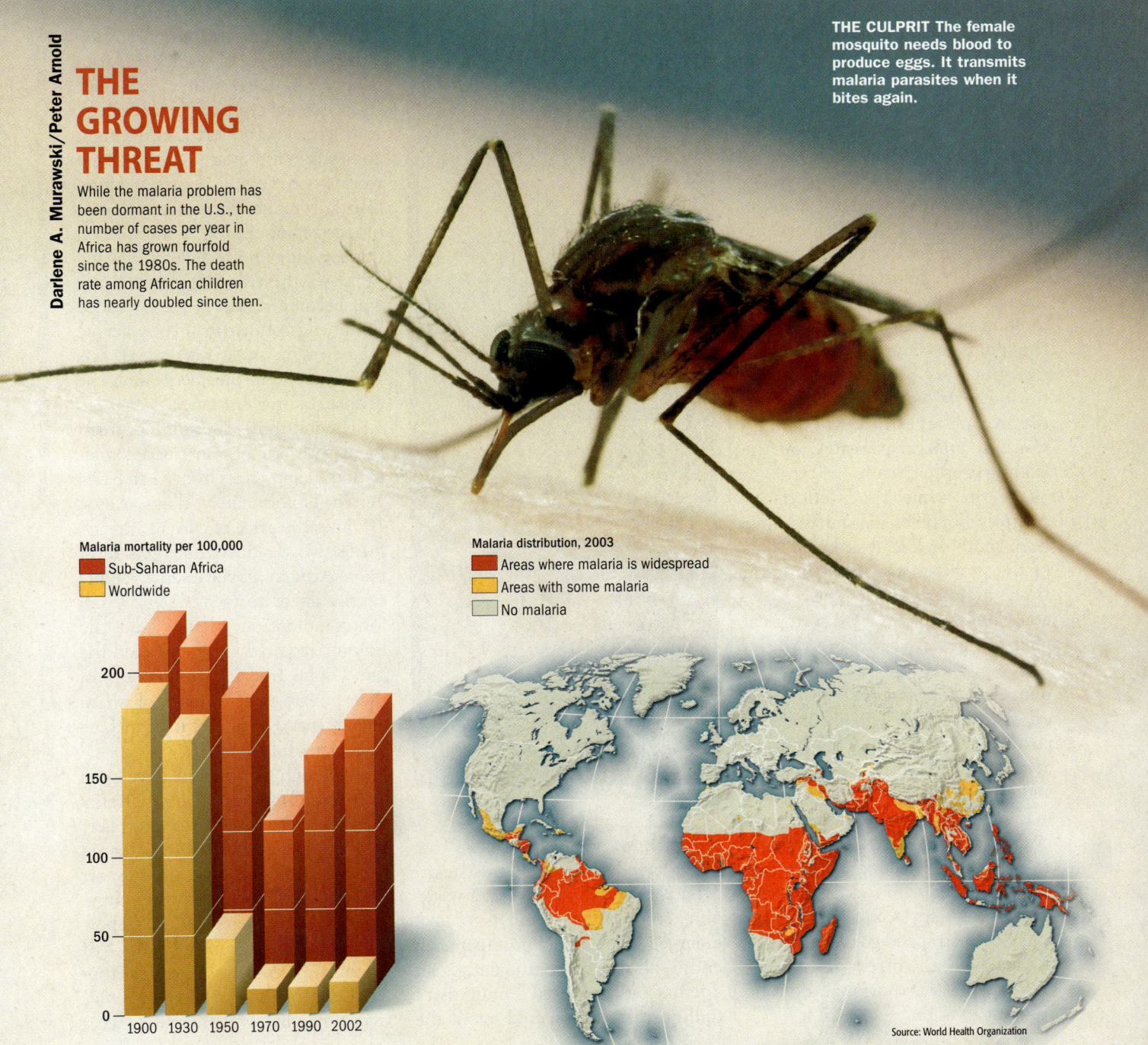

Darlene A. Murawski/Peter Arnold

THE GROWING THREAT

While the malaria problem has been dormant in the U.S., the number of cases per year in Africa has grown fourfold since the 1980s. The death rate among African children has nearly doubled since then.

THE CULPRIT The female mosquito needs blood to produce eggs. It transmits malaria parasites when it bites again.

Malaria mortality per 100,000
- Sub-Saharan Africa
- Worldwide

200
150
100
50
0
1900 1930 1950 1970 1990 2002

Malaria distribution, 2003
- Areas where malaria is widespread
- Areas with some malaria
- No malaria

Source: World Health Organization

You might expect that one bout of malaria would lead to lifelong protection against the disease. But for complicated reasons, that is not the case. The illness tends to be less severe in adults who are continually exposed to the parasites. But when young children become infected, they are much more likely to suffer severe anemia and convulsions that may lead to permanent brain damage and death.

For decades, the best treatment for malaria was a relatively cheap and effective medication called chloroquine, which was discovered in Germany in 1934. But by the 1970s, the drug had been used so widely to treat all kinds of fevers, not just those caused by malaria, that the malaria parasites became resistant. So doctors had to turn to a second medication, called sulfadoxine-pyrimethamine, or SP, for short. Within five years, however, the parasites started to develop resistance to SP as well. Today resistance to both drugs is on the rise in parts of Africa, where drug-resistant malaria parasites are the leading cause of death.

At the same time, efforts to control anopheles mosquitoes have been more or less abandoned. Part of the problem was the realization that malaria could never be completely wiped out from tropical regions the way it had been in the U.S. and other countries in temperate zones. There was also a growing backlash against DDT, a pesticide that is highly effective at attacking mosquitoes but whose widespread use in agriculture killed many fish, beneficial insects, and birds. Although only small amounts of DDT are needed to control malaria—usually in indoor-spraying campaigns—its toxic reputation made cash-strapped governments in Africa, which often must rely heavily on international donors, hesitant to use it.

SLOWING THE SPREAD

The tools for fighting malaria are already at hand. It's just a matter of getting them out to those who need it.

TREATED NETS Sprayed with insecticide, they act as traps; mosquitoes are attracted by CO2 and killed on contact.

SWEET WORMWOOD A drug made from this Chinese herb cures 90% of patients within three days, but it is in short supply.

DDT When the poison is sprayed on or inside a hut, it kills mosquitoes without doing a lot of harm to the environment.

There Is a Silver Lining

So much for how things got so bad. The silver lining to all this heartache is that the outlines of a workable solution have at long last emerged. No one is promising an end to all deaths from malaria. But doctors estimate that hundreds of millions of people could avoid the illness and the death rate could be cut in half. The catch: Although astonishingly inexpensive (at least by the industrial world's standards), an effective response is still beyond the financial resources of the poorest nations of the world, particularly those in Africa. There simply can be no progress without help from the developed world.

To be successful, any antimalaria campaign must do two things: treat the illness and prevent the transmission of parasites. Several studies in Africa have proved that combination therapy (using several types of drugs at once), in which at least one of the medications comes from a plant called sweet wormwood, easily destroys drug-resistant malarial parasites in the bloodstream. Using combination therapy, often in the same pill, greatly decreases the risk that the parasites will become resistant. As an added bonus, artemisinin, the active ingredient in sweet wormwood, acts very quickly, further decreasing the chances of drug resistance.

The full three-day course of treatment with artemisinin-based combination therapy costs from $1 to $10 a person. Unfortunately, that's at least 10 times the price of current, though ineffective, treatment programs. Most poor African governments simply cannot afford to foot the entire bill for combination therapy and the training required to give it. And the same holds true for the majority of their private citizens, many of whom already spend a third of their income on malaria treatment.

Although nearly every developed country and most major international aid groups have said they are ready to help pay for artemisinin-based treatment in Africa, that support has not always been forthcoming. Some health experts believe a report about the many benefits of artemisinin-containing drugs from the U.S. Institute of Medicine will, over time, dissolve any reluctance.

Malaria struck 300 million in one year, killing as many as 3 million.

Stop Mosquitoes Before They Bite

And what about prevention? Many African countries are working to distribute low-cost insecticide-soaked mosquito nets. These serve as traps for mosquitoes, which are attracted by the carbon dioxide that sleepers exhale and are then killed by the insecticide. The nets are portable, so they can be taken along by their owners. In villages where at least 80% of pregnant women and children under age 5 sleep beneath insecticide-sprayed mosquito nets, the rate of illness for all residents has dropped dramatically. Unfortunately, only 1% or 2% of people in malarial zones sleep under mosquito nets. Also, most nets need to be retreated every six months, and they are less effective in areas where anopheles mosquitoes bite all day long instead of just at night.

Another effective method of reducing transmission is to spray DDT inside huts and other buildings. Intriguingly, DDT is often better at repelling mosquitoes than killing them. This requires much less pesticide than was once sprayed on crops and swamps. An international antipesticide treaty that took effect in May 2004 makes an exception for the use of DDT in malarial areas. But some health experts are worried that the complicated process to get permission to use DDT will limit the pesticide's effectiveness.

Recent experience in South Africa shows just how well DDT can work. In 1996, the South African government, under pressure from environmental groups, decided to stop its use of DDT in residential spraying. Instead the government would use pesticides that contained safer types of chemicals. Unfortunately, it turned out that many anopheles mosquitoes in South Africa were resistant to those chemicals. The number of cases of malaria, which had been hovering between 8,000 and 13,000 a year, grew steadily worse, and by the year 2000 it had reached 64,000 cases, with 423 deaths. When the government reintroduced DDT spraying, the number of cases fell almost immediately.

Even environmentalists had to admit that DDT was necessary. "I wasn't very happy about it," says Gerhard Verdoorn, chairman of South Africa's Endangered Wildlife Trust, a conservation group which had earlier lobbied the South African government to drop the pesticide and now helps train DDT sprayers. "We can't just look after animals and not care if people die."

That's the kind of attitude that will make a difference in the battle against malaria. The know-how to control the disease already exists. What is not so clear is whether there is the necessary commitment—financial and political—to make it happen.

—**Updated 2005, from TIME, July 26, 2004**

RESPONDING AND THINKING CRITICALLY

Respond

1. How do you feel about the severity of the malaria outbreak in Africa and the response to treat it?

Recall and Interpret

2. (a)Approximately how many people become ill with malaria each year? (b)Why is this particularly tragic?

3. (a)By how much has the number of malaria cases grown in Africa since the 1980s? (b)What are the economic implications of a malaria outbreak?

4. (a)What causes someone to contract malaria? (b)How have the medicines used to treat the disease both failed and succeeded?

Analyze and Evaluate

5. (a)What does the writer claim are two things an anti-malaria campaign must do? (b)In what way do these things represent cause-and-effect situations?

6. (a)What effect does the chemical DDT have on wildlife? (b)Based on evidence from the text, do you think the writer is for or against the use of DDT in the fight against malaria? How do you know?

Connect

7. Do you think the benefits of DDT outweigh the risks? Explain.

8. How do you think the spread and response to an epidemic like malaria is different now than it would have been in eighteenth-century England?

from *A Dictionary of the English Language* and *Letter to Lord Chesterfield*

MEET SAMUEL JOHNSON

Samuel Johnson once said in his typically blunt but humorous way, "No man but a blockhead ever wrote except for money." Money was, in fact, a problem for Johnson throughout most of his life. Although he was one of the greatest writers of his time, he often had to struggle to make ends meet.

A Difficult Childhood Born in Lichfield in 1709, Samuel Johnson was the son of a bookseller. In his infancy, he contracted tuberculosis of the lymph nodes. The disease left him deaf in one ear, nearly blind in one eye, and badly scarred. Despite these health problems, Johnson grew to be an exceptionally bright student. According to his mother, he could memorize almost instantly whatever he read. In his late teens, Johnson managed to scrape together enough money to attend Oxford University, but he could not afford to complete his education there. His time at college was marked by intense poverty and he was forced to leave without obtaining a degree. From the time he left school until his father died in 1731, little is known about Johnson except that he most likely suffered from acute mental depression.

> *"Dictionaries are like watches; the worst is better than none, and the best cannot be expected to go quite true."*
>
> —Samuel Johnson

Literary Success and Financial Strain After Oxford, Johnson unsuccessfully tried his hand at a number of jobs. At the age of twenty-six, he settled down and married a widow about twenty years his senior. Then he opened a school. He had difficulty keeping students, however, and within two years, he closed the school and moved to London. Soon after arriving there, Johnson began to earn his living by writing. He contributed essays to the *Gentlemen's Magazine* and attracted critical attention with his poem "London," which condemned certain political leaders and vices of the time. This success was soon followed by others, such as *The Rambler*, a short-lived but influential magazine that Johnson founded. Although these works brought Johnson acclaim, they did not earn him much money.

Further Success—and Compensation Johnson's fortunes began to change when he reached his thirties. It was then that a bookseller commissioned him to write an English language dictionary. Johnson and six assistants worked for more than eight years to gather and produce the almost 40,000 entries that *A Dictionary of the English Language* contains. The sheer scope of the task—it had taken a French academy forty years to complete a comparable French dictionary—clinched Johnson's reputation as a scholar.

When Johnson was in his fifties, he was at last freed from his financial difficulties when King George III granted him a pension for life. In his later years, Johnson continued to work, editing an edition of *Lives of the English Poets*, a series of biographical and critical essays. Johnson died in 1784 at the age of seventy-five and was buried in Westminster Abbey.

Samuel Johnson was born in 1709 and died in 1784.

Literature Online **Author Search** For more about Samuel Johnson, go to www.glencoe.com.

Connecting to the Texts

Samuel Johnson's preface to *A Dictionary of the English Language* points out that language is constantly changing and evolving. As you read, think of some slang phrases that were once popular among your peers but that you now no longer use.

Building Background

Johnson's *A Dictionary of the English Language* was published in 1755 in London. Hoping for financial support, Johnson dedicated his *Plan of the Dictionary* to Lord Chesterfield, a statesman and patron of many struggling writers. Although Chesterfield paid some initial attention and offered his advice, he soon lost interest in the project and never provided Johnson with any funding. Johnson was forced to use much of his own income from the *Dictionary* to pay the small staff who copied his work by hand, pasted revisions, and produced the pages. Shortly after the work was published, however, Chesterfield wrote complimentary reviews of the *Dictionary,* presumably in the hope of persuading Johnson to dedicate the work to him. The praise provoked Johnson, whose letter of response has become famous.

Setting Purposes for Reading

Big Idea The English Enlightenment and Neoclassicism

As you read the selections, note Johnson's use of reason as the guiding force behind his opinions.

Literary Element Voice

Voice is the distinctive use of language that conveys to the reader the personality of a writer or narrator. Voice is determined by elements of style such as word choice and tone. Johnson's voice is characterized by precise diction, or word choice; by the use of sarcasm; and by long sentences balanced by parallel structures.

- See Literary Terms Handbook, p. R19.

Literature Online Interactive Literary Elements Handbook To review or learn more about the literary elements, go to www.glencoe.com.

Reading Strategy Distinguishing Fact and Opinion

Facts are statements that can be verified or proven true. **Opinions** express beliefs, ideas, and feelings, and as such, they cannot be verified. A good reader uses prior knowledge and logic to recognize whether the author is presenting information as verifiable truth. As you read the selection, notice how Johnson gets his opinions across—even in the traditionally factual text of a dictionary.

Reading Tip: Compiling Emotional Language You can often spot an author's opinion by his or her use of emotional words. As you read, keep track of emotional language.

Vocabulary

vigilance (vij′ ə ləns) *n.* careful watchfulness; p. 651 *Keeping up to date with clothing fashions requires a certain amount of vigilance.*

intuitive (in tōō′ ə tiv) *adj.* known or perceived without deliberate thought; p. 651 *The young man had an intuitive gift for playing the piano.*

immutably (i mū′ tə blē) *adv.* unchangeably; permanently; p. 651 *Although Perkins had retired as governor years earlier, his name was immutably linked to that office.*

aggregated (ag′ rə gā′ təd) *adj.* collected; gathered into a whole; p. 651 *The neighborhood's crime statistics were aggregated in a report and sent to the mayor's office.*

exultation (eg′ zul tā′ shən) *n.* joy; elation; p. 655 *Winning the marathon filled Peter with feelings of pride and exultation.*

Vocabulary Tip: Antonyms Antonyms are words that have opposite or nearly opposite meanings. For example, *contempt* and *praise* are antonyms.

OBJECTIVES
In studying these selections, you will focus on the following:
- analyzing literary periods
- analyzing an author's voice and tone
- distinguishing fact and opinion

from

A Dictionary of the English Language

Trompe L'Oeil with Writing Materials. Evert Collier. Oil on canvas, 18½ x 25½ in. Victoria and Albert Museum, London.

Samuel Johnson

from The Preface

In hope of giving longevity to that which its own nature forbids to be immortal, I have devoted this book, the labor of years, to the honor of my country, that we may no longer yield the palm of philology[1] without a contest to the nations of the continent. The chief glory of every people arises from its authors. Whether I shall add anything by my own writings to the reputation of English literature must be left to time. Much of my life has been lost under the pressures of disease; much has been trifled away; and much has always been spent in provision for the day that was passing over me; but I shall not think my employment useless or ignoble if, by my assistance, foreign nations and distant ages gain access to the propagators[2] of knowledge and understand the teachers of truth, if my labors afford light to the repositories[3] of science and add celebrity to Bacon, to Hooker, to Milton, and to Boyle.[4]

When I am animated by this wish, I look with pleasure on my book, however defective, and deliver it to the world with the spirit of a man that has endeavored well. That it will

---

1. A *palm* leaf is a symbol for excellence or victory; *philology* is the study of language.

2. As used here, *propagators* are people who spread knowledge.
3. *Repositories* are storehouses.
4. Francis *Bacon*, Richard *Hooker*, John *Milton*, and Robert *Boyle* are writers and scholars whom Johnson quotes throughout his dictionary.

Reading Strategy **Distinguishing Fact and Opinion** *Is this statement a fact or an opinion? Do you agree with it? Why or why not?*

Big Idea **The English Enlightenment and Neoclassicism** *What statement is Johnson making about the place of language, ideas, and education in world culture?*

immediately become popular I have not promised to myself. A few wild blunders and risible[5] absurdities, from which no work of such multiplicity was ever free, may for a time furnish folly with laughter and harden ignorance in contempt; but useful diligence will at last prevail, and there never can be wanting some who distinguish desert; who will consider that no dictionary of a living tongue ever can be perfect, since while it is hastening to publication, some words are budding, and some falling away; that a whole life cannot be spent upon syntax and etymology,[6] and that even a whole life would not be sufficient; that he, whose design includes whatever language can express, must often speak of what he does not understand; that a writer will sometimes be hurried by eagerness to the end and sometimes faint with weariness under a task which Scaliger[7] compares to the labors of the anvil and the mine; that what is obvious is not always known, and what is known is not always present; that sudden fits of inadvertency[8] will surprise **vigilance,** slight avocations[9] will seduce attention, and casual eclipses will darken learning; and that the writer shall often in vain trace his memory at the moment of need for that which yesterday he knew with **intuitive** readiness and which will come uncalled into his thoughts tomorrow.

In this work, when it shall be found that much is omitted, let it not be forgotten that much likewise is performed; and though no book was ever spared out of tenderness to the author, and the world is little solicitous to know whence proceeded the faults of that which it condemns; yet it may gratify curiosity to inform it that the *English Dictionary* was written with little assistance of the learned and without any patronage of the great; not in the soft obscurities of retirement or under the shelter of academic bowers,[10] but amidst inconvenience and distraction, in sickness and in sorrow. It may repress the triumph of malignant[11] criticism to observe that if our language is not here fully displayed, I have only failed in an attempt which no human powers have hitherto completed. If the lexicons[12] of ancient tongues, now **immutably** fixed and comprised in a few volumes, are yet, after the toil of successive ages, inadequate and delusive; if the **aggregated** knowledge and cooperating diligence of the Italian academicians did not secure them from the censure of Beni;[13] if the embodied critics of France, when fifty years had been spent upon their work, were obliged to change its economy[14] and give their second edition another form, I may surely be contented without the praise of perfection, which, if I could obtain, in this gloom of solitude, what would it avail me? I have protracted my work till most of those whom I wished to please have sunk into the grave, and success and miscarriage are empty sounds: I therefore dismiss it with frigid tranquility, having little to fear or hope from censure or from praise. ◢

---

5. *Risible* means "laughable" or "comical."
6. *Syntax* is sentence structure, and *etymology* is word history.
7. *Scaliger* refers to J. J. Scaliger (1540–1609), a scholar who suggested that criminals be sentenced to writing dictionaries.
8. *Inadvertency* means "heedlessness" or "negligence."
9. *Avocations* are hobbies or other diversions.

Literary Element Voice *What does this statement tell you about the author's personality?*

Vocabulary

vigilance (vij´ ə ləns) *n.* careful watchfulness
intuitive (in tōō´ ə tiv) *adj.* known or perceived without deliberate thought

---

10. By *bowers,* Johnson means "idealized settings."
11. In this case, *malignant* means "having an evil or negative influence."
12. *Lexicons* are dictionaries.
13. Paola *Beni* severely criticized the Italian Academy's dictionary.
14. Here, *economy* means "organization."

Literary Element Voice *What qualities of Johnson's voice does this statement convey?*

Vocabulary

immutably (i mū´ tə blē) *adv.* unchangeably; permanently
aggregated (ag´ rə gā´ təd) *adj.* collected; gathered into a whole

from
A Dictionary of the English Language

ANTHO′ LOGY. *n.* 1. A collection of flowers. 2. A collection of poems.

CLUB. *n.* An assembly of good fellows, meeting under certain conditions.

> What right has any man to meet in factious *clubs* to vilify the government?
>> Dryden, *Medal, Dedication*.

IMA′ GINATION. *n.* 1. Fancy; the power of forming ideal pictures; the power of representing things absent to one's self or others. 2. Conception; image in the mind; idea. 3. Contrivance; scheme.

KIND. *adj.* Benevolent; filled with general good-will.

> By the *kind* gods, 'tis most ignobly done
> To pluck me by the beard.
>> Shakespeare, *King Lear*.

LEXICO′ GRAPHER. *n.* A writer of dictionaries; a harmless drudge that busies himself in tracing the original and detailing the signification of words.

MAN. *n.* 1. Human being.

> The king is but a *man* as I am; the violet smells to him as it doth to me; the element shows to him as it doth to me, all his senses have but human conditions.
>> Shakespeare.

2. Not a woman. 3. Not a boy. 4. A word of familiarity bordering on contempt. 5. Not a beast.

MO′ PPET. *n.* A puppet made of rags.

Dr. Samuel Johnson's house in London, designed by Johnson.

NA′ TURE. *n.* 1. An imaginary being supposed to preside over the material and animal world. 2. The constitution of an animated body.

> We're not ourselves,
> When *nature*, being oppressed, commands the mind
> To suffer with the body.
>> Shakespeare, *King Lear*.

3. Disposition of mind; temper. 4. The regular course of things. 5. Natural affection, or reverence; native sensations. 6. Sort; species. 7. Physics; the science which teaches the quality of things.

OATS. *n.* A grain, which in England is generally given to horses, but in Scotland supports the people.

PA′ STERN. *n.* The knee of a horse.

> I will not change my horse with any that treads on four *pasterns*.[1]
>> Shakespeare, *Henry V*.

PA′ TRON. *n.* One who countenances, supports, or protects. Commonly a wretch who supports with insolence and is paid with flattery.

PE′ NSION. *n.* An allowance made to anyone without an equivalent. In England it is generally understood to mean pay given to a state hireling for treason to his country.

PE′ PPERMINT. *n.* Mint eminently hot.

SLO′ THFUL. *adj.* Idle; lazy; sluggish; inactive; indolent; dull of motion.

> The desire of the *slothful* killeth him; for his hands refuse to labor.
>> Proverbs, 21:25.

SMOKE. *n.* The visible effluvium, or sooty exhalation, from anything burning.

SNEEZE. *n.* Emission of wind audibly by the nose.

WIT. *n.* 1. The powers of the mind; the mental faculties; the intellects. This is the original signification. 2. Imagination; quickness of fancy. 3. Sentiments produced by quickness of fancy. 4. A man of fancy. 5. A man of genius. 6. Sense; judgment. 7. In the plural, sound mind; intellect not crazed. 8. Contrivance; stratagem; power of expedients.

X. A letter which, though found in Saxon words, begins no word in the English language.

YAWN. *v.* 1. To gape; to oscitate; to have the mouth opened involuntarily by fumes, as in sleepiness.

YOUTH. *n.* The part of life succeeding to childhood and adolescence; the time from fourteen to twenty-eight.

---

1. A *pastern* is actually part of a horse's foot. When an acquaintance asked Johnson why he had defined it as a *knee,* he answered, "Ignorance, Madam, pure ignorance."

Reading Strategy Distinguishing Fact and Opinion
What opinion is hidden within this "factual" definition?

Big Idea The English Enlightenment and Neoclassicism *This definition is nearly twice as long as any of the others in this listing. What does this suggest about Johnson's view of the human mind and reason?*

Dr. Johnson in the Anteroom of Lord Chesterfield, Waiting for an Audience, 1748.
Edward Matthew Ward. Oil on canvas, 106 x 139.4 cm. Tate Gallery, London.

Letter to Lord Chesterfield

Samuel Johnson

To the Right Honorable the Earl of Chesterfield

February 7, 1755

My Lord,

    I have been lately informed, by the proprietor of the *World*,[1] that two papers, in which my *Dictionary* is recommended to the public, were written by your Lordship. To be so distinguished is an honor, which, being very little accustomed to favors from the great, I know not well how to receive, or in what terms to acknowledge.

---

1. The *World* was the newspaper in which Chesterfield praised the *Dictionary.*

When, upon some slight encouragement, I first visited your Lordship, I was overpowered, like the rest of mankind, by the enchantment of your address,[2] and could not forbear to wish that I might boast myself *le vainqueur du vainqueur de la terre*,[3] that I might obtain that regard for which I saw the world contending; but I found my attendance so little encouraged that neither pride nor modesty would suffer me to continue it. When I had once addressed your Lordship in public, I had exhausted all the art of pleasing which a retired and uncourtly scholar can possess. I had done all that I could; and no man is well pleased to have his all neglected, be it ever so little.

Seven years, my Lord, have now passed since I waited in your outward rooms, or was repulsed from your door; during which time I have been pushing on my work through difficulties of which it is useless to complain and have brought it at last to the verge of publication without one act of assistance, one word of encouragement, or one smile of favor. Such treatment I did not expect, for I never had a patron before.

The shepherd in Virgil grew at last acquainted with Love and found him a native of the rocks.[4] Is not a patron, my Lord, one who looks with unconcern on a man struggling for life in the water and, when he has reached ground, encumbers him with help? The notice which you have been pleased to take of my labors, had it been early, had been kind; but it has been delayed till I am indifferent and cannot enjoy it; till I am solitary and cannot impart it; till I am known and do not want it.

I hope it is no very cynical asperity[5] not to confess obligations where no benefit has been received or to be unwilling that the public should consider me as owing that to a patron which Providence has enabled me to do for myself.

Having carried on my work thus far with so little obligation to any favorer of learning, I shall not be disappointed though I should conclude it, if less be possible, with less; for I have been long wakened from that dream of hope in which I once boasted myself with so much **exultation**, my Lord,

Your Lordship's most humble,
most obedient servant,
Sam. Johnson

---

2. In this context, *address* means "manner of speaking; conversation."
3. The French phrase *le vainqueur du vainqueur de la terre* (lə van′ koer doo van′ koer də lä tāer) means "the conqueror of the conqueror of the earth."
4. *[The shepherd . . . rocks.]* This is a reference to a work by the Roman poet Virgil (70–19 B.C.) in which a shepherd complains that love was born among jagged rocks.
5. Here, *asperity* means "bitterness."

Reading Strategy Distinguishing Fact and Opinion *Is this a statement of fact or of opinion? How do you know?*

Literary Element Voice *Describe Johnson's voice in this passage. What statement is Johnson actually making to Lord Chesterfield?*

Vocabulary

exultation (eg′ zul tā′ shən) *n.* joy; elation

RESPONDING AND THINKING CRITICALLY

Respond

1. What is your impression of Johnson after reading excerpts from his works?

Recall and Interpret

2. (a)In the first paragraph of the preface to *A Dictionary of the English Language*, what purpose does Johnson say he hopes the dictionary will fulfill? (b)How might the definitions in the dictionary help fulfill this purpose?

3. (a)Which of the definitions from Johnson's dictionary are sarcastic? (b)Why might Johnson have decided to include these definitions?

4. (a)Summarize the first two paragraphs of Johnson's letter to Lord Chesterfield. (b)What functions do these paragraphs serve?

5. (a)In the fourth paragraph of the letter, to whom does Johnson compare himself? (b)How does this comparison help express Johnson's attitude toward Lord Chesterfield?

Analyze and Evaluate

6. (a)What is the overall tone of the preface to *A Dictionary of the English Language*? (b)What does this suggest about Johnson?

7. Which style of definition do you prefer: the straightforward or the sarcastic? Why?

8. Do you agree with Johnson's response to Chesterfield's praise, or do you feel he should have handled the situation differently? Give reasons for your response.

Connect

9. Contemporary dictionaries are compiled by large groups of writers and editors. What might be some of the benefits of a dictionary written by such a group? What might be some of the drawbacks?

10. **Big Idea** The English Enlightenment and Neoclassicism What characteristics of Johnson's works suggest the influence of the English Enlightenment? How might Johnson's style contradict the principles of reason?

LITERARY ANALYSIS

Literary Element Voice

The **voice** of a literary work is the distinctive use of language that conveys to the reader the personality of a writer or narrator. Voice is determined by elements of style such as word choice and tone. Johnson's voice is marked by long, elegant sentences; precise diction; and an expertly controlled sarcastic wit.

1. In the preface to the *Dictionary* or in the letter to Lord Chesterfield, find an example of a long, elegant sentence that Johnson uses to witty or sarcastic effect.

2. Which word choices in the second paragraph of the letter to Lord Chesterfield do you find particularly effective? Why?

3. What aspects of Johnson's personality are revealed in the letter?

Review: Tone

As you learned on page 255, **tone** is an author's attitude toward his or her subject matter. Tone is conveyed through elements such as word choice, punctuation, sentence structure, and figures of speech. The tone of Samuel Johnson's "Letter to Lord Chesterfield," although outwardly respectful, contains more than a hint of angry sarcasm.

Partner Activity With a partner, use a chart like this one to paraphrase Johnson's polite tone into his not-so-polite intended meaning.

| **Text:** "To be so distinguished is an honor, which, being very little accustomed to favors from the great, I know not well how to receive . . . " | **Meaning:** Johnson has no idea how to respond to Chesterfield's praise because he has had so little praise from him up to this point. |

Reading Strategy ## Distinguishing Fact and Opinion

When you **distinguish fact and opinion**, you determine whether information can be verified and proved true.

1. (a)Concerning fact and opinion, how does Johnson's dictionary differ from most standard dictionaries today? (b)Why might the dictionary form be especially fitting for Johnson's style of expression?

2. Use your notes to pick out the emotional words in the following sentences from the selections.

   (a)"a harmless drudge that busies himself in tracing the original and detailing the signification of words." (from the *Dictionary*)

   (b)"I was overpowered, like the rest of mankind, by the enchantment of your address". (from "Letter to Lord Chesterfield")

   (c)"for I have been long wakened from that dream of hope in which I once boasted myself with so much exultation". (from "Letter to Lord Chesterfield")

Vocabulary **Practice**

Practice with Antonyms Choose the antonym for each vocabulary word listed in the first column.

1. exultation   **a.** sorrow   **b.** terror

2. immutably   **a.** endlessly   **b.** temporarily

3. vigilance   **a.** scorn   **b.** inattentiveness

4. intuitive   **a.** serene   **b.** obtuse

5. aggregated   **a.** infuriated   **b.** scattered

Academic Vocabulary

Here is a word from the vocabulary list on page R82.

invest (in vest′) *v.* to commit money in the interest of earning a financial return

Practice and Apply
How might it have helped Johnson if Lord Chesterfield had **invested** in the dictionary?

Writing About Literature

Compare and Contrast Style An author's **style** refers to his or her choice and arrangement of language. How does the style of Johnson's "Letter to Lord Chesterfield" differ from the style we generally use in letter writing today?

In a few paragraphs, compare Johnson's style in his letter to the style of a modern letter, focusing on the following points: formality of language and tone, length and structure of sentences, and salutation and closing. Then write a paragraph containing your thoughts as to what the different styles suggest about society then and now.

Before you draft, follow the path shown here to help you organize your essay.

Introduction: Present the issue and your opinion on it at the end of your introduction.

Body Paragraphs: Compare
• formality of language and tone
• length and structure of sentences
• salutation and closing of the two types of letters

Conclusion: Summarize your main points and add any additional insight.

After you complete your draft, meet with a peer reviewer to evaluate each other's work and to suggest revisions. Then proofread and edit your draft for errors in spelling, grammar, and punctuation.

Internet Connection

The Internet provides free access to many reference resources. Make a list of the most useful sites for dictionaries, encyclopedias, thesauruses, databases, and other specialized resources you can find. Compile your list with those of your classmates and post the master list in your classroom or school library.

Literature Online **Web Activities** For eFlashcards, Selection Quick Checks, and other Web activities, go to www.glencoe.com.

Grammar Workshop

Language Usage

▶ **Correcting Pronoun-Antecedent Agreement**

A **pronoun** substitutes for a noun and should always refer to a clear noun, or **antecedent.** Remember that pronouns should agree in number and gender with the antecedent to which they refer.

▶ **Test-Taking Tip**

To check for pronoun-antecedent agreement when writing for a test, read the sentence to yourself. Sentences that need correction often sound strange or confusing.

▶ **Language Handbook**

For more about pronouns and antecedents, see Language Handbook, pp. R49–R50.

Literature Online
eWorkbooks To link to the Grammar and Language eWorkbook, go to www.glencoe.com.

OBJECTIVES
• Understand pronoun-antecedent agreement.
• Recognize rules of grammar.

Correcting Pronoun-Antecedent Agreement

"The notice which you have been pleased to take of my labors, had it been early, had been kind; but it has been delayed till I am indifferent and cannot enjoy it."

—Samuel Johnson, from "Letter to Lord Chesterfield"

Connecting to Literature In the quotation above, Samuel Johnson uses the pronoun *it* in place of the noun *notice*. When you speak or write, make sure that every **pronoun** you use has a clear **antecedent,** or noun to which the pronoun refers. Avoid these common problems in pronoun-antecedent agreement:

Problems

1. **A weak or vague pronoun antecedent**
   The *Dictionary* was well received, which was Johnson's reward.

2. **A pronoun that refers to more than one antecedent.**
   Johnson and Chesterfield disagreed about the value of the *Dictionary*, and he would not finance the work.

Solutions

• Clarify the antecedent of the pronoun.
  1. The *Dictionary* received much critical acclaim, which was Johnson's reward.

  2. Johnson and Chesterfield disagreed about the value of the *Dictionary*, and Chesterfield would not finance the work.

• Substitute a noun for the pronoun.
  1. The *Dictionary's* warm critical reception was Johnson's reward.

  2. Chesterfield disagreed with Johnson about the value of the *Dictionary*, and he would not finance the work.

Exercise

Revise for Clarity Rewrite the following sentences to correct pronoun-antecedent errors. Add any necessary information.

1. Johnson told Lord Chesterfield that he should not take credit for the work.
2. Lord Chesterfield's neglect of Johnson did not reflect well on him.
3. The letter was extremely sarcastic, but did Chesterfield recognize it?
4. The writing was filled with complex sentences, which made it seem formal.
5. Johnson's *Dictionary* was revolutionary, which received mixed reactions.

from *The Life of Samuel Johnson*

MEET JAMES BOSWELL

For years, the biographer and diarist James Boswell's accomplishments were overshadowed by those of Samuel Johnson, the literary giant about whom he wrote. Before the twentieth century, Boswell was often regarded as little more than an adequate reporter. The discovery of Boswell's journals in the 1920s and 1930s, however, revealed his rare insight and his important role in the development of the modern biography.

Early Life Boswell was born in 1740 in Edinburgh, Scotland, the son of well-to-do parents. As a child he disliked the school he attended, so his father provided him with private tutors. Boswell received an excellent education in the arts and law, but he did not want to become a lawyer like his father. Instead, he was drawn to the theater and the arts. In 1760, at the age of twenty, he ran away to London, but his father soon brought him back home. Father and son struck a bargain: James could return to London as soon as he passed his law exams, so at the age of twenty-two he passed his exams and happily set out.

A Literary Friendship Boswell loved the life of the city. He made a point of introducing himself to London's intellectual elite and quickly became a part of it. His wealthy background and personal charm afforded him access to the upper crust of London society. He met such notable figures of the time as painter Joshua Reynolds, writer Oliver Goldsmith, and political reformer John Wilkes. In a London bookshop, he also met the famous man of letters Samuel Johnson, and one of the great friendships of English literary history began. At the time they met, Boswell was only twenty-two. Johnson was fifty-three.

Travels Abroad Shortly after meeting Johnson, Boswell toured Europe, spending time in Corsica, a Mediterranean island. His account of his tour across Corsica, published when he was twenty-eight, was both a popular and a critical success.

At twenty-nine, Boswell married and moved back to Scotland to practice law. Though he could see Johnson only occasionally, the two wrote to each other and, when Boswell was in his early thirties, they toured the Scottish Highlands and the Hebrides Islands, off the western coast of Scotland, together. Boswell later published his journal from the tour. However, he is best known for *The Life of Samuel Johnson.* His sharp memory and eye for detail allow readers a vivid look into the life of not just Samuel Johnson, but also of Boswell himself.

> *"We cannot tell the precise moment when friendship is formed. As in filling a vessel drop by drop, there is at last a drop which makes it run over; so in a series of kindnesses there is at last one which makes the heart run over."*
>
> —James Boswell

While he was proud of his literary efforts, Boswell nevertheless regarded himself as a personal failure. He died in 1795, at the age of fifty-four, never to realize the impact his work would have on English literature.

James Boswell was born in 1740 and died in 1795.

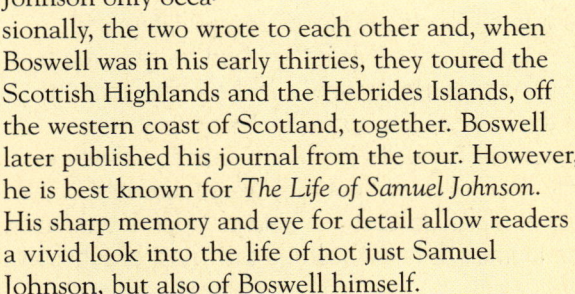

Literature Online **Author Search** For more about James Boswell, go to www.glencoe.com.

Connecting to the Biography

The following selection begins by describing Boswell's first meeting with Samuel Johnson, the greatest literary celebrity of his day. As you read the excerpt, think about the following questions:

- Popular media often feature stories about famous people. Are they mostly positive or mostly negative?
- Is there anyone in the public eye whom you admire? For what reasons do you admire him or her?

Building Background

Throughout his friendship with Johnson, Boswell kept detailed journals in which he recorded his conversations with his illustrious friend. Boswell later used these journals, as well as information he gathered by interviewing Johnson's friends and acquaintances, to write the story of Johnson's life. For years it was believed that Boswell's journals had been destroyed shortly after his death, but they were recovered in the 1920s at Malahide Castle in Ireland. Upon examination of the journals, scholars learned that most of Johnson's conversations, the true spice of Boswell's biography, had been copied almost directly from Boswell's initial recording of them in his journals.

Setting Purposes for Reading

Big Idea The English Enlightenment and Neoclassicism

As you read this selection, notice Boswell's emphasis on Samuel Johnson's intellectual rigor, strongly held opinions, and force of personality.

Literary Element Biography

A **biography** is a nonfiction account of a person's life and personality, written by someone other than the subject. Using such resources as interviews, diaries, journals, and letters, the biographer describes major events in the subject's life and provides insight into the subject's character. As you read the selection, notice how the biographer is himself a character in the story of Johnson's life.

- See Literary Terms Handbook, p. R2.

Reading Strategy Evaluating Credibility

To analyze what you read, you must sometimes **evaluate the credibility** of the author or source. In a biography such as Boswell's *The Life of Samuel Johnson*, you must read carefully to separate facts from opinions and detect **bias,** or an inclination toward an opinion or position. Ask yourself if the author seems reliable. How can you tell?

Reading Tip: Taking Notes As you read, take notes on examples of bias within the text.

Vocabulary

veneration (ven´ ə rā´ shən) *n.* deep respect or reverence; p. 661 *The visiting dignitary was met with veneration and cheering crowds.*

zealous (zel´ əs) *adj.* filled with intense, enthusiastic devotion; p. 664 *The principal is zealous about the need for art in the school.*

impetuous (im pech´ ōō əs) *adj.* characterized by rushing headlong into things; impulsive; p. 665 *Guillermo has an impetuous nature that allows him to talk to complete strangers.*

precept (prē´ sept) *n.* a rule intended as a guide for conduct or action; p. 665 *Regular attendance and punctuality are two of our club's precepts.*

ingenuity (in´ jə nōō´ ə tē) *n.* cleverness; inventiveness; p. 666 *Jackson's brilliant model for the science fair was just one example of his ingenuity.*

Vocabulary Tip: Denotation and Connotation Denotation is the literal or dictionary meaning of a word. Connotation is the suggested or implied meaning.

Literature Online Interactive Literary Elements Handbook To review or learn more about the literary elements, go to www.glencoe.com.

OBJECTIVES
In studying this selection, you will focus on the following:
- understanding the historical period
- analyzing biography
- evaluating credibility of sources

from The Life of Samuel Johnson

James Boswell

Boswell Meets Johnson 1763

This is to me a memorable year; for in it I had the happiness to obtain the acquaintance of that extraordinary man whose memoirs I am now writing, an acquaintance which I shall ever esteem as one of the most fortunate circumstances in my life.

Though then but two-and-twenty, I had for several years read his works with delight and instruction and had the highest reverence for their author, which had grown up in my fancy into a kind of mysterious **veneration,** by figuring to myself a state of solemn elevated abstraction in which I supposed him to live in the immense metropolis of London. . . .

Mr. Thomas Davies the actor, who then kept a bookseller's shop in Russel Street, Covent Garden, told me that Johnson was very much his friend and came frequently to his house, where he more than once invited me to meet him, but by some unlucky accident or other, he was prevented from coming to us. . . .

At last, on Monday the sixteenth of May, when I was sitting in Mr. Davies's back parlor, after having drunk tea with him and Mrs. Davies, Johnson unexpectedly came into the shop; and Mr. Davies having perceived him through the glass door in the room in which we were sitting, advancing towards us—he announced his awful[1] approach to me, somewhat in the manner of an actor in the part of Horatio, when he addresses Hamlet on the

1. Here, *awful* means "awe-inspiring."

appearance of his father's ghost,[2] "Look, my Lord, it comes." I found that I had a very perfect idea of Johnson's figure, from the portrait of him painted by Sir Joshua Reynolds soon after he had published his *Dictionary*, in the attitude of sitting in his easy chair in deep meditation, which was the first picture his friend did for him, which Sir Joshua very kindly presented to me, and from which an engraving has been made for this work. Mr. Davies mentioned my name and respectfully introduced me to him. I was much agitated; and recollecting his prejudice against the Scotch, of which I had heard much, I said to Davies, "Don't tell where I come from." "From Scotland," cried Davies roguishly. "Mr. Johnson," said I, "I do indeed come from Scotland, but I cannot help it." I am willing to flatter myself that I meant this as light pleasantry to sooth and conciliate him, and not as a humiliating abasement[3] at the expense of my country. But however that might be, this speech was somewhat unlucky; for with that quickness of wit for which he was so remarkable, he seized the expression "come from Scotland," which I used in the sense of being of that country; and, as if I had said that I had come away from it, or left, retorted, "That, Sir, I find, is what a very great many of your countrymen cannot help." This stroke stunned me a good deal; and when we had sat down, I felt myself not a little embarrassed and apprehensive of what might come next. He then addressed himself to Davies: "What do you think of Garrick?[4] He has refused me an order[5] for the play for Miss Williams[6] because he knows the house will be full and that an order would be worth three shillings." Eager to take any opening to get into conversation with him,

I ventured to say, "Oh, Sir, I cannot think Mr. Garrick would grudge such a trifle to you." "Sir," said he, with a stern look, "I have known David Garrick longer than you have done, and I know no right you have to talk to me on the subject." Perhaps I deserved this check; for it was rather presumptuous in me, an entire stranger, to express any doubt of the justice of his animadversion[7] upon his old acquaintance and pupil. I now felt myself much mortified and began to think that the hope which I had long indulged of obtaining his acquaintance was blasted. And, in truth, had not my ardor been uncommonly strong, and my resolution uncommonly persevering, so rough a reception might have deterred me forever from making any further attempts. Fortunately, however, I remained upon the field not wholly discomfited[8] and was soon rewarded by hearing some of his conversation, of which I preserved the following short minute,[9] without marking the questions and observations by which it was produced.

"People," he remarked, "may be taken in once, who imagine that an author is greater in private life than other men. Uncommon parts require uncommon opportunities for their exertion.

"In barbarous society, superiority of parts is of real consequence. Great strength or great wisdom is of much value to an individual. But in more polished times there are people to do everything for money; and then there are a number of other superiorities, such as those of birth and fortune and rank that dissipate[10] men's attention and leave no extraordinary share of respect for personal and intellectual superiority. This is wisely ordered by Providence[11] to preserve some equality among mankind.

---

2. In William Shakespeare's *Hamlet*, Act 1, scene 4, Horatio announces to his friend Hamlet the appearance of Hamlet's father's ghost.
3. An *abasement* is a humbling.
4. David *Garrick* (1717–1779) was considered the greatest Shakespearean actor of his time.
5. In this context, an *order* is a free ticket.
6. Garrick gave a benefit performance for his impoverished friend, the poet Anna *Williams* (1706–1783), who was also a friend of Johnson's.

Literary Element Biography *Why does Johnson's remark "stun" Boswell?*

7. An *animadversion* (a′ nə mad′ vər′ zhən) is an unfavorable remark or criticism.
8. When Boswell says he was not *wholly discomfited*, he means he was not completely frustrated or thwarted.
9. In this instance, a *minute* is a record or a summary.
10. *Dissipate* means "waste."
11. *Providence* is divine guidance.

Literary Element Biography *What is Boswell saying about his reporting of this conversation?*

Big Idea The English Enlightenment and Neoclassicism *How do Johnson's comments in this paragraph reflect Enlightenment ideas?*

Samuel Johnson with James Boswell at home in Boer Court. Hand-colored engraving.

Viewing the Art: Does this image of Johnson (left) capture his personality as Boswell describes it? Explain your answer.

"Sir, this book [*The Elements of Criticism*,[12] which he had taken up] is a pretty essay and deserves to be held in some estimation, though much of it is chimerical."[13]

Speaking of one who with more than ordinary boldness attacked public measures and the royal family, he said, "I think he is safe from the law, but he is an abusive scoundrel; and instead of applying to my Lord Chief Justice to punish him, I would send half a dozen footmen[14] and have him well ducked.[15]

"The notion of liberty amuses the people of England and helps to keep off the *taedium vitae*.[16] When a butcher tells you that his heart bleeds for his country, he has, in fact, no uneasy feeling.

"Sheridan[17] will not succeed at Bath with his oratory. Ridicule has gone down before him, and I doubt,[18] Derrick is his enemy.

"Derrick may do very well as long as he can outrun his character, but the moment his character gets up with him, it is all over."

It is, however, but just to record, that some years afterwards, when I reminded him of this sarcasm, he said, "Well, but Derrick has now got a character that he need not run away from."

I was highly pleased with the extraordinary vigor of his conversation and regretted that I was drawn away from it by an engagement at another place. I had, for a part of the evening, been left alone with him and had ventured to make an observation now and then, which he received very civilly; so that I was satisfied that though there was a roughness in his manner, there was no ill nature in his disposition. Davies followed me to the door, and when I complained to him a little of the hard blows which the great man had given me, he kindly took upon him to console me by saying, "Don't be uneasy. I can see he likes you very well."

---

12. *The Elements of Criticism* was written by Scottish jurist and philosopher Henry Home, Lord Kames (1696–1782).
13. *Chimerical* (ki mer′ i kəl) means "whimsical" or "fanciful."
14. *Footmen* were servants.
15. Ducking in water was a type of punishment.
16. *Taedium vitae* (tī′ dē əm vē′ tī) is Latin for "weariness of life."
17. *Sheridan* is Thomas Sheridan (1719–1788), an Irish-born actor.
18. In this context, *doubt* means "fear" or "suspect."

Reading Strategy Evaluating Credibility *What is Boswell implying about Johnson's opinions of others?*

Johnson's Character

The character of Samuel Johnson has, I trust, been so developed in the course of this work that they who have honored it with a perusal[19] may be considered as well acquainted with him. As, however, it may be expected that I should collect into one view the capital and distinguishing features of this extraordinary man, I shall endeavor to acquit myself of that part of my biographical undertaking, however difficult it may be to do that which many of my readers will do better for themselves.

His figure was large and well formed, and his countenance[20] of the cast of an ancient statue; yet his appearance was rendered strange and somewhat uncouth by convulsive cramps, by the scars of that distemper[21] which it was once imagined the royal touch[22] could cure, and by a slovenly[23] mode of dress. He had the use only of one eye; yet so much does mind govern and even supply the deficiency of organs, that his visual perceptions, as far as they extended, were uncommonly quick and accurate. So morbid was his temperament that he never knew the natural joy of a free and vigorous use of his limbs: when he walked, it was like the struggling gait of one in fetters;[24] when he rode, he had no command or direction of his horse but was carried as if in a balloon. That with his constitution and habits of life he should have lived seventy-five years is a proof that an inherent *vivida vis*[25] is a powerful preservative of the human frame.

Man is, in general, made up of contradictory qualities; and these will ever shew[26] themselves in strange succession, where a consistency in appearance at least, if not reality, has not been attained by long habits of philosophical discipline. In proportion to the native vigor of the mind, the contradictory qualities will be the more prominent and more difficult to be adjusted; and, therefore, we are not to wonder that Johnson exhibited an eminent example of this remark which I have made upon human nature. At different times, he seemed a different man, in some respects; not, however, in any great or essential article, upon which he had fully employed his mind, and settled certain principles of duty, but only in his manners and in the display of argument and fancy in his talk. He was prone to superstition, but not to credulity.[27] Though his imagination might incline him to a belief of the marvelous and the mysterious, his vigorous reason examined the evidence with jealousy. He was a sincere and **zealous** Christian, of high Church-of-England and monarchical principles, which he would not tamely suffer to be questioned; and had, perhaps, at an early period, narrowed his mind somewhat too much, both as to religion and politics. His being impressed with the danger of extreme latitude in either, though he was of a very independent spirit, occasioned his appearing somewhat unfavorable to the prevalence of that noble freedom of sentiment which is the best possession of man. Nor can it be denied that he had many prejudices, which, however, frequently suggested many of his pointed sayings that rather shew a playfulness of fancy than any settled malignity. He was steady and inflexible in maintaining the obligations of religion and morality, both from a regard for the order of society and from a veneration for the Great Source[28] of all order; correct, nay, stern in his taste; hard to please and easily

---

19. A *perusal* is a careful reading.
20. Boswell refers to Johnson's *countenance,* or facial features.
21. The disease that Boswell refers to as *distemper* was scrofula, tuberculosis of the lymphatic glands.
22. Because of a popular but mistaken belief that scrofula could be cured by the *royal touch,* Johnson was taken to London at the age of two to be touched by Queen Anne.
23. *Slovenly* means "untidy" or "sloppy."
24. *Fetters* are chains or shackles on the ankles or feet.
25. *Vivida vis* (vē′ vē dä wēs) means "life force."
26. *Shew* means "show."

27. *Credulity* means "a willingness to believe without sufficient evidence; gullibility."
28. The *Great Source* refers to God as the provider.

Reading Strategy Evaluating Credibility *Do you think Boswell can or cannot be trusted to give an accurate description of the "differences" in Johnson's personality? Explain.*

Vocabulary

zealous (zel′ əs) adj. filled with intense, enthusiastic devotion

Literary Element Biography *As a biographer, what does Boswell expect from his readers?*

offended; **impetuous** and irritable in his temper, but of a most humane and benevolent heart, which shewed itself not only in a most liberal charity, as far as his circumstances would allow, but in a thousand instances of active benevolence. He was afflicted with a bodily disease, which made him often restless and fretful, and with a constitutional melancholy, the clouds of which darkened the brightness of his fancy and gave a gloomy cast to his whole course of thinking. We, therefore, ought not to wonder at his sallies[29] of impatience and passion at any time, especially when provoked by obtrusive[30] ignorance or presuming petulance,[31] and allowance must be made for his uttering hasty and satirical sallies even against his best friends. And, surely, when it is considered, that, "amidst sickness and sorrow," he exerted his faculties in so many works for the benefit of mankind, and particularly that he achieved the great and admirable *Dictionary* of our language, we must be astonished at his resolution. The solemn text "of him to whom much is given, much will be required" seems to have been ever present to his mind, in a rigorous sense, and to have made him dissatisfied with his labors and acts of goodness, however comparatively great, so that the unavoidable consciousness of his superiority was, in that respect, a cause of disquiet. He suffered so much from this, and from the gloom which perpetually haunted him and made solitude frightful, that it may be said of him, "If in this life only he had hope, he was of all men most miserable."[32] He loved praise when it was

In him were united a most logical head with a most fertile imagination, which gave him an extraordinary advantage in arguing. . . .

brought to him but was too proud to seek for it. He was somewhat susceptible of[33] flattery. As he was general and unconfined in his studies, he cannot be considered as master of any one particular science; but he had accumulated a vast and various collection of learning and knowledge, which was so arranged in his mind as to be ever in readiness to be brought forth. But his superiority over other learned men consisted chiefly in what may be called the art of thinking, the art of using his mind, a certain continual power of seizing the useful substance of all that he knew and exhibiting it in a clear and forcible manner; so that knowledge, which we often see to be no better than lumber[34] in men of dull understanding, was, in him, true, evident, and actual wisdom. His moral **precepts** are practical, for they are drawn from an intimate acquaintance with human nature. His maxims[35] carry conviction, for they are founded on the basis of common sense and a very attentive and minute survey of real life. His mind was so full of imagery that he might have been perpetually a poet; yet it is remarkable, that, however rich his prose is in this respect, his poetical pieces, in general, have not much of that splendor, but are rather distinguished by strong sentiment and acute observation conveyed in harmonious and energetic verse, particularly in heroic couplets.[36] Though usually grave, and even awful, in his deportment, he possessed uncommon and peculiar powers of wit and humor; he frequently indulged himself in colloquial pleasantry; and the heartiest merri-

---

29. *Sallies* are outbursts.
30. *Obtrusive* means "pushy in a rude or bold manner."
31. *Petulance* is bad temper.
32. ["*If . . . miserable.*"] is based on I Corinthians 15:19: "If in this life only we have hope in Christ, we are of all men most miserable."

Literary Element Biography *How would you describe Boswell's tone here? In your opinion, is Boswell just trying to make his friend look good, or is his comment accurate?*

Vocabulary

impetuous (im pech′ oo əs) *adj.* characterized by rushing headlong into things; impulsive

---

33. *Susceptible of* means "easily affected by."
34. Here, *lumber* means "useless material."
35. *Maxims* are sayings that express moral principles or rules of conduct.
36. *Heroic couplets* consist of paired rhyming lines written in iambic pentameter.

Big Idea The English Enlightenment and Neoclassicism *In what way might Boswell's version of Samuel Johnson be said to epitomize the age of the Enlightenment?*

Vocabulary

precept (prē′ sept) *n.* a rule intended as a guide for conduct or action

Oliver Goldsmith, Irish playwright, poet and dramatist, with James Boswell, diarist, and Dr. Samuel Johnson, poet, critic and lexicographer.

ment was often enjoyed in his company, with this great advantage, that as it was entirely free from any poisonous tincture[37] of vice or impiety,[38] it was salutary[39] to those who shared in it. He had accustomed himself to such accuracy in his common conversation that he at all times expressed his thoughts with great force and an elegant choice of language, the effect of which was aided by his having a loud voice and a slow, deliberate utterance. In him were united a most logical head with a most fertile imagination, which gave him an extraordinary advantage in arguing: for he could reason close or wide, as he saw best for the moment. Exulting in his intellectual strength and dexterity, he could, when he pleased, be the greatest sophist[40] that ever contended in the lists of declamation,[41] and

from a spirit of contradiction and a delight in shewing his powers, he would often maintain the wrong side with equal warmth and **ingenuity,** so that when there was an audience, his real opinions could seldom be gathered from his talk; though when he was in company with a single friend, he would discuss a subject with genuine fairness. But he was too conscientious to make error permanent and pernicious[42] by deliberately writing it, and in all his numerous works, he earnestly inculcated[43] what appeared to him to be the truth, his piety being constant and the ruling principle of all his conduct.

Such was Samuel Johnson, a man whose talents, acquirements, and virtues were so extraordinary that the more his character is considered, the more he will be regarded by the present age, and by posterity, with admiration and reverence. ᴧ

---

37. *Tincture* means "trace" or "tinge."
38. *Impiety* means "lack of reverence."
39. *Salutary* means "conducive to health or well-being."
40. A *sophist* is one who is skilled in using deceptive arguments.
41. Here, a *declamation* is a speech.

Literary Element Biography *Based on Boswell's description in this passage, what do you think it would be like to be in Johnson's presence when he "expressed his thoughts"?*

---

42. *Pernicious* means "destructive."
43. *Inculcated* means "encouraged by persistent teaching or indoctrination."

Vocabulary

ingenuity (in′ jə nōō′ ə tē) *n.* cleverness; inventiveness

RESPONDING AND THINKING CRITICALLY

Respond

1. What was your impression of Johnson during his first meeting with Boswell? Did your impression of him change as you read more about him? Explain why or why not.

Recall and Interpret

2. (a)How did Boswell meet Johnson? (b)Why might Boswell have felt so nervous during that first meeting?

3. (a)How did Johnson reply to Boswell's statement, "I . . . come from Scotland, but I cannot help it"? (b)What was your impression of Johnson based on this reply?

4. (a)Name an aspect of Johnson's personality that Boswell finds objectionable. (b)How does Boswell's overall description excuse this trait?

Analyze and Evaluate

5. (a)What parts of Boswell's description of Johnson's physical appearance are objective, or factual—and which are subjective, or personal opinion? (b)Why might Boswell have included both types of descriptions?

6. (a)Describe the tone of Boswell's criticisms of Johnson. (b)What does this tone suggest about Boswell's opinion of Johnson?

7. (a)What do the quotations that Boswell provides reveal about Johnson's personality? (b)What do they reveal about Boswell himself?

8. In your opinion what was Boswell's purpose in writing about Johnson? Support your opinion with evidence from the work.

9. (a)How might Johnson's friendship have been helpful to Boswell as a biographer? (b)What difficulties might the friendship have posed?

10. How might the portrayal of Johnson have differed had it been written by an enemy instead of a friend?

Connect

11. **Big Idea** **The English Enlightenment and Neoclassicism** In what ways does Boswell's biography exemplify the guiding principles of the Enlightenment?

PRIMARY VISUAL ARTIFACT

Johnson's Portrait

Sir Joshua Reynolds (1723–1792) was one of the most important portrait painters and art critics of

his day, as well as the first president of Britain's Royal Academy. Throughout his life, Reynolds befriended many writers and thinkers, including Samuel Johnson and political theorist Edmund Burke. His portraits of his friends rank among his best. This famous painting of Johnson, completed around 1775, captures many of the physical characteristics, and suggests many of the personality traits, that Boswell describes in his biography.

Group Activity Discuss the following questions with your classmates.

1. (a)What do you find most striking about this portrait? (b)In what ways is Reynolds's method of representation similar to Boswell's?

2. Based on Boswell's description, does this seem like a true likeness? Explain.

Literary Element Biography

Before *The Life of Samuel Johnson*, **biographies** generally focused on describing an individual's major life events and accomplishments. Boswell's attempt to provide, in his words, a "view of [Johnson's] mind" was instrumental in developing the modern approach to biography, with its emphasis on analyzing the forces that shape personality.

1. (a)At what points in the selection does Boswell examine the forces that helped shape Johnson's opinions and behavior? (b)What are these forces?

2. In your opinion, does Boswell provide convincing reasons for Johnson's behavior? Support your opinion with evidence from the selection.

Review: Style

As you learned on page 415, **style** is the combination of expressive qualities that distinguish an author's work, including word choice and the length and arrangement of sentences, as well as the use of figurative language and imagery.

Read this passage from the preface to *A Dictionary of the English Language* by Samuel Johnson.

> "In this work, when it shall be found that much is omitted, let it not be forgotten that much likewise is performed; and though no book was ever spared out of tenderness to the author, and the world is little solicitous to know whence proceeded the faults of that which it condemns; yet it may gratify curiosity to inform it that the *English Dictionary* was written with little assistance of the learned and without any patronage of the great . . . "

Use a Venn diagram to show how Boswell's and Johnson's writing styles are alike and different.

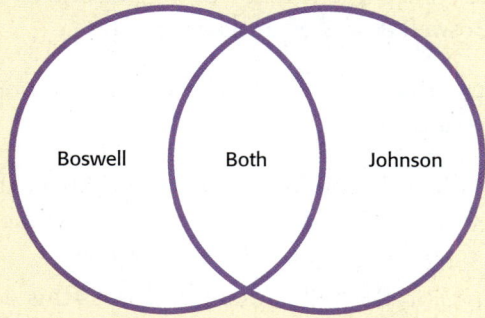

Reading Strategy Evaluating Credibility

Writers select words according to their connotations, which carry emotional or implied meanings, as well as their denotations, or dictionary definitions. Looking at word choices helps you determine a writer's attitude toward a topic. In James Boswell's account of Samuel Johnson's life, he makes every attempt to be fair. But his comments are often based upon his own subjective perspective. For each of the following phrases from the selection, decide whether the statement is objective (fact) or subjective (opinion).

1. "his appearance was rendered strange and somewhat uncouth"

2. "He had the use only of one eye"

3. "I had, for a part of the evening, been left alone with him"

Vocabulary Practice

Practice with Denotation and Connotation
Determine whether each vocabulary word below has a positive, negative, or neutral connotation. In some cases, a word might have both positive and negative connotations depending on its context. If you need help, use a dictionary or thesaurus.

1. veneration
    a. positive   **b.** neutral   **c.** negative

2. zealous
    a. positive   **b.** neutral   **c.** negative

3. impetuous
    a. positive   **b.** neutral   **c.** negative

4. precept
    a. positive   **b.** neutral   **c.** negative

5. ingenuity
    a. positive   **b.** neutral   **c.** negative

Writing About Literature

Analyze Genre Elements Many critics thought Boswell's portrayal of Johnson was too realistic because it described Johnson's shortcomings as well as his virtues. In your opinion, should biographers include a person's negative qualities? Do circumstances ever warrant withholding negative information? Write a brief essay in which you analyze these issues and state your opinion of them. Use evidence from the selection to support your opinion.

Before you begin drafting, create a list of reasonable arguments for and against your position. Support each argument with as much evidence from the text as you can. Then use the strongest arguments in support of your position as your essay's main ideas. Use the arguments against as counterarguments to which you should respond. Use a two-column chart like the one below to organize your thoughts.

Arguments and Evidence	
In Support	In Opposition
Main Ideas Evidence	Counterarguments Evidence

After you complete your draft, meet with a peer reviewer to evaluate each other's work and to suggest revisions. Then proofread and edit your draft for errors in spelling, grammar, and punctuation.

Literary Criticism

According to Samuel Johnson, "The business of the biographer is often to pass slightly over those performances and incidents which produce vulgar greatness, to lead the thoughts into domestic privacies, and display the minute details of daily life." Meet with a partner to discuss whether Boswell passes over Johnson's greatness to show the "minute details" of his life.

Boswell's Language and Style

Using Parenthetical Expressions In this selection from *The Life of Samuel Johnson*, Boswell often uses parenthetical expressions in order to add clarity and further information to his sentences. Parenthetical expressions are usually enclosed by commas, dashes, or parentheses. Generally, they are used to increase the richness, texture, and variety of a piece of writing. Consider, for example, the following passage:

> Mr. Thomas Davies the actor, <u>who then kept a bookseller's shop in Russel Street, Covent Garden</u>, told me that Johnson was very much his friend and came frequently to his house, <u>where he more than once invited me to meet him</u>, but by some unlucky accident or other, he was prevented from coming to us.

Note how these two underlined parenthetical expressions effectively convey information that increases the reader's comprehension of the setting and characters.

Activity Scan this selection from *The Life of Samuel Johnson* in search of other examples of parenthetical expressions. Try to determine what these expressions add to each sentence. Compile your findings in a chart like the one below.

Parenthetical Expressions	Value of Expression

Revising Check

Parenthetical Expressions The use of parenthetical expressions is an important factor to consider when revising your own writing. With a partner, go through your analysis of biography and note places where a parenthetical expression could be used to make your sentences more effective.

Literature Online **Web Activities** For eFlashcards, Selection Quick Checks, and other Web activities, go to www.glencoe.com.

from

Samuel Johnson

W. Jackson Bate

Winner of the Pulitzer Prize

Building Background

Walter Jackson Bate was awarded two Pulitzer Prizes during his distinguished career. He won the second prize in 1978 for his vividly written life of Samuel Johnson. The following excerpt from that work describes James Boswell's family background and his relationship with Samuel Johnson.

Set a Purpose for Reading

Read to learn more about Boswell's life and his famed biography of Johnson.

Reading Strategy

Determining Main Idea and Supporting Details

Determining the main idea means finding the most important thought in a paragraph or a selection which is developed through the use of **supporting details**, such as examples, reasons, facts, or descriptions. As you read, take notes to help you determine the main idea and supporting details.

Main Idea	Supporting Details

On Monday, May 16, when he[1] dropped into the small bookshop kept by his friend Tom Davies, there occurred one of the famous meetings in literary history, which began an acquaintance that was ultimately to result in one of the masterpieces of world literature—James Boswell's *Life of Johnson* (1791). The admiring young Scot was the son of Alexander Boswell, Laird of Auchinleck, a man about Johnson's age, who had studied law at Leyden and was now a judge on the Scottish bench. Though Boswell's name, because of his great work, was to become a household word not long after his death, he himself was drastically underrated until our own generation. He has proved, at the very least, to be a far more complicated person than was ever imagined. The most celebrated literary discovery of this century was the vast journal—or series of journals—he kept through most of his life, chronicling with complete frankness his own personal experiences and, more important, recording conversations and interviews with noted people he met. When published, the writings—*The Private Papers of*

---

1. *He* refers to James Boswell.

James Boswell from Malahide Castle (1928–34)— filled eighteen volumes, and they were later to be supplemented by other material. The conversations in the *Life of Johnson,* together with those in Boswell's earlier *Journal of a Tour to the Hebrides with Samuel Johnson* (1785), are carved from this enormous collection of diaries.

We should remind ourselves (it is often forgotten) how extremely young Boswell was when he met Johnson—he was only twenty-two; Johnson was fifty-three—just as we should remind ourselves that he had many interests, and spent most of his adult life as an able and busy lawyer in Edinburgh, visiting London only on vacations. In some ways, he was even younger than twenty-two at this time, and was generally to remain younger than his years. The identity for which the young Boswell was searching—and continued to search—was one that could define itself against the example of his father, Lord Auchinleck, who was firm and moralistic, a Whig[2] and a Presbyterian, and who proudly spoke broad Scots. In reaction, the son was all the father was not: romantically imaginative, promiscuous, impulsively idealistic and open-natured, pliable,[3] and with an impressionable genius for mimicry.

In his search for identity, a shadow in the background was always there to make him uneasy if he allowed himself to think of it. There was a strain of mental instability in his family; and Boswell's own younger brother John, after the age of nineteen, was to suffer from marked insanity for most of his remaining life. The stability for which Boswell was always to crave was something that his gregarious[4] nature could acquire only through others. And his profoundest enjoyment, if not at the start, certainly as the years passed, was the company, example, and if possible the approval, of older men whom he admired—men of acknowledged standing who were also interesting in themselves, knew the world, and, like Johnson, symbolized the moral rectitude he wanted desperately to impose on his own wayward nature.

Hence his injunctions to himself in his journal to identify with admired models, and acquire a stronger mind and character ("*be* Johnson"). At first the ideals suggest conventional notions of sophistication and elegance. After arriving in London, for example, he writes, "I felt strong dispositions to *be a Mr. Addison.*"[5] Months later— he has by now met and talked a good deal with Johnson—the rather frightened youth is to set off for Harwich to get the boat to Holland, where he is to study law. And the models now, basically so different from each other (the father from whom he is in part fleeing, Lord Chesterfield,[6] and Johnson), show what he really wants most to acquire—inner strength, reserve, calmness, and courage: "[Be] like Father, grave . . . composed. . . . Go abroad with a manly resolution. . . . Never despair. . . . Study [to be] like Lord Chesterfield, *manly. . . . Resemble Johnson . . . your mind will strengthen*" (August 1763); or, later in the year, "*Be* like the Duke of Sully." As he approaches and enters his thirties, there are moments of satisfaction (when he says "you," he is addressing himself—a common practice in his diaries, and typical of his attempt at detachment):

"You felt yourself . . . *like a Johnson* in comparison of former days" (1766). "Was *powerful* like Johnson, and very much satisfied with myself" (1767). "I was in such a frame as to *think myself an Edmund Burke*"[7] (1774). "Fancied myself like Burke, and drank moderately . . ." (1775).

One of the touching entries is near the end, toward the close of his life. Much of his despair—he is now fifty—is that he felt he had no more inner strength to meet difficulties now, when he needed it badly, than he had as a youth—that he seemed to have gone through life "without any addition to my character from my having had the friendship of Dr. Johnson and many eminent men."

Many readers assume that he was constantly in Johnson's presence. But during the twenty-one

---

2. The *Whig* party was the dominant political faction in England at the time.
3. *Pliable* means "changeable."
4. *Gregarious* means "outgoing" or "social."

5. Joseph *Addison* (1672–1719) was a famed essayist.
6. *Lord Chesterfield* (1694–1773) was a statesman and the patron of many writers.
7. *Edmund Burke* (1729–1797) was a conservative British political thinker and statesman.

James Boswell: Caricature, Boswell's tour of the Hebrides. May 1786.

years he knew Johnson, the total number of days he spent in Johnson's company amounted to 325, plus another 101 during their trip to Scotland and the Hebrides[8] in 1773.

Even so, by 1772—ten years after he met Johnson—he had accumulated what he justly called "a vast treasure of his conversation at different times," and decided that he would someday try to write a life of Johnson using these materials. It was to be a new kind of biography—a "life in Scenes," as though it were a kind of drama. And when the "life in Scenes" did appear, nothing comparable to it had existed. Nor has anything comparable been written since, because that special union of talents, opportunities, and subject matter has never been duplicated. If there were writers who had Boswell's opportunities of knowing their subject as well, they have not had his unusual combination of talents. If they had his talents, they have lacked his opportunities. The talents include his gift for empathy and

dramatic imitation, his ability to draw people out and get them to talk freely, his astonishing memory for conversations, his zest and gusto, his generous capacity for admiration, and his sheer industry as a reporter—qualities that are by no means often found together. Bringing these qualities into focus and sustaining his industry was his prevailing sense of what he called "the *waste* of good if it be not preserved," of the rapid erosion and loss of human experience through life's enemy, time, and the need to rescue it as far as possible through the recorded word. But the final indispensable element in Boswell's great work is Johnson himself. Fascinating as they are, the interviews with others—David Hume, Voltaire, Rousseau, the elder Pitt[9]—rarely approach in range of topics and personal interest any section of equal length dealing with Johnson.

---

8. The *Hebrides* are islands off the western coast of Scotland.

9. *David Hume* (1711–1776) was a Scottish philosopher. *Voltaire* (1694–1778) and Jean-Jacques *Rousseau* (1712–1778) were famed French writers and philosophers. William *Pitt* (1708–1778) was a powerful British statesman and orator.

The picture of Johnson, which for better or worse remains permanently imprinted because of this classic work, is inevitably, given the circumstances, somewhat specialized. Most important, it is a picture of Johnson in his later years. The first half of Johnson's life occupies little more than a tenth of the work. Less than a quarter takes him up to fifty-three, when his life was more than two-thirds over; and a full half of the book is devoted to Johnson's last eight years, from sixty-seven to seventy-five. There are also personal sides of Johnson even after fifty-three of which Boswell could never know, but of which others—above all, Mrs. Thrale[10]—knew or suspected a great deal, though they did not always care to proclaim their knowledge. Moreover, it is a very masculine world in which Boswell presents him—the world of The Club and the taverns. In addition, he saw Johnson through the spectacles of his own romantic Toryism,[11] with the result that Johnson has been—and perhaps will unfortunately always be—viewed as an "arch-conservative." Even his minor dramatic touches have proved permanent:

for example, his exaggerated insertion of "Sir" before so many of Johnson's remarks, as if to give them a kind of thunderous and formal authority; or his decision to change his references to him from "Mr. Johnson" to "Dr. Johnson," with the result that Johnson alone, of all great writers who have ever received a doctor's degree, is forever known to most people as "Dr. Johnson." (Ironically Johnson himself—according to Hawkins[12]—rather disliked being called Dr. Johnson. At least, as even Boswell once admitted, he hardly ever assumed it in formal notes or on cards—"but called himself Mr. Johnson"; and when Boswell once noticed a letter addressed to him with the title "Esquire," and said he thought it a title inferior to "Doctor," Johnson "checked me, and seemed pleased with it.") Yet whatever its limitations, large or small, the work remains unique among all writings by one human being about another—unique in the way Boswell himself foresaw when he decided as a mature man to undertake it: that is, in the drama, fidelity, and range of interests in the conversation of one of the most fascinating individuals in history. ॐ

---

10. Hester *Thrale* (1741–1821) and her husband Henry Thrale were Johnson's friends and traveling companions.
11. The principles of the English Tory party, which opposed those of the Whigs, are known as *Toryism*.

---

12. Sir John *Hawkins* (1719–1789) was a close friend and biographer of Johnson.

RESPONDING AND THINKING CRITICALLY

Respond

1. After having read this excerpt, does Boswell's biography of Johnson seem more or less reliable? Explain.

Recall and Interpret

2. (a)According to Bate, how was Boswell different from his father? (b)In his diary, what did Boswell repeatedly urge himself to do? (c)What does this suggest about Boswell's character?

3. What talents made Boswell an extraordinary biographer?

Analyze and Evaluate

4. (a)According to Bate, what change did Boswell often make to Johnson's remarks? (b)How have these types of changes affected people's perceptions of Johnson?

5. (a)What is the main idea of this excerpt? (b)Do you think Bate adequately developed and supported the main idea with details? Why or why not?

Connect

6. Society's views of biography as a genre have changed since Boswell's time. What do you think is most important in a biography, factual evidence or dramatic appeal? Explain.

7. **Big Idea** The English Enlightenment and Neoclassicism In what ways do Boswell's life and work embody the principles of the Enlightenment? In what ways do they deviate from these principles?

OBJECTIVES
- Read to enhance understanding of British history and culture.
- Analyze the historical context that shapes elements of a literary work.
- Determine the main ideas and supporting details of a literary work.

Writing Workshop

Persuasive Essay

 Taking a Stand on an Issue

The Writing Process

In this workshop, you will follow the stages of the writing process. At any stage, you may think of new ideas to include and better ways to express them. Feel free to return to earlier stages as you write.

Prewriting

Drafting

Revising

Focus Lesson:
Appropriate Tone

Editing and Proofreading

Focus Lesson:
Parallelism

Presenting

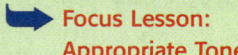
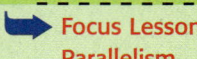

Writing Models For models and other writing activities, go to www.glencoe.com.

OBJECTIVES

- Write a persuasive essay that takes a stand on an issue.
- Include a clearly stated thesis supported by precise and relevant evidence.

"I repeat, let no man talk to me of these and the like expedients till he hath at least some glimpse of hope that there will ever be some hearty and sincere attempt to put them in practice."

—Jonathan Swift, from *A Modest Proposal*

Connecting to Literature In *A Modest Proposal*, Swift uses satire to take a stand on the issue of Irish poverty and, specifically, England's attitudes toward it. Through his satire, Swift attempts to persuade his English audience of the danger of their attitudes by illustrating the horrible result if these attitudes were carried to an extreme, but logical, outcome. In a persuasive essay, the writer takes a position on an issue and attempts to persuade the audience through reasoned arguments. To write a successful essay, you will need to learn the goals of persuasive writing and the strategies for achieving those goals.

Rubric: Features of Persuasive Essays

Goals	Strategies
To present a clearly stated opinion to a target audience	☑ Choose an issue with opposing viewpoints
	☑ Choose your side of the issue and clarify your position
To present relevant evidence in a logically organized argument	☑ Defend your position with appropriate reasons, specific details, and evidence presented in a logical order
	☑ Use rhetorical devices, such as parallelism, to strengthen your argument
To anticipate and address audience concerns and counterarguments	☑ Present your views and respond to opposing views in a reasonable voice and tone
To use persuasion as an instrument for action or change	☑ Persuade your audience to act in response to your position

Real-World Connection

Logical reasoning and relevant evidence form the backbone of a strong argument. Some arguments in the real world, however, rely on emotional rather than logical appeals—for example, television, radio, and print advertisements.

> **Assignment**
>
> Write a persuasive essay to defend your position on a controversial issue you care about. As you move through the stages of the writing process, keep your audience and purpose in mind.
>
> **Audience:** peers, school faculty, or community members
>
> **Purpose:** to persuade others to think about and act on your issue in a certain way

Analyzing a Professional Model

In the following speech given at the outbreak of World War II, future prime minister Winston Churchill attempts to persuade the British people that war has become necessary. As you read, note Churchill's firm position on this controversial issue and his support of that position. Pay close attention to the comments in the margin. They point out features that you may want to include in your own persuasive essay.

War Speech, September 3, 1939 by Winston Churchill

In this solemn hour it is a consolation to recall and to dwell upon our repeated efforts for peace. All have been ill-starred, but all have been faithful and sincere. This is of the highest moral value—and not only moral value, but practical value—at the present time, because the wholehearted concurrence of scores of millions of men and women, whose cooperation is indispensable and whose comradeship and brotherhood are indispensable, is the only foundation upon which the trial and tribulation of modern war can be endured and surmounted. This moral conviction alone affords that ever-fresh resilience which renews the strength and energy of people in long, doubtful and dark days. Outside, the storms of war may blow and the lands may be lashed with the fury of its gales, but in our own hearts this Sunday morning there is peace. Our hands may be active, but our consciences are at rest.

We must not underrate the gravity of the task which lies before us or the temerity of the ordeal, to which we shall not be found unequal. We must expect many disappointments, and many unpleasant surprises, but we may be sure that the task which we have freely accepted is one not beyond the compass and the strength of the British Empire and the

Thesis

Clarify your issue and identify your position in a thesis statement.

Emotional Appeal

Stir the audience's emotions by personalizing your issue.

Logical Appeal

Cite reasons that guide your audience through the logic of your position.

French Republic. The Prime Minister said it was a sad day, and that is indeed true, but at the present time there is another note which may be present, and that is a feeling of thankfulness that, if these great trials were to come upon our Island, there is a generation of Britons here now ready to prove itself not unworthy of the days of yore and not unworthy of those great men, the fathers of our land, who laid the foundations of our laws and shaped the greatness of our country.

This is not a question of fighting for Danzig or fighting for Poland. We are fighting to save the whole world from the pestilence of Nazi tyranny and in defense of all that is most sacred to man. This is no war of domination or imperial aggrandizement or material gain; no war to shut any country out of its sunlight and means of progress. It is a war, viewed in its inherent quality, to establish, on impregnable rocks, the rights of the individual, and it is a war to establish and revive the stature of man. Perhaps it might seem a paradox that a war undertaken in the name of liberty and right should require, as a necessary part of its processes, the surrender for the time being of so many of the dearly valued liberties and rights. In these last few days the House of Commons has been voting dozens of Bills which hand over to the executive our most dearly valued traditional liberties. We are sure that these liberties will be in hands which will not abuse them, which will use them for no class or party interests, which will cherish and guard them, and we look forward to the day, surely and confidently we look forward to the day, when our liberties and rights will be restored to us, and when we shall be able to share them with the peoples to whom such blessings are unknown.

Supporting Evidence

Use specific details to illustrate a point.

Ethical Appeal

Appeal to the audience's sense of right and wrong to gain support for your position.

Counterarguments

Refute opposing arguments to strengthen your own position.

Rhetorical Devices

Use rhetorical devices such as repetition and parallelism to add force to your argument.

Reading-Writing Connection Think about the writing techniques that you just encountered and try them out in the persuasive essay you write.

Prewriting

Explore Issues Is there a school policy that you consider unfair or a procedure in your community that you think should be updated or changed? Perhaps you hold a position on an issue that you believe has not yet been given proper attention. Think of an issue that is important to you, that is controversial, and that can be debated logically.

Clarify Your Position and Create a Call for Action Once you have chosen an issue, decide on and clarify your position on it. Write a thesis statement in which you identify your issue and present your concise position. Then consider your purpose for persuading your audience. Do you want to change opinions or offer a new perspective for people to consider? Do you want ultimately to persuade your audience to act in a certain way? Develop a call for action, or a statement that expresses what you want your audience to do regarding the issue.

Address Your Audience Pay particular attention to your target audience. If your audience is likely to agree with your position, you may use your argument as a means to underscore your shared position and to effect action. If your audience is likely to disagree, tailor your background information, evidence, and tone to address that audience's needs and to anticipate potential objections. If your audience is unfamiliar with your issue or position, provide adequate background that explains why your issue is important and why your position deserves attention.

Organize Your Argument Organize your argument in a logical, coherent way. Order of importance is usually an effective way to organize a persuasive essay. For example, to make an immediate impact on your readers, start with your most important supporting evidence. Or, to leave your readers thinking about your strongest evidence, build up to your most important evidence.

Use one of the graphic organizers below to help you outline your essay.

Types of Appeals

▶ **Logical Appeal** reaches an audience through reason.

▶ **Emotional Appeal** stirs an audience's feelings by personalizing the issue.

▶ **Ethical Appeal** focuses on an audience's sense of right and wrong.

Test Prep

Essay tests often require you to take a stand on an issue. Choose a position you can support with facts, reasons, and examples.

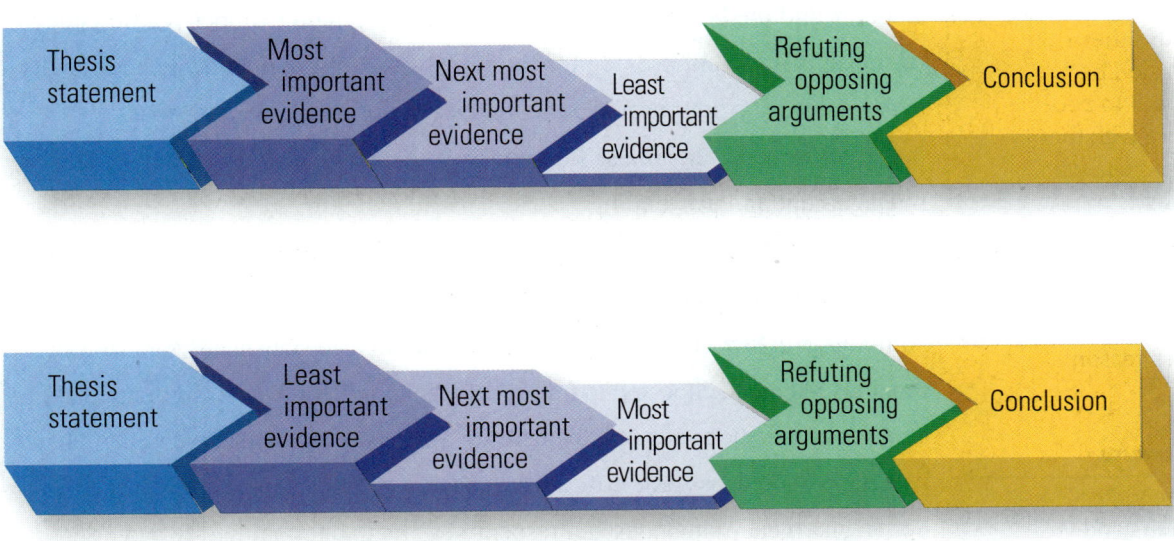

Drafting

Go with the Flow As you develop your argument, you may think of new or better reasons and supporting evidence to include. Feel free to adjust your original outline as necessary. Reread your draft periodically, checking to see that you maintain a reasonable tone and that you firmly support your reasons with logical evidence.

Analyzing a Workshop Model

Here is a final draft of a persuasive essay. Read the essay and answer the questions in the margin. Use the answers to these questions to guide you as you write.

Background

How does the writer raise awareness of the issue?

Thesis

How might this thesis and call to action be persuasive both to people who agree with the writer and to those who may not at first?

Logical Appeal

Why does this reason make sense?

Counterarguments

How does the writer show an understanding of both sides of the issue?

State of Emergency: It Could Happen to Us

Lately, disasters have become a regular occurrence: wildfires blazing on the West Coast, hurricanes flooding the Gulf Coast, and even tornadoes ravaging our own state. Disturbingly, Linden High School has not updated its emergency management and response plan in more than twenty years. More disturbingly, school officials currently do not intend to review the plan, even though they admit it is outdated. Officials have cited expense as the main reason, yet Linden High intends to approve a request from the Athletic Department to build a new football field this summer. Before updating costly athletic facilities, Linden School should consider the broader needs of its students and the best use of its limited funds. Updating Linden's emergency response plan would provide for the safety of *all* Linden students and faculty, make recovery from possible emergencies faster and less expensive in the future, and encourage students to take an active role in emergency management and prevention.

The fact that Linden High has managed to avoid a major disaster so far does not mean that the school is now, or will be, prepared to face one in the future. Although it is true that large-scale natural disasters are statistically rare in communities like ours, choosing to inform Linden's staff and students of potential emergency situations can only be helpful. This is not to say that we will or should become paranoid, as some critics have suggested. Instead, we should pay attention to emergency situations and response efforts in our community and elsewhere to learn the best ways to deal with crises.

The cost of updating Linden's emergency response plan may seem expensive at first; however, in the long run it would save money, recovery time, and possibly lives. One of the first steps in updating the response plan would involve locating and addressing current hazards. For example, John Gupta, principal of nearby Colgate High School, hired a building inspector as part of an emergency-plan update. The inspector installed fire-resistant walls in the electrical closet. Although the procedure was costly, the expense proved to be justified when a fire broke out in the room a year later. As Gupta noted, "the new walls kept the fire contained. A $2,000 renovation saved the whole school from going up in flames." The renovation probably saved hundreds of thousands of dollars and countless lives. In fact, the *Linden Times* noted that similar updates prevented almost $800,000 in property damage in Linden last year alone. Besides, although some preventive measures are expensive, many are not. "Planning in advance, keeping extra supplies, and creating routine procedures such as practice drills cost little but are extremely effective," noted Linden fire chief John Rodriguez. A preventive approach improves the ability to respond to emergencies and decreases the need to respond overall.

Focusing on updating the emergency response plan would offer students an active role in preventing and managing emergency situations. Staff and student volunteers could ideally work together to determine potential emergency situations; prepare call lists, evacuation procedures, and practice drills; and communicate how to respond to emergencies through school meetings and simulations. Designating a group of trained student responders would encourage students to take responsibility for their own safety and that of others. In this way, they would gain valuable life skills.

Instead of putting off emergency-response planning, Linden High needs to take responsibility for the safety of its students and staff before an emergency occurs. By updating our current plan, we could save lives and money; we would encourage students to take an active role in public safety; and we would decrease the number of emergency situations overall. Why not learn from our nation's recent disasters and avoid repeating past mistakes?

Supporting Evidence
How does this example illustrate the main point of the paragraph?

Emotional Appeal
Why might this statement sway readers to respond personally to the issue presented?

Organization
Why might the writer give this reason last?

Rhetorical Devices
How are parallel structure and repetition effectively used in the conclusion?

Revising

Use the rubric below to help you evaluate and strengthen your essay.

Rubric: Writing a Persuasive Essay
☑ Do you choose a controversial issue and present a clearly stated thesis?
☑ Do you present logical reasons and relevant supporting evidence?
☑ Do you organize your reasons logically and effectively?
☑ Do you anticipate and address audience concerns and counterarguments?
☑ Do you present your views and respond to opposing views in a reasonable and formal tone?
☑ Do you use rhetorical devices, such as parallelism, to strengthen your argument?

► **Focus Lesson**

Appropriate Tone

As you revise, use an appropriate tone to make your argument clear, reasonable, and convincing. Avoid sounding angry or sarcastic. Maintain a respectful, formal, and reasonable tone throughout your essay to show that your position is fair and worth considering.

Draft:

Some guys can't stop complaining that talking about emergencies will make everyone paranoid, but that's nonsense. They don't know what's happening in the real world. Let's keep our minds on emergency situations and response efforts in our community and elsewhere.

Revision:

This is not to say that we will or should become paranoid, as some critics have suggested.[1] Instead, we should pay attention to emergency situations and response efforts in our community and elsewhere[2] to learn the best ways to deal with crises.

1: Use a formal tone, avoiding contractions, slang, and colloquial language.

2: Use a reasonable, respectful tone to address opposing arguments.

Traits of Strong Writing

Ideas message or theme and the details that develop it

Organization arrangement of main ideas and supporting details

Voice writer's unique way of using tone and style

Word Choice vocabulary a writer uses to convey meaning

Sentence Fluency rhythm and flow of sentences

Conventions correct spelling, grammar, usage, and mechanics

Presentation the way words and design elements look on a page

For more information on using the Traits of Strong Writing, see pages R33–R34 of the Writing Handbook.

Editing and Proofreading

Get It Right When you have completed the final draft of your essay, proofread it for errors in grammar, usage, mechanics, and spelling. Refer to the Language Handbook, pages R46–R60, as a guide.

> ### Focus Lesson
>
> ## Parallelism
>
> Parallelism is the use of the same grammatical form to express ideas similar in content and function. To create parallel structure, balance each element in a series of words, phrases, or sentences. For example, balance nouns with nouns and participle phrases with participle phrases. Writers often use parallelism as a rhetorical device to add sophistication to an argument, to clarify a relationship between ideas, or to emphasize a point.

Original: Phrases similar in content and function are expressed using different grammatical forms.

Lately, disasters have become a regular occurrence: <u>wildfires on the West Coast</u>, <u>hurricanes flooding the Gulf Coast</u>, and even <u>fatal tornadoes</u>.

Improved: Make phrases parallel by balancing grammatical forms.

Lately, disasters have become a regular occurrence: <u>wildfires blazing on the West Coast</u>, <u>hurricanes flooding the Gulf Coast</u>, and even <u>tornadoes ravaging our own state</u>.

Presenting

The Power of Presentation How you present your persuasive essay depends on your audience and how you want to address your issue. If your essay focuses on an issue in the community, you may want to send it to the editor of a local newspaper. If it focuses on a school-related issue, you may wish to present it aloud at a student council meeting. Whichever way you present your essay, be sure that you have a clean, final copy that follows your teacher's guidelines.

Writer's Portfolio

Place a copy of your persuasive essay in your portfolio to review later.

Speaking, Listening, and Viewing Workshop

Persuasive Speech

Delivering a Persuasive Speech

Connecting to Literature Jonathan Swift used his satirical essay *A Modest Proposal* to convince and persuade others of his beliefs. Sometimes, such as in informal or everyday situations, a written essay may not be the best way to persuade others to agree with you. Instead, you may want to speak to your audience directly. A good way to accomplish this task is to prepare and deliver a persuasive speech. The goal of a persuasive speech is to convince listeners to adopt a particular opinion, or to take some action regarding an issue. This type of speech should be built on structured, logical arguments and should use solid evidence to support those arguments.

> ▶ **Assignment** Plan and deliver a persuasive speech.

Types of Persuasive Speeches

There are four basic types of persuasive speeches. A persuasive speech can propose the following:

Fact The speaker makes a claim as if it were a fact, although it is not necessarily. *A teen curfew will lower crime rates throughout the city.*

Problem The speaker claims something is a serious problem deserving immediate attention. *Teenagers with nothing to do may take part in vandalism and other crimes.*

Policy The speaker asserts that one course of action is better than another. *We should introduce a curfew for teenagers because parental supervision alone is not enough.*

Value The speaker argues the merits of one opinion by providing another opinion. Unlike fact, problem, and policy propositions, a value proposition appeals to emotion rather than reason. *Since older teenagers are more responsible, the curfew should only apply to younger teens.*

Before drafting your speech, decide which type of persuasive speech will best suit your purpose.

Planning Your Presentation

You need to organize your persuasive speech and develop a coherent structure to get your message across to listeners. Below is a chart that describes guidelines and techniques for writing an effective persuasive speech.

Structure	Purpose	Techniques
Introduction	States your topic and position.	• Choose a topic and position you have strong feelings about. • Identify your listeners—their mood, background, and attitude. • Make your first words powerful and engaging.
Body or Argument	Supports your position with strong reasons and convincing evidence presented in a logical order.	• Cite statistics and/or quote a respected authority. • Use established truths, such as historical and scientific facts. • Share personal experiences.

Using Visual Media

Consider using graphics to emphasize important points in your speech. A chart or graph can make facts and statistics easier to understand. A photograph can add emotional impact to your message.

Rehearsing

Practice giving your speech alone, perhaps in front of a mirror, and in front of family members or friends. Ask them for feedback on your performance. Then revise your speech on the basis of your audience's reactions and suggestions.

As you rehearse, use these verbal and nonverbal presentation techniques.

Techniques for Delivering a Persuasive Speech

Verbal Techniques	Nonverbal Techniques
☑ **Delivery** Speak from the heart; don't read your speech.	☑ **Eye Contact** Maintain eye contact with your audience. Refer to your notes only when necessary.
☑ **Pace** Speak at a moderate speed, but use your voice to emphasize main points.	☑ **Posture** Stand tall with your head straight, but be natural.
☑ **Clarity** Speak clearly and distinctly. Pronounce all words carefully.	☑ **Gestures** Use gestures and facial expressions to convey meaning and reinforce your ideas.

OBJECTIVES
- Prepare and deliver a persuasive speech.
- Provide feedback on a presentation.
- Analyze types of persuasive speeches.

For Independent Reading

DURING THE RESTORATION AND THE EIGHTEENTH CENTURY, THE NOVEL WAS considered a new and shocking literary genre. The novel began to take shape in the eighteenth century; in the nineteenth and twentieth centuries, the novel evolved into one of the crowning glories of English literature.

Daniel Defoe is often credited with writing the first English novel, *Robinson Crusoe* (1719). In Defoe's novel, the shipwrecked Crusoe survives on a Caribbean island for twenty-eight years with a few supplies and a prisoner he calls Friday. All but ignored by the upper classes because Defoe himself was only a middle-class merchant, *Robinson Crusoe* was welcomed by shopkeepers, apprentices, servants, and the country at large. Since Defoe's time, the popularity of novels has never diminished.

Pamela, or Virtue Rewarded

by Samuel Richardson (1740)

In *Pamela*, Richardson is the "editor" of a collection of letters and journals penned by fifteen-year-old Pamela Andrews, a maidservant in a wealthy household, and five acquaintances. These entries take the reader through Pamela's relationship with Mr. B., the son of Pamela's late employer. Mr. B. is in hot pursuit of Pamela, but she repeatedly rejects his advances because of her desire to remain chaste. Despite Mr. B.'s unorthodox method of wooing, including imprisoning her, Pamela finally falls in love with him and the two are married. During the latter part of the novel, Pamela attempts to explain her decision to her fellow letter writers.

The History of Tom Jones, a Foundling

by Henry Fielding (1749)

Considered by many to be Fielding's greatest novel, *Tom Jones* seems like a precursor to the modern-day soap opera. The reader follows Tom from childhood to adulthood and witnesses the growth of his love for his childhood sweetheart, Sophia, a character likely based on Fielding's wife. As one might expect, the course of true love does not run smoothly, and the characters must overcome many obstacles. Before the two are united, they travel all over the country, giving the reader a picture of England in the mid-1700s. Fielding wrote that his purpose in writing *Tom Jones* was "to recommend goodness and innocence" and that he had "endeavored to laugh mankind out of their favorite follies and vices."

"It is one of the good jokes of literature that we reach the third book of Tristram Shandy *before the hero is born. But not all readers see why the joke is good. The entire structure of the work depends on the fact that the starting point is not Tristram's birth but his begetting."*

—D. W. Jefferson, "*Tristram Shandy* and the Tradition of Learned Wit"

"The great aim of Sterne was to give as true a picture as possible of real human beings as they are in themselves, not as they imagine themselves to be, nor as others judge them to be by their actions and outward behavior alone. This meant the shifting of emphasis from the external to the internal event, from the patterned plot artificially conceived and imposed on the characters, to the free evocation of the fluid, ever-changing process of being."

—A. A. Mendilow in "The Revolt of Sterne,"
from *Time and the Novel*, 1952.

The Life and Opinions of Tristram Shandy, Gentleman

by Laurence Sterne (1759–1767)

Tristram Shandy has been described as strange, tedious, silly, and downright nasty. Yet it has also been called an important forerunner of the stream-of-consciousness novel and psychological fiction. Despite critics' differing opinions, *Tristram Shandy* was enormously popular with the public. In nine volumes, Sterne depicts the life of Shandy (whose name means "half crazy"). The book defies all conventions: events occur out of order, stories are unfinished, and some pages are even left blank.

From the Glencoe Literature Library

Gulliver's Travels

by Jonathan Swift

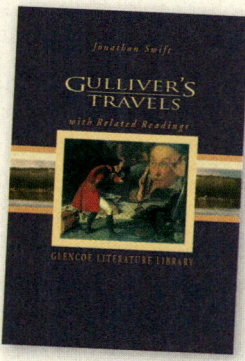

Gulliver's Travels describes the journeys of Dr. Lemuel Gulliver, ship's surgeon, world traveler, and reporter. Gulliver visits strange lands that are inhabited by various bizarre creatures, from six-inch-high Lilliputians to the giant Brobdingnagians and the savage and brutal Yahoos. By contrasting these creatures with humans, Swift highlights human weakness and societal ills.

Reading: Fiction

Carefully read the following passage. Use context clues to help you define any words with which you are unfamiliar. Pay close attention to the use of figurative language and tone. Then, on a separate sheet of paper, answer the questions that follow.

from *The Battle of the Books* by Jonathan Swift

line

[U]pon the highest corner of a large window there dwelt a certain spider, swollen up to the first magnitude by the destruction of infinite numbers of flies, whose spoils lay scattered before the gates of his palace, like human bones before the cave of some giant. . . . In this mansion he had for some time dwelt in peace and plenty, without danger to

5   his person by swallows from above, or to his palace by brooms from below: when it was the pleasure of fortune to conduct thither a wandering bee, to whose curiosity a broken pane in the glass had discovered itself, and in he went; where . . . he at last happened to alight upon one of the outward walls of the spider's citadel; which, yielding to the unequal weight, sunk down to the very foundation. Thrice he endeavored to force his passage, and

10   thrice the center shook. The spider within, feeling the terrible convulsion, supposed at first that nature was approaching to her final dissolution; or else, that Beelzebub, with all his legions, was come to revenge the death of many thousands of his subjects whom his enemy had slain and devoured. However, he at length valiantly resolved to issue forth and meet his fate. Meanwhile the bee had acquitted himself of his toils, and, posted

15   securely at some distance, was employed in cleansing his wings, and disengaging them from the ragged remnants of the cobweb. By this time the spider was adventured out, when, beholding the chasms, the ruins, and dilapidations of his fortress, he was very near his wits' end; he stormed and swore like a madman, and swelled till he was ready to burst. . . . "A plague split you," said he . . . "is it you, with a vengeance, that have made

20   this litter here? . . . " "Good words, friend," said the bee having now pruned himself, and being disposed to droll. . . . "Sirrah," replied the spider, "if it were not for breaking an old custom in our family, never to stir abroad against an enemy, I should come and teach you better manners." "I pray have patience," said the bee, "or you'll spend your substance, and, for aught I see, you may stand in need of it all, toward the repair of your house."

25   "Rogue, rogue," replied the spider, "yet methinks you should have more respect to a person whom all the world allows to be so much your betters. " . . . At this the spider, having swelled himself into the size and posture of a disputant, began his argument in the true spirit of controversy. . . .

"Not to disparage myself," said he, "by the comparison with such a rascal, what art
thou but a vagabond without house or home, without stock or inheritance? born to no
possession of your own, but a pair of wings and a drone-pipe. Your livelihood is a
universal plunder upon nature. . . . "

"I am glad," answered the bee, "to hear you grant at least that I am come honestly by
my wings and my voice; for then, it seems, I am obliged to Heaven alone for my flights
and my music. . . . I visit indeed all the flowers and blossoms of the field and garden; but
whatever I collect thence enriches myself, without the least injury to their beauty, their
smell, or their taste. . . . [O]ne insect furnishes you with a share of poison to destroy
another . . . producing nothing at all but flybane and a cobweb."

1. Which of the following literary elements is
Jonathan Swift using in the phrase *the destruction
of infinite numbers of flies*, in line 2?
(A) allusion
(B) metaphor
(C) simile
(D) hyperbole
(E) motif

2. Which of the following literary elements is Swift
using in the phrase *like human bones before the cave
of some giant*, in line 3?
(A) conceit
(B) hyperbole
(C) simile
(D) metaphor
(E) aside

3. At first what does the spider assume is happening
as the bee attempts to free itself?
(A) The world is ending.
(B) A sparrow has come to eat him.
(C) A broom is sweeping away his web.
(D) A fly has landed in his web.
(E) A bee has landed in his web.

4. Which of the following literary elements is Swift
using in the phrase *Beelzebub, with all his legions,
was come to revenge the death of many thousands of
his subjects*, in lines 11–12?
(A) allusion
(B) metaphor
(C) simile
(D) hyperbole
(E) motif

5. From the context, what do you conclude that the
word *acquitted*, in line 14, means?
(A) exonerated
(B) explained
(C) freed
(D) imprisoned
(E) prosecuted

6. Which of the following literary elements is Swift
using in the phrase *he stormed and swore like a
madman*, in line 18?
(A) allusion
(B) metaphor
(C) simile
(D) hyperbole
(E) motif

7. Which of the following literary elements is Swift using in the phrase *swelled till he was ready to burst*, in lines 18–19?
(A) allusion
(B) metaphor
(C) simile
(D) hyperbole
(E) motif

8. Why does the spider claim to be unable to attack the bee?
(A) The spider is afraid of the bee.
(B) The spider has been wounded.
(C) The spider must rebuild his web.
(D) There is no time for the spider to attack.
(E) A family tradition prevents the spider.

9. From the context, what do you conclude that the word *substance*, in line 23, means?
(A) basis
(B) matter
(C) theme
(D) thought
(E) understanding

10. What does the spider fear that he will do by comparing himself to the bee?
(A) cause controversy
(B) disparage himself
(C) lose his inheritance
(D) become a vagabond
(E) become a disputant

11. How does the bee counter the assertion that he is *a universal plunder upon nature*, in lines 31–32?
(A) The bee says that heaven gave it its flights and music.
(B) The bee says that the spider is more wicked.
(C) The bee says that it can fly and sing, and the spider cannot.
(D) The bee says that the spider cannot create anything.
(E) The bee says that it does not destroy what it collects.

12. From the context, what do you conclude that the word *furnishes*, in line 37, means?
(A) supplies
(B) removes
(C) confiscates
(D) undermines
(E) collects

13. Which of the following is the most prominent literary element in this passage?
(A) repetition
(B) symbol
(C) allegory
(D) apostrophe
(E) personification

14. According to your reading of this passage, what do you conclude that the overall tone of this piece is?
(A) angry
(B) humorous
(C) skeptical
(D) sinister
(E) knowing

15. From your reading of this selection, what do you think the author's main purpose is?
(A) to persuade
(B) to instruct
(C) to inform
(D) to entertain
(E) to describe

Literature Online **Unit Assessment** To prepare for the unit test, go to www.glencoe.com.

Vocabulary Skills: Sentence Completion

For each item in the Vocabulary Skills section, choose the word or words that best complete the sentence.

1. The violent _____ of the English Civil War ended with the execution of King Charles I.
   (A) bombast
   (B) discord
   (C) precept
   (D) ingenuity
   (E) esteem

2. The harsh ten years after the end of the English Civil War were marked by _____ Puritan rule.
   (A) diverse
   (B) jovial
   (C) zealous
   (D) aggregated
   (E) loath

3. After the restoration of the _____ to the throne, British literature became increasingly secular.
   (A) negligence
   (B) exultation
   (C) indictment
   (D) complaisance
   (E) monarch

4. The Enlightenment sprang, in part, from a newfound _____ of the power of reason by writers and philosophers.
   (A) stratagem
   (B) cavalcade
   (C) veneration
   (D) indictment
   (E) negligence

5. Although the leaders of the Puritan Commonwealth attempted to _____ Royalist sentiment, in the end they failed.
   (A) subdue
   (B) elate
   (C) disabuse
   (D) mourn
   (E) commend

6. Slowly it became clear that the Puritan Commonwealth was not a benevolent purveyor of liberty but instead was _____ and oppressive.
   (A) reconciled
   (B) superfluous
   (C) impetuous
   (D) intuitive
   (E) malicious

7. Enlightenment thinkers rejected _____ and unsound ideas while embracing the ancient works of Western civilization.
   (A) immutable
   (B) jovial
   (C) diverse
   (D) irrational
   (E) aggregated

8. The Restoration led to a reversal of the ban on theater, music, and other _____ that were popular at the time.
   (A) diversions
   (B) edifices
   (C) vigilance
   (D) stratagems
   (E) negligence

9. Enlightenment thinkers showed great _____ for reason and the natural sciences.
   (A) bombast
   (B) sustenance
   (C) negligence
   (D) esteem
   (E) magnitude

10. Many artists, expecting a renewal of royal patronage, were _____ by the restoration of the king.
   (A) elated
   (B) confounded
   (C) mourned
   (D) disabused
   (E) commended

Grammar and Writing Skills: Paragraph Improvement

Read carefully through the opening paragraphs from the first draft of a student's persuasive essay. Pay close attention to the writer's use of **parallelism, pronouns,** and **commas**. Then, on a separate sheet of paper, answer the questions below.

(1) Many in our community claim that their property taxes are too high. (2) They claim that the government takes too much, and they have claimed that they are voiceless in the way those taxes are spent. (3) These complaints while genuinely felt should not be acted upon by city or county officials.

(4) The property taxes in Hansen County are some of the lowest in the state. (5) All of the surrounding counties including Green Rain, Regal, South Regal, and Smith. outrank Hansen in property taxes by several percentage points. (6) Furthermore, Hansen County has the lowest rate of taxation in the state, and it is unmatched in all adjacent states.

(7) Many argue that our property taxes are used to fund unnecessary expenditures, such as pay increases for county employees and unwarranted road improvements. (8) The facts, however, tell a different story. (9) Twenty-seven percent of the property taxes collected approximately ten times the amount spent on road construction goes directly toward the purchase of essentials for the functioning of the public schools. (10) These essentials include heating, and air conditioning, textbooks, school lunches, busing, and computers. (11) Without these funds students will be underserved and undereducated; they will be left without a proper training in technology; current texts will not be available; some will go hungry during the day, while others will be unable to attend school at all. (12) These taxes are absolutely necessary to the future of these students.

1. Which is the best revision of sentence 2?
  (A) They claim that the government takes too much. And they have claimed that they are voiceless in the way those taxes are spent.
  (B) They claim that the government takes too much, and they have claimed that they are voiceless.
  (C) They have claimed that they are voiceless in the way those taxes are spent.
  (D) They claim that the government takes too much, and they claim that they are voiceless in the way those taxes are spent.
  (E) They claim that the government takes too much; they are voiceless in the way they spend those taxes.

2. Which is the best revision of sentence 3?
  (A) These complaints should not be acted upon by city or county officials.
  (B) These complaints, while genuinely felt, should not be acted upon by city or county officials.
  (C) Genuinely felt complaints should not be acted upon by city or county officials.
  (D) City or county officials should not act upon genuinely felt complaints.
  (E) City or county officials have acted upon these genuinely felt complaints.

3. Which is the best revision of sentence 5?
- **(A)** All of the surrounding counties—including Green Rain, Regal, South Regal, and Smith—outrank Hansen in property taxes by several percentage points.
- **(B)** The surrounding counties outrank Hansen in property taxes by several percentage points.
- **(C)** All of the surrounding counties outranks Hansen in property taxes by several points.
- **(D)** All of the surrounding counties, including Green Rain, and Regal, and South Regal, and Smith, outrank Hansen in property taxes by several percentage points.
- **(E)** Delete this sentence.

4. Which is the best revision of sentence 6?
- **(A)** Also, Hansen County has the lowest rate of taxation in the state, and it is unmatched in all adjacent states.
- **(B)** Furthermore, Hansen County has the lowest rate of taxation in the state, and this rate is unmatched in all adjacent states.
- **(C)** Furthermore, Hansen County has the lowest rate of taxation in the state.
- **(D)** It is also unmatched in all adjacent states.
- **(E)** Hansen County has the lowest rate.

5. Sentences 7 and 8 are an example of which persuasive technique?
- **(A)** call to action
- **(B)** supporting evidence
- **(C)** counterargument
- **(D)** ethical appeal
- **(E)** emotional appeal

6. Which trait of strong writing is the student demonstrating in sentence 8?
- **(A)** ideas
- **(B)** organization
- **(C)** voice
- **(D)** word choice
- **(E)** sentence fluency

7. Which is the best revision of sentence 9?
- **(A)** Twenty-seven percent of the property taxes collected—approximately ten times the amount spent on road construction—goes directly toward the purchase of essentials for the functioning of the public schools.
- **(B)** Twenty-seven percent of property taxes go to purchase essentials for public schools.
- **(C)** Twenty-seven percent of the property taxes collected is spent on road construction.
- **(D)** Taxes are used for essentials for public schools.
- **(E)** Approximately ten times the amount spent on road construction goes directly toward the purchase of essentials for public schools.

8. Which is the best revision of sentence 10?
- **(A)** These essentials include heating and air conditioning, textbooks and school lunches, busing and computers.
- **(B)** These essentials include heating and air conditioning, textbooks, school lunches, busing, and computers.
- **(C)** Some of these essentials include heating, and air conditioning, textbooks, school lunches, busing, and computers.
- **(D)** Essentials include heat, air conditioning, textbooks, lunches, busing, and computers.
- **(E)** Delete this sentence.

9. Which error appears in sentence 11?
- **(A)** incorrect use of semicolons
- **(B)** fragment
- **(C)** lack of pronoun-antecedent agreement
- **(D)** lack of subject-verb agreement
- **(E)** incorrect parallelism

10. What should the author conclude this essay with?
- **(A)** counterargument
- **(B)** strongest argument
- **(C)** response to counterargument
- **(D)** supporting evidence
- **(E)** background

Essay

What do you think was the most important long-term effect of the Enlightenment? Write a short persuasive essay stating your opinion supported by evidence from this unit and any background knowledge you have. As you write, keep in mind that your essay will be checked for **ideas, organization, voice, word choice, sentence fluency, conventions,** and **presentation.**

The Hay Wain, 1821. John Constable. National Gallery, London, UK.

The Triumph of

ROMANTICISM

1750–1837

Looking Ahead

Toward the end of the 1700s, industrial and political revolution overturned traditional ways of life in Europe. Bold, new ideas were beginning to challenge the belief in reason associated with the Enlightenment. In time, many of these ideas would form part of Romanticism, a broad movement in art and thought that valued feeling and imagination over reason. British Romantic writers found inspiration in nature, folk culture, the medieval past, and their own passions.

Keep the following questions in mind as you read:

 What were the essential features of Romanticism?

How did Romantic writers respond to nature?

What conception of the imagination did Romanticism express?

OBJECTIVES
In learning about the age of English Romanticism, you will focus on the following:
- analyzing the characteristics of the literary period and the issues that influenced the writers of that period
- evaluating the influences of the historical period that shaped literary characters, plots, settings, and themes
- connecting literature to historical contexts, current events, and your own experiences

TIMELINE

1750–1837

BRITISH LITERATURE

1750   **1790**

1751
Thomas Gray's "Elegy Written in a Country Churchyard" is published anonymously

1765
Bishop Percy publishes *Reliques of Ancient English Poetry*

1765
First gothic novel, Horace Walpole's *The Castle of Otranto*, is published

1786
Robert Burns publishes *Poems, Chiefly in the Scottish Dialect*

1786
William Beckford publishes *Vathek*

1792
Mary Wollstonecraft publishes *A Vindication of the Rights of Woman*

1794
Ann Radcliffe publishes *The Mysteries of Udolpho*

1794
William Blake publishes *Songs of Innocence and Experience*

1798
William Wordsworth and Samuel Taylor Coleridge publish *Lyrical Ballads*

1799
William Wordsworth begins *The Prelude*

BRITISH EVENTS

1750   **1790**

1753
Britain and its colonies celebrate January 1 as New Year's Day for the first time

1769
James Watt invents modern high-pressure steam engine

1771
Sir Richard Arkwright builds first water-powered cotton mill

1776 ▲
American colonists declare their independence from Britain; Adam Smith publishes *The Wealth of Nations*

1781
British surrender at Yorktown ends American Revolution ▶

1788
British establish first colony in Australia

1795
Mungo Park explores Niger River in Africa

1798
Thomas Malthus publishes *An Essay on the Principle of Population*

1802
British purchase Elgin Marbles

1805
British defeat Napoleon's naval forces at Trafalgar

1807
Britain outlaws slave trade

WORLD EVENTS

1750   **1790**

1752
First U.S. hospital opens in Philadelphia

1752
Benjamin Franklin proves that lightning is electricity

1754
French and Indian War begins in North America

1755
Moscow University established in Russia

1789
French Revolution begins with storming of the Bastille prison

1793
Eli Whitney invents the cotton gin in the U.S. ▶

1793
French King Louis XVI executed by revolutionaries

◀ **1794**
Toussaint L'Ouverture leads Haitian revolts against France and Spain

1804
Napoleon Bonaparte proclaimed emperor of France

Literature Online **Timeline** Visit www.glencoe.com for an interactive timeline.

Frigate *Macedonian* captured by frigate *United States,* 1812.

1810

1813
Jane Austen publishes *Pride and Prejudice*

1814
First historical novel, Sir Walter Scott's *Waverley,* is published

1815
Jane Austen publishes *Emma*

1817
Samuel Taylor Coleridge's *Biographia Literaria* is published

1818
John Keats publishes *Endymion* ▼

1818
George Gordon, Lord Byron publishes *Childe Harold's Pilgrimage*

1818
First science fiction novel, Mary Shelley's *Frankenstein,* is published

1820
Percy Bysshe Shelley publishes *Prometheus Unbound*

1824
George Gordon, Lord Byron publishes *Don Juan* ▼

1810

1811
Prince of Wales becomes regent

1811
Luddites destroy machinery

1812
War between United States and Great Britain begins

1814
George Stephenson designs first steam locomotive ▼

1819
Peterloo Massacre takes place

1824
England purchases Singapore and Malaya

1830
First public railway line opens in Britain

1810

1810
Father Hidalgo leads Mexican revolt against Spain

1812
Grimm brothers publish *Children's and Household Tales*

1815
Napoleon defeated at Waterloo, ending Napoleonic Wars

1814–1815
Congress of Vienna meets

1817
In Africa, Shaka becomes chief of Zulus

1819 ▶
Simón Bolívar leads Venezuelan revolt against Spain

1821
Greece revolts against Turkey and declares its independence

1830
France occupies Algeria

Napoleon

Reading Check

Analyzing Graphic Information What new types of fiction first appeared during the Romantic Period?

BY THE NUMBERS

BRITISH COTTON CONSUMPTION, 1800–1900

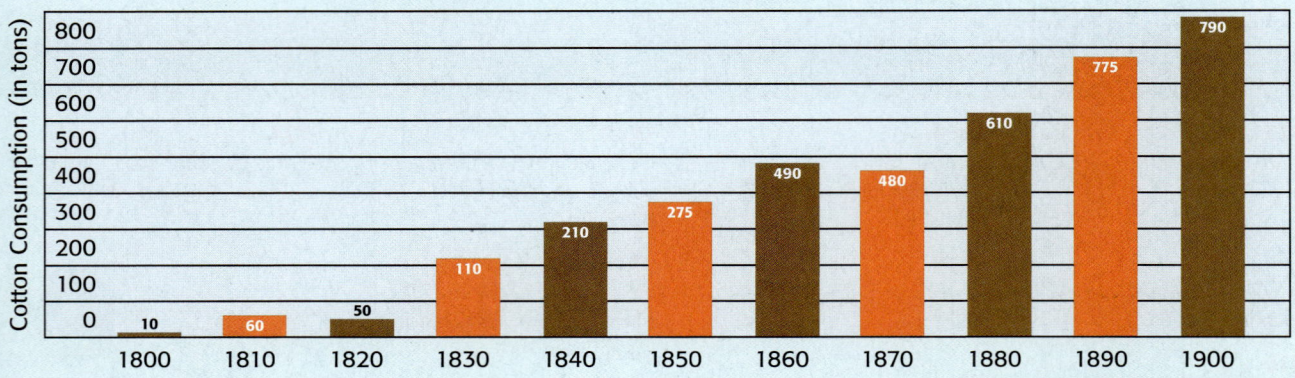

Cotton Consumption (in tons)

Year	Value
1800	10
1810	60
1820	50
1830	110
1840	210
1850	275
1860	490
1870	480
1880	610
1890	775
1900	790

Source *Historical Statistics of the United States*

The Cost of Gentility

In the late 1700s, the word *genteel* referred to a well-bred person. Gentility, which made a family socially acceptable, was closely related to economic status and lifestyle, and was reflected in the number and quality of one's servants, horses, carriages, and houses. The following list presents what a family could afford at various income levels.

100 pounds per year
- One ill-paid servant

300 pounds per year
- Two servants

400 pounds per year
- Three servants (including a cook)

500 pounds per year
- Gentility on a tight budget

700–1,000 pounds per year
- A carriage

More than 4,000 pounds per year
- A second house in London for the social season

TRAVEL EXPENSES

A genteel young Englishman's education was not complete until he had experienced the Grand Tour, a European trip that could last three to four years. Money went much further on the Continent than in England. One British traveler of the late 1700s estimated that a tourist could live better on 100 pounds a year in Italy than on 500 pounds a year in England.

MILITARY EXPANSION

Between 1793 and 1815, England spent 1,650,000,000 pounds on warfare. By the time of the Battle of Waterloo (1815), the British army had grown to about 250,000 men, more than six times its size at the time of the French Revolution (1789). The British navy had grown even faster, from 16,000 men to more than 140,000.

POPULATION BOOM

Between 1760 and 1815, England's population grew five times as fast as during the preceding fifty years. One reason was falling mortality rates from epidemic diseases such as plague.

POLICING LONDON

In 1829 Parliament passed the Metropolitan Police Act, and Sir Robert Peel set up a constabulary for London. London's first police (called "Bobbies" or "Peelers" after Sir Robert) were required to be younger than 35, at least 5 feet 5 inches tall, in good health, and able to read and write. They were required to walk a beat of twenty miles a day, seven days a week.

GROWTH OF RAILROADS

The first public railway line opened in 1830 and extended 32 miles between the British cities of Liverpool and Manchester. Pulling a 40-ton train, the locomotive sped along at 16 miles per hour. Within 20 years, locomotives were able to reach 50 miles per hour, an incredible speed at the time.

BEING THERE

In the late 1700s, manufacturing began to assume a larger role in the British economy. As a result, industrial towns began to spread over England's landscape. To escape what they saw as a growing blight of factories and slums, many Romantic writers fled to remote areas such as the Lake District.

 A *Hungerford Stairs,* c.1810. George Shepherd. Guildhall Library, Corporation of London.

 B *London's Royal Exchange,* 1809. Thomas Rowlandson.

 C *Flatford Mill,* 1817. John Constable. Tate Gallery, London.

 **Maps in Motion** Visit www.glencoe.com for an interactive map.

Reading Check

Analyzing Graphic Information:

1. About how many times larger was the British navy in 1815 than it had been in 1789?

2. At top speed, how long would it have taken the first train to travel from Liverpool to Manchester in 1830?

3. In what part of England is the Lake District located?

The Triumph of

ROMANTICISM

1750–1837

Historical, Social, and Cultural Forces

The Industrial Revolution

Beginning in Britain in the late 1700s, the Industrial Revolution brought a shift from economies based on farming and handmade goods to economies based on manufacturing by machines in industrial factories. Coal and steam replaced wind and water as new sources of energy and power. Cities and towns grew as people moved from the country to work in factories. This process produced wealth for a few factory owners but widespread misery for their workers, who struggled with long hours, bad working conditions, poverty, slums, and disease.

The American and French Revolutions

The late 1700s was a period of growing political unrest that culminated in a series of revolutions. In 1776 Britain's American colonists declared their independence, resulting in a long war before the United States of America won its freedom in 1781. The French Revolution began in 1789 as a democratic protest against royal despotism and an idealistic assertion of human equality. Yet, once in power, the revolutionary government in France resorted to brutality, leading to the execution of thousands during the Reign of Terror.

Latin American Revolutions

In the early 1790s, the ideals of the American and French Revolutions began to spread throughout Latin America. In France's colony of Saint Domingue (present-day Haiti), enslaved Africans took up arms under the leadership of Toussaint L'Ouverture, winning independence in 1804. Beginning in 1810, a widespread series of revolts took place against Spanish rule in Latin America. By 1824, Argentina, Chile, Mexico, Peru, Uruguay, Paraguay, Colombia, Venezuela, and Bolivia had become independent.

The Napoleonic Wars

In 1793 revolutionary France declared war on Britain. From that point until 1815, with no more than a brief respite, Britain and France were engaged in the Napoleonic Wars. Napoleon Bonaparte—a brilliant

The Hero of Trafalgar, 1898. Orford Smith. Color lithograph.

young Corsican and one of the most successful military commanders in history—first championed the French Revolution and then seized power himself, becoming emperor of France in 1804. The British naval commander Horatio Nelson became a national hero when he shattered Napoleon's fleet at the battle of Trafalgar in 1805. Britain continued to fight Napoleon on land and sea until his defeat at the climactic Battle of Waterloo in 1815.

Romanticism

Romanticism sprang from a reaction against Enlightenment values. While the Enlightenment praised reason and its limits, the Romantics were fascinated by extreme physical sensations and mental states—even terror and madness. Romantic works are filled not with moderation and social cohesion but with exotic extremes, whimsy and caprice, nightmares and visions, innocent children, lone wanderers, and quests after the unattainable. The skeptical intellectual is the representative figure of the Enlightenment; for the Romantics, it is the sublimely inspired poet.

Unlike Enlightenment thinkers, the Romantics did not view feelings as untrustworthy or distracting. On the contrary, they valued expressions of feelings as authentic. Someone who was capable of feeling deeply demonstrated a natural human sympathy both to nature and to the feelings of others.

> *"It is the addition of strangeness to beauty that constitutes the romantic character in art."*
>
> —Walter Pater

Romantic poets were particularly suspicious of the Enlightenment view of nature: that it obeyed mechanical laws and that it could be mastered. In Romanticism, nature is always active, vital, and spontaneous. For many Romantics, true enlightenment came not from isolating oneself in bookish studies, but rather from nature. "Nature" for the Romantics included scenery, especially wilderness, and an interest in the natural state of people. For instance, the simplicity of common people—the songs they sang and the stories they told—inspired poets, as did children. Imagining what primitive people might have been like in a state of nature gave rise to the Romantic ideal of the "noble savage," a human being of instinctive goodness. Above all, Romantic writers placed their trust in instinct and the power of the imagination.

PREVIEW **Big Ideas** of The Triumph of Romanticism

1 The Stirrings of Romanticism

During the later 1700s, dissident voices began to challenge the rule of rationalism and the values of civilization that underpinned the Enlightenment. New movements in literature, which would soon develop into Romanticism, emphasized the importance of feelings and imagination over reason.

See pages 700–701.

2 Nature and the Imagination

As the Industrial Revolution began to transform Britain into a nation of cities and factories, Romantics sought inspiration in the beauty of the natural world, the simple lives of ordinary workers, the innocence of childhood, and the mysterious and supernatural.

See pages 702–703.

3 The Quest for Truth and Beauty

A second generation of English Romantics succeeded the first, inheriting many of the enthusiasms and values of their predecessors. During their tragically brief lives, Lord Byron, Percy Shelley, and John Keats each actively pursued the elusive Romantic ideals of truth and beauty.

See pages 704–705.

The Stirrings of Romanticism

he bold attempts of Enlightenment thinkers to find reason and order in the world—indeed, in the whole universe—inspired an equally bold reaction against those qualities. The reaction became Romanticism.

> *"Man was born free, and everywhere he is in chains."*
>
> —Jean-Jacques Rousseau, *The Social Contract*

The "State of Nature"

Interested in getting at the root causes of things, including human nature, several Enlightenment thinkers speculated about what humans in a "state of nature" might be like. One of the most influential of these thinkers was Jean-Jacques Rousseau, a Swiss who spent much of his adult life in France. He believed that humans were born naturally good, curious, and content with satisfying just their basic needs. According to Rousseau, society corrupts us so that we instead desire status, idleness, and luxuries. Can we ever regain the primitive innocence and happiness of the "noble savage"? Rousseau thought not, but he did believe in educating children in a more natural way. His ideal education would be more "natural" in two ways, both by allowing the child to be outside in nature and by attending to the unfolding of each child's inner nature as he or she develops. He believed such education would produce upstanding citizens who would be confident in their own abilities and opinions. Rousseau became an important catalyst for the new generation of Romantic writers.

Sensibility and the Emotions

Young writers increasingly wanted to reduce the Enlightenment's emphasis on reason. One solution was to replace it with a kind of sympathetic feeling called "sensibility." While seventeenth-century physician William Harvey might have discovered that the source for the circulation of the blood was the heart, the Romantics were far more interested in the way the heart represents the origin of emotion than in its mechanics. This cult of sensibility first emphasized the physical reactions we have when our hearts are moved—blushing, turning pale, and fainting. They read these visible movements of the blood as signs of inner moral sympathy and virtue.

The Imagination

Another warm, Romantic antidote to the cool reason of the Enlightenment was the imagination, which blends sensory impressions with fantasy. Enlightenment thinkers had tended to dismiss the imagination, either because they wanted to analyze pure experience in their scientific experiments or because they were interested in purely logical arguments in their philosophical searches for fundamental truths. Romantic writers valued precisely that quality of the imagination that Enlightenment writers had despised: its ability to fuse sights and sounds from wildly different kinds of experience in ways that defy sense. In fact the Romantics embraced the irrational ecstasies and horrors of the imagination. The poet William Blake (see page 754), for example, believed that imagination, rather than science, held the secrets of the universe. As he asserted, "Vision or Imagination is a Representation of what Eternally Exists, Really and Unchangeably."

The Pre-Romantics

The early years of this era saw several writers who straddled both Enlightenment values and the emerging ideals of Romanticism. Thomas Gray used Neoclassical techniques in his poetry, such as elevated language and classical forms, while embracing

The Ancient of Days. Frontispiece, plate 1, from *Europe, a Prophecy,* 1794. William Blake. The Pierpont Morgan Library, New York.

a love of nature and a belief in the common man—important ideals of later Romantic poets. Despite his acceptance in high society, Robert Burns wrote of the lives of common people in Scottish dialect characteristic of peasants and farmers. Perhaps the most famous pre-Romantic writer of all, William Blake was not content with the prevailing Neo-classical values of his day and focused on supernatural elements and imaginative experimentation thereby forging a style all his own.

A proverb is a short statement that expresses a truth. Blake wrote the following proverbs as a counterpart to the book of Proverbs in the Bible.

from *Proverbs of Hell* from *The Marriage of Heaven and Hell* by William Blake

No bird soars too high, if he soars with his own wings.
A dead body revenges not injuries.
The most sublime act is to set another before you.
If the fool would persist in his folly he would become wise.
Folly is the cloke of knavery.
Shame is Pride's cloke.
Prisons are built with stones of Law, Brothels with bricks of Religion.
The pride of the peacock is the glory of God.
The lust of the goat is the bounty of God.
The wrath of the lion is the wisdom of God.
The nakedness of woman is the work of God.
Excess of sorrow laughs. Excess of joy weeps.
The roaring of lions, the howling of wolves, the raging of the stormy sea, and the destructive sword, are portions of eternity too great for the eye of man.

Reading Check

Comparing and Contrasting How do Blake's ideas oppose Enlightenment values?

erhaps the most profound disagreement between Enlightenment and Romantic writers was their differing reactions to nature. What is it for? Is it good or bad? What should we do with it?

What Is Nature?

To Enlightenment thinkers, disorderly nature seemed meant for humans to tame. Nature could be made more productive in farms run on rational principles. Nature could be made more rational by being analyzed and studied in laboratories. Nature could be made more beautiful in orderly gardens with straight paths and clear views.

The answers to these questions seemed more complicated to writers a few generations later when the face of nature was literally changing. Cities and towns were sprawling into the countryside, railroads began to crisscross the landscape, smoke-belching factories were springing up. Had human intervention really made nature more rational or more beautiful? And what did these changes say about the humans who had caused them?

> "*Heaven lies about us in our infancy!*"
>
> —William Wordsworth

Romantics preferred their nature wild and untamed. Their landscape gardens, for example, kept a space for wilderness, with winding paths through tangled woods leading to sudden, startling views. Instead of the arranged prettiness of an ornamental garden, they preferred the sublime experience of the Swiss Alps, where the overwhelming scale of nature inspires awe rather than mere appreciation. In his poem "The Tables Turned," William Wordsworth (see page 780) recommended that we shut our books and lift our eyes to the natural world around us: "Enough of science and of art; / Close up those barren leaves; / Come forth, and bring with you a heart / That watches and receives."

The Child and the Common Man

Who led the most natural life? One answer for the Romantics was children, because they had not yet been educated by school or society. Long before the Enlightenment, thinkers had viewed children as deficient adults precisely because they had not yet been transformed by education. The Romantics, however, saw in children innocence and imagination rather than ignorance. Another group whose lives and culture had not been distorted by civilized values was the common people. Writers of the period became interested in imagining the experiences and impressions of ordinary folk.

In 1798, two young poets, William Wordsworth and Samuel Taylor Coleridge (see page 799), decided to publish a book of poetry, called *Lyrical Ballads,* that experimented with these new ideas. Their poems for the most part are written in the simple verse form of folk ballads or hymns. They use informal vocabulary, not ornate language. Their subjects, too, are drawn from the lives of uneducated people: a little girl whose brothers and sisters have died, an old Indian woman, a mentally deficient boy, an old sailor, a father going for a walk with his young son.

Dreams and Nightmares

Many Romantic writers shared a critical attitude toward the methods and promised benefits of science. Wordsworth, for instance, was concerned about our motivations in studying nature: "Our meddling intellect / Mis-shapes the beauteous forms of things; /— We murder to dissect." This Romantic indictment of how science deforms nature took life in the gothic novel *Frankenstein* by Mary Shelley (see page 833). As a result of views like these, many Romantics were fascinated by subjects that science could not explain. Coleridge contributed a long poem to *Lyrical Ballads* that includes nightmarish scenes set among the icebergs of the Antarctic. He later claimed that his famous poem "Kubla Khan" appeared to him in a drug-induced dream vision. By focusing on the irrational and unnatural, Romantic writers hoped to embrace the full scope of human experience, including the pains and pleasures of the heart and the dark recesses of the mind.

Cloud Study, Horizon of Trees. John Constable. Royal Academy of Arts, London.

from the Preface to *Lyrical Ballads* by William Wordsworth

The principal object, then, which I proposed to myself in these poems was to choose incidents and situations from common life, and to relate or describe them, throughout, as far as was possible, in a selection of language really used by men; . . . Low and rustic life was generally chosen, because in that condition, the essential passions of the heart find a better soil in which they can attain their maturity, are less under restraint, and speak a plainer and more emphatic language; because in that condition of life our elementary feelings co-exist in a state of greater simplicity, and, consequently, may be more accurately contemplated, and more forcibly communicated; because the manners of rural life germinate from those elementary feelings; and, from the necessary character of rural occupations, are more easily comprehended; and are more durable; and lastly, because in that condition the passions of men are incorporated with the beautiful and permanent forms of nature.

Reading Check

Analyzing Cause and Effect How did Wordsworth and Coleridge's interest in common life influence their poetry?

or the Romantics, the deepest human experiences were often moments of intense communication between their inner selves and the world around them. They sought these experiences by falling in love, writing poetry, and fighting for causes they believed in.

The Revolutionary Spirit

In 1789 the French Revolution seemed to offer young people a chance to realize these dreams. Wordsworth and Coleridge, among many others, responded to the ideals of "Liberty, Equality, Fraternity" and were infused with enthusiasm for the revolutionary cause. As Wordsworth exulted (in lines later included in his long autobiographical narrative poem *The Prelude*), "Bliss was it in that dawn to be alive, / But to be young was very heaven!" When these ideals seemed betrayed by the bloody excesses of the Reign of Terror, both men slipped into conservative views. The next generation of Romantics, such as Percy Bysshe Shelley (see page 850), who had been inspired by Wordsworth's and Coleridge's youthful political radicalism, felt betrayed and continued to support revolt both at home and abroad.

The Spirit of Nationalism

The Romantic interest in folk culture had important political as well as literary consequences. Many English Romantics, whose education had been steeped in the classics, were particularly stirred by the struggles of the Greek people to win independence from Turkish rule. The Romantic poet George Gordon, Lord Byron (see page 842) donated money to the Greek cause, founded an artillery unit, and died en route to fight beside the Greeks.

Exotic Places and Times

For the Romantics, a great part of the attraction of foreign lands was the glamour of their cultures. Such places held the allure of the unknown and the exotic. Actual travel was not always necessary. The Romantics could feed their imaginations with the writings of travelers to the Near East and other far-away places. Literature with exotic settings—whether experienced or imagined—proved very popular with Romantic writers and audiences. Other remote and beautiful spots appealed to them as well. The highlands of Scotland and the Swiss and Italian Alps, for example, with their rough peaks and raging torrents, provided the settings for Mary Shelley's *Frankenstein*.

The past, too, offered exotic surprises. Many Romantic writers bypassed the familiar, sunlit eras of Greece and Rome for darker, more mysterious periods. In particular, the medieval "Dark Ages" appealed to them. The Romantics were inspired by the same qualities of the Middle Ages that the Enlightenment thinkers despised—Gothic wildness, age-old ritual, and strange beliefs. Beginning in 1765 with Horace Walpole's *The Castle of Otranto*, literature with medieval settings, such as weird landscapes and haunted castles, created a literary form, the gothic novel.

> *"Much have I traveled in the realms of gold . . ."*
>
> —John Keats
> "On First Looking into Chapman's Homer"

The Poetic Quest

It is not surprising that in an age so conscious of its own rebellion, Romantic poets above all reflected on their role in culture. Many poets in this period, most notably Wordsworth and Shelley, wrote manifestos declaring the supremacy of poetry. Others wrote poems that seem to be allegories of the grand poetic quest for beauty and truth that guided many Romantic poets. One such poet who sought to capture exuberance and beauty was John Keats (see page 865). In his brief life, he traveled far in his imagination. Some of his most famous sonnets are about the ability of books to transport him to the magical realms of the imagination. Sublime thoughts demand sublime forms of expression, Romantic poets thought. They were thrilled to take on this challenge.

Percy Bysshe Shelley, 1845. Joseph Severn. Oil on canvas. Keats-Shelley Memorial House, Rome.

from *A Defense of Poetry* by Percy Bysshe Shelley

The most unfailing herald, companion, and follower of the awakening of a great people to work a beneficial change in opinion or institution, is Poetry. At such periods there is an accumulation of the power of communicating and receiving intense and impassioned conceptions respecting man and nature. The persons in whom this power resides, may often, as far as regards many portions of their nature, have little apparent correspondence with that spirit of good of which they are the ministers. But even whilst they deny and abjure, they are yet compelled to serve, the Power which is seated on the throne of their own soul. It is impossible to read the compositions of the most celebrated writers of the present day without being startled with the electric life which burns within their words. They measure the circumference and sound the depths of human nature with a comprehensive and all-penetrating spirit, and they are themselves perhaps the most sincerely astonished at its manifestations, for it is less their spirit than the spirit of the age. Poets are the hierophants [interpreters] of an unapprehended inspiration, the mirrors of the gigantic shadows which futurity casts upon the present, the words which express what they understand not; the trumpets which sing to battle, and feel not what they inspire: the influence which is moved not, but moves. Poets are the unacknowledged legislators of the World.

Reading Check

Analyzing Cause and Effect In Shelley's view, what links poetry with revolution?

WRAP—UP

Why It Matters

Many of Romanticism's core values, such as the spiritual power of nature, the importance of the imagination, and the dignity of the artist, have become a permanent part of our civilization. Today's environmental movements and creative arts programs are part of the cultural legacy of Romanticism.

The Romantics helped change the way our civilization regards children. Before the Romantic period, children were seen simply as immature adults. Romantics such as Rousseau, Blake, and Wordsworth, however, attached a central importance to what they saw as the unique experiences of childhood.

Romanticism also shaped our vision of the medieval period. Since the Renaissance, most people had viewed the Middle Ages as a time of "Gothic" barbarism, but the Romantics saw the medieval past as a glamorous era of knights and ladies, fairies and wizards, dragons and quests.

When it spread to the United States, European Romanticism helped influence American literature, inspiring writers such as Ralph Waldo Emerson, Henry David Thoreau, Edgar Allan Poe, Nathaniel Hawthorne, and Herman Melville.

 **Literature Online Big Ideas** Link to Web resources to further explore the Big Ideas at www.glencoe.com.

Cultural Links

- Largely ignored in his own time, William Blake has had a great influence on modern writers, particularly poets, including William Butler Yeats, Theodore Roethke, and Allen Ginsberg.

- The gothic novel and the historical novel, types of fiction that remain very popular today, made their first appearance during the Romantic period.

- Often cited as the first science fiction novel, Mary Shelley's *Frankenstein* helped establish the image of the brilliant, but mad, scientist that is still a feature of popular culture. As an artificial human made from flesh (not machinery, like a robot), Frankenstein's monster is perhaps the first android in literature.

You might try using this study organizer to keep track of the literary elements you learn in this unit.

FOLDABLES Study Organizer **BOUND BOOK**

Reader-Response Journal

Connect to Today

Use what you have learned about the period to do one of these activities.

1. Speaking/Listening Neoclassicism valued tradition, society, and reason; Romanticism valued experiment, the individual, and emotion. Working with several other students, hold a panel discussion on which of these value systems is a better guide to life.

2. Visual Literacy Mary Shelley's novel *Frankenstein* has become one of the most familiar Romantic literary works. Create a visual collage showing the different ways in which Victor Frankenstein and his monster have been portrayed visually in such popular media as illustrated books, stage plays, movies, television programs, comic books, graphic novels, and video games.

OBJECTIVES
- Hold a panel discussion.
- Create a visual collage.

Literature Online Study Central Visit www.glencoe.com and click on Study Central to review English Romanticism.

The Stirrings of Romanticism

Autumn Leaves, 1856. Sir John Everett Millais. Manchester Art Gallery, UK.

"To see a World in a Grain of Sand,
And a Heaven in a Wild Flower,
Hold Infinity in the palm of your hand,
And Eternity in an hour."

—William Blake, "Auguries of Innocence"

Elegy Written in a Country Churchyard

MEET THOMAS GRAY

"I shall be but a shrimp of an author," Thomas Gray noted late in his life, reflecting on the small number of works he had published. If measured only by quantity, Gray's output of poetry was indeed small. He allowed only thirteen of his poems to be published during his lifetime. Gray's reputation as an author was more secure than he imagined, however, for if he wrote little, he also wrote remarkably well. His "Elegy Written in a Country Churchyard" remains one of the best-loved poems in the English language.

> "['Elegy Written in a Country Churchyard'] *abounds with images that find a mirror in every mind, and with sentiments to which every bosom returns an echo.*"
>
> —Samuel Johnson, "The Life of Gray"

A Good Education Gray was born in 1716 in London to a doting mother and a violent, uncaring father. His mother wanted to provide her only son (the sole survivor of twelve children) with a good education and a stable life away from his father. She sent him at the age of eight to study at Eton, a prestigious boarding school. There, Gray formed enduring friendships with Richard West, the son of a prominent lawyer, and Horace Walpole, the wealthy son of a powerful English politician.

After Eton, Gray attended Cambridge University, but interrupted his studies for two years to tour Europe with Walpole. Gray returned to Cambridge at the age of twenty-five to complete his studies and stayed on to become a resident scholar.

The Secluded Poet Gray led a quiet life, maintaining close relationships with only a handful of people. Among them was his mother, whom he often visited in the village of Stoke Poges, where she moved after his father's death. Gray came to love the natural beauty of the village and the quiet life of its people. In its peaceful surroundings he worked on two of his best poems: a sonnet on the death of his friend Richard West and "Elegy Written in a Country Churchyard," which took him nine years to complete. Gray did not plan to publish the elegy, but he had little choice in the matter. He showed it to Walpole, who shared it with friends, and an imperfect copy of the poem made its way to the editor of a popular periodical. When Gray learned that the *Magazine of Magazines* planned to print the poem without his permission, he quickly published an accurate version. Gray's "Elegy Written in a Country Churchyard" came out in February 1751 to almost immediate acclaim. Because he felt that a gentleman should not accept payment for writing poetry, he let his publisher keep all the profits.

A Perfectionist at Work At the age of forty-one, Gray was offered the position of poet laureate of England, but he turned down the honor. A perfectionist, Gray wrote very slowly and feared that as poet laureate he would have to produce works at a rate that would compromise his standards. Gray died at Cambridge at the age of fifty-five, after a long illness. He was buried in Stoke Poges next to his mother.

Thomas Gray was born in 1716 and died in 1771.

Literature Online Author Search For more about Thomas Gray, go to www.glencoe.com.

Connecting to the Poem

In this poem, Gray contemplates a village graveyard and thinks of those who are buried there. As you read, consider the following questions:

- How much is a person's life affected by fate and circumstance?
- How would you like people to remember you?

Building Background

Gray's "Elegy" shows the influence of two types of poetry popular in the 1700s. One type was the **elegy**, a poem that laments a death or some other great loss. The elegy was common in classical Greek and Latin poetry, to which Gray and other poets looked for models. The other type was "landscape" poetry, in which the speaker's natural surroundings evoke melancholy musings on life and death. Gray's "Elegy" belongs to a subdivision of this type, "graveyard" poetry, in which the evocative scene is set in a cemetery.

Setting Purposes for Reading

Big Idea The Stirrings of Romanticism

As you read, look for elements in the poem that emphasize emotion, the imagination, and nature.

Literary Element Epitaph

An **epitaph** is a brief statement, often inscribed on a gravestone, that commemorates a dead person. As you read the poem, pay particular attention to the epitaph at the end. Ask yourself how the epitaph relates to the rest of the poem.

- See Literary Terms Handbook, p. R6.

Literature Online **Interactive Literary Elements Handbook** To review or learn more about the literary elements, go to www.glencoe.com.

Reading Strategy Interpreting Imagery

Imagery refers to the word pictures that writers create to evoke an emotional response. In creating imagery, writers use sensory details that appeal to sight, hearing, touch, taste, or smell. **Interpreting imagery** involves analyzing these word pictures and determining the kind of emotional responses the images evoke in the reader.

Reading Tip: Taking Notes Use a chart to make associations between images, the senses to which they appeal, and the feelings they suggest.

Image (line)	Appeals to Sense of...	Emotional Response

Vocabulary

pomp (pomp) *n.* splendid or dignified display; p. 711 *The pomp of the graduation ceremony emphasized its significance.*

inevitable (i nev′ ə tə bəl) *adj.* incapable of being avoided or prevented; certain; p. 711 *Realizing that defeat was inevitable, the candidate conceded the election.*

genial (jē′ nē əl) *adj.* giving warmth and comfort; pleasant or cheerful; p. 712 *The genial host enthusiastically greeted his guests.*

uncouth (un kōōth′) *adj.* crude; lacking polish, culture, or refinement; p. 713 *The uncouth couple chatted during the performance.*

kindred (kin′ drid) *adj.* like; allied; similar; p. 713 *Wanting desperately to win, the athletes shared kindred emotions.*

Vocabulary Tip: Analogies An analogy is a relationship between two pairs of words.

OBJECTIVES

In studying this selection, you will focus on the following:
- analyzing literary genres
- analyzing elegy and epitaph
- interpreting imagery

Stoke Poges Church, 1864. Jasper Francis Cropsey. Oil on board, 11.75 x 19 in. Johnny van Haeften Gallery, London.

Elegy Written in a Country Churchyard

Thomas Gray

The curfew tolls the knell of parting day,
The lowing° herd wind slowly o'er the lea,°
The plowman homeward plods his weary way,
And leaves the world to darkness and to me.

5   Now fades the glimmering landscape on the sight,
And all the air a solemn stillness holds,
Save where the beetle wheels his droning flight,
And drowsy tinklings lull the distant folds;

Save that from yonder ivy-mantled tower
10 The moping owl does to the moon complain
Of such, as wandering near her secret bower,°
Molest her ancient solitary reign.

2 **lowing:** the sound a cow makes; **lea:** a meadow

11 **bower:** a shelter of leafy branches

Reading Strategy **Interpreting Imagery** *What mood does the cluster of images in the first stanza create?*

Beneath those rugged elms, that yew tree's shade,
Where heaves the turf in many a moldering heap,
15 Each in his narrow cell forever laid,
The rude° forefathers of the hamlet sleep.

The breezy call of incense-breathing Morn,
The swallow twittering from the straw-built shed,
The cock's shrill clarion° or the echoing horn,°
20 No more shall rouse them from their lowly bed.

For them no more the blazing hearth shall burn,
Or busy housewife ply her evening care;
No children run to lisp their sire's return,
Or climb his knees the envied kiss to share.

25 Oft did the harvest to their sickle yield,
Their furrow oft the stubborn glebe° has broke;
How jocund° did they drive their team afield!
How bowed the woods beneath their sturdy stroke!

Let not Ambition mock their useful toil,
30 Their homely joys, and destiny obscure;°
Nor Grandeur hear with a disdainful smile
The short and simple annals° of the poor.

The boast of heraldry,° the **pomp** of power,
And all that beauty, all that wealth e'er gave,
35 Awaits alike the **inevitable** hour.
The paths of glory lead but to the grave.

Nor you, ye proud, impute° to these the fault,
If Memory o'er their tomb no trophies° raise,
Where through the long-drawn aisle and fretted vault°
40 The pealing anthem swells the note of praise.

Can storied urn° or animated° bust
Back to its mansion call the fleeting breath?
Can Honor's voice provoke° the silent dust,
Or Flattery soothe the dull cold ear of Death?

---

16 **rude:** uncultured; unrefined

19 **clarion:** a crowing sound; **echoing horn:** a hunter's horn

26 **glebe:** soil
27 **jocund** (jo′ kənd): cheerfully; lightheartedly

30 **obscure:** undistinguished

32 **annals:** descriptive accounts or histories

33 **heraldry:** Here, *heraldry* means "nobility."

37 **impute:** attribute
38 **trophies:** memorials to military heroes, usually depicting arms taken from the enemy
39 **fretted vault:** an arched church ceiling adorned with carving in decorative patterns
41 **storied urn:** a funeral urn depicting the life of the deceased and often inscribed with a legend; **animated:** lifelike
43 **provoke:** bring to life

Big Idea **The Stirrings of Romanticism** *How does this stanza reflect the emergence of Romanticism?*

Vocabulary

pomp (pomp) *n.* splendid or dignified display
inevitable (i nev′ ə tə bəl) *adj.* incapable of being avoided or prevented; certain

45   Perhaps in this neglected spot is laid
       Some heart once pregnant with celestial fire;
       Hands that the rod of empire might have swayed,
       Or waked to ecstasy the living lyre.

       But Knowledge to their eyes her ample page
50   Rich with the spoils of time did ne'er unroll;
       Chill Penury° repressed their noble rage,
       And froze the **genial** current of the soul.

       Full many a gem of purest ray serene,
       The dark unfathomed° caves of ocean bear:
55   Full many a flower is born to blush unseen,
       And waste its sweetness on the desert air.

       Some village Hampden,° that with dauntless breast
       The little tyrant of his fields withstood;
       Some mute inglorious Milton° here may rest,
60   Some Cromwell° guiltless of his country's blood.

       The applause of listening senates to command,
       The threats of pain and ruin to despise,
       To scatter plenty o'er a smiling land,
       And read their history in a nation's eyes,

65   Their lot forbade: nor circumscribed° alone
       Their growing virtues, but their crimes confined;
       Forbade to wade through slaughter to a throne,
       And shut the gates of mercy on mankind,

       The struggling pangs of conscious truth to hide,
70   To quench the blushes of ingenuous° shame,
       Or heap the shrine of Luxury and Pride
       With incense kindled at the Muse's flame.°

       Far from the madding° crowd's ignoble strife,
       Their sober wishes never learned to stray;
75   Along the cool sequestered° vale of life
       They kept the noiseless tenor° of their way.

---

51 Penury (pen′ yə rē): extreme poverty

54 unfathomed: of uncertain depth

57 Hampden: John Hampden (1594–1643), an English Parliamentary leader who opposed Charles I over unfair taxation
59 Milton: John Milton (1608–1674), a renowned English poet
60 Cromwell: Oliver Cromwell (1599–1658), an English statesman and general who was responsible for much bloodshed

65 circumscribed: limited; restricted

70 ingenuous: innocent; naive

72 incense kindled at the Muse's flame: Here, *incense* means "praise," and *the Muse* stands for a poet or poetry, so this phrase means "poetic praise."
73 madding: acting as if mad; frenzied
75 sequestered: sheltered; secluded
76 tenor: course; direction

Big Idea   **The Stirrings of Romanticism** *What aspect of Romanticism having to do with the poor is evident in this stanza?*

Reading Strategy   **Interpreting Imagery** *What two images are contrasted in this stanza?*

Vocabulary

genial (jē′ nē əl) *adj.* giving warmth and comfort; pleasant or cheerful

The Harvest Wagon.
George Stubbs. Oil on board, 66 x 96.5 cm. Roy Miles Fine Paintings, London.

Yet even these bones from insult to protect
Some frail memorial still erected nigh,
With **uncouth** rhymes and shapeless sculpture decked,
80   Implores the passing tribute of a sigh.

Their name, their years, spelt by the unlettered Muse,°
The place of fame and elegy supply:
And many a holy text around she strews,
That teach the rustic moralist to die.

81 **unlettered Muse:** uneducated poet; Gray is referring to the tombstone engraver

85   For who to dumb Forgetfulness a prey,
This pleasing anxious being e'er resigned,
Left the warm precincts of the cheerful day,
Nor cast one longing lingering look behind?

On some fond breast the parting soul relies,
90   Some pious drops the closing eye requires;
Even from the tomb the voice of Nature cries,
Even in our ashes live their wonted° fires.

92 **wonted:** customary; usual

For thee, who mindful of the unhonored dead
Dost in these lines their artless tale relate;
95   If chance, by lonely contemplation led,
Some **kindred** spirit shall inquire thy fate,

Vocabulary

uncouth (un kōōth′) *adj.* crude; lacking polish, culture, or refinement
kindred (kin′ drid) *adj.* like; allied; similar

Haply° some hoary-headed swain° may say,
"Oft have we seen him at the peep of dawn
Brushing with hasty steps the dews away
100   To meet the sun upon the upland lawn.

"There at the foot of yonder nodding beech
That wreathes its old fantastic roots so high,
His listless° length at noontide would he stretch
And pore upon the brook that babbles by.

105   "Hard by yon wood, now smiling as in scorn,
Muttering his wayward° fancies he would rove,
Now drooping, woeful wan, like one forlorn,
Or crazed with care, or crossed in hopeless love.

"One morn I missed him on the customed hill,
110   Along the heath° and near his favorite tree;
Another came; nor yet beside the rill°
Nor up the lawn nor at the wood was he;

"The next with dirges° due in sad array
Slow through the churchway path we saw him borne.
115   Approach and read (for thou canst read) the lay,°
Graved on the stone beneath yon aged thorn."°

The Epitaph

Here rests his head upon the lap of Earth
A youth to Fortune and to Fame unknown.
Fair Science frowned not on his humble birth,
120   *And Melancholy marked him for her own.*

Large was his bounty, and his soul sincere,
Heaven did a recompense as largely send:
He gave to Misery all he had, a tear;
He gained from Heaven ('twas all he wished) a friend.

125   *No farther seek his merits to disclose,*
Or draw his frailties from their dread abode
(There they alike in trembling hope repose),
The bosom of his Father and his God.

97	**Haply:** perhaps; **hoary-headed swain:** a white-haired countryman
103	**listless:** lacking in energy; sluggish
106	**wayward:** irregular; unpredictable; erratic
110	**heath:** a stretch of land covered with heather or wild shrubs
111	**rill:** a small stream or brook
113	**dirges:** songs of mourning
115	**lay:** a poem
116	**thorn:** a hawthorn, a thorny tree with white or pink flowers

Literary Element   Epitaph   *Some critics maintain that Gray wrote his own epitaph at the end of the poem. If so, what do these lines tell you about Gray?*

RESPONDING AND THINKING CRITICALLY

Respond

1. (a)What emotions did you experience while reading Gray's elegy? (b)What lines or images prompted these emotions?

Recall and Interpret

2. (a)In lines 17–28, what sights, sounds, and feelings does the speaker say the dead have left behind? (b)What do these **images** have in common?

3. (a)In lines 45–64, what does the speaker speculate some of the country people might have become if they had been able to fulfill their potential? (b)What kept them from fulfilling their potential?

4. (a)Summarize the speaker's feelings about the dead. (b)How does the speaker hope readers will feel about the people buried in the churchyard?

Analyze and Evaluate

5. In your opinion, what is the main **theme** of this poem? Use specific lines or phrases to support your answer.

6. (a)What does the person described in the epitaph have in common with the other people described in the elegy? (b)What evidence can you find in the poem that Gray described himself in the epitaph?

7. (a)Do you find Gray's elegy to be sad, hopeful, or both? (b)Some critics have judged Gray's elegy to be overly sentimental. Do you agree with this criticism? Explain.

Connect

8. If you were to rewrite the elegy for modern American readers, what famous people would you choose to take the place of Hampden, Milton, and Cromwell? Explain your choices.

9. Big Idea **The Stirrings of Romanticism** How does "Elegy Written in a Country Churchyard" demonstrate that writers at this time were beginning to focus on emotion, imagination, and nature rather than on reason, science, and classical literature? Use details from the poem to support your answer.

LITERARY ANALYSIS

Literary Element Epitaph

An **epitaph** may describe the merits and accomplishments of a person who has died, or it may take the form of an appeal from the dead to those who pass by the grave. A number of writers have composed their own epitaphs.

1. What form does the epitaph at the end of the poem take?

2. Assuming that Gray has written his own epitaph, how does he choose to be remembered?

Review: Elegy

As you learned on page 446, an **elegy** is a poem mourning the death of an individual or a lament for a tragic event. In the eighteenth century, the so-called Graveyard School of English poets wrote elegies that were general reflections on death and immortality and combined somber imagery of human impermanence with philosophical speculation.

Group Activity Meet with a small group and discuss the following questions:

1. What characteristics make Gray's elegy an example of the Graveyard School?

2. What does Gray's "Elegy" mourn? Does it just lament the loss of one individual or does it go beyond this? Cite evidence from the poem to support your response.

READING AND VOCABULARY

Reading Strategy | **Interpreting Imagery**

In his elegy, Gray often uses contrasting imagery. For example, the noise of the "madding crowd's ignoble strife" is contrasted with the "noiseless tenor" of village life, which is pictured as a journey through a "cool sequestered vale" (lines 73–76).

1. Identify an example of contrasting imagery in lines 105–108.

2. How does Gray's use of contrasting images contribute to the meaning of the poem?

Vocabulary | Practice

Practice with Analogies Choose the word that best completes each analogy.

1. obligatory : necessary :: certain :
   a. uncouth
   b. pomp
   c. genial
   d. inevitable

2. cold : hostile :: warm :
   a. kindred
   b. genial
   c. inevitable
   d. uncouth

3. simplicity : plainness :: magnificence :
   a. pomp
   b. genial
   c. uncouth
   d. kindred

4. rare : common :: refined :
   a. genial
   b. kindred
   c. uncouth
   d. pomp

5. restless : serene :: unlike :
   a. inevitable
   b. kindred
   c. pomp
   d. uncouth

Academic Vocabulary

Here is a word from the vocabulary list on page R82. This word will help you think, write, and talk about the selection.

minimized (min′ ə mīzd′) *v.* reduced to the least degree of importance, size, or value

Practice and Apply
In what ways has society **minimized** the importance of the poor, humble rustics represented in Gray's elegy?

WRITING AND EXTENDING

Writing About Literature

Respond to Setting The **setting** is the time and place in which a literary work takes place. Write a brief essay analyzing the effect of the setting on the mood and theme of Gray's elegy. Discuss the following questions as you develop your essay.

- How does the darkness of the churchyard contribute to the mood?

- What other elements in the setting affect the mood and theme of the poem?

Before you begin your first draft, complete a chart similar to the one below, in which you analyze various details of the setting. Comment on how each detail contributes to the mood or the theme.

Detail of Setting	Contribution to Mood and Theme
darkness of churchyard	gives the poem a melancholy mood
silence in the air	suggests a lonely feeling

When you complete your first draft, get together with a peer reviewer. Evaluate each other's drafts and suggest improvements. Then proofread and edit your revised copy for errors in spelling, grammar, and punctuation before producing a final version.

Listening and Speaking

In his elegy, Gray personifies many qualities, such as ambition, grandeur, memory, and honor. Meet with a small group and have each member assume the role of one of these qualities. Staying within your assigned role, discuss Gray's view of the people buried in the churchyard.

Literature Online **Web Activities** For eFlashcards, Selection Quick Checks, and other Web activities, go to www.glencoe.com.

Burns's Poetry

MEET ROBERT BURNS

Scottish author Robert Burns was famous both for his songwriting and his poetry. Still celebrated as a Scottish national hero, he wrote simple lyrics that continue to capture the imagination of readers around the world. He had a keen ear for the speech of his native land, and in his work he employed its characteristic sound to impart a fresh vitality to English literature.

> "My heart's in the Highlands, my
>   heart is not here,
> My heart's in the Highlands a-chasing
>   the deer."
>
> —Robert Burns

Peasant-Poet Burns was born on a farm in southwestern Scotland to poor, uneducated peasants. As a boy, he worked on the farm and attended school infrequently. Whatever education Burns obtained came mainly from reading. His favorite writers were Shakespeare and Pope. Burns's mother, uneducated but imaginative, taught him the ballads, legends, and songs of the Scottish peasants. These songs inspired him to write poetry of his own.

After the death of his father, Burns quickly developed his gift for expressing emotions of love, friendship, and amusement in verse. He also attempted to keep the family farm going, but failed. Soon, however, his fortunes changed for the better. At the age of twenty-seven, he published *Poems, Chiefly in the Scottish Dialect*, a work that enjoyed immediate success with simple farmers and sophisticated critics alike. Burns then temporarily gave up farming and moved to Edinburgh. There, he played the role expected of him—that of a gifted but uncultured rustic.

Labor of Love In 1788 Burns left Edinburgh and settled on a farm in Ellisland, Dumfriesshire. When his friend James Johnson planned to compile a definitive anthology of Scottish folk songs, he asked Burns to help him, and Burns jumped at the chance. He threw himself wholeheartedly into the project and for the next three years roamed the countryside collecting, editing, and writing lyrics for many old Scottish tunes, thus preserving the rhythms and accents of his native tongue. Considering this work to be a labor of love, he declined payment, even refusing to allow his name to appear in the collection. In doing so, he created difficulties for scholars, who have found it almost impossible to determine where some of the original folk songs leave off and Burns's contributions begin.

Sadly enough, Burns's devotion to his country and to the peasant life was the cause of his early death. He had developed a heart disease from overly strenuous work on his father's farm as a boy, and he finally succumbed to it at the age of thirty-seven. But Burns the poet lives on in spirit when every year on New Year's Eve people join hands and sing his beautiful song "Auld Lang Syne."

Robert Burns was born in 1759 and died in 1796.

Literature Online **Author Search** For more about Robert Burns, go to www.glencoe.com.

Connecting to the Poems

Burns's poems celebrate the joy of being human, of loving, working, appreciating nature, and laughing with friends. As you read, consider how important it is to have plans for the future.

Building Background

Robert Burns's poetry flourished during a time when the English-controlled British government was trying to subdue Scottish patriotism by depriving Scots of civil liberties. The favorable reception of Burns's *Poems, Chiefly in the Scottish Dialect* did much to restore a sense of pride in his fellow Scots, and Burns's later preservation of traditional Scottish songs raised him to the status of folk hero. His work reflects his familiarity with Scottish peasant life as well as his deep connection with nature. Burns is said to have composed "To a Mouse" after turning up a mouse's nest while plowing and saving the mouse from the spade of the boy who was holding the horses.

Setting Purposes for Reading

Big Idea The Stirrings of Romanticism

As you read, notice how Burns's poems reflect the importance of feelings, imagination, and sensitivity to nature.

Literary Element Dialect

Dialect is a variety of language that is characteristic of a particular region or group of people. Burns wrote many poems in Lowland Scots, a dialect of English. Watch for words with apostrophes. Sometimes, an apostrophe indicates missing letters: for example, the apostrophe in *tim'rous* stands for the letter *o* in the word *timorous*.

- See Literary Terms Handbook, p. R4.

Literature Online **Interactive Literary Elements Handbook** To review or learn more about the literary elements, go to www.glencoe.com.

Reading Strategy Monitoring Comprehension

Monitoring your comprehension means thinking about whether you are understanding what you read. Reading and understanding Burns's dialect is like breaking a code. First, read each poem silently, using the margin notes for help. Then read each poem aloud, listening to its sounds and rhythms. Check your understanding by paraphrasing each stanza, or restating it in your own words.

Reading Tip: Taking Notes Use a chart to record difficult passages and your paraphrases of them.

Passage	Paraphrase
"Should auld acquaintance be forgot"	Should we forget our old friends?

Vocabulary

dominion (də min′ yən) *n.* control or the exercise of control; p. 720 *Gandhi spearheaded a movement to put an end to England's dominion over India.*

bleak (blēk) *adj.* cold; harsh; raw; p. 721 *The bleak wind howled through the chinks in the doors and window frames.*

foresight (fôr′ sīt′) *n.* preparation or concern for the future; p. 721 *His grandfather's foresight in saving money helped pay for Randall's education.*

Vocabulary Tip: Synonyms Words that have the same or nearly the same meaning are called synonyms. For example, the words *eradicate* and *eliminate* are synonyms.

OBJECTIVES
In studying these selections, you will focus on the following:
- relating literature to the historical period
- analyzing dialect
- monitoring comprehension

Droving the Hills, 1891. Joseph Denovan Adam. Oil on canvas, 30 x 50 in. Sotheby's Picture Library, London.

John Anderson, My Jo

Robert Burns

John Anderson, my jo,[1] John,
  When we were first acquent,
Your locks[2] were like the raven,
  Your bonnie brow was brent;[3]
5 But now your brow is beld,[4] John,
  Your locks are like the snow,
But blessings on your frosty pow,[5]
  John Anderson, my jo!

John Anderson, my jo, John,
10   We clamb the hill thegither,
And mony a canty[6] day, John,
  We've had wi' ane anither;
Now we maun[7] totter down, John,
  And hand in hand we'll go,
15 And sleep thegither at the foot,
  John Anderson, my jo!

1. *"Jo"* is an altered form of *joy,* here meaning "dear" or "sweetheart."
2. *Locks* are hair.
3. *Brent* means "smooth" or "unwrinkled."
4. *Beld* means "bald."
5. *Pow* means "head."
6. *Canty* means "cheerful."
7. *Maun* means "must."

Reading Strategy Monitoring Comprehension *The word* but *in line 5 signals a contrast. How do the second four lines in this stanza contrast with the first four?*

To a Mouse

Robert Burns

Town Mouse and Country Mouse, from *Aesop's Fables.*
Edward Julius Detmold (1883–1957). Private collection.

*On Turning Her Up in Her Nest
with the Plow, November, 1785*

Wee, sleekit,° cow'rin', tim'rous beastie,
O, what a panic's in thy breastie!
Thou need na start awa sae hasty
    Wi' bickering brattle!°
5 I wad be laith° to rin an' chase thee
    Wi' murd'ring pattle!°

I'm truly sorry man's **dominion**
Has broken Nature's social union
An' justifies that ill opinion
10   Which makes thee startle
At me, thy poor, earthborn companion
    An' fellow mortal!

1 sleekit: sleek

4 bickering brattle: the sudden sounds of a scamper
5 wad be laith: would be loath, or reluctant
6 pattle: plowstaff, small paddle or spade with a long handle, used to clean a plow

---

Literary Element Dialect *How would you restate this sentence in Standard English?*

Literary Element Dialect *Why do you think Burns mainly uses Standard English and not Scottish dialect in this stanza?*

Vocabulary

dominion (də min′ yən) *n.* control or the exercise of control

I doubt na, whiles,° but thou may thieve;
What then? poor beastie, thou maun° live!
15 A daimen-icker in a thrave°
    'S a sma' request:
I'll get a blessin' wi' the lave°
    An' never miss 't!

Thy wee-bit housie, too, in ruin!
20 Its silly wa's° the win's are strewin'!
An' naething, now, to big° a new ane
    O' foggage° green!
An' **bleak** December's winds ensuin',
    Baith snell° an' keen!

25 Thou saw the fields laid bare an' waste,
An' weary winter comin' fast,
An' cozie here, beneath the blast,
    Thou thought to dwell,
Till crash! the cruel coulter° past
30   Out through thy cell.

That wee bit heap o' leaves an' stibble°
Has cost thee mony a weary nibble!
Now thou's turned out, for a' thy trouble,
    But° house or hald,°
35 To thole° the winter's sleety dribble
    An' cranreuch° cauld!

But, Mousie, thou art no thy lane°
In proving **foresight** may be vain:
The best laid schemes o' mice an' men
40   Gang aft a-gley°
An' lea'e° us nought but grief an' pain
    For promised joy.

Still thou art blest, compared wi' me!
The present only toucheth thee:
45 But, och! I backward cast my e'e
    On prospects drear!
An' foward, tho' I canna see,
    I guess an' fear!

13	**whiles:** sometimes
14	**maun:** must
15	**daimen-icker in a thrave:** an occasional ear of corn in a bundle
17	**lave:** remainder
20	**silly wa's:** weak walls
21	**big:** build
22	**foggage:** moss
24	**snell:** bitter; severe
29	**coulter:** a plowshare, a blade attached to a plow
31	**stibble:** stubble
34	**But:** without; **hald:** an obsolete form of *hold,* meaning "shelter"
35	**thole:** endure
36	**cranreuch:** frost
37	**no thy lane:** not alone
40	**Gang aft a-gley:** go often awry; turn out badly
41	**lea'e:** leave

Reading Strategy Monitoring Comprehension *How would you paraphrase these lines?*

Vocabulary

bleak (blēk) *adj.* cold; harsh; raw
foresight (fôr´sīt´) *n.* preparation or concern for the future

Auld Lang Syne

Robert Burns

Should auld acquaintance be forgot,
    And never brought to min'?
Should auld acquaintance be forgot,
    And auld lang syne?[1]

5   For auld lang syne, my dear.
      For auld lang syne,
      We'll tak a cup o' kindness yet,
      For auld lang syne.

We twa hae run about the braes,[2]
10   And pu'd the gowans[3] fine;
But we've wander'd mony a weary foot
    Sin' auld lang syne.

We twa hae paidled i' the burn,[4]
    From morning sun till dine;
15   But seas between us braid hae roar'd[5]
    Sin' auld lang syne.

And there's a hand, my trusty fiere,[6]
    And gie's a hand o' thine;
And we'll tak a right guid-willie waught,[7]
20   For auld lang syne.

And surely ye'll be your pint-stowp,[8]
    And surely I'll be mine;
And we'll tak a cup o' kindness yet
    For auld lang syne.

1. *Auld lang syne* means "old long ago."
2. *Braes* are hills.
3. *Pu'd the gowans* means "pulled the daisies."
4. *Hae paidled i' the burn* means "have paddled in the stream."
5. *Braid hae roar'd* means "broad have roared."
6. *Fiere* means "friend."
7. *Tak a right guid-willie waught* means "take a good drink."
8. *Ye'll be your pint-stowp* means "you'll pay for your pint."

Big Idea **The Stirrings of Romanticism** *How does this stanza suggest the importance of human relationships and emotions?*

RESPONDING AND THINKING CRITICALLY

Respond

1. Which lines from the poems did you find most memorable? Why?

Recall and Interpret

2. (a)Summarize what the speaker says in the second stanza of "John Anderson, My Jo." (b)What does "the hill" **symbolize**, or represent? What does "sleep" represent?

3. (a)What has the speaker done to the mouse in "To a Mouse"? (b)What reasons does the speaker give for regretting what has happened?

4. (a)Whom does the speaker address in "Auld Lang Syne"? (b)What is the speaker's attitude toward friendship and old times?

Analyze and Evaluate

5. What does the second stanza in "To a Mouse" seem to suggest about the speaker's view of the relationship between nature and human beings? Explain.

6. (a)What lesson does the mouse's experience teach, according to the speaker? (b)What is **ironic**, or unexpected, about the ideas in the last stanza of the poem?

Connect

7. How good a friend would the speaker in "Auld Lang Syne" make? Support your answer.

8. **Big Idea** The Stirrings of Romanticism Why do you think Burns's poems appealed so much to Scottish peasants?

LITERARY ANALYSIS

Literary Element Dialect

Dialects may differ in pronunciation, grammar, vocabulary, and spelling from standard forms of language.

1. Use Standard English to reword several stanzas from the poems. Which version of each stanza do you prefer? Why?

2. Why do you think Burns chose to write his poems in his native dialect, Lowland Scots, rather than in Standard English?

Review: Rhyme Scheme

As you learned on page 266, **rhyme scheme** refers to the pattern that end rhymes form in a stanza or a poem. You indicate the rhyme scheme by assigning a different letter of the alphabet to each new rhyme.

Group Activity Meet with a small group to identify the rhyme scheme for the first stanza in each poem. Complete a chart like the one shown below:

"John Anderson, My Jo"

John	*a*
acquent	*b*
raven	
brent	
John	
snow	
pow	
jo	

Reading Strategy Monitoring Comprehension

Efficient readers **monitor their comprehension** by having mental conversations with themselves as they read. They notice when something does not make sense, and they apply strategies to aid comprehension, such as paraphrasing, that are appropriate to the work and their own learning style. Review the chart you created on page 718 and then answer the following questions:

1. How would you paraphrase lines 19–20 in "To a Mouse"?

2. How does paraphrasing specific lines and stanzas help you to understand them better?

Vocabulary Practice

Practice with Synonyms Find the synonym for each vocabulary word listed in the first column. Use a dictionary or a thesaurus if you need help.

1. dominion   **a.** protection   **b.** rule

2. bleak   **a.** oppressive   **b.** radiant

3. foresight   **a.** recollection   **b.** prescience

Academic Vocabulary

Here are two words from the vocabulary list on page R82.

appreciate (ə prē′ shē āt′) *v.* to recognize the value of or be thankful for

eventual (i ven′ chōō əl) *adj.* happening at an unspecified time in the future; ultimate

Practice and Apply

1. How do the speakers in Burns's poems show that they **appreciate** the good things in life?

2. What **eventual** hardships does the speaker foresee for the mouse in "To a Mouse"?

Writing About Literature

Compare Theme and Tone The **theme** of a literary work is its most important or central idea, often expressed as a general statement about life. The **tone** is a reflection of the author's attitude toward the subject of a work of literature, conveyed through such elements as structure, figures of speech, and word choice. Write a brief essay comparing the theme and tone of each of these poems. As you develop your essay, discuss the following questions:

- What is the theme of each poem? Is the theme stated directly or revealed gradually through events, dialogue, or description?

- How would you describe the tone of each poem? Is it affectionate, protective, friendly, nostalgic, or something else?

Before you begin your first draft, complete a chart like the one below. Develop these ideas in your essay.

	Theme	Tone
"John Anderson, My Jo"		
"To a Mouse"		
"Auld Lang Syne"		

After you complete your draft, meet with a peer reviewer to evaluate each other's work and to suggest revisions. Then proofread and edit your draft for errors in spelling, grammar, and punctuation.

Internet Connection

With a partner, look on the Internet for information on Scottish dialects, such as Lowland Scots, identifying characteristic words, grammatical constructions, idioms, and pronunciations. When you have completed your research, create a visual to display your findings and use it in presenting an oral report to your classmates.

Literature Online Web Activities For eFlashcards, Selection Quick Checks, and other Web activities, go to www.glencoe.com.

from *A Vindication of the Rights of Woman*

MEET MARY WOLLSTONECRAFT

When Mary Wollstonecraft wrote *A Vindication of the Rights of Woman,* she became the mother of the feminist movement and launched a struggle that would continue for more than two centuries. Through her writing, Wollstonecraft exposed injustices, challenged a society dominated by white, upper-class males, and promoted social improvement.

Awakening to Social Injustice Wollstonecraft was born in London to a violent, alcoholic father who squandered the family's fortune. Her childhood was filled with anxiety and fear, and she quickly realized the subservient role of women: her mother was abused and submissive, and her brother was well educated, while she was not. Wollstonecraft resented her family and the inequalities that existed between the sexes.

Controversial Writer With limited opportunities to support herself and her family, Wollstonecraft tried the few professions available to middle-class women—governess, lady's companion, and educator. While a governess, Wollstonecraft wrote her first novel, *Mary, A Fiction.* The novel is a cultural critique of a patriarchal and aristocratic society. It was published by Joseph Johnson, who later hired Wollstonecraft to be a reviewer for his journal, *Analytical Review,* and introduced her to the political theorist William Godwin, whom Wollstonecraft later married.

At the *Analytical Review,* Wollstonecraft continued to write educational tracts, believing that through education women would become an integral part of society. She published her first controversial work, *A Vindication of the Rights of Men,* anonymously in 1790, and she continued her work on education and politics with the publication of *A Vindication of the Rights of Woman* in 1792. She called for a "revolution in female manners" and for a world in which women would not be limited to menial labor or relegated to the dependent roles of wife,

companion, or governess. Despite her radical determination "to loudly demand Justice for one half of the human race," the work was well received.

> "[I]t is a farce to call any being virtuous whose virtues do not result from the exercise of its own reason. This was Rousseau's opinion respecting men: I extend it to women."
>
> —Mary Wollstonecraft

A Troubled Life Although neither Wollstonecraft nor William Godwin believed in marriage, their bond was strong. However, their life together was cut short when Wollstonecraft died just eleven days after giving birth to her daughter Mary, who would become Mary Shelley, author of *Frankenstein.* Godwin was devastated by Wollstonecraft's death and decided to publish her unfinished novel, in which she documented "the misery and oppression, peculiar to women, that arise out of the partial laws and customs of society." Since then, her writings have been praised for their influence on the women's rights movement.

Mary Wollstonecraft was born in 1759 and died in 1797.

Literature Online **Author Search** For more about Mary Wollstonecraft, go to www.glencoe.com.

Connecting to the Essay

Although the fight for women's rights began centuries ago and the movement has made great strides, discrimination still exists. Wollstonecraft used her pen to voice her opinions. As you read her essay, consider whether gender equality is possible.

Building Background

The French Revolution broke out in 1789—an event that some people in England embraced and some denounced. British statesman and orator Edmund Burke published *Reflections on the Revolution in France,* defending the existing social order and aristocracy. Wollstonecraft attacked Burke's views in *A Vindication of the Rights of Men,* citing the widespread corruption and the social and economic inequality in England. In the essay, she mentioned the rights of women— a subject that would be developed in *A Vindication of the Rights of Woman* (a *vindication* is a justification or defense).

Setting Purposes for Reading

Big Idea The Stirrings of Romanticism

As you read, notice how Wollstonecraft challenges the values of her time and calls for change.

Literary Element Thesis

The **thesis** is the statement of the proposition to be proved in a nonfiction persuasive essay. A thesis may be stated directly or implied and is usually expressed toward the beginning of the essay. To persuade readers to accept the thesis, the writer must then present convincing evidence, which may include facts, reasons, and well-supported opinions.

• See Literary Terms Handbook, p. R18.

Literature Online Interactive Literary Elements Handbook To review or learn more about the literary elements, go to www.glencoe.com.

Reading Strategy Evaluating Argument

Argument is a type of writing in which logic and reason are used to persuade the reader. **Evaluating argument** means judging the argument and the credibility of the writer based on how well he or she establishes authority and supports the thesis with convincing evidence.

Reading Tip: Taking Notes Use a chart like the one below to record the reasoning behind Wollstonecraft's argument. Determine whether her reasons are credible.

Argument	Support	Credibility

Vocabulary

indignation (in′ dig nā′ shən) *n.* anger aroused by something unjust or mean; p. 727 *My indignation at our unfair treatment could not be appeased.*

rational (rash′ ən əl) *adj.* able to reason; sensible; p. 727 *Though she was angered by the idea, the woman remained rational as she expressed her point of view.*

faculty (fak′ əl tē) *n.* capacity of the mind; ability; aptitude; p. 729 *Kathleen possessed the faculty to solve difficult math problems.*

congenial (kən jēn′ ē əl) *adj.* compatible; agreeable; p. 730 *The congenial couple loved and respected each other.*

condescend (kon′ di send′) *v.* to lower oneself; p. 730 *She wouldn't condescend to cheating on the test.*

Vocabulary Tip: Connotation and Denotation The connotation of a word is its implied meaning or the idea that is associated with it. A word's literal meaning is its denotation.

OBJECTIVES
In studying this selection, you will focus on the following:
• analyzing literary periods
• identifying theses
• evaluating arguments

from
A Vindication
of the
Rights of Woman

Mary Wollstonecraft

from the Introduction

After considering the historic page and viewing the living world with anxious solicitude,[1] the most melancholy emotions of sorrowful **indignation** have depressed my spirits, and I have sighed when obliged to confess that either nature has made a great difference between man and man or that the civilization which has hitherto taken place in the world has been very partial. I have turned over various books written on the subject of education and patiently observed the conduct of parents and the management of schools, but what has been the result?—a profound conviction that the neglected education of my fellow creatures is the grand source of the misery I deplore and that women, in particular, are rendered weak and wretched by a variety of concurring causes, originating from one hasty conclusion. The conduct and manners of women, in fact, evidently prove that their minds are not in a healthy state, for like the flowers which are planted in too rich a soil, strength and usefulness are sacrificed to beauty, and the flaunting leaves, after having pleased a fastidious eye, fade, disregarded on the stalk, long before the season when they ought to have arrived at maturity. One cause of this barren blooming I attribute to a false system of education, gathered from the books written on this subject by men who, considering females rather as women than human creatures, have been more anxious to make them alluring mistresses than affectionate wives and **rational** mothers, and the understanding of the sex has been so bubbled[2] by this specious homage[3] that the civilized women of the present century, with a few exceptions, are only anxious to inspire love when they ought to cherish a nobler ambition and by their abilities and virtues exact respect. . . .

Yet, because I am a woman, I would not lead my readers to suppose that I mean violently to agitate[4] the contested question respecting the quality or inferiority of the sex, but as the subject lies in my way, and I cannot pass it over without subjecting the main tendency of my reasoning to misconstruction, I shall stop a moment to deliver, in a few words, my opinion. In the government of the physical world, it is observable that the female in point of strength is, in general,

---

1. *Solicitude* is care or concern.

---

2. Here, *bubbled* means "fooled" or "deceived."
3. *Specious homage* means "deceptively attractive honor or respect."
4. Wollstonecraft uses *agitate* to mean "discuss, debate, or push forward as a question to be settled."

inferior to the male. This is the law of nature, and it does not appear to be suspended or abrogated[5] in favor of woman. A degree of physical superiority cannot, therefore, be denied—and it is a noble prerogative! But not content with this natural preeminence,[6] men endeavor to sink us still lower merely to render us alluring objects for a moment, and women, intoxicated by the adoration which men, under the influence of their senses, pay them, do not seek to obtain a durable interest in their hearts or to become the friends of the fellow creatures who find amusement in their society.

I am aware of an obvious inference:[7] from every quarter have I heard exclamations against masculine women, but where are they to be found? If by this appellation[8] men mean to inveigh against their ardor[9] in hunting, shooting, and gaming, I shall most cordially join in the cry; but if it be against the imitation of manly virtues, or, more properly speaking, the attainment of those talents and virtues, the exercise of which ennobles the human character, and which raise females in the scale of animal being, when they are comprehensively termed mankind; all those who view them with a philosophic eye must, I should think, wish with me, that they may every day grow more and more masculine. . . .

My own sex, I hope, will excuse me if I treat them like rational creatures instead of flattering their *fascinating* graces and viewing them as if they were in a state of perpetual childhood, unable to stand alone. I earnestly wish to point out in what true dignity and human happiness consists—I wish to persuade women to endeavor to acquire strength, both of mind and body, and to con-

The Woman of Fashion, 1883–1885. James Jacques Joseph Tissot. Oil on canvas, 148.3 x 103 cm. Private collection.

Viewing the Art: What might Wollstonecraft think of the women pictured? Why?

vince them that the soft phrases, susceptibility of heart, delicacy of sentiment,[10] and refinement of taste are almost synonymous with epithets[11] of weakness and that those beings who are only the objects of pity and that kind of love which has been termed its sister will soon become objects of contempt. . . .

The education of women has, of late, been more attended to than formerly; yet they are still reckoned a frivolous sex and ridiculed or pitied by the writers who endeavor by satire or instruction to improve them. It is acknowledged that they spend many of the first years

---

5. *Abrogated* means "abolished."
6. Here, *superiority, prerogative,* and *preeminence* are synonymous.
7. An *inference* is a conclusion based on something known or assumed.
8. An *appellation* is a name or description; here, it refers to the word *masculine* in the previous sentence.
9. *Inveigh against their ardor* means "to speak vehemently against women's enthusiasm for."

---

10. *Sentiment* refers to emotion or feelings.
11. *Epithets* are descriptive words.

of their lives in acquiring a smattering of accomplishments; meanwhile, strength of body and mind are sacrificed to libertine[12] notions of beauty, to the desire of establishing themselves—the only way women can rise in the world—by marriage. And this desire making mere animals of them, when they marry, they act as such children may be expected to act: they dress; they paint, and nickname God's creatures. Surely these weak beings are only fit for a seraglio![13] Can they be expected to govern a family with judgment or take care of the poor babes whom they bring into the world?

If then it can be fairly deduced from the present conduct of the sex, from the prevalent fondness for pleasure which takes place of ambition and those nobler passions that open and enlarge the soul, that the instruction which women have hitherto received has only tended, with the constitution of civil society, to render them insignificant objects of desire—mere propagators[14] of fools!—if it can be proved that in aiming to accomplish them, without cultivating their understandings, they are taken out of their sphere of duties and made ridiculous and useless when the short-lived bloom of beauty is over, I presume that *rational* men will excuse me for endeavoring to persuade them to become more masculine and respectable.

Indeed, the word *masculine* is only a bugbear.[15] There is little reason to fear that women will acquire too much courage or fortitude, for their apparent inferiority with respect to bodily strength must render them, in some degree, dependent on men in the various relations of life, but why should it be increased by prejudices that give a sex to virtue and confound simple truths with sensual reveries? . . .[16]

12. *Libertine* means "morally unrestrained."
13. A *seraglio* (si ral´ yō) is a harem.
14. *Propagators* are those who produce offspring.
15. A *bugbear* is an object of needless fear.
16. *Reveries* are daydreams.

Literary Element   Thesis *Is this deduction merely a restatement of the thesis, or is it a further conclusion based on the reasons and evidence used to support the thesis? Explain.*

from Chapter 2

. . . Youth is the season for love in both sexes, but in those days of thoughtless enjoyment, provision should be made for the more important years of life when reflection takes place of sensation. But Rousseau,[17] and most of the male writers who have followed his steps, have warmly inculcated[18] that the whole tendency of female education ought to be directed to one point: to render them pleasing.

Let me reason with the supporters of this opinion who have any knowledge of human nature, do they imagine that marriage can eradicate[19] the habitude of life? The woman who has only been taught to please will soon find that her charms are oblique sunbeams and that they cannot have much effect on her husband's heart when they are seen every day, when the summer is passed and gone. Will she then have sufficient native energy to look into herself for comfort and cultivate her dormant[20] **faculties**? Or is it not more rational to expect that she will try to please other men, and in the emotions raised by the expectation of new conquests, endeavor to forget the mortification her love or pride has received? When the husband ceases to be a lover—and the time will inevitably come—her desire of pleasing will then grow languid[21] or become a spring of bitterness, and love, perhaps the most evanescent[22] of all passions, gives place to jealousy or vanity.

I now speak of women who are restrained by principle or prejudice. Such women, though they would shrink from an intrigue with real

17. *Rousseau* is Jean-Jacques Rousseau (1712–1778), a French philosopher who believed humanity is essentially good but is corrupted by society.
18. *Inculcated* means "taught" or "frequently repeated."
19. *Eradicate* means "get rid of."
20. *Dormant* means "in a state of rest or inactivity."
21. *Languid* means "faint" or "weak."
22. *Evanescent* means "likely to vanish."

Reading Strategy   Evaluating Argument *Why does Wollstonecraft refer to Rousseau? How does the reference help to develop her credibility and argument?*

Vocabulary

faculty (fak´ əl tē) *n.* capacity of the mind; ability; aptitude

abhorrence, yet, nevertheless, wish to be convinced by the homage of gallantry that they are cruelly neglected by their husbands, or days and weeks are spent in dreaming of the happiness enjoyed by **congenial** souls till their health is undermined and their spirits broken by discontent. How then can the great art of pleasing be such a necessary study? It is only useful to a mistress; the chaste wife and serious mother should only consider her power to please as the polish of her virtues, and the affection of her husband as one of the comforts that render her talk less difficult and her life happier. But whether she be loved or neglected, her first wish should be to make herself respectable and not to rely for all her happiness on a being subject to like infirmities with herself.

The worthy Dr. Gregory[23] fell into a similar error. I respect his heart but entirely disapprove of his celebrated legacy to his daughters. . . .

He actually recommends dissimulation[24] and advises an innocent girl to give the lie to her feelings and not dance with spirit, when gaiety of heart would make her feet eloquent without making her gestures immodest. In the name of truth and common sense, why should not one woman acknowledge that she can take more exercise than another or, in other words, that she has a sound constitution. And why, to damp innocent vivacity, is she darkly to be told that men will draw conclusions which she little thinks of? Let the libertine draw what inference he pleases, but I hope that no sensible mother will restrain the natural frankness of youth by instilling such indecent cautions. Out of the abundance of the heart, the mouth speaketh, and a wiser than Solomon[25] hath said that the heart should be made clean and not trivial

ceremonies observed, which it is not very difficult to fulfill with scrupulous exactness when vice reigns in the heart.

Women ought to endeavor to purify their heart, but can they do so when their uncultivated understandings make them entirely dependent on their senses for employment and amusement, when no noble pursuit sets them above the little vanities of the day or enables them to curb the wild emotions that agitate a reed over which every passing breeze has power? To gain the affections of a virtuous man, is affectation necessary? Nature has given woman a weaker frame than man, but to ensure her husband's affections, must a wife, who by the exercise of her mind and body whilst she was discharging the duties of a daughter, wife, and mother, has allowed her constitution to retain its natural strength, and her nerves a healthy tone, is she, I say, to **condescend** to use art and feign a sickly delicacy in order to secure her husband's affection? Weakness may excite tenderness and gratify the arrogant pride of man, but the lordly caresses of a protector will not gratify a noble mind that pants for, and deserves to be respected. Fondness is a poor substitute for friendship! . . .

If all the faculties of woman's mind are only to be cultivated as they respect her dependence on man; if, when a husband be obtained, she have arrived at her goal, and meanly proud, rests satisfied with such a paltry crown, let her grovel contentedly, scarcely raised by her employments above the animal kingdom; but, if, struggling for the prize of her high calling, she look beyond the present scene, let her cultivate her understanding without stopping to consider what character the husband may have whom she is destined to marry. Let her only determine, without being too anxious about present happiness, to acquire the qualities that ennoble a rational being, and a rough inelegant husband may shock her taste without destroying her peace of mind. She will not model her soul

---

23. *Dr. Gregory* is John Gregory (1724–1773), a Scottish physician who wrote the book *A Father's Legacy to His Daughters.*
24. *Dissimulation* is pretense.
25. *Solomon,* king of Israel during the tenth century B.C., was known for his wisdom.

Big Idea The Stirrings of Romanticism *How does this statement reflect Romanticism's criticism of traditional values?*

Vocabulary

congenial (kən jēn′ ē əl) *adj.* compatible; agreeable

Reading Strategy Evaluating Argument *Is this statement an effective refutation of the views of Rousseau and Dr. Gregory? Explain.*

Vocabulary

condescend (kon′ di send′) *v.* to lower oneself

Portrait of Helen Gow, c. 1901–1910. Alexander Mann. Oil on canvas. Private collection.

to suit the frailties of her companion, but to bear with them: his character may be a trial, but not an impediment to virtue. . . .

These may be termed Utopian[26] dreams. Thanks to that Being who impressed them on my soul and gave me sufficient strength of mind to dare to exert my own reason, till, becoming dependent only on him for the support of my virtue, I view with indignation the mistaken notions that enslave my sex.

I love man as my fellow; but his scepter, real or usurped, extends not to me, unless the reason of an individual demands my homage; and even then the submission is to reason, and not to man. In fact, the conduct of an accountable being must be regulated by the operations of its own reason, or on what foundation rests the throne of God?

It appears to me necessary to dwell on these obvious truths because females have been insulated, as it were, and while they have been stripped of the virtues that should clothe humanity, they have been decked with artificial graces that enable them to exercise a short-lived tyranny. Love, in their bosoms, taking place of every nobler passion, their sole ambition is to be fair, to raise emotion instead of inspiring respect; and this ignoble desire, like the servility in absolute monarchies, destroys all strength of character. Liberty is the mother of virtue, and if women be, by their very constitution, slaves, and not allowed to breathe the sharp invigorating air of freedom, they must ever languish like exotics[27] and be reckoned beautiful flaws in nature. ❧

---

26. *Utopian* means "impossibly ideal."

27. *Languish like exotics* means "to grow weak or droop like plants out of their natural environment."

Literary Element   Thesis   *What analogy is Wollstonecraft using here to support her thesis? In your opinion, is it a valid analogy? Explain.*

RESPONDING AND THINKING CRITICALLY

Respond

1. Do you think you would have found Wollstonecraft's arguments convincing if you had lived during the late eighteenth century? Explain.

Recall and Interpret

2. (a)In the introduction, what does Wollstonecraft say has resulted from women's neglected education? (b)What does she urge women to do? Why?

3. (a)What comparisons does Wollstonecraft make between women and children? (b)What do these comparisons reveal about women's status?

4. (a)What marital problems result when women are taught only to please men? (b)Why does Wollstonecraft think it is important for women to fully cultivate all their faculties?

5. (a)Summarize the ideas Wollstonecraft presents in the last paragraph. (b)What do you think she means by "Liberty is the mother of virtue"?

Analyze and Evaluate

6. (a)How would you describe Wollstonecraft's tone? (b)Is her tone likely to persuade readers to adopt her point of view? Explain.

7. In describing the relationship between men and women, Wollstonecraft says, "Fondness is a poor substitute for friendship!" Do you agree? Explain.

8. (a)What superiority does Wollstonecraft concede to men? (b)Why does she claim that this one difference does not make one sex worthier than the other? Does her admission of this difference weaken or strengthen her argument? Explain.

Connect

9. **Big Idea** The Stirrings of Romanticism (a)How does Wollstonecraft's essay challenge the values of British society during her time period? (b)How does her essay predict change?

DAILY LIFE AND CULTURE

Women's Roles in Society

Eighteenth-century British society was divided along class and gender lines. Women were not allowed to vote, own property, or receive an equal education. With few career options—teacher, seamstress, governess, or lady's companion—marriage was the primary goal for most upper-class women. Marriage was a legal and economic contract, and for most women it was the only means of social advancement. Most aristocratic women did not attend school but were taught by their governess to be docile, fashionable, moral, and marriageable. Their daily lessons might include reading Shakespearean sonnets, learning to sing and play the harpsichord, and refining their needlework. Their most important lessons focused on manners and morality.

Educational opportunities were determined by the station and rank a child was born into; therefore, lower-class girls were the least educated group in England. While some attended Christian charity schools, little time was spent on lessons. The girls spun, sewed, wove, and did farmwork in exchange for religious and moral instruction. When the girls were old enough for employment, they usually worked full-time as maids and seamstresses.

Group Activity Discuss these questions with your classmates.

1. Do you think Wollstonecraft was justified in writing A *Vindication of the Rights of Woman*? Explain.

2. How do women's roles differ today? How have these differences affected modern life?

Literary Element · Thesis

A well-crafted **thesis** alone is not enough to persuade readers. In order to be convincing, the writer must present compelling evidence, such as facts, statistics, examples, and expert opinions, to support the thesis.

1. What is the thesis of *A Vindication of the Rights of Woman*?

2. How does Wollstonecraft support her thesis? Give specific examples from the essay.

Review: Allusion

As you learned on page 520, an **allusion** is an indirect reference to a well-known person, place, or event from history, music, art, or another literary work. Discovering the meaning of an allusion can be essential to understanding a work of literature. In her essay, Wollstonecraft alludes to Sir Thomas More's book *Utopia.*

Partner Activity Work with a partner and use the Internet to research information on Thomas More's *Utopia.* Look up the meaning of the title, where the word originated, and how it is used today. Then determine why Wollstonecraft would say that her ideas "may be termed Utopian dreams."

Young Woman Sewing by Lamplight, 1825. Georg Friedrich Kersting. Oil on canvas, 40.3 x 34.2 cm. Private collection.

Reading Strategy · Evaluating Argument

In addition to establishing her credibility, Wollstonecraft builds her arguments logically so that the reader is led to the same conclusion she has reached. One type of reasoning she uses effectively is cause and effect.

1. (a) What makes Wollstonecraft qualified to write on the topic of women's rights? (b) How does she establish her credibility?

2. According to Wollstonecraft, what is the main cause of the "weak and wretched" state of women in late-eighteenth-century society?

Vocabulary · Practice

Practice with Connotation and Denotation
Read each sentence below and determine whether the boldfaced word has a positive, negative, or neutral connotation.

1. She debated her points in a logical, **rational** manner.
   a. positive   **b.** negative   **c.** neutral

2. Despite the rain, the bride and groom remained **congenial.**
   a. positive   **b.** negative   **c.** neutral

3. The professor was intelligent, but he tended to **condescend** toward his students.
   a. positive   **b.** negative   **c.** neutral

4. The old man retained his mental **faculties.**
   a. positive   **b.** negative   **c.** neutral

5. The man expressed his hostile **indignation** when asked to share his table in the restaurant.
   a. positive   **b.** negative   **c.** neutral

Academic Vocabulary

Here is a word from the vocabulary list on page R82.

prohibit (prō hib′ it) *v.* to forbid one from doing something

Practice and Apply
According to Wollstonecraft, what did men **prohibit** women from doing?

Writing About Literature

Analyze Thesis Wollstonecraft uses complex sentence structures and an elaborate style that may be difficult for modern readers to understand. In a few paragraphs, summarize the essay and paraphrase Wollstonecraft's thesis so readers today can easily grasp her ideas.

To help you organize your summary, write an outline of the main points in the selection. Be sure to include the main idea and supporting evidence for each of Wollstonecraft's arguments.

I. Paraphrase Thesis
  A.
  B.
II. Summary of Introduction
  A.
  B.
  C.
III. Summary of Chapter 2
  A.
  B.
  C.

After you complete your draft, meet with a peer reviewer to evaluate each other's work and to suggest revisions. Then proofread and edit your draft for errors in spelling, grammar, and punctuation.

Literary Criticism

Scholar Barbara Caine asserts that "Wollstonecraft made no attempt to deny sexual difference" but demanded that difference "cease to be seen and expressed in hierarchical terms." In a paragraph, explain Caine's distinction and show how her assertion is illustrated in Wollstonecraft's essay.

Wollstonecraft's Language and Style

Using Italics Writers use italics—letters that slant to the right—to distinguish certain words. Italics are most frequently used for the titles of works of literature or art, names of newspapers and magazines, foreign words and phrases that are not often used in English, and for words that represent themselves. Often Wollstonecraft uses italics for emphasis. By italicizing a word or phrase, she signals to the reader that the word or phrase is essential to her idea or point of view. Consider the effect of the italicized word *fascinating* in the passage below.

"My own sex, I hope, will excuse me if I treat them like rational creatures instead of flattering their *fascinating* graces and viewing them as if they were in a state of perpetual childhood, unable to stand alone."

Here, Wollstonecraft italicizes the word *fascinating* to emphasize her sarcastic attack against the hollow flattery men often use to treat women as children.

Activity Create a chart using the headings below to list more examples of Wollstonecraft's use of italics for emphasis and to analyze their effects.

Sentence with Italicized Word	Analysis of the Effect of Italicized Word

Revising Check

Italics Avoid overusing italics for emphasis when writing. If used sparingly, italics for emphasis can be effective. However, when they are overused, the emphasis is lost, and the italics become distracting. Show emphasis in other ways, such as varying your sentence structure and word choice. With a partner, go through your analysis of Wollstonecraft's thesis and note places where italics or other means of achieving emphasis could improve your essay.

Literature Online Web Activities For eFlashcards, Selection Quick Checks, and other Web activities, go to www.glencoe.com.

Vocabulary Workshop

Word Origins and Word Parts

Understanding Greek and Latin Roots, Prefixes, and Suffixes

"My own sex, I hope, will excuse me if I treat them like rational creatures instead of flattering their *fascinating* graces and viewing them as if they were in a state of perpetual childhood, unable to stand alone."

—Mary Wollstonecraft, from *A Vindication of the Rights of Woman*

Connecting to Literature Almost a third of the words in this sentence from *A Vindication of the Rights of Woman* are derived from Latin. Examples include *excuse* (from *excusare*, "to explain"), *rational* (from *ratio*, "reason"), *fascinating* (from *fascinum*, "witchcraft"), *viewing* (from *videre*, "to see"), and *perpetual* (from *perpetere*, "continual"). Many English words trace their origins to Latin or Greek, and becoming familiar with a few common word parts—**prefixes**, **suffixes**, and **roots**—can help you determine the meanings of unfamiliar words.

Prefixes and suffixes are word parts that are added to base words—words that can stand alone—or to roots. Prefixes are added at the beginning, and suffixes are placed at the end. Roots cannot stand alone and must have prefixes, suffixes, or both added. So, for example, the word *excuse* is made up of the Latin prefix *ex-* ("from") and the root *caus* ("cause"). Here are some common Greek and Latin prefixes, roots, suffixes, and their meanings:

Prefixes	Roots	Suffixes
auto- self, same	*bio* life	*-ate* cause to be
contra- against	*dic(t)* say	*-cide* killing
dis- opposite	*gen* birth, race	*-graph* writing
im- / in- not	*phono* sound	*-ible* inclined to, capable of
re- back, again	*scrib* write	*-ion* state, condition

Exercise

Using a dictionary and the chart above, find the origin of the word parts and the definition of each of the following words. Notice how the Greek or Latin word parts contribute to the English meaning.

1. phonograph
2. autobiography
3. genocide
4. contradiction
5. distensible

► **Vocabulary Terms**

A **prefix** is a word part that is added to the beginning of a root or base word to create a new meaning; a **suffix** is added to the end. Unlike a base word, a root cannot stand alone.

► **Test-Taking Tip**

When you find an unfamiliar word in a reading passage, break it into its word parts. Then think of words you know that are made up of the same word parts. Identifying familiar roots can be especially helpful.

► **Reading Handbook**

For more about word parts and word origins, see Reading Handbook, p. R20.

eFlashcards For eFlashcards and other vocabulary activities, go to www.glencoe.com.

OBJECTIVES
- Learn to recognize common Greek and Latin word parts.
- Use word parts to understand unfamiliar words.

Preview the Article

"Raising Their Voices" examines the rise of feminism and new opportunities for women in Arab countries.

1. Read the **subheads,** or the headlines between paragraphs. What clues do these subheads give you about the content of the article?

2. What do you already know about feminism? How can you apply your prior knowledge to the article?

Set a Purpose for Reading

Read to learn about the changing roles of women in the Middle East.

Reading Strategy

Identifying Problem and Solution
When you **identify problems and solutions** while reading, you examine issues the writer presents and evaluate how these issues might be resolved. As you read, think about the problems associated with gender inequality discussed in "Raising Their Voices." Then think about how Arab women are attempting to solve these problems. Use a chart like the one below to organize your thoughts.

Problem	Possible Solution
Half of Arab women still cannot read.	The number of women enrolled in schools is steadily rising.

OBJECTIVES
- Skim text for overall impression and particular information.
- Analyze problems and solutions within a text.
- Read and evaluate informational text.

TIME

Raising Their Voices

Savvy, optimistic and ambitious, a new generation of Arab women is speaking out, forging its own brand of feminism— and slowly reshaping Arab society.

By JEFF CHU

DOZENS OF MEN SCURRY AROUND A SUBURBAN CAIRO art gallery, carrying out the rapid-fire orders issued by a tall, imposing woman in black jeans and a cream cashmere sweater. "Everyone out of the way!" barks director Inas El Degheidi, scanning the set to make sure everything is in place for the next scene in *Women in Search of Freedom,* her film about the harsh lives of female migrant workers. Even in a cosmopolitan city like Cairo, most Arab men aren't used to being bossed around by a woman, but El Degheidi's confrontational style does not faze her crew; they "are used to my way by now," she says. So are audiences: The veteran Egyptian filmmaker is known for training her camera on problems that male-dominated Arab society tries to keep under wraps—marital infidelity and a legal system that's tougher on women accused of adultery than on men. "Issues need to be brought to the surface," the director says, "to create a healthy social dialogue."

Provocative? You bet. El Degheidi, 46, belongs to a rising generation of Arab women who are challenging the conservatism and sexism of the Middle East, where some 90% of the population is Muslim and females are rarely treated as equals. Across the region, these women are using their growing prominence to push for women's rights, and overcoming real obstacles in the process. In Jordan, Queen Rania is lobbying for a progressive agenda—and upsetting traditionalists. In the tiny oil-rich nation of Qatar, Sheika Mouza, the wife of the country's king, has become the architect of an educational expansion that's giving women new choices. And all over the Arab world, smart, ambitious, effective women in all fields—politics, business, arts, sports—are helping to claim a larger role for women in all walks of life.

HISTORY
EL Degheidi's films are informed by the "residue" of past discrimination.

Barry Iverson

Daring to Speak Out

El Degheidi is one of eight children from a conservative, middle-class family. She and her sisters "were restricted in all our comings and goings," she says. "This discrimination must have left some residue," including a deep curiosity about relations between men and women. But probing society's fault lines can be hazardous to one's health. Some of El Degheidi's films have earned her death threats from Islamic militants. "There are people now who want to hush any loud voice with a different opinion," El Degheidi says.

Especially if the voice belongs to a woman. In January 2004, Lubna Olayan, Saudi Arabia's best-known businesswoman, spoke before an audience of men and women at an economic forum without wearing a head scarf, leading Saudi Arabia's top cleric to condemn her "shameful behavior." The topic of her speech: pursuing change while preserving core values. "To progress," Olayan said, "we have no choice but to embrace change." Throughout the Arab world, legions of young women are doing just that, studying at universities (more than half of undergraduates in Kuwait, Saudi Arabia, and Qatar are female), and preparing for a society in which it's normal for women to be called "doctor" or "entrepreneur" in addition to—and sometimes instead of—"wife" and "mother." But they don't see change as an abandonment of duty. Rather, it means choice. The right to choose, say, whether to wear a veil in public is as much a part of a woman's emancipation as the right to vote. The veil is no barrier to hijab-wearing leaders like Sheika Mouza; not wearing one is likewise no obstacle to Queen Rania.

HEAD-ON Moukalled, who tackles topics such as Afghan refugees, says many Arabs "don't want to face problems that need to be dealt with."

Ayman Mroueh

One sign of change is the growing public role being taken by the wives of Arab leaders. (No Arab country is ruled by a woman.) The steps may seem small, but in these conservative cultures, they are important. In 2002, when Bahrain held its first election in over 25 years, Sheika Sabeeka, the King's wife, led a campaign to encourage women to vote. When Morocco's King Mohammed VI wed Salma Bennani that year, he gave her the title "Princess." Before that, spouses of Morocco's kings had rarely been seen, let alone honored with titles. And the King has also spoken out on women's rights. Syrian President Bashar Assad's wife, Asma, travels with her husband and promotes the cause of microfinance—small loans for entrepreneurial women who would otherwise be unable to obtain credit. Her mother-in-law made just a handful of appearances during the 30-year rule of the current President's father, Hafez.

Women in Government

Women are also a growing presence in the official ranks of government. In 2003, after the people of Qatar approved a constitution giving women the right to vote and run for office, the Persian Gulf state got its first female Cabinet member. Tunisia's Cabinet has six women; Jordan's has three. But "patriarchy is still there," says Jordan's Asma Khader, a women's-rights activist and high government official. Women hold less than 6% of the region's parliamentary seats (the global average is nearly 16%). The United Arab Emirates and Kuwait bar women from voting or running for parliament. Morocco has the highest rate of female representation—women hold 35 of the 325 seats in the Chamber of Representatives—and reserves 30 seats for women. That the half-female electorate only voted five

SELF-ESTEEM Yassine urges women to be "more positive and proactive."

Etienne Boyer/SIPA

women into at-large seats shows how hard it is to crack a male-run system. "Women in the Arab world are still operating in male-dominated societies with stale traditions," says Haifa al Kaylani. She is the founder of the Arab International Women's Forum, a networking group. Says Khader:

"Women's [political] participation and equal rights are still not accepted by some extremist groups and religious interpretations."

Some governments have defied such dissenters, expanding women's legal rights. Egyptian President Hosni Mubarak, for example, has ruled that children born to Egyptian mothers would be considered Egyptian; previously, only fathers passed on citizenship. Moroccan lawmakers have approved King Mohammed VI's reforms of the country's personal-status code. Women were given the right to ask for divorce, the minimum marriage age for girls rose from 15 to 18, and polygamy was strictly limited.

Education: "The Bones of the Body"

Morocco's Nadia Yassine is a mother of four, grandmother of one, and the daughter of fundamentalist leader Sheik Abdel-Salam Yassine. As spokeswoman for his Justice and Charity Party, she is perhaps the most visible fundamentalist feminist in the Arab world.

Her hair tucked under a tight head scarf and her body cloaked in a flowing robe, Yassine, 45, hardly fits the West's image of a feminist—but neither she nor her more liberal counterparts claim to be Western-style feminists. "I adapted my feminism from Islam, not Western culture," she says. Her inspiration comes partly from Islam's history. Muhammad was "a true feminist," she says. His favorite wife, Aisha, a revered Islamic-law expert, led an

army into battle. Discrimination "is a homegrown malady," Yassine says. "We can find solutions derived from our own culture, our own value system."

Perhaps the most potent solution is education. "We have to unveil the Arab woman's mind," says Egyptian activist Nawal El Saadawi. Though half of Arab women still cannot read and 4 million girls are not in school, education rates have risen rapidly across the region. In Bahrain, Jordan, Lebanon, the United Arab Emirates, and the Palestinian territories, enrollment rates for girls and boys are equal among primary-school-age children. In a 2003 values survey, Saudi women ranked learning third, behind only faith and family in importance. In Qatar, where Sheika Mouza, the second of the ruler's three wives, has led a drive to build a world-class educational system, including branches of Cornell University's medical school and Texas A&M's petrochemical college, more than 70% of undergrads are women.

In Kuwait, the numbers are about the same—and girls' desire to perform is so strong that "if we left admission to grades, we would have almost 100% girls," says Fayzah al-Kharafi, a chemistry professor at Kuwait University. Al-Kharafi, 57, knows how education can break down barriers. A trailblazer in Arab higher education, she has racked up impressive firsts at K.U.—first woman to get a scientific Ph.D. there; first female science professor; and, in 1993, first woman to lead

"The lives of Arab women are still not what they should be."

—DIANA MOUKALLED, editor, Future TV international news

ROYAL PREROGATIVE Mouza has used her power to transform education in Qatar.

Barry Iverson

an Arab-world university when she was named president. She gave up that job in 2002 because she missed the classroom, where she says she can have a bigger role in pushing students to pursue academic excellence. "Education is the bones of the body," she says. "We cannot live without it. It gives more opportunities. Women are prepared for all jobs in society."

But once they have diplomas, can they get those jobs? In Saudi Arabia, women make up 55% of undergraduates, but only 15% of the labor force. Those who venture beyond traditional working-women's sectors like health care and education are greeted by male skepticism. Architect Nadia Bakhurji recalls how hard it was to win funding for her Riyadh firm. Men doubted her trustworthiness, purely due to her gender. "One man said, 'Don't you have a husband? A male figure we can deal with? Between you and me, what if we don't get our money back?'" she says. "They don't have as much faith in you because you're a woman." She pressed on, thinking of her mother, who wed at 14 and

never realized her dream of entering politics. "The best she could do was to concentrate on her children," Bakhurji says. "She boosted me. She told me, 'You're a star.'" Her persistence paid off in 1996, when she won the backing of billionaire investor Prince Alwaleed bin Talal bin Abdulaziz al Saud. His willingness to bet on a business-woman shows an openness that Bakhurji, 36, hopes will soon be the norm. Her generation "will have a knock-on effect" on her son's, she says. "The next generation is going to be far more accustomed to seeing their mothers as work-oriented and high achievers."

Getting the Message Out

Role models matter, agrees Nawal El Moutawakel, who was the only woman on Morocco's Olympic team in 1984, when she won the 400-meter hurdles and became the first Arab woman to strike Games gold. Now an International Olympic Committee member, she notes that "it's becoming something very usual" for Arab women to have a medal-winning presence in the male-dominated sports world.

El Moutawakel, 41, says her success—and that of athletes who have followed her—has opened doors and minds even for those who will never set foot on an Olympic track. She points to the Run for Fun, a 10-km race she organizes in Casablanca each May, as one symbol of the larger public space now becoming available to women. In 2003, 12,000 women—"all sizes, all ages, all dress codes, Olympic champions, members of parliament, grandmothers"—took part. "We don't exclude men; they come to help," says El Moutawakel, laughing. "But I want to push for women to understand the importance of participation."

It's not always easy to get that message to the ordinary citizen, especially when women have not had a real voice in society for so many generations. Says Assilah al-Harthy, the first female executive with Oman's national oil firm: "We need to teach people that they can speak out, that they have a choice. People may not understand the first time or the second time, but they will start asking, 'Why, where, when?'"

It helps if they hear others speaking out. The Arab media—more influential than ever, due in part to the growing use of satellite dishes, jokingly called the national flower in several countries—has broadened debate through the work of journalists such as Diana Moukalled. She is the editor of Lebanon-based Future TV's international news, and the Arab world's only female roving reporter. "The media has a great role to play in putting the spotlight on issues, providing a platform for women, and educating people," says Moukalled, 33, producer of about 30 hour-long documentaries. Her work is sometimes shelved; pro-Saddam Hussein sentiments in the region killed a show about Iraq's Kurds, made before the Iraq war started in 2003. "We all know there is censorship," she says. "But so many have made it on air, stirring discussions about important issues."

That women are viewing, reading, and talking is itself progress. "The lives of Arab women are still not what they should be," Moukalled says, "[but] things are moving forward." Calls for change are getting louder. In January 2004, 300 Saudi women signed a petition to Saudi Arabia's Crown Prince demanding reform, including more women in government and the relaxation of restrictions on their daily lives. Though the petition was mostly ignored by the country's rulers, the petition was a big step.

The changes may not be fast or radical by Western standards. But the women of the Arab world respond: We are not in the West. "We've always heard from the West, 'Broaden your horizons!' And we have," says Sheika Hanadi al-Thani, who heads an investment company for women in Qatar. "Now it's time for us to tell the West, 'You think outside your box.' Be patient, be more understanding of the context." "We are moving in the right direction," says al-Harthy. "But we can't go too fast. Change is not easy to take."

It's easier when many move together—a theme in El Degheidi's film. *Women in Search of Freedom* focuses on three women from different Arab lands who find themselves in a foreign country and seek strength from each other. The journey of today's Arab women is much the same. Some may be conservative, others more liberal, but as they progress, venturing into territory that's foreign to many in their society, they'll need unity to succeed. El Degheidi, for one, is sure who will succeed. "Don't be afraid to break barriers," she says to her Arab sisters. "You will be the winner in the end."

—Updated 2005, from TIME International, February 23, 2004

RESPONDING AND THINKING CRITICALLY

Respond

1. How did you respond to the differences in gender equality in Arab society?

Recall and Interpret

2. (a)What problems in Arab society does filmmaker Inas El Degheidi attempt to bring out into the open? (b)What is different about the new generation of Arab women?

3. (a)What response has El Degheidi's work received? (b)What does this imply about the attitude that some people in Arab societies have toward feminists and women's issues?

4. (a)What is one example of an Arab leader's wife's attempt to influence change in society and politics? (b)Name three male Arab leaders mentioned in the article who are sympathetic to women's rights. What have they done to improve the status of women?

Analyze and Evaluate

5. (a)Why does Nadia Yassine say her feminism is "from Islam, not Western culture"? (b)How might Islamic feminism differ from Western feminism?

6. (a)What is the ratio of women undergraduates to women in the labor force in Saudi Arabia? (b)What might account for this discrepancy?

7. (a)How has journalist Diana Moukalled used the media to call attention to the fight for women's rights? (b)How does censorship affect her work?

Connect

8. How does the role of women in late-eighteenth-century English society compare with the role of women in Arab societies today?

from *The Diary of Fanny Burney*

MEET FANNY BURNEY

"To have some account of my thoughts, manners, acquaintances, and actions, when the hour arrives at which time is more nimble than memory, is the reason which induces me to keep a Journal—a Journal in which, I must confess, my *every* thought must open my whole heart." Fanny Burney began keeping a diary at age fifteen and continued writing in it for seventeen years, documenting her "wonderful, surprising, and interesting adventures . . . hopes, fears, reflections, and dislikes."

A Young Talent Burney was born in 1752 and moved to London when she was eight. Two years later her mother died, leaving her distraught and in perpetual need of her father's love and approval. She found comfort in her family, friends, and books. Though Burney claims she was "unable to read at the age of eight," she began writing when she was ten, and by her mid-teens had completed her first novel, *The Adventures of Caroline Evelyn*. However, Burney burned all her manuscripts on her fifteenth birthday in obedience to her father, who felt that being "a scribbler" was too frivolous for her.

> *"To a heart formed for friendship and affection the charms of solitude are very shortlived."*
>
> —Fanny Burney

A Secret Author Though she destroyed her manuscripts, Burney didn't stop writing. In 1778 she secretly published *Evelina*, the sequel to her first novel. Praised for its lively social observations, the book's central theme focused on women's roles in society. As she did in later works, Burney satirized class structure, the struggle for power, and the abuse of wealth.

For six months readers raved about the book while trying to guess the identity of the author. When they eventually discovered that Burney was the author, her life changed forever. Burney soon became a popular guest of literary groups, and her proud father introduced her to several members of London's upper class, including Dr. Samuel Johnson. Despite her success, Burney remained shy.

Court Life In 1782 Burney published *Cecilia*. Though she was praised by critics, she made little money, and at thirty, her family thought of her as a spinster with no secure future. In 1786 Burney reluctantly accepted a position in the court of Queen Charlotte. While at court, she documented King George's madness and court happenings in her diaries and letters, marking her place as an important historian. However, she grew increasingly depressed. Burney was released from service five years later after growing ill, and in 1793 she married Alexandre Jean-Baptiste Piochard d'Arblay—a French Catholic—with the begrudging consent of her father. Their son Alexander was born a year later. In 1810 Burney was diagnosed with breast cancer, and determined to live, underwent a mastectomy. Her last novel, *The Wanderer; or Female Difficulties*, was published in 1812.

Burney died in 1840, and she willed her manuscripts to her niece Charlotte Barrett, who later published Burney's *Diaries and Letters*. The publication renewed interest in Burney, and she is now regarded as an important historian and novelist who did much to further women's fiction writing.

Fanny Burney was born in 1752 and died in 1840.

Literature Online **Author Search** For more about Fanny Burney, go to www.glencoe.com.

Connecting to the Diary

In the following diary entries, Burney expresses her excitement about the success of her book and the speculation about its authorship. When her secret is discovered, she claims it is her most important day. What event has changed your life? How would you write about it?

Building Background

In 1740, twelve years before Burney was born, Samuel Richardson published what many consider to be the first English novel, *Pamela*. This **epistolary novel**—or novel told through letters—about a virtuous teenage servant girl was an overnight success praised by everyone from ministers to respected literary figures such as Alexander Pope. Consequently, Burney had reason to feel pleased and excited when early reviews of *Evelina*—also an epistolary novel about a virtuous young girl—compared it favorably with *Pamela*.

Setting Purposes for Reading

Big Idea The Stirrings of Romanticism

As you read, look for hints that Burney and the people she describes are coming to value individuals over society and to prefer feelings and imagination to reason.

Literary Element Wit

Today, **wit** is the exhibition of cleverness and humor in writing. In the sixteenth and seventeenth centuries, people considered wit the expression of truth in a surprising way, such as by pointing out a meaningful resemblance between seemingly dissimilar things. While reading Burney's diary entries, look for ways she uses wit in her descriptions of events and people.

• See Literary Terms Handbook, p. R19.

Literature Online **Interactive Literary Elements Handbook** To review or learn more about the literary elements, go to www.glencoe.com.

Reading Strategy Analyzing Cultural Context

After it was discovered that Burney wrote *Evelina*, she was invited to several meetings and dinners and met many literary figures and important families. As you read Burney's diary entries, look for references to other literary figures and conversations about books and the arts.

Reading Tip: Taking Notes Use a chart to record Burney's descriptions of her role as an author, her meetings with other literary figures, and her conversations about the arts. Note what these descriptions reveal about society and the times.

Literary Figures	Conversations	Role as Author	My Understanding of Society

Vocabulary

profound (prə found′) *adj.* characterized by deep understanding or insight; p. 744 *Her profound statement about life stunned us all.*

zenith (zē′ nith) *n.* a peak; the greatest point; p. 744 *The zenith of her career was the day her first novel was published.*

sanguine (sang′ gwin) *adj.* confident; optimistic; p. 746 *She was not sanguine about the success of her play.*

droll (drōl) *adj.* amusingly odd; p. 746 *He was a droll character and always amused us.*

confound (kən found′) *v.* to confuse; to bewilder; p. 748 *I am confounded by society's attitude toward women.*

Vocabulary Tip: Word Parts The definitions of word parts can often help you determine the meaning of unfamiliar words.

OBJECTIVES
In studying this selection, you will focus on the following:
• analyzing literary periods
• understanding and analyzing wit
• analyzing cultural context

from
The Diary of
Fanny Burney

Fanny Burney

On the Dunes (Lady Shannon and Kitty), 1900–1910.
Sir James Jebusa Shannon. Oil on canvas, 73 3/8 x 56 3/8 in.
Smithsonian American Art Museum, Washington, DC.

JANUARY, 1778. This year was ushered in by a grand and most important event! At the latter end of January, the literary world was favored with the first publication of the ingenious, learned, and most **profound** Fanny Burney! I doubt not but this memorable affair will, in future times, mark the period whence chronologers will date the **zenith** of the polite arts in this island!

This admirable authoress has named her most elaborate performance *Evelina; or, a Young Lady's Entrance into the World.*

Perhaps this may seem a rather bold attempt and title for a female whose knowledge of the world is very confined and whose inclinations, as well as situation, incline her to a private and domestic life. All I can urge is that I have only presumed to trace the accidents and adventures to which a "young woman" is liable; I have not pretended to show the world what it actually *is,* but what it *appears* to a girl of seventeen, and so far as that, surely any girl who is past seventeen may safely do?

My little book, I am told, is now at all the circulating libraries. I have an exceeding odd sensation when I consider that it is now in the power of *any* and *every* body to read what I so carefully hoarded even from my best friends, till this last month or two, and that a work which was so lately lodged, in all privacy, in my bureau, may now be seen by every butcher and baker, cobbler and tinker, throughout the three kingdoms, for the small tribute of a threepence.

Literary Element Wit *How is Burney using wit in this sentence?*

Vocabulary

profound (prə found′) *adj.* characterized by deep understanding or insight

zenith (zē′ nith) *n.* a peak; the greatest point

Big Idea The Stirrings of Romanticism *What social values is Burney reflecting?*

My aunt and Miss Humphries[1] being settled at this time at Brompton,[2] I was going thither with Susan to tea, when Charlotte[3] acquainted me that they were then employed in reading *Evelina* to the invalid, my cousin Richard.

This intelligence gave me the utmost uneasiness—I foresaw a thousand dangers of a discovery—I dreaded the indiscreet warmth of all my confidants. In truth, I was quite sick with apprehension and was too uncomfortable to go to Brompton, and Susan carried my excuses.

Upon her return, I was somewhat tranquilized, for she assured me that there was not the smallest suspicion of the author and that they had concluded it to be the work of a *man!*

Finding myself more safe than I had apprehended, I ventured to go to Brompton next day. On my way upstairs, I heard Miss Humphries in the midst of Mr. Villars's letter of consolation upon Sir John Belmont's rejection of his daughter;[4] and just as I entered the room, she cried out, "How pretty that is!"

How much in luck would she have thought herself had she known *who* heard her!

In a private confabulation[5] which I had with my Aunt Anne, she told me a thousand things that had been said in its praise and assured me that they had not for a moment doubted that the work was a *man's*.

I must own I suffered great difficulty in refraining from laughing upon several occasions—and several times, when they praised what they read, I was on the point of saying, "You are very good!" and so forth, and I could scarcely keep myself from making acknowledgments and bowing my head involuntarily. However, I got off perfectly safe.

It seems, to my utter amazement, Miss Humphries has guessed the author to be Anstey, who wrote the *Bath Guide!*[6] How improbable and how extraordinary a supposition! But they have both of them done it so much honor that, but for Richard's anger at Evelina's bashfulness, I never could believe they did not suspect me.

CHESINGTON,[7] JUNE 18.   Here I am, and here I have been this age, though too weak[8] to think of journalizing; however, as I never had so many curious anecdotes to record, I will not, at least this year, the first of my appearing in public, give up my favorite old hobbyhorse.[9]

I came hither the first week in May. My recovery, from that time to this, has been slow and sure; but as I could walk hardly three yards in a day at first, I found so much time to spare that I could not resist treating myself with a little private sport with *Evelina*, a young lady whom I think I have some right to make free with. I had promised Hetty[10] that *she* should read it to Mr. Crisp, at her own particular request; but I wrote my excuses and introduced it myself.

I told him it was a book which Hetty had taken to Brompton to divert my cousin Richard during his confinement. He was so indifferent about it that I thought he would not give himself the trouble to read it and often embarrassed me by unlucky questions, such as, "If it was reckoned clever?" and "What I thought of it?" and "Whether folks laughed at it?" I always evaded any direct or satisfactory answer; but he was so totally free from any idea of suspicion that my perplexity escaped his notice.

At length, he desired me to begin reading to him. I dared not trust my voice with the little introductory ode,[11] for as *that* is no romance, but the sincere effusion[12] of my heart, I could as soon read aloud my own letters, written in my own name and character. I therefore skipped it

---

1. *Miss Humphries* was a housekeeper and friend to Burney's cousin Richard's family.
2. Burney's great-aunts lived in the countrified district of *Brompton*.
3. *Susan* and *Charlotte* were Burney's younger sisters.
4. [*Mr. Villars's letter . . . his daughter*] refers to a scene in *Evelina*.
5. Here, a *confabulation* refers to a conversation or chat.
6. *Anstey* is Christopher Anstey (1724–1805), a poet whose novel, *The New Bath Guide,* was written in verse and satirized life in Bath.

Reading Strategy   Analyzing Cultural Context
Why does everyone seem to think a man wrote Evelina?

7. The Burneys were frequent visitors to *Chesington* Hall, the home of family friend Samuel Crisp.
8. Burney was *weak* because she had been ill and had been sent to Chesington to recuperate.
9. Burney uses *hobbyhorse* to mean "pastime."
10. *Hetty* was Burney's older sister.
11. An *ode* is a lyric poem that is serious or lofty in subject, feeling, and style.
12. An *effusion* is an outpouring.

Reading Strategy   Analyzing Cultural Context
Why does Crisp ask Burney such questions? What do the questions reveal about the culture of the time?

and have so kept the book out of his sight that, to this day, he knows not it is there. Indeed, I have since heartily repented that I read *any* of the book to him, for I found it a much more awkward thing than I had expected. My voice quite faltered when I began it, which, however, I passed off for the effect of remaining weakness of lungs, and, in short, from an invincible embarrassment, which I could not for a page together repress, the book, by my reading, lost all manner of spirit.

Nevertheless, though he has by no means treated it with the praise so lavishly bestowed upon it from other quarters, I had the satisfaction to observe that he was even greedily eager to go on with it, so that I flatter myself the *story* caught his attention; and, indeed, allowing for my *mauling*[13] reading, he gave it quite as much credit as I had any reason to expect. But now that I was sensible of my error in being my own mistress of the ceremonies, I determined to leave to Hetty the third volume and therefore pretended I had not brought it. He was in a delightful ill humor about it, and I enjoyed his impatience far more than I should have done his forbearance. Hetty, therefore, when she comes, has undertaken to bring it.

Well, I cannot but rejoice that I published the book, little as I ever imagined how it would fare; for hitherto it has occasioned me no small diversion, and *nothing* of the disagreeable sort. But I often think a change *will* happen, for I am by no means so **sanguine** as to suppose such success will be uninterrupted. Indeed, in the midst of the greatest satisfaction that I feel, an inward *something* which I cannot account for

> "*I flatter myself the story caught his attention; and, indeed, allowing for my mauling reading, he gave it quite as much credit as I had any reason to expect.*"

prepares me to expect a reverse; for the more the book is drawn into notice, the more exposed it becomes to criticism and remark.

JULY 25.   Mrs. Cholmondeley[14] has been reading and praising *Evelina*, and my father is quite delighted at her approbation[15] and told Susan that I could not have had a greater compliment than making two such women my friends as Mrs. Thrale[16] and Mrs. Cholmondeley, for they were severe and knowing and afraid of praising *à tort et à travers*,[17] as their opinions are liable to be quoted.

Mrs. Thrale said she had only to complain it was too short. She recommended it to my mother to read!—how **droll**!—and she told her she would be much entertained with it, for there was a great deal of human life in it, and of the manners of the present times, and added that it was written "by somebody who knows the top and the bottom, the highest and the lowest of mankind." She has even lent her set to my mother, who brought it home with her!

AUGUST 3.   I now come to last Saturday evening when my beloved father came to Chesington, in full health, charming spirits, and all kindness, openness, and entertainment.

---

13. *Mauling* means "rough" or "mangled."

14. *Mrs. Cholmondeley* (chum′ lē) was a hostess who had influence in fashionable society.
15. *Approbation* is approval or praise.
16. *Mrs. Thrale* is Hester Thrale, a prominent society hostess and the wife of Henry Thrale, a wealthy member of Parliament.
17. The French phrase *à tort et à travers* (à tôr′ ā ä trä vāər′) means "at random" or "haphazardly."

Reading Strategy   Analyzing Cultural Context
What does Mrs. Thrale value about Evelina?

Vocabulary

sanguine (sang′ gwin) *adj*. confident; optimistic

Vocabulary

droll (drōl) *adj*. amusingly odd

In his way hither, he had stopped at Streatham,[18] and he settled with Mrs. Thrale that he would call on her again in his way to town and carry me with him! And Mrs. Thrale said, "We all long to know her."

I have been in a kind of twitter ever since, for there seems something very formidable in the idea of appearing as an authoress! I ever dreaded it, as it is a title which must raise more expectations than I have any chance of answering. Yet I am highly flattered by her invitation and highly delighted in the prospect of being introduced to the Streatham society.

My dear father communicated this intelligence, and a great deal more, with a pleasure that almost surpassed that with which I heard it, and he seems quite eager for me to make another attempt. He desired to take upon himself the communication to my Daddy Crisp,[19] and as it is now in so many hands that it is possible accident might discover it to him, I readily consented.

Sunday evening, as I was going into my father's room, I heard him say, "The variety of characters—the variety of scenes—and the language—why she has had very little education but what she has given herself—less than any of the others!" and Mr. Crisp exclaimed, "Wonderful!—it's wonderful!"

I now found what was going forward and therefore deemed it most fitting to decamp.[20]

About an hour after, as I was passing through the hall, I met my daddy [Crisp]. His face was all animation and archness; he doubled his fist at me and would have stopped me, but I ran past him into the parlor.

Before supper, however, I again met him, and he would not suffer me to escape; he caught both my hands, and looked as if he would have looked me through, and then exclaimed, "Why, you little hussy—you young devil!—aren't you ashamed to look me in the face, you *Evelina,* you! Why, what a dance have you led me about it! Young friend, indeed! Oh, you little hussy, what tricks have you served me!"

---

18. *Streatham* was the site of Mr. and Mrs. Thrale's country house.
19. *Daddy Crisp* was Burney's nickname for Samuel Crisp.
20. *Decamp* means "to leave suddenly."

Reading Strategy Analyzing Cultural Context
Why would Mrs. Thrale say everyone longed to meet Burney?

LONDON, AUGUST. I have now to write an account of the most consequential day I have spent since my birth, namely, my Streatham visit.

Our journey to Streatham was the least pleasant part of the day, for the roads were dreadfully dusty, and I was really in the fidgets from thinking what my reception might be and from fearing they would expect a less awkward and backward kind of person than I was sure they would find.

Mr. Thrale's house is white and very pleasantly situated in a fine paddock.[21] Mrs. Thrale was strolling about and came to us as we got out of the chaise.

She then received me, taking both my hands, and with mixed politeness and cordiality[22] welcoming me to Streatham. She led me into the house and addressed herself almost wholly for a few minutes to my father, as if to give me an assurance she did not mean to regard me as a show or to distress or frighten me by drawing me out. Afterwards she took me upstairs and showed me the house and said she had very much wished to see me at Streatham and should always think herself much obliged to Dr. Burney for his goodness in bringing me, which she looked upon as a very great favor.

Visual Vocabulary
A *chaise* (shāz) is a light, open carriage used for pleasure or traveling

But though we were some time together and though she was so very civil, she did not *hint* at my book, and I love her much more than ever for her delicacy in avoiding a subject which she could not but see would have greatly embarrassed me.

When we returned to the music room, we found Miss Thrale was with my father. Miss Thrale is a very fine girl, about fourteen years of age, but cold and reserved, though full of knowledge and intelligence.

Soon after, Mrs. Thrale took me to the library; she talked a little while upon common topics, and then, at last, she mentioned *Evelina.*

---

21. A *paddock* is a small field or pasture.
22. *Cordiality* is friendliness or graciousness.

Literary Element Wit *In what clever way does Burney describe her feelings about her visit to Streatham?*

"Yesterday at supper," said she, "we talked it all over and discussed all your characters, but Dr. Johnson's[23] favorite is Mr. Smith. He declares the fine gentleman *manqué*[24] was never better drawn, and he acted him all the evening, saying, 'he was all for the ladies'! He repeated whole scenes by heart. I declare I was astonished at him. Oh, you can't imagine how much he is pleased with the book; he 'could not get rid of the rogue,' he told me. But was it not droll," said she, "that I should recommend to Dr. Burney and tease him so innocently to read it?"

I now prevailed upon Mrs. Thrale to let me amuse myself, and she went to dress. I then prowled about to choose some book, and I saw, upon the reading table, *Evelina*—I had just fixed upon a new translation of Cicero's *Laelius* when the library door was opened, and Mr. Seward[25] entered. I instantly put away my book because I dreaded being thought studious and affected. He offered his service to find anything for me and then, in the same breath, ran on to speak of the book with which I had myself "favored the world"!

The exact words he began with I cannot recollect, for I was actually **confounded** by the attack; and his abrupt manner of letting me know he was *au fait*[26] equally astonished and provoked me. How different from the delicacy of Mr. and Mrs. Thrale!

When we were summoned to dinner, Mrs. Thrale made my father and me sit on each side of her. I said that I hoped I did not take Dr. Johnson's place—for he had not yet appeared.

---

23. *Dr. Johnson* is Samuel Johnson (1709–1784), who wrote *A Dictionary of the English Language* and was one of the most highly respected literary figures of his time.
24. The French word *manqué* (man kā′) means "unfulfilled" or "frustrated in realizing one's ambitions or capabilities."
25. *Mr. Seward* was a friend of the Thrales.
26. The French phrase *au fait* (ō fā′) means "well instructed in" or "thoroughly conversant with" a given topic. Burney uses it here to show that Mr. Seward knows she wrote *Evelina*.

Big Idea The Stirrings of Romanticism *Why would Burney not want to be considered studious or to be seen reading Cicero?*

Vocabulary

confound (kən found′) *v.* to confuse; to bewilder

"No," answered Mrs. Thrale, "he will sit by you, which I am sure will give him great pleasure."

Soon after we were seated, this great man entered. I have so true a veneration for him that the very sight of him inspires me with delight and reverence, notwithstanding the cruel infirmities to which he is subject; for he has almost perpetual convulsive movements, either of his hands, lips, feet, or knees, and sometimes all together.

Mrs. Thrale introduced me to him, and he took his place. We had a noble dinner and a most elegant dessert. Dr. Johnson, in the middle of dinner, asked Mrs. Thrale what was in some little pies that were near him.

"Mutton," answered she, "so I don't ask you to eat any, because I know you despise it."

"No, madam, no," cried he. "I despise nothing that is good of its sort, but I am too proud now to eat of it. Sitting by Miss Burney makes me very proud today!"

"Miss Burney," said Mrs. Thrale, laughing, "you must take great care of your heart if Dr. Johnson attacks it; for I assure you he is not often successless."

"What's that you say, madam?" cried he. "Are you making mischief between the young lady and me already?"

A little while after, he drank Miss Thrale's health and mine and then added:

" 'Tis a terrible thing that we cannot wish young ladies well without wishing them to become old women!"

"But some people," said Mr. Seward, "are old and young at the same time, for they wear so well that they never look old."

"No, sir, no," cried the doctor, laughing, "that never yet was; you might as well say they are at the same time tall and short. I remember an epitaph to that purpose, which is in ——"

(I have quite forgot what—and also the name it was made upon, but the rest I recollect exactly:)

Reading Strategy Analyzing Cultural Context *Why is Burney so excited to meet Dr. Johnson?*

Big Idea The Stirrings of Romanticism *How does Dr. Johnson's comment reflect the values many were beginning to challenge at this time?*

The Bridge Party. Edgar Bundy. Private collection.

"——— lies buried here;
So early wise, so lasting fair,
That none, unless her years you told,
Thought her a child or thought her old."

Mrs. Thrale then repeated some lines in French, and Dr. Johnson some more in Latin. An epilogue of Mr. Garrick's[27] to *Bonduca*[28] was then mentioned, and Dr. Johnson said it was a miserable performance, and everybody agreed it was the worst he had ever made.

"And yet," said Mr. Seward, "it has been very much admired; but it is in praise of English valor, and so I suppose the subject made it popular."

"I don't know, sir," said Dr. Johnson, "anything about the subject, for I could not read on till I came to it. I got through half a dozen lines, but I could observe no other subject than eternal dullness. I don't know what is the matter with David; I am afraid he is grown superannuated,[29] for his prologues[30] and epilogues used to be incomparable."

"Nothing is so fatiguing," said Mrs. Thrale, "as the life of a wit; he and Wilkes[31] are the two oldest men of their ages I know, for they have both worn themselves out by being eternally on the rack to give entertainment to others."

"David, madam," said the doctor, "looks much older than he is; for his face has had double the business of any other man's; it is never at rest; when he speaks one minute, he has quite a different countenance to what he assumes the next; I don't believe he ever kept the same look for half an hour together in the whole course of his

---

27. David *Garrick* (1717–1779) was considered the greatest Shakespearean actor of his time.
28. *Bonduca* was a play written at the beginning of the seventeenth century by the English dramatist John Fletcher.
29. *Superannuated* means "ineffective because of advanced age."
30. As used here, *prologues* are poems used to introduce plays.
31. *Wilkes* is John Wilkes (1727–1797), a British political reformer.

The Bibliophilist's Haunt or Creech's Bookshop, William Fettes Douglas. City of Edinburgh Museums and Art Galleries, Scotland.

Viewing the Art: In Fanny Burney's day and in our own, book buyers and readers have been intrigued by books with anonymous authors. Why do you think this is the case?

life; and such an eternal, restless, fatiguing play of the muscles must certainly wear out a man's face before its real time."

"Oh, yes," cried Mrs. Thrale, "we must certainly make some allowance for such wear and tear of a man's face."

We left Streatham at about eight o'clock, and Mr. Seward, who handed me into the chaise, added his interest to the rest, that my father would not fail to bring me again next week to stay with them for some time. In short, I was loaded with civilities from them all. And my ride home was equally happy with the rest of the day, for my kind and most beloved father was so happy in *my* happiness and congratulated me so sweetly that he could, like myself, think on no other subject.

Yet my honors stopped not here; for Hetty, who, with her *sposo,*[32] was here to receive us, told me she had lately met Mrs. Reynolds, sister of Sir Joshua[33] and that she talked very much and

very highly of a new novel called *Evelina,* though without a shadow of suspicion as to the scribbler. And not contented with her own praise, she said that Sir Joshua, who began it one day when he was too much engaged to go on with it, was so much caught that he could think of nothing else and was quite absent all the day, not knowing a word that was said to him, and when he took it up again, found himself so much interested in it that he sat up all night to finish it!

Sir Joshua, it seems, vows he would give fifty pounds to know the author! I have also heard, by the means of Charles,[34] that other persons have declared they *will* find him out!

This intelligence determined me upon going myself to Mr. Lowndes[35] and discovering what sort of answers he made to such curious inquirers as I found were likely to address him. But as I did not dare trust myself to speak, for I felt that I

---

32. *Sposo* is Italian for *husband.*

33. *Sir Joshua* is Sir Joshua Reynolds (1723–1792), an important British portrait painter.
34. *Charles* was Burney's brother.
35. *Mr. Lowndes* was the publisher of *Evelina.*

should not be able to act my part well, I asked my mother to accompany me.

We introduced ourselves by buying the book, for which I had a commission from Mrs. G——. Fortunately, Mr. Lowndes himself was in the shop, as we found by his air of consequence and authority, as well as his age, for I never saw him before.

The moment he had given my mother the book, she asked if he could tell her who wrote it.

"No," he answered. "I don't know myself."

"Pho, pho," said she, "you mayn't choose to tell, but you must know."

"I don't, indeed, ma'am," answered he. "I have no honor in keeping the secret, for I have never been trusted. All I know of the matter is that it is a gentleman of the other end of the town."

My mother made a thousand other inquiries, to which his answers were to the following effect: that for a great while, he did not know if it was a man or a woman, but now he knew that much and that he was a master of his subject and well versed in the manners of the times.

"For some time," continued he, "I thought it had been Horace Walpole's,[36] for he once published a book in this snug manner, but I don't think it is now. I have often people come to inquire of me who it is, but I suppose he will come out soon, and then, when the rest of the world knows it, I shall. Servants often come for it from the other end of the town, and I have asked them divers questions myself, to see if I could get at the author, but I never got any satisfaction."

Just before we came away, upon my mother's still further pressing him, he said, with a most important face, "Why, to tell you the truth, madam, I have been informed that it is a piece of real secret history, and in that case, it will never be known."

This was too much for me; I grinned irresistibly and was obliged to look out at the shop door till we came away.

STREATHAM, SUNDAY, AUG. 23. I know not how to express the fullness of my contentment at this sweet place. All my best expectations are exceeded, and you know they were not very moderate. If, when my dear father comes, Susan and Mr. Crisp were to come too, I believe it would require at least a day's pondering to enable me to form another wish.

Our journey was charming. The kind Mrs. Thrale would give courage to the most timid. She did not ask me questions or catechize[37] me upon what I knew or use any means to draw me out but made it her business to draw herself out— that is, to start subjects, to support them herself, and to take all the weight of the conversation, as if it behoved her to find me entertainment. But I am so much in love with her that I shall be obliged to run away from the subject or shall write of nothing else.

When we arrived here, Mrs. Thrale showed me my room, which is an exceeding pleasant one, and then conducted me to the library, there to divert myself while she dressed.

Miss Thrale soon joined me, and I begin to like her. Mr. Thrale was neither well nor in spirits all day. Indeed, he seems not to be a happy man, though he has every means of happiness in his power. But I think I have rarely seen a very rich man with a light heart and light spirits.

Dr. Johnson was in the utmost good humor. ☙

---

36. *Horace Walpole* (1717–1797) was a British writer and historian.

Big Idea **The Stirrings of Romanticism** *What qualities of Evelina's author does Mr. Lowndes value?*

---

37. *Catechize* means "to methodically question or examine."

Literary Element **Wit** *How is Burney using wit to express her happiness?*

RESPONDING AND THINKING CRITICALLY

Respond

1. What questions would you like to ask Fanny Burney or the people she mentions?

Recall and Interpret

2. (a)Why does Burney think people may consider her book a "bold attempt and title"? (b)What is her response to these thoughts?

3. (a)Why does Burney at first avoid Brompton? (b)What conflicting emotions does she experience at Brompton? Why?

4. (a)According to Burney, how does Crisp feel about *Evelina* after she has read some of it to him? (b)Why might Burney have been so nervous about reading her novel to him? Why might his approval be important to her?

5. (a)What is Burney's motivation for going to see Mr. Lowndes? (b)Do you think she is satisfied with what she learns at the shop? Support your answer with evidence from the text.

Analyze and Evaluate

6. Why might Burney wish to keep her authorship of *Evelina* secret? Use evidence from the selection to support your opinion.

7. (a)How did the publication of *Evelina* change Burney's life? (b)How does she reflect on this change in her diary?

Connect

8. **Big Idea** The Stirrings of Romanticism
Romanticism values feelings and imagination over reason. How does Burney express her feelings in her diary?

LITERARY ANALYSIS

Literary Element Wit

Did you smile at Burney's description of herself as "the ingenious, learned, and most profound Fanny Burney"? If so, you were reacting to her **wit**, or cleverness.

1. Find two other examples of wit in Burney's diary entries. What makes each one witty?

2. Restate one of the witty passages to make its underlying meaning clear.

Writing About Literature

Apply Form and Theme Burney is thrilled to dine with Samuel Johnson, one of her literary heroes. What would it be like to have dinner with one of your heroes? Imagine the event and write a diary entry about it.

Literature Online **Web Activities** For eFlashcards, Selection Quick Checks, and other Web activities, go to www.glencoe.com.

READING AND VOCABULARY

Reading Strategy Analyzing Cultural Context

To understand Burney's diary entries, it is helpful to understand the cultural context of the time.

Partner Activity With a classmate, discuss the types of people Burney meets as well as the events and discussions she describes. What do these things tell you about societal values at the time?

Vocabulary Practice

Practice with Word Parts Match each vocabulary word below with the definition of its word part. Use a dictionary if you need help.

1. droll
2. profound
3. confound
4. zenith
5. sanguine

a. prefix, "before"
b. root, "high overhead"
c. suffix, "to pour"
d. root, "imp"
e. root, "blood"

Grammar Workshop

Sentence Structure

Avoiding Dangling Modifiers

"Finding myself more safe than I had apprehended, I ventured to go to Brompton next day."

—Fanny Burney, from *The Diary of Fanny Burney*

Connecting to Literature Fanny Burney introduces this sentence from her diary with a verbal phrase. The modifier *Finding myself more safe than I had apprehended* adds information about why she made the trip. However, sometimes a writer uses such modifiers incorrectly, confusing the reader. A **dangling modifier** doesn't relate to anything in the sentence. To avoid dangling modifiers, make sure the connection between modifiers and the words they modify is clear.

Problem	**Dangling modifier**
	Curious about the identity of the author, the book was a topic of conversation everywhere.
	Curious about the identity of the author is an example of a **phrase** that erroneously modifies a word in the main clause of a sentence—in this case, the noun *book*. The sentence appears to say that the book was curious about the identity of the author.

Solution 1 Add a noun to which the dangling modifier can refer.

Curious about the identity of the author, people in the town made the book a topic of conversation everywhere.

Solution 2 Move the modifier into the main clause.

The book was a topic of conversation everywhere among people curious about the identity of the author.

Exercise

Revise for Clarity Rewrite the following sentences to correct any dangling modifiers. If a sentence needs no revision, write *correct*.

1. Seeking to remain anonymous, the book was published without Fanny Burney's name.

2. Intensely personal, Burney wrote the diary to express her thoughts and feelings.

3. Excited and curious, many were eager to read *Evelina*.

4. After reading *Evelina*, high praise was given to the author by Mrs. Cholmondeley.

5. Both popular forms of entertainment, people living in eighteenth-century England enjoyed reading books and going to the theater.

▶ **Recognizing Dangling Modifiers**

A **dangling modifier** does not logically modify any word in a sentence.

▶ **Test-Taking Tip**

To avoid dangling modifiers, think about the meaning of the sentence. Make sure each phrase modifies a word close to it.

▶ **Language Handbook**

For more about sentence structure, see Language Handbook, pp. R50–R51.

Literature Online
eWorkbooks To link to the Grammar and Language eWorkbook, go to www.glencoe.com.

OBJECTIVES
- Identify dangling modifiers.
- Recognize and correct errors in writing.

Blake's Poetry

MEET WILLIAM BLAKE

Poet, artist, and mystic—William Blake was not content with the prevailing neoclassical values of his day. His interest in the supernatural and his imaginative experimentation classify him as pre-Romantic. Blake was defiantly unique, and some of his contemporaries considered him insane. As poet William Wordsworth said of the unworldly Blake, "there is something in the madness of this man which interests me more than the sanity of Lord Byron and Walter Scott."

> *"Poetry fettered fetters the human race. Nations are destroyed, or flourish, in proportion as their poetry, painting, and music are destroyed or flourish!"*
>
> —William Blake

Strange and Humble Beginnings Blake grew up in London, surrounded by the grit and poverty of the new industrial age. From early childhood, Blake spoke of having religious visions of angels and prophets; these visions would continue throughout his life. When, at age ten, he expressed a desire to become a painter, his parents sent him to a drawing school. At the age of fifteen, Blake was apprenticed to an engraver—an artisan who cuts or carves designs into wood blocks or metal sheets from which prints can be made.

When he was twenty-five, Blake married Catherine Boucher, an uneducated woman whom he later taught to read and trained as an engraver. She accepted his eccentric lifestyle and intense spirituality. "I have very little of Mr. Blake's time," she once told a friend, lightheartedly. "He is always in Paradise." The couple was befriended by a group of progressive artists who admired Blake's fervent imagination and helped him publish his first book of poems when he was twenty-six. Soon after, Blake started his own print shop, taking his younger brother, Richard, as his apprentice. Tragically, Richard fell ill and died in the winter of 1787. As he sat by his brother's bedside, Blake claimed that he saw his brother's spirit joyously clap its hands and ascend toward heaven.

A Creative Fervor The late 1780s and early 1790s found Blake at the peak of his creative powers. He discovered a new method of relief etching on copperplates, which he called "illuminated printing." Blake, with the help of Catherine, used this technique to beautifully illustrate and hand-paint nearly all of his books. Unfortunately, this method was so complex and time-consuming that relatively few copies of his work were produced; the surviving originals are ranked among the art treasures of the world. In 1794 Blake published a volume of lyric poems called *Songs of Innocence and Experience*. Blake described this work as "shewing the two contrary states of the human soul." As he grew older, Blake became more and more caught up in his mystical faith and visions of a heavenly world. His later work demonstrates his ever-deepening reflections on God, humankind, and the power of the imagination. As he famously wrote, "If the doors of perception were cleansed every thing would appear to man as it is, infinite."

William Blake was born in 1757 and died in 1827.

Literature Online **Author Search** For more about William Blake, go to www.glencoe.com.

Connecting to the Poems

Blake's poems explore the relationship between the innocence of youth and the often jaded world of experience. As you read, think about the following questions:

- Does the way you perceive the world change as you grow older?
- Do you think there are drawbacks to leaving the world of innocence?

Building Background

Blake first wrote *Songs of Innocence* and then added *Songs of Experience* as a counterpoint and complement. Subsequently, both volumes were published as one book. As these titles suggest, part of Blake's mystical vision is to view the universe in contrasts. The poems in *Songs of Innocence* examine good, passivity, and reason; those in the companion volume explore evil, violence, and unreasonable emotion. Blake's view of the world was influenced by the Industrial Revolution. In the late eighteenth century, machinery and manufacturing began to dominate Britain's economy. Blake felt that these changes were dehumanizing to laborers, especially to children, who were regularly forced to work long hours at dangerous jobs.

Setting Purposes for Reading

Big Idea The Stirrings of Romanticism

As you read, note how Blake favors imagination over deductive reasoning.

Literary Element Symbol

A **symbol** is a person, an animal, a place, an object, or an event within a text that exists on a literal level but also represents something on a figurative level. A symbol may have multiple layers of meanings or associations. The meaning of any symbol is determined by its textual surroundings.

- See Literary Terms Handbook, p. R18.

Literature Online **Interactive Literary Elements Handbook** To review or learn more about the literary elements, go to www.glencoe.com.

Reading Strategy Visualizing

To **visualize** means to use your imagination to form pictures of the setting, characters, and action. As you read, pay close attention to sensory details and descriptions and your responses to them. Then compare and contrast your visualizations with Blake's own engraved representations of his poems.

Reading Tip: Comparing and Contrasting Use Venn diagrams like the one below to compare and contrast the most prominent elements of your visualizations with Blake's engravings. In the left part of the diagram, write down the images, colors, and any other sensory details that you experienced that differ from Blake's engravings. Next, in the right part of the diagram, record all of the elements that are present in the engravings but that were absent from your visualization. Then, in the diagram's overlapping portion, record all of the elements common to both the engravings and to your visualizations. Complete a Venn diagram for each poem.

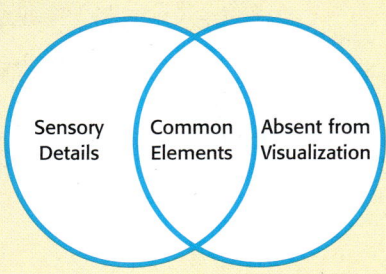

Sensory Details — Common Elements — Absent from Visualization

Child laborers at the Alioin towel mill, England.

OBJECTIVES

In studying these selections, you will focus on the following:
- analyzing historical context
- analyzing symbols, stanzas, and meter
- visualizing

A Poison Tree, Plate 49 from *Songs of Innocence and Experience.*
c. 1815–1826. William Blake. Etching, ink, and watercolor.
Fitzwilliam Museum, University of Cambridge.

A Poison Tree

William Blake

I was angry with my friend;
I told my wrath, my wrath did end.
I was angry with my foe;
I told it not, my wrath did grow.

5   And I watered it in fears,
Night and morning with my tears;
And I sunnèd[1] it with smiles,
And with soft deceitful wiles.

And it grew both day and night,
10   Till it bore an apple bright.
And my foe beheld it shine,
And he knew that it was mine,

And into my garden stole
When the night had veiled the pole;[2]
15   In the morning glad I see
My foe outstretched beneath the tree.

---

1. The accent on *e* shows that the word *sunnèd* is pronounced with two syllables.
2. *Pole* means "sky" or "heavens."

Literary Element   **Symbol** *What symbol is alluded to in this line?*

Literary Element   **Symbol** *How are the poison tree and the apple connected?*

The Lamb

William Blake

The Shepherd, 1789. William Blake. Etching, ink and watercolor. The Huntington Library, Art Collections, and Botanical Gardens, San Marino, CA.

Little Lamb, who made thee?
  Dost thou know who made thee?
Gave thee life and bid thee feed
By the stream and o'er the mead;[1]
5   Gave thee clothing of delight,
Softest clothing, woolly bright;
Gave thee such a tender voice,
Making all the vales rejoice!
    Little Lamb, who made thee?
10   Dost thou know who made thee?

    Little Lamb, I'll tell thee,
    Little Lamb, I'll tell thee!
He[2] is callèd by thy name,
For he calls himself a Lamb.
15   He is meek and he is mild;
He became a little child.
I a child and thou a lamb,
We are callèd by his name.
    Little Lamb, God bless thee!
20   Little Lamb, God bless thee!

---

1. Here, *mead* means "meadow."
2. *He* refers to Jesus Christ.

Reading Strategy **Visualizing** *How do you picture this scene? Do you see it as calm or turbulent?*

The Tyger, 1794–1795. William Blake. Etching, ink and watercolor. The Huntington Library, Art Collections, and Botanical Gardens, San Marino, CA.

The Tyger

William Blake

Tyger! Tyger! burning bright
In the forests of the night,
What immortal hand or eye
Could frame thy fearful symmetry?[1]

5   In what distant deeps[2] or skies
Burnt the fire of thine eyes?
On what wings dare he aspire?
What the hand dare seize the fire?

And what shoulder, and what art,
10   Could twist the sinews of thy heart?
And when thy heart began to beat,
What dread hand? and what dread feet?

What the hammer? what the chain?
In what furnace was thy brain?
15   What the anvil? what dread grasp
Dare its deadly terrors clasp?

When the stars threw down their spears
And watered heaven with their tears,
Did he smile his work to see?
20   Did he who made the Lamb make thee?

Tyger! Tyger! burning bright
In the forests of the night,
What immortal hand or eye
Dare frame thy fearful symmetry?

1. In this context, *symmetry* means "well-proportioned form."
2. *Deeps* means "ocean" or "abyss."

Reading Strategy **Visualizing** *How does the description in the first four lines create a striking image?*

Big Idea **The Stirrings of Romanticism** *How do these lines reflect Blake's concerns about the industrialization of society?*

RESPONDING AND THINKING CRITICALLY

Respond

1. Which of these poems did you find the most compelling? Why?

Recall and Interpret

2. (a)Briefly summarize what happens to the speaker's anger with a friend and a foe in "A Poison Tree." (b)Why, in your opinion, does the speaker deal with his anger in this way?

3. (a)In the first ten lines of "The Lamb," what questions does the speaker ask the lamb? (b)According to the speaker, what three things has the lamb been given? (c)What do these lines reveal about the speaker's attitude toward the lamb?

4. (a)In "The Tyger," what question does the speaker ask in lines 1–5 and in lines 21–24? How do these questions differ? (b)From these questions, what can you infer about the speaker's attitude toward the Tyger?

5. (a)In lines 13–16, to whom does the speaker compare the Tyger's creator? (b)What images does the speaker use to create this metaphor?

Analyze and Evaluate

6. (a)At the end of "A Poison Tree," how does the speaker feel? (b)Do you think it is appropriate for the speaker to feel this way? Explain.

7. (a)How is "The Tyger" similar to "The Lamb"? How are the poems different? (b)What do you think is gained by reading these poems together?

Connect

8. **Big Idea** **The Stirrings of Romanticism** How do these poems embody a shift away from reason and convention and toward imagination and individualism?

LITERARY ANALYSIS

Literary Element Symbol

One key to understanding **symbols** is to think associatively. In Blake's poems, note how imagery and tone are used to narrow and eliminate some associations in order to specifically define the symbols.

1. (a)What ideas do you associate with a tree and an apple? (b)In "A Poison Tree," what do you think the apple and the tree symbolize?

2. (a)What ideas or characteristics do you associate with a lamb and a tiger? (b)What do you think the lamb and the Tyger symbolize?

Writing About Literature

Compare and Contrast Theme Theme is the main idea about life in a work of literature. In your opinion, what is the theme of "The Lamb"? What is the theme of "The Tyger"? In a short paragraph, compare and contrast the themes of these poems. Be sure to cite evidence to support your claims.

READING AND VOCABULARY

Reading Strategy Visualizing

Visualizing may help you comprehend the actions or mannerisms of a character and a speaker's attitude toward what he or she is describing.

1. Which images or actions were easiest to visualize in "A Poison Tree"? Explain.

2. What images from "The Tyger" helped you understand the speaker's attitude toward his or her subject matter?

Academic Vocabulary

Here is a word from the vocabulary list on page R82.

implicit (im plis′ it) *adj.* something that is understood but unstated; implied

Practice and Apply
What is the **implicit** meaning of the last line in "A Poison Tree"?

Literary Element Stanza

A **stanza** is a group of lines forming a unit in a poem. A stanza in a poem is similar to a paragraph in prose. Some of the most common types of stanzas are the couplet, or two-line stanza; the tercet, which has three lines; and the quatrain, which has four. As you read these poems, note how Blake uses the quatrain and the natural break provided by the stanza to transition from one concept or thought to another.

- See Literary Terms Handbook, p. R17.

Reading Strategy Analyzing Historical Context

Analyzing historical context involves gathering background information and exploring social forces that influenced the writing of a literary work. As you read these poems, use your background knowledge of the Industrial Revolution to better understand the context in which these poems were written.

LONDON

William Blake

I wander thro' each charter'd[1] street,
Near where the charter'd Thames does flow,
And mark in every face I meet
Marks of weakness, marks of woe.

5   In every cry of every Man,
In every Infant's cry of fear,
In every voice, in every ban,[2]
The mind-forg'd manacles[3] I hear.

How the Chimney-sweeper's cry
10   Every black'ning Church appalls;
And the hapless[4] Soldier's sigh
Runs in blood down Palace walls.

But most thro' midnight streets I hear
How the youthful Harlot's[5] curse
15   Blasts the new born Infant's tear,
And blights with plagues the Marriage hearse.

1. Here, *chartered* means "controlled."

2. *Ban* refers to a legal prohibition, a public curse, or a marriage announcement.
3. *Manacles* means "shackles."

4. *Hapless* means "deserving pity."

5. *Harlot* means "prostitute."

Reading Strategy Analyzing Historical Context *What does this suggest to you about the conditions in London at the time?*

THE CHIMNEY SWEEPER
from Songs of Innocence

William Blake

The Chimney Sweeper, plate 7 (Bentley 12) from Songs of Innocence and of Experience 1789-94. William Blake. Raised etching. Yale Center for British Art, Paul Mellon Collection, New Haven, CT.

When my mother died I was very young,
And my father sold me while yet my tongue
Could scarcely cry "'weep! 'weep! 'weep! 'weep!"[1]
So your chimneys I sweep, & in soot I sleep.

5   There's little Tom Dacre, who cried when his head,
That curl'd like a lamb's back, was shav'd: so I said
"Hush, Tom! never mind it, for when your head's bare
You know that the soot cannot spoil your white hair."

And so he was quiet, & that very night,
10 As Tom was a-sleeping, he had such a sight!—
That thousands of sweepers, Dick, Joe, Ned, & Jack,
Were all of them lock'd up in coffins of black.

And by came an Angel who had a bright key,
And he open'd the coffins & set them all free;
15 Then down a green plain leaping, laughing, they run,
And wash in a river, and shine in the Sun.

Then naked & white, all their bags left behind,
They rise upon clouds and sport in the wind;
And the Angel told Tom, if he'd be a good boy,
20 He'd have God for his father, & never want joy.

And so Tom awoke; and we rose in the dark,
And got with our bags & our brushes to work.
Tho' the morning was cold, Tom was happy & warm;
So if all do their duty they need not fear harm.

---

1. "'weep . . . 'weep" is the child's attempt to say "sweep!" as a chimney sweeper would have.

Reading Strategy   Analyzing Historical Context   *Why does the speaker of the poem work as a chimney sweeper?*

Big Idea   The Stirrings of Romanticism   *What role does the imagination play in these lines?*

THE CHIMNEY SWEEPER
from *Songs of Experience*

William Blake

A little black thing among the snow,
Crying "'weep! 'weep!" in notes of woe!
"Where are thy father & mother? say?"
"They are both gone up to the church to pray.

5   "Because I was happy upon the heath,
And smil'd among the winter's snow,
They clothed me in the clothes of death,
And taught me to sing the notes of woe.

"And because I am happy & dance & sing,
10   They think they have done me no injury,
And are gone to praise God & his Priest & King,
Who make up a heaven of our misery."

The Chimney Sweeper, Plate 37 from *Songs of Innocence and of Experience,* c. 1815–26. William Blake. Etching, ink and watercolor. Fitzwilliam Museum, University of Cambridge, England.

Reading Strategy Analyzing Historical Context *What social institutions is the speaker commenting upon in these lines? How does the speaker view these institutions?*

RESPONDING AND THINKING CRITICALLY

Respond

1. What was the strongest emotion that you felt as you read these poems?

Recall and Interpret

2. (a)What does the speaker in "London" claim to hear in "every voice, in every ban"? (b)What specific people does the speaker mention?

3. (a)At the end of "The Chimney Sweeper" from *Songs of Innocence*, why is Tom "happy"? (b)What is the message of this poem?

4. (a)In "The Chimney Sweeper" from *Songs of Experience*, how is the child clothed and what is the child taught to sing? (b)What does this imply about innocence?

Analyze and Evaluate

5. (a)In the last stanza of "London," what effect does the "youthful harlot's curse" have on the newborn child? (b)What does this symbolize?

6. What makes "London" a song of experience, rather than a song of innocence?

7. (a)In "The Chimney Sweeper" from *Songs of Innocence*, what two settings are contrasted? (b)In "The Chimney Sweeper" from *Songs of Experience*, what is the predominant setting? (c)What do the settings of both poems suggest about the relationship between youth and experience?

Connect

8. **Big Idea** **The Stirrings of Romanticism** What elements of Romanticism are most evident in these poems? Explain.

DAILY LIFE AND CULTURE

Chimney Sweeps and Child Labor

The Industrial Revolution in Great Britain during the middle part of the eighteenth century fundamentally altered familial and societal structures. New large-scale manufacturing techniques and tools required a large urban labor force. Tragically, children were regularly forced into dangerous, unhealthy, and cruel environments, for little or no pay. Like the chimney sweeps depicted in Blake's poems, these children were nearly always from poor families. In fact, many of them were orphans.

As a result of the alarming conditions in the factories, mines, and mills, an act was passed in 1833 that provided for the inspection of these facilities. These inspections resulted in the Factory Act of 1847, which limited the number of hours children could work. Subsequent acts followed throughout the nineteenth century, as did greater interest in reforming societal ills. By the start of the twentieth century, child labor had all but vanished in Britain.

Sweep! From "Cries of London," c. 1840. Guildhall Art Gallery, London.

Group Activity Discuss these questions with a group of classmates.

1. Why do you think parents might allow their children to be subjected to harsh factory conditions?

2. Does Blake's depiction of London seem accurate? Explain.

LITERARY ANALYSIS

Literary Element Stanza

A **stanza** is a unified group of lines within a larger poem. A stanza serves a similar function to a paragraph in prose. Blake often writes in quatrains, which are one of the most commonly occurring stanzas in English lyric poetry. Think about how each quatrain forms a self-contained idea while simultaneously adding to the poem as a whole.

1. In "London," what is the connection between the first two stanzas and the last two stanzas?
2. Describe what happens in each stanza of "The Chimney Sweeper" from *Songs of Innocence*.

Review: Meter

As you learned on page 431, **meter** is the regular pattern of stressed and unstressed syllables that gives a line of poetry a predictable rhythm. The basic unit of meter is the **foot**. A foot usually contains one stressed syllable (marked ´) and one or more unstressed syllables (marked ˘).

Partner Activity Meet with another classmate and try to determine the meter in "London" and both "Chimney Sweeper" poems. First, read each stanza aloud and try to figure out where the stresses fall. Remember that the meter of a poem is not always regular. Then, on a separate sheet of paper, rewrite the stanza, marking stressed and unstressed syllables. Finally, based on your **scansion**, label the meter using the appropriate terminology. For a list of all of the terms used to define the different types of meter, refer to the Literary Terms Handbook, page R10.

A View in Regent's Park in 1831, from *The Progress of Steam.* Henry Thomas Alken. City of Westminster Archive Centre, London.

READING AND VOCABULARY

Reading Strategy Analyzing Historical Context

Writers are influenced by their environments, cultures, and experiences. Some writers, such as Blake, choose to overtly tackle the social issues and problems of their day. Often, in order to **analyze historical context**, you must bring your own knowledge of historical events to bear on a text. If you have trouble answering these questions, reread the biography on page 754 and Building Background on page 755, as well as the Unit Four introduction.

1. How does Blake characterize the urban environment of London?
2. Cite several instances from these poems that illustrate Blake's concern for the poor and destitute.
3. (a)According to the poems, how were children sometimes treated during this era? (b)Does this treatment differ from that in our own time? Explain.

Academic Vocabulary

Here are two words from the vocabulary list on page R82.

abandon (ə ban′ dən) *v.* to desert, or leave behind completely

widespread (wīd′ spred′) *adj.* something that is common to a large area; prevalent

Practice and Apply

1. Why do you think the child in "The Chimney Sweeper" from *Songs of Innocence* was **abandoned**?
2. Why do you think Blake depicted **widespread** misery in London?

Writing About Literature

Explore Author's Purpose An author typically writes to accomplish one or more of the following purposes: to persuade, to inform, to explain, to entertain, or to describe. What do you think Blake's purpose was in writing *Songs of Innocence and Experience*? Write a brief essay in which you try to establish the poet's purpose or purposes. Use evidence from the poems to defend your position. Remember that before you can figure out a text's purpose, you have to identify its main message and its target audience or audiences. You might organize your essay like this.

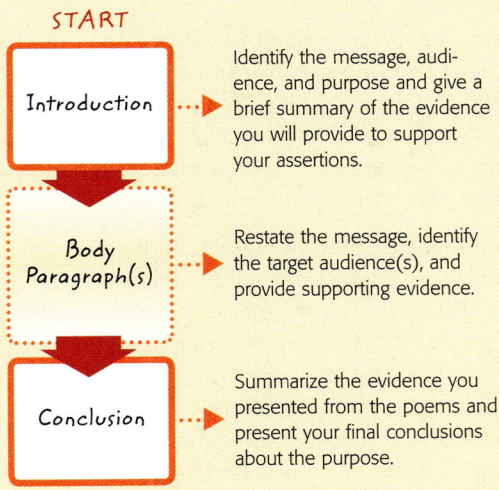

START

Introduction → Identify the message, audience, and purpose and give a brief summary of the evidence you will provide to support your assertions.

Body Paragraph(s) → Restate the message, identify the target audience(s), and provide supporting evidence.

Conclusion → Summarize the evidence you presented from the poems and present your final conclusions about the purpose.

FINISH

After you complete your draft, meet with a peer reviewer to evaluate each other's work and to suggest revisions. Then proofread and edit your draft for errors in spelling, grammar, and punctuation.

Interdisciplinary Activity: Art

Blake considered himself a painter and engraver as much as he considered himself a poet. Many of the themes and beliefs common to Blake's poetry are also present in his visual work. Meet with a few classmates to research Blake's paintings and engravings. Consult Blake's images on the preceding pages and the Literary History on pages 766–767 and use the Internet and a library to find color examples of Blake's work. Once your research is complete, present your findings to the class.

Blake's Language and Style

Using Parallelism and Repetition In the poems from *Songs of Innocence and Experience*, Blake often uses parallelism and repetition to add rhetorical force, emphasize and draw connections between certain ideas, and increase the musicality of his poems. For example, observe how Blake's use of parallelism and repetition in "The Lamb" adds to the poem's force and lilting musical quality:

> Little lamb, who made thee?
> Dost thou know who made thee?
> Gave thee life and bid thee feed
> By the stream and o'er the mead;
> Gave thee clothing of delight,
> Softest clothing, woolly bright;
> Gave thee such a tender voice,
> Making all the vales rejoice!
> Little lamb, who made thee?
> Dost thou know who made thee?

Notice some of Blake's uses of repetition and parallelism:

Example	Literary Device
"Little lamb, who made thee?" lines 1 and 9	Repetition
"Gave thee life…Gave thee clothing…Gave thee such a tender voice" lines 3–7	Parallelism

Activity Create a chart of your own, listing more examples of repetition and parallelism in Blake's poems. Try to determine what each example contributes to the poem as a whole.

Revising Check

Parallelism and Repetition With a partner, go through your analysis of Blake's purpose and note places where parallelism and repetition could be used to strengthen connections between ideas and to make your arguments more effective.

Literature Online Web Activities For eFlashcards, Selection Quick Checks, and other Web activities, go to www.glencoe.com.

The Two Sides of Blake

> "*Improvement makes straight roads; but the crooked roads without improvement are roads of genius.*"
> —William Blake, "Proverbs of Hell"

MANY CREATIVE INDIVIDUALS EXCEL IN different art forms. Michelangelo, the Italian Renaissance artist, was a painter, sculptor, and poet. Victor Hugo, the French artist, was a poet, novelist, and painter. One of the greatest examples of this powerful urge to create is William Blake, who was not only a poet but a highly skilled engraver and painter also.

Early Influences

Blake grew up in an unconventional atmosphere of religious piety, enthusiasm, and vision. His parents encouraged Blake's individuality and artistic interests. At age ten, he began a lifelong study of the great Italian and German Renaissance artists. At fifteen, he was apprenticed to study the art of engraving.

When Blake's apprenticeship as an engraver ended, he enrolled in the Royal Academy of Art. There Blake scorned the orthodox rules and conventions based on

Nebuchadnezzar, 1795. William Blake. Colored engraving, Tate Gallery, London.

Greek and Roman traditions. He also rejected drawing from models, dead or alive. In his copy of William Wordsworth's poetry, Blake noted, "Natural Objects always did & now do weaken, deaden & obliterate Imagination in Me." Essentially, Blake believed that art should be created directly from the imagination rather than drawn from the observation of nature.

Visionary Art

All pictorial art consists of five elements: line, shape, color, tone, and texture. Blake's affinity for medieval art led him to value line as the preeminent element of his artistic style. He also condemned any technique—brushwork or shadowing—that made the contours of a painting "soft" or unclear.

Throughout his career, Blake's favorite creative subjects were drawn from religious works, such as the Bible, Milton's *Paradise Lost*, and Dante's *Divine Comedy*, which he was illustrating at the time of his death. Blake's knowledge of the Bible and Medieval and Renaissance art led him to create some of his most startling images. For instance, the ink and watercolor painting *Nebuchadnezzar* is remarkably frightening. It illustrates an episode from the biblical Book of Daniel in which a Babylonian king goes mad and acts like a beast. The image of the tortured king, rendered in bulky horror, presents a warning against pride and reflects Blake's fear of kings. Note how the lines of the engraving are stark and clear yet provide a ghastly texture.

In addition, many of Blake's engravings and artworks are pictorial representations of his poems. In *Infant Joy*, an early work from the 1789 version of *Songs of Innocence*, Blake presents the poem, as well as the figures of a mother, child, and angel encircled by a partly opened bud; a closed bud, in the lower right of the illustration, balances the three figures. Poet and critic Kathleen Raine notes how "the tendrils of his 'wandering vine'" suggest the energy and spontaneity that runs through all of life.

Late in life, Blake accepted a commission to illustrate the biblical Book of Job. *The Lord Answering Job Out of the Whirlwind* illustrates Job's repentance before God. Here, Blake's mastery of engraving can be seen in the

Infant Joy, 1815–1826. William Blake. Colored etching.
Fitzwilliam Museum, University of Cambridge, UK.

wrote, "or be enslaved by another Man's. I will not reason & compare: my business is to Create." In his engravings, paintings, and poetry, Blake lived by his own rules and blazed his own imaginative path.

The Lord Answering Job Out of the Whirlwind. 1825. William Blake. Copper engraving. Tate Gallery, London.

majestic, circular lines of the whirlwind surrounding the Lord and endowing Him with a textured weight. The swirl is echoed in the sketchy figures above the plate itself. Interestingly, the figure of God is reminiscent of Michelangelo's famous painting of *God Creating Adam* on the ceiling of the Sistine Chapel.

Blake's overarching belief was that reason stifles vision and inspiration. This was the cornerstone of his artistic credo. "I must Create a System," he once

Literature Online **Literary History** For more about the art and poetry of William Blake, go to www.glencoe.com.

RESPONDING AND THINKING CRITICALLY

1. Which engraving or painting do you think is the most interesting? Explain.

2. Look back at Blake's illustrations that accompany his poems on pages 756–762. How do his engravings enhance the content of his poems?

3. Why do you think an artist would want to explore two different art forms, such as painting and poetry?

OBJECTIVES
• Read to enhance understanding of literary periods and movements.

• Read to see the connection between art and poetry.

from *Pride and Prejudice*

MEET JANE AUSTEN

A clergyman's daughter, Jane Austen never traveled beyond her middle-class circle of family and acquaintances, typical of England's villages. The lives of these small town residents became the inspiration for Austen's most memorable works.

> *"3 or 4 families in a country village is the very thing to work on."*
>
> —Jane Austen, on novel writing

Family Life Jane Austen was born in 1775 to a minister, George Austen, and his wife, Cassandra. Although the Austens had a comfortable income, they were not considered rich, especially since there were seven children in the family. While not always able to provide financially for their children, Austen's parents encouraged Jane and her siblings to have a passion for learning. Her father owned a library of over five hundred books, and Austen later wrote that her family were "great novel readers, and not ashamed of being so." The Austens often produced stories, verses, and short plays to amuse themselves. As a result, Austen began writing at an early age to entertain her family, reading her satirical sketches aloud.

By the time she was twenty, she had written an early version of her novel *Sense and Sensibility* and soon afterward began the manuscripts that eventually became *Pride and Prejudice* and *Northanger Abbey*. Years later, she revised and expanded these manuscripts, which were well received when they were published. During the remainder of her brief life, she wrote three more novels—*Mansfield Park*, *Emma*, and *Persuasion*.

Marriage and Manners In an age when genteel young women could not seek gainful employment, marriage meant financial security. The pressure to marry was strong, and Austen examines that pressure throughout her work with a witty and satirical eye. Although Austen never married, she is believed to have had a brief engagement in 1802 with a twenty-one-year-old suitor from her village, until she broke the engagement a day after it was formed. Some historians speculate that Austen, while traveling with her family, fell in love with another man who died soon afterward. Little is known about these aspects of Austen's life, as her sister Cassandra was fiercely protective of her and destroyed many of Austen's private letters and correspondence once the author died.

While Austen's novels were popular with the public and many of her fellow authors, it was only after her death that she received critical acclaim. Sir Walter Scott wrote in his journal, in an entry dated March 14, 1826, "Also read again, and for the third time at least, Miss Austen's very finely written novel of *Pride and Prejudice*. That young lady had a talent for describing the involvement and feelings and characters of ordinary life which is to me the most wonderful I ever met with."

Jane Austen was born in 1775 and died in 1817.

Literature Online Author Search For more about Jane Austen, go to www.glencoe.com.

Connecting to the Novel

Pride and Prejudice tells the story of a middle-class family living in eighteenth-century England. The mother of the family, Mrs. Bennet, makes it her purpose in life to find husbands for her five daughters. In this time period, women were expected to marry young. Marriages were often based on financial arrangements rather than love. As you read, think about how marriage has changed since Jane Austen's time.

Building Background

Women rarely owned property in eighteenth-century England. Instead, property and other finances usually belonged to the husband or father. For this reason, even though the Bennet family is middle-class, it is necessary for the daughters to marry into wealth. After the death of Mr. Bennet, the family's estate would go to another male relative instead of Mrs. Bennet or their daughters.

Setting Purposes for Reading

Big Idea **The Stirrings of Romanticism**

As you read, look for clues about which characters show attitudes of Romanticism—such as valuing individualism and feeling over reason—and which preserve Enlightenment attitudes, valuing reason and self-control.

Literary Element Dialogue

Dialogue is conversation between characters in a literary work. Through dialogue, a writer reveals the feelings, thoughts, and intentions of characters, sets up conflicts, and moves the plot forward. Much of the dialogue in *Pride and Prejudice* reveals the relationships between characters.

- See Literary Terms Handbook, p. R4.

Literature Online **Interactive Literary Elements Handbook** To review or learn more about the literary elements, go to www.glencoe.com.

Reading Strategy Analyzing Characterization

When you **analyze characterization,** you look critically at how the thoughts, actions, and motives of a character are revealed. In **direct characterization,** the author tells something outright about a character's personality. In **indirect characterization,** the author suggests traits by describing a character's words, thoughts, actions, or appearance, as well as the reactions of other characters.

Reading Tip: Taking Notes Create a character map like the one shown below to analyze characters.

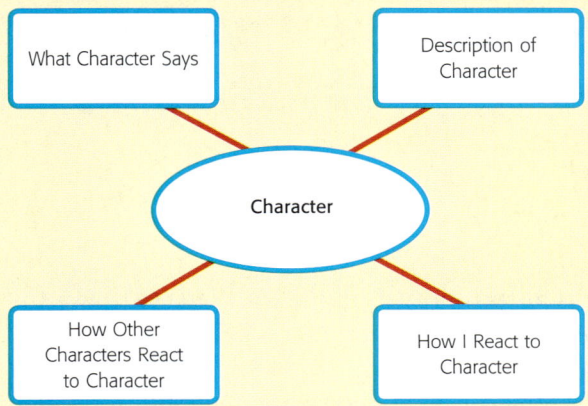

Vocabulary

hypocritical (hip′ ə krit′ i kəl) *adj.* pretending to believe one thing but doing the opposite; p. 772 *It is hypocritical to urge others to recycle when you don't do the same.*

acquaintance (ə kwānt′ əns) *n.* the state of being familiar with; p. 772 *I did not know Mary well; I had only just made her acquaintance.*

emphatic (em fat′ ik) *adj.* with strong emphasis; p. 772 *My mother was emphatic about having us call home if we were going to stay out late.*

Vocabulary Tip: Word Origins Word origins are the history and development of a word.

OBJECTIVES
In studying this selection, you will focus on the following:
- analyzing literary periods
- evaluating dialogue and point of view
- analyzing characterization

Promenade. Constant-Emile Troyon. Oil on canvas. Courtesy of Thomas Brod and Patrick Pilkington. Private collection.

from Pride and Prejudice

Jane Austen

Chapter 1

It is a truth universally acknowledged that a single man in possession of a good fortune must be in want of a wife.

However little known the feelings or views of such a man may be on his first entering a neighborhood, this truth is so well fixed in the minds of the surrounding families that he is considered as the rightful property of some one or other of their daughters.

"My dear Mr. Bennet," said his lady to him one day, "have you heard that Netherfield Park is let at last?"

Mr. Bennet replied that he had not.

"But it is," returned she; "for Mrs. Long has just been here, and she told me all about it."

Mr. Bennet made no answer.

"Do not you want to know who has taken it?" cried his wife impatiently.

"*You* want to tell me, and I have no objection to hearing it."

This was invitation enough.

"Why, my dear, you must know, Mrs. Long says that Netherfield is taken by a young man of large fortune from the north of England; that he came down on Monday in a chaise and four[1] to see the place, and was so much delighted with it that he agreed with Mr. Morris immediately; that he is to take possession before Michaelmas,[2] and some of his servants are to be in the house by the end of next week."

"What is his name?"

"Bingley."

"Is he married or single?"

"Oh! Single, my dear, to be sure! A single man of large fortune; four or five thousand a year.[3] What a fine thing for our girls!"

"How so? How can it affect them?"

"My dear Mr. Bennet," replied his wife, "how can you be so tiresome! You must know that I am thinking of his marrying one of them."

"Is that his design in settling here?"

---

1. A *chaise and four* is an elegant coach drawn by four horses.
2. *Michaelmas* [mik′ əl məs] is September 29, the feast of the archangel Michael, which is celebrated mainly in England.
3. A yearly income of *four or five thousand* pounds was then a fairly large sum of money probably acquired from land holdings and investments.

Literary Element Dialogue *What does this dialogue reveal about the relationship between Mr. and Mrs. Bennet?*

Reading Strategy Analyzing Characterization *How does Austen reveal Mrs. Bennet's character?*

"Design! Nonsense, how can you talk so! But it is very likely that he *may* fall in love with one of them, and therefore you must visit him as soon as he comes."

"I see no occasion for that. You and the girls may go, or you may send them by themselves, which perhaps will be still better, for as you are as handsome as any of them, Mr. Bingley might like you the best of the party."

"My dear, you flatter me. I certainly *have* had my share of beauty, but I do not pretend to be anything extraordinary now. When a woman has five grown-up daughters, she ought to give over thinking of her own beauty."

"In such cases, a woman has not often much beauty to think of."

"But, my dear, you must indeed go and see Mr. Bingley when he comes in the neighborhood."

"It is more than I engage for,[4] I assure you."

"But consider your daughters. Only think what an establishment it would be for one of them. Sir William and Lady Lucas are determined to go, merely on that account, for in general you know they visit no newcomers. Indeed you must go, for it will be impossible for *us* to visit him if you do not."

"You are overscrupulous[5] surely. I dare say Mr. Bingley will be very glad to see you; and I will send a few lines by you to assure him of my hearty consent to his marrying whichever he chooses of the girls, though I must throw in a good word for my little Lizzy."

"I desire you will do no such thing. Lizzy is not a bit better than the others; and I am sure she is not half so handsome as Jane, nor half so good-humored as Lydia. But you are always giving *her* the preference."

"They have none of them much to recommend them," replied he; "they are all silly and ignorant like other girls, but Lizzy has something more of quickness than her sisters."

"Mr. Bennet, how can you abuse your own children in such a way? You take delight in vexing me. You have no compassion on my poor nerves."

"You mistake me, my dear. I have a high respect for your nerves. They are my old friends. I have heard you mention them with consideration these twenty years at least."

"Ah! You do not know what I suffer."

"But I hope you will get over it, and live to see many young men of four thousand a year come into the neighborhood."

"It will be no use to us if twenty such should come, since you will not visit them."

"Depend upon it, my dear, that when there are twenty, I will visit them all."

Mr. Bennet was so odd a mixture of quick parts, sarcastic humor, reserve, and caprice, that the experience of three and twenty years had been insufficient to make his wife understand his character. *Her* mind was less difficult to develop. She was a woman of mean[6] understanding, little information, and uncertain temper. When she was discontented, she fancied herself nervous. The business of her life was to get her daughters married; its solace was visiting and news.

Chapter 2

Mr. Bennet was among the earliest of those who waited on Mr. Bingley. He had always intended to visit him, though to the last always assuring his wife that he should not go; and till the evening after the visit was paid, she had no knowledge of it. It was then disclosed in the following manner. Observing his second daughter employed in trimming a hat, he suddenly addressed her with, "I hope Mr. Bingley will like it, Lizzy."

"We are not in a way to know *what* Mr. Bingley likes," said her mother resentfully, "since we are not to visit."

"But you forget, Mama," said Elizabeth, "that we shall meet him at the assemblies,[7] and that Mrs. Long has promised to introduce him."

"I do not believe Mrs. Long will do any such thing. She has two nieces of her own. She is

---

4. *Engage for* means "plan to undertake."
5. *Overscrupulous* means "overly concerned about social niceties."

6. *Mean* means "low" or "poor."
7. *Assemblies* are public dances.

Reading Strategy Analyzing Characterization *How does Austen characterize Lizzie as she introduces her?*

Big Idea The Stirrings of Romanticism *Does this description make Mr. Bennet seem like part of the Romantic Age or of the Enlightenment? Explain.*

Literary Element Dialogue *What purpose does this dialogue serve?*

a selfish, **hypocritical** woman, and I have no opinion of her."

"No more have I," said Mr. Bennet; "and I am glad to find that you do not depend on her serving you."

Mrs. Bennet deigned not to make any reply; but unable to contain herself, began scolding one of her daughters.

"Don't keep coughing so, Kitty, for heaven's sake! Have a little compassion on my nerves. You tear them to pieces."

"Kitty has no discretion in her coughs," said her father; "she times them ill."

"I do not cough for my own amusement," replied Kitty fretfully.

"When is your next ball to be, Lizzy?"

"Tomorrow fortnight."[8]

"Aye, so it is," cried her mother, "and Mrs. Long does not come back till the day before; so, it will be impossible for her to introduce him, for she will not know him herself."

"Then, my dear, you may have the advantage of your friend, and introduce Mr. Bingley to *her*."

"Impossible, Mr. Bennet, impossible, when I am not acquainted with him myself; how can you be so teasing?"

"I honor your circumspection. A fortnight's **acquaintance** is certainly very little. One cannot know what a man really is by the end of a fortnight. But if *we* do not venture, somebody else will; and after all, Mrs. Long and her nieces must stand their chance; and therefore, as she will think it an act of kindness, if you decline the office, I will take it on myself."

The girls stared at their father. Mrs. Bennet said only, "Nonsense, nonsense!"

"What can be the meaning of that **emphatic** exclamation?" cried he. "Do you consider the

Three Gentlemen Greeting Each Other. Richard Dighton (1795-1880). Watercolor and ink wash over pencil. Private collection. Bonhams, London.

forms of introduction, and the stress that is laid on them, as nonsense? I cannot quite agree with you *there*. What say you, Mary, for you are a young lady of deep reflection, I know, and read great books, and make extracts."

Mary wished to say something very sensible, but knew not how.

"While Mary is adjusting her ideas," he continued, "let us return to Mr. Bingley."

"I am sick of Mr. Bingley," cried his wife.

"I am sorry to hear *that*; but why did not you tell me so before? If I had known as much this morning, I certainly would not have called on him. It is very unlucky; but as I have actually paid the visit, we cannot escape the acquaintance now."

The astonishment of the ladies was just what he wished—that of Mrs. Bennet perhaps surpassing the rest—though when the first tumult of joy was over, she began to declare that it was what she had expected all the while.

---

8. *Tomorrow fortnight* means "two weeks from tomorrow."

"How good it was in you, my dear Mr. Bennet! But I knew I should persuade you at last. I was sure you loved your girls too well to neglect such an acquaintance. Well, how pleased I am! And it is such a good joke, too, that you should have gone this morning, and never said a word about it till now."

"Now, Kitty, you may cough as much as you choose," said Mr. Bennet; and, as he spoke, he left the room, fatigued with the raptures of his wife.

"What an excellent father you have, girls," said she, when the door was shut. "I do not know how you will ever make him amends for his kindness; or me either, for that matter. At our time of life it is not so pleasant, I can tell you, to be making new acquaintances everyday; but for your sakes, we would do anything. Lydia, my love, though you *are* the youngest, I dare say Mr. Bingley will dance with you at the next ball."

"Oh!" said Lydia stoutly, "I am not afraid; for though I *am* the youngest, I'm the tallest."

The rest of the evening was spent in conjecturing how soon he would return Mr. Bennet's visit, and determining when they should ask him to dinner.

Chapter 3

Not all that Mrs. Bennet, however, with the assistance of her five daughters, could ask on the subject was sufficient to draw from her husband any satisfactory description of Mr. Bingley. They attacked him in various ways—with barefaced questions, ingenious suppositions, and distant surmises—but he eluded the skill of them all; and they were at last obliged to accept the secondhand intelligence of their neighbor Lady Lucas. Her report was highly favorable. Sir William had been delighted with him. He was quite young, wonderfully handsome, extremely agreeable, and to crown the whole, he meant to be at the next assembly with a large party. Nothing could be more delightful! To be fond of dancing was a certain step toward falling in love; and very lively hopes of Mr. Bingley's heart were entertained.

"If I can but see one of my daughters happily settled at Netherfield," said Mrs. Bennet to her husband, "and all the others equally well married, I shall have nothing to wish for."

In a few days Mr. Bingley returned Mr. Bennet's visit, and sat about ten minutes with him in his library. He had entertained hopes of being admitted to a sight of the young ladies, of whose beauty he had heard much; but he saw only the father. The ladies were somewhat more fortunate, for they had the advantage of ascertaining from an upper window that he wore a blue coat and rode a black horse.

An invitation to dinner was soon afterward dispatched, and already had Mrs. Bennet planned the courses that were to do credit to her housekeeping, when an answer arrived which deferred it all. Mr. Bingley was obliged to be in town[9] the following day, and consequently unable to accept the honor of their invitation, etc. Mrs. Bennet was quite disconcerted. She could not imagine what business he could have in town so soon after his arrival in Hertfordshire;[10] and she began to fear that he might be always flying about from one place to another, and never settled at Netherfield as he ought to be. Lady Lucas quieted her fears a little by starting the idea of his being gone to London only to get a large party for the ball, and a report soon followed that Mr. Bingley was to bring twelve ladies and seven gentlemen with him to the assembly. The girls grieved over such a number of ladies; but were comforted the day before the ball by hearing that, instead of twelve, he had brought only six with him from London, his five sisters and a cousin. And when the party entered the assembly room, it consisted of only five altogether; Mr. Bingley, his two sisters, the husband of the eldest, and another young man.

Mr. Bingley was good-looking and gentlemanlike; he had a pleasant countenance, and easy, unaffected manners. His sisters were fine women,

---

9. *In town* refers to London.
10. *Hertfordshire* [härt′ fərd shər] is an English county just north of London.

Big Idea The Stirrings of Romanticism *Does this description of Mr. Bingley make him seem to fit the Romantic Age or the Enlightenment? Explain.*

Reading Strategy Analyzing Characterization *What does this description of Mrs. Bennet's concerns add to her characterization?*

with an air of decided fashion. His brother-in-law, Mr. Hurst, merely looked the gentleman; but his friend Mr. Darcy soon drew the attention of the room by his fine, tall person, handsome features, noble mien—and the report which was in general circulation within five minutes after his entrance of his having ten thousand a year. The gentlemen pronounced him to be a fine figure of a man, the ladies declared he was much handsomer than Mr. Bingley, and he was looked at with great admiration for about half the evening, till his manners gave a disgust which turned the tide of his popularity; for he was discovered to be proud, to be above his company, and above being pleased; and not all his large estate in Derbyshire[11] could then save him from having a most forbidding, disagreeable countenance, and being unworthy to be compared with his friend.

Mr. Bingley had soon made himself acquainted with all the principal people in the room; he was lively and unreserved, danced every dance, was angry that the ball closed so early, and talked of giving one himself at Netherfield. Such amiable qualities must speak for themselves. What a contrast between him and his friend! Mr. Darcy danced only once with Mrs. Hurst and once with Miss Bingley, declined being introduced to any other lady, and spent the rest of the evening in walking about the room, speaking occasionally to one of his own party. His character was decided. He was the proudest, most disagreeable man in the world, and everybody hoped that he would never come there again. Among the most violent against him was Mrs. Bennet, whose dislike of his general behavior was sharpened into particular resentment by his having slighted one of her daughters.

Elizabeth Bennet had been obliged by the scarcity of gentlemen to sit down for two dances; and during part of that time, Mr. Darcy had been standing near enough for her to overhear a conversation between him and Mr. Bingley, who came from the dance for a few minutes to press his friend to join it.

"Come, Darcy," said he, "I must have you dance. I hate to see you standing about by yourself in this stupid manner. You had much better dance."

"I certainly shall not. You know how I detest it, unless I am particularly acquainted with my partner. At such an assembly as this, it would be insupportable. Your sisters are engaged, and there is not another woman in the room whom it would not be a punishment to me to stand up with."

"I would not be so fastidious as you are," cried Bingley, "for a kingdom! Upon my honor, I never met with so many pleasant girls in my life as I have this evening; and there are several of them you see uncommonly pretty."

"*You* are dancing with the only handsome girl in the room," said Mr. Darcy, looking at the eldest Miss Bennet.

"Oh! She is the most beautiful creature I ever beheld! But there is one of her sisters sitting down just behind you, who is very pretty, and I dare say, very agreeable. Do let me ask my partner to introduce you."

"Which do you mean?" and turning round, he looked for a moment at Elizabeth, till catching her eye, he withdrew his own and coldly said, "She is tolerable; but not handsome enough to tempt *me*; and I am in no humor at present to give consequence to young ladies who are slighted by other men. You had better return to your partner and enjoy her smiles, for you are wasting your time with me."

Mr. Bingley followed his advice. Mr. Darcy walked off; and Elizabeth remained with no very cordial feelings toward him. She told the story, however, with great spirit among her friends; for she had a lively, playful disposition, which delighted in anything ridiculous.

The evening altogether passed off pleasantly to the whole family. Mrs. Bennet had seen her eldest daughter much admired by the Netherfield party. Mr. Bingley had danced with her twice, and she had been distinguished by his sisters.

---

11. *Derbyshire* [där′ bi shər] is a county in north-central England.

Big Idea   The Stirrings of Romanticism *Does Mr. Darcy seem to be part of the Romantic Age or the Enlightenment? Explain.*

Literary Element   Dialogue *What does this dialogue reveal about Mr. Darcy's character?*

Reading Strategy   Analyzing Characterization *How does this paragraph contribute to the characterization of Elizabeth?*

Jane was as much gratified by this as her mother could be, though in a quieter way. Elizabeth felt Jane's pleasure. Mary had heard herself mentioned to Miss Bingley as the most accomplished girl in the neighborhood; and Catherine and Lydia had been fortunate enough to be never without partners, which was all that they had yet learned to care for at a ball. They returned therefore in good spirits to Longbourn, the village where they lived, and of which they were the principal inhabitants. They found Mr. Bennet still up. With a book he was regardless of time, and on the present occasion he had a good deal of curiosity as to the event of an evening which had raised such splendid expectations. He had rather hoped that all his wife's views on the stranger would be disappointed, but he soon found that he had a very different story to hear.

"Oh, my dear Mr. Bennet"—as she entered the room—"we have had a most delightful evening, a most excellent ball. I wish you had been there. Jane was so admired, nothing

Two Women Reading in an Interior. Jean Georges Ferry. Gavin Graham Gallery, London.

could be like it. Everybody said how well she looked, and Mr. Bingley thought her quite beautiful, and danced with her twice. Only think of *that*, my dear; he actually danced with her twice; and she was the only creature in the room that he asked a second time. First of all, he asked Miss Lucas. I was so vexed to see him stand up with her; but, however, he did not admire her at all: indeed, nobody can, you know; and he seemed quite struck with Jane as she was going down the dance. So, he inquired who she was, and got introduced, and asked her for the two next. Then, the two third he danced with Miss King, and the two fourth with Maria Lucas, and the two fifth with Jane again, and the two sixth with Lizzy, and the Boulanger—"[12]

"If he had had any compassion for *me*," cried her husband impatiently, "he would not have danced half so much! For God's sake, say no more of his partners. Oh, that he had sprained his ankle in the first dance!"

"Oh! My dear," continued Mrs. Bennet, "I am quite delighted with him. He is so excessively handsome! And his sisters are charming women. I never in my life saw anything more elegant than their dresses. I dare say the lace upon Mrs. Hurst's gown—"

Here she was interrupted again. Mr. Bennet protested against any description of finery. She was therefore obliged to seek another branch of the subject, and related, with much bitterness of spirit and some exaggeration, the shocking rudeness of Mr. Darcy.

"But I can assure you," she added, "that Lizzy does not lose much by not suiting *his* fancy; for he is a most disagreeable, horrid man, not at all worth pleasing. So high and so conceited that there was no enduring him! He walked here, and he walked there, fancying himself so very great! Not handsome enough to dance with! I wish you had been there, my dear, to have given him one of your set-downs.[13] I quite detest the man."

---

12. When a gentleman asked a lady to dance, the couple danced a two-dance set, except in the case of more complex or exhausting dances, such as the *Boulanger* [boō län zhā´]. The *two third* is the third two-dance set, the *two fourth* is the fourth, and so on.
13. *Set-downs* means "snubbing remarks" or "rebuffs."

RESPONDING AND THINKING CRITICALLY

Respond

1. Which character do you find most interesting? Why?

Recall and Interpret

2. (a)According to the opening paragraph, what "truth" is "universally acknowledged"? (b)What is Austen implying about society here?

3. (a)Who has rented Netherfield Park? (b)Why is this important to Mrs. Bennet?

4. (a)Summarize the reasons that Bingley draws approval at the local assembly. (b)Why does Darcy first attract the attention of the room?

5. (a)What girl does Bingley show a preference for? Why? (b)What might this reveal about Bingley's character?

Analyze and Evaluate

6. (a)How is the opening paragraph ironic? (b)How does the irony hint at the plot events that follow?

7. (a)Identify the narrator's tone, or attitude toward the subject. (b)Toward which character(s) does she seem most sympathetic?

8. (a)Which character seems to most display the trait of pride? (b)Which most displays prejudice? Explain.

Connect

9. **Big Idea** **The Stirrings of Romanticism** Which character exemplifies most strongly the values of the Romantic era? Explain.

PRIMARY VISUAL ARTIFACT

Marriage, Behind the Scenes

William Hogarth (1697–1764) was a Romantic artist known mostly for his satirical paintings and engravings. Hogarth's work focused on issues of the middle class and often criticized the hypocrisy of society. His work greatly influenced Romantic literature of the time. Completed in 1745, this famous painting, from a series titled *Marriage à la Mode*, shows a young man and woman as their families prepare a marriage contract to confirm the financial details of their arranged marriage.

Group Activity Discuss the following questions with your classmates.

1. How has Hogarth depicted the young couple (seen on the left)? What does he seem to be saying about their relationship?

2. What elements expressed in this painting are reminiscent of ideas and themes in *Pride and Prejudice*?

The Marriage Settlement, (first of six from *Marriage à la Mode* series), 1742–44. William Hogarth. Oil on canvas, 90.8 x 69.9 cm. National Gallery, London.

Literary Element Dialogue

In the eighteenth century, novels were chiefly descriptive. Action and dialogue were mainly tools of drama on stage. Jane Austen was the first major British writer to make extensive use of both action and dialogue in fiction. As an omniscient, or all-knowing, narrator, Austen often makes direct statements about her characters' personalities. However, she then reveals her characters' personalities in action and in conversation. Austen's dialogue is also realistic, in keeping with her characters' backgrounds and traits. For example, Mr. Bennet is intentionally witty, and Mrs. Bennet is not witty at all, though she often makes us laugh.

1. Identify three remarks or actions by Mr. Bennet that support the direct statements made about him at the close of Chapter 1. Then do the same for Mrs. Bennet.

2. What do we learn about Bingley's and Darcy's personalities in Chapter 3? What specific actions and lines of dialogue help reveal their personalities?

Review: Point of View

As you learned on page 276, **point of view** is the relationship of the narrator to the story. The third-person omniscient narrator, or all-knowing point of view, is not a character in the story but someone who stands outside the story and comments on the action. A third-person omniscient narrator knows everything about the characters and events and may reveal details that the characters themselves could not reveal.

Group Activity Meet with a group of classmates and discuss how point of view is used throughout the selection from *Pride and Prejudice*. Then, record specific instances where the omniscient point of view is used by the narrator and determine its significance in the selection. Use a chart like the one below.

Examples	Significance

Reading Strategy Analyzing Characterization

Sometimes a narrator directly reveals details about a character; other times these character traits are implied. For example, Chapter 1 of *Pride and Prejudice* explicitly states that Mrs. Bennet is "a woman of mean understanding, little information, and uncertain temper." However, Mrs. Bennet's actions also imply that she is a foolish person, without explicitly stating it.

1. What do we learn about each main character's personality in this excerpt from *Pride and Prejudice*?

2. How does the author reveal these character traits directly and indirectly throughout the selection?

Vocabulary Practice

Practice with Word Origins Match each word with its corresponding etymology. Use a dictionary for assistance.

1. hypocritical   **a.** Latin root, meaning "to make known"

2. emphatic   **b.** Greek root, meaning "exhibit"

3. acquaintance   **c.** Greek root, meaning "actor"

Actors Rosamund Pike (left) as Jane Bennet and Keira Knightley as Elizabeth Bennet from the 2005 filming of *Pride and Prejudice*.

JANE AUSTEN **777**

Writing About Literature

Analyze Genre Elements Satire is writing that comments, sometimes humorously, on human flaws, ideas, social customs, or institutions. The purpose of satire may be to reform or to entertain. Write a brief essay describing how Jane Austen satirizes some aspect of society, such as the effort to marry well, the impact of gossip, the effect of wealth on people's behavior, or the importance of physical appearance and social rank. Use textual evidence from the selection to defend your position. Follow this writing path as you draft your essay.

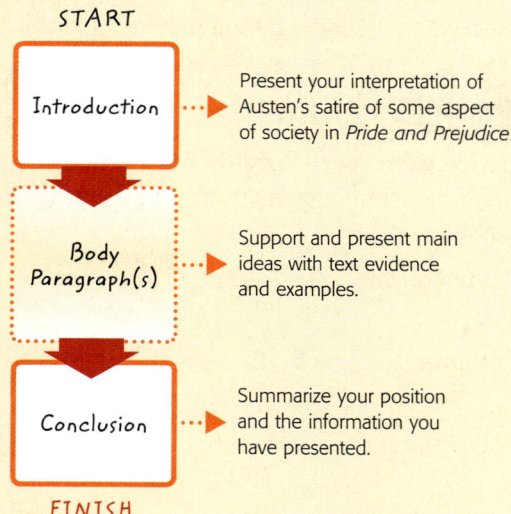

START

Introduction ····▸ Present your interpretation of Austen's satire of some aspect of society in *Pride and Prejudice*.

Body Paragraph(s) ····▸ Support and present main ideas with text evidence and examples.

Conclusion ····▸ Summarize your position and the information you have presented.

FINISH

After you complete your draft, exchange papers with a partner. Review each other's work and suggest revisions. Then, proofread your draft for errors.

Performing

In groups of three, assign one student the role of Mr. Bennet, one the role of Mrs. Bennet, and the third student the role of the Bennet sisters. Perform the scene from Chapter 2 on pages 771–773, practicing the subtle comic effects Austen creates with the dialogue. Focus on the clarity and timing of your gestures and facial expressions.

Literature Online Web Activities For eFlashcards, Selection Quick Checks, and other Web activities, go to www.glencoe.com.

Austen's Language and Style

Adding Narrator Commentary In *Pride and Prejudice*, Jane Austen often incorporates the opinions and observations of the third-person narrator. **Narrator commentary** is a specific type of narrative style in which the author allows the narrator to make comments on situations in the text. Consider the following example:

> "Mr. Bennet was among the earliest of those who waited on Mr. Bingley. He had always intended to visit him, though to the last always assuring his wife that he should not go; and till the evening after the visit was paid, she had no knowledge of it."

Notice how Austen creates wry, understated narrative by contrasting the narrator's comments with Mr. Bennet's actions.

Observe some of the narrator commentary Austen creates:

Narrator Commentary	Ideas Emphasized
1. "he was looked at with great admiration for about half the evening, till his manners gave disgust which turned the tide of his popularity"	1. The narrator echoes in a lightly mocking way the voice of the community, whose approval is fickle and selfish.
2. "Here she was interrupted again. Mr. Bennet protested against any description of finery."	2. The narrator contributes to the sharp, witty tone.

Activity Create a similar chart of your own. Identify as many examples of narrator commentary from *Pride and Prejudice* as you can, and explain how each example adds to the conflict and theme.

Revising Check

Narrator Commentary When you revise your essay on satire, see if you can incorporate examples of narrator commentary from *Pride and Prejudice* to emphasize themes and important points. This will add light humor to your essay and entertain as well as inform readers.

PART 2

Nature and the Imagination

The Bard, c.1817. John Martin. Oil on canvas, 50 x 39.96 in. Yale Center
for British Art, Paul Mellon Collection, New Haven, CT.

"*Poetry is the spontaneous overflow of powerful feelings: it takes its
origin from emotion recollected in tranquility.*"

—William Wordsworth, preface to *Lyrical Ballads*

Wordsworth's Poetry

MEET WILLIAM WORDSWORTH

William Wordsworth was a true literary pioneer. He defied the conventions of his time by insisting that poetry should express deep feelings about everyday experiences. In the process, he influenced a generation of poets and helped revolutionize English poetry.

Passion for Nature Wordsworth was born in England's Lake District, a land of breathtaking scenery. Early in life, he suffered two tragedies: the sudden death of his mother when he was eight and the death of his father about five years later. The orphaned Wordsworth children were separated. William and his brothers boarded with a couple near the school the boys attended, and their sister, Dorothy, lived with relatives. Though Wordsworth grieved over the loss of his parents, he came to love school, the people of the Lake District, and the land. The passion he developed for poetry, for simple country living, and for the natural world was to influence him for the rest of his life.

> *"Come forth into the light of things, Let Nature be your Teacher."*
>
> —William Wordsworth

Rebel in France Wordsworth furthered his education at Cambridge University, graduating at the age of twenty-one. While visiting France, he became caught up in the spirit of the French Revolution, which he viewed as a struggle for social justice. He also fell in love with a French woman named Annette Vallon. Though he wanted to stay with her, lack of money forced him to return to England. The next few years were difficult ones for Wordsworth. He felt guilty about leaving Vallon, disillusioned by the increasing violence in France, and disappointed by the poor critical response to

his volumes of poetry *An Evening Walk* and *Descriptive Sketches*. Lacking a purpose for his future, he teetered on the brink of mental collapse.

Literary Acclaim When Wordsworth was in his mid-twenties, however, his fortunes changed. He inherited money from a friend, was given a cottage in the Lake District, and was reunited with his sister, Dorothy, who was his dear friend and confidant. Soon afterward, he met Samuel Taylor Coleridge, and this meeting resulted in what is probably the most significant friendship in all of English literature. With the companionship and support of his sister and his friend, Wordsworth began to devote himself to writing poetry. He soon established his reputation as a leading young poet with a slim volume of poems entitled *Lyrical Ballads*, first published in 1798. That book, which includes Wordsworth's poem "Lines Composed a Few Miles Above Tintern Abbey" and Coleridge's *The Rime of the Ancient Mariner*, became the cornerstone of English Romanticism.

Wordsworth continued to write throughout his long life, which he spent in the Lake District with his sister and his wife, Mary. His masterpiece, *The Prelude*, a long autobiographical poem, was published after his death.

William Wordsworth was born in 1770 and died in 1850.

Literature Online **Author Search** For more about William Wordsworth, go to www.glencoe.com.

Connecting to the Poems

In the following poems, Wordsworth describes his experiences of nature and their effect on his life. As you read, think about what you can derive from appreciating nature.

Building Background

In 1800 Wordsworth added a preface to the second edition of *Lyrical Ballads* to explain his new approach to poetry. Wordsworth's innovative ideas clashed with those of his predecessors: Swift, Pope, and Johnson, the giants of Neoclassicism. They believed poetry should be an art that engages the mind more than the heart; it should be calculated rather than spontaneous, witty rather than emotional. Wordsworth, on the other hand, suggested that all good poetry springs from the "spontaneous overflow of powerful feelings" that the poet "recollect[s] in tranquility." He felt that the language of poetry should be simple and natural.

Setting Purposes for Reading

Big Idea Nature and the Imagination

As you read, consider what these poems suggest about the relationship between humans and the natural world.

Literary Element Enjambment

Enjambment is the continuation of a sentence in a poem from one line to the next. Wordsworth often uses enjambment in his poetry, as in these lines from "It Is a Beauteous Evening, Calm and Free":

> Listen! The mighty Being is awake,
> And doth with his eternal motion make
> A sound like thunder—everlastingly.

As you read, notice additional examples of this technique.

- See Literary Terms Handbook, p. R5.

Literature Online **Interactive Literary Elements Handbook** To review or learn more about the literary elements, go to www.glencoe.com.

Reading Strategy Identifying Genre: Romantic Poetry

In Wordsworth's view, Romantic poetry differed from Neoclassical poetry in its emphasis on spontaneity, its expression of powerful feelings, and its use of simple language.

....

Reading Tip: Taking Notes Use a web diagram to list examples of Romantic traits in Wordsworth's poems.

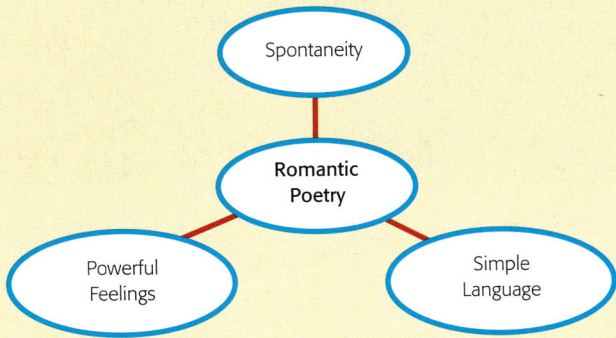

Vocabulary

sordid (sôr′ did) *adj.* filthy; selfish; greedy; mean; p. 782 *Putting himself before others, he used any means to achieve his sordid goals.*

piety (pī′ ə tē) *n.* devoutness; reverence; p. 783 *With heartfelt piety, he bowed his head upon entering the cathedral.*

secluded (si klōō′ did) *adj.* shut off from others; undisturbed; p. 786 *By hiding in a secluded thicket, the fox eluded the hunters.*

repose (ri pōz′) *v.* lie at rest; rest from work or toil; p. 786 *Worn out from work, the farmer reposed for a while under a shady tree.*

Vocabulary Tip: Word Origins and Antonyms Many dictionaries provide the **etymology,** or the history of a word, along with the word's definition.

Words that are opposite in meaning are antonyms.

OBJECTIVES
In studying these selections, you will focus on the following:
- analyzing literary periods
- analyzing enjambment

- understanding genre
- evaluating diction
- analyzing sensory details

The Dissolute Household, 1668. Jan Steen. Oil on canvas. Victoria and Albert Museum, London.

The World Is Too Much with Us

William Wordsworth

The world is too much with us; late and soon,
Getting and spending, we lay waste our powers;
Little we see in Nature that is ours;
We have given our hearts away, a **sordid** boon![1]
5   This Sea that bares her bosom to the moon;
The winds that will be howling at all hours,
And are up-gathered now like sleeping flowers;
For this, for everything, we are out of tune;
It moves us not.—Great God! I'd rather be
10   A Pagan[2] suckled in a creed[3] outworn;
So might I, standing on this pleasant lea,[4]
Have glimpses that would make me less forlorn;
Have sight of Proteus[5] rising from the sea;
Or hear old Triton[6] blow his wreathèd horn.

1. A *boon* is a gift.
2. Here, a *Pagan* is a believer in the ancient Greek or Roman gods of mythology.
3. A *creed* is any statement of faith or principles.
4. A *lea* (lē) is a meadow.
5. In Greek mythology, Proteus (prō′ tē əs), an old man and a prophet, would rise from the sea and assume many forms.
6. *Triton* (trīt′ ən) is the son of the sea god Neptune, who makes the sound of the ocean by blowing through his conch-shell horn.

Big Idea **Nature and the Imagination** *Why is the inability to be moved by nature tragic to the speaker?*

Vocabulary

sordid (sôr′ did) *adj.* filthy; selfish; greedy; mean

It Is a Beauteous Evening, Calm and Free

William Wordsworth

It is a beauteous evening, calm and free,
The holy time is quiet as a Nun
Breathless with adoration; the broad sun
Is sinking down in its tranquility;
5 The gentleness of heaven broods o'er the Sea:
Listen! the mighty Being is awake,
And doth with his eternal motion make
A sound like thunder—everlastingly.
Dear Child![1] dear Girl! that walkest with me here,
10 If thou appear untouched by solemn thought,
Thy nature is not therefore less divine:
Thou liest in Abraham's bosom[2] all the year,
And worship'st at the Temple's inner shrine,
God being with thee when we know it not.

1. *Dear Child* refers to Caroline, Wordsworth's daughter with Annette Vallon.
2. According to a Jewish tradition, souls on their way to heaven rest with *Abraham*, a father of the Hebrew people, enjoying a state of bliss.

My Heart Leaps Up

William Wordsworth

My heart leaps up when I behold
A rainbow in the sky:
So was it when my life began;
So is it now I am a man;
5 So be it when I shall grow old,
    Or let me die!
The Child is father of the Man;
And I could wish my days to be
Bound each to each by natural **piety**.

Literary Element **Enjambment** *What does Wordsworth achieve by using enjambment in lines 1 and 2?*

Vocabulary

piety (pī′ ə tē) *n.* devoutness; reverence

A View of Westminster with the Royal Barge and Other Shipping. Joseph Nicholls. Oil on canvas, 61 x 111.7 cm. Private collection.

Composed Upon Westminster Bridge,
September 3, 1802

William Wordsworth

Earth has not anything to show more fair:
Dull would he be of soul who could pass by
A sight so touching in its majesty:
This City now doth, like a garment, wear
5   The beauty of the morning; silent, bare,
Ships, towers, domes, theaters, and temples lie
Open unto the fields, and to the sky;
All bright and glittering in the smokeless air.
Never did sun more beautifully steep
10   In his first splendor, valley, rock, or hill;
Ne'er saw I, never felt, a calm so deep!
The river glideth at his own sweet will:
Dear God! the very houses seem asleep;
And all that mighty heart is lying still!

Reading Strategy   **Identifying Genre: Romantic Poetry**
What emotion does this poem convey?

RESPONDING AND THINKING CRITICALLY

Respond

1. Which poem did you like best? Why?

Recall and Interpret

2. (a)According to line 2 of "The World Is Too Much with Us," with what activities are people preoccupied? How does this preoccupation change people's lives? (b)What does the speaker think of this change?

3. (a)In lines 2–3 of "It Is a Beauteous Evening, Calm and Free," to what does the speaker compare the evening? (b)What does this **simile** suggest about the speaker's attitude toward nature?

4. (a)In "My Heart Leaps Up," what natural phenomenon does the speaker admire? (b)What qualities are usually associated with this phenomenon?

5. (a)In "Composed Upon Westminster Bridge," when does the speaker describe London? (b)Why is that time of day significant?

Analyze and Evaluate

6. (a)What is the **theme,** or main idea about life, of "The World Is Too Much with Us"? (b)Is this theme still relevant to life today? Explain.

7. Restate the paradox in line 7 of "My Heart Leaps Up." In what sense does that statement seem contradictory? In what sense is it true?

8. What is the poetic form of "Composed Upon Westminster Bridge"? Which other Wordsworth poems use the same form?

Connect

9. **Big Idea** **Nature and the Imagination** How does Wordsworth view the relationship between humans and the natural world? Explain.

LITERARY ANALYSIS

Literary Element **Enjambment**

Poets may use enjambed lines to emphasize rhyming words or to create a conversational tone, breaking lines where people would pause in conversation.

1. What lines of "The World Is Too Much with Us" are enjambed? What rhymes do the line breaks emphasize?

2. What purposes do the three examples of enjambment in the first eight lines of "It Is a Beauteous Evening, Calm and Free" serve?

Writing About Literature

Respond to Tone Tone is a reflection of the writer's attitude toward a subject as conveyed through such elements as word choice, punctuation, sentence structure, and figures of speech. Choose one of the four poems you have just read. In a short essay, identify the poem's tone and explain how it is conveyed.

Literature Online **Web Activities** For eFlashcards, Selection Quick Checks, and other Web activities, go to www.glencoe.com.

READING AND VOCABULARY

Reading Strategy **Identifying Genre: Romantic Poetry**

Wordsworth's poems reflect the characteristics that distinguish Romantic poetry. Review the web diagram you made on page 781, and then answer the following questions.

1. What elements in these poems reflect Wordsworth's idea that poetry springs from "the spontaneous overflow of powerful feelings"?

2. To what extent is the language in these poems simple and natural?

Vocabulary **Practice**

Practice with Word Origins Match each vocabulary word with the meaning of its Latin root. Use a dictionary if you need help.

1. sordid   a. dutiful

2. piety   b. dirt

Literary Element Diction

Diction refers to an author's word choice, or use of appropriate words to convey a particular meaning. Diction is particularly important in poetry, which uses language more economically than most prose does. As you read, notice Wordsworth's diction and consider its effects.

- See Literary Terms Handbook, p. R5.

Reading Strategy Analyzing Sensory Details

In creating effective images, writers use **sensory details,** or descriptions that appeal to one or more of the five senses: sight, hearing, touch, taste, and smell. Like diction and sentence structure, sensory details influence the tone and meaning of a literary work.

LINES COMPOSED A FEW MILES ABOVE TINTERN ABBEY

William Wordsworth

Five years have past; five summers, with the length
Of five long winters! and again I hear
These waters, rolling from their mountain springs
With a soft inland murmur. Once again
5 Do I behold these steep and lofty cliffs,
That on a wild **secluded** scene impress
Thoughts of more deep seclusion; and connect
The landscape with the quiet of the sky.
The day is come when I again **repose**

Reading Strategy Analyzing Sensory Details *This poem was inspired by Wordsworth's two visits to the ruins of a medieval abbey located in an area of Wales known for its striking beauty. Which details in the first eight lines help you visualize the scene?*

Vocabulary

secluded (si klōō′ did) *adj.* shut off from others; undisturbed
repose (ri pōz′) *v.* lie at rest; rest from work or toil

Interior of Tintern Abbey.
Thomas Girtin.
Watercolor on paper.
Private collection.

10   Here, under this dark sycamore, and view
       These plots of cottage ground, these orchard tufts,
       Which at this season, with their unripe fruits,
       Are clad in one green hue, and lose themselves
       'Mid groves and copses.[1] Once again I see
15   These hedgerows,[2] hardly hedgerows, little lines
       Of sportive wood run wild; these pastoral farms,
       Green to the very door; and wreaths of smoke
       Sent up, in silence, from among the trees!
       With some uncertain notice, as might seem
20   Of vagrant dwellers in the houseless woods,
       Or of some hermit's cave, where by his fire
       The hermit sits alone.

                    These beauteous forms,
       Through a long absence, have not been to me
       As is a landscape to a blind man's eye;
25   But oft, in lonely rooms, and 'mid the din
       Of towns and cities, I have owed to them
       In hours of weariness, sensations sweet,

---

1. *Copses* are thick, dense growths of small trees or bushes.
2. *Hedgerows* are rows of bushes, shrubs, or trees that serve
as fences or boundaries.

Literary Element Diction *What does the phrase "unripe fruits" suggest about the time of year?*

Big Idea Nature and the Imagination *What comforts the speaker while he is in the city?*

Felt in the blood, and felt along the heart;
And passing even into my purer mind,
30   With tranquil restoration—feelings, too,
Of unremembered pleasure: such, perhaps,
As have no slight or trivial influence
On that best portion of a good man's life,
His little, nameless, unremembered, acts
35   Of kindness and of love. Nor less, I trust,
To them I may have owed another gift,
Of aspect more sublime; that blessed mood,
In which the burthen[3] of the mystery,
In which the heavy and the weary weight
40   Of all this unintelligible[4] world,
Is lightened—that serene and blessed mood,
In which the affections gently lead us on—
Until, the breath of this corporeal[5] frame
And even the motion of our human blood
45   Almost suspended, we are laid asleep
In body, and become a living soul;
While with an eye made quiet by the power
Of harmony, and the deep power of joy,
We see into the life of things.
                                        If this
50   Be but a vain belief, yet, oh! how oft—
In darkness and amid the many shapes
Of joyless daylight; when the fretful stir
Unprofitable, and the fever of the world,
Have hung upon the beatings of my heart—
55   How oft, in spirit, have I turned to thee,
O sylvan Wye![6] thou wanderer through the woods,
How often has my spirit turned to thee!

        And now, with gleams of half-extinguished thought,
With many recognitions dim and faint,
60   And somewhat of a sad perplexity,
The picture of the mind revives again;
While here I stand, not only with the sense
Of present pleasure, but with pleasing thoughts
That in this moment there is life and food
65   For future years. And so I dare to hope,
Though changed, no doubt, from what I was when first

---

3. *Burthen* is a variant form of *burden*.
4. *Unintelligible* means "incapable of being understood."
5. *Corporeal* means "bodily."
6. *Sylvan* means "wooded"; the *Wye* is the river whose banks
   Wordsworth walked during his visits.

Big Idea **Nature and the Imagination** *What type of relationship with nature do these lines suggest?*

I came among these hills; when like a roe[7]
I bounded o'er the mountains, by the sides
Of the deep rivers, and the lonely streams,
70 Wherever nature led—more like a man
Flying from something that he dreads than one
Who sought the thing he loved. For nature then
(The coarser pleasures of my boyish days,
And their glad animal movements all gone by)
75 To me was all in all—I cannot paint
What then I was. The sounding cataract[8]
Haunted me like a passion; the tall rock,
The mountain, and the deep and gloomy wood,
Their colors and their forms, were then to me
80 An appetite; a feeling and a love,
That had no need of a remoter charm,
By thought supplied, nor any interest
Unborrowed from the eye. That time is past,
And all its aching joys are now no more,
85 And all its dizzy raptures. Not for this
Faint[9] I, nor mourn nor murmur; other gifts
Have followed; for such loss, I would believe,
Abundant recompense.[10] For I have learned
To look on nature, not as in the hour
90 Of thoughtless youth; but hearing oftentimes
The still, sad music of humanity,
Nor harsh nor grating, though of ample power
To chasten and subdue. And I have felt
A presence that disturbs me with the joy
95 Of elevated thoughts; a sense sublime
Of something far more deeply interfused,
Whose dwelling is the light of setting suns,
And the round ocean and the living air,
And the blue sky, and in the mind of man;
100 A motion and a spirit, that impels
All thinking things, all objects of all thought,
And rolls through all things. Therefore am I still
A lover of the meadows and the woods
And mountains; and of all that we behold
105 From this green earth; of all the mighty world

---

7. A *roe* is a small Eurasian deer found in lightly forested regions.
8. A *cataract* is a large waterfall.
9. Here, *faint* means "to lose heart; become depressed."
10. *Recompense* means "compensation; repayment."

Literary Element Diction *What do the words* roe *and* bounded *suggest about the speaker's former reaction to nature?*

Literary Element Diction *How does this image contrast with the image of "the sounding cataract" in line 76?*

Tintern Abbey, 1794. Joseph Mallord William Turner. Tate Gallery, London.

Of eye and ear—both what they half create,
And what perceive; well pleased to recognize
In nature and the language of the sense,
The anchor of my purest thoughts, the nurse,
110   The guide, the guardian of my heart, and soul
Of all my moral being.

                     Nor perchance,
If I were not thus taught, should I the more
Suffer my genial spirits[11] to decay;
For thou art with me here upon the banks
115   Of this fair river; thou my dearest Friend,[12]
My dear, dear Friend, and in thy voice I catch
The language of my former heart and read
My former pleasures in the shooting lights
Of thy wild eyes. Oh! yet a little while
120   May I behold in thee what I was once,
My dear, dear Sister! and this prayer I make,

---

11. Here, *suffer* means "to allow"; *genial spirits* means "vital energies."
12. *My dearest Friend* refers to Wordsworth's sister, Dorothy, who accompanied him on this walking tour.

Big Idea   **Nature and the Imagination** *What does nature mean to the speaker?*

Knowing that Nature never did betray
The heart that loved her; 'tis her privilege,
Through all the years of this our life, to lead
125 From joy to joy; for she can so inform[13]
The mind that is within us, so impress
With quietness and beauty, and so feed
With lofty thoughts, that neither evil tongues,
Rash judgments, nor the sneers of selfish men,
130 Nor greetings where no kindness is, nor all
The dreary intercourse of daily life,
Shall e'er prevail against us, or disturb
Our cheerful faith, that all which we behold
Is full of blessings. Therefore let the moon
135 Shine on thee in thy solitary walk;
And let the misty mountain winds be free
To blow against thee: and, in after years,
When these wild ecstasies shall be matured
Into a sober pleasure; when thy mind
140 Shall be a mansion for all lovely forms,
Thy memory be as a dwelling place
For all sweet sounds and harmonies; oh! then,
If solitude, or fear, or pain, or grief,
Should be thy portion, with what healing thoughts
145 Of tender joy wilt thou remember me,
And these my exhortations! Nor, perchance—
If I should be where I no more can hear
Thy voice, nor catch from thy wild eyes these gleams
Of past existence—wilt thou then forget
150 That on the banks of this delightful stream
We stood together; and that I, so long
A worshipper of Nature, hither came
Unwearied in that service; rather say
With warmer love—oh! with far deeper zeal
155 Of holier love. Nor wilt thou then forget
That after many wanderings, many years
Of absence, these steep woods and lofty cliffs,
And this green pastoral landscape, were to me
More dear, both for themselves and for thy sake!

13. Here, *inform* means "to inspire."

Literary Element Diction *What does the diction in this passage suggest about city life?*

Big Idea Nature and the Imagination *What does the speaker suggest about the relationship between humans and nature in lines 155–159?*

RESPONDING AND THINKING CRITICALLY

Respond

1. Which lines of this poem did you find most meaningful? Which lines would you like to clarify or ask questions about?

Recall and Interpret

2. (a)Describe the **setting** of the poem. What sights and sounds does the speaker mention in lines 1–22? (b)What is the speaker's attitude toward the sights and sounds around him?

3. (a)How many years have passed since the speaker's first visit to the countryside overlooking Tintern Abbey? (b)Why has the speaker so often "returned in spirit" to these powerful scenes since his first visit?

4. (a)In what ways has the speaker changed since his first visit? How does he look upon nature now? (b)How does the speaker feel about the changes he sees in himself since his first visit?

5. (a)Who accompanies the speaker on his return visit? (b)How does the presence of a companion

enhance the speaker's pleasure in returning to this particular place?

Analyze and Evaluate

6. Is this poem about nature, about human nature, or about both? Explain your opinion, citing lines from the poem to support your ideas.

7. In what ways is this poem like prose? What elements are "poetic"?

8. In line 152, the speaker says that he is a "worshipper of Nature." In your opinion, does the speaker worship nature only, or does he worship something more? Give examples to support your opinion.

Connect

9. **Big Idea** **Nature and the Imagination** Compare "Lines Composed a Few Miles Above Tintern Abbey" with "It Is a Beauteous Evening, Calm and Free." Consider Wordsworth's attitude toward nature and the enjoyment of nature. What similarities do you see in these poems?

PRIMARY SOURCE QUOTATION

Evaluating a Literary Rebel

Francis Jeffrey, a literary critic, expressed the following opinions about Wordsworth's poetry in articles published in the *Edinburgh Review* in 1807 and 1814. As you read the excerpts, note this critic's reaction to Wordsworth's poetry and Romanticism.

"With Mr. Wordsworth and his friends, it is plain that their peculiarities of diction are things of choice, and not of accident. They write as they do, upon principle and system; and it evidently costs them much pains to keep down to the standard which they have proposed for themselves."

"The new poets are just as great borrowers as the old; only that, instead of borrowing from the more popular passages of their illustrious predecessors, they have preferred furnishing themselves from vulgar ballads and plebean nurseries."

"If Mr. Wordsworth, instead of confining himself almost entirely to the society of . . . cottagers and little children . . . had condescended to mingle a little more with the people that were to read and judge [his book], we cannot help thinking that its texture might have been considerably improved."

Group Activity Discuss the following questions with your classmates. Cite evidence from Wordsworth's poems for support.

1. What is Jeffrey's evaluation of Wordsworth's diction?

2. What criticism does Jeffrey level at Wordsworth in the last quotation? How might Wordsworth have responded?

LITERARY ANALYSIS

Literary Element Diction

Through his **diction,** or word choice, Wordsworth rebelled against the strict demands of Neoclassicism. Instead of using "poetic" language, he tried to use simple and natural language, which reflected the speech patterns of ordinary people.

1. In "Tintern Abbey," does Wordsworth fulfill his intention to write poetry "in a selection of language really spoken" by people? Explain.

2. How does the diction in this poem reflect Wordsworth's aesthetic principles and reinforce his ideas?

Review: Lyric Poetry

As you learned on page 449, **lyric poetry** expresses a speaker's personal thoughts and feelings. Lyric poems are usually short and musical, and they emphasize the experience of emotion.

Partner Activity With a partner, answer these questions:

1. Review the four poems by Wordsworth that precede "Lines Composed a Few Miles Above Tintern Abbey." In what ways are these poems examples of lyric poetry?

2. (a)In what way is "Lines Composed a Few Miles Above Tintern Abbey" an example of a lyric poem? (b)What is the verse form of this poem?

READING AND VOCABULARY

Reading Strategy Analyzing Sensory Details

By using **sensory details,** Wordsworth creates images, or word pictures, that evoke emotional responses in the reader. Review the examples of sensory details that you noted while reading the poems, and then answer the following questions.

1. To which senses do most of the sensory details in "Tintern Abbey" appeal? Identify images that appeal to the sense of touch.

2. Which sensory details evoke negative emotions about life in London?

3. How does the use of sensory details reinforce the theme of this poem? Cite examples to support your opinion.

Vocabulary Practice

Practice with Antonyms Find the antonym for each vocabulary word below. Use a dictionary or a thesaurus if you need help.

1. secluded   **a.** crowded   **b.** isolated

2. repose   **a.** relax   **b.** toil

Academic Vocabulary

Here are two words from the vocabulary list on page R82.

accompany (ə kumʹ pə nē) *v.* to join or follow

highlight (hīʹ lītʹ) *v.* to point out or place emphasis on

Practice and Apply
1. What did Wordsworth gain when his sister **accompanied** him to Tintern Abbey?
2. What themes does Wordsworth often **highlight** in his poetry?

Writing About Literature

Analyze Sound Devices Poets use the following sound devices to create a sense of rhythm or a musical quality, to emphasize particular words or phrases, or to reinforce meaning:

- **alliteration,** the repetition of consonant sounds at the beginning of words
- **assonance,** the repetition of the same or similar vowel sounds in stressed syllables that end with different consonant sounds
- **consonance,** the repetition of consonant sounds, typically at the end of non-rhyming words

In a brief essay, identify examples of these sound devices in "Lines Composed a Few Miles Above Tintern Abbey" and explain their purpose. Use a graphic organizer like the one shown below to help you organize your ideas.

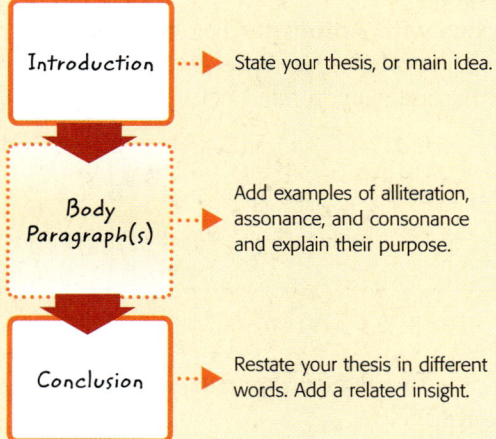

Introduction → State your thesis, or main idea.

Body Paragraph(s) → Add examples of alliteration, assonance, and consonance and explain their purpose.

Conclusion → Restate your thesis in different words. Add a related insight.

After you complete your draft, meet with a peer reviewer to evaluate each other's work and to suggest revisions. Then edit and proofread your draft for errors in spelling, grammar, and punctuation.

Reading Further

If you enjoyed reading these poems by William Wordsworth, you might enjoy these books.

Collection: *William Wordsworth: Selected Poetry,* edited by Stephen Gill and Duncan Wu, contains an excellent sampling of Wordsworth's poetry.

Critical Biography: *Wordsworth* by Margaret Drabble is a brief, clear study of Wordsworth's life and work.

Wordsworth's Language and Style

Keeping Language Simple Wordsworth believed that the language of poetry should be simple and natural. Notice the diction in the opening lines of "The World Is Too Much with Us":

> The world is too much with us; late and soon,
> Getting and spending, we lay waste our powers;
> Little we see in Nature that is ours;
> We have given our hearts away, a sordid boon!

Wordsworth expresses his ideas in simple, clear language, using only one- or two-syllable words. The "voice" is that of someone talking to a friend. The chart below identifies other examples of Wordsworth's diction and explains its effect.

Simple Language	Effect
"So was it when my life began; / So is it now I am a man; / So be it when I shall grow old" ("My Heart Leaps Up")	One-syllable words reinforce the continuity (from past to present to future) of the speaker's devotion to nature's beauty.
"Dear God! the very houses seem asleep" ("Composed Upon . . . ")	A simple personification conveys London's stillness in the morning.
"let the moon / Shine on thee in thy solitary walk; / And let the misty mountain winds be free / to blow against thee" ("Tintern Abbey")	Two simple images convey the speaker's advice to his sister.

Activity Scan Wordsworth's poems for other examples of simple, natural language. List each example and explain its effect. Then share your list with your classmates.

Revising Check

Simple Language Work with a partner to review your essay about Wordsworth's use of sound devices. Look for places where you might make your word choice clearer and more direct by substituting simple and natural words for abstract or difficult ones. Revise your essay to strengthen the diction.

Literature Online Web Activities For eFlashcards, Selection Quick Checks, and other Web activities, go to www.glencoe.com.

from *The Journals of Dorothy Wordsworth*

MEET DOROTHY WORDSWORTH

The depth of Dorothy Wordsworth's devotion to her brother William, the great Romantic poet, and of his devotion to her can be illustrated by a striking entry in one of Dorothy's journals that describes the events surrounding William's marriage to his childhood sweetheart, Mary Hutchinson. On the night before he was to be married, William entrusted Dorothy with the wedding ring, presumably for safekeeping. On the morning of the wedding she returned it to him. Recalling that moment in her journal, she wrote, "I gave him the wedding ring—with how deep a blessing! I took it from my forefinger where I had worn it the whole of the night before—he slipped it again onto my finger, and blessed me fervently." Modern readers might view this revelation as odd, and apparently so did the editors of the first edition of Dorothy's journals, who chose to omit it when the journals were published after her death. In fact, however, Mary was Dorothy's oldest friend. Neither woman was jealous of the other. After William married, Dorothy lived with him and his wife and helped them raise their children.

> "We walked to Rydale. It was very pleasant—Grasmere lake a beautiful image of stillness, clear as glass, reflecting all things. . . . The church and buildings, how quiet they were!"
>
> —Dorothy Wordsworth
> from *The Grasmere Journals*

Three Writers, One Soul Dorothy Wordsworth was born on Christmas Day. When she was six years old, her mother died, and Dorothy was separated from her brothers and sent to live with relatives because it was thought that an all-male household was not a fit place to raise a young girl. Many years later, Dorothy was reunited with her brother William. Dorothy and William enjoyed a deep friendship with the poet Samuel Taylor Coleridge, with whom they walked and talked daily for a number of years. The three were so close that Dorothy once described the trio as "three persons with one soul."

Observer of Nature Although Dorothy wrote some poetry, her best writing is found in her journals and letters. Her *Alfoxden Journal 1798* and *The Grasmere Journals 1800–1803* offer a remarkably detailed and rich view of English cottage life in the first part of the nineteenth century and provide valuable insights into her relationship with her brother and her influence on his poetry. Dorothy's journal writing (which, according to her, she pursued "because I shall give William pleasure by it") shows her to be a keen observer of nature and of the people around her. One biographer has called her "probably . . . the most distinguished of English writers who never wrote a line for the general public."

Later Years When Dorothy Wordsworth was in her mid-sixties, she fell seriously ill with arteriosclerosis. She became an invalid, and the disease apparently affected her mind. She remained in this debilitated state for more than twenty years until her death at the age of eighty-three.

Dorothy Wordsworth was born in 1771 and died in 1855.

Literature Online **Author Search** For more about Dorothy Wordsworth, go to www.glencoe.com.

Connecting to the Journal

Have you ever come across a scene in nature so extraordinary that you wanted to share it with someone? In one of Dorothy Wordsworth's journal entries, she describes her reaction to seeing a ribbon of daffodils growing along the shore of a lake in the English countryside. As you read, think about these questions:

- What makes a natural scene memorable for you?
- What thoughts does such a scene inspire?

Building Background

In 1799 William and Dorothy Wordsworth, together with their brother John, a sea captain home on leave, settled in the rustic village of Grasmere. They lived modestly in Dove Cottage, a small house covered in the summer with the green leaves and colorful flowers of a scarlet bean plant that climbed the cottage's exterior. Their property included a small orchard and garden and a boat on Grasmere Lake. From 1800 to 1803, Dorothy recorded descriptions of village life in and around Grasmere. William Wordsworth often turned to Dorothy's journals for inspiration as well as for details for his poems. The journal entry you are about to read, written in the spring of 1802, inspired William to write the poem "I Wandered Lonely as a Cloud," the first stanza of which is reprinted on the next page.

Setting Purposes for Reading

Big Idea Nature and the Imagination

As you read, notice how Dorothy Wordsworth's observations reflect the Romantics' admiration for nature, and how nature was the ideal stimulus for the imagination.

Literary Element Journal

A **journal** is a daily record of events kept by a participant in those events or by a witness to them. Journals can provide interesting details about people's daily lives and can also be an important source of historical information. As you read, think about the information this journal entry reveals about Dorothy's relationship to William and her influence on his poetry.

- See Literary Terms Handbook, p. R9.

Reading Strategy Analyzing Mood

Mood is the emotional quality that a writer creates in a literary work. A writer's style, including subject matter, choice of language, setting, and tone, as well as figurative language and sound devices, such as rhyme and rhythm, contribute to a work's mood. **Analyzing mood** means discovering how these components work together. As you read Dorothy Wordsworth's journal entry, notice how she creates mood.

....

Reading Tip: Taking Notes Use a chart similar to the one below to record examples of Wordsworth's style that contribute to the mood of the journal entry.

Example	Style Element	Description of Mood
"The wind seized our breath..."	personification	violent weather

Literature Online Interactive Literary Elements Handbook To review or learn more about the literary elements, go to www.glencoe.com.

OBJECTIVES
In studying this selection, you will focus on the following:
- analyzing literary movements
- understanding the characteristics of journal writing
- identifying and analyzing mood

from *The Journals of* *Dorothy Wordsworth*

Dorothy Wordsworth

THURSDAY, APRIL 15. It was a threatening misty morning—but mild. We [Dorothy and William] set off after dinner from Eusemere. Mrs. Clarkson went a short way with us but turned back. The wind was furious, and we thought we must have returned. We first rested in the large boathouse, then under a furze bush opposite Mr. Clarkson's; saw the plough going in the field. The wind seized our breath; the lake was rough. There was a boat by itself floating in the middle of the bay below Water Millock. We rested again in the Water Millock lane. The hawthorns are black and green, the birches here and there greenish, but there is yet more of purple to be seen on the twigs. We got over into a field to avoid some cows—people working, a few primroses by the roadside wood-sorrel flowers, the anemone, scentless violets, strawberries, and that starry yellow flower which Mrs. C. calls pile wort. When we were in the woods beyond Gowbarrow Park, we saw a few daffodils[1] close to the waterside. We fancied that the lake had floated the seeds ashore and that the

I wandered lonely as a cloud

That floats on high o'er vales and hills,

When all at once I saw a crowd,

A host of golden daffodils,

Beside the lake, beneath the trees,

Fluttering and dancing in the breeze.

—William Wordsworth

little colony had so sprung up. But as we went along there were more and yet more, and at last under the boughs of the trees, we saw that there was a long belt of them along the shore, about the breadth of a country turnpike road. I never saw daffodils so beautiful. They grew among the mossy stones about and about them; some rested their heads upon these stones as on a pillow for weariness, and the rest tossed and reeled and danced and seemed as if they verily laughed with the wind that blew upon them over the lake. They looked so gay, ever glancing, ever changing. This wind blew directly over the lake to them. There was here and there a little knot and a few stragglers a few yards higher up, but they were so few as not to disturb the simplicity and unity and life of that one busy highway. We rested again and again. The bays were stormy, and we heard the waves at different distances and in the middle of the water like the sea.

---

1. The *daffodil*, also called the trumpet narcissus, has a brilliant yellow flower with a trumpet-shaped central crown.

Literary Element Journal *How might the details in this paragraph have inspired William Wordsworth to write "I Wandered Lonely as a Cloud"?*

Reading Strategy Analyzing Mood *What mood is created by this personification of the daffodils?*

Big Idea Nature and the Imagination *The Romantics valued the unity and simplicity of nature. What principle of Romanticism is illustrated here by Wordsworth's imaginative treatment of nature?*

RESPONDING AND THINKING CRITICALLY

Respond

1. What aspect or detail of this journal entry did you find most interesting? Explain.

Recall and Interpret

2. (a)Describe the journey the Wordsworths take. (b)What weather conditions do they encounter and what stops do they make?

3. (a)What kinds of observations does the author record in this journal entry? (b)What do these observations suggest about her attitude toward nature?

Analyze and Evaluate

4. (a)What human qualities does the author give to the daffodils? (b)How does this use of **personification** help the reader visualize the daffodils?

5. Identify several sensory images in the journal entry and evaluate how well each one helps you imagine what the author is describing.

Connect

6. Do you think you appreciate the natural world in the same way Dorothy and William Wordsworth did? Explain.

7. **Big Idea** **Nature and the Imagination** The Romantics often found spiritual strength in the natural world, especially as the Industrial Revolution and urbanization increased the distance between humanity and nature. What indications of this do you find in Dorothy Wordsworth's journal?

LITERARY ANALYSIS

Literary Element Journal

Journals provide a glimpse into what life was like during a certain time period.

1. What does the journal entry reveal about the time and place in which Dorothy, William, and Coleridge lived?

2. What does the journal entry suggest about Dorothy Wordsworth's values and outlook on life? Use details from the entry to support your ideas.

Writing About Literature

Compare and Contrast Imagery Find and study a complete copy of "I Wandered Lonely as a Cloud." In a short essay, compare the images and discuss the apparent influence of Dorothy's journal on William's poem.

READING AND VOCABULARY

Reading Strategy Analyzing Mood

Mood, the emotional quality of a literary work, encompasses both **tone**, the attitude a writer takes toward the subject, and **atmosphere**, which refers to the physical qualities of the work's setting.

1. What mood is conveyed in the journal entry and what details help convey this mood?

2. How does the first line of William Wordsworth's poem alter the mood of Dorothy's journal entry?

Academic Vocabulary

Here is a word from the vocabulary list on page R82.

complement (kom′ plə ment′) *n.* something that completes or makes up a whole

Practice and Apply

How did Dorothy Wordsworth serve as a **complement** to her brother William?

Literature Online **Web Activities** For eFlashcards, Selection Quick Checks, and other Web activities, go to www.glencoe.com.

Kubla Khan and The Rime of the Ancient Mariner

MEET SAMUEL TAYLOR COLERIDGE

Tales such as *Robinson Crusoe* and the *Arabian Nights* enthralled young Samuel Taylor Coleridge, and from an early age, he felt drawn to the worlds of fantasy and the exotic.

A Lonely and Friendless Youth Coleridge was born at Ottery St. Mary, Devonshire. His father was the village vicar, an unworldly but popular figure. He died when Coleridge was only nine years old. Lonely and friendless, Coleridge retreated into books and his own vivid imagination where he nurtured dreams of a better future for himself. He spent much time alone outdoors, and once, after running away after a fight and collapsing on a riverbank, spent the night there and almost froze to death. As a result, he contracted a painful case of rheumatism that plagued him for the rest of his life. At the time, opium was a standard medical treatment for such a condition, and in the course of easing his persistent attacks, Coleridge grew to depend on the drug and lamented his addiction. "Yet to my fellow men," he wrote, "I may say that I was seduced into the accursed Habit ignorantly."

While at Cambridge University, Coleridge became inspired by the democratic ideals of the French Revolution. Along with several friends, including the poet Robert Southey, he joined in a movement to establish an ideal community in the United States that would be removed from war and intolerance and would give all citizens an equal voice in the government. Coleridge, Southey, and others planned to set up their community by the Susquehanna River in Pennsylvania. However, the utopian group disintegrated, and Coleridge moved with his wife, Sarah (Southey's wife's sister), and their new baby back to England to live in a small village in Somerset.

A Turning Point When Coleridge was twenty-five, he met the poet William Wordsworth. They became good friends, and Wordsworth and his sister Dorothy moved to Somerset to be near Coleridge. The two poets spent endless hours in each other's company and soon began their famous collaboration on *Lyrical Ballads*, which was published in 1798 and included Coleridge's *The Rime of the Ancient Mariner*. For Coleridge, this period was the happiest of his life.

> "Not the poem which we have read, but that to which we return, with the greatest pleasure, possesses the genuine power, and claims the name of essential poetry."
>
> —Samuel Taylor Coleridge

Poet and Critic By his early thirties, Coleridge had turned most of his attention to writing prose essays and treatises on literary and religious subjects. Despite illness, depression, and drug addiction, Coleridge produced an extraordinary body of work. He became the greatest literary critic of his age, known particularly for his perceptive commentary on the plays of Shakespeare and his *Biographia Literaria*, a spiritual autobiography and a brilliant exposition of the romantic ideals of art and life.

Samuel Taylor Coleridge was born in 1772 and died in 1834.

Literature Online **Author Search** For more about Samuel Taylor Coleridge, go to www.glencoe.com.

Connecting to the Poem

Throughout history, writers and artists have written about utopias, dreamscapes, and fantastic places. In "Kubla Khan," Coleridge envisions an exotic, foreign locale from the past. As you read, think about the following questions:

- Why are we simultaneously excited and frightened by the exotic and the unknown?
- How do imagination and creativity help us to understand other people, places, or situations?

Building Background

At the time when Coleridge wrote "Kubla Khan," he had been taking opium to ease the pain of his rheumatism, and, to distract his troubled mind, he was reading a travel book called *Purchas His Pilgrimage* by Samuel Purchas (1613). He fell asleep after reading a passage relating how Kubla Khan, the thirteenth-century founder of the Mongol dynasty in China, built a beautiful palace amid a tropical paradise. According to Coleridge, during his three-hour nap he literally dreamed up three hundred lines of poetry "without any sensation or consciousness of effort." On waking, he began writing the poem but was interrupted by a visitor. When he returned to his work an hour later, he could not remember the rest, and the poem remains an unfinished fragment.

Setting Purposes for Reading

Big Idea **Nature and the Imagination**

The Romantics were fascinated with the realm of dreams and nightmares, visions and creative madness. As you read, notice how these elements are intertwined in "Kubla Khan."

Literary Element **Alliteration**

Alliteration is a literary device in which words or stressed syllables beginning with the same sound—usually a consonant sound—are repeated; for example, "meandering with a mazy motion." As you read, look for examples of alliteration.

- See Literary Terms Handbook, p. R1.

Reading Strategy **Analyzing Cause-and-Effect Relationships**

A **cause** is an action or event that makes something happen; an **effect** is the result of that action or event. In a complicated narrative poem such as "Kubla Kahn," it is important to pay close attention to the ways in which events unfold over the course of each stanza in order to determine the cause-and-effect relationships.

Reading Tip: Noting Causes and Effects Use a chart to record the causes and effects you discover as you read.

Cause	Effect
• Kubla Khan issued a decree.	• Walls and towers were built. • Gardens were planted.

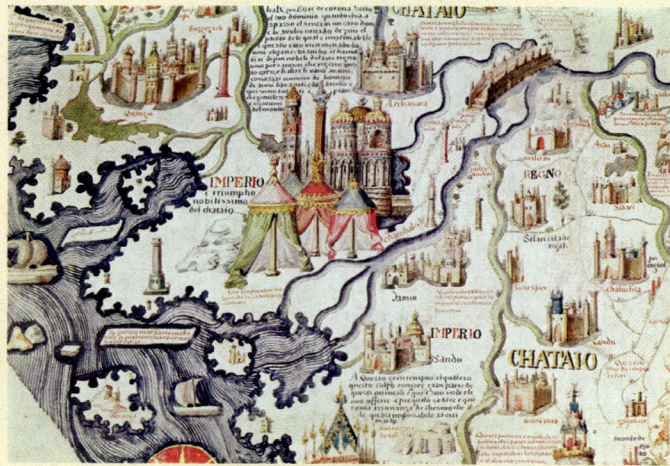

Map showing Cambuluc, the capital of Kubla Khan's Mongol Empire. British Museum, London.

Literature Online **Interactive Literary Elements Handbook** To review or learn more about the literary elements, go to www.glencoe.com.

OBJECTIVES
In studying this selection, you will focus on the following:
- analyzing literary periods
- analyzing alliteration
- analyzing cause-and-effect relationships

Kubla Khan, in an elephant sedan, and his following on a big game and bird hunt, c. 1412. Studio of the Boucicaut Master. Illumination.

KUBLA KHAN

Samuel Taylor Coleridge

In Xanadu° did Kubla Khan°
A stately pleasure dome decree:°
Where Alph,° the sacred river, ran
Through caverns measureless to man
5   Down to a sunless sea.
So twice five miles of fertile ground
With walls and towers were girdled round:
And there were gardens bright with sinuous rills,°
Where blossomed many an incense-bearing tree;
10 And here were forests ancient as the hills,
Enfolding sunny spots of greenery.

But oh! that deep romantic chasm which slanted
Down the green hill athwart a cedarn cover!°
A savage place! as holy and enchanted
15 As e'er beneath a waning moon was haunted
By woman wailing for her demon lover!
And from this chasm, with ceaseless turmoil seething,
As if this earth in fast thick pants were breathing,
A mighty fountain momently° was forced:
20 Amid whose swift half-intermitted° burst
Huge fragments vaulted like rebounding hail,
Or chaffy grain beneath the thresher's flail:
And 'mid these dancing rocks at once and ever
It flung up momently the sacred river.

1 **Xanadu** (zaʹ nə do͞oʹ) is perhaps an altered form of *Xamdu* (also *Shang-tu*), a residence of Kubla Khan. **Kubla Khan** (1215–1294), the grandson of Genghis Khan, conquered China and became the first khan, or ruler, of the Mongol dynasty.
2 **Decree** means "order." Kubla Khan ordered that a pleasure dome be built.
3 Coleridge probably named the river **Alph** in reference to the Greek river Alpheus.
8 **Sinuous rills** means "winding streams."

13 **Athwart a cedarn cover** means "across a covering of cedars."

19 **Momently** means "from moment to moment."
20 **Intermitted** means "interrupted."

Literary Element **Alliteration** *Identify five examples of alliteration in lines 1–5 of this poem.*

Kubla Khan with Marco Polo in Peking, 1375. Bibliothèque Nationale, Paris.

25   Five miles meandering with a mazy motion
Through wood and dale the sacred river ran,
Then reached the caverns measureless to man,
And sank in tumult to a lifeless ocean:
And 'mid this tumult Kubla heard from far
30   Ancestral voices prophesying war!
      The shadow of the dome of pleasure
      Floated midway on the waves;
      Where was heard the mingled measure°
      From the fountain and the caves.
35   It was a miracle of rare device,°
A sunny pleasure dome with caves of ice!

      A damsel with a dulcimer°
      In a vision once I saw:
      It was an Abyssinian° maid,
40   And on her dulcimer she played,
      Singing of Mount Abora.°
      Could I revive within me
      Her symphony and song,
      To such a deep delight 'twould win me,
45   That with music loud and long,
I would build that dome in air,
That sunny dome! those caves of ice!
And all who heard should see them there,
And all should cry, Beware! Beware!
50   His flashing eyes, his floating hair!
Weave a circle round him thrice,
And close your eyes with holy dread,
For he° on honeydew hath fed,
And drunk the milk of Paradise.

33 Here, **measure** means "tune or melody; a rhythmic sound."

35 Here, **device** means "design."

37 A **dulcimer** (dul´ sə mər) is a stringed musical instrument.

39 **Abyssinian** means "from Abyssinia," the former name of Ethiopia in East Africa.

41 **Mount Abora** is probably a reference to Mount Amara in Ethiopia.

53 The words **his, him,** and **he** in lines 50–53 all refer to the speaker of the poem.

Reading Strategy Analyzing Cause-and-Effect Relationships
What causes the speaker to have this vision?

Big Idea Nature and the Imagination *How does this passage indicate the power of the imagination?*

RESPONDING AND THINKING CRITICALLY

Respond

1. How did you respond to the place described?

Recall and Interpret

2. (a)Describe the pleasure dome and its setting in lines 1–11. (b)How would you describe the mood of the first stanza?

3. (a)Identify images from the first stanza that suggest that the pleasure dome and its surroundings are bright and beautiful. (b)Identify images from the second stanza that suggest the surroundings are dark and dangerous. (c)What does the contrast between these stanzas suggest to you about the nature of the pleasure dome?

4. (a)What do the "Ancestral voices" in line 30 predict? (b)How is this prediction at odds with the description of the pleasure dome from the first stanza? (c)What might this suggest about people's creations?

Analyze and Evaluate

5. (a)What can you infer about the speaker's character from lines 49–54? (b)Why might the speaker think that people would be filled with "holy dread" upon seeing him?

6. (a)What might the "damsel with a dulcimer" symbolize to the poet? (b)What do you think the "honeydew" and the "milk of Paradise" symbolize?

7. (a)What does Coleridge's use of contrasting images contribute to your understanding of the poem? (b)What do you think is the theme of this poem?

Connect

8. **Big Idea** **Nature and the Imagination** What characteristics of "Kubla Khan" strike you as dreamlike? Explain.

LITERARY ANALYSIS

Literary Element **Alliteration**

Poets often use **alliteration** to emphasize certain words, to create a musical quality, to help establish the prevailing mood of a poem, or to reinforce meaning.

1. Explain the cumulative effect of the alliterative words in lines 15–16.

2. (a)Point out all the instances of alliteration in lines 42–46. (b)Why do you think Coleridge uses this device in these lines?

Literary Criticism

Scholar Kenneth Burke maintains that "Kubla Khan" is in "perfect form," the first stanza presenting a thesis (main idea); the second, an antithesis (opposite idea); and the third, a fusion of the thesis and antithesis (resolution). Write a brief analysis of the structure of the poem and include an explanation of why you agree or disagree with Burke.

Literature Online **Web Activities** For eFlashcards, Selection Quick Checks, and other Web activities, go to www.glencoe.com.

READING AND VOCABULARY

Reading Strategy **Analyzing Cause-and-Effect Relationships**

A cause is an event or action that results in an **effect**. Analyzing **causes and effects** in literature can help you to better remember and understand what is happening.

1. What are the effects of the mighty fountain that erupts from the chasm?

2. What would happen if the speaker could remember the "damsel's dulcimer" song?

Academic Vocabulary

Here is a word from the vocabulary list on page R82.

consist (kən sist′) *v.* be made up; be formed

Practice and Apply
Does "Kubla Khan" **consist** mainly of description or narration? Explain.

| LITERATURE PREVIEW | READING PREVIEW |

Connecting to the Poem

Do you ever think of life as a journey? In *The Rime of the Ancient Mariner*, the narrator recounts his adventure at sea. During this voyage, he learns difficult lessons about nature and humanity.

- Have you ever learned a valuable life lesson by experiencing hardship or encountering difficulty?
- Do you think it is important for people to share their tales of adversity and pain?

Building Background

The Rime of the Ancient Mariner is an account of a sea voyage to distant places, with crime, death, and inhuman suffering as parts of the ghastly adventure. Initially Wordsworth collaborated with Coleridge on the composition of the poem. Before dropping out of the joint venture, Wordsworth suggested several memorable details, including the shooting of the albatross and the ship's navigation by dead men.

Setting Purposes for Reading

Big Idea Nature and the Imagination

As you read, examine the way in which the mariner interacts with both the fantastic and the ordinary.

Literary Element Narrative Poetry

Narrative poetry is verse that tells a story. Narrative poems have characters, settings, and narrators who describe a series of events, much like the narrator in a novel or short story. Many narrative poems also have literary elements such as figurative language and dialogue. A narrative poem may be written in any verse form and may be rhymed or unrhymed. In this work, Coleridge chose to use a ballad stanza structure and rhyme scheme.

- See Literary Terms Handbook, p. R11.

Reading Strategy Reviewing

To **review** is to reread or to think over what you have read in order to help you organize ideas and remember details. Try to separate main events from supporting description.

Reading Tip: Summarizing Summarizing what happens in each part of the poem will help you to understand its plot. Coleridge has done some of this work for you by putting a brief summary, which he calls the *argument*, in marginal glosses. You should rewrite and incorporate Coleridge's notes into your own summary. *The Rime of the Ancient Mariner* has seven parts. As you read, write a summary for each part.

Vocabulary

dismal (diz′ məl) *adj.* dark and gloomy; p. 808 *It was a dismal afternoon, and I was glad I could stay indoors, where it was warm and bright.*

penance (pen′ əns) *n.* an act of self-punishment to show repentance for a sin; p. 820 *In the Greek tragedy, Oedipus puts out his own eyes as penance for having killed his father.*

impart (im pärt′) *v.* to give; donate; p. 823 *Uncle Simon loves to impart little bits of wisdom to all of us at family dinners.*

Vocabulary Tip: Context Clues Clues to the meanings of unfamiliar words can often be found in the surrounding text.

Literature Online Interactive Literary Elements Handbook To review or learn more about the literary elements, go to www.glencoe.com.

Jewelled binding with 275 jewels. Sangorski & Sutcliffe. Illuminated manuscript, 330 x 240 x 30 mm.

OBJECTIVES
In studying this selection, you will focus on the following:
- analyzing literary periods
- analyzing narrative poetry
- using reviewing as a reading strategy

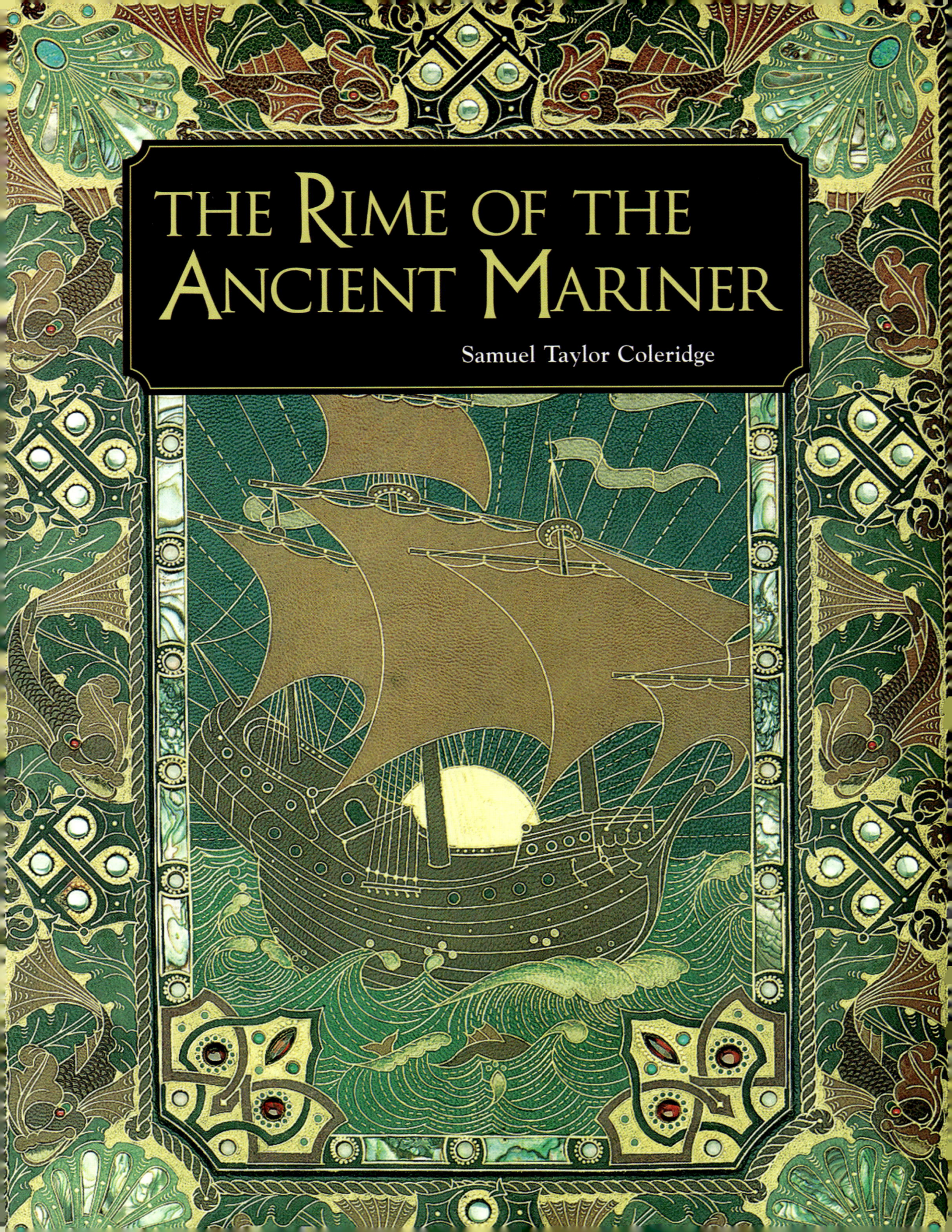

THE RIME OF THE ANCIENT MARINER

Samuel Taylor Coleridge

ARGUMENT

How a Ship, having passed the Equator, was driven by storms to the cold Country towards the South Pole; and how from thence she made her course to the tropical Latitude of the Great Pacific Ocean; and of the strange things that befell; and in what manner the Ancient Mariner came back to his own Country.

PART I

It is an ancient Mariner,
And he stoppeth one of three.
"By thy long gray beard and glittering eye,
Now wherefore stopp'st thou me?

5   "The Bridegroom's doors are opened wide,
And I am next of kin;
The guests are met, the feast is set:
May'st hear the merry din."

He holds him with his skinny hand,
10   "There was a ship," quoth he.
"Hold off! unhand me, graybeard loon!"
Eftsoons° his hand dropped he.

He holds him with his glittering eye—
The Wedding Guest stood still,
15   And listens like a three years' child:
The Mariner hath his will.

The Wedding Guest sat on a stone:
He cannot choose but hear;
And thus spake on that ancient man,
20   The bright-eyed Mariner.

An ancient Mariner meeteth three Gallants bidden to a wedding feast and detaineth one.

The Wedding Guest is spellbound by the eye of the old seafaring man and constrained to hear his tale.

---

12. *Eftsoons* means "at once."

Literary Element Narrative Poetry *To whom does the Mariner address his tale? What is the setting of their meeting?*

Big Idea Nature and the Imagination *What elements of the supernatural are at work in this stanza?*

Mariner recounts story to wedding guest, 1875. Gustave Doré. Engraving.

Viewing the Art: How does the body language of the Mariner and the Wedding Guest reflect their emotions? Explain.

"The ship was cheered, the harbor cleared,
Merrily did we drop
Below the kirk,° below the hill,
Below the lighthouse top.

25 "The Sun came up upon the left,
Out of the sea came he!
And he shone bright, and on the right
Went down into the sea.

"Higher and higher every day,
30 Till over the mast at noon°—"
The Wedding Guest here beat his breast,
For he heard the loud bassoon.

The bride hath paced into the hall,
Red as a rose is she;
35 Nodding their heads before her goes
The merry minstrelsy.°

The Wedding Guest he beat his breast,
Yet he cannot choose but hear;
And thus spake on that ancient man,
40 The bright-eyed Mariner.

The Mariner tells how the ship sailed southward with a good wind and fair weather, till it reached the Line. [The line is the equator.]

The Wedding Guest heareth the bridal music; but the Mariner continueth his tale.

---

23. *Kirk* is Scottish for church.
30. In this line, Coleridge is saying the sun's position indicates that the ship has reached the equator.
36. A *minstrelsy* is a group of musicians.

"And now the Storm Blast came, and he
Was tyrannous and strong:
He struck with his o'ertaking wings,
And chased us south along.

45   "With sloping masts and dipping prow,°
As who pursued with yell and blow
Still treads the shadow of his foe,
And forward bends his head,
The ship drove fast, loud roared the blast,
50   And southward aye° we fled.

"And now there came both mist and snow,
And it grew wondrous cold:
And ice, mast-high, came floating by,
As green as emerald.

55   "And through the drifts the snowy clifts°
Did send a **dismal** sheen:
Nor shapes of men nor beasts we ken°—
The ice was all between.

"The ice was here, the ice was there,
60   The ice was all around:
It cracked and growled, and roared and howled,
Like noises in a swound!°

"At length did cross an Albatross,
Thorough the fog it came;
65   As if it had been a Christian soul,
We hailed it in God's name.

The ship driven by a storm toward the South Pole.

The land of ice, and of fearful sounds, where no living thing was to be seen.

Till a great sea bird, called the Albatross, came through the snow-fog, and was received with great joy and hospitality.

---

45. A *mast* is a vertical pole that supports a ship's sails, and the *prow* is the forward part of a ship's hull.
50. *Aye* means "ever."
55. *Clifts* means "crevices."
57. *Ken* means "saw; identified."
62. A *swound* is a swoon or fainting fit.

Big Idea Nature and the Imagination *How does the use of personification here reflect the Romantic idea that the imagination is a force within the individual that reacts to the natural world?*

Big Idea Nature and the Imagination *What is the effect of this personification?*

Vocabulary

dismal (diz′ məl) *adj.* dark and gloomy

"It ate the food it ne'er had eat,
And round and round it flew.
The ice did split with a thunder-fit;
70   The helmsman steered us through!

"And a good south wind sprung up behind;
The Albatross did follow,
And every day, for food or play,
Came to the mariners' hollo!

75   "In mist or cloud, on mast or shroud,°
It perched for vespers° nine;
Whiles all the night, through fog-smoke white,
Glimmered the white Moonshine."

"God save thee, ancient Mariner!
80   From the fiends that plague thee thus!—
Why look'st thou so?"°—"With my crossbow
I shot the Albatross."

PART II

"The Sun now rose upon the right:°
Out of the sea came he,
85   Still hid in mist, and on the left
Went down into the sea.

"And the good south wind still blew behind,
But no sweet bird did follow,
Nor any day for food or play
90   Came to the mariners' hollo!

"And I had done a hellish thing,
And it would work 'em woe:
For all averred,° I had killed the bird
That made the breeze to blow.
95   'Ah, wretch!' said they, 'the bird to slay,
That made the breeze to blow!'

And lo! the Albatross proveth a bird of good omen, and followeth the ship as it returned northward through fog and floating ice.

The ancient Mariner inhospitably killeth the pious bird of good omen.

His shipmates cry out against the ancient Mariner for killing the bird of good luck.

---

75. A *shroud* is a rope that supports the mast of a ship.
76. Here, *vespers* means "evenings."
79–81. The words *["God . . . so?"]* are spoken by the Wedding Guest.
83. This line indicates that the ship is heading north.
93. *Averred* means "asserted; affirmed."

Reading Strategy   **Reviewing** *What happens in this last stanza? Why does the Guest interrupt the Mariner?*

Literary Element   **Narrative Poetry** *Does the Mariner offer any motivation for what he has done? Explain.*

The albatross is shot by arrow, 1875.
Gustave Doré. Engraving.

"Nor dim nor red, like God's own head,
The glorious Sun uprist:°
Then all averred, I had killed the bird
100   That brought the fog and mist.
' 'Twas right,' said they, 'such birds to slay,
That bring the fog and mist.'

"The fair breeze blew, the white foam flew,
The furrow° followed free;
105   We were the first that ever burst
Into that silent sea.

"Down dropped the breeze, the sails dropped down,
'Twas sad as sad could be;
And we did speak only to break
110   The silence of the sea!

"All in a hot and copper sky,
The bloody Sun, at noon,
Right up above the mast did stand,
No bigger than the Moon.

115   "Day after day, day after day,
We stuck, nor breath nor motion;
As idle as a painted ship
Upon a painted ocean.

"Water, water, everywhere,
120   And all the boards did shrink;
Water, water, everywhere,
Nor any drop to drink.

"The very deep did rot: O Christ!
That ever this should be!
125   Yea, slimy things did crawl with legs
Upon the slimy sea.

But when the fog cleared off, they justify the same, and thus make themselves accomplices in the crime.

The fair breeze continues; the ship enters the Pacific Ocean and sails northward, even till it reaches the Line.

The ship hath been suddenly becalmed.

And the Albatross begins to be avenged.

---

98. *Uprist* means "arose."
104. The *furrow* is the ship's wake.

"About, about, in reel and rout°
The death-fires° danced at night;
The water, like a witch's oils,
130 Burned green and blue and white.

"And some in dreams assurèd were
Of the Spirit that plagued us so;
Nine fathom deep he had followed us
From the land of mist and snow.

135 "And every tongue, through utter drought,
Was withered at the root;
We could not speak, no more than if
We had been choked with soot.

"Ah! well a-day! what evil looks
140 Had I from old and young!
Instead of the cross, the Albatross
About my neck was hung.

A Spirit had followed them; one of the invisible inhabitants of this planet, neither departed souls nor angels. . . . They are very numerous, and there is no climate or element without one or more.

The shipmates, in their sore distress, would fain throw the whole guilt on the ancient Mariner: in sign whereof they hang the dead sea bird round his neck.

The ancient Mariner beholdeth a sign in the element afar off.

PART III

"There passed a weary time. Each throat
Was parched, and glazed each eye.
145 A weary time! a weary time!
How glazed each weary eye,
When looking westward, I beheld
A something in the sky.

"At first it seemed a little speck,
150 And then it seemed a mist;
It moved and moved, and took at last
A certain shape, I wist.°

"A speck, a mist, a shape, I wist!
And still it neared and neared:
155 As if it dodged a water sprite,
It plunged and tacked and veered.

---

127. *In reel and rout* means "in riotous, whirling movements."
128. *Death-fires* are luminous glowings supposedly seen over dead bodies.
152. *Wist* means "knew."

Big Idea Nature and the Imagination *How do lines 125–130 demonstrate the Mariner's imagination at work?*

Reading Strategy Reviewing *Why would the Mariner's shipmates hang the albatross around his neck?*

SAMUEL TAYLOR COLERIDGE **811**

"With throats unslaked,° with black lips baked,
We could nor laugh nor wail;
Through utter drought all dumb we stood!
160   I bit my arm, I sucked the blood,
And cried, 'A sail! a sail!'

"With throats unslaked, with black lips baked,
Agape° they heard me call:
Gramercy!° they for joy did grin,
165   And all at once their breath drew in,
As they were drinking all.

"See! see! (I cried) she tacks no more!
Hither to work us weal;°
Without a breeze, without a tide,
170   She steadies with upright keel!

"The western wave was all aflame.
The day was well nigh done!
Almost upon the western wave

At its nearer approach, it seemeth him to be a ship; and at a dear ransom he freeth his speech from the bonds of thirst.

A flash of joy;

And horror follows. For can it be a ship that comes onward without wind or tide?

---

157. *Unslaked* means "unrelieved of thirst."
163. *Agape* means "with mouths open in wonder."
164. *Gramercy* is an exclamation of surprise or sudden feeling similar to "Have mercy on us!"
168. *Work us weal* means "do us good; benefit us."

Rested the broad bright Sun;
175 When that strange shape drove suddenly
Betwixt us and the Sun.

"And straight° the Sun was flecked with bars,
(Heaven's Mother send us grace!)
As if through a dungeon grate he peered
180 With broad and burning face.

"Alas! (thought I, and my heart beat loud)
How fast she nears and nears!
Are those *her* sails that glance in the Sun,
Like restless gossameres?°

185 "Are those *her* ribs through which the Sun
Did peer, as through a grate?
And is that Woman all her crew?
Is that a Death? and are there two?
Is Death that woman's mate?

190 "*Her* lips were red, *her* looks were free,
Her locks were yellow as gold:
Her skin was as white as leprosy,
The Nightmare Life-in-Death was she,
Who thicks man's blood with cold.

195 "The naked hulk alongside came,
And the twain were casting dice;
'The game is done! I've won! I've won!'
Quoth she, and whistles thrice.

"The Sun's rim dips; the stars rush out:
200 At one stride comes the dark;
With far-heard whisper, o'er the sea,
Off shot the specter bark.°

"We listened and looked sideways up!
Fear at my heart, as at a cup,
205 My lifeblood seemed to sip!
The stars were dim, and thick the night,
The steersman's face by his lamp gleamed white;

It seemeth him but the skeleton of a ship.

And its ribs are seen as bars on the face of the setting Sun. The Specter-Woman and her Death mate, and no other on board the skeleton ship.

Like vessel, like crew!

Death and Life-in-Death have diced for the ship's crew, and she (the latter) winneth the ancient Mariner.

No twilight within the courts of the Sun.

At the rising of the Moon,

177. Here, *straight* means "immediately."
184. *Gossameres* (or gossamers) are fine films of cobwebs.
202. *Specter bark* means "ghost ship."

Big Idea Nature and the Imagination *How does the strange ship represent the supernatural?*

Reading Strategy Reviewing *What happens in this stanza?*

From the sails the dew did drip—
Till clomb° above the eastern bar
210 The hornèd Moon,° with one bright star
Within the nether° tip.

"One after one, by the star-dogged Moon,°
Too quick for groan or sigh,
Each turned his face with a ghastly pang,
215 And cursed me with his eye.

"Four times fifty living men,
(And I heard nor sigh nor groan)
With heavy thump, a lifeless lump,
They dropped down one by one.
220 "The souls did from their bodies fly—
They fled to bliss or woe!
And every soul, it passed me by,
Like the whiz of my crossbow!"

PART IV

"I fear thee, ancient Mariner!
225 I fear thy skinny hand!
And thou art long, and lank, and brown,
As is the ribbed sea-sand.

"I fear thee and thy glittering eye,
And thy skinny hand, so brown."—
230 "Fear not, fear not, thou Wedding Guest!
This body dropped not down.

"Alone, alone, all, all alone,
Alone on a wide, wide sea!
And never a saint took pity on
235 My soul in agony.

One after another, .

His shipmates drop down dead.

But Life-in-Death begins her work on the ancient Mariner.

The Wedding Guest feareth that a Spirit is talking to him;

But the ancient Mariner assureth him of his bodily life, and proceedeth to relate his horrible penance.

---

209. *Clomb* means "climbed."
210. A *hornèd Moon* is a crescent moon.
211. *Nether* means "lower."
212. Sailors believed that a *star-dogged Moon* was a sign of impending evil.

Reading Strategy Reviewing *What happens to the Mariner's shipmates and why?*

Literary Element Narrative Poetry *What image does this line recall? What does this suggest?*

Reading Strategy Reviewing *Why is the Wedding Guest frightened?*

Death and Life play dice on skeleton ship, 1875. Gustave Doré. Engraving.

Viewing the Art: Do you think this engraving captures the mood and atmosphere of the scene in the poem? Why or why not?

"The many men, so beautiful!
And they all dead did lie:
And a thousand thousand slimy things
Lived on; and so did I.

240　"I looked upon the rotting sea,
And drew my eyes away;
I looked upon the rotting deck,
And there the dead men lay.

"I looked to heaven, and tried to pray;
245　But or° ever a prayer had gushed,
A wicked whisper came, and made
My heart as dry as dust.

"I closed my lids, and kept them close,
And the balls like pulses beat;
250　For the sky and the sea, and the sea and the sky
Lay like a load on my weary eye,
And the dead were at my feet.

He despiseth the creatures of the calm.

And envieth that they should live, and so many lie dead.

245.　Here, *or* means "before."

"The cold sweat melted from their limbs,
Nor rot nor reek did they:
255   The look with which they looked on me
Had never passed away.

"An orphan's curse would drag to hell
A spirit from on high;
But oh! more horrible than that
260   Is the curse in a dead man's eye!
Seven days, seven nights, I saw that curse,
And yet I could not die.

"The moving Moon went up the sky,
And nowhere did abide:
265   Softly she was going up,
And a star or two beside—

"Her beams bemocked the sultry main,°
Like April hoarfrost° spread;
But where the ship's huge shadow lay,
270   The charmèd water burned alway°
A still and awful red.

"Beyond the shadow of the ship,
I watched the water snakes:
They moved in tracks of shining white,
275   And when they reared, the elfish light
Fell off in hoary° flakes.

"Within the shadow of the ship
I watched their rich attire:
Blue, glossy green, and velvet black,
280   They coiled and swam; and every track
Was a flash of golden fire.

"O happy living things! no tongue
Their beauty might declare:
A spring of love gushed from my heart,
285   And I blessed them unaware:
Sure my kind saint took pity on me,
And I blessed them unaware.

267. This line means "Her moonbeams mocked the hot sea."
268. *Hoarfrost* is frost, especially the white coating it forms on surfaces.
270. *Alway* means "all along."
276. *Hoary* means "white."

Reading Strategy   **Reviewing** *What has the Mariner seen for the last seven days and seven nights and what has he tried to do? Look back at line 244.*

"The selfsame moment I could pray;
And from my neck so free
290   The Albatross fell off, and sank
Like lead into the sea."

The spell begins to break.

PART V

"Oh sleep! it is a gentle thing,
Beloved from pole to pole!
To Mary Queen the praise be given!
295   She sent the gentle sleep from Heaven
That slid into my soul.

"The silly° buckets on the deck,
That had so long remained,
I dreamed that they were filled with dew;
300   And when I awoke, it rained.

By grace of the holy Mother, the ancient Mariner is refreshed with rain.

"My lips were wet, my throat was cold,
My garments all were dank;
Sure I had drunken in my dreams,
And still my body drank.

305   "I moved, and could not feel my limbs:
I was so light—almost
I thought that I had died in sleep,
And was a blessèd ghost.

"And soon I heard a roaring wind:
310   It did not come anear;
But with its sound it shook the sails
That were so thin and sere.°

He heareth sounds and seeth strange sights and commotions in the sky and the element.

"The upper air burst into life!
And a hundred fire-flags sheen,°
315   To and fro they were hurried about!
And to and fro, and in and out,
The wan° stars danced between.

---

297. Here, *silly* means "useless."
312. *Sere* means "worn."
314. *Fire-flags* may refer to the aurora australis, or southern
lights. *Sheen* means "shone."
317. *Wan* means "faint; dull" (compared with the fire-flags).

Literary Element   Narrative Poetry *How does the Mariner's action contribute unwittingly to his salvation?*

Literary Element   Narrative Poetry *How has the Mariner's situation changed?*

"And the coming wind did roar more loud,
And the sails did sigh like sedge;°
320   And the rain poured down from one black cloud;
The Moon was at its edge.

"The thick black cloud was cleft,° and still
The Moon was at its side:
Like waters shot from some high crag,
325   The lightning fell with never a jag,
A river steep and wide.

"The loud wind never reached the ship,
Yet now the ship moved on!
Beneath the lightning and the Moon
330   The dead men gave a groan.

"They groaned, they stirred, they all uprose,
Nor spake, nor moved their eyes;
It had been strange, even in a dream,
To have seen those dead men rise.

335   "The helmsman steered, the ship moved on;
Yet never a breeze up-blew;
The mariners all 'gan work the ropes,
Where they were wont° to do;
They raised their limbs like lifeless tools—
340   We were a ghastly crew.

"The body of my brother's son
Stood by me, knee to knee:
The body and I pulled at one rope,
But he said nought to me."

345   "I fear thee, ancient Mariner!"
"Be calm, thou Wedding Guest!
'Twas not those souls that fled in pain,
Which to their corses° came again,
But a troop of spirits blessed:

350   "For when it dawned—they dropped their arms,
And clustered round the mast;
Sweet sounds rose slowly through their mouths,
And from their bodies passed.

The bodies of the ship's crew are inspired, and the ship moves on; [Inspired means "breathed life into" or "animated by divine or supernatural influence."]

But not by the souls of the men, nor by demons of earth or middle air, but by a blessed troop of angelic spirits, sent down by the invocation of the guardian saint.

---

319. *Sedge* is marsh grass.
322. *Cleft* means "split."
338. *Wont* means "accustomed."
348. *Corses* are corpses.

Big Idea   Nature and the Imagination *What is the Mariner's explanation for the crew's revival?*

"Around, around, flew each sweet sound,
355 Then darted to the Sun;
Slowly the sounds came back again,
Now mixed, now one by one.

"Sometimes a-dropping from the sky
I heard the skylark sing;
360 Sometimes all little birds that are,
How they seemed to fill the sea and air
With their sweet jargoning!°

"And now 'twas like all instruments,
Now like a lonely flute;
365 And now it is an angel's song,
That makes the heavens be mute.

"It ceased; yet still the sails made on
A pleasant noise till noon,
A noise like of a hidden brook
370 In the leafy month of June,
That to the sleeping woods all night
Singeth a quiet tune.

"Till noon we quietly sailed on,
Yet never a breeze did breathe:
375 Slowly and smoothly went the ship,
Moved onward from beneath.

"Under the keel nine fathom deep,
From the land of mist and snow,
The Spirit slid: and it was he
380 That made the ship to go.
The sails at noon left off their tune,
And the ship stood still also.

"The Sun, right up above the mast,
Had fixed her to the ocean:
385 But in a minute she 'gan stir,
With a short uneasy motion—
Backwards and forwards half her length
With a short uneasy motion.

"Then like a pawing horse let go,
390 She made a sudden bound:
It flung the blood into my head,
And I fell down in a swound.

The lonesome Spirit from the South Pole carries on the ship as far as the Line, in obedience to the angelic troop, but still requireth vengeance.

---

362. *Jargoning* means "warbling."

Reading Strategy Reviewing *Summarize what has happened so far in Part V.*

"How long in that same fit I lay,
I have not to declare;
395 But ere my living life returned,
I heard, and in my soul discerned
Two voices in the air.

" 'Is it he?' quoth one, 'Is this the man?
By him who died on cross,
400 With his cruel bow he laid full low
The harmless Albatross.

" 'The Spirit who bideth by himself
In the land of mist and snow,
He loved the bird that loved the man
405 Who shot him with his bow.'

"The other was a softer voice,
As soft as honeydew:
Quoth he, 'The man hath penance done,
And **penance** more will do.' "

The Polar Spirit's fellow demons, the invisible inhabitants of the element, take part in his wrong; and two of them relate, one to the other, that penance long and heavy for the ancient Mariner hath been accorded to the Polar Spirit, who returneth southward.

PART VI

FIRST VOICE

410 " 'But tell me, tell me! speak again,
Thy soft response renewing—
What makes that ship drive on so fast?
What is the ocean doing?'

SECOND VOICE

" 'Still as a slave before his lord,
415 The ocean hath no blast;°
His great bright eye most silently
Up to the Moon is cast—

" 'If he may know which way to go;
For she guides him smooth or grim.
420 See, brother, see! how graciously
She looketh down on him.'

---

415. *Blast* means "wind."

Literary Element Narrative Poetry *Who are these voices and why are they important?*

Vocabulary

penance (pen′ əns) *n.* an act of self-punishment to show repentance for a sin

Angels remove the curse, 1875. Gustave Doré. Engraving.

FIRST VOICE

> " 'But why drives on that ship so fast,
> Without or wave or wind?'

SECOND VOICE

> " 'The air is cut away before,
> 425 And closes from behind.'

> " 'Fly, brother, fly! more high, more high!
> Or we shall be belated:°
> For slow and slow that ship will go,
> When the Mariner's trance is abated.'

> 430 "I woke, and we were sailing on
> As in a gentle weather:
> 'Twas night, calm night, the moon was high;
> The dead men stood together.

> "All stood together on the deck,
> 435 For a charnel-dungeon° fitter:
> All fixed on me their stony eyes,
> That in the Moon did glitter.

> "The pang, the curse, with which they died,
> Had never passed away:
> 440 I could not draw my eyes from theirs,
> Nor turn them up to pray.

> "And now this spell was snapped: once more
> I viewed the ocean green,
> And looked far forth, yet little saw
> 445 Of what had else been seen—

> "Like one, that on a lonesome road
> Doth walk in fear and dread,
> And having once turned round walks on,
> And turns no more his head;
> 450 Because he knows, a frightful fiend
> Doth close behind him tread.

> "But soon there breathed a wind on me,
> Nor sound nor motion made:
> Its path was not upon the sea,
> 455 In ripple or in shade.

The Mariner hath been cast into a trance; for the angelic power causeth the vessel to drive northward faster than human life could endure.

The supernatural motion is retarded; the Mariner awakes, and his penance begins anew.

The curse is finally expiated.
[Expiated means "paid for" or "made amends for."]

---

427. *Belated* means "made late."
435. A *charnel-dungeon* is a burial vault.

Literary Element Narrative Poetry *How do these lines signal a new phase of the story?*

"It raised my hair, it fanned my cheek
Like a meadow-gale of spring—
It mingled strangely with my fears,
Yet it felt like a welcoming.

460   "Swiftly, swiftly flew the ship,
Yet she sailed softly too:
Sweetly, sweetly blew the breeze—
On me alone it blew.

"Oh! dream of joy! is this indeed
465   The lighthouse top I see?
Is this the hill? is this the kirk?
Is this mine own countree?

"We drifted o'er the harbor bar,°
And I with sobs did pray—
470   O let me be awake, my God!
Or let me sleep alway.

"The harbor bay was clear as glass,
So smoothly it was strewn!
And on the bay the moonlight lay,
475   And the shadow of the Moon.

"The rock shone bright, the kirk no less,
That stands above the rock:
The moonlight steeped in silentness
The steady weathercock.

480   "And the bay was white with silent light,
Till, rising from the same,
Full many shapes, that shadows were,
In crimson colors came.

"A little distance from the prow
485   Those crimson shadows were:
I turned my eyes upon the deck—
Oh, Christ! what saw I there!

"Each corse lay flat, lifeless and flat,
And, by the holy rood!°
490   A man all light, a seraph° man,
On every corse there stood.

And the ancient Mariner beholdeth his native country.

The angelic spirits leave the dead bodies,

And appear in their own forms of light.

---

468. A *harbor bar* is a bank of sand across the mouth of a harbor, obstructing navigation.
489. The *holy rood* is the cross symbolizing the Christian faith.
490. A *seraph* is an angel of the highest rank.

Literary Element   Narrative Poetry   *Who are these characters?*

"This seraph band, each waved his hand:
It was a heavenly sight!
They stood as signals to the land,
495　　Each one a lovely light;

"This seraph band, each waved his hand,
No voice did they **impart**—
No voice; but oh! the silence sank
Like music on my heart.

500　　"But soon I heard the dash of oars,
I heard the Pilot's° cheer;
My head was turned perforce° away,
And I saw a boat appear.

"The Pilot and the Pilot's boy,
505　　I heard them coming fast:
Dear Lord in Heaven! it was a joy
The dead men could not blast.

"I saw a third—I heard his voice:
It is the Hermit good!
510　　He singeth loud his godly hymns
That he makes in the wood.
He'll shrieve° my soul, he'll wash away
The Albatross's blood."

Hermit saves the Mariner, 1875. Gustave Doré. Engraving.

PART VII

"This Hermit good lives in that wood
515　　Which slopes down to the sea.
How loudly his sweet voice he rears!
He loves to talk with mariners
That come from a far countree.

"He kneels at morn, and noon, and eve—
520　　He hath a cushion plump:
It is the moss that wholly hides
The rotted old oak stump.

The Hermit of the wood

---

501. A *pilot* is a person who steers ships in and out of a harbor.
502. *Perforce* means "of necessity."
512. To *shrieve* is to hear confession and grant forgiveness.

Reading Strategy　Reviewing *What role does the Mariner think the Hermit will play?*

Vocabulary

impart　(im pärt´) *v.* to give; donate

SAMUEL TAYLOR COLERIDGE　**823**

"The skiff° boat neared: I heard them talk,
'Why, this is strange, I trow!°
525 Where are those lights so many and fair,
That signal made but now?'

" 'Strange, by my faith!' the Hermit said—
'And they answered not our cheer!°
The planks looked warped! and see those sails,
530 How thin they are and sere!
I never saw aught° like to them,
Unless perchance it were

" 'Brown skeletons of leaves that lag
My forest brook along;
535 When the ivy tod° is heavy with snow,
And the owlet whoops to the wolf below,
That eats the she-wolf's young.'

" 'Dear Lord! it hath a fiendish look—
(The Pilot made reply)
540 I am a-feared'—'Push on, push on!'
Said the Hermit cheerily.

"The boat came closer to the ship,
But I nor spake nor stirred;
The boat came close beneath the ship,
545 And straight° a sound was heard.

"Under the water it rumbled on,
Still louder and more dread:
It reached the ship, it split the bay;
The ship went down like lead.

550 "Stunned by that loud and dreadful sound,
Which sky and ocean smote,°
Like one that hath been seven days drowned
My body lay afloat;
But swift as dreams, myself I found
555 Within the Pilot's boat.
"Upon the whirl, where sank the ship,

Approacheth the ship with wonder.

The ship suddenly sinketh.

The ancient Mariner is saved in the Pilot's boat.

---

523. A *skiff* is a small seagoing boat, used for sailing or rowing.
524. *Trow* means "suppose" or "believe."
528. Here, *cheer* means "shout of welcome."
531. *Aught* means "anything."
535. An *ivy tod* is a bush of ivy.
545. Here, *straight* means "immediately."
551. *Smote* means "struck."

Big Idea **Nature and the Imagination** *How are the images from nature in this stanza similar to other images you have already encountered in the poem?*

The boat spun round and round;
And all was still, save that the hill
Was telling of the sound.

560 "I moved my lips—the Pilot shrieked
And fell down in a fit;
The holy Hermit raised his eyes,
And prayed where he did sit.

"I took the oars: the Pilot's boy,
565 Who now doth crazy go,
Laughed loud and long, and all the while
His eyes went to and fro.
'Ha! ha!' quoth he, 'full plain I see,
The Devil knows how to row.'

570 "And now, all in my own countree,
I stood on the firm land!
The Hermit stepped forth from the boat,
And scarcely he could stand.

" 'O shrieve me, shrieve me, holy man!'
575 The Hermit crossed his brow.°
'Say quick,' quoth he, 'I bid thee say—
What manner of man art thou?'

"Forthwith this frame of mine was wrenched
With a woeful agony,
580 Which forced me to begin my tale;
And then it left me free.

"Since then, at an uncertain hour,
That agony returns:
And till my ghastly tale is told,
585 This heart within me burns.

"I pass, like night, from land to land;
I have strange power of speech;
That moment that his face I see,
I know the man that must hear me:
590 To him my tale I teach.
"What loud uproar bursts from that door!

The ancient Mariner earnestly entreateth the Hermit to shrieve him; and the penance of life falls on him.

And ever and anon throughout his future life an agony constraineth him to travel from land to land,

---

575. *Crossed his brow* means "made the sign of the cross on his forehead."

Literary Element Narrative Poetry *How do those in the boat react to the Mariner's movement? Why do you think they react this way?*

Reading Strategy Reviewing *Why must the Mariner tell his tale and why must the Wedding Guest listen?*

SAMUEL TAYLOR COLERIDGE **825**

The wedding guests are there:
But in the garden bower the bride
And bridemaids singing are:
595   And hark the little vesper bell,
Which biddeth me to prayer!

"O Wedding Guest! this soul hath been
Alone on a wide, wide sea:
So lonely 'twas, that God himself
600   Scarce seemèd there to be.

"O sweeter than the marriage feast,
'Tis sweeter far to me,
To walk together to the kirk
With a goodly company!—

605   "To walk together to the kirk,
And all together pray,
While each to his great Father bends,
Old men, and babes, and loving friends
And youths and maidens gay!

610   "Farewell, farewell! but this I tell
To thee, thou Wedding Guest!
He prayeth well, who loveth well
Both man and bird and beast.

"He prayeth best, who loveth best
615   All things both great and small;
For the dear God who loveth us,
He made and loveth all."

The Mariner, whose eye is bright,
Whose beard with age is hoar,
620   Is gone: and now the Wedding Guest
Turned from the bridegroom's door.

He went like one that hath been stunned,
And is of sense forlorn:°
A sadder and a wiser man,
625   He rose the morrow morn.

Albatross from cover binder. Sangorski and
Sutcliffe, London.

And to teach, by his own example, love
and reverence to all things that God
made and loveth.

---

623. *Of sense forlorn* means "stripped of his senses."

Big Idea **Nature and the Imagination** *How does nature
inform the moral of the Mariner's tale?*

Literary Element **Narrative Poetry** *According to the last
stanza, what does the Wedding Guest do now? How has he
been changed by his experience?*

RESPONDING AND THINKING CRITICALLY

Respond

1. (a)What images remain in your mind from this poem? Explain. (b)What still puzzles you about this poem? Write your answer in the form of a question.

Recall and Interpret

2. (a)What sin or crime does the Mariner say he has committed? (b)What happens to the ship after this deed? (c)How do the Mariner's fellow crewmen single him out for punishment?

3. (a)Who is aboard the skeleton ship in Part III and what are they doing? (b)What is the result of their activity?

4. (a)What comparison does the Mariner make between himself, the water snakes, and the dead men in lines 236–239? (b)How does his view of these water snakes change at the end of Part IV in lines 272–291? (c)How does the Mariner change with this realization?

5. (a)In Part IV what happens when the Mariner prays? (b)In lines 402–409 what does the lonesome Polar Spirit decide and why? (c)What broader idea might this symbolize?

Analyze and Evaluate

6. (a)Do you think the Mariner is responsible for what happens to the ship? Why or why not? (b)Do you think the Mariner's punishment fits his crime? Explain.

7. Coleridge added side notes to help the reader better follow the plot. Do you think they are helpful? Why or why not?

8. Coleridge once wrote that a reader must put aside his or her understanding of reality and accept the writer's world. Identify three details in the poem that helped you accept the story as real.

Connect

9. **Big Idea** **Nature and the Imagination** How does this poem exemplify Romantic ideas about nature and the imagination?

Literary Element ## Narrative Poetry

Traditionally, there are three main types of **narrative poetry:** the epic, the romance, and the ballad. Epic poems, like *Beowulf* (see page 24), are long poems written in a formal style that often trace the story of a noble and courageous hero. Romances are similar to epics and often recount the exploits of heroic knights. *Sir Gawain and the Green Knight* (see page 174) is one example. The ballad is a shorter narrative poem that is written in the form of a song.

1. Explain Coleridge's use of a frame story to present the tale of the Mariner's adventure.

2. (a)How would you characterize the Mariner? (b)Why do you think Coleridge wrote this poem in the ballad form?

3. (a)What incident sparks the conflict of the story? (b)What incident serves as the climax?

Review: Ballad Stanza

As you learned on page 210, a **literary ballad** is written in imitation of folk ballads but has a known author. The writer may employ a **ballad stanza** and rhyme scheme, as well as archaic diction to achieve this effect.

Partner Activity Meet with another classmate and talk about Coleridge's use of the elements of folk ballads in *The Rime of the Ancient Mariner*. Construct a chart like the one below, citing at least one example from the poem for each of the bulleted elements.

Ballad Element	Example
• Quatrains of alternating 4 and 3 stressed syllables	
• Rhyme scheme of *abcb*	
• Iambic meter	
• Repeated lines or refrains	
• Use of slant rhymes	
• Archaic spellings	

SAMUEL TAYLOR COLERIDGE **827**

READING AND VOCABULARY

Reading Strategy Reviewing

Summarizing the main ideas, supporting details, actions, and plot of a literary work as you review that work will aid your understanding of it.

1. Summarize each of the seven parts of *The Rime of the Ancient Mariner*.

2. Write a summary of the whole poem in two or three sentences.

Vocabulary Practice

Practice with Context Clues Use the context clues in each sentence below to choose the vocabulary word from *The Rime of the Ancient Mariner* that best completes each sentence.

1. The Mariner wants the Hermit, as a holy man, to tell him what _____ he must pay to atone for his sin.
   a. dismal   **b.** penance   **c.** impart

2. By his deeds as well as his words, the father tried to _____ a sense of morality in his children.
   a. penance   **b.** dismal   **c.** impart

3. Set after a global war, the movie paints a _____ picture of a civilization that has crumbled.
   a. penance   **b.** dismal   **c.** impart

Academic Vocabulary

Here are two words from the vocabulary list on page R82.

predominant (pri dom′ ə nənt) *adj.* most frequent; most noticeable

crucial (krōō′ shəl) *adj.* critical; of extreme importance

Practice and Apply

1. What are the **predominant** images in *The Rime of the Ancient Mariner*?

2. Is suspending your disbelief **crucial** to appreciating this poem? Explain.

WRITING AND EXTENDING

Writing About Literature

Evaluate Contemporary Relevance Two expressions from Coleridge's poems that have entered our language are "searching for one's Xanadu" from "Kubla Khan" and "an albatross hanging around one's neck" from *The Rime of the Ancient Mariner*. Use the context of each poem to decide what these sayings mean. Then write a paragraph about each expression, giving examples of how each one could be used today.

Before you begin writing, go through the poems and collect evidence that supports your view about the meaning of each expression. Organize your thoughts about each expression in a three-column chart like the one below.

Expression	Context	Meaning

After you complete your paragraphs, meet with a peer reviewer to evaluate each other's work and to suggest revisions. Then proofread and edit your paragraphs for errors in spelling, grammar, and punctuation.

Learning for Life

Write a memo to a movie producer in which you discuss why *The Rime of the Ancient Mariner* would make a great movie. Outline the major events of the adventure, identifying who, what, when, and where. Give suggestions for adapting the poem into a movie, including recommendations for actors who could play the leading roles. Give reasons why these actors would be appropriate. You might also suggest a location for shooting the film.

 **Web Activities** For eFlashcards, Selection Quick Checks, and other Web activities, go to www.glencoe.com.

Informational Text

Portrait of a Gentleman (thought to be Thomas Cavendish). Attributed to John Bettes the Younger. Oil on panel. Private collection.

from

In Patagonia

Bruce Chatwin

Hawthornden Prize Winner

Building Background

In 1591 a British fleet under the command of Thomas Cavendish sailed from Plymouth, England, on a voyage to the Pacific Ocean. The trip would end in disaster. As a result of bad weather, ill luck, and a series of miscalculations, many in the fleet's crew were lost. This disaster may have provided some of the inspiration for Samuel Taylor Coleridge's *The Rime of the Ancient Mariner*. The following selection, from Bruce Chatwin's prize-winning book *In Patagonia*, describes the circumstances surrounding the disaster.

Set a Purpose for Reading

Read to discover the historical basis for Coleridge's *The Rime of the Ancient Mariner*.

Evaluating Historical Influences

Evaluating historical influences involves gathering and examining the background information related to the writing of a literary work. As you read, take notes on the parallels between the historical events and the events in Coleridge's poem. Use a two-column chart like the one below.

Literary Work	Historical Events
Ancient Mariner's voyage	Voyage of the Desire

On October 30th 1593,[1] the ship *Desire*, of 120 tons, limping home to England, dropped anchor in the river at Port Desire, this being her fourth visit since Thomas Cavendish[2] named the place in her, his flagship's, honor, seven years before.

The captain was now John Davis, a Devon man, the most skilled navigator of his generation. Behind him were three Arctic voyages in search of the North-West Passage. Before him were two books of seamanship and six fatal cuts of a Japanese pirate's sword.

Davis had sailed on Cavendish's Second Voyage "intended for the South Sea." The fleet left Plymouth on August 26th 1591, the Captain-General in the galleon *Leicester*; the other ships were the *Roebuck*, the *Desire*, the *Daintie*, and the *Black Pinnace*, the last so named for having carried the corpse of Sir Philip Sydney.[3]

Cavendish was puffed up with early success, hating his officers and crew. On the coast of Brazil,

---

1. Although Chatwin cites the year 1593, 1592 is more likely based on the chronology of the voyage.
2. *Thomas Cavendish* (1555–1592) was a famed explorer who led the third circumnavigation of the globe.
3. A *pinnace* is a small sailing ship. *Sir Philip Sydney* (1554–1586) was an Elizabethan poet, courtier, and soldier.

he stopped to sack[4] the town of Santos. A gale scattered the ships off the Patagonian coast, but they met up, as arranged, at Port Desire.

The fleet entered the Magellan Strait[5] with the southern winter already begun. A sailor's frostbitten nose fell off when he blew it. Beyond Cape Froward, they ran into north-westerly gales and sheltered in a tight cove with the wind howling over their mastheads. Reluctantly, Cavendish agreed to revictual[6] in Brazil and return the following spring.

On the night of May 20th, off Port Desire, the Captain-General changed tack[7] without warning. At dawn, the *Desire* and the *Black Pinnace* were alone on the sea. Davis made for port, thinking his commander would join him as before, but Cavendish set course for Brazil and thence to St. Helena.[8] One day he lay down in his cabin and died, perhaps of apoplexy,[9] cursing Davis for desertion: "This villain that hath been the death of me."

Davis disliked the man but was no traitor. The worst of the winter over, he went south again to look for the Captain-General. Gales blew the two ships in among some undiscovered islands, now known as the Falklands.

This time, they passed the Strait and out into the Pacific. In a storm off Cape Pilar, the *Desire* lost the *Pinnace*, which went down with all hands. Davis was alone at the helm, praying for

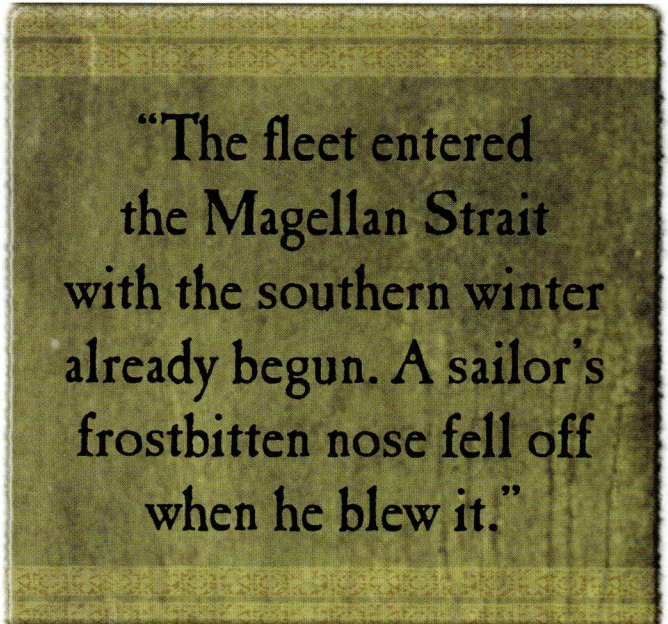

"The fleet entered the Magellan Strait with the southern winter already begun. A sailor's frostbitten nose fell off when he blew it."

a speedy end, when the sun broke through the clouds. He took bearings, fixed his position, and so regained the calmer water of the Strait.

He sailed back to Port Desire, the crew scurvied and mutinous and the lice lying in their flesh, "clusters of lice as big as peason, yea, and some as big as beanes." He repaired the ship as best he could. The men lived off eggs, gulls, baby seals, scurvy grass and the fish called *pejerrey*. On this diet they were restored to health.

Ten miles down the coast, there was an island, the original Penguin Island, where the sailors clubbed twenty thousand birds to death. They had no natural enemies and were unafraid of their murderers. John Davis ordered the penguins dried and salted and stowed fourteen thousand in the hold.

On November 11th a war-party of Tehuelche Indians[10] attacked "throwing dust in the ayre, leaping and running like brute beasts, having vizzards on their faces like dogs' faces, or else their faces are dogs' faces indeed." Nine men died in the skirmish, among them the chief mutineers, Parker and Smith. Their deaths were seen as the just judgment of God.

The *Desire* sailed at nightfall on December 22nd and set course for Brazil where the Captain hoped to provision with cassava[11] flour. On January 30th he made land at the Isle of Plasencia, off Rio de Janeiro. The men foraged for fruit and vegetables in gardens belonging to the Indians.

---

4. Here, *sack* means "pillage."
5. The *Magellan Strait* connects the Atlantic and Pacific Oceans near the southern tip of South America.
6. *Revictual* means to "resupply with food."
7. Here, *tack* means "course."
8. *St. Helena*, first discovered in 1502, was a British island colony and port of call off the southwestern coast of Africa.
9. *Apoplexy* is a stroke.

---

10. The *Tehuelche Indians* were a nomadic group that inhabited Patagonia.
11. *Cassava* is a tuber, or a plant with bulky, underground stems, that can be dried and milled into flour.

Six days later, the coopers[12] went with a landing party to gather hoops for barrels. The day was hot and the men were bathing, unguarded, when a mob of Indians and Portuguese attacked. The Captain sent a boat crew ashore and they found the thirteen men, faces upturned to heaven, laid in a rank with a cross set by them.

John Davis saw pinnaces sailing out of Rio harbor. He made for open sea. He had no other choice. He had eight casks of water and they were fouled.

As they came up to the Equator, the penguins took their revenge. In them bred a "loathsome worme" about an inch long. The worms ate everything, iron only excepted—clothes, bedding, boots, hats, leather lashings, and live human flesh. The worms gnawed through the ship's side and threatened to sink her. The more worms the men killed, the more they multiplied.

Around the Tropic of Cancer, the crew came down with scurvy. Their ankles swelled and their chests, and their parts swelled so horribly that "they could neither stand nor lie nor go."

The Captain could scarcely speak for sorrow. Again he prayed for a speedy end. He asked the men to be patient; to give thanks to God and accept his chastisement. But the men were raging mad and the ship howled with the groans and curses of the dying.

Map of the Magellan Straits, from Cosmographie Universelle, 1555. Guillaume Le Testu. Watercolor on paper. Ministry of Defense, Service Historique de l'Armee de Terre, France.

Only Davis and a ship's boy were in health, of the seventy-six who left Plymouth. By the end there were five men who could move and work the ship.

And so, lost and wandering on the sea, with topsails and spritsails torn, the rotten hulk drifted, rather than sailed, into the harbor of Berehaven on Bantry Bay[13] on June 11th 1593. The smell disgusted the people of that quiet fishing village. . . .

---

12. *Coopers* repair and build wooden barrels or casks.

13. *Bantry Bay* is in southwest Ireland.

"The Southern Voyage of John Davis" appeared in Hakluyt's[14] edition of 1600. Two centuries passed and another Devon man, Samuel Taylor Coleridge, set down the 625 controversial lines of *The Ancient Mariner*, with its hammering repetitions and story of crime, wandering, and expiation.[15]

John Davis and the Mariner have these in common: a voyage to the Black South, the murder of a bird or birds, the nemesis which follows, the drift through the tropics, the rotting ship, the curses of dying men. Lines 236–9 are particularly resonant of the Elizabethan voyage:

> The many men so beautiful!
> And they all dead did lie:
> And a thousand, thousand slimy things
> Lived on and so did I.

In *The Road to Xanadu*, the American scholar John Livingston Lowes traced the Mariner's victim to a "disconsolate Black Albitross" shot by one Hatley, the mate of Captain George Shelvocke's privateer in the eighteenth century. Wordsworth had a copy of this voyage and showed it to Coleridge when the two men tried to write the poem together. . . .

Lowes demonstrated how the voyages in Hakluyt and Purchas[16] fuelled Coleridge's imagination. "The mighty great roaring of ice" that John Davis witnessed on an earlier voyage off Greenland reappears in line 61: "It cracked and growled and roared and howled." But he did not, apparently, consider the likelihood that Davis's voyage to the Strait gave Coleridge the backbone for his poem. ∾

---

14. Richard *Hakluyt* (1552–1616) was a British geographer and chronicler of British exploration. The second edition of his nautical record was completed and released between 1598 and 1600.

15. *Expiation* is the act of making atonement.

16. Samuel *Purchas* (1577–1626) chronicled British nautical discoveries, continuing the work of Hakluyt. His work was a favorite of Coleridge's.

RESPONDING AND THINKING CRITICALLY

Respond

1. In your opinion, what aspects of this account most resemble the events in Coleridge's poem? Explain.

Recall and Interpret

2. (a)As he died, what did Cavendish accuse Davis of? Describe the events that led to the accusation. (b)Why do you think Cavendish came to this conclusion?

3. (a)For what reason did the crew kill the penguins on Penguin Island? (b)Why do you think they needed so many penguins?

Analyze and Evaluate

4. Based on the descriptions in this passage, do you agree with Chatwin that the killing of the penguins provided Coleridge's inspiration for the killing of the albatross? Explain.

5. (a)Why do you think Davis told the crew to accept God's "chastisement"? (b)In what ways does Davis's notion of divine punishment echo the themes of Coleridge's poem?

Connect

6. Based on the chart you made while reading, do you believe that these events gave Coleridge "the backbone for his poem," as Chatwin claims? Support your opinion with evidence from this selection and from *The Rime of the Ancient Mariner*.

OBJECTIVES
- Evaluate the historical influences that shape elements of a literary work.
- Connect a literary work, including character, plot, and setting, to its historical context.

from the Introduction to
Frankenstein

MEET MARY SHELLEY

The daughter of two celebrated writers and social thinkers, Mary Shelley might have been destined for literary stardom even if she had never met and married the great Romantic poet Percy Bysshe Shelley. No one could have predicted, however, that at age eighteen she would write *Frankenstein*, a novel that in its day far outstripped the popularity of her famous husband's poetry.

Mary Shelley was the daughter of the radical philosopher William Godwin and Mary Wollstonecraft Godwin, whose well-known writings included one of England's first treatises on women's rights. Nevertheless, Shelley's childhood was not a happy one. Her brilliant mother died from complications following childbirth; her father remarried a woman with a family of her own and little time for her stepdaughter. However, Shelley did get to meet many British intellectuals of the day. Young admirers of William Godwin's writings often gathered at the philosopher's home; one of these literary lights was Percy Bysshe Shelley, the man who was to become her husband.

> *"Nothing contributes so much to tranquilize the mind as a steady purpose—a point on which the soul may fix its intellectual eye."*
>
> —Mary Shelley

Literary Life The Shelleys' life together was romantic but troubled. Only one of their children survived past infancy, Mary Shelley suffered a breakdown, and her husband was sometimes unfaithful. Still, the Shelleys were passionate about many of the same things, including literature and languages. They often read together, usually the classics, sharing their responses at length.

In 1816 the couple traveled across Europe to Switzerland and took up residence near Lord Byron—who at the time, unlike Percy Shelley, was a glamorous celebrity. It was during their stay in Switzerland that Mary Shelley began writing the book that became one of the best-known gothic novels of all time. Published anonymously two years later, *Frankenstein; or, The Modern Prometheus* tells the now familiar story of a "mad" scientist, Dr. Frankenstein, who gives life to a creature made from parts of corpses. Although Frankenstein's "monster" is sensitive and kind, his appearance arouses hatred and fear, dooming him to misery. The novel was an instant hit, and Britain was buzzing with speculations (all wrong) about its author. Mary Shelley was highly pleased with its success, but her happiness was short-lived: in 1822 her twenty-nine-year-old husband died.

New Mission Mary Shelley devoted much of the rest of her life to establishing her late husband's reputation as one of the great English poets. Her efforts were successful. A complete collection of Shelley's works, painstakingly edited by his widow, was published in 1847, and Shelley's poetry began to receive the critical acclaim that it now enjoys. Mary Shelley continued to write to support herself. Her later works, however, never matched *Frankenstein* in originality of conception or emotional power. That masterpiece remains popular with readers to this day—a testament to the overwhelming power and scope of her imagination.

Mary Shelley was born in 1797 and died in 1851.

Literature Online **Author Search** For more about Mary Shelley, go to www.glencoe.com.

Connecting to the Essay

In this essay, Mary Shelley examines the creative process and describes what inspired her to write *Frankenstein.* As you read, think about the following questions:

- What moments of creative inspiration have you experienced?
- What might have triggered these experiences?

Building Background

In 1831, when the novel *Frankenstein* was being prepared for a new edition, the publishers asked Mary Shelley to write an introduction that answered the question so many still asked: How could a young woman of eighteen have created a novel so far removed from her own experience? Mary Shelley's Introduction offers fascinating insights into the genesis of a literary work.

Setting Purposes for Reading

Big Idea Nature and the Imagination

As you read, consider the importance of nature and the imagination to this Romantic writer.

Literary Element Gothic Novel

Mary Shelley's *Frankenstein* is a **gothic novel.** A gothic novel has a gloomy, ominous setting and elements of mystery, horror, or the supernatural. The first gothic novel, *The Castle of Otranto,* was written by Horace Walpole (1717–1797) and tells the eerie and horrifying story of a royal family's demise. This novel sparked a fascination with not only gothic writing, but gothic painting and architecture as well. As you read the introduction to *Frankenstein,* look for gothic elements.

- See Literary Terms Handbook, p. R7.

Literature Online Interactive Literary Elements Handbook To review or learn more about the literary elements, go to www.glencoe.com.

Reading Strategy Activating Prior Knowledge

You derive meaning from a literary work by relating what you read to what you already know. To better understand this selection, you must draw upon your **prior knowledge** about the act of writing, the creative process, and the story of *Frankenstein.*

Reading Tip: Taking Notes On a chart like the one below, record the connections you make between your prior knowledge and the events the author describes.

Event	Prior Knowledge
Mary Shelley struggled to find an idea for a ghost story.	I, too, sometimes have writer's block.

Vocabulary

incite (in sīt′) *v.* to urge or provoke; p. 836 *The angry speaker nearly incited a riot.*

illustrious (i lus′ trē əs) *adj.* famous and distinguished; p. 838 *The illustrious author gave a series of lectures about her life and work.*

relinquish (ri ling′ kwish) *v.* to give up; to put aside; to abandon; p. 838 *Jamal's grandfather decided to relinquish his driving privileges.*

acute (ə kūt′) *adj.* sharp; intense; p. 839 *A swollen appendix caused him acute pain.*

transient (tran′ shənt) *adj.* lasting only a brief time; temporary; p. 839 *Because of the cool climate, that region has only a transient growing season.*

Vocabulary Tip: Word Parts You can often figure out the meaning of an unfamiliar word by analyzing its parts: its root, prefix, or suffix.

OBJECTIVES
In studying this selection, you will focus on the following:
- analyzing literary periods
- understanding the gothic novel
- activating prior knowledge

from The Introduction to Frankenstein

Mary Shelley

The publishers of the Standard Novels, in selecting *Frankenstein* for one of their series, expressed a wish that I should furnish them with some account of the origin of the story. I am the more willing to comply because I shall thus give a general answer to the question so very frequently asked me—how I, then a young girl, came to think of and to dilate[1] upon so very hideous an idea.

It is true that I am very averse to bringing myself forward in print, but as my account will only appear as an appendage[2] to a former production, and as it will be confined to such topics as have connection with my authorship alone, I can scarcely accuse myself of a personal intrusion.

It is not singular that, as the daughter of two persons of distinguished literary celebrity, I should very early in life have thought of writing. As a child I scribbled, and my favorite pastime during the hours given me for recreation was to "write stories." Still, I had a dearer pleasure than this, which was the formation of castles in the air—the indulging in waking dreams—the following up trains of thought, which had for their subject the formation of a succession of imaginary incidents. My dreams were at once more fantastic and agreeable than my writings. In the latter I was a close imitator—rather doing as others had done than putting down the suggestions of my own mind. What I wrote was intended at least for one other eye—my childhood's companion and friend; but my dreams were all my own. I accounted for them to nobody; they were my refuge when annoyed—my dearest pleasure when free.

I lived principally in the country as a girl and passed a considerable time in Scotland. I made occasional visits to the more picturesque parts, but my habitual residence was on the blank and dreary northern shores of the Tay, near Dundee. Blank and dreary on retrospection, I call them; they were not so to me then. They were the aerie[3] of freedom and the pleasant region where unheeded I could commune with the creatures of my fancy. I wrote then, but in a most commonplace style. It was beneath the trees of the grounds belonging to our house, or on the bleak sides of the woodless mountains near, that my true compositions, the airy flights of my imagination, were born and fostered. I did not make myself the heroine of my tales. Life appeared to

---

1. Here, *dilate* means "to speak or write at length."
2. An *appendage* is an addition or accompaniment.

Reading Strategy Activating Prior Knowledge *Why might publishers ask authors to describe the origin of their stories?*

3. An *aerie* is a nest or retreat.

Castle. Victor Hugo (1802–1885). British Museum, London.

Viewing the Art: How would you describe the atmosphere in this painting? How does it compare with the setting in which Shelley found herself?

me too commonplace an affair as regarded myself. I could not figure to myself that romantic woes or wonderful events would ever be my lot; but I was not confined to my own identity, and I could people the hours with creations far more interesting to me at that age than my own sensations.

After this my life became busier, and reality stood in place of fiction. My husband, however, was from the first very anxious that I should prove myself worthy of my parentage and enroll myself on the page of fame. He was forever **inciting** me to obtain literary reputation, which

even on my own part I cared for then, though since I have become infinitely indifferent to it. At this time he desired that I should write, not so much with the idea that I could produce anything worthy of notice, but that he might himself judge how far I possessed the promise of better things hereafter. Still I did nothing. Traveling, and the cares of a family, occupied my time; and study, in the way of reading or improving my ideas in communication with his far more cultivated mind, was all of literary employment that engaged my attention.

In the summer of 1816, we visited Switzerland and became the neighbors of Lord Byron.[4] At first we spent our pleasant hours on the lake or wandering on its shores; and Lord Byron, who was writing the third canto[5] of *Childe Harold,*[6] was the only one among us who put his thoughts

Big Idea **Nature and the Imagination** *In what ways was Shelley's childhood conducive to her future career as a novelist?*

Reading Strategy **Activating Prior Knowledge** *Why did Mary Shelley's husband have such high expectations of her?*

Vocabulary

incite (in sīt´) *v.* to urge or provoke

4. George Gordon, *Lord Byron* (1788–1824) was an English Romantic poet.
5. A *canto* is a division of a long poem.
6. *Childe Harold's Pilgrimage* is one of Byron's best-known poems.

upon paper. ==These, as he brought them successively to us, clothed in all the light and harmony of poetry, seemed to stamp as divine the glories of heaven and earth,== whose influences we partook with him.

But it proved a wet, ungenial summer, and incessant rain often confined us for days to the house. Some volumes of ghost stories translated from the German into French fell into our hands. There was the *History of the Inconstant Lover,* who, when he thought to clasp the bride to whom he had pledged his vows, found himself in the arms of the pale ghost of her whom he had deserted. There was the tale of the sinful founder of his race whose miserable doom it was to bestow the kiss of death on all the younger sons of his fated house, just when they reached the age of promise. His gigantic, shadowy form, clothed like the ghost in *Hamlet,* in complete armor, but with the beaver up, was seen at midnight, by the moon's fitful beams, to advance slowly along the gloomy avenue. The shape was lost beneath the shadow of the castle walls; but soon a gate swung back, a step was heard, the door of the chamber opened, and he advanced to the couch of the blooming youths, cradled in healthy sleep. Eternal sorrow sat upon his face as he bent down and kissed the forehead of the boys, who from that hour withered like flowers snapped upon the stalk. I have not seen these stories since then, but their incidents are as fresh in my mind as if I had read them yesterday.

"We will each write a ghost story," said Lord Byron, and his proposition was acceded[7] to. There were four of us.[8] The noble author[9] began a tale, a

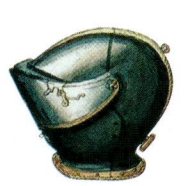

Visual Vocabulary
In a suit of armor, a *beaver* is a moveable piece on the helmet that protects the face.

A Nightmare. Theodor M. von Holst, (1810–44). Oil on canvas. Private collection.

fragment of which he printed at the end of his poem of Mazeppa. Shelley, more apt to embody ideas and sentiments in the radiance of brilliant imagery and in the music of the most melodious verse that adorns our language than to invent the machinery of a story, commenced one founded on the experiences of his early life. Poor Polidori had some terrible idea about a skull-headed lady who was so punished for peeping through a keyhole— what to see I forget: something very shocking and wrong, of course; but when she was reduced to a worse condition than the renowned Tom of Coventry,[10] he did not know what to do with her and was obliged to dispatch her to the tomb of the

---

7. *Acceded* means "consented."
8. The *four of us* consisted of the Shelleys, Byron, and John Polidori, Byron's personal physician.
9. The *noble author* refers to Byron.

Big Idea **Nature and the Imagination** *Why was nature important to Lord Byron?*

Literary Element **Gothic Novel** *What elements in these stories are characteristic of gothic novels?*

---

10. According to legend, Peeping *Tom of Coventry* lost his eyes as punishment for looking at Lady Godiva when she rode naked through Coventry.

Illustration from *Frankenstein* by Mary Shelley. Theodor M. von Holst. Engraving. Private collection.

Capulets,[11] the only place for which she was fitted. The **illustrious** poets also, annoyed by the platitude[12] of prose, speedily **relinquished** their uncongenial task.

I busied myself *to think of a story*—a story to rival those which had excited us to this task. One which would speak to the mysterious fears of our nature and awaken thrilling horror—one to make the reader dread to look round, to curdle the blood, and quicken the beatings of the heart. If I did not accomplish these things, my ghost story would be unworthy of its name. I thought and pondered—vainly. I felt that blank incapability of invention which is the greatest misery of authorship, when

---

11. The *tomb of the Capulets* was the setting of Romeo's and Juliet's deaths in Shakespeare's play.
12. *Platitude* means "lack of originality; dullness; triteness."

dull Nothing replies to our anxious invocations.[13] "Have you thought of a story?" I was asked each morning, and each morning I was forced to reply with a mortifying negative.

Everything must have a beginning, to speak in Sanchean phrase,[14] and that beginning must be linked to something that went before. The Hindus give the world an elephant to support it, but they make the elephant stand upon a tortoise. Invention, it must be humbly admitted, does not consist in creating out of void, but out of chaos; the materials must, in the first place, be afforded: it can give form to dark, shapeless substances but cannot bring into being the substance itself. In all matters of discovery and invention, even of those that appertain to the imagination, we are continually reminded of the story of Columbus and his egg.[15] Invention consists in the capacity of seizing on the capabilities of a subject and in the power of molding and fashioning ideas suggested to it.

Many and long were the conversations between Lord Byron and Shelley, to which I was a devout but nearly silent listener. During one of these, various philosophical doctrines were discussed, and among others the nature of the principle of life, and whether there was any probability of its ever being discovered and communicated. They talked of the experiments of Dr. Darwin[16] (I speak not of what the doctor really did or said that he did, but, as more to my purpose, of what was then spoken of as having been done by him), who preserved a piece of vermicelli[17] in a glass case till by some extraordinary means it began to move with voluntary motion. Not thus, after all, would life be given. Perhaps a corpse would be reanimated; galvanism[18] had given

---

13. *Invocations* are prayers or appeals to a higher power.
14. *Sanchean phrase* refers to Cervantes's *Don Quixote*, in which the character of Sancho Panza often uses proverbs to express common sense.
15. In response to claims that others could have discovered the New World before him, *Columbus* challenged guests at a banquet to make an *egg* stand on end. When nobody could do it, he tapped one end of the egg flat and stood it on the table, bolstering his claim that the others could only follow his lead.
16. *Dr.* Erasmus *Darwin* was a physician and scientist and the grandfather of the famous naturalist Charles Darwin.
17. *Vermicelli* (vur′ mə chel′ ē) is a long, slender noodle thinner than spaghetti.
18. Here, *galvanism* may refer to the use of electricity to stimulate muscle tissue.

token of such things: perhaps the component parts of a creature might be manufactured, brought together, and endued with vital warmth.

Night waned upon this talk, and even the witching hour had gone by before we retired to rest. When I placed my head on my pillow, I did not sleep, nor could I be said to think. My imagination, unbidden, possessed and guided me, gifting the successive images that arose in my mind with a vividness far beyond the usual bounds of reverie. I saw—with shut eyes, but **acute** mental vision—I saw the pale student of unhallowed arts kneeling beside the thing he had put together. I saw the hideous phantasm[19] of a man stretched out, and then, on the working of some powerful engine, show signs of life and stir with an uneasy, half-vital motion. Frightful must it be, for supremely frightful would be the effect of any human endeavor to mock the stupendous mechanism of the Creator of the world. His success would terrify the artist; he would rush away from his odious handiwork, horror-stricken. He would hope that, left to itself, the slight spark of life which he had communicated would fade, that this thing which had received such imperfect animation would subside into dead matter, and he might sleep in the belief that the silence of the grave would quench forever the **transient** existence of the hideous corpse which he had looked upon as the cradle of life. He sleeps; but he is awakened; he opens his eyes; behold, the horrid thing stands at his bedside, opening his curtains and looking on him with yellow, watery, but speculative eyes.

I opened mine in terror. The idea so possessed my mind that a thrill of fear ran through me, and I wished to exchange the ghastly image of my fancy for the realities around. I see them still: the very room, the dark parquet, the closed shutters with the moonlight struggling through, and the sense I had that the glassy lake and white high Alps were beyond. I could not so easily get rid of my hideous phantom; still it haunted me. I must try to think of something else. I recurred to my ghost story—my tiresome, unlucky ghost story! Oh! If I could only contrive one which would frighten my reader as I myself had been frightened that night!

Swift as light and as cheering was the idea that broke in upon me. "I have found it! What terrified me will terrify others; and I need only describe the specter which had haunted my midnight pillow." On the morrow I announced that I had *thought of a story*. I began that day with the words "It was on a dreary night of November," making only a transcript of the grim terrors of my waking dream.

At first I thought but of a few pages, of a short tale, but Shelley urged me to develop the idea at greater length. I certainly did not owe the suggestion of one incident, nor scarcely of one train of feeling, to my husband, and yet but for his incitement, it would never have taken the form in which it was presented to the world. From this declaration I must except the preface. As far as I can recollect, it was entirely written by him.

And now, once again, I bid my hideous progeny[20] go forth and prosper. I have an affection for it, for it was the offspring of happy days, when death and grief were but words,[21] which found no true echo in my heart. Its several pages speak of many a walk, many a drive, and many a conversation, when I was not alone; and my companion[22] was one who, in this world, I shall never see more. But this is for myself; my readers have nothing to do with these associations. . . . ❧

Visual Vocabulary
A *parquet* (pär kāʹ) floor is made of wooden pieces, often of different colors, worked into a geometric pattern or mosaic.

---

19. A *phantasm* is an image or illusion.

20. *Progeny* means "offspring, or the product of a creative effort."
21. [*when death . . . words*] Shelley is referring to a time before the deaths of her husband and two of her children.
22. Shelley's *companion* was her husband, who died in a boating accident in 1822.

RESPONDING AND THINKING CRITICALLY

Respond

1. What insights or ideas about the writing process did this selection give you?

Recall and Interpret

2. (a)Why does Shelley write this account of the origin of her story even though she claims she is "averse to bringing [her]self forward in print"? (b)What does this contradiction tell you about her personality?

3. (a)According to the second paragraph, what childhood activity did Shelley find more agreeable than writing? (b)How did Shelley's parents and husband influence her as a writer?

4. (a)Describe the events that led up to Shelley's idea for the plot of *Frankenstein.* (b)Do these factors support her theories about invention? Explain.

Analyze and Evaluate

5. Do you agree with Shelley's assessment of what is needed for invention? Why or why not?

6. Shelley was not alone when she conceived of and wrote *Frankenstein.* What part did other writers play in her success?

Connect

7. Shelley sought to appeal to "the mysterious fears of our nature and awaken thrilling horror." What books or movies have you read or seen that meet this description?

8. **Big Idea** **Nature and the Imagination** How does Shelley suggest that imagination is more important than reason?

LITERARY ANALYSIS

Literary Element Gothic Novel

The trappings of gothic fiction include haunted castles, clanking chains, mysterious graveyards, and restless spirits. Originally the term **gothic novel** referred only to works with a medieval atmosphere or setting. Gradually, however, its meaning expanded to refer to any work that featured terror or gloom.

1. Describe the gothic elements of Shelley's waking dream that inspired *Frankenstein.*

2. In your opinion, what accounts for the popularity of gothic novels today?

Literary Criticism

Author Brian W. Aldiss argues that the Introduction to *Frankenstein* contains evidence that the novel should be classified as science fiction (fiction in which scientific facts or theories inform the plot). With a partner, list elements from the introduction that support Aldiss's opinion.

Literature Online **Web Activities** For eFlashcards, Selection Quick Checks, and other Web activities, go to www.glencoe.com.

READING AND VOCABULARY

Reading Strategy Activating Prior Knowledge

When you read, you filter the words on a page through your prior experience and knowledge. Review the chart you made on page 834.

1. What prior knowledge helped you the most in understanding this selection?

2. Which aspects of the selection do you wish you'd known more about prior to reading the text?

Vocabulary Practice

Practice with Word Parts Match each vocabulary word with the definition of its Latin root. Use a dictionary if you need help.

1. incite   **a.** to leave behind

2. relinquish   **b.** to make bright

3. acute   **c.** to put in motion

4. illustrious   **d.** to sharpen

5. transient   **e.** to cross, pass by

PART 3

The Quest for Truth and Beauty

La Belle Dame Sans Merci, 1893. John Williams Waterhouse. Oil on canvas,
44.09 x 31.89 in. Hessisches Landesmuseum, Darnstadt, Germany.

*"I am certain of nothing but the holiness of the heart's affections and
the truth of imagination—what the imagination seizes as beauty must
be truth—whether it existed before or not."*

—John Keats

Byron's Poetry

MEET GEORGE GORDON, LORD BYRON

George Gordon, Lord Byron—aristocrat, poet, member of Parliament, athlete, expatriate, and freedom fighter—was perhaps the most colorful figure of his day.

> *"Be thou the rainbow to the storms of life,*
> *The evening beam that smiles the*
>   *clouds away,*
> *And tints to-morrow with prophetic ray!"*
>
> —Lord Byron, *The Bride of Abydos*

Descended from two noble but flamboyant and violent families, Byron inherited his title and a large estate at the age of ten, when his great-uncle, known as the "Wicked Lord," died. Byron had been born with a clubfoot, and the physical suffering and acute embarrassment it caused him profoundly affected his temperament. "No action of Lord Byron's life—scarce a line he has written—but was influenced by his personal defect," Mary Shelley wrote. To compensate for this impairment, Byron succeeded in becoming a masterful swimmer, horseman, boxer, cricket player, and fencer.

Literary Celebrity As a student at Cambridge University, Byron was known for his lavish lifestyle and flamboyant behavior; he even kept a tame bear as a pet. After graduating from Cambridge, he embarked upon an adventurous journey, traveling on horseback across Portugal and Spain and on to distant lands that few Englishmen had visited, including Asia Minor (present-day Turkey) and mountainous Albania. While traveling, he worked his adventures into his poetry, including the first part of his long poem *Childe Harold's Pilgrimage*, which made him the toast of London society at age twenty-four.

In his own words, "I awoke one morning and found myself famous."

His books sold well, and he influenced art and fashion, as well as literature, with his flamboyant style. In addition, as a member of the House of Lords, he championed liberal political causes. For example, he bravely defended the rebelling Nottingham weavers, whose jobs were threatened by new textile machines.

Soon, however, this extraordinarily handsome poet—with brown curly hair, fine features, and intensely brilliant eyes—saw his fame turn to notoriety. Personal scandals plagued him as he pursued a self-indulgent lifestyle with many love affairs.

Poet in Exile At twenty-eight, Byron exiled himself from England, never to return. He briefly lived in Switzerland, where he spent time with the Shelleys, and then settled in Italy. There, he composed *Don Juan*, a verse satire that describes the adventures of a licentious, though naive, young man. Always an outspoken defender of personal and political freedom, Byron died of fever shortly after his thirty-sixth birthday, having exhausted his energies training Greek troops fighting for independence from the Turks. His efforts in support of the Greek independence movement made him a national hero in Greece. Byron influenced a host of eminent writers, including Goethe in Germany, Balzac in France, Pushkin and Dostoevsky in Russia, and Hawthorne, Melville, and Poe in the United States.

Lord Byron was born in 1788 and died in 1824.

Literature Online **Author Search** For more about Lord Byron, go to www.glencoe.com.

Connecting to the Poems

What makes you admire something or someone? In these poems, Lord Byron admires the strength of the sea and the beauty of a woman. As you read, think about the following questions:

- Why are people fascinated by violent natural events, such as volcanoes, tsunamis, and hurricanes?
- Which objects or events stir intense feelings in you that are difficult to express?

Building Background

In medieval times, *childe* referred to a young nobleman who was a candidate for knighthood. Byron applied that title to the hero of *Childe Harold's Pilgrimage* to suggest the character's inner nobility and his quest for meaning. Sick of society, Harold embarks on a series of journeys across Europe, only to encounter more disillusionment in the wake of the Napoleonic Wars. As Byron describes him, Childe Harold is "the wandering outlaw of his own dark mind."

"She Walks in Beauty," a lovely lyric poem originally written for music, was inspired by the sight of the poet's cousin by marriage, the beautiful Lady Wilmot Horton. She appeared at a party dressed in a black mourning gown decorated with spangles, or bits of sparkling material.

Setting Purposes for Reading

Big Idea The Quest for Truth and Beauty

As you read, notice how these poems reflect Romantic ideals of beauty.

Literary Element Juxtaposition

Juxtaposition refers to the placing of two or more distinct elements of a literary work—for example, words, phrases, images, lines, or passages—next to or close to one another. For example, in line 7 of "Apostrophe to the Ocean," Byron uses this technique to contrast the speaker's future and his past: "From all I may be, or have been before." As you read, look for other examples of this technique and consider its effects.

- See Literary Terms Handbook, p. R9.

Reading Strategy Analyzing Figurative Language

When you **analyze figurative language**, you examine language that is not meant to be interpreted literally but is used for descriptive effect, often to suggest ideas. First, identify figures of speech, or specific devices of figurative language such as metaphor, simile, and personification. Then determine what each device contributes to the work.

Reading Tip: Identifying Figurative Language Use a chart to record examples of figurative language and to describe their function in the poems.

Example	Type	Function
"like a drop of rain" (line 16, "Apostrophe to the Ocean")	simile	suggests the insignificance of humans

Vocabulary

spurn (spurn) *v.* to reject or drive off; p. 845 *Members of Congress spurned the unqualified nominee.*

arbiter (är′ bə tər) *n.* a judge; p. 846 *Public opinion is the final arbiter in a debate between two candidates.*

mar (mär) *v.* to spoil or damage; p. 846 *The walls of that building were marred with graffiti.*

Vocabulary Tip: Analogies Analogies are comparisons based on relationships between words and ideas.

Literature⬤nline **Interactive Literary Elements Handbook** To review or learn more about the literary elements, go to www.glencoe.com.

OBJECTIVES
In studying these selections, you will focus on the following:
- analyzing literary periods
- analyzing juxtaposition
- interpreting figurative language

The Florentine Girl (The Artist's Daughter), c. 1827.
Henry Howard. Oil on canvas, 965 x 610 mm.
Tate Gallery, London

She Walks in Beauty

George Gordon, Lord Byron

She walks in beauty, like the night
　　Of cloudless climes[1] and starry skies;
And all that's best of dark and bright
　　Meet in her aspect[2] and her eyes:
5　　Thus mellowed to that tender light
　　Which heaven to gaudy day denies.

One shade the more, one ray the less,
　　Had half impaired the nameless grace
Which waves in every raven tress,
10　　Or softly lightens o'er her face;
Where thoughts serenely sweet express
　　How pure, how dear their dwelling place.

And on that cheek, and o'er that brow,
　　So soft, so calm, yet eloquent,
15　　The smiles that win, the tints that glow,
　　But tell of days in goodness spent,
A mind at peace with all below,
　　A heart whose love is innocent!

---

1. Here, *climes* means "climates" or "atmospheres."
2. Here, *aspect* means "appearance" or "face."

Reading Strategy　Analyzing Figurative Language
What does the speaker suggest about the woman by using this simile?

from Childe Harold's Pilgrimage

George Gordon, Lord Byron

Apostrophe to the Ocean

There is a pleasure in the pathless woods;
There is a rapture on the lonely shore;
There is society, where none intrudes,
By the deep sea, and music in its roar.
5 I love not man the less, but nature more,
From these our interviews, in which I steal°
From all I may be, or have been before,
To mingle with the universe, and feel
What I can ne'er express, yet cannot all conceal.

10 Roll on, thou deep and dark blue ocean—roll!
Ten thousand fleets sweep over thee in vain;
Man marks the earth with ruin—his control
Stops with the shore. Upon the watery plain
The wrecks are all thy deed, nor doth remain
15 A shadow of man's ravage, save his own,
When, for a moment, like a drop of rain,
He sinks into thy depths with bubbling groan,
Without a grave, unknelled,° uncoffined, and unknown.

His steps are not upon thy paths—thy fields
20 Are not a spoil for him—thou dost arise
And shake him from thee; the vile strength he wields
For earth's destruction thou dost all despise,
Spurning him from thy bosom to the skies,
And send'st him, shivering in thy playful spray
25 And howling, to his gods, where haply° lies
His petty hope in some near port or bay,
And dashest him again to earth—there let him lay.

6 **steal:** to depart quietly

18 **unknelled:** without the ringing of church bells

25 **haply:** perhaps

Reading Strategy **Analyzing Figurative Language** *What does the personification in this passage reveal about the ocean and the speaker?*

Vocabulary

spurn (spurn) *v.* to reject or drive off

The armaments which thunderstrike the walls
Of rock-built cities, bidding nations quake
30 And monarchs tremble in their capitals,
The oak leviathans,° whose huge ribs make
Their clay° creator the vain title take
Of lord of thee and **arbiter** of war—
These are thy toys, and as the snowy flake,
35 They melt into thy yeast° of waves, which **mar**
Alike the Armada's pride or spoils of Trafalgar.°

Thy shores are empires, changed in all save thee—
Assyria, Greece, Rome, Carthage,° what are they?
Thy waters washed them power while they were free,
40 And many a tyrant since; their shores obey
The stranger, slave, or savage; their decay
Has dried up realms to deserts—not so thou,
Unchangeable, save to thy wild waves' play.
Time writes no wrinkle on thine azure° brow;
45 Such as creation's dawn beheld, thou rollest now.

Thou glorious mirror, where the Almighty's form
Glasses itself° in tempests; in all time,
Calm or convulsed—in breeze, or gale, or storm,
Icing the pole, or in the torrid clime°
50 Dark-heaving—boundless, endless, and sublime—
The image of eternity—the throne
Of the Invisible; even from out thy slime
The monsters of the deep are made; each zone°
Obeys thee; thou goest forth, dread, fathomless, alone.

55 And I have loved thee, Ocean! and my joy
Of youthful sports was on thy breast to be
Borne, like thy bubbles, onward: from a boy
I wantoned° with thy breakers°—they to me
Were a delight—and if the freshening sea
60 Made them a terror, 'twas a pleasing fear,
For I was as it were a child of thee,
And trusted to thy billows far and near,
And laid my hand upon thy mane—as I do here.

31 **leviathans:** large ships
32 **clay:** human

35 **yeast:** the foam or froth of troubled waters
36 **Armada…Trafalgar:** a Spanish fleet that sailed against England in 1588 and was destroyed, as were most of the French ships captured by Lord Nelson at the Spanish cape of Trafalgar in 1805
38 **Assyria, Greece, Rome, Carthage:** powerful ancient empires

44 **azure:** sky blue

47 **Glasses itself:** reflects

49 **torrid clime:** the intensely hot area near the equator

53 **zone:** a climatic region of the earth

58 **wantoned:** frolicked **breakers:** large waves

Literary Element **Juxtaposition** *What does the speaker suggest about the ocean's power by juxtaposing the phrases "oak leviathans" and "huge ribs" (line 31) with "thy toys" and "the snowy flake"?*

Big Idea **The Quest for Truth and Beauty** *How does the speaker suggest the ocean is divine?*

Vocabulary

arbiter (är′ bə tər) *n.* a judge
mar (mär) *v.* to spoil or damage

RESPONDING AND THINKING CRITICALLY

Respond

1. What new ideas about nature and beauty did these poems suggest to you?

Recall and Interpret

2. (a)What qualities besides beauty does the woman in "She Walks in Beauty" have? (b)What can you infer about the speaker's feelings toward her?

3. (a)In lines 1–36 of "Apostrophe to the Ocean," how does the speaker portray the relationship between the ocean and human beings? (b)What do these lines suggest about the ability of human beings to master nature?

4. (a)In lines 37–54 of "Apostrophe to the Ocean," how does the speaker contrast the nature of the ocean with the fortunes of human beings? (b)What can you infer about the speaker's views on humans and the ocean from this contrast?

Analyze and Evaluate

5. What **images** in "She Walks in Beauty" best communicate to you the woman's beauty?

6. (a)In the last stanza of "Apostrophe to the Ocean," how does the speaker describe his boyhood relationship with the ocean? (b)What do the first and last stanzas reveal about the speaker?

7. Byron wrote *Childe Harold's Pilgrimage* in Spenserian stanzas, a verse form named after Edmund Spenser. (a)What is the **rhyme scheme** of each stanza? (b)What effects does Byron achieve with the longer ninth line of each stanza?

Connect

8. **Big Idea** **The Quest for Truth and Beauty** In "She Walks in Beauty," what is the main idea that Byron conveys about physical beauty?

LITERARY ANALYSIS

Literary Element **Juxtaposition**

By using **juxtaposition**, poets can create unexpected pairings and stunning contrasts.

1. In lines 17–18 of "She Walks in Beauty," why does the speaker juxtapose phrases about the subject's mind and heart?

2. What examples of juxtaposition in "Apostrophe to the Ocean" did you find most effective?

Writing About Literature

Respond to Author's Craft Byron's "Apostrophe to the Ocean" expresses admiration and awe in response to something in the world outside himself. An **apostrophe** is a figure of speech in which a speaker addresses an absent or dead person or something nonhuman as if it were able to respond. Brainstorm a list of people from the past or natural forces that you admire. Then, compose an apostrophe to one of these subjects.

Literature Online **Web Activities** For eFlashcards, Selection Quick Checks, and other Web activities, go to www.glencoe.com.

READING AND VOCABULARY

Reading Strategy **Analyzing Figurative Language**

When you **analyze the figurative language** in a poem, you can often detect the work's tone.

1. In the last line of "Apostrophe to the Ocean," what does the word *mane* suggest about the ocean?

2. How would you contrast the tone of "Apostrophe to the Ocean" with that of "She Walks in Beauty"?

Vocabulary **Practice**

Practice with Analogies Choose the word that best completes each analogy.

1. spurn : snub :: obscure :

   a. confuse   **b.** upset   **c.** display

2. arbiter : judge :: error :

   a. correction   **b.** disclaimer   **c.** blunder

3. mar : repair :: insult :

   a. offend   **b.** extol   **c.** denigrate

The Byronic Hero

> "Mad—bad—and dangerous to know."
>
> —Lady Caroline Lamb, on Lord Byron

GEORGE GORDON, LORD BYRON WAS ONLY thirty-six when he died. His brief life was marked by bold adventure, lascivious scandal, and artistic accomplishment. His work and lifestyle profoundly influenced the culture of his time.

When Byron published the first two cantos of *Childe Harold's Pilgrimage* in 1812, he became famous overnight. The speaker of this long poem is an unconventional outsider, a moody, passionate, mysterious wanderer. In short, he is a Byronic hero— an antihero, alienated and rebellious. Byron himself embodied many of these traits, and the archetype that he created has become ingrained in literature and popular culture.

Characteristics of the Byronic Hero

Literary critics have defined the Byronic hero in various ways, but most agree on the archetype's essential characteristics.

Rebellious The Byronic hero is a rebel, an individualist who questions and rejects society's laws, conventions, and morality. As the model for this type of figure, Byron might have looked to Melmoth the Wanderer, the title character of a highly popular gothic novel, or Napoleon Bonaparte, the mysterious commoner who became emperor of France and whose genius was to transform it into a great European power.

Alienated The Byronic hero disdains society and social conventions. He rejects the assumption that the upper classes, the nobility, or the gentry—people of wealth, rank, and privilege—deserve advantages in life solely because of their ancestry. He is often an outcast or outlaw who supports the democratic ideals of a meritocracy.

Manfred on the Jungfrau, 1840–61. Ford Madox Brown. Oil on canvas. Manchester Art Gallery, England.

Gloomy The Byronic hero is darkly handsome, melancholy, moody, and mysterious. He can never be happy, even when good things happen. He is difficult to portray because the reader must sympathize with him, yet he must be rather unpleasant. One of Byron's characters, Manfred, carries an air of melancholy that grows out of a mysterious, "half-maddening sin." Byronic heroes often have unexplained pasts that intensify their air of mystery and hint at great sorrow.

Bold The Byronic hero is arrogant and defiant. He trusts in his superior abilities. Byron's heroes are effective, almost superhuman leaders who overcome obstacles and formidable, even supernatural, opponents. This confidence helps make the Byronic hero an endearing character to the reader.

Dangerous The Byronic hero is ultimately self-destructive. Unlike traditional heroes, the Byronic hero is unlikely to live happily ever after. That is his charm and his tragedy. Appealing as he may be to the various women who cross his path, he cannot be faithful to them. He is either incapable of such fidelity, or his wandering destiny keeps him from lasting attachments.

The Legacy of the Byronic Hero

Besides the dark, brooding characters that he created, Byron himself left a lasting impact on European culture. His style and persona mirrored the tastes of the day—his portrait in Albanian dress (see page 842) shows the era's fascination with the exotic. The famed Russian poet Alexander Pushkin, an enthusiastic admirer of Byron's, had himself painted in a similarly exotic costume. Eugène Delacroix, the French painter, became such a devotee of Byron's that the topics of several of his large pictures are based on Byron's poems. As if they were making a pilgrimage, artists followed in Byron's footsteps, traveling throughout Europe, the Middle East, and North Africa and painting exotic street scenes and portraits of Arab chieftains and commoners.

Composers have immortalized several Byronic heroes as well. *The Corsair Overture* by Hector Berlioz became a popular ballet based on a Byronic hero, while Berlioz's *Harold in Italy* grew out of Byron's first major work, *Childe Harold's Pilgrimage.* Inspired by the Byronic hero Manfred, Robert Schumann wrote the *Manfred Overture*, and Peter Ilich Tchaikovsky wrote the *Manfred Symphony.*

Still, the most significant effect of the Byronic hero has been in literature. Many nineteenth-century novels feature brooding, mysterious characters, such as Mr. Rochester in Charlotte Brontë's *Jane Eyre* and Heathcliff in Emily Brontë's *Wuthering Heights.* In modern times, the Byronic hero has been a regular feature of popular culture, appearing in Harlequin romances, comic books, and detective stories. The Byronic hero has also found his way to the big screen. In spaghetti westerns, Clint Eastwood famously portrayed nameless gunslingers and roving outlaws, characters who embodied the archetype of the Byronic hero. Perhaps pop culture's most well-known example of the Byronic hero, though, is James Dean's title role in *Rebel Without a Cause.*

Lord Byron Reposing in the House of a Fisherman Having Swum the Hellespont, c. 18th–19th century. Sir William Allan. Roy Miles Fine Paintings, London.

Literature Online **Literary History** For more about the Byronic hero, go to www.glencoe.com.

RESPONDING AND THINKING CRITICALLY

1. What are the characteristics of a Byronic hero?

2. In what ways is the Byronic hero similar to and different from the traditional hero?

3. Why do you think the Byronic hero has endured in literature, movies, and art?

4. Choose a contemporary character from a comic book, movie, novel, story, or play and discuss how that character exemplifies the Byronic hero.

OBJECTIVES
- Connect literature to historical contexts, current events, and personal experience.
- Evaluate literature for its historical significance and universality.
- Understand the Byronic hero.

Shelley's Poetry

MEET PERCY BYSSHE SHELLEY

Many of our modern stereotypes of poets are derived from the life and character of Percy Shelly. He died young; he was politically radical and indifferent to the social norms of his age; he was passionate and often intemperate; and in his poems, he celebrated nature's transcendence while embracing its inherent gloom.

> *"Poets are the unacknowledged legislators of the World."*
>
> —Percy Bysshe Shelley

"Mad Shelley" Born in 1792, Shelley was the son of a country squire and an heir to a wealthy estate. He was the oldest child in a family mostly of girls. He was adored by his sisters and indulged by his father, who was unsure how to manage his unruly son. At age ten, when he attended Syon House Academy, however, he was often ridiculed. When he switched to Eton at twelve, the boys there treated him worse, calling him "Mad Shelley" and playing practical jokes on him. Shelley retreated into fantasy, writing gothic poems and melodramatic romances. He also began to gravitate toward political literature that opposed hypocrisy and injustice.

At eighteen, Shelley entered University College, Oxford, where he met his lifelong friend and biographer Thomas Hogg. The two were expelled only six months later, however, after they circulated and refused to admit authorship of the pamphlet *The Necessity of Atheism.* Shelley then traveled to London, where he met, and eventually eloped with, Harriet Westbrook. Both Shelley's family and Harriet's were opposed to the marriage. As a result, the couple had to fend for themselves with little money. After moving from place to place, they went to Dublin, Ireland.

Emerging Poet By 1813 Shelley had returned to London, where he published his first major work, *Queen Mab,* a prophetic poem that condemns war, the monarchy, and the church. That same year Harriet gave birth to their first of two children. Shelley, though, was soon to fall in love with Mary Godwin, the daughter of his mentor, radical philosopher William Godwin, and author Mary Wollstonecraft. Just before his twenty-second birthday, Shelley left for Europe with Mary. They spent the summer of 1816 on the shores of Lake Geneva, in Switzerland, where Shelley met and befriended George Gordon, Lord Byron. After two years of traveling and writing, they returned to England. Soon after their return, Harriet drowned herself. Percy and Mary were then married.

In 1818, seeking a more healthful climate, relief from his creditors, and increased proximity to Lord Byron, Shelley moved his household to Italy. In Italy, Shelley wrote some of his best poetry and essays. Yet, tragedy loomed. He and Mary lost two of their own children, and Mary suffered a severe nervous breakdown. Then, just prior to his thirtieth birthday, Shelley drowned in a boating accident. "You were all brutally mistaken about Shelley," wrote his grief-stricken friend Lord Byron. "[He was] the best and least selfish man I ever knew."

Percy Bysshe Shelley was born in 1792 and died in 1822.

Literature Online **Author Search** For more about Percy Bysshe Shelley, go to www.glencoe.com.

Connecting to the Poem

In "Ozymandias," the remains of an ancient Egyptian statue inspire a meditation on the impermanence of worldly power and the unrelenting passage of time. What do you feel is the most enduring kind of contribution a person can make?

Building Background

Ozymandias is the Greek name for Ramses II, the pharaoh who ruled Egypt during the thirteenth century B.C. Much of our knowledge of Ramses is derived from the large-scale monuments built to glorify his reign.

Shelley wrote "Ode to the West Wind" in 1819 in a forest beside the Arno River near Florence, Italy. "To a Skylark" celebrates the European skylark, a small bird thought to have one of the most beautiful songs of all the larks. What's more, the skylark sings only in flight—often when it is too high to be seen.

Setting Purposes for Reading

Big Idea **The Quest for Truth and Beauty**

As you read, consider how Shelley presents Romantic ideas about beauty, nature, and political radicalism.

Literary Element **Irony**

Irony takes several forms, all arising from a contrast between appearance and reality. In **verbal irony**, words that appear to mean one thing actually mean the opposite. In **situational irony**, the outcome of a situation is the opposite of what one expected. **Dramatic irony** exists when the audience or reader knows something that a character does not know. As you read "Ozymandias," try to determine what purpose irony is serving in the poem.

- See Literary Terms Handbook, p. R9.

Literature Online **Interactive Literary Elements Handbook** To review or learn more about the literary elements, go to www.glencoe.com.

Reading Strategy **Drawing Conclusions About Meaning**

A **conclusion** is a general statement about a number of specific examples. In a work of literature, these specific examples are the literary elements, rhetorical devices, main ideas, or themes presented by the author. By analyzing these specific examples, a reader can draw a valid conclusion about the meaning of the literary work.

Reading Tip: Taking Notes As you read, note specific examples in the poem that might aid you in drawing a conclusion about its meaning. Write down each example, describe it, and then label the line in which it appears. After recording your examples, draw a conclusion about the poem's meaning.

Vocabulary

dirge (durj) *n.* a song sung in grief; a mournful hymn; p. 855 *During the ceremony, a dirge was sung in honor of the missing soldiers.*

cleave (klēv) *v.* to tear or rip; to split something apart; p. 856 *It was quite easy for the axe to cleave the soft wood.*

tumult (tōō′ məlt) *n.* disorder; an uproar; p. 857 *After the show, there was a great tumult outside the theater.*

satiety (sə tī′ ə tē) *n.* a feeling of weariness or even dislike of something caused by satisfying an appetite or desire for it in excess; p. 860 *Diners suffered satiety after the enormous meal.*

Vocabulary Tip: Synonyms Synonyms are words that have the same or similar meanings. Note that synonyms are always the same part of speech.

OBJECTIVES

In studying these selections, you will focus on the following:
- analyzing literary periods
- analyzing irony
- drawing conclusions about meaning
- analyzing diction
- recognizing author's purpose

Memnonium, Thebes, from *David Roberts in Egypt and Nubia*, 1848. L. Haghe. Color lithograph. Institute of Civil Engineers.

Ozymandias

Percy Bysshe Shelley

I met a traveler from an antique land
Who said: Two vast and trunkless legs of stone
Stand in the desert . . . Near them, on the sand,
Half sunk, a shattered visage[1] lies, whose frown,
5   And wrinkled lip, and sneer of cold command,
Tell that its sculptor well those passions read
Which yet survive, stamped on these lifeless things,
The hand[2] that mocked[3] them, and the heart[4] that fed:
And on the pedestal these words appear:
10   "My name is Ozymandias, king of kings:
Look on my works, ye Mighty, and despair!"
Nothing beside remains. Round the decay
Of that colossal wreck, boundless and bare
The lone and level sands stretch far away.

1. A *visage* is a face.

2. Here, *hand* refers to the hand of the sculptor.
3. *Mocked* means "imitated" or "derided."
4. *Heart* refers to the heart of Ozymandias.

Literary Element   **Irony** *What is ironic about the statue's inscription? What does the irony suggest about the theme of the poem?*

RESPONDING AND THINKING CRITICALLY

Respond

1. What is your opinion of Ozymandias? Give reasons for your answer.

Recall and Interpret

2. (a)At the start of the poem, what does the traveler describe? (b)What specific details help you visualize what is being described?

3. (a)What words appear on the pedestal? (b)What do these words suggest about Ozymandias's personality and character?

4. (a)How does the traveler describe the area surrounding the ruins? (b)What does this description suggest about the nature of power and fame?

Analyze and Evaluate

5. (a)In your opinion, for what purposes did Shelley write this poem? (b)How successful was he? Explain.

6. (a)Why do you think Shelley uses "a traveler from an antique land" as the storyteller within the poem? (b)What is the effect of having both a speaker and a storyteller? Explain.

Connect

7. **Big Idea** **The Quest for Truth and Beauty**
How are Shelley's political radicalism and Romantic ideals evident in this poem? Explain.

LITERARY ANALYSIS

Literary Element Irony

Irony can be used in many different ways in a literary work. It can be used to support the theme or main idea. It can add humor, increase suspense, or create a surprise. In "Ozymandias," there are several different examples of irony that help advance the poem's theme.

1. Find examples of irony in "Ozymandias." What type of irony is illustrated by each example? Explain.

2. How does the irony support the theme of the poem?

Literary Criticism

Scholar Donald H. Reiman, summing up Shelley's own philosophy, asserts that Shelley "dedicated his efforts to the destruction of tyranny in all its forms." What evidence can you find of that dedication in "Ozymandias"? Share your thoughts with a partner. Be sure to refer to specific lines or ideas from the poem as you discuss Shelley's philosophy.

Literature Online **Web Activities** For eFlashcards, Selection Quick Checks, and other Web activities, go to www.glencoe.com.

READING AND VOCABULARY

Reading Strategy Drawing Conclusions About Meaning

Much of the evidence needed to draw accurate conclusions about a literary work is not explicitly stated. Therefore, it is often necessary for the reader to infer the meaning from various elements within the work.

1. What do you think is the meaning of the poem "Ozymandias"?

2. In support of your opinion, list three specific examples from the poem.

Academic Vocabulary

Here are two words from the vocabulary list on page R82.

utilize (ū′ tə līz′) *v.* to put to practical use or service.

brief (brēf) *adj.* short in length; abrupt

Practice and Apply
1. How does Shelley **utilize** irony in the poem?
2. What is Shelley saying about the **brief** nature of human life?

Literary Element Diction

Diction is an author's word choice, or the use of appropriate words to convey a particular meaning. Diction is particularly important in poetry, which uses language more economically than most prose does. As you read "Ode to the West Wind" and "To a Skylark" pay attention to Shelley's use of diction.

• See Literary Terms Handbook, p. R5.

Reading Strategy Recognizing Author's Purpose

To **recognize an author's purpose** means to recognize an author's intent. An author typically writes to accomplish one or more of the following purposes: to persuade, to instruct, to inform or explain, to entertain, to describe, or to tell a story.

Ode *to the* West Wind

Percy Bysshe Shelley

1

O wild West Wind, thou breath of Autumn's being,
Thou, from whose unseen presence the leaves dead
Are driven, like ghosts from an enchanter fleeing,

Yellow and black and pale and hectic red,°
5 Pestilence-stricken multitudes: O Thou,
Who chariotest° to their dark wintry bed

The wingèd seeds, where they lie cold and low,
Each like a corpse within its grave, until
Thine azure° sister of the Spring° shall blow

4 hectic red: like the flushed cheeks that are symptomatic of tuberculosis and other wasting diseases
6 chariotest: conveys in a chariot

9 azure: sky blue **sister of the Spring:** the south wind

Literary Element Diction *If Shelley had used "sky blue" instead of "azure," would line 9 sound more formal or more like everyday speech?*

10　Her clarion° o'er the dreaming earth and fill
　　(Driving sweet buds like flocks to feed in air)
　　With living hues and odors plain and hill:

　　Wild Spirit, which art moving everywhere;
　　Destroyer and preserver; hear, oh, hear!

2

15　Thou on whose stream, 'mid the steep sky's commotion,
　　Loose clouds like Earth's decaying leaves are shed,
　　Shook from the tangled boughs of Heaven and Ocean,°

　　Angels° of rain and lightning: there are spread
　　On the blue surface of thine aery surge,
20　Like the bright hair uplifted from the head

　　Of some fierce Maenad,° even from the dim verge
　　Of the horizon to the zenith's height,
　　The locks of the approaching storm. Thou **dirge**

　　Of the dying year, to which this closing night
25　Will be the dome of a vast sepulchre,°
　　Vaulted with all thy congregated might

　　Of vapors, from whose solid atmosphere
　　Black rain and fire and hail will burst: oh, hear!

3

　　Thou who didst waken from his summer dreams
30　The blue Mediterranean where he lay
　　Lulled by the coil of his crystalline streams,

　　Beside a pumice° isle in Baiae's bay,°
　　And saw in sleep old palaces and towers
　　Quivering within the wave's intenser day,

35　All overgrown with azure moss and flowers
　　So sweet the sense faints picturing them! Thou
　　For whose path the Atlantic's level powers

---

10 clarion: trumpet call

17 the tangled boughs of Heaven and Ocean: a metaphor for the way in which clouds are formed by a suspension of water (**Ocean**) in air (**Heaven**)
18 Angels: messengers

21 Maenad (mē′ nad): in Greek mythology, a female worshiper of Dionysus, the god of wine and wild revelry

25 sepulchre (se′ pəl kər): a tomb

32 pumice (pə′ məs): a light, porous volcanic rock **Baiae's** (bī′ ēz) **bay:** a small seaport in a volcanic area near Naples, Italy, which had been a tourist resort in ancient Roman times. Shelley had taken a boat trip there in 1818 and observed its underwater ruins.

Literary Element **Diction** *What tone does this metaphor help create?*

Vocabulary

dirge (durj) *n.* a song sung in grief; a mournful hymn

Snow Storm at Sea, 1842. Joseph Mallord William Turner. Oil on canvas, 91½ x 122 cm. Tate Gallery, London.

Cleave themselves into chasms, while far below
The sea-blooms and the oozy woods which wear
40   The sapless foliage of the ocean, know

Thy voice and suddenly grow grey with fear
And tremble and despoil themselves:° oh, hear!

39–42 The sea-blooms . . . despoil themselves: the vegetation at the bottom of the sea changes with the seasons **despoil:** to undress; here, referring to a loss of vegetation

Literary Element   **Diction** *Why might Shelley have chosen the word* oozy?

Vocabulary

cleave (klēv) *v.* to tear or rip; to split something apart

4

If I were a dead leaf thou mightest bear;
If I were a swift cloud to fly with thee;
45 A wave to pant beneath thy power and share

The impulse° of thy strength, only less free
Than thou, O Uncontrollable! If even
I were as in my boyhood and could be

The comrade of thy wanderings over Heaven,
50 As then, when to outstrip thy skiey speed
Scarce seemed a vision, I would ne'er have striven

As thus with thee in prayer in my sore need.
Oh, lift me as a wave, a leaf, a cloud!
I fall upon the thorns of life! I bleed!

55 A heavy weight of hours has chained and bowed
One too like thee: tameless and swift and proud.

5

Make me thy lyre,° even as the forest is:
What if my leaves are falling like its own!
The **tumult** of thy mighty harmonies

60 Will take from both a deep, autumnal tone,
Sweet, though in sadness. Be thou, Spirit fierce,
My spirit! Be thou me, impetuous one!

Drive my dead thoughts over the universe
Like withered leaves to quicken a new birth!
65 And by the incantation° of this verse,

Scatter, as from an unextinguished hearth
Ashes and sparks, my words among mankind!
Be through my lips to unawakened Earth

The trumpet of a prophecy! O Wind,
70 If Winter comes, can Spring be far behind?

---

46 impulse: a sudden force that causes motion, such as a push

57 lyre (līr): a harp, in this case probably an Aeolian harp, a stringed instrument that produces musical sounds when the wind passes over its strings

65 incantation: a ritual recitation or chanting, usually of a magic charm or spell

---

Reading Strategy Recognizing Author's Purpose *What do these lines suggest about Shelley's purpose for writing this poem?*

Vocabulary

tumult (too′ məlt) *n.* disorder; an uproar

Wheatfield with Lark, 1888. Vincent van Gogh. Oil on canvas. Rijksmuseum, Amsterdam.

To a Skylark

Percy Bysshe Shelley

Hail to thee, blithe° Spirit!
    Bird thou never wert,
That from Heaven, or near it,
    Pourest thy full heart
5 In profuse° strains of unpremeditated° art.

Higher still and higher
    From the earth thou springest
Like a cloud of fire;
    The blue deep thou wingest,
10 And singing still dost soar, and soaring ever singest.

1 **blithe:** carefree; lighthearted

5 **profuse:** plentiful; given freely or abundantly; **unpremeditated:** done without plan or forethought

---

Literary Element   Diction *How does the diction in these lines affect their sound?*

In the golden lightning
    Of the sunken sun,
O'er which clouds are bright'ning,
    Thou dost float and run—
15 Like an unbodied joy whose race is just begun.

The pale purple even°
    Melts around thy flight;
Like a star of Heaven,
    In the broad daylight
20 Thou art unseen, but yet I hear thy shrill delight,

Keen° as are the arrows
    Of that silver sphere,°
Whose intense lamp narrows
    In the white dawn clear
25 Until we hardly see—we feel that it is there.

All the earth and air
    With thy voice is loud,
As, when night is bare,
    From one lonely cloud
30 The moon rains out her beams, and Heaven is overflowed.

What thou art we know not;
    What is most like thee?
From rainbow clouds there flow not
    Drops so bright to see
35 As from thy presence showers a rain of melody.

Like a poet hidden
    In the light of thought,
Singing hymns unbidden,
    Till the world is wrought
40 To sympathy with hopes and fears it heeded not:

Like a high-born maiden
    In a palace tower,
Soothing her love-laden
    Soul in secret hour
45 With music sweet as love, which overflows her bower:°

16 **even:** evening

21 **Keen:** sharp

22 **silver sphere:** the planet Venus, also called the morning star because it is visible just before or at sunrise

45 **bower:** a private room or bedroom

Big Idea **The Quest for Truth and Beauty** *How does Shelley's description of the skylark in this line mimic the Romantic quest for truth and beauty?*

Like a glowworm golden
    In a dell° of dew,
Scattering unbeholden
    Its aerial hue
50 Among the flowers and grass, which screen it from the view!

Like a rose embowered
    In its own green leaves,
By warm winds deflowered,
    Till the scent it gives
55 Makes faint with too much sweet those heavy-wingèd thieves:

Sound of vernal° showers
    On the twinkling grass,
Rain-awakened flowers,
    All that ever was
60 Joyous and clear and fresh, thy music doth surpass:

Teach us, Sprite or Bird,
    What sweet thoughts are thine:
I have never heard
    Praise of love or wine
65 That panted forth a flood of rapture so divine.

Chorus Hymeneal,°
    Or triumphal chant,
Matched with thine would be all
    But an empty vaunt,°
70 A thing wherein we feel there is some hidden want.

What objects are the fountains°
    Of thy happy strain?°
What fields or waves or mountains?
    What shapes of sky or plain?
75 What love of thine own kind? What ignorance of pain?

With thy clear keen joyance°
    Languor° cannot be:
Shadow of annoyance
    Never came near thee:
80 Thou lovest—but ne'er knew love's sad **satiety**.

47 **dell:** a small, deep valley

56 **vernal:** occurring in the spring

66 **Chorus Hymeneal** (hī′ mə nē′ əl): a wedding song that comes from the name Hymen, the Greek god of marriage

69 **vaunt:** a boast

71 **fountains:** sources

72 **strain:** a melody

76 **joyance:** rejoicing; delight
77 **Languor** (lang′ gər): lack of energy or spirit; weariness

---

Literary Element   Diction *How does the word* panted *affect the connotation of this line?*

Vocabulary

satiety (sə tī′ ə tē) *n.* a feeling of weariness or even dislike of something caused by satisfying an appetite or desire for it in excess

Waking or asleep,
　　Thou of death must deem°
Things more true and deep
　　Than we mortals dream,
85　Or how could thy notes flow in such a crystal stream?

We look before and after,
　　And pine for what is not:
Our sincerest laughter
　　With some pain is fraught;
90　Our sweetest songs are those that tell of saddest thought.

Yet if we could scorn
　　Hate and pride and fear;
If we were things born
　　Not to shed a tear,
95　I know not how thy joy we ever should come near.

Better than all measures
　　Of delightful sound,
Better than all treasures
　　That in books are found,
100　Thy skill to poet were, thou scorner of the ground!

Teach me half the gladness
　　That thy brain must know,
Such harmonious madness
　　From my lips would flow
105　The world should listen then—as I am listening now.

82　**deem:** to think, believe, or judge

Reading Strategy　**Recognizing Author's Purpose** *In what ways do lines 101–104 suggest both Shelley's Romanticism and his purpose for writing this poem?*

The Large Lark, 1731-1743. Mark Catesby.
Academy of Natural Sciences of Philadelphia, PA.

RESPONDING AND THINKING CRITICALLY

Respond

1. Which of these poems more effectively invokes the natural world? Explain.

Recall and Interpret

2. (a)Sections 1–3 of "Ode to the West Wind" describe how the wind affects three aspects of nature. What are those aspects? (b)What do these descriptions reveal about the speaker's view of the West Wind?

3. (a)What does the speaker suggest in the final line of "Ode to the West Wind"? (b)What do you think the West Wind **symbolizes**, or represents for the speaker?

4. (a)In lines 1–30 of "To a Skylark," what words or images help you imagine the skylark's flight and song? (b)Describe the speaker's attitude toward the skylark.

5. (a)To what people or things does the speaker compare the skylark in lines 31–60? (b)What qualities of the skylark do these comparisons suggest?

Analyze and Evaluate

6. (a)What effect does Shelley create with his use of apostrophe in "Ode to the West Wind"? (b)Do you think this technique makes the poem more powerful? Explain.

7. In "To a Skylark," what effect does the rhyme scheme create?

Connect

8. **Big Idea** The Quest for Truth and Beauty
What ideas about truth and beauty do these poems convey?

YOU'RE THE CRITIC: Different Viewpoints

Are Shelley's Ideas Juvenile?

Read the two excerpts of literary criticism below. T. S. Eliot was one of the most important twentieth-century poets and critics. J. B. Priestley was a popular twentieth-century British novelist, dramatist, and essayist. Eliot and Priestley disagree about the merits of the ideas Shelley presents in his poetry. As you read, try to determine your position on the issues they raise.

"Shelley's views I positively dislike. . . . When the doctrine, theory, belief, or 'view of life' presented in a poem is one which the mind of the reader can accept as coherent, mature, and founded on the facts of experience, it interposes no obstacle to the reader's enjoyment, whether it be one that he accept or deny, approve or deprecate. When it is one which the reader rejects as childish or feeble, it may, for a reader of well-developed mind, set up an almost complete check."

—T. S. Eliot

"[W]hen he is in full flight . . . his poetry is marvelous in its innocence and loveliness . . . as if it belonged to—and is indeed celebrating— some future Golden Age. . . . What any generous youth, preferably in rebellion against tyranny and injustice, imagines for a few minutes . . . goes soaring and glittering and singing through volume after volume of Shelley."

—J. B. Priestley

Group Activity Discuss the following questions with classmates. Refer to the excerpts and cite evidence from Shelley's poems for support.

1. (a)Why does Eliot argue that Shelley's views prevent enjoyment of the poems? (b)How might Priestley respond to Eliot's criticism?

2. With which critic do you agree more? Explain.

LITERARY ANALYSIS

Literary Element Diction

The **diction** used by a poet is closely connected to the mood that is created in the poem. For example, writers who choose plain, unadorned, straightforward language may create an unromantic, matter-of-fact mood. Writers who use florid, dense language or a great deal of figurative or connotative language will create a far different tone in their writing. In poetry, diction creates the rhymes, rhythms, and other sound devices that can contribute to the mood.

1. (a)How would you describe the diction in "Ode to the West Wind" and "To a Skylark"? (b)In your opinion, what effect does the diction have on the mood of each poem?

2. In each poem, how does Shelley's use of rhythm and rhyme affect the mood?

Review: Rhyme Scheme

As you learned on page 266, the **rhyme scheme** of a poem is the pattern that is formed in a stanza by the rhymes at the end of each line. "Ode to the West Wind" is written in the terza rima form. Shelley borrowed this poetic form from Dante and other Italian literary sources.

Partner Activity Meet with another classmate and explore the rhyme scheme of terza rima. The rhyme scheme is designated by assigning a different letter of the alphabet to each new rhyme. Make a note of any other patterns or poetic forms that you notice.

READING AND VOCABULARY

Reading Strategy Recognizing Author's Purpose

Often the author's purpose is directly related to the theme of a poem. Identifying the theme of a literary work can help you **recognize the author's purpose**. To determine the theme, pay close attention to the main ideas, supporting details, rhetorical strategies, and any literary elements the writer uses.

1. What do you think Shelley's purpose was for writing each of these poems?

2. What is the **theme**, or message about life, of each poem? How does the theme of each relate to Shelley's purpose? Explain.

Vocabulary Practice

Practice with Synonyms Choose the synonym for each vocabulary word below.

1. dirge
   a. hymn   **b.** funeral   **c.** barge
2. cleave
   a. fall   **b.** split   **c.** join
3. tumult
   a. peace   **b.** calm   **c.** disorder
4. satiety
   a. hollowness   **b.** glut   **c.** emptiness

Academic Vocabulary

Here are two words from the vocabulary list on page R82.

displace (dis plās′) *v.* to replace; to take the place of something

thereby (thār bī′) *adv.* by the means of; in that way

Practice and Apply

1. In "Ode to the West Wind," what does the speaker say **displaces** his "dead thoughts" in line 63?

2. If the speaker of "To a Skylark" learned "half the gladness" (line 101) of the lark, what would he gain **thereby**?

Writing About Literature

Evaluate Author's Craft Not all readers have admired Shelley's poetry. Some critics have found his work to be too sentimental. Do you agree or disagree? In a few paragraphs, support or challenge the notion that Shelley's poems are too sentimental. Draw upon your knowledge of Romanticism as well as your own personal taste. Give examples from the poems to support your view.

Before you begin writing, be sure to determine the position you will take and to find evidence in support of that position. Use a chart like the one below to organize your main ideas and supporting evidence.

Guidelines for Persuasive Writing			
Introduce the issue	State your opinion	Support your position	Draw your conclusions
Describe the issue, and supply any background needed to help readers understand it.	Take your stand in a clear, direct thesis statement.	Present your evidence—facts, opinions, or both—responding to opposing viewpoints.	End by summarizing your ideas.

After you complete your draft, meet with a peer reviewer to evaluate each other's work and to suggest revisions. Then proofread and edit your draft for errors in spelling, grammar, and punctuation.

Literature Groups

Each of Shelley's poems examines someone's desire or attempt to create something meaningful. In your group, review what Ozymandias wanted to build and what the speakers of "Ode to the West Wind" and "To a Skylark" want to create. Discuss what Shelley says about each of their desires, motivations, and attempts, and determine the poet's attitude toward each. Then develop a statement about creativity that you think sums up the message in these poems. Share your ideas with other groups.

Shelley's Language and Style

Using Exclamation Points In "Ozymandias," "Ode to the West Wind," and "To a Skylark," Shelley uses exclamation points to show strong feeling, to indicate a forceful command, and to add variety to his poems. Consider how his use of exclamation points increases the intensity and the declarative force of the following lines from "Ode to the West Wind":

Line 14: "Destroyer and preserver; hear, oh, hear!"
Line 36: "So sweet the sense faints picturing them!"
Line 54: "I fall upon the thorns of life! I bleed!"

Notice Shelley's purposes for using exclamation points in the chart below.

Exclamation	Purpose
Line 14	command
Line 36	strong emotion
Line 54	strong emotion

Activity Create a chart of your own, listing more examples of exclamation points in these three poems. For each exclamation, determine the purpose it serves in the line in which it appears.

Revising Check

Exclamation Points The use of exclamation points in formal writing should be kept to a minimum. There are very few instances when this type of punctuation is needed. However, there are times when it can be effective. For example, exclamations can create a humorous effect, draw the reader's attention to an idea introduced by a quotation, or strengthen the response to a counterargument. With a partner, go through your persuasive essay about Shelley's sentimentality. Note places where an exclamation point might be useful and remove any unnecessary examples.

Literature Online Web Activities For eFlashcards, Selection Quick Checks, and other Web activities, go to www.glencoe.com.

Keats's Poetry

MEET JOHN KEATS

"**M**ortality," wrote John Keats, "weighs heavily on me like unwilling sleep." Keats wrote these words at age twenty-one, soon after launching his poetic career. Within five years, he was dead. To say he made the most of his time would be an understatement. No other poet—not even Chaucer, Shakespeare, or Milton—progressed so far by the age of twenty-five.

> "*O for ten years, that I may overwhelm Myself in poesy; so I may do the deed That my own soul has to itself decreed.*"
>
> —John Keats, from "Sleep and Poetry"

Young Keats Keats was affected by death at an early age. When he was eight, his father died after falling from a horse; when he was fourteen, his mother died of tuberculosis. He took no special interest in literature until he was fifteen. With the encouragement of his mentor, Charles Cowden Clarke, Keats immersed himself in reading.

No sooner had Keats awakened to literature than he was pulled out of school by his practical-minded guardian and apprenticed to the pharmacist-surgeon Thomas Hammond, with whom Keats studied medicine. Keats continued to read and study with Clarke, however, and at age twenty-one Keats abandoned medicine for poetry.

The Soul's Decree Up to that time, Keats had written few poems—and certainly none of artistic importance. Then, after spending an entire night with Clarke reading from the poet George Chapman's lively translation of Homer, Keats produced his first major poem: "On First Looking into Chapman's Homer." Leigh Hunt, a political radical, successful author, and friend of Keats's, published the poem and others by Keats in his journal, the *Examiner*. With Hunt's help, Keats found a publisher for his first book when he was only twenty-one. It sold poorly and received mixed reviews.

In the summer of 1818, Keats embarked on a walking tour of the northern British Isles. After slogging for days in pouring rain, he came down with the first symptoms of tuberculosis and returned to London. There he found that his brother Tom was gravely ill with the disease. Keats became Tom's devoted caregiver until Tom died that December. About the same time, Keats met and fell in love with Fanny Brawne. They became engaged, but their relationship was tormented by Keats's illness, poverty, and strict devotion to his work.

1819 came to be known as Keats's Great Year as a poet. Despite physical and emotional strain, Keats wrote the greatest works of his career: *The Eve of St. Agnes*, "La Belle Dame sans Merci," the great odes, and *Lamia*, among others. Within five years after he had begun writing poetry, Keats was a master. Nonetheless, time was running out. By the fall, Keats's tuberculosis made it impossible for him to sustain his creative momentum. In a desperate attempt to prolong his life, he sailed the next September for Italy. Just six months later, he died in Rome and was buried there. At his request, his marker bears no name—just this epitaph: "Here lies one whose name was writ in water."

John Keats was born in 1795 and died in 1821.

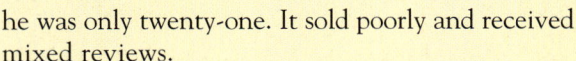

Literature Online Author Search For more about John Keats, go to www.glencoe.com.

Connecting to the Poems

Do you ever worry that life is too short for you to fulfill all your goals and aspirations? As you read, think about the following questions:

- How might an illness or family hardship prevent you from fulfilling your goals?
- How might a heightened awareness of your mortality *help* you fulfill your goals and aspirations?

Building Background

Keats's letters reveal his evolving struggle with the problem of evil and suffering in the world and show his refusal to be comforted by religious absolutes or abstract philosophy. In a letter from 1817, Keats used the term "negative capability" to describe the necessity of the poet to be objective by restraining the urge to define and control his or her subject. Negative capability allowed one to exist within "uncertainties, Mysteries, doubts, without any irritable reaching after fact & reason." In such instances, said Keats, "Beauty overcomes every other consideration."

Setting Purposes for Reading

Big Idea The Quest for Truth and Beauty

As you read, notice how the poems reflect the Romantic ideals of truth and beauty.

Literary Element Form

Form refers to the structure that governs a literary genre. "La Belle Dame sans Merci" ("The Beautiful Woman Without Pity") is a **ballad**—a narrative poem that recounts a dramatic episode (see page 208). "When I Have Fears That I May Cease to Be" is a **Shakespearean sonnet**—a fourteen-line poem typically in iambic pentameter with a set rhyme scheme (see page 253).

- See Literary Terms Handbook, p. R7.

Literature Online **Interactive Literary Elements Handbook** To review or learn more about the literary elements, go to www.glencoe.com.

Reading Strategy Applying Background Knowledge

When you **apply background knowledge,** you use what you already know about an author to help you understand his or her writing. As you read the poems, think about the biographical and background information about Keats that you read earlier.

Reading Tip: Drawing Conclusions Use a graphic organizer like the one below to draw conclusions about Keats's poems based on your background knowledge.

Passage:		Background:		Conclusion:
"When I have fears that I may cease to be / Before my pen has gleaned my teeming brain"	**+**	Keats contracted tuberculosis at the age of twenty-four and knew he didn't have much longer to live. His father, mother, and brother died during his lifetime.	**=**	Despite his youth, it is understandable that Keats was obsessed with the subject of mortality.

Vocabulary

loitering (loi′ tər ing) *adj.* standing or lingering idly about a place; p. 868 *The shop owner did not like people loitering around his entrance if they were not going to buy anything.*

glean (glēn) *v.* to collect slowly and carefully; to gather crops left on a field after reaping; p. 869 *Although he sometimes thought his coursework was irrelevant, Jared had gleaned more useful knowledge than he realized.*

teeming (tēm′ ing) *adj.* full; at the point of overflowing; p. 869 *The teeming river was in danger of flooding the town.*

Vocabulary Tip: Context Clues Context clues are the words and phrases surrounding an unfamiliar word. You can use these clues to figure out the meaning of the unfamiliar word.

OBJECTIVES

In studying these selections, you will focus on the following:
- analyzing literary periods
- analyzing poetic forms
- applying background knowledge

La Belle Dame sans Merci

John Keats

La Belle Dame Sans Merci, 1865. Walter Crane. Private collection.

O what can ail thee, knight-at-arms,
    Alone and palely **loitering**?
The sedge[1] has wither'd from the lake,
    And no birds sing.

5 O what can ail thee, knight-at-arms,
    So haggard, and so woe-begone?
The squirrel's granary[2] is full,
    And the harvest's done.

I see a lily on thy brow,
10   With anguish moist and fever dew,
And on thy cheeks a fading rose
    Fast withereth too.

I met a lady in the meads,[3]
    Full beautiful—a fairy's child,
15 Her hair was long, her foot was light,
    And her eyes were wild.

I made a garland for her head,
    And bracelets too, and fragrant zone;[4]
She look'd at me as she did love,
20   And made sweet moan.

I set her on my pacing steed,
    And nothing else saw all day long,
For sidelong would she bend and sing
    A fairy's song.

25 She found me roots of relish sweet,
    And honey wild, and manna dew,[5]
And sure in language strange she said
    "I love thee true."

She took me to her elfin grot,[6]
30   And there she wept and sigh'd full sore,
And there I shut her wild wild eyes
    With kisses four.

And there she lulled me asleep,
    And there I dream'd—Ah! woe betide!
35 The latest[7] dream I ever dream'd
    On the cold hill side.

I saw pale kings and princes too,
    Pale warriors, death-pale were they all;
They cried, "La Belle Dame sans Merci
40   Hath thee in thrall!"[8]

I saw their starved lips in the gloam,[9]
    With horrid warning gaped wide,
And I awoke, and found me here,
    On the cold hill's side.

45 And this is why I sojourn[10] here,
    Alone and palely loitering,
Though the sedge is wither'd from the lake,
    And no birds sing.

---

1. *Sedge* refers to reedy, grasslike plants often found on wet ground or in water.
2. A *granary* is a place for storing grain.
3. *Meads* is an old-fashioned way of saying "meadowlands."
4. *Zone* is an old-fashioned term for "belt" or "girdle."

Literary Element   **Form** *What makes lines 9–12 a ballad stanza? How does it deviate from the traditional ballad form?*

Vocabulary

loitering (loi′ tər ing) *adj.* standing or lingering idly about a place

5. *Manna dew* is the sweet juice from the European ash tree and certain other plants. According to Exodus 16:13–36, *manna* is also the food that God miraculously provided for the Israelites.
6. *Grot* means "cave" or "grotto."
7. *Latest* here means "last."
8. *In thrall* means "enslaved."
9. *Gloam* means "twilight."
10. A *sojourn* is a visit or temporary stay.

Big Idea   **The Quest for Truth and Beauty** *How does the plight of the knight-at-arms reflect the Romantic quest for beauty?*

On Hounslow Heath, exhibited 1770. Richard Wilson. Oil on canvas, 425 x 527 cm. Tate Gallery, London.

WHEN I HAVE FEARS THAT I MAY CEASE TO BE

John Keats

When I have fears that I may cease to be
　　Before my pen has **gleaned** my **teeming** brain,
Before high-piled books, in charactery,[1]
　　Hold like rich garners[2] the full-ripened grain;
5　When I behold, upon the night's starred face,
　　Huge cloudy symbols of a high romance,
And think that I may never live to trace
　　Their shadows, with the magic hand of chance;
And when I feel, fair creature of an hour,
10　　That I shall never look upon thee more,
Never have relish in the fairy power
　　Of unreflecting love—then on the shore
Of the wide world I stand alone, and think
Till love and fame to nothingness do sink.

1. *Charactery* means "characters" or "symbols," in other words, letters of the alphabet.
2. *Garners* are storehouses for grain.

Reading Strategy Applying Background Knowledge *What is the speaker afraid of losing here? How does your background knowledge help you interpret these lines?*

Vocabulary

glean (glēn) *v.* to collect slowly and carefully; to gather crops left on a field after reaping

teeming (tēm´ ing) *adj.* full; at the point of overflowing

RESPONDING AND THINKING CRITICALLY

Respond

1. (a)Which poem did you prefer? (b)What did this poem leave you thinking or wondering?

Recall and Interpret

2. (a)In "La Belle Dame sans Merci," what does the speaker ask the knight-at-arms in the first two stanzas? (b)How does the time of year reflect the knight's physical and emotional state?

3. (a)Summarize the story the knight tells in reply. (b)What do the knight's words reveal about him?

4. (a)Summarize the speaker's main fears in "When I Have Fears . . ." (b)What do these fears reveal about the speaker's values and goals?

Analyze and Evaluate

5. (a)How do you interpret the knight's dream in "La Belle Dame sans Merci"? (b)In your opinion, why does the knight stay "on the cold hill's side"?

6. (a)What happens to the speaker's fears in "When I Have Fears . . ."? (b)What tone is established in the concluding couplet?

Connect

7. **Big Idea** **The Quest for Truth and Beauty** (a)How does "La Belle Dame sans Merci" exemplify the Romantic quest for beauty? (b)How does "When I Have Fears . . ." exemplify the Romantic quest for truth?

LITERARY ANALYSIS

Literary Element Form

The **forms** of "La Belle Dame sans Merci" and "When I Have Fears . . ." contribute to the meaning of each poem.

1. (a)How is the ballad form appropriate to the subject and theme of "La Belle Dame sans Merci"? (b)How do the first and last stanzas contribute to the poem?

2. (a)In "When I Have Fears . . .," what is the focus of each quatrain? (b)How does the final couplet resolve the issues in the three quatrains?

Literary Criticism

Scholars have variously interpreted "La Belle Dame sans Merci" as a poem about (1) the enslavement of the poet by his muse, or source of inspiration, (2) Keats's concern that his love for Fanny Brawne was lessening his poetic powers, and (3) the seductive power of beauty and literary fame. In a brief essay, explain your intepretation of the poem.

Literature Online Web Activities For eFlashcards, Selection Quick Checks, and other Web activities, go to www.glencoe.com.

READING AND VOCABULARY

Reading Strategy Applying Background Knowledge

Use your background knowledge about Keats to answer the following questions.

1. How does the sonnet "When I Have Fears . . ." illustrate Keats's principle of negative capability?

2. What aspect of Keats's life is it possible to see in "La Belle Dame sans Merci"?

Vocabulary Practice

Practice with Context Clues Identify the context clue that best helps you determine the meaning of the underlined vocabulary word.

1. Mr. Thomas liked his workers to be busy; he never tolerated loitering if there was work to do.
  a. busy   **b.** tolerated

2. During autumn, the farmer gleaned corn from his fields.
  a. autumn   **b.** corn

3. When I began writing my essay, my brain was teeming with so many ideas.
  a. essay   **b.** many

Connecting to the Poem

How can you capture a moment in time? In Keats's poem, young lovers painted on a vase are forever caught in a merry chase. As you read, think about the following questions:

- Have you ever admired a work of art in which a moment in time has been captured and suspended?
- Have you ever felt a sense of sadness and anticlimax after a pleasurable experience?

Building Background

The artistic tradition of painted pottery in ancient Greece can be traced back to the city of Corinth in the seventh century B.C. There, painters began to cover vases with black silhouetted shapes, often the forms of animals. As the style spread to Athens, it evolved to include narrative scenes based on Greek mythology. The appearance of an Athenian vase—black figures on a red clay background—became famous. In Keats's day, archeological excavations in the Mediterranean region produced many examples of painted urns, creating interest throughout Europe in all things classical. "Ode on a Grecian Urn" may have been inspired by such an urn.

Setting Purposes for Reading

Big Idea **The Quest for Truth and Beauty**

As you read, notice how Keats finds the Romantic ideals of truth and beauty in the Grecian urn.

Literary Element **Ode**

An **ode** is a long, serious lyric poem that is elevated in tone and style. Some odes celebrate a person, quality, or object, while others are private meditations. Nearly all odes use **apostrophe,** or the poetic figure of speech in which an idea, inanimate object, or absent person is directly addressed. As you read, note how Keats addresses the Grecian urn and the figures painted on it.

- See Literary Terms Handbook, p. R12.

Reading Strategy **Evaluating Rhetorical Devices**

Rhetorical devices are techniques writers use to manipulate language for effect or to evoke an emotional response in the reader. Rhetorical devices include questions, exclamations, and repetition. A **rhetorical question** is one to which no answer is expected because the answer is obvious. **Exclamations** and **repetition** call attention to particular ideas. **Parallelism** is the repetition of words, phrases, or sentences that have the same grammatical form. As you read, notice how these rhetorical devices enhance the poem.

....

Reading Tip: Taking Notes Use a chart similar to the one below to record the rhetorical devices in the poem.

Example	Rhetorical Device
Line 9 "What mad pursuit? What struggle to escape?"	rhetorical question

Vocabulary

deities (dē′ ə tēz) n. gods or goddesses; divinities; p. 872 *The streets downtown are named after ancient Greek and Roman deities.*

desolate (des′ ə lit) adj. destitute of inhabitants; deserted; p. 873 *After the hurricane, John returned to find his hometown desolate.*

Vocabulary Tip: Word Origins Dictionary entries often include the etymology of a word, which is its history and origin.

Literature Online **Interactive Literary Elements Handbook** To review or learn more about the literary elements, go to www.glencoe.com.

OBJECTIVES
In studying this selection, you will focus on the following:
- analyzing literary periods
- analyzing an ode
- evaluating rhetorical devices

Ode on a Grecian Urn

John Keats

1

Thou still unravished bride of quietness,
 Thou foster child of silence and slow time,
Sylvan° historian, who canst thus express
 A flowery tale more sweetly than our rhyme:
5 What leaf-fringed legend haunts about° thy shape
 Of **deities** or mortals, or of both,
  In Tempe or the dales of Arcady?°
What men or gods are these? What maidens loath?°
 What mad pursuit? What struggle to escape?
10 What pipes and timbrels?° What wild ecstasy?

2

Heard melodies are sweet, but those unheard
 Are sweeter; therefore, ye soft pipes, play on;
Not to the sensual° ear, but, more endeared,
 Pipe to the spirit ditties° of no tone:
15 Fair youth, beneath the trees, thou canst not leave
 Thy song, nor ever can those trees be bare;
  Bold Lover, never, never canst thou kiss,
Though winning near the goal—yet, do not grieve;
 She cannot fade, though thou hast not thy bliss,
20 Forever wilt thou love, and she be fair!

3 **Sylvan** means "of the woods."

5 **Haunts about** means "surrounds."

7 **Tempe** is a beautiful valley. **Arcady** (Arcadia) is a mountainous region. Both are in Greece and have traditionally been considered ideal rustic landscapes.
8 **Loath** means "reluctant."
10 **Timbrels** are ancient percussion instruments similar to tambourines.

13 **Sensual** means "physical or bodily."
14 **Ditties** are short, simple songs.

Literary Element Ode *To whom does "Thou" refer? What figure of speech common to odes is Keats using in the first two lines of the poem?*

Reading Strategy Evaluating Rhetorical Devices *What rhetorical devices does Keats use in these lines? What is the purpose of these devices?*

Vocabulary

deities (dē′ ə tēz) *n.* gods or goddesses; divinities

Women carrying water, 6th century B.C. Black figure Attic hydria from Vulci.

3

Ah, happy, happy boughs! that cannot shed
    Your leaves, nor ever bid the Spring adieu;
And, happy melodist, unwearied,
    Forever piping songs forever new;
25 More happy love! more happy, happy love!
    Forever warm and still to be enjoyed,
      Forever panting, and forever young;
All breathing human passion far above,
    That leaves a heart high-sorrowful and cloyed,°
30   A burning forehead, and a parching tongue.

4

Who are these coming to the sacrifice?
    To what green altar, O mysterious priest,
Lead'st thou that heifer lowing at the skies,
    And all her silken flanks with garlands dressed?
35 What little town by river or seashore,
    Or mountain-built with peaceful citadel,°
      Is emptied of this folk, this pious morn?
And, little town, thy streets forevermore
    Will silent be; and not a soul to tell
40   Why thou art **desolate**, can e'er return.

5

O Attic shape! Fair attitude! with brede°
    Of marble men and maidens overwrought,°
With forest branches and the trodden weed;
    Thou, silent form, dost tease us out of thought
45 As doth eternity: Cold Pastoral!°
    When old age shall this generation waste,
      Thou shalt remain, in midst of other woe
Than ours, a friend to man, to whom thou say'st,
    "Beauty is truth, truth beauty"—that is all
50   Ye know on earth, and all ye need to know.

29 **Cloyed** means "oversatisfied; burdened by excess."

36 A **citadel** is a fortress.

41 **Attic** refers to the simple, graceful style characteristic of Attica, or Athens, Greece. **Brede** refers to an interwoven or braided design.
42 Here, **overwrought** means "with the surface decorated."
45 **Pastoral** refers to an artwork depicting the life of a shepherd or simple rural life in general.

Big Idea   The Quest for Truth and Beauty *How does Keats's equation of truth and beauty represent a principle of Romantic idealism?*

Vocabulary

desolate (des′ ə lit) *adj.* destitute of inhabitants; deserted

RESPONDING AND THINKING CRITICALLY

Respond

1. What images of the Grecian urn do you find most striking? Explain.

Recall and Interpret

2. (a)What metaphors does the speaker use to describe the urn in lines 1–3? (b)What do the metaphors reveal about the speaker's view of the urn?

3. Why might an "unheard" melody be sweeter than a "heard melody" (see lines 11–12)?

4. (a)What people and things does the speaker address in the second and third stanzas? (b)Why does the speaker envy them? Cite evidence from the poem.

Analyze and Evaluate

5. An **oxymoron** is a figure of speech in which contradictory ideas are combined for effect, as in the phrase "wise fool." Explain the oxymoron in the final stanza. What is its effect?

6. (a)Why do you think Keats found comfort and solace by contemplating the figures painted on the urn? (b)What can you infer about Keats's views concerning the purpose of art?

Connect

7. **Big Idea** **The Quest for Truth and Beauty**
How have later artists and thinkers reacted to the Romantic idealism of Keats's identification of truth with beauty?

LITERARY ANALYSIS

Literary Element   Ode

A **Horatian ode,** named for the Roman poet Horace, has a regular pattern of stanzas and a rhyme scheme. "Ode on a Grecian Urn" is considered a Horatian ode. Keats believed that the poet should subordinate his own identity in order to enable the ode's subject to emerge fully. He called this quality "negative capability."

1. (a)What are the structure and rhyme scheme of "Ode on a Grecian Urn"? (b)How does Keats create variations on the form?

2. How does Keats achieve negative capability in "Ode on a Grecian Urn"?

Writing About Literature

Apply Form Using Keats's "Ode on a Grecian Urn" as your inspiration and model, write an ode to an inanimate object in which you address the topics of art, time, truth, and beauty. You may use the Horatian form if you wish.

READING AND VOCABULARY

Reading Strategy   Evaluating Rhetorical Devices

In poetry, **rhetorical devices,** such as **rhetorical questions, parallelism,** and **exclamation,** can enhance the lyric quality and the sound of a poem, especially when it is read aloud.

1. Explain the use of parallelism in stanza 3 and describe its effect.

2. What is the effect of the rhetorical questions in stanza 4?

Vocabulary   Practice

Practice with Word Origins Match each vocabulary word with its corresponding Latin root word. Use a dictionary for assistance.

1. deities   **a.** *sōlus,* meaning "alone"

2. desolate   **b.** *deus,* meaning "a god"

Literature Online **Web Activities** For eFlashcards, Selection Quick Checks, and other Web activities, go to www.glencoe.com.

Comparing Literature *Across Time and Place*

Connecting to the Reading Selections

The cyclical nature of the seasons inspires the four works compared here—an English Romantic poem, a series of Japanese haiku, a poem by a writer of the Harlem Renaissance, and a memoir by a contemporary American writer. Together, they show an awareness of how a few small details in nature can lead to broader reflections on life.

England, 1819

John Keats
To Autumn ....poem 876
Vitality in the third season

Japan, c. 1675

Matsuo Bashō
Haiku for Four Seasons ....haiku 880
Seasons—each a self-contained world

United States, 1925

Countee Cullen
To John Keats, Poet, At Springtime ....poem 882
Thawing of winter; explosion of spring

United States, 1974

Annie Dillard
Untying the Knot
from *Pilgrim at Tinker Creek* ....reflective narrative 884
Locating oneself in the circle of life

COMPARING THE `Big Idea` The Quest for Truth and Beauty

Poets from around the world have conveyed a sense of rapture and ecstasy in exploring natural beauty. They have found transcendent power in small details, often drawing connections between humanity and the weather, the animal kingdom, and physical landscapes.

COMPARING Nature Imagery

Scenes from nature can focus on the energetic and colorful, or the bleak and unforgiving. Images, or word pictures, that describe concrete sensory details in nature also function as springboards to larger meanings in these selections by Keats, Bashō, Cullen, and Dillard.

COMPARING Literary Traditions

Nature has been the theme and inspiration for works throughout history. It provides a dramatic backdrop to evaluate the place of humans in the world. As civilization becomes more technological and urban, writers continue to explore the way nature coexists and contrasts with these developments.

LITERATURE PREVIEW

Connecting to the Poem

Do certain seasons inspire certain moods? For example, consider the way you might feel during the first few days of spring after a long, cold winter. In "To Autumn," Keats describes the ripe fullness of autumn. As you read, think about the following questions:

- Which moods and feelings do you commonly associate with autumn?
- How might a season indicate both growth and decay?

Building Background

Keats wrote "To Autumn" in September 1819 and described it in a letter to J. H. Reynolds a few days later: "How beautiful the season is now. . . . I never lik'd stubble fields so much as now—Aye better than the chilly green of the spring. Somehow a stubble plain looks warm—in the same way that some pictures look warm—this struck me so much in my Sunday's walk that I composed upon it."

Setting Purposes for Reading

Big Idea **The Quest for Truth and Beauty**

Note how this poem reflects the Romantic focus on the beauty of the natural world.

Literary Element **Imagery**

Imagery refers to the word pictures that writers create to evoke an emotional response in the reader. In creating effective images, writers use **sensory details,** or descriptions that appeal to one or more of the five senses. As you read "To Autumn," note the vivid images Keats presents and the sensory details that appeal to the reader's sense of sight, hearing, touch, taste, and smell.

- See Literary Terms Handbook, p. R9.

Literature Online Interactive Literary Elements Handbook To review or learn more about the literary elements, go to www.glencoe.com.

READING PREVIEW

Reading Strategy Analyzing Sound Devices

Sound devices are the techniques used to appeal to the ear—that is, to enhance rhythm, to emphasize particular sounds, or to add to the musical quality of the writing. When you **analyze sound devices,** you examine specific sound devices independently in order to better understand a poem as a whole. **Assonance** is a sound device in which the same or similar vowel sounds are repeated. **Consonance** occurs when consonant sounds are repeated, typically at the ends of non-rhyming words. **Alliteration** is the repetition of consonant sounds at the beginnings of words. **Onomatopoeia** is the use of a word or phrase to imitate or suggest the sound of the word it describes.

Reading Tip: Determining Patterns In order to determine the pattern of a poem's sound effects, note individual examples of different effects as you read. Organize your findings in a chart like the one below.

Sound Device	Examples
Assonance	line 7: "the hazel shells"
Consonance	
Alliteration	
Onomatopoeia	

Vocabulary

conspiring (kən spīr′ ing) *adj.* planning or plotting secretly; p. 877 *Maria saw her brothers whispering behind the shed, and she knew they were conspiring against her.*

furrow (fur′ ō) *n.* a long, narrow trench in the ground made by a plow; a rut, groove, or wrinkle; p. 878 *When my father is in a serious mood, a deep furrow lines his forehead.*

Vocabulary Tip: Synonyms Synonyms are words that have the same or similar meanings.

OBJECTIVES
In studying this selection, you will focus on the following:
- analyzing literary periods
- identifying imagery
- analyzing sound devices

An Autumn Lane. Edward W. Waite. Burlington Paintings, London.

To Autumn

John Keats

1

Season of mists and mellow fruitfulness,
    Close bosom-friend of the maturing sun;
Conspiring with him how to load and bless
    With fruit the vines that round the thatch-eaves run;
5 To bend with apples the mossed cottage-trees,
    And fill all fruit with ripeness to the core;
        To swell the gourd, and plump the hazel shells
With a sweet kernel; to set budding more,
    And still more, later flowers for the bees,
10   Until they think warm days will never cease,
        For Summer has o'er-brimmed their clammy cells.

2

    Who hath not seen thee oft amid thy store?
        Sometimes whoever seeks abroad may find
    Thee sitting careless on a granary[1] floor,
15   Thy hair soft-lifted by the winnowing[2] wind;
    Or on a half-reaped **furrow** sound asleep,
        Drowsed with the fume of poppies, while thy hook[3]
            Spares the next swath[4] and all its twinèd flowers:
    And sometimes like a gleaner[5] thou dost keep
20   Steady thy laden head across a brook;
        Or by a cider-press, with patient look,
            Thou watchest the last oozings, hours by hours.

3

    Where are the songs of Spring? Ay, where are they?
        Think not of them, thou hast thy music, too—
25 While barred[6] clouds bloom the soft-dying day,
        And touch the stubble-plains with rosy hue;
    Then in a wailful choir the small gnats mourn
        Among the river sallows,[7] borne aloft
           Or sinking as the light wind lives or dies;
30 And full-grown lambs loud bleat from hilly bourn;[8]
        Hedge crickets sing; and now with treble soft
        The redbreast whistles from a garden croft,[9]
           And gathering swallows twitter in the skies.

---

1. A *granary* is a storehouse for grain.
2. *Winnowing* is a process of separating wheat grain from chaff, or husks, by blowing away the chaff, which is lighter.
3. A *hook* is a curved blade used to cut grain.
4. A *swath* is a row or area of grain to be cut.
5. A *gleaner* is one who gathers grain left in the field by the reapers.
6. *Barred* means "streaked."
7. *Sallows* are low-growing willow trees.
8. *Bourn* means "region."
9. A *croft* is a small piece of enclosed land, often near a house.

Literary Element Imagery *What image does Keats use here to describe autumn? Which senses does he appeal to?*

Reading Strategy Analyzing Sound Devices *How do the sound devices in these lines contribute to the poem?*

Vocabulary

furrow (fur′ō) *n.* a long, narrow trench in the ground made by a plow; a rut, groove, or wrinkle

AFTER YOU READ

RESPONDING AND THINKING CRITICALLY

Respond

1. Which images remain in your mind after reading the poem?

Recall and Interpret

2. (a)In the first stanza, what have autumn and the sun conspired to do? (b)List examples of personification in the second stanza. (c)In what ways do these images differ from those in the first stanza?

3. (a)Cite three instances in which the spirit of autumn is personified as a farm girl. (b)What view of autumn does this personification suggest?

4. (a)According to the speaker, who sings the songs of autumn, and when do they sing? (b)Why might this be an appropriate time for autumn's music?

Analyze and Evaluate

5. (a)What are some of the descriptive details that help create a sense of abundance? (b)Why might Keats have used these images?

6. (a)What examples of imagery do you find in "To Autumn"? (b)What do these details contribute to your appreciation of the poem?

Connect

7. **Big Idea** The Quest for Truth and Beauty
Keats wrote that "if poetry comes not as naturally as the leaves to a tree, it had better not come at all." In other words, human creations such as poetry should be modeled on the effortless beauty of nature. In your opinion, does "To Autumn" fulfill this Romantic ideal? Explain.

LITERARY ANALYSIS

Literary Element Imagery

The **imagery,** or word pictures, a writer creates includes **sensory details** and **figurative language** that evoke an emotional response.

1. What types of figurative language does Keats use in "To Autumn"? Give examples from the text.

2. How does Keats's use of imagery match your expectations of a description of autumn? How is it different?

Writing About Literature

Evaluate Author's Craft Write two or three paragraphs about the imagery in one of the other Keats poems you read in this unit. Use passages from the poem to show how his imagery appeals to each of the various senses. You might also discuss how other literary devices help Keats to create or underscore the sensory impressions he conveys with his imagery.

Literature Online **Web Activities** For eFlashcards, Selection Quick Checks, and other Web activities, go to www.glencoe.com.

READING AND VOCABULARY

Reading Strategy Analyzing Sound Devices

Sound devices—such as alliteration, assonance, consonance, and onomatopoeia—are the techniques in poetry used to appeal to the ear. Refer to the chart you made on page 876, and then answer the following questions.

1. In the second stanza, which sound devices reinforce the image of autumn (as a farm girl) sleeping? Explain.

2. Line 24 responds to the question in line 23. How might the sound devices in line 24 contribute to the tone and meaning of the response?

Vocabulary Practice

Practice with Synonyms Choose the synonym that best replaces the underlined vocabulary word in each sentence below.

1. She saw the girls conspiring against her.
   a. wondering   **b.** plotting   **c.** attempting

2. The tractor wheel left a deep furrow in the rain-soaked cornfield.
   a. wrinkle   **b.** hole   **c.** trench

BEFORE YOU READ

Building Background

Matsuo Bashō is considered the master of the haiku—a Japanese poetic form that traditionally draws a comparison between two images and consists of seventeen syllables spread out over three lines—five syllables in the first, seven in the second, and five in the third.

Born in 1644 in the Iga province of Japan, Bashō originally led the life of a samurai. But when his master died suddenly in 1666, Bashō changed paths, leaving his samurai training to travel and pursue writing, eventually moving to the capital city Edo, now Tokyo.

In 1684 Bashō set out on foot and, with the barest essentials, hiked across Japan, recording his experiences in nature in journals. Bashō suggested, "Learn about a pine tree from a pine tree, and a bamboo plant from a bamboo plant." In 1694 Bashō died in Osaka while on a journey.

Literature Online **Author Search** For more about Matsuo Bashō, go to www.glencoe.com.

Haiku for Four Seasons

Matsuo Bashō
Translated by Makoto Ueda

Spring

Ran no ka ya The fragrant orchid:
Chō no tsubasa ni Into a butterfly's wings
Takimono su It breathes the incense.

Summer

Hi no michi ya Toward the sun's path
Aoi katamuku Hollyhock flowers turning
Satsuki-ame In the rains of summer.

Evening Snow at Asuka-yama, from the series *Eight Views of the Environs of Edo,* 1837–1838. Ando Hiroshige. Color woodblock print. The Cleveland Museum of Art, OH.

Autumn

Kareeda ni	On a bare branch
Karasu no tomarikeri	A crow is perched—
Aki no kure	Autumn evening.

Winter

Fuyu no hi ya	The winter sun—
Bajō ni kōru	Frozen on the horse,
Kagebōshi	My shadow.

Quickwrite

Study the images in one of Bashō's haiku. Then write a paragraph comparing or contrasting these images about the season. How did the poem make you rethink one of the seasons? Discuss the insights you gained from the comparison.

Building Background

Born in 1903, Countee Cullen embodied the ideals of the Harlem Renaissance while writing poetry that connected with English Romanticism. In 1925 Cullen published *Color,* his first volume of poems, which included "To John Keats, Poet, At Springtime." Cullen wrote the bulk of his most powerful work during the 1920s. In his early writings, Cullen strove to be considered a great poet rather than a black poet. Writers have argued on both sides of this question—some believe that literary criticism should not consider race, while others believe a writer's work should not be removed from his or her racial identity. Cullen sought to prove that blacks could write as well as whites in the same poetic forms. He died in 1946.

Literature Online Author Search For more about Countee Cullen, go to www.glencoe.com.

To John Keats, Poet, At Springtime

Countee Cullen

I cannot hold my peace, John Keats;
There never was a spring like this;
It is an echo, that repeats
My last year's song and next year's bliss.
5   I know, in spite of all men say
Of Beauty, you have felt her most.
Yea, even in your grave her way
Is laid. Poor, troubled, lyric ghost,
Spring never was so fair and dear
10   As Beauty makes her seem this year.

I cannot hold my peace, John Keats;
I am as helpless in the toil
Of Spring as any lamb that bleats[1]
To feel the solid earth recoil
15   Beneath his puny legs. Spring beats
Her tocsin[2] call to those who love her,
And lo! the dogwood petals cover
Her breast with drifts of snow, and sleek
White gulls fly screaming to her, and hover
20   About her shoulders, and kiss her cheek,
While white and purple lilacs muster
A strength that bears them to a cluster
Of color and odor; for her sake
All things that slept are now awake.

---

1. *Bleats* refers to the cries of a lamb.
2. *Tocsin* means "a bell that sounds an alarm."

Garden in May, 1895. Maria Oakey Dewing.
Oil on canvas, 23 ⅝ x 32 ½ in. Smithsonian
American Art Museum, Washington, DC.

25   And you and I, shall we lie still,
       John Keats, while Beauty summons us?
       Somehow I feel your sensitive will
       Is pulsing up some tremulous[3]
       Sap road of a maple tree, whose leaves
30   Grow music as they grow, since your
       Wild voice is in them, a harp that grieves
       For life that opens death's dark door.
       Though dust, your fingers still can push
       The Vision Splendid to a birth,
35   Though now they work as grass in the hush
       Of the night on the broad sweet page of
             the earth.

       "John Keats is dead," they say, but I
       Who hear your full insistent cry
       In bud and blossom, leaf and tree,
40   Know John Keats still writes poetry.
       And while my head is earthward bowed
       To read new life sprung from your shroud,
       Folks seeing me must think it strange
       That merely spring should so derange
45   My mind. They do not know that you,
       Johns Keats, keep revel[4] with me, too.

---

3. *Tremulous* means "trembling or shaking."
4. *Revel* means "unrestrained joy or celebration."

Discussion Starter

Countee Cullen expresses his enthusiasm for both the writings of Keats and spring in this poem. How well does he express his feelings? How do the poem's form and language add to or detract from Cullen's message? Discuss these questions with a group of classmates.

Building Background

"I was what they called a live wire. I was shooting off sparks," noted writer Annie Dillard on her youth. She channeled her energy into writing that displays a sharp focus on details in nature and the underlying unity in life. After college, Dillard settled in Roanoke, Virginia, near Tinker Creek, which became the subject of the book that propelled her literary career. In 1971 Dillard nearly died from pneumonia; this experience inspired her to appreciate life and the natural world more fully. What came of her journals from this time was the personal, reflective narrative *Pilgrim at Tinker Creek*.

The book was published in 1974 and won the Pulitzer Prize for nonfiction in 1975.

Critics saw a distinct American voice emerge from Dillard's journals, comparing her work to that of the American naturalist and famed journal writer Henry David Thoreau. Her work also conveys religious themes, as she considers the work of a grand creator reflected in both the unity and diversity and joy and suffering in nature.

Literature Online Author Search For more about Annie Dillard, go to www.glencoe.com.

Untying the Knot
from *Pilgrim at Tinker Creek*

Annie Dillard

Yesterday I set out to catch the new season, and instead I found an old snakeskin. I was in the sunny February woods by the quarry; the snakeskin was lying in a heap of leaves right next to an aquarium someone had thrown away. I don't know why that someone hauled the aquarium deep into the woods to get rid of it; it had only one broken glass side. The snake found it handy, I imagine; snakes like to rub against something rigid to help them out of their skins, and the broken aquarium looked like the nearest likely object. Together the snakeskin and the aquarium made an interesting scene on the forest floor. It looked like an exhibit at a trial—circumstantial evidence—of a wild scene, as though a snake had burst through the broken side of the aquarium, burst through his ugly old skin, and disappeared, perhaps straight up in the air, in a rush of freedom and beauty.

The snakeskin had unkeeled scales,[1] so it belonged to a nonpoisonous snake. It was roughly five feet long by the yardstick, but I'm not sure

---

1. *Unkeeled scales* means that the snake does not have a ridge down the center of its scales. Unkeeled scales appear shiny and smooth.

because it was very wrinkled and dry, and every time I tried to stretch it flat it broke. I ended up with seven or eight pieces of it all over the kitchen table in a fine film of forest dust.

The point I want to make about the snakeskin is that, when I found it, it was whole and tied in a knot. Now there have been stories told, even by reputable scientists, of snakes that have deliberately tied themselves in a knot to prevent larger snakes from trying to swallow them—but I couldn't imagine any way that throwing itself into a half hitch would help a snake trying to escape its skin. Still, ever cautious, I figured that one of the neighborhood boys could possibly have tied it in a knot in the fall, for some whimsical boyish reason, and left it there, where it dried and gathered dust. So I carried the skin along thoughtlessly as I walked, snagging it sure enough on a low branch and ripping it in two for the first of many times. I saw that thick ice still lay on the quarry pond and that the skunk cabbage was already out in the clearings, and then I came home and looked at the skin and its knot.

The knot had no beginning. Idly I turned it around in my hand, searching for a place to untie; I came to with a start when I realized I must have turned the thing around fully ten times. Intently, then, I traced the knot's lump around with a finger; it was continuous. I couldn't untie it any more than I could untie a doughnut; it was a loop without beginning or end. These snakes *are* magic, I thought for a second, and then of course I reasoned what must have happened. The skin had been pulled inside-out like a peeled sock for several inches; then an inch or so of the inside-out part—a piece whose length was coincidentally equal to the diameter of the skin—had somehow been turned right-side out again, making a thick lump whose edges were lost in wrinkles, looking exactly like a knot.

So. I have been thinking about the change of seasons. I don't want to miss spring this year.

> "I could no more catch spring by the tip of the tail than I could untie the apparent knot in the snakeskin . . . Both are continuous loops."

I want to distinguish the last winter frost from the out-of-season one, the frost of spring. I want to be there on the spot the moment the grass turns green. I always miss this radical revolution; I see it the next day from a window, the yard so suddenly green and lush I could envy Nebuchadnezzar[2] down on all fours eating grass. This year I want to stick a net into time and say "now," as men plant flags on the ice and snow and say, "here." But it occurred to me that I could no more catch spring by the tip of the tail than I could untie the apparent knot in the snakeskin; there are no edges to grasp. Both are continuous loops.

I wonder how long it would take you to notice the regular recurrence of the seasons if you were the first man on earth. What would it be like to live in open-ended time broken only by days and nights? You could say, "it's cold again; it was cold before," but you couldn't make the key connection and say, "it was cold this time last year," because the notion of "year" is precisely the one you lack. Assuming that you hadn't yet noticed any orderly progression of heavenly bodies, how long would you have to live on earth before you could feel with any assurance that any one particular long period of cold would, in fact, end? "While the earth remaineth, seedtime and harvest, and cold and heat, and summer and winter, and day and night shall not cease": God makes this guarantee very early in Genesis to a people whose fears on this point had perhaps not been completely allayed.

It must have been fantastically important, at the real beginnings of human culture, to conserve and relay this vital seasonal information, so that the people could anticipate dry or cold seasons,

---

2. *Nebuchadnezzar* (c. 630–561 B.C.) was the great king and military strategist of Babylonia. He was rumored to have gone mad and lived like a wild animal for seven years (see William Blake's famous illustration on page 766).

and not huddle on some November rock hoping pathetically that spring was just around the corner. We still very much stress the simple fact of four seasons to schoolchildren; even the most modern of modern new teachers, who don't seem to care if their charges can read or write or name two products of Peru, will still muster some seasonal chitchat and set the kids to making paper pumpkins, or tulips, for the walls. "The people," wrote Van Gogh in a letter, "are very sensitive to the changing seasons." That we are "very sensitive to the changing seasons" is, incidentally, one of the few good reasons to shun travel. If I stay at home I preserve the illusion that what is happening on Tinker Creek is the very newest thing, that I'm at the very vanguard and cutting edge of each new season. I don't want the same season twice in a row; I don't want to know I'm getting last week's weather, used weather, weather broadcast up and down the coast, old-hat weather.

But there's always unseasonable weather. What we think of the weather and behavior of life on the planet at any given season is really all a matter of statistical probabilities; at any given point, anything might happen. There is a bit of every season in each season. Green plants—deciduous green leaves—grow everywhere, all winter long, and small shoots come up pale and new in every season. Leaves die on the tree in May, turn brown, and fall into the creek. The calendar, the weather, and the behavior of wild creatures have the slimmest of connections. Everything overlaps smoothly for only a few weeks each season, and then it all tangles up again. The temperature, of course, lags far behind the calendar seasons, since the earth absorbs and releases heat slowly, like a leviathan[3] breathing. Migrating birds head south in what appears to be dire panic, leaving mild weather and fields full of insects and seeds; they reappear as if in all eagerness in January, and poke about morosely in the snow. Several years ago our October woods

---

3. *Leviathan* means something "very large, as a whale," and is an allusion to a monstrous sea creature mentioned in the Bible.

would have made a dismal colored photograph for a sadist's[4] calendar: a killing frost came before the leaves had even begun to brown; they drooped from every tree like crepe, blackened and limp. It's all a chancy, jumbled affair at best, as things seem to be below the stars.

Time is the continuous loop, the snakeskin with scales endlessly overlapping without beginning or end, or time is an ascending spiral if you will, like a child's toy Slinky. Of course we have no idea which arc on the loop is our time, let alone where the loop itself is, so to speak, or down whose lofty flight of stairs the Slinky so uncannily walks.

The power we seek, too, seems to be a continuous loop. I have always been sympathetic with the early notion of a divine power that exists in a particular place, or that travels about over the face of the earth as a man might wander—and when he is "there" he is surely not here. You can shake the hand of a man you meet in the woods; but the spirit seems to roll along like the mythical hoop snake with its tail in its mouth. There are no hands to shake or edges to untie. It rolls along the mountain ridges like a fireball, shooting off a spray of sparks at random, and will not be trapped, slowed, grasped, fetched, peeled, or aimed. "As for the wheels,[5] it was cried unto them in my hearing, O wheel." This is the hoop of flame that shoots the rapids in the creek or spins across the dizzy meadows; this is the arsonist of the sunny woods: catch it if you can. ∾

---

4. A *sadist* derives gratification from being cruel to others.
5. *"As for the wheels . . ."* is a passage from the Bible, Ezekiel 10:13, addressing a vision of God on Earth.

Quickwrite

Dillard uses an image of a curled-up piece of snakeskin as a springboard to discuss the continuity of life. Essay writers often identify an engaging image or anecdote from their experience and then develop it into a broader reflection on life. How does Dillard develop the metaphor of the snakeskin? Write a paragraph on this topic, citing details from the text.

Wrap-Up: Comparing Literature Across Time and Place

- **To Autumn**
  by John Keats
- **Haiku for Four Seasons**
  by Matsuo Bashō
- **To John Keats, Poet, At Springtime**
  by Countee Cullen
- **Untying the Knot from Pilgrim at Tinker Creek**
  by Annie Dillard

A Cherry Blossom Viewing Picnic. Edo screen painting. Brooklyn Museum of Art, NY.

COMPARING THE `Big Idea` The Quest for Truth and Beauty

Group Activity Keats, Bashō, Cullen, and Dillard express sentiments about nature that range from breathless enthusiasm to quiet, sober meditation. Read the quotations below. In a group, discuss the following questions.

1. How do you think each of these writers would define truth and beauty? Which writer's outlook is most compelling to you? Explain.

2. What do each of these writers search for through their writings on nature?

> *"Hedge crickets sing; and now with treble soft
> The redbreast whistles from a garden croft,"*
>
> —Keats, "To Autumn"

> *"On a bare branch
> A crow is perched"*
>
> —Bashō, "Haiku for Four Seasons"

> *". . . whose leaves
> Grow music as they grow, since your
> Wild voice is in them, a harp that grieves"*
>
> —Cullen, "To John Keats, Poet, At Springtime"

> *"Everything overlaps smoothly for only a few weeks each season, and then it all tangles up again."*
>
> —Dillard, "Untying the Knot" from *Pilgrim at Tinker Creek*

COMPARING Nature Imagery

Writing Write a brief essay in which you compare the imagery in two or more of the selections. Base your comparison on the sensory qualities of the images and how they contribute to the work's message about life. Refer to evidence from the selections you chose in your response.

COMPARING Literary Traditions

Speaking and Listening Research a tradition of nature writing in nonfiction or poetry. You may choose journals and reflective narratives, or poetry. Research the forces that influenced the writing and present your findings to the class in an oral presentation.

OBJECTIVES
- Compare works about nature from different genres and cultures.
- Analyze imagery and sensory details.
- Research literary traditions.

Writing Workshop

Reflective Essay

 Reflecting on a Poetic Theme

"I never saw daffodils so beautiful. They grew among the mossy stones about and about them; some rested their heads upon these stones as on a pillow for weariness."

—Dorothy Wordsworth, from *The Journals of Dorothy Wordsworth*

Connecting to Literature In her journal, Dorothy Wordsworth reflects on an enjoyable walk that she took through a field of daffodils and offers an insight about her observations. In a reflective essay, a writer describes an experience or observation to better understand what it means personally and what it might teach others. A reflective essay may also describe a personal response to literature and explore the meaning of a reading experience. To write an effective essay, you will need to learn the goals of reflective writing and the strategies to achieve those goals.

Rubric: Features of Reflective Essays About Poetic Themes

Goals	Strategies
To share your personal reflections about the meaning of a poem	☑ Draw comparisons between specific personal experiences and universal literary themes ☑ Quote lines from the poem as evidence to support your ideas
To explain your observations and ideas in a logical order	☑ Clearly organize your ideas from beginning to end
To present a vivid description	☑ Use concrete details to describe personal responses and observations and to make an experience come alive
To connect with an audience	☑ Use first-person point of view ☑ Use a thoughtful, conversational tone to develop a personal writing voice

---

The Writing Process

In this workshop, you will follow the stages of the writing process. At any stage, you may think of new ideas to include and better ways to express them. Feel free to return to earlier stages as you write.

Prewriting

- - - - - - - - - - - -

Drafting

- - - - - - - - - - - -

Revising

➡ Focus Lesson: Varying Sentence Structure

Editing and Proofreading

➡ Focus Lesson: Using Active and Passive Voice

Presenting

- - - - - - - - - - - -

Writing Models For models and other writing activities, go to www.glencoe.com.

OBJECTIVES

- Write a reflective essay exploring the personal significance of a poem.
- Use descriptive details and a conversational style to connect personal experience to a broader theme or belief.

Real-World Connection

Perhaps you have already been asked to reflect on a personal experience for a job interview or in a college admissions essay. The point of reflection is to help someone else understand why an experience is meaningful to you and what your insights suggest about you as a person.

> ▶ **Assignment**
>
> Write a reflective essay in which you interpret the meaning of a poem, explore its personal significance, and connect that significance to a broader theme or belief. As you move through the stages of the writing process, keep your audience and purpose in mind.
>
> **Audience:** teacher, classmates, and peers familiar with the chosen poem
>
> **Purpose:** to explain an interpretation of a poem and support it with personal experience

Analyzing a Professional Model

In the essay below, poet Robin Becker reflects on the significance of her experience as an adolescent reading William Wordsworth's "Lines Composed a Few Miles Above Tintern Abbey." As you read the passage, pay close attention to the comments in the margin. They point out features you might want to include in your own reflective essay.

From *"Wordsworth"* by Robin Becker

Wordsworth is full of loss. So are adolescents. At thirteen, before I'd thought much about poetry, Miss Bickley asked us to feel the undertow of longing in the first-person voice. Reading aloud, she instructed us to listen to the unrhymed iambic pentameter, the word and phrasal repetitions, and the syntax of "Tintern Abbey." (Lousy in math and science, I thought, *I can do this*.) I learned to listen for "Once again" and "How oft," the moody signals and backward-looking words that triggered descriptions of Wordsworth's countryside and of the "lonely rooms" in which he sought consolation. With his semicolons and dashes, he built winding sentences, and though I couldn't always follow the grammar (*"Oh yeah?"* was penciled in a margin of my old *Norton* anthology), I liked the sound, the poem's steady iambic music. What I understood of "voice" I gathered from trying to leap—with Wordsworth—from concrete ("A lover of the meadows and the woods") to abstract ("soul / Of all my moral being") and to follow the poem's argument, which I felt, at the time, was a parable for how to grow up.

    As a city kid, I knew only two rural landscapes: my beloved Camp Greylock in the Adirondacks and Wordsworth's rustic woodland. Onto his

First-Person Point of View

Use the pronoun *I* to "speak" directly to your reader.

Literary Interpretation

Explore the personal meaning of the poem in the introduction.

Tintern Abbey. Samuel Palmer. Watercolor, 11 ⅛ x 19 ⅜ in. Victoria and Albert Museum, London.

Descriptive Details

Use concrete details to make the experience of reading a poem come alive.

sensuous descriptions of childhood ("when like a roe / I bounded o'er the mountains") I transposed my own tomboyhood: perishable, vagabond. I identified with the poet's fall from "thoughtless youth," and I remember liking "the still, sad music of humanity" for its mournfulness. Did we discuss the sibilance? The assonance? I don't recall. But certain phrases— "the din / Of towns and cities" and "greetings where no kindness is" and "The dreary intercourse of daily life"—pleased me enormously, for they evoked my own scorn for the hypocrisy and tedium of grown-ups and gave me an ally in literature.

Writing Voice

Use a conversational tone to help readers sense that a real person is communicating with them.

Another surprise: The poem turned out to have a love interest! Chaste but not austere, Wordsworth's affection for his sister, Dorothy, provided the second half of the poem with memorable metaphors:

> . . . when thy mind
> Shall be a mansion for all lovely forms,
> Thy memory be as a dwelling place
> For all sweet sounds and harmonies. . . .

Supporting Evidence

Cite lines from the poem to support your interpretation of the poem's meaning and themes.

Wordsworth's great fortune in having an intimate friend ("For thou art with me here upon the banks / Of this fair river; thou, my dearest Friend, / My dear, dear Friend") with whom to share his thoughts did not escape me; I, too, longed for a companionable pal. . . . At thirteen, I was consoled.

Conclusion

Reveal the personal significance of the poem and connect your experience to broader themes and beliefs.

Reading-Writing Connection Think about the writing techniques that you just encountered and try them out in the reflective essay you write.

Prewriting

Explore Ideas Your essay is more likely to turn out well if you choose a poem that is interesting and meaningful. Think about which poem from this unit made the deepest impression on you. Consider connections you might draw between the poem and your own experience.

Reflect on Poetic Themes Writing a reflective essay about a poetic theme involves more than describing the experience of reading a poem. As you reflect on a poem, consider the following questions:

• **What Does the Poem Mean?** Become familiar with the poem's main ideas and images. Picture what the poem is saying.

• **Why Is It Significant to Me?** Think about your personal responses to the poem. How does understanding the poem help you better understand yourself, your beliefs, and the human experience in general?

• **How Does the Poem Connect to a Broader Theme?** What insight about human experience did you learn from your reflection?

Gather Details Note the images, phrases, and lines in the poem that express the theme or message you will focus on. Examine the poetic elements that also contribute to the theme, such as meter, rhyme, and other sound devices. Then explore how the poem relates to your own observations and experience and use vivid details to develop your description.

Make a Plan As you plan your essay, keep in mind that you will need to connect the poem to personal observation and experience. You may find it helpful to explore the poem's meaning chronologically, moving through the poem from beginning to end. Here is a chart one student used to outline a reflective essay about the poem "Ozymandias" by Percy Bysshe Shelley.

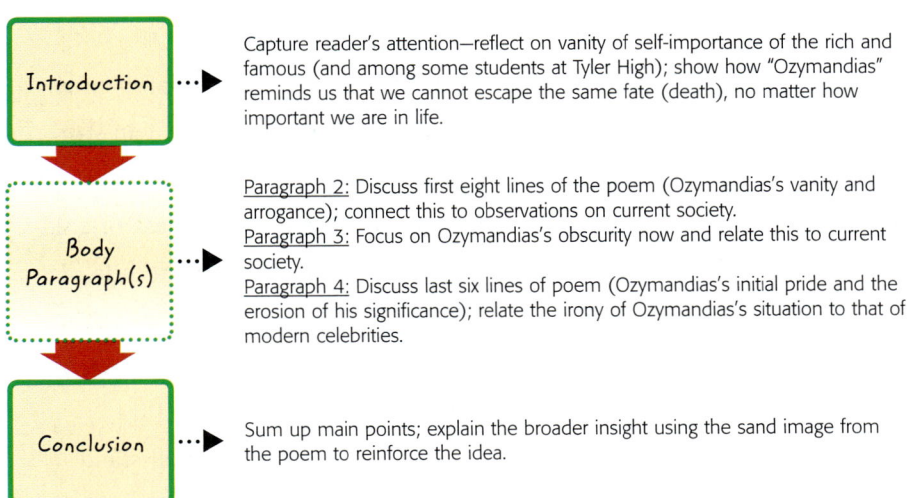

Introduction ····▶ Capture reader's attention—reflect on vanity of self-importance of the rich and famous (and among some students at Tyler High); show how "Ozymandias" reminds us that we cannot escape the same fate (death), no matter how important we are in life.

Body Paragraph(s) ····▶ Paragraph 2: Discuss first eight lines of the poem (Ozymandias's vanity and arrogance); connect this to observations on current society.
Paragraph 3: Focus on Ozymandias's obscurity now and relate this to current society.
Paragraph 4: Discuss last six lines of poem (Ozymandias's initial pride and the erosion of his significance); relate the irony of Ozymandias's situation to that of modern celebrities.

Conclusion ····▶ Sum up main points; explain the broader insight using the sand image from the poem to reinforce the idea.

> **Test Prep**
>
> When you take an essay test, allow some time in the beginning to outline your ideas and figure out the best organization.

Drafting

From Plan to Paper When you begin your first draft, use your outline as a guide to help you balance your specific reflections on the poem with more general conclusions and insights. As you write, however, be open to new observations about the poem and your personal responses.

Analyzing a Workshop Model

Here is a final draft of a reflective essay. Read the essay and answer the questions in the margin. Use the answers to these questions to guide you as you write.

The Eroding Sands of Time

Some people matter and some people don't—or so many would have us believe. Nothing is easier to overestimate than the importance of one's own existence on Earth. In our culture today, that sense of importance is frequently based on how much wealth or fame someone has: celebrities, in particular, often act superior to others. They also tend to confuse their current status with some kind of lasting fame or immortality. I've also seen this exaggerated sense of importance reflected in the attitudes and actions of high-profile politicians and even some students at Tyler High. These people think they are much more influential than they really are in the long run. In "Ozymandias," Percy Bysshe Shelley shows how even one of the greatest pharaohs of ancient Egypt comes to ruin and nothingness. The poem's theme is still relevant today; whether one is a pharaoh or a peasant, a president or a prom queen, we cannot escape the same fate.

Shelley devotes the first eight lines of his sonnet to describing the statue of Ozymandias, which is actually the Greek name for the Egyptian pharaoh Ramses II. The speaker in the poem, who is observing the statue, can still see the passions, power, and majesty of this great ruler reflected in the ruins of the statue. The speaker notices especially the "frown" and "sneer of cold command" carved on the ruler's face. This sneer represents the attitude of Ramses when he was at the height of his power. He, like the wealthy person in a new sport-utility vehicle or the successful politician of the moment, was riding high—building, creating, transforming, and feeling invincible.

Yet the statue is broken in two parts. Only the legs of stone still stand upright, and, "Near them, on the sand, / Half sunk, a shattered visage lies . . ."

First-Person Point of View

How does using first-person point of view affect the tone of this essay?

Literary Interpretation

How does interpreting the poetic theme here make the introduction more effective?

Organization

Why might the writer choose to focus on the beginning of the poem in the first body paragraph?

Supporting Evidence

How do the quotations from the poem strengthen the writer's personal insights?

Shelley's choppy description broken by commas emphasizes the image of Ozymandias's shattered face. Despite his former power, Ozymandias now lies in pieces. His commanding sneer and "wrinkled lip" have crumbled, and the once imposing statue threatens to turn back to dust. However mighty he was at one time, Ramses' power and influence were only temporary. He is no longer important, just as today's celebrities will soon be forgotten.

The last six lines of the poem emphasize the irony of the situation. Beginning with "My name is Ozymandias," an inscription on the pedestal warns everyone about the greatness of this man. I can't help thinking this is a bit like the proclamations of famous people who walk into a restaurant and tell their name to the host, as if that gesture alone should allow them to skip the line formed by everyone else who is waiting for a table. The inscription goes on to tell others to look on the mighty works of Ozymandias and "despair," as though his works will forever dwarf those of anyone else. Similarly, rappers today often boast of their success in their songs, only to fall out of the spotlight a short time later. This poem makes it clear that the inscription and Ozymandias's fate are two different things. Thousands of years later, Ozymandias is just a broken statue. His success was a fleeting thing. The "lone and level sands"—or death and oblivion—are the fate that lies ahead for everyone. Time reduces, erodes, and obscures all human achievements, whether they are the accomplishments of a political figure, a celebrity, or an ordinary person.

If Ozymandias could have known the fate of his statue, would he have boasted? Perhaps everyone should look at Ozymandias and rethink his or her own importance. Worldly fame and importance do not last; the sands of time run out for all.

Descriptive Details

What effect do the descriptive details have on the reader?

Organization

Why are the personal observations and ideas easy to follow?

Conclusion

How do these final reflections wrap up the essay?

Revising

Peer Review E-mail the draft of your essay to one or more peer reviewers. They can provide comments in a separate document and offer suggestions for revisions.

Use the rubric below to evaluate and strengthen your essay.

Traits of Strong Writing

Ideas message or theme and the details that develop it

Organization arrangement of main ideas and supporting details

Voice writer's unique way of using tone and style

Word Choice vocabulary a writer uses to convey meaning

Sentence Fluency rhythm and flow of sentences

Conventions correct spelling, grammar, usage, and mechanics

Presentation the way words and design elements look on a page

For more information on using the Traits of Strong Writing, see pages R33–R34 of the Writing Handbook.

Rubric: Writing a Reflective Essay

☑ Do you present your personal reflections about the meaning of a poem?

☑ Do you connect with your audience through first-person point of view and a conversational tone?

☑ Do you present your observations in a logical order?

☑ Do you use descriptive details and cite lines from the poem?

☑ Do you draw comparisons between personal experience and broader themes?

▶ **Focus Lesson**

Varying Sentence Structure

Vary the length and structure of your sentences to make your writing more lively and rhythmical. Simple sentences are sometimes short and sound direct and straightforward. Compound, complex, and compound-complex sentences are often longer and may alter the pace of your writing. An interrogative sentence can heighten the dramatic effect. See the sentence draft and revision from the student workshop model below.

Draft: The sentences of the paragraph have very similar structures and lengths and create a dull, predictable rhythm.

If Ozymandias had known his statue's fate, he would not have boasted. If people looked at Ozymandias, they would rethink their own importance.

Revision: Vary sentence length and structure to enliven the writing.

If Ozymandias could have known the fate of his statue, would he have boasted?[1] Perhaps everyone should look at Ozymandias and rethink his or her own importance.[2]

1: Use an interrogative sentence for variation and heightened dramatic effect.

2: Use a simple sentence to sound straightforward.

Editing and Proofreading

Get It Right When you have completed the final draft of your essay, proofread it for errors in grammar, usage, mechanics, and spelling. Refer to the Language Handbook, page R32, as a guide.

▶ **Focus Lesson**

Using Active and Passive Voice

A sentence in the active voice shows the subject acting. The action of the sentence flows forward: *The traveler describes the ruins of an ancient statue.* A sentence in the passive voice "hides" the actor in the sentence and makes the action weak and indirect: *The ruins of an ancient statue were described.* To make passive-voice sentences clearer and more dramatic, rewrite them in the active voice as you edit. You will need to rearrange the word order so that the noun in the subject position is the actor in the sentence.

Original: The passive voice diminishes the impact of the sentence.

All human achievements are reduced, eroded, and obscured by time.

Improved: Use the active voice to make the sentence more direct and powerful.

Time reduces, erodes, and obscures all human achievements.

Identifying Passive Voice

The passive voice consists of a form of the auxiliary verb *be* together with the past participle of the verb. Note these examples:

• *Ozymandias is remembered.* [present]

• *Ozymandias was remembered.* [past]

• *Ozymandias was being remembered.* [past progressive]

Read Aloud

Read your writing aloud to catch errors, such as typos, that you would not have noticed otherwise.

Presenting

Final Details Is your essay inviting to read? Make handwritten papers neat and legible. If you are working on a computer, follow your teacher's guidelines for formatting your final draft. For example, check that you are using the appropriate type size and spacing. Remember, appearance counts.

Writer's Portfolio

Place a copy of your reflective essay in your portfolio to review later.

Speaking, Listening, and Viewing Workshop

Reflective Presentation

Delivering a Reflective Presentation on a Poetic Theme

Connecting to Literature "The idea of talking about poetry is not to get to the bottom of it, but to clarify it, to make it more a part of what you and other people know and will remember. . . . What a poem makes you feel helps you make sense of it by making the poem part of your own experience. . . . Go slow, be simple and clear, and say how it seems to you and what exact words and lines in the poem your ideas and feelings come from."
—Kenneth Koch and Kate Farrell, from *Talking about Poetry*

Poets Kenneth Koch and Kate Farrell offer some sound strategies for sharing your reflections on a poem in an oral presentation. When you reflect on a poem or other literary work, you think about what the poem means to you and explore how the literature has shaped your thoughts and beliefs. As you deliver a reflective presentation on a poetic theme, you tell these ideas to others—a live audience—in order to explain what that poem has taught you and what it might teach others.

> **Assignment** Plan and deliver a reflective presentation based on a poetic theme from Unit Four.

Ozymandias
I met a traveler from an antique land
Who said: Two vast and trunkless legs of stone
Stand in the desert . . . Near them, on the sand,
Half sunk, a shattered visage lies, whose frown
And wrinkled lip, and sneer of cold command,

Planning Your Presentation

When you reflected on a poetic theme in your Writing Workshop essay, you were addressing an audience of readers. However, when you deliver your reflective presentation, you will be addressing an audience of listeners. Adapt your essay into a presentation by following these guidelines:

- Read your reflective essay aloud to a peer. Discuss which ideas you should keep or delete. What thoughts and feelings will your audience find most memorable?
- Do not rely on your written essay to deliver your reflective presentation. Instead, jot down key words and ideas on index cards. Refer to your notes as a speaking prompt.
- Include quotations and visual images in your presentation to illustrate key ideas and to make your topic lively and interesting. If you are reflecting on a short poem such as "Ozymandias" by Percy Bysshe Shelley, you might write the entire poem on an index card and read it aloud at the start of your presentation.

Presenting Visual Media

Visual media, such as photographs, a collage, drawings, or a computer slide show, can explain ideas to your audience and make your presentation more interesting. Check to be sure that your visual media enhance your presentation by practicing with your props beforehand. Use the checklist below as a guide:

☑ Have I remembered not to block the visuals while presenting?
☑ Do I use color in my presentation?
☑ Do I face the audience and not the visuals?
☑ Have I used at least twenty-four point font for any text on slides and overheads?
☑ Do I vary the tone of my visual media, incorporating both humor and serious images when appropriate?

Active Listening Tips

Invite your audience to follow these guidelines for effective listening:
- Prepare to listen.
- Note the topic and recall what you already know about it.
- Pay attention to the structure of the message.
- Take notes.
- Ask questions, aloud or silently.
- Listen for feelings as well as thoughts.

Rehearsing

One way to become a better speaker is to watch others present. Borrow techniques that seem effective and adapt them for your own presentation. If possible, browse video and audio clips of famous speeches or literary presentations.

Techniques for Delivering a Reflective Presentation

Verbal Techniques	Nonverbal Techniques
☑ **Pace** Speak at a moderate speed but vary the rate and use pauses to convey your meaning.	☑ **Eye Contact** Make frequent eye contact with the audience; if you are nervous, you may look slightly above the crowd instead.
☑ **Pronunciation** Speak clearly, pronouncing all the words precisely.	☑ **Facial Expressions** Vary your facial expressions to reflect the tone and mood of what you are saying.
☑ **Tone** Speak in an animated voice to entertain your listeners and keep everyone interested.	☑ **Visual Aids** Use photographs, collages, drawings, or computer presentations to enhance your speech.

OBJECTIVES
- Deliver a reflective presentation to an audience.
- Speak effectively to explain and justify ideas to peers.

For Independent Reading

DESPITE SOME INITIAL CRITICISM, THE NOVEL BECAME WIDELY ACCEPTED DURING THE Romantic period, inspiring a dramatic increase in fiction writing in the 1800s. Though authors used a wide range of styles, including gothic, historical, and Romantic, the basis of the novel was reality. In fact, Sir Walter Scott in 1824 defined the novel as "a fictitious narrative . . . accommodated to the ordinary train of human events."

Frankenstein

by Mary Shelley (1818)

In his attempt to create a human being, Victor Frankenstein assembles body parts from corpses and ultimately gives life to a monster. This epistolary novel (or novel of letters) about the experiments of Dr. Frankenstein combines romance and science fiction to create one of the most famous gothic novels of the time. *Frankenstein*, however, transcends the gothic fascination with the supernatural to explore the nature of evil and the possible consequences of mechanization in the new industrial age. Mary Shelley, the wife of the Romantic poet Percy Bysshe Shelley, conceived the idea for the story after reading ghost stories and experiencing a terrifying nightmare.

Emma

by Jane Austen (1815)

In her time, Jane Austen was nearly alone in writing the **novel of manners**, a realistic, usually satiric novel that examines the behavior and outlook of a particular social class. *Emma* is generally considered her most accomplished work, masterfully focusing on village life. The main character, Emma Woodhouse, amuses herself by making matches between her friends. With many humorous twists, this novel of manners charts Emma's journey toward greater self-awareness and, ultimately, love.

"*Scott's main achievement was to get people to realize that history was not just a list of political and religious dates denoting events that seemed to have happened of their own accord; instead he showed how history was the product of human decisions, human drama. Scott knew that his historical novels were nothing but educated guesses at what those human choices and human dramas really involved, but he persuaded us that the properly educated guess was the lesser lie than the flat denial of the human element.*"

—Nathan Uglow

Ivanhoe

by Sir Walter Scott (1819)

Sir Walter Scott's novels were immensely popular during his lifetime. After completing a series of Scottish historical novels, he turned his focus to England in *Ivanhoe*, his tale of a Saxon knight who returns home from the Crusades to marry his love, Rowena. A true product of the Romantic age, Scott incorporated his fascination with the marvelous and uncommon into his work. Because of his emphasis on history, Scott is often regarded as the inventor of the historical novel. His work later influenced Charles Dickens and James Fenimore Cooper.

From the Glencoe Literature Library

Sense and Sensibility

by Jane Austen

This classic novel tells the story of the Dashwood sisters, Elinor and Marianne, who face romantic adventures and misfortunes and try to protect each other as only sisters can.

Pride and Prejudice

by Jane Austen

Austen's novel tells the story of Elizabeth Bennet and Fitzwilliam Darcy and the stubborn pride and foolish prejudice that threaten to keep them apart.

Test Preparation and Practice

English–Language Arts

Reading: Nonfiction

Carefully read the following passage. Use context clues to help you define any words with which you are unfamiliar. Pay close attention to the author's purpose and her use of figurative language and argument. Then, on a separate sheet of paper, answer the questions.

from *A Vindication of the Rights of Woman* by Mary Wollstonecraft

line

I once knew a weak woman of fashion, who was more than commonly proud of her delicacy and sensibility. She thought a distinguishing taste and puny appetite the height of all human perfection, and acted accordingly. I have seen this weak sophisticated being neglect all the duties of life, yet recline with self-complacency on a sofa, and boast of her want of appetite as a proof of delicacy that
5 extended to, or, perhaps, arose from, her exquisite sensibility; for it is difficult to render intelligible such ridiculous jargon. . . .

Women are everywhere in this deplorable state; for, in order to preserve their innocence, as ignorance is courteously termed, truth is hidden from them, and they are made to assume an artificial character before their faculties have acquired any strength. Taught from their infancy that beauty is
10 woman's scepter, the mind shapes itself to the body, and roaming round its gilt cage, only seeks to adore its prison. Men have various employments and pursuits which engage their attention, and give a character to the opening mind; but women, confined to one, and having their thoughts constantly directed to the most insignificant part of themselves, seldom extend their views beyond the triumph of the hour. . . .

15 This argument branches into various ramifications. Birth, riches, and every extrinsic advantage that exalt a man above his fellows, without any mental exertion, sink him in reality below them. In proportion to his weakness, he is played upon by designing men, till the bloated monster has lost all traces of humanity. . . . Educated in slavish dependence, and enervated by luxury and sloth, where shall we find men who will stand forth to assert the rights of man, or claim the privilege of moral
20 beings, who should have but one road to excellence? Slavery to monarchs and ministers, which the world will be long in freeing itself from, and whose deadly grasp stops the progress of the human mind, is not yet abolished.

Let not men then in the pride of power, use the same arguments that tyrannic kings and venal ministers have used, and fallaciously assert that woman ought to be subjected because she has
25 always been so. . . .

[I]f women be educated for dependence, that is, to act according to the will of another fallible being, and submit, right or wrong, to power, where are we to stop? Are they to be considered as vicegerents allowed to reign over a small domain, and answerable for their conduct to a higher tribunal, liable to error?

line

line   It will not be difficult to prove that such delegates will act like men subjected by fear, and make
30   their children and servants endure their tyrannical oppression. As they submit without reason, they
will, having no fixed rules to square their conduct by, be kind, or cruel, just as the whim of the
moment directs; and we ought not to wonder if sometimes, galled by their heavy yoke, they take a
malignant pleasure in resting it on weaker shoulders. . . .

     For man and woman, truth, if I understand the meaning of the word, must be the same; yet the
35   fanciful female character, so prettily drawn by poets and novelists, demanding the sacrifice of truth
and sincerity, virtue becomes a relative idea, having no other foundation than utility, and of that utility
men pretend arbitrarily to judge, shaping it to their own convenience.

1. From the context, what do you conclude that the word *want* in line 4 means?
   A. need
   B. lack
   C. plan
   D. desire

2. Which of the following best describes the tone of the phrase *as ignorance is courteously termed*, in lines 7–8?
   F. sad
   G. sympathetic
   H. ironic
   J. bitter

3. Which type of figurative language is Wollstonecraft using in the phrase *beauty is woman's scepter* in lines 9–10?
   A. simile
   B. personification
   C. metaphor
   D. metaphysical conceit

4. What does Wollstonecraft claim "seeks to adore its prison" in lines 10–11?
   F. the ignorant woman's mind
   G. a beautiful woman's scepter
   H. a gilt cage
   J. an artificial character

5. According to Wollstonecraft in lines 12–14, what is the effect of women's having only one employment?
   A. They direct their thoughts to insignificant things.
   B. They open their minds and develop character.
   C. They develop insignificant character traits.
   D. They seldom extend their views past the present.

6. According to Wollstonecraft, what sinks a man below his fellows?
   F. advantage without mental exertion
   G. riches and every advantage
   H. the ramifications of argument
   J. weakness

7. From the context, what do you conclude that the word *enervated*, in line 18, means?
   A. strengthened
   B. frightened
   C. excited
   D. weakened

8. To whom does the word *delegates*, in line 30, refer?
   F. husbands
   G. women
   H. kings
   J. tyrants

9. Which of the following is the main idea of the paragraph that begins on line 30?
   A. Men and women are naturally tyrannical.
   B. Tyranny is unavoidable in the household.
   C. Women are not capable of tyrannical behavior.
   D. The effects of tyranny are never isolated.

10. From the context, what do you conclude that the word *drawn*, in line 36, means?
   F. created
   G. closed
   H. drained
   J. confused

11. On the basis of this passage, with which of the following statements do you think Wollstonecraft would be most likely to agree?
   A. Equality between the sexes is impossible.
   B. Truth is based on utility.
   C. Arbitrary power cannot be justified.
   D. Innocence is the most desirable condition.

12. On the basis of this passage, what do you think the overall tone of this essay is?
   F. ironic
   G. authoritative
   H. humorous
   J. sarcastic

13. From your reading of this selection, what do you think the author's main purpose was?
   A. to persuade
   B. to instruct
   C. to inform
   D. to entertain

14. What is the main idea of this passage?
   F. Men and women must be treated differently.
   G. There is no such thing as truth.
   H. Inequality and tyranny are needless evils.
   J. Women are more adept than men.

Literature Online **Unit Assessment** To prepare for the Unit test, go to www.glencoe.com.

902 UNIT 4 THE TRIUMPH OF ROMANTICISM

Vocabulary Skills: Sentence Completion

For each item in the Vocabulary Skills section, choose the word or words that best complete the sentence.

1. During the Romantic period, writers chose to _____ the _____ mind embraced by the Enlightenment in favor of the imagination and intuition.
   A. relinquish . . . dismal
   B. spurn . . . rational
   C. cleave . . . acute
   D. repose . . . congenial

2. During the 1700s, England's _____ over the Americas came to an end.
   F. dirge
   G. faculty
   H. penance
   J. dominion

3. Many of the Romantic writers at first embraced the political and cultural _____ and revolution of their day.
   A. tumult
   B. satiety
   C. teeming
   D. foresight

4. Romantic poets, including Keats and Shelley, believed in the _____ but transcendent power of the natural world.
   F. hypocritical
   G. bleak
   H. conspiring
   J. transient

5. William Blake's unconventional poetics, behavior, and religious beliefs confounded many of his _____.
   A. arbiters
   B. faculties
   C. furrows
   D. acquaintances

6. The radicalism of many of the Romantics _____ anger and indignation among _____ traditional thinkers and critics.
   F. incited . . . emphatically
   G. imparted . . . pomp
   H. loitered . . . deities
   J. relinquished . . . desolate

7. Many historians think that the American and French revolutions were the _____ outcome of royal mismanagement.
   A. uncouth
   B. inevitable
   C. illustrious
   D. kindred

8. The Romantics believed that the imagination was the most judicial and accurate _____ of the world.
   F. piety
   G. dirge
   H. arbiter
   J. indignation

9. There was _____ discontentment among the poor in response to the conditions of the Industrial Revolution.
   A. genial
   B. illustrious
   C. sordid
   D. acute

10. Mary Shelley's most famous fiction presents a disturbing and _____ view of humanity.
    F. bleak
    G. congenial
    H. transient
    J. kindred

Grammar and Writing Skills: Paragraph Improvement

In the following excerpt from a student draft of a reflective essay, you will find underlined phrases and sentences. The number beneath each underlined phrase corresponds to a numbered question on the next page. Each question will prompt you to replace an underlined phrase. If you think the original should not be changed, choose "NO CHANGE."

At the end of the passage, you will also find a boxed number. This number refers to a question about a specific paragraph or to the essay as a whole.

Both the boxed number and the numbers that appear beneath underlined phrases or sentences refer to question numbers, *not* to the sequence of sentences or paragraphs.

As you read, pay close attention to the writer's use of modifiers, punctuation, and voice.

[1]

How can the world be made up of contradictions? Good and evil, light and dark, and tragedy and comedy are all at odds, and yet exist as parts of a greater whole! These contradictions are what William Blake was wrestling with as he wrote "The Tyger." This poem depicts the violence and power of a Tyger, and the awe the speaker feels for it. Enthralled by the Tyger's force, the poem is propelled by an electric and rhythmic cadence. The poet also intended the piece as a contrast and complement to the delightful and innocent Lamb, from his Songs of Innocence. The contrast of these elements—*innocence* and *experience,* as embodied by these animals—is a compelling symbol for the world in which we live.

[2]

In the first stanza, a question is posed by the speaker. This question, the backbone of the poem's theme, animates the whole purpose of both innocence and experience: "What immortal hand or eye / Could frame thy fearful symmetry?" Here Blake is asking, "What could produce such a frightening thing?" He is also asking, "How can the Tyger's nature, which contradicts that of the Lamb's, exist?" This is the "fearful symmetry" to which Blake is referring. In fact, symmetry is employed throughout the *Songs of Innocence and Experience* with complex echoes and counterargument. The interaction between the worlds of innocence and experience evokes many thoughts. It prompts exploration. It prompts the kinds of questions that only I ask when I see violence, or unhappiness, or when I consider natural disasters or calamities caused by human beings. I wonder how these things can exist in a world with so much potential for good.

10

1. A. NO CHANGE
   B. *Good* and *evil, light* and *dark,* and *tragedy* and *comedy* are all at odds, and yet exist as parts of a greater whole!
   C. Good and evil, light and dark, and tragedy and comedy are all at odds and yet exist as parts of a greater whole.
   D. Good and evil; light and dark; tragedy and comedy; are all at odds, and yet exist as parts of a greater whole.

2. F. NO CHANGE
   G. Enthralled by the Tyger's force; the poem is propelled by an electric, rhythmic cadence.
   H. Enthralled by the Tyger's force. The poem is propelled by an electric, and rhythmic cadence.
   J. Enthralled by the Tyger's force, Blake made the poem seem propelled by an electric and rhythmic cadence.

3. A. NO CHANGE
   B. delightful and innocent Lamb from his *Songs of Innocence.*
   C. *delightful, innocent* Lamb, from *Songs of Innocence.*
   D. "delightful" and "innocent" Lamb—from his Songs of Innocence.

4. F. NO CHANGE
   G. innocence and experience as embodied by these animals. Is a *compelling* symbol for the *world* in which we live.
   H. *innocence* and *experience* as embodied by these animals—is a *compelling* symbol for the *world* in which we live.
   J. innocence and experience, as embodied by these animals—is a compelling symbol for the world in which we live.

5. A. NO CHANGE
   B. A question is posed in the first stanza.
   C. In the first stanza, the speaker poses a question.
   D. In the first stanza: a question is posed.

6. F. NO CHANGE
   G. animated the whole purpose of both innocence and experience:
   H. *animates* a purpose of innocence and experience:
   J. animates the whole purpose of both "innocence" and "experience."

7. A. NO CHANGE
   B. Nevertheless, Blake is asking,
   C. Actually here Blake is asking.
   D. Here, actually, Blake is asking;

8. F. NO CHANGE
   G. In fact, with complex echoes and counterargument, symmetry is employed throughout the *Songs of Innocence and Experience*
   H. In fact, symmetry is employed throughout the *Songs of Innocence and Experience*
   J. symmetry is employed throughout the *Songs of Innocence and Experience* with complex echoes and counterargument.

9. A. NO CHANGE
   B. Only it prompts the kinds of questions that I ask when I see violence
   C. It prompts the kinds of questions that I ask only when I see violence
   D. It prompts the questions that only I ask when I see violence

10. Which of the following would be the most logical topic for paragraph 3?
   F. Blake's poetic influences
   G. discussion of stanzas after the first stanza
   H. examination of the relationship between "The Tyger" and "The Lamb"
   J. examination of symbolism in "The Lamb"

Essay

Which poem from this unit affected you most? Write a reflective essay in which you discuss how the poem changed you, how it relates to your personal experience, and what the universal themes in the poem are. As you write, keep in mind that your essay will be checked for **ideas, organization, voice, word choice, sentence fluency, conventions,** and **presentation.**

The Bayswater Omnibus, 1895. George William Joy. Oil on canvas, 47½ x 78¼ in. Museum of London.

The Victorian Age

1837–1901

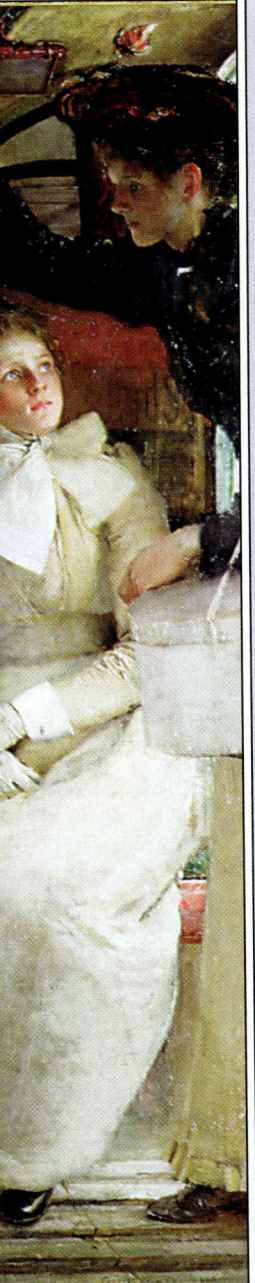

Looking Ahead

During the sixty-four-year reign of Queen Victoria, Britain experienced unprecedented economic and technological growth and dramatic political and social change. Britain became "the workshop of the world." About a quarter of the world's people lived within the British Empire. A growing social consciousness stirred reforms. Some Victorian writers felt an optimistic promise in the era; others saw the menace of a world driven by inhuman forces.

Keep the following questions in mind as you read:

◆ How were Britain and the British Empire changing during the Victorian age?

◆ What conditions helped stimulate Victorian optimism?

◆ How did the mood of later Victorian writers change?

OBJECTIVES
In learning about the Victorian age, you will focus on the following:
- analyzing the characteristics of Victorian literature and how issues of the period influenced writers
- evaluating the influences of the historical period that shaped literary characters, plots, settings, and themes in Victorian literature
- connecting Victorian literature to historical contexts, current events, and your own experiences

Timeline 1837–1901

Charles Darwin

BRITISH LITERATURE

1835

1841
Humorous weekly *Punch* is founded

1847
Emily Brontë publishes *Wuthering Heights*

1847
Charlotte Brontë publishes *Jane Eyre*

1850
Alfred Tennyson becomes poet laureate

1859
Charles Darwin publishes *On the Origin of Species*

1859
Edward FitzGerald publishes *Rubáiyát of Omar Khayyám*

1861
Charles Dickens publishes *Great Expectations*

1862
Christina Rossetti publishes *Goblin Market* ▼

1865

1865
Lewis Carroll publishes *Alice's Adventures in Wonderland*

1866
Gerard Manley Hopkins becomes a Roman Catholic

1867
Matthew Arnold publishes *New Poems*

BRITISH EVENTS

1835

1837
Victoria is crowned queen

1838
Chartists demand political reforms

1839
First real bicycle is invented in Scotland

1840
Queen Victoria marries Prince Albert

1841
Hong Kong comes under British sovereignty

1845
Irish Potato Famine begins

1851
Great Exhibition is held ▶

1854
Britain enters Crimean War

1857
Indian Mutiny breaks out

1861
Prince Albert dies

1862
John Hanning Speke identifies source of the Nile

1865

Crystal Palace

1865
Joseph Lister initiates antiseptic surgery

WORLD EVENTS

1835

1837
John Deere invents the steel plow in the U.S.

1848
Revolutions break out in Europe

1848
German philosophers Marx and Engels write *Communist Manifesto*

1856
Remains of Neanderthal man are discovered in Germany ▶

1861
Alexander II emancipates Russian serfs

1865

1865
American Civil War ends

1866
Alfred Nobel invents dynamite

1868
Meiji restoration occurs in Japan

Literature Online **Timeline** Visit www.glencoe.com for an interactive timeline.

The Mad Tea Party, John Tenniel. The Pierpont Morgan Library, New York.

1885

1878
Thomas Hardy publishes *The Return of the Native*

1882
Robert Louis Stevenson publishes *Treasure Island*

1884
First volume of *Oxford English Dictionary* is published

1894
First issue of *The Yellow Book* is published

1895
The Importance of Being Earnest by Oscar Wilde is produced

1896
A. E. Housman publishes *A Shropshire Lad*

1897
Bram Stoker publishes *Dracula*

1898
H. G. Wells publishes *The War of the Worlds* ▶

1885

1866
Great Eastern lays first successful transatlantic cable

1869
Debtors' prisons abolished

1876
Queen Victoria is proclaimed Empress of India

1885
General Gordon is killed at Khartoum

1897
Queen Victoria celebrates her Diamond Jubilee

1899
Boer War begins in South Africa

1901
Commonwealth of Australia established ▶

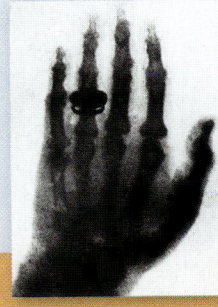

1901
Queen Victoria dies; Edward VII becomes king

1885

1874
First Impressionist exhibition is held in Paris

1876
Alexander Graham Bell invents the telephone in the U.S. ▼

1885
Leopold II of Belgium acquires Congo in Africa

1888
Wilhelm II becomes emperor of Germany

1895
Italian engineer Guglielmo Marconi invents wireless telegraphy

1895 ▲
German physicist Wilhelm Röntgen discovers X rays

1899
Austrian psychoanalyst Sigmund Freud publishes *The Interpretation of Dreams*

1900
Boxer Rebellion breaks out in China

1901
First Nobel Prizes are awarded

Reading Check

Analyzing Graphic Information For how many years was Queen Victoria a widow?

By the Numbers

Growth in the British Electorate, 1832–1884

Through a series of reform bills, the number of male voters in Britain greatly increased during the Victorian age. Women would have to wait until the twentieth century to win the right to vote.

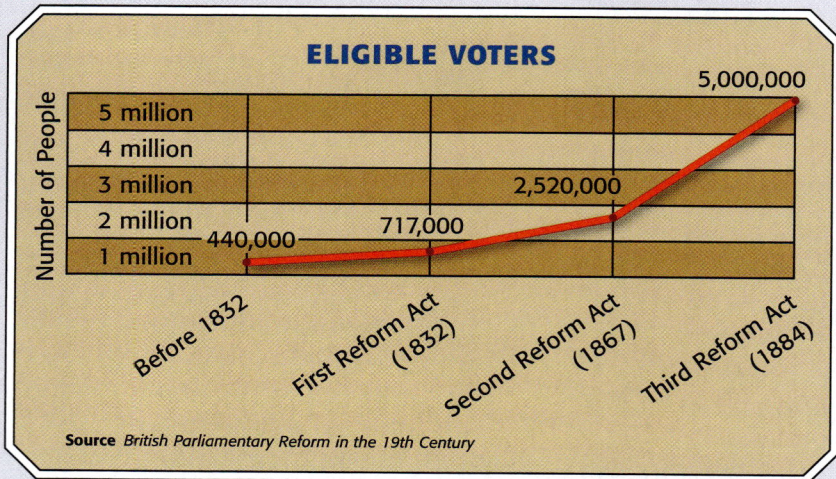

ELIGIBLE VOTERS

Number of People

5 million			
4 million			
3 million			2,520,000
2 million	440,000	717,000	
1 million			

5,000,000

Before 1832 · First Reform Act (1832) · Second Reform Act (1867) · Third Reform Act (1884)

Source *British Parliamentary Reform in the 19th Century*

THE GREAT EXHIBITION OF 1851

Queen Victoria officially opened the "Great Exhibition of the Works of Industry of All Nations"—the first world's fair—at noon on May 1, 1851, in the mammoth Crystal Palace erected in London's Hyde Park.

- The Crystal Palace was 1,848 feet long and 408 feet wide. The central transept was 108 feet high.

- Built of prefabricated sections, the building's iron frame held 896,000 square feet of glass.

- More than half of the almost 14,000 exhibitors at the Great Exhibition were from Britain and the British Empire.

- More than 6,200,000 visitors attended the exhibition— 478,773 in the last week alone—before it closed on October 11, 1851.

- Entrance fees alone brought in 424,418 pounds, 15 shillings. As a result, the Great Exhibition made a large profit.

- Among the displays on the grounds of the Great Exhibition were the first life-size models of extinct creatures that scientists had only named a few years earlier: dinosaurs.

SETTLING AUSTRALIA

Between 1788 and 1868, Britain sent more than 160,000 convicts to Australia. The First Fleet consisted of 11 small ships carrying 736 criminals. Their average age was 27. The oldest male was in his sixties; the youngest was 9. The youngest female was 13; the oldest, 84.

HOME LIGHTING

Before the electric light was invented, candles and oil lamps lighted homes. Both needed constant attention. One estate employed 3 or more men cutting candlewicks, removing wax drips, cleaning glass lamp chimneys, and filling lamps. Even a modest home could have some 20 or more lamps.

CHILD MORTALITY

In 1839 nearly half the funerals in London were for children younger than 10 years old.

SERVANTS

In Victorian Britain, having at least one servant was a mark of middle-class respectability. In 1891 servants made up 16 percent of the British work force.

EDUCATION

Elementary education was not compulsory in Britain until 1880. In 1871 more than 19 percent of the men and 26 percent of the women getting married could not sign their names in their parish register. Twenty years later, both of these figures had dropped to around 7 percent.

HUNTING

The Victorian upper class spent a lot of time shooting game animals on their estates. During a three-day period in 1864, hunters at one estate killed 4,045 pheasants, 3,902 rabbits, 860 hares, 59 woodcocks, and 28 creatures described as "various."

Being There

The Victorian age was a period of great expansion for the British Empire. Along with other European powers, the British engaged in a fierce competition for African colonies. The vast Indian subcontinent became "the Jewel in the Crown" of Queen Victoria, who was declared Empress of India in 1876. Britain's annexation of Australia continued throughout the Victorian age, until the entire island continent was part of the British Empire.

B *The Last of England,* Ford Madox Brown, 1852–1855. Oil on panel. Birmingham Museums and Art Gallery, United Kingdom.

C *The British Raj Great Indian Peninsular Terminus,* unknown artist, nineteenth century. Watercolor on paper. British Library, London, United Kingdom.

A *View of Harbour Street, Kingston, Jamaica,* after James Hakewill, nineteenth century. Engraving. Private collection.

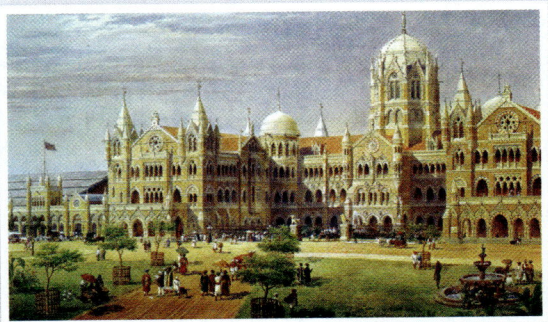

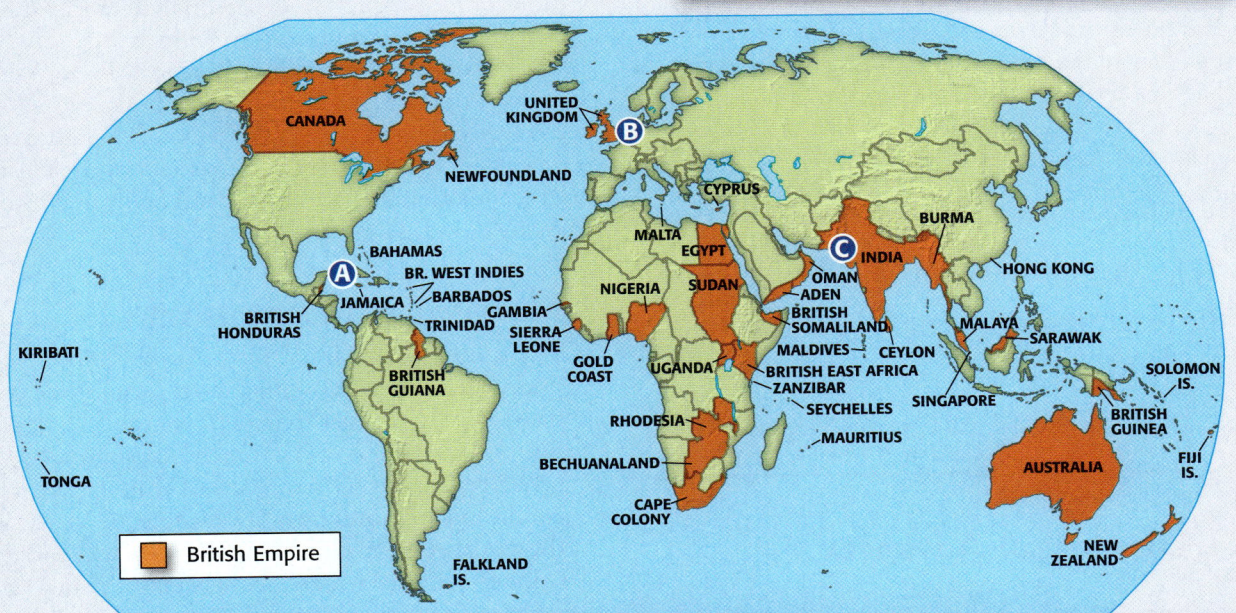

British Empire

Reading Check

Analyzing Graphic Information:

1. About how many times greater was the British electorate after 1884 than it had been before 1832?

2. Approximately how many exhibitors at the Great Exhibition were from Britain and the British Empire?

3. On what continent did the British Empire have the smallest amount of territory?

Literature online **Maps in Motion** Visit www.glencoe.com for an interactive map.

The Victorian Age

1837–1901

Historical, Social, and Cultural Forces

Queen Victoria and Her Empire

Victoria came to the British throne in 1837 as a girl of eighteen; at her death in 1901, most of her subjects had never known any other ruler. Personally, Victoria was most interested in her own family—her husband, Prince Albert, and their nine children. As "mother of the empire," however, she also played a major symbolic role in unifying Britain's widespread colonies.

The British had begun to settle Australia in 1788. Britain was also a major player in the European scramble to colonize Africa. Above all, in India, Britain consolidated and expanded its rule in what had begun as a privately funded enterprise under the East India Company. By Queen Victoria's sixtieth anniversary Diamond Jubilee in 1897, she ruled one-quarter of the world's population.

> "The British Empire is under Providence the greatest instrument for good that the world has seen."
>
> —Lord Curzon, Viceroy of India

Technological Advances

Britain's imperial success was aided by technological strength. Victorian life literally sped up. For untold centuries, the fastest speeds possible—and then only for the rich—were achieved with horses and sailing ships. Steam power democratized speed. By the end of the century, locomotives could reach fifty miles per hour and steamships, fifteen knots. Both provided regular and relatively inexpensive transportation.

Many nineteenth-century inventions similarly changed the fabric and structure of daily life. Cast iron and elevators enabled people to build taller buildings; transatlantic telegraph wires and telephones meant people communicated more quickly and widely; the new aniline dyes meant people dressed more brightly. Electric light made streets safer and theatrical performances more thrilling. The discovery of vaccines and the pasteurization of milk improved health. Canned food fed soldiers and arctic explorers while bringing variety to the limitations of locally produced, seasonal diets. For the first time, photographs preserved memories. To the Victorians, speed and other technological innovations seemed to promise a better world in many respects. As the Victorian historian Thomas Babington Macaulay wrote, "every improvement of the means of locomotion benefits mankind morally and intellectually as well as materially."

Marxism and Darwinism

The stunning changes of Victorian life came at a price. The visible signs of material progress seemed to many contemporaries to underscore the lack of progress on other fronts. Governmental committees published reports on such subjects as child labor laws, conditions in mines, and sewer projects. Many of these reports, known as Blue Books because of the color of their covers, had real effects on public opinion and the laws. Despite mountains of data, however, many people felt the lack of an overarching theory to make sense of the huge changes they had witnessed. In this cultural climate, two men provided theories that continue to influence us today.

German-born philosopher Karl Marx moved to London in 1849 after being exiled from Paris for his political radicalism. In Britain, he drew on the information contained in the Blue Books to write his most famous and influential book, *Das Kapital* ("Capital"), which first began to appear in English in 1886. Marx believed that class warfare was inevitable. According to Marx, all property and the means of production should be held in common, and all means of subsistence should be shared out equally: "From each according to his abilities, to each according to his needs."

Marx intended his ideas to have earth-shaking political and social consequences; the British naturalist Charles Darwin did not. He published his book *On the Origin of Species by Means of Natural Selection* in 1859, but the seeds of it had been planted more than twenty years earlier on an expedition to gather biological specimens. Darwin's long-term observations and speculations led him to view all living organisms—from pine trees and codfish to human beings—as governed by the same natural laws. For Darwin, the mechanism of evolution was controlled by blind chance; there was no agent

Postcard illustrating the British Empire, c. 1919. Rykoff Collection.

behind the changes and no intended goal. By the end of the century, contemporary interpreters of Darwin claimed evolution implied progress. They used biological notions of "the survival of the fittest" (not Darwin's words) to justify the power of the rich, an application known as Social Darwinism. Darwin himself loathed controversy, however, and was not interested in applying his theories to human social policy.

PREVIEW Big Ideas of the Victorian Age

1 Optimism and the Belief in Progress

During the Victorian era, Britain developed a huge empire. The resulting material success, coupled with technological advances and social reforms, encouraged an optimistic belief in progress that was reflected in some Victorian literature.

See pages 914–915.

2 The Emergence of Realism

In the mid-1800s, a reaction to Romanticism began to appear in both art and literature. Known as Realism, this new movement aimed to explore contemporary life and ordinary experience. Focusing on individuals dealing with everyday problems, Victorian Realist writers often sought to reform society.

See pages 916–917.

3 Disillusionment and Darker Visions

By the late 1800s, a movement called Naturalism developed out of Realism. Like Realists, Naturalists presented contemporary people and their problems as accurately as possible. However, Naturalists tended toward extreme pessimism, suggesting that fate was predetermined and meaningless.

See pages 918–919.

Optimism and the Belief in Progress

Just like styles of clothing, beliefs and ideals go out of fashion—and then often come back in again. Victorian values have been sneered at off and on for more than a century, but they show no sign of disappearing.

Victorian Values

Three of the most typical Victorian ideals were self-improvement, moral earnestness, and the value of work. In the bestselling *Self-Help,* published in 1859, Samuel Smiles preached a gospel of thrift, hard work, and patience: "Honorable industry travels the same road with duty; and Providence has closely linked both with happiness." Moral earnestness defined the work of Queen Victoria's favorite contemporary writer, her poet laureate, Alfred, Lord Tennyson (see page 922). After the death of her husband Prince Albert in 1861, the queen cherished Tennyson's long, thoughtful poem *In Memoriam,* which struggles to affirm the survival of love despite death and religious doubts.

> *"Not what I have, . . . but what I do is my kingdom."*
>
> —Thomas Carlyle, *Sartor Resartus*

The Middle-Class Public

The middle-class virtues of Victorian individualism seemed to define a new aristocracy of merit. Making something of oneself required guidance and effort. The well-to-do middle classes spent a lot of money on reading for self-improvement—and there was much new material for them to read. Periodicals were crammed with serialized novels, book reviews, travel writing, current events, and other educational pieces. Several Victorian novelists, including Charles Dickens (see page 984) and William Makepeace Thackeray, edited their own journals that also published their work, ridding themselves of the burdens of patronage.

The Expansion of Democracy

Many British workers were literate and—thanks to cheaper books, municipally funded lending libraries, and Mechanics' Institutes (workingmen's colleges)—were exposed to new ideas. During this period, continental Europe experienced many violent political upheavals, coups, and revolutions, but Britain did not. One reason for this lies in the greater ability of the British to change through political means in response to pressures from below.

Although Victorian Britain was officially a representative democracy, the right to vote at the beginning of the queen's reign was very limited. Nonetheless, there was a marked trend toward increasing representation and social mobility. In 1832 the First Reform Bill brought the vote to middle-class men. In 1867 the Second Reform Bill enfranchised many workingmen, doubling the electorate. By the end of the nineteenth century, women could vote in most local elections. It was not until the end of World War I, however, that all men over twenty-one and women over thirty could vote. Many people felt that real economic, social, and political mobility was increasingly possible. These signs of hope spread throughout the empire.

Imperialism

Britain gained its empire more through commercial expansion than through military conquest. British colonial rule did not aim at centralized control, and there could be considerable variation in local government. Colonial New Zealand, for example, in 1893 became the first country in the world to give the vote to all adults regardless of sex or race. British institutions—including the army, the civil service, and the law—offered some inclusion and mobility to colonials. Mohandas Gandhi, for example, was born in India and admitted to the British bar in London in 1889. His legal work to end discrimination against Indians in South Africa, another British colony, started him on his path to become the leader of the movement for Indian independence. There is no doubt that British colonial rule could be officious and insensitive. But many people in Victorian Britain truly believed they were bringing their colonial subjects the benefits of Western civilization.

Queen Victoria Opening the 1862 Exhibition after Crystal Palace Moved to Sydenham. Joseph Nash. Private collection.

One of the most influential critics of Victorian culture was the essayist and historian Thomas Carlyle.

from *Past and Present* by Thomas Carlyle

All true Work is sacred; in all true Work, were it but true hand-labor, there is something of divineness. Labor, wide as the Earth, has its summit in Heaven. Sweat of the brow; and up from that to sweat of the brain, sweat of the heart; which includes all Kepler calculations, Newton meditations, all Sciences, all spoken Epics, all acted Heroisms, Martyrdoms,—up to that "Agony of bloody sweat," which all men have called divine! O brother, if this is not "worship," then I say, the more pity for worship; for this is the noblest thing yet discovered under God's sky. Who art thou that complainest of thy life of toil? Complain not. Look up, my wearied brother; see thy fellow Workmen there, in God's Eternity; surviving there, they alone surviving: sacred Band of the Immortals, celestial Bodyguard of the Empire of Mankind.

Reading Check

Interpreting Why did Victorians such as Carlyle value work?

For the Victorians, in an age of transition where all the old values seemed in the process of being demolished, life was lived amid a babble of conflicting opinions. Whom should they trust?

The Road to Wealth

At the beginning of the Industrial Revolution, the British economic theorist Adam Smith put forward the idea that a nation of individuals free to pursue their own economic self-interest without governmental interference would ultimately produce a stronger, wealthier nation. To give moral justification to such self-interest, the Victorian thinkers Jeremy Bentham and John Stuart Mill came up with the theory of Utilitarianism—the view that the ethical value of an activity is measured by the extent of its usefulness. Utilitarianism strongly influenced the ethical decisions that Victorians made in political and economic life. Many factory owners and businessmen, particularly in the industrial north of Britain, became strong advocates for putting free-market and Utilitarian doctrines into practice.

> "The greatest happiness of the greatest number is the foundation of morals and legislation."
>
> —Jeremy Bentham

Free-market economic policy had visible consequences. Victorian Britain, whose population doubled during the first half of the 1800s, had more money than ever before, and more poor people than ever before. Did a forward-moving nation have a responsibility to help the poorest people among them, who produced no wealth but consumed resources? Quite a few people argued that the answer was no. Proponents of self-help thought it was self-evident that it was one's own fault if one was poor. Extreme Utilitarians argued that one poor person's starvation was more than offset by the full stomach of a person capable of producing something beneficial for society. Social Darwinists, erroneously believing they were supported by Charles Darwin's writings on evolution, claimed that aid to the unfit was, in fact, unnatural. Artificially prolonging the life of the unfit, they believed, weakened a whole society.

Voices of Reform

Equally determined Victorian voices spoke out on behalf of the poor and helpless. Carlyle, for example, passionately exposed the underlying flaws in Victorian society, warning of Britain's moral, as well as literal, starvation. His writings inspired many writers and reformers, including Karl Marx and the novelist Charles Dickens.

Doctors, ministers, journalists, and private philanthropists organized many charitable organizations, including the Ladies' Society for the Education and Employment of the Female Poor, the Society for the Prevention of Cruelty to Animals, and the Young Men's Christian Association (YMCA). Reformers within Parliament used Blue Book reports to educate the well-to-do middle class about the poor. Reports on, for example, child labor in coal mines, were widely read, leading to reform laws.

The Novel and the Condition of England

In 1845 Benjamin Disraeli chose to write a novel to persuade the wealthy to unite "the two nations" of England—the rich and the poor. In her novel *North and South,* Elizabeth Gaskell used Britain's geography to explain its economic divisions. Many other authors wrote novels to represent, in a socially realistic way, the "Condition of England." They set their novels in factory towns. Their characters were working-class mill-hands, clerks, seamstresses—or lower-class people, such as paupers. Plots partially depended on romance but also included riots among workers and meetings to discuss working conditions. Victorian novels proved to be powerful instruments for instructing middle-class readers. As they sat in their parlors, these readers began to imagine the humanity of those whom they might never meet.

The Docks at Cardiff, 1894. Lionel Walden. Oil on canvas. Musée d'Orsay, Paris.

from *Hard Times* by Charles Dickens

"Now, what I want is, Facts. Teach these boys and girls nothing but Facts. Facts alone are wanted in life. Plant nothing else, and root out everything else. You can only form the minds of reasoning animals upon Facts: nothing else will ever be of any service to them. This is the principle on which I bring up my own children, and this is the principle on which I bring up these children. Stick to Facts, Sir!"

The scene was a plain, bare, monotonous vault of a school-room, and the speaker's square forefinger emphasized his observations by underscoring every sentence with a line on the schoolmaster's sleeve. The emphasis was helped by the speaker's square wall of a forehead, which had his eyebrows for its base, while his eyes found commodious cellarage in two dark caves, overshadowed by the wall. The emphasis was helped by the speaker's mouth, which was wide, thin, and hard set. The emphasis was helped by the speaker's voice, which was inflexible, dry, and dictatorial. The emphasis was helped by the speaker's hair, which bristled on the skirts of his bald head, a plantation of firs to keep the wind from its shining surface, all covered with knobs, like the crust of a plum pie, as if the head had scarcely warehouse-room for the hard facts stored inside. The speaker's obstinate carriage, square coat, square legs, square shoulders,—nay, his very neckcloth, trained to take him by the throat with an unaccommodating grasp, like a stubborn fact, as it was,—all helped the emphasis.

"In this life, we want nothing but Facts, Sir; nothing but Facts!"

The speaker, and the schoolmaster, and the third grown person present, all backed a little, and swept with their eyes the inclined plane of little vessels then and there arranged in order, ready to have imperial gallons of facts poured into them until they were full to the brim.

Reading Check

Analyzing Cause and Effect Why did Victorian writers move in the direction of Realism?

Disillusionment and Darker Visions

ne of the most admirable characteristics of the Victorians was their capacity for self-criticism. Even at the height of Victorian optimism—when technological and material progress seemed to many people to be limitless—doubting voices already were heard.

Pessimism and Naturalism

The young Thomas Carlyle worried that, in an age that worshiped machinery, people too would grow "mechanical in head and in heart, as well as in hand." Carlyle's fellow cultural critic John Ruskin, in a series of letters addressed to British "workmen and laborers," looked around and saw a savage world: a "yelping, carnivorous crowd, mad for money and lust, tearing each other to pieces, and starving each other to death." The ugliness and brutality of the Victorian age prompted many painful questions: What could replace traditions as they disappeared? What would unify the country when religious feeling weakened? Could human nature and society improve indefinitely? Could they, in fact, change at all?

The Realist novel, which had proved itself so effective in rousing emotion, began to seem too good at raising falsely comforting feelings such as sentimentality or smugness. A new generation of novelists were influenced in part by Darwinism to look for inevitable natural, rather than spiritual, forces guiding the course of human life. In France, for example, the novelist Émile Zola wrote novels according to a set of beliefs called Naturalism. Naturalistic novels, plays, and poems tend to present a grim, almost fatalistic view of the world, in which mostly lower-class characters are trapped by circumstances beyond their control for reasons that they cannot determine. Zola's goal was to use the novel almost as a scientific instrument. He observed that he was subjecting his fictional characters to "the same analytical examination that surgeons perform on corpses." For novelists fol-

lowing in the path of Zola, clinical knowledge of the human condition replaced teary sympathy.

Other writers who did not identify themselves with Naturalism nonetheless shared a tendency toward a somber realization of life's randomness. The late Victorian writer Thomas Hardy (see page 1003) wrote many poems as "Satires of Circumstance." We could not, he believed, even flatter ourselves that gods cared about us enough to torment us; our life here was merely a cosmic joke of happenstance.

> *"How arrives it joy lies slain,*
> *And why unblooms the best hope*
> *   ever sown?"*
>
> —Thomas Hardy, "Hap"

Decadent Literature

As the nineteenth century drew to a close, a new mood arose in Victorian culture. Referred to as *decadence* (meaning "decline" or "decay"), this new cultural spirit was, like Naturalism, a reaction to the prevailing optimism of the Victorian age. Naturalist writers, however, had hoped that their literary works could influence people's opinions. By contrast, Decadent writers rejected the idea that works of art had to serve any useful purpose. Among the most notorious of the Decadents was Oscar Wilde, an Irish-born comic genius who enjoyed upending Victorian values—but always with a subversively serious intent. As Wilde wrote, "There is no such thing as a moral or an immoral book. Books are well written, or badly written. That is all." Partaking in the growing disillusionment at the end of the Victorian age, Decadent writers disdained and despised the consolations of religion and bourgeois life. They embraced life's futility through extremes of style, whether in dress, behavior, or their literary work.

The Doubt: "Can These Drying Bones Live?", c. 1855. Henry Alexander Bowler. Tate Gallery, London.

In the following poem, Thomas Hardy compares nature's dark forces to subalterns, a term for junior officers in the British army.

"The Subalterns" by Thomas Hardy

I

"Poor wanderer," said the leaden sky,
   "I fain would lighten thee,
But there be laws in force on high
   Which say it must not be."

II

—"I would not freeze thee, shorn one," cried
   The North, "knew I but how
To warm my breath, to slack my stride;
   But I am ruled as thou."

III

—"To-morrow I attack thee, wight,"
   Said Sickness. "Yet I swear
I bear thy little ark no spite,
   But am bid enter there."

IV

—"Come hither, Son," I heard Death say;
   "I did not will a grave
Should end thy pilgrimage to-day,
   But I, too, am a slave!"

V

We smiled upon each other then,
   And life to me wore less
Of that fell look it wore ere when
   They owned their passiveness.

Reading Check

Comparing and Contrasting How did Naturalism differ from Realism?

Wrap–Up

Why It Matters

The fundamental problems and questions that Victorians faced, and the solutions they attempted, are still with us. Most visible are the material changes; for example, the ways in which nineteenth-century cities were organized. Like us, the Victorians were consumers with an enormous appetite for innovations and material goods—often absurd and unnecessary.

The newly complicated nineteenth-century world made more evident the need for educated and involved citizens. Social reforms and increasing democratization are two important trends of the Victorian age. We still puzzle over how large a role government should have in helping the poor. Darwinism is still hotly debated today.

Above all, we have inherited from the Victorians an uneasy faith in ourselves. We share both their hopefulness about progress and their doubts about ever achieving it.

 Literature Online **Big Ideas** Link to Web resources to further explore the Big Ideas at www.glencoe.com.

Cultural Links

◆ The Victorian poet Gerard Manley Hopkins became an important influence on modern literature in English after an edition of his works was first published in 1918.

◆ Charlotte Brontë's *Jane Eyre* inspired Jean Rhys's novel *Wide Sargasso Sea*, which tells the story of Mr. Rochester's first wife. *Jack Maggs*, a novel by the contemporary Australian writer Peter Carey, retells Dickens's *Great Expectations*.

◆ Lewis Carroll has had a large influence on modern culture, including words he coined (such as *chortle*), and on literary works, such as the fiction of the Argentine writer Jorge Luis Borges.

You might try using this study organizer to take notes on the people, settings, and events you read about in this unit.

 **THREE-TAB BOOK**

Connect to Today ◆ Use what you have learned about the period to do one of these activities.

1. Speaking/Listening Select one of the important questions that the Victorians debated (for example: Is the purpose of art to be beautiful or useful? What is the responsibility of the government toward the underprivileged?). Hold a panel discussion in which you and your fellow students explore your own attitudes about this question.

2. Visual Literacy Beginning with Lewis Carroll's own drawings and the famous illustrations by the Victorian cartoonist John Tenniel, Carroll's *Alice* books have been very popular with artists. Create a visual display of different treatments of Carroll's books and discuss with other students the effects of differences in culture and medium.

OBJECTIVES
- Conduct a debate.
- Create a visual display.

Literature Online **Study Central** Visit www.glencoe.com and click on Study Central to review the Victorian age.

Part 1
Optimism and the Belief in Progress

Queen Victoria in Her Coronation Robes, 1887. Chromolithograph.
From a book celebrating the queen's Golden Jubilee.

"'*Tis only noble to be good.*
Kind hearts are more than coronets,
And simple faith than Norman blood."

—Alfred, Lord Tennyson, "Lady Clara Vere de Vere"

Tennyson's Poetry

MEET ALFRED, LORD TENNYSON

Not an average child, Alfred Tennyson produced a six-thousand-line epic poem by the age of twelve. He also wrote poems in the styles of Alexander Pope, Sir Walter Scott, and John Milton before his teen years. Throughout his life, Tennyson would turn to poetry whenever he felt troubled. As he said in one of his poems, "for the unquiet heart and brain / A use in measured language lies."

Tennyson had great need of such solace. His father, a clergyman, had a long history of mental instability. When Tennyson's grandfather considered the clergyman unfit to take over the family dynasty—thereby virtually disinheriting him—Tennyson's father turned to drugs and alcohol. He often took out his bitter disappointment on the family.

> *"I suffered what seemed to me to shatter all my life so that I desired to die rather than live."*
>
> —Alfred, Lord Tennyson

Early Struggles At age eighteen, Tennyson joined his older brother at Cambridge University. Although he was painfully shy, his poetry brought him to the attention of an elite group of students known as "The Apostles." Thriving on their affection and support, Tennyson gained confidence in his abilities. His closest friend was Arthur Henry Hallam, a brilliant and popular student who later became engaged to Tennyson's sister. While at Cambridge, Tennyson published *Poems, Chiefly Lyrical*, and he accompanied Hallam and other Apostles to Spain to support the unsuccessful revolt against Ferdinand VII.

In 1831 Tennyson left Cambridge to be with his father, whose health was failing. After his father's death, Tennyson decided to pursue a career in poetry rather than return to school. His early volumes of poetry drew mixed reviews, however, and Tennyson was hurt by some stinging criticism. Then, in 1833, he learned that Arthur Hallam had died suddenly of a stroke. Tennyson fell into a deep and long depression. Nearly a decade passed before he published any poetry. However, he wrote some of his most significant poems during this period, perfecting his craft during what he later called his "ten years' silence."

Literary Renown When he was thirty-two, Tennyson brought out a new book of poems. This time, almost all of the reviews were positive. Fame came in 1850 with the publication of *In Memoriam A. H. H.*, a long cycle of poems about his grief over the loss of Hallam. That same year, Queen Victoria appointed Tennyson to succeed William Wordsworth as poet laureate. Finally confident about his future, Tennyson married Emily Sellwood, his fiancée of fourteen years.

For the rest of his life, Tennyson enjoyed remarkable prestige. His books could be found in the home of nearly every English reader. To his contemporaries, Tennyson was the great consoling voice of their age.

Alfred, Lord Tennyson was born in 1809 and died in 1892.

Literature Online **Author Search** For more about Alfred, Lord Tennyson, go to www.glencoe.com.

Connecting to the Poems

Modern readers turn to Tennyson's poetry for its heart-breaking beauty and haunting sense of the transitory nature of life. Like all great artists, Tennyson pondered the meaning of life and death. As you read, think about how one copes with the tragic loss of a relative or friend.

Building Background

In Memoriam A. H. H. Within a few days of Arthur Hallam's death in 1833, Tennyson wrote an **elegy**, or poem of lament, about this loss. He continued writing elegies over the next seventeen years, eventually collecting them under the title *In Memoriam A. H. H.*

"Crossing the Bar" At eighty-one Tennyson wrote this poem, and just a few days before his death he asked that it be placed at the end of every edition of his work.

"Tears, Idle Tears" This lyric is from Tennyson's first long narrative poem, *The Princess*, which explores the role of women in society. Tennyson wrote "Tears, Idle Tears" at Tintern Abbey, the setting of Wordsworth's famous poem.

Setting Purposes for Reading

Big Idea Optimism and the Belief in Progress

As you read, consider to what extent these poems reflect the belief in optimism that characterized the Victorian age.

Literary Element Rhythm

Rhythm refers to the pattern of beats created by the arrangement of stressed and unstressed syllables in lines of verse. For example, in the following line from *In Memoriam A. H. H.*, the second, fourth, sixth, and eighth syllables are stressed:

> Ă hánd thăt cán bĕ cláspĕd nŏ móre—

As you read these poems, notice the rhythm and consider its effect.

- See Literary Terms Handbook, p. R15.

Reading Strategy Analyzing Mood

To **analyze mood**, identify the elements that work together to create the emotional quality of a literary work. These elements include diction, imagery, and figurative language as well as rhythm, rhyme, repetition, and other sound devices.

....

Reading Tip: Analyzing Mood As you read, use a diagram like the one below to help you identify the elements that create mood.

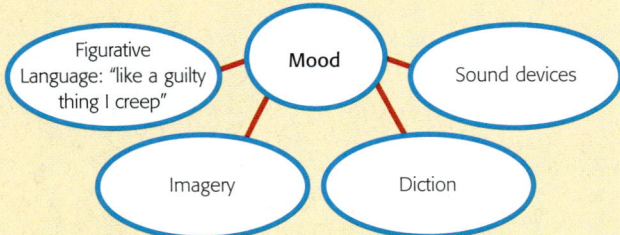

Vocabulary

license (lī′ səns) *n.* freedom used irresponsibly; p. 925 *Jen often took license with her sister's belongings, "borrowing" them without asking.*

sloth (slôth) *n.* inactivity; laziness; p. 925 *Active and energetic, she resented her husband's idleness and sloth.*

diffusive (di fū′ siv) *adj.* spread out or widely scattered; p. 927 *A diffusive energy surged through the stadium as the players ran onto the field.*

feigned (fānd) *adj.* pretended; imagined; p. 929 *Is your interest in this offer genuine or feigned?*

....

Vocabulary Tip: Analogies Analogies are comparisons based on relationships between words and ideas.

Literature Online **Interactive Literary Elements Handbook** To review or learn more about the literary elements, go to www.glencoe.com.

OBJECTIVES

In studying these selections, you will focus on the following:
- analyzing literary periods
- understanding rhythm
- analyzing mood

London Twilight from the Adelphi. Christopher Richard Wynne Nevinson (1889–1946). Oil on canvas, 44.5 x 59 cm.

from *In Memoriam A. H. H.*

Alfred, Lord Tennyson

7

Dark house, by which once more I stand
  Here in the long unlovely street,°
  Doors, where my heart was used to beat
So quickly, waiting for a hand,

5 A hand that can be clasped no more—
  Behold me, for I cannot sleep,
  And like a guilty thing I creep
At earliest morning to the door.

2 long unlovely street: Wimpole Street in London, where Arthur Henry Hallam lived after he left Cambridge

He is not here; but far away
10   The noise of life begins again,
And ghastly through the drizzling rain
On the bald street breaks the blank day.

27

I envy not in any moods
The captive void of noble rage,
The linnet° born within the cage,
That never knew the summer woods;

3 **linnet:** a small bird

5   I envy not the beast that takes
His **license** in the field of time,
Unfettered by the sense of crime,
To whom a conscience never wakes;

Nor, what may count itself as blest,
10   The heart that never plighted troth°
But stagnates in the weeds of **sloth;**
Nor any want-begotten rest.°

10 **plighted troth:** "pledged loyalty" or "became engaged to marry"

12 **want-begotten rest:** leisure that comes from a lack of commitment (as opposed to a rest that is earned through struggle)

I hold it true, whate'er befall;
I feel it, when I sorrow most;
15   'Tis better to have loved and lost
Than never to have loved at all.

54

O, yet we trust that somehow good
Will be the final goal of ill,
To pangs of nature, sins of will,
Defects of doubt, and taints of blood;°

3–4 These two lines specify four types of ills: *pangs of nature* (physical pain), *sins of will* (moral transgressions), *defects of doubt* (spiritual shortcomings), and *taints of blood* (inherited flaws).

5   That nothing walks with aimless feet;
That not one life shall be destroyed,
Or cast as rubbish to the void,
When God hath made the pile complete;

Reading Strategy   Analyzing Mood *What feelings does the setting evoke in the speaker?*

Reading Strategy   Analyzing Mood *Why does the poet include this image?*

Big Idea   Optimism and the Belief in Progress *What Victorian belief do these lines reflect?*

Vocabulary

license (lī′ səns) *n.* freedom used irresponsibly
sloth (slôth) *n.* inactivity; laziness

That not a worm is cloven° in vain;
10   That not a moth with vain desire
      Is shriveled in a fruitless fire,
Or but subserves° another's gain.

Behold, we know not anything;
      I can but trust that good shall fall
15   At last—far off—at last, to all,
And every winter change to spring.

So runs my dream; but what am I?
      An infant crying in the night;
      An infant crying for the light,
20   And with no language but a cry.

9 **cloven:** split

12 **subserves:** "promotes" or "assists"

106

Ring out, wild bells, to the wild sky,
      The flying cloud, the frosty light:
      The year is dying in the night;
Ring out, wild bells, and let him die.

5   Ring out the old, ring in the new,
      Ring, happy bells, across the snow:
      The year is going, let him go;
Ring out the false, ring in the true.

Ring out the grief that saps the mind,
10   For those that here we see no more;
      Ring out the feud of rich and poor,
Ring in redress to all mankind.

Ring out a slowly dying cause,
      And ancient forms of party strife;°
15   Ring in the nobler modes of life,
With sweeter manners, purer laws.

14 **party strife:** antagonism or a dispute between sides or factions

Ring out the want, the care, the sin,
      The faithless coldness of the times;
      Ring out, ring out my mournful rhymes,
20   But ring the fuller minstrel in.

Reading Strategy   **Analyzing Mood** *How does the mood of this section change in the final stanza?*

Literary Element   **Rhythm** *What effect does the rhythm of this passage create?*

Ring out false pride in place and blood,
    The civic slander and the spite;
    Ring in the love of truth and right,
Ring in the common love of good.

25 Ring out old shapes of foul disease;
    Ring out the narrowing lust of gold;
    Ring out the thousand wars of old,
Ring in the thousand years of peace.

Ring in the valiant man and free,
30   The larger heart, the kindlier hand;
    Ring out the darkness of the land,
Ring in the Christ that is to be.

                    130
Thy voice is on the rolling air
    I hear thee where the waters run;
    Thou standest in the rising sun,
And in the setting thou art fair.

5   What art thou then? I cannot guess;
    But though I seem in star and flower
    To feel thee some **diffusive** power,
I do not therefore love thee less.

My love involves the love before;
10   My love is vaster passion now;
    Tho' mix'd with God and Nature thou,
I seem to love thee more and more.

Far off thou art, but ever nigh;°
    I have thee still, and I rejoice;
15   I prosper, circled with thy voice;
I shall not lose thee tho' I die.

13 **nigh:** near

Big Idea   Optimism and the Belief in Progress *What positive changes does
the speaker hope for in the new year?*

Reading Strategy   Analyzing Mood *What feelings does the speaker convey in
these lines?*

Vocabulary

diffusive (di fū′ siv) *adj.* spread out or widely scattered

Hove Beach with Fishing Boats, c.1824. John Constable. Oil on paper laid on canvas. Victoria and Albert Museum, London.

Crossing the Bar   Alfred, Lord Tennyson

Sunset and evening star,
    And one clear call for me!
And may there be no moaning of the bar,[1]
    When I put out to sea,

5   But such a tide as moving seems asleep,
    Too full for sound and foam,
When that which drew from out the boundless deep
    Turns again home.

Twilight and evening bell,
10   And after that the dark!
And may there be no sadness of farewell,
    When I embark;

For though from out our bourne[2] of Time and Place
    The flood[3] may bear me far,
15   I hope to see my Pilot face to face
    When I have crossed the bar.

1. A *bar,* or sandbar, is a ridge of sand formed by the action of tides or currents.

2. *Bourne* means "boundary."
3. *Flood* means "rising tide."

Literary Element **Rhythm** *How does the rhythm reinforce the meaning of these lines?*

Tears, Idle Tears

from *The Princess*

Alfred, Lord Tennyson

Recalling the Past, 1888. Carlton Alfred Smith. Watercolor on paper. The Stapleton Collection.

Tears, idle[1] tears, I know not what they mean,
Tears from the depth of some divine despair
Rise in the heart, and gather to the eyes,
In looking on the happy autumn fields,
5   And thinking of the days that are no more.

Fresh as the first beam glittering on a sail,
That brings our friends up from the underworld,
Sad as the last which reddens over one
That sinks with all we love below the verge;[2]
10   So sad, so fresh, the days that are no more.

Ah, sad and strange as in dark summer dawns
The earliest pipe of half-awakened birds
To dying ears, when unto dying eyes
The casement[3] slowly grows a glimmering square;
15   So sad, so strange, the days that are no more.

Dear as remembered kisses after death,
And sweet as those by hopeless fancy **feigned**
On lips that are for others; deep as love,
Deep as first love, and wild with all regret;
20   O Death in Life, the days that are no more.

1. Here, *idle* means "having no basis or reason."

2. *Verge* refers to the horizon.

3. A *casement* is a window that opens outward.

Reading Strategy   Analyzing Mood   *How does the phrase "autumn fields" convey a feeling of loss?*

Reading Strategy   Analyzing Mood   *What feelings does Tennyson convey by describing the past as "Death in Life"?*

Vocabulary

feigned   (fānd)   *adj.* pretended; imagined

RESPONDING AND THINKING CRITICALLY

Respond

1. Which lines from these poems did you find the most memorable? Why?

Recall and Interpret

2. (a)In section 27 of *In Memoriam*, to what does the speaker compare those people who have never loved anyone? (b)What do these **metaphors** lead the speaker to conclude about lost love?

3. (a)In "Crossing the Bar," what is compared to a sea voyage? (b)What phrases and **images** suggest this comparison?

4. (a)In lines 16–19 of "Tears, Idle Tears," to what does the speaker compare "the days that are no more"? (b)How do these **similes** illustrate line 20?

Analyze and Evaluate

5. How would you describe the **tone** of "Crossing the Bar"? What words and phrases create this tone?

6. Sum up the speaker's attitude toward the past in "Tears, Idle Tears." Compare that attitude to the one expressed by the speaker of *In Memoriam*.

7. How does the title of "Tears, Idle Tears" relate to its **theme**, or main idea?

Connect

8. **Big Idea** **Optimism and the Belief in Progress** Tennyson's contemporaries found *In Memoriam* very inspirational. Explain how the speaker of this poem evolves through stages of grief, progressing to more positive emotions. Cite specific lines from the poem to support your response.

LITERARY ANALYSIS

Literary Element Rhythm

Meter is a type of **rhythm** in which the alteration between stressed and unstressed syllables is predictable and regular.

1. What is the metrical pattern of *In Memoriam*?

2. What is the effect of using regular rhythms in poems that concern grief and loss?

Writing About Literature

Evaluate Author's Craft In poetry, **author's craft** refers to how a poet uses elements such as word choice, imagery, rhythm, and rhyme to create certain effects. In a short essay, identify examples of repetition in *In Memoriam* and "Tears, Idle Tears." Which ideas does the poet emphasize through repetition?

Literature **Online** **Web Activities** For eFlashcards, Selection Quick Checks, and other Web activities, go to www.glencoe.com.

READING AND VOCABULARY

Reading Strategy Analyzing Mood

Refer to the diagram you created on page 923, and then answer the following questions.

1. How would you describe the mood of "Crossing the Bar"?

2. What details in the speaker's surroundings help create the mood?

Vocabulary Practice

Practice with Analogies Choose the word that best completes each analogy.

1. generous : miserly :: feigned :
   a. charitable   **b.** real
2. irritation : annoyance :: sloth :
   a. laziness   **b.** frenzy
3. fear : fright :: license :
   a. liberty   **b.** faith
4. wild : tame :: diffusive :
   a. scattered   **b.** contained

Connecting to the Poem

Which of your achievements do you love to relive in memory? In Tennyson's poem, the speaker remembers his glorious adventures and longs to resume his voyages. As you read, think about whether it is important to experience as much of life as possible.

Building Background

Like *In Memoriam*, "Ulysses" was inspired by Arthur Hallam's death. Tennyson said that the poem expresses "the feeling about the need of going forward and braving the struggle of life." Ulysses is the Roman name for the Greek hero Odysseus, whose exploits are portrayed in Homer's epic poems, the *Iliad* and the *Odyssey*. Odysseus, the king of Ithaca, spent ten years fighting in the Trojan War. After the fall of Troy, Odysseus wandered for ten more years throughout the Mediterranean world, encountering mythical creatures and facing great perils. At last, he returned to Ithaca to reestablish himself as king and was reunited with his faithful wife, Penelope, and his son, Telemachus (tə le′ mə kəs). In "Ulysses," Tennyson carries the story of Odysseus further, presenting the thoughts of the old king who longs for one last adventure.

Setting Purposes for Reading

Big Idea Optimism and the Belief in Progress

As you read, consider the Victorian values that Ulysses and his son might reflect.

Literary Element Assonance and Consonance

Assonance is the repetition of similar vowel sounds within non-rhyming words, as in this line from *In Memoriam*: "His license in the field of time." **Consonance** is the repetition of consonant sounds within or at the ends of non-rhyming words, as in this line from "Crossing the Bar": "The flood may bear me far." As you read, notice other examples of these sound devices.

• See Literary Terms Handbook, pp. R2 and R4.

Reading Strategy Analyzing Tone

When you **analyze tone**, you think critically about how the writer's attitude toward a subject is conveyed through such elements as diction, sentence structure, imagery, and figures of speech. As you read, pause from time to time to consider the poet's attitude toward Ulysses.

Reading Tip: Determining Tone Use a web like the one below to help you identify the elements that convey tone.

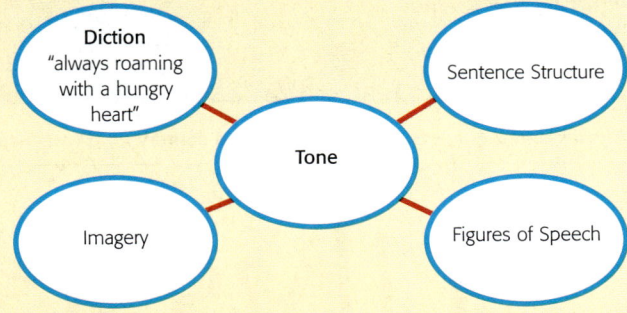

Diction "always roaming with a hungry heart" — Tone — Sentence Structure — Imagery — Figures of Speech

Vocabulary

prudence (prōōd′ əns) *n.* sound judgment; careful management; p. 933 *Please use prudence in deciding how to invest the money.*

abide (ə bīd′) *v.* remain; p. 934 *Though his power and wealth were lost, his family and friends abided.*

Vocabulary Tip: Context Clues To figure out the meaning of an unfamiliar word, look for clues in the surrounding words or sentences.

Literature⬤nline Interactive Literary Elements Handbook To review or learn more about the literary elements, go to www.glencoe.com.

OBJECTIVES
In studying this selection, you will focus on the following:
• analyzing literary periods

• identifying assonance, consonance, and alliteration
• analyzing tone

Ulysses and the Sirens. Roman mosaic, 3rd century A.D. Musee National du Bardo, Tunis, Tunisia.

Ulysses

Alfred, Lord Tennyson

It little profits that an idle king,
By this still hearth, among these barren crags,°
Matched with an agèd wife, I mete and dole
Unequal laws° unto a savage race,
5   That hoard and sleep and feed, and know not me.

    I cannot rest from travel; I will drink
Life to the lees.° All times I have enjoyed
Greatly, have suffered greatly, both with those
That loved me, and alone; on shore, and when
10   Through scudding° drifts the rainy Hyades°
Vexed the dim sea. I am become a name;
For always roaming with a hungry heart
Much have I seen and known—cities of men
And manners, climates, councils, governments,
15   Myself not least, but honored of them all—

2 **barren crags:** here, the rugged landscape of Ithaca, the Greek island where Ulysses lives
4 **Unequal laws:** rewards and punishments

7 **lees:** sediment found at the bottom of wine and other liquids. To "drink to the lees" is to drink to the last drop.

10 **scudding:** wind-driven. **Hyades** (hī′ə dēz′): a cluster of stars. When they rose, it was believed that rain would soon follow.

Literary Element   **Assonance and Consonance** *Which words contain the short i sound? Which words contain the g sound?*

And drunk delight of battle with my peers,
Far on the ringing plains of windy Troy.°
I am a part of all that I have met;
Yet all experience is an arch wherethrough
20 Gleams that untraveled world, whose margin fades
Forever and forever when I move.
How dull it is to pause, to make an end,
To rust unburnished, not to shine in use!
As though to breathe were life! Life piled on life
25 Were all too little, and of one to me
Little remains; but every hour is saved
From that eternal silence, something more,
A bringer of new things; and vile it were
For some three suns to store and hoard myself,
30 And this gray spirit yearning in desire
To follow knowledge like a sinking star,
Beyond the utmost bound of human thought.

    This is my son, mine own Telemachus,
To whom I leave the scepter and the isle—
35 Well-loved of me, discerning to fulfill
This labor, by slow **prudence** to make mild
A rugged people, and through soft degrees
Subdue them to the useful and the good.
Most blameless is he, centered in the sphere
40 Of common duties, decent not to fail
In offices of tenderness, and pay
Meet° adoration to my household gods,
When I am gone. He works his work, I mine.

    There lies the port; the vessel puffs her sail;
45 There gloom the dark broad seas. My mariners,
Souls that have toiled and wrought and thought with me—
That ever with a frolic welcome took
The thunder and the sunshine, and opposed
Free hearts, free foreheads—you and I are old;
50 Old age hath yet his honor and his toil;
Death closes all; but something ere the end,
Some work of noble note, may yet be done,
Not unbecoming men that strove with Gods.
The lights begin to twinkle from the rocks;
55 The long day wanes; the slow moon climbs; the deep

16–17 battle . . . Troy: the Trojan War, which the Greeks won after a ten-year siege

Print of the ship of Ulysses.

42 Meet: fitting; proper

Moans round with many voices. Come, my friends,
'Tis not too late to seek a newer world.
Push off, and sitting well in order smite
The sounding furrows;° for my purpose holds
60 To sail beyond the sunset, and the baths
Of all the western stars,° until I die.
It may be that the gulfs will wash us down;
It may be we shall touch the Happy Isles,°
And see the great Achilles,° whom we knew.
65 Though much is taken, much **abides**; and though
We are not now that strength which in old days
Moved earth and heaven, that which we are, we are—
One equal temper of heroic hearts,
Made weak by time and fate, but strong in will
70 To strive, to seek, to find, and not to yield.

59 sounding furrows: crashing waves.

60–61 baths . . . stars: reference to
the ancient belief that the stars descended
into a sea or river that encircled Earth.
63 Happy Isles: in Greek mythology,
the place where mortals favored by the
gods are sent to dwell after they die.
64 Achilles (ə kiʹ lēz): the greatest
warrior in the Greek assault on Troy.

Reading Strategy **Analyzing Tone** *Which words and phrases in these lines
convey a tone of admiration?*

Big Idea **Optimism and the Belief in Progress** *What values does this line
affirm?*

Vocabulary

abide (ə bīdʹ) *v.* remain

RESPONDING AND THINKING CRITICALLY

Respond

1. What questions would you ask Ulysses if he were alive today?

Recall and Interpret

2. (a)How does Ulysses spend his time at home? (b)How does he feel about his life at home? Use evidence from the poem to support your answer.

3. (a)What does Ulysses miss from his past? (b)Sum up Ulysses' thoughts and feelings about aging. Support your answer with evidence from the poem.

4. (a)What does Ulysses want his band of followers to do with him? (b)Why might Tennyson have chosen to wait until late in the poem before revealing whom Ulysses is addressing in his monologue?

Analyze and Evaluate

5. How do you interpret lines 18–21 of the poem?

6. (a)How does Ulysses regard his son's approach to life? (b)Which character would you rather have as a ruler—Ulysses or Telemachus? Why?

7. (a)What arguments does Ulysses present to persuade his listeners to join him? (b)Do you find his arguments persuasive? Explain why or why not.

Connect

8. **Big Idea** Optimism and the Belief in Progress Which Victorian values does Ulysses embody? Which values does his son reflect?

VISUAL LITERACY: Fine Art

Odysseus in Art and Literature

Tennyson was not the first artist to be fascinated by Odysseus—nor would he be the last. This fearless, wily hero has inspired countless works of art throughout the ages, ranging from the ancient Greek red-figure vase shown at the right (ca. 500 B.C.) to James Joyce's modern novel *Ulysses* (1922) and Romare Bearden's contemporary collage *The Return of Odysseus* (1977).

The vase depicts a scene from Homer's *Odyssey*. The sirens were enchantresses who lived on an island. They lured passing sailors to destruction with irresistibly beautiful songs. To resist this fate, Odysseus had his crew plug their ears with wax and tie him to the mast. He listened in anguish as his boat passed the sirens' island.

Group Activity Discuss the following questions with your classmates.

1. What do the artist's Odysseus and Tennyson's Ulysses have in common?

2. Why do you think Odysseus has inspired countless artists over time?

Attic red-figured stamnos of Siren, 5th century B.C. British Museum, London.

Literary Element Assonance and Consonance

Tennyson is often praised for the musical patterns of his poetry. To help create these patterns, he sometimes uses **assonance** and **consonance**. For example, in line 5 of "Ulysses," he uses assonance, repeating long e sounds: "That hoard and sleep and feed, and know not me"; in line 17, he uses consonance, repeating the n and r sounds: "Far on the ringing plains of windy Troy."

1. Find other examples of assonance and consonance in "Ulysses."

2. How does Tennyson's use of assonance and consonance contribute to the overall effect of the poem?

Review: Alliteration

As you learned on page 800, **alliteration** is the repetition of consonant sounds at the beginnings of words, as in the line "On the bald street breaks the blank day." Like assonance and consonance, alliteration is used to create rhythmic or musical effects.

Partner Activity Meet with a classmate to identify examples of alliteration in "Ulysses." Use a two-column chart like the one below to record your examples and describe their effects.

Example	Effect
lines 6-7 "I will drink / Life to the lees."	Creates rhythm; emphasizes the idea that Ulysses enjoys life to the fullest.

Reading Strategy Analyzing Tone

A writer's **tone** may convey a variety of attitudes such as sympathy, irony, admiration, sadness, or bitterness. To **analyze the tone** of "Ulysses," focus on elements such as diction, imagery, and figurative language. In the following lines, for example, the image of fading light gives the speaker's words a sad, urgent tone:

> The lights begin to twinkle from the rocks;
> The long day wanes;

Review the web you completed on page 931, and then answer the following questions.

1. How would you describe the overall tone of this poem?

2. What details in the poem contribute to this tone?

Vocabulary Practice

Practice with Context Clues For each sentence below, identify the context clue that most suggests the meaning of the underlined vocabulary word.

1. The true hero acts not with rashness, but with prudence.

a. true   b. hero   c. rashness

2. Even though heroes die, their messages abide, never fading away.

a. die   b. never fading   c. away

Academic Vocabulary

Here are two words from the vocabulary list on page R82.

incline (in klīn´) v. have a particular tendency or bent of mind

conceive (kən sēv´) v. to hold as one's opinion

Practice and Apply
1. In your opinion, does Tennyson **incline** toward joyful or sorrowful subjects? Explain.
2. How does Tennyson's Ulysses **conceive** of old age?

Writing About Literature

Respond to Theme In his poems, Tennyson often expresses ideas about life in thematic statements, such as "'Tis better to have loved and lost / Than never to have loved at all" and "I will drink / Life to the lees." Find another such statement in one of the Tennyson poems you have read and write a journal entry explaining whether you agree with it. Discuss how the idea relates to your own experience or that of someone you know. Before you begin writing, organize your thoughts in a graphic organizer like the one below.

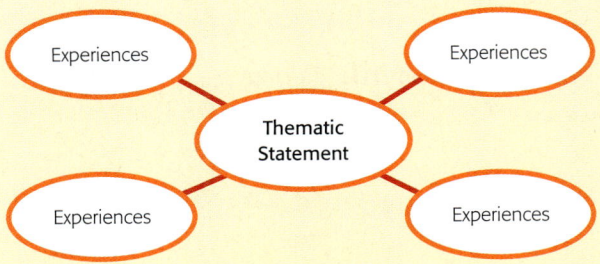

Literature Groups

"Ulysses" takes the form of a **dramatic monologue**—a dramatic poem in which the speaker describes a crucial moment in his or her life to a silent listener. In the process, the speaker reveals much about his or her own character. With a small group, discuss the character of Ulysses as Tennyson portrays him. Consider his attitude toward his family and the people of Ithaca, the value he places on his past experiences, his dreams for the future, his description of Telemachus, and his efforts to inspire his crew. Focus on the following questions, using evidence from the poem to support your interpretations:

- Is Ulysses irresponsible for wanting to leave his wife, son, and homeland to go on one last voyage, or is he just being true to his nature as a hero?

- Is his plan in the best interest of his people?

- How do you think his family will react?

Create a group statement of opinion and explain your ideas to the rest of your class.

Tennyson's Language and Style

Using Capitalization in Poetry You probably have mastered many of the rules of capitalization for formal writing. For example, you know that you capitalize the first word of a sentence, the pronoun *I*, and proper nouns and adjectives. These rules of capitalization also apply to poetry. In addition, in traditional poems, the first word of each line is capitalized.

To some degree, capitalization reflects the conventions of the time. During the Victorian age, poets and prose writers sometimes capitalized common nouns for emphasis or to indicate personification. For example, in the following passages from "Locksley Hall," Tennyson capitalizes the common nouns *time, life, nature, honor,* and *vision*:

"Love took up the glass of Time,"
"Love took up the harp of Life,"
"Nay, but Nature brings thee solace;"
"the hurt that Honor feels,"
"Saw the Vision of the world,"

Activity Create a chart listing examples of capitalized words in the poems by Tennyson you have just read. Consider the following categories:

- Proper nouns

- The first word of a line

- Personified or emphasized nouns

Revising Check

Capitalization Proper capitalization is important to consider when revising your own writing. With a partner, go through the journal entry you wrote about a thematic statement in Tennyson's poems. Look for words that should be capitalized and revise your entry to correct these errors. Then, imagine that you were writing during the Victorian age. Circle nouns that you might have capitalized for emphasis.

Literature Online Web Activities For eFlashcards, Selection Quick Checks, and other Web activities, go to **www.glencoe.com**.

Comparing Literature Across Time and Place

Connecting to the Reading Selections

The line between love and heartache is thin, delicate, and often defies logic. The following poems by Elizabeth Barrett Browning and Edna St. Vincent Millay, letter by Simone de Beauvoir, and song by John Lennon and Paul McCartney investigate the necessity of love and its power to change lives.

England, 1850

Elizabeth Barrett Browning
Sonnet 43.. sonnet **939**
A love for all time

United States, 1931

Edna St. Vincent Millay
Love Is Not All: It Is Not Meat nor Drink.... poem **943**
Love—a necessity or an indulgence?

France, 1947

Simone de Beauvoir
Simone de Beauvoir to Nelson Algren................. letter **944**
The frenetic fervor of a new relationship

England, 1965

John Lennon and Paul McCartney
In My Life.. song **946**
Love in the past and in the present

COMPARING THE Big Idea Optimism and the Belief in Progress

Barrett Browning's poem describes an idealized love and reflects an optimism unburdened by certain realities of her life and times. The four selections here express idealistic views of the adventure and power of romance, while also presenting realistic hurdles between lovers.

COMPARING Theme of Passionate Love

The themes of love and desire have produced some of history's most memorable literature. The selections you are about to read explore the presence and absence of love in one's life.

COMPARING Historical Contexts

The manner in which love is expressed in a poem, a song, or a letter can depend upon historical context. For example, at one point it was fashionable to write religious love poems. This is not the case today.

Sonnet 43

MEET ELIZABETH BARRETT BROWNING

The eldest child of a wealthy country squire, Elizabeth Barrett Browning spent her childhood playing in the countryside and reading. In fact, by the age of ten, Elizabeth Barrett Browning had read a stunning array of literature, from the histories of classical Greece and Rome to Shakespeare's plays. Reflecting on her youth, Browning said, "Books and dreams were what I lived in and domestic life only seemed to buzz gently around, like bees about the grass."

Hope End Barrett grew up on a lush, opulent country estate called "Hope End." Her father derived his wealth from sugar plantations in Jamaica. The business turned sour, however, while Barrett was still a youth and the family adopted a more modest lifestyle. When she was fifteen, Barrett suffered a spinal injury, which, along with a chronic problem with her lungs, left her bedridden for much of her life. Despite her poor health, Barrett became one of the most successful and versatile poets in Victorian England. Her work was characterized by enthusiasm, directness, and a warmly felt sense of social responsibility. Still, Barrett's family life was difficult, and she struggled to cope with the tragic drowning in 1840 of her favorite brother, Edward. Additionally, her contact with the outside world was restricted by her over-protective father, who forbade any of his eleven children to marry. By the age of thirty-five, Barrett was confined to her bedroom in the family's London home because of both her health and her father's wishes.

> *"I tell you hopeless grief is passionless."*
>
> —Elizabeth Barrett Browning

A Great Love Story Despite her confinement, Barrett became well known for her published verses. When her poems came to the attention of the fledgling poet Robert Browning, he immediately wrote her a telegram declaring, "I love your verses with all my heart, dear Miss Barrett. I do, as I say, love these books with all my heart—and I love you too." In contrast to Barrett's bedridden existence, Browning led an active social life. Six years her junior, Browning was determined and brash. He boldly began to visit Barrett despite her father's disapproval. The two eloped in 1846, moved quickly to Italy, and settled at Casa Guidi, an old stone house in Florence. In Italy, the couple had a child they nicknamed "Pen," and Barrett Browning became an avid player in politics, supporting the *risorgimento* movement that sought to unify the country. In 1850 Barrett Browning published *Sonnets from the Portuguese*, perhaps her most famous collection.

While her love poems still thrill readers, Browning, like other Victorian writers, also wrote literature intended to spark social reform. Her 1857 book-length poem *Aurora Leigh* was groundbreaking. The work critiques the treatment of women in Victorian society by telling the story of an independent, artistic heroine. Of the poem, Virginia Woolf wrote, "Aurora Leigh, with her passionate interest in social questions, her conflict as artist and woman, her longing for knowledge and freedom, is the true daughter of her age."

Elizabeth Barrett Browning was born in 1806 and died in 1861.

Literature Online **Author Search** For more about Elizabeth Barrett Browning, go to www.glencoe.com.

LITERATURE PREVIEW

READING PREVIEW

Connecting to the Sonnet

In the following sonnet, Barrett Browning explores the way she experiences love. As you read the poem, think about the following questions:

- How would you define love? Is love the same as romance?
- Is love a luxury, or a basic human need, like air and water?

Building Background

Elizabeth Barrett Browning wrote forty-four sonnets describing the fear, excitement, and hope she felt when, after years of ill health that left her bedridden, she fell in love. Barrett Browning waited until three years after her marriage to slip the sonnets into her husband's coat pocket. Robert Browning, her husband, was so impressed with the sonnets that he insisted she publish them. Not wanting to share her private feelings with the public, she published the cycle of sonnets under the misleading title *Sonnets from the Portuguese*, hoping people would think the poems were translations rather than expressions of her own emotions.

Setting Purposes for Reading

Big Idea Optimism and the Belief in Progress

As you read, notice how Barrett Browning's poem reflects the optimism and belief in progress of her day. Also, consider how the sonnet relates to the themes addressed by other Victorian writers, including marriage.

Literary Element Repetition

Repetition is the recurrence of sounds, words, phrases, lines, or stanzas in a poem. This literary device builds a sense of unity in a work and calls attention to particular ideas.

- See Literary Terms Handbook, p. R15.

Reading Strategy Analyzing Style

To **analyze style** means to break down the expressive qualities of a work in order to help reveal the author's attitude and purpose in writing. Word choice, figurative language, and imagery are key elements that help create style. In addition, identifying genre, poetic form, and subject matter can help you to understand certain stylistic choices. For instance, you may expect something different from a sonnet than from a haiku. Also, context matters—you might interpret a religious metaphor in a love poem differently from the same metaphor in a poem about war.

Reading Tip: Connecting Style and Theme As you read, identify the stylistic elements the poet employs. Ask yourself how these elements reflect the poem's theme. Keep track of these elements in a graphic organizer like the one below.

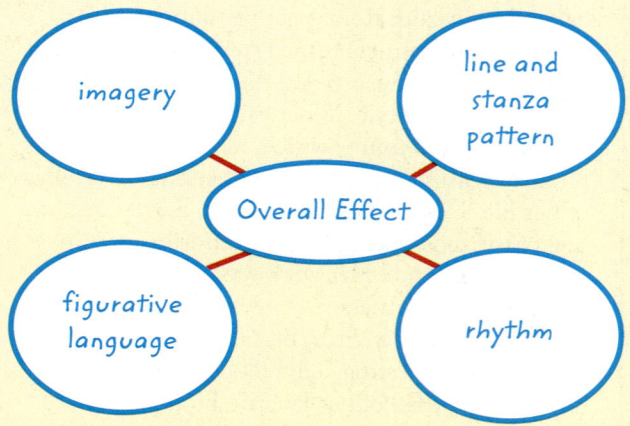

Literature Online **Interactive Literary Elements Handbook** To review or learn more about the literary elements, go to www.glencoe.com.

OBJECTIVES
In studying this selection, you will focus on the following:
- analyzing literary genres

- analyzing repetition
- analyzing style

Sonnet 43

Elizabeth Barrett Browning

The Painter's Honeymoon, c.1863–4. Lord Frederic Leighton. Oil on canvas, 83.8 x 77.5 cm. Museum of Fine Art, Boston.

How do I love thee? Let me count the ways.
I love thee to the depth and breadth and height
My soul can reach, when feeling out of sight
For the ends of Being and ideal Grace.
5 I love thee to the level of every day's
Most quiet need, by sun and candlelight.
I love thee freely, as men strive for Right;
I love thee purely, as they turn from Praise.
I love thee with the passion put to use
10 In my old griefs, and with my childhood's faith.
I love thee with a love I seemed to lose
With my lost saints—I love thee with the breath,
Smiles, tears, of all my life!—and, if God choose,
I shall but love thee better after death.

Reading Strategy   Analyzing Style   *What do these images of the sun and candlelight suggest about the speaker's feelings?*

RESPONDING AND THINKING CRITICALLY

Respond

1. The speaker of "Sonnet 43" expresses her love in a variety of "ways." Which of these "ways" do you find most compelling? Explain.

Recall and Interpret

2. (a)Paraphrase how the speaker describes her love in lines 1–8. (b)What do these lines reveal about the nature of the speaker's love?

3. (a)How does the speaker describe her love in lines 9–12? (b)What can you infer about the speaker's past from these lines?

4. (a)How long does the speaker expect her love to last? (b)What line or lines in the poem support your interpretation?

Analyze and Evaluate

5. (a)How would you describe the speaker's **tone,** or attitude toward the subject? (b)What does the speaker's tone seem to suggest about her character and personality?

6. Evaluate the advantages and disadvantages of a love as strong as the speaker's in the poem.

Connect

7. Do you think this poem is too personal or that the language and imagery is too outdated to be of interest to modern-day readers? Explain.

8. **Big Idea** **Optimism and the Belief in Progress** How does this poem reflect an optimistic outlook and a belief in progress? Explain.

LITERARY ANALYSIS

Literary Element Repetition

Repetition in a literary work often helps to highlight important concepts.

1. (a)Identify repeated words and phrases as well as syntactical repetition in Barrett Browning's poem. (b)What is the effect of this repetition?

2. How does this repetition relate to the professed purpose of the poem?

Writing About Literature

Apply Form Try your hand at writing your own love sonnet. Begin with Barrett Browning's first line, and then write thirteen lines describing something that you love. The poem you create can be serious or humorous. Use figurative language and end the sonnet with a conclusion. To review the sonnet form, see pages 252–253.

Literature Online **Web Activities** For eFlashcards, Selection Quick Checks, and other Web activities, go to www.glencoe.com.

READING AND VOCABULARY

Reading Strategy Analyzing Style

The style of a work can be a window into the writer's purpose. Review the web you created to analyze the stylistic features of the sonnet.

1. What distinguishes the style of this sonnet? Cite examples from the text.

2. How does the use of concrete imagery and abstract concepts contribute to the poem's message?

Academic Vocabulary

Here are two words from the vocabulary list on page R82.

straightforward (strāt′ fôr′ wərd) *adj.* a clear, honest report; basic

compile (kəm pīl′) *v.* to pull together comments from a variety of sources

Practice and Apply

1. Are the emotions in this poem presented in a **straightforward** manner? Explain.

2. How does the poem **compile** Barrett Browning's feelings for Robert Browning?

BEFORE YOU READ

Building Background

To a generation of Americans who came of age during the Roaring Twenties, the poet Edna St. Vincent Millay was a symbol of the modern woman: young, independent, free-spirited, energetic, and beautiful. In fact, the line "My candle burns at both ends" from one of Millay's poems became a motto for the age.

After graduating from college, she moved to Greenwich Village, a section of New York City renowned for its artists, intellectuals, and eccentric atmosphere. There she worked as an actress, fell in and out of love, and wrote. In 1921 she traveled to Europe and spent two years as a correspondent for *Vanity Fair* magazine. Upon returning to New York, she met and fell in love with Eugen Boissevain, a businessman whom she married several months later. In 1923, when she was thirty-one, she won the Pulitzer Prize for Poetry.

Literature Online **Author Search** For more about Edna St. Vincent Millay, go to www.glencoe.com.

Love Is Not All: It Is Not Meat nor Drink

Edna St. Vincent Millay

Love is not all: it is not meat nor drink
Nor slumber nor a roof against the rain;
Nor yet a floating spar to men that sink
And rise and sink and rise and sink again;
5   Love can not fill the thickened lung with breath,
Nor clean the blood, nor set the fractured bone;
Yet many a man is making friends with death
Even as I speak, for lack of love alone.
It well may be that in a difficult hour,
10   Pinned down by pain and moaning for release,
Or nagged by want past resolution's power,
I might be driven to sell your love for peace,
Or trade the memory of this night for food.
It well may be. I do not think I would.

Discussion Starter

Millay's poem explores both the power and the inability of love to sustain an individual. The speaker in the poem expresses both emotional and rational responses to love. Which type of response to love does the speaker most value? Discuss this question with a group of classmates and cite examples from the poem to support your views.

BEFORE YOU READ

Building Background

French existentialist Simone de Beauvoir is best known for her 1949 feminist classic *The Second Sex* and her lifelong friendship with philosopher and Nobel Prize–winning author Jean-Paul Sartre. Beauvoir also wrote many successful works of fiction, which explored existentialist themes of alienation and the individual's relationship with the world. In 1947 Beauvoir began an unlikely and passionate relationship with Nelson Algren, the gritty Chicago writer. Their seventeen-year romance is well-documented by the letters they sent to each other across the Atlantic Ocean.

As World War II drew to a close, Beauvoir traveled to the United States to lecture at college campuses. On this trip, she met Algren who introduced Beauvoir to the pervasive poverty, the distressed working class, and the bohemian Wicker Park neighborhood of Chicago. The day Beauvoir returned to Paris after her trip, she wrote the following letter. The two later traveled and lived together. In the end, they went their separate ways. Of her relationship with Algren, Beauvoir wrote, "To explore an unfamiliar country is work, but to possess it through the love of an appealing foreigner is a miracle."

Literature Online **Author Search** For more about Simone de Beauvoir, go to www.glencoe.com.

Simone de Beauvoir to Nelson Algren

Sunday, 18 Mai 1947

My Precious beloved Chicago man,[1]

I think of you in Paris, in Paris I miss you. The whole journey was marvelous. We had nearly no night since we went to the East. At Newfoundland the sun began to set, but five hours later it was rising in Shannon, above a sweet green Irish landscape. Everything was so beautiful and I had so much to think that I hardly slept. This morning at 10 (it was 6 by your time), I was in the heart of Paris. I hoped the beauty of Paris would help me to get over my sadness; but it did not. First, Paris is not beautiful today. It is gray and cloudy; it is Sunday, the streets are empty, and everything seems dull, dark, and dead. Maybe it is my heart which is dead to Paris. My heart is yet in New York, at the corner of Broadway where we said goodbye; it is in my Chicago home, in my own warm place against your loving heart. I suppose in two or three days it will be a bit different. I must be concerned again by all the French intellectual and politic life, by my work and my friends. But today I don't even wish to get interested in all these things; I feel lazy and tired, and I can enjoy only memories. My beloved one, I don't know why I waited so long before

---

1. *"My Precious beloved Chicago man"* refers to Nelson Algren.

Alone. Emilio Longoni. Casa di Livorno, Milan, Italy.

saying I loved you. I just wanted to be *sure* and not to say easy, empty words. But it seems to me now love was there since the beginning. Anyway, now it is here, it is love and my heart aches. I am happy to be so bitterly unhappy because I know you are unhappy, too, and it is sweet to have a part of the same sadness. With you pleasure was love, and now pain is love too. We must know every kind of love. We'll know the joy of meeting again. I want it, I need it, and I'll get it. Wait for me. I wait for you. I love you more even than I said, more maybe than you know. I'll write very often. Write to me very often too. I am your wife forever.

Your Simone

I read the whole book[2] and I like it *very* much. I'll have it translated, sure. Kisses and kisses and kisses. It was so sweet when you kissed me. I love you.

---

2. The book Beauvoir refers to is Algren's novel *The Man with the Golden Arm,* which won the first National Book Award for fiction.

Quickwrite

A common adage is "Absence makes the heart grow fonder." How do you think Beauvoir would react to this adage? Do you think this saying is true? Write a paragraph exploring these questions. Cite evidence from the letter and the Building Background feature in your answer.

BEFORE YOU READ

Building Background

The Beatles emerged from the English city of Liverpool to take the world by storm. The Fab Four's lineup included John Lennon, Paul McCartney, George Harrison, and Ringo Starr. Influenced by American rock n' roll, the Beatles perfected the art of the pop song. As they grew as musicians, their songs became more complex and emotionally revealing. One of the first songs to demonstrate such growth was "In My Life," a song written by guitarist and singer John Lennon for the 1965 album *Rubber Soul.* Lennon remarked, "'In My Life' was, I think, my first real, major piece of work. Up until then it had all been glib and throwaway."

The song originally contained a catalog of specific memories from Lennon's youth, but Lennon edited the song to speak more generally about the experience of love, memory, and life.

Though Lennon wrote "In My Life," both he and McCartney collaborated on most of the songs they wrote. Sometimes this collaboration consisted of one slightly revising the other's songs, and at other times one would complete the other's song fragments. Due to an agreement made during the early years of the band, Lennon and McCartney are credited for all songs that one or both of them wrote and royalties were split equally.

Literature Online **Author Search** For more about the Beatles, go to www.glencoe.com.

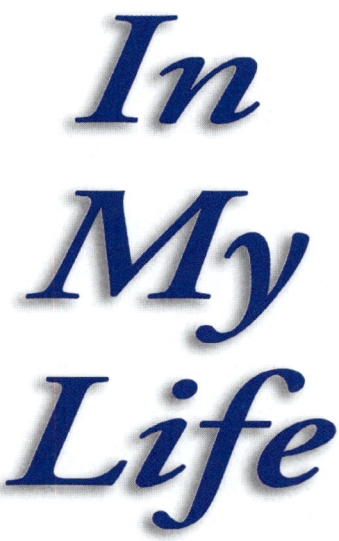

In My Life

John Lennon and
Paul McCartney

There are places I remember all my life,
Though some have changed,
Some forever, not for better,
Some have gone and some remain.

5　All these places had their moments
With lovers and friends I still can recall.
Some are dead and some are living.
In my life I've loved them all.

But of all these friends and lovers,
10　There is no one compares with you,
And these mem'ries lost their meaning
When I think of love as something new.

Though I know I'll never lose affection
For people and things that went before,
15　I know I'll often stop and think about them,
In my life I'll love you more.

Though I know I'll never lose affection
For people and things that went before,
I know I'll often stop and think about them,
20　In my life I'll love you more.
In my life I'll love you more.

Discussion Starter ....

How is this song structured? How are songs similar to poems? What qualities associated with poetry are at work in this song? Discuss these questions in a group. If a recording of the song is available, listen to it to enrich your understanding of the lyrics.

Wrap-Up: Comparing Literature Across Time and Place

- *Sonnet 43*
  by Elizabeth Barrett Browning
- *Love Is Not All: It Is Not Meat nor Drink*
  by Edna St. Vincent Millay
- *Simone de Beauvoir to Nelson Algren*
  by Simone de Beauvoir
- *In My Life*
  by John Lennon and Paul McCartney

COMPARING THE Big Idea Optimism and the Belief in Progress

Writing What purpose does love serve in society? Does love inspire innovation and bring about a better quality of life? Does a belief in love go hand in hand with a belief in progress? Write a brief essay comparing the arguments made by these four writers.

COMPARING Theme of Passionate Love

Group Activity With a group of classmates, read and discuss the following quotations. Ask yourselves, how does each quotation characterize love? How does love affect each speaker? Is love eternal or can love change over time? Is love a necessity or an indulgence?

> *"I love thee with a love I seemed to lose / With my lost saints"*
> —Barrett Browning, Sonnet 43

> *"Love can not fill the thickened lung with breath, Nor clean the blood, nor set the fractured bone;"*
> —Millay, "Love Is Not All: It Is Not Meat nor Drink"

> *"With you pleasure was love, and now pain is love too."*
> —Beauvoir, "Simone de Beauvoir to Nelson Algren"

> *"And these mem'ries lost their meaning When I think of love as something new."*
> —Lennon and McCartney, "In My Life"

Online Romance. Illustration. Farida Zaman.

COMPARING Historical Contexts

Speaking and Listening Writers are influenced by their surroundings. Barrett Browning's poem is a product of her upbringing in Victorian England. Millay's poem mirrors her frenetic lifestyle during the Roaring Twenties. Beauvoir's letter reflects the bohemian values of her day. Lennon and McCartney's song is influenced by sudden stardom. Research the historical backdrop of one of the selections and give a short oral report to your class about how the context helps you better understand the writer's portrayal of love and passion.

OBJECTIVES
- Compare poems, a letter, and a song about love from different cultures and eras.
- Analyze the theme of passionate love in literature.
- Evaluate how historical context influences your understanding of literature and music.

Preview the Article

"What Is Love?" examines whether love is culturally acquired or genetically programmed.

1. How does love influence traditions and institutions in our culture?

2. Based on the photographs on pages 949 and 950, what point do you think the writer is going to make about love?

Set a Purpose for Reading

Read to learn about scientific studies on the origin of love.

Reading Strategy

Examining Connotation and Denotation
A word's **denotation** is its literal meaning, or its dictionary definition. **Connotation** refers to the suggested or implied meanings associated with a word beyond its literal meaning. As you read, examine how the writer uses connotation and denotation.

Example Sentence	"Love is mushy; science is hard."
Connotation or Denotation	Connotations: mushy; hard
Overall Effect	The author implies that science comes from reason and love comes from emotion.

OBJECTIVES
- Read to examine how a writer uses denotation and connotation.
- Analyze informational text using appropriate comprehension strategies.

TIME

What Is LOVE?

After centuries of ignoring the subject as too vague and mushy, scientists have undergone a change of heart about the tender passion.

By PAUL GRAY

What is this thing called love? What? Is this thing called love? What is this thing called? Love.

HOWEVER PUNCTUATED, Cole Porter's simple question begs an answer. Love's symptoms are familiar enough: a drifting mooniness in thought and behavior, the mad conceit that the entire universe has rolled itself up into the person of the beloved, a conviction that no one on earth has ever felt so torrentially about a fellow creature before. Love is ecstasy and torment, freedom and slavery. Poets and songwriters would be in a fine mess without it. Plus, it makes the world go round.

Until recently, scientists wanted no part of it. The reason for this avoidance, this reluctance to study what is probably life's most intense emotion, is not difficult to track down. Love is mushy; science is hard. Anger and fear, feelings that have been considerably researched in the field and the lab, can be quantified through measurements: pulse and breathing rates, muscle contractions, a whole spider web of involuntary responses. Love does not register as definitively on the instruments; it leaves a blurred fingerprint that could be mistaken for anything from indigestion to a manic attack. Anger and fear have direct roles—fighting or running—in the survival of the species. But romantic love, and all the attendant sighing and swooning and sonnet writing, has struck many pragmatic investigators as beside the point.

So biologists and anthropologists assumed that it would be fruitless, even frivolous, to study love's origins, the way it was encoded in our genes or imprinted in our brains. Serious scientists simply assumed that romantic love was really all in the head, put there five or six centuries ago when civilized societies first found enough spare time to indulge in flowery prose. The task of writing the book of love was ceded to playwrights, poets, and pulp novelists.

But in recent years, scientists across a broad range of disciplines have had a change of heart about love. The amount of research expended on the tender passion has

UNITED STATES
Valentine's Day

Romantic rituals in the West have evolved into the bestowal of flowers, candy, and other sweet nothings. But the absence of such gift giving in poorer cultures does not, anthropologists are learning, mean the absence of romance.

never been more intense. To explain this rise in interest, some point to the growing number of women scientists and suggest that they may be more willing than their male colleagues to take love seriously. Says researcher Elaine Hatfield: "When I was back at Stanford in the 1960s, they said studying love and human relationships was a quick way to ruin my career. Why not go where the real work was being done: on how fast rats could run?" Whatever the reasons, science seems to have come around to a view that nearly everyone else has always taken for granted: Romance is real. It is not merely a conceit; it is bred into our biology.

Getting to this point logically is harder than it sounds. The love-as-cultural-delusion argument has long seemed unassailable. What actually accounts for the emotion, according to this scenario, is that people long ago made the mistake of taking fanciful literary notions seriously. Among the prime suspects are the 12th-century French troubadours who more or less invented the Art of Courtly Love, an elaborate and artificial ritual for idle aristocrats.

Ever since then, the injunction to love and to be loved has hummed nonstop through popular culture; it is a dominant theme in music, films, novels, magazines, and nearly everything shown on TV. Love is a formidable and thoroughly proved commercial engine; people will buy and do almost anything that promises them a chance at the bliss of romance.

But does all this mean that love is merely a phony emotion that we picked up because our culture celebrates it? Psychologist Lawrence Casler, author of *Is Marriage Necessary?*, forcefully thinks so, at least at first: "I don't believe love is part of human nature, not for a minute. There are social pressures at work." Then a shadow falls over his certainty. "Even if it is a part of human nature, like crime or violence, it's not necessarily desirable."

Well, love either is or is not intrinsic to our species; having it both ways leads nowhere. And the contention that romance is an entirely acquired trait—the revenge of overly imaginative love poets on those who would take them literally—has always rested on some flimsy premises.

Why, for example, has romantic love—that odd collection of tics and impulses—lasted over the centuries? Most mass hallucinations, such as the 17th-century tulip mania in Holland (when the popularity of tulips pushed the price of a single bulb sky high), flame out fairly rapidly when people realize the absurdity of what they have been doing and come to their senses. When people in love come to their senses, they tend to orbit with added energy around each other and look more helplessly loopy and self-besotted. If romance were purely a figment, unsupported by any rational or sensible evidence, then surely most folks would be immune to it by now. Look around. It hasn't happened. Love is still in the air.

And it may be far more widespread than even romantics imagined. Those who argue that love is a cultural fantasy have tended to do

CHINA
Courtship on Horseback

On the plains of Xinjiang, mounted Kazakh suitors play Catch the Maiden. He chases her in pursuit of a kiss. If he succeeds, she goes after him with a riding crop.

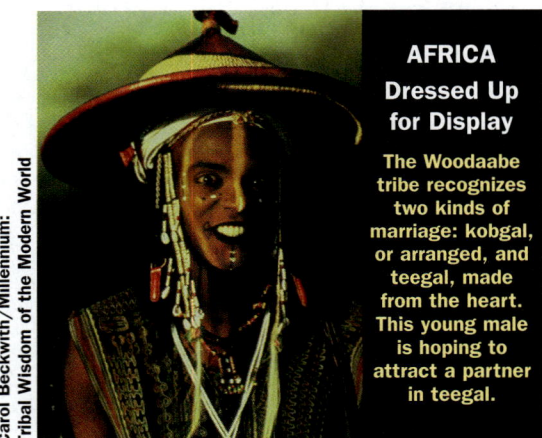

AFRICA Dressed Up for Display

The Woodaabe tribe recognizes two kinds of marriage: kobgal, or arranged, and teegal, made from the heart. This young male is hoping to attract a partner in teegal.

so from a Eurocentric and class-driven point of view. Romance, they say, arose thanks to circumstances peculiar to the West: leisure time, a decent amount of creature comforts, a certain level of refinement in the arts and letters. Romantic love was for aristocrats, not for peasants.

But a study conducted by anthropologists William Jankowiak of the University of Nevada-Las Vegas and Edward Fischer of Tulane University found evidence of romantic love in at least 147 of the 166 cultures they studied. This discovery, if borne out, should pretty well wipe out the idea that love is an invention of the Western mind rather than a biological fact. Says Jankowiak: "It is, instead,

a universal phenomenon, a panhuman characteristic that stretches across cultures. Societies like ours have the resources to show love through candy and flowers, but that does not mean that the lack of resources in other cultures indicates the absence of love."

Some scientists are not startled by this contention. One of them is anthropologist Helen Fisher, a research associate at the American Museum of Natural History. Says Fisher: "I've never *not* thought that love was a very primitive, basic human emotion, as basic as fear, anger, or joy. It is so evident. I guess anthropologists have just been busy doing other things."

Among the things anthropologists—often knobby-kneed gents in safari shorts—tended to do in the past was ask questions about courtship and marriage rituals. This now seems a classic example, as the old song has it, of looking for love in all the wrong places. In many cultures, love and marriage do not go together. Weddings can have all the romance of corporate mergers,

signed and sealed for family or territorial interests. This does not mean, Jankowiak insists, that love does not exist in such cultures; it erupts in clandestine forms, "a phenomenon to be dealt with."

But if science is going to probe and prod and then announce that we are all scientifically fated to love—and to love preprogrammed types—by our genes and chemicals, then a lot of people would just as soon not know. If there truly is a biological predisposition to love, as more and more scientists are coming to believe, then it follows that there is also an amazing diversity in the ways humans have chosen to express the feeling. The cartoon images of cavemen bopping cavewomen over the head and dragging them home by their hair? Love. Helen of Troy, subjecting her adopted city to 10 years of ruinous siege? Love. Romeo and Juliet? Ditto. Joe in Accounting making a fool of himself around the water cooler over Susan in Sales? Love. Like the universe, the more we learn about love, the more preposterous and mysterious it is likely to appear.

Updated 2005, from TIME, February 15, 1993

RESPONDING AND THINKING CRITICALLY

Respond

1. How did the article influence your preconceptions about the origin of love?

Recall and Interpret

2. (a) Why have scientists traditionally been reluctant to study the concept of love? (b) Who took on the "task of writing the book of love"?

3. (a) Paraphrase the "love-as-cultural-delusion" argument. (b) What facts tend to refute this argument?

4. (a) According to some modern anthropologists, why are courtship and marriage rituals the wrong places to look for the origins of love? (b) Where do modern scientists look for the origin of love?

Analyze and Evaluate

5. (a) Why do you think the writer chose to use the introductory quote by Cole Porter? (b) What is the significance of the quote?

6. (a) Why do some theorists think love is a fantasy of the West? (b) How does the study by Jankowiak and Fischer prove this theory wrong?

7. If romantic love is genetically programmed, what selective advantage does it afford the human species?

Connect

8. How do you think Victorian writers would have responded to the modern scientific view that love is biologically determined?

Hopkins's Poetry

MEET GERARD MANLEY HOPKINS

Like many artists and writers, Gerard Manley Hopkins did not know fame during his lifetime. In fact, his poetry was not published until 1918, nearly thirty years after his death. For this reason, Hopkins was long viewed as a twentieth-century poet, although in recent decades scholars and publishers have considered his poems in their original Victorian context—all the better to understand and appreciate the extent of Hopkins's innovation and accomplishment as a poet.

From Highgate to High Church The first of nine children, Hopkins was born into a middle-class Anglican family who shared a love of literature, art, and music. He began writing as a child and won a poetry prize when he was fifteen. After a brilliant career at the Highgate School in London, Hopkins entered Oxford University in 1863. There he studied Latin and Greek and was also exposed to the newest ideas in poetry and theology. These pursuits fostered in Hopkins a dual interest in rich, imagistic verse and in rich, imagistic religion—the latter of which led him first to High Church Anglicanism and then to Roman Catholicism and the Jesuit priesthood. As a result of his conversion, Hopkins suffered a painful and enduring estrangement from his Protestant family.

> "The world is charged with the grandeur of God.
> It will flame out, like shining from shook foil."
>
> —Gerard Manley Hopkins

The Poet Priest Soon after his conversion, Hopkins burned most of his poems in a display of religious devotion. For seven years he wrote no new poetry. Then, in 1875, one of his superiors suggested that he write a poem about five nuns exiled for their faith who had drowned in the shipwreck of the *Deutschland*. "The Wreck of the Deutschland" was rejected for publication due to its unconventional style but sparked in Hopkins a renewed interest in writing poetry—which he would continue to do for the remaining fourteen years of his life.

In much of Hopkins's early poetry, the meeting of the mind and nature leads directly to a transcendent awareness of God in all things—an awareness expressed fervently and poignantly in his 1877 poem "God's Grandeur."

Late in life, however, Hopkins produced a series of "terrible sonnets" which express despair at the poet's inability to fully escape the prison of the self. This despair created for Hopkins a frustrating dilemma: isolation from the very God who made each human unique—and, therefore, isolated from one another.

Hopkins's priestly life was varied and full. His duties took him, among other places, to the slums of industrial England, where he witnessed the misery of the poor and the devastation of the natural environment. His last five years were spent teaching Greek and Latin at the Catholic University in Dublin and writing some of his most striking poetry.

Gerard Manley Hopkins was born in 1844 and died in 1889.

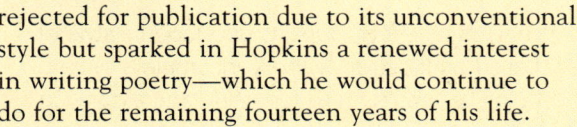

Literature Online **Author Search** For more about Gerard Manley Hopkins, go to www.glencoe.com.

Connecting to the Poems

Are human beings a part of nature or apart from it? In these poems, Hopkins suggests that both may be true. As you read, think about these questions:

- What actions do you take that affect the natural environment?
- When in your life have you felt most a part of the natural world?

Building Background

Gerard Manley Hopkins believed that each human being was characterized by an intricate and utterly unique design—a kind of spiritual fingerprint that he called "inscape." This notion also extended to his poetry. He once said that "design, pattern, or what I am in the habit of calling 'inscape' is what I above all aim at in poetry."

To create such an effect, Hopkins developed a style of poetry based on irregular rhythms, incomplete syntax, and echoing devices such as repetition and alliteration. The resulting roughness, he believed, captured not only the complex design of the human mind but also its jolting movements as it perceives and reflects on an object in nature.

Setting Purposes for Reading

Big Idea Optimism and the Belief in Progress

Another word for *progress*—a central Victorian ideal—is *change*. As you read these poems, consider how change can be both beautiful and sad.

Literary Element Sprung Rhythm

Hopkins's central poetic innovation was a technique he called **sprung rhythm**. Sprung rhythm is a kind of meter in which each foot contains one stressed syllable (the first) and any number of unstressed syllables. This meter has four kinds of feet: the stressed monosyllable (´), the trochee (´ ˘), the dactyl (´ ˘ ˘), and the first paeon (´ ˘ ˘ ˘). Additional unstressed syllables are also permitted.

- See Literary Terms Handbook, p. R17.

Reading Strategy Monitoring Comprehension

To **monitor comprehension,** note whether you fully grasp the author's meaning as you read. If not, you can use strategies to help you understand the text. These strategies include reading more slowly, rereading difficult passages, and using a graphic organizer.

Reading Tip: Charting Meaning As you read, use a two-column chart to clarify the meaning of difficult phrases. Use footnotes, a dictionary, or your own prior knowledge to help you.

Difficult Phrase	Simplified Meaning
"dappled things"	"blotched or spotted things"

Vocabulary

dappled (dap´ əld) *adj.* marked with spots; p. 953 *A ray of sun warmed the fawn's dappled coat.*

fallow (fal´ ō) *n.* land plowed but left unseeded; p. 953 *The fallow field lay brown and empty, waiting for next year's seeds.*

blight (blīt) *n.* a disease caused by parasites that makes plants and trees wither and die; p. 954 *A blight in the region killed thousands of saplings.*

Vocabulary Tip: Word Origins Many words in English come from words in other languages. Understanding word origins can help you figure out the meaning of unfamiliar words.

Literature Online **Interactive Literary Elements Handbook** To review or learn more about the literary elements, go to www.glencoe.com.

OBJECTIVES

In studying these selections, you will focus on the following:
- analyzing literary time periods
- analyzing sprung rhythm
- monitoring comprehension

The Sower, 1888. Vincent van Gogh. Oil on canvas, 64 x 80.5 cm. Rijksmuseum, Netherlands.

Pied Beauty

Gerard Manley Hopkins

Glory be to God for **dappled** things—
    For skies of couple-color as a brinded° cow;
        For rose-moles° all in stipple° upon trout that swim;
Fresh-firecoal chestnut-falls;° finches' wings;
5   Landscape plotted and pieced°—fold,° **fallow**, and plow;
        And áll trádes, their gear and tackle and trim.°

All things counter,° original, spare, strange;
    Whatever is fickle, freckled (who knows how?)
        With swift, slow; sweet, sour; adazzle, dim;
10 He fathers-forth° whose beauty is past change:
                Praise him.

2 brinded: streaked or spotted.
3 rose-moles: marks of a reddish color.
stipple: a method of painting that uses small dots of color to produce gradations of tone
4 fresh-firecoal: *fresh-firecoal chestnut-falls* describes the glowing color of chestnuts newly stripped of their husks.
5 Landscape plotted and pieced: the patchwork pattern created by dividing land into fields. **fold:** an enclosed area for sheep
6 trim: equipment or clothing.
7 counter: contrary or opposite
10 fathers-forth: creates

Reading Strategy   **Monitoring Comprehension** *How does your prior knowledge of the word* couple *help you understand the meaning of this unusual phrase?*

Vocabulary
....

dappled (dap′ əld) *adj.* marked with spots
fallow (fal′ ō) *n.* land plowed but left unseeded

The Wild Wood, Autumn. Alfred Oliver (d 1943). Private collection.

Spring and Fall: To a Young Child

Gerard Manley Hopkins

Márgarét, are you gríeving
Over Goldengrove unleaving?°
Leáves líke the things of man, you
With your fresh thoughts care for, can you?
5   Áh! ás the heart grows older
It will come to such sights colder
By and by, nor spare a sigh
Though worlds of wanwood leafmeal° lie;
And yet you wíll weep and know why.
10   Now no matter, child, the name:
Sórrow's spríngs áre the same.
Nor mouth had, no nor mind, expressed
What heart heard of, ghost° guessed:
It ís the **blight** man was born for,
15   It is Margaret you mourn for.

2 **Goldengrove unleaving:** a grove of trees losing its leaves in autumn

8 **wanwood leafmeal:** a ground covering of crushed, decomposing, pale-colored autumn leaves

13 **ghost:** the spirit or soul

Literary Element   **Sprung Rhythm** *Which three syllables are stressed in this line? What type of foot does each stressed syllable begin?*

Big Idea   **Optimism and the Belief in Progress** *How do these lines express the flip side of Victorian optimism?*

Vocabulary

blight (blīt) *n.* a disease caused by parasites that makes plants and trees wither and die

RESPONDING AND THINKING CRITICALLY

Respond

1. Do you think the same person could be the speaker of both poems, or is it likely that the speakers are two different people? Give reasons for your answer.

Recall and Interpret

2. (a)In the first stanza of "Pied Beauty," for what specific things does the speaker glorify God? (b)What do the speaker's choices suggest about his concept of beauty?

3. (a)In the second stanza of "Pied Beauty," for what does the speaker praise God? (b)Explain the comparison the speaker makes between God's beauty and the beauty of the world.

4. (a)In "Spring and Fall," how does the speaker first explain Margaret's grief? How does he later explain it? (b)What can you infer about the speaker's

philosophy of life, death, and the aging process? Use details from the poem to support your answer.

Analyze and Evaluate

5. In your opinion, why does Hopkins include examples from trade (*gear, tackle,* and *trim*) in his praise of pied beauty?

6. In "Pied Beauty," how does Hopkins's use of **imagery,** or word pictures, help to convey the poem's **theme,** or main idea?

7. Do you agree with the point of view expressed in lines 5–9 of "Spring and Fall"? Why or why not?

Connect

8. | Big Idea | **Optimism and the Belief in Progress** The Victorians felt that it was their prerogative to bend nature to their own purposes. How does "Pied Beauty" counter this idea?

LITERARY ANALYSIS

| Literary Element | Sprung Rhythm

Hopkins chose to use **sprung rhythm** because "it is nearest to the rhythm of prose, that is, the native and natural rhythm of speech."

1. In your opinion, does sprung rhythm resemble natural, everyday speech? Support your answer, using specific examples from the poems.

2. Do you think sprung rhythm captures the movement of the mind as it sees and registers what it perceives? Explain.

Listening and Speaking

With a partner, take turns reading the two poems aloud. Before you begin, reread the definition of sprung rhythm in the Literary Element feature on page 952. Also pay attention to the way each poem sounds—specifically, the use of end rhyme and alliteration in each poem.

Literature Online **Web Activities** For eFlashcards, Selection Quick Checks, and other Web activities, go to www.glencoe.com.

READING AND VOCABULARY

| Reading Strategy | Monitoring Comprehension

Remember that when you **monitor comprehension,** you pay special attention to parts of the text you don't understand.

Reread "Spring and Fall." What line or phrase seemed difficult the first time you read it but is much clearer now? Explain.

| Vocabulary | Practice

Practice with Word Origins Use a dictionary with etymologies to help you match each vocabulary word to the description of its origin.

a. blight **b.** dappled **c.** fallow

1. Old English word for a skin condition

2. Old English word meaning "a piece of plowed land"

3. Middle English word that describes a color

Jabberwocky

MEET LEWIS CARROLL

Considered a dull lecturer by many of his students and a marginally important mathematician by his colleagues at Oxford University, Charles Lutwidge Dodgson might, on the surface, seem an uninteresting fellow. Yet this quiet, painfully shy man published some of the wittiest children's fiction ever written. Under the pen name Lewis Carroll, Dodgson became world famous, particularly for two books that for generations have captivated children and adults alike: *Alice's Adventures in Wonderland* and *Through the Looking Glass and What Alice Found There*.

An Inventive Youth The son of a church rector, Dodgson was the third child and oldest son in a family of eleven children. The Dodgson children lived in an isolated country village and had few friends outside the family, but they found many ways to amuse themselves. From an early age, Dodgson entertained his younger siblings by performing magic tricks and marionette shows and by writing poetry and word games for the family's homemade magazines.

As a teenager, Dodgson spent four years at the Rugby School. These were unhappy years, as Dodgson's shyness and frequent ill health made him a target for bullying. The young scholar found more success at Oxford University, where he excelled in mathematics and classical studies. Graduating first in his class in mathematics, Dodgson was granted a scholarship and assumed a post as a lecturer in mathematics. As a condition of this scholarship, Dodgson was also ordained a deacon, but a severe stammer kept him from seeking a career in preaching.

Play Makes Perfect Even though Dodgson spent twenty-six years teaching math at Oxford, he was bored by the work. In the company of children, however, Dodgson was neither bored nor shy. He was able to speak to children without stammering, and he loved to entertain young visitors—often the children of fellow faculty members—by inventing games, performing magic tricks, giving puppet shows, and telling stories. Much to Dodgson's own surprise, one of these stories eventually became *Alice in Wonderland*.

> *"In a desperate attempt to strike out some new line of fairy-lore, I had sent my heroine straight down a rabbit-hole, to begin with, without the least idea what was to happen afterwards."*
>
> —Lewis Carroll

Alice was not Dodgson's first publication, however. Between 1854 and 1856, several of Dodgson's comical and satirical works appeared in national publications. Then, in 1856, a poem called "Solitude" was printed under the pseudonym "Lewis Carroll." In typical word-play fashion, Dodgson had created this name by translating his given name into Latin—Carolus Ludovicus—then reversing the names and translating them back into English. He used the pseudonym on all of his non-academic works, although Dodgson also published a good number of scholarly works under his given name.

Lewis Carroll was born in 1832 and died in 1898.

Literature Online Author Search For more about Lewis Carroll, go to www.glencoe.com.

Connecting to the Poem

Lewis Carroll's flights of fancy resulted in some very compelling inventions. As you read, think about why the notion of inventing new things is so compelling to human beings.

Building Background

Dodgson often entertained the young daughters of Henry George Liddell, the dean of his college. On a summer day in 1862, Dodgson and a friend took the girls on a boat trip up the river Thames. Dodgson told an especially amusing tale that afternoon, and young Alice Liddell begged him to write it down for her. Eventually some writers who read the manuscript persuaded Dodgson to revise and expand his story for publication. In 1865 he published the story as *Alice's Adventures in Wonderland.* Six years later he published a sequel, *Through the Looking Glass and What Alice Found There,* which includes the poem "Jabberwocky."

Setting Purposes for Reading

Big Idea Optimism and the Belief in Progress

Among other things, the Victorians invented the train, the toilet, the vacuum cleaner, the stamp, and cola. As you read, notice how Victorian inventiveness extended itself to the world of verse as well.

Literary Element Nonsense Verse

Nonsense verse is humorous poetry that defies logic—or, at first glance, appears to. Nonsense verse usually has a strong rhythm and contains made-up words. These words—like *galumphing* in "Jabberwocky"—often use **onomatopoeia,** or a technique of using words whose sounds suggest their meanings.

- See Literary Terms Handbook, p. R12.

Literature Online **Interactive Literary Elements Handbook** To review or learn more about the literary elements, go to www.glencoe.com.

Reading Strategy Clarifying Meaning

To **clarify the meaning** of a nonsense word (also called **nonce words**), you can use both context and syntax. For example, if a character is "galumphing into the forest," both the *-ing* form of the nonsense word and the clue "into the forest" would tell you that *galumphing* is a way of walking or running.

Reading Tip: Analyzing Syntax When you come across a confusing phrase or sentence, clarify the syntax by labeling the nonsense words' parts of speech.

ADJ.   ADJ. N.
'Twas brillig, and the slithy toves
     V   V   N
Did gyre and gimble in the wabe. . . .

THE SHOWER OF CARDS.

Alice and the Cards. First published in 1865.

OBJECTIVES

In studying this selection, you will focus on the following:
- analyzing literary genres
- identifying characteristics of nonsense verse
- clarifying meaning by analyzing syntax

Jabberwocky

Lewis Carroll

'Twas brillig, and the slithy toves
    Did gyre and gimble in the wabe;
All mimsy were the borogoves,
    And the mome raths outgrabe.

5   "Beware the Jabberwock, my son!
    The jaws that bite, the claws that catch!
Beware the Jubjub bird, and shun
    The frumious Bandersnatch!"

He took his vorpal sword in hand:
10   Long time the manxome foe he sought—
So rested he by the Tumtum tree,
    And stood awhile in thought.

And as in uffish thought he stood,
    The Jabberwock, with eyes of flame,
15   Came whiffling through the tulgey wood,
    And burbled as it came!

One, two! One, two! And through and through
    The vorpal blade went snicker-snack!
He left it dead, and with its head
20   He went galumphing back.

"And hast thou slain the Jabberwock?
    Come to my arms, my beamish boy!
O frabjous day! Callooh! Callay!"
    He chortled in his joy.

25   'Twas brillig, and the slithy toves
    Did gyre and gimble in the wabe;
All mimsy were the borogoves,
    And the mome raths outgrabe.

The Jabberwock, 19th century. John Tenniel. Illustration.

RESPONDING AND THINKING CRITICALLY

Respond

1. Which lines in the poem struck you as particularly amusing? Why?

Recall and Interpret

2. (a)What warnings does the father give his son? (b)What do these warnings suggest about the setting of the poem?

3. (a)Summarize what happens in stanzas 3–5. (b)What do these events reveal about the boy's character?

4. (a)How does the father respond to his son's actions? (b)Why do you think he responds in this manner?

Analyze and Evaluate

5. (a)Describe the poem's meter (or rhythm) and rhyme scheme. (b)What effects are created by these devices?

6. (a)How would you describe the poem's atmosphere? (b)Does the atmosphere change? Explain your answer citing specific evidence from the poem.

7. (a)Why do you think Carroll repeats the first stanza at the end of the poem? (b)What is the effect of this repetition?

Connect

8. **Big Idea** **Optimism and the Belief in Progress** What Victorian attitudes might Carroll be mocking, or satirizing, in this poem?

LITERARY ANALYSIS

Literary Element **Nonsense Verse**

Carroll provided "definitions" for many of the nonce words in "Jabberwocky." For example, he defined a "tove" as a type of badger that had short horns and "lived chiefly on cheese" and "slithy" as a combination of "slimy" and "lithe" that means "smooth and active." For each nonce word below, write one or two real words that are suggested by its sound.

1. brillig **2.** mimsy **3.** raths

4. frumious **5.** uffish **6.** frabjous

Performing

In a small group, use a combination of mime, dance, music, or visual arts to create a multimedia performance of "Jabberwocky." As part of your planning, go over the poem together and recall possible meanings for the nonce words. Use this discussion to help you decide what each creature and setting should look and sound like.

Literature Online **Web Activities** For eFlashcards, Selection Quick Checks, and other Web activities, go to www.glencoe.com.

READING AND VOCABULARY

Reading Strategy **Clarifying Meaning**

Remember that you can use context and syntactical clues to clarify possible meanings of nonce words in the poem.

Partner Activity Copy the first stanza of the poem. Label each nonce word with a part of speech (*N, V, ADJ,* or *ADV*). Now rewrite the stanza, substituting a real word of the same part of speech for each nonce word. Read your new stanza aloud to a partner. Discuss similarities and differences in your interpretations.

Academic Vocabulary

Here is a word from the vocabulary list on page R82.

coherent (kō hēr′ ənt) *adj.* logically consistent

Practice and Apply
Even though "Jabberwocky" is a nonsense poem, do you find it **coherent**? Why?

Jabberwocky

Wanda Coleman

Budding Scholar, Henry Herman Roseland (1866–1950). Private collection.

Building Background

Wanda Coleman, a prize-winning African American poet and novelist, had a transformative experience when she read Lewis Carroll's *Alice's Adventures in Wonderland* and *Through the Looking Glass.* In particular, Carroll's poem "Jabberwocky" helped her make sense of the realities of racial discrimination. In her world, as in Alice's, nothing was ever as it seemed.

Set a Purpose for Reading

Read to discover how reading a literary classic influenced a future writer.

Analyzing Literary Influences

Analyzing literary influences involves examining the ways that literary works affect writers. As you read, take notes about the influence of Lewis Carroll's poem on Coleman. Use a cause-and-effect diagram like the one below to help you.

Cause	Effect
Coleman feels like an outsider.	She turns to reading.

The stultifying[1] intellectual loneliness of my Watts upbringing was dictated by my looks—dark skin and unconkable kinky hair. Being glowered at was a constant state of being. The eyes of adults and children alike immediately informed me that some unpleasant *ugliness* had entered their sphere and spoiled their pleasure because of its close and onerous[2] proximity. I recall one such moment very strongly: a white man was standing in front of me at such an angle that I was momentarily uncertain what he was frowning at. I turned to look behind me and saw nothing.

I have come to mark such moments—as they have recurred throughout my life—as indicative of the significance of physical likeness, beyond the issue of physical beauty: of the importance of "mirror image" (a phrase that recurs in one form or another in my poetry); in the ongoing dialogue of race, as I've struggled to grasp and respond to what others *assume* when their eyes are directed at or on me. I find the shifts in visual context as infuriating now as they were in childhood. The act of wading through stereotypes, in order to

---

1. *Stultifying* means "negating" or "dulling."
2. *Onerous* means "troublesome."

become clearly visible in the larger society, corresponds exactly to that moment when Lewis Carroll's Alice steps through that looking glass.

Incapable of imagining my world, removed from it by gender and race as well as by time and place, Lewis Carroll had nevertheless provided me with a means (and an attitude) with which to assess, evaluate, and interpret my own journey through this bizarre actuality of late-twentieth-century America, where nothing is ever as it seems. I was a *Negro* child—yet this book, and its poem "Jabberwocky," served singularly to buoy my self-esteem, constantly under assault by my Black peers, family members, and the world outside.

I found the rejection unbearable and—encouraged by my parents to read—sought an escape in books, which were usually hard to come by. In the South Central Los Angeles of the 1950s and 1960s, there were only three Black-owned bookstores, and I would not discover them until early adulthood. In my childhood there was no Harlem Renaissance, no Black arts movement; I did not encounter the poems of Paul Laurence Dunbar and James Weldon Johnson[3] except at church socials and in the early 1960s, during Negro History "week" celebrations. There were no images of Black children *of any age* in the American literature I encountered. The sole exception was "Little Black Sambo," whom I immediately rejected upon finding the book on my desk in the first grade—along with equally boring books featuring Dick, Jane, and Spot. There was no way in which I could "identify" with these strange images of children. I was born and raised in the white world of Southern California; it gave birth to me, but excluded me. Even the postwar Watts of the poet Arna Bontemps,[4] and the South Central Los Angeles that would riot in 1965, were predominantly working-class white neighborhoods with small Black enclaves.

Whenever my father visited public libraries, he allowed me to roam the stacks. This was my Wonderland. I was immediately enthralled with the forbidden world of adult literature, hidden away in leather-bound tomes I was neither able to reach nor allowed to touch. I hungered to enter, and my appetite had no limits. I plowed through Papa's dull issues of *National Geographic* and Mama's tepid copies of *Reader's Digest* and *Family Circle* in desperation, starved. At age ten I consumed the household copy of the complete works of Shakespeare. Although the violence was striking, and *Hamlet* engrossing (particularly Ophelia), I was too immature to appreciate the Bard until frequent rereadings in my mid-teens.

On Christmas, thereabouts, I received Johanna Spyri's[5] *Heidi* as a well-intended gift. I had exhausted our teensy library, and my father's collections of *Knight* and *Esquire*. . . . Between my raids on the adults-only stuff, there was nothing but *Heidi*, reread in desperation until I could quote chunks of the text, mentally squeezing it for what I imagined to be hidden underneath. One early spring day, my adult cousin Rubyline came by the house with a nourishing belated Christmas gift: an illustrated collection of *Alice's Adventures in Wonderland and Through the Looking-Glass*. (She also gave me my first *Roget's*—which I still use—on my twelfth birthday in 1958.) In love with poetry since kindergarten, my "uffish" vows were startlingly renewed.

---

5. *Johanna Spyri* (1829–1901) was a Swiss writer.

The Children's Encyclopedia, James McDonald (b.1956). Oil on canvas. Private collection. Bourne Gallery, Reigate, Surrey, UK.

---

3. *Paul Laurence Dunbar* (1872–1906) was an African American poet and novelist. *James Weldon Johnson* (1871–1938) was an African American poet and leading member of the National Association for the Advancement of Colored People.
4. *Arna Bontemps* (1902–1973) was an African American novelist, historian, and poet.

I promptly retired *Heidi* and steeped myself in Alice to an iambic spazz.

In the real world I was an outsider, but in the stories and poems of Carroll I *belonged*. Why? Perhaps because when he freed Alice in the mirror, he also freed my imagination and permitted me to imagine myself living in an adventure, sans[6] the constraints of a racist society. If a drink or a slice of cake could transform her, alter her shape and size, the next leap for me was the most illogically logical of all: *Why not a transformation of her skin color?* In my frequent rereadings of Alice, I rewrote her as me.

"Jabberwocky" was and remains one of only a dozen poems I've ever loved enough to memorize. It heads the very long list of my favorite

> *"If a drink or a slice of cake could transform her . . . Why not a transformation of her skin color?"*

childhood poems, along with Poe's "Raven," Service's "Cremation of Sam McGee," Byron's "Prisoner of Chillon," Coleridge's "Rime of the Ancient Mariner," Henley's "Invictus," and E. A. Robinson's "Richard Cory."[7] To the astute reader, Carroll's lasting influence on my poetry is easily discerned. Many have referred to "Jabberwocky" as nonsense, but in my Los Angeles childhood, it made absolutely one hundred percent perfect sense. And within the context of Los Angeles today, that "nonsense" is dangerously and exhilaratingly profound.

---

6. *Sans* is a French word that means "without."

7. Edgar Allan *Poe* (1809–1849) was an American poet and fiction writer; Robert *Service* (1874–1958) was a Canadian poet; Lord *Byron* (1788–1824) and Samuel Taylor *Coleridge* (1772–1834) were British Romantic poets; William Ernest *Henley* (1849–1903) was a British critic and poet; and Edwin Arlington *Robinson* (1869–1935) was an American poet.

RESPONDING AND THINKING CRITICALLY

Respond

1. Which details in this essay did you find most interesting? Why?

Recall and Interpret

2. (a)How did Coleman's peers, family members, and strangers treat her as a child? (b)How did reading the poem "Jabberwocky" help buoy her self-esteem?

3. (a)Why did Coleman feel at home in Carroll's stories and poems? (b)What does the question, *"Why not a transformation of her skin color?"* reveal about Coleman's response to Alice?

Analyze and Evaluate

4. What does Coleman's exploration of magazines, the "forbidden world of adult literature," and her rereading of *Heidi* suggest about her personality and environment?

5. (a)Which words in this essay establish a comparison between reading and eating? (b)What does this comparison suggest about Coleman's regard for reading?

6. Why does Coleman maintain that "Jabberwocky" is meaningful rather than nonsensical?

Connect

7. What is the best book you have ever read? How can reading be a transformative experience?

OBJECTIVES
- Analyze literary influences.
- Construct graphic organizers.

Part 2
Realism and Naturalism

On Strike, c. 1891. Sir Hubert von Herkomer.
Oil on canvas. Royal Academy of Arts, London.

"It is a dreadful thing for the greatest and most necessary part of a very rich nation to live a hard life without dignity, knowledge, comforts, delights or hopes in the midst of plenty—which plenty they make."

—Gerard Manley Hopkins

The Age of the Novel

> "The person, be it gentleman or lady, who has not pleasure in a good novel, must be intolerably stupid."
>
> —Jane Austen, *Northanger Abbey*

WHILE THE NOVEL WAS BORN IN THE eighteenth century, it was not until the nineteenth century that the novel came of age. Many social factors converged to propel the novel to the forefront of the literary world. First, literacy rates for England's growing middle class rose sharply, increasing readership and creating new markets for the nineteenth-century novelist. Second, the emergence of libraries in the mid-1800s allowed greater access to literature. Most of these libraries were subscription libraries that charged customers an annual usage fee, with the restriction of borrowing one book at a time. At the forefront of this emergence was businessman Charles Edward Mudie. He wielded a tremendous amount of clout in the literary world because his library purchased thousands of copies of new books to loan to its customers. During this time, novels were often published in three volumes, called "triple-decker" novels, so publishers and subscription libraries could charge readers for each volume. Mudie strictly enforced this three-volume format rule.

Third, innovations in the publishing industry gave rise to inexpensive literary magazines which published complete novels in a series of short monthly installments. In fact, the serial novel became the most popular trend in the nineteenth century. Interestingly, some authors completed their novels before publication, but others, such as Charles Dickens, used the reactions of their reading public to shape the story's events. Dickens, Wilkie Collins, William Thackeray, and Thomas Hardy all published several novels in serial form.

Finally, the novel was a new and evolving literary form; novelists from this period did not suffer from an "anxiety of influence." Thus, the novel form allowed

The Artful Dodger picking a pocket to the amazement of Oliver Twist, c. 1837–8. George Cruikshank. Book illustration. Private collection.

writers to experiment with several new genres, such as the comic novel or the sporting novel. Jane Austen and William Thackeray continued an eighteenth-century trend, writing romance novels and novels of manners. Wilkie Collins shaped the gothic novel into the suspenseful but more realistic sensation novel or crime fiction. Two other important genres of the nineteenth century were the social-problem novel and the Regionalist novel.

Social-Problem Novels

Social-problem novels, also called "Condition of England" novels, drew attention to social ills in an attempt to spark reform. For instance, Charles Dickens's novels *Hard Times* and *Oliver Twist* reveal the poverty and exploitation of London's lower classes, and his novel *Bleak House* focuses on the corruption in England's legal system. Elizabeth Gaskell also wrote several novels urging social reform, and her first novel, *Mary Barton*, depicts the harsh, miserable conditions of the working-class people in her own rural community. In the preface to the work, Gaskell wrote, "Whatever public effort can do in the way of legislation, or private effort in the way of merciful deeds, of helpless love in the way of a widow's mites, should be done, and that speedily." Social-problem novelists opposed blind optimism in progress, and by presenting a realistic account of the negative effects of the Industrial Revolution, they raised public consciousness and triggered social reforms throughout the late 1800s.

Regionalist Novels

Another popular genre was the Regionalist novel, which employs a detailed setting that is often modeled on a real, usually rural, location. Regionalist novels are examples of Realism in the sense that they emphasize accurate rather than romantic settings and explore how place influences characters and events. This type of fiction is further characterized by the use of local dialect, references to specific natural or physical landmarks, incorporation of the community's political or social values, and parody of local characters. For example, Thomas Hardy set all of his novels in the fictional county of Wessex, which was based on the real county of Dorset and the town of Dorchester near his childhood home. Charlotte and Emily Brontë both created haunting backdrops in *Jane Eyre* and *Wuthering Heights* that echo the Yorkshire moors where they grew up.

Nineteenth-century publishing trends, such as the serial novel, may not remain popular today, but their enduring impact was the firm establishment of a public market for literature. Toward the end of the

Philip in Church, c. 1862. Frederick Walker. Gouache on paper, 179.92 x 144.88 in. The Tate Museum, London.

nineteenth century, free public libraries began to replace subscription libraries, ensuring that literature would remain widely available.

Literature Online **Literary History** For more about the age of the novel, go to www.glencoe.com.

RESPONDING AND THINKING CRITICALLY

1. What changes occurred in the nineteenth-century literary market?

2. (a) What types of issues do social-problem novels address? (b) Identify some contemporary novels or films that serve a similar function.

3. Compare and contrast the way social-problem novels and Regionalist novels reflect the emerging focus on Realism in the nineteenth century.

OBJECTIVES
- Read to connect Victorian novels to history.
- Understand how trends in publishing and readership affect literature.

from *Jane Eyre*

MEET CHARLOTTE BRONTË

The daughter of an Irish-born clergyman, Charlotte Brontë grew up in the tiny village of Haworth on the edge of the bleak Yorkshire moors. Although her childhood was somewhat dismal and lonely, these experiences would later inspire her greatest stories and novels.

> *"It is in vain to say human beings ought to be satisfied with tranquility: they must have action; and they will make it if they cannot find it."*
>
> —Charlotte Brontë, from *Jane Eyre*

A Family Curse Born in 1816, Charlotte Brontë experienced tragedy at a young age. Her mother died in 1821. Not long afterward her two older sisters, Maria and Elizabeth, succumbed to tuberculosis and typhus, both brought on by their stay at a poorly run girls' boarding school. This school later became the model of Charlotte's Lowood School in *Jane Eyre*. In the gloomy parsonage behind the church where their father worked, the four remaining Brontë children offset their unhappy, isolated lives by spinning tales of imaginary worlds and exotic characters. From this childhood play came a wealth of later creativity: Charlotte, Anne, and Emily all won distinction as writers; their brother Branwell became a painter. Nevertheless, their lives were tragically shortened by what seemed like a family curse, tuberculosis: Branwell died of it in September 1848; Emily, just a few months later; and Anne succumbed the following year.

Instant Literary Success Despite the specter of death that haunted her family, Charlotte was able to produce a number of poems and novels, including the novel *Jane Eyre*. Charlotte published *Jane Eyre* in 1847 under the pen name Currer Bell, but the book was an instant success that soon drew its author from anonymity. Charlotte was then free to publish other novels, including some that had been rejected before. She also became the subject of one of the Victorian era's most famous biographies, *The Life of Charlotte Brontë* by Elizabeth Gaskell, herself a well-known novelist.

An absorbing tale, *Jane Eyre* blends Realism and Romanticism in recounting, with the detail typical of Victorian fiction, the life of its title character from childhood on. Like Dickens's *Oliver Twist*, *Jane Eyre* first faces life as a penniless young orphan. The story is Brontë's most memorable work, and it leaves a lasting impression of the power of her writing. Virginia Woolf once wrote, "All her force, and it is the more tremendous for being constricted, goes into the assertion, 'I love,' 'I hate,' 'I suffer.'"

Charlotte Brontë, the only one of her siblings to reach the age of thirty, died of tuberculosis in March 1855, less than a year after she was married. She was not yet thirty-nine years old.

Charlotte Brontë was born in 1816 and died in 1855.

Literature Online **Author Search** For more about Charlotte Brontë, go to www.glencoe.com.

Connecting to the Story

In this excerpt from *Jane Eyre,* the young Jane is sent away to school after living with her cruel aunt. As you read, think about how those around you would describe your personality. Is this an accurate representation of who you really are?

Building Background

At the beginning of the novel, Jane Eyre is a ten-year-old orphan left in the care of her aunt, Mrs. Sarah Reed. Mrs. Reed and her children, Eliza, Georgiana, and John, treat Jane with great cruelty. Jane, who is treated like a maid and ordered around by the housekeeper, Bessie, is blamed and punished whenever the Reed children misbehave. During one of these punishments, Mrs. Reed locks Jane in the red room, where Jane's uncle died. Jane is frightened and begs to be let out of the room. Mrs. Reed refuses and Jane becomes so upset she passes out. When she awakes, a physician is standing over her. He recommends that Jane be sent away to a boarding school because she is so miserable living with the Reed family. The selection you are about to read begins when Jane first meets Mr. Brocklehurst, the headmaster of the school.

Setting Purposes for Reading

Big Idea Disillusionment and Darker Visions

As you read, think about the conditions a young orphan in Victorian England would have faced.

Literary Element Description

Description is a detailed portrayal of a person, a place, an object, or an event. Good descriptive writing appeals to the senses through imagery.

• See Literary Terms Handbook, p. R4.

Reading Strategy Analyzing Characterization

Characterization is the method a writer uses to reveal the personality of a character. In **direct characterization,** the writer makes explicit statements about a character. In **indirect characterization,** the writer reveals a character through his or her words, thoughts, and actions and through what other characters think and say about that character.

Reading Tip: Taking Notes As you read, note examples of both direct and indirect characterization in the selection from *Jane Eyre.*

Vocabulary

vacant (vā′ kənt) *adj.* empty; p. 969 *The house was vacant for months until a family finally moved in.*

scrutiny (skrōōt′ ən ē) *n.* close watch or examination; p. 970 *The suspect's activities were under close scrutiny by the police.*

advocate (ad′ və kāt′) *v.* to support or argue for; p. 972 *I advocate environmental protection since I firmly believe in recycling.*

retaliation (ri tal′ ē ā′ shən) *n.* getting even with; revenge; p. 973 *Doing well on the exam is the best retaliation for not doing well on the paper.*

subside (səb sīd′) *v.* to give way or end; p. 974 *The fear I felt about graduation eventually subsided, and I eagerly awaited the challenges ahead.*

Vocabulary Tip: Context Clues Context clues are the words and sentences around an unfamiliar word that help you figure out the word's meaning.

Literature Online Interactive Literary Elements Handbook To review or learn more about the literary elements, go to www.glencoe.com.

OBJECTIVES
In studying this selection, you will focus on the following:
• recognizing the characteristics of literary genres such as the novel
• analyzing an author's use of description
• evaluating characterization

from

Jane Eyre

Charlotte Brontë

A Girl Writing. Henriette Browne. Oil color on canvas, 74 cm. x 92 cm. Victoria and Albert Museum, London.

*I*t was the fifteenth of January, about nine o'clock in the morning. Bessie was gone down to breakfast; my cousins had not yet been summoned to their mama; Eliza was putting on her bonnet and warm garden coat to go and feed her poultry, an occupation of which she was fond, and not less so of selling the eggs to the housekeeper and hoarding up the money she thus obtained. She had a turn for traffic, and a marked propensity for saving, shown not only in the vending of eggs and chickens but also in driving hard bargains with the gardener about flower roots, seeds, and slips of plants, that functionary having orders from Mrs. Reed to buy from this young lady all the products of her parterre[1]

she wished to sell; and Eliza would have sold the hair off her head if she could have made a handsome profit thereby. As to her money, she first secreted it in odd corners, wrapped in a rag or an old curl paper;[2] but some of these hoards having been discovered by the housemaid, Eliza, fearful of one day losing her valued treasure, consented to entrust it to her mother, at a usurious[3] rate of interest—fifty or sixty percent, which interest she exacted every quarter, keeping her accounts in a little book with anxious accuracy.

---

1. A *parterre* is a garden in which the flowerbeds are arranged to form a pattern.

2. *Curl paper* is a small piece of paper used for curling hair.
3. *Usurious* means "excessive."

Reading Strategy Analyzing Characterization *How does Brontë reveal Eliza's character in this passage?*

Georgiana sat on a high stool, dressing her hair at the glass, and interweaving her curls with artificial flowers and faded feathers, of which she had found a store in a drawer in the attic. I was making my bed, having received strict orders from Bessie to get it arranged before she returned (for Bessie now frequently employed me as a sort of under-nurserymaid,[4] to tidy the room, dust the chairs, etc.). Having spread the quilt and folded my nightdress, I went to the windowseat to put in order some picture books and doll's-house furniture scattered there; an abrupt command from Georgiana to let her playthings alone (for the tiny chairs and mirrors, the fairy plates and cups were her property) stopped my proceedings, and then, for lack of other occupation, I fell to breathing on the frostflowers with which the window was fretted, and thus clearing a space in the glass through which I might look out on the grounds, where all was still and petrified under the influence of a hard frost.

From this window were visible the porter's[5] lodge and the carriage road, and just as I had dissolved so much of the silver-white foliage veiling the panes as left room to look out, I saw the gates thrown open and a carriage roll through. I watched it ascending the drive with indifference; carriages often came to Gateshead, but none ever brought visitors in whom I was interested. It stopped in front of the house, the doorbell rang loudly, the newcomer was admitted. All this being nothing to me, my **vacant** attention soon found livelier attraction in the spectacle of a little hungry robin, which came and chirruped on the twigs of the leafless cherry tree nailed against the wall near the casement. The remains of my breakfast of bread and milk stood on the table, and having crumbled a morsel of roll, I was tugging at the sash to put out the crumb on the windowsill when Bessie came running upstairs into the nursery.

"Miss Jane, take off your pinafore;[6] what are you doing there? Have you washed your hands and face this morning?" I gave another tug before I answered, for I wanted the bird to be secure of its bread; the sash yielded, I scattered the crumbs, some on the stone sill, some on the cherry-tree bough, then, closing the window, I replied:

"No, Bessie; I have only just finished dusting."

"Troublesome, careless child! And what are you doing now? You look quite red, as if you had been about some mischief; what were you opening the window for?"

I was spared the trouble of answering, for Bessie seemed in too great a hurry to listen to explanations; she hauled me to the washstand, inflicted a merciless but happily brief scrub on my face and hands with soap, water, and a coarse towel; disciplined my head with a bristly brush, denuded me of my pinafore, and then hurrying me to the top of the stairs, bid me go down directly, as I was wanted in the breakfast room.

I would have asked who wanted me; I would have demanded if Mrs. Reed was there, but Bessie was already gone, and had closed the nursery door upon me. I slowly descended. For nearly three months, I had never been called to Mrs. Reed's presence; restricted so long to the nursery, the breakfast, dining, and drawing rooms were become for me awful regions, on which it dismayed me to intrude.

I now stood in the empty hall; before me was the breakfast-room door, and I stopped, intimidated and trembling. What a miserable little poltroon[7] had fear, engendered of unjust punishment, made of me in those days! I feared to return to the nursery, and feared to go forward to the parlor; ten minutes I stood in agitated hesitation. The vehement ringing of the breakfast-room bell decided me; I *must* enter.

"Who could want me?" I asked inwardly, as with both hands I turned the stiff door handle which, for a second or two, resisted my efforts.

---

4. The *under-nurserymaid* helps take care of the nursery—the part of the house where children sleep, play, and study.
5. A *porter* is someone who works at the door or gate to let people inside.

Vocabulary

vacant (vā′ kənt) *adj.* empty

---

6. A *pinafore* is a sleeveless housedress worn over a dress.
7. *Poltroon* means "a complete coward."

"What should I see beside Aunt Reed in the apartment? A man or a woman?" The handle turned, the door unclosed, and passing through and curtseying low, I looked up at—a black pillar!—such, at least, appeared to me, at first sight, the straight, narrow, sable-clad shape standing erect on the rug; The grim face at the top was like a carved mask, placed above the shaft by way of capital.

Mrs. Reed occupied her usual seat by the fireside; she made a signal to me to approach; I did so, and she introduced me to the stony stranger with the words: "This is the little girl respecting whom I applied to you."

He, for it was a man, turned his head slowly towards where I stood, and having examined me with the two inquisitive-looking gray eyes which twinkled under a pair of bushy brows, said solemnly, and in a bass voice: "Her size is small; what is her age?"

"Ten years."

"So much?" was the doubtful answer; and he prolonged his **scrutiny** for some minutes. Presently he addressed me:

"Your name, little girl?"

"Jane Eyre, sir."

In uttering these words, I looked up: he seemed to me a tall gentleman, but then I was very little; his features were large, and they and all the lines of his frame were equally harsh and prim.

"Well, Jane Eyre, and are you a good child?"

Impossible to reply to this in the affirmative; my little world held a contrary opinion. I was silent. Mrs. Reed answered for me by an expressive shake of the head, adding soon, "Perhaps the less said on that subject the better, Mr. Brocklehurst."

"Sorry indeed to hear it! She and I must have some talk," and bending from the perpendicular, he installed his person in the armchair, opposite Mrs. Reed's. "Come here," he said.

I stepped across the rug; he placed me square and straight before him. What a face he had, now that it was almost on a level with mine! what a great nose! and what a mouth! and what large prominent teeth!

"No sight so sad as that of a naughty child," he began, "especially a naughty little girl. Do you know where the wicked go after death?"

"They go to hell," was my ready and orthodox answer.

"And what is hell? Can you tell me that?"

"A pit full of fire."

"And should you like to fall into that pit, and to be burning there forever?"

"No, sir."

"What must you do to avoid it?"

I deliberated a moment; my answer, when it did come, was objectionable: "I must keep in good health, and not die."

"How can you keep in good health? Children younger than you die daily. I buried a little child of five years old only a day or two since—a good little child, whose soul is now in heaven. It is to be feared the same could not be said of you, were you to be called hence."

Not being in a condition to remove his doubts, I only cast my eyes down on the two large feet planted on the rug, and sighed, wishing myself far enough away.

"I hope that sigh is from the heart, and that you repent of ever having been the occasion of discomfort to your excellent benefactress."

"Benefactress! benefactress!" said I, inwardly. "They all call Mrs. Reed my benefactress; if so, a benefactress is a disagreeable thing."

"Do you say your prayers night and morning?" continued my interrogator.

"Yes, sir."

"Do you read your Bible?"

"Sometimes."

"With pleasure? Are you fond of it?"

"I like Revelations, and the book of Daniel, and Genesis and Samuel, and a little bit of Exodus, and some parts of Kings and Chronicles, and Job and Jonah."

"And the Psalms? I hope you like them?"

"No, sir."

Vocabulary

scrutiny (skrōōt′ ən ē) *n.* close watch or examination

Four Girls and a Dog on a Bridge Over the Debdon Burn. Henry Hetherington Emmerson. Watercolor on paper. Cragside House, Northumberland, UK.

I was about to propound a question, touching the manner in which that operation of changing my heart was to be performed, when Mrs. Reed interposed, telling me to sit down; she then proceeded to carry on the conversation herself.

"Mr. Brocklehurst, I believe I intimated in the letter which I wrote to you three weeks ago that this little girl has not quite the character and disposition I could wish; should you admit her into Lowood school, I should be glad if the superintendent and teachers were requested to keep a strict eye on her, and above all, to guard against her worst fault, a tendency to deceit. I mention this fact in your hearing, Jane, that you may not attempt to impose on Mr. Brocklehurst."

Well might I dread, well might I dislike Mrs. Reed, for it was her nature to wound me cruelly; never was I happy in her presence: however carefully I obeyed, however strenuously I strove to please her, my efforts were still repulsed and repaid by such sentences as the above. Now, uttered before a stranger, the accusation cut me to the heart: I dimly perceived that she was already obliterating hope from the new phase of existence which she destined me to enter; I felt, though I could not have expressed the feeling, that she was sowing aversion and unkindness along my future path; I saw myself transformed under Mr. Brocklehurst's eye into an artful, obnoxious child, and what could I do to remedy the injury?

"Nothing, indeed!" thought I, as I struggled to repress a sob, and hastily wiped away some tears, the impotent evidences of my anguish.

"No? Oh, shocking! I have a little boy, younger than you, who knows six Psalms by heart; and when you ask him which he would rather have, a gingerbread nut[8] to eat or a verse of a Psalm to learn, he says: 'Oh! the verse of a Psalm! Angels sing Psalms'; says he, 'I wish to be a little angel here below'; he then gets two nuts in recompense for his infant piety."

"Psalms are not interesting," I remarked.

"That proves you have a wicked heart; and you must pray to God to change it, to give you a new and clean one, to take away your heart of stone and give you a heart of flesh."

---

8. A *gingerbread nut* is the fruit of the doum tree, or gingerbread tree, named because the fruit tastes like gingerbread.

Literary Element Description *How does Mrs. Reed's description of Jane foreshadow Jane's future treatment at Lowood?*

"Deceit is, indeed, a sad fault in a child," said Mr. Brocklehurst; "it is akin to falsehood, and all liars will have their portion in the lake burning with fire and brimstone; she shall, however, be watched, Mrs. Reed; I will speak to Miss Temple and the teachers."

"I should wish her to be brought up in a manner suiting her prospects," continued my benefactress; "to be made useful, to be kept humble; as for the vacations, she will, with your permission, spend them always at Lowood."

"Your decisions are perfectly judicious, madam," returned Mr. Brocklehurst. "Humility is a Christian grace, and one peculiarly appropriate to the pupils of Lowood; I, therefore, direct that especial care shall be bestowed on its cultivation among them. I have studied how best to mortify in them the worldly sentiment of pride; and, only the other day, I had a pleasing proof of my success. My second daughter, Augusta, went with her mama to visit the school, and on her return she exclaimed: 'Oh, dear papa, how quiet and plain all the girls at Lowood look; with their hair combed behind their ears, and their long pinafores, and those little holland[9] pockets outside their frocks—they are almost like poor people's children! And,' said she, 'they looked at my dress and mama's as if they had never seen a silk gown before.'"

"This is the state of things I quite approve," returned Mrs. Reed. "Had I sought all England over, I could scarcely have found a system more exactly fitting a child like Jane Eyre. Consistency, my dear Mr. Brocklehurst; I **advocate** consistency in all things."

"Consistency, madam, is the first of Christian duties, and it has been observed in every arrangement connected with the establishment of Lowood: plain fare, simple attire, unsophisticated accommodations, hardy and active habits; such is the order of the day in the house and its inhabitants."

"Quite right, sir. I may then depend upon this child being received as a pupil at Lowood, and there being trained in conformity to her position and prospects?"

"Madam, you may; she shall be placed in that nursery of chosen plants—and I trust she will show herself grateful for the inestimable privilege of her election."

"I will send her, then, as soon as possible, Mr. Brocklehurst; for, I assure you, I feel anxious to be relieved of a responsibility that was becoming too irksome."

"No doubt, no doubt, madam, and now I wish you good morning. I shall return to Brocklehurst Hall in the course of a week or two; my good friend, the archdeacon,[10] will not permit me to leave him sooner. I shall send Miss Temple notice that she is to expect a new girl, so that there will be no difficulty about receiving her. Good-bye."

"Good-bye, Mr. Brocklehurst; remember me to Mrs. and Miss Brocklehurst, and to Augusta and Theodore, and Master Broughton Brocklehurst."

"I will, madam. Little girl, here is a book entitled the 'Child's Guide'; read it with prayer, especially that part containing 'an account of the awfully sudden death of Martha G—, a naughty child addicted to falsehood and deceit.'"

With these words Mr. Brocklehurst put into my hand a thin pamphlet sewed in a cover, and having rung for his carriage, he departed.

Mrs. Reed and I were left alone. Some minutes passed in silence; she was sewing, I was watching her. Mrs. Reed might be at that time some six-or seven-and-thirty; she was a woman of robust frame, square shouldered and strong limbed, not tall, and, though stout, not obese; she had a somewhat large face, the underjaw being much developed and very solid; her brow was low, her chin large and prominent, mouth and nose sufficiently regular; under her light eyebrows glimmered an eye devoid of ruth;[11] her skin was dark and opaque, her hair nearly flaxen; her constitution was sound as a bell—illness never came near her; she was an exact, clever manager; her household and tenantry[12] were thoroughly under her control; her children, only, at times defied her authority, and laughed it to scorn;

---

9. *Holland* refers to a type of linen or heavy cotton first made in Holland.

Vocabulary

advocate (ad′ və kāt′) *v.* to support or argue for

---

10. The *archdeacon,* in the Church of England, is a church official ranking just below a bishop. He assists the bishop in his duties.
11. *Ruth* is compassion or pity.
12. *Tenantry* refers to tenant farmers on Mrs. Reed's estate.

she dressed well, and had a presence and port[13] calculated to set off handsome attire.

Sitting on a low stool, a few yards from her armchair, I examined her figure; I perused her features. In my hand I held the tract, containing the sudden death of the Liar, to which narrative my attention had been pointed as to an appropriate warning. What had just passed; what Mrs. Reed had said concerning me to Mr. Brocklehurst; the whole tenor of their conversation, was recent, raw, and stinging in my mind; I had felt every word as acutely as I had heard it plainly, and a passion of resentment fomented now within me.

Mrs. Reed looked up from her work; her eye settled on mine, her fingers at the same time suspended their nimble movements.

"Go out of the room; return to the nursery," was her mandate. My look or something else must have struck her as offensive, for she spoke with extreme though suppressed irritation. I got up; I went to the door; I came back again; I walked to the window, across the room, then close up to her.

Speak I must; I had been trodden on severely, and *must* turn, but how? What strength had I to dart **retaliation** at my antagonist? I gathered my energies and launched them in this blunt sentence:

"I am not deceitful: if I were, I should say I loved *you*, but I declare I do not love you; I dislike you the worst of anybody in the world except John Reed; and this book about the liar you may give to your girl, Georgiana, for it is she who tells lies, and not I."

Mrs. Reed's hands still lay on her work inactive; her eye of ice continued to dwell freezingly on mine.

"What more have you to say?" she asked, rather in the tone in which a person might address an opponent of adult age than such as is ordinarily used to a child.

That eye of hers, that voice stirred every antipathy I had. Shaking from head to foot, thrilled with ungovernable excitement, I continued.

"I am glad you are no relation[14] of mine; I will never call you aunt again as long as I live. I will never come to see you when I am grown up; and if anyone asks me how I liked you, and how you treated me, I will say the very thought of you makes me sick and that you treated me with miserable cruelty."

"How dare you affirm that, Jane Eyre?"

"How dare I, Mrs. Reed? How dare I? Because it is the *truth*. You think I have no feelings, and that I can do without one bit of love or kindness; but I cannot live so, and you have no pity. I shall remember how you thrust me back— roughly and violently thrust me back—into the red room,[15] and locked me up there, to my dying day; though I was in agony, though I cried out, while suffocating with distress, 'Have mercy! Have mercy, Aunt Reed!' And that punishment you made me suffer because your wicked boy struck me—knocked me down for nothing. I will tell anybody who asks me questions this exact tale. People think you a good woman, but you are bad; hard-hearted. *You* are deceitful!"

Ere I had finished this reply, my soul began to expand, to exult, with the strangest sense of freedom, of triumph, I ever felt. It seemed as if an invisible bond had burst, and that I had struggled out into unhoped-for liberty. Not without cause was this sentiment: Mrs. Reed looked frightened; her work had slipped from her knee; she was lifting up her hands, rocking herself to and fro, and even twisting her face as if she would cry.

> *"People think you a good woman, but you are bad; hard-hearted. You are deceitful!"*

---

13. *Port* is a way of carrying oneself.

Reading Strategy Analyzing Characterization *Based on the characterization in this paragraph, what kind of person do you think Mrs. Reed is?*

Reading Strategy Analyzing Characterization *How does this passage reveal Jane's character?*

Vocabulary

retaliation (ri tal′ ē ā′ shən) n. getting even with; revenge

---

14. *Relation* here means "blood relation." Mrs. Reed is Jane's aunt by marriage.

15. The *red room* is a room with red furnishings. When Jane was younger, Mrs. Reed unjustly punished her by locking her in that room, in which Jane's uncle had died.

She is Witty to Talk With. Helen Jackson. Watercolor on paper, 50.8 x 43.1 cm. Private collection. The Maas Gallery, London.

"Jane, you are under a mistake; what is the matter with you? Why do you tremble so violently? Would you like to drink some water?"

"No, Mrs. Reed."

"Is there anything else you wish for, Jane? I assure you, I desire to be your friend."

"Not you. You told Mr. Brocklehurst I had a bad character, a deceitful disposition; and I'll let everybody at Lowood know what you are, and what you have done."

"Jane, you don't understand these things; children must be corrected for their faults."

"Deceit is not my fault!" I cried out in a savage, high voice.

"But you are passionate, Jane, that you must allow; and now return to the nursery—there's a dear—and lie down a little."

"I am not your dear. I cannot lie down; send me to school soon, Mrs. Reed, for I hate to live here."

"I will indeed send her to school soon," murmured Mrs. Reed, sotto voce;[16] and gathering up her work, she abruptly quitted the apartment.

I was left there alone—winner of the field. It was the hardest battle I had fought, and the first victory I had gained. I stood awhile on the rug, where Mr. Brocklehurst had stood, and I enjoyed my conqueror's solitude. First, I smiled to myself and felt elated; but this fierce pleasure **subsided** in me as fast as did the accelerated throb of my pulses. A child cannot quarrel with its elders, as I had done, cannot give its furious feelings uncontrolled play, as I had given mine, without experiencing afterward the pang of remorse and the chill of reaction. A ridge of lighted heath,[17] alive, glancing, devouring, would have been a meet[18] emblem of my mind when I accused and menaced Mrs. Reed; the same ridge, black and blasted after the flames are dead, would have represented as meetly my subsequent condition, when half an hour's silence and reflection had shown me the madness of my conduct, and the dreariness of my hated and hating position. ❧

---

16. *Sotto voce* means "in an undertone." The expression, from Italian, literally means "under the voice."
17. *Lighted heath* is moorland that has caught fire.
18. *Meet* means "suitable or appropriate."

Big Idea **Disillusionment and Darker Visions** *Why do you think Brontë chose these images to describe Jane's feelings?*

Vocabulary

subside (səb sīd´) *v.* to give way or end

RESPONDING AND THINKING CRITICALLY

Respond

1. Imagine you faced a situation similar to Jane Eyre's. How would you have reacted?

Recall and Interpret

2. (a)With what duties is Jane often employed in the nursery? (b)What does this reveal about her role in the Reed household?

3. (a)How does Mrs. Reed describe Jane to Mr. Brocklehurst? (b)How might her comments affect the way Mr. Brocklehurst treats Jane?

4. (a)How does Mrs. Reed want Jane to be brought up? (b)What does this reveal about Mrs. Reed and her relationship with Jane?

5. (a)How does Jane behave after the departure of Mr. Brocklehurst? (b)What changing feelings does Jane experience after her conversation with Mrs. Reed? Why does she feel this way?

Analyze and Evaluate

6. (a)What sort of person is Mr. Brocklehurst? (b)What ironic contrasts do the details about Augusta Brocklehurst's visit to Lowood reveal about Lowood and the Brocklehursts?

7. (a)Why do you think Mrs. Reed wants to be Jane's friend at the end of the selection? (b)How does Brontë use imagery in this scene to represent opposite sides of the argument?

8. (a)What characteristics does Jane Eyre seem to possess throughout the selection? (b)What differences do you perceive between young Jane and the older Jane who narrates the story?

Connect

9. **Big Idea** **Disillusionment and Darker Visions** What does Jane Eyre's situation reveal about how Victorian novelists attempted to create social change?

DAILY LIFE AND CULTURE

Orphans in Victorian England

Sanitation was poor during the Victorian age and there was a lack of treatment for diseases that would be cured easily today. As a result, the average life span for men and women was twenty-six years, and even younger in urban areas. For these reasons, orphaned children like Jane Eyre were not uncommon in Victorian England.

Some orphans, like Jane, were taken into the care of family or distant relatives. However, those without any family usually went to workhouses, as shown in Charles Dickens's novel *Oliver Twist* (see page 985). Conditions in these workhouses were harsh, and children were forced to work long hours with no pay, receiving only meager amounts of food and a place to sleep. There were no laws in place to protect children from cruel treatment at this time.

Group Activity Discuss these questions with your classmates.

1. How do you feel about the limitations placed upon and lack of opportunities for children like Jane Eyre?

2. Why do you think novels such as *Jane Eyre* brought attention to the situation of orphans? Explain.

Orphans, 1879. George Aldolphus Storey. Oil on canvas, 103.5 x 128 cm. Private collection.

LITERARY ANALYSIS

Literary Element **Description**

Description reveals details about people and places in a story and often shapes how a reader feels about events in the text. Writers can use description to develop the **mood,** or emotional quality, of a literary work. Description also reveals the **tone,** or the attitude of the author (or narrator) toward his or her subject.

1. What qualities are revealed about Jane, Mrs. Reed, and Mr. Brocklehurst through description?

2. How does the narrator's description of her surroundings show how she feels about them?

3. What is the overarching mood of the excerpt?

Review: Point of View

As you learned on page 276, **point of view** is the standpoint from which a story is told. In a story with **first-person point of view,** the narrator is a character in the story and uses the words *I* and *me,* as in the selection from *Jane Eyre.* Sometimes, a narrator retells events that have already happened. For example, in *Jane Eyre,* an adult narrator is recalling the events of her childhood.

Partner Activity Work with a partner to find evidence in *Jane Eyre* that an adult narrator is retelling past events. Then determine what is revealed about the adult Jane Eyre through her recollection of childhood events. Use a chart like the one below to take notes.

Example Sentence	What the Reader Learns
"Well, Jane Eyre, and are you a good child?" Impossible to reply to this in the affirmative; my little world held a contrary opinion.	The adult narrator knows she was isolated and alone in the Reed household and made to feel that she was not a good girl. A child narrator might not be able to express those feelings or even recognize the situation.

READING AND VOCABULARY

Reading Strategy **Analyzing Characterization**

Authors use **characterization** to shape the way a reader views the characters and their actions. As you read about a character, remember that by carefully selecting details, an author controls the impression the reader forms. Find examples of characterization in the selection from *Jane Eyre* that use the following techniques. Then describe what each passage reveals about the character.

1. a direct statement

2. a character's actions

3. a character's physical appearance

Vocabulary **Practice**

Practice with Context Clues Use context clues to identify the definition of each underlined vocabulary word.

1. Her <u>vacant</u> stare led me to believe she was not paying attention.
   - **a.** blank
   - **b.** cautious
   - **c.** disagreeable
   - **d.** careful

2. After months of <u>scrutiny</u>, I decided to invest in the stock company.
   - **a.** anticipation
   - **b.** discussion
   - **c.** enjoyment
   - **d.** analysis

3. I <u>advocate</u> the use of pesticides in farming because it helps to keep the crops free from insects.
   - **a.** help
   - **b.** support
   - **c.** criticize
   - **d.** consider

4. Beth's methods of <u>retaliation</u> were unfair because her attacks were unprovoked.
   - **a.** arrangement
   - **b.** wrongdoing
   - **c.** payback
   - **d.** satisfaction

5. Once the rain <u>subsided</u>, we were able to put our umbrellas away.
   - **a.** flooded
   - **b.** responded
   - **c.** grew
   - **d.** went away

Writing About Literature

Evaluate Author's Craft Brontë creates rich, detailed images in her writing that enhance what readers understand about her characters. In a few paragraphs, summarize how the various images Brontë uses throughout the excerpt from *Jane Eyre* help you understand the three main characters in the selection: Jane, Mrs. Reed, and Mr. Brocklehurst.

To help you organize your summary, first write an outline of the images you find. Be sure to include the thesis of your essay and supporting evidence. Draw quotes from the text to support your ideas.

> I. Thesis
>   A.
>   B.
>
> II. Imagery and Jane
>   A.
>   B.
>   C.
>
> III. Imagery and Mrs. Reed
>   A.
>   B.
>   C.
>
> IV. Imagery and Mr. Brocklehurst
>   A.
>   B.
>   C.

After you complete your draft, meet with a peer reviewer to evaluate each other's work and to suggest revisions. Then proofread and edit your draft for errors in spelling, grammar, and punctuation.

Internet Connection

Use the Internet to research information about the Brontë family's life and legacy. Then compare and contrast various scholars' views on each sister's talents and contributions to literature. Present your findings to your class.

Literature Online **Web Activities** For eFlashcards, Selection Quick Checks, and other Web activities, go to www.glencoe.com.

Brontë's Language and Style

Using Colons A colon can introduce a list, a formal quotation, or material that explains, illustrates, or restates the preceding material. Brontë uses colons in her writing to introduce quotations and illustrative material. Consider the effect of the colons in the passage below.

> "So much?" was the doubtful answer; and he prolonged his scrutiny for some minutes. Presently he addressed me:
>   "Your name, little girl?"
>   "Jane Eyre, sir."
>   In uttering these words, I looked up: he seemed to me a tall gentleman, but then I was very little;

The first colon in this passage introduces what Mr. Brocklehurst says to Jane. The second introduces material that explains or illustrates the first part of the sentence—it tells what Jane saw when she looked up.

Activity Scan the text for other colons and determine the function of each one. Then add your examples and explanations to a chart like the one below.

Example	Function of Colon
She introduced me to the stony stranger with the words: "This is the little girl respecting whom I applied to you."	Introduces a quotation

Revising Check

Colons Modern colon usage differs somewhat from Brontë's. Colons are not often used to introduce quotations now. Remember that a colon should follow a complete sentence. For example, "We need the following: a camp stove, a lantern, and two canteens" is correct. It would be incorrect to write "We need: a camp stove, a lantern, and two canteens." Keep this in mind as you review your essay on Brontë's use of images. Make sure you have used colons correctly and look for places where you might add them to clarify and improve your work.

Grammar Workshop

Sentence Structure

▶ **Understanding Adverb Clauses**

An **adverb clause** tells *when, where, how, why, to what extent,* or *under what conditions* about the main clause of the sentence. It is introduced with a **subordinating conjunction**.

▶ **Test-Taking Tip**

To identify an adverb clause during a test, first determine how many pairs of subjects and predicates are in the sentence. If there is more than one, then the sentence has multiple clauses. If an independent clause functions as an adverb, then it is an adverb clause.

▶ **Language Handbook**

For more about adverb clauses, see Language Handbook, pp. R46–R47.

eWorkbooks To link to the Grammar and Language eWorkbook, go to www.glencoe.com.

Using Adverb Clauses

"Ere I had finished this reply, my soul began to expand, to exult, with the strangest sense of freedom, of triumph, I ever felt."
—Charlotte Brontë, from *Jane Eyre*

Connecting to Literature The above sentence from *Jane Eyre* can be broken into two clauses: a main clause (also called an independent clause) and a subordinate clause (also called a dependent clause). The main clause, "my soul began to expand, to exult, with the strangest sense of freedom, of triumph, I ever felt," includes a subject and a predicate, and it expresses a complete thought. The subordinate clause, "Ere I had finished this reply," also includes a subject and a predicate, but it depends on the main clause to complete its meaning.

One type of subordinate clause, an **adverb clause**, modifies a verb, an adjective, or an adverb and comes either before or after the main clause in a sentence. When the adverb clause comes first, it should be separated from the main clause by a comma. An adverb clause always begins with a **subordinating conjunction**, such as *after, although, as, because, how, if, than, that,* or *while.*

Examples:

- When Mr. Brocklehurst came to visit, Mrs. Reed announced she was sending Jane away.

[The adverb clause tells *when* and modifies the verb *was sending.*]

- If Jane could be free from Mrs. Reed, she was content to go away to Lowood.

[The adverb clause tells *under what conditions* and modifies the verb *was content.*]

- Charlotte Brontë believed in the importance of a woman's education before many others shared her views.

[The adverb clause tells *when* and modifies the verb *believed.*]

Exercise

Identify the adverb clause in each of the following sentences.

1. When she opened the window, Jane threw out breadcrumbs to feed the birds.
2. Before Jane went away to Lowood, she lived with the cruel Reed family.
3. The Brontë sisters created memorable literary works before they died.
4. If medical technology were better, there would not have been so many orphaned children in Victorian England.

OBJECTIVES
- Understand adverb clauses.
- Analyze sentence structure.

My Last Duchess

MEET ROBERT BROWNING

From early in his career, English poet Robert Browning explored the darker aspects of human nature. His real self seemed completely at odds with the poet who embraced Realism and wrote about murder, madness, jealousy, deceit, and corruption. He had a pleasant demeanor, and he was a loving, devoted husband and father.

"It is the glory and good of Art
That Art remains the one way possible
Of speaking truth,—to mouths like
*   mine, at least."*

—Robert Browning

"The Poet of Men's Souls" Browning was an expert at dissecting the hearts and minds of his characters. This analytical bent was encouraged early in life by his parents. Although he attended various schools, Browning's education was gained mostly at home, where he lived with his parents until he married at age thirty-four. After spending one year at London University, Browning embarked on a writing career. Unfortunately, Browning's high expectations were quickly dashed by critics who mocked his poems and ignored his plays altogether.

Many of Browning's first poems were published in *Monthly Repository*, the most radical middle-class journal of its time. Its editor, the Unitarian W. J. Fox, espoused radical political, social, and economic reforms. Browning's close involvement with Fox and his intellectual circle exposed the poet to ideas that would not reach most of the English literati until the 1840s and 1850s.

One person who did admire Browning's work was a popular poet named Elizabeth Barrett (see page 939). After several months of correspondence, they met in person. Browning soon declared his love for Barrett, but she was reluctant to marry because of her poor health and the opposition of her overbearing father. In 1846, however, the couple eloped to Italy and settled in Florence, where they remained for the next fifteen years.

Recognition and Success The marriage between Barrett and Browning proved to be a happy one. Barrett Browning recovered her health, and in 1849 she gave birth to a son. When she died in 1861, Browning and his son moved back to England, where he finally began to receive the recognition he deserved. Another edition of his collected poems was requested in 1863, and his next book of poems, *Dramatis Personae* (1864), reached two editions. After the publication of *The Ring and the Book* (1868), a blank-verse dramatic poem based on a murder trial in Rome in 1698, Browning became a much sought-after celebrity.

Browning never remarried, even though he survived his wife by nearly thirty years. He claimed that his "heart was buried in Florence." On his last trip to Italy, he developed bronchitis. After learning of the favorable reviews of his last book of verse, Browning smiled and muttered, "How gratifying." He died a few hours later.

Robert Browning was born in 1812 and died in 1889.

Literature Online **Author Search** For more about Robert Browning, go to www.glencoe.com.

Connecting to the Poem

What kind of person is angered by kindness? In Browning's poem, a Duke reveals his extreme irritation over his late wife's generous, outgoing nature. As you read the poem, think about how jealousy and possessiveness affect relationships.

Building Background

During his teens, Browning devoted much time to studying the poems of Percy Bysshe Shelley (see page 850). Browning's first published work, *Pauline,* was clearly influenced by Shelley's confessional style. One reviewer commented on the "intense and morbid self-consciousness" that the poem displayed. Embarrassed by such criticism, Browning decided to avoid exposing himself in his poetry. He began to use speakers who were fictional or historical characters. He had refined this technique by the time he wrote "My Last Duchess," which is loosely based on the life of the Duke of Ferrara, a sixteenth-century Italian duke whose wife died under mysterious circumstances.

Setting Purposes for Reading

Big Idea The Emergence of Realism

As you read, notice how Realism's focus on the actual life of individuals, with all their flaws exposed, is displayed in "My Last Duchess."

Literary Element Dramatic Monologue

Dramatic monologue is a form of dramatic poetry in which the speaker addresses a silent listener. Unlike traditional poetry in which the speaker of a poem often speaks for the poet, the speaker of the dramatic monologue is a separate character, with his or her own distinct personality, much like a character in a story or play. As you read the poem, examine how the speaker reveals his personality through what he says.

● See Literary Terms Handbook, p. R5.

Literature Online Interactive Literary Elements Handbook To review or learn more about the literary elements, go to www.glencoe.com.

Reading Strategy Clarifying Meaning

To **clarify meaning** is to examine confusing parts of a text in order to make sense of them. When you read a poem set during the Renaissance, such as "My Last Duchess," you may encounter archaic or difficult vocabulary, imagery, and line breaks that hinder comprehension. Adjust your reading rate, reread, and paraphrase to clarify what you don't understand.

....

Reading Tip: Paraphrasing Important Ideas Use a chart to paraphrase important ideas in the poem.

Lines	Key Details	Paraphrase
1–4	Duchess painted, wall, as if alive, Frà Pandolf	That's a painting of my former duchess on the wall. It's so lifelike. The artist Frà Pandolf painted it quickly, and there it is.

Vocabulary

countenance (koun´ tə nəns) *n.* someone's face; the expression on someone's face; p. 981 *Bright blue eyes complemented his cheerful countenance.*

trifling (trī´ fling) *n.* treating someone or something as unimportant; showing a lack of proper respect; p. 982 *The judge lost patience with his trifling.*

munificence (mū nif´ ə səns) *n.* great generosity; p. 982 *Through the munificence of an anonymous donor, the fundraiser was a success.*

Vocabulary Tip: Word Origins A word's origin explains its history and illustrates how the word relates to other words in English and other languages. In a dictionary, a word's origin usually appears in brackets.

OBJECTIVES
In studying this selection, you will focus on the following:
● relating literary works and authors to their eras
● analyzing dramatic monologue
● clarifying meaning

The Duchess of Berri, c.1825. Sir Thomas Lawrence.
Oil on canvas. Musée Crozatier, Le Puy-en-Velay, France.

My Last Duchess

Robert Browning

That's my last Duchess painted on the wall,
Looking as if she were alive. I call
That piece a wonder, now: Frà Pandolf's[1] hands
Worked busily a day, and there she stands.
5 Will 't please you sit and look at her? I said
"Frà Pandolf" by design,[2] for never read
Strangers like you that pictured **countenance**,
The depth and passion of its earnest glance,
But to myself they turned (since none puts by[3]
10 The curtain I have drawn for you, but I)
And seemed as they would ask me, if they durst,[4]
How such a glance came there; so, not the first
Are you to turn and ask thus. Sir, 'twas not
Her husband's presence only, called that spot
15 Of joy into the Duchess' cheek: perhaps
Frà Pandolf chanced to say, "Her mantle[5] laps
Over my lady's wrist too much," or "Paint
Must never hope to reproduce the faint
Half-flush that dies along her throat." Such stuff
20 Was courtesy, she thought, and cause enough

1. *Frà* (frä), meaning "brother," is the Italian title given to members of a religious order of friars. Frà Pandolf is an imaginary artist and friar.
2. *By design* here means "intentionally."
3. *Puts by* means "sets aside" or "draws open."
4. *Durst* means "dared."
5. A *mantle* is a cloak.

Literary Element Dramatic Monologue *What do you learn about the speaker and the setting of the poem from the title and the opening lines?*

Vocabulary

countenance (koun′ tə nəns) *n.* someone's face; the expression on someone's face

For calling up that spot of joy. She had
A heart—how shall I say?—too soon made glad,
Too easily impressed; she liked whate'er
She looked on, and her looks went everywhere.
25 Sir, 'twas all one! My favor[6] at her breast,
The dropping of the daylight in the West,
The bough of cherries some officious[7] fool
Broke in the orchard for her, the white mule
She rode with round the terrace—all and each
30 Would draw from her alike the approving speech,
Or blush, at least. She thanked men—good! but thanked
Somehow—I know not how—as if she ranked
My gift of a nine-hundred-years-old name
With anybody's gift. Who'd stoop to blame
35 This sort of **trifling**? Even had you skill
In speech—(which I have not)—to make your will
Quite clear to such an one, and say, "Just this
Or that in you disgusts me; here you miss,
Or there exceed the mark"—and if she let
40 Herself be lessoned so, nor plainly set
Her wits to yours, forsooth,[8] and made excuse,
—E'en then would be some stooping; and I choose
Never to stoop. Oh, sir, she smiled, no doubt,
Whene'er I passed her; but who passed without
45 Much the same smile? This grew; I gave commands;
Then all smiles stopped together. There she stands
As if alive. Will 't please you rise? We'll meet
The company below, then. I repeat,
The Count your master's known **munificence**
50 Is ample warrant that no just pretense
Of mine for dowry will be disallowed;[9]
Though his fair daughter's self, as I avowed
At starting, is my object. Nay, we'll go
Together down, sir! Notice Neptune,[10] though,
55 Taming a sea horse, thought a rarity,
Which Claus of Innsbruck[11] cast in bronze for me!

6. A *favor* here refers to a gift presented as a sign of one's love, such as a piece of jewelry or a decorative ribbon.

7. The word *officious* (ə fi′ shəs) today means "interfering" or "meddlesome." However, an archaic meaning is "kind and helpful."

8. *Forsooth* is an archaic word meaning "in truth."

9. The duke is saying here that he feels assured that the Count will approve his claim for a generous dowry.

10. *Neptune* is the god of the sea in Roman mythology. Note that the duke is referring to a sculpture of Neptune.

11. *Claus of Innsbruck* (inz′ brook) is an imaginary sculptor. Innsbruck, Austria, is the site of Emperor Maximilian's tomb, known for its bronze work.

Reading Strategy Clarifying Meaning *In your own words, explain what the speaker is saying in this sentence (lines 25–31). What do these lines reveal about the duchess and the speaker?*

Big Idea The Emergence of Realism *Does Browning's presentation of the speaker show Realism or Romanticism? Explain.*

Vocabulary

trifling (trī′ fling) *n.* treating someone or something as unimportant; showing a lack of proper respect

munificence (mū nif′ ə səns) *n.* great generosity

RESPONDING AND THINKING CRITICALLY

Respond

1. If you could ask the speaker one question, what would it be and why?

Recall and Interpret

2. (a)What is the speaker showing the visitor? (b)How does he account for "that spot of joy" on the duchess's cheek?

3. (a)Summarize the speaker's description of the duchess's character and behavior. (b)From this description, what can you infer about his attitude toward her?

4. Who is the visitor and why has he come to see the speaker? Support your response with evidence from the poem.

Analyze and Evaluate

5. (a)What words in the poem explain why the speaker didn't tell the duchess how her behavior affected him? (b)What does this decision reveal about his personality?

6. (a)What do you think happened to the duchess? What evidence from the poem suggests this? (b)Why do you think Browning does not explicitly state what happened to the duchess?

Connect

7. **Big Idea** **The Emergence of Realism**
Newspaper accounts of real, scandalous, and violent events had become readily available to readers in Browning's time. How may Browning have been trying to compete for the same audience with the poem "My Last Duchess"?

LITERARY ANALYSIS

Literary Element **Dramatic Monologue**

The speaker of a **dramatic monologue** describes a crucial moment in his or her life to someone who makes no response or comment. As we "listen in" on this one-sided conversation, we gain insight into the speaker's character and learn his or her viewpoint about the subject being discussed. The speaker can be a fictional or historical figure, always clearly distinct from the poet.

1. Does the speaker come across as a sympathetic or unsympathetic character? Explain.

2. How do you think the listener reacted to the speaker's description of his wife? Explain.

Listening and Speaking

Read "My Last Duchess" aloud to a classmate. Before you begin, think about how you can use your voice, facial expressions, and gestures to make your reading dramatic.

Literature Online **Web Activities** For eFlashcards, Selection Quick Checks, and other Web activities, go to www.glencoe.com.

READING AND VOCABULARY

Reading Strategy **Clarifying Meaning**

Review the ideas you recorded in your paraphrasing chart from page 980.

1. What gift does the duke refer to in line 33? Why does the duke believe that the duchess did not appreciate this gift?

2. What reference at the end of the poem suggests that the duke's new wife could meet with the same fate as the former duchess?

Vocabulary **Practice**

Practice with Word Origins Use a dictionary to match each vocabulary word with the definition of its origin.

1. trifling
2. munificence
3. countenance

a. Latin, "generous"
b. Latin, "hold together"
c. Old French, "to mock or trick"

from *Oliver Twist*

MEET CHARLES DICKENS

Charles Dickens was the most beloved British author of the Victorian age, and more than a hundred years after his death, his work is still popular, both in print and in dramatic and musical versions. The magic that millions still find in Dickens's novels can be traced, at least in part, to the eccentric and colorful array of characters that he created: villainous Fagin of *Oliver Twist*, miserly Scrooge of *A Christmas Carol*, shiftless Mr. Micawber of *David Copperfield*, and bitter Miss Havisham of *Great Expectations*. Like most Realist authors, Dickens based his characters on his own experience. In fact, many people believe that his father was the model for Micawber and that his mother inspired Mrs. Nickleby in *Nicholas Nickleby*.

Birth and Early Life Dickens was born in Portsmouth in southern England, the second of eight children. His father was a clerk who worked for the navy. During his childhood, Dickens's family repeatedly moved to escape creditors. When his father was finally sent to a debtors' prison,

Dickens, then twelve, began working in a warehouse pasting labels on pots of shoe polish. After a sudden inheritance improved the family's fortunes, Dickens found work as a lawyer's clerk and then as a shorthand reporter in the law courts.

Literary Triumphs Dickens's literary career began with the success of *Sketches by Boz,* a collection of brief scenes about life in the city that he wrote for a London newspaper. *Boz* led to *The Pickwick Papers,* his first novel, which like much of his work, was published in weekly or monthly installments. Prompted by his success, Dickens married Catherine Hogarth in 1836, and they eventually had ten children. Dickens was a prolific writer. He published fifteen major novels, in addition to a plethora of stories, essays, poems, and travel notes.

> *"I don't profess to be profound; but I do lay claim to common sense."*
>
> —Charles Dickens, *David Copperfield*

Dickens and his wife separated in 1858, and about this time, he began to read his work publicly in both London and the United States. His readings were mobbed by adoring fans. Despite failing health, Dickens kept a frenetic schedule of writing, reform activities, attending theatricals, and readings. His energy, which had always seemed boundless to friends, began to wane, and his farewell reading tour exhausted him. He died in 1870, leaving an unfinished novel, *The Mystery of Edwin Drood.*

Dickens intended his novels as a means of social reform. Human welfare could not keep pace with the technological advances of his time, and Dickens did much to expose evil byproducts of industrialization: child labor, debtors' prisons, ruinous financial speculation, inhuman legal procedures, and mismanagement of schools, orphanages, prisons, and hospitals.

Charles Dickens was born in 1812 and died in 1870.

Literature Online **Author Search** For more about Charles Dickens, go to www.glencoe.com.

Connecting to the Story

Dickens was aware of many of the social problems of his day and wrote to call attention to them. As you read, think about the following questions:

- If you were a writer, what social problems would you want to call attention to today?
- How else might you call attention to today's social issues?

Building Background

Dickens's novels present a panorama of human nature and of Victorian life. The following selection from *Oliver Twist* introduces Oliver, an orphan who must depend on the mercies of public support. When he turns nine, Oliver becomes too old for the orphanage. He is taken by Mr. Bumble, a parish official, to a workhouse, a kind of prison where the poor must work for a meager upkeep. When we meet him, Oliver has been given a slice of bread so that he will not look hungry when he appears before the parish board of directors to be introduced to his new home.

Setting Purposes for Reading

Big Idea The Emergence of Realism

As you read, note how Dickens re-creates the dismal living conditions of poor orphans and highlights specific areas in need of reform.

Literary Element Exposition

Exposition is part of the **plot** of a fictional work. The plot begins with exposition, which introduces the story's characters, setting, and conflict. Chapter One of *Oliver Twist* deals with his birth and his mother's death. Chapter Two, of which this selection is a part, is also part of the exposition. As you read, notice what this excerpt tells you about Oliver and his circumstances.

- See Literary Terms Handbook, p. R6.

Literature Online **Interactive Literary Elements Handbook** To review or learn more about the literary elements, go to www.glencoe.com.

Reading Strategy Connecting to Contemporary Issues

Connecting means linking what you read to events in your own life, to world events, or to other selections you have read. Associating details from literature with those from current events can help you further understand what you read.

Reading Tip: Creating a Double-Entry Journal As you read, use a double-entry journal to ask and answer questions that link this excerpt to contemporary issues.

Questions	Answers

Vocabulary

demolition (dem′ ə lish′ ən) *n.* the state of being demolished or obliterated; p. 986 *When the demolition derby was over, all the cars were destroyed.*

extraordinary (iks trôr′ də ner′ ē) *adj.* very unusual or remarkable; p. 987 *Dressing up dogs as children produces an extraordinary sight.*

philosophical (phil′ ə sof′ i kəl) *adj.* concerned with the deeper meaning of life; p. 987 *Jenny liked to discuss philosophical matters with her father.*

inseparable (in sep′ ər ə bəl) *adj.* linked so closely that it is almost impossible to separate; p. 988 *The sisters were inseparable.*

Vocabulary Tip: Word Parts Studying the parts of a word—prefixes, roots, and suffixes—can sometimes help you understand an unfamiliar word's meaning and its part of speech.

OBJECTIVES

In studying this selection, you will focus on the following:
- analyzing the cultural and historical context of a literary work
- understanding the function of exposition and satire
- understanding the importance of connecting to contemporary issues

from

Oliver Twist

Charles Dickens

Oliver had not been within the walls of the workhouse a quarter of an hour, and had scarcely completed the **demolition** of a second slice of bread, when Mr. Bumble, who had handed him over to the care of an old woman, returned; and, telling him it was a board night, informed him that the board had said he was to appear before it forthwith.

Not having a very clearly defined notion of what a live board was, Oliver was rather astounded by this intelligence, and was not quite certain whether he ought to laugh or cry. He had no time to think about the matter, however; for

Literary Element Exposition *What does this passage tell you about Oliver's character?*

Mr. Bumble gave him a tap on the head, with his cane, to wake him up, and another on the back to make him lively; and bidding him follow, conducted him into a large whitewashed room, where eight or ten fat gentlemen were sitting round a table. At the top of the table, seated in an armchair rather higher than the rest, was a particularly fat gentleman with a very round, red face.

"Bow to the board," said Bumble. Oliver brushed away two or three tears that were lingering in his eyes, and seeing no board but the table, fortunately bowed to that.

"What's your name, boy?" said the gentleman in the high chair.

Oliver was frightened at the sight of so many gentlemen, which made him tremble; and the beadle[1] gave him another tap behind, which made him cry: and these two causes made him answer in a very low and hesitating voice; whereupon a gentleman in a white waistcoat[2] said he was a fool. Which was a capital way of raising his spirits, and putting him quite at his ease.

"Boy," said the gentleman in the high chair, "listen to me. You know you're an orphan, I suppose?"

"What's that, sir?" inquired poor Oliver.

"The boy *is* a fool—I thought he was," said the gentleman in the white waistcoat.

"Hush!" said the gentleman who had spoken first. "You know you've got no father or mother, and that you were brought up by the parish, don't you?"

"Yes, sir," replied Oliver, weeping bitterly.

"What are you crying for?" inquired the gentleman in the white waistcoat. And to be sure it was very **extraordinary**. What *could* the boy be crying for?

"I hope you say your prayers every night," said another gentleman in a gruff voice; "and pray for the people who feed you, and take care of you—like a Christian."

"Yes, sir," stammered the boy. The gentleman who spoke last was unconsciously right. It would have been *very* like a Christian, and a marvellously good Christian, too, if Oliver had prayed for the people who fed and took care of *him*. But he hadn't, because nobody had taught him.

"Well! You have come here to be educated, and taught a useful trade," said the red-faced gentleman in the high chair.

"So you'll begin to pick oakum[3] tomorrow morning at six o'clock," added the surly one in the white waistcoat.

For the combination of both these blessings in the one simple process of picking oakum, Oliver bowed low by the direction of the beadle, and was then hurried away to a large ward, where, on a rough, hard bed, he sobbed himself to sleep. What a noble illustration of the tender laws of England! They let the paupers go to sleep!

Poor Oliver! He little thought, as he lay sleeping in happy unconsciousness of all around him, that the board had that very day arrived at a decision which would exercise the most material influence over all his future fortunes. But they had. And this was it:

The members of this board were very sage, deep, **philosophical** men; and when they came to turn their attention to the workhouse, they found out at once, what ordinary folks would never have discovered—the poor people liked it! It was a regular place of public entertainment for the poorer classes; a tavern where there was nothing to pay; a public breakfast, dinner, tea, and supper all the year round; a brick and mortar Elysium, where it was all play and no work. "Oho!" said the board, looking very knowing,

---

1. A *beadle* is a minor officer of a parish, or church district.
2. A *waistcoat* (wes ′ kət) is a vest.

Literary Element   Exposition *How do the gentlemen treat Oliver?*

Vocabulary

extraordinary (iks trôr′ də ner′ ē) *adj.* very unusual or remarkable

---

3. To *pick oakum* is to tear apart old rope for the stringy fiber that was used in sealing the seams of boats.

Literary Element   Exposition *What does this passage tell you about how Oliver was treated in the past?*

Reading Strategy   Connecting to Contemporary Issues *Oliver is forced to work at a menial job for virtually no pay. To what modern global economic issue can you connect Oliver's situation?*

Vocabulary

philosophical (phil′ ə sof′ i kəl) *adj.* concerned with the deeper meaning of life

"we are the fellows to set this to rights; we'll stop it all, in no time." So they established the rule, that all poor people should have the alternative (for they would compel nobody, not they), of being starved by a gradual process in the house, or by a quick one out of it. With this view, they contracted with the water-works to lay on an unlimited supply of water; and with a corn-factor to supply periodically small quantities of oatmeal; and issued three meals of thin gruel a day, with an onion twice a week, and half a roll on Sundays. They made a great many other wise and humane regulations, having reference to the ladies, which it is not necessary to repeat; kindly undertook to divorce poor married people, in consequence of the great expense of a suit in Doctors' Commons; and, instead of compelling a man to support his family, as they had theretofore done, took his family away from him, and made him a bachelor! There is no saying how many applicants for relief, under these last two heads, might have started up in all classes of society, if it had not been coupled with the workhouse; but the board were long-headed men, and had provided for this difficulty. The relief was **inseparable** from the workhouse and the gruel; and that frightened people.

For the first six months after Oliver Twist was removed, the system was in full operation. It was rather expensive at first, in consequence of the increase in the undertaker's bill, and the necessity of taking in the clothes of all the paupers, which fluttered loosely on their wasted, shrunken forms, after a week or two's gruel. But the number of workhouse inmates got thin as well as the paupers; and the board were in ecstasies.

The room in which the boys were fed, was a large stone hall, with a copper[4] at one end; out of which the master, dressed in an apron for the purpose, and assisted by one or two women, ladled the gruel at meal-times. Of this festive composition each boy had one porringer,[5] and no more—except on occasions of great public rejoicing, when he had two ounces and a quarter of bread besides. The bowls never wanted washing. The boys polished them with their spoons till they shone again; and when they had performed this operation (which never took very long, the spoons being nearly as large as the bowls), they would sit staring at the copper, with such eager eyes, as if they could have devoured the very bricks of which it was composed; employing themselves, meanwhile, in sucking their fingers most assiduously, with the view of catching up any stray splashes of gruel that might have been cast thereon. Boys have generally excellent appetites. Oliver Twist and his companions suffered the tortures of slow starvation for three months. At last they got so voracious and wild with hunger, that one boy, who was tall for his age, and hadn't been used to that sort of thing (for his father had kept a small cook's shop), hinted darkly to his companions, that unless he had another basin of gruel *per diem*, he was afraid he might some night happen to eat the boy who slept next him, who happened to be a weakly youth of tender age. He had a wild, hungry eye; and they implicitly believed him. A council was held; lots were cast who should walk up to the master after supper that evening and ask for more; and it fell to Oliver Twist.

The evening arrived, the boys took their places. The master, in his cook's uniform, stationed himself at the copper, his pauper assistants ranged themselves behind him; the gruel was served out; and a long grace was said over the short commons.[6] The gruel disappeared; the boys whispered to each other, and winked at Oliver; while his next neighbors nudged him. Child as he was, he was desperate with hunger, and reckless with misery. He rose from the table; and

---

4. A *copper* is a large boiler for cooking, originally made of copper.

Big Idea The Emergence of Realism *How does Dickens view the treatment of the poor?*

Big Idea The Emergence of Realism *What situation is Dickens targeting for reform?*

Vocabulary

inseparable (in sep′ ər ə bəl) *adj.* linked so closely that it is almost impossible to separate

---

5. A *porringer* is a small, shallow bowl with a handle.
6. A *common* is a ration or allowance of food.

Literary Element Exposition *How does this passage hint at a future conflict for Oliver?*

advancing to the master, basin and spoon in hand, said, somewhat alarmed at his own temerity,—

"Please, sir, I want some more."

The master was a fat, healthy man; but he turned very pale. He gazed in stupefied astonishment on the small rebel for some seconds; and then clung for support to the copper. The assistants were paralyzed with wonder, the boys with fear.

"What!" said the master at length, in a faint voice.

"Please, sir," replied Oliver, "I want some more."

The master aimed a blow at Oliver's head with the ladle, pinioned him in his arms, and shrieked aloud for the beadle.

The board were sitting in solemn conclave,[7] when Mr. Bumble rushed into the room in great excitement, and addressing the gentleman in the high chair, said,—

"Mr. Limbkins, I beg your pardon, sir! Oliver Twist has asked for more!"

There was a general start. Horror was depicted on every countenance.

"For *more*!" said Mr. Limbkins. "Compose yourself, Bumble, and answer me distinctly. Do I understand that he asked for more, after he had eaten the supper allotted by the dietary?"[8]

"He did, sir," replied Bumble.

"That boy will be hung," said the gentleman in the white waistcoat. "I know that boy will be hung."

Nobody controverted the prophetic gentleman's opinion. An animated discussion took place. Oliver was ordered into instant confinement; and a bill was next morning pasted on the outside of the gate, offering a reward of five pounds to anybody who would take Oliver Twist off the hands of the parish. In other words, five

Oliver Asks for More. Harold Copping. Color lithograph. Illustration for "Character Sketches from Dickens" compiled by B.W. Matz, 1924. Private collection.

pounds and Oliver Twist were offered to any man or woman who wanted an apprentice[9] to any trade, business, or calling.

"I never was more convinced of anything in my life," said the gentleman in the white waistcoat, as he knocked at the gate and read the bill next morning: "I never was more convinced of anything in my life, than I am that that boy will come to be hung." ♋

---

7. A *conclave* is a private meeting.
8. A *dietary* is a daily ration or allowance of food.

Reading Strategy Connecting to Contemporary Issues *What does this passage tell you about the goal of the board members? Name some similar contemporary circumstances.*

---

9. An *apprentice* is a trainee who works in return for instruction in an art or trade.

RESPONDING AND THINKING CRITICALLY

Respond

1. What was your first reaction to Oliver's plight?

Recall and Interpret

2. What circumstances lead the gentlemen of the board to think Oliver a fool?

3. (a)How does the gentleman in the white waistcoat respond to Oliver's weeping? (b)What does the man's reaction reveal about him?

4. (a)How does the staff respond to Oliver's request for more food? (b)Why do they respond this way?

Analyze and Evaluate

5. (a)How does the description of the gentlemen on the board compare to the description of the work-house boys? (b)What does this comparison suggest about the gentlemens' true motivations?

6. (a)What does Dickens suggest is the official attitude toward the poor? (b)What does the board think of its own efforts on behalf of the poor?

7. What is implied by the prediction that Oliver will be hung and by the bill that is posted on the gate?

8. What theme is implied by the excerpt from *Oliver Twist*? Explain.

Connect

9. **Big Idea** **The Emergence of Realism** Do you think literature is an effective way to call attention to social problems? Explain.

YOU'RE THE CRITIC: Different Viewpoints

Was Dickens Too Melodramatic?

Dickens loved the theater. In fact, critics often detect a sense of melodrama in Dickens's writing. A melodrama is usually a play, but the term can apply to any work that has a strong conflict, appeals principally to the emotions, and arouses strong feelings of horror or pity. The characters are usually flat and either extremely good or extremely wicked. Read the following comments by two critics on Dickens's use of melodrama.

"Some parts of [Oliver Twist] are so crude and of so clumsy a melodrama, that one is almost tempted to say that Dickens would have been greater without it. . . . It is by far the most depressing of all his books; it is in some ways the most irritating; yet its ugliness gives the last touch of honesty to all that spontaneous and splendid output."
—G. K. Chesterton

"The typical Dickens novel . . . always exists round a framework of melodrama. The last thing anyone ever remembers about the books is their central story. . . .

Of course it would be absurd to say that Dickens is a vague or merely melodramatic writer. Much that he wrote is extremely factual, and in the power of evoking visual images he has probably never been equaled. When Dickens has once described something you see it for the rest of your life."
—George Orwell

Group Activity Discuss the following questions with classmates. Refer to the quotations on this page and cite evidence from the *Oliver Twist* excerpt.

1. Do these critics view Dickens's melodrama as positive or negative? Explain.

2. In general, do you think the excerpt from *Oliver Twist* is melodramatic? Explain.

Literary Element Exposition

The reader learns quite a lot about Oliver and his circumstances in the **exposition** included in this excerpt.

1. What is the setting of this excerpt?

2. What is Oliver's situation?

3. What is the reader expected to feel for Oliver? For Mr. Bumble?

4. What is the major conflict of this excerpt and how is it resolved?

Review: Satire

As you learned on page 565, **satire** is writing that comments, sometimes humorously, on human flaws, ideas, social customs, or institutions. The purpose of satire may be to reform, entertain, or both. Some satiric devices are irony, hyperbole, and understatement.

Partner Activity Meet with another classmate and discuss the satire in this excerpt from *Oliver Twist*. Then, working with your partner, create an organizer that shows the satiric devices Dickens uses. Jot down page and line numbers.

Satiric Devices in *Oliver Twist*		
Irony	Exaggeration	Understatement

Reading Strategy Connecting to Contemporary Issues

In this excerpt from *Oliver Twist*, Dickens shines a harsh light on the treatment of orphans in Victorian times, but have times changed?

1. How are orphans taken care of today?

2. Estimates of the number of orphans worldwide vary but are all high. What are some reasons today for the high number of orphans in the world?

3. Do you think orphans are treated more humanely today than they were in Dickens's time? Explain your answer.

Vocabulary Practice

Practice with Word Parts Identify the meaning of the underlined part of each vocabulary word. Use a dictionary if necessary.

1. <u>de</u>molition   **a.** for   **b.** down

2. extra<u>ordin</u>ary   **a.** order   **b.** painful

3. <u>phil</u>osophical   **a.** difficult   **b.** loving

4. insepar<u>able</u>   **a.** talented   **b.** capable of

Academic Vocabulary

Here are two words from the vocabulary list on page R82.

deviate (dē′ vē āt′) *v.* to turn aside from a path or course

supplement (sup′ lə mənt) *n.* an addition to something to make up for a deficiency

Practice and Apply

1. How does Oliver **deviate** from accepted rules in regards to meals?

2. Why were the gentlemen opposed to giving the orphans a **supplement** to their diet?

British child star Mark Lester as Oliver Twist asking for some more gruel during the filming of *Oliver,* 1967.

Writing About Literature

Analyze Cultural and Historical Context Write an essay to demonstrate how Dickens, as represented by the excerpt from *Oliver Twist*, exemplifies his era in the ideas he explores. First identify the period. Then state several characteristics of the time; include cultural values, class relationships, and social concerns. For each characteristic of the period, give examples from the excerpt from *Oliver Twist*.

As you explore the topic, list the characteristics of the period in one column and the treatment of those characteristics in *Oliver Twist* in a second column.

Characteristics of Period	Treatment
Economics: Rapid Industrialization	Economics: Orphans forced to labor in work-shops

As you write, follow the path below.

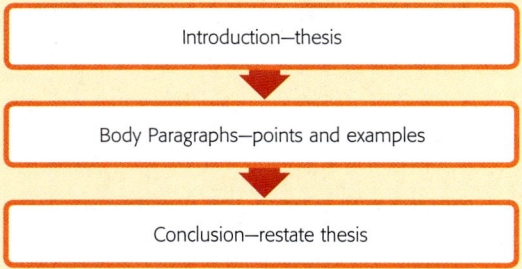

After you complete your draft, meet with a peer reviewer to evaluate each other's work and to suggest revisions. Then proofread and edit your draft for errors in spelling, grammar, and punctuation.

Learning for Life

Research organizations that help poor, orphaned, or starving children in your town, county, parish, or state; make a plan on how to help address this problem, either individually or as a group.

Literature Online Web Activities For eFlashcards, Selection Quick Checks, and other Web activities, go to www.glencoe.com.

Dickens's Language and Style

Using Interjections An interjection is a word or phrase that expresses emotion or exclamation. Dickens uses a number of interjections, all followed by an exclamation point. For instance, note the interjection in the following passage: "Poor Oliver! He little thought, as he lay sleeping in happy unconsciousness of all around him, that the board had that very day arrived at a decision . . ." In writing, a mild interjection is usually followed by a comma. A strong interjection is followed by an exclamation point. An interjection is not the same as direct address, in which persons are addressed in speaking, reading, or writing.

Note how Dickens uses both interjections and direct address in *Oliver Twist*:

Interjections	Direct Address
Hush!	"Boy,"
Well!	"Mr. Limbkins,"
What!	"Sir,"
Oho!	

Activity On a separate sheet of paper, supply the following sentences with one of the interjections from the list below.

hush, wow, help, well, ouch, ah

1. _____, the service is starting.

2. _____! Is it really worth that much?

3. _____! You stepped on my foot.

4. _____, it's your phone ringing; not mine.

5. _____! He wasn't very friendly.

6. _____! The kitchen is on fire.

Revising Check

Interjections Use interjections sparingly in your writing, except for places where they capture emotion in a way that direct address cannot. Check the paper you wrote on cultural and historical context to see if you used interjections, and, if so, evaluate their purpose. Consider if using direct address would be a better choice.

Vocabulary Workshop

Word Origins

Understanding Political and Historical Terms

"In other words, five pounds and Oliver Twist were offered to any man or woman who wanted an apprentice to any trade, business, or calling."

—Charles Dickens, from *Oliver Twist*

Connecting to Literature Whether you are reading historical or political documents, or literature like *Oliver Twist*, you will likely encounter words that come from other languages. Much of the English language, including words we still use today, originated in Greek and Latin. For example, in the above quote, the word *apprentice* comes from the Latin root *apprendere*, meaning "to learn."

Understanding difficult material, such as historical and political terms, will be easier if you know a word's origin, or **etymology**. The following entry lists the etymology of the word *history*.

history (his′ tə rē) *n.* a record of events: *a history of pop music.*
[Latin *historia* inquiry, history]

- What does the Latin root word mean?
- How does the word's etymology relate to its modern meaning?

The following dictionary entry of the word *political* shows how a word can have a root, prefix, or suffix that comes from another language.

political (pə li′ ti kəl) *adj.* of, relating to, or concerned with government: *a political campaign* [Greek *polis* city + *-al* relating to]

- What suffix is added to this root?
- What other words contain this root or suffix?

Exercise

Working in groups, use a dictionary to find the etymologies of the following words. Record your answers in a chart like the one below.

Word	Etymology	Relevance to Modern Use
abolish	Latin, *abolēre,* "to do away with"	means to get rid of something
academy		
aristocrat		
merit		
moratorium		
per diem		

► **Vocabulary Terms**

A word's **etymology** is its history, development, and origin. By studying a word's etymology, you can learn how its use has evolved over time.

► **Test-Taking Tip**

By knowing a few common Latin and Greek prefixes and suffixes, you will be able to guess the meaning of many unfamiliar words you may encounter on standardized tests.

► **Reading Handbook**

For more about word origins, see Reading Handbook, p. R20.

Literature Online
eFlashcards For eFlashcards and other vocabulary activities, go to www.glencoe.com.

OBJECTIVES
- Trace the etymology of terms used in political science and history.
- Use knowledge of Greek and Latin roots, prefixes, and suffixes to understand complex words.

Dover Beach

MEET MATTHEW ARNOLD

The nineteenth century brought enormous changes to England. Yet, rapid economic and industrial progress had its price. In his poetry and prose, Matthew Arnold addressed the deep sense of loss and futility felt by many as a result of the economic and social changes that swept across Europe.

An Uninspired Student Arnold grew up as the son of the most renowned educator in early Victorian England, the headmaster of the famous Rugby School. However, to his somber father's dismay, the young Arnold neglected his studies and instead showed more interest in fanciful clothes and social repartee. Nevertheless, at eighteen, he managed to win the Rugby poetry prize as well as a scholarship to Oxford University. Oxford failed to turn Arnold into a serious student, however. But in his mid-twenties Arnold surprised his family and friends by publishing two volumes of melancholy and profoundly serious verse. Because Arnold was a perfectionist, he published the volumes anonymously; he later withdrew them from circulation because he was dissatisfied with his writing. After marrying Fanny Lucy Wightman in 1851, Arnold accepted an appointment as an inspector of schools in order to support his family. For thirty-five years he traveled over England's wretched roads and stayed at dreary inns in order to inspect the dismal schools of the period.

> *"The best poetry will be found to have a power of forming, sustaining, and delighting us, as nothing else can."*
>
> —Matthew Arnold

An Ars Poetica In 1853 Arnold published his third book of poems, *Poems: A New Edition*, which was the first to bear his name. In the preface to this book, Arnold delivered his famous dictum—poetry should not only express an author's feelings but should also "animate and ennoble" its readers. Thus, for Arnold, literature served an aesthetic and social function.

In 1857 Arnold was elected to the poetry chair at Oxford University. There he gave a series of lectures presenting his ideas on poetry, society, and education in general. As inspector of schools, Arnold studied the British and European educational systems closely. He concluded that all young children should receive a broad education in both the arts and the sciences. The goal of such an education, he felt, was "to enable a man to know himself and the world."

A Critic Is Born As Arnold wrote more prose, he wrote less poetry. In 1867 he published *New Poems*, his last major publication as a poet. From that point on, Arnold focused on social, political, and literary criticism almost exclusively. One of Arnold's best-known critical works was *Culture and Anarchy*, published in 1869. In this volume, Arnold repeated his belief that literature and culture were as necessary to society as religion. A few years later, Arnold wrote four books specifically on religion and its place in a society that was fascinated by science. Toward the end of Arnold's life, he traveled to the United States, where he lectured to enthusiastic audiences and continued to write.

Matthew Arnold was born in 1822 and died in 1888.

Literature Online **Author Search** For more about Matthew Arnold, go to www.glencoe.com.

Connecting to the Poem

The poem "Dover Beach" is Arnold's response to the changes and fears of his time, and yet its message is universal. As you read, think about the following questions:

- Have you ever felt uncertain about the future?
- What comforts you when you are sad or lonely? How do you deal with loss in your own life?

Building Background

The town of Dover, England, which is famous for its chalk-white cliffs, is only about twenty miles from France, which lies across the Strait of Dover. Many critics believe that Arnold visited the town on his honeymoon in 1851. At that time, Arnold was adjusting not only to married life but also to his new position as inspector of schools. In addition, like other Victorians, he was adjusting to the transition in England from an age of faith to an age of science and technology. Scientific discoveries seemed to challenge traditional religious beliefs, and Arnold addressed some of these profound social and religious changes in "Dover Beach."

Setting Purposes for Reading

Big Idea **Disillusionment and Darker Visions**

As you read this selection, note the language and phrases Arnold uses to convey a dark vision of the world and a sense of impermanence.

Literary Element **Meter**

Meter is the regular pattern of stressed and unstressed syllables that gives a line of poetry a more or less predictable rhythm. The basic unit of meter is known as a **foot**, which usually consists of one or two stressed syllables (marked ´) and one or more unstressed syllables (marked ˘). As you read Arnold's poem, pay attention to the rhythm and to the way in which the stressed and unstressed syllables in each stanza are arranged.

- See Literary Terms Handbook, p. R10.

Literature Online **Interactive Literary Elements Handbook** To review or learn more about the literary elements, go to www.glencoe.com.

Reading Strategy **Comparing and Contrasting Imagery**

Imagery describes the word pictures that writers create to evoke an emotional response in readers. In creating effective images, writers use sensory details, or descriptions that appeal to one or more of the five senses: sight, hearing, touch, taste, and smell. When you **compare and contrast,** you note the similarities and differences between two or more things. As you read, watch for various images of permanence and impermanence that create tension and convey a sense of loss.

Reading Tip: Noting Imagery Use a chart to record the imagery that you find in the poem.

Images of Permanence	Images of Impermanence
the cliffs of England stand, / Glimmering and vast, out in the tranquil bay.	on the French Coast the light / Gleams and is gone.

A Seaside View. David Cox. Watercolor on paper. Private collection.

OBJECTIVES
In studying this selection, you will focus on the following:
- analyzing literary periods
- analyzing meter
- comparing and contrasting imagery

DOVER BEACH

Matthew Arnold

The sea is calm tonight.
The tide is full, the moon lies fair
Upon the straits[1]—on the French coast the light
Gleams and is gone; the cliffs of England stand,
5 Glimmering and vast, out in the tranquil bay.
Come to the window, sweet is the night air!
Only, from the long line of spray
Where the sea meets the moon-blanched land,
Listen! you hear the grating roar
10 Of pebbles which the waves draw back, and fling,
At their return, up the high strand,[2]
Begin, and cease, and then again begin,
With tremulous cadence[3] slow, and bring
The eternal note of sadness in.

15 Sophocles[4] long ago
Heard it on the Aegean,[5] and it brought
Into his mind the turbid[6] ebb and flow
Of human misery; we
Find also in the sound a thought,
20 Hearing it by this distant northern sea.

The Sea of Faith
Was once, too, at the full, and round earth's shore
Lay like the folds of a bright girdle[7] furled.
But now I only hear
25 Its melancholy, long, withdrawing roar,
Retreating, to the breath
Of the night wind, down the vast edges drear
And naked shingles[8] of the world.

Ah, love, let us be true
30 To one another! for the world, which seems
To lie before us like a land of dreams,
So various, so beautiful, so new,
Hath really neither joy, nor love, nor light,
Nor certitude, nor peace, nor help for pain;
35 And we are here as on a darkling[9] plain
Swept with confused alarms of struggle and flight,
Where ignorant armies clash by night.

1. *Straits* refers to the Strait of Dover, a narrow channel separating England and France.

2. A *strand* is a shore.

3. *Tremulous* means "trembling." *Cadence* is a rhythmic rise and fall.

4. *Sophocles* was a Greek dramatist who lived during the fifth century B.C.
5. The *Aegean* is the arm of the Mediterranean Sea between Greece and Turkey.
6. *Turbid* means "confusing" or "in a state of turmoil."

7. A *girdle* is anything that girds, or encircles, such as a belt or sash worn around the waist.

8. *Shingles* are beaches covered with water-worn pebbles.

9. Something that is *darkling* is characterized by darkness.

Reading Strategy Comparing and Contrasting Imagery *How does the description of the sea change over the course of this stanza?*

RESPONDING AND THINKING CRITICALLY

Respond

1. What image or images made the deepest impression on you? Why?

Recall and Interpret

2. (a)What does the speaker see from the window in lines 1–6? (b)What does the speaker hear in lines 7–14? (c)Describe the shift in mood from the beginning of this stanza to the end.

3. (a)What emotion does the speaker associate with the sound of waves? (b)According to the poem, what does Sophocles hear? (c)Why does the speaker make this allusion to Sophocles?

4. (a)How does the speaker describe the "Sea of Faith"? (b)What does this suggest about faith?

Analyze and Evaluate

5. (a)According to the speaker, in what ways has the world not changed since the time of Sophocles? (b)Do you agree or disagree with this assertion? Explain.

6. What words or images suggest that the speaker of the poem still has hope?

7. (a)What is the theme, or main idea, of the poem? (b)In your opinion, do the images of the shoreline effectively convey the theme? Explain.

Connect

8. **Big Idea** **Disillusionment and Darker Visions** How might being "true to one another" help in a world of struggle and pain?

LITERARY ANALYSIS

Literary Element | Meter

Meter often gives clues to the meaning and mood of a poem.

1. (a)What is the dominant foot in the first two lines of the poem? (b)How does the breakdown of this regularity contribute to the poem's meaning?

2. How does the meter in the first two stanzas support the imagery?

Literary Criticism

The American critic Lionel Trilling saw Arnold as the Victorian most ahead of his time:

> Perhaps more than any other man of his time and nation he perceived the changes that were taking place in the conditions of life and in the minds of men to bring into being the world we now know.

To what changes "in the conditions of life and in the minds of men" was Arnold responding in "Dover Beach"? In a paragraph, describe the attitude of the poem toward these changes.

Literature Online **Web Activities** For eFlashcards, Selection Quick Checks, and other Web activities, go to www.glencoe.com.

READING AND VOCABULARY

Reading Strategy | Comparing and Contrasting Imagery

A poem's images are often clues to the deeper meaning of the work.

1. (a)Compare and contrast the images of light and darkness that appear in the first and last stanzas of the poem. (b)Explain what each might symbolize.

2. Compare and contrast the imagery used to portray each body of water mentioned in the poem.

Academic Vocabulary

Here is a word from the vocabulary list on page R82.

incorporate (in kôr′ pə rāt′) v. to blend into something that already exists

Practice and Apply
How does Arnold **incorporate** images of the sea in "Dover Beach"?

Housman's Poetry

MEET A. E. HOUSMAN

Solitary and brilliant, Alfred Edward Housman was known during his life for both his classical scholarship and his somber poetry. Much of Housman's poetic fame, though, came late in his life, resulting both from his own emotional upheavals and from the changes in tastes that represented the first steps in the transformation of the Victorians into Moderns.

"With rue my heart is laden
For golden friends I had,
For many a rose-lipped maiden
And many a lightfoot lad."

—A. E. Housman
from *A Shropshire Lad*

A Shropshire Lad The oldest of seven children, Housman loved learning and sharing knowledge with others, especially his younger brothers and sisters, whom he tutored throughout childhood. One anecdote in particular stands out: to demonstrate a lesson on astronomy, Housman had his siblings stand together on the front lawn. There, each took on the role of a celestial body and, under his direction, moved about according to the patterns and laws of the solar system.

At the center of this active, happy home life was Housman's mother. Her death—sadly, occurring on the young poet's twelfth birthday—was an emotional shock that affected Housman for years. Housman was a gifted student of the classics and, as a result, won a scholarship to St. John's College, Oxford. At first he did well. However, during a period of emotional struggle, and what some have characterized as a nervous breakdown, he failed his final examinations. He had to return the following

year and received a lesser "pass" degree. Housman then took a civil service job in London, working in the same office as his friend Moses Jackson, whom he had met in Oxford. On his own, Housman continued to study the Greek and Latin classics in the British Museum reading room and began to publish impressive scholarly articles. These articles eventually resulted in his being made chair of Greek and Latin at University College, London, in 1892.

Grief and Poetry That same year, Moses Jackson's brother, Adalbert, died of typhoid. After Moses's departure several years earlier for a teaching career in India, Adalbert had become Housman's closest companion. His death prompted a poetic outpouring from Housman and sparked his greatest work: *A Shropshire Lad.* This collection of sixty-three poems is tragic in tone and addresses the themes of death, aging, and loss.

In 1911 Housman became professor of Latin at Trinity College, Cambridge—a position he retained until his death. After the release of *A Shropshire Lad,* Housman's poetic output dwindled considerably. He released only one other book, *Last Poems,* during the remainder of his life. These poems are representative of Housman's understanding of the purpose of all great poetry, to "transfuse emotion" and to "entangle the reader in a net of thoughtless delight."

A. E. Housman was born in 1859 and died in 1936.

Literature Online **Author Search** For more about A. E. Housman, go to www.glencoe.com.

Connecting to the Poems

In your own life, how do you deal with tragedy? The speaker in each of the following poems describes memories of heartache and loss. As you read, think about the following questions:

- How do you think your accomplishments in life will affect the way people remember you?
- How might age alter the way you view your relationships with others?

Building Background

As a child, Housman was encouraged by his mother to recite passages from the King James Bible. The simplicity and eloquence of its language strongly impressed him. Other works that influenced Housman include Greek and Latin lyric poetry as well as traditional English and Scottish folk ballads, whose language, structure, and rich subject matter sparked Housman's own creativity. Housman used Shakespeare's songs and the lyrical works of William Blake and the German poet Heinrich Heine as models for the poems in *A Shropshire Lad,* in which both "To an Athlete Dying Young" and "When I Was One-and-Twenty" appear. Yet many of Housman's favorite themes—passing youth, early death, unhappy love, the indifference of nature—derive from the disappointments and pains of his own youth.

Setting Purposes for Reading

Big Idea **Disillusionment and Darker Visions**

Notice how Housman's poems adhere to the notions of Realism while expressing an inherent pessimism.

Literary Element **Lyric Poetry**

Lyric poetry expresses a speaker's personal thoughts and feelings and is typically short and musical. While the subject of a lyric poem might be an object, a person, or an event, the emphasis of the poem is on the experience of emotion.

- See Literary Terms Handbook, p. R10.

Reading Strategy **Connecting to Personal Experience**

Connecting to personal experience means relating what you read to events in your own life. When you connect personal experience to a text, you gain a greater understanding of that text.

Reading Tip: Taking Notes Use a chart to connect your personal experience with the poems.

Text	My Experience	Significance
"To an Athlete Dying Young" Lines 11–12: "And early though the laurel grows / It withers quicker than the rose."	I was a more agile athlete when I was younger. I'm not nearly as fast as I used to be.	Housman's poem seems to reflect the real world accurately.

Vocabulary

threshold (thresh′ hōld′) *n.* doorway; entranceway; p. 1000 *The groom carried the bride over the threshold.*

fleet (flēt) *adj.* swift; fast; p. 1000 *Most of the children were fleet of foot.*

rue (rōō) *n.* sorrow; remorse; p. 1001 *He felt nothing but rue about the day he bought the broken down motorcycle.*

Vocabulary Tip: Analogies Analogies compare words based on the relationship between each pair's meaning.

Literature Online **Interactive Literary Elements Handbook** To review or learn more about the literary elements, go to www.glencoe.com.

OBJECTIVES
In studying these selections, you will focus on the following:
- analyzing literary periods
- analyzing lyric poetry
- connecting to personal experience

To an Athlete Dying Young

A. E. Housman

The Victor, 1898. Ottilie Wilhelmina Roederstein. Tempera on paperboard, 91 x 69.8 cm. Private collection.

The time you won your town the race
We chaired you through the market-place;
Man and boy stood cheering by,
And home we brought you shoulder-high.

5   Today, the road all runners come,
Shoulder-high we bring you home,
And set you at your **threshold** down,
Townsman of a stiller town.

Smart lad, to slip betimes[1] away
10   From fields where glory does not stay
And early though the laurel[2] grows
It withers quicker than the rose.

Eyes the shady night has shut

Cannot see the record cut,[3]
15   And silence sounds no worse than cheers
After earth has stopped the ears:

Now you will not swell the rout[4]
Of lads that wore their honors out,
Runners whom renown outran
20   And the name died before the man.

So set, before its echoes fade,
The **fleet** foot on the sill of shade,
And hold to the low lintel[5] up
The still-defended challenge-cup.

25   And round that early-laureled head
Will flock to gaze the strengthless dead,
And find unwithered on its curls
The garland briefer than a girl's.

---

1. Here, *betimes* means "early in life."
2. *Laurel* is the symbol for victory; in ancient Greece and Rome, victorious athletes were crowned with laurel wreaths.

Literary Element Lyric Poetry *In what ways has Housman made these lines musical? What other element of lyric poetry do you see at work in these lines?*

Vocabulary

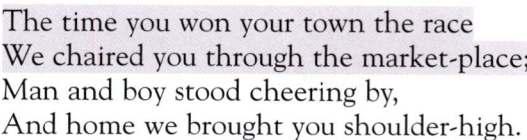

threshold (thresh′ hōld′) *n.* doorway; entranceway

---

3. *Cut* means "broken" or "outdone."
4. In this instance, a *rout* is a particular group or class of people.
5. A *lintel* is an architectural piece spanning, and usually bearing the weight, above a door.

Vocabulary

fleet (flēt) *adj.* swift; fast

When I Was One-and-Twenty

A. E. Housman

Lovers in a Café. Gottardt Kuehl. Galerie Berko, Brussels, Belgium.

When I was one-and-twenty
    I heard a wise man say,
"Give crowns and pounds and guineas[1]
    But not your heart away;
5 Give pearls away and rubies
    But keep your fancy free."
But I was one-and-twenty,
    No use to talk to me.
When I was one-and-twenty
10   I heard him say again,
"The heart out of the bosom
    Was never given in vain;
'Tis paid with sighs a plenty
    And sold for endless **rue**."
15 And I am two-and-twenty,
    And oh, 'tis true, 'tis true.

---

1. *Crowns*, *pounds*, and *guineas* are British units of currency.

Reading Strategy   Connecting to Personal Experience   *In what ways, if any, does the feeling in these lines relate to your personal experiences?*

Vocabulary

rue (rōō) *n.* sorrow; remorse

RESPONDING AND THINKING CRITICALLY

Respond

1. Which of these poems could you relate to the most? Explain.

Recall and Interpret

2. (a)In "To an Athlete Dying Young," compare the two occasions on which the athlete is brought home "shoulder high." What has happened to him in each case? (b)Why do you think Housman juxtaposes these two events in the poem?

3. (a)Summarize the commentary and advice the speaker gives in lines 9–28 in "To an Athlete. . . . " (b)From this, what can you infer about the speaker's attitudes toward youth, fame, and death? Explain the basis for your inference.

4. (a)In "When I Was One-and-Twenty" what advice does the wise man give the speaker? How does the speaker respond to this advice? (b)Why do you think the speaker responds in this way?

5. (a)How does the speaker's attitude change during the course of "When I Was One-and-Twenty"? (b)What do you think causes this change?

Analyze and Evaluate

6. (a)Briefly describe the meter and rhyme scheme in "To an Athlete Dying Young." (b)Do you think these elements are well suited to the poem's subject matter? Explain.

7. (a)In "When I Was One-and-Twenty," what is ironic about the experience the speaker describes? (b)How does the speaker's use of repetition reinforce this irony?

Connect

8. **Big Idea** **Disillusionment and Darker Visions** Briefly describe how the themes of both these poems represent Naturalism's pessimistic view of the world.

LITERARY ANALYSIS

Literary Element Lyric Poetry

The word *lyric* comes from *lyre,* a stringed instrument that was used to accompany poetry in ancient Greece. In English verse, poems are considered lyric if they are musical and emotional and if they deemphasize narrative elements. Usually this means that the poem will use rhyme, meter, or some other musical device. In addition, lyric poetry will often explore an emotionally charged subject.

1. Describe the personal thoughts and emotions expressed by each poem's speaker.

2. From the two poems you have read, why do you think Housman is considered an important lyric poet of the Victorian period? Use specific examples from the poems to support your views.

Writing About Literature

Respond to Tone How did the tone of these poems affect you? Write a brief letter to the speaker of one of the poems in which you explain the thoughts and feelings you experienced as you read.

READING AND VOCABULARY

Reading Strategy Connecting to Personal Experience

Connecting personal experience to a text can make reading more fulfilling. Based on your own experiences, do these poems seem like accurate representations of real-life situations? Explain.

Vocabulary Practice

Practice with Analogies Choose the word that best completes each analogy.

1. canal : ocean :: threshold :
   a. pedestrian   **b.** building   **c.** bolt

2. dim : bright :: fleet :
   a. slow   **b.** quick   **c.** group

3. make : create :: rue :
   a. hope   **b.** reinvent   **c.** regret

Literature Online **Web Activities** For eFlashcards, Selection Quick Checks, and other Web activities, go to www.glencoe.com.

Hardy's Poetry

MEET THOMAS HARDY

When Thomas Hardy was apprenticed to an architect at age sixteen, a minister denounced him for trying to rise above his class. However, the young man had even higher ambitions than the minister suspected. Each morning Hardy rose early and studied literature before going to the office. His hunger for learning eventually led to a distinguished writing career. Although it was criticized at first, Hardy's "self-taught" style gave his writing a stern, authentic voice—a voice that captured the mood of the late Victorian age without pandering to the literary fashions of the time.

> *"My opinion is that a poet should express the emotion of all the ages and the thought of his own."*
>
> —Thomas Hardy

Seeds of Naturalism Hardy was born and grew up in Higher Bockhampton, a small village in the county of Dorset in southwest England that would play an integral role in his literary career. The region is agricultural, and across its rugged surface stand monuments of the past: Saxon and Roman ruins, as well as the great boulders of Stonehenge. Hardy often set his writing in this bleakly beautiful landscape to emphasize nature's indifference to human suffering. This view of nature as an indifferent, implacable force is the foundation of Naturalism, which Hardy was among the first great English writers to espouse.

Having completed his apprenticeship, Hardy moved to London to work as an architect. He hoped to become a poet and spent his free time visiting museums and theaters and writing poetry. Magazines rejected his verse, however, so Hardy focused on fiction. He returned to Dorset and wrote his first novel while working as an architect. Although publishers rejected the manuscript, writer George Meredith encouraged Hardy to continue writing fiction. His third novel, *Under the Greenwood Tree,* met with success in 1874 and enabled him to devote himself to writing.

Return to Poetry At age thirty, Hardy met Emma Gifford, whom he married four years later. At first the marriage was happy, but the couple gradually drifted apart. The difficulty of sustaining love in marriage became an important theme in Hardy's work, and his later novels were often criticized for their frank portrayal of relationships between men and women. Although Hardy was hurt by the attacks, the publicity boosted book sales. However, a particularly harsh review of *Tess of the d'Urbervilles* (1891) led Hardy to declare, "Well, if this sort of thing continues, no more novel-writing for me. A man must be a fool to deliberately stand up to be shot at." When his novel *Jude the Obscure* (1895) elicited even more outrage, Hardy decided never to write another novel, turning instead to his first passion, poetry. In the next three decades, he wrote nearly a thousand poems.

Hardy's wife died in 1912, ending decades of estrangement, but filling Hardy with regret and remorse. He expressed these feelings in "Poems of 1912–1913," often considered the peak of his achievement. Hardy wrote prolifically until the final months of his life.

Thomas Hardy was born in 1840 and died in 1928.

Literature Online **Author Search** For more about Thomas Hardy, go to www.glencoe.com.

Connecting to the Poems

In these poems, Hardy composes three variations on the subject of death. As you read, think about the following questions:

- Has a winter landscape ever reminded you of death?
- Are war deaths always heroic?
- How would you prefer to be remembered after your death?

Building Background

In a headnote to "The Man He Killed," Hardy noted that the speaker in the poem is a man who recently returned home to Dorset, England, from the South African War. Also known as the Boer War, this conflict between Great Britain and the Afrikaans, Dutch settlers in South Africa, lasted from 1899 to 1902. In Hardy's lifetime, Great Britain was the largest imperialist nation in the world; by the end of the 1800s, Britain controlled nearly one-quarter of Earth's land surface. The South African War, in conjunction with British armed conflicts in Eastern Europe, Asia, Africa, and the Middle East, provoked criticism against imperialist policies. Although Hardy claimed to be "quite outside politics," he voiced his opposition to war.

Setting Purposes for Reading

Big Idea **Disillusionment and Darker Visions**

As you read the poems, identify ideas that reflect Hardy's Naturalism, such as realistic details, pessimism, and a belief in the futility of human endeavors.

Literary Element **Irony**

Irony is a contrast or discrepancy between expectation and reality. **Verbal irony** occurs when a person says one thing but means another. **Situational irony** occurs when the actual outcome of a situation is the opposite of, or completely different from, what was expected. As you read the poems, look for Hardy's use of both verbal and situational irony.

- See Literary Terms Handbook, p. R9.

Reading Strategy **Making Generalizations**

When you draw conclusions about a writer's beliefs and ideas from specific details in a text, you are **making generalizations.** Generalizations help you make connections between a literary work and universal themes.

To make generalizations, ask yourself the following questions as you read:

- What is the author's **tone,** or attitude, toward his or her subject?
- How do the events or ideas in the literary work relate to my prior knowledge and background information?
- How might the characters or events represent a broader theme or idea?

Reading Tip: Taking Notes Use a chart similar to the one below to record a detail from each of the poems and the generalization you draw from each detail.

	"The Darkling Thrush"	"The Man He Killed"	"Ah, Are You Digging on My Grave?"
Detail	"and every spirit upon earth / Seemed fervorless as I"		
Generalization	The twentieth century begins with a universal feeling of pessimism.		

Literature ♦ **nline** **Interactive Literary Elements Handbook** To review or learn more about the literary elements, go to www.glencoe.com.

OBJECTIVES
In studying these selections, you will focus on the following:
- analyzing literary periods and themes
- analyzing irony and dramatic monologue
- making generalizations

The Darkling Thrush

Thomas Hardy

Tawny Thrush. John James Audubon. 1833.

I leant upon a coppice[1] gate
    When Frost was specter-gray,
And Winter's dregs made desolate
    The weakening eye of day.
5 The tangled bine-stems[2] scored the sky
    Like strings of broken lyres,
And all mankinds that haunted nigh
    Had sought their household fires.

The land's sharp features seemed to be
10   The Century's corpse[3] outleant,[4]
His crypt the cloudy canopy,
    The wind his death-lament.
The ancient pulse of germ[5] and birth
    Was shrunken hard and dry,
15 And every spirit upon earth
    Seemed fervorless as I.

At once a voice arose among
    The bleak twigs overhead
In a full-hearted evensong
20   Of joy illimited;[6]
An aged thrush, frail, gaunt, and small,
    In blast-beruffled plume,[7]
Had chosen thus to fling his soul
    Upon the growing gloom.

25 So little cause for carolings
    Of such ecstatic sound
Was written on terrestrial things
    Afar or nigh around,
That I could think there trembled through
30   His happy good-night air
Some blessed Hope, whereof he knew
    And I was unaware.

---

1. A *coppice* is a small wood or thicket.
2. *Bine-stems* are the stems of a climbing plant.
3. *The Century's corpse* refers to the passing of the nineteenth century (Hardy first published this poem on Dec. 29, 1900).
4. *Outleant* means "leaned out" or "outstretched."
5. Here, *germ* means "seed" or "bud."
6. *Illimited* means "unlimited."
7. *Blast-beruffled plume* refers to the bird's feathers, which were disturbed or made to stand on end by a gust of wind.

Reading Strategy Making Generalizations *Based on the metaphor in these lines, how would you describe the speaker's attitude toward the nineteenth century?*

Literary Element Irony *Reread the last four lines. What is ironic about the song of the thrush?*

Two Soldiers at Arras, 1917. John Singer Sargent. Watercolor on paper. Christie's Images.

THE
MAN
HE
KILLED

Thomas Hardy

"Had he and I but met
By some old ancient inn,
We should have sat us down to wet[1]
Right many a nipperkin![2]

5 "But ranged as infantry,
And staring face to face,
I shot at him as he at me,
And killed him in his place.

"I shot him dead because—
10 Because he was my foe,
Just so: my foe of course he was;
That's clear enough; although

"He thought he'd 'list,[3] perhaps,
Off-hand like—just as I—
15 Was out of work—had sold his traps[4]—
No other reason why.

"Yes; quaint and curious war is!
You shoot a fellow down
You'd treat if met where any bar is,
20 Or help to half-a-crown."[5]

---

1. Here, *wet* means "drink."
2. *Nipperkin* is a colloquial word for a small glass of ale.
3. Here, *'list* means "enlist in the army."
4. *Traps* are personal belongings.
5. A *half-a-crown* is a coin formerly used in Great Britain.

Reading Strategy   Making Generalizations *What generalization can you make about the speaker's feelings toward the soldier he killed?*

Big Idea   Disillusionment and Darker Visions
How is the speaker's ironic attitude toward war in the final stanza an example of Naturalism?

"Ah, Are You Digging on My Grave?"

Thomas Hardy

Treasured Pets. Albert Ludovici. Anthony Mitchell Paintings, Nottingham, UK.

"Ah, are you digging on my grave
    My loved one?—planting rue?"[1]
—"No: yesterday he went to wed
One of the brightest wealth has bred.
5 'It cannot hurt her now,' he said,
    'That I should not be true.' "

"Then who is digging on my grave?
    My nearest dearest kin?"
—"Ah, no: they sit and think, 'What use!
10 What good will planting flowers produce?
No tendance[2] of her mound can loose
    Her spirit from Death's gin.' "[3]

"But some one digs upon my grave?
    My enemy?—prodding sly?"
15 —"Nay: when she heard you had passed the Gate
That shuts on all flesh soon or late,
She thought you no more worth her hate,
    And cares not where you lie."

"Then, who is digging on my grave?
20   Say—since I have not guessed!"
—"O it is I, my mistress dear,
Your little dog, who still lives near,
And much I hope my movements here
    Have not disturbed your rest?"

25 "Ah, yes! *You* dig upon my grave . . .
    Why flashed it not on me
That one true heart was left behind!
What feeling do we ever find
To equal among human kind
30   A dog's fidelity!"

"Mistress, I dug upon your grave
    To bury a bone, in case
I should be hungry near this spot
When passing on my daily trot.
35 I am sorry, but I quite forgot
    It was your resting-place."

---

1. *Rue* is a type of ornamental plant; the word can also mean "sorrow."
2. *Tendance* means "tending" or "looking after."
3. Here, *gin* means "trap."

Reading Strategy Making Generalizations *Based on the first three stanzas, what generalization can you make about the speaker's relationships?*

Literary Element Irony *How is the dog's "apology" ironic?*

RESPONDING AND THINKING CRITICALLY

Respond

1. Which of these poems did you like best? Explain.

Recall and Interpret

2. (a)Describe the speaker's emotional response to the thrush's song in "The Darkling Thrush." (b)Does the song inspire the speaker to be hopeful? Explain.

3. (a)In "The Man He Killed," what does the speaker think would have happened if he had met the man at the inn? (b)What actually happened? Why?

4. (a)In "Ah, Are You Digging on My Grave?" how does the woman react when she first learns who is digging on her grave? (b)What can you infer about nature from the digger's response? Explain.

Analyze and Evaluate

5. In literature, the attribution of human thoughts and emotions to nature or to non-human objects or animals is called the **pathetic fallacy.** In your opinion, is Hardy guilty of this fallacy in "The Darkling Thrush"? Explain.

6. (a)In your opinion, why might Hardy have written "Ah, Are You Digging on My Grave?" as a **dialogue**? (b)How do the dialogue and the rhyme scheme enhance the poem's irony?

Connect

7. **Big Idea** **Disillusionment and Darker Visions** How do these three poems illustrate the literary movement known as Naturalism?

LITERARY ANALYSIS

Literary Element **Irony**

The term **irony** derives from a character in Greek comedy called the *eiron*, meaning "dissembler" or "deceiver." The *eiron* spoke in understatement and pretended to be dimwitted to fool enemies. The current literary use of irony retains this idea of "dissembling." In **verbal irony,** what a character or speaker says is often nearly the opposite of what is meant. **Situational irony** occurs when an outcome is vastly different from what was expected.

1. Explain the verbal irony in the words "Had chosen thus to fling his soul / Upon the growing gloom" in "The Darkling Thrush."

2. In "The Man He Killed," what details suggest that the speaker employs verbal irony when he uses the word *quaint* to describe war?

3. Identify two examples of situational irony in "Ah, Are You Digging on My Grave?"

Review: Dramatic Monologue

As you learned on page 980, **dramatic monologue** is a form of dramatic poetry in which the speaker addresses a silent listener—and in the process reveals much about his or her character. "The Man He Killed" is an example of a dramatic monologue. The reader is the silent listener to the speaker's narrative and receives the speaker's moral lesson at the end of the monologue.

Group Activity Meet with a small group and create a chart similar to the one below to demonstrate what the reader learns about the speaker through his monologue.

Element of Dramatic Monologue	Effect on Reader
personal tone	inspires identification and compassion

1. What does the reader learn about the personality and character of the speaker in "The Man He Killed"?

2. What moral or lesson does the speaker convey in this poem?

Reading Strategy Making Generalizations

You can **make generalizations** by drawing conclusions about themes and ideas in Hardy's poems. Think about the background information you have about Hardy and what themes or ideas Hardy might be conveying in each poem.

1. Based on "The Darkling Thrush," what generalization can you make about Hardy's view of the relationship between humans and nature?

2. What evidence in "The Man He Killed" supports the generalization that Hardy viewed war as dehumanizing and absurd?

3. Although the three poems portray different speakers in different situations, each speaker expresses a similar view of human life. What generalizations about Hardy's philosophy of life can you make based on the three poems?

Academic Vocabulary

Here are two words from the vocabulary list on page R82.

military (mil′ ə ter′ ē) *adj.* characteristic of or pertaining to armed forces

neutral (noo′ trəl) *adj.* not taking a position or side in a conflict or dispute

Practice and Apply

1. How did the speaker's **military** experience motivate his actions in "The Man He Killed"?
2. Does the speaker in "The Man He Killed" maintain a **neutral** tone throughout the poem? Explain.

Writing About Literature

Explore Author's Purpose Author's purpose refers to an author's intent in writing a literary work. Typically, authors write for one or more of the following reasons: to persuade, to inform, to explain, to entertain, or to describe.

Hardy once said: "Poetry is emotion put into measure." Based on this quotation, your background knowledge of Hardy, and the poems you just read, write a brief essay exploring the author's purpose in one of the three poems. Keep in mind that an author often has more than one purpose for writing a poem. As you draft, follow the writing path below.

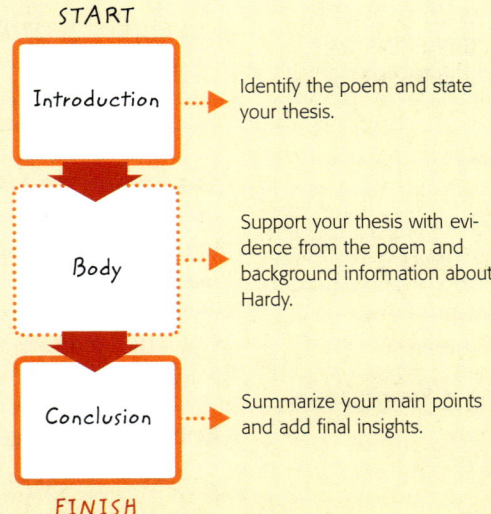

START

Introduction — Identify the poem and state your thesis.

Body — Support your thesis with evidence from the poem and background information about Hardy.

Conclusion — Summarize your main points and add final insights.

FINISH

When you are finished with your draft, edit and proofread it for errors in spelling, grammar, and punctuation.

Reading Further

To read more by Thomas Hardy, look for the following books.

Poetry: *The Essential Hardy,* edited by Joseph Brodsky, contains some of Hardy's best poems.

Short Stories: *Outside the Gates of the World: Selected Short Stories,* edited by John Bayley and Jan Jedrzejewski, presents some of Hardy's short fiction.

Literature Online Web Activities For eFlashcards, Selection Quick Checks, and other Web activities, go to www.glencoe.com.

Writing Workshop

Literary Analysis

 Analyzing a Poem

Connecting to Literature Matthew Arnold wrote not only literature but also **literary criticism**, or studies concerned with interpreting, analyzing, and evaluating other works of literature. In literary analysis—a type of literary criticism—the reader studies the specific parts of a piece of literature to determine how they work together to express a theme or deeper meaning. To write a successful essay, you will need to learn the goals of literary analysis writing and the strategies for achieving those goals.

Rubric: Features of a Literary Analysis

Goals	Strategies
To analyze specific elements of the poem	☑ Show how diction, rhythm, tone, mood, sound devices, imagery, and figurative language contribute to the theme
To write a concise thesis statement	☑ Introduce your thesis, or your interpretation of the theme ☑ In the conclusion, restate your thesis and summarize your analysis
To support the analysis with evidence	☑ Cite examples from the poem ☑ Draw your own conclusions and interpret your evidence
To organize your main points in a logical, effective order	☑ Organize your major points according to the chronological order of the poem or in order of importance

The Writing Process

In this workshop, you will follow the stages of the writing process. At any stage, you may think of new ideas to include and better ways to express them. Feel free to return to earlier stages as you write.

Prewriting

- - - - - - - - - - - - - -

Drafting

- - - - - - - - - - - - - -

Revising

- - - - - - - - - - - - - -

➡ Focus Lesson: Rewriting Wordy Sentences

Editing and Proofreading

➡ Focus Lesson: In-Text Quotations from Poems

Presenting

- - - - - - - - - - - - - -

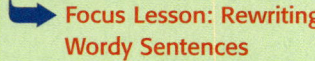

Writing Models For models and other writing activities, go to www.glencoe.com.

OBJECTIVES
- Write a literary analysis on how particular elements of a poem express a broader theme or deeper meaning.
- Support your analysis with textual evidence, and draw and interpret your own conclusions for your reader.

> ### Assignment
>
> Write a literary analysis that examines how particular elements of a poem express a broader theme or deeper meaning. As you move through the stages of the writing process, keep your audience and purpose in mind.
>
> **Audience:** teacher, classmates, and peers
>
> **Purpose:** to analyze the deeper meaning or theme of a poem

Analyzing a Professional Model

In his essay, "Hardy and the Poetry of Isolation," critic and educator David Perkins studies themes of isolation and alienation in Thomas Hardy's poetry, including "The Man He Killed." As you read the following passage, note how Perkins analyzes the elements of the poem to reveal a deeper theme. Pay close attention to the comments in the margin. They point out features that you might want to include in your own literary analysis essay.

From "Hardy and the Poetry of Isolation"
by David Perkins

Perhaps Hardy's most successful exploration of the common mental attitude which permits men to slough their questionings occurs in "The Man He Killed." Here the extreme surface simplicity, the short, almost jingling meters, the colloquial idiom, the total absence of stock poetic associations, the unwillingness to employ the glitter of poetic phrase, bespeak a rigid artistic discipline and integrity in which all has been subordinated to an interplay of character and incident. The situation, of course, is simply that in battle two soldiers, "ranged as infantry, / And staring face to face" (lines 5–6), have fired on each other, and the survivor narrates that event. The poem turns on the character of the speaker revealed in his reactions to what has taken place. The speaker begins by stating that he had no personal quarrel with the man he killed. This naturally raises the question of why he killed him, and, pondering the question, the speaker can only say that it was "Because he was my foe" (line 10). But he seems unsure and unsatisfied, and hence reiterates the explanation: "my foe of course he was; / That's clear enough" (lines 11–12). We are introduced, then, to a rather simple type of person, incapable of thinking past stock and ready-made answers

Thesis

Clearly state your thesis, present an interpretation, and include the author's name and the title of the work.

Supporting Evidence

Support your thesis with main points based on your conclusions.

Supporting Evidence

Support your main points with quotations accurately cited from the text.

("he was my foe"), well-meaning and troubled by having killed a man toward whom he felt no rancor. At once the speaker goes on to recognize that the man was not his "foe" at all, but simply a man who happened, like himself, to have drifted into the army:

> "He thought he'd 'list, perhaps,
> Off-hand like—just as I—
> Was out of work—had sold his traps—
> No other reason why. (lines 13–16)

At this point, the speaker having identified himself with the man he killed, convention would seem to suggest a revulsion from the killing, and a direct attack on war and the meaningless slaughter it involves. But this would take the poem outside the limited feeling and moral awareness of the speaker. Instead the speaker merely concludes:

> "Yes; quaint and curious war is!
> You shoot a fellow down
> You'd treat if met where any bar is,
> Or help to half-a-crown." (lines 17–20)

The summing up leading to the conclusion that war is "quaint and curious" suggests that the speaker has resolved his problem and will be no more troubled by it. But in the reader the aroused sense of wrong is in no way satisfied by the words "quaint and curious." Instead, by the drastic understatement of the last stanza, Hardy forces the reader to face up to the situation more or less on his own, and exacts that "full look at the worst" which is a necessary prelude to any possible "Better." Hence it is by the limitations of the speaker that the poem makes its point. But the limitations of the speaker give an additional edge of irony to the poem. For the irony is not simply that two men who have no quarrel should fire on each other, being trapped in the blind moilings of the "Immanent Will." There is the further irony that a decent man, such as the speaker, should not be more disturbed, should be able to appease his discomfort with the words "quaint and curious."

Reading-Writing Connection Think about the writing techniques that you have just encountered and try them out in the literary analysis you write.

Prewriting

Choose a Poem Think about the poems from the unit that you found moving or interesting. The more strongly you feel about a work, the more you will have to say about it.

Analyze the Poem Reread the poem several times paying attention to the form, content, and meaning.

▶ **Explore Interpretations** Review your notes about the poem. Are you still wondering about any passages, ideas, or themes? What is your interpretation? Consider how your classmates interpreted the poem differently. Notice that less obvious interpretations often make more interesting analyses.

▶ **Analyze Important Elements** Consider specific elements of the poem, such as speaker, imagery, structure, mood, sound devices, and figurative language. How do these elements enhance the poem's meaning?

Selection	"My Last Duchess," a poem by Robert Browning
Summary	duke and a count's emissary discuss the duke's possible marriage to the count's daughter
Speaker	the duke (dramatic monologue/first-person perspective)
Figurative Language	personification of the painting ("there she stands"); metaphors of ownership ("that piece," "my gift," "my object")
Imagery	the duke's speculation on Frà Pandolf's relationship with the duchess (to make her blush)
Structure	56 lines with regular rhythm, meter, and rhyme
Tone	duke's jealous, vengeful tone
Theme/ Meaning	strategies to flaunt power ultimately undermine it

Narrow Your Thesis Once you have a grasp on the meaning and themes of your poem, summarize your topic and your main idea in one or two sentences. Include the name of the poem, the name of the author, and the meaning or theme you will discuss. Feel free to revise or limit your thesis as you write your draft.

Draw Conclusions and Elaborate Be sure to support your main points with relevant evidence and precise examples from the poem. Then draw conclusions and explain to readers how the evidence supports your points and thesis.

Make a Plan In the body of your essay, organize your main points in an effective, logical order. If you are analyzing a change that occurs in the poem, use chronological order. If you organize your analysis around essential literary elements, you may wish to use order of importance. Revise the order as you write.

Literary Present Tense

Use the present tense when you write about literature. Although the poem you analyze was written long ago, the text is continuously being introduced to new readers and is being reinterpreted by those already familiar with the poem.

Test Prep

Essay tests often include an unfamiliar poem or passage to be read and analyzed quickly. Before writing, read the text closely to help you form your thesis and main points. Return to the text, as you write, to find evidence.

Drafting

Present and Support Your Points Present your major points in a straight-forward, logical way, and support them with direct evidence from the poem. As you discuss more complex interpretations and connections, be sure to explain the significance of your evidence to the reader, clarifying how it supports your thesis.

Analyzing a Workshop Model

Here is a final draft of a literary analysis. Read the essay and answer the questions in the margin. Use the answers to these questions to guide you as you write.

Power and Possession in "My Last Duchess"

Background
Why would the writer summarize the poem in the introduction?

Thesis
What makes this statement an effective thesis?

Literary Elements
How does the use of personification strengthen the analysis?

Supporting Evidence
Why might the writer quote the poem directly here?

In his poem, "My Last Duchess," Robert Browning portrays the discussion between a duke and an emissary from a count over the duke's possible marriage to the count's daughter. The duke pauses to show the emissary a painting of the former duchess. Throughout his monologue, the duke flaunts his power by calling attention to his possessions, emphasizing his title and position, and revealing the consequences for those who resist his control. Through the duke's first-person perspective, his arrogant, jealous tone, and the figurative language in "My Last Duchess," Browning reveals how the very strategies the duke uses to attain and demonstrate his power undermine that power in the end.

In the opening lines of the poem, the duke begins by confiding in the emissary, discussing his painting and its artist as if to show off his powerful position and valuable possessions. Rather than refer to the portrait as a *painting*, the duke speaks of it as "my last Duchess painted on the wall" (line 1), personifying the image as though it actually were his wife and not just a picture of her. The personification continues as he notes, "there she stands" (line 4) having drawn back the curtain only he controls ("none puts by / The curtain . . . but I," lines 9–10). By personifying the painting, the duke appears to possess not just the painting but also, literally, the woman.

In addition, the duke dares to expose this power relationship, although there is no clear indication that the emissary has asked or even cares about the painting (or about the former duchess). The duke says "Strangers like you . . . seemed as they would ask me, if they durst, / How such a glance came there;" followed by "so, not the first / Are you to turn and ask thus" (lines 7–13). Whether or not the emissary *does* ask about the duchess, the duke's lengthy confession reveals not only his power but his arrogance.

"My Last Duchess" is a dramatic monologue in which the duke controls the discussion and tells only his version of events. Yet, through his monologue, the duke reveals his jealous and tyrannical nature, probably hurting his chance for remarriage. When the duke describes the painting in detail, his admiration for artist Frà Pandolf's work gives way to jealousy. The duke speculates on how the artist may have made the duchess blush for the painting by complimenting her: "perhaps / Frà Pandolf chanced to say . . . 'Paint / Must never hope to reproduce the faint / Half-flush that dies along her throat'" (lines 15–19). The duke's tone and speculation reveal his jealous suspicion at the thought of someone's having any power at all over what he feels is his alone.

This desire for complete control over the duchess becomes clear as the duke explains their relationship through a series of metaphors related to possession. The duke views her "approving speech" and "blush" as gifts that should be reserved for him alone, in return for his "gift of a nine-hundred-years-old name" (line 33). Even the duchess's "thanking" others threatens the duke, as the gesture represents both a "gift" from the duchess to another man and her autonomy. As the duke confesses, he refused to discuss his jealousy with her or "let / Herself be lessoned so, nor plainly set / Her wits to yours" (lines 39–41). He then explains, "—E'en then would be some stooping; and I choose / Never to stoop" (lines 42–43). The statements reinforce that the duke sees the duchess as his property. Any reasoning with her would imply she were an equal, and that would undermine the duke's power. Echoing his statement from line 2, he finally says of the painting, "There she stands / As if alive" (lines 46–47). The repetition and the duke's satisfied tone suggest that the painting is a perfect compromise; the duchess has literally become his object.

As the duke negotiates terms for the future marriage, he affirms that, despite talk of the dowry, the "fair daughter's self, as I avowed / At starting, is my object" (lines 52–53). At this point, the duke's use of the word *object* is clearly ironic; he means it literally. By flaunting his power and rank, the duke exposes himself to the emissary as a jealous tyrant. Like Neptune, the sea god he admires, the duke must dominate, and is therefore likely to destroy, anything that compromises his power.

Exposition

Main Point
What makes this a strong main point?

Literary Elements
What is the purpose of this sentence?

Supporting Evidence
How are the quotations presented so they do not interrupt the flow of thought?

Supporting Evidence
How does elaboration of the evidence in this paragraph strengthen the analysis?

Organization
What is the general organization of the paper? Why is it effective for this analysis?

Conclusion
What makes this a strong conclusion?

Revising

Use the rubric below to help you evaluate and strengthen your essay.

Traits of Strong Writing

Ideas message or theme and the details that develop it

Organization arrangement of main ideas and supporting details

Voice writer's unique way of using tone and style

Word Choice vocabulary a writer uses to convey meaning

Sentence Fluency rhythm and flow of sentences

Convention correct spelling, grammar, usage, and mechanics

Presentation the way words and design elements look on a page

For more information on using the Traits of Strong Writing, see pages R33–R34 of the Writing Handbook.

Rubric: Writing a Literary Analysis Essay

☑ Do you show how specific elements of the poem contribute to the overall meaning or theme?

☑ Does your essay have a concise thesis statement that includes your interpretation of the theme or the effect to be analyzed?

☑ Do you cite direct evidence from the poem to support your points?

☑ Do you elaborate on your main points, draw your own conclusions, and interpret the significance of your evidence clearly?

☑ Do you organize your main points in a logical, effective order?

▶ **Focus Lesson**

Rewriting Wordy Sentences

The most effective writing is straightforward, clear, and concise. Unnecessary wordiness often creates confusion and distracts readers. This is not to say that all sentences should be short or simple but that every word, sentence, and paragraph should count. When revising, omit redundant or unnecessary words and rewrite abstract, flowery sentences in a more straightforward style.

Draft:

At this point, <u>there is no doubt but that</u>[1] the duke's use of the word *object* is clearly ironic; <u>the reason why is that</u>[1] <u>the duke</u>[2] means it literally. The duke <u>is a man who,</u>[1] by flaunting his power and rank, exposes himself to the emissary as a jealous tyrant and <u>despot.</u>[3]

Revision:

At this point, the duke's use of the word *object* is clearly ironic; he means it literally. By flaunting his power and rank, the duke exposes himself to the emissary as a jealous tyrant.

1. <u>Avoid needless words or phrases.</u>
2. <u>Use pronouns to eliminate unnecessary repetition.</u>
3. <u>Delete redundant words and phrases.</u>

Editing and Proofreading

Get It Right When you have completed the final draft of your essay, proofread it for errors in grammar, usage, mechanics, and spelling. Refer to the Language Handbook, pages R46–R60, as a guide.

Exposition

> ## Focus Lesson

In-Text Quotations from Poems

As with prose, enclose a direct quotation from a poem in quotation marks. Cite the line or line range in parentheses after the quotation, outside the quotation marks, and before the final punctuation. To indicate a line break, separate one line from the next with a slash mark with a space on each side. Use single quotation marks for quotations within quotations and be sure to match the original text exactly.

Long Quotations

If you are quoting more than three lines of poetry, set them off as a long quotation (indented ten letter spaces). Do not use quotation marks unless they appear in the original poem. Cite line numbers in parentheses and place the citation *after* the end punctuation.

Original: The quotation does not indicate the line break, and the citation is not punctuated or placed correctly.

Echoing his statement from line 2, he finally says of the painting, "There she stands As if alive 46–47."

Improved: The quotation is punctuated and cited correctly.

Echoing his statement from line 2, he finally says of the painting, "There she stands / As if alive" (lines 46–47).

Presenting

One Last Look After revising and editing your essay, read it once more to make sure it is presentable. Check to see that all quotations are accurate and complete and that they are cited properly.

The Duchess of Berri, c.1825. Sir Thomas Lawrence. Oil on canvas. Musée Crozatier, Le Puy-en-Velay, France.

Writer's Portfolio

Place a clean copy of your literary analysis essay in your portfolio to review later.

Speaking, Listening, and Viewing Workshop

Oral Response

Delivering an Oral Response to Literature

Connecting to Literature Poetry is open to many interpretations. After reading a thought-provoking poem like "The Man He Killed," readers often enjoy discussing their thoughts and reactions. A group discussion is a useful way for people to share their responses to literature and enhance their understanding of a piece of writing.

> ▶ **Assignment** In groups, respond to and discuss the major themes present in a literary work from Unit Five.

Organizing a Discussion Group

Assign roles to people in your group, such as facilitator and recorder. Each group member is equally responsible for discussion.

This chart will help you understand these roles:

Preparing for Discussion
Think about what ideas and responses you would like to share with your group members and be ready to support these views with evidence from the text. Remember to present your ideas in a logical order.

Role	Duties
Leader/Facilitator	• introduces the discussion topic • invites each participant to speak • keeps the discussion focused and interactive • keeps track of the time • helps participants arrive at a consensus
Group Participants (All)	• form ideas and questions about the literature before the discussion • contribute throughout the discussion • support any opinions with facts • avoid repeating what has been said earlier • listen carefully to other group members • evaluate opinions of others • respect the opinions of others
Recorder	• keeps track of the most important points • helps the group leader form conclusions based on the discussion • helps summarize the discussion

Effective Listening

In a discussion group it is important to be an effective listener as well as an effective speaker. You can gain valuable insights about a text from listening to the opinions of other group members. Good listening involves much more than just hearing the words of a speaker. When you listen well, you understand, evaluate, and remember what you hear so you are better able to respond to a speaker's thoughts.

Try these techniques to improve your listening skills:

Prepare to listen. Clear your mind of other thoughts and focus on the speaker, keeping a comfortable level of eye contact. Do not glance around the room, look through papers, or let your mind wander. Maintain your concentration the entire time the speaker is talking.

Note the topic and recall what you already know about it. It is easier to understand and remember information about a subject you are familiar with. Connect the subject to information you have read about or discussed before. But don't assume you already know it all. Listen with an open mind.

Ask questions, aloud or silently. If you don't understand a point a speaker is trying to make, ask questions. Even when you do understand, ask yourself silent questions to evaluate what you hear. Active listening involves evaluating a speaker's message, especially for bias or faulty information.

Listen for feelings as well as thoughts. Pay attention to the speaker's tone, expressions, gestures, and posture. Often *how* something is said reveals much about *what* is said.

Techniques for Delivering and Listening to an Oral Response to Literature

Verbal Techniques	Nonverbal Techniques
☑ **Pace** Allow each group member time to voice his or her opinion before moving on to the next topic.	☑ **Listen** Remain quiet until it is your turn to speak.
☑ **Discuss** Ask open-ended questions to promote discussion.	☑ **Poise** Use nonverbal communication such as nodding and eye contact to show you understand what the speaker is saying.
☑ **Evaluate** After discussion, take some time to evaluate how well you worked together as a group.	☑ **Gestures** Avoid nervous habits and other movements that may distract the speaker.

Time Limits

Set time limits for your group to ensure there's enough time for each idea or topic to be discussed.

OBJECTIVES
- Orally express and explain ideas about literature.
- Encourage group members to contribute ideas and viewpoints.

For Independent Reading

NOVELS DOMINATED THE LITERARY SCENE IN VICTORIAN TIMES, AND MANY BECAME wildly popular, turning their authors into celebrated public figures. Some of these works first appeared over several months as magazine installments. This delayed gratification only served to increase the public's interest, as readers waited eagerly for each new installment to appear.

Many of these novels, though, offered more than simple entertainment; they offered serious social commentary as well as insightful portraits of Victorian lives. Unlike the previous era's Romantic fictions, these novels were intended to be realistic depictions of life in Victorian England.

English Novelist Charles Dickens

Great Expectations

by Charles Dickens (1860–1861)

One of Dickens's most notable achievements, *Great Expectations* was also one of his last, completed just nine years before his death. The work explores the childhood and youth of Philip Pirrip, or Pip, as he is called, and the hardships he endures, largely at the hands of others. Told from a first-person perspective, the novel is an exploration of Pip's own mind and a depiction of the inequalities and the loss of human worth in England during the Industrial Revolution.

Middlemarch: A Study of Provincial Life

by George Eliot (1871–1872)

George Eliot was the pen name of Mary Ann Evans, one of the most prominent Victorian novelists. *Middlemarch,* widely considered Eliot's best novel, is true to its subtitle, for it offers a detailed and riveting portrait of provincial England in the nineteenth century, giving readers a glimpse of every class of society, from landed gentry to laborers. The plot revolves around the frustrations of its two main characters. A Victorian woman vainly seeking intellectual fulfillment, Dorothea Brooke resorts to marrying scholarly but pompous Edward Casaubon. Meanwhile, Tertius Lydgate, an idealistic young doctor, faces ruin and disgrace brought on by his beautiful but thoughtless wife.

"[Jane Eyre], indeed, is a book after our own heart. . . . The story is not only of singular interest, naturally evolved, unflagging to the last, but it fastens itself upon your attention, and will not leave you. The book closed, the enchantment continues. . . . Reality—deep, significant reality—is the great characteristic of the book. It is an autobiography,—not, perhaps, in the naked facts and circumstances, but in the actual suffering and experience. The form may be changed, and here and there some incidents invented; but the spirit remains such as it was. The machinery of the story may have been borrowed, but by means of this machinery the authoress is unquestionably setting forth her own experience."

—George Henry Lewes, *Fraser's Magazine*, December 1847

Actress Charlotte Gainsbourg as Jane Eyre, 1996

English novelist Charlotte Brontë, c. 1840.

Jane Eyre

by Charlotte Brontë (1847)

Charlotte Brontë intertwines elements of Romanticism and Realism in her first published novel, *Jane Eyre*. As she tells the romantic tale of a poor, orphaned governess and her wealthy, brooding employer, Brontë provides lyrical glimpses into English provincial life. Given the realities of her world, Jane Eyre must choose between her romantic impulses and her moral duty. As a fine Victorian woman, she chooses the latter, with very dramatic—and romantic—results.

From the Glencoe Literature Library

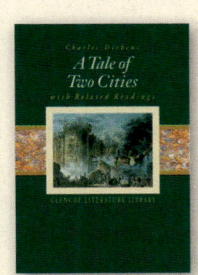

A Tale of Two Cities

by Charles Dickens

This classic novel follows Charles Darnay during the tumultuous and bloody years leading up to the French Revolution.

The Return of the Native

by Thomas Hardy

Clym Yeobright, returning to his native region of England, marries a woman bent on leaving.

Wuthering Heights

by Emily Brontë

A story of revenge, love, and obsession set in the desolate Yorkshire district of England, near the end of the eighteenth century.

Reading: Fiction

Carefully read the following passage. Use context clues to help you define any words with which you are unfamiliar. Pay close attention to the use of figurative language, argument, and the author's purpose. Then, on a separate sheet of paper, answer the questions on pages 1023–1024.

from *The New Railway* from *Dombey and Son* by Charles Dickens

line

The first shock of a great earthquake had, just at that period, rent the whole neighborhood to its center. Traces of its course were visible on every side. Houses were knocked down; streets broken through and stopped; deep pits and trenches dug in the ground; enormous heaps of earth and clay thrown up; buildings that were undermined and shaking, propped by great beams of wood. . . .

5 Everywhere were bridges that led nowhere; thoroughfares that were wholly impassable; Babel towers of chimneys, wanting half their height; temporary wooden houses and enclosures, in the most unlikely situations; carcasses of ragged tenements, and fragments of unfinished walls and arches, and piles of scaffolding, and wildernesses of bricks, and giant forms of cranes, and tripods straddling above nothing. There were a hundred thousand shapes and substances of incompleteness, wildly mingled

10 out of their places, upside down, burrowing in the earth, aspiring in the air, moldering in the water, and unintelligible as any dream. . . .

In short, the yet unfinished and unopened railroad was in progress; and from the very core of all this dire disorder, trailed smoothly away, upon its mighty course of civilization and improvement.

But as yet, the neighborhood was shy to own the railroad. . . . Nothing was the better for it, or

15 thought of being so. If the miserable waste ground lying near it could have laughed, it would have laughed it to scorn, like many of the miserable neighbors.

Staggs's Gardens was uncommonly incredulous. It was a little row of houses, with little squalid patches of ground before them, fenced off with old doors, barrel staves . . . and dead bushes; with bottomless tin kettles and exhausted iron fenders, thrust into the gaps. Here, the Staggs's Gardeners

20 trained scarlet beans, kept fowls and rabbits, erected rotten summer-houses (one was an old boat), dried clothes, and smoked pipes. . . . Staggs's Gardens was regarded by its population as a sacred grove not to be withered by railroads; and so confident were they generally of its long outliving any such ridiculous inventions, that the master chimney-sweeper at the corner, who was understood to take the lead in the local politics of the Gardens, had publicly declared that on the occasion of the

25 railroad opening, if ever it did open, two of his boys should ascend the flues of his dwelling, with instructions to hail the failure with derisive jeers from the chimney-pots.

* * *

There was no such place as Staggs's Gardens. It had vanished from the earth. Where the old rotten summer-houses once had stood, palaces now reared their heads, and granite columns of

gigantic girth opened a vista to the railway world beyond. . . . The old by-streets now swarmed with
30   passengers and vehicles of every kind. . . .

        As to the neighborhood which had hesitated to acknowledge the railroad in its struggling days,
that had grown wise and penitent . . . and now boasted of its powerful and prosperous relation. There
were railway patterns in its drapers' shops, and railway journals in the windows of its newsmen. There
were railway hotels, coffee-houses, lodging-houses, boarding-houses; railway plans, maps, views,
35   wrappers, bottles, sandwich-boxes, and timetables. . . . There was even railway time observed in
clocks, as if the sun itself had given in. Among the vanquished was the master chimney-sweeper . . .
who now lived in a stuccoed house three stories high, and gave himself out, with golden flourishes
upon a varnished board, as contractor for the cleansing of railway chimneys by machinery.

1. From the context, what do you conclude that the
word *rent*, in line 1, means?
(A) hired
(B) torn
(C) paid
(D) chartered
(E) withheld

2. Which of the following literary elements is
Dickens using in the phrase *Babel towers of
chimneys*, in lines 5–6?
(A) allusion
(B) alliteration
(C) simile
(D) understatement
(E) personification

3. Which of the following literary elements is
Dickens using in the phrase *There were a hundred
thousand shapes and substances of incompleteness*, in
line 9?
(A) allusion
(B) metaphor
(C) simile
(D) hyperbole
(E) personification

4. Which of the following literary elements is
Dickens using in the phrase *unintelligible as any
dream*, in line 11?
(A) allusion
(B) metaphor
(C) simile
(D) hyperbole
(E) personification

5. According to the second paragraph, to what does
the word *earthquake*, in line 1, refer?
(A) the effects of the unfinished railroad
(B) the effects of long-term neglect
(C) the poverty in this particular urban area
(D) the destruction of a prosperous urban area
(E) the destruction of a civilization

6. To what does the pronoun *its* in line 13 refer?
(A) civilization
(B) the railway
(C) disorder
(D) the neighborhood
(E) Staggs's Gardens

7. In lines 22–26, how does Dickens reveal the
master chimney-sweeper's personality?
(A) by direct characterization
(B) by indirect characterization
(C) in metaphors
(D) as a symbol
(E) by personification

8. What can you infer from the master chimney-
sweeper's actions in lines 22–26?
(A) He believes that the railroad will help
improve commerce in Staggs's Gardens.
(B) He is unaware of the railroad's existence.
(C) He is in favor of the destruction of Staggs's
Gardens.
(D) He has never seen a railroad before.
(E) He assumes that the railroad will fail.

9. Which of the following literary elements is Dickens using in the phrase *palaces now reared their heads*, in line 28?
  (A) allusion
  (B) metaphor
  (C) simile
  (D) hyperbole
  (E) personification

10. From the context, what do you conclude that the word *penitent*, in line 32, means?
  (A) angry
  (B) perfect
  (C) unsure
  (D) repentant
  (E) vengeful

11. Which of the following literary elements is Dickens using in the phrase *as if the sun itself had given in*, in line 36?
  (A) allusion
  (B) metaphor
  (C) simile
  (D) hyperbole
  (E) personification

12. What is the tone of the last sentence in this passage?
  (A) unsure
  (B) melancholic
  (C) ironic
  (D) bitter
  (E) sympathetic

13. From what point of view is this passage written?
  (A) first person
  (B) second person
  (C) third-person omniscient
  (D) third-person limited
  (E) ironic

14. On the basis of this passage, which of the following ideas do you think Dickens would most likely agree with?
  (A) It was a terrible crime for Staggs's Gardens to have been destroyed.
  (B) The risks associated with progress far outweigh any potential benefits.
  (C) Technological progress can bring many social and economic benefits.
  (D) There is no such thing as progress.
  (E) The railroads are a destructive force and have little merit.

15. What is the overall tone of this passage?
  (A) unsure
  (B) melancholic
  (C) ironic
  (D) bitter
  (E) confrontational

Literature Online **Unit Assessment** To prepare for the Unit test, go to www.glencoe.com.

1024 UNIT 5 THE VICTORIAN AGE

Vocabulary Skills: Sentence Completion

For each item in the Vocabulary Skills section, choose the word or words that best complete the sentence.

1. In many ways, the pessimism of the Naturalist movement was meant to _____ the Romantic view of nature.
   (A) rue
   (B) advocate
   (C) blight
   (D) redress
   (E) dapple

2. Many in England failed to consider the _____ and widespread negative effects of the British Empire on the peoples that Britain colonized.
   (A) philosophical
   (B) extraordinary
   (C) vacant
   (D) dappled
   (E) trifling

3. The rise of literary Realism was _____ from Victorian social reform movements.
   (A) philosophical
   (B) fleet
   (C) vacant
   (D) dappled
   (E) inseparable

4. Victorian society, in general, opposed moral _____ and approved of personal restraint.
   (A) retaliation
   (B) demolition
   (C) license
   (D) threshold
   (E) countenance

5. The misery caused by the Industrial Revolution in poor urban areas resulted in greatly increased governmental _____ and oversight.
   (A) threshold
   (B) scrutiny
   (C) munificence
   (D) demolition
   (E) countenance

6. Realism was both a reaction against the Romantic movement and a means through which to _____ social reform.
   (A) advocate
   (B) subside
   (C) rue
   (D) blight
   (E) diffuse

7. Thomas Hardy's pessimism was a/an _____ conviction that arose partly from his experiences.
   (A) fleet
   (B) inseparable
   (C) dappled
   (D) trifling
   (E) philosophical

8. Victorian writers stood at the _____ of the modern era and, as a result, expressed many modern ideas.
   (A) munificence
   (B) retaliation
   (C) threshold
   (D) countenance
   (E) demolition

9. As the Romantic movement _____, so did the portrayal of nature as benevolent and divine.
   (A) subsided
   (B) retaliated
   (C) blighted
   (D) feigned
   (E) rued

10. Some critics consider Dickens's writing melodramatic and his subjects occasionally _____ or silly.
    (A) vacant
    (B) trifling
    (C) dappled
    (D) fleet
    (E) extraordinary

Grammar and Writing Skills: Paragraph Improvement

Read carefully through the opening paragraphs from the first draft of a student's literary analysis. Pay close attention to the writer's use of **clauses, quotations,** and **punctuation.** Then on a separate sheet of paper, answer the questions on pages 1026–1027.

(1) *In Matthew Arnold's brilliant, melancholy poem "Dover Beach" the speaker describes the physical sensations that he associates with the sea and the emotions that these sensations arouse.* (2) *Although the poem begins with imagery that is entirely derived from observation it expands to incorporate a broad subject.* (3) *The speaker states, "The sea is calm tonight. The tide is full, the moon lies fair Upon the straits" (lines 1–3).* (4) *These lines, however, serve only to initiate a powerful meditation on the nineteenth century's greatest intellectual struggles.*

(5) *The majority of the first stanza is fixed on one principle: simple observation of the physical world.* (6) *The final lines of this stanza, though, foreshadow the philosophical probing of the remaining stanzas.* (7) *"Begin, and cease, and then again begin, With tremulous cadence slow," writes Arnold, "and bring The eternal note of sadness in" (lines 12–14).* (8) *These lines, which describe the sounds of pebbles being washed up and down the shore, attract attention, and ensure recognition of the pebbles' symbolic importance.* (9) *The pebbles are our miseries.*

(10) *The next stanza confirms this symbol: "Into his mind the turbid ebb and flow / Of human misery (lines 17–18)."* (11) *Although this image seems to imply that the sea represents life the speaker changes course, thereby complicating the poem's theme.* (12) *The speaker claims, "The Sea of Faith / Was once, too, at the full" (lines 21–22).* (13) *The sea has become something explicitly more than simply "the sea."* (14) *It has come to represent the recession of belief and a place from which the speaker may contemplate humanity's earthly life.*

1. Which error, if any, appears in sentence 1?
   (A) The appositive *"Dover Beach"* is not set off with commas.
   (B) The title of the poem is quoted.
   (C) The long introductory phrase lacks a comma at the end.
   (D) A comma separates two adjectives.
   (E) No error appears in the sentence.

2. Which is the best way to revise sentence 2?
   (A) Insert a comma after *begins*.
   (B) Insert a semicolon after *observation*.
   (C) Insert commas after *Although* and *imagery*.
   (D) Insert a comma after *observation*.
   (E) Make no change.

3. Which is the best way to revise sentence 3?
- **(A)** The speaker states, "The sea is calm tonight. The tide is full, the moon lies fair Upon the straits (lines 1–3)."
- **(B)** The speaker states, *The sea is calm tonight. The tide is full, the moon lies fair Upon the straits* (lines 1–3).
- **(C)** The speaker states, "The sea is calm tonight. The tide is full, the moon lies fair Upon the straits."
- **(D)** The speaker states, "The sea is calm tonight. / The tide is full, the moon lies fair / Upon the straits" (lines 1–3).
- **(E)** Make no change.

4. Which error, if any, appears in sentence 7?
- **(A)** The citation appears outside quotation marks.
- **(B)** *Cease* is not capitalized.
- **(C)** *Cadence* is not capitalized.
- **(D)** Slash marks do not separate lines of poetry.
- **(E)** No error appears in the sentence.

5. Which is the best way to revise sentence 8?
- **(A)** Delete the comma after *attention*.
- **(B)** Change *which* to *that*.
- **(C)** Insert a comma after *recognition*.
- **(D)** Delete the comma after *lines*.
- **(E)** Make no change.

6. Which trait of strong writing is the student demonstrating in sentence 9?
- **(A)** ideas
- **(B)** oganization
- **(C)** voice
- **(D)** word choice
- **(E)** sentence fluency

7. Which error, if any, appears in sentence 10?
- **(A)** The colon should be a comma.
- **(B)** A citation appears within a quotation.
- **(C)** The slash mark is unnecessary.
- **(D)** The word *symbol* is unnecessary.
- **(E)** No error appears in the sentence.

8. Which error, if any, appears in sentence 11?
- **(A)** The subject and the verb do not agree.
- **(B)** No comma appears after the introductory clauses.
- **(C)** This is a sentence fragment.
- **(D)** This is a comma splice (run-on sentence).
- **(E)** No error appears in the sentence.

9. Which would be the most logical topic for an additional concluding paragraph?
- **(A)** a discussion of the stanzas following those already discussed
- **(B)** Arnold's poetic influences
- **(C)** an examination of the historical importance of Dover Beach
- **(D)** an examination of the literary importance of Arnold's poem "Dover Beach"
- **(E)** an explanation of the author's feelings about "Dover Beach"

10. Which sentence would make the strongest conclusion?
- **(A)** Without the power of faith, as Arnold so powerfully demonstrates, there can be no hope in a world where "ignorant armies clash by night."
- **(B)** The miseries we experience today are the same as those experienced in Arnold's day.
- **(C)** In "Dover Beach," Arnold elegantly weaves together observations of the natural world with a discussion of the erosion of faith during the Victorian era.
- **(D)** "Dover Beach" forces readers to observe their own smallness in relation to the larger world and the way in which that world is filled with the "eternal note of sadness."
- **(E)** Arnold's "Dover Beach" is unsurpassed in its examination of nature's power to inspire.

Essay

Write a short literary analysis of a poem from this unit. Be sure to support your opinions with evidence from the text of the poem. As you write, keep in mind that your essay will be checked for **ideas, organization, voice, word choice, sentence fluency, conventions,** and **presentation.**

THE MODERN AGE

1901–1950

VB 1921

Looking Ahead

When the twentieth century began, Britain was at the height of its power. During the next half century, the British endured bitter class conflict, two world wars, global economic depression, and growing demands for independence among the colonial peoples they ruled. This period of profound change also witnessed the emergence of powerful Modernist writers, who modified and broke with the forms and traditions of British literature.

Keep the following questions in mind as you read:

▶ How did World Wars I and II impact British literature?

▶ How was class conflict represented in British literature?

▶ How did attitudes toward the British Empire begin to change during this period?

▶ What were some major characteristics of Modernism?

OBJECTIVES

In learning about the Modern age, you will focus on the following:

- analyzing the characteristics of modern literature and how issues of the period influenced writers
- evaluating the influences of the historical forces that shaped literary characters, plots, settings, and themes in modern literature
- connecting modern literature to historical contexts, current events, and your own experiences

TIMELINE

1901–1950

BRITISH LITERATURE

1900

1901
Rudyard Kipling publishes *Kim*

1907
Rudyard Kipling wins Nobel Prize in Literature

1913
George Bernard Shaw's *Pygmalion* is first produced

1914
Modernist journal *Blast* begins publication ▼

1917
William Butler Yeats publishes *The Wild Swans at Coole*

1918
Siegfried Sassoon publishes *Counter-Attack*

1920

1920
Wilfred Owen's *Collected Poems* is published

1922
Katherine Mansfield publishes *The Garden Party*

1922
T. S. Eliot publishes *The Waste Land*

1922
James Joyce publishes *Ulysses*

BRITISH EVENTS

1900

1901
Queen Victoria dies; Edward VII becomes king

1902
Boer War ends in South Africa

1903
Women's Social and Political Union is formed

1909
Old-age pension is introduced

1912
Luxury liner *Titanic* sinks

1915
Germans sink British liner *Lusitania*

1916
Easter Rebellion occurs in Dublin

1918 ▲
British women over the age of thirty gain voting rights

1920

1922
Irish Free State is established

1922
BBC begins radio broadcasts

1924
First Labour government is formed

WORLD EVENTS

1900

1903
In the U.S., Orville and Wilbur Wright make first successful airplane flight

1905
Einstein publishes special theory of relativity ▼

1911
Manchu Dynasty falls in China; Chinese republic is proclaimed

1914
World War I begins

1914
Panama Canal opens

1917
United States enters World War I

1917
Russian Revolution removes czar from power

1918
World War I ends

1922 ▲
King Tut's tomb is discovered in Egypt

Literature Online Timeline Visit www.glencoe.com for an interactive timeline.

1925

1925 ▲
George Bernard Shaw wins Nobel Prize in Literature

1929
Virginia Woolf publishes *A Room of One's Own*

1930
W. H. Auden publishes *Poems*

1931
Virginia Woolf publishes *The Waves* ▼

1940

1945
George Orwell publishes *Animal Farm* ▶

1945
Elizabeth Bowen publishes *The Demon Lover*

1946
Dylan Thomas publishes *Deaths and Entrances*

1948
T. S. Eliot wins Nobel Prize in Literature

1949
George Orwell publishes *Nineteen Eighty-four*

1925

1926
General strike begins

1928
Alexander Fleming discovers penicillin

1936
King Edward VIII abdicates; George VI becomes king

1940

◀ **1940**
Winston Churchill becomes prime minister

1940
Battle of Britain begins

1945
Clement Attlee becomes prime minister

1946
National Health Service is established

1947
Princess Elizabeth marries Duke of Edinburgh

1925

1927 ▲
Charles Lindbergh makes first transatlantic solo flight

1929
Great Depression begins

1930
Gandhi leads Salt March in India

1933
Adolf Hitler becomes German chancellor

1936
Spanish Civil War begins

1937
Japan invades China

1939
World War II begins

1940

1942
Nazi "final solution" establishes death camps for Jews

1945
United States drops atomic bombs on two Japanese cities; World War II ends

1945
United Nations is established

1947
India and Pakistan gain independence

Reading Check

Analyzing Graphic Information What major British literary works were published in 1922?

BY THE NUMBERS

World War I Casualties

ALLIED POWERS					
	TOTAL FORCES	**TOTAL DEATHS**	**WOUNDED**	**PRISONERS AND MISSING**	**TOTAL CASUALTIES**
Russia	12,000,000	1,700,000	4,950,000	2,500,000	9,150,000
British Empire	8,904,467	908,371	2,090,212	191,652	3,190,235
France	8,410,000	1,357,800	4,266,000	537,000	6,160,800
Italy	5,615,000	650,000	947,000	600,000	2,197,000
United States	4,355,000	116,516	204,002	4,500	323,018

CENTRAL POWERS					
	TOTAL FORCES	**TOTAL DEATHS**	**WOUNDED**	**PRISONERS AND MISSING**	**TOTAL CASUALTIES**
Germany	11,000,000	1,773,700	4,216,058	1,152,800	7,142,558
Austria-Hungary	7,800,000	1,200,000	3,620,000	2,200,000	7,020,000

Source *U.S. War Department, reprinted in* Encyclopaedia Britannica

SINKING OF THE *TITANIC*

On the night of April 14, 1912, the British luxury liner *Titanic* struck an iceberg in the North Atlantic and sank two hours and forty minutes later. Of the 2,224 passengers and crew aboard, more than 1,500 people drowned or froze to death in the icy water.

THE EVACUATION OF DUNKIRK

In late May 1940, a rapid German advance trapped a large force of British and French troops at Dunkirk on the French coast. Using a fleet of 41 large destroyers and 900 civilian boats, which ferried troops to the larger vessels, the British rescued 338,000 British and French troops.

PACKAGES FROM HOME

During World War I, British civilians sent their troops 1,742,947 scarves, 1,574,155 pairs of mittens, 6,145,673 hospital bags, 12,258,536 bandages, and 16,000,000 books.

PANDEMIC

In 1918 and 1919, an influenza epidemic spread around the world with devastating results. In Britain, 228,000 people died, the highest death rate since a cholera epidemic in 1849. It has been estimated that 22 million people—or more than twice the number of people killed in World War I—died from influenza.

BOMB DAMAGE

At the end of World War II, in 1945, 700,000 London-area houses damaged by German bombs and rockets still needed repair. There were also 42,000 houses too damaged to be habitable.

VACATION TIME

During the 1920s, 1,500,000 British workers received a vacation with pay. By 1938, this figure had doubled. The Holidays with Pay Act (1938) increased the number of British workers entitled to paid vacations to 11 million in the following year.

CLASS AND DIET

A 1937 survey showed that an average middle-class family ate 12% less bread and flour, 16% fewer potatoes, and half as much margarine as an average working-class family. An average middle-class family ate nearly 36% more meat, more than twice as much fish and fresh milk, 68% more eggs, and 56% more butter than an average working-class family.

BEING THERE

A Bomb damage in central London, October 1941. Achille Beltrame. Engraving in Italian newspaper *La Domenica del Corriere*.

During World War I, the principal area of combat for British troops was the Western Front, where parallel systems of trenches stretched from the North Sea to the border of Switzerland.

B The Entrance Hall, Savoy Hotel, London, c. 20th century. English School. Coloured lithograph. Bibliothèque des Arts Décoratifs, Paris.

C English trenches along the Western Front in WWI.

Literature Online **Maps in Motion** Visit www.glencoe.com for an interactive map.

Reading Check

Analyzing Graphic Information

1. What was the total number of British forces engaged in World War I who died of wounds, disease, or other causes?

2. Compared with workers in the 1920s, how many additional British workers received paid vacations in 1939 as a result of the Holidays with Pay Act?

3. In what country was most of the Western Front located?

THE MODERN AGE

1901–1950

Historical, Social, and Cultural Forces

The British Empire

At its peak in the early twentieth century, the British Empire ruled about one-quarter of the world's people. Increasing nationalism in the colonies, however, challenged British rule. Ireland, Britain's first colony, became the independent Irish Free State in 1922 (with the important exception of six northern counties). India and Pakistan became independent after World War II. As Britain's former colonies gained independence, the proud boast that the "sun never set" on the British Empire was no longer true.

World War I

In the early twentieth century, a series of political crises and a continent-wide arms race brought tensions in Europe to a head. Leaders were willing to use war as a way to preserve their power. The British viewed Germany's sudden invasion of Belgium in 1914 as a threat and declared war. Britain and the other Allied Powers, France and Russia, were soon engaged with the Central Powers, Germany, Austria-Hungary, and Turkey, in a war fought on several continents. It was a war of mud, blood, and barbed wire, made more deadly by new tanks, machine guns, flamethrowers, and poison gas. Before the war ended in November 1918, millions of people had been killed, and the economic, social, and political order of Europe had been devastated. Monarchies in Russia, Germany, and Austria-Hungary were overthrown. The conflict was particularly disturbing to Europeans because it brought a violent end to a period many had viewed as an era of progress. As British Foreign Minister Sir Edward Grey observed at the war's outset, "The lamps are going out all over Europe; we shall not see them lit again in our lifetime."

The 1920s and the Great Depression

During the war, Britain had lost many of the markets for its industrial products to the United States and Japan. Industries such as coal, steel, and textiles declined after the war, leading to a rise in unemployment. In 1921 two million British workers were unemployed. Britain soon rebounded, however, and experienced limited prosperity from 1925 to 1929. This relatively prosperous period came to an abrupt end with the Great Depression, a major economic collapse that began when the stock market crashed in the United States in October 1929. Deflation, or falling prices, caused bankruptcies, and thousands of companies and millions of individuals were financially ruined. During 1932, the worst year of the Great Depression, nearly one British worker in every four was unemployed.

"We shall not flag or fail. We shall go on to the end."

—Winston Churchill, speech, June 4, 1940

World War II

Europe's postwar economic and political problems encouraged the rise of dictatorships in many countries. In Germany, Adolf Hitler and the Nazi Party gained power by appeals to nationalism and ethnic hatred. Beginning in 1936, Nazi Germany began a policy of territorial expansion that would soon lead to war. On September 1, 1939, German forces attacked Poland, forcing Britain and France to declare war on Germany. World War II had begun. Germany soon overran much of Europe, including France, leaving Britain isolated and vulnerable. In May 1940 Winston Churchill became British prime minister and through his wartime speeches expressed the stubborn, heroic determination of the British people to continue the fight. Beginning in early September 1940, the German air force, the *Luftwaffe*, subjected Britain to the first sustained bombing of civilian targets in the history of warfare. For months, British cities were bombed nightly. Although thousands of people were killed or injured, and enormous damage was done, British morale remained high throughout the war, which continued until the surrenders of Germany and Japan in 1945.

Battle between German and British airplanes, 1916. Bayrisches Armeemuseum, Ingolstadt, Germany.

Postwar Britain: New Priorities

The end of World War II left Britain with massive economic problems and bitter class conflict. In elections immediately after the war, the Labour Party, which promised far-reaching economic reforms, gained a landslide victory. In 1946 the new government passed legislation providing government aid to help the unemployed, the sick, and the aged. The Labour government also created a system of national health care that ensured medical services for everyone. The cost of building a welfare state that would take care of its own citizens forced Britain to reduce expenses abroad. This meant the dismantling of the British Empire. Britain was no longer able to afford the cost of being a world power.

PREVIEW **Big Ideas** of the Modern Age

1 Class, Colonialism, and the Great War

In the first half of the twentieth century, Britain's political and economic power was challenged by class conflict at home, resistance to British colonialism abroad, and the outbreak of World War I. British writers responded to this period of political and social upheaval that profoundly changed Britain's life and culture.

See pages 1036–1037.

2 Modernism

World War I was a devastating and futile bloodbath that decimated a generation and shattered European civilization. Responding to the chaos and barbarism of the war, British writers attempted to find meaning in both traditional literary forms and the innovative movement known as Modernism.

See pages 1038–1039.

3 World War II and Its Aftermath

The growth of dictatorships during the 1920s and 1930s led to World War II. The British and their Allies defeated the Axis powers, but postwar Britain, under economic and political pressure, dismantled its colonial empire. These years brought a deep sense of cultural anxiety and disillusionment that permeated British writing.

See pages 1040–1041.

Class, Colonialism, and the Great War

People's expectations and opportunities are shaped by several factors. One of the most important is the social and economic class to which they belong. This was certainly true of Britain in the early twentieth century, when challenges to the traditional British class structure were just beginning to be heard.

Class Conflict

As the Victorian politician and novelist Benjamin Disraeli observed, the British upper and lower classes formed "two nations . . . as ignorant of each other's habits, thoughts, and feelings, as if they were of different planets; who are . . . fed by different food, are ordered by different manners, and are not governed by the same laws." By the early twentieth century, people of diverse groups had begun to question Britain's traditional social values. Trade unions grew, and their leaders began to agitate for a radical change to the economic system. In 1900 a new political party was formed, the Labour Party, which dedicated itself to the interests of workers. By midcentury, a group of writers known as the Angry Young Men were voicing their suspicion and resentment of the static British establishment and bitterly attacking its manners, snobbery, and hypocrisy.

> "The argument of the broken window pane is the most valuable argument in modern politics."
>
> —Emmeline Pankhurst

Women's Rights

Women composed another disaffected group that began to seek greater political power. The suffrage movement in Britain, which had long been working peacefully to secure votes for women, took a bold new direction after Emmeline Pankhurst founded the Women's Social and Political Union (WSPU) in 1903.

Under the leadership of Pankhurst and her daughters, British suffragettes used unusual publicity stunts to call attention to their demands. They pelted government officials with eggs, chained themselves to lampposts, burned railroad cars, and smashed the windows of fashionable department stores. The British government finally relented and gave women over thirty the right to vote in 1918; ten years later, the voting age for women was lowered to twenty-one.

British Imperialism

Throughout the 1800s, Britain had continued to expand its overseas territories, in part to provide markets for British goods to replace those lost to growing commercial rivals such as Germany and the United States. Some British writers, such as Rudyard Kipling (see page 1068) defended colonialism. In a celebrated poem, he admonished, "Take up the White Man's burden— / The savage wars of peace— / Fill full the mouth of Famine / And bid the sickness cease." Other writers, such as George Orwell (see page 1077), were far more critical of British imperialism. Orwell, a colonial police officer in Burma, witnessed abuses of power that oppressed him "with an intolerable sense of guilt."

The Great War

With no historical precedent for the scale of the bloodshed and destructiveness of World War I, the British referred to it simply as the Great War. The chief battlefield for British troops, known as the Western Front, stretched for hundreds of miles across northern France. From parallel systems of defensive trenches protected with barbed wire, enemy armies faced each other across "no-man's-land," a wilderness of shell craters and rubble. The battles of the Great War were vast, prolonged bloodbaths. In 1916, on the first day of the Battle of the Somme, 60,000 British soldiers were killed or wounded. By the time the battle was over in mid-November, British losses amounted to more than 400,000.

The Food Queue, c. 20th century. C. R. W. Nevinson. Pastel on brown paper. Imperial War Museum, London.

Vera Brittain wrote an autobiographical account of the years 1900 to 1925, called Testament of Youth. *Her fiancé, Roland, and her brother Edward were killed in battle. In the following passage, she writes of her feelings when the war finally ended on November 11, 1918.*

from *Testament of Youth* by Vera Brittain

I detached myself from the others and walked slowly up Whitehall, with my heart sinking in a sudden cold dismay. Already this was a different world from the one that I had known during four life-long years, a world in which people would be light-hearted and forgetful, in which themselves and their careers and their amusements would blot out political ideals and great national issues. And in that brightly lit, alien world I should have no part. All those with whom I had really been intimate were gone; not one remained to share with me the heights and the depths of my memories. As the years went by and youth departed and remembrance grew dim, a deeper and ever deeper darkness would cover the young men who were once my contemporaries.

For the time I realized, with all that full realization meant, how completely everything that had hitherto made up my life had vanished with Edward and Roland, with Victor and Geoffrey. The War was over; a new age was beginning; but the dead were dead and would never return.

Reading Check

Analyzing Cause and Effect Why do you think the end of World War I failed to make Vera Brittain feel elated?

Modernism is a historical term that refers to a literary and artistic movement that developed in the early 1900s and continued throughout the 1940s. Although there were forerunners to Modernism in the late nineteenth century, it did not fully emerge until the years just before, and immediately following, World War I.

Groundbreaking Ideas

New scientific ideas in biology, psychology, and physics strongly influenced the development of Modernism. In the late nineteenth century, Charles Darwin's biological theory of evolution had already challenged traditional beliefs about the origin and nature of human beings. Around 1900, the psychological theories of Sigmund Freud, emphasizing the role of the unconscious in human personality, questioned accepted attitudes about human behavior. At about the same time, Albert Einstein's special and general theories of relativity established new relationships among space, time, and energy, overturning the familiar Newtonian laws of physics, including the concept of a three-dimensional universe.

"Nothing can be brought to an end in the unconscious; nothing is past or forgotten."

—Sigmund Freud, *The Interpretation of Dreams*

Modern Art

During the first part of the Modernist period, artists ceased trying to create realistic depictions of the world around them. The painters Georges Braque and Pablo Picasso developed a style of art called Cubism, in which the shapes of objects or people were angular, geometric, or fragmented. Sometimes different sides of a subject were shown simultaneously. Both artists went on to work in other styles after the end of

World War I, but their early work influenced later artists. Another artistic movement, called Surrealism, was influenced by Freud's emphasis on the subconscious and the role of dreams in human behavior. Surrealist artists such as René Magritte and Salvador Dalí created dreamlike images in their paintings, as in Dalí's famous work *The Persistence of Memory*, with its melting, distorted timepieces.

Modernist Literature

The work of early Modernist writers was influenced by contemporary movements in the arts. For example, the Imagist poets, who appeared around the time of World War I, used techniques that resembled Cubism's presentation of an object from several perspectives. The horrors of the war and the alienation of modern life gave Modernist writing a dark tone of disillusionment bordering on despair. This bleak sense of spiritual emptiness is memorably conveyed in T. S. Eliot's poem *The Waste Land*, one of the major literary works of Modernism. Modernist poets, such as Eliot (see page 1117), abandoned established meters to experiment with free verse. Modernism also produced a revolution in prose fiction, such as the short stories and novels of James Joyce (see page 1138) and the novels of Virginia Woolf (see page 1149). Both Joyce and Woolf incorporated the new ideas of psychology into their fiction, using the literary technique known as stream of consciousness to reflect a character's free-flowing thoughts, feelings, and memories.

Joyce took the stream-of-consciousness technique to its limits in *Ulysses* (1922), creating a book that is simultaneously realistic, symbolic, poetic, didactic, comic, ironic, and mythic. Since Joyce, writers have had to think differently about the nature of the novel.

The subject matter of literature changed too. With the shock of the war, technological advances, and greater social freedom, writers realized that they could and should write about *anything*. No subject was too dignified or undignified, too familiar or remote, to appear in a modern poem or novel.

Room in the second Post-Impressionist Exhibition in 1912 showing the works of Henri Matisse. Roger Fry. Oil on wood, 20.19 x 24.76 in. Louvre, Paris.

The epic novel Ulysses, *by James Joyce, is the fictional account of the life of several Dublin citizens over the course of one day—June 16, 1904. The following passage focuses on one of the major characters, Leopold Bloom, and presents his interior monologue during a walk through the city.*

from *Ulysses* by James Joyce

Mr Bloom came to Kildare street. First I must. Library.

Straw hat in sunlight. Tan shoes. Turnedup trousers. It is. It is.

His heart quopped softly. To the right. Museum. Goddesses. He swerved to the right.

Is it? Almost certain. Won't look. Wine in my face. Why did I? Too heady. Yes, it is. The walk. Not see. Not see. Get on.

Making for the museum gate with long windy strides he lifted his eyes. Handsome building. Sir Thomas Deane designed. Not following me?

Didn't see me perhaps. Light in his eyes.

The flutter of his breath came forth in short sighs. Quick. Cold statues quiet there. Safe in a minute.

No, didn't see me. After two. Just at the gate.

My heart!

His eyes beating looked steadfastly at cream curves of stone. Sir Thomas Deane was the Greek architecture.

Look for something I.

His hasty hand went quick into a pocket, took out, read unfolded Agendath Netaim. Where did I?

Busy looking for.

He thrust back quickly Agendath.

Afternoon she said.

I am looking for that. Yes, that. Try all pockets. Handker. *Freeman.* Where did I? Ah, yes. Trousers. Purse. Potato. Where did I?

Hurry. Walk quietly. Moment more. My heart.

His hand looking for the where did I put found in his hip pocket soap lotion have to call tepid paper stuck. Ah, soap there! Yes. Gate.

Safe!

Reading Check

Interpreting How does this passage reflect the influence of psychology on literature during the Modern era?

What is worth fighting and dying for? The disillusionment that resulted from World War I left many British people, particularly intellectuals, writers, and artists, with the opinion that traditional ideas of military heroism and national honor were worthless concepts. As the world's dictators grew more ruthless and aggressive in the 1930s, however, democratic nations such as Britain had to stand up to these totalitarian regimes or risk being taken over.

"Do not let us speak of darker days; let us rather speak of sterner days. These are not dark days: these are great days—the greatest days our country has ever lived."

—Winston Churchill, speech, October 1941

Wartime Britain

After the fall of France in June 1940, only the British stood between Nazi Germany and the conquest of Europe. To gain control of the skies over Britain in preparation for an invasion, the Germans began a massive bombing campaign against British cities. Under the determined leadership of their wartime prime minister, Winston Churchill (see page 1166), the British remained defiant despite nightly German air raids, which the British referred to as the Blitz. Britain's Royal Air Force fought back heroically, soon inflicting major losses on the German bombers and effectively putting an end to the planned invasion of Britain. As Churchill memorably observed of the RAF, "Never in the field of human conflict was so much owed by so many to so few." German bombing raids and later rocket attacks took a terrible toll on British lives, however, and left large parts of some of Britain's major cities, particularly London, in ruins. Among the most vivid depictions of London during the Blitz are those contained in the fiction of Elizabeth Bowen (see page 1174).

By the end of 1941, Britain was no longer fighting alone but had been joined by the Soviet Union and the United States. Together, the Allies succeeded in defeating Germany and Japan by August 1945. However, the wartime alliance between the Soviet Union and the West collapsed when the Nazi threat had been eliminated, and the Americans and Soviets soon became rivals in a Cold War for control of the postwar world. With these superpowers in possession of atomic weapons, there was a new threat of nuclear world war. Everyone had witnessed in horror the devastating effects of the atomic bombs dropped on Japan. Fear of a nuclear holocaust was pervasive. The Cold War and its constant threat of global annihilation loomed over postwar Britain.

Postwar Britain

Britain's recovery from World War II was slow and challenging. The country was virtually bankrupt. Because of shortages, food rationing was increased. Coal rationing did not end until 1958. For a long time, Britain remained a hungry and cold nation. Two world wars also hastened the end of the British Empire. After World War II, the first in a long line of British colonies and dependencies became independent. India and Pakistan gained independence in 1947, followed a year later by Ceylon (Sri Lanka), Burma (Myanmar), and Palestine (Israel). Many British, both at home and abroad, found their country's diminished status to be a blow to national pride. For many others, however, the loss of Britain's colonies was a relief. After the hardship of two world wars, a group of reformers renounced the failed ideals of the past and saw a new opportunity to help all British citizens by alleviating economic and social injustice.

After the war, the Labour government set out to create a modern welfare state—a state in which the government takes responsibility for providing people with basic services. In 1946 the National Insurance Act and the National Health Service Act were passed to provide funds to those in need and health care for everyone. The British welfare state became the model for most western European countries after the war.

Shelterers in the Tube, 1941. Henry Moore. Pencil, pen and ink, watercolour and crayon on paper, 38¹⁄₁₀ x 22 in. Tate Gallery, London.

from *George Orwell's Wartime Diary*

10 September, 1940

Can't write much of the insanities of the last few days. It is not so much that the bombing is worrying in itself as that the disorganization of traffic, frequent difficulty of telephoning, shutting of shops whenever there is a raid on etc etc, combined with the necessity of getting on with one's ordinary work, wear one out and turn life into a constant scramble to catch up lost time. . . .

The delayed-action bombs are a great nuisance, but they appear to be successful in locating most of them and getting all the neighboring people out until the bomb shall have exploded. All over South London, little groups of disconsolate-looking people wandering about with suitcases and bundles, either people who have been ren-dered homeless or, in more cases, who have been turned out by the authorities because of an unexploded bomb. . . .

Most of last night in the public shelter, having been driven there by recurrent whistle and crash of bombs not very far away at intervals of about a quarter of an hour. Frightful discomfort owing to overcrowding, though the place was well-appointed, with electric light and fans. People, mostly elderly working class, grousing bitterly about the hardness of the seats and the longness of the night, but no defeatist talk.

Reading Check

Comparing and Contrasting How does the tone of the excerpt from Churchill's speech on page 1040 contrast with that of Orwell's diary?

WRAP-UP

Why It Matters

World War I was a cultural watershed for twentieth-century Britain. The war decimated a generation of young men, and many of the survivors were haunted by the horrors of the Western Front, where the traditional view of war as heroic adventure became a grimly ironic absurdity. As the poet Philip Larkin observed, "Never such innocence again."

Modernism fundamentally changed the way people looked at the world around them. Modernist artists transformed familiar objects into exotic new shapes or explored the content of dreams. Modernist writers, such as T. S. Eliot and James Joyce, broke away from traditional literary forms and values to create the classics of a new literature wherein reality might be redefined not by fidelity to exterior appearances but by the patterns of myth or the flow of the subconscious mind.

Cultural Links

▶ The word *quark*, coined by physicist Murray Gell-Mann as a name for a fundamental subatomic particle, was taken from a passage in James Joyce's novel *Finnegans Wake*.

 Literature⊙nline Big Ideas Link to Web resources to further explore the Big Ideas at www.glencoe.com.

▶ Virginia Woolf's *A Room of One's Own* influenced and inspired the modern generation of feminists, who sympathized with Woolf's view that women, especially women artists, need privacy and financial independence.

▶ The term *newspeak*, derived from the name of the language invented by George Orwell in his novel *Nineteen Eighty-four*, has been widely used to refer to messages expressed in the media that are deliberately misleading and contradictory for the purpose of controlling public opinion. The adjective *Orwellian* is used to describe features of totalitarian governments.

▶ In a famous speech delivered in 1946, Winston Churchill introduced the phrase "iron curtain" to refer to the political barrier isolating the nations controlled by the Soviet Union after World War II.

You might try using this study organizer to keep track of the big ideas in this unit.

 **THREE-POCKET BOOK**

Connect to Today ▶ Use what you have learned about the period to do one of these activities.

1. Speaking/Listening Could World War I have been prevented? In a small group, research and discuss the factors that led to the war and the measures that could have been taken to avoid this conflict.

2. Visual Literacy Working with other students, create an exhibit that illustrates and explains Modernism. You can use examples from literature, fine art, music, architecture, or interior design.

OBJECTIVES
● Conduct a discussion.
● Create a visual display.

Literature⊙nline Study Central Visit www.glencoe.com and click on Study Central to review the Modern age.

PART 1

Class, Colonialism, and the Great War

La Mitrailleuse, 1915. Christopher R. W. Nevinson. Tate Gallery, London.

"What passing-bells for these who die as cattle?
Only the monstrous anger of guns."

—Wilfred Owen, *"Anthem for Doomed Youth"*

Comparing Literature Across Time and Place

Connecting to the Reading Selections

What is the best way to respond to a person in need? The four selections compared here—a short story by Katherine Mansfield, an essay by Bessie Head, a parable from the Bible, and verses from the Qur'an—explore this issue and offer insights about life.

England, 1922

Katherine Mansfield
A Cup of Tea..short story 1045
A chance meeting—a painful realization

Botswana, Africa, 1967

Bessie Head
Village People ....essay 1054
Sharing the individual's pain

England, 1611

King James Version of the Bible
The Parable of Lazarus and the Rich Man ....parable 1057
The tables turned

Arabia, c. 650

from the Qur'an
What is true generosity? .... sacred text 1059

COMPARING THE [Big Idea] Class, Colonialism, and the Great War

Wealth and poverty can generate rigid classes that divide people and erode society. The writers of these selections examine the misery of poverty, the power of wealth, and the true meaning of compassion.

COMPARING Tone

Tone is a reflection of the writer's attitude toward a subject as conveyed through such elements as word choice, punctuation, sentence structure, and figures of speech. These four selections reflect different attitudes toward poverty and the poverty-stricken.

COMPARING Past and Present

Though advances in technology have improved the quality of life for many people throughout the world today, the widening gulf between the haves and the have-nots is still a grim reality. These selections reveal how different cultures of the past viewed wealth and poverty.

A Cup of Tea

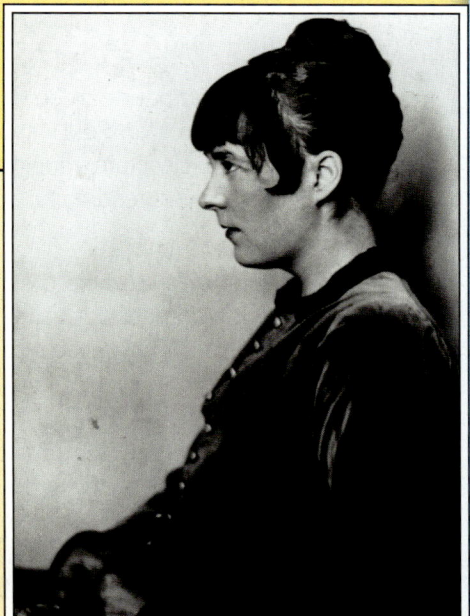

MEET KATHERINE MANSFIELD

Katherine Mansfield lived for only thirty-four years, but in her short life she became one of the greatest short story writers and an innovator in the form. Her stories have been called delicate, beautiful, and profound. She revolutionized the concept of the short story, moving it away from the strictures of plot and external action. She was able to capture the meaning of a relationship in a series of sensations, illuminating the inner truth of a character's life.

> *"Life is, all at one and the same time, far more mysterious and far simpler than we know."*
>
> —Katherine Mansfield

Setbacks and Success Born Katherine Mansfield Beauchamp in Wellington, New Zealand, she was the daughter of a domineering father and an aloof mother. As a young child, Mansfield was nurtured primarily by her maternal grandmother. She tasted her first literary success at age nine: first prize in a school composition contest. When she was fourteen, her family sailed to London, and she enrolled in Queen's College. There, she edited the school magazine and, to her delight, discovered such authors as Oscar Wilde.

Mansfield returned briefly to New Zealand, but in 1908 moved to England for good. Her life there got off to a rough start. She married hastily, then left her husband after only a few days, suffered a miscarriage, and became increasingly disillusioned. Then in 1911 her life improved—Mansfield published her first book and met the man who would become her second husband, John Middleton Murry, editor of two magazines in which she published her stories. Though a member of a literary circle that included D. H. Lawrence and Virginia

Woolf, Mansfield often felt alienated from it, and she criticized the intellectual snobbery she perceived in some of her artist friends.

The death of her soldier brother in 1915 affected Mansfield deeply. Dedicating herself to preserving her memories of him and their shared childhood, she wrote a series of short stories that beautifully portray her family life in New Zealand. Regarded today as masterpieces of the short-story form, these stories were published in 1920 in the collection *Bliss and Other Stories*.

Illness and Critical Acclaim Never in good health, Mansfield contracted tuberculosis in her early thirties. Despite her illness, she continued to write, producing some of her best works, including "A Cup of Tea," while desperately seeking a cure for her illness. During this period, she published the critically acclaimed collection *The Garden Party*. She completed her last story only months before her death. Two more collections of stories, *The Dove's Nest* and *Something Childish*, were published posthumously. Literary historian Saralyn Daly offered this assessment of Mansfield's work: "In her variety of treatment, depth of perception, and formal precision, but most of all in the continuing aliveness and immediate relevance of her stories, rests [Mansfield's] claim to a place in literary history."

Katherine Mansfield was born in 1888 and died in 1923.

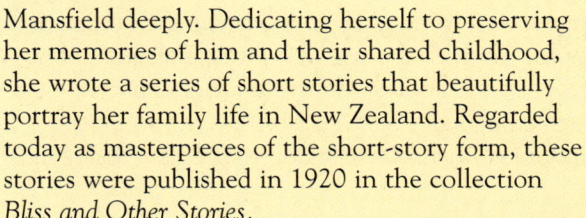 **Author Search** For more about Katherine Mansfield, go to www.glencoe.com.

Connecting to the Story

What motivates someone to be charitable toward a person in need? In Mansfield's short story, the main character helps a destitute young woman she meets on the street. As you read, think about the following questions:

- What prompts you to help others?
- What acts do you consider altruistic, or done with unselfish regard for the good of others?

Building Background

This short story is set in England at the beginning of the twentieth century. At this time, people from different social classes did not socialize with one another, and it was considered improper for upper-class women to work inside or outside the home.

Mansfield is credited with writing a new kind of short story—one more concerned with the emotions and psychological makeup of its characters than those of the past. Through the use of images, dialogue, monologue, and metaphors, Mansfield focused on her characters' emotional states, subtle shifts of mood, and **epiphanies**—that is, their sudden, significant realizations.

Setting Purposes for Reading

Big Idea Class, Colonialism, and the Great War

As you read, consider what this story suggests about the upper class and class conflict in early-twentieth-century Britain.

Literary Element Motivation

A character's **motivation** is his or her reason for acting, thinking, or feeling in a certain way. This motivation may be stated in the story or implied. As you read, consider the motivations of the characters in this story.

- See Literary Terms Handbook, p. R11.

Literature Online **Interactive Literary Elements Handbook** To review or learn more about the literary elements, go to www.glencoe.com.

Reading Strategy Connecting to Contemporary Issues

One reason that great literature endures is that generations of readers recognize its relevance to their own times. When you **connect literature to contemporary issues,** you relate events and issues in a story to those in society today.

Reading Tip: Identifying Connections Use a chart to record connections between Mansfield's story and contemporary issues.

Event in Story	Contemporary Issue
A stranger asks Rosemary for money.	Homeless people today sometimes ask passersby for handouts.

Vocabulary

quaint (kwānt) *adj.* pleasingly unusual or odd; p. 1047 *Tourists are amused to find a quaint bungalow nestled among the downtown skyscrapers.*

odious (ō′ dē əs) *adj.* causing hate, disgust, or repugnance; p. 1048 *The odious sight of the garbage dump offended us.*

exotic (ig zot′ ik) *adj.* strangely beautiful or fascinating; p. 1048 *I had never before seen that exotic flower, with its unusual leaves and petals.*

retort (ri tôrt′) *v.* to reply in a witty, quick, or sharp manner; p. 1052 *When her father refused to agree with her, the frustrated teen retorted sarcastically, "You always take my side."*

Vocabulary Tip: Analogies An analogy is a likeness between two things that are unlike in other ways.

OBJECTIVES

In studying this selection, you will focus on the following:
- analyzing literary periods
- analyzing motivation
- connecting literature to contemporary issues

Marguerite Kelsey, 1928. Meredith Frampton. Oil on canvas, 120.8 x 141.2 cm. Tate Gallery, London.

A Cup of Tea

Katherine Mansfield

Rosemary Fell was not exactly beautiful. No, you couldn't have called her beautiful. Pretty? Well, if you took her to pieces . . . But why be so cruel as to take anyone to pieces? She was young, brilliant, extremely modern, exquisitely well dressed, amazingly well read in the newest of the new books, and her parties were the most delicious mixture of the really important people and . . . artists—**quaint** creatures, discoveries of hers, some of them too terrifying for words, but others quite presentable and amusing.

Literary Element **Motivation** *Why do you think Rosemary invites "really important people" to her parties?*

Vocabulary

quaint (kwānt) *adj.* pleasingly unusual or odd

KATHERINE MANSFIELD **1047**

Rosemary had been married two years. She had a duck[1] of a boy. No, not Peter—Michael. And her husband absolutely adored her. They were rich, really rich, not just comfortably well off, which is **odious** and stuffy and sounds like one's grandparents. But if Rosemary wanted to shop she would go to Paris as you and I would go to Bond Street.[2] If she wanted to buy flowers, the car pulled up at that perfect shop in Regent Street, and Rosemary inside the shop just gazed in her dazzled, rather **exotic** way, and said: "I want those and those and those. Give me four bunches of those. And that jar of roses. Yes, I'll have all the roses in the jar. No, no lilac. I hate lilac. It's got no shape." The attendant bowed and put the lilac out of sight, as though this was only too true; lilac was dreadfully shapeless. "Give me those stumpy little tulips. Those red and white ones." And she was followed to the car by a thin shopgirl staggering under an immense white paper armful that looked like a baby in long clothes. . . .

One winter afternoon she had been buying something in a little antique shop in Curzon Street. It was a shop she liked. For one thing, one usually had it to oneself. And then the man who kept it was ridiculously fond of serving her. He beamed whenever she came in. He clasped his hands; he was so gratified he could scarcely speak. Flattery, of course. All the same, there was something . . .

"You see, madam," he would explain in his low respectful tones, "I love my things. I would rather not part with them than sell them to someone who does not appreciate them, who has not that fine feeling which is so rare. . . ." And, breathing deeply, he unrolled a tiny square of blue velvet and pressed it on the glass counter with his pale fingertips.

Today it was a little box. He had been keeping it for her. He had shown it to nobody as yet. An exquisite little enamel box with a glaze so fine it looked as though it had been baked in cream. On the lid a minute[3] creature stood under a flowery tree, and a more minute creature still had her arms around his neck. Her hat, really no bigger than a geranium petal, hung from a branch; it had green ribbons. And there was a pink cloud like a watchful cherub floating above their heads. Rosemary took her hands out of her long gloves. She always took off her gloves to examine such things. Yes, she liked it very much. She loved it; it was a great duck. She must have it. And, turning the creamy box, opening and shutting it, she couldn't help noticing how charming her hands were against the blue velvet. The shopman, in some dim cavern of his mind, may have dared to think so too. For he took a pencil, leaned over the counter, and his pale bloodless fingers crept timidly towards those rosy, flashing ones, as he murmured gently: "If I may venture to point out to madam, the flowers on the little lady's bodice."[4]

"Charming!" Rosemary admired the flowers. But what was the price? For a moment the shopman did not seem to hear. Then a murmur reached her. "Twenty-eight guineas,[5] madame."

"Twenty-eight guineas." Rosemary gave no sign. She laid the little box down; she buttoned her gloves again. Twenty-eight guineas. Even if one is rich . . . She looked vague.[6] She stared at a plump teakettle like a plump hen above the shopman's head, and her voice was dreamy as she answered: "Well, keep it for me—will you? I'll . . ."

But the shopman had already bowed as though keeping it for her was all any human being could ask. He would be willing, of course, to keep it for her forever.

---

1. Here, *duck* probably means "a darling" or "a dear," although it could also mean "funny thing" or "odd but harmless person."
2. *Bond Street*—as well as *Regent Street* and *Curzon Street* mentioned later—was, and continues to be, an elegant London street lined with shops that sell expensive items.

Big Idea **Class, Colonialism, and the Great War** *What does Mansfield criticize about Rosemary?*

Vocabulary

odious (ō′ dē əs) *adj.* causing hate, disgust, or repugnance

exotic (ig zot′ ik) *adj.* strangely beautiful or fascinating

---

3. *Minute* means "tiny."
4. A *bodice* is the fitted part of a dress from the waist to the shoulder.
5. A *guinea* was a unit of money equal to one pound and one shilling (or twenty-one shillings).
6. Here, *vague* means "uncertain."

Literary Element **Motivation** *Why does Rosemary remove her gloves to examine the enamel box?*

The discreet door shut with a click. She was outside on the step, gazing at the winter afternoon. Rain was falling, and with the rain it seemed the dark came too, spinning down like ashes. There was a cold bitter taste in the air, and the new-lighted lamps looked sad. Sad were the lights in the houses opposite. Dimly they burned as if regretting something. And people hurried by, hidden under their hateful umbrellas. Rosemary felt a strange pang. She pressed her muff to her breast; she wished she had the little box, too, to cling to. Of course, the car was there. She'd only to cross the pavement. But still she waited. There are moments, horrible moments in life, when one emerges from shelter and looks out, and it's awful. One oughtn't to give way to them. One ought to go home and have an extra-special tea. But at the very instant of thinking that, a young girl, thin, dark, shadowy—where had she come from?—was standing at Rosemary's elbow and a voice like a sigh, almost like a sob, breathed: "Madame, may I speak to you a moment?"

"Speak to me?" Rosemary turned. She saw a little battered creature with enormous eyes, someone quite young, no older than herself, who clutched at her coat collar with reddened hands, and shivered as though she had just come out of the water.

"M-madame," stammered the voice. "Would you let me have the price of a cup of tea?"

"A cup of tea?" There was something simple, sincere in that voice; it wasn't in the least the voice of a beggar. "Then have you no money at all?" asked Rosemary.

"None, madam," came the answer.

"How extraordinary!" Rosemary peered through the dusk, and the girl gazed back at her. How more than extraordinary! And suddenly it

> ## "Supposing she took the girl home? . . . what would happen? It would be thrilling."

seemed to Rosemary such an adventure. It was like something out of a novel by Dostoevsky,[7] this meeting in the dusk. Supposing she took the girl home? Supposing she did do one of those things she was always reading about or seeing on the stage, what would happen? It would be thrilling. And she heard herself saying afterwards to the amazement of her friends: "I simply took her home with me," as she stepped forward and said to that dim person beside her: "Come home to tea with me."

The girl drew back startled. She even stopped shivering for a moment. Rosemary put out a hand and touched her arm. "I mean it," she said, smiling. And she felt how simple and kind her smile was. "Why won't you? Do. Come home with me now in my car and have tea."

"You—you don't mean it, madam," said the girl, and there was pain in her voice.

"But I do," cried Rosemary. "I want you to. To please me. Come along."

The girl put her fingers to her lips and her eyes devoured Rosemary. "You're—you're not taking me to the police station?" she stammered.

"The police station!" Rosemary laughed out. "Why should I be so cruel? No, I only want to make you warm and to hear—anything you care to tell me."

Hungry people are easily led. The footman held the door of the car open, and a moment later they were skimming through the dusk.

"There!" said Rosemary. She had a feeling of triumph as she slipped her hand through the velvet strap. She could have said, "Now I've got you," as she gazed at the little captive she had netted. But of course she meant it kindly. Oh,

---

7. Fyodor *Dostoevsky,* a Russian writer who is considered one of the world's greatest novelists, often dramatized moral and psychological issues and wrote of the poor.

Reading Strategy Connecting to Contemporary Issues
How might a wealthy person today respond to a poor person's request for pocket change?

Literary Element Motivation *Why does Rosemary invite the young woman home?*

Firelight. Norman Hepple (1908–1994). Oil on canvas. Private collection.

Viewing the Art: How would you describe the woman's expression? Why might Rosemary have a similar expression?

more than kindly. She was going to prove to this girl that—wonderful things did happen in life, that—fairy godmothers were real, that—rich people had hearts, and that women *were* sisters. She turned impulsively, saying: "Don't be frightened. After all, why shouldn't you come back with me? We're both women. If I'm the more fortunate, you ought to expect . . ."

But happily at that moment, for she didn't know how the sentence was going to end, the car stopped. The bell was rung, the door opened, and with a charming, protecting, almost embracing movement, Rosemary drew the other into the hall. Warmth, softness, light, a sweet scent, all those things so familiar to her she never even thought about them, she watched that other receive. It was fascinating. She was like the little rich girl in her nursery with all the cupboards to open, all the boxes to unpack.

"Come, come upstairs," said Rosemary, longing to begin to be generous. "Come up to my room." And, besides, she wanted to spare this poor little thing from being stared at by the servants; she decided as they mounted the stairs she would not even ring for Jeanne, but take off her things by herself. The great thing was to be natural!

And "There!" cried Rosemary again, as they reached her beautiful big bedroom with the curtains drawn, the fire leaping on her wonderful lacquer furniture, her gold cushions and the primrose and blue rugs.

The girl stood just inside the door; she seemed dazed. But Rosemary didn't mind that.

"Come and sit down," she cried, dragging her big chair up to the fire, "in this comfy chair. Come and get warm. You look so dreadfully cold."

"I daren't, madam," said the girl, and she edged backwards.

"Oh, please,"—Rosemary ran forward—"you mustn't be frightened, you mustn't, really. Sit down, and when I've taken off my things we shall go into the next room and have tea and be cosy. Why are you afraid?" And gently she half pushed the thin figure into its deep cradle.

But there was no answer. The girl stayed just as she had been put, with her hands by her sides and her mouth slightly open. To be quite sincere, she looked rather stupid. But Rosemary wouldn't acknowledge it. She leaned over her, saying: "Won't you take off your hat? Your pretty hair is all wet. And one is so much more comfortable without a hat, isn't one?"

There was a whisper that sounded like "Very good, madam," and the crushed hat was taken off.

"Let me help you off with your coat, too," said Rosemary.

Big Idea Class, Colonialism, and the Great War *What does this passage suggest about the disparity between Rosemary's world and her guest's?*

Big Idea Class, Colonialism, and the Great War *What can you conclude about Rosemary's attitude toward her guest?*

The girl stood up. But she held on to the chair with one hand and let Rosemary pull. It was quite an effort. The other scarcely helped her at all. She seemed to stagger like a child, and the thought came and went through Rosemary's mind, that if people wanted helping they must respond a little, just a little, otherwise it became very difficult indeed. And what was she to do with the coat now? She left it on the floor, and the hat too. She was just going to take a cigarette off the mantelpiece when the girl said quickly, but so lightly and strangely: "I'm very sorry, madam, but I'm going to faint. I shall go off, madam, if I don't have something."

"Good heavens, how thoughtless I am!" Rosemary rushed to the bell.

"Tea! Tea at once! And some brandy immediately!"

The maid was gone again, but the girl almost cried out. "No, I don't want no brandy. I never drink brandy. It's a cup of tea I want, madam." And she burst into tears.

It was a terrible and fascinating moment. Rosemary knelt beside her chair.

"Don't cry, poor little thing," she said. "Don't cry." And she gave the other her lace handkerchief. She really was touched beyond words. She put her arm round those thin, birdlike shoulders.

Now at last the other forgot to be shy, forgot everything except that they were both women, and gasped out: "I can't go on no longer like this. I can't bear it. I shall do away with myself. I can't bear no more."

"You shan't have to. I'll look after you. Don't cry any more. Don't you see what a good thing it was that you met me? We'll have tea and you'll tell me everything. And I shall arrange something. I promise. *Do* stop crying. It's so exhausting. Please!"

The other did stop just in time for Rosemary to get up before the tea came. She had the table placed between them. She plied the poor little creature with everything, all the sandwiches, all the bread and butter, and every time her cup was empty she filled it with tea, cream and sugar. People always said sugar was so nourishing. As for herself she didn't eat; she smoked and looked away tactfully so that the other should not be shy.

And really the effect of that slight meal was marvelous. When the tea table was carried away a new being, a light, frail creature with tangled hair, dark lips, deep, lighted eyes, lay back in the big chair in a kind of sweet languor,[8] looking at the blaze. Rosemary lit a fresh cigarette; it was time to begin.

"And when did you have your last meal?" she asked softly.

But at that moment the door handle turned.

"Rosemary, may I come in?" It was Philip.

"Of course."

He came in. "Oh, I'm so sorry," he said, and stopped and stared.

"It's quite all right," said Rosemary smiling. "This is my friend, Miss—"

"Smith, madam," said the languid[9] figure, who was strangely still and unafraid.

"Smith," said Rosemary. "We are going to have a little talk."

"Oh, yes," said Philip. "Quite," and his eye caught sight of the coat and hat on the floor. He came over to the fire and turned his back to it. "It's a beastly afternoon," he said curiously, still looking at that listless figure, looking at its hands and boots, and then at Rosemary again.

"Yes, isn't it?" said Rosemary enthusiastically. "Vile."

Philip smiled his charming smile. "As a matter of fact," said he, "I wanted you to come into the library for a moment. Would you? Will Miss Smith excuse us?"

The big eyes were raised to him, but Rosemary answered for her. "Of course she will." And they went out of the room together.

"I say," said Philip, when they were alone. "Explain. Who is she? What does it all mean?"

Rosemary, laughing, leaned against the door and said: "I picked her up in Curzon Street. Really. She's a real pick-up. She asked me for the price of a cup of tea, and I brought her home with me."

---

8. *Languor* means "a dreamy, lazy mood or quality."
9. *Languid* means "lacking energy or vitality."

Literary Element Motivation *Whose needs are uppermost in Rosemary's mind?*

Literary Element Motivation *Why does the young woman identify herself as "Smith"?*

"But what on earth are you going to do with her?" cried Philip.

"Be nice to her," said Rosemary quickly. "Be frightfully nice to her. Look after her. I don't know how. We haven't talked yet. But show her—treat her—make her feel—"

"My darling girl," said Philip, "you're quite mad, you know. It simply can't be done."

"I knew you'd say that," **retorted** Rosemary. "Why not? I want to. Isn't that a reason? And besides, one's always reading about these things. I decided—"

"But," said Philip slowly, and he cut the end of a cigar, "she's so astonishingly pretty."

"Pretty?" Rosemary was so surprised that she blushed. "Do you think so? I—I hadn't thought about it."

"Good Lord!" Philip struck a match. "She's absolutely lovely. Look again, my child. I was bowled over when I came into your room just now. However . . . I think you're making a ghastly mistake. Sorry, darling, if I'm crude and all that. But let me know if Miss Smith is going to dine with us in time for me to look up *The Milliner's Gazette*."[10]

"You absurd creature!" said Rosemary, and she went out of the library, but not back to her bedroom. She went to her writing room and sat down at her desk. Pretty! Absolutely lovely! Bowled over! Her heart beat like a heavy bell.

---

10. A *milliner* is one who makes or sells women's hats. A *gazette* is a newspaper.

Big Idea Class, Colonialism, and the Great War *How would you characterize the upper-class marriage portrayed in this story?*

Vocabulary

retort (ri tôrt´) *v.* to reply in a witty, quick, or sharp manner

Pretty! Lovely! She drew her check book towards her. But no, checks would be no use, of course. She opened a drawer and took out five pound notes, looked at them, put two back, and holding the three squeezed in her hand, she went back to her bedroom.

Half an hour later Philip was still in the library, when Rosemary came in.

"I only wanted to tell you," said she, and she leaned against the door again and looked at him with her dazzled exotic gaze, "Miss Smith won't dine with us tonight."

Philip put down the paper. "Oh, what's happened? Previous engagement?"

Rosemary came over and sat down on his knee. "She insisted on going," said she, "so I gave the poor little thing a present of money. I couldn't keep her against her will, could I?" she added softly.

Rosemary had just done her hair, darkened her eyes a little, and put on her pearls. She put up her hands and touched Philip's cheeks.

"Do you like me?" said she, and her tone, sweet, husky, troubled him.

"I like you awfully," he said, and he held her tighter. "Kiss me."

There was a pause.

Then Rosemary said dreamily, "I saw a fascinating little box today. It cost twenty-eight guineas. May I have it?"

Philip jumped her on his knee. "You may, little wasteful one," said he.

But that was not really what Rosemary wanted to say.

"Philip," she whispered, and she pressed his head against her bosom, "am I *pretty*?" ❧

Literary Element Motivation *What is the real reason why Rosemary cut Miss Smith's visit short?*

AFTER YOU READ

RESPONDING AND THINKING CRITICALLY

Respond

1. Do you sympathize with Rosemary? Why or why not?

Recall and Interpret

2. (a)Why does Rosemary enjoy shopping at the antique store? (b)How would you **characterize** Rosemary from her thoughts and actions while she is shopping?

3. (a)Describe Curzon Street as it appears to Rosemary. (b)What do Rosemary's impressions of Curzon Street suggest about her emotional state?

4. (a)What does Rosemary ask her husband at the end of the story? (b)What does her question to Philip reveal about their relationship? Use details from the story to explain your answer.

Analyze and Evaluate

5. "I picked her up in Curzon Street," Rosemary explains to Philip. "She's a real pick-up." In what ways is Miss Smith like the other things Rosemary picks up on Curzon Street? How is she different?

6. (a)What do you think is the **climax** in this story? (b)How does this event contribute to the story?

7. (a)Why might Mansfield have used dashes and ellipses in the story? (b)Do you find them effective? Explain.

Connect

8. **Big Idea** **Class, Colonialism, and the Great War** What do you think is Mansfield's opinion of the upper class? Do you think she was sympathetic to the plight of the lower class? Support your answers with details from the story.

LITERARY ANALYSIS

Literary Element **Motivation**

Revealing characters' **motivations** helps to make the characters believable and their actions realistic.

1. What does Rosemary believe is her reason for helping Miss Smith? What is her real motive?

2. Why does Philip discourage his wife from helping Miss Smith? Why do you think he comments on Miss Smith's beauty?

Interdisciplinary Activity: Math

The enamel box Rosemary wishes to buy costs twenty-eight guineas. Rosemary gives Miss Smith three pound notes. What is the difference between her gift and the price of the box? Find out how much twenty-eight guineas and three pounds in the early 1900s would equal today in U.S. dollars. What do your discoveries tell you about Rosemary's "generosity" toward Miss Smith?

Literature Online **Web Activities** For eFlashcards, Selection Quick Checks, and other Web activities, go to www.glencoe.com.

READING AND VOCABULARY

Reading Strategy **Connecting to Contemporary Issues**

Review the chart you made on page 1046, and then answer the following questions.

1. In your experience, how do most people behave toward the homeless today?

2. How has the role of women in society changed since the time of this story?

Vocabulary **Practice**

Practice with Analogies Complete each analogy.

1. stiff : formal :: quaint :
   a. ancient   **b.** unusual   **c.** foreign

2. unpleasant : enjoyable :: odious :
   a. repulsive   **b.** intense   **c.** attractive

3. shout : yell :: retort :
   a. reply   **b.** sing   **c.** whisper

4. cloudy : overcast :: exotic :
   a. predictable   **b.** unusual   **c.** typical

BEFORE YOU READ

Building Background

At age thirteen, Bessie Head discovered that she had been born in a mental hospital and that she was really the daughter of a wealthy white woman and a Zulu man. She had been raised by foster parents and then sent to a mission school outside Durban, South Africa. Fortunately, her biological mother had provided for her education, and Head was able to remain in school where she acquired a lifelong love of reading.

After leaving school, she taught, worked as a reporter, and married fellow journalist Harold Head, with whom she had a son. Soon after, they divorced, and Head moved from South Africa to Botswana with her son.

There, she worked as a teacher, market gardener, and writer until she died suddenly of hepatitis.

Head wrote the following selection from "Village People" during her first years living in Serowe, Botswana, in the mid-1960s. At that time, Serowe was a village of 33,000 people who "all live in mud huts," according to Head. Botswana, a neighboring country of South Africa, has a limited supply of fresh water and experiences periodic droughts.

Literature⊙nline **Author Search** For more about Bessie Head, go to www.glencoe.com.

Village People

Bessie Head

Poverty has a home in Africa—like a quiet second skin. It may be the only place on earth where it is worn with an unconscious dignity. People do not look down at your shoes which are caked with years of mud and split so that the toes stick out. They look straight and deeply into your eyes to see if you are friend or foe. That is all that matters. To some extent I think that this eye-looking, this intense human awareness, is a reflection of the earth all about. There is no end to African sky and to African land. One might say that in its vastness is a certain kind of watchfulness that strips man down to his simplest form. If that is not so, then there must be some other, unfathomable reason for the immense humanity and the extreme gentleness of the people of my village.

Poverty here has majority backing.[1] Our lives are completely adapted to it. Each day we eat a porridge of millet[2] in the morning; a thicker millet porridge with a piece of boiled meat at midday; and at evening we repeat breakfast. We use our heads to transport almost everything: water from miles and miles, bags of corn and maize, and firewood.

This adaptation to difficult conditions in a permanently drought-stricken country is full of calamity.[3] Babies die most easily of starvation and malnutrition: and yet, within this pattern

---

1. [*Poverty . . . backing.*] More people here are poverty-stricken than not.
2. *Millet* is a type of cereal grass whose grain is used for food.
3. A *calamity* is a catastrophe causing terrible loss and pain.

Cookie, Annie Mavata, 1956. Dorothy Kay. Oil on canvas, 69 x 57 cm. Pretoria Art Museum, Pretoria, South Africa.

of adaptation people crowd in about the mother and sit, sit in heavy silence, absorbing the pain, till, to the mother, it is only a dim, dull ache folded into the stream of life. It is not right. There is a terrible mindlessness about it. But what alternative? To step out of this mindless safety, and face the pain of life alone when the balance is heavily weighted down on one side, is for certain to face a fate far worse. Those few who have are insane in a strange, quiet, harmless way: walking all about the village, freely. Only by their ceaseless muttering and half-clothed bodies are they distinguishable from others. It is not right, as it is negative merely to strive for existence. There must be other ingredients boiling in the pot. Yet how? We are in the middle of nowhere. Most communication is by ox cart or sledge. Poverty also creates strong currents of fear and anxiety. We are not outgoing. We tend to push aside all new intrusions. We live and survive by making as few demands as possible. Yet, under the deceptive peace around us we are more easily confused and torn apart than those with the capacity to take in their stride the width and the reach of new horizons.

BESSIE HEAD **1055**

Do we really retain the right to develop slowly, admitting change only in so far as it keeps pace with our limitations, or does change descend upon us as a calamity? I merely ask this because, anonymous as we are, in our favor is a great credit balance of love and warmth that the gods somewhere should count up. It may be that they overlook desert and semidesert places. I should like to remind them that there are people here too who need taking care of.

The Old Woman

She was so frail that her whole body swayed this way and that like a thin stalk of corn in the wind. Her arms were as flat as boards. The flesh hung loosely, and her hands which clutched the walking stick were turned outwards and knobbled with age. Under her long dress also swayed the tattered edges of several petticoats. The ends of two bony stick-legs peeped out. She had on a pair of sand-shoes. The toes were all sticking out, so that the feet flapped about in them. She wore each shoe on the wrong foot, so that it made the heart turn over with amusement.

Yet she seemed so strong that it was a shock when she suddenly bent double, retched and coughed emptily, and crumbled to the ground like a quiet sigh.

"What is it, Mmm? What is the matter?" I asked.

"Water, water," she said faintly.

"Wait a minute. I shall ask at this hut here if there is any water."

"What is the matter?" they asked.

"The old lady is ill," I said.

"No," she said curtly. "I am not ill. I am hungry."

The crowd laughed in embarrassment that she should display her need so nakedly. They turned away; but old ladies have no more shame left. They are like children. They give way to weakness and cry openly when they are hungry.

"Never mind," I said. "Hunger is a terrible thing. My hut is not far away. This small child will take you. Wait till I come back, then I shall prepare food for you."

Then, it was late afternoon. The old lady had long passed from my mind when a strange young woman, unknown to me, walked into the yard with a pail of water on her head. She set it down outside the door and squatted low.

"Good-day. How are you?" I said.

She returned the greeting, keeping her face empty and carefully averted. It is impossible to say: what do you want? Whom are you looking for? It is impossible to say this to a carefully averted face and a body that squats quietly, patiently. I looked at the sky, helplessly. I looked at the trees. I looked at the ground, but the young woman said nothing. I did not know her, inside or out. Many people I do not know who know me, inside and out, and always it is this way, this silence.

A curious neighbor looked over the hedge.

"What's the matter?" she asked.

I turned my eyes to the sky again, shrugging helplessly.

"Please ask the young woman what she wants, whom she is looking for."

The young woman turned her face to the neighbor, still keeping it averted, and said quietly:

"No, tell her she helped our relative who collapsed this morning. Tell her the relatives discussed the matter. Tell her we had nothing to give in return, only that one relative said she passes by every day on her way to the water tap. Then we decided to give a pail of water. It is all we have."

Tell them too. Tell them how natural, sensible, normal is human kindness. Tell them, those who judge my country, Africa, by gain and greed, that the gods walk about her barefoot with no ermine and gold-studded cloaks. ❧

Discussion Starter

In your opinion, is Head disillusioned by the events that take place or are her ideals reinforced by them? Discuss this question in a small group. Use specific details from the essay to support your opinions. Then share your conclusions with the class.

BEFORE YOU READ

Building Background

The King James Version of the Bible was the first English-language translation to receive widespread, lasting acceptance among English-speaking people. It consists of the books of the Old Testament, originally in Hebrew, and the New Testament, originally in Greek.

A **parable** is an illustrative story answering a question or pointing to a moral or religious lesson. The most famous parables are those told by Jesus, such as the one you are about to read. In this parable, Lazarus, whose name comes from the Hebrew word meaning "God Has Helped," is a diseased beggar. At that time many people believed that the diseased and destitute were to blame for their afflictions, perhaps because they or an ancestor had sinned. This parable also mentions Father Abraham, an Old Testament patriarch regarded as the founder of the Hebrew people.

The Parable of the Rich Man. Frans Francken the Younger. Musée Municipal, Cambrai, France.

The Parable of Lazarus and the Rich Man

from the *King James Version of the Bible*

There was a certain rich man, which was clothed in purple and fine linen, and fared sumptuously every day:

And there was a certain beggar named Lazarus, which was laid at his gate, full of sores,

And desiring to be fed with the crumbs which fell from the rich man's table: moreover the dogs came and licked his sores.

And it came to pass, that the beggar died, and was carried by the angels into Abraham's bosom: the rich man also died, and was buried;

And in hell he lift up his eyes, being in torments, and seeth Abraham afar off, and Lazarus in his bosom.

And he cried and said, Father Abraham, have mercy on me, and send Lazarus, that he may dip the tip of his finger in water, and cool my tongue; for I am tormented in this flame.

But Abraham said, Son, remember that thou in thy lifetime receivedst thy good things and likewise Lazarus evil things: but now he is comforted, and thou art tormented.

And beside all this, between us and you there is a great gulf fixed: so that they which would pass from hence to you cannot; neither can they pass to us, that *would come* from thence.

Then he said, I pray thee therefore, father, that thou wouldest send him to my father's house:

For I have five brethren; that he may testify unto them, lest they also come into this place of torment.

Abraham saith unto him, They have Moses and the prophets; let them hear them.

And he said, Nay, father Abraham: but if one went unto them from the dead, they will repent.

And he said unto him, If they hear not Moses and the prophets, neither will they be persuaded, though one rose from the dead. ❧

—Luke 16:19–31

Quickwrite ....

How do you respond to the role reversal that takes place in this parable? What does the parable imply about the lives of Lazarus and the rich man, and how does that lesson apply to all humans? Write a paragraph in which you address these questions.

BEFORE YOU READ

Building Background

The Arabic word *Qur'an*, which means "recitation" or "reading aloud," refers to the holy book of Islam. Muslims believe that the Qur'an is the sacred word of Allah, or God, and the authoritative guide to life. According to Muslim belief, Allah directly revealed the Qur'an to Muhammad (A.D. 570–632).

This prophet was born into a merchant family in the Arabian city of Mecca (in present-day Saudi Arabia) and was orphaned when he was about six years old. Around the year 610, Muhammad began to experience visions in a hillside cave where he meditated at night and heard a voice proclaiming, "You are the Messenger of God." Two years later Muhammad began to share his divine messages, which called upon him to preach a new religion marked by devotion to a single deity, by upright and pious conduct, and by generosity to those in need. Many merchants at that time felt Muhammad's preaching threatened their lifestyle and businesses, while others disagreed with Muhammad because they believed in multiple gods. In 622 Muhammad was forced to flee from Mecca to the city of Medina. Eight years later, however, he returned to Mecca in triumph. Islam spread rapidly after his death in 632.

About twenty years later, the Qur'an was written down in standard text. The Qur'an identifies the five "pillars of Islam," or the core practices that devout Muslims follow: acknowledging Allah as the only God, praying five times a day, fasting from dawn to dusk during the holy month of Ramadan, giving alms—or donations—to the poor, and undertaking a pilgrimage to Mecca once in a lifetime, if the believer has the means.

from the Qur'an

Translated by N. J. Dawood

Attend to your prayers, render the alms levy, and kneel with those who kneel. (2:43)

Those that give their wealth for the cause of God and do not follow their almsgiving with taunts and insults shall be rewarded by their Lord; they shall have nothing to fear or to regret. (2:262)

As for those needy men who, being wholly pre-occupied with fighting for the cause of God, cannot travel the land in quest of trading ventures: the ignorant take them for men of wealth on account of their modest behavior. But you can recognize them by their look—they never importune men for alms. Whatever alms you give are known to God. (2:273)

You shall never be truly righteous until you give in alms what you dearly cherish. The alms you give are known to God. (3:92)

God does not love arrogant and boastful men, who are themselves tight-fisted and enjoin others to be tight-fisted; who conceal the riches which God of His bounty has bestowed upon them (We have prepared a shameful punishment for the unbelievers) . . . (4:37)

Alms shall be only for the poor and the destitute; for those that are engaged in the management of alms and those whose hearts are sympathetic to the Faith; for the freeing of slaves and debtors; for the advancement of God's cause; and for the traveler in need. That is a duty enjoined by God. God is all-knowing and wise. (9:60)

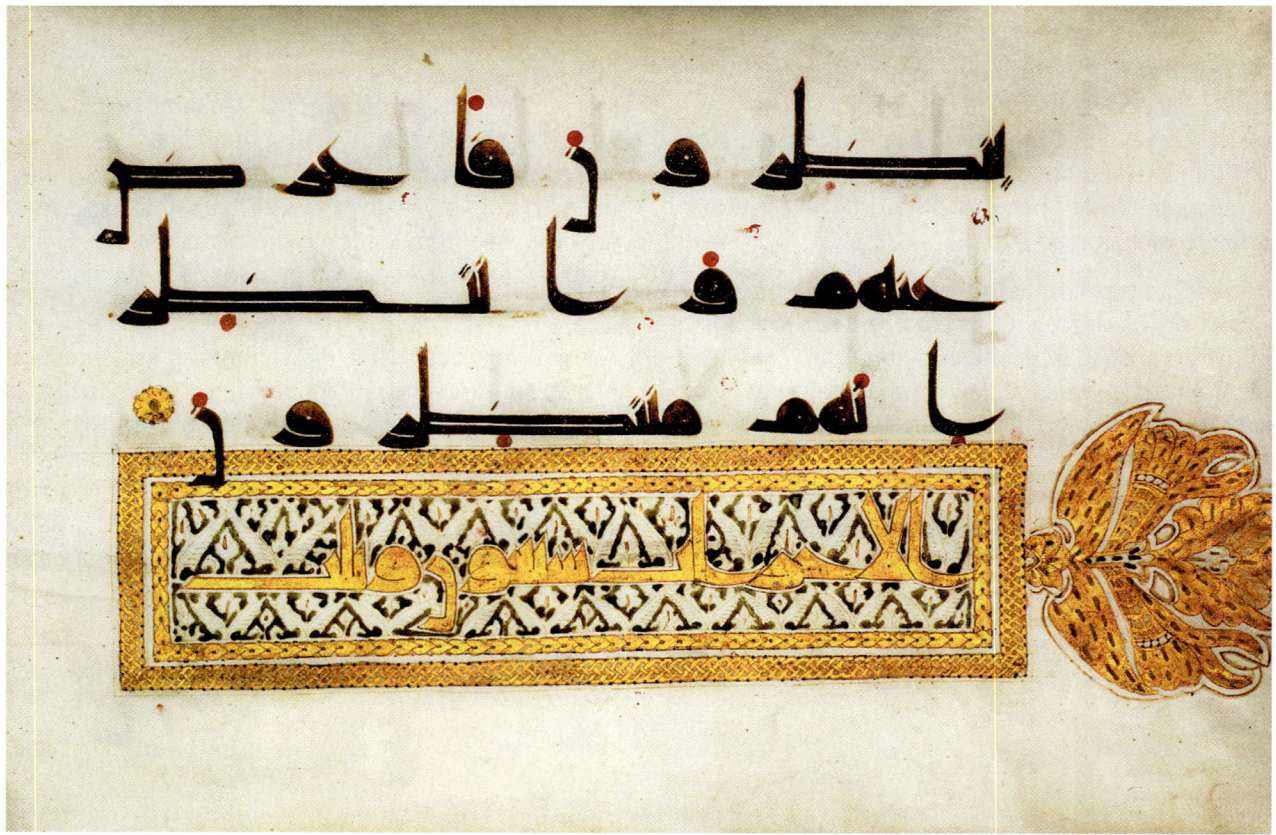

Fragment from the Qur'an. Iraq or Syria, 9th–10th century. Ink and gold leaf on parchment, 21.5 x 32.5 cm. Museum für Islamische Kunst, Staatliche Museen zu Berlin, Germany.

The true believers, both men and women, are friends to one another. They enjoin what is just and forbid what is evil; they attend to their prayers, and render the alms levy, and obey God and His apostle. On these God will have mercy. God is mighty and wise. (9:71)

Tell My servants, those who are true believers, to be steadfast in prayer and to give alms in private and in public, before that day arrives when all trading shall cease and friendships be no more. (14:31)

Give to the near of kin their due, and also to the destitute and to the traveler in need. Do not squander your substance wastefully, for the wasteful are Satan's brothers; and Satan is ever ungrateful to his Lord. (17:27)

You are called upon to give in the cause of God. Some among you are ungenerous; yet whoever is ungenerous to this cause is ungenerous to himself. Indeed, God does not need you, but you need Him. If you pay no heed, He will replace you by others who shall bear no resemblance to yourselves. (47:38)

Have you thought of him that denies the Last Judgment? It is he who turns away the orphan and has no urge to feed the destitute. (107:1)

Discussion Starter

Which verses from the Qur'an convey the Muslim attitude toward compassion and generosity? How is the message in this selection similar and dissimilar from those in the other selections in this Comparing Literature feature? Consider how the message is conveyed in each selection. Discuss these questions with a group of classmates.

- **A Cup of Tea**
  by Katherine Mansfield

- **Village People**
  by Bessie Head

- **The Parable of Lazarus and the Rich Man**
  King James Version of the Bible

- **from the Qur'an**

COMPARING THE [Big Idea] Class, Colonialism, and the Great War

Writing Read the following quotations. Then write a brief essay in which you compare the messages about class conflict and the insights about life conveyed in two or more of the selections.

> "'Come, come upstairs,' said Rosemary, longing to begin to be generous."
>
> —Mansfield, "A Cup of Tea"

> "Tell them, those who judge my country, Africa, by gain and greed, that the gods walk about her barefoot with no ermine and gold-studded cloaks."
>
> —Head, "Village People"

> "Son, remember that thou in thy lifetime receivedst thy good things, and likewise Lazarus evil things: but now he is comforted, and thou art tormented."
>
> —King James Version of the Bible

> "whoever is ungenerous to this cause is ungenerous to himself."
>
> —Qur'an

Thoughts of a Hungry Man. Emilio Longoni. Oil on canvas, 74.8 x 61.02 in. Museo Civico, Biella, Italy.

COMPARING Tone

Group Activity With a small group of your classmates, discuss each of the above quotations. How would you describe the tone of each quotation?

COMPARING Past and Present

Visual Display How does British culture today view wealth and poverty? Does that view differ from the one suggested by Mansfield's short story? Research the ways in which Britain currently addresses the needs of the poor. Then create a visual display, such as a chart or a collage, to represent your findings.

OBJECTIVES
- Compare and contrast authors' messages.
- Analyze tone.

- Compare and contrast cultures.

Media Link to Class, Colonialism, and the Great War

"Down and Out in Europe" examines the reasons behind the rise of homelessness in Europe and what is being done to solve the problem.

1. Scan the **subheads,** or smaller headlines within the article. What clues do they give you about the content of the article?

2. Examine the photograph on page 1064. Based on this image, do you think homelessness in Europe is a serious problem? Explain.

Set a Purpose for Reading

Read to learn how homelessness has become a major concern for many European countries and what solutions have been proposed to help alleviate the problem.

Reading Strategy

Analyzing Text Structure
When you **analyze text structure,** you determine a pattern of organization within a piece of writing. Most informational texts are organized by chronological order, cause-and-effect order, or compare-and-contrast order. Use a chart similar to the one below to identify the pattern in each subsection of the article.

Subsection	Homeless Women
Organizational Pattern	
Explanation	

OBJECTIVES
- Read to analyze how a writer uses text structure.
- Relate informational text to literary and historical periods

TIME

Down and Out In Europe

The number of homeless in Western Europe is at its highest level in 50 years—and rising. What should be done?

By APARISIM GHOSH

BIG SID TELLS LIES. DURING THE COURSE OF A SINGLE three-hour conversation on a London street corner, he relates his life story four times, each version more fantastical than the last. In one, he swims to the middle of the Thames in midwinter to rescue a drowning dog. In another, he defeats a band of armed skinheads with his bare hands. Sid is a black man who says his parents came to Britain from the Caribbean. But the specific biographical details he serves up vary so dramatically he might easily be talking about three or four completely different people; the narrative of inconsistencies mounts as he works his way through a two-liter bottle of hard cider. By the halfway point, he's contradicting himself almost every other sentence, and lapsing into incoherent repetitions of his two favorite phrases: "short-term" and "long-term."

Depending on which version of the saga you believe, Big Sid was born in South London, or in Yorkshire—a county in England; he's a high school dropout or played football at college; he was married (and divorced) twice, or never. He may be 35, or 40. He claims to be utterly alone in the world, an orphan with no relatives at all, but asked if he will allow himself to be photographed for this article, he balks. "I have family, man," he says, his high voice abruptly dropping to an embarrassed whisper. "I don't want them to pick up your magazine and see me in this condition."

His condition is the one certain, cruel, truth about Big Sid: he is homeless. On this bitterly cold winter night, he will make a bed of flattened cardboard boxes in the recessed doorway of a music store, squeeze into a fluorescent green sleeping bag that's too small for his angular 6-foot-6-inch frame, and rest his bald head on an old mail carrier's sack that contains his every possession. He's been sleeping on the streets for much of his adult life,

WHERE THE HOMELESS ARE

FEANTSA, a Brussels-based umbrella body of homeless organizations, estimates that over 3 million people in Western Europe are homeless. Numbers for specific countries are hard to get. Some countries simply don't bother to count, while others have different definitions for homelessness. The numbers below are estimates based on data from government and private sources

HIGH RATES >3 per 1,000	MEDIUM RATES 1-3 per 1,000	LOW RATES <1 per 1,000
United Kingdom	Austria	Sweden
Germany	Finland	Greece
France	Belgium	
	Netherlands	
	Denmark	

NOTE: NO CREDIBLE DATA IS AVAILABLE FOR THE EUROPEAN COUNTRIES NOT LISTED.

> **❝** That Europe's homelessness problem is roughly the same as America's **IS A SHOCK**. After all, Europe sees itself as kinder, gentler, and more socially responsible than the U.S. **❞**

wandering from city to city. Once or twice a year, he will go to a shelter for homeless people, to get out of nasty weather or to have a doctor look at the sores on his feet. But these interludes rarely last more than a few days because Sid finds constant human company stressful, and is deeply suspicious of anything that smacks of officialdom. "The shelters are okay for short-term, for a bath and medical treatment," he says, "but they aren't for long-term, man, not for me."

A Huge Challenge

Finding long-term solutions for people like Big Sid is an enormous—and growing—challenge for Western Europe, where homelessness has quietly been climbing to levels not seen since the end of World War II. Hard numbers are scarce, but according to the European Federation of National Organizations Working with the Homeless (FEANTSA), a Brussels-based group of homeless organizations, at least 3 million Western Europeans are homeless. And between one-fifth and one-third of them are members of homeless families. Only a small number, less than 10%, sleep on the streets like Big Sid. Most

huddle into shelters or temporary housing, live in shacks, or bed down in the homes of friends and family. Think homelessness is an American problem? Think again. As a percentage of population, it's as bad in Europe as it is in the U. S., where there are an estimated 2 million homeless, according to Dennis Culhane, a social-policy expert at the University of Pennsylvania.

That Europe's homelessness problem is roughly the same as America's—and that one of the fastest-growing segments of Europe's homeless population is families—is a shock. After all, Europe sees itself as kinder, gentler, and more socially responsible than the U.S. The continent has an extensive, expensive social safety net that's designed to help and protect its most vulnerable citizens—the kind of people who are thrown to the wolves in winner-take-all America. But that might just be the point: It's easier to be homeless in Europe, where even the down-and-out get social-welfare checks.

Activists and experts, however, don't like to make a direct cause-and-effect connection between welfare and homelessness. They point, instead, to inadequate and

sometimes senseless social-welfare policies that throw money at the problem but don't do enough to move the homeless from the streets and shelters into jobs and permanent housing. "The safety net is failing some of the most vulnerable sections of European society," says Freek Spinnewijn, FEANTSA's director. "A lot of people are falling through—people with mental-health problems, drug and alcohol problems, and people who have suffered [from] abuse."

Homeless Women

Most homeless people in Europe are single or separated men, like Big Sid. But voluntary agencies say the fastest-growing segments among the homeless are like Christelle: young, female, and part of a family. The explanations range from the predictable (the scarcity of jobs) to the counterintuitive (women's independence may be a contributor: more assertive women are more likely to dump abusive husbands and move into homeless shelters). When the numbers were small, Europe did well by homeless families and women, giving them priority in temporary and permanent government housing. But as their numbers swell, housing is being stretched thin. Spinnewijn says that single women with children make up the majority of homeless families in Europe. "One of the main reasons for the increasing number of homeless families is divorce," says Spinnewijn. "There has been a rise in the number of divorces, and often, divorced women with children find it very difficult to have an economically sustainable life."

Christelle, originally from northwestern France, has been living in a Paris shelter for five months. According to the French government's rules, she can only stay six months, which means she must find a new place to stay. Christelle is worried about the deadline, but is optimistic that she will have a job and an apartment soon. With no friends in Paris and what appears to be a distant relationship with her family, who live several hours away, she contacted a social-aid worker who placed her in a shelter.

Résumé in hand, she goes out each day looking for work. "I'd like a job in the hospitality industry, maybe as a receptionist," she says. But the job market is tight, and so she tries to hide her circumstances from possible employers, to duck prejudice against homeless people. "Nobody knows I don't have my own home, and I don't tell them," she says. That includes her husband from whom she is separated, and her family. When she calls her parents, she lets them believe she has a place to live.

The music of Jennifer Lopez plays on the radio in the background, and Christelle says what she'd really like to do is live in the U.S. "I dream of Los Angeles," she says. "Things just seem better there." But for the moment, it's enough to care for her daughter and keep going out every day looking for a job. "When I was young I would see people from shelters and thought it must not be easy to live like that, without a place of your own," she says with an awkward smile. "Now I know."

Heading for a Normal Life

It's hard to know what is tormenting the short, stocky man slouched on a bench in a Berlin metro station at 11 P.M. one freezing winter night. His blue eyes are bloodshot from alcohol, his brown beard mottled. Asked for his name by a worker from the Berlin City Mission—a homeless organization—he comes up with "O'Brien," although he's plainly German. He agrees to be taken to a shelter run by the Mission, which is sponsored by the Lutheran Church. There, he is required to surrender the black table lamp that he jealously guards at all times. He's then handed a bowl of hot soup, but screams out that he wants spaghetti. After some soothing words from the kitchen volunteers, he begrudgingly takes his bowl of soup to the almost-empty dining room.

A drunken tantrum is nothing more than a small nuisance for those who work with the homeless. Volunteers routinely encounter hostility, even violence, particularly from men who sleep on the streets. "Those who've been on the streets for years get very uncomfortable when they are suddenly in a confined space, surrounded by lots of people," says Susan Fallis. She is the project manager at a West London hostel, one of several run by the charity Broadway. "They are suspicious and angry, and get put off by even the simplest things."

Residents at Fallis's hostel are provided hot meals, clean bedrooms, even well-being services like foot massages and aromatherapy. If any of the residents are substance abusers, they are encouraged to sign up for government programs to help them. The hostel receives around $940 a week from the British government for each of its 30-odd residents. It also charges them a small fee, about $15 a week, for things like electricity, water, and gas. It's a small amount they can afford to pay from their welfare checks. The fee has another function: It is meant to help residents deal with simple real-world chores like paying bills. "They need to take small steps toward a normal life," Fallis says.

Money Isn't Enough

Europe's traditional response to homelessness has been to throw money at the problem, in the form of benefits. Unemployed single French citizens over the age of 25 and with no children are entitled to an allowance of around $480 a month. In Britain, people can claim $60–96 per week in unemployment benefits. In Germany, the homeless are entitled to an allowance of $11 a day. Social researchers know that "it's not a matter of giving someone [money each month] and expecting them to find a place to live and make a life," says Martin Hirsch. He is the president of Emmaus France, a voluntary organization that runs shelters and provides housing across the country. "Money isn't enough for people with problems—physical,

STREET LIFE: A homeless man beds down for the night in central London.

Philip Hollis

psychological—who can't take care of themselves."

Can Europe fix its homelessness problem? Not before it acknowledges that the problem is far more serious than officials currently admit. Social researchers say an accurate count of the homeless is as crucial as an accurate national census. Central governments would be smart to pass that job on to local authorities; they're closer to the problem and better able to quantify it. This is shown by the experience of Germany's states, which under German law are responsible for dealing with homelessness. As a result, Germany provides the most accurate picture of the problem among the major European countries. After peaking at 590,000 in 1997, the number of homeless Germans fell to 390,000 in 2000. The decline also suggests that local authorities do a better job, not just of counting the homeless but of getting them off the streets.

Other countries are coming around to the idea that workable solutions for homelessness must come from local authorities. England's Homelessness Act came into force in 2002, requiring each of its 354 local-government housing authorities to develop a homelessness plan.

So far, the response from voluntary groups has been mixed. Alastair Jackson, director of policy for the housing organization Shelter, says the law has already "improved the quality of help" available to homeless people. But he and others worry that better coordination and cooperation among central and local governments and volunteer organizations must take place. And yes, European governments will still need to throw more money at the problem—to pay for more affordable housing, more shelters, and for the detox, rehabilitation, and therapies many homeless people need to overcome their serious personal problems.

Big Sid doesn't think that's possible. It's been two weeks since he went to a shelter, and now he's back on the streets of London after a trip to the beach resort of Brighton where he begged on the streets for money. He's still telling tall tales, but they've taken on a much darker tone, with him playing the victim instead of the hero. The villains, inevitably, are representatives of the state, from doctors in public hospitals who don't give him the medicines he wants to police officers who beat him up for no reason. "Governments hurt people," he says, recounting years of abuse he endured—or did he?—in a state-run correctional school 20 years ago. "Government programs are all short-term, and nothing good comes of short-term." Finding long-term solutions for the Big Sids of Europe may be the hardest part of dealing with homelessness.

—Updated 2005, from TIME International, February 10, 2003

RESPONDING AND THINKING CRITICALLY

Respond

1. What do you think can be done to solve the problem of homelessness in Europe and in our own society?

Recall and Interpret

2. (a)Who is "Big Sid"? (b)Aside from his homelessness, what problems does Big Sid appear to be suffering from?

3. (a)What is the estimated number of Western Europeans who are homeless? (b)Why is it "easier" to be homeless in Europe than in the United States?

4. (a)Why are women the fastest-growing segment of the homeless population? (b)Why do you think those who have suffered abuse or have mental health issues are more likely to be homeless?

Analyze and Evaluate

5. (a)What kind of assistance is available to the homeless in Europe? (b)Why do most social researchers believe that providing money is not enough to eradicate homelessness?

6. (a)What possible solutions for homelessness does the writer suggest? (b)What evidence does the writer cite to support the viability of these suggestions?

7. (a)What kinds of text structures are used in "Down and Out in Europe"? (b)How does the structure show the short- and long-term effects of homelessness?

Connect

8. How do the profiles of homeless people in this article help you understand the class divisions in Katherine Mansfield's story "A Cup of Tea"?

The Modern British Short Story

> *"Short-story writers see by the light of the flash; theirs is the art of the only thing that one can be sure of—the present moment."*
>
> —Nadine Gordimer,
> from "The Flash of Fireflies"

DURING THE SECOND HALF OF THE NINETEENTH century, the short story gained international popularity. Pioneers of the form included Hawthorne, Poe, and Irving in the United States; Balzac, Flaubert, and Maupassant in France; and Turgenev, Tolstoy, and Chekhov in Russia. Yet in Victorian England the climate that fostered the development of the novel stifled that of the short story. Story writer and critic H. E. Bates wrote that the short story "cannot tolerate a weight of words or a weight of moral teaching, and it is highly significant that these two factors are dominant characteristics of the Victorian English novel." Around 1880, however, the British began to seriously question the Victorian values and conventions that had unified their country (and empire) for the last fifty years. Writer Frank O'Connor suggests that the short story is typically a product of a fragmented society. Thus, as the Victorian world fell apart, writers focused on the individual and the present moment rather than on society and historical continuity. Suddenly, the concentrated form of the short story made sense.

Toward Realism

British fiction during the 1880s and 1890s reflects the transition from Victorian literary conventions to twentieth-century Realism.

The short stories of Thomas Hardy, for instance, reflect a melancholy attitude and a shift toward Realism; yet, the reality Hardy presents is undermined by the artificiality of the Victorian language he uses. Similarly, Rudyard Kipling's short stories were criticized for their focus on brief episodes and use of literary "tricks." Indeed, the short story form was widely criticized as too episodic and formulaic to contain any moral force. Joseph Conrad's short stories, on the other hand, unite the aims of Realism and Romanticism by using concrete, realistic details to suggest deeper symbolic and philosophical meaning. According to critic Charles E. May, it was Conrad who, "because of the profundity of his vision and the subtlety of his use of language, effectively made the transition" and mastered the modern short story form.

Modernism

Both public literacy and the availability of reading material increased drastically during the Victorian and early modern periods. These factors broadened

Conversation Piece, 1912. Vanessa Bell. Oil on panel. University of Hull Art Collection, Humberside, UK. ©1961 Estate of Vanessa Bell, courtesy of Henrietta Garnett.

and fractured the reading public; writers could no longer take for granted a unified audience. The growing alienation between the artist and society during the 1890s became the dominant force of the Modernist movement. Many Modernist writers deliberately opposed popular tastes and trends.

After the turn of the century, prevailing assumptions about the individual, faith, history, materialism, and knowledge shattered. Writers no longer saw reality as a recognizable constant; rather, reality depended on each person's fragmented perception of it. "Look within," suggested Virginia Woolf. Woolf and other writers, including Katherine Mansfield, James Joyce, and D. H. Lawrence, concentrated on writing about "an ordinary mind on an ordinary day"—that is, about the mental consciousness of a character. Sigmund Freud's psychoanalysis contributed to this focus on the internal life and spurred literary innovations, such as stream-of-consciousness writing.

Furthermore, many modern short stories are known for depicting seemingly trivial "slices of life" that depend on important moments and the manipulation of mood rather than plot to reveal meaning. For example, in his stories, Joyce established theme through realistic detail and atmosphere. He often used **epiphany**—or a moment of revelation in which something commonplace is seen in a new light—to unify and bring his stories to a close.

Mid-Twentieth-Century Style

The events of the early twentieth century, particularly the world wars and the Great Depression, irrevocably destroyed many British conventions and

Front cover of the prospectus for The Yellow Book, *1894. Aubrey Beardsley. Lithograph. Private collection.* The Yellow Book *was an influential British literary magazine.*

ideals. Like earlier Modernist writers, Elizabeth Bowen and Graham Greene wrote stories that focused on the internal psychological and moral struggles within characters. However, Bowen and Greene often linked their characters to contemporary political and social settings.

For the modern short story writer, any subject will do, and nothing needs to "happen." Yet, due to the constraints of the form, every detail must contribute to a story's meaning. As William Faulkner noted, "In a short story . . . almost every word has to be almost exactly right."

Literature Online **Literary History** For more about the modern British short story, go to www.glencoe.com.

Miss Youghal's Sais

MEET RUDYARD KIPLING

Rudyard Kipling reportedly read in a magazine that he had died. Kipling's literary reputation has suffered a similar fate, having been buried and resurrected numerous times both in his lifetime and since his death. Readers critical of Kipling are uncomfortable with his staunch defense of British imperialism, which grew from his sincere belief that it was Britain's duty to introduce European culture to societies he believed to be less civilized. Supporters of Kipling admire the keen observations that characterize his depiction of Anglo-Indian life and find inspiration in the themes of courage, self-sacrifice, and loyalty in his works.

Childhood Influences Born to English parents living in Bombay, India, Kipling grew up speaking Hindustani better than English. His happy childhood in India made a deep impression on him and contributed to his romantic treatment of India in his fiction. When he was only five years old,

Kipling was sent to live with a hired foster family in England—a common practice among British families living in India. It was an unhappy experience for Kipling, who felt deserted by his parents. At the age of twelve, he was enrolled at the United Services College, a boarding school in Devon. His experiences there instilled in him an admiration for individualism, discipline, and order—qualities that strongly influenced his thinking and writing in later years.

> *"The magic of Literature lies in the words, and not in any man."*
>
> —Rudyard Kipling

Literary Success At seventeen, Kipling returned to India, where he worked as a journalist. He traveled widely and began to publish his first stories and poems about military life and Indian culture under British rule. In 1889 Kipling returned to England and continued his successful and prolific writing career.

In 1892 Kipling married American Caroline Balestier and settled in Vermont. Over the next few years, he wrote extensively, including the novels *Captains Courageous* and *Kim*, as well as his beloved children's classic *The Jungle Book* and its sequel, *The Second Jungle Book*. Kipling returned to England in 1897.

A Genius of Narrative In 1907 Kipling became the first English author to be awarded the Nobel Prize in Literature. At the award ceremony, Kipling was praised as "the greatest genius in the realm of narrative that [England] has produced in our times." In later years, however, Kipling's defense of British imperialism became unfashionable among more liberal-minded thinkers in England, and his popularity declined. English novelist George Orwell's assessment of Kipling's literary reputation echoed the debate that continues today: "I worshipped [him] at thirteen, loathed him at seventeen, enjoyed him at twenty, despised him at twenty-five, and now again rather admire him."

Rudyard Kipling was born in 1865 and died in 1936.

Literature Online **Author Search** For more about Rudyard Kipling, go to www.glencoe.com.

Connecting to the Story

This story is about the lengths to which some people will go to be near the person they love. As you read, think about what you would be willing to sacrifice to win the love of someone you care about.

Building Background

For more than one hundred years prior to gaining independence in 1947, India was a colony of the British Empire. When India was a colony, most aspects of Indian society were dominated by the British. Kipling's literature, which reflects this imperialism, has drawn attacks from critics. Yet even those who condemn Kipling's political attitudes have come to recognize the respect he showed for native cultures and the careful attention he gave to detailing Indian life. The story you are about to read was written early in Kipling's career, during the time he spent in India working as a journalist. It was published in one of his first collections of short stories, *Plain Tales from the Hills*.

Setting Purposes for Reading

Big Idea Class, Colonialism, and the Great War

As you read "Miss Youghal's *Sais*," look for details that reveal Kipling's attitude toward Indian culture and the British presence in India.

Literary Element Narrator

In literary works such as stories, novels, and narrative poems, the **narrator** is the person who tells the story. The narrator may be a character in the story or someone outside the story. In "Miss Youghal's *Sais*," the narrator is a character in the story. As you read, look for details that reveal who the narrator is, how he is related to the protagonist (hero), and what purpose he serves.

• See Literary Terms Handbook, p. R11.

Interactive Literary Elements Handbook To review or learn more about the literary elements, go to www.glencoe.com.

Reading Strategy Identifying Assumptions

An **assumption** is an idea or belief that one takes for granted without any actual proof. As you read, watch for characters in this story who make assumptions that color their perception of the events that take place.

Reading Tip: Taking Notes Look for assumptions as you read and note which ones change during the course of the action.

Character	Assumption	Change

Vocabulary

unsavory (un sā′ vər ē) *adj.* sinister; morally questionable; p. 1071 *The unsavory stranger curled his lip and stared with cold, piercing eyes at the frightened children.*

compensation (kom′ pən sā′ shən) *n.* something that offsets, counterbalances, or makes up for; p. 1073 *Seeing her favorite performer in person was compensation enough for the problems Linda encountered getting to the concert.*

suppressing (sə pres′ ing) *n.* prohibiting publication or circulation; censoring; p. 1073 *Fearing a backlash from voters, the politician favored suppressing news of the tax increases he planned.*

farce (färs) *n.* a humorous drama in which the situation and characters are greatly exaggerated; p. 1074 *The farce we performed featured jealous lovers, mistaken identity, meddling parents, and silly complications.*

Vocabulary Tip: Word Parts You can figure out the meanings of some unfamiliar words by examining their parts.

OBJECTIVES
In studying this selection, you will focus on the following:
• analyzing literary periods

• analyzing narrator and conflict
• identifying assumptions

Miss Youghal's Sais

Rudyard Kipling

Pushkar Blues (2), c. 21st century. Bella Easton. Oil on panel, 153.6 x 137 cm. Private collection.

When Man and Woman are agreed, what can the Kazi[1] do?
—*Proverb.*

Some people say that there is no romance in India. Those people are wrong. Our lives hold quite as much romance as is good for us. Sometimes more.

Strickland was in the Police, and people did not understand him; so they said he was a doubtful sort of man and passed by on the other side. Strickland had himself to thank for this. He held the extraordinary theory that a Policeman in India should try to know as much about the natives as the natives themselves. Now, in the whole of Upper India there is only one man who can pass for Hindu or Mahommedan,[2] hide-dresser or priest, as he pleases. He is feared and respected by the natives from the Ghor Kathri[3] to the Jamma Musjid;[4] and he is supposed to have the gift of invisibility and executive control over many Devils. But this has done him no good in the eyes of the Indian Government.

Strickland was foolish enough to take that man for his model; and, following out his absurd theory, dabbled in **unsavory** places which no respectable man would think of exploring—all among the native riff-raff. He educated himself in this peculiar way for seven years, and people could not appreciate it. He was perpetually "going Fantee"[5] among natives, which, of course, no man with any sense believes in. He was initiated into the *Sat Bhai*[6] at Allahabad[7] once, when he was on leave; he knew the Lizzard-Song of the Sansis,[8] and the *Hálli-Hukk* dance, which is a religious can-can[9] of a startling kind. When a man knows who dance the *Hálli-Hukk*, and how, and when, and where, he knows something to be proud of. He has gone deeper than the skin. But Strickland was not proud, though he had helped once, at Jagadhri,[10] at the Painting of the Death Bull, which no Englishman must even look upon; had mastered the thieves'-patter of the *chángars*; had taken a Eusufzai[11] horse-thief alone near Attock; and had stood under the sounding-board of a Border mosque and conducted service in the manner of a Sunni Mollah.[12]

His crowning achievement was spending eleven days as a *faquir* or priest in the gardens of Baba Atal at Amritsar,[13] and there picking up the threads of the great Nasiban Murder Case. But people said, justly enough, "Why on earth can't Strickland sit in his office and write up his diary, and recruit, and keep quiet, instead of showing up the incapacity of his seniors?" So the Nasiban Murder Case did him no good departmentally; but, after his first feeling of wrath, he returned to his outlandish custom of prying into native life. When a man once acquires a taste for this particular amusement, it abides with him all his days. It is the most fascinating thing in the world—Love not excepted. Where other men took ten days to

---

1. A *kazi* (kä′ zē) is a civil judge.
2. A *Mahommedan* is a Muslim.
3. The *Ghor Kathri* (gōr kä trē′), in the city of Peshawar, Pakistan, was once a Buddhist monastery and was later a sacred Hindu temple.
4. The *Jamma Musjid* (jä′ mä mäs jid′) is the Principal Mosque in Delhi. A mosque (mosk) is the Muslim place of worship.
5. *Going Fantee* (făn′ tē) means "mixing with the natives and conforming to their habits."

Literary Element Narrator *What does the narrator reveal about his attitude toward life and romance in these lines?*

Reading Strategy Identifying Assumptions *What assumptions of the British in India does this comment reveal?*

Big Idea Class, Colonialism, and the Great War *What attitude toward Indian culture is expressed in this sentence?*

Vocabulary

unsavory (un sā′ vər ē) *adj.* sinister; morally questionable

---

6. *Sat Bhai* (sät bī′) literally means "seven brothers."
7. *Allahabad* (al′ ə hə bad′), a city in north-central India, is a Hindu pilgrimage site.
8. The *Sansis* (sän sēz′) are a low-caste people of the Indian state of Punjab (pun jäb′). The caste system is a rigid social division characterized by hereditary status, hereditary occupation, and fixed social barriers.
9. The *can-can* is a Parisian dance characterized by exaggerated high kicking.
10. *Jagadhri* (jä gä′ drē) is a town in the Punjab.
11. The *Eusufzai* (ū soof′ zī) are a tribe of northwest Pakistan.
12. A *Sunni Mollah* (soo′ nē mə lä′) is a Muslim religious leader or teacher.
13. *Amritsar* (äm′ rit′ ser) is a city in northwestern India and the center of the Sikh (sēk) faith. Sikhs believe in one God and are disciples of the ten gurus (goo′ rooz), or teachers.

Literary Element Narrator *What is the narrator's attitude toward Strickland's accomplishments?*

the Hills, Strickland took leave for what he called *shikar*,[14] put on the disguise that appealed to him at the time, stepped down into the brown crowd, and was swallowed up for a while. He was a quiet, dark young fellow— spare, black-eyed—and, when he was not thinking of something else, a very interesting companion. Strickland on Native Progress as he had seen it was worth hearing. Natives hated Strickland; but they were afraid of him. He knew too much.

When the Youghals came into the station, Strickland—very gravely, as he did every-thing—fell in love with Miss Youghal; and she, after a while, fell in love with him because she could not understand him. Then Strickland told the parents; but Mrs. Youghal said she was not going to throw her daughter into the worst paid department in the Empire, and old Youghal said, in so many words, that he mistrusted Strickland's ways and works, and would thank him not to speak or write to his daughter any more. "Very well," said Strickland, for he did not wish to make his lady-love's life a burden. After one long talk with Miss Youghal he dropped the business entirely.

The Youghals went up to Simla[15] in April.

In July Strickland secured three months' leave on "urgent private affairs." He locked up his house—though not a native in the Province would wittingly have touched "Estreekin Sahib's"[16] gear for the world—and went down to see a friend of his, an old dyer, at Tarn Taran.

Here all trace of him was lost, until a *sais*[17] or groom met me on the Simla Mall with this extraordinary note:

---

14. *Shikar* (shē kar') means "hunting."
15. From 1865 to 1939, *Simla* (sĕm' lä) was India's summer capital and is still a popular summer resort.
16. In colonial India, *Sahib* (sä hēb') was a respectful form of address for a European man.
17. A *sais* (sä ēs') is a servant who attends to horses; a groom, or an attendant who follows on foot behind a mounted rider or carriage.

Reading Strategy   **Identifying Assumptions** *What assumptions does the narrator make about Miss Youghal and her knowledge of Strickland?*

Literary Element   **Narrator** *Who is the narrator? How do you know?*

DEAR OLD MAN,—Please give bearer a box of cheroots[18]—Supers, No. 1, for preference. They are freshest at the Club. I'll repay when I reap-pear; but at present I'm out of society.—Yours,
E. STRICKLAND.

I ordered two boxes, and handed them over to the *sais* with my love. That *sais* was Strickland, and he was in old Youghal's employ, attached to Miss Youghal's Arab. The poor fellow was suffering for an English smoke, and knew that, whatever happened, I should hold my tongue till the business was over.

Visual Vocabulary
An *Arab* is an Ara-bian horse prized for its speed and purity of breed.

Later on, Mrs. Youghal, who was wrapped up in her servants, began talking at houses where she called of her paragon among *saises*—the man who was never too busy to get up in the morning and pick flowers for the breakfast-table, and who blacked—actually *blacked*—the hooves of his horse like a London coachman! The turn-out[19] of Miss Youghal's Arab was a wonder and a delight. Strickland— Dulloo, I mean—found his reward in the pretty things that Miss Youghal said to him when she went out riding. Her parents were pleased to find she had forgotten all her foolishness for young Strickland, and said she was a good girl.

Strickland vows that the two months of his service were the most rigid mental discipline he has ever gone through. Quite apart from the little fact that the wife of one of his fellow-*saises* fell in love with him and then tried to poison him with arsenic because he would have nothing to do with her, he had to school him-self into keeping quiet when Miss Youghal went out riding with some man who tried to flirt with her, and he was forced to trot behind carrying the blanket and hearing every word! Also, he had to keep his temper when he was

---

18. *Cheroots* (shə rōōts') are cigars.
19. *Turn-out* refers to the horse's carriage or other equipment or furnishings.

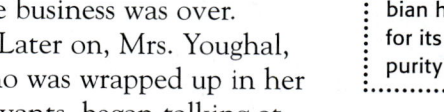

Big Idea   **Class, Colonialism, and the Great War** *Why might Mrs. Youghal be proud that her daughter's* sais *blacked the horse's hooves?*

slanged[20] in the theater porch by a policeman—especially once when he was abused by a Naik[21] he had himself recruited from Isser Jang village—or, worse still, when a young subaltern[22] called him a pig for not making way quickly enough.

But the life had its **compensations**. He obtained great insight into the ways and thefts of *saises*—enough, he says, to have summarily convicted half the population of the Punjab if he had been on business. He became one of the leading players at knuckle-bones,[23] which all *jhampánies*[24] and many *saises* play while they are waiting outside the Government House[25] or the Gaiety Theater of nights; he learned to smoke tobacco that was three-fourths cowdung; and he heard the wisdom of the grizzled Jemadar [26] of the Government House grooms. Whose words are valuable. He saw many things which amused him; and he states, on honor, that no man can appreciate Simla properly till he has seen it from the *sais*'s point of view. He also says that, if he chose to write all he saw his head would be broken in several places.

Strickland's account of the agony he endured on wet nights, hearing the music and seeing the lights in "Benmore," with his toes tingling for a waltz and his head in a horse-blanket, is rather amusing. One of these days Strickland is going to write a little book on his experiences. That book will be worth buying, and even more worth **suppressing**.

Indian Girl, 1991. Penelope Anstice. Oil on board. Private collection.

Thus he served faithfully as Jacob served for Rachel;[27] and his leave was nearly at an end when the explosion came. He had really done his best to keep his temper in the hearing of the flirtations I have mentioned; but he broke down at last. An old and very distinguished General took Miss Youghal for a ride, and began that specially offensive "you're-only-a-little-girl" sort of flirtation—most difficult for a woman to turn aside deftly, and most maddening to listen to. Miss Youghal was shaking with fear at the things he said in the hearing of her *sais*. Dulloo—Strickland—stood it as long as he could. Then he caught hold of the General's bridle, and, in most fluent English, invited him to step off and be flung over the cliff. Next minute Miss Youghal began to cry, and Strickland saw that he had hopelessly given himself away, and everything was over.

---

20. *Slanged* means "attacked with abusive language."
21. A *Naik* (nä ēk´) is a corporal of the native infantry.
22. A *subaltern* is a junior military officer.
23. *Knuckle-bones* is a game played by tossing and catching sheep bones.
24. *Jhampánies* (jäm pän´ ēz) are bearers of a jampan, a chair that is designed to hold one person and is carried on poles by men.
25. The *Government House* is the residence of a governor or the owner or manager of an estate.
26. A *Jemadar* (jə mə där´) is the head of a group of servants.

Big Idea **Class, Colonialism, and the Great War** *How might the thought expressed here reflect Kipling's own experiences in India?*

Literary Element **Narrator** *What does this sentence suggest about the narrator?*

Vocabulary

compensation (kom´ pən sā´ shən) *n.* something that offsets, counterbalances, or makes up for

suppressing (sə pres´ ing) *n.* prohibiting publication or circulation; censoring

---

27. *Jacob served for Rachel* refers to Genesis 29:15–40 in the Bible, in which Jacob served Rachel's father, Laban, for fourteen years in return for Rachel's hand in marriage.

The General nearly had a fit, while Miss Youghal was sobbing out the story of the disguise and the engagement that was not recognized by the parents. Strickland was furiously angry with himself, and more angry with the General for forcing his hand; so he said nothing, but held the horse's head and prepared to thrash the General as some sort of satisfaction. But when the General had thoroughly grasped the story, and knew who Strickland was, he began to puff and blow in the saddle, and nearly rolled off with laughing. He said Strickland deserved a V.C.,[28] if it were only for putting on a *sais's* blanket. Then he called himself names, and vowed that he deserved a thrashing, but he was too old to take it from Strickland. Then he complimented Miss Youghal on her lover. The scandal of the business never struck him; for he was a nice old man, with a weakness for flirtations. Then he laughed again, and said that old Youghal was a fool. Strickland let go of the cob's[29] head, and suggested that the General had better help them if that was his opinion. Strickland knew Youghal's weakness for men with titles and letters after their names and high official position. "It's rather like a forty-minute **farce**," said the General, "but, begad, I *will* help, if it's only to escape that tremendous thrashing I deserve. Go along to your home, my *sais*-Policeman, and change into decent kit,[30] and I'll attack Mr. Youghal. Miss Youghal, may I ask you to canter home and wait?"

* * *

About seven minutes later there was a wild hurroosh[31] at the Club. A *sais*, with blanket and head-rope, was asking all the men he knew: "For Heaven's sake lend me decent clothes!" As the men did not recognize him, there were some peculiar scenes before Strickland could get a hot bath, with soda in it, in one room, a shirt here, a collar there, a pair of trousers elsewhere, and so on. He galloped off, with half the Club wardrobe on his back, and an utter stranger's pony under him, to the house of old Youghal. The General, arrayed in purple and fine linen, was before him. What the General had said Strickland never knew, but Youghal received Strickland with moderate civility; and Mrs. Youghal, touched by the devotion of the transformed Dulloo, was almost kind. The General beamed and chuckled, and Miss Youghal came in, and, almost before old Youghal knew where he was, the parental consent had been wrenched out, and Strickland had departed with Miss Youghal to the telegraph office to wire for his European kit. The final embarrassment was when a stranger attacked him on the Mall and asked for the stolen pony.

In the end, Strickland and Miss Youghal were married, on the strict understanding that Strickland should drop his old ways, and stick to Departmental routine, which pays best and leads to Simla. Strickland was far too fond of his wife, just then, to break his word, but it was a sore trial to him; for the streets and the bazaars, and the sounds in them, were full of meaning to Strickland, and these called to him to come back and take up his wanderings and his discoveries. Some day I will tell you how he broke his promise to help a friend. That was long since, and he has, by this time, been nearly spoiled for what he would call *shikar*. He is forgetting the slang, and the beggar's cant,[32] and the marks, and the signs, and the drift of the undercurrents, which, if a man would master, he must always continue to learn.

But he fills in his Departmental returns beautifully. ◆

---

28. *V.C.,* or the Victoria Cross, is a British military decoration bestowed for conspicuous bravery in battle.
29. A *cob* is a short-legged stout variety of horse.
30. Here, *kit* means "outfit or uniform."
31. Here, a *hurroosh* is a commotion.

Reading Strategy Identifying Assumptions *Why does the general laugh so hard?*

Vocabulary

farce (färs) *n.* a humorous drama in which the situation and characters are greatly exaggerated

32. *Cant* means "language, jargon, or manner of speaking."

Big Idea Class, Colonialism, and the Great War *What conventional attitude toward British life in India is expressed here?*

Literary Element Narrator *What does this comment reveal about the narrator's attitude toward Indian culture?*

RESPONDING AND THINKING CRITICALLY

Respond

1. Do you think this story has a happy ending? Why or why not?

Recall and Interpret

2. (a)Explain how Strickland has put into practice his theory about his job. (b)What do his past adventures reveal about his personality and character?

3. (a)What job does Strickland take on in Simla? Why? (b)What are the challenges and rewards of the job?

4. (a)How does the incident with the general lead to the final outcome of the story? (b)Do you think Strickland expected this outcome? Explain.

5. (a)How is Strickland's life changed by his marriage? (b)What can you infer about his attitude toward his new life?

Analyze and Evaluate

6. Evaluate the importance of the story's setting. How does it affect the sequence of events? Explain, using specific examples from the story.

7. (a)Why might Kipling have included the proverb at the beginning of the story? (b)Do you agree with the sentiment expressed in the proverb? Why or why not?

Connect

8. **Big Idea** Class, Colonialism, and the Great War (a)What political issues of the time are reflected in this story? (b)What can you infer about Kipling's attitude toward these issues? Use evidence from the story to support your opinion.

Literary Element Narrator

The **narrator** of a story is important for several reasons. The events in a story unfold through his or her eyes and ears. An author's choice of narrator establishes a particular **point of view** from which the events are seen. The narrator can also dictate the **tone** of a story. Finally, a narrator can comment on the characters and events and inform the reader of ideas or **themes** the author wishes to convey. Review "Miss Youghal's *Sais*" and the answers you gave to the Literary Element questions that appear at the bottom of each page of the selection. Then answer these questions:

1. (a)Who is the narrator of this story? How do you know? (b)What seems to be his relationship to Strickland? What evidence in the story leads you to this conclusion?

2. (a)What can you infer about the narrator's personality and character from his comments and opinions? (b)How do his comments and opinions affect your perception of the other characters and the events that take place?

Review: Conflict

As you learned on page 23, **conflict** is the struggle between two opposing forces: the protagonist and the antagonist. The **protagonist** is the central character in a story. An **antagonist** is a person or force that opposes the protagonist. Generally, the reader is meant to sympathize with the protagonist and to be critical or fearful of the antagonist(s).

Partner Activity With a partner, review the events of "Miss Youghal's *Sais*." Then answer these questions:

1. (a)Who is the protagonist of this story? (b)Who are the antagonists?

2. (a)What is the nature of the conflict between these opposing forces? (b)Is the conflict **external** or **internal**? Why?

3. (a)Identify the **climax.** How does it serve as a turning point and lead to the resolution? (b)How is the conflict resolved?

Reading Strategy Identifying Assumptions

The characters in "Miss Youghal's *Sais*" make **assumptions** about events and other characters that help the reader understand how the characters relate to one another. Use the Reading Strategy notes in your chart on page 1069 and your knowledge of the selection to answer these questions.

1. (a)What assumptions does the narrator make about the methods Strickland employs in his job? (b)How is the narrator both critical and admiring of Strickland's methods?

2. (a)What do the Youghals assume about Strickland's character? (b)When and how do their assumptions change?

3. (a)What assumption does Strickland make about the General when he observes him with Miss Youghal? (b)What causes him to change his assumption?

4. At the end of the story, do you think the narrator assumes that Strickland has made the right decision and that his marriage is a happy one? Explain.

Vocabulary Practice

Practice with Word Parts Use your knowledge of word parts and a dictionary to help you answer the questions.

1. What is the meaning of the word created by removing the prefix *un-* from the word *unsavory*?
   a. caring   **b.** devoutly   **c.** appetizing

2. Which word shares the same Latin root as *compensation*?
   a. dispense   **b.** peninsula   **c.** compete

3. Which word shares the same Latin root as *suppressing*?
   a. prescient   **b.** supply   **c.** compression

4. Which suffix can be used to create an adjective from the base word *farce*?
   a. -tion   **b.** -ical   **c.** -ive

Writing About Literature

Analyze Cultural and Historical Context In a brief essay, discuss how Kipling uses the historical and cultural context of the **setting** in "Miss Youghal's *Sais*" to provide information about India under British rule. You may want to review the biography on page 1068 and Building Background on page 1069 before you begin.

Begin your essay by stating the main point you wish to make about Kipling's use of setting. In the body of the essay, offer examples of details from the story that describe both Indian and British life. Using evidence from the story, conclude the essay with your own estimation of Kipling's attitude toward Indian life and the British presence in India. Use a graphic organizer to help you organize your ideas.

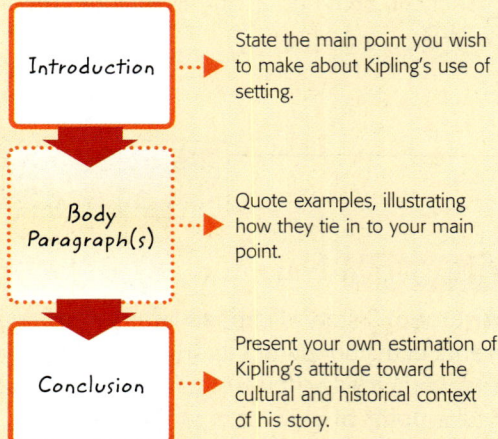

Introduction	State the main point you wish to make about Kipling's use of setting.
Body Paragraph(s)	Quote examples, illustrating how they tie in to your main point.
Conclusion	Present your own estimation of Kipling's attitude toward the cultural and historical context of his story.

After completing your draft, meet with a peer reviewer to evaluate each other's work and suggest revisions. Then edit and proofread your draft for errors in spelling, grammar, and punctuation.

Interdisciplinary Activity: History

Kipling wrote from the point of view of an Englishman in colonial India. Research the history of the English presence in India. Why was Britain there? How was the English presence perceived by Indians? What is the state of relations between the two nations today? In a brief essay, summarize your findings.

Literature**Online** **Web Activities** For eFlashcards, Selection Quick Checks, and other Web activities, go to www.glencoe.com.

Shooting an Elephant

MEET GEORGE ORWELL

Have you ever heard the expression "Big Brother is watching you"? It comes from George Orwell's *Nineteen Eighty-Four*, a novel in which Big Brother, an all-powerful ruler, watches and controls every aspect of people's lives. According to Orwell, "The moral to be drawn from this dangerous nightmare situation is a simple one: *Don't let it happen. It depends on you.*" Orwell took this idea to heart, serving as the "conscience of his generation," according to critic V. S. Pritchett.

> *"Every line of serious work that I have written since 1936 has been written, directly or indirectly, against totalitarianism."*
>
> —George Orwell
> from "Why I Write"

Developing Social Consciousness Orwell—whose real name was Eric Blair—was born in Motihari, India, where his father worked for the British government. Orwell's parents were lower-middle-class people who scraped together enough money to send Orwell to English prep schools. When he attended private school in England, he was distinguished from the other boys by both his brilliance and his relative poverty. He found that the boys from wealthy families were treated better than he was. Being a victim of class distinctions during his school days made Orwell sympathetic to the working class and other victims of injustice, a sympathy that influenced his writing.

After graduation, Orwell did not pursue a university education; instead, he applied to become a member of the Indian Imperial Police. At nineteen, he sailed to Burma (now Myanmar), where he spent the next five years working as a police officer. While on leave in England, Orwell decided, at the age of twenty-four, to resign his post in Burma and pursue a writing career. He wrote that his experiences in Burma had left him with "an immense weight of guilt. . . . I wanted to submerge myself, to get right down among the oppressed, to be one of them and on their side against their tyrants." Orwell did this by donning rags and wandering the streets of the impoverished East End of London. He spent the next year in Paris, working as a dishwasher in French hotels and restaurants and writing articles about his experiences in Burma and his views on unemployment and poverty.

Writer and Activist By his late twenties, Orwell had published only a few pieces; his book *Down and Out in Paris and London*, a fictionalized account of actual incidents in the Paris and London slums, had already been rejected three times by publishers. Disheartened, he decided to take a "regular job" and accepted a teaching position at an English school for boys. But Orwell's literary fortunes soon changed. His book was published, it sold well, and his writing career was under way.

In 1936 Orwell was dispatched to report on the Spanish civil war, but caught up in the cause, he joined a combat unit to fight fascism. His wartime experiences and later work as a British Broadcasting Corporation radio broadcaster intensified Orwell's fear of government authority and censorship. He later wrote that a government's changing of historical fact to suit its needs "frightens me much more than bombs." His last two novels, *Animal Farm* and *Nineteen Eighty-Four*, express this fear.

George Orwell was born in 1903 and died in 1950.

Literature**Online** **Author Search** For more about George Orwell, go to www.glencoe.com.

Connecting to the Essay

In this essay, Orwell recalls an incident when he felt forced to act against his better judgment. As you read, think about the following questions:

- How does peer pressure affect your behavior?
- How much of human behavior is motivated by the fear of being laughed at?

Building Background

To understand the superior attitude prevalent among the British in Burma at the time Orwell was living there, it is helpful to know that Britain then had colonies and territories in nearly every part of the world. The empire was so vast, in fact, that the British proudly proclaimed, "The sun never sets on the British Empire," meaning that even as the sun set in one part of the empire, it was sure to be rising or still shining in another.

When Orwell was in Burma, elephants were important draft animals. They were used to move timber and other heavy materials, and Southeast Asian logging operations used them extensively because they could lift felled trees with their trunks. An elephant was trained and handled by one man, called a *mahout*, who often became the elephant's inseparable companion.

Setting Purposes for Reading

Big Idea Class, Colonialism, and the Great War

As you read, look for evidence of class conflict and the effects of British colonialism in Burma in the 1920s.

Literary Element Symbol

A **symbol** is a person, animal, place, object, or event that exists on a literal level within a work but also represents something on a figurative level. As you read the essay, examine how Orwell develops the symbolic meaning of the elephant.

- See Literary Terms Handbook, p. R18.

Reading Strategy Analyzing Evidence

When you **analyze evidence**, you consider the facts, examples, and reasons a writer uses to support his or her opinion. After considering the evidence, you can evaluate the validity of the writer's opinion.

Reading Tip: Taking Notes Use a chart to keep track of the evidence Orwell presents to support his opinions.

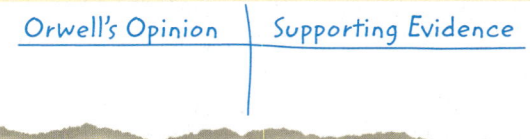

Orwell's Opinion	Supporting Evidence

Vocabulary

supplant (sə plant´) *v.* to take the place of, often unfairly; p. 1080 *Wishing to supplant the king, the prince plotted against him.*

despotic (des pot´ ik) *adj.* tyrannical; oppressive; p. 1080 *The despotic ruler raised taxes for his own personal gain.*

labyrinth (lab´ ə rinth´) *n.* a place containing winding, interconnected passages; p. 1080 *Jessie quickly became lost in the labyrinth.*

squalid (skwol´ id) *adj.* dirty or broken-down due to poverty or neglect; p. 1080 *The family's squalid living conditions were a direct cause of the infant's illness.*

garish (gār´ ish) *adj.* excessively bright; flashy; gaudy; p. 1082 *The garish party decorations were in poor taste.*

Vocabulary Tip: Analogies Analogies are comparisons based on relationships between words.

Literature Online **Interactive Literary Elements Handbook** To review or learn more about the literary elements, go to www.glencoe.com.

OBJECTIVES
In studying this selection, you will focus on the following:
- relating British literature to its historical context
- analyzing symbols and thesis
- analyzing evidence

An Indian elephant and his mahout with a fortress on a hill and palm trees behind, mid-19th century. Elizabeth Sophia Forbes. Woolwork panel. Dreweatt Neate Fine Art Auctioneers, Newbury, England.

Shooting an Elephant

George Orwell

In Moulmein, in lower Burma, I was hated by large numbers of people—the only time in my life that I have been important enough for this to happen to me. I was subdivisional police officer of the town, and in an aimless, petty[1] kind of way anti-European feeling was very bitter. No one had the guts to raise a riot, but if a European woman went through the bazaars alone somebody would probably spit betel juice[2] over her dress. As a police officer I was an obvious target and was baited whenever it seemed safe to do so. When a nimble[3] Burman tripped me up on the football field and the referee (another Burman) looked the other way, the crowd yelled with hideous laughter. This happened more than once. In the end the sneering[4] yellow faces of young men that met me everywhere, the insults hooted after me when I was at a safe distance, got badly on my nerves. The young Buddhist priests were the worst of all. There were several thousands of them in the town and none of them seemed to have anything to do except stand on street corners and jeer at Europeans.

---

1. *Petty* means "trivial" or "insignificant."
2. *Betel juice* consists of leaves and nuts of the betel palm mixed with mineral lime.
3. Here, *nimble* means "agile" or "quick-moving."

4. *Sneering* means "scornful."

Reading Strategy   Analyzing Evidence *What evidence supports Orwell's statement that "anti-European feeling was very bitter"?*

All this was perplexing and upsetting. For at that time I had already made up my mind that imperialism[5] was an evil thing and the sooner I chucked up my job and got out of it the better. Theoretically—and secretly, of course—I was all for the Burmese and all against their oppressors, the British. As for the job I was doing, I hated it more bitterly than I can perhaps make clear. In a job like that you see the dirty work of Empire at close quarters. The wretched prisoners huddling in the stinking cages of the lockups, the gray, cowed faces of the long-term convicts, the scarred buttocks of the men who had been flogged with bamboos—all these oppressed me with an intolerable sense of guilt. But I could get nothing into perspective. I was young and ill-educated and I had had to think out my problems in the utter silence that is imposed on every Englishman in the East. I did not even know that the British Empire is dying, still less did I know that it is a great deal better than the younger empires that are going to supplant it. All I knew was that I was stuck between my hatred of the empire I served and my rage against the evil-spirited little beasts who tried to make my job impossible. With one part of my mind I thought of the British Raj[6] as an unbreakable tyranny, as something clamped down, *in saecula saeculorum*,[7] upon the will of prostrate[8] peoples; with another part I thought that the greatest joy in the world would be to drive a bayonet into a Buddhist priest's guts. Feelings like these are the normal by-products of imperialism; ask any Anglo-Indian official, if you can catch him off duty.

---

5. *Imperialism* is the policy of extending a nation's authority by acquisition of territory.
6. *British Raj* (räj) refers to the British Empire in the East; *raj* is a Hindu word meaning "rule."
7. *In saecula saeculorum* means "forever and ever."
8. Here, *prostrate* means "completely overcome"; "helpless."

Literary Element Symbol *What do the prisoners symbolize for Orwell?*

Big Idea Class, Colonialism, and the Great War
Summarize the conflicting feelings that Orwell identifies as "the normal by-products of imperialism."

Vocabulary

supplant (sə plant′) *v.* to take the place of, often unfairly

One day something happened which in a roundabout way was enlightening. It was a tiny incident in itself, but it gave me a better glimpse than I had had before of the real nature of imperialism—the real motives for which **despotic** governments act. Early one morning the subinspector at a police station the other end of the town rang me up on the phone and said that an elephant was ravaging the bazaar. Would I please come and do something about it? I did not know what I could do, but I wanted to see what was happening and I got on to a pony and started out. I took my rifle, an old .44 Winchester and much too small to kill an elephant, but I thought the noise might be useful *in terrorem*.[9] Various Burmans stopped me on the way and told me about the elephant's doings. It was not, of course, a wild elephant, but a tame one which had gone "must."[10] It had been chained up, as tame elephants always are when their attack of "must" is due, but on the previous night it had broken its chain and escaped. Its mahout,[11] the only person who could manage it when it was in that state, had set out in pursuit, but had taken the wrong direction and was now twelve hours' journey away, and in the morning the elephant had suddenly reappeared in the town. The Burmese population had no weapons and were quite helpless against it. It had already destroyed somebody's bamboo hut, killed a cow, and raided some fruit-stalls and devoured the stock; also it had met the municipal rubbish van and, when the driver jumped out and took to his heels, had turned the van over and inflicted violences upon it.

The Burmese subinspector and some Indian constables were waiting for me in the quarter where the elephant had been seen. It was a very poor quarter, a **labyrinth** of **squalid** bamboo huts,

---

9. The Latin phrase *in terrorem* means "to terrify."
10. Here, *must* refers to the state of frenzy a male animal periodically undergoes during mating season.
11. A *mahout* (mə hout′) is an elephant keeper.

Literary Element Symbol *What might the elephant symbolize?*

Vocabulary

despotic (des pot′ ik) *adj.* tyrannical; oppressive
labyrinth (lab′ ə rinth′) *n.* a place containing winding, interconnected passages
squalid (skwol′ id) *adj.* dirty or broken-down due to poverty or neglect

thatched with palm leaf, winding all over a steep hillside. I remember that it was a cloudy, stuffy morning at the beginning of the rains. We began questioning the people as to where the elephant had gone and, as usual, failed to get any definite information. That is invariably the case in the East; a story always sounds clear enough at a distance, but the nearer you get to the scene of events the vaguer it becomes. Some of the people said that the elephant had gone in one direction, some said that he had gone in another, some professed not even to have heard of any elephant. I had almost made up my mind that the whole story was a pack of lies, when we heard yells a little distance away. There was a loud, scandalized cry of "Go away, child! Go away this instant!" and an old woman with a switch[12] in her hand came round the corner of a hut, violently shooing away a crowd of naked children. Some more women followed, clicking their tongues and exclaiming; evidently there was something that the children ought not to have seen. I rounded the hut and saw a man's dead body sprawling in the mud. He was an Indian, a black Dravidian coolie,[13] almost naked, and he could not have been dead many minutes. The people said that the elephant had come suddenly upon him round the corner of the hut, caught him with its trunk, put its foot on his back and ground him into the earth. This was the rainy season and the ground was soft, and his face had scored a trench a foot deep and a couple of yards long. He was lying on his belly with arms crucified and head sharply twisted to one side. His face was coated with mud, the eyes wide open, the teeth bared and grinning with an expression of unendurable agony. (Never tell me, by the way, that the dead look peaceful. Most of

> "It had already destroyed somebody's bamboo hut, killed a cow, and raided some fruitstalls and devoured the stock . . ."

the corpses I have seen looked devilish.) The friction of the great beast's foot had stripped the skin from his back as neatly as one skins a rabbit. As soon as I saw the dead man I sent an orderly to a friend's house nearby to borrow an elephant rifle. I had already sent back the pony, not wanting it to go mad with fright and throw me if it smelt the elephant.

The orderly came back in a few minutes with a rifle and five cartridges, and meanwhile some Burmans had arrived and told us that the elephant was in the paddy fields[14] below, only a few hundred yards away. As I started forward practically the whole population of the quarter flocked out of the houses and followed me. They had seen the rifle and were all shouting excitedly that I was going to shoot the elephant. They had not shown much interest in the elephant when he was merely ravaging their homes, but it was different now that he was going to be shot. It was a bit of fun to them, as it would be to an English crowd; besides they wanted the meat. It made me vaguely uneasy. I had no intention of shooting the elephant—I had merely sent for the rifle to defend myself if necessary—and it is always unnerving to have a crowd following you. I marched down the hill, looking and feeling a fool, with the rifle over my shoulder and an ever-growing army of people jostling at my heels. At the bottom, when you got away from the huts, there was a metaled road and beyond that a miry[15] waste of paddy fields a thousand yards across, not yet ploughed but soggy from the first rains and dotted with coarse grass. The elephant was standing eight yards from the road, his left side towards us. He took not the slightest notice of the crowd's approach. He was tearing up bunches of grass, beating them against his knees to clean them and stuffing them into his mouth.

I had halted on the road. As soon as I saw the elephant I knew with perfect certainty that I ought not to shoot him. It is a serious matter to

---

12. Here, a *switch* is a slender, flexible rod, twig, or stick used for whipping.
13. A *Dravidian* is a person from southern India who speaks the Dravidian language. A *coolie* is an unskilled laborer.

Literary Element   Symbol   *What might the Dravidian coolie symbolize?*

14. *Paddy fields* are rice fields.
15. *Miry* means "swampy."

shoot a working elephant—it is comparable to destroying a huge and costly piece of machinery—and obviously one ought not to do it if it can possibly be avoided. And at that distance, peacefully eating, the elephant looked no more dangerous than a cow. I thought then and I think now that his attack of "must" was already passing off; in which case he would merely wander harmlessly about until the mahout came back and caught him. Moreover, I did not in the least want to shoot him. I decided that I would watch him for a little while to make sure that he did not turn savage again, and then go home.

But at that moment I glanced round at the crowd that had followed me. It was an immense crowd, two thousand at the least and growing every minute. It blocked the road for a long distance on either side. I looked at the sea of yellow faces above the **garish** clothes— faces all happy and excited over this bit of fun, all certain that the elephant was going to be shot. They were watching me as they would watch a conjurer[16] about to perform a trick. They did not like me, but with the magical rifle in my hands I was momentarily worth watching. And suddenly I realized that I should have to shoot the elephant after all. The people expected it of me and I had got to do it; I could feel their two thousand wills pressing me forward, irresistibly. And it was at this moment, as I stood there with the rifle in my hands, that I first grasped the hollowness, the futility[17] of the white man's dominion in the East. Here was I, the white man with his gun, standing in front of the unarmed native crowd—seemingly the leading actor of the piece; but in reality I was only an absurd puppet pushed to and fro by the will of those yellow faces behind. I perceived in this moment that when the white man turns tyrant it is his own freedom that he destroys. He

becomes a sort of hollow, posing dummy, the conventionalized figure of a sahib.[18] For it is the condition of his rule that he shall spend his life in trying to impress the "natives," and so in every crisis he has got to do what the "natives" expect of him. He wears a mask, and his face grows to fit it. I had got to shoot the elephant. I had committed myself to doing it when I sent for the rifle. A sahib has got to act like a sahib; he has got to appear resolute, to know his own mind and do definite things. To come all that way, rifle in hand, with two thousand people marching at my heels, and then to trail feebly away, having done nothing—no, that was impossible. The crowd would laugh at me. And my whole life, every white man's life in the East, was one long struggle not to be laughed at.

---

16. A *conjurer* is a magician.
17. *Futility* means "ineffectiveness" or "uselessness."

Reading Strategy   Analyzing Evidence *What evidence in this paragraph supports Orwell's certainty that he "ought not to shoot" the elephant?*

Vocabulary

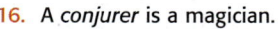

garish (gār′ ish) *adj.* excessively bright; flashy; gaudy

---

18. *Sahib* is a title similar to *sir* that Indian people once used when speaking to or of a European.

Big Idea   Class, Colonialism, and the Great War *How does this statement epitomize Orwell's perception of the absurdity of British colonialism?*

But I did not want to shoot the elephant. I watched him beating his bunch of grass against his knees, with that preoccupied grandmotherly air that elephants have. It seemed to me that it would be murder to shoot him. At that age I was not squeamish about killing animals, but I had never shot an elephant and never wanted to. (Somehow it always seems worse to kill a *large* animal.) Besides, there was the beast's owner to be considered. Alive, the elephant was worth at least a hundred pounds; dead, he would only be worth the value of his tusks, five pounds, possibly. But I had got to act quickly. I turned to some experienced-looking Burmans who had been there when we arrived, and asked them how the elephant had been behaving. They all said the same thing: he took no notice of you if you left him alone, but he might charge if you went too close to him.

It was perfectly clear to me what I ought to do. I ought to walk up to within, say, twenty-five yards of the elephant and test his behavior. If he charged, I could shoot; if he took no notice of me, it would be safe to leave him until the mahout came back. But also I knew that I was going to do no such thing. I was a poor shot with a rifle and the ground was soft mud into which one would sink at every step. If the elephant charged and I missed him, I should have about as much chance as a toad under a steamroller. But even then I was not thinking particularly of my own skin, only of the watchful yellow faces behind. For at that moment, with the crowd watching me, I was not afraid in the ordinary sense, as I would have been if I had been alone. A white man mustn't be frightened in front of "natives"; and so, in general, he isn't frightened. The sole thought in my mind was that if anything went wrong those two thousand Burmans would see me pursued, caught, trampled on, and reduced to a grinning corpse like that Indian up the hill. And if that happened it was quite probable that some of them would laugh. That would never do. There was only one alternative. I shoved the cartridges into the magazine and lay down on the road to get a better aim.

Reading Strategy Analyzing Evidence *What evidence does Orwell present to justify his decision to shoot the elephant?*

The crowd grew very still, and a deep, low, happy sigh, as of people who see the theater curtain go up at last, breathed from innumerable throats. They were going to have their bit of fun after all. The rifle was a beautiful German thing with cross-hair sights. I did not then know that in shooting an elephant one would shoot to cut an imaginary bar running from ear-hole to ear-hole. I ought, therefore, as the elephant was sideways on, to have aimed straight at his ear-hole; actually I aimed several inches in front of this, thinking the brain would be further forward.

When I pulled the trigger I did not hear the bang or feel the kick—one never does when a shot goes home—but I heard the devilish roar of glee that went up from the crowd. In that instant, in too short a time, one would have thought, even for the bullet to get there, a mysterious, terrible change had come over the elephant. He neither stirred nor fell, but every line of his body had altered. He looked suddenly stricken, shrunken, immensely old, as though the frightful impact of the bullet had paralyzed him without knocking him down. At last, after what seemed a long time—it might have been five seconds, I dare say—he sagged flabbily to his knees. His mouth slobbered. An enormous senility seemed to have settled upon him. One could have imagined him thousands of years old. I fired again into the same spot. At the second shot he did not collapse but climbed with desperate slowness to his feet and stood weakly upright, with legs sagging and head drooping. I fired a third time. That was the shot that did for him. You could see the agony of it jolt his whole body and knock the last remnant of strength from his legs. But in falling he seemed for a moment to rise, for as his hind legs collapsed beneath him he seemed to tower upward like a huge rock toppling, his trunk reaching skywards like a tree. He trumpeted, for the first and only time. And then down he came, his belly towards me, with a crash that seemed to shake the ground even where I lay.

I got up. The Burmans were already racing past me across the mud. It was obvious that the elephant would never rise again, but he was not dead. He was breathing very rhythmically with long rattling gasps, his great mound of a side painfully rising and falling. His mouth was wide open—I could see far down into caverns of pale pink throat. I waited a long time for him to die,

Leg Rowing Race, 1922. A canoe is propelled by leg power in a boat race event on a river in Burma.

but his breathing did not weaken. Finally I fired my two remaining shots into the spot where I thought his heart must be. The thick blood welled out of him like red velvet, but still he did not die. His body did not even jerk when the shots hit him, the tortured breathing continued without a pause. He was dying, very slowly and in great agony, but in some world remote from me where not even a bullet could damage him further. I felt that I had got to put an end to that dreadful noise. It seemed dreadful to see the great beast lying there, powerless to move and yet powerless to die, and not even to be able to finish him. I sent back for my small rifle and poured shot after shot into his heart and down his throat. They seemed to make no impression. The tortured gasps continued as steadily as the ticking of a clock.

In the end I could not stand it any longer and went away. I heard later that it took him half an hour to die. Burmans were bringing dahs[19] and baskets even before I left, and I was told they had stripped his body almost to the bones by the afternoon.

Afterwards, of course, there were endless discussions about the shooting of the elephant. The owner was furious, but he was only an Indian and could do nothing. Besides, legally I had done the right thing, for a mad elephant has to be killed, like a mad dog, if its owner fails to control it. Among the Europeans opinion was divided. The older men said I was right, the younger men said it was a damn shame to shoot an elephant for killing a coolie, because an elephant was worth more than any damn Coringhee[20] coolie. And afterwards I was very glad that the coolie had been killed; it put me legally in the right and it gave me a sufficient pretext for shooting the elephant. I often wondered whether any of the others grasped that I had done it solely to avoid looking a fool.

---

19. *Dahs* are heavy Burmese knives.

Literary Element Symbol *What might the elephant symbolize in this passage?*

---

20. *Coringhee* is a port in southeastern India.

Big Idea Class, Colonialism, and the Great War *How does this paragraph reflect the distorted values of British colonialism?*

RESPONDING AND THINKING CRITICALLY

Respond

1. Which scene in the essay made the strongest impression on you? Explain.

Recall and Interpret

2. (a)According to Orwell, what attitude did the Burmese have toward him and the other Europeans? (b)What do you think accounts for this attitude?

3. (a)Describe how Orwell carried out his plan of action. Why did it take so long? What did he want to avoid at all costs? (b)What role did the crowd play in determining the elephant's fate?

4. (a)How do the reactions of both older and younger Europeans to the shooting of the elephant compare with Orwell's realization at the end of the essay? (b)Looking back, what judgments does Orwell seem to be making about himself and about British imperialism?

Analyze and Evaluate

5. (a)Analyze Orwell's reasons for changing his mind about shooting the elephant. (b)Explain what his change of mind suggests about his character at the time of the incident.

6. What effects are created by Orwell's lengthy, detailed description of the elephant's fate?

7. How does Orwell's perspective on the incident differ from that of the crowd of Burmese natives?

Connect

8. **Big Idea** **Class, Colonialism, and the Great War** According to Orwell, what is the **paradox**, or apparent contradiction, at the heart of colonialism? How does the essay illustrate this paradox?

YOU'RE THE CRITIC: Different Viewpoints

Who Is the Greater Victim?

Read the two excerpts of literary criticism below. Notice how each critic emphasizes a different aspect of Orwell's complexity.

"The key to the moral content of 'Shooting an Elephant' lies in a chain of identifications made by the narrator, beginning with his identification of the trampled Dravidian with the victim of the crucifixion. . . . All of these identifications (Dravidian with Jesus, elephant with Dravidian, narrator with elephant) come together with an earlier image, that of the humiliated Burmese in the [i]mperial jail, the 'prostrate peoples' victimized by Empire."

—Thomas Bertonneau

"[The narrator of 'Shooting an Elephant'] is the target of physical and verbal abuse for the native population. A pivotal opposition, between individual and group, is established immediately, one that will reverberate through the narrative."

—Peter Marks

1. Both critics agree that the narrator is a victim, but each emphasizes a different aspect of the victimization. What is the difference in emphasis between the two critics?

2. (a)In your opinion, who is more victimized by the British Empire—persons such as the young Orwell, who must enforce the laws, or the native population, who must obey the laws? (b)How does each critic answer this question?

Burmese woman driving, Rangoon, Burma, 1922.

Literary Element Symbol

Symbols in literature often represent something abstract. For example, in "Shooting an Elephant," the elephant might symbolize the British Empire. Both are large, powerful, fearsome things that are dying a slow death.

1. If the elephant is a symbol for the British Empire, what might the elephant's behavior suggest about the way the British rulers have treated the Burmese people?

2. (a)What do you think Orwell himself might symbolize for the people of the town? (b)How does this symbolism help explain the fact that he is "hated by large numbers of people"?

Review: Thesis

As you learned on page 726, the **thesis** is the main idea, or statement to be proved, in a work of nonfiction. A thesis may be stated or implied. The author must support the thesis with evidence in the form of reasons and examples.

Partner Activity Meet with a classmate and discuss the thesis of Orwell's essay. Create a web diagram similar to the one below. In the center circle, write the thesis. If the thesis is stated, quote it from the essay; if the thesis is implied, paraphrase it in your own words. Then, in the surrounding circles, write evidence that supports the thesis.

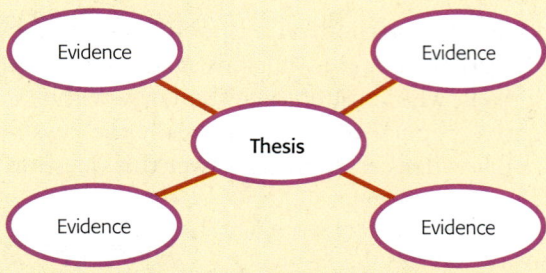

Reading Strategy Analyzing Evidence

Analyzing evidence is one way to test the validity of an author's thesis. The facts, examples, and reasons presented by the author determine whether the reader is convinced by the author's thesis or opinions.

1. (a)Identify an opinion that Orwell expresses. (b)List three pieces of evidence that support that opinion.

2. Does Orwell convince you of his belief that both the rulers and the ruled are victims of British imperialism? Explain.

Vocabulary Practice

Practice with Analogies Choose the word that best completes each analogy below.

1. lively : somber :: garish :
   a. ugly
   b. bright
   c. luminous
   d. subdued

2. ill : sick :: squalid :
   a. well-maintained
   b. dirty
   c. stormy
   d. peaceful

3. uproot : remove :: supplant :
   a. position
   b. add
   c. beseech
   d. displace

4. cruel : kind :: despotic :
   a. tyrannical
   b. democratic
   c. overbearing
   d. kingly

5. path : lane :: labyrinth :
   a. crooked
   b. winding
   c. maze
   d. puzzle

Academic Vocabulary

Here is a word from the vocabulary list on page R82. This word will help you think, write, and talk about the selection.

administrate (ad min′ is trāt′) *v.* to manage or supervise

Practice and Apply
In what way did the narrator help the British Empire **administrate** the lives of the Burmese people?

Writing About Literature

Explore Author's Purpose The author's purpose is the author's intent in writing a literary work. Authors usually write for one or more of the following purposes: to persuade, to inform, to explain, to entertain, or to describe. Write a brief essay in which you discuss Orwell's purpose in writing "Shooting an Elephant." Consider the following questions as you develop your essay.

- How does Orwell feel about his job?

- What is Orwell's attitude concerning British imperialism in Burma?

- Does Orwell offer a solution to the problems caused by imperialism? If so, what is it?

Before you begin to write, you might want to organize your ideas in a chart similar to the one below.

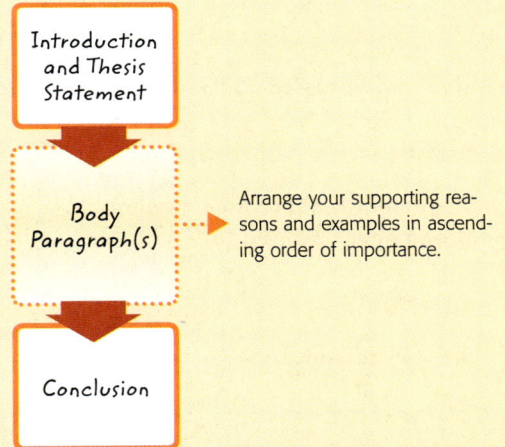

Introduction and Thesis Statement

Body Paragraph(s) — Arrange your supporting reasons and examples in ascending order of importance.

Conclusion

After you complete your draft, meet with a classmate to evaluate each other's work and to suggest revisions. Then proofread and edit your work for errors in spelling, grammar, and punctuation.

Listening and Speaking

With a partner, role-play an interview that a reporter might conduct with Orwell after the incident described in "Shooting an Elephant." Invent appropriate questions the reporter might ask, as well as answers that Orwell would be likely to give.

Orwell's Language and Style

Using Dashes In "Shooting an Elephant," Orwell frequently uses dashes. Authors commonly use dashes to indicate a sudden interruption or a shift in thought, or to set off an appositive or explanatory statement, as in the following sentence.

"I had no intention of shooting the elephant—I had merely sent for the rifle to defend myself if necessary—and it is always unnerving to have a crowd following you."

Consider the following purposes for which Orwell uses dashes.

Example	Purpose
"In Moulmein, in lower Burma, I was hated by large numbers of people—the only time in my life that I have been important enough for this to happen to me."	explanatory statement
"Theoretically—and secretly, of course—I was all for the Burmese and all against their oppressors, the British."	to introduce words the author wants to emphasize

Activity Scan "Shooting an Elephant" for other examples of dashes. Make a list of these examples and indicate the purpose of each usage. Consider whether the dash emphasizes an idea, indicates a break in thought, or sets off an appositive or an appositive phrase—a word or phrase that identifies or gives more detailed information about another word.

Revising Check

Dashes When revising your own writing, it is important to consider your marks of punctuation. With a partner, review your essay on Orwell's purpose for writing. Revise your writing by including dashes in places where they would enhance your intended meaning.

Literature Online **Web Activities** For eFlashcards, Selection Quick Checks, and other Web activities, go to www.glencoe.com.

Grammar Workshop

Sentence Structure

► **Using Commas with Coordinating Conjunctions**

Use a comma before independent clauses beginning with *but* and *and* unless the clauses are very short.

- The story was interesting, but it was just too long.

To avoid confusion, use a comma before clauses beginning with *for*.

- She offered the book, for Sam wanted to read it.

► **Test-Taking Tip**

Before handing in a written test, make sure your coordinating conjunctions correctly show how ideas are connected.

► **Language Handbook**

For more on coordinating conjunctions, see Language Handbook, p. R47.

eWorkbooks To link to the Grammar and Language eWorkbook, go to www.glencoe.com.

OBJECTIVES
- Use coordinating conjunctions correctly.
- Apply standard rules for punctuating independent clauses.

Using Coordinating Conjunctions

"No one had the guts to raise a riot, but if a European woman went through the bazaars alone somebody would probably spit betel juice over her dress."

—George Orwell, from "Shooting an Elephant"

Connecting to Literature In the quotation above, George Orwell uses a coordinating conjunction to combine two thoughts and clearly show the connection between them. A **conjunction** is a word that joins single words or groups of words. A **coordinating conjunction** joins words or groups of words that have equal importance in a sentence. Use them to link choppy sentences or join the parts of a sentence. Some common coordinating conjunctions are *and, but, or, nor, for, yet,* and *so.*

Examples

Use *and* or *or* to connect similar sentence elements:

> Orwell was often taunted <u>and</u> harassed by the Burmese people.

Use *but, yet,* or *nor* to connect contrasting sentence parts:

> Orwell says, "I was not squeamish about killing animals, <u>but</u> I had never shot an elephant and never wanted to."

Use *for* or *so* to show cause and effect between ideas:

> He was miserable, <u>for</u> he was caught between two cultures.

Exercise

Inserting Conjunctions Combine the sentence parts by using one of the coordinating conjunctions in parentheses. Write your answers on a separate sheet of paper.

1. In his short story, Orwell uses direct language (and, so) appeals to the reader's emotions.
2. He hated the British raj (so, but) also disliked Burmese nationalism.
3. Burma was once part of the British Empire, (but, for) it gained its independence in 1948.
4. Orwell had to investigate an elephant that had killed a man, (yet, for) that was part of his job.
5. He would have to shoot the elephant, (or, yet) the natives would laugh at him.

The Soldier

MEET RUPERT BROOKE

Rupert Brooke was handsome, charming, intelligent, privileged, and beloved—a "young Apollo," as one friend described him. Winston Churchill said of Brooke, "He was all that one would wish England's noblest sons to be." Because of his early death in World War I, he has remained that golden young poet forever, and it is partly because of his early death that his reputation as a poet survives.

> "The thoughts to which [Brooke] gave expression . . . will be shared by many thousands of young men."
>
> —Winston Churchill

A Privileged Youth Brooke was born in the town of Rugby, and he had all the advantages of a well-to-do upbringing. He went to the prestigious Rugby School, where his father was headmaster. He studied Latin and Greek, and he began to write poetry at the age of nine. Brooke had a childlike sense of wonder. He was full of vitality and energy, and he possessed an air of confidence and unselfconscious ease. Brooke was a gifted student, but he was also skilled at athletics, excelling at soccer, cricket, tennis, and swimming. As expected, he went on to King's College, Cambridge, in 1906 and soon counted among his friends such notable intellectuals as writer Virginia Woolf (see page 1149), economist John Maynard Keynes, and poet William Butler Yeats (see page 1106).

After graduating from Cambridge in 1909, Brooke spent time traveling and writing. During his late teens and early twenties, he went to Italy, Germany, the United States, and Canada. Then he departed for the South Sea islands of Hawaii, Samoa, Fiji, and Tahiti. His poetry at this time was mostly concerned with the topics of love and nature. Brooke's idealistic preoccupation with rural motifs earned him and his friends the moniker "neo-pagans." In Tahiti, Brooke appeared to have found a place that was perfectly suited to both his ideals and his artistic sensibility.

War Breaks Out Brooke was never happier than while he was in Tahiti, but he decided to return to England during the spring of 1914. A few months later, World War I began, and like many men his age, Brooke immediately volunteered for service. As a member of the Royal Navy Volunteer Reserve, Brooke was dispatched to Antwerp, Belgium; however, he saw no military action because the area surrounding Antwerp was not being contested at the time. During this period, he produced his best-known poetry, the five war sonnets entitled "Nineteen Fourteen," of which "The Soldier" is perhaps the most famous and openly patriotic. In February 1915 Brooke's company was ordered to set sail for the Dardanelles for the Gallipoli campaign. In Cairo, however, Brooke suffered through bouts of sunstroke and dysentery. Then he contracted blood poisoning from a small insect bite. He died on April 23 on a hospital ship in the Aegean Sea and was buried on the Greek island of Skyros. Ironically, his death brought him almost immediate fame as both a poet and a symbol of innocent youth struck down by war.

Rupert Brooke was born in 1887 and died in 1915.

Literature Online **Author Search** For more about Rupert Brooke, go to www.glencoe.com.

Connecting to the Poem

What does a person owe his country? What values are worth fighting for? In Brooke's poem, the speaker demonstrates his love for his country. As you read the poem, think about the following questions.

- How would you define the word *patriot*?
- What are the positive and negative aspects of being idealistic about war and death?

Building Background

British soldiers in World War I faced a terrible paradox. Even though they felt a strong urge to fight in order to preserve and defend the world they knew, the horrors of the war increasingly led them to become disillusioned with their cause. At the beginning of the war, most English soldiers believed in the justness of their cause and sought to reassure their families back home to keep up morale. In fact, one soldier, in his haste to assure his wife of the worthiness of the war, complained of depressing letters from the homefront and wrote, "It is just these people who have suffered nothing who make the most fuss." When the horrors of World War I became widely known, Brooke's idealistic poetry suffered a loss of popularity. It was not until after World War II that his work rose again in the public's esteem.

Setting Purposes for Reading

Big Idea Class, Colonialism, and the Great War

In the first half of the twentieth century, the power of the British Empire was challenged by colonial unrest and World War I. As you read the poem, consider the poet's attitude toward war especially in light of what you know today about such catastrophic events.

Literary Element Mood

Mood is the emotional quality of a literary work that is conveyed through description and evocative language. Mood differs from atmosphere, which is concerned mainly with the physical qualities that contribute to mood, such as time, place, and weather.

- See Literary Terms Handbook, p. R11.

Reading Strategy Applying Background Knowledge

Background knowledge refers to what you already know about the historical, social, and cultural forces that help shape a literary work. The ideas expressed in Brooke's poems were shaped in part by the attitudes and conditions of the world in which he lived. Becoming familiar with those attitudes and conditions and their influence on Brooke can help you gain a better understanding and appreciation of his poetry.

Reading Tip: Taking Notes Reread the biography of Brooke on page 1089 and the Building Background feature on this page, noting details that describe attitudes of his time and the war he faced. Use a chart like the one shown here to jot down some of those details. As you read his poem, look for ideas that may have been influenced by the attitudes and conditions you have noted. Add these examples to your chart.

Attitudes and Conditions	Details in Poem
1. World War I begins.	1. "If I should die," suggests that the speaker understands that he may die in the war.
2.	2.

Literature Online Interactive Literary Elements Handbook To review or learn more about the literary elements, go to www.glencoe.com.

OBJECTIVES
In studying this selection, you will focus on the following:
- analyzing the historical period
- analyzing mood
- applying background knowledge

THE SOLDIER

Rupert Brooke

A Group of Soldiers, 1917. C. R. W. Nevinson. Oil on canvas.
Imperial War Museum, London.

If I should die, think only this of me:
    That there's some corner of a foreign field
That is forever England. There shall be
    In that rich earth a richer dust concealed;
5   A dust whom England bore, shaped, made aware,
    Gave, once, her flowers to love, her ways to roam,
A body of England's, breathing English air,
    Washed by the rivers, blest by suns of home.

And think, this heart, all evil shed away,
10   A pulse in the eternal mind, no less
    Gives somewhere back the thoughts by England given;
Her sights and sounds; dreams happy as her day;
    And laughter, learnt of friends; and gentleness,
    In hearts at peace, under an English heaven.

Reading Strategy   Applying Background Knowledge *Why do you think the speaker is willing to fight?*

Big Idea   Class, Colonialism, and the Great War *According to the speaker, what will be the outcome of the war?*

RESPONDING AND THINKING CRITICALLY

Respond

1. Do you find this poem inspiring or naive? Explain.

Recall and Interpret

2. (a)If the speaker should die, how does he wish to be remembered? (b)What does this reveal about his values and attitudes toward his homeland?

3. (a)According to the speaker, what will happen to his heart? (b)What does the second stanza suggest about the speaker's attitude toward life and death?

Analyze and Evaluate

4. What universal theme do you see in "The Soldier"?

5. How does the use of imagery help you better understand the poem's theme? Support your answer using specific examples from the poem.

Connect

6. **Big Idea** **Class, Colonialism, and the Great War** What does "The Soldier" suggest to you about how people in England might have viewed the war at its start?

LITERARY ANALYSIS

Literary Element Mood

Mood is created by a number of elements, including a writer's choice of language, subject matter, setting, and tone, as well as sound devices such as rhyme and rhythm.

1. Describe the mood of "The Soldier."

2. What words or phrases help to create the mood?

Writing About Literature

Analyze Genre Elements "The Soldier" is an **Italian sonnet,** in which the octave presents a situation that the sestet comments upon. In a brief essay, evaluate how the form helps add structure to the poem. What situation does the octave present? What comment does the sestet provide? Do you agree with Brooke's message? Cite examples to support your opinion.

Prince Henry, or Harry, the Duke of Gloucester, son of King George V of England, with his colleagues at military camp in 1917.

READING AND VOCABULARY

Reading Strategy Applying Background Knowledge

By applying what you know to what you read, you can gain a better understanding of how social conditions and historical forces shape a literary work.

1. (a)According to lines 5–8, what did England do for the speaker? (b)How does this view make sense, given what you know about Brooke's life?

2. Brooke wrote this poem early in the war and had not seen any real combat. How does knowing this add to your understanding of the poem?

Academic Vocabulary

Here are two words from the vocabulary list on page R82.

draft (draft) *n.* the process or method of selecting one or more individuals from a group for some, usually compulsory, service.

statistic (stə tis′ tik) *n.* one viewed as a nameless item of statistical information

Practice and Apply

1. Do you think Brooke would have supported a military **draft**? Explain.

2. Do you think Brooke viewed the death of a soldier as a meaningless **statistic**? Explain.

Dreamers

MEET SIEGFRIED SASSOON

In January 1916, England's First Battalion dug itself into a line of trenches along the river Somme in France and waited to stage the British army's largest offensive of the Great War. Siegfried Sassoon was a transportation officer for the First Battalion, and in April of that year he proved himself a courageous soldier. He successfully rescued a number of wounded comrades while under heavy fire in no-man's-land and was awarded the Military Cross for valor. This selfless—and extremely dangerous—act of heroism and other forays into enemy territory earned him the nickname Mad Jack.

Early Life Born to a family of considerable wealth and privilege in 1886, Sassoon grew up on a country estate near Warminster, Kent, and spent his leisure time playing cricket and golf. Sassoon was educated at home by a private tutor until he reached the age of fourteen, and then he attended the New Beacon School. In 1902 he enrolled at Marlborough College, ostensibly to study law, but he became interested in writing poetry. He later went to Clare College, Cambridge, to pursue studies in history but did not complete a degree. Instead, he wrote poetry and self-published *Poems,* his first of ten collections to appear in print before he enlisted in the army and was sent to France.

The Making of a Pacifist Poet The First Battle of the Somme began on July 1 and resulted in over 57,000 British casualties on the first day. It is still considered the bloodiest single day of fighting in British military history. Five days later Sassoon captured a German trench by himself and was recommended for the Victoria Cross. Later that month he became afflicted with acute gastroenteritis and was evacuated to England, an action that saved his life. The Battle of the Somme resulted in over one million casualties, and the horrors of such bloodshed forever changed the way Sassoon viewed war.

> *"I am not protesting against the conduct of the war, but against the political errors and insincerities for which the fighting men are being sacrificed."*
>
> —Siegfried Sassoon

While Sassoon was recuperating in a military hospital, his horror and disgust at what he perceived to be the senseless slaughter of the war turned him into a pacifist. However, he felt guilty that his fellow countrymen were still fighting and dying, and he returned to the front only to be shot in the shoulder and hospitalized once again. At the encouragement of another pacifist, the philosopher Bertrand Russell, Sassoon decided to voice his opposition to the war in a letter to newspapers.

Along with other antiwar poets, such as his friend Wilfred Owen, Sassoon was able to poignantly convey the suffering and express the thoughts and feelings of the lost generation of British soldiers who succumbed to the brutal bloodbath of World War I.

Siegfried Sassoon was born in 1886 and died in 1967.

Literature Online Author Search For more about Siegfried Sassoon, go to www.glencoe.com.

Connecting to the Poem

There are probably a number of things you do each day that you might consider commonplace or boring—showering, going to school, waiting in line in the cafeteria. As you read, think about these questions:

- Have you ever been faced with a task so unpleasant that you would gladly welcome a return to your ordinary habits?
- What circumstances might make you appreciate the mundane aspects of your daily life?

Building Background

As World War I dragged on and the casualties mounted, veteran soldiers became weary and disheartened. Many lost their motivation and felt a stark sense of separation from those at home who could not be expected to comprehend the terror of trench warfare. Some soldiers felt so alienated from their families that they passed up opportunities to visit home on leave. Many other soldiers were disgusted by war accounts that glossed over the horrors of battle that they had endured. They felt that the patriotic tributes to heroism portrayed a false picture of the senseless atrocities of war. Much of the war poetry written during this period reflects the soldiers' feelings of abandonment and disillusionment.

Setting Purposes for Reading

Big Idea **Class, Colonialism, and the Great War**

As you read the poem, consider how World War I redefined notions of normalcy for both civilians and soldiers.

Literary Element **Title**

The **title** of a literary work is the first clue about the work's meaning. The title may help to explain the setting, provide insight into the theme, or describe the action that will take place in the work. Before you read this poem, consider what it might be about based on the title.

- See Literary Terms Handbook, p. R18.

Reading Strategy Comparing and Contrasting Imagery

To **compare** two things is to focus on their similarities, while to **contrast** them is to focus on their differences. **Imagery** refers to the word pictures that a writer uses to evoke emotions in the reader through the use of vivid sensory details. As you read, look for Sassoon's use of contrasting image patterns.

Reading Tip: Taking Notes Use a chart similar to the one below to list contrasting images of war and civilian life.

Images of Civilian Life	Images of War
"firelit homes, clean beds, and wives"	"foul dugouts, gnawed by rats"

Vocabulary

destiny (des′ tə nē) n. fate; what will necessarily happen; p. 1095 *Convinced that fame was her destiny, Wilma felt little need to practice her act.*

feud (fūd) n. lengthy, bitter conflict or dispute; p. 1095 *The tribal leaders had engaged in a number of feuds that made a lasting peace nearly impossible.*

fatal (fāt′ əl) adj. causing death, destruction, or harm; p. 1095 *After weeks of deliberation, the jury delivered a fatal verdict.*

Vocabulary Tip: Context Clues Sometimes the context, or surrounding words and phrases, of an unfamiliar word can provide clues to the word's meaning.

Literature Online **Interactive Literary Elements Handbook** To review or learn more about the literary elements, go to www.glencoe.com.

OBJECTIVES
In studying this selection, you will focus on the following:
- analyzing literary movements and genres
- analyzing a work's title
- comparing and contrasting imagery

Wounded at the Roadside. Benjamin Strasser. Heeresgeschichtliches Museum, Vienna, Austria.

DREAMERS

Siegfried Sassoon

Soldiers are citizens of death's gray land,
    Drawing no dividend from time's tomorrows.
In the great hour of **destiny** they stand,
    Each with his **feuds**, and jealousies, and sorrows.
5 Soldiers are sworn to action; they must win
    Some flaming, **fatal** climax with their lives.
Soldiers are dreamers; when the guns begin
    They think of firelit homes, clean beds, and wives.

I see them in foul dugouts, gnawed by rats,
10   And in the ruined trenches, lashed with rain,
Dreaming of things they did with balls and bats,
    And mocked by hopeless longing to regain
Bank-holidays, and picture shows, and spats,
    And going to the office in the train.

Literary Element   Title *How do these two lines explain and expand the title of the poem?*

Vocabulary

destiny (des′ tə nē) *n.* fate; what will necessarily happen
feud (fūd) *n.* lengthy, bitter conflict or dispute
fatal (fāt′ əl) *adj.* causing death, destruction, or harm

RESPONDING AND THINKING CRITICALLY

Respond

1. What is your reaction to the things soldiers dream about during war?

Recall and Interpret

2. (a)How does the speaker describe the soldiers in the first stanza? (b)From this description, what can you infer about the speaker's attitude toward the circumstances of a soldier's life?

3. (a)According to the speaker, what do soldiers dream about? (b)How do these dreams contrast with the reality of war?

Analyze and Evaluate

4. (a)Why does the speaker include routine tasks, such as "going to the office in the train," among the civilian comforts that the soldiers long for? (b)What moral, or lesson, might Sassoon be conveying to his readers?

5. (a)How does Sassoon convey his disillusionment with war in the poem? (b)Who or what has determined the soldiers' "destiny"?

6. The speaker says that soldiers "must win / Some flaming, fatal climax with their lives." In your opinion, are wars ever won? Explain.

Connect

7. **Big Idea** **Class, Colonialism, and the Great War** How does "Dreamers" reflect the cultural trauma experienced by the British people during and after the Great War?

LITERARY ANALYSIS

Literary Element Title

A good **title** stimulates the reader's interest and curiosity about a literary work. The title can state or imply the subject or theme of the work, provide a clue to its meaning, or give the reader a sense of the period or setting. A title may be understated, ironic, or paradoxical.

1. What is the typical connotation of the word *dreamer*?

2. How does the poem contradict the expectations that the reader derives from the title?

Internet Connection

Conduct Internet and library research to find firsthand accounts of soldiers' experiences in World War I. How do these accounts compare with the experiences expressed in "Dreamers"? Share your findings and your insights with the class.

Literature Online **Web Activities** For eFlashcards, Selection Quick Checks, and other Web activities, go to www.glencoe.com.

READING AND VOCABULARY

Reading Strategy Comparing and Contrasting Imagery

"Dreamers" is composed of two contrasting image patterns—the worlds of military and civilian life.

1. Cite examples of images in the poem that represent the contrasting worlds of war and peace.

2. What generalizations can you make about these contrasting image patterns?

Vocabulary Practice

Practice with Context Clues Identify the context clue that helps reveal the meanings of the bold-faced vocabulary words.

1. The soldier's **destiny** was determined by the nature of war.
   a. soldier's   **b.** determined

2. The warring factions' **feuds** went back for several generations.
   a. warring factions   **b.** generations

3. The doctor told her patient that his disease was **fatal** and he only had six months to live.
   a. doctor   **b.** six months to live

Dulce et Decorum Est

MEET WILFRED OWEN

One day in January 1917, Lieutenant Wilfred Owen and his men marched six miles over shell-pocked roads and through flooded trenches. The mud was so thick and deep in places that a number of Owen's men became stuck and had to slip out of their waders to free themselves. They continued their march with freezing and bleeding feet while suffering enemy machine-gun fire and heavy shelling. When it appeared that circumstances couldn't get worse, German soldiers fired canisters of chlorine gas at them. Through his gas mask, Owen watched one of his men choke to death in a sea-green cloud of poison. This was the incident that inspired Owen's poem "Dulce et Decorum Est."

> "My subject is War, and the pity of war. I am not concerned with Poetry. The Poetry is in the Pity."
>
> —Wilfred Owen

Soldier and Poet Owen was born to a working-class family in Oswestry, England, in 1893. He attended school at the Birkenhead Institute and graduated from the Shrewsbury Technical School. Owen gained entrance to the University of London but could not afford the tuition. To help pay for his schooling, he took a job as an assistant to the vicar of Dunsden. However, he soon became disenchanted with his position and went to France to teach English. When Britain entered World War I, Owen enlisted in the British army and left for the front to fight for his country.

One night, after falling into a fifteen-foot shell hole and badly banging his head, Owen experienced unrelenting headaches, which he believed were a result of a concussion. For two months he fought the headaches and the Germans under punishing conditions until doctors diagnosed his illness as "shell shock." Unable to lead his regiment, Owen was transported to Craiglockhart War Hospital in Edinburgh, Scotland, for treatment. When fellow soldier and poet Siegfried Sassoon arrived at the hospital, the two became friends and exchanged poems. Sassoon helped the younger poet by introducing him to Robert Ross, a London editor. Although critics would later point out that Owen's poems exhibited greater range and technical superiority, Owen was humble about comparing himself to Sassoon. "I am not worthy to light his pipe," he wrote to his mother.

A Posthumous Legacy Owen was more sensitive and compassionate about his subject than many other war poets of the time, and he developed a direct, outspoken style that broke with the conventions of the day. When he was young, he admired the poetry of Keats and Shelley. However, the poet that probably had the greatest impact on his work was Sassoon. Wilfred Owen would go on to become one of England's most admired war poets, but he would not live long enough to see his poems in print. Tragically, he was killed in battle one week before the end of the war, and the bulk of his poems were posthumously published by Sassoon in the 1920s.

Wilfred Owen was born in 1893 and died in 1918.

Literature Online **Author Search** For more about Wilfred Owen, go to www.glencoe.com.

Connecting to the Poem

Popular images of war in movies and recruitment ads often depict soldiers in triumph and battle campaigns as glorious adventures. As you read, think about the following questions:

- What do you imagine war is really like?
- Is it always honorable and glorious to die for one's country?

Building Background

During World War I, new technologies brought unprecedented dangers to soldiers and civilians alike. In most previous wars, soldiers had relied on single-shot rifles, hand-to-hand combat, or limited artillery. However, during the Great War, machine guns and tanks killed more efficiently and caused considerably more destruction. Chemicals such as mustard gas, chlorine gas, and phosphorous poisoned and maimed troops. Mortars, which were capable of firing their shells more than a half mile, decimated fighting forces and civilian centers. For the first time in the history of warfare, entire companies of soldiers could be destroyed before they could draw their weapons or catch sight of their enemies.

Setting Purposes for Reading

Big Idea Class, Colonialism, and the Great War

The strength and confidence of Britain as a military power came under increasing scrutiny as the war progressed. As you read, consider how the suffering and deaths of large numbers of soldiers might have affected morale in the field and eroded support at home.

Literary Element Verse Paragraph

Verse paragraphs and prose paragraphs have a similar function—to convey a main idea that is supported by details. Unlike a stanza, a verse paragraph does not have a fixed number of lines. Verse paragraphs are indicated on the page by a blank space between groups of lines.

- See Literary Terms Handbook, p. R19.

Reading Strategy Recognizing Author's Purpose

An **author's purpose** is usually one of the following: to persuade, to inform or explain, to entertain, to describe, or to tell a story. Nonfiction writers often state their purposes explicitly, but novelists and poets tend to imply their purposes. Critically examining the title, tone, theme, and figurative language in "Dulce et Decorum Est" can help you determine Owen's purpose.

Reading Tip: Asking Questions As you read, ask yourself the following questions:

- Why does Owen use a Latin quotation from Horace for his title?
- Why does the speaker repeat Horace's quotation in the final two lines of the poem?
- How does the speaker's **tone** help fulfill Owen's purpose?
- What do the **similes** and **metaphors** in the poem tell you about Owen's attitude toward war?

Vocabulary

trudge (truj) *v.* to walk wearily or laboriously; p. 1099 *After the loss, the coach made the entire football team trudge behind the bus for a mile.*

ecstasy (ek′ stə sē) *n.* a state beyond reason or self-control; p. 1099 *The musicians moved the audience to a state of collective ecstasy.*

vile (vīl) *adj.* repulsive or disgusting; p. 1099 *When the landlord unlocked the door, he was met by a vile odor that came from the kitchen.*

Vocabulary Tip: Synonyms Words that have the same or similar meanings are called synonyms. Note that synonyms are always the same part of speech.

Literature Online **Interactive Literary Elements Handbook** To review or learn more about the literary elements, go to www.glencoe.com.

OBJECTIVES
In studying this selection, you will focus on the following:
- analyzing literary periods and genres
- analyzing verse paragraphs
- recognizing author's purpose

1098 UNIT 6 THE MODERN AGE

DULCE ET DECORUM EST

Wilfred Owen

Bent double, like old beggars under sacks,
Knock-kneed, coughing like hags, we cursed through sludge,
Till on the haunting flares we turned our backs
And towards our distant rest began to **trudge**.
5   Men marched asleep. Many had lost their boots
But limped on, blood-shod. All went lame; all blind;
Drunk with fatigue; deaf even to the hoots
Of tired, outstripped Five-Nines[1] that dropped behind.

Gas! GAS! Quick, boys!—An **ecstasy** of fumbling,
10   Fitting the clumsy helmets[2] just in time;
But someone still was yelling out and stumbling
And flound'ring like a man in fire or lime . . .
Dim, through the misty panes and thick green light,
As under a green sea, I saw him drowning.

15   In all my dreams, before my helpless sight,
He plunges at me, guttering, choking, drowning.

If in some smothering dreams you too could pace
Behind the wagon that we flung him in,
And watch the white eyes writhing in his face,
20   His hanging face, like a devil's sick of sin;
If you could hear, at every jolt, the blood
Come gargling from the froth-corrupted lungs,
Obscene as cancer, bitter as the cud
Of **vile**, incurable sores on innocent tongues,—
25   My friend, you would not tell with such high zest
To children ardent[3] for some desperate glory,
The old Lie: *Dulce et decorum est
Pro patria mori.*[4]

1. *Five-Nines* were artillery shells used during World War I.

2. *Clumsy helmets* are gas masks.

3. *Ardent* means eager.

4. Written by Horace, *Dulce . . . mori* means "It is sweet and honorable to die for one's country."

Big Idea   Class, Colonialism, and the Great War   *How do these similes challenge the notion that war is glorious?*

RESPONDING AND THINKING CRITICALLY

Respond

1. How did you feel when the speaker addresses the reader in the final verse paragraph?

Recall and Interpret

2. (a)In the first verse paragraph, how does the speaker describe the soldiers' retreat? (b)What do you learn about their physical and mental condition?

3. (a)Summarize the speaker's description of what happens to one of the soldiers. (b)What does the description suggest about the speaker's attitude toward the war?

4. (a)What theme, or message, do you think the speaker wants to convey in lines 25–28? (b)What evidence has been presented by the speaker earlier in the poem to prove his contention that the Latin quotation is a lie?

Analyze and Evaluate

5. (a)Explain the **metaphor** in line 6. (b)What sound effects make this metaphor particularly effective?

6. (a)What **similes** does the speaker use to describe the dying soldier in the final verse paragraph? (b)What is the cumulative effect of these similes?

7. (a)Why are the children in line 26 so eager for "desperate glory"? (b)Why do you think Owen describes the glory as "desperate"?

Connect

8. **Big Idea** **Class, Colonialism, and the Great War** Most of Owen's poems were published after the war. How do you think most people in Britain would have reacted to "Dulce et Decorum Est" when they first read it? Do you think the poem may have affected their opinions about the war effort? Explain.

LITERARY ANALYSIS

Literary Element **Verse Paragraph**

While poems written before the twentieth century usually contain stanzas, many contemporary poems are made up of **verse paragraphs.**

1. What is the function of the first two verse paragraphs of "Dulce et Decorum Est"?

2. How do lines 15–16 function as a transitional verse paragraph?

3. What is the main idea of the final verse paragraph?

Writing About Literature

Respond to Title In his title, Owen quotes the ancient Roman poet Horace. At the end of the poem, the title is repeated. In a one-paragraph response, explain why you think Owen invoked Horace's words.

READING AND VOCABULARY

Reading Strategy **Recognizing Author's Purpose**

Sometimes an author will have more than one purpose for writing. However, authors generally consider one purpose more important than the others.

1. What do you think was Owen's main purpose in writing "Dulce et Decorum Est"?

2. How do Owen's **tone** and **figurative language** contribute to his purpose?

Vocabulary **Practice**

Practice with Synonyms Identify the synonym for each vocabulary word below.

1. trudge   **a.** smell   **b.** plod

2. ecstasy   **a.** rapture   **b.** drain

3. vile   **a.** pathetic   **b.** offensive

Literature Online **Web Activities** For eFlashcards, Selection Quick Checks, and other Web activities, go to www.glencoe.com.

Informational Text

The World War I Yorkshire Trench system built by 49th West Riding Division near the Yser Canal at Boesinghe, Belgium.

from The Great War and Modern Memory

Paul Fussell

Winner of the National Book Award

Building Background

Paul Fussell was born in California in 1924. His experiences fighting as an infantryman in World War II profoundly influenced his beliefs about the meaning of war, its causes, and its relationship to literature and the arts. In the following excerpt, from his National Book Award–winning *The Great War and Modern Memory*, Fussell describes the trenches that spanned the Western Front during World War I. (See map on page 1033.)

Set a Purpose for Reading

Read to learn about the experiences of soldiers and the trenches in which they lived and fought during World War I.

Reading Strategy

Synthesizing Information

To **synthesize** means to draw information from multiple sources in order to come to a conclusion. As you read, take notes about the lives of the soldiers in the trenches. Include in your notes information drawn from other sources in this unit, including poetry. Then use this information to come to a conclusion about life in the trenches. Use an evaluation chart like the one below.

Information About Trench Life	Evidence	Conclusion

Henri Barbusse[1] estimates that the French front alone contained about 6250 miles of trenches. Since the French occupied a little more than half the line, the total length of the numerous trenches occupied by the British must come to about 6000 miles. We thus find over 12,000 miles of trenches on the Allied side alone. When we add the trenches of the Central Powers, we arrive at a figure of about 25,000 miles, equal to a trench sufficient to circle the earth. Theoretically it would have been possible to walk from Belgium to Switzerland entirely below ground, but although the lines were "continuous," they were not entirely seamless: occasionally mere shell holes or fortified strong-points would serve as a connecting link. Not a few survivors have performed the heady imaginative exercise of envisioning the whole line at once. Stanley Casson is one who, imagining the whole line from his position on the ground, implicitly submits the whole preposterous conception to the criterion of the "normally" rational and intelligible. As he remembers, looking back from 1935,

---

1. *Henri Barbusse* (1873–1935) was a French infantryman and novelist.

Our trenches stood on a faint slope, just overlooking German ground, with a vista of vague plainland below. Away to right and left stretched the great lines of defense as far as eye and imagination could stretch them. I used to wonder how long it would take for me to walk from the beaches of the North Sea to that curious end of all fighting against the Swiss boundary; to try to guess what each end looked like; to imagine what would happen if I passed a verbal message, in the manner of the parlor game, along to the next man on my right to be delivered to the end man of all up against the Alps. Would anything intelligible at all emerge?

Another imagination has contemplated a similar absurd transmission of sound all the way from north to south. Alexander Aitken[2] remembers the Germans opposite him celebrating some happy public event in early June, 1916, presumably either the (ambiguous) German success at the naval battle of Jutland (May 31–June 1) or the drowning of Lord Kitchener, lost on June 5 when the cruiser *Hampshire* struck a mine and sank off the Orkney Islands.[3] Aitken writes, "There had been a morning in early June when a tremendous tin-canning and beating of shell-gongs had begun in the north and run south down their lines to end, without doubt, at Belfort and Mulhausen[4] on the Swiss frontier." Impossible to believe, really, but in this mad setting, somehow plausible.

2. *Alexander Aitken* (1895–1967) was a soldier, war memoirist, and famed mathematician.
3. The *naval battle of Jutland,* which took place off the coast of Denmark, was the only major naval battle of the war. It ended without a decisive victor. *Lord Kitchener* (1850–1916) was a British field marshal and secretary of state for war. The *Orkney Islands* sit off the northeast coast of Scotland.
4. *Belfort,* the capital of the Territoire de Belfort in eastern France, was successfully defended by the allies during World War I. *Mulhausen* is an industrial town in northeastern France.

"When all is said and done," Sassoon[5] notes, "the war was mainly a matter of holes and ditches." And in these holes and ditches extending for ninety miles, continually, even in the quietest times, some 7000 British men and officers were killed and wounded daily, just as a matter of course. "Wastage," the Staff called it.

There were normally three lines of trenches. The front-line trench was anywhere from fifty yards or so to a mile from its enemy counterpart. Several hundred yards behind it was the support trench line. And several hundred yards behind that was the reserve line. There were three kinds of trenches: firing trenches, like these; communication trenches, running roughly perpendicular to the line and connecting the three lines; and "saps," shallower ditches thrust out into No Man's Land, providing access to forward

5. Siegfried *Sassoon* was one of the Trench Poets (see page 1093).

Soldier cleaning a trench in the Champagne region of France.

A French front line trench from WWI.

distance: that would have been to invite enfilade[8] fire. Every few yards a good trench zig-zagged. It had frequent traverses designed to contain damage within a limited space. Moving along a trench thus involved a great deal of weaving and turning. The floor of a proper trench was covered with wooden duckboards, beneath which were sumps a few feet deep designed to collect water. The walls, perpetually crumbling, were supported by sandbags, corrugated iron, or bundles of sticks or rushes. Except at night and in half-light, there was of course no looking over the top except through periscopes, which could be purchased in the "Trench Requisites" section of the main London department stores. The few snipers on duty during the day observed No Man's Land through loopholes cut in sheets of armor plate.

The entanglements of barbed wire had to be positioned far enough out in front of the trench to keep the enemy from sneaking up to grenade-throwing distance. Interestingly, the two novelties that contributed most to the personal menace of the war could be said to be American inventions. Barbed wire had first appeared on the American frontier in the late nineteenth century for use in restraining animals. And the machine gun was the brainchild of Hiram Stevens Maxim (1840–1916), an American who, disillusioned with native patent law, established his Maxim Gun Company in England and began manufacturing his guns in 1889. He was finally knighted for his efforts. At first the British regard for barbed wire was on a par with Sir Douglas Haig's[9]

observation posts, listening posts, grenade-throwing posts, and machine gun positions. The end of a sap was usually not manned all the time: night was the favorite time for going out. Coming up from the rear, one reached the trenches by following a communication trench sometimes a mile or more long. It often began in a town and gradually deepened. By the time pedestrians reached the reserve line, they were well below ground level.

A firing trench was supposed to be six to eight feet deep and four or five feet wide. On the enemy side a parapet[6] of earth or sandbags rose about two or three feet above the ground. A corresponding "parados"[7] a foot or so high was often found on top of the friendly side. Into the sides of trenches were dug one- or two-man holes ("funk-holes"), and there were deeper dugouts, reached by dirt stairs, for use as command posts and officers' quarters. On the enemy side of a trench was a fire-step two feet high on which the defenders were supposed to stand, firing and throwing grenades, when repelling attack. A well-built trench did not run straight for any

---

6. A *parapet* is a wall used to protect soldiers.
7. The *parados* was the side of the trench that faced away from the enemy.

8. *Enfilade* is gunfire directed at a position from that position's flank.
9. *Sir Douglas Haig* (1861–1928) was a British field marshal and commander in chief of British forces in France.

A view of the German Trench Avenue on the Western Front, showing the elaborate construction erected by the Germans.

understanding of the machine gun. In the autumn of 1914, the first wire Private Frank Richards saw emplaced before the British positions was a single strand of agricultural wire found in the vicinity. Only later did the manufactured article begin to arrive from England in sufficient quantity to create the thickets of mock-organic rusty brown that helped give a look of eternal autumn to the front.

The whole British line was numbered by sections, neatly, from right to left. A section, normally occupied by a company, was roughly 300 yards wide. One might be occupying front-line trench section 51; or support trench S 51, behind it; or reserve trench SS 51, behind both. But a less formal way of identifying sections of trench was by place or street names with a distinctly London flavor. *Piccadilly* was a favorite; popular also were *Regent Street* and *Strand*; junctions were *Hyde Park Corner* and *Marble Arch*. Directional and traffic control signs were everywhere in the trenches, giving the whole system the air of a parody modern city, although one literally "underground."

RESPONDING AND THINKING CRITICALLY

Respond

1. In what way has this passage changed your understanding of life in the trenches? Explain.

Recall and Interpret

2. (a)According to Fussell, what did the British staff refer to as "Wastage"? (b)Why do you think they used this term?

3. (a)How did the British identify sections of the trench when speaking informally? (b)For what reason do you think they did this?

Analyze and Evaluate

4. (a)For what reason might Fussell describe the two instances of the "transmission of sound all the way from north to south"? (b)In your opinion, why are these anecdotes effective?

5. (a)How are the trenches like a "modern city"? (b)In your opinion, how successful is Fussell's description of the trenches? Explain.

Connect

6. In what ways does Fussell's description of trench life resemble the descriptions in the poetry of Rupert Brooke, Wilfred Owen, and Siegfried Sassoon? Based on these similarities and your evaluation chart on page 1101, what conclusions can you draw about life in the trenches?

OBJECTIVES
- Read to enhance understanding of history and British culture.
- Evaluate the historical influences that shape elements of a literary work.

PART 2
Modernism

The Arrival, ca. 1913. Christopher R. W. Nevinson. Oil on canvas, 30 x 25 in. Tate Gallery, London.

"The most beautiful thing we can experience is the mysterious. It is the source of all art and science."

—Albert Einstein, "What I Believe"

Yeats's Poetry

MEET WILLIAM BUTLER YEATS

William Butler Yeats (yāts) is universally regarded as one of the greatest poets of the twentieth century. Born into an Anglo-Irish Protestant family in the Dublin suburb of Sandymount, Yeats loved to read and daydream as a child, especially during his summers at his grandparents' home in County Sligo, where he rode his pony about the scenic countryside and discovered Irish folklore and mythology.

Irish Romantic The son of a distinguished portrait painter, Yeats briefly studied painting but turned to writing poetry in his teens. His early work was influenced by the Romantics, particularly William Blake. Yeats even dressed the part of the romantic young poet, wearing a flowing tie, brown velvet jacket, and his father's old cape and wide-brimmed hat.

When Yeats was twenty-three, he published his first book of verse, and soon afterward a young woman named Maud Gonne arrived at his home to tell him that his poetry had moved her deeply. This meeting began Yeats's long obsession with Gonne, an actress and Irish patriot who inspired him to join the fight to free Ireland from British rule.

Although Gonne refused Yeats's many marriage proposals, she haunted his imagination and became a central figure in his poetry. Yeats did not end his pursuit of her until 1916, more than twenty years after they had first met. He later wrote that it was a "miserable love affair" and that he might as well have been offering his heart to a statue in a museum. Fortunately, Yeats found contentment in 1917, when he married Georgie Hyde-Lees.

Yeats combined his passions for literature and for Irish nationalism by joining the Celtic Revival, a cultural and political movement dedicated to Irish independence and to the use of Irish folklore in literature. He also presided over the Irish National Theatre Society at the Abbey Theatre in Dublin with his friend and patron, Augusta, Lady Gregory, and the playwright J. M. Synge. Yeats contributed many of his own plays to this theater, including *The Land of Heart's Desires*. He hoped to unite Catholics and Protestants in Ireland through a national literature that transcended religious differences.

"We should write out our own thoughts in as nearly as possible the language we thought them in, as though in a letter to an intimate friend."

—William Butler Yeats

From Romantic to Modernist In middle age, when Yeats reread the poems of his youth, he found "little but romantic convention, unconscious drama." He began to write in a less romantic style that more closely resembled natural speech. His poetry became less dreamlike and more energetic; his imagery became more economical and his tone more conversational. "Sentimentality," he declared, "is deceiving oneself; rhetoric is deceiving other people." Yeats received the Nobel Prize in Literature in 1923.

William Butler Yeats was born in 1865 and died in 1939.

Literature Online Author Search For more about William Butler Yeats, go to www.glencoe.com.

Connecting to the Poems

In these poems, Yeats reveals his thoughts and feelings about a special place and a special person. As you read, think about the following questions:

- Where would you like to go to find peace and renewal?
- How would you describe this place of peace?

Building Background

Yeats's early poems "The Lake Isle of Innisfree" and "When You Are Old" are romantic, lyrical, and dreamlike. "The Lake Isle of Innisfree" was influenced by Yeats's reading of *Walden* by Henry David Thoreau, a nineteenth-century American writer, who described his retreat from the city to a simple cabin by a forest pond. Yeats wrote his poem after the sight of a small fountain in a shop window in London brought the sound of Sligo's lake water lapping back into his consciousness.

Setting Purposes for Reading

Big Idea Modernism

The Modernist poets were fascinated with contrast and the tension between opposites. As you read, notice how Yeats's early poetry reflects this characteristic.

Literary Element Rhyme Scheme

The pattern that end rhymes form in a stanza or poem is known as its **rhyme scheme**. The rhyme scheme is designated by assigning a different letter of the alphabet to each new rhyme.

- See Literary Terms Handbook, p. R15.

Literature Online **Interactive Literary Elements Handbook** To review or learn more about the literary elements, go to www.glencoe.com.

Reading Strategy Drawing Conclusions About Author's Meaning

Drawing conclusions is part of the process of inferring, or making informed guesses about what an author suggests. Because poets often suggest meaning rather than state it directly, drawing conclusions is essential to constructing meaning in a poem. When you draw a conclusion, you make a general statement that is supported by evidence.

Reading Tip: Taking Notes Use a chart like the one below to record conclusions you draw from the details presented in the poems.

Details	Conclusions
The speaker plans to build a small cabin, raise bees, and plant beans.	The speaker dreams of a simple life close to nature.

Juliette Drouet, 1883. Jules Bastien-Lepage. Oil on canvas, 36 x 31 cm. Musée Victor Hugo, Paris.

OBJECTIVES
In studying these selections, you will focus on the following:
- analyzing literary periods
- analyzing rhyme scheme
- drawing conclusions about author's meaning

The Lake Isle of Innisfree
William Butler Yeats

I will arise and go now, and go to Innisfree,[1]
And a small cabin build there, of clay and wattles[2] made:
Nine bean-rows will I have there, a hive for the honeybee,
And live alone in the bee-loud glade.[3]

5 And I shall have some peace there, for peace comes
      dropping slow,
Dropping from the veils of the morning to where the
      cricket sings;
There midnight's all a glimmer, and noon a purple glow,
And evening full of the linnet's[4] wings.

I will arise and go now, for always night and day
10 I hear lake water lapping with low sounds by the shore;
While I stand on the roadway, or on the pavements gray,
I hear it in the deep heart's core.

1. *Innisfree* is an island in County Sligo. Yeats had wanted to go to Innisfree since hearing of it as a child.
2. *Wattles* are walls made of twigs.
3. A *glade* is an open space in the forest.
4. A *linnet* is a small brown songbird.

When You Are Old
William Butler Yeats

When you[1] are old and gray and full of sleep,
And nodding by the fire, take down this book,
And slowly read, and dream of the soft look
Your eyes had once, and of their shadows deep;

5 How many loved your moments of glad grace,
And loved your beauty with love false or true,
But one man loved the pilgrim soul in you,
And loved the sorrows of your changing face;

And bending down beside the glowing bars,[2]
10 Murmur, a little sadly, how Love fled
And paced upon the mountains overhead
And hid his face amid a crowd of stars.

1. Some critics think that the *you* Yeats is addressing is Maud Gonne, the woman he loved and who rejected his proposals of marriage. However, this poem is actually a free translation of Pierre de Ronsard's sonnet to *his* love Hélène (see page 460).

2. *Glowing bars* refers to the grate in front of the fireplace.

Literary Element   **Rhyme Scheme** *Which lines rhyme in this stanza?*

RESPONDING AND THINKING CRITICALLY

Respond

1. Would you like to live in Innisfree or a place like it? Why or why not?

Recall and Interpret

2. (a) List three details from "The Lake Isle of Innisfree" that describe this special place. (b) What can you infer about this place from the speaker's description of it?

3. (a) What does the speaker hear "in the deep heart's core"? (b) What do you think it means to hear something in this manner?

4. (a) According to the speaker in "When You Are Old," how does his love differ from that of others? (b) What might you infer about the relationship between the woman and the speaker?

Analyze and Evaluate

5. In "The Lake Isle of Innisfree," what do you think Innisfree **symbolizes**, or represents, for the speaker?

6. In "When You Are Old," what does the **personification** of love seem to suggest about the woman? About the speaker's love for the woman?

7. Evaluate the speaker's **tone**, or attitude toward the subject, in "When You Are Old." Does the speaker seem disillusioned? Why or why not? Use details from the poem to support your answer.

Connect

8. **Big Idea** **Modernism** What contrasts does the speaker suggest in these poems?

LITERARY ANALYSIS

Literary Element **Rhyme Scheme**

In these poems, Yeats adopts the traditional form of the lyric with a recurring pattern of rhyming sounds.

1. What is the rhyme scheme of "When You Are Old"?

2. How does the rhyme help reinforce the meaning?

Writing About Literature

Compare and Contrast Poems "When You Are Old" is based on Pierre de Ronsard's poem "To Hélène" (see page 460). Reread both poems and then write a brief essay in which you compare and contrast the poems' forms, tone, and content.

A Lakeside Gathering. Henry Boddington. Gavin Graham Gallery, London.

READING AND VOCABULARY

Reading Strategy **Drawing Conclusions About Author's Meaning**

Drawing conclusions helps you find connections among the details in a poem and see the larger picture.

1. Will the speaker in "The Lake Isle of Innisfree" ever really go to Innisfree? Explain.

2. In "When You Are Old," what does the speaker want the woman to feel as she reads the poem? What clues support your conclusion?

Academic Vocabulary

Here is a word from the vocabulary list on page R82.

liberal (lib rəl´) *adj.* generous; giving freely

Practice and Apply
Is the speaker in "When You Are Old" **liberal** or ungenerous? Explain.

Literature Online **Web Activities** For eFlashcards, Selection Quick Checks, and other Web activities, go to www.glencoe.com.

Sailing to Byzantium
and *The Second Coming*

Connecting to the Poems

In "Sailing to Byzantium," the speaker describes a timeless realm of the imagination; in "The Second Coming," the speaker utters a grim prophecy triggered by trends he observes in the modern world. As you read, think about the following questions:

- What place would you choose to symbolize the kingdom of the imagination?
- Are conditions in the world getting better or worse?

Building Background

The Byzantine Empire was the name of the eastern, or Greek, division of the Roman Empire. The capital city of Byzantium was a great center of artistic activity during the Middle Ages. Yeats regarded Byzantium as a holy city of the imagination, a perfect blend of the practical, the spiritual, and the artistic.

"The Second Coming" is based on Yeats's theory that cycles of history and nature occur every two thousand years. During this time, one civilization evolves and decays, eventually replaced by another. The title of the poem alludes to the New Testament prediction of Christ's return to Earth at the end of the world, after a time of terror and chaos.

Setting Purposes for Reading

Big Idea Modernism

Yeats exerted enormous influence on the Modernist poets, particularly in his use of symbolism. As you read, notice the symbolic richness of these poems.

Literary Element Structure

Structure is the framework or general plan of a literary work. Structure refers to the relationship of the parts of a work to one another and to the whole piece. As you read, notice the structure of these poems.

- See Literary Terms Handbook, p. R17.

Reading Strategy Analyzing Figurative Language: Metaphor

Analyzing is the process of looking critically at the separate parts of a literary work in order to understand the whole. When you **analyze metaphors**, you identify figures of speech that make comparisons without using the words *like* or *as*. You then consider what the poet achieves by using metaphors instead of literal language.

Reading Tip: Identifying Metaphors As you read, record your interpretations of the metaphors in the poems.

Vocabulary

artifice (är′ tə fis) *n.* trickery; deception; p. 1111 *Her friendly attitude was a mere artifice.*

anarchy (an′ ər kē) *n.* a complete lack of political order; chaos; p. 1113 *Mobs of citizens rioted, storming the capitol and ushering in a state of anarchy.*

conviction (kən vik′ shən) *n.* a strong belief; p. 1113 *Is it your conviction that writing helps one think better?*

vex (veks) *v.* disturb; trouble; irritate; p. 1113 *Eager to catch her train, she was vexed by the waiter's slow service.*

Vocabulary Tip: Context Clues You can often figure out the meanings of unfamiliar words by looking for clues in the **context**, or the surrounding words and sentences.

Literature Online **Interactive Literary Elements Handbook** To review or learn more about the literary elements, go to www.glencoe.com.

OBJECTIVES
In studying these selections, you will focus on the following:
- analyzing literary periods
- analyzing figurative language and meter
- understanding the structure of poetry

SAILING TO BYZANTIUM

William Butler Yeats

I

That is no country for old men. The young
In one another's arms, birds in the trees
—Those dying generations—at their song,
The salmon-falls,[1] the mackerel-crowded
    seas,
5   Fish, flesh, or fowl, commend all summer
    long
Whatever is begotten, born, and dies.
Caught in that sensual music all neglect
Monuments of unaging intellect.

II

An aged man is but a paltry[2] thing,
10   A tattered coat upon a stick, unless
Soul clap its hands and sing, and louder
    sing
For every tatter in its mortal dress,
Nor is there singing school but studying
Monuments of its own magnificence;
15   And therefore I have sailed the seas and
    come
To the holy city of Byzantium.

III

O sages[3] standing in God's holy fire
As in the gold mosaic of a wall,
Come from the holy fire, perne in a gyre,[4]
20   And be the singing-masters of my soul.
Consume my heart away; sick with desire
And fastened to a dying animal
It knows not what it is; and gather me
Into the **artifice** of eternity.

IV

25   Once out of nature I shall never take
My bodily form from any natural thing,
But such a form as Grecian goldsmiths
    make
Of hammered gold and gold enameling
To keep a drowsy Emperor awake;[5]
30   Or set upon a golden bough to sing
To lords and ladies of Byzantium
Of what is past, or passing, or to come.

---

1. *Salmon-falls* are the rapids in rivers that salmon swim up to spawn.
2. *Paltry* means "worthless."
3. *Sages* are the wise men pictured on the walls of the churches in Byzantium.
4. *Perne in a gyre* means to spin around in a spiral motion. Yeats associated gyres with the spinning of fate; here, the speaker asks the images on the wall to come down and spin him into their timeless state of being.
5. *But such a form . . . awake* refers to something Yeats once read about: An emperor in Byzantium had a tree made of gold and silver upon which artificial birds sat and sang.

Literary Element   Structure *How might the last two stanzas of this poem contrast with the first two?*

Vocabulary

artifice (är′ tə fis) *n.* trickery; deception

The New Planet, 1921. Konstantin Fiodorvich Juon. Tempera on cardboard, 71 x 101 cm. Tretjakov Gallery, Moscow.

The Second Coming

William Butler Yeats

Turning and turning in the widening gyre[1]
The falcon cannot hear the falconer;
Things fall apart; the center cannot hold;
Mere **anarchy** is loosed upon the world,

5   The blood-dimmed tide is loosed, and everywhere
The ceremony of innocence is drowned;
The best lack all **conviction**, while the worst
Are full of passionate intensity.

Surely some revelation is at hand;
10   Surely the Second Coming is at hand.
The Second Coming! Hardly are those words out
When a vast image out of *Spiritus Mundi*[2]
Troubles my sight: somewhere in sands of the desert
A shape with lion body and the head of a man,[3]
15   A gaze blank and pitiless as the sun,
Is moving its slow thighs, while all about it
Reel shadows of the indignant desert birds.
The darkness drops again; but now I know
That twenty centuries of stony sleep[4]
20   Were **vexed** to nightmare by a rocking cradle,[5]
And what rough beast, its hour come round at last,
Slouches towards Bethlehem[6] to be born?

---

1. A *gyre* is a circular form or motion.
2. The Latin phrase *Spiritus Mundi* means "Spirit of the World." Yeats
   believed that all people are connected through this spirit and that it
   constitutes the collective, inherited body of myths and symbols
   common to all cultures.
3. [*A shape . . . man*] This figure is meant to resemble the Egyptian
   sphinx.
4. [*That twenty . . . sleep*] The speaker is referring to the two-thousand-
   year period before the birth of Christ.
5. *Rocking cradle* refers to the birth of the infant Jesus.
6. *Bethlehem* was the birthplace of Jesus Christ.

Literary Element   Structure *With which image in the first part of
this poem does the image of "the indignant desert birds" contrast?*

Big Idea   Modernism *What might the "rough beast" symbolize?*

Vocabulary

anarchy (an′ ər kē) *n.* a complete lack of political order; chaos
conviction (kən vik′ shən) *n.* a strong belief
vex (veks) *v.* disturb; trouble; irritate

RESPONDING AND THINKING CRITICALLY

Respond

1. What line or lines from the poems made the strongest impression on you? Why?

Recall and Interpret

2. (a)What is the country described in the first stanza of "Sailing to Byzantium" like? (b)Why does the speaker travel to Byzantium?

3. (a)In lines 17–24 of "Sailing to Byzantium," what does the speaker ask the sages to do? (b)Why do you think the speaker makes these requests?

4. (a)In "The Second Coming," how does the speaker describe the state of the world and human affairs in the first stanza? (b)What seems to be the speaker's attitude toward this situation?

5. (a)According to the speaker, where is the "rough beast" going? (b)Why is it going there?

Analyze and Evaluate

6. In "Sailing to Byzantium," how would you describe the speaker's attitude toward aging and death?

7. Evaluate the **mood** of "The Second Coming." How does the speaker's **tone**, or attitude toward the subject, contribute to that mood?

8. Yeats wrote "The Second Coming" shortly after the end of World War I. What relationship can you see between the devastation of war and the events described in this poem?

Connect

9. **Big Idea** Modernism Explain how Yeats uses the notions of song and singing in a symbolic way in "Sailing to Byzantium."

VISUAL LITERACY: Graphic Organizer

Organizing Details in Poetry

You can often use graphic organizers to record details in a literary work and your ideas about them. For example, you might organize the details in "The Second Coming" in a diagram like the one below. Copy this organizer on a separate sheet of paper and fill it in.

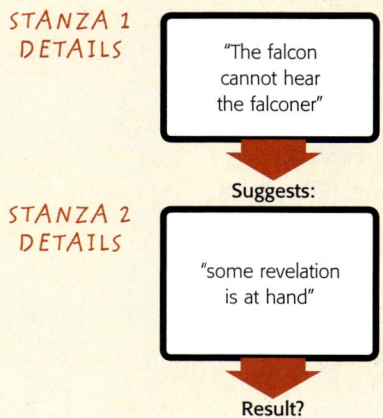

STANZA 1 DETAILS

"The falcon cannot hear the falconer"

Suggests:

STANZA 2 DETAILS

"some revelation is at hand"

Result?

Group Activity Discuss the following questions with classmates. Refer to your graphic organizer and cite evidence from "The Second Coming" for support.

1. Do the details in the first stanza lead you to conclude that the "Second Coming" is at hand? Explain.

2. Yeats does not indicate what will result *after* the "rough beast" is born in Bethlehem. What do you imagine will happen then?

3. How will the "rough beast" differ from Christ?

Literary Element Structure

Structure refers to the sequence of thoughts and images that work together to impart the meaning of a poem.

1. In what way is the structure of "Sailing to Byzantium" symmetrical?

2. How would you describe the structure of "The Second Coming"? Consider the subject matter of each stanza.

Review: Meter

As you learned on page 995, meter refers to a regular pattern of stressed and unstressed syllables that gives a line of poetry a predictable rhythm. In "Sailing to Byzantium," Yeats uses **iambic pentameter**, meaning that each line of verse usually contains five feet in which a stressed syllable follows an unstressed one.

An octave is a stanza that consists of eight lines. **Ottava rima** is a stanza written in iambic pentameter with an *ababababcc* rhyme scheme.

1. Copy a stanza from "Sailing to Byzantium." Scan the meter and mark the rhyme scheme. Is the stanza written in ottava rima? Explain.

2. What effects do the meter and rhyme scheme create in "Sailing to Byzantium"? Give examples.

The Great Sphinx against the Great Pyramid of Cheops, Egypt.

Reading Strategy Analyzing Figurative Language: Metaphor

When you **analyze metaphors**, you look critically at examples of this figure of speech to determine what they contribute to the poem as a whole.

1. In "Sailing to Byzantium," to what does the speaker compare "an aged man" in line 10? What does this comparison suggest?

2. Why is the metaphor of a "dying animal" in line 22 effective?

3. In "The Second Coming," what is "the ceremony of innocence" in line 6?

Vocabulary Practice

Practice with Context Clues Use context clues to figure out the meaning of the boldfaced vocabulary word in each sentence below.

1. An ingenious **artifice**, her kind attitude was a clever cover.
   a. decoration   **b.** deception   **c.** harmony

2. Some frontier towns were in a state of **anarchy** until federal marshals and judges arrived.
   a. lawlessness   **b.** poverty   **c.** starvation

3. You must stand up for your **convictions** when others challenge them.
   a. beliefs   **b.** plans   **c.** excuses

4. The teacher was **vexed** when the blaring horns from passing cars interrupted his lecture.
   a. confident   **b.** confused   **c.** irritated

Academic Vocabulary

Here is a word from the vocabulary list on page R82. This word will help you think, write, and talk about the selections.

erode (i rōd′) *v.* wear away; eat into

Practice and Apply
What evidence suggests that Yeats's Romantic views **eroded** after World War I?

Writing About Literature

Evaluate Author's Craft Write an essay evaluating Yeats's use of metaphor. Support your assessment with evidence from "The Lake Isle of Innisfree," "When You Are Old," "Sailing to Byzantium," and "The Second Coming."

As you draft, follow the writing guide shown below to keep your essay on track.

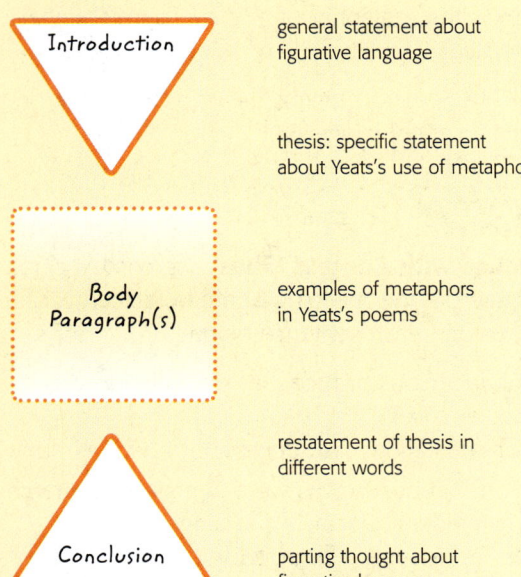

Introduction — general statement about figurative language

— thesis: specific statement about Yeats's use of metaphor

Body Paragraph(s) — examples of metaphors in Yeats's poems

— restatement of thesis in different words

Conclusion — parting thought about figurative language

After you complete your draft, meet with a peer reviewer to evaluate each other's work and to suggest revisions. Then proofread and edit your draft for errors in spelling, grammar, and punctuation.

Reading Further

For more by and about Yeats, look for these collections:

- *Fairy and Folk Tales of Ireland*, edited by W. B. Yeats, is a collection of Irish legends, folktales, and songs.

- *William Butler Yeats: A Collection of Criticism*, edited by Patrick J. Keane, provides insights into Yeats's poetry and life.

- *Collected Poems* by W. B. Yeats contains most of Yeats's poetic output over his lifetime.

Literature Online Web Activities For eFlashcards, Selection Quick Checks, and other Web activities, go to www.glencoe.com.

Yeats's Language and Style

Using Conjunctions A conjunction is a word that joins single words or groups of words. In his poetry, Yeats frequently uses conjunctions to indicate relationships between words and clauses.

"I will arise **and** go now, **and** go to Innisfree,"

"**While** I stand on the roadway, **or** on the pavements gray, / I hear it in the deep heart's core."

"The best lack all conviction, **while** the worst / Are full of passionate intensity."

In the first example above, the word *and* is a **coordinating conjunction,** or one that joins words or groups of words of equal grammatical weight. The speaker's arising and his going to Innisfree are equally important. Similarly, the phrases "on the roadway" and "on the pavements gray," joined by the coordinating conjunction *or*, have equal weight. The word *while* is a **subordinating conjunction,** or one that joins two clauses so as to make one grammatically dependent on the other.

The chart below lists coordinating conjunctions, correlative conjunctions (those that work in pairs), and common subordinating conjunctions.

Conjunctions		
Coordinating	**Correlative**	**Subordinating**
and or but so nor yet for	Both . . . and either . . . or just as . . . so neither . . . nor not only . . . but (also) whether . . . or	although when as where because while if once so unless

Activity List other examples of conjunctions in Yeats's poems. For each conjunction, explain in your own words the relationship expressed.

Revising Check

Conjunctions With a partner, go through your essay about Yeats's use of metaphor and note places where you might clarify relationships by using conjunctions.

Preludes

MEET T. S. ELIOT

In 1917 customers of Lloyds Bank on London's Queen Henrietta Street might have been surprised to learn that the shy young American they knew as Mr. Eliot the banker was known in literary circles as T. S. Eliot the poet. Eliot's supervisors at the bank knew that he wrote poetry, but they dismissed his writing as a curious hobby. In reality, poetry was far more than just a hobby to Eliot, and by the time he left the bank eight years later, he was one of the leading poets and critics of his age.

> *"The experience of a poem is the experience both of a moment and of a lifetime."*
>
> —T. S. Eliot

Education and Groundbreaking Poems

Thomas Stearns Eliot was born in St. Louis, Missouri, to a prominent family that traced its roots to Puritan New England. An excellent student, Eliot studied philosophy and literature at Harvard University, the Sorbonne in Paris, and Oxford University in England. While still in school, he began writing poetry, composing such groundbreaking poems as "Preludes" and "The Love Song of J. Alfred Prufrock." In London, he met poet Ezra Pound, who immediately recognized his genius and brought Eliot's work to the attention of various publishers. Pound praised Eliot's Modernist verse and encouraged him to continue writing.

Eliot decided to stay in England. At age twenty-six, he married a British woman named Vivienne Haigh-Wood. Soon after, she became seriously ill; to pay for her mounting medical expenses, Eliot took on a number of jobs, including the position at Lloyds Bank. After work he wrote poetry and, to supplement his income, literary essays and reviews. These articles had an impact far beyond his expectations, helping to shape literary criticism for years to come. Unfortunately, as Eliot's reputation grew, so did his personal problems. His wife's illness, their financial difficulties, and his long workdays took a physical and mental toll on him, and at the age of thirty-three he was close to collapse. While resting for a few months in a Swiss sanatorium, he worked on *The Waste Land,* a long poem about the spiritual breakdown of the modern world. It proved to be one of the most influential poems of the twentieth century.

Spiritual Renewal and International

Acclaim At the age of thirty-six, Eliot left Lloyds to become an editor at Faber & Faber, a London publishing house. He also continued to write, composing a number of distinguished poems and plays. In his late thirties, Eliot became a British citizen. Always a deeply spiritual man, Eliot was also baptized into the Church of England. His later poems, such as "Ash Wednesday" and *Four Quartets,* show the influence of his conversion to Anglo-Catholicism. At the age of sixty, Eliot received the Nobel Prize in Literature. He died in London sixteen years later. At the time of his death, many considered Eliot the most important poet and critic writing in the English language.

T. S. Eliot was born in 1888 and died in 1965.

Literature Online Author Search For more about T. S. Eliot, go to www.glencoe.com.

Connecting to the Poem

In "Preludes," T. S. Eliot describes a city street on a winter evening and the following morning. As you read the poem, think about the following questions:

- What sights, sounds, and feelings do you experience while walking down a city street?
- How do your associations with the city compare with those that Eliot describes?

Building Background

T. S. Eliot often built his poems around images that capture the essence of a time, place, and mood, much as good photographs do. Eliot's poems often include **allusions** to other literary works or historical events, and they juxtapose religious imagery with trivial elements including popular songs, nursery rhymes, and jingles.

In music, preludes are short pieces that introduce longer, more complex compositions. The poem "Preludes" describes a city much like the St. Louis neighborhood of Eliot's childhood. To Eliot, the physical decay of a city represented a deeper moral and spiritual decay. This theme runs throughout much of his work.

Setting Purposes for Reading

Big Idea Modernism

As you read, think about how "Preludes" illustrates a sense of alienation and despair that is characteristic of Modernist poetry.

Literary Element Imagery

Imagery consists of the word pictures that writers create to evoke a particular emotional response. In creating effective images, writers use **sensory details,** or descriptions that appeal to one or more of the five senses (sight, hearing, touch, taste, and smell). As you read "Preludes," note the images Eliot presents.

- See Literary Terms Handbook, p. R9.

Literature Online **Interactive Literary Elements Handbook** To review or learn more about the literary elements, go to www.glencoe.com.

Reading Strategy Analyzing Style

Style consists of the expressive qualities that distinguish an author's work, including word choice, the length and arrangement of sentences, and the use of figurative language and imagery. To analyze style, look at these qualities separately to determine the meaning of the work as a whole. Analyzing style can also reveal an author's tone and purpose in writing.

Reading Tip: Taking Notes As you read "Preludes," look for stylistic elements that help reveal Eliot's attitude toward his subject and his purpose in writing this poem. Organize your examples in a chart like this one:

Stylistic Devices	Eliot's Attitude
Word Choice	The impersonal connotation of the word "passageways" hints at a negative attitude toward the sight described.
Figurative Language	
Imagery	

Vocabulary

constitute (kon′ stə tōōt′) v. make up; form; p. 1120 *An hour for lunch constituted our only break from the all-day seminar.*

infinitely (in′ fə nit lē) adv. boundlessly; endlessly; p. 1120 *The unending array of obstructions made solving the puzzle infinitely complicated.*

Vocabulary Tip: Synonyms Words that have the same or nearly the same meaning are called synonyms. The words *withered* and *shriveled,* for example, are synonyms.

OBJECTIVES
In studying this selection, you will focus on the following:
- identifying characteristics of Modernist poetry
- interpreting imagery
- analyzing author's style

Preludes

T. S. Eliot

Tower Bridge, from the limited-edition portfolio *London,* published 1909. Photogravure. Alvin Langdon Coburn. Private collection.

I

The winter evening settles down
With smell of steaks in passageways.
Six o'clock.
The burnt-out ends of smoky days.
5 And now a gusty shower wraps
The grimy scraps
Of withered leaves about your feet
And newspapers from vacant lots;
The showers beat
10 On broken blinds and chimney-pots,[1]
And at the corner of the street
A lonely cab-horse steams and stamps.

And then the lighting of the lamps.

II

The morning comes to consciousness
15 Of faint stale smells of beer
From the sawdust-trampled[2] street
With all its muddy feet that press
To early coffee-stands.

With the other masquerades[3]
20 That time resumes,
One thinks of all the hands
That are raising dingy shades
In a thousand furnished rooms.[4]

1. *Chimney-pots* are pipes that protrude from chimney tops.

2. *Sawdust-trampled* refers to the sawdust that many bars and shops sprinkled on their floors to absorb dirt and spilled drinks. The sawdust has been carried into the streets on the soles of people's shoes.

3. Here, a *masquerade* is a pretense or act.

4. *Furnished rooms* are cheap, one-room apartments that come with beds and other basic pieces of furniture.

Reading Strategy Analyzing Style *What effect does Eliot's word choice have on your impression of this scene?*

Literary Element Imagery *To what senses do the images in lines 15–18 appeal? What emotions do these images evoke?*

III

You tossed a blanket from the bed,
25 You lay upon your back, and waited;
You dozed, and watched the night revealing
The thousand sordid images
Of which your soul was **constituted;**
They flickered against the ceiling.
30 And when all the world came back
And the light crept up between the shutters
And you heard the sparrows in the gutters,
You had such a vision of the street
As the street hardly understands;
35 Sitting along the bed's edge, where
You curled the papers from your hair,
Or clasped the yellow soles of feet
In the palms of both soiled hands.

IV

His soul stretched tight across the skies
40 That fade behind a city block,
Or trampled by insistent feet
At four and five and six o'clock;
And short square fingers stuffing pipes,
And evening newspapers, and eyes
45 Assured of certain certainties,
The conscience of a blackened street
Impatient to assume the world.

I am moved by fancies that are curled
Around these images, and cling:
50 The notion of some **infinitely** gentle
Infinitely suffering thing.

Wipe your hand across your mouth, and laugh;
The worlds revolve like ancient women
Gathering fuel in vacant lots.

Big Idea Modernism *In what sense do the words* sordid *and* soul *contrast with one another? What comment is Eliot making in lines 27–28 about contemporary life?*

Vocabulary

constitute (kon′ stə tōōt′) *v.* make up; form
infinitely (in′ fə nit lē) *adv.* boundlessly; endlessly

RESPONDING AND THINKING CRITICALLY

Respond

1. What images in "Preludes" did you find especially vivid?

Recall and Interpret

2. (a)What sights, sounds, and odors are described in the first prelude? (b)What mood do these images evoke?

3. (a)What images are described in the second prelude? (b)What do these images have in common?

4. (a)In the fourth prelude, what moves the speaker? (b)What does this tell you about the speaker?

5. (a)Explain the progression of time from the first prelude to the fourth prelude. (b)How does this progression illustrate the revolving of the worlds described in lines 53–54?

Analyze and Evaluate

6. (a)To what does the speaker compare the revolving of the worlds? (b)In your own words, explain what this simile means. (c)How does it help sum up the main point of the poem?

7. (a)What parts of the preludes were most meaningful to you? (b)What parts were most challenging to understand? In each case, explain why.

Connect

8. **Big Idea** **Modernism** (a)Cite examples from "Preludes" that illustrate characteristics of Modernist poetry. (b)Do you like Modernist poetry, traditional forms, or both? Support your opinion with reasons.

LITERARY ANALYSIS

Literary Element **Imagery**

In "Preludes," Eliot creates a series of word pictures that present a dreary view of twentieth-century urban life.

1. (a)To what sense do the images in lines 2–4 and line 15 appeal? To what other sense(s) might these images appeal? (b)Are the images pleasant? Explain.

2. (a)Cite examples of images from the poem that appeal to sight, hearing, and touch. (b)What emotions do these images evoke?

Internet Connection

What does T. S. Eliot have to do with the musical *Cats*? How did his hometown of St. Louis honor him? Why did he ask to be buried in East Coker, England? Using Eliot's name as a keyword, surf the Internet to answer these questions or others you may have about Eliot. While you're online, visit an Eliot chat room to discover what other students think of him or to post a question about his work. Share what you learn with your classmates.

READING AND VOCABULARY

Reading Strategy **Analyzing Style**

Review the Reading Strategy notes you wrote down while reading "Preludes." Note how the word choices, figurative language, and structure of the poem contribute to its theme.

1. Which words from the poem convey a dreary or pessimistic attitude?

2. Line 13 contains no emotionally charged words, yet it conveys a melancholy attitude. Explain how the placement and construction of this sentence might account for this attitude.

Vocabulary **Practice**

Practice with Synonyms Identify the synonym for each vocabulary word listed in the first column. Use a dictionary or a thesaurus if you need help.

1. constituted   **a.** composed   **b.** substituted

2. infinitely   **a.** conditionally   **b.** limitlessly

Literature Online **Web Activities** For eFlashcards, Selection Quick Checks, and other Web activities, go to www.glencoe.com.

The Rocking-Horse Winner

MEET D. H. LAWRENCE

David Herbert Lawrence helped to define modern literature with his carefully constructed, highly original, and socially conscious novels and short stories. Yet his attitudes about life and writing were often in direct contrast to the opinions held by society at the time.

Turmoil and Controversy

Lawrence was born in a small mining village near Nottingham, England, to an illiterate coal miner and a retired schoolteacher mother. As a young child, Lawrence suffered a severe attack of pneumonia from which he never fully recovered. This affliction, however, enabled him to escape from a life of work in the coal mines. Instead, he attended school on a scholarship but was forced to abandon his education at sixteen to work as a clerk in a factory. After a short time, however, Lawrence again fell ill. While recuperating, he formed a close friendship with Jessie Chambers, a local farmer's daughter. Soon Lawrence became a pupil-teacher, later earning a teacher's certificate at University College, Nottingham. Encouraged by Jessie, he also started writing poetry and fiction.

Lawrence's mid-twenties were turbulent: He broke with Jessie, his mother died, his first novels were published, and he decided to give up teaching and support himself solely by writing. During this time, Lawrence fell in love and eloped with a German woman named Frieda von Richtofen. For the next two years, the couple traveled extensively throughout Europe. Frieda became the prototype for many of Lawrence's best-known heroines.

The onset of the First World War forced Lawrence and his wife to return to England, where at first they settled on the south coast. Because of Frieda's nationality and Lawrence's outspoken criticism of the war, however, many local residents suspected them of being spies. Persecuted, they were forced to live on the run, traveling throughout England until the end of the war.

During this time, Lawrence published a novel called *The Rainbow*, which was seized by the police and declared obscene. Throughout his career, Lawrence's work so scandalized the public that some of his books were banned.

> *"Be still when you have nothing to say; when genuine passion moves you, say what you've got to say, and say it hot."*
>
> —D. H. Lawrence

Writer in Exile Disgusted with England, Lawrence and his wife left for Italy in 1919 and spent the rest of their lives traveling in search of an ideal society—as well as a warm climate for Lawrence's respiratory illnesses. The couple settled for several years in Taos, New Mexico, where Lawrence fell ill and found that he was in the late stages of tuberculosis. They returned to Italy, and Lawrence finished his last and most controversial novel, *Lady Chatterley's Lover*. From Italy, Frieda took him to France in search of a cure. During this time he wrote "The Rocking-Horse Winner," as well as many other short stories. Lawrence died at the age of forty-five with Frieda at his bedside.

D. H. Lawrence was born in 1885 and died in 1930.

Literature Online **Author Search** For more about D. H. Lawrence, go to www.glencoe.com.

Connecting to the Story

Do you agree or disagree with the saying "Money can't buy happiness"? In "The Rocking-Horse Winner," Lawrence explores how the desire for money affects one family. As you read, think about the following questions:

- Would your life be better if you had more material things?
- How would you define *luck*?

Building Background

"The Rocking-Horse Winner" takes place in England in the early part of the twentieth century. At that time, social classes were quite distinct, and many people who were not born wealthy lived beyond their means in an effort to attain the prestige of a higher social class.

This story mentions many popular horse races held in England, including the Ascot (run at Ascot Heath) and the St. Leger (held at Doncaster every September). The Turf Commission is a committee of the Jockey Club—an organization dedicated to the improvement of thoroughbred racing. The Turf Commission operates a bank in which bettors can deposit money for future bets.

Setting Purposes for Reading

Big Idea Modernism

As you read, consider how this story reflects Lawrence's concerns about society's emphasis on money.

Literary Element Foreshadowing

Foreshadowing is the author's use of hints or clues to prepare readers for events that will happen later in a story. Mood, atmosphere, events, physical objects, and even character traits can foreshadow later events. As you read, look for examples of foreshadowing.

- See Literary Terms Handbook, p. R7.

Literature Online Interactive Literary Elements Handbook To review or learn more about the literary elements, go to www.glencoe.com.

Reading Strategy Making Inferences About Characters

Making inferences involves making educated guesses about what an author implies or suggests. Because authors often do not directly state what they want readers to know, making inferences is essential to constructing meaning. In reading Lawrence's story, you must examine details about the characters and then infer what they believe, how they feel, and why they act as they do.

Reading Tip: Taking Notes Use a chart to record your inferences about the characters in the story.

| Details | Inferences About Characters |

Vocabulary

parry (par′ ē) *v.* to respond, as to a question or argument, by warding off or diverting; p. 1127 *Instead of answering directly, she parried the question by telling an amusing story.*

obstinately (ob′ stə nit lē′) *adv.* in a manner not yielding to argument, persuasion, or reason; inflexibly; p. 1129 *Obstinately remaining silent, he fixed his eyes on the floor.*

reiterate (rē it′ ə rāt′) *v.* to say or do again; to repeat; p. 1130 *I reiterated the question because he seemed not to hear it.*

emancipate (i man′ sə pāt′) *v.* to free; to liberate; p. 1133 *The governor pardoned several criminals, emancipating them from prison.*

Vocabulary Tip: Analogies Analogies are comparisons based on relationships between ideas.

OBJECTIVES
In studying this selection, you will focus on the following:
- analyzing literary periods
- understanding foreshadowing and motivation
- making inferences about characters

The Rocking-Horse Winner

D. H. Lawrence

There was a woman who was beautiful, who started with all the advantages, yet she had no luck. She married for love, and the love turned to dust. She had bonny[1] children, yet she felt they had been thrust upon her, and she could not love them. They looked at her coldly, as if they were finding fault with her. And hurriedly she felt she must cover up some fault in herself. Yet what it was that she must cover up she never knew. Nevertheless, when her children were present, she always felt the centre of her heart go hard. This troubled her, and in her manner she was all the more gentle and anxious for her children, as if she loved them very much. Only she herself knew that at the centre of her heart was a hard little place that could not feel love, no, not for anybody. Everybody else said of her: "She is such a good mother. She adores her children." Only she herself, and her children themselves, knew it was not so. They read it in each other's eyes.

There were a boy and two little girls. They lived in a pleasant house, with a garden, and they had discreet servants, and felt themselves superior to anyone in the neighbourhood.

Although they lived in style, they felt always an anxiety in the house. There was never enough money. The mother had a small income, and the father had a small income, but not nearly enough for the social position which they had to keep up. The father went into town to some office. But though he had good prospects, these prospects never materialised. There was always the grinding sense of the shortage of money, though the style was always kept up.

At last the mother said: "I will see if *I* can't make something." But she did not know where to begin. She racked her brains, and tried this thing and the other, but could not find anything successful. The failure made deep lines come into her face. Her children were growing up, they would have to go to school. There must be more money, there must be more money. The father,

who was always very handsome and expensive in his tastes, seemed as if he never *would* be able to do anything worth doing. And the mother, who had a great belief in herself, did not succeed any better, and her tastes were just as expensive.

And so the house came to be haunted by the unspoken phrase: *There must be more money! There must be more money!* The children could hear it all the time, though nobody said it aloud. They heard it at Christmas, when the expensive and splendid toys filled the nursery. Behind the shining modern rocking-horse, behind the smart doll's house, a voice would start whispering: "There *must* be more money! There *must* be more money!" And the children would stop playing, to listen for a moment. They would look into each other's eyes, to see if they had all heard. And each one saw in the eyes of the other two that they too had heard. "There *must* be more money! There *must* be more money!"

It came whispering from the springs of the still-swaying rocking-horse, and even the horse, bending his wooden, champing head, heard it. The big doll, sitting so pink and smirking in her new pram,[2] could hear it quite plainly, and seemed to be smirking all the more self-consciously because of it. The foolish puppy, too, that took the place of the teddy bear, he was looking so extraordinarily foolish for no other reason but that he heard the secret whisper all over the house: "There *must* be more money!"

Yet nobody ever said it aloud. The whisper was everywhere, and therefore no one spoke it. Just as no one ever says: "We are breathing!" in spite of the fact that breath is coming and going all the time.

"Mother," said the boy Paul one day, "why don't we keep a car of our own? Why do we always use uncle's, or else a taxi?"

"Because we're the poor members of the family," said the mother.

"But why *are* we, mother?"

"Well—I suppose," she said slowly and bitterly, "it's because your father has no luck."

The boy was silent for some time.

---

1. *Bonny* means "good-looking; robust."

Reading Strategy Making Inferences About Characters *What effect might the mother's attitude have on her children?*

Big Idea Modernism *What does Lawrence criticize about middle-class life?*

---

2. A *pram* (short for *perambulator*) is a baby carriage.

Reading Strategy Making Inferences About Characters *Do the children really hear the secret whispers? Explain.*

"Is luck money, mother?" he asked, rather timidly.

"No, Paul. Not quite. It's what causes you to have money."

"Oh!" said Paul vaguely. "I thought when Uncle Oscar said *filthy lucker,* it meant money."

"*Filthy lucre*³ does mean money," said the mother. "But it's lucre, not luck."

"Oh!" said the boy. "Then what *is* luck, mother?"

"It's what causes you to have money. If you're lucky you have money. That's why it's better to be born lucky than rich. If you're rich, you may lose your money. But if you're lucky, you will always get more money."

"Oh! Will you? And is father not lucky?"

"Very unlucky, I should say," she said bitterly.

The boy watched her with unsure eyes.

"Why?" he asked.

"I don't know. Nobody ever knows why one person is lucky and another unlucky."

"Don't they? Nobody at all? Does *nobody* know?"

"Perhaps God. But He never tells."

"He ought to, then. And aren't you lucky either, mother?"

"I can't be, if I married an unlucky husband."

"But by yourself, aren't you?"

"I used to think I was, before I married. Now I think I am very unlucky indeed."

"Why?"

"Well—never mind! Perhaps I'm not really," she said.

The child looked at her to see if she meant it. But he saw, by the lines of her mouth, that she was only trying to hide something from him.

"Well, anyhow," he said stoutly, "I'm a lucky person."

"Why?" said his mother, with a sudden laugh.

He stared at her. He didn't even know why he had said it.

"God told me," he asserted, brazening⁴ it out.

"I hope He did, dear!" she said, again with a laugh, but rather bitter.

"He did, mother!"

"Excellent!" said the mother, using one of her husband's exclamations.

The boy saw she did not believe him; or rather, that she paid no attention to his assertion. This angered him somewhere, and made him want to compel her attention.

He went off by himself, vaguely, in a childish way, seeking for the clue to "luck." Absorbed, taking no heed of other people, he went about with a sort of stealth, seeking inwardly for luck. He wanted luck, he wanted it, he wanted it. When the two girls were playing dolls in the nursery, he would sit on his big rocking-horse, charging madly into space, with a frenzy that made the little girls peer at him uneasily. Wildly the horse careered,⁵ the waving dark hair of the boy tossed, his eyes had a strange glare in them. The little girls dared not speak to him.

When he had ridden to the end of his mad little journey, he climbed down and stood in front of his rocking-horse, staring fixedly into its lowered face. Its red mouth was slightly open, its big eye was wide and glassy-bright.

"Now!" he would silently command the snorting steed. "Now, take me to where there is luck! Now take me!"

And he would slash the horse on the neck with the little whip he had asked Uncle Oscar for. He *knew* the horse could take him to where there was luck, if only he forced it. So he would mount again and start on his furious ride, hoping at last to get there. He knew he could get there.

"You'll break your horse, Paul!" said the nurse.

"He's always riding like that! I wish he'd leave off!" said his elder sister Joan.

But he only glared down on them in silence. Nurse gave him up. She could make nothing of him. Anyhow, he was growing beyond her.

---

3. *Lucre* (lōō′ kər) is Latin for "profit." Here, it refers to money, especially that gained through greed or dishonesty.

Big Idea Modernism *What does Lawrence imply about the mother's values?*

Reading Strategy Making Inferences About Characters *How might the mother's answer influence Paul?*

Reading Strategy Making Inferences About Characters *What is Paul's mother trying to hide?*

---

4. Here, *brazening* means "stating confidently."
5. *Careered* means "rushed forward."

Literary Element Foreshadowing *What might Paul's frenzied riding foreshadow?*

One day his mother and his Uncle Oscar came in when he was on one of his furious rides. He did not speak to them.

"Hallo, you young jockey! Riding a winner?" said his uncle.

"Aren't you growing too big for a rocking-horse? You're not a very little boy any longer, you know," said his mother.

But Paul only gave a blue glare from his big, rather close-set eyes. He would speak to nobody when he was in full tilt. His mother watched him with an anxious expression on her face.

At last he suddenly stopped forcing his horse into the mechanical gallop and slid down.

"Well, I got there!" he announced fiercely, his blue eyes still flaring, and his sturdy long legs straddling apart.

"Where did you get to?" asked his mother.

"Where I wanted to go," he flared back at her.

"That's right, son!" said Uncle Oscar. "Don't you stop till you get there. What's the horse's name?"

"He doesn't have a name," said the boy.

"Gets on without all right?" asked the uncle.

"Well, he has different names. He was called Sansovino last week."

"Sansovino, eh? Won the Ascot. How did you know this name?"

"He always talks about horse-races with Bassett," said Joan.

The uncle was delighted to find that his small nephew was posted with all the racing news. Bassett, the young gardener, who had been wounded in the left foot in the war and had got his present job through Oscar Cresswell, whose batman[6] he had been, was a perfect blade of the "turf."[7] He lived in the racing events, and the small boy lived with him.

Oscar Cresswell got it all from Bassett.

"I only know the winner," said the boy.

"Master Paul comes and asks me, so I can't do more than tell him, sir," said Bassett, his face terribly serious, as if he were speaking of religious matters.

"And does he ever put anything on a horse he fancies?"

"Well—I don't want to give him away—he's a young sport, a fine sport, sir. Would you mind asking him himself? He sort of takes a pleasure in it, and perhaps he'd feel I was giving him away, sir, if you don't mind."

Bassett was serious as a church.

The uncle went back to his nephew and took him off for a ride in the car.

"Say, Paul, old man, do you ever put anything on a horse?" the uncle asked.

The boy watched the handsome man closely.

"Why, do you think I oughtn't to?" he **parried.**

"Not a bit of it! I thought perhaps you might give me a tip for the Lincoln."

The car sped on into the country, going down to Uncle Oscar's place in Hampshire.

"Honour bright?"[8] said the nephew.

"Honour bright, son!" said the uncle.

"Well, then, Daffodil."

"Daffodil! I doubt it, sonny. What about Mirza?"

"I only know the winner," said the boy. "That's Daffodil."

"Daffodil, eh?"

There was a pause. Daffodil was an obscure horse comparatively.

"Uncle!"

"Yes, son?"

"You won't let it go any further, will you? I promised Bassett."

---

6. A *batman* is a British army orderly, or personal attendant.

7. A *blade of the "turf"* is a horse-racing fan.

Reading Strategy Making Inferences About Characters *What are your first impressions of Uncle Oscar?*

---

8. *Honour bright* is an expression used to declare that one is speaking the truth (as in "on your honour").

Reading Strategy Making Inferences About Characters *What does this detail suggest about Bassett?*

Vocabulary

parry (par′ ē) *v.* to respond, as to a question or argument, by warding off or diverting

"Bassett be damned, old man! What's he got to do with it?"

"We're partners. We've been partners from the first. Uncle, he lent me my first five shillings,[9] which I lost. I promised him, honour bright, it was only between me and him; only you gave me that ten-shilling note I started winning with, so I thought you were lucky. You won't let it go any further, will you?"

The boy gazed at his uncle from those big, hot, blue eyes, set rather close together. The uncle stirred and laughed uneasily.

"Right you are, son! I'll keep your tip private. Daffodil, eh? How much are you putting on him?"

"All except twenty pounds,"[10] said the boy. "I keep that in reserve."

The uncle thought it a good joke.

"You keep twenty pounds in reserve, do you, you young romancer? What are you betting, then?"

"I'm betting three hundred," said the boy gravely. "But it's between you and me, Uncle Oscar! Honour bright?"

The uncle burst into a roar of laughter.

"It's between you and me all right, you young Nat Gould,"[11] he said, laughing. "But where's your three hundred?"

"Bassett keeps it for me. We're partners."

"You are, are you! And what is Bassett putting on Daffodil?"

"He won't go quite as high as I do, I expect. Perhaps he'll go a hundred and fifty."

"What, pennies?" laughed the uncle.

"Pounds," said the child, with a surprised look at his uncle. "Bassett keeps a bigger reserve than I do."

Between wonder and amusement Uncle Oscar was silent. He pursued the matter no further, but he determined to take his nephew with him to the Lincoln races.

"Now, son," he said, "I'm putting twenty on Mirza, and I'll put five on for you on any horse you fancy. What's your pick?"

"Daffodil, uncle."

"No, not the fiver on Daffodil!"

"I should if it was my own fiver," said the child.

"Good! Good! Right you are! A fiver for me and a fiver for you on Daffodil."

The child had never been to a race-meeting before, and his eyes were blue fire. He pursed his mouth tight and watched. A Frenchman just in front had put his money on Lancelot. Wild with excitement, he flayed his arms up and down, yelling *"Lancelot! Lancelot!"* in his French accent.

Daffodil came in first, Lancelot second, Mirza third. The child, flushed and with eyes blazing, was curiously serene. His uncle brought him four five-pound notes, four to one.

"What am I to do with these?" he cried, waving them before the boy's eyes.

"I suppose we'll talk to Bassett," said the boy. "I expect I have fifteen hundred now; and twenty in reserve; and this twenty."

His uncle studied him for some moments.

"Look here, son!" he said. "You're not serious about Bassett and that fifteen hundred, are you?"

"Yes, I am. But it's between you and me, uncle. Honour bright?"

"Honour bright all right, son! But I must talk to Bassett."

"If you'd like to be a partner, uncle, with Bassett and me, we could all be partners. Only, you'd have to promise, honour bright, uncle, not to let it go beyond us three. Bassett and I are lucky, and you must be lucky, because it was your ten shillings I started winning with. . . ."

Uncle Oscar took both Bassett and Paul into Richmond Park for an afternoon, and there they talked.

"It's like this, you see, sir," Bassett said. "Master Paul would get me talking about racing events, spinning yarns, you know, sir. And he was always keen on knowing if I'd made or if I'd

---

9. *Shillings* were British coins worth one twentieth of a pound.

10. *Pounds* are currency used in Britain. Twenty pounds in the mid-1920s would be worth about $1,000 today.

11. *Nat Gould* was a sports journalist who often wrote about horse racing.

Reading Strategy Making Inferences About Characters *Why does Paul reveal his prediction about the race to Uncle Oscar?*

Reading Strategy Making Inferences About Characters *Why does Paul feel so peaceful?*

Reading Strategy Making Inferences About Characters *Why does Paul not want Uncle Oscar to reveal the partnership?*

Horse Race #14. Robert McIntosh.

lost. It's about a year since, now, that I put five shillings on Blush of Dawn for him: and we lost. Then the luck turned, with that ten shillings he had from you: that we put on Singhalese. And since that time, it's been pretty steady, all things considering. What do you say, Master Paul?"

"We're all right when we're sure," said Paul. "It's when we're not quite sure that we go down."

"Oh, but we're careful then," said Bassett.

"But when are you *sure?*" smiled Uncle Oscar.

"It's Master Paul, sir," said Bassett in a secret, religious voice. "It's as if he had it from heaven. Like Daffodil, now, for the Lincoln. That was as sure as eggs."

"Did you put anything on Daffodil?" asked Oscar Cresswell.

"Yes, sir. I made my bit."

"And my nephew?"

Bassett was **obstinately** silent, looking at Paul.

"I made twelve hundred, didn't I, Bassett? I told uncle I was putting three hundred on Daffodil."

"That's right," said Bassett, nodding.

"But where's the money?" asked the uncle.

"I keep it safe locked up, sir. Master Paul he can have it any minute he likes to ask for it."

"What, fifteen hundred pounds?"

"And twenty! And *forty*, that is, with the twenty he made on the course."

"It's amazing!" said the uncle.

"If Master Paul offers you to be partners, sir, I would, if I were you: if you'll excuse me," said Bassett.

Vocabulary

obstinately (ob′ stə nit lē′) *adv.* in a manner not yielding to argument, persuasion, or reason; inflexibly

Oscar Cresswell thought about it.

"I'll see the money," he said.

They drove home again, and, sure enough, Bassett came round to the garden-house with fifteen hundred pounds in notes. The twenty pounds reserve was left with Joe Glee, in the Turf Commission deposit.

"You see, it's all right, uncle, when I'm *sure!* Then we go strong, for all we're worth. Don't we, Bassett?"

"We do that, Master Paul."

"And when are you sure?" said the uncle, laughing.

"Oh, well, sometimes I'm *absolutely* sure, like about Daffodil," said the boy; "and sometimes I have an idea; and sometimes I haven't even an idea, have I, Bassett? Then we're careful, because we mostly go down."

"You do, do you! And when you're sure, like about Daffodil, what makes you sure, sonny?"

"Oh, well, I don't know," said the boy uneasily. "I'm sure, you know, uncle; that's all."

"It's as if he had it from heaven, sir," Bassett **reiterated.**

"I should say so!" said the uncle.

But he became a partner. And when the Leger was coming on Paul was "sure" about Lively Spark, which was a quite inconsiderable horse. The boy insisted on putting a thousand on the horse, Bassett went for five hundred, and Oscar Cresswell two hundred. Lively Spark came in first, and the betting had been ten to one against him. Paul had made ten thousand.

"You see," he said, "I was absolutely sure of him."

Even Oscar Cresswell had cleared two thousand.

"Look here, son," he said, "this sort of thing makes me nervous."

"It needn't, uncle! Perhaps I shan't be sure again for a long time."

"But what are you going to do with your money?" asked the uncle.

"Of course," said the boy, "I started it for mother. She said she had no luck, because father

is unlucky, so I thought if I was lucky, it might stop whispering."

"What might stop whispering?"

"Our house. I *hate* our house for whispering."

"What does it whisper?"

"Why—why"—the boy fidgeted—"why, I don't know. But it's always short of money, you know, uncle."

"I know it, son, I know it."

"You know people send mother writs,[12] don't you, uncle?"

"I'm afraid I do," said the uncle.

"And then the house whispers, like people laughing at you behind your back. It's awful, that is! I thought if I was lucky——"

"You might stop it," added the uncle.

The boy watched him with big blue eyes, that had an uncanny cold fire in them, and he said never a word.

"Well, then!" said the uncle. "What are we doing?"

"I shouldn't like mother to know I was lucky," said the boy.

"Why not, son?"

"She'd stop me."

"I don't think she would."

"Oh!"—and the boy writhed in an odd way—"I *don't* want her to know, uncle."

"All right, son! We'll manage it without her knowing."

They managed it very easily. Paul, at the other's suggestion, handed over five thousand pounds to his uncle, who deposited it with the family lawyer, who was then to inform Paul's mother that a relative had put five thousand pounds into his hands, which sum was to be paid out a thousand pounds at a time, on the mother's birthday, for the next five years.

"So she'll have a birthday present of a thousand pounds for five successive years," said Uncle Oscar. "I hope it won't make it all the harder for her later."

Paul's mother had her birthday in November. The house had been "whispering" worse than

---

Reading Strategy Making Inferences About Characters *Why is Uncle Oscar nervous?*

Vocabulary

reiterate (rē it′ ə rāt′) *v.* to say or do again; to repeat

---

12. Here, *writs* are legal notices demanding payment for outstanding bills.

Big Idea Modernism *What does this whispering suggest about society's values?*

5 O'Clock Cowboy. P. J. Crook (b. 1945). Acrylic on wood, 43 x 53 cm. Private collection.

Viewing the Art: How would you describe the mood of this work? How does it compare with the mood of the story?

ever lately, and, even in spite of his luck, Paul could not bear up against it. He was very anxious to see the effect of the birthday letter, telling his mother about the thousand pounds.

When there were no visitors, Paul now took his meals with his parents, as he was beyond the nursery control. His mother went into town nearly every day. She had discovered that she had an odd knack of sketching furs and dress materials, so she worked secretly in the studio of a friend who was the chief "artist" for the leading drapers.[13] She drew the figures of ladies in furs and ladies in silk and sequins for the newspaper advertisements. This young woman artist earned several thousand pounds a year, but Paul's mother only made several hundreds, and she was again dissatisfied. She so wanted to be first in something, and she did not succeed, even in making sketches for drapery advertisements.

She was down to breakfast on the morning of her birthday. Paul watched her face as she read her letters. He knew the lawyer's letter. As his mother read it, her face hardened and became more expressionless. Then a cold, determined look came on her mouth. She hid the letter under a pile of others, and said not a word about it.

---

13. *Drapers* are dealers in cloth and other dry goods.

Horse Race #5. Robert McIntosh.

"Didn't you have anything nice in the post for your birthday, mother?" said Paul.

"Quite moderately nice," she said, her voice cold and absent.

She went away to town without saying more.

But in the afternoon Uncle Oscar appeared. He said Paul's mother had had a long interview with the lawyer, asking if the whole five thousand could not be advanced at once, as she was in debt.

"What do you think, uncle?" said the boy.

"I leave it to you, son."

"Oh, let her have it, then! We can get some more with the other," said the boy.

Reading Strategy Making Inferences About Characters *What reaction from his mother was Paul hoping for?*

"A bird in the hand is worth two in the bush, laddie!" said Uncle Oscar.

"But I'm sure to *know* for the Grand National; or the Lincolnshire; or else the Derby. I'm sure to know for *one* of them," said Paul.

So Uncle Oscar signed the agreement, and Paul's mother touched the whole five thousand. Then something very curious happened. The voices in the house suddenly went mad, like a chorus of frogs on a spring evening. There were certain new furnishings, and Paul had a tutor. He was *really* going to Eton,[14] his father's school, in the following autumn. There were flowers in the winter, and a blossoming of the luxury Paul's mother had been used to. And yet the voices in the house, behind the sprays of mimosa and almond-blossom, and from under

14. *Eton* is a prestigious private school in England.

the piles of iridescent cushions, simply trilled and screamed in a sort of ecstasy: "There *must* be more money! Oh-h-h; there *must* be more money. Oh, now, now-w! Now-w-w—there *must* be more money!—more than ever! More than ever!"

It frightened Paul terribly. He studied away at his Latin and Greek with his tutor. But his intense hours were spent with Bassett. The Grand National had gone by: he had not "known," and had lost a hundred pounds. Summer was at hand. He was in agony for the Lincoln. But even for the Lincoln he didn't "know," and he lost fifty pounds. He became wild-eyed and strange, as if something were going to explode in him.

"Let it alone, son! Don't you bother about it!" urged Uncle Oscar. But it was as if the boy couldn't really hear what his uncle was saying.

"I've got to know for the Derby! I've got to know for the Derby!" the child reiterated, his big blue eyes blazing with a sort of madness.

His mother noticed how overwrought he was.

"You'd better go to the seaside. Wouldn't you like to go now to the seaside, instead of waiting? I think you'd better," she said, looking down at him anxiously, her heart curiously heavy because of him.

But the child lifted his uncanny blue eyes.

"I couldn't possibly go before the Derby, mother!" he said. "I couldn't possibly!"

"Why not?" she said, her voice becoming heavy when she was opposed. "Why not? You can still go from the seaside to see the Derby with your Uncle Oscar, if that's what you wish. No need for you to wait here. Besides, I think you care too much about these races. It's a bad sign. My family has been a gambling family, and you won't know till you grow up how much damage it has done. But it has done damage. I shall have to send Bassett away, and ask Uncle Oscar not to talk racing to you, unless you promise to be reasonable about it: go away to the seaside and forget it. You're all nerves!"

"I'll do what you like, mother, so long as you don't send me away till after the Derby," the boy said.

"Send you away from where? Just from this house?"

"Yes," he said, gazing at her.

"Why, you curious child, what makes you care about this house so much, suddenly? I never knew you loved it."

He gazed at her without speaking. He had a secret within a secret, something he had not divulged, even to Bassett or to his Uncle Oscar.

But his mother, after standing undecided and a little bit sullen for some moments, said:

"Very well, then! Don't go to the seaside till after the Derby, if you don't wish it. But promise me you won't let your nerves go to pieces. Promise you won't think so much about horse-racing and *events*, as you call them!"

"Oh no," said the boy casually. "I won't think much about them, mother. You needn't worry. I wouldn't worry, mother, if I were you."

"If you were me and I were you," said his mother, "I wonder what we *should* do!"

"But you know you needn't worry, mother, don't you?" the boy repeated.

"I should be awfully glad to know it," she said wearily.

"Oh, well, you *can*, you know. I mean, you *ought* to know you needn't worry," he insisted.

"Ought I? Then I'll see about it," she said.

Paul's secret of secrets was his wooden horse, that which had no name. Since he was **emancipated** from a nurse and a nursery-governess, he had had his rocking-horse removed to his own bedroom at the top of the house.

"Surely you're too big for a rocking-horse!" his mother had remonstrated.[15]

"Well, you see, mother, till I can have a *real* horse, I like to have *some* sort of animal about," had been his quaint answer.

---

15. *Remonstrated* means "objected."

Reading Strategy Making Inferences About Characters *What does this passage reveal about the mother's insights into her son?*

Vocabulary

emancipate (i man′ sə pāt′) *v.* to free; to liberate

Literary Element Foreshadowing *What mood does this detail create? What might this mood foreshadow?*

Reading Strategy Making Inferences About Characters *What can you conclude about Paul's mother?*

"Do you feel he keeps you company?" she laughed.

"Oh yes! He's very good, he always keeps me company, when I'm there," said Paul.

So the horse, rather shabby, stood in an arrested prance in the boy's bedroom.

The Derby was drawing near, and the boy grew more and more tense. He hardly heard what was spoken to him, he was very frail, and his eyes were really uncanny. His mother had sudden strange seizures of uneasiness about him. Sometimes, for half an hour, she would feel a sudden anxiety about him that was almost anguish. She wanted to rush to him at once, and know he was safe.

Two nights before the Derby, she was at a big party in town, when one of her rushes of anxiety about her boy, her first-born, gripped her heart till she could hardly speak. She fought with the feeling, might and main, for she believed in common sense. But it was too strong. She had to leave the dance and go downstairs to telephone to the country. The children's nursery-governess was terribly surprised and startled at being rung up in the night.

"Are the children all right, Miss Wilmot?"

"Oh yes, they are quite all right."

"Master Paul? Is he all right?"

"He went to bed as right as a trivet. Shall I run up and look at him?"

"No," said Paul's mother reluctantly. "No! Don't trouble. It's all right. Don't sit up. We shall be home fairly soon." She did not want her son's privacy intruded upon.

"Very good," said the governess.

It was about one o'clock when Paul's mother and father drove up to their house. All was still. Paul's mother went to her room and slipped off her white fur cloak. She had told her maid not to wait up for her. She heard her husband downstairs, mixing a whisky and soda.

And then, because of the strange anxiety at her heart, she stole upstairs to her son's room. Noiselessly she went along the upper corridor. Was there a faint noise? What was it?

She stood, with arrested muscles, outside his door, listening. There was a strange, heavy, and

yet not loud noise. Her heart stood still. It was a soundless noise, yet rushing and powerful. Something huge, in violent, hushed motion. What was it? What in God's name was it? She ought to know. She felt that she knew the noise. She knew what it was.

Yet she could not place it. She couldn't say what it was. And on and on it went, like a madness.

Softly, frozen with anxiety and fear, she turned the door handle.

The room was dark. Yet in the space near the window, she heard and saw something plunging to and fro. She gazed in fear and amazement.

Then suddenly she switched on the light, and saw her son, in his green pyjamas, madly surging on the rocking-horse. The blaze of light suddenly lit him up, as he urged the wooden horse, and lit her up, as she stood, blonde, in her dress of pale green and crystal, in the doorway.

"Paul!" she cried. "Whatever are you doing?"

"It's Malabar!" he screamed in a powerful, strange voice. "It's Malabar!"

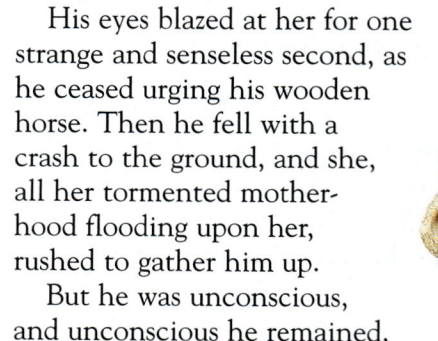

His eyes blazed at her for one strange and senseless second, as he ceased urging his wooden horse. Then he fell with a crash to the ground, and she, all her tormented motherhood flooding upon her, rushed to gather him up.

But he was unconscious, and unconscious he remained, with some brain-fever. He talked and tossed, and his mother sat stonily by his side.

"Malabar! It's Malabar! Bassett, Bassett, I *know*! It's Malabar!"

Literary Element   Foreshadowing *What might this description foreshadow?*

Literary Element   Foreshadowing *What feelings does this description evoke? What does it suggest might happen?*

So the child cried, trying to get up and urge the rocking-horse that gave him his inspiration.

"What does he mean by Malabar?" asked the heart-frozen mother.

"I don't know," said the father stonily.

"What does he mean by Malabar?" she asked her brother Oscar.

"It's one of the horses running for the Derby," was the answer.

And, in spite of himself, Oscar Cresswell spoke to Bassett, and himself put a thousand on Malabar: at fourteen to one.

The third day of the illness was critical: they were waiting for a change. The boy, with his rather long, curly hair, was tossing ceaselessly on the pillow. He neither slept nor regained consciousness, and his eyes were like blue stones. His mother sat, feeling her heart had gone, turned actually into a stone.

In the evening, Oscar Cresswell did not come, but Bassett sent a message, saying could he come up for one moment, just one moment? Paul's mother was very angry at the intrusion, but on second thoughts she agreed. The boy was the same. Perhaps Bassett might bring him to consciousness.

The gardener, a shortish fellow with a little brown moustache and sharp little brown eyes, tiptoed into the room, touched his imaginary cap to Paul's mother, and stole to the bedside, staring with glittering, smallish eyes at the tossing, dying child.

"Master Paul!" he whispered. "Master Paul! Malabar came in first all right, a clean win. I did as you told me. You've made over seventy thousand pounds, you have; you've got over eighty thousand. Malabar came in all right, Master Paul."

"Malabar! Malabar! Did I say Malabar, mother? Did I say Malabar? Do you think I'm lucky, mother? I knew Malabar, didn't I? Over eighty thousand pounds! I call that lucky, don't you, mother? Over eighty thousand pounds! I knew, didn't I know I knew? Malabar came in all right. If I ride my horse till I'm sure, then I tell you, Bassett, you can go as high as you like. Did you go for all you were worth, Bassett?"

"I went a thousand on it, Master Paul."

"I never told you, mother, that if I can ride my horse, and *get there*, then I'm absolutely sure—oh, absolutely! Mother, did I ever tell you? I *am* lucky!"

"No, you never did," said his mother.

But the boy died in the night.

And even as he lay dead, his mother heard her brother's voice saying to her: "My God, Hester, you're eighty-odd thousand to the good, and a poor devil of a son to the bad. But, poor devil, poor devil, he's best gone out of a life where he rides his rocking-horse to find a winner."

"It's Malabar! Bassett . . . I know!"

Reading Strategy Making Inferences About Characters *Why does the mother believe that Bassett might be able to help Paul?*

Big Idea Modernism *What does this passage suggest about love and money in modern society?*

RESPONDING AND THINKING CRITICALLY

Respond

1. What went through your mind at the end of the story?

Recall and Interpret

2. (a)How does the mother feel about her children at the beginning of the story? (b)Do you think her feelings for Paul change over the course of the story? Explain.

3. (a)What does the house whisper? (b)Why might only the children hear what the house is whispering?

4. (a)How does Paul use the rocking horse to gain luck? (b)What might the rocking horse **symbolize** to Paul?

5. (a)How does Paul arrange to give his mother his winnings? (b)What does Paul's mother's reaction to the gift of money reveal about her?

Analyze and Evaluate

6. In your opinion, should anyone be held responsible for what happens to Paul? Explain.

7. This story is written almost like a fairy tale. Do you find this **style** effective? Why or why not?

8. This story has an **omniscient**, or all-knowing, narrator. How might the story change if it were told from the point of view of Paul or his mother?

Connect

9. **Big Idea** Modernism What effect does society's emphasis on money have on the characters in this story?

LITERARY ANALYSIS

Literary Element Foreshadowing

Foreshadowing often helps to build suspense or interest in a story. It makes readers predict what will happen and encourages them to keep reading to see if their predictions prove to be correct.

1. Cite several examples of foreshadowing from the story. What later events do these examples predict?

2. What events does the title of the story foreshadow?

Review: Motivation

As you learned on page 1046, **motivation** refers to a character's reason for acting, thinking, or feeling in a certain way. A character's motivation may be stated directly or only implied.

Partner Activity Meet with a partner to discuss what the following passage reveals about Paul's motivation. Then answer the questions.

"Well, anyhow," he said stoutly, "I'm a lucky person."

"Why?" said his mother, with a sudden laugh.

He stared at her. He didn't even know why he had said it.

"God told me," he asserted, brazening it out.

"I hope He did, dear!" she said, again with a laugh, but rather bitter.

1. What is Paul's motivation for seeking luck?

2. What prompts Paul to claim that God told him he was lucky?

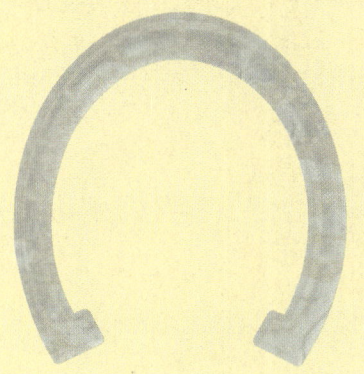

READING AND VOCABULARY

Reading Strategy Making Inferences About Characters

Making inferences about the characters in a story can help you understand their actions and discover the author's theme, or message about life.

1. What can you infer about Paul and the other children from their reactions to the whispering house?

2. What is the theme of this story? Which character's statement from the story sums up the theme? Explain.

Vocabulary Practice

Practice with Analogies Choose the word that best completes each analogy.

1. emancipate : enslave :: admire :
   a. detest
   c. worship
   b. love
   d. esteem

2. parry : confront :: tow :
   a. suspend
   c. push
   b. pull
   d. bury

3. reiterate : repeat :: examine :
   a. negate
   c. overlook
   b. inspect
   d. ignore

4. obstinately : inflexibly :: courageously :
   a. valiantly
   c. timidly
   b. indignantly
   d. lethargically

Academic Vocabulary

Here are two words from the vocabulary list on page R82. These words will help you think, write, and talk about the selection.

distort (dis tôrt′) *v.* to alter the natural meaning or shape of an object or idea

sum (sum) *n.* an amount of money

Practice and Apply

1. How does Paul's mother **distort** the definition of *luck*?

2. What **sum** do you think would have satisfied Paul's mother?

WRITING AND EXTENDING

Writing About Literature

Analyze Character Characterization can be direct or indirect. With direct characterization, the author states facts about a character's personality; with indirect characterization, the author reveals a character's personality by providing details about the character's appearance, words, thoughts, and actions or by telling what other characters say about that character. Write a character sketch that describes the traits that Paul or his mother exhibit in the story. First, fill in a web like the one below to help you take notes on your character.

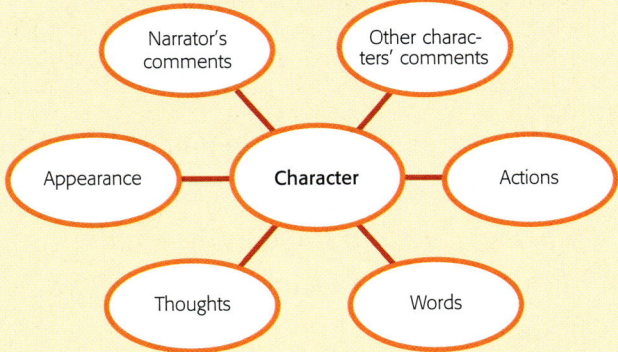

After you complete your draft, meet with a peer reviewer to evaluate each other's work and to suggest revisions. Then proofread and edit your draft for errors in spelling, grammar, and punctuation.

Literature Groups

Both Bassett and Uncle Oscar know about Paul's betting and help him to place his bets. Is it irresponsible of them to let Paul continue even after he becomes upset about not winning? Discuss this question in a small group, keeping in mind that both adults profit from Paul's "luck." Also think about Bassett's description of Paul's gift and Uncle Oscar's initial hesitations. Why might they keep their actions secret from Paul's mother? Discuss both sides of the argument, citing details from the selection. Share your ideas with other groups.

Literature Online **Web Activities** For eFlashcards, Selection Quick Checks, and other Web activities, go to www.glencoe.com.

Araby

MEET JAMES JOYCE

Although James Joyce was born and grew up in Dublin, Ireland, and set all of his work there, he found the voice to write about the city only in exile. Leaving Dublin (the city Joyce termed "the center of paralysis") allowed him the distance to imaginatively re-create the city in his fiction.

> *"Welcome, O life! I go to encounter for the millionth time the reality of experience and to forge in the smithy of my soul the uncreated conscience of my race."*
>
> —James Joyce

Early Exile The oldest of ten children, Joyce was born into an affluent Catholic family that sank into poverty due to his father's heavy drinking and irresponsibility. However, Joyce did have happy memories of his father, especially from the time they lived on North Richmond Street—the setting of "Araby." Joyce's father often walked the streets of Dublin with young James, telling stories about the people who lived there.

Although Joyce received most of his education in Catholic schools, he later rebelled against Catholicism and what he felt was the stifling environment of Dublin. After graduating from Dublin's University College in 1902, Joyce left Dublin for Paris to seek freedom from narrow religious and social conventions. When his mother contracted a fatal illness, he returned to Ireland and began working on the stories that would become *Dubliners*. In 1904 he met and fell in love with Nora Barnacle, an uneducated but witty and intelligent working-class girl whom he persuaded to leave Ireland with him for good. She became his lifelong companion.

A Struggling Genius Moving throughout Europe, Joyce spent most of his time in Trieste, Paris, Zurich, and Rome, teaching languages and writing in his spare time. Although he was convinced of his own genius, Joyce's frankness and his experiments with form made it difficult for him to get his writing published. When his work did get published, it was often considered scandalous and was banned by censors. As a result, Joyce earned very little income from his writing until his later years. In addition to publishing difficulties and poverty, he suffered from severe eye diseases and endured over twenty operations—some of which left him temporarily blind.

By the end of his life, Joyce was recognized as one of the most innovative and influential writers of the twentieth century. He experimented with language, plot, and characterization, focusing on the inner reality of his characters through the literary technique known as stream of consciousness. He gained acclaim for his autobiographical novel *A Portrait of the Artist as a Young Man*, as well as for his finely crafted stories in *Dubliners*. A perfectionist who was devoted to his art, Joyce spent seven years writing his masterpiece, *Ulysses*. Joyce's fiction represents Dublin as a microcosm for all human experience.

James Joyce was born in 1882 and died in 1941.

Literature Online **Author Search** For more about James Joyce, go to www.glencoe.com.

Connecting to the Story

In "Araby," a young boy embarks on a quest and comes to a startling realization. Have you ever looked forward to an important event that turned out differently from what you expected? Think about the following questions:

- How did the actual event compare with your expectations?
- How might anticipation of the event diminish its significance when the event finally occurs?

Building Background

Realistic and gritty, the content of *Dubliners* discouraged potential publishers and printers. After myriad rejections and more than nine years after original negotiations began, a London firm finally agreed to print the book. During printing, however, parts of the manuscript were lost, and more than two hundred of Joyce's corrections were never made.

Setting Purposes for Reading

Big Idea Modernism

As you read "Araby," notice how Joyce derives meaning from both traditional and innovative literary movements and techniques.

Literary Element Epiphany

An **epiphany** is a moment of sudden realization of the true meaning of a situation, person, or object. Joyce was an innovator in the use of this technique and suggested that these glimpses offered a kind of revelation into a character. With an epiphany, a character has an intuitive moment in which a simple or commonplace thing is seen in a new light that triggers a deeper insight into the world or the inner life of the character. As you read the story, look for the narrator's epiphany.

- See Literary Terms Handbook, p. R6.

Literature Online Interactive Literary Elements Handbook To review or learn more about the literary elements, go to www.glencoe.com.

Reading Strategy Making and Verifying Predictions

When you **make predictions,** you make educated guesses about what will happen later in a selection. You then **verify predictions** by looking for textual evidence that confirms their accuracy. As you read, make predictions about later events and the outcome of "Araby" and verify the accuracy of your predictions.

Reading Tip: Taking Notes Use a chart like the one below to make and verify predictions as you read.

Prediction	Evidence for Prediction	Verification

Vocabulary

imperturbable (im′ pər tur′ bə bəl) *adj.* not easily excited or disturbed; calm; p. 1141 *The guard was imperturbable despite the boys' attempts to goad him to anger.*

diverge (dī vurj′) *v.* to move in different directions from a common point; to branch out; p. 1141 *When the detective asked about the thief's identity, the witnesses' stories diverged.*

converge (kən vurj′) *v.* to come together in a common interest or conclusion; to center; p. 1142 *Revelers converge on Times Square every New Year's Eve.*

impinge (im pinj′) *v.* to strike or dash; to collide; p. 1142 *He felt the blast of the bass impinge on his eardrums.*

amiability (ā′ mē ə bil′ ə tē) *n.* kindliness; friendliness; p. 1142 *Mrs. Lorca's amiability made her popular in the neighborhood.*

Vocabulary Tip: Antonyms Antonyms are words that have opposite or nearly opposite meanings.

OBJECTIVES
In studying this selection, you will focus on the following:
- analyzing literary periods
- analyzing epiphany and symbol
- making and verifying predictions

Araby

James Joyce

A Glasgow Close. Joan Eardley (1921–1963). Oil on canvas, 24 x 20 in.
Hunterian Art Gallery, University of Glasgow, Scotland.

North Richmond Street, being blind,[1] was a quiet street except at the hour when the Christian Brothers' School set the boys free. An uninhabited house of two stories stood at the blind end, detached from its neighbors in a square ground. The other houses of the street, conscious of decent lives within them, gazed at one another with brown **imperturbable** faces. The former tenant of our house, a priest, had died in the back drawing room. Air, musty from having been long enclosed, hung in all the rooms, and the waste room behind the kitchen was littered with old useless papers. Among these I found a few paper-covered books, the pages of which were curled and damp: *The Abbot*, by Walter Scott, *The Devout Communicant* and *The Memoirs of Vidocq*.[2] I liked the last best because its leaves were yellow. The wild garden behind the house contained a central apple tree and a few straggling bushes under one of which I found the late tenant's rusty bicycle pump. He had been a very charitable priest; in his will he had left all his money to institutions and the furniture of his house to his sister.

When the short days of winter came dusk fell before we had well eaten our dinners. When we met in the street the houses had grown somber. The space of sky above us was the color of ever-changing violet and towards it the lamps of the street lifted their feeble lanterns. The cold air stung us and we played till our bodies glowed. Our shouts echoed in the silent street. The career of our play brought us through the dark muddy lanes behind the houses where we ran the gantlet[3] of the rough tribes from the cottages, to the back doors of the dark dripping gardens where odors arose from the ashpits, to the dark odorous stables where a coachman smoothed and combed the horse or shook music from the buckled harness. When we returned to the street, light from the kitchen windows had filled the areas. If my uncle was seen turning the corner we hid in the shadow until we had seen him safely housed. Or if Mangan's sister came out on the doorstep to call her brother in to his tea we watched her from our shadow peer up and down the street. We waited to see whether she would remain or go in and, if she remained, we left our shadow and walked up to Mangan's steps resignedly. She was waiting for us, her figure defined by the light from the half-opened door. Her brother always teased her before he obeyed and I stood by the railings looking at her. Her dress swung as she moved her body and the soft rope of her hair tossed from side to side.

Every morning I lay on the floor in the front parlor watching her door. The blind was pulled down to within an inch of the sash so that I could not be seen. When she came out on the doorstep my heart leaped. I ran to the hall, seized my books and followed her. I kept her brown figure always in my eye and, when we came near the point at which our ways **diverged**, I quickened my pace and passed her. This happened morning after morning. I had never spoken to her, except for a few casual words, and yet her name was like a summons to all my foolish blood.

Her image accompanied me even in places the most hostile to romance. On Saturday evenings when my aunt went marketing I had to go to carry some of the parcels. We walked through the flaring streets, jostled by drunken men and bargaining women, amid the curses of laborers, the shrill litanies[4] of shopboys who stood on guard by the barrels of pigs' cheeks, the nasal chanting of street singers, who sang a *come-you-all* about

---

1. Here, *blind* means "dead-end."
2. *The Abbot* is a historical novel; *The Devout Communicant* is a religious manual; *The Memoirs of Vidocq* is the story of a French detective.
3. *Gantlet* [or *gauntlet*] refers to an outdated punishment in which the offender was made to run between two rows of men who struck at him with switches or weapons as he passed. Here, it means "a series of challenges."

Vocabulary

imperturbable (im′ pər tur′ bə bəl) *adj.* not easily excited or disturbed; calm

---

4. As it is used here, *litany* is a repetitive announcement to attract customers.

Reading Strategy Making and Verifying Predictions
Based on the narrator's description of Mangan's sister, what do you think his feelings for her are?

Vocabulary

diverge (dī vurj′) *v.* to move in different directions from a common point; to branch out

O'Donovan Rossa,[5] or a ballad about the troubles in our native land. These noises **converged** in a single sensation of life for me: I imagined that I bore my chalice safely through a throng of foes. Her name sprang to my lips at moments in strange prayers and praises which I myself did not understand. My eyes were often full of tears (I could not tell why) and at times a flood from my heart seemed to pour itself out into my bosom. I thought little of the future. I did not know whether I would ever speak to her or not or, if I spoke to her, how I could tell her of my confused adoration. But my body was like a harp and her words and gestures were like fingers running upon the wires.

One evening I went into the back drawing room in which the priest had died. It was a dark rainy evening and there was no sound in the house. Through one of the broken panes I heard the rain **impinge** upon the earth, the fine incessant needles of water playing in the sodden beds. Some distant lamp or lighted window gleamed below me. I was thankful that I could see so little. All my senses seemed to desire to veil themselves and, feeling that I was about to slip from them, I pressed the palms of my hands together until they trembled, murmuring: *O love! O love!* many times.

At last she spoke to me. When she addressed the first words to me I was so confused that I did not know what to answer. She asked me was I going to *Araby*.[6] I forget whether I answered yes or no. It would be a splendid bazaar, she said; she would love to go.

—And why can't you? I asked.

---

5. A *come-you-all* is a ballad; *O'Donovan Rossa* was a nineteenth-century Irish nationalist.
6. *Araby* was a bazaar held in 1894 in Dublin.

While she spoke she turned a silver bracelet round and round her wrist. She could not go, she said, because there would be a retreat[7] that week in her convent.[8] Her brother and two other boys were fighting for their caps and I was alone at the railings. She held one of the spikes, bowing her head towards me. The light from the lamp opposite our door caught the white curve of her neck, lit up her hair that rested there and, falling, lit up the hand upon the railing. It fell over one side of her dress and caught the white border of a petticoat, just visible as she stood at ease.

—It's well for you, she said.

—If I go, I said, I will bring you something.

What innumerable follies laid waste my waking and sleeping thoughts after that evening! I wished to annihilate the tedious intervening days. I chafed against the work of school. At night in my bedroom and by day in the classroom her image came between me and the page I strove to read. The syllables of the word *Araby* were called to me through the silence in which my soul luxuriated and cast an Eastern enchantment over me. I asked for leave to go to the bazaar on Saturday night. My aunt was surprised and hoped it was not some Freemason[9] affair. I answered few questions in class. I watched my master's face pass from **amiability** to sternness; he hoped I was not beginning to idle. I could not call my wandering thoughts together. I had hardly any patience with the serious work of life which, now that it stood between me and my desire, seemed to me child's play, ugly monotonous child's play.

On Saturday morning I reminded my uncle that I wished to go to the bazaar in the evening. He was fussing at the hall stand, looking for the hat brush, and answered me curtly:

—Yes, boy, I know.

As he was in the hall I could not go into the front parlor and lie at the window. I left the house in bad humor and walked slowly towards

---

7. A *retreat* is a group withdrawal for prayer and meditation.
8. Here, a *convent* is a school run by an order of Catholic nuns.
9. The *Freemasons* are part of a secret fraternity whose members are primarily Protestant.

A Meeting, 1884. Maria Bashkirtseff. Oil on canvas, 195 x 177 cm. Musée d'Orsay, Paris.

the school. The air was pitilessly raw and already my heart misgave me.

When I came home to dinner my uncle had not yet been home. Still it was early. I sat staring at the clock for some time and, when its ticking began to irritate me, I left the room. I mounted the staircase and gained the upper part of the house. The high cold empty gloomy rooms liberated me and I went from room to room singing. From the front window I saw my companions playing below in the street. Their cries reached me weakened and indistinct and, leaning my forehead against the cool glass, I looked over at the dark house where she lived. I may have stood there for an hour, seeing nothing but the brown-clad figure cast by my imagination, touched discreetly by the lamplight at the curved neck, at the hand upon the railings and at the border below the dress.

When I came downstairs again I found Mrs. Mercer sitting at the fire. She was an old garrulous woman, a pawnbroker's widow, who collected used stamps for some pious purpose. I had to endure the gossip of the tea table. The meal was prolonged beyond an hour and still my uncle did not come. Mrs. Mercer stood up to go: she was sorry she couldn't wait any longer, but it was after eight o'clock and she did not like to be out late, as the night air was bad for her. When she had gone I began to walk up and down the room, clenching my fists. My aunt said:

—I'm afraid you may put off your bazaar for this night of Our Lord.

At nine o'clock I heard my uncle's latchkey in the hall door. I heard him talking to himself and

Reading Strategy Making and Verifying Predictions
How does the aunt's statement undermine what Araby symbolizes for the narrator? What might her casual remark foreshadow for the rest of the story?

JAMES JOYCE   **1143**

La Gare, 1991. P. J. Crook. Acrylic on canvas and wood, 116.8 x 91.4 cm. Private collection.

Viewing the Art: How would you describe the atmosphere of this work? What scene does it remind you of in the story? Why?

heard the hall stand rocking when it had received the weight of his overcoat. I could interpret these signs. When he was midway through his dinner I asked him to give me the money to go to the bazaar. He had forgotten.

—The people are in bed and after their first sleep now, he said.

I did not smile. My aunt said to him energetically:

—Can't you give him the money and let him go? You've kept him late enough as it is.

My uncle said he was very sorry he had forgotten. He said he believed in the old saying: *All work and no play makes Jack a dull boy.* He asked me where I was going and, when I had told him a second time he asked me did I know *The Arab's Farewell to His Steed.*[10] When I left the kitchen he was about to recite the opening lines of the piece to my aunt.

I held a florin[11] tightly in my hand as I strode down Buckingham Street towards the station. The sight of the streets thronged with buyers and glaring with gas recalled to me the purpose of my journey. I took my seat in a third-class carriage of a deserted train. After an intolerable delay the train moved out of the station slowly. It crept onward among ruinous houses and over the twinkling river. At Westland Row Station a crowd of people pressed to the carriage doors; but the porters moved them back, saying that it was a special train for the bazaar. I remained alone in the bare carriage. In a few minutes the train drew up beside an improvised wooden platform. I passed out on to the road and saw by the lighted dial of a clock that it was ten minutes to ten. In front of me was a large building which displayed the magical name.

I could not find any sixpenny entrance and, fearing that the bazaar would be closed, I passed in quickly through a turnstile, handing a shilling to a weary-looking man. I found myself in a big hall girdled at half its height by a gallery. Nearly all the stalls were closed and the greater part of the hall was in darkness. I recognized a silence like that which pervades a church after a service. I walked into the center of the bazaar timidly. A few people were gathered about the stalls which were still open. Before a curtain, over which the words *Café Chantant*[12] were written in colored lamps, two men were counting money on a salver.[13] I listened to the fall of the coins.

Remembering with difficulty why I had come I went over to one of the stalls and examined porcelain vases and flowered tea sets. At the door of the stall a young lady was talking and laughing with two young gentlemen. I remarked their English accents and listened vaguely to their conversation.

—O, I never said such a thing!
—O, but you did!
—O, but I didn't!
—Didn't she say that?
—Yes. I heard her.
—O, there's a . . . fib!

Observing me the young lady came over and asked me did I wish to buy anything. The tone of her voice was not encouraging; she seemed to have spoken to me out of a sense of duty. I looked humbly at the great jars that stood like eastern guards at either side of the dark entrance to the stall and murmured:

—No, thank you.

The young lady changed the position of one of the vases and went back to the two young men. They began to talk of the same subject. Once or twice the young lady glanced at me over her shoulder.

I lingered before her stall, though I knew my stay was useless, to make my interest in her wares seem the more real. Then I turned away slowly and walked down the middle of the bazaar. I allowed the two pennies to fall against the sixpence in my pocket. I heard a voice call from one end of the gallery that the light was out. The upper part of the hall was now completely dark.

Gazing up into the darkness I saw myself as a creature driven and derided by vanity; and my eyes burned with anguish and anger. ❧

---

10. [*The . . . Steed*] is a sentimental poem by Caroline Norton.
11. A *florin* was a coin worth two shillings, which, at the time, equaled about fifty cents.

12. *Café Chantant* was a popular café that provided musical entertainment.
13. A *salver* is a tray commonly used to serve food and drinks.

Literary Element Epiphany *What is the boy's epiphany in the final passage of the story? How does the conversation between the "young lady" and the "two young gentlemen" help bring about the boy's epiphany?*

RESPONDING AND THINKING CRITICALLY

Respond

1. (a)What were your feelings toward the narrator at the end of the story? (b)Were you surprised by the outcome? Explain.

Recall and Interpret

2. (a)Describe the neighborhood in the opening scene of the story. (b)What does the **personification** of the houses in the first paragraph tell you about the people who live in the neighborhood?

3. (a)At what time of day does the narrator see Mangan's sister? When does he think of her? (b)How well does the narrator know her, and upon what do his feelings seem to be based?

4. (a)What causes the narrator to be delayed in going to the bazaar? (b)Based on the uncle's words and actions, what sort of relationship does he seem to have with his nephew?

Analyze and Evaluate

5. Explain at least two reasons why you think Araby becomes so important to the narrator. What might the bazaar represent to him?

6. (a)What do the narrator's illusions and disillusions tell you about his personality? (b)Why do you think the narrator buys nothing from the stall with the porcelain vases?

7. What broader message or theme might Joyce be revealing through the story?

Connect

8. **Big Idea** **Modernism** How does Joyce connect traditional symbols and images to the modern world in "Araby"?

LITERARY ANALYSIS

Literary Element **Epiphany**

Earlier writers had used and discussed the occurrence of a character's sudden revelation or recognition, referring to it as "the moment," but Joyce gave the term **epiphany** a spiritual dimension. The name derives from a Greek word denoting the manifestation of a deity. Joyce remarked that the "something" that triggers an epiphany is its "soul, its whatness [that] leaps to us from the vestment of its appearance." Note how the narrator's epiphany affords him a spiritual insight into himself and the world.

1. Where does the narrator's epiphany occur in the story and what events trigger the epiphany?

2. (a)What revelation does the epiphany offer the narrator about the world? (b)What spiritual revelation does the epiphany give the narrator about himself?

Review: Symbol

As you learned on page 1078, a **symbol** is any object, person, place, or experience that exists on a literal level but also represents something beyond itself, on a figurative level.

Partner Activity Meet with a partner to discuss the meaning of the religious symbols in the passage below. Then answer the questions that follow.

"I imagined that I bore my chalice safely through a throng of foes. Her name sprang to my lips at moments in strange prayers and praises which I myself did not understand. . . . I did not know whether I would ever speak to her or not or, if I spoke to her, how I could tell her of my confused adoration."

1. In Roman Catholic dogma, the chalice is the vessel that holds the consecrated wine transformed by the priest into the blood of Christ. In this passage, what does the chalice symbolize?

2. How does Mangan's sister function as a symbol in this passage?

Reading Strategy — Making and Verifying Predictions

As you read the story, you **made predictions** about what would happen. Look back at the chart you made for the Reading Tip on page 1139 and verify the accuracy of your predictions. Reread parts of the story that give clues to the ending that you may have missed during your first reading.

1. What clues throughout the story suggest that the narrator might be exaggerating the significance of his relationship with Mangan's sister?

2. How did the narrator form his initial concept of Araby as a place of mystery and delight?

3. How might the narrator's daily life have led him to create romantic fantasies about Mangan's sister and about Araby?

Vocabulary Practice

Practice with Antonyms Choose the best antonym for each vocabulary word below.

1. impinge   **a.** collide   **b.** separate

2. diverge   **a.** unite   **b.** divert

3. amiability   **a.** kindliness   **b.** animosity

4. imperturbable   **a.** calm   **b.** volatile

5. converge   **a.** intersect   **b.** divide

Academic Vocabulary

Here is a word from the vocabulary list on page R82.

whereby (hwār bī′) *adv.* by, through, or in accordance with

Practice and Apply
What were the circumstances **whereby** the narrator achieved his epiphany?

Writing About Literature

Analyze Imagery The literary critic Edmund Wilson compared what happens in Joyce's fiction to what goes on in the mind just before sleep: "Images or words in the conscious mind take on an ominous significance . . . incidents swell with meaning." Choose an image pattern that occurs throughout "Araby" and analyze how the significance of the imagery "swells" or changes as the story progresses. For example, think about the interplay between light and dark imagery, the role of religious imagery, or the function of the exotic imagery used to describe Araby. Write a brief essay in which you cite examples of the image pattern you have chosen from the beginning, middle, and end of the story. Show how the pattern increases in significance as the story progresses toward the narrator's epiphany at the climax of the story. As you draft your essay, use the following model.

Introduction — Give necessary background. In your one- or two-sentence thesis, describe the image pattern you will analyze and how its significance increases as the story progresses.

Body Paragraph(s) — Cite examples from the text. Explain how the examples support your thesis.

Conclusion — Sum up your main points. Explain how the increasing significance of the imagery relates to the narrator's epiphany and theme of the story.

After you complete your draft, meet with a peer reviewer to evaluate each other's work and to suggest revisions. Then proofread and edit your essay for errors in spelling, grammar, and punctuation.

Literary Criticism

Critics Cleanth Brooks Jr. and Robert Penn Warren assert that the narrator of "Araby" continues to be troubled as an adult by the disparity between the real and the ideal that he recognized as a boy in the story; otherwise, his experience at the bazaar would no longer matter to him. With a partner, share your opinion of this interpretation. Support your opinion with evidence from the story.

Vocabulary Workshop

Word Parts

▶ **Vocabulary Terms**
An **etymology** is a word's origin. You can find the origins of most words in a dictionary.

▶ **Test-Taking Tip**
When faced with an unfamiliar word in a reading passage, break it into its parts. Then think of familiar words that include those parts.

▶ **Reading Handbook**
For more about word parts and word origins, see Reading Handbook, p. R20.

eFlashcards For eFlashcards and other vocabulary activities, go to www.glencoe.com.

OBJECTIVES
• Use word parts to help you understand math and science terms.
• Verify word meanings by using a dictionary.

Understanding Unfamiliar Math and Science Terms

"I held a florin tightly in my hand as I strode down Buckingham Street towards the station."

—James Joyce, from "Araby"

Connecting to Literature The word *florin* in the quotation above comes from the Latin *flor-* meaning "flower." The coin was originally made in Florence and was stamped with the image of a lily. The common English words *flour*, *flourish*, and *Florida* also come from this Latin root.

Examples

You can figure out the meaning of many math and science terms if you know some common word parts. Study the word parts and their definitions in the chart below.

Roots		Suffixes	
astr/o	star	*-crat*	ruler
auto	self	*-escence*	becoming
flor	flower	*-grapher*	writer
ge/o	earth	*-nomy*	laws/knowledge
tele	distant	*-metry*	measure

Exercise

Answer the following questions by combining a word part from each column above. Consult a dictionary to check your answers.

1. What word describes a branch of mathematics that deals with lines, angles, and solids?
2. What word means "blossoming"?
3. What do you call someone who sends long-distance messages?
4. What word describes the scientific study of the objects in outer space?
5. What word describes a ruler with unlimited power?

Woolf's Works

MEET VIRGINIA WOOLF

As a child, Virginia Woolf was tutored by one of the most prominent intellectuals and literary critics in England—her father, Sir Leslie Stephen. Following in his footsteps, Woolf began her career as an essayist and critic. She went on, however, to write some of the most untraditional and influential novels of the early twentieth century. Her work was a deliberate attempt to break the conventions of fiction, and she challenged the way traditional novels presented the flow of time and individual experience. She saw life not as a neatly arranged series of events but as a process we live every day. To be faithful to this idea, Woolf's fiction avoids plot as we know it and instead swirls through the consciousness of characters, revealing the essence of their lives.

> *"A woman must have money and a room of her own if she is to write fiction."*
>
> —Virginia Woolf, "A Room of One's Own"

Bloomsbury Virginia Woolf, born Adeline Virginia Stephen, was the next to youngest in a family of four children. At the age of thirteen, her mother died, a loss that plunged Woolf into a deep depression. Woolf periodically suffered serious mental breakdowns for the rest of her life. After the death of her father, when she was in her early twenties, Woolf, her brother, and her two sisters moved to the Bloomsbury district of London. Soon Woolf had made her mark as an essayist and critic for the *Times Literary Supplement*. The home of Woolf and her sister Vanessa, a painter, quickly became a center of English intellectual activity and a salon that attracted eminent authors and thinkers, such as E. M. Forster, George Bernard Shaw, and economist John Maynard Keynes.

This loose collection of artists and thinkers, dubbed the Bloomsbury Group, shared a passion for the arts and an intense dislike of the restrictions of Victorian England.

The Hogarth Press The outbreak of World War I caused Woolf's depression to recur, despite her progression as a writer and the publication of her first novel, *The Voyage Out* (1915). Hoping a new artistic outlet would restore her health, she and her husband, essayist and journalist Leonard Woolf, set up a printing press in the basement of Hogarth House, their home. From this humble beginning grew one of the most important publishing ventures of the day—Hogarth Press. The press became a leading force in the popularization of modern, experimental literature and philosophy, publishing the writing of such important literary figures as Katherine Mansfield and T. S. Eliot and such influential thinkers as Sigmund Freud. Hogarth Press also published Woolf's own novels, including *Mrs. Dalloway* and *To the Lighthouse*, two of her most popular, respected, and experimental works.

When Woolf was in her late fifties, she lost her last battle with mental illness. In 1941 she drowned herself in the river near her home in Sussex. Yet, her legacy lies in her innovative style as well as her passion for women's equality.

Virginia Woolf was born in 1882 and died in 1941.

Literature Online **Author Search** For more about Virginia Woolf, go to www.glencoe.com.

Connecting to the Essay

In this excerpt from "A Room of One's Own," Woolf describes the negative effects of traditional roles on women's lives. As you read, think about the following questions:

- How have the roles of women changed since Woolf's time?
- How do you think society views the "ideal woman"? What qualities is she expected to possess?

Building Background

Woolf wrote the essay "A Room of One's Own" during a time in which England's woman suffrage movement had won substantial victories. In 1918 the English government extended the right to vote to all British female citizens over the age of thirty. In 1928, a year before "A Room of One's Own" was published, the voting age for women was lowered to twenty-one. Woolf was an active supporter of the suffrage movement and other women's rights movements of the time even though many of the intellectuals she associated with scorned the agitation for increased women's rights. "A Room of One's Own" is based on "Women and Fiction," a series of lectures she delivered at Newnham and Girton colleges, Cambridge. In these lectures, she discussed the educational, social, and financial disadvantages that she believed had prevented women of the past from becoming successful writers.

Setting Purposes for Reading

Big Idea Modernism

Modernism represented a break with both literary and social traditions. As you read, examine how Woolf's essay reflects these changes.

Literary Element Argument

Argument is a type of persuasive writing in which logic or reason is used to try to influence a reader's ideas or actions. As you read Woolf's essay, examine how she constructs her argument about the obstacles faced by women writers.

- See Literary Terms Handbook, p. R2.

Reading Strategy Analyzing Tone

When you **analyze tone,** you think critically about how the writer's attitude toward a subject is conveyed through such elements as diction, sentence structure, imagery, and figures of speech.

Reading Tip: Interpreting Tone As you read, pause from time to time to consider Woolf's attitude toward the idea that women are inherently incapable of creating great art.

Vocabulary

guffaw (gu fô′) v. to laugh loudly and boisterously; p. 1153 *He guffawed at Marvin's ridiculous suggestion.*

thwart (thwôrt) v. to prevent from doing or achieving something; p. 1154 *The criminal was able to thwart detectives for several years.*

hinder (hin′ dər) v. to make difficult the progress of; to hold back; p. 1154 *If the drought continues, it will hinder the growth of corn.*

dilemma (di lem′ ə) n. a situation requiring a choice between equally undesirable alternatives; p. 1154 *When I was admitted to only the colleges I least wanted to attend, I faced the dilemma of choosing which offer to accept.*

morbid (môr′ bid) adj. overly sensitive to death and decay; not cheerful or wholesome; p. 1154 *People who suffer from depression are usually inclined toward morbid and unhappy thoughts.*

Vocabulary Tip: Word Origins Word origins include the history and development of a word.

Literature Online **Interactive Literary Elements Handbook** To review or learn more about the literary elements, go to www.glencoe.com.

OBJECTIVES
In studying this selection, you will focus on the following:
- understanding Modernism
- interpreting an author's argument
- analyzing tone

from *A Room of One's Own*

Virginia Woolf

The Music Room, 30 Strandgade, 1907. Vilhelm Hammershoi. Oil on canvas. Private collection.

Here am I asking why women did not write poetry in the Elizabethan age, and I am not sure how they were educated; whether they were taught to write; whether they had sitting-rooms to themselves; how many women had children before they were twenty-one; what, in short, they did from eight in the morning till eight at night. They had no money evidently; according to Professor Trevelyan[1] they were married whether they liked it or not before they were out of the nursery, at fifteen or sixteen very likely. It would have been extremely odd, even upon this

---

1. *Professor Trevelyan* was a British historian and author who often wrote about the history of England.

showing, had one of them suddenly written the plays of Shakespeare, I concluded, and I thought of that old gentleman, who is dead now, but was a bishop, I think, who declared that it was impossible for any woman, past, present, or to come, to have the genius of Shakespeare. He wrote to the papers about it. He also told a lady who applied to him for information that cats do not as a matter of fact go to heaven, though they have, he added, souls of a sort. How much thinking those old gentlemen used to save one! How the borders of ignorance shrank back at their approach! Cats do not go to heaven. Women cannot write the plays of Shakespeare.

Be that as it may, I could not help thinking, as I looked at the works of Shakespeare on the shelf, that the bishop was right at least in this; it would have been impossible, completely and entirely, for any woman to have written the plays of Shakespeare in the age of Shakespeare. Let me imagine, since facts are so hard to come by, what would have happened had Shakespeare had a wonderfully gifted sister, called Judith, let us say. Shakespeare himself went, very probably—his mother was an heiress—to the grammar school, where he may have learnt Latin—Ovid, Virgil, and Horace[2]—and the elements of grammar and logic. He was, it is well known, a wild boy who poached[3] rabbits, perhaps shot a deer, and had, rather sooner than he should have done, to marry a woman in the neighborhood, who bore him a child rather quicker than was right. That escapade[4] sent him to seek his fortune in London. He had, it seemed, a taste for the theater; he began by holding horses at the stage door. Very soon he got work in the theater, became a successful actor, and lived at the hub of the universe, meeting everybody, knowing everybody, practicing

his art on the boards,[5] exercising his wits[6] in the streets, and even getting access to the palace of the queen. Meanwhile his extraordinarily gifted sister, let us suppose, remained at home. She was as adventurous, as imaginative, as agog[7] to see the world as he was. But she was not sent to school. She had no chance of learning grammar and logic, let alone of reading Horace and Virgil. She picked up a book now and then, one of her brother's perhaps, and read a few pages. But then her parents came in and told her to mend the stockings or mind the stew and not moon[8] about with books and papers. They would have spoken sharply but kindly, for they were substantial people who knew the conditions of life for a woman and loved their daughter—indeed, more likely than not she was the apple of her father's eye. Perhaps she scribbled some pages up in an apple loft on the sly, but was careful to hide them or set fire to them. Soon, however, before she was out of her teens, she was to be betrothed[9] to the son of a neighboring wool stapler. She cried out that marriage was hateful to her, and for that she was severely beaten by her father. Then he ceased to scold her. He begged her instead not to hurt him, not to shame him in this matter of her marriage. He would give her a chain of beads or a fine petticoat, he said; and there were tears in his eyes. How could she disobey him? How could she break his heart? The force of her own gift alone drove her to it. She made up a small parcel of her belongings, let herself down by a rope one summer's night and took the road to London. She was not seventeen. The birds that sang in the hedge were not more musical than she was. She had the quickest fancy, a gift like her brother's, for the tune of words. Like him, she had a taste

---

2. *Ovid,* *Virgil,* and *Horace* were famous poets from ancient Rome who were commonly studied by students.
3. Here, *poached* means "hunted illegally."
4. An *escapade* is an unconventional adventure.

Reading Strategy Analyzing Tone *How would you characterize Woolf's tone in this passage?*

Literary Element Argument *Why does Woolf tell the story of the bishop? Why does she imagine that Shakespeare had a sister?*

---

5. Here, *on the boards* means "onstage."
6. As it is used here, *wits* means "intelligence."
7. *Agog* means "full of interest or anticipation."
8. Here, *moon* means "to wander or pass time aimlessly."
9. *Betrothed* means "engaged to be married."

Literary Element Argument *What contrast is Woolf drawing here?*

Reading Strategy Analyzing Tone *What is the tone of these questions? How do they demonstrate Woolf's attitude toward her subject?*

A Maid with a Pail in the Backyard, c. 1660/61. Pieter de Hooch. Oil on canvas, 48.2 x 42.9 cm. Private collection.

for the theater. She stood at the stage door; she wanted to act, she said. Men laughed in her face. The manager—a fat, loose-lipped man—**guffawed.** He bellowed something about poodles dancing and women acting—no woman, he said, could possibly be an actress. He hinted—you can imagine what. She could get no training in her craft. Could she even seek her dinner in a tavern or roam the streets at midnight? Yet her genius was for fiction and lusted to feed abundantly upon the lives of men and women and the study of their ways. At last—for she was very young, oddly like Shakespeare the poet in her face, with the same gray eyes and rounded brows—at last Nick Greene the actor-manager took pity on her; she found herself with child by that gentleman and so—who shall measure the heat and violence of the poet's heart when caught and tangled in a woman's body?—killed herself one winter's night and lies buried at some crossroads where the omnibuses[10] now stop outside the Elephant and Castle.

That, more or less, is how the story would run, I think, if a woman in Shakespeare's day had had Shakespeare's genius. But for my part, I agree with the deceased bishop, if such he was—it is unthinkable that any woman in Shakespeare's day should have had Shakespeare's genius. For genius like Shakespeare's is not born among laboring, uneducated, servile people. It was not born in England among the Saxons and the Britons. It is not born today among the working classes. How, then, could it have been born among women whose work began, according to Professor Trevelyan, almost before they were out of the nursery, who were forced to it by their parents and held to it by all the power of law and custom? Yet genius of a sort must have existed among women as it must have existed among the working classes. Now and again an Emily Brontë or a Robert Burns[11] blazes out and proves its presence. But certainly it never got itself on to

10. *Omnibuses* is another term for "buses."

11. *Brontë* overcame the obstacle of being a woman, and *Burns* overcame the obstacle of being from the working class; both became famous writers.

Big Idea **Modernism** *How does this statement represent a break with traditional beliefs?*

Interior with Sewing Woman, early 19th century. Ascribed to Fedor Petrovich Tolstoi. Oil on canvas, 42 x 46.8 cm. Tretjakov Gallery, Moscow.

paper. When, however, one reads of a witch being ducked, of a woman possessed by devils, of a wise woman selling herbs, or even of a very remarkable man who had a mother, then I think we are on the track of a lost novelist, a suppressed poet, of some mute and inglorious Jane Austen,[12] some Emily Brontë who dashed her brains out on the moor or mopped and mowed about the highways crazed with the torture that her gift had put her to. Indeed, I would venture to guess that Anon,[13] who wrote so many poems without signing them, was often a woman. It was a woman Edward FitzGerald,[14] I think, suggested who made the ballads and the folk songs, crooning them to her children, beguiling her spinning with them, or the length of the winter's night.

This may be true or it may be false—who can say?—but what is true in it, so it seemed to me, reviewing the story of Shakespeare's sister as I had made it, is that any woman born with a great gift in the sixteenth century would certainly have gone crazed, shot herself, or ended her days in some lonely cottage outside the village, half witch, half wizard, feared and mocked

at. For it needs little skill in psychology to be sure that a highly gifted girl who had tried to use her gift for poetry would have been so **thwarted** and **hindered** by other people, so tortured and pulled asunder by her own contrary instincts, that she must have lost her health and sanity to a certainty. No girl could have walked to London and stood at a stage door and forced her way into the presence of actor-managers without doing herself a violence and suffering an anguish which may have been irrational—for chastity[15] may be a fetish invented by certain societies for unknown reasons—but were none the less inevitable. Chastity had then, it has even now, a religious importance in a woman's life, and has so wrapped itself round with nerves and instincts that to cut it free and bring it to the light of day demands courage of the rarest. To have lived a free life in London in the sixteenth century would have meant for a woman who was poet and playwright a nervous stress and **dilemma** which might well have killed her. Had she survived, whatever she had written would have been twisted and deformed, issuing from a strained and **morbid** imagination. And undoubtedly, I thought, looking at the shelf where there are no plays by women, her work would have gone unsigned. ❧

---

15. *Chastity* is the quality or state of being morally pure.

Literary Element   **Argument** *How does Woolf's argument support this statement?*

Vocabulary

thwart (thwôrt) *v.* to prevent from doing or achieving something

hinder (hin′ dər) *v.* to make difficult the progress of; to hold back

dilemma (di lem′ ə) *n.* a situation requiring a choice between equally undesirable alternatives

morbid (môr′ bid) *adj.* overly sensitive to death and decay; not cheerful or wholesome

---

12. *[Some . . . Austen]* alludes to a line from Thomas Gray's "Elegy Written in a Country Churchyard," which reads, "Some mute inglorious Milton here may rest." (See page 710.)
13. *Anon* is the abbreviation for "Anonymous."
14. *Edward FitzGerald* was an English poet and translator.

RESPONDING AND THINKING CRITICALLY

Respond

1. What was your response to Woolf's argument?

Recall and Interpret

2. (a)How does Woolf feel about the bishop's comments about women? (b)Summarize and explain the extended **analogy** in the second paragraph that Woolf uses to support her view.

3. (a)In the third paragraph, who is "Anon"? (b)What point does Woolf make through the use of this name?

Analyze and Evaluate

4. What is the main message of Woolf's essay?

5. (a)In your opinion, was Woolf's primary purpose to inform, persuade, entertain, or disprove the views of others? Explain. (b)Do you believe Woolf effectively fulfills her purpose? Why or why not?

6. (a)What effect does Woolf create with the use of long paragraphs? (b)How might the essay be affected if shorter paragraphs were used?

7. (a)How do you think a sixteenth-century Englishman might define the "ideal woman"? (b)In your opinion, are Woolf's views still relevant today? Explain.

Connect

8. **Big Idea** **Modernism** How does Woolf's essay reflect the Modernist break with tradition?

LITERARY ANALYSIS

Literary Element **Argument**

An **argument** is an opinion supported by carefully chosen facts and logical reasoning.

1. (a)Summarize Professor Trevelyan's and the unnamed bishop's comments about women, as presented in the first paragraph. (b)What point might Woolf be making by including the comment about cats?

2. (a)In the fourth paragraph, what fate does Woolf believe a gifted sixteenth-century woman would have suffered? (b)What evidence does Woolf offer in support of her view?

Writing About Literature

Evaluate Author's Craft In the second paragraph, Woolf uses a highly original analogy, or comparison, to support her ideas about women. In a few paragraphs, analyze the analogy. In your opinion, does the analogy effectively make Woolf's point? Explain.

READING AND VOCABULARY

Reading Strategy **Analyzing Tone**

Writers use a variety of literary elements to craft **tone**, including text structure and imagery.

1. At what points in the essay is Woolf sarcastic?

2. In your opinion, what is the overall tone of the essay? Support your opinion with passages and ideas from the selection.

Vocabulary **Practice**

Practice with Word Origins Match each vocabulary word below with its etymology. Use a dictionary if necessary.

1. guffaw   **a.** Greek root, meaning "ambiguous proposition"

2. thwart   **b.** Latin root, meaning "diseased"

3. hinder   **c.** Middle English root, meaning "to cross"

4. dilemma   **d.** Old English root, meaning "in the way"

5. morbid   **e.** Scottish origin, imitating the sound of laughter

from *Mrs. Dalloway*

LITERATURE PREVIEW

Connecting to the Novel

In this excerpt from Virginia Woolf's novel *Mrs. Dalloway*, the title character reflects upon events in her past. As you read, think about the following questions:

- Have you ever made a decision you later regretted? What did you do about the decision?
- Have you ever had your train of thought suddenly interrupted by your surroundings?

Building Background

The novel *Mrs. Dalloway* follows one day in the life of its title character, Clarissa Dalloway. The story takes place in June 1923, several years after the end of World War I. The reader learns about Clarissa's former fiancé, Peter Walsh, whom Clarissa rejected at the age of eighteen; her husband Richard Dalloway, the man Clarissa chose over Peter; and Hugh Whitbread, a childhood friend whose wife is constantly ill. Clarissa's interactions with these characters and her internal monologue reveal a sense of regret over past decisions. The excerpt you are about to read comes from the beginning of the novel, when Clarissa takes a morning walk before preparing for the large party she is to host that evening.

Setting Purposes for Reading

Big Idea Modernism

As you read, note how Woolf's Modernist narrative style presents a psychoanalytic portrait of Clarissa Dalloway.

Literary Element Stream of Consciousness

Stream of consciousness is a method of writing that imitates human thought with a continuous and formless flow of ideas, feelings, observations, and memories. As you read the excerpt from *Mrs. Dalloway*, pay attention to how this method helps reveal insights into Clarissa Dalloway and her view of the world.

- See Literary Terms Handbook, p. R17.

READING PREVIEW

Reading Strategy Visualizing

To **visualize** means to use your imagination to form pictures of the setting, characters, and action based on the details you read. By visualizing, you can put together important parts of the story and immerse yourself in the action that takes place.

Reading Tip: Asking Questions When you visualize, you should ask yourself such basic questions as how does this setting, character, or object look? Who is in this scene? Where are the characters in relation to one another and their surroundings?

Vocabulary

solemn (sol′ əm) *adj.* serious; somber; p. 1157 *Once we heard the bad news, everyone's mood became solemn.*

presumably (pri zoo′ mə blē) *adv.* by reasonable assumption; p. 1159 *Presumably, you have studied for the test since it is a large part of your grade.*

ailment (āl′ mənt) *n.* sickness or affliction; p. 1159 *A doctor can prescribe medication to cure your ailment.*

perpetual (pər pech′ oo əl) *adj.* constantly occurring; p. 1160 *My sister and I cannot agree on anything; our arguments are perpetual.*

cordial (kôr′ jəl) *adj.* personable and likeable; p. 1161 *His cordial personality showed he was warm and sincere.*

Vocabulary Tip: Synonyms Words that have the same meaning are called synonyms.

Literature Online Interactive Literary Elements Handbook To review or learn more about the literary elements, go to www.glencoe.com.

OBJECTIVES

In studying this selection, you will focus on the following:
- recognizing the characteristics of the Modernist novel
- understanding stream-of-consciousness writing and description
- analyzing the events of a literary work through visualizing

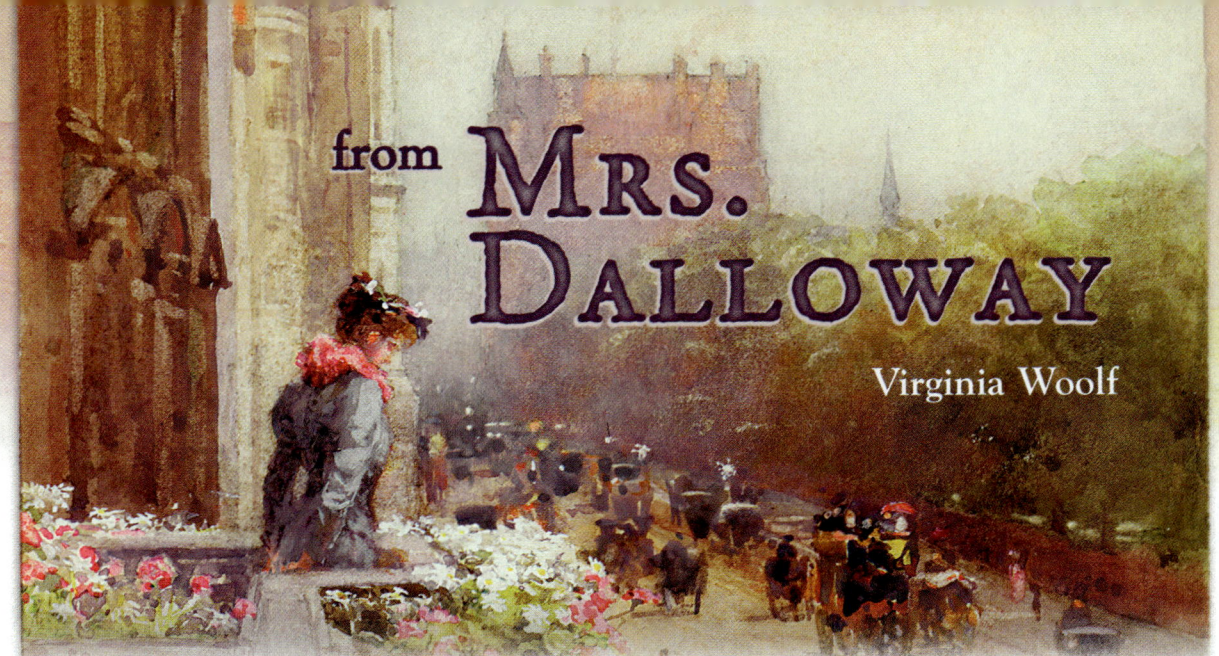

from MRS. DALLOWAY

Virginia Woolf

Piccadilly in June, 1892. Rose Maynard Barton. Watercolor on paper. Private collection.

Mrs. Dalloway said she would buy the flowers herself.

For Lucy had her work cut out for her. The doors would be taken off their hinges; Rumpelmayer's men were coming. And then, thought Clarissa Dalloway, what a morning—fresh as if issued to children on a beach.

What a lark! What a plunge! For so it had always seemed to her, when, with a little squeak of the hinges, which she could hear now, she had burst open the French windows and plunged at Bourton[1] into the open air. How fresh, how calm, stiller than this of course, the air was in the early morning; like the flap of a wave; the kiss of a wave, chill and sharp and yet (for a girl of eighteen as she then was) **solemn,** feeling as she did, standing there at the open window, that something awful was about to happen; looking at the flowers, at the trees with the smoke winding off them and the rooks rising, falling; standing and looking until Peter Walsh said, "Musing among the vegetables?"—was that it?—"I prefer men to cauliflowers"—was that it? He must have said it at breakfast one morning when she had gone out on to the terrace—Peter Walsh. He would be back from India one of these days, June or July, she forgot which, for his letters were awfully dull; it was his sayings one remembered; his eyes, his pocket-knife, his smile, his grumpiness and, when millions of things had utterly vanished—how strange it was!—a few sayings like this about cabbages.

She stiffened a little on the kerb,[2] waiting for Durtnall's van to pass. A charming woman, Scrope Purvis thought her (knowing her as one does know people who live next door to one in Westminster); a touch of the bird about her, of the jay, blue-green, light, vivacious, though she was over fifty, and grown very white since her illness. There she perched, never seeing him, waiting to cross, very upright.

For having lived in Westminster—how many years now? over twenty,—one feels even in the midst of the traffic, or waking at night, Clarissa was positive, a particular hush, or solemnity; an indescribable pause; a suspense (but that might be her heart, affected, they said, by influenza) before Big Ben strikes. There! Out it boomed. First a warning, musical; then the hour, irrevocable. The leaden circles dissolved in the air. Such fools we are, she thought, crossing

---

1. *Bourton,* also called Bourton-on-the-Water, is a village in southeast Britain.

Literary Element Stream of Consciousness *What brings Clarissa back to these thoughts?*

Vocabulary

solemn (sol′ əm) *adj.* serious; somber

2. *Kerb* is a variant spelling of "curb."

Reading Strategy Visualizing *How does Woolf create a visual image with this sound?*

The Bird's Nest. Edward Killingworth Johnson. Private collection.

Victoria Street.[3] For Heaven only knows why one loves it so, how one sees it so, making it up, building it round one, tumbling it, creating it every moment afresh; but the veriest frumps, the most dejected of miseries sitting on doorsteps (drink their downfall) do the same; can't be dealt with, she felt positive, by Acts of Parliament[4] for that very reason: they love life. In people's eyes, in the swing, tramp, and trudge; in the bellow and the uproar; the carriages, motor cars, omnibuses, vans, sandwich men shuffling and swinging; brass bands; barrel organs; in the triumph and the jingle and the strange high singing of some aeroplane overhead was what she loved; life; London; this moment of June.

For it was the middle of June. The War[5] was over, except for some one like Mrs. Foxcroft at the Embassy last night eating her heart out because that nice boy was killed and now the old Manor House must go to a cousin; or Lady Bexborough who opened a bazaar, they said, with the telegram in her hand, John, her favorite, killed; but it was over; thank Heaven—over. It was June. The King and Queen were at the Palace. And everywhere, though it was still so early, there was a beating, a stirring of galloping ponies, tapping of cricket bats; Lords, Ascot, Ranelagh[6] and all the rest of it; wrapped in the soft mesh of the grey-blue morning air, which, as the day wore on, would unwind them, and set down on their lawns and pitches the bouncing ponies, whose forefeet just struck the ground and up they sprung, the whirling young men, and laughing girls in their transparent muslins who, even now, after dancing all night, were taking their absurd woolly dogs for a run; and even now, at this hour, discreet old dowagers[7] were shooting out in their motor cars on errands of mystery; and the shopkeepers were fidgeting in their windows with their paste and diamonds, their lovely old sea-green brooches in eighteenth-century settings to tempt Americans (but one must economise, not buy things rashly for Elizabeth), and she, too, loving it as she did with an absurd and faithful passion, being part of it, since her people were courtiers once in the time of the Georges,[8] she, too, was going that very night to kindle and illuminate; to give her party. But how strange on entering the Park, the silence; the mist; the hum; the slow-swimming happy ducks; the pouched birds waddling; and who should be coming along with his back against the Government buildings, most appropriately, carrying a despatch box stamped with the Royal Arms, who but Hugh Whitbread; her old friend Hugh—the admirable Hugh!

---

3. *Victoria Street* is a major street in London, with landmarks such as Big Ben, Westminster Cathedral, and Buckingham Palace.
4. *Acts of Parliament* are laws created by the British Parliament.
5. *The War* refers to World War I.

6. *Lords, Ascot, Ranelagh* refers to Lord's Cricket Ground, Ascot Racecourse, and Ranelagh Gardens, each a famous site in or near London.
7. *Dowagers* are elderly women, usually of a high social class.
8. *Courtiers . . . time of the Georges* means that Clarissa's ancestors were attendants to the royal court of the eighteenth-century kings of England (George I, George II, and George III).

Literary Element Stream of Consciousness *What might this interruption in Clarissa's train of thought indicate about her personality?*

"Good-morning to you, Clarissa!" said Hugh, rather extravagantly, for they had known each other as children. "Where are you off to?"

"I love walking in London," said Mrs. Dalloway. "Really it's better than walking in the country."

They had just come up—unfortunately—to see doctors. Other people came to see pictures; go to the opera; take their daughters out; the Whitbreads came "to see doctors." Times without number Clarissa had visited Evelyn Whitbread in a nursing home. Was Evelyn ill again? Evelyn was a good deal out of sorts, said Hugh, intimating by a kind of pout or swell of his very well-covered, manly, extremely handsome, perfectly upholstered body (he was almost too well dressed always, but **presumably** had to be, with his little job at Court) that his wife had some internal **ailment**, nothing serious, which, as an old friend, Clarissa Dalloway would quite understand without requiring him to specify. Ah yes, she did of course; what a nuisance; and felt very sisterly and oddly conscious at the same time of her hat. Not the right hat for the early morning, was that it? For Hugh always made her feel, as he bustled on, raising his hat rather extravagantly and assuring her that she might be a girl of eighteen, and of course he was coming to her party to-night, Evelyn absolutely insisted, only a little late he might be after the party at the Palace to which he had to take one of Jim's boys,—she always felt a little skimpy beside Hugh; schoolgirlish; but attached to him, partly from having known him always, but she did think him a good sort in his own way, though Richard was nearly driven mad by him, and as for Peter Walsh, he had never to this day forgiven her for liking him.

She could remember scene after scene at Bourton—Peter furious; Hugh not, of course, his match in any way, but still not a positive imbecile as Peter made out; not a mere barber's block.

When his old mother wanted him to give up shooting or to take her to Bath[9] he did it, without a word; he was really unselfish, and as for saying, as Peter did, that he had no heart, no brain, nothing but the manners and breeding of an English gentleman, that was only her dear Peter at his worst; and he could be intolerable; he could be impossible; but adorable to walk with on a morning like this.

(June has drawn out every leaf on the trees. The mothers of Pimlico[10] gave suck to their young. Messages were passing from the Fleet to the Admiralty. Arlington Street and Piccadilly[11] seemed to chafe the very air in the Park and lift its leaves hotly, brilliantly, on waves of that divine vitality which Clarissa loved. To dance, to ride, she had adored all that.)

For they might be parted for hundreds of years, she and Peter; she never wrote a letter and his were dry sticks; but suddenly it would come over her, If he were with me now what would he say?—some days, some sights bringing him back to her calmly, without the old bitterness; which perhaps was the reward of having cared for people; they came back in the middle of St. James's Park on a fine morning—indeed they did. But Peter—however beautiful the day might be, and the trees and the grass, and the little girl in pink—Peter never saw a thing of all that. He would put on his spectacles, if she told him to; he would look. It was the state of the world that interested him; Wagner, Pope's[12] poetry, people's characters eternally, and the defects of her own soul. How he scolded her! How they argued! She would marry a Prime Minister and stand at the top of a staircase; the perfect hostess he called her

9. *Bath* is a popular resort town in southwestern Britain.
10. *Pimlico* is another name for a friarbird, and is also the name of a district in London.
11. *Piccadilly* refers to Piccadilly Circus, an intersection of five streets in a busy section of London.
12. *Wagner* refers to the German composer Richard Wagner (1813–1883), and *Pope* refers to the English poet Alexander Pope (1688–1744).

Their Majesties' Return from Ascot, 1925. Alfred Munnings. Oil on canvas, 148.0 x 244.5 cm. Tate Gallery, London.

(she had cried over it in her bedroom), she had the makings of the perfect hostess, he said.

So she would still find herself arguing in St. James's Park, still making out that she had been right—and she had too—not to marry him. For in marriage a little licence, a little independence there must be between people living together day in day out in the same house; which Richard gave her, and she him. (Where was he this morning for instance? Some committee, she never asked what.) But with Peter everything had to be shared; everything gone into. And it was intolerable, and when it came to that scene in the little garden by the fountain, she had to break with him or they would have been destroyed, both of them ruined, she was convinced; though she had borne about with her for years like an arrow sticking in her heart the grief, the anguish; and then the horror of the moment when some one told her at a concert that he had married a woman met on the boat going to India![13] Never should she forget all that! Cold, heartless, a prude, he called her. Never could she understand how he cared. But those Indian women did presumably—silly, pretty, flimsy nincompoops. And she wasted her pity. For he was quite happy, he assured her—perfectly happy, though he had never done a thing that they

talked of; his whole life had been a failure. It made her angry still.

She had reached the Park gates. She stood for a moment, looking at the omnibuses in Piccadilly.

She would not say of any one in the world now that they were this or were that. She felt very young; at the same time unspeakably aged. She sliced like a knife through everything; at the same time was outside, looking on. She had a **perpetual** sense, as she watched the taxi cabs, of being out, out, far out to sea and alone; she always had the feeling that it was very, very dangerous to live even one day. Not that she thought herself clever, or much out of the ordinary. How she had got through life on the few twigs of knowledge Fräulein Daniels gave them she could not think. She knew nothing; no language, no history; she scarcely read a book now, except memoirs in bed; and yet to her it was absolutely absorbing; all this; the cabs passing; and she would not say of Peter, she would not say of herself, I am this, I am that.

Her only gift was knowing people almost by instinct, she thought, walking on. If you put her in a room with some one, up went her back like a cat's; or she purred. Devonshire House, Bath House, the house with the china cockatoo, she had seen them all lit up once; and remembered Sylvia, Fred, Sally Seton—such hosts of people;

---

13. *India* was a British colony from the mid-1700s to 1947.

Reading Strategy **Visualizing** *What details might Clarissa have left out from this depiction?*

Vocabulary

perpetual (pər pech′ o͞o əl) *adj.* constantly occurring

In the Park (St. James's Park), 1912. Malcolm Drummond. Southampton City Art Gallery, Hampshire, UK.

*Fear no more the heat o' the sun
Nor the furious winter's rages.*[16]

This late age of the world's experience had bred in them all, all men and women, a well of tears. Tears and sorrows; courage and endurance; a perfectly upright and stoical bearing. Think, for example, of the woman she admired most, Lady Bexborough, opening the bazaar.

There were Jorrocks' *Jaunts and Jollities*; there were *Soapy Sponge* and Mrs. Asquith's *Memoirs* and *Big Game Shooting in Nigeria,* all spread open. Ever so many books there were; but none that seemed exactly right to take to Evelyn Whitbread in her nursing home. Nothing that would serve to amuse her and make that indescribably dried-up little woman look, as Clarissa came in, just for a moment **cordial;** before they settled down for the usual interminable talk of women's ailments. How much she wanted it—that people should look pleased as she came in, Clarissa thought and turned and walked back towards Bond Street, annoyed, because it was silly to have other reasons for doing things. Much rather would she have been one of those people like Richard who did things for themselves, whereas, she thought, waiting to cross, half the time she did things not simply, not for themselves; but to make people think this or that; perfect idiocy she knew (and now the policeman held up his hand) for no one was ever for a second taken in. Oh if she could have had her life over again! she thought, stepping on to the pavement, could have looked even differently! ❧

and dancing all night; and the wagons plodding past to market; and driving home across the Park. She remembered once throwing a shilling into the Serpentine.[14] But every one remembered; what she loved was this, here, now, in front of her; the fat lady in the cab. Did it matter then, she asked herself, walking towards Bond Street,[15] did it matter that she must inevitably cease completely; all this must go on without her; did she resent it; or did it not become consoling to believe that death ended absolutely? but that somehow in the streets of London, on the ebb and flow of things, here, there, she survived, Peter survived, lived in each other, she being part, she was positive, of the trees at home; of the house there, ugly, rambling all to bits and pieces as it was; part of people she had never met; being laid out like a mist between the people she knew best, who lifted her on their branches as she had seen the trees lift the mist, but it spread ever so far, her life, herself. But what was she dreaming as she looked into Hatchards' shop window? What was she trying to recover? What image of white dawn in the country, as she read in the book spread open:

---

14. The *Serpentine* is a lake in Hyde Park, London.
15. *Bond Street* is a street in London full of expensive shops.

Big Idea Modernism *What do you think Clarissa is trying to "recover"? What were the Modernists trying to recover?*

16. *"Fear no more . . . "* is a quotation from a song in Shakespeare's play *Cymbeline.*

Big Idea Modernism *How does this thought relate to Modernist beliefs?*

Vocabulary

cordial (kôr′ jəl) *adj.* personable and likeable

RESPONDING AND THINKING CRITICALLY

Respond

1. What images presented in this stream-of-consciousness narrative were the most startling? Explain.

Recall and Interpret

2. (a)What is the setting of this excerpt? (b)How does setting affect the stream-of-consciousness narrative?

3. (a)Describe the sights and sounds Clarissa experiences on her morning walk. (b)What does the reader learn about Clarissa through these images?

4. (a)What event is taking place that evening? (b)How does this event, and other details from the novel, show Clarissa's priorities?

5. (a)Why did Clarissa choose to marry Richard instead of Peter? (b)Why do you think this information is not revealed immediately?

Analyze and Evaluate

6. (a)How do you think Clarissa feels about her husband and daughter? (b)Why does a reader learn more about a character from his or her thoughts and actions than from dialogue?

7. How do the last lines of the excerpt represent an overall theme in *Mrs. Dalloway*?

Connect

8. **Big Idea** **Modernism** How does the narrative structure of *Mrs. Dalloway* differ from other stories or novels you have read?

PRIMARY SOURCE QUOTATION

Evaluating an Innovator

The following review of *Mrs. Dalloway* was written by John W. Crawford, a literary critic of Woolf's time. It has been excerpted from the May 10, 1925, edition of *The New York Times*. As you read the quotation, notice the groundbreaking qualities that Crawford finds in Woolf's novel.

"Virginia Woolf is almost alone . . . in the intricate yet clear art of her composition. Clarissa's day, the impressions she gives and receives, the memories and recognitions which stir in her, the events which are initiated remotely and engineered almost to touching distance of the impervious Clarissa, capture in a definitive matrix the drift of thought and feeling in a period, the point of view of a class, and seem almost to indicate the strength and weakness of an entire civilization."

Group Activity Discuss the following questions with your classmates.

1. What does Crawford consider Woolf's strengths as a writer? Refer to specific examples in *Mrs. Dalloway* that support Crawford's idea.

2. How does Clarissa Dalloway represent society, according to Crawford? Explain.

3. Do you agree with Crawford's assessment of *Mrs. Dalloway*? Support your answer with examples from the selection.

Virginia Woolf in a Deckchair, 1912. Vanessa Bell. Oil on board, 35.5 x 24 cm. London, Sotheby's. Copyright 1961 Estate of Virginia Bell. Courtesy of Henrietta Garnett.

Literary Element | Stream of Consciousness

Stream of consciousness is a term originated by American psychologist William James to describe human thought as a continuous flow of observation and reflection; our minds jump without apparent logic and without rest from one thought to another. Stories using stream of consciousness as a method of narration change topic suddenly and illogically in order to imitate these shifts in thought. The author seldom speaks directly to the reader but allows characters to reveal themselves through their thoughts. Stream of consciousness can be written in first or third person.

1. In what way is the excerpt from *Mrs. Dalloway* a stream-of-consciousness narrative?

2. Find at least two examples of sudden shifts in the narrative that imitate the way the mind jumps from one thought to another.

3. How would this excerpt be different had it been written in first-person point of view instead of third-person point of view?

Review: Description

As you learned on page 967, **description** reveals details about people and places in a story and often shapes how a reader feels about events in the text. Writers can use description to develop the **mood**, or emotional quality, of a literary work. Description also reveals the **tone**, or the attitude of the author (or narrator) toward his or her subject.

Partner Activity Work with a partner to find examples of description in *Mrs. Dalloway*. Then determine what description reveals about the tone of the excerpt. Use a chart like the one below to take notes.

Description	Tone
"How fresh, how calm . . . standing there at the open window, that something awful was about to happen . . ."	The narrator sets a peaceful tone but also creates anticipation that something awful will happen.

Reading Strategy | Visualizing

Visualizing provides clues about a character's motives and beliefs. Through visualizing, you can put yourself in the situation of the main characters and understand their actions. Examine how visualization reveals the intentions of Clarissa Dalloway by answering the following questions.

1. What kind of mental image of Clarissa Dalloway did you create?

2. How does visualization help you understand the motives and feelings of Mrs. Dalloway?

Vocabulary | Practice

Practice with Synonyms Identify the synonym for each vocabulary word. Use a dictionary or a thesaurus if you need help.

1. solemn   **a.** skeptical   **b.** somber

2. presumably   **a.** decently   **b.** likely

3. ailment   **a.** cure   **b.** disease

4. perpetual   **a.** recurring   **b.** halting

5. cordial   **a.** enjoyable   **b.** friendly

Academic Vocabulary

Here are two words from the vocabulary list on page R82.

notwithstanding (not′ with stan′ ding) *prep.* despite

forthcoming (fôrth′ kum′ ing) *adj.* candid, open for discussion

Practice and Apply

1. **Notwithstanding** his absence, why does Clarissa Dalloway still think about Peter Walsh?

2. How **forthcoming** is Woolf in presenting Clarissa's thoughts to the reader?

Writing About Literature

Respond to Conflict Woolf shares the thoughts and values of her main character through a rambling associative process. Thus, she subtly reveals the conflicts Clarissa Dalloway encounters. When **internal conflict** is present, a struggle takes place within the mind of a character who is torn between opposing feelings, desires, or goals. In a few paragraphs, summarize how Woolf reveals the internal conflict of Clarissa Dalloway.

To help you organize your summary, first organize your thoughts in an outline. Be sure to list supporting evidence for each main idea. Don't forget to include a concise thesis that directly responds to your topic and to use topic sentences. Remember to draw quotations from the text where necessary and to explain how those quotations support your assertions.

I. **Introduction**
  A. Topic of Essay
  B. Thesis Statement

II. **First Body Paragraph:** Clarissa Dalloway
  A. **Topic Sentence:** State a conflict Mrs. Dalloway encountered.
  B. **Evidence:** Provide evidence indicating that the conflict is internal.
  C. **Analysis:** Explain how your evidence supports your topic sentence.

III. **Conclusion**
  A. Reiterate Thesis
  B. Concluding Thought or Judgment

After you complete your draft, meet with a peer reviewer to evaluate each other's work and to suggest revisions. Then proofread and edit your draft for errors in spelling, grammar, and punctuation.

Performing

Pantomime is a kind of dramatic performance in which events are acted out onstage to a voice-over or a narrative chorus. Work in a group to act out the scene between Hugh Whitbread and Clarissa Dalloway on page 1159. Have one group member play Clarissa, another Hugh, while a third group member voices the thoughts and opinions of Clarissa. Present your scene to the class.

Woolf's Language and Style

Using Gerunds A gerund is a verb form that ends in -*ing* and is used in the same ways a noun is used. While gerunds look like verbs and the verb form called a participle, they are always either subjects or objects. Woolf uses gerunds to create imagery that is full of details and a sense of continuing action. Consider the effect of the gerunds in the passage below:

"And everywhere, though it was still so early, there was a beating, a stirring of galloping ponies, tapping of cricket bats;"

Notice how gerunds in the selection contribute to the images Woolf creates. Her language is both descriptive and immediate.

Use of Gerund	Effect of Emphasis
"...there was a (beating,) a (stirring) of galloping ponies, (tapping) of cricket bats"	Woolf shows that Clarissa Dalloway is focused on the action in the scene before her and emphasizes the continuous movement of the London setting.

Also, note that *galloping* is not a gerund; it is used as an adjective to describe the ponies.

Activity Scan the excerpt from *Mrs. Dalloway* for other gerunds or gerund phrases. Determine the significance of each example and the effect created by the use of a gerund.

Revising Check

Gerunds Avoid overusing gerunds in your writing. If used sparingly, they can create a sense of action within a scene. However, when they are overused, gerunds can be distracting. Try to balance the use of gerunds with the use of verbs or other nouns.

Literature Online **Web Activities** For eFlashcards, Selection Quick Checks, and other Web activities, go to www.glencoe.com.

PART 3

World War II and Its Aftermath

It's a Long, Long Way, 1941. Henry Lamb. Oil on canvas. South African National Gallery, Cape Town.

"What is absurd and monstrous about war is that men who have no personal quarrel should be trained to murder one another in cold blood."

—Aldous Huxley, *"Words and Behavior"*

Be Ye Men of Valor

MEET WINSTON CHURCHILL

"Blood, toil, tears, and sweat." These unforgettable words of Winston Churchill were not merely a rallying cry, but his approach to life. He is perhaps one of the most renowned prime ministers of Great Britain, inspiring a nation and leading it to victory in the face of World War II.

> *"You ask, what is our aim? I can answer in one word: Victory—victory at all costs, victory in spite of all terror; victory, however long and hard the road may be."*
>
> —Winston Churchill

Lasting Influences Churchill's childhood profoundly influenced his beliefs and career (in addition to his political positions, Churchill was a soldier, journalist, writer, historian, and painter). Born to Lord Randolph Churchill, a conservative member of Parliament, and the American heiress Jennie Jerome, Churchill was unable to form a bond with either of his parents, particularly his aloof father, whom he greatly admired. From an early age he was fascinated with soldiers and historic battles, and his father enrolled him in England's Royal Military College at Sandhurst. After graduation Churchill served as a junior officer in the British army and later as a war correspondent in Cuba, India, and South Africa. After his famous escape from a Pretoria prisoner-of-war camp, Churchill used the profits from his writings and lectures to pursue a career in politics. Throughout his career—even after his father's death—Churchill's political interests would mirror those of his father.

Political Career Churchill's military experience and his background as a writer gave him a unique advantage in the political realm. He served in numerous positions in Parliament, including home secretary, first lord of the Admiralty, minister of munitions, secretary of state for war and air, and secretary for the colonies. In 1940 Churchill became prime minister just as the Germans invaded Belgium—a post he held until the end of the war and the defeat of the Axis powers.

A Literary Knight At the age of seventy-one, Churchill was voted out of office as prime minister, but he was reelected six years later. In 1953 he was knighted and awarded the Nobel Prize in Literature for his work on history and politics, *The Second World War* (published in six volumes, 1948–1953), in particular. Ten years later Churchill left public office to spend his last years writing, painting, and traveling. The scope of his achievements impacted not only England but the entire world.

Winston Churchill was born in 1874 and died in 1965.

Literature Online **Author Search** For more about Winston Churchill, go to www.glencoe.com.

Connecting to the Speech

Early in Churchill's career as prime minister, his courage was tested by World War II. What major event has tested your courage? As you read, think about the following questions:

- How did you respond to the event?
- If you could relive the experience, how might you respond differently?

Building Background

During World War II, Churchill inspired the English people with his words of patriotism and hope. Delivered on May 19, 1940, "Be Ye Men of Valor" was Churchill's first radio broadcast to the British public as prime minister. In the speech Churchill insists on victory, and he refuses to negotiate or compromise with Adolf Hitler.

Initially Churchill believed Britain would be fighting the Nazis alone. "There is one thing that will bring Hitler down, and that is an absolutely devastating, exterminating attack by very heavy bombers from this country upon the Nazi homeland," Churchill wrote, describing the bombing plan. He was still carrying out these strategies when the United States joined the war after the attack on Pearl Harbor in 1941.

Setting Purposes for Reading

Big Idea World War II and Its Aftermath

As you read, notice how Churchill inspires confidence and courage in the British people.

Literary Element Rhetoric

Rhetoric is the art of using language to present facts and ideas in order to persuade an audience. As you read Churchill's speech, notice how he combines logic, emotion, and artful phrases to inform the public about the German advance and to express his confidence in his troops and the Allied cause.

- See Literary Terms Handbook, p. R15.

Reading Strategy Distinguishing Fact and Opinion

A **fact** is a statement that can be proved true. An **opinion,** however, is a statement of someone's personal beliefs or feelings, and it cannot be proved.

Reading Tip: Taking Notes Use a chart to distinguish facts from opinions in Churchill's speech.

Facts	Opinions
"our heavy bombers are striking nightly . . ."	"It would be foolish, however, to disguise the gravity of the hour."

Vocabulary

ravage (rav′ ij) *v.* to lay waste to; to destroy; p. 1169 *The air raids will ravage the city, destroying churches, homes, and factories.*

grapple (grap′ əl) *v.* to attempt to deal with; to struggle; p. 1169 *He grappled with the idea of conceding but realized victory was the only option.*

imperious (im pēr′ ē əs) *adj.* imperative; urgent; p. 1171 *The nation faced imperious problems and needed to utilize all of its resources to survive.*

indomitable (in dom′ ə tə bəl) *adj.* incapable of being subdued or overcome; p. 1171 *The captain infused an indomitable spirit in his men.*

Vocabulary Tip: Context Clues Context clues are words and sentences surrounding an unfamiliar word that can help you determine the meaning of that word.

Literature Online Interactive Literary Elements **Handbook** To review or learn more about the literary elements, go to www.glencoe.com.

OBJECTIVES
In studying this selection, you will focus on the following:
- reading and analyzing a historic speech
- understanding rhetoric and rhetorical devices
- distinguishing fact and opinion

Prime Minister Churchill inspects a bomb crater.

Be Ye Men of Valor

Winston Churchill

I speak to you for the first time as Prime Minister in a solemn hour for the life of our country, of our Empire, of our Allies,[1] and, above all, of the cause of Freedom. A tremendous battle is raging in France and Flanders. The Germans, by a remarkable combination of air bombing and heavily armored tanks, have broken through the French defenses north of the Maginot Line,[2] and strong columns of their armored vehicles are **ravaging** the open country, which for the first day or two was without defenders. They have penetrated deeply and spread alarm and confusion in their track. Behind them there are now appearing infantry in lorries,[3] and behind them, again, the large masses are moving forward. The regroupment of the French armies to make head against, and also to strike at, this intruding wedge has been proceeding for several days, largely assisted by the magnificent efforts of the Royal Air Force.

We must not allow ourselves to be intimidated by the presence of these armored vehicles in unexpected places behind our lines. If they are behind our Front, the French are also at many points fighting actively behind theirs. Both sides are therefore in an extremely dangerous position. And if the French Army, and our own Army, are well handled, as I believe they will be; if the French retain that genius for recovery and counter-attack for which they have so long been famous; and if the British Army shows the dogged endurance and solid fighting power of which there have been so many examples in the past—then a sudden transformation of the scene might spring into being.

It would be foolish, however, to disguise the gravity[4] of the hour. It would be still more foolish to lose heart and courage or to suppose that well-trained, well-equipped armies numbering three or four millions of men can be overcome in the space of a few weeks, or even months, by a scoop, or raid of mechanized vehicles, however formidable.[5] We may look with confidence to the stabilization of the Front in France, and to the general engagement of the masses, which will enable the qualities of the French and British soldiers to be matched squarely against those of their adversaries.[6] For myself, I have invincible confidence in the French Army and its leaders. Only a very small part of that splendid army has yet been heavily engaged; and only a very small part of France has yet been invaded. There is good evidence to show that practically the whole of the specialized and mechanized forces of the enemy have been already thrown into the battle; and we know that very heavy losses have been inflicted upon them. No officer or man, no brigade or division, which **grapples** at close quarters with the enemy, wherever encountered, can fail to make a worthy contribution to

> "No officer or man, no brigade or division, which grapples at close quarters with the enemy, wherever encountered, can fail to make a worthy contribution to the general result."

---

1. At the date of this speech, Britain's allies were France and several smaller countries that were occupied by German troops.
2. The *Maginot Line* was a heavily fortified line of defense in France that was assembled to stave off the Germans.
3. *Lorries* are British motor trucks.

Big Idea World War II and Its Aftermath *How do Churchill's opening lines reflect the attitude of the British during World War II?*

Reading Strategy Distinguishing Fact and Opinion
What major fact is Churchill talking about? In his opinion, how should the British deal with that fact?

Vocabulary

ravage (rav′ ij) *v.* to lay waste to; to destroy

---

4. Here, *gravity* means "seriousness" or "importance."
5. *Formidable* means "arousing fear or dread."
6. *Adversaries* are opponents.

Vocabulary

grapple (grap′ əl) *v.* to attempt to deal with; to struggle

WINSTON CHURCHILL **1169**

the general result. The Armies must cast away the idea of resisting behind concrete lines or natural obstacles, and must realize that mastery can only be regained by furious and unrelenting assault. And this spirit must not only animate the High Command, but must inspire every fighting man.

In the air—often at serious odds—often at odds hitherto thought overwhelming —we have been clawing down three or four to one of our enemies; and the relative balance of the British and German Air Forces is now considerably more favorable to us than at the beginning of the battle. In cutting down the German bombers, we are fighting our own battle as well as that of France. My confidence in our ability to fight it out to the finish with the German Air Force has been strengthened by the fierce encounters which have taken place and are taking place. At the same time, our heavy bombers are striking nightly at the taproot[7] of German mechanized power, and have already inflicted serious damage upon the oil refineries on which the Nazi effort to dominate the world directly depends.

We must expect that as soon as stability is reached on the Western Front, the bulk of that hideous apparatus of aggression which gashed Holland into ruin and slavery in a few days, will be turned upon us. I am sure I speak for all when I say we are ready to face it; to endure it; and to retaliate against it—to any extent that the unwritten laws of war permit. There will be many men, and many women, in this island who when the ordeal comes upon them, as come it will, will feel comfort, and even a pride—that they are sharing the perils of our lads at the Front—soldiers, sailors, and airmen, God bless them—and are drawing away from them a part at least of the onslaught they have to bear. Is not this the appointed time for all to make the utmost exertions in their power? If the battle is to be won, we must provide our men with ever-increasing quantities of the weapons and ammunition they need. We must have, and have quickly, more airplanes, more tanks, more

Prime Minister Winston Churchill and Brendan Bracken survey bomb damage to the Houses of Parliament, London.
Viewing the Art: How does seeing this photograph of actual war damage add to your appreciation of the speech?

---

7. As it is used here, *taproot* means "the most important part."

Reading Strategy Distinguishing Fact and Opinion
Which elements of this paragraph are fact and which are opinion?

shells, more guns. There is **imperious** need for these vital munitions. They increase our strength against the powerfully armed enemy. They replace the wastage of the obstinate[8] struggle; and the knowledge that wastage will speedily be replaced enables us to draw more readily upon our reserves and throw them in now that everything counts so much.

Our task is not only to win the battle—but to win the War. After this battle in France abates[9] its force, there will come the battle for our island—for all that Britain is, and all that Britain means. That will be the struggle. In that supreme emergency we shall not hesitate to take every step, even the most drastic, to call forth from our people the last ounce and the last inch of effort of which they are capable. The interests of property, the hours of labor, are nothing compared with the struggle for life and honor, for right and freedom, to which we have vowed ourselves.

I have received from the Chiefs of the French Republic, and in particular from its **indomitable** Prime Minister, M. Reynaud, the most sacred pledges that whatever happens they will fight to the end, be it bitter or be it glorious. Nay, if we fight to the end, it can only be glorious.

Having received His Majesty's commission, I have found an administration of men and women of every party and of almost every point of view. We have differed and quarreled in the past; but now one bond unites us all—to wage war until victory is won, and never to surrender ourselves to servitude and shame, whatever the cost and the agony may be. This is one of the most awe-striking periods in the long history of France and Britain. It is also beyond doubt the most sublime. Side by side, unaided except by their kith and kin in the great Dominions and by the wide Empires which rest beneath their shield—side by side, the British and French peoples have advanced to rescue not only Europe but mankind from the foulest and most soul-destroying tyranny which has ever darkened and stained the pages of history. Behind them—behind us—behind the armies and fleets of Britain and France—gather a group of shattered States and bludgeoned[10] races: the Czechs, the Poles, the Norwegians, the Danes, the Dutch, the Belgians—upon all of whom the long night of barbarism will descend, unbroken even by a star of hope, unless we conquer, as conquer we must; as conquer we shall.

Today is Trinity Sunday.[11] Centuries ago words were written to be a call and a spur to the faithful servants of Truth and Justice: "Arm yourselves, and be ye men of valor, and be in readiness for the conflict; for it is better for us to perish in battle than to look upon the outrage of our nation and our altar. As the Will of God is in Heaven, even so let it be."[12] ❧

---

8. *Obstinate* means "stubborn."
9. *Abates* means "reduces in intensity."

---

10. As it is used here, *bludgeoned* means "bullied or beaten."
11. *Trinity Sunday* is the first Sunday after Pentecost (the fiftieth day after Easter) in the Christian calendar.
12. In this quotation from 1 Maccabees 3:58–60, Judas Maccabeus, the leader of a Jewish rebellion during the second century B.C., urges his army before a battle against the Syrians, who then ruled Judaea.

RESPONDING AND THINKING CRITICALLY

Respond

1. If you had been listening to the live broadcast of this speech as a British citizen, how might you have felt? Explain.

Recall and Interpret

2. (a)What does Churchill describe in the first paragraph? (b)What emotions does he convey with his use of descriptive language?

3. (a)How does Churchill describe the British and French armies? (b)Why might he describe them this way?

4. (a)What information does Churchill report about Holland? (b)How does this information support his argument that Britain's men and women must prepare to fight?

Analyze and Evaluate

5. Is Churchill's use of **loaded words**—language that expresses strong emotion—effective? Explain.

6. Churchill ends his speech with a quote: "it is better for us to perish in battle than to look upon the outrage of our nation and our altar." (a)What outrage might he be referring to? (b)Is this an effective end to his speech? Explain. (c)Do you agree with his assertion? Why or why not?

Connect

7. **Big Idea** **World War II and Its Aftermath** Churchill chooses to foster the idea that war is a noble, even a sublime, effort. Why do you think he portrays war in this manner?

LITERARY ANALYSIS

Literary Element **Rhetoric**

Common rhetorical devices include **rhetorical questions,** or questions to which no answer is expected; **parallelism,** in which words, phrases, or sentences are balanced in structure; and **loaded words,** which appeal to emotion.

Does Churchill appeal primarily to emotions or to intellect? How might this choice have helped persuade his audience?

Writing About Literature

Analyze Structure In one sentence, summarize what Churchill is hoping to persuade his listeners to do or believe. Next, outline the speech, showing how his argument progresses from beginning to end. Then, in two or three paragraphs, evaluate the way in which he structures his argument. Does his arrangement of ideas make his speech persuasive? Be sure to support your opinion with evidence.

Literature Online **Web Activities** For eFlashcards, Selection Quick Checks, and other Web activities, go to www.glencoe.com.

READING AND VOCABULARY

Reading Strategy **Distinguishing Fact and Opinion**

Distinguishing fact and opinion enables listeners and readers to evaluate the information they receive.

Does Churchill rely more heavily on facts or on opinions to persuade his audience? Explain. Why does Churchill include his opinions in his speech?

Vocabulary **Practice**

Practice with Context Clues Based on the context clues, choose the vocabulary word that best completes each sentence.

a. ravaged   **c.** grapple
b. imperious   **d.** indomitable

1. They _____ our home, destroying everything.

2. He delivered the _____ message to the anxious general—Paris had fallen.

3. They will need to _____ with the problem until they reach an agreement.

4. They began to fear that their adversaries were _____ and unconquerable.

Vocabulary Workshop

Denotation and Connotation

Recognizing Loaded Words

"We must expect that as soon as stability is reached on the Western Front, the bulk of that hideous apparatus of aggression which gashed Holland into ruin and slavery in a few days, will be turned upon us."

—Winston Churchill, from "Be Ye Men of Valor"

Connecting to Literature In this excerpt from his World War II speech, Winston Churchill's language is charged with conviction. He appeals to the British people directly, using a persuasive tone and words loaded with emotion. Highly charged phrases such as "hideous apparatus of aggression" and "gashed Holland into ruin and slavery" helped Churchill mobilize the British people to fight a brutal war. While his **loaded words** helped inspire a country's commitment to a necessary action, people often use such words to manipulate public opinion for their personal, political, or commercial gain.

- **Bias** is language that expresses a one-sided point of view. The **connotations** of words reveal an author's bias. Note how Churchill states his positive bias directly, giving his words honesty and authority.
  For myself, I have <u>invincible confidence</u> in the French Army and its leaders.

- **Hyperbole** is a statement that uses exaggeration for effect.
  After this battle in France abates its force, there will come the battle for our island—for <u>all that Britain is</u>, and <u>all that Britain means</u>.

- **Propaganda** is language used to influence the public. It often includes bias and hyperbole and may distort the truth.
  Nay, if we <u>fight to the end</u>, it can only be <u>glorious</u>.

▶ **Vocabulary Terms**

Loaded words express strong opinions or emotions. Some reveal **bias,** or prejudice. **Hyperbole** is the use of exaggeration to make a point. **Propaganda** is language that may distort the truth to be persuasive.

▶ **Test-Taking Tip**

When you read test passages, consider the author's purpose and point of view. Look for evidence in the text that indicates the author's position.

▶ **Reading Handbook**

For more about denotation and connotation, see Reading Handbook, p. R20.

OBJECTIVES
- Identify intended effects of persuasive language.
- Recognize influence of propaganda.

Exercise

For each of the following quotations from speeches by Churchill, underline the loaded words and identify the persuasive techniques being used. Write your answers on a separate piece of paper.

1. "Never in the field of human conflict was so much owed by so many to so few."
2. "Upon this battle depends the survival of Christian civilization."
3. "I have nothing to offer but blood, toil, tears and sweat."
4. "[W]e would rather see London laid in ruins and ashes than that it should be tamely and abjectly enslaved."

The Demon Lover

MEET ELIZABETH BOWEN

Elizabeth Bowen once said, "If you look at life one way, there is always cause for alarm." Though she may have experienced more causes for alarm than most people, Bowen maintained her sense of perspective and her composure throughout her life. In view of the many hardships she faced at an early age, this strong sense of self and her world no doubt came in very handy.

A Difficult Childhood Born into the Anglo-Irish gentry, Elizabeth Dorothea Cole Bowen spent her early childhood in Dublin and at Kildorrey. Before her eighth birthday, Bowen's father was hospitalized with a long-term illness, and she and her mother left for England to live with family. Five years later her mother died of cancer. Bowen was then taken in by her aunts on the Kentish sea-coast of England and sent to a boarding school.

When World War I broke out, Bowen, still in her teens, went to work in an Irish hospital for soldiers suffering from shell shock, or what is now typically referred to as post-traumatic stress syndrome.

> *"I feel happiest, in the sense of poetic truth, in the short story. Yet if I wrote only short stories, I should feel I was shrinking."*
>
> —Elizabeth Bowen

The Literary Life After World War I, the twenty-year-old Bowen began to write. She published her first collection of short stories, *Encounters*, in 1923 at the age of twenty-four. She also married Alan Cameron. The couple lived together for a number of years in London. By the time she was thirty, Bowen had become associated with the renowned Bloomsbury Group, which included such literary heavyweights as Virginia Woolf and E. M. Forster.

In 1930 Bowen inherited her family's home, Bowen's Court, in County Cork, Ireland. But she remained in London until 1940, when, as part of her job with the English Ministry of Information, she was posted in Dublin. Her function was to send back to England reports on the Irish people's sentiments about World War II. Bowen moved into Bowen's Court in 1952, but after a few years she moved back to London, where she would reside for the rest of her life.

Bowen's work was influenced by the grim changes World War II brought to English life. The brooding silence of London's abandoned bomb-torn neighborhoods fills many of her works, including her novel *The Heat of the Day*. Many of her short stories, such as "The Demon Lover" and "The Cat Jumps," also subtly weave in supernatural elements. Her work is filled with small but powerful details and an unfailingly accurate sense of time and place.

Bowen's most effective work deals with Britain's upper class. Her stories won her a reputation as an acute observer of both human nature and English society. Her work lives on at least in part because of her flair for description and her particular gift for revealing subtle changes of light, sound, landscape, and human emotion.

Elizabeth Bowen was born in 1899 and died in 1973.

Literature Online **Author Search** For more about Elizabeth Bowen, go to www.glencoe.com.

Connecting to the Story

In Bowen's short story, a woman is unexpectedly and frighteningly confronted by her past. As you read, think about the following questions:

- What makes a story or movie scary?
- Have you ever experienced a suspenseful or uncertain moment? How did it make you feel?

Building Background

This story, which is based loosely on a gothic ballad, takes place during World War II during the German bombing of London known as the Blitz. On fifty-seven consecutive nights, the German Luftwaffe bombed London in an effort to obliterate the city and destroy the fighting spirit of Britain's people. Many families moved to the country to get out of harm's way. Those who could not afford to move had to take shelter where they could find it. The story also contains a flashback to World War I, when the main character became engaged to a young soldier.

Setting Purposes for Reading

Big Idea   World War II and Its Aftermath

As you read "The Demon Lover," take note of the setting, as well as the main character's dark pessimism and overwhelming sense of foreboding.

Literary Element   Flashback

A **flashback** is an interruption in the chronological order of a narrative to show an event that happened earlier. This gives readers information that may help them to figure out the main events of a story. As you read, examine how details from the flashback frame the rest of the story.

- See Literary Terms Handbook, p. R7.

Literature Online **Interactive Literary Elements Handbook** To review or learn more about the literary elements, go to www.glencoe.com.

Reading Strategy   Analyzing Sensory Details

In creating effective images, writers use **sensory details,** or descriptions that appeal to one or more of the five senses: sight, hearing, touch, taste, and smell. Like diction and sentence structure, sensory details influence the tone and meaning of a literary work.

Reading Tip: Using Your Senses Create a chart like the one below to keep track of the senses you use as you read "The Demon Lover."

Image or Description	Senses
"it had been a steamy, showery day"	touch

Vocabulary

prosaic (prō zā′ ik) *adj.* commonplace; ordinary; p. 1177 *The students' more prosaic expectations were upset by the instructor's nontraditional approach.*

intermittent (in′ tər mit′ ənt) *adj.* alternately starting and stopping; p. 1178 *During the storm, weather bulletins interrupted regular programming on an intermittent basis.*

precipitately (pri sip′ ə tət′ lē) *adv.* without deliberation; hastily; abruptly; p. 1178 *Rushing out of the store, Cal precipitately knocked the vase off the shelf.*

emanate (em′ ə nāt′) *v.* to come forth from a source; to issue; p. 1181 *On Thanksgiving Day, wonderful smells emanate from the kitchen.*

impassively (im pas′ iv lē) *adv.* in an emotionless manner; p. 1181 *Surprisingly, the patient accepted the grim diagnosis impassively.*

Vocabulary Tip: Word Origins Learning the origin of words can help you build vocabulary and decipher unfamiliar words.

OBJECTIVES
In studying this selection, you will focus on the following:
- analyzing literary periods
- analyzing flashback
- analyzing sensory details

The Gallery, 1952. Leonard Campbell Taylor. Oil on canvas. Private collection.

The Demon Lover

Elizabeth Bowen

Towards the end of her day in London Mrs. Drover went round to her shut-up house to look for several things she wanted to take away. Some belonged to herself, some to her family, who were by now used to their country life. It was late August; it had been a steamy, showery day: at the moment the trees down the pavement glittered in an escape of humid yellow afternoon sun.

Against the next batch of clouds, already piling up ink-dark, broken chimneys and parapets[1] stood out.

1. A *parapet* is a low, protective railing or wall along the edge of a roof or balcony.

Reading Strategy Analyzing Sensory Details *In what ways does this paragraph appeal to your senses?*

In her once familiar street, as in any unused channel, an unfamiliar queerness had silted up;[2] a cat wove itself in and out of railings, but no human eye watched Mrs. Drover's return. Shifting some parcels under her arm, she slowly forced round her latchkey in an unwilling lock, then gave the door, which had warped, a push with her knee. Dead air came out to meet her as she went in.

The staircase window having been boarded up, no light came down into the hall. But one door, she could just see, stood ajar, so she went quickly through into the room and unshuttered the big window in there. Now the **prosaic** woman, looking about her, was more perplexed[3] than she knew by everything that she saw, by traces of her long former habit of life—the yellow smoke stain up the white marble mantelpiece, the ring left by a vase on the top of the escritoire; the bruise in the wall-paper where, on the door being thrown open widely, the china handle had always hit the wall. The piano, having gone away to be stored, had left what looked like claw marks on its part of the parquet.[4] Though not much dust had seeped in, each object wore a film of another kind; and, the only ventilation being the chimney, the whole drawing room smelled of the cold hearth. Mrs. Drover put down her parcels on the escritoire and left the room to proceed upstairs; the things she wanted were in a bedroom chest.

Visual Vocabulary
An *escritoire* is a writing table or desk.

She had been anxious to see how the house was—the part-time caretaker she shared with some neighbors was away this week on his holiday, known to be not yet back. At the best of times he did not look in often, and she was never sure that she trusted him.

There were some cracks in the structure, left by the last bombing,[5] on which she was anxious to keep an eye. Not that one could do anything—

A shaft of refracted[6] daylight now lay across the hall. She stopped dead and stared at the hall table—on this lay a letter addressed to her.

She thought first—then the caretaker *must* be back. All the same, who, seeing the house shuttered, would have dropped a letter in at the box? It was not a circular,[7] it was not a bill. And the post office redirected, to the address in the country, everything for her that came through the post. The caretaker (even if he *were* back) did not know she was due in London today—her call here had been planned to be a surprise—so his negligence in the manner of this letter, leaving it to wait in the dusk and the dust, annoyed her. Annoyed, she picked up the letter, which bore no stamp. But it cannot be important, or they would know . . . She took the letter rapidly upstairs with her, without a stop to look at the writing till she reached what had been her bedroom, where she let in light. The room looked over the garden and other gardens: the sun had gone in; as the clouds sharpened and lowered, the trees and rank[8] lawns seemed already to smoke with dark. Her reluctance to look again at the letter came from the fact that she felt intruded upon—and by someone contemptuous[9] of her ways. However, in the tenseness preceding the fall of rain she read it: it was a few lines.

Dear Kathleen: You will not have forgotten that today is our anniversary, and the day we said. The years have gone by at

---

2. Here, *silted up* means "built up."
3. *Perplexed* means "bewildered" or "puzzled."
4. *Parquet* is inlaid wood, often of different colors, that is worked into geometric patterns or mosaic and is used especially for flooring.

5. *The last bombing* indicates that the story takes place during World War II.
6. *Refracted* means "coming in at an angle."
7. Here, a *circular* is a printed advertisement.
8. As it is used here, *rank* means "overgrown with weeds."
9. *Contemptuous* means "scornful."

Big Idea World War II and Its Aftermath *Why is Mrs. Drover unable to do anything about her crumbling house?*

Reading Strategy Analyzing Sensory Details *What does this description of the lawns and garden contribute to the story's overall mood?*

once slowly and fast. In view of the fact that nothing has changed, I shall rely upon you to keep your promise. I was sorry to see you leave London, but was satisfied that you would be back in time. You may expect me, therefore, at the hour arranged. Until then . . .   K.

Mrs. Drover looked for the date: it was today's. She dropped the letter on to the bedsprings, then picked it up to see the writing again—her lips, beneath the remains of lipstick, beginning to go white. She felt so much the change in her own face that she went to the mirror, polished a clear patch in it and looked at once urgently and stealthily[10] in. She was confronted by a woman of forty-four, with eyes starting out under a hat brim that had been rather carelessly pulled down. She had not put on any more powder since she left the shop where she ate her solitary tea. The pearls her husband had given her on their marriage hung loose round her now rather thinner throat, slipping in the V of the pink wool jumper her sister knitted last autumn as they sat round the fire. Mrs. Drover's most normal expression was one of controlled worry, but of assent.[11] Since the birth of the third of her little boys, attended by a quite serious illness, she had had an **intermittent** muscular flicker to the left of her mouth, but in spite of this she could always sustain a manner that was at once energetic and calm.

Turning from her own face as **precipitately** as she had gone to meet it, she went to the chest where the things were, unlocked it, threw up the lid and knelt to search. But as rain began to come crashing down she could not keep from looking over her shoulder at the stripped bed on which the letter lay. Behind the blanket of rain the clock of the church that still stood struck six—with rapidly

heightening apprehension she counted each of the slow strokes. "The hour arranged . . . My God," she said, "*what* hour? How should I . . . ? After twenty-five years . . ."

The young girl talking to the soldier in the garden had not ever completely seen his face. It was dark; they were saying good-bye under a tree. Now and then—for it felt, from not seeing him at this intense moment, as though she had never seen him at all—she verified his presence for these few moments longer by putting out a hand, which he each time pressed, without very much kindness, and painfully, on to one of the breast buttons of his uniform. That cut of the button on the palm of her hand was, principally, what she was to carry away. This was so near the end of a leave from France that she could only wish him already gone. It was August 1916.[12] Being not kissed, being drawn away from and looked at intimidated Kathleen till she imagined spectral[13] glitters in the place of his eyes. Turning away and looking back up the lawn she saw, through branches of trees, the drawing-room window alight: she caught a breath for the moment when she could go running back there into the safe arms of her mother and sister, and cry: "What shall I do, what shall I do? He has gone."

Hearing her catch her breath, her fiancé said, without feeling: "Cold?"

"You're going away such a long way."

"Not so far as you think."

"I don't understand?"

"You don't have to," he said. "You will. You know what we said."

---

10. *Stealthily* means "secretly."
11. Here, *assent* means "resignation."

12. *August 1916* indicates that this flashback takes place during the First World War.
13. *Spectral* means "ghostly."

Literary Element   Flashback   *What clues indicate that a flashback is beginning?*

Reading Strategy   Analyzing Sensory Details   *What does the pain Mrs. Drover experiences here suggest to you about her relationship with the young soldier?*

St. Paul's Cathedral from Ludgate Circus, London, England. John Atkinson Grimshaw.

"But that was—suppose you—I mean, suppose."

"I shall be with you," he said, "sooner or later. You won't forget that. You need do nothing but wait."

Only a little more than a minute later she was free to run up the silent lawn. Looking in through the window at her mother and sister, who did not for the moment perceive her, she already felt that unnatural promise drive down between her and the rest of all human kind. No other way of having given herself could have made her feel so apart, lost and foresworn.[14] She could not have plighted a more sinister troth.[15]

Kathleen behaved well when, some months later, her fiancé was reported missing, presumed killed. Her family not only supported her but were able to praise her courage without stint[16] because they could not regret, as a husband for her, the man they knew almost nothing about. They hoped she would, in a year or two, console herself—and had it been only a question of

---

14. Here, *foresworn* means "abandoned."
15. [*She . . . troth.*] She could not have pledged herself to a more evil promise.
16. To praise without *stint* is to praise generously and without reservation.

Literary Element Flashback *What does the soldier's promise suggest about the letter Kathleen receives?*

consolation things might have gone much straighter ahead. But her trouble, behind just a little grief, was a complete dislocation from everything. She did not reject other lovers, for these failed to appear: for years she failed to attract men—and with the approach of her thirties she became natural enough to share her family's anxiousness on this score. She began to put herself out, to wonder; and at thirty-two she was very greatly relieved to find herself being courted by William Drover. She married him, and the two of them settled down in this quiet, arboreal[17] part of Kensington:[18] in this house the years piled up, her children were born and they all lived till they were driven out by the bombs of the next war. Her movements as Mrs. Drover were circumscribed,[19] and she dismissed any idea that they were still watched.

As things were—dead or living the letter writer sent her only a threat. Unable, for some minutes, to go on kneeling with her back exposed to the empty room, Mrs. Drover rose from the chest to sit on an upright chair whose back was firmly against the wall. The desuetude[20] of her former bedroom, her married London home's whole air of being a cracked cup from which memory, with its reassuring power, had either evaporated or leaked away, made a crisis—and at just this crisis the letter writer had, knowledgeably, struck. The hollowness of the house this evening canceled years on years of voices, habits,

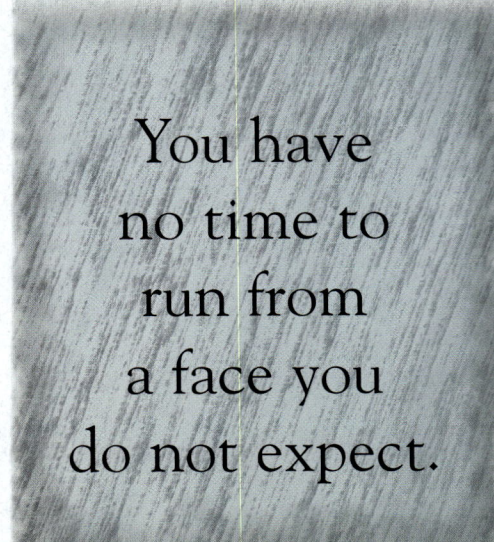

You have no time to run from a face you do not expect.

and steps. Through the shut windows she only heard rain fall on the roofs around. To rally[21] herself, she said she was in a mood—and for two or three seconds shutting her eyes, told herself that she had imagined the letter. But she opened them—there it lay on the bed.

On the supernatural side of the letter's entrance she was not permitting her mind to dwell. Who, in London, knew she meant to call at the house today? Evidently, however, this had been known. The caretaker, *had* he come back, had had no cause to expect her: he would have taken the letter in his pocket, to forward it, at his own time, through the post. There was no other sign that the caretaker had been in—but, if not? Letters dropped in at doors of deserted houses do not fly or walk to tables in halls. They do not sit on the dust of empty tables with the air of certainty that they will be found. There is needed some human hand—but nobody but the caretaker had a key.

Under circumstances she did not care to consider, a house can be entered without a key. It was possible that she was not alone now. She might be being waited for, downstairs. Waited for—until when? Until "the hour arranged." At least that was not six o'clock: six has struck.

She rose from the chair and went over and locked the door.

The thing was, to get out. To fly? No, not that: she had to catch her train. As a woman whose utter dependability was the keystone of her family life she was not willing to return to the country, to her husband, her little boys and her sister, without the objects she had come up to fetch. Resuming work at the chest she set about making up a number of parcels in a rapid, fumbling-decisive way. These, with her

---

17. *Arboreal* indicates that there were many trees where they lived.
18. *Kensington* is a wealthy district in London.
19. *Circumscribed* means "restricted."
20. *Desuetude* (des′ wə tood′) means "in a state of disuse."

Big Idea World War II and Its Aftermath *In what way might Mrs. Drover's home represent the whole of London?*

---

21. Here, *rally* means "to calm and encourage."

shopping parcels, would be too much to carry; these meant a taxi—at the thought of the taxi her heart went up and her normal breathing resumed. I will ring up the taxi now; the taxi cannot come too soon: I shall hear the taxi out there running its engine, till I walk calmly down to it through the hall. I'll ring up—But no: the telephone is cut off . . . She tugged at a knot she had tied wrong.

The idea of flight . . . He was never kind to me, not really. I don't remember him kind at all. Mother said he never considered me. He was set on me, that was what it was—not love. Not love, not meaning a person well. What did he do, to make me promise like that? I can't remember—But she found that she could.

She remembered with such dreadful acuteness that the twenty-five years since then dissolved like smoke and she instinctively looked for the weal[22] left by the button on the palm of her hand. She remembered not only all that he said and did but the complete suspension of *her* existence during that August week. I was not myself—they all told me so at the time. She remembered—but with one white burning blank as where acid has dropped on a photograph: *under no conditions* could she remember his face.

So, wherever he may be waiting, I shall not know him. You have no time to run from a face you do not expect.

The thing was to get to the taxi before any clock struck what could be the hour. She would slip down the street and round the side of the square to where the square gave on the main road. She would return in the taxi, safe, to her own door, and bring the solid driver into the house with her to pick up the parcels from room to room. The idea of the taxi driver made her decisive, bold: she unlocked her door, went to the top of the staircase and listened down.

She heard nothing—but while she was hearing nothing the *passé*[23] air of the staircase was disturbed by a draft that traveled up to her face.

It **emanated** from the basement: down there a door or window was being opened by someone who chose this moment to leave the house.

The rain had stopped; the pavements steamily shone as Mrs. Drover let herself out by inches from her own front door into the empty street. The unoccupied houses opposite continued to meet her look with their damaged stare. Making towards the thoroughfare and the taxi, she tried not to keep looking behind. Indeed, the silence was so intense—one of those creeks of London silence exaggerated this summer by the damage of war—that no tread could have gained on hers unheard. Where her street debouched[24] on the square where people went on living, she grew conscious of, and checked, her unnatural pace. Across the open end of the square two buses **impassively** passed each other: women, a perambulator, cyclists, a man wheeling a barrow signalized, once again, the ordinary flow of life. At the square's most populous corner should be—and was—the short taxi rank. This evening, only one taxi—but this, although it presented its blank rump, appeared already to be alertly waiting for her. Indeed, without looking round the driver started his engine as she panted up from behind and put her hand on the door. As she did so, the clock struck seven. The taxi faced the main road: to make the trip back to her house it would have to turn—she had settled back on the seat and the taxi *had* turned before she, surprised by its knowing movement, recollected that she had not "said where." She leaned forward to scratch at the glass panel that divided the driver's head from her own.

The driver braked to what was almost a stop, turned round and slid the glass panel back: the jolt of this flung Mrs. Drover forward till her

Visual Vocabulary
A *perambulator* is a baby carriage.

---

22. A *weal* is a bruise or mark on the skin; a welt.
23. As it is used here, *passé* means "stale."

Literary Element Flashback *How is this sentiment reflected in the soldier's past behavior?*

24. *Debouched* (di bōōshd´) means "emerged."

Vocabulary

emanate (em´ ə nāt´) *v.* to come forth from a source; to issue
impassively (im pas´ iv lē) *adv.* in an emotionless manner

The Strand by Night, 1937. Christopher Richard Wynne Nevinson. Bradford Art Galleries and Museums, West Yorkshire, UK.

face was almost into the glass. Through the aperture[25] driver and passenger, not six inches between them, remained for an eternity eye to eye. Mrs. Drover's mouth hung open for some seconds before she could issue her first scream. After that she continued to scream freely and to beat with her gloved hands on the glass all round as the taxi, accelerating without mercy, made off with her into the hinterland[26] of deserted streets.

---

25. An *aperture* (ap′ ər chər) is an opening.

26. Here, *hinterland* means "remoteness."

Reading Strategy   Analyzing Sensory Details *What details in this passage contribute to the ominous mood?*

RESPONDING AND THINKING CRITICALLY

Respond

1. What was your reaction to the conclusion of this story? Explain.

Recall and Interpret

2. (a)How does Bowen describe Mrs. Drover's house in the beginning of the story? (b)Describe the atmosphere the setting creates.

3. (a)How does Mrs. Drover react to finding the letter on the hall table? (b)What does her reaction suggest about her personality and way of life?

4. (a)What does Mrs. Drover do after reading the letter? (b)What does her reaction to the contents of the letter indicate about her relationship with the writer and her feelings about him?

Analyze and Evaluate

5. (a)Mrs. Drover cannot, under *any* circumstances, remember her fiancé's face. What does this suggest to you? (b)How does this detail contribute to the story's mood?

6. What do you think happens to Mrs. Drover at the end? Explain.

Connect

7. **Big Idea** **World War II and Its Aftermath** (a)Why do you think Bowen chose war-torn London as the setting for this story? (b)In your opinion, how might both world wars have affected Mrs. Drover's emotional health?

LITERARY ANALYSIS

Literary Element Flashback

Reread the **flashback** sequence on pages 1178–1180. Then answer the questions about how the information from the flashback helped you better understand Mrs. Drover's present-day situation.

1. How did Mrs. Drover's younger self really feel when her fiancé was presumed dead? How did the "sinister troth" affect her?

2. Do you think Bowen's use of the flashback interrupts the flow of the story, or does it intensify the suspense? Explain.

Writing About Literature

Analyze Plot In a suspenseful story, unresolved conflicts create feelings of curiosity, uncertainty, and even dread. Write a brief essay about the threat to the central character in "The Demon Lover," analyzing those elements that help produce suspense.

Literature Online **Web Activities** For eFlashcards, Selection Quick Checks, and other Web activities, go to www.glencoe.com.

READING AND VOCABULARY

Reading Strategy Analyzing Sensory Details

Review your chart cataloging the sensory details of the story and answer the following questions.

1. (a)What sensory details does Bowen use to describe her London house? (b)How do the details contribute to the story's creepy atmosphere?

2. (a)What sensory details does Bowen use to describe the day on which the story takes place? (b)How do these details create suspense?

Vocabulary Practice

Practice with Word Parts Using the definitions of the foreign words below, select the English word that is derived from each one. Use a dictionary for help.

1. *Passivus* (Latin): "capable of feeling"
   a. intermittent   **b.** impassively

2. *Emanare* (Latin): "to flow"
   a. precipitately   **b.** emanate

3. *Prosa* (Latin): "straightforward"
   a. prosaic   **b.** precipitately

4. *Praecipitatus* (Latin): "thrown down headlong"
   a. intermittent   **b.** precipitately

Musée des Beaux Arts and The Unknown Citizen

MEET W. H. AUDEN

For much of the middle part of the twentieth century, Wystan Hugh Auden was hailed as the greatest poet of his generation—the successor to T. S. Eliot and William Butler Yeats. His poetry was brilliant and political. Auden often used traditional formal techniques to explore modern social and spiritual concerns. His prolific output and versatile abilities helped clear the way for a new poetic style in the post–World War II period.

> *"Poetry makes nothing happen. It survives in the valley of its saying."*
>
> —W. H. Auden

The Auden Group Born in York, the son of a distinguished doctor, the young Auden had no particular literary ambitions; he had originally planned to become a mining engineer. His absorbing interest during childhood and adolescence was science, primarily biology. However, by 1922 he discovered a knack for poetry—publishing his first poem two years later, at the age of seventeen. After entering Oxford in 1925, Auden famously declared to his English tutor that he planned to become "a great poet."

While at Oxford, Auden became friends with a group of some of the brightest young poets in England, including Stephen Spender, Cecil Day-Lewis, and Louis MacNeice. Auden's influence in this illustrious group was so great that it was known as the "Auden Group," and later dubbed by journalists and critics as the Auden Generation. After college Auden began teaching in Scotland and England. A somewhat eccentric teacher, he was nonetheless liked by his students. Soon after Auden began teaching, his first book of verse was published. By the age of twenty-five, with the publication of a second volume, Auden had made a mark on the literary landscape. At the time, his poems were characterized, in part, by his belief that poetry could act as a kind of therapy, performing a function similar to psychoanalysis.

An American Citizen Although his writing was primarily psychological, Auden, like many of his contemporaries, was active in the politics of his day. "I am not one of those who believe that poetry need or even should be directly political," he wrote, "but in a critical period such as ours, I do believe that the poet must have direct knowledge of the major political events." He went to Spain in 1937 during the Spanish Civil War, hoping to aid the Loyalists in their fight against fascism. This visit inspired the poem *Spain,* one of Auden's most famous works. In 1938, just before the start of World War II, Auden moved to the United States. "The attractiveness of America to a writer is its openness," he said. Auden became a U.S. citizen in 1946. The next year he won the Pulitzer Prize for *The Age of Anxiety.*

In the late 1940s, Auden divided his time between Europe and the United States. From 1956 to 1961, he was professor of poetry at Oxford University. Throughout the rest of his life he continued to write, creating a diverse body of work that includes not only poetry but also drama, criticism, blues music, musical librettos, and nonsense verse.

W. H. Auden was born in 1907 and died in 1973.

Literature Online **Author Search** For more about W. H. Auden, go to www.glencoe.com.

Connecting to the Poems

In the following poems, Auden expresses his ideas on human suffering and individuality. As you read, think about the following questions:

- Do you think people are immune to the suffering and loss of other people?
- In a world where we shop at the same stores, watch the same TV shows, and in general have so much in common, how do people retain their individuality?

Building Background

The title of the poem "Musée des Beaux Arts" refers to the Royal Museum of Fine Arts in Brussels, Belgium. This museum owns the painting *The Fall of Icarus,* to which Auden refers in his poem (see page 1186). This painting, by Pieter Brueghel the Elder, the great sixteenth-century Flemish artist, depicts Brueghel's interpretation of the Greek myth of Icarus. In this myth, Icarus and his father, Daedalus, escape from prison by making artificial wings of feathers and wax, which they fasten to their shoulders. Daedalus warns Icarus not to fly too close to the sun because it could melt the wax, but Icarus ignores his father's warning and falls to his death. In Brueghel's rendition, Icarus's legs are disappearing into the sea in a corner of the painting; the rest of the scene has nothing to do with him.

Setting Purposes for Reading

Big Idea World War II and Its Aftermath

As you read, notice how Auden addresses human isolation, cultural anxiety, and disillusionment with society.

Literary Element Irony

Irony is the contrast or discrepancy between appearance and reality. Irony can take several forms: **verbal irony** in a poem exists when the speaker says one thing, but the poet clearly means something different; **dramatic irony** occurs when the audience or reader knows something that the speaker of the poem or one of its characters does not know. As you read, pay attention to Auden's use of irony.

- See Literary Terms Handbook, p. R9.

Reading Strategy Clarifying Meaning

To **clarify meaning** means to focus on difficult sections of a text in order to understand them better. Often this involves rereading, summarizing, and asking questions.

Reading Tip: Asking Questions As you read Auden's poems, ask yourself the following questions:

- What is the stanza basically saying?
- How could I restate these lines to improve my comprehension?
- What does this image seem to represent? Why might the poet have included it?

Vocabulary

reverently (rev′ rənt lē) *adv.* respectfully; with deep affection or veneration; p. 1186 *The child spoke reverently about his favorite teacher.*

forsaken (fôr sāk′ ən) *adj.* deserted or lonely; p. 1186 *The windswept mountains are a forsaken place during the winter.*

sensible (sen′ sə bəl) *adj.* having good judgment or sound thinking; p. 1188 *Most commentators agreed that the jury's decision was well reasoned and very sensible.*

Vocabulary Tip: Analogies Analogies compare words based on the relationship between each pair's meaning.

Literature Online **Interactive Literary Elements Handbook** To review or learn more about the literary elements, go to www.glencoe.com.

OBJECTIVES
In studying these selections, you will focus on the following:
- analyzing literary periods
- analyzing irony and diction
- clarifying meaning

The Fall of Icarus, c. 1558–1566. Pieter Brueghel the Elder. Oil on canvas, 73.7 x 111.8 cm. Musée Royaux des Beaux-Arts de Belgique, Brussels, Belgium.

Musée des Beaux Arts

W. H. Auden

About suffering they were never wrong,
The Old Masters:[1] how well they understood
Its human position; how it takes place
While someone else is eating or opening a window or just walking dully along;
5 How, when the aged are **reverently,** passionately waiting
For the miraculous birth, there always must be
Children who did not specially want it to happen, skating
On a pond at the edge of the wood:
They never forgot
10 That even the dreadful martyrdom must run its course
Anyhow in a corner, some untidy spot
Where the dogs go on with their doggy life and the torturer's horse
Scratches its innocent behind on a tree.

In Bruegel's *Icarus*, for instance: how everything turns away
15 Quite leisurely from the disaster; the ploughman may
Have heard the splash, the **forsaken** cry,
But for him it was not an important failure; the sun shone
As it had to on the white legs disappearing into the green
Water; and the expensive delicate ship that must have seen
20 Something amazing, a boy falling out of the sky,
Had somewhere to get to and sailed calmly on.

---

1. *The Old Masters* refers to great European artists of the sixteenth to eighteenth centuries.

Literary Element Irony *What is ironic about the ship sailing "calmly on"?*

Vocabulary

reverently (rev′ rənt lē) *adv.* respectfully; with deep affection or veneration
forsaken (fôr sāk′ ən) *adj.* deserted or lonely

Motor Manufacturing – Empire buying makes busy factories, 1928. Poster. Victoria and Albert Museum, London.

The Unknown Citizen

W. H. Auden

(To JS/07/M/378
This Marble Monument Is Erected by the State)[1]

He was found by the Bureau of Statistics to be
One against whom there was no official complaint,
And all the reports on his conduct agree
That, in the modern sense of an old-fashioned word, he was a saint,
5   For in everything he did he served the Greater Community.
Except for the War till the day he retired
He worked in a factory and never got fired,
But satisfied his employers, Fudge Motors Inc.
Yet he wasn't a scab[2] or odd in his views,
10   For his Union reports that he paid his dues,
(Our report on his Union shows it was sound)
And our Social Psychology workers found
That he was popular with his mates and liked a drink.
The Press are convinced that he bought a paper every day
15   And that his reactions to advertisements were normal in every way.
Policies taken out in his name prove that he was fully insured,
And his Health-card shows he was once in hospital but left it cured.
Both Producers Research and High-Grade Living declare
He was fully **sensible** to the advantages of the Installment Plan
20   And had everything necessary to the Modern Man,
A phonograph, a radio, a car, and a frigidaire.
Our researchers into Public Opinion are content
That he held the proper opinions for the time of year;
When there was peace, he was for peace; when there was war, he went.
25   He was married and added five children to the population,
Which our Eugenist[3] says was the right number for a parent of his generation,
And our teachers report that he never interfered with their education.
Was he free? Was he happy? The question is absurd:
Had anything been wrong, we should certainly have heard.

---

1. A quotation or a short inscription at the beginning of a poem is called an *epigraph*.
2. A *scab* is slang for someone who does not want to join a union.
3. A *Eugenist* is someone who studies or supports the hereditary enhancement of the human race by controlled breeding.

Literary Element   Irony *How do you know that this passage is ironic?*

Big Idea   World War II and Its Aftermath *Do you think Auden believes that this is all people in the modern world need? What do you think he is suggesting in these lines?*

Vocabulary

sensible (sen′ sə bəl) *adj.* having good judgment or sound thinking

RESPONDING AND THINKING CRITICALLY

Respond

1. What is your opinion of Auden's portrayal of humanity in both poems?

Recall and Interpret

2. (a)According to the speaker in "Musée des Beaux Arts," what did the "Old Masters" understand about suffering? (b)What do the dogs do and how does "the torturer's horse" behave? (c)What does this suggest about nature's reaction to human suffering?

3. (a)What "disaster" occurs in the second stanza? (b)According to the speaker of the poem, how does "everything" in Brueghel's painting react to this disaster?

4. (a)In "The Unknown Citizen," how is the citizen described? (b)What effect does the epigraph have on the poem as a whole?

5. (a)What questions are posed at the end of "The Unknown Citizen"? (b)Why does the speaker state that these questions are "absurd"? Consider the identity of the speaker.

Analyze and Evaluate

6. (a)What is the message of "Musée des Beaux Arts"? (b)Do you agree with this message? Explain.

7. (a)How does Auden use **imagery** to convey his ideas about suffering in "Musée des Beaux Arts"? (b)Which image do you believe is most effective? Explain.

8. (a)What is the message of "The Unknown Citizen"? (b)Do you agree or disagree with this message?

Connect

9. **Big Idea** **World War II and Its Aftermath** In what ways do these poems suggest the disillusionment of British writers during this time?

VISUAL LITERACY: Graphic Organizer

Visualizing Auden's Arguments

A sound argument must be supported by convincing evidence. While not all poems contain an overt argument, those that do can be evaluated in much the same way that a persuasive or analytical essay is evaluated. For example, in Auden's "Musée des Beaux Arts" the poet is making an overt argument about the nature of human suffering and the way in which others respond to suffering that is not their own. While less overt, Auden is also making an argument in "The Unknown Citizen" concerning dehumanization in contemporary society.

To understand and evaluate Auden's arguments, reread the poems and compile any evidence presented by the poet. Use this evidence to complete a chart like the one on the right. Then answer the questions.

Poet's Argument	Supporting Evidence	My Evaluation of the Argument
	"how it takes place / While someone else is eating or opening a window or just walking dully along"	

1. In what ways are the arguments in both of these poems similar?

2. How does Auden use Brueghel's painting to support his argument in "Musée des Beaux Arts"?

3. Do you agree or disagree with Auden's arguments regarding human nature? Explain.

Literary Element Irony

Irony is an important element to identify and analyze because it can completely shade the message of a literary work. For example, if you do not grasp the irony in Auden's "The Unknown Citizen" you will miss the main message of the poem.

1. Find several examples of **dramatic irony** in "Musée des Beaux Arts" and explain how they support the poem's theme.

2. Cite several examples of **verbal irony** in "The Unknown Citizen" and explain how they help to convey the poem's message.

Review: Diction

As you learned on page 854, an author's word choice, or use of appropriate words to convey a particular meaning, is called **diction**. Good writers choose their words carefully to express their intended meaning precisely. Diction is particularly important in poetry, which uses language more economically than most prose does. In "Musée des Beaux Arts," Auden deliberately uses language that is plain, straightforward, even earthy—as when he describes a corner "where the dogs go on with their doggy life." In this example, Auden's diction creates an unromantic matter-of-fact tone.

Partner Activity Work with a partner to answer the following questions.

1. Find another example of mundane or earthy language in "Musée des Beaux Arts." What effect is created by this choice of language?

2. In your opinion, how does Auden's diction help convey the **theme,** or message about life, of "Musée des Beaux Arts"?

Reading Strategy Clarifying Meaning

The meaning of a poem can sometimes be difficult to determine. Poets often use figurative and elevated language, rhetorical devices, and narrative techniques to convey their meaning. When the meaning of a passage in a literary work is not entirely clear to you, it is important to ask yourself questions about that passage and rephrase it in your own words so that you can gain a better understanding of the work.

1. Paraphrase lines 10–13 of "Musée des Beaux Arts." In what ways do these lines contribute to the theme of the poem?

2. (a)Examine lines 24–26 in "The Unknown Citizen." What does the citizen do? (b)How would you describe the tone of these lines?

Vocabulary Practice

Practice with Analogies Choose the word that best completes each analogy. To complete an analogy, decide on the relationship represented by the first pair of words. Then, apply that relationship to the second set of words.

1. **violently : peacefully :: reverently :**
   a. disrespectfully **b.** happily **c.** swiftly

2. **bold : brave :: forsaken :**
   a. unhealthy **b.** desolate **c.** meaningful

3. **vivid : bright :: sensible :**
   a. cluttered **b.** sensational **c.** reasonable

Academic Vocabulary

Here are two words from the vocabulary list on page R82.

colleague (kol´ ēg) *n.* an academic or professional peer; an associate

adjacent (ə jā´ sənt) *adj.* directly next to; nearby

Practice and Apply

1. In "The Unknown Citizen," what do the citizen's **colleagues** think of him?

2. In Brueghel's painting, what is depicted **adjacent** to Icarus's falling body?

Writing About Literature

Respond to Theme The **theme** of a literary work is its main idea, which is sometimes expressed as a general statement about life. Some works have a **stated theme,** like "Musée des Beaux Arts." Others, like "The Unknown Citizen," have an **implied theme.** Write a short response essay in which you analyze and evaluate the themes of both poems.

Before you begin drafting your essay, it is important to determine what you think the theme of each poem is, your opinion of these themes, and how well you feel each theme is developed. Use a graphic organizer like the one below.

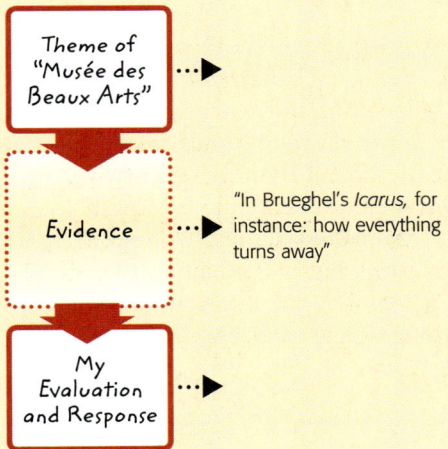

"In Brueghel's *Icarus,* for instance: how everything turns away"

After you complete your draft, meet with a peer reviewer to evaluate each other's work and to suggest revisions. Then proofread and edit your draft for errors in spelling, grammar, and punctuation.

Literary Criticism

Even when his subject matter was serious, Auden delighted in changing the tone in his poems from somber to light and amusing. One critic, commenting on Auden's early work, noted the poet's "crazy wit" and "delight in playing with words." Auden himself claimed that many writers do not appreciate "the basic frivolity of art. People do not understand that it is possible to believe in a thing and ridicule it at the same time." Do you think that these quotations accurately describe Auden's work? In a paragraph or two, analyze one of Auden's poems in light of these quotations.

Auden's Language and Style

Using Colons In "Musée des Beaux Arts" and "The Unknown Citizen," Auden uses colons for multiple reasons. The colon is typically used to introduce a list; to introduce material that illustrates, explains, adds to, or restates preceding material; or to introduce a long, formal quotation. Consider the way in which Auden is using the colon in the following lines:

> "Was he free? Was he happy? The question is absurd:
> Had anything been wrong, we should certainly have heard."

In this example, Auden uses the colon to introduce new material that adds information to the previous statement.

Activity Reread the poems, taking note of all of the instances in which Auden uses a colon and the way in which each colon is used. Then, create a two-column chart like the one below:

Examples	Purpose
"The Unknown Citizen," lines 28–29: "Was he free? Was he happy? The question is absurd: Had anything been wrong, we should certainly have heard."	The colon is used to introduce new material that adds information to the previous statement.

Revising Check

Colons It is very important to know how to use the colon correctly. Its misuse can lead to cluttered or confusing sentences. With a partner, go through your response to the themes in Auden's poems and note places where a colon might be appropriate or places where you may have used one incorrectly. Revise your draft to improve sentence fluency.

Literature Online Web Activities For eFlashcards, Selection Quick Checks, and other Web activities, go to www.glencoe.com.

A Shocking Accident

MEET GRAHAM GREENE

Among the finest writers of postwar Britain, Graham Greene produced a string of popular spy thrillers, which he called his "entertainments," as well as more serious works of literature. The grandnephew of Victorian writer Robert Louis Stevenson, Greene was a masterful storyteller who achieved both popular and critical success.

Headmaster's Son Greene grew up in Hertfordshire, north of London. He attended the exclusive Berkhamsted School, of which his father was headmaster, and came to detest the brutalities of boarding-school life, especially since he was often tormented for being the headmaster's son. At seventeen he suffered an emotional breakdown and ran away. Later, recalling his tortured years at the school, Greene wrote: "One met for the first time characters, adult and adolescent, who bore about them the genuine quality of evil."

As a result of running away from boarding school, Greene spent six months under the care of a London psychoanalyst, who also happened to be a writer. Later Greene would call these months the happiest time of his life. Not only did he escape the hated boarding school, but he began to write for himself with the encouragement of the sympathetic doctor. The experience also sparked Greene's lifelong interest in psychoanalysis.

Writing and Spying Greene attended Oxford University and, upon graduation in 1925, published a volume of poetry. For the next few years, he worked as a journalist, eventually finding himself on the staff of one of Britain's best newspapers, the London *Times*. After several years, he resigned to become a full-time writer. With the publication of *The Man Within* (1929), Greene established himself as a novelist. Not long afterward came two major novels: *Brighton Rock* (1938) and *The Power and the Glory* (1940).

Along with many other English authors, Greene served in British intelligence during World War II. His experience helped him in the writing of his spy novels, many of which were turned into popular films. Greene also found there was plenty to spy on in his own society. A careful observer, he was attentive to the smallest details: "You're there, listening to every word, but part of you is observing. Everything is useful to a writer, you see—every scrap, even the longest and most boring of luncheon parties."

> "The great advantage of being a writer is that you can spy on people."
>
> —Graham Greene

Literary Success A convert to Roman Catholicism, Greene often treated moral and religious themes in his more serious fiction. He also was a worldwide traveler and is noted for his realistic depiction of Cold War and colonial politics in novels like *The Heart of the Matter* (1948), *The Quiet American* (1956), and *The Comedians* (1966). In addition, he produced such humorous satires as *Our Man in Havana* (1958), a parody of his own spy thrillers.

Graham Greene was born in 1904 and died in 1991.

Literature Online **Author Search** For more about Graham Greene, go to www.glencoe.com.

Connecting to the Story

Has a shocking situation ever caused you to laugh? In Greene's short story, an unfortunate accident becomes a source of humor for others. As you read, think about the following questions:

- Why do people sometimes find humor in shocking situations?
- Is it important for your friends to react to situations in the same way you do?

Building Background

"A Shocking Accident" draws on Greene's early school experiences and reflects his more satirical side. In England, "public schools" are expensive private schools: the term *public* merely dates back to a time when these schools were the first schools opened outside the home. Two prestigious public schools mentioned in this story are Marlborough and Rugby.

Setting Purposes for Reading

Big Idea World War II and Its Aftermath

During the years after World War II, a sense of cultural anxiety and disillusionment permeated British writing. As you read, consider which aspects of British society Greene criticizes or satirizes in this story.

Literary Element Character

A **character** is a person or animal portrayed in a literary work. Less important characters, known as **minor characters,** are used by a writer to "fill out" a scene, to provide dialogue, or to further the plot in some way. As opposed to **main characters,** who are typically fully developed, minor characters display few personality traits and generally act in a consistent manner. As you read, consider how you would classify each character in this story.

- See Literary Terms Handbook, p. R3.

Literature Online **Interactive Literary Elements Handbook** To review or learn more about the literary elements, go to www.glencoe.com.

Reading Strategy Recognizing Bias

Recognizing bias involves identifying statements that are prejudiced or those that strongly support only one side of an issue. As you read, look for examples of bias on the part of the narrator and the characters in this story.

Reading Tip: Taking Notes Use a chart to record examples of bias in the story.

Example of Bias	Explanation

Vocabulary

callousness (kal´ əs nəs) *n.* hardness in mind or feelings; insensitivity; p. 1195 *The reporters showed callousness in interviewing the mourners at the funeral.*

commiseration (kə miz´ ə rā´ shən) *n.* a feeling or expression of sympathy; compassion; p. 1195 *Those players who grumbled about the referee's calls received no commiseration from their coach.*

intrinsically (in trin´ zik lē) *adv.* inherently; in its very nature; p. 1196 *The head of the social services department believes that people are intrinsically good.*

brevity (brev´ ə tē) *n.* shortness in speech or writing; p. 1196 *By deleting unnecessary words, you give your writing brevity, clarity, and force.*

appease (ə pēz´) *v.* to bring to a state of peace or quiet; to satisfy; p. 1197 *Sometimes, only a bottle of warm milk can appease a crying baby.*

Vocabulary Tip: Synonyms Words that have the same or nearly the same meaning are called synonyms.

OBJECTIVES
In studying this selection, you will focus on the following:
- analyzing literary periods
- analyzing characters
- recognizing bias

The Apple-Tub, 1992. Ditz. Private collection.

A Shocking Accident

Graham Greene

1

Jerome was called into his housemaster's[1] room in the break between the second and the third class on a Thursday morning. He had no fear of trouble, for he was a warden—the name that the proprietor and headmaster of a rather expensive preparatory school had chosen to give to approved, reliable boys in the lower forms[2] (from a warden one became a guardian and finally before leaving, it was hoped for Marlborough or Rugby, a crusader). The housemaster, Mr. Wordsworth, sat behind his desk with an appearance of perplexity[3] and apprehension.[4] Jerome had the odd impression when he entered that he was a cause of fear.

"Sit down, Jerome," Mr. Wordsworth said. "All going well with the trigonometry?"

"Yes, sir."

"I've had a telephone call, Jerome. From your aunt. I'm afraid I have bad news for you."

"Yes, sir?"

"Your father has had an accident."

"Oh."

Mr. Wordsworth looked at him with some surprise. "A serious accident."

"Yes, sir?"

Jerome worshipped his father: the verb is exact. As man re-creates God, so Jerome re-created his father—from a restless widowed author into a mysterious adventurer who traveled in far places—Nice, Beirut, Majorca, even the Canaries. The time had arrived about his eighth birthday when Jerome believed that his

---

1. A *housemaster* is a teacher who supervises a residence hall of a boys' school.
2. Here, *forms* means "grades."
3. *Perplexity* is the state of being puzzled or confused.
4. Here, *apprehension* means "dread."

Literary Element   **Character** *How does Jerome react to the news of his father's accident?*

father either "ran guns"[5] or was a member of the British Secret Service. Now it occurred to him that his father might have been wounded in "a hail of machine-gun bullets."

Mr. Wordsworth played with the ruler on his desk. He seemed at a loss how to continue. He said, "You know your father was in Naples?"

"Yes, sir."

"Your aunt heard from the hospital today."

"Oh."

Mr. Wordsworth said with desperation, "It was a street accident."

"Yes, sir?" It seemed quite likely to Jerome that they would call it a street accident. The police of course had fired first; his father would not take human life except as a last resort.

"I'm afraid your father was very seriously hurt indeed."

"Oh."

"In fact, Jerome, he died yesterday. Quite without pain."

"Did they shoot him through the heart?"

"I beg your pardon. What did you say, Jerome?"

"Did they shoot him through the heart?"

"Nobody shot him, Jerome. A pig fell on him." An inexplicable convulsion took place in the nerves of Mr. Wordsworth's face; it really looked for a moment as though he were going to laugh. He closed his eyes, composed his features and said rapidly as though it were necessary to expel the story as quickly as possible, "Your father was walking along a street in Naples when a pig fell on him. A shocking accident. Apparently in the poorer quarters of Naples they keep pigs on their balconies. This one was on the fifth floor. It had grown too fat. The balcony broke. The pig fell on your father."

Mr. Wordsworth left his desk rapidly and went to the window, turning his back on Jerome. He shook a little with emotion.

Jerome said, "What happened to the pig?"

5. *Ran guns* means "smuggled firearms and ammunition."

Literary Element Character *Why does this thought pop into Jerome's mind?*

Literary Element Character *What is Mr. Wordsworth trying to hide?*

2

This was not **callousness** on the part of Jerome, as it was interpreted by Mr. Wordsworth to his colleagues (he even discussed with them whether, perhaps, Jerome was yet fitted to be a warden). Jerome was only attempting to visualize the strange scene to get the details right. Nor was Jerome a boy who cried; he was a boy who brooded,[6] and it never occurred to him at his preparatory school that the circumstances of his father's death were comic—they were still part of the mystery of life. It was later, in his first term at his public school, when he told the story to his best friend, that he began to realize how it affected others. Naturally after that disclosure he was known, rather unreasonably, as Pig.

Unfortunately his aunt had no sense of humor. There was an enlarged snapshot of his father on the piano; a large sad man in an unsuitable dark suit posed in Capri with an umbrella (to guard him against sunstroke), the Faraglione rocks forming the background. By the age of sixteen Jerome was well aware that the portrait looked more like the author of *Sunshine and Shade* and *Rambles in the Balearics* than an agent of the Secret Service. All the same he loved the memory of his father: he still possessed an album filled with picture-postcards (the stamps had been soaked off long ago for his other collection), and it pained him when his aunt embarked with strangers on the story of his father's death.

"A shocking accident," she would begin, and the stranger would compose his or her features into the correct shape for interest and **commiseration**. Both reactions, of course, were false, but it was terrible for Jerome to see how suddenly, midway in her rambling discourse,[7]

6. *Brooded* means "pondered unhappily."
7. As it is used here, *discourse* means "story."

Big Idea World War II and Its Aftermath *What does Greene criticize about British public schools?*

Vocabulary

callousness (kal′ əs nəs) *n.* hardness in mind or feelings; insensitivity

commiseration (kə miz′ ə rā′ shən) *n.* a feeling or expression of sympathy; compassion

the interest would become genuine. "I can't think how such things can be allowed in a civilized country," his aunt would say. "I suppose one has to regard Italy as civilized. One is prepared for all kinds of things abroad, of course, and my brother was a great traveler. He always carried a water filter with him. It was far less expensive, you know, than buying all those bottles of mineral water. My brother always said that his filter paid for his dinner wine. You can see from that what a careful man he was, but who could possibly have expected when he was walking along the Via Dottore Manuele Panucci on his way to the Hydrographic[8] Museum that a pig would fall on him?" That was the moment when the interest became genuine.

Jerome's father had not been a very distinguished writer, but the time always seems to come, after an author's death, when somebody thinks it worth his while to write a letter to the *Times Literary Supplement* announcing the preparation of a biography and asking to see any letters or documents or receive any anecdotes from friends of the dead man. Most of the biographies, of course, never appear—one wonders whether the whole thing may not be an obscure form of blackmail and whether many a potential writer of a biography or thesis finds the means in this way to finish his education at Kansas or Nottingham.[9] Jerome, however, as a chartered accountant, lived far from the literary world. He did not realize how small the menace[10] really was, or that the danger period for someone of his father's obscurity had long passed. Sometimes he rehearsed the method of recounting his father's death so as to reduce the comic element to its smallest dimensions—it would be of no use to refuse information, for in that case the biographer would undoubtedly visit his aunt who was living to a great old age with no sign of flagging.[11]

It seemed to Jerome that there were two possible methods—the first led gently up to the accident, so that by the time it was described the listener was so well prepared that the death came really as an anticlimax. The chief danger of laughter in such a story was always surprise. When he rehearsed this method Jerome began boringly enough.

"You know Naples and those high tenement buildings? Somebody once told me that the Neapolitan[12] always feels at home in New York just as the man from Turin[13] feels at home in London because the river runs in much the same way in both cities. Where was I? Oh, yes. Naples, of course. You'd be surprised in the poorer quarters what things they keep on the balconies of those sky-scraping tenements—not washing, you know, or bedding, but things like livestock, chickens or even pigs. Of course the pigs get no exercise whatever and fatten all the quicker." He could imagine how his hearer's eyes would have glazed by this time. "I've no idea, have you, how heavy a pig can be, but these old buildings are all badly in need of repair. A balcony on the fifth floor gave way under one of those pigs. It struck the third floor balcony on its way down and sort of ricocheted into the street. My father was on the way to the Hydrographic Museum when the pig hit him. Coming from that height and that angle it broke his neck." This was really a masterly attempt to make an **intrinsically** interesting subject boring.

The other method Jerome rehearsed had the virtue of **brevity**.

"My father was killed by a pig."

"Really? In India?"

"No, in Italy."

"How interesting. I never realized there was pig-sticking in Italy. Was your father keen on polo?"

In course of time, neither too early nor too late, rather as though, in his capacity as a

---

8. *Hydrographic* means "relating to the scientific analysis of the physical conditions of water."
9. *Nottingham,* a city in central England, is home to several universities.
10. A *menace* is a threat.
11. *Flagging* means "weakening."

Reading Strategy   Recognizing Bias
What bias does Jerome's aunt reveal in this passage?

---

12. A *Neapolitan* is one who lives in Naples, Italy.
13. *Turin* is a city in Italy.

Vocabulary

intrinsically (in trin′ zik lē) *adv.* inherently; in its very nature

brevity (brev′ ə tē) *n.* shortness in speech or writing

chartered accountant, Jerome had studied the statistics and taken the average, he became engaged to be married: to a pleasant fresh-faced girl of twenty-five whose father was a doctor in Pinner.[14] Her name was Sally, her favorite author was still Hugh Walpole,[15] and she had adored babies ever since she had been given a doll at the age of five which moved its eyes and made water. Their relationship was contented rather than exciting, as became the love affair of a chartered accountant; it would never have done if it had interfered with the figures.

One thought worried Jerome, however. Now that within a year he might himself become a father, his love for the dead man increased; he realized what affection had gone into the picture-postcards. He felt a longing to protect his memory, and uncertain whether this quiet love of his would survive if Sally were so insensitive as to laugh when she heard the story of his father's death. Inevitably she would hear it when Jerome brought her to dinner with his aunt. Several times he tried to tell her himself, as she was naturally anxious to know all she could that concerned him.

"You were very small when your father died?"

"Just nine."

"Poor little boy," she said.

"I was at school. They broke the news to me."

"Did you take it very hard?"

"I can't remember."

"You never told me how it happened."

"It was very sudden. A street accident."

"You'll never drive fast, will you, Jemmy?" (She had begun to call him "Jemmy.") It was too late then to try the second method—the one he thought of as the pig-sticking one.

They were going to marry quietly in a registry office and have their honeymoon at Torquay.[16] He avoided taking her to see his aunt until a week before the wedding, but then the night came, and he could not have told himself whether his apprehension was more for his father's memory or the security of his own love.

The moment came all too soon. "Is that Jemmy's father?" Sally asked, picking up the portrait of the man with the umbrella.

"Yes, dear. How did you guess?"

"He has Jemmy's eyes and brow, hasn't he?"

"Has Jerome lent you his books?"

"No."

"I will give you a set for your wedding. He wrote so tenderly about his travels. My own favorite is *Nooks and Crannies*. He would have had a great future. It made that shocking accident all the worse."

"Yes?"

Jerome longed to leave the room and not see that loved face crinkle with irresistible amusement.

"I had so many letters from his readers after the pig fell on him." She had never been so abrupt before.

And then the miracle happened. Sally did not laugh. Sally sat with open eyes of horror while his aunt told her the story, and at the end, "How horrible," Sally said. "It makes you think, doesn't it? Happening like that. Out of a clear sky."

Jerome's heart sang with joy. It was as though she had **appeased** his fear forever. In the taxi going home he kissed her with more passion than he had ever shown and she returned it. There were babies in her pale blue pupils, babies that rolled their eyes and made water.

"A week today," Jerome said, and she squeezed his hand. "Penny for your thoughts, my darling."

"I was wondering," Sally said, "what happened to the poor pig?"

"They almost certainly had it for dinner," Jerome said happily and kissed the dear child again. ◖

---

14. *Pinner* is a town in England.
15. *Hugh Walpole* was an English novelist.
16. *Torquay* is a town in southwestern England.

Literary Element Character *What conflict must Jerome resolve?*

Literary Element Character *What kind of person is Sally?*

Literary Element Character *What does Sally's question reveal about her?*

Vocabulary

appease (ə pēz´) *v.* to bring to a state of peace or quiet; to satisfy

RESPONDING AND THINKING CRITICALLY

Respond

1. How did you react when you learned what had happened to Jerome's father? Do you think your reaction was appropriate? Why or why not?

Recall and Interpret

2. (a)When Jerome first hears about his father's accident, what does he assume has happened? Why? (b)What actually happened in the accident?

3. (a)How do Mr. Wordsworth and others react to the story of the accident? (b)Why might it pain Jerome to hear his aunt tell the story to strangers?

4. (a)How does Sally react to the aunt's story? (b)What does her reaction suggest about her character?

Analyze and Evaluate

5. Compare the methods Jerome devises for telling the story of the accident. In your opinion, why does he devise these two different methods?

6. Find an example of **situational irony** in the story and evaluate the effect it creates.

7. (a)What **theme,** or message about life, do you think Greene wanted to convey through this story? (b)Do you agree with this message? Why or why not?

Connect

8. **Big Idea** **World War II and Its Aftermath** Which aspects of British society does this story criticize or satirize? Support your response with evidence from the story.

LITERARY ANALYSIS

Literary Element **Character**

In this story Jerome is the main character, and the other characters are minor. Characters that show varied and sometimes contradictory traits are called **round;** characters who reveal only a single personality trait are called **flat.**

1. Is Jerome a round or a flat character? Explain.

2. Is he static or dynamic? Give reasons for your answer.

Writing About Literature

Analyze Comic Devices Humor is the quality of a work that makes it amusing or comic. Sometimes humor comes from the plot of the work and involves situational irony or exaggerated or ridiculous events. Sometimes humor is derived from the characters themselves or from the use of language, including exaggeration, understatement, puns, sarcasm, and verbal irony. Write a brief essay in which you identify the comic devices in "A Shocking Accident" and explain how they add humor to the story.

Literature Online **Web Activities** For eFlashcards, Selection Quick Checks, and other Web activities, go to www.glencoe.com.

READING AND VOCABULARY

Reading Strategy **Recognizing Bias**

Review the chart you created on page 1193 and then answer the following questions.

1. What is the narrator's attitude toward Jerome's way of life?

2. How does the narrator describe Jerome's fiancée, Sally? What can you conclude about the narrator's attitude toward people like her?

Vocabulary **Practice**

Practice with Synonyms Find the synonym for each vocabulary word from "A Shocking Accident." Use a dictionary or a thesaurus if you need help.

1. callousness   **a.** self-pity   **b.** insensitivity

2. commiseration   **a.** harshness   **b.** sympathy

3. intrinsically   **a.** essentially   **b.** fervently

4. brevity   **a.** aptitude   **b.** concision

5. appease   **a.** satisfy   **b.** provoke

Grammar Workshop

Sentence Structure

Avoiding Run-on Sentences

"'You can see from that what a careful man he was, but who could possibly have expected when he was walking along the Via Dottore Manuele Panucci on his way to the Hydrographic Museum that a pig would fall on him?'"

    —Graham Greene, from "A Shocking Accident"

Connecting to Literature In the passage above, Graham Greene presents connected ideas in a **compound sentence**—a sentence with two or more main clauses. The conjunction *but* separates the two main clauses, and it prevents a **run-on sentence,** or two or more complete sentences written as though they were one sentence.

Run-on sentences The clauses of run-on sentences have no punctuation between them or are separated only by a comma.

> *Jerome's friends tease him thoughtlessly they don't understand his difficulty dealing with his father's bizarre accident.*

Solution A Break the sentence into two sentences.

> *Jerome's friends tease him thoughtlessly. They don't understand his difficulty dealing with his father's bizarre accident.*

Solution B Separate the clauses with a semicolon.

> *Jerome's friends tease him thoughtlessly; they don't understand his difficulty dealing with his father's bizarre accident.*

Solution C Add a comma and a coordinating conjunction.

> *Jerome's friends tease him thoughtlessly, <u>for</u> they don't understand his difficulty dealing with his father's bizarre accident.*

Exercise

Revising for Clarity Correct each of the following run-on sentences.

1. Jerome admired his father in fact, he worshipped him.
2. Jerome did not cry, he brooded.
3. Mr. Wordsworth tried to hide a laugh, Jerome found the accident mysterious rather than funny.
4. Sally recognized Jerome's father's photograph she had not read Jerome's father's books.

▶ **Commas and Coordinating Conjunctions**

Use a comma before conjunctions when they join clauses that could stand on their own as complete sentences.

- Jerome dreads his aunt's talks, and he wishes he could avoid them.

▶ **Coordinating Conjunctions**

and	or
but	so
for	yet
nor	

▶ **Test-Taking Tip**

To avoid run-on sentences when writing for a test, review sentences that present more than one thought. Add correct punctuation and necessary conjunctions.

▶ **Language Handbook**

For more about sentence structure, see Language Handbook, pp. R50–R51.

Literature Online
eWorkbooks To link to the Grammar and Language eWorkbook, go to www.glencoe.com.

OBJECTIVES
- Analyze and correct run-on sentences.
- Structure sentences to clarify meaning.

Fern Hill and *Do Not Go Gentle into That Good Night*

MEET DYLAN THOMAS

Dylan Thomas once wrote, "A poet is a poet for such a very tiny bit of his life; for the rest, he is a human being." Thomas certainly tried to live his life to the fullest. He loved parties; he was an entertaining conversationalist; and he enjoyed speaking and reading his poems in public.

> *"A good poem is a contribution to reality. The world is never the same once a good poem has been added to it."*
>
> —Dylan Thomas

Early Success Born in Swansea (swän′ zē), South Wales, Thomas was the son of a farmer's daughter and an English teacher. He attended the Swansea grammar school, where he gained a wide breadth of knowledge of English poetry, though he was an average student in most subjects. He displayed an early aptitude for writing poetry, submitting "decent verse" to his school newspaper when he was only eleven years old.

At age seventeen, Thomas decided not to continue his education and took a job at the local newspaper, writing book and theater reviews. When he was nineteen, he published his first poem in the *New English Weekly*, and within the year he was publishing a poem every month in various literary journals. At age twenty, he published his first book of poetry, *Eighteen Poems*, for which he received instant critical acclaim. At such a young age, he had already gained a literary reputation for the "wildness" of his imagery, for his use of sound and rhythm, and for his exploration of the inner workings of the mind.

In 1934 Thomas left Wales to live the freewheeling life of a writer in London. To support himself he worked as a journalist, actor, screenwriter, and broadcaster for the British Broadcasting Corporation. During this period he wrote several volumes of short stories and memoirs in addition to poetry. One of his most famous and popular works, "A Child's Christmas in Wales," was a memoir of his childhood in Swansea.

In 1937 Thomas married and then returned to Wales, settling in the small picturesque fishing village of Laugharne, Carmarthenshire. He and his wife, Caitlin, and their three children lived in a converted boathouse overlooking the sea—a setting that inspired many of his poems.

Poet and Performer In 1950, Thomas made his first visit to the United States to embark on a series of whirlwind poetry-reading and speaking tours at American universities. Considered one of the best performers of poetry in modern times, he was idolized by the literary establishment. In 1953, during his third tour of America, he collapsed in New York after a party celebrating his thirty-ninth birthday. He fell into a coma and died several days later of complications from alcoholism.

Shortly before his death Thomas completed *Under Milk Wood*, a radio play celebrating daily life in a small Welsh village. Thomas, who saw himself as a modern-day descendant of the English Romantics, remains best known for his radiant and resonant verse.

Dylan Thomas was born in 1914 and died in 1953.

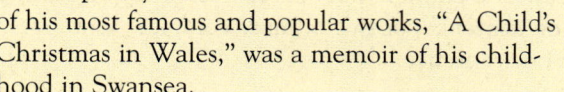

Literature Online **Author Search** For more about Dylan Thomas, go to www.glencoe.com.

Connecting to the Poems

Thomas's childhood in Wales provided material for much of his poetry. As you read, think about the following questions:

- What is your favorite childhood memory?
- How do you feel about the passing of time?

Building Background

"Fern Hill," one of Thomas's most acclaimed poems, is a fine example of his characteristic use of original images, rich symbols, and dazzling language. This poem was inspired by vacation visits to Fernhill Farm, the home of his aunt Ann Jones. Thomas also enjoyed a particularly close relationship with his father, whom he addressed in "Do Not Go Gentle into That Good Night." The elder Thomas, who was blind, encouraged his son's writing, and Thomas composed many of his early poems seated at his father's desk in the study at their family home in Swansea.

Setting Purposes for Reading

Big Idea World War II and Its Aftermath

Though he wrote after World War II, when gloom and disillusionment permeated Britain, Thomas sought to affirm the basic values of home and family. As you read, consider how these poems reflect those values.

Literary Element Assonance and Consonance

The repetition of nearby vowel sounds in stressed syllables is called **assonance,** as in the phrase *my wild life* or *stay in the same place*. The repetition of consonant sounds, typically within or at the end of nonrhyming words, is called **consonance,** as in these echoing *d* sounds in Yeats's "The Second Coming": "The blood-dimmed tide is loosed." As you read, notice these techniques and consider their effects.

- See Literary Terms Handbook, pp. R2 and R4.

Literature Online **Interactive Literary Elements Handbook** To review or learn more about the literary elements, go to www.glencoe.com.

Reading Strategy Analyzing Figures of Speech

Analyzing figures of speech involves looking critically at specific devices or kinds of figurative language, such as metaphor, personification, simile, or symbol. Another figurative device that occurs less often is known as **oxymoron**. It combines two contradictory terms, as in the phrase "darkness visible" in Milton's *Paradise Lost*.

Reading Tip: Charting Figures of Speech Use a chart to record your interpretations of figures of speech in these poems.

Figure of speech	Interpretation
Simile: "happy as the grass was green"	Joy was intrinsic to the speaker as a child.

Vocabulary

hail (hāl) *v.* acclaim; pay tribute to; p. 1202 *A crowd gathered to hail the championship team on its triumphant return.*

spellbound (spel′ bound) *adj.* fascinated; affected as if by enchantment; p. 1203 *Roger stared as if spellbound at the flickering colored lights on the water.*

heedless (hēd′ lis) *adj.* careless; not paying attention; p. 1203 *Ignoring the ranger's warnings, the heedless boys dragged their sleds to the top of the steep hill.*

frail (frāl) *adj.* delicate; fragile; p. 1204 *The frail old men, with their canes and walkers, sat on benches outside the nursing home.*

Vocabulary Tip: Using Context Clues You can often figure out the meanings of unfamiliar words by looking at their context, or the surrounding words and sentences.

OBJECTIVES

In studying these selections, you will focus on the following:
- analyzing literary periods
- analyzing assonance, consonance, and form
- analyzing figures of speech

FERN HILL

Dylan Thomas

Now as I was young and easy under the apple boughs
About the lilting[1] house and happy as the grass was green,
    The night above the dingle[2] starry,
      Time let me **hail** and climb
5   Golden in the heydays of his[3] eyes,
And honored among wagons I was prince of the apple towns
And once below a time I lordly had the trees and leaves
      Trail with daisies and barley
    Down the rivers of the windfall light.

10 And as I was green and carefree, famous among the barns
About the happy yard and singing as the farm was home,
    In the sun that is young once only,
      Time let me play and be
    Golden in the mercy of his means,
15 And green and golden I was huntsman and herdsman, the calves
Sang to my horn, the foxes on the hills barked clear and cold,
      And the sabbath rang slowly
    In the pebbles of the holy streams.

1. *Lilting* means "lively" or "cheerful."
2. A *dingle* is a small wooded valley.
3. A *heyday* is the prime of one's existence; *his* refers to Time.

Reading Strategy   Analyzing Figures of Speech *What does this personification suggest about time?*

Big Idea   World War II and Its Aftermath *What do the images in this stanza imply about the speaker's home and family?*

Vocabulary

hail (hāl) *v.* acclaim; pay tribute to

All the sun long it was running, it was lovely, the hay
20 Fields high as the house, the tunes from the chimneys, it was air
    And playing, lovely and watery
      And fire green as grass.
    And nightly under the simple stars
As I rode to sleep the owls were bearing the farm away,
25 All the moon long I heard, blessed among stables, the nightjars[4]
    Flying with the ricks,[5] and the horses
      Flashing into the dark.

And then to awake, and the farm, like a wanderer white
With the dew, come back, the cock on his shoulder: it was all
30   Shining, it was Adam and maiden,[6]
      The sky gathered again
    And the sun grew round that very day.
So it must have been after the birth of the simple light
In the first, spinning place, the **spellbound** horses walking warm
35   Out of the whinnying green stable
      On to the fields of praise.

And honored among foxes and pheasants by the gay house
Under the new made clouds and happy as the heart was long,
    In the sun born over and over,
40   I ran my **heedless** ways,
    My wishes raced through the house high hay
And nothing I cared, at my sky blue trades, that time allows
In all his tuneful turning so few and such morning songs
    Before the children green and golden
45   Follow him out of grace,[7]

Nothing I cared, in the lamb white days, that time would take me
Up to the swallow thronged loft by the shadow of my hand,
    In the moon that is always rising,
      Nor that riding to sleep
50   I should hear him fly with the high fields
And wake to the farm forever fled from the childless land.
Oh as I was young and easy in the mercy of his means,
    Time held me green and dying
    Though I sang in my chains like the sea.

4. *Nightjars* are nocturnal birds.
5. *Ricks* are haystacks.

6. *Adam and maiden* refers to the biblical Adam and Eve in the Garden of Eden.

7. *[Follow . . . grace]* is a reference to Adam's fall from grace and innocence.

Literary Element   Assonance and Consonance *What examples of consonance do you see in these lines?*

Reading Strategy   Analyzing Figures of Speech *What was the speaker like as a child?*

Vocabulary

spellbound (spel′ bound) *adj.* fascinated; affected as if by enchantment
heedless (hēd′ lis) *adj.* careless; not paying attention

Do Not Go Gentle into That Good Night

Dylan Thomas

Old Man Walking in a Rye Field, 1905. Laurits Andersen Ring. Oil on canvas, 68 x 56 cm.

Do not go gentle into that good night,
Old age should burn and rave at close of day;
Rage, rage against the dying of the light.

Though wise men at their end know dark is right,
5 Because their words had forked no lightning they
Do not go gentle into that good night.

Good men, the last wave by, crying how bright
Their **frail** deeds might have danced in a green bay,
Rage, rage against the dying of the light.

10 Wild men who caught and sang the sun in flight,
And learn, too late, they grieved it on its way,
Do not go gentle into that good night.

Grave men, near death, who see with blinding sight
Blind eyes could blaze like meteors and be gay,
15 Rage, rage against the dying of the light.

And you, my father, there on the sad height,
Curse, bless, me now with your fierce tears, I pray.
Do not go gentle into that good night.
Rage, rage against the dying of the light.

Literary Element Assonance and Consonance *What examples of assonance does this line contain?*

Reading Strategy Analyzing Figures of Speech *What kinds of words might fork lightning?*

Vocabulary

frail (frāl) *adj.* delicate; fragile

RESPONDING AND THINKING CRITICALLY

Respond

1. Which of the two poems do you identify with more? Why?

Recall and Interpret

2. (a)In the first four stanzas of "Fern Hill," how does the speaker describe himself and his life? (b)What can you infer about the speaker's view of youth from these stanzas?

3. (a)What has the speaker lost in the last stanza of "Fern Hill"? (b)In your opinion, what are the speaker's "chains"?

4. (a)What four types of people are mentioned in "Do Not Go Gentle into That Good Night"? (b)Why does each rage against death?

Analyze and Evaluate

5. What might Fern Hill **symbolize** for the speaker?

6. In your opinion, does the speaker in "Do Not Go Gentle into That Good Night" express greater love by urging his father to rage than by wishing him a peaceful death? Explain.

7. What might dark and light **symbolize** in "Do Not Go Gentle into That Good Night"?

Connect

8. **Big Idea** World War II and Its Aftermath How do these poems affirm the values of home and family?

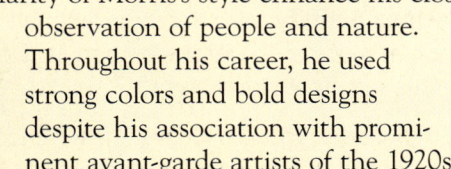

VISUAL LITERACY: Fine Art

Illustrating the Welsh Countryside

Sir Cedric Morris (1889–1982) spent his formative years in and around Swansea. Largely self-taught, he painted portraits, still lifes, and landscapes. After attending the Académie Delacluse in Paris for one term, he enlisted in the British army at the outbreak of World War I. In the oil painting titled *Llanmadoc Hill, Gower Peninsula, 1928*, he depicts a typical farm and outbuildings set among the hills that distinguish the Welsh countryside. The simplicity and clarity of Morris's style enhance his close observation of people and nature. Throughout his career, he used strong colors and bold designs despite his association with prominent avant-garde artists of the 1920s.

Group Activity Discuss the following questions with a small group of your classmates.

1. What is the mood of this painting? How does Morris convey this mood?

2. Which details in "Fern Hill" does the painting call to mind?

Llanmadoc Hill, Gower Penninsula, 1928.
Sir Cedric Morris. Oil on canvas, 65.4 x 81.2 cm.
Glynn Vivian Art Gallery, Swansea, Wales.

Literary Element **Assonance and Consonance**

Both **assonance** and **consonance**, together with other sound devices such as alliteration (the repetition of initial consonant sounds), contribute to a poem's musical qualities.

1. What examples of assonance do lines 1–2, 10, and 49–50 of "Fern Hill" contain?

2. Point out examples of consonance in lines 5, 11, and 46 of "Fern Hill."

3. What instances of **alliteration** can you find in these poems?

4. What effects do these sound devices produce?

Review: Form

As you learned on page 465, form is the structure a literary work takes. Dylan Thomas chose to use the **villanelle** form for his poem "Do Not Go Gentle into That Good Night." This intricate form contains nineteen lines divided into five tercets (three-line stanzas), each with the rhyme scheme *aba*, and a final quatrain (four-line stanza) with the rhyme scheme *abaa*. The first line is repeated as a **refrain** at the end of the second and fourth stanzas. The last line of the first stanza is repeated at the end of the third and fifth stanzas. Both lines reappear as the final two lines of the poem.

Partner Activity With another classmate, discuss Thomas's use of the villanelle form in "Do Not Go Gentle into That Good Night."

1. How does Thomas weave lines 1 and 3 into the sentence structures of stanzas 2, 3, 4, and 5?

2. What purpose do the **refrains** serve in this poem?

3. Why might Thomas have chosen this highly structured form for such a personal and moving subject?

Reading Strategy **Analyzing Figures of Speech**

By **analyzing figures of speech**, such as simile, metaphor, personification, symbol, and oxymoron, you can explore the theme of a poem and the author's purpose for writing.

1. In "Fern Hill," how is time **personified**? How would you interpret the speaker's views of the passage of time?

2. In "Do Not Go Gentle into That Good Night," what does the **oxymoron** "blinding sight" (line 13) suggest?

3. How might the father's "fierce tears" (line 17) both curse and bless the speaker?

Vocabulary **Practice**

Practice with Context Clues Using clues in each sentence, choose the correct definition for each boldfaced vocabulary word below.

1. The audience looked **spellbound** as the acrobat prepared for her death-defying leap.
   a. restless   **b.** patient   **c.** entranced

2. My elderly aunt, who is **frail,** is afraid of falling down.
   a. foreign   **b.** retired   **c.** delicate

3. The class gathered to **hail** the spelling champion.
   a. interview   **b.** criticize   **c.** acclaim

4. The **heedless** driver disregarded traffic signals.
   a. bewildered   **b.** inattentive   **c.** angry

Academic Vocabulary

Here is a word from the vocabulary list on page R82. This word will help you think, write, and talk about the selections.

layer (lā′ ər) *n.* a single thickness

Practice and Apply
In "Fern Hill," how does the theme of the passage of time take on deeper **layers** of meaning?

Writing About Literature

Compare and Contrast Theme and Tone Even though "Fern Hill" and "Do Not Go Gentle into That Good Night" share such elements as figurative language, sound devices, and light and dark imagery, the two poems differ in theme and tone. Write a brief essay in which you compare and contrast these elements.

Before you write, plan your essay carefully. Follow the writing path shown below to organize your ideas.

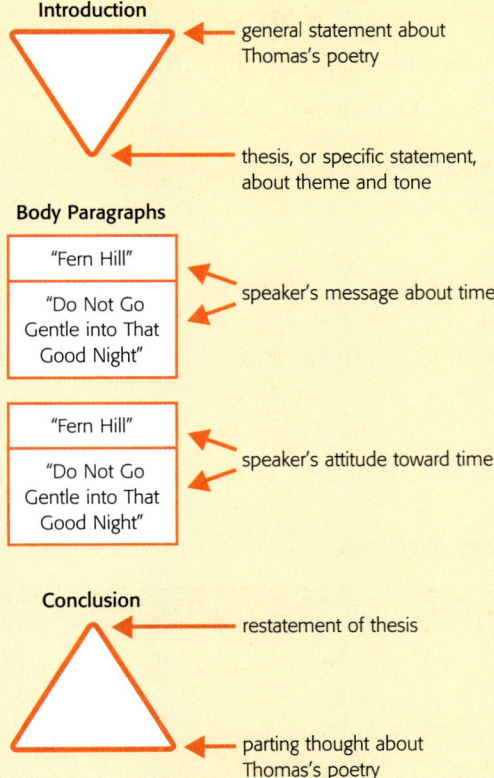

Introduction
← general statement about Thomas's poetry
← thesis, or specific statement, about theme and tone

Body Paragraphs
"Fern Hill"
"Do Not Go Gentle into That Good Night"
← speaker's message about time

"Fern Hill"
"Do Not Go Gentle into That Good Night"
← speaker's attitude toward time

Conclusion
← restatement of thesis
← parting thought about Thomas's poetry

When you're done writing, proofread and edit your draft for errors in spelling, grammar, and punctuation.

Listening and Speaking

Dylan Thomas was famous for his expressive public readings of his poems. Choose one of the two poems in this lesson and read it aloud. Practice intonations and pauses and consider adding gestures and facial expressions to bring the poem to life. When you feel you're ready to perform, present your reading of the poem to the class.

Thomas's Language and Style

Using Repetition in Structure Dylan Thomas uses repetition skillfully in these poems. For example, in "Do Not Go Gentle into That Good Night," he repeats lines one and three as dictated by the villanelle form. In stanzas two through five, Thomas repeats the structure, focusing each stanza on a different group of people who rage against death: the wise, the good, the wild, and the grave.

In "Fern Hill," Thomas also uses repetition to link details and strengthen structure. For example, notice the use of repetition and parallelism in the first and second stanzas:

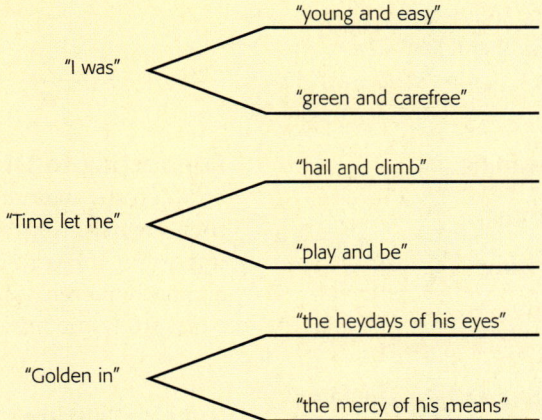

"I was"
"young and easy"
"green and carefree"

"Time let me"
"hail and climb"
"play and be"

"Golden in"
"the heydays of his eyes"
"the mercy of his means"

Activity Add to the graphic above, identifying the details the speaker links by repeating "it was" in stanzas 3 and 4 and "nothing I cared" in stanzas 5 and 6. Why do you think time seems to pass differently for children and for adults?

Revising Check

Repetition Repetition and parallelism can be effective ways to strengthen the structure of your own writing. With a partner, review your essay comparing and contrasting theme and tone in Thomas's poems. Revise your writing by using repetition to link details or support the structure.

Literature Online **Web Activities** For eFlashcards, Selection Quick Checks, and other Web activities, go to www.glencoe.com.

Writing Workshop

Short Story

 Creating and Resolving a Conflict

"His leave was nearly at an end when the explosion came. He had really done his best to keep his temper in the hearing of the flirtations . . . but he broke down at last."

—Rudyard Kipling, from "Miss Youghal's *Sais*"

Connecting to Literature In "Miss Youghal's *Sais*," Kipling presents a conflict between the main character, Strickland, and Miss Youghal's parents. Kipling then creates an interesting resolution to this situation. In a short story, your most important job is to create and resolve a conflict. To do this, you must also think about characters, setting, and other fictional elements. To write a successful short story, study the features in the chart below.

Rubric: Features of Short Story Writing

Goals	Strategies
To tell a story by creating and resolving a conflict	☑ Introduce characters with an interesting conflict
	☑ Present a series of events that builds and resolves the conflict
To present interesting characters in a clearly defined setting	☑ Use specific details and sensory images
	☑ Use dialogue to bring characters to life
To create a clear, coherent series of events that make up the plot	☑ Use chronological order
	☑ Link words, paragraphs, and sentences with transitions
To entertain the reader from beginning to end	☑ Create interest at the beginning, build up tension or conflict, include a clear climax, and end in a satisfying way

The Writing Process

In this workshop, you will follow the stages of the writing process. At any stage, you may think of new ideas to include and better ways to express them. Feel free to return to earlier stages as you write.

Prewriting

Drafting

Revising

➤ Focus Lesson: Using Action Verbs

Editing and Proofreading

➤ Focus Lesson: Correcting Sentence Fragments

Presenting

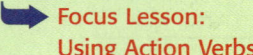

Writing Models For models and other writing activities, go to www.glencoe.com.

OBJECTIVES
- Write a short story with a specific conflict and resolution.
- Present a clear series of events and a climax.
- Maintain a consistent point of view.

Real-World Connection

Because the success of your story depends on your ability to resolve the story's conflict in a plausible and creative way, you develop creative problem-solving skills as you write—skills required for many jobs.

> **Assignment**
>
> Write a short story in which you create and resolve a clear conflict.
>
> ---
>
> **Audience:** your peers, classmates, and teacher
>
> **Purpose:** to entertain by presenting all the elements of a good short story, including setting, characters, and plot—events, conflict, rising action, climax, and resolution.

Analyzing a Professional Model

The unnamed narrator of this modern short story by Indian writer R. K. Narayan tells the story of a loose cobra in a family's yard. Notice how the narrator presents the conflict, intensifies it, and resolves it in an ambiguous, but satisfying, way. The comments in the margin below point out features you might want to include in your own story.

"A Snake in the Grass" by R. K. Narayan

On a sunny afternoon, when the inmates of the bungalow were at their siesta, a cyclist rang his bell at the gate frantically and announced: "A big cobra has got into your compound. It crossed my wheel." He pointed to its track under the gate, and resumed his journey.

The family consisting of the mother and her four sons assembled at the gate in great agitation. The old servant, Dasa, was sleeping in the shed. They shook him out of his sleep and announced to him the arrival of the cobra. "There is no cobra," he replied and tried to dismiss the matter. They swore at him and forced him to take an interest in the cobra. "The thing is somewhere here. If it is not found before the evening, we will dismiss you. Your neglect of the garden and the lawns is responsible for all these dreadful things coming in." Some neighbors dropped in. They looked accusingly at Dasa: "You have the laziest servant on earth," they said. "He ought to keep the surroundings tidy." "I have been asking for a grass-cutter for months," Dasa said. In one voice they ordered him to manage with the available things and learn not to make demands. He persisted. They began to speculate how much it would

Conflict

Grab your reader's interest by introducing the conflict early.

Point of View

Maintain a consistent point of view throughout the story.

Dialogue

Add natural-sounding dialogue to reveal characters' backgrounds, personalities, and motives, or to advance the plot.

cost to buy a grass-cutter. A neighbor declared that you could not think of buying any article made of iron till after the war. He chanted banalities of wartime prices. The second son of the house asserted that he could get anything he wanted at controlled prices. The neighbor became eloquent about the black market. A heated debate followed. The rest watched in apathy. At this point the college boy of the house butted in with: "I read in an American paper that 30,000 people die of snake bite every year." Mother threw up her arms in horror and arraigned Dasa. The boy elaborated the statistics. "I have worked it out, 83 a day. That means every twenty minutes someone is dying of cobra bite. As we have been talking here, one person has lost his life somewhere." Mother nearly screamed on hearing it. The compound looked sinister. The boys brought in bamboo sticks and pressed one into the hands of the servant also. He kept desultorily poking it into the foliage with a cynical air. "The fellow is beating about the bush," someone cried aptly. They tucked up their dhoties, seized every available knife and crowbar, and began to hack the garden. Creepers, bushes, and lawns were laid low. What could not be trimmed was cut to the root. The inner walls of the house brightened with the unobstructed glare streaming in. When there was nothing more to be done Dasa asked triumphantly, "Where is the snake?"

Fictional Elements: Setting

Use concrete details, sensory images, and figurative language to describe setting.

An old beggar cried for alms at the gate. They told her not to pester when they were engaged in a snake hunt. On hearing it the old woman became happy. "You are fortunate. It is God Subramanya who has come to visit you. Don't kill the snake." Mother was in hearty agreement: "You are right. I forgot all about the promised Abhishekam. This is a reminder." She gave a coin to the beggar, who promised to send down a snake-charmer as she went. Presently an old man appeared at the gate and announced himself as a snake-charmer. They gathered around him. He spoke to them of his life and activities and his power over snakes. They asked admiringly: "How do you catch them?" "Thus," he said, pouncing upon a hypothetical snake on the ground. They pointed the direction in which the cobra had gone and asked him to go ahead. He looked helplessly about and said: "If you show me the snake, I'll at once catch it. Otherwise what can I do? The moment you see it again, send for me. I live nearby." He gave his name and address and departed.

At five in the afternoon, they threw away their sticks and implements and repaired to the veranda to rest. They had turned up every stone in the garden and cut down every grass blade and shrub, so that the tiniest insect coming into the garden should have no cover. They were loudly discussing the various measures they would take to protect themselves against reptiles in the future, when Dasa appeared before them carrying a water-pot whose mouth was sealed with a slab of stone. He put the pot down and said: "I have caught him in this. I saw him peeping out of it. . . . I saw him before he could see me." He explained at length the strategy he had employed to catch and seal up the snake in the pot. They stood at a safe distance and gazed on the pot. Dasa had the glow of a champion on his face. "Don't call me an idler hereafter," he said. Mother complimented him on his sharpness and wished she had placed some milk in the pot as a sort of religious duty. Dasa picked up the pot cautiously and walked off saying that he would leave the pot with its contents with the snake-charmer living nearby. He became the hero of the day. They watched him in great admiration and decided to reward him adequately.

It was five minutes since Dasa was gone when the youngest son cried: "See there!" Out of a hole in the compound wall a cobra emerged. It glided along towards the gate, paused for a moment to look at the gathering in the veranda with its hood half open. It crawled under the gate and disappeared along a drain. When they recovered from the shock they asked, "Does it mean that there are two snakes here?" The college boy murmured: "I wish I had taken the risk and knocked the water-pot from Dasa's hand; we might have known what it contained."

Rising Action

Present a series of events that intensifies the conflict.

Climax

Be sure to include a clear climax, or the most exciting or suspenseful moment in your story.

Resolution

Present an interesting, satisfying, or surprising resolution.

Reading-Writing Connection Think about the writing techniques that you have just encountered and try them out in the short story you write.

Prewriting

Pace the Story

Pacing means telling story events at an effective rate. A good story usually builds slowly to a climax, then quickly comes to a resolution.

Gather Ideas Find ideas by observing. For example, perhaps you notice a new person riding the bus you take. What makes this stranger stand out? Imagine different scenarios: Where is the person going? Why? What if . . . ? Start with the observation, and then use your imagination to develop the conflict and events.

Imagine Characters and Setting Who is your story about? Will you show conflict through two opposing characters? Consider what the characters look like; how they speak, move, and behave; and what they want or are trying to achieve. Then decide where and when the story will take place.

Add Dialogue Add natural-sounding dialogue to reveal a character's background, personality, and motives, or to present the conflict or events.

Plan the Plot The plot, or sequence of events, is what happens in a story. Keep the plot focused on the conflict. An **external conflict** occurs when a character struggles against an outside force, such as another character, society, or the environment. An **internal conflict** occurs when the character struggles with his or her feelings. Before writing, fill out a story map like the one below.

Setting • Time: • Place:	Characters
Problem/Conflict:	
Main Events: 1. 2. 3. **Climax:**	
Resolution:	

Choose the Point of View The **point of view** is the perspective from which a story is told. The *narrator*, the person who tells the story, may be a character in the story or someone unnamed outside of the story.

Drafting

Create Paragraphs As you draft, create separate paragraphs for separate events. If you include dialogue, start a new paragraph each time the speaker changes.

Analyzing a Workshop Model

Here is a final draft of a student's short story. Read the story and answer the questions in the margin. Use the answers to these questions to guide you as you write.

A Prior Engagement

Every Saturday afternoon for years, Eudora Stills invited herself to our house for tea. A well-known busybody and a remarkably bad judge of character, she held my mother captive for hours, repeating the same gossip. How my mother tolerated her none of us understood.

One Saturday, however, Eudora didn't call. My mother set out tea and warm, golden scones just the same. Finally, she coaxed my father to walk to Eudora's house to check on her. When he returned, he said, "Well, she's not dead." He added with a sly grin, "She's engaged!" He explained that Eudora had been seeing Brandon Mites, a man we all distrusted, for almost a year. When he proposed to Eudora, she said yes, just like that. Worse, she was planning to pick up and move east with this well-known cheat.

Hearing the news, my mother grew somber. "I'm surprised Eudora never told me," she said to no one in particular.

When Eudora came over to discuss her move with my mother, she proudly flashed her large but ill-fitting, and possibly fake, diamond ring. After Eudora left, my mother remained seated in the living room, picking at a scone until evening fell. My dad reminded her to make supper.

The next night I saw my mother peering into the bathroom sink drain. She lifted the stopper and pulled out Eudora's diamond ring. We both knew what trouble that spelled. How could Eudora tell her fiancé she'd lost it? He'd drop her for sure. My mother slipped the ring into her pocket. Then she stunned me by saying, "I guess that's that for Brandon Mites."

When Eudora came the next Saturday, I knew my mother hadn't told her about the ring. A week later, when Eudora confessed in a panicked voice that she had lost the ring, my mother offered tea and sympathy but nothing more. A month later, when Eudora told my mother that the engagement was over, all I heard my mother say was "Scone?"

Conflict

How does the opening create interest and introduce the conflict?

Rising Action

How do events intensify the conflict or make the story more interesting?

Point of View

Who is narrating the events of the story? Is the narrative point of view consistent? Explain.

Climax

What is the high point of tension, or turning point, of the story?

Resolution

Is this a satisfying ending? Explain.

Revising

Use the rubric below to evaluate your writing.

Rubric: Writing an Effective Short Story

☑ Do you present and resolve a conflict?

☑ Do you create a clear series of events?

☑ Do you build up tension or intensify the conflict, present a clear climax, and end with a satisfying resolution?

☑ Do you present events in chronological order and link them with transitions?

☑ Do you use a consistent point of view?

☑ Do you use dialogue to reveal characters or advance the plot?

Focus Lesson

Using Action Verbs

An action verb tells what someone or something does. Action verbs can express either physical action (*She flashed her ring at me*) or mental action (*She stunned me*). For the most impact in your short story, use precise and vivid action verbs, such as *muttered* and *pounced*, instead of state-of-being verbs, such as *was* and *had been*. Also avoid the passive voice, which consists of a form of *to be* plus a past participle.

Draft:

Every Saturday afternoon for years Eudora Stills was over to our house for tea. A well-known busybody and a remarkably bad judge of character, she was always holding my mother captive for hours. How my mother tolerated her was understood by none of us.

Revision:

Every Saturday afternoon for years, Eudora Stills <u>invited herself</u>[1] to our house for tea. A well-known busybody and a remarkably bad judge of character, she <u>held</u>[2] my mother captive for hours, repeating the same gossip. How my mother tolerated her <u>none of us understood.</u>[3]

1: <u>Use action verbs to convey precise information.</u>

2: <u>Replace wordy constructions with precise verbs.</u>

3: <u>Use the active voice whenever possible.</u>

Editing and Proofreading

Get It Right When you have completed the final draft of your story, proofread it for errors in grammar, usage, mechanics, and spelling. Refer to the Language Handbook, pages R46–R60, as a guide.

> **Focus Lesson**

Correcting Sentence Fragments

A sentence fragment results from punctuating an incomplete sentence as if it were a complete sentence. Review your work to make sure that each sentence includes a subject and a complete verb, and correct any subordinate clauses you punctuated as complete sentences. Note that professional writers sometimes use sentence fragments intentionally to create an effect. For example, fragments can emphasize a point or make dialogue sound realistic. Nevertheless, use them carefully. In most of your writing, and especially on tests, avoid sentence fragments.

Problem: The sentence uses a verb form that cannot stand alone.

My dad <u>reminding</u> her to make supper.

Solution 1: Add a helping verb.

My dad <u>was reminding</u> her to make supper.

Solution 2: Change the form of the verb.

My dad <u>reminded</u> her to make supper.

Problem: A sentence has no verb and does not express a complete thought.

When he proposed to Eudora, she said yes. Just like that.

Solution 1: If the fragment adds emphasis or interest, you can let it stand.

Solution 2: Eliminate the fragment by combining it with the previous sentence.

When he proposed to Eudora, <u>she said yes, just like that.</u>

Punctuating Dialogue

Use quotation marks around the speaker's exact words only, and always place a period or comma *inside* closing quotation marks:

When he returned, he said, "Well, she's not dead."

Presenting

Create a Literary Magazine Work with your class and your teacher to collect all the students' short stories and assemble them in a booklet. You might also want to make an electronic version of your literary magazine to store on a school computer.

Writer's Portfolio

Place a copy of your short story in your portfolio to review later.

Speaking, Listening, and Viewing Workshop

Oral Interpretation

Delivering an Oral Interpretation of a Short Story

Using a Model

Try brainstorming an interpretation of your own short story before you begin working on a story from Unit Six. When you think about the choices you made in your own writing, you can understand and evaluate the choices another writer made in his or her work.

Connecting to Literature When you deliver an oral interpretation of a short story, you examine the themes, style, and literary devices the author chose and consider why he or she chose them. By sharing your thoughts and opinions about a short story, you can connect your own experiences to what you have read and share these ideas with others.

> **Assignment** Plan and deliver an oral interpretation of a short story you have read in Unit Six.

First, take time to reflect on and evaluate the short story you have chosen. Decide which major themes in the story you want to share with your audience. Ask yourself, how did the story make me feel after reading it? In what ways did I feel differently about life or relationships because of the story? These questions can help you begin to form your interpretation of a short story.

Preparing to Present

When you wrote your own short story, you decided on a conflict and how the main characters could resolve it. When you present your interpretation of a short story, you will discuss the author's intentions by analyzing the story's conflict and showing how its resolution shapes the story's themes.

As you prepare your interpretation, ask yourself:

- What universal themes are present in this story?
- How does style—sentence structure, word choice, tone—impact the way I read this story?
- How does the narrator and point of view affect what I know about this work?
- Are there any symbols or images that relate to my main ideas about the story?
- How does this story compare with other works written during this time period?

Rehearsing

It's a good idea to practice your oral interpretation of a short story with a partner before presenting to the class. You can provide each other with feedback in order to make your presentations stronger. Your partner can also give you suggestions about what visual media may be appropriate for your interpretation.

Including Visual Media

Visual media such as a drawing of the characters, a photograph of the setting, or a video clip of the author can attract the interest of your audience as well as support the major ideas of your interpretation. Try to include at least two pieces of visual media in your interpretation.

Gaining the Attention of Your Audience

By creating an interesting introduction, you will gain and keep your audience's attention. For example, you might begin by asking a rhetorical question or by sharing a brief personal anecdote that relates to the story.

Techniques for Delivering an Oral Interpretation of a Short Story

Verbal Techniques	Nonverbal Techniques
☑ **Volume** Vary the volume of your voice as needed, but speak loud enough so the audience can hear you.	☑ **Eye Contact** Direct eye contact with members of the audience will show you are knowledgeable and confident in your presentation.
☑ **Pace** When quoting the short story you have chosen, let the punctuation guide your pacing—pause for colons and semicolons; change the tone of your voice for question marks and exclamation points.	☑ **Gestures** Use gestures to emphasize important ideas in your interpretation.
☑ **Tone** In order to set a strong, fierce tone, speak loudly; speaking softly will create a quieter, softer tone.	☑ **Visual Aids** Use photographs or drawings that express elements of the story's setting, images, or characters.

OBJECTIVES
- Use appropriate speaking strategies in oral interpretation.
- Speak effectively to explain and justify ideas to peers.

For Independent Reading

THE NOVEL, WHICH HAD COME TO PROMINENCE DURING THE VICTORIAN PERIOD, continued to dominate the literary scene in the early half of the twentieth century. Many novels from this period reveal and criticize the destructive influences of colonial power on society and on the individual. The emphasis on the individual as well as on character development and motivation reflected a continued interest in the theories of psychoanalysis.

Heart of Darkness

by Joseph Conrad (1902)

In this tale, Charles Marlow, a thoughtful sailor, tells of his physical and psychological journey up the Congo River. He is attempting to reach the Inner Station to relieve Mr. Kurtz, the agent for a company that trades in ivory. The trip takes Marlow through the African jungle, where he encounters widespread inefficiency and cruelty at various company stations. When Marlow arrives at the Inner Station, he discovers that Kurtz rules the native population with force and brutality. Marlow takes the agent aboard his steamboat, but Kurtz is ill and cannot be saved.

A Passage to India

by E. M. Forster (1924)

Set in turn-of-the-century India, this three-part novel explores several themes including the relationship between the power of the earth and the imagination and the relationship between East (India) and West (Britain). In the novel, Adela Quested, a young Englishwoman eager to discover the "real" India, visits the country and befriends the respected Dr. Aziz. After a cultural misunderstanding, she accuses him of attacking her. He is imprisoned, but during the ensuing trial, she withdraws her charges. One of Aziz's British friends, Mr. Fielding, defends Aziz. However, when Mr. Fielding befriends Adela, the friendship between the two men ends. Several years later, Dr. Aziz encounters Mr. Fielding, but they cannot find common ground. Their ethnic and social differences become all too clear.

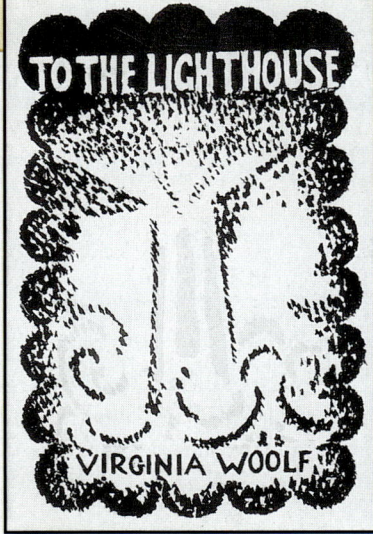

"I must say, despite my notorious grave reservations concerning Virginia Woolf, that the most original of the bunch is To the Lighthouse. *It is the best book of hers that I know. Her character drawing has improved. Mrs. Ramsay almost amounts to a complete person."*

—Arnold Bennett, *Evening Standard*, June 23, 1927

"To the Lighthouse . . . is a book of interrelationships among people. . . . Those who reject To the Lighthouse *as inferior to* Mrs. Dalloway. *. . . must fail to notice the richer qualities of mind and imagination and emotion which Mrs. Woolf, perhaps not wanting them, omitted from* Mrs. Dalloway.*"*

—Louis Kronenberger, *The New York Times*, May 8, 1927

To the Lighthouse

by Virginia Woolf (1927)

This novel, written in stream of consciousness, is driven by character and imagination, rather than a strict narrative. On Scotland's Isle of Skye, where the Ramsay family has a summer residence, Mr. and Mrs. Ramsay play out the roles traditionally expected of them. Mr. Ramsay, a once famous philosopher, smugly exhibits his rational approach to life while Mrs. Ramsay attends to her guests, her children, and her husband's ego. Woolf reveals the flaws of British society and of the Ramsays by contrasting them with Lily Briscoe, an artist who is a guest of the family.

From the Glencoe Literature Library

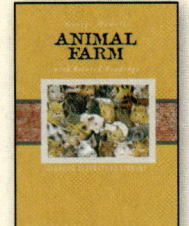

Animal Farm

by George Orwell

Written as a fable, this novel presents a satire of Communist Russia and its revolution.

All Quiet on the Western Front

by Erich Maria Remarque

This novel depicts the horrors of World War I from a German soldier's viewpoint.

The Time Machine *and* The War of the Worlds

by H. G. Wells

The Time Machine tells of a scientist who travels into the future. *The War of the Worlds* is the story of a Martian invasion of Earth.

Reading: Essay

Carefully read the following passage. Use context clues to help you define any words with which you are unfamiliar. Pay close attention to the use of figurative language, character, the main idea, and the author's purpose. Then, on a separate sheet of paper, answer the questions on pages 1221–1222.

"Old Mrs. Grey" by Virginia Woolf

line

There are moments even in England, now, when even the busiest, most contented suddenly let fall what they hold—it may be the week's washing. Sheets and pyjamas crumble and dissolve in their hands, because, though they do not state this in so many words, it seems silly to take the washing round to Mrs. Peel when out there over the fields over the hills, there is no washing; no pinning of

5 clothes to lines; mangling and ironing; no work at all, but boundless rest. Stainless and boundless rest; space unlimited; untrodden grass; wild birds flying; hills whose smooth uprise continue that wild flight.

Of all this however only seven foot by four could be seen from Mrs. Grey's corner. That was the size of her front door which stood wide open, though there was a fire burning in the grate. The fire looked like a small spot of dusty light feebly trying to escape from the embarrassing pressure of the

10 pouring sunshine.

Mrs. Grey sat on a hard chair in the corner looking—but at what? Apparently at nothing. She did not change the focus of her eyes when visitors came in. Her eyes had ceased to focus themselves; it may be that they had lost the power. They were aged eyes, blue, unspectacled. They could see, but without looking. She had never used her eyes on anything minute and difficult; merely upon faces,

15 and dishes and fields. And now at the age of ninety-two they saw nothing but a zigzag of pain wriggling across the door, pain that twisted her legs as it wriggled; jerked her body to and fro like a marionette. Her body was wrapped round the pain as a damp sheet is folded over a wire. The wire was spasmodically jerked by a cruel invisible hand. She flung out a foot, a hand. Then it stopped. She sat still for a moment.

20 In that pause she saw herself in the past at ten, at twenty, at twenty-five. She was running in and out of a cottage with eleven brothers and sisters. The line jerked. She was thrown forward in her chair.

"All dead. All dead," she mumbled. "My brothers and sisters. And my husband gone. My daughter too. But I go on. Every morning I pray God to let me pass."

The morning spread seven foot by four green and sunny. Like a fling of grain the birds settled on

25 the land. She was jerked again by another tweak of the tormenting hand.

"I'm an ignorant old woman. I can't read or write, and every morning when I crawls down stairs, I say I wish it were night; and every night, when I crawls up to bed, I say, I wish it were day. I'm only an ignorant old woman. But I prays to God: O let me pass. I'm an ignorant old woman—I can't read or write."

30 So when the color went out of the doorway, she could not see the other page which is then lit up; or hear the voices that have argued, sung, talked for hundreds of years.

The jerked limbs were still again.

"The doctor comes every week. The parish doctor now. Since my daughter went, we can't afford Dr. Nicholls. But he's a good man. He says he wonders I don't go. He says my heart's nothing but

35 wind and water. Yet I don't seem able to die."

So we—humanity—insist that the body shall still cling to the wire. We put out the eyes and the ears; but we pinion it there, with a bottle of medicine, a cup of tea, a dying fire, like a rook on a barn door; but a rook that still lives, even with a nail through it.

---

1. According to the context, what does the word *boundless* in line 5 most nearly mean?
(A) unconscious
(B) beautiful
(C) finishing
(D) endless
(E) bright

2. Which of the following literary elements is Woolf using in line 6 in the phrases *untrodden grass; wild birds flying; hills whose smooth uprise continue that wild flight?*
(A) personification
(B) idiom
(C) foreshadowing
(D) imagery
(E) epiphany

3. Which of the following literary elements is Woolf using in lines 9–10 in the phrase *dusty light feebly trying to escape from the embarrassing pressure of the pouring sunshine?*
(A) metaphor
(B) simile
(C) personification
(D) idiom
(E) symbol

4. Which device is Woolf using in the phrase *Apparently at nothing* in line 11?
(A) sentence fragment
(B) rhetorical question
(C) parallelism
(D) repetition
(E) figurative language

5. According to the context, what does the word *minute* in line 14 most nearly mean?
(A) convoluted
(B) a short period of time
(C) distant
(D) academic
(E) small

6. Which of the following literary elements is Woolf using in the phrase *jerked her body to and fro like a marionette* in lines 16–17?
(A) metaphor
(B) simile
(C) personification
(D) idiom
(E) symbol

7. Which of the following literary elements is Woolf using in *Like a fling of grain the birds settled on the land* in lines 24–25?
(A) metaphor
(B) simile
(C) personification
(D) idiom
(E) symbol

8. What sound device is Woolf using in the phrase *tweak of the tormenting hand* in line 25?
   (A) consonance
   (B) assonance
   (C) rhyme
   (D) onomatopoeia
   (E) alliteration

9. What is the dialogue beginning in line 26 an example of?
   (A) apostrophe
   (B) onomatopoeia
   (C) dialect
   (D) idiom
   (E) rhetoric

10. To what does the word *voices* in line 31 refer?
   (A) writers and their works
   (B) birdsong
   (C) Mrs. Grey's childhood
   (D) Mrs. Grey's siblings and husband
   (E) the world outside Mrs. Grey's home

11. Which of the following literary elements is being used in the phrase *He says my heart's nothing but wind and water* in lines 34–35?
   (A) metaphor
   (B) simile
   (C) personification
   (D) idiom
   (E) epiphany

12. Which of the following best describes Mrs. Grey's character?
   (A) dynamic
   (B) minor
   (C) round
   (D) direct
   (E) static

13. Which of the following best describes the overall mood of this passage?
   (A) hopeful
   (B) grim
   (C) humorous
   (D) witty
   (E) boisterous

14. From which point of view is this passage narrated?
   (A) first person
   (B) second person
   (C) third-person omniscient
   (D) third-person limited
   (E) ironic

15. Which of the following best summarizes this essay's main idea?
   (A) Without fail, life always brings new experiences.
   (B) Life is sometimes harsh and can feel like a prison.
   (C) Human dignity is always derived from the family.
   (D) All people have the right to a happy domestic life.
   (E) Life must always come to an end.

Literature Online **Unit Assessment** To prepare for the Unit test, go to www.glencoe.com.

1222 UNIT 6   THE MODERN AGE

Vocabulary Skills: Sentence Completion

For each item in the Vocabulary Skills section, choose the word or words that best complete the sentence.

1. The bloody stalemate that emerged during World War I completely _____ Europe.
   (A) retorted
   (B) grappled
   (C) appeased
   (D) converged
   (E) ravaged

2. The unreasonable restrictions imposed on Germany at the end of World War I were _____ related to the rise of Hitler and the start of World War II.
   (A) intrinsically
   (B) impassively
   (C) heedlessly
   (D) odiously
   (E) reverently

3. Many in Germany held the conviction that its _____ was to _____ the rule of the British Empire.
   (A) labyrinth . . . brevity
   (B) feud . . . ecstasy
   (C) destiny . . . supplant
   (D) farce . . . compensation
   (E) vileness . . . amiability

4. Modernism _____ radically from the literary movements of the Victorian period.
   (A) supplanted
   (B) commiserated
   (C) trudged
   (D) hailed
   (E) diverged

5. While the Realists were reacting to the _____ conditions of urban life, the Modernists were, in part, reacting to the horrors of mechanized war.
   (A) squalid
   (B) spellbound
   (C) imperturbable
   (D) dogged
   (E) exotic

6. The start of the twentieth century was marred by the rise of numerous _____ European governments.
   (A) quaint
   (B) intermittent
   (C) despotic
   (D) prosaic
   (E) sensible

7. Many of the heads of Europe were _____ of the threat posed by Nazi Germany.
   (A) callous
   (B) heedless
   (C) sensible
   (D) unsavory
   (E) quaint

8. The _____ spirit of the British was demonstrated during the Blitz, in which London was destroyed by bombing.
   (A) imperious
   (B) garish
   (C) forsaken
   (D) indomitable
   (E) frail

9. Although the Nazis _____ Europe for years, the continent was eventually emancipated from Nazism.
   (A) frail
   (B) suppressed
   (C) exotic
   (D) emanated
   (E) despotic

10. During the first half of the twentieth century, Modernism was _____ by many critics, who recognized the movement's great inventiveness.
    (A) precipitated
    (B) converged
    (C) hailed
    (D) impinged
    (E) retorted

Grammar and Writing Skills: Paragraph Improvement

Read carefully through the opening paragraphs from the first draft of a student's short story. Pay close attention to **sentence structure, punctuation,** and the writer's **use of conjunctions.** Then on a separate sheet of paper, answer the questions on pages 1224–1225.

---

(1) There were three things that really upset Frank Mead, the first was rudeness. (2) He couldn't stand it when someone spoke out of turn, cut in line, or failed to adhere to proper driving etiquette, he absolutely hated cell phones. (3) Second, Frank hated books. "Just a lot of dead people," Frank would say. (4) For good measure he'd add, "yet they're boring too." (5) Third, and most important, Frank hated to work. (6) Few ever saw Frank walked up stairs or lift anything larger than a lunch pail. (7) However, his disdain for work was made far more complicated by the fact that the region's busiest construction firm employed him.

(8) As of late, the firm for which he worked—Big Briggs—was busier than ever. (9) Big Briggs had landed an account with a very small, but very wealthy, private college. (10) The dean of this college, it turns out, was a rabid hockey fan, his love for the sport had started to influence his duties as dean. (11) At official dinners, during lectures, and even at commencement ceremonies—this year's ceremony was notably bad—he found ways in which to introduce pucks, sticks, nets, and goalies.

(12) That fall, the college had received an unexpected and very generous donation, the dean immediately earmarked the money for the building of an expansive hockey rink. (13) This rink, it was hoped, would become the envy of even professional teams, to the dean, this meant great prestige. (14) Big Briggs was contracted within days of the donation, and with that contract came Frank Mead.

---

1. Which is the best revision of sentence 1?
(A) The three things that really upset Frank Mead were rudeness.
(B) There were three things that really upset Frank Mead. The first was rudeness.
(C) There were three things that really upset Frank Mead; The first was rudeness.
(D) Rudeness really upset Frank Mead.
(E) Frank Mead was really upset by rudeness.

2. Which error appears in sentence 2?
(A) sentence fragment
(B) lack of subject-verb agreement
(C) lack of pronoun-antecedent agreement
(D) run-on sentence
(E) No error appears.

3. Which is the best revision of sentence 4?
- **(A)** For good measure he'd add, yet they're boring.
- **(B)** For good measure he would add, "yet they're boring too."
- **(C)** For good measure he'd add, "And they're boring too."
- **(D)** He'd add, "yet they're boring too."
- **(E)** He would add, "yet they're boring too."

4. Which error appears in sentence 6?
- **(A)** run-on sentence
- **(B)** sentence fragment
- **(C)** incorrect verb form
- **(D)** incorrect parallelism
- **(E)** misplaced modifier

5. What are the dashes in sentence 8 used to do?
- **(A)** set off an appositive phrase
- **(B)** emphasize an idea
- **(C)** indicate a break in thought
- **(D)** complicate the sentence structure
- **(E)** provide unnecessary information

6. Which is the best revision of sentence 10?
- **(A)** A rabid hockey fan the dean of this college.
- **(B)** The dean of this college was, it turns out, a rabid hockey fan, yet his love for the sport was influencing his duties as dean.
- **(C)** The dean of this college was a rabid hockey fan; His love for the sport was influencing him.
- **(D)** The dean of this college was, it turns out, a rabid hockey fan, and his love for the sport was influencing his duties as dean.
- **(E)** The dean of this college was, it turns out, a rabid hockey fan, however his love for the sport was influencing his duties as dean.

7. What are the dashes in sentence 11 used to do?
- **(A)** set off an appositive phrase
- **(B)** emphasize an idea
- **(C)** indicate a break in thought
- **(D)** complicate the sentence structure
- **(E)** provide essential information

8. Which error appears in sentence 12?
- **(A)** run-on sentence
- **(B)** sentence fragment
- **(C)** incorrect coordinating conjunction
- **(D)** incorrect parallelism
- **(E)** improper use of dialogue

9. Which is the best revision of sentence 13?
- **(A)** This rink, it was hoped, would become the envy of even professional teams, but to the dean this meant great prestige.
- **(B)** This rink—it was hoped—would become the envy of even professional teams, to the dean this meant prestige.
- **(C)** This rink would become the envy of even professional teams, this meant great prestige.
- **(D)** This rink, it was hoped, would become the envy of even professional teams; to the dean, this meant great prestige.
- **(E)** To the dean this meant great prestige.

10. This passage includes which parts of a plot?
- **(A)** exposition and rising action
- **(B)** exposition, rising action, and climax
- **(C)** rising action, climax, and falling action
- **(D)** exposition, rising action, climax, falling action, and resolution
- **(E)** only the resolution

Essay

In "The Second Coming," William Butler Yeats wrote the following:

> Things fall apart; the center cannot hold;
> Mere anarchy is loosed upon the world,
> The blood-dimmed tide is loosed, and everywhere
> The ceremony of innocence is drowned;
> The best lack all conviction, while the worst
> Are full of passionate intensity.

Write a short essay in which you explore the continuing relevance and validity of this passage for us today. As you write, keep in mind that your essay will be checked for **ideas, organization, voice, word choice, sentence fluency, conventions,** and **presentation.**

The Light Programme, 2002. Mark Copeland. Oil on canvas, 12.20 x 16.14 in. Private collection.

An International Literature

1950–Present

Looking Ahead

For the British, the period after World War II was marked by declining status abroad and enormous changes at home. The British Empire was gradually dismantled, and former British colonies struggled to adjust to home rule. Britain's economy sputtered, and the traditional class system no longer seemed secure. Responding to these upheavals, writers in Britain and in its former colonies produced a great outpouring of literature.

Keep the following questions in mind as you read:

▶ What are some major characteristics of contemporary British literature?

▶ What problems resulted from the collapse of the British Empire?

▶ What factors helped make English a global language?

OBJECTIVES

In learning about contemporary British literature, you will focus on the following:

- analyzing the characteristics of contemporary British literature and how issues of the period influenced writers
- evaluating the influences of the historical forces that shaped literary characters, plots, settings, and themes in contemporary literature
- connecting contemporary literature to historical contexts, current events, and your own experiences

Timeline

1950–Present

Muriel Spark

BRITISH LITERATURE

1950

1952
Nadine Gordimer publishes
The Soft Voice of the Serpent

1953
Samuel Beckett's play
Waiting for Godot is produced

1954
William Golding publishes
Lord of the Flies

1956
John Osborne's *Look Back
in Anger* is produced

1957
Stevie Smith publishes
Not Waving but Drowning

1958
Chinua Achebe publishes
Things Fall Apart

1960

1961
Muriel Spark publishes
The Prime of Miss Jean Brodie

1963
National Theatre
Company opens

1966
Tom Stoppard's play
*Rosencrantz and Guildenstern
Are Dead* is produced

1970
Ted Hughes publishes *Crow*

1978
Iris Murdoch publishes
The Sea, the Sea

1979
V. S. Naipaul publishes
A Bend in the River

BRITISH EVENTS

1950

1952
George VI dies; Elizabeth II
becomes queen ▼

1953
James Watson and Francis
Crick reveal the double
helical structure of the
DNA molecule

1954
Wartime food rationing ends

1959
The first Hovercraft crosses
the English Channel

1960

1962 ▲
The Beatles have their first
hit single, "Love Me Do"

1969
Violence erupts in Northern
Ireland

1973
Britain joins the European
Economic Community

1978
First "test-tube" baby is born

1979
Margaret Thatcher becomes
the first woman to serve as
prime minister

WORLD EVENTS

1950

1953
Edmund Hillary and Tenzing
Norgay climb Mt. Everest

1956
Suez Crisis occurs in Egypt

1957
The former British colony of
Ghana gains independence

1957
The Soviet Union launches
Sputnik I, the first Earth-
orbiting satellite ◄

1960

1961
Soviet cosmonaut Yuri
Gagarin becomes the first
human in space

1963
President John F. Kennedy
is assassinated ►

1966
China's Cultural Revolution
begins

1969
U.S. *Apollo XI* spacecraft
lands on the Moon

1975
Vietnam War ends

Literature Online Timeline Visit www.glencoe.com
for an interactive timeline.

The Old Vic Theatre in London

1980

1981
Salman Rushdie publishes
Midnight's Children

1985
Margaret Atwood publishes
The Handmaid's Tale

1986
Wole Soyinka wins
Nobel Prize in Literature

1990
Derek Walcott
publishes *Omeros*

1991
Nadine Gordimer wins
Nobel Prize in Literature

1992
Derek Walcott wins
Nobel Prize in Literature

1995
Seamus Heaney wins
Nobel Prize in Literature

1996
New Globe Theatre opens

2000

2000
Seamus Heaney publishes
translation of *Beowulf*

2000
Zadie Smith publishes
White Teeth ▶

2001
V. S. Naipaul wins
Nobel Prize in Literature

2005
Harold Pinter wins
Nobel Prize in Literature

1980

1981
Prince Charles marries
Lady Diana Spencer

1982
Britain defeats Argentina
in Falklands War

1986
Andrew Lloyd Webber's
musical *Phantom of
the Opera* premieres

1988
Terrorists blow up an airliner
over Lockerbie, Scotland

1994
The Chunnel opens,
providing a railway tunnel
under the English Channel
to link England with France

1997
Princess Diana is killed in
a car accident

British forensic officers
gather evidence.

2005 ▲
Terrorist bombings in
London claim more than
fifty lives

1980

1981
The first case of AIDS
is reported

1989
Germany opens
Berlin Wall ▶

1989
Chinese government
suppresses the Tiananmen
Square protests

1991
The Soviet Union
is dissolved

1993
The European Union
is established

1994
Nelson Mandela is elected
president of South Africa

2000

2001
Terrorist attacks destroy
the World Trade Center
in New York

2003
Iraq War begins

2004 ▲
A massive tsunami
devastates Southeast Asia

2005
Hurricane Katrina devastates
New Orleans and parts of
the Gulf Coast region

Reading Check

Analyzing Graphic Information How long did food
rationing continue in Britain after the end of World
War II in 1945?

By the Numbers

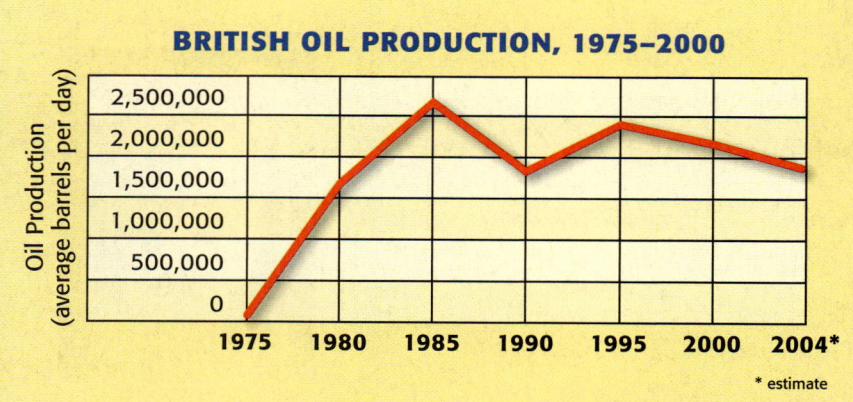

BRITISH OIL PRODUCTION, 1975–2000

Oil Production (average barrels per day)

2,500,000
2,000,000
1,500,000
1,000,000
500,000
0

1975   1980   1985   1990   1995   2000   2004*

* estimate

Source *Energy Information Administration*

In 1975 Britain began oil production in the North Sea, the arm of the Atlantic Ocean that separates the British Isles from the European mainland. Oil production boomed during the 1980s and 1990s. However, after peaking in the late 1990s, North Sea oil has declined. Some analysts predict that production will remain stagnant or continue to decrease—creating concern over the supply of oil.

End of Empire

Listed below are some of the former British colonies and dependencies that achieved home rule after World War II. (The country's former name is in parentheses.)

India—1947
Pakistan—1947
Sri Lanka (Ceylon)—1948
Myanmar (Burma)—1948
Israel (Palestine)—1948
Ghana (Gold Coast)—1957
Cyprus—1960
Nigeria—1960
Tanzania (Tanganyika)—1961
Jamaica—1962
Trinidad and Tobago—1962
Uganda —1962
Kenya—1963
Zambia (Northern Rhodesia)—1964
Malawi (Nyasaland)—1964
Malta—1964
Guyana (British Guiana)—1966
Botswana (Bechuanaland)—1966
Lesotho—1966
Fiji and Tonga—1970
Bahamas—1973
Belize—1981
Brunei—1984

IMMIGRATION

In the late twentieth century, the ethnic make-up of Britain began to change when immigrants, mostly from the West Indies, began to arrive. In 1948, 547 immigrants from Jamaica arrived; by 1955 that number had increased to 18,561. Immigrants from the Indian subcontinent and then from Asia, Africa, and the Middle East followed.

CONSUMER SPENDING

Between 1955 and 1960, the number of British people who owned refrigerators rose from 6 percent to 16 percent; those owning washing machines, from 25 percent to 44 percent; and those owning automobiles, from 18 percent to 32 percent. Shopping in postwar Britain became Americanized with more than 800 supermarkets opening in Britain between 1956 and 1961.

EDUCATION

One of the major changes in postwar Britain was the establishment of a system of comprehensive schools, or secondary schools that admit pupils from all ability levels. In 1971, 34 percent of British secondary school students attended comprehensive schools; by 1980, that figure had risen to 80 percent.

INFLATION

Inflation was a serious economic problem for Britain in the postwar period. During the two centuries between 1754 and 1954, prices rose six times. Prices tripled, however, in the twenty-year span between 1956 and 1976.

ENGLISH SPEAKERS

Approximately 350 million people throughout the world speak English as a first language, and another 450 million use it as a second language. About one-seventh of the world's population speaks English, and that number continues to rise.

Being There

After World War II, the sun did set over the British Empire, which dissolved into the Commonwealth of Nations. This federation of nations voluntarily recognizes the British monarchy as a symbol of their economic alliance and collaborates on economic and social policies. Today, the Commonwealth (shown in orange on the map below) comprises fifty-three countries, including Canada, Australia, India, Pakistan, Nigeria, and South Africa.

B *Kano State, Nigeria, 2002.*

C *Hanbury Street, London, 1996.*

A *An elephant walks down a street amid traffic as it rains in Bombay, 2005.*

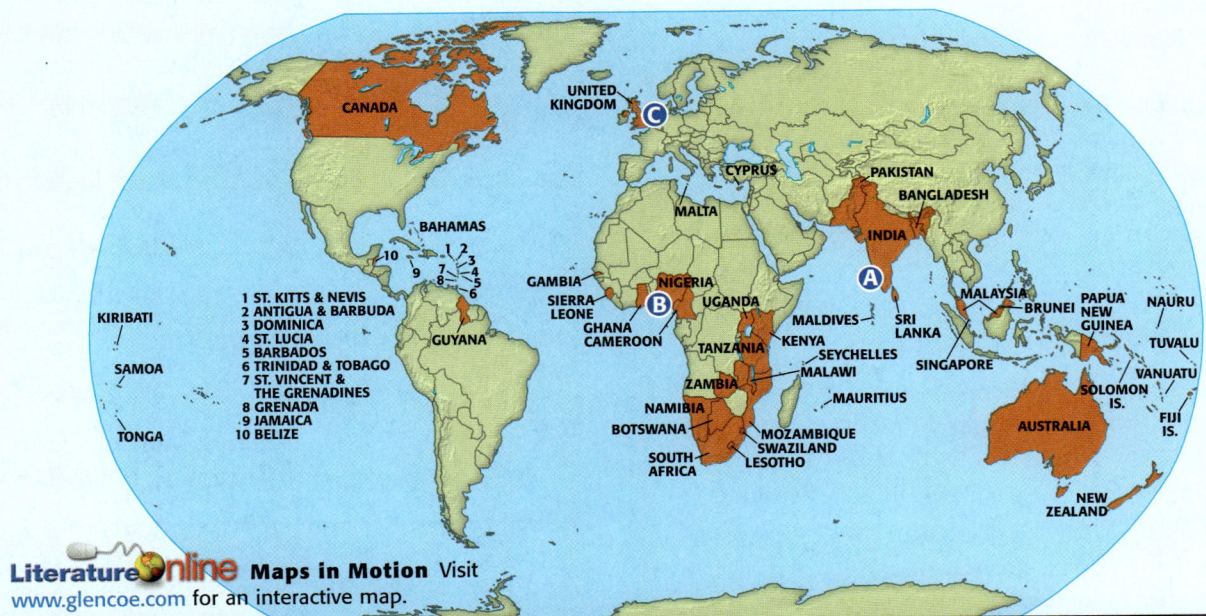

Literature Online **Maps in Motion** Visit www.glencoe.com for an interactive map.

Reading Check

Analyzing Graphic Information:

1. About how many times greater was West Indian immigration to Britain in 1955 than it had been in 1948?

2. Approximately how many people throughout the world speak English as a first or second language?

3. Which continents have countries that belong to the British Commonwealth of Nations?

An International Literature

Historical, Social, and Cultural Forces

Domestic and Foreign Problems

The end of World War II left Britain saddled with serious economic problems. After a landslide victory in 1946, the Labour Party instituted a series of programs to strengthen the economy. The government assumed responsibility for housing, pensions, unemployment, and the nation's railroads and mines. A national health program made medical care available to everyone. The British welfare state became the model for many other postwar European countries.

Another thorny problem involved relations with Britain's neighbor, Ireland. In the late 1960s, violence erupted in Northern Ireland between the Protestant Unionists, who wanted to remain in the United Kingdom, and the Catholic Nationalists, who wanted to break with Britain and join the Republic of Ireland. In the 1970s and 1980s terrorists from the Irish Republican Army carried out bombings in Britain.

End of the Empire

To strengthen its economy, Britain was forced to reduce expenses abroad. To do so, Britain gradually agreed to the demands of many of its colonies for home rule. Colony by colony, the British Empire was thus dismantled.

In Asia and Africa, the new nations created from former British colonies faced an array of formidable problems, including overpopulation, poverty, and ethnic and religious strife. In India, for example, despite government efforts, the population grew at the alarm-ing rate of more than two percent each year during the 1950s and 1960s. This growth wreaked havoc on the economy, increasing poverty in that new nation. Moreover, conflicts among India's religious groups often erupted in violence.

Newly created African nations struggled to resolve the tension between modern and traditional lifestyles. Some African leaders supported Western-style capitalism. Others, such as Julius Nyerere (ni rär´ ē) of Tanzania, followed what they deemed traditional African socialism in which the community had ownership rights. Nyerere believed that Tanzania's economic and political life should imitate that found in a traditional African community, or a village inhabited by an extended family.

> *"To be free is not merely to cast off one's chains, but to live in a way that respects and enhances the freedom of others."*
>
> —Nelson Mandela, from
> *Long Walk to Freedom*

Though South Africa had been independent since 1910, its political system remained controlled by whites. In the late 1940s, South African whites codified the laws separating whites and blacks into a system of racial segregation known as *apartheid* ("apartness"). Under the leadership of the African National Congress (ANC), blacks in South Africa demonstrated against legalized segregation. The government brutally repressed these demonstrations, sentencing ANC leader Nelson Mandela to life imprisonment in 1964. Under the administration of anti-apartheid President F. W. de Klerk, Mandela was released from prison in 1990.

Joining Europe

The loss of its colonial empire brought Britain closer to its Western European allies. As the Cold War developed between the two superpowers, the United States and the Soviet Union, Britain sought security by joining the North Atlantic Treaty Organization (NATO), a defensive alliance formed in 1949. Britain also sought closer economic ties with the nations of Western Europe. In 1973 Britain joined the free-trade zone of the European Economic Community (EEC), or Common Market, despite uncertainty over the consequences of this step. Britain's political ties to the continent grew stronger when the EEC morphed into the European Union in 1993.

Julius Nyerere carried by supporters, 1961.

PREVIEW **Big Ideas** of An International Literature

1	Making and Remaking Traditions

Since the end of World War II, Britain has struggled through an identity crisis with few parallels in its long history. Every British cultural trait and tradition, from the monarchy to the stiff upper lip, seemed called into question. In the process, contemporary British writers created variations and innovations upon traditional literary forms and themes.

See pages 1234–1235.

2	Colonialism and Postcolonialism

Throughout the twentieth century, agitation for independence had been growing in various parts of the vast British Empire. Beginning in 1947, with the partition of British India into the independent states of India and Pakistan, a long succession of former colonies declared independence. Writers in these new nations broadened the scope of English literature in both subject matter and style.

See pages 1236–1237.

3	Globalization

One of the most important cultural legacies of the British Empire was the establishment of English as a global language, used by an estimated 800 million people worldwide by the end of the twentieth century. As a result, contemporary literature in English is enriched by the voices and experiences of writers from a great variety of cultures throughout the world.

See pages 1238–1239.

Early in the twentieth century, Britain was supreme among the nations of the world. Fifty years later, with its empire lost, Britain's preeminence disappeared, and British confidence eroded. Both internally and externally, Britain found it had to achieve a new identity.

An Identity Crisis

For most of the British people, the loss of the empire produced few shock waves. To ordinary people in Britain—rather than the relatively small number of the middle and upper classes who had served as colonial administrators—the British Empire had always been a rather distant, if glorious, prospect. Even if the empire had been remote, however, its loss seemed ominous and darkly symbolic of British decline.

In addition to the dissolution of the British Empire, economic woes contributed to the alarming sense that something was very wrong. Economic recovery after World War II was painfully slow. Burdened with heavy debt and a shortage of goods, postwar Britain imposed a program of austerity on its war-weary citizens. Fresh fruit, canned goods, meat, and butter were among the rationed foods. Persistently high rates of unemployment triggered bitter labor disputes, fueling fears that joblessness might be a permanent condition in Britain. By the mid-1970s, inflation was increasing faster than at any time since the war. The economy fluctuated under the direction of prime ministers Margaret Thatcher and John Major in the 1980s and 1990s. Under Tony Blair, Britain continued to face daunting economic challenges, exacerbated by rising security costs because of terrorist threats.

Shift in Values

Meanwhile, various social changes generated widespread anxiety. The youth rebellion that affected American society in the 1960s had its counterpart in Britain. Many British, particularly older people, objected to the increasing "permissiveness" they observed in mass media, including advertising, movies, television, and popular music. The relationship among the long-established classes of English society began to break down as the power of the common people increased. Nothing in postwar Britain seemed safe and secure.

> *"I thought it would last my time—*
> *The sense that, beyond the town,*
> *There would always be fields and*
> *farms . . . "*
>
> —Philip Larkin, "Going, Going"

Contemporary British Literature

After decades of Modernist innovation, British poets after World War II were free to reexamine literary tradition. Ted Hughes's poetry looked beyond the Modernists to create a vision of nature that combines beauty and brutality.

Many of the greatest prose writers working today are British novelists. Indian-born author Salman Rushdie's *Midnight's Children* has been universally hailed for its innovative postmodern take on Indian history. Zadie Smith's novel *White Teeth* (2000) was a critically acclaimed postmodern narrative about immigrant communities in London. Kazuo Ishiguro's novels, including *The Remains of the Day* (1989) and *Never Let Me Go* (2005), are more straightforward narratives infused with subtle emotion. Other writers from the Commonwealth, including South African Nobel laureate J. M. Coetzee and Englishmen Ian McEwen and Julian Barnes, have been consistently lauded for their varied works in prose.

Beginning in the mid-1950s, an extraordinary group of playwrights revolutionized the British theater. Samuel Beckett's play *Waiting for Godot* (1953) became an instant classic of absurdist drama. In plays such as *The Caretaker* (1960) and *The Homecoming* (1965), Harold Pinter (see page 1271) created characters unable to communicate and devoid of love.

My Parents, 1977. David Hockney. Tate Gallery, London.

"Thistles" by Ted Hughes

Against the rubber tongues of cows and the hoeing
   hands of men
Thistles spike the summer air
Or crackle open under a blue-black pressure.

Every one a revengeful burst
Of resurrection, a grasped fistful
Of splintered weapons and Icelandic frost thrust up

From the underground stain of a decayed Viking.
They are like pale hair and the gutturals of dialects.
Every one manages a plume of blood.

Then they grow grey, like men.
Mown down, it is a feud. Their sons appear,
Stiff with weapons, fighting back over the same ground.

Reading Check

Comparing and Contrasting How would you compare Hughes's view of nature with that of traditional Romantics?

Colonialism and Postcolonialism

F rom the earliest days of the British Empire, many of its colonies struggled to gain independence. Though most of these early struggles failed, the American Revolution, of course, proved a notable exception.

British Colonial Rule

During the nineteenth and early twentieth centuries, Britain colonized large portions of the world. Markedly different from earlier and more limited British colonialism, especially in Africa and Asia, this "new imperialism" aimed at total control over vast territories. Although based on economic exploitation and influenced by racist attitudes toward colonial peoples, British imperialism also promoted humanitarian goals, such as building railroads, telegraphs, schools, and hospitals. In a poem written in 1899, British poet Rudyard Kipling coined the phrase "the white man's burden" to capture this odd blend of racism and humanitarianism inherent in British imperialism.

> "People go to Africa and confirm what they already have in their heads and so they fail to see what is there in front of them."
>
> —Chinua Achebe

Throughout the British Empire, however, even well-intentioned administrators and zealous missionaries often came into conflict with colonial peoples. In a series of novels that includes his masterpiece, *Things Fall Apart* (1958), Nigerian writer Chinua Achebe (see page 1304) describes the devastating effect of colonialism and Christianity on the traditional African way of life.

Problems of Independence

As the British Empire collapsed, independence brought serious problems to former British colonies. For example, British India consisted of two countries, one Hindu (India) and the other Muslim (Pakistan). When India and Pakistan became independent in 1947, millions of people fled across the new borders, with Hindus streaming toward India and Muslims toward Pakistan. In the ensuing violence, more than a million people perished. Mohandas Gandhi, the renowned Indian nationalist leader and advocate of nonviolence, was assassinated by a Hindu militant on January 30, 1948.

During the 1950s and 1960s, many former British colonies in Africa achieved independence, but their national spirit was undermined by ethnic clashes. Civil warfare was a tragic aftermath of colonialism. In building colonial empires, Britain and other European powers had drawn up the boundaries of African nations with little regard to the inhabitants' ethnic diversity.

In South Africa, the process of achieving political independence for non-whites was complicated by apartheid, the official system of racial segregation in force since the late 1940s. After decades of resistance, apartheid was finally overturned, and in 1994 free elections brought Nelson Mandela to power as the first black president of South Africa. Among the most outspoken critics of South African racism were the writers Doris Lessing (see page 1284) and Nadine Gordimer (see page 1295).

Postcolonial Literature

Many writers from former British colonies, including Achebe, Wole Soyinka, Derek Walcott, and V. S. Naipaul, have addressed the political and social problems that continue to plague these countries even after independence. Postcolonial writers constantly grapple with the tension between native and colonial cultures while addressing themes of identity, racism, and cultural dominance. Because English is so widely spoken, many postcolonial writers have felt compelled to adopt this language even if it's not their native tongue.

A wooden carving of a car with a European and his driver, c. 20th century. Zaire Luba. Museum of Central Africa, Tervuren, Belgium.

In the nineteenth century, the British had boasted that "the sun never set" on their worldwide empire. After World War II, as colony after colony became independent, Britain's national prestige was dealt a severe blow.

"Homage to a Government" by Philip Larkin

Next year we are to bring the soldiers home
For lack of money, and it is all right.
Places they guarded, or kept orderly,
Must guard themselves, and keep themselves orderly.
We want the money for ourselves at home
Instead of working. And this is all right.

It's hard to say who wanted it to happen,
But now it's been decided nobody minds.
The places are a long way off, not here.
Which is all right, and from what we hear

The soldiers there only made trouble happen.
Next year we shall be easier in our minds.

Next year we shall be living in a country
That brought its soldiers home for lack of money.
The statues will be standing in the same
Tree-muffled squares, and look nearly the same.
Our children will not know it's a different country.
All we can hope to leave them now is money.

Reading Check

Analyzing Cause and Effect According to the speaker in Larkin's poem, why did Britain give up its colonies?

What does the term *English literature* convey to you? In the Middle Ages, the term applied only to the writings produced on an island off the northwest coast of Europe. Even three hundred years ago, in the early stages of the British Empire, the meaning of the term extended only to the works created by British colonists in New England and Virginia. Today, writers throughout the world create masterpieces in English. How did this extraordinary turn of events come about?

Movement of Peoples

From its beginning more than three centuries ago, the British Empire spurred the migration of people. Emigrants left Britain to settle in India, Canada, Australia, New Zealand, South Africa, and a host of other British colonies.

> *"I am a word in a foreign language."*
>
> —Margaret Atwood, "Disembarking at Quebec"

People also moved from one colony to another within the British Empire in search of work on plantations or in mines. The family of writer V. S. Naipaul (see page 1331) emigrated from British India to Trinidad in the West Indies. In *Prologue to an Autobiography*, Naipaul describes his complex heritage: "There was a migration from India to be considered, a migration within the British Empire. There was my Hindu family, with its fading memories of India; there was India itself. And there was Trinidad, with its past of slavery, its mixed population, its racial antagonisms, and its changing political life."

Exporting English

During its heyday as an empire-builder, Britain exported many goods, from cotton products and cricket bats to policies and laws. Undoubtedly, the most important British export was the English language itself. It traveled widely in the three centuries during which Britain ruled much of the world. The emergence of Britain's former colony, the United States of America, as a superpower after World War II also contributed to the global dominance of English.

A Global Literature

Just as improvements and innovations in transportation and technology have enabled people from different countries to communicate more easily, the spread of the English language and British culture throughout the world has given rise to an international literature in English. The Nobel Prize in Literature serves as a yardstick to measure the increase in the number of writers throughout the world creating works in English. Before World War II, only one Nobel laureate writing in English, the Indian writer Rabindranath Tagore (rə bin′ drə nät′ tə gôr′), was neither British, Irish, nor American. Since World War II, Nobel laureates writing in English include Patrick White from Australia, Nadine Gordimer and J. M. Coetzee from South Africa, Wole Soyinka from Nigeria, and Derek Walcott and V. S. Naipaul from the Caribbean.

In the twenty-first century, with all its advances in technology, the world seems to be a smaller place. Nevertheless, literature remains a major source of understanding and entertainment, just as it was in the times of Chaucer, Shakespeare, and Keats. Throughout this worldwide community, the global village, people continue to look to British literature for a glorious tradition that is still growing and seeking new directions.

Britain Seen from the North, 1981. Tony Cragg. Plastic and mixed media, 173.22 x 314.96 x 3.93 in. Tate Gallery, London.

Among the themes addressed by the writers of this global literature in English are the effects of colonialism, the nature of cultural identity, and the experience of crossing boundaries, either geographical or historical. Published in 1981, Salman Rushdie's novel Midnight's Children *opens with this account of the narrator's birth at the exact moment when India became independent.*

from *Midnight's Children* by Salman Rushdie

I was born in the city of Bombay . . . once upon a time. No, that won't do, there's no getting away from the date: I was born in Doctor Narlikar's Nursing Home on August 15th, 1947. And the time? The time matters, too. Well then: at night. No, it's important to be more . . . On the stroke of midnight, as a matter of fact. Clock-hands joined palms in respectful greeting as I came. Oh, spell it out, spell it out: at the precise instant of India's arrival at independence, I tumbled forth into the world. There were gasps. And, outside the window, fireworks and crowds. A few seconds later, my father broke his big toe; but his accident was a mere trifle when set beside what had befallen me in the benighted moment, because thanks to the occult tyrannies of those blandly saluting clocks I had been mysteriously handcuffed to history, my destinies indissolubly chained to those of my country. For the next three decades, there was to be no escape. Soothsayers had prophesied me, newspapers celebrated my arrival, politicos ratified my authenticity. I was left entirely without a say in the matter.

Reading Check

Interpreting Why might some writers from former British colonies feel "handcuffed to history," as does Rushdie's narrator?

Wrap-Up

Why It Matters

English is the main or official language in more than sixty nations and is used on every continent. The reasons for the spread of English point to the influence of the once global British Empire and the emergence of the United States as a world power. The spread of the English language has created a vast audience for traditional British literature. More important, it has provided an opportunity for writers throughout the world to create modern classics in the English language. Drawing upon their cultural traditions and life experiences, these writers have broadened and enriched British literature.

The Modernist movement had run its course when World War II ended. Postmodernism, with its emphasis on literature as a self-consciously artificial form, influenced postwar literature in Britain (Julian Barnes's novel *Flaubert's Parrot* is one notable example), but much contemporary British poetry and fiction adapted traditional literary forms. British drama is perhaps the genre richest in innovation, as the plays of Samuel Beckett, John Osborne, Harold Pinter, and Wole Soyinka attest.

 **Big Ideas** Link to Web resources to further explore the Big Ideas at **www.glencoe.com**.

Cultural Links

▶ In his recent translation of *Beowulf*, Seamus Heaney stated that he sought to evoke the traditional English that he heard as a child in Northern Ireland.

▶ In his book-length narrative poem *Omeros*, Derek Walcott invests his tale of a Caribbean fisherman's voyage to his ancestral African home with allusions to the Homeric epics.

▶ V. S. Naipaul's novel *A Bend in the River* is a postcolonial account of the African region first described by Joseph Conrad in his novel *Heart of Darkness* (1902).

You might try using this study organizer to explore the different literary genres in this unit.

FOLDABLES Study Organizer **FOUR-TAB BOOK**

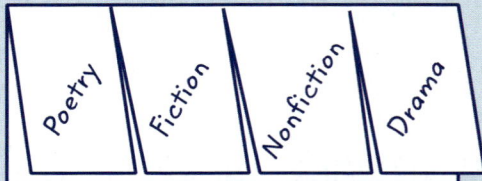

Connect to Today

Use what you have learned about the period to do one of these activities.

1. Speaking/Listening Working with other students, research the political, social, and cultural legacy of the British Empire for both Britain and its former colonies. Hold a panel discussion to explore the positive and negative effects of British imperialism.

2. Visual Literacy Research the Festival of Britain and create a display showing some of its buildings, artifacts, and attractions. Held in 1951, that festival commemorated the centennial of the Great Exhibition.

OBJECTIVES
- Hold a panel discussion.
- Create a display.

Literature Online Study Central Visit **www.glencoe.com** and click on Study Central to review contemporary British literature.

The British Isles:
Making and Remaking Traditions

Untitled, from a series of five, 1973. Tim Mara. Silkscreen print, 34.76 x 34.76 in.
Wolverhampton Art Gallery, West Midlands, UK.

*"You're hurt because everything's changed. Jimmy's hurt because
everything's the same. And neither of you can face it."*

—Alison in John Osborne's *Look Back in Anger*

Not Waving but Drowning

MEET STEVIE SMITH

Florence Margaret Smith got her nickname Stevie as a young girl when she and a friend were riding horses in a London park. Smith's horse was slow, and she rose in the saddle to urge it on. A few boys playing in the park saw her unsuccessful attempt to speed her mount and taunted, "Come on, Steve," referring to Steve Donaghue, a famous jockey of the day. Smith's companion loved the joke and began referring to Smith as Steve. Other friends soon were affectionately calling the petite, jockey-sized woman Stevie. The name stuck for the rest of her life.

Smith grew up with her mother, her aunt, and her older sister in a suburb of London. When Smith was three years old, her father deserted the family to become a sailor. Smith was a smart but unmotivated student. Her sister once noted that although Smith shirked school work, she could "get to the heart of the matter in two ticks."

> "The times will just have to enlarge themselves to make room for me, won't they?"
>
> —Stevie Smith

The World of Work Not considered academically suited for college, Smith attended secretarial school and soon got a job as the secretary for the head of a publishing firm. She worked there for thirty years, supporting herself and her aunt, who lived with her for her entire life. In her spare time, Smith wrote poetry and read prodigiously, keeping a log of what she read and copying down passages that stimulated or impressed her.

Smith had her first poems published in a magazine in 1935. With this success, she approached an editor at a publishing house with a collection of her poems. The editor told Smith that before she was likely to get a book of poetry published she needed to "go away and write a novel." Smith did just that, completing her book in about six weeks. Against the advice of the editor who had encouraged Smith, the publishing house turned down Smith's novel. However, another publisher soon accepted it. *A Novel on Yellow Paper* was published in 1937 and a book of Smith's poetry was published soon afterward.

The Pendulum of Popularity Smith achieved sudden fame that launched her to the center of London's literary circles. She continued writing prose, but poetry was her real love. In fact, Smith's prose often exhibits the musicality and rhythm of poetry. One short story she wrote had such perfect meter that she later had it published as a poem, adding only line breaks and stanza divisions.

World War II interrupted Smith's writing career. She served as a volunteer fire-watcher during the nighttime air raid attacks on London. After the war, Smith's poetry didn't sell, and her publisher was reluctant to print her new work. Smith's popularity resurged in the late 1950s, however, and in the 1960s she received awards for her poems. In 1969 Queen Elizabeth honored her by giving her the Gold Medal for Poetry. A few years later, Smith died of an inoperable brain tumor.

Stevie Smith was born in 1902 and died in 1971.

Literature Online **Author Search** For more about Stevie Smith, go to www.glencoe.com.

Connecting to the Poem

"Not Waving but Drowning" is about a man who has faced substantial difficulties in life. As you read the poem, think about how people respond when they notice someone in trouble.

- What makes it easy or difficult to help someone in trouble?
- Do you think people are more likely to show callousness or compassion to someone in trouble?

Building Background

Smith believed that "a poet should get on with his work and not be bothered by what his status is in the community." By following this principle, Smith developed a unique and independent style that differed greatly from that of her contemporaries. One of her most distinctive styles was the use of humorous verse to express what were in fact profoundly serious themes. Another distinctive characteristic was her use of her own sketches (which she referred to as "doodles") to illustrate her poems.

Setting Purposes for Reading

Big Idea Making and Remaking Traditions

As you read, notice how Smith uses both conventional poetic forms, including rhyme and meter, and unconventional elements in the poem.

Literary Element Speaker

In prose fiction, the narrator is the person, object, or force telling the story. In poetry, this role is taken by the **speaker.** The speaker may or may not be the poet. As you read "Not Waving but Drowning," identify the different speakers who make statements in this poem.

- See Literary Terms Handbook, p. R17.

Literature Online Interactive Literary Elements Handbook To review or learn more about the literary elements, go to www.glencoe.com.

Reading Strategy Questioning

Questioning is a reading strategy that involves asking yourself specific questions to aid your comprehension.

Reading Tip: Asking Questions Make three or more copies of a diagram like the one below. As you read each stanza of "Not Waving but Drowning," fill in a copy of the diagram to ask and answer questions about the poem. If you wish, you can fill in more than one diagram per stanza.

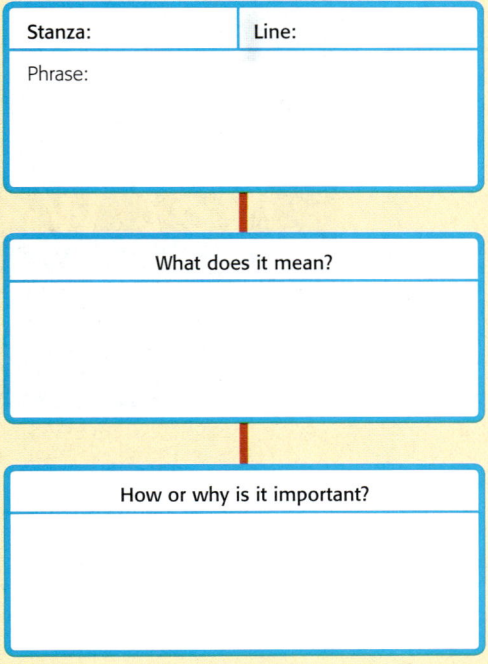

Stanza:	Line:
Phrase:	

What does it mean?

How or why is it important?

OBJECTIVES
In studying this selection, you will focus on the following:
- analyzing genre elements
- analyzing speaker
- asking questions about the text

Not Waving but Drowning

Stevie Smith

Nobody heard him, the dead man,
But still he lay moaning:
I was much further out than you thought
And not waving but drowning.

5   Poor chap, he always loved larking[1]
And now he's dead
It must have been too cold for him his heart gave way,
They said.

Oh, no no no, it was too cold always
10   (Still the dead one lay moaning)
I was much too far out all my life
And not waving but drowning.

---

1. Here, *larking* means "engaging in harmless pranks."

Literary Element   **Speaker** *Who is speaking in these two lines?*

Reading Strategy   **Questioning** *What connotations does the word* cold *have here?*

RESPONDING AND THINKING CRITICALLY

Respond

1. Did the subject of the poem match what you predicted the poem would be about, based on its title? Why or why not?

Recall and Interpret

2. (a)In the first stanza, what statement does the dead man make? (b)Do you think he had tried to communicate this thought while he was living? Explain.

3. (a)In the second stanza, what do "they" believe caused the man's death? (b)In your opinion, who are "they"? What do you infer about their relationship with the drowned man?

4. (a)In the first line of the third stanza, why does the man say, "no no no"? (b)In your own words, explain what he means in this stanza.

Analyze and Evaluate

5. (a)Which words and phrases in the poem have double meanings? (b)What do these plays on words suggest about the dead man's ability to be understood by others?

6. Do you think this poem is tragic, comic, both, or something else? Explain.

Connect

7. **Big Idea** **Making and Remaking Traditions**
(a)What poetic conventions does "Not Waving but Drowning" employ? (b)In what ways is this poem unconventional? (c)How does the tension between poetic traditions and innovations relate to the message of the poem?

LITERARY ANALYSIS

Literary Element **Speaker**

On the surface, "Not Waving but Drowning" is a simple poem. There are no long, complex words, and the phrasing is conversational. But identifying the different speakers starts to reveal layers of complexity.

1. Identify the different speakers in the poem. In which lines are each person speaking?

2. What clues helped you figure out who was speaking and when there was a shift in speakers?

Writing About Literature

Evaluate Author's Craft Write a brief review of "Not Waving but Drowning." Begin by summarizing Smith's main message in this poem and then explain the literary devices she uses to get this message across. End your review by stating your opinion of the poem. Does reading this poem make you interested in reading more of Smith's poetry? Explain why or why not.

Literature Online **Web Activities** For eFlashcards, Selection Quick Checks, and other Web activities, go to www.glencoe.com.

READING AND VOCABULARY

Reading Strategy **Questioning**

To understand poetry, you need to ask questions not only as you read a poem but also as you analyze it.

1. What connotations do the following words have in the context of this poem: *Too far out* in line 11 and *drowning* in the title, line 4, and line 12. How do these words add to the meaning of the poem?

2. In terms of his ability to communicate, has anything changed for the man over the course of the poem? Explain your answer.

Academic Vocabulary

Here is a word from the vocabulary list on page R82.

circumstance (sur′ kəm stans′) *n.* a condition or fact that accompanies an event

Practice and Apply
Summarize the **circumstances** related to the title of the poem.

At the Pitt-Rivers

MEET PENELOPE LIVELY

Have you ever wondered how your life might have changed if you had made a different decision at a critical turning point? In her autobiographical novel *Making It Up*, Penelope Lively imagines alternate life paths, exploring what might have happened if her family, fleeing Cairo, Egypt, during World War II, had headed for South Africa instead of their actual destination, Palestine. Would the ship on which they sailed have been torpedoed, as so many other ships had been? She also wonders what would have happened if she had had children at a younger age than she did, if her husband-to-be had been sent to fight in the Korean War, if she had married a different man, or if she had gone on an archaeological dig as a student. Did the choices she made cut off more rewarding paths, or did they avert disasters?

> *"It seems to me that the challenge of writing novels and short stories is to transcend and translate personal experience . . ."*
>
> —Penelope Lively

Childhood Upheaval Lively was born in Cairo and spent much of her childhood there. Her father, a bank manager, was so busy that she rarely saw him, and her mother was often occupied with social engagements. As a child Lively spent most of her time with a young English woman named Lucy, who started out as her nurse and then became her governess. Lively had no formal education until 1945, when she was sent to a boarding school in England after her parents divorced. Already dealing with the trauma of parental neglect, Lively now had to endure permanent separation from Lucy, to whom she had become attached. She saw England as "not home at all—a mysterious, grey, wet place where it rained all the time."

Literary Pursuits After graduating from high school, Lively went on to college, earning a degree in history at Oxford. She married Jack Lively, a university professor, and they had two children. She and her husband had a long and happy marriage until his death in 1998. While raising her children, Lively began writing children's books. Her first published novel, *Astercote*, is about modern English villagers who fear the return of the medieval plague. She has written more than twenty novels for children, set mostly in rural England and concerned with the significance of memory and history.

By the mid-1970s, Lively began shifting her focus to literature for adults, although she continued to write for children well into the 1980s. "I began to feel that I was in danger of writing the same children's books over and over again," she explains. "More than that, I'd exhausted the ways in which I could explore my own preoccupations and interests within children's books." Her adult novels continue to explore the themes of the past and memory, but in the context of how such themes can affect one's philosophy or perspective on life. Lively won the Booker Prize for her novel *Moon Tiger* in 1987.

Penelope Lively was born in 1933.

Literature Online **Author Search** For more about Penelope Lively, go to www.glencoe.com.

Connecting to the Story

In this story, the narrator observes a couple and speculates about their lives. As you read, think about the following questions:

- What can you learn about strangers by observing their behavior, expressions, and moods?
- How might your impression of someone else's relationship influence your own relationships?

Building Background

The setting of this story is the Pitt Rivers Museum of Anthropology and World Archaeology, located at Oxford University. The Pitt Rivers Museum was established in 1884, when Lieutenant-General Pitt Rivers donated his considerable collection of artifacts (more than 18,000 objects) to the university. The museum now has more than half a million objects, most of them on display, filling cluttered cases and identified with small handwritten labels. One of its holdings is a three-floors-high totem pole, which is mentioned in the story.

Setting Purposes for Reading

Big Idea **Making and Remaking Traditions**

As you read, notice how the author creates an unconventional love story.

Literary Element **Vernacular**

Vernacular is the ordinary speech of a particular country or region. It is more casual and informal than cultivated, formal speech and includes slang and **dialect**. Another important feature of vernacular is the use of **idiom**—a grammatical construction peculiar to a particular language. In its departure from literal meaning, idiom is close to metaphor, as in the expression "catch his eye." As you read the story, examine how Lively uses vernacular language to reveal characteristics of the narrator's background and personality.

- See Literary Terms Handbook, p. R19.

Literature Online **Interactive Literary Elements Handbook** To review or learn more about the literary elements, go to www.glencoe.com.

Reading Strategy   Synthesizing

When you **synthesize**, you combine various details or simple ideas to arrive at a more complex idea. Synthesizing information helps you reach a deeper understanding of a literary text.

....

Reading Tip: Taking Notes In a chart, record significant details from the story, as well as relevant background information. Synthesize your information and details to gain new insights into the story.

Details in Story	Pitt-Rivers is in Oxford
Background Information	
Synthesis	

Vocabulary

benign (bi nīn′) *adj.* pleasant and friendly; p. 1249 *Hoping to reassure the patient, the nurse gave him a benign smile.*

explicit (eks plis′ it) *adj.* plainly and clearly expressed; definite; p. 1250 *The children had explicit instructions to return to the house.*

compulsory (kəm pul′ sər ē) *adj.* obligatory; required; p. 1250 *He did not want to take mid-terms, but the tests were compulsory.*

radiant (rā′ dē ənt) *adj.* beaming, as with joy, love, or energy; p. 1251 *The bride was radiant as she looked at her new husband.*

envious (en′ vē əs) *adj.* feeling jealous or discontented because of the good fortune or superior abilities of another; p. 1252 *Jeremy was envious of his brother's amazing athletic ability.*

Vocabulary Tip: Connotation and Denotation
The denotation of a word is its literal, dictionary definition. Its connotation is what it suggests, beyond the literal definition.

OBJECTIVES

In studying this selection, you will focus on the following:
- relating literature to historical periods
- understanding vernacular
- synthesizing information

At the Pitt-Rivers

Penelope Lively

Man and Woman in an Art Gallery. Lincoln Seligman. Private Collection.

They've got this museum in Oxford, called the Pitt-Rivers; I spend a lot of time there. It's a weird place, really weird, stuff from all over the world crammed into glass cases like some kind of mad junk-shop—native things from New Guinea and Mexico and Sumatra and wherever you like to think of. Spears and stone axes and masks and a thousand different kinds of fish-hook. And bead jewelery and peculiar musical instruments. And a great totem from Canada. You can learn a lot there about what people get up to: it makes you think. Mostly it's pretty depressing—umpteen different nasty ways of killing each other.

I didn't start going there to learn anything; just because it was a nice quiet place to mooch around[1] and be on my own, Saturdays, or after school. It got to be a kind of habit. There aren't often people there—the odd art student, a few kids gawping at the shrunken heads, one or two serious-looking blokes wandering around. The porter's usually reading the *Sun*[2] or having a snooze; there's not a lot of custom. The Natural History Museum is a bigger draw; you have to go through that to get into the Pitt-Rivers. You'll always get an audience for a dinosaur and a few nasty-looking jellyfish in formalin.[3] Actually I'm partial to the Natural History Museum myself; that makes you think, too. All those fossils, and then in the end you and me. I had a go at reading *The Origin of Species*[4] last term, not that I got very far. There's a room upstairs in the museum where Darwin's friend—Huxley—had this great

---

1. To *mooch around* is British slang for "to idle away time."

2. The *Sun* is a British tabloid newspaper.
3. *Formalin* is a trademark for a clear watery solution of formaldehyde (a disinfectant and preservative) with a small amount of methanol (a poisonous liquid alcohol).
4. *The Origin of Species* is a book by Charles Darwin that explains his theory of evolution by natural selection.

argument with that bishop[5] and the rest of them. It says so on the door. I like that, it seems kind of respectful. Putting up a plaque to an argument, instead of just JOE SOAP WAS BORN HERE or whatever. It should be done more often.

It was in the Natural History Museum—underneath the central whale—that I first saw her, and since my mind was on natural selection I thought she wasn't all that good an example of it. I remember thinking that it was funny it doesn't seem to operate with girls, so you got them getting prettier and prettier, because good-looking girls have a better deal than bad-looking ones, you've only got to observe a bit to see that. I always notice girls, to see if they're pretty or not, and she wasn't. She wasn't specially ugly; just very ordinary—you wouldn't look at her twice. She was sitting on a bench, watching the entrance.

All the girls I know—at school or round where I live—are either attractive or they're not. If they're attractive they have lots of blokes after them and if they're not they don't. It's as simple as that. If they're attractive just looking at them makes you think of all sorts of things, imagine what it would be like and so forth, and if they're not then it doesn't really occur to you, except in so far as it occurs to you a good deal of the time, actually. This girl was definitely not attractive. In the first place she was in fact quite old, not far off thirty, I should think, and in the second she hadn't got a nice figure; her legs were kind of dumpy and she didn't have pretty hair or anything like that. I gave her a look, just automatically, to check, and then didn't bother with her.

Until I came alongside, where I could see her face clearly, and then I looked again. And again. She still wasn't pretty, but she had the most beautiful expression I've ever seen in my life. She glowed; that's the only way I can put it. She

sat there with her hands in her lap, watching the door, and radiating away so that in a peculiar fashion it made you feel good just to look at her, a bit like you were joining in how she felt. Stupid, I daresay, but that's how it was.

And I thought to myself: oh ho . . . I mean, I've seen films and I've read books and I know a bit about things.

As a matter of fact I've been in love myself twice. The first time was with a girl in my class at school and I suppose it was a bit of a trial run, really, I mean I'm not altogether sure how much I was feeling it but it seemed quite important when it was going on. The second time was last year, when I was fifteen. She came to stay with her married sister who lives round the corner from us and though it's months and months ago now I still feel quite faint and weak when I go past the house.

Oh ho, I thought. I felt kindly—sort of **benign**—and a bit curious to see what the bloke would be like. I thought he couldn't be much because of her not being pretty. I mean, in films you can always tell who's going to fall for who because they'll be the two good-lookers and while I'm not saying real life's like that there is a way people match each other, isn't there, you've only got to look round at married people. Let me hasten to say that I'm not all that good-looking myself, only about B+. Not too bad, but not all that marvelous either.

But he didn't show up and I wanted to get on into the Pitt-Rivers, so I left her there, waiting. What I haven't said is that one of the things I go to the Pitt-Rivers for is to write poetry. I write quite a lot of poetry. I could do it at home—I often do—and it's not that I'm coy or anything, my parents know about it and they're quite interested, but I just like the idea of having a special place to go to. It's quiet there, and a bit odd like I've said, and nobody takes any notice of me.

Sometimes I feel I'm getting somewhere with this poetry, and other times it looks to me pretty awful. I showed a few poems to our English master and he was very helpful: he said what was good and pointed out where I'd used words badly, or not worked out what I was thinking very well,

---

5. In 1860 Bishop Samuel Wilberforce lost a famous debate with Thomas Henry Huxley over the issue of evolution.

Reading Strategy Synthesizing *What new understanding do you gain about the narrator by synthesizing his comments in this paragraph?*

Reading Strategy Synthesizing *What new side of the narrator is revealed through his observations of the woman in the museum?*

Vocabulary

benign (bi nīn′) *adj.* pleasant and friendly

Portrait of Keith Henderson in a Black Hood, 1902. Maxwell Ashby Armfield. 16.5 x 17.5 cm. Collection of Andrew McIntosh Patrick, UK.

so that was quite encouraging. He's a nice bloke. I like his lessons. He's very good at explaining poetry. I mean, I think poetry's amazingly difficult: sometimes you read a thing again and again and you just can't see what the hell the person's getting at. He reads all sorts of poetry to us, our English master, and you really get the hang of it after a bit—hard stuff like Hopkins[6] and The Hound of Heaven,[7] and Donne.[8] He read us some of those Donne poems about love the other day which are all very **explicit** and I must say first time round I hadn't quite got the point—

'Licence my roving hands . . .' and so forth—but he wasn't embarrassed or anything, our English master, and when you realize that it's not geography he's talking about, the poet, then as a matter of fact I think that poem's lovely.[9] I got a bit fed up with the way some of my mates were sniggering about it, being all-knowing; truth to tell I doubt if they know any more than I do, it's all just show. And that's a beautiful poem: I mean, if anything makes it clear that there's nothing wrong about sex, that poem does, they ought to make it **compulsory** reading for some people.

---

6. *Hopkins* refers to the British poet Gerard Manley Hopkins (1844–1889).
7. "The Hound of Heaven" is a poem by British poet Francis Thompson (1859–1907).
8. *Donne* refers to John Donne (1572–1631), an Anglican cleric and poet.

Vocabulary

explicit (eks plis′ it) *adj.* plainly and clearly expressed; definite

---

9. The Donne poem referred to here is "Elegy XIX: On My Mistress Going to Bed."

Reading Strategy Synthesizing *What new insight about the narrator do you gain from a synthesis of the details in this passage?*

Vocabulary

compulsory (kəm pul′ sər ē) *adj.* obligatory; required

Anyway, I went on into the Pitt-Rivers and I was up on the first floor, in a favorite corner of mine among the arrow-heads, when I saw her again, and I must say I got quite a shock. Because the man with her was an old bloke: he was older than my father, fiftyish and more, he must have been at least twenty years older than her. So I reckoned I must have made a mistake. Not that at all.

They were talking, though I couldn't hear what they were saying because they were on the far side of the gallery. They stopped in front of a case and I could see their faces quite clearly. They stood there looking at each other, not talking anymore, and I realized I hadn't made a mistake after all. Absolutely not. They didn't touch each other, they just stood and looked; it seemed like ages. I don't imagine they knew I was there.

And that time I was shocked. Really shocked. I don't mind telling you, I thought it was disgusting. He was an ordinary-looking person—he might have been a schoolmaster or something, he wore those kind of clothes, old trousers and sweater, and he had greyish hair, a bit long. And there was she, and as I've said she wasn't pretty, not at all, but she had this marvelous look about her, and she was years and years younger.

It was because of him, I realized, that she had that look.

I didn't like it at all. I got up, from where I was sitting, with quite a clatter to make sure they heard me and I went stumping off out of the museum. I wasn't going to write any more poetry that day, I could see. I went off home and truth to tell I didn't really think much more about them, that man and the girl, mainly because of being rather disgusted, like I said.

A couple of weeks later they were there again. They were on the ground floor, at the back, by the rush matting[10] and ceremonial gear for with-it tribesmen, leaning up against a glass case that they weren't looking into, and talking. At least he was talking, quiet and serious, and she was listening, and nodding from time to time. I was busy with some thinking I wanted to do, and I tried not to take any notice of them; I mean, they were neither here nor there as far as I was concerned, none of my business, though I still thought it was a bit creepy. I couldn't see *why*, frankly. You fancy people your own age, and that's all there is to it, is what I thought. What I'd always thought.

So I ignored them, except that I couldn't quite. I kept sneaking a look, every now and then, and the more I did the more I felt kind of friendly towards them; I liked them. Which was a bit weird considering they didn't know I even existed—they certainly weren't interested in *me*—so it was a pretty one-sided kind of relationship. I thought he seemed like a nice bloke, whatever you thought about him and her and all that. It was something about the way he smiled, and the way he told her things (not that I ever heard a word they said, I wasn't eavesdropping, not ever, let's be quite clear about that) that made her look interested and say things back and so on. I thought it was obvious they like talking to each other, quite apart from anything else. I thought that was nice.

I only took out that girl I mentioned—the one who came to stay with her sister—once, and as a matter of fact we couldn't find much to talk about. I was still in love with her—no doubt about that—but it was a bit sticky, I don't mind admitting. In fact I was quite glad when it was time to take her back to her sister's. In many ways the best part was just thinking about her.

Every time I looked at the girl—the Pitt-Rivers one, that is—I found myself imagining what it must be like being able to feel that you've made someone look like that. **Radiant**, like she was. Which is what that bloke must have been able to feel. I found myself putting myself in his place, as it were, and wondering. I've done a lot of wondering about things like

---

Big Idea Making and Remaking Traditions *How does the couple in the story violate the narrator's traditional concept of love?*

Reading Strategy Synthesizing *Based on what you already know about the narrator, why do you think he has begun to change his negative attitude toward the couple?*

Vocabulary

radiant (rā′ dē ənt) *adj.* beaming, as with joy, love, or energy

---

10. *Rush* is a type of marsh plant with cylindrical, often hollow stems; it is used to make chair bottoms and mats. The term *rush matting* refers to mats made out of rush.

Museum Arch II, 2003. Pam Ingalls.

that—everybody does, I suppose—but mostly it's been more kind of basic. Now, I began to think I didn't really know anything. Looking at those two—watching them, if you like—was a bit like seeing something go on behind a thick glass window, so it was half removed from you. You could see but not hear, hear but not touch, or whatever. I could see, but I didn't know.

I suppose you could say I was envious, in a funny kind of way. I don't mean jealous in that I fancied the girl, or anything like that. As I've said already, she wasn't pretty, or even attractive. And I wasn't **envious** like you might be envious of someone for being happier than you are, because I'm not specially unhappy, as it happens. I think I was envious of them for being what they were—as though one fossil creature might

be envious of a more evolved kind of fossil creature, which of course is a stupid idea.

When I was in the Pitt-Rivers again I looked for them, quite deliberately, but they weren't there. I was disappointed, though I pretended to myself it really didn't matter. I wondered about why they went there in the first place; I mean, people have to meet each other somewhere but why *there*? It doesn't exactly spring to mind as a romantic spot. I supposed there were reasons they didn't want to meet somewhere obvious and public: maybe he was married, I thought, or maybe she was, even. I wondered if that was the only place they met, or did they have others. Once walking through the botanical gardens, I found myself looking for them in the big glasshouses there.

Literary Element Vernacular *What does the idiom* spring to mind *mean? Why might the writer have chosen to use an idiomatic expression here?*

I know the inside of the Pitt-Rivers pretty well by now. Considering it's not anthropology or ethnology or whatever I went there for in the first place, it's quite surprising what a lot I could tell you about the things people believe and do. Primitive people, that is—what the Pitt-Rivers calls primitive people. And I think it's all very sad, actually: sad because it's like children, not understanding how things work and getting it all wrong, and carving each other up because of it a lot of the time. It does actually make you feel things get better—wars and bombs and everything notwithstanding. Nobody wants to go on being a child all their lives.

I was thinking about this—looking at a case full of particularly loony stuff to do with witchcraft—when I saw them again. At least I saw her first, standing by the totem with her hands in her coat pockets, and I didn't have to look at the door to know he'd arrived: her face told you that. He came up to her and gave her a kind of hug—arm round her shoulders and then quickly off again—and they wandered away up the stairs, heads together, talking.

I didn't follow them; it had been nice to see them again, and know they were there, and that was it. I was busy on a poem I'd been writing and unpicking and rewriting for some time. It was a poem about an old man sitting on a bench in a park and getting into conversation with a boy—someone around my age—and they swap opinions and observations (it's all dialogue, this poem, like a long conversation) and it's not till the end you realize they're the same person. It sounds either corny, or pretentious, I know; and what I could never decide was whether to have it as though the old man's looking back, or the boy's kind of projecting forward—imagining himself, as it were. So I went on fiddling about with this, and didn't really think much about the man and the girl, until I saw it was latish and there was no one else in the museum except me and some feet on the wooden floor of the gallery overhead, walking round and round, round and round. Two pairs of feet. They'd been doing that for ages, I realized; I'd been hearing them without registering.

I saw them go past—just their heads, above the glass cases—and something wasn't right. They weren't talking. She had her arm through his, and she was looking straight in front of her, and when I saw her face I had a nasty kind of twinge in my stomach. Because she was miserable. Once, she looked at him, and they both managed a bleak sort of smile. And then they walked on, round the gallery again, and next time past they still weren't talking, just holding on to each other like that, like people who're ill, or very old. And then the attendant rang the bell, and I heard them come down the stairs, and they came past me and went out into the Natural History Museum.

I went after them. I saw them stop—under the central whale, just where I first saw her—and then they did say something to each other. I couldn't see her face; she had her back to me. He went off then, on his own, out through the main entrance, quickly, and she sat down on a bench. For a moment or two she just sat staring at that wretched whale, and then she felt in her bag and got out a comb and did her hair, as though that might help. And then she dropped the comb and didn't seem to have noticed, even, because she just sat; she didn't bother to pick it up or anything. I could see her face then, and I hope I don't ever see anyone look so unhappy again. I truly hope that.

I don't know what had happened. I never will. Somehow, I don't think they were ever going to see each other again, but why . . . well, that's their concern, just like the rest of it was, except that in this peculiar way I'd come to feel it was mine too. I didn't think there was anything disgusting about them anymore, or creepy—I hadn't for a long time. I suppose you could say I'd learned something else in the Pitt-Rivers, by accident. I never did go on with that poem. I tore it up, as far as it had got; I wasn't so sure anymore about that conversation, that there could even be one, or not like I'd been imagining, anyway. ❧

Reading Strategy Synthesizing *What new understanding do you reach about the couple's relationship when you synthesize the details in this paragraph?*

Reading Strategy Synthesizing *Why do you think the narrator feels personally involved in the couple's lives?*

RESPONDING AND THINKING CRITICALLY

Respond

1. What would you have liked to ask the narrator at the end of the story?

Recall and Interpret

2. (a)Why does the narrator spend so much time at the Pitt-Rivers? (b)What might this suggest about his home life?

3. (a)Why is the narrator shocked and disgusted at first by the relationship between the two people? (b)What does this reveal about his attitude toward love?

4. (a)Why is the narrator envious of the couple— especially of the older man? (b)What does the narrator learn about love by watching the couple?

Analyze and Evaluate

5. (a)Consider the scene in which the two people appear to separate permanently. Explain how the author indicates that both of them suffer greatly at this moment. (b)How does the narrator react to their separation?

6. (a)What evidence in the story suggests that the two people have an emotional and intellectual, rather than a physical, relationship? (b)What do you think is the most likely reason that the couple decided to end their relationship?

Connect

7. The narrator tears up the poem he has been writing, realizing that the opinions and observations in it are no longer valid. Have you ever had an experience that forced you to reevaluate one of your beliefs or assumptions about life? Explain.

8. **Big Idea** **Making and Remaking Traditions** What elements of Lively's style make this story different from others you have read in this textbook? Explain.

PRIMARY SOURCE QUOTATION

The Functions of Fiction

Read the two comments by Penelope Lively below. Notice how each quotation expresses Lively's attitudes toward life, memory, and the functions of fiction.

> *"I have never come to terms with life, and I wouldn't wish anyone else to do so; if fiction is to help at all in the process of living, it is by illuminating its conflicts and ambiguities."*

> *"I don't imagine that I am ever going to find the answer to the questions prompted by the workings of memory; all I can do is pose these questions in fictional form and see what happens."*

Group Activity Discuss the following questions with a group of classmates. Refer to the quotations and cite evidence from "At the Pitt-Rivers" for support.

1. (a)According to the first quotation, what does Lively believe to be the function of fiction? (b)How does "At the Pitt-Rivers" fulfill this function?

2. (a)How might the "workings of memory" have contributed to Lively's ideas in this story? (b)According to Lively, how does she use memory in her fiction?

Literary Element Vernacular

The use of the **vernacular** gives an informal feel to a work of literature. For example, in "At the Pitt-Rivers," the narrator addresses the reader as if he were having a casual conversation with a friend.

1. (a)How does the narrator use the vernacular to describe his first impressions of the young woman? (b)What characteristics does the narrator's vernacular speech reveal about himself?

2. (a)Choose one paragraph from the story that has examples of vernacular language and reword it into Standard English. (b)How does the tone of the reworded paragraph compare to the tone of the original?

3. When the narrator is talking about the first time he was in love, he calls it a "trial run." How would you explain this idiom to someone who is just learning English?

Review: Narrator

As you learned on page 1069, a **narrator** is the voice that tells the story in a work of fiction. Sometimes, the narrator is a character in the story; at other times, the narrator is an observer outside the story.

Partner Activity Meet with a classmate and discuss the narrator in "At the Pitt-Rivers." Is he a character in the story, an outside observer, or a combination of both? To help in your analysis, complete a graphic organizer like the one below.

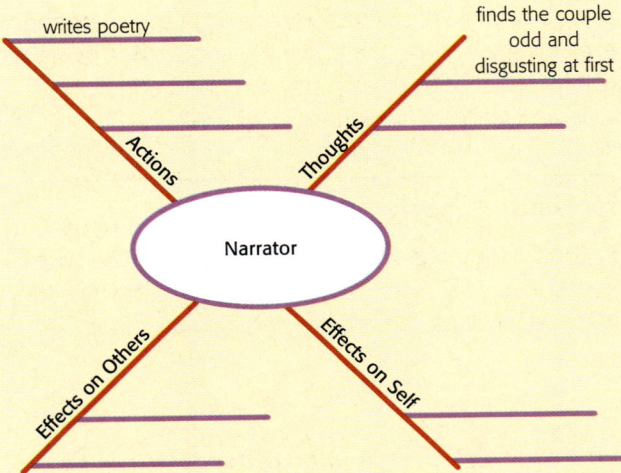

writes poetry

finds the couple odd and disgusting at first

Actions

Thoughts

Narrator

Effects on Others

Effects on Self

Reading Strategy Synthesizing

Synthesizing story details, footnote information, background information, biographical information about the author, and your own prior knowledge can help you interpret a story. Review the chart you created on page 1247.

1. What details can you synthesize from the story to characterize the narrator as a lonely introvert who is deprived of love?

2. What interpretation of the narrator's thought processes and behavior can you synthesize from the many references to his reading habits in the text?

Vocabulary Practice

Practice with Connotation and Denotation
Decide whether each boldfaced vocabulary word below has a positive, negative, or neutral connotation based on the context of each word.

1. Sandra was quite **explicit** when she told us to be at the restaurant by noon.
   a. positive   **b.** negative   **c.** neutral

2. Watching the happy couple made me **envious** because I had never been in such a happy relationship.
   a. positive   **b.** negative   **c.** neutral

3. She didn't mind writing papers, but she never liked taking the **compulsory** final exams.
   a. positive   **b.** negative   **c.** neutral

4. With **benign** smiles, the two neighbors nodded to each other as they passed.
   a. positive   **b.** negative   **c.** neutral

5. Happy to be on his own at last, Jack was **radiant** as he greeted friends and family at his housewarming party.
   a. positive   **b.** negative   **c.** neutral

Writing About Literature

Apply Style Lively makes heavy use of vernacular that reflects the narrator's background and culture. Write a short story of your own in which you similarly use vernacular to reveal a narrator or character's culture and experience. Use the following questions to help you develop your story:

- What is the cultural setting of your story? How does your main character fit into that culture?

- What types of vernacular—idioms, dialect, slang— would your character use in speech? What types of punctuation—dashes, parentheses, ellipses, abbreviations—would help express the character's use of vernacular in narration or dialogue?

- How can you use vernacular to enhance your readers' understanding of your characters and plot?

Before you draft, organize the elements of your story in a chart similar to the one below.

Setting	
Characters	
Narrator/Point of View	
Plot/Conflict	
Theme	
Voice	
Style	

When you have finished your first draft, get together with a classmate. Read each other's stories aloud, and then discuss the use of vernacular and recommend improvements. After you revise your draft, proofread it for errors in spelling, grammar, and punctuation.

Learning for Life

In a public place such as a mall, park, or restaurant, discreetly observe strangers. Take notes, reflecting on their behavior and making inferences about their lives. Then, write an essay about the value of doing such an activity.

Lively's Language and Style

Using Colons Authors most often use colons to introduce a list or an important phrase or clause in a sentence. Note how Lively's use of colons in "At the Pitt-Rivers" contributes to the distinctive voice and style of the narrator.

> "I showed a few poems to our English master and he was very helpful: he said what was good and pointed out where I'd used words badly, or not worked out what I was thinking very well, so that was quite encouraging."

In the example above, the colon introduces the comments of the English master. The use of the colon here is unconventional. Most writers would have used a semicolon or a dash or would have begun a new sentence. Notice some other examples of Lively's use of colons in the story:

Quotation	Effect of Colon
"You can learn a lot there about what people get up to: it makes you think."	The clause after the colon restates the information before it, reinforcing the point.
"At least I saw her first, standing by the totem with her hands in her coat pockets, and I didn't have to look at the door to know he'd arrived: her face told you that."	The clause after the colon supplies the reason that explains the statement before the colon.

Activity Create a chart similar to the one above. Then scan "At the Pitt-Rivers" for other examples of Lively's use of colons, listing these examples in the chart and explaining what you think Lively accomplishes by using colons. What does Lively's use of colons add to the style and voice of her writing?

Revising Check

Colons With a partner, review the short story you wrote. Revise your story by including colons in places where they would clarify your meaning or enhance your style.

Literature Online **Web Activities** For eFlashcards, Selection Quick Checks, and other Web activities, go to www.glencoe.com.

Comparing Literature *Across Time and Place*

Connecting to the Reading Selections

Through inspiration, persuasion, instruction, and example, parents try to influence their children's lives. The three selections compared here—poems by Seamus Heaney (shā′ məs hē′ nē) and Li-Young Lee, respectively, and a memoir by Michael Ondaatje (än da′ jā)—provide different insights about parent-child relationships.

Seamus Heaney
Follower .... poem 1258
Role reversal

England, 1966

Li-Young Lee
Mnemonic .... poem 1262
The power of memory

United States, 1986

Michael Ondaatje
Photograph from ***Running in the Family*** .... memoir 1264
"Absolutely perfect for each other"

Canada, 1982

COMPARING THE Big Idea Making and Remaking Traditions

As seen in the poetry of Seamus Heaney, contemporary British literature often blends the innovative with the traditional. Like Heaney, Lee and Ondaatje also mix the new with the old as they explore the past as both a gift and a burden.

COMPARING Profiles

Parents sometimes urge their children toward certain paths in life and dissuade them from others. In the selections compared here, the writers explore their parents' influence on their personalities. In portraying their parents, the writers create profiles of themselves as well.

COMPARING Cultures

To some extent, any writer's views reflect the values of his or her culture. Heaney's background is rural Irish Catholic; Lee's, Chinese-American; and Ondaatje's, Sri Lankan and Canadian. These cultures have left their mark on the writers of these selections.

Follower

MEET SEAMUS HEANEY

Seamus Heaney is one of the most honored and popular poets writing today. His collections of poems have sold in the tens of thousands, and his poetry readings draw enthusiastic crowds throughout the world.

> *"Be true to your own solitude, true, true to your own secret knowledge"*
>
> —Seamus Heaney

Poet and Teacher Born to Roman Catholic parents, Heaney was raised in County Derry, Northern Ireland, in what he once described as "a farming household with enlightened values and a special sense of worth." The eldest of nine children, he became aware at a very early age of his homeland's violent history. His education led him away from rural life at the age of twelve when he won a scholarship to St. Columb's College, a Catholic boarding school. He described this transition as moving from "the earth of farm labor to the heaven of education."

An avid reader, he began writing poetry when he was a student at Queen's University in Belfast. After graduating, he continued developing his poetry while supporting himself by teaching secondary school. He has said that he has "a poetic, protective notion that his poetry should not be a meal ticket." Later he taught at Queens University and the University of California at Berkeley, the University of Oxford, and Harvard University, where he joined the faculty in 1982. In 1984 he was named Boylston Professor of Rhetoric and Oratory at Harvard, a prestigious position that allows him to spend several months of the year in Dublin, writing and enjoying time with his wife and children.

Heaney's first volume of poems, *Death of a Naturalist* (1966), contains the acclaimed poem "Follower." Though his early poems show the influence of Robert Frost, they take for their subject domestic rural life in Northern Ireland. In fact, the greatest influence on Heaney's work is his Irish heritage.

Nobel Laureate Deeply rooted in the Irish countryside, Heaney's poetry depicts the people, crafts, politics, history, and the myths of his native land, particularly the bitter conflicts between Ireland and England over the independence and unification of the divided Irish state. Heaney's fascination with archaic lore extends beyond Irish forebears to Danes, Normans, and Vikings, who battled for control of the British Isles during the Anglo-Saxon period. In 2000 his magnificent translation of the epic poem *Beowulf* earned critical and popular acclaim. Heaney is also an accomplished essayist on poetry and both modern and ancient Irish history.

Heaney's poetry is known for its phrasing, which is fresh and striking, and for its vivid imagery, which is often tactile, energetic, and violent. In 1995, in recognition of his many achievements as a poet, Heaney was awarded the Nobel Prize in Literature. According to critic Richard Tillinghast, Heaney's poetry serves as a "powerful tonic" against the disillusionment and alienation expressed by many contemporary writers.

Seamus Heaney was born in 1939.

Literature Online **Author Search** For more about Seamus Heaney, go to www.glencoe.com.

Connecting to the Poem

In "Follower," the speaker describes a complicated father-son relationship. As you read, think about the following questions:

- When you were a child, what adults did you regard as role models, and why?
- What does the popular saying "What goes around comes around" mean?

Building Background

Seamus Heaney has said that his poetry is a "quest for precision and definition." His poems are rich with description, which he calls "the living speech of a landscape I was born with." Unlike many other poets of his generation, Heaney often structures his poetry around traditional forms (such as stanzas based on rhyme) and sets his poems in rural areas that are similar to the ones he knew as a child. His poems are often compared to those of William Wordsworth, the Romantic poet who wrote about the harmony and beauty of nature. Heaney has said that "Wordsworth was lucky and . . . I was lucky in having this kind of rich, archetypal subject matter as part of growing up."

Setting Purposes for Reading

Big Idea **Making and Remaking Traditions**

As you read, consider what is traditional and what is original in this poem.

Literary Element **Slant Rhyme**

Slant rhyme is an approximate or near rhyme. For example, the repetition of the *ck* consonant sound in the words *sock* and *pluck* forms a slant rhyme. As you read, identify other examples of slant rhyme and consider their effects.

- See Literary Terms Handbook, p. R16.

Literature Online **Interactive Literary Elements Handbook** To review or learn more about the literary elements, go to www.glencoe.com.

Reading Strategy Making Generalizations

Making generalizations involves generating statements that can apply to more than one item or group. Making generalizations is part of the process of inferring.

Reading Tip: Taking Notes Use a chart to record your generalizations based on the details in Heaney's poem.

Detail	Generalization
"I was a nuisance, tripping, falling / Yapping always."	Children sometimes feel that they are in the way.

Irish countryside in Limavady District, Northern Ireland.

OBJECTIVES
In studying this selection, you will focus on the following:
- analyzing genre elements
- identifying slant rhyme
- making generalizations

Follower

Seamus Heaney

Ploughing. Nancy Smith (flourished 1940–1950).
Transport poster. Stapleton Collection, UK.

My father worked with a horse plow,
His shoulders globed like a full sail strung
Between the shafts and the furrow.[1]
The horses strained at his clicking tongue.

5   An expert. He would set the wing
And fit the bright steel-pointed sock.[2]
The sod rolled over without breaking.
At the headrig,[3] with a single pluck

Of reins, the sweating team turned round
10 And back into the land. His eye
Narrowed and angled at the ground,
Mapping the furrow exactly.

I stumbled in his hobnailed[4] wake,[5]
Fell sometimes on the polished sod;
15 Sometimes he rode me on his back
Dipping and rising to his plod.

I wanted to grow up and plow,
To close one eye, stiffen my arm.
All I ever did was follow
20 In his broad shadow round the farm.

I was a nuisance, tripping, falling,
Yapping always. But today
It is my father who keeps stumbling
Behind me, and will not go away.

---

1. A *furrow* is a trench made by a plow.
2. A *sock* is the blade of a plow.
3. A *headrig* is the mechanism on a plow that turns the blade used to cut the soil.

4. A *hobnail* is a short nail with a thick head that protects the soles of shoes.
5. A *wake* is the visible trail left by a moving body, such as the trail left by a ship as it cuts through water.

Literary Element   Slant Rhyme   *What example of slant rhyme is found in this stanza?*

RESPONDING AND THINKING CRITICALLY

Respond

1. What are your impressions of the speaker in this poem? Explain.

Recall and Interpret

2. (a)In stanzas 1–3, what task does the speaker describe? (b)How does he feel about the way his father performs this task? What words or phrases reveal the speaker's feelings toward his father?

3. (a)As a child, what did the speaker wish to become when he grew up? (b)What does the speaker's reflection on this desire suggest?

4. (a)Who is the follower in lines 1–22? In lines 22–24? (b)Make inferences about the changes that the father and the son have undergone. How have these changes affected their relationship?

Analyze and Evaluate

5. Heaney's poetry is often praised for its vivid imagery. (a)Which words and phrases in this poem suggest images of the sea and sailing? (b)Why do you think Heaney uses this image pattern?

6. In stanzas 4 and 6, how does the **repetition** of forms of "stumble" help reveal the changes the father and son have undergone?

7. Why might the speaker feel haunted by the memory of his father?

Connect

8. **Big Idea** **Making and Remaking Traditions** In what ways is "Follower" a traditional poem? In what ways does it depart from tradition? Explain.

LITERARY ANALYSIS

Literary Element Slant Rhyme

Slant rhyme is based on **assonance**, the repetition of a vowel sound, or **consonance**, the repetition of a consonant sound at the ends of words.

1. What examples of slant rhyme can you find in "Follower"?

2. Contrast the true rhymes in the poem with the slant rhymes you identified. How might you explain the difference between the two types of rhyme?

Writing About Literature

Respond to Theme Heaney's autobiographical poem develops a theme, or message, about the past. What do you think the last sentence of the poem means? What might the "stumbling" father who will not go away symbolize? Write a paragraph or two to support your interpretation.

Literature Online **Web Activities** For eFlashcards, Selection Quick Checks, and other Web activities, go to www.glencoe.com.

READING AND VOCABULARY

Reading Strategy Making Generalizations

To **make a generalization,** ask yourself what broad statement is supported by the particular details in a poem.

1. What general statement can you make about the lives of rural Irish farmers like the speaker's father?

2. Based on the poem, what generalization can you make about parent-child relationships?

Academic Vocabulary

Here are two words from the vocabulary list on page R82.

element (el′ ə mənt) *n.* a part of a complex whole

role (rōl) *n.* a character assigned or taken on

Practice and Apply
1. In "Follower," Heaney sometimes uses irregular rhythm. What effect does this **element** create?
2. How do the speaker and his father switch **roles** in the poem?

Building Background

Li-Young Lee is a successful poet and gifted autobiographer. Born in Jakarta, Indonesia, Lee has lived in a variety of places throughout the world, ranging from Macau to Pennsylvania. Currently, he resides in Chicago.

Li-Young Lee's father briefly served as the personal physician to Chinese leader Mao Tse-tung (**mou´ dzə´ doong´**) but the Chinese Revolution forced Lee's family to flee China and move to Indonesia. There, Lee's father helped found a university but was arrested by President Sukarno, mainly for teaching Western ideas, philosophy, and religion, including the Bible. The family escaped to Hong Kong, where Lee's father became a successful preacher. In 1964 the family immigrated to a Pennsylvania town, where Lee's father continued his work as a preacher. Lee devoted a large portion of his memoir, *The Winged Seed* (1995), to exploring his relationship with his father, who died in 1980.

The poem "Mnemonic" appeared in *Rose,* Lee's first volume of poetry, published in 1986. The word *mnemonic* refers to a device—such as an acronym, a slogan, a jingle, or a rhyme—that helps one remember something. Lee's poetry often explores the power of memory and identity. He typically writes in free verse with powerful, evocative imagery.

Literature Online **Author Search** For more about Li-Young Lee, go to www.glencoe.com.

Mnemonic

Li-Young Lee

 # 49. Gerrit Greve. 1995.

I was tired. So I lay down.
My lids grew heavy. So I slept.
Slender memory, stay with me.

I was cold once. So my father took off his blue sweater.
5 He wrapped me in it, and I never gave it back.
It is the sweater he wore to America,
this one, which I've grown into, whose sleeves are too long,
whose elbows have thinned, who outlives its rightful owner.
Flamboyant blue in daylight, poor blue by daylight,
10 it is black in the folds.

A serious man who devised complex systems of numbers
    and rhymes
to aid him in remembering, a man who forgot nothing,
    my father
would be ashamed of me.
Not because I'm forgetful,
15 but because there is no order
to my memory, a heap
of details, uncatalogued, illogical.
For instance:
God was lonely. So he made me.
20 My father loved me. So he spanked me.
It hurt him to do so. He did it daily.
The earth is flat. Those who fall off don't return.
The earth is round. All things reveal themselves to men
    only gradually.

I won't last. Memory is sweet.
25 Even when it's painful, memory is sweet.

Once, I was cold. So my father took off his blue sweater.

Discussion Starter

How does the blue sweater trigger memories about the speaker's father in "Mnemonic"? What does the poem suggest about the relationship between generations? Discuss these questions with a small group of classmates.

Building Background

The works of Michael Ondaatje, a Canadian novelist and poet of Dutch-Ceylonese descent, appeal to a general audience and have earned him wide recognition. The following selection is from his memoir *Running in the Family,* which he wrote in 1982 after visiting Ceylon (now Sri Lanka), the island country just southeast of India. He had enjoyed a happy childhood in Ceylon, even though his parents divorced in 1948; in 1952 Ondaatje followed his mother, brother, and sister to London, where he attended college. Dissatisfied with the curriculum, however, he left London at the age of nineteen to join his brother in Montreal, and graduated from the University of Toronto in 1965. During these years he quickly excelled at writing both prose and poetry, publishing his first volume of poetry, *The Dainty Monsters,* in 1967.

In 1992 Ondaatje won the Booker Prize, the most prestigious British award for fiction, for *The English Patient.* This novel was later adapted into a film that won the Academy Award for Best Picture in 1996. It tells the story of the relationship between a nurse and a severely burned patient in Italy near the end of World War II.

A **memoir** is a type of narrative nonfiction that presents the story of a specific period in the writer's life. It's generally written from the first-person point of view and emphasizes the narrator's experiences during this time period. A memoir may also reveal the impact of historical events on the writer's life. Memoirs differ from autobiographies in that autobiographies usually encompass the events of the writer's entire life. In recent years, memoirs have become increasingly popular and have been written by established authors and novices alike.

Literature⦿nline Author Search For more about Michael Ondaatje, go to www.glencoe.com.

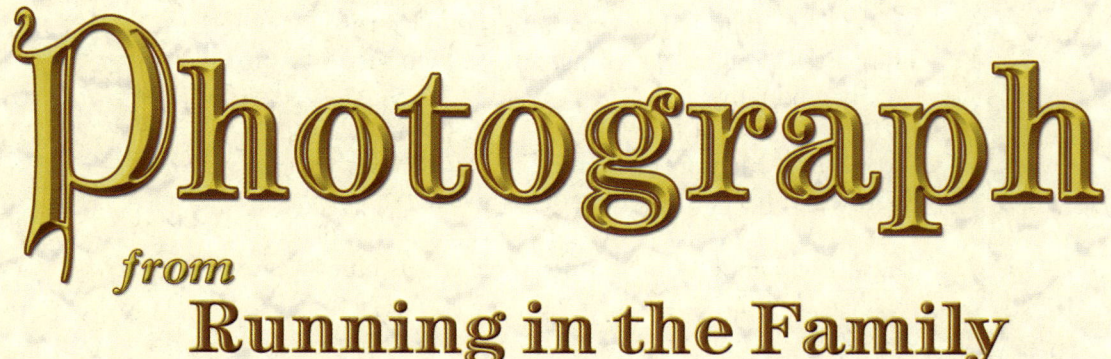

Photograph

from

Running in the Family

Michael Ondaatje

My Aunt pulls out the album and there is the photograph I have been waiting for all my life. My father and mother together. May 1932.

They are on their honeymoon and the two of them, very soberly dressed, have walked into a photographic studio. The photographer is used to wedding pictures. He has probably seen every pose. My father sits facing the camera, my mother stands beside him and bends over so that her face is in profile on a level with his. Then they both begin to make hideous faces.

My father's pupils droop to the south-west corner of his sockets. His jaw falls and resettles into a groan that is half idiot, half shock. (All this is emphasized by his dark suit and well-combed hair.) My mother in white has twisted her lovely features and stuck out her jaw and upper lip so that her profile is in the posture of a monkey. The print is made into a postcard and sent through the mails to various friends. On the back my father has written *"What we think of married life."*

Everything is there, of course. Their good looks behind the tortured faces, their mutual humor, and the fact that both of them are hams of a very superior sort. The evidence I wanted that they were absolutely perfect for each other. My father's tanned skin, my mother's milk paleness, and this theater of their own making.

It is the only photograph I have found of the two of them together. ❧

WHAT WE THINK OF MARRIED LIFE

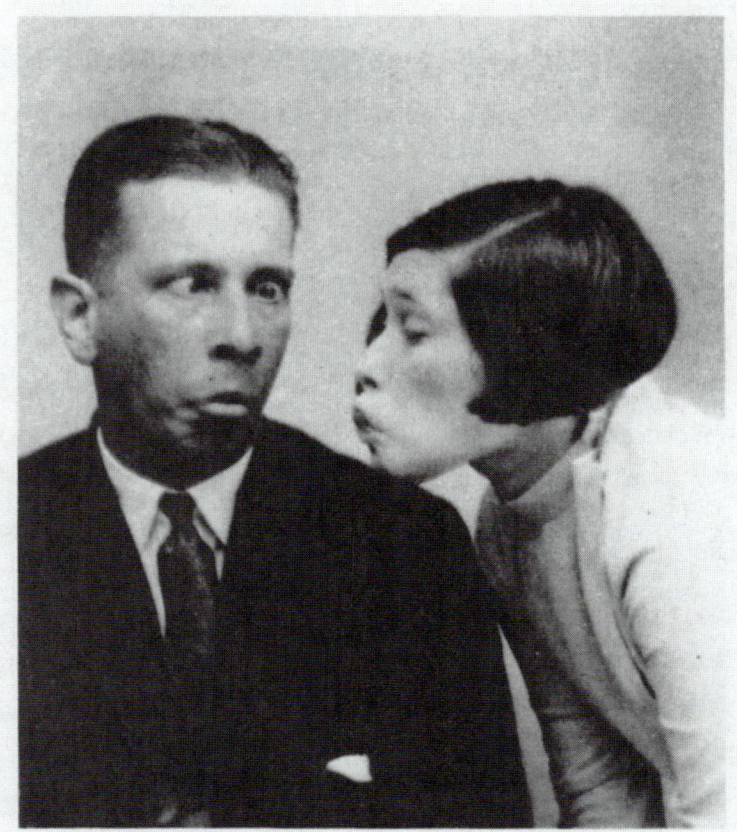

Photo of author's parents taken on their honeymoon.

Quickwrite

In this selection, Ondaatje reconstructs the context of a photograph of his parents. Why is it important to him to reconstruct his parents' past? What does he discover about his parents from examining the old photograph of them (shown here)? Write a paragraph in which you explain your views.

- *Follower*
  by Seamus Heaney

- *Mnemonic*
  by Li-Young Lee

- *Photograph* from *Running in the Family*
  by Michael Ondaatje

COMPARING THE [Big Idea] Making and Remaking Traditions

Group Activity In exploring the past as both a gift and a burden, the writers of these selections blend the original and the traditional. With a small group of classmates, discuss what is fresh and new about each of these selections and what is traditional. Consider both form and content, and cite evidence from the selections to support your points.

COMPARING Profiles

Writing Read the following quotations from the selections. Then write a brief essay in which you compare two of the quotations in terms of what they reveal about both the parent or parents and the writer. Which profile emerges as most vivid and compelling? Cite additional evidence from the selections to support your points.

> *"All I ever did was follow*
> *In his broad shadow round the farm."*
>
> —Heaney, "Follower"

> *"He wrapped me in it, and I never gave it back.*
> *It is the sweater he wore to America."*
>
> —Lee, "Mnemonic"

> *" . . . the fact that both of them are hams of a very*
> *superior sort. The evidence I wanted that they were*
> *absolutely perfect for each other."*
>
> —Ondaatje, *Running in the Family*

Study for a Family Group. Henry Moore. Bronze. Private collection.

COMPARING Cultures

Visual Display Each of the writers represented in these selections grew up in a distinct culture that to some extent colored his perspective. Using Internet and library resources, research one of the cultures represented in these selections to learn more about its view of parent-child relationships. Then represent your findings in a visual display such as an illustration or a collage.

OBJECTIVES
- Conduct a group discussion.
- Analyze profiles.

- Create a visual display.

Wind

MEET TED HUGHES

In 1984 the British government took the world by surprise when it named Ted Hughes as its poet laureate. The honor usually goes to a poet who writes conservative, mainstream verse. Hughes's poetry, however, is sometimes controversial and dark. He often portrayed nature as fiercely beautiful and violent.

A Love of Nature and Wild Places Hughes grew up in the rugged landscape of Yorkshire, England. From a young age, he loved being out in nature, hiking, hunting, and fishing. He began writing poetry in high school, and after graduating and gaining admission to Cambridge University on scholarship, he deferred his enrollment for two years to serve in the Royal Air Force. He had a post as a radio mechanic at a radar station in a remote area on the east coast of England. With a lot of time on his hands, Hughes read and reread Shakespeare. By the time his term of service was up, he knew all the plays intimately.

At Cambridge, Hughes began as an English major but later changed his major to anthropology. Although he always planned to be a poet, he loved studying folklore and felt it gave him good background for his writing. After graduating in 1954, Hughes took a number of odd jobs in London, devoting his free time to writing. He worked as a night security guard at a steel mill, washed dishes at a zoo cafeteria, taught, and worked as a gardener.

> *"Maybe all poetry . . . is a revealing of something that the writer doesn't actually want to say, but desperately needs to communicate."*
>
> —Ted Hughes

About a year after Hughes graduated, he met American postgraduate student Sylvia Plath, who would later become a famous poet. They fell in love and were married four months later.

Life on a Roller Coaster Plath made a practice of submitting her poems to many different magazines and was often published. Soon, she was typing up Hughes's poetry and submitting it as well. Plath entered several dozen of Hughes's poems in a poetry contest sponsored by a major publisher and a panel of distinguished U.S. poets chose Hughes as the winner among almost three hundred entrants. The prize was the publication of Hughes's first book, *Hawk in the Rain*, which received good reviews and even won another prestigious award several years later. The poem "Wind" appeared in that collection.

Literary Success The publication of *Hawk in the Rain*, when Hughes was only twenty-seven, launched his career as a poet. After Plath died in 1963, Hughes focused on teaching and raising their children, Frieda and Nicholas. His writing career continued and, over his lifetime, Hughes wrote more than two dozen books of poetry, sixteen children's books, and more than a dozen plays.

Ted Hughes was born in 1930 and died in 1998.

Literature Online **Author Search** For more about Ted Hughes, go to www.glencoe.com.

Connecting to the Poem

Throughout his poetry, Hughes portrays nature as a violent, vivid, gripping force. As you read the poem, think about the following questions:

- What feelings and moods do you associate with the wind?
- How can the wind be helpful to people? How can it be harmful?

Building Background

"Wind" is set in Yorkshire, the wild and sometimes inhospitable region of England where Hughes grew up. Many of Hughes's poems celebrate the unbridled energy of nature, treating it as an almost magical force that can release the power of human emotion. His poems also explore the adversarial relationship between people and nature as well as people's isolation from both nature and one another.

Setting Purposes for Reading

Big Idea Making and Remaking Traditions

Notice the ways in which "Wind" follows literary tradition and the ways in which it is a nontraditional poem.

Literary Element Personification

Personification is a figure of speech in which a nonhuman thing is given human characteristics. For example, if you say "the trees are sighing in the wind" you are personifying the trees because people sigh. As you read "Wind," notice how Hughes uses personification.

- See Literary Terms Handbook, p. R13.

Reading Strategy Analyzing Language

Analyzing language involves noticing the word choices and figures of speech a poet uses to determine what makes a poem especially effective.

....

Reading Tip: Taking Notes Use a chart like the one below to record and analyze words, phrases, and figures of speech in the poem.

Line	Word, Phrase, or Figure of Speech	Why Effective
1	far out at sea	It's surprising to think of a house far out at sea.

Vocabulary

flounder (floun′ dər) v. struggle to obtain footing; p. 1269 *I slipped in the mud and was floundering, flinging my arms in circles.*

luminous (l$\overline{oo}$′ mə nəs) adj. emitting a glowing light; p. 1269 *The moon on the horizon was luminous and orange like a jack-o'-lantern.*

grimace (grim′ is) n. a look of pain or disgust; p. 1269 *The grimace on my teacher's face told me my answer wasn't even close.*

....

Vocabulary Tip: Analogies Analogies highlight relationships between pairs of words. Completing word analogies can help reinforce your understanding of new vocabulary words.

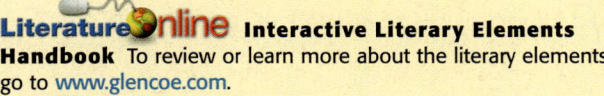

Literature Online Interactive Literary Elements Handbook To review or learn more about the literary elements, go to www.glencoe.com.

OBJECTIVES
In studying this selection, you will focus on the following:
- analyzing genre elements
- analyzing personification
- analyzing language

Wind

Ted Hughes

Bitter Wind. Carel Weight. Oil on board. Private collection.

*T*his house has been far out at sea all night,
The woods crashing through darkness, the booming hills,
Winds stampeding the fields under the window
Floundering black astride and blinding wet

5   Till day rose; then under an orange sky
The hills had new places, and wind wielded
Blade-light, **luminous** black and emerald,
Flexing like the lens of a mad eye.

At noon I scaled along the house-side as far as
10   The coal-house door. Once I looked up—
Through the brunt wind[1] that dented the balls of my eyes
The tent of the hills drummed and strained its guy rope,[2]

The fields quivering, the skyline a **grimace**,
At any second to bang and vanish with a flap:
15   The wind flung a magpie[3] away and a black-
Back gull bent like an iron bar slowly. The house

Rang like some fine green goblet in the note
That any second would shatter it.[4] Now deep
In chairs, in front of the great fire, we grip
20   Our hearts and cannot entertain book, thought,

Or each other. We watch the fire blazing,
And feel the roots of the house move, but sit on,
Seeing the window tremble to come in,
Hearing the stones cry out under the horizons.

1. A *brunt wind* is a wind of shockingly great force.
2. A *guy rope* is a cord or cable used for steadying or guiding.

3. A *magpie* is a kind of bird.

4. The phrase *rang like some fine green goblet* refers to the fact that most objects will vibrate at set frequencies, based on size, shape, and material. If, for example, a singer produces a note that is the natural frequency of a glass goblet, the goblet will begin to vibrate and may shatter.

Reading Strategy   Analyzing Language   *Which two words in this line appeal to the sense of hearing? What do you imagine when you read this line?*

Vocabulary

flounder (floun′ dər) *v.* struggle to obtain footing
luminous (lo͞o′ mə nəs) *adj.* emitting a glowing light
grimace (grim′ is) *n.* a look of pain or disgust

RESPONDING AND THINKING CRITICALLY

Respond

1. What image or idea in this poem did you find most interesting or surprising? Explain.

Recall and Interpret

2. (a)According to the speaker, where has the house been during the night? (b)How do you know that this is a figurative description?

3. What effect has the wind had on the landscape, the house, and the people who live there? Support your answers with specific evidence from the poem.

Analyze and Evaluate

4. (a)How does Hughes change or mix metaphors in this poem? (b)Does this mixing of metaphors bother you? Why or why not?

5. (a)What symbolism do you see in this poem? Consider the problem or conflict the poem centers on and the images used in the poem. (b)Which stylistic or literary device is most effective in illustrating the symbolism?

Connect

6. **Big Idea** **Making and Remaking Traditions** (a)In what ways do Hughes's word choices, sound effects, or style make this poem traditional? (b)In what ways do they make the poem nontraditional?

LITERARY ANALYSIS

Literary Element Personification

Not only can the use of **personification** make descriptions vivid, it can also help intensify the drama of a work of literature.

1. How is the wind personified in the first stanza? What does the wind do and what effect does this action have on the landscape?

2. How does Hughes's use of personification in describing the wind and the house intensify the sense of a power differential in this poem? How does this help bring out the poem's theme?

Performing

Read "Wind" aloud several times, paying close attention to punctuation to help bring out the meaning. Practice different ways of using cadence, pacing, and pauses to reinforce ideas. Once you have decided how to read the poem aloud, think about ways of adding sound effects to increase the drama. After you've planned your approach and rehearsed, perform your dramatic reading for the class.

Literature Online **Web Activities** For eFlashcards, Selection Quick Checks, and other Web activities, go to www.glencoe.com.

READING AND VOCABULARY

Reading Strategy Analyzing Language

In writing this poem about the wind, Hughes has chosen many words that sound like what they describe. This use of language is called **onomatopoeia.** Refer to the chart you made on page 1268. Then answer these questions.

1. In line 2, why might the words *crashing* and *booming* be better suited to the poem than common synonyms, such as *falling* and *loud*?

2. Find two more examples of onomatopoeia in this poem. Explain why you think these word choices are particularly effective.

Vocabulary Practice

Practice with Analogies Choose the word that best completes each analogy below.

1. noisy : quiet :: luminous :
   a. light   b. dim   c. unlucky

2. quiver : tremble :: flounder :
   a. favor   b. flash   c. thrash

3. laughter : humor :: grimace :
   a. triumph   b. success   c. pain

That's All

MEET HAROLD PINTER

Harold Pinter was a twenty-seven-year-old actor when he received a phone call from a friend, a drama student at Bristol University, who had an assignment to direct a production. The friend asked Pinter to write a play. Although currently making a living by acting, Pinter had already done some writing: he'd had a few of his poems published in a literary magazine and was working on an autobiographical novel. However, Pinter had never written a play, and his friend had a tight deadline—the play had to be ready in six days. Pinter not only met the deadline; he exceeded it, finishing the one-act play in four days.

> *"Firstly and finally, and all along the line, you write because there's something you want to write, have to write. For yourself."*
>
> —Harold Pinter

An Actor Turns Playwright This one-act play, called *The Room*, was a success at Bristol University and another drama school associated with the university decided to put on the play, entering it into a drama competition. An influential critic gave *The Room* a favorable review. About a month later, an independent producer who had read about Pinter's play in a newspaper contacted Pinter to see if he had any other works completed. Pinter, encouraged by the praise he had received for *The Room*, had already written two more plays. The producer bought options on one of the two. Pinter's career as a playwright had begun.

When Pinter began writing plays, he drew heavily on his experience as an actor. This experience helped him pace his plays and write what he referred to as "speakable dialogue." He also drew on his experience writing poetry, which helped him craft dialogue to help convey his characters' underlying emotions.

A Distinguished Career After the modest success of *The Room*, Pinter wrote nine plays in six years. His first major success was *The Caretaker*, which was produced when Pinter was thirty-one. This full-length play, which was nominated for a Tony award, appeared on Broadway in New York. By 1964, when he wrote the short play, or sketch, *That's All*, Pinter had won three more important awards. About his short plays Pinter said, "There is no real difference between my sketches and my plays. In both I am interested primarily in people. I want to present living people to the audience, worthy of their interest basically because they are, they exist."

Since writing *That's All*, Pinter has written dozens of sketches, plays, screenplays, and radio and television dramas. He has also published his own poetry and collected the poetry of others in anthologies. In 2005 Pinter won the Nobel Prize in Literature.

Harold Pinter was born in 1930.

Literature Online **Author Search** For more about Harold Pinter, go to www.glencoe.com.

Connecting to the Play

Harold Pinter's play *That's All* is a seemingly casual conversation between two women. As you read the play, think about the following questions:

- Do conversations always have a clear purpose?
- Do people usually converse in organized, coherent sentences and paragraphs?

Building Background

Pinter's plays are characterized by unexplained circumstances and an atmosphere of menace. His characters, typically engaged in a struggle for survival or identity, are often unable to communicate clearly because they do not understand their needs, feelings, or motivations. They engage in small talk, begin thoughts without finishing them, and do not listen carefully to one another. However, through reticence, understatement, and silent pauses, they unknowingly disclose their inner thoughts, which emerge from beneath their banal remarks.

Setting Purposes for Reading

Big Idea Making and Remaking Traditions

Notice the ways in which Pinter's play breaks away from traditional drama.

Literary Element Theater of the Absurd

Pinter, along with other playwrights such as Samuel Beckett, Jean Genet, and Eugène Ionesco, is often associated with the literary movement known as the **theater of the absurd.** Arising from the disillusionment of two world wars, these avant-garde playwrights depict life as illogical, futile, and meaningless. They often ignore or parody the conventions of traditional drama, such as unified plot, coherent dialogue, or clear character motivation. As you read *That's All,* analyze the dialogue between the two women to discover its underlying meaning.

- See Literary Terms Handbook, p. R18.

Reading Strategy Making Inferences About Characters

Making inferences about characters involves putting together clues from their dialogue or actions to draw conclusions about the characters that are not directly stated. You might make inferences about the characters' feelings, motivations, or ideas; you also might infer what the characters or their lives symbolize.

....

Reading Tip: Taking Notes *That's All* presents two characters who talk about a third person who does not appear in the play. Make a web diagram similar to the one below for each character. Use your web to record the inferences you make about the characters as you read the play.

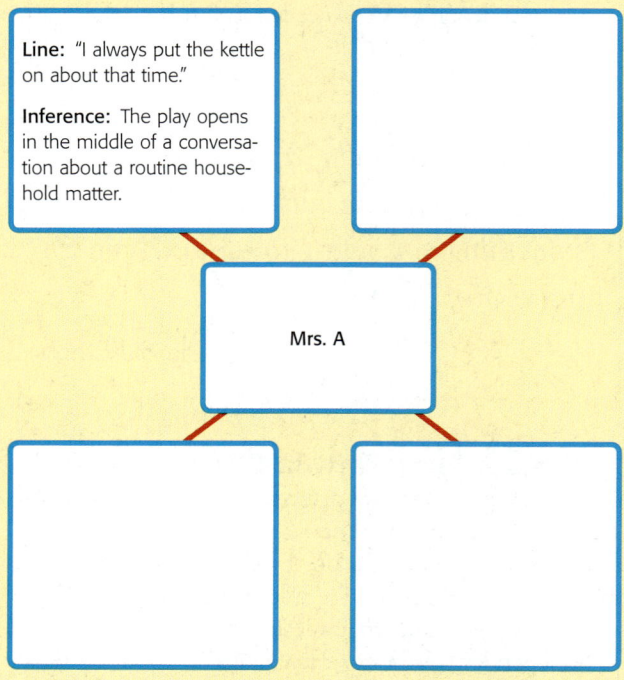

Line: "I always put the kettle on about that time."

Inference: The play opens in the middle of a conversation about a routine household matter.

Mrs. A

Literature Online **Interactive Literary Elements Handbook** To review or learn more about the literary elements, go to www.glencoe.com.

OBJECTIVES
In studying this selection, you will focus on the following:
- analyzing genre elements
- analyzing the theater of the absurd
- making inferences about characters

That's All

Harold Pinter

MRS. A. I always put the kettle on about that time.

MRS. B. Yes. [*Pause.*]

MRS. A. Then she comes round.

MRS. B. Yes. [*Pause.*]

MRS. A. Only on Thursdays.

MRS. B. Yes. [*Pause.*]

MRS. A. On Wednesdays I used to put it on. When she used to come round. Then she changed it to Thursdays.

MRS. B. Oh yes.

MRS. A. After she moved. When she used to live round the corner, then she always came in on Wednesdays, but then when she moved she used to come down to the butcher's on Thursdays. She couldn't find a butcher up there.

MRS. B. No.

MRS. A. Anyway, she decided she'd stick to her own butcher. Well, I thought, if she can't find a butcher, that's the best thing.

MRS. B. Yes. [*Pause.*]

MRS. A. So she started to come down on Thursdays. I didn't know she was coming down on Thursdays until one day I met her in the butcher.

MRS. B. Oh yes.

MRS. A. It wasn't my day for the butcher. I don't go to the butcher on Thursday.

MRS. B. No, I know. [*Pause.*]

MRS. A. I go on Friday.

MRS. B. Yes. [*Pause.*]

MRS. A. That's where I see you.

MRS. B. Yes. [*Pause.*]

MRS. A. You're always in there on Fridays.

MRS. B. Oh yes. [*Pause.*]

MRS. A. But I happened to go in for a bit of meat, it turned out to be a Thursday. I wasn't going in for my usual weekly on Friday. I just slipped in, the day before.

MRS. B. Yes.

MRS. A. That was the first time I found out she couldn't find a butcher up there, so she decided to come back here, once a week, to her own butcher.

MRS. B. Yes.

MRS. A. She came on Thursday so she'd be able to get meat for the weekend. Lasted her till Monday, then from Monday to Thursday they'd have fish. She can always buy cold meat, if they want a change.

MRS. B. Oh yes. [*Pause.*]

MRS. A. So I told her to come in when she came down after she'd been to the butcher's and I'd put a kettle on. So she did. [*Pause.*]

MRS. B. Yes. [*Pause.*]

MRS. A. It was funny because she always used to come in Wednesdays. [*Pause.*] Still, it made a break. [*Long pause.*]

MRS. B. She doesn't come in no more, does she? [*Pause.*]

MRS. A. She comes in. She doesn't come in so much, but she comes in. [*Pause.*]

MRS. B. I thought she didn't come in. [*Pause.*]

MRS. A. She comes in. [*Pause.*] She just doesn't come in so much. That's all. ❧

Big Idea Making and Remaking Traditions *What do you think Pinter's use of pauses here is intended to indicate about the conversation between Mrs. A and Mrs. B?*

Reading Strategy Making Inferences About Characters *Based on this information, what can you infer about the friendship between Mrs. A and the unnamed woman?*

Literary Element Theater of the Absurd *What elements of the theater of the absurd can you detect in this dialogue?*

RESPONDING AND THINKING CRITICALLY

Respond

1. What did you think of the dialogue in the play? In what ways does it resemble conversations you have had or overheard?

Recall and Interpret

2. (a)What are the two women in this play talking about? (b)Based on their conversation, what can you infer about Mrs. A's life?

3. (a)How does Mrs. A learn that the unnamed woman visits the butcher shop on a different day of the week? (b)What can you infer about the attitude of the woman toward her visits to Mrs. A?

4. (a)What does Mrs. B ask Mrs. A toward the end of the play? How does Mrs. A respond? (b)What attitudes or feelings can you infer from Mrs. A's response?

Analyze and Evaluate

5. (a)Why do you think Pinter named these characters as he did? (b)Do you think the names strengthen the message of the play? Explain.

6. (a)Why do you think Pinter chose the title *That's All* for this sketch? (b)Why do you think he ended the sketch with these words?

7. (a)In your opinion, is this short play a comedy? Explain. (b)Can you detect a tragic undercurrent in the play? Explain.

Connect

8. **Big Idea** **Making and Remaking Traditions** In what way might the dialogue in *That's All* be more realistic than the dialogue in much traditional drama?

LITERARY ANALYSIS

Literary Element **Theater of the Absurd**

To portray what they see as the fundamental absurdity of life, playwrights of this school often write fragmented dialogue interrupted by long silences between lonely characters desperately seeking meaning or identity.

1. What is Mrs. A desperately searching for in this play? How does she try to deceive herself that she has found what she is looking for?

2. What does Mrs. B force Mrs. A to admit at the end of the play? What motive might Mrs. B have for shattering Mrs. A's illusions?

Writing About Literature

Evaluate Author's Craft Sometimes the best way to understand and evaluate an author's craft is to imitate it. Write a one-page play in which Mrs. A and the unnamed woman have tea together at Mrs. A's house. Develop the conversation so that it closely resembles the style of the dialogue in *That's All.*

Literature Online **Web Activities** For eFlashcards, Selection Quick Checks, and other Web activities, go to www.glencoe.com.

READING AND VOCABULARY

Reading Strategy **Making Inferences About Characters**

To understand the theme of the play, you must make inferences about the characters and their lives. Look at the web diagram you made on page 1272, and then answer the following questions.

1. What can you infer about the relationship between Mrs. A and Mrs. B?

2. What point do you think Pinter is making about the majority of human relationships?

Academic Vocabulary

Here is a word from the vocabulary list on page R82.

constant (kon′ stənt) *adj.* unchanging or continually recurring

Practice and Apply
What does Mrs. A prefer to keep **constant** in her life?

British Drama—From the Drawing Room to the Kitchen Sink

"What do I know of man's destiny? I could tell you more about radishes."

—Samuel Beckett, from "Enough"

THE LATE TWENTIETH CENTURY WAS A PERIOD OF extraordinary richness for British drama, when exciting young playwrights forged bold new paths for theater in England. The devastation of World War II had a major impact on these developments. Despite social reforms enacted by the Labour Party in the aftermath of the war, widespread bitterness and frustration remained in British society. Wartime rationing of clothing, gasoline, and food continued into the 1950s. College educations failed to lead to meaningful jobs. An anger born of desire for social change and intensified by Britain's slow postwar recovery was reflected in many British novels and plays of the early 1950s. John Osborne was the playwright who first dramatized this bitterness. When his play *Look Back in Anger* opened on May 8, 1956, it challenged audiences with a working-class hero, his brutal language, and the rage he expressed toward the traditional British class system.

Scene from *Waiting for Godot,* 1994.

Kitchen-Sink Drama

The successful British playwrights of the 1930s and 1940s, such as Noel Coward and W. Somerset Maugham, crafted witty, formulaic plays often described as "drawing-room comedies" since the action frequently took place in a living, or drawing, room. Their upper class characters spoke in refined accents and employed servants. To the audiences of such plays, *Look Back in Anger* came as a distinct shock.

Osborne's working-class hero in the play, Jimmy Porter, marries above his social status. University educated, he still sells candy in a street market because he can't find a job equal to his schooling or his ego. Frustrated, he verbally attacks his wife, her upper-middle-class background, and, by extension, the entire British class system. Porter's furious, self-pitying rants stunned audiences and gave rise to the term "Angry Young Men," which soon categorized a group of young writers who attacked British society in their plays and novels.

Look Back in Anger also features a realistic setting—a squalid one-room apartment—that represented a new type of play dealing with working-class life, the "kitchen-sink drama." Other notable kitchen-sink dramatists included Arnold Wesker, whose early plays depict Jewish working-class life in London, and Shelagh Delaney, whose best-known play, *A Taste of Honey,* presents the experiences of a working-class girl struggling with single motherhood.

Absurdists and Contemporaries

Another important work of postwar British drama is the Irish-born playwright Samuel Beckett's *Waiting for Godot* (1952). Beckett's tragicomic play presents characters who are clown-like vagrants repeating senseless phrases in an unending round of pointless activity. Drama critic Martin Esslin used the term "theater of the absurd" to describe postwar plays that express "bewilderment, anxiety, and wonder in the face of an inexplicable universe." The term draws from the writings of Albert Camus, who explored the theories of existentialism in questioning if there was a point to life. Reflecting postwar pessimism, Beckett's plays—including *End Game* and *Happy Days*—emphasize inaction and futility. Among the British playwrights influenced by Beckett, who won the Nobel Prize in Literature in 1969, are Tom Stoppard and Harold Pinter.

Czech-born playwright Tom Stoppard became famous with *Rosencrantz and Guildenstern Are Dead*, a play based on two minor characters in *Hamlet*. His other important works include *The Real Inspector Hound* (a parody of the conventions of stage thrillers), *Jumpers* (a satire of academics), and *Arcadia* (a time-traveling play about thermodynamics, fractals, and chaos theory). Stoppard displays a strong theatrical sense as well as an understanding of modern science and modern ethics. Using puns and other kinds of word play, he creates plays that provoke and amuse.

Harold Pinter is a prolific writer who explores the mysteries and underlying meanings in everyday dialogue. His first full-length play, *The Birthday Party*, was followed by *The Caretaker*, *The Homecoming*, *Betrayal*, and numerous screenplays. Unlike Beckett, Pinter writes plays that have the appearance of Realism.

Rosencrantz and Guildenstern Are Dead, 1995.

What links Pinter to Beckett is his use of dialogue, which employs a variety of strategies—from the banalities of small talk to extended silences—to highlight the difficulties of communication. In 2005 Pinter won the Nobel Prize in Literature. In his Nobel Lecture he notes, "Truth in drama is forever elusive. You never quite find it but the search for it is compulsive. The search is clearly what drives the endeavor."

Contemporary British drama continues to investigate political and social issues. British dramatist Caryl Churchill has written political plays that express socialist and feminist themes. *Top Girls*, one of Churchill's best-known plays, introduces famous women from legend and history, such as the medieval figure Pope Joan and the Victorian traveler Isabella Bird, into an analysis of contemporary feminism. Today, British playwrights continue to push the boundaries of theme, form, and production.

Literature Online **Literary History** For more about postwar British drama, go to www.glencoe.com.

RESPONDING AND THINKING CRITICALLY

1. How do you think you would have responded if you had been in the audience when *Look Back in Anger* was first produced?

2. What do you think marked the major change between prewar and postwar British drama?

3. What are some of the essential features of late twentieth-century British drama?

OBJECTIVES
- Compare and contrast the characteristics of drama over time.
- Connect drama to historical context.

What We Lost

MEET EAVAN BOLAND

Eavan Boland's early life was marked by the disruptions of moving from place to place and the struggles associated with learning where one belongs. In 1950, at the age of five, she left her native Ireland when her father became ambassador to the Court of St. James in London. She vividly remembers the anti-Irish hostility she faced from Londoners at the time as well as the feelings of isolation and humiliation that such cruelty prompted in her.

Cultural Isolation In 1956 her father was named Irish ambassador to the United Nations, and again Boland found herself uprooted in a move that took her family clear across the Atlantic to New York City. Boland enrolled in the Convent of the Sacred Heart School, and she thought New York was a "beautiful, bizarre city." However, her new surroundings did little to diminish her feeling that she was an outsider. It was at this time that she found hints of an emerging aesthetic that would shape her work as a writer: the deepening "feeling that your reality is an inner rather than an outer" experience.

In 1959 Boland returned to Ireland to go to boarding school at Holy Child Convent in Killiney, County Dublin, where she stayed until 1962. Again she felt chillingly distant from her own culture because of her long absence. She did not speak Gaelic and her upbringing in London and New York set her apart. Nevertheless, it was an important time for her as she became reacquainted with Ireland, and she found that her loneliness was conducive to writing.

Family Influences Boland was not exactly alone when it came to seriously exploring her artistic side, though. Her mother, Frances Kelly Boland, was an accomplished painter who had studied with the postexpressionists in Paris in the 1930s. While Boland insists that both her parents "were profoundly influential" on her work, her mother

promoted the kind of confidence that would help Boland challenge the male-dominated literary traditions of Ireland.

> *"The idea of a poetry which can fathom silences, follow the outsider's trail—that draws me in."*
>
> —Eavan Boland

Teacher and Writer After graduating from Holy Child, Boland worked as a hotel housekeeper and used her wages to publish a chapbook entitled *23 Poems* (1962). She went on to study English at Trinity College, Dublin, during the next four years, earning a first-class honors degree. Boland taught for a while at Trinity but felt she "was completely unsuited to being an academic." However, she has lectured at the School of Irish Studies in Dublin since the late 1960s and writes reviews and articles for the *Irish Times*. Since 1996 she has taught graduate level workshops in poetry in the Stanford Creative Writing Program in California.

Eavan Boland was born in 1944.

Literature Online **Author Search** For more about Eavan Boland, go to www.glencoe.com.

Connecting to the Poem

Many people find that family memories become more valuable as time passes. What stories do you know about your parents' or grandparents' generation? As you read this poem, ask yourself how family memories can be preserved.

Building Background

In her 1995 book of prose *Object Lessons,* Boland writes about the life of her grandmother, a woman she knows almost nothing about. In the book, Boland constructs a story that intimately ties her own life together with that of her grandmother while revealing the parallel construction of Boland's own persona as poet, wife, and mother in the traditional, male-dominated literary world. Boland doesn't need every detail of her grandmother's life to build a convincing and meaningful portrait of the woman. It is precisely because she is freed from the historical facts and precedents that she can also chart a convincing course as an Irish woman poet.

Setting Purposes for Reading

Big Idea Making and Remaking Traditions

As you read, think about how the poem departs from traditional poetic conventions.

Literary Element Voice

The author's distinctive use of language to convey the speaker's personality to the reader is referred to as **voice.** Various elements of style can determine a writer's voice. These elements may include sentence structure, word choice, sound devices, pace, and tone. As you read the poem, determine if you can "hear" a distinct voice emerging from the piece.

● See Literary Terms Handbook, p. R19.

Literature Online Interactive Literary Elements Handbook To review or learn more about the literary elements, go to www.literature.glencoe.com.

Reading Strategy Clarifying Meaning

Rereading passages in a literary work can help to clarify the meaning of the text. Characters' identities, the sequence or cause of events, challenging language, or even puzzling ideas may become clearer when you slowly reread the material. While reading the poem, make notes about where the meaning of the poem becomes vague; then reread these sections.

Reading Tip: Taking Notes Even if the meaning of a text isn't clear from the start, read all the way to the end the first time through. Information presented earlier in the piece may become more understandable once you consider all the details. As you read Boland's poem, make a chart like the one below to help you clarify meaning.

Difficult Line or Phrase	Possible Meaning	Meaning After Rereading
The distance is a crystal earshot	The surroundings are frozen and glistening.	Crystal suggests something hard and clear.

Rack Picture for William Malcolm Bunn, 1882. John Frederick Peto. Oil on canvas, 24 x 20 in. Smithsonian American Art Museum, Washington, DC.

OBJECTIVES
In studying this selection, you will focus on the following:
● analyzing literary periods
● analyzing voice
● clarifying meaning

What We Lost

Eavan Boland

Marion McLean. Ian Fleming. Oil on canvas. The Fleming-Wyfold Art Foundation.

It is a winter afternoon.
The hills are frozen. Light is failing.
The distance is a crystal earshot.
A woman is mending linen in her kitchen.

5   She is a countrywoman.
Behind her cupboard doors she hangs sprigged,
stove-dried lavender in muslin.[1]
Her letters and mementos and memories

1. *Muslin* is a strong, often sheer cotton fabric.

Literary Element   Voice *What do these short opening sentences contribute to the speaker's voice?*

are packeted in satin at the back with
10   gaberdine and worsted and
the cambric² she has made into bodices;³
the good tobacco silk for Sunday Mass.

She is sewing in the kitchen.
The sugar-feel of flax is in her hands.
15   Dusk. And the candles brought in then.
One by one. And the quiet sweat of wax.

There is a child at her side.
The tea is poured, the stitching put down.
The child grows still, sensing something of importance.
20   The woman settles and begins her story.

Believe it, what we lost is here in this room
on this veiled evening.
The woman finishes. The story ends.
The child, who is my mother, gets up, moves away.

25   In the winter air, unheard, unshared,
the moment happens, hangs fire, leads nowhere.
The light will fail and the room darken,
the child fall asleep and the story be forgotten.

The fields are dark already.
30   The frail connections have been made and are broken.
The dumb-show⁴ of legend has become language,
is becoming silence and who will know that once

words were possibilities and disappointments,
were scented closets filled with love letters
35   and memories and lavender hemmed into muslin,
stored in sachets,⁵ aired in bed linen;

and traveled silks and the tones of cotton
tautened into bodices, subtly shaped by breathing;
were the rooms of childhood with their griefless peace,
40   their hands and whispers, their candles weeping brightly?

2. *Gaberdine, worsted,* and *cambric*
   are particular kinds of cloth.
3. A *bodice* is the upper part of a
   woman's dress.

4. A *dumb-show* is a part of a
   play presented in gestures
   without words.

5. *Sachets* are small perfumed
   bags placed in drawers to scent
   clothing during storage.

Reading Strategy   Clarifying Meaning *Reread the context surrounding this line after you've finished the poem. What was lost?*

Literary Element   Voice *How has sentence length changed from the opening lines of the poem? How does that change affect the voice?*

RESPONDING AND THINKING CRITICALLY

Respond

1. What is your reaction to the loss expressed by the speaker?

Recall and Interpret

2. (a)Who is "the woman" in the poem? (b)Why doesn't the speaker describe her more fully?

3. (a)List three of the fabrics mentioned in the early stanzas of the poem. (b)How do these concrete things contrast with what was lost?

4. (a)To whom is the woman's story told, and with what results? (b)Is the story important? Explain.

Analyze and Evaluate

5. (a)The events in the poem take place before the speaker is born. What effect is created by the vivid and immediate descriptions of these scenes? (b)Is the poet effective at drawing you into the visual aspects of the past? Explain.

6. The last line ends with a question mark. Reread the end of the poem to determine where the question begins. Rephrase the question in your own words. What is being asked?

Connect

7. Do you think that family history, particularly a family's stories and traditions, is important to who we are as individuals? Explain.

8. **Big Idea** **Making and Remaking Traditions** In this poem, how does Boland depart from traditional poetic techniques? Consider rhyme, sound effects, and rhythm.

LITERARY ANALYSIS

Literary Element **Voice**

A piece of writing can be magical when a reader can hear an original **voice** coming from the page. Of course the words are silent, but their placement and their rhythms can make a kind of verbal music that is distinctive.

1. Choose a stanza from "What We Lost" and explain specifically how word choice, pace, or other elements contribute to the voice in that stanza.

2. Characterize the overall voice you hear in the poem and provide examples to support your opinion.

Writing About Literature

Respond to Mood The emotional quality of a literary work is referred to as its **mood.** Much like voice, the writer's choice of language, subject matter, setting, and tone, as well as sound devices such as rhyme and rhythm, contribute to creating mood. In a brief essay, discuss the mood of "What We Lost." Provide evidence from the poem to support your opinions.

Literature Online **Web Activities** For eFlashcards, Selection Quick Checks, and other Web activities, go to www.glencoe.com.

READING AND VOCABULARY

Reading Strategy **Clarifying Meaning**

Rereading a passage that appears difficult at first can often unlock its meaning. However, it helps to identify parts of the text that seem clear, so that you can weigh your interpretations of difficult sections against them.

Using the chart you made on page 1279, choose a passage that was unclear at first and re-examine it in relation to parts of the poem that seem absolutely clear to you. What is your interpretation of the difficult passage now? Explain.

Academic Vocabulary

Here is a word from the vocabulary list on page R82.

denote (di nōt´) *v.* serve as an indication of

Practice and Apply
What do you think the packets of love letters **denote** about the woman in the poem's past?

Part 2

Around the World: Extending and Evaluating Traditions

Man's Natural World, c. 20th century. Sir Peter Scott. Oil on canvas. Private collection.

"The English language is nobody's special property. It is the property of the imagination: it is the property of the language itself."

—Derek Walcott

A Mild Attack of Locusts

MEET DORIS LESSING

After visiting South Africa in 1956, Doris Lessing was escorted to the airport by two police officers and told never to return. She was banned for twenty-five years from entering South Africa and Southern Rhodesia (now Zimbabwe) because of her political views and her opposition to apartheid, South Africa's former official policy of racial segregation. Throughout her life, Lessing has caused a stir with her novels and her clearly articulated political views.

An Uncomfortable Childhood Lessing was born to English parents in Persia (now Iran), where her father had been a captain in the British Army. In 1924 Lessing's parents moved to the British colony in the African country of Southern Rhodesia, where Lessing would spend the next twenty-five years of her life.

Lessing has described her childhood as a mixture of some pleasure and more pain. Only excursions into the natural world provided Lessing with some relief from the strict governance of her mother, who was determined to raise a "proper" daughter. As a young adolescent, Lessing was sent to an all-girls' school in the nation's capital, Salisbury. Miserable, she dropped out at the age of thirteen, ending her formal education.

> "I wasn't thinking about being a writer then—I was just thinking about how to escape."
>
> —Doris Lessing

An Unbounded Career Soon after dropping out of school, Lessing left home and began working— first as a nursemaid, then later as a typist. By her early twenties, Lessing had been married twice, and at age thirty she left her second husband to live in England with her son.

Lessing took with her to England the manuscript of her first novel, *The Grass Is Singing,* and with its publication, she began a successful career as a novelist. Much of Lessing's work is autobiographical, based upon her experiences in Africa and as a mother and wife bound by social expectations. Her stories set in Africa chronicle the struggle between native black Africans and the white colonials who claimed their land.

Critics have tried to label Lessing both a feminist and a writer about race relations, but Lessing dislikes such labels. Unlike some of her contemporaries, who enjoy the fame that accompanies a writing career, Lessing claims she prefers not to give book tours and interviews. She once said to an interviewer, "I told my publishers it would be far more useful for everyone if I stayed at home, writing another book."

In addition to her numerous novels (which include a five-volume science fiction series), Lessing has also published several collections of short stories, as well as poetry, essays, travel writings, and two autobiographical works. In 1995 Lessing visited South Africa for the first time since being forcibly removed in 1956. Recognized at last as a significant and revolutionary writer, Lessing was, on this occasion, welcomed with open arms.

Doris Lessing was born in 1919.

Literature Online **Author Search** For more about Doris Lessing, go to www.glencoe.com.

Connecting to the Story

All human communities must cope with hazards of nature—earthquakes, tornadoes, hurricanes, and the like. As you read, think about the following questions:

- What natural hazards do the people of your community face?
- How does your family or school prepare for and protect against these hazards?

Building Background

Lessing was five when her father moved the family to a vast, remote farm in Southern Rhodesia, where he hoped to grow rich by raising maize, or corn. In spite of her mother's energetic efforts to create a refined life in this rough settlement, the farm did not yield the wealth her father had anticipated.

One of the many hazards of farming in this region were locusts. The name *locust* refers to a number of jumping insects, including the periodical cicada (sə kā′ də)—which appears every seven, thirteen, or seventeen years—and the true locust, a migratory grasshopper. Locusts severely damage crops wherever they swarm.

Setting Purposes for Reading

Big Idea Colonialism and Postcolonialism

Southern Rhodesia (now Zimbabwe) declared independence from Britain in 1923. As you read "A Mild Attack of Locusts," look for aspects of British colonialism that persist several decades later, when the story takes place.

Literary Element Theme

Theme refers to a central idea about life that is expressed in a work of literature. A work can have more than one theme, and these themes may be universal—widely held across human cultures. A theme is different from a topic. A topic is a broad category, such as "hardship," whereas a theme conveys a complete idea *about* a topic; for example, "Hardship is best met with a sense of humor."

- See Literary Terms Handbook, p. R18.

Reading Strategy Analyzing Conflict

Conflict is the central struggle in a story or drama. This struggle might be between two or more people, between people and nature, or between people and their own feelings. To analyze conflict, determine whether a character is struggling against something on the outside, something on the inside, or both. Then watch to see how—or whether—each conflict is resolved.

....

Reading Tip: Identifying Conflict As you read, use a graphic organizer like the one below to identify conflicts in the story.

Outside Force ← Character → Inner Feelings

Vocabulary

acrid (ak′ rid) *adj.* burning, biting, or irritating to the taste or smell; p. 1287 *Where is that acrid stench coming from?*

irremediable (ir i mē′ dē ə bəl) *adj.* not subject to remedy or cure; p. 1289 *The tornado left irremediable damage in its wake.*

imminent (im′ ə nənt) *adj.* about to happen; impending; p. 1291 *A clap of thunder told us that a rainstorm was imminent.*

Vocabulary Tip: Word Origins Many words in English derive from, or come from, words in other languages. Knowing a word's origin can help you better understand its meaning.

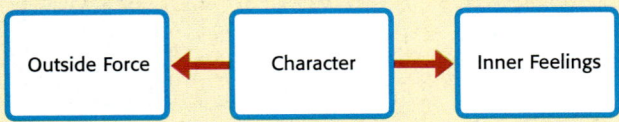 **Interactive Literary Elements Handbook** To review or learn more about the literary elements, go to www.glencoe.com.

OBJECTIVES
In studying this selection, you will focus on the following:
- analyzing genre elements
- identifying themes
- analyzing conflicts

DORIS LESSING **1285**

A Mild Attack of Locusts

Doris Lessing

Swarm of desert locusts.

The rains that year were good; they were coming nicely just as the crops needed them—or so Margaret gathered[1] when the men said they were not too bad. She never had an opinion of her own on matters like the weather, because even to know about what seems a simple thing like the weather needs experience. Which Margaret had not got.

The men were Richard her husband, and old Stephen, Richard's father, a farmer from way back; and these two might argue for hours whether the rains were ruinous or just ordinarily exasperating. Margaret had been on the farm three years. She still did not understand how they did not go bankrupt altogether, when the men never had a good word for the weather, or the soil, or the government. But she was getting to learn the language. Farmers' language. And

they neither went bankrupt nor got very rich. They jogged along doing comfortably.

Their crop was maize. Their farm was three thousand acres on the ridges that rise up toward the Zambesi escarpment[2]—high, dry wind-swept country, cold and dusty in winter, but now, in the wet season, steamy with the heat rising in wet soft waves off miles of green foliage. Beautiful it was, with the sky blue and brilliant halls of air, and the bright green folds and hollows of country beneath, and the mountains lying sharp and bare twenty miles off across the rivers. The sky made her eyes ache; she was not used to it. One does not look so much at the sky in the city she came from. So that evening when Richard said: "The government is sending out warnings that locusts are expected, coming down from the breeding grounds up North," her instinct was to look about her at the trees.

---

1. As it is used here, *gathered* means "concluded."

2. The *Zambesi escarpment* is a series of steep cliffs along the Zambesi River in southern Africa.

Insects—swarms of them—horrible! But Richard and the old man had raised their eyes and were looking up over the mountain. "We haven't had locusts in seven years," they said. "They go in cycles, locusts do." And then: "There goes our crop for this season!"

But they went on with the work of the farm just as usual until one day they were coming up the road to the homestead for the midday break, when old Stephen stopped, raised his finger and pointed: "Look, look, there they are!"

Out ran Margaret to join them, looking at the hills. Out came the servants from the kitchen. They all stood and gazed. Over the rocky levels of the mountain was a streak of rust-colored air. Locusts. There they came.

At once Richard shouted at the cookboy. Old Stephen yelled at the houseboy. The cookboy ran to beat the old ploughshare[3] hanging from a tree branch, which was used to summon the laborers at moments of crisis. The houseboy ran off to the store to collect tin cans, any old bit of metal. The farm was ringing with the clamor of the gong; and they could see the laborers come pouring out of the compound, pointing at the hills and shouting excitedly. Soon they had all come up to the house, and Richard and old Stephen were giving them orders—Hurry, hurry, hurry.

And off they ran again, the two white men with them, and in a few minutes Margaret could see the smoke of fires rising from all around the farmlands. Piles of wood and grass had been prepared there. There were seven patches of bared soil, yellow and oxblood color and pink, where the new mealies[4] were just showing, making a film of bright green; and around each drifted up thick clouds of smoke. They were throwing wet leaves on to the fires now, to make it **acrid** and black. Margaret was watching the hills. Now there was a long, low cloud advancing, rust-color still, swelling forward and out as she looked. The telephone was ringing. Neighbors—quick, quick, there come the locusts. Old Smith had had his crop eaten to the ground. Quick, get your fires started. For of course, while every farmer hoped the locusts would overlook his farm and go on to the next, it was only fair to warn each other; one must play fair. Everywhere, fifty miles over the countryside, the smoke was rising from myriads[5] of fires. Margaret answered the telephone calls, and between calls she stood watching the locusts. The air was darkening. A strange darkness, for the sun was blazing—it was like the darkness of a veldt[6] fire, when the air gets thick with smoke. The sunlight comes down distorted,[7] a thick, hot orange. Oppressive it was, too, with the heaviness of a storm. The locusts were coming fast. Now half the sky was darkened. Behind the reddish veils in front, which were the advance guards of the swarm, the main swarm showed in dense black cloud, reaching almost to the sun itself.

Margaret was wondering what she could do to help. She did not know. Then up came old Stephen from the lands. "We're finished, Margaret, finished! Those beggars can eat every leaf and blade off the farm in half an hour! And it is only early afternoon—if we can make enough smoke, make enough noise till the sun goes down, they'll settle somewhere else perhaps. . . ." And then: "Get the kettle going. It's thirsty work, this."

So Margaret went to the kitchen, and stoked up the fire, and boiled the water. Now, on the tin roof of the kitchen she could hear the thuds and bangs of falling locusts, or a scratching slither as one skidded down. Here were the first of them. From down

---

3. A *ploughshare* is the cutting blade of a plow.
4. A *mealie* is an ear of corn.

5. *Myriads* means "a great or countless number."
6. The *veldt* (velt, felt) is a rolling grassland region in southern Africa that has scattered bushes and trees.
7. Here, *distorted* means "unnatural in appearance."

Reading Strategy Analyzing Conflict *What external conflict does everyone on the farm face? What additional internal conflict does Margaret face?*

Big Idea Colonialism and Postcolonialism *What does the locust crisis reveal about the relationship between the landowners and the laborers?*

Reading Strategy Analyzing Conflict *What competing feelings or desires is Margaret struggling with?*

Vocabulary

acrid (ak′ rid) *adj.* burning, biting, or irritating to the taste or smell

Brown Locust Swarm, South Africa

on the lands came the beating and banging and clanging of a hundred gasoline cans and bits of metal. Stephen impatiently waited while one gasoline can was filled with tea, hot, sweet and orange-colored, and the other with water. In the meantime, he told Margaret about how twenty years back he was eaten out, made bankrupt, by the locust armies. And then, still talking, he hoisted up the gasoline cans, one in each hand, by the wood pieces set cornerwise across each, and jogged off down to the road to the thirsty laborers. By now the locusts were falling like hail on to the roof of the kitchen. It sounded like a heavy storm. Margaret looked out and saw the air dark with a crisscross of the insects, and she set her teeth and ran out into it—what the men could do, she could. Overhead the air was thick, locusts everywhere. The locusts were flopping against her, and she brushed them off, heavy red-brown creatures, looking at her with their beady old-men's eyes while they clung with hard, serrated[8] legs. She held her breath with disgust and ran through into the house. There it was even more like being in a heavy storm. The iron roof was reverberating,[9] and the clamor of iron from the lands was like

thunder. Looking out, all the trees were queer and still, clotted with insects, their boughs weighed to the ground. The earth seemed to be moving, locusts crawling everywhere, she could not see the lands at all, so thick was the swarm. Toward the mountains it was like looking into driving rain— even as she watched, the sun was blotted out with a fresh onrush of them. It was a half-night, a perverted blackness.

Then came a sharp crack from the bush—a branch had snapped off. Then another. A tree down the slope leaned over and settled heavily to the ground. Through the hail of insects a man came running. More tea, more water was needed. She supplied them. She kept the fires stoked and filled cans with liquid, and then it was four in the afternoon, and the locusts had been pouring across overhead for a couple of hours. Up came old Stephen again, crunching locusts underfoot with every step, locusts clinging all over him; he was cursing and swearing, banging with his old hat at the air. At the doorway he stopped briefly, hastily pulling at the clinging insects and throwing them off, then he plunged into the locust-free living room.

"All the crops finished. Nothing left," he said.

But the gongs were still beating, the men still shouting, and Margaret asked: "Why do you go on with it, then?"

"The main swarm isn't settling. They are heavy with eggs. They are looking for a place to settle and lay. If we can stop the main body settling on our farm, that's everything. If they get a chance to lay their eggs, we are going to have everything eaten flat with hoppers[10] later on." He picked a stray locust off his shirt and split it down with his thumbnail—it was clotted inside with eggs.

---

8. *Serrated* means "jagged" or "saw-toothed."
9. *Reverberating* means "echoing."

Reading Strategy **Analyzing Conflict** *How does Margaret handle her ignorance and fear?*

---

10. *Hoppers* are baby locusts.

"Imagine that multiplied by millions. You ever seen a hopper swarm on the march? Well, you're lucky."

Margaret thought an adult swarm was bad enough. Outside now the light on the earth was a pale, thin yellow, clotted with moving shadows; the clouds of moving insects thickened and lightened like driving rain. Old Stephen said, "They've got the wind behind them, that's something."

"Is it very bad?" asked Margaret fearfully, and the old man said emphatically: "We're finished. This swarm may pass over, but once they've started, they'll be coming down from the North now one after another. And then there are the hoppers—it might go on for two or three years."

Margaret sat down helplessly, and thought: Well, if it's the end, it's the end. What now? We'll all three have to go back to town. . . . But at this, she took a quick look at Stephen, the old man who had farmed forty years in this country, been bankrupt twice, and she knew nothing would make him go and become a clerk in the city. Yet her heart ached for him, he looked so tired, the worry lines deep from nose to mouth. Poor old man. . . . He had lifted up a locust that had got itself somehow into his pocket, holding it in the air by one leg. "You've got the strength of a steel-spring in those legs of yours," he was telling the locust, good-humoredly. Then, although he had been fighting locusts, squashing locusts, yelling at locusts, sweeping them in great mounds into the fires to burn for the last three hours, nevertheless he took this one to the door and carefully threw it out to join its fellows, as if he would rather not harm a hair of its head. This comforted Margaret; all at once she felt irrationally cheered. She remembered it was not the first time in the last three years the man had announced their final and **irremediable** ruin.

"Get me a drink, lass," he then said, and she set the bottle of whisky by him.

In the meantime, out in the pelting storm of insects, her husband was banging the gong, feeding the fires with leaves, the insects clinging to him all over—she shuddered. "How can you bear to let

them touch you?" she asked. He looked at her, disapproving. She felt suitably humble—just as she had when he had first taken a good look at her city self, hair waved and golden, nails red and pointed. Now she was a proper farmer's wife, in sensible shoes and a solid skirt. She might even get to letting locusts settle on her—in time.

Having tossed back a whisky or two, old Stephen went back into the battle, wading now through glistening brown waves of locusts.

Five o'clock. The sun would set in an hour. Then the swarm would settle. It was as thick overhead as ever. The trees were ragged mounds of glistening brown.

Margaret began to cry. It was all so hopeless—if it wasn't a bad season, it was locusts; if it wasn't locusts, it was army-worm[11] or veldt fires. Always something. The rustling of the locust armies was like a big forest in the storm; their settling on the roof was like the beating of the rain; the ground was invisible in a sleek, brown, surging tide—it was like being drowned in locusts, submerged by the loathsome brown flood. It seemed as if the roof might sink in under the weight of them, as if the door might give in under their pressure and these rooms fill with them—and it was getting so dark . . . she looked up. The air was thinner; gaps of blue showed in the dark, moving clouds. The blue spaces were cold and thin—the sun must be setting. Through the fog of insects she saw figures approaching. First old Stephen, marching bravely along, then her husband, drawn and haggard with weariness. Behind them the servants. All were crawling all over with insects. The sound of the gongs had stopped. She could hear nothing but the ceaseless rustle of a myriad wings.

The two men slapped off the insects and came in.

"Well," said Richard, kissing her on the cheek, "the main swarm has gone over."

"For the Lord's sake," said Margaret angrily, still half-crying, "what's here is bad enough, isn't it?" For although the evening air was no longer black and thick, but a clear blue, with a pattern of insects whizzing this way and that across it,

Reading Strategy **Analyzing Conflict** *What new insight do we gain about old Stephen's struggle against the locusts?*

Vocabulary

irremediable (ir i mē′ dē ə bəl) *adj.* not subject to remedy or cure

11. An *army-worm* is any of various insect larvae that travel in groups and destroy vegetation.

Literary Element **Theme** *How does Richard's attitude differ from Margaret's?*

Under the Acacia Tree, 1991. Tilly Willis. Oil on board, 25 x 35 cm. Private collection.
Viewing the Art: What sense of the story's setting do you get from this painting?

everything else—trees, buildings, bushes, earth, was gone under the moving brown masses.

"If it doesn't rain in the night and keep them here—if it doesn't rain and weight them down with water, they'll be off in the morning at sunrise."

"We're bound to have some hoppers. But not the main swarm—that's something."

Margaret roused herself, wiped her eyes, pretended she had not been crying, and fetched them some supper, for the servants were too exhausted to move. She sent them down to the compound to rest.

She served the supper and sat listening. There is not one maize plant left, she heard. Not one. The men would get the planters out the moment the locusts had gone. They must start all over again.

But what's the use of that, Margaret wondered, if the whole farm was going to be crawling with hoppers? But she listened while they discussed the new government pamphlet that said how to defeat the hoppers. You must have men out all the time, moving over the farm to watch for movement in the grass. When you find a patch of hoppers, small lively black things, like crickets, then you dig trenches around the patch or spray them with poison from pumps supplied by the government. The government wanted them to cooperate in a world plan for eliminating this plague forever. You should attack locusts at the source. Hoppers, in short. The men were talking as if they were planning a war, and Margaret listened, amazed.

Reading Strategy   Analyzing Conflict *Why do you think the men go about resolving their conflict with the locusts in this manner?*

In the night it was quiet; no sign of the settled armies outside, except sometimes a branch snapped, or a tree could be heard crashing down.

Margaret slept badly in the bed beside Richard, who was sleeping like the dead, exhausted with the afternoon's fight. In the morning she woke to yellow sunshine lying across the bed—clear sunshine, with an occasional blotch of shadow moving over it. She went to the window. Old Stephen was ahead of her. There he stood outside, gazing down over the bush. And she gazed, astounded—and entranced, much against her will. For it looked as if every tree, every bush, all the earth, were lit with pale flames. The locusts were fanning their wings to free them of the night dews. There was a shimmer of red-tinged gold light everywhere.

She went out to join the old man, stepping carefully among the insects. They stood and watched. Overhead the sky was blue, blue and clear.

"Pretty," said old Stephen, with satisfaction.

Well, thought Margaret, we may be ruined, we may be bankrupt, but not everyone has seen an army of locusts fanning their wings at dawn.

Over the slopes, in the distance, a faint red smear showed in the sky, thickened and spread. "There they go," said old Stephen. "There goes the main army, off south."

And now from the trees, from the earth all round them, the locusts were taking wing. They were like small aircraft, maneuvering for the take-off, trying their wings to see if they were dry enough. Off they went. A reddish brown steam was rising off the miles of bush, off the lands, the earth. Again the sunlight darkened.

And as the clotted branches lifted, the weight on them lightening, there was nothing but the black spines of branches, trees. No green left, nothing. All morning they watched, the three of them, as the brown crust thinned and broke and dissolved, flying up to mass with the main army, now a brownish-red smear in the southern sky. The lands which had been filmed with green, the new tender mealie plants, were stark and bare. All the trees stripped. A devastated landscape. No green, no green anywhere.

By midday the reddish cloud had gone. Only an occasional locust flopped down. On the ground were the corpses and the wounded. The African laborers were sweeping these up with branches and collecting them in tins.

> There is not one maize plant left... Not one.

"Ever eaten sun-dried locust?" asked old Stephen. "That time twenty years ago, when I went broke, I lived on mealie meal and dried locusts for three months. They aren't bad at all—rather like smoked fish, if you come to think of it."

But Margaret preferred not even to think of it.

After the midday meal the men went off to the lands. Everything was to be replanted. With a bit of luck another swarm would not come traveling down just this way. But they hoped it would rain very soon, to spring some new grass, because the cattle would die otherwise—there was not a blade of grass left on the farm. As for Margaret, she was trying to get used to the idea of three or four years of locusts. Locusts were going to be like bad weather, from now on, always **imminent.** She felt like a survivor after war—if this devastated and mangled countryside was not ruin, well, what then was ruin?

But the men ate their supper with good appetites.

"It could have been worse," was what they said. "It could be much worse." ❧

Literary Element Theme *How has Margaret's view of the locusts changed?*

Big Idea Colonialism and Postcolonialism *What message about history itself might Lessing want to convey?*

Vocabulary

imminent (im′ ə nənt) *adj.* about to happen; impending

RESPONDING AND THINKING CRITICALLY

Respond

1. How might you have felt if you had seen these locusts approaching your home?

Recall and Interpret

2. (a)Why doesn't Margaret understand how the farm does not go bankrupt? (b)What can you infer about the nature of "farmer's language"? Why?

3. (a)According to Stephen, why do the farmers continue fighting the locusts even after the insects have already destroyed the crops? (b)What does Stephen's reason for continuing to fight the locusts suggest about his claim that the farmers are "finished"?

4. (a)Why does Margaret cry at the end of the first day? (b)Why is Margaret so disturbed by the locusts? Why aren't the farmers as upset as she is?

Analyze and Evaluate

5. Why might people who live in the city have a different attitude toward nature than those who live in the country?

6. (a)What words and phrases best help you to picture the locusts fanning their wings in the morning? (b)In your opinion, what do these images add to the story?

7. Lessing's fiction has been called "deeply autobiographical." Reread the background information on page 1285. What elements of her life might Lessing have used in this story?

Connect

8. **Big Idea** Colonialism and Postcolonialism
Lessing writes that "I believe that the chief gift from Africa to writers . . . is the continent itself. . . . Africa gives you the knowledge that man is a small creature, among other creatures, in a large landscape." How does Lessing communicate this feeling of smallness in "A Mild Attack of Locusts"?

PRIMARY VISUAL ARTIFACT

Locust Swarms

The species of locust featured in Lessing's story is known as the desert locust. Desert locusts are short-horned grasshoppers (family *Acrididae*) that  are known to change their behavior and form swarms of adults or bands of hoppers. Swarms typically fly with the wind at a speed of about 16–19 kilometers an hour and can travel up to 130 kilometers a day. Locust swarms can vary from less than one square kilometer to several hundred square kilometers.

There can be at least 40 million and sometimes as many as 80 million locust adults in each square kilometer of swarm. A very small part of an average swarm eats the same amount of food in one day as about ten elephants, twenty-five camels, or 2,500 people.

Group Activity Discuss the following questions with your classmates.

1. Find a short passage in "A Mild Attack of Locusts" that this photo might be used to illustrate.

2. How does the photo help you understand Margaret's feelings of hopelessness and despair?

Literary Element | Theme

A story's **theme,** or central message about life, is sometimes **stated,** or expressed directly. More often, though, the theme is **implied,** or revealed gradually through events, dialogue, description, or a character's actions. Remember, though, that works of literature can have more than one theme. Because of this, a story might directly express one theme and then imply a range of others.

One way to identify a story's theme is to ask yourself what the main character learns during the course of the story. What does the character think or believe at the story's outset? How, at the end of the story, has this perspective changed? Usually, the lesson learned by the main character has a strong connection to the message the author hopes to send the reader.

1. What stated theme appears in the first paragraph of the story?

2. What lesson about farming does Margaret learn from her experiences in the story?

3. What more general lesson about life—what implied theme—can you extrapolate from the lesson Margaret learns?

Review: Title

As you learned on page 1094, the **title** of a literary work may serve a number of purposes. It may help to explain the setting, provide insight into the theme, or describe the action that will take place in the work. The title "A Mild Attack of Locusts" serves several purposes. First, it describes what will happen in the story—there will be a swarm of locusts. Second, it describes the farmers' reaction to the attack, which they say was not as bad as it might have been. Lessing's title is also an example of **understatement,** a declaration that presents something as being less important than it really is, thereby focusing the reader's attention on something the author wants to emphasize.

Group Activity Discuss the following questions with a group of classmates.

1. In what way is the title "A Mild Attack of Locusts" an understatement? What idea does Lessing wish to emphasize?

2. Come up with another title for this story. Why do you think your alternate title is appropriate?

Reading Strategy | Analyzing Conflict

When conflict is **external,** a struggle occurs between a character and some outside force, such as a person or a group of people, nature, or society. When conflict is **internal,** a character struggles with two or more competing feelings or desires. Review the chart you completed on page 1285.

1. What external force does Margaret struggle against?

2. With what internal feelings does Margaret struggle?

3. In your opinion, which of these conflicts is more central to the story? Why?

Vocabulary | Practice

Practice with Word Origins Match each word below with the correct description of its origin. Use a dictionary to help you.

1. acrid	**a.** from a Latin word meaning "to heal"
2. imminent	**b.** from a Latin word meaning "to threaten"
3. irremediable	**c.** from a Latin word meaning "edge"

Academic Vocabulary

Here are two words from the vocabulary list on page R82.

consume (kən sōōm´) v. 1. to destroy completely; to do away with 2. to absorb completely; to obsess

overall (ō´ vər ôl´) adj. including everything; total

Practice and Apply

1. In your opinion, which is the greater threat to Margaret: that which is **consuming** the farm, or that which **consumes** her thoughts? Explain.

2. How do the initial words and behaviors of the men contradict their **overall** attitude toward the locusts?

Writing About Literature

Compare and Contrast Characters "A Mild Attack of Locusts" can be read as one family's battle against a natural calamity. Each member of the family, however, responds to the calamity differently. Write a brief essay in which you compare and contrast the response of Margaret, Richard, and Stephen to the threat—and the reality—of the locust swarm.

Before you begin, you may want to create a diagram like this one for each character.

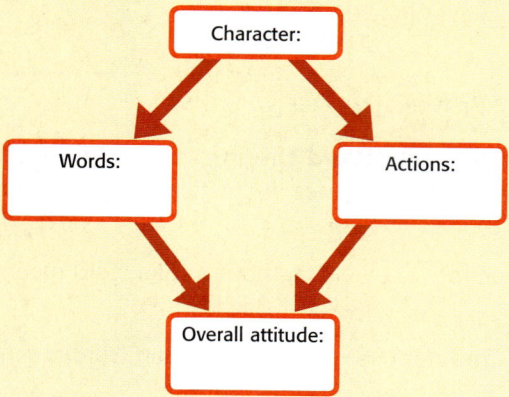

Character:

Words:

Actions:

Overall attitude:

After you complete your draft, meet with a peer reviewer to read each other's work and to offer suggestions for revision. Be sure to proofread your draft for errors in spelling, grammar, and punctuation.

Internet Connection

Locust swarms are a major hazard for farmers in Africa, the Middle East, and southwest Asia. What other natural hazards threaten farms in southern Africa, where "A Mild Attack of Locusts" is set? What are some natural hazards that threaten farms in other regions of the world, such as Europe, Central America, and the South Pacific? Conduct an Internet search to find answers to these questions. Present your findings to the class in a brief oral report.

Lessing's Language and Style

Comparing with *Like* and *As* In "A Mild Attack of Locusts," Lessing communicates the impact of the locust swarm on the farm by comparing the insects' appearance and movements to other objects or events. Consider, for example, these sentences from the story:

"The rustling of the locust armies was <u>like</u> a big forest in the storm."

"It seemed <u>as if</u> the roof might sink in under the weight of them."

Although both sentences make comparisons, the signal words differ according to the sentence structure. *Like,* a preposition, is used to introduce a prepositional phrase; *as* and *as if,* subordinating conjunctions, introduce subordinate clauses.

Both forms of comparison help an author describe an experience from a particular character's point of view. That is, they create subjective images while also communicating objective happenings. In the comparisons above, Lessing effectively evokes the claustrophobic feeling Margaret is experiencing—while also communicating the literal sound and weight of the swarming insects.

Activity Scan the story for other examples of comparisons using *like, as,* or *as if.* Explain whether the linking word in each example introduces a prepositional phrase or a subordinate clause. Then explain which kind of comparison, in your opinion, creates more vivid, effective images and why.

Revising Check

Comparing Words Because "A Mild Attack of Locusts" is told from Margaret's point of view, many of the comparisons in the story give hints about Margaret's attitude toward what is happening. With a partner, review your essay comparing and contrasting characters' responses to the swarm. How might you incorporate one or two comparisons from the story as textual support for your discussion of Margaret's response? How might you use one or two original comparisons to describe the responses of the men?

Literature Online **Web Activities** For eFlashcards, Selection Quick Checks, and other Web activities, go to www.glencoe.com.

The Train from Rhodesia

MEET NADINE GORDIMER

Nadine Gordimer grew up in a South Africa that was divided along racial lines. Born in a mining town near the capital, Johannesburg, Gordimer was the daughter of wealthy parents of European descent. As a member of the white minority—and in the care of an overprotective mother—Gordimer was sheltered from the harsher effects of apartheid, South Africa's official policy of racial segregation (which was abolished in the early 1990s). During frequent trips to the library, the young Gordimer began reading about the injustices suffered by her black compatriots, and as her awareness of their problems grew, so did her desire to help.

> "I did not, at the beginning, expect to earn a living by being read. I wrote as a child out of the joy of apprehending life through my senses—the look and scent and feel of things."
>
> —Nadine Gordimer

In Black and White Gordimer began writing by the age of nine, and her first story was published in a Johannesburg magazine when she was only fifteen. Gordimer has referred to herself as a "natural writer"—one who never made a conscious decision to write.

As Gordimer matured, her writing became more consciously concerned with the dehumanizing effects of racial prejudice. Throughout the 1950s and 1960s, Gordimer published novels and collections of short stories that explored issues related to apartheid: the narrow-mindedness of small-town life, the psychology of the master/servant relationship, the paranoia resulting from colonialism, and the superficial liberalism of her privileged peers.

Writing and Politics Gordimer is often praised for her skillful handling of sensitive political and social themes. Her writing is distinguished by a dispassionate tone that is free from sentimentality or bias. To achieve objectivity, Gordimer often presents several different, opposing perspectives on an event or situation in her stories. Gordimer claims that an author can transcend his or her own politics but still remain engaged in the political realities of the time.

Although several of her books were banned in South Africa before the demise of apartheid, Gordimer, unlike many of her contemporaries, refused to go into exile. Gordimer has periodically left South Africa for lecture tours and teaching assignments in the United States, but she has remained a citizen of her native country to this day. She is a long-time member of the African National Congress, the nation's governing political party since 1994, and is a founding member of the Congress of South African Writers. Gordimer has received many awards for her work, including the Nobel Prize in Literature in 1991.

Nadine Gordimer was born in 1923.

Literature Online **Author Search** For more about Nadine Gordimer, go to www.glencoe.com.

Connecting to the Story

Have you ever traveled someplace where you felt a distinct divide between tourists and local people? As you read "The Train from Rhodesia," think about the following questions:

- How should tourists treat local people?
- How can tourists both help and hurt developing nations?

Building Background

"The Train from Rhodesia" takes place sometime during the early or mid-1900s at an African train station where black merchants have gathered to sell their wares to white passengers. Under apartheid, blacks in South Africa could not vote in national elections, own property, or live in areas reserved for whites. Denied basic rights, many blacks lived in abject poverty, eking out a living by selling goods to white tourists. The prices of these goods were rarely fixed; instead, buyer and seller bargained, or haggled, over prices.

Setting Purposes for Reading

Big Idea Colonialism and Postcolonialism

As you read "The Train from Rhodesia," notice how the physical separation of characters symbolizes a broader social barrier between groups of people.

Literary Element Setting

Setting refers to the time and place in which the events of a story occur. The setting of a story can include not only physical surroundings, but also the ideas, customs, values, and beliefs of the people who live there. As you read this story, observe the ways in which various characters perceive and interact with their surroundings.

- See Literary Terms Handbook, p. R16.

Literature Online **Interactive Literary Elements Handbook** To review or learn more about the literary elements, go to www.glencoe.com.

Reading Strategy Visualizing

When you **visualize**, you form mental pictures of what is happening in the story based on the details provided by the narrator. This strategy can be useful when the narrator presents the story from multiple points of view. Picturing the story's setting or events in your mind's eye can help you determine when the point of view, or perspective, is shifting from one character to another.

Reading Tip: Taking Notes As you read, note how certain objects or events appear—and who is viewing them.

Appearance or Effect	Observer
"The train came out of the red horizon and bore down toward them over the single straight track."	the stationmaster

Vocabulary

vendor (ven′ dər) n. one who sells goods; p. 1297 *The vendor offered a selection of sandwiches and drinks.*

career (kə rēr′) v. to move or run with a swift headlong motion; to rush or dash along; p. 1299 *The children careered toward the playground with squeals of delight.*

wryly (rī′ lē) adv. in a twisted or distorted manner; p. 1301 *Her face twisted wryly with displeasure.*

sinew (sin′ ū) n. a tendon; p. 1301 *The sculpture represented every muscle and sinew in the athlete's body.*

Vocabulary Tip: Context Clues You can figure out the meaning of an unfamiliar word by looking for clues in the surrounding words or sentences.

OBJECTIVES
In studying this selection, you will focus on the following:
- connecting literature to historical contexts
- analyzing setting and symbol
- visualizing details

The Refreshment Car. Poster, 1928. Victoria and Albert Museum, London.

The Train from Rhodesia

Nadine Gordimer

The train came out of the red horizon and bore down toward them over the single straight track. The stationmaster came out of his little brick station with its pointed chalet roof, feeling the creases in his serge[1] uniform in his legs as well. A stir of preparedness rippled through the squatting native **vendors** waiting in the dust; the face of a carved wooden animal, eternally surprised, stuck out of a sack.

---

1. *Serge* is a twilled cloth.

Literary Element   **Setting** *In what physical surroundings is this story set?*

Vocabulary

vendor (ven′ dər) *n.* one who sells goods

The stationmaster's barefoot children wandered over. From the gray mud huts with the untidy heads that stood within a decorated mud wall, chickens, and dogs with their skin stretched like parchment over their bones, followed the piccanins[2] down to the track. The flushed and perspiring west cast a reflection, faint, without heat, upon the station, upon the tin shed marked "Goods," upon the walled kraal,[3] upon the gray tin house of the stationmaster and upon the sand, that lapped all around, from sky to sky, cast little rhythmical cups of shadow, so that the sand became the sea, and closed over the children's black feet softly and without imprint.

The stationmaster's wife sat behind the mesh of her verandah. Above her head the hunk of a sheep's carcass moved slightly, dangling in a current of air.

They waited.

The train called out, along the sky; but there was no answer; and the cry hung on: I'm coming . . . I'm coming . . .

The engine flared out now, big, whisking a dwindling body behind it; the track flared out to let it in.

Creaking, jerking, jostling, gasping, the train filled the station.

Here, let me see that one—the young woman curved her body further out of the corridor window. Missus? smiled the old boy, looking at the creatures he held in his hand. From a piece of string on his gray finger hung a tiny woven basket; he lifted it, questioning. No, no, she urged, leaning down toward him, across the height of the train, toward the man in the piece of old rug; that one, that one, her hand commanded. It was a lion, carved out of soft dry wood that looked like spongecake; heraldic,[4] black and white, with impressionistic detail burnt in. The old man held

it up to her still smiling, not from the heart, but at the customer. Between its Vandyke teeth, in the mouth opened in an endless roar too terrible to be heard, it had a black tongue. Look, said the young husband, if you don't mind! And round the neck of the thing, a piece of fur (rat? rabbit? meerkat?); a real mane, majestic, telling you somehow that the artist had delight in the lion.

Visual Vocabulary
Vandyke means "V-shaped," as in a Vandyke beard.

All up and down the length of the train in the dust the artists sprang, walking bent, like performing animals, the better to exhibit the fantasy held toward the faces on the train. Buck, startled and stiff, staring with round black and white eyes. More lions, standing erect, grappling[5] with strange, thin, elongated warriors who clutched spears and showed no fear in their slits of eyes. How much, they asked from the train, how much?

Give me penny, said the little ones with nothing to sell. The dogs went and sat, quite still, under the dining car, where the train breathed out the smell of meat cooking with onion.

A man passed beneath the arch of reaching arms meeting gray-black and white in the exchange of money for the staring wooden eyes, the stiff wooden legs sticking up in the air; went along under the voices and the bargaining, interrogating the wheels. Past the dogs; glancing up at the dining car where he could stare at the faces, behind glass, drinking beer, two by two, on either side of a uniform railway vase with its pale dead flower. Right to the end, to the guard's van, where the stationmaster's children had just collected their mother's two loaves of bread; to the engine itself, where the stationmaster and the driver stood talking against the steaming complaint of the resting beast.

The man called out to them, something loud and joking. They turned to laugh, in a twirl of

---

2. *Piccanins* is a name some people used for black children in Africa.
3. A *kraal* is an enclosure for livestock.
4. The lion is *heraldic* because it resembles the rearing lions often found on coats of arms (or family crests). Heraldry is the craft of describing and representing coats of arms.

Reading Strategy Visualizing *Visualize the arrangement in space of the woman and the old man. What does it tell you about their relationship?*

---

5. *Grappling* means "wrestling."

Literary Element Setting *What two worlds, or settings, are divided by the window? What do these two worlds represent?*

Compartment C, Car 293, 1938. Edward Hopper. Oil on canvas.

steam. The two children **careered** over the sand, clutching the bread, and burst through the iron gate and up the path through the garden in which nothing grew.

Passengers drew themselves in at the corridor windows and turned into compartments to fetch money, to call someone to look. Those sitting inside looked up: suddenly different, caged faces, boxed in, cut off, after the contact of outside. There was an orange a piccanin would like. . . . What about that chocolate? It wasn't very nice. . . .

A young girl had collected a handful of the hard kind, that no one liked, out of the chocolate box, and was throwing them to the dogs, over at the dining car. But the hens darted in, and swallowed the chocolates, incredibly quick and accurate, before they had even dropped in the dust, and the dogs, a little bewildered,

looked up with their brown eyes, not expecting anything.

—No, leave it, said the girl, don't take it. . . .

Too expensive, too much, she shook her head and raised her voice to the old boy, giving up the lion. He held it up where she had handed it to him. No, she said, shaking her head. Three-and-six?[6] insisted her husband, loudly. Yes baas! laughed the boy. *Three-and-six?*—the young man was incredulous. Oh leave it—she said. The young man stopped. Don't you want it? he said, keeping his face closed to the boy. No, never mind, she said, leave it. The old native kept his head on one side, looking at them sideways, holding the lion. Three-and-six, he murmured, as old people repeat things to themselves.

The young woman drew her head in. She went into the coupé[7] and sat down. Out of the window, on the other side, there was nothing;

Big Idea Colonialism and Postcolonialism *How does this sentence portray European colonists in Africa?*

Vocabulary

career (kə rēr′) *v.* to move or run with a swift headlong motion; to rush or dash along

6. *Three-and-six* is three shillings and sixpence, the equivalent today of somewhere between five and twenty American dollars, depending on the exact time the story takes place.
7. On British trains, a *coupé* is a half-compartment at the end of a passenger car with only one row of seats.

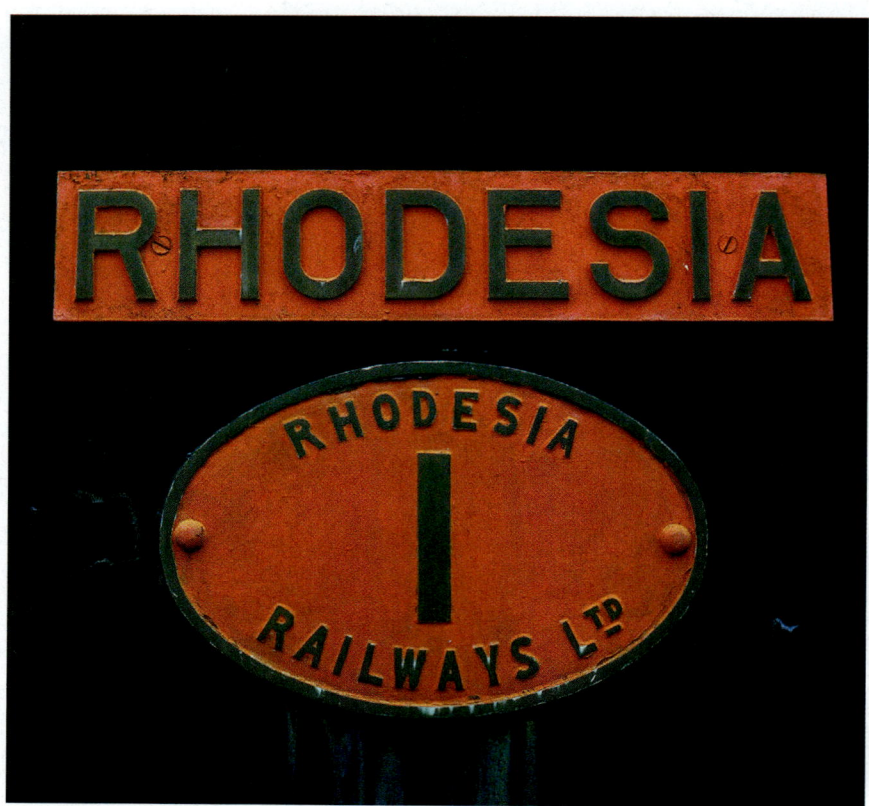

train, clinging to the observation platforms, or perhaps merely standing on the iron step, holding the rail; but on the train, safe from the one dusty platform, the one tin house, the empty sand.

There was a grunt. The train jerked. Through the glass the beer drinkers looked out, as if they could not see beyond it. Behind the fly-screen, the stationmaster's wife sat facing back at them beneath the darkening hunk of meat.

There was a shout. The flag drooped out. Joints not yet coordinated, the segmented body of the train heaved and bumped back against itself. It began to move; slowly the scrolled chalet moved past it, the yells of the natives, running alongside, jetted up into the air, fell back at different levels. Staring wooden faces waved drunkenly, there, then gone, questioning for the last time at the windows. Here, one-and-six baas!—As one automatically opens a hand to catch a thrown ball, a man fumbled wildly down his pocket, brought up the shilling and sixpence and threw them out; the old native, gasping, his skinny toes splaying the sand, flung the lion.

The piccanins were waving, the dogs stood, tails uncertain, watching the train go: past the mud huts, where a woman turned to look, up from the smoke of the fire, her hand pausing on her hip.

The stationmaster went slowly in under the chalet.

The old native stood, breath blowing out the skin between his ribs, feet tense, balanced in the sand, smiling and shaking his head. In his opened palm, held in the attitude of receiving, was the retrieved shilling and sixpence.

sand and bush; a thorn tree. Back through the open doorway, past the figure of her husband in the corridor, there was the station, the voices, wooden animals waving, running feet. Her eye followed the funny little valance of scrolled wood that outlined the chalet roof of the station; she thought of the lion and smiled. That bit of fur round the neck. But the wooden buck, the hippos, the elephants, the baskets that already bulked out of their brown paper under the seat and on the luggage rack! How will they look at home? Where will you put them? What will they mean away from the places you found them? Away from the unreality of the last few weeks? The man outside. But he is not part of the unreality; he is for good now. Odd . . . somewhere there was an idea that he, that living with him, was part of the holiday, the strange places.

Outside, a bell rang. The stationmaster was leaning against the end of the train, green flag rolled in readiness. A few men who had got down to stretch their legs sprang on to the

---

Literary Element **Setting** *What realization about an artifact and its setting does the woman have?*

Big Idea Colonialism and Postcolonialism *What is implied in this passage about the European colonialists' attitude toward, and understanding of, native black Africans?*

The blind end of the train was being pulled helplessly out of the station.

The young man swung in from the corridor, breathless. He was shaking his head with laughter and triumph. Here! he said. And waggled the lion at her. One-and-six!

What? she said.

He laughed. I was arguing with him for fun, bargaining—when the train had pulled out already, he came tearing after. . . . One-and-six Baas! So there's your lion.

She was holding it away from her, the head with the open jaws, the pointed teeth, the black tongue, the wonderful ruff of fur facing her. She was looking at it with an expression of not seeing, of seeing something different. Her face was drawn up, **wryly,** like the face of a discomforted child. Her mouth lifted nervously at the corner. Very slowly, cautious, she lifted her finger and touched the mane, where it was joined to the wood.

But how could you, she said. He was shocked by the dismay of her face.

Good Lord, he said, what's the matter?

If you wanted the thing, she said, her voice rising and breaking with the shrill impotence of anger, why didn't you buy it in the first place? If you wanted it, why didn't you pay for it? Why didn't you take it decently, when he offered it? Why did you have to wait for him to run after the train with it, and give him one-and-six? One-and-six!

She was pushing it at him, trying to force him to take it. He stood astonished, his hands hanging at his sides.

But you wanted it! You liked it so much?

—It's a beautiful piece of work, she said fiercely, as if to protect it from him.

You liked it so much! You said yourself it was too expensive—

Oh *you*—she said, hopeless and furious. *You.* . . . She threw the lion on to the seat.

He stood looking at her.

She sat down again in the corner and, her face slumped in her hand, stared out of the window. Everything was turning round inside her. One-and-six. One-and-six. One-and-six for the wood and the carving and the **sinews** of the legs and the switch of the tail. The mouth open like that and the teeth. The black tongue, rolling, like a wave. The mane round the neck. To give one-and-six for that. The heat of shame mounted through her legs and body and sounded in her ears like the sound of sand pouring. Pouring, pouring. She sat there, sick. A weariness, a tastelessness, the discovery of a void made her hands slacken their grip, atrophy[8] emptily, as if the hour was not worth their grasp. She was feeling like this again. She had thought it was something to do with singleness, with being alone and belonging too much to oneself.

She sat there not wanting to move or speak, or to look at anything, even; so that the mood should be associated with nothing, no object, word or sight that might recur and so recall the feeling again. . . . Smuts blew in grittily, settled on her hands. Her back remained at exactly the same angle, turned against the young man sitting with his hands drooping between his sprawled legs, and the lion, fallen on its side in the corner.

The train had cast the station like a skin. It called out to the sky, I'm coming, I'm coming; and again, there was no answer. ❧

---

8. Here, *atrophy* means "go slack; weaken."

Big Idea **Colonialism and Postcolonialism** *What epiphany, or sudden realization, does the woman experience in this passage?*

Reading Strategy **Visualizing** *What does the body language of each character symbolize?*

RESPONDING AND THINKING CRITICALLY

Respond

1. Were you surprised by the woman's reaction to her husband's "bargain"? Explain.

Recall and Interpret

2. (a)At the beginning of the story, who is waiting for the train? (b)How do these people differ from the passengers?

3. (a)Describe the artifact the old man wants to sell to the woman. (b)What does the description of the artifact imply about its value?

4. (a)Why does the woman decide against buying the carved lion? (b)What does her reaction to her husband's "bargain" suggest about her new perspective?

Analyze and Evaluate

5. The man is confused by the woman's reaction to the purchase. How would you explain to him what she is feeling?

6. What might the train from Rhodesia **symbolize**, or represent, in this story?

7. Gordimer does not use quotation marks to set off the dialogue in this story. How does this aspect of her style affect your reading of the story?

Connect

8. **Big Idea** Colonialism and Postcolonialism
How might the economics at work in this story be viewed as a microcosm, or small-scale representation, of colonial economics?

LITERARY ANALYSIS

Literary Element Setting

In a sense, "The Train from Rhodesia" is a story about setting itself—and about what happens when two very different settings collide. Occupying the world *inside* the train—the European world of tourism and travel—are the woman who admires the merchant's carved lion and the husband who haggles over it "for fun." Occupying the world *outside* the train—the African world of hungry dogs and gray mud huts—is the vendor himself, and others like him, whose livelihood depends upon the "sport" of haggling. As the woman interacts with this foreign setting and its inhabitants, she comes to realize that she lives in a fantasy world and that the real world exists outside the train. By juxtaposing these two settings, Gordimer also invites the reader to expand or revise his or her view of Africa—to consider how it has been altered, and in some ways infected, by its colonial history.

1. Why do you think Gordimer does not specify the exact time and place of the story?

2. One result of the contact between the two worlds is that the lion carving becomes cheapened. What else—or who else—becomes cheapened in the transaction? Explain.

Review: Symbol

As you learned on page 1078, a **symbol** is any object, person, place, or experience that exists on a literal level but also represents something beyond itself. Clues to the symbolism in a story can sometimes be found in the title. For example, "The Train from Rhodesia" suggests that the train itself is a key symbol in Gordimer's story. Stories are not limited to a single symbol, however. Often, objects and events that occur around the central symbol extend or deepen the symbolic power of the story as a whole.

Group Activity Read each quotation from the story in the three examples below. Then discuss possible symbolic meanings of the boldfaced words.

1. "From a piece of string on his gray finger hung a tiny woven basket; he lifted it, questioning. No, no, she urged, **leaning down toward him,** across the height of the train . . . that one, that one, her hand commanded. It was a **lion,** carved out of soft dry wood . . . "

2. "All up and down the length of the train in the dust **the artists** sprang, walking bent, like performing animals, the better to exhibit the fantasy held toward the **faces on the train.**"

3. "The **train** had cast the **station** like a skin."

Reading Strategy — Visualizing

In the same way that an artist arranges people and objects on a canvas, an author arranges people and objects in the space of a story's setting. **Visualizing** these spatial arrangements can help you understand the relationships and conflicts between characters. It can also help you keep track of shifting perspectives, or points of view.

Read each passage from the story below, visualizing the scene being described. Then identify the perspective or the relationship suggested by the description.

1. "Creaking, jerking, jostling, gasping, the train filled the station." (page 1298)

2. "Back through the open doorway, past the figure of her husband in the corridor, there was the station, the voices, wooden animals waving, running feet." (page 1300)

Vocabulary — Practice

Practice with Context Clues For each sentence below, identify the context clues that help you determine the meaning of the boldfaced vocabulary word.

1. The **vendor** searched through his bag of wares to find the item the shopper requested.
   a. searched   **b.** bag   **c.** wares

2. The roller coaster crawled up to the peak and then **careered** toward the ground with thrilling speed.
   a. crawled   **b.** toward   **c.** speed

3. The baby screwed his face up **wryly** and then spat out the spinach.
   a. screwed   **b.** spat   **c.** spinach

4. The muscles and **sinews** in the cheetah's hind legs flexed as the large cat prepared to leap.
   a. cheetah's   **b.** flexed   **c.** cat

Writing About Literature

Analyze Figurative Language Throughout "The Train from Rhodesia," Gordimer personifies the train. It "calls out," "gasps," and "breathes," among other actions. In a brief essay, analyze Gordimer's use of personification in the story. Why do you think she chooses to describe the train this way? What does the personification add to the story? How effective is it? As you write, follow the path below.

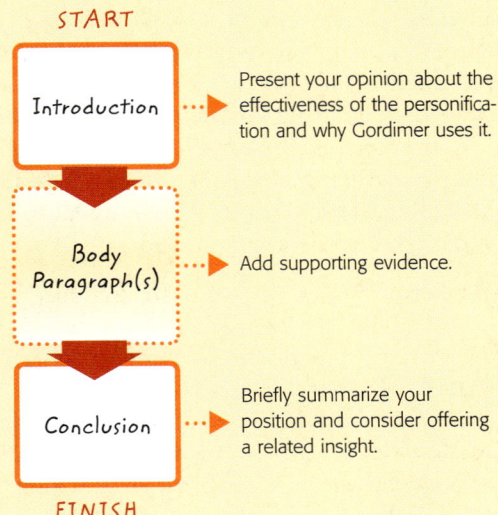

START

Introduction ····▶ Present your opinion about the effectiveness of the personification and why Gordimer uses it.

Body Paragraph(s) ····▶ Add supporting evidence.

Conclusion ····▶ Briefly summarize your position and consider offering a related insight.

FINISH

After you complete your draft, exchange papers with a peer reviewer. Use your peer's suggestions to revise your work. Be sure to proofread your final draft for errors in spelling, grammar, and punctuation.

Interdisciplinary Activity: History

Investigate the major political changes that have occurred in Rhodesia during Gordimer's lifetime. Using a history book, an encyclopedia, or the Internet, find answers to the following questions:

- What effects did British rule have on the native people of Rhodesia?

- When did Northern Rhodesia and Southern Rhodesia become Zambia and Zimbabwe?

- How are these countries governed now?

Take notes on your answers and use them to present a brief oral report to your class.

Dead Men's Path

MEET CHINUA ACHEBE

Nigerian author Chinua Achebe (chē nōō′ ə ə chā′ bā) is considered one of Africa's finest fiction writers. A "strange, early tribute" helped inspire him to pursue a writing career. When he was a university student in Nigeria, a retired English ambassador visited the school and read aloud an amusing limerick Achebe had written. At the time, Achebe had not thought about becoming a writer, but he said, "when I heard my name and nonsense poem recited . . . you could have knocked me over with a feather."

A member of the Ibo (ē′ bō) tribe, Achebe grew up in the village of Ogidi, where his father taught at the local missionary school. His parents, who were devout Protestants, gave him the name Albert. While studying at the University College at Ibadan (which was also the alma mater of prominent Nigerian writer Wole Soyinka), Achebe rejected his European name and adopted the African name Chinualumogu, meaning "My spirit come fight for me." He majored in English literature and decided he wanted to become a writer.

> "At the University I read some appalling European novels about Africa . . . and realized that our story could not be told for us by anyone else."
>
> —Chinua Achebe

Crusader for Biafra From 1954 to 1963, Achebe worked as a producer for the Nigerian Broadcasting Company (NBC) in Lagos, the Nigerian capital. While holding this position, he began his career as a writer with the publication of *Things Fall Apart* (1958), an immediate triumph. In this novel, Achebe explores the traumatic effects of African contact with Western ways. The protagonist of the novel is a proud village leader who refuses to adopt Western culture.

After Nigeria gained independence from England in 1960, Achebe was one of many who grew disillusioned with the new government, a military dictatorship, and attempted to establish a separate nation in eastern Nigeria called Biafra. As chairman of the Biafra National Guidance Committee, Achebe traveled abroad with other writers, seeking support for the Biafran cause. In the ensuing civil war, approximately one million Ibo died fighting for independence, many from disease and starvation. The collapse of Biafra and its reunification with Nigeria in 1970 prompted Achebe to retire from political life and live abroad, devoting himself to writing and teaching.

Acclaimed Novelist In the late 1970s, when Nigeria once again became a republic, Achebe returned to his native country. A car accident near Lagos in 1990 left him paralyzed below the waist and confined to a wheelchair. He then accepted a teaching position at Bard College in New York.

Achebe's fiction, remarkable for its psychological depth and social insight, is popular throughout the world. In addition to *Things Fall Apart,* his novels include *No Longer at Ease* (1960), *Arrow of God* (1964), *A Man of the People* (1966), and *Anthills of the Savannah* (1987).

Chinua Achebe was born in 1930.

Literature Online **Author Search** For more about Chinua Achebe, go to www.glencoe.com.

Connecting to the Story

History often involves the age-old struggle between the new and the old, the modern and the traditional. Achebe's story reflects this conflict. As you read, think about the following questions:

- What do the words *modern* and *traditional* suggest to you?
- Is progress always a good thing?

Building Background

This story is set in a mission school near a small village in Nigeria in 1949. At that time, Nigeria was still a British colony, and Western ideas were sweeping across Africa. Mission schools sought to give students a solid academic education and to instruct them in Christian beliefs and traditions so that they would put aside the pagan ways of their ancestors. Many of Achebe's stories depict the effects of Western cultures on African traditions. He wrote: "We have been subjected—and have subjected ourselves too—to this period during which we have accepted everything alien as good and practically everything local or native as inferior."

Setting Purposes for Reading

Big Idea Colonialism and Postcolonialism

As you read "Dead Men's Path," consider what happens when old African ways come into conflict with new Western ideas.

Literary Element Conflict

A **conflict,** or struggle between two opposing forces, is central to all plots. In an **external conflict,** the main character struggles against an outside force. This force may be another character, society, nature, or fate. As you read, notice the external conflict in this story.

- See Literary Terms Handbook, p. R4.

Literature Online Interactive Literary Elements Handbook To review or learn more about the literary elements, go to www.glencoe.com.

Reading Strategy Analyzing Characterization

When you **analyze characterization,** you identify the main qualities that make up a character's personality and then determine how they affect events in the story. **Characterization** refers to the methods that authors use to reveal characters. These methods include describing a character's appearance, actions, speech, and thoughts.

Reading Tip: Mapping Character Use a web to map the character of Michael Obi. Create additional webs for Obi's wife and the village priest.

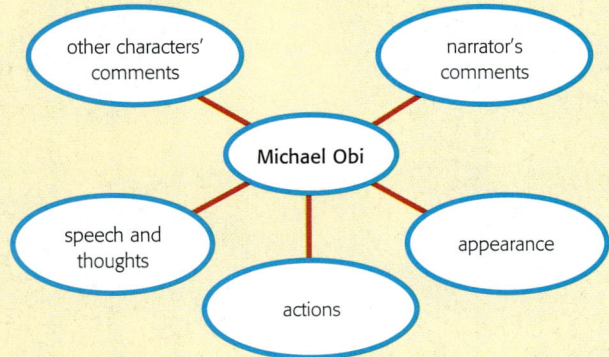

Vocabulary

pivotal (piv′ ət əl) *adj.* of central or vital importance; p. 1306 *Maria's experiences in the army were pivotal in developing her character.*

denigration (den′ i grā′ shən) *n.* defamation of one's character or reputation; slander; p. 1307 *The leader suffered ongoing denigration from his enemies and a hostile press.*

superannuated (soo′ pər an′ ū ā′ tid) *adj.* out of date; p. 1307 *The teenager considered her mother old-fashioned and her taste in clothes superannuated.*

Vocabulary Tip: Analogies Analogies are comparisons based on relationships between ideas.

OBJECTIVES
In studying this selection, you will focus on the following:
- analyzing literary periods
- understanding conflict
- analyzing characterization

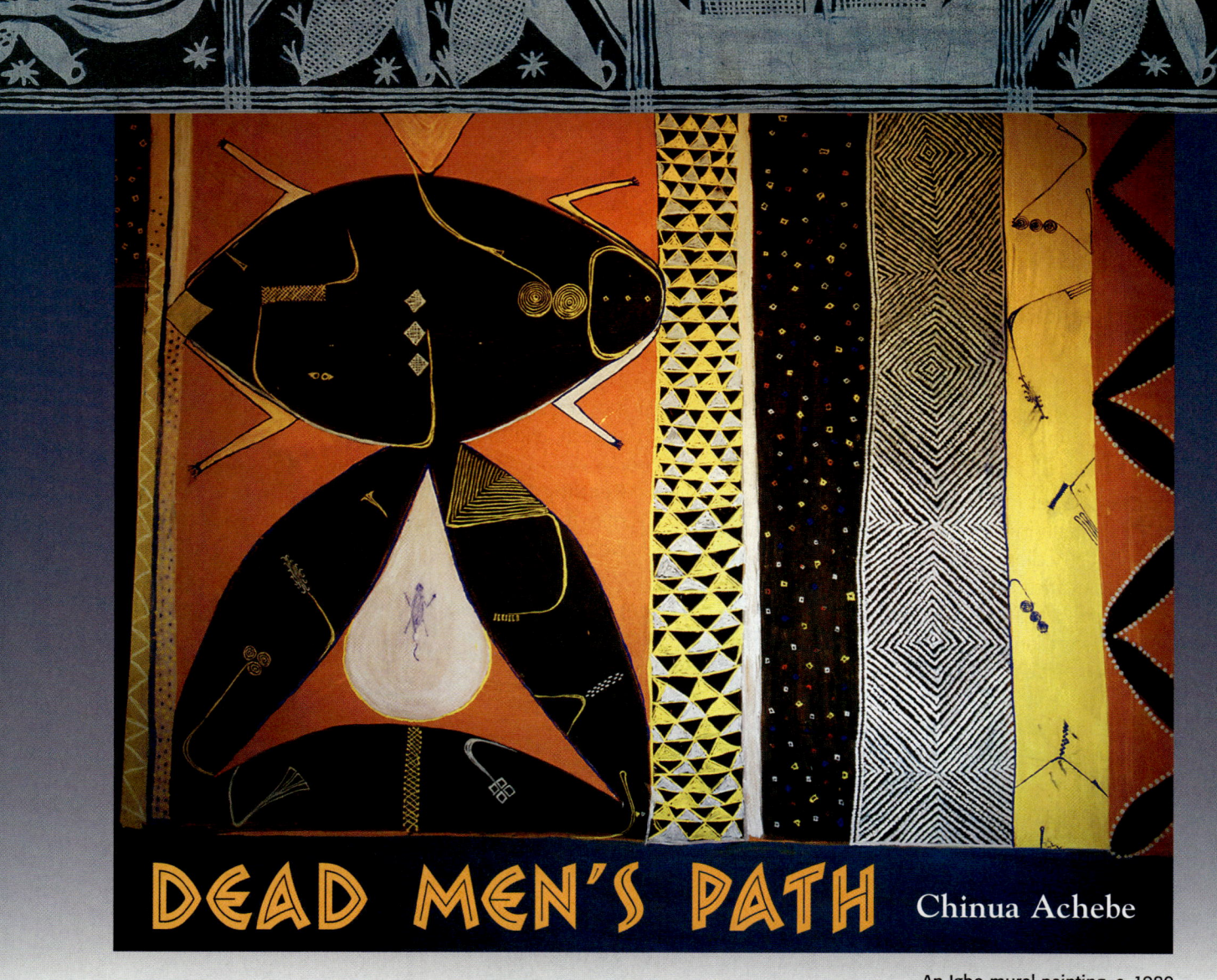

DEAD MEN'S PATH

Chinua Achebe

An Igbo mural painting, c. 1980.

Michael Obi's hopes were fulfilled much earlier than he had expected. He was appointed headmaster of Ndume Central School in January 1949. It had always been an unprogressive school, so the Mission authorities decided to send a young and energetic man to run it. Obi accepted this responsibility with enthusiasm. He had many wonderful ideas and this was an opportunity to put them into practice. He had had sound secondary school education which designated him a "**pivotal**

teacher" in the official records and set him apart from the other headmasters in the mission field. He was outspoken in his condemnation[1] of the narrow views of these older and often less-educated ones.

"We shall make a good job of it, shan't we?" he asked his young wife when they first heard the joyful news of his promotion.

---

1. *Condemnation* means "the act of severely disapproving of something."

Vocabulary

pivotal (piv′ ət əl) *adj.* of central or vital importance

Reading Strategy Analyzing Characterization *What strengths and weaknesses does Obi bring to his job?*

"We shall do our best," she replied. "We shall have such beautiful gardens and everything will be just *modern* and delightful . . ." In their two years of married life she had become completely infected by his passion for "modern methods" and his **denigration** of "these old and **superannuated** people in the teaching field who would be better employed as traders in the Onitsha[2] market." She began to see herself already as the admired wife of the young headmaster, the queen of the school.

The wives of the other teachers would envy her position. She would set the fashion in everything . . . Then, suddenly, it occurred to her that there might not be other wives. Wavering between hope and fear, she asked her husband, looking anxiously at him.

"All our colleagues are young and unmarried," he said with enthusiasm which for once she did not share. "Which is a good thing," he continued.

"Why?"

"Why? They will give all their time and energy to the school."

Nancy was downcast. For a few minutes she became skeptical about the new school; but it was only for a few minutes. Her little personal misfortune could not blind her to her husband's happy prospects. She looked at him as he sat folded up in a chair. He was stoop-shouldered and looked frail. But he sometimes surprised people with sudden bursts of physical energy. In his present posture, however, all his bodily strength seemed to have retired behind his deep-set eyes, giving them an extraordinary power of penetration. He was only twenty-six, but looked thirty or more. On the whole, he was not unhandsome.

"A penny for your thoughts, Mike," said Nancy after a while, imitating the woman's magazine she read.

"I was thinking what a grand opportunity we've got at last to show these people how a school should be run."

Ndume School was backward in every sense of the word. Mr. Obi put his whole life into the work, and his wife hers too. He had two aims. A high standard of teaching was insisted upon, and the school compound[3] was to be turned into a place of beauty. Nancy's dream-gardens came to life with the coming of the rains, and blossomed. Beautiful hibiscus and allamanda hedges in brilliant red and yellow marked out the carefully tended school compound from the rank neighborhood bushes.

One evening as Obi was admiring his work he was scandalized to see an old woman from the village hobble right across the compound, through a marigold flower bed and the hedges. On going up there he found faint signs of an almost disused path from the village across the school compound to the bush on the other side.

"It amazes me," said Obi to one of his teachers who had been three years in the school, "that you people allowed the villagers to make use of this footpath. It is simply incredible." He shook his head.

"The path," said the teacher apologetically, "appears to be very important to them. Although it is hardly used, it connects the village shrine with their place of burial."

"And what has that got to do with the school?" asked the headmaster.

"Well, I don't know," replied the other with a shrug of the shoulders. "But I remember there was a big row[4] some time ago when we attempted to close it."

---

2. *Onitsha* is a commercial city in Nigeria.

Big Idea Colonialism and Postcolonialism *How has modernization affected young Nigerians like Obi's wife?*

Vocabulary

denigration (den´ i grā´ shən) *n.* defamation of one's character or reputation; slander
superannuated (soo͞´ pər an´ ū ā´ tid) *adj.* out of date

3. A *compound* is a group of buildings.
4. As it is used here, a *row* (rou) is a noisy disturbance or quarrel.

Reading Strategy Analyzing Characterization *What does this detail reveal about Obi?*

"That was some time ago. But it will not be used now," said Obi as he walked away. "What will the Government Education Officer think of this when he comes to inspect the school next week? The villagers might, for all I know, decide to use the schoolroom for a pagan[5] ritual during the inspection."

Heavy sticks were planted closely across the path at the two places where it entered and left the school premises. These were further strengthened with barbed wire.

Three days later the village priest of *Ani* called on the headmaster. He was an old man and walked with a slight stoop. He carried a stout walking stick which he usually tapped on the floor, by way of emphasis, each time he made a new point in his argument.

"I have heard," he said after the usual exchange of cordialities, "that our ancestral footpath has recently been closed . . . "

"Yes," replied Mr. Obi. "We cannot allow people to make a highway of our school compound."

"Look here, my son," said the priest bringing down his walking stick, "this path was here before you were born and before your father was born. The whole life of this village depends on it. Our dead relatives depart by it and our ancestors visit us by it. But most important, it is the path of children coming in to be born . . . "

Mr. Obi listened with a satisfied smile on his face.

"The whole purpose of our school," he said finally, "is to eradicate just such beliefs as that. Dead men do not require footpaths. The whole idea is just fantastic. Our duty is to teach your children to laugh at such ideas."

"What you say may be true," replied the priest, "but we follow the practices of our fathers. If you reopen the path we shall have nothing to quarrel about. What I always say is: let the hawk perch and let the eagle perch." He rose to go.

"I am sorry," said the young headmaster. "But the school compound cannot be a thoroughfare. It is against our regulations. I would suggest your constructing another path, skirting our premises. We can even get our boys to help in building it. I don't suppose the ancestors will find the little detour too burdensome."

"I have no more words to say," said the priest, already outside.

Two days later a young woman in the village died in childbed. A diviner[6] was immediately consulted and he prescribed heavy sacrifices to propitiate[7] ancestors insulted by the fence.

Obi woke up next morning among the ruins of his work. The beautiful hedges were torn up not just near the path but right round the school, the flowers trampled to death and one of the school buildings pulled down . . . That day, the white Supervisor came to inspect the school and wrote a nasty report on the state of the premises but more seriously about the "tribal-war situation developing between the school and the village, arising in part from the misguided zeal[8] of the new headmaster." ❧

---

5. *Pagan* means "relating to a religion that involves many gods."

Literary Element Conflict *What conflict does Obi's assertion set in motion?*

Reading Strategy Analyzing Characterization *What does the village priest value?*

---

6. A *diviner* is a fortune teller.
7. To *propitiate* is to appease.
8. *Zeal* is earnest enthusiasm.

Literary Element Conflict *How does the Supervisor's assessment of the conflict differ from Obi's?*

RESPONDING AND THINKING CRITICALLY

Respond

1. Were you surprised by the end of the story? Why or why not?

Recall and Interpret

2. (a)What do the Obis hope to accomplish when they take charge of the school? (b)How might the path stand in the way of what Mr. Obi has set out to accomplish?

3. (a)Why is the path important to the villagers? (b)What can you infer about the villagers' attitudes toward their ancestors and their heritage? Support your inference with evidence from the story.

4. (a)What **proverb**, or short saying, does the village priest tell Mr. Obi he always says? (b)What message is the village priest trying to convey to Mr. Obi through this proverb?

Analyze and Evaluate

5. (a)What qualities do you think are important in a headmaster? (b)Which of these qualities do you think Mr. Obi possesses?

6. How well does Achebe express the differences between modern and traditional values? Do you think he is fair in his portrayal? Explain.

7. With his training and attitudes, do you think Mr. Obi could have reacted any differently to the problems he encountered? Explain.

Connect

8. Big Idea **Colonialism and Postcolonialism** What does this story suggest about the way people should treat another culture's traditional beliefs?

DAILY LIFE AND CULTURE

Life in a Nigerian Village

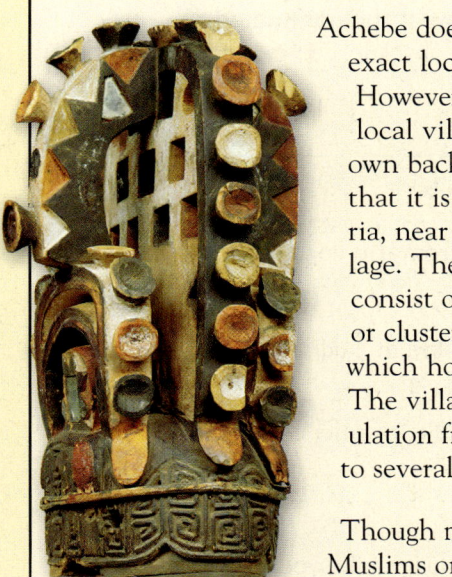

Achebe does not specify the exact location of his story. However, the habits of the local villagers—and Achebe's own background—suggest that it is set in eastern Nigeria, near a traditional Ibo village. These villages usually consist of several compounds, or clusters of huts, each of which houses a single family. The villages can range in population from several hundred to several thousand.

Though most Nigerians are Muslims or Christians, ancient tribal beliefs still persist. The Ibo, for example, traditionally believed in a god so powerful that he had to be approached through lesser deities, each affiliated with

a different Ibo village. The Ibo view death as the transition between the human and the spirit world. After a sojourn in the spirit world, the soul is believed to be reborn into a new life.

Each village is served by a priest or priestess who advises in spiritual matters and presides over religious rituals and ceremonies. Additionally, people known as diviners seek to discern and report the will of the gods. The diviner's message from the gods guides decision-making for the individual and the community.

Group Activity Discuss the following questions with your classmates.

1. Which aspects of traditional Ibo life are reflected in "Dead Men's Path"?

2. What evidence does the story provide of the importance of the diviner in village life?

Igbo mask with knobbed headgear.

Literary Element Conflict

In an **external conflict,** the main character is not always a "good" character, nor is the outside force with which he or she struggles always "bad."

1. What is the outside force with which Obi struggles?

2. How is the external conflict resolved?

3. How might the story have ended if Obi had followed the village priest's advice?

Review: Irony

As you learned on page 851, **irony** is a contrast or discrepancy between expectation and reality. **Situational irony** occurs when the outcome of a situation is the opposite of what someone expected.

Partner Activity With a partner, identify and explain the ironies in this story. Use a diagram like the following to record your information.

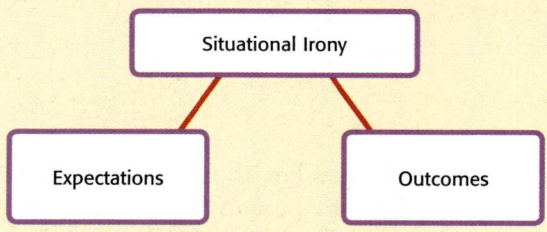

Situational Irony

Expectations   Outcomes

Igbo mask, Leja Village

Reading Strategy Analyzing Characterization

As you **analyze characterization,** remember that by carefully selecting details, an author controls the reader's impression of a character. Review the character web you completed on page 1305, and then answer the following questions.

1. What are Michael Obi's chief personality traits?

2. Choose one of Obi's actions listed in your web. How does that action help drive the plot forward?

3. What are Obi's wife's main qualities?

4. Who is more tolerant, Obi or the village priest? Explain.

Vocabulary Practice

Practice with Analogies Choose the word that best completes each analogy.

1. extraneous : irrelevant :: pivotal :
   a. central **b.** dispensable **c.** ambiguous

2. explication : interpretation :: denigration :
   a. integration **b.** instigation **c.** defamation

3. superficial : shallow :: superannuated :
   a. desultory **b.** obsolete **c.** extensive

Academic Vocabulary

Here are two words from the vocabulary list on page R82.

consequent (kon′ sə kwent′) *adj.* following as a result of

regulate (reg′ yə lāt′) *v.* to rule, control, or direct

Practice and Apply

1. What happens because of the young woman's death in childbirth and the villagers' **consequent** distress?

2. How does Obi attempt to **regulate** the villagers' activities?

Writing About Literature

Respond to Theme Almost every culture has characteristic **proverbs** and other sayings that express rules of conduct or make general observations about life. Chinua Achebe is well-known for incorporating Ibo proverbs into his fiction. For example, the proverb spoken by the village priest, "let the hawk perch and let the eagle perch," provides the nugget of wisdom that might have resolved the conflict amicably in this story. Create a brief dialogue between any two characters in this story. In the dialogue, have one of the characters say a proverb.

First, brainstorm with a group of classmates a list of themes that the story conveys about topics such as *ambition, tradition, innovation,* or *compromise.* Then, choose one of these themes and discuss images from nature that might help illustrate the message. You might want to organize your thoughts in a graphic.

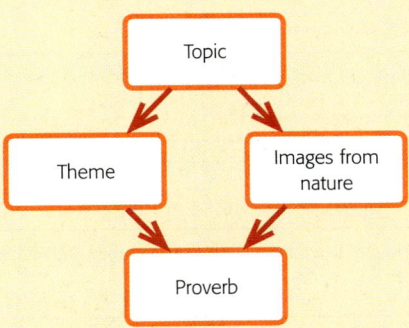

Finally, write down several possible proverbs, and then choose one that is catchy, clear, and concise to incorporate into your dialogue. Exchange your completed dialogue with a classmate and offer suggestions for revision. Then proofread your work for errors in spelling, grammar, and punctuation.

Learning for Life

Imagine that you have been asked to write a classified advertisement for Obi's successor at Ndume Central School. What qualifications should the next headmaster have? Keep in mind what the mission authorities would want for their school as you write your ad.

Achebe's Language and Style

Punctuating Dialogue Conversation between characters in a literary work is known as **dialogue.** Authors usually indicate dialogue by placing quotation marks before and after each character's words. Sometimes, though, a character's words are interrupted with an attribution, or an identifying phrase. Consider, for example, this sentence from "Dead Men's Path":

"Yes," **replied Mr. Obi.** "We cannot allow people to make a highway of our school compound."

This attribution is a simple one, identifying Mr. Obi as the speaker. Other attributions may provide additional information about the speaker's actions, manner, or audience, as in the following examples:

A: "It amazes me," **said Obi to one of his teachers who had been three years in the school,** "that you people allowed the villagers to make use of this footpath."

B: "The path," **said the teacher apologetically,** "appears to be very important to them."

C: "Look here, my son," **said the priest bringing down his walking stick,** "this path was here before you were born and before your father was born."

In example A, the prepositional phrase "to one of his teachers . . ." identifies the person addressed. In example B, the adverb *apologetically* tells how the teacher speaks. And in example C, the participial phrase "bringing down his walking stick" describes the speaker's accompanying actions.

Activity Scan the story for additional examples of attributions in the dialogue and explain what each attribution conveys to the reader.

Revising Check

Attributions Using attributions can add clarity and vividness to your dialogue. With a partner, review the dialogue you created for the Writing About Literature assignment. Note places where the insertion of an attribution would make the dialogue clearer or provide needed context. Revise your draft accordingly.

Vocabulary Workshop

Distinct Meanings

▶ **Vocabulary Terms**

Homophones are words that are pronounced the same yet have completely different meanings and spellings.

▶ **Test-Taking Tip**

To decipher the meaning of a homophone, look for context clues. These clues will help you tell what meaning is intended.

▶ **Reading Handbook**

For more about vocabulary development, see Reading Handbook, p. R20.

eFlashcards For eFlashcards and other vocabulary activities, go to www.glencoe.com.

OBJECTIVES
• Recognize homophones.
• Use homophones correctly in context.

Understanding Homophones

"'What will the Government Education Officer think of this when he comes to inspect the school next week?'"

> —Chinua Achebe, from "Dead Men's Path"

Connecting to Literature In this passage from "Dead Men's Path," Chinua Achebe uses the homophone *week*. **Homophones** are words that have different meanings and spellings yet share the same pronunciation. *Week* is a homophone because it has two meanings that are spelled differently but pronounced the same. For example, *week* means "a series of seven days" and *weak* means "frail."

Here is a brief list of homophones:

Word	Meaning	Example
bear	an animal; to cope	The brown *bear* came dangerously close to camp.
bare	lacking clothing	The doctor examined his *bare* shoulder.
break	to crack, split, or smash	Enslaved people endeavored to *break* their bonds.
brake	to stop a movement	The negligent driver failed to *brake* for the pedestrian.
piece	a part of something	I completed the last *piece* of the puzzle.
peace	tranquility	During war, people long for *peace*.
stairs	a series of steps	Take the *stairs* because it's quicker than the elevator.
stares	fixed gazes	The new student was intimidated by the *stares* of the class.
scent	an odor	The *scent* of oranges makes me feel refreshed.
cent	a denomination of money	I wouldn't pay one *cent* to see that movie.
sent	shipped off	I *sent* her to the store for some milk.

When you are unsure about the meaning of a homophone, use context clues to decipher the meaning or consult a dictionary. Remember, a computer's spell-check program cannot identify incorrect homophones. Because a computer cannot discern the meaning you intend, it will only tell you whether the word is spelled correctly. By carefully proofreading your work, you will eliminate any mistakes with homophones.

Exercise

Choose the correct homophone in each sentence.

1. Michael Obi was enthralled with knew / new ways of doing things.
2. Michael Obi did not want to hear / here what the tribal priest had to say.
3. Michael and his wife, Nancy, lost sight / site of the sacred values of African culture.
4. I found "Dead Men's Path" to be an interesting and thoughtful tail / tale.

Telephone Conversation

MEET WOLE SOYINKA

Wole Soyinka (wä′ lä shä ying′ ka) has earned an international reputation as one of the most distinguished and powerful voices for social change and human rights. His plays, poetry, novels, and essays have not only helped to introduce the world to the traditions and folklore of Africa, but they have also exposed Nigeria's struggles with colonial rule, oppression and injustice, dictatorship, modernization, and civil war. As Soyinka has said, "Books and all forms of writing have always been objects of terror to those who seek to suppress the truth."

"I have one abiding religion—human liberty . . . my writing grows more and more preoccupied with the theme of the oppressive boot, the irrelevance of the color of the foot that wears it and the struggle for individuality."

—Wole Soyinka

Cultural Conflicts Soyinka was born in Nigeria when it was still under British rule. His parents were educators and were able to provide him with a strong English education. Soyinka's grandfather taught him about African tradition and the Yoruba gods and folklore, which influenced his later writing. Thus, from an early age, Soyinka was keenly aware of the cultural conflicts between African tradition and British modernization. Soyinka's lifelong political activism was inspired during his childhood by the independence movement in Nigeria and a revolt against a tax on women led by his mother. Soyinka graduated from college in England in 1958 and returned to Nigeria in 1960, shortly after the country gained its independence.

A Voice of Truth In 1966 a military coup overthrew the freely elected Nigerian government. The next year, a section of the country seceded, forming the Republic of Biafra, and the Nigerian civil war began. In the same year, Soyinka was falsely accused of helping the Biafrans buy jet fighters and was imprisoned for more than two years. The military government kept him in solitary confinement in a four-by-eight-foot cell. To save his sanity and communicate with his supporters, Soyinka manufactured his own ink and began a diary using anything he could find to write on—toilet paper, cigarette packages, and book pages. These notes were later published in *The Man Died: Prison Notes of Wole Soyinka*. Although Soyinka was released in 1969, it would not be the last time he found himself in legal trouble. More than two decades later, he was charged with treason for criticizing the government and sentenced to death, forcing Soyinka into self-imposed exile for four years.

In 1986 Soyinka became the first African to receive the Nobel Prize in Literature, which was a mixed blessing for him. He remarked, "It has such a prestige and such a hold on people's imagination in all corners and on all levels that you become the property of the world."

Wole Soyinka was born in 1934.

Literature Online **Author Search** For more about Wole Soyinka, go to www.glencoe.com.

Connecting to the Poem

In the poem, the speaker recounts a conversation in which a potential tenant's race becomes an issue with a landlord. As you read, think about the following questions:

- Have you ever faced some type of discrimination?
- How did you react to the situation? What emotions did you experience?

Building Background

African tradition was an important part of Soyinka's childhood and has played an essential and recurring role in his work. In 1960 Soyinka began researching Yoruba drama and folklore, and his novels, plays, and poetry blend these traditions with traditional European form. "Telephone Conversation" reflects his ability as a playwright to create dramatic dialogue that uses irony and humor to satirize an encounter with racial prejudice.

Setting Purposes for Reading

Big Idea Colonialism and Postcolonialism

As you read, notice how Soyinka uses imagery and dialogue to record an encounter with racial prejudice.

Literary Element Free Verse

Poetry that has no fixed pattern of meter, rhyme, line length, or stanza arrangement is called **free verse.** As you read Soyinka's poem, notice how he uses techniques such as repetition and alliteration to create lyrical patterns; also note his use of irony and imagery to emphasize meaning and capture the formlessness, prejudice, and discrimination that he perceives in modern life.

- See Literary Terms Handbook, p. R7.

Literature Online **Interactive Literary Elements Handbook** To review or learn more about the literary elements, go to www.glencoe.com.

Reading Strategy Connecting to Contemporary Issues

Connecting means linking what you read to events in your own life, to world events, or to other selections you have read. To **connect to contemporary issues,** compare how issues in a text have been treated over time and how they are treated today.

Reading Tip: Comparing and Contrasting Use a Venn diagram to compare today's issues of racism and prejudice with those in "Telephone Conversation."

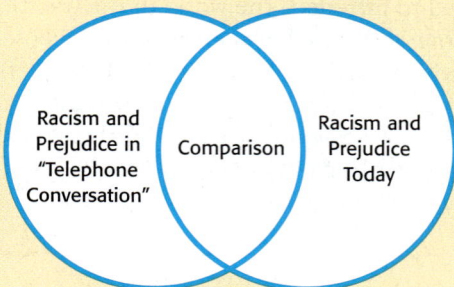

Racism and Prejudice in "Telephone Conversation" — Comparison — Racism and Prejudice Today

Vocabulary

rancid (ran´ sid) *adj.* having an offensive or foul odor or taste; p. 1316 *The rancid food smelled like garbage.*

revelation (rev´ ə lā´ shən) *n.* the act of making something known; something that is revealed; p. 1316 *Her revelation brought attention to the way society discriminated against women.*

assent (ə sent´) *v.* to agree to something after consideration; concur; p. 1316 *He would assent only after he carefully analyzed all of his options.*

friction (frik´ shən) *n.* the clashing between two people or groups of opposed views; p. 1316 *After their argument, the friction between the couple was evident to us all.*

Vocabulary Tip: Synonyms Synonyms are words that have the same or nearly the same meaning.

OBJECTIVES
In studying this selection, you will focus on the following:
- analyzing genre elements
- analyzing free verse
- connecting to contemporary issues

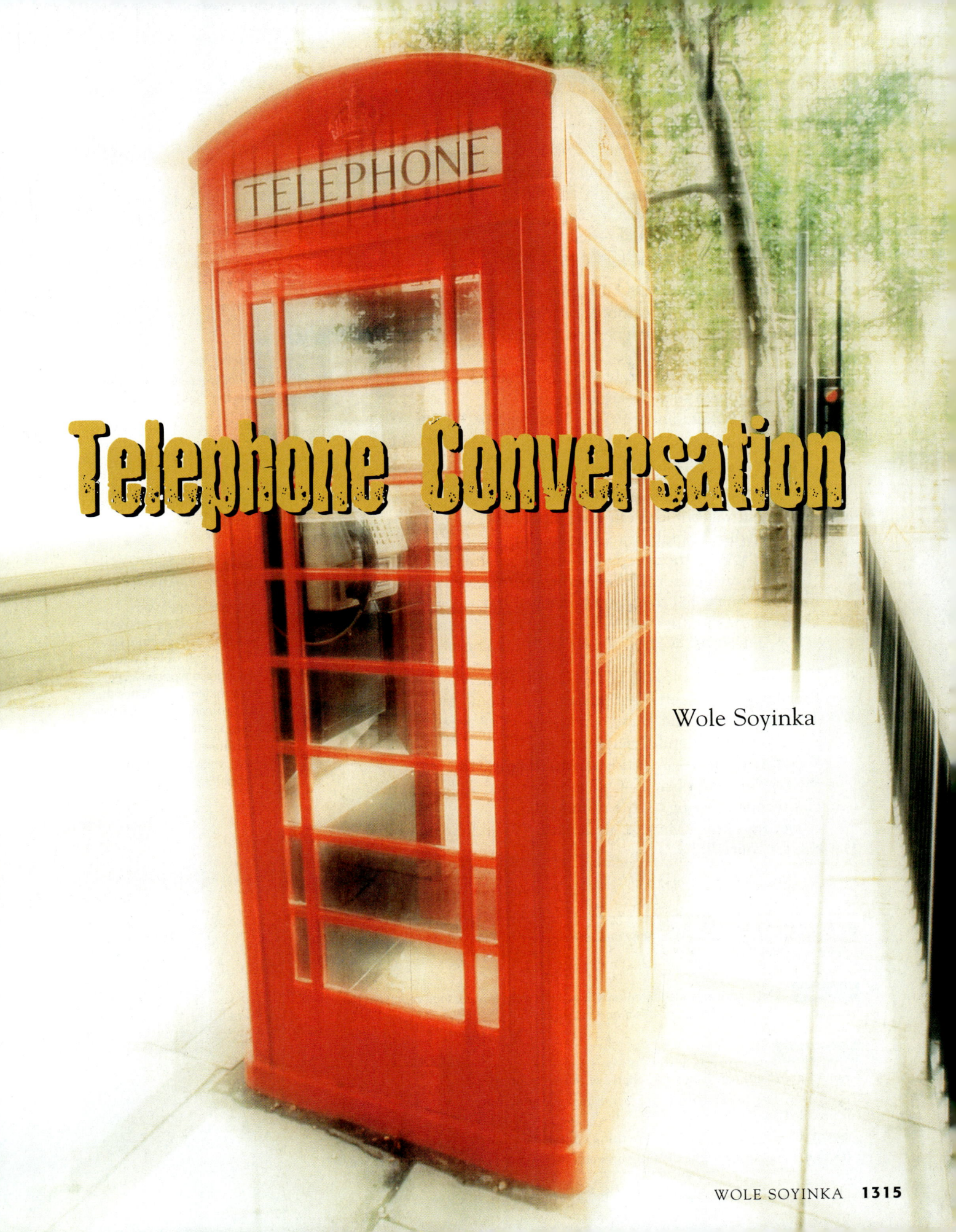

Telephone Conversation

Wole Soyinka

The price seemed reasonable, location
Indifferent. The landlady swore she lived
Off premises. Nothing remained
But self-confession. "Madam," I warned,
5 "I hate a wasted journey—I am—African."
Silence. Silenced transmission of
Pressurized good breeding. Voice, when it came,
Lipstick-coated, long gold-rolled
Cigarette-holder pipped. Caught I was, foully.

10 "HOW DARK?" . . . I had not misheard . . . "ARE YOU LIGHT
OR VERY DARK?" Button B. Button A. Stench
Of **rancid** breath of public hide-and-speak.
Red booth. Red pillar-box.[1] Red double-tiered
Omnibus[2] squelching tar. It *was* real! Shamed
15 By ill-mannered silence, surrender
Pushed dumbfoundment to beg simplification.
Considerate she was, varying the emphasis—

"ARE YOU DARK? OR VERY LIGHT?" **Revelation** came.
"You mean—like plain or milk chocolate?"
20 Her **assent** was clinical, crushing in its light
Impersonality. Rapidly, wavelength adjusted,
I chose, "West African sepia"[3]—and as an afterthought,
"Down in my passport." Silence for spectroscopic
Flight of fancy,[4] till truthfulness clanged her accent
25 Hard on the mouthpiece. "WHAT'S THAT?" conceding[5]
"DON'T KNOW WHAT THAT IS." "Like brunette."

"THAT'S DARK, ISN'T IT?" "Not altogether.
Facially, I am brunette, but madam, you should see
The rest of me. Palm of my hand, soles of my feet
30 Are a peroxide blond. **Friction**, caused—
Foolishly madam—by sitting down, has turned
My bottom raven black—One moment madam!"—sensing
Her receiver rearing on the thunderclap
About my ears—"Madam," I pleaded, "Wouldn't you rather
35 See for yourself?"

1. A *pillar-box* is a mailbox.
2. A *double-tiered omnibus* is a bus that has two levels.

3. *Sepia* is a brownish gray to dark olive brown color.

4. A spectroscope is an instrument scientists use to examine the spectrum, or range, of colors in white light. The phrase "spectroscopic flight of fancy" indicates that the woman has paused to consider the range of colors she knows.

5. Here, *conceding* means "admitting."

Literary Element Free Verse *How does the beginning of this selection defy traditional poetic conventions?*

Big Idea Colonialism and Postcolonialism *How does this passage represent the cultural conflict created by colonialism and racism?*

Vocabulary

rancid (ran′ sid) *adj.* having an offensive or foul odor or taste
revelation (rev′ ə lā′ shən) *n.* the act of making something known; something that is revealed
assent (ə sent′) *v.* to agree to something after consideration; concur
friction (frik′ shən) *n.* the clashing between two people or groups of opposed views

RESPONDING AND THINKING CRITICALLY

Respond

1. (a)What is your opinion of the landlady? (b)How might you respond if someone asked you a question similar to the one the landlady asks the speaker?

Recall and Interpret

2. (a)What is the "self-confession" the speaker makes to the landlady? (b)What does his confession imply about his past experience? Explain.

3. (a)What question does the landlady ask the speaker? (b)**Verbal irony** occurs when the meaning of a statement is the reverse of what is meant. How is the word "considerate" in line 17 an example of verbal irony?

4. (a)How does the telephone conversation end? (b)What does the speaker's final plea suggest about his attitude toward the landlady?

5. (a)How would you describe the content of the telephone conversation in lines 18–33? (b)How would you characterize the speaker and the landlady from their conversation and the speaker's comments?

Analyze and Evaluate

6. Humor often points out human failings and the irony found in many situations. How effective is Soyinka's use of humor in presenting the gravity of racism? Explain.

7. How does Soyinka's style help address the sensitive issue of racism? Consider his use of humor, irony, and imagery.

Connect

8. **Big Idea** **Colonialism and Postcolonialism** Soyinka became the first African writer to win a Nobel Prize. How might poems such as "Telephone Conversation" broaden the scope of English literature?

LITERARY ANALYSIS

Literary Element Free Verse

Many twentieth-century poets, striving to emphasize the relationship between form and meaning in a poem, have written in **free verse** to capture the formlessness that they perceive in modern life.

1. Why might Soyinka have wanted this poem to follow natural speech patterns? Explain.

2. From what past tradition might Soyinka be trying to break? Explain.

Writing About Literature

Analyze Tone The **tone** of a text expresses the author's attitude toward his or her subject and audience. Tone is conveyed through word choice, punctuation, structure, and figures of speech. Write a brief essay analyzing the tone of "Telephone Conversation." Consider how the tone of the poem changes as it progresses and examine what that change implies.

Literature Online **Web Activities** For eFlashcards, Selection Quick Checks, and other Web activities, go to www.glencoe.com.

READING AND VOCABULARY

Reading Strategy Connecting to Contemporary Issues

Artists continue to respond to racism and prejudice today.

1. (a)How does Soyinka address the presence of racism and prejudice? (b)Do you think this type of racism still exists? Explain.

2. (a)How do other contemporary artists, such as writers and musicians, address these issues? (b)How do their views and ideas compare with Soyinka's work?

Vocabulary Practice

Practice with Synonyms Identify the synonym for each vocabulary word below.

1. rancid **a.** clean **b.** rotten

2. revelation **a.** insight **b.** reality

3. assent **a.** assure **b.** agree

4. friction **a.** discord **b.** harmony

Two Sheep

MEET JANET FRAME

In 1947 Janet Frame voluntarily checked into a mental institution. Mistakenly diagnosed as schizophrenic, she spent the next eight years in and out of hospitals. In her autobiography, she describes this dark, bleak existence: "I inhabited a territory of loneliness which I think resembles that place where the dying spend their time before death, and from where those who do return living to the world bring inevitably a unique point of view that is a nightmare, a treasure, and a lifelong possession." In fact, Frame's lifelong love of creative writing provided her with an emotional outlet; while hospitalized, she published her first collection of short stories, *The Lagoon*. Amazingly, Frame was scheduled to receive a frontal lobotomy, an operation in which doctors cut nerve fibers in the brain, potentially leaving the patient in a permanently vegetative state. Just before the procedure, however, Frame's doctors informed her that *The Lagoon* had won a prestigious literary award. They cancelled the surgery, and Frame was discharged from the hospital.

> *"It is little wonder that I value writing as a way of life when it actually saved my life."*
>
> —Janet Frame, from *An Autobiography*

Family Misfortunes Janet Frame was born in Dunedin, a city bordering the Pacific Ocean on the southeastern coast of New Zealand. Her father was a railroad worker, and her mother wrote poetry, which she sold to neighbors. After several moves, the family settled in the small town of Oamaru. A shy child, Frame spent her time reading and writing. She became acquainted with illness and tragedy at an early age; her brother had epilepsy, and two of her sisters drowned during childhood. As a young adult, Frame trained to become a teacher. But on the morning she was to receive her final evaluation for certification, she panicked. Greeted by the headmaster and inspector at the start of class, she asked to be excused for a moment, and, as she reported in her autobiography, "I walked out of the room and out of the school, knowing I would never return."

No "Mad Genius" Frame's subsequent breakdown, which led to her numerous stays in psychiatric wards, proved to be a turning point in her life. Following the critical success of *The Lagoon*, she went on to pursue a productive writing career. Readers and critics who knew of Frame's hospitalizations dubbed her a "mad genius," believing that her creative powers sprang from mental instability, but Frame (and a team of London doctors) proved them wrong. During the late 1950s, while living in London, Frame sought an explanation for the loneliness and depression that plagued her at times. After submitting to several interviews and a psychiatric evaluation, she was told that she was not schizophrenic and was not mentally ill.

In her prolific career, Frame published not only short stories but also novels, poetry, and a three-volume autobiography. New Zealand film director Jane Campion adapted Frame's autobiography into the film *An Angel at My Table*. As her fame increased, Frame traveled internationally to promote her work, and lived for brief periods of time in both England and the United States. She returned permanently to her birthplace, Dunedin, in 1997.

Janet Frame was born in 1924 and died in 2004.

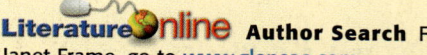 **Author Search** For more about Janet Frame, go to www.glencoe.com.

Connecting to the Fable

In the following fable, Frame uses two talking sheep on their way to a slaughterhouse to teach a life lesson. As you read, think about the following questions:

- If you could see into the future, how do you think it would change your life?
- Do you think that "ignorance is bliss"?

Building Background

Early in her writing career, Frame devoted herself to writing Realist stories. In 1963, however, she turned her attention to allegory. The fable "Two Sheep" was first published in *You Are Now Entering the Human Heart* (1983). A **fable** is a short, often simple story intended to teach a lesson about human behavior. The moral or lesson is usually implied by the plot of the story and then stated explicitly at the end. "Two Sheep" is an example of a beast fable, in which animals talk and act like representative human types. Like many other fables, "Two Sheep" is not set in any specific time or place. Unlike most fables, the moral or lesson is not stated, leaving the reader to infer it.

Setting Purposes for Reading

Big Idea Globalization

As you read, look for ways in which this story illustrates the rich diversity of contemporary English literature.

Literary Element Anthropomorphism

Anthropomorphism is the practice of ascribing human form or characteristics to nonhuman objects or animals. This element is often found in fables, where the main characters are commonly animals that have the ability to speak and think. As you read "Two Sheep," note the various ways in which the animals behave like humans.

- See Literary Terms Handbook, p. R1.

Literature Online **Interactive Literary Elements Handbook** To review or learn more about the literary elements, go to www.glencoe.com.

Reading Strategy Identifying Sequence

To **identify sequence** is to recognize the pattern of organization that a writer uses to present information. In narrative writing, writers often use chronological, or time, order to present a sequence of events in the order in which they happen.

....

Reading Tip: Making a Sequence Chart As you read, identify and record the sequence of events. When you finish reading, study the sequence of events to help determine the moral or lesson of the story.

> *Sequence of Events in "Two Sheep"*
>
> 1. Two sheep are traveling to the saleyards. The first one knows that they are to be slaughtered. The second does not.
> 2.

Vocabulary

pall (pôl) *n.* an atmosphere of dark and gloom; p. 1321 *The rain clouds overhead cast a pall on our picnic.*

barren (bar′ ən) *adj.* having little or no vegetation; bare; p. 1321 *The barren landscape was devoid of all plant life.*

unperturbed (un pər turbd′) *adj.* undisturbed; not troubled; p. 1322 *Dressed in a warm, furry parka, Tom was unperturbed by the subzero temperature.*

Vocabulary Tip: Word Origins A word's origin explains its history and illustrates how the word relates to other words in English and other languages. In a dictionary, a word's origin usually appears in brackets.

OBJECTIVES
In studying this selection, you will focus on the following:
- analyzing genre elements
- recognizing anthropomorphism
- identifying sequence

Two Sheep

Janet Frame

Two sheep were traveling to the saleyards. The first sheep knew that after they had been sold their destination was the slaughterhouse at the freezing works. The second sheep did not know of their fate. They were being driven with the rest of the flock along a hot dusty valley road where the surrounding hills leaned in a sun-scorched wilderness of rock, tussock,[1] and old rabbit warrens.[2] They moved slowly, for the drover[3] in his trap was in no hurry, and had even taken one of the dogs to sit beside him while the other scrambled from side to side of the flock, guiding them.

"I think," said the first sheep who was aware of their approaching death, "that the sun has never shone so warm on my fleece, nor, from what I see with my small sheep's eye, has the sky seemed so flawless, without seams or tucks or cracks or blemishes."

"You are crazy," said the second sheep who did not know of their approaching death. "The sun is warm, yes, but how hot and dusty and heavy my wool feels! It is a burden to go trotting along this oven shelf. It seems our journey will never end."

"How fresh and juicy the grass appears on the hill!" the first sheep exclaimed. "And not a hawk in the sky!"

"I think," replied the second sheep, "that something has blinded you. Just look up in the

---

1. A *tussock* is a clump or tuft of grass.
2. *Warrens* are places where rabbits are kept and bred.
3. A *drover* is one who drives sheep.

Literary Element Anthropomorphism *What human characteristics are attributed to the sheep?*

Reading Strategy Identifying Sequence *What attitude does each sheep express toward his surroundings? What seems odd or ironic about their respective attitudes?*

sky and see those three hawks waiting to swoop and attack us!"

They trotted on further through the valley road. Now and again the second sheep stumbled.

"I feel so tired," he said. "I wonder how much longer we must walk on and on through this hot dusty valley?"

But the first sheep walked nimbly and his wool felt light upon him as if he had just been shorn. He could have gamboled like a lamb in August.

"I still think," he said, "that today is the most wonderful day I have known. I do not feel that the road is hot and dusty. I do not notice the stones and grit that you complain of. To me the hills have never seemed so green and enticing, the sun has never seemed so warm and comforting. I believe that I could walk through this valley forever, and never feel tired or hungry or thirsty."

"Whatever has come over you?" the second sheep asked crossly. "Here we are, trotting along hour after hour, and soon we shall stand in our pens in the saleyards while the sun leans over us with its branding irons and our overcoats are such a burden that they drag us to the floor of our pen where we are almost trampled to death by the so dainty feet of our fellow sheep. A fine life that is. It would not surprise me if after we are sold we are taken in trucks to the freezing works and killed in cold blood. But," he added, comforting himself, "that is not likely to happen. Oh no, that could never happen! I have it on authority that even when they are trampled by their fellows, sheep do not die. The tales we hear from time to time are but malicious rumors, and those vivid dreams which strike us in the night as we sleep on the sheltered hills, they are but illusions. Do you not agree?" he asked the first sheep.

They were turning now from the valley road, and the saleyards were in sight, while drawn up in the siding on the rusty railway lines, the red trucks stood waiting, spattered inside with sheep and cattle dirt and with white chalk marks, in cipher,[4] on the outside. And still the first sheep did not reveal to his companion that they were being driven to certain death.

When they were jostled inside their pen the first sheep gave an exclamation of delight.

"What a pleasant little house they have let to us! I have never seen such smart red-painted bars, and such four-square corners. And look at the elegant stairway which we will climb to enter those red caravans for our seaside holiday!"

"You make me tired," the second sheep said. "We are standing inside a dirty pen, nothing more, and I cannot move my feet in their nicely polished black shoes but I tread upon the dirt left by sheep which have been imprisoned here before us. In fact I have never been so badly treated in all my life!" And the second sheep began to cry. Just then a kind elderly sheep jostled through the flock and began to comfort him.

"You have been frightening your companions, I suppose," she said angrily to the first sheep. "You have been telling horrible tales of our fate. Some sheep never know when to keep things to themselves. There was no need to tell your companion the truth, that we are being led to certain death!"

But the first sheep did not answer. He was thinking that the sun had never blessed him with so much warmth, that no crowded pen had ever seemed so comfortable and luxurious. Then suddenly he was taken by surprise and hustled out a little gate and up the ramp into the waiting truck, and suddenly too the sun shone in its true colors, battering him about the head with gigantic burning bars, while the hawks congregated above, sizzling the sky with their wings, and a **pall** of dust clung to the **barren** used-up hills, and everywhere was commotion, pushing, struggling, bleating, trampling.

"This must be death," he thought, and he began to struggle and cry out.

The second sheep, having at last learned that he would meet his fate at the freezing works,

---

4. Here, *in cipher* means "in code."

Literary Element Anthropomorphism *What human failing is revealed by the second sheep's denials?*

Reading Strategy Identifying Sequence *In what way does the arrival of the third sheep advance the plot of the story?*

Vocabulary

pall (pôl) *n.* an atmosphere of dark and gloom
barren (bar′ ən) *adj.* having little or no vegetation; bare

stood **unperturbed** now in the truck with his nose against the wall and his eyes looking through the slits.

"You are right," he said to the first sheep. "The hill has never seemed so green, the sun has never been warmer, and this truck with its neat red walls is a mansion where I would happily spend the rest of my days."

But the first sheep did not answer. He had seen the approach of death. He could hide from it no longer. He had given up the struggle and was lying exhausted in a corner of the truck. And when the truck arrived at its destination, the freezing works, the man whose duty it was to unload the sheep noticed the first lying so still in the corner that he believed it was dead.

"We can't have dead sheep," he said. "How can you kill a dead sheep?"

So he heaved the first sheep out of the door of the truck onto the rusty railway line.

"I'll move it away later," he said to himself. "Meanwhile here goes with this lot."

And while he was so busy moving the flock, the first sheep, recovering, sprang up and trotted away along the line, out the gate of the freezing works, up the road, along another road, until he saw a flock being driven before him.

"I will join the flock," he said. "No one will notice, and I shall be safe."

While the drover was not looking, the first sheep hurried in among the flock and was soon trotting along with them until they came to a hot dusty road through a valley where the hills leaned in a sun-scorched wilderness of rock, tussock, and old rabbit warrens.

By now he was feeling very tired. He spoke for the first time to his new companions.

"What a hot dusty road," he said. "How uncomfortable the heat is, and the sun seems to be striking me for its own burning purposes."

The sheep walking beside him looked surprised.

"It is a wonderful day," he exclaimed. "The sun is warmer than I have ever known it, the hills glow green with luscious grass, and there is not a hawk in the sky to threaten us!"

"You mean," the first sheep replied slyly, "that you are on your way to the saleyards, and then to the freezing works to be killed."

The other sheep gave a bleat of surprise.

"How did you guess?" he asked.

"Oh," said the first sheep wisely, "I know the code. And because I know the code I shall go around in circles all my life, not knowing whether to think that the hills are bare or whether they are green, whether the hawks are scarce or plentiful, whether the sun is friend or foe. For the rest of my life I shall not speak another word. I shall trot along the hot dusty valleys where the hills are both barren and lush with spring grass.

"What shall I do but keep silent?"

And so it happened, and over and over again the first sheep escaped death, and rejoined the flock of sheep who were traveling to the freezing works. He is still alive today. If you notice him in a flock, being driven along a hot dusty road, you will be able to distinguish him by his timidity, his uncertainty, the frenzied expression in his eyes when he tries, in his condemned silence, to discover whether the sky is at last free from hawks, or whether they circle in twos and threes above him, waiting to kill him. ❧

Literary Element Anthropomorphism *Considering the first sheep's response here, what has he gained from his experiences?*

Reading Strategy Identifying Sequence *As a result of all the things that have happened to him in the story, what does the first sheep resolve to do? Why do you think he reaches this conclusion?*

RESPONDING AND THINKING CRITICALLY

Respond

1. What aspects of this fable did you enjoy most? Why?

Recall and Interpret

2. (a)At the beginning of the story, what does the first sheep know that the second sheep does not? (b)How does the first sheep's knowledge at the beginning affect his perception of his surroundings?

3. (a)How does the first sheep perceive the sun and the hawks after he's been taken by surprise and hustled into the truck? (b)What accounts for the first sheep's change in perception as he stands in the truck?

4. (a)How does the first sheep escape "certain death" at the freezing works? (a)In what way does he not really escape?

5. (a)At the end of the story, what does the first sheep say his life will be like? (b)How will observers be able to distinguish him from the other

sheep traveling to the freezing works? (c)What do these admissions reveal about his attitude toward what he has learned?

Analyze and Evaluate

6. (a)What does the first sheep literally mean when he says, "I know the code"? (b)What might knowing the code mean symbolically? (c)In what ways might one's life be affected by knowing the code?

7. (a)What is the moral of this fable? (b)In your opinion, how effectively does the author convey this moral? Explain.

Connect

8. (a)Do you think the first sheep would have been better off or worse off had he not known his fate? Explain. (b)How are people affected by knowing their fate?

9. **Big Idea** **Globalization** Why might Frame's fable appeal to a variety of worldwide cultures?

VISUAL LITERACY: Photography

Against the Flock

The setting and characters of "Two Sheep" share similarities with Frame's native New Zealand. New Zealand has a population of 3.5 million people, but 60 million sheep. It is one of the major producers of sheep and exporters of wool worldwide. Sheep tend to be timid, remain in flocks, and have almost no protection against predators. These characteristics enhance their literary significance and symbolism. Fables often advance the notion that sheep are innocent, defenseless, and easily led astray. The major themes in Frame's writing, however, complicate any simple reading of the sheep in her story.

1. (a)How does this photo fit traditional perceptions of sheep and what they symbolize? (b)How might this photo relate to the message in Frame's fable?

2. (a)In her fable, how does Frame play with the notion that sheep typically symbolize innocence and defenselessness? (b)Does the photo reinforce or contradict Frame's understanding of conformity? Explain.

Flock of sheep in roadway near Naseby, South Island, New Zealand.

Literary Element Anthropomorphism

Assigning human traits to animal characters in a fable allows writers to teach valuable lessons about life in an engaging, entertaining, and inoffensive way. Review the behavior of the sheep in the fable you have just read.

1. What general human traits or characteristics do the sheep possess?

2. What specific attitudes, emotions, and opinions do they express? Support your answer with examples from the fable.

3. The second sheep convinces himself that being killed at the freezing works "is not likely to happen." Does this seem like a typical human reaction to the concept of approaching death? Explain.

Review: Diction

As you learned on page 854, **diction,** an author's choice of words, is an important component of an author's voice or style. (Other components include sentence structure, choice of sensory details, and use of figures of speech.) In "Two Sheep," Janet Frame uses simple words and dialogue to tell her story.

Partner Activity With a partner, answer these questions:

1. (a)Why is simple language appropriate for a children's fable? (b)In what other ways besides diction does "Two Sheep" resemble a children's fable?

2. (a)In what significant way is "Two Sheep" more like an adult fable than a children's fable? (b)Would using more difficult or sophisticated language increase or decrease the effectiveness of "Two Sheep"? Explain.

Reading Strategy Identifying Sequence

The sequence of events in "Two Sheep" tells a deceptively simple story about a sheep who escapes the slaughterhouse accidentally. The author uses the events in the story (and the characters' reactions to those events) to reveal lessons about life. Review the sequence of events that you recorded in your sequence chart on page 1319.

1. Identify the three events in the story that trigger significant changes in the development or direction of the plot. Explain the significance of each of these events.

2. (a)What observations about life are expressed or implied as the story progresses? (b)What morals or lessons are taught through these observations?

Vocabulary Practice

Practice with Word Origins Match each vocabulary word below with its origin. Use a dictionary if you need help.

1. pall
2. barren
3. unperturbed

a. Middle Welsh *brynar,* meaning "fallow land"

b. Middle English meaning "cloak"

c. root word from Latin *perturbare,* meaning "to throw into confusion"

Academic Vocabulary

Here are two words from the vocabulary list on page R82.

final (fīn' əl) *adj.* at the end; last; ultimate

potential (pə ten' shəl) *n.* possibility; capability

Practice and Apply
1. What **final** destination was intended for the sheep?
2. How did the **potential** for escaping this destination become a reality for the first sheep?

Writing About Literature

Analyze Genre Elements Think of a useful lesson about life that you would like to teach. Then write your own fable, constructing a plot that conveys this truth in a creative way. Your story should be simple and easy to read. Your main characters may be animals or any other nonhumans, but they should possess human characteristics. End your story by explicitly stating the moral. Use a graphic organizer like the one below to plan your story.

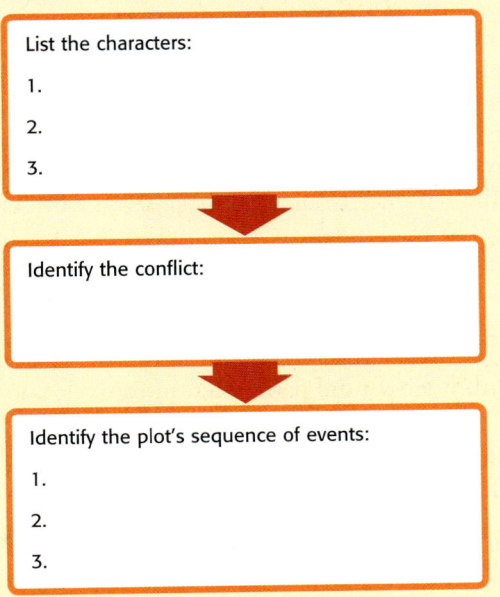

List the characters:

1.

2.

3.

Identify the conflict:

Identify the plot's sequence of events:

1.

2.

3.

Draft your fable, relating the events of the plot according to the sequence you created. Conclude your fable by explicitly stating the moral. After completing the draft, meet with a peer reviewer to evaluate each other's work and to suggest revisions. Then edit and proofread your draft for errors in spelling, grammar, and punctuation.

Listening and Speaking

Readers theater is a presentation in which readers use their voices, facial expressions, and controlled gestures and stances to convey the tone, mood, and action of a work. With a small group of classmates, give a readers theater presentation of "Two Sheep." Assign solo speaking roles to individual members of the group for each of the four characters who speak dialogue in the story, as well as a narrator. After practicing, perform your presentation for the class.

Frame's Language and Style

Using Participles A participle is a verb form that can function as an adjective. Present participles end in *-ing* (*traveling*), and past participles often end in *-ed* (*traveled*) or are irregular (*breaking*, but *broken*). A **participial phrase** is a participle and any complements or modifiers. Participial phrases always act as adjectives. (Be careful not to mistake **gerunds** for participles. Gerunds end in *-ing*, but they function as *nouns.*) When a participle is part of a verb phrase, the participle functions as a *verb*, not an *adjective*. Examine these examples from the story you have just read.

- *Two sheep* **were traveling** *to the saleyards.* (verb phrase)
- *The* **traveling sheep** *were hot and tired.* (present participle as adjective)
- **Having traveled there before**, *they knew the way.* (participial phrase as adjective)
- **Traveling** *was difficult for the sheep.* (gerund as subject)

Note how Frame uses participles and participial phrases as adjectives in "Two Sheep."

Participle	Effectiveness
freezing works	*Freezing works* is a chilling description.
surrounding hills	*Surrounding hills* creates a claustrophobic feeling.

Activity Write a brief paragraph in which you describe an activity or event (for example, playing a game or attending a dance) and include participles used as adjectives. Choose participles that help readers picture your description more vividly.

Revising Check

Participles Work with a partner to revise the word choices you made in the fable you wrote. Find places to add or substitute participles used as adjectives.

Literature Online **Web Activities** For eFlashcards, Selection Quick Checks, and other Web activities, go to www.glencoe.com.

Grammar Workshop

Mechanics

Using Commas with Nonessential Elements

"They were turning now from the valley road, and the saleyards were in sight, while drawn up in the siding on the rusty railway lines, the red trucks stood waiting, spattered inside with sheep and cattle dirt and with white chalk marks, in cipher, on the outside."

—Janet Frame, from "Two Sheep"

Connecting to Literature In her fable "Two Sheep," author Janet Frame uses commas to set off **nonessential elements**, or additional information that interrupts the flow of thought in a sentence. The interruption may be an expression, a comment, a definition, a clarification, supplementary information, or a name. For example, Frame separates "in cipher" in the quotation above, because it is an adjective phrase and the rest of the sentence would still make sense without it.

In determining whether an element is truly essential to the meaning of the sentence, ask yourself if the element fundamentally changes the meaning of the sentence. If it does not, then set if off with commas.

Problem 1 Missing commas with nonessential participles, infinitives, and their phrases

The second sheep moved slowly for they were in no hurry and didn't know what awaited them.

Solution *The second sheep moved slowly, for they were in no hurry and didn't know what awaited them.*

Problem 2 Missing commas with nonessential adjective clauses

Janet Frame who was a talented writer published her first short story collection while she was hospitalized.

Solution *Janet Frame, who was a talented writer, published her first short story collection while she was hospitalized.*

Problem 3 Missing commas with interjections, conjunctive adverbs, and parenthetical expressions.

The sheep in fact is forced to realize the dual nature of reality.

Solution *The sheep, in fact, is forced to realize the dual nature of reality.*

Exercise

Rewrite the following sentences, adding commas where needed.

1. The author of the story Janet Frame led a troubled life.

2. Frame scheduled to have an operation won a literary prize and was released from the hospital.

3. We can however learn from the themes present in "Two Sheep."

▶ **Understanding Nonessential Elements**

Nonessential elements are additional information in a sentence that interrupt the flow of thought. Nonessential elements should be separated from the rest of a sentence by a comma.

▶ **Test-Taking Tip**

When looking over a written test, check to see that no commas are missing. The meaning of a sentence may seem clear to you, but missing commas can make it unclear to a reader.

▶ **Language Handbook**

For more on using commas, see the Language Handbook, pp. R54–R55.

Literature Online

eWorkbooks To link to the Grammar and Language eWorkbook, go to www.glencoe.com.

OBJECTIVES
- Learn how to identify nonessential elements.
- Recognize correct punctuation.

from *Tales of the Islands*

MEET DEREK WALCOTT

Inspired by their schoolteacher mother, Derek Walcott and his twin brother, Roderick, enjoyed reading literature and improvising plays at an early age. Both boys grew up to be writers, following in the footsteps of their father, an amateur poet and artist who died when the boys were only a year old.

> *"The fate of poetry is to fall in love with the world."*
>
> —Derek Walcott

A Young Poet Derek Walcott grew up in a middle-class family on the Caribbean island of Saint Lucia. His father worked for the government and his mother was an elementary school teacher. The arts were valued highly in the Walcott home, and in this enriched environment, Walcott quickly developed a lasting love of art and language. By the time he was eight years old, he had decided to become a poet. In his youth he began a practice of writing a poem a day in the notebooks his mother gave him for this purpose. She also guided him by giving him famous poems to copy and imitate. In this way, Walcott began to internalize different forms of poetry and gain an appreciation of sound devices, rhythm, and cadence.

As a teenager, Walcott had several of his poems published in a local newspaper. When he was eighteen, he borrowed two hundred dollars from his mother and used it to publish his first book of poetry, which he then sold on the streets of Castries, his hometown and the capital of Saint Lucia. The book, *25 Poems*, received good reviews, and Walcott was soon able to pay his mother back for the loan.

Caribbean Theater Although he continued writing poetry, Walcott soon became involved in theater. In 1950 he helped found the Saint Lucia Arts Guild, for which he wrote several plays. He received a fellowship to study theater in New York City in 1958. He continued his involvement with Caribbean theater when he moved to Trinidad in 1959, founding with his brother the Trinidad Theatre Workshop. Walcott's plays often incorporate Caribbean folktales or local history. About writing these plays, Walcott has said, "The great challenge for me was to write as powerfully as I could without writing down to the audience, so that the large emotions could be taken in by a fisherman or a guy on the street, even if he didn't understand every line."

Walcott has written more than thirty plays; *Ti-Jean and His Brothers* (1958) and *Dream on Monkey Mountain* (1967) are two of the most famous. In addition, he wrote an epic poem, *Omeros* (1990), which is based on Homer's *Odyssey*. Walcott received the Nobel Prize in Literature in 1992. In addition to writing poetry and plays, Walcott paints and teaches, dividing his time between the Caribbean and the United States.

Derek Walcott was born in 1930.

Literature Online **Author Search** For more about Derek Walcott, go to www.glencoe.com.

Connecting to the Poem

Leaving a beloved place is the subject of this poem from Walcott's series of poems entitled "Tales of the Islands." As you read the poem, think about the following questions:

- What feelings have you had about leaving a place that you love?
- What wishes have you had related to the place, its future, and your relationship to the place?

Building Background

Saint Lucia is a small island in the eastern Caribbean. It was settled by the French in 1635 and was taken over by the British in 1814. The Europeans cut down forests along the coastal plains to cultivate sugar on large plantations. In the 1700s and early 1800s enslaved Africans were brought to work on the plantations. After slavery was outlawed by Great Britain in 1838, plantation owners brought Asians, especially from the subcontinent of India, to work as indentured servants. The island finally gained independence in 1979.

Setting Purposes for Reading

Big Idea Colonialism and Postcolonialism

Notice the ways in which Walcott refers to French Creole customs and incorporates English literary tradition in this poem.

Literary Element Imagery

The word pictures in a work of literature are called **imagery.** Such images appeal to one or more of the five senses and evoke an emotional response in the reader. Notice the sense that Walcott appeals to the most with the imagery in this poem.

- See Literary Terms Handbook, p. R9.

Literature Online **Interactive Literary Elements Handbook** To review or learn more about the literary elements, go to www.glencoe.com.

Reading Strategy Evaluating Sound Devices

Sound devices include a variety of techniques that writers use to appeal to the ear and to add a musical quality to their writing. Some common sound devices include repetition, rhyme, alliteration, assonance, and caesura. Use the Literary Terms Handbook to review the definition of each of these devices.

Reading Tip: Taking Notes Use a chart like the one below to record examples of the different sound devices in this poem.

Device	Line	Example
Assonance	Epigraph	The vowel sounds in the second syllable of *Adieu* and the first syllable of *foulard* are the same.
Alliteration		
Caesura		
Repetition		
Internal Rhyme		
End Rhyme		

Vocabulary

precipice (pres′ ə pis) *n.* a very steep or overhanging mass of rock as on a cliff; p. 1329 *The precipice plunged into the sea, without even a beach at its base.*

fidelity (fi del′ ə tē) *n.* the quality or state of being faithful; p. 1329 *The fidelity of a true friend is priceless.*

Vocabulary Tip: Synonyms Synonyms are words that have the same or nearly the same meaning.

OBJECTIVES

In studying this poem, you will focus on the following:
- analyzing genre elements
- analyzing imagery
- evaluating sound devices

from
Tales of the Islands

Derek Walcott

Chapter X

"Adieu foulard . . ."[1]

I watched the island narrowing the fine
Writing of foam around the **precipices** then
The roads as small and casual as twine
Thrown on its mountains; I watched till the plane
5 Turned to the final north and turned above
The open channel with the gray sea between
The fishermen's islets[2] until all that I love
Folded in cloud; I watched the shallow green
That broke in places where there would be reef,
10 The silver glinting on the fuselage,[3] each mile
Dividing us and all **fidelity** strained
Till space would snap it. Then, after a while
I thought of nothing; nothing, I prayed, would change;
When we set down at Seawell[4] it had rained.

1. *Adieu foulard* (ə dyü fo͞o
lärd′) is from a folk song
traditionally sung on Saint
Lucia when friends or family
members leave the island.
Adieu is French for "good-bye,"
and a *foulard* is a neckerchief
worn by the people of Saint
Lucia.

2. *Islets* are little islands.

3. A *fuselage* is the central body
of the aircraft.

4. *Seawell* is a city in Barbados.

Literary Element   **Imagery** *From this image, determine where the
speaker is in relation to the roads and mountains.*

Vocabulary

precipice (pres′ ə pis) *n.* a very steep or overhanging mass of rock as
on a cliff
fidelity (fi del′ ə tē) *n.* the quality or state of being faithful

RESPONDING AND THINKING CRITICALLY

Respond

1. What images did you find to be most powerful? Explain.

Recall and Interpret

2. (a)What is the setting of this poem? (b)What is the speaker's attitude toward the subject? What clues helped you figure out the speaker's attitude?

3. (a)What does the speaker pray for in line 13? (b)What does this prayer imply about his feelings as he leaves the island?

Analyze and Evaluate

4. (a)Count the number of lines and analyze the rhyme scheme of this poem. Use this information to identify the form of the poem. (b)In what ways does this poem fit this traditional form? How does it depart from the form?

5. (a)Near the end of the poem, how does the tone change? (b)Do you think this change adds meaning to the poem? Explain.

Connect

6. **Big Idea** Colonialism and Postcolonialism Although English is the official language of Saint Lucia, many people there also speak French Creole. (a)How does the poem pay homage to Saint Lucia's alternate language? (b)How does the poem fit into the tradition of English classics?

LITERARY ANALYSIS

Literary Element Imagery

Images can appeal to any of the five senses. They can be simple references to color, odor, taste, sound, or texture. They can also be more complex, incorporating similes or metaphors.

1. Evaluate Walcott's use of simile in lines 3–4. What comparison is being made? Does this simile help you better envision the scene? Explain.

2. Evaluate Walcott's use of metaphor in lines 11–12. Which sense or senses are being appealed to and what is being likened to what? Does this metaphor help you better understand the speaker's feelings? Explain.

Interdisciplinary Activity: Art

Reread the poem from "Tales of the Islands" several times to help you focus on the poem's tone and mood. Use colored pencils or chalk to illustrate the poem, choosing colors to create a piece of art that depicts both the images in the poem and the tone and the mood of the piece. Share your artwork with the class.

READING AND VOCABULARY

Reading Strategy Evaluating Sound Devices

Refer to the chart you made on page 1328 for examples of assonance and alliteration from the poem. Then answer these questions.

1. How does the use of assonance affect the pace of the poem?

2. Why do you think Walcott uses alliteration at specific points in this poem? Do you think these lines convey dramatic tension or serve some other purpose? Explain.

Vocabulary Practice

Practice with Synonyms Identify the synonym for each vocabulary word below.

1. fidelity   a. faithfulness   b. faithlessness

2. precipice   a. cliff   b. valley

Literature Online Web Activities For eFlashcards, Selection Quick Checks, and other Web activities, go to www.glencoe.com.

B. Wordsworth

MEET V. S. NAIPAUL

V. S. (Vidiadhar Surajprasad) Naipaul chose to become a writer at age eleven because he thought of writing as a noble occupation. However, writing did not come easily for Naipaul. "I do not believe in natural genius. I do not believe in the spontaneous outpouring of the soul. Style is essentially a matter of hard thinking," Naipaul once told writer and poet Derek Walcott in an interview.

Early Years and Education Naipaul was born on the Caribbean island of Trinidad. His grandparents on both sides of his family had come to the West Indies from India as indentured servants. Within a few decades, Naipaul's mother's family had achieved wealth; his father's family had not. However, education was important to his father's family, and Naipaul's father completed school and got a job writing for a Trinidad newspaper. The family moved numerous times, as Naipaul's father changed jobs frequently.

Despite his disrupted childhood, Naipaul was able to gain a good education graduating from Trinidad's most prestigious school. In 1950 he won a government scholarship to attend Oxford University, and he graduated in 1953 with a degree in English.

A Literary Life in London After graduating, Naipaul moved to London. There he got a part-time job with the British Broadcasting Company (BBC) editing and presenting a weekly radio program about literature that was designed for a Caribbean audience. When Naipaul wasn't working on his radio program, he worked toward his goal of becoming a writer. Naipaul's first literary works were based on memories of his years in Trinidad. The novels *The Mystic Masseur* (1957) and *The Suffrage of Elvira* (1958) and the short story collection *Miguel Street* (which contains the story "B. Wordsworth") were well-received by critics and readers. But Naipaul's status as a great author was secured with the publication of *A House for Mr.*

Biswas (1961). The novel's title character is based on Naipaul's father and the work presents a fictionalized account of Naipaul's childhood in Trinidad.

> "A book should speak to you directly. You should be able to pick up things in your own experience and if you can't pick things up, then for you, the book has failed, I think."
>
> —V. S. Naipaul

A Cosmopolitan Writer In 1960 the government of Trinidad gave Naipaul a grant to return to the Caribbean. Based on his travels, he wrote a nonfiction book, *The Middle Passage*, detailing his views of the region. This book was the first of many nonfiction books Naipaul wrote documenting his travels through India, the Middle East, Africa, and the Caribbean. Many of his novels, too, are set in developing nations struggling to form new national identities after the end of colonialism.

Naipaul has won numerous prizes, including the Nobel Prize in Literature in 2001.

V. S. Naipaul was born in 1932.

Literature Online Author Search For more about V. S. Naipaul, go to www.glencoe.com.

Connecting to the Story

The following story describes a friendship that develops between a young boy and an older man who claims they both are poets. As you read the story, think about the following questions:

- To be a good poet, what qualities does a person need to have?
- Must a poet necessarily write poetry, or are there other ways a person can be a poet?

Building Background

"B. Wordsworth" is set in the city of Port-of-Spain, which is the capital city of the Caribbean island of Trinidad, now known as the Republic of Trinidad and Tobago. The population of Port-of-Spain is close to 50,000. People of many different backgrounds live in the city, including people of African descent, people of European descent, people of mixed heritage, and people from the subcontinent of India whose families moved to Trinidad in the 1800s as indentured servants. Formerly a British colony, Trinidad and Tobago became an independent republic in 1962.

Setting Purposes for Reading

Big Idea **Globalization**

As you read, notice details that make this story both specific to a particular place and universal.

Literary Element **Dialect**

Dialect is a variation of a language that is spoken in a particular region or by a particular group of people. Dialects may differ from the standard form of a language in vocabulary, pronunciation, or grammar. As you read, note how the dialect used by the characters differs from Standard English.

- See Literary Terms Handbook, p. R4.

Literature Online **Interactive Literary Elements Handbook** To review or learn more about the literary elements, go to www.glencoe.com.

Reading Strategy **Drawing Conclusions About Meaning**

Drawing conclusions about meaning means making a generalization about the main idea, or theme, of a story from the clues supplied by the author. These clues can be found in the dialogue of the characters, in the narrator's commentary, and in the specific details used to describe the setting.

....

Reading Tip: Taking Notes Use a chart similar to the one below to write down clues that you think may help you draw conclusions about the meaning of this story.

Detail	Meaning

Vocabulary

hospitable (hos′ pi′ tə bəl) *adj.* offering generous and cordial welcome to guests; p. 1333 *A hospitable person is gracious when people come to visit.*

constellation (kon′ stə lā′ shən) *n.* any of eighty-eight groups of stars, many of which traditionally represent characters and objects in ancient mythology; p. 1335 *We could identify several constellations when we studied the patterns of stars in the night sky.*

patronize (pā′ trə nīz′) *v.* to be a customer of; p. 1336 *They preferred to patronize locally owned stores rather than large chain stores.*

distill (dis til′) *v.* to extract the essence of; p. 1336 *Distilling information means expressing it in as few words as possible.*

Vocabulary Tip: Analogies Analogies are comparisons based on relationships between ideas.

OBJECTIVES
In studying this selection, you will focus on the following:
- analyzing genre elements
- analyzing dialect
- drawing conclusions about meaning

Landscape, Trinidad, c. 1921. James Wilson Morrice. Oil on canvas, 74 x 92.2 cm. Art Gallery of Toronto.

B. Wordsworth

V. S. Naipaul

Three beggars called punctually every day at the **hospitable** houses in Miguel Street. At about ten an Indian came in his dhoti[1] and white jacket, and we poured a tin of rice into the sack he carried on his back. At twelve an old woman smoking a clay pipe came and she got a cent. At two a blind man led by a boy called for his penny. Sometimes we had a rogue.[2] One day a man called and said he was hungry. We gave him a meal. He asked for a cigarette and wouldn't go until we had lit it for him. That man never came again.

The strangest caller came one afternoon at about four o'clock. I had come back from school and was in my home-clothes. The man said to me, "Sonny, may I come inside your yard?"

He was a small man and he was tidily dressed. He wore a hat, a white shirt, and black trousers.

I asked, "What do you want?"

He said, "I want to watch your bees."

We had four small gru-gru palm trees and they were full of uninvited bees.

---

1. A *dhoti* is a loincloth worn by Hindu men in India.
2. One might be described as a *rogue* if one is somehow different or set apart from a group. *Rogue* can also mean a beggar.

Visual Vocabulary
Gru-gru palm trees are spiny-trunked palms that grow in the West Indies.

I ran up the steps and shouted, "Ma, it have a man outside here. He say he want to watch the bees."

My mother came out, looked at the man, and asked in an unfriendly way, "What you want?"

The man said, "I want to watch your bees."

His English was so good, it didn't sound natural, and I could see my mother was worried.

She said to me, "Stay here and watch him while he watch the bees."

The man said, "Thank you, Madam. You have done a good deed today."

He spoke very slowly and very correctly as though every word was costing him money.

We watched the bees, this man and I, for about an hour, squatting near the palm trees.

The man said, "I like watching bees. Sonny, do you like watching bees?"

I said, "I ain't have the time."

He shook his head sadly. He said, "That's what I do, I just watch. I can watch ants for days. Have you ever watched ants? And scorpions, and centipedes, and *congorees*[3]—have you watched those?"

I shook my head.

I said, "What you does do, mister?"

He got up and said, "I am a poet."

I said, "A good poet?"

He said, "The greatest in the world."

"What's your name, mister?"

"B. Wordsworth."

"B for Bill?"

"Black. Black Wordsworth. White Wordsworth[4] was my brother. We share one heart. I can watch a small flower like the morning glory and cry."

I said, "Why you does cry?"

"Why, boy? Why? You will know when you grow up. You're a poet, too, you know. And when you're a poet you can cry for everything."

I couldn't laugh.

He said, "You like your mother?"

"When she not beating me."

He pulled out a printed sheet from his hip-pocket and said, "On this paper is the greatest poem about mothers and I'm going to sell it to you at a bargain price. For four cents."

I went inside and I said, "Ma, you want to buy a poetry for four cents?"

My mother said, "Tell that blasted man to haul his tail away from my yard, you hear."

I said to B. Wordsworth, "My mother say she ain't have four cents."

B. Wordsworth said, "It is the poet's tragedy."

And he put the paper back in his pocket. He didn't seem to mind.

I said, "Is a funny way to go round selling poetry like that. Only calypsonians[5] do that sort of thing. A lot of people does buy?"

He said, "No one has yet bought a single copy."

"But why you does keep on going round, then?"

He said, "In this way I watch many things, and I always hope to meet poets."

I said, "You really think I is a poet?"

"You're as good as me," he said.

And when B. Wordsworth left, I prayed I would see him again.

About a week later, coming back from school one afternoon, I met him at the corner of Miguel Street.

He said, "I have been waiting for you for a long time."

I said, "You sell any poetry yet?"

He shook his head.

He said, "In my yard I have the best mango tree in Port of Spain. And now the mangoes are ripe and red and very sweet and juicy. I have waited here for you to tell you this and to invite you to come and eat some of my mangoes."

He lived in Alberto Street in a one-roomed hut placed right in the center of the lot. The yard seemed all green. There was the big mango tree. There was a coconut tree and there was a plum tree. The place looked wild, as though it

---

3. *Congorees* is a West Indian term for "millipedes" (long, many-legged arthropods).

4. *White Wordsworth* is a reference to the English poet William Wordsworth (1770–1850).

Literary Element Dialect *How does the boy's dialect differ from Standard English? List two specific differences.*

Big Idea Globalization *What does this statement tell you about the globalization of English?*

5. *Calypsonians* are folk musicians who sing calypso music—satirical street ballads native to Trinidad and Tobago that are often improvised.

Reading Strategy Drawing Conclusions About Meaning *Why do you think the boy wants to see B. Wordsworth again?*

wasn't in the city at all. You couldn't see all the big concrete houses in the street.

He was right. The mangoes were sweet and juicy. I ate about six, and the yellow mango juice ran down my arms to my elbows and down my mouth to my chin and my shirt was stained.

My mother said when I got home, "Where you was? You think you is a man now and could go all over the place? Go cut a whip for me."

She beat me rather badly, and I ran out of the house swearing that I would never come back. I went to B. Wordsworth's house. I was so angry, my nose was bleeding.

B. Wordsworth said, "Stop crying, and we will go for a walk."

I stopped crying, but I was breathing short. We went for a walk. We walked down St. Clair Avenue to the Savannah[6] and we walked to the racecourse.

B. Wordsworth said, "Now, let us lie on the grass and look up at the sky, and I want you to think how far those stars are from us."

I did as he told me, and I saw what he meant. I felt like nothing, and at the same time I had never felt so big and great in all my life. I forgot all my anger and all my tears and all the blows.

Visual Vocabulary
Orion the Hunter is the constellation named for a mythological giant hunter.

When I said I was better, he began telling me the names of the stars, and I particularly remembered the **constellation** of Orion the Hunter, though I don't really know why. I can spot Orion even today, but I have forgotten the rest.

Then a light was flashed into our faces, and we saw a policeman. We got up from the grass.

The policeman said, "What you doing here?"

B. Wordsworth said, "I have been asking myself the same question for forty years."

We became friends, B. Wordsworth and I. He told me, "You must never tell anybody about me and about the mango tree and the coconut tree and the plum tree. You must keep that a secret. If you tell anybody, I will know, because I am a poet."

I gave him my word and I kept it.

I liked his little room. It had no more furniture than George's[7] front room, but it looked cleaner and healthier. But it also looked lonely.

One day I asked him, "Mister Wordsworth, why you does keep all this bush in your yard? Ain't it does make the place damp?"

He said, "Listen, and I will tell you a story. Once upon a time a boy and girl met each other and they fell in love. They loved each other so much they got married. They were both poets. He loved words. She loved grass and flowers and trees. They lived happily in a single room, and then one day, the girl poet said to the boy poet, 'We are going to have another poet in the family.' But this poet was never born, because the girl died, and the young poet died with her, inside her. And the girl's husband was very sad, and he said he would never touch a thing in the girl's garden. And so the garden remained, and grew high and wild."

I looked at B. Wordsworth, and as he told me this lovely story, he seemed to grow older. I understood his story.

We went for long walks together. We went to the Botanical Gardens and the Rock Gardens. We climbed Chancellor Hill in the late afternoon and watched the darkness fall on Port of Spain, and watched the lights go on in the city and on the ships in the harbor.

He did everything as though he were doing it for the first time in his life. He did everything as though he were doing some church rite.

---

6. *Savannah* is a two-hundred-acre park in Port-of-Spain, Trinidad, that includes a racecourse.

Reading Strategy Drawing Conclusions About Meaning
What does the boy learn from B. Wordsworth in this passage?

Vocabulary

constellation (kon′ stə lā′ shən) *n.* any of eighty-eight groups of stars, many of which traditionally represent characters and objects in ancient mythology

7. *George* is a character in Naipaul's book of short stories *Miguel Street*.

Literary Element Dialect *What difference do you detect between the speech of the policeman and that of B. Wordsworth?*

Reading Strategy Drawing Conclusions About Meaning
What does this statement indicate about B. Wordsworth's philosophy of life?

He would say to me, "Now, how about having some ice cream?"

And when I said yes, he would grow very serious and say, "Now, which café shall we **patronize**?" As though it were a very important thing. He would think for some time about it, and finally say, "I think I will go and negotiate the purchase with that shop."

The world became a most exciting place.

One day, when I was in his yard, he said to me, "I have a great secret which I am now going to tell you."

I said, "It really secret?"

"At the moment, yes."

I looked at him, and he looked at me. He said, "This is just between you and me, remember. I am writing a poem."

"Oh." I was disappointed.

He said, "But this is a different sort of poem. This is the greatest poem in the world."

I whistled.

He said, "I have been working on it for more than five years now. I will finish it in about twenty-two years from now, that is, if I keep on writing at the present rate."

"You does write a lot, then?"

He said, "Not any more. I just write one line a month. But I make sure it is a good line."

I asked, "What was last month's good line?"

He looked up at the sky, and said, *"The past is deep."*

I said, "It is a beautiful line."

B. Wordsworth said, "I hope to **distill** the experiences of a whole month into that single line of poetry. So, in twenty-two years, I shall have written a poem that will sing to all humanity."

I was filled with wonder.

Our walks continued. We walked along the seawall at Docksite one day, and I said, "Mr.

Watching, 1995. Betye Saar. Mixed media on metal, 13½ x 9½ in. Courtesy of Michael Rosenfeld Gallery, New York.

Wordsworth, if I drop this pin in the water, you think it will float?"

He said, "This is a strange world. Drop your pin, and let us see what will happen."

The pin sank.

I said, "How is the poem this month?"

But he never told me any other line. He merely said, "Oh, it comes, you know. It comes."

Or we would sit on the seawall and watch the liners come into the harbor.

But of the greatest poem in the world I heard no more.

I felt he was growing older.

"How you does live, Mr. Wordsworth?" I asked him one day.

He said, "You mean how I get money?"

When I nodded, he laughed in a crooked way.

He said, "I sing calypsos in the calypso season."

"And that last you the rest of the year?"

"It is enough."

"But you will be the richest man in the world when you write the greatest poem?"

He didn't reply.

One day when I went to see him in his little house, I found him lying on his little bed. He looked so old and so weak, that I found myself wanting to cry.

He said, "The poem is not going well."

He wasn't looking at me. He was looking through the window at the coconut tree, and he was speaking as though I wasn't there. He said, "When I was twenty I felt the power within myself." Then, almost in front of my eyes, I could see his face growing older and more tired. He said, "But that—that was a long time ago."

And then—I felt it so keenly, it was as though I had been slapped by my mother. I could see it clearly on his face. It was there for everyone to see. Death on the shrinking face.

He looked at me, and saw my tears and sat up.

He said, "Come." I went and sat on his knees.

He looked into my eyes, and he said, "Oh, you can see it, too. I always knew you had the poet's eye."

He didn't even look sad, and that made me burst out crying loudly.

He pulled me to his thin chest, and said, "Do you want me to tell you a funny story?" and he smiled encouragingly at me.

But I couldn't reply.

He said, "When I have finished this story, I want you to promise that you will go away and never come back to see me. Do you promise?"

I nodded.

He said, "Good. Well, listen. That story I told you about the boy poet and the girl poet, do you remember that? That wasn't true. It was something I just made up. All this talk about poetry and the greatest poem in the world, that wasn't true, either. Isn't that the funniest thing you have heard?"

But his voice broke.

I left the house, and ran home crying, like a poet, for everything I saw.

I walked along Alberto Street a year later, but I could find no sign of the poet's house. It hadn't vanished, just like that. It had been pulled down, and a big, two-storied building had taken its place. The mango tree and the plum tree and the coconut tree had all been cut down, and there was brick and concrete everywhere.

It was just as though B. Wordsworth had never existed. ❧

> "When I have finished this story, I want you to promise that you will go away and never come back to see me."

Reading Strategy Drawing Conclusions About Meaning
In your opinion, what is B. Wordsworth's motivation for extracting this promise from the boy?

Reading Strategy Drawing Conclusions About Meaning
What lesson has B. Wordsworth taught the boy by denying the truth of his stories? Why does the boy run home crying?

RESPONDING AND THINKING CRITICALLY

Respond

1. What was the main emotion you felt at the end of the story? Explain.

Recall and Interpret

2. (a)How does B. Wordsworth's request differ from the requests of the others who visit "the hospitable houses of Miguel Street"? (b)What does this request suggest about him? How does it set him apart from the others?

3. (a)Who does B. Wordsworth say is his brother? What do they have in common, according to B. Wordsworth? (b)In what ways does the thing B. Wordsworth and his "brother" share make them both poets?

4. (a)What are some of the things B. Wordsworth and the narrator do together? (b)What does B. Wordsworth teach the narrator to value?

5. (a)What does B. Wordsworth tell the narrator on his deathbed? How does the narrator respond to B. Wordsworth's revelation? (b)How has the narrator become "like a poet"?

Analyze and Evaluate

6. Is this story unique to Trinidad, or does it contain universal qualities? How might a different setting change the story?

7. How would you describe B. Wordsworth's perspective on poetry?

Connect

8. Naipaul has said that a reader should see elements of his or her own experience in a story. Does B. Wordsworth remind you of anyone you've ever known? What influence did this person have on your life?

9. **Big Idea** **Globalization** How does this story demonstrate that twentieth-century English is a global language?

Literary Element ## Dialect

Authors incorporate **dialect** into their writing for various reasons. They might include dialect to help convey a sense of place or the social context of the character. Review the story, looking for examples of dialect, and then answer the following questions.

1. In terms of grammar and vocabulary, how does the dialect spoken by some characters in this story differ from Standard English?

2. Which characters in the story use dialect and which use Standard English? What does this speech difference tell you about the characters?

3. What difference do you notice between the boy's speech when he is narrating the story and when he is engaged in dialogue with the other characters? What might account for this difference?

Review: Foreshadowing

As you learned on page 1123, **foreshadowing** is an author's use of clues to prepare readers for events that will happen later in a story.

Partner Activity Meet with a classmate and find two or more examples of foreshadowing in this story. What do you think each example foreshadows? Working with your partner, create a chart similar to the one below in which you list the examples of foreshadowing you have found.

Examples of Foreshadowing	What the Example Foreshadows
"You will know when you grow up . . . And when you're a poet you can cry for everything."	After his last meeting with B. Wordsworth, the boy "ran home crying, like a poet, for everything I saw."

Reading Strategy **Drawing Conclusions About Meaning**

Authors sometimes state the theme, or meaning, of a work directly. More often, however, they give readers hints, or clues, and expect them to draw their own conclusions about the meaning of a work. Review the chart you made on page 1332, and then answer the following questions.

1. What conclusions can you draw about the influence B. Wordsworth has upon the narrator in the story?

2. Why do you think B. Wordsworth confesses to the narrator at their final meeting that his stories about himself are false?

Vocabulary **Practice**

Practice with Analogies Choose the word that best completes each analogy.

1. stars : constellation :: ship :
   a. fleet   **b.** port   **c.** galley
2. kind : good-hearted :: hospitable :
   a. healing   **b.** hostile   **c.** generous
3. instill : remove :: distill :
   a. extract   **b.** dilute   **c.** inject
4. patronize : favor :: despise :
   a. humiliate   **b.** hate   **c.** acclaim

Academic Vocabulary

Here are two words from the vocabulary list on page R82.

normal (nôr′ məl) *adj.* conforming to an accepted standard, model, or pattern

occur (ə kur′) *v.* to take place or come to pass

Practice and Apply

1. In what way is B. Wordsworth not a **normal** visitor to the houses on Miguel Street?
2. What **occurs** in the final paragraph of the story?

Writing About Literature

Analyze Character Write a character sketch of B. Wordsworth. Before you begin to write, review the story, considering the following factors:

• how the narrator describes B. Wordsworth

• how other characters see B. Wordsworth

• the words and actions of B. Wordsworth

• how B. Wordsworth describes himself

• B. Wordsworth's deathbed confession

If any of the details you find about B. Wordsworth appear contradictory, consider what the contradictions may reveal about his character. Follow the writing path below to help you organize your essay.

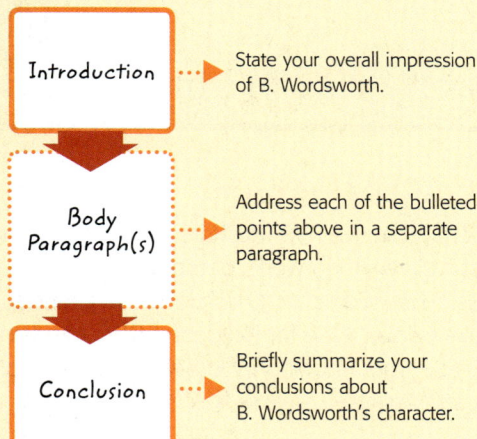

Introduction ····▶ State your overall impression of B. Wordsworth.

Body Paragraph(s) ▶ Address each of the bulleted points above in a separate paragraph.

Conclusion ····▶ Briefly summarize your conclusions about B. Wordsworth's character.

When you complete your draft, proofread and edit it to correct any errors in grammar, spelling, and punctuation.

Literature Groups

The last line of the story says, "It was just as though B. Wordsworth had never existed." In a small group, discuss the **irony** of this statement by addressing the following questions: How does it seem as if B. Wordsworth had never existed? In what ways might B. Wordsworth have had a lasting effect that he hadn't even considered? Share a summary of your ideas with other groups.

Literature Online **Web Activities** For eFlashcards, Selection Quick Checks, and other Web activities, go to www.glencoe.com.

The Gateway to India.

from

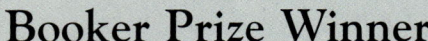

Imaginary homelands

Salman Rushdie

Booker Prize Winner

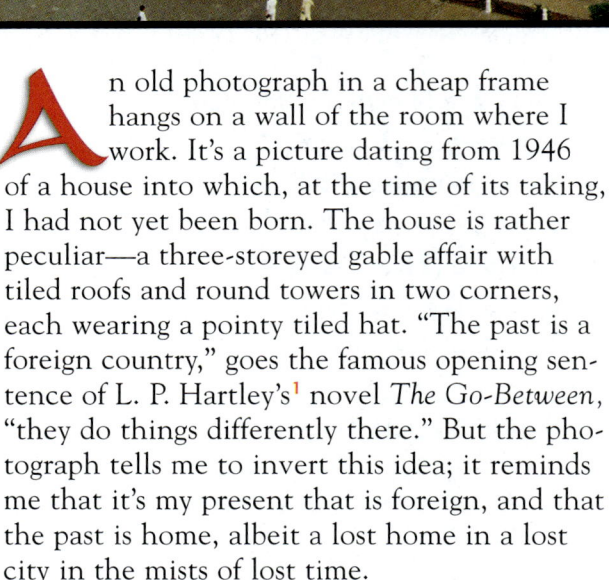

Building Background

Indian-born author Salman Rushdie has written some of the most well-regarded works of the past twenty-five years. His novel *Midnight's Children* was awarded the prestigious Booker Prize for Fiction in 1981. The following excerpt is from *Imaginary Homelands,* a book of criticism and essays.

Set a Purpose for Reading

Read to understand a novelist's perspective on writing in this new global age.

Reading Strategy

Identifying Assumptions and Ambiguity

An **assumption** is an idea or a belief that a person takes for granted without any actual proof. **Ambiguity** is the state of having more than one meaning. Use a two-column chart, like the one below, to help you to identify assumptions and ambiguities as you read the essay.

Assumptions	Ambiguities

An old photograph in a cheap frame hangs on a wall of the room where I work. It's a picture dating from 1946 of a house into which, at the time of its taking, I had not yet been born. The house is rather peculiar—a three-storeyed gable affair with tiled roofs and round towers in two corners, each wearing a pointy tiled hat. "The past is a foreign country," goes the famous opening sentence of L. P. Hartley's[1] novel *The Go-Between*, "they do things differently there." But the photograph tells me to invert this idea; it reminds me that it's my present that is foreign, and that the past is home, albeit a lost home in a lost city in the mists of lost time.

A few years ago I revisited Bombay, which is my lost city, after an absence of something like half my life. Shortly after arriving, acting on an impulse, I opened the telephone directory and looked for my father's name. And, amazingly, there it was; his name, our old address, the unchanged telephone number, as if we had never gone away to the unmentionable country across

---

1. *L. P. Hartley* (1895–1972) was an English critic, novelist, and short story writer.

the border. It was an eerie discovery. I felt as if I were being claimed, or informed that the facts of my faraway life were illusions, and that this continuity was the reality. Then I went to visit the house in the photograph and stood outside it, neither daring nor wishing to announce myself to its new owners. (I didn't want to see how they'd ruined the interior.) I was overwhelmed. The photograph had naturally been taken in black and white; and my memory, feeding on such images as this, had begun to see my childhood in the same way, monochromatically. The colors of my history had seeped out of my mind's eye; now my other two eyes were assaulted by colors, by the vividness of the red tiles, the yellow-edged green of cactus-leaves, the brilliance of bougainvillea creeper.[2] It is probably not too romantic to say that that was when my novel *Midnight's Children* was really born; when I realized how much I wanted to restore the past to myself, not in the faded grays of old family-album snapshots, but whole, in CinemaScope and glorious Technicolor.

Bombay is a city built by foreigners upon reclaimed land; I, who had been away so long that I almost qualified for the title, was gripped by the conviction that I, too, had a city and a history to reclaim.

It may be that writers in my position, exiles or emigrants or expatriates, are haunted by some sense of loss, some urge to reclaim, to look back, even at the risk of being mutated into pillars of salt. But if we do look back, we must also do so in the knowledge—which gives rise to profound uncertainties—that our physical alienation from India almost inevitably means that we will not be capable of reclaiming precisely the thing that was lost; that we will, in short, create fictions, not actual cities or villages, but invisible ones, imaginary homelands, Indias of the mind.

Writing my book in North London, looking out through my window on to a city scene totally unlike the ones I was imagining on to paper, I was constantly plagued by this problem, until I felt obliged to face it in the text, to make clear that (in spite of my original . . . ambition to unlock the gates of lost time so that the past reappeared as it actually had been, unaffected by

the distortions of memory) what I was actually doing was a novel of memory and about memory, so that my India was just that: "my" India, a version and no more than one version of all the hundreds of millions of possible versions. I tried to make it as imaginatively true as I could, but imaginative truth is simultaneously honorable and suspect, and I knew that my India may only have been one to which I (who am no longer what I was, and who by quitting Bombay never became what perhaps I was meant to be) was, let us say, willing to admit I belonged. . . .

So literature can, and perhaps must, give the lie to official facts. But is this a proper function of those of us who write from outside India? Or are we just dilettantes[3] in such affairs, because we are not involved in their day-to-day unfolding, because by speaking out we take no risks, because our personal safety is not threatened? What right do we have to speak at all?

My answer is very simple. Literature is self-validating. That is to say, a book is not justified by its author's worthiness to write it, but by the quality of what has been written. There are terrible books that arise directly out of experience, and extraordinary imaginative feats dealing with themes which the author has been obliged to approach from the outside.

Literature is not in the business of copyrighting certain themes for certain groups. And as for risk: the real risks of any artist are taken in the work, in pushing the work to the limits of what is possible, in the attempt to increase the sum of what it is possible to think. Books become good when they go to this edge and risk falling over it—when they endanger the artist by reason of what he has, or has not *artistically* dared.

So if I am to speak for Indian writers in England I would say this, paraphrasing G. V. Desani's[4] H. Hatterr: The migrations of the fifties and sixties happened. "We are. We are here." And we are not willing to be excluded from any part of our heritage; which heritage includes . . . the right of any member of this post-diaspora[5]

---

2. *Bougainvillea creeper* is a tropical ornamental plant.

3. Here, *dilettantes* means "amateurs" or "those with a superficial understanding."
4. *G. V. Desani* (1909–2000) was an Indian novelist and journalist. His best-known work is the novel *All About H. Hatterr.*
5. *Diaspora* means "the scattering of a people from their homeland."

community to draw on its roots for its art, just as all the world's community of displaced writers has always done.

Let me override at once the faintly defensive note that has crept into these last few remarks. The Indian writer, looking back at India, does so through guilt-tinted spectacles. (I am of course, once more, talking about myself.) I am speaking now of those of us who emigrated . . . and I suspect that there are times when the move seems wrong to us all. . . . Sometimes we feel that we straddle two cultures; at other times, that we fall between two stools. But however ambiguous and shifting this ground may be, it is not an infertile territory for a writer to occupy. If literature is in part the business of finding new angles at which to enter reality, then once again our distance, our long geographical perspective, may provide us with such angles. Or it may be that that is simply what we must think in order to do our work. . . .

England's Indian writers are by no means all the same type of animal. Some of us, for instance, are Pakistani. Others Bangladeshi. Others West, or East, or even South African. And V. S. Naipaul, by now, is something else entirely. This word "Indian" is getting to be a pretty scattered concept. Indian writers in England include political exiles, first-generation migrants, affluent expatriates whose residence here is frequently temporary, naturalized Britons, and people born here who may never have laid eyes on the subcontinent. Clearly, nothing that I say can apply across all these categories. But one of the interesting things about this diverse community is that, as far as Indo-British fiction is concerned, its existence changes the ball game, because that fiction is in future going to come as much from addresses in London, Birmingham and Yorkshire as from Delhi or Bombay.

One of the changes has to do with attitudes towards the use of English. Many have referred to the argument about the appropriateness of this language to Indian themes. And I hope all of us share the view that we can't simply use the language in the way the British did; that it needs remaking for our own purposes. Those of us who do use English do so in spite of our ambiguity towards it, or perhaps because of that, perhaps because we can find in that linguistic struggle a reflection of other struggles taking place in the real world, struggles between the cultures within ourselves and the influences at work upon our societies. To conquer English may be to complete the process of making ourselves free.

But the British Indian writer simply does not have the option of rejecting English, anyway. His children, her children, will grow up speaking it, probably as a first language; and in the forging of a British Indian identity the English language is of central importance. It must, in spite of everything, be embraced. (The word "translation" comes, etymologically, from the Latin for "bearing across." Having been borne across the world, we are translated men. It is normally supposed that something always gets lost in translation; I cling, obstinately, to the notion that something can also be gained.)

To be an Indian writer in this society is to face, every day, problems of definition. What does it mean to be "Indian" outside India? How can culture be preserved without becoming ossified?[6] How should we discuss the need for change within ourselves and our community

---

6. Here, *ossified* means "rigidly conventional."

without seeming to play into the hands of our racial enemies? What are the consequences, both spiritual and practical, of refusing to make any concessions to Western ideas and practices? What are the consequences of embracing those ideas and practices and turning away from the ones that came here with us? These questions are all a single, existential question. How are we to live in the world?

I do not propose to offer, prescriptively, any answers to these questions; only to state that these are some of the issues with which each of us will have to come to terms.

To turn my eyes outwards now, and to say a little about the relationship between the Indian writer and the majority white culture in whose midst he lives, and with which his work will sooner or later have to deal:

In common with many Bombay-raised middle-class children of my generation, I grew up with an intimate knowledge of, and even sense of friendship with, a certain kind of England: a dream-England. . . . I wanted to come to England. I couldn't wait. And to be fair, England has done all right by me; but I find it a little difficult to be properly grateful. I can't escape the view that my relatively easy ride is not the result of the dream-England's famous sense of tolerance and fair play, but of my social class, my freak fair skin and my "English" English accent. Take away any of these, and the story would have been very different. Because of course the dream-England is no more than a dream. . . .

As Richard Wright[7] found long ago in America, black and white descriptions of society are no longer compatible. Fantasy, or the mingling of fantasy and naturalism, is one way of dealing with these problems. It offers a way of echoing in the form of our work the issues faced by all of us: how to build a new, "modern" world out of an old, legend-haunted civilization, an old culture which we have brought into the heart of a newer one. But whatever technical solutions we may find, Indian writers in these islands, like others who have migrated into the north from the south, are capable of writing from a kind of double perspective: because they, we, are at one and the same time insiders and outsiders in this society. This stereoscopic vision[8] is perhaps what we can offer in place of "whole sight." ◖

---

7. *Richard Wright* (1908–1960) was an African American novelist.
8. *Stereoscopic vision* refers to the combining of two images— often photographs of the same thing taken at slightly different angles—into a single three-dimensional image, with the aid of a stereoscope.

RESPONDING AND THINKING CRITICALLY

Respond

1. In what ways has this essay changed your understanding of the effects of globalization on literature?

Recall and Interpret

2. (a)When Rushdie revisited his childhood home in Bombay, what realization did he have? (b)What metaphor does Rushdie use to examine his feelings? Explain.

3. (a)According to Rushdie, what "can, and perhaps must," literature do? (b)In his opinion, what have displaced writers always done?

4. How does Rushdie describe England and his life there?

Analyze and Evaluate

5. (a)Rushdie claims that Indian writers cannot use English "in the way the British did" and "that it needs remaking." Why does Rushdie say this? (b)Do you agree with this claim? Why or why not?

6. (a)Briefly state the main ideas of this essay. (b)With which ideas do you agree? With which do you disagree? Explain your reasoning.

Connect

7. How is the "stereoscopic vision" described by Rushdie at the end of this essay demonstrated by other writers in this unit?

OBJECTIVES
- Read to enhance understanding of history and British culture.
- Identify and analyze an author's unstated assumptions based on explicitly stated information.

Games at Twilight

MEET ANITA DESAI

Many of Anita Desai's novels brilliantly portray life in India, its past and present, and the struggles that many Indians, especially women and children, face. Her novels and short stories are often full of vivid imagery and ornate detail. As Nobel Prize–winning novelist J. M. Coetzee has stated, "Desai's strength as a writer has always been her eye for detail . . . her gift for telling metaphor, and above all her feel for the sun and sky, heat and dust, for the elemental reality of central India."

A Distinct Genius Desai was born Anita Mazumdar in Mussoorie, India, north of Delhi, to a German mother and an Indian father. Hers was a family of bookworms, and she treasured the amount of time and privacy she had as a child to read and dream. "I grew up in a home where three languages were spoken together— Hindi, English, and German—but English was my literary language—the one I read and wrote in. I am grateful for that because it opened to me the literature of the world and I made myself at home in it and was not restricted to any one region." Desai came to appreciate each language for "its own distinct genius." She found English the most flexible of languages, however, and the one in which she could best work "to convey the rhythms, accents, tones, and pace of Indian life."

Desai began to write in English at the age of seven, publishing her first story at age nine. After graduating with a B.A. in English literature from Delhi University in 1957,

she married Ashvin Desai, a businessman; they later had four children.

In 1963, when she was twenty-six, Desai published her first novel, *Cry, the Peacock,* which deals with the oppression of Indian women. *Where Shall We Go This Summer?* also explores the theme of despairing women. Many of her novels, such as *Bye-Bye Blackbird* and *Fire on the Mountain,* focus on the profound cultural changes that India has experienced since the dissolution of the British Empire.

> *"I believe literature and art really contain the essence of life and the world, uncover its innermost secrets and present those truths that one might ordinarily miss or ignore, and so [are] closer to the truth than life itself."*
>
> —Anita Desai

An International Teacher In addition to several collections of short stories, Desai has published some books for children, acquiring a strong international reputation as a children's writer. In 1987 she came to the United States to teach creative writing at Smith College in Massachusetts. Since that time she has alternated between living and teaching in the United States and in India. She is also a Fellow of England's Royal Society of Literature.

Anita Desai was born in 1937.

Literature Online Author Search For more about Anita Desai, go to www.glencoe.com.

Connecting to the Story

What were some of your favorite games as a child? When you played, how important was winning? As you read, think about the following questions:

- Who sets rules for children's games? Can they change?
- If you win a game, what, exactly, have you achieved?

Building Background

A counting-out game is a simple game, played by an indeterminate number of participants, usually for the purpose of choosing a person to be "it" in the playing of another, different game. Many countries around the world have their own versions of counting-out games, and some games have seemingly endless variations. Some of the most common of these games are Rock, Paper, Scissors; Odd or Even; coin flipping; drawing straws; or counting-out rhymes such as "Eeny, Meeny, Miny, Mo" or (in England) "Tinker, Tailor, Soldier, Sailor." The game played by the children near the start of "Games at Twilight" is an example of a counting-out game.

Setting Purposes for Reading

Big Idea Globalization

As you read, notice how the Indian culture in the story reflects British influences.

Literary Element Point of View

Point of view is the standpoint from which a story is told. In a first-person story, the narrator is a character in the story. In a third-person story, the narrator stands outside the story and describes the characters and actions. As you read "Games at Twilight," consider how the narrator's relationship to the story affects the telling of it.

- See Literary Terms Handbook, p. R13.

Literature Online Interactive Literary Elements Handbook To review or learn more about the literary elements, go to www.glencoe.com.

Reading Strategy Connecting to Personal Experience

You can bring your own **personal experiences** and world knowledge to bear on any reading situation to help you understand and assess what is happening. This is especially useful when you read literature in which cultural comparisons are explicit or implicit.

Reading Tip: Taking Notes Use a chart to list similarities and differences you note between your experiences and those of characters in the story.

Similarities	Differences

Vocabulary

stridently (strīd′ ənt lē) *adv.* in a harsh, grating manner; p. 1346 *Len's classmates stridently denounced his opinion.*

defunct (di fungkt′) *adj.* no longer existing or active; dead; p. 1348 *The little mom-and-pop grocery store that used to be on our corner is now defunct.*

temerity (tə mer′ ə tē) *n.* excessive or reckless boldness; rashness; p. 1348 *We were amazed at Linda's temerity as she faced down the bullies.*

fray (frā) *n.* a heated dispute or contest; p. 1349 *The game of dodgeball had already degenerated into a free-for-all before George entered the fray.*

lugubrious (loo gōō′ brē əs) *adj.* excessively mournful or sorrowful; p. 1351 *The little girl's expression as she held her broken doll was so lugubrious that I couldn't help but sympathize.*

Vocabulary Tip: Word Parts Knowledge of prefixes, suffixes, and roots can help you understand unfamiliar words.

OBJECTIVES
In studying this selection, you will focus on the following:
- analyzing literary periods
- evaluating point of view
- connecting to personal experiences

Games at Twilight

Anita Desai

Girl on a Swing, India, 2000. Andrew Macara. Oil on canvas, 63.5 x 76.2 cm. Private collection.

It was still too hot to play outdoors. They had had their tea, they had been washed and had their hair brushed, and after the long day of confinement in the house that was not cool but at least a protection from the sun, the children strained to get out. Their faces were red and bloated with the effort, but their mother would not open the door, everything was still curtained and shuttered in a way that stifled the children, made them feel that their lungs were stuffed with cotton wool and their noses with dust and if they didn't burst out into the light and see the sun and feel the air, they would choke.

"Please, ma, please," they begged. "We'll play in the veranda and porch—we won't go a step out of the porch."

"You will, I know you will, and then—"

"No—we won't, we won't," they wailed so horrendously that she actually let down the bolt of the front door so that they burst out like seeds from a crackling, overripe pod into the veranda, with such wild, maniacal[1] yells that she retreated to her bath and the shower of talcum powder and the fresh sari[2] that were to help her face the summer evening.

They faced the afternoon. It was too hot. Too bright. The white walls of the veranda glared **stridently** in the sun. The bougainvillea[3] hung about it, purple and magenta, in livid balloons. The garden outside was like a tray made of beaten brass, flattened out on the red gravel and the stony soil in all shades of metal—aluminum, tin, copper, and brass. No life stirred at this arid time of day—the birds still drooped, like dead fruit, in the papery tents of the trees; some squirrels lay limp on the wet earth under the garden tap. The outdoor dog lay stretched as if dead on the veranda mat, his paws and ears and tail all reaching out like dying travelers in search of water. He rolled his eyes at the children—two white marbles rolling in the purple sockets, begging for sympathy—and attempted to lift his tail in a wag but could not. It only twitched and lay still.

Then, perhaps roused by the shrieks of the children, a band of parrots suddenly fell out of the eucalyptus tree, tumbled frantically in the

---

3. *Bougainvillea* is a woody, tropical vine with flowers.

---

1. *Maniacal* means "marked by excessive enthusiasm."
2. A *sari* is an outer garment worn mainly by Hindu women.

Little Indian Girl with a Leaf, 1998. Penelope Anstice. Oil on canvas. Private collection.

still, sizzling air, then sorted themselves out into battle formation and streaked away across the white sky.

The children, too, felt released. They too began tumbling, shoving, pushing against each other, frantic to start. Start what? Start their business. The business of the children's day which is—play.

"Let's play hide-and-seek."

"Who'll be It?"

"You be It."

"Why should I? You be—"

"You're the eldest—"

"That doesn't mean—"

The shoves became harder. Some kicked out. The motherly Mira intervened. She pulled the boys roughly apart. There was a tearing sound of cloth but it was lost in the heavy panting and angry grumbling and no one paid attention to the small sleeve hanging loosely off a shoulder.

"Make a circle, make a circle!" she shouted, firmly pulling and pushing till a kind of vague circle was formed. "Now clap!" she roared and, clapping, they all chanted in melancholy unison: "Dip, dip, dip—my blue ship—" and every now and then one or the other saw he was safe by the way his hands fell at the crucial moment—palm on palm, or back of hand on palm—and dropped out of the circle with a yell and a jump of relief and jubilation.

Raghu was It. He started to protest, to cry "You cheated—Mira cheated—Anu cheated—" but it was too late, the others had all already streaked away. There was no one to hear when he called out, "Only in the veranda—the porch—Ma said—Ma *said* to stay in the porch!" No one had stopped to listen, all he saw were their brown legs flashing through the dusty shrubs, scrambling up brick walls, leaping over compost heaps and hedges, and then the porch stood empty in the purple shade of the bougainvillea and the garden was as empty as before; even the limp squirrels had whisked away, leaving everything gleaming, brassy and bare.

Only small Manu suddenly reappeared, as if he had dropped out of an invisible cloud or from a bird's claws, and stood for a moment in the center of the yellow lawn, chewing his finger and near to tears as he heard Raghu shouting, with his head pressed against the veranda wall, "Eighty-three, eighty-five, eighty-nine, ninety . . ." and then made off in a panic, half of him wanting to fly north, the other half counseling south. Raghu turned just in time to see the flash of his white shorts and the uncertain skittering of his red sandals, and charged after him with such a blood-curdling yell that Manu stumbled over the hosepipe, fell into its rubber coils, and lay there weeping, "I won't be It—you have to find them all—all—All!"

"I know I have to, idiot," Raghu said, superciliously kicking him with his toe. "You're dead," he said with satisfaction, licking the beads of perspiration off his upper lip, and then stalked off in search of worthier prey, whistling spiritedly so that the hiders should hear and tremble.

Ravi heard the whistling and picked his nose in a panic, trying to find comfort by burrowing the

Reading Strategy Connecting to Personal Experience
Based on your memories of childhood, do the children's pent-up energy and eagerness to play seem believable? Explain.

ANITA DESAI **1347**

finger deep-deep into that soft tunnel. He felt himself too exposed, sitting on an upturned flowerpot behind the garage. Where could he burrow? He could run around the garage if he heard Raghu come—around and around and around—but he hadn't much faith in his short legs when matched against Raghu's long, hefty, hairy footballer legs. Ravi had a frightening glimpse of them as Raghu combed the hedge of crotons and hibiscus,[4] trampling delicate ferns underfoot as he did so. Ravi looked about him desperately, swallowing a small ball of snot in his fear.

The garage was locked with a great heavy lock to which the driver had the key in his room, hanging from a nail on the wall under his work shirt. Ravi had peeped in and seen him still sprawling on his string-cot in his vest and striped underpants, the hair on his chest and the hair in his nose shaking with the vibrations of his phlegm-obstructed snores. Ravi had wished he were tall enough, big enough to reach the key on the nail, but it was impossible, beyond his reach for years to come. He had sidled away and sat dejectedly on the flowerpot. That at least was cut to his own size.

But next to the garage was another shed with a big green door. Also locked. No one even knew who had the key to the lock. That shed wasn't opened more than once a year when Ma turned out all the old broken bits of furniture and rolls of matting and leaking buckets, and the white anthills were broken and swept away and Flit sprayed into the spiderwebs and rat holes so that the whole operation was like the looting of a poor, ruined, and conquered city. The green leaves of the door sagged. They were nearly off their rusty hinges. The hinges were large and made a small gap between the door and the walls—only just large enough for rats, dogs, and, possibly, Ravi to slip through.

Ravi had never cared to enter such a dark and depressing mortuary[5] of **defunct** household goods seething with such unspeakable and alarming animal life but, as Raghu's whistling grew angrier and sharper and his crashing and storming in the hedge wilder, Ravi suddenly slipped off the flowerpot and through the crack and was gone. He chuckled aloud with astonishment at his own **temerity** so that Raghu came out of the hedge, stood silent with his hands on his hips, listening, and finally shouted "I heard you! I'm coming! *Got* you—" and came charging round the garage only to find the upturned flowerpot, the yellow dust, the crawling of white ants in a mud hill against the closed shed door—nothing. Snarling, he bent to pick up a stick and went off, whacking it against the garage and shed walls as if to beat out his prey.

Ravi shook, then shivered with delight, with self-congratulation. Also with fear. It was dark, spooky in the shed. It had a muffled smell, as of graves. Ravi had once got locked into the linen cupboard and sat there weeping for half an hour before he was rescued. But at least that had been a familiar place, and even smelled pleasantly of starch, laundry, and, reassuringly, of his mother. But the shed smelled of rats, anthills, dust, and spiderwebs. Also of less definable, less recognizable horrors. And it was dark. Except for the white-hot cracks along the door, there was no light. The roof was very low. Although Ravi was small, he felt as if he could reach up and touch it with his fingertips. But he didn't stretch. He hunched himself into a ball so as not to bump into anything, touch or feel anything. What might there not be to touch him and feel him as he stood there, trying to

---

4. *Crotons* and *hibiscus* are tropical plants.

5. A *mortuary* is a place where dead bodies are kept before burial.

Literary Element Point of View *Note the shift in point of view. What about this new point of view suggests that Ravi has become the main character?*

Big Idea Globalization *Football, known as soccer in the United States, is a part of British culture that caught on in the colonies. Explain why this detail about Raghu might be significant.*

Literary Element Point of View *What have you found out about Ravi in this section so far that you could not learn if the story were told from a different point of view?*

Vocabulary

defunct (di fungkt′) *adj.* no longer existing or active; dead

temerity (tə mer′ ə tē) *n.* excessive or reckless boldness; rashness

Abstract Day, 2005. Lou Wall. Private collection.

see in the dark? Something cold, or slimy—like a snake. Snakes! He leaped up as Raghu whacked the wall with his stick—then, quickly realizing what it was, felt almost relieved to hear Raghu, hear his stick. It made him feel protected.

But Raghu soon moved away. There wasn't a sound once his footsteps had gone around the garage and disappeared. Ravi stood frozen inside the shed. Then he shivered all over. Something had tickled the back of his neck. It took him a while to pick up the courage to lift his hand and explore. It was an insect—perhaps a spider— exploring *him*. He squashed it and wondered how many more creatures were watching him, waiting to reach out and touch him, the stranger.

There was nothing now. After standing in that position—his hand still on his neck, feeling the wet splodge of the squashed spider gradually dry—for minutes, hours, his legs began to tremble with the effort, the inaction. By now he could see enough in the dark to make out the large solid shapes of old wardrobes, broken buckets, and bedsteads piled on top of each other

around him. He recognized an old bathtub—patches of enamel glimmered at him and at last he lowered himself onto its edge.

He contemplated slipping out of the shed and into the **fray**. He wondered if it would not be better to be captured by Raghu and be returned to the milling crowd as long as he could be in the sun, the light, the free spaces of the garden, and the familiarity of his brothers, sisters, and cousins. It would be evening soon. Their games would become legitimate. The parents would sit out on the lawn on cane basket chairs and watch them as they tore around the garden or gathered in knots to share a loot of mulberries or black, teeth-splitting *jamun*[6] from the garden trees. The gardener would fix the hosepipe to the water tap and water would fall lavishly through the air to the ground, soaking the dry yellow grass and the red gravel and arousing the sweet, the intoxicating scent of water on dry earth—that loveliest scent in the world. Ravi sniffed for a whiff of it. He half rose from the bathtub, then heard the despairing scream of one of the girls as Raghu bore down upon her. There was the sound of a crash, and of rolling about in the bushes, the shrubs, then screams and accusing sobs of, "I touched the den—" "You did not—" "I did—" "You liar, you did *not*" and then a fading away and silence again.

---

6. *Jamun* is a tropical fruit.

Reading Strategy | Connecting to Personal Experience
How might these "legitimate" games be different from the game the children have been playing?

Vocabulary

fray (frā) *n.* a heated dispute or contest

Ravi sat back on the harsh edge of the tub, deciding to hold out a bit longer. What fun if they were all found and caught—he alone left unconquered! He had never known that sensation. Nothing more wonderful had ever happened to him than being taken out by an uncle and bought a whole slab of chocolate all to himself, or being flung into the soda man's pony cart and driven up to the gate by the friendly driver with the red beard and pointed ears. To defeat Raghu—that hirsute,[7] hoarse-voiced football champion—and to be the winner in a circle of older, bigger, luckier children—that would be thrilling beyond imagination. He hugged his knees together and smiled to himself almost shyly at the thought of so much victory, such laurels.[8]

There he sat smiling, knocking his heels against the bathtub, now and then getting up and going to the door to put his ear to the broad crack and listening for sounds of the game, the pursuer and the pursued, and then returning to his seat with the dogged determination of the true winner, a breaker of records, a champion.

It grew darker in the shed as the light at the door grew softer, fuzzier, turned to a kind of crumbling yellow pollen that turned to yellow fur, blue fur, gray fur. Evening. Twilight. The sound of water gushing, falling. The scent of earth receiving water, slaking its thirst in great gulps and releasing that green scent of freshness, coolness. Through the crack Ravi saw the long purple shadows of the shed and the garage lying still across the yard. Beyond that, the white walls of the house. The bougainvillea had lost its lividity, hung in dark bundles that quaked and twittered and seethed with masses of homing sparrows. The lawn was shut off from his view. Could he hear the children's voices? It seemed to him that he could. It seemed to him that he could hear them chanting, singing, laughing. But what about the game? What had happened? Could it be over? How could it when he was still not found?

It then occurred to him that he could have slipped out long ago, dashed across the yard to the veranda, and touched the "den." It was necessary to do that to win. He had forgotten. He had only remembered the part of hiding and

trying to elude[9] the seeker. He had done that so successfully, his success had occupied him so wholly that he had quite forgotten that success had to be clinched by that final dash to victory and the ringing cry of "Den!"

With a whimper he burst through the crack, fell on his knees, got up and stumbled on stiff, benumbed legs across the shadowy yard, crying heartily by the time he reached the veranda so that when he flung himself at the white pillar and bawled, "Den! Den! Den!" his voice broke with rage and pity at the disgrace of it all and he felt himself flooded with tears and misery.

Out on the lawn, the children stopped chanting. They all turned to stare at him in amazement. Their faces were pale and triangular in the dusk. The trees and bushes around them stood inky and sepulchral, spilling long shadows across them. They stared, wondering at his reappearance, his passion, his wild animal howling. Their mother rose from her basket chair and came towards him, worried, annoyed, saying, "Stop it, stop it, Ravi. Don't be a baby. Have you hurt yourself?" Seeing him attended to, the children went back to clasping their hands and chanting "The grass is green, the rose is red . . . ."

But Ravi would not let them. He tore himself out of his mother's grasp and pounded across the lawn into their midst, charging at them with his head lowered so that they scattered in surprise. "I won, I won, I won," he bawled, shaking his head so that the big tears flew. "Raghu didn't find me. I won, I won—"

It took them a minute to grasp what he was saying, even who he was. They had quite forgotten him. Raghu had found all the others long ago. There had been a fight about who was to be It next. It had been so fierce that their mother had emerged from her bath and made them change to another game. Then they had played another and another. Broken mulberries from the tree and eaten them. Helped the driver wash the car when their father returned from work. Helped the gardener water the beds till he roared at them and swore he would complain to their parents. The

---

7. *Hirsute* means "covered with hair."
8. *Laurels* means "glory and honor."

9. To *elude* is to escape from.

Reading Strategy Connecting to Personal Experience
Do you think Ravi's predicament in this passage is believable? Explain.

Children's Play (detail), 1987. Shanti Panchal. Watercolor on paper, 130 x 100 cm. Private collection.

parents had come out, taken up their positions on the cane chairs. They had begun to play again, sing and chant. All this time no one had remembered Ravi. Having disappeared from the scene, he had disappeared from their minds. Clean.

"Don't be a fool," Raghu said roughly, pushing him aside, and even Mira said, "Stop howling, Ravi. If you want to play, you can stand at the end of the line," and she put him there very firmly.

The game proceeded. Two pairs of arms reached up and met in an arc. The children trooped under it again and again in a **lugubrious** circle, ducking their heads and intoning[10]

10. *Intoning* is chanting.

"The grass is green,
The rose is red;
Remember me
When I am dead, dead, dead,
dead . . ."

And the arc of thin arms trembled in the twilight, and the heads were bowed so sadly, and their feet tramped to that melancholy refrain so mournfully, so helplessly, that Ravi could not bear it. He would not follow them, he would not be included in this funereal game. He had wanted victory and triumph—not a funeral. But he had been forgotten, left out, and he would not join them now. The ignominy[11] of being forgotten—how could he face it? He felt his heart go heavy and ache inside him unbearably. He lay down full length on the damp grass, crushing his face into it, no longer crying, silenced by a terrible sense of his insignificance.

11. *Ignominy* means "humiliation and dishonor."

RESPONDING AND THINKING CRITICALLY

Respond

1. What is your overall impression of the children and their games throughout the story? Explain.

Recall and Interpret

2. (a)What are the children doing at the beginning of the story? (b)What does the children's behavior at the beginning tell you about the relationships among them?

3. (a)Where does Ravi hide? Why does he choose that place? (b)What idea builds in Ravi's mind as he hides?

4. (a)What does Ravi suddenly realize he must do to win the game? (b)In your opinion, why is Ravi crying as he leaves his hiding place and heads for the "den"?

Analyze and Evaluate

5. (a)How do the other children tend to treat Ravi throughout the story? Why do you think this is so? (b)How does the dialogue help to convey these relationships?

6. (a)Why does Ravi *not* win the game? (b)If Ravi had managed to win the game, do you think he would have received "so much victory, such laurels" as he dreams of? Explain.

7. (a)How does Ravi react to the other children's behavior toward him at the end? (b)What seems to affect him more deeply, not winning or having been forgotten? Explain.

Connect

8. **Big Idea** Globalization Cite elements in this story that demonstrate the effects of globalization. Does any element maintain a uniquely Indian flavor? Explain.

VISUAL LITERACY: Graphic Organizer

Two Sides of Childhood

Adults often speak fondly of the joys of childhood, but as Desai's story demonstrates, childhood has its share of insecurities and fears as well. How you ultimately view childhood may be determined by how you remember and weigh these ups and downs. Construct a Venn diagram, like the one shown below. In one circle, jot words and images that reflect the positive side of childhood; in the other circle, jot words and images that reflect the negative side. In the overlap, note anything that seems both positive and negative about childhood.

Group Activity With a partner, answer these questions about childhood in relation to "Games at Twilight."

1. Add to the diagram at least one positive and one negative aspect about childhood based on the lives of Ravi and the other children in "Games at Twilight."

2. In your opinion, is Ravi experiencing a particularly unhappy childhood? Explain.

3. Do you think the feelings of isolation and rejection that Ravi experiences are unique to childhood or are they feelings that one experiences throughout life? Explain. How might an adult's reaction to these feelings differ from that of a child?

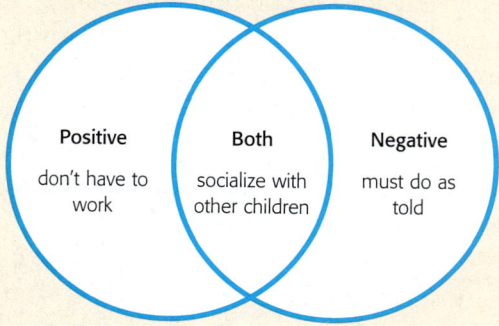

Positive — don't have to work

Both — socialize with other children

Negative — must do as told

Literary Element ## Point of View

In a story written from the **third-person limited** point of view, the narrator stands outside the story and reveals the thoughts, feelings, and observations of only one, or a limited number, of characters. In a story written from the **third-person omniscient,** or all knowing, point of view, the narrator knows everything about the characters and events and may reveal details that the characters themselves could not reveal.

1. From which point of view is "Games at Twilight" written, third-person limited or omniscient? How can you tell?

2. How does the point of view affect this story? What might have been different if the story had been told from a different point of view?

Review: Mood

As you learned on page 1090, **mood** is the emotional quality of a literary work. Choice of language, subject matter, setting, and tone, as well as such sound devices as rhyme and rhythm, contribute to the mood of a work.

Partner Activity Meet with another classmate and discuss how the mood changes during the course of this story. Construct a graphic organizer like the one below, in order to trace the sequence of moods in the story and to note which events and literary elements create these moods.

MOODS IN "GAMES AT TWILIGHT"

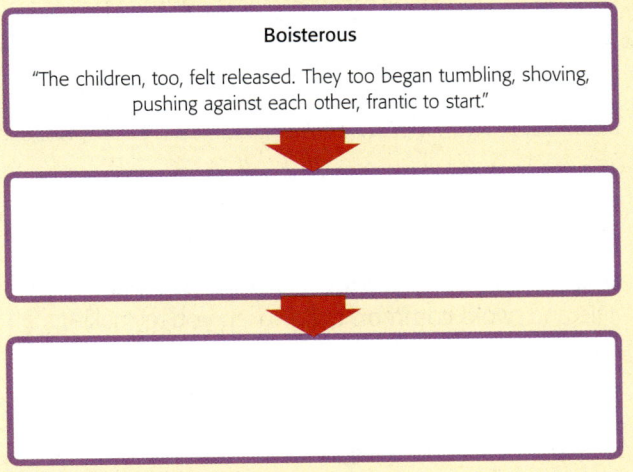

Boisterous

"The children, too, felt released. They too began tumbling, shoving, pushing against each other, frantic to start."

Reading Strategy ## Connecting to Personal Experience

You can use your personal experiences and knowledge of the world to help you understand what you read. By relating your own experiences to a text, you can identify more closely with the characters, setting, or conflicts. Think about your own childhood experiences as you answer the following questions.

1. Do you think Desai effectively captures the emotions of a child in this situation? Explain.

2. If you had been one of Ravi's siblings, what might you have said to him when he reappeared in the yard?

Vocabulary ## Practice

Practice with Word Parts Based on the definitions of the vocabulary words and your knowledge of word parts, answer the questions below.

1. Which word has a negative prefix?
   a. stridently   **b.** defunct   **c.** fray

2. Which word has an adverb-forming suffix?
   a. lugubrious   **b.** temerity   **c.** stridently

3. Which word has no added prefix or suffix?
   a. fray   **b.** temerity   **c.** defunct

4. Which word has a suffix that forms an adjective?
   a. stridently   **b.** lugubrious   **c.** fray

Academic Vocabulary

Here are two words from the vocabulary list on page R82.

area (ār′ ē ə) *n.* a part of a space; a geographical region

conduct (kon′ dukt) *v.* to manage, control, or direct

Practice and Apply

1. What **area** of the property does Ravi hide in?
2. How does Raghu **conduct** his search for the children during the game?

Writing About Literature

Evaluate Author's Craft Anita Desai uses **figurative language** in this story to create vivid impressions in the reader's mind. For example, she uses a **simile** when she states that the children "burst out [of the door] like seeds from a crackling, overripe pod." Identify three vivid similes or **metaphors** in the story. Write several paragraphs in which you explain how they make the scene clearer or more interesting. Follow the writing path shown below.

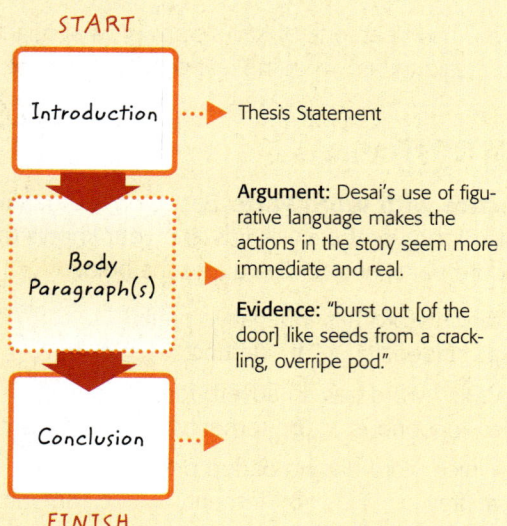

START

Introduction ····▶ Thesis Statement

Body Paragraph(s) ····▶ **Argument:** Desai's use of figurative language makes the actions in the story seem more immediate and real.

Evidence: "burst out [of the door] like seeds from a crackling, overripe pod."

Conclusion ····▶

FINISH

After you complete your draft, meet with a peer reviewer to evaluate each other's work and to suggest revisions. Then proofread and edit your draft for errors in spelling, grammar, and punctuation.

Literature Groups

In a small group, discuss the role of the games in this story. How do the children interact as they play? What social skills do they practice and learn? As a group, decide if the games have a positive or a negative influence on the children in the story. Share your group's opinion with the class.

Desai's Language and Style

Comparing by Degrees Most adjectives have three degrees of comparison. **Positive** is used to describe one person or thing (*sweet, wonderful*); **comparative** is used to describe one of two persons or things (*sweeter, more wonderful*); and **superlative** is used to describe one of three or more persons or things (*sweetest, most wonderful*). Note that the adverbs *more* and *most* are used with adjectives when the *-er* or *-est* endings would be cumbersome: *wonderfulest*.

In the passage from the story below, the word *eldest* functions as a superlative adjective because it describes one child among several.

> "'Let's play hide-and-seek.'"
> "Who'll be It"
> "You be It."
> "Why should I? You be—"
> "You're the eldest—'"

Activity In this chart are a number of adjectives used by Desai in "Games at Twilight." Complete the chart, filling in the degrees that are missing. Then, add three adjectives of your own choosing from "Games at Twilight" and fill in the missing degrees.

Positive	Comparative	Superlative
	wilder	
	angrier	
terrible		
	luckier	
necessary		
	better	
		loveliest

Revising Check

Degrees of Comparison It is important to be specific and avoid common traps when you're making comparisons. For example, the sentence "She was the best of the two," should be "She was the better of the two." With a partner, go through your evaluation of Desai's figurative language and note where more precise comparisons would make your meaning clearer. Then revise your draft accordingly.

Elegy for the Giant Tortoises

MEET MARGARET ATWOOD

"I began as a profoundly apolitical writer," Canadian poet and novelist Margaret Atwood once told *Ms.* magazine, "but then I began to do what all novelists and some poets do: I began to describe the world around me." Over the course of her more than forty years as an author, Atwood's unblinking description of the world as she sees it has won her legions of fans all over the globe.

A Split Personality Atwood was born in Ottawa, Ontario, the daughter of an entomologist. She spent the better part of her first seven years in the forested bush of northwestern Quebec, where her father was doing research on insects. The family lived far from civilization for much of each year, which meant Atwood grew up without many playmates, movies, or even a consistently working radio. As a result she learned to read at an early age, and she has been a voracious reader ever since.

During the coldest months of the year, the family packed up and moved to various cities. This trundling back and forth between forest solitude and the bustle of the city, Atwood would later claim, endowed her with the split personality necessary to become a poet. Even as a very young child she wrote stories, comic books, and plays, but it wasn't until years later that she decided to dedicate her life to writing. When she was seven years old, Atwood and her family relocated to Toronto, Ontario, where she spent her entire adolescence. She had a rather normal high school experience until her fourth year when she suddenly and without warning transformed into a poet. As she describes it, she was walking home from school one day when, "a large invisible thumb descended from the sky and pressed down on the top of my head. A poem formed. . . . It was a gift, this poem—a gift from an anonymous donor."

Atwood studied at the University of Toronto and went on to get her master's degree from Radcliffe College in Massachusetts. She was only in her mid-twenties when her poetry collection *The Circle Game* won the prestigious Governor General's Literary Award for Poetry. Perhaps as a result of her early years in the bush, many of Atwood's poems, including those in *The Circle Game*, explore themes of humankind's precarious relationship with the natural world. She published a number of volumes of poetry in the years that followed, as well as several collections of short stories. It has been as a novelist, however, that Atwood has made her greatest mark upon the literary world.

> "I hope that people will finally come to realize that there is only one 'race'—the human race—and that we are all members of it."
>
> —Margaret Atwood

Atwood's Women Margaret Atwood's novels are peopled with strong women who have complicated, and often troubled, emotional lives. Much of her work dissects modern life through a frankly feminist lens. Atwood's probing insights into human behavior have made her one of the most popular and critically acclaimed writers of her time.

Margaret Atwood was born in 1939.

Literature Online Author Search For more about Margaret Atwood, go to www.glencoe.com.

Connecting to the Poem

What is our responsibility to the environment? As you read the poem, think about the following questions:

- Why do you think people, businesses, and governments might ignore the potential long-term implications of pollution, habitat destruction, and other environmental problems?
- What are some activities people can do on a daily basis to improve the environment?

Building Background

Her early experiences in the Canadian wilderness focused Atwood's attention on nature. "Later on I studied chemistry and botany and zoology," she recalls, "and if I hadn't been a writer I'd have gone on with that." Atwood believes that the struggle to survive in nature is a theme that runs throughout Canadian literature. She sees herself as a strongly nationalistic Canadian writer and views Canadian literature as distinct from its American and British counterparts. She believes that a single unifying and defining symbol or theme identifies each country or culture. For the United States, it is the frontier, and for England, it is the island. For Canada, Atwood believes, this defining theme is survival.

Setting Purposes for Reading

Big Idea Globalization

Atwood's work reflects a global perspective, an acknowledgment of the many nations and cultures that make up the modern world. As you read "Elegy for the Giant Tortoises," consider the serious global issues at the poem's core.

Literary Element Alliteration

Alliteration is the repetition of consonant sounds at the beginnings of words. It can be used to reinforce meaning or create a musical effect. As you read "Elegy for the Giant Tortoises," listen for the sounds of repeated consonants and try to figure out the poet's intention in using them.

- See Literary Terms Handbook, p. R1.

Reading Strategy Interpreting Imagery

Imagery refers to the word pictures that writers create to evoke an emotional response. In creating effective images, writers use **sensory details,** or descriptions that appeal to one or more of the five senses.

Reading Tip: Focusing on Images As you read, note the images in the poem and what they might mean.

Vocabulary

withering (with′ ər ing) v. becoming dry; shriveling from lack of moisture; p. 1357 *The bunch of grapes I left on the picnic table were withering from the heat.*

periphery (pə rif′ ər ē) n. the outward or farthest boundary; p. 1358 *The girls were dancing together in the middle of the room while the boys hung back on the periphery.*

plodding (plod′ ding) v. walking heavily and/or slowly; p. 1358 *The tired mule was plodding through the yard dragging the broken plow behind him.*

lumbering (lum′ bər ing) v. moving heavily and clumsily; p. 1358 *The old dog came lumbering up the steps.*

obsolete (ob′ sə lēt′) adj. no longer in use; outdated; p. 1358 *The new computers made the old ones obsolete.*

Vocabulary Tip: Synonyms Synonyms are words that have the same or similar meanings. Note that synonyms are always the same part of speech.

Literature Online **Interactive Literary Elements Handbook** To review or learn more about the literary elements, go to www.glencoe.com.

OBJECTIVES
In studying this selection, you will focus on the following:
- analyzing genre elements
- analyzing alliteration
- interpreting imagery

Fantaise, 1975. Peter Kinsley. Private collection.

Elegy for the Giant Tortoises

Margaret Atwood

Let others pray for the passenger pigeon,
the dodo,[1] the whooping crane, the eskimo:
everyone must specialize

I will confine myself to a meditation
5   upon the giant tortoises
    withering finally on a remote island.

---

1. A *dodo* was a heavy flightless bird, now extinct.

Big Idea   **Globalization**   *What might the passenger pigeon, dodo, whooping crane, and Eskimo (Inuit) have in common?*

Vocabulary

withering (wi<u>th</u>′ ər ing) *v.* becoming dry; shriveling from lack of moisture

I concentrate in subway stations,
in parks, I can't quite see them,
they move to the **peripheries** of my eyes

10 but on the last day they will be there;
already the event
like a wave travelling shapes vision:

on the road where I stand they will materialize,
plodding past me in a straggling line
15 awkward without water

their small heads pondering
from side to side, their useless armor
sadder than tanks and history,

in their closed gaze ocean and sunlight paralyzed,
20 **lumbering** up the steps, under the archways
toward the square glass altars

where the brittle gods are kept,
the relics of what we have destroyed,
our holy and **obsolete** symbols.

Reading Strategy Interpreting Imagery *What does the speaker mean by the statement that the ocean and sunlight are "paralyzed" in the tortoise's closed gaze?*

Vocabulary

periphery (pə rif′ ər ē) *n.* the outward or farthest boundary
plodding (plod′ ding) *v.* walking heavily and/or slowly
lumbering (lum′ bər ing) *v.* moving heavily and clumsily
obsolete (ob′ sə lēt′) *adj.* no longer in use; outdated

RESPONDING AND THINKING CRITICALLY

Respond

1. What was your emotional response to the poem's ending? Why?

Recall and Interpret

2. (a)Where does the speaker go to concentrate on the tortoises? (b)Are these appropriate places to go? Explain.

3. (a)To what does the speaker compare the tortoise's shell? (b)What point does the speaker seem to be making with this comparison?

4. Where does the speaker imply we will have to go to see tortoises in the future? Why?

Analyze and Evaluate

5. (a)What emotions do you think Atwood wanted to evoke in readers with this poem? (b)What might have been her purpose in writing the poem?

6. (a)To what does the poet compare the museum in the final two stanzas? (b)Why do you think Atwood uses this particular comparison?

Connect

7. **Big Idea** **Globalization** How might the theme of this poem be said to reflect global concerns?

LITERARY ANALYSIS

Literary Element Alliteration

Alliteration is the repetition of consonants or consonant sounds at the beginnings of words in close proximity to one another. In "Elegy for the Giant Tortoises," Atwood uses alliteration to reinforce rhythm and musicality and to emphasize particular points.

1. Listen to the way the phrase "subway station" sounds in line 7. What does this sound reinforce given the context of the stanza?

2. What sort of rhythm do the phrases "plodding past" (line 14) and "side to side" (line 17) create?

Reading Further

If you would like to read more by Margaret Atwood, you might enjoy these works:

- In the novel *The Blind Assassin* (winner of the prestigious Booker Prize), Atwood uses multiple story lines to take readers on a complicated and often hilarious journey.
- The poems in *The Circle Game* look at human beings against the backdrop of the natural world.

READING AND VOCABULARY

Reading Strategy Interpreting Imagery

By **interpreting** the **imagery** in the poem, you may note that the speaker suggests a person should not pray for all species; it is necessary to specialize.

1. Why do you think Atwood uses the images of prayer and church to make her point?

2. (a)Identify three images in the poem that relate to war. (b)How do you interpret the significance of these images?

Vocabulary Practice

Practice with Synonyms Identify the synonym for each vocabulary word below.

1. lumbering	**a.** shambling	**b.** sidling
2. plodding	**a.** stuttering	**b.** laboring
3. periphery	**a.** border	**b.** center
4. withering	**a.** festering	**b.** wilting
5. obsolete	**a.** out-dated	**b.** new

Literature Online **Web Activities** For eFlashcards, Selection Quick Checks, and other Web activities, go to www.glencoe.com.

Preview the Article

"Music Goes Global" examines the rise of global music, a kind of music that has no language barriers.

1. Examine the title. What might "global" mean in this context?

2. Read the *deck*, or the sentence in large type that appears underneath the headline. What connection might the writer make between music and traditions?

Set a Purpose for Reading

Read to learn how music can establish cultural identity and serve as a universal language.

Reading Strategy

Activating Prior Knowledge
When you recall information and personal experiences that are uniquely your own, you are **activating prior knowledge.**

As you read "Music Goes Global," ask yourself how the article relates to your prior knowledge and experiences. Create a chart like the one below.

Questions	Prior Knowledge
How does the topic of the article relate to my personal interests?	

OBJECTIVES
- Make connections between prior knowledge and a text.
- Explore life experiences related to subject area content.

TIME

Music Goes Global

From Kingston to Cape Town, from New Delhi to New York, musicians are rocking old traditions. Your world will never be the same.

By CHRISTOPHER JOHN FARLEY

IT'S EARLY EVENING IN KINGSTON. THE SLUMBERING HILLS that surround the capital of Jamaica are covered in warm blankets of shadows. It has been a season of heat—the sugarcane crop is shriveling for lack of rain and the streets are dusty and dry. The heat makes tensions rise.

Independence Day is coming, the anniversary of Jamaica's emergence from the control of Britain. Outside club Asylum, one of the city's most popular night spots, young Jamaicans have begun to gather. Inside, things are slow as the drone of foreign acts—Britney Spears, Whitney Houston, 'N Sync—echoes across the empty dance floor. But out on the streets, kids are making their own scene, to their own sounds. Ragga (a rap-influenced form of reggae) booms out of parked cars. Young Jamaican men with white scarves tied around their heads vibrate to the music—some of which are songs of protest.

It is a scene like those that nowadays are taking place in cities all over the planet—in Tokyo, in Cape Town, in Reykjavik. In such ways, in such places, a fresh sound in global music is being born. It's the beating heart of a new world.

Bob Marley, the great Jamaican reggae star, once posed the question "Won't you help me sing these songs of freedom?" Music can be a tool: for relaxation, for stimulation, for communication—and for social change. In fact, it is often a rhythm of resistance: against war, against social injustice, against government corruption.

The U.S., in this one-superpower age, has perhaps never been so dominant—economically, militarily, culturally. That strength attracts immigrants, who bring with them new forms of music. That strength also inspires competition. Musicians and performers in other countries, mindful of American influence, assert their national identities and culture and create new musical genres they can call their own: garage in Britain, kwaito in South Africa, ever evolving forms of reggae in Jamaica. America may be the world's policeman, but citizens of the world—and the New Americans who have come here—have turned up their car stereos and are dancing like never before.

The quest for change has often been a family affair: many top global-music performers, including Nigeria's Femi Kuti (son of Fela), Jamaica's Ziggy Marley (son of Bob) and Brazil's Max de Castro (son of Wilson Simonal), are the children of musical pioneers. In recent years around the world, old traditions have been revived, remolded, and returned to prominence by a new generation and new technology. In Tijuana, Mexico, young DJs have crossed traditional norteno (a polka-like music) with not-at-all-traditional techno to create a fresh genre, Nortec. In Bogota, Colombia, the rock duo Aterciopelados mixed old-time accordion-driven vallenato with clubland drum-'n'-bass beats. In Rio de Janeiro, Brazil, the great chanteuse Marisa Monte smoothly blended samba and art-pop.

Centuries of customs have changed in just decades. In the 1940s and '50s, radio brought the music of the outside world to much of Africa for the first time. In the 1970s, audiocassette tapes made it possible for Third World musicians to spread their own music quickly, cheaply, and profitably. Acts like the Congo's Papa Wemba became continent-wide superstars.

In the 21st century, the Internet has opened up the world to itself. In the distant past—say, a decade ago—global-music fans had to wait for a record label to decide whether to distribute a foreign artist in their country. A few years later, Internet file-sharing services were allowing users to listen to whatever they wanted, anywhere they chose, anytime they pleased. Today, online music stores tend to have wider and more diverse inventories than their bricks-and-mortar counterparts.

The we-are-the-world maxim is this: music is the universal language. For the mainstream record industry in the U.S., however, music in

WYCLEF JEAN

SHAKIRA

DE CASTRO

Paulo Fridman/TIME

Todd France/CORBIS

Nick Baratta for Teen People

languages other than English often wasn't considered universal; it was controversial.

Richie Valens hit it big with "La Bamba" in 1959. The music industry didn't wholeheartedly embrace another Latin rocker until Santana's late-in-life success in 1999. After that, tongues became untied. Wyclef Jean's platinum hip-hop CDs, *The Carnival* and *The Ecleftic*, mixed English and Haitian Creole. Christina Aguilera, who launched her career singing English-language teen pop, recorded a CD entirely in Spanish. Increasingly, world-beaters are collaborating and connecting with one another. Colombian rocker Shakira had a CD executive-produced by Cuban-American Emilio Estefan Jr. that drew from Argentine tango.

SHIRLEY
MANSON

Phil Knott/Camerapress/Retna

MARC ANTHONY

Niels Van Iperenn/Retna

ZIGGY MARLEY

Fred Prouser/Reuters

HIKARU

Michael Halsband/TIME

MIKE D

Michael Lavine/CORBIS

Musicians performing in different languages often strike similar chords. Listen to the intense, undulant wail of Assane Ndiaye on the song "Nguisstal," a track on *Streets of Dakar: Generation Boul Fale*, a compilation of young Senegalese acts. *Boul fale* is a Wolof phrase that means, loosely, "Never mind." The American punk group Nirvana's great album of teen angst was also titled *Nevermind*. Alienation, it seems, is a nation without borders.

The new global music doesn't exclude America. After all, one of America's biggest rock stars of the past few years was Dave Matthews, a white African; the Japanese pop star Utada Hikaru hailed from Manhattan. The old-school term *world music* is a joke, a wedge, a way of separating English-language performers from the rest of the planet. But there has always been crossover. In 1958 Dean Martin scored a hit with the Italian tune "Volare"; in 1967 Frank Sinatra recorded an album of songs by Brazilian composer Antonio Carlos (Tom) Jobim. Elvis Presley's "Can't Help Falling in Love" is based on the 18th century French ballad "Plaisir d'amour."

Pop music and global music aren't mutually exclusive categories. In the 1980s Paul Simon, David Byrne, and Peter Gabriel blended world beats. Later, Sting scored a hit with Algerian rai star Cheb Mami, Lauryn Hill covered Bob Marley on MTV Unplugged, and Britney Spears made a habit of working with Swedish songwriter Max Martin. Over the years, Madonna's sound—and style—has been inspired by many cultures.

Lyrics are important, but they don't have to matter. Even when Bob Dylan, arguably America's finest lyricist, mumbles through a number, the poetry of his words comes out in the phrasing. "How does it feel?" Dylan famously asked on "Like a Rolling Stone." We may not have known exactly what he meant, but we knew how it felt. Today's musicians have taken that lesson to heart. Thom Yorke of the British band Radiohead wrote some songs for his classic album *Kid A* by cutting up lyric sheets and pulling lines out of a top hat. The Icelandic band Sigur Ros sang some songs in a made-up tongue it called Hopelandic.

Many of today's global musicians move back and forth from their native tongues to English, on the same album, sometimes on the same song. There's a sense that geography doesn't have to equal destiny. The Tokyo-based rock trio the Brilliant Green produced a CD almost entirely in Japanese. It was recorded in Tokyo. The CD's title? *Los Angeles*.

Listening to music in an unfamiliar tongue can be more thrilling than listening to a song whose lyrics are instantly understandable. That's because if you can connect

FASSIE

Michael Halsband/TIME

DAVE MATTHEWS

Robert Delahanty/CORBIS

ATERCIOPELADOS

Ted Thai/TIME

with another person beyond lyrics, beyond language, then you have engaged in a kind of telepathy. You have managed to escape the everyday realm of ordinary communication and entered a place where souls communicate directly. It's cooler than instant messaging. Cherif Mbaw is a Senegalese singer-guitarist living in Paris; the songs on his brilliant CD *Kham Kham* are in his native Wolof. But when Mbaw, with his beatific tenor, soars into a passage of staccato vocals and jittery guitar work on "Saay Saay," you know exactly what he means even if you don't know what he's saying. His intent is in his inflection; his eloquence is in his emotion. Boundaries fall away.

Is a sense of cultural uniqueness lost in the global-pop blender? If they are grooving to America's latest pop star in Kingston, is there anywhere to hide? The first years of the 21st century have been haunted by the specter of globalization. Our star-spangled world with its parade of powerful letters—the U.N., the WTO, the IMF—hammers the diversity of the planet into homogenized goop. But the Colombian duo Aterciopelados insists on recording its CDs in its hometown of Bogotá. And Max de Castro projects blown-up images of old Brazilian LPs at some of his concerts to remind audiences of his country's heritage. Many new global artists have the curiosity to wander the earth with their music and the integrity to stay connected to their homelands. This is the help Marley asked for. These are freedom songs.

It's getting hot in club Asylum, but the dancers just keep on going. At this club and ones like it around the world—in Sao Paulo, in Dakar, in Havana, in New York City—Independence Day is every night.

— Updated 2005,
from TIME (Special Issue), Fall, 2001

RESPONDING AND THINKING CRITICALLY

Respond

1. What was your reaction to the music described in the article? How is it different from or similar to the music you listen to?

Recall and Interpret

2. (a)What is "global music"? (b)Why do you think this kind of music has become popular?

3. (a)How is music a tool? (b)How does it allow musicians to "assert their national identities"?

4. (a)How did technology inspire a global music revolution? (b)How has technology continued to make access to music easier?

Analyze and Evaluate

5. (a)What similarities does the writer point out between American and world music? (b)What effect does this point have on his argument?

6. (a)How did your prior experiences and personal interests relate to the article? (b)Explain whether the writer assumes readers have a prior knowledge of music. Cite specific examples from the text.

Connect

7. How does this article connect global music to some of the themes in contemporary British literature?

Writing Workshop

Critical Review

 Evaluating a Literary Work

> *"The real risks of any artist are taken in the work, in pushing the work to the limits of what is possible. . . . Books become good when they go to this edge and risk falling over it."*
>
> —Salman Rushdie, from *Imaginary Homelands*

Connecting to Literature In this passage, Salman Rushdie discusses what, in his opinion, an artist must successfully attempt in order to create great literature. More narrowly, in a critical review you examine what an artist has attempted to achieve in a particular work and evaluate his or her relative success, citing specific strengths and weaknesses to support your opinion. To write a successful critical review, learn the goals of critical writing and the strategies for achieving those goals.

Rubric: Features of Critical Reviews

Goals	Strategies
To make a statement about a story's literary merits	☑ Develop a thesis for expressing your overall critical judgment of the story
To support with evidence a personal evaluation of the story	☑ Analyze and assess important literary elements in the story to show that your thesis is valid
	☑ Include direct evidence from the story, such as examples and quotations, to support your evaluation
To present a logically organized critical review of the story	☑ Summarize the basic plot and state your thesis in the introduction
	☑ State your reasons and supporting evidence in your body paragraphs
	☑ Restate your thesis and make a recommendation about the story
To persuade the reader to accept your evaluation of the story	☑ In the conclusion, consider readers' expectations and address opposing viewpoints

---

The Writing Process

In this workshop, you will follow the stages of the writing process. At any stage, you may think of new ideas to include and better ways to express them. Feel free to return to earlier stages as you write.

Prewriting

Drafting

Revising

 Focus Lesson: Adding Evidence to Support a Viewpoint

Editing and Proofreading

 Focus Lesson: Correcting Verb Tense

Presenting

Writing Models For models and other writing activities, go to www.glencoe.com.

OBJECTIVES
- Write a critical review to analyze the literary merits of a short story and to persuade a reader to accept your evaluation of the story.
- Develop a thesis and support it with reasons and direct evidence.

Real-World Connection

In the real world, critics of the arts have earned praise and scorn in equal measure. Both attitudes reflect the amount of power critics hold in determining the success of a work. As you write your own review, make sure that your judgment is as fair, honest, and informed as possible.

> ▶ **Assignment**
>
> Write a critical review in which you analyze the literary merits of a short story and make a critical evaluation of the story. As you move through the stages of the writing process, keep your audience and purpose in mind.
>
> **Audience:** peers and others who may be interested in the story
>
> **Purpose:** to evaluate a story and convince an audience of the validity of your evaluation

Analyzing a Professional Model

In this critical review, *New York Times* writer Selden Rodman reviews V. S. Naipaul's collection of short stories *Miguel Street*, praising the story "B. Wordsworth" in particular. As you read the review, notice how Rodman makes a critical evaluation and supports it with examples and evidence from the text. Pay close attention to the comments in the margin. They point out features that you may want to include in your own critical review.

from *"Catfish Row, Trinidad"* by Selden Rodman

The mystifying things about Trinidad writers—most recently Samuel Selvon, Geoffrey Holder, and the present author—is why they ever leave the island. Existence in this corner of the British West Indies may not be paradise, but compared with the slums of London or New York, this is life among those who know how to live it. Certainly it has never a dull moment. V. S. Naipaul, born in Trinidad of Hindu parents and educated at Oxford, proved he knew the region in his novel, "The Mystic Masseur." He proves it again with these short, delightful sketches of Miguel Street, the Catfish Row of Port of Spain. . . .

The finest of this really fine collection of portraits is the one entitled "B. Wordsworth." B stands for Black, and it is about a poet who wanders in one day just to "watch the bees" and who answers a policeman who asks what he's doing lying on his back in a public place, "I have been asking myself the same question for forty years." The young narrator takes this character to meet his mother:

Conversational Tone

Share your opinions using a natural voice and a conversational tone.

Introduction

In your introduction, include the author and the title of the work you are to review, as well as your thesis, or overall critical judgment of the work.

Plot Summary

Give a brief plot summary so that readers unfamiliar with the work will understand your review.

Direct Quotations

Support your evaluation with critical evidence, including examples and direct quotations.

"He pulled out a printed sheet from his hip-pocket and said, 'On this paper is the greatest poem about mothers and I'm going to sell it to you at a bargain price. For four cents.'

"I went inside and I said, 'Ma, you want to buy a poetry for four cents?'

"My mother said, 'Tell that blasted man to haul his tail away from my yard, you hear?'

"I said to B. Wordsworth, 'My mother say she ain't have four cents.'

"B. Wordsworth said, 'It is the poet's tragedy.'"

He put the paper back in his pocket. He didn't seem to mind. The ending of this little classic is a sad one. But the prevailing mood of the stories is comic, and most of the characters fulfill themselves through their idiosyncrasies—a fact which brings us back to the original question.

Opposing Viewpoints

Answer possible objections to your evaluation to persuade your reader that your opinion is balanced.

Conclusion

Sum up your review and give your recommendation in your conclusion.

In the final chapter the narrator is about to join his fellow story-tellers abroad ("The Americans gave me a visa after making me swear I wouldn't overthrow their government by armed force"). In the airport lounge, filled with haughty tourists in sun-glasses looking "too rich, too comfortable," he wishes he had never got a scholarship. Wouldn't it be interesting now to have a novel about one of these children of nature in our frigid cities—and then, the native's return?

Reading-Writing Connection Think about the writing techniques that you have just encountered and try them out in the critical review you write.

Prewriting

Choose a Story Choose a story from Unit Seven that left you with a strong positive or negative impression.

Examine and Evaluate Your Story After you choose a story, reread it several times. Try to determine the author's purpose for writing the story and which literary elements are used to achieve the desired effects. Ask yourself:

▶ What is the author trying to achieve? Did he or she meet this goal? How?

▶ What is the theme of the story and how is it conveyed?

▶ What is the plot like? Is it believable? Is it engaging or suspenseful? Why?

▶ How does the setting affect the story?

▶ How are the characters developed? Are they believable? Do they undergo significant change?

▶ In your opinion, what element is most important to the overall success or failure of the story?

Develop a Thesis What is your overall opinion of the story? Distill that opinion into a clear, one- or two-sentence thesis statement that presents and explains your overall critical judgment of the story.

Identify Critical Evidence Remember that a critical review involves more than just stating your opinion; you need to give logical reasons why your opinion is valid and deserves your audience's consideration.

Outline Your Review Create an outline to organize your ideas. Follow the basic structure of an essay and include any background information your audience may need.

Discuss Your Ideas Once you finish organizing your ideas, share your evaluation and outline with a partner. Partners should also help each other clarify their theses, organize their reasons, and identify additional supporting evidence from the story.

Review the Reviews

Sharpen your critical sense by reading book and film reviews published in current newspapers and magazines. Notice the voice and tone of the reviews, the evaluations presented, and how those evaluations are supported.

Agree to Disagree

Your opinions about a story will probably be different from those of others. Use the variance to your advantage. A second opinion may cause you to consider aspects of a story you had overlooked.

Introduction	Give the story's title and author. Summarize the plot briefly. State your overall critical judgment in your thesis.	"The Train from Rhodesia" by Nadine Gordimer Thesis: Through realistic description and full characterization, Gordimer shows how the complex and pervasive force of racism damages the victim, the oppressor, and those caught in between.
Body Paragraphs	Focus on the major elements that contribute to the story's success or failure. State your opinions, support them with reasons.	Gordimer uses vivid descriptions and a detached voice to suggest the existence of racism, using rich characterization to powerfully show how it affects the characters.
Conclusion	Restate your evaluation and make a recommendation to the reader.	Although Gordimer's subtlety and complex characters may be frustrating at first, most readers will find her story powerful and almost haunting.

Drafting

Stay Flexible As you draft your review, use your outline as a guide but be flexible as your evaluation evolves. You may change your opinion about the story as you explore it on a deeper level and the author's purpose and effects become clearer.

Analyzing a Workshop Model

Here is a final draft of a critical review. Read the review and answer the questions in the margin. Use the answers to these questions to guide you as you write your own review.

"The Train from Rhodesia": A Subtle but Powerful Message

Introduction

What makes this a strong introduction?

Plot Summary

Does this plot summary provide enough information for the reader? Explain.

Thesis

What details make this an appropriate thesis for a critical review?

Tone

How would you describe the tone of the review?

Example

Why might the writer include this example but not quote the passage directly here?

"The Train from Rhodesia" by South African writer Nadine Gordimer is a haunting story that explores the damaging effects of racism in a subtle but powerful way. Gordimer begins the story with a rich description of an African train station just as a train pulls in. The story revolves around a seemingly trivial event: a young woman is interested in buying a carved lion from a native artist but decides it is too expensive. Without her knowledge, her husband bargains with the artist and buys the carving at a much cheaper price. He then gives the carving to his wife, pleased with his success. Through realistic description and full characterization, "The Train from Rhodesia" shows how the complex and pervasive forces of colonialism and racism damage the victim, the oppressor, and those caught in between.

It is easy to get caught up in Gordimer's vivid images. From the very first line, we are *there,* feeling the train bearing down on the station, seeing and hearing it "creaking, jerking, jostling, gasping." Through the precise descriptions, we also see and hear the evidence of blatant racial tension at the station and on the train, without any mention of it directly. At the station, the native vendors are "squatting" and "waiting in the dust." The stationmaster's "barefoot" children approach the train, where they are enclosed in shadows. These images focus on the low, almost hidden, position of the native Africans and hint at an unspoken divide between the black natives and the white travelers on the train. On the train, we hear needier native children begging the travelers for a penny, an orange, or a chocolate; a moment later we see a young girl throwing a handful of unwanted chocolates to the dogs instead. No words are exchanged between the girl and the children, and the narrator does not explain or comment on the action. This type of subtlety and detachment throughout the story makes the events and interactions especially disturbing.

Perhaps the most compelling aspect of Gordimer's story, though, is her sharp characterization of people, both black and white, who encounter the complex but familiar issue of racism in one way or another. As a contrast to the girl with the candy, Gordimer paints the wife as sympathetic and self-aware. When she examines the carving, the wife is able to see past the object to the artistry of the "heraldic" lion and the dignity and satisfaction of the artist. The wife sees the lion's mouth "opened in an endless roar too terrible to be heard" and its fur mane, "a real mane, majestic, telling you somehow that the artist had delight in the lion." Here, again, Gordimer's realistic details suggest much more than they actually describe.

At the same time, however, Gordimer weaves contrasting details into the narrative, exposing contradictions in the characters. From the limited third-person perspective, we learn the wife's intimate thoughts, her sympathy toward the artist, for example, but also her more automatic, conventional attitudes. She sees the adult artist selling his wares on the train as an "old boy"—at that time a conventional, but condescending, racial description. Whatever respect the wife has for the artist, she always speaks gruffly to him in person, in a commanding, almost annoyed tone. The artist, a minor character, conforms to the racist social conventions as well, though unlike the wife he has little choice. He calls the wife "Missus" and the husband "Baas" (boss) more out of the need to make a sale than out of respect, and he smiles "not from the heart, but at the customer." When the husband pays the artist after bargaining for a cheaper price, the artist, "smiling and shaking his head," appears more happy than humiliated, at least for the moment. Simply speaking, the money, as little as it is, is presently more useful to him than the lion.

Gordimer's detached tone and complex, often contradictory, characters may leave some readers frustrated. The ending of the story asks more questions than it answers, yet one theme becomes clear: the lingering effects of colonialism and racism are damaging to all those involved, no matter which side of the color line they're on. Read "The Train from Rhodesia" and you'll find that Gordimer's vivid images and powerful characters stay with you long after you finish the story.

Persuasion/Exposition

Connection to Thesis
How does this information strengthen the writer's review?

Organization
How are the first two body paragraphs organized? Why is this an effective way of organizing the review?

Direct Quotations
What do the direct quotations here add to the review that a summarized example might not?

Opposing Viewpoints
How does telling readers that they might be "frustrated" with the story help support the writer's evaluation? Explain.

Conclusion
What makes this a strong conclusion?

Revising

Use the rubric below to help you evaluate and strengthen your review.

Rubric: Writing an Effective Critical Review

☑ Do you make a statement about your overall judgment of a story's literary merits?

☑ Do you support your evaluation with reasons, examples, and direct quotations?

☑ Do you present a logically organized critical review of the story?

☑ Do you address readers' expectations and opposing viewpoints and persuade the reader to accept your evaluation of the story?

▶ Focus Lesson

Adding Evidence to Support a Viewpoint

To persuade your audience that your viewpoint is valid, check to be sure that you fully support your viewpoint with reasons and that you back up those reasons with examples and direct quotations.

Draft:

Perhaps the most compelling aspect of Gordimer's story, though, is her sharp characterization of people, both black and white, who encounter the complex but familiar issue of racism in one way or another. As a contrast to the girl with the candy, the wife is sympathetic and self-aware.

Revision:

Perhaps the most compelling aspect of Gordimer's story, though, is her sharp characterization of people, both black and white, who encounter the complex but familiar issue of racism in one way or another. As a contrast to the girl with the candy, Gordimer paints the wife as sympathetic and self-aware. When she examines the carving, the wife is able to see past the object to the artistry of the "heraldic" lion and the dignity and satisfaction of the artist.[1] The wife sees the lion's mouth "opened in an endless roar too terrible to be heard" and its fur mane, "a real mane, majestic, telling you somehow that the artist had delight in the lion."[2] Here, again, Gordimer's realistic details suggest much more than they actually describe.[3]

1: Add examples from the text.   **2: Add direct quotations.**

3: Show how your evidence supports your thesis.

Editing and Proofreading

Get It Right When you have completed the final draft of your review, proofread it for errors in grammar, usage, mechanics, and spelling. Refer to the Language Handbook, pages R46–R60, as a guide.

> **Focus Lesson**

Correcting Verb Tense

When you write a critical review—or when you write about a literary work in general—use the present tense. This is called the **literary present tense.** Although the story you are reviewing was written in the past, the text will be new for unfamiliar readers, and it will reveal new ways of looking at the story for those who are familiar with it.

Original: The statement describing the story uses the past tense.

As a contrast to the girl with the candy, Gordimer painted the wife as sympathetic and self-aware.

Improved: Even when the literary action you describe technically happened in the past, use the literary present tense.

As a contrast to the girl with the candy, Gordimer paints the wife as sympathetic and self-aware.

Original: The statement about the story, like the quotation, is in the past tense.

One of the first images occurred at the station, where the stationmaster's barefoot children watched the train and wandered over as shadows "closed over the children's black feet softly and without imprint."

Improved: Do not change the tense of the quoted material but write your own material in the present tense.

One of the first images occurs at the station, where the stationmaster's barefoot children watch the train and wander over as shadows "closed over the children's black feet softly and without imprint."

Presenting

Take One Last Look Before you turn in your critical review, take one last look to make sure that it is free of errors. Give it an interesting title and check to be sure that you have followed your teacher's guidelines regarding length, spacing, and content.

Citing Titles

When you edit your review, check to be sure that the title of your text is properly spelled, capitalized, and punctuated.

- **Stories and poems are in quotation marks:**

  "The Train from Rhodesia"

  "Wind"

- **Novels, books, plays, movies, and art-works are italicized (or underlined):**

  Miguel Street

  That's All

Writer's Portfolio

Place a clean copy of your critical review in your portfolio to review later.

Speaking, Listening, and Viewing Workshop

Critical Review

Delivering a Critical Review

Connecting to Literature A critical review is a way to share your impressions about a work of literature. When you deliver a critical review, you evaluate what a writer attempted to achieve and whether you feel he or she succeeded. You encounter different kinds of critical reviews nearly every day, sometimes without even realizing it. A critical review can take the form of a newspaper editorial, a book review in a magazine, or a commentary on a radio or news broadcast.

> ▶ **Assignment** In groups, plan and deliver a critical review in the style of a television or radio broadcast.

Planning Your Presentation

There are a variety of ways you can arrange to record the audio and visual elements of your review. For example, you can use a home video camera to create a talk show–style newscast or a hand-held tape recorder to develop a radio broadcast. However, your radio or television broadcast does not have to be complicated. You might simply pretend to have an "on-air" set and present your review to an audience of your classmates.

Preparing to Present

- Decide which parts of your critical review you want to share with your audience. In a radio or television format, you may not have enough time to cover everything. Therefore, limit your presentation to your most important points.
- Before presenting, read your critical review several times to remember the key events in the order they appear. Don't try to memorize the words verbatim; avoid simply reading the review aloud.
- Experiment with gestures, facial expressions, and postures to show excitement, dismay, and other emotions. Try practicing in front of a mirror before you record your presentation.
- Consider playing background music as part of your presentation. If you are planning a television broadcast, incorporate sound effects, graphics, or additional visual media.

Presenting

Begin by giving your audience a brief synopsis of what you are reviewing, but don't give away the entire plot. You may want to grab the attention of your audience by asking a question, for example, "Do you ever wonder what would have happened if you had to move to another country? The boy in this story found out."

Most importantly, relax and enjoy yourself. If you're tense, your audience will sense it. If you forget an important detail, add it later, simply saying, "There's something else you need to know."

Techniques for Delivering a Critical Review

Verbal Techniques	Nonverbal Techniques
☑ **Volume** Speak loudly and clearly.	☑ **Eye Contact** Make direct eye contact with the audience. When other group members are speaking, make eye contact with them.
☑ **Pace** You will need to speak slowly enough for your audience to understand you, especially when pronouncing unfamiliar words.	☑ **Gestures** Use gestures to emphasize important ideas in your critical review.
☑ **Tone** Vary the tone of your voice to keep your audience interested, particularly if you're presenting a radio recording.	☑ **Visual Aids** Use photographs or drawings related to your critical review. If presenting a radio broadcast, describe these photographs or other visual media to listeners.
☑ **Emphasis** Stress important points of your review, perhaps by using transitional phrases such as *most importantly*.	

Technology Skills

If you decide to record your presentation, there are many resources available to provide technology assistance. Both the Internet and the library are valuable resources for technology help. Additionally, your school may have an audio-visual department that can provide assistance.

OBJECTIVES
- Deliver an oral critique of a literary work.
- Develop appropriate speaking strategies in the classroom.
- Use a variety of media to share ideas and information.

For Independent Reading

ENGLISH LITERATURE IN THE LATTER HALF OF THE TWENTIETH CENTURY BECAME increasingly global and far more inclusive. Women and minority writers—groups that had been largely excluded from critical examination—produced acclaimed works of fiction, poetry, and drama.

Through literature, colonized peoples began to find a means by which to explore issues related to colonialism, such as race and cultural identity. Also, writing became increasingly experimental and innovative, as genres, traditions, and national boundaries blurred or were abandoned altogether.

Waiting for Godot

by Samuel Beckett (1952)

This play, which is Beckett's most well known, is one of the leading works of the twentieth-century dramatic movement known as the theater of the absurd. Structured in two acts, *Waiting for Godot* is stripped bare of theatrical pretense; the stage is empty during much of the play except for four characters and a leafless tree. The main characters, Vladimir and Estragon, are unsure of their purpose but are convinced that they are waiting for an unseen, possibly nonexistent character named Godot.

Midnight's Children

by Salman Rushdie (1981)

Declared by the Booker Prize committee the best British novel to win the Booker Prize in the last twenty-five years, *Midnight's Children* begins in 1947, on the first night of India's independence. At the stroke of midnight, 1,001 children are born with unusual gifts and a deep connection to their new nation. This controversial and often difficult novel combines elements of magical realism, myth, family drama, and the modern history of India in the postcolonial period. The novel follows the life of midnight's child Saleem Sinai, whose strange and difficult life is inextricably bound to the history of India and Pakistan.

"The literary map of India is about to be redrawn. . . . Serious English-language novelists from India (often called Indo-Anglians), or those from abroad who use Indian material, have steered a steady course between . . . two vast, mutually obliterating realities. . . . What this fiction has been missing is a different kind of ambition, something just a little coarse, a hunger to swallow India whole and spit it out. . . . Now, in Midnight's Children, Salman Rushdie has realized that ambition. . . . This is a book to accept on its own terms, and an author to welcome into world company."

—Clark Blaise, *The New York Times*, April 19, 1981

Possession: A Romance

by A. S. Byatt (1990)

Brilliantly weaving together multiple storylines and genres, Byatt's novel explores the relationships between the past and the present, writers and their readers, and women and men. *Possession*, which won the Booker Prize in 1990, focuses on two young literary scholars, Roland Michell and Maud Bailey, who uncover a secret romance that existed between two poets from the Victorian age. Through letters and manuscripts, Michell and Bailey piece together this hidden history, which forces them to reevaluate the meaning of their own lives and scholarship.

From the Glencoe Literature Library

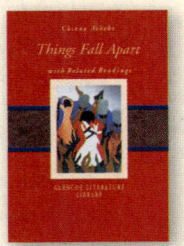

Things Fall Apart

by Chinua Achebe

As Britain's imperial ambitions extend into Africa, a centuries-old way of life vanishes and Okonkwo, a figure of heroic proportions, meets his moving, tragic end.

Nectar in a Sieve

by Kamala Markandaya

Nectar in a Sieve explores painful and disturbing aspects of poverty and a village's transformation from agriculture to industry.

A House for Mr. Biswas

by V. S. Naipaul

Set in Trinidad, this novel draws largely from the author's own childhood experiences as a Hindu Indian living in what was then a British colony.

Reading: Poetry

Carefully read the following poem. Use context clues to help you define any words with which you are unfamiliar. Pay close attention to the poem's form, use of figurative language, and sound devices. Then, on a separate sheet of paper, answer the questions on pages 1377–1378.

"Winding Up" by Derek Walcott

line

I live on the water,
alone. Without wife and children,
I have circled every possibility
to come to this:

5   a low house by grey water,
with windows always open
to the stale sea. We do not choose such things,

but we are what we have made.
We suffer, the years pass,
10   we shed freight but not our need

for encumbrances. Love is a stone
that settled on the sea-bed
under grey water. Now, I require nothing

from poetry but true feeling,
15   no pity, no fame, no healing. Silent wife,
we can sit watching grey water,

and in a life awash
with mediocrity and trash
live rock-like.

20   I shall unlearn feeling,
unlearn my gift. That is greater
and harder than what passes there for life.

1. From which point of view is this poem written?
   (A) first person
   (B) second person
   (C) third-person limited
   (D) third-person omniscient
   (E) third-person expansive

2. Which of the following literary elements is Walcott using in lines 5 and 6?
   (A) personification
   (B) idiom
   (C) foreshadowing
   (D) imagery
   (E) epiphany

3. What sound device are the words *stale sea*, in line 7, an example of?
   (A) consonance
   (B) assonance
   (C) rhyme
   (D) onomatopoeia
   (E) alliteration

4. The pronoun *we*, in lines 7–10, refers to the speaker and what or whom else?
   (A) the sea
   (B) all humanity
   (C) poetry
   (D) the speaker's wife and children
   (E) the speaker's home

5. From the context, what do you conclude that the word *encumbrances*, in line 11, most nearly means?
   (A) movements
   (B) changes
   (C) burdens
   (D) graces
   (E) exchanges

6. Which of the following literary elements is Walcott using in the clause *Love is a stone*, in line 11?
   (A) metaphor
   (B) simile
   (C) personification
   (D) flashback
   (E) paradox

7. Which of the following two sound devices appear in line 12?
   (A) consonance and onomatopoeia
   (B) consonance and personification
   (C) alliteration and consonance
   (D) assonance and meter
   (E) meter and rhyme

8. What does the phrase *silent wife*, in line 15, refer to?
   (A) the speaker
   (B) the sea
   (C) freight
   (D) poetry
   (E) mediocrity

9. The end words in lines 17 and 18 are an example of which of the following sound devices?
   (A) alliteration
   (B) onomatopoeia
   (C) meter
   (D) rhythm
   (E) slant rhyme

10. What does the phrase *my gift*, in line 21, refer to?
    (A) feeling
    (B) mediocrity
    (C) poetry
    (D) life
    (E) loneliness

11. Which of the following best describes the form of this poem?
    (A) sonnet
    (B) blank verse
    (C) terza rima
    (D) free verse
    (E) villanelle

12. Which of the following describes the majority of this poem's stanzas?
    (A) couplets
    (B) tercets
    (C) quatrains
    (D) octaves
    (E) sestets

13. Which of the following best describes the conflict that appears in this poem?
  (A) internal
  (B) external
  (C) man versus nature
  (D) man versus fate
  (E) man versus man

14. Which of the following best describes the overall mood of this poem?
  (A) hopeful
  (B) resigned
  (C) desperate
  (D) comic
  (E) ironic

15. Which of the following statements best describes the theme of this poem?
  (A) It is best to avoid committing oneself emotionally to other people.
  (B) Peace of mind is available only to those who have no hope.
  (C) Life is awash in mediocrity.
  (D) Sometimes it is best to resign oneself to life and accept it as it is.
  (E) Fame is not worth pursuing.

Literature Online **Unit Assessment** To prepare for the unit test, go to www.glencoe.com.

1378 UNIT 7 AN INTERNATIONAL LITERATURE

Vocabulary Skills: Sentence Completion

For each item in the Vocabulary Skills section, choose the word or words that best complete the sentence.

1. As English became a global language, those groups that had been on the _____ of the British Empire began to create influential and widely read works.
   (A) temerity
   (B) periphery
   (C) friction
   (D) sinew
   (E) denigration

2. After the war, many young people _____ opposed Britain's cultural traditions, which they felt were both _____ and out of touch.
   (A) hospitably . . . envious
   (B) wryly . . . explicit
   (C) stridently . . . luminous
   (D) hospitably . . . radiant
   (E) stridently . . . superannuated

3. The collapse of the British Empire was a/an _____ event in the development of English literature in the postwar period.
   (A) acrid
   (B) unperturbed
   (C) pivotal
   (D) defunct
   (E) barren

4. By the middle of the twentieth century, it was clear that the faults of the British Empire were _____, and its collapse was likely.
   (A) rancid
   (B) withering
   (C) envious
   (D) plodding
   (E) irremediable

5. Although many effects of the British Empire's collapse were _____, there were also some serious negative consequences, such as the rise of apartheid in South Africa.
   (A) benign
   (B) imminent
   (C) compulsory
   (D) lugubrious
   (E) plodding

6. When England's economic woes threatened to cause the country to _____, the government established a modern welfare state that provided, among other things, universal health care.
   (A) distill
   (B) patronize
   (C) career
   (D) lumber
   (E) flounder

7. Although many writers in the postwar generation rejected the past, some demonstrated a great _____ to traditional forms, topics, and techniques.
   (A) fray
   (B) vendor
   (C) precipice
   (D) fidelity
   (E) revelation

8. Economic and social problems caused a deep _____ to be cast across postwar Britain.
   (A) friction
   (B) assent
   (C) temerity
   (D) pall
   (E) fray

9. As the Cold War deepened and the threat of a nuclear disaster seemed _____, Britain, the United States, and other Western European nations formed NATO.
   (A) imminent
   (B) radiant
   (C) luminous
   (D) withering
   (E) lugubrious

10. To many critics, the appearance of a global postcolonial body of English literature was a _____ that radically altered their previously held assumptions.
    (A) temerity
    (B) revelation
    (C) vendor
    (D) sinew
    (E) denigration

Grammar and Writing Skills: Paragraph Improvement

Carefully read the opening paragraphs from the first draft of a student's critical review. Pay close attention to **verb tense, punctuation,** and **organization.** Then, on a separate sheet of paper, answer the questions on pages 1380–1381.

(1) Doris Lessing's "A Mild Attack of Locusts" is a smartly constructed fable that explores the ability of some people to survive in the face of nature's unforgiving and often destructive power. (2) Lessing who spent much of her young life on a farm in Africa begins by describing the story's three principal characters, the farm on which they live, and their struggles against bankruptcy. (3) This struggle is thrown into high relief by a government announcement that swarms of locusts were expected. (4) With strong character development, compelling dialogue, and vivid sensory details, Lessing illustrates how personal histories affect individual perceptions of nature's threat.

(5) The story's three main characters—Margaret; her husband, Richard; and Richard's father, old Stephen—all had different perceptions. (6) Each character bases their perceptions on their own experiences. (7) For example, Margaret, who is not from a farming background, is horrified by the swarming locusts. (8) On seeing her husband covered in locusts, she asks, "How can you bear to let them touch you?" (9) Later Margaret is shown crying, thinking that "it was all so hopeless—if it wasn't a bad season, it was locusts." (10) This was not the response, though, of either her husband or old Stephen. (11) Throughout A Mild Attack of Locusts, Richard and old Stephen waver between statements of total despair and actions that suggest hope. (12) While this might create the impression that these characters are inconsistent, their behavior is actually the result of something altogether different. (13) In particular, old Stephen who has been bankrupted twice in the past acts hopeful but sounds despairing.

1. Which is the best way to revise sentence 2?
(A) Insert commas after *life* and after *Africa.*
(B) Delete both commas in the sentence.
(C) Delete *who spent much of her young life on a farm.*
(D) Insert commas before *who* and after *Africa.*
(E) Insert a comma after *begins.*

2. Which is the best way to revise sentence 3?
(A) Change *were* to *are.*
(B) Change *is* to *was.*
(C) Delete *that swarms of locusts were expected.*
(D) Insert *to come* after *expected.*
(E) Make no change.

3. Which is the best revision of sentence 5?
(A) All three main characters—Margaret, her husband Richard, and Richard's father, old Stephen—had different perceptions.
(B) The story's three main characters—Margaret; her husband, Richard; and Richard's father, old Stephen—all have different perceptions.
(C) The story's three main characters: Margaret; her husband, Richard; and Richard's father, old Stephen, all had different perceptions.
(D) Margaret, her husband Richard, and Richard's father, old Stephen, had different perceptions.
(E) Make no change.

4. Which is the best revision of sentence 6?

(A) Each character bases their perceptions on personal experience.

(B) Each character bases their perceptions on his or her experience.

(C) Each character's perceptions are based on their experience.

(D) Each character bases his or her perceptions on personal experience.

(E) All characters base their perceptions on his or her experience.

5. Which persuasive technique appears in sentences 8 and 9?

(A) rhetorical question

(B) thesis statement

(C) evidence from the text

(D) addressing opposing viewpoints

(E) plot summary

6. Which is the best revision of sentence 10?

(A) This is not the response, though, of either her husband or old Stephen.

(B) This was not the response though of either her husband or old Stephen.

(C) This was not the response—though—of either her husband or old Stephen.

(D) Old Stephen, though, did not respond this way.

(E) Though this was not the response of either her husband or old Stephen.

7. Which error appears in sentence 11?

(A) *A Mild Attack of Locusts* does not have quotation marks around it.

(B) This is a run-on (comma splice) sentence.

(C) The subject and verb disagree.

(D) This is a sentence fragment.

(E) No error appears.

8. Which persuasive technique appears in sentence 12?

(A) rhetorical question

(B) thesis statement

(C) evidence from the text

(D) addressing opposing viewpoints

(E) plot summary

9. Which is the best revision of sentence 13?

(A) In particular, old Stephen who has been bankrupted twice in the past acted hopeful but sounded despairing.

(B) In particular; old Stephen who has been bankrupted twice in the past acts hopeful but sounds despairing.

(C) In particular, old Stephen who has been bankrupted twice in the past.

(D) In particular, old Stephen: who has been bankrupted twice in the past acts hopeful but sounds despairing.

(E) In particular, old Stephen, who has been bankrupted twice in the past, acts hopeful but sounds despairing.

10. Which of the following should the author present next in this essay?

(A) examples of how dialogue illustrates each character's perception of nature

(B) details from Lessing's time spent on an African farm

(C) a comparison between the setting in this story and those in similar works

(D) an analysis of the rhetorical devices used in this story

(E) an evaluation of Lessing's use of sound devices in this story

Essay

Write a critical review of one selection from this unit. Analyze how imagery, rhetorical devices, and figurative language function in the work and what ideas these devices help convey. As you write, keep in mind that your essay will be checked for **ideas, organization, voice, word choice, sentence fluency, conventions,** and **presentation.**

REFERENCE SECTION

▶ **Literary Terms Handbook** **R1**

▶ **Reading Handbook** **R20**
    Vocabulary Development R20
    Comprehension Strategies R21
    Literary Response R23
    Analysis and Evaluation R24

▶ **Foldables™** **R26**

▶ **Writing Handbook** **R30**
    The Writing Process R30
    Using the Traits of Strong Writing R33
    Writing Modes R35
    Research Paper Writing R36

▶ **Business Writing** **R42**

▶ **Language Handbook** **R46**
    Grammar Glossary R46
    Mechanics R53
    Spelling R58

▶ **Test-Taking Skills Handbook** **R61**

Glossary/Glosario **R64**

Academic Word List **R82**

Index of Skills **R85**

Index of Authors and Titles **R100**

Index of Art and Artists **R104**

Acknowledgments **R108**

LITERARY TERMS HANDBOOK

A

Act A major unit of a drama, or play. Modern dramas generally have one, two, or three acts. Older dramas, including Shakespeare's, often have five acts. Acts may be divided into one or more scenes.

See also DRAMA, SCENE.

Allegory A literary work in which all or most of the characters, settings, and events stand for ideas, qualities, or figures beyond themselves. The overall purpose of an allegory is to teach a moral lesson. Bunyan's *The Pilgrim's Progress* is an allegory in which Vanity Fair represents the world and the Celestial City symbolizes heaven.

See pages 154, 533.
See also SYMBOL.

Alliteration The repetition of consonant sounds, generally at the beginnings of words. Alliteration can be used to emphasize words, reinforce meaning, or create a musical effect. Note the repeated *s* and *d* sounds in the following line from Hopkins's "Pied Beauty":

> With <u>s</u>wift, <u>s</u>low; <u>s</u>weet, <u>s</u>our; a<u>d</u>azzle, <u>d</u>im;

See pages 276, 800, 936.
See also SOUND DEVICES.

Allusion A reference to a well-known character, place, or situation from history, music, art, or another work of literature. Discovering the meaning of an allusion can often be essential to the understanding of a work. W. H. Auden alludes to the Greek myth of Icarus in his poem "Musée des Beaux Arts."

See pages 520, 600, 733.

Ambiguity The state of having more than one meaning. The richness of literary language lies in its ability to evoke multiple layers of meaning.

See also CONNOTATION.

Analogy A comparison that shows similarities between two things that are otherwise dissimilar. A writer may use an analogy to explain something unfamiliar by comparing it to something familiar. Shakespeare pokes fun at analogies in "Sonnet 130," claiming, "My mistress' eyes are nothing like the sun."

See also METAPHOR, SIMILE.

Anapest A metrical foot of three syllables in which two unstressed syllables are followed by a stressed one (˘˘´). In the following line from Siegfried Sassoon's "Does It Matter?" the feet are divided by slashes:

> ˘ ˘ ´ / ˘ ˘ ´ / ˘ ˘ ´
> You can drink / and forget / and be glad. . . .

See also FOOT, METER, SCANSION.

Anecdote A brief account of an interesting happening. Essayists often use anecdotes to support their opinions, clarify their ideas, get the reader's attention, or entertain. Biographers often include anecdotes to illustrate points about their subjects. Boswell's *The Life of Samuel Johnson* contains an anecdote about the first time Boswell was introduced to Johnson by Thomas Davies.

Antagonist A person or a force that opposes the protagonist, or central character, in a story or drama. The reader is generally meant not to sympathize with the antagonist. In *Beowulf,* Grendel is an antagonist.

See also CONFLICT, PROTAGONIST.

Anthropomorphism The assignment of human characteristics to gods, animals, or inanimate objects. It is a key element in fables, where the main characters are often animals. The sheep in Janet Frame's "Two Sheep" have human characteristics.

See page 1319.
See also FABLE.

Aphorism A short, pointed statement that expresses a wise or clever observation about human experience, such as Pope's saying from *An Essay on Criticism*:

> We think our fathers fools, so wise we grow;
> Our wiser sons, no doubt, will think us so.

See also EPIGRAM.

Apostrophe A figure of speech in which a speaker addresses an inanimate object, an idea, or an absent person. In Percy Bysshe Shelley's "Ode to the West Wind," the speaker addresses the wind.

See page 271.
See also PERSONIFICATION.

Archetype A symbol, a character, an image, or a story pattern that recurs frequently in literature and evokes strong responses, often based on unconscious memory. The story of a hero who embarks on a dangerous quest is a recurring story in literature and film. Sir Gawain in *Sir Gawain and the Green Knight* embarks on an archetypal journey.

See pages 173, 205.
See also SYMBOL.

Argument   A type of persuasive writing in which logic or reason is used to try to influence a reader's ideas or actions. In *A Vindication of the Rights of Woman,* Mary Wollstonecraft presents a powerful argument for the education of women. *Argument* can also refer to a prose summary or synopsis of what is in a story or play. This type of argument appears at the beginning of Coleridge's *The Rime of the Ancient Mariner.*

See pages 124, 352, 425, 456, 603, 726, 1150.
See also PERSUASION.

Aside   In a play, a character's comment that is directed to the audience or another character but is not heard by any other characters on the stage. Asides, which are rare in modern drama, reveal what a character is thinking or feeling. An example occurs in Act 1, scene 4, of Shakespeare's *Macbeth.*

> King.   My worthy Cawdor!
> Macbeth. [*Aside.*] The Prince of Cumberland!
>   That is a step
> On which I must fall down, or else o'erleap.

See also SOLILOQUY.

Assonance   The repetition of the same or similar vowel sounds in stressed syllables that end with different consonant sounds. For example, the long *i* sound is repeated in the opening line from Ben Jonson's "On My First Son":

> Farewell, thou child of my right hand, and joy; . . .

See pages 931, 1201.
See also SOUND DEVICES.

Atmosphere   The dominant emotional feeling of a literary work that contributes to the mood. Orwell's description of the natives' dislike of him in "Shooting an Elephant" builds an atmosphere of suspense and foreboding.

See page 316.
See also MOOD.

Author's purpose   An author's intent in writing a literary work. Authors typically write for one or more of the following purposes: to persuade, to inform, to explain, to entertain, or to describe. John Bunyan wrote *The Pilgrim's Progress* to provide moral instruction.

See pages 154, 280, 288, 573, 609, 854, 1098.
See also DICTION, STYLE, THEME.

Autobiography   The story of a person's life written by that person. Autobiographies can give insights into the author's view of himself or herself and of the society in which he or she lived. *The Book of Margery Kempe* is the autobiography of a medieval woman.

See page 146.
See also BIOGRAPHY, DIARY, MEMOIR, NONFICTION.

B

Ballad   A narrative song or poem. Folk ballads, which usually recount an exciting or dramatic episode, were passed down by word of mouth for generations before being written down. Literary ballads are written in imitation of folk ballads but have a known author. Coleridge's *The Rime of the Ancient Mariner* is a literary ballad. "Bonny Barbara Allan" is a folk ballad.

See pages 208–209, 210, 827.
See also FOLKLORE, NARRATIVE POETRY, ORAL TRADITION.

Ballad stanza   A quatrain, or four-line stanza, in which the first and third lines have four stressed syllables, and the second and fourth lines have three stressed syllables. Only the second and fourth lines rhyme. Although the basic foot in this stanza is the iamb ($\smile\,\prime$), there tend to be many irregularities, as in this stanza from "Get Up and Bar the Door."

> It fell about the Martinmas time,
> And a gay time it was then,
> When our goodwife got puddings to make,
> And she's boiled them in the pan.

See pages 210, 827.
See also QUATRAIN, SCANSION.

Bias   An inclination toward a certain opinion or position on a topic, possibly stemming from prejudice.

See pages 1173, 1193.
See also NONFICTION.

Biography   An account of a person's life written by someone other than the subject. Biographies have been written of many of the writers in this book. Boswell's *The Life of Samuel Johnson* is a famous example.

See page 660.
See also AUTOBIOGRAPHY, DIARY, JOURNAL, MEMOIR.

Blank verse Poetry or lines of dramatic verse written in unrhymed iambic pentameter. Each line has five feet, with each foot made up of an unstressed syllable followed by a stressed syllable. Because blank verse may attempt to imitate spoken English, every line need not be perfectly regular. Most of Shakespeare's characters speak in blank verse—as Macbeth does, for example, when he addresses the floating dagger in Act 2, scene 1:

　　And on thy blade and dudgeon gouts of blood,

See also FOOT, IAMBIC PENTAMETER, SCANSION.

Byronic hero *See HERO.*

C

Cadence The rhythmic rise and fall of language when it is spoken or read aloud.
See also FREE VERSE, METER.

Caesura A pause in a line of poetry, usually near the middle of a line, with two stressed syllables before and two after, creating a strong rhythm. A caesura is used to produce variations in meter and to draw attention to certain words. Some pauses are indicated by punctuation, others by phrasing or meaning. In the lines below, from Tennyson's *In Memoriam A. H. H.*, the caesuras are marked by double vertical lines.

　　Ring out the old, || ring in the new,
　　Ring, happy bells, || across the snow;

See also RHYTHM.

Carpe diem A Latin phrase meaning "seize the day"; in other words, "make the most of each moment." In *carpe diem* poems, the speaker emphasizes the shortness of life—usually to persuade a young woman to yield to love while she still has her youth and beauty. Andrew Marvell's poem "To His Coy Mistress" is a famous example.

See pages 456, 478.

Cavalier poetry The work of a group of English poets in the 1600s who were loyal to the monarchy. Cavalier poetry is generally intended to entertain rather than to instruct. It is characterized by regular rhythmic patterns, carefully structured stanzas, and simple but eloquent language. Love is a popular theme. Herrick, Suckling, and Lovelace were Cavalier poets.

See pages 452–453.

Character A person portrayed in a literary work. A **main character** is central to the story and is typically fully developed. A **minor character** displays few personality traits and is used to help develop the story. Characters who show varied and sometimes contradictory traits, such as Rosemary in Katherine Mansfield's "A Cup of Tea," are called **round**. Characters who reveal only one personality trait, such as the narrator's mother in V. S. Naipaul's "B. Wordsworth," are called **flat**. A **stereotype**, or stock character, is typically flat. A **dynamic character**, such as Paul in D. H. Lawrence's "The Rocking-Horse Winner," grows and changes during the story. A **static character** remains basically the same throughout a story. Things happen to the character, but he or she does not change.

See pages 210, 1123, 1193, 1272.
See also CHARACTERIZATION, STEREOTYPE.

Characterization The methods a writer uses to reveal the personality of a character. In **direct characterization**, the writer makes explicit statements about a character, as D. H. Lawrence does in "The Rocking-Horse Winner." In **indirect characterization**, the writer reveals a character through his or her words, thoughts, and actions and through what other characters think and say about that character, as in the characterization of the young woman in Gordimer's "The Train from Rhodesia."

See pages 93, 140, 539, 769, 967, 1305.
See also CHARACTER.

Cliché A word or phrase that is so overused that it is virtually meaningless. "Dead as a doornail," "piece of cake," and "last but not least" are all clichés.

Climax *See PLOT.*

Colloquialism Informal language used in everyday conversation but not in formal writing or speech. In Mansfield's "A Cup of Tea," Miss Smith is speaking colloquially when she says, "I can't go on no longer . . . I can't bear no more."

See also DIALECT, VERNACULAR.

Comedy A type of drama that is humorous and often has a happy ending. A **heroic comedy** focuses on the exploits of a larger-than-life hero.

See also DRAMA, FARCE, HUMOR, PARODY, SATIRE, WIT.

Comic relief A humorous scene, event, or speech in a serious drama. It provides relief from emotional intensity while at the same time highlighting the seriousness of the story. The porter scene in Shakespeare's *Macbeth* (Act 2, Scene 3) is a famous example.

Conceit An elaborate figure of speech that makes a comparison between two significantly different things. The conceit draws an analogy between some object from nature or everyday life and the subject or theme of a poem. Often a conceit is lengthy and dominates a passage or an entire poem. A **metaphysical conceit** is an intellectual comparison—rather than one based on nature—that can develop a wide range of ideas and capture a broad range of emotions. In Sir Thomas Wyatt's "Whoso List to Hunt," the conceit compares romance with deer hunting.

See page 438.
See also ANALOGY, EXTENDED METAPHOR, METAPHYSICAL POETRY, SIMILE.

Conflict The central struggle between two opposing forces in a story or drama. An **external conflict** exists when a character struggles against some outside force, such as another person, nature, society, or fate. An **internal conflict** is a struggle that takes place within the mind of a character who is torn between opposing feelings, desires, or goals. In Desai's "Games at Twilight," the conflict is largely internal. In Achebe's "Dead Men's Path," the conflict is mostly external.

See pages 23, 79, 191, 530, 1075, 1285, 1305.
See also ANTAGONIST, PLOT, PROTAGONIST.

Connotation The suggested or implied meanings associated with a word beyond its dictionary definition, or denotation. A word can have a positive, negative, or neutral connotation.

See pages 271, 611, 948.
See also AMBIGUITY, DENOTATION, FIGURATIVE LANGUAGE.

Consonance The repetition of consonant sounds, typically at the end of nonrhyming words and preceded by different vowel sounds, as in this succession of echoing *d* sounds in William Butler Yeats's "The Second Coming":

The bloo**d**-dimme**d** ti**d**e is loose**d**, . . .

See pages 931, 1201.
See also SOUND DEVICES.

Couplet Two consecutive, rhymed lines of poetry that follow the same rhythmic pattern. The last two lines of Shakespeare's "Sonnet 29" are a couplet:

For thy sweet love rememb'red such wealth brings
That then I scorn to change my state with kings.

See also HEROIC COUPLET, RHYME, SONNET.

Crisis *See PLOT.*

D

Dactyl A three-syllable metrical foot, in which the first syllable is stressed and the following two are unstressed. The following line from Tennyson's "Tears, Idle Tears" has a basic dactylic rhythm:

Tears, idle/ tears, I know/ not what they/ mean,

See also FOOT, METER, SCANSION.

Denotation The literal, or dictionary, meaning of a word.

See pages 271, 611, 948.
See also CONNOTATION.

Dénouement *See PLOT.*

Description A detailed portrayal of a person, a place, an object, or an event. Good descriptive writing appeals to the senses through imagery. Anita Desai's "Games at Twilight" begins with an effective description of a hot afternoon.

See pages 967, 1156.
See also FIGURATIVE LANGUAGE, IMAGERY.

Dialect A variation of a language spoken by a particular region or class. Dialects may differ from the standard form of a language in vocabulary, pronunciation, or grammatical form. In Naipaul's story "B. Wordsworth," the narrator and his mother speak a dialect of English.

I ran up the steps and shouted, "Ma, it have a man outside here. He say he want to watch the bees."

See pages 718, 1332.
See also VERNACULAR.

Dialogue Conversation between characters in a literary work. Dialogue can contribute to characterization, create mood, advance the plot, and develop theme.

See page 769.

Diary An individual's daily record of impressions, events, or thoughts, written for personal use rather than for publication. Samuel Pepys's diary, written between 1660 and 1669, is a famous example.

See page 553.
See also JOURNAL.

Diction A writer's choice of words; an important element in the writer's "voice" or style. Skilled writers choose their words carefully to convey a particular meaning or feeling.

See pages 786, 854, 1190, 1324.
See also AUTHOR'S PURPOSE, CONNOTATION, STYLE, TONE, VOICE.

Dimeter A line of verse consisting of two feet.

See also FOOT, METER, SCANSION.

Drama A story intended to be performed by actors before an audience. The script of a dramatic work, or play, often includes the author's instructions to the actors and director, known as stage directions. A drama may be divided into acts, which may also be broken up into scenes, indicating changes in location or the passage of time.

See also ACT, COMEDY, PROPS, SCENE, STAGE DIRECTIONS, TRAGEDY.

Dramatic irony *See IRONY.*

Dramatic monologue A form of dramatic poetry in which a speaker addresses a silent listener. The speaker may be a fictional or historical figure and is clearly distinct from the poet. Robert Browning's poem "My Last Duchess" is a dramatic monologue.

See pages 980, 1008.
See also DRAMATIC POETRY, MONOLOGUE.

Dramatic poetry Poetry in which characters are revealed through dialogue and monologue, as well as through description. Hardy's "Ah, Are You Digging on My Grave?" is an example of dramatic poetry.

See also DIALOGUE, DRAMATIC MONOLOGUE.

Dramatic structure The structure of a serious play. Common elements are exposition, rising action, climax, falling action, and resolution.

See also PLOT.

Dynamic character *See CHARACTER.*

E

Elegy A poem mourning a death or another great loss. Tennyson's *In Memoriam A. H. H.* is an elegy.

See pages 446, 715.

End rhyme The rhyming of words at the ends of lines, as in Housman's "To an Athlete Dying Young."

End-stopped line A line of poetry that contains a complete thought, thus requiring a semicolon or period at the end, as in Blake's "A Poison Tree":

> I was angry with my friend;
> I told my wrath, my wrath did end.

See also ENJAMBMENT.

Enjambment The continuation of a sentence from one line of a poem to another, without a pause, as in the following lines from Shakespeare's "Sonnet 116":

> Let me not to the marriage of true minds
> Admit impediments; love is not love
> Which alters when it alteration finds . . .

Enjambment enables poets to create a conversational tone, breaking lines at points where people would normally pause in conversation yet still maintaining the unity of thought.

See page 781.
See also RHYTHM.

Epic A long narrative poem that recounts the adventures of a larger-than-life hero. This **epic hero** is usually a man of high social status who embodies the ideals of his people. He is often of great historical or legendary importance. Epic plots typically involve supernatural events, long time periods, distant journeys, and life-and-death struggles between good and evil. Works such as *Beowulf* are called **folk epics** because they have no certain authorship and arise, usually through storytelling, from the collective experiences of a people. **Literary epics,** such as John Milton's *Paradise Lost,* are written by known authors.

See pages 20–21, 52.
See also LEGEND, MYTH, ORAL TRADITION.

Epigram A short, witty verse or saying. Samuel Taylor Coleridge defined *epigram* with an epigram of his own:

> What is an Epigram? A dwarfish whole,
> Its body brevity, and wit its soul.

See also APHORISM.

Epigraph A quotation from another work or source that suggests the theme or main idea of the work at hand. It is often up to the reader to determine how the quoted work relates to the literature it introduces. An epigraph generally serves as an introductory passage at the beginning of a literary work. Kipling's "Miss Youghal's *Sais*" begins with an epigraph.

Epilogue   A concluding statement or section added to a work of literature.

Epiphany   A moment of sudden understanding of the true meaning of a situation, a person, or an object. In Katherine Mansfield's "A Cup of Tea," Rosemary Fell's realization that her husband finds Miss Smith pretty is an epiphany.

See page 1139.

Epistle   Any letter, such as Johnson's "Letter to Lord Chesterfield." Often the term is applied to a more literary work than the informal communication written by most people. Pope called the four poems that make up *An Essay on Man* "verse epistles."

Epitaph   A brief statement commemorating a dead person, often inscribed on a gravestone. Thomas Gray's "Elegy Written in a Country Churchyard" ends with an epitaph, as does Malory's *Le Morte d'Arthur.*

See page 709.
See also ELEGY.

Epithet   A word or brief phrase used to characterize a person, place, or thing. Royal epithets are common: Good Queen Bess, Richard the Lionheart, Edward the Black Prince, Charles the Bold, and Philip the Good, for example.

Essay   A short piece of nonfiction writing on any topic. The purpose of the essay is to communicate an idea or opinion. A **formal essay** is serious and impersonal, often with the purpose of instructing or persuading. Typically, the author strikes a serious tone and develops a main idea, or thesis, in a logical, highly organized way. An **informal** or **personal essay** entertains while it informs, usually in light, conversational style. Bacon's "Of Studies" is a formal essay. Addison and Steele wrote informal essays for *The Spectator.*

See pages 547, 591, 612–613.
See also NONFICTION, THESIS.

Exaggeration   *See HYPERBOLE.*

Exemplum   A brief story used as an example to illustrate a moral point. Chaucer's "The Pardoner's Tale" is an exemplum.

See also ANECDOTE, FABLE.

Exposition   *See PLOT.*

Extended metaphor   A metaphor that compares two unlike things in various ways throughout a paragraph, a stanza, or an entire selection.

See page 603.
See also METAPHOR.

F

Fable   A short, often humorous tale intended to teach a lesson about human behavior or to give advice about how to behave. Many fables end by stating the moral, or lesson to be learned, while others leave it up to the reader to infer the moral. In a **beast fable,** animals talk and act like humans.

See also LEGEND, MORAL, PARABLE, THEME.

Fairy tale   A type of folktale that features supernatural elements, such as spirits, talking animals, and magic.

See also FOLKTALE.

Falling action   *See PLOT.*

Fantasy   A literary work that is set in an unreal world and that often concerns incredible characters and events. There are elements of fantasy in Swift's *Gulliver's Travels.*

See also SCIENCE FICTION.

Farce   A type of comedy with ridiculous situations, characters, or events.

See also COMEDY, HUMOR, PARODY, SATIRE.

Fiction   A narrative in which situations and characters are invented by the writer. Some aspects of a fictional work may be based on fact or experience. Fictional works include short stories, novels, and plays.

See also DRAMA, NONFICTION, NOVEL, SHORT STORY.

Figurative language   Language used for descriptive effect in order to convey ideas or emotions. Figurative expressions are not literally true but express some truth beyond the literal level. Figurative language is especially common in poetry.

See pages 260, 312, 843, 1107.
See also FIGURE OF SPEECH.

Figure of speech   A specific kind of figurative language such as metaphor, personification, or simile.

See also CONNOTATION, FIGURATIVE LANGUAGE, METAPHOR, OXYMORON, PERSONIFICATION, SIMILE, SYMBOL.

Flashback An interruption in the chronological order of a narrative to describe an event that happened earlier. A flashback gives readers information that may help explain the main events of a story. Elizabeth Bowen's "The Demon Lover" includes a flashback.

See page 1175.
See also FORESHADOWING.

Flash-forward An interruption in the chronological sequence of a narrative to leap forward in time.

See also FLASHBACK.

Flat character *See CHARACTER.*

Foil A character whose attitudes, beliefs, or behavior differ significantly from those of another character. Often a foil is a minor character who serves, through contrast, to emphasize the distinctive characteristics of the main character.

See page 352.
See also ANTAGONIST, CHARACTER, CHARACTERIZATION, PROTAGONIST.

Folklore Traditional beliefs, customs, stories, songs, and dances of a culture. Folklore is passed down through oral tradition and is based on the concerns of ordinary people. There are elements of folklore in *Beowulf*.

See also BALLAD, EPIC, FOLKTALE, LEGEND, MYTH, ORAL TRADITION.

Folktale A traditional story passed down orally long before being written down. Folktales include animal stories, trickster stories, fairy tales, myths, legends, and tall tales.

See also FOLKLORE.

Foot The basic unit in the measurement of a line of metrical poetry. A foot usually contains one stressed syllable (´) and one or more unstressed syllables (˘). The basic metrical feet are the **anapest** (˘ ˘ ´), **dactyl** (´ ˘ ˘), **iamb** (˘ ´), **spondee** (´ ´), and **trochee** (´ ˘).

See also METER, RHYTHM, SCANSION, STANZA.

Foreshadowing An author's use of clues to prepare readers for events that will happen later in a story. D. H. Lawrence prepares the reader for future happenings by stating at the beginning of "The Rocking-Horse Winner" that there was "always an anxiety in the house. There was never enough money."

See pages 1123, 1338.
See also FLASHBACK, PLOT, SUSPENSE.

Form The structure of a poem. Many modern writers use loosely structured poetic forms instead of following traditional or formal patterns. These poets vary the lengths of lines and stanzas, relying on emphasis, rhythm, pattern, or the placement of words and phrases to convey meaning.

See pages 465, 866, 1206.
See also FREE VERSE, RHYTHM, STANZA, STRUCTURE.

Formal essay *See ESSAY.*

Frame story A story that surrounds another story or that serves to link several stories together. The frame is the outer story, which usually precedes and follows the inner, more important story. Chaucer's *The Canterbury Tales* is a frame story. The pilgrimage is the outer story, or frame, unifying the tales or inner stories told by the pilgrims.

See also STRUCTURE.

Free verse Poetry that has no fixed pattern of meter, rhyme, line length, or stanza arrangement. T. S. Eliot's "Preludes" is an example of free verse. Although poets who write free verse ignore traditional rules, they use techniques such as repetition and alliteration to create musical patterns in their poems.

See page 1314.
See also FORM, METER, RHYME, RHYTHM, STANZA.

G–H

Genre A category or type of literature. Examples of genres are poetry, drama, fiction, and nonfiction.

See page 781.

Gothic novel A novel that has a gloomy, foreboding setting and contains strong elements of horror, mystery, and the supernatural. English writer Horace Walpole is credited with writing the first gothic novel, *The Castle of Otranto*, in 1765. *Gothic* originally referred to a style of architecture in western Europe during the Middle Ages. Since the setting of Walpole's novel is a medieval castle, the term was applied to this type of writing.

See page 834.
See also NOVEL.

Haiku An ancient Japanese form of poetry that has three lines and seventeen syllables. The first and third lines have five syllables each; the middle line has seven syllables. Usually about nature, a traditional haiku uses striking imagery to evoke an insight or capture a mood.

See also IMAGERY.

Heptameter A metrical line of seven feet.

See also FOOT, METER, SCANSION.

Hero The chief character in a literary work, typically one whose admirable qualities or noble deeds arouse admiration. Although the word *hero* is applied only to males in traditional usage—*heroine* being the term used for females—modern usage applies the term to either gender. A **Byronic hero** is the unconventional, brooding, romantic character popularized by Lord Byron in some of his verse.

See pages 20–21, 52, 848–849.
See also EPIC, LEGEND, MYTH, PROTAGONIST, TRAGEDY.

Heroic couplet A pair of rhymed lines in iambic pentameter that work together to express an idea or make a point. A heroic couplet is based on the poetic form used by ancient Greek and Roman poets in their heroic epics. The following lines from Pope's *An Essay on Man* form a heroic couplet:

> And, spite of pride, in erring reason's spite,
> One truth is clear, Whatever is, is right.

See page 587.
See also IAMBIC PENTAMETER, METER, RHYTHM.

Heroic stanza A group of four poetic lines (a quatrain) in iambic pentameter having a rhyme scheme of *abab*, also known as the **elegiac stanza**. Gray's "Elegy Written in a Country Churchyard" features heroic, or elegiac, stanzas.

See also IAMBIC PENTAMETER, QUATRAIN, RHYME SCHEME.

Hexameter Line of verse consisting of six feet.

See also FOOT, METER, SCANSION.

Historical fiction Fiction that sets characters against the backdrop of a period other than the author's own. Some works of historical fiction include actual historical people along with fictitious characters. Defoe's *A Journal of the Plague Year* is historical fiction.

See page 623.
See also FICTION, NOVEL.

Historical narrative A work of nonfiction that tells the story of important historical events or developments. Bede's *The Ecclesiastical History of the English*

People tells of the influence of the Christian church on English civilization.

See page 83.
See also HISTORY, NONFICTION.

History A factual account of real events that occurred in the past. Typically, a history is arranged chronologically and seeks to provide an objective description of what happened.

See also HISTORICAL FICTION, NONFICTION.

Hubris Extreme pride or arrogance. Hubris often results in the downfall of a protagonist who violates a human, natural, or divine law. In his sonnet "Ozymandias," Percy Bysshe Shelley provides a concise portrait of hubris in the doomed king whose empire lies in ruins around him.

See also TRAGEDY.

Humor The quality of a literary work that makes the characters and their situations seem funny, amusing, or silly. Humor often points out human failings and the irony found in many situations. Humorous language includes sarcasm, exaggeration, and verbal irony.

See page 124.
See also COMEDY, FARCE, PARODY, PUN, SATIRE, WIT.

Hymn A lyric poem or song addressed to a divine being or expressing religious sentiments.

See also LYRIC.

Hyperbole A figure of speech that uses exaggeration to express strong emotion, to make a point, or to evoke humor. The following passage from Andrew Marvell's "To His Coy Mistress" contains hyperbole:

> An hundred years should go to praise
> Thine eyes, and on thy forehead gaze; . . .

See pages 475, 1173.
See also FIGURATIVE LANGUAGE, UNDERSTATEMENT.

I

Iamb A two-syllable metrical foot consisting of one unstressed syllable and one stressed syllable, as in the word *divide*.

Iambic pentameter A poetic meter in which each line is composed of five feet (**pentameter**); each foot—known as an **iamb**—consists of one unstressed syllable (˘) followed by one stressed syllable (´). In order to imitate the natural flow of spoken English, poets using iambic pentameter often vary its rhythm. The following line from Spenser's "Sonnet 75" is a perfect example of this metrical form:

> ˘ ´ ˘ ´ ˘ ´ ˘ ´
> But came / the tide, / and made / my pains /
> ˘ ´
> his prey.

See also BLANK VERSE, FOOT, HEROIC COUPLET, METER, RHYTHM, SCANSION.

Idiom An expression whose meaning is different from the literal meaning of the words that make it up. Phrases such as "catch his eye," "turn the tables," "over the hill," and "keep tabs on" are idiomatic expressions understood by native speakers but often puzzling to nonnative speakers. Idioms can add realism to dialogue in a story and contribute to characterization.

See page 1185.
See also DIALECT.

Imagery The "word pictures" that writers create to evoke an emotional response. In creating effective images, writers use **sensory details**, or descriptions that appeal to one or more of the five senses: sight, hearing, touch, taste, and smell. Note Yeats's use of imagery in "The Lake Isle of Innisfree."

See pages 593, 709, 876, 995, 1094, 1118, 1328, 1356.
See also FIGURATIVE LANGUAGE.

Informal essay *See ESSAY.*

Interior monologue A technique that records a character's emotions, memories, and opinions. Interior monologue contributes to the stream-of-consciousness effect. Joyce's "Araby" contains interior monologue.

See also STREAM OF CONSCIOUSNESS.

Internal conflict *See CONFLICT.*

Internal rhyme Rhyme that occurs within a single line of poetry. Poets use internal rhyme to convey meaning, to evoke mood, or simply to create a musical effect.

See also RHYME.

Inversion Reversal of the usual word order for emphasis or variety. Writers use inversion to maintain rhyme scheme or meter, or to emphasize certain words. In the first line that follows from Gray's "Elegy Written in a Country Churchyard," the verb (*fades*) comes before the subject

(*landscape*), a reversal of the usual order. In the second line, the object (*stillness*) comes before the verb (*holds*).

> Now fades the glimmering landscape on the
> sight,
> And all the air a solemn stillness holds, . . .

See page 543.
See also STYLE.

Irony A contrast or discrepancy between appearance and reality. **Situational irony** exists when the outcome of a situation is the opposite of expectations, as in Hardy's poem "Ah, Are You Digging on My Grave?" **Verbal irony** occurs when the meaning of a statement is the reverse of what is meant, as in Swift's *A Modest Proposal*. **Dramatic irony** occurs when readers or viewers know something that the characters do not.

See pages 116, 404, 584, 851, 1004, 1310.

J–L

Journal A daily record of events kept by a participant in those events or a witness to them. A journal is usually less intimate than a diary, emphasizing events rather than emotions. Dorothy Wordsworth's journal, kept from 1800 to 1803, provides a glimpse into English country life.

See page 796.
See also DIARY, NONFICTION.

Juxtaposition The placing of two or more distinct things side by side in order to contrast or compare them. It is commonly used to evoke an emotional response in the reader.

See page 843.

Kenning A descriptive figure of speech that takes the place of a common noun, especially in Anglo-Saxon and Norse poetry. In *Beowulf*, for example, the sea is described as the "whale road."

See also FIGURATIVE LANGUAGE.

Legend A traditional story handed down from the past, based on actual people and events, and tending to become more exaggerated and fantastical over time. Often legends celebrate the heroic qualities of a national or cultural leader. Legends about King Arthur and his knights of the Round Table have evolved from a real warrior who led the British in battle in the eighth century A.D.

See page 197.
See also FOLKLORE, FOLKTALE, HERO, ORAL TRADITION.

Literary criticism A type of writing in which the writer analyzes and evaluates a literary work.

Lyric poetry Poetry that expresses a speaker's personal thoughts and feelings. A lyric poem is usually short and creates a single, unified impression. William Wordsworth's "The World Is Too Much with Us" is an example of a lyric poem.

See pages 449, 793, 999.
See also POETRY.

M

Maxim A short saying that contains a general truth or gives practical advice, particularly about morality and behavior. Also known as an adage or aphorism.

See also APHORISM.

Melodrama A melodrama is usually a play, but it can be any work that has a strong conflict and appeals primarily to the emotions. In a melodrama, the characters are either extremely good or extremely wicked.

See also DRAMA.

Memoir A type of narrative nonfiction that presents the story of a period in the writer's life. It is usually written from the first-person point of view and emphasizes the narrator's own experience of this period. It may also reveal the impact of significant historical events on his or her life.

See also AUTOBIOGRAPHY, BIOGRAPHY.

Metaphor A figure of speech that compares or equates two seemingly unlike things to help readers perceive the first thing more vividly. In contrast to a simile, a metaphor implies the comparison instead of stating it directly; hence there is no use of connectives such as *like* or *as*. The lines below from Sir Philip Sidney's "Sonnet 39" contain metaphors:

> **Come sleep! O sleep, the certain knot of peace,**
> **The baiting place of wit, the balm of woe, . . .**

See pages 294, 603, 843, 1110.
See also EXTENDED METAPHOR, FIGURATIVE LANGUAGE, SIMILE.

Metaphysical poetry The work of a group of seventeenth-century English poets led by John Donne. Metaphysical poetry is written in a conversational style, emphasizes complex meanings, contains unusual imagery, and extends the range of metaphors into areas of science, religion, and learning.

See pages 428–429.
See also CONCEIT, METAPHOR.

Meter A regular pattern of stressed (´) and unstressed (˘) syllables that gives a line of poetry a more or less predictable rhythm. The basic unit of meter is the foot, consisting of one or two stressed syllables and/or one or two unstressed syllables. The iamb, for example, consists of two syllables: one unstressed followed by one stressed. The length of a metrical line can be expressed in terms of the number of feet it contains:

> **dimeter, two feet**
> **trimeter, three feet**
> **tetrameter, four feet**
> **pentameter, five feet**
> **hexameter, six feet**
> **heptameter, seven feet**

The following lines from Marlowe's "The Passionate Shepherd to His Love" are in iambic tetrameter:

> **Come live / with me, / and be / my love,**
> **And we / will all / the plea / sures prove.**

See pages 431, 764, 995, 1115.
See also FOOT, IAMBIC PENTAMETER, RHYTHM, SCANSION.

Metonymy A figure of speech in which a word or phrase is substituted for another that is related. For example, the executive branch of the British government is often referred to as Downing Street, where the prime minister lives in London.

See also FIGURATIVE LANGUAGE.

Miracle play A medieval religious drama presenting a story from the Bible or the lives of the saints; also called a **mystery play.**

See pages 152–153.
See also MORALITY PLAY.

Mock-epic An imitation epic, or long narrative poem, that makes fun of the trivial values of a society by using elevated language to describe a mundane event. Pope's "The Rape of the Lock" is a mock-epic.

See page 593.
See also EPIC.

Modernism A term applied to a variety of twentieth-century artistic movements that shared a desire to break with the past. In addition to technical experimentation, Modernist playwrights, writers, and artists in the first half of the twentieth century were interested in the irrational or inexplicable, as well as in the workings of the unconscious mind. The poetry of T. S. Eliot, with its new subject matter, diction, and metrical patterns, came to define Modernism. Other Modernist writers include Virginia Woolf and James Joyce.

See pages 1038–1039.
See also STREAM OF CONSCIOUSNESS.

Monologue   A long speech by a character in a literary work, spoken either to others or as if alone.

See also DRAMATIC MONOLOGUE, SOLILOQUY.

Mood   The emotional quality of a literary work. A writer's choice of language, subject matter, setting, and tone, as well as sound devices such as rhyme and rhythm, contribute to creating mood. *Mood* is a broader term than *tone,* which refers to the attitude of a writer toward the subject matter or the audience. It also differs from *atmosphere,* which is concerned mainly with the physical qualities that contribute to a mood, such as time, place, and weather. The mood of Defoe's *A Journal of the Plague Year* is somber.

See pages 74, 169, 796, 923, 1090, 1353.
See also ATMOSPHERE, SETTING, TONE.

Moral   A practical lesson about right and wrong conduct taught in a fable or parable.

See also FABLE, PARABLE.

Morality play   A medieval religious play popular in the 1400s and 1500s. The plays centered on the moral struggles of everyday people and were designed to teach lessons about salvation and the struggle between virtue and vice. Characters were personifications of abstract qualities such as vice, virtue, mercy, ignorance, and poverty. *Everyman* is a morality play.

See pages 152–153.
See also MIRACLE PLAY.

Motif   A significant word, phrase, image, description, idea, or other element repeated throughout a literary work and related to the theme. Luck is a motif in D. H. Lawrence's "The Rocking-Horse Winner."

See pages 337, 442.
See also THEME.

Motivation   The stated or implied reason for a character's actions. Motivation may be an external circumstance or an internal moral or emotional impulse. In Doris Lessing's "A Mild Attack of Locusts," farmers are moved to action by the desire to save their crops from locusts.

See pages 1046, 1136.

Myth   A traditional story that deals with goddesses, gods, heroes, and supernatural forces. A myth may explain a belief, a custom, or a force of nature. Milton's *Paradise Lost* has mythic elements.

See also EPIC, FOLKLORE, LEGEND, ORAL TRADITION.

N

Narrative   Writing or speech that tells a story. Narratives may be fiction or nonfiction, prose or poetry.

See also NARRATIVE POETRY, NARRATOR.

Narrative poetry   Verse that tells a story. **Ballads**, **epics**, and **romances** are all types of narrative poetry. "The Rime of the Ancient Mariner" by Samuel Taylor Coleridge is a narrative poem.

See page 804.
See also BALLAD, DRAMATIC MONOLOGUE, EPIC, NARRATIVE.

Narrator   The person who tells a story. The narrator may be a character in the story, as in James Joyce's "Araby," or outside the story, as in Doris Lessing's "A Mild Attack of Locusts."

See pages 1069, 1255.
See also NARRATIVE, PERSONA, POINT OF VIEW, SPEAKER.

Naturalism   A literary movement characterized by a belief that people are part of the natural world and have little control over their own lives. Writers such as Hardy and Lawrence focused on the powerful economic, social, and environmental forces that shape the lives of individuals.

See pages 918–919.
See also REALISM.

Neoclassicism   A term often applied to English literature of the Neoclassical period, from 1660 to the end of the eighteenth century. This period, which is also known as the Age of Reason, corresponds to Unit Three in the text. Neoclassical writers valued order, reason, balance, and clarity over emotion. The work of Alexander Pope is an example of Neoclassicism.

See also RESTORATION AGE.

Nonfiction Literature that deals with real people, places, and events. Among the categories of nonfiction are biographies, autobiographies, and essays.

See also AUTOBIOGRAPHY, BIOGRAPHY, ESSAY, FICTION, HISTORY, MEMOIR.

Nonsense verse Humorous poetry that defies logic. It usually has a strong rhythm and contains made-up words known as **nonce words**. Lewis Carroll's "Jabberwocky" is nonsense verse.

See page 957.

Novel A book-length fictional prose narrative having a plot, characters, setting, and a theme. A short novel is often called a **novella**.

See pages 964–965.
See also FICTION, PLOT, SHORT STORY.

Novel of manners A realistic work that deals with the conventions and values of a particular society or social class, such as those depicted in Jane Austen's novels of nineteenth-century English country life.

O

Octave The first eight lines of a **Petrarchan,** or **Italian,** sonnet. The octave usually presents a situation, an idea, or a question.

See also SONNET.

Octet A group of eight lines in a poem.

Ode A serious lyric poem, dignified and sincere in tone and style. Some odes celebrate a person, an event, or even a power; others are more private meditations. A **Horatian ode**, named for the Roman poet Horace, has a regular stanza pattern and rhyme scheme. An **irregular ode** has no set rhyme scheme or stanza pattern. John Keats's "Ode on a Grecian Urn" is considered a Horatian ode.

See page 871.
See also LYRIC POETRY.

Onomatopoeia The use of a word or phrase that imitates or suggests the sound of what it describes. The words *mew*, *crack*, *swish*, *hiss*, *caw*, and *buzz* are onomatopoeic words. "The murmurous haunt of flies on summer eves," is an example of an onomatopoeic line from Keats's "Ode to a Nightingale," evoking the sound of flies.

See pages 876, 957.
See also SOUND DEVICES.

Oral tradition The passing of literature by word of mouth from one generation to the next. Oral literature is a way of recording the past, glorifying leaders, and teaching morals and traditions to young people.

See also BALLAD, EPIC, FOLKLORE, FOLKTALE, LEGEND, MYTH.

Ottava rima A stanza of eight lines written in iambic pentameter with the rhyme scheme *abababcc*. Yeats's "Sailing to Byzantium" is written in ottava rima.

See page 1115.
See also IAMBIC PENTAMETER, RHYME SCHEME, STANZA.

Oxymoron A figure of speech in which opposite ideas are combined. Examples are "bright darkness," "wise fool," and "hateful love." Milton's description of hell in *Paradise Lost* as "darkness visible" is an example of an oxymoron.

See page 1201.
See also FIGURATIVE LANGUAGE, PARADOX.

P–Q

Parable A simple story pointing to a moral or religious lesson. It differs from a fable in that the characters are people instead of animals.

See page 1057.
See also FABLE, MORAL.

Paradox A situation or statement that seems to be impossible or contradictory but is nevertheless true, literally or figuratively. The fifth line of Elizabeth I's poem "On Monsieur's Departure" contains two paradoxes:

I am and not, I freeze and yet am burned,

See page 470.
See also OXYMORON.

Parallelism The use of a series of words, phrases, or sentences that have similar grammatical form. Parallelism shows the relationship between ideas and helps emphasize thoughts. Johnson's letter to Lord Chesterfield contains parallelism:

I have been pushing on my work through difficulties of which it is useless to complain and have brought it at last to the verge of publication without one act of assistance, one word of encouragement, or one smile of favor.

See pages 284, 422.
See also REPETITION.

Parody A humorous imitation of a literary work that aims to point out the work's shortcomings. A parody may imitate the plot, characters, or style of another work, usually through exaggeration. Shakespeare's "Sonnet 130" is a parody of Renaissance love poetry.

See page 575.
See also COMEDY, FARCE, HUMOR, SATIRE.

Pastoral Poetry that idealizes the simple lives of shepherds in a rural setting. Pastoral poems often exaggerate the rural pleasures and the innocence of country people living in harmony with nature. An example of pastoral poetry is Marlowe's "The Passionate Shepherd to His Love."

See page 276.

Pathetic fallacy The attribution of human thoughts and emotions to nature or to nonhuman objects or animals. In "The Tyger," William Blake speaks of the stars as if they were capable of human feeling:

> When the stars threw down their spears
> And watered heaven with their tears

The pathetic fallacy is a type of personification but refers specifically to feelings, not to all human qualities.

See also PERSONIFICATION.

Pentameter A metrical line of five feet.

See also BLANK VERSE, FOOT, METER.

Persona The person created by the author to tell a story. Whether the story is told by an omniscient narrator or by one of the characters, the author of the work often adopts a persona—a personality different from his or her real one. The attitudes and beliefs of the persona may not be the same as those of the author. Jonathan Swift is the author of *Gulliver's Travels*; however, the first-person narrator, Lemuel Gulliver, is the voice through which Swift chose to tell his story.

See also NARRATOR, POINT OF VIEW.

Personification A figure of speech in which an animal, an object, a force of nature, or an idea is given human characteristics. Yeats personifies love in these lines from "When You Are Old":

> Murmur, a little sadly, how Love fled
> And paced upon the mountains overhead
> And hid his face amid a crowd of stars.

See pages 517, 1268.
See also APOSTROPHE, FIGURATIVE LANGUAGE, PATHETIC FALLACY.

Persuasion Writing, usually nonfiction, that attempts to convince readers to think or act in a particular way. Writers of persuasive works use appeals to logic or emotion and other techniques to sway their readers. Mary Wollstonecraft's *A Vindication of the Rights of Woman* is an excellent example of persuasive writing.

See also ARGUMENT.

Petrarchan sonnet *See SONNET.*

Play *See DRAMA.*

Plot The sequence of events in a short story, novel, or drama. Most plots deal with a problem and develop around a **conflict,** a struggle between opposing forces. The plot begins with **exposition,** which introduces the story's characters, setting, and situation. The **rising action** adds complications to the conflicts, or problems, leading to the **climax,** or **crisis,** the point of highest emotional pitch. The climax gives way rapidly to its logical result in the **falling action** and finally to the **resolution** (sometimes called the **dénouement**), in which the final outcome is revealed.

See page 369.
See also CONFLICT.

Poetry A form of literary expression that differs from prose in emphasizing the line, rather than the sentence, as the unit of composition. Many other traditional characteristics of poetry apply to some poems but not to others. Some of these characteristics are emotional, imaginative language; use of metaphor, simile, and other figures of speech; division into stanzas; and the use of rhyme and regular patterns of meter.

See also FIGURATIVE LANGUAGE, FREE VERSE, METER, PROSE, RHYME, STANZA.

Point of view The standpoint from which a story is told. In a story with **first-person** point of view, the narrator is a character in the story and uses the words *I* and *me,* as in James Joyce's "Araby." In a story told from **third-person** point of view, the narrator is someone who stands outside the story and describes the characters and action, as in D. H. Lawrence's "The Rocking-Horse Winner." **Third-person omniscient,** or all-knowing point of view, means that the narrator knows everything about the characters and events and may reveal details that the characters themselves could not reveal. If the narrator describes events as only one character perceives them, as in Elizabeth Bowen's "The Demon Lover," the point of view is called **third-person limited.** An **objective** point of view is that of a narrator who presents a story in a completely impersonal way, describing only external aspects of characters and events and never directly referring to thoughts or emotions.

See pages 276, 777, 976, 1345.
See also NARRATOR, SPEAKER.

Postmodernism A broad contemporary movement in art, music, film, literature, and other cultural areas that is viewed as growing out of or replacing Modernism. Many of the characteristic features of postmodernist literature extend or exaggerate tendencies of Modernism. For example, Modernist writers turned away from the apparent objectivity of Realism; postmodernists go further, introducing a frankly artificial, self-conscious playfulness into their works.

See also MODERNISM.

Prologue An introductory section of a play, a speech, or another literary work. Chaucer's *The Canterbury Tales* contains a long prologue.

See also EPILOGUE.

Propaganda Written or spoken material designed to bring about a change or to damage a cause through use of emotionally charged words, name-calling, or other techniques.

See page 1173.

Props A theater term (a shortened form of *properties*) for articles used in a stage play or movie or television set.

See also DRAMA.

Prose Written language that is not versified. Novels, short stories, and essays are usually written in prose.

See also POETRY.

Protagonist The central character in a literary work, around whom the main conflict revolves. Generally, the audience is meant to sympathize with the protagonist.

See page 1075.
See also ANTAGONIST, CONFLICT, HERO, PLOT.

Proverb A saying that expresses some truth about life or contains some bit of popular wisdom such as "faint heart never won fair lady," "marry in haste, repent at leisure," or "out of sight, out of mind."

See also APHORISM, EPIGRAM.

Psalm A song of praise most commonly found in the biblical book of Psalms. David, king of Israel around 1000 B.C., wrote many of these psalms. Occasionally a modern poet will title his or her poem a psalm.

See page 421.

Pun A humorous use of words that are similar in sound (*merry* and *marry*) or of a word with several meanings. In Shakespeare's *Romeo and Juliet*, when Mercutio is fatally wounded, he says, "Ask for me tomorrow, and you shall find me a grave man," meaning both "serious" and "dead."

Puritan writing The work of early seventeenth-century writers who supported the Puritan cause. John Milton and John Bunyan were two major Puritan writers.

See pages 508–509.

Quatrain A stanza of four lines.

See also BALLAD STANZA, COUPLET, HEROIC STANZA, SESTET, STANZA.

R

Rationalism A philosophy that values reason over feeling or imagination. It was most influential during the Neoclassical period.

See also NEOCLASSICISM, ROMANTICISM.

Realism A literary movement first prominent in the late nineteenth and early twentieth centuries. Realism seeks to portray life as it is really lived. Realistic fiction often focuses on middle- or working-class conditions and characters, often with reformist intent. Charles Dickens was a Realist writer.

See pages 916–917.
See also NATURALISM.

Refrain A line or lines repeated regularly, usually in a poem or song. In Dylan Thomas's "Do Not Go Gentle into That Good Night," the line "Rage, rage against the dying of the light" serves as a refrain.

See also REPETITION.

Regionalism An emphasis on themes, characters, customs, and settings of a particular geographical region. Thomas Hardy wrote regional novels set in southwest England.

See also DIALECT, VERNACULAR.

Repetition   The recurrence of sounds, words, phrases, lines, or stanzas in a speech or literary work. Repetition increases the sense of unity in a work and can draw attention to particular ideas.

See pages 871, 940.
See also PARALLELISM, REFRAIN.

Renaissance   A word meaning "rebirth." The Renaissance in Europe marked a transition from the medieval period to the modern world. The height of the English Renaissance occurred in the late sixteenth and early seventeenth centuries, when William Shakespeare was active.

Resolution   *See PLOT.*

Restoration Age   The short period immediately following the restoration of the Stuarts to the throne in 1660. The age is marked by the return of drama to the English stage.

Rhetoric   The art of using language—often in public speaking—to present facts and ideas in order to persuade. **Rhetorical devices** are techniques writers use to manipulate language for effect or to evoke an emotional response in the reader. These may include repetition, parallelism, analogy, logic, and the skillful use of connotation and anecdote. Effective rhetoric often appeals to logic, emotion, morality, or authority. A **rhetorical question** is a question to which no answer is expected or the answer is obvious.

See pages 871, 1167.
See also ANALOGY, ANECDOTE, ARGUMENT, CONNOTATION, PARALLELISM, REPETITION.

Rhyme   The repetition of the same stressed vowel sounds and any succeeding sounds in two or more words. **End rhyme** occurs at the ends of lines of poetry. **Internal rhyme** occurs within a single line.

See also RHYME SCHEME, SLANT RHYME.

Rhyme scheme   The pattern that end rhymes form in a stanza or a poem. Rhyme scheme is designated by the assignment of a different letter of the alphabet to each new rhyme. The rhyme scheme of the following lines from Thomas Hardy's "The Man He Killed" is *abab*:

"Had he and I but met	*a*
By some old ancient inn,	*b*
We should have sat us down to wet	*a*
Right many a nipperkin!	*b*

See pages 266, 450, 723, 863, 1107.
See also RHYME.

Rhythm   The pattern of beats created by the arrangement of stressed and unstressed syllables, especially in poetry. Rhythm gives poetry a musical quality, can add emphasis to certain words, and may help convey the poem's meaning. Rhythm can be regular, with a predictable pattern or meter, or irregular. Note the regular rhythm in the following lines from A. E. Housman's "To an Athlete Dying Young":

> The time you won your town the race
> We chaired you through the market-place;

See page 923.
See also IAMBIC PENTAMETER, METER, SCANSION, SPRUNG RHYTHM.

Rising action   *See PLOT.*

Romance   Historically, a term used to describe long narrative works about the exploits and love affairs of chivalric heroes such as King Arthur and Sir Lancelot. The term *romance* can also be applied to any story that involves noble heroes, idealized love, or fantastic events that seem remote from everyday life. Sir Thomas Malory's *Le Morte d'Arthur* is a romance.

See pages 16–17.
See also LEGEND.

Romanticism   An artistic movement that began in Europe and valued imagination and feeling over intellect and reason. The works of William Wordsworth, Coleridge, Byron, and Keats represent the height of Romantic poetry. This time period corresponds to Unit Four in this text.

Round character   *See CHARACTER.*

Run-on line   *See ENJAMBMENT.*

S

Sarcasm   The use of bitter or caustic language to point out shortcomings or flaws.

See also IRONY, SATIRE.

Satire   Writing that exposes to ridicule the vices or follies of people or societies through devices such as hyperbole, understatement, and irony. The purpose of satire may be to reform or to entertain. Swift's *A Modest Proposal* is a famous satirical essay whose purpose was to reform England's policy toward Ireland.

See pages 565, 991.
See also COMEDY, HYPERBOLE, IRONY, PARODY, UNDERSTATEMENT, WIT.

Scansion The analysis of the meter of a line of verse. To scan a line of poetry means to note the stressed and unstressed syllables and to divide the line into its feet, or rhythmic units. Stressed syllables are marked (´) and unstressed syllables (ˇ). Note the scansion of these lines from Byron's "She Walks in Beauty":

> She walks / in beau / ty, like / the night
> Of cloud / less climes / and star / ry skies; . . .

Since each line has four feet and the rhythm is iambic, the lines can be described as iambic tetrameter.

See also FOOT, METER, RHYTHM.

Scene A subdivision of an act in a play. A scene is shorter than an act.

See also ACT, DRAMA.

Science fiction Fiction that deals with the impact of science and technology—real or imagined—on society and on individuals. Sometimes occurring in the future, science fiction commonly portrays space travel, exploration of other planets, and possible future societies.

Sensory details See IMAGERY.

Septet A stanza of seven lines.

Sestet A six-line stanza.

See also SONNET.

Setting The time and place in which the events of a literary work occur. Setting includes not only the physical surroundings but also the ideas, customs, values, and beliefs of a particular time and place. Setting often helps create an atmosphere or a mood. Setting plays an important part in Lessing's "A Mild Attack of Locusts."

See page 1296.
See also ATMOSPHERE, MOOD.

Shakespearean songs Shakespeare used songs in his plays to heighten the drama, making what is merry merrier or what is sad sadder. His plays include love songs, nonsense songs, and **dirges**, songs that mourn a death.

See page 301.

Shakespearean sonnet See SONNET.

Short story A brief fictional narrative that generally includes the following major elements: setting, characters, plot, point of view, and theme.

See pages 1066–1067.
See also FICTION, NOVEL, PLOT.

Simile A figure of speech that uses *like* or *as* to compare seemingly unlike things. In the following example from Andrew Marvell's "To His Coy Mistress," the poet compares his love's complexion to dew:

> Now, therefore, while the youthful hue
> Sits on thy skin like morning dew,

See pages 294, 298, 843.
See also ANALOGY, FIGURATIVE LANGUAGE, METAPHOR.

Slant rhyme An approximate rhyme occurring when words include sounds that are similar but not identical (*jackal* and *buckle*). Slant rhyme typically involves some variation of **consonance** (the repetition of similar consonant sounds) or **assonance** (the repetition of similar vowel sounds). In "Follower," Seamus Heaney features slant rhyme in word pairs such as *sock/pluck* and *plow/furrow*.

See page 1259.
See also RHYME.

Soliloquy In drama, a long speech by a character who is alone on stage. A soliloquy reveals the private thoughts and emotions of that character. In Act 3, scene 1 of Shakespeare's *Macbeth*, Macbeth delivers a soliloquy that begins

> To be thus is nothing, but to be safely thus—
> Our fears in Banquo stick deep, . . .

See page 305.
See also ASIDE, DRAMATIC MONOLOGUE, MONOLOGUE.

Sonnet A lyric poem of fourteen lines, typically written in iambic pentameter and usually following strict patterns of stanza divisions and rhymes. The **Shakespearean**, or **English**, sonnet consists of three **quatrains**, or four-line stanzas, followed by a **couplet**, or pair of rhyming lines. The rhyme scheme is typically *abab, cdcd, efef, gg*. The couplet often presents a conclusion to the issues or questions presented in the three quatrains. Like a Shakespearean sonnet, the **Spenserian sonnet** has three quatrains and a couplet, but it follows the rhyme scheme *abab bcbc cdcd ee*. This interlocking rhyme scheme pushes the sonnet toward the final couplet, which makes a key point or comment. In the **Petrarchan**, or **Italian**, sonnet, fourteen lines are divided into two stanzas, the eight-line **octave** and the six-line **sestet**. The sestet usually responds to a question or situation posed by the octave. The rhyme scheme for the octave is typically *abbaabba*; for the sestet, the rhyme scheme is typically *cdecde*.

See pages 252–253.
See also COUPLET, LYRIC POETRY, RHYME SCHEME, STANZA.

Sonnet sequence A series of sonnets focused on a particular theme. Elizabeth Barrett Browning's *Sonnets from the Portuguese* is a sonnet sequence.

See also SONNET.

Sound devices Techniques used, especially in poetry, to appeal to the ear. Writers use sound devices to enhance the sense of rhythm, to emphasize particular sounds, or to add a musical quality to their work.

See pages 276, 876, 1328.
See also ALLITERATION, ASSONANCE, CONSONANCE, ONOMATOPOEIA, RHYME.

Speaker The person who is speaking in a poem, similar to a narrator in a work of prose. Sometimes the speaker's voice is that of the poet, sometimes that of a fictional person or even a thing. The speaker's words communicate a particular tone, or attitude, toward the subject of the poem. One should never assume that the speaker and the writer are identical, however. For example, the speaker in "My Last Duchess" is *not* the poet, Robert Browning.

See pages 280, 1243.
See also DRAMATIC MONOLOGUE, NARRATOR, TONE.

Spenserian stanza A nine-line poetic stanza composed of eight lines of iambic pentameter and one of iambic hexameter, with the rhyme scheme *ababbcbcc*. Byron used this stanza in "Childe Harold's Pilgrimage."

See also IAMBIC PENTAMETER, METER.

Spondee A metrical foot of two stressed syllables.

See also FOOT, METER.

Sprung rhythm A kind of irregular rhythm in which each foot has one stressed syllable, usually the first, and a varied number of unstressed syllables. Gerard Manley Hopkins, who invented the term and the technique, believed this to be the rhythm of natural speech.

See page 952.
See also METER, RHYTHM.

Stage directions Instructions written by a playwright to describe the appearance and actions of characters, as well as the sets, costumes, and lighting.

See also DRAMA.

Stanza A group of lines forming a unit in a poem or song. A stanza in a poem is similar to a paragraph in prose. Typically, stanzas in a poem are separated by a line of space.

See page 760.
See also BALLAD STANZA, COUPLET, HEROIC STANZA, QUATRAIN, SONNET, SPENSERIAN STANZA.

Static character See CHARACTER.

Stereotype A character who is not developed as an individual but instead represents a collection of traits and mannerisms supposedly shared by all members of a group.

See also CHARACTER.

Stream of consciousness The literary representation of a character's free-flowing thoughts, feelings, and memories. Stream-of-consciousness writing does not always employ conventional sentence structure or other rules of grammar and usage. Virginia Woolf and James Joyce often used stream of consciousness in their works.

See page 1156.

Structure The particular order or pattern a writer uses to present ideas. Narratives commonly follow a chronological order, while the structure of persuasive or expository writing may vary. Listing detailed information, using cause and effect, or describing a problem and then offering a solution are some other ways a writer can present a topic. The structure of *The Canterbury Tales* allowed Chaucer to represent a wide variety of characters and social classes.

See pages 255, 565, 1062, 1110.
See also FORM.

Style The expressive qualities that distinguish an author's work, including word choice and the length and arrangement of sentences, as well as the use of figurative language and imagery. Style can reveal an author's attitude and purpose in writing.

See pages 415, 615, 668, 940, 1118.
See also AUTHOR'S PURPOSE, DICTION, FIGURATIVE LANGUAGE, IMAGERY, TONE.

Subject The topic of a literary work.

Suspense A feeling of curiosity, uncertainty, or even dread about what is going to happen next in a story. Writers increase the level of suspense by creating a threat to the central character and raising questions in a reader's mind about the outcome of a conflict. Suspense is especially important in the plot of an adventure or a mystery story. Anita Desai builds suspense in "Games at Twilight" as the young boy waits to be discovered in the shed.

See also PROTAGONIST.

Symbol Any object, person, place, or experience that exists on a literal level but also represents something else, usually something abstract. The lamb is a symbol of innocence in Blake's "The Lamb."

See pages 755, 1078, 1146, 1302.
See also ALLEGORY, FIGURATIVE LANGUAGE.

Symbolist poetry A kind of poetry that emphasizes suggestion and inward experience instead of explicit description. Originating in France in the late 1800s, the symbolist poets influenced twentieth-century writers such as William Butler Yeats, T. S. Eliot, and Virginia Woolf.

See also MODERNISM.

Synecdoche A figure of speech in which a part is used for the whole or a whole is used for a part. In this line from the book of Revelation in the Bible, "All nations, and kindreds, and people, and tongues," *tongues* (a part) is used for the whole (languages).

See also METONYMY.

T

Tercet A stanza of three rhyming lines.
See also STANZA.

Terza rima A verse form consisting of a sequence of interlocking three-line stanzas, or tercets. The first and third lines of the first stanza rhyme, and the second line provides the rhyme for the first and third lines of the next stanza, forming the rhyme scheme *aba, bcb, cdc,* and so on. The beginning of Shelley's "Ode to the West Wind" (page 854) illustrates terza rima.

See page 863.

Tetrameter A metrical line of four feet.
See also FOOT, METER.

Theater of the absurd Drama, primarily of the 1950s and 1960s, that presents a series of scenes in which the characters—often confused and anxious—exist in a meaningless world. Harold Pinter is a leading English dramatist of absurdist and other plays.

See pages 1272, 1276–1277.
See also DRAMA.

Theme The message of a story, poem, novel, or play. Some works have a **stated theme**, which the author expresses directly. More commonly, works have an **implied theme**, which is revealed gradually through events, dialogues, or description. A literary work may have more than one theme. Some themes are universal, meaning that they are widely held ideas about life. Themes and **subjects** are different. The subject of a work might be love; the theme would be what the writer says about love—for example, love is cruel; love is wonderful; love is fleeting.

See pages 74, 301, 305, 436, 438, 575, 1285.
See also AUTHOR'S PURPOSE, MORAL.

Thesis The main idea of a work of nonfiction. The thesis may be stated directly or implied. The thesis of Francis Bacon's "Of Studies" is that books have multiple uses and readers have multiple needs and capabilities.

See pages 726, 1086.
See also NONFICTION.

Third-person point of view See POINT OF VIEW.

Title The name given to a literary work. The title can help explain the setting, provide insight into the theme, or describe the action that will take place in the work.

See pages 1094, 1293.

Tone An author's attitude toward his or her subject matter or the audience. Tone is conveyed through elements such as word choice, punctuation, sentence structure, and figures of speech. A writer's tone might convey a variety of attitudes such as sympathy, amusement, or superiority. The tone of Thomas Hardy's "Ah, Are You Digging on My Grave?" is one of bittersweet humor.

See pages 116, 255, 263, 301, 561, 656, 931, 1150.
See also AUTHOR'S PURPOSE, NARRATOR, SPEAKER, STYLE, VOICE.

Tragedy A play in which a main character suffers a downfall. That character, the **tragic hero,** is typically a person of dignified or heroic stature. The downfall may result from outside forces or from a weakness within the character, which is known as a **tragic flaw.** In Shakespeare's *Macbeth*, Macbeth's tragic flaw is excessive ambition.

See page 388.
See also DRAMA, HERO, HUBRIS.

Tragic hero *See TRAGEDY.*

Trimeter A metrical line of three feet.

See also FOOT, METER.

Trochee A metrical foot made up of one stressed and one unstressed syllable. The line below, from Shakespeare's *Macbeth*, has four trochees and can be described as trochaic tetrameter.

  Double, / double, / toil and / trouble;

See also FOOT, METER.

U–W

Understatement Language that makes something seem less important than it really is. Understatement may be used to add humor or to focus the reader's attention on something the author wants to emphasize.

See also HYPERBOLE.

Vernacular Ordinary speech of a particular country or region. Vernacular is more casual than cultivated, formal speech. Slang, dialect, and idiom are commonly included as part of the vernacular. Writers often employ vernacular to enhance the realism of their narrative or dialogue. The narrator in Penelope Lively's story "At the Pitt-Rivers" uses vernacular.

See page 1247.
See also DIALECT, IDIOM, REGIONALISM.

Verse paragraph A group of lines in a poem that form a unit. Unlike a stanza, a verse paragraph does not have a fixed number of lines. While poems written before the twentieth century usually contain stanzas, many contemporary poems are made up of verse paragraphs. Verse paragraphs help to organize a poem into thoughts, as paragraphs help to organize prose.

See page 1098.
See also STANZA.

Villanelle A nineteen-line poem divided into five tercets, or stanzas of three lines, each with the rhyme scheme *aba*, and a final quatrain with the rhyme scheme *abaa*. The first line is repeated as a refrain at the end of the second and fourth stanzas. The last line of the first stanza is repeated at the end of the third and fifth stanzas. Both lines reappear as the final two lines of the poem. This six-stanza form was originally used in French pastoral poetry. Thomas's "Do Not Go Gentle into That Good Night" is a villanelle.

See page 1206.
See also QUATRAIN, REFRAIN, STANZA.

Voice The distinctive use of language that conveys the author's or narrator's personality to the reader. Voice is determined by elements of style such as word choice and tone.

See pages 649, 1279.
See also AUTHOR'S PURPOSE, DICTION, NARRATOR, STYLE, TONE.

Wit An exhibition of cleverness and humor. Jonathan Swift, Alexander Pope, and Lewis Carroll are authors famous for their wit.

See page 743.
See also COMEDY, HUMOR, SATIRE.

The Reading Process

Being an active reader is a crucial part of being a lifelong learner. It is also an ongoing task. Good reading skills are recursive; that is, they build on each other, providing the tools you'll need to understand text, to connect selections to your own life, to interpret ideas and themes, and to read critically.

Vocabulary Development

To develop a rich vocabulary, consider these four important steps:

- **Read** a wide variety of texts.
- **Enjoy** and engage in wordplay and word investigation.
- **Listen** carefully to how others use words.
- **Participate** regularly in good classroom discussions.

Using context to discover meaning

When you look at the words and sentences surrounding a new word, you are using context. **Look** before, at, and after a new word or phrase. **Connect** what you know with what an author has written. Then **guess** at a possible meaning. **Try again** if your guess does not make sense. Consider these strategies for using context:

- Look for a synonym or an antonym nearby to provide a clue to the word's meaning.
- Notice if the text relates the word's meaning to another word.
- Check for a description of an action associated with the word.
- Try to find a general topic or idea related to the word.

Using word parts and word origins

Consider these basic elements when taking a word apart to determine meaning:

- **Base words** Locate the most basic part of a word to predict a core meaning.
- **Prefixes** Look at syllables attached before a base that add to or change a meaning.
- **Suffixes** Look at syllables added to the end of a base word that create new meanings.

Also consider **word origins**—Latin, Greek, and Anglo-Saxon roots—that are the basis for much of English vocabulary. Knowing these roots can help you determine derivations and spellings, as well as meanings in English.

Using reference materials

When using context and analyzing word parts do not help to unlock the meaning of a word, go to a reference source such as a dictionary, a glossary, a thesaurus, or even the Internet. Use these tips:

- **Locate** a word by using the guide words at the top of the pages.
- **Look** at the parts of the reference entry, such as part of speech, definition, or synonym.
- **Choose** between multiple meanings by thinking about what makes sense.
- **Apply** the meaning to what you're reading.

Distinguishing between meanings

Determining subtle differences between word meanings also aids comprehension. **Denotation** refers to the dictionary meaning or meanings of a word. **Connotation** refers to an emotion or underlying value that accompanies a word's dictionary meaning. The word *fragrance* has a different connotation from the word *odor,* even though the denotation of both words is "smell."

Comprehension Strategies

Because understanding is the most critical reading task, lifelong learners use a variety of reading strategies before, during, and after reading to ensure their comprehension.

Establishing and adjusting purposes for reading

To establish a purpose for reading, preview or **skim** a selection by glancing quickly over the entire piece, reading headings and subheadings, and noticing the organizational pattern of the text.

If you are reading to learn, solve a problem, or perform a task involving complex directions, consider these tips:

- Read slowly and carefully.
- Reread difficult passages.
- Take careful notes or construct a graphic.

Adjust your strategies as your purpose changes. To locate specific information in a longer selection, or to enjoy an entertaining plot, you might allow yourself a faster pace. Know when to speed up or slow down to maintain your understanding.

Drawing on personal background

When you recall information and personal experiences that are uniquely your own, you **draw on your personal background.** By thus **activating prior knowledge,** and combining it with the words on a page, you create meaning in a selection. To expand and extend your prior knowledge, share it interactively in classroom discussions.

Monitoring and modifying reading strategies

Check or **monitor your understanding** as you read, using the following strategies:

- Summarize
- Clarify
- Question
- Predict what will come next

You can use these four important steps once or twice in an easy, entertaining passage or after every paragraph in a conceptually dense nonfiction selection. As you read, think about asking interesting questions, rather than passively waiting to answer questions your teacher may ask later.

All readers find that understanding sometimes breaks down when material is difficult. Consider these steps to modify or change your reading strategies when you don't understand what you've read:

- Reread the passage.
- Consult other sources, including text resources, teachers, and other students.
- Write comments or questions on another piece of paper for later review or discussion.

Constructing graphic organizers

Graphic organizers, such as charts, maps, and diagrams, help you construct ideas in a visual way so you can remember them later. Look at the following model. Like a Venn diagram, which compares and contrasts two ideas or characters, a **semantic features analysis** focuses on the discriminating features of ideas or words. The items or ideas you want to compare are listed down the side, and the discriminating features are listed across the top. In each box use a + if the feature or characteristic applies to the item or a − if the feature or characteristic does not apply.

People in Government	Elected	Appointed	Passes Laws	Vetoes Laws
President	+	−	−	+
State Governor	+	−	−	+
Supreme Court Justice	−	+	−	−
Secretary of Defense	−	+	−	−

A **flowchart** helps you keep track of the sequence of events. Arrange ideas or events in a logical, sequential order. Then draw arrows between your ideas to indicate how one idea or event flows into another. Look at the following flowchart to see how you might show the chronological sequence of a story. Use a flowchart to make a **change frame,** recording causes and effects in sequence to illustrate how something changed.

A **web** can be used for a variety of purposes as you read a selection.

- To **map out the main idea and details** of a selection, put the main idea in the middle circle and, as you read, add supporting details around the main thought.
- To **analyze a character in a story,** put the character's name in the middle and add that character's actions, thoughts, reputation, plot involvement, and personal development in the surrounding circles.
- To **define a concept,** put a word or an idea in the middle circle and then add a more general category, descriptions, examples, and non-examples in the surrounding circles.

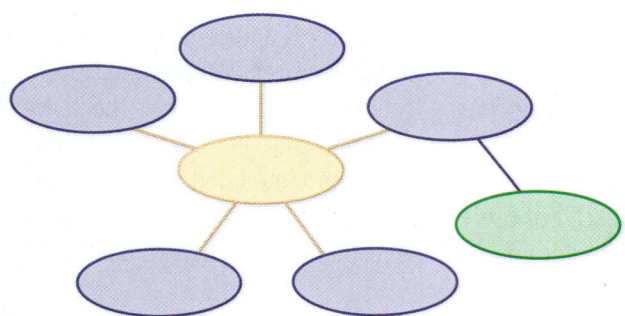

Analyzing text structures

To follow the logic and message of a selection and to remember it, analyze the **text structure,** or organization of ideas, within a writer's work. In narrative as well as in informational text, writers may embed one structure within another, but it is usually possible to identify one main pattern of organization. Recognizing the pattern of organization can help you discover the writer's purpose and will focus your attention on the important ideas in the selection. **Look for signal words** to point you to the structure.

- **Chronological order** often uses words such as *first, then, after, later,* and *finally.*
- **Cause-and-effect order** can include words or phrases such as *therefore, because, subsequently,* or *as a result of.*
- **Comparison-contrast order** may use words or phrases such as *similarly, in contrast, likewise,* or *on the other hand.*

Interpreting graphic aids

Graphic aids provide an opportunity to see and analyze information at a glance. Charts, tables, maps, and diagrams allow you to analyze and compare information. Maps include a compass rose, legend, and scale to help you interpret direction, symbols, and size. Charts and graphs compare information in categories running horizontally and vertically.

Tips for Reading Graphic Aids

- Examine the title, labels, and other explanatory features.
- Apply the labels to the graphic aid.
- Interpret the information.

Look carefully at the models below.

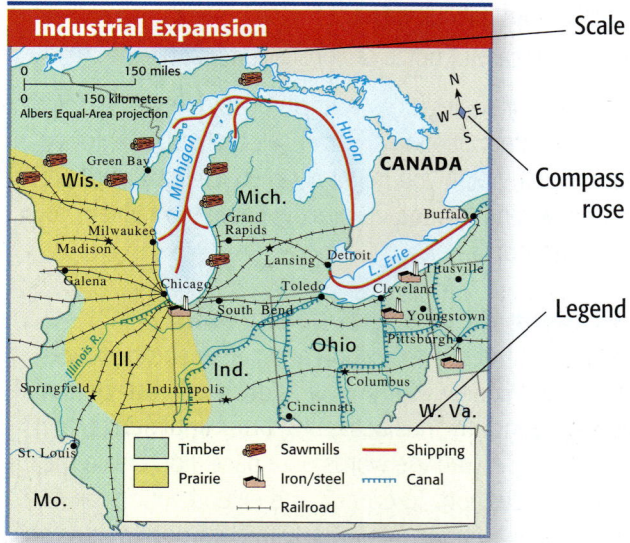

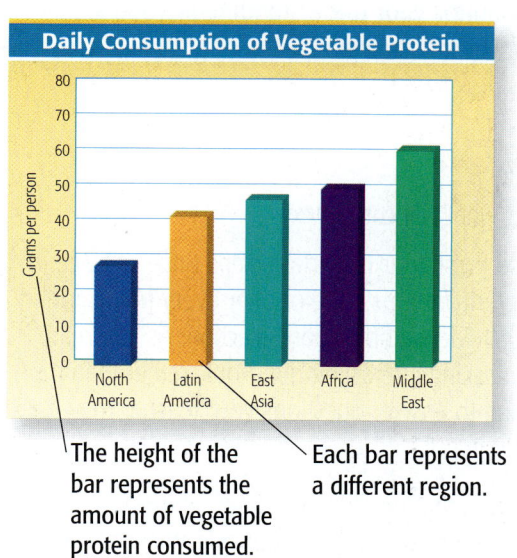

The height of the bar represents the amount of vegetable protein consumed.

Each bar represents a different region.

Sequencing

The order in which thoughts are arranged is called a **sequence**. A good sequence is one that is logical, given the ideas in a selection. **Chronological order, spatial order,** and **order of importance** are common forms of sequencing. Think about the order of a writer's thoughts as you read and pay particular attention to sequence when **following complex written directions**.

Summarizing

A summary is a short restatement of the main ideas and important details of a selection. Summarizing what you have read is an excellent tool for understanding and remembering a passage.

Tips for Summarizing

- Identify the **main ideas** or most important thoughts within a selection.
- Determine the essential **supporting details.**
- Relate all the main ideas and the essential details in a **logical sequence.**
- **Paraphrase**—that is, use your own words.
- Answer **who, what, why, where,** and **when** questions when you summarize.

The best summaries can easily be understood by someone who has not read the selection. If you're not sure whether an idea is a main idea or a detail, try taking it out of your summary. Does your summary still sound complete?

Drawing inferences and supporting them

An **inference** involves using your reason and experience to come up with an idea based on what a writer implies or suggests but does not directly state. The following strategic reading behaviors are examples of inference:

- **Making a prediction** is taking an educated guess about what a text will be about based on initial clues a writer provides.
- **Drawing a conclusion** is making a general statement you can explain with reason or with supporting details from a text.
- **Making a generalization** is generating a statement that can apply to more than one item or group.

What is most important when inferring is to be sure that you have accurately based your thoughts on supporting details from the text as well as on your own knowledge.

Reading silently for sustained periods

When you read for long periods of time, your task is to avoid distractions. Check your comprehension regularly by summarizing what you've read so far. Using study guides or graphic organizers can help get you through difficult passages. Take regular breaks when you need them and vary your reading rate with the demands of the task.

Synthesizing information

You will often need to read across texts; that is, in different sources, combining or **synthesizing** what you've learned from varied sources to suit your purposes. Follow these suggestions:

- Understand the information you've read in each source.
- Interpret the information.
- Identify similarities and differences in ideas or logic.
- Combine like thoughts in a logical sequence.

Literary Response

Whenever you share your thoughts and feelings about something you've read, you are responding to text. While the way you respond may vary with the type of text you read and with your individual learning style, as a strategic reader you will always need to adequately support your responses with proof from the text.

Responding to informational and aesthetic elements

When you respond both intellectually *and* emotionally, you connect yourself with a writer and with other people. To respond in an intellectual way, ask yourself if the ideas you have read are logical and well supported. To respond emotionally, ask yourself how you feel about those ideas and events. Choose a way to respond that fits your learning style. Class discussions, journal entries, oral interpretations, enactments, and graphic displays are some of the many ways to share your thoughts and emotions about a writer's work.

Comparing responses with authoritative views

Critics' reviews may encourage you to read a book, see a movie, or attend an event. They may also warn you that whatever is reviewed is not acceptable entertainment or is not valued by the reviewer. Deciding whether to value a review depends on the credibility of the reviewer and also on your own personal views and feelings. Ask yourself the following questions:

- What is the reviewer's background?
- What qualifies the reviewer to write this evaluation?
- Is the review balanced? Does it include both positive and negative responses?
- Are arguments presented logically?
- Are opinions supported with facts?
- What bias does this reviewer show?
- Do I agree? Why or why not?

Analysis and Evaluation

Good readers want to do more than recall information or interpret thoughts and ideas. When you read, read critically, forming opinions about characters and ideas, and making judgments using your own prior knowledge and information from the text.

Analyzing characteristics of texts

To be a critical reader and thinker, start by analyzing the characteristics of the text. Think about what specific characteristics make a particular selection clear, concise, and complete. Ask yourself these questions:

- What **pattern of organization** has this writer used to present his or her thoughts? Cause/effect? Comparison/contrast? Problem/solution? Does this organization make the main ideas clear or vague? Why?
- What word order, or **syntax,** gives force and emphasis to this writer's ideas? Does the grammatical order of the words make ideas sound complete, or is the sentence structure confusing?
- What **word choices** reveal this writer's tone, or attitude about the topic? Is the language precise or too general? Is it economical and yet descriptive?

Evaluating the credibility of sources

Evaluating the credibility of a source involves making a judgment about whether a writer is knowledgeable and truthful. Consider the following steps:

- **Decide on the writer's purpose or motive.** What will the writer gain if you accept his or her ideas or if you act on his or her suggestions?
- **Investigate the writer's background.** How has the writer become an authority in his or her field? Do others value what he or she says?
- **Evaluate the writer's statements.** Is the writer's information factual? Can it be proved? Are opinions clearly stated as such? Are they adequately supported with details so that they are valid? Are any statements nonfactual? Check to be sure.

Analyzing logical arguments and modes of reasoning

When you analyze works you've read, ask yourself whether the reasoning behind a writer's works is logical. Two kinds of logical reasoning are

Inductive Reasoning By observing a limited number of particular cases, a reader arrives at a general or universal statement. This logic moves from the specific to the general.

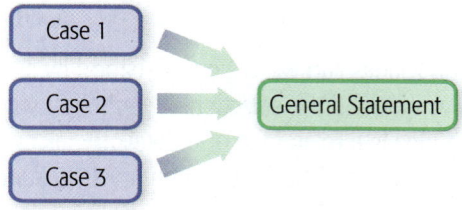

Deductive Reasoning This logic moves from the general to the specific. The reader takes a general statement and, through reasoning, applies it to specific situations.

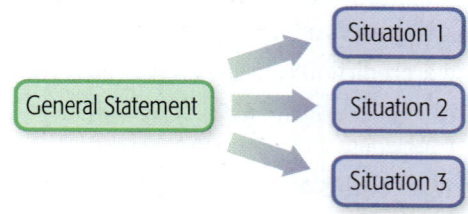

Faulty reasoning, on the other hand, is vague and illogical. Look for either/or reasoning or oversimplified statements when analyzing faulty reasoning. Failure to understand a writer's work may be the result of poorly presented, unsupported arguments, sequenced in a haphazard way.

A writer shows **bias** when he or she demonstrates a strong personal, and sometimes unreasonable, opinion. Look for bias when evaluating editorials, documentaries, and advertisements.

Writers use **persuasive techniques** when they try to get readers to believe a certain thing or act in a particular way. A writer may have a strong personal bias and still compose a persuasive essay that is logical and well supported. On the other hand, deceptive arguments can be less than accurate in order to be persuasive. Read carefully to judge whether a writer's bias influences his or her writing in negative or positive ways.

 ## Reading and Thinking with Foldables™

by Dinah Zike, M.Ed., Creator of Foldables™

Using Foldables™ Makes Learning Easy and Enjoyable

Anyone who has paper, scissors, and a stapler or some glue can use Foldables in the classroom. Just follow the illustrated step-by-step directions. Check out the following sample:

 **Reading Objective:** to understand how one character's actions affect other characters in a short story

Use this Foldable to keep track of what the main character does and how his or her actions affect the other characters.

1. Place a sheet of paper in front of you so that the short side is at the top. Fold the paper in half from top to bottom.

2. Fold in half again, from side to side, to divide the paper into two columns. Unfold the paper so that the two columns show.

3. Draw a line along the column crease. Then, through the top layer of paper, cut along the line you drew, forming two tabs.

4. Label the tabs *Main character's actions* and *Effects on others.*

5. As you read, record the main character's actions under the first tab. Record how each of those actions affects other characters under the second tab.

> Practice reading and following step-by-step directions.

> Illustrations make directions easier to follow.

> Become an active reader, tracking and reorganizing information so that you can better comprehend the selection.

Short Story

 **Reading Objective:** to analyze a short story on the basis of its literary elements

As you read, use the following Foldable to keep track of five literary elements in the short story.

1. Stack three sheets of paper with their top edges about a half-inch apart. Be sure to keep the side edges straight.

2. Fold up the bottom edges of the paper to form six tabs, five of which will be the same size.

3. Crease the paper to hold the tabs in place and staple the sheets together along the crease.

4. Turn the sheets so that the stapled side is at the top. Write the title of the story on the top tab. Label the five remaining tabs *Setting, Characters, Plot, Point of View,* and *Theme.*

5. Use your Foldable as you read the short story. Under each labeled tab, jot down notes about the story in terms of that element.

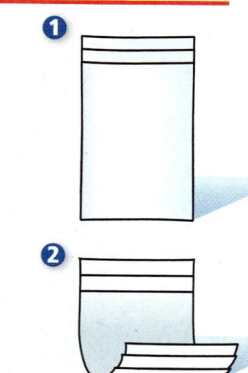

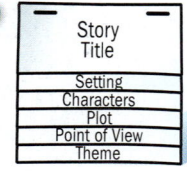

You may adapt this simple Foldable in several ways.

■ Use it with dramas, longer works of fiction, and some narrative poems—wherever five literary elements are present in the story.

■ Change the labels to focus on something different. For example, if a story or a play has several settings, characters, acts, or scenes, you could devote a tab to each one.

Drama

 **Reading Objective:** to understand conflict and plot in a drama

As you read the drama, use the following Foldable to keep track of conflicts that arise and ways that those conflicts are resolved.

1. Place a sheet of paper in front of you so that the short side is at the top. Fold the paper in half from side to side.

2. Fold the paper again, one inch from the top as shown here.

3. Unfold the paper and draw lines along all of the folds. This will be your chart.

4. At the top, label the left column *Conflicts* and the right column *Resolutions.*

5. As you read, record in the left column the various conflicts that arise in the drama. In the right column, explain how each conflict is resolved by the end of the drama.

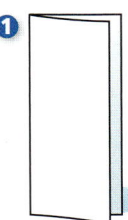

You may adapt this simple Foldable in several ways.

■ Use it with short stories, longer works of fiction, and many poems—wherever conflicts and their resolutions are important.

■ Change the labels to focus on something different. For example, you could record the actions of two characters, or you could record the thoughts and feelings of a character before and after the story's climax.

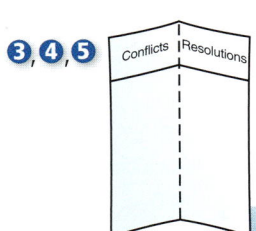

Lyric Poem

Reading Objective: to interpret the poet's message by understanding the speaker's thoughts and feelings

As you read the poem, use the following Foldable to help you distinguish between what the speaker *says* and what the poet *means*.

1. Place a sheet of paper in front of you so that the short side is at the top. Fold the paper in half from top to bottom.

2. Fold the paper in half again from left to right.

3. Unfold and cut through the top layer of paper along the fold line. This will make two tabs.

4. Label the left tab *Speaker's Words.* Label the right tab *Poet's Meaning.*

5. Use your Foldable to jot down notes on as you read the poem. Under the left tab, write down key things the speaker says. Under the right tab, write down what you think the poet means by having the speaker say those things.

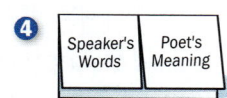

You may adapt this simple Foldable in several ways.

- Use it to help you visualize the images in a poem. Just replace *Speaker's Words* with *Imagery* and replace *Poet's Meaning* with *What I See.*

- Replace the label *Speaker's Words* with *Speaker's Tone* and under the tab write adjectives that describe the tone of the speaker's words.

- If the poem you are reading has two stanzas, you might devote each tab to notes about one stanza.

Informational Text

 **Reading Objective:** to understand and remember ideas in informational text

As you read a nonfiction selection, use this Foldable to help you identify what you already know about the topic, what you might want to know about it, and what you learn about it from the selection.

1. Hold a sheet of paper in front of you so that the short side is at the top. Fold the bottom of the paper up and the top down to divide the paper into thirds.

2. Unfold the paper and turn it so that the long side is at the top. Draw lines along the folds and label the three columns *Know, Want to Know,* and *Learned.*

3. Before you read the selection, write what you already know about the topic under the left heading and what you want to know about it under the middle heading. As you read, jot down what you learn about the topic under the last heading.

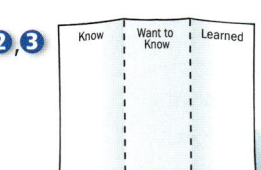

You may adapt this simple Foldable in several ways.

- Use it with magazine and newspaper articles, textbook chapters, reference articles, and informational Web sites—anything you might read to look for information.

- Use this three-part Foldable to record information from three sources. Label each column with the name of one source and write notes from that source under its heading.

- For a two-column Foldable, just fold the sheet of paper in half. For four columns, fold it in half and then in half again.

The Writing Process

Writing is a process with five stages: *prewriting, drafting, revising, editing/ proofreading,* and *publishing/presenting.* These stages often overlap, and their importance, weight, and even their order vary according to your needs and goals. Because writing is recursive, you almost always have to double back somewhere in this process, perhaps to gather more information or to reevaluate your ideas.

The Writing Process

Prewriting → Drafting → Revising → Editing/ Proofreading → Publishing/ Presenting

Prewriting

The prewriting stage includes coming up with ideas, making connections, gathering information, defining and refining the topic, and making a plan for a piece of writing.

Tips for prewriting

- Begin with an interesting idea (*what* you will write about).
- Decide the purpose of the writing (*why* you are writing).
- Identify the audience (for *whom* you are writing).
- Explore your idea through a technique such as freewriting, clustering, making diagrams, or brainstorming.

  Freewriting is writing nonstop for a set time, usually only five or ten minutes. The idea is to keep pace with your thoughts, getting them on paper before they vanish. Freewriting can start anywhere and go anywhere.

  Clustering begins with writing a word or phrase in the middle of a sheet of paper. Circle the word or phrase; then think of related words and ideas. Write them in bubbles connected to the central bubble. As you cluster, connect related ideas. The finished cluster will be a diagram of how your ideas can be organized.

  Brainstorming is creating a free flow of ideas with a group of people—it's like freewriting with others. Start with a topic or question; encourage everyone to join in freely. Accept all ideas without

judgment and follow each idea as far as it goes. You can evaluate the ideas later.

- Search for information in print and nonprint sources.
- If you are writing a personal essay, all of the information may come from your own experiences and feelings. If you are writing a report or a persuasive essay, you will probably need to locate pertinent factual information and take notes on it. Besides library materials, such as books, magazines, and newspapers, you will want to use the Internet and other online resources. You may also want to interview people with experience or specialized knowledge related to your topic.
- As you gather ideas and information, jot them down on note cards to use as you draft.
- Evaluate all ideas and information to determine or fine-tune the topic.
- Organize information and ideas into a plan that serves as the basis for writing.
- Develop a rough outline reflecting the method of organization you have chosen. Include your main points and supporting details.
- Find and include missing information or ideas that might add interest or help accomplish the purpose of the writing.

Drafting

In this stage you translate into writing the ideas and information you gathered during prewriting. Drafting is an opportunity to explore and develop your ideas.

Tips for drafting

- Follow the plan made during prewriting but be flexible. New and better ideas may come to you as you develop your ideas; be open to them.
- Transform notes and ideas into related sentences and paragraphs, but don't worry about grammar or mechanics. At this point, it is usually better to concentrate on getting your ideas on paper. You might want to circle or annotate ideas or sections that need more work.
- Determine the tone or attitude of the writing.
- Try to formulate an introduction that will catch the interest of your intended audience.

Revising

In this stage, review and evaluate your draft to make sure it accomplishes its purpose and speaks to its intended audience. When revising, interacting with a peer reviewer can be especially helpful.

Using peer review

Ask one or more of your classmates to read your draft. Here are some specific ways in which you can direct their responses:

- Have readers tell you in their own words what they have read. If you do not hear your ideas restated, you will want to revise for clarity.
- Ask readers to tell you what parts of your writing they liked best and why.
- Discuss the ideas in your writing with your readers. Add any new insights you gain to your revision.
- Ask readers for suggestions about things such as organization and word choice.

You may want to take notes on your readers' suggestions so you will have a handy reference as you revise.

Tips for the peer reviewer

When you are asked to act as a reviewer for a classmate's writing, the following tips will help you do the most effective job:

- Read the piece all the way through—without commenting—to judge its overall effect.
- Tell the writer how you responded to the piece. For example, did you find it informative? interesting? amusing?
- Ask the writer about parts you don't understand.
- Think of questions to ask that will help the writer improve the piece.
- Be sure that your suggestions are constructive.
- Help the writer make improvements.
- Answer the writer's questions honestly. Think about how you would like someone to respond to you.

Tips for revising

- Be sure you have said everything you wanted to say. If not, *add.*
- If you find a section that does not relate to your topic, *cut it.*
- If your ideas are not in a logical order, *rearrange* sentences and paragraphs.
- *Rewrite* any unclear sentences.
- Evaluate your introduction to be sure it creates interest, leads the reader smoothly into your topic, and states your main idea. Also evaluate your conclusion to be sure it either summarizes your writing or effectively brings it to an end.
- Evaluate your word choices. Choose vivid verbs and precise nouns. Use a thesaurus to help you.
- Consider the comments of your peer reviewer. Evaluate them carefully and apply those that will help you create a more effective piece of writing.

Editing/Proofreading

In the editing/proofreading stage, you polish your revised draft and proofread it for errors in grammar and spelling. Use this proofreading checklist to help you check for errors and use the proofreading symbols in the chart below to mark places that need corrections.

- ☑ Have I avoided run-on sentences and sentence fragments and punctuated sentences correctly?
- ☑ Have I used every word correctly, including plurals, possessives, and frequently confused words?
- ☑ Do verbs and subjects agree? Are verb tenses correct?

- ☑ Do pronouns refer clearly to their antecedents and agree with them in person, number, and gender?
- ☑ Have I used adverb and adjective forms and modifying phrases correctly?
- ☑ Have I spelled every word correctly and checked the unfamiliar ones in a dictionary?

Publishing/Presenting

There are a number of ways you can share your work. You could publish it in a magazine, a class anthology, or another publication, or read your writing aloud to a group. You could also join a writers' group and read one another's works.

Proofreading Symbols

Symbol	Example	Meaning
⊙	Lt Brown	Insert a period.
∧	No one came to the party.	Insert a letter or a word.
≡	I enjoyed paris.	Capitalize a letter.
/	The Class ran a bake sale.	Make a capital letter lowercase.
‿	The campers are home sick.	Close up a space.
ⓢⓟ	They visited N.Y. ⓢⓟ	Spell out.
∧ ⌃	Sue please come I need your help.	Insert a comma or a semicolon.
∪	He enjoyed feild day.	Transpose the position of letters or words.
#	alltogether	Insert a space.
ℰ	We went to to Boston.	Delete letters or words.
⌄⌄ ⌄	She asked, Whos coming?	Insert quotation marks or an apostrophe.
/ = /	mid January	Insert a hyphen.
¶	"Where?" asked Karl. "Over there," said Ray.	Begin a new paragraph.

Using the Traits of Strong Writing

What are some basic terms you can use to discuss your writing with your teacher or classmates? What should you focus on as you revise and edit your compositions? Check out the following seven terms, or traits, that describe the qualities of strong writing. Learn the meaning of each trait and find out how using the traits can improve your writing.

Ideas The message or the theme and the details that develop it

Writing is clear when readers can grasp the meaning of your ideas right away. Check to see whether you're getting your message across.

- ☑ Does the title suggest the theme of the composition?
- ☑ Does the composition focus on a single narrow topic?
- ☑ Is the thesis—the main point or central idea—clearly stated?
- ☑ Do well-chosen details elaborate your main point?

Organization The arrangement of main ideas and supporting details

An effective plan of organization points your readers in the right direction and guides them easily through your composition from start to finish. Find a structure, or order, that best suits your topic and writing purpose. Check to see whether you've ordered your key ideas and details in a way that keeps your readers on track.

- ☑ Are the beginning, middle, and end clearly linked?
- ☑ Is the internal order of ideas easy to follow?
- ☑ Does the introduction capture your readers' attention?
- ☑ Do sentences and paragraphs flow from one to the next in a way that makes sense?
- ☑ Does the conclusion wrap up the composition?

Voice A writer's unique way of using tone and style

Your writing voice comes through when your readers sense that a real person is communicating with them. Readers will respond to the **tone** (or attitude) that you express toward a topic and to the **style** (the way that you use language and shape your sentences). Read your work aloud to see whether your writing voice comes through.

- ☑ Does your writing sound interesting?
- ☑ Does your writing reveal your attitude toward your topic?
- ☑ Does your writing sound like you—or does it sound like you're imitating someone else?

Word Choice The vocabulary a writer uses to convey meaning

Words work hard. They carry the weight of your meaning, so make sure you choose them carefully. Check to see whether the words you choose are doing their jobs well.

- ☑ Do you use lively verbs to show action?
- ☑ Do you use vivid words to create word pictures in your readers' minds?
- ☑ Do you use precise words to explain your ideas simply and clearly?

Sentence Fluency The smooth rhythm and flow of sentences that vary in length and style

The best writing is made up of sentences that flow smoothly from one sentence to the next. Writing that is graceful also sounds musical–rhythmical rather than choppy. Check for sentence fluency by reading your writing aloud.

- ☑ Do your sentences vary in length and structure?
- ☑ Do transition words and phrases show connections between ideas and sentences?
- ☑ Does parallelism help balance and unify related ideas?

Conventions Correct spelling, grammar, usage, and mechanics

A composition free of errors makes a good impression on your readers. Mistakes can be distracting, and they can blur your message. Try working with a partner to spot errors and correct them. Use this checklist to help you.

- ☑ Are all words spelled correctly?
- ☑ Are all proper nouns—as well as the first word of every sentence—capitalized?
- ☑ Is your composition free of sentence fragments?
- ☑ Is your composition free of run-on sentences?
- ☑ Are punctuation marks—such as apostrophes, commas, and end marks—inserted in the right places?

Presentation The way words and design elements look on a page

Appearance matters, so make your compositions inviting to read. Handwritten papers should be neat and legible. If you're using a word processor, double-space the lines of text and choose a readable font. Other design elements– such as boldfaced headings, bulleted lists, pictures, and charts–can help you present information effectively as well as make your papers look good.

Preparing a manuscript

Follow the guidelines of the Modern Language Association when you prepare the final copy of your research paper.

- **Heading** On separate lines in the upper left-hand corner of the first page, include your name, your teacher's name, the course name, and the date.
- **Title** Center the title on the line below the heading.
- **Numbering** Number the pages one-half inch from the top of the page in the right-hand corner. Write your last name before each page number after the first page.
- **Spacing** Use double spacing throughout.
- **Margins** Leave one-inch margins on all sides of every page.

Writing Modes

Writing may be classified as expository, descriptive, narrative, or persuasive. Each of these classifications, or modes, has its own purpose.

Expository Writing

Expository writing gives instructions, defines or explains new terms or ideas, explains relationships, compares one thing or opinion with another, or explains how to do something. Expository essays usually include a thesis statement in the introduction.

- ☑ Does the opening contain attention-grabbing details or intriguing questions to hook the reader?
- ☑ Have I provided sufficient information to my audience in a clear and interesting way?
- ☑ Have I checked the accuracy of the information I have provided?
- ☑ Are my comparisons and contrasts clear and logical?

Descriptive Writing

Description re-creates an experience primarily through the use of sensory details. A writer should strive to create a single impression that all the details support. To do so requires careful planning as well as choices about order of information, topic sentences, and figurative language.

- ☑ Did I create interest in my introduction?
- ☑ Are my perspective and my subject clearly stated in my topic sentence?
- ☑ Did I organize details carefully and consistently?
- ☑ Did I order information effectively?
- ☑ Have I chosen precise, vivid words?
- ☑ Do transitions clearly and logically connect the ideas?
- ☑ Have I created a strong, unified impression?

Narrative Writing

Narrative writing, whether factual or fictional, tells a story and has these elements: characters, plot, point of view, theme, and setting. The plot usually involves a conflict between a character and an opposing character or force.

- ☑ Did I introduce characters and a setting?
- ☑ Did I develop a plot that begins with an interesting problem or conflict?
- ☑ Did I build suspense, lead the reader to a climax, and end with a resolution?
- ☑ Did I use dialogue to move the story along?

Persuasive Writing

Persuasive writing expresses a writer's opinion. The goal of persuasion is to make an audience change its opinion and, perhaps, take action. Effective persuasive writing uses strong, relative evidence to support its claims. This kind of writing often requires careful research, organization, and attention to language.

- ☑ Did I keep my audience's knowledge and attitudes in mind from start to finish?
- ☑ Did I state my position in a clear thesis statement?
- ☑ Have I included ample supporting evidence?
- ☑ Have I addressed opposing viewpoints?
- ☑ Have I avoided errors in logic?

WRITING HANDBOOK **R35**

Research Paper Writing

More than any other type of paper, research papers are the product of a search—a search for data, for facts, for informed opinions, for insights, and for new information.

Selecting a topic

- If a specific topic is not assigned, choose a topic. Begin with the assigned subject or a subject that interests you. Read general sources of information about that subject and narrow your focus to some aspect of it that interests you. Good places to start are encyclopedia articles and the tables of contents of books on the subject. A computerized library catalog will also display many subheads related to general topics. Find out if sufficient information about your topic is available.

- As you read about the topic, develop your paper's central idea, which is the purpose of your research. Even though this idea might change as you do more research, it can begin to guide your efforts. For example, if you were assigned the subject of the Civil War, you might find that you're interested in women's roles during that war. As you read, you might narrow your topic down to women who went to war, women who served as nurses for the Union, or women who took over farms and plantations in the South.

Conducting a broad search for information

- Generate a series of researchable questions about your chosen topic. Then research to find answers to your questions.

- Among the many sources you might use are the card catalog, the computer catalog, the *Reader's Guide to Periodical Literature* (or an electronic equivalent), newspaper indexes, and specialized references such as biographical encyclopedias.

- If possible, use primary sources as well as secondary sources. A **primary source** is a firsthand account of an event–for example, the diary of a woman who served in the army in the Civil War is a primary source. **Secondary sources** are sources written by people who did not experience or influence the event. Locate specific information efficiently by using the table of contents, indexes, chapter headings, and graphic aids.

Developing a working bibliography

If a work seems useful, write a **bibliography card** for it. On an index card, write down the author, title, city of publication, publisher, date of publication, and any other information you will need to identify the source. Number your cards in the upper right-hand corner so you can keep them in order.

Following are model bibliography, or source, cards.

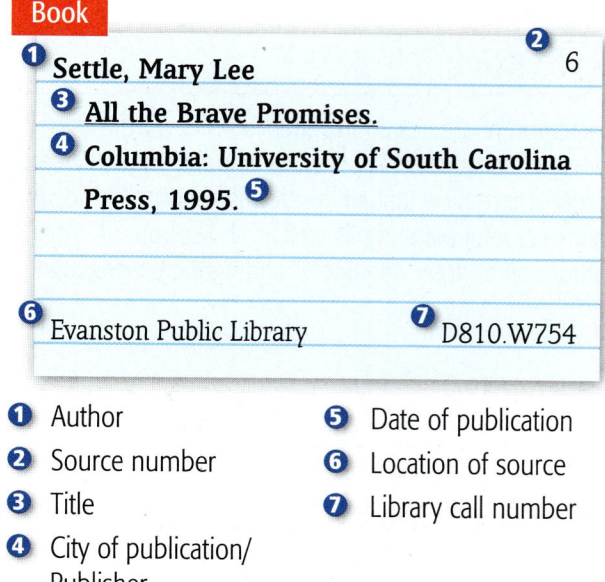

0 Author
2 Source number
3 Title
4 City of publication/Publisher
5 Date of publication
6 Location of source
7 Library call number

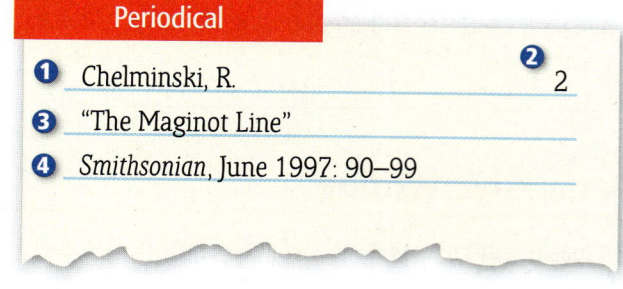

0 Author
2 Source number
3 Title
4 Title of magazine/date/page number(s)

Online source

① "Job Hunting Resources" ② 6
③ The Career Building Network
④ CareerBuilder
⑤ 14 Feb. 2002
⑥ http://www.careerbuilder.com

① Title	④ Sponsoring organization
② Source number	⑤ Date of access
③ Title of database	⑥ URL

Evaluating your sources

Your sources should be **a**uthoritative, **r**eliable, **t**imely, and **s**uitable (**arts**).

- The source should be **authoritative.** The author should be well-known in the field. An author who has written several books or articles about a subject or who is frequently quoted may be considered an authority. You might also consult *Book Review Index* and *Book Review Digest* to find out how other experts in the field have evaluated a book or an article.

- The source should be **reliable.** If possible, avoid material from popular magazines in favor of that from more scholarly journals. Be especially careful to evaluate material from online sources. For example, the Web site of a well-known university is more reliable than that of an individual. (You might also consult a librarian or your instructor for guidance in selecting reliable online sources.)

- The source should be **timely.** Use the most recent material available, particularly for subjects of current importance. Check the publication date of books as well as the month and year of periodicals.

- The source should be **suitable,** or **appropriate.** Consider only material that is relevant to the purpose of your paper. Do not waste time on books or articles that have little bearing on your topic. If you are writing on a controversial topic, you should include material that represents more than one point of view.

Compiling and organizing note cards

Careful notes will help you to organize the material for your paper.

- As you reread and study sources, write useful information on index cards. Be sure that each note card identifies the source (use the number of the bibliography card that corresponds to each source).

- In the lower right-hand corner of the card, write the page number on which you found the information. If one card contains several notes, write the page number in parentheses after the relevant material.

- Three helpful ways to take notes are paraphrasing, summarizing, and quoting directly.

  1. **Paraphrase** important details that you want to remember; that is, use your own words to restate specific information.

  2. **Summarize** main ideas that an author presents. When you summarize several pages, be sure to note the page on which the material begins and the page on which it ends—for example, 213–221.

  3. **Quote** the exact words of an author only when the actual wording is important. Be careful about placing the author's words in quotation marks.

- Identify the subject of each note card with a short phrase written in the upper left.

> Avoid **plagiarism**—presenting an author's words or ideas as if they were your own. Remember that you must credit the source not only for material directly quoted but also for any facts or ideas obtained from the source.

See the sample note card below, which includes information about careers and goals from three pages.

> *Careers and goals*   12
> Many people "crave work that will
> spark... excitement and energy."
> (5) Sher recognizes that a career does
> not necessarily satisfy a person's aim
> in life. (24) She also offers advice on
> how to overcome obstacles that people
> experience in defining their goals. (101)

- Organize your note cards to develop a **working outline.** Begin by sorting them into piles of related cards. Try putting the piles together in different ways that suggest an organizational pattern. (If, at this point, you discover that you do not have enough information, go back and do further research.) Many methods of organization are possible. You might also combine methods of organization.

Developing a thesis statement

A thesis statement tells what your topic is and what you intend to say about it—for example, "World War II changed the lives of African Americans and contributed to the rise of the civil rights movement."

- Start by examining your central idea.
- Refine it to reflect the information that you gathered in your research.
- Next, consider your approach to the topic. What is the purpose of your research? Are you proving or disproving something? illustrating a cause-and-effect relationship? offering a solution to a problem? examining one aspect of the topic thoroughly? predicting an outcome?
- Revise your central idea to reflect your approach.
- Be prepared to revise your thesis statement if necessary.

Drafting your paper

Consult your working outline and your notes as you start to draft your paper.

- Concentrate on getting your ideas down in a complete and logical order.
- Write an introduction and a conclusion. An effective introduction creates interest, perhaps by beginning with a question or a controversial quotation; it should also contain your thesis statement. An effective conclusion will summarize main points, restate your thesis, explain how the research points to important new questions to explore, and bring closure to the paper.

Documenting sources

Since a research paper, by its nature, is built on the work of others, you must carefully document all the sources you have used.

- Name the sources of words, ideas, and facts that you borrow.
- In addition to citing books and periodicals from which you take information, cite song lyrics, letters, and excerpts from literature.
- Also credit original ideas that are expressed graphically in tables, charts, and diagrams, as well as the sources of any visual aids you may include, such as photographs.
- You need not cite the source of any information that is common knowledge, such as "John F. Kennedy was assassinated in 1963 in Dallas, Texas."

In-text citations The most common method of crediting sources is with parenthetical documentation within the text. Generally a reference to the source and page number is included in parentheses at the end of each quotation, paraphrase, or summary of information borrowed from a source. An in-text citation points readers to a corresponding entry in your **works-cited list**—a list of all your sources, complete with publication information, that will appear as the final page of your paper. The Modern Language Association (MLA) recommends the following guidelines for crediting sources in text. You may wish to refer to the *MLA Handbook for Writers of Research Papers* by Joseph Gibaldi for more information and examples.

- **Put in parentheses the author's last name and the page number where you found the information.**

    An art historian has noted, "In Wood's idyllic farmscapes, man lives in complete harmony with Nature; he is the earth's caretaker" (Corn 90).

- **If the author's name is mentioned in the sentence, put only the page number in parentheses.**

    Art historian Wanda Corn has noted, "In Wood's idyllic farmscapes, man lives in complete harmony with Nature; he is the earth's caretaker" (90).

- **If no author is listed, put the title or a shortened version of the title in parentheses. Include a page number if you have one.**

    Some critics believe that Grant Wood's famous painting *American Gothic* pokes fun at small-town life and traditional American values ("Gothic").

Compiling a list of works cited

At the end of your text, provide an alphabetized list of published works or other sources cited.

- Include complete publishing information for each source.
- For magazine and newspaper articles, include the page numbers. If an article is continued on a different page, use + after the first page number.
- For online sources, include the date accessed.
- Cite only those sources from which you actually use information.
- Arrange entries in alphabetical order according to the author's last name. Write the last name first. If no author is given, alphabetize by title.
- For long entries, indent five spaces every line after the first.

How to cite sources

On the next three pages, you'll find sample style sheets that can help you prepare your list of sources—the final page of the research paper. Use the one your teacher prefers.

MLA Style

MLA style is most often used in English and social studies classes. Center the title *Works Cited* at the top of your list.

Source	Style
Book with one author	Witham, Barry B. *The Federal Theatre Project: A Case Study.* New York: Cambridge UP, 2003. ["UP" is an abbreviation for "University Press."].
Book with two or three authors	Hoy, Pat C., II, Esther H. Schor, and Robert DiYanni. *Women's Voices: Visions and Perspectives.* New York: McGraw-Hill, 1990. [If a book has more than three authors, name only the first author and then write "et al." (Latin abbreviation for "and others").]
Book with editor(s)	Komunyakaa, Yusef, and David Lehman, eds. *The Best American Poetry 2003.* New York: Scribners, 2003.
Book with an organization or a group as author or editor	Smithsonian Institution. *Aircraft of the National Air and Space Museum.* Washington: Smithsonian Institution Press, 1998.
Work from an anthology	Cofer, Judith Ortiz. "Tales Told Under the Mango Tree." *Hispanic American Literature.* Ed. Nicolas Kanellos. New York: HarperCollins, 1995. 34–44.
Introduction in a published book	Weintraub, Stanley. Introduction. *Great Expectations.* By Charles Dickens. New York: Signet, 1998. v–xii.
Encyclopedia article	"Jazz." *Encyclopaedia Britannica.* 15th ed. 1998.
Weekly magazine article	Franzen, Jonathan. "The Listener." *New Yorker* 6 Oct. 2003: 85–99.
Monthly magazine article	Quammen, David. "Saving Africa's Eden." *National Geographic* Sept. 2003: 50–77.
Newspaper article	Dionne, E. J., Jr. "California's Great Debate." *Washington Post* 26 Sept. 2003: A27. [If no author is named, begin the entry with the title of the article.]
Internet	"Visit Your Parks." *National Park Service.* 1 Oct. 2003. National Park Service, U.S. Dept. of the Interior. 3 Nov. 2003 <http://www.nps.gov/parks.html>.
Online magazine article	Martin, Richard. "How Ravenous Soviet Viruses Will Save the World." *Wired Magazine* 11.10 (October 2003). 17 Oct. 2003 <http://www.wired.com/wired/archive/11.10/phages.html>.
Radio or TV program	"Orcas." *Champions of the Wild.* Animal Planet. Discovery Channel. 21 Oct. 2003.
Videotape or DVD	Hafner, Craig, dir. *The True Story of Seabiscuit.* DVD. A & E Home Video, 2003. [For a videotape (VHS) version, replace "DVD" with "Videocassette."]
Interview	Campeche, Tanya. E-mail interview. 25 Feb. 2004. [If an interview takes place in person, replace "E-mail" with "Personal"; if it takes place on the telephone, use "Telephone."]

CMS Style

CMS style was created by the University of Chicago Press to meet its publishing needs. This style, which is detailed in *The Chicago Manual of Style* (CMS), is used in a number of subject areas. Center the title *Bibliography* at the top of your list.

Source	Style
Book with one author	Witham, Barry B. *The Federal Theatre Project: A Case Study.* New York: Cambridge University Press, 2003.
Book with multiple authors	Hoy, Pat C., II, Esther H. Schor, and Robert DiYanni. *Women's Voices: Visions and Perspectives.* New York: McGraw-Hill, 1990. [If a book has more than ten authors, name only the first seven and then write "et al." (Latin abbreviation for "and others").]
Book with editor(s)	Komunyakaa, Yusef, and David Lehman, eds. *The Best American Poetry 2003.* New York: Scribners, 2003.
Book with an organization or a group as author or editor	Smithsonian Institution. *Aircraft of the National Air and Space Museum.* Washington, DC: Smithsonian Institution Press, 1998.
Work from an anthology	Cofer, Judith Ortiz. "Tales Told Under the Mango Tree." *Hispanic American Literature,* edited by Nicolas Kanellos, 34–44. New York: HarperCollins, 1995.
Introduction in a published book	Dickens, Charles. *Great Expectations.* New introduction by Stanley Weintraub. New York: Signet, 1998.
Encyclopedia article	[Credit for encyclopedia articles goes in your text, not in your bibliography.]
Weekly magazine article	Franzen, Jonathan. "The Listener." *New Yorker,* October 6, 2003, 85–99.
Monthly magazine article	Quammen, David. "Saving Africa's Eden." *National Geographic,* September 2003, 50–77.
Newspaper article	Dionne, E. J., Jr. "California's Great Debate." *Washington Post,* September 26, 2003, A27. [Credit for unsigned newspaper articles goes in your text, not in your bibliography.]
Internet	U.S. Dept. of the Interior. "Visit Your Parks." *National Park Service.* http://www.nps.gov/parks.html.
Online magazine article	Martin, Richard. "How Ravenous Soviet Viruses Will Save the World." *Wired Magazine* 11.10 (October 2003). http://www.wired.com/wired/archive/11.10/phages.html.
Radio or TV program	[Credit for radio and TV programs goes in your text, not in your bibliography.]
Videotape or DVD	Hafner, Craig, dir. *The True Story of Seabiscuit.* A & E Home Video, 2003. DVD. [For a videotape (VHS) version, replace "DVD" with "Videocassette."]
Interview	[Credit for interviews goes in your text, not in your bibliography.]

APA Style

The American Psychological Association (APA) style is commonly used in the sciences. Center the title *References* at the top of your list.

Source	Style
Book with one author	Witham, B. B. (2003). *The federal theatre project: A case study.* New York: Cambridge University Press.
Book with multiple authors	Hoy, P. C., II, Schor, E. H., & DiYanni, R. (1990). *Women's voices: Visions and perspectives.* New York: McGraw-Hill. [If a book has more than six authors, list the first six authors and then write "et al." (Latin abbreviation for "and others").]
Book with editor(s)	Komunyakaa, Y., & Lehman, D. (Eds.). (2003). *The best American poetry 2003.* New York: Scribners.
Book with an organization or a group as author or editor	Smithsonian Institution. (1998). *Aircraft of the National Air and Space Museum.* Washington, DC: Smithsonian Institution Press.
Work from an anthology	Cofer, J. O. (1995). Tales told under the mango tree. In N. Kanellos (Ed.), *Hispanic American Literature* (pp. 34–44). New York: HarperCollins.
Introduction in a published book	[Credit for introductions goes in your text, not in your references.]
Encyclopedia article	Jazz. (1998). In *Encyclopaedia Britannica.* (Vol. 6, pp. 519–520). Chicago: Encyclopaedia Britannica.
Weekly magazine article	Franzen, J. (2003, October 6). The listener. *The New Yorker,* 85–99.
Monthly magazine article	Quammen, D. (2003, September). Saving Africa's Eden. *National Geographic,* 204, 50–77.
Newspaper article	Dionne, E. J., Jr. (2003, September 26). California's great debate. *The Washington Post,* p. A27. [If no author is named, begin the entry with the title of the article.]
Internet	U.S. Dept. of Interior, National Park Service. (2003, October 1). *National Park Service.* Visit your parks. Retrieved October 17, 2003, from http://www.nps.gov/parks.html
Online magazine article	Martin, R. (2003, October). How ravenous Soviet viruses will save the world. *Wired Magazine,* 11.10. Retrieved October 17, 2003, from http://www.wired.com/wired/archive/11.10/phages.html
Radio or TV program	Orcas. (2003, October 21). *Champions of the wild* [Television series episode]. Animal Planet. Silver Spring, MD: Discovery Channel.
Videotape or DVD	Hafner, C. (Director). (2003). *The true story of Seabiscuit* [DVD]. A & E Home Video. [For a videotape (VHS) version, replace "DVD" with "Videocassette."]
Interview	[Credit for interviews goes in your text, not in your references.]

BUSINESS WRITING

Business writing is a specialized form of expository writing. Business writing might include documents such as letters, memorandums, reports, briefs, proposals, and articles for business publications. Business writing must be clear, concise, accurate, and correct in style and usage.

Letter of Application

One form of business writing that follows a conventional format is a letter of application. A letter of application can be used when applying for a job, an internship, or a scholarship. In most cases, the letter is intended to accompany a résumé or an application. Because detailed information is usually included in the accompanying form, a letter of application should provide a general overview of your qualifications and the reasons you are submitting an application. A letter of application should be concise. You should clearly state which position you are applying for and then explain why you are interested and what makes you qualified. The accompanying material should speak for itself.

32 South Street
Austin, Texas 78746
May 6, 20___

Melissa Reyes
City Life magazine
2301 Davis Avenue
Austin, Texas 78764

❶ Re: Internship

Dear Ms. Reyes:

    I am a junior at City High School and editor of the City High Herald. I ❷ am writing to apply for your summer internship at City Life magazine. As a journalism student and a longtime fan of your magazine, I feel that an internship with your magazine would provide me with valuable experience in the field of journalism. I believe that my role with the City High Herald ❸ has given me the skills necessary to be a useful contributor to your magazine this summer. In addition, my enclosed application shows that I ❹ am also a diligent worker.
    I thank you for considering my application for your summer internship, and I hope to be working with you in the coming months.

Sincerely,

Anne Moris

Anne Moris

❶ The optional subject line indicates the topic of the letter.

❷ The writer states her purpose directly and immediately.

❸ The writer comments briefly on her qualifications.

❹ The writer makes reference to the accompanying material.

Activity: Choose a local business where you might like to work. Write a letter of application for an internship at that business. Assume that you will be submitting this letter along with a résumé or an internship application that details your experience and qualifications.

Résumé

The purpose of a résumé is to provide the employer with a comprehensive record of your background information, related experience, and qualifications. Although a résumé is intended to provide a great deal of information, the format is designed to provide this information in the most efficient way possible.

All résumés should include the following information: a heading that provides your name and contact information; a job goal or a career objective; your education information; your work experience; other related experience; and relevant activities, associations, organizations, or projects that you have participated in. You may also want to include honors that you have received and list individuals whom the employer can contact for a reference. When listing work experience, be sure to give the name of the employer, your job title, and a few brief bulleted points describing your responsibilities.

---

❶ Jane Wiley
909 West Main Street, Apt. #1
Urbana, Illinois 61802
(217) 555-0489 • jane@internet.edu

Goal
Seeking position in television news production

❷ **Education**
Junior standing in the College of Communications at the University of Illinois, Urbana-Champaign
2000 Graduate of City High School

Honors
Member of National Honor Society

Activities
❸ Member, Asian American Association: 2001–Present
Environmental Committee Chairperson, Asian American Association: August 2002–May 2003

Work Experience
❹ Radio Reporter, WPGU, 107.1 FM, Champaign, Illinois: May 2002–Present
❺ • Rewrote and read stories for afternoon newscasts
• Served as field reporter for general assignments

Cashier, Del's Restaurant, Champaign, Illinois: May 2002–August 2002
• Responsible for taking phone orders
• Cashier for pickup orders

Assistant Secretary, Office of Dr. George Wright, Woodstock, Illinois: May 2001–August 2001
• Answered phones
• Made appointments

---

❶ Header includes all important contact information.

❷ All important education background is included.

❸ Related dates are included for all listed activities.

❹ Job title is included along with the place of employment.

❺ Job responsibilities are briefly listed.

Activity: Create an outline that lists the information that you would want to include in a résumé. Use a word processor if possible.

Job Application

When applying for a job, you usually need to fill out a job application. When you fill out the application, read the instructions carefully. Examine the entire form before beginning to fill it out. Write neatly and fill out the form completely, providing all information directly and honestly.

If a question does not apply to you, indicate that by writing *n/a,* short for "not applicable." Keep in mind that you will have the opportunity to provide additional information in your résumé, in your letter of application, or during the interview process.

❶ **Please type or print neatly in blue or black ink.**

❷ **Name:** _____ **Today's date:** _____
Address: _____
Phone #: _____ **Birth date:** _____ **Sex:** ____ **Soc. Sec. #:** _____

****

Job History (List each job held, starting with the most recent job.)

❸ 1. Employer: _____ Phone #: _____
Dates of employment: _____
Position held: _____
Duties: _____

❹ 2. Employer: _____ Phone #: _____
Dates of employment: _____
Position held: _____
Duties: _____

****

Education (List the most recent level of education completed.)

_____

****

Personal References:

1. Name: _____ Phone #: _____
Relationship: _____

2. Name: _____ Phone #: _____
Relationship: _____

❶ The application provides specific instructions.
❷ All of the information requested should be provided in its entirety.
❸ The information should be provided neatly and succinctly.
❹ Experience should be stated accurately and without embellishment.

Activity: Pick up a job application from a local business or use the sample application above. Complete the application thoroughly. Fill out the application as if you were actually applying for the job. Be sure to pay close attention to the guidelines mentioned above.

Memos

A memorandum (memo) conveys precise information to another person or a group of people. A memo begins with a leading block. It is followed by the text of the message. A memo does not have a formal closing.

TO: All Employees
FROM: Jordan Tyne, Human Resources Manager
❶ SUBJECT: New Human Resources Assistant Director
DATE: November 3, 20__

❷ Please join me in congratulating Leslie Daly on her appointment as assistant director in the Human Resources Department. Leslie comes to our company with five years of experience in the field. Leslie begins work on Monday, ❸ November 10. All future general human resource inquiries should be directed to Leslie.

Please welcome Leslie when she arrives next week.

❶ The topic of the memo is stated clearly in the subject line.

❷ The announcement is made in the first sentence.

❸ All of the important information is included briefly in the memo.

Business E-mail

E-mail is quickly becoming the most common form of business communication. While e-mail may be the least formal and most conversational method of business writing, it shouldn't be written carelessly or too casually. The conventions of business writing—clarity, attention to your audience, proper grammar, and the inclusion of relevant information—apply to e-mail.

An accurate subject line should state your purpose briefly and directly. Use concise language and avoid rambling sentences.

To: LiamS@internet.com
From: LisaB@internet.com
CC: EricC@internet.com
Date: January 7, 8:13 A.M.
❶ Subject: New Product Conference Call

Liam,

❷ I just wanted to make sure that arrangements have been made for next week's conference call to discuss our new product. The East Coast sales team has already scheduled three sales meetings at the end of the month with potential buyers, so it's important that our sales team is prepared to talk about the product. Please schedule the call when the manufacturing director is available, ❸ since he will have important information for the sales team.

Lisa

❶ Subject line clearly states the topic.

❷ The purpose is stated immediately and in a conversational tone.

❸ Important details are included in a brief, direct fashion.

Activity: Write an e-mail to your coworkers. Inform them of a change in company procedure that will affect them. State the specific information that they need to know. Indicate to your coworkers whether action needs to be taken on their part.

Grammar Glossary

This glossary will help you quickly locate information on parts of speech and sentence structure.

A

Absolute phrase. *See* Phrase.

Abstract noun. *See* Noun chart.

Action verb. *See* Verb.

Active voice. *See* Voice.

Adjective A word that modifies a noun or pronoun by limiting its meaning. Adjectives appear in various positions in a sentence. (The *gray* cat purred. The cat is *gray*.)

Many adjectives have different forms to indicate **degree of comparison**. *(short, shorter, shortest)*

The **positive degree** is the simple form of the adjective. *(easy, interesting, good)*

The **comparative degree** compares two persons, places, things, or ideas. *(easier, more interesting, better)*

The **superlative degree** compares more than two persons, places, things, or ideas. *(easiest, most interesting, best)*

A **predicate adjective** follows a linking verb and further identifies or describes the subject. (The child is *happy*.)

A **proper adjective** is formed from a proper noun and begins with a capital letter. Many proper adjectives are created by adding these suffixes: *-an, -ian, -n, -ese,* and *-ish. (Chinese, African)*

Adjective clause. *See* Clause chart.

Adverb A word that modifies a verb, an adjective, or another adverb by making its meaning more specific. When modifying a verb, an adverb may appear in various positions in a sentence. (Cats *generally* eat less than dogs. *Generally,* cats eat less than dogs.) When modifying an adjective or another adverb, an adverb appears directly before the modified word. (I was *quite* pleased that they got along *so* well.) The word *not* and the contraction *-n't* are adverbs. (Mike *wasn't* ready for the test today.) Certain adverbs of time, place, and degree also have a negative meaning. (He's *never* ready.)

Some adverbs have different forms to indicate degree of comparison. *(soon, sooner, soonest)*

The **comparative** degree compares two actions. *(better, more quickly)*

The **superlative** degree compares three or more actions. *(fastest, most patiently, least rapidly)*

Adverb clause. *See* Clause chart.

Antecedent. *See* Pronoun.

Appositive A noun or a pronoun that further identifies another noun or pronoun. (My friend *Julie* lives next door.)

Appositive phrase. *See* Phrase.

Article The adjective *a, an,* or *the.*

Indefinite articles (*a* and *an*) refer to one of a general group of persons, places, or things. (I eat *an* apple *a* day.)

The **definite article** (*the*) indicates that the noun is a specific person, place, or thing. (*The* alarm woke me up.)

Auxiliary verb. *See* Verb.

B

Base form. *See* Verb tense.

C

Clause A group of words that has a subject and a predicate and that is used as part of a sentence. Clauses fall into two categories: *main clauses,* which are also called *independent clauses,* and *subordinate clauses,* which are also called *dependent clauses.*

A **main clause** can stand alone as a sentence. There must be at least one main clause in every sentence. (*The rooster crowed,* and *the dog barked.*)

A **subordinate clause** cannot stand alone as a sentence. A subordinate clause needs a main clause to complete its meaning. Many subordinate clauses begin with subordinating conjunctions or relative pronouns. (*When Geri sang her solo,* the audience became quiet.) The chart on the next page shows the main types of subordinate clauses.

TYPES OF SUBORDINATE CLAUSES

Clause	Function	Example	Begins with . . .
Adjective clause	Modifies a noun or pronoun	Songs *that have a strong beat* make me want to dance.	A relative pronoun such as *which, who, whom, whose,* or *that*
Adverb clause	Modifies a verb, an adjective, or an adverb	*Whenever Al calls me,* he asks to borrow my bike.	A subordinating conjuction such as *after, although, because, if, since, when,* or *where*
Noun clause	Serves as a subject, an object, or a predicate nominative	*What Philip did* surprised us.	Words such as *how, that, what, whatever, when, where, which, who, whom, whoever, whose,* or *why*

Collective noun. *See* Noun chart.

Common noun. *See* Noun chart.

Comparative degree. *See* Adjective; Adverb.

Complement A word or phrase that completes the meaning of a verb. The four basic kinds of complements are *direct objects, indirect objects, object complements,* and *subject complements.*

A **direct object** answers the question *What?* or *Whom?* after an action verb. (Kari found a *dollar.* Larry saw *Denise.*)

An **indirect object** answers the question *To whom? For whom? To what?* or *For what?* after an action verb. (Do *me* a favor. She gave the *child* a toy.)

An **object complement** answers the question *What?* after a direct object. An object complement is a noun, a pronoun, or an adjective that completes the meaning of a direct object by identifying or describing it. (The director made me the *understudy* for the role. The little girl called the puppy *hers.*)

A **subject complement** follows a subject and a linking verb. It identifies or describes a subject. The two kinds of subject complements

are *predicate nominatives* and *predicate adjectives.*

A **predicate nominative** is a noun or pronoun that follows a linking verb and tells more about the subject. (The author of "The Raven" is *Poe.*)

A **predicate adjective** is an adjective that follows a linking verb and gives more information about the subject. (Ian became *angry* at the bully.)

Complex sentence. *See* Sentence.

Compound preposition. *See* Preposition.

Compound sentence. *See* Sentence.

Compound-complex sentence. *See* Sentence.

Conjunction A word that joins single words or groups of words.

A **coordinating conjunction** (*and, but, or, nor, for, yet, so*) joins words or groups of words that are equal in grammatical importance. (David *and* Ruth are twins. I was bored, *so* I left.)

Correlative conjunctions (*both . . . and, just as . . . so, not only . . . but also, either . . . or, neither . . . nor, whether . . . or*) work in pairs to join words and groups of words

of equal importance. (Choose *either* the muffin *or* the bagel.)

A **subordinating conjunction** (*after, although, as if, because, before, if, since, so that, than, though, until, when, while*) joins a dependent idea or clause to a main clause. (Beth acted *as if* she felt ill.)

Conjunctive adverb An adverb used to clarify the relationship between clauses of equal weight in a sentence. Conjunctive adverbs are used to replace *and* (*also, besides, furthermore, moreover*); to replace *but* (*however, nevertheless, still*); to state a result (*consequently, therefore, so, thus*); or to state equality (*equally, likewise, similarly*). (Ana was determined to get an A; *therefore*, she studied often.)

Coordinating conjunction. *See* Conjunction.

Correlative conjunction. *See* Conjunction.

D

Declarative sentence. *See* Sentence.

Definite article. *See* Article.

Demonstrative pronoun. *See* Pronoun.

Direct object. *See* Complement.

E

Emphatic form. *See* Verb tense.

F

Future tense. *See* Verb tense.

G

Gerund A verb form that ends in *-ing* and is used as a noun. A gerund may function as a subject, the object of a verb, or the object of a preposition. (*Smiling* uses fewer muscles than *frowning.* Marie enjoys *walking.*)

Gerund phrase. *See* Phrase.

I

Imperative mood. *See* Mood of verb.

Imperative sentence. *See* Sentence chart.

Indicative mood. *See* Mood of verb.

Indirect object. *See* Complement.

Infinitive A verb form that begins with the word *to* and functions as a noun, an adjective, or an adverb. (No one wanted *to answer.*) Note: When *to* precedes a verb, it is not a preposition but instead signals an infinitive.

Infinitive phrase. *See* Phrase.

Intensive pronoun. *See* Pronoun.

Interjection A word or phrase that expresses emotion or exclamation. An interjection has no grammatical connection to other words. Commas follow mild ones; exclamation points follow stronger ones. (*Well,* have a good day. *Wow!*)

Interrogative pronoun. *See* Pronoun.

Intransitive verb. *See* Verb.

Inverted order In a sentence written in *inverted order,* the predicate comes before the subject. Some sentences are written in inverted order for variety or special emphasis. (Up the beanstalk *scampered Jack.*) The subject also generally follows the predicate in a sentence that begins with *here* or *there.* (*Here was* the solution to his problem.) Questions, or interrogative sentences, are generally written in inverted order. In many questions, an auxiliary verb precedes the subject, and the main verb follows it. (*Has* anyone *seen* Susan?) Questions that begin with *who* or *what* follow normal word order.

Irregular verb. *See* Verb tense.

L

Linking verb. *See* Verb.

M

Main clause. *See* Clause.

Mood of verb A verb expresses one of three moods: indicative, imperative, or subjunctive.

The **indicative mood** is the most common. It makes a statement or asks a question. (We *are* out of bread. *Will* you *buy* it?)

The **imperative mood** expresses a command or makes a request. (*Stop* acting like a child! Please *return* my sweater.)

The **subjunctive mood** is used to express, indirectly, a demand, suggestion, or statement of necessity (I demand that he *stop* acting like a child. It's necessary that she *buy* more bread.) The subjunctive is also used to state a condition or wish that is contrary to fact. This use of the subjunctive requires the past tense. (If you *were* a nice person, you *would return* my sweater.)

N

Nominative pronoun. *See* Pronoun.

Noun A word that names a person, a place, a thing, or an idea. The chart on this page shows the main types of nouns.

TYPES OF NOUNS

Noun	Function	Examples
Abstract noun	Names an idea, a quality, or a characteristic	capitalism, terror
Collective noun	Names a group of things or persons	herd, troop
Common noun	Names a general type of person, place, thing, or idea	city, building
Compound noun	Is made up of two or more words	checkerboard, globe-trotter
Noun of direct address	Identifies the person or persons being spoken to	*Maria,* please stand.
Possessive noun	Shows possession, ownership, or the relationship between two nouns	my *sister's* room
Proper noun	Names a particular person, place, thing, or idea	Cleopatra, Italy, Christianity

Noun clause. *See* Clause chart.

Noun of direct address. *See* Noun chart.

Number A noun, pronoun, or verb is *singular* in number if it refers to one; *plural* if it refers to more than one.

O

Object. *See* Complement.

P

Participle A verb form that can function as an adjective. Present participles always end in *-ing.* (The woman comforted the *crying* child.) Many past participles end in *-ed.* (We bought the beautifully *painted* chair.) However, irregular verbs form their past participles in some other way. (Cato was Caesar's *sworn* enemy.)

Passive voice. *See* Voice.

Past tense. *See* Verb tense.

Perfect tense. *See* Verb tense.

Personal pronoun. *See* Pronoun, Pronoun chart.

Phrase A group of words that acts in a sentence as a single part of speech.

An **absolute phrase** consists of a noun or pronoun that is modified by a participle or participial phrase but has no grammatical relation to the complete subject or predicate. (*The vegetables being done,* we finally sat down to eat dinner.)

An **appositive phrase** is an appositive along with any modifiers. If not essential to the meaning of the sentence, an appositive phrase is set off by commas. (Jack plans to go to the jazz concert, *an important musical event.*)

A **gerund phrase** includes a gerund plus its complements and modifiers. (*Playing the flute* is her hobby.)

An **infinitive phrase** contains the infinitive plus its complements and modifiers. (It is time *to leave for school.*)

A **participial phrase** contains a participle and any modifiers necessary to complete its meaning. (The woman *sitting over there* is my grandmother.)

A **prepositional phrase** consists of a preposition, its object, and any modifiers of the object. A prepositional phrase can function as an adjective, modifying a noun or a pronoun. (The dog *in the yard* is very gentle.) A prepositional phrase may also function as an adverb when it modifies a verb, an adverb, or an adjective. (The baby slept *on my lap.*)

A **verb phrase** consists of one or more auxiliary verbs followed by a main verb. (The job *will have been completed* by noon tomorrow.)

Positive degree. *See* Adjective.

Possessive noun. *See* Noun chart.

Predicate The verb or verb phrase and any objects, complements, or modifiers that express the essential thought about the subject of a sentence.

A **simple predicate** is a verb or verb phrase that tells something about the subject. (We *ran.*)

A **complete predicate** includes the simple predicate and any words that modify or complete it. (We *solved the problem in a short time.*)

A **compound predicate** has two or more verbs or verb phrases that are joined by a conjunction and share the same subject. (We *ran to the park and began to play baseball.*)

Predicate adjective. *See* Adjective; Complement.

Predicate nominative. *See* Complement.

Preposition A word that shows the relationship of a noun or pronoun to some other word in the sentence. Prepositions include *about, above, across, among, as, behind, below, beyond, but, by, down, during, except, for, from, into, like, near, of, on, outside, over, since, through, to, under, until, with.* (I usually eat breakfast *before* school.)

A **compound preposition** is made up of more than one word. *(according to, ahead of, as to, because of, by means of, in addition to, in spite of, on account of)* (We played the game *in spite of* the snow.)

Prepositional phrase. *See* Phrase.

Present tense. *See* Verb tense.

Progressive form. *See* Verb tense.

Pronoun A word that takes the place of a noun, a group of words acting as a noun, or another pronoun. The word or group of words that a pronoun refers to is called its **antecedent.** (In the following sentence, *Mari* is the antecedent of *she. Mari likes Mexican food, but she doesn't like Italian food.*)

A **demonstrative pronoun** points out specific persons, places, things, or ideas. *(this, that, these, those)*

An **indefinite pronoun** refers to persons, places, or things in a more general way than a noun does. *(all, another, any, both, each, either, enough, everything, few, many, most, much, neither, nobody, none, one, other, others, plenty, several, some)*

An **intensive pronoun** adds emphasis to another noun or pronoun. If an intensive pronoun is omitted, the meaning of the sentence will be the same. *(Rebecca herself decided to look for a part-time job.)*

An **interrogative pronoun** is used to form questions. *(who? whom? whose? what? which?)*

A **personal pronoun** refers to a specific person or thing. Personal pronouns have three cases: nominative, possessive, and objective. The case depends upon the function of the pronoun in a sentence. The first chart on this page shows the case forms of personal pronouns.

A **reflexive pronoun** reflects back to a noun or pronoun used earlier in the sentence, indicating that the same person or thing is involved.

(We told ourselves to be patient.) A **relative pronoun** is used to begin a subordinate clause. *(who, whose, that, what, whom, whoever, whomever, whichever, whatever)*

Proper adjective. *See* Adjective.

Proper noun. *See* Noun chart.

R

Reflexive pronoun. *See* Pronoun.

Relative pronoun. *See* Pronoun.

S

Sentence A group of words expressing a complete thought. Every sentence has a subject and a predicate. Sentences can be classified by function or by structure. The second chart on this page shows the categories by function; the following subentries describe the categories by structure. *See also* Subject; Predicate; Clause.

A **simple sentence** has only one main clause and no subordinate clauses. *(Alan found an old violin.)*

A simple sentence may contain a compound subject or a compound predicate or both. *(Alan and Teri found an old violin. Alan found an old violin and tried to play it. Alan and Teri found an old violin and tried to play it.)* The subject and the predicate can be expanded with adjectives, adverbs, prepositional phrases, appositives, and verbal phrases. As long as the sentence has only one main clause, however, it remains a simple sentence. *(Alan, rummaging in the attic, found an old violin.)*

A **compound sentence** has two or more main clauses. Each main clause has its own subject and predicate, and these main clauses are usually joined by a comma and a coordinating conjunction. *(Cats meow, and dogs bark, but ducks quack.)* Semicolons may also be used to join the main clauses in a compound sentence. *(The helicopter landed; the pilot had saved four passengers.)*

A **complex sentence** has one main clause and one or more

PERSONAL PRONOUNS

Case	Singular Pronouns	Plural Pronouns	Function in Sentence
Nominative	I, you, she, he, it	we, you, they	subject or predicate nominative
Objective	me, you, her, him, it	us, you, them	direct object, indirect object, or object of a preposition
Possessive	my, mine, your, yours, her, hers, his, its	our, ours, your, yours, their, theirs	replacement for the possessive form of a noun

TYPES OF SENTENCES

Sentence Type	Function	Ends with . . .	Examples
Declarative sentence	Makes a statement	A period	I did not enjoy the movie.
Exclamatory sentence	Expresses strong emotion	An exclamation point	What a good writer Consuela is!
Imperative sentence	Makes a request or gives a command	A period or an exclamation point	Please come to the party. Stop!
Interrogative sentence	Asks a question	A question mark	Is the composition due today?

subordinate clauses. (*Since the movie starts at eight, we should leave here by seven-thirty.*)

A **compound-complex sentence** has two or more main clauses and at least one subordinate clause. (*If we leave any later, we may miss the previews, and I want to see them.*)

Simple predicate. *See* Predicate.

Simple subject. *See* Subject.

Subject The part of a sentence that tells what the sentence is about.

A **simple subject** is the main noun or pronoun in the subject. (*Babies* crawl.*)

A **complete subject** includes the simple subject and any words that modify it. (*The man from New Jersey* won the race.*) In some sentences, the simple subject and the complete subject are the same. (*Birds* fly.*)

A **compound subject** has two or more simple subjects joined by a conjunction. The subjects share the same verb. (*Firefighters* and *police officers* protect the community.*)

Subjunctive mood. *See* Mood of verb.

Subordinate clause. *See* Clause.

Subordinating conjunction. *See* Conjunction.

Superlative degree. *See* Adjective; Adverb.

T

Tense. *See* Verb tense.

Transitive verb. *See* Verb.

V

Verb A word that expresses action or a state of being. (*cooks, seem, laughed*)

An **action verb** tells what someone or something does. Action verbs can express either physical or mental action. (Crystal *decided* to *change* the tire herself.)

A **transitive verb** is an action verb that is followed by a word or words that answer the question *What?* or *Whom?* (I *held* the baby.)

An **intransitive verb** is an action verb that is not followed by a word that answers the question *What?* or *Whom?* (The baby *laughed.*)

A **linking verb** expresses a state of being by linking the subject of a sentence with a word or an expression that identifies or describes the subject. (The lemonade *tastes* sweet. He *is* our new principal.) The most commonly used linking verb is *be* in all its forms (*am, is, are, was, were, will be, been, being*). Other linking verbs include *appear, become, feel, grow, look, remain, seem, sound, smell, stay, taste.*

An **auxiliary verb**, or helping verb, is a verb that accompanies the main verb to form a verb phrase. (I *have been* swimming.) The forms of *be* and *have* are the most common auxiliary verbs: (*am, is, are, was, were, being, been; has, have, had, having*). Other auxiliaries include *can, could, do, does, did, may, might, must, shall, should, will, would.*

Verbal A verb form that functions in a sentence as a noun, an adjective, or an adverb. The three kinds of verbals are gerunds, infinitives, and

participles. *See* Gerund; Infinitive; Participle.

Verb tense The tense of a verb indicates when the action or state of being occurs. All the verb tenses are formed from the four principal parts of a verb: a base form (*talk*), a present participle (*talking*), a simple past form (*talked*), and a past participle (*talked*). A **regular verb** forms its simple past and past participle by adding *-ed* to the base form. (*climb, climbed*) An **irregular verb** forms its past and past participle in some other way. (*get, got, gotten*)

In addition to present, past, and future tenses, there are three perfect tenses.

The **present perfect tense** expresses an action or a condition that occurred at some indefinite time in the past. This tense also shows an action or a condition that began in the past and continues into the present. (She *has played* the piano for four years.)

The **past perfect tense** indicates that one past action or condition began *and* ended before another past action started. (Andy *had finished* his homework before I even began mine.)

The **future perfect tense** indicates that one future action or condition will begin *and* end before another future event starts. Use *will have* or *shall have* with the past participle of a verb. (By tomorrow, I *will have finished* my homework, too.)

The **progressive form** of a verb expresses a continuing action with any of the six tenses. To make the progressive forms, use the appropriate tense of the verb *be* with the present participle of the main verb. (She *is swimming*. She *has been swimming.*)

The **emphatic form** adds special force, or emphasis, to the present and past tense of a verb. For the emphatic form, use *do, does,* or *did* with the base form. (Toshi *did want* that camera.)

Voice The **voice** of a verb shows whether the subject performs the action or receives the action of the verb.

A verb is in the **active voice** if the subject of the sentence performs the action. (The referee *blew* the whistle.)

A verb is in the **passive voice** if the subject of the sentence receives the action of the verb. (The whistle *was blown* by the referee.)

Mechanics

This section will help you use correct capitalization, punctuation, and abbreviations in your writing.

Capitalization

This section will help you recognize and use correct capitalization in sentences.

Rule: Capitalize the first word in any sentence, including direct quotations and sentences in parentheses unless they are included in another sentence.

> **Example:** She said, "Come back soon."
>
> Emily Dickinson became famous only after her death. (She published only six poems during her lifetime.)

Rule: Always capitalize the pronoun *I* no matter where it appears in the sentence.

> **Example:** Some of my relatives think that I should become a doctor.

Rule: Capitalize proper nouns, including

a. names of individuals and titles used in direct address preceding a name or describing a relationship.

> **Example:** George Washington; Dr. Morgan; Aunt Margaret

b. names of ethnic groups, national groups, political parties and their members, and languages.

> **Example:** Italian Americans; Aztec; the Republican Party; a Democrat; Spanish

c. names of organizations, institutions, firms, monuments, bridges, buildings, and other structures.

> **Example:** Red Cross; Stanford University; General Electric; Lincoln Memorial; Tappan Zee Bridge; Chrysler Building; Museum of Natural History

d. trade names and names of documents, awards, and laws.

> **Example:** Microsoft; Declaration of Independence; Pulitzer Prize; Sixteenth Amendment

e. geographical terms and regions or localities.

> **Example:** Hudson River; Pennsylvania Avenue; Grand Canyon; Texas; the Midwest

f. names of planets and other heavenly bodies.

> **Example:** Venus; Earth; the Milky Way

g. names of ships, planes, trains, and spacecraft.

> **Example:** USS *Constitution*; *Spirit of St. Louis*; *Apollo 11*

h. names of most historical events, eras, calendar items, and religious names and items.

> **Example:** World War II; Age of Enlightenment; June; Christianity; Buddhists; Bible; Easter; God

i. titles of literary works, works of art, and musical compositions.

> **Example:** "Why I Live at the P.O."; *The Starry Night*; *Rhapsody in Blue*

j. names of specific school courses.

> **Example:** Advanced Physics; American History

Rule: Capitalize proper adjectives (adjectives formed from proper nouns).

> **Example:** Christmas tree; Hanukkah candles; Freudian psychology; American flag

Punctuation

This section will help you use these elements of punctuation correctly.

Rule: Use a **period** at the end of a declarative sentence or a polite command.

Example: I'm thirsty.

Example: Please bring me a glass of water.

Rule: Use an **exclamation point** to show strong feeling or after a forceful command.

Example: I can't believe my eyes!

Example: Watch your step!

Rule: Use a **question mark** to indicate a direct question.

Example: Who is in charge here?

Rule: Use a **colon**

a. to introduce a list (especially after words such as *these, the following,* or *as follows*) and to introduce material that explains, restates, or illustrates previous material.

Example: The following states voted for the amendment: Texas, California, Georgia, and Florida.

Example: The sunset was colorful: purple, orange, and red lit up the sky.

b. to introduce a long or formal quotation.

Example: It was Mark Twain who stated the following proverb: "Man is the only animal that blushes. Or needs to."

c. in precise time measurements, biblical chapter and verse references, and business letter salutations.

Example:
3:35 P.M.	7:50 A.M.
Gen. 1:10–11	Matt. 2:23
Dear Ms. Samuels:	Dear Sir:

Rule: Use a **semicolon**

a. to separate main clauses that are not joined by a coordinating conjunction.

Example: There were two speakers at Gettysburg that day; only Lincoln's speech is remembered.

b. to separate main clauses joined by a conjunctive adverb or by *for example* or *that is.*

Example: Because of the ice storm, most students could not get to school; consequently, the principal canceled all classes for the day.

c. to separate the items in a series when these items contain commas.

Example: The students at the rally came from Senn High School, in Chicago, Illinois; Niles Township High School, in Skokie, Illinois; and Evanston Township High School, in Evanston, Illinois.

d. to separate two main clauses joined by a coordinating conjunction when such clauses already contain several commas.

Example: The designer combined the blue silk, brown linen, and beige cotton into a suit; but she decided to use the yellow chiffon, yellow silk, and white lace for an evening gown.

Rule: Use a **comma**

a. between the main clauses of a compound sentence.

Example: Ryan was late getting to study hall, and his footsteps echoed in the empty corridor.

b. to separate three or more words, phrases, or clauses in a series.

Example: Mel bought carrots, beans, pears, and onions.

c. between coordinate modifiers.

Example: That is a lyrical, moving poem.

d. to set off parenthetical expressions, interjections, and conjunctive adverbs.

Example: Well, we missed the bus again.

Example: The weather is beautiful today; however, it is supposed to rain this weekend.

e. to set off nonessential words, clauses, and phrases, such as:
—adverbial clauses

Example: Since Ellen is so tall, the coach assumed she would be a good basketball player.

—adjective clauses

Example: Scott, who had been sleeping, finally woke up.

—participles and participial phrases

Example: Having found what he was looking for, he left.

—prepositional phrases

Example: On Saturdays during the fall, I rake leaves.

—infinitive phrases

Example: To be honest, I'd like to stay awhile longer.

—appositives and appositive phrases

Example: Ms. Kwan, a soft-spoken woman, ran into the street to hail a cab.

f. to set off direct quotations.

Example: "My concert," Molly replied, "is tonight."

g. to set off an antithetical phrase.

Example: Unlike Tom, Rob enjoys skiing.

h. to set off a title after a person's name.

Example: Margaret Thomas, Ph.D., was the guest speaker.

i. to separate the various parts of an address, a geographical term, or a date.

Example: My new address is 324 Indian School Road, Albuquerque, New Mexico 85350.

I moved on March 13, 1998.

j. after the salutation of an informal letter and after the closing of all letters.

Example: Dear Helen,   Sincerely,

k. to set off parts of a reference that direct the reader to the exact source.

Example: You can find the article in the *Washington Post*, April 4, 1997, pages 33–34.

l. to set off words or names used in direct address and in tag questions.

Example: Yuri, will you bring me my calculator?

Lottie became a lawyer, didn't she?

Rule: Use a **dash** to signal a change in thought or to emphasize parenthetical material.

Example: During the play, Maureen—and she'd be the first to admit it—forgot her lines.

Example: There are only two juniors attending—Mike Ramos and Ron Kim.

Rule: Use **parentheses** to set off supplemental material. Punctuate within the parentheses only if the punctuation is part of the parenthetical expression.

Example: If you like jazz (and I assume you do), you will like this CD. (The soloist is Miles Davis.)

Example: The upper Midwest (which states does that include?) was hit by terrible floods last year.

Rule: Use **brackets** to enclose information that you insert into a quotation for clarity or to enclose a parenthetical phrase that already appears within parentheses.

Example: "He serves his [political] party best who serves the country best." —*Rutherford B. Hayes*

Example: The staircase (which was designed by a famous architect [Frank Lloyd Wright]) was inlaid with ceramic tile.

Rule: Use **ellipsis points** to indicate the omission of material from a quotation.

Example: ". . . Neither an individual nor a nation can commit the least act of injustice against the obscurest individual. . . ."
—*Henry David Thoreau*

Rule: Use **quotation marks**

a. to enclose a direct quotation, as follows:

Example: "Hurry up!" shouted Lisa.

When a quotation is interrupted, use two sets of quotation marks.

Example: "A *cynic*," wrote Oscar Wilde, "is someone who knows the price of everything and the value of nothing."

Use single quotation marks for a quotation within a quotation.

Example: "Did you say 'turn left' or 'turn right'?" asked Leon.

In writing dialogue, begin a new paragraph and use a new set of quotation marks every time the speaker changes.

Example: "Do you really think the spaceship can take off?" asked the first officer.
"Our engineer assures me that we have enough power," the captain replied.

b. to enclose titles of short works, such as stories, poems, essays, articles, chapters, and songs.

Example: "The Lottery" [short story]
"Provide, Provide" [poem]
"Civil Disobedience" [essay]

c. to enclose unfamiliar slang terms and unusual expressions.

Example: The man called his grandson a "rapscallion."

d. to enclose a definition that is stated directly.

Example: *Gauche* is a French word meaning "left."

Rule: Use **italics**

a. for titles of books, lengthy poems, plays, films, television series, paintings and sculptures, long

musical compositions, court cases, names of newspapers and magazines, ships, trains, airplanes, and spacecraft. Italicize and capitalize articles *(a, an, the)* at the beginning of a title only when they are part of the title.

Example: *E.T.* [film]; *The Piano Lesson* [play]
The Starry Night [painting]
the *New Yorker* [magazine]
Challenger [spacecraft]
The Great Gatsby [book]
the *Chicago Tribune* [newspaper]

b. for foreign words and expressions that are not used frequently in English.

Example: Luciano waved good-bye, saying, *"Arrivederci."*

c. for words, letters, and numerals used to represent themselves.

Example: There is no *Q* on the telephone keypad.

Example: Number your paper from *1* through *10.*

Rule: Use an **apostrophe**

a. for a possessive form, as follows:

Add an apostrophe and *-s* to all singular nouns, plural nouns not ending in *-s*, singular indefinite pronouns, and compound nouns. Add only an apostrophe to a plural noun that ends in *-s*.

Example: the tree's leaves
the man's belt
the bus's tires
the children's pets
everyone's favorite
my mother-in-law's job
the attorney general's decision
the baseball player's error
the cats' bowls

If two or more persons possess something jointly, use the possessive form for the last person named. If they possess it individually, use the possessive form for each one's name.

Example: Ted and Harriet's family
Ted's and Harriet's bosses
Lewis and Clark's expedition
Lewis's and Clark's clothes

b. to express amounts of money or time that modify a noun.

Example: two cents' worth

Example: three days' drive (You can use a hyphenated adjective instead: a three-day drive.)

c. in place of omitted letters or numerals.

Example: haven't [have not]   the winter of '95

d. to form the plural of letters, numerals, symbols, and words used to represent themselves. Use an apostrophe and -*s*.

Example: You wrote two 5's instead of one.

Example: How many *s*'s are there in Mississippi?

Example: Why did he use three *!*'s at the end of the sentence?

Rule: Use a **hyphen**

a. after any prefix joined to a proper noun or proper adjective.

Example: all-American   pre-Columbian

b. after the prefixes *all-, ex-,* and *self-* joined to any noun or adjective, after the prefix *anti-* when it joins a word beginning with *i,* after the prefix *vice-* (except in some instances such as *vice president*), and to avoid confusion between words that begin with *re-* and look like another word.

Example: ex-president
self-important
anti-inflammatory
vice-principal
re-creation of the event
recreation time
re-pair the socks
repair the computer

c. in a compound adjective that precedes a noun.

Example: a bitter-tasting liquid

d. in any spelled-out cardinal or ordinal numbers up to *ninety-nine* or *ninety-ninth,* and with a fraction used as an adjective.

Example: twenty-three   eighty-fifth
one-half cup

e. to divide a word at the end of a line between syllables.

Example: air-port   scis-sors
fill-ing   fin-est

Abbreviations

Abbreviations are shortened forms of words.

Rule: Use only one period if an abbreviation occurs at the end of a sentence. If the sentence ends with a question mark or an exclamation point, use the period and the second mark of punctuation.

Example: We didn't get home until 3:30 A.M.

Example: Did you get home before 4:00 A.M.?

Example: I can't believe you didn't get home until 3:30 A.M.!

Rule: Capitalize abbreviations of proper nouns and abbreviations related to historical dates.

Example: John Kennedy Jr.   P.O. Box 333
800 B.C.   A.D. 456   1066 C.E.

Use all capital letters and no periods for most abbreviations of organizations and government agencies.

Example: CBS   CIA   IBM
NFL   MADD   GE
FBI

Spelling

The following basic rules, examples, and exceptions will help you master the spellings of many words.

Forming Plurals

English words form plurals in many ways. Most nouns simply add -s. The following chart shows other ways of forming plural nouns and some common exceptions to the pattern.

General Rules for Forming Plurals		
If the word ends in	**Rule**	**Examples**
ch, s, sh, x, z	add -es	glass, glasses
a consonant + *y*	change *y* to *i* and add -es	caddy, caddies
a vowel + *y* or *o*	add only -s	cameo, cameos monkey, monkeys
a consonant + *o* common exceptions	generally add -es but sometimes add only -s	potato, potatoes cello, cellos
f or *ff* common exceptions	add -s change *f* to *v* and add -es	cliff, cliffs hoof, hooves
lf	change *f* to *v* and add -es	half, halves

A few plurals are exceptions to the rules in the previous chart, but they are easy to remember. The following chart lists these plurals and some examples.

Special Rules for Forming Plurals	
Rule	**Examples**
To form the plural of most proper names and one-word compound nouns, follow the general rules for plurals.	Cruz, Cruzes Mancuso, Mancusos crossroad, crossroads
To form the plural of hyphenated compound nouns or compound nouns of more than one word, make the most important word plural.	mother-in-law, mothers-in-law attorney general, attorneys general
Some nouns have unusual plural forms.	goose, geese child, children
Some nouns have the same singular and plural forms.	moose scissors pants

Adding Prefixes

When adding a prefix to a word, keep the original spelling of the word. Use a hyphen only when the original word is capitalized or with the prefixes *all-, ex-,* and *self-* joined to a noun or adjective.

    co + operative = cooperative
    inter + change = interchange
    pro + African = pro-African
    ex + partner = ex-partner

Suffixes and the Silent *e*

Many English words end in a silent letter *e*. Sometimes the *e* is dropped when a suffix is added. When adding a suffix that begins with a consonant to a word that ends in silent *e*, keep the *e*.

    like + ness = likeness   sure + ly = surely
    COMMON EXCEPTIONS awe + ful = awful;
    judge + ment = judgment

When adding a suffix that begins with a vowel to a word that ends in silent *e*, usually drop the *e*.

    believe + able = believable
    expense + ive = expensive
    COMMON EXCEPTION mile + age = mileage

When adding a suffix that begins with *a* or *o* to a word that ends in *ce* or *ge*, keep the *e* so the word will retain the soft *c* or *g* sound.

    notice + able = noticeable
    courage + ous = courageous

When adding a suffix that begins with a vowel to a word that ends in *ee* or *oe*, keep the final *e*.

    see + ing = seeing   toe + ing = toeing

Drop the final silent *e* after the letters *u* or *w*.

    argue + ment = argument
    owe + ing = owing

Keep the final silent *e* before the suffix *-ing* when necessary to avoid ambiguity.

    singe + ing = singeing

Suffixes and the Final *y*

When adding a suffix to a word that ends in a consonant + *y*, change the *y* to *i* unless the suffix begins with *i*. Keep the *y* in a word that ends in a vowel + *y*.

    try + ed = tried   fry + ed = fried
    stay + ing = staying   display + ed = displayed
    copy + ing = copying   joy + ous = joyous

Adding *-ly* and *-ness*

When adding *-ly* to a word that ends in a single *l*, keep the *l*, but when the word ends in a double *l*, drop one *l*. When the word ends in a consonant + *le*, drop the *le*. When adding *-ness* to a word that ends in *n*, keep the *n*.

    casual + ly = casually
    practical + ly = practically
    dull + ly = dully
    probable + ly = probably
    open + ness = openness
    mean + ness = meanness

Doubling the Final Consonant

Double the final consonant in words that end in a consonant preceded by a single vowel if the word is one syllable, if it has an accent on the last syllable that remains there even after the suffix is added, or if it is a word made up of a prefix and a one-syllable word.

    stop + ing = stopping
    admit + ed = admitted
    replan + ed = replanned

Do not double the final consonant if the accent is not on the last syllable or if the accent shifts when the suffix is added. Also do not double the final consonant if the final consonant is *x* or *w*. If the word ends in a consonant and the suffix begins with a consonant, do not double the final consonant.

    benefit + ed = benefited
    similar + ly = similarly
    raw + er = rawer
    box + like = boxlike
    friend + less = friendless
    rest + ful = restful

Forming Compound Words

When joining a word that ends in a consonant to a word that begins with a consonant, keep both consonants.

    out + line = outline
    after + noon = afternoon
    post + card = postcard
    pepper + mint = peppermint

ie and *ei*

Learning this rhyme can save you many misspellings: "Write *i* before *e* except after *c*, or when sounded like *a* as in *neighbor* and *weigh*." There are many exceptions to this rule, including *seize, seizure, leisure, weird, height, either, neither, forfeit.*

-cede, -ceed, and *-sede*

Because of the relatively few words with *sēd* sounds, these words are worth memorizing.

These words use *-cede:* **accede, precede, secede.**
One word uses *-sede:* **supersede.**
Three words use *-ceed:* **exceed, proceed, succeed.**

Succeeding on Tests

This section is designed to help you prepare for both classroom and standardized tests. You will become familiar with the various formats of tests and the types of questions you will be required to answer.

Preparing for Classroom Tests

This section will help you learn how to prepare for classroom tests.

Thinking ahead

- Write down information about an upcoming test—when it will be given, what it will cover, and so on—so you can plan your study time effectively.
- Review your textbook, quizzes, homework assignments, class notes, and handouts. End-of-chapter review questions often highlight key points from your textbook.
- Develop your own questions about main ideas and important details, and practice answering them. Writing your own practice tests is an excellent way to get ready for a real test.
- Make studying into an active process. Rather than simply rereading your notes or a chapter in your textbook, try to create a summary of the material. This can be an outline, a list of characters, or a time line. Try to include details from both your lecture notes and your textbook reading so you will be able to see connections between the two.
- Form study groups. Explaining information to a peer is one of the best ways to learn the material.
- Sleep well the night before a test. Spreading your study time over several days should have given you enough confidence to go to bed at your regular time the night before a test.
- Remember that eating well helps you remain alert. Students who eat a regular meal on the morning of a test generally score higher than those who do not.

Taking objective tests

Many of the tests you take in your high school classes will be objective tests, meaning that they ask questions that have specific correct answers. Time is often limited for these tests, so be sure to use your time efficiently.

- First, read the directions carefully. If anything is unclear, ask questions.
- Try to respond to each item on the test, starting with the easier ones.
- Skip difficult questions rather than dwelling on them. You can always come back to them at the end of the test.
- Try to include some time to review your test before turning it in.

Below are tips for answering specific kinds of objective test items:

Kind of item	Tips
Multiple-choice	Read all the answer choices provided before choosing one; even if the first one seems nearly correct, a later choice may be a better answer. Be cautious when choosing responses that contain absolute words such as *always, never, all,* or *none.* Since most generalizations have exceptions, absolute statements are often incorrect.
True/False	If *any* part of the item is false, the correct answer must be "false."
Short-answer	Use complete sentences to help you write a clear response.
Fill-in	Restate fill-ins as regular questions if you are not sure what is being asked.
Matching	Note in the directions whether some responses can be used more than once or not used at all.

Taking subjective (essay) tests

You will also take subjective tests during high school. Typically, these tests ask questions that require you to write an essay. Your grade is based more on how well you are able to make your point than on whether you choose a correct answer.

- When you receive the test, first read it through. If there are several questions, determine how much time to spend on each question.

- Begin your answer by jotting down ideas on scratch paper for several minutes. Read the test question again to make sure you are answering it. Then create a rough outline from which you can create your essay.

- Start your essay with a thesis statement in the first paragraph and follow with paragraphs that provide supporting evidence. Give as much information as possible, including examples and illustrations where appropriate.

- Finish your essay with a conclusion, highlighting the evidence you have provided and restating your thesis.

- You will probably not have time to revise and recopy your essay. After you are finished writing, spend any remaining time proofreading your answer and neatly making any necessary corrections.

Preparing for Standardized Tests

Standardized tests are designed to be administered to very large groups of students, not just those in a particular class. Three of the most widely known standardized tests, all part of the college application process, are the ACT, the PSAT, and the SAT. The strategies in this handbook refer specifically to the PSAT and SAT tests, but they also can apply to preparing for the ACT and other standardized tests.

The PSAT is generally administered to students in the eleventh grade, though some schools offer it to students in the tenth grade as well. This test is designed to predict how well you will do on the SAT. For most students, the PSAT is simply a practice test. Those who perform exceptionally well on the eleventh grade PSAT, however, will qualify for National Merit Scholarship competition.

The SAT consists of the SAT-I: Reasoning Test and a variety of SAT-II: Subject Tests. The SAT-I is a three-hour test that evaluates your general verbal and mathematics skills. The SAT-II: Subject Tests are hour-long tests given in specific subjects and are designed to show specifically how much you have learned in a particular subject area.

Tips for taking standardized tests

Standardized tests are often administered outside of regular class time and require registration. Ask your teacher or guidance counselor how you can register early to ensure that you can take the test at a time and location most convenient for you. In addition, follow these tips:

- Skip difficult questions at first. Standardized tests are usually timed, so first answer items you know. You can return later to those you skipped.

- Mark only your answers on the answer sheet. Most standardized tests are scored by a computer, so stray marks can be read as incorrect answers.

- Frequently compare the question numbers on your test with those on your answer sheet to avoid putting answers in the wrong spaces.

- If time permits, check your answers. If you are not penalized for guessing, fill in answers for any items you might have skipped.

Preparing for the PSAT and the SAT-I

The verbal sections of the PSAT and SAT-I contain sentence completion items and reading comprehension questions.

Sentence completion

Sentence completion items provide a sentence with one or two blanks and ask you to select the word or pair of words that best fits in the blank(s). Here is some general information to help you with these questions on the PSAT and SAT-I.

- Start by reading the sentence and filling in your own word to replace the blank. Look for words that show how the word in the blank is related to the rest of the sentence–*and, but, since, therefore, although.*

- Do not read the sentence with the words from each answer choice inserted. This may leave you with several choices that "sound good."

- Once you have chosen your own word to fill in the blank, pick the word from the answer choices that is closest in meaning to your word.

- If you have trouble coming up with a specific word to fill in the blank, try to determine whether the word should be positive or negative. Even this bit of information can help you eliminate some answer choices. If you can eliminate even one answer choice, take a guess at the correct answer.

Reading comprehension

Reading comprehension questions on the PSAT and SAT-I measure your ability to understand and interpret what you read. Each reading passage is followed by a series of questions. Here are some points to keep in mind when working with these questions:

- You get points for answering questions correctly, not for reading passages thoroughly. Therefore, it is to your advantage to read the passages quickly and spend your time working on the questions.

- After quickly reading a passage, briefly summarize it. This will help you answer general questions, which are based on the passage as a whole.

- To answer specific questions based on details included in the passage, return to the passage to find the correct answers. Reading Comprehension is like an open-book test: you are expected to look at the passage while answering the questions.

- Reading Comprehension passages almost never include controversial opinions. Therefore, an answer choice like "advocated the overthrow of the government" is very likely to be incorrect.

- If you can eliminate even one answer choice, take a guess at the correct answer.

Taking Essay Tests

Writing prompts, or long essay questions, include key words that signal the strategy you will use to bring your ideas into sharp focus. Similarly, these key words also appear in constructed responses, or short essay questions.

Key Word	Strategy
Analyze	To **analyze** means to systematically and critically examine all parts of an issue or event.
Classify or categorize	To **classify** or **categorize** means to put people, things, or ideas into groups, based on a common set of characteristics.
Compare and contrast	To **compare** is to show how things are similar or alike. To **contrast** is to show how things are different.
Describe	To **describe** means to present a sketch or an impression. Rich detail, especially details that appeal to the senses, flesh out a description.
Discuss	To **discuss** means to systematically write about all sides of an issue or event.
Evaluate	To **evaluate** means to make a judgment and support it with evidence.
Explain	To **explain** means to clarify or make plain.
Illustrate	To **illustrate** means to provide examples or to show with a picture or another graphic.
Infer	To **infer** means to read between the lines or to use knowledge or experience to draw conclusions, make generalizations, or form a prediction.
Justify	To **justify** means to prove or to support a position with specific facts and reasons.
Predict	To **predict** means to tell what will happen in the future based on an understanding of prior events and behaviors.
State	To **state** means to briefly and concisely present information.
Summarize	To **summarize** means to give a brief overview of the main points of an event or issue.
Trace	To **trace** means to present the steps or stages in a process or an event in sequential or chronological order.

GLOSSARY/GLOSARIO

Pronunciation Key

This glossary lists the vocabulary words found in the selections in this book. The definition given is for the word as it is used in the selection; you may wish to consult a dictionary for other meanings of these words. The key below is a guide to the pronunciation symbols used in each entry.

a	at	ō	hope	ng	sing
ā	ape	ô	fork, all	th	thin
ä	father	oo	wood, put	th	this
e	end	ōō	fool	zh	treasure
ē	me	oi	oil	ə	ago, taken, pencil, lemon, circus
i	it	ou	out	′	indicates primary stress
ī	ice	u	up	′	indicates secondary
o	hot	ū	use		

ENGLISH	ESPAÑOL
A	**A**

abide (ə bīd′) *v.* remain; **p. 934**	**abide/permanecer** *v.* subsistir; **p. 934**
abundantly (ə bun′ dənt lē) *adv.* plentifully; **p. 417**	**abundantly/abundantemente** *adv.* en gran cantidad; cuantiosamente; **p. 417**
acquaintance (ə kwānt′ əns) *n.* the state of being familiar with; **p. 772**	**acquaintance/conocido(a)** *s.* persona con quien se tiene trato o relación, sin ser amistad; **p. 772**
acrid (ak′ rid) *adj.* burning, biting, or irritating to the taste or smell; **p. 1287**	**acrid/acre** *adj.* irritante, amargo o desagradable al gusto y al olfato; **p. 1287**
acute (ə kūt′) *adj.* sharp; intense; **p. 839**	**acute/agudo** *adj.* punzante; intenso; **p. 839**
admonish (ad mon′ ish) *v.* to warn; to reprimand; **p. 76**	**admonish/amonestar** *v.* advertir; reprender; **p. 76**
adversary (ad′ vər ser′ ē) *n.* opponent; enemy; **p. 117**	**adversary/adversario** *s.* oponente; enemigo; **p. 117**
adversity (ad vur′ sə tē) *n.* a state of hardship; misfortune; **p. 163**	**adversity/adversidad** *s.* momento de gran dificultad; infortunio; desgracia; **p. 163**
advocate (ad′ və kāt′) *v.* to support or argue for; **p. 972**	**advocate/abogar** *v.* defender o hablar a favor de alguien; **p. 972**
aggregated (ag′ rə gā′ təd) *adj.* collected; gathered into a whole; **p. 651**	**aggregated/agregado** *adj.* sumado; unido a un todo; **p. 651**

ailment (āl´ mənt) *n.* sickness or affliction; **p. 1159**

allaying (ə lā´ ing) *adj.* putting at rest; relieving; **p. 472**

alteration (ôl´ tə rā´ shən) *n.* change; modification; **p. 295**

amends (ə mendz´) *n.* something done or given to make up for injury, loss, etc.; **p. 365**

amiability (a´ mē ə bil´ ə tē) *n.* kindliness; friendliness; **p. 1142**

anarchy (an´ ər kē) *n.* a complete lack of political order; chaos; **p. 1113**

antidote (an´ ti dōt´) *n.* a medicine used to counteract the effects of a poison; any counteracting remedy; **p. 394**

appall (ə pôl´) *v.* to fill with horror and shock; **p. 362**

appease (ə pēz´) *v.* to bring to a state of peace or quiet; to satisfy; **p. 1197**

arbiter (är´ bə tər) *n.* a judge; **p. 846**

arrogance (ar´ ə gəns) *n.* overbearing pride or self-importance; **p. 134**

artifice (är´ tə fis) *n.* trickery; deception; **p. 1111**

aspire (əs pīr´) *v.* to strive for; **p. 87**

assent (ə sent´) *v.* to agree to something after consideration; concur; **p. 1316**

avarice (av´ ər is) *n.* greed; **p. 381**

awry (ə rī´) *adj.* wrong; in a faulty way; **p. 307**

B

balm (bäm) *n.* a healing ointment; a soothing application; **p. 273**

barren (bar´ ən) *adj.* having little or no vegetation; bare; **p. 1321**

beguile (bi gīl´) *v.* to mislead by trickery; to deceive; **p. 420**

benign (bi nīn´) *adj.* pleasant and friendly; **p. 1249**

bitter (bit´ ər) *adj.* hard to bear; causing pain; **p. 261**

blanch (blanch) *v.* to turn white or become pale; **p. 78**

ailment/dolencia *s.* enfermedad o aflicción; **p. 1159**

allaying/calmar *v.* tranquilizar; aplacar; **p. 472**

alteration/alteración *s.* cambio; modificación; **p. 295**

amends/reparación *s.* desagravio, compensación o satisfacción por una ofensa, daño o injuria; **p. 365**

amiability/afabilidad *s.* amabilidad, cordialidad; **p. 1142**

anarchy/anarquía *s.* desconcierto o desorganización por ausencia de una autoridad; **p. 1113**

antidote/antídoto *s.* medicina usada para contrarrestar los efectos de una substancia venenosa; contraveneno; **p. 394**

appall/consternar *v.* horrorizar, conmocionar; **p. 362**

appease/apaciguar *v.* aquietar; tranquilizar o calmar; **p. 1197**

arbiter/árbitro(a) *s.* persona que actúa como un juez en un conflicto; **p. 846**

arrogance/arrogancia *s.* altanería, demasiado orgullo o soberbia; **p. 134**

artifice/artificio *s.* habilidad; arte o ingenio con lo que algo está hecho; **p. 1111**

aspire/aspirar *v.* anhelar; **p. 87**

assent/acordar *v.* determinar o deliberar individualmente; estar de acuerdo; **p. 1316**

avarice/avaricia *s.* codicia; **p. 381**

awry/mal *adj.* contrariamente a lo previsto o a lo deseado; **p. 307**

B

balm/bálsamo *s.* sustancia medicinal; ungüento que alivia; **p. 273**

barren/yermo *adj.* que tiene poca o ninguna vegetación; pelado; **p. 1321**

beguile/embaucar *v.* despistar mediante trampas; engañar; **p. 420**

benign/benigno(a) *adj.* afable, benévolo, piadoso; **p. 1249**

bitter/amargado(a) *adj.* que guarda resentimiento por frustraciones o disgustos; **p. 261**

blanch/blanqueado(a) *adj.* decoloración; **p. 78**

bleak (blēk) *adj.* cold; harsh; raw; **p. 721**

blight (blīt) *n.* a disease caused by parasites that makes plants and trees wither and die; **p. 954**

blithe (blīth) *adj.* carefree; lighthearted; **p. 187**

bombast (bom′ bast) *n.* pretentious language; **p. 548**

brandish (bran′ dish) *v.* to shake or swing threateningly, as a weapon; **p. 203**

brevity (brev′ ə tē) *n.* shortness in speech or writing; **p. 1196**

C

calamity (kə lam′ ə tē) *n.* disaster; extreme misfortune; **p. 307**

callousness (kal′ əs nəs) *n.* hardness in mind or feelings; insensitivity; **p. 1195**

career (kə rēr′) *v.* to move or run with a swift headlong motion; to rush or dash along; **p. 1299**

cavalcade (kav′ əl kād′) *n.* a ceremonial procession; **p. 555**

censure (sen′ shər) *n.* strong disapproval; condemnation as wrong; **p. 302**

chaste (chāst) *adj.* pure; virtuous; modest; **p. 471**

cleave (klēv) *v.* to tear or rip; to split something apart; **p. 856**

commend (kə mend′) *v.* to praise; to express approval of; **p. 589**

commiseration (kə miz′ ə rā′ shən) *n.* a feeling or expression of sympathy; compassion; **p. 1195**

compensation (kom′ pən sā′ shən) *n.* something that offsets, counterbalances, or makes up for; **p. 1073**

complaisance (kəm plā′ səns) *n.* a willingness to please, be gracious, or be courteous; **p. 618**

composure (kəm pō′ zhər) *n.* a calm or tranquil state of mind; **p. 149**

compulsory (kəm pul′ sər ē) *adj.* obligatory; required; **p. 1250**

concede (kən sēd′) *v.* to admit as true; acknowledge; **p. 128**

concord (kon′ kôrd) *n.* an agreement of interests or feelings; **p. 257**

bleak/ helado(a) *adj.* crudo; brutal; riguroso; **p. 721**

blight/roya *s.* hongo parásito que ataca plantas y árboles; **p. 954**

blithe/alegre *adj.* despreocupado; tranquilo **p. 187**

bombast/lenguaje pomposo *s.* expresiones ostentosas o pedantes; **p. 548**

brandish/blandir *v.* levantar o mover de modo amenazante, como un arma; **p. 203**

brevity/brevedad *s.* corta extensión o duración de un discurso o escrito; **p. 1196**

C

calamity/calamidad *s.* desgracia; infortunio; **p. 307**

callousness/insensibilidad *s.* dureza al pensar o actuar; crueldad; **p. 1195**

career/apresurarse *v.* moverse o correr de prisa; avanzar con rapidez; **p. 1299**

cavalcade/cabalgata *s.* desfile ceremonial; **p. 555**

censure/censura *s.* reprobación; crítica o juicio negativos; **p. 302**

chaste/puro(a) *adj.* casto; modesto; virtuoso; **p. 471**

cleave/partir *v.* rajar o hender; dividir algo en dos o más partes; **p. 856**

commend/elogiar *v.* ensalzar; alabar; **p. 589**

commiseration/conmiseración *s.* sentimiento o expresión de compasión; lástima; **p. 1195**

compensation/compensación *s.* algo que se da para compensar, remunerar o retribuir algo; **p. 1073**

complaisance/afabilidad *s.* amabilidad; deseo de complacer o ser cortés; **p. 618**

composure/compostura *s.* estado mental de tranquilidad o calma; **p. 149**

compulsory/obligatorio(a) *adj.* que tiene que ser hecho, cumplido u obedecido; **p. 1250**

concede/conceder *v.* admitir; reconocer, convenir; **p. 128**

concord/pacto *s.* acuerdo, convenio, lo que se decide entre dos partes; **p. 257**

condescend (kon´ di send´) *v.* to lower oneself; p. 730

confining (kən´ fīn ing) *adj.* restricting; limiting; p. 625

confound (kən found´) *v.* to confuse; to defeat or overthrow; to bewilder; p. 597, 748

congeal (kən jēl´) *v.* harden; thicken; p. 267

congenial (kən jēn´ ē əl) *adj.* compatible; agreeable; p. 730

congregation (kong´ grə gā´ shən) *n.* a group of people who gather for religious worship; p. 439

conjecture (kən jek´ chər) *v.* to infer from inconclusive evidence; to guess; p. 575

conspiring (kən spīr´ ing) *adj.* planning or plotting secretly; p. 877

constant (kon´ stənt) *adj.* never stopping, continuous; faithful, steadfast; p. 466

constellation (kon´ stə lā´ shən) *n.* any of eighty-eight groups of stars, many of which traditionally represent characters and objects in ancient mythology; p. 1335

constitute (kon´ stə tōōt´) *v.* make up; form; p. 1120

contemplation (kon´ təm plā´ shən) *n.* careful thought or consideration; meditation; p. 440

continual (kən tin´ ū əl) *adj.* ongoing; repeated frequently; p. 261

converge (kən vurj´) *v.* to come together in a common interest or conclusion; to center; p. 1142

conviction (kən vik´ shən) *n.* a strong belief; p. 1113

copiously (kō´ pē əs lē) *adv.* plentifully; p. 175

cordial (kôr´ jəl) *adj.* personable and likeable; p. 1161

countenance (koun´ tə nəns) *n.* someone's face; the expression on someone's face; p. 981

covetousness (kuv´ it əs nəs) *n.* great desire for something belonging to another; p. 440

condescend/condescender *v.* dignarse; acceder; p. 730

confining/restrictivo *adj.* que restringe; p. 625

confound/confundir *v.* turbar; desconcertar; p. 597, 748

congeal/congelar(se) *v.* solidificar(se); cuajar(se); espesar(se); p. 267

congenial/compatible *adj.* afín; que concuerda; p. 730

congregation/congregación *s.* grupo de personas que se reúne para orar; p. 439

conjecture/conjeturar *v.* inferir sin evidencias suficientes o claras; suponer; p. 575

conspiring/conspirar *v.* unirse o aliarse para preparar una acción contra algo; p. 877

constant/constante *adj.* que se repite continuamente; que permanece igual; que no deja de hacer lo empezado; p. 466

constellation/constelación *s.* uno de ochenta y ocho grupos de estrellas, que en muchos casos representan personajes y objetos de la mitología antigua; p. 1335

constituted/constituió *v.* formó; compuso; p. 1120

contemplation/contemplación *s.* consideración o reflexión cuidadosa; meditación; p. 440

continual/continuo(a) *adj.* constante; sin interrupción; p. 261

converge/converger *v.* llegar a una conclusión o interés común; dirigirse a un mismo punto; p. 1142

conviction/convicción *s.* ideas en las que se cree firmemente; p. 1113

copiously/copiosamente *adv.* de modo abundante; p. 175

cordial/cordial *adj.* afectuoso, amable; p. 1161

countenance/semblante *s.* cara; expresión del rostro; p. 981

covetousness/codicia *s.* deseo intenso de obtener algo que pertenece a otro; p. 440

D

dappled (dap′ əld) *adj.* marked with spots; **p. 953**

dauntless (dônt′ lis) *adj.* daring; not easily discouraged; **p. 186**

deem (dēm) *v.* regard as; consider; **p. 272**

deference (def′ ər əns) *n.* courteous respect; **p. 569**

deftly (deft′ lē) *adv.* skillfully; nimbly; **p. 122**

defunct (di fungkt′) *adj.* no longer existing or active; dead; **p. 1348**

defy (di fī′) *v.* to resist; to refuse to cooperate with; **p. 627**

deities (dē′ ə tēz) *n.* gods or goddesses; divinities; **p. 872**

deluge (del′ ūj) *n.* anything that overwhelms as if by a flood; **p. 523**

demolition (dem′ ə lish′ ən) *n.* the state of being demolished or obliterated; **p. 986**

denigration (den′ i grā′ shən) *n.* defamation of one's character or reputation; slander; **p. 1307**

desolate (des′ ə lit) *adj.* destitute of inhabitants; deserted; **p. 873**

despotic (des pot′ ik) *adj.* tyrannical; oppressive; **p. 1080**

destiny (des′ tə nē) *n.* fate; what will necessarily happen; **p. 1095**

diffusive (di fū′ siv) *adj.* spread out or widely scattered; **p. 927**

digress (dī′ gres) *v.* to stray from the main subject; **p. 570**

dilemma (di lem′ ə) *n.* a situation requiring a choice between equally undesirable alternatives; **p. 1154**

diligently (dil′ ə jənt lē) *adv.* persistently; **p. 86**

direful (dīr′ fəl) *adj.* terrible; dreadful; **p. 320**

dirge (durj) *n.* a song sung in grief; a mournful hymn; **p. 855**

disabuse (dis′ ə būz′) *v.* to free from a falsehood or misconception; **p. 590**

discern (di surn′) *v.* to perceive; to detect; **p. 523**

D

dappled/moteado(a) *adj.* adornado con manchas o lunares; **p. 953**

dauntless/intrépido *adj.* sin miedo; atrevido; **p. 186**

deem/considerar *v.* estimar; juzgar; **p. 272**

deference/deferencia *s.* tratamiento cortés o respetuoso; **p. 569**

deftly/diestramente *adv.* hábilmente; ágilmente; **p. 122**

defunct/difunto *adj.* que ya no existe; muerto; **p. 1348**

defying/desafiante *adj.* que se niega a cooperar; **p. 627**

deities/deidades *s.* dioses o diosas; divinidades; **p. 872**

deluge/diluvio *s.* torrente; algo que abruma o cae como un diluvio; **p. 523**

demolition/demolición *s.* derribo o destrucción; **p. 986**

denigration/denigración *s.* acción de ofender o desacreditar a alguien; calumnia; **p. 1307**

desolate/desolado(a) *adj.* falto de habitantes; desierto; **p. 873**

despotic/déspota *adj.* tiránico; opresivo; **p. 1080**

destiny/destino *n.* fortuna; encadenamiento de sucesos necesario e inevitable; **p. 1095**

diffusive/difuso(a) *adj.* difundido o esparcido; **p. 927**

digress/divagar *v.* desviarse del tema principal; **p. 570**

dilemma/dilema *s.* situación de duda en la que hay que elegir; **p. 1154**

diligently/diligentemente *adv.* de modo persistente; **p. 86**

direful/espantoso(a) *adj.* terrible; atroz; **p. 320**

dirge/endecha *s.* canción triste o de lamento; himno fúnebre; **p. 855**

disabuse/desengañar *v.* sacar a alguien del error; **p. 590**

discern/discernir *v.* percibir; detectar; **p. 523**

discord/emphatic

discord (dis′ kôrd) *n.* a lack of agreement or harmony; **p. 589**

discourse (dis′ kôrs′) *n.* verbal communication in speech or writing; **p. 285**

discreet (dis krēt′) *adj.* having or showing careful judgment in speech and action; prudent; **p. 102**

discretion (dis kresh′ ən) *n.* good judgment; **p. 426**

disdainful (dis dān′ fəl) *adj.* feeling or showing contempt; scornful; **p. 107**

dismal (diz′ məl) *adj.* dark and gloomy; **p. 808**

disperse (dis purs′) *v.* to scatter about; distribute widely; **p. 132**

distill (dis til′) *v.* to extract the essence of; **p. 1336**

diverge (dī vurj′) *v.* to move in different directions from a common point; to branch out; **p. 1141**

diverse (di vurs′) *adj.* markedly different; **p. 535**

diversion (di vur′ zhən) *n.* an amusement; an entertainment; **p. 605**

divulge (di vulj′) *v.* to make known; disclose; **p. 148**

doleful (dōl′ fəl) *adj.* sad; **p. 200**

dominion (də min′ yən) *n.* control or the exercise of control; **p. 720**

doom (do͞om) *n.* that which cannot be escaped; death, ruin, or destruction; **p. 295**

droll (drōl) *adj.* amusingly odd; **p. 746**

dwell (dwel) *v.* to live as a resident; **p. 213**

E

ecstasy (ek′ stə sē) *n.* a state beyond reason or self-control; **p. 1099**

edifice (ed′ ə fis) *n.* a building, especially a large one; **p. 604**

elate (i lāt′) *v.* to make happy; **p. 608**

emanate (em′ ə nāt′) *v.* to come forth from a source; to issue; **p. 1181**

emancipate (i man′ sə pāt′) *v.* to free; to liberate; **p. 1133**

emphatic (em fat′ ik) *adj.* with strong emphasis; **p. 772**

discordia/enfático(a)

discord/discordia *s.* sin acuerdo en las opiniones; sin armonía; **p. 589**

discourse/discurso *s.* comunicación oral o escrita; **p. 285**

discreet/discreto *adj.* cuidadoso al hablar o actuar; prudente; **p. 102**

discretion/discreción *s.* tacto, sensatez; **p. 426**

disdainful/desdeñoso *adj.* que siente o muestra desprecio; **p. 107**

dismal/sombrío(a) *adj.* con poca luz y melancólico; **p. 808**

disperse/dispersar(se) *v.* separado; extendido o repartido; **p. 132**

distill/destilar *v.* extraer la esencia; **p. 1336**

diverge/divergir *v.* moverse en diferentes direcciones desde un punto común; desviarse; **p. 1141**

diverse/diverso *adj.* patentemente diferente; **p. 535**

diversion/diversión *s.* entretenimiento; distracción; **p. 605**

divulge/divulgar *v.* dar a conocer; revelar; **p. 148**

doleful/afligido *adj.* triste; **p. 200**

dominion/dominio *s.* poder o control sobre algo; **p. 720**

doom/sino *s.* fuerza desconocida que actúa sobre las cosas y determina sucesos; fatalidad; **p. 295**

droll/risible *adj.* chistoso; cómico; raro; **p. 746**

dwell/residir *v.* habitar, morar; **p. 213**

E

ecstasy/éxtasis *s.* arrobamiento; un estado más allá de razón o dominio de sí mismo; **p. 1099**

edifice/edificio *s.* construcción alta; se refiere particularmente a un edificio alto y de aspecto imponente; **p. 604**

elate/regocijar *v.* hacer feliz; **p. 608**

emanate/emanar *v.* salir de una fuente; expedir; **p. 1181**

emancipate/emancipar *v.* liberar; poner en libertad; **p. 1133**

emphatic/enfático(a) *adj.* que se expresa con énfasis; **p. 772**

endure (en door´) *v.* bear; tolerate; put up with; **p. 426**

enmity (en´ mə tē) *n.* ill will; hostility; **p. 420**

envious (en´ vē əs) *adj.* feeling jealous or discontented because of the good fortune or superior abilities of another; **p. 1252**

esteem (es tēm´) *n.* favorable opinion; **p. 549**

estimable (es´ tə mə bəl) *adj.* deserving of esteem; admirable; **p. 102**

execute (ek´ sə kūt´) *v.* to carry out; to put into effect; **p. 285**

exotic (ig zot´ ik) *adj.* strangely beautiful or fascinating; **p. 1048**

explicit (eks plis´ it) *adj.* plainly and clearly expressed; definite; **p. 1250**

exploit (eks´ ploit) *n.* bold deed; **p. 376**

expound (iks pound´) *v.* to set forth in detail; explain; **p. 86**

extraordinary (iks trôr´ də ner´ ē) *adj.* very unusual or remarkable; **p. 987**

exultation (eg´ zul tā´ shən) *n.* joy; elation; **p. 655**

F

faculty (fak´ əl tē) *n.* capacity of the mind; ability; aptitude; **p. 729**

fallow (fal´ ō) *n.* land plowed but left unseeded; **p. 953**

farce (färs) *n.* a humorous drama in which the situation and characters are greatly exaggerated; **p. 1074**

fatal (fāt´ əl) *adj.* causing death, destruction, or harm; **p. 1095**

feigned (fānd) *adj.* pretended; imagined; **p. 929**

feud (fūd) *n.* lengthy, bitter conflict or dispute; **p. 1095**

fidelity (fi del´ ə tē) *n.* the quality or state of being faithful; **p. 1329**

flee (flē) *v.* to run away; **p. 261**

fleet (flēt) *adj.* swift; fast; **p. 1000**

flounder (floun´ dər) *v.* struggle to obtain footing; **p. 1269**

endure/soportar *v.* resistir; tolerar; aguantar; **p. 426**

enmity/enemistad *s.* hostilidad; **p. 420**

envious/envidioso(a) *adj.* que siente dolor o pesar del bien de otros; que desea lo que no posee; **p. 1252**

esteem/estima *s.* opinión o actitud favorable; aprecio; **p. 549**

estimable/estimable *adj.* que merece aprecio; admirable; **p. 102**

execute/ejecutar *v.* llevar a cabo; realizar; **p. 285**

exotic/exótico(a) *adj.* extrañamente hermoso o fascinante; **p. 1048**

explicit/explícito(a) *adj.* que expresa claramente y determinadamente; **p. 1250**

exploit/hazaña *s.* proeza; **p. 376**

expound/exponer *v.* presentar en detalle; explicar; **p. 86**

extraordinary/extraordinario(a) *adj.* que excede lo normal o lo ordinario; **p. 987**

exultation/exultación *s.* júbilo; regocijo; **p. 655**

F

faculty/facultad *s.* capacidad mental; habilidad; aptitud; **p. 729**

fallow/barbecho *s.* tierra arada y sin sembrar para dejarla descansar; **p. 953**

farce/farsa *s.* comedia humorística en la que se exagera la situación de los personajes; **p. 1074**

fatal/crucial *adj.* que es decisivo o muy importante porque condiciona el desarrollo de algo; **p. 1095**

feigned/fingido(a) *adj.* simulado; imaginado; **p. 929**

feuds/contiendas. *adj.* lidia, pelea; disputa o discusión; **p. 1095**

fidelity/fidelidad *s.* lealtad y constancia que se debe a las ideas, afectos, obligaciones; **p. 1329**

flee/huir *v.* escapar(se); **p. 261**

fleet/ligero(a) *adj.* apresurado; rápido; **p. 1000**

floundering/tambaleando *v.* moviéndose como si fuese a caer; **p. 1269**

flourish (flur′ ish) *v.* to exist at the peak of development or achievement; to thrive; **p. 77**

folly (fol′ ē) *n.* foolishness; an irrational and useless undertaking; **p. 303**

foremost (fôr′ mōst′) *adj.* ahead of all others or in the first position; **p. 216**

foresight (fôr′ sīt′) *n.* preparation or concern for the future; **p. 721**

forged (fôrjd) *adj.* formed or shaped, often with blows or pressure after heating; **p. 25**

forsaken (fôr sāk′ ən) *adj.* deserted or lonely; **p. 1186**

frail (frāl) *adj.* delicate; fragile; **p. 1204**

fray (frā) *n.* a heated dispute or contest; **p. 1349**

friction (frik′ shən) *n.* the clashing between two people or groups of opposed views; **p. 1316**

frivolous (friv′ ə ləs) *adj.* not serious; silly; **p. 87**

furrow (fur′ ō) *n.* a long, narrow trench in the ground made by a plow; a rut, groove, or wrinkle; **p. 878**

G

garish (gār′ ish) *adj.* excessively bright; flashy; gaudy; **p. 1082**

genial (jē′ nē əl) *adj.* giving warmth and comfort; pleasant or cheerful; **p. 712**

glean (glēn) *v.* to collect slowly and carefully; to gather crops left on a field after reaping; **p. 869**

grapple (grap′ əl) *v.* to attempt to deal with; to struggle; **p. 1169**

gratify (grat′ ə fī′) *v.* to satisfy; indulge; **p. 121**

grimace (grim′ is) *n.* a look of pain or disgust; **p. 1269**

guffaw (gu fô′) *v.* to laugh loudly and boisterously; **p. 1153**

H

hail (hāl) *v.* acclaim; pay tribute to; **p. 1202**

heedless (hēd′ lis) *adj.* careless; not paying attention; **p. 1203**

flourish/florecer *v.* alcanzar el máximo desarrollo o progreso; prosperar; **p. 77**

folly/locura *s.* disparate; hecho o dicho imprudentes o insensatos; **p. 303**

foremost/primer(o-a) *adj.* antes de todo, destacado o en primer lugar; **p. 216**

foresight/previsión *s.* preparación o preocupación para atender contingencias o evitar males futuros; **p. 721**

forged/forjado *adj.* formado o moldeado, a menudo mediante golpes o presión después de calentarse; **p. 25**

forsaken/desolado(a) *adj.* despoblado, desierto; **p. 1186**

frail/frágil *adj.* delicado; débil; **p. 1204**

fray/riña *s.* disputa o contienda ardiente; **p. 1349**

friction/fricción *n.* enfrentamientos o desacuerdos entre personas o colectividades; **p. 1316**

frivolous/frívolo *adj.* que no es serio; tonto; **p. 87**

furrow/surco *s.* hendidura hecha en la tierra con el arado; ranura; arruga en la cara; **p. 878**

G

garish/chillón *adj.* excesivamente brillante; llamativo; **p. 1082**

genial/cordial *adj.* afectuoso y amable; agradable y amistoso; **p. 712**

glean/cosechar *v.* conseguir o lograr resultados luego de trabajar por ellos; recoger cultivos cuando están maduros; **p. 869**

grapple/forcejear *v.* tratar de resolver; luchar; **p. 1169**

gratify/gratificar *v.* satisfacer; complacer; **p. 121**

grimace/mueca *s.* mirada de dolor o disgusto; **p. 1269**

guffaw/carcajear *v.* reír a carcajadas o vulgarmente; **p. 1153**

H

hail/vitorear *v.* ovacionar; aclamar; **p. 1202**

heedless/indiferente *adj.* despreocupado; sin prestar atención; **p. 1203**

hinder (hin′ dər) *v.* to make difficult the progress of; to hold back; **p. 1154**

hospitable (hos′ pi tə bəl) *adj.* offering generous and cordial welcome to guests; **p. 1333**

hue (hū′) *n.* color, shade, or tint; **p. 477**

hypocritical (hip′ ə krit′ i kəl) *adj.* pretending to believe one thing but doing the opposite; **p. 772**

I

illustrious (i lus′ trē əs) *adj.* famous and distinguished; **p. 838**

imminent (im′ ə nənt) *adj.* about to happen; impending; **p. 1291**

immutably (i mū′ tə blē) *adv.* unchangeably; permanently; **p. 651**

impart (im pärt′) *v.* to give; donate; **p. 823**

impassively (im pas′ iv lē) *adv.* in an emotionless manner; **p. 1181**

impediment (im ped′ ə mənt) *n.* an obstruction; an obstacle; **p. 286**

imperious (im pēr′ ē əs) *adj.* imperative; urgent; **p. 1171**

imperturbable (im′ pər tur′ bə bəl) *adj.* not easily excited or disturbed; calm; **p. 1141**

impetuous (im pech′ ōō əs) *adj.* characterized by rushing headlong into things; impulsive; **p. 665**

impinge (im pinj′) *v.* to strike or dash; to collide; **p. 1142**

incensed (in sensd′) *v.* to make enraged; filled with anger; **p. 356**

incite (in sīt′) *v.* to urge or provoke; **p. 836**

inconstancy (in kon′ stən sē) *n.* changeable nature; disloyalty; **p. 471**

indictment (in dīt′ mənt) *n.* a formal accusation; **p. 537**

indignation (in′ dig nā′ shən) *n.* anger aroused by something unjust or mean; **p. 727**

indissoluble (in′ di sol′ yə bəl) *adj.* incapable of being broken; permanent; **p. 353**

indomitable (in dom′ ə tə bəl) *adj.* incapable of being subdued or overcome; **p. 1171**

hinder/estorbar *v.* impedir el progreso; obstaculizar; **p. 1154**

hospitable/hospitalario *adj.* que acoge a sus huéspedes con amabilidad y generosidad; **p. 1333**

hue/matiz(ces) *s.* color, grado o tono; **p. 477**

hypocritical/hipócrita *adj.* persona que finge ideas, sentimientos o cualidades diferentes de los que tiene en realidad; **p. 772**

I

illustrious/ilustre *adj.* famoso y distinguido; **p. 838**

imminent/inminente *adj.* que está por ocurrir; próximo; **p. 1291**

immutably/inmutablemente *adv.* de un modo que no cambia; permanentemente; **p. 651**

impart/impartir *v.* dar; repartir; **p. 823**

impassively/impasiblemente *adv.* sin mostrar emoción; **p. 1181**

impediment/impedimento *s.* obstáculo; tropiezo; **p. 286**

imperious/imperioso *adj.* imperativo; urgente; **p. 1171**

imperturbable/imperturbable *adj.* que no se emociona o molesta fácilmente; calmado; **p. 1141**

impetuous/impetuoso *adj.* apresurado; impulsivo; **p. 665**

impinge/tropezar *v.* golpear; chocar; **p. 1142**

incensed/indignado(a) *adj.* enfadado; irritado; **p. 356**

incite/incitar *v.* urgir o provocar; **p. 836**

inconstancy/inconstancia *s.* falta de estabilidad y permanencia; facilidad para cambiar de opinión, de amigos, etc.; **p. 471**

indictment/acusación *s.* denuncia formal; **p. 537**

indignation/indignación *s.* ira provocada por algo injusto o malo; **p. 727**

indissoluble/indisoluble *adj.* que no se puede desunir o separar; **p. 353**

indomitable/indomable *adj.* incapaz de ser gobernado o sometido; rebelde; **p. 1171**

inevitable (i nev′ ə tə bəl) *adj.* incapable of being avoided or prevented; certain; **p. 711**

infamous (in′ fə məs) *adj.* having a bad reputation; notorious; **p. 31**

infinitely (in′ fə nit lē) *adv.* boundlessly; endlessly; **p. 1120**

infirmity (in fur′ mə tē) *n.* weakness; state of being feeble or unable; **p. 310**

ingenuity (in′ jə noo′ ə tē) *n.* cleverness; inventiveness; **p. 666**

inseparable (in sep′ ər ə bəl) *adj.* linked so closely that it is almost impossible to separate; **p. 988**

insipid (in sip′ id) *adj.* lacking interest; dull; **p. 548**

instigation (in′ stə gā′ shən) *n.* the act of inciting or urging on; **p. 148**

intermittent (in′ tər mit′ ənt) *adj.* alternately starting and stopping; **p. 1178**

intrepid (in trep′ id) *adj.* fearless; courageous; **p. 177**

intrinsically (in trin′ zik lē) *adv.* inherently; in its very nature; **p. 1196**

intuitive (in too′ ə tiv) *adj.* known or perceived without deliberate thought; **p. 651**

inveterate (in vet′ ə rit) *adj.* firmly established; deep-rooted; **p. 606**

irrational (i rash′ ən əl) *adj.* lacking reason; ill-advised; **p. 619**

irremediable (ir i mē′ dē ə bəl) *adj.* not subject to remedy or cure; **p. 1289**

J

jeopardy (jep′ ər dē) *n.* danger; **p. 203**

jest (jest) *n.* an utterance or act offered humorously or mockingly; **p. 432**

jovial (jō′ vē al) *adj.* full of good humor; genial and playful; **p. 358**

K

keen (kēn) *adj.* having a sharp edge or point; **p. 303**

inevitable/inevitable *adj.* que no se puede evitar o prevenir; **p. 711**

infamous/infame *adj.* desacreditado; de mala reputación; **p. 31**

infinitely/infinitamente *adv.* ilimitadamente; sin termino; **p. 1120**

infirmity/enfermedad *s.* padecimiento; dolencia o alteración de la salud; **p. 310**

ingenuity/ingenio *s.* talento; inventiva; **p. 666**

inseperable/inseparable *adj.* persona estrechamente unida a otra por vínculos de amor o amistad; imposible de separar; **p. 988**

insipid/insípido *adj.* falto de interés; soso; **p. 548**

instigation/instigación *s.* acto de incitar o impulsar; **p. 148**

intermittent/intermitente *adj.* que se inicia y se detiene alternativamente; **p. 1178**

intrepid/intrépido *adj.* temerario; valiente; **p. 177**

intrinsically/intrínsecamente *adv.* de modo inherente o esencial; dentro de su misma naturaleza; **p. 1196**

intuitive/intuitivo *adj.* que se piensa o percibe de inmediato sin necesidad de razonar; **p. 651**

inveterate/arraigado *adj.* firmemente establecido; crónico; empedernido; **p. 606**

irrational/irracional *adj.* absurdo; incoherente; **p. 619**

irremediable/irremediable *adj.* que no se puede evitar o remediar; **p. 1289**

J

jeopardy/riesgo *s.* peligro; **p. 203**

jest/broma *s.* lo que se hace o se dice para que alguien se ría sin mala intención; **p. 432**

jovial/jovial *adj.* de buen humor; alegre y festivo; **p. 358**

K

keen/agudo(a) *adj.* que tiene un punto o filo afilado; **p. 303**

kindred (kin′ drid) *adj.* like; allied; similar; **p. 713**

L

labyrinth (lab′ ə rinth′) *n.* a place containing winding, interconnected passages; **p. 1080**

lament (lə ment′) *n.* expression of sorrow; song or literary composition that mourns a loss or death; **p. 25**

languish (lang′ gwish) *adj.* dispirited; lacking vitality; **p. 272**

license (lī′ səns) *n.* freedom used irresponsibly; **p. 925**

loath (lōth) *adj.* reluctant; unwilling; **p. 556**

loitering (loi′ tər ing) *adj.* standing or lingering idly about a place; **p. 868**

lugubrious (loo goo′ brē əs) *adj.* excessively mournful or sorrowful; **p. 1351**

lumbering (lum′ bər ing) *v.* moving heavily and clumsily; **p. 1358**

luminous (loo′ mə nəs) *adj.* emitting a glowing light; **p. 1269**

M

magnitude (mag′ nə tood′) *n.* greatness of size or extent; **p. 580**

malicious (mə lish′ əs) *adj.* deliberately harmful; **p. 559**

mar (mär) *v.* to spoil or damage; **p. 846**

meek (mēk) *adj.* mild; gentle; **p. 261**

monarch (mon′ ərk′) *n.* one who rules over a state or a territory, usually by hereditary right, as a king or a queen; **p. 550**

morbid (môr′ bid) *adj.* overly sensitive to death and decay; not cheerful or wholesome; **p. 1154**

mortal (môrt′ əl) *adj.* destined to die; **p. 268**

mourn (môrn) *v.* to show or feel sadness; grieve; **p. 544**

kindred/semejante *adj.* casi igual; análogo; similar; **p. 713**

L

labyrinth/laberinto *s.* lugar que tiene pasajes o recovecos interconectados; **p. 1080**

lament/lamento *s.* expresión de pesar; canción o composición literaria que expresa dolor por una pérdida o muerte; **p. 25**

languished/lánguido(a) *adj.* falto de ánimo; sin fuerzas; **p. 272**

license/libertinaje *s.* abuso de la libertad sin tener en cuenta a los demás; **p. 925**

loath/reacio *adj.* que se opone a hacer algo; remiso; **p. 556**

loitering/vagando *v.* andar libre y sin rumbo; holgazaneando; **p. 868**

lugubrious/lúgubre *adj.* afligido, sombrío o tétrico; **p. 1351**

lumbering/moverse pesadamente *frase verbal.* moviéndose trabajosa y torpemente; **p. 1358**

luminous/luminoso(a) *adj.* que despide luz; **p. 1269**

M

magnitude/magnitud *s.* de gran tamaño o extensión; **p. 580**

malicious/malicioso *adj.* que provoca daño deliberadamente; **p. 559**

mar/estropear *v.* maltratar o deteriorar; **p. 846**

meek/sumiso(a) *adj.* dócil; obediente; **p. 261**

monarch/monarca *s.* el que rige un estado o territorio, usualmente por derecho heredado, como un rey o reina; **p. 550**

morbid/mórbido *adj.* muy sensible a la muerte o descomposición; que no es saludable ni alegre; **p. 1154**

mortal/mortal *adj.* que ha de morir; **p. 268**

mourn/acongojar *v.* mostrar tristeza o dolor por la muerte de alguien; lamentar una pérdida; **p. 544**

munificence (mū nif′ ə səns) *n.* great generosity;
   p. 982

mute (mūt) *adj.* unable to speak; refraining from
   producing vocal sounds; **p. 256**

myriad (mir′ ē əd) *n.* a great or countless number;
   p. 524

N

negligence (neg′ li jəns) *n.* an air of careless ease or
   casualness; **p. 618**

O

oblivion (ə bliv′ ē ən) *n.* a state of forgetting;
   p. 309

obsolete (ob′ sə lēt′) *adj.* no longer in use; outdated; **p. 1358**

obstinately (ob′ stə nit lē′) *adv.* in a manner not
   yielding to argument, persuasion, or reason;
   inflexibly; **p. 1129**

odious (ō′ dē əs) *adj.* causing hate, disgust, or
   repugnance; **p. 1048**

oppressed (ə prest′) *adj.* burdened; weighed down;
   p. 626

P

pageant (paj′ ənt) *n.* an elaborately staged drama or
   spectacular exhibition; **p. 310**

pall (pôl) *n.* an atmosphere of dark and gloom;
   p. 1321

parry (par′ ē) *v.* to respond, as to a question or
   argument, by warding off or diverting; **p. 1127**

passion (pash′ ən) *n.* powerful emotion; love;
   p. 544

patronize (pā′ trə nīz′) *v.* to be a customer of;
   p. 1336

peerless (pēr′ lis) *adj.* unrivaled; without equal;
   p. 329

penance (pen′ əns) *n.* an act of self-punishment to
   show repentance for a sin; **p. 820**

munificence/munificencia *s.* gran generosidad;
   p. 982

mute/mudo(a) *adj.* incapacidad que impide el habla;
   sin palabras, sin voz o sin sonidos; **p. 256**

myriad/miríada *s.* multitud o infinidad de personas,
   cosas o asuntos; **p. 524**

N

negligence/neglicencia *s.* actitud de descuido o
   indiferencia; **p. 618**

O

oblivion/inconsciencia *s.* estado en que la persona no
   se da cuenta de las cosas; **p. 309**

obsolete/obsoleto(a) *adj.* desusado, inadecuado;
   anticuado, caduco; **p. 1358**

obstinately/obstinadamente *adv.* de modo que no
   cede a ningún razonamiento o persuasión;
   inflexiblemente; **p. 1129**

odious/odioso(a) *adj.* que causa odio, disgusto, o
   repugnancia; **p. 1048**

oppressed/oprimido *adj.* agobiado; abatido; **p. 626**

P

pageant/espectáculo *s.* función o diversión públicas;
   p. 310

pall/palio *s.* manto; atmósfera obscura y sombría;
   p. 1321

parry/esquivar *v.* desviar la conversación cuando no se
   quiere tratar un tema; **p. 1127**

passion/pasión *s.* sentimiento intenso; afección;
   p. 544

patronize/ir a un negocio *v.* ser cliente de un
   negocio; **p. 1336**

peerless/incomparable *adj.* sin par; sin igual;
   p. 329

penance/penitencia *s.* acto realizado para mostrar
   arrepentimiento por los pecados; **p. 820**

perceive/prophetic

perceive (pər sēv´) *v.* to become aware of; comprehend; **p. 156**

peril (per´ əl) *n.* risk of injury, loss, or destruction; **p. 201**

periphery (pə rif´ ər ē) *n.* the outward or farthest boundary; **p. 1358**

pernicious (pər nish´ əs) *adj.* destructive; deadly; **p. 375**

perpetual (pər pech´ ōō əl) *adj.* constantly occurring; **p. 1160**

pertain (pər tān´) *v.* to be connected to or have relevance to; **p. 385**

philosophical (phil´ ə sof´ i kəl) *adj.* concerned with the deeper meaning of life; **p. 987**

piety (pī´ ə tē) *n.* devoutness; reverence; **p. 783**

pivotal (piv´ ət əl) *adj.* of central or vital importance; **p. 1306**

plenteous (plen´ tē əs) *adj.* abundant; fruitful; **p. 328**

plodding (plod ing) *v.* walking heavily and/or slowly; **p. 1358**

pomp (pomp) *n.* splendid or dignified display; **p. 711**

precept (prē´ sept) *n.* a rule intended as a guide for conduct or action; **p. 665**

precipice (pres´ ə pis) *n.* a very steep or overhanging mass of rock as on a cliff; **p. 1329**

precipitately (pri sip´ ə tət´ lē) *adv.* without deliberation; hastily; abruptly; **p. 1178**

predominance (pri dom´ ə nəns) *n.* the state of being most important, common, or noticeable; **p. 348**

presumably (pri zōō´ mə blē) *adv.* by reasonable assumption; **p. 1159**

prevail (pri vāl´) *v.* be in general use; succeed; **p. 467**

prevarication (pri var´ ə kā shən) *n.* the act of evading the truth; lying; **p. 111**

prodigious (prə dij´ əs) *adj.* great in size, number, or degree; enormous; **p. 627**

profound (prə found´) *adj.* characterized by deep understanding or insight; **p. 744**

prophetic (prə fet´ ik) *adj.* having the quality of foretelling future events; **p. 324**

percibir/profético

perceive/percibir *v.* ser consciente de algo; comprender; **p. 156**

peril/peligro *s.* riesgo de herida, pérdida o destrucción; **p. 201**

periphery/periferia *s.* espacio que rodea un núcleo cualquiera; **p. 1358**

pernicious/pernicioso(a) *adj.* perjudicial; gravemente dañoso; **p. 375**

perpetual/perpetuo(a) *adj.* que dura y permanece; **p. 1160**

pertain/relacionar *v.* que está conectado o asociado a algo; **p. 385**

philosophical/filosófico(a) *adj.* relacionado a los aspectos esenciales de la vida; **p. 987**

piety/piedad *s.* devoción; reverencia; **p. 783**

pivotal/central *adj.* de enorme importancia; **p. 1306**

plenteous/abundante *adj.* en gran cantidad; copioso; **p. 328**

plodding/caminar trabajosamente *frase verbal;* moviéndose lenta y pesadamente, con trabajo; **p. 1358**

pomp/pompa *s.* acompañamiento suntuoso y solemne; **p. 711**

precept/precepto *s.* regla o pauta de comportamiento o acción; **p. 665**

precipice/precipicio *s.* despeño o caída violenta y profunda, casi vertical; **p. 1329**

precipitately/precipitadamente *adv.* sin pensarlo; apresuradamente; abruptamente; **p. 1178**

predominance/predominancia *s.* condición de ser lo más importante, común o notorio; **p. 348**

presumably/es de suponer *adv.* se puede conjeturar o calcular según los indicios; **p. 1159**

prevail/prevalecer *v.* perdurar, subsistir; sobresalir, tener superioridad; **p. 467**

prevarication/engaño *s.* acto de evadir la verdad; mentira; **p. 111**

prodigious/descomunal *adj.* extraordinario en tamaño, número o grado; enorme; **p. 627**

profound/profundo *adj.* que se caracteriza por una gran comprensión o conocimiento; **p. 744**

prophetic/profético *adj.* que tiene la cualidad de anticipar futuros sucesos; **p. 324**

prosaic (prō zā′ ik) *adj.* commonplace; ordinary; **p. 1177**

provoke (prə vōk′) *v.* to call forth; to stir to action or feeling; **p. 344**

prowess (prou′ is) *n.* superior ability; skill; **p. 401**

prudence (prōōd′ əns) *n.* sound judgment; careful management; **p. 933**

prudent (prōōd′ ənt) *adj.* cautious; careful; **p. 120**

purge (purj) *n.* the process of getting rid of impurities or undesirable elements; **p. 393**

Q

quaint (kwānt) *adj.* pleasingly unusual or odd; **p. 1047**

quench (kwench) *v.* to put out; to extinguish; **p. 557**

R

radiant (rā′ dē ənt) *adj.* beaming, as with joy, love, or energy; **p. 1251**

rancid (ran′ sid) *adj.* having an offensive or foul odor or taste; **p. 1316**

rancor (rang′ kər) *n.* bitter malice or resentment; **p. 77**

rational (rash′ ən əl) *adj.* able to reason; sensible; **p. 727**

ravage (rav ij′) *v.* to lay waste to; to destroy; **p. 1169**

reckoning (rek′ ən ing) *n.* a settlement of accounts; **p. 156**

reconciled (rek′ ən sīld) *adj.* brought to acceptance of; **p. 537**

redress (ri dres′) *v.* to set right; to remedy; **p. 379**

refined (ri fīnd′) *adj.* freed from imperfections; improved; **p. 434**

reiterate (rē it′ ə rāt′) *v.* to say or do again; to repeat; **p. 1130**

relinquish (ri ling′ kwish) *v.* to give up; put aside; to abandon; **p. 838**

repentance (ri pent′ əns) *n.* feeling of sorrow for wrongdoing; remorse; **p. 327**

prosaic/prosaico *adj.* común; ordinario o vulgar; **p. 1177**

provoke/provocar *v.* mover o incitar; inducir a alguien a que haga algo; **p. 344**

prowess/destreza *s.* habilidad para hacer algo bien hecho; arte o primor; **p. 401**

prudence/prudencia *s.* buen juicio; sensatez; **p. 933**

prudent/prudente *adj.* cuidadoso; cauto; **p. 120**

purge/purga *s.* eliminación de impurezas o elementos inconvenientes; **p. 393**

Q

quaint/pintoresco(a) *adj.* agradablemente raro o peculiar; **p. 1047**

quench/extinguir *v.* apagar; aplacar; **p. 557**

R

radiant/radiante *adj.* brillante, como con alegría, amor, o energía; **p. 1251**

rancid/rancio(a) *adj.* que ha adquirido olor o sabor más fuertes, mejorándose o echándose a perder; **p. 1316**

rancor/rencor *s.* fuerte resentimiento u odio; **p. 77**

rational/racional *adj.* que es capaz de razonar; sensible; **p. 727**

ravage/asolar *v.* arruinar; destruir; **p. 1169**

reckoning/ajuste de cuentas *s.* calcular ganancias y pérdidas; **p. 156**

reconciled/reconciliado *adj.* que ha aceptado o perdonado; **p. 537**

redress/reparar *v.* arreglar; remediar o corregir; **p. 379**

refine/refinar *v.* eliminar impurezas; hacer más fino o más puro; **p. 434**

reiterate/reiterar *v.* decir o hacer de nuevo; repetir; **p. 1130**

relinquish/renunciar *v.* ceder; rendirse; abandonar; **p. 838**

repentance/arrepentimiento *s.* pena o pesar de haber hecho algo; remordimiento; **p. 327**

replenish (ri plen′ ish) v. to refill or make complete again; to add a new supply to; **p. 417**

repose (ri pōz′) v. lie at rest; rest from work or toil; **p. 786**

reprove (ri pro͞ov′) v. to scold or correct, usually gently or out of kindness; **p. 126**

respite (res′ pit) n. a delay or extension; **p. 158**

restrain (ri strān′) v. to hold back; restrict; **p. 149**

retaliation (ri tal′ ē ā′ shən) n. getting even with; revenge; **p. 973**

retort (ri tôrt′) v. to reply in a witty, quick, or sharp manner; **p. 1052**

revelation (rev′ ə lā′ shən) n. the act of making something known; something that is revealed; **p. 1316**

reverently (rev′ rənt lē) adv. respectfully; with deep affection or veneration; **p. 1186**

rue (ro͞o) n. sorrow; remorse; **p. 1001**

S

sanguine (sang′ gwin) adj. confident; optimistic; **p. 746**

satiety (sə tī′ ə tē) n. a feeling of weariness or even dislike of something caused by satisfying an appetite or desire for it in excess; **p. 860**

scorn (skôrn) v. to reject as contemptible or unworthy; **p. 272**

scruple (skro͞o′ pəl) n. a moral or ethical principle that restrains action; **p. 347**

scrutiny (skro͞ot′ ən ē) n. close watch or examination; **p. 970**

secluded (si klo͞o′ did) adj. shut off from others; undisturbed; **p. 786**

sensible (sen′ sə bəl) adj. having good judgment or sound thinking; **p. 1188**

shroud (shroud) n. burial cloth; **p. 30**

siege (sēj) n. blockade; the surrounding of a fortified place by an opposing army intending to invade it; **p. 396**

sinew (sin′ ū) n. a tendon; **p. 1301**

slander (slan′ dər) v. to utter false or malicious statements about; **p. 148**

replenish/reabastecer v. llenar o completar de nuevo; agregar o volver a surtir; **p. 417**

repose/reposar v. permanecer en quietud; descansar en medio de un trabajo o fatiga; **p. 786**

reprove/reprender v. corregir, regañar o amonestar a alguien desaprobando su conducta; **p. 126**

respite/pausa s. postergación o intervalo; **p. 158**

restrain/refrenar v. aguantar; reprimir; **p. 149**

retaliation/represalia s. revancha por una agresión; venganza; **p. 973**

retort/replicar v. responder en una manera ingeniosa, rápida, o aguda; **p. 1052**

revelation/revelación s. descubrimiento de algo secreto u oculto; manifestación de algo oculto; **p. 1316**

reverently/reverentemente adv. con respeto; que muestra veneración; **p. 1186**

rue/arrepentir(se) v. sentir gran pena por algo; desear que algo no hubiera ocurrido; **p. 1001**

S

sanguine/optimista adj. confiado; esperanzado; **p. 746**

satiety/hartazgo s. sensación de molestia o cansancio que puede darse por la satisfacción completa o excesiva, esp. de comida o bebida; **p. 860**

scorn/despreciar v. desairar, desdeñar; no apreciar el valor de algo; **p. 272**

scruple/escrúpulo s. principio moral o ético que limita una acción; **p. 347**

scrutiny/escrutinio s. examen y averiguación exacta de algo; **p. 970**

secluded/apartado(a) adj. retirado, separado, remoto; **p. 786**

sensible/sensato(a) adj. prudente, de buen juicio, que piensa antes de actuar; **p. 1188**

shroud/mortaja s. tela o paño para el entierro; **p. 30**

siege/sitio s. asedio; cerco puesto a una plaza o fortaleza para combatirla o apoderarse de ella; **p. 396**

sinew/tendón s. tejido fibroso; **p. 1301**

slander/calumniar v. desacreditar; difamar; **p. 148**

sloth (slôth) *n.* laziness; **p. 285**

solemn (sol′ əm) *adj.* serious; somber; **p. 1157**

solicitous (sə lis′ ə təs) *adj.* full of concern; **p. 98**

sordid (sôr′ did) *adj.* filthy; selfish; greedy; mean; **p. 782**

spellbound (spel′ bound) *adj.* fascinated; affected as if by enchantment; **p. 1203**

spite (spīt) *n.* desire to annoy or harm; ill will; **p. 466**

spurn (spurn) *v.* to reject or drive off; **p. 845**

squalid (skwol′ id) *adj.* dirty or broken down due to poverty or neglect; **p. 1080**

stalking (stô′ king) *v.* tracking; pursuing; **p. 261**

stealthy (stel′ thē) *adj.* secret; sly; **p. 339**

stratagem (strat′ ə jəm) *n.* a deception; a military tactic designed to surprise an enemy; **p. 595**

stridently (strīd′ ənt lē) *adv.* in a harsh, grating manner; **p. 1346**

strife (strīf) *n.* unrest or violent conflict; **p. 477**

subdue (səb dōō′) *v.* conquer; overcome; quiet; **p. 268, 544**

subside (səb sīd′) *v.* to give way or end; **p. 974**

subterranean (səb′ tə rā′ nē ən) *adj.* below the earth's surface; underground; **p. 528**

suffice (sə fīs′) *v.* to be enough for; **p. 137**

superannuated (sōō′ pər an′ ū ā′ tid) *adj.* out of date; **p. 1307**

superfluous (soo pur′ flōō əs) *adj.* beyond what is necessary; **p. 549**

supplant (sə plant′) *v.* to take the place of, often unfairly; **p. 1080**

suppressed (sə presd′) *adj.* subdued; held back; **p. 256**

suppressing (sə pres′ ing) *n.* prohibiting publication or circulation; censoring; **p. 1073**

surfeited (sur′ fit əd) *adj.* overfed; **p. 340**

sustenance (sus′ tə nəns) *n.* food or other items that support life; **p. 566**

sloth/flojera *s.* pereza; **p. 285**

solemn/solemne *adj.* serio, formal; grave, sombrío; **p. 1157**

solicitous/solícito *adj.* preocupado o interesado; deseoso de servir; **p. 98**

sordid/sórdido(a) *adj.* sucio; mísero; avariento; mezquino; **p. 782**

spellbound/embelesado(a) *adj.* fascinado; que arroba y cautiva los sentidos; **p. 1203**

spite/malicia *s.* mala intención; maldad; **p. 466**

spurn/rechazar *v.* despreciar; ahuyentar; **p. 845**

squalid/mísero *adj.* sucio o deteriorado debido a la pobreza y el descuido; **p. 1080**

stalking/acechando *v.* observar y mirar a escondidas; vigilar o aguardar; **p. 261**

stealthy/furtivo(a) *adj.* hecho a escondidas; sigiloso; **p. 339**

strategem/estratagema *s.* engaño o fingimiento; ardid de guerra para conseguir un objetivo; **p. 595**

stridently/estridentemente *adv.* de modo áspero y chirriante; **p. 1346**

strife/conflicto *n.* combate, contienda, disputa; **p. 477**

subdue/someter *v.* conquistar; subyugar; pacificar; **p. 268, 544**

subside/decaer *v.* calmar(se), pasar(se); **p. 974**

subterranean/subterráneo *adj.* que opera o existe bajo la superficie; debajo de la tierra; **p. 528**

suffice/bastar *v.* ser suficiente; **p. 137**

superannuated/anticuado *adj.* pasado de moda o fuera de uso; **p. 1307**

superfluous/superfluo *adj.* innecesario; sobrante; **p. 549**

supplant/suplantar *v.* tomar el lugar de; **p. 1080**

suppressed/contenido(a) *adj.* reprimir; refrenar; **p. 256**

suppressing/supresión *s.* prohibición de la publicación o circulación; censura; **p. 1073**

surfeited/saciado(a) *adj.* harto; que ha satisfecho el apetito con comida y bebida; **p. 340**

sustenance/sustento *s.* alimento y otros medios que conservan la vida; **p. 566**

T

teeming (tēm′ ing) *adj.* full; at the point of overflowing; **p. 869**

temerity (tə mer′ ə tē) *n.* excessive or reckless boldness; rashness; **p. 1348**

tempest (tem′ pist) *n.* a violent storm; a violent outburst or disturbance; **p. 295**

threshold (thresh′ hōld′) *n.* doorway; entranceway; **p. 1000**

thwart (thwôrt) *v.* to prevent from doing or achieving something; **p. 1154**

transgress (trans gres′) *v.* to break or violate a law; to go beyond a limit; **p. 522**

transient (tran′ shənt) *adj.* lasting only a brief time; temporary; **p. 839**

treachery (treach′ ər ē) *n.* willful betrayal of trust; treason; **p. 257**

tread (tred) *v.* to walk or step upon; **p. 296**

trifling (trī′ fling) *n.* treating someone or something as unimportant; showing a lack of proper respect; **p. 982**

trudge (truj) *v.* to walk wearily or laboriously; **p. 1099**

tumult (tōō′ məlt) *n.* disorder; an uproar; **p. 857**

tyrant (tī′ rənt) *n.* a cruel, oppressive ruler; a ruler with unlimited power; **p. 302**

U

unconfined (un kən fīnd′) *adj.* not shut in; unrestricted; **p. 472**

uncouth (un kōōth′) *adj.* crude; lacking polish, culture, or refinement; **p. 713**

unperturbed (un pər turbd′) *adj.* undisturbed; not troubled; **p. 1322**

unsavory (un sā′ vər ē) *adj.* sinister; morally questionable; **p. 1071**

usurper (ū surp′ ər) *n.* one who seizes the power, position, or rights of another by force; **p. 402**

T

teeming/rebosante *adj.* muy lleno; lleno en grado extremo; **p. 869**

temerity/temeridad *s.* excesivo atrevimiento o imprudencia; audacia; **p. 1348**

tempest/tempestad *s.* tormenta fuerte y violenta; agitación de los ánimos; **p. 295**

threshold/umbral *s.* entrada; parte inferior o escalón; **p. 1000**

thwart/obstruir *v.* impedir que se haga o logre algo; **p. 1154**

transgress/transgredir *v.* violar una ley; sobrepasar un límite; **p. 522**

transient/transitorio *adj.* que tan sólo dura un tiempo breve; temporal; **p. 839**

treachery/traición *s.* acción que rompe la confianza o fidelidad; deslealtad; **p. 257**

tread/pisar *v.* caminar o poner el pie encima; **p. 296**

trifling/jugando (con) *v.* tratar algo o a alguien sin la consideración o el respeto que merece; no respetar o burlarse de alguien; **p. 982**

trudge/caminar (con dificultad) *frase verbal* marchar penosamente y con mucho trabajo; **p. 1099**

tumult/tumulto *s.* confusión; alboroto; **p. 857**

tyrant/tirano(a) *s.* gobernante que abusa de su poder y autoridad de manera injusta; quien tiene el poder absoluto; **p. 302**

U

unconfined/ilimitado(a) *adj.* que no tiene límites; sin restricciones **p. 472**

uncouth/tosco(a) *adj.* burdo, grosero; sin delicadeza, cultura o educación; **p. 713**

unperturbed/imperturbable *adj.* sereno; tranquilo; **p. 1322**

unsavory/ultrajante *adj.* ofensivo; deshonroso; **p. 1071**

usurper/usurpador *s.* quien toma el poder, la posición o los derechos de otro mediante la fuerza; **p. 402**

V

vacant (vā′ kənt) *adj.* empty; **p. 969**

vain (vān) *adj.* conceited; excessively pleased with oneself; **p. 268**

valor (val′ ər) *n.* courage and boldness, as in battle; bravery; **p. 257**

vendor (ven′ dər) *n.* one who sells goods; **p. 1297**

veneration (ven′ ə rā′ shən) *n.* deep respect or reverence; **p. 661**

vex (veks) *v.* disturb; trouble; irritate; **p. 1113**

vigilance (vij′ ə ləns) *n.* careful watchfulness; **p. 651**

vile (vīl) *adj.* repulsive or disgusting; **p. 1099**

W

wan (won) *adj.* pale; **p. 272**

withering (with′ ər ing) *v.* becoming dry; shriveling from lack of moisture; **p. 1357**

writhing (rīth′ ing) *adj.* twisting, as in pain; **p. 31**

wryly (rī′ lē) *adv.* in a twisted or distorted manner; **p. 1301**

Z

zealous (zel′ əs) *adj.* filled with intense, enthusiastic devotion; **p. 664**

zenith (zē′ nith) *n.* a peak; the greatest point; **p. 744**

V

vacant/desocupado(a) *adj.* vacío; **p. 969**

vain/vanidoso(a) *adj.* presuntuoso; deseo excesivo de mostrar las cualidades y de que se le reconozcan y alaben; **p. 268**

valor/valentía *s.* hecho heroico con arrojo y coraje; bravura; **p. 257**

vendor/vendedor *s.* el que vende algo; **p. 1297**

veneration/veneración *s.* profundo respeto o adoración; **p. 661**

vex/enfadar *v.* disgustar; enojar; irritar; **p. 1113**

vigilance/vigilancia *s.* atención cuidadosa; **p. 651**

vile/repugnante *adj.* asqueroso o desagradable; **p. 1099**

W

wan/pálido(a) *adj.* decolorado; **p. 272**

withering/marchitando *v.* ponerse mustio; resecarse y perder frescura; **p. 1357**

writhing/retorcido *adj.* que flexiona el cuerpo, como cuando se siente dolor; **p. 31**

wryly/tergiversadamente *adv.* de modo distorsionado o enredado; **p. 1301**

Z

zealous/fervoroso *adj.* lleno de entusiasmo y devoción; **p. 664**

zenith/cenit *s.* apogeo; punto máximo; **p. 744**

ACADEMIC WORD LIST

The list of words that appears on this page and the following pages represents a research-based collection of words that are commonly used in academic texts. The purpose of the list is to present students with the basics of a working academic vocabulary, one that will prove useful in reading, writing, and research in many areas of study. Many of these words also appear throughout the Glencoe Language Arts program.

Sublist One

analysis
approach
area
assessment
assume
authority
available
benefit
concept
consistent
constitutional
context
contract
create
data
definition
derived
distribution
economic
environment
established
estimate
evidence
export
factors
financial
formula
function
identified
income
indicate
individual

interpretation
involved
issues
labor
legal
legislation
major
method
occur
percent
period
policy
principle
procedure
process
required
research
response
role
section
sector
significant
similar
source
specific
structure
theory
variables

Sublist Two

achieve
acquisition
administration

affect
appropriate
aspects
assistance
categories
chapter
commission
community
complex
computer
conclusion
conduct
consequences
construction
consumer
credit
cultural
design
distinction
elements
equation
evaluation
features
final
focus
impact
injury
institute
investment
items
journal
maintenance
normal

obtained
participation
perceived
positive
potential
previous
primary
purchase
range
region
regulations
relevant
resident
resources
restricted
security
select
site
sought
strategies
survey
text
traditional
transfer

Sublist Three

alternative
circumstances
comments
compensation
components
consent
considerable

constant
constraints
contribution
convention
coordination
core
corporate
corresponding
criteria
deduction
demonstrate
document
dominant
emphasis
ensure
excluded
framework
funds
illustrated
immigration
implies
initial
instance
interaction
justification
layer
link
location
maximum
minorities
negative
outcomes
partnership

philosophy
physical
proportion
published
reaction
registered
reliance
removed
scheme
sequence
sex
shift
specified
sufficient
task
technical
techniques
technology
validity
volume

Sublist Four

access
adequate
annual
apparent
approximated
attitudes
attributed
civil
code
commitment
communication
concentration
conference
contrast
cycle
debate
despite
dimensions
domestic
emerged
error

ethnic
goals
granted
hence
hypothesis
implementation
implications
imposed
integration
internal
investigation
job
label
mechanism
obvious
occupational
option
output
overall
parallel
parameters
phase
predicted
principal
prior
professional
project
promote
regime
resolution
retained
series
statistics
status
stress
subsequent
sum
summary
undertaken

Sublist Five

academic
adjustment

alter
amendment
aware
capacity
challenge
clause
compounds
conflict
consultation
contact
decline
discretion
draft
enable
energy
enforcement
entities
equivalent
evolution
expansion
exposure
external
facilitate
fundamental
generated
generation
image
liberal
license
logic
marginal
medical
mental
modified
monitoring
network
notion
objective
orientation
perspective
precise
prime
psychology

pursue
ratio
rejected
revenue
stability
styles
substitution
sustainable
symbolic
target
transition
trend
version
welfare
whereas

Sublist Six

abstract
accurate
acknowledged
aggregate
allocation
assigned
attached
author
bond
brief
capable
cited
cooperative
discrimination
display
diversity
domain
edition
enhanced
estate
exceed
expert
explicit
federal
fees
flexibility

furthermore
gender
ignored
incentive
incidence
incorporated
index
inhibition
initiatives
input
instructions
intelligence
interval
lecture
migration
minimum
ministry
motivation
neutral
nevertheless
overseas
preceding
presumption
rational
recovery
revealed
scope
subsidiary
tapes
trace
transformation
transport
underlying
utility

Sublist Seven

adaptation
adults
advocate
aid
channel
chemical
classical

comprehensive
comprise
confirmed
contrary
converted
couple
decades
definite
deny
differentiation
disposal
dynamic
eliminate
empirical
equipment
extract
file
finite
foundation
global
grade
guarantee
hierarchical
identical
ideology
inferred
innovation
insert
intervention
isolated
media
mode
paradigm
phenomenon
priority
prohibited
publication
quotation
release
reverse
simulation
solely
somewhat

submitted
successive
survive
thesis
topic
transmission
ultimately
unique
visible
voluntary

Sublist Eight

abandon
accompanied
accumulation
ambiguous
appendix
appreciation
arbitrary
automatically
bias
chart
clarity
conformity
commodity
complement
contemporary
contradiction
crucial
currency
denote
detected
deviation
displacement
dramatic
eventually
exhibit
exploitation
fluctuations
guidelines
highlighted
implicit
induced

inevitably
infrastructure
inspection
intensity
manipulation
minimized
nuclear
offset
paragraph
plus
practitioners
predominantly
prospect
radical
random
reinforced
restore
revision
schedule
tension
termination
theme
thereby
uniform
vehicle
via
virtually
visual
widespread

Sublist Nine

accommodation
analogous
anticipated
assurance
attained
behalf
bulk
ceases
coherence
coincide
commenced
concurrent

confined
controversy
conversely
device
devoted
diminished
distorted
duration
erosion
ethical
format
founded
incompatible
inherent
insights
integral
intermediate
manual
mature
mediation
medium
military
minimal
mutual
norms
overlap
passive
portion
preliminary
protocol
qualitative
refine
relaxed
restraints
revolution
rigid
route
scenario
sphere
subordinate
supplementary
suspended
team

temporary
trigger
unified
violation
vision

Sublist Ten

adjacent
albeit
assembly
collapse
colleagues
compiled
conceived
convinced
depression
encountered
enormous
forthcoming
inclination
integrity
intrinsic
invoked
levy
likewise
nonetheless
notwithstanding
odd
ongoing
panel
persistent
posed
reluctant
so-called
straightforward
undergo
whereby

> References beginning with R refer to handbook pages.

Literary Concepts

Absurd, Theater of the. *See* Theater of the Absurd.

Act R1

Allegory 154, 169, 533, 539, R1

Alliteration 192, 276, 278, 451, 794, 800, 803, 876, 936, 1206, 1356, 1359, R1

Allusion 520, 530, 600, 733, 1118, R1

Ambiguity 1340, R1

Analogy 23, 52, 89, 124, 140, 197, 206, 210, 217, 260, 264, 271, 274, 289, 438, 442, 444, 475, 479, 553, 561, 593, 600, 843, 847, 923, 999, 1046, 1078, 1123, 1137, 1155, 1185, 1190, 1268, 1305, 1332, R1

Anapest R1, R7

Anecdote R1

Antagonist 191, 1075, R1

Anthropomorphism 1319, 1324, R1

Antithesis 601

Aphorism R1

Apostrophe 271, 274, R1

Archetype 172, 191, 205, R1–R2

Argument 124, 140, 352, 368, 425, 427, 428, 443, 456, 458, 603, 674, 733, 1150, 1155, 1189, R2

Aside 305, 336, R2

Assonance 794, 876, 931, 936, 1201, 1206, 1261, R2

Assumption 1069, 1076, 1340

Atmosphere 316, 336, 798, R2

Attributions 1311

Author's craft 22, 58, 82, 92, 145, 196, 254, 259, 265, 270, 275, 279, 283, 292–293, 336, 351, 414, 424, 430, 445, 455, 464, 469, 474, 479, 516, 532, 542, 546, 552, 564, 574, 585, 586, 602, 614, 623, 628, 648, 659, 708, 717, 725, 742, 754, 768, 780, 795, 799, 833, 842, 847, 850, 865, 879, 922, 930, 939, 951, 956, 966, 977, 979, 984, 994, 998, 1003, 1045, 1068, 1077, 1089, 1093, 1097,

1106, 1116, 1117, 1122, 1138, 1149, 1155, 1166, 1174, 1184, 1192, 1200, 1242, 1245, 1246, 1258, 1267, 1271, 1275, 1278, 1284, 1295, 1304, 1313, 1318, 1327, 1331, 1344, 1354, 1355

Author's meaning 1107, 1109

Author's purpose 115, 154, 169, 170, 280, 282, 288, 573, 609, 765, 854, 863, 1009, 1087, 1098, 1100, R2, R24

Author's style 53, 141, 170, 192, 289, 313, 405, 443, 531, 540, 562, 585, 601, 615, 620, 621, 643, 657, 668, 669, 734, 765, 778, 794, 864, 937, 977, 992, 1087, 1116, 1164, 1191, 1207, 1256, 1294, 1311, 1325, 1354

Autobiography 146, R2

Ballad 866, R2

   folk 208–209

   literary 827

Ballad stanza 210, 217, 827, R2

Bias 1173, 1193, 1198, R2, R25

Biography 660, 668, 794, R2–R3

Blank verse 315, 405, R3

Byronic hero 848–849

   See also Hero.

Cadence R3

Caesura 591, R3

Caricature 620

Carpe diem 453, 456, 458, 478, R3

Cavalier poetry 452–453, R3

Character 210, 217, 218–225, 387, 405, 620, 1123, 1137, 1193, 1198, 1210, 1212, 1272, 1275, 1294, 1305, 1339, R3

   See also Characterization; Stereotype.

   dynamic 217, R3

   flat 1198, R3

   foil 352, 368, R7

   main 1193, R3

   minor 1193, R3

   round 1198, R3

   static 217, R3

Characterization 93, 140, 539, 769, 777, 967, 976, 1053, 1137, 1305, 1310, R3

   direct 115, 539, 769, 967, 1137, R3

   indirect 115, 539, 769, 967, 1137, R3

Chronicle 83

Classicism 452–453

Cliché R3

Climax 369, 1053, 1075, 1211, 1213

   See also Plot.

Closed couplet 591

Colloquialism R3

Comedy R3

   heroic R3

Comic devices 1198

Comic relief 351, R4

Conceits 428, 442, R4

   elaborate 452

   metaphysical 428, 438, 442, R4

Conclusion 851, 853

Conflict 351, 1208–1215, 1285, R13

   external 23, 52, 79, 191, 530, 1075, 1212, 1293, 1305, 1310, R4

   internal 23, 52, 79, 191, 530, 1075, 1164, 1212, 1293, R4

Connotation 271, 274, 611, 660, 668, 726, 733, 948, 1173, 1247, 1255, R4, R20

Consonance 794, 876, 931, 936, 1201, 1206, 1261, R4

Context 55, 58

   cultural 10–11, 68, 242–243, 409, 463, 506–507, 698–699, 743, 752, 912–913, 992, 1034–1035, 1061, 1076, 1232–1233, 1257, 1266

   historical 10–11, 193, 242–243, 506–507, 698–699, 760, 764, 912–913, 938, 947, 992, 1034–1035, 1076, 1232–1233

   social 10–11, 242–243, 506–507, 698–699, 912–913, 1034–1035, 1232–1233

Conversational style 452

Couplet 253, 300, 591, R4, R16

   closed 591

   end-stopped 591

   heroic 453, 585, 591

Crisis. *See* Plot.

Cultural context 10–11, 68, 242–243, 409, 454, 463, 506–507, 643, 698–699, 743, 752, 912–913, 992,

1034–1035, 1061, 1076, 1232–1233, 1257, 1266

Dactyl R4, R7

Denotation 271, 274, 611, 660, 668, 726, 733, 948, 1173, 1247, 1255, R4, R20

Dénouement (resolution) 369
    See also Plot.

Description 967, 976, 1163, R4
    spatial order 531

Dialect 718, 723, 1247, 1332, 1338, R4

Dialogue 53, 170, 205, 562, 769, 777, 778, 1209, 1212, 1215, 1311, R4

Diary 553, 561, R4

Diction 405, 585, 786, 793, 854, 863, 1190, 1324, R5

Dimeter R5

Drama R5
    absurdists 1277
    classical Greek 20–21
    contemporary 1277
    kitchen-sink 1276
    medieval 152–153

Dramatic irony 116, 123, 404, 851, 1004, 1185, 1190
    See also Irony.

Dramatic monologue 937, 980, 983, 1008, R5

Dramatic poetry R5

Dramatic structure R5

Dynamic character 217, R3

Elegy 446, 448, 709, 715, 923, R5

Emotional appeals 427, 675

End rhyme R5, R15

End-stopped couplet 591, R5

English language
    Middle English 90–91
    Old English 80, 90

English (Shakespearean) Sonnet 252, 253, 866, R16

Enjambment 781, 785, R5

Epic. *See also* Mock-epic.
    folk R5
    form 20–21
    hero 21, 52, 53, R5
    literary R5

Epigram 587, R5

Epigraph R5

Epilogue R6

Epiphany 1046, 1067, 1139, 1146, R6

Epistle 743, R6

Epistolary novel 743

Epitaph 709, 715, R6

Epithet R6

Essay 284, 591, 612
    formal 551, 612–613, R6
    informal (personal) 547, 551, 613, R6
    periodical 615

Ethical appeals 676

Exaggeration 573
    See also Hyperbole.

Exclamation 871, 874

Exemplum 116, 141, R6

Exposition 369, 985, 991
    See also Plot.

Extended metaphor 603, 609, R6

Fable 1319, R6

Fairy tale R6

Falling action 369
    See also Plot.

Fantasy R6

Farce R6

Fiction R6
    historical 623, 628

Figurative language 260, 263, 600, 843, 879, 1303, R6
    apostrophe 271, 274, R1
    hyperbole 475, 478, 1173, R8
    metaphor 294, 297, 312, 431, 930, 1098, 1100, 1354, R10
    oxymoron 874, 1201, 1206, R12
    personification 123, 274, 297, 312, 431, 437, 517, 519, 1109, 1206, 1268, 1270, R13
    simile 294, 297, 298, 300, 312, 431, 930, 1098, 1100, 1354, R16
    symbol 51, 297, R18

Figure of speech 294, 437, 1201, 1206, R6

Flashback 1175, 1183, R7

Flash-forward R7

Flat character 1198
    See also Character.

Foil 352, 368, R7

Folk ballads 208–209

Folklore R7

Folktale R7

Foot 431, 764, 995, R7

Foreshadowing 1123, 1136, 1338, R7

Form 465, 752, 866, 870, 874, 942, 1206, R7
    epic 20–21

Formal essay 551, 612–613
    See also Essay.

Frame story 93, R7

Free verse 1314, 1317, R7

Genre 21, 150, 217, 264, 406, 540, 669, 778, 781, 785, 1092, 1277, 1325, R7

Gothic novel 834, 840, R7

Greek drama, classical 20–21

Haiku R7–R8

Heptameter R8

Hero
    Byronic 848–849, R8
    epic 21, 52, 53, R5

Heroic comedy R3

Heroic couplet 453, 585, R8

Heroic stanza R8

Hexameter R8

Historical context 10–11, 193, 242–243, 506–507, 698–699, 760, 764, 829–832, 912–913, 938, 947, 992, 1034–1035, 1076, 1232–1233

Historical fiction 623, 628, R8

Historical influences 5, 670, 829

Historical narrative 83, 89, R8

History R8

Horatian ode 874

Hubris R8

Humor 124, 140, 573, 1198, R8

Hymn R8

Hyperbole 475, 478, 1173, R8

Iamb R7, R8

Iambic pentameter 252, 1115, R8–R9

Idiom 1247, R9

Imagery 116, 150, 274, 437, 562, 600, 715, 798, 847, 875, 876, 879, 887, 930, 955, 995, 997, 1094, 1096, 1118, 1121, 1147, 1189, 1328, 1330, 1356, 1359, R9

Implied theme 454, 463, 575, 1191, 1293, R18

Informal (personal) essay 547, 551, 613
    See also Essay.

Interior monologue R9

Internal rhyme R9, R15

Inversion 313, 543, R9

Irony 573, 1339

dramatic 116, 123, 404, 851, 1004, 1185, 1190, R9

situational 116, 123, 404, 584, 851, 1004, 1008, 1198, 1310, R9

verbal 116, 404, 584, 1006, 1185, 1190, 1317, R9

Irregular ode R12

Italian (Petrarchan) Sonnet 252, 253, 517, 1092, R16

Journal 796, 798, R9

Juxtaposition 843, 847, R9

Kenning R9

Legend 192, 197, 205, R9

Literary ballad 827
    See also Ballad.

Literary criticism 18, 123, 264, 265, 297, 405, 441, 443, 583, 669, 734, 803, 840, 853, 862, 870, 990, 997, 1085, 1147, 1191, 1367, 1372–1373, R10, R24

Literary history 20–21, 90–91, 152–153, 208–209, 252–253, 314–315, 428–429, 452–453, 612–613, 766–767, 848–849, 964–965, 1066–1067, 1276–1277

Literary influences 960

Literary traditions 875, 887

Loaded words 1172, 1173

Logical appeals 675

Lyric poetry 449, 450, 793, 999, 1002, R10

Main character 1193, R3
    See also Character.

Maxim R10

Medieval drama 152–153

Meditative tone 452

Melodrama R10

Memoir 1264, R10

Metaphor 294, 297, 312, 431, 930, 1098, 1100, 1115, 1354, R10
    extended 603, 609

Metaphysical conceit 428, 438, 442, R4

Metaphysical poetry 428–429, R10

Meter 252, 436, 450, 930, 997, 1115, R10
    foot 431, 764, 995

Metonymy R10

Minor character 1193, R3

Miracle plays 152–153, R10

Mock-epic 593, 600, R10

Modernism 1038, 1066, R10–R11

Monologue R11

Mood 74, 79, 80, 169, 205, 278, 796, 798, 923, 930, 976, 1090, 1092, 1163, 1282, 1353, R11

Moral R11

Morality plays 153, R11

Motif 313, 337, 351, 442, 478, R11

Motivation 1046, 1053, 1136, R11

Mystery plays 152–153, R10

Myth R11

Narrative R11
    historical 83, 89

Narrative poetry 804, 827, R11

Narrator 1069, 1075, 1255, R11
    omniscient 1136

Narrator commentary 778

Naturalism R11

Nature imagery 875, 887

Neoclassicism R11

Nonce words (nonsense words) 957, R11

Nonfiction R12

Nonsense verse 957, 959, R12

Novel R12
    epistolary 743
    Gothic 834, 840
    Regionalist 965
    social-problem 964–965

Novella R12

Novel of manners R12

Octave 253, 517, R12
    See also Sonnet.

Octet R12

Ode 459, 871, 874, R12
    Horatian 874, R12
    irregular R12

Omniscient narrator 1136
    See also Narrator.

Onomatopoeia 876, 957, 1270, R12

Oral tradition R12

Ottava rima 1115, R12

Oxymoron 874, 1201, 1206, R12

Parable 1057, R12

Paradox 269, 470, 473, 1085, R12

Parallelism 284, 288, 289, 422, 591, 601, 765, 871, 874, 1172, R12

Parody 294, 575, 584, R13

Pastoral R13

Pathetic fallacy R13

Patterns 876

Pentameter R13

Periodical essay 615

Persona 573, R13

Personal essay 613
    See also Essay.

Personification 123, 274, 312, 431, 437, 517, 519, 1109, 1146, 1206, 1268, 1270, R13

Persuasion R13

Petrarchan Sonnet 252, 253, 517, 1092
    See also Sonnet.

Plays 154, 316 *See also* Drama.
    miracle 152–153
    morality 153
    mystery 152–153

Plot 368, 387, 1183
    climax 369, 1053, 1075, 1211, 1213, R13
    conflict R13
    exposition 369, 985, 991, R13
    falling action 369, R13
    resolution 369, 1211, 1213, R13
    rising action 369, 1211, 1213, R13

Poetry 74, 80, 93, 116, 124, 260, 266, 425, 1109, R13
    See also Sonnet.
    Cavalier 452–453
    lyric 449, 793, 999, 1002
    metaphysical 428–429
    narrative 804, 827
    Romantic 781

Point of view 278, 777, 1075, 1212, 1213, 1345
    first-person 276, 889, 892, 976, R13
    objective R14
    third-person 276, 1353, R13
    third-person limited R14
    third-person omniscient 1353, R13

Postmodernism R14

Prologue R14

Propaganda 1173, R14

Props R14

Prose R14

Protagonist 191, 1075, R14

Proverbs 1309, 1311, R14

Psalm R14

Pun 304, R14

Puritan writing R14

Quatrains 253, R14, R16

Rationalism R14

Realism 916, 1066, R14

Refrain 304, 1206, R14

Regionalism R14

Regionalist novel 965

Renaissance R15

Repetition 289, 765, 871, 940, 942, 1207, 1261, R15

Resolution 369, 1211, 1213
    See also Plot.

Restoration Age R15

Rhetoric 1167, 1172, R15

Rhetorical devices 289, 676, 679, 871, 874, R15
    analogy R1
    exclamations 871, 874
    parallelism 284, 288, 289, 422, 601, 681, 765, 871, 874, R12
    repetition 289, 765, 871, 940, R15

Rhetorical question 871, 874, 1172, R15

Rhyme 465
    end R5, R15
    internal R9, R15
    slant 1259, 1261, R16

Rhyme scheme 252, 266, 269, 450, 723, 847, 863, 1107, R15

Rhythm 465, 923, 930, R15
    sprung 952, 955

Rising action 369, 1211, 1213
    See also Plot.

Romance R15

Romanticism R15

Romantic poetry 781, 785

Round character 1198
    See also Character.

Run-on line. *See* Enjambment.

Sarcasm R15

Satire 565, 573, 778, 991, R15

Scansion 764, R16

Scene R16

Science fiction R16

Sensory details 786, 793, 876, 879, 1118, 1175, 1183
    See also Imagery.

Septet R16

Sequence 23, 52, 1319, 1324
    See also Sonnet sequence.

Sestet 253, 517, R16
    See also Sonnet.

Setting 53, 531, 716, 1076, 1210, 1296, 1302, R16

Shakespearean songs R16

Shakespearean sonnet 252, 253, 866
    See also Sonnet.

Shakespeare's Theater 314–315

Short story 1066–1067, 1208–1215, 1256, R16

Simile 294, 297, 298, 300, 312, 431, 930, 1098, 1100, 1354, R16

Situational irony 116, 123, 404, 584, 851, 1004, 1008, 1198, 1310
    See also Irony.

Slant rhyme 1259, 1261, R16

Social context 10–11, 242–243, 506–507, 698–699, 912–913, 1034–1035, 1232–1233

Social-problem novel 964–965

Soliloquy 305, 336, R16

Song 301

Sonnet 266
    English (Shakespearean) 252, 253, 866, R16
    Italian (Petrarchan) 252, 253, 517, 1092, R16
    meter and rhyme patterns 252
    Spenserian 252, 253, R16

Sonnet sequence 271, R17

Sound devices 458, 879, 1328, 1330, R17
    alliteration 192, 276, 278, 451, 794, 800, 876, 936, 1356, 1359, R1
    assonance 794, 876, 931, 936, R2
    consonance 794, 876, 931, 936, R4
    onomatopoeia 876, 957, 1270, R12

Spatial order 531, R23

Speaker 280, 451, 1243, 1245, R17

Spenserian sonnet 252, 253, R16

Spenserian stanza R17

Spondee R7, R17

Sprung rhythm 952, 955, R17

Stage directions R17

Stanza 760, 763, R17

Stated theme 1191, 1293, R18

Static character 217
    See also Character.

Stereotype R17
    See also Character.

Stream of consciousness 1156, 1163, R17

Structure 1110, 1115, 1172, R17

Style 53, 141, 170, 192, 289, 313, 405, 415, 422, 443, 531, 540, 562, 585, 601, 615, 620, 621, 643, 657, 668, 669, 734, 765, 778, 864, 937, 940, 942, 1116, 1118, 1121, 1136, 1256, R17, R33

Subject R18

Suspense R18

Symbol 51, 297, 458, 755, 759, 1078, 1086, 1146, 1302, R18

Symbolist poetry R18

Symbolize 723, 862, 1109, 1136, 1205, 1302

Synecdoche R18

Tercet R18

Terza rima R18

Tetrameter R18

Theater
    of the absurd 1272, 1275, 1277, R18
    Shakespeare's 314–315

Theme 54, 74, 80, 141, 301, 304, 305, 423, 436, 438, 584, 591, 715, 752, 759, 863, 930, 937, 938, 940, 947, 955, 1075, 1198, 1207, 1261, 1285, 1311
    implied 454, 463, 575, 1191, 1293, R18
    stated 1191, 1293, R18
    universal 454, 463

Thesis 352, 726, 733, 1086, R18

Third-person point of view. *See* Point of view.

Title 1094, 1096, 1100, 1293, R18

Tone 116, 123, 255, 258, 263, 269, 301, 304, 436, 468, 561, 573, 628, 656, 785, 798, 930, 931, 936, 976, 1002, 1004, 1044, 1061, 1075, 1098, 1100, 1109, 1150, 1155, 1163, 1207, 1317, R18, R33
    meditative 452

Tragedy 388, 404, R18–R19

Tragic flaw R19

Tragic hero 316, 388, 404, 405
    See also Tragedy.

Translations 173

Trimeter R19

Trochee R7, R19

Understatement 478, 573, 1293, R19

Universal theme 454, 463

Verbal irony 116, 404, 584, 1006, 1185, 1190, 1317
    See also Irony.

INDEX OF SKILLS

Vernacular 1247, 1255, R19

Verse epistle 587

Verse paragraph 1098, 1100, R19

Villanelle 1206, R19

Voice 305, 312, 649, 656, 1279, 1282, R19, R33

Wit 743, 752, R19

Reading and Critical Thinking

Activating prior knowledge 197, 206, 834, 840, 1360, R21
See also Connecting to personal experience.

Ambiguity, identifying 1340

Analyzing 1, 72, 79, 89, 115, 123, 139, 144, 150, 168, 190, 195, 205, 217, 258, 263, 269, 274, 278, 282, 287, 297, 300, 304, 311, 336, 351, 368, 387, 403, 409, 412, 422, 427, 436, 441, 448, 450, 458, 468, 473, 478, 519, 529, 538, 545, 551, 560, 573, 575, 591, 599, 609, 620, 628, 647, 656, 667, 673, 715, 723, 732, 741, 752, 759, 763, 776, 785, 792, 798, 803, 827, 832, 840, 847, 853, 862, 870, 874, 879, 930, 935, 942, 950, 955, 959, 962, 975, 983, 990, 997, 1002, 1008, 1053, 1065, 1075, 1085, 1092, 1096, 1100, 1104, 1109, 1114, 1121, 1146, 1155, 1162, 1172, 1183, 1189, 1198, 1205, 1245, 1254, 1261, 1270, 1275, 1282, 1292, 1302, 1309, 1317, 1323, 1330, 1338, 1343, 1352, 1359, 1363
argument 352, 368, 603, 610
cause-and-effect relationships 146, 150, 388, 404, 644, 800, 803
Cavalier poetry 453
characteristics of texts R24
characterization 769, 777, 967, 976, 1305, 1310
conflict 1285, 1293
contrasting images 255
cultural context 68, 409, 743, 752
evidence 1078, 1086
figurative language 843, 847, 1110, 1115
figures of speech 294, 297, 431, 1201, 1206
historical context 193, 760, 764

imagery 116
language 1268, 1270
literary influences 960
logical reasoning R24–R25
Medieval theater 153
Metaphors 1110, 1115
Metaphysical poetry 429
mood 796, 798, 923, 930
objectivity 116
persuasive techniques R25
sensory details 786, 1175, 1183
setting 53
sound devices 276, 278, 458, 876, 879
style 942, 1118, 1121
syntax 957, R24
text structure 255, 258, 415, 423, 565, 574, 1062, R22
theme 141
tone 116, 123, 931, 936, 1150, 1155
word choice R24

Applying background knowledge 316, 336, 465, 468, 866, 870, 1090, 1092

Argument
analyzing 352, 368, 603, 610
evaluating 124, 140, 456, 458, 726, 733

Asking questions 1156, 1185

Assessing 387

Assumptions, identifying 1069, 1076, 1340

Author's background, investigating R24

Author's beliefs, drawing conclusions 423, 427, 553, 561

Author's craft, evaluating 336, 351

Authors' culture, comparing and contrasting 68

Author's meaning, drawing conclusions 1107, 1109

Author's purpose, recognizing 154, 169, 854, 863, 1098, 1100, R24

Author's statements, evaluating R24

Background knowledge, applying 316, 336, 465, 468, 866, 870, 1090, 1092

Bias, recognizing 1193, 1198, R25

Big Idea
A Bard for the Ages 243, 246–247
Class, Colonialism, and the Great War 1035, 1036–1037

Colonialism and Postcolonialism 1233, 1236–1237
Disillusionment and Darker Visions 913, 918–919
The Emergence of Realism 913, 916–917
The English Enlightenment and Neoclassicism 507, 512–513
The Epic Warrior 11, 12–13
Globalization 1233, 1238–1239
Humanists and Courtiers 243, 244–245
Making and Remaking Traditions 1233, 1234–1235
Modernism 1035, 1038–1039
Nature and the Imagination 699, 702–703
Optimism and the Belief in Progress 913, 914–915
The Power of Faith 11, 14–15
Puritanism and the Civil War 507, 508–509
The Quest for Truth and Beauty 699, 704–705
The Restoration 507, 510–511
The Sacred and the Secular 243, 248–249
The Stirrings of Romanticism 699, 700–701
The World of Romance 11, 16–17
World War II and Its Aftermath 1035, 1040–1041

Big Idea treatments, comparing and contrasting 54, 68, 454, 463, 621, 643, 875, 887, 938, 947, 1044, 1061, 1257, 1266

Building background 23, 55, 58, 74, 83, 93, 116, 124, 146, 154, 172, 193, 197, 210, 255, 260, 266, 271, 276, 280, 284, 294, 301, 305, 316, 337, 352, 369, 388, 406, 415, 425, 438, 446, 456, 459, 460, 461, 465, 470, 475, 517, 520, 533, 543, 547, 553, 565, 587, 593, 603, 615, 623, 629, 635, 639, 649, 660, 670, 709, 718, 726, 743, 755, 769, 781, 796, 800, 804, 829, 834, 843, 851, 866, 871, 876, 880, 882, 884, 923, 931, 940, 943, 944, 946, 952, 957, 960, 967, 980, 985, 995, 999, 1004, 1046, 1054, 1057,

1059, 1069, 1078, 1090, 1094, 1098, 1101, 1107, 1110, 1118, 1123, 1139, 1150, 1156, 1167, 1175, 1185, 1193, 1201, 1243, 1259, 1263, 1264, 1268, 1272, 1279, 1285, 1296, 1305, 1314, 1319, 1328, 1332, 1340, 1345, 1356

Cause-and-effect order R22

Cause-and-effect relationships, analyzing 146, 150, 388, 404, 644, 800, 803

Characteristics of texts, analyzing R24

Characterization, analyzing 769, 777, 967, 976, 1305, 1310

Characters
 comparing and contrasting 849
 making inferences about 1123, 1137, 1272, 1275
 mapping 1305
 responding to 210, 217, 387

Chronological order 423, R22, R23

Clarifying meaning 260, 264, 952, 957, 959, 980, 983, 1185, 1190, 1279, 1282

Comparing and contrasting 1314
 Authors' culture 68
 Big Idea treatments 54, 68, 454, 463, 621, 643, 875, 887, 938, 947, 1044, 1061, 1257, 1266
 characters 849
 cultures 54, 68, 454, 463, 621, 643, 1044, 1061, 1257, 1266
 genres 21, 91, 153, 209, 253, 315, 406, 429, 453, 613, 767, 849, 965, 1067, 1277
 historical contexts 938, 947
 imagery 875, 887, 995, 997, 1094, 1096
 literary traditions 875, 887
 profiles 1257, 1266
 speakers 280, 282
 style 621, 643
 themes 54, 423, 454, 463, 938, 947
 tone 269, 1044, 1061
 visualizations 755

Comparison-contrast order R22

Comprehension, monitoring 172, 192, 547, 551, 718, 724, 952, 955

Conclusions, drawing 209, 298, 300, 305, 312, 423, 427, 553, 561, 851, 853, 866, 1107, 1109, 1332, 1339, R23

Conflict, analyzing 1285, 1293

Connecting
 to the Big Idea 51, 72, 79, 89, 115, 123, 139, 144, 150, 168, 190, 195, 205, 217, 258, 263, 269, 271, 274, 276, 278, 280, 282, 287, 297, 300, 304, 311, 336, 351, 368, 387, 403, 409, 422, 427, 436, 441, 448, 450, 458, 468, 473, 478, 519, 529, 538, 545, 551, 553, 560, 565, 573, 575, 591, 599, 609, 620, 628, 656, 667, 673, 715, 723, 732, 752, 759, 763, 776, 785, 792, 798, 803, 827, 840, 847, 853, 862, 870, 874, 879, 930, 935, 942, 955, 959, 975, 980, 990, 997, 1002, 1008, 1053, 1075, 1085, 1092, 1096, 1100, 1109, 1114, 1121, 1146, 1155, 1162, 1172, 1183, 1189, 1198, 1205, 1245, 1254, 1261, 1270, 1275, 1282, 1292, 1302, 1309, 1317, 1323, 1330, 1332, 1338, 1352, 1359, 1363
 to contemporary issues 51, 623, 628, 741, 985, 991, 1046, 1053, 1314, 1317
 to personal experience 142, 266, 269, 999, 1002, 1345, 1353, R21
 to reading selections 23, 54, 74, 83, 93, 116, 124, 146, 154, 172, 197, 210, 255, 260, 266, 284, 294, 301, 305, 316, 412, 415, 425, 438, 446, 454, 456, 465, 470, 475, 517, 520, 533, 543, 547, 587, 593, 603, 615, 621, 623, 647, 649, 660, 709, 718, 726, 743, 755, 769, 781, 796, 800, 804, 832, 834, 843, 851, 866, 871, 875, 876, 923, 931, 938, 940, 950, 952, 957, 962, 967, 980, 985, 995, 999, 1004, 1044, 1046, 1065, 1069, 1078, 1090, 1094, 1098, 1104, 1107, 1110, 1118, 1123, 1139, 1150, 1156, 1167, 1175, 1185, 1193, 1201, 1243, 1257, 1259, 1268, 1272, 1279, 1285, 1296, 1305, 1314, 1319, 1328, 1343, 1345, 1356

Connotation, examining 271, 274, 948

Contrasting images, analyzing 255

Credibility, evaluating 150, 337, 351, 660, 668, R24

Cultures, comparing and contrasting 54, 68, 454, 463, 621, 643, 1044, 1061, 1257, 1266

Cultural context, analyzing 68, 752

Denotation, examining 271, 274, 948

Determining
 main idea and supporting details 284, 288, 670
 patterns 876

Distinguishing fact and opinion 410, 649, 657, 1167, 1172

Drawing conclusions 209, 298, 300, 866, R23
 about author's beliefs 423, 427, 553, 561
 about author's meaning 1107, 1109
 about meaning 851, 853, 1332, 1339
 about theme 305, 312

Evaluating 51, 72, 79, 89, 115, 123, 139, 144, 168, 190, 195, 205, 217, 258, 263, 269, 274, 276, 282, 287, 297, 300, 304, 311, 336, 368, 387, 403, 409, 412, 422, 427, 436, 441, 448, 450, 468, 473, 478, 519, 529, 538, 545, 551, 560, 573, 575, 591, 599, 609, 620, 628, 647, 656, 667, 673, 715, 723, 732, 741, 752, 759, 763, 776, 785, 792, 798, 803, 827, 832, 840, 847, 853, 862, 870, 879, 930, 935, 942, 950, 955, 959, 975, 983, 990, 997, 1002, 1008, 1053, 1065, 1075, 1078, 1085, 1092, 1096, 1100, 1104, 1109, 1114, 1121, 1146, 1155, 1162, 1172, 1183, 1189, 1198, 1205, 1245, 1254, 1261, 1270, 1275, 1282, 1292, 1302, 1309, 1317, 1323, 1338, 1343, 1352, 1359, 1363
 argument 124, 140, 456, 458, 726, 733
 author's craft 336, 351
 author's statements R24
 credibility 150, 337, 351, 660, 668, R24
 historical influences 5, 670, 829, 960, 1042
 imagery 150
 rhetorical devices 871, 874
 sound devices 1328, 1330

Evidence, analyzing 1078, 1086

Examining
 connotation 271, 274, 948
 denotation 271, 274, 948

Fact and opinion, distinguishing 410, 649, 657, 1167, 1172

Faulty reasoning, recognizing R25

Figurative language

analyzing 843, 847, 1110, 1115
identifying 843
Figures of speech, analyzing 294, 297, 431, 1201, 1206
Generalizations, making 615, 620, 1004, 1009, 1259, 1261, R23
Genres
comparing/contrasting 21, 91, 153, 209, 253, 315, 406, 429, 453, 613, 767, 849, 965, 1067, 1277
identifying (Romantic poetry) 781, 785
Graphic organizers 644, R21–R22
character (map) 769
chart 23, 69, 74, 83, 124, 172, 197, 255, 263, 264, 266, 276, 280, 294, 305, 352, 369, 387, 388, 406, 410, 415, 425, 431, 438, 446, 451, 456, 465, 475, 517, 533, 547, 553, 565, 603, 623, 709, 948, 1046, 1078, 1118, 1247, 1259, 1268, 1296, 1328, 1332, 1345, 1360
checklist 337
compare-contrast chart 280
concept web 931, 940, 1305
continuum 116
diagram 52, 260, 1243
double-entry journal 985
Foldables 18, 250, 514, 706, 920, 1042, 1240, R26–R29
idea web 284
map 1, 2
mood graphic 169
paraphrase chart 587
response-evidence chart 210
sequence chart 1319
Venn diagram 755, 1314
web diagram 191, 1272
word web 271
Historical context
analyzing 193, 760, 764
comparing and contrasting 938, 947
Historical influences, evaluating 5, 670, 829, 960, 1042
Identifying
ambiguity 1340
assumptions 1069, 1076, 1340
clues 575
figurative language 843, 1110
genre: Romantic poetry 781, 785

main ideas (in poems) 253
problem and solution 517, 519, 736
sequence 23, 52, 1319, 1324
Imagery
analyzing and evaluating 150
comparing and contrasting 875, 887, 995, 997, 1094, 1096
interpreting 593, 600, 709, 716, 1356, 1359
Independent reading 228–229, 423, 492–493, 684–685, 898–899, 1009, 1020–1021, 1116, 1218–1219, 1359, 1374–1375
Inferring. See Making inferences.
Information, synthesizing 1101, 1247, 1255, R23
Interpreting 51, 72, 79, 89, 115, 123, 139, 144, 150, 168, 190, 195, 205, 217, 258, 263, 269, 274, 276, 282, 287, 297, 300, 304, 311, 336, 351, 368, 387, 403, 409, 412, 422, 427, 436, 441, 448, 450, 458, 468, 473, 478, 519, 529, 538, 545, 551, 560, 573, 575, 591, 599, 609, 620, 628, 647, 656, 667, 673, 715, 723, 732, 741, 752, 759, 763, 776, 785, 792, 798, 803, 827, 832, 840, 847, 853, 862, 870, 874, 879, 930, 935, 942, 950, 955, 959, 962, 975, 983, 990, 997, 1002, 1008, 1053, 1065, 1075, 1078, 1085, 1092, 1096, 1100, 1104, 1109, 1114, 1121, 1146, 1155, 1162, 1172, 1183, 1189, 1198, 1205, 1245, 1254, 1261, 1270, 1275, 1282, 1292, 1302, 1309, 1317, 1319, 1330, 1338, 1343, 1352, 1359, 1363
imagery 593, 600, 709, 716, 1356, 1359
tone 1150
Investigating, author's background R24
Language, analyzing 1268, 1270
Literary criticism 18, 123, 265, 297, 405, 583, 669, 1367, R24
Literary influences, analyzing 960
Literary response R237
Literary traditions, comparing and contrasting 875, 887
Logical reasoning
analyzing R24–R25
deductive reasoning R24
inductive reasoning R24

Logical sequence R23
Main ideas 352
determining 284, 288, 670, R23
determining (in poems) 253
Making generalizations 615, 620, 1004, 1009, 1259, 1261, R23
Making inferences 449, 451, R23
about characters 1123, 1137, 1272, 1275
about theme 74, 80, 438, 442, 575, 584
Making predictions 1139, 1147, R23
Mapping, characters 1305
Meaning
clarifying 260, 264, 952, 957, 959, 980, 983, 1185, 1190, 1279, 1282
drawing conclusions about 851, 853, 1332, 1339
restating 260
Metaphors
analyzing 1110, 1115
identifying 1110
Modes of reasoning, analyzing R24–R25
Monitoring comprehension 172, 192, 547, 551, 718, 724, 952, 955, R21
Mood
analyzing 796, 798, 923, 930
responding to 80
Objectivity, analyzing 116
Order of importance sequence R23
Paraphrasing 93, 115, 473, 587, 592, 980, R23, R37
Pattern of organization, analyzing R24
Patterns, determining 876
Persuasive techniques, analyzing R25
Predicting 369, 387
Predictions
making 1139, 1147, R23
verifying 1139
Previewing 3, 69, 142, 410, 475, 479, 644, 736, 948, 1062, 1360
Primary sources 485, 792, 1162, 1254
Prior knowledge, activating 197, 206, 834, 840, 1360, R21
Problem and solution, identifying 517, 519, 736
Profiles, comparing and contrasting 1257, 1266

Questioning 446, 448, 543, 547, 1098, 1243, 1245

Reading check 7, 13, 15, 17, 239, 241, 245, 247, 249, 503, 505, 509, 511, 513, 695, 697, 701, 703, 705, 909, 911, 915, 917, 919, 1031, 1033, 1037, 1039, 1041, 1231, 1235, 1237, 1239

Reading graphical information 8, 9, 240, 241, 504, 505, 698, 699, 910, 911, 1032, 1033, 1230, 1231, R22

Reading process R20–R25

Recalling 51, 72, 79, 89, 115, 123, 139, 144, 150, 168, 190, 195, 205, 217, 258, 263, 269, 274, 276, 282, 287, 297, 300, 304, 311, 336, 351, 368, 387, 403, 409, 412, 422, 427, 436, 441, 448, 450, 458, 468, 473, 478, 519, 529, 538, 545, 551, 560, 573, 575, 591, 599, 609, 620, 628, 647, 656, 667, 673, 715, 723, 732, 741, 752, 759, 763, 776, 785, 792, 798, 803, 827, 832, 840, 847, 853, 862, 870, 874, 879, 930, 935, 942, 950, 955, 959, 962, 975, 983, 990, 997, 1002, 1008, 1053, 1065, 1075, 1078, 1085, 1092, 1096, 1100, 1104, 1109, 1114, 1121, 1146, 1155, 1162, 1172, 1183, 1189, 1198, 1205, 1245, 1254, 1261, 1270, 1275, 1282, 1292, 1302, 1309, 1317, 1319, 1330, 1338, 1343, 1352, 1359, 1363

Recognizing
  Author's purpose 154, 169, 854, 863, 1098, 1100, R24
  bias 1193, 1198, R25
  faulty reasoning R25

Responding 51, 72, 79, 89, 115, 123, 139, 144, 150, 168, 190, 195, 205, 217, 258, 263, 269, 274, 276, 282, 287, 297, 300, 304, 311, 336, 351, 368, 387, 403, 412, 422, 427, 436, 441, 448, 450, 458, 468, 473, 478, 490, 519, 529, 538, 545, 551, 560, 573, 575, 591, 599, 609, 620, 628, 647, 656, 667, 673, 715, 723, 732, 741, 752, 759, 763, 776, 785, 792, 798, 803, 827, 832, 840, 847, 853, 862, 870, 874, 879, 930, 935, 942, 950, 955, 959, 962, 975, 983, 990, 997, 1002, 1008, 1053, 1065, 1075, 1078, 1085, 1092, 1096, 1100, 1104, 1109, 1114, 1121, 1146, 1155, 1162, 1172, 1183, 1189, 1198, 1205, 1245, 1254, 1261, 1270, 1275, 1282, 1292, 1302, 1309, 1317, 1319, 1330, 1338, 1343, 1352, 1359, 1363
  to characters 210, 217
  to literature R23
  to mood 80
  to tone 301, 304

Restating, meaning 260

Reviewing 804, 828

Rhetorical devices, evaluating 871, 874

Semantic features analysis R21

Sensory details, analyzing 786, 1175, 1183

Sequence R23
  identifying 23, 52, 1319, 1324
  logical R23

Setting, analyzing 53

Setting purpose for reading 23, 69, 72, 83, 93, 116, 124, 142, 146, 154, 172, 193, 197, 210, 255, 260, 266, 271, 276, 280, 284, 294, 301, 305, 316, 406, 410, 415, 425, 438, 446, 456, 465, 470, 475, 517, 520, 533, 543, 547, 553, 565, 585, 593, 603, 623, 644, 649, 660, 670, 709, 718, 726, 736, 743, 755, 769, 781, 796, 800, 804, 829, 834, 843, 851, 866, 871, 876, 923, 931, 940, 948, 952, 957, 960, 967, 980, 985, 995, 999, 1004, 1046, 1062, 1069, 1090, 1094, 1098, 1101, 1107, 1110, 1118, 1139, 1150, 1156, 1167, 1175, 1185, 1193, 1201, 1243, 1259, 1268, 1272, 1279, 1285, 1296, 1305, 1314, 1319, 1328, 1332, 1340, 1345, 1356, 1360, R21

Signal words R22

Silent reading R23

Skimming R21

Sound devices
  analyzing 276, 278, 458, 876, 879
  evaluating 1328, 1330

Spatial order 423, 531, R23

Speakers, comparing and contrasting 280, 282

Style
  analyzing 942, 1118, 1121
  comparing and contrasting 621, 643

Subheads, reading 736, 1062

Summarizing 83, 89, 425, 517, 533, 539, 804, R23

Supporting details, determining 284, 288, 670, R23

Syntax, analyzing 957, R24

Synthesizing information 1101, 1247, 1255, R23

Text structure
  analyzing 255, 258, 415, 423, 565, 574, 1062, R22
  cause-and-effect order 423, R22
  chronological order 423, R22
  comparison-contrast order 423, R22
  spatial order 423, 531, R23

Theme
  analyzing 141
  comparing and contrasting themes 54, 423, 454, 463, 938, 947
  drawing conclusions about 305, 312
  making inferences 74, 80, 438, 442, 575, 584

Thesis 284, 352
  See also Main ideas.

Tone
  analyzing 116, 123, 931, 936, 1150, 1155
  comparing and contrasting 269, 1044, 1061
  interpreting 1150
  responding to 301, 304

Verifying predictions 1139

Visualizations, comparing and contrasting 755

Visualizing 520, 530, 755, 759, 1156, 1163, 1296, 1303

Who, what, why, where, and when questions R23

Word choice, analyzing R24

Vocabulary

Academic vocabulary 52, 80, 140, 169, 192, 206, 278, 282, 300, 404, 437, 442, 448, 451, 458, 479, 519, 530, 539, 561, 574, 584, 592, 600, 610, 657, 716, 724, 733, 753, 764, 793, 798, 803, 828, 853, 863, 936, 942, 959, 991, 997, 1009, 1086, 1092, 1109, 1115, 1137, 1147, 1163, 1190, 1206, 1245, 1261, 1275, 1282, 1293, 1310, 1324, 1339, 1353, R82–R84

Analogies 23, 52, 74, 80, 89, 124, 140, 197, 206, 210, 217, 260, 264, 271, 274, 438, 442, 444, 475, 479, 553, 561, 593, 600, 709, 716, 843, 847, 923, 930, 999, 1002, 1046, 1053, 1078, 1086, 1123, 1137, 1185, 1190, 1268, 1270, 1305, 1310, 1332, 1339, R1

Anglo-Saxon word parts 73, 154

Antonyms 146, 352, 368, 520, 530, 543, 545, 615, 620, 649, 657, 781, 793, 1139, 1147

Base words R20

Connotation 271, 274, 611, 660, 668, 726, 733, 1247, 1255, R4, R20

Context clues 116, 123, 305, 312, 388, 404, 425, 427, 470, 473, 585, 592, 603, 610, 804, 828, 866, 870, 931, 936, 967, 976, 1094, 1096, 1110, 1115, 1167, 1172, 1201, 1206, 1296, 1303, R20
   contrast 207
   example 207
   restatement 207
   synonym 207

Denotation 271, 274, 611, 660, 668, 726, 733, 1247, 1255, R4, R20

Etymology 266, 301, 337, 547, 781, 993, 1148

Greek roots (word parts) 154, 304, 735

Homophones 1312

Latin roots (word parts) 154, 169, 304, 539, 735

Math and science terms 1148

Middle English word parts 90–91, 169, 304

Old English roots 73, 304

Political and historical terms 993

Prefixes 533, 623, 735, 832, R20

Roots 533, 623, 735, 832, 1148

Suffixes 316, 336, 533, 623, 735, 832, 1148, R20

Synonyms 93, 115, 172, 192, 207, 255, 258, 294, 297, 369, 387, 415, 423, 431, 437, 465, 468, 541, 565, 574, 584, 718, 724, 851, 863, 876, 879, 1098, 1100, 1118, 1121, 1156, 1163, 1193, 1198, 1314, 1317, 1328, 1330, 1356, 1359

Thesaurus
   dictionary style 541
   traditional style 541

Vocabulary reference materials R20
   thesaurus 541

Word origins 73, 83, 266, 269, 301, 304, 337, 351, 547, 551, 735, 769, 777, 781, 785, 847, 871, 952, 955, 980, 983, 993, 1150, 1155, 1175, 1285, 1293, 1319, 1324, R20

Word parts 73, 154, 169, 284, 288, 316, 336, 533, 539, 623, 735, 743, 752, 832, 840, 985, 991, 1069, 1076, 1148, 1183, 1345, 1353, R20

Writing

Action verbs 1214

Active voice 895

Analysis
   of cultural context 463, 1061
   literary 1010–1017
   personal 889
   style 643
   theme 947

Analyzing
   character 1137, 1339
   comic devices 1198
   couplets 300
   cultural context 463, 992, 1061
   figurative language 1303
   genre elements 150, 217, 264, 540, 669, 778, 1092, 1325
   historical context 992
   humor 1198
   imagery 1147
   mood 278
   plot 1183
   poem for literary analysis 1013
   professional writing model 219–220, 675–676, 889–890, 1011–1012, 1209–1211, 1365–1366
   setting 53, 531
   sound devices 192, 458, 794
   style 643
   theme 141
   thesis 734
   tone 437, 931, 1317
   workshop writing model 222–223, 483, 678–679, 892–893, 1014–1015, 1212–1213, 1368–1369

APA-citation style R41

Appeals

   emotional 675, 677, 678
   ethical 676, 677
   logical 675, 677, 678

Applying
   form 752, 874
   style 1256
   theme 752

Argument 674 *See also* Persuasive Writing.
   organizing 677

Audience 219, 481, 675, 677, 889, 1011, 1209, 1365

Author's craft
   evaluating 336, 351, 479, 574, 585, 601, 628, 864, 879, 977, 1116, 1155, 1245, 1275, 1354
   responding to 847

Author's purpose, exploring 115, 170, 1009, 1087

Background 678, 1014

Bibliography, working R36–R37

Bibliography card R36

Blank verse 405

Brainstorming 847, 1311, 1367, R30

Business e-mail R45

Business writing
   business e-mail R45
   job application R44
   letter of application R42
   memos R45
   résumé R43

Call for action 677

Character
   analyzing 1137, 1339
   comparing/contrasting 1294
   describing 1210, 1212
   responding to 620

Chronological order, clarifying with 1219

Citing, titles 1371

Citing sources 489

Clarifying with chronological order 1219

Climax 1211, 1213

Clustering R30

CMS-citation style R40

Comic devices, analyzing 1198

Comparing/contrasting characters 1294

ideas 610
imagery 798
motifs 313
poems 1109
profiles 1266
style 657
theme 423, 724, 759
theme and tone 1207
tone 269, 468, 724
Conclusion 220, 486, 893, 1012, 1015,
1366, 1369
draw and elaborate 1013
Conflict
creating and resolving 1208–1215
responding to 1164
Connecting, to thesis 1369
Contemporary relevance,
evaluating 206, 519, 828
Conventions R34
Conversational tone 223, 890, 1365
Counterarguments 676, 679
Creative writing
blank verse 405
classified advertisement 1311
dialogue 222–223, 562, 1209, 1212
diary entry 752
epitaph 448
memo 827
ode 874
scripted version of poems 282
short story 1208–1215, 1256
sonnets 942
Critical evidence, identifying 1367
Critical review 1364–1371
Cultural context, analysis 463
Describing
character 1210
setting 1210
Descriptive details 220, 221, 222, 223,
224, 890, 893
Descriptive essay 218–225
Descriptive writing 80, 520, 560, 562,
R35
Details
descriptive 220, 222, 223, 890, 893
organizing 221, 891
summarizing with 517
Dialogue 222–223, 562, 1209, 1212
punctuating 1215, 1311

Direct quotations 485, 489, 1011, 1017,
1366, 1369, R37
Documenting sources 487, R36,
R38–R41
Drafting 222–223, 483–486, 678–679,
892–893, 1014–1015, 1212–1213,
1368–1369, R31
Draw conclusions 1013
Editing 225, 489, 681, 895, 1017, 1215,
1371, R32
Elaboration 1013
with anecdotes 220
with descriptive details 222, 224
Emotional appeal 675, 677, 679
Essay 284
descriptive 218–224
persuasive 674–681
reflective 888–895
Ethical appeal 676, 677
Evaluating
argument 443
author's craft 336, 351, 479, 574, 585,
601, 628, 864, 879, 977, 1116, 1155,
1245, 1275, 1354
contemporary relevance 206, 519,
828
a literary work (critical review)
1364–1371
rhetorical devices 289
sound devices 451
sources 481, 487, R37
Evidence. See Supporting evidence.
Examples, in critical review 1368
Exploring author's purpose 115, 170,
765, 1009, 1087
Expository writing 53, 170, 192, 206,
217, 218, 224, 264, 274, 300, 423, 437,
443, 451, 458, 468, 479, 480–489, 519,
585, 592, 601, 610, 620, 628, 657, 669,
724, 765, 785, 794, 879, 887, 937, 977,
992, 1009, 1087, 1100, 1116, 1137, 1147,
1183, 1191, 1198, 1256, 1303, 1354,
1364–1371, R35
Fictional elements, describing 1210
Figurative language, analyzing 1303
First-person point of view 889, 892
Flexibility 1368
Form, applying 752, 874, 942
Freewriting R30

Genre elements, analyzing 150, 217,
264, 540, 669, 778, 1092, 1325
Graphic organizer
chart 53, 192, 221, 264, 313, 437, 479,
669, 716, 724, 828, 992, 1311, 1354
cluster diagram 481
concept web 937, 1137
diagram 1294
double-entry journal 985
prewriting 53, 206, 531, 540, 677,
734, 1325, 1339
Venn diagram 610
Heading R34
Historical investigation 480–489
Humor, analyzing 1198
Ideas R33
compare/contrast 610
describing 221
exploring 481, 891
finding 221, 1212
Imagery 274, 437, 562, 798
analyzing 1147
comparison 887
Impression
clarifying 221
dominant 223
Information, searching for R36
Introduction 219, 1365, 1368
Inversion 313
Issues, exploring 677
Job application R44
Journal, double-entry 985
Journalists' Questions 481
Letter 610
Letter of application R42
Literary analysis 1010–1017
Literary criticism 264, 297, 405, 443,
734, 803, 840, 870, 997, 1085, 1191
Literary elements 1012, 1014, 1015
Literary interpretation 889, 892
Literary present tense 1013, 1371
Literary research paper, historical
investigation 480–489
Logical appeal 675, 677
Main idea 253, 284
Main point 1015
Manuscript guidelines 225, 489, 681,
895, 1017, 1215, 1371, R34
Margins R34

Memo R45
   writing 827
MLA-citation style R39
Mood
   analyzing 278
   responding to 80, 1282
Narration 1208–1215
Narrative writing R35
Note cards 482, R37
Note taking. *See* Research paper.
Numbering R34
Opposing point of view 1366, 1369
Organization 223, 443, 484, 677, 679,
   891, 892, 893, 1012, 1013, 1015, 1369,
   R33
Outlining 170, 289, 443, 482, 891, 1164,
   1367, R37–R38
Pace of story 1212
Paragraphs 1212
   organization 610
   structure 484
   transitions 488–489
Paraphrasing 217, 482, 656, R37
Passive voice 895
Peer review 224, 488, 894, R31
Personal analysis 889
Personal opinions, for critical
   review 1367
Persuasive writing 427, 674–681, 683,
   1364–1371, R35
Plagiarism 482, R37
Plot
   analyzing 1183
   planning 1212
   responding to 368
Plot summary 1365, 1368
Poems, comparing/contrasting 1109
Point of view 1209, 1212, 1213
   adding evidence to support 1370
   first-person 889, 892
   opposing 1366, 1369
Presentation R34
Presenting 225, 489, 681, 895, 1017,
   1215, 1371, R32
Present tense 1013
Prewriting 221, 481–482, 677, 891, 1013,
   1212, 1367, R30
Primary sources 485, 792, 1162, 1254,
   R36

Professional writing model,
   analyzing 219–220, 675–676,
   889–890, 1011–1012, 1209–1211,
   1365–1366
Proofreading 225, 489, 681, 895, 1017,
   1215, 1371, R32
Proofreading symbols R32
Publishing R32
Punctuating, titles 1371
Purpose 219, 481, 675, 889, 1011, 1209,
   1365
Quickwrite 57, 459, 462, 638, 642, 881,
   886, 945, 1058, 1265
Quotations
   direct 485, 489, 1011, 1017, 1366,
   1369, R37
   literary 484
   long 1017
Quoting sources 482
   punctuating 489, 1017, R37
Reflection 891
Reflective essay 888–895
Research paper 480–489, 992, R36–R41
Resolution 1211, 1213
Responding
   to argument 368
   to author's craft 847
   to character 620
   to conflict 1164
   to imagery 274, 437, 562
   to mood 80, 1282
   to plot 368
   to setting 716
   to theme 448, 592, 937, 1191, 1261,
   1311
   to title 1100
   to tone 785, 1002
Response essay 1191
Résumé R43
Review 1245
Revising 53, 141, 170, 192, 224, 289, 313,
   443, 488–489, 531, 540, 585, 601, 669,
   680, 765, 778, 794, 864, 894, 937, 977,
   992, 1016, 1087, 1116, 1191, 1207, 1214,
   1256, 1294, 1311, 1325, 1354, 1370, R31
Rhetorical devices 676, 679
   evaluating 289
Rising action 1211, 1213

Rubrics 218, 224, 480, 488, 674, 680,
   888, 894, 1010, 1016, 1208, 1214, 1364,
   1370
Satiric writing 574, 778
Secondary sources 485, R36
Selecting, poem for literary
   analysis 1013
Sentence fluency R34
Sentence fragments 1215
Sentences
   compound 1199
   run-on 1199
   short, choppy 225
   wordy 1016
Sentence structure, varying 894
Setting
   analyzing 53, 531
   describing 1210
   responding to 716
Short story 1208–1215
Sound devices
   analyzing 192, 458
   evaluating 451
Sources
   documenting 487, R36, R38–R41
   evaluating 481, 487, R37
   Internet 657, 724, 1121, 1294
   paraphrasing 482, R37
   primary 485
   punctuating quotations 489, R37
   quoting 482, 489, R37
   secondary 485
   summarizing 482, R37
   using variety of 481, 487
Spacing R34
Style R33
   analysis 643
   applying 1256
   comparing/contrasting 657
Subject 219, 222
   choosing 221
Summarizing 734, 977, 1164
   information 484, 517
   plot 1365, 1368
   sources 482, R37
Supporting evidence 679, 890, 892,
   1011, 1012, 1014, 1015, 1367
   adding 1370
   details 483, 676
   quotations 484, 485, R37

Theme
    analyzing 141, 947
    applying 752
    comparing/contrasting 423, 724, 759, 1207
    responding to 448, 592, 937, 1191, 1261, 1311
Thesis 482, 483, 675, 677, 678, 1011, 1014, 1368
    analyzing 734
    connecting to 1369
    developing 1367
    narrowing 1013
Thesis statement R38
Title R34
    citing 1371
    punctuating 1371
    responding to 1100
Tone R33
    comparing/contrasting 269, 468, 724, 1207
    conversational 223, 890, 1365
    responding to 785, 1002
    using appropriate 680
Topic
    finding 481
    narrowing 481
    selecting R36
Traits of Strong Writing 224, 488, 680, 894, 1016, 1214, 1370, R33–R34
Transitions 488–489
Verb tense 1371
Voice 890, R33
Word choice 585, R24, R33
Wordy sentences 1016
Works-cited list 482, 487, 489, R38
Workshop model, analyzing 222–223, 483, 678–679, 892–893, 1014–1015, 1213, 1368–1369
Writing about literature 53, 80, 115, 141, 150, 170, 192, 206, 217, 264, 269, 274, 278, 289, 300, 313, 351, 368, 404, 423, 427, 437, 443, 448, 451, 458, 468, 479, 519, 531, 540, 562, 574, 584, 592, 601, 610, 620, 628, 657, 669, 716, 724, 734, 752, 759, 765, 778, 785, 794, 798, 828, 847, 864, 874, 879, 930, 937, 942, 977, 992, 1002, 1009, 1087, 1092, 1100, 1109, 1116, 1137, 1147, 1155, 1164, 1183, 1191, 1198, 1207, 1245, 1256, 1261, 1275, 1282, 1294, 1303, 1311, 1317, 1325, 1339, 1354
Writing process R30–R41

Grammar

Abbreviations R57
Active voice 895
    See also Voice.
Adjective 170, 562, R46
    comparative degree 1354, R46
    positive degree 1354, R46
    predicate R46
    proper R46
    superlative degree 1354, R46
Adverb 562, R46
    comparative degree R46
    conjunctive R47
    superlative degree R46
Adverb clause 978
    See also Clause.
Agreement
    pronoun-antecedent 658
    subject-verb 290
Antecedent 658
    See also Pronoun.
Apostrophe R56–R57
Appositives R46
Articles
    definite R46
    indefinite R46
Brackets R55
Capitalization R53
    in poetry 937
Clause
    adjective R47
    adverb R47
    main R46
    noun R47
    subordinate R46, R47
Colon 977, 1191, 1256, R54
Comma R54–R55
    with coordinating conjunctions 1088, 1199
    with nonessential elements 1326
    serial 540
Comma splice 225
Comparative degree 1354, R46
Complement
    direct object R47
    indirect object R47
    object complement R47
    predicate adjective R47
    predicate nominative R47
    subject complement R47
Compound words, forming R59
Conjunction
    coordinating 1088, 1116, 1199, R47
    correlative 443, R47
    subordinating 978, 1116, R47
Conjunctive adverb R47
Connotation 271, 274, 611, 1173, R4, R20
Coordinating conjunction 1116, R47
    using commas with 1088, 1199
Dangling modifiers 753
Dash 1087, R55
Degrees of comparison 1354, R46
Denotation 271, 274, 611, 1173, R4, R20
Dialogue, punctuating 1311
Diction 405, 585
Direct object. *See* Complement.
Doubling final consonant R59
Ellipsis points R56
Exclamation point 864, R54
Gerund 1164, 1325, R48
Hyphen R57
Indirect object. *See* Complement.
Infinitive R48
    split 562
Interjection 992, R48
Inverted order R48
Italics 734, R56
    for titles 1371
Literary present tense 1371
Modifiers, dangling 753
Mood of verb
    imperative mood R48
    indicative mood R48
    subjunctive mood R48
Nonessential elements 1326
Noun 562, R48
    abstract R48
    collective R48
    common R48
    compound R48
    noun of direct address R48
    possessive R48
    proper R48
Noun clause. *See* Clause.
Number R49

Object complement. *See* Complement.
Parallelism (parallel structure) 601, 681, 765
Parentheses R55
Parenthetical expressions 669
Participle 1325, R49
Parts of speech
   adjectives 170, 562, R46
   adverbs 562, R46
   nouns 562, R48
   pronouns 53, R49
   verbs 93, 151, 192, 562, R51
Period R54
Phrase
   absolute R49
   appositive R49
   gerund R49
   infinitive 562, R49
   participial 1325, R49
   prepositional R49
   verb R49
Plurals, forming R58
Positive degree 1354, R46
Possessive 53
Possessive noun. *See* Noun.
Predicate 93
   complete R49
   compound R49
   simple R49
Prefixes
   forming R59
Preposition
   compound R49
Prepositional phrase. *See* Phrase.
Present tense 1013 *See* also Verb tense.
   literary 1371
Pronoun 658, R49
   antecedent R49
   demonstrative R49
   indefinite 141, R49–R50
   intensive R50
   interrogative R50
   nominative R50
   objective R50
   personal R50
   possessive 53, R50
   reflexive R50
   relative R50
Pronoun-antecedent agreement 658
Punctuation R54–R57

of dialogue 1215, 1311
of quotations from sources 489, R37
of titles 1371
Question mark R54
Quotation marks R56
   for author's words R37
   in titles 1371
Run-on sentences 1199
Semicolon 225, 289, R54
Sentence
   complex R50–R51
   compound 1199, R50
   compound-complex R51
   declarative R50
   exclamatory R50
   imperative R50
   interrogative R50
   run-on 1199
   short, choppy 225
   simple R50
   wordy 1016
Sentence fragments 1215
Sentence structure 894, 1199, 1294, R50–R51
Serial commas 540
Simple language 794
Spelling, rules, examples, and exceptions for R58–R60
Split infinitive 562
Subject
   complete R51
   compound R51
   simple 93, R51
Subject-verb agreement 290
Subjunctive mood. *See* Mood of verb.
Suffixes
   and final *y* R59
   and silent *e* R59
Superlative degree 1354, R46
Verb 93, R51
   action 192, 1214, R51
   agreement, subject-verb 290
   auxiliary R51
   intransitive 192, R51
   irregular 151, R51
   linking R51
   regular R51
   transitive 192, R51
Verbal R51
Verb tense 1371

emphatic form R52
future R51
of irregular verb 151, R51
past R51
perfect R51
present R51
progressive form R51
of regular verb 151, R51
Voice (of verb)
   active voice R52
   passive voice 895, R52
Word choice 585, R24
Word comparison 1294
Wordy sentences 1016

Speaking, Listening, and Viewing

Active listening 897, 955
Advertising campaign 289
Audience, for oral presentation 1217, 1373
Brainstorming 1216
Building background 63, 406
Compare/contrast, value systems 706
Critical review, delivering 1372–1373
Critical viewing 168, 190, 250, 406, 409, 529, 560, 585, 667, 767, 776, 935, 1205, 1292, 1323
Debate 250, 540, 920
Discussion Starter 61, 67, 460, 634, 883, 943, 946, 1056, 1060, 1263
Effective listening 1019
Expository presentation 226–227
Graphic organizer
   chart 1114, 1189
   concept map 287
   storyboard 51
   text diagram 311
   Venn diagram 1352
Group discussion 18, 51, 52, 61, 67, 68, 79, 190, 250, 287, 311, 436, 460, 463, 491, 514, 540, 573, 583, 584, 609, 706, 715, 716, 777, 887, 920, 947, 1018, 1019, 1042, 1061, 1114, 1240
Listening 897, 955, 1019
Literary criticism 18, 123, 441, 583, 669, 853, 862, 990, 1085, 1147, 1372–1373
Literature groups 141, 479, 551, 592, 864, 937, 1137, 1339, 1354

Multimedia presentation 490–491
Nonverbal techniques 227, 491, 683, 897, 1019, 1217, 1373
Oral presentation
  advertising campaign 289
  of critical review 1372–1373
  literary criticism 18, 583
  movie review 585
  on nature writing tradition 887
  oral interpretation of short story 1216–1217
  oral response to literature 1018–1019
  persuasive speech 682–683
  photo-essay 226–227
  readers theater 1325
  reflective presentation 896–897
  of satirical proposal 574
  scripted version of poems 282
  of Shakespeare's songs 289
  of song 451
  visual aids 289, 1240
Oral research report 643, 947, 1294
  with visual aids 18, 531, 724
Panel discussion 706, 1240
Performing
  dialogue 53, 170, 562, 778, 1325
  dramatic reading 89, 983, 1207, 1270
  multimedia performance 959
  pantomime 601, 1164
  scripted version of poems 282
  Shakespeare's songs 304
  song 451
Planning
  critical review 1372
  multimedia presentation 491
  oral interpretation 897
  reflective presentation 897
Readers theater 1325
Reading aloud 955
Rehearsing 53, 89, 170, 227, 491, 683, 897, 1217
Role playing 716, 1087
Technology skills, for recording presentation 1373
Time limits 1019
Tone (of voice) 301
Verbal techniques 227, 491, 683, 897, 1019, 1217, 1373
Visual aids

in multimedia presentations (exhibits) 490, 491
in oral research reports 531, 724
in presentations 18, 226, 227, 289, 514, 1240
Visual display
  of artistic treatments of literary works 920
  in characterization 250
  collage 706
  concept 287
  in cultural comparisons 68, 406–409, 1061, 1266
  multimedia 1042
Visual media
  for oral interpretation 1217
  for persuasive speech 683
  for reflective presentation 897

Research, Test-Taking, and Study Skills

ACT R62
APA-citation style R41
Bibliography, working R36–R37, R40
Bibliography card R36
CMS-citation style R40
Documenting sources 487, R36, R38–R41
Essay tests R61, R63
  See also Writing tests.
Evaluating sources 481, 487, R24, R37
Fill-in tests R61
Grammar tests
  paragraph improvement 234–235, 498–499, 690–691, 904–905, 1026–1027, 1224–1225, 1380–1381
Graphic organizers 644, 677, 866, 991, 1191, 1255, 1311, 1325, 1353, R21
  analogy/relationship chart 444
  bound book 250, 706
  cause-and-effect chart 800
  cause-and-effect diagram 960
  cause-and-effect organizer 146, 150, 388
  change frame R21
  character analysis web 769, R22
  charts 23, 53, 69, 73, 74, 83, 124, 140, 141, 142, 172, 192, 193, 197, 205, 206, 255, 263, 264, 266, 276, 294, 305,

313, 352, 369, 387, 388, 405, 406, 410, 415, 425, 431, 437, 438, 446, 451, 456, 465, 475, 479, 517, 531, 533, 540, 543, 547, 553, 561, 565, 591, 600, 603, 623, 656, 669, 670, 709, 716, 718, 724, 726, 736, 743, 777, 796, 827, 843, 876, 977, 1004, 1008, 1018, 1087, 1339, 1354
  checklist 154, 337
  cluster diagram 481
  compare-contrast chart 280
  concept map 287
  concept web 404, 539, 923, 931, 940, 1086, 1137, 1305, R22
  continuum 116
  diagram 52, 260, 1243, 1294
  double-entry journal 985
  etymology chart 993
  evaluation chart 1101
  figures of speech chart 1201
  flowchart R21
  Foldables 18, 250, 514, 706, 920, 1042, 1240, R26–R29
  main idea web 284, R22
  mood graphic 169
  outline chart 734
  for poetry details 1114
  response-evidence chart 210
  semantic chart 611, R21
  sequence chart 1319
  storyboard 51
  text diagram 311
  three-column chart 828, 980, 999, 1069, 1139, 1189, 1268, 1279, 1328
  three-pocket book 1042
  three-tab book 920
  timeline 6–7, 238–239, 502–503, 694–695, 908–909, 1030–1031, 1228–1229
  two-column chart 829, 832, 936, 948, 952, 976, 992, 995, 1046, 1078, 1092, 1107, 1118, 1123, 1167, 1175, 1193, 1247, 1256, 1259, 1296, 1332, 1338, 1340, 1345, 1360
  Venn diagram 610, 668, 755, 1314, 1352
  web diagrams 191, 288, 584, 609, 781, 1272, R22
  word web 271
Information, searching for R36

Internet research 80, 192, 313, 473, 545, 657, 724, 977, 1096, 1121, 1266, 1294
Internet sources 657, 724, 1096, 1266
Keyword search 80, 313, 1121
Matching tests R61
MLA-citation style R39
Multiple-choice tests R61
Note cards 482, R37
Note taking 18, 23, 51, 52, 53, 69, 73, 74, 83, 116, 124, 140, 141, 142, 150, 154, 169, 172, 191, 192, 193, 197, 205, 250, 255, 260, 263, 264, 266, 271, 276, 284, 287, 288, 294, 305, 311, 313, 337, 352, 369, 387, 388, 404, 405, 406, 410, 415, 425, 431, 437, 438, 444, 446, 451, 456, 465, 475, 479, 481, 482, 514, 517, 531, 533, 539, 540, 543, 547, 553, 561, 565, 584, 591, 600, 603, 609, 611, 623, 644, 656, 660, 668, 669, 670, 677, 706, 709, 716, 718, 724, 726, 734, 736, 743, 755, 769, 777, 781, 796, 800, 827, 828, 832, 843, 851, 866, 876, 920, 923, 948, 952, 960, 967, 977, 980, 985, 991, 992, 993, 995, 999, 1004, 1008, 1018, 1042, 1046, 1069, 1078, 1087, 1090, 1101, 1107, 1110, 1118, 1123, 1137, 1139, 1167, 1189, 1193, 1243, 1247, 1256, 1259, 1272, 1279, 1294, 1296, 1305, 1311, 1314, 1319, 1325, 1328, 1332, 1338, 1339, 1340, 1345, 1352, 1353, 1354, 1360, R21–R22
Objective tests R61
    See also Grammar tests; Reading tests; Vocabulary tests.
Observation 1256
Paraphrasing sources 482, R37
Plagiarism 482, R37
Primary sources 485, 792, 1162, 1254, R36
PSAT R62–R63
Quotations
    direct 485, R37

literary 484
    long 1017
Quoting sources 482
    punctuation 489, R37
Reading comprehension questions R63
Reading tests
    essay 1220–1222
    fiction 686–688, 1022–1024
    nonfiction 230–232, 494–496, 900–902
    poetry 1376–1378
References lists R41
Research reports 480–489, 992, R36–R41
    Internet 313, 473, 545, 724, 977, 1096, 1121, 1294
    oral 887
    with visual aids 531
SAT R62–R63
Secondary sources 485, R36
Sentence completion items R62–R63
Short-answer tests R61
Sources
    documenting 487, R36, R38–R41
    evaluating 481, 487, R24, R37
    Internet 657, 724, 1096, 1121, 1266, 1294
    paraphrasing 437, 482
    primary 485
    punctuation for quotations 489, R37
    quoting 482, 489, R37
    secondary 485
    summarizing 482, 517, R37
    variety 481, 487
Standardized tests R62–R63
Subjective (essay) tests. *See* Essay tests.
Summarizing sources 482, R37
Test practice 891, R61–R63
    grammar 234–235, 498–499, 690–691, 904–905, 1026–1027, 1224–1225, 1380–1381
    reading 230–232, 494–496,

686–688, 900–902, 1022–1024, 1220–1222, 1376–1378
    vocabulary 233, 496, 689, 903, 1025, 1223, 1379
    writing 235, 499, 691, 905, 1027, 1225, 1381
Test-taking tips 73, 151, 207, 290, 444, 541, 611, 658, 677, 735, 753, 978, 993, 1013, 1088, 1148, 1173, 1199, 1312, 1326
Thesis 482, 483
Thesis statement R38
Topic
    finding 481
    narrowing 481
    selecting R36
True/false tests R61
Vocabulary tests, sentence
    completion 233, 496, 689, 903, 1025, 1223, 1379
Works-cited list 482, 487, 489, R38, R39
Writing tests
    critical review 1381
    descriptive essay 235
    expository essay 499
    literary analysis 1027
    persuasive essay 691
    reflective essay 905
    short essay 1225

Interdisciplinary Activities

Anthropology 531
Art 258, 765, 1330
Daily life and culture 139, 403, 538, 599, 732, 763, 975, 1309
History 192, 473, 993, 1303
Math 1053, 1148
Music 304
Political science 993
Psychology 206
Science 1148
Sociology 531

INDEX OF AUTHORS AND TITLES

A

Achebe, Chinua 1304
Addison, Joseph 614
"Ah, Are You Digging on My Grave?" 1003
All the world's a stage, from As You Like It 305
Araby 1138
Areopagitica, from 509
Arnold, Matthew 994
At the Pitt-Rivers 1246
Atwood, Margaret 1355
Auden, W. H. 1184
Auld Lang Syne 717
Austen, Jane 768
Autumn 880

B

B. Wordsworth 1331
Bacon, Sir Francis 283, 494
Bashō, Matsuo 880
Bate, Walter Jackson 670
Batter my heart, three-personed God 249
Battle of Maldon, The, from 13
Battle of the Books, The, from 686
Battle of the Pelennor Fields, The, from The Lord of the Rings: The Return of the King, from 58
Be Ye Men of Valor 1166
Beauvoir, Simone de 944
Becker, Robin 889
Bede, The Venerable 82, 230
Behn, Aphra 542
Beowulf, from 22
Blake, William 701, 754, 760, 766–767
Blow, Blow, Thou Winter Wind 301
Boland, Eavan 1278
Bonny Barbara Allan 210
Book of Margery Kempe, The, from 145
Boswell, James 659
Bowen, Elizabeth 1174
Brief History of Heroes, A 69
Brittain, Vera 1037
Brontë, Charlotte 966
Brooke, Rupert 1089

Browning, Elizabeth Barrett 939
Browning, Robert 979
Bunyan, John 532
Burney, Fanny 742
Burns, Robert 717
Byron, George Gordon, Lord 842

C

Camus, Albert 639
Canterbury Tales, The, from 91, 92, 116, 124
Carlyle, Thomas 915
Carpe Diem 459
Carroll, Lewis 956
Catfish Row, Trinidad, from 1365
Chatwin, Bruce 829
Chaucer, Geoffrey 91, 92, 116, 124
Childe Harold's Pilgrimage, from 842
Chimney Sweeper, The, from Songs of Experience 760
Chimney Sweeper, The, from Songs of Innocence 760
Chu, Jeff 142, 736
Churchill, Winston 675, 1166
Coleman, Wanda 960
Coleridge, Samuel Taylor 799
Collected Beowulf, The, from 62
Composed Upon Westminster Bridge, September 3, 1802 780
Constant Lover, The 464
Creation of Adam and Eve, The, from 15
Crossing the Bar 922
Cullen, Countee 882
Cup of Tea, A 1045

D

Darkling Thrush, The 1003
Dead Men's Path 1304
Death Be Not Proud 430
Death by Mosquito 644
Death of Humbaba, The, from Gilgamesh 55
Defence of Poesie, A, from 245
Defense of Poetry, A, from 705

Defoe, Daniel 622
Demon in the Freezer, The, from 629
Demon Lover, The 1174
Desai, Anita 1344
Diary of Fanny Burney, The, from 742
Diary of Samuel Pepys, The, from 552
Dickens, Charles 917, 984, 1022
Dictionary of the English Language, A, from 648
Dillard, Annie 884
Distant Mirror, A, from 193
Do Not Go Gentle into That Good Night 1200
Donne, John 249, 430, 438
Dover Beach 994
Down and Out in Europe 1062
Dreamers 1093
Dryden, John 546
Dulce et Decorum Est 1097

E

Ecclesiastical History of the English People, The, from 82, 230
Elegy for the Giant Tortoises 1355
Elegy Written in a Country Churchyard 708
Eliot, T. S. 1117
Elizabeth I 254
Epigrams 586
Essay of Dramatic Poesy, An, from 546
Essay on Man, An, from 586
Everyman, from 154
Eve's Apology, from Salve Deus Rex Judaeorum 424

F

Farley, Christopher John 1360
Fear No More the Heat o' the Sun 301
Fern Hill 1200
Follower 1258
Frame, Janet 1318
Frankenstein, from the Introduction to 833
Fussell, Paul 1101

G

Games at Twilight 1344
Genesis, from the King James Version of
    the Bible, from 414
George Orwell's Wartime Diary,
    from 1041
Get Up and Bar the Door 210
Ghosh, Aparisim 1062
Gilgamesh, from 55
Gordimer, Nadine 1295
Gorman, Christine 644
Gray, Paul 948
Gray, Thomas 708
Great War and Modern Memory, The,
    from 1101
Greene, Graham 1192
Gulliver's Travels, from 575

H

Haiku for Four Seasons 880
Hard Times, from 917
Hardy, Thomas 919, 1003
Hardy and the Poetry of Isolation,
    from 1011
Head, Bessie 1054
Heaney, Seamus 1258
Henry, William A., III 410
Herrick, Robert 455
Hinds, Gareth 62
History of the Peloponnesian War,
    from 635
Homage to a Government 1237
Homer 513
Hopkins, Gerard Manley 951
Horace 459
House Unlocked, A, from 219
Housman, A. E. 998
How Soon Hath Time 516
Hughes, Ted 1235, 1267
Hunt, Tristram 69

I

Imaginary Homelands, from 1340
In Memoriam A. H. H., from 922
In My Life 946
In Patagonia, from 829
It Is a Beauteous Evening, Calm and
    Free 780

J

Jabberwocky (Carroll) 956
Jabberwocky (Coleman) 960
Jane Eyre, from 966
John Anderson, My Jo 717
Johnson, Samuel 648
Jonson, Ben 445, 449
Journal of the Plague Year, A, from 622
Journals of Dorothy Wordsworth, The,
    from 795
Joyce, James 1138

K

Keats, John 865, 871, 876
Kempe, Margery 145
Khayyám, Omar 461
King James Version of the Bible,
    from 414, 1057
Kipling, Rudyard 1068
Kubla Khan 799

L

La Belle Dame sans Merci 865
Lake Isle of Innisfree, The 1106
Lanyer, Aemilia 424
Lamb, The 754
Larkin, Philip 1237
Lawrence, D. H. 1122
Le Morte d'Arthur, from 17, 196
Lee, Li-Young 1262
Lennon, John 946
Lessing, Doris 1284
Letter to Her Daughter 602
Letter to Lord Chesterfield 648
Letter to Nelson Algren 944
Life of Samuel Johnson, The, from 659
Lines Composed a Few Miles Above
    Tintern Abbey 786
Lively, Penelope 219, 1246
London 760
Lord of the Rings, The, from 58
Love Is Not All: It Is Not Meat nor
    Drink 943
Lovelace, Richard 469
Lover Showeth How He Is Forsaken,
    The 259
Lyrical Ballads, from the Preface to 703

M

Macbeth, The Tragedy of 316
Malory, Sir Thomas 17, 196
Man He Killed, The 1003
Mansfield, Katherine 1045
Marlowe, Christopher 275
Marvell, Andrew 474
McCartney, Paul 946
Meditation 17 438
Midnight's Children, from 1239
Midsummer Night's Spectacle 410
Mild Attack of Locusts, A 1284
Millay, Edna St. Vincent 943
Milton, John 509, 516, 520
Miss Youghal's Sais 1068
Mnemonic 1262
Modest Proposal, A 564
Montagu, Lady Mary Wortley 602
Mrs. Dalloway, from 1156
Musée des Beaux Arts 1184
Music Goes Global 1360
My Heart Leaps Up 780
My Last Duchess 979

N

Naipaul, V. S. 1331
Narayan, R. K. 1209
New Railway, The, from 1022
Not Waving but Drowning 1242
Nymph's Reply to the Shepherd, The 279

O

Ode on a Grecian Urn 871
Ode to the West Wind 854
Odyssey, from 513
Of Cunning, from 494
Of Studies 283
Old Mrs. Grey 1220
Oliver Twist, from 984
On Her Loving Two Equally 542
On Monsieur's Departure 254
On My First Son 445
Ondaatje, Michael 1264
Orwell, George 1041, 1077
Orwell's Wartime Diary, from 1041
Our revels now are ended, from The
    Tempest 305
Owen, Wilfred 1097
Ozymandias 850

INDEX OF AUTHORS AND TITLES

P

Parable of Lazarus and the Rich Man, The, from the King James Version of the Bible 1057
Paradise Lost, from 520
Pardoner's Tale, The, from 116
Passionate Shepherd to His Love, The 275
Past and Present, from 915
Pepys, Samuel 552
Perkins, David 1011
Petrarch 253
Photograph, from Running in the Family 1264
Pied Beauty 951
Pilgrim at Tinker Creek, from 884
Pilgrim's Progress, The, from 532
Pinter, Harold 1271
Plague, The, from 639
Poison Tree, A 754
Pope, Alexander 513, 586, 593
Preludes 1117
Preston, Richard 629
Pride and Prejudice, from 768
Prologue, The, from 92
Proverbs of Hell from The Marriage of Heaven and Hell, from 701
Psalm 23 from the King James Version of the Bible 414

Q

Qur'an, from the 1059

R

Raising Their Voices 736
Raleigh, Sir Walter 279
Rape of the Lock, The, from 593
Richard III, from 247
Rime of the Ancient Mariner, The 799
Roads Now Taken, The 142
Rocking-Horse Winner, The 1122
Rodman, Selden 1365
Ronsard, Pierre de 460
Room of One's Own, A, from 1149
Rosenthal, Daniel 406
Rubáiyát, from the 461
Rushdie, Salman 1239, 1340

S

Sailing to Byzantium 1110
Salve Deus Rex Judaeorum, from 424
Samuel Johnson, from 670
Sassoon, Siegfried 1093
Satire Against Mankind, A, from 511
Seafarer, The 74
Second Coming, The 1110
Shakespeare, William 247, 292, 298, 301, 305, 316
Shakespeare on Screen, from 406
She Walks in Beauty 842
Shelley, Mary 833
Shelley, Percy Bysshe 705, 850, 854
Shocking Accident, A 1192
Shooting an Elephant 1077
Sidney, Sir Philip 245, 270
Simone de Beauvoir to Nelson Algren 944
Sir Gawain and the Green Knight, from 172
Sir Patrick Spens 210
Smith, Stevie 1242
Snake in the Grass, A 1209
Soldier, The 1089
Song 430
Song: To Celia 449
Sonnet XII (Petrarch) 253
Sonnet 29 (Shakespeare) 298
Sonnet 30 (Spenser) 265
Sonnet 31 (Sidney) 270
Sonnet 39 (Sidney) 270
Sonnet 43 (Browning) 939
Sonnet 73 (Shakespeare) 298
Sonnet 75 (Spenser) 265
Sonnet 116 (Shakespeare) 292
Sonnet 130 (Shakespeare) 292
Soyinka, Wole 1313
Spectator, The, from 614
Speech to the Troops at Tilbury 254
Spenser, Edmund 265
Spring 880
Spring and Fall: To a Young Child 951
Steele, Sir Richard 614
Subalterns, The 919
Suckling, Sir John 464
Summer 880
Swift, Jonathan 564, 575, 686

T

Tales of the Islands, from 1327
Tears, Idle Tears 922
Telephone Conversation 1313
Tennyson, Alfred, Lord 922, 931
Testament of Youth, from 1037
That's All 1271
Thistles 1235
Thomas, Dylan 1200
Throne of Blood, from Shakespeare on Screen 406
Thucydides 635
To a Mouse 717
To a Skylark 854
To Althea, from Prison 469
To an Athlete Dying Young 998
To Autumn 876
To Be, or Not to Be, from Hamlet 305
To Hélène 460
To His Coy Mistress 474
To John Keats, Poet, At Springtime 882
To Lucasta, Going to the Wars 469
To the Virgins, to Make Much of Time 455
Tolkien, J. R. R. 58
Tragedy of Macbeth, The 316
Train from Rhodesia, The 1295
Tuchman, Barbara 193
Two Sheep 1318
Tyger, The 754

U

Ulysses (Tennyson) 931
Ulysses, from (Joyce) 1039
Unknown Citizen, The 1184
Untying the Knot, from Pilgrim at Tinker Creek 884

V

Valediction: Forbidding Mourning, A 430
Village People 1054
Vindication of the Rights of Woman, A, from 725, 900
Voyage to Brobdingnag, A, from Gulliver's Travels, from 580
Voyage to Lilliput, A, from Gulliver's Travels, from 575

W

Walcott, Derek 1327, 1376
War Speech, September 3, 1939 675
What Is Love? 948
What We Lost 1278
When I Consider How My Light Is Spent 516
When I Have Fears That I May Cease to Be 865
When I Was One-and-Twenty 998

When You Are Old 1106
Whoso List to Hunt 259
Why So Pale and Wan, Fond Lover? 464
Wife of Bath's Tale, The 124
Wilmot, John 511
Wind 1267
Winding Up 1376
Winter 880
Wollstonecraft, Mary 725, 900
Woolf, Virginia 1149, 1156, 1220

Wordsworth, from 889
Wordsworth, Dorothy 795
Wordsworth, William 703, 780, 783, 784, 786
World Is Too Much with Us, The 780
Wyatt, Sir Thomas 262

Y

Yeats, William Butler 1106, 1108, 1110, 1112

INDEX OF ART AND ARTISTS

A

Adam, Joseph Denovan, *Droving the Hills* 719

Allan, Sir William, *Lord Byron reposing in the house of a fisherman having swum the Hellespont* 849

Angelico, Fra, *Annunciation (detail)* 424

Angelico, Fra, *Heaven from the Last Judgement (detail)* 167

Anstice, Penelope, *Little Indian Girl with a Leaf* 1347

Anstice, Penelope, *Indian Girl* 1073

Armfield, Maxwell Ashby, *Portrait of Keith Henderson in a Black Hood* 1250

Audubon, John James, *Tawny Thrush* 1005

B

Bailly, David, *Vanitas* 249

Barker, John Joseph, *Irish Emigrants* 571

Barton, Rose Maynard, *Piccadilly in June* 1157

Bashkirtseff, Maria, *A Meeting* 1143

Bastien-Lepage, Jules, *At Harvest Time* 213

Bastien-Lepage, Jules, *Juliette Drouet* 1107

Beale, Mary, *Portrait of Aphra Behn* 542

Beardsley, Aubrey Vincent, *Front cover of the prospectus for 'The Yellow Book'* 1067

Beardsley, Aubrey Vincent, *How Morgan LeFay Gave a Shield to Sir Tristam* 196

Beardsley, Aubrey, *The Battle of the Beaux and the Belles* 594

Bell, Vanessa, *Conversation Piece* 1066

Bell, Vanessa, *Interior with Table* 1028

Bell, Vanessa, *Virginia Woolf in a Deckchair* 1162

Bindon, Francis, *Portrait of Jonathan Swift* 584

Blake, William, *A Poison Tree* 756

Blake, William, *Elohim Creating Adam* 416

Blake, William, *Infant Joy* 767

Blake, William, *Judgement of Adam and Eve* 523

Blake, William, *Nebuchadnezzar* 766

Blake, William, *Satan in his Original Glory* 524

Blake, William, *The Ancient of Days* 701

Blake, William, *The Chimney Sweeper, Plate 7* 761

Blake, William, *The Chimney Sweeper, Plate 37* 762

Blake, William, *The Lord Answering Job out of a Whirlwind* 767

Blake, William, *The Shepherd* 757

Blake, William, *The Tyger* 758

Blake, William, *Winter* 303

Bloemaert, Abraham, *Shepherd and Shepherdess* 281

Boddington, Henry, *A Lakeside Gathering* 1109

Bordone, Paris, *Two Lovers* 449

Bosch, Hieronymus, *The Ship of Fools* 558

Botticelli, Sandro, *Flora, detail from the Primavera* 457

Boucher, Francois, *Madame de Pompadour* 596

Boucher, Francois, *Shepherd Piping to a Shepherdess* 276

Bower, Edward, *A Cavalier* 452

Bowler, Henry Alexander, *The Doubt: "Can These Drying Bones Live?"* 919

Braun, Georg, and Franz Hogenberg, *Bird's eye view of Canterbury* 99

Breu the Elder, Joerg, *Saint Bernard exorcising an evil spirit; Death of Saint Bernard of Clairvaux* 147

Bridges, Fidelia, *Untitled* 875

Broderick, Muriel, *The Beginnings of the Christmas Play* 152

Brown, Ford Madox, *Chaucer at the Court of Edward III* 136

Brown, Ford Madox, *Manfred of the Jungfrau* 848

Brown, Ford Madox, *The Last of England* 911

Browne, Henriette, *A Girl Writing* 968

Brueghel the Elder, Pieter, *The Fall of Icarus* 1186

Bundy, Edgar, *The Bridge Party* 749

Burgh, Lydia de, *Portrait of Queen Elizabeth II wearing coronation robes and the Imperial State Crown* 1236

C

Carmontelle, Louis Carrogis, *Laurence Sterne* 685

Carpaccio, Vittore, *Saint Ursula dreams of her coming martyrdom, announced by an angel* 435

Carrick, John Mulcaster, *The Death of Arthur* 203

Carrington, Dora, *Baroque Harmony in the Ice Off the Labrador Coast* 77

Cattermole, George, *Macbeth instructing the murderers employed to kill Banquo* 357

Christus, Petrus, *The Last Judgment* 157

Clark, Joseph, *Waifs and Strays* 566

Coburn, Alvin Langdon, *Tower Bridge* 1119

Collier, Edwaert, *Still Life with Inkstand and Books* 286

Collier, Edwaert, *Trompe l'oeil with Writing Materials* 650

Constable, John, *Cloud Study, Horizon of Trees* 703

Constable, John, *Flatford Mill* 697

Constable, John, *The Hay Wain* 692–693

Constable, John, *Hove Beach with Fishing Boats* 928

Cope, Charles West, *The Pilgrim Fathers: Departure of a Puritan Family for New England* 506

Copeland, Mark, *The Light Programme* 1226

Copping, Harold, *Oliver Asks for More* 989

Couder, Louis-Charles Auguste, *Siege of Yorktown, October 17th, 1836* 694

Cox, David, *A Seaside View* 995

Cragg, Tony, *Britain Seen from the North* 1239

Crane, Walter, *La Belle Dame Sans Merci* 867

Creti, Donato, *Astronomical Observation: Venus* 272

Crook, P. J., *5 O'Clock Cowboy* 1131

Crook, P. J., *La Gare* 1144

Cropsey, Jasper Francis, *Stoke Poges Church* 710

Cruikshank, George, *The Artful Dodger picking a pocket to the amazement of Oliver Twist* 964

D

Danckerts, Hendrick, *John Rose Presenting the First English-Grown Pineapple to Charles II* 511

Decamps, Alexandre Gabriel, *The Witches in Macbeth* 322

De Morgan, William, *Three ceramic tiles depicting a ship sailing at sunset* 75

Detmold, Edward Julius, *Town Mouse and the Country Mouse* 720

Dewing, Maria Oakey, *Garden in May* 883

di Brera, Pinacoteca, *Two Lovers* 449

Dighton, Richard, *Three Gentlemen Greeting Each Other* 772

Ditz, *The Apple-Tub* 1194

Doré, Gustave, *Albatross is shot by arrow (detail)* 810

Doré, Gustave, *Angels remove the curse* 820

Doré, Gustave, *Cursed ship is sent to the equator where crew perish* 812

Doré, Gustave, *Death and Life play dice on skeleton ship* 815

Doré, Gustave, *Death on a Pale Horse* 624

Doré, Gustave, *Hermit saves the Mariner* 823

Doré, Gustave, *London Traffic Jam* 559

Doré, Gustave, *Mariner recounts story to wedding guest* 807

Doré, Gustave, *Satan's Flight Through Chaos* 529

Doré, Gustave, *Satan Smitten by Michael, from Book IV of Paradise Lost* 502

Droeshout, Martin, *Detail of a Portrait of William Shakespeare* 291

Drummond, Malcolm, *In the Park (St. James's Park)* 1161

Douglas, William Fettes, *The Bibliophilist's Haunt or Creech's Bookshop* 750

Dyke, Anthony van, *Charles I of England* 453

E

Eardley, Joan, *A Glasgow Close* 1140

Easton, Bella, *Pushkar Blues (2)* 1070

Emmerson, Henry Hetherington, *Four Girls and a Dog on a Bridge Over the Debdon Burn* 971

Eves, Reginald-Grenville, *Thomas Hardy* 1003

F

Faed, John, *Shakespeare and His Friends* 549

Ferry, Jean Georges, *Two Women Reading in an Interior* 775

Fildes, Sir Luke, *Applicants for Admission to a Casual Ward* 568

Fleming, Ian, *Marion McLean* 1280

Folingsby, George Frederick, *John Bunyan in Prison* 532

Forbes, Elizabeth Sophia, *An Indian Elephant and His Mahout* 1079

Fragonard, Jean-Honore, *The Stolen Kiss* 476

Frampton, Meredith, *Marguerite Kelsey* 1047

Francken the Younger, Frans, *The Parable of the Rich Man* 1057

Frith, William Powell, *Sir Roger de Coverly and Addison with "The Saracen's Head"* 616

Fry, Roger, *Room in the second Post-Impressionist Exhibition in 1912 showing the works of Henri Matisse* 1039

Fuseli, Henry, *Lady Macbeth Sleepwalking* 391

Fuseli, Henry, *Prospero* 312

Fuseli, Henry, *Three Witches* 324

Fuseli, Henry, *Lady Macbeth Seizing the Daggers* 341

G

Gardiner, Clive, *Motor Manufacturing—Empire buying makes busy factories* 1187

Giorgione (Da Castelfranco, Giorgio), *Double Portrait* 299

Girtin, Thomas, *Interior of Tintern Abbey* 787

Greve, Gerrit, *# 49* 1262

Grimshaw, John Atkinson, *St. Paul's Cathedral from Ludgate Circus, London, England* 1179

H

Hammershøi, Vilhelm, *The Music Room, 30 Strandgade* 1151

Harden, John, *Dorothy Wordsworth in a Wheelchair* 795

Haydon, Benjamin Robert, *Portrait of William Wordsworth* 780

Hayman, Francis, *Robert Lovelace preparing to abduct Clarissa Harlowe* 503

Heere, Lucas de, *The Family of Henry VIII: An Allegory of the Tudor Succession* 236

Hepple, Norman, *Firelight* 1050

Herkomer, Sir Hubert von, *On Strike* 963

Hilliard, Nicholas, *A Young Man Leaning Against a Tree Among Roses* 261

Hilliard, Nicolas, *Henry Percy, 9th Earl of Northumberland* 252

Hilton, William, *John Keats* 865

Hiroshige, Ando, *Evening Snow at Asuka-yama* 881

Hockney, David, *My Parents* 1235

Hoefnage, Joris, *A Fete at Bermondsey* 241

Hogarth, William, *David Garrick as Richard III* 247

Hogarth, William, *Family Party* 505

Hogarth, William, *The Marriage Settlement* 776

Hogarth, William, *O' The Roast Beef of Olde England* 536

Hogarth, William, *Southwark Fair* 538

Holbein the Younger, Hans, *Lady in a White Cap* 463

Holmes, Mabelle Linnea, *The Coming of the Norsemen in 1000 AD* 78

Holst, Theodore M. von, *A Nightmare* 837

Hooch, Pieter de, *A Maid with a Pail in the Backyard* 1153

Hopper, Edward, *Compartment C, Car 293* 1299

Howard, Henry, *The Florentine Girl (The Artist's Daughter)* 844

Hugo, Victor, *Castle* 836

Humphrey, Ozias, *Portrait of Jane Austen* 768

I

Ingalls, Pam, *Museum Arch II* 1252

Ingres, Jean Auguste Dominique, *Paolo and Francesca* 268

J

Jackson, Helen, *She is Witty to Talk With* 974

Jerichau, Holger, *A View of Benares* 1070

Jervas, Charles, *Jonathan Swift* 564

Johnson, Edward Killingworth, *The Bird's Nest* 1158

Joy, George William, *The Bayswater Omnibus* 906

Juon, Konstantin Fiodorvich, *The New Planet* 1112

K

Kay, Dorothy, *Cookie, Annie Mavata* 1055

Kersting, Georg Friedrich, *Young Woman Sewing by Lamplight* 733

Killingbeck, Benjamin, *Earl and Countess of Ossory and Their Children at Ampthill Park* 505

Kinley, Peter, *Fantaise* 1357

Knyff, Leonard, *The Southeast Prospect of Hampton Court* 241

Koch, Joseph Anton, *Macbeth and the Witches* 374

Kropp, Steve, *Horse Race* 1124

Kuehl, Gottardt, *Lovers in a Café* 1001

L

Lamb, Henry, *It's a Long, Long Way* 1165

Lawrence, Sir Thomas, *The Duchess of Berri* 981

Le Testu, Guillaume, *Map of the Magellan Straits* 831

Leal, Juan de Valdes, *Allegory of Death (In Ictu Oculi)* 162

Leighton, Lord Frederic, *The Painter's Honeymoon* 941

Longoni, Emilio, *Alone* 945

Longoni, Emilio, *Thoughts of a Hungry Man* 1061

Ludovici, Albert, *Treasured Pets* 1007

M

Macara, Andrew, *Girl on a Swing* 1346

Maclise, Daniel, *The Banquet Scene from Macbeth* 361

Mann, Alexander, *Portrait of Helen Gow* 731

Mara, Tim, *Untitled* 1241

Martin, John, *The Bard* 779

Martin, John, *The Fallen Angels Entering Pandemonium* 527

Master of Saint Severin, *The Exorcism of the Demon* 145

McDonald, James, *The Children's Encyclopedia* 961

McIntosh, Robert, *Horse Race # 14* 1128

McIntosh, Robert, *Horse Race # 5* 1132

Mij, Hieronymus van der, *A Girl at a Window holding a Bunch of Grapes* 296

Mileham, Harry, *Chaucer, the Knight and the Squire from 'The Pardoner's Prologue' of 'The Canterbury Tales'* 119

Millais, Sir John Everett, *Autumn Leaves* 707

Moore, Henry, *Shelterers in the Tube* 1041

Morrice, James Wilson, *Landscape, Trinidad* 1333

Morris, Sir Cedric, *Llanmadoc Hill, Gower Peninsula* 1205

Munnings, Alfred, *Their Majesties' Return from Ascot* 1160

N

Nash, Joseph, *Queen Victoria Opening the 1862 Exhibition after Crystal Palace moved to Sydenham* 915

Nasmyth, Alexander, *Tantallon Castle with the Bass Rock* 211

Nebot, Balthazar, *Covent Garden Market* 513

Nevinson, Christopher Richard Wynne, *A Group of Soldiers* 1091

Nevinson, Christopher Richard Wynne, *La Mitrailleuse* 1043

Nevinson, Christopher Richard Wynne, *London Twilight from the Adelphi* 924

Nevinson, Christopher Richard Wynne, *The Arrival* 1105

Nevinson, Christopher Richard Wynne, *The Food Queue* 1037

Nevinson, Christopher Richard Wynne, *The Strand by Night* 1182

Nicholls, Joseph, *A View of Westminster with the Royal Barge and Other Shipping* 784

Nicholson, William, *Sir Walter Scott* 899

O

Oliver, Alfred, *The Wild Wood* 954

Oliver, Isaac, *Edward Herbert, 1st Baron Herbert of Cherbury* 245

Oliver, Issac, *Portrait of Frances Howard, Countess of Essex and Somerset* 252

Opie, John, *Mary Wollstonecraft (Mrs. William Godwin)* 725

P

Palmer, Samuel, *Tintern Abbey* 890

Panchal, Shanti, *Children's Play (detail)* 1351

Peake, Robert, *Queen Elizabeth I Being Carried in Procession* 251

Pereda, Antonio, *Allegory of Fleeting Time* 413

Peto, John Frederick, *Rack Picture for William Malcolm Bunn* 1279

Pettie, John, *Two Strings to her Bow* 544

Phillips, Thomas, *Lord Byron* 842

Phillips, Thomas, *William Blake* 754

Pierre, Christian, *The Temptress* 426

Pond, Arthur, *Portrait of Thomas Gray* 708

R

Raven, John Samuel, *Caregg Cennen Castle* 382

Redoute, Pierre Joseph, *Camellia Japonica* 277

Reibisch, Friedrich Martin von, *Illustration of a Knight and Horse in Armor* 130

Reibisch, Friedrich Martin von, *Two Knights Fighting with Swords* 193

Reynolds, Sir Joshua, *Portrait of Francis Russell, the Marpuess of Tavistock* 467

Reynolds, Sir Joshua, *Portrait of Samuel Johnson* 667

Richardson, Jonathan, *Alexander Pope* 586

Richardson, Jonathan, *Sir Richard Steele* 614

Riesener, Henri Francois, *Babet and His Son* 447

Ring, Laurits Andersen, *Old Man Walking in a Rye Field* 1204

Rodin, Auguste, *The Thinker* 590

Roerich, Nikolai, *Visitors from Overseas* 50

Roederstein, Ottilie Wilhelmina, *The Victor* 1000

Romney, George, *Macbeth and the Witches* 372

Roseland, Henry Herman, *Budding Scholar* 960

Ross, Thomas, *The City Weir, Bath, looking towards Walcot* 127

Rossetti, Dante Charles Gabriel, *The Death of Lady Macbeth* 397

Rowlandson, Thomas, *Customers in the coffee house in Salisbury Market-Place* 617

Rowlandson, Thomas, *London's Royal Exchange* 697

Rowlandson, Thomas, *Young Ladies' Finishing School* 613

Ruskin, John, *Study of a dragon's head after Michelangelo* 44

S

Saar, Betye, *Watching* 1336

Sargent, John Singer, *Ellen Terry as Lady Macbeth* 331

Sargent, John Singer, *Two Soldiers of Arras* 1006

Scott, Sir Peter, *Man's Natural World* 1283

Seligman, Lincoln, *Man and Woman in an Art Gallery* 1248

Severn, Joseph, *Percy Bysshe Shelley* 705

Shannon, Sir James Jebusa, *On the Dunes (Lady Shannon and Kitty)* 744

Shepherd, George, *Hungerford Stairs* 697

Smith, Carlton Alfred, *Recalling the Past* 929

Smith, Nancy, *Ploughing* 1260

Smith, Orford, *The Hero of the Trafalgar* 698

Steen, Jan, *The dissolute household* 782

Stiepanoff, Alexei, *The Love Song* 466

Stokes, Adrian, *Young Girl and the Angel of Death* 161

Stone, Henry, *Triple portrait of King Charles I* 515

Storey, George Aldolphus, *Orphans* 975

Stothard, Thomas, *The Pilgrimage to Canterbury* 96

Strasser, Benjamin, *Wounded at the Roadside* 1095

Stroop, Dirck, *Charles II's entry into London on the day before his Coronation in 1661* 554

Stubbs, George, *The Harvest Wagon* 713

T

Taylor, Leonard Campbell, *The Gallery* 1176

Tenniel, John, *The Jabberwocky* 958

Tenniel, John, *The Mad Tea Party* 909

Tissot, James Jacques Joseph, *The Woman of Fashion* 728

Troyon, Constant-Emile, *Promenade* 770

Turner, Joseph Mallord William, *Snow Storm at Sea* 856

Turner, Joseph Mallord William, *Tintern Abbey* 790

U

Unknown, Artist, *Anne Boleyn* 262

Unknown, Artist, *Elizabeth I* 256

Unknown, Artist, *Promenading Noblemen (detail)* 295

Unknown, Artist, *The Triumph of Death* 155

V

Valdés Leal, Juan de, *Allegory of Death (In Ictu Oculi)* 462

Valkenborch, Frederick van, *A Market Scene with Fruit and Vegetable Sellers* 432

Van Gogh, Vincent, *The Sower* 953

Van Gogh, Vincent, *Wheatfield with Lark* 858

Varley, John, *Conway Castle* 349

Vroom, Hendrik Cornelisz, *Sea Battle Between the Spanish Armada and English Naval Forces* 242

W

Wagstaff, Charles Edward, *Portrait of John Dryden* 546

Waite, Edward W., *An Autumn Lane* 877

Walden, Lionel, *The Docks at Cardiff* 917

Walker, Frederick, *Philip in Church* 965

Wall, Lou, *Abstract Day* 1349

Wallis, Henry, *Dr. Johnson at Cave's the Publisher* 500

Wallis, Henry, *The Room in Which Shakespeare Was Born* 293

Ward, Edward Matthew, *Dr. Johnson in the Anteroom of Lord Chesterfield, Waiting for an Audience* 654

Waterhouse, John William, *La Belle Dame Sans Merci* 841

Waterhouse, John William, *The Soul of the Rose* 273

Way, Andrew John Henry, *The Wealth of Autumn* 875

Weight, Carel, *Bitter Wind* 1269

West, Benjamin, *Cromwell Dissolving the Long Parliament* 509

Willis, Tilly, *Under the Acacia Tree* 1290

Willison, George, *James Boswell* 659

Wilson, Richard, *On Hounslow Heath* 869

Wingfield, James D., *An Interior at Hampton Court* 607

Wootton, John, *Macbeth and the Three Witches* 317

Wright of Derby, Joseph, *The Old Man and Death* 168

Wright, Joseph of Derby, *The Orrery* 563

Z

Zaman, Farida, *Online Romance* 947

Zincke, Christian Friedrich, *Miniature of Joseph Addison* 614

ACKNOWLEDGMENTS

Unit 1

"The Battle of Maldon" from *An Anthology of Old English Poetry,* edited by Charles W. Kennedy, translated by Charles W. Kennedy, copyright © 1960 by Oxford University Press, Inc. Used by permission of Oxford University Press, Inc.

From "The Creation of Adam and Eve" from *Everyman and Medieval Miracle Plays,* edited by A. C. Cawley. Reprinted by permission of Everyman's Library, Northburgh House, 10 Northburgh Street, London EC1V 0AT.

From *Beowulf,* translated by Burton Raffel, copyright © 1963 renewed © 1991 by Burton Raffel. Used by permission of Dutton Signet, a division of Penguin Group (USA) Inc.

Excerpt from *Gilgamesh: A Verse Narrative* by Herbert Mason. Copyright © 1970 by Herbert Mason. Reprinted by permission of Houghton Mifflin Company. All rights reserved.

Excerpt from "The Battle of the Pelennor Fields" from *The Lord of the Rings* by J. R. R. Tolkien, edited by Christopher Tolkien. Copyright © 1954, 1955, 1965, 1966 by J. R. R. Tolkien. Copyright © renewed 1982, 1983 by Christopher R. Tolkien, Michael H. R. Tolkien, John F. R. Tolkien and Priscilla M. A. R. Tolkien. Copyright © renewed 1993, 1994 by Christopher R. Tolkien, John F. R. Tolkien and Priscilla M. A. R. Tolkien. Reprinted by permission of Houghton Mifflin Company. All rights reserved.

"The Seafarer" from *Poems and Prose from the Old English,* translated by Burton Raffel. Edited by Alexandra H. Olsen and Burton Raffel. Copyright © 1998 by Yale University. Reprinted by permission of Yale University Press.

From *The Canterbury Tales* by Geoffrey Chaucer, translated by Neville Coghill. Reproduced with permission of Curtis Brown Group Ltd, London on behalf of the Estate of Neville Coghill. Copyright © Neville Coghill 1952.

From *The Book of Margery Kempe,* translated by Tony D. Triggs. Reprinted by permission of the Continuum International Publishing Group.

From *The Complete Works of the Gawain Poet* by John Gardner. Copyright © 1965 by The University of Chicago. Reprinted by permission of The University of Chicago Press.

Excerpt from *Sir Gawain and the Green Knight,* translated with an introduction by Brian Stone (Penguin Classics, 1959). Copyright © Brian Stone, 1959, 1964, 1974. Reprinted by permission of Penguin Group (UK).

From A Distant Mirror by Barbara W. Tuchman, copyright © 1978 by Barbara W. Tuchman. Used by permission of Alfred A. Knopf, a division of Random House, Inc.

Reprinted with the permission of Scribner, an imprint of Simon & Schuster Adult Publishing Group, from *Le Morte d'Arthur* by Sir Thomas Malory, edited by R. M. Lumiansky. Copyright © 1982 by R. M. Lumiansky.

From *A House Unlocked* by Penelope Lively, copyright © 2001 by Penelope Lively. Used by permission of Grove/Atlantic, Inc.

Unit 2

From *Shakespeare on Screen,* reproduced by permission of Curtis Brown Group Ltd, London on behalf of Daniel Rosenthal. Copyright © Daniel Rosenthal 1957.

From *Rubáiyát of Omar Khayyám* translated by Edward FitzGerald, copyright © 1983 by St. Martin's Press, LLC, and reprinted with permission.

Unit 3

Excerpt from *The History of the Peloponnesian War* by Thucydides, translated by Rex Warner, with an introduction and notes by M. I. Finley (Penguin Classics 1954, Revised edition 1972). Translation copyright © Rex Warner, 1954. Introduction and Appendices copyright © M. I. Finley, 1972. Reprinted by permission of Penguin Group (UK) and The Random House Group Ltd.

From *The Plague* by Albert Camus, translated by Stuart Gilbert, copyright 1948 by Stuart Gilbert. Used by permission of Alfred A. Knopf, a division of Random House, Inc.

Excerpt from *Samuel Johnson* by Walter Jackson Bate. Copyright © 1975, 1977 by Walter Jackson Bate. Reprinted by permission of William B. Goodman.

Unit 4

Abridged from *In Patagonia* by Bruce Chatwin. Copyright © 1977 by Bruce Chatwin. Used by permission of Simon & Schuster Adult Publishing Group.

"To John Keats Poet at Springtime" from *On These I Stand* by Countee Cullen. Copyrights held by Amistad Research Center, Tulane University, administered by Thompson and Thompson, Brooklyn, NY.

"Untying the Knot" from *Pilgrim at Tinker Creek* by Annie Dillard. Copyright © 1974 by Annie Dillard. Reprinted by permission of HarperCollins Publishers.

"On Wordsworth," by Robin Becker, from *First Loves: Poets Introduce the Essential Poems That Captivated and Inspired Them.* Reprinted by permission of Robin Becker.

Unit 5

"Sonnet XXX" of *Fatal Interview* by Edna St. Vincent Millay. From *Collected Poems,* HarperCollins. Copyright © 1931, 1958 by Edna St. Vincent Millay and Norma Millay Ellis. All rights reserved. Used by permission of Elizabeth Barnett, literary executor.

"In My Life" © 1965 Sony/ATV Tunes LLC. All rights administered by Sony/ATV Music Publishing, 8 Music Square West, Nashville, TN 37203. All rights reserved. Used by permission

"The Darkling Thrush," "The Man He Killed" and "Ah, Are You Digging on My Grave?" reprinted with the permission of Scribner, an imprint of Simon & Schuster Adult Publishing Group, from *The Complete Poems of Thomas Hardy,* edited by James Gibson. Copyright © 1978 by Macmillan London Ltd.

From Perkins, David. "Hardy and the Poetry of Isolation" ELH 26:2 (1959), 253–270. Copyright © The Johns Hopkins University Press. Reprinted with the permission of The Johns Hopkins University Press.

Unit 6

The extract from Vera Brittain's *Testament of Youth* is reproduced by permission of Mark Bostridge and Rebecca Williams, her literary executors.

Excerpt from *The Collected Essays, Journalism and Letters of George Orwell, Volume II: My Country Right or Left, 1940-1943,* copyright © 1968 by Sonia Brownell Orwell and renewed 1996 by Mark Hamilton, reprinted by permission of Harcourt, Inc.

"A Cup of Tea" from *The Short Stories of Katherine Mansfield* by Katherine Mansfield, copyright 1923 by Alfred A. Knopf, a division of Random House, Inc. and renewed 1951 by John Middleton Murry. Used by permission of Alfred A. Knopf, a division of Random House, Inc.

"Village People" copyright © Bessie Head, *Tales of Tenderness and Power,* Ad. Donker 1989. Reprinted by permission of Johnson & Alcock Ltd.

From *The Koran: With a Parallel Arabic Text* translated with notes by N. J. Dawood (Penguin Books, 1990). Copyright © N. J. Dawood, 1956, 1959, 1966, 1968, 1974, 1990. Reprinted by permission of Penguin Group (UK).

"Shooting an Elephant" from *Shooting an Elephant and Other Essays* by George Orwell, copyright 1950 by Sonia Brownell Orwell and renewed 1978 by Sonia Pitt-Rivers, reprinted by permission of Harcourt, Inc.

"Dulce et Decorum Est" by Wilfred Owen, from *The Collected Poems of Wilfred Owen*, copyright © 1963 by Chatto & Windus, Ltd. Reprinted by permission of New Directions Publishing Corp.

From *The Great War and Modern Memory* by Paul Fussell, copyright © 1975 by Oxford University Press, Inc. Used by permission of Oxford University Press, Inc.

"The Lake Isle of Innisfree" and "When You Are Old" reprinted with the permission of Scribner, an imprint of Simon & Schuster Adult Publishing Group, from *The Collected Works of W. B. Yeats, Volume I: The Poems, Revised*, edited by Richard J. Finneran (New York: Scribner, 1997)

"Sailing to Byzantium" reprinted with the permission of Scribner, an imprint of Simon & Schuster Adult Publishing Group, from *The Collected Works of W. B. Yeats, Volume I: The Poems, Revised*, edited by Richard J. Finneran. Copyright © 1928 by The Macmillan Company; copyright renewed © 1956 by Georgie Yeats.

"The Second Coming" reprinted with the permission of Scribner, an imprint of Simon & Schuster Adult Publishing Group, from *The Collected Works of W. B. Yeats, Volume I: The Poems, Revised*, edited by Richard J. Finneran. Copyright © 1924 by The Macmillan Company; copyright renewed © 1952 by Georgie Yeats.

"The Rocking-Horse Winner" by D. H. Lawrence, copyright © 1933 by the Estate of D. H. Lawrence, renewed © 1961 by Angelo Ravagli and C. M. Weekley, Executors of the Estate of Frieda Lawrence, from *Complete Stories of D. H. Lawrence* by D. H. Lawrence. Used by permission of Viking Penguin, a division of Penguin Putnam, Inc.

Excerpt from *Mrs. Dalloway* by Virginia Woolf, copyright 1925 by Harcourt, Inc. and renewed 1953 by Leonard Woolf, reprinted by permission of the publisher.

Excerpt from *A Room of One's Own* by Virginia Woolf, copyright 1929 by Harcourt, Inc., and renewed 1957 by Leonard Woolf, reprinted by permission of the publisher.

"The Demon Lover" from *The Collected Stories of Elizabeth Bowen* by Elizabeth Bowen, copyright © 1981 by Curtis Brown, Ltd., Literary Executors of the Estate of Elizabeth Bowen. Used by permission of Alfred A. Knopf, a division of Random House, Inc.

"Musée des Beaux Arts" copyright 1940 & renewed 1968 by W. H. Auden, "The Unknown Citizen" copyright 1940 & renewed 1968 by W. H. Auden, from *Collected Poems* by W. H. Auden. Used by permission of Random House, Inc.

"A Shocking Accident," copyright © 1957 by Graham Greene, from *Collected Stories of Graham Greene*, by Graham Greene. Used by permission of Viking Penguin, a division of Penguin Group (USA).

"Fern Hill" by Dylan Thomas, from *The Poems of Dylan Thomas*, copyright © 1945 by The Trustees for the Copyrights of Dylan Thomas. Reprinted by permission of New Directions Publishing Corp.

"Do Not Go Gentle into That Good Night" by Dylan Thomas, from *The Poems of Dylan Thomas*, copyright © 1952 by Dylan Thomas. Reprinted by permission of New Directions Publishing Corp.

"A Snake in the Grass" by R. K. Narayan, from *Under the Banyan Tree* by R. K. Narayan, copyright © 1985 by R. K. Narayan. Used by permission of Viking Penguin, a division of Penguin Group (USA) Inc.

"Old Mrs. Grey" from *The Death of the Moth and Other Essays* by Virginia Woolf, copyright 1942 by Harcourt, Inc. and renewed 1970 by Marjorie T. Parsons, Executrix, reprinted by permission of the publisher.

Unit 7

"Thistles" from *Wodwo* by Ted Hughes. Copyright © 1961 by Ted Hughes. Reprinted by permission of HarperCollins Publishers.

Excerpts from *Midnight's Children,* © 1980 by Salman Rushdie, by permission of The Wylie Agency.

"Not Waving, But Drowning" by Stevie Smith, from *Collected Poems of Stevie Smith*, copyright © 1972 by Stevie Smith. Reprinted by permission of New Directions Publishing Corp.

"At the Pitt-Rivers" from *A Pack of Cards and Other Stories* by Penelope Lively. Copyright © 1978, 1980, 1981, 1982, 1984, 1985, 1986 by Penelope Lively. Used by permission of Grove/Atlantic, Inc.

"Follower" from *Poems 1965–1975* by Seamus Heaney. Copyright © 1980 by Seamus Heaney. Reprinted by permission of Farrar, Straus & Giroux, Inc.

"Mnemonic" by Li-Young Lee. Reprinted by permission of BOA Editions and The Permissions Company.

"Photograph" "Photo of Parents" from *Running in the Family* by Michael Ondaatje. Copyright © 1982 by Michael Ondaatje. Used by permission of W. W. Norton & Company, Inc.

"Wind" from *Selected Poems 1957–1967* by Ted Hughes. Copyright © 1956 by Ted Hughes. Reprinted by permission of HarperCollins Publishers.

"That's All" from *Complete Plays: Three* by Harold Pinter. Copyright © 1978 by H. Pinter Ltd. Used by permission of Grove/Atlantic, Inc.

"What We Lost" from *Outside History: Selected Poems 1980–1990* by Eavan Boland. Copyright © 1990 by Eavan Boland. Used by permission of W. W. Norton & Company, Inc.

"A Mild Attack of Locusts" from *The Habit of Loving* by Doris Lessing. Copyright © 1957 by Doris Lessing. Reprinted by permission of HarperCollins Publishers.

"The Train from Rhodesia" by Nadine Gordimer, reprinted by the permission of Russell & Volkening, as agents for the author. Copyright © 1950 by Nadine Gordimer, renewed 1978 by Nadine Gordimer.

"Dead Men's Path," copyright © 1972, 1973 by Chinua Achebe, from *Girls at War and Other Stories* by Chinua Achebe. Used by permission of Doubleday, a division of Random House, Inc.

"Telephone Conversation" copyright © 1962 by Wole Soyinka. Reprinted with permission by Melanie Jackson Agency, LLC.

"Two Sheep" from *Snowman Snowman* by Janet Frame. Copyright © 1962, 1963 by Janet Frame. Reprinted by permission of George Braziller, Inc.

Chapter X, "Adieu foulard . . ." from "Tales of the Islands" from *Collected Poems 1948–1984* by Derek Walcott. Copyright © 1986 by Derek Walcott. Reprinted by permission of Farrar, Straus & Giroux Inc.

ACKNOWLEDGMENTS

"B. Wordsworth" from *Miguel Street* by V. S. Naipaul, copyright © 1959 by V. S. Naipaul. Used by permission of Alfred A. Knopf, a division of Random House, Inc.

Excerpts from *Imaginary Homelands,* © 1991 by Salman Rushdie, by permission of The Wylie Agency.

"Games at Twilight" from *Games at Twilight and Other Stories* by Anita Desai. Copyright © 1978 by Anita Desai. Reproduced by permission of the author c/o Rogers, Coleridge & White, Ltd., 20 Powis Mews, London W11 1JN.

"Elegy for the Giant Tortoises" reprinted by permission of Margaret Atwood, copyright © 1968, 1976 by Margaret Atwood. Currently available in the US in *Selected Poems*, 1965–1975, published by Houghton Mifflin, © 1976.

From "Catfish Row, Trinidad" by Selden Rodman. *New York Times*, May 15, 1960. Copyright © 1960 by The New York Times Co. Reprinted with permission.

Reference Section

Content from The Academic Word List, developed at the School of Linguistics and Applied Language Studies at Victoria University of Welllington, New Zealand, is reprinted by permission of Averil Coxhead. http://language.massey.ac.nz/staff/awl/index.shtml.

Maps

Mapping Specialists, Inc.

Photography

Cover CORBIS; **vi** THE KOBAL COLLECTION/NEW LINE CINEMA; **vii** Southampton City Art Gallery, Hampshire, UK/Bridgeman Art Library; **viii** Musee Conde, Chantilly, France,Giraudon/Bridgeman Art Library; **ix** Art Resource, NY; **x** Lambeth Palace Library, London, UK/Bridgeman Art Library; **xii** AKG Images; **xiii** Private Collection/Bridgeman Art Library; **xix** (t)E. T. Archive; **xix** (b) Mary Evans Picture Library; **xv** RÈunion des MusÈes Nationaux/Art Resource, NY; **xvii** Neue Pinakothek/AKG Images; **xxi** Mary Evans Picture Library; **xxii** Charles Plante Fine Arts English/Bridgeman Art Library; **xxiv** Tretjakov Gallery/Photo: akg-images; **xxix** Joseph Nicholls/Private Collection, Christie's Images Ltd/Bridgeman Art Library; **xxvi** Geoffrey Clements/CORBIS; **xxx** Museo Nazionale di Villa Giulia, Rome, Italy/Nimatallah/Art Resource, NY; **xxxii** John Singer Sargent/Tate Gallery, London/Art Resource, NY; **xxxiii** Min. Defense - Service Historique de l'Armee de Terre,France, Giraudon/Bridgeman Art Library; **xxxiv** Getty Images; **xxxv** (b)Andrew Brookes/CORBIS; **xxxv** (tr)Getty Images; **xxxv** (tl)Stockbyte; **3** Photodisc; **4–5** Musee de la Tapisserie, Bayeux, France, With special authorisation of the city of Bayeux/Bridgeman Art Library; **6** (t)Erich Lessing/ Art Resource, NY; **6** (c)HIP/Art Resource, NY; **6** (b)Aachen Cathedral Treasury, Aachen, Germany, Bildarchiv Steffens/Bridgeman Art Library; **7** (tl)Museum of London, UK/Bridgeman Art Library; **7** (cr)Fishmongers' Hall, London, UK/ Bridgeman Art Library; **7** (cl)Dept. of the Environment, London, UK/Bridgeman Art Library; **7** (cr)Art Resource, NY; **7** (tr)British Library, London, UK/ Bridgeman Art Library; **7** (b)Centre Historique des Archives Nationales, Paris, France, Archives Charmet/Bridgeman Art Library; **9** (tl)HIP/Art Resource, NY; **9** (tr)British Library, London, UK/Bridgeman Art Library; **9** (b)Simon Bening/ British Library, London, UK/Bridgeman Art Library; **10** The Pierpont Morgan Library/Art Resource, NY; **13** British Museum, London, UK/Bridgeman Art Library; **15** Angelo Hornak/CORBIS; **17** HIP/Art Resource, NY; **19** Werner Forman/Art Resource, NY; **20** Werner Forman/Art Resource, NY; **21** HIP/Art Resource, NY; **22** Werner Forman/Art Resource, NY; **24** Schloss Charlottenburg, Berlin/Bridgeman Art Library; **25** Werner Forman/CORBIS; **26** Bryan and Cherry Alexander; **27** Werner Forman/Art Resource, NY; **28** By Permission of The British Library; **29** R. Sheridan/Ancient Art & Architecture Collection; **30** Musee Conde, Chantilly, France,Giraudon/Bridgeman Art Library; **31** akg-images/Werner Forman; **32** British Museum/Michael Holford; **33** CM Dixon/HIP/The Image Works; **34** Art Resource, NY; **35** Ted Spiegel/ CORBIS; **36** Richard T. Nowitz/CORBIS; **37** 2004 Werner Forman/TopFoto/The Image Works; **39** Werner forman/CORBIS; **40** Werner Forman Archives; **41** Werner Forman/CORBIS; **42** National Museum of Iceland, Reykjavik, Iceland/ Bridgeman Art Library; **43** Werner Forman/CORBIS; **44** Abbot Hall Art Gallery, Kendal, Cumbria, UK/Bridgeman Art Library; **45** The British Museum; **46** Nationalmuseet, Copenhagen/Bridgeman Art Library, London; **47** Archivo Iconografico, S.A./CORBIS; **48** Erich Lessing/Art Resource, NY; **49** Ted Spiegel/ CORBIS; **50** Scala/Art Resource, NY; **51** Jerry Bingham and George Cox; **54** (t)British Museum, London, UK, Boltin Picture Library/Bridgeman Art Library; **54** (b)Jerry Bingham and George Cox; **54** (tc)Erich Lessing/Art Resource, NY; **54** (bc)The Collected Beowulf. All Artwork Copyright .c1999-2000 Gareth Hinds. Reproduced by permission of Candlewick Press, Inc.; **55** Michael Holford; **56** Erich Lessing/Art Resource, NY; **57** Ancient Art & Architecture; **58** Hulton Archive/Getty Images; **59–61** THE KOBAL COLLECTION/NEW LINE CINEMA; **62–67** The Collected Beowulf. All Artwork Copyright .c1999–2000 Gareth Hinds. Reproduced by permission of Candlewick Press, Inc.; **71** (tl)CORBIS; **71** (br)Bridgeman Art Library; **71** (tr)Bridgeman Art Library; **71–72** CORBIS; **72** (b)Getty Images; **75** William De Morgan/The De Morgan Centre, London/Bridgeman Art Library; **76** Bibliotheque Nationale, Paris, France/ Bridgeman Art Library; **77** first printed in The Art of Dora Carrington, Herbert Press, 1994; **78** Mabelle Linnea Holmes/Jamestown-Yorktown Educational Trust, VA/Bridgeman Art Library; **81** British Library, London, UK/Bridgeman Art Library; **82** The Art Archive/British Library; **84** British Library, London/ Bridgeman Art Library; **86** Kungl. Bernadotte-Biblioteket (The Royal Collection); **87** Ronald Sheridan/Ancient Art & Architecture; **90** Bridgeman Art Library/Getty Images; **91** Getty Images; **92** British Library/akg-images; **94** akg-images; **96–97** Thomas Stothard, Tate Gallery, London/Art Resource, NY; **99** akg-images; **101** By courtesy of The Board of Trustees of the Victoria & Albert Museum, London/ET Archive, London/SuperStock; **103–104** PrivateCollection/ Bridgeman Art Library; **106–108** Huntington Library and Art Gallery, San Marino, CA/Bridgeman Art Library; **111** Jupiter Images; **112** Art Resource, NY; **114** akg-images/British Library; **117** Archivo Iconografico, S.A./CORBIS; **118** The Huntington Library, Art Collections, and Botanical Gardens, San Marino, California/Bridgeman Art Library; **119** Private Collection/Bridgeman Art Library; **121** Ronald Sheridan/Ancient Art & Architecture; **122** Private Collection/ Bridgeman Art Library; **125** The Huntington Library, Art Collections, and Botanical Gardens, San Marino, CA/SuperStock; **127** Thomas Ross/Victoria Art Gallery, Bath and North East Somerset Council/Bridgeman Art Library; **128** Gianni Dagli Orti/CORBIS; **129** Archivo Iconografico, S.A./CORBIS; **130** Stapleton Collection/CORBIS; **133** Musee Conde, Chantilly, France/Giraudon/ Art Resource, NY; **134** Canterbury Cathedral, Kent, UK/Bridgeman Art Library; **136** Tate Gallery, London/Art Resource, NY; **138** Biblioteca Marciana, Venice, Italy/Giraudon/Art Resource, NY; **139** Stapleton Collection/CORBIS; **143** Xurxo Lobato; **144** (t)Shamil Zhumatov/Reuters; **144** (b)Kent News & Pictures; **145** Scala/Art Resource, NY; **147** Erich Lessing/Art Resource, NY; **149** Bibliotheque Municipale, Boulogne-sur-Mer, France/Giraudon/Art Resource, NY; **152** Muriel Broderick/The Illustrated London News Picture Library, London, UK/Bridgeman Art Library; **153–155** Giraudon/Art Resource, NY; **157** Bildarchiv Preussischer Kulturbesitz/Art Resource, NY; **158** Erich Lessing/Art Resource, NY; **161** Giraudon/Art Resource, NY; **162** Scala/Art Resource, NY; **167** Museo di San Marco dell'Angelico, Florence, Italy, Giraudon/The Bridgeman Art Library International; **168** Wadsworth Atheneum, Hartford. The Ella Gallup Sumner and Mary Catlin Sumner Collection Fund; **171** Archivo Iconografico,S.A./ CORBIS; **174** Erich Lessing/Art Resource, NY; **176** Ron Sheridan/Ancient Art & Architecture Collection, Ltd; **177** The Pierpont Morgan Library/Art Resource, NY; **178** The British Library; **179** E. T. Archive; **180** British Library, London/ Bridgeman Art Library; **182** The Art Archive/University Library Heidelberg/ Dagli Orti; **184** A.M. Rosati/Art Resource, NY; **186** North Wind Picture Archives; **188** AKG Berlin/SuperStock; **190** HIP/Art Resource, NY; **193** Stapleton Collection/CORBIS; **194** British Library, London, Great Britain/Erich Lessing/Art

Resource, NY; **196** Archivo Icconografico,S.A./CORBIS; **198** Lambeth Palace Library, London, UK/Bridgeman Art Library; **199** Bridgeman Art Library; **200** Bibliotheque Nationale, Paris, France/Bridgeman Art Library; **203** Fine Art Photographic Library/CORBIS; **208** Ancient Art & Architecture Collection, Ltd; **209** Stapleton Collection/CORBIS; **211** National Gallery of Scotland, Edinburgh, Scotland/Bridgeman Art Library; **213** Sotheby's/AKG Images; **215** Victoria and Albert Museum, London/Art Resource, NY; **223** (l)Stock Image/SuperStock; **223** (r)Alamy; **226** Huntington Library and Art Gallery, San Marino, CA/Bridgeman Art Library; **228** (r)Musee des Antiquities Nationales, St. Germain-en-Laye, France/Bridgeman Art Library; **228** (l)courtesy Professor Bernard J Muir; **229** (l)Galleria Sabauda, Turin, Italy/Scala/Art Resource, NY; **229** File photo; **229** (t)Private Collection, The Stapleton Collection/Bridgeman Art Library; **236–237** Lucas de Heere/National Museum and Gallery of Wales, Cardiff/Bridgeman Art Library; **238** (cl)Ancient Art & Architecture Collection Ltd; **238** (t)Ancient Art & Architecture Collection Ltd; **238** (br)Time Life Pictures/Getty Images; **238** (bl)Gianni Dagli Orti/CORBIS; **238** (cr)Nicolas Hilliard, British Museum, London, UK/Bridgeman Art Library; **239** (t)Newberry Library/Stock Montage; **239** (bl)Getty Images; **239** (br)Seattle Art Museum/CORBIS; **239** (c)Bildarchiv Preussischer Kulturbesitz/Art Resource, NY; **241** (b)Hoefnagel Joris/Hatfield House, Hertfordshire, UK/Bridgeman Art Library; **241** (t)National Portrait Gallery, London, UK/Bridgeman Art Library; **241** (c)Leonard Knyff/Yale Center for British Art, Paul Mellon Collection/Bridgeman Art Library; **242** Erich Lessing/Art Resource, NY; **245** Isaac Oliver/Powis Castle, Wales, UK/Bridgeman Art Library; **247** William Hogarth/Walker Art Gallery, National Museums Liverpool/Bridgeman Art Library; **249** Erich Lessing/Art Resource, NY; **251** Robert Peake/Private Collection/Bridgeman Art Library; **252** (r)Victoria & Albert Museum, London/Art Resource, NY; **252** Nicholas Hilliard/Rijksmuseum, Amsterdam, Holland/Bridgeman Art Library; **254** Woburn Abbey/Bridgeman Art Library/Christie's Images Ltd; **256** National Portrait Gallery of London; **259** Francesco Bartolozzi/Private Collection, The Stapleton Collection/Bridgeman Art Library; **261** Victoria and Albert Museum, London/Art Resource, NY; **262** National Portrait Gallery of London/SuperStock; **265** Private Collection, Philip Mould, Historical Portraits Ltd, London, UK/Bridgeman Art Library; **267** O'Shea Gallery, London/Bridgeman Art Library; **268** RÈunion des MusÈes Nationaux/Art Resource, NY; **270** National Portrait Gallery of London; **272** Scala/Art Resource, NY; **273** Christie's Images Ltd; **275** Getty Images; **276** Francois Boucher/Wallace Collection, London, UK/Bridgeman Art Library; **277** Fitzwilliam Museum, University of Cambridge/Bridgeman Art Library; **279** Kunsthistorisches Museum, Vienna, Austria/Bridgeman Art Library; **281** Abraham Bloemaert/Collection of the Earl of Pembroke, Wilton House, Wilts/Bridgeman Art Library; **283** Getty Images; **285** First Image; **286** Edwaert Collier/Private Collection/Bridgeman Art Library; **291** Nathan Benn/CORBIS; **292** Mary Evans Picture Library; **293** Tate Gallery, London/Art Resource, NY; **295** RÈunion des MusÈes Nationaux/Art Resource, NY; **296** Sotheby's/akg-images; **298** Masterfile; **299** Giorgione, (Giorgio da Castelfranco)/Palazzo Venezia, Rome,Italy/Bridgeman Art Library; **303** William Blake/Tate Gallery/Art Resource, NY; **306** AKG Images; **308** Erich Lessing/Art Resource, NY; **312** Henry Fuseli/York Museums Trust (York Art Gallery), UK/Bridgeman Art Library; **314** Ancient Art & Architecture Collection Ltd; **315** Hulton-Deutsch Collection/CORBIS; **317** Rafael Valls Gallery, London/Bridgeman Art Library (c)PunchStock; **322** Wallace Collection, London, UK/Bridgeman Art Library; **324** Royal Shakespeare Theater Collection, London, Great Britain/Erich Lessing/Art Resource, NY; **326** Gianni Dagli Orti/CORBIS; **331** John Singer Sargent/Tate Gallery, London/Art Resource, NY; **335** Palazzo Ducale, Venice, Italy/Erich Lessing/Art Resource, NY; **341** Tate Gallery, London/Art Resource, NY; **346** Victoria & Albert Museum, London/Art Resource, NY; **349** Agnew & Sons, London/Bridgeman Art Library; **350** © Staatliche Kunstsammlungen Dresden, Germany/The Bridgeman Art Library International; **357** Victoria & Albert Museum, London/Bridgeman Art Library; **361** E. T. Archive; **364** Victoria & Albert Museum, London, UK/Bridgeman Art Library; **372** Folger Shakespeare Library, Washington, DC/Art Resource, NY; **374** Landesmuseum Ferdinandeum, Innsbruck, Austria/Snark/Art Resource, NY; **375** National Geographic/Getty Images; **379** Spike Mafford/Getty Images; **382** Christie's Images Ltd; **391** The Louvre, Paris, France/Scala/Art Resource, NY; **397** Dante Charles Gabriel Rossetti/Ashmolean Museum, University of Oxford, UK/Bridgeman Art Library; **402** Dagli Orti/The Art Archive; **403** Agnew & Sons, London/Bridgeman Art Library; **406–407** Toho/The Kobal Collection; **408** (l)Toho/The Kobal Collection; **408** (r)Leeds Museums and Art Galleries (City Museum) UK/Bridgeman Art Library; **409** Toho/The Kobal Collection; **411** David Cooper/TIME; **412** (l)David Blue/TIME; **412** (r)Michael Daniel/TIME; **413** Erich Lessing/Art Resource, NY; **414** AKG Images; **416** Tate Gallery, London/Art Resource, NY.; **418** AKG Images; **421** The Art Archive/Anagni Cathedral Italy/Dagli Orti (A); **424** Fra Angelico/Prado, Madrid, Spain/Bridgeman Art Library; **426** Private Collection of Christian Pierre/SuperStock; **428** Erich Lessing/Art Resource, NY; **429** Private Collection Agnew's, London, UK/Bridgeman Art Library; **430** Private Collection/Bridgeman Art Library; **432** Frederick van Valkenborch/Private Collection, Rafael Valls Gallery, London, UK/Bridgeman Art Library; **433** Science Museum, London, Great Britain/HIP/Art Resource, NY; **435** Accademia, Venice, Italy/Erich Lessing/Art Resource, NY; **439** Private Collection/Bridgeman Art Library; **441** Angelo Hornak/CORBIS; **442** akg-images/Amelot; **445** National Portrait Gallery of London; **447** Musee des Beaux-Arts, Rouen, France/Erich Lessing/Art Resource, NY; **449** Pinacoteca di Brera, Milan, Italy/Erich Lessing/Art Resource, NY; **452** (l)Edward Bower/Dunster Castle, Somerset, UK, National Trust Photographic Library/John Hammond/Bridgeman Art Library; **453** Scala/Art Resource, NY; **454** (t)Victoria & Albert Museum, London/Art Resource, NY; **454** (tc)Erich Lessing/Art Resource, NY; **454** (bc)Erich Lessing/Art Resource, NY; **454** (b)Seattle Art Museum/CORBIS; **455** Hulton Archive/Getty Images; **457** Sandro Botticelli/Galleria degli Uffizi, Florence, Italy/Bridgeman Art Library; **459–460** Erich Lessing/Art Resource, NY; **462** Seattle Art Museum/CORBIS; **463** National Trust/Art Resource, NY; **464** National Portrait Gallery of London; **466** Fine Art Photographic Library, London/Art Resource, NY; **467** Peter Willi/Bridgeman Art Library; **469** Getty Images; **471** Private Collection/Bridgeman Art Library; **474** Private Collection, Ken Welsh/Bridgeman Art Library; **476–478** Erich Lessing/Art Resource, NY; **486** Foto Marburg/Art Resource, NY; **487** Robbie Jock/CORBIS; **490** (l)Danny Lehman/CORBIS; **490** (r)Jim Zuckerman/CORBIS; **492** (l)Private Collection, The StapletonCollection,;/Bridgeman Art Library; **492** (r)Private Collection/Bridgeman Art Library; **493** File photo; **493** File photo; **493** File photo; **493** Christie's Images Ltd; **500–501** Getty Images; **502** (tl)Private Collection/Bridgeman Art Library; **502** (bl)The Art Archive/Album/J. Enrique Molina; **502** (br)Werner Forman/Art Resource, NY; **502** (cr)Time Life Pictures/Getty Images; **502** (tr)Private Collection/Bridgeman Art Library; **502** (cl)Royal Society, London, UK/Bridgeman Art Library; **503** (t)Southampton City Art Gallery, Hampshire, UK/Bridgeman Art Library; **503** (c)R.R.McIan, City of Edinburgh Museums and Art Galleries, Scotland/Bridgeman Art Library; **503** (b)Bildarchiv Preussischer Kulturbesitz/Art Resource, NY; **505** (t)Mary Evans Picture Library; **505** (b) Benjamin Killingbeck/Private Collection, Ackermann and Johnson Ltd, London, UK/Bridgeman Art Library; **505** (c)Christie's Images Ltd/Bridgeman Art Library; **506** National Gallery of Victoria, Melbourne, Australia/Bridgeman Art Library; **509** Benjamin West/Montclair Art Museum, New Jersey, USA/Bridgeman Art Library; **511** Stapleton Collection/CORBIS; **513** Tate Gallery, London/Art Resource, NY; **515** Victoria & Albert Museum, London/Art Resource, NY; **516** Image Select/Art Resource, NY; **523** The Huntington Library, Art Collections, and Botanical Gardens, San Marino, California/SuperStock; **524–527** Tate Gallery, London/Art Resource, NY; **529** Chris Hellier/CORBIS; **532** National Gallery of Victoria, Melbourne, Australia/Bridgeman Art Library; **536** William Hogarth/Tate Gallery, London/Art Resource, NY; **538** Erich Lessing/Art Resource, NY; **542** St. Hilda's College, Oxford, UK/Bridgeman Art Library; **544–549** Bridgeman Art Library; **552** National Portrait Gallery of London/SuperStock; **554–555** Museum of London, UK/Bridgeman Art Library; **556** Culver Pictures, Inc.; **557** Guildhall Art Gallery, Corporation of London/Bridgeman Art Library; **558** Culver Pictures, Inc.; **559** Snark/Art Resource, NY; **560** Hulton Archive/Getty Images; **563** Derby Museum and Art Gallery, UK/Bridgeman Art Library; **564** National Portrait Gallery of London/SuperStock; **566** Sotheby's/akg-images; **568** Royal Holloway and Bedford New College, Surrey/Bridgeman Art Library; **569** R.

Sheridan/Ancient Art and Architecture; **571** Victoria Art Gallery, Bath and North East Somerset Council/Bridgeman Art Library; **577** Mary Evans Picture Library; **579** Image Select/Art Resource, NY; **581** Private Collection/Image Select/Art Resource, NY; **584** Francis Bindon/Royal Hospital Chelsea, London, UK/ Bridgeman Art Library; **586** Yale Center for British Art, Paul Mellon Collection, USA/Bridgeman Art Library; **588** Louvre, Paris, France/Scala/Art Resource, NY; **590** Réunion des Musées Nationaux/Art Resource, NY; **594** The Barber Institute of Fine Arts, University of Birmingham/Bridgeman Art Library; **596** Louvre, Paris, France/Réunion des Musées Nationaux/Art Resource, NY; **599** Image Select/Art Resource, NY; **602** Gervase Spencer/Victoria & Albert Museum/E. T. Archive; **607** Haynes Fine Art Gallery, Broadway, UK/Fine Art Photographic Library, London/Art Resource, NY; **612** Archivo Iconografico, S.A./CORBIS; **613** Museum of London UK/Bridgeman art Library; **614** (t)Christian Friedrich Zincke/Lincolnshire County Council, Usher Gallery, Lincoln, UK/Bridgeman Art Library; **614** (b)Jonathan Richardson/National Gallery of Victoria, Melbourne, Australia/Bridgeman Art Library; **616** William Powell Frith/Guildhall Art Gallery, Corporation of London, UK/Bridgeman Art Library; **617** Mary Evans Picture Library; **619** Bettmann/CORBIS; **621** (t)Frontispiece to 'London's Remembrancer' by John Bell/Private Collection/ Bridgeman Art Library; **621** (b)Gustavo Gilabert/CORBIS; **621** (tc)Mediscan/ CORBIS; **621** (bc)Private Collection, Richard Philp, London/Bridgeman Art Library; **624** Mary Evans Picture Library; **626** Getty Images; **627** North Wind Picture Archives; **629** Karen Kasmauski/CORBIS; **631** CDC/PHIL/CORBIS; **633** Mediscan/CORBIS; **637–640** Bildarchiv Preussischer Kulturbesitz/Art Resource, NY; **645** Darlene A. Murawski/Peter Arnold; **646** (t)Mark Edwards/Still Pictures/Peter Arnold; **646** (c)Andy Crump/Who/Photo Researchers; **646** (b)Joe Alexander/AFP; **648** Bridgeman Art Library; **650** Victoria & Albert Museum, London/Art Resource, NY; **652** John Bethell/Bridgeman Library, London/New York; **654** Edward Matthew Ward/Tate Gallery, London/Art Resource, NY; **659** Scottish National Portrait Gallery, Edinburgh/Bridgeman Art Library; **661** Michael Nicholson/CORBIS; **663** Mary Evans Picture Library; **666** Bettmann/CORBIS; **667** Tate Gallery, London/Art Resource, NY; **670–672** Bettmann/CORBIS; **676** Snark/Art Resource, NY; **681** Warren Faldley/CORBIS; **684** (r)Private Collection/Bridgeman Art Library; **684** (l)E. T. Archive; **685** (r)file photo; **685** Culver Pictures, Inc.; **685** (l)Musee Conde, Chantilly, France,Giraudon/Bridgeman Art Library; **692–693** National Gallery Collection; By kind permission of the Trustees of the National Gallery, London/CORBIS; **694** (t)The Art Archive/British Museum; **694** (bl)The Art Archive/Musèe du Nouveau Monde La Rochelle/Dagli Orti; **694** (c)Rèunion des Musèes Nationaux/Art Resource, NY; **694** (br)Bettmann/CORBIS; **695** (tcr)The Pierpont Morgan Library/Art Resource, NY; **695** (t)Smithsonian American Art Museum, Washington, DC/Art Resource, NY; **695** (bcl)Private Collection/Bridgeman Art Library; **695** (bcr)The Art Archive/Museo Bolivar Caracas/Dagli Orti]; **695** The Art Archive/Musèe du Ch,teau de Versailles/Dagli Orti; **695** (tcl)John Keats/ Private Collection/Bridgeman Art Library; **697** (c)Historical Picture Archive/ CORBIS; **697** (t) George ShepherdGuildhall Library, Corporation of London, UK/Bridgeman Art Library; **697** (b)The Art Archive/Tate Gallery London/John Webb; **698** Fine Art Photographic Library/CORBIS; **701** The Pierpont Morgan Library/Art Resource, NY; **703** Royal Academy of Arts, London, UK/Bridgeman Art Library; **705** Joseph Severn/Keats-Shelley Memorial House, Rome, Italy/ Bridgeman Art Library; **707** Manchester Art Gallery, UK/Bridgeman Art Library; **708** Arthur Pond/Arthur Fitzwilliam Museum, University of Cambridge, UK/ Bridgeman Art Library; **710** Jasper Francis Cropsey/Johnny van Haeften Gallery, London, UK/Bridgeman Art Library; **713** George Stubbs/Roy Miles Fine Paintings/Bridgeman Art Library; **717** Mary Evans Picture Library; **719** Sotheby's Transparency Library; **720** Private Collection/Bridgeman Art Library/ SuperStock; **722** Mary Evans Picture Library; **725** Tate Gallery, London/Art Resource, NY; **728–731** Bridgeman Art Library; **733** Neue Pinakothek/AKG Images; **737** Barry Iverson; **738** Ayman Mroueh; **739** Etienne Boyer/SIPA; **740** Barry Iverson; **742** Mary Evans Picture Library; **744** Smithsonian American Art Museum, Washington, DC/Art Resource, NY; **747** Bridgeman Art Library; **749** Fine Art Photographic Library, London/Art Resource, NY; **750** City of Edinburgh Museums and Art Galleries, Scotland/Bridgeman Art Library; **754** National Portrait Gallery, London/SuperStock; **755** The Art Archive; **756** Fitzwilliam Museum, University of Cambridge/Bridgeman Art Library; **757–758** The Huntington Library, Art Collections, and Botanical Gardens, San Marino, CA/ SuperStock; **761** Yale Center for British Art, Paul Mellon Collection, USA/ Bridgeman Art Library; **762** Blake, William/Fitzwilliam Museum, University of Cambridge, UK/Bridgeman Art LibraryMERCHANDISE; **763** Guildhall Art Gallery, London, Great Britain/HIP/Art Resource, NY; **764** City of Westminster Archive Centre, London, UK/Bridgeman Art Library; **766** Tate Gallery, London/ Art Resource, NY; **767** (l)William Blake/Fitzwilliam Museum, University of Cambridge, UK/Bridgeman Art Library; **767** (r)Tate Gallery, London/Art Resource, NY; **768** Ozias Humphrey/Private Collection/Bridgeman Art Library; **770** Courtesy of Thomas Brod and Patrick Pilkington/Bridgeman Art Library; **772** Bonhams, London, UK/Bridgeman Art Library; **775** Gavin Graham Gallery, London, UK/Bridgeman Art Library; **776** Erich Lessing/Art Resource, NY; **777** Working Title Films/ZUMA/CORBIS; **779** John Martin/Yale Center for British Art, Paul Mellon Collection, USA, Paul Mellon Collection/Bridgeman Art Library; **780** Benjamin Robert Haydon/National Portrait Gallery, London, UK, Giraudon/Bridgeman Art Library; **782** Victoria & Albert Museum, London/Art Resource, NY; **784** Joseph Nicholls/Private Collection, Christie's Images Ltd/ Bridgeman Art Library; **787** Thomas Girtin/Private Collection, Agnew's, London, UK/Bridgeman Art Library; **790** Tate Gallery, London/Bridgeman Art Library; **793** The Art Archive/Culver Pictures; **795** Abbot Hall Art Gallery, Kendal, Cumbria, UK/Bridgeman Art Library; **796** Bryan Reinhart/Masterfile; **799** National Portrait Gallery of London; **800** British Museum, London, UK/ Bridgeman Art Library; **801–802** Bibliotheque Nationale, Paris/AKG Images; **805** Christie's Images Ltd; **807–823** E. T. Archive; **826** Christie's Images Ltd; **829** Christie's Images Ltd/Bridgeman Art Library; **831** Min. Defense - Service Historique de l'Armee de Terre,France, Giraudon/Bridgeman Art Library; **833** National Portrait Gallery, London/SuperStock; **836** British Museum/E. T. Archive; **837** (r)Private Collection, Christie's Images Ltd/Bridgeman Art Library; **837** The Stapleton Collection/Bridgeman Art Library; **838** Private Collection/ Bridgeman Art Library; **839** Yelagin Island Palace, St. Petersburg, Russia/ Bridgeman Art Library; **841** Hessisches Landesmuseum, Darmstadt, Germany/ Bridgeman Art Library; **842** National Portrait Gallery, London/SuperStock; **844** Tate Gallery, London/Art Resource, NY; **848** Manchester Art Gallery, UK/ Bridgeman Art Library; **849** Sir William Allan/Roy Miles Fine Paintings/ Bridgeman Art Library; **850** Getty Images; **852** Mary Evans Picture Library; **856** Tate Gallery, London/SuperStock; **858** Rijksmuseum Vincent Van Gogh, Amsterdam, The Netherlands/Bridgeman Art Library; **861** Academy of Natural Sciences of Philadelphia/CORBIS; **863** National Portrait Gallery/akg-images; **865** William Hilton/Lincolnshire County Council, Usher Gallery, Lincoln, UK/ Bridgeman Art Library; **867** Walter Crane/Bridgeman Art Library; **869** Tate Gallery, London/Art Resource, NY; **872** Museo Nazionale di Villa Giulia, Rome, Italy/Nimatallah/Art Resource, NY; **875** (t)Smithsonian American Art Museum, Washington, DC/Art Resource, NY; **875** (bc)Smithsonian American Art Museum, Washington, DC/Art Resource, NY; **875** (b)Church of Santi Nicola e Cataldo Lecce, Puglia, Italy/Bridgeman Art Library; **875** (tc)Giraudon/Art Resource, NY; **877** Fine Art Photographic Library, London/Art Resource, NY; **880** Victoria & Albert Museum, London/Bridgeman Art Library; **881** Christie's Images Ltd/CORBIS; **883** Smithsonian American Art Museum, Washington, DC/ Art Resource, NY; **884** Joe McDonald/CORBIS; **887** Brooklyn Museum of Art/ CORBIS; **890** Victoria and Albert Museum, London/Art Resource, NY; **893** Erich Lessing/Art Resource, NY; **898** (r)Getty Images; **898** (l)Everett Collection; **898** (r)Aaron Haupt; **899** File photo; **899** (t)Christie's Images Ltd; **899** (l)William Nicholson/Scottish National Portrait Gallery, Edinburgh, Scotland/Bridgeman Art Library; **906–907** George William Joy/Museum of London, UK/Bridgeman Art Library; **908** (tc)The Art Archive/British Museum/Eileen Tweedy; **908** (t)Mary Evans Picture Library; **908** (b)Bildarchiv Preussischer Kulturbesitz/Art Resource, NY; **908** (bc)CORBIS; **909** (cw from top)The Pierpont Morgan Library/Art Resource, NY; **909** (cw from top)Giraudon/Art Resource, NY; **909** (cw from top)Getty Images; **909** (cw from top)Mary Evans Picture Library; **909** (cw from top)Bettmann/CORBIS; **911** (t)Ford Madox Brown/Birmingham Museums and Art Gallery/Bridgeman Art Library; **911** (bl)James Hakewill/

Private Collection, Christie's Images Ltd/Bridgeman Art Library; **911** (br)British Library, London, UK/Bridgeman Art Library; **913** Rykoff Collection/CORBIS; **915** Joseph Nash/Private Collection, Bonhams, London, UK/Bridgeman Art Library; **917** RÈunion des MusÈes Nationaux/Art Resource, NY; **919** Tate Gallery, London/Art Resource, NY; **921** The Art Archive/Dagli Orti; **922** National Portrait Gallery of London; **924** Christie's Images Ltd; **928** Victoria & Albert Museum, London/Art Resource, NY; **929** The Stapleton Collection/Bridgeman Art Library; **932** Musee National du Bardo, Tunis, Tunisia/Erich Lessing/Art Resource, NY; **933** Underwood & Underwood/CORBIS; **934** Erich Lessing/Art Resource, NY; **935** British Museum, London, Great Britain/Erich Lessing/Art Resource, NY; **936** Musee National du Bardo, Tunis, Tunisia/Erich Lessing/Art Resource, NY; **938** (b)Bettmann/CORBIS; **938** (bc)Tate Gallery, London/Art Resource, NY; **938** (t)Fine Art Photographic Library, London/Art Resource, NY; **938** (tc)Ricco/Maresca Gallery/Art Resource, NY; **939** John Brett/Private Collection/Bridgeman Art Library; **941** Museum of Fine Arts, Boston, Charles H. Bayley Picture and Painting Fund; **945** Alinari/Art Resource, NY; **947** Images.com/CORBIS; **949** (t)Sandi Fellman; **949** (b)Jay Dickman; **950** Carol Beckwith/Millennium Tribal Wisdom of the Modern World; **951** Getty Images; **951** Getty Images; **953** Erich Lessing/Art Resource, NY; **954** Fine Art Photographic Library, London/Art Resource, NY; **956** Christ Church College, Oxford by N. Herkomer/E. T. Archive; **957** Mary Evans Picture Library/The Image Works; **957** Mary Evans Picture Library/The Image Works; **958** Mary Evans Picture Library; **960** Private Collection, Christie's Images Ltd/Bridgeman Art Library; **961** Private Collection, Bourne Gallery, Reigate, Surrey/Bridgeman Art Library; **963** Sir Hubert von Herkomer/Royal Academy of Arts, London, UK/Bridgeman Art Library; **964** Image Select/Art Resource, NY; **965** Erich Lessing/Art Resource, NY; **966** Getty Images; **968** Victoria & Albert Museum, London/Art Resource, NY; **971** Cragside House, Northumberland, UK, National Trust Photographic Library/Derrick E. Witty,/Bridgeman Art Library; **974** Private Collection, The Maas Gallery, London, UK/Bridgeman Art Library; **975** Christie's Images Ltd; **979** National Portrait Gallery, London/SuperStock; **981** Musee Crozatier, Le Puy-en-Velay, France/Bridgeman Art Library; **984** Hulton Archive/Getty Images; **986** Private Collection, Barbara Singer/Bridgeman Art Library; **989** Private Collection/Bridgeman Art Library; **991–994** Getty Images; **995** Charles Plante Fine Arts English/Bridgeman Art Library; **998** Hulton-Deutsch Collection/CORBIS; **1000** AKG Images; **1001** Galerie Berko, Brussels, Belgium/Fine Art Photographic Library, London/Art Resource, NY; **1003** Reginald-Grenville Eves, Towner Art Gallery, Eastbourne, East Sussex, UK/Bridgeman Art Library; **1005** Geoffrey Clements/CORBIS; **1006** Christie's Images Ltd/Bridgeman Art Library; **1007** Fine Art Photographic Library, London/Art Resource, NY; **1017** Musee Crozatier, Le Puy-en-Velay, France/Bridgeman Art Library; **1020** (r)Aaron Haupt; **1020** Hulton Archive/Getty Images; **1021** (l)Getty Images; **1021** (t)The Everett Collection; **1028–1029** Tate Gallery, London/Art Resource, NY; **1030** (t)Percy Wyndham Lewis/Stapleton Collection, UK/Bridgeman Art Library; **1030** (b)The Art Archive/Culver Pictures; **1030** (bc)Scala/Art Resource, NY; **1030** (tc)Snark/Art Resource, NY; **1031** (tl)Sava Botzaris/Private Collection, Bonhams, London, UK/Bridgeman Art Library; **1031** (tc)Vanessa Bell/Private Collection, The Stapleton Collection/Bridgeman Art Library; **1031** (bc)Getty Images; **1031** (b)The Art Archive/Culver Pictures; **1031** (tr) Joy and John Halas & Batchelor Collection Ltd./Bridgeman Art Library; **1033** (tr)Bibliotheque des Arts Decoratifs, Paris, France, Archives Charmet/Bridgeman Art Library; **1033** (tl)The Art Archive/Domenica del Corriere/Dagli Orti; **1033** (b)Snark/Art Resource, NY; **1035** Erich Lessing/Art Resource, NY; **1037** The Art Archive/Imperial War Museum; **1039** RÈunion des MusÈes Nationaux/Art Resource, NY; **1041–1043** Tate Gallery, London/Art Resource, NY; **1044** (t)Ignace Henri Jean Fantin-Latour/Fitzwilliam Museum, University of Cambridge, UK/Bridgeman Art Library; **1044** (tc) Bildarchiv Preussischer Kulturbesitz/Art Resource, NY; **1044** (bc) Scala/Art Resource, NY; **1044** (b) Indianapolis Museum of Art, USA, Gift of Mr. and Mrs. Harrison Eiteljorg/Bridgeman Art Library; **1045** Topical Press Agency/Getty Images; **1047** Tate Gallery, London/Art Resource, NY; **1050** Private Collection/Bridgeman Art Library, London; **1055** Pretoria Art Museum, Pretoria, South Africa; **1057** Giraudon Art Resource, NY; **1060** Bildarchiv Preussischer Kulturbesitz/Art Resource, NY; **1061** Alinari/Art Resource, NY; **1064** Phillip Hollas/TIME; **1066** Vanessa Bell/University of Hull Art Collection, Humberside, UK/Bridgeman Art Library; **1067** Aubrey Beardsley/Private Collection/Bridgeman Art Library; **1068** John Collier/Bateman's, East Sussex, UK, National Trust Photographic Library/John Hammond/Bridgeman Art Library; **1070** Private Collection/Bridgeman Art Library; **1072** Robert Maier/Animals, Animals; **1073** Private Collection/Bridgeman Art Library; **1077** AKG Images/London; **1079** Dreweatt Neate Fine Art Auctioneers, Newbury/Bridgeman Art Library; **1082** Joe McDonald/Animals, Animals; **1084** Hulton-Deutsch Collection/CORBIS; **1085** Bettmann/CORBIS; **1089** Mary Evans Picture Library; **1091** Imperial War Museum/E. T. Archive; **1092** Bettmann/CORBIS; **1093** George C. Beresford/Beresford/Getty Images; **1095** Erich Lessing/Art Resource, NY; **1097** Getty Images; **1101** Colin Woodbridge/Alamy; **1102** Archives Larousse, Paris, France,Giraudon/Bridgeman Art Library; **1103** POPPERFOTO/Alamy; **1104** BETTMAN/CORBIS; **1105** Tate Gallery, London/Art Resource, NY; **1106** Getty Images; **1107** MusÈe Victor Hugo/akg-images; **1109** Fine Art Photographic Library, London/Art Resource, NY; **1111** Hagia Sophia, Istanbul, Turkey/Erich Lessing/Art Resource, NY; **1112** Tretjakov Gallery/akg-images; **1115** Paul Almasy/CORBIS; **1117** Alfred Eisenstaedt/Time Life Pictures/Getty Images; **1119** Private Collection/The Stapleton Collection Bridgeman Art Library; **1122** Getty Images; **1124** Images.com/CORBIS; **1129** CORBIS; **1131** Private Collection/Bridgeman Art Library; **1132** CORBIS; **1134** Wernher Krutein/Liaison International; **1136** Hulton Getty/Liaison Agency; **1138** UPI/Bettmann/CORBIS; **1140** Hunterian Art Gallery, University of Glasgow; **1143** Musee d'Orsay/Art Resource, NY; **1144** Private Collection/Bridgeman Art Library; **1149** George C. Beresford/Getty Images; **1153–1154** akg-images; **1157** Private Collection/Chris Beetles/Bridgeman Art Library; **1158** Fine Art Photographic Library, London/Art Resource, NY; **1160** Tate Gallery, London/Art Resource, NY; **1161** Southampton City Art Gallery, Hampshire, UK/Bridgeman Art Library; **1162** Sotheby's/akg-images; **1165** Henry Lamb/South African National Gallery, Cape Town, South Africa/Bridgeman Art Library; **1166** Art Resource, NY; **1168** Archive Photos; **1170** Getty Images; **1174** Mary Evans Picture Library/Robin Adler; **1176** Private Collection/Bridgeman Art Library; **1177** William Morris Gallery, Walthamstow, UK/Bridgeman Art Library; **1179** Fine Art Photographic Library/CORBIS; **1181** Hulton-Deutsch Collection/CORBIS; **1182** Bradford Art Galleries and Museums, West Yorkshire, UK/Bridgeman Art Library; **1184** Jerry Cooke/Time & Life Pictures/Getty Images; **1186** Musee Royaux des Beaux-Arts de Belgique, Brussels, Belgium/Bridgeman Art Library; **1187** Victoria & Albert Museum, London/Art Resource, NY; **1192** Bettmann/CORBIS; **1194** Private Collection/Bridgeman Art Library; **1200** Getty Images; **1202** Horace Bristol/CORBIS; **1204** Christie's Images Ltd/SuperStock; **1205** Sir Cedric Morris/Glynn Vivian Art Gallery, Swansea, Wales/Bridgeman Art Library; **1210** ZIGMUND LESZCZYNSKI/Animals, Animals; **1213** CORBIS; **1217** Alamy Images; **1218** (t)Bettmann/CORBIS; **1218** (br)Aaron Haupt; **1218** (bl)Hulton-Deutsch Collection/CORBIS; **1219** (t)Christie's Images Ltd; **1219** (b)file photo; **1219** (cl)Mary Evans Picture Library; **1219** (cr)File photo; **1219** (c)File photo; **1226–1227** Mark Copelad/Private Collection, Portal Gallery Ltd/Bridgeman Art Library; **1228** (t)Alexander Moffat/Scottish National Portrait Gallery, Edinburgh, Scotland/Bridgeman Art Library; **1228** (br)Bettmann/CORBIS; **1228** (cl)Lydia de Burgh/Government of Northern Ireland, Stormont, N. Ireland/Bridgeman Art Library; **1228** (cr)Getty Images; **1229** (tl)London, UK, Boltin Picture Library/Bridgeman Art Library; **1229** (b)Wolfgang Kaehler/CORBIS; **1229** (tr)MC PHERSON COLIN/CORBIS SYGMA; **1229** (cr)Benjamin Lowy/CORBIS; **1229** (cl)Sion Touhig/CORBIS; **1231** (br)Kim Sayer/CORBIS; **1231** (bl)DESMOND BOYLAN/Reuters/CORBIS; **1231** (t)Getty Images; **1233** Bettmann/CORBIS; **1235** Tate Gallery, London/Art Resource, NY; **1237** Werner Forman/Art Resource, NY; **1239** Tate Gallery, London/Art Resource, NY; **1241** Tim Mara/Wolverhampton Art Gallery, West Midlands, UK/Bridgeman Art Library; **1242** Getty Images; **1244** Arthur Tress/Photonica; **1246** Getty Images; **1248** Private Collection/Bridgeman Art Library; **1250** Collection of Andrew McIntosh Patrick, UK/Bridgeman Art Library; **1252** Pam Ingalls/CORBIS; **1254** Getty Images; **1257** (t)Henry Herbert La Thangue/Oldham Art Gallery, Lancashire, UK/Bridgeman Art Library; **1257** (c)Bettmann/CORBIS; **1257** (b)Daniel Nevins/SuperStock; **1259** Geray Sweeney/CORBIS; **1260** Stapleton Collection, UK/Bridgeman Art Library; **1262** Gerrit Greve/CORBIS; **1265** From Running in the Family by Michael Ondaatje.Copyright **1982** by Michael Ondaatje. Used by permission of W.W. Norton & Company, Inc; **1266** Scala/Art Resource, NY; **1267** Henri Cartier-Bresson/Magnum Photos; **1269** Carel Weight/Private Collection/Bridgeman Art Library; **1271** Derek Hudson/Getty Images; **1273** Owen Franken/CORBIS; **1276–1277** Robbie Jack/CORBIS; **1278** Kevin Casey; **1279** Smithsonian American Art Museum, Washington, DC/Art Resource, NY; **1280** The Fleming-Wyfold Art Foundation/Bridgeman Art Library; **1283** Sir Peter Scott/ Private Collection/Bridgeman Art Library; **1284** Hulton Getty Images/Tony Stone Images; **1286** Ancient Art & Architecture; **1288** Philip Richardson; Gallo Images/ CORBIS; **1290** Bridgeman Art Library; **1292** Pierre Holtz/Reuters/CORBIS; **1295** Fay Goodwin/Network/SABA; **1297** Victoria & Albert Museum, London/Art Resource, NY; **1298** Hulton Getty/Liaison Agency; **1299** Geoffrey Clements/ CORBIS; **1300** africanpictures.net; **1304** Miriam Berkley; **1306** Margaret Courtney-Clarke/CORBIS; **1306–1308** The Newark Museum/Art Resource, NY; **1309** Bowers Museum of Cultural Art/CORBIS; **1310** Christie's Images Ltd/ CORBIS; **1313** Jacques Langevin/CORBIS SYGMA; **1315** Miguel S. Salmeron/FPG International; **1318** Time Life Syndication/Henry Grossman; **1320** Adrian Burke/ CORBIS; **1322** Shiko Nakano/Photonica; **1323** John Carnemolla/Australian Picture Library/CORBIS; **1327** Pressens Bild/Globe Photos; **1329** Yann Arthus-Bertrand/CORBIS; **1331** MC PHERSON COLIN/CORBIS SYGMA; **1333** (t)Art Gallery of Ontario, Toronto, Canada/Bridgeman Art Library; **1333** (b)John N. Trager; **1335** Space Telescope Science Institute/CORBIS; **1336** Steve Peck/ Courtesy of Michael Rosenfeld Gallery, New York City; **1340** Robert Holmes/ CORBIS; **1342** Simon Reddy/Alamy; **1344** Sophie Bassouls/CORBIS SYGMA; **1346–1347** Private Collection/Bridgeman Art Library; **1349** Lou Wall/CORBIS; **1351** Private Collection/Bridgeman Art Library; **1355** Anthony Loew/Time Life Pictures/Getty Images; **1357** Private Collection, Bonhams,London,UK/Bridgeman Art Library; **1361** (t)Paulo Fridman/TIME; **1361** (c)Todd France/CORBIS; **1361** (b)Nick Baratta for Teen People; **1362** (tl)Phil Knott/Camerapress/Retna; **1362** (b)Michael Lavine/CORBIS; **1362** (bc)Michael Halsband/TIME; **1362** (tr)Niels Van Iperenn/Retna; **1362** (tc)Fred Prouser/Reuters; **1363** (l)Michael Halsband/TIME; **1363** (c)Robert Delahanty/CORBIS; **1363** (r)Ted Thai/TIME; **1366** Chris Ballentine/Alamy Images; **1373** Nancy Sheehan/Photo Edit; **1374** Aaron Haupt; **1374** (tl) Thierry Orban/CORBIS SYGMA; **1374** (b) Colin McPherson/CORBIS; **1375** (cl) BASSOULS SOPHIE/CORBIS SYGMA; **1375** (cr)file photo; **1375** (t)Bettmann/CORBIS; **1375** (b)file photo; **1375** (c)file photo.